C000177882

Chambers *Universal Learners'* Dictionary

International Students' Edition

EFL Adviser: Tom McArthur

Assistant Editors: C M Schwarz, G W Davidson,
M A Seaton, J W Graham, R J Sherrard, P Cairns

Chambers *Universal Learners'* Dictionary

Edited by E M Kirkpatrick

Pronunciation under the direction of
Professor David Abercrombie and Alan Kemp
of the Department of Linguistics,
University of Edinburgh

International Students' Edition

CHAMBERS

© 1980 W & R Chambers Ltd Edinburgh

Reprinted 1983, 1984, 1985, 1986, 1987

We have made every effort to mark as such all words which we believe to be trademarks. We should also like to make it clear that the presence of a word in the dictionary, whether marked or unmarked, in no way affects its legal status as a trademark.

All rights reserved. No part of this publication may be reproduced, stored in a retrieval system, or transmitted in any form or by any means, electronic, mechanical, photocopying, recording or otherwise, without the prior permission of W & R Chambers Ltd.

ISBN 0 550 10634 0 paperback

Printed in Great Britain by
Richard Clay Ltd, Bungay, Suffolk

Contents

Preface

Chambers Universal Learners' Dictionary has been specially created for learners of English who already have some knowledge of English and who are at the stage of requiring particular help with how to use the language. Copious and detailed examples of usage have, therefore, been given to show words in their usual context. These examples are interesting, modern and lively and will encourage the student to become familiar with English usage.
Another feature of the dictionary which will help the learner to use English correctly is the inclusion of labels which indicate in what kind of situation a particular word is suitable. Learners of English as a foreign language often have difficulty with this aspect of English.
The aim of this dictionary is to provide comprehensive information in as simple a form as possible. This is shown in the simply-worded definitions, in the clear and uncomplicated pronunciation scheme, and in the helpful grammatical information which has been provided at the individual entries in such a way that it is easy to understand immediately. This is a dictionary which individual learners will be able to use by themselves without necessarily relying on the help of a teacher.

Arrangement of Entries

To be able to use an individual dictionary it is important to know how the information is arranged. Different dictionaries have different ways of arranging the material provided. The following instructions will help the user to make full use of this particular dictionary.

Headwords

Each separate entry in the dictionary begins with a word in bold (or black) type which is placed further out into the margin than the other words in the column, *eg* **almost, must, real**. These words are called **headwords**, being the chief words in the entries, and are arranged in alphabetical order.
Sometimes you will find words in the list of headwords which are followed by a small number, *eg* **bear**^{1}. These numbers have been used to mark words which have the same form as each other and so look exactly the same. Sometimes they are pronounced in the same way as each other, *eg* **light**^{1}, **light**^{2}, **light**^{3}, and sometimes they are pronounced differently, *eg* **lead**^{1} [liːd], **lead**^{2} [led].
Sometimes a word appears in the list of headwords which is not actually defined there. Instead of a definition you will find a cross-reference to where the word is defined. So in the list of headwords you will find **naval** *see* **navy** because **naval** is defined at **navy** from which it is formed. Similarly you will find **barmaid** *see* **bar** in the list of headwords since **barmaid** is defined at **bar**.
In some cases words appear in the list of headwords which are not explained in the text of the dictionary but in the Appendices, the section at the end of the dictionary. In such cases cross-references have been given in the list of headwords, *eg* **Venezuela, Venezuelan** *see* Appendix 2.
Many of the words which are defined in the dictionary do not appear as headwords because words and phrases which belong to the same word-family as a particular headword are listed under it. These include:

Derivatives

Derivatives are words which are formed from the headword or from the main part of the headword by adding a suffix or ending. So you will find **accurately** and **accuracy** under the headword **accurate**, **absurdity** and **absurdness** under **absurd**, **naughtily** under

naughty. Some derivatives, such as those just mentioned, are not defined since their meanings are obvious from the headword.

Derivatives which have been defined are given in alphabetical order and begin on a separate line to make them easier to find in the entry, *eg* **moody** under **mood**, **perishable** under **perish**. Derivatives which are not defined but which have been given an example of usage are also in alphabetical order and begin on a separate line, *eg* **abdominal** and **adjustment**.

Compounds

After the derivatives you will find a list of compounds in alphabetical order. Compounds are words which are made up of two elements — the headword, or a derivative of the headword, plus another word, *eg* **air-conditioned**, **air hostess**, **airmail** and **airy-fairy** are all under the headword **air**, and **national anthem** and **nation-wide** are under the headword **nation**. As you will see from these words some compounds are hyphenated (*eg* **air-conditioned**), some are one word, and some are two words — in English it is often a matter of personal choice whether compounds are hyphenated or not. All have been given a grammatical label. Two-word compounds which do not begin with the headword, *eg* **grand piano, upright piano**, are often treated as phrases.

Note Compounds formed from phrasal verbs (see under **Phrases** below) are not always defined separately. Frequently they are placed in a bracket after the appropriate verb, *eg* **take off** . . . 2 *vi* . . . *The plane took off for Rome* (*nc* **take-off**).

Phrases

Following the compounds is a list of phrases in alphabetical order. Phrases are groups of words containing the headword or a derivative of the headword, *eg* **dead set on**, **dead to the world** under **dead**; **not at all**, **not that** under **not**; **pop the question**, **pop up** under **pop**; **in relation to** under **relate**. The words **a** and **the** at the beginning of a phrase have been ignored for purposes of alphabetical order, *eg* **a far cry**, **the Bar**.

Phrases are not always listed under the first word of the phrase, *eg* **pay through the nose** appears under **nose**. If the phrase is not listed under the first word of the phrase you should try looking up the other words in the phrase. Often a phrase is listed under the word which is considered to be the most important word in the phrase. There will often be a cross-reference, *eg* at **pay** you will find **pay through the nose** *see* **nose**. Grammatical labels have not been given for phrases except for phrasal verbs.

Phrases which are made up of verbs plus adverbs or prepositions and act in the same way as verbs are called **phrasal verbs**, *eg* **come across** under **come**; **put up with** under **put**; **take in** under **take**. For further information on these see **Grammatical labels** below.

The Entries

Spelling and alternative forms of words

If we look at the actual form of headwords and derivatives it will be seen that more than one spelling is sometimes given. Many verbs in English can be spelt with either **-ize** or **-ise** as their ending. Which you use is a matter of choice. This dictionary gives the **-ize** spelling first but indicates that the **-ise** form is quite acceptable in the following way: **realize**, **-ise**; **baptize**, **-ise**; **centralize**, **-ise**. Derivatives of such verbs have the alternative form indicated simply by **-s-** since derivatives of a word are assumed to follow the spelling pattern of that word, *eg* **realization**, **-s-**. The **-ize** spelling is common particularly in American English.

Note Some verbs do not have an **-ize** form and can only be spelt with **-ise**, *eg* **advise**, **supervise**.

Some words which can be spelt correctly in more than one way sometimes appear in the dictionary like this: **acknowledg(e)ment**. This indicates that this word is correctly spelt with or without **(e)** and so both **acknowledgement** and **acknowledgment** are acceptable. Sometimes both spellings have been written out in full, separated by a comma, *eg* **omelette**, **omelet**.

Sometimes alternative forms of phrases have been shown by the use of an oblique (/), *eg* **all/just the same**. This means that **all the same** and **just the same** have the same meaning.

Pronunciation

The headword is followed immediately by a group of letters or symbols in square brackets and in roman (ordinary) type. This shows the pronunciation of the word. The pronunciation scheme is explained in detail on pp xv-xix.

All headwords have been given pronunciation but not all derivatives *etc* have. Frequently these have just been given stress marks to indicate which part of the word should be emphasized when being pronounced, *eg* '**neatly**. For further information on stress marks see p. xvii.

Grammatical labels

Labels giving grammatical information, *eg* parts of speech, are in *italic* type. If the part of speech label comes immediately after one of the numbers in a series of definitions then the label applies only to the definition with that number:

accident 1 *nc* an unexpected happening, often harmful, causing injury *etc.* **2** *nu* chance.

This indicates that the first meaning of **accident** is a countable noun and the second meaning of **accident** is an uncountable noun. Similarly at **provide** we have:

provide 1 *vt* to give or supply. **2** *vi* to supply or prepare what is necessary.

This indicates that the first meaning of **provide** is a transitive verb and that the second meaning is an intransitive verb. If the part of speech label applies to all of the numbered definitions following it the label comes before the numbering sequence begins, *ie* before the number **1**:

admire *vt* **1** to look at with great pleasure and often to express this pleasure. **2** to have a very high opinion of (someone or something).

This indicates that both meanings of **admire** are transitive verbs. For further information on the position of labels see p xiii. A full list of labels and abbreviations is given on p xx.

Labelling of nouns

Learners of English frequently have difficulty in deciding which nouns may be used in the plural form and which may not. It is sometimes very difficult even for those whose mother tongue is English to make such decisions. However to give as much help as possible to the user of the dictionary we have labelled the nouns in the following ways.

nc This is short for *noun countable* and means that a noun (or a particular meaning) labelled in this way may be used in the plural form, *eg* **daisy**, **drum** or **notice 1**.

nu This is short for *noun uncountable* and means that a noun (or a particular meaning) labelled in this way may not be used in the plural form, *eg* **information**, **luggage**, **movement 2** and **3**.

ncu This is short for *noun countable and uncountable* and means that a noun (or a particular meaning) labelled in this way may or may not take a plural form depending on the meaning, *eg* **movement 1**.

nc (*no pl*) This is short for *noun countable* (*no plural*) and indicates that a noun labelled in this way could take a plural form but in practice does not, *eg* **buzz 2**, **small screen**, **time 5**.

n sing This is short for *noun singular.* A noun labelled in this way is one that looks plural in form but in fact is treated as singular, being accompanied by a singular verb, *eg* **mumps**, **mathematics**.

n pl This is short for *noun plural.* A noun labelled in this way is one which is plural in form and is accompanied by a plural verb, *eg* **scissors**.

n This is short for *noun* and is the label used where the question of countability is not relevant, *eg* in titles such as **Home Office**, **Christendom** *etc.*

(*attrib*) When used in the labelling of nouns this is short for *attributively* and means that the noun (or particular meaning) labelled in this way is commonly used as an adjective before another noun. Many nouns in English can be used as adjectives in this way. Usually the label (*attrib*) has been placed before an example of usage showing the noun used as an adjective. So at the first meaning of the noun **dance** we have given two examples of the word used as a noun: *Have you done this dance before?*; *Will you have the next dance with me?*; and two examples of the noun used as an adjective: (*attrib*) *dance music*; (*attrib*) *dance steps.* Sometimes the noun labelled (*attrib*) will be joined by a hyphen to the word it describes, *eg* **shopping** and **shipping** as in **shopping-basket**, **shipping-agent**. Where a particular noun is always, or almost always, used as an adjective the whole noun and not just an example of usage is labelled, *eg* **casement** (*usu attrib*).

pl This is short for *plural*. The plural forms of nouns have been given where these are irregular (*ie* where they do not just add **s** or **es**), *eg* **mouse** – *pl* **mice**; where there might be some doubt as to whether the plural is regular or not, *eg* **house** – *pl* **houses**; where there are common spelling problems, *eg* **flamingo** – *pl* **flamingo(e)s** (the bracket shows that both **flamingoes** and **flamingos** are possible), **folio** – *pl* **folios**; and where there are alternative plurals, *eg* **fish** – *pls* **fish**, (*rare*) **fishes**. Alternative plurals are usually given in order of frequency, *ie* the more common form coming first. In some cases where more than one plural form has been given it indicates that certain meanings of the noun have a different plural form from other meanings, *eg* **foot** – *pl* **feet** (*defs 1–3*), **foot** (*def 3*), *ie* the first, second and third meanings of **foot** all take the plural form **feet** but the third meaning can also take the plural form **foot**.

fem This is short for *feminine* and indicates that the word following this label is the word applied to the female equivalent of the word before the label, *eg* **abbot** – *fem* **abbess**; **conductor 3** (*fem* **conductress**).

(*with cap*) This is short for *with capital* and indicates that the noun labelled in this way is spelt with a capital letter, eg **arts** (*often with cap*), **artillery 2** (*often with cap*), **president** (*with cap in titles*).

(*in cmpds*) This is short for *in compounds* and indicates that the word labelled in this way is used as a part of another word or compound, *eg* **boat 3** as in **gravy-boat**, **box** as in **matchbox** or **letterbox**, **pan 1** as in **frying-pan**. See also section on labelling of adjectives below.

Labelling of verbs and phrasal verbs

(a) **Verbs** are labelled in the following way:

vt This is short for *verb transitive* and means that a verb (or a particular meaning) labelled in this way takes a direct object, *eg* **include** as in *Does that include him?*; **invent** as in *Who invented the telephone?*

vi This is short for *verb intransitive* and means that a verb (or a particular meaning) labelled in this way does not take a direct object, *eg* **reappear** as in *She suddenly reappeared*; **appeal** as in *He appealed to the judge*; **apologize** as in *She apologized to him for being late.*

vti This is short for *verb transitive and intransitive* and means that a verb (or a particular meaning) labelled in this way is capable of either taking or not taking a direct object, *eg* **dance** as in *She began to dance as soon as she heard the music* and in *Can you dance the waltz?*

v refl This is short for *verb reflexive* and means that the verb (or a particular meaning) labelled in this way is followed by a reflexive pronoun, *ie* a pronoun object that refers back to the subject, as in **abandon 2** *v refl . . . He abandoned himself to despair.*

pt, ptp These are short for *past tense, past participle* and have been given at the beginning of some verb entries. Where the past tense and past participle are the same they appear like this: **flee** – *pt, ptp* **fled**. Otherwise they have been separated, *eg* **come** – *pt* **came**: *ptp* **come**. Past tenses and past participles have been given for irregular (strong) verbs, *eg* **fight** – *pt, ptp* **fought**; **fly** – *pt* **flew**: *ptp* **flown**, or for verbs whose past tense or past participle might cause difficulty because of spelling, *eg* **abet** – *pt, ptp* **abetted**; **abhor** – *pt, ptp* **abhorred**; **grab** – *pt, ptp* **grabbed**.

Some verbs are shown as having more than one past tense and past participle. This sometimes indicates that the verb has alternative past tenses and past participles, *eg* the past tense of **cleave** is either **cleft**, **cleaved** or **clove** and similarly the past participle is either **cleft** or **cloven**. Usually these are given in order of frequency, *ie* the most common form is placed first.

In some cases where more than one past tense and past participle have been given it indicates that certain meanings of the verb have a different past tense and past participle from other meanings, *eg* **hang** – *pt, ptp* **hung** (*defs 1, 2, 4, 5, 6, 7*), **hanged** (*def 3*), *ie* all meanings except the third meaning have **hung** as the past tense and past participle but the third meaning has **hanged** as the past tense and past participle.

prp This is short for *present participle.* Present participles have been given only where the spelling is not obvious from that of the past tense. So you will find that **travelling** has not been given as it is assumed to follow the spelling pattern of **travelled**. However such present participles as **running** have been given as help is needed with the spelling and this help is not given by the past tense **ran** or the past participle **run**.

(*not used with* **is, was** *etc and* **-ing**) This means that verbs (or meanings of verbs) labelled in this way are not usually found in the progressive tenses. Thus you say *He knows everything,* but not *He is knowing everything.* Likewise you say *I do not understand what he is saying,* but not *I am not understanding what he is saying,* and *That sounded like a car,* but not *That was sounding like a car.*

(b) **Phrasal verbs** (see under **Phrases** above) are labelled in the following way:

vi A phrasal verb labelled *vi* is simply a phrase which acts like an intransitive verb. Examples are **go off** as in *The little boy was injured when the rifle went off in his hand* and **set to** as in *They set to and finished the work the same day.*

vt fus This is short for *verb transitive fused.* A fused transitive phrasal verb is a phrase which acts like a transitive verb and whose object can never come between the verb and its accompanying preposition, *eg* **spy on** as in *Our next-door neighbours are always spying on us.* A fused phrasal verb may be made up of a verb plus an adverb and preposition, *eg* **put up with** where the adverb and the preposition cannot be separated from each other or from the verb itself by the object, as in *I cannot put up with all this noise.* You cannot say *I cannot put all this noise up with* or *I cannot put up all this noise with.*

vt sep This is short for *verb transitive separable.* A separable transitive phrasal verb is a phrase which acts like a transitive verb whose object can either come between the verb and its accompanying adverb or after the accompanying adverb, *eg* **put aside**. You can say either *She put aside her work* or *She put her work aside.* If the object is a pronoun it must come between the verb and the adverb. You must say *She put it aside.* You cannot say *She put aside it.*

vt oblig sep This is short for *verb transitive obligatorily separated.* This refers to a separable transitive phrasal verb in which the object must come between the verb and adverb, *eg* **push around** = to treat roughly. You say, in this sense, *He pushes his young brother around,* not *He pushes around his young brother.*

vt usu sep This is short for *verb transitive usually separated.* This refers to a separable phrasal verb in which the object usually comes between the verb and adverb, *eg* **bring round** as in *The smelling salts brought him round* and *Smelling salts usually bring unconscious people round.* It is possible but unusual to say *Smelling salts bring round unconscious people.*

Note Not all phrases consisting of verbs and prepositions or adverbs have been treated as phrasal verbs. Verb phrases consisting of verb plus object followed by preposition plus object have not usually been treated as phrasal verbs but as ordinary phrases and so do not have grammatical labels, *eg* **put (someone) off (something)**, **put (something) down to (something)**.

Sometimes a preposition or adverb which (usually) accompanies a certain verb has been placed in brackets after it, *eg* **abstain** (*often with* **from**), **accord 1** (*with* **with**), **pose[1] 2** (*with* **as**).

Labelling of adjectives

(*attrib*) This is short for *attributive* and means that an adjective (or a particular meaning) labelled in this way comes before the noun which it describes, *eg* all the meanings of **advance** or **dead 3**. So you can say *He made an advance payment,* but not *The payment he made was advance*; *This is an advance copy of this book,* but not *The copy of this book is advance*; *He came to a dead stop,* but not *The stop he came to was dead*; *There was a dead silence,* but not *The silence was dead.*

(*pred*) This is short for *predicative* and means that an adjective (or a particular meaning) labelled in this way does not come before the noun which it describes, *eg* all the meanings of **asleep** or **dead 2**. So you can say *The people are asleep,* but not *The asleep people were not disturbed by the noise*; *My foot is asleep,* but not *My asleep foot is uncomfortable*; *The engine is dead,* but not *They are trying to repair his dead engine.*

Sometimes certain adjectives are accompanied by a particular preposition. This has been indicated in the labelling of the adjectives, *eg* **deaf 2** is labelled (*pred with* **to**) *He was deaf to all our arguments,* **bad 5** is labelled (*pred with* **for**) *Smoking is bad for your health,* and **good 4** is labelled (*with* **at** *or* **with** *when pred*) *He's good at tennis*; *He's good with children.*

Most adjectives in English can be either attributive or predicative. In this dictionary adjectives which are not labelled (*attrib*) or (*pred*) can be used in either position and are usually accompanied by examples indicating this, *eg* **deaf 1** *She has been deaf since birth*; *a deaf old man.*

(*neg*) This is short for *negative.* The negative form of some adjectives has been given simply by placing after the adjective the prefix which makes the adjective negative, *eg* **abashed** (*neg* **un-**); the first meaning of **friendly** (*neg* **un-**). Some negative forms have been thought to need separate articles and these have been cross-referred from the positive form, *eg* **appropriate** . . . *See also* **inappropriate**; **able** . . . *See also* **unable**; **fertile** . . . *See also* **infertile**.

(*compar*), (*superl*) These are short for *comparative* and *superlative.* The comparative and superlative forms have been given only where these are irregular, *eg* **good** – *compar* **better**: *superl* **best**.

(*in cmpds*) This is short for *in compounds* and indicates that the word labelled in this way is used as part of another word or compound, *eg* **-bodied** as in **able-bodied**, **full-bodied**; **Anglo-** as in **Anglo-American**.

Other labels

Often there is a label in italic type in brackets which does not refer to any aspect of grammar. Such labels tell you, for example, which field or subject a word belongs to or in what kind of situation a particular word is suitable.

The most helpful way to deal with these is to list in alphabetical order all those labels which are in need of explanation.

(*Amer*) This is short for *American* and means that the word labelled in this way is the American equivalent of a British word.

(i) Sometimes it is used to indicate that the word following the label is the American spelling of a word, *eg* **colour**, (*Amer*) **color**. This means that **colour** is the British, and **color** the American, way of spelling it.

The American spelling has been given only for the headword, and derivatives are assumed to follow the spelling pattern of the headword; *eg* since **colour** has the American equivalent **color** it follows that **coloured**, **colourful**, **colouring** are spelt **colored**, **colorful**, **coloring** in American English.

(ii) Sometimes the (*Amer*) label is used to indicate that what follows is the American pronunciation of a word, *eg* **tomato** [tə'maːtou, (*Amer*) -'mei-].

(iii) Sometimes the (*Amer*) label is used to show that the word (or particular meaning) labelled in this way is the American equivalent of a British word, *ie* that in America the thing being defined is called something completely different from what it is called in Britain, *eg* **faucet** (*Amer*) a tap[2]; **hood 3** (*Amer*) the bonnet of a car.

(iv) Sometimes the (*Amer*) label is used to indicate that the word in bold (or black) type following the label is the American equivalent of a British word, *eg* **pavement** (*Amer* **sidewalk**).

(*arch*) This is short for *archaic* and means that the word (or particular meaning) labelled in this way is no longer commonly used in modern English although it was common in the past, *eg* **knave 2** = a dishonest person.

(*Brit*) This is short for *British* and is used to indicate something which is specifically British, *eg* **Premium Bond, sausage roll**.

(*derog*) This is short for *derogatory* and means that the word (or particular meaning) labelled in this way is used only when the user is expressing disapproval or scorn of the person or thing about which he is speaking or writing, *eg* **brat** (*derog*) a child; **bookworm** (*sometimes derog*) a person who reads a lot.

(*dial*) This is short for *dialectal* and indicates that the word (or particular meaning) labelled in this way is a word used only in some parts of Britain and so is a part of a British dialect, *eg* **wee**.

(*euph*) This is short for *euphemistic* and means that the word (or particular meaning) labelled in this way is a more pleasant, less direct way of expressing something that is unpleasant in some way, *eg* **pass away** (*euph*) to die; **breathe one's last** (*euph*) to die.

(*facet*) This is short for *facetious* and means that the word (or particular meaning) labelled in this way is intended to be funny or humorous, *eg* **wherewithal**. Often a word which can be used facetiously can also be used in formal English where no humour is intended, *eg*

palatial. This can either be used as a formal adjective from **palace** or as a facetious word to describe something large and magnificent, so we have labelled this (*formal or facet*).

(*fig*) This is short for *figurative* and means that the word (or particular meaning) labelled in this way is not used in a literal, ordinary way, *eg* **make someone's hackles rise** (*fig*) to make someone angry. As a human being does not actually have hackles which rise when he is angry this phrase is clearly not literal.

Sometimes it is only an example of usage that is labelled (*fig*), *eg* **bring down** to cause to fall: *The storm brought all the trees down*; (*fig*) *That will bring down the dictator.* The (*fig*) label here is to show that the dictator will be defeated and that he will not physically fall down.

(*formal*) This means that the word (or particular meaning) labelled in this way is usually used in formal situations or contexts. It is very important to label such words, *eg* **countenance** *nc* (*formal*) the face, as the use of formal words in an ordinary or informal situation (or the use of informal words in a very formal situation) is a common error when learners are speaking English. You would use the word **countenance** only when intending to be very formal.

As will be seen from the note on (*facet*) many nouns marked (*formal*) can also be used facetiously in an ordinary or informal way.

Some words are used in very formal situations indeed and these have been labelled (*very formal*), *eg* **palpable**.

Some words which are not particularly formal but which have a less formal, more commonly used equivalent have been labelled (*more formal than*), *eg* **acquire** is labelled (*more formal than* **get**); **regret** is labelled (*more formal than* **be sorry**).

Similarly some words have been labelled (*less formal than*), *eg* **phone** (*less formal than* **telephone**).

(*hist*) This is short for *historical* and means that the word (or particular meaning) labelled in this way refers to something that is no longer to be found, used *etc*, but which was quite common in the past, *eg* **chariot**, **gibbet**.

(*inf*) This is short for *informal* and means that the word (or particular meaning) labelled in this way is used only in an informal situation or context, *eg* **pal** (*inf*) a friend; **tipsy** (*inf*) slightly drunk. You would never use **pal** or **tipsy** in a formal situation. You would particularly not use such language when writing a formal letter.

(*ironic*) This indicates that a word (or particular meaning) labelled in this way means the opposite of what it seems to be saying, *eg* **pretty 2** (*ironic*) fine: *This is a pretty mess!*; **fine 8** (*ironic*) wonderful: *This is a fine state of affairs!*

(*legal*) This means that the word (or particular meaning) labelled in this way applies to a term used in matters dealing with law, *eg* **the accused**, **the burden of proof**.

(*liter*) This is short for *literary* and means that the word (or particular meaning) labelled in this way is usually found in English literature, *eg* poems, novels, plays *etc*, rather than in ordinary speech or writing, *eg* **bondage** (*liter*) slavery; **bough** (*liter*) a branch of a tree; **breast 3** (*liter*) heart or feelings.

(*loosely*) This means that the word (or particular meaning) labelled in this way is used in an inexact or loose way, *eg* **boat 1** a small vessel for travelling over water. **2** (*loosely*) a larger vessel for the same purpose; a ship; **hundreds of 1** several hundred. **2** (*loosely*) very many.

(*offensive*) This means that the word (or particular meaning) labelled in this way should not be used unless the user is intending to be very insulting, *eg* **nigger** (*offensive*) a Negro; **papist** (*offensive*) a Roman Catholic.

(*old*) This means that the word (or particular meaning) labelled in this way applies to something which is no longer commonly used although it was in the past. It refers to words and things more recent than those labelled (*arch*) or (*hist*), *eg* **boudoir, gramophone**.

(*orig*) This is short for *originally* and indicates that the word (or particular meaning) labelled in this way originally had a meaning other than its modern meaning, *eg* **card-carrying 1** openly showing support for or membership of an organization, point of view *etc*. **2** (*orig*) holding a membership card of a political party *etc*.

® This symbol, which is placed immediately after the word to which it refers, indicates that a word labelled in this way is a registered trademark, *ie* that it is a name which may be used to refer only to a particular article made by a particular company (who have registered the name) and may not be used to refer to an article, however similar, made by another company, *eg* **Tannoy®**, **Xerox®**, **Valium®**.

(*sl*) This is short for *slang* and means that the word (or particular meaning) labelled in this way is used only in very informal situations or contexts. The term slang in this dictionary is used for words that are more informal than those marked informal. Words marked slang must never be used in formal situations and particularly not when writing formal letters, *eg* **booze** (*sl*) alcoholic drink.

(*tech*) This is short for *technical* and means that the word (or particular meaning) labelled in this way is used in a particular specialist field. Words labelled (*tech*) often have a more commonly used, less technical, equivalent, *eg* **caries** (*tech*) decay or rottenness of the bones or *esp* the teeth; **campanology** (*tech*) (the study of) bell-ringing.

Some words or meanings are labelled (*not a tech term*). This means that the word labelled in this way, *eg* **painkiller**, is not the term used by specialists.

(*vulg*) This is short for *vulgar* and means that the word (or particular meaning) labelled in this way is acceptable only in some situations and by certain sections of society. Many people find such words indecent and are offended by their use, *eg* **cunt** (*vulg*) the female sexual organs.

Position of labels

If the label applies to all of the meanings of a particular part of speech of a word in an entry the label comes before the numbering sequence begins, *ie* before the number **1**:

animate *vt* (*formal*) **1** to make lively. **2** to be the cause of.

This indicates that both the meanings of the verb **animate** are formal.

If the label applies to more than one part of speech in an entry the label is repeated before the numbering sequence, if any, of each new part of speech:

accord (*formal*) **1** *vi* (*with* **with**) to agree with. **2** *vt* to grant or give to (a person). – *nu* (*formal*) agreement.

This indicates that all meanings of **accord**, whether it is a verb or a noun, are formal.

If the label is placed immediately after one of the numbers in a definition it indicates that the label applies only to the meaning immediately following:

address *vt* **1** to put a name and address on (an envelope *etc*). **2** (*formal*) to speak or write to. – *nc* **1** the name of the house, street, town *etc* where a person lives. **2** (*formal*) a speech.

This indicates that only the second meaning of the verb **address** and the second meaning of the noun **address** are formal.

If there is a label after one of the numbers in a definition and there is also a label which comes before the whole numbering sequence then both labels apply to the definition so labelled:

superficial *adj* (*formal*) **1** on, or affecting, the surface only. **2** (*sometimes derog*) not thorough. **3** (*derog*) (of a person) incapable of deep thought or feeling.

This indicates that all the meanings of **superficial** are formal, that the second meaning is always formal and sometimes derogatory, and that the third meaning is always both formal and derogatory.

Of course, where there is no numbering sequence it is obvious that the label applies to the word or part of speech labelled, *eg* **fragrant** (*formal*) having a sweet smell.

Where more than one label is given within the same bracket all labels apply, *eg* **supercilious** (*formal derog*) contemptuous or disdainful. This indicates that **supercilious** is both formal and derogatory.

Definitions

After the headword or derivative, pronunciation and part of speech comes the definition, which gives the meaning of the word or phrase in simple words and is in roman (ordinary) type.

Some words, *eg* **obvious**, have only one meaning but many have more than one meaning, *eg* **again** *adv* **1** once more or another time. **2** as in a previous condition, situation *etc*. **3** in addition. **4** on the other hand. It will be seen from this example that individual meanings are numbered in bold **1**, **2**, **3**, **4** *etc*. The meanings are arranged as far as possible in order of frequency, *ie* with the most common meaning coming first and the least common last.

Sometimes two meanings have been put together in one definition by the use of brackets, *eg* **move 1** *vti* to (cause to) change position or go from one place to another; **movement 1** *ncu* (an act of) changing position or going from one point to another.

Some words, *eg* **open**, can be more than one part of speech. In such cases the most common part of speech with its definition is given first, followed by other parts of speech with their definitions. The parts of speech (with their numbered definitions) are separated from each other by a dash (–), *eg* **open** *adj* **1** allowing things or people to go, or be taken or put, through, in or out; not shut. **2** allowing the inside to be seen. **3** ready for business; able to be used. **4** which can be entered, seen *etc* by anyone. **5** (of cloth *etc*) with (wide) spaces between the threads . . . *etc.* – *vti* **1** to make or become open. **2** to begin. **3** to start, begin business *etc.*

Examples of usage

Very often after a definition, and separated from it by a colon (:), you will find a sentence or phrase (or several of them) in italics showing how the word which has just been defined is commonly used. Where more than one example of a particular meaning of a word has been given, the examples are separated from each other by a semi-colon (;), *eg* **now** *adv* **1** (at) the present time: *I am living in England now*; *Now would be a good time to go to France.* **2** . . .
We have given a large number of examples in this dictionary since it is extremely important that learners of English should learn how words are used as well as how they are pronounced and what they mean.

Where an example of usage, for some reason, requires further explanation than that provided by the basic definition, a short explanatory phrase has been given in roman (ordinary) type in brackets preceded by the symbol (=) meaning 'is equal to': *eg* under **ability** *to the best of my ability* (= as well as I can); under **ovation** *They gave the president a standing ovation* (= They stood and applauded him).

Other information

At the end of some entries you will find that your attention has been directed to other entries by means of cross-references, in some cases to words which are the negative or opposite of the headword or of one of its derivatives, *eg* **accurate** . . . *See also* **inaccurate**, in other cases to words which are connected with the headword in some way, *eg* to words which are part of its word-family, *eg* **ability** . . . *See also* **disable**, **inability**, **unable**.

Pronunciation

The pronunciation of every headword and of many other words has been given in square brackets immediately after the word.

The variety of English pronunciation that has been used as a model in this dictionary is that which is commonly known as **Received Pronunciation** or **RP**. The symbols used for the transcriptions are those of the alphabet of the International Phonetic Association (IPA); they are explained in the table below. The particular style of transcription used in this dictionary is that which is known as the 'simplified' or 'extra-broad' IPA transcription of English, devised by Daniel Jones and recommended by him for use in teaching English to foreign learners.

Pronunciation key

symbol	example	
a	[bag]	**bag**
aː	[baːθ]	**bath**
e	[hed]	**head**
i	[milk]	**milk**
iː	[fiːl]	**feel**
o	[boks]	**box**
oː	[hoːl]	**hall**
u	[fut]	**foot**
uː	[bluː]	**blue**
ʌ	[lʌv]	**love**
ə	[ˈribən]	**ribbon**
əː	[fəːst]	**first**
ã	[avãˈgaːd]	**avant-garde**
ẽ	[pẽsˈnei]	**pince-nez**
õ	[reizõˈdetr]	**raison d'être**

Note The symbols ã, ẽ and õ are used for the vowels of the French words **blanc**, **vin** and **bon** respectively.

symbol	example	
ai	[fain]	**fine**
au	[laud]	**loud**
ei	[pein]	**pain**
eə	[heə]	**hair**
iə	[hiə]	**here**
oi	[dʒoin]	**join**
ou	[gou]	**go**
uə	[puə]	**poor**
p	[peidʒ]	**page**
b	[boːl]	**ball**
t	[ˈteibl]	**table**
d	[dog]	**dog**
k	[kik]	**kick**

g	[get]	**get**
m	[mad]	**mad**
n	[neim]	**name**
ŋ	[baŋ]	**bang**
l	[leik]	**lake**
r	[reis]	**race**
f	[fi:t]	**feet**
v	[vois]	**voice**
θ	[θiŋ]	**thing**
ð	[ðou]	**though**
s	[seif]	**safe**
z	[zu:]	**zoo**
ʃ	[ʃip]	**ship**
ʒ	['meʒə]	**measure**
h	[ha:f]	**half**
w	[weit]	**wait**
j	[jʌŋ]	**young**
x	[lox]	**loch**
tʃ	[tʃi:z]	**cheese**
dʒ	['dʒakit]	**jacket**

The pronunciation of every headword is indicated by a phonetic transcription immediately after the word.

The pronunciation of derivatives, whether defined or undefined, generally follows the pattern of the headword, and in such cases no transcription is given for the derivatives. Consider the following examples:

ornate [o:'neit] *adj* with a lot of ornament . . . **or'nately** *adv.* **or'nateness** *nu.*
(This means that **ornately** is to be pronounced [o:'neitli], and **ornateness** [o:'neitnis].)

partner ['pa:tnə] *nc* **1** a person who shares the ownership of . . .
'partnership 1 *ncu* the state of being or becoming partners . . .
(This means that **partnership** is to be pronounced ['pa:tnəʃip].)

Where there is a change of pronunciation, *eg* in cases where a vowel in a headword is unstressed but the corresponding vowel in a derivative is stressed, the change in pronunciation is indicated by a transcription of all or part of the derivative, as can be seen in the following examples:

angel ['eindʒəl] *nc* **1** a messenger or attendant of God . . .
angelic [an'dʒelik] *adj* like an angel . . .

partial ['pa:ʃəl] *adj* **1** not complete . . .
ˌparti'ality [-ʃi'aləti] *nu* **1** a liking for . . .
(It is to be understood that the part of the derivative which is not transcribed is to be pronounced in the same way as the corresponding part of the headword: thus **partiality** is to be pronounced [pa:ʃi'aləti].)

There are three exceptions to these rules:

(i) Where a derivative has a different stress pattern from that of the headword, but this change in stress pattern does not cause any other change in the pronunciation of the word, no transcription is given for the derivative, as in the following example:

anecdote ['anikdout] *nc* a short, interesting or amusing story . . .
ˌanec'dotal *adj* like, of, or full of, anecdotes . . .
(From this, it can be assumed that **anecdotal** is to be pronounced [anik'doutl].)

Note For an explanation of the use of stress marks to indicate the pronunciation of vowels, see the section on Stress below.

(ii) Where a derivative has a different stress pattern from that of the headword, with an unstressed 'weak' vowel in the derivative corresponding to a stressed vowel in the headword, the pronunciation of the unstressed vowel is predictable, and therefore no transcription is given to indicate the change, as in the examples which follow:

acid ['asid] *adj* sharp or sour . . .
a'cidity *nu* the quality of containing acid . . .
(**Acidity** is to be pronounced [ə'sidəti], but no transcription is given to indicate the change from ['a-] to [ə-], as this is entirely predictable following the rules of English pronunciation.)

prophecy ['profəsi] **1** *nu* the power of foretelling the future . . .
pro'phetic [-'fe-] *adj* of or concerning prophecy . . .
(**Prophetic** is to be pronounced [prə'fetik], but again the change from ['pro-] to [prə-] is not indicated because it is predictable from the change in stress pattern.)

rhetoric ['retərik] *nu* **1** the art of speaking . . .
rhe'torical [-'to-] *adj.*
(The word **rhetorical** is to be pronounced [ri'torikəl]: again the change from ['re-] to [ri-] is predictable from the change in stress pattern.)

The commonest correspondences between vowels in stressed syllables and 'weak' vowels in unstressed syllables can be summarized as follows:
in a position corresponding to stressed [a, aː, o, oː, ʌ, əː, ei, ou], one usually finds unstressed [ə];
in a position corresponding to stressed [e, i, iː], one usually finds unstressed [i];
in a position corresponding to stressed [uː], one often finds unstressed [u].

(iii) Undefined words which are derivatives of words which are themselves derivatives can be assumed to follow the pronunciation pattern of the word from which they are derived rather than the pronunciation of the headword, and so their pronunciation has not been indicated by a transcription:

prophecy ['profəsi] **1** *nu* the power of foretelling the future . . .
pro'phetic [-'fe-] *adj* of or concerning prophecy . . . **pro'phetically** *adv.*
(Thus **prophetically** is to be pronounced [prə'fetikəli], following the pattern of **prophetic** not the pattern of the headword **prophecy**.)

In the case of compounds, the elements which together make up the compound are generally to be pronounced in the same way as they would be if they were independent words, *eg* **home** = [houm], **work** = [wəːk], **homework** = ['houmwəːk].
However, in the case of the combining elements **-body**, **-land**, **-man**, and **-men**, it is to be assumed that they have [ə] as their vowel when unstressed unless otherwise shown in a transcription. Thus we have **everybody**, **Highland**, **fireman** (= [-bədi], [-lənd], [-mən]) but **bogeyman** [-man], **bogeymen** [-men], **busybody** [-bodi] and **overland** [-land].

Note See Appendix 9 for the pronunciation of many common suffixes and combining elements.

Stress

A stress mark denoting primary stress (') is placed just before that syllable in each word which is pronounced with greatest force or stress; this symbol is used both in the bold words and inside the square brackets, *eg* **abate** [ə'beit]; **a'batement**.
A stress mark denoting secondary stress (ˌ) is placed just before that syllable (if any) in a word

which is pronounced with a certain degree of stress, but with less than primary stress. This symbol is only used on the words in bold, *eg* **ˌabdiˈcation**, since one of the functions of the secondary stress mark is to indicate that a particular syllable in a derivative has a certain degree of stress and that the vowel of that syllable should be the same as the corresponding stressed vowel of the headword rather than being replaced by an unstressed 'weak' vowel. Where the pronunciations of derivatives are indicated by transcriptions, such information is not necessary, and it will moreover be obvious from the vowel symbols in the transcriptions which syllables have secondary stress since these syllables will contain the 'full' vowels of stressed syllables rather than the unstressed 'weak' vowels listed above. Consider the following examples:

providence [ˈprovidəns] *ncu* (an event showing) God's care for all creatures . . .
  ˌproviˈdential [-ˈdenʃəl] *adj* fortunate . . .
(This means that **ˌproviˈdential** is to be pronounced [proviˈdenʃəl]; without the secondary stress, this would be [prəviˈdenʃəl].)

aspire [əˈspaiə] *vi* to try very hard to reach . . .
  ˌaspiˈration [aspi-] *nc* an ambition . . .
(This means that **aspiration** is to be pronounced [aspiˈreiʃən], not [əspiˈreiʃən]; although the secondary stress on the first syllable is clear from the presence of [a] rather than [ə] in the transcription, it is also marked on the bold word along with the primary stress to show the full stress pattern of the word.)

anonymous [əˈnoniməs] *adj* without the name of the author . . .
  anonymity [anəˈniməti] *nu* the state of not making one's name known . . .
(That the first syllable has secondary stress is clear from the presence of the vowel [a] rather than [ə] in the pronunciation, and therefore secondary stress is not marked on the bold word.)

Primary (and sometimes also secondary) stress is also indicated in certain other cases:

(i) on two-word, unhyphenated compounds, when the stress pattern is not the normal one of secondary on the first element followed by primary on the second element (*eg* **false alarm** [ˌfoːlsəˈlaːm]). Therefore, stress is indicated on *eg* **ˈfairy light**, **ˈluncheon voucher**, and (at **eˈstate-car**) **ˈstation wagon**. The same principle applies to the marking of stress on phrasal verbs, which have the same 'normal' pattern of secondary stress on the first element followed by primary stress on the second element; therefore, stress is not usually shown on verbs such as **fall apart** [ˌfoːləˈpaːt], **fall away** [ˌfoːləˈwei], *etc* which have this stress pattern, but is shown on verbs such as **ˈfall for** and **ˈfall on/upon** which do not have it. (Note that in the case of phrasal verbs comprising more than one particle, the primary stress is generally on the first particle, as in **go ˈback on, put ˈup with** *etc.*)
In cases where abbreviations are given, the stress pattern of the abbreviation is again secondary followed by primary (*eg* **JP** = **ˌJˈP**) unless otherwise shown, and it can also be assumed that the pronunciation of the abbreviation is merely that of the individual letters (see Appendix 7). However, rare exceptions can be found, for example **VAT** [viːeiˈtiː, vat].

(ii) on phrases where it was felt that some clarification of the stress pattern was necessary, for example on many phrases where there is only one (primary) stress in the entire phrase, despite its containing more than one word, *eg* **by far** (not **ˈby ˈfar** or **ˌby ˈfar**), **ˈdown with** (not **ˈdown ˈwith** or **ˌdown ˈwith**), and in cases where the position of the stress(es) would be difficult for a foreign learner to predict, *eg* **ˌfar ˌbe it from ˈme, the ˈfact of the matter**.

(iii) in examples of usage given at entries marked (*in cmpds*), where the example given is not entered elsewhere in the dictionary, *eg ˌevil-ˈminded, ˌevil-ˈsmelling* (at **evil-** under **evil**), and *ˌAnglo-Aˈmerican* (at **Anglo-**). Note that in these cases, the stress pattern is given for the adjective in predicative position; when used attributively, and especially when followed by a word with primary stress on the first syllable, the stress pattern would typically change as follows:
  ˈfoul and ˌevil-ˈsmelling; an ˌevil-smelling ˈliquid.

Thus, at certain other entries, we find, for example, *an ˌeight-page ˈdocument* (at **eight-** under **eight**) and *a ˌfour-sided ˈfigure* (at **-sided** under **side**).

(iv) exceptionally, where stress changes with meaning, as is the case with **fag-end** (definition 1 = *ˈfag-end*; definition 2 = *ˌfag-ˈend*).

American pronunciation

There are many differences between Received Pronunciation and the particular variety of American English pronunciation (referred to after this as **Amer**) with which it has been compared in this dictionary, and a number of these differences have been indicated in the text. However, certain patterns of difference are more easily stated as general rules which the user can himself apply, and these are indicated below:

[r] **Amer** pronounces those **r**'s which **RP** generally does not, for example in word-final position, *eg* **acquire** [(*Amer*) əˈkwaiər], or before a consonant, *eg* **absorb** [(*Amer*) əbˈzo:rb].

[a:] **Amer** tends to pronounce the vowel symbolized [a:] in **RP**, except before [r], as a sound similar to **RP** [a], *eg* **advance** [(*Amer*) ədˈvans].

[o] **Amer** pronounces the vowel symbolized [o] in **RP** as a sound similar to **RP** [a:] in many cases, *eg* **got** [(*Amer*) ga:t], but in some cases, mostly where **RP** [o] is followed by [f, θ, s, r, g, ŋ], as a sound similar to **RP** [o:], *eg* **dog** [(*Amer*) do:g], **coffee** [(*Amer*) ˈko:fi].

[ju:] After the sounds [t, d, n, l, s], **Amer** has [u:] where **RP** has [ju:], *eg* **tune** [(*Amer*) tu:n], **new** [(*Amer*) nu:]. (In **RP**, [u:] is more common than [ju:] after [l]).

[əri] **Amer** gives greater stress than **RP** does to endings in **-ary** and **-ory**, and often also **-ery**. This *usu* gives rise to pronunciations which are slightly different from **RP**, *eg* **monetary** [(*Amer*) -teri], **confectionery** [(*Amer*) -neri], **obligatory** [(*Amer*) -to:ri].

[ail] **Amer** pronounces the endings of the majority of **-ile** words [-əl] as opposed to **RP**'s [-ail], as in, for example, **fragile** [(*Amer*) -dʒəl], **hostile** [(*Amer*) -təl]. In some cases, *eg* **infantile** and **juvenile**, [-ail] is most frequent in **Amer** also, with [-əl] occurring less frequently; and certain words, *eg* **gentile**, are always pronounced [-ail] in both **Amer** and **RP**. An exception to all these patterns, however, is **mercantile** [(*Amer*) -ti:l].

[i] Where **RP** has [i] in final position, **Amer** has [i:], *eg* **happy** [(*Amer*) ˈhapi:].

Labels and Abbreviations used in Dictionary

abbrev	abbreviation
adj	adjective
adv	adverb
Amer	American
approx	approximately
arch	archaic
attrib	attributive, attributively
aux	auxiliary
biol	biology
bot	botany
Brit	British
chem	chemistry
chess	—
cmpds	compounds
compar	comparative
conj	conjunction
dated sl	dated slang
def	definition
derog	derogatory
dial	dialectal
drama	—
E	East
econ	economics
eg	for example
esp	especially
etc	*et cetera*, and so on
euph	euphemistic
facet	facetious
fem	feminine
fig	figurative
formal	—
Fr	French
geog	geography
geol	geology
geom	geometry
gram	grammar
hist	historical
ie	that is
imper	imperative
in cmpds	in compounds
inf	informal
infin	infinitive
interj	interjection
ironic	—
L	Latin
legal	—
liter	literary
masc	masculine
math	mathematics
med	medical
mil	military
modal aux	modal auxiliary
music	—
myth	mythology
n	noun
N	North
naut	nautical
nc	noun countable
ncs	nouns countable
ncu	noun countable and uncountable
ncus	nouns countable and uncountable
neg	negative
no cap	no capital
no pl	no plural
n pl	noun plural
ns	nouns
n sing	noun singular
nu	noun uncountable
nus	nouns uncountable
offensive	—
old	—
orig	originally
passive	—
pers	person
pfx	prefix
philos	philosophy
phot	photography
phys	physics
pl	plural
polit	politics
pred	predicative
prep	preposition
pron	pronoun
prp	present participle
prt	present tense
psych	psychology
pt	past tense
ptp	past participle
®	registered trademark
rare	—
relative pron	relative pronoun
relig	religion
S	South
S Africa	South Africa
Scottish	—
sl	slang
superl	superlative
tech	technical
US	United States (of America)
usu	usually
v	verb
vi	verb intransitive
v refl	reflexive verb
vt	verb transitive
vt fus	verb transitive fused
vti	verb transitive and intransitive
vt oblig sep	verb transitive obligatorily separated
vt sep	verb transitive separable
vt usu sep	verb transitive usually separated
vulg	vulgar
W	West
with cap	with capital

Aa

a, an [ə(n)] *adj* (indefinite article. The form **a** is used before words beginning with a consonant *eg* *a boy*, or consonant sound *eg a union*; the form **an** is used before words beginning with a vowel *eg an owl*, or vowel sound *eg an honour*.) **1** one: *There is a boy in the garden*; *I'd like a (glass of) beer*; *Is he a friend of yours?* (= one of your friends); *I've just won a hundred pounds* (= £100); *He'll be here in half an hour*; *It took me an hour and a half to get there.* **2** any; every: *An owl can see in the dark*; *A dog has four legs.* **3** used in certain expressions referring to one person, thing *etc*: *He's such a nice man*; *What a lovely day it has been!*; *How big a town is Glasgow?* (= How big is Glasgow?). **4** used in certain phrases denoting quantities *etc*: *a few books*; *a lot of money*: *I need a little more time*; *I only have a few.* **5** for each; per: *These shoes are £10 a pair*; *We earn £2 an hour.* **6** used with certain nouns which refer to an action or a state: *I must have a wash*; *He has a good knowledge of French.* **7** (used *esp* with people's names) one particular; a certain: *There's a Mr Brown outside who would like to speak to you.*

A-Z/A to Z [eitə'zed] *nc* a small book of information in alphabetical order, *esp* a guide to the streets of a town or city.

A1 [ei'wʌn] *adj* (*inf*: *usu pred*) of the highest quality; very good: *This material is A1.*

aback [ə'bak] : **taken aback** surprised and *usu* rather upset: *She was taken aback by his rudeness.*

abandon [ə'bandən] **1** *vt* to leave, not intending to return to: *She abandoned the child*; *They abandoned the stolen car*; (*fig*) *He abandoned the whole idea.* **2** *v refl* (*liter or formal*) to give (oneself) completely to: *He abandoned himself to despair.* – *nu* (*formal*) uncontrolled freedom of action: *He danced with gay abandon.*

a'bandoned *adj* **1** (*formal*: *usu attrib*) immoral; shameless: *an abandoned young woman.* **2** (*attrib*) having been left without any intention of returning to or reclaiming: *The police found the abandoned car.*

abase [ə'beis] *vt* (*usu refl*: *liter*) to make (oneself) humble: *He abased himself in the presence of the emperor.* **a'basement** *nu.*

abashed [ə'baʃt] *adj* (*usu pred*: *neg* **un-**) embarrassed: *He was rather abashed at all the compliments he received.*

abate [ə'beit] *vi* (*formal*) to become less: *The noise/storm gradually abated.*

a'batement *nu* (*formal*) making or becoming less: *the abatement of the storm.*

abattoir ['abətwaː, (*Amer*) abə'twaːr] *nc* (*formal*) a place where animals are killed for food; a slaughterhouse.

abbess *see* **abbot**.

abbey ['abi] *nc* **1** the building(s) in which a Christian (*usu* Roman Catholic) group of monks or nuns lives. **2** the church now or formerly belonging to it: *Westminster Abbey.*

abbot ['abət] – *fem* **abbess** ['abes] – *nc* the male head of an abbey (*def 1*).

abbreviate [ə'briːvieit] *vt* (*formal*) to shorten (a word, phrase *etc*): *Frederick is often abbreviated to Fred.*

ab,brevi'ation **1** *nc* a shortened form of a word *etc*: *Maths is an abbreviation of mathematics.* **2** *nu* (*formal*) the act of shortening (a word *etc*): *He was annoyed by the abbreviation of his name to Fred.*

ABC [eibiː'siː] **1** *nu* the alphabet: *The child has not learnt his ABC.* **2** *nu* the simplest and most basic knowledge: *the ABC of engineering.* **3** *nc* a table of information *etc* arranged alphabetically, *esp* a railway timetable.

abdicate ['abdikeit] **1** *vti* to leave or give up the position and authority of a king or queen: *The king abdicated (the throne) in favour of his son.* **2** *vt* (*formal*) to leave or give up (responsibility, power *etc*): *He abdicated all responsibility for the work to his elder son.* **,abdi'cation** *ncu.*

abdomen ['abdəmən] *nc* (*tech*) the part of the body between the hips and the lower ribs.

ab'dominal [-'do-] *adj* (*tech*: *esp attrib*): *an abdominal operation*; *severe abdominal pain.*

abduct [əb'dʌkt] *vt* (*formal*) to take (someone) away against his will *usu* by trickery or violence; to kidnap: *The president has been abducted.* **ab'duction** [-ʃən] *ncu.*

aberration [abə'reiʃən] *ncu* (*formal*) a departure from, or variation of, the correct or usual way of thinking or behaving: *He had a mental aberration*; *These printing errors were caused by the computer's aberrations.*

abet [ə'bet] – *pt, ptp* **a'betted** – *vt* (*esp legal*) to help or encourage (someone) to do something wrong: *He abetted his cousin in robbing the bank.*

aid and abet *see* **aid**.

abeyance [ə'beiəns] : **in a'beyance** (*formal*) left undecided *usu* for a short time: *The matter was left in abeyance*; *The office of president was in abeyance for several months.*

abhor [əb'hoː] – *pt, ptp* **ab'horred** – *vt* (*formal*: not used with **is, was** *etc* and **-ing**) to look on, or think of, with horror; to hate very much: *The headmaster abhors violence.*

ab'horrence [-'ho-] *nu* (*formal*): *He has an abhorrence of violence.*

ab'horrent [-'ho-] *adj* (*formal*: *usu pred with* **to**) hateful: *Fighting was abhorrent to him.*

abide [ə'baid] – *pt, ptp* **abode** [ə'boud] (*def 2*) – **1** *vt* (*in neg with* **could, can**) to put up with; to tolerate: *I can't abide noisy people.* **2** *vi* (*liter*) to live: *She abode by a lake.*

a'biding *adj* (*formal*: *attrib*) lasting; continuing: *an abiding love.*

a'bide by *vt fus* – *pt, ptp* **a'bided** (*formal*) to act according to; to be faithful to: *They must abide by the rules of the game*; *You must abide by your decision.*

ability [ə'biləti] **1** *nu* the power, knowledge *etc* to do something: *She doesn't have the ability to do the job properly*; *I shall do the job to the best of my ability* (= as well as I can). **2** *nc* a skill: *a man of many abilities.*

See also **disable, inability, unable**.

abject ['abdʒekt] *adj* (*attrib*) miserable; wretched: *The widow lives in abject poverty*; *an abject apology.* **'abjectly** *adv.*

abjure [əb'dʒuə] *vt* (*liter*) to swear to give up; to swear to leave for ever: *The nun abjured worldly pleasures.*

ablaze [ə'bleiz] *adj* (*pred*) **1** burning strongly: *The building was ablaze when the fire brigade arrived.* **2** (*fig*) very bright: *The street was ablaze with lights.*

able ['eibl] *adj* **1** (*pred*) having enough strength, knowledge *etc* to do something: *He was able to open the door*; *He was able to answer the question*; *He was able to speak French*; *He will come if he is able.* **2** clever and skilful; capable: *a very able nurse*; *He is the most able of our pupils*; *The lawyer put forward an able defence of his client.* **'ably** *adv.* *See also* **ability, unable**.

ablutions [ə'blu:ʃənz] *n pl* (*formal or facet*) the washing of the body: *He's performing his ablutions.*

abnormal [ab'no:məl] *adj* not normal: *His behaviour is abnormal for a child of his age*; *an abnormal reaction.* **ˌabnor'mality** [-'ma-] *ncu.*
ab'normally *adv*: *It is abnormally cold for this time of year.*

aboard [ə'bo:d] *adv, prep* on (to) or in(to) (a means of transport): *We were aboard for several hours*; *He went aboard the ship/train/aircraft.*

abode [ə'boud] *nc* (*liter or facet*) a house or the place where someone lives: *the abode of kings*; *Come to my humble abode.* – *v see* **abide**.

abolish [ə'boliʃ] *vt* to put an end to (a custom, law *etc*): *We must abolish the death penalty.*
ˌabo'lition [a-] *nu* the act of abolishing, *esp* (*hist*) slavery.
ˌabo'litionist [a-] *nc* a person who tries to abolish something, *esp* (*hist*) slavery: *William Wilberforce was one of the great abolitionists of the nineteenth century.*

A-bomb ['eibom] *nc* an atomic bomb.

abominable [ə'bominəbl] *adj* very bad; terrible: *That's an abominable way to treat your own son*; *What abominable weather*; *I found his treatment of his mother abominable.* **a'bominably** *adv.*

abominate [ə'bomineit] *vt* (*formal*) to hate very much; to detest: *He abominates cruelty.* **ˌabomi'nation** *ncu.*

aborigine [abə'ridʒini] *nc* an original inhabitant of a country, *esp* of Australia. **ˌabo'riginal** *adj.*

abort [ə'bo:t] **1** *vti* (*often tech*) to lose or bring about the loss of (an unborn child) from the womb: *The doctors decided to abort the foetus because it was deformed*; *The doctor aborted her when she was three months pregnant*; *She aborted when she was four months pregnant.* **2** *vti* (of a plan *etc*) to (cause to) come to nothing or become useless. **3** *vt* to stop or abandon (a space mission, *eg* the firing of a rocket) before it is completed.
a'bortion [-ʃən] **1** *ncu* the stopping of the development of an unborn child: *The girl wanted (to have) an abortion*; *Abortion is against some people's principles.* **2** *nc* (*formal*) something completely useless or unsuccessful: *This scheme has proved to be a complete abortion.*
a'bortive [-tiv] *adj* unsuccessful: *They made an abortive attempt to climb the mountain*; *All government attempts to prevent the strike were abortive.*

abound [ə'baund] *vi* (*formal*) **1** (*with* **in**) to have plenty of: *The east coast abounds in good farming land.* **2** to be very plentiful: *Sheep abound on these hills*; *Fish abound in these waters.*
See also **abundance**.

about [ə'baut] **1** *prep* on the subject of: *a story about a boy*; *We talked about our plans*; *What's the book about?* **2** *prep, adv* (*sometimes* **round about**) near (in place, time, size *etc*): *He lives about five miles away*; *It happened about five years ago*; *He arrived (round) about six o'clock*; *The box is just about big enough*; *somewhere round about Glasgow.* **3** *prep, adv* in different directions; here and there; to many places: *The children ran about (the garden) happily*; *Do stop rushing about.* **4** *prep, adv* in or on some part (of a place *etc*): (*inf*) *Is there any food about the place?*; *There were several people sitting about the room*; (*inf*) *You'll find him somewhere about*; *You must try to enter when there is no-one about.* **5** *prep, adv* around or surrounding: *She wore a coat about her shoulders*; *Trees grew about the house*; *He lay asleep with his clothes scattered about.* **6** *adv* (in military commands *etc*) in the opposite direction: *About turn!*
be a'bout to to be going to (perform an action): *He is (just) about to answer the question*; *I am about to leave the office.*
bring about *see* **bring**.
come about *see* **come**.
go about *see* **go**.
month, week *etc* **about** every alternate month, week *etc*: *I go to Manchester and Birmingham week about* (= One week I go to Manchester and one week I go to Birmingham).

above [ə'bʌv] *prep* **1** in a higher position than: *There is a picture above the fireplace*; *He lives in a flat above his shop*; (*fig*) *He puts her happiness above everything else.* **2** greater than: *The child's intelligence is above average.* **3** too good for: *She is above doing something like that*; *The police must be above suspicion*; *You must not be above asking for help.* – *adv* **1** higher up: *seen from above.* **2** (in a book *etc*) earlier or higher up on the page: *See above.*
aˌbove-'board *adj* (*pred*) open and honourable; not secret: *We must keep the whole affair above-board*; *I think it is all above-board.*
above all most importantly: *He is strong, brave and, above all, honest.*
above a person's head *see* **head**.
be, get (a bit) a'bove oneself to have or acquire too high an opinion of oneself; to be or become very conceited: *She's got a bit above herself since she went to live in that district.*

abrasion [ə'breiʒən] *nc* (*formal*) an injury caused by scraping or grazing the skin: *He was suffering from minor abrasions after the accident.*
a'brasive [-siv] *adj* **1** (*usu attrib*: *formal or tech*) tending to make surfaces rough when rubbed on to them: *An abrasive material is unsuitable for cleaning baths.* **2** (*formal*) (of people, their actions *etc*) extremely annoying and irritating: *I find his manner of speaking abrasive*; *an abrasive manner.* – *nc* something used for scraping or rubbing a surface: *Sandpaper is an abrasive*; *He used an abrasive to remove the rust from his car.*

abreast [ə'brest] *adv* side by side: *They walked along the road three abreast.*
keep abreast of to remain up to date with: *keeping abreast of recent scientific developments.*

abridge [ə'bridʒ] *vt* (*formal*) to make (*esp* a book) shorter.
a'bridged *adj* shortened: *an abridged version of his novel.* **a'bridg(e)ment** *ncu* (*formal*).

abroad [ə'bro:d] *adv* **1** in or to another country: *He has just returned from (being) abroad*; *He lived abroad for many years.* **2** (*liter*) over a wide area: *They spread the news abroad.* **3** (*formal*) current; going around: *There's a rumour abroad that he's coming soon.* **4** (*liter*) out of doors or free: *Witches go abroad in the hours of darkness.*

abrogate ['abrəgeit] *vt* (*very formal*) to finish or put an end to (a law, custom *etc*): *The new government abrogated many laws made by the previous government.* **ˌabro'gation** *nu.*

abrupt [ə'brʌpt] *adj* **1** (*usu attrib*) sudden; unexpected: *The car came to an abrupt halt; an abrupt change of direction.* 2 (of a person's manner of speaking *etc*) rude or sharp: *She always sounds abrupt on the telephone; an abrupt manner.* **a'bruptly** *adv.* **a'bruptness** *nu.*

abscess ['abses] *nc* a painful swelling, containing pus, in a part of the body: *He has a bad abscess under that tooth.*

abscond [əb'skond] *vi* (*formal*) to go away secretly, *esp* in order to escape the law: *He absconded with the firm's money.*

absent ['absənt] *adj* 1 not present: *Johnny was absent from school with a cold; Let us drink a toast to absent friends.* 2 (*formal*) (of a look *etc*) not noticing what is happening; inattentive: *She had rather an absent look on her face.* – [əb'sent] *v refl* (*formal*) to stay away from: *He absented himself from the meeting.*

'absence 1 *nu* the condition of not being present: *His absence was noticed.* 2 *nc* a time during which a person *etc* is not present: *After an absence of five years he returned home.* 3 *nu* non-existence or lack: *the absence of noise.*

ˌabsen'tee *nc* a person who is not present, *esp* frequently (*eg* at work, school *etc*): *Absentees have a bad effect on a firm's economy;* (*attrib*) *He's an absentee landlord and very rarely visits his estate.*

ˌabsen'teeism *nu* being often absent from work *etc* without good reason: *Absenteeism is a problem in some industries.*

'absently *adv* in an absent (*def 2*) manner: *She stared absently out of the window while the teacher was talking.*

ˌabsent-'minded *adj* not noticing what is going on around one because one is thinking deeply: *an absent-minded professor; He seems very absent-minded today.* **ˌabsent-'mindedly** *adv.* **ˌabsent-'mindedness** *nu.*

absolute ['absəlu:t] *adj* 1 (*attrib*) complete: *absolute honesty; Absolute nonsense!* 2 (*formal*) not subject to the laws; without any limits: *an absolute monarch; His power was absolute.*

ˌabso'lutely *adv* completely: *I agree with you absolutely; It is absolutely impossible for me to go.*

absolute zero (*tech*) theoretically, the lowest possible temperature, *approx* −273°C.

absolution *see* **absolve**.

absolve [əb'zolv] *vt* 1 (*formal or legal*) to make free or release (from a promise, duty or blame): *The soldier was absolved from returning to his regiment; He was absolved of all blame.* 2 (*relig*) to release (from sin) and give God's forgiveness to.

absolution [absə'lu:ʃən] *nu* forgiveness, *esp* forgiveness of sins as declared by a priest: *The priest granted the man absolution after he confessed his sins.*

absorb [əb'zo:b] *vt* 1 (*formal*) to soak up: *The cloth absorbed the ink I had spilled;* (*fig*) *You must absorb as much information as possible.* 2 (*often in passive*) to take up the whole attention of (a person): *He was completely absorbed in his book; His work absorbed all his energies.*

ab'sorbent *adj* (*formal*) able to soak up: *Absorbent paper is useful in the kitchen.*

ab'sorption [-'zo:p-] *nu* the act of absorbing or being absorbed: (*formal*) *the absorption of the liquid; his absorption in his book.*

abstain [əb'stein] *vi* (*often with* **from**) not to do, take *etc* (something): *He abstained (from voting in the election);* (*formal*) *He abstained from alcohol.*

ab'stainer *nc* a person who abstains.

ab'stention [-'sten-] *ncu* the act of abstaining: *At the election of the new chairman the voting was six for, three against, and two abstentions;* (*formal*) *his abstention from alcohol.*

See also **abstinent**.

abstemious [əb'sti:miəs] *adj* (*formal*) taking little food, drink *etc*: *She was being very abstemious as she was trying to lose weight; an abstemious young man.* **ab'stemiously** *adv.* **ab'stemiousness** *nu.*

abstention *see* **abstain**.

abstinent ['abstinənt] *adj* (*formal*: *esp pred*) abstaining, *esp* from alcoholic drink: *Since his car crash he has been completely abstinent.* **'abstinence** *nu.*

See also **abstain**.

abstract ['abstrakt] *adj* 1 (of a noun) referring to something which exists as an idea and which is not physically real: *Truth, poverty and bravery are abstract nouns; Truth is abstract.* 2 (of painting, sculpture *etc*) concerned with colour, shape, texture *etc* rather than showing things as they really appear: *an abstract sketch of a vase of flowers; Modern art is often rather abstract.* 3 (*formal*) concerned with ideas and theory rather than actual examples: *an abstract argument; His reasoning seems very abstract.* – *nc* 1 an abstract painting, sculpture *etc*: *He always paints abstracts.* 2 (*formal*) a summary (of a book, article *etc*): *Could I have an abstract of your article on industrial diseases?* – [ab'strakt] *vt* (*formal*) to take out or away: *It's possible to abstract several good points from this discussion.*

ab'stracted *adj* (*formal or liter*) occupied in thought: *an abstracted gaze; she seemed abstracted.*

ab'stractedly *adv.*

ab'straction [-ʃən] (*formal*) 1 *nu* the act of abstracting: *the abstraction of the information from his report.* 2 *nu* the state of being occupied in thought: *He pretended to be listening to me but his abstraction was obvious.* 3 *nc* an abstract quality *eg* truth, poverty, bravery *etc*: *He is too much concerned with abstractions and not with facts.*

in the 'abstract in theory and not in practice: *He always tries to deal with problems in the abstract and never thinks of the practical details.*

See also **concrete**.

abstruse [əb'stru:s] *adj* (*formal*) difficult to understand: *I find his arguments rather abstruse; abstruse reasoning.* **ab'struseness** *nu.*

absurd [əb'sə:d] *adj* unreasonable or ridiculous: *These demands are absolutely absurd; She's wearing an absurd hat.* **ab'surdly** *adv.* **ab'surdity** *ncu.* **ab'surdness** *nu.*

abundance [ə'bʌndəns] *nu* (*formal*) a large amount: *an abundance of food; There was food in abundance at the party.*

a'bundant *adj* (*usu attrib*) plentiful: *an abundant supply of food; abundant proof.*

a'bundantly *adv* to a great extent; very: *abundantly clear.*

abuse [ə'bju:z] *vt* 1 (*formal*) to use wrongly, *usu* with harmful results: *She abused her privileges by taking too long a holiday.* 2 (*esp old*) to insult or speak roughly to someone: *She abused the servants.* – [ə'bju:s] 1 *nu* insulting language: *He shouted a stream of abuse at her.* 2 *ncu* (*formal*) the wrong use of something: *This toy has been subjected to a lot of abuse.*

a'busive [-siv] *adj* using insulting language: *He wrote an abusive letter to the manager; The tone of his letter was rather abusive.* **a'busively** *adv.* **a'busiveness** *nu.*

See also **disuse, misuse**.

abut [ə'bʌt] – *pt, ptp* **a'butted** – *vi* (*formal*: *usu with* **on** (**to**)) to be joined or connected to something at one side or end: *My house abuts on (to) the cement works.*

abysmal [ə'bizməl] *adj* very great (*usu* in a bad sense); very bad: *abysmal ignorance*: *The weather is abysmal.* **a'bysmally** *adv*.

abyss [ə'bis] *nc* (*liter*) a very large and deep hole: *He fell into an abyss on Everest*; (*fig formal*) *an abyss of despair.*

academy [ə'kadəmi] *nc* **1** a higher school for special study: *Academy of Music*; *Naval Academy.* **2** a society to encourage science, art *etc*: *The Royal Academy.* **3** in Scotland, a type of senior school.

academic [akə'demik] *adj* **1** (*attrib*) of or concerning study *esp* in schools, colleges *etc*: *There is a shortage of academic jobs*; *She does not wish to work in a factory – she wants an academic career.* **2** theoretical rather than practical or useful: *That idea is only of academic interest*; *The question of whether you should emigrate is completely academic – with your qualifications you would not get a job.* – *nc* (*sometimes derog*) a university or college teacher.

ˌaca'demically [akə'de-] *adv*: *She is not academically well-qualified.*

accede [ək'siːd] : **ac'cede to** *vt fus* (*formal*) to agree to: *He acceded to my request.*

accede to the throne to become king or queen: *She acceded to the throne in 1952.*

See also **accession**.

accelerate [ək'seləreit] **1** *vi* to increase speed: *The driver accelerated* (= made his car go faster) *to pass the other car*; *The car accelerated downhill.* **2** *vt* (*formal*) to make (something) happen sooner: *The cold weather accelerated the end of the holiday season.* **acˌcele'ration** *nu*.

ac'celerator *nc* a pedal, lever *etc* that controls the speed or acceleration of a machine: *He put his foot on the accelerator.*

See also **decelerate**.

accent ['aksənt] **1** *nc* (a mark used to show) the stress on a syllable: *The accent is on the second syllable.* **2** *nc* a mark used to show the pronunciation of a letter in certain languages: *Put an accent on the e in début.* **3** *nu* (*fig*) emphasis: *The accent must be on hard work.* **4** *nc* a special way of pronouncing words in a particular area or way of life: *a Yorkshire accent*; *an educated accent.* – [ək'sent] *vt* to pronounce with stress or emphasis: *The second syllable is accented.*

accentuate [ək'sentjueit] *vt* to emphasize or make more evident: *That white dress accentuates her pale skin.* **acˌcentu'ation** *nu*.

accept [ək'sept] *vt* **1** to take (something offered): *He accepted the gift*; (*fig*) *He accepted the responsibility.* **2** to believe in or agree to: *We accept your account of what happened*; *It's accepted that we'll vote tomorrow.*

ac'ceptable *adj* (*neg* **un-**) **1** satisfactory: *The decision should be acceptable to most people*; *an acceptable compromise.* **2** pleasing: *a very acceptable gift.* **ac'ceptably** *adv*.

ac'ceptance *ncu*: *the acceptance of a gift*; *We have had few acceptances to our party invitations.*

ac'cepted *adj* generally recognized or approved: *It is an accepted fact that the world is round.*

access ['akses] **1** *nu* (*formal*) way or right of approach or entry: *We gained access to the house through a window.* **2** *nu* (*formal*) way or right to meet (someone) or use (something): *I have access to the President at any time*; *Senior students have access to the library at weekends.* **3** *nc* (*liter or old*) a sudden attack: *an access of rage.*

ac'cessible *adj* (*usu pred*) (of a person or place) able to be reached or approached easily: *His house is accessible only on foot.* **acˌcessi'bility** *nu*.

See also **inaccessible**.

accession [ək'seʃən] **1** *ncu* a coming to the position of king or queen: *in the year of the Queen's accession (to the throne).* **2** *nc* (*formal*) an addition: *There are several new accessions to the books in the library.*

See also **accede**.

accessory [ək'sesəri] *nc* **1** something additional (*eg* a handbag, scarf, shoes *etc* to the main part of a woman's clothing, or a radio, seat-covers *etc* to a car): *She wore matching accessories.* **2** (*legal*) a person who helps somebody, *esp* a criminal: *His accessories escaped punishment.*

accessory before, after the fact (*legal*) a person who helps a criminal before or after the crime has been committed.

accident ['aksidənt] **1** *nc* an unexpected happening, often harmful, causing injury *etc*: *He had an accident at work*; *There has been a road accident.* **2** *nu* chance: *I met her by accident.*

ˌacci'dental [-'den-] *adj* happening by chance or accident: *Their meeting was accidental*; *an accidental omission.* – *nc* (*music*) a sharp, flat or natural not in the key-signature.

ˌacci'dentally [-'den-] *adv* by chance; by accident: *She met him accidentally*; *I accidentally left my keys in the door.*

acclaim [ə'kleim] *vt* (*formal*) **1** to applaud or welcome enthusiastically: *The footballer was acclaimed by the fans.* **2** to declare (someone) ruler, winner *etc* by enthusiastic approval: *They acclaimed him king.* – *nu* (*formal*) enthusiastic approval: *He acknowledged the acclaim of the crowd.*

acclamation [aklə'meiʃən] *nu* (*formal*) a noisy demonstration of applause, agreement, approval *etc*: *He was chosen leader by acclamation of the crowd and not by a secret ballot.*

acclimatize, -ise [ə'klaimətaiz] *vti* (*formal*) to make or become accustomed to a new climate, new surroundings *etc*: *It took him several months to become acclimatized to the heat.* **acˌclimati'zation, -s-** *nu*.

accolade ['akəleid, (*Amer*) akə'leid] *nc* (*formal*) official praise or approval: *He received the accolade of the government.*

accommodate [ə'komədeit] **1** *vti* to find or be a place for: *The house could accommodate two families.* **2** *vt* (*formal*: *with* **with**) to supply (someone) with: *The bank accommodated him with a loan of £100.* **3** *vt* (*formal*) to oblige: *They did their best to accommodate him by carrying out his wishes.* **4** *vt* (*formal*) to make suitable; to make to fit: *He tried to accommodate his way of life to hers.*

ac'commodating *adj* (*formal*) obliging; helpful: *She is a very accommodating person*; *She is always most accommodating.*

acˌcommo'dation *nu* **1** room(s) in a house or hotel in which to live, *esp* for a short time: *It is difficult to find accommodation in London in August.* **2** space for something: *There is accommodation for your car behind the hotel.*

accompany [ə'kʌmpəni] *vt* **1** (*more formal than* **go with**) to go, be or do with (someone or something): *He accompanied her to the door*; *Steak is* *often accompanied by red wine.* **2** to play a musical instrument to go along with (a singer *etc*): *He accompanied her on the piano.*

ac'companiment *ncu* something that accompanies: *She used to play the piano accompaniment to silent films.*

ac'companist *nc* a person who plays a musical accompaniment.

accomplice [ə'kʌmplis, (*Amer*) -'kom-] *nc* a person who helps another, *esp* in crime: *The thief's accomplice warned him that the police were coming.*

accomplish [ə'kʌmpliʃ, (*Amer*) -'kom-] *vt* (*formal*) to complete (something) successfully: *Have you accomplished your task?*

ac'complished *adj* skilled: *He's an accomplished singer/liar; He's very accomplished (at playing the piano).*

ac'complishment **1** *nu* (*formal*) finishing; completion: *The accomplishment of the task took several months.* **2** *nc* a special skill: *She has many different accomplishments.*

accord [ə'ko:d] (*formal*) **1** *vi* (*with* **with**) to agree with: *His story accords with what I saw happen.* **2** *vt* to grant or give to (a person): *They accorded the president great respect; We shall accord you a warm welcome.* – *nu* (*formal*) agreement: *That is not in accord with your original statement; We are completely in accord as to how we should act.* – *See also* **of one's own accord, with one accord** *below.*

ac'cordance: in ac'cordance with (*formal*) in agreement with: *The money will be given out in accordance with his instructions.*

ac'cordingly *adv* **1** in agreement (with the circumstances *etc*): *Find out what has happened and act accordingly.* **2** (*formal*) therefore: *He was very worried about the future of the firm and accordingly he did what he could to help.*

according to **1** as said or told by: *the Gospel according to St Mark; According to John, the bank closes at 3 p.m.* **2** (*formal*) in agreement with: *He acted according to his promise.* **3** in the order of: *The books are arranged according to their subjects.* **4** in proportion to: *You will be paid according to the amount of work you have done.*

of one's own accord of one's own free will: *He did it of his own accord, without being forced to.*

with one accord (*formal*) (everybody) in agreement: *With one accord they stood up to cheer him.*

accordion [ə'ko:diən] *nc* a musical instrumeent with bellows, a keyboard or set of buttons, and metal reeds.

accost [ə'kost] *vt* (*formal*) to approach and speak to, *esp* in an unfriendly or sexual way: *I was accosted in the street by four men with guns; A prostitute accosted him outside the theatre.*

account [ə'kaunt] *nc* **1** a statement of money owing: *Send me an account!* **2** (*usu in pl*) a record of money received and spent: *You must keep your accounts in order;* (*attrib*) *an account book.* **3** an arrangement by which a person keeps his money in a bank: *I have (opened) an account with the local bank; Your bank account is overdrawn* (= you owe the bank money). **4** an arrangement by which a person makes a regular (*eg* monthly) payment instead of paying at the time of buying: *I have an account at Smiths; I do all my shopping on account.* **5** a description or explanation (of something that has happened): *He gave me a full account of his holiday.*

ac'countable *adj* (*pred*) responsible: *He is accountable to me for his actions.*

ac'countancy *nu* the work of an accountant: *He is studying accountancy.*

ac'countant *nc* a keeper or inspector of (money) accounts: *He employs an accountant to deal with his income tax.*

ac'count for *vt fus* **1** to give a reason for; to explain: *I can account for the mistake.* **2** (*formal*) to settle or deal with successfully: *The army accounted for large numbers of the enemy.*

by all accounts in the opinion of most people: *By all accounts, he's an excellent golfer.*

call/bring (someone) to account to demand an explanation from (someone): *He was called to account for his ridiculous behaviour; The criminal must be brought to account.*

give a good account of oneself to do well: *He gave a good account of himself (during the match).*

on ac'count of because of: *She stayed indoors on account of the bad weather.*

on my, his *etc* **account** because of or for my, his *etc* sake: *You don't have to leave early on my account.*

on no account not for any reason: *On no account must you open that door.*

take (something) into account, take account of (something) to consider (something which is part of the problem *etc*): *We must take his illness into account when assessing his work.*

turn to (good) account to use (a situation *etc*) to one's advantage: *I'm sure I'll be able to turn this money to good account.*

See also **unaccountable**.

accredited [ə'kreditid] *adj* (*formal: with* **with** *when pred*) officially recognized: *the Queen's accredited representative; He is accredited with writing the most comprehensive work on Wordsworth.*

accrue [ə'kru:] *vi* (*formal*) **1** to come as a natural result or development (from): *Many benefits accrued from his new job.* **2** (of money) to be added: *Interest will accrue to your bank account.*

accumulate [ə'kju:mjuleit] *vti* (*more formal than* **gather**) (*usu* of things) to gather or be gathered together in a large quantity: *It's amazing how many books we've accumulated; Rubbish accumulates very quickly in our house.*

ac'cumulation **1** *nu* (*usu* of things) the act of gathering together in a large quantity: *The accumulation of money is very satisfying.* **2** *nc* a collection or large quantity: *an accumulation of rubbish.*

ac'cumulator *nc* a type of electric battery.

accurate ['akjurət] *adj* **1** exactly right: *That is an accurate drawing; All his answers were accurate.* **2** making no mistakes: *He is an accurate person; Is your watch accurate?* **'accurately** *adv.* **'accuracy** *nu.*

See also **inaccurate.**

accursed [ə'kə:sid] *adj* (*old or liter*) **1** under a curse. **2** hateful; damned.

accuse [ə'kju:z] *vt* (*with* **of**) to state (that someone has done something wrong): *They accused him of stealing the car; He was accused of murder.*

,accu'sation [a-] *ncu*: *Their accusations proved false; the accusation of an innocent man.*

the ac'cused *n sing or pl* (*legal*) the person(s) accused in a court of law: *The accused was found not guilty.*

accustom [ə'kʌstəm] *vt* (*usu refl: formal*) to make (someone) familiar with or used to: *He soon accustomed himself to the idea.*

ac'customed *adj* (*formal*: *attrib*) usual: *He took his accustomed seat.*

ac'customed to (*neg* **un-**) familiar with or used to: *I am not accustomed to being treated like that.*

ace [eis] *nc* 1 the one in playing-cards: *the ace of spades.* 2 a person who is expert at anything: *He's an ace with a rifle.* 3 a serve in tennis in which the ball is not touched by the opposing player. – *adj* (*inf*: *attrib*) expert; very good: *an ace cameraman.*

within an ace of (*fig*) very near to: *He was within an ace of success.*

acetic [ə'siːtik] : **acetic acid** *nu* the acid in vinegar.

acetylene [ə'setəliːn] *nu* a kind of gas used for giving light and heat: *a cylinder of acetylene*; (*attrib*) *acetylene welding.*

ache [eik] *nc* (*often in cmpds*) a continuous pain: *I have a headache*; *I suffer from backache*; *I have an ache in my stomach*; (*fig*) *the heartache of losing a child.* – *vi* 1 to be in continuous pain: *My tooth aches*; (*fig*) *My heart aches for her.* 2 (*often with* **for**: *inf*) to want very much: *He was aching for a cigarette*; *I was aching to tell him the good news.*

achieve [ə'tʃiːv] *vt* to gain or reach successfully: *He has achieved his ambition.*

a'chievement *ncu*: *his achievements as a sportsman*; *the achievement of his ambition.*

acid ['asid] *adj* 1 (of taste) sharp or sour: *These oranges are rather acid*; *Lemons and limes are acid fruits.* 2 sarcastic: *acid humour*; *His comments were rather acid.* – *nu* a substance, containing hydrogen, which will dissolve metals *etc*: *She spilled some acid which burned a hole in her dress*; *Vinegar contains acid.*

a'cidity *nu* the quality of containing acid or too much acid: *She suffers from acidity of the stomach.*

'acid test *nc* a test or investigation that proves or disproves the worth, value *etc* of something: *His invention seems a good idea but the acid test will be whether it actually works.*

ack'nowledge [ək'nolidʒ] *vt* 1 to admit as being fact: *He acknowledged defeat*; *He acknowledged that I was right.* 2 to say (*usu* in writing) that one has received (something): *He acknowledged the letter*; *She acknowledged receipt of the parcel.* 3 to give thanks for: *He acknowledged their help in his speech.* 4 (*formal*) to greet someone: *He acknowledged her by lifting his hat.*

acknowledg(e)ment 1 *nu* the act of acknowledging: *He was knighted in acknowledgement of his services to the company.* 2 *nc* something sent, done *etc* to acknowledge (a letter, gift, person *etc*): *I sent her a birthday gift but received no acknowledgement.*

acme ['akmi] *nc* (*formal*: *no pl*) the top or highest point: *the acme of perfection.*

acne ['akni] *nu* a common skin disease with pimples: *Acne is common among young people.*

acorn ['eikoːn] *nc* the fruit of the oak tree.

acoustic [ə'kuːstik] *adj* 1 (*esp attrib*) having to do with hearing or with sound: *This hall has acoustic problems.* 2 (*attrib*) not using electricity to produce sound: *an acoustic guitar.*

a'coustics 1 *n pl* the characteristics (*eg* of a room or hall) which make hearing in it good or bad: *The acoustics of the large hall are very bad.* 2 *n sing* the science of sound: *He is studying acoustics*; *Acoustics is his special subject.*

acquaint [ə'kweint] *vt* (*formal*) 1 to make (*usu* oneself) familiar (with): *You must acquaint yourself with the layout of the building.* 2 to inform (a person) of: *Have you acquainted her with your plans?*

acquaintance 1 *nc* a person whom one knows slightly. 2 *nu* (*formal*) (*usu* slight) knowledge: *My acquaintance with her dates from 1968*; *His acquaintance with the works of Shakespeare is slight.*

be ac'quainted with to know or be familiar with: *I'm not acquainted with her father*; *He was already acquainted with the new plans.*

make someone's acquaintance to get to know someone; to become friendly with someone: *I made her acquaintance when on holiday in France.*

acquiesce [akwi'es] *vi* (*formal*) to agree: *After a lot of persuasion, he finally acquiesced.* **acqui'escence** *nu.* **acqui'escent** *adj.*

acqui'esce in *vt fus* (*formal*) to accept: *He acquiesced in the plan.*

acquire [ə'kwaiə] *vt* (*more formal than* **get**) to get: *He acquired a knowledge of English*: *She acquired shares in the company*; *The firm has acquired a reputation for dishonesty.*

acquisition [akwi'ziʃən] (*formal*) 1 *nu* the act of acquiring: *the acquisition of more land*: *the acquisition of more teachers.* 2 *nc* something acquired: *She was proud of her acquisitions at the sale.*

acquisitive [ə'kwizətiv] *adj* (*formal*) eager to get possessions: *The magpie is an acquisitive bird.*

ac'quisitiveness *nu.*

acquit [ə'kwit] – *pt*, *ptp* **ac'quitted** – *vt* to declare (an accused person) to be innocent: *The judge acquitted her of murder*; *She was acquitted on a charge of murder.*

acquittal *ncu* (*legal*) (a) freeing from an accusation: *He was released from prison following his acquittal.*

ac'quit oneself to carry out one's task *etc*; to conduct oneself: *He acquitted himself well in the debate.*

acre ['eikə] *nc* a measure of land, 4840 square yards (4046·9 square metres).

'acreage [-ridʒ] *nu* the number of acres in a piece of land: *What is the acreage of this field?*

acrid ['akrid] *adj* harsh in smell or taste: *The acrid smell of smoke filled the room*; *The smell was acrid and unpleasant.*

acrimony ['akriməni, (*Amer*) -mouni] *nu* (*formal*) bitterness of feeling or speech.

'acrimonious [-'mou-] *adj* (*formal*): *They're having a very acrimonious dispute.*

acrobat ['akrəbat] *nc* a person in a circus *etc* who performs gymnastics. **ˌacro'batic** *adj.*

ˌacro'batics *n pl* acrobatic performances.

acronym ['akrənim] *nc* a word formed from the initial letters of other words (*eg radar* for *ra*dio *d*etecting *a*nd *r*anging).

across [ə'kros] *prep* 1 to the other side (of); from one side to the other side of: *He took her across the road*; *She ran across the field*; *They came across the room.* 2 at the other side (of): *The butcher's shop is across the street*: *She lives across the road from me.* – *adv* to the other side or to the speaker's side: *She's coming across to see me.*

across the board *see* **board**.

acrostic [ə'krostik] *nc* a poem or puzzle in which the first or last letters of each line, taken in order, spell a word or a sentence.

act [akt] 1 *vi* to do something: *It's time the government acted to lower taxes*; *The police must act quickly.* 2 *vi* to behave: *He acted foolishly at the meeting.* 3 *vti* to perform (a part) in a play: *He's acted (the part of Romeo) in many theatres*; (*fig*) *I* *thought he was dying, but he was only acting* (= pretending). – *nc* **1** something done: *Running away is an act of cowardice; He committed many cruel acts.* **2** (*often with cap*) a law: *Acts of Parliament.* **3** a section of a play: *'Hamlet' has five acts.* **4** (a group of people giving) an entertainment: *I'm in an act called 'The Smith Family'.* – *See also* **act** *in phrases below.*

acting *adj* (*attrib*) temporarily carrying out the duties of: *He is acting president of the society.*

'actor – *fem also* **'actress** – *nc* a performer in a play.

'act as *vt fus* to do the work or duties of: *He acts as head of department when his boss is away; This sofa also acts as a bed.*

ˌact for *see* **act on behalf of**.

act on/(*formal*) **upon** *vt fus* **1** to do something following the advice, instructions *etc* of someone: *I am acting on the advice of my lawyer; Have you acted on his instructions/suggestions?* **2** to have an effect on: *Certain acids act on metal.*

act on behalf of (*often legal*)/**act for** to do something for (someone else); to act as the representative of (someone): *My lawyer is acting on my behalf; He is also acting on behalf of my mother; She is acting for the headmaster in his absence.*

act up *vi* (*inf*) to behave or act badly or wrongly: *That child always acts up when his father is away; My car always acts up on a long journey; My injured leg is acting up again.*

act upon *see* **act on**.

in the 'act (of) at the exact moment (of doing something): *He was caught in the act (of stealing my car); I was in the very act of leaving when he arrived.*

put on an act to pretend: *I thought she had hurt herself but she was only putting on an act.*

action ['akʃən] **1** *ncu* something done: *Your actions were rather hasty; Action, not talking, is necessary if we are to defeat the enemy; You must take action immediately to prevent trouble; The firemen are ready to go into action as soon as they hear the alarm.* **2** *nc* a movement or gesture: *Tennis needs a good wrist action.* **3** *nc* a legal case: *He brought an action for divorce against his wife.* **4** *nu* the events (of a play, film *etc*): *The action of the play takes place on an island.* **5** *nc* the mechanism (of a watch *etc*). **6** *ncu* a battle; fighting: *He was killed in action; Our troops fought an action against the enemy.*

'actionable *adj* (*formal*) liable to be the subject of a legal case: *His insulting remarks are actionable; an actionable statement.*

'action stations 1 *n pl* positions taken up by soldiers in readiness for a battle *etc.* **2** *nu* (*fig*) a state of readiness for activity: *Action stations! The concert is about to begin!*

in 'action 1 working: *Is your machine still in action?* **2** performing *etc*: *He saw his favourite footballer in action last week.*

out of action not working: *My car's out of action this week; (inf) I'm out of action with a sore back.*

activate ['aktiveit] *vt* (*formal*) to put into force or operation: *The smoke activated the fire alarms.* **2** (*tech*) to make radioactive.

See also **reactivate**.

active ['aktiv] *adj* **1** energetic or lively; able to work *etc*: *At seventy, he's no longer very active; The volcano is no longer very active; He's a very active child.* **2** (busily) involved: *She's active in the Communist Party; She is an active supporter of women's rights.* **3** (*usu attrib*) causing an effect or effects: *Yeast is an active ingredient of bread.* **4** (*pred*) in force: *The rule banning women members is still active in some men's clubs.* **5** (*gram*) of the form of a verb in which the subject performs the action of the verb: *The dog bit the man.* **'activeness** *nu.*

'actively *adv*: *actively engaged in politics.*

ac'tivity 1 *nu* the state of being active or lively: *The streets are full of activity this morning.* **2** *nc* something which one does: *His activities include fishing and golf.*

See also **inactive, passive**.

actor, actress *see* **act**.

actual ['aktʃuəl] *adj* (*usu attrib*) real; existing; not imaginary: *In actual fact he is not as stupid as you think he is; What was the actual result of your discussion?*

ˌactu'ality [-'a-] *ncu* (a) reality: *the actuality of the situation.*

'actually *adv* **1** really: *Are you actually going now?; She actually saw the accident happen.* **2** in fact: *Actually, I'm doing something else this evening.*

actuary ['aktjuəri] *nc* a person who calculates the risks and prices of insurance. **ˌactu'arial** [-'eə-] *adj.*

actuate ['aktjueit] *vt* (*formal*: *usu in passive*) to cause (a person) to do something: *He is actuated by love of money.*

acumen ['akjumen] *nu* (*formal*) sharpness or quickness of understanding: *He is noted for his business acumen.*

acupuncture ['akjupʌŋktʃə] *nu* a method of treating illness *etc* by sticking needles into the patient's skin at certain points.

acute [ə'kjuːt] *adj* **1** (of a disease *etc*) severe but not lasting very long: *He had an acute attack of indigestion; They think his illness is acute rather than chronic.* **2** very great: *She suffered acute disappointment; There is an acute shortage of teachers; Her disappointment was acute.* **3** quick-witted or shrewd: *As a businessman, he's very acute; He made an acute observation.* **4** (of the senses) keen, good or sharp: *My hearing's very acute; acute hearing.* **a'cuteness** *nc.*

a'cutely *adv* to a great extent: *She is acutely aware of her lack of qualifications.*

acute accent *nc* a mark (´) over a vowel in some languages to show its pronunciation (*eg* **é** in French).

acute angle *nc* an angle of less than ninety degrees.

See also **chronic**.

ad [ad] (*inf*) short for **advertisement**: *I'll put an ad in the newspaper.*

adage ['adidʒ] *nc* (*formal*) a saying or proverb.

adamant ['adəmənt] *adj* (*formal*) determined or insistent: *He was adamant in his refusal; She was adamant that she had not seen him; an adamant refusal.*

Adam's apple [adəmz'apl] *nc* the part which sticks out slightly from the front of the neck in male human beings.

adapt [ə'dapt] *vti* to make suitable or to alter (so as to fit): *This paint has been specially adapted for use in dry climates; She always adapted easily to new circumstances; He has adapted the play for television.*

a'daptable *adj* (*usu pred*) (of a person or thing) willing or able to change to fit in with different circumstances: *Children are usually very adaptable.* **aˌdapta'bility** *nu.*

ˌ**adap'tation** [a-] **1** *nu* the act of adapting: *the adaptation of his play for radio.* **2** *nc* something adapted, *esp* the arrangement of a story for television, cinema *etc.*

a'daptor *nc* a device which enables an electrical plug of one type to be used in a socket of another type, or several plugs to be used in the same socket at the same time.

add [ad] **1** *vt* (*often with* **to**) to put (one thing) to or with (another): *You have only to add water; He added water to his whisky; Have you added in the cost of transport?* **2** *vti* (*math*: *often with* **to, together, up**) to find the total of (various numbers): *He can't add properly; Add these figures together; Add 124 to 356; He added up the column of figures.* **3** *vt* to say something extra: *He explained, and added that he was sorry.* **4** *vi* (*with* **to**) to increase: *The news added to our happiness; They have added to their family; His illness had added to their difficulties.*

addendum [ə'dendəm] – *pl* **ad'denda** [-də] – *nc* (*formal*) something added, *esp* to a book, statement *etc.*

ad'dition 1 *nu* the act of adding: *The child is not good at addition; Have you checked the addition of the bill?* **2** *nc* something added: *They've had an addition to the family.*

ad'ditional *adj*: *This has meant additional work for me.*

'additive [-tiv] *nc* (*formal*) a substance which is added, *esp* to food: *Certain additives are harmful.*

add up *vi* (*inf*) to seem sensible or logical: *I don't understand his behaviour – it just doesn't add up.* – *See also* **add** (*def 2*).

adder ['adə] *nc* the only type of poisonous snake found wild in Britain.

addict ['adikt] *nc* a person who has become dependent on something, *esp* drugs: *a drug addict*; (*loosely*) *a television addict.*

ad'dicted *adj* (*pred*: *often with* **to**) **1** dependent on (*esp* a drug): *He is addicted to heroin; She can't give up alcohol – she's addicted.* **2** (*loosely*) very fond of: *He's addicted to ice-cream.* **ad'diction** [-ʃən] *nc.*

addition, additive *see* **add**.

address [ə'dres] *vt* **1** to put a name and address on (an envelope *etc*): *Please address the parcel clearly.* **2** (*formal*) to speak or write to: *I shall address my remarks to you only.* – [(*Amer*) 'adres] *nc* **1** the name of the house, street, town *etc* where a person lives: *'What is his address?' 'His address is 30 Main St, Edinburgh.'* **2** (*formal*) a speech: *He made a long and boring address.*

'addresˌsee [ad-] *nc* (*formal*) the person to whom a letter *etc* is addressed: *I cannot read the name of the addressee.*

ad'dress oneself to (*formal or liter*) to give one's attention to (a person or action): *He addressed himself to his task with enthusiasm.*

adenoids ['adənoidz] *n pl* swollen tissue at the back of the nose: *The child has had his adenoids removed.*

'adeˌnoidal *adj* **1** of the adenoids. **2** producing a sound typical of someone with adenoids: *an adenoidal voice.*

adept [ə'dept] *adj* (*usu pred*) highly skilled: *He's very adept at keeping his balance.* – ['adept] *nc* (*formal*) an expert.

adequate ['adikwət] *adj* sufficient; enough: *He does not earn a large salary but it is adequate for his needs; He received an adequate salary.*

'adequately *adv.* **'adequacy** *nu* (*formal*). *See also* **inadequate**.

adhere [əd'hiə] *vi* (*formal*) **1** (*often with* **to**) to stick (to): *This tape doesn't adhere (to the floor) very well.* **2** (*with* **to**) to be or remain loyal (to): *I'm adhering to my principles.* **ad'herence** *nu.*

ad'herent *nc* (*formal*) a follower; supporter: *an adherent of Marx.*

adhesion [əd'hi:ʒən] *nu* the act or quality of adhering (to).

ad'hesions *n pl* (*med*) a condition in which pieces of body tissue which are normally separate stick together, or the pieces themselves: *She suffered from adhesions after the operation to remove her appendix.*

ad'hesive [-siv] *adj* (*usu attrib*) able to adhere; sticky: *adhesive tape.* – *ncu* a substance which makes things stick: *The tiles would not stick as he was using the wrong adhesive.*

ad hoc [ad'hok] *adj* (*usu attrib*) (of a committee *etc*) arranged for a particular purpose: *an ad hoc meeting of the board of directors; That was an ad hoc decision which will not necessarily apply to future cases.*

adieu [ə'dju:] – *pls* **a'dieux** [-z], **a'dieus** – *interj, nc* (*liter*) goodbye!: *He bade her adieu for ever; his last adieu.*

adjacent [ə'dʒeisənt] *adj* (*with* **to** *when pred*) lying next (to): *We had adjacent rooms in the hotel; They have bought the house adjacent to mine.*

adjective ['adʒiktiv] *nc* a word which describes a noun: *a red flower; air which is cool.* ˌ**adjec'tival** [-'tai-] *adj.*

adjoin [ə'dʒoin] *vti* (*formal*) to be next to or joined to (each other): *His house adjoins the church; Their gardens adjoin.*

adjourn [ə'dʒə:n] **1** *vti* to stop (a meeting *etc*), intending to continue it at another time or place: *We shall adjourn (the meeting) until Wednesday.* **2** *vi* (*formal*) to go to another place: *Let us adjourn to the drawing-room.* **a'djournment** *ncu.*

adjudicate [ə'dʒu:dikeit] *vti* (*formal*) to act as a judge (in an artistic competition *etc*): *He adjudicates at musical festivals throughout the country.* **aˌdjudi'cation** *ncu.* **a'djudicator** *nc.*

adjunct ['adʒʌŋkt] *nc* (*formal*) something (often less important) added: *Running a garage is only an adjunct to his main business of selling cars.*

adjust [ə'dʒʌst] (*more formal than* **change**) **1** *vti* (*often with* **to**) to change in order to become more suitable: *He soon adjusted to his new way of life.* **2** *vt* to change (the position of, setting of): *Adjust the setting of the alarm clock!; He adjusted his hat.*

a'djustable *adj* able to be adjusted: *This car has adjustable seats; The seats are adjustable.*

-adjusted (*in cmpds*) suited or adapted (to circumstances *etc*): *a very well-adjusted young man.*

a'djustment *ncu*: *Some adjustment is necessary; The adjustments made to the machine were expensive.*

adjutant ['adʒutənt] *nc* a military officer who assists a commanding officer.

ad-lib ['ad'lib] – *pt, ptp* ˌ**ad-'libbed** – *vti* to say (something), *esp* in a speech, play *etc*, that is not written or prepared: *He forgot his speech and had to ad-lib.*

ad lib *adj* not written or prepared: *an ad lib speech; His speech was entirely ad lib.* – *adv* **1** without being prepared: *He spoke ad lib for ten minutes on pollution.* **2** (*inf*) without limit; freely:

He borrows books ad lib from his friends.

administer [əd'ministə] *vt* **1** to govern or manage: *He administers the sales force and the finances of the company.* **2** to carry out (the law *etc*). **3** (*formal*) to give (medicine, help *etc*): *The doctor administered drugs to the patient; The priest administered the last rites to the dying man.*

ad'ministrate [-streit] *vti* (*formal*) to govern or manage: *Who administrates your financial affairs?*

adˌmini'stration 1 *nu* management: *He's in charge of administration at the factory; The chief judge is responsible for the administration of justice.* **2** *nc* (the people who carry on) the government of a country *etc*: *the Labour administration of 1964.*

administrative [-strətiv, (*Amer*) -streitiv] *adj*: *He holds an administrative post in the company; a great deal of administrative ability; His duties are mainly administrative.*

ad'ministrator [-strei-] *nc* a person who works in (an) administration.

admirable *see* **admire**.

admiral ['admərəl] *nc* (*with cap in titles*) in the British navy, (a person of) the rank next below Admiral of the Fleet: *He is an admiral now; Admiral McGregor.* – *See also* Appendix 3.

Admiral of the Fleet *nc* (a person of) the highest rank in the British navy. – *See also* Appendix 3.

the 'Admiralty the government office which manages the navy and its business.

admire [əd'maiə] *vt* **1** to look at with great pleasure and often to express this pleasure: *I've just been admiring your new car.* **2** to have a very high opinion of (something or someone): *I admire John's courage; She admires John for his courage.*

'admirable ['admə-] *adj* worthy of being admired; extremely good: *an admirable knowledge of antiques; His behaviour during the trouble was admirable.*

'admirably ['admə-] *adv* extremely well: *He's admirably suited to the job.*

admiration [admi'reiʃən] *nu*: *I have great admiration for her courage; They were filled with admiration at the football team's performance.*

ad'mirer *nc* **1** one who admires (someone or something): *He is an admirer of Mozart.* **2** a man who is attracted by a particular woman: *She has many admirers.*

ad'miring *adj* (*usu attrib*): *She gave him an admiring glance.* **ad'miringly** *adv.*

admission *see* **admit**.

admit [əd'mit] – *pt, ptp* **ad'mitted** – *vt* **1** (*formal*) to allow to enter: *He admitted the visitor to the drawing-room; This ticket admits one person.* **2** to say that one recognizes or accepts the truth of: *He admitted (that) he was wrong.* **3** (*formal*: *with* **of**: not used with **is, was** *etc* and **-ing**) to allow: *This admits of no other explanation.*

ad'missible [-səbl] *adj* (*formal or legal*) allowable: *Is this evidence admissible in court?; admissible evidence.*

ad'mission [-ʃən] **1** *nu* the act of admitting or being admitted: *They charge £1 for admission.* **2** *ncu* (an) act of accepting the truth of (something): *an admission of guilt.*

ad'mittance *nu* (*formal*) (the right or permission of) entrance: *This ticket gives admittance to the theatre; The burglars gained admittance through the kitchen window.*

ad'mittedly *adv* as is generally accepted: *Admittedly, she is not well.*

See also **inadmissible**.

admonish [əd'moniʃ] *vt* (*formal*) to scold or speak disapprovingly of (someone) because he has done wrong: *The judge admonished the young man for fighting in the street.* **ˌadmo'nition** [ad-] *ncu.* **ad'monitory** *adj.*

ado [ə'du:]: **without more/further ado** (*formal*) without any more fuss and bother: *He stopped talking and left without further ado.*

adolescent [adə'lesnt] *adj* in the stage between childhood and adulthood. – *nc* a person at this stage of life: *Adolescents often quarrel with their parents.*

ˌado'lescence *nu* the time between childhood and adulthood.

adopt [ə'dopt] *vt* **1** to take (a child of other parents) as one's own: *Since they had no children of their own they decided to adopt a little girl.* **2** to take (something) as one's own: *After going to France he soon adopted the French way of life; The government had had to adopt new financial policies.* **3** to choose formally (a political candidate *etc*): *He has been adopted as Liberal candidate for Manchester.*

a'doption [-ʃən] *ncu* (an act of) adopting.

a'doptive [-tiv] *adj* (*attrib*) as a result of or by adoption: *his adoptive father.*

adore [ə'do:] *vt* **1** (not used with **is, was** *etc* and **-ing**) to love or like very much: *He adores his children; She adores going to the theatre.* **2** (*relig*) to worship.

a'dorable *adj* worthy of being adored: *an adorable little baby; That puppy is adorable.* **a'dorably** *adv.*

ˌado'ration [adə-] *nu* worship or great love.

a'doring *adj* (*usu attrib*): *an adoring smile; adoring parents.* **a'doringly** *adv.*

adorn [ə'do:n] *vt* (*formal*) to make beautiful, often with decorations or ornamentation: *Their house is adorned with beautiful antique ornaments.*

a'dornment *nu* (*formal*) decoration or ornament.

adrenalin [ə'drenəlin] *nu* (*tech*: *Amer* **ˌepi'nephrine**) a hormone which stimulates the heart and raises the blood pressure: *Fear increases the amount of adrenalin in the body.*

adrift [ə'drift] *adj* (*pred*), *adv* drifting: *adrift on the open sea; (fig) adrift in London.*

adroit [ə'droit] *adj* skilful: *We admired his adroit handling of the boat; His handling of the difficult situation was most adroit.* **a'droitly** *adv.* **a'droitness** *nu.*

adulation [adju'leiʃən] *nu* (*formal*) excessive flattery: *The teenager's adulation of the pop-group worried her parents.* **'adulatory** *adj.*

adult ['adʌlt, (*esp Amer*) ə'dʌlt] *adj* **1** (*usu attrib*) fully grown: *an adult gorilla.* **2** mature or grown-up: *adult behaviour; Her behaviour was not very adult.* – *nc* **1** a fully-grown human being: *That film is suitable only for adults.* **2** a fully-grown animal, bird *etc.*

adulterate [ə'dʌltəreit] *vt* (*formal*) to make (something) impure by mixing in something else: *This expensive wine has been adulterated with wine of a poorer quality.* **aˌdulte'ration** *nu.*

adultery [ə'dʌltəri] *nu* sexual intercourse between a husband and a woman who is not his wife or between a wife and a man who is not her husband: *She divorced her husband because of his adultery with his secretary.*

a'dulterer – *fem* **a'dulteress** – *nc* a person who commits adultery.

a'dulterous *adj* (*usu attrib*) of or involving

adultery: *an adulterous relationship.*

advance [əd'vaːns] **1** *vti* to move forward: *The army advanced towards the town; The angry townspeople advanced on the town hall;* (*formal*) *Is it possible to advance the date of the wedding?; Our plans are advancing well; He married the boss's daughter to advance his chances of promotion.* **2** *vt* (*formal*) to give or make (a suggestion, proposal *etc*): *He advanced a new scheme for saving money.* **3** *vt* to supply (someone) with (money) on credit: *The bank will advance you £500.* – **1** *ncu* moving forward or progressing: *We've halted the enemy's advance; The builder made no advance on the house during the winter; Great advances in medicine have been made in this century.* **2** *nc* a payment made before the normal time, often to cover initial expenses: *We'll give the author an advance of £200 on this book; Can I have an advance on my salary?* **3** *nu* increase: *The auctioneer asked if there was any advance on £300 for the table.* **4** *nc* (*usu in pl*) an attempt at (*esp* sexual) seduction: *She had difficulty in escaping his advances.* – *adj* (*attrib*) **1** made *etc* before the necessary or agreed time: *He made an advance payment.* **2** made beforehand: *an advance booking.* **3** (of a book *etc*) sent or received before the publication date: *He sent me an advance copy of his novel.* **4** (of a section of an army *etc*) sent ahead of the main group or force: *the advance guard.*

ad'vanced *adj* having made a lot of progress in a given way; at a high level: *The building is in an advanced state of decay; an advanced Latin course; Her illness is so far advanced that it is now incurable.*

ad'vancement *nu* (*formal*) **1** progress: *His researches contributed to the advancement of chemistry.* **2** promotion: *Your advancement in this firm has been rapid.*

in ad'vance 1 before(hand): *Can you pay me in advance?* **2** in front: *I've been sent on in advance (of the main force).*

advantage [əd'vaːntidʒ] **1** *ncu* (a) gain or benefit: *There are several advantages in being self-employed; There's no advantage in losing your temper.* **2** *nu* in tennis, the first point gained after deuce.

advantageous [advən'teidʒəs] *adj* (*usu attrib*) having or giving an advantage: *Because of his experience he was in an advantageous position for promotion.* **ˌadvan'tageously** *adv.*

have an/the advantage (over) to be in a better or more advantageous position (than): *As she already knew French, she had an advantage over the rest of the class.*

take advantage of 1 to make use of (a situation, person *etc*) in such a way as to benefit oneself: *You must take advantage of the hot weather – it won't last long; He took full advantage of all his business opportunities.* **2** (*formal or liter*) to seduce; to use (someone) sexually: *He took advantage of her in the woods.*

to ad'vantage 1 in a way that shows the good qualities clearly: *Her dress shows off her figure to advantage.* **2** in a way that brings profit: *He's turned his previous experience to advantage in his new business.*

See also **disadvantage**.

advent ['advent] *nu* (*formal*) **1** coming or arrival: *the advent of space travel.* **2** (*with cap: relig*) a time of preparation, including the four Sundays before Christmas, for the coming birth of Christ: *Advent is a Christian festival;* (*attrib*) *an Advent calendar.*

adventure [əd'ventʃə] **1** *nc* a bold or exciting undertaking or experience: *He wrote a book about his adventures in the jungle; Alice's Adventures in Wonderland.* **2** *nu* the excitement of risk or danger: *His love of adventure encouraged him to join the expedition.*

ad'venturer – *fem* **ad'venturess** – *nc* **1** a person who seeks adventure. **2** (*often derog*) a person who seeks his fortune by risky and/or dishonest means: *Don't lend him any money – he's just an adventurer.*

ad'venturous *adj* (*neg* **un-**) liking or eager for adventure(s): *That child is too adventurous; The adventurous boy fell from the roof of the derelict building.* **ad'venturously** *adv.*

adverb ['advəːb] *nc* a word used before or after a verb, before an adjective or preposition, or with another adverb to show time, manner, place, degree *etc*: *Yesterday he looked more carefully in the drawer, and there he found a very small key with a hole right through it.* **ad'verbial** *adj.* **ad'verbially** *adv.*

adversary ['advəsəri] *nc* (*formal*) an opponent; an enemy: *his adversary in the chess match; The adversaries fought with swords.*

adverse ['advəːs] *adj* (*attrib*) unfavourable: *adverse circumstances; adverse criticism.* **'adversely** *adv.*

ad'versity *ncu* (*formal or liter*) misfortune or hardship: *She remained optimistic in the face of all adversity; She overcame all adversities.*

advert ['advəːt] short for **advertisement**: *I saw your advert in yesterday's newspaper.*

advertise ['advətaiz] *vti* to make (something) known to the public by any of various methods: *I've advertised (my house) in the newspaper; They advertised on TV for volunteers.*

advertisement [əd'vəːtismənt, (*Amer*) advər'taizmənt] *nc* (*also* **ad** [ad], **advert** ['advəːt]) a film, newspaper announcement, poster *etc* making something known, *esp* in order to persuade people to buy it: *an advertisement for toothpaste on television; She replied to my advertisement for domestic help; He put an advertisement in the paper.*

'advertiser 1 *nc* a person who advertises. **2** *n* (*with cap*) a word often used in the titles of newspapers: *the Newtown Advertiser.*

advice [əd'vais] **1** *nu* suggestions to a person about what he should do: *You must seek legal advice if you want a divorce; Let me give you a piece of advice.* **2** *nc* (*formal*) formal notice about an account *etc*: *I have not yet received this month's advice from the bank.*

advise [əd'vaiz] *vt* **1** to give advice to; to recommend: *My lawyer advises me (to buy the house); He advises buying the house.* **2** (*formal: usu with* **of**) to inform: *This letter is to advise you of our interest in your suggestion.*

ad'visable *adj* (*pred*) (of actions) wise: *The doctor does not think it advisable for you to drink.* **adˌvisa'bility** *nu.*

-advised (*in cmpds*) **1** (of actions *etc*) considered and thought out: *an ill-advised action.* **2** (of people) recommended or guided: *He was well-advised to sell his house when prices were high.*

ad'visedly [-zid-] *adv* (*formal*) after careful consideration: *I tell you this advisedly and in strictest confidence.*

ad'viser, ad'visor *nc* a person who advises: *our foreign language adviser.*

ad'visory *adj* (*usu attrib*) **1** giving advice: *an*

advisory leaflet. **2** able or qualified to give advice: *He acted in an advisory capacity.*
See also **inadvisable**.

advocate ['advəkət] *nc* **1** in Scotland, a lawyer with a similar function to a barrister. **2** a supporter; a person who is in favour (of): *an advocate of reform.* – [-keit] *vt* (*formal*) to speak in favour of; to recommend: *He advocated increasing the charges.*
'advocacy [-kəsi] *nu* **1** the work or rôle of a (legal) advocate. **2** (*formal*) recommendation or support of: *His advocacy of this action has a selfish motive.*

aegis ['i:dʒis]: **under the aegis of** (*formal*) with the (moral or financial) support of (someone): *under the aegis of the British government.*

aeon, eon ['i:on] *nc* (*formal or facet*) an extremely long period of time; an age: *in aeons past; We seem to have waited aeons for the train.*

aerated ['eiəreitid] *adj* (*attrib*) (of a liquid) having gas or air put into it: *aerated waters.*

aerial ['eəriəl] *nc* (*Amer* **an'tenna**) a wire or rod (or a set of these) able to send or receive radio waves *etc*: *a television aerial.* – *adj* (*attrib*) in or from the air: *aerial photography.*

aerie *see* **eyrie**.

aero- [eərou] (*in cmpds*) air, flying *etc*, as in **aerodynamics**.

aerobatics [eərə'batiks] *n pl* acrobatics performed by an aircraft or high in the air.

aerodrome ['eərədroum] *nc* a place (*usu* private or military) where aircraft are kept and from which they operate.

aerodynamics [eərədai'namiks] *n sing* the study of forces acting on objects in the air: *Aerodynamics is an interesting subject.* **ˌaerody'namic** *adj.*

aeronautics [eərə'no:tiks] *n sing* the science or practice of flying: *Aeronautics is becoming popular.*
ˌaero'nautical *adj.*

aeroplane ['eərəplein] *nc* (*often abbrev* **plane**: *Amer* **'airplane**) a machine for flying which is heavier than air and has wings.

aerosol ['eərəsol] *nc* **1** a mixture of liquid or solid particles and gas under pressure which is released from a container in the form of a mist: *Many deodorants come in the form of aerosols*; (*attrib*) *an aerosol spray.* **2** the container of this mixture: *Don't throw that aerosol on the fire!*

aesthetic, (*Amer*) **esthetic** [is'θetik] *adj* (*formal*) **1** (*pred*) artistic and pleasing to the eye: *That armchair is comfortable but not very aesthetic.* **2** (*attrib*) of beauty or its appreciation: *She has no aesthetic sense.*
aes'thetics *n sing* the study or principles of beauty or the fine arts.

afar [ə'fa:] *adv* (*liter*) from, at or to a distance: *The three wise men came from afar; Afar off he saw the spires of the city.*

affable ['afəbl] *adj* pleasant and easy to talk to: *an affable young man; I find him very affable.* **'affably** *adv.* **ˌaffa'bility** *nu.*

affair [ə'feə] *nc* **1** happenings *etc* which are connected with a particular person or thing: *the Kennedy affair; the Suez affair.* **2** (*loosely*) a thing: *The new machine is a weird-looking affair.* **3** (*often in pl*) business; concern(s): *The prime minister is busy with affairs of state; financial affairs; Where I go is entirely my own affair.* **4** a love affair: *His wife found out about his affair with his secretary.*
state of affairs *see* **state**[1].

affect [ə'fekt] *vt* **1** to act or have an effect on: *Rain affects the grass; The weather affected her decision; His heavy drinking is beginning to affect his liver; The disease is affecting his eyesight; His kidneys have been affected by the disease.* **2** to move the feelings of: *She was deeply affected by the news of her father's death.* **3** (*formal*) to pretend to feel: *She affected grief.*
ˌaffec'tation [a-] *ncu* (an example of) insincere or unnatural behaviour *etc*: *Her silly affectations annoy me.*
af'fected *adj* **1** not natural: *He has an affected way of talking.* **2** behaving *etc* in such a way: *He is such an affected young man; She is rather affected.*
af'fecting *adj* (*formal*) able to affect emotionally: *an affecting poem; I find his poetry affecting.*
See also **unaffected**.

affection [ə'fekʃən] **1** *nu* liking or fondness: *I have great affection for her, but she never shows any affection towards me.* **2** *nc* a feeling of fondness: *He replaced the old boyfriend in her affections.*
af'fectionate [-nət] *adj* having or showing affection: *an affectionate child; She is very affectionate towards her mother; an affectionate letter.*
af'fectionately *adv.*

affidavit [afi'deivit] *nc* (*legal*) a written declaration on oath: *You must swear an affidavit.*

affiliated [ə'filieitid] *adj* (*formal*) connected with or joined to (a larger group *etc*) as a member: *That union is affiliated to the engineering union; an affiliated branch of the union.*
afˌfili'ation (*formal*) **1** *nu* the act of becoming connected with or joined to (as a member). **2** *nc* a connection with (an organization *etc*): *His new job prevents him from having any affiliation with a political party.*

affinity [ə'finəti] *nc* (*formal*) **1** a feeling of attraction towards or liking for (a person, thing *etc*): *He had an affinity for cats.* **2** a closeness in relationship, form *etc*: *There is a distinct affinity between these two languages.*

affirm [ə'fə:m] *vt* (*formal*: not *usu* used with **is, was** *etc* and **-ing**) to state something positively and firmly: *Despite all the policeman's questions the lady continued to affirm that she was innocent.*
ˌaffir'mation [a-] *ncu.*
af'firmative [-tiv] *adj, nu* (*formal*) saying or indicating yes to a question, suggestion *etc*: *He gave an affirmative nod; a reply in the affirmative.*

affix [ə'fiks] *vt* (*formal*) to attach (something) to an object *etc*: *Affix the stamp in the top right-hand corner of the envelope; Affix it to the envelope.* – ['afiks] *nc* (*formal*) an addition, *esp* (*gram*) one at the beginning (**prefix**) or end (**suffix**) of a word: *unintelligible; affliction; illegal.*

afflict [ə'flikt] *vt* (*formal*) to give pain or distress to (a person *etc*): *She is continually afflicted by/with headaches; afflicted by/with grief.*
af'fliction [-ʃən] *ncu* (*formal*): *Her migraine is a great affliction to her.*

affluent ['afluənt] *adj* (*formal*) wealthy: *the affluent society; He is becoming more and more affluent.*
'affluence *nu* (*formal*) wealth: *His affluence did not preclude him from enjoying simple things.*

afford [ə'fo:d] *vt* **1** (*usu with* **can, could**) to be able to spend enough money, time *etc* on or for something: *I can't afford* (*to buy*) *a new car; I can only afford two days for painting the room.* **2** (*usu with* **can, could**) to be able to do (something) without causing oneself trouble, difficulty *etc*: *She couldn't afford to be rude to her employer no matter how rude he was to her.* **3** (*formal*) to give: *That will afford him little pleasure.*

affray [ə'frei] *nc* (*legal or formal*) a fight: *an affray in a public house.*

affront [ə'frʌnt] *nc* an insult, *usu* one made in public: *His remarks were obviously intended as an affront to her.* – *vt* to insult or offend, *usu* in public; to cause to feel embarrassed and offended: *We were affronted by the offhand way in which they treated us.*

afield [ə'fi:ld] : **far afield** (*liter*) far away from (home *etc*): *He left home at the age of twenty and travelled far afield.*

aflame [ə'fleim] *adj* (*pred*) in flames or burning: *The whole house was aflame in a few minutes*; (*fig*) *aflame with desire.*

afloat [ə'flout] *adj* (*pred*) **1** floating: *We've got the boat afloat at last.* **2** at sea: *life afloat.*

afoot [ə'fut] *adj* (*pred*) in progress or happening: *There is a scheme afoot to improve recreational facilities in the area.*

aforesaid [ə'fo:sed], **aforementioned** [əfo:-'menʃənd] *adjs* (*formal or legal*) said, named *etc* before (*usu* in an earlier part of a document).

afraid [ə'freid] *adj* (*pred*) **1** feeling fear or being frightened (of a person, thing *etc*): *He's afraid of his mother*; *He is afraid of going out alone*; *The child is not afraid of the dark*; *She was afraid to go.* **2** sorry (to have to say that): *I'm afraid I don't agree with you*; *I'm afraid the cat is dead.*

See also **unafraid**.

afresh [ə'freʃ] : **start afresh** (*formal*) to start from the beginning again: *There are so many changes in this that we'll just have to start the whole thing afresh.*

Africa, African *see* Appendix 2.

Afrikaans [afri'ka:ns, (*Amer also*) -'ka:nz] *n, adj* (of) one of two official languages of South Africa (the other being English), having its origins in seventeenth-century Dutch. – *See also* Appendix 2.

Afro- [afrou] (*in cmpds*) African: ˌ*Afro-A'merican.*

aft [a:ft] *adv* (*naut*) near or towards the stern (of a ship).

after ['a:ftə] *prep* **1** later in time or place than: *He drinks port after dinner*; *After the car came a bus.* **2** following (*often indicating repetition*): *I've told you time after time*; *one thing after another*; *night after night.* **3** behind: *Shut the door after you!*; *He always leaves a trail of confusion after him.* **4** in search or pursuit of: *He ran after the bus.* **5** considering; because or in spite of: *After all I've done you'd think he'd make an effort*; *It's sad to fail after all that work.* **6** in imitation of or following (the style, version *etc* of): *This painting is after* (*the style of*) *Constable.* – *adv* (*usu* **'afterwards**) later in time or place: *They arrived soon after.* – *conj* later than the time when: *After she died we moved house twice.*

after- (*in cmpds*) later in time: *an afterthought.*

'afters *n sing* (*inf*) dessert; pudding: *What's for afters?*

'aftercare *nu* (*formal*) medical care *etc* given to someone after a period of treatment, a surgical operation *etc*: *Aftercare is particularly important for elderly patients.*

'afterlife *nc* (*formal*) a life after death.

'aftermath [-maθ] *nc* the situation *etc* resulting from an important, *esp* unpleasant, event: *The country is still recovering from the aftermath of the war.*

'afterwards *adv* later or after something else has happened or happens: *He told me afterwards that he had not enjoyed the film.*

after all 1 (used when giving a reason for doing something *etc*) taking everything into consideration: *I won't invite him. After all, I don't really know him.* **2** in spite of everything that has/had happened, been said *etc*: *It turns out he went by plane after all.*

be 'after (*inf*) to be looking for or hoping to be given something: *When she came in here she was definitely after something*; *What are you after?*; *The police are after him.*

afternoon [a:ftə'nu:n] *ncu* the time between morning and evening: *He arrived in the afternoon*; *I'll be seeing him tomorrow afternoon*; *He works for us three afternoons a week*; (*The*) *early afternoon would be a convenient time to see him*; *He is leaving on Tuesday afternoon*; (*attrib*) *afternoon tea.*

afternoon tea *see* **tea**.

this afternoon *see* **this**.

again [ə'gen] *adv* **1** once more or another time: *Say that again!*; *He hit the child again and again*; *He never saw her again*; *Don't do that again!* **2** as in a previous condition, situation *etc*: *He has been abroad but he is home again now.* **3** in addition: *He earns twice as much again as she does.* **4** (*formal*: *usu with* **then**) on the other hand: *Then again, perhaps he does want to come.*

against [ə'genst] *prep* **1** in opposition to: *They fought against the enemy*; *His action was against the law*; *He spoke out against the new law*; *He couldn't be heard against the background of noise.* **2** compared with; in contrast to: *The trees were black against the evening sky.* **3** touching or in contact with: *He stood with his back against the wall.* **4** in collision or violent contact with: *The rain beat against the window*; *He fell against the wall.* **5** in order to protect against: *The child had a vaccination against tuberculosis.*

agate ['ageit] *ncu* a semi-precious stone made of layers of quartz of various colours: *agate in a silver setting*; (*attrib*) *an agate brooch.*

age [eidʒ] **1** *nu* the amount of time during which a person or thing has existed: *He went to school at the age of six* (*years*); *'What age is she?' 'She is three years old.'* **2** *nc* (*often with cap*) a particular period of time: *This machine was the wonder of the age*; *He is studying the social conditions of the Middle Ages.* **3** *nu* the quality of being old: *This wine will improve with age.* **4** *nu* the later time of life: *With the wisdom of age he regretted the mistakes he had made in his youth.* **5** *nc* (*inf*: *usu in pl*) a very long time: *We've been waiting* (*for*) *ages for a bus.* – *v* – *prp*

'ag(e)ing – *vti* **1** to (cause to) grow old: *Wine is aged in barrels and then in bottles.* **2** to (cause to) look old: *He has aged a lot since I last saw him*; *His troubles have aged him.*

aged [eidʒd] (*def 1*), ['eidʒid] (*def 2*) *adj* **1** (*pred*) of the age of: *a child aged five.* **2** (*attrib*) old: *an aged man.*

'ageless *adj* never growing old or never looking older: *an ageless film actress*; *ageless beauty*; *Her beauty seems ageless.*

'age-old *adj* (*attrib*) done, known *etc* for a very long time: *an age-old custom.*

the aged ['eidʒid] old people: *care for the aged.*

age of consent *see* **consent**.

('come) of 'age (to be) old enough to be considered legally an adult (in Britain aged eighteen or over).

agency *see* **agent**.

agenda [ə'dʒendə] *nc* a list of things to be done, *esp* at a meeting: *What's on the agenda this morning?*

agent ['eidʒənt] *nc* **1** (*formal when of people*) a person or thing that acts or is the cause of something that happens: *Certain chemical cleaning agents harm skin*; *She was the agent of his despair.* **2** a person who acts for someone in business *etc*: *an agent for a manufacturing company*; *a house agent*; *a theatrical agent.* **3** (*esp* **secret agent**) a spy: *an agent for the Russians.*

'**agency 1** *nc* the office or business of an agent: *The employment agency will get you a job*; *He owns an advertising agency.* **2** *nu* (*formal*) the act of causing or being active in something: *I detected his agency in the trouble in the office.*

by/through the agency of (*formal*) by the action of: *The meeting was arranged through the agency of a friend.*

aggravate ['agrəveit] *vt* **1** (*formal*) to make worse: *His bad temper aggravated the situation.* **2** (*inf*) to make (someone) angry or impatient: *She was aggravated by the child's constant questions.* ˌ**aggra'vation** *nu.*

aggregate ['agrigət] *nu* **1** (*tech*) a material such as pieces of rock added to cement to make concrete. **2** a total: *What is the aggregate of goals from the two football matches?*

on 'aggregate collecting a number of findings *etc* together and treating them as a whole: *On aggregate of the goals scored in both matches, the opposing team are the winners.*

aggressive [ə'gresiv] *adj* ready to attack or oppose; quarrelsome: *a most aggressive boy*; *That child is so aggressive that he is always fighting at school*; (*fig*) *He is not aggressive enough to succeed in business.* **ag'gressively** *adv.* **ag'gressiveness** *nu.*

ag'gression [-ʃən] *ncu* (a feeling of) hostility: *His actions showed his aggression.*

ag'gressor *nc* (*formal*) (in a war *etc*) the party which attacks first: *He is the aggressor in all the fights at school.*

aggrieved [ə'gri:vd] *adj* (*formal*) unhappy or hurt because of unjust treatment: *He felt aggrieved at/over his friend's distrust*; *He was the aggrieved party in the divorce case.*

aghast [ə'ga:st] *adj* (*pred*: *formal*) struck with horror: *He stared aghast at the scene of destruction in front of him*; *She was aghast at the cruel treatment of the child.*

agile ['adʒail] *adj* active; able to move and change direction quickly and easily: *The antelope is a very agile animal*; *He is very agile.* **a'gility** [-'dʒi-] *nu.*

agitate ['adʒiteit] **1** *vt* to make (someone) excited and anxious: *His presence agitated her.* **2** *vi* to try to arouse public feeling and action: *That group is agitating for prison reform.* **3** *vt* (*formal*) to shake or stir: *The tree was agitated violently by the wind.*

'**agitated** *adj.*

ˌ**agi'tation** *nu*: *in a state of agitation*; *agitation for women's rights.*

'**agitator** *nc* a person who tries constantly to stir up public feeling: *a political agitator.*

aglow [ə'glou] *adj* (*liter*: *pred*) bright and glowing with colour or warmth: *The trees were aglow with the colours of autumn*; *Her face was aglow with health.*

agnostic [ag'nostik] *adj, nc* (of) a person who believes that it is impossible to know whether God exists or not: *He is a confirmed agnostic*; *agnostic principles.* **ag'nosticism** [-sizəm] *nu.*

ago [ə'gou] *adv* at a certain time in the past: *I went to France two years ago*; *Long ago, men lived in caves*; *I knew him many years ago*; *How long ago did he leave?*

agog [ə'gog] *adj* (*pred*) eager and excited: *We were all agog at the news*; *agog with excitement.*

agony ['agəni] *ncu* great pain or suffering: *The dying man was in agony*; (*fig*) *She suffered agonies of regret over her decision.*

'**agonized, -s-** *adj* (*usu attrib*: *usu fig*) showing agony: *He had an agonized expression on his face as he lost the tennis match.*

'**agonizing, -s-** *adj* causing agony: *an agonizing pain*; *an agonizing decision*; *The pain was agonizing.* '**agonizingly, -s-** *adv.*

agree [ə'gri:] – *pt, ptp* **a'greed** – *vi* (not *usu* used with **is, was** *etc* and **-ing** (*defs 3-6*)) **1** (*often with* **with**) to think or say the same (as): *He and I usually agree*; *I agreed with them that we should try again*; (*fig*) *The newspaper report does not agree with what he told us.* **2** (*often with* **to**) to say that one will do or allow something: *He agreed to go*; *He agreed to our request.* **3** (*often with* **on**) to discuss and come to the same decision: *We agreed on a date for our next holiday*; *We agreed that June would be the best time.* **4** (*with* **with**) to be good for (*usu* one's health): *Cheese does not agree with me.* **5** to be happy and friendly together: *John and his wife don't agree.* **6** (*gram*: *often with* **with**) to be in an appropriate tense, case, person *etc*: *The verb must agree with its subject*; *The verb and subject have to agree.*

a'greeable 1 *adj* (*formal*) pleasant: *She seems very agreeable*; *She is a most agreeable person.* **2** *adj* (*pred*) willing to agree: *Are you agreeable to (doing) that?*

a'greeably *adv* pleasantly: *I was agreeably surprised by the cheapness of the restaurant prices.*

a'greement 1 *nu* the state of agreeing: *We are all in agreement.* **2** *nc* a business, political *etc* arrangement, spoken or written: *You have broken our agreement*; *We have signed an agreement*; *He has come to/reached an agreement with his friend about sharing a car.*

strike an agreement *see* **strike**.

See also **disagree**.

agriculture ['agrikʌltʃə] *nu* (the science of) the cultivation of land: *He is studying agriculture.*

ˌ**agri'cultural** *adj*: *an agricultural college.*

ˌ**agri'culturalist** *nc.*

aground [ə'graund] *adj* (*pred*), *adv* (of ships) (stuck) on the bed of the sea *etc* in shallow water: *The ship was aground on a sandbank*; *Our boat ran aground at the mouth of the river.*

aha! [a:'ha:] *interj* expressing satisfaction and triumph, *usu* at suddenly understanding something, seeing what one has been searching for *etc*: *Aha! Now I understand!*; *Aha! There it is!*

ahead [ə'hed] *adv* (*often with* **of**) **1** in front: in advance: *He went on ahead of me*; *Is Australian time ahead of British time?* **2** more successful: *We are well ahead (of all our rivals) at present.*

get, go, look ahead *see* **get, go, look**.

aid [eid] *ncu* (*more formal or tech than* **help**) (an) act of giving help: *Rich countries give aid to developing countries*; *The teacher uses visual aids*; *Poor people are sometimes given legal aid by the government to help them pay the expenses of law cases*; *He came to my aid when my car broke down.* – *vt* (*formal*) to help: *I was greatly aided in my search by the kindness of the library staff.*

aid and abet (*legal or facet*) to provide help and encouragement in some bad or illegal activity: *His* *wife aids and abets him in his dishonest deeds.*

in 'aid of as a financial help to (a charity *etc*): *The collection is in aid of the blind.*

what is (something) in aid of? (*Brit inf*) for what reason or purpose is something being done *etc*: *What is all this fuss in aid of?*

ail [eil] (*old*) **1** *vi* to be ill: *The old lady has been ailing for some time.* **2** *vt* to trouble: *What ails you?*

'ailment *nc* an illness, *usu* not serious or dangerous: *Children often have minor ailments.*

aim [eim] **1** *vti* (*usu with* **at, for**) to point or direct something at; to try to hit or reach *etc*: *He picked up the rifle and aimed it at the target*; *He aimed a blow at her head*; (*fig*) *He is aiming for the top of his profession.* **2** *vi* (*with* **to, at**) to plan or intend: *He aims to finish the book next week*; *He aims at finishing the job tomorrow.* – **1** *nu* the act of or skill at aiming: *His aim is excellent.* **2** *nc* what a person intends to do: *My aim is to become prime minister.*

'aimless *adj* (*usu attrib*) without purpose: *an aimless life.* **'aimlessness** *nu.*

'aimlessly *adv*: *We found her wandering aimlessly about.*

take aim (*sometimes with* **at**) to aim (*def 1*): *He took (careful) aim before he fired*; *He took aim at the target.*

ain't *see* **be, have**.

air [eə] **1** *nu* the mixture of gases we breathe; the atmosphere: *Mountain air is pure.* **2** *nu* the space above the ground; the sky: *Birds fly through the air.* – *See also* **by air** *below.* **3** *nu* (*formal*) appearance or look: *The house had an air of neglect.* **4** *nc* (*old*: *music*) a tune: *She played a simple air on the piano.* – *vt* **1** to expose to the air in order to dry or make more fresh *etc*: *to air linen.* **2** (*fig*) to make known: *He loved to air his grievances.*

'airily *adv* in a light-hearted manner: *She airily dismissed all objections.* **'airiness** *nu.*

'airing **1** *nu* exposure to air: *She brought out the spare sheets for airing.* **2** *nc* a short walk *etc* in the open air: *She took the baby for an airing.* **3** *nc* (*fig*) a period of exposure to general notice: *He gave his views an airing whenever he had the opportunity.*

'airless *adj* **1** (of weather) still and windless: *It was a hot, airless night.* **2** (of a room *etc*) stuffy and without air: *The room was so airless that several people fainted*; *an airless room.*

'airy *adj* **1** with plenty of (fresh) air: *an airy room*; *This room is nice and airy.* **2** (*attrib*) light-hearted and not serious: *He has an airy disregard for authority.*

'airborne *adj* (*formal*: *usu pred*) in the air or flying: *We were airborne five minutes after boarding the plane.*

ˌair-con'ditioned *adj* having air-conditioning: *an air-conditioned building*; *The building is air-conditioned throughout.*

ˌair-con'ditioning *nu* a method of providing a room, building *etc* with air of a controlled temperature and humidity: *Our air-conditioning has broken down.*

'aircraft – *pl* **'aircraft** – *nc* any of several types of machine for flying in the air: *Enemy aircraft have been seen over London.*

'aircraft carrier *nc* a ship which carries aircraft and which aircraft can use for landing and taking off.

'airfield *nc* an area of ground (with buildings *etc*) where (*usu* military) aircraft are kept and from which they fly.

'air force *nc* the part of the armed services which uses aircraft: *the army, navy and air force.*

'air-gun *nc* a gun that is worked by air under pressure.

'air hostess *nc* a young woman who looks after passengers in an aircraft.

'airing-cupboard *nc* a heated cupboard in which clothes *etc* are put to become completely dry and warm.

'airlift *nc* an operation to move cargo or people, carried out by air, *esp* in a time of war or natural disaster.

'airline *nc* (a company that owns) a regular air transport service: *My father is the chairman of an airline*; *Which airline are you travelling by?*

'airliner *nc* a (*usu* large) aircraft for carrying passengers.

'air-lock *nc* a bubble in a pipe which prevents liquid from flowing along it: *There's no water coming out of the garden hose – there must be an air-lock in it.*

'airmail *nu* **1** a system of carrying mail by air: *I shall send this parcel by airmail.* **2** mail carried by air: (*attrib*) *an airmail letter.*

'airman *nc* a member of an air force: *British airmen.*

'airplane *nc* (*Amer*) an aeroplane.

'airport *nc* a place where passenger aircraft arrive and depart, with buildings for customs, waiting-rooms *etc.*

'air-raid *nc* an attack by aircraft.

'airship *nc* an aircraft that is lighter than air and can be steered *etc.*

'air-space *nu* the part of the sky directly above a country which is considered as part of the country.

'air terminal *nc* **1** a place in a town centre connected by a bus service to a nearby airport. **2** a building containing the arrival and departure areas at an airport.

'airtight *adj* (of a container *etc*) into or through which air cannot pass: *It is difficult to make a room completely airtight*; *an airtight seal on a bottle.*

'airway *nc* a regular course followed by aircraft.

'airworthy *adj* in good condition for flying: *Is that plane airworthy?*; *few airworthy planes.* **'airworthiness** *nu.*

ˌairy-'fairy *adj* (*inf derog*) fanciful without being based on fact or real conditions *etc*: *He has airy-fairy ideas about the brotherhood of man*; *The scheme seems rather airy-fairy.*

airs and graces (*derog*) behaviour in which a person acts as if he is better or more important than others: *In spite of all her airs and graces she had very few talents.*

ˌair-sea 'rescue combined use of aircraft and boats in the rescue of people from the sea.

by 'air in an aircraft: *He often travels by air.*

in the air (*inf*) **1** uncertain or undecided: *The whole plan is rather in the air.* **2** being generally considered, thought or talked about: *It's in the air that they may get married.*

on the air broadcasting (regularly) on radio or television.

put on airs/give oneself airs to behave as if one is better or more important than others: *She gives herself such airs that everyone dislikes her.*

take the air (*old or facet*) to go for a walk.

aisle [ail] *nc* **1** a passage between rows of seats *etc*, *esp* in a church: *the aisle in a cinema*; *The bride walked up the aisle.* **2** the side part of the inside of a church.

ajar [ə'dʒaː] *adj* (*pred*) partly open: *The door was ajar when I returned.*

akimbo [ə'kimbou] *adj* (*placed immediately after noun*) with hand on hip and elbow bent outward: *She stood with arms akimbo.*

akin [ə'kin] *adj* (*pred*: *often with* **to**) similar in nature: *This problem is akin to the one we had last year.*

alabaster ['aləbaːstə] *nu, adj* (of) a white semi-transparent stone used for ornaments *etc*: *a lamp of alabaster*; *an alabaster ash-tray.*

à la carte [alaː'kaːt] *adv, adj* (of a meal) with each dish on the menu chosen and priced separately: *I always eat à la carte so that I can choose how much I want*; *an à la carte menu.*

alacrity [ə'lakrəti] *nu* (*formal*) quick and cheerful willingness to do something: *He obeyed with alacrity.*

alarm [ə'laːm] **1** *nu* (*more formal than* **fear**) sudden fear: *We did not share her alarm at the suggestion.* **2** *nc* something that gives warning of danger, attracts attention *etc*: *Sound/raise the alarm*; *a fire-alarm*; (*attrib*) *an alarm clock.* – *vt* to make (someone) afraid: *The least sound alarms the old lady.*

a'larming *adj* disturbing or causing fear: *an alarming rise in the number of road accidents*; *an alarming piece of news*; *That news is rather alarming.* **a'larmingly** *adv.*

a'larmist *nc* (*formal*) a person who is too much inclined to expect trouble: *alarmists who forecast the end of the world.*

alas! [ə'las] *interj* (*old, liter or facet*) used to express grief: *Alas, he died young!*

albatross ['albətros] *nc* a large long-winged sea-bird of the southern oceans, related to the gull family.

albino [al'biːnou, (*Amer*) -'bai-] – *pl* **al'binos** – *nc, adj* (a person or animal) with no natural colour in the skin, hair or eyes: *My cat is an albino*; *Albino rabbits are white with pink eyes.*

album ['albəm] *nc* **1** a book with blank pages for holding photographs, stamps *etc.* **2** a long-playing gramophone record: *I haven't got the group's latest album.*

albumen ['albjumən] *nu* (*tech*) the white part of an egg.

alchemy ['alkəmi] *nu* (*hist*) the early form of chemistry, one of whose aims was to discover how to make gold from other metals. **'alchemist** *nc.*

alcohol ['alkəhol] *nu* (drinks containing) liquid made by the fermentation or distillation of sugar: *This beer contains a high proportion of alcohol*; *I never drink alcohol – I drink orange juice.*

ˌalco'holic *adj* **1** of or containing alcohol: *Is cider alcoholic?*; *alcoholic drinks.* **2** (*attrib*) caused by alcohol: *Her face had an alcoholic flush.* – *nc* a person who suffers from a dependence on alcohol and drinks too much: *He drinks a lot but he is not actually an alcoholic.*

'alcoholism *nu* the condition suffered by an alcoholic: *Alcoholism is more common than drug addiction.*

alcove ['alkouv] *nc* a small section of a room *etc* formed by part of the wall being set back.

alderman ['oːldəmən] *nc* **1** in England, a member of a town, county or borough council next in rank to the mayor. **2** in the US, a member of the governing body of a city.

ale [eil] **1** *ncu* the name given to certain kinds of beer: *two pints of ale*; *We make various ales.* **2** *nc* a glass of ale.

'alehouse *nc* (*old*) an inn or public house.

alert [ə'ləːt] *adj* **1** quick-thinking: *He's a very alert child*; *She's very old now but she's still very alert.* **2** (*pred*: *with* **to**) watchful and aware: *You must be alert to the dangers around you.* – *nc* a signal to be ready for action. – *vt* to make (someone) alert; to warn: *The sound of gunfire alerted us to our danger.*

a'lertly *adv.* **a'lertness** *nu.*

on the alert on the watch (for): *We were all on the alert for any sound that might tell us where he was.*

alfresco [al'freskou] *adj, adv* (*formal*) held *etc* in the open air: *an alfresco meal*; *We often eat alfresco in the summer.*

algae ['aldʒiː] *n pl* a group of simple plants which includes seaweed.

algebra ['aldʒibrə] *nu* (*math*) a method of calculating using letters and signs to represent numbers.

ˌalge'braic [-'breiik] *adj.*

Algeria, Algerian *see* Appendix 2.

alias ['eiliəs] *nc* a false name: *What alias did the crook use this time?*; *They keep changing aliases.* – *adv* using as a false name: *John Smith, alias Peter Jones.*

alibi ['alibai] *nc* **1** the fact or a statement that a person accused of a crime was somewhere else when it was committed: *Has he an alibi for the night of the murder?* **2** (*loosely*) an excuse: *He had no alibi for his failure to arrive home on time.*

alien ['eiliən] *adj* (*attrib*) foreign: *an alien land*; *alien customs.* – *See also* **alien to** *below.* – *nc* a foreigner: *Aliens are not welcome there.*

'alienate [-neit] *vt* (*formal*) **1** to make someone feel unfriendly to one or strange: *He alienated his wife by his cruelty to her.* **2** to turn away: *He alienated her affections.* **ˌalie'nation** *nu.*

'alien to not in keeping with; unfamiliar to: *Unkindness was alien to his gentle nature.*

alight[1] [ə'lait] – *pt, ptp* **a'lighted** – *vi* (*formal*) **1** to get down from or out of: *to alight from a horse/car.* **2** (*with* **on**) to settle or land on: *The bird alighted on the fence*; (*fig*) *His eye alighted on the letter.*

alight[2] [ə'lait] *adj* (*pred*) on fire: *The stove was still alight*; (*fig*) *His eyes were alight with joy.*

set (something) alight to cause (something) to start burning: *The boys set the pile of rubbish alight.*

align [ə'lain] **1** *vt* (*tech*) to put in a straight line or in parallel lines: *Did the mechanic align the wheels of the car?* **2** *v refl* (*formal*) to support one side in an argument, politics *etc*: *He aligned himself with the rebels.*

a'lignment *ncu* **1** (*tech*) arrangement in a line or in parallel lines: *He checked the alignment of the car's wheels.* **2** (*formal*) arrangement of groups in politics *etc*: *New political alignments are forming in Europe.*

See also **non-aligned, realign**.

alike [ə'laik] *adj* (*pred*: *neg* **un-**) like one another; similar: *Twins are often very alike.* – *adv* in the same way: *He treated all his children alike.*

alimentary [ali'mentəri] : **alimentary canal** *nc* (*tech*) the passage for the digestion of food in animals, including the gullet, stomach and intestines.

alimony ['alimәni, (*Amer*) -mouni] *nu* (*legal*) an allowance for support made to a wife by her husband when they are legally separated: *The judge ordered him to pay his wife a large sum of money as alimony.*

alive [ə'laiv] *adj* (*pred*) **1** living and not dead:

Queen Victoria was still alive in 1900. **2** full of activity: *The town was alive with policemen on the day of the march.*

a'live to aware of: *He was alive to the dangers of the situation.*

See also **live**².

alkali ['alkəlai] *ncu* a substance, the opposite of acid, such as soda or potash.

'alkaline [-lain] *adj*: *He took some alkaline powder for his sore stomach.*

all [o:l] *adj, pron* **1** the whole (of): *He ate all the cake; He has spent all of his money; I know all!* **2** every one (of a group) when taken together: *They were all present; All men are equal; All must go.* – *adv* entirely: *It is all gone; He lives all alone; The bride was (dressed) all in white.* **2** much; even more: *Your low pay is all the more reason to find a new job; I feel all the better for a hot bath.*

all- (*in cmpds: formal*) wholly and completely: *all-powerful.*

ˌall-'clear *nc* (*usu with* **the**) a signal or formal statement that a time of danger, illness *etc* is over or no longer expected: *They sounded the all-clear after the air-raid; The doctor has given me the all-clear at last.*

'all-in *adj* (*attrib*) **1** with nothing left out: *an all-in price.* **2** with nothing forbidden: *all-in wrestling.*

'all-out *adj* (*attrib*) using the greatest effort possible: *an all-out attempt to break the world record.*

'all-round *adj* (*attrib*) **1** including or applying to every part, person, thing *etc*: *an all-round pay rise.* **2** good at all parts of a subject *etc*: *an all-round sportsman.*

ˌall-'rounder *nc* a person who is good at many kinds of sport *etc.*

'all-time *adj* (*attrib*) of the whole period of time up to the present: *an all-time great* (= one of the greatest that ever existed); *one of his all-time successes.*

above all *see* **above**.

after all *see* **after**.

all alone *see* **alone**.

all along the whole time (that something was happening): *I knew it all along; I realized all along that he was dishonest.*

all at once 1 all at the same time: *Don't eat those cakes all at once!* **2** suddenly: *All at once the light went out.*

all in 1 (*inf*) exhausted: *He was all in after the game.* **2** with everything included: *Is that the price all in?* – *See also* **all-in** *above.*

all in all considering everything: *We haven't done badly, all in all.*

all of a sudden suddenly: *All of a sudden there was a loud explosion.*

all over 1 over the whole of (a person, thing *etc*): *My car is dirty all over.* **2** finished: *The excitement's all over now.* **3** everywhere: *We've been looking all over for you!* **4** (*inf*) exactly what one would expect from (a person *etc*): *Isn't that just Peter all over!* **5** (*inf*) covered with: *My coat is all over mud!*

all 'over with finished with; completed or dealt with: *Oh, that problem's all over with now.*

all right 1 unhurt; not ill or in difficulties *etc*: *You look ill. Are you all right?* **2** an expression of agreement to do something: *'Will you come?' 'Oh, all right.'*

all there 1 (*inf: usu with neg*) completely sane: *I don't think he's all there.* **2** (*inf*) having an alert, intelligent mind and good ideas: *She's all there when it comes to looking after her own interests.*

at 'all (*used for emphasis in negs*) in any way, amount or circumstances: *I don't do that at all; I am not at all happy about the situation.* – *See also* **not at all** *under* **not**.

first of all *see* **first**.

in 'all in total, when everything is added up: *I spent three hours in all waiting for buses last week.*

in all conscience, honesty, innocence *see* **conscience, honesty, innocence**.

once and for all *see* **once**.

allay [ə'lei] *vt* (*formal*) to make less: *He allayed her fears.*

allege [ə'ledʒ] *vt* (*usu formal*) to say, *esp* in making a legal statement, without giving proof: *He alleged that he had been with the accused on the night of the murder.*

allegation [ali'geiʃən] *nc* (*formal*) a statement or act of stating without giving proof that a person has done something wrong *etc*: *His allegations about her behaviour are untrue; He submitted his allegation to the police in writing.*

allegiance [ə'li:dʒəns] *nu* (*formal*) a duty to support and obey (a person, group, idea *etc*): *I have no allegiance to any political party; We owe allegiance to the Queen.*

allegory ['aligəri, (*Amer*) -go:ri] *ncu* (a story in) a style of writing in which the characters represent ideas, types of personality etc: *In this allegory Sin is defeated in battle by Conscience.* **ˌalle'gorical** [-'go-] *adj.*

allergy ['alədʒi] *nc* **1** an unusual sensitiveness of the body which causes certain people to be affected in a bad way by something *usu* harmless: *The rash on her face is caused by an allergy to eggs/cats/grass.* **2** (*inf fig*) a dislike: *She has an allergy to hard work.*

allergic [-'lə:-] *adj* (*with* **to** *when pred*) affected in a bad way by (certain) things: *He is allergic to certain flowers; He has an allergic condition;* (*fig*) *He is allergic to work.*

alleviate [ə'li:vieit] *vt* (*formal*) to make an improvement by lessening (pain *etc*): *The drugs will alleviate the pain; Her conversation alleviated the dullness of the evening somewhat.* **alˌlevi'ation** *nu.*

alley ['ali] *nc* **1** (*often* **'alleyway**) a narrow street in a city *etc* (*usu* not wide enough for vehicles). **2** a long narrow area used for the games of bowling or skittles: *a bowling alley.*

blind alley *see* **blind**.

alliance, allied *see* **ally**.

alligator ['aligeitə] *nc* a kind of large reptile closely related to the crocodile, found mainly in the rivers of the warmer parts of America.

alliteration [əlitə'reiʃən] *nu* the repetition of the same sound at the beginning of two or more words close together, as in *Sing a Song of Sixpence.*

allocate ['aləkeit] *vt* (*formal*) **1** to give (to someone) for his own use: *He allocated a room to each student.* **2** to set apart (for a particular purpose): *They allocated £500 to the project.*

ˌallo'cation (*formal*) **1** *nu* the act of allocating: *The allocation of money is the responsibility of the committee.* **2** *nc* whatever is allocated to one person, purpose *etc*: *The child ate his allocation of chocolate all at once.*

allot [ə'lot] – *pt, ptp* **al'lotted** – *vt* (*formal*) to give (each person) a fixed share of or place in (something): *They have allotted all the money to the different people who applied; He was allotted a small part of the work.*

al'lotment 1 *nc* (*Brit*) a small part of a larger piece of public ground rented to a person to grow vegetables *etc* in his spare time. 2 *nu* (*formal*) the act of allotting: *the allotment of money.*

allow [ə'lau] 1 *vt* not to forbid or prevent: *He allowed me to enter; Playing football on Sundays is not allowed.* 2 *vi* (*with* **for**) to take into consideration when judging or deciding (*esp* a future possibility): *These figures allow for price rises; We must allow for an emergency.* 3 *vt* to give, *esp* for a particular purpose or regularly: *They allowed three days for the journey; His father allows him too much money.* 4 *vt* (*formal*) to admit: *He allowed that it had been a mistake.*

al'lowable *adj* able to be admitted or accepted: *an allowable excuse; Is smoking allowable here?*

al'lowance *nc* 1 a fixed sum or quantity given regularly: *His father made him an allowance of £20 a month; She has a generous dress allowance from her parents.* 2 something (*usu* a quantity) allowed: *This dress pattern has a seam allowance of 1 cm.*

make allowance for to take into consideration when deciding *etc*: *We've made allowance for the fact that everyone has different tastes.*

make allowances for (a person) to judge (a person) less severely, or expect less of (them), than other people: *We must make allowances for Mary – she is not well.*

alloy ['aloi] *ncu* a mixture of two or more metals.

allude [ə'lu:d] *vi* (*formal with* **to**) to speak of indirectly or mention in passing: *He did not allude to the remarks made by the previous speaker.*

al'lusion [-ʒən] *ncu* (*formal*) (the act of making) an (often indirect) mention of or reference to: *The play was full of allusions to the author's own life; The prime minister made no allusion to the war in his speech.*

allure [ə'ljuə] *nu* (*formal*) (the quality of) attraction or charm: *the allure of the stage; the allure of foreign countries.* – *vt* (*formal*) to tempt or attract by promises *etc.* **al'luring** *adj.*

allusion *see* **allude.**

alluvial [ə'lu:viəl] *adj* (*tech*: *esp attrib*) consisting of earth, sand *etc* carried down to low land by rivers: *alluvial plains.*

ally [ə'lai] *vti* to join by political agreement, marriage, friendship *etc*: *Small countries must ally themselves with larger countries in order to survive; The two companies allied with each other to increase profits.* – ['alai] *nc* a state, person *etc* allied with another: *The two countries were allies at that time; She made an ally of the new girl.*

al'liance 1 *ncu* joining or connection: *I am working in alliance with the government.* 2 *nc* an agreement or treaty by which people, countries *etc* ally themselves with one another: *This alliance ended the war; Our company has entered into an alliance with a French company.*

'allied ['a-] *adj* 1 (*attrib*) joined by political agreement or treaty: *The allied forces entered the country.* 2 (*pred with* **with**) together with; joined to: *Her beauty allied with her intelligence made her a successful model.* 3 (*pred with* **to**) related to; resembling: *The ape is closely allied to man.*

almanac ['o:lmənak] *nc* a calendar *usu* with information about the phases of the moon *etc.*

almighty [o:l'maiti] *adj* 1 (*relig*) having complete power: *almighty God; God is almighty;* (*facet*) *our almighty headmaster.* 2 (*inf*: *attrib*) very great: *We had an almighty row.*

the Almighty God.

almond ['a:mənd] *nc* 1 (*also* **'almond tree**) a kind of tree related to the peach: (*attrib*) *almond blossom.* 2 the kernel of its fruit: *The cake had raisins and almonds in it;* (*attrib*) *almond essence.*

almost ['o:lmoust] *adv* nearly but not quite: *She is almost five years old; We are almost at our destination; He is almost completely recovered; She almost fell under a moving car.*

alms [a:mz] *n pl* (*old*) money *etc* given to the poor.

aloft [ə'loft] *adv* 1 (*liter*) in the sky; above one's head: *He held the banner aloft.* 2 (*naut*) above the deck or up the mast of a ship: *The sailors were sent aloft.*

alone [ə'loun] *adv* 1 with no-one else; by oneself: *He lived alone; She is alone in believing that he is innocent.* 2 (*formal or for emphasis*) only: *He alone can remember; He would be respected for that one thing alone.*

all alone completely by oneself: *He has been all alone since the death of his wife.*

leave, let alone *see* **leave, let.**

along [ə'loŋ] *prep* 1 from one end to the other; in the direction of the length of: *He walked along several streets; Part of the wall runs along the river.* 2 at a point at the end or on the length of: *There's a post-box somewhere along this street.* – *adv* 1 onwards or forward: *He ran along beside me; Come along, please!* 2 at a point on the length of or at the (other) end of a corridor, road, river *etc*: *He lives somewhere along here; I'll be along* (= I'll be there) *in five minutes.* 3 with some verbs, indicates informality or casualness of intention *etc*: *Do come along to the party if you are free!; I always take along a thermos flask when I go on a long journey.*

a,long'side *prep, adv* beside or close to (the side of a ship, a pier *etc*): *He berthed alongside his friend's boat.*

all, get, go along *see* **all, get, go.**

aloof [ə'lu:f] *adj* (*usu pred*) keeping oneself apart or at a distance from other people: *I kept aloof from the whole business; People find the new teacher rather aloof.* **a'loofness** *nu.*

aloud [ə'laud] *adv* so as can be heard: *He read the letter aloud; He cried aloud when the doctor touched his wound.*

alpha ['alfə] *n* the first letter of the Greek alphabet (**A, α**).

alphabet ['alfəbit] *nc* the letters of a written language arranged in order: *I have learned all the letters of the Greek alphabet.*

,alpha'betical [-'be-] *adj* of the alphabet: *in alphabetical order.* **,alpha'betically** *adv.*

alpine ['alpain] *adj* (*attrib*) (*often with cap*) of the Alps or other high mountains: *alpine flowers.*

already [o:l'redi] *adv* 1 before a particular time; previously: *I had already gone when Tom arrived; I don't want to go to London – I've been there already this week.* 2 now or before the expected time: *Are you leaving already?; He hasn't gone already, has he?; You're not going already, are you?*

also ['o:lsou] *adv* in addition or besides; too: *He is studying German but he is also studying French; I know him also; I don't like him. Also I think he's a fool; Not only does he swim well but he also skis well.*

'also-ran *nc* (*inf often derog*) an unsuccessful or unimportant person (*esp* compared with someone else): *He was an also-ran in the race for promotion; He is a bit of an also-ran.*

altar ['o:ltə] *nc* 1 in some Christian churches the table on which the bread and wine are consecrated during the celebration of communion: *The bride* *and groom stood before the priest at the altar.* **2** a table *etc* on which offerings are made to a god.

alter ['o:ltə] *vti* to make or become different; to change: *Will you alter this dress (to fit me)?; The town has altered a lot in the last two years.*

ˌalteˈration 1 *nu* the act of changing: *Alteration of the shop-front is still in progress.* **2** *nc* the change which is made: *The alterations he has made to the play have not improved it.*

altercation [o:ltə'keiʃən] *ncu (formal or facet)* (an) argument or quarrel in words: *A noisy altercation was in progress between the two politicians.*

alternate ['o:ltəneit] *vti (formal)* to use, do *etc* by turns, repeatedly, one after the other: *John alternates between teaching and studying; He tried to alternate red and yellow tulips along the path as he planted them; He alternates reading with/and watching television.* – [o:l'tə:nət] *adj* **1** coming, happening *etc* in turns, one after the other: *The water came in alternate bursts of hot and cold.* **2** every second (day, week *etc*): *He came to visit us on alternate Tuesdays; My friend and I take the children to school on alternate days.*

al'ternately [-'tə:nət-] *adv* one (state, feeling, person *etc*) after the other: *She felt alternately hot and cold; Wet days and dry days came alternately that week.* **alter'nation** *nu.*

alternative [o:l'tə:nətiv] *adj* offering a choice of a second possibility: *An alternative arrangement can be made if my plans don't suit you.* – *nc* **1** a choice between two (or loosely more) things or possibilities: *Do we have any alternative in this case?; You leave me no alternative but to dismiss you.* **2** either (or loosely any) of these: *I don't like fish. Is there an alternative on the menu?*

al'ternatively *adv* as an alternative: *I thought we'd all have fish. Alternatively, I could have fish and you two could have roast beef.*

although [o:l'ðou] *conj* **1** in spite of the fact that: *Although he hurried, the shop was closed when he got there.* **2** *(old: more usu* **though**) if or even if: *I would not marry you although you were the last man on earth.*

altimeter ['altimi:tə, *(Amer)* al'timitər] *nc* an instrument for measuring altitude.

altitude ['altitju:d] *nu (more tech than* **height**) height above sea-level, *esp* great height: *What is the altitude of the ski-resort?; I'm not used to living at this altitude.*

alto ['altou] – *pl* **'altos** – *nc* **1** (a singer having) a singing voice of the lowest pitch for a woman (*also* **con'tralto**) and the highest pitch for a man: *She is an alto; His alto is quite good; (attrib) an alto voice.* **2** in music, a part written for a voice at this pitch: *The alto is rather difficult; (attrib) the alto part.* – *adv* with an alto voice: *He sings alto.*

altogether [o:ltə'geðə] *adv* **1** completely: *I'm not altogether satisfied.* **2** on the whole and considering everything: *I'm wet, I'm tired and I'm cold. Altogether I'm not feeling very cheerful.*

altruism ['altruizəm] *nu (formal)* an unselfish concern for the good of others.

ˌaltru'istic *adj (formal)* showing altruism: *He acted from an altruistic desire to make sure everyone else was all right.*

aluminium [alju'miniəm], *(Amer)* **aluminum** [ə'lu:minəm] *nu, adj* (of) an element (symbol **Al**), a light, silver-coloured metal used in making saucepans *etc*: *pans made of aluminium; aluminium foil.*

always ['o:lweiz] *adv* **1** at all times: *I always work hard; He is almost always right; I'll always remember her.* **2** continually or repeatedly: *He is always making mistakes; He always went home at five o'clock.* **3** *(usu with* **can/could**) if no other course of action seems better: *If you don't like it, you can always go home; You could always ask your father if your mother doesn't know the answer.*

am *see* **be**.

amalgam [ə'malgəm] *ncu (tech)* a mixture, *esp* of metals: *The dentist mixed the amalgam before filling the patient's teeth with it.*

a'malgamate [-meit] *vti (formal)* to join or mix together (*esp* of business companies): *The small firm had to amalgamate with the larger one or go bankrupt.* **aˌmalga'mation** *ncu.*

amass [ə'mas] *vti (formal)* to gather or collect in a large quantity: *He amassed a fortune; He amassed an enormous quantity of information.*

amateur ['amətə, *(Amer)* -tʃər] *nc* **1** a person who takes part in a sport *etc* without being paid for it: *The tennis tournament was open only to amateurs; (attrib) an amateur golfer; (attrib) an amateur tournament.* **2** someone who does something for the love of it and not for money: *For an amateur, he was quite a good photographer; (attrib) amateur photography.* **3** *(inf)* a person who is not very skilful at something: *I don't want to have my watch mended by a bunch of amateurs!*

ˌama'teurish [-'tə:-] *adj (derog)* not very skilful: *He made an amateurish attempt at carpentry.*

amaze [ə'meiz] *vt* to surprise greatly: *His stupidity amazed me; I was amazed at his stupidity.*

a'mazement *nu* great surprise: *To my amazement, he had never heard of her.*

a'mazing *adj* surprising; astonishing: *an amazing sight; It is amazing that you have not heard of him.*

a'mazingly *adv* **1** in an amazing manner; very surprisingly: *Amazingly, the injured man survived.* **2** to a very surprising extent: *The number of people killed by this dangerous practice is amazingly small.*

ambassador [am'basədə] – *fem* **am'bassadress** – *nc* **1** the government minister appointed to act for his government in another country: *the British Ambassador to Italy.* **2** *(fig)* a representative: *He is the firm's ambassador at such meetings.* **amˌbassa'dorial** [-'do:-] *adj (formal).*

amber ['ambə] *nu, adj* (of) a hard yellow or brownish substance, formed from resin, used in making jewellery *etc*: *made of amber; an amber brooch.*

ambidext(e)rous [ambi'dekstrəs] *adj (pred)* able to use both hands equally well: *His parents are both left-handed but he is ambidextrous.* **ˌambi'dext(e)rously** *adv.*

ambience ['ambiəns] *nu (formal)* surroundings; surrounding influence or atmosphere: *I like the ambience of French cafés.*

'ambient *adj (attrib formal)* (of air, temperature *etc*) surrounding: *The ambient temperature of the nursery should be 20° C.*

ambiguous [am'bigjuəs] *adj (neg* **un-**) having more than one possible meaning; *(loosely)* not very clear: *After the cat caught the mouse, it died is an ambiguous statement* (*ie* it is not clear whether *it* = the cat or = the mouse); *His statement was rather ambiguous; The prisoner's statement is very ambiguous in places.* **am'biguously** *adv.*

ˌambi'guity [-'gju:-] **1** *nu* uncertainty of meaning: *There is a degree of ambiguity in his remarks.* **2**

nc an ambiguous word or statement: *His speech was full of ambiguities.*
am'biguousness *nu* uncertainty of meaning: *The ambiguousness of his letter confused her.*

ambition [am'biʃən] **1** *ncu* the desire for success, fame, power *etc*: *He is full of ambition and energy; He will never realize all his ambitions.* **2** *nc* the desire eventually to become or do something special: *His ambition is to be Prime Minister; He has always had an ambition to go to Moscow; He at last achieved/realized his ambition to sail round the world.*
am'bitious *adj* (*neg* **un-**) **1** having ambition: *an ambitious man; He is very ambitious.* **2** showing ambition (but often not completely successful in achieving an aim): *an ambitious piece of work; That plan is too ambitious.* **am'bitiously** *adv.*
am'bitiousness *nu* the quality which a thing or person has when ambitious: *They were amazed at the ambitiousness of his scheme.*

amble ['ambl] *vi* to walk without hurrying: *We were ambling along enjoying the scenery.* – *nu* a slow, unhurried walk.

ambulance ['ambjuləns] *nc* a vehicle for carrying the sick and injured to hospital *etc*: *Call an ambulance – this man is very ill!*

ambush ['ambuʃ] *vt* to wait in hiding for and make a surprise attack on: *They planned to ambush the enemy as they marched towards the capital.* – *nc* **1** an attack made in this way. **2** the group of people making the attack. **3** the place in which they hide.

ameliorate [ə'mi:liəreit] *vti* (*formal*) to make or become better: *You will not ameliorate the situation by giving long explanations.* **a͵melio'ration** *nu.*

amenable [ə'mi:nəbl] *adj* (*formal*: *pred*) ready to accept advice or guidance: *I am quite amenable to your suggestions; I always find her most amenable.*

amend [ə'mend] *vt* **1** (*formal*) to correct or improve: *We shall amend the error as soon as possible.* **2** to change slightly: *The author is amending the text for the new edition.*
a'mendment *ncu* (a) change (*usu* in something written, *esp* a law *etc*): *amendments to the text.*
make amends to do something to improve the situation after doing something wrong, stupid *etc*: *He gave her a present to make amends for his rudeness.*
See also **emend**.

amenity [ə'mi:nəti] *nc* something that makes life more pleasant or convenient: *This part of town has a lot of amenities – good shops, parks etc.*

America, American *see* Appendix 2.

amethyst ['aməθist] *ncu* a purple semi-precious stone: *He bought her a huge amethyst;* (*attrib*) *an amethyst pendant.*

Amharic *see* Appendix 2.

amiable ['eimiəbl] *adj* likeable; pleasant and good-tempered: *John is a very amiable young man; She seems very amiable to him.* **͵amia'bility** *nu.*
'amiably *adv* in a good-tempered manner: *He smiled amiably.*

amicable ['amikəbl] *adj* (*formal*) friendly: *The dispute was settled in a very amicable manner; She was very amicable last night.* **'amicably** *adv.*

amid, amidst [ə'mid(st)] *preps* (*often liter*) in the middle of; among: *Amid all the confusion, the real point of the meeting was lost; He felt small and insignificant amidst the vast shadows of the forest.*

amiss [ə'mis] *adj* (*liter, old or formal*: *pred*) wrong: *What's amiss with that machine today?*
take (something) amiss (*formal*) to be upset or offended by something: *He took it amiss that I had not consulted him before acting; I was anxious that you should not take my words amiss.*

ammo ['amou] *short for* **ammunition**.

ammonia [ə'mouniə] *nu* **1** a strong-smelling gas made of hydrogen and nitrogen. **2** a solution of this gas in water, used for cleaning *etc.*

ammunition [amju'niʃən] *nu* **1** (*inf abbrev* **ammo** ['amou]) things used in the firing of a gun *etc* (*eg* bullets, gunpowder, shells): *How long will the soldiers' ammunition last?* **2** (*fig*) facts *etc* used against someone in an argument: *She used my words as ammunition against me later.*

amnesia [am'ni:ziə] *nu* (*med*) loss of memory: *After falling on his head he suffered from amnesia for several weeks.*

amnesty ['amnəsti] *ncu* (*formal*) a general pardon given to people who have done wrong *esp* against the government: *The murderer was released under the amnesty declared by the new president.*

amok [ə'mok], **amuck** [ə'mʌk]: **run amok/amuck** to rush about madly, attacking everybody and everything: *The prisoner ran amok and killed two prison officers.*

among, (*also, esp Brit*) **amongst** [ə'mʌŋ(st)] *prep* **1** in the middle of: *a house among the trees.* **2** in shares or parts to each person (in a group *etc*): *Divide the chocolate among you; We only had one programme amongst the three of us.* **3** in the group of: *Among his novels, this is the best.*

amoral [ei'morəl] *adj* not interested in or concerned with questions of right and wrong: *It is difficult to prevent her from stealing, as she is totally amoral; an amoral young woman.*
See also **immoral**.

amorous ['amərəs] *adj* (*formal*) **1** (*attrib*) showing (sexual) love: *He gave the blonde an amorous glance.* **2** ready or inclined to love: *He is a very amorous young man; He gets amorous when he's had a glass of wine.*

amount [ə'maunt] *vi* (*with* **to**) **1** to add up to: *The bill amounted to £5.* **2** to be equal to: *Borrowing money and not returning it amounts to stealing.* – *nc* a quantity, *esp* of money: *a large amount of money in the bank; a vast amount of experience.*

ampère ['ampeə] *nc* (*also* **amp** [amp]) (*tech*: *often abbrev* **A** *when written*) the unit by which an electric current is measured.

ampersand ['ampəsand] *nc* (*formal*) a name for the symbol **&** meaning 'and'.

amphibian [am'fibiən] *nc* **1** (*tech*) a creature that spends part of its life on land and part in water: *Frogs are amphibians.* **2** a vehicle designed to move on land or in the water. **3** an aircraft designed to fly from land or water.
am'phibious *adj* **1** (*tech*) living on land and in water: *amphibious creatures; Frogs are amphibious.* **2** (*formal*: *attrib*) used or carried out on land and on or in water: *An amphibious attack was launched on the seaport; an amphibious vehicle.*

amphitheatre, (*Amer*) **amphitheater** ['amfiθiətə] *nc* (*hist*) an oval or circular building with rows of seats surrounding a central space, *usu* used as a theatre.

ample ['ampl] *adj* **1** (*more formal than* **enough**) (more than) enough: *There is ample space for four people; Three days will be ample (time) for the journey.* **2** large: *an ample bosom.*
'amply *adv*: *He was amply repaid for his efforts.*

amplify ['amplifai] *vt* **1** (*formal*) to make larger, *esp* by adding details to: *Could you amplify your original report?* 2 to make (the sound from a radio, record-player *etc*) louder by using an amplifier. ˌ**amplifi'cation** [-fi-] *ncu*.

'**amplifier** *nc* a piece of equipment for increasing the strength or power-level of electric currents *esp* so as to increase loudness: *You need a new amplifier for your stereo equipment.*

'**amplitude** [-tju:d] *nu* (*formal*) largeness or size.

amputate ['ampjuteit] *vti* (*formal or tech*) (of a surgeon *etc*) to cut off (an arm or leg *etc*): *They are going to have to amputate (his left leg).* ˌ**ampu'tation** *ncu*.

amuck *see* **amok**.

amuse [ə'mju:z] *vt* 1 to make (someone) laugh: *The comedian amused the audience greatly; I was amused at/by the monkey's antics.* 2 to interest or give pleasure to (for a time): *They amused themselves playing cards; How will they amuse the children on a wet afternoon?*

a'**musement** 1 *nu* the state of being amused or of finding something funny: *a smile of amusement; The teacher slipped on a banana skin to the great amusement of the children.* 2 *nc* an entertainment or interest: *amusements for a wet afternoon;* (*attrib*) *amusement arcade.*

a'**musing** *adj* rather funny or humorous: *an amusing story; I find him very amusing.* a'**musingly** *adv*.

an *see* **a**.

anachronism [ə'nakrənizəm] (*formal*) 1 *ncu* the mistake (made *esp* in writing a historical novel, play *etc*) of including a reference to an idea, object *etc* which did not exist at the time written about, *eg* mentioning a clock in a story of ancient Rome. 2 *nc* something which is old-fashioned and out of place in the modern world: *The British aristocracy is often considered an anachronism today.* aˌ**nachro'nistic** *adj*.

anaemia, (*Amer*) **anemia** [ə'ni:miə] *nu* (*med*) a medical condition caused by not having enough red cells in the blood: *Anaemia is common during pregnancy.*

a'**naemic** *adj* 1 (*med: usu pred*) suffering from anaemia: *She has been anaemic for years.* 2 (*fig*) pale or weak: *The room was decorated in an anaemic shade of pink.*

anaesthetic, (*Amer*) **anesthetic** [anəs'θetik] *nc* a substance, used in surgery *etc*, that causes lack of feeling in a part of the body (a **local anaesthetic**) or unconsciousness (a **general anaesthetic**): *to be under an anaesthetic.*

ˌ**anaes'thesia** [-'θi:ziə, (*Amer*) -ʒə] *nu* (*tech*) loss of consciousness or of feeling caused by an anaesthetic.

anaesthetist [ə'ni:sθətist, (*Amer*) ə'nes-] *nc* the doctor responsible for giving an anaesthetic to the patient during a surgical operation.

anaesthetize, -ise [ə'ni:sθətaiz, (*Amer*) ə'nes-] *vt* to make (someone) unable to feel pain *etc* (by giving an anaesthetic to): *The patient has been anaesthetized – you can operate now.*

anagram ['anəgram] *nc* a word, phrase or sentence formed from the letters of another: *Flit on, cheering angel is an anagram of Florence Nightingale.*

anal *see* **anus**.

analogy [ə'nalədʒi] 1 *nc* (*formal*) a likeness or similarity in some ways: *There is an analogy between the gills of a fish and the lungs of an animal.* 2 *nu* reasoning from similar cases: *By analogy with last year's results, we can guess what will happen this year.*

a'**nalogous** [-gəs] *adj* (*usu pred with* **to**) similar or alike in some ways: *I've looked at several cases analogous to ours.*

analysis [ə'naləsis] – *pl* **a'nalyses** [-si:z] – 1 *ncu* (a) detailed examination of something (a sentence, a chemical compound *etc*) *esp* by breaking it up into the parts of which it is made: *The chemist is making an analysis of the poison; We must make a close analysis of the situation.* 2 *nc* (*esp Amer*) psycho-analysis: *He is undergoing analysis for his emotional problems.*

analyse, (*Amer*) **analyze** ['anəlaiz] *vt* 1 to examine the nature of (something) *esp* by breaking up (a whole) into the parts of which it is made: *The children are analysing sentences; The doctor analysed the blood sample; You must analyse the sales figures.*

analyst ['anəlist] *nc* 1 a person who analyses: *a chemical analyst in a laboratory.* 2 (*esp Amer*) a psychiatrist.

analytical [anə'litikl] *adj* (*attrib*) using or based on analysis: *an analytical report on the problem; He has an analytical mind.*

anarchy ['anəki] *nu* 1 the absence or failure of government: *Total anarchy followed the defeat of the government.* 2 (*loosely*) disorder and confusion: *His classroom was in a continual state of anarchy.*

'**anarchist** *nc* 1 a person who believes that governments are unnecessary or undesirable. 2 a person who tries to overturn the government by violence. 3 a person who tries to cause disorder of any kind. '**anarchism** *nu*.

anathema [ə'naθəmə] *ncu* (*formal*) something or someone hated: *Strong drink is (an) anathema to him.*

anatomy [ə'natəmi] *nu* 1 the science of the structure of the (*usu* human) body, *esp* the study of the body by cutting up dead animal and human bodies: *He is studying anatomy;* (*attrib*) *anatomy students/lectures.* 2 (*loosely: often facet*) the structure of the body: *His fall left him with a pain in several parts of his anatomy.*

anatomical [anə'tomikl] *adj* (*tech*) concerned with the parts of the body: *no anatomical abnormality.* ˌ**ana'tomically** *adv*.

a'**natomist** *nc* a person who specializes in anatomy.

ancestor ['ansistə, (*Amer*) -ses-] – *fem* (*old*) '**ancestress** – *nc* a person who was a member of one's family a long time ago and from whom one is descended: *Raleigh is an ancestor of mine.*

an'cestral [-'ses-] *adj* (*attrib*) of one's ancestors: *his ancestral home.*

'**ancestry** *nc* a line of ancestors coming down to one's parents: *He is of noble ancestry.*

anchor ['aŋkə] *nc* 1 something, *usu* a heavy piece of metal with points which dig into the sea-bed, used to hold a boat in one position. 2 (*fig*) anything that holds someone or something steady: *He leaned over the cliff, using a bush as an anchor.* – *vti* to hold (a boat *etc*) steady (with an anchor): *They have anchored (the boat) near the shore;* (*fig*) *The climbers were anchored to each other by a rope.*

'**anchorage** [-ridʒ] *nc* a place which is safe, or used, for anchoring boats: *a sheltered anchorage.*

at 'anchor (of a ship) anchored: *The ship lay at anchor in the bay.*

weigh anchor *see* **weigh**.

anchovy ['antʃəvi] *nc* a small kind of Mediterranean fish of the herring family, used in cooking as a decoration and to add flavour: *fillets of anchovy*; (*attrib*) *anchovy sauce.*

ancient ['einʃənt] *adj* **1** (*usu attrib*) relating to times long ago, *esp* before the collapse of Rome in AD 476: *ancient history.* **2** very old: *He was wearing an ancient, worn-out sweater*; *That book is ancient.* – *nc* (*liter or facet*) an old person: *The porter was an ancient who looked very frail.*

ancient history *nu* **1** history of times long ago. **2** (*facet*) a recent fact *etc* that is very well-known: *'Did you know he had emigrated?' 'Yes, that's ancient history!'*

the ancients people who lived in ancient times: *the wisdom of the ancients.*

and [ənd, and] *conj* **1** joining two statements, pieces of information *etc*: *I opened the door and went inside*; *The hat was blue and red*; *a man and woman*; *a mother and child.* **2** in addition to: *2 and 2 makes 4*; *Time and time again I told him to stop.* **3** as a result of which: *Go away and I shall never speak to you again*; *Try hard and you will succeed.* **4** (*inf*) used instead of 'to' of the infinitive of a verb: *Do try and come!*

anecdote ['anikdout] *nc* (*formal*) a short, interesting or amusing story, *esp* a true one: *He told us slanderous anecdotes about politicians that he knew.*

ˌanec'dotal *adj* (*formal*) like, of, or full of anecdotes: *He has a relaxed, anecdotal prose-style.*

anemone [ə'neməni] *nc* a kind of flower related to the buttercup, *usu* red, blue or purple.

aneroid ['anəroid]: **aneroid barometer** *nc* a barometer in which the pressure of the air is measured without the use of a liquid.

anesthetic *see* **anaesthetic**.

anew [ə'nju:] *adv* (*old or liter*) again; freshly: *The world, in spring, seems to be born anew.*

angel ['eindʒəl] *nc* **1** a messenger or attendant of God: *The angels announced the birth of Christ to the shepherds*; *The little girl played an angel in the Christmas play.* **2** (*fig*) a very good or beautiful person: *She's an absolute angel about helping us.*

angelic [an'dʒelik] *adj* like an angel, *esp* very good: *a little boy with an angelic expression*; *He looks angelic, but he is often very naughty.* **an'gelically** *adv.*

anger ['aŋgə] *nu* a violent, bitter feeling (against someone or something): *He was filled with anger about the way he had been treated.* – *vt* (*formal*) to make someone angry: *His words angered her very much.*

'angry *adj* **1** feeling or showing anger: *He was so angry that he was unable to speak*; *He regretted his angry words*; *He gets angry over nothing*; *She got angry at the children and hit them*; *She is angry with him*; (*fig*) *The sky looks angry – it is going to rain.* **2** red and sore-looking: *He has an angry cut over his left eye*; *That cut looks angry.* **'angrily** *adv.*

angle[1] ['aŋgl] *nc* **1** the (amount of) space between two straight lines or surfaces that meet: *a sharp angle*; *an angle of 90°.* **2** (*inf*) a point of view: *What's your angle on this matter?*; *from a journalist's angle.* – *vt* **1** to direct or point something at an angle: *He angled the camera up towards the ceiling.* **2** to give (an account of news *etc*) in such a way as to suit a particular point of view or appeal to a certain group *etc*: *This programme is angled at five- to seven-year-olds.*

angular ['aŋgjulə] *adj* **1** (*attrib*) having an angle or angles: *an angular building.* **2** (of a person) thin and bony: *She is tall and angular*; *an angular young man.* **ˌangularity** [-'la-] *nu.*

angle[2] ['aŋgl] *vi* to use a rod and line to try to catch fish: *angling for trout.* **2** (*with* **for**: *usu derog*) to try to get something by indirect means: *I think he is angling for a free meal*; *She is angling for compliments.*

'angler *nc* a person who fishes with a rod and line. **'angling** *nu.*

Anglican ['aŋglikən] *nc, adj* (a member) of the Church of England: *an Anglican bishop*; *He is not a Roman Catholic – he is an Anglican.*

anglicize, -ise ['aŋglisaiz] *vt* (*formal*) to make English or more like English: *to anglicize the pronunciation of a French word*; *After living in England for ten years, he had become very anglicized.*

Anglo- [aŋglou] (*in cmpds*) English: *ˌAnglo-A'merican*; *ˌAnglo-'Scottish.*

anglophile ['aŋgləfail] *adj, nc* (*formal*) (of) a person who likes or admires the English people.

anglophobia [aŋglə'foubiə] *nu* (*formal*) a hatred or fear of England and the English.

'anglophobe *nc* a person who hates or fears the English.

Anglo-Saxon [aŋglou'saksən] **1** *nc* one of the original Germanic settlers in England or southern Scotland. **2** *n, adj* Old English. – *adj* **1** of the Anglo-Saxons. **2** of English-speaking people generally.

angora [aŋ'go:rə] *nc* a kind of goat, cat or rabbit with long silky hair. **2** *nu, adj* (of) the wool made from the hair of an angora goat or rabbit.

angry *see* **anger**.

anguish ['aŋgwiʃ] *nu* (*formal*) very great pain of body or mind; agony: *The woman suffered terrible anguish when her child was ill.*

'anguished *adj* (*usu attrib*: *often facet*) suggesting suffering, *usu* of mind: *He was concentrating hard, with an anguished expression on his face.*

angular, angularity *see* **angle**[1].

animal ['animəl] *nc* **1** a living being which can feel things and move freely: *man and other animals*; *the higher animals*; (*attrib*) *animal life.* **2** an animal other than man: *a book on man's attitude to animals*; (*attrib*) *animal, not human, instincts.*

animate ['animeit] *vt* (*formal*) **1** to make lively: *Joy animated his face.* **2** to be the cause of: *His actions were animated by revenge.* – [-mət] *adj* living: *an animate object*; *Is the object animate or inanimate?*

'animated [-mei-] *adj* **1** lively: *An animated discussion followed his speech*; *The discussion was animated.* **2** made to move as if alive: *animated dolls/cartoons.* **ˌani'mation** *nu.*

See also **inanimate**.

animosity [ani'mosəti] *ncu* (*formal*) (a) strong dislike or hatred: *The rivals had regarded one another with animosity for years*; *She felt a strong animosity towards her new neighbour.*

ankle ['aŋkl] *nc* the (area around the) joint connecting the foot and leg: *She has broken her ankle*; *She has slim ankles*; (*attrib*) *ankle socks.*

annals ['anlz] *n pl* (*esp tech*) yearly historical accounts of events: *This king is mentioned several times in the annals of the period*; (*fig*) *one of the most shocking stories in the annals of crime.*

annex [ə'neks] *vt* (*formal*) **1** to take possession of *eg* a country. **2** to add or attach: *She annexed a report of the meeting to her letter.* – ['aneks] (*also* **'annexe**) *nc* a building added to, or used as an addition to, another building: *a hotel annexe.* ˌ**annex'ation** [a-] *nu* (*formal*).

annihilate [ə'naiəleit] *vt* (*formal*) to destroy completely: *The epidemic annihilated the population of the town.* **anˌnihi'lation** *nu.*

anniversary [anə'vəːsəri] *nc* the day of the year on which something once happened and is (*esp* officially) remembered: *We celebrated our fifth wedding anniversary*; *Yesterday was the third anniversary of our arrival in this country*; (*attrib*) *an anniversary dinner.*

annotate ['anəteit] *vt* (*formal*) to add notes, explanations *etc* to (a book *etc*): *This copy has been annotated by the author.* ˌ**anno'tation** *ncu.*

announce [ə'nauns] *vt* **1** to make known publicly: *Mary and John have announced their engagement.* **2** to make known the arrival or entrance of: *When I arrived, the servant announced me*; *He announced the next singer.*

an'nouncement *ncu*: *He wishes to make an important announcement*; *The announcement of their engagement surprised everyone.*

an'nouncer *nc* a person who introduces programmes or reads the news on radio or television.

annoy [ə'noi] *vt* to make (someone) rather angry or impatient: *Please go away and stop annoying me!*

an'noyance **1** *nc* something which annoys: *That noise has been an annoyance to me for weeks!* **2** *nu* the state of being annoyed: *He was red in the face with annoyance.*

an'noyed *adj* made angry: *My mother is annoyed with me*; *She is annoyed at arriving late*; *He was annoyed at her remarks*; *She was annoyed by the laughter of the children*; *an annoyed frown.*

an'noying *adj* causing annoyance: *He has several annoying habits*; *She's very annoying.* **an'noyingly** *adv.*

annual ['anjuəl] *adj* (*usu attrib*) **1** happening every year: *The flower-show is an annual event.* **2** of one year: *What is his annual salary?* – *nc* **1** a book of which a new edition is published every year: *Many children's annuals are published near Christmas.* **2** a plant that lives for only one year.

'annually *adv*: *His salary is increased annually.*

an'nuity [-'njuː-] *nc* (*formal*) payment made each year for a certain time (*usu* the life of the person receiving it): *He has retired from work and receives an annuity from his former employers.*

annul [ə'nʌl] – *pt, ptp* **an'nulled** – *vt* (*formal*) to declare (that something is) not valid and cancel (*esp* a marriage or legal contract): *Their marriage was annulled by the Pope.* **an'nulment** *ncu.*

annum *see* **per annum** *under* **per**.

anode ['anoud] *nc* (*tech*) the point at which an electric current enters a battery *etc.*

See also **cathode**.

anoint [ə'noint] *vt* (*formal*) to smear or cover with ointment or oil *esp* in a religious ceremony: *anointed by a priest.*

anomaly [ə'noməli] *nc* something unusual or different from the normal (and *usu* less satisfactory): *There are many anomalies in the pay-structure*; *A pub with no beer is quite an anomaly!* **a'nomalous** *adj.*

anon [ə'non] short for **anonymous**, when used instead of the name of the author of a poem *etc.*

anonymous [ə'nonəməs] *adj* without the name of the author, giver *etc* being known or given: *The giver of the prizes wished to remain anonymous*; *an anonymous author.* **a'nonymously** *adv.*

anonymity [anə'niməti] *nu* (*formal*) the state of not making one's name known: *He was careful to preserve his anonymity.*

anorak ['anərak] *nc* a hooded waterproof jacket: *Most children wear anoraks in the winter.*

another [ə'nʌðə] *adj, pron* **1** a different (thing or person): *This letter isn't from Tom – it's from another friend of mine*; *The coat I bought was dirty, so the shop gave me another.* **2** (one) more of the same kind: *Have another biscuit!*; *You didn't tell me you wanted another of those!*; *He thinks he's another Shakespeare.*

See also **one another** *under* **one**.

answer ['aːnsə] *nc* **1** something said, written or done that is caused by a question asked, an action carried out *etc* by another person: *She refused to give an answer to his questions*; *When she criticized his driving, his answer was to drive faster than ever.* **2** the solution to a problem: *The answer to your transport difficulties is to buy a car.* – **1** *vti* to make an answer to a question, problem, action *etc*: *Answer my questions, please*; *Why don't you answer the letter?* **2** *vt* to act in a fixed manner as an answer to (the door/bell/telephone *etc*), *ie* to open the door, pick up the telephone *etc*: *He answered the telephone promptly as soon as it rang*; *Could you answer the door, please?* **3** *vti* (*formal*) to be suitable or all that is necessary (for): *This will answer my requirements.* **4** *vt* (*often with* **to**) to be the same as or correspond to (a description *etc*): *The police have found a man answering (to) that description.* – *See also* **answer for** *below.*

'answerable *adj* (*pred*: *usu with* **to, for**) to have the responsibility: *I will be answerable to you for his good behaviour* (= I will see that he behaves well); *She is answerable for the whole project.*

'answer for *vt fus* **1** (*often with* **to**) to bear the responsibility or be responsible for (something): *I'll answer to your mother for your safety.* **2** to suffer or be punished (for something): *You'll answer for your rudeness one day!*

ant [ant] *nc* a type of small insect, related to bees, wasps *etc*, and often thought of as very hard-working.

'ant-hill *nc* a mound or heap of earth built as a nest by ants.

antagonist [an'tagənist] *nc* (*formal*) an opponent or enemy: *He glared at his antagonist across the conference table.*

an'tagonism *nu* (*formal*) unfriendliness or opposition: *He sensed their antagonism immediately he entered the room.*

anˌtago'nistic *adj* (*formal*) (*with* **to** *or* **towards** *when pred*) unfriendly or opposed: *an antagonistic attitude*; *He is antagonistic towards me and my ideas.* **anˌtago'nistically** *adv.*

an'tagonize, -ise *vt* (*formal*) to make an enemy or opponent of (someone): *You are antagonizing her by your rudeness.*

Antarctic [ant'aːktik] *adj* (*attrib*) of the area round the South Pole: *an Antarctic expedition.*

the Antarctic the area round the South Pole: *Scott of the Antarctic.*

ante- [anti] (*in cmpds*) before; (in place) as in **ante-room**; (in time) as in **antedate**.

antecedents [anti'siːdənts] *n pl* (*formal*) (information about) the origins, history *etc* of (a person or thing): *What are his antecedents?*

antedate [anti'deit] *vt* (*formal*) **1** to belong to an earlier period than: *Shakespeare's plays antedate the modern type of stage.* **2** to put a date on (a document *etc*) that is earlier than the actual date:

She must have antedated that cheque.

antediluvian [antidi'lu:viən] *adj* (*fig facet*) very old or old-fashioned (*literally*, old enough to have existed *etc* before Noah's Flood): *My grandmother has antediluvian ideas on the upbringing of children*; *Her ideas are rather antediluvian.*

antelope ['antəloup] – *pls* **'antelopes, 'antelope** – *nc* any of several types of quick-moving, graceful, horned animal related to the goat and cow: *I shot two antelopes*; *a herd of antelope.*

antenatal [anti'neitl] *adj* (*formal*: *attrib*) before birth: *Good antenatal care reduces the number of infant deaths.*

antenna [an'tenə] – *pls* **an'tennae** [-ni:] (*def 1*), **an'tennas** (*def 2*) – *nc* **1** a feeler of an insect. **2** (*Amer*) an aerial (for a radio *etc*).

anteroom ['antirum] *nc* (*formal*) a room opening into another and more important room: *He was kept waiting in the anteroom for some time before being admitted to the throne room to see the king.*

anthem ['anθəm] *nc* a piece of music for a church choir *usu* with words from the Bible. **2** (*loosely*) a song of praise generally.

anthology [an'θolədʒi] *nc* a collection of pieces of poetry or prose: *an anthology of love poems.*

anthracite ['anθrəsait] *nu* a kind of very hard coal that burns almost without any smoke or flames: *This stove burns anthracite*; (*attrib*) *an anthracite stove* (= a stove that burns anthracite).

anthrax ['anθraks] *nu* a deadly disease of sheep and cattle that may be given to man.

anthropology [anθrə'polədʒi] *nu* the study of human society, customs, beliefs *etc.* **ˌanthropo'logical** [-'lo-] *adj.* **ˌanthro'pologist** *nc.*

anti- [anti] (*in cmpds*) **1** against, as in **anti-aircraft**. **2** the opposite of, as in **anticlockwise**.

anti-aircraft [anti'eəkra:ft] *adj* (*mil*: *attrib*) used to fight against enemy aircraft: *anti-aircraft defences.*

antibiotic ['antibai'otik] *nc* a medicine which is used to kill the bacteria that cause disease: *Penicillin was one of the earliest antibiotics.*

antibody ['antibodi] *nc* (*tech*) a substance produced in *eg* the human body, which fights bacteria *etc*: *Babies have few antibodies against infection.*

anticipate [an'tisəpeit] *vt* **1** to expect (something): *I'm not anticipating any trouble*; *I'm anticipating a large crowd of people at tonight's meeting.* **2** to see what is going to be wanted, required *etc* in the future and do what is necessary before the situation occurs: *A businessman must try to anticipate what his customers will want.* **3** (*formal*) to do something before (someone else): *When they reached their destination, the British explorers found that they had been anticipated by the French.*

anˌtici'pation *nu* **1** the act of anticipating (a person, thing *etc*): *His anticipation of the question meant that he was ready to answer it.* **2** the act of looking forward to (an event *etc*) with hope, pleasure *etc*: *I'm looking forward to the concert with great anticipation.*

anticlimax [anti'klaimaks] *nc* a dull or disappointing ending to a play, activity *etc* after increasing excitement or interest: *After all the weeks of preparation and excitement, Mary found the concert itself a bit of an anticlimax.*

anticlockwise [anti'klokwaiz] *adv, adj* moving in the opposite direction to that in which the hands of a clock move: *The wheels turn anticlockwise*; *They turn in an anticlockwise direction.*

antics ['antiks] *n pl* odd, silly or amusing behaviour: *The children laughed at the monkey's antics.*

anticyclone [anti'saikloun] *nc* a circling movement of air or wind around an area of high air pressure, *usu* causing calm weather.

antidote ['antidout] *nc* **1** (*tech*) a medicine *etc* which is given to prevent a poison acting on a person *etc*: *If you are bitten by a poisonous snake, you have to be given an antidote*; *There is no known antidote for this weedkiller*; *This is an antidote against snake-bites.* **2** (*fig*) anything that prevents something bad: *Laughter is a good antidote for arrogance.*

antifreeze ['antifri:z] *ncu* a substance which is added to a liquid, *usu* water (*eg* in the radiator of a car engine), to prevent it from freezing.

antihistamine [anti'histəmi:n] *nc* (*tech*) a medicine which is used to treat hay fever and other allergies: *He has stopped sneezing because he is on antihistamines.*

antipathy [an'tipəθi] *ncu* (*formal*) (a) strong dislike: *I feel a great antipathy towards him*; *There is a great deal of antipathy between them.*

ˌantipa'thetic [-'θe-] *adj* (*very formal*: *with* **to, towards** *when pred*) feeling antipathy (towards a person *etc*): *an antipathetic attitude*; *antipathetic to/towards modern methods of education.*

antipodes [an'tipədi:z] *n pl* places on the earth's surface exactly opposite each other (*esp* Australia and New Zealand, which are opposite to Europe).

antique [an'ti:k] *adj* **1** old and *usu* valuable: *an antique chair.* **2** (*derog*) old or old-fashioned: *an antique car*; *That car is positively antique.* – *nc* something made long ago (*usu* more than a hundred years ago) which is valuable or interesting: *He collects antiques*; *That chair is an antique*; (*attrib*) *an antique shop* (= a shop where antiques are sold).

antiquarian [anti'kweəriən] *adj* (*usu attrib*) related to (the study of) antiques or antiquities: *an antiquarian bookshop.* – *nc* an antiquary.

antiquary ['antikwəri] *nc* a person who studies, collects, or buys and sells antiques.

antiquated ['antikweitid] *adj* (*derog*) old or out of fashion: *an antiquated car*; *It is rather antiquated now.*

antiquity [an'tikwəti] (*formal*) **1** *nu* ancient times, *esp* those of the ancient Greeks and Romans: *I enjoy reading stories about the gods and heroes of antiquity.* **2** *nu* great age: *a statue of great antiquity* (= a very old statue). **3** *nc* something remaining from ancient times (*eg* a statue, a vase): *an exhibition of Roman antiquities.*

anti-semitic [antisə'mitik] *adj* (*formal*) hating the Jews. **ˌanti-'semitism** [-'se-] *nu.*

antiseptic [anti'septik] *ncu, adj* (of) a substance that destroys bacteria (*eg* in a wound) or prevents their growth: *You ought to put some antiseptic on that cut*; *an antiseptic cream.*

antisocial [anti'souʃəl] *adj* **1** against the welfare of the community *etc*: *It is antisocial to drop rubbish in the street*; *antisocial habits.* **2** not wanting the company of others: *Since his wife died, he has become more and more antisocial*; *He is rather an antisocial young man.*

antithesis [an'tiθəsis] – *pl* **an'titheses** [-si:z] – (*formal*) **1** *nc* the direct opposite of: *Evil is the antithesis of good.* **2** *ncu* (an example of) the contrasting of two ideas, words *etc* in a sentence, speech *etc*; *To err is human, to forgive divine is an example of antithesis.*

antler ['antlə] *nc* (the branch of) a deer's horn: *A stag has antlers.*

antonym ['antənim] *nc* (*formal*) a word opposite in meaning to another word: *Big and small are antonyms.*

an'tonymy [-'to-] *nu* (*formal*) the state of being antonyms: *Big and small are examples of antonymy.*

anus ['einəs] *nc* (*tech*) the lower opening of the alimentary canal through which waste substances pass. **'anal** *adj.*

anvil ['anvil] *nc* a block, *usu* of iron, on which metal objects (*eg* horse-shoes) are hammered into shape: *the blacksmith's anvil.*

anxiety *see* **anxious**.

anxious ['aŋkʃəs] *adj* **1** worried about what may happen or have happened: *I'm anxious about the future; She is anxious about her father's health; an anxious mother.* **2** (*attrib*) causing worry, fear or uncertainty: *That was an anxious moment when you almost fell over the cliff.* **3** (*pred: with* **to**) wanting very much to do, have *etc* (something): *He's very anxious to please.* **'anxiously** *adv.*

anxiety [aŋ'zaiəti] **1** *ncu* (something which causes) worry: *That is a great anxiety to me; The mother was filled with anxiety about her child's health.* **2** *nu* strong desire: *his anxiety to please.*

any ['eni] **1** *pron, adj* one (person, thing *etc*), no matter which; (*pl*) some (people, things *etc*) no matter which: *It doesn't matter which book you give me – I'll take any of them; I'll take any book; You don't need to choose which books to give me – I'll take any (books) you have.* **2** *pron, adj* (in questions and negative sentences *etc*) one; (*pl*) some: *There is supposed to be a key to open this door but I can't find any; John has been to some interesting places but I've never been to any; Have you been to any interesting places?; We have hardly any coffee left; without any trouble at all.* **3** *adj* every: *Any schoolboy could tell you the answer.* – *adv* at all; (even) by a small amount: *Is this book any better than the last one?; I don't think his writing has improved any.*

'anybody, 'anyone *pron* **1** (in questions, and negative sentences *etc*) some person: *Is anybody there?; I can't see anybody; Have you appointed anyone to the job yet?* **2** any person, no matter which: *Anyone could tell you the answer to that.*

'anyhow *adv* **1** nevertheless; in spite of what has been or might be said, done *etc*: *I don't think you can do it, but you can try anyhow; Anyhow, even if the problem does arise, it won't affect us.* **2** (*inf*; *also* **'any old how**) in a careless way; in an untidy state: *Books were piled on shelves any old how.*

anyone *see* **anybody**.

'anything *pron* **1** (in questions, and negative sentences *etc*) some thing: *Can you see anything?; I can't see anything.* **2** a thing of any kind: *You can buy anything you like; 'What would you like for your birthday?' 'Anything will do.'*

'anyway *adv* nevertheless; in spite of what has been or might be said, done *etc*: *My mother says I can't go to the party but I'm going anyway; Anyway, even if she refuses permission I still intend to go.*

'anywhere *adv* in any place at all: *Have you seen my gloves anywhere?; I can't find them anywhere; 'Where will I put these?' 'Anywhere will do.'*

any a'mount of (*inf*) a great deal of: *You'll have no difficulty in buying green velvet – there's any amount of it on sale in the shops.*

at 'any rate 1 whatever may happen or have happened: *It's a pity it has started to rain, but at any rate we can still enjoy ourselves at the cinema.* **2** that is to say; at least: *He is a very good artist, at any rate for someone who is colour-blind; The Queen is coming to see us – at any rate, that's what John says.*

get anywhere *see* **get somewhere** *under* **get**.

in 'any case nevertheless; in spite of what has been or might be said, done *etc*: *I don't believe the story but I'll check it in any case; In any case, even if the problem can be solved it won't be easy.*

apart [ə'pa:t] *adv* **1** separated by a certain distance: *The trees were planted three metres apart; He stood with his feet apart; The two political parties will never agree – their policies are too far apart.* **2** (*with* **from**) to one side; away from: *She sat apart from the other people.*

a'part from except for: *I can't think of anything I need, apart from a car.* – *See also* **apart** (*def 2*) *above.*

come apart *vi* to break into pieces: *The book came apart in my hands; My jacket is coming apart at the seams.*

take apart 1 *vt sep* to separate (something) into the pieces from which it is made: *He took the engine apart.* **2** *vt oblig sep* (*sl*) to deal with or criticize (a person, plan *etc*) severely: *If you hand in work like that, the teacher will take you apart.*

tell apart *vt oblig sep* (*usu with* **can, cannot** *etc*) to recognize the difference between; to distinguish: *I cannot tell the twins apart; Can you tell them apart?*

apartheid [ə'pa:teit] *nu* (the policy of) keeping people of different races apart by making them live in separate areas *etc.*

apartment [ə'pa:tmənt] *nc* **1** a room, *usu* rented, in a private house, occupied separately by a particular person or group of people. **2** (*Amer*) a flat. **3** (*formal or Amer*) a single room in a house: *a five-apartment house* (= a house with five rooms plus a kitchen and a bathroom). **4** (*in pl: Brit*) a set of rooms, *usu* rented, for living in.

apathy ['apəθi] *nu* (*formal*) a lack of interest or enthusiasm: *The club closed down because of the apathy of the members; his apathy towards his work.*

ˌapa'thetic [-'θe-] *adj* (*formal*) showing or feeling apathy: *an apathetic young woman; an apathetic attitude; She was very apathetic towards the idea.* **ˌapa'thetically** *adv.*

ape [eip] *nc* a large monkey with little or no tail. – *vt* to imitate (a person's behaviour *etc*): *Children often ape their parents.*

aperitif [əperi'ti:f] *nc* a drink, *esp* alcoholic, taken before a meal.

aperture ['apətjuə] *nc* **1** (*formal*) an opening or hole: *There's a slight aperture under that window that causes a draught.* **2** (the size of) the opening (*eg* in a camera) through which light passes.

apex ['eipeks] – *pls* **'apexes, apices** ['eipisi:z] – *nc* the highest point or tip (of something): *the apex of a triangle;* (*fig formal*) *the apex of a person's career.*

aphid ['eifid] , (*rare*) **aphis** ['eifis] – *pls* **'aphids**, (*rare*) **'aphides** [-di:z] – *nc* (*formal*) a very small insect that lives on plants, *esp* a greenfly.

aphrodisiac [afrə'diziak] *nc, adj* (*formal or tech*) (of) a substance that causes sexual excitement: *Nutmeg is considered an aphrodisiac; an aphrodisiac effect.*

apiary ['eipiəri] *nc* a place (containing several hives) where bees are kept.

apiece [ə'pi:s] *adv* (*formal*) to, for, by *etc* each one of a group: *These toys cost fifty pence apiece.*

aplomb [ə'plom] *nu* (*formal*) self-confidence; assurance: *She carried out her duties as hostess with great aplomb.*

apocryphal [ə'pokrəfəl] *adj* (*formal*) said to be true but probably not: *an apocryphal story; I think that story is apocryphal.*

apologetic *see* **apologize**.

apologize, -ise [ə'polədʒaiz] *vi* to express regret or say that one is sorry, for having done something wrong, for a fault *etc*: *I apologize for not coming sooner; I must apologize to her for his rudeness.*

a,polo'getic [-'dʒetik] *adj* showing regret or saying one is sorry for having done something wrong *etc*: *He gave an apologetic smile; He was very apologetic about the mess.* **a,polo'getically** *adv.*

a'pology *nc* an expression of regret for having done something wrong *etc*: *Please accept my apology/my humble apologies for not arriving on time; He made his apologies for not attending.*

an a'pology for (*inf*) an example of (something) of poor quality *etc*; *That's rather an apology for an essay; an apology for a car.*

apoplexy ['apəpleksi] *nu* (*old*) the loss of the power to feel, move *etc* due to damage to a blood-vessel in the brain: *He died of apoplexy.*

,apo'plectic [-'plektik] *adj* **1** (*attrib*) suffering from or affected by apoplexy: *an apoplectic fit.* **2** red and angry: *He was apoplectic with rage.*

apostle [ə'posl] *nc* **1** (*often with cap*) a man sent out to preach the gospel in the early Christian church, *esp* one of the twelve disciples of Christ: *Matthew and Mark were apostles.* **2** (*formal*) a person who tries to raise support for a (new) cause: *He is an apostle of European unity.*

apostolic [apə'stolik] *adj* (*formal*: *usu attrib*) **1** of the apostles. **2** of the Pope: *the Apostolic See.*

apostrophe [ə'postrəfi] *nc* a mark (**'**) which is used to show that a letter or letters has/have been omitted from a word, and which is also used in possessive phrases and in the plurals of letters: *the boy's coat; the boys' coats; There are two n's in 'cannot' but only one in 'can't'.*

apothecary [ə'poθəkəri] *nc* (*old*) a person who makes and sells drugs and medicines.

appal, (*Amer*) **appall** [ə'po:l] – *pt, ptp* **ap'palled** – *vt* to horrify or shock: *I was appalled at how ill he looked; I was appalled by the child's rudeness.* **ap'palling** *adj.* **ap'pallingly** *adv.*

apparatus [apə'reitəs] – *pls* **,appa'ratus, ,appa'ratuses** – *ncu* machinery, tools or equipment: *chemical apparatus; a piece of gymnastic apparatus; This is an apparatus for stretching leather; (fig) the apparatus of local government.*

apparel [ə'parəl] *nu* (*old or liter*) clothing: *the fine apparel of the prince.*

apparent [ə'parənt] *adj* **1** (*pred*) easy to see; evident: *It is quite apparent to all of us that you haven't done your work properly.* **2** (*formal*) seeming but perhaps not real: *His apparent unwillingness would disappear if we paid him enough; His ability is more apparent than real.*

ap'parently *adv*: *They are apparently not coming; Apparently he is not feeling well.*

apparition [apə'riʃən] **1** *nc* something strange or remarkable, *esp* a ghost: *She thought she saw an apparition in the ruined castle.* **2** *nu* (*formal*) the sudden coming into view of something or someone, *esp* something supernatural: *She screamed at the sudden apparition of the ghostly figure.*

appeal [ə'pi:l] *vi* **1** (*often with* **to**) to ask (someone) earnestly for something: *She appealed to him for help; She appealed to me to help her; He appealed for support.* **2** (*usu legal*) to take a case one has lost to a higher court *etc*; to ask (a referee, judge *etc*) for a new decision: *He appealed against a three-year sentence; Now that you have been convicted you must appeal; They appealed to the football league against the referee's decision; It was not clear who had won, so they appealed to the referee.* **3** (*with* **to**) to be pleasing: *This place appeals to me.* – **1** *ncu* (the act of making) a request (for help, a decision *etc*): *The Christmas appeal raised £500 for charity; He made a last appeal for help; The judge rejected his appeal; The prime minister made an appeal to the country for calm during the crisis.* **2** *nu* attraction: *Music holds little appeal for me; Swimming has lost its appeal for me.*

ap'pealing *adj* **1** (*neg* **un-**) pleasing: *an appealing little girl; The idea of going abroad is very appealing.* **2** (*usu attrib*) showing that a person wishes help *etc*: *She gave me an appealing look.*

appear [ə'piə] **1** *vi* to become able to be seen; to come into view: *A man suddenly appeared round the corner of the street.* **2** *vi* to arrive at or come into (a place *etc*): *He never appears before nine o'clock; He appeared in time for dinner.* **3** *vi* to come before or present oneself/itself before the public or (*legal*) a judge *etc*: *He is appearing at our local theatre; His latest novel appeared last week; He appeared before Judge Scott.* **4** *vti* to look or seem as if (something is the case): *It appears that he is wrong; He appears to be wrong; She appears a little upset.*

ap'pearance **1** *nu* what can be seen (of a person, thing *etc*): *You could see he was poor by his appearance; From his appearance he seemed very wealthy.* **2** *nu* (*formal*) the state of seeming to be the case: *This has the appearance of truth.* **3** *nc* the act of coming into view or coming into a place: *The thieves ran off at the sudden appearance of two policemen.* **4** *nc* the act of coming before or presenting oneself/itself before the public or (*legal*) a judge *etc*: *He is making his first appearance at our local theatre; This is his third appearance before the magistrate.*

keep up appearances to behave in such a way as to hide the truth (*esp* something bad or unpleasant) from other people: *They haven't much money but they buy expensive clothes in order to keep up appearances.*

put in, make an appearance to attend (a meeting, party *etc*) *usu* only for a short time: *I don't want to stay for the whole meeting, but I'll put in an appearance at the beginning.*

to, by, from all appearances judging by, or basing one's opinion on, what can be seen *etc*: *He is to all appearances a happy man; By all appearances, they are very much in love.*

appease [ə'pi:z] *vt* (*formal*) to calm or satisfy (a person, desire *etc*) *usu* by giving what was asked for or is needed: *His hunger was soon appeased; She appeased his curiosity by explaining the situation to him.* **ap'peasement** *nu.*

appellation [apə'leiʃən] *nc* (*formal*) a name or title: *His official appellation was Chief of Police but everyone called him the Chief.*

append [ə'pend] *vt* (*formal*) to add (something) to a document, letter *etc*: *Appended is a note of my expenses; Have you appended your signature to your written statement?*

ap'pendage [-didʒ] *nc* **1** (*formal*) something which is added or attached to a document, letter *etc.* **2** (*biol*) something which is attached to and forms part of the body: *Arms, legs and tails are appendages*; (*facet or derog*) *the king and all his appendages* (= the less important people who accompany him).

appendicitis [əpendi'saitis] *nu* the inflammation of the appendix in the body which *usu* causes pain and often requires the removal of the appendix by surgery.

appendix [ə'pendiks] – *pls* **ap'pendixes** *or* **ap'pendices** [-si:z] (*def 1*), **ap'pendixes** (*def 2*) – *nc* **1** a section, *usu* containing extra information, added at the end of a book, document *etc.* **2** a narrow tube leading from the large intestine: *She's had her appendix removed.*

appertain [apə'tein] *vi* (*formal*: *with* **to**) to belong or relate to (something): *There are certain privileges appertaining to this post.*

appetite ['apitait] *ncu* a desire for food: *He hasn't much* (*of an*) *appetite*; *He has a good appetite*; (*fig*) *He has a great appetite for work.*

'appetizer, -s- *nc* (*esp Amer*) something eaten or drunk before or at the beginning of a meal in order to increase the appetite: *They ate smoked salmon as an appetizer.*

'appetizing, -s- *adj* (*neg* **un-**) which increases the appetite: *an appetizing smell*; *That smells appetizing!*

applaud [ə'plo:d] *vt* **1** to praise or show approval, by clapping the hands: *to applaud a speech/a singer.* **2** (*formal*) to express approval of: *I applaud your decision to study medicine.*

ap'plause [-z] *nu* praise or approval, expressed by clapping: *The Prime Minister received great applause at the end of his speech*; *A round of applause followed his speech.*

apple ['apl] *nc* a round fruit (*usu* with a green or red skin) which can be eaten: *The child was eating an apple*; (*attrib*) *an apple tree*; (*attrib*) *an apple tart*; *a slice of apple.*

the apple of someone's eye (*inf*) a person or thing which is greatly loved: *She is the apple of her father's eye.*

in ˌapple-pie 'order (*inf*) neat and tidy, with everything in its correct place: *Her desk is always in apple-pie order.*

upˌset someone's/the 'apple cart (*inf*) to bring into disorder (a person's *etc*) plans: *The football team were doing very well when their best player upset the apple cart by breaking his leg.*

apply [ə'plai] **1** *vt* (*formal*) (*with* **to**) to put (something) on or against something else: *to apply ointment to a cut.* **2** *vti* (*formal*) (*with* **to, against**) to use (something) for some purpose: *to apply force to a door that will not open*; *He applied his knowledge of the country to planning their escape*; *How will he apply this knowledge?* **3** *vi* (*with* **for**) to ask for (something) formally: *You could apply* (*to the manager*) *for a job*; *He applied to the government for financial help.* **4** (*with* **to**: not used with **is, was** *etc* and **-ing**) to concern or be relevant to: *This rule does not apply to him.*

ap'pliance [ə'plai-] *nc* an instrument or tool used for a particular job: *A washing-machine is an electrical appliance.*

'applicable ['apli-] *adj* (*formal*: *pred*) that concerns or is relevant to: *This rule is not applicable* (*to me*). **ˌapplica'bility** *nu.*

'applicant ['apli-] *nc* a person who applies (for a job *etc*): *There were two hundred applicants for the job of editor.*

ˌappli'cation [apli-] **1** *ncu* (a) formal request (for a job *etc*): *Have you sent in your application for a place at the university?*; *We have had several applications for the new job*; *on application to the headmaster.* **2** *nu* (*formal*) the use of something for some purpose: *the practical application of the scientific discovery in medicine*; *the application of a rule to a particular situation*; *The application of this cream to your face is supposed to make you look younger.* **3** *nu* (*formal*) hard work: *He has got a good job through/by sheer application.* **4** *nc* (*formal*) an ointment *etc* applied to a cut, wound *etc*: *An application made from wild plants quickly healed the wound.*

ap'plied *adj* (*attrib*) put to practical use, rather than simply theoretical: *applied science/mathematics/linguistics.*

apply oneself, one's mind (*with* **to**) to give one's full attention or energy (to a task *etc*): *If that child would only apply himself he could pass his exams*; *I shall apply my mind to the problem.*

See also **inapplicable**.

appoint [ə'point] *vt* **1** to give (a person) a job or position: *They appointed him manager*; *They have appointed a new manager.* **2** (*formal*) to fix or agree on (a time for something): *to appoint a time for a meeting.*

ap'pointed *adj* (*attrib*: *formal*) fixed: *the appointed time for a meeting*; *He arrived before the appointed time.*

ap'pointment **1** *ncu* (an) arrangement to meet someone: *I made an appointment to see him*; *You can see the doctor only by appointment.* **2** *ncu* the act of appointing (a person) to a job or position: *The appointment of a new manager improved efficiency*; (*attrib*) *an appointments committee.* **3** *nc* the job or position to which a person is appointed: *His appointment was for one year only.*

apportion [ə'po:ʃən] *vt* (*formal*) to divide and hand (something) out in fair shares: *He apportioned his property among his children*: (*fig*) *It is difficult to apportion blame in this case.*

apposite ['apəzit] *adj* (*formal*: *with* **to** *when pred*) suitable; appropriate: *Some of them were talking nonsense, but John made some apposite remarks*; *Your remarks are not apposite to the current situation.* **'appositely** *adv.* **'appositeness** *nu.*

appraise [ə'preiz] *vt* (*formal*) to decide the value, quality, ability *etc* (of a person, thing *etc*): *It is difficult to appraise his suitability for the job.*

ap'praisal *ncu.*

ap'praising *adj* (*attrib*): *She gave him an appraising look.*

appreciate [ə'pri:ʃieit] (not used with **is, was** *etc* and **-ing** (*defs 1–3*)) **1** *vt* to be grateful for (something): *I appreciate all your hard work.* **2** *vt* to value (someone or something) highly; to understand or enjoy (something): *He doesn't appreciate poetry*; *Mothers are very often not appreciated.* **3** *vt* (*formal*) to know and understand (something); to be aware of (something): *I appreciate your difficulties but I cannot help.* **4** *vi* (*formal*) to increase in value: *My house has appreciated* (*in value*) *considerably over the last ten years.*

ap'preciable [-ʃəbl] *adj* (*formal*) noticeable; considerable: *There has been no appreciable improvement in the patient's health*; *The increase in heating costs is appreciable.*

ap'preciably [-ʃəbli] *adv* (*formal*): *This winter is appreciably colder than last winter.*

apˌpreci'ation 1 *nu* gratefulness; thanks: *I wish to show my appreciation for what you have done.* **2** *ncu* the act or state of valuing, enjoying or understanding (something): *He has a deep appreciation of poetry.* **3** *nu* (*formal*) the state of knowing or being aware of (something): *I have some appreciation of your problems.* **4** *nu* (*formal*) an increase in value. **5** *nc* an essay, newspaper article *etc* which describes the qualities of something: *an appreciation of a new book.*

ap'preciative [-ʃətiv] *adj* (*neg* **un-**) grateful; showing thanks: *an appreciative audience*; (*formal*) *They were appreciative of his hard work.*

ap'preciatively *adv.*

apprehend [apri'hend] *vt* **1** (*formal*) to arrest: *The police apprehended the thief.* **2** (*old*: not used with **is, was** *etc* and **-ing**) to understand: *I apprehend the meaning of your words.*

ˌappre'hension [-ʃən] **1** *ncu* (*more formal than* **fear**) fear; anxiety: *I view the new plans with some apprehension.* **2** *nu* (*formal*) arrest: *the apprehension of the thieves.* **3** *nu* (*formal*: *with* **a(n)**) understanding: *He has a clear apprehension of our problems.*

ˌappre'hensive [-siv] *adj* anxious; worried: *I am rather apprehensive about my interview for the job*; *She is apprehensive for the safety of her child who has been kidnapped*; *She wore rather an apprehensive expression.* **ˌappre'hensively** *adv.* **ˌappre'hensiveness** *nu.*

apprentice [ə'prentis] *nc* a (*usu* young) person who is learning a trade: *He couldn't fix my washing-machine – he was only an apprentice*; (*attrib*) *an apprentice electrician.* – *vt* (*formal*) to make someone an apprentice: *His father apprenticed him to an engineer.*

ap'prenticeship *ncu* the state of being, or the time during which a person is, an apprentice: *He is serving his apprenticeship as a mechanic.*

apprise [ə'praiz] *vt* (*formal*: *with* **of**) to inform (a person) of (an event *etc*): *Have you apprised him of the change in your circumstances?*

approach [ə'proutʃ] **1** *vti* to come near (to): *The car approached* (*the traffic lights*) *at top speed*; *Christmas is approaching.* **2** *vt* (*formal*) to speak to (someone) in order to ask for something: *I can approach my father for money.* **3** *vt* (*formal*) to be almost the equal of (a person) in ability *etc*: *No writer can begin to approach Shakespeare in greatness.* – *nc* **1** the act of coming near: *The boys ran off at the approach of a policeman.* **2** (*formal*) a road, path *etc* leading to a place: *All the approaches to the village were blocked by snow.* **3** (*often pl*) an attempt to obtain or attract a person's help, interest, friendship *etc*: *They have made an approach/approaches to the government for help*; *Their approaches for financial help proved unsuccessful*; *That fellow makes approaches to* (= he tries to become (sexually) friendly with) *every woman he meets.*

ap'proachable *adj* **1** friendly; ready to listen (to problems, questions *etc*): *He's a very approachable person*; *I find him very approachable.* **2** (*pred*) that can be reached: *In the winter the village is sometimes not approachable by road.*

See also **unapproachable**.

approbation [aprə'beiʃən] *nu* (*formal*) approval; good opinion: *His bravery received the approbation of the whole town.*

appropriate [ə'proupriət] *adj* (*formal*: *with* **to** *when pred*) suitable; proper: *Her clothes were appropriate to the occasion*; *Complain to the appropriate authority.* – [-eit] *vt* (*formal*) **1** to take (something) as one's own: *He appropriated the best bedroom*; *He has appropriated the firm's money for his own uses.* **2** to put (money *etc*) aside for a particular purpose: *The committee appropriated money for building new houses.* **apˌpropri'ation** *nu.*

ap'propriately *adv* suitably: *They were all appropriately dressed for the occasion.*

ap'propriateness *nu.*

See also **inappropriate, misappropriate**.

approve [ə'pruːv] **1** *vi* (*often with* **of**) to be pleased with or think well of (a person, thing *etc*): *I approve of your decision*; *You've bought a new house? I approve.* **2** *vt* (*formal*) to agree to or permit (something): *The committee approved the plan.*

ap'proval *nu* the act or state of agreeing to or being pleased with (a person, thing *etc*): *This proposal meets with my approval*; *It has the approval of the whole committee*; *I'll give my approval to it.* – *See also* **on approval** *below.*

ap'proving *adj* (*attrib*) showing approval: *She gave him an approving smile.*

ap'provingly *adv*: *The old lady smiled approvingly at the boy when he politely opened the door.*

ap'proved school *nc* (in Britain until 1969) a state school for young people who have broken the law.

on ap'proval to be sent or given back to a shop *etc* if not satisfactory: *She bought two dresses on approval.*

See also **disapprove**.

approximate [ə'proksimət] *adj* very nearly correct or accurate; not intended to be absolutely correct: *Give me an approximate answer!*; *Can you give me an approximate price for the job?*; *Her answer to the sum was only approximate.* – [-meit] *vi* to come close to (something) in value, accuracy *etc*: *Your story approximates to the truth but it is not completely accurate.*

ap'proximately *adv* nearly; more or less: *There will be approximately five hundred people present.*

apˌproxi'mation (*formal*) **1** *nc* a figure, answer *etc* which is not (intended to be) exact: *This figure is just an approximation.* **2** *nu* the process of estimating a figure *etc*: *We decided on a price by a process of approximation.*

apricot ['eiprikot] *nc, adj* (of) an orange-coloured fruit like a small peach: *We had apricots for dessert*; *She wore an apricot-coloured dress.*

April ['eiprəl] *n* the fourth month of the year, the month following March: *She is leaving sometime in April*; *He is coming on April 23* (said as 'on April (the) twenty-third' or 'on the twenty-third of April'); *He is coming on the 23rd/twenty-third of April*; *She died last April.*

April fool *nc* the victim of a trick or joke on April 1, April Fools' Day.

apron ['eiprən] *nc* **1** a piece of cloth, plastic *etc* worn over the front of the clothes for protection against dirt *etc*: *Put on your apron before you start preparing the dinner.* **2** something like an apron in shape, *eg* a hard surface for aircraft on an airfield: *the apron in front of the airport building.* **3** the part of the stage in a theatre which is in front of the curtain: (*attrib*) *an apron stage.*

apropos [aprə'pou]: **ˌapro'pos of** (*formal*) concerning; with regard to: *What did he say apropos of the new project?*

apt [apt] *adj* **1** (*pred*: *with* **to**) likely: *He is apt to get angry if you ask a lot of questions.* **2** (*formal*) suitable: *That was an apt remark!*; *That remark was most apt.* **3** (*formal*: *usu attrib*) clever; quick to learn: *He is an apt student.*

'aptly *adv* in a suitable or appropriate way: *Life is not getting easier, as John very aptly remarked yesterday.*

'aptness *nu* the state of being suitable or quick to learn: *the aptness of the remark*; *The success of the course depends on the aptness of the student.*

aptitude ['aptitju:d] *ncu* (*formal*) (*sometimes with* **for**) (a) talent or ability: *He has/shows an aptitude for mathematics.*

aqua- [akwə] (*in cmpds*) of water, as in **aqualung**.

aqualung ['akwəlʌŋ] *nc* an apparatus worn by divers on their backs which supplies them with oxygen to breathe.

aquamarine [akwəmə'ri:n] *nc, adj* (of) a bluish-green precious stone.

aquarium [ə'kweəriəm] – *pls* **a'quariums, a'quaria** – *nc* a glass tank, or a building containing tanks, for keeping fish and other water animals.

Aquarius [ə'kweəriəs] *n* a sign of the zodiac, the Water-carrier: *People born between January 21 and February 19 are said to be born under the sign of Aquarius.*

aquatic [ə'kwatik] *adj* (*formal*: *attrib*) living, growing, or taking place in water: *aquatic plants/sports.*

aqueduct ['akwidʌkt] *nc* a type of bridge which is used to carry water (*eg* a canal) across a valley *etc.*

aquiline ['akwilain] *adj* curved like an eagle's beak: *an aquiline nose.*

Arab ['arəb] *nc* a person who is one of the peoples of the Middle East: (*attrib*) *an Arab sheikh.* – *See also* Appendix 2.

Arabia, Arabian *see* Appendix 2.

'Arabic *n, adj* (of) one of the main languages used in the countries of the Middle East, and also as the religious language of Islam. – *See also* Appendix 2.

Arabic numerals 1, 2, 3 *etc*, as opposed to Roman numerals, I, II, III *etc.*

arable ['arəbl] *adj* (*formal or tech*) on which crops are grown: *arable land*; *He owns an arable farm*; *Is this land arable?*

arbiter ['a:bitə] *nc* (*formal*) **1** a person who has the power, influence *etc* to make decisions about something: *They are arbiters of fashion.* **2** (*rare*) an arbitrator.

arbitrary ['a:bitrəri] *adj* **1** not decided by rules or laws but by a person's own opinion: *He made a rather arbitrary decision to close the local cinema without consulting other people*; *His decision was completely arbitrary.* **2** (*attrib*) (of a person) who uses power without thinking of other people's opinions, feelings *etc*: *An arbitrary ruler is unpopular with his subjects.*

'arbitrarily *adv* in an arbitrary way: *I wish the manager would stop making decisions so arbitrarily.*

arbitrate ['a:bitreit] *vti* (*formal*) to act as an arbitrator in a dispute *etc*: *He has been asked to arbitrate in the dispute between the workers and management.*

ˌarbi'tration *nu* the making of a decision by an arbitrator: *The dispute has gone/was taken to arbitration.*

'arbitrator *nc* a person who makes a decision or judgement in a dispute *etc.*

arbour, (*Amer*) **arbor** ['a:bə] *nc* (*formal or liter*) a shady place among trees, *usu* with a seat, *esp* one in a garden.

arc [a:k] *nc* **1** a part of the line which forms a circle or other curve. **2** a curve of bright light formed by a strong electric current passing across a space between two objects that conduct electricity.

'arc-lamp, 'arc-light *ncs* a lamp in which the source of light is an electric arc.

arcade [a:'keid] *nc* **1** a covered walk or passage *usu* with shops *etc*: *a shopping arcade.* **2** (*loosely*) a large hall, building *etc* with stalls *etc*: *an amusement arcade.*

arch [a:tʃ] *nc* **1** the top part of a window, door *etc* or a support for a roof *etc* which is built in the shape of a curve. **2** a monument which is shaped like an arch: *the Marble Arch in London.* **3** anything that is like an arch in shape: *The rainbow formed an arch in the sky*; *The soldiers made an arch with their swords for their captain and his bride to walk under.* **4** the raised part of the sole of the foot: *He suffers from fallen arches.* – *vti* to (cause to) be in the shape of an arch: *The cat arched its back*; *The rainbow arched across the sky.*

arched *adj* in the shape of an arch or having arches: *an arched doorway/passage.*

'archway *nc* an arched passage, door or entrance.

arch- [a:k, a:tʃ] (*in cmpds*) main, chief or most important, as in **archangel, archbishop**.

archaeology [a:ki'olədʒi] *nu* the study of objects belonging to ancient times (*eg* buildings, tools *etc* found in the earth). **ˌarchae'ologist** *nc.*

ˌarchaeo'logical [-'lo-] *adj*: *archaeological research/remains/findings.*

archaic [a:'keiik] *adj* (of words *etc*) no longer in common use: *Methinks is an archaic word*; *It is archaic.*

'archaism *nc* (*formal*) an archaic word or expression.

archangel [a:keindʒəl] *nc* a chief angel: *the archangel Gabriel.*

archbishop [a:tʃ'biʃəp] *nc* (*with cap in titles*) (the status of) a chief bishop: *the Archbishop of Westminster*; *a meeting of archbishops and bishops.*

arch'bishopric [-rik] **1** *nc* the area over which an archbishop has control. **2** *nu* the position or rank of an archbishop.

archer ['a:tʃə] *nc* a person who shoots with a bow and arrows.

'archery *nu* the art or sport of shooting with a bow.

archipelago [a:ki'pelәgou] – *pl* **ˌarchi'pelago(e)s** – *nc* (*tech*) a group of islands.

architect ['a:kitekt] *nc* a person who designs buildings *etc*: *Who was the architect who drew these plans?*; (*fig*) *John was the architect of this scheme.*

'architecture [-tʃə] *nu* **1** the art of designing buildings: *He's studying architecture.* **2** any particular style of building or the buildings built in a particular style: *classical architecture*; *I don't like modern architecture.* **ˌarchi'tectural** *adj.*

archives ['a:kaivz] *n pl* (a place for keeping) old documents *etc*: *There are many valuable books in the firm's archives.*

'archivist [-ki-] *nc* (*tech*) a person who looks after archives.

archway *see* **arch**.

Arctic ['a:ktik] *adj* **1** (*attrib*) of the area round the

North Pole: *the Arctic wilderness.* **2** (*no cap*) very cold: *arctic conditions.*

the Arctic the area round the North Pole: *The expedition set off towards the Arctic.*

ardent ['a:dənt] *adj* enthusiastic; passionate: *He is an ardent supporter of that political party; He is an ardent lover; He is not as ardent in his support as he used to be.* **'ardently** *adv.*

ardour, (*Amer*) **ardor** ['a:də] *nu* (*formal*) enthusiasm; passion: *So great was his patriotic ardour that he would willingly have died for his country; She was quite overcome by her lover's ardour.*

arduous ['a:djuəs, (*Amer*) -dʒu-] *adj* (*formal*) difficult; needing hard work: *This is an arduous task; This task is arduous.* **'arduously** *adv.* **'arduousness** *nu.*

are *see* **be**.

area ['eəriə] **1** *ncu* the extent or size of a flat surface: *This garden is twelve square metres in area.* **2** *nc* a place; part (of a town *etc*): *Do you live in this area?* **3** *nc* a subject, activity or topic: *Do you have any experience in this area?; an area of dispute.*

arena [ə'ri:nə] *nc* **1** any place for a public show, contest *etc*: *an arena at a horse-show;* (*hist*) *The gladiators fought in the arena.* **2** (*fig*) any place or sphere in which arguments, debates *etc* take place: *The town hall is the arena for tonight's political debate; the political arena.*

aren't *see* **be**.

Argentina, Argentine, Argentinian *see* Appendix 2.

argue ['a:gju:] **1** *vi* (*with* **with** someone, **about** something) to quarrel with (a person) or discuss (something) with a person in a not very friendly way: *I'm not going to argue; The two brothers are always arguing with each other; Will you children stop arguing about whose toy that is!* **2** *vi* (*formal: with* **for, against**) to suggest reasons for or for not doing something: *I argued for accepting the plan; He argued against our joining the Common Market.* **3** *vt* (*with* **into, out of**) to persuade (a person) (not) to do something: *I'll try to argue him into going; He argued her out of buying the dress.* **4** *vti* (*formal*) to try to prove something by giving reasons; to be or give evidence for: *She argued the point very cleverly; These buried ruins argue the existence of an earlier civilization.*

'arguable *adj* (*neg* **un-**) able to be argued about: *It is arguable that he would have been better to go; That is an arguable point.*

'arguably *adv* it could be argued that (something is the case); (*loosely*) possibly; probably: *He is arguably the best Prime Minister we have ever had.*

'argument *nc* **1** a quarrel or unfriendly discussion: *They are having an argument about/over whose turn it is.* **2** the reasons for or against (an idea etc): *The argument for/against going.* **3** the theme or subject of a book *etc*: *a philosophical argument.*

ˌargu'mentative [-'mentətiv] *adj* (*derog*) fond of arguing: *He is so argumentative that he has few friends; an argumentative mood/old man.*

aria ['a:riə] *nc* (*music*) a song for one voice, *eg* in an opera.

arid *adj* (*formal*) **1** dry; not having water: *an arid desert; The soil is rather arid.* **2** (*fig*) without result: *an arid discussion; The discussion was arid.* **a'ridity, 'aridness** *nus.*

Aries ['eəri:z] *n* a sign of the zodiac, the Ram: *People born between March 21 and April 20 are said to be born under the sign of Aries.*

arise [ə'raiz] – *pt* **arose** [ə'rouz] : *ptp* **arisen** [ə'rizn] – *vi* **1** (*formal*) to come into being: *A strong wind arose; We can come earlier if the need arises; These problems have arisen as a result of your carelessness.* **2** (*with* **from, out of**) to result from or be caused by (something); *Are there any matters arising from the minutes?; This problem arises out of our earlier decision.* **3** (*old, liter or formal*) to get up or stand up: *'Arise, Sir Knight!'*

aristocracy [arə'stokrəsi] *nc* in some countries, *eg* Britain, the highest social class, who *usu* own land: *Dukes and earls are members of the aristocracy.*

'aristocrat [-krat, (*Amer*) ə'ristəkrat] *nc* a member of the aristocracy.

ˌaristo'cratic [-'kra-, (*Amer*) əristə'kratik] *adj* (of people, behaviour *etc*) proud and noble-looking: *an aristocratic manner; She looks very aristocratic.* **ˌaristo'cratically** *adv.*

arithmetic [ə'riθmətik] *nu* the art of counting by numbers.

arithmetical [ariθ'metikl] *adj*: *arithmetical problems.*

Ark [a:k] : **the Ark** the boat in which Noah lived during the Flood: *The animals went into the Ark two by two.*

arm[1] [a:m] **1** *nc* the part of the body between the shoulder and the hand: *He has broken both his arms; She was holding a large box in her arms.* **2** *nc* anything shaped like or similar to this: *She sat on the arm of the chair.* **3** *nc* the part of a coat *etc* which covers an arm; the sleeve: *This shirt is too long in the arms for me; There's a hole in the arm of this sweater.* **4** *nu* (*formal fig*) strength or power: *the arm of the law.* **5** *nc* (*often with cap*) a section of the army, navy *etc*: *the Fleet Air Arm.*

-armed (*in cmpds*) having (a certain number or type of) arm(s): *a one-armed man.*

'armful *nc* as much as a person can hold in one arm or in both arms: *an armful of flowers/clothes.*

'armband *nc* a strip of cloth *etc* worn round the arm: *The people all wore black armbands as a sign of mourning.*

'armchair *nc* a chair with arms at each side. – *adj* (*attrib*) having no practical experience: *an armchair critic/politician.*

'arm-hole *nc* the opening at the shoulder of a coat, shirt, sweater *etc* through which the arm is put: *The arm-holes of this coat are too tight.*

'armpit *nc* the hollow under the arm at the shoulder.

ˌarm-in-'arm *adv, adj* (*pred*) (of two or more people) with arms linked together: *They walked along arm-in-arm.*

the (long) arm of the law (*inf*) the power or authority of the police force: *Although the criminal moved to another town, the long arm of the law soon caught up with him.*

chance one's arm *see* **chance**.

keep at arm's length to avoid becoming too friendly with someone: *She keeps her new neighbours at arm's length.*

with open arms with a very friendly welcome: *He greeted them with open arms; They welcomed the new plans with open arms.*

arm[2] [a:m] (*formal*) **1** *vt* to give weapons to (a person *etc*): *to arm the police.* **2** *vti* to prepare for battle, war *etc*: *They armed for battle;* (*fig*) *He armed himself with all the facts before the meeting.*

armed *adj* **1** having a weapon or weapons: *An armed man robbed the bank; Armed forces entered* *the country*; (*fig*) *He went to the meeting armed with all the information he needed.* **2** (of a weapon) prepared for use in war *etc*: *The torpedo is fully armed.*

arms *n pl* **1** weapons: *British policemen do not usually carry arms.* **2** a design *etc* which is used as the symbol of a town, family *etc* (*see also* **coat of arms**).

be up in arms to be very angry and make a great protest (about something): *He is up in arms about the decision to close the road.*

take up arms (*often with* **against**) to begin fighting: *The peasants took up arms against the dictator.*

See also **unarmed**.

Armada [aːˈmaːdə]: **the Armada** (*hist*) the fleet of Spanish ships sent to attack England in 1588.

armament [ˈaːməmənt] *ncu* (*formal*: *usu in pl*) equipment for war, *eg* the guns, bombs, shells *etc* of a ship, aeroplane, tank *etc.*

armistice [ˈaːmistis] *nc* (an agreement) stopping fighting (in a war, battle *etc*): *An armistice was declared*; (*attrib*) *Armistice day.*

armour, (*Amer*) **armor** [ˈaːmə] *nu* **1** (*hist*) a metal suit or covering worn by knights *etc* as a protection against injury while fighting: *a suit of armour.* **2** (*mil*) a metal covering to protect ships, tanks *etc* against damage from weapons. **3** (*mil*) vehicles that have armour and guns, *eg* tanks.

ˈarmoured *adj* (*attrib*: *mil*) **1** (of vehicles *etc*) protected by armour: *an armoured car.* **2** made up of armoured vehicles: *an armoured division of an army.*

ˈarmoury *nc* (*mil*) the place where weapons are made or kept.

ˌarmour-ˈplated *adj* (*mil*) protected with a covering of iron or steel.

army [ˈaːmi] *nc* **1** a large number of men armed and organized for war: *The two armies met at dawn.* **2** (*often with cap*) the army of a particular country: *My son is in the Army.* **3** a large number (of people *etc*): *An army of tourists/workmen appeared.*

aroma [əˈroumə] *nc* (*formal*) the (*usu* pleasant) smell that a substance has or gives off: *the aroma of coffee.*

aromatic [arəˈmatik] *adj* (*formal*) having a sweet or pleasant smell: *aromatic herbs.*

arose *see* **arise**.

around [əˈraund] **1** *prep, adv* on all sides of or in a circle about (a person, thing *etc*): *Flowers grew around the tree*; *The children danced around the snowman*; *There were flowers all around.* **2** *prep, adv* here and there; at or to several places (in a house, room, town *etc*): *Clothes had simply been left lying around* (*the house*); *I'll just wander around for a while.* **3** *prep* near to (a time, place *etc*): *I'll meet you around three o'clock.* **4** *adv* in the opposite direction: *Turn around!* **5** *adv* somewhere near: *If you need me, I'll be somewhere around.*

have ˌbeen aˈround (*inf*) to have a great deal of experience of life: *I've been around – I know what people are like.*

See also **round**.

arouse (əˈrauz] *vt* (*formal*) **1** to cause or give rise to (something): *His actions aroused my suspicions/anger.* **2** to cause (a person) to become awake or active: *He was aroused from a deep sleep. See also* **rouse**.

arrange [əˈreindʒ] *vt* **1** to put (things *etc*) in some sort of order: *Arrange these books in alphabetical order*; *She arranged the flowers in a vase.* **2** to plan or make decisions (about future events): *We have arranged a meeting for next week*; *I have arranged with John to meet him in Glasgow*; *I have arranged for you to meet her tomorrow.* **3** to make (a piece of music) suitable for particular voices or instruments: *This music has been arranged for choir and orchestra.*

arˈrangement **1** *nu* the act of putting (things *etc*) in some order: *The arrangement of goods in the shop window is done by our sales staff*; *She is good at flower-arrangement.* **2** *ncu* the order, pattern *etc* which results from things being arranged: *I like the arrangement of the furniture in this room*; *The flower-arrangements in this hotel are always beautiful.* **3** *nc* agreement (about something): *We'll have to come to some arrangement about this*; *They've finally come to some sort of arrangement about sharing expenses.* **4** *ncu* (the act of making) a piece of music suitable for particular voices or instruments: *That is a beautiful arrangement of that tune.*

arˈrangements *n pl* plans; decisions; preparations *etc*: *Have you made any arrangements for a meeting with him?*; *The funeral arrangements have all been made.*

arrant [ˈarənt] *adj* (*formal or liter*: *attrib*) (of someone or something) bad to a great degree: *That is arrant nonsense*; *He is an arrant liar.*

array [əˈrei] **1** *nc* things, people *etc* arranged in some order: *an array of jars of sweets*; *an array of soldiers*; *an impressive array of facts.* **2** *nu* (*formal*) fine clothes: *They were all dressed up in holiday array.* – *vt* **1** to put (things, people *etc*) in some order for battle, show *etc*: *soldiers arrayed for battle.* **2** (*formal*: *usu in passive*) to dress (oneself) *eg* in fine clothes: *The king was arrayed in his coronation robes.*

arrears [əˈriəz] *n pl* money which should have been paid because it is owed but which has not been paid: *The district council are trying to collect all the rent arrears*; (*formal fig*) *After I came back from holiday I had to cope with arrears of work.*

in arrears not up to date (*eg* in payments): *He is in/has fallen into arrears with his rent*; (*fig*) *I am now in arrears with my work.*

arrest [əˈrest] *vt* **1** to capture or take hold of (a person) because he or she has broken the law: *The police arrested the thief.* **2** (*formal*) to catch or attract (a person's attention): *My attention was arrested by a sudden movement.* **3** (*formal*) to stop: *Economic difficulties arrested the growth of industry.* – *nc* **1** the act of arresting or being arrested (*eg* by the police): *The police made several arrests during the football match.* **2** (*tech*) a stopping of action: *Cardiac arrest is another term for heart failure. – See also* **under arrest** *below.*

arˈresting *adj* **1** striking; attracting the attention: *an arresting view.* **2** (*formal*: *attrib*) (of a policeman) who makes an arrest: *Who was the arresting officer?*

under arrest in the position of having been arrested: *You are under arrest*; *The thief was placed under arrest.*

arrive [əˈraiv] *vi* **1** to reach (a place, the end of a journey *etc*): *They arrived home last night*; *What time do you expect them to arrive?*; *The parcel arrived yesterday.* **2** (*inf*) to be successful: *Now that he has been invited to lunch with the Prime Minister, he feels he has really arrived. – See also* **arrive at** *below.*

arˈrival **1** *nu* the act of arriving: *I was greeted by*

my sister on my arrival. 2 *nc* a person, thing *etc* who has arrived: *You must be the new arrival; I wish he would stop calling our baby the new arrival.*
ar'rive at *vt fus* to reach (a place *etc*): *We arrived at the station as the train was leaving;* (*fig*) *The committee failed to arrive at a decision;* (*fig*) *We both arrived at the same conclusion.*

arrogant ['arəgənt] *adj* extremely proud; thinking that one is much more important than other people: *An arrogant young man; an arrogant manner; He is so arrogant.* **'arrogantly** *adv.* **'arrogance** *nu.*

arrow ['arou] *nc* 1 a thin, straight stick with a point, which is fired from a bow. 2 anything like an arrow in shape, *eg* a sign used to show which way to go or to show the position of something: *You can't get lost – just follow the arrows.*

arse [a:s] *nc* (*vulg*) (*Amer* **ass**) the buttocks.

arsenal ['a:sənl] *nc* a factory or store for weapons, ammunition *etc.*

arsenic ['a:snik] *nu* 1 an element (symbol **As**) which is used to make certain poisons. 2 a poison made with arsenic: *He killed his wife with arsenic.*

arson ['a:sn] *nu* (*formal*) the crime of setting fire to (a building *etc*) on purpose: *He was convicted of arson.*

art [a:t] 1 *nu* the study of painting and sculpture: *I'm studying art at school;* (*attrib*) *art college.* 2 *nu* examples of painting and sculpture: *Do you like modern art?;* (*attrib*) *an art gallery.* 3 *nu* the creation or expression of beauty in the form of painting, sculpture, music, literature *etc*: *Ballet is a form of art.* 4 *ncu* an ability or skill which is due more to practice than learning (often contrasted with science); the (best) way of doing something: *the art of conversation/war; Is cookery an art or a science?* 5 *nc* (*usu in pl*: *old*) cleverness or skill used in a bad way; tricks: *In spite of all his arts, he failed to persuade the girl to come to his room.*
'artful *adj* (*usu attrib*) clever; having a lot of skill (*usu* in a bad sense): *an artful thief.* **'artfully** *adv.* **'artfulness** *nu.*
'artless *adj* (*formal*: *usu attrib*) simple and natural in manner; honest; not trying to deceive people: *A child's artless questions sometimes embarrass people; artless beauty.* **'artlessly** *adv.* **'artlessness** *nu.*
arts *n pl* (*often with cap*) certain subjects studied at university, *eg* languages, literature, history: *the Faculty of Arts; Master of Arts.*
the Arts literature, music, painting *etc*: *a great patron of the Arts.*
black art *see* **black**.
fine art *see* **fine**[1].
See also **artist, artiste**.

artefact, artifact ['a:tifakt] *nc* (*formal or tech*) an object made by man (as opposed to something which occurs naturally): *Watches, chairs and statues are artefacts whereas trees and stones are not.*

artery ['a:təri] *nc* 1 a tube that carries blood from the heart through the body: *He is suffering from hardening of the arteries.* 2 any main route of travel and transport *eg* a road, railway, river *etc.*
arterial [a:'tiəriəl] *adj* (*attrib*) of or like an artery: *He suffers from arterial disease; arterial roads.*

artful *see* **art**.

arthritis [a:'θraitis] *nu* a medical condition in which there is a swelling at a place in the body where two or more bones join (*eg* the elbow, knee, wrist) causing pain and great difficulty in moving: *He suffers from arthritis.*
ar'thritic [-'θri-] 1 *nc, adj* (a person who is) suffering from arthritis: *She has been an arthritic for more than ten years; an arthritic old lady; She's a bit arthritic now.* 2 *adj* of or caused by arthritis: *arthritic swelling; Do you think that the swelling is arthritic in origin?*

artichoke ['a:titʃouk] *nc* a thistle-like plant with large flower-heads, parts of which can be eaten: *We started the meal with artichokes;* (*attrib*) *Artichoke hearts* (= the bottom part of the flower-heads) *are a great delicacy.*
Jerusalem artichoke [dʒə'ru:sələm] *nc* a type of plant whose roots can be eaten.

article ['a:tikl] *nc* 1 (*formal*) a thing or an object: *This shop sells articles of all kinds; Several articles of clothing were found at the scene of the murder.* 2 a piece of writing in a newspaper or magazine: *He has written an article on Shakespeare for a literary magazine.* 3 (*formal*: *usu in pl*) (one of) the separate parts of clauses of a document, agreement *etc*: *articles of apprenticeship.* 4 (*gram*) **the** (the definite article) or **a/an** (the indefinite article).

articulate [a:'tikjuleit] *vti* (*formal*) to speak or pronounce (something), clearly and distinctly: *The teacher articulated* (*his words*) *very carefully.*
– [-lət] *adj* 1 able to express one's thoughts clearly: *His lectures are always extremely interesting – he is such an articulate young man; He is so articulate.* 2 (of speech) pronounced clearly and distinctly: *Articulate speech is essential for a teacher.* **ar'ticulately** [-lət-] *adv.* **ar'ticulateness** [-lət-] *nu.*
ar,ticu'lation *nu* the way in which a person speaks or pronounces (something): *His articulation is poor.*
articulated lorry *nc* a lorry in two parts, the cab or front section of which can turn at an angle to the main part, making it easier to turn corners.
See also **inarticulate**.

artifact *see* **artefact**.

artificial [a:ti'fiʃəl] *adj* 1 made by man; not natural; not real: *I dislike artificial flowers; Are these flowers artificial or real?; The colour of this dress looks different in artificial light than in daylight; He walks with a limp because he has an artificial leg.* 2 not genuine; (behaving) in a way which is not natural: *He speaks with a very artificial accent; It sounds artificial.* **arti'ficially** *adv.* **,artifici'ality** [-ʃi'a-], **,arti'ficialness** *nus.*
artificial respiration *nu* (*tech*) the process of forcing air into and out of the lungs *eg* of a person who has almost drowned: *He gave/administered artificial respiration to the man who had fallen into the sea.*

artillery [a:'tiləri] *nu* 1 large guns. 2 (*often with cap*) the part of an army which looks after and fires such guns: *the Royal Artillery.*

artisan ['a:tizan, (*Amer*) -zn] *nc* (*formal*) a skilled workman: *Carpenters are artisans.*

artist ['a:tist] *nc* 1 a person who paints pictures: *Monet was a famous artist.* 2 a person who is skilled at some particular thing, *esp* one of the fine arts *eg* sculpture: *She is a well-known stained-glass artist;* (*inf*) *Our cook is an artist at making cheap meals look expensive.* 3 a singer, dancer, actor *etc*; an artiste: *He announced the names of the artists who were taking part in the show.*
ar'tistic *adj* 1 liking or skilled in painting, music

etc: *an artistic young woman*; *She is very artistic.* **2** beautiful; created or done with skill and good taste: *That flower-arrangement looks very artistic*; *The pianist gave a very artistic performance of the new work.* **ar'tistically** *adv.*

'artistry *nu* (*formal*) artistic skill: *the artistry of a great painter or musician.*

artiste [aː'tiːst] *nc* (*formal*) a person who performs in a theatre, circus *etc*: *a troupe of circus artistes.*

artless *etc see* **art**.

as [az] *conj* **1** (only used with a verb which describes a continuous action) when; while; during or at a particular time: *I met John as I was coming home*; *We'll be able to talk as we go.* **2** because; for the reason that: *As I am leaving tomorrow, I've bought you all a present.* **3** in the same way that: *If you are not sure how to behave, do as I do.* **4** used to introduce a statement of what the speaker knows or believes to be the case: *As you know I'll be leaving tomorrow.* **5** although; even though; it doesn't matter how much: *Old as I am, I can still fight*; *Try as you may, you will never succeed*; *Much as I want to, I cannot go.* **6** used to refer to something which has already been stated and apply it to another person: *Tom is Welsh, as are Dick and Harry*; *He is very stupid, as are all the members of his family.* – *adv* used in comparisons, *eg* the first *as* in the following example: *The bread was as hard as a brick.* – *prep* **1** used in comparisons, *eg* the second *as* in the following example: *The bread was as hard as a brick.* **2** (with certain verbs *eg* **regard, treat, describe, accept**) used to introduce a word or phrase which describes the subject or object of a sentence: *I am regarded by some people as a bit of a fool*; *Why won't you accept me as your friend?*; *He treats me as an idiot.* **2** like: *He was dressed as a woman.* **4** in the position of: *He is greatly respected both as a person and as a politician.*

'as for (used when turning to a new subject of discussion *etc* after talking about someone or something else) with regard to; concerning: *The thief was caught by the police almost immediately. As for the stolen jewels, they were found in a dustbin.*

'as from/'as of (*formal*) starting at (a particular time): *As from tomorrow, I'll start work half an hour earlier.*

as 'if/as 'though 1 in a way that would be correct or appropriate if (something else were true): *He treats me as if I were a fool*; *He acted as if he were mad*; *He spoke as though he knew all about our plans when in fact he knew nothing about them.* **2** in a way that suggests that (something is about to happen *etc*): *He opened his mouth as if to speak*; *He stood up as if to leave*; *You look as if you are going to be sick – perhaps you should go home.*

as good as *see* **good.**

as it were (*formal*) in a way, to some extent *etc*: *I'm a sort of unpaid adviser, as it were, to the committee.*

as long as *see* **long**.

as of *see* **as from**.

as though *see* **as if**.

'as to (*formal*) as far as (something) is concerned; with regard to: *Since the room is painted purple, we haven't much choice as to the colour of the carpet*; *I'm willing to read his book, but as to publishing it, that's a different matter*; *We now have the plans of the new church. As to the hall, there is simply not enough money at present.*

asbestos [az'bestos] *nu, adj* (of) a mineral that will not burn and which is used to make clothing *etc* which can protect against fire: *This suit is* (*made of*) *asbestos*; *an asbestos suit.*

ascend [ə'send] *vti* (*formal*) to climb, go, or rise up: *They ascended the hill*; *The smoke ascended into the air.*

a'scendancy/a'scendency *nu* (*very formal*) (the position of having) control or power over (a person *etc*): *They have the ascendancy over the other political groups.*

a'scent [-t] (*formal*) **1** *nu* the act of climbing, going up or rising: *The ascent of Mount Everest proved too difficult for him.* **2** *nc* (a path *etc* that has) a steep slope upwards: *They had great difficulty in climbing the steep and slippery ascent.*

ascend the throne (*formal*) to be crowned king or queen.

ascertain [asə'tein] *vt* (*formal*) to find out: *Is there any way of ascertaining whether or not what he says is true?*; *Can we ascertain the truth of his statement?*

ˌascer'tainable *adj.*

ascetic [ə'setik] *adj* (*formal*) avoiding or limiting pleasure and comfort, *esp* for religious reasons: *Monks and nuns are ascetic*; *They lead ascetic lives.* – *nc* an ascetic person.

a'scetically *adv.* **a'sceticism** [-sizəm] *nu.*

ascribe [ə'skraib] *vt* (*formal*) to think of (something) as done, made or caused by (someone or something): *He ascribed his success to the help of his friends*; *The play was wrongly ascribed to Shakespeare.* **a'scribable** *adj.*

asexual [ei'sekʃuəl] *adj* (*formal*) without involving sex: *asexual reproduction*: *Their relationship is entirely asexual.*

ash[1] [aʃ] **1** *nc* (*also* **'ash tree**) a kind of forest tree with smooth grey bark and black buds: *That tree is an ash*; (*attrib*) *an ash wood.* **2** *nu, adj* (of) its wood: *a table made of ash*; *an ash stick.*

ash[2] [aʃ] *ncu* the dust *etc* that remains after anything is burnt: *You're dropping cigarette ash on the carpet!*; *Sweep away the ashes when you are cleaning the fireplace.*

'ashen *adj* (*formal*) (of someone's face *etc*) ash-coloured; very pale: *her ashen looks*; *She looked ashen when she heard the news of his death.*

'ashes *n pl* the remains of a human body after cremation: *Her ashes were scattered on the sea.*

'ashtray *nc* a dish or other container for cigarette ash: *Don't drop ash on the carpet – use the ashtray!*

ashamed [ə'ʃeimd] *adj* (*pred*: *neg* **un-**) feeling shame: *He was ashamed of his bad work*; *He was ashamed to admit his mistake*; *He felt ashamed of himself.*

ashore [ə'ʃoː] *adv* on or on to the shore: *The sailor went ashore.*

Asia, Asian *see* Appendix 2.

aside [ə'said] *adv* on or to one side: *They stood aside to let her pass*; *He took her aside and told her the news.* – *nc* words spoken (*esp* by an actor) which other people (on the stage) are not supposed to hear: *She whispered an aside to him.*

put aside *vt sep* (*often with* **for**) to keep (something) for a particular person or occasion: *Would you put this book aside for me and I'll collect it later*; *We have put aside the dress you ordered.*

ask [aːsk] **1** *vti* to put a question: *I asked her where to go*; *He asked me what the time was*; *Ask the price of that scarf*; *If you don't know, you must ask*; *Ask him about the arrangements for tomorrow's meeting.* **2** *vti* (*sometimes with* **for**) to state one's wish or need (for something) to a person: *I asked her to* *help me; I asked (him) for a day off; Can I ask a favour of you?* **3** *vt* to invite: *He asked her (to come) to his house.*

'ask after *vt fus* to make inquiries about the state of: *She asked after his father.*

'ask for *vt fus* **1** to express a wish to see or speak to (someone): *When he telephoned he asked for you; He is very ill and keeps asking for his daughter.* **2** (*inf*) to behave as if inviting (something unpleasant): *Going out in cold weather without a coat is just asking for trouble; She asked for all she got.*

for the 'asking you may have (something) simply by asking (for it): *This table is yours for the asking.*

askance [ə'skans]: **look askance at** (*formal*) to look at or consider with suspicion: *She looked askance at any offers of help.*

askew [ə'skjuː] *adv, adj* (*pred*) not straight or level: *That painting is hanging askew; Her hat is all askew.*

asleep [ə'sliːp] *adj* (*pred*) **1** sleeping: *They remained asleep despite the noise; The baby is asleep.* **2** (*inf*) of arms and legs *etc*, numb: *My foot's asleep.*

fall asleep to pass into a state of being asleep: *He fell asleep eventually.*

asparagus [ə'sparəgəs] *nu* **1** the young shoots of a type of plant which are eaten as a vegetable: *a bunch of asparagus*; (*attrib*) *asparagus soup.* **2** the plant: *He is growing asparagus in his garden.*

aspect ['aspekt] *nc* **1** a part of something to be thought or talked about: *We must consider every aspect of the problem.* **2** (*formal*) the direction in which a building *etc* faces: *As the house had a southerly aspect it was very sunny.* **3** (*formal*) look or appearance: *His face had a frightening aspect.*

asperity [a'sperəti] *nu* (*very formal*) **1** (of manner or temper) harshness or bitterness: *Her friends were surprised by the asperity of her reply.* **2** (of weather) bitter coldness: *We were not prepared for the asperity of last winter.*

aspersions [ə'spəːʃənz, (*Amer*) -ʒənz]: **cast aspersions (on)** (*formal*) to make damaging criticism (about): *I did not mean to cast aspersions on your ability.*

asphalt ['asfalt, (*Amer*) -foːlt] *nu* a mixture containing tar, used to make roads, pavements, roofs *etc*: *The workmen are laying asphalt*; (*attrib*) *an asphalt roof.*

asphyxiate [əs'fiksieit] *vti* (*formal*) to stop (someone) breathing; to suffocate (by smoke, fumes *etc*): *The fireman was asphyxiated by the dense smoke.*

as'phyxia [-ə], **as,phyxi'ation** *nus* (*formal*) suffocation: *He died from asphyxia/asphyxiation.*

aspic ['aspik] *nu* a kind of jelly made from meat, fish *etc*: *chicken in aspic; herring in aspic.*

aspirant *see* **aspire**.

aspirate ['aspirət] *nc* (*formal*) the sound of the letter **h**: *Some people cannot pronounce aspirates.* – [-reit] *vt* (*formal*) to make the sound of the letter **h**.

aspire [ə'spaiə] *vi* (*formal: usu with* **to**) to try very hard to reach (something difficult, ambitious *etc*): *He aspired to the position of president.*

'aspirant ['aspi-, (*Amer*) ə'spairənt] *nc* (*very formal*) a person who aspires.

,aspi'ration [aspi-] *nc* (*often in pl*) an ambition: *He has aspirations to greatness.*

aspirin ['aspərin] *ncu* a (tablet of a) kind of pain-killing drug: *The child has a fever – give her some/an aspirin.*

ass[1] [as] *nc* **1** a donkey. **2** (*derog*) a stupid person: *What an ass he is!*

ass[2] [as] *nc* (*inf Amer*) arse.

assail [ə'seil] *vt* (*formal: often fig*) to attack: *He was assailed with questions; He was assailed by doubts.*

as'sailant *nc* (*formal*) a person who attacks: *His assailant came up behind him in the dark.*

assassinate [ə'sasineit] *vt* to murder, *esp* for political reasons: *The president was assassinated by terrorists.* **as,sassi'nation** *ncu.*

as'sassin *nc* (*formal*) a person who assassinates (someone).

assault [ə'soːlt] *vt* **1** to attack, *esp* suddenly: *The youths assaulted the night watchman; The soldiers assaulted the castle under cover of darkness.* **2** to rape: *He was sent to prison for assaulting a seven-year-old girl.* – **1** *nc* a (sudden) attack: *They made a night assault on the fortress*; (*fig*) *His speech was a vicious assault on their principles.* **2** *ncu* (an act of) rape: *The man was found guilty of making an assault on his stepdaughter.*

assault and battery (*legal*) an attack (on a person) in which physical force is used.

assay ['asei] *ncu* (*tech*) (a) test (of metal or ore) to find out its quality or what it is made of: *On assay the gold was found to be very impure.* – [ə'sei] *vti* (*tech*) to make such a test (on a metal *etc*): *The ore was assayed and found to be of high quality.*

assemble [ə'sembl] (*formal*) **1** *vi* (of people) to come together: *The crowd assembled in the hall.* **2** *vt* to call or bring together: *He assembled his family and told them of his plan; She assembled the facts for her essay.* **3** *vt* to put together (a machine *etc*): *He assembled the model aeroplane in less than two hours.*

as'semblage [-blidʒ] *nc* (*formal*) a collection (of people or things).

as'sembly **1** *nc* a collection of people (*usu* for a particular purpose): *a legislative assembly; The headmaster made an announcement at assembly* (= at a meeting of staff and pupils of a school); (*attrib*) *an assembly hall.* **2** *nu* the act of assembling: *The assembly of the parts of the machine took several hours.*

as'sembly line *nc* a continuous series of machines and workers through which an article, product *etc* passes in the process of its manufacture.

assent [ə'sent] *nu* (*formal*) agreement: *The Queen gave the royal assent to the new parliamentary bill.* – *vi* (*formal*: *with* **to**) to agree: *They assented to the proposal to widen the road.*

assert [ə'səːt] *vt* **1** (*formal*) to say definitely: *She asserted that she would not go.* **2** to insist on: *He asserted his independence/innocence; They asserted their right to disagree.* **as'sertion** [-ʃən] *ncu.*

as'sertive [-tiv] *adj* inclined to make assertions or assert oneself: *She's so assertive that she'll achieve her ambitions; a very assertive young woman.*

as'sert oneself to state one's opinions confidently and act in a way that will make people take notice of one: *You must assert yourself more if you want promotion.*

assess [ə'ses] *vt* (*formal*) **1** to decide the value, power *etc* of (something or someone): *Can you assess my chances of winning?* **2** to fix an amount (to be paid in tax *etc*): *My income has been assessed wrongly.* **as'sessment** *ncu.*

as'sessor *nc* (*formal*) a person who assesses, *esp* for taxation.

asset ['aset] *nc* anything useful or valuable; an

advantage: *He is a great asset to the company.*

'assets *n pl* the total property, money *etc* of a person, company *etc*: *The company is in financial trouble because its debts are greater than its assets.*

assiduous [ə'sidjuəs, (*Amer*) -dʒu-] *adj* (*formal*) **1** hard-working: *He is a most assiduous student; He is most assiduous.* **2** (*attrib*) careful and precise: *He pays assiduous attention to detail.* **as'siduously** *adv.* **assiduity** [asi'dju:əti], **as'siduousness** *nus* (*formal*).

assign [ə'sain] *vt* (*formal*) **1** to give to someone as his share or duty: *They assigned the task to us; The most important people were assigned the most comfortable chairs.* **2** to order or appoint: *He assigned three men to the job.* **3** to fix (a time or place): *The teacher assigned Wednesday evening to meeting the parents.*

ˌassig'nation [asig-] *nc* (*formal*) an appointment or arranged meeting, *esp* of lovers: *He made an assignation with his secretary.*

as'signment (*formal*) **1** *nc* a duty assigned to someone: *You must complete this assignment by tomorrow.* **2** *nu* the act of assigning: *He is in charge of the assignment of work.*

assimilate [ə'siməleit] *vt* (*formal*) to take in and digest: *Plants assimilate food from the earth*; (*fig*) *I can't assimilate all these facts at once.* **asˌsimi'lation** *nu.*

assist [ə'sist] *vt* (*often formal*) to help: *The junior doctor assisted the surgeon at the operation.*

as'sistance *nu* help: *Will you give me some assistance?*

as'sistant *nc* **1** a person who assists; a helper: *laboratory assistant*; (*attrib*) *An assistant headmaster is one rank below a headmaster.* **2** a person who serves in a shop *etc*: *There are not enough assistants in this department.*

assizes [ə'saiziz] *n pl* (*hist*) a kind of law court in England.

associate [ə'sousieit] **1** *vt* to join or connect in the mind: *She always associated warm weather with holidays by the sea.* **2** *vti* (*formal*) (*usu with* **with**) to join (with someone) in friendship or work: *They don't usually associate (with each other) after office hours; I refuse to associate with thieves.* – [-ət] *adj* (*attrib*) **1** having a lower position or rank: *He's only an associate member of the society; an associate professor.* **2** joined or connected with: *At the conference they met members of associate organizations.* – *nc* a (business) colleague or partner: *I like him but not his associates.*

asˌsoci'ation *nc* **1** a club, society *etc*: *Many associations are breaking up for lack of money.* **2** (*formal*) a friendship or partnership: *Your firm and mine have had a very friendly association for many years.* **3** a connection in the mind: *The house had too many associations with her dead husband for her to be happy in it.*

Association football *nu* (*usu abbrev*) **soccer** ['sokə]) the game played under the rules of the Football Association.

in asˌsoci'ation with (*formal*) together with: *We are acting in association with the London branch of our firm.*

See also **dissociate**.

assorted [ə'so:tid] *adj* mixed; of or containing various different kinds: *assorted colours; a bag of assorted sweets; These flower seeds are assorted.*

as'sortment *nc* a mixture or variety: *an assortment of garments at the jumble sale.*

assuage [ə'sweidʒ] *vt* (*formal or liter*) to ease or make (pain, hunger *etc*) less: *Her grief could not be assuaged.*

assume [ə'sju:m] *vt* **1** to take or accept as true: *I assume (that) you'd like time to decide.* **2** (*formal*) to take upon oneself or accept (authority, responsibility *etc*): *He assumed the rôle of leader in the emergency.* **3** (*formal*) to put on (a disguise, particular appearance *etc*): *He assumed a look of horror when he heard the news.*

as'sumed *adj* **1** pretended; not genuine: *a look of assumed astonishment/innocence; His look of astonishment was assumed; He is going under an assumed name* (= He is not using his real name). **2** generally accepted: *the prisoner's assumed innocence.*

as'sumption [-'sʌmp-] **1** *nc* something assumed: *You're making an assumption which might not be true; We are going/working on the assumption that* (= We are assuming that) *the work will be finished tomorrow; I was under the assumption that* (= I was assuming that) *you were coming tomorrow.* **2** *nu* (*formal*) the act of assuming: *His assumption of the leadership proved disastrous.*

as'suming (that) taking it as true (that): *Assuming (that) you're right we'll make a great deal of money from this project.*

assure [ə'ʃuə] *vt* **1** to state positively (that): *I assured him (that) the house was empty.* **2** (*formal*) to make (someone) sure: *You may be assured that we shall do all we can to help; We are assured of your innocence.* **3** (*formal*) to insure: *Does this insurance policy assure you against accident?*

as'surance **1** *nu* confidence: *I envy him his assurance.* **2** *nc* a promise: *He gave me his assurance that he would help.* **3** *nu* (*formal*) insurance: *life assurance.*

as'sured *adj* certain and confident: *an assured young woman; He always seems very assured.*

as'suredly [-rid-] *adv* (*old*) certainly.

asterisk ['astərisk] *nc* a star-shaped mark (*) used in printing, *esp* to show an added note.

asthma ['asmə, (*Amer*) 'azmə] *nu* an illness which makes breathing difficult: *He can't play tennis because he suffers from asthma.*

asthmatic [as'matik, (*Amer*) az-] **1** *nc, adj* (a person who is) suffering from asthma: *He is a chronic asthmatic; an asthmatic patient.* **2** *adj* of or caused by asthma: *an asthmatic wheeze.*

astigmatism [a'stigmətizəm] *nu* (*tech*) (a condition in which there is) a defect in the eye which causes bad eyesight: *He wears spectacles to correct his astigmatism; He has an astigmatism in his right eye.*

ˌastig'matic [-'ma-] *adj* (*usu pred*): *He is astigmatic rather than short-sighted.*

astir [ə'stə:] *adj* (*pred*) having got up out of bed in the morning: *The whole household was astir early.*

astonish [ə'stoniʃ] *vt* (not *usu* used with **is, was** *etc* and **-ing**) to surprise greatly: *I was astonished by his ignorance.*

a'stonishing *adj*: *an astonishing sight; Their enthusiasm for the new project was astonishing.*

a'stonishment *nu*: *To my astonishment she burst into tears; She looked at him in astonishment.*

astound [ə'staund] *vt* to make (someone) very surprised: *I was astounded to hear of his imprisonment.*

a'stounding *adj*: *an astounding piece of news; It is astounding to hear that he has been promoted.*

astrakhan [astrə'kan] *nu, adj* (of) lamb-skin with

closely curled wool: *My hat is (made of) astrakhan; an astrakhan coat.*

astray [ə'strei]: **go astray** to go away from the right direction; to become lost: *The letter has gone astray.*

lead astray to cause to go away from the right direction: *We were led astray by an inaccurate map*; (*fig*) *He's not a bad boy, but his friends lead him astray.*

astride [ə'straid] *prep* with legs on each side of: *She sat astride the horse.* – *adv* (with legs) apart: *He stood with legs astride.*

astringent [ə'strindʒənt] *adj* **1** sharp and sarcastic: *an astringent remark*; *I found her remarks rather astringent.* **2** causing the tissues of the body, *eg* the skin, to draw together: *astringent liquid*; *It has astringent properties.* – *nc* a type of astringent liquid *etc* put on the face to close the pores of the skin: *She uses an astringent every morning.*

a'stringency *nu.*

astro- [astrou] (*in cmpds*) of stars: ˌ*astro'physics.*

astrology [ə'strolədʒi] *nu* the study of the stars and their influence on people's lives: *I don't believe in astrology.* **a'strologer** *nc.* **astrological** [astrə'lodʒikl] *adj.*

astronaut ['astrəno:t] *nc* a person who travels in space: *Who was the first astronaut to land on the moon?*

astronomy [ə'stronəmi] *nu* the study of the stars and their movements: *He is studying astronomy*; (*attrib*) *astronomy lectures.* **a'stronomer** *nc.*

astronomic(al) [astrə'nomik(l)] *adj* **1** (of numbers or amounts) very large: *An astronomical number of people were killed in the war*; *The cost of the new building was astronomical.* **2** (*usu attrib*) of astronomy: (*formal*) *astronomical observations.*

astute [ə'stju:t] *adj* clever and cunning: *an astute remark/businessman.* **a'stuteness** *nu.*

asunder [ə'sʌndə] *adv* (*formal*) apart or into pieces: *The rock split asunder.*

asylum [ə'sailəm] **1** *nu* (*formal*) safety; protection: *He was granted political asylum.* **2** *nc* (*old*) a home for people who are mentally ill: *Asylums are now called mental hospitals.*

asymmetrical [asi'metrikl] *adj* (*usu pred*) not symmetrical: *The sides of that house are asymmetrical.*

at [at] *prep* showing **1** position: *They are not at home*; *She lives at 33 Forest Road*; *I saw him at a distance.* **2** direction: *He looked at her*; *She shouted at the boys in the garden.* **3** time: *He arrived at ten o'clock*; *The children came at the first sound of the bell.* **4** state or occupation: *The countries are at war*; *She is at work.* **5** pace or speed: *They climbed the hill at a walk*; *He drove at 120 kilometres per hour.* **6** cost: *bread at 20 pence a loaf.*

at 'all (*usu in neg*) in any way: *I don't like it at all*; *I'm not at all sure*; *Has he contacted you at all?*

at 'last in the end; after a delay: *The old man opened the door at last*; *At last we discovered what had happened.*

at 'length 1 in detail: *He described the play at great length.* **2** (*formal*) at last: *At length the wedding day arrived.*

at long last in the end; after a long delay: *At long last the rain stopped*; *At long last the new carpet was delivered.*

at 'once immediately: *Do it at once!*

ate *see* **eat**.

atheism ['eiθiizəm] *nu* the belief that there is no God.

'atheist *nc* a person who does not believe in God.

ˌ**athe'istic** *adj.*

athlete ['aθli:t] *nc* a person who is good at sport, *esp* running, jumping *etc*: *All the family were outstanding athletes.*

ath'letic [-'le-] *adj* **1** (*attrib*) of athletics: *He is taking part in the athletic events.* **2** good at athletics; strong and able to move easily and quickly: *He looks very athletic*; *an athletic young man.*

ath'letics [-'le-] *n sing* the sports of running, jumping *etc* or competitions in these.

atlas ['atləs] *nc* a book of maps: *My atlas is out of date.*

atmosphere ['atməsfiə] **1** *nu* the air surrounding the earth: *The atmosphere in the city is polluted.* **2** *nc* any surrounding feeling: *There was a friendly atmosphere in the village.*

ˌ**atmos'pheric** [-'fe-] *adj* (*usu attrib*): *atmospheric disturbance.*

ˌ**atmos'pherics** [-'fe-] *n pl* (*tech*) (on a radio *etc*) noises caused by electrical disturbances in the air.

atmospheric pressure *nu* the pressure exerted by the atmosphere at the surface of the earth, due to the weight of the air.

atoll ['atol] *nc* a ring-shaped island or reef made of coral.

atom ['atəm] *nc* **1** (*tech*) the smallest part of an element. **2** (*fig*) anything very small: *There's not an atom of truth in what she says.*

a'tomic [-'to-] *adj* (*usu attrib*) **1** using atomic power: *an atomic power station.* **2** of an atom: *atomic particle.*

atom(ic) bomb *nc* a bomb using atomic energy.

atomic energy *nu* very great energy obtained by breaking up the atoms of some substances.

atomic power *nu* power (for making electricity *etc*) obtained from atomic energy.

atomize, -ise ['atəmaiz] *vt* (*formal*) to break something down into its separate atoms: *Perfume is atomized when it is sprayed from its container.*

'atomizer, -s- *nc* (*formal*) a container from which liquid can be released in a fine spray.

atone *vi* (*formal*: *usu with* **for**) to do something good to show that one is sorry for doing something bad: *He tried to atone for his sins.* **a'tonement** *ncu.*

atrocious [ə'trouʃəs] *adj* **1** (*often inf*) very bad: *We had atrocious weather on holiday*; *Your handwriting is atrocious.* **2** (*attrib*: *formal*) extremely cruel: *an atrocious crime.*

a'trociousness *nu* the quality of being atrocious.

atrocity [ə'trosəti] **1** *nu* atrociousness. **2** *nc* an extremely cruel and wicked act: *The invading army committed many atrocities on innocent women and children.*

atrophy ['atrəfi] *vti* (*tech*) (*usu* of part of the body) to (cause to) become weak and useless: *The muscles in her leg have atrophied.* – *nu* (*tech*) wasting away: *She is suffering from atrophy of the muscles.*

attach [ə'tatʃ] *vt* to fasten or join to: *I'll attach my comments to this page*; (*fig*) *I don't attach much importance to it.*

at'tached *adj* **1** joined or connected: *the attached cheque*; *You will find my cheque attached.* **2** (*pred*: *with* **to**) fond of: *I'm very attached to my brother.*

at'tachment 1 *nu* the act of attaching or state of being attached. **2** *nc* something attached: *There are several attachments for this food-mixer.* **3** *nc* (*formal*: *with* **for/to**) liking or affection: *He has a special attachment for this town.*

attaché [əˈtaʃei, (*Amer*) atəˈʃei] *nc* a junior official in an embassy.

attaché-case [əˈtaʃikeis] *nc* a small case for documents *etc*.

attack [əˈtak] **1** *vt* to make a sudden, violent attempt to hurt somebody or something: *He attacked me with a knife*; (*facet*) *He attacked the steak with gusto.* **2** *vt* to speak or write against: *The Prime Minister's policy was attacked in the newspapers.* **3** *vti* (in games) to attempt to score (a goal). – **1** *ncu* an act or the action of attacking: *The brutal attack killed the old man*; *an attack on personal liberties*; *That footballer regularly played in attack.* **2** *nc* a sudden bout of illness: *He's had another heart attack*; *He's recovering from an attack of 'flu.*

attain [əˈtein] *vt* (*formal*) **1** to gain; to succeed in achieving: *He attained a place at university*; *He attained all his ambitions.* **2** to reach: *He attained the shore after a long swim*; *He attained the age of twenty-one.* **atˈtainable** *adj* (*neg* **un-**).

atˈtainment (*formal*) **1** *nc* something one has attained, *esp* a particular skill: *a man of great attainments.* **2** *nu* the act of attaining: *The attainment of wealth did not make him happy.*

attempt [əˈtempt] *vt* (*more formal than* **try**) **1** to try (to do something): *He attempted to reach the dying man, but did not succeed.* **2** to make an effort to do, complete *etc* (something): *She attempted the crossword*; *He did not attempt the last question in the exam.* – *nc* **1** a try: *She failed in her attempt to swim the Channel*; *He made an attempt on Everest*: *She made no attempt to run away*; *My attempts at sewing have been very unsuccessful.* **2** an attack: *They made an attempt on his life but he survived.*

attend [əˈtend] **1** *vt* to go to or be present at: *He attended the meeting.* **2** *vi* (*formal*: *with* **to**) to listen or give attention to: *Attend carefully to what the lecturer is saying!* **3** *vt* (*esp* of doctors) to look after and care for: *He attended her all through her illness.* **4** *vt* (*formal*) to go with (someone or something) to help or serve them: *The queen was attended by her ladies*; (*fig*) *Our arrival was attended by many problems.*

atˈtendance **1** *nu* the act of attending: *His attendance at the wedding surprised the family.* **2** *ncu* the number of people attending: *Attendances at the concerts went down after the price of tickets increased.*

atˈtendant *nc* a person who attends someone; a servant: *a cloakroom attendant*; *a car-park attendant.* – *adj* (*usu attrib*: *formal*) (of circumstances, conditions *etc*) going along with; accompanying: *The snow and its attendant bad roads delayed the funeral*; *The delay and its attendant inconvenience angered the holiday-makers.*

in atˈtendance in the position of helping or serving: *She limped in with her nurse in attendance*; *There was no doctor in attendance at the road accident.*

attention [əˈtenʃən] **1** *nu* careful notice: *He called my attention to the problem*; *He tried to attract my attention*; *He'll give your letter his attention when he returns*; *Pay attention to your teacher!* **2** *nu* care: *That broken leg needs urgent attention.* **3** *nu* concentration of the mind: *His attention wanders.* **4** *nu* (in the army *etc*) a position in which one stands very straight with hands by the sides and feet together: *He stood to attention.* **5** *nc* (*formal*: *usu in pl*) an act of kindness: *They paid her various little attentions.*

atˈtentive [-tiv] *adj* giving attention: *The children were very attentive when the teacher was speaking*; *He is very attentive to her needs*; *an attentive class of schoolchildren.*

atˈtentively [-tiv-] *adv*: *They listened attentively to what she was saying.* **atˈtentiveness** *nu*.

attest [əˈtest] *vti* (*formal*) to say or show that something is true: *The witnesses attested to the good character of the accused.*

ˌattesˈtation [ates-] (*formal*) **1** *nu* the act of attesting. **2** *nc* something which attests; a testimony: *The good exam results were an attestation to the skill of the teachers.*

atˈtested *adj* (*tech*) of cattle, officially certified free from tuberculosis *etc*: *He has an attested herd of cattle*; *Is his herd fully attested?*

attic [ˈatik] *nc* a room at the top of a house under the roof: *They store old furniture in the attic*; (*attrib*) *attic window.*

attire [əˈtaiə] *nu* (*formal*) clothing: *in formal attire.* – *vt* (*formal*) to dress: *She was attired in red silk.*

attitude [ˈatitjuːd] *nc* **1** a way of thinking or acting *etc*: *What is your attitude to politics?*; *I find your attitude unhelpful.* **2** (*formal*) a position of the body: *The artist painted the model in various attitudes.*

strike an attitude *see* **strike**.

attorney [əˈtəːni] *nc* **1** a person who has the legal power (**power of attorney**) to act for another person. **2** (*Amer*) a lawyer.

attract [əˈtrakt] *vt* **1** to cause (someone or something) to come towards: *A magnet attracts iron*; (*fig*) *I tried to attract her attention.* **2** to arouse (someone's) liking or interest: *She attracted all the young men in the neighbourhood.*

atˈtraction [-ʃən] **1** *nu* the act or power of attracting: *magnetic attraction*; *She had no attraction for him.* **2** *nc* something that attracts: *The attractions of the holiday resort include sandy beaches and two golf-courses.*

atˈtractive [-tiv] *adj* (*neg* **un-**) **1** pleasant and good-looking: *She is an attractive girl*; *She is young and attractive.* **2** likeable; having attraction: *That is an attractive proposition*; *He found the proposition attractive.* **atˈtractively** *adv*. **atˈtractiveness** *nu*.

attribute [əˈtribjut] *vt* **1** (*formal*) to think of as being written, made *etc* by: *The play is attributed to Shakespeare.* **2** to think of as being caused by: *He attributed his illness to the cold weather.* – [ˈatribjuːt] *nc* a quality that is a particular part of a person or thing: *Intelligence is not one of his obvious attributes.*

atˈtributable *adj* (*pred*: *with* **to**) that can be attributed: *His illness was directly attributable to the damp house.*

attribution [atriˈbjuːʃən] *ncu* (*formal*): *The attribution of the play to Shakespeare was obviously wrong.*

atˈtributive [-tiv] **1** *adj* (*formal*) expressing an attribute. **2** *nu, adj* (*gram*) (a noun) used, in front of a noun, as an adjective: *a mountain stream.* **3** *adj* (*gram*) (of an adjective) always placed before the noun to which it refers: *a mere child.*

attrition [əˈtriʃən] : **a war of attrition** a war in which the enemy is made gradually weaker by some means or another.

aubergine [ˈoubəʒiːn] (*Amer* **ˈeggplant**) **1** *ncu* a dark purple fruit used as a vegetable: *Have some/an aubergine.* **2** *nc* the plant which produces this fruit.

auburn ['o:bən] *adj* (of hair) reddish-brown in colour: *She has auburn hair*; *Her hair is auburn.*

auction ['o:kʃən] *nc* a public sale in which each thing is sold to the person who offers the highest price: *They held an auction*; *He sold the house by auction.* – *vt* to sell something in this way: *He auctioned all his furniture before emigrating.*

ˌauctio'neer *nc* a person who is in charge of selling things at an auction.

audacious [o:'deiʃəs] *adj* (*formal*) bold and daring; showing no fear: *This is an audacious plan*; *Her audacious replies embarrassed her mother*; *That child is so audacious.*

au'dacity [-'dasə-] *ncu* (*formal*): *He had the audacity to ignore my letter*; *You have to admire his audacity.*

audible ['o:dəbl] *adj* able to be heard: *When the microphone broke her voice was barely audible*; *a scarcely audible remark.* **ˌaudi'bility** *nu.* *See also* **inaudible**.

audience ['o:diəns] *nc* **1** a group of people watching or listening to a performance *etc*: *The audience at the concert consisted of young people only*; *a television audience.* **2** (*formal*) a formal interview with someone important *eg* a king: *He sought an audience with the Pope.*

audio- [o:diou] (*in cmpds*) of sound or hearing, as in **audio-typist**.

audio-typist ['o:dioutaipist] *nc* a typist who types from a recording on a tape-recorder *etc*.

audio-visual [o:diou'viʒuəl] : **audio-visual aids** *n pl* films, recordings *etc* used in teaching.

audit ['o:dit] *nc* (*tech*) an official examination of financial accounts: *the annual audit.* – *vt* (*tech*) to examine financial accounts officially: *The firm's accounts were audited last month.*

'auditor *nc* a person who audits accounts.

audition [o:'diʃən] *nc* a trial performance for an actor, singer, musician *etc*: *She had an audition for the part of Lady Macbeth.* – *vti* to (cause to) take part in an audition: *He's auditioned forty people already*; *She auditioned for the part of Ophelia but did not get it.*

auditorium [o:di'to:riəm] – *pls* **ˌaudi'toria** [-ə] , **ˌaudi'toriums** – *nc* (*tech*) the part of a theatre, hall *etc* where the audience sits.

aught [o:t] *pron* (*old or dial*) anything: *Did you hear aught about it?*

augment [o:g'ment] *vt* (*formal*) to increase in amount or make bigger in size or number: *He tried to augment his income by writing novels.* **ˌaugmen'tation** *ncu.*

augur ['o:gə] : **augur well, ill** (*formal*) to be a good or bad sign for the future: *His school progress report augurs well for his academic career.*

August ['o:gəst] *n* the eighth month of the year, the month following July: *He is coming to visit us in August*; *He is coming on August 23* (said as 'on August (the) twenty-third' or 'on the twenty-third of August'); *He is coming on the 23rd/twenty-third of August*; *It happened last August.*

august [o:'gʌst] *adj* (*formal*: *usu attrib*) full of nobility and dignity: *The judge was an august figure in his robes.*

aunt [a:nt] *nc* (*with cap in names*) the sister of one's father or mother, or the wife of one's uncle: *My Aunt Anne died last week*; *The child went to the circus with her favourite aunt.*

'auntie, 'aunty ['a:nti] *nc* (*inf*: *with cap in names*) an aunt: *Auntie Jean*; *Where's your auntie?*

au pair [ou'peə] *nc* a girl who goes abroad to live with a family and help with children, housework *etc* in order to learn the language: *They have a different au pair every three months*; (*attrib*) *Our au pair girl is very efficient.*

aura ['o:rə] *nc* (*formal*) a particular feeling, air or atmosphere: *There was an aura of mystery about her.*

aural ['o:rəl] *adj* (*formal*: *attrib*) of the ear: *His aural faculties were damaged by the explosion.* *See also* **oral**.

au revoir [ourə'vwa:] *interj* goodbye.

aurora [o:'ro:rə] : **aurora borealis** [bo:ri'eilis] , **aurora australis** [o'streilis] *n* (*tech*) coloured lights seen in the sky near the North/South Poles (*also* **Northern/Southern lights**).

auspices ['o:spisiz]: **under the auspices of** (*formal*) arranged or encouraged by (a society *etc*): *This exhibition is being held under the auspices of the Arts Council.*

au'spicious [-ʃəs] *adj* (*formal*) giving hope of success: *You haven't made a very auspicious start to your new job.* *See also* **inauspicious**.

austere [o:'stiə] *adj* (*formal*) **1** severely simple and plain: *He leads an austere way of life*; *His way of life is rather austere.* **2** without decoration: *That is an austere building*; *That building is rather austere.*

au'stereness, au'sterity [-'ste-] *nus.*

Australia, Australian *see* Appendix 2.

Austria, Austrian *see* Appendix 2.

authentic [o:'θentik] *adj* (*formal*) true, real or genuine: *Are your documents authentic or faked?*; *These are authentic certificates.*

au'thenticate [-keit] *vt* (*formal*) to prove something true or genuine: *Has his signature been authenticated?*

auˌthenti'cation *ncu* (*formal*) (an act of) authenticating: *The authentication of his certificates was a mere formality.*

ˌauthen'ticity [-sə-] *nu* the quality of being authentic: *He doubts the authenticity of my passport.*

author ['o:θə] – *fem* **'author, 'authoress** – *nc* **1** the writer of a book, article, play *etc*: *He used to be a well-known author but his books are out of print now.* **2** (*formal*) the creator or beginner of anything: *God, the author of our being*; *Who is the author of this practical joke?*

'authorship *nu* the state or fact of being an author: *The authorship of the novels was a matter for conjecture*; *Authorship brought him few rewards.*

authority [o:'θorəti] **1** *nu* the power or right to do something: *He gave me the authority to act on his behalf*; *I have no authority to do that.* **2** *nc* a person who is an expert, or a book that can be referred to, on a particular subject: *He is a great authority on Roman history.* **3** *nc* (*usu in pl*) the person or people who have power in an administration *etc*: *The authorities would not allow public meetings.* **4** *nu* (*formal*) a natural quality in a person which makes him able to control and influence people: *Napoleon was a man of authority.*

auˌthori'tarian *adj* (*formal*) considering obedience to authority more important than personal freedom: *authoritarian parents*; *His parents are very authoritarian*; *an authoritarian government.* – *nc* a person who has authoritarian views: *He is an authoritarian with old-fashioned views.*

au'thoritative [-tətiv, (*Amer*) -teitiv] *adj* said or written by an expert or a person in authority: *I* *cannot give you an authoritative opinion; His comments sounded very authoritative.*

authorize, -ise ['o:θəraiz] *vt* (*formal*) **1** to give (someone) the power or right to do something: *I authorized him to sign the documents.* **2** to give permission for something: *I authorized the payment of £100 to John Smith.* **ˌauthori'zation, -s-** *ncu.*

See also **unauthorized**.

auto- [o:tou] (*in cmpds*) for or by oneself or itself, as in **autobiography**.

auto ['o:tou] short for **automobile**.

autobiography [o:təbai'ogrəfi] *nc* the story of a person's life written by himself: *His autobiography was published just before he died.* **ˌauto-bio'graphic(al)** [-'gra-] *adj.*

autocrat ['o:təkrat] *nc* a ruler who has total control: *The Tsars of Russia were autocrats.*

autocracy [o:'tokrəsi] *ncu* (*formal*) government by an autocrat.

ˌauto'cratic *adj* **1** having absolute power: *an autocratic ruler/government.* **2** expecting complete obedience: *She has a very autocratic father; He is too autocratic.*

autograph ['o:təgra:f] *nc* a person's signature, *esp* as a souvenir: *May I have your autograph?; She collected autographs of film stars.* – *vt* to write one's name on (*esp* for a souvenir): *The actor autographed her programme.*

automatic [o:tə'matik] *adj* **1** (of a machine *etc*) working by itself: *She has an automatic washing-machine; Is the machine automatic?* **2** (of an action) unconscious; without thinking: *an automatic response; Her response was completely automatic.* – *nc* **1** something (*eg* a washing-machine) which works automatically. **2** a self-loading gun: *He has two automatics and a rifle.*

'automated [-mei-] *adj* working by automation: *a fully automated process; Is the process fully automated?*

ˌauto'matically *adv* **1** in an automatic way: *This machine works automatically.* **2** without thinking: *He answered automatically, as he was thinking about something else.*

ˌauto'mation *nu* (in factories *etc*) the use of machines, *esp* to work other machines: *Automation has resulted in some skilled people losing their jobs.*

automaton [o:'tomətən] – *pls* **au'tomata** [-tə] , **au'tomatons** – *nc* **1** a human-shaped machine that can be operated to move by itself. **2** a person who acts like a machine.

automobile ['o:təməbi:l, (*Amer*) o:təmə'bi:l] *nc* (*Amer: often abbrev* **'auto** ['o:tou] – *pl* **'autos**) a motor-car.

autonomy [o:'tonəmi] *nu* (*formal*) **1** the power or right of a country *etc* to govern itself. **2** a state of independent control: *The business has complete autonomy.*

au'tonomous *adj* (*formal*) **1** self-governing: *an autonomous region; It is completely autonomous.* **2** having independent control: *The school is run on autonomous principles.*

autopsy ['o:topsi] *nc* (*tech*) a medical examination of a body after death: *The autopsy proved he had been poisoned.*

autumn ['o:təm] *ncu* (*Amer* **fall**) the season of the year when leaves change colour and fall, September to October or November in cooler northern regions: *These flowers wither in autumn; Her book will be published in the autumn* (= the autumn of this year); *in the autumn of 1930; He came to see us last autumn* (= the autumn of last year); (*attrib*) *autumn colours* (= the colours of leaves in autumn); (*attrib*) *a lovely autumn evening; We have had a series of very wet autumns recently; Autumn is my favourite season.*

autumnal [o:'tʌmnəl] *adj* (*formal*) of or like autumn: *autumnal colours; The weather is quite autumnal today.*

auxiliary [o:g'ziljəri] *adj* (*attrib*) **1** helping: *She is employed as an auxiliary nurse.* **2** additional: *The hospital has an auxiliary power supply.* – *nc* **1** a helper: *She is employed as an auxiliary in the hospital.* **2** (*gram: also* **auxiliary verb**) a verb that helps to form different verb tenses, *eg have, be etc*: *I shall go; He has gone.*

avail [ə'veil]: **a'vail oneself (of)** (*formal*) to make use of: *You must avail yourself of any financial support you can get.*

of no/little avail, to no/little avail (*formal*) of no or little use or effect: *He tried to revive her but to no avail; His efforts were of little avail.*

available [ə'veiləbl] *adj* (*neg* **un-**) able or ready to be used: *The halls are available on Saturday night; The book will not be available until late March; All the available money has been used.* **aˌvaila'bility** *nu.*

avalanche ['avəla:nʃ] *nc* **1** a fall of snow and ice down a mountain: *Two skiers were buried by the avalanche.* **2** a large number: *an avalanche of letters.*

avant-garde [avã'ga:d] *adj* (*formal*) of the most modern and advanced ideas in art, literature, music *etc*: *His poetry is too avant-garde for me; avant-garde writers.*

avarice ['avəris] *nu* (*formal*) strong desire for money, expensive things *etc*; greed: *He looked at the gold coins with avarice; His avarice for money increased as he grew older.*

ˌava'ricious [-ʃəs] *adj* (*formal*): *an avaricious old miser; He is so avaricious.*

avenge [ə'vendʒ] *vt* (*formal*) to take revenge for a wrong on behalf of someone else: *He avenged his brother/his brother's death.* **a'venger** *nc.*

See also **revenge, vengeance**.

avenue ['avinju:] **1** *nc* a road, often with trees along either side. **2** *n* (*with cap: often abbrev* **Ave.** *when written*) a word used in the names of certain roads or streets: *His address is 14 Swan Avenue.* **3** *nc* (*formal fig*) a means or way: *We had no avenue of escape.*

average ['avəridʒ] *nc* (*math*) the numerical result of adding several amounts together and dividing the total by the number of amounts: *The average of 3, 7, 9 and 13 is 8* (= 32÷4). – *adj* **1** (*attrib*) obtained by finding the average of amounts *etc*: *average price; The average temperature today was 20°C.* **2** ordinary; usual; not extreme: *The average person is not very wealthy; His work is about average* (= no better and no worse than the work of others). – *vt* **1** to find the average of. **2** to form an average: *The walkers averaged twenty miles a day.*

average out 1 *vt sep* to work out the average result: *He averaged out his expenses at £10 per day; He averaged them out.* **2** *vi* (*with* **at**) to result in as an average: *His car's petrol consumption averaged out at ten gallons a week.*

averse [ə'və:s] *adj* (*pred: with* **to**) having a dislike for (something): *I'm not averse to working hard.*

a'version [-ʃən, (*Amer*) -ʒən] (*formal*) **1** *nu* a

feeling of dislike: *He has an aversion to smoking.* 2 *nc* something disliked: *Whisky is one of his pet aversions.*

avert [ə'və:t] *vt* (*formal*) 1 to turn away, *esp* one's eyes: *She averted her eyes from the dead animal.* 2 to prevent: *His quick thinking averted disaster.*

aviary ['eiviəri] *nc* a place in which birds are kept.

aviation [eivi'eiʃən] *nu* 1 (the science or practice of) flying in aircraft. 2 the industry concerned with aircraft manufacture, design *etc*: *He is looking for a job in aviation*; (*attrib*) *the aviation industry.*

avid ['avid] *adj* (*formal*) eager or greedy: *avid readers of historical novels*; *She was avid for information.* **'avidly** *adv.* **a'vidity** *nu.*

avocado [avə'ka:dou] – *pl* **ˌavo'cados** – 1 *ncu* (*also* **avocado pear**) a kind of pear-shaped tropical fruit: *They began the meal with avocado with prawns*; *She bought two avocados.* 2 *nc* the tree which produces this fruit.

avoid [ə'void] *vt* to keep away from (a place, person or thing): *He drove carefully to avoid the holes in the road*; *Avoid introducing her to my wife.*

a'voidance *nu.*

a'voidable *adj* (*neg* **un-**: *usu attrib*): *I shall not make any avoidable changes to my plans.*

avoirdupois [avwa:du'pwa:] *nu* the system of measuring weights in pounds (*lb*) and ounces (*oz*).

avow [ə'vau] *vt* (*very formal*) to state openly: *He avowed his intention of resigning*; *She avowed that she would never return to her husband.*

a'vowal *ncu* (*very formal*) (a) definite statement: *He made an open avowal of his feelings.*

a'vowed *adj* (*attrib*: *formal*) stated: *His avowed policy was to make a great deal of money.*

avuncular [ə'vʌŋkjulə] *adj* (*formal*: *usu attrib*) 1 like an uncle, *ie* kind, well-meaning *etc*: *He gave an avuncular smile.* 2 of an uncle: *He takes his avuncular responsibilities seriously.*

await [ə'weit] *vt* (*formal*) to wait for: *You must await the arrival of his letter.*

awake [ə'weik] – *pt* **awoke** [ə'wouk]: *ptps* **a'waked, a'woke** – *vt* (*formal*) to rouse (someone) from sleep: *I awoke him at seven o'clock.* – *vi* (*formal*) to stop sleeping: *He awoke suddenly.* – *adj* (*pred*) not asleep: *Is he awake yet?*

a'waken *vti* 1 (*formal*) to awake: *I was awakened by the song of the birds.* 2 to start a feeling (of interest, guilt *etc*): *His interest was awakened by the lecture.* **a'wakening, a'waking** *ncus.*

a'waken to *vt fus* (*formal*) to become aware of: *It was a long time before he awakened to the danger around him.*

be a'wake to to be aware of: *Do you think they're fully awake to the problems involved?*

wide awake *see* **wide**.

award [ə'wo:d] *vt* 1 to give (someone something that they have won or deserved): *They awarded her first prize.* 2 (*legal*) to give: *He was awarded damages of £2000.* – *nc* something awarded: *The film awards were presented annually.*

aware [ə'weə] *adj* 1 (*pred*) knowing (about) or conscious (of): *She became aware of a peculiar smell*; *Is he aware of the problem?*; *Are they aware that I'm coming?* 2 knowing and being concerned about what is happening: *She's not politically aware*; *a politically aware young woman.*

a'wareness *nu.*

away [ə'wei] *adv* 1 to or at a distance from the person speaking or the person or thing spoken about: *He lives three miles away*; *His arrival is still six hours away*; *Go away!*; *Take it away!* 2 in the opposite direction: *She turned away so that he would not see her tears.* 3 (gradually) into nothing: *The noise died away.* 4 continuously: *They worked away until dark.* 5 (of a football match *etc*) not on the home ground: *The team is playing away this weekend.* – *adj* (*attrib*) *an away match.*

a'way with (him *etc***)!** (*arch*) take (him *etc*) away!

far and away *see* **far**.

right away *see* **right**.

straight away *see* **straight**.

awe [o:] *nu* (*formal*) wonder and fear: *She holds her teacher in awe*; *The child looked in awe upon the queen.* – *vt* (*usu in passive*: *formal*) to fill with awe: *He was awed by the whole situation.*

'awe-inspiring, 'awesome *adjs* (*formal*) causing awe: *an awe-inspiring sight*; *The waterfall was awe-inspiring.*

'awestruck *adj* (*formal*: *usu pred*) filled with awe: *She was awestruck by the beauty of the mountains.* See *also* **overawe**.

awful ['o:ful] *adj* 1 (*inf*: *attrib*) very great: *I'm in an awful rush today.* 2 (*inf*) very bad: *This book is awful*; *I have an awful headache.* 3 (*formal*) terrible or dreadful: *His death was an awful experience for his wife.*

'awfully *adv* (*inf*) very (much): *I'm awfully glad to see you*; *It's an awfully good book*; *Thanks awfully!* **'awfulness** *nu.*

awhile [ə'wail] *adv* (*often liter*) for a short time: *Can you stay awhile?*

awkward ['o:kwəd] *adj* 1 not graceful or elegant: *an awkward boy*; *an awkward movement*; *He is awkward in his movements.* 2 difficult or causing difficulty, inconvenience *etc*: *It's an awkward cupboard to reach*; *He asked an awkward question*; *There was an awkward silence when the child broke the expensive vase*; *I couldn't explain the situation over the telephone. It was a bit awkward – there was someone else in the room.*

'awkwardly *adv* 1 in a clumsy or inelegant way: *He handles a tennis racket very awkwardly.* 2 in a difficult position: *I can see you are awkwardly placed.* **'awkwardness** *nu.*

awl [o:l] *nc* a pointed tool for making small holes, *esp* in leather.

awning ['o:niŋ] *nc* a covering (of canvas *etc*) to give shelter from sun or rain, often in front of a shop, hotel *etc*: *The greengrocer has baskets of fruit and vegetables outside his shop under the awning.*

awoke *see* **awake**.

awry [ə'rai] *adj* (*pred*) crooked; in disorder: *His tie was all awry.* – *adv* wrong or not as intended: *His plans went awry.*

axe, (*Amer*) **ax** [aks] *nc* a tool with a (long) handle and a metal blade for cutting down trees and cutting wood *etc* into pieces: *He chopped down the tree with a huge axe.* – *vt* 1 to get rid of; to dismiss: *They've axed 50% of their staff*; *They axed the plan for the new swimming-pool.* 2 to make less or reduce (costs, services *etc*): *Government spending in education has been axed.*

have an 'axe to grind to have a personal, often selfish, reason for being involved in something: *I have no axe to grind – I just want to help you.*

axiom ['aksiəm] *nc* (*formal*) a fact or statement which is definitely true and accepted as a principle or rule.

ˌ**axio'matic** [-'matik] *adj* (*formal*): *It is axiomatic that a circle is round*; *an axiomatic statement.*

axis ['aksis] – *pl* **axes** ['aksiːz] – *nc* **1** the real or imaginary line on which a thing turns (as the axis of the earth, from North Pole to South Pole, around which the earth turns). **2** a fixed line used as a reference, as in a graph: *He plotted the temperatures on the horizontal axis.*

axle ['aksl] *nc* the pin or rod on which a wheel turns: *The garage mechanic found a crack in the back axle of the car.*

ay(e)[1] [ai] *interj* (*old or dial*) yes.

aye *nc* a vote in favour (of something).

the ayes the people who vote in favour: *The ayes have it!* (= they have won the vote).

ay(e)[2] [ei] *adv* (*arch or liter*) always.

azure ['aʒə] *nu, adj* (of) a light blue colour: *the azure of the sky*; *azure skies.*

Bb

babble ['babl] *vi* **1** to talk quickly and indistinctly: *The speaker was babbling in a language I couldn't understand.* **2** (*inf*) to talk foolishly: *What are you babbling about now?* **3** (*liter or formal*) to make a continuous and indistinct noise (like a stream *etc*): *The stream babbled over the pebbles.* – *nu* such talk or noises: *A low babble of noise arose when the teacher left the classroom*; (*liter or formal*) *The babble of the stream could be faintly heard.*

babe [beib] *nc* **1** (*liter*) a baby: *She was just a babe in arms* (= a small baby not yet able to walk) *when the war began.* **2** *see* **baby** (*def 4*).

babel ['beibl, (*Amer*) 'babl] *nu* (*sometimes with* **a**: *formal*) (a scene of) noise and confusion: *The market-place was a veritable babel on a Saturday morning.*

baboon [bə'buːn, (*Amer*) ba-] *nc* a kind of large monkey with a dog-like face.

baby ['beibi] *nc* **1** a very young child: *Some babies cry during the night*; (*attrib*) *She has a baby boy.* **2** the youngest of a group: *At 17, he was the baby of the football team.* **3** (*derog*) a person (often a child) who acts like a baby or in a very childish way: *That boy is such a baby that he cries when he hurts himself slightly.* **4** (*sl: esp Amer, often* **babe**) a girl or young woman. – *vt* to treat (someone) as if he or she were a baby: *They babied the youngest member of the family all his life.*

'**babyhood** *nu* the time or state of being a baby: *She has had a scar on her face since babyhood.*

'**babyish** *adj* (*derog*) **1** like a baby; not mature: *That child was so babyish that he cried every day at school.* **2** of clothes *etc*, suitable for a baby: *She insists on dressing her eight-year-old daughter in babyish clothes.*

'**baby buggy/carriage** *nc* (*Amer*) a pram.

baby grand *nc* a small grand piano: *We have a baby grand in our sitting-room.*

'**baby-minder** *nc* a full-time professional baby-sitter, *usu* someone who looks after children in her own house *eg* when the children's mothers are at work: *She takes her child to a baby-minder on her way to work.*

'**baby-sit** *vi* to remain in a house to look after a child while its parents are out: *She baby-sits for her friends every Saturday.*

'**baby-sitter** *nc* a person who does this: *She can't go to the party – she can't get a baby-sitter.*

bachelor ['batʃələ] *nc* an unmarried man: *He will never marry – he's a confirmed bachelor* (= he has no intention of ever marrying); (*attrib*) *a bachelor flat/apartment* (= a flat/apartment suitable for one person).

'**bachelorhood** *nu* (*formal*) the time or state of being a bachelor: *He enjoys bachelorhood too much to get married.*

Bachelor of Arts, Science *etc* a person who has passed examinations of a particular level in Arts or Science *etc* at a university.

bacillus [bə'siləs] – *pl* **ba'cilli** [-lai] – *nc* (*tech*) a rod-shaped bacterium, *esp* one causing disease: *Dysentery is caused by bacilli.*

back [bak] *nc* **1** in man, the part of the body from the neck to the bottom of the spine: *She lay on her back*; *He has broken his back.* **2** in animals, the upper part of the body: *She put the saddle on the horse's back.* **3** the part of anything that is opposite to the front or furthest from the front: *They are painting the back of the house*; *the back of the picture*; *She sat at the back of the hall*; (*attrib*) *He delivers milk at the back door.* **4** in football, hockey *etc* a player who plays behind the forwards. – *adj* (*attrib*) of an earlier date: *Before you leave that job you must collect your back pay* (= salary or wages that you have already earned). – *adv* **1** to, or at, the place or person from which a person or thing came: *I went back to London*; *She took the damaged book back to the shop*; *He is just back* (= he has just returned) *from his holidays*; *He gave the car back to its owner.* **2** away (from something); not near (something): *Move back! Let the ambulance get to the injured man*; *Keep back from me or I'll hit you!* **3** towards the back (of something), away from the front (of something): *Sit back in your chair – don't sit on the edge of it.* **4** in return; in response to: *If he kicks you, kick him back*; *When the teacher is scolding you, don't answer back.* **5** to, or in, the past: *far back in ancient times*; (*inf*) *I saw him a few years back* (= a few years ago); *Think back to your childhood.* – **1** *vti* to (cause to) move backwards: *He backed (his car) out of the garage*; *The child backed away from his father in terror.* **2** *vt* to help or support: *Will you back me against the others?* **3** *vt* to bet or gamble on: *I backed your horse to win but it lost.* **4** *vt* to put a back on: *I've backed this picture with a sheet of cardboard so that the edges will not curl up.*

-backed (*in cmpds*) having a (certain kind of) back: *These books are cloth-backed*; *a hump-backed bridge.*

'**backer** *nc* a person who supports another in business *etc*, *esp* with money: *Who is the backer of the new theatre?*

'**backing** *nu* support *eg* in the form of money: *They had the backing of their parents in this decision*; *The firm gave backing to his new project.*

'**backless** *adj* having no back: *She was wearing a backless dress*; *Her new dress is backless.*

'**backache** *ncu* (a) pain in the back: *My backache is getting worse*; *I suffer from backache.*

ˌ**back-'bencher** *nc* in Britain, a member of Parliament who does not hold any of the more important government positions: *He used to be a junior minister but he is now only a back-bencher.*

'backbite *vi* (*liter*) to speak evil of, and criticize, a person when he is not present.

'backbiting *nu*: *Constant backbiting by her colleagues led to her resignation.*

'backbone 1 *nc* the spine: *the backbone of a herring.* **2** *nc* (*fig*) the chief support: *The older employees are the backbone of the industry.* **3** *nu* firmness and strength of character: *A coward has no backbone.*

'backbreaking *adj* (*usu attrib*) (of a task *etc*) very difficult or requiring very hard work: *Digging the garden is a backbreaking job.*

'backchat *nu* (*inf*) answering back rudely; cheek; impertinence: *The new office boy is always giving backchat to the older employees.*

'back-cloth *nc* the painted cloth used as background on a stage: *A pantomime usually requires a bright and colourful back-cloth*; (*formal fig*) *The ski-ing competitions took place against the magnificent back-cloth of the Alps.*

,back'date *vt* **1** to put an earlier date on (a cheque *etc*): *He should have paid his bill last month and so he has backdated the cheque.* **2** to make payable from a date in the past: *Our rise in pay was backdated to April.*

'backdrop *nc* a back-cloth: *A forest scene was the backdrop in his latest play*; (*formal fig*) *The castle looked impressive against the backdrop of the mountains.*

,back'fire *vi* **1** (of a motor-car *etc*) to make a loud bang because of unburnt gases in the exhaust system: *The child was frightened when the car backfired.* **2** (of a plan *etc*) to have unexpected results, often opposite to the intended results: *His scheme backfired (on him), and he lost a lot of money.*

'background *nc* **1** the space behind the principal or most important figures or objects of a picture *etc*: *He always paints ships against a background of stormy skies*; *I like the figures in the foreground of that picture but I don't like the trees in the background*; (*fig*) *His wife helps him a lot although she always stays in the background*; (*fig*) *The younger daughter is more beautiful than her sister but she is always kept in the background.* **2** a series of happenings that go before, and help to explain, an event *etc*: *Have you explained the background to the situation?*; (*attrib*) *Have you any background information?* **3** a person's origins, education *etc*: *She was ashamed of her humble background*; *They decided to marry, despite the differences in their backgrounds.*

'backhand 1 *nc* in tennis *etc*, (the ability to make) a stroke or shot with the back of one's hand turned towards the ball: *She won the match with a clever backhand*; *His backhand is very strong*; (*attrib*) *a backhand stroke.* **2** *nu* writing with the letters sloping backwards: *I can always recognize her backhand*; (*attrib*) *His backhand writing was difficult to read.* – *adv* in a way that uses (a) backhand: *She played the stroke backhand*; *She writes backhand.*

,back'handed *adj* **1** (*usu attrib*) made with, or using, a backhand: *a backhanded stroke* **2** having a possible second meaning: *a backhanded compliment* (= a compliment that could be taken as an insult); *That compliment was rather backhanded.*

'backhander *nc* (*inf*) a bribe: *He won the contract for his firm by giving a backhander to the official.*

'backlash *nc* (*no pl*) an unpleasant and often violent reaction to an action, situation, theory *etc*: *There was a backlash against the government's financial policy.*

'backlog *nc* a pile of uncompleted work *etc* which has collected: *There is a backlog of orders because of the strike.*

,back-'number *nc* **1** an out-of-date copy or issue of a magazine *etc*: *He collects back-numbers of comic magazines.* **2** (*fig inf*) a person or thing which is out of date or no longer useful: *That actress is a real back-number now.*

,back-'pedal 1 *vti* to turn the pedals (on a bike *etc*) backwards. **2** *vi* to reverse one's opinion or course of action *etc*: *He was forced to back-pedal and say the opposite of what he said originally.*

'backroom *adj* (*attrib*) working unseen by the public: *Special effects on television are produced by the backroom boys.*

back seat *see* **take a back seat, back-seat driver** *below.*

'backside *nc* (*inf*) the bottom or buttocks: *He sits on his backside all day long and does no work.*

'backslide *vi* (*formal*) to become bad, evil, worse *etc* after some improvement: *He improved slightly but was apt to backslide unless he was supervised.*

'backstage *adj* (*attrib*) **1** at the back of a theatre stage: *She has a backstage job.* **2** (*fig*) out of the public view: *The public do not know about backstage dealings of the government.* – *adv* at, or to, the back of a theatre stage: *We went backstage after the show.*

'backstroke *nc* (*no pl*) in swimming, a stroke made when lying on one's back in the water: *The child is better at backstroke than at breaststroke*; *He has a strong backstroke.*

'backtrack *vi* (*usu fig*) to go back the way one came: *He was forced to backtrack on hearing the new evidence.*

'backwash *nc* **1** a backward current *eg* that following a ship's passage through the water: *The backwash of the steamer almost overturned the small boat.* **2** (*formal*) the unintentional results of an action, situation *etc*: *The backwash of that firm's financial troubles affected the employees of several other firms.*

'backwater *nc* **1** a stretch of river not in the main stream, where the water does not move very much. **2** (*usu derog*) a place not affected by what is happening in the world outside, *usu* because of its isolation: *The village where he lives now is rather a backwater.*

'backwoods *n pl* forest or uncultivated country: *The backwoods of Canada*; (*fig derog*) *He lives in the backwoods of Kent.*

,back'yard *nc* **1** (*Brit*) an area (often paved) at the back of a house *etc*: *He is building a boat in his backyard.* **2** (*esp Amer*) a garden at the back of a house *etc*: *He grows vegetables in his backyard.*

back down *vi* to give up one's opinion, claim *etc*: *She backed down in the face of strong opposition.*

'back of (*Amer inf*) behind: *He parked back of the store.*

the back of beyond *see* **beyond**.

back on to *vt fus* (of a building *etc*) to have its back next to (something): *My house backs on to the racecourse.*

back out 1 *vi, vt sep* to move out backwards: *He opened the garage door and backed (his car) out.* **2** *vi* (*fig*) to withdraw from a promise *etc*: *You promised to help – you mustn't back out now!*

ˌ**back-seat 'driver** a passenger in the back seat of a car *etc* who gives unwanted advice on how to drive it: *Very often back-seat drivers cannot drive*; (*fig*) *His plans are always being delayed by the back-seat drivers in his department.*

back up *vt sep* to support or encourage: *The new evidence backed up my arguments*; *Her husband never seems to back her up.*

be glad to see the back of (*inf*) to be pleased when someone or something unpleasant is no longer present or causing a problem *etc*: *I'll be glad to see the back of her – she's so bad-tempered!*; *She was glad to see the back of that unreliable old car.*

behind someone's back *see* **behind**.

break the back of *see* **break**.

get off someone's back (*inf*) to stop annoying someone: *Get off my back! I can't work if you keep on criticizing me.*

get one's own back *see* **own**.

go back on *see* **go**.

have one's back to the wall (*formal*) to be in a very difficult or desperate situation: *He certainly has his back to the wall as he has lost his job and cannot find another one.*

put one's back into (*inf*) to do (something) with all one's strength: *He really put his back into making the business profitable.*

put someone's back up (*inf*) to anger someone: *He put my back up with his boasting.*

take a back seat (*fig*) to take an unimportant position: *At these discussions he always takes a back seat and listens to others talking.*

turn one's back on *see* **turn**.

backgammon ['bakgamən] *nu* a game for two players, played on a board with dice and fifteen pieces each: *Do you play backgammon?*

backward ['bakwəd] *adj* **1** (*attrib*) aimed or directed backwards: *He left without a backward glance*; *She took a backward jump.* **2** less advanced in mind or body than is normal for one's age: *a backward child*; *He is backward for his age.* **3** (*derog*) late in developing a modern culture, mechanization *etc*: *That part of Britain is still very backward*; *the backward peoples of the world.*

'backwardness *nu*.

'backwards, (*rarer*) **'backward** *advs* **1** towards the back: *He glanced backwards.* **2** with one's back facing the direction one is going in: *The child walked backwards into a lamp-post.* **3** in the opposite way to that which is usual: *Can you count from 1 to 10 backwards?* (= starting at 10 and counting to 1). **4** from a better to worse state: *Instead of progressing, we're going backwards.*

backwards and forwards in one direction and then in the opposite direction: *The dog ran backwards and forwards across the grass*; *This part of the weaving machine moves backwards and forwards very rapidly.*

bend/fall over backwards (*inf*) to try very hard; to make a great effort: *He bent over backwards to get us two tickets for the football international.*

know backwards *see* **know**.

bacon ['beikən] *nu* the flesh of the back and sides of a pig, salted and dried, used as food: *Would you like (some) bacon and eggs for breakfast?*

bacteria [bak'tiəriə] – *sing* **bac'terium** [-əm] – *n pl* (*tech*) organisms not able to be seen except under a microscope, found in great numbers in rotting matter, in air, in soil and in living bodies, some being the germs of disease: *His throat infection was caused by bacteria.*

bacˌteri'ology [-'olədʒi] *nu* the study of bacteria.

bacˌterio'logical [-'lo-] *adj.*

bacˌteri'ologist *nc* a person who is an expert in bacteriology: *He is a bacteriologist in the local hospital.*

bactrian *see* **camel**.

bad [bad] – *compar* **worse** [wəːs] – *superl* **worst** [wəːst] – *adj* **1** not good; not efficient; not satisfactory: *He is a bad driver*; *She is a bad manager*; *His eyesight is bad*; *That was a bad decision*; *They are bad at tennis* (= they play tennis badly); *Many people are bad at spelling.* **2** wicked; immoral: *He is a bad man*; *He has done some bad things*; *That woman is bad*; *You bad girl!* **3** unpleasant: *bad news*; *The weather is bad.* **4** rotten: *a bad apple*; *This meat is bad.* **5** (*pred*: *with* **for**) causing harm or injury: *Smoking is bad for your health*; *Drinking alcohol is bad for your liver*; *Children must not be given everything they want – it is bad for them.* **6** (of a part of the body) painful, or in a weak state: *He can't walk very well – he has a bad leg*; *She has a bad heart*; *How is your bad back?*; *I have a bad head* (= headache) *today.* **7** unwell: *the patient is feeling quite bad today*; (*inf*) *Is the patient very bad?* **8** (of something undesirable) serious or severe: *There has been a bad accident*; *How bad is your headache?*; *That was a bad mistake.* **9** (of a debt) not likely to be paid: *The firm loses a great deal of money every year from bad debts.*

'baddy *nc* (*inf*) a person who is evil, or a criminal, in a war, crime story *etc*: *Sometimes the baddies seem to have all the luck, but the goodies usually win in the end.*

'badly – *compar* **worse**; *superl* **worst** – *adv* **1** not well, efficiently or satisfactorily: *He plays tennis very badly.* **2** to a serious or severe extent: *He badly needs a haircut*; *My leg is hurting badly*; *The dress is badly stained.* **'badness** *nu.*

bad temper *see* **temper** (*def 1*).

badly off not having much *esp* money: *We can't go on holiday – we are too badly off*; *We are not badly off for cups but we don't have enough plates.*

feel bad (about something) to feel upset or ashamed about something: *I feel bad about forgetting to telephone you.*

go bad to become rotten: *This meat has gone bad.*

go from bad to worse to get into an even worse condition *etc* than before: *Things are going from bad to worse for the firm – not only are we losing money but there's going to be a strike as well.*

in a bad way (*inf*) very ill, in serious trouble *etc*; *You'll be in a bad way if you lose your job*; *He's in a bad way – he might die.*

not bad (*inf*) quite good: *'Is she a good swimmer?' 'She's not bad.'*

too bad unfortunate: *It's too bad that your holiday was cancelled*; *I'm sorry I can't come, but it's just too bad* (= nothing can be done about it).

bade *see* **bid**.

badge [badʒ] *nc* a mark, emblem or ornament showing rank, occupation, or membership of a society, team *etc*: *a school badge on a blazer*; *a badge on a policeman's helmet.*

badger ['badʒə] *nc* a burrowing animal of the weasel family. – *vt* to annoy or worry *usu* by asking questions, or requesting something, repeatedly: *He badgered the authorities until they gave him a new passport.*

badminton ['badmintən] *nu* a game played on a court with a shuttlecock and rackets: *I don't play tennis but I play badminton*; (*attrib*) *a badminton match.*

baffle ['bafl] *vt* to bewilder or be too difficult for (a person): *I was baffled by her attitude towards her husband*; *The police have not solved the crime – they are completely baffled by it.*

'baffling *adj*: *a baffling crime*; *I find her attitude to the situation completely baffling.*

bag [bag] *nc* **1** (*often in cmpds*) a container made of soft material (*eg* cloth, animal skin, plastic *etc*): *She carried a small bag*; *a handbag*; *a shopping-bag.* **2** the amount contained in a bag: *two bags of sugar.* **3** a quantity of fish or game caught: *Did you get a good bag today?* – *See also* **bags** *below.* – *v* – *pt, ptp* **bagged** – *vt* **1** (*formal*) to put into a bag: *Will you bag the potatoes?* **2** (*inf*) to kill (game): *I've bagged two rabbits and a pheasant today.* **3** (*inf*) to obtain or reserve (a seat, place *etc*): *Please bag a front seat for me before the crowds arrive!*

'baggy *adj* loose, like an empty bag: *He wears baggy trousers*; *Those trousers are far too baggy.*

bags *n pl* **1** a style of baggy trousers: *Oxford bags.* **2** (*with* **of**: *inf*) a large amount of: *He's got bags of money.*

bag and baggage with all one's belongings, equipment *etc*: *She left him bag and baggage.*

in the bag (*inf*) as good as done or complete (in the desired way): *Your appointment as director is in the bag.*

let the cat out of the bag *see* **cat**.

baggage ['bagidʒ] *nu* a traveller's suitcases, bags *etc*; luggage: *He sent his baggage on in advance*; *You can take only a certain amount of baggage on an aircraft*; (*attrib*) *the baggage compartment.*
See also **bag**.

bagpipes ['bagpaips] *n pl* a wind instrument consisting of a bag fitted with pipes, played in Scotland *etc*: *He wants to learn to play the bagpipes.*

bah! [ba:] *interj* used to show disgust or contempt: *Bah! What a mess!*

Bahasa Indonesia *see* Appendix 2.

bail[1] [beil] *nu* a sum of money which is given to a court of law to get an untried prisoner out of prison until the time of his trial, and which acts as security for his return: *bail of £500*; *She paid £300 bail for her son and lost the money when he did not appear for trial.*

bail out *vt sep* to set (a person) free by giving such money to a court of law: *They won't allow you to bail out someone accused of murder.* – *See also* **bale out** *under* **bale**[2].

stand/go bail for (*legal*) to provide bail for (someone): *Her father refused to stand bail for her when she was arrested on a drugs charge.*

bail[2] [beil] *nc* one of the cross-pieces laid on the top of the wicket in cricket.

bail[3] *see* **bale**[2].

bailiff ['beilif] *nc* **1** in England, an officer who assists a sheriff, with certain legal powers: *The bailiffs took possession of the bankrupt man's house.* **2** a person who manages an estate or a farm *etc* for its owner: *He lives in London and employs a bailiff to look after his farm in Devon.*

bait [beit] *nu* **1** food used to attract fish, animals *etc* which one wishes to catch, kill *etc*: *Before he went fishing he dug up some worms for bait.* **2** (*fig*) something intended to attract or tempt: *The policewoman acted as bait for the attacker who had murdered a woman the night before.* – *vt* **1** to put bait on or in (a hook, trap *etc*): *He baited his fishing hook with a fly*; *He baited the mousetrap with cheese.* **2** (*formal*) to tease unkindly; to annoy: *They baited the new boy at school unmercifully.*

-baiting (*in cmpds*) making dogs attack (a bear, bull *etc*): *'bear-baiting*; *'bull-baiting.*

rise to the bait *see* **rise**.

baize [beiz] *nu* a type of coarse woollen cloth, often green, *usu* used for covering billiard-tables, card-tables *etc.*

bake [beik] **1** *vti* to cook in an oven using either no liquid or fat, or only a very little of these, in the cooking process: *I'm going to bake (bread) today*; *She baked the ham*; *The cake was baking in the oven.* **2** *vti* to dry or harden by the heat of the sun or of fire: *The sun is baking the ground dry*; *The pottery was left to bake in the hot sun.* **3** *vi* (*inf*) to become very hot: *I'm baking in this heat.*

baked *adj*: *baked ham*; *freshly baked bread*; *Is that ham baked or boiled?*

'baker *nc* **1** a person who bakes: *He is a qualified baker*; *She is a good baker.* **2** a baker's shop: *Where is the nearest baker?*

'baker's *nc* a baker's shop: *I'm just going to the baker's.*

'bakery *nc* a place where baking is done and/or where bread, cakes *etc* are sold: *There's no bread today – there's a strike at the bakery*; *I bought some cakes at the bakery.*

'baking *nu* **1** the act or art of cooking bread, cakes *etc*: *She is good at baking.* **2** the things baked: *She put the baking away in tins.*

'baking powder *nu* a powder used to make cakes *etc* rise: *This sponge cake is very flat – you can't have used enough baking powder.*

baking soda, *also* **bicarbonate of soda** (*inf abbrev* **bicarb** ['baika:b]) *nu* a white powder, sodium bicarbonate, used in baking powder and as a cure for indigestion.

a baker's dozen (*old inf*) thirteen.

balance ['baləns] **1** *nc* a weighing instrument, *esp* one with two dishes hanging from a beam supported in the middle. **2** *nu* a state of physical steadiness in which weight is evenly distributed: *Keep your balance on the tightrope*; *The child was walking along the wall when he lost his balance and fell*; (*fig*) *The design lacks balance.* **3** *nu* state of mental or emotional steadiness: *It happened while the balance of her mind was disturbed*; *You must retain a sense of balance if you are going to make a success of the job.* **4** *nc* the amount by which the two sides of a financial account (money spent and money received) differ: *I have a balance* (= amount remaining) *of £100 in my bank account*; *a large bank balance*; *I'll pay a deposit now and give you the balance* (= the remainder of the money owed) *next week*; *the country's balance of payments.* – **1** *vti* (of two sides of a financial account) to make or be equal: *You must learn to balance your accounts*; *I can't get these accounts to balance.* **2** *vti* to make or keep steady by means of an even distribution of weight: *She balanced the jug of water on her head*; *The girl balanced on her toes*; *Children on a seesaw should be about the same weight, so that each balances the other*; (*fig*) *In the architects' design the wing on one side of the house was balanced by the stables on the other side.* **3** *vt* to compare (one thing with another) in one's mind: *You must balance the good points against the bad points and then make your decision.*

'balance sheet *nc* a paper showing a summary

and balance of financial accounts.

a balanced diet a diet which contains all the vitamins *etc* essential for health: *A balanced diet includes fruit and vegetables.*

balance of power the (even) distribution of political and military power between nations.

in the balance in an undecided or uncertain state: *Her fate is (hanging) in the balance.*

off balance not steady: *He hit me while I was off balance.*

on 'balance having taken everything into consideration and compared advantages and disadvantages *etc*: *It was difficult to decide which of the two was the better tennis player but on balance I think Miss Smith was.*

See also **imbalance**.

balcony ['balkəni] *nc* **1** a platform, with a wall or railing, built out from the wall of a building: *All the rooms in that hotel have balconies.* **2** in theatres *etc*, an upper floor or gallery: *We sat in the balcony of the cinema*; (*attrib*) *balcony seats.*

bald [bo:ld] *adj* **1** (of people) with little or no hair on the head: *He has been bald since he was forty*; *a bald head*; *He is going bald* (= becoming bald). **2** (of birds, animals) without feathers, fur *etc*: *The dog had a bald patch on its back*; *The parrot is nearly bald.* **3** (*fig*) bare or plain: *He gave a bald statement of the facts*; *His account was rather bald.*

'balding *adj* becoming bald: *He is already balding, although he is only thirty*; *a balding middle-aged man.*

'baldly *adv* in a bare or plain way: *He answered her questions baldly but adequately.*

'baldness *nu*: *a cure for baldness*; *the baldness of his statement.*

bale[1] [beil] *nc* a large bundle of goods or material (cloth, hay *etc*) tied together: *a bale of cotton.* – *vt* to make into bales: *She watched them baling the hay.*

bale[2] [beil] *vt* (*also* **bail**) to clear (water out of a boat with buckets *etc*): *Several gallons of water were baled out of the boat.*

bale out 1 *vi* to parachute from a plane in an emergency. **2** *vi, vt sep* to clear water out of a boat: *We shall have to bale (the water/boat) out.* – *See also* **bail out** *under* **bail**[1].

baleful ['beilful] *adj* (*formal or liter*: *usu attrib*) **1** evil or harmful: *a baleful influence.* **2** full of hate: *He wore a baleful expression.*

'balefully *adv*: *She glared balefully at him.*

balk, baulk [bo:(l)k] *vi* (*formal*: *with* **at**) to refuse to act in a particular way: *He agreed to help them in their plan, but balked at telling lies*; *I balked at spending all that money on a dress.*

Balkan, Balkans *see* Appendix 2.

ball[1] [bo:l] *nc* **1** anything roughly round in shape: *a ball of wool*; *meatballs and spaghetti in tomato sauce.* **2** a round or roundish object used in games: *a tennis ball*; *a golf ball.*

balls! *interj* (*vulg*) rubbish!; nonsense!

,ball-'bearing 1 *nc* (*usu in pl*) in machinery *etc*, one of the small steel balls that sit loosely in grooves and help the revolving of one part over another by lessening friction. **2** *nu* (*tech*) a bearing in which friction is lessened by such balls.

'ballcock *nc* in a cistern, a valve which is shut or opened by the rise or fall of a floating ball.

'ballpoint *nc* a pen having a tiny ball as the writing point: *He always uses a ballpoint*; (*attrib*) *a ballpoint pen.*

the ball of one's foot, thumb the fleshy part of the sole of the foot behind the big toe or at the base of the thumb: *She danced on the balls of her feet*; *The knife made a deep cut in the ball of his thumb.*

on the ball (*inf*) quick, alert and up-to-date: *The manager is increasing profits because he's really on the ball.*

play ball with (*inf*) to work or act together with; to cooperate with: *If you play ball with us you will make a lot of money.*

start/set, keep the ball rolling (*inf*) to start or keep something going, *esp* a conversation: *He can be relied on to start the ball rolling at parties.*

ball[2] [bo:l] *nc* a formal dance: *a ball at the palace*; (*attrib*) *She wore a ball-gown.*

'ballroom *nc* a large room where balls *etc* are held: *the ballroom of the castle*; (*attrib*) *ballroom dancing.*

have a ball (*inf*) to have a good time; to enjoy oneself.

ballad ['baləd] *nc* **1** a simple poem in verses of two or four lines, telling a story: *The Ballad of Sir Patrick Spens.* **2** such a poem set to music. **3** a simple, often sentimental, song: *Older people prefer ballads to pop music.*

ballast ['baləst] *nu* something heavy placed in a ship *etc* to keep it steady when it has no cargo: *After unloading their catch, the fishing-boats took on gravel as ballast.*

ballerina [balə'ri:nə] *nc* a female (often principal) ballet-dancer: *Pavlova was a famous ballerina.*

ballet ['balei, (*Amer*) ba'lei] **1** *nc* a theatrical performance of dancing with set steps and mime, often telling a story: *Swan Lake is my favourite ballet.* **2** *nu* the art of dancing in this way: *She is taking lessons in ballet*; (*attrib*) *a ballet class.* **3** *nc* a group of dancers who perform ballet(s): *A member of the Royal Ballet.*

ballistics [bə'listiks] *n sing* (*tech*) the science of things (*eg* rockets, bullets *etc*) forcibly thrown.

ballistic missile *nc* a missile guided for part of its course but falling like an ordinary bomb.

balloon [bə'lu:n] *nc* **1** a large bag, made of light material and filled with a gas lighter than air, *esp* formerly carrying passengers or goods in a basket hanging below: *The balloon was invented before the aeroplane.* **2** a small version of the same, with no basket, used as a toy or decoration for parties *etc*: *They decorated the dance-hall with balloons.* **3** in a strip cartoon *etc*, a balloon-shaped outline enclosing words spoken.

ballot ['balət] *nc* a method of voting in secret by marking a paper and putting it into a box: *They held a ballot to choose a new chairman*; *The question was decided by ballot*; (*attrib*) *ballot-box*; (*attrib*) *ballot-paper.* – *vi* (*formal*) to vote or choose by ballot: *They balloted for two new committee members.*

ballyhoo [bali'hu:, (*Amer*) 'balihu:] *nu* (*inf derog*) noisy or sensational advertising or publicity: *There was a lot of ballyhoo about the president's visit.*

balm [ba:m] *ncu* **1** (a) pleasant-smelling oil or ointment used in healing or soothing pain. **2** (*formal fig*) something that soothes: *The music was balm to my ears.*

'balmy[1] *adj* soothing; mild: *balmy air*; *The air is balmy tonight.* **balminess** *nu.*

balmy[2] *see* **barmy**.

balsa ['bo:lsə] **1** *nc* (*also* **'balsa tree**) a tropical American tree. **2** *nu, adj* (*often* **'balsa-wood**) (of) its very lightweight wood: *His model aeroplane is* *made of balsa*; *a balsa-wood model.*

balsam ['bo:lsəm] *nu* a pleasant-smelling liquid resin or resin-like substance obtained from certain trees: *He inhaled balsam when he had a bad cold.*

balustrade [balə'streid] *nc* a row of pillars on a balcony, staircase *etc*, joined by a rail: *an elegant balustrade.*

bamboo [bam'bu:] *nu, adj* (of) a type of gigantic grass with hollow, jointed, woody stems: *furniture made of bamboo*; *bamboo furniture.*

bamboozle [bam'bu:zl] *vt* (*inf*) to confuse completely and often deceive: *The motorist was completely bamboozled by the road-signs and took the wrong turning.*

ban [ban] *nc* an order that a certain thing may not be done: *There is a ban on smoking downstairs in the bus.* – *v* – *pt, ptp* **banned** – *vt* to forbid: *The government banned publication of his book*; *He was banned from entering the school grounds.*

banal [bə'na:l, (*Amer*) 'beinl] *adj* (*formal*) lacking originality or interest: *The speaker's banal remarks added nothing to the discussion*; *His comments were dull and banal.* **ba'nality** [-'na-] *ncu.*

banana [bə'na:nə] *nc* **1** the long curved fruit, yellow-skinned when ripe, of a type of very large tropical tree: *He ate a banana*; (*attrib*) *a banana skin.* **2** the tree.

band[1] [band] *nc* **1** (*often in cmpds*) a strip of cloth, metal *etc* to put round something *eg* to hold something in place or to keep several things together: *The tennis player wore a headband*; *He wore a black armband at the funeral*; *a rubber band*; *The waistband of these trousers is too tight.* **2** a stripe of a colour or material which is different from its background or surroundings: *Her grey skirt had a band of red in it*; *It's possible to see bands of several different colours in a rainbow.* **3** in radio *etc*, a group of frequencies or wavelengths: *the medium waveband.*

band[2] [band] *nc* **1** a number of persons forming a group for a purpose: *a band of robbers*; *a band of football supporters.* **2** a body of musicians (*esp* wind and percussion players): *a brass band*; *a dance band.* – *vi* to unite or gather together for a purpose: *The teachers banded together to oppose the new headmaster.*

'bandmaster *nc* the conductor of a musical (*esp* brass) band: *the bandmaster of a military band.*

'bandsman ['bandz-] *nc* a member of a musical (*esp* brass) band: *a bandsman in a military band.*

'bandstand *nc* a platform where bands play music out of doors.

,jump on the 'bandwagon (*derog*) to take part in something, or show an interest in something, only because it is fashionable or because it is going to be of some (financial) advantage to oneself: *When oil was discovered in the North Sea a lot of companies jumped on the bandwagon*; *When tourists first began to visit the island he jumped on the bandwagon and built several hotels.*

bandage ['bandidʒ] *ncu* (a piece of) cloth for binding up a wound, or a broken bone: *She had a bandage on her injured finger*; *The nurse fetched a roll of bandage.* – *vt* to cover with a bandage: *The doctor bandaged the boy's foot.*

bandit ['bandit] *nc* an outlaw or robber, *esp* as a member of a gang: *They were attacked by bandits in the mountains.*

bandy[1] ['bandi]: **bandy words** (*formal*) to argue (with someone): *I won't waste time bandying words with you!*

bandy[2] ['bandi] *adj* **1** (*sometimes derog*) (of legs) bent outwards at the knee: *She wears long skirts to hide her bandy legs*; *Her legs are a bit bandy.* **2** (*also* **bandy-'legged** [-'legid]) (of a person) having bandy legs: *a bandy-legged football player*; *She is bandy-legged.*

bane [bein]: **the bane** the source or cause of evil, harm or trouble: *The new manager is the bane of my existence.*

bang [baŋ] *nc* **1** a sudden loud noise: *The door shut with a bang.* **2** a blow or knock: *I got a bang on the head from a falling branch.* **3** (*Amer*: *usu in pl*) (a piece of) a fringe of hair: *Are bangs still in fashion?* **4** (*sl*) an act of sexual intercourse. – *vti* **1** to close with a sudden loud noise: *He banged the door*; *The door banged shut in the wind.* **2** to hit or strike violently, often making a loud noise: *The child banged his drum*; *He banged on the door*; *He banged the book down angrily on the table*; *The car banged me on the leg.* **3** to (cause to) make a sudden loud noise: *He blew into the paper bag, then banged it*; *We could hear the fireworks banging away in the distance.* **4** (*sl*) to have sexual intercourse (with).

'banger *nc* **1** an explosive firework: *The child was frightened by the bangers at the firework display.* **2** (*Brit inf*) a sausage: *bangers and beans.* **3** (*Brit inf*) an old car in poor condition: *He bought an old banger just to get to work every day.*

bang in the middle (*inf*) right in the middle (of something): *He walked in bang in the middle of a family quarrel*; *He fell down bang in the middle of the road.*

bang up to date (*inf*) right up to date: *That hairstyle's bang up to date.*

Bangladesh, Bangladeshi *see* Appendix 2.

bangle ['baŋgl] *nc* a rigid type of bracelet worn on the arm or leg: *gold bangles.*

banish ['baniʃ] *vt* (*formal*) **1** to send away (*usu* from a country), *esp* as a punishment: *He was banished (from the country) for treason.* **2** to put (thoughts *etc*) out of one's mind: *The child could not banish her fear of the dark.* **'banishment** *nu.*

banister ['banistə] *nc* **1** (*often in pl*) the handrail of a staircase and the posts supporting it: *Children love sliding down banisters.* **2** one of the posts supporting the handrail.

banjo ['bandʒou] – *pl* **'banjo(e)s** – *nc* a stringed musical instrument similar to the guitar: *He plays the banjo*; *Play me a tune on the banjo.*

bank[1] [baŋk] *nc* **1** a mound or ridge (of earth *etc*): *There's a good view from the top of this bank*; *The child climbed the bank to pick flowers*; *a bank of snow at each side of the road.* **2** the ground at the edge of a river, lake *etc*: *The river's overflowed its banks.* **3** a raised area of sand under the sea: *a sand-bank*; *Dogger Bank is a fishing-ground in the North Sea.* **4** a mass (of cloud, mist or fog): *Suddenly we saw a bank of fog over the motorway.* – **1** *vti* (*often with* **up**) to form into a bank or banks: *The earth was banked up against the wall of the house*; *Snow always banks up quickly against our back door.* **2** *vt* (*often with* **up**) to cover (a fire) with a large amount of coal, to prevent much air getting in and to keep it burning: *Bank (up) the fire before you go to bed.* **3** *vti* to tilt (an aircraft *etc*) while turning.

bank[2] [baŋk] *nc* **1** a place where money is lent or exchanged, or put for safety and/or to acquire interest: *He has plenty of money in the bank*; *I must go to the bank today*; *I borrowed some money from my child's bank* (= a small box *etc* for putting in money which one is saving). **2** a place for storing other valuable material: *A blood bank is a place where blood is kept for use in medicine.* – **1** *vi* to do one's banking business: *I bank with the bank in the centre of town.* **2** *vt* to put into a bank: *Be sure to bank the money before 3 o'clock.*

'banker *nc* a person who owns or manages a bank.

bank balance *see* **balance** (*def 4*).

'bank book *nc* a book recording money deposited in, or withdrawn from, a bank.

'banker's card *nc* (*also* **'cheque card**) a card issued by a bank guaranteeing that the holder's cheques (up to a certain limit) will be paid: *The shop would not accept the girl's cheque in payment of the dress until she showed her banker's card.*

bank holiday *nc* a day on which banks are closed (and which is often also a public holiday): *Is this a bank holiday? All the shops are closed*; (*attrib*) *bank-holiday Monday.*

'bank-note *nc* a piece of paper issued by a bank, used as money: *She was counting a pile of bank-notes when the robbers entered the bank.*

'bank on *vt fus* (*inf*) to rely on: *I'm banking on his help to run the disco*; *Don't bank on me – I'll probably be late.*

bank[3] [baŋk] *nc* a collection of rows (of instruments *etc*): *The modern pilot has banks of instruments and switches to operate.*

bankrupt ['baŋkrʌpt] *adj* **1** unable to pay one's debts: *the bankrupt garage-owner*; *He has been declared bunkrupt.* **2** (*formal*: *pred with* **of**) without; lacking in: *He was absolutely bankrupt of original ideas.* – *nc* a person who is unable to pay his debts. – *vt* to make bankrupt: *His wife's extravangance soon bankrupted him.*

'bankruptcy *nu*: *His extravagance resulted in bankruptcy*; (*formal*) *bankruptcy of ideas.*

banner ['banə] *nc* **1** a military flag. **2** a large strip of cloth, *usu* hung between two poles, bearing a slogan *etc*: *Many of the demonstrators were carrying banners saying 'Higher wages for all'*; (*fig*) *Everything the government did was done under the banner of civil rights.*

banner headline *nc* in a newspaper, a headline in very large type, *usu* going across the whole width of the page: *The news of the birth of the royal baby was given banner headlines.*

banns [banz] *n pl* a public announcement of a couple's intention to marry: *The banns of their marriage were put up outside the registry office.*

banquet ['baŋkwit] *nc* a feast or ceremonial dinner at which speeches are often made: *the Lord Mayor's banquet.*

bantam ['bantəm] *nc* a small variety of domestic fowl: *She keeps bantams as well as ordinary hens*; (*attrib*) *a bantam cock.*

banter ['bantə] *nu* friendly teasing: *The boy in hospital was cheered up by the noisy banter of his friends.*

baptize, -ise [bap'taiz] *vt* to dip (a person) in water, or sprinkle (someone) with water, as a symbol of acceptance into the Christian church, *usu* also giving him a name: *Jesus was baptized by John*; *She was baptized Mary but calls herself Jane.*

'baptism [-tizəm] *ncu* (an act of) baptizing: *the baptism of the baby*; (*fig*) *his baptism as a soldier.*

bap'tismal *adj* (*attrib*): *his baptismal name.*

baptism of fire a first experience of something, *usu* something difficult, frightening *etc*: *The soldier never recovered from his baptism of fire in his first day in the trenches.*

bar [ba:] *nc* **1** a rod or oblong piece (*esp* of a solid substance): *a gold bar*; *a five-bar gate*; *a bar of soap/chocolate*; *There are iron bars on the basement windows.* **2** a broad line or band: *The blue material had bars of red running through it.* **3** a bolt: *There's a bar on the door.* **4** a counter at which articles of a particular kind are sold: *a sandwich bar*; *a snack bar*; *a milk bar.* **5** a counter across which drinks are served: *Your whisky is on the bar.* **6** a public house: *I'll meet you in the Argyll Bar at 6 p.m.* **7** a measured division in music, containing a certain number of beats: *Sing the first ten bars.* **8** (*formal*) something which prevents (something happening): *His poverty is a bar to his ambition.* **9** (*formal*) a bank of sand *etc* at the mouth of a river. **10** the rail between the judge's seat and the rest of the court, at which the prisoner stands to be charged or sentenced: *The prisoner at the bar collapsed when he was sentenced to ten years' imprisonment.* – *See also* **the Bar** *below.* **11** an addition to a (military) medal, often to show that it has been won twice: *DSO and bar.* – *v* – *pt, ptp* **barred** – *vt* **1** to fasten with a bar: *Bar the door and lock it.* **2** to prevent from entering; to ban: *He's been barred from the club for his bad behaviour.* **3** to prevent (from doing something): *My lack of money bars me from going on holiday.* – *prep* (*inf*) except: *All bar one of the family had flu last winter.*

'barring *prep* (*inf*) except; without: *Barring accidents* (= unless there is an accident) *he will be there*; *Everyone agreed, barring Mary.*

'barmaid, 'barman, (*mainly Amer*) **'bartender** [-tendə] *nc* a person who serves at the bar of a public-house or hotel.

the Bar barristers as a whole: *The Bar is a highly respected profession.*

be called to the Bar (*formal*) to become a barrister: *He was called to the Bar three years ago.*

barb [ba:b] *nc* **1** a backward-facing point on an arrowhead, fishing-hook *etc*: *The barb of the fishing-hook stuck in his foot.* **2** (*formal*) a witty but hurtful remark: *She tried to ignore the barbs of her jealous friend.*

barbed *adj* having barbs: *a barbed arrow*; *a barbed remark*; *That remark was rather barbed.*

barbed wire *nu* wire with sharp points at intervals, used for making fences *etc*: *I tore my skirt on that barbed wire*; (*attrib*) *a barbed-wire fence.*

barbarous ['ba:bərəs] *adj* (*formal derog*) **1** uncultured and uncivilized: *He disliked the barbarous habits of his companions*; *Some eighteenth century practices would be considered barbarous nowadays.* **2** brutal: *They made a barbarous assault on the women.* **'barbarousness** *nu.*

bar'barian [-'beəriən] *nc* an uncultured and uncivilized person: (*hist*) *The barbarians attacked the Roman settlements*; (*derog*) *He has the manners of a barbarian.* – *adj* (*esp attrib*) uncivilized and uncultured: *barbarian tribes*; *barbarian customs.*

bar'baric [-'barik] *adj* barbarous.

'barbarism (*formal*) **1** *nu* the state of being uncivilized *etc.* **2** *nc* a bit of barbarous behaviour, *esp* an incorrect or inelegant expression in speech.

bar'barity [-'ba-] **1** *nu* the state of being barbarous. **2** *nc* a barbarous act: *The barbarities committed by the invaders were never forgotten.*

barbecue ['ba:bikju:] *nc* **1** a framework for grilling meat *etc* over a charcoal fire: *We cooked the steak on a barbecue.* **2** a social entertainment in the open air, at which food is barbecued: *We were invited to* *a barbecue.* – *vt* to cook on a barbecue: *He barbecued enough steak for twelve people.*

barber ['ba:bə] *nc* **1** a person who cuts men's hair, shaves their beards *etc.* **2** a barber's shop: *Where is the nearest barber?*

'barber's *nc* a barber's shop: *He is going to the barber's.*

barbiturate [ba:'bitjurət] *nc* (*tech*) a drug for calming the nerves or producing sleep, *usu* taken as a pill: *He killed himself by taking an overdose of barbiturates.*

bard [ba:d] *nc* (*liter or formal*) a poet: *Robert Burns is Scotland's most famous bard.*

bare [beə] *adj* **1** uncovered or naked: *bare skin*; *The hot sun burned her bare arms*; *The child was completely bare when they found him*; *bare floors* (= floors without rugs or carpets); *bare walls* (= walls without wallpaper, decoration *etc*). **2** empty: *bare shelves*; *The cupboard is completely bare* (*of food*). **3** of trees *etc*, without leaves: *In winter many trees are bare*; *bare trees.* **4** worn thin; threadbare: *a bare carpet*; *The carpet is a bit bare.* **5** (*attrib*) basic; essential: *the bare necessities of life.* – *vt* to uncover: *The boxer bared his chest*; *The dog bared its teeth in anger.*

'barely *adv* scarcely or only just: *We have barely enough food*; *He's barely arrived, and you already want him to go!*

'bareness *nu*: *the bareness of the trees in winter.*

'bareback *adv, adj* (*attrib*) without a saddle: *I enjoy riding bareback*; *She goes bareback riding.*

'barefaced *adj* (*attrib*) openly impudent: *That was a barefaced lie.*

'barefoot(ed) *adj, adv* not wearing shoes or socks *etc*: *The children go barefoot all summer*; *barefoot(ed) children*; *As the beach was so stony, few of the children were barefoot(ed).*

,bare'headed *adj, adv* not wearing a hat *etc*: *The women were forced to work bareheaded under the hot sun*; *bareheaded women*; *Few of the women were bareheaded.*

,bare'legged [-'legid] *adj, adv* having the legs not covered by trousers, tights *etc*: *The stupid girl arrived for the hike barelegged and wearing sandals*; *barelegged children.*

bargain ['ba:gin] *nc* **1** something bought cheaply and giving good value for money: *This carpet was a real bargain*; (*attrib*) *I bought this at a bargain price.* **2** an agreement made between people (about buying or selling something, or about doing something): *I'll make a bargain with you*; *The two presidents have struck a bargain with each other.* – *vi* to argue about or discuss a price, the terms of an agreement *etc*: *I bargained with him and finally got the price down to £5.*

'bargain for *vt fus* (*often in neg*) to expect or take into consideration: *I didn't bargain for everyone arriving at once*; *He got much more than he bargained for when he started arguing with her.*

drive a (hard) bargain *see* **drive**.

into the bargain in addition; besides: *First I broke my leg, and then I got flu into the bargain!*

barge [ba:dʒ] *nc* a flat-bottomed boat, used on rivers and canals: *Coal was sometimes carried on barges.* – *vi* **1** to move (about) clumsily: *He barged about the room.* **2** to bump (into): *He barged into me and didn't even apologize.* **3** (*inf*: *with* **in(to)**) to push one's way (into) rudely: *She barged in without knocking.*

baritone ['baritoun] *nc* **1** (a singer with) a deep male voice between base and tenor: *He is/has a good baritone*; (*attrib*) *a baritone voice.* **2** in music, a part written for a voice at this pitch: *The baritone is rather difficult*; (*attrib*) *the baritone part.* – *adv* with a baritone voice: *He sings baritone.*

bark[1] [ba:k] *nc* the short, sharp cry of a dog, fox *etc.* – **1** *vi* to make this sound: *The dog barked when I knocked at the door.* **2** *vti* to utter abruptly: *She barked a reply*; *There's no need to bark at me just because you're annoyed.*

bark up the wrong tree (*inf*) to get the wrong idea (about something): *You're barking up the wrong tree if you think the judge will be sympathetic.*

his bark is worse than his bite (*inf*) he sounds angry but he does not actually do anything harmful: *The old man next door is always shouting at the children but his bark is worse than his bite.*

bark[2] [ba:k] *nu* the covering of the trunk and branches of a tree: *The deer have eaten all the bark off that tree.* – *vt* to take the skin off (part of the body) by accident: *I barked my shin on the table.*

bark[3] *see* **barque**.

barley ['ba:li] *nu* a type of grain used for food and for making beer and whisky: *The farmer has harvested his barley*; (*attrib*) *barley water.*

barley sugar *nu* a kind of hard sweet made by melting and cooling sugar.

barmaid, barman *see* **bar**.

barmy, balmy[2] ['ba:mi] *adj* (*Brit sl*) crazy: *She's gone barmy!*; *a barmy old woman.*

barn [ba:n] *nc* **1** a building in which grain, hay *etc* are stored: *The farmer keeps his tractor in the barn.* **2** (*fig*) a large, inconvenient, uncomfortable building: *They live in a great barn of a house four miles from here.*

barnacle ['ba:nəkl] *nc* a kind of small shellfish that sticks to rocks and the bottoms of ships.

barometer [bə'romitə] *nc* an instrument which measures the weight or pressure of the atmosphere and indicates changes of weather: *The barometer is falling* (= the level of mercury in the barometer is falling) – *it is going to rain*; (*formal fig*) *Public opinion polls act as a barometer of confidence in the government.* **barometric** [barə'metrik] *adj* (*tech*: *attrib*): *barometric pressure.*

baron ['barən] *nc* **1** (*with cap in titles*) in Britain, (the status of) a nobleman next in rank below a viscount: *He was made a baron*; *Baron Scott of Sidcup.* **2** (*with cap in titles*) in some European countries, (the status of) a noble of similar rank: *Baron Rothschild.* **3** (*inf*) a powerful person: *a newspaper baron.*

'baroness *nc* (*with cap in titles*) **1** (the status of) a baron's wife. **2** (the status of) a lady holding a baronial title in her own right.

ba'ronial [-'rou-] *adj* (*attrib*) **1** of a baron: *a baronial court.* **2** in or of a style of architecture imitating that of old castles: *That mansion is built in baronial style.*

'barony *nc* the rank or land of a British baron.

baronet ['barənit] *nc* (the status of) a holder of the lowest British title that can be passed on to an heir.

'baronetcy *nc* the rank of a baronet.

barque, bark[3] [ba:k] *nc* (*hist or liter*) a type of sailing ship.

barracks ['barəks] *n sing or pl* a building or buildings for housing soldiers: *He was confined to barracks* (= he was not allowed to leave the barracks) *for striking an officer.*

barrage ['bara:ʒ, (*Amer*) bə'ra:ʒ] *nc* **1** something (*esp* heavy gunfire) that hinders, or keeps back, an enemy: *a barrage of gunfire.* 2 (*formal fig*) an overwhelming number: *a barrage of questions.* 3 a man-made barrier across a river.

barrel ['barəl] *nc* 1 a container made of curved pieces of wood bound with hoops; a metal container of similar shape: *The barrels contain beer.* 2 the amount contained by a barrel: *a barrel of beer.* 3 a long, hollow, cylindrical shape, *esp* the tube-shaped part of a gun: *The bullet jammed in the barrel of the gun.*

barren ['barən] *adj* (*formal*) 1 not able to produce crops, fruit *etc*: *That old apple-tree is barren*; *barren old fruit trees.* 2 bare and without crops *etc*: *a barren landscape*; *That part of the world is cold and barren.* 3 (*esp liter*) (of women) incapable of having children. 4 (*fig*: *esp attrib*) not producing results: *a barren discussion.* **'barrenness** *nu.*

barricade [bari'keid] *nc* a barrier (often temporary and quickly constructed) put up to block a street *etc*: *The police put up barricades to keep back the crowds during the procession.* – *vt* 1 to block something (*eg* a street) with a barricade. 2 (*often with* **in(to)**) to shut (*eg* oneself) away behind a barrier: *He's barricaded himself into an office on the third floor.*

barrier ['bariə] *nc* 1 something put up as a defence or protection: *The police put up barriers to keep back the crowds.* 2 (*fig*) something that keeps things *etc* apart or causes difficulty: *The bitterness of their quarrel caused a barrier between the former friends*; *He found his deafness a barrier to promotion.*

barrister ['baristə] *nc* in England, a lawyer qualified to present cases in court.

barrow[1] ['barou] *nc* 1 a wheelbarrow: *He wheeled the barrow into the garden.* 2 a small (*usu* two-wheeled) cart, pushed by hand, from which goods are often sold in markets *etc*: *I bought this fruit from that barrow over there.*

'barrow boy *nc* a man or boy who sells goods from a barrow.

barrow[2] ['barou] *nc* (*hist*) a large mound over an ancient grave or burial ground: *The archaeologists are investigating that barrow.*

bartender *see* **bar**.

barter ['ba:tə] *vti* (*formal*) to trade by giving (one thing) in exchange (for another): *The bandits bartered gold for guns*; (*fig*) *She bartered away her freedom for money when she married him.* – *nu* (*formal*) 1 the act of bartering: *Barter is no longer common.* 2 goods given or used in bartering: *Some tribes use sea-shells as barter.*

basalt ['baso:lt] *nu* any of certain types of dark-coloured rock.

base[1] [beis] *nc* 1 the foundation or support (of something); the line or surface on which a geometrical figure is regarded as standing: *The base of this triangle is 5 centimetres long*; *The base of the statue is made of stone*; (*fig*) *He used the novel as a base for the film.* 2 the lowest part (of something): *There were snowdrops round the base of the tree.* 3 the main ingredient of a mixture: *This paint has oil as a base.* 4 a headquarters, starting-point *etc*, sometimes containing living accommodation: *He lives on the army base two miles away*; *They used Edinburgh as a base for their travels in Scotland.* 5 the number on which a system of numbers is founded: *The decimal system uses 10 as a base.* 6 in baseball or rounders, any of the fixed points between which the players run: *He got back to base in record time.* 7 (*chem*) a substance which reacts with an acid to form a salt *etc.* – *vt* 1 to use as a foundation *etc*: *This house is based on solid rock*; *I base my opinion on the evidence.* 2 to use as a headquarters, starting-point *etc*: *Our group was based in Paris.*

'baseless *adj* without a base, foundation, reason *etc*: *a baseless claim*; *His accusations are totally baseless.*

See also **basic**.

base[2] [beis] *adj* (*formal*) mean, wicked or worthless: *base desires/motives*; (*liter*) *Is he base enough to do such a thing!* **'basely** *adv* **'baseness** *nu.*

base metal *ncu* (a) non-precious metal: *Long ago people tried to turn base metals into gold.*

See also **debase**.

baseball ['beisbo:l] *nu* an American game played with bat and ball by two teams of nine people: *He plays baseball, not football*; (*attrib*) *a baseball match.*

basement ['beismənt] *nc* the lowest floor of a building, *usu* below ground level: *She lives in a basement*; (*attrib*) *a basement flat.*

bash [baʃ] *vt* (*inf*: *sometimes with* **in**) to beat or smash (in): *He bashed his head against the wall*; *The soldiers bashed in the door.* – *nc* (*inf*) 1 a heavy blow: *He gave the door a bash with his foot.* 2 a dent: *The car had a bash on its nearside door.*

bash on/ahead (with) *vi* (*sl*) to go on doing something *esp* in a careless or inattentive way: *In spite of his father's advice he bashed on with the painting.*

have a bash at (*inf*) to make an attempt at: *Although he was not a handyman, he had a bash at mending the lock.*

bashful ['baʃful] *adj* lacking confidence; shy: *a bashful young girl*; *a bashful smile*; *He is too bashful to ask a girl to go to the cinema.* **'bashfully** *adv.* **'bashfulness** *nu.*

basic ['beisik] *adj* 1 of, or forming, the main part or foundation of something: *The basic recipe doesn't include all the things that I actually use*; *Your basic theory is wrong*; *The idea of forgiveness is basic to Christian belief*; *10 is the basic number in the decimal system*; *His basic salary isn't good but he gets commission.* 2 (*inf*) restricted to a fundamental level, elementary: *His education was very basic*; *He has only a very basic knowledge of French.* – *nc* (*usu in pl*: *inf*) something which forms the base (of a theory, mixture *etc*): *She doesn't seem to have grasped the basics of the subject.*

'basically *adv* with reference to what is basic; fundamentally: *She seems rather strict, but basically* (= in reality) *she's very nice*; *Her job, basically, is to deal with foreign customers.*

See also **base**[1].

basin ['beisn] *nc* 1 a bowl in a bathroom, toilet *etc* for washing oneself in: *a wash-hand basin.* 2 a wide, open dish for mixing or preparing food in: *a pudding-basin.* 3 a basinful: *a basin of hot water.* 4 the area drained by a river: *the basin of the Nile.* 5 the deep part of a harbour: *There were four yachts anchored in the harbour basin.*

'basinful *nc* the amount contained by a basin: *a basinful of water.*

basis ['beisis] – *pl* **'bases** [-si:z] *nc* 1 (*fig*) that on which a thing rests or is founded: *This idea is the basis of my argument*; *On the basis of what he said, I'd guess he'll make a success of it.* 2 (*formal*) the most important ingredient of a mixture: *The basis of bread is flour.*

bask [ba:sk] *vi* **1** to lie (*esp* in warmth or sunshine): *The seals basked in the warm sun.* **2** to enjoy and take great pleasure (in): *He basked in the approval of his friends.*

basket ['ba:skit] *nc* **1** (*often in cmpds*) a container made of strips of wood, rushes *etc* woven together: *She carried a large basket; a shopping-basket; a waste-paper basket.* **2** the amount contained by a basket: *a basket of fruit.* **3** a net into which the ball is thrown in basket-ball.

'basketball *nu* a game in which goals are scored by throwing a ball into a net on a high post: *He plays basketball.*

'basketry *nu* basketwork.

'basketwork *nu* **1** articles made of plaited rushes *etc*: *One stall at the sale of work sold only basketwork*; (*attrib*) *a basketwork chair.* **2** the art of making these: *The children learned basketwork at school.*

bass[1] [beis] – *pl* **'basses** – *nc* **1** (a singer having) a male voice of the lowest pitch: *The choir needs some new basses; He has a good bass*; (*attrib*) *a bass song.* **2** in music, a part written for a voice or instrument of the lowest pitch: *The bass of this piece is very difficult*; (*attrib*) *the bass part.* – *adv* with a bass voice: *He sings bass.*

bass[2] [bas] – *pl* **bass**, (*rare*) **'basses** – *nc* a type of fish of the perch family.

bassoon [bə'su:n, (*Amer*) ba-] *nc* a woodwind musical instrument which gives a very low sound: *She plays the bassoon; He played a tune on the bassoon.*

bas'soonist *nc* a person who plays the bassoon.

bastard ['ba:stəd] *nc* **1** (*usu offensive*) a child born of parents not married to each other. **2** (*vulg*: used to show anger, annoyance, sympathy *etc*) a person: *He's a really mean bastard; The poor bastard doesn't have much luck.* – *adj* **1** (*attrib*: *usu offensive*) born of parents not married to each other: *a bastard son.* **2** (*formal*: *usu attrib*) not genuine or pure, often due to being made up of parts which come from different sources: *a bastard style of architecture which combines modern and classical designs.*

'bastardize, -ise, *vt* (*formal*) to make not genuine or pure.

'bastardized *adj*: *a bastardized form of French.*

baste[1] [beist] *vt* to drop fat or butter over (roasting meat *etc*): *Baste the joint to prevent it from burning.*

baste[2] [beist] *vt* to sew temporarily and loosely, with long stitches: *Baste the hem before you sew it properly.*

bastion ['bastjən, (*Amer*) 'bastʃən] *nc* **1** (*hist*) a part of a fortification which sticks out: *The defenders of the castle manned the bastions.* **2** (*formal fig*) a person, place or thing which acts as a defence: *He's one of the last bastions of the old leisurely way of life; The remoteness of the village was a bastion against tourists.*

bat[1] [bat] *nc* **1** a shaped piece of wood *etc* for striking the ball in cricket, baseball, table-tennis *etc.* **2** (*inf*) a batsman: *He is the best bat in the team.* – *v* – *pt, ptp* **batted** – **1** *vi* to use a bat: *He bats with his left hand.* **2** *vt* to strike (the ball) with a bat: *He batted the ball into the crowd.*

'batsman ['bats-] *nc* a person who bats in cricket.

off one's own bat (*inf*) completely by oneself (without help): *He must be very clever to have made it all off his own bat; He did it off his own bat, without consulting anyone else first.*

bat[2] [bat] *nc* a mouse-like animal which flies, *usu* at night.

'batty *adj* (*inf*) crazy: *That old man is completely batty; She is batty about cats* (= she is very fond of cats); *a batty old man.*

bat[3] [bat] – *pt, ptp* **'batted** – *vt* (*inf*) to flutter or wink (an eyelid or eye): *The new secretary was always batting her eyelids at the boss; He didn't bat an eye* (= show surprise, shock *etc*) *when I told him he was sacked.*

batch [batʃ] *nc* a quality or number of things or people, got ready, delivered *etc*, all at one time: *a batch of bread/cakes/documents; The children arrived at the party in batches of three or four.*

bated ['beitid]: **with bated breath** (*fig*: *sometimes facet*) breathing only slightly, due to anxiety, excitement *etc*: *The crowd watched with bated breath as the fireman brought the child down the ladder; I'll wait with bated breath to see what happens when you arrive.*

bath [ba:θ] – *pl* **baths** [ba:ðz] – *nc* **1** a large container for holding water in which to wash the whole body: *I'll fill the bath with water for you.* **2** an act of washing in a bath: *I think I'll have a bath tonight; She has cold baths three times a week.* **3** (a container of) liquid *etc* in which something is immersed, processed *etc*: *A bird bath; Photographic paper is put into three different baths during developing; a bath of dye.* – *vti* to wash in a bath: *I'll bath the baby; She bathed in cold water.*

,bath'chair (*also* **bath chair**) *nc* a kind of wheeled chair for an invalid, *orig* with three wheels.

'bathroom *nc* **1** a room in a house *etc* which contains a bath: *We've installed a new bathroom*; (*attrib*) *bathroom scales.* **2** (*esp Amer*) a lavatory.

baths *n pl* (*usu with* **the**) a public swimming pool.

bath salts *see* **salt**.

have a bath/(*formal*) **take a bath** to bath oneself: *I'm filthy – I must have a bath.*

bathe [beið] **1** *vt* to put a part of one's body (*eg* the feet or hands) into water for washing or to lessen pain: *He bathed his feet to get the dirt off; I'll bathe your wounds.* **2** *vi* to go swimming (in the sea *etc*): *She bathes in the sea every day.* – *nc* an act of swimming (in the sea): *a midnight bathe.*

'bather *nc* a person who goes swimming (in the sea or in a swimming-pool): *Three bathers have drowned.*

'bathing *nu* (*often attrib or in cmpds*) the activity of going into water to swim: *The children love bathing; Bring your bathing-suit/bathing-costumes and bathing-cap.*

'bathed in (*liter or formal*) covered with: *The hills are bathed in sunlight.*

batik ['batik] *nu* a method of dyeing patterns on cloth by waxing certain areas so that they remain uncoloured.

batman ['batmən] – *pl* **'batmen** – *nc* an army officer's servant.

baton ['batn, (*Amer*) ba'ton] *nc* **1** a short, heavy stick, carried by a policeman as a weapon. **2** a light, slender stick used when conducting an orchestra or choir: *The conductor raised his baton.*

batsman *see* **bat**[1].

battalion [bə'taljən] *nc* a large body of foot soldiers, made up of several companies, forming part of a brigade: *the pipe band of the 2nd Battalion, the Black Watch.*

batten ['batn] *nc* **1** a piece of wood used for keeping other pieces in place: *These strips are all fastened* *together with a long batten.* **2** in ships, a strip of wood used to fasten down the hatches.

batten down *vt sep* to fasten with battens: *The sailors battened down the hatches at the first sign of the storm.*

batter[1] ['batə] *vt* to beat with blow after blow: *He was battered to death with a large stick*; (*fig*) *The ship was battered by rain and wind.*

'battering-ram *nc* (*hist*) a large wooden beam with a metal head used in war for battering down walls.

batter[2] ['batə] *nu* eggs, milk, flour *etc* beaten together for use in cooking: *She prepared the batter for the pancakes.*

battery ['batəri] **1** *nc* a series of two or more electric cells arranged to produce, or store, a current: *This torch needs a new battery.* **2** *nc* an arrangement of cages in which laying hens *etc* are kept. **3** *nu* (*legal*) *see* **assault and battery** *under* **assault**. **4** *nc* a group of large guns (and the people manning them). **5** *nc* (*fig*) a long or large (often confusing) series: *He fired a battery of questions at me*; *This plane has a whole battery of different instruments.*

battle ['batl] *nc* a fight between opposing armies or individuals: *That was the last battle of the war*; (*fig*) *the battle for promotion*; (*fig*) *a battle for first place in the tennis tournament.* – *vi* (*formal*) to fight: *They battled fiercely until dawn*; (*fig*) *She had battled against ill-health for many years*; (*fig*) *They battled for first place.*

'battleax(e) *nc* **1** (*hist*) an axe used in battle. **2** (*inf derog*) an unpleasant, domineering woman: *She's a real old battleaxe!*

'battle-cry *nc* **1** a shout in battle: *The troops rallied at the sound of their battle-cry.* **2** a slogan: *'Down with war' is the battle-cry of the pacifists.*

'battlefield *nc* the place where a battle is, or was, fought: *After the battle, the bodies of dead soldiers covered the battlefield.*

'battleship *nc* a heavily armed and armoured warship.

do battle (*often fig*) to fight: *I'm going home to do battle with my parents about my career.*

battlement ['batlmənt] *nc* (*often in pl*) in castles *etc* a wall or parapet with openings for firing from.

batty *see* **bat**[2].

bauble ['bo:bl] *nc* (*often derog*) a small, *usu* almost worthless, ornament or piece of jewellery: *Christmas tree baubles*; *Only one of these rings is made of diamonds – the rest are just baubles.*

baulk *see* **balk**.

bawdy ['bo:di] *adj* vulgar and coarse: *He told some bawdy jokes*; *The songs he sang at the party were rather bawdy.*

bawl [bo:l] *vti* (*derog*) to shout or cry loudly: *He bawled something rude at me from the gate*; (*inf*) *That baby's been bawling all night.* – *nc* (*derog*) a loud cry or shout: *A bawl from the door announced his friend's arrival.*

bay[1] [bei] *nc* (*often found with cap in place-names*) a wide inward bend of a coastline: *The yacht anchored in the bay*; *Botany Bay.*

bay[2] [bei] *nc* (*usu in cmpds*) a separate compartment, area or room *etc* (*usu* one of several) set aside for a special purpose: *This area is a parking-bay for doctors' cars*; *the loading-bay in the warehouse*; *The child is in the sick-bay* (= a room in a school *etc* for ill children *etc*).

bay window *nc* a window jutting out from a room beyond the line of the wall.

bay[3] [bei] *adj* (*attrib*) (of horses) reddish-brown in colour. – *nc* a bay horse.

bay[4] [bei] *nc* (*also* **'bay tree**) another name for the laurel tree, whose leaves (**'bay leaves**) are used in seasoning meat *etc* and (traditionally) in making victory wreaths.

bay[5] [bei] *nu* (*also* **'baying**) the deep cry of hunting-dogs. – *vi* (*esp* of large dogs) to bark: *The hounds bayed at the fox.*

hold/keep (something or someone) at bay to fight off or keep (*eg* hunger or an enemy) from overcoming (*usu* oneself): *I'm just managing to hold disaster at bay*; *The boxer managed to keep his opponent at bay.*

bayonet ['beiənit] *nc* a knife-like instrument of steel fixed to the end of a rifle barrel. – *v* – *pt, ptp* **'bayoneted** – *vt* (*formal*) to stab with a bayonet.

bazaar [bə'za:] *nc* **1** an Eastern market place. **2** a sale of goods of various kinds, *esp* home-made or second-hand: *Are you coming to the church bazaar?*

bazooka [bə'zu:kə] *nc* a weapon consisting of a long tube that launches a small rocket with an explosive head.

be [bi:] – *prt* **am** [am], **are** [a:], **is** [iz]: *pt* **was** [woz], **were** [wə:]: *prp* **'being**: *ptp* **been** [bi:n, (*Amer*) bin]: *subjunctive* **were** [wə:]: *short forms* **I'm** [aim] (**I am**), **you're** [juə] (**you are**), **he's** [hi:z] (**he is**), **she's** [ʃi:z] (**she is**), **it's** [its] (**it is**), **we're** [wiə] (**we are**), **they're** [ðeə] (**they are**): *neg short forms* **isn't** ['iznt] (**is not**), **aren't** [a:nt] (**are not**), **ain't** [eint] (*inf or facet*) (**am/is/are not**), **wasn't** ['woznt] (**was not**), **weren't** [wə:nt] (**were not**) – *aux* (only used with **is, was** *etc* and **-ing** when forming a passive) **1** used with a present participle to form the progressive or continuous tenses: *I'm reading*; *I am being followed*; *What were you saying?* **2** used with a present participle to form a type of future tense: *I'm going to London next week.* **3** used with a past participle to form the passive voice: *He was shot*; *Fish are often found in this river.* **4** used with an infinitive to express several ideas, *eg* necessity: *When am I to leave?*; purpose: *The letter is to tell us he's coming*; a possible future happening: *If he were to lose, I'd win*; possibility or impossibility: *It's nowhere to be seen*; (*formal*) fate; unpredictable happenings: *After his accident, he was never to walk again.* – *vi* (only used with **is, was** *etc* and **-ing** when referring to temporary states of behaviour) used in giving or asking for information about the existence or state of something or someone: *I am Mr Smith*; *Is he alive?*; *She wants to be an actress*; *They're in the garden*; *The money will be ours*; *There was a reason for my anger*; *They are being silly.*

'being 1 *nu* existence; life: *when did the Roman Empire come into being?* **2** *nc* any living person or thing: *beings from outer space.*

as it were *see* **as**.

the ˌbe-all and 'end-all the final aim apart from which nothing is of any real importance: *This job isn't the be-all and end-all of existence.*

if it hadn't been/wasn't for, hadn't it been for *see* **for**.

-to-'be (*in cmpds*) future: *the bride-to-be*; *my husband-to-be.*

beach [bi:tʃ] *nc* the sandy or stony shore of a sea or lake: *Children love playing on the beach.* – *vt* to drive or pull (a boat *etc*) up on to a beach: *We'll beach the boat here and continue on foot.*

'beach ball *nc* a large light ball used in games on the beach.
'beachcomber *nc* a person who searches beaches for things of value, interest *etc.*
'beachwear *nu* clothes, *eg* a swimming costume, swimming-trunks *etc*, for wearing on the beach.
beacon ['bi:kən] *nc* **1** a fire on a high place, *orig* used as a sign of danger: *Beacons were lit on the hillsides in time of war.* **2** a type of light, fire *etc* that warns of danger, *eg* the light in a lighthouse. **3** a radio station or transmitter that sends out signals to guide shipping or aircraft.
bead [bi:d] *nc* a little ball of glass *etc* strung with others in a necklace, rosary *etc*: *She's wearing two strings of wooden beads*; (*fig*) *There were beads of sweat on his forehead.* **'beaded** *adj.*
'beady *adj* (of eyes) small and bright: *the beady eyes of the blackbird*; *The man's eyes were small and beady.*
beagle ['bi:gl] *nc* a type of small hunting-dog.
beak [bi:k] *nc* the hard, horny (*usu* pointed) part of a bird's mouth with which it gathers food: *The heron's long, sharp beak is used for catching fish*; *The thrush had a worm in its beak.*
beaker ['bi:kə] *nc* **1** a large drinking-glass or cup: *a beaker of hot milk.* **2** a deep glass container used in chemistry: *That beaker contains acid.*
beam [bi:m] *nc* **1** a long straight piece of wood, often used in ceilings *etc* as a support. **2** a ray of light *etc*: *a beam of sunlight*; *a moonbeam*; (*fig*) *A beam* (= a smile) *of pleasure lit up her face.* **3** the greatest width of a ship or boat. **4** the part of a set of scales from which the weighing-pans hang. – **1** *vi* to smile or grin broadly: *She beamed with delight.* **2** *vti* (*tech*) to send out (rays of light, radio waves *etc*): *The sun was beaming brightly*; *This transmitter beams radio waves all over Britain.*
off the beam (*inf*) off course or target; inaccurate: *Our original estimate was a long way off the beam.*
bean [bi:n] *nc* **1** any one of several kinds of pod-bearing plant or its seed: *runner beans*; *French beans.* **2** the bean-like seed of other plants: *coffee beans.*
full of beans (*inf*) full of energy; very cheerful: *She has been ill but she is full of beans now.*
not to have a bean (*inf*) to have no money: *Could you lend me fifty pence? I haven't (got) a bean with me.*
bear[1] [beə] – *pt* **bore** [bo:] *ptp* **borne** [bo:n] (*in passive of def 3,* **born** [bo:n]) – **1** *vt* (*usu in neg with* **cannot, could not** *etc*) to put up with or endure: *He was unable to bear the pain any longer*; *I couldn't bear it if he left*; *I can't bear this noise any longer.* **2** *vt* to be strong enough for; to be able to support: *Will the table bear my weight?*; (*fig*) *It doesn't bear thinking about* (= It's too unpleasant to think about). **3** *vt* to produce (children): *She has borne (him) several children*; *She was born on July 7.* **4** *vt* (*formal*) to carry: *He was borne shoulder-high after his victory.* **5** *vt* (*formal*) to have or show: *He was once attacked by a dog, and he bears the scars to this day*; *The statue bears an inscription*; *The cheque bore his signature.* **6** *vi* to turn or fork: *The road bears left here*; *You must bear right at the next junction.* **7** *v refl* (*formal*) to behave (*usu* well): *He bore himself well at the trial.* **8** *vt* (*formal*) to have (a feeling) towards (someone): *No-one knew of the love she bore him*; *I bear you no ill-will.*
'bearable *adj* (*usu pred*) able to be endured: *Sometimes this job is quite bearable.*
'bearer *nc* (*formal*) a person or thing that bears: *I'm the bearer of bad news*; *The bearers will carry your luggage on the expedition*; *Six bearers carried him to the grave.*
'bearing 1 *nu* (*formal*) manner, way of standing *etc*: *He has a very military bearing.* **2** *nc* (*usu in pl*: sometimes short for **ˌball-'bearings**) a part of a machine that has another part moving in or on it. **3** *nc* the direction of one thing or person with respect to another: *The ship's bearing is 55°* (= fifty-five degrees) *west of the Scilly Isles.*
'bearings *n pl* location, place on a map *etc*; *The island's bearings are 10° North, 24° West.*
bear down on/(*formal*) **upon** *vt fus* to approach quickly and often threateningly: *The angry teacher bore down on the child.* **2** to exert pressure on: *The weight is bearing down on my chest.*
bear fruit 1 to produce fruit: *These pear trees bore no fruit this year.* **2** (*formal fig*) to produce results: *I hope your hard work will bear fruit.*
bear in mind *see* **mind**.
bear no resemblance (to) to have no similarity (to); to look unlike: *She bears no resemblance to her sister*; *She and her sister bear no resemblance.*
bear out *vt sep* (*formal*) to support or confirm: *This bears out what you said*; *If you put in a complaint about him, I will bear you out.*
bear up *vi* to keep up courage, strength *etc* (under strain): *She's bearing up well after her shock.*
ˌbear 'with *vt fus* (*formal*) to be patient with (someone): *Bear with me for a minute, and you'll see what I mean.*
bear witness *see* **witness**.
be borne in (up)on someone (*formal*) to be impressed on a person's mind: *It was gradually borne in (up)on me that I had no chance of succeeding.*
find/get one's bearings (*often fig*) to find one's position with reference to *eg* a known landmark: *If we can find this hill, I'll be able to get my bearings*; *He'll soon find his bearings in his new job.*
have a bearing on (*formal*) to have a connection with or have importance regarding: *This has no bearing on the question we're discussing.*
lose one's bearings (*often fig*) to become uncertain of one's position: *He's confused me so much that I've lost my bearings completely.*
See also **unbearable**.
bear[2] [beə] *nc* a large heavy animal with thick fur and hooked claws.
'bearskin 1 *ncu, adj* (of) the skin of a bear: *There's a bearskin on his wall*; *a hat made from bearskin*; *a bearskin rug.* **2** *nc* a tall fur cap worn as part of some military uniforms.
beard [biəd] **1** *ncu* the hair that grows on the chin (*usu* of a man, but also on *eg* goats): *He has a beard*; *He always looks as if he has three days' growth of beard.* **2** *nc* a group of hair-like tufts on an ear of corn: *the beard on barley.*
'bearded *adj*: *I like bearded men*; *He's bearded now.*
beard (someone) in his den (*formal fig*) to face (someone) openly or boldly; to confront (someone): *I bearded the boss in his den because I was determined to get a decision.*
bearer, bearing *see* **bear**[1].
bearskin *see* **bear**[2].
beast [bi:st] *nc* **1** a four-footed (*esp* large) animal: *the beasts of the jungle*; *a beast of burden* (= an

animal used for carrying or pulling). **2** (*inf*) a cruel, brutal person: *Who is the beast that's been attacking children?* **3** (*Brit inf*) an unpleasant person: *Arthur is a beast for refusing to come!*

'beastly *adj* **1** like a beast in actions or behaviour: *He's a beastly creature.* **2** (*Brit inf*) disagreeable: *What a beastly thing to do!*; *The weather is really beastly today.* **'beastliness** *nu*.

See also **bestial**.

beat [bi:t] – *pt* **beat**: *ptp* **'beaten** – **1** *vti* to strike or hit repeatedly: *Beat the carpet*; *Beat the drum*; *Look at the waves beating the shore*; *The child was beaten* (= punished by being spanked or struck with a stick *etc*) *for misbehaviour.* **2** *vt* to win against; to defeat: *She beat me in a contest*; (*inf*) *The problem has got him beaten* (= he is unable to solve it); (*inf*) *It beats* (= puzzles) *me how you can walk so fast.* **3** *vt* to mix thoroughly with a whisk, fork *etc*: *Beat an egg*; *Beat the cake mixture.* **4** *vti* to (cause to) move in a regular rhythm: *Large birds usually beat their wings more slowly than small birds do*; *My heart is beating faster than usual.* **5** *vti* to strike (bushes, heather *etc*) to force birds or animals into the open for shooting *etc*: *They were beating the bushes for pheasants.* **6** *vt* to mark or indicate (musical time) with a baton *etc*: *A conductor beats time for an orchestra.* – *See also* **beat** *in phrases below.* – *nc* **1** a regular stroke, or its sound, *eg* of a clock, a piece of music *etc*: *I like the beat of that song.* **2** a regular or usual course or circuit: *a policeman's beat*; *a postman's beat.*

'beaten *adj* **1** overcome; defeated: *the beaten army*; *the beaten football team*; *He looked tired and beaten.* **2** (*attrib*) mixed thoroughly: (*a*) *beaten egg.* **3** (*attrib*) shaped by hammering: *beaten copper.*

'beater *nc* a person or thing that beats or is used for beating: *Do you use an electric beater when you're cooking?*; *a grouse beater.*

'beating *ncu* (an) act of beating: *The beating of the rain on the window woke me up early*; *The schoolboy was given a beating for laziness.*

beat about the bush to approach a subject in an indirect way, without coming to the point or making any decision: *He always beats about the bush when I ask him a question.*

beat down 1 *vi* (of the sun) to give out great heat: *The sun's rays beat down on us in the desert.* **2** *vt sep* to reduce (the price of something) by bargaining: *We managed to beat the price down by £5.* **3** *vt sep* to force (a person) to lower a price: *We tried to beat him down but we had to pay the full price in the end.*

'beat it (*Brit sl*: *often interj*) to go away: *Beat it, or I'll hit you!*; *She told her little brother to beat it.*

beat off *vt sep* to succeed in overcoming or preventing: *The old man beat off the youths who attacked him*; *He beat the attack off easily.*

beat a (hasty) retreat to go away in a hurry: *The children beat a hasty retreat when they saw the headmaster.*

beat up *vt sep* to punch, kick or hit (a person) severely and repeatedly: *They beat my brother up and left him for dead*; *He beat up an old lady.*

off the beaten track away from main roads, centres of population *etc*: *There's no bus service to their house – it's off the beaten track.*

take a beating (*inf*) to be badly defeated: *Our football team took a terrible beating last Saturday.*

beatific [bi:ə'tifik] *adj* (*liter*) expressing great happiness: *a beatific smile*; *The child's smile was beatific.*

beating *see* **beat**.

beau [bou] – *pl* **beaux** [-z] – *nc* **1** (*old or facet*) a boyfriend or (male) lover: *Who is her latest beau?* **2** (*old*) a very finely- or too-carefully-dressed man. *See also* **belle**.

beauty ['bju:ti] **1** *nu* a quality very pleasing to the eye, ear *etc*: *This picture has great beauty*; *Her beauty is undeniable.* **2** *nc* a woman or girl having such a quality: *She was a great beauty in her youth.* **3** *nc* (*inf*) something (or someone) very good or remarkable: *His new car is a beauty!*; (*ironic*) *The black eye he got was a real beauty!*

'beauteous [-tiəs] *adj* (*attrib*: *liter*): *a beauteous lady.*

'beautiful *adj*: *a beautiful woman*; *Those roses are beautiful*; *beautiful piano music.*

'beautifully *adv*: *beautifully dressed*; *She sings beautifully.*

'beautify [-fai] *vt* (*formal*: *sometimes facet*) to make beautiful, often by decorating: *She beautified herself before going to the dance.*

'beauty queen *nc* a girl or woman who is voted the most beautiful in a contest: *She was a beauty queen several times before being chosen as Miss World.*

'beauty spot *nc* **1** a place of great natural beauty: *We visited many of Wales's beauty spots.* **2** (*old*) a mark (often artificial) on the face, intended to emphasize beauty.

beaver ['bi:və] **1** *nc* an animal with strong front teeth, living on land and in water, noted for its skill in damming streams. **2** *nu, adj* (of) its fur: *a hat made of beaver*; *a beaver coat.*

beaver away (at) *vi* (*inf*) to keep busily working (at some task): *He beavers away all day* (*at the job*) *but he never seems to get anything done.*

becalmed [bi'ka:md] *adj* (of a sailing ship *etc*) unable to move because of lack of wind: *The yacht was becalmed when the wind dropped*; *a becalmed fleet.*

became *see* **become**.

because [bi'koz] *conj* for the reason that: *She won because she's best*; *I can't go because I am ill*; *Because I was ill, I lost my job*; *'Why aren't you going?' 'Because I don't want to.'*

be'cause of on account of; by reason of: *I can't walk because of my broken leg*; *He stopped work because of ill-health.*

beck [bek]: **at someone's beck and call** always ready and waiting to carry out someone's order or wishes: *He has many servants at his beck and call*; *She always has plenty of men at her beck and call.*

beckon ['bekən] *vti* to summon or call (someone) towards oneself by making a sign (to) *usu* with the fingers: *Beckon your friend over so that I can speak to him*; *She beckoned to him to join her*; (*fig*) *I'd like to sit and read, but the housework beckons!*

become [bi'kʌm] – *pt* **became** [bi'keim]: *ptp* **be'come** – **1** *vi* to come to be; to grow to be: *His job became increasingly difficult*; *Her coat has become badly torn*; *She has become even more beautiful.* **2** *vi* (of people) to grow up to be; to qualify or take a job as: *She became a nun*; *He became a doctor.* **3** *vi* (*with* **of**) to happen to: *What became of her son?*; *What's become of my jacket?* **4** *vt* (*formal or old*) to suit or look attractive on (someone): *That dress really becomes her.*

be'coming *adj* **1** (*formal*) attractive: *Your new hat is very becoming*; *a very becoming dress.* **2** (*pred*: *formal or old*) suitable (to): *He made a speech becoming* (*to*) *the occasion.*

be'comingly *adv* (*formal*) attractively: *The girl is becomingly modest.*
See also **unbecoming**.

bed [bed] *nc* **1** a piece of furniture, or a place, to sleep on: *The child goes to bed at six o'clock; The doctor sat on the bed to examine the child; He fell asleep as soon as he got into bed; The child sleeps in a small bed; The dog sleeps on a bed of straw.* **2** the channel (of a river) or floor (of a sea) *etc.* **3** (*sometimes in cmpds*) a plot in a garden: *a bed of flowers; a flower-bed.* **4** a place in which anything rests; a foundation: *standing on a bed of stone.* **5** a layer: *a bed of chalk below the surface.*
-bedded (*in cmpds*) having (a certain number or type of) bed(s): *a double-bedded room; a twin-bedded room.*
'bedding *nu* **1** mattress, bedclothes *etc*: *We have enough beds for the guests but not enough bedding.* **2** straw *etc* for cattle *etc* to sleep on. **3** the process of planting young plants outside in flower-beds *etc*: *The bedding of the strawberry plants took two hours.*
'bedclothes [-klouðz, (*Amer*) -klouz] *n pl* sheets, blankets *etc*: *He pulled the bedclothes up over his head.*
'bedcover *nc* a top cover for a bed: *We bought matching bedcovers for the two beds.*
'bedpan *nc* a vessel for urine and faeces, used when a person cannot get out of bed because of illness *etc.*
'bedridden *adj* in bed permanently or for a long period because of age or sickness: *She has been bedridden since the car accident; a bedridden invalid.*
'bedrock *nu* **1** (*tech*) the solid rock forming the lowest layer underneath soil or rock fragments. **2** (*fig*) the lowest state or level: *His financial position was bad enough but it's reached bedrock now.*
'bedroom *nc* a room for sleeping in: *We have three bedrooms in our house.*
'bedside *nc* the place or position next to a person's bed: *Her son was at her bedside when she died;* (*attrib*) *a bedside table;* (*attrib*) *That doctor has a good bedside manner.*
'bedsit (*inf*)/ˌ**bed-'sitter**/ˌ**bed-'sitting-room** *ncs* a single room (*usu* rented) for both eating and sleeping in: *Students often live in bedsitters.*
'bedspread *nc* a top cover for a bed: *Please remove the bedspread before you get into bed.*
'bedstead [-sted] *nc* the frame of a bed: *Place the mattress on the bedstead.*
'bedtime *nu* the time at which one normally goes to bed: *Seven o'clock is the children's bedtime;* (*attrib*) *a bedtime story.*
bed and board lodging and food: *Bed and board is £5 per day.*
bed and breakfast lodging for the night, and breakfast only (not lunch or dinner).
bed of roses (*inf*) an easy or comfortable place, job *etc*: *Life is not a bed of roses.*
bed down *vi, vt sep* (*inf*) to (cause to) settle in bed in preparation for sleep: *They bedded down for the night; We'll bed the children down for the night; We bedded them down early.*
bed out *vt sep* to transfer (young plants) into outdoor flower-beds: *Have you bedded out those flowers yet?; I bedded them out yesterday.*
go to bed 1 to get into bed: *I'm sleepy – I think I'll go to bed now; What time do you usually go to bed?* **2** (*often with* **with**; *euph*) to have sexual intercourse with; to have a love affair with: *He is going to bed with his secretary.*
make a bed *see* **make**.

bedevilled [bi'devld] *adj* (*formal*: *pred*) cursed (with bad luck *etc*): *Our plans have been bedevilled by a series of disasters.*

bedlam ['bedləm] *ncu* (a place of) noise, confusion or uproar: *This place is bedlam when everyone speaks at once.*

bedraggled [bi'dragld] *adj* (*formal*) (of people *etc*) very wet and untidy: *We arrived home bedraggled after a walk in the rain; a bedraggled dog.*

bee [bi:] *nc* **1** any of several types of four-winged insect related to wasps and ants, *esp* the insect that makes honey. **2** (*esp Amer*) a meeting for combined work and enjoyment: *a knitting bee.*
'beehive *nc* a box in which bees are kept, and where they store their honey. – *adj* (*attrib*) like a dome-shaped beehive: *a beehive hairstyle.*
'beeswax ['bi:zwaks] *nu* the yellowish solid substance produced by bees for making their cells, and used in polishing wood.
a bee in one's bonnet (*inf*) an idea which has become fixed in one's mind: *She has a bee in her bonnet about going to America.*
ˌ**make a 'bee-line for** (*inf*) to take the most direct way to; to go immediately to: *Fred always makes a bee-line for the prettiest girl at a party.*
See also **bumble-bee**.

beech [bi:tʃ] **1** *nc* (*also* **'beech tree**) a kind of forest tree with smooth silvery bark and small nuts: *That tree is a beech;* (*attrib*) *a beech forest.* **2** *nu, adj* (of) its wood: *a door made of beech; beech panelling.*

beef [bi:f] *nu* **1** the flesh of a bull, cow or ox, used as food: *We prefer beef to pork.* **2** (*inf*) fat (*usu* too much): *He has a lot of beef on him.*
'beefy *adj* **1** (*usu attrib*) of or like beef: *This soup has a beefy taste.* **2** (*inf*) having a lot of fat or muscle: *a huge, beefy man; She's quite beefy.*
'beefeater *nc* a man of the king's or queen's bodyguard, who is also a guard of the Tower of London.
beef tea *nu* the juice of chopped beef, sometimes taken by sick people: *The invalid was given beef tea.*

beehive *see* **bee**.

been *see* **be**.

beer [biə] **1** *ncu* a type of alcoholic drink made from malted barley flavoured with hops: *She doesn't like beer; We produce four different beers in this brewery.* **2** *nc* a glass of beer: *He ordered two beers and a whisky.*
'beery *adj* (*inf*) **1** of or like beer: *a beery smell; This room smells beery.* **2** (of a person) showing that one has been drinking beer: *a huge beery nose.*
small beer (*formal*) something unimportant: *This is small beer compared with the work he usually does.*

beeswax *see* **bee**.

beet [bi:t] *ncu* a plant with a round or carrot-shaped root, one variety (**red beet**, *usu* **'beetroot**) used as food (*esp* in salads), another (**'sugar beet**) as a source of sugar.

beetle ['bi:tl] *nc* an insect with four wings, the front pair being hard and horny and forming a cover for the back pair: *A black beetle scurried across the bare floorboards.*

beetling ['bi:tliŋ] *adj* (*formal*) jutting or sticking out; overhanging: *beetling cliffs; His eyebrows were black and beetling.*

beetroot *see* **beet**.

befall [bi'fo:l] – *pt* **befell** [bi'fel] : *ptp* **be'fallen** –

(*formal*) **1** *vt* to happen to (a person or thing): *A disaster has befallen her.* **2** *vi* (*esp* in the Bible) to happen: *And so, it befell that they went to a far country.*

befit [bi'fit] – *pt, ptp* **be'fitted** – *vt* (*formal*) to be suitable to; to be fitting or right for: *His speech befitted the occasion.* **be'fitting** *adj.*

before [bi'fo:] *prep* **1** earlier than: *She was born before the war; They left before breakfast; I saw him two days before the wedding; She visited her mother before leaving; He'll come before very long.* **2** (*formal*) in the presence of: *The criminal appeared before the judge; The child had to appear before the headmaster.* **3** in front of: *She was before me in the queue; He is before me in the list of people to be promoted; 9 comes before 10.* **4** (*formal*) rather than; in preference to: *Honour before wealth.* – *adv* earlier: *I've seen you before somewhere.* – *conj* **1** earlier than the time when: *I'll phone before I come; She died before she reached the hospital; Before I go, I must phone my parents.* **2** rather than; in preference to: *I would die before I would betray my country.*

be'forehand [-hand] *adv* before the time when something else is done: *If you're coming, let me know beforehand.*

befriend [bi'frend] *vt* (*formal*) to take (someone) as a friend: *The old man befriended her when she was lonely.*

beg [beg] – *pt, ptp* **begged** – *vti* **1** to ask for (money, food *etc, usu* in the street): *The old man was so poor that he had to beg in the street; The tramp begged me for money; He begged five pounds from me.* **2** (*sometimes with* **of**: *formal*) to ask (someone) desperately or earnestly: *I beg you not to do it; Don't do it – I beg of you!*

'beggar *nc* **1** a person who lives by begging: *The beggar asked for money for food.* **2** (*inf*: *often affectionately*) a rascal: *Cheeky beggar!* – *vt* (*formal*) to make very poor: *He was beggared by the collapse of his firm.*

'beggarly *adj* (*formal*: *esp attrib*) very poor; worthless: *a beggarly sum of money.*

beggar description (*formal*) to be so great in some way that the speaker's words cannot describe (it): *This essay's so bad that it beggars description; Her beauty beggared description.*

be ˌgoing (a-)'begging (*inf*) to be unclaimed, unsold or unwanted: *I'll have the last cake if it's going begging.*

beg the question (*formal*) to take for granted the very point that needs to be proved: *Your statement begs the question of whether we get any money.*

beg to differ (*formal*) to disagree: *You may think that he should get the job but I beg to differ.*

began *see* **begin**.

beget [bi'get] – *pt* **begot** [bi'got], (*arch*) **begat** [bi'gat]: *ptp* **begotten** [bi'gotn] – *vt* **1** (*arch*) to be the father of: *Abraham begat Isaac.* **2** (*formal fig*) to cause: *They begot a great deal of ill-will.*

beggar, beggarly *etc see* **beg**.

begin [bi'gin] – *prp* **be'ginning**: *pt* **began** [bi'gan]: *ptp* **begun** [bi'gʌn] – *vti* to come, or bring, into being; to start; to commence: *The meeting begins at 8 o'clock; I began this book yesterday; He began to talk; She began walking; She is beginning to hate him; Begin at question 1 and answer all the questions.* **be'ginning** *ncu.*

be'ginner *nc* someone who is just learning how to do something: *'Does he paint well?' 'He's not bad for a beginner.'*

to be'gin with 1 at first: *I didn't like him to begin with, but now he's one of my best friends.* **2** firstly: *There are many reasons why I don't like her – to begin with, she doesn't tell the truth.*

begot, begotten *see* **beget**.

begrudge [bi'grʌdʒ] *vt* (*formal*) to envy (someone something) or be unwilling that (someone should have something): *I begrudge him his success; I begrudge him that cake.*

be'grudging *adj* (*formal*: *attrib*) unwilling: *She gave him a begrudging smile.* **be'grudgingly** *adv.* *See also* **grudge**.

beguile [bi'gail] *vt* (*formal*) **1** to cheat or to lead by deception (into): *He was beguiled into buying the fake antique.* **2** to occupy (time) pleasantly: *He beguiled (away) the time with gardening.* **3** to charm or amuse (a person): *She beguiled the children with stories.*

be'guiling *adj* charming: *a beguiling smile.* **be'guilingly** *adv.*

begun *see* **begin**.

behalf [bi'ha:f]: **on be'half of (someone) 1** (*formal*) speaking (or writing) for other people, as well as for oneself: *I am speaking on behalf of all our members.* **2** for, or in the interests of: *I'm collecting on behalf of the blind; He is acting on his own behalf; She replied on John's behalf.*

behave [bi'heiv] **1** *vi, v refl* to act in a suitable way; to be orderly, obedient *etc*: *If you come, you must behave (yourself); The child always behaves (himself) at his grandmother's.* **2** *vi* to act or react (well, badly *etc*): *He behaved badly at bedtime; He always behaves like a gentleman; Some people do not behave normally when they are worried.* **3** *vi* (*formal*) (of people or things) to act in response to something done or happening: *Some metals behave differently when heated.*

be'haviour, (*Amer*) **be'havior** [-jə] *nu* **1** way of behaving: *A school is judged by the behaviour of its pupils.* **2** (of people or things) actions or reactions (to what is done or happens): *the behaviour of rats when they are attacked; He's studying the behaviour of metals in acids.*

ˌwell-, ˌbadly- *etc* **be'haved** *adj* good (bad *etc*) in manners or conduct: *Badly-behaved children annoy everyone; That little girl is always very well-behaved.*

be on one's best behaviour to be trying to behave oneself well: *He was on his best behaviour because he wanted a present on his birthday.*

See also **misbehave**.

behead [bi'hed] *vt* to cut off the head of (*usu* a person): *King Henry VIII of England had several of his wives beheaded.* **be'heading** *ncu.*

beheld *see* **behold**.

behest [bi'hest] *nc* (*arch or formal*) a command: *He was shot at the King's behest.*

behind [bi'haind] *prep* **1** at or towards the back of: *Stand behind the door!; They were standing behind him.* **2** remaining after: *Tourists always leave so much litter behind them; I wish you wouldn't leave such a mess behind you!* **3** (*inf*) in support; encouraging: *We're right behind him on this point.* **4** less good than: *He's well behind the others in his knowledge of the subject.* – *adv* **1** at the back; in the rear: *coming up behind; following behind.* **2** (*also* **be'hindhand** [-hand]) not up to date; late: *He's behind with his work.* **3** remaining: *He left the book behind when he went; We stayed behind after the others to say goodbye to the headmaster; He has gone abroad but he has left his wife and child behind.* – *nc* (*euph*) the buttocks: *The child's mother smacked him on his behind.*

behind someone's back (*inf*) without someone's knowledge or permission: *He sometimes bullies his sister behind his mother's back.*

behold [bi'hould] – *pt, ptp* **beheld** [bi'held] – (not used with **is, was** *etc* and **-ing**) **1** *vt* (*liter*) to see; to observe: *What a sight to behold!* **2** *vti* (*liter or arch: usu in imperative*) to look: *Behold! A stranger has followed us.* **be'holder** *nc*.

beholden [bi'houldən]: **be'holden to** (*formal*) owing a debt or favour to; being grateful to: *Does his kindness to you make you beholden to him?*; *I won't be beholden to you!*

behove [bi'houv]: **it behoves (one)** (*formal*) it is right or necessary for (one to do something): *I have already accepted the invitation, so it behoves me to go.*

beige [beiʒ] **1** *nu, adj* (of) a pale pinkish-yellow colour: *She wore a beige hat.* **2** *nu* something (*eg* material, paint *etc*) beige in colour: *She was dressed in beige.*

being *see* **be**.

belabour, (*Amer*) **belabor** [bi'leibə] *vt* (*formal*) **1** to beat thoroughly: *He belaboured me with a big stick.* **2** to discuss at too great length: *They belaboured the point for hours but came to no decision.*

belated [bi'leitid] *adj* (*formal*) happening, coming *etc*, late or too late: *a belated birthday card*; *belated thanks*; *My thanks are belated but sincere.*

be'latedly *adv*: *We thanked him belatedly for his kindness.*

belch [beltʃ] **1** *vi* to give out air noisily from the stomach through the mouth: *He belched after eating too much.* **2** *vt* (*often with* **out**) (of a chimney, volcano *etc*) to throw (out) violently: *factory chimneys belching (out) smoke.* – *nc* an act of belching: *He gave a loud belch.*

beleaguered [bi'li:gəd] *adj* (*formal*) under attack: *a beleaguered castle*; *The city was beleaguered.*

belfry ['belfri] *nc* the part of a (church) tower in which bells are hung.

Belgian, Belgium *see* Appendix 2.

belie [bi'lai] – *prp* **be'lying**: *ptp* **be'lied** – *vt* (*formal*) to give a false idea or impression of (something): *His innocent face belies his cunning.*

belief *see* **believe**.

believe [bi'li:v] *vt* (not used with **is, was** *etc* and **-ing**) **1** to regard (something) as true: *I believe his story*; *She believed what he told her*; *He believed that she was sorry.* **2** to trust (a person), accepting what he says as true: *I believe you.* **3** to have an idea (that); to think (that): *I believe he's coming tomorrow.* – *See also* **believe in** *below*.

be'lief [-f] **1** *nu* faith or trust: *I do not share your belief in his ability*; *To the best of my belief* (= in my sincere opinion) *I have never seen him before.* **2** *nc* (*often in pl*) something believed: *My belief is that he's not dead*; *Christian beliefs.*

be'lievable *adj*.

be'liever *nc* **1** a person who has (*esp* religious) beliefs: *He is a true believer.* **2** a person who recognizes the value or advantage of something: *He is a great believer in having breakfast in bed on Sunday.*

be'lieve in *vt fus* **1** to accept the existence of (something) as a fact: *Do you believe in ghosts?* **2** to recognize the value or advantage of (something): *Some doctors believe in a low-fat diet*; *He believes in capital punishment.* **3** to have faith in the ability *etc* of (someone): *He will achieve his ambition – he really believes in himself.*

make believe *see* **make**.

See also **disbelief, unbelievable, unbeliever**.

belittle [bi'litl] *vt* (*formal*) to make to seem small or unimportant (*usu* by harsh criticism): *She tried to belittle his achievements by saying that she could do better.*

bell [bel] *nc* **1** a hollow object, *usu* of metal, which gives a ringing sound when struck by the clapper inside: *the church bells.* **2** any other mechanism for giving a ringing sound: *Our doorbell is broken.* **3** the sound made by a bell: *Did you hear the bell?*

'bell-bottom(ed) *adj* (of trousers) widely flared at the bottom of the leg.

'bell-bottoms *n pl* trousers with bell-bottomed legs.

ring a bell *see* **ring**[2].

belladonna [belə'donə] **1** *ncu* (*old*) the plant deadly nightshade, all parts of which are poisonous. **2** *nu* the drug prepared from it.

belle [bel] *nc* (*old*) the most beautiful lady at a dance *etc*: *the belle of the ball*; *the belle of New York.*

See also **beau**.

bellicose ['belikous] *adj* (*liter*) warlike or quarrelsome: *a bellicose nation*; *His facial expression was unpleasantly bellicose.*

belligerent [bi'lidʒərənt] *adj* **1** unfriendly; hostile: *She gave me a belligerent stare*; *We tried to be friendly towards her but she is very belligerent and quarrelsome.* **2** (*formal*) waging war: *belligerent nations.* – *nc* (*formal*) a nation or person waging war: *We are the belligerents in this situation.*

bel'ligerence *nu*. **bel'ligerently** *adv*.

bellow ['belou] *vti* **1** (of a bull) to roar. **2** (of people) to roar like a bull: *The headmaster bellowed at the children.* – *nc* an act of roaring.

bellows ['belouz] *n pl* an instrument for making a current of air and directing it on to a fire, into organ pipes *etc*.

belly ['beli] *nc* **1** (*inf of people*) the part of the body between the breast and the thighs, containing the bowels: *the horse's belly*; *I've a pain in my belly.* **2** the bulging interior of anything similar in shape *etc*: *the belly of a ship.*

'belly-laugh *nc* a loud, deep laugh: *the belly-laughs of the rugby players in the bar.*

belly out *vi* (*formal*) to swell out: *The yacht's sails bellied out in the strong wind.*

have ˌhad a 'bellyful of (*sl*) to have had a quantity of (something) which is enough, or more than enough; to be tired of: *I've had a bellyful of your arguments!*

belong [bi'loŋ] *vi* (not used with **is, was** *etc* and **-ing**) **1** (*with* **to**) to be the property of: *This book belongs to me*; *The furniture belongs to my mother.* **2** (*with* **to**) to be a native, member *etc* of: *I belong to Glasgow*; *Britain belongs to the EEC.* **3** (*with* **with**) to go along or together with: *This page belongs with all the others*; *This shoe belongs with that shoe.* **4** (*sometimes with* **in**) to have a correct place: *These shoes belong in the cupboard*; *I feel that I belong here.*

be'longings *n pl* personal possessions: *She can't have gone away – all her belongings are still here.*

beloved [bi'lʌvid] *adj* (*old or formal*) much loved: *my beloved country*; *This house was beloved by my mother*; *He was beloved of everyone.* – *nc* (*old*) a person very dear to one: *My beloved left me for another.*

below [bəˈlou] *prep* lower in position, rank, standard *etc* than: *Her skirt reached below her knees*; *A captain ranks below a major*; *That work is below his usual standard.* – *adv* in a lower place: *He's waiting down below*; *We looked down from the mountain at the houses (down) below.*

belt [belt] *nc* **1** (*sometimes in cmpds*) a long (narrow) piece of leather, cloth *etc* used to keep clothing, weapons *etc* in place: *a trouser-belt*; *a gunbelt*; *She wore a leather belt round her waist.* **2** a similar object used to connect and set in motion the wheels of a piece of machinery: *The belt of my vacuum-cleaner is broken.* **3** a zone or region of country *etc*: *an industrial belt*; *You can't build houses there – it's a green belt* (= an area of grassland near a town or city); *He is very wealthy and lives in the stockbroker belt.* – *vt* **1** to fasten (*eg* trousers) with a belt: *He belted his trousers on rapidly.* **2** to strike (*usu* a person) with a belt: *The teacher belted the naughty pupils.* **3** (*sl*) to strike or beat (not necessarily with a belt): *I'll belt you if you do that again!*

'belted *adj* **1** (*formal*: *attrib*) (of an earl) wearing a ceremonial belt. **2** (*attrib*) (of an animal *etc*) marked with a band of different colour: *a belted Galloway* (= a breed of cow).

'belting *nc* (*sl*) a thrashing: *I got a belting from my Dad for being cheeky.*

bemoan [biˈmoun] *vt* (*formal*) to moan about or lament (something): *He bemoaned his fate in being born the younger son.*

bemused [biˈmjuːzd] *adj* (*formal*) bewildered or greatly puzzled: *The old lady was bemused by the traffic rushing past in the city*; *His face had a bemused look.*

bench [bentʃ] *nc* **1** a long (*usu* wooden) seat: *a park bench.* **2** a work-table for a carpenter, technician *etc*: *a workbench.* – *See also* **the bench** *below.*

back-bencher, front-bencher *see* **back, front**.

the bench the judge(s) or magistrates of a court of law: *You'll be appearing before the bench in January.*

bend [bend] – *pt, ptp usu* **bent** [bent] (but *on one's* **'bended knees**) – **1** *vti* to make, become, or be, angled or curved: *Please bend your arm*; *Can you bend your knee?*; *He bent his head in prayer*; *She bent down to pick up the coin*; *The road bends to the right along here*; *He was so strong that he could bend an iron bar*; (*fig*) *He bends the rules* (= he alters the rules) *to suit himself.* **2** *vt* (*old or formal*) to force (someone) to do what one wants: *He bent me to his will.* – *nc* a curve or angle in a road, piece of metal *etc*: *The car crash happened at the bend in the road.*

the bends agonizing pains, *esp* in the joints, affecting divers when they surface too quickly.

'bent on (*formal*) determined on: *The firm seems bent on destruction*; *He is bent on winning.*

beneath [biˈniːθ] *prep* **1** (*old or formal*) in a lower position than; under; below: *He buried the body beneath the floorboards*; *beneath her coat.* **2** not worthy of: *It is beneath my dignity to do that.* – *adv* (*old or formal*) below or underneath: *They stood helplessly on the cliff-top watching the boat breaking up on the rocks beneath.*

benediction [benəˈdikʃən] *ncu* (*relig*) (a) prayer giving blessing.

benefactor [ˈbenəfaktə] *nc* (*formal*) a person who gives friendly help, often in the form of money: *He is my friend and benefactor*; *The benefactor who gave money to the orphanage did not wish his name to be known.*

benefice [ˈbenəfis] *nc* (*formal*) a post as vicar, rector *etc* and the income (from land, buildings *etc*) which goes with it.

beneficial [benəˈfiʃəl] *adj* (*formal*) having good results or effects: *Fresh air is beneficial to your health*; *the beneficial effects of a holiday.*

ˌbeneˈficiary [-ʃəri, (*Amer*) -ʃieri] *nc* (*legal*) a person who receives a gift *etc* (*usu* in a will): *Under my aunt's will, my sister and I were the only beneficiaries.*

benefit [ˈbenəfit] **1** *ncu* something good to receive; an advantage: *He got a lot of benefit from their friendship*; *the benefit of experience*; *all the benefits of fresh air and exercise*; *There's no benefit to be had from changing jobs now.* **2** *nc* a performance at a theatre or game *etc* at which profits go to one player or to charity: *This game is a benefit for John Anderson.* **3** *ncu* (a) payment under a state insurance scheme *etc*: *child/sickness/unemployment benefit(s).* – *v* – *pt, ptp* **'benefited** – **1** *vi* (*usu with* **from** *or* **by**) to gain advantage: *He benefited greatly from the advice.* **2** *vt* (*formal*) to do good to: *The long rest benefited her.*

give (someone) the benefit of the doubt to assume that someone is innocent or is telling the truth because there is not enough evidence to be sure that he is not doing so: *I am not sure whether his story is true or not but I'll give him the benefit of the doubt.*

benevolence [biˈnevələns] *nu* (*formal*) kindness, generosity and desire to do good.

beˈnevolent *adj* (*formal*) **1** (of individual people) being kind and wishing (someone) well: *a benevolent father*; *His intentions were benevolent.* **2** (*attrib*) (of an organization *etc*) charitable and generous: *the Police Benevolent Fund.*

beˈnevolently *adv.*

Bengali *see* Appendix 2.

benign [biˈnain] *adj* **1** (*formal*) (of people, their actions *etc*) kind; well-wishing: *a benign old man*; *His smile was benign.* **2** (*formal fig*) pleasant; mild: *The weather was very benign.* **3** (*med*) not fatal: *a benign tumour*; *The tumour proved benign.*

beˈnignly *adv*: *smiling benignly.*

bent[1] *see* **bend**.

bent[2] [bent] *nc* (*formal*) a natural inclination or liking for: *He's of a studious bent*; *He has a bent for mathematics.*

benzene [ˈbenziːn] *nu* a liquid hydrocarbon obtained from coal tar.

'benzine [-ziːn] *nu* a motor fuel obtained from petroleum.

'benzol(e) [-zol] *nu* unrefined benzene, used as a motor fuel.

bequeath [biˈkwiːð] *vt* (*legal or formal*) to leave (personal belongings) by will: *She bequeathed £100 to charity.*

bequest [biˈkwest] *nc* **1** an act of bequeathing: *He made several bequests.* **2** anything bequeathed in someone's will: *I received a bequest in my uncle's will.*

bereaved [biˈriːvd] *adj* (*attrib*) very sad, having lost, through death, someone dear to one: *a bereaved mother.*

beˈreavement *ncu*: *She sent a letter of sympathy on his bereavement*; *Bereavements are common in very large families.*

the bereaved (*formal*) a person who is, or people who are, bereaved: *The minister tried to comfort the bereaved.*

bereft [biˈreft] *adj* (*pred with* **of**: *formal or arch*)

having had someone or something taken away: *bereft of life; bereft of speech; bereft of hope.*
See also **bereaved**.

beret ['berei, (*Amer*) bə'rei] *nc* a round cap made of soft material, often worn as part of a uniform: *In some parts of France many of the men wear berets.*

berry ['beri] *nc* (*often in cmpds*) a kind of small (often juicy) fruit: *holly berry; strawberry; Those berries are poisonous.*

berserk [bə'sə:k, (*Amer*) 'bə:sə:k] *adj* (*usu pred*) violently insane: *He went berserk when he heard of his son's imprisonment.*

berth [bə:θ] *nc* **1** a sleeping-place in a ship *etc*: *Have you booked a berth on the Queen Elizabeth II?* **2** a place in a port *etc* where a ship or boat can be moored or tied up. – *vti* to moor (a ship): *The ship has berthed in London.*

beseech [bi'si:tʃ] – *pt, ptp* **besought** [bi'so:t] – *vt* (*arch or formal*) to beg (for): *He beseeched her to marry him; Don't kill him – I beseech you!*
be'seeching *adj* (*formal*: *usu attrib*): *She gave him a beseeching look.*

beset [bi'set] – *pt, ptp* **be'set** – *vt* (*usu in passive*: *liter*) to attack on all sides: *They were beset by thieves;* (*fig*) *He was constantly beset by worries.*

beside [bi'said] *prep* **1** by the side of or near: *He stood beside the window; She sat beside her sister.* **2** compared with: *She looks ugly beside her sister.*
be'sides *prep* in addition to: *Is anyone coming besides John?* – *adv* **1** also; moreover: *These shoes are expensive – besides, they're too small.* **2** in addition: *She has three sons and an adopted one besides.*
be be'side oneself (with) to be in a state of very great, uncontrolled anger, excitement or other emotion: *She was beside herself with excitement as the day of her holiday approached; She was beside herself with jealousy when her sister got married.*
be beside the point (*formal*) to have no connection with the subject being discussed; to be irrelevant: *You will have to go. Whether you want to go is beside the point.*

besiege [bi'si:dʒ] *vi* **1** to surround (*eg* a town) with an army in order to force (it) to surrender. **2** (*fig*: *with* **with**) to overwhelm (not necessarily in an unfriendly way) with: *The reporters besieged me with questions about the plane crash.*

besotted [bi'sotid] *adj* (*with* **with** *when pred*) very much in love (with): *He's besotted with a girl in London; He looked at her with a besotted expression.*

besought *see* **beseech**.

bespatter [bi'spatə] *vt* (*formal*) to sprinkle with mud, dirt *etc*: *The motor-cyclists were bespattered with mud.*

bespoke [bi'spouk] *adj* (*attrib*: *formal*) **1** (of clothes *etc*) ordered to be made: *a bespoke suit.* **2** making (clothes *etc*) to order: *a bespoke tailor.*

best [best] *adj, pron* (something which is) good to the greatest extent: *the best book on the subject; the best (that) I can do; She is the best painter I know; That is my best china; She is my best friend; He sends his best wishes; Which method is (the) best?; She was sorry that they had to part but it was all for the best; To the best of my knowledge* (= as far as I know) *he is not coming back; The roses are at their best in June.* – *adv* in the most excellent way; in the best manner: *She sings best (of all).* – *vt* (*formal*) to defeat: *He was bested in the argument.*
best man *nc* the bridegroom's attendant at a wedding.
ˌbest'seller *nc* something (*usu* a book) which sells very many copies: *Ernest Hemingway wrote several bestsellers.*
'best-selling *adj* (*attrib*) selling very many copies: *a best-selling book.*
all the best! (used as a toast, as a farewell *etc*) I hope that you may be happy, successful *etc.*
the ˌbest of it 'is (that) the most amusing thing is (that): *And the best of it is, he wasn't going to get the job anyway!*
the best part of (*inf*) most of; nearly (all of): *I've read the best part of two hundred books on the subject.*
do one's best to try as hard as possible: *He'll do his best to be here on time, but he may be late.*
for the 'best likely or intended to have the best results possible in a particular situation: *We don't want to send the child away to school but we're doing it for the best.*
get the best of to win, or get some advantage from, (a fight, argument *etc*): *He was shouting a lot, but I think I got the best of the argument.*
I, we *etc* **had 'best** it would be best for me, us *etc* to: *I'd best go, or I'll be late.*
make the best of it to do all one can to turn a failure, disaster *etc* into something successful: *She is disappointed at not getting into university but she'll just have to make the best of it and find a job.*
put one's best foot forward (*formal*) to make the best attempt possible: *If you put your best foot forward you will complete the work in time.*
See also **good, well, better**.

bestial ['bestjəl, (*Amer*) 'bestʃəl] *adj* (*liter or formal*) savage or like an animal: *bestial behaviour.*
bestiality [besti'aləti] *ncu.*
See also **beast**.

bestir [bi'stə:] – *pt, ptp* **be'stirred** – *v refl* (*liter*) to move to action: *Bestir yourself!*
See also **stir**.

bestow [bi'stou] *vt* (*formal*: *with* **on**) to give (*esp* a title, award *etc*) to someone: *The Queen bestowed a knighthood on him.* **be'stowal** *ncu.*

bet [bet] – *pts, ptps* **bet, 'betted** – *vti* (*often with* **on**) to gamble (*usu* with money) *eg* on a racehorse, or on whether or not something will happen in a certain way: *I'm betting (a pound) on that horse; I bet you can't* (= I challenge you to) *stand on your hands; I('ll) bet you were* (= You must have been) *angry!* – *nc* **1** an act of betting; a wager: *I won my bet.* **2** a sum of money betted: *Place your bets, gentlemen!*
hedge one's bets *see* **hedge**.
take a bet (*often with* **on**) to bet: *Are you willing to take a bet on whether he'll come or not?*

beta ['bi:tə, (*Amer*) 'beitə] *n* the second letter of the Greek alphabet (Β, β).

betake [bi'teik] – *pt* **betook** [bi'tuk] : *ptp* **be'taken** – *v refl* (*liter or facet*) to take (oneself) somewhere: *I betook myself to London.*

betide [bi'taid] : **ˌwoe be'tide him, you** *etc* (*liter or facet*) he, you *etc* will regret it: *Woe betide you if you forget!*

betook *see* **betake**.

betray [bi'trei] *vt* **1** to act disloyally or treacherously towards (*esp* a person who trusts one) *eg* by making secrets about him known *esp* to an enemy: *He betrayed his own brother (to the enemy);* (*formal*) *The general betrayed the king's trust by organizing a rebellion.* **2** (*formal*) to give away (a secret *etc*); to disclose: *Never betray a confidence!* **3** (*formal*) to show (signs of): *Her pale face betrayed her fear; His voice betrayed the fact that he was drunk.* **be'trayal** *ncu.* **be'trayer** *nc.*

betroth [bi'trouð, (*Amer*) bi'tro:θ] *vt* (*formal or old*: *often in passive*) to promise in marriage: *She was betrothed to her husband at the age of twenty*; *They were betrothed for five years before they got married.* **be'trothal** *ncu*.

be'trothed *nc* (*formal*) the person to whom one is betrothed: *May I introduce you to my betrothed?*

better ['betə] *adj* **1** good to a greater extent: *Yours is better than mine*; *His chances of winning are better than mine*; *He has a better car than I do*; *The weather's much better than it was yesterday.* **2** (*pred*) stronger in health; recovered (from an illness): *I feel better today than I did last week*; *She's completely better now.* **3** (*pred*) preferable: *Better to do it now than later*; *It is better to leave your job than wait to be sacked.* – *adv* well to a greater extent: *He sings better now than he did before*; *He sings better than her.* – *pron* someone or something which is good to a greater extent than the other (of two people or things): *He's the better of the two.* – *nc* (*esp in pl*: *often facet*) someone higher in social position, rank *etc*: *Don't be rude to your betters!* – **1** *vt* to beat; to improve on: *He's bettered all previous records*; *She has bettered her last year's time for the race.* **2** *vti* to improve: *She tried to better herself* (= improve her social *etc* position) *by marrying a rich man*; (*formal*) *The situation has bettered a little.*

'betterment *nu* (*formal*) improvement; advancement: *This research is for the betterment of our lives.*

one's better half *see* **half**.

better off richer; happier in some way: *He'd be better off working as a miner*; *She'd be better off if she divorced him*; *You'd be better off without him.*

the better part of (*inf*) most of: *He talked for the better part of an hour.*

get the better of to overcome; to win (against): *He got the better of his opponent/the argument.*

I, we *etc* **had 'better** it would be wise(r) for me, us *etc* to (do something): *You'd better stop while you're winning*; *We'd better go home now.*

know better *see* **know**.

See also **good, best, well**.

between [bi'twi:n] *prep* **1** in, to, through or across the space dividing two people, places, times *etc*: *between the car and the pavement*; *between 2 o'clock and 2.30*; *You must not eat between meals if you want to lose weight.* **2** concerning the relationship of two things or people: *the love between mother and child*; *the difference between right and wrong.* **3** by the combined action of; working together: *They managed it between them*; *We bought the house between us.* **4** part to one (person or thing), part to (the other): *Divide the chocolate between you*; *She shared the cake between John and Mary.*

between you and me/between ourselves in confidence: *Between you and me, I think he's rather nice*; *Just between ourselves, I think he has gone away.*

few and far between *see* **few**.

ˌin be'tween times at intervals between other events: *She does not eat much at meal times but eats a lot in between times.*

betwixt [bi'twikst] *prep* (*arch*) between.

bevel ['bevəl] *nc* (*esp tech*) **1** a slanting edge (rather than a sharp corner): *A chisel has a bevel on its cutting edge.* **2** a piece of wood *etc* with this type of edge. – *v* – *pt, ptp* **'bevelled**, (*Amer usu*) **'beveled** – *vt* (*tech*) to give a bevel or slant to (something): *The joiner bevelled the edge of the shelf.*

'bevelled *adj*: *bevelled glass.*

beverage ['bevərid ʒ] *nc* (*formal*) a drink, *esp* tea, coffee, or other non-alcoholic drink.

bevy ['bevi] *nc* **1** a flock or gathering (of birds). **2** (*fig*) a group (of women or girls): *a bevy of girls round the swimming-pool.*

bewail [bi'weil] *vt* (*liter*) to wail about or be sorrowful about: *He bewailed his misfortune.*

beware [bi'weə] – used mostly in the imperative and the infinitive – **1** *vti* (*usu with* **of**) to be careful (of): *Beware of the dog*; *Beware of thieves*; (*formal*) *Beware lest he bite you*; *Beware the Ides of March!* **2** *vi* to be careful: *He told them to beware.*

bewilder [bi'wildə] *vt* to amaze or puzzle: *She was completely bewildered when her husband suddenly left her*; *The child was bewildered by the mathematics that was taught at her new school.*

be'wilderment *nu*.

bewitch [bi'witʃ] *vt* to cast a spell on, or affect by magic: *The wizard bewitched the children*; *She bewitched us with her smile.* **be'witching** *adj*.

beyond [bi'jond] *prep* **1** on the farther side of: *My house is just beyond those trees.* **2** farther on than (something) in time or place: *I can't see beyond the next street*; *I cannot plan beyond tomorrow.* **3** out of the range, reach, power *etc* of: *beyond help/understanding/one's strength*; *How he exists on his income is beyond me*; *She is beyond caring* (= she no longer cares because she is too tired *etc*) *about her appearance.* **4** other than; apart from: *What is there to say beyond what's already been said?*

the back of beyond (*inf*: *derog*) a very remote place: *They live at the back of beyond, somewhere in the Australian bush.*

beyond a joke past the limit of being humorous: *His attitude towards women is beyond a joke.*

beyond compare (*liter*) impossible to compare, having no equal: *His achievements are beyond compare.*

beyond one's means too expensive(ly): *A painting by Picasso is beyond my means*; *He lives well beyond his means* (= he spends more money than he earns).

bi- [bai] (*in cmpds*) **1** two, as in **bilateral**. **2** twice, as in **bi-annual**. **3** (happening) every second (week, month *etc*), as in **bi-monthly** (*def 1*).

bi-annual [bai'anjuəl] *adj* (*formal*) happening twice a year: *a bi-annual event*; *The dinner is bi-annual, not annual.* **ˌbi-'annually** *adv*.

bias ['baiəs] **1** *ncu* favouring of one or other (side in an argument *etc*) rather than remaining neutral; prejudice: *He has a bias against people of different races*; *Her choice certainly showed bias.* **2** *nc* a weight on or in an object (*eg* a bowl for playing bowls) making it move in a particular direction. – *v* – *pt, ptp* **'bias(s)ed** – *vt* to influence (*usu* unfairly): (*formal*) *He biased the result by paying the judge*; *He was biased by the report in the newspapers.*

'bias(s)ed *adj* (*neg* **un-**) favouring one side rather than another: *a biased judgement*; *His attitude is biased.*

bias binding *nu* a type of material used for finishing off hems, seams *etc*.

bib [bib] *nc* **1** a cloth *etc* tied under a child's chin to catch spilt food *etc*: *Plastic bibs can be dangerous.* **2** the top part of an apron or overalls, covering the chest.

Bible ['baibl] **1** *n* (*with* **the**) the sacred writings of the Christian Church, consisting of the Old and New Testaments. **2** *nc* (*often no cap*) a book containing these writings: *He had a Bible in his* hand. **3** *nc* (*no cap*: *inf facet*) a highly-detailed book, regarded as a reliable reference: *This book is the car mechanic's bible.*

biblical ['biblikəl] *adj* (*often with cap*) of or like the Bible: *biblical references*; *His language is very biblical.*

bibliography [bibli'ogrəfi] *nc* **1** a list of books by one author or on one subject: *a bibliography of Ibsen's writings*; *a bibliography of nuclear physics.* **2** a list, *usu* at the back of a book, of those books which have been mentioned in the text. ˌ**bibli'ographer** *nc.* ˌ**biblio'graphic(al)** [-'gra-] *adj.*

bibliophile ['bibliəfail] *nc* (*formal*) a person who likes books very much and collects them.

bicarbonate [bai'ka:bənət] *ncu* a chemical compound containing a double proportion of carbon dioxide.

bicarbonate of soda (*inf abbrev* **bicarb** ['baika:b]) *see* **baking soda**.

bicentenary [baisen'ti:nəri, (*Amer*) bai'sentəneri], (*formal*) **bicentennial** [baisen'teniəl] *nc* a two-hundredth anniversary: *the bicentenary of American independence*; (*attrib*) *the bicentenary celebrations.*

biceps ['baiseps] *n pl* the large muscles in the front of the upper arm: *The weight-lifter has enormous biceps.*

bicker ['bikə] *vi* to keep on quarrelling (about small things): *They're always bickering about details*; *Those two children bicker constantly.*

bicycle ['baisikl] *nc* (*often abbrev* **bike** [baik], **cycle** ['saikl]) a pedal-driven vehicle with two wheels and a seat: *She was on her bicycle*; *He is teaching his child to ride a bike*; *He came by bike.* – *vi* (*usu abbrev* **'cycle**) to ride a bicycle: *He bicycled slowly up the hill.*

bid [bid] – *pt* **bade** [bad] (*defs 4, 5*): *ptp* **'bidden** (*defs 4, 5*); *pt, ptp* **bid** (*defs 1, 2, 3*) – **1** *vti* to offer (an amount of money) at an auction: *John bid (£500) for the painting.* **2** *vti* (in card-games) to state in advance the number of tricks a player will try to win: *I bid four spades.* **3** *vi* (*with* **for**) (in building *etc*) to state a price (for a contract): *My firm is bidding for the contract for the new road.* **4** *vt* (*liter or formal*) to tell (someone) to (do something): *He bade me enter.* **5** *vt* (*liter or formal*) to express a wish, a greeting *etc* (to someone): *I bid you good morning*; *He bade me farewell.* – *nc* **1** an offer of a price: *a bid of £10.* **2** a statement of how many tricks one hopes to win at cards: *a bid of three hearts.* **3** an attempt (to obtain): *He made a bid for freedom but was captured*; *He made a bid to attract the votes of the young people.* **'bidder** *nc.* **'bidding** *nu.*

'biddable *adj* (*inf*) obedient: *He's a very biddable child*; *That dog is very biddable.*

See also **outbid**.

bide [baid] : **bide one's time** to wait for a good opportunity: *I'm just biding my time until he makes a mistake.*

bidet ['bi:dei] *nc* a low basin for washing the genital area: *Not all bathrooms have a bidet.*

biennial [bai'eniəl] *adj* **1** (*esp attrib*: *formal*) happening once in every two years: *a biennial event.* **2** (of plants *etc*) lasting for two years: *Wallflowers are biennial*; *a biennial plant.* – *nc* a plant that flowers only in the second year of its life, and then dies.

bi'ennially *adv.*

bier [biə] *nc* (*old*) a type of wooden stretcher for carrying dead people to the grave.

bifocal [bai'foukəl] *adj* (of lenses) having two points of focus, which help people to see things close at hand and things far away.

bi'focals *n pl* spectacles with bifocal lenses.

big [big] *adj* **1** large in size: *He has a big car*; *They live in a big house*; *Is this room big enough?*; (*fig*) *He has not much money but he has big ideas.* **2** (*attrib*) important: *a big event in publishing*; *He's a big man in banking*; *This is your big day.* – *adv* (*inf*) in a big way; on a large scale: *We must think big*; *He likes to talk big* (= to boast).

'biggish *adj* (*inf*: *usu attrib*) quite big: *We have a biggish house.*

big game *nu* large animals (*usu* lions, tigers *etc*) that are hunted: *He hunts big game in Africa*; (*attrib*) *a big game hunter.*

'bigwig *nc* (*inf*: *often derog*) a person of importance: *He's a bigwig in local government.*

bigamy ['bigəmi] *nu* marriage to two wives or two husbands at once (a crime in some countries): *He's been charged with committing bigamy.* **'bigamist** *nc.* **'bigamous** *adj.*

bigot ['bigət] *nc* a person who constantly and stubbornly holds a particular point of view *etc*: *He is a religious bigot.*

'bigoted *adj*: *She is so bigoted that she will not speak to people who are not of her religion*; *He's a very bigoted man.*

'bigotry *nu* (*formal*) bigoted attitude or behaviour.

bijou ['bi:ʒu:] *adj* (*formal or facet*) small and elegant: *Bijou detached houses for sale.*

bike *see* **bicycle**.

bikini [bi'ki:ni] *nc* a brief two-piece swimming costume for women.

bilateral [bai'latərəl] *adj* (*esp attrib*: *formal*) affecting, signed, or agreed, by two sides, countries *etc*: *a bilateral agreement.*

bilberry ['bilbəri] *nc* **1** a shrub with a dark blue berry. **2** one of its berries.

bile [bail] *nu* **1** a yellowish thick bitter fluid in the liver. **2** (*liter*) anger or irritability.

bilious ['biljəs] *adj* **1** of, or affected by, too much bile: *She has had a bilious attack*; *I feel rather bilious.* **2** (*derog*) (of some colours) unpleasantly strong, often resembling the colour of bile: *bilious yellow*; *bilious green*; *That colour is rather bilious.*

'biliousness *nu*: *After eating too much I had an attack of biliousness.*

bilge [bildʒ] **1** *nc* the broadest part of a ship's bottom. **2** *nu* filth or rubbish such as collects there. **3** *nu* (*fig inf*) nonsense: *Don't talk bilge!*

bilingual [bai'liŋgwəl] *adj* **1** written or spoken in two languages: *a bilingual dictionary.* **2** speaking two languages equally well: *He's bilingual in English and French*; *a bilingual waiter.*

bilious, biliousness *see* **bile**.

bill[1] [bil] *nc* a bird's beak: *a bird with a yellow bill.*

bill[2] [bil] *nc* **1** an account of money owed for goods *etc*: *I received an electricity bill today*; *Have you paid your bill?*; *He footed* (= paid) *the bill for the meal.* **2** (*with cap in particular titles*) a draft of a proposed law: *This is the draft of the new bill*; *the Industrial Relations Bill*; *Has the Women's Rights Bill become law yet?* **3** (*Amer*) a banknote: *a five-dollar bill.* **4** (*formal*) a poster used for advertising: *Stick no bills on this wall!* – *vt* **1** to send an account (to someone): *We'll bill you next month for your purchases.* **2** to bring to the attention of the public by poster or other advertisement: *She's billed as America's greatest singer.*

'billboard *nc* a large board on which advertising posters are displayed: *He stuck posters on the billboard.*

'billfold *nc* (*Amer*) a wallet for paper money: *a billfold full of dollars.*

bill of exchange a written order for payment of a certain sum of money to a particular named person on a certain future date.

bill of fare (*formal or facet*) a menu: *What's our bill of fare for tonight?*

bill of sale a formal legal paper stating transfer of ownership.

fill the bill (*inf*) to be suitable; to be exactly what is required: *We are looking for a holiday cottage and this will fill the bill.*

foot the bill *see* **bill** (*def 1*) *above.*

billet ['bilit] *nc* a private house *etc* where soldiers are given food and lodging. – *v* – *pt, ptp* **'billeted** – *vt* to give lodging to (*eg* soldiers): *The men are billeted in the church hall.*

billet-doux [bilei'du:] – *pl* **ˌbillets-'doux** [-z] – *nc* (*old or facet*) a love-letter.

billiards ['biljədz] *n sing* a game played with long thin sticks (**cues**) and balls, on a table with pockets at the sides and corners: *Do you play billiards?*; (*attrib*) *a billiards match.*

billiard- (*in cmpds*): *a 'billiard-table*; *a 'billiard-ball.*

billion ['biljən] – *pls* **'billion** (*defs 1, 3*), **'billions** (*defs 2, 3*) – *nc* **1** (preceded by **a**, a number, or a word signifying a quantity) often in the UK, the number 1 000 000 000 000; in the US and often in the UK, the number 1 000 000 000: *a billion*; *one billion*; *two billion*; *several billion.* **2** often in the UK, the figure 1 000 000 000 000; in the US and often in the UK, the figure 1 000 000 000. **3** a billion pounds or dollars: *The sum involved amounts to several billion(s).* – *adj* (preceded by **a**, a number, or a word signifying a quantity: *usu attrib*) often in the UK, 1 000 000 000 000 in number; in the US and often in the UK, 1 000 000 000 in number: *a billion stars*; *a few billion stars.*

billion- (*in cmpds*) having a billion (of something): *Is there such a thing as a billion-dollar banknote?*

'billionth 1 *nc* one of a billion equal parts. **2** *nc, adj* (the) last of a billion (people, things *etc*) or (the person, thing *etc*) in an equivalent position.

'billions of 1 several billion: *billions of dollars.* **2** (*loosely*) lots of: *He has read billions of books.*

See also Appendix 1.

billow ['bilou] *nc* (*liter*) a large wave.

'billowy *adj* (*esp attrib*): *billowy waves*; (*fig*) *a billowy skirt.*

billow out *vi* to move in a way similar to large waves: *The sails billowed out in the strong wind*; *Her skirt billowed out in the breeze.*

billycan ['bilikan] *nc* (*inf abbrev* **'billy**) a metal tin used for cooking in or eating and drinking from, *esp* when camping.

billy-goat ['biligout] *nc* a male (*usu* adult) goat. *See also* **nanny-goat**.

bi-monthly [bai'mʌnθli] *adj, adv* **1** (happening) once in every two months. **2** (happening) twice a month.

bin [bin] *nc* (*often in cmpds*) a container (*usu* metal or plastic, often large) in which corn *etc* is stored or rubbish is collected: *a waste-paper bin*; *a dustbin.*

binary ['bainəri] *adj* (*math*) consisting of two.

the binary system the system of writing and calculating with numbers which uses only two digits (0 and 1) and has 2 as a base (101 = 1 four, 0 twos, 1 unit = 5).

bind [baind] – *pt, ptp* **bound** [baund] – *vt* **1** to tie up (with string, strips of cloth, bandage etc): *The doctor bound up the old man's leg with elastic bandage*; *The robbers bound up the bank manager with rope.* **2** to fasten together and put a cover on the pages of (a book): *Bind this book in leather.* **3** (*formal*) to make (someone) swear or promise (to do something): *This contract binds you to pay me £100.*

'binder *nc* **1** a person who binds books. **2** a harvesting-machine that binds grain as it cuts it.

'binding 1 *ncu* anything that binds. **2** *nc* the covering in which the leaves of a book are fixed: *leather binding.*

-bound (*in cmpds*) **1** (of a book) having a binding of a particular kind: *leather-bound books*; *cloth-bound volumes.* **2** prevented from making progress by a particular thing: *The ship was fogbound/icebound*; *snowbound cars*; *the strike-bound docks.*

bind (someone) over *vt oblig sep* (*legal*) to make (someone) legally obliged (*eg* to appear in court, to behave well): *The magistrate did not fine him but bound him over for three months.*

See also **bound**[2].

bingo ['biŋgou] *nu* a gambling game using cards with numbered squares: *She goes to bingo every night*; *Do you play bingo?*; (*attrib*) *a bingo-hall.*

binoculars [bi'nokjuləz] *n pl* an instrument for making distant objects look nearer, with separate eyepieces for each eye: *The hunter looked at the deer on the hillside through his binoculars.*

bio- [baiou] (*in cmpds*) life or living things, as in **biodegradable**.

biochemistry [baiə'kemistri] *nu* the chemistry of living things: *He is studying the biochemistry of the blood*; (*attrib*) *a biochemistry lecture.* **ˌbio'chemist** *nc.*

ˌbio'chemical [-mikəl] *adj*: *a biochemical reaction.*

biodegradable [baiədi'greidəbl] *adj* (*formal*) able to be separated into individual parts by bacteria: *All vegetable matter is biodegradable*; *biodegradable materials.*

biography [bai'ogrəfi] **1** *nc* a written account by someone of another person's life: *He has written a biography of Nelson.* **2** *nu* this type of writing: *Some people prefer biography to fiction.* **bi'ographer** *nc.* **ˌbio'graphic(al)** [-'gra-] *adj.*

biology [bai'olədʒi] *nu* the science of living things: *human biology*; *In biology, the schoolchildren studied the working of a sheep's heart*; (*attrib*) *a biology lesson.* **bio'logical** [-'lo-] *adj.* **bio'logically** [-'lo-] *adv.* **bi'ologist** *nc.*

biological warfare *nu* the use of germs as a weapon.

bionics [bai'oniks] *n sing* **1** the use of biological principles in the design of computers *etc.* **2** (*loosely*) the use of electronics in human medicine, *eg* heart valves, artificial limbs *etc.*

bi'onic *adj* of or using bionics.

bipartite [bai'pa:tait] *adj* (*attrib*: *formal*) involving, or agreed by, two countries *etc*: *a bipartite agreement.*

biped ['baiped] *nc* (*formal*) an animal with two feet (*eg* man).

biplane ['baiplein] *nc* an aeroplane with two sets of wings, one above the other.

birch [bə:tʃ] **1** *nc* (*also* **'birch tree**) a kind of small tree with pointed leaves valued for its wood: *That tree is a birch*; (*attrib*) *birch leaves.* **2** *nu, adj* (of) its wood: *a desk made of birch*; *a birch desk.* **3** *nc* a rod made of birch branches, formerly used in giving punishment: *Some people want to bring back the birch* (= to have the birch used as punishment again). – *vt* to flog or beat (someone) with a birch rod (as a punishment): *Many people consider it cruel to birch criminals.*

bird [bə:d] *nc* **1** a two-legged feathered creature, with a beak and two wings, with which most can fly: *Kiwis and ostriches are birds which cannot fly.* **2** (*sl: sometimes derog*) a girl: *Who's that bird over there?*; *That's his new bird* (= girlfriend).

'bird-fancier *nc* a person who breeds birds: *Our neighbour is a bird-fancier and has built a new aviary.*

ˌbird's-eye 'view *nc* **1** a general view from above: *a bird's-eye view of London from an aeroplane.* **2** a summary (of a subject): *His report gives a bird's-eye view of the problem.*

'bird-watcher *nc* someone who studies birds by observing them closely. **'bird-watching** *nu.*

Biro® ['bairou] *nc* a type of ballpoint pen.

birth [bə:θ] **1** *ncu* (an) act of coming into the world; being born: *A doctor could not be present at the birth of her son*; *She had a difficult birth*; *She's been deaf since birth*; *There were six hundred births here last year.* **2** *nu* descent or place of birth: *She's Scots by birth.* **3** *nu* (*formal*) the beginning: *the birth of a new era*; *the birth of civilization.*

'birth control *nu* prevention of the conception of children: *The pill is one method of birth control*; *They keep having children because they don't practise birth control.*

'birthday *nc* the anniversary of the day on which a person was born: *She celebrated her twentieth birthday yesterday*; *Today is his birthday*; (*attrib*) *a birthday party/card.*

'birthmark *nc* a permanent mark on the skin at or from birth: *She has a red birthmark on her face.*

'birthplace *nc* the place where a person *etc* was born: *Have you visited Shakespeare's birthplace?*; (*fig*) *the birthplace of the steam engine.*

'birthrate *nc* the number of births per head of population over a given period: *The birthrate in many countries has decreased with the introduction of the contraceptive pill.*

'birthright *ncu* (*often fig*) the rights one may claim by birth: *Freedom of speech is part of man's birthright.*

give birth (to) (*formal*) (of a mother) to produce (a baby) from the womb: *She gave birth last night*; *She has given birth to two sets of twins*; (*fig*) *He has given birth to several brilliant ideas.*

biscuit ['biskit] *nc* **1** (*Amer* **'cookie**) a crisp, sweet piece of dough baked in small flat cakes. **2** a similar savoury flat cake. **3** (*Amer*) a small soft round cake.

take the biscuit (*inf*) to be worse than everything else: *His latest piece of impertinence really takes the biscuit!*

bisect [bai'sekt] *vt* (*geom*) to cut into two equal parts: *A diagonal line across a square bisects it.*

bisexual [bai'sekʃuəl] *adj* **1** having the sexual organs of both male and female. **2** sexually attracted to both males and females.

bishop ['biʃəp] *nc* **1** (*with cap in titles*) (the status of) a Christian clergyman in charge of a group of churches, *usu* in a large city or area: *the Bishop of Lincoln*; *He was made a bishop in 1967.* **2** one of the pieces in chess.

'bishopric [-rik] *nc* **1** the post or position of bishop. **2** the area under the charge of a bishop: *in the bishopric of Lincoln.*

bison ['baisn] – *pls* **'bison**, (*rare*) **'bisons** – *nc* **1** the American buffalo: *a herd of bison.* **2** the large European wild ox.

bit[1] [bit] *nc* **1** a small piece: *a bit of bread*; *There's a bit of this machine missing.* **2** (*inf*) a piece of any size: *Let me give you a bit of advice.* **3** (*inf*) a short time: *Wait a bit longer.*

'bitty (*inf*) *adj* made up of small, unrelated pieces: *We had a very bitty conversation*; *His essay was rather bitty.*

a bit (*inf*) (*sometimes with* **of**) a little; slightly; rather: *I'm a bit tired*; *The dress is a bit too tight*; *He's a bit of a fool.*

bit by bit gradually: *Move the pile of rocks bit by bit, not all at once.*

do one's bit (*inf*) to take one's share in a task: *Each of us will have to do his bit if we are to finish the job in time.*

every bit as *see* **every.**

in, to 'bits in(to) *usu* small pieces: *The broken mirror lay in bits on the floor*; *The toy just fell to bits*; *The child pulled the flowers to bits*; *It came to bits in my hand*; *He loves taking his car to bits.*

not a 'bit of it! not at all!; don't mention it!

bit[2] *see* **bite.**

bit[3] [bit] *nc* a tool with a cutting edge (*usu* fitted into a drill and turned at high speed).

bit[4] [bit] *nc* the part of a bridle which a horse holds in its mouth.

take the bit between one's teeth to go ahead and tackle a problem seriously and determinedly, acting on one's own: *I took the bit between my teeth and asked her if she was lying.*

bitch [bitʃ] *nc* **1** the female of the dog, wolf or fox. **2** (*derog sl*) a (bad-tempered or unpleasant) woman: *Joan is a real bitch!* – *vi* (*inf*) to make unpleasant comments (about someone or something): *She's always bitching about how badly she's treated.*

'bitchy *adj* (*usu* of women) fond of making unpleasant comments about people: *She is sometimes very bitchy about her colleagues.*

bite [bait] – *pt* **bit** [bit] : *ptp* **bitten** ['bitn] – **1** *vti* to seize, grasp or tear (something) with the teeth or jaws: *He bit into the apple*; *The dog bit his leg*; *He was bitten by a mosquito*; (*fig*) *He's been bitten by the urge to travel.* **2** *vi* (of a tool *etc*) to grip: *The drill won't bite (into this wood) very well.* – *nc* **1** an act of biting or the piece or place bitten: *He took a bite from the apple*; *He ate the whole cake in three bites*; *Your dog gave me a nasty bite*; *She has a mosquito bite on her leg.* **2** (*inf: no pl*) a small amount of food: *Come and have a bite (to eat) with us.* **3** the nibble of a fish on the end of one's line: *I've been fishing for hours without a bite.*

'biting *adj* (*usu attrib*) **1** very cold and causing discomfort: *a biting wind.* **2** (*fig*) wounding or hurtful: *a biting remark.*

bite the dust (*inf fig*) to fail; to be unsuccessful: *That's another scheme that's bitten the dust.*

bitter ['bitə] *adj* **1** having a sharp, acid taste like lemons *etc*, and sometimes unpleasant: *These plums are bitter*; *a bitter orange.* **2** full of pain or sorrow: *She learned from bitter experience*; *She* *feels very bitter*; *bitter disappointment.* **3** (*usu attrib*) hostile; full of hatred or opposition: *bitter enemies*; *a great deal of bitter opposition to his scheme.* **4** very cold: *a bitter wind*; *That wind is cold and bitter.* – *nu* a kind of beer: *Two pints of bitter, please.*

'bitterly *adv*: *bitterly disappointed*; *bitterly opposed to the wedding*; *bitterly cold.*

'bitterness *nu.*

'bitters *n pl* a liquid made from bitter herbs or roots, and mixed with certain alcoholic drinks.

'bittersweet *adj* (*usu fig*: *usu attrib*) pleasant and unpleasant, or bitter and sweet, at the same time: *a bittersweet love affair.*

a bitter pill (to swallow) (*formal*) something difficult to accept: *She found his betrayal a bitter pill to swallow.*

until/till/to the bitter end up to the very end, however unpleasant *etc*: *The play was very boring but we stayed until the bitter end*; *Although the party was very noisy we stayed to the bitter end.*

bitumen ['bitjumin] *nu* a black, sticky substance obtained from petroleum and used in road-making.

bi'tuminous [-'tju:mi-] *adj* containing bitumen.

bivouac ['bivuak] – *pt, ptp* **'bivouacked** – *vi* to camp out at night without a tent. – *nc* (the site of) a camp without tents.

bi-weekly [bai'wi:kli] *adj, adv* **1** (happening *etc*) once every two weeks. **2** (happening *etc*) twice each week.

bizarre [bi'za:] *adj* (*formal*) odd or very strange: *a bizarre turn of events*; *You look really bizarre in that costume!*

blab [blab] – *pt, ptp* **blabbed** – *vti* (*sl*) (*sometimes with* **out**) to tell something that one is not supposed to tell: *He blabbed to the enemy*; *He blabbed the story all round the town.*

black [blak] *adj* **1** of the colour in which these words are printed: *black paint*; *The walls were painted black.* **2** without light: *a very black night*; *The night was black and starless.* **3** (*inf*) dirty: *Your hands are black!*; *black hands from lifting coal.* **4** without milk: *black coffee/tea*; *I take my coffee black.* **5** (*attrib*) sad or deep: *black despair.* **6** (*attrib*) evil: *black magic.* **7** (*usu attrib*) bad-tempered: *She gave him a black look.* **8** (*often offensive*: *currently acceptable in the US, S Africa etc*) Negro, of African, West Indian descent. **9** (*esp S Africa*) coloured; of mixed descent (increasingly used by people of mixed descent to refer to themselves). **10** (*pred*) (during a strike *etc*) banned by a trade-union: *This cargo is black, so we can't touch it.* – **1** *ncu* (any shade of) the colour in which these words are printed: *Black and white are opposites*; *We produce a variety of blacks.* **2** *ncu* something (*eg* material, paint *etc*) black in colour: *I've used up all the black.* **3** *nc* (*often with cap*: *often offensive*: *currently acceptable in the US, S Africa etc*) a Negro; a person of African, West Indian *etc* descent. – *vt* **1** to make black: *I blacked his eye* (= gave him a black eye) *in the fight.* **2** to clean with black polish: *He blacked his shoes.* **3** to ban work on: *This type of cargo has been blacked by the strikers.* – *See also* **black out** *below.* **'blackness** *nu.*

'blacken **1** *vti* to make or become black or very dark in colour: *The sky blackened before the storm.* **2** *vt* to make to seem bad: *She blackened his character.* **3** *vt* to clean with black polish: *He blackened his boots.*

'blackish *adj* fairly black; close to black: *He was watching some large blackish birds in a field.*

black art/magic *nu* magic performed for evil reasons: *He tries to practise black magic.*

'blackberry *nc* a very dark-coloured fruit growing (*usu* wild) on a bush: *We had blackberries and cream for dessert.* – *See also* **go blackberrying** *below.*

'blackbird *nc* a dark-coloured bird of the thrush family.

'blackboard *nc* a dark-coloured board for writing on in chalk (used *esp* in schools).

black box *nc* a built-in machine for automatic recording of the details of a plane's flight: *They hope to find out the cause of the air crash when they find the black box.*

black bread *nu* bread made from rye flour.

,black'currant *nc* **1** a garden bush grown for its small black fruit. **2** its fruit: *She bought four kilos of blackcurrants*; (*attrib*) *blackcurrant jam.*

black eye *nc* an eye with bad bruising around it (*eg* from a punch): *George gave me a black eye when we were fighting.*

blackguard ['blaga:d] *nc* (*old or formal*) a worthless and evil person: *Take your hands off my wife, you blackguard!*

'blackhead *nc* a small black-topped lump in a pore of the skin, *esp* of the face.

black ice *nu* a type of ice which is very difficult to see, making roads dangerous to drive on *etc.*

'blackleg *nc* (*derog*) a person willing to work when his fellow-workers are on strike: *After the strike the workers refused to work with the blackleg.* – *vi* to act as a blackleg: *He blacklegged during the strike.*

'blacklist *nc* a list of people suspected, not approved of, out of favour *etc.* – *vt* to put (a person *etc*) on such a list: *They blacklisted him because he was a member of a left-wing political party.*

'blackmail *vt* to obtain money illegally from (a person), *usu* by threatening to make known something which the victim wants to keep secret. – *nu* the act of blackmailing: *money got by blackmail.* **'blackmailer** *nc.*

Black Maria [mə'raiə] *nc* (*inf*) a prison van: *The policemen took the three suspects to the police station in a Black Maria.*

black market *ncu* (a place for) the illegal buying and selling, at high prices, of goods that are scarce, rationed *etc*: *He made a fortune selling coffee on the black market*; (*attrib*) *black market goods.*

black marketeer *nc* a person who sells goods on the black market.

'blackout *nc* **1** a period of darkness produced by putting out, or concealing, all lights: *Accidents increase during a blackout*; (*fig*) *There has been a blackout of news* (= a ban on, or interruption of, news) *about the coup.* **2** a period of unconsciousness: *He had several blackouts during his illness.* – *See also* **black out**.

black pudding *see* **pudding**.

black sheep *nc* a member of a family or group who is unsatisfactory in some way: *My brother has always been the black sheep of the family because he has been in prison several times.*

'blacksmith *nc* a person who makes and repairs by hand things made of iron: *The blacksmith made a new shoe for the horse.*

be in someone's black books *see* **book**.

black and blue (*inf*) badly bruised: *He has*

beaten the child black and blue.

black and white 1 (of television *etc*) having no colours except black, white and shades of grey. 2 definitely either good or bad: *He's inclined to regard things in terms of black and white.* – *See also* **in black and white** *below.*

black out *vi* to lose consciousness: *He blacked out for almost a minute.* – *See also* **blackout**.

ˌgo 'blackberrying to gather blackberries: *Let's go blackberrying tomorrow.*

in black and white in writing or print: *Would you put that down in black and white?*

bladder ['bladə] *nc* 1 the bag-like part of the body in which the urine collects. 2 a thin bag stretched by filling with air or liquid (*eg* the inner lining of a football).

blade [bleid] *nc* 1 the cutting part of a knife, sword *etc*: *His penknife has several different blades.* 2 the flat part of a leaf *etc*: *a blade of grass.* 3 the flat part of an oar.

blame [bleim] *vt* 1 to consider the responsibility for something bad as belonging to a particular person, thing *etc*: *I blame the wet road for the accident*; *You can't blame the accident on him.* 2 to find fault with (a person): *I don't blame you for wanting to leave.* – *nu* the responsibility (for something bad): *She always puts the blame on me*; *He always takes the blame for everything that goes wrong.*

'blameless *adj* (*formal*) innocent: *He led a blameless life*; *Although the boy had not broken the window himself, he was not entirely blameless.*

'blameworthy *adj* (*formal*: *usu pred*) deserving blame: *Although he caused the accident he is not blameworthy as it was unavoidable.*

be to blame (for) to be responsible (for an unfortunate happening): *She's to blame for all this mess!*

blanch [bla:ntʃ] 1 *vti* (*formal*) to make or become white: *She blanched with fear.* 2 *vt* to put (fruit, vegetables *etc*) into boiling water for a few seconds: *Blanch the beans before freezing them*; *Blanch the almonds to remove the skins from them.*

blancmange [blə'monʒ] *ncu* a jelly-like pudding made with milk.

bland [bland] *adj* 1 (of food *etc*) so mild as to be almost tasteless: *He's on a diet of bland food for his ulcer*; *That soup is very bland.* 2 (*usu pred*) (of people, their actions *etc*) mild or (too) gentle in manner: *That man is so bland that he irritates me.* 3 (*usu attrib*) (of people, their actions *etc*) showing no emotion: *His bland smile showed nothing of what he felt.* **'blandly** *adv.* **'blandness** *nu.*

blank [blaŋk] *adj* 1 (of paper) without writing or marks: *a blank sheet of paper*; *This paper is completely blank.* 2 expressionless: *His face was completely blank*; *a blank look.* 3 (of a wall) having no door, window *etc.* – *nc* 1 (*often fig*) an empty space: *My mind was a blank*: *There was a blank on the wall after we took down the picture.* 2 (in forms *etc*) a space left to be filled (with a signature *etc*): *Fill in all the blanks!* 3 a blank cartridge: *The soldier fired a blank.*

'blankly *adv* with a blank expression, often showing lack of understanding: *He looked at me blankly when I asked him about his brother.*

'blankness *nu.*

blank cartridge *nc* a cartridge without a bullet.

blank cheque *nc* 1 a signed cheque on which the sum to be paid has not been entered. 2 (*no pl*: *fig*) permission to do what one feels is necessary with complete freedom: *He's given me a blank cheque to carry out my plan.*

blank verse *nu* unrhymed poetry.

go blank to become empty: *My mind went blank when the police questioned me.*

blanket ['blaŋkit] *nc* 1 a warm covering made of wool *etc* (for a bed, or sometimes used as a garment by American Indians *etc*): *The child pulled the blanket over his head before falling asleep.* 2 (*fig*) something which covers like a blanket: *a blanket of snow.* – *adj* (*attrib*) covering all of a group of things: *a blanket agreement/instruction.* – *v* – *pt, ptp* **'blanketed** – *vt* 1 to cover, as if with a blanket: *The hills were blanketed in snow.* 2 (*with* **out**) to shut out completely: *This will blanket out the sound.*

blare [bleə] (*often with* **out**) 1 *vi* (of *eg* a trumpet) to sound loudly: *They could hear the trumpets blaring in the distance.* 2 *vti* to sound loudly and often harshly: *The radio was blaring out (pop music) constantly.* – 1 *nu* the sound of a trumpet. 2 *nc* (*no pl*) a loud or harsh sound: *the blare of pop music.*

blarney ['bla:ni] *nu* (*inf*) pleasant words or flattery: *Irish blarney.*

blasé ['bla:zei, (*Amer*) bla:'zei] *adj* no longer excited by pleasures which excite less experienced people: *She's very blasé about flying to New York because she's done it so often.*

blaspheme [blas'fi:m] *vi* (*formal*) 1 to speak without respect about God, religion *etc.* 2 to swear, using the name of God *etc.* **blas'phemer** *nc.*

blasphemous ['blasfəməs] *adj* (*formal*) (of speech or writing about God, religion *etc*) irreverent and without respect.

'blasphemy [-fəmi] *ncu* speaking or writing in this way.

blast [bla:st] *nc* 1 a strong, sudden stream (of air): *a blast of cold air.* 2 a loud sound made by a wind instrument, car horn *etc*: *One blast of the trumpet awakened all the soldiers.* 3 an explosion, or the strong wave of air spreading out from it: *He was knocked down by the blast from the explosion.* – 1 *vt* to tear (apart, open *etc*) by an explosion: *The door was blasted off its hinges.* 2 *vt* (*formal*) to wither or destroy: *The crops were blasted by the storm.* 3 *vti* (*often with* **out**) to come or be sent out, very loudly: *Music (was being) blasted out from the radio.* – *interj* (*inf*) showing anger: *Blast (it)!*

'blasted *adj* (*attrib*) 1 (*inf*) damned; annoying: *What a blasted mess you've made!* 2 (*formal*) withered and destroyed: *a blasted heath.*

'blasting *nu* in mining *etc*, the breaking up of rock *etc* by explosives: *Dynamite is sometimes used in blasting.*

'blast furnace *nc* a furnace for melting iron ore using blasts of hot air.

at full blast at full power, speed *etc*: *He had the radio going at full blast* (= as loud as possible).

blast off *vi* (of rockets, spacecraft *etc*) to take off and start to rise (*nc* **'blast-off**).

blatant ['bleitənt] *adj* (*formal*) very obvious; shameless: *a blatant lie*; *blatant disrespect*; *His satisfaction at my misfortune was quite blatant.* **'blatantly** *adv.*

blaze[1] [bleiz] *nc* 1 a bright light or fire: *A neighbour rescued her from the blaze.* 2 (*no pl*) an outburst (of anger, emotion *etc*): *He shouted at them in a blaze of fury.* 3 a bright display: *a blaze of colour.* – *vi* to burn; to shine brightly: *The fire blazed all night*; *The sun blazed in the sky.*

'blazing *adj* **1** burning brightly: *a blazing fire.* **2** (*inf*) extremely angry: *He was blazing when he heard what had happened*; *They had a blazing row as soon as their visitors had gone home.*

blaze[2] [bleiz]: **blaze a trail** (*fig formal*) to lead or show the way towards something new: *His discoveries blazed a trail in the field of nuclear power.*

blazer ['bleizə] *nc* a type of jacket, often part of a school uniform.

blazon ['bleizn] *vt* (*formal*) to display very obviously: *His name was blazoned all over the newspapers.*

bleach [bli:tʃ] *nu* liquid *etc* used for whitening clothes *etc* or removing stains: *Use bleach on this sheet to take the stains out!* – **1** *vti* to take out, or lose, colour; to whiten: *The sun has bleached his red shirt*; *His hair bleached in the sun.* **2** *vt* to remove stains by use of bleach: *She bleached his white shirt.*

bleak [bli:k] *adj* **1** cold and unsheltered: *a bleak landscape*; *The moors are bleak and barren.* **2** not hopeful: *a bleak outlook for the future*; *His future looks rather bleak.*

bleary-eyed [bliəri'aid] *adj* having red-rimmed eyes (*esp* due to lack of sleep): *He was bleary-eyed the morning after the party*; *He had a bleary-eyed appearance.*

bleat [bli:t] *vi* to make the noise of a sheep, lamb or goat: *The lamb bleated for its mother*; *Oh, do stop bleating about being tired!*

bleed [bli:d] – *pt, ptp* **bled** [bled] – **1** *vi* to lose blood: *He was bleeding badly from a large cut.* **2** *vt* to take blood from: *Doctors used to bleed their patients to try to cure their illnesses.* **3** *vt* to draw sap from (a tree). **4** *vt* (*inf*) to obtain money from by force, illegal means *etc*, over a period of time: *He bled me of all my money.*

'bleeding *adj* **1** losing blood: *a bleeding wound.* **2** (*inf*: *offensive to many people*: *attrib*) used for emphasis: *Get out of the bleeding way!*

my heart bleeds for you 1 (*formal*) I sympathize with you: *My heart bleeds for you in your distress.* **2** (*ironic*) I have no sympathy for you whatsoever: *You've too much money? My heart bleeds for you!*

bleep [bli:p] *nc* **1** a short, high-pitched burst of sound, often of radio waves. **2** (*also* **'bleeper**) a small instrument for making this sound, used *eg* to call a doctor in hospital when needed: *Call Dr Smith on his bleep!* – *vi* to make a short, high-pitched sound, *usu* by electronic means: *Satellites bleep as they circle the earth.*

blemish ['blemiʃ] *nc* (*formal*) a stain, mark or fault: *a blemish on an apple*; *She has several blemishes on her skin*; *That left a blemish on his reputation.* – *vt* (*formal*) to spoil: *Her beauty was blemished by a large scar.*

blend [blend] *vti* (*more formal or tech than* **mix**) **1** to mix together: *Blend the eggs and milk together.* **2** (*fig*) to mix or be mixed, giving a good result: *These two colours blend rather well.* – *nc* a mixture: *a fine blend of tea*; (*fig*) *a pleasant blend of charm and simplicity.*

'blender *nc* a machine for mixing things together, *esp* in cooking.

'blending *nu* mixing together: *blending of colours.*

bless [bles] – *pt* **blessed**: *ptps* **blessed, blest** – *vt* **1** to pronounce holy: *Bless the bread and wine.* **2** to ask God to show favour to: *Bless this ship.*

blessed ['blesid] *adj* **1** (*relig or liter*) holy: *the Blessed Virgin.* **2** (*inf euph*) damned: *She's hit every blessed one!* **'blessedly** [-sid-] *adv.* **'blessedness** [-sid-] *ncu.*

'blessing *nc* **1** a wish or prayer for happiness or success: *The priest gave them his blessing.* **2** any cause of happiness: *Her daughter was a great blessing to her.*

be 'blessed with [blest] (*formal or facet*) to be fortunate in having: *She's been blessed with many children.*

a blessing in disguise something that has proved to be fortunate after seeming unfortunate: *His death in the road accident was a blessing in disguise as he was slowly dying of cancer.*

blew *see* **blow**.

blight [blait] **1** *nu* a disease in plants that withers them: *potato blight.* **2** *nc* (*formal*) a thing that spoils: *There's a blight on all my efforts.* – *vt* **1** to cause to wither: *The frost has blighted my potatoes.* **2** (*formal*) to bring to nothing: *That has blighted our hopes.*

blind [blaind] *adj* **1** not able to see: *a blind man*; *Is he blind?* **2** (*pred with* **to**) unable to understand, to see or to notice: *He was blind to the dangers*; *She is blind to his faults.* **3** (*usu attrib*) hiding what is beyond: *a blind turning in the road.* **4** (*attrib*) of or for blind people: *a blind school.* **5** (*usu attrib*) having no doors, windows or other openings: *a blind wall.* **6** (*attrib*) extreme; without thinking: *blind haste/panic/fury.* – *nc* **1** a screen to prevent light coming through a window *etc*: *The sunlight is too bright – pull the blind down!* **2** (*inf*) something intended to mislead or deceive: *He did that as a blind.* – *See also* **the blind** *below.* – *vt* **1** to make blind: *He was blinded in the war.* **2** (of a bright light *etc*) to prevent from seeing clearly for a moment: *I was blinded by the car headlights.*

'blinding *adj* (*esp attrib*) **1** tending to make blind: *a blinding shower of sparks.* **2** tending to prevent from seeing clearly for a moment: *He shone a blinding light into my face.* **3** sudden: *He realized, in a blinding flash, that she was the murderer.*

'blindly *adv.* **'blindness** *nu.*

blind alley *nc* **1** an alley with only one opening. **2** (*fig*) a situation without any way out: *This is a blind alley of a job.*

blind date *nc* (an informal social appointment with) someone of the opposite sex whom one has never met before: *She first met her husband on a blind date*; *He was her blind date.*

'blindfold *nc* a piece of cloth *etc* put over the eyes to prevent someone from seeing: *The kidnappers put a blindfold over the child's eyes.* – *vt* to put a blindfold on (some person or animal). – *adj* (*pred*), *adv* with the eyes covered by a cloth *etc*: *She was blindfold when she came into the room.*

'blind spot *nc* **1** any matter about which one always shows lack of understanding: *She seems to have a blind spot about physics.* **2** an area which is impossible or difficult to see (from a car *etc*) due to an obstruction (*eg* the window frame of the car).

blind drunk (*inf*) completely drunk.

the blind leading the blind one inexperienced or incompetent person telling another about something: *My teaching you about politics will be a case of the blind leading the blind.*

not a 'blind bit of (*inf*) not any: *Her comments didn't make a blind bit of difference to his attitude.*

turn a blind eye *see* **turn**.

blink [bliŋk] 1 *vti* to move (the eyelids) rapidly up and down: *It is impossible to stare for a long time without blinking.* 2 *vi* (*formal or liter*) (of a light) to shine unsteadily. – *nc* a rapid movement of the eyelids.

'blinkers *n pl* leather flaps on a bridle preventing a horse from seeing sideways.

bliss [blis] *nu* (*formal or liter*) very great happiness: *heavenly bliss*; *the bliss of a young married couple.* **'blissful** *adj*. **'blissfully** *adv*.

blister ['blistə] *nc* 1 a thin bubble on the skin, containing liquid: *My feet have blisters after walking so far.* 2 a similar spot on any surface: *Look at the blisters on that paintwork.* – *vti* to (cause to) rise in a blister or blisters: *His skin blisters easily*; *The heat blistered the paint.*

blithe [blaið] *adj* (*liter*) happy and light-hearted: *She is merry and blithe*; *a blithe young girl.* **'blithely** *adv*.

blitz [blits] *nc* a sudden, vigorous attack, *orig* in war: (*inf*) *I'll make a blitz on my washing today.* – *vt* to make such an attack on (*usu* in war): *They blitzed London during the war.*

blizzard ['blizəd] *nc* a blinding storm of wind and snow: *Two climbers are missing after yesterday's blizzard.*

bloated ['bloutid] *adj* swollen and puffed out: *She felt bloated after eating so much*; *a bloated feeling.*

blob [blob] *nc* a (*usu* small) shapeless mass of liquid *etc*: *a blob of paint*; *a blob of wax.*

bloc [blok] *nc* a group of nations *etc* who have an interest or purpose in common: *the European trade bloc.*

block [blok] *nc* 1 a mass of wood or stone *etc*, *usu* flat-sided: *Blocks of stone are often used in building.* 2 (*often in cmpds*) a piece of wood used for certain purposes: *a chopping-block*; *a child's building blocks.* 3 a connected group of houses, offices *etc*: *a block of flats*; *an office/apartment block.* 4 a barrier: *The police set up a road block to catch the thieves.* 5 (*esp Amer*) a group of buildings bounded by four streets: *I'll take a walk round the block.* 6 (*Amer*) the length of one of these four sides: *My house is five blocks away.* 7 an area of seating in a theatre *etc*: *We're sitting in block A.* 8 (*hist*) a large piece of wood on which a person laid his head when being beheaded. – *vt* to make (progress) difficult or impossible: *A snowdrift blocked his path*; *The opposition blocked the passage of the bill through parliament.*

bloc'kade [-'keid] *nc* something which blocks every approach to a place by land or sea. – *vt*: *The ships blockaded the town.*

'blockage [-kidʒ] 1 *nc* something causing a pipe *etc* to be blocked: *There's a blockage in the pipe, so the water has stopped flowing*; *He is suffering from a blockage in a blood-vessel.* 2 *nu* the state of being blocked: *Don't put rubbish in the sink – it causes blockage of the drains.*

blocked *adj* obstructed or closed by some sort of block (*def* 4): *I have a bad cold – my nose is blocked*; *The sink drain is blocked with tea-leaves*; *a blocked drain.*

block capital/letter *nc* a capital letter written in imitation of printed type (*eg* those in NAME, the first letter of a sentence *etc*). – *See also* **upper case** *under* **case**[2].

'blockhead *nc* (*inf*) a stupid person.

bloke [blouk] *nc* (*Brit inf*) a man: *I've seen that bloke somewhere before.*

blond [blond] – *fem* **blonde** – *adj* having light-coloured hair: *a blond child.*

blonde *nc* a woman with light-coloured hair: *Last night I took a blonde to dinner.*

blood [blʌd] *nu* 1 the red fluid pumped through the body by the heart: *Blood poured from the wound in his side.* 2 descent or ancestors, *esp* royal or aristocratic: *He is of royal blood.* 3 (*inf or liter*) temper: *His behaviour really made by blood boil* (= made me very angry); *His blood is up* (= He is very angry).

'bloodless *adj* 1 (*liter*: *usu attrib*) without the shedding of blood: *a bloodless victory.* 2 (*not a tech term*: *usu pred*) having fewer red blood cells than normal; anaemic: *She is definitely bloodless.* 3 (*formal or liter*) uninteresting; having no energy: *a bloodless young man.*

'bloody *adj* 1 stained with blood: *a bloody shirt*; *His clothes were torn and bloody.* 2 bleeding: *a bloody nose.* 3 (*formal or liter*) murderous and cruel: *a bloody battle*; *The last battle was the most bloody.* 4 (*inf*: *offensive to many people*: *attrib*) used for emphasis: *That bloody car ran over my foot!*

'bloodbath *nc* (*formal or liter*) a battle *etc* during which many people are killed: *The Battle of the Somme was a bloodbath.*

'bloodcurdling *adj* (*esp attrib*) terrifying and horrible: *a blood-curdling scream.*

'blood dónor *nc* a person who gives blood for use by another person in transfusion *etc*.

'blood group/type *nc* any one of the types into which human blood is classified: *Her blood group is O.*

'blood heat *nu* the normal temperature of human blood (about 37° Centigrade, 98° Fahrenheit).

'bloodhound *nc* a large dog with a very good sense of smell, used for tracking.

'blood-poisoning *nu* an infection of the blood: *He is suffering from blood-poisoning.*

'blood pressure *ncu* the (amount of) pressure of the blood on the walls of the blood-vessels: *The nurse will take your blood pressure*; *The excitement will raise his blood pressure.*

'bloodshed *nu* (*formal*) deaths or shedding of blood: *There was much bloodshed in the battle.*

'bloodshot *adj* (of eyes) full of red lines and inflamed with blood: *My eyes are bloodshot because of lack of sleep*; *bloodshot eyes.*

'blood sports *n pl* those sports in which animals are killed: *Fox-hunting is one of the common blood sports.*

'bloodstained *adj* stained with blood: *a blood-stained bandage*; *The murderer's clothes were blood-stained.*

'bloodstock *nu* thoroughbred horses.

'bloodstream *nu* the blood flowing through the body: *She died because the poison entered her bloodstream.*

'bloodthirsty *adj* 1 eager to kill people: *a blood-thirsty warrior*; *That general is cruel and bloodthirsty.* 2 (of a film *etc*) full of scenes in which there is much killing. **'bloodthirstiness** *nu*.

'blood-vessel *nc* any of the tubes in the body through which the blood flows: *He has burst a blood-vessel.*

ˌbloody-'minded *adj* (*inf derog*) deliberately awkward or uncooperative: *I wish he wouldn't be so bloody-minded – he should just do what he is told*; *a bloody-minded old fool.* **ˌbloody-'mindedness** *nu*.

in cold blood while free from excitement or passion: *He killed his son in cold blood.*

bloom [blu:m] (*formal*) **1** *nc* a flower: *These blooms are withering now.* **2** *nu* the state of flowering: *The flowers are in bloom.* **3** *nu* (*often fig*) freshness or perfection: *in the bloom of youth.* – *vi* **1** to flower: *The roses are blooming; Daffodils bloom in the spring.* **2** to flourish: *She was ill but she's blooming now.*

'blooming *adj* **1** flowering: *a blooming plant.* **2** flourishing: *in blooming health; You're looking blooming today.* **3** (*inf euph: attrib*) cursed, damned, or extremely: *What a blooming stupid thing to do; The blooming idiot!*

bloomer ['blu:mə] *nc* (*Brit inf*) a mistake: *Putting the letter in the wrong envelope was a bloomer.*

bloomers ['blu:məz] *n pl* **1** (*hist*) a woman's garment, like short loose trousers gathered at the knee, worn for games *etc.* **2** (*old or inf facet*) knickers, *esp* of the kind that reach to the knee.

blossom ['blosəm] **1** *nc* a flower, *esp* of a fruit tree: *What a beautiful blossom!* **2** *nu* all such flowers considered together: *apple blossom.* – *vi* **1** (*formal*) to develop flowers: *My plant has blossomed.* **2** (*fig formal*) to flourish; to prosper: *She blossomed into a beautiful woman.* **'blossoming** *adj.*

blot [blot] *nc* **1** a spot or stain (often of ink): *The child's exercise book was full of blots.* **2** something ugly; something which spoils something beautiful or good: *a blot on the landscape; a blot on his reputation.* – *v* – *pt, ptp* **'blotted** – *vt* **1** to spot or stain, *esp* with ink: *I blotted this sheet of paper in three places when my nib broke.* **2** to dry with blotting-paper: *Blot your signature before you fold the paper.* – *See also* **blot out** *below.*

'blotter *nc* a pad or sheet of blotting-paper.

'blotting-paper *nu* soft paper used for drying up ink.

blot one's copybook to make a bad mistake: *He has really blotted his copybook by being late for the interview.*

blot out *vt sep* **1** to hide from sight: *The rain blotted out the view.* **2** to conceal from memory: *I've blotted out all memory of that terrible day.*

blotch [blotʃ] *nc* a discoloured mark (often large) on paper, skin *etc*: *Those red blotches on her face are very ugly.*

blotched, 'blotchy *adjs* having or covered in blotches.

blouse [blauz] *nc* a woman's (often loose) garment for the upper half of the body: *She wore a skirt and blouse.*

blow[1] [blou] *nc* **1** (*more formal than* **hit**) a stroke or knock: *He received a blow on the head.* **2** a sudden misfortune: *Her husband's death was a real blow.*

come to blows (with) to begin to fight (with) *usu* with fists: *The two boys often quarrel but they don't usually come to blows (with each other).*

strike a blow for *see* **strike**.

blow[2] [blou] – *pt* **blew** [blu]: *ptp* **blown** – **1** *vi* (of a current of air) to be moving: *The wind blew more strongly.* **2** *vt* (of *eg* wind) to cause (something) to move in a given way: *The explosion blew off the lid; Blow away all the dust!* **3** *vi* to be moved by the wind or a current of air: *The door must have blown shut.* **4** *vi* to drive air (upon or into): *Please blow into this tube!* **5** *vt* to make a sound by means of (a musical instrument *etc*): *He blew the horn loudly.* **6** *vti* to burst or break: *Take care not to blow a fuse; The fuse has blown.* **7** *vi* to breathe heavily after exercise *etc*: *The horse was blowing slightly after the race.* – *See also* **blow** *in phrases below.*

'blowy *adj* (*inf*) windy: *It's very blowy on the beach today; a blowy day.*

'blowhole *nc* a breathing-hole (through the ice for seals *etc*) or a nostril (*esp* on the head of a whale *etc*).

'blow-lamp, 'blow-torch *ncs* a lamp for aiming a very hot flame at a particular spot: *The joiner burned the paint off the wood with a blow-lamp.*

'blowout *nc* **1** the bursting of a car tyre: *That's the second blowout I've had with this car.* **2** (on *eg* an oil rig) a violent escape of gas *etc.* **3** (*sl*) a huge feast: *We had a blowout on his birthday.*

'blowpipe *nc* a tube from which a dart (often poisonous) is blown.

blow-up *see* **blow up** (*def 4*).

blow one's nose to clear the nose by breathing out sharply through it into a handkerchief.

blow one's top (*inf*) to become very angry: *She blew her top when he arrived home late.*

blow out *vt sep* to extinguish or put out (a flame *etc*) by blowing: *The wind blew out the candle; The child blew out the match.*

blow over *vi* to pass and become forgotten: *The trouble will soon blow over.*

blow the gaff *see* **gaff**.

blow up 1 *vi, vt sep* to break into pieces, or be broken into pieces, by an explosion: *The bridge blew up/was blown up; The soldiers blew the factory up.* **2** *vt sep* to fill with air or a gas: *He blew up the balloon; He blew the tyre up with difficulty.* **3** *vi* (*inf*) to lose one's temper: *If he says that again I'll blow up.* **4** *vt sep* to enlarge (a photograph *etc*) (*nc* **'blow-up**). **5** *vt sep* (*sl*) to scold or speak to (someone) angrily: *She blew me up for arriving late.*

blubber ['blʌbə] *nu* the fat of whales and other sea animals. – *vi* (*inf*) to weep noisily: *Stop blubbering and act like a man!*

bludgeon ['blʌdʒən] *vt* (*formal*) **1** to strike repeatedly with something heavy and blunt. **2** to force (often by repeated arguments *etc*): *She bludgeoned me into doing something which I didn't want to do.* – *nc* a short stick with a heavy end.

blue [blu:] *adj* **1** of the colour of a cloudless sky: *blue paint; Her eyes are blue.* **2** vulgarly sexual: *blue jokes; His jokes were a bit blue; a blue film.* **3** (*inf: pred*) sad or depressed: *I'm feeling blue today.* – **1** *ncu* (any shade of) the colour of a cloudless sky: *That is a beautiful blue.* **2** *ncu* a blue paint, material *etc*: *We'll have to get some more blue.* **3** *nu* (*liter*) the sky or the sea: *The balloon floated off into the blue.* **4** *nc* an award given to a person, *esp* at Oxford or Cambridge Universities, who has represented his college *etc* in sports. **5** *nc* such a person: *He's a Cambridge blue.*

'blueness *nu.*

'bluish *adj* quite blue; close to blue: *a bluish green; Her eyes are bluish.*

'bluebell *nc* **1** the wood hyacinth, which has blue, bell-shaped flowers. **2** in Scotland and N England, the harebell.

'bluebottle *nc* a kind of large house-fly with a blue abdomen: *There's a bluebottle buzzing round the kitchen.*

ˌblue'collar *adj* (*attrib*) (of workers) wearing overalls and working in factories *etc*: *Bluecollar workers are demanding the same pay as office staff.*

'blueprint *nc* a detailed photographic plan of work to be carried out: *the blueprints for a new aircraft; (fig) a blueprint for success.*

'bluestocking *nc* (*often derog*) a very educated

woman; a woman who is interested in serious, intellectual subjects: *She never comes to parties – she's too much of a bluestocking.*

ˌ**blue-eyed 'boy** (*derog*) a favourite: *He will get promotion – he's the boss's blue-eyed boy.*

the blues 1 (*inf*) low spirits; depression: *He's got the blues today but he's usually cheerful.* **2** a form of jazz music with sad themes, of American Negro origin.

once in a blue moon very seldom: *He visits his mother once in a blue moon.*

out of the blue without warning: *He arrived out of the blue, without phoning first.*

bluff[1] [blʌf] *adj* rough, hearty and frank: *His manner was bluff and friendly; He's a bluff old man who doesn't hesitate to say what he thinks.* **'bluffness** *nu.*

bluff[2] [blʌf] *vti* to deceive, or try to deceive, by pretending to have something (*eg* an advantage) that one does not have: *He bluffed his way through the exam without actually knowing anything; He's only bluffing.* – *nc* an act of bluffing: *Her bluff did not deceive them.*

bluff[3] [blʌf] *nc* a steep cliff, *esp* along a seashore or river.

blunder ['blʌndə] *vi* **1** to stumble (about or into something): *In the darkness, he blundered into the door.* **2** to make a (bad) mistake: *He really blundered when he insulted the boss's wife.* – *nc* a (bad) mistake: *They made a real blunder when they insulted the President.*

blunderbuss ['blʌndəbʌs] *nc* an old-fashioned short hand-gun with a wide-mouthed barrel.

blunt [blʌnt] *adj* **1** (of objects) having no point or sharp edge: *a blunt knife; This razor-blade is blunt.* **2** (of people) (sometimes unpleasantly) straightforward or frank in speech: *He has a blunt manner; She was very blunt, and said that she did not like him.* – *vt* **1** to make less sharp: *This knife has been blunted by years of use;* (*fig*) *The bad news has blunted my appetite;* (*fig*) *My pay rise will blunt the effect of the tax increases.*

'bluntly *adv.* **'bluntness** *nu.*

blur (blɜ:] *nc* something not clearly seen: *Everything is just a blur when I take my spectacles off.* – *v* – *pt, ptp* **blurred** – *vti* to make or become unclear: *The rain blurred my vision; The issue was blurred by the lack of information.* **blurred, blurry** *adjs.*

blurb [blɜ:b] **1** *nc* (*inf*) a publisher's description of a book, *usu* printed on the jacket. **2** *nu* (*derog*) material advertising things for sale *etc*: *That travel company keeps sending me blurb about holidays abroad.*

blurt [blɜ:t]: **blurt out** *vt sep* to say (something) suddenly or without thinking of the effect or result: *He blurted out the whole story; He blurted the truth out.*

blush [blʌʃ] *nc* a red glow on the skin caused by shame, embarrassment *etc.* – *vi* to show shame, embarrassment *etc* by growing red in the face: *That girl blushes easily.*

bluster ['blʌstə] *vi* to speak in a boasting, angry or threatening way (*usu* with little effect): *He's only blustering, since he can't really carry out his threats.* – *nu* this type of speech. **'blustering** *adj, nu.*

'blustery *adj* (of the wind) blowing in irregular, strong gusts: *Yesterday the weather was very blustery; a blustery day.*

boa ['bouə] *nc* **1** (*usu* **boa constrictor**) a kind of large snake that kills by winding itself round its prey. **2** a long scarf-like garment (*usu* made of feathers).

boar [bo:] **1** *nc* a male pig (*esp* the wild variety). **2** *nu* its flesh.

board [bo:d] **1** *nc* a strip of timber: *The windows of the old house had boards nailed across them.* **2** *nc* (*often in cmpds*) a flat piece of wood *etc* for a special purpose: *notice-board; chessboard; diving-board.* **3** *nu* meals: *We paid for board and lodging.* **4** *nc* an official group of persons controlling or administering an organization *etc*: *He is on the school's board of directors.* **5** *nc* (*usu in pl*) a sheet of stiff material, *esp* for binding books. – **1** *vt* to enter, or get on to (a *usu* passenger-carrying vehicle, ship, plane *etc*): *This is where we board the bus; They boarded the Birmingham train; The pirates boarded* (= climbed aboard in order to capture) *the ship.* **2** *vi* to live temporarily and take meals (in someone else's house): *He boards at Mrs Smith's during the week.* **3** *vt* to have (someone) to stay under such an arrangement (*usu* for money): *She can board three students.* – *See also* **board up** *below.*

'boarder *nc* a person who temporarily lives, and takes his meals, in someone else's house.

above-board *see* **above**.

across-the-board *see* **across the board** *below.*

'boarding-house *nc* a house where people live and take meals as paying guests: *She runs a boarding-house.*

'boarding-pass *nc* a card or piece of paper which allows one to go on board a plane.

'boarding-school *nc* a school which provides accommodation and food as well as instruction.

'boardroom *nc* a room in which the meetings of a board of directors *etc* are held.

across the board (*with hyphen when attrib*) applying in all cases: *They were awarded wage increases across the board;* (*attrib*) *an across-the-board increase in wages.*

board up *vt sep* to cover with boards: *board up a hole.*

go by the board (*inf*) to be abandoned or thrown aside: *All my plans went by the board when I lost my job.*

on 'board on, or in, a ship, plane *etc*: *There were fifty people on board when the ship sank.*

boast [boust] **1** *vi* to talk with too much pride: *He was always boasting about how clever his son was.* **2** *vt* (*formal*) to possess proudly: *Our office boasts the finest view for miles.* – *nc* **1** the words used in talking proudly about something: *His boast is that he has never yet lost a match.* **2** (*formal*) the thing about which one speaks proudly: *Her beauty was the boast of the town.* **'boastful** *adj.* **'boastfully** *adv.* **'boastfulness, 'boasting** *nus.*

boat [bout] *nc* **1** a small vessel for travelling over water: *We'll cross the stream by boat; We hired a rowing-boat.* **2** (*loosely*) a larger vessel for the same purpose; a ship: *We're going to cross the Atlantic in a passenger boat.* **3** (*usu in cmpds*) a serving-dish shaped like a boat: *a gravy-boat.* – *vi* (*also* **go boating**) to sail about in a small boat for pleasure: *They are boating on the Thames; We go boating every Sunday.*

'boathook *nc* a metal hook fixed to a pole, for pulling or pushing a boat.

'boathouse *nc* a covered place where boats are stored *etc.*

'boatman *nc* a man in charge of a small boat in which fare-paying passengers are carried.

'**boat train** *nc* a train taking passengers to or from a ship.

in the same boat (*inf fig*) in the same, *usu* difficult, position or circumstances: *We're all in the same boat as far as low wages are concerned.*

boater ['boutə] *nc* a round, stiff straw hat: *He wore a blazer and a boater.*

boatswain, bosun ['bousn] *nc* an officer who looks after a ship's boats, ropes, sails *etc.*

bob[1] [bob] *pt, ptp* **bobbed** – **1** *vi* to move (up and down): *The cork was bobbing about in the water.* **2** *vi* (*old*) to curtsy. – *nc* a curtsy.

bob[2] [bob] *pl* **bob** – *nc* (*old inf*) a shilling piece.

bobbin ['bobin] *nc* a (*usu* wooden) reel or spool for winding thread *etc*: *There's no thread left on the bobbin.*

bobby ['bobi] *nc* (*Brit inf*) a policeman: *Ask the bobby for directions.*

bobsleigh ['bobslei], **bobsled** ['bobsled] *ncs* a vehicle on metal runners used in crossing (and sometimes racing on) snow and ice.

bode [boud]: **bode ill/well** (*formal*) to be an omen of or to foretell bad or good fortune: *This bodes well for the future.*

bodice ['bodis] *nc* the part of a woman's or child's dress covering the upper part of the body (not the arms): *The dress had a fitted bodice and a full skirt; The child's skirt was attached to a bodice.*

bodied, bodily *see* **body**.

bodkin ['bodkin] *nc* a large blunt needle.

body ['bodi] **1** *nc* the whole frame of a man or animal including the bones and flesh: *Athletes have to look after their bodies.* **2** *nc* the frame of a man or animal, not including the head (and sometimes not including the arms or legs): *His body was badly burned in the accident but his face was unhurt.* **3** *nc* a dead person: *The battlefield was covered with bodies.* **4** *nc* (*no pl*) the main part of anything: *in the body of the hall.* **5** *nc* a mass: *a huge body of evidence.* **6** *nc* a group of persons considered to be acting as one: *He's a member of several professional bodies.* **7** *nu* the quality of being strong and substantial: *This wine has very little body* (= strength and flavour); *This shampoo will give your hair some body.*

-bodied (*in cmpds*) having (a) body (of a certain kind): *a ˌmetal-bodied 'car; an ˌable-bodied 'man; a ˌfull-bodied 'wine.*

'**bodily** *adj* (*attrib*) of the body: *You must satisfy your bodily needs.* – *adv* by the entire (physical) body: *They lifted him bodily and carried him off.*

'**bodyguard** *nc* a guard or guards to protect (*esp* an important person): *the president's bodyguard.*

'**bodywork** *nu* the outer casing of a car *etc*: *The bodywork of his new car has rusted already.*

boffin ['bofin] *nc* (*inf sometimes derog*) a scientist: *These boffins are always thinking up ridiculous ideas.*

bog [bog] *ncu* very wet ground; marsh.

'**boggy** *adj*: *boggy ground; The path is boggy.*

be bogged down to be hindered in movement; to be prevented from making progress: *The tractor keeps getting bogged down in the mud;* (*fig*) *I'm getting bogged down in all this paperwork.*

bogey[1], **bogy** ['bougi] *nc* **1** (*myth*: *also* '**bogeyman,** '**bogyman** [-man] – *pls* '**bogeymen,** '**bogymen** [-men]) an evil spirit, ghost *etc.* **2** something specially feared: *Flying has always been a bogey to her.*

See also **bogie**.

boggle ['bogl] (*inf*) **1** *vi* to be almost overcome with amazement: *The mind boggles!* **2** *vt* (*Amer*) to amaze: *It boggles my mind!*

bogie, bogey[2] ['bougi] *nc* a four- or six-wheeled frame supporting part of a long vehicle, *eg* a railway carriage.

bogus ['bougəs] *adj* false; not genuine: *She was fooled by his bogus identity card; His foreign accent was bogus.*

bogy *see* **bogey**[1].

bohemian [bə'hi:miən] *nc* a person who lives in a way which is less restricted than most people's lives, taking no notice of conventional rules of behaviour. – *adj*: *The art teacher seemed rather bohemian to the rest of the staff; his bohemian habits.*

boil[1] [boil] **1** *vti* to turn rapidly from liquid to vapour when heated: *I'm boiling the water; The water's boiling.* **2** *vi* to contain something which is boiling: *The kettle's boiling* (= the water in the kettle is boiling). **3** *vti* to cook by boiling in water *etc*: *The potatoes have boiled; I've boiled the potatoes.* **4** *vi* (*inf*) to be hot: *I'm boiling in this thick coat!* **5** *vi* (*inf*) to be angry: *I was boiling when I saw the mess they had made.* – *See also* **boil over** *below.*

'**boiler** *nc* a vessel in which water is heated or steam is produced: *The central-heating boiler is broken.*

'**boilersuit** *nc* a pair of overalls: *The workman was wearing a boilersuit.*

'**boiling-point** *nc* the temperature at which something boils: *What is the boiling-point of water?*

boil over *vi* to boil and overflow: *The pan of water boiled over and spilt on the floor.*

on, to the boil at or towards boiling-point: *The kettle's on the boil; Bring the water to the boil; The milk's coming to the boil.*

boil[2] [boil] *nc* an inflamed swelling on the skin: *His neck is covered with boils.*

boisterous ['boistərəs] *adj* wild and noisy: *a boisterous party/child; He is very boisterous today.*

bold [bould] *adj* **1** daring or fearless: *The soldiers thought of a bold plan of attack.* **2** (*old or formal*) impudent: *Would you think me bold if I asked how much your hat cost?; a bold remark.* **3** striking and well-marked: *a dress with bold stripes.* **4** (of type) thick and clear, **like this**. '**boldly** *adv.* '**boldness** *nu.*

bold as brass (*inf*) very cheeky: *She walked in late as bold as brass.*

if I may be/make so bold (as to) (*formal*) if I may dare (to do or say something): *If I may be so bold as to speak frankly, I find your comments offensive.*

bolero ['bolərou] – *pl* '**boleros** – *nc* a short jacket with no fastening.

Bolivia, Bolivian *see* Appendix 2.

bollard ['bola:d] *nc* **1** a post used on a traffic island or to keep traffic away from a certain area: *They have closed off the pedestrian shopping area with bollards.* **2** a short post on a wharf or ship round which ropes are fastened.

bolshie, bolshy ['bolʃi] *adj* (*derog sl*) deliberately uncooperative or unhelpful: *He gets very bolshie when asked to do something he doesn't agree with; She's in a bolshy mood.*

bolster ['boulstə] *nc* a long, often round pillow. – *v* – *pt, ptp* '**bolstered** – *vt* (*often with* **up**) to prop up; to support: *We're getting a loan to bolster (up) the economy.*

bolt [boult] *nc* **1** a bar to fasten a door *etc*: *The burglars couldn't get in because of the bolt which I'd* *fitted.* 2 a thick round bar of metal, often with a screw thread for a nut: *nuts and bolts.* 3 a flash of lightning. 4 a roll (of cloth): *a bolt of silk.* – 1 *vt* to fasten with a bolt: *He bolted the door.* 2 *vt* to swallow hastily: *The child bolted her food.* 3 *vi* to go away very fast: *The horse bolted in terror.*

'bolthole *nc* a place into which an animal runs to escape: *a rabbit's bolthole*; (*fig*) *There's a secret bolthole behind this wall so that we can escape.*

ˌbolt(-)'upright *adv* absolutely upright: *She sat bolt upright in the chair with her back very straight.*

a bolt from the blue a sudden, unexpected happening: *His resignation was a bolt from the blue.*

ˌmake a 'bolt for it to (attempt to) run away very fast: *The prisoners made a bolt for it when the guard wasn't looking.*

bomb [bom] *nc* a hollow case containing explosives or other harmful material: *The enemy dropped a bomb on the factory and blew it up.* – 1 *vt* to drop bombs on; to place bombs in *etc*: *London was bombed several times.* 2 *vi* (*sl*) to fail miserably: *The play bombed on the first night.*

'bomber *nc* 1 an aeroplane built for bombing. 2 a person who bombs: *Bombers have caused many deaths in Northern Ireland.*

'bombshell *nc* (*fig*) a piece of startling and often very bad news: *His resignation was a real bombshell.*

'bombsite *nc* an area in a town where a bomb has exploded and left only ruins.

go like a bomb (*sl*) 1 to move very fast: *My car goes like a bomb.* 2 to sell extremely well; to be very successful: *These pop-records go like a bomb*; *The party is going like a bomb.*

bombard [bəm'baːd] *vt* 1 to attack with artillery: *They bombarded the town.* 2 to direct questions *etc* at: *The reporters bombarded the film star with questions.* **bom'bardment** *ncu.*

bombastic [bom'bastik] *adj* (*formal*) fond of pompous, meaningless talk: *bombastic prose.*

bona fide [bounə'faidi] *adv, adj* (*esp attrib*) genuine(ly) or legal(ly): *It's a bona fide agreement*; *He has a bona fide excuse*; *He travelled bona fide.*

bonanza [bə'nanzə] *nc* (*inf*) a sudden increase (in profits *etc*): *Shopkeepers in seaside towns enjoy a bonanza in hot summers.*

bond [bond] *nc* 1 (*usu in pl*: *liter*) something used for tying (*esp* a person): *They released the prisoner from his bonds.* 2 (*fig*) something that unites or joins people together: *a bond of friendship.* 3 a written promise to pay a sum of money, *usu* by a certain date. – *See also* **premium bond**. 4 (*formal*) a join (*esp* by a sticky, glue-like substance). – *vti* to join or to be joined by adhesive: *This glue will bond plastic to wood.*

bonded store/warehouse *nc* a warehouse where goods are kept until customs or other duty on them is paid.

in'bond awaiting (in a bonded warehouse) payment of customs duty: *The whisky is in bond.*

bondage ['bondidʒ] *nu* (*liter*) slavery: *Peasants were kept in bondage by their masters.*

bone [boun] 1 *nu* the hard substance forming the skeleton of man, animals *etc*: *Bone decays far more slowly than flesh.* 2 *nc* a piece of this substance: *She broke two of the bones in her foot*; *All that was left of the corpse was the bones*; (*fig*) *the bare bones* (= the basic parts) *of her argument.* – *vt* to take the bones out of (fish *etc*): *Get the butcher to bone the joint of beef.*

-boned (*in cmpds*) having (a particular kind of) bones: *a small-boned person.*

boned *adj* with bones removed: *boned fish.*

'bony *adj* 1 (*attrib*) like bone: *a bony substance.* 2 full of bones: *bony fish*; *This fish is very bony.* 3 thin: *bony fingers; She is tall and bony.*

bone china *nu* china in whose manufacture the ashes of burnt bones are used.

ˌbone-'dry *adj* (*usu pred*) completely dry: *'Are those sheets damp?' 'No, they're bone-dry.'*

bone meal *nu* ground bones, used as fertilizer *etc.*

bone idle (*inf*) very lazy: *He could find a job but he's bone idle.*

a bone of contention a cause of argument or quarrelling: *Who should inherit their uncle's estate was a bone of contention between the two men for many years.*

have a bone to pick with (someone) to have something to disagree or argue about, with (a person): *I've (got) a bone to pick with you.*

make no bones about to have no hesitation about (stating or doing something openly): *They made no bones about (telling us) how they felt.*

to the bone 1 thoroughly and completely: *I was chilled to the bone.* 2 to the minimum: *I've cut my expenses to the bone.*

bonfire ['bonfaiə] *nc* a large fire in the open air, often built to celebrate something: *Many people in Britain have bonfires on November 5*; (*attrib*) *bonfire night.*

bonnet ['bonit] *nc* 1 (*usu* baby's or (old) woman's) head-dress fastened under the chin *eg* by strings. 2 (*Amer* **hood**) the cover of a motor-car engine *etc*: *Lift the bonnet and have a look at the engine.*

bonny ['boni] *adj* 1 in Scotland, pretty and attractive: *a bonny girl*; *She's very bonny*; *a bonny dress.* 2 healthy-looking and attractive: *a bonny baby.*

bonus ['bounəs] *nc* 1 an addition to the sum due as interest, dividend, or wages: *a production bonus.* 2 something unexpected or extra: *The extra two days holiday was a real bonus.*

bony *see* **bone**.

boo [buː] – *pl* **boos** – *nc, interj* a derisive shout, made *eg* by a disapproving crowd, or by a person trying to startle another: *He ignored the boos of the crowd*; *He crept up behind her and shouted 'Boo!'.* – *v* – *3rd pers sing prt* **boos**: *pt, ptp* **booed** – *vti* to make such a sound at a person *etc*: *The crowd booed (him).*

boob [buːb] *nc* 1 (*inf*) a mistake: *Forgetting to invite her to the party was a real boob.* 2 (*sl: usu in pl*) a woman's breast. – *vi* (*inf*) to make a mistake: *You've boobed again.*

booby ['buːbi] *nc* (*arch*) a stupid person.

'booby prize *nc* a prize for the lowest score *etc*: *John came last and got the booby prize.*

'booby-trap *nc* 1 something laid as a trap, *eg* a bucket of water put above a door so as to fall on the person who opens the door. 2 a bomb or mine made to look like something harmless.

book [buk] *nc* 1 a number of sheets of paper (*esp* printed) bound together: *Where's my exercise book!* 2 a piece of writing, bound and covered: *I've written a book on Shakespeare.* 3 a record of bets: *to keep/make a book.* 4 a small card folder containing stamps, matches *etc*: *a book of matches*; *a book of stamps.* 5 the words of an opera: *She wrote the music and he wrote the book.* – *See also* **books** *below.* – 1 *vti* to buy or reserve (a ticket, seat *etc*) for a play *etc*: *I've booked four seats* *for Friday's concert*; *Can we book in advance?* **2** *vt* to hire in advance: *We've booked the orchestra to appear here on Saturday.* **3** *vt* to charge with a legal offence: *He was booked for speeding.* – *See also* **book in** *below.*

'bookable *adj* (*usu pred*) able to be reserved in advance: *Are these seats bookable?*

'bookie *nc* (*inf*) a bookmaker.

'bookish *adj* (*derog*) having, or showing, too much fondness for reading: *She's a very bookish child.*

'booklet [-lit] *nc* a small, thin book: *They have published a booklet about the history of the town.*

books *n pl* records, *eg* of a business: *My accountant looks after my books.*

'bookbinding *nu* putting the covers on books. **'bookbinder** *nc.*

'bookcase *nc* a set of shelves for books.

'bookend *nc* (*usu in pl*) one of a pair of (*usu* heavy) objects used to keep a row of books upright.

'booking-office *nc* an office where travel tickets *etc* are sold: *There was a queue at the station booking-office.*

'book-keeping *nu* the keeping of accounts. **'book-keeper** *nc.*

'bookmaker *nc* a professional betting man who takes bets and pays winnings.

'bookmark *nc* something put in a book to mark a particular page: *He used a bus-ticket as a bookmark.*

'bookstall *nc* a small shop in a station *etc* where books *etc* are sold.

'bookworm *nc* (*inf*: *sometimes derog*) a person who reads a lot.

'be in someone's 'good/'bad/'black books to be in or out of favour with someone: *The salesman has been in the manager's good books since he increased last year's sales*; *Even since he forgot about her birthday he has been in her black books.*

booked up 1 having every ticket sold: *The theatre is booked up for the season.* **2** fully engaged; completely busy: *I'm booked up till August.*

book in 1 *vi* to sign one's name on the list of guests at an hotel *etc*: *We have booked in at the Royal Hotel.* **2** *vt sep* to reserve a place for (someone) in a hotel *etc*: *My aunt is coming to stay so I've booked her in at the nearest hotel.*

bring to book (*formal*) to make (a person) explain, or suffer for, his behaviour.

by the book strictly according to the rules: *She always does things by the book.*

in 'my book in my opinion: *In my book your behaviour was perfectly justified.*

boom[1] [bu:m] *nc* a sudden increase in a business *etc*: *There's been a boom in the sales of TV sets.* – *vi* to increase suddenly (and become more profitable): *Business is booming this week.*

'boom town *nc* a suddenly prosperous town: *The discovery of gold in the area changed the quiet market town into a boom town overnight.*

boom[2] [bu:m] *vi* (*often with* **out**) to make a hollow sound, like a large drum or gun: *His voice boomed out over the loudspeaker.* – *nc* such a sound: *the boom of the guns.*

boom[3] [bu:m] *nc* **1** a pole by which the bottom edge of a sail is kept stretched. **2** a barrier across a harbour entrance. **3** a long pole for an overhead microphone.

boomerang ['bu:məraŋ] *nc* a curved piece of wood used by Australian aborigines, so balanced that, when thrown to a distance, it returns to the thrower. – *vi* (*formal*) (of an act, plan *etc*) to go wrong and do harm to the person who did or thought of it: *His evil plot boomeranged on him.*

boon[1] [bu:n] *nc* a thing to be thankful for; a blessing: *It's been a real boon to have a car this week.*

boon[2] [bu:n]: **boon companion** *nc* (*formal*) a person whose company one enjoys very much: *They used to be boon companions but now they are enemies.*

boor [buə] *nc* (*derog*) a coarse, ill-mannered person: *He's such a boor that I wouldn't invite him to my party.*

'boorish *adj*: *boorish manners/young men*; *His behaviour was extremely boorish.*

boost [bu:st] *vt* to expand; to make greater; to improve: *We've boosted the sales figures*; *It's boosted his reputation.* – *nc* **1** a piece of help, encouragement *etc*: *This publicity will give our sales a real boost.* **2** a push upwards: *Give me a boost up over the wall.*

'booster *nc* **1** a person or thing that boosts: *That was a real morale booster for me* (= That made me feel more cheerful and optimistic). **2** a device for increasing power, force *etc*: *I've fixed a booster on the TV aerial to improve the signal.* **3** the first stage of a rocket that works by several stages. **4** a later dose of vaccine *etc* which increases the effect of an earlier one: *a booster against polio*; (*attrib*) *a booster shot* (= injection) *against tetanus.*

boot[1] [bu:t] *nc* **1** a covering for the foot and lower part of the leg, *usu* made of leather *etc*: *I've bought a pair of suede boots.* **2** (*Amer* **trunk**) a place for luggage in a motor-car *etc*: *Put my case in the boot please.* **3** (*inf*) a kick: *He gave the ball such a boot that it disappeared from view.* – *vt* (*inf*) **1** to kick: *He booted the ball out of the goal.* **2** (*sl*) (*with* **out**) to throw (someone) out by force: *He was booted out of his last job.*

'bootlegger *nc* a person who smuggles alcoholic liquor.

give, get the boot (*sl*) to dismiss (someone) or to be dismissed (*usu* from a job): *He got the boot for always being late.*

put the boot in (*sl*: *often fig*) to attack (someone) viciously and unfairly: *When the firm was unable to pay higher wages the employees put the boot in and went on strike although they knew it would bankrupt the firm.*

boot[2] [bu:t]: **to 'boot** (*formal*) in addition; also: *She is beautiful, and wealthy to boot.*

bootee [bu:'ti:] *nc* a (usu knitted woollen) boot for a baby.

booth [bu:ð, (*Amer*) -θ] *nc* **1** a tent or stall, *esp* at a fair: *the fortuneteller's booth.* **2** (*sometimes in cmpds*) a small compartment for a given purpose: *a phone booth*; *a polling-booth.*

bootlegger *see* **boot**[1].

booty ['bu:ti] *nu* goods taken from *eg* an enemy by force (*esp* in wartime): *The soldiers shared the booty among themselves*; *The police found the burglars' booty hidden in the cellar.*

booze [bu:z] *nu* (*sl*) alcoholic drink: *Have you got enough booze for the party?* – *vi* (*sl*) to drink alcoholic drinks: *He's been boozing since the pub opened.*

'boozer *nc* (*sl*) **1** a drinker of alcohol: *He's known to be a boozer.* **2** a public house: *He goes to the boozer every Friday night.*

borax ['bo:raks] *nu* a mineral compound, found as a salty crust on the shores of certain lakes, used for cleaning *etc.* **bo'racic** [-sik] *adj.*

border ['bo:də] *nc* **1** the edge of a particular thing: *the border of a picture/handkerchief.* **2** the boundary of a country: *They'll ask for your passport at the border*; (*attrib*) *a border patrol.* **3** a flower bed round the edge of a lawn *etc*: *a flower border*; *a border of pansies.* – *vi* (*with* **on**) to come near to or lie on the border of: *Germany borders on France*; (fig) *This borders on the ridiculous.*

'**borderline** *adj* (*fig*) doubtful; on the border between one thing and another: *He was a borderline case, so we gave him an additional exam to see if he would pass it.* – *nc* the border between one thing and another: *He was on the borderline between passing and failing.*

the Borders the area of Scotland near its boundary with England.

bore[1] [bo:] *vt* to make (a hole *etc* in something) by using a drill, by digging *etc*: *He bored a hole in the kitchen wall*; *They bored a tunnel under the sea.* – *nc* the size of the hollow barrel of a gun.

'**borehole** *nc* a hole made by boring, *esp* to find oil *etc.*

bore[2] [bo:] *vt* to make (someone) feel tired and uninterested, by being dull *etc*: *He bores everyone with stories about his travels.* – *nc* a dull, boring person or thing: *He's such a bore*; *It's a bore to have to go out again.*

'**boredom** *nu* the state of being bored.

'**boring** *adj*: *a boring job*; *This book is boring.*

bore[3] *see* **bear**[1].

bore[4] [bo:] *nc* a tidal wave which moves quickly up certain rivers.

born, borne *seq* **bear**[1].

borough ['bʌrə, (*Amer*) 'bə:rou] *nc* **1** (*Brit hist*) a town with a corporation and special privileges granted by royal charter. **2** any of the thirty-two local government areas into which Greater London is divided (excluding the City of London).

borough council *nc* in the UK, a district or parish council which has kept its historical title of 'borough', and whose chairman is called 'mayor'.

See also **burgh**.

borrow ['borou] *vt* **1** to take (something, often money) temporarily with the intention of returning it: *He borrowed a book from the library*; *She borrowed £1 from a friend.* **2** to adopt (words *etc*) from another language: *English borrows words from French.* '**borrower** *nc.*

'**borrowing 1** *nu* the taking of something temporarily with the intention of returning it: *The borrowing of money is not a good idea.* **2** *nc* a word *etc* adopted from another language: *Déjà vu is a borrowing from French.*

borstal ['bo:stl] **1** *nc* an institution where criminals who are under a certain age are sent. **2** *nu* (*loosely*) imprisonment in such a place: *John Smith got six months' borstal for beating up the old lady.*

bosom ['buzəm] *nc* **1** (*euph or old*) a woman's breasts: *She has a large bosom.* **2** (*euph*) the chest: *She held him tenderly to her bosom.* **3** (*fig*) the centre; the innermost part: *in the bosom of his family.* **4** (*liter*) the heart; the inner feelings: *Pity stirred within his bosom.* – *adj* (*formal*: *attrib*) intimate; close: *a bosom friend.*

boss[1] [bos] *nc* (*inf*) the master or manager: *He's the boss of the factory but his employees prefer the under-manager.* – *vt* (*usu with* **about/around**) to order: *Stop bossing everyone about!*

'**bossy** *adj* liking to order others about. '**bossily** *adv.* '**bossiness** *nu.*

boss[2] [bos] *nc* (*hist*) a round decoration in the centre of a shield *etc.*

See also **embossed**.

bosun *see* **boatswain**.

botany ['botəni] *nu* the scientific study of plants.

bo'tanic(al) [-'ta-] *adj.*

'**botanist** *nc* a person who studies botany.

botanic(al) gardens *n sing or pl* a public park for the growing of native and foreign plants.

botch [botʃ] *nc* (*inf*) a messy, badly done piece of work *etc*: *He made a botch of mending the table.* – *vt* (*inf*) to do (something) badly: *He really botched the job.*

both [bouθ] *adj, pron* the two; the one and the other: *We both went*; *Both (the) men are dead*; *The men are both dead*; *Both are dead.*

both . . . and not only . . . but also: *He's both rich and handsome*; *She has been successful both as a novelist and as a playwright.*

bother ['boðə] **1** *vt* to annoy or worry: *It bothers me that this situation can arise*; *Stop bothering me!* **2** *vi* to take the trouble: *Don't bother to write – it isn't necessary.* **1** *nu* trouble, nuisance or worry: *I had no bother finding your house*; *If it's no bother we'll come tomorrow.* **2** *nc* (*no pl*) something or someone that causes bother: *What a bother all this is!* – *interj* used to express mild annoyance: *Bother! I've cut my finger.*

'**bothersome** *adj* (*formal*) causing bother or annoyance: *a bothersome cough*; *That noise is very bothersome.*

bottle ['botl] *nc* **1** a hollow narrow-necked container for holding liquids *etc*: *a lemonade bottle*; *There are six pills left in this bottle.* **2** the amount contained in a bottle: *He drank three bottles of milk*; *The baby is crying for its bottle.* – *vt* to put into bottles: *Who bottled this wine?* – *See also* **bottle up** *below.*

'**bottle-feed** *vti* to feed a baby (with milk *etc*) from a bottle with a teat on it. ,**bottle-'fed** *adj.*

,**bottle-'green** *nu, adj* (of) a very dark green colour: *a bottle-green dress.*

'**bottleneck** *nc* a place where slowing down or stopping of progress occurs, *esp* a narrow part of a road which becomes very crowded with traffic: *There's a bottleneck where the motorway ends and the ordinary road begins*; *The strike has created a bottleneck in the assembly department.*

bottle up *vt sep* to prevent (*eg* one's feelings) from becoming known or obvious: *Don't bottle up your anger – tell him what's annoying you.*

bottom ['botəm] **1** *nu* the lowest part of anything: *The ship sank to the bottom of the sea*; (*attrib*) *It's on the bottom shelf.* **2** *nc* (the person in) the position of the least clever in a class *etc*: *He's (at) the bottom of the class.* **3** *nc* the upper part of the body on which a person sits. **4** *nc* the outside of the hull of a ship.

'**bottomless** *adj* (*formal*) very deep: *a bottomless pit*; *The lake is said to be bottomless.*

at 'bottom in reality: *At bottom, he's really a very shy person.*

be at the bottom of to be the cause of (*usu* something bad): *Who's at the bottom of these nasty rumours?*

bottom gear *see* **gear**.

get to the bottom of to discover the explanation of the real facts of (a mystery *etc*): *I'll get to the bottom of this somehow.*

boudoir ['bu:dwa:] *nc* (*old*) a lady's private sitting-room or bedroom.

bough [bau] *nc* (*liter*) a branch of a tree: *She sat* *under the bough of an apple tree.*

bought *see* **buy**.

boulder ['bouldə] *nc* a large rock or stone: *A boulder rolled down the mountain and killed the climber.*

boulevard ['buːləvaːd] (*esp in the US*) **1** *nc* a broad street, sometimes lined with trees. **2** *n* (*with cap*) a word often used in the names of such streets: *Our address is 121 Granger Boulevard.*

bounce [bauns] **1** *vti* to (cause to) spring or jump back from a solid surface, like a rubber ball thrown against a wall: *She was bouncing up and down with excitement*; *She bounced the ball over the net.* **2** *vi* (*inf*) (of a cheque) to be sent back unpaid, because of lack of money in a bank account: *I hope he doesn't try to cash that cheque today – it'll bounce unless I put some more money in my bank.* – **1** *nc* (of a ball *etc*) an act of springing back: *With one bounce the ball went over the net.* **2** *nu* (*inf*) energy and liveliness: *She has a lot of bounce.*

'**bouncing** *adj* (*usu attrib*) strong and lively: *a bouncing baby.*

bound[1] see **bind**.

bound[2] [baund] : **-bound** (*in cmpds*) going in a particular direction: *I'm homeward-bound*; *west-bound traffic.*

'**bound for** ready to go to or on the way to: *I'm bound for Africa.*

'**bound to 1** certain to: *He's bound to notice your mistake.* **2** obliged to: *I felt bound to mention it.*

ˌ**bound 'up in** busy or interested in: *He's very bound up in his work.*

ˌ**bound 'up with** closely concerned or connected with: *My personal finances are bound up with the future of the whole business.*

See also **-bound** *under* **bind**.

bound[3] [baund] *nc* (*formal*: *usu in pl*) limits of some kind: *This is beyond the bounds of co-incidence*; *His greed knows no bounds.* – *vt* (*formal or liter*) to surround or form the boundary of: *Great Britain is bounded by water on every side.*

'**boundless** *adj* tremendous; vast; having no limit: *He has boundless energy*; *She has boundless faith in her husband's ability*; *His strength is boundless.*

out of bounds outside the permitted area or limits: *The cinema was out of bounds for the boys from the local boarding-school.*

bound[4] [baund] *nc* a spring; a jump; a leap: *He reached me in one bound.* – *vi* to move in this way: *The dog bounded over eagerly to where I was sitting.*

by leaps and bounds *see* **leap**.

boundary ['baundəri] *nc* **1** an often imaginary line separating one thing from another: *the boundary between two towns*; (*fig*) *the boundary between the possible and the impossible.* **2** (in cricket) a hit which crosses the boundary line round the field, scoring four runs.

boundless *see* **bound**[3].

bounty ['baunti] **1** *nu* (*formal*) generosity in giving. **2** *nc* (*formal*) something given out of generosity: *He's given a bounty to the poor people of the town.* **3** *nc* in some countries, a reward given as encouragement (*eg* to kill or capture dangerous animals, criminals *etc*): *There's a bounty for foxes in some countries.*

'**bountiful,** '**bounteous** [-tiəs] *adjs* (*formal*: *usu attrib*) **1** generous: *bounteous gifts.* **2** plentiful: *a bountiful crop of wheat.*

bouquet [bu'kei] **1** *nc* a bunch of flowers arranged in a certain way, given as a gift, carried by a bride *etc*: *The little girl gave a bouquet to the Queen.* **2** *ncu* (*formal*) the perfume of wine: *This wine has an excellent bouquet.*

bourgeois ['buəʒwaː] *nc* (*derog*) **1** a person lacking in good taste, culture *etc.* **2** a member of the middle class. – *adj* (*derog*) lacking in good taste, culture *etc*: *His taste in furniture is very bourgeois*; *bourgeois attitudes.*

the ˌ**bourgeoi'sie** [-'ziː] *n pl* (*derog*) **1** people who are lacking in good taste, culture *etc.* **2** members of the middle class.

bout [baut] *nc* **1** a period or spell (of): *a violent bout of coughing*; *a severe bout of flu.* **2** a (*usu* boxing) contest: *a bout of fifteen five-minute rounds.*

boutique [buː'tiːk] *nc* a fashionable, *usu* small shop, *esp* one selling clothes: *She prefers small boutiques to large stores.*

bovine ['bouvain] *adj* **1** of or like a cow, ox *etc*: *bovine tuberculosis.* **2** (*derog*) (of people) dull or stupid: *She's become so bovine since she gave up work*; *a bovine expression.*

bow[1] [bau] **1** *vti* to bend (the head and often also the upper part of the body) forwards in greeting a person *etc*: *He bowed to the ladies*; *They bowed their heads in prayer.* **2** *vi* (*formal*: *with* **to**) to submit (to) or accept: *They've bowed to the inevitable*; *I bow to your superior knowledge.* – *nc* a bowing movement (of the head or body): *He made a bow to the ladies.*

bowed *adj* (*often with* **down**) bent downwards, *eg* by the weight of something: *The bowed heads of the praying women*; *The trees were bowed down with apples*; (*fig*) *He was bowed down by the huge responsibility.*

bow[2] [bou] *nc* **1** a springy curved rod bent by a string, by which arrows are shot: *He shot the deer with a bow and arrow.* **2** a rod with horsehair stretched along it, by which the strings of a violin *etc* are sounded. **3** a looped knot of ribbon, leather, nylon *etc* as in a bow tie, shoelace *etc*: *Tie your belt in a bow*; *Her dress is decorated with bows.*

bow tie *nc* a kind of tie for a man, made or tied in (the shape of) a bow (*def 3*).

bow window *nc* a curved bay window.

bow[3] [bau] *nc* (*often in pl*) the front part of a ship or boat, which cuts through the water when the ship *etc* is moving forwards: *The waves broke over the bows of the boat.*

bowel ['bauəl] *nc* **1** (*usu in pl*) the part of the food-processing or digestive system below the stomach; the intestines: *The surgeon removed part of her bowel*; *Have the child's bowels moved* (= Has the child defecated) *today?* **2** (*fig*: *in pl*) the inside of something, *esp* when deep: *in the bowels of the ship/the earth.*

bower ['bauə] *nc* (*liter*) **1** a place in a garden made shady by overhanging plants, trees *etc.* **2** a lady's private sitting-room.

bowl[1] [boul] *nc* a wooden ball rolled along the ground in playing bowls. – *See also* **bowls** *below.* – **1** *vi* (*formal*) to play bowls: *The old men bowl every day.* **2** *vti* to deliver or send (a ball) towards the batsman in cricket: *He bowled the ball so swiftly that the batsman missed it*; *He bowled the first over.* **3** *vt* to put (a batsman) out by hitting the wicket with the ball: *Smith was bowled for eighty-five* (= Smith was put out after making eighty-five runs).

'**bowler**[1] *nc* **1** a person who bowls in cricket *etc.* **2** a person who plays bowls.

'bowling *nu* the game of skittles, bowls or something similar.

bowls *n sing* a game played on a smooth green with bowls having a bias: *We often play bowls on Sunday afternoons*; *Let's have a game of bowls*; *Bowls is my favourite game.*

'bowling-alley *nc* **1** a long narrow set of wooden boards along which one bowls at skittles. **2** a building which contains several of these.

'bowling-green *nc* a smooth piece of grassland for playing bowls.

bowl along *vi* (*inf*) to speed along smoothly: *He bowled along in his new car.*

bowl over *vt sep* to knock down: *I was bowled over in the rush for the door*; (*fig*) *His generosity bowled me over.*

bowl[2] [boul] *nc* **1** (*often in cmpds*) a round, deep dish *eg* for mixing or serving food *etc*: *a baking-bowl*; *a soup bowl.* **2** the amount contained in such a dish: *I had three bowls of soup.* **3** a round hollow part, *esp* of a tobacco pipe, a spoon *etc*: *The bowl of this spoon is dirty.*

bowler[1] *see* **bowl**[1].

bowler[2] ['boulə] *nc* (*also* **bowler hat**) a type of hard, round felt hat: *The bank manager always wears a bowler when going to work.*

bowling *see* **bowl**[1].

box[1] [boks] **1** *nc* (*often in cmpds*) a case (*usu* of wood, metal or plastic, and with a lid) for holding something: *a wooden box*; *a black box*; *a matchbox*; *a letterbox.* **2** *nc* the amount contained in a box: *She ate three boxes of chocolates.* **3** *nc* in a theatre *etc*, a group of seats separated from the rest of the audience. **4** *ncu* a type of evergreen shrub or small tree: *a hedge of box.* **5** *nu, adj* (*also* **'boxwood**) (of) its hard wood. – *vt* (*formal*) to put (something) into boxes: *Will you box these apples?* – *See also* **box in** *below.*

'Boxing day *n* December 26, the day after Christmas day.

'box number *nc* a number used *eg* in a newspaper advertisement instead of a full address to which letters *etc* are to be sent: *There was no telephone number in the advertisement – only a box number*; *When I write to my husband in the army I use a PO* (= Post Office) *box number.*

'box office *nc* a ticket office in a theatre, concert-hall *etc*: *There's a queue at the box office for tonight's show.*

box in *vt sep* to block up (someone's exit): *My car's boxed in between yours and Peter's.*

box up *vt sep* (*inf*) to enclose or shut up in a small, uncomfortable space: *I'm boxed up in this tiny office all day*; (*fig*) *She keeps her feelings boxed up and you don't know what she's thinking.*

box the compass to name the thirty-two points of the compass, first clockwise and then anti-clockwise.

box[2] [boks] *vti* to fight (someone) with the fists: *Years ago, fighters used to box without wearing padded gloves.* – *nc* a blow on the ear with the hand.

'boxer[1] *nc*: *He's a champion boxer.*

'boxing *nu* the sport of fighting with the fists.

'boxing-glove *nc* a boxer's padded glove.

box someone's ears to strike someone on the ears: *The man boxed his son's ears for being impertinent.*

boxer[1] *see* **box**[2].

boxer[2] ['boksə] *nc* a medium-sized breed of dog with smooth brown hair.

boy [boi] *nc* **1** a male child: *He was only a boy when he died*; *She has three girls and one boy* (= son). **2** (*in cmpds*) a male (often adult) who does a certain job: *a cowboy*; *a paper-boy.*

'boyhood *nu* the time of being a boy: *He had a very happy boyhood*; (*attrib*) *boyhood memories.*

'boyish *adj* like a boy in appearance, manner *etc*: *boyish good looks*; *His appearance was boyish.*

'boyishly *adv.* **'boyishness** *nu.*

'boyfriend *nc* a girl's favourite male friend or usual male companion.

Boy Scout *see* **scout**.

boycott ['boikot] *vt* to refuse to have any social or business dealings with (a firm, country *etc*): *The trade unions have boycotted that firm because the workers are not members of a union.* – *nc* a ban on or refusal to deal with a firm *etc*: *Trade with that country is under boycott.*

bra [bra:] short for **brassière**.

brace [breis] *nc* **1** something that draws together and holds tightly: *He wears a brace to straighten his teeth.* **2** a pair or couple *usu* of game-birds: *a brace of pheasants.* – *vt* (*often refl*) to make firm or steady: *He braced himself for the struggle.*

'braces *n pl* (*also* **pair of braces** *nc*) (*Amer* **su'spenders**) straps over the shoulders for holding up the trousers.

'bracing *adj* healthy or filling with energy: *bracing sea air*; *I find this climate bracing.*

bracelet ['breislit] *nc* an ornament worn round the wrist or arm: *a gold bracelet.*

bracken ['brakən] *nu* the most common British fern: *The deer ran through the bracken.*

bracket ['brakit] *nc* **1** (*usu in pl*) in writing or printing, marks (*eg* ( ), [ ], { } , ⟨ ⟩ *etc*) used to enclose or group together one or more words, symbols *etc.* **2** a number of people regarded as a particular group: *He's in a very high tax bracket.* **3** a support for a shelf *etc*: *The shelf fell down because the brackets were not strong enough.* – *v* – *pt, ptp* **'bracketed** – *vt* **1** to enclose (words *etc*) by brackets. **2** (*sometimes with* **together**) to group together (similar or equal people or things): *All those books can be bracketed together in the category of fiction*; *Don't bracket me with him just because we work for the same company.*

brackish ['brakiʃ] *adj* (*formal*) (of water) tasting slightly of salt, often unpleasantly.

brag [brag] – *pt, ptp* **bragged** – *vi* to talk (about something) with too much pride; to boast: *He is always bragging that he is the best fighter.* – *nc* such talk: *He did not fulfil his brag that he could drink ten pints of beer.*

'braggart [-gət] *nc* (*old or formal*) a person who brags.

braid [breid] *vt* to plait or wind together (*esp* strands of hair): *Her mother braided her hair.* – **1** *nu* threads *etc* twisted together and used as decoration on uniforms, dresses *etc*: *There is gold braid on the admiral's uniform.* **2** *nc* a narrow piece (of hair *etc*) made by plaiting: *Her braids were tied with pink ribbon.*

braille [breil] *nu* a system of printing for the blind, using raised dots: *She has been taught to read braille.*

brain [brein] **1** *ncu* a greyish substance within the head; the centre of the nervous system: *The surgeon had to operate on her brain*; (*inf*) *He blew his brains out* (= shot himself through the head) (*attrib*) *brain surgery*; (*attrib*) *brain injury.* **2** *ncu* (*often in pl*) cleverness; intelligence; the mind:

She has a good brain; a man of very little brain; You've plenty of brains – why don't you use them! **3** *nc* (*inf*) a clever person: *He's one of the best brains in the country.* – *vt* (*sl*) to hit (someone) on the head with great force: *When the thief broke in I brained him with a hammer.*

'brainless *adj* (*inf*) stupid: *a brainless idiot; He's absolutely brainless.*

'brainy *adj* (*inf*) clever: *The elder child is the brainy one of the family; She's brainy.*

'brainchild *nc* a favourite theory, invention *etc* thought up by a particular person: *This entire process is Dr Smith's brainchild.*

'brain drain *nu* the loss of experts to another country (*usu* in search of better salaries *etc*): *As a result of the brain drain Britain does not have enough doctors.*

'brainstorm *nc* **1** a sudden mental disturbance: *He had a brainstorm and murdered his wife.* **2** (*Amer inf*) a brainwave.

'brainteaser *nc* a difficult puzzle.

'brainwash *vt* to force (a person) to obey, conform, confess *etc* by putting great (psychological) pressure on him: *The terrorists brainwashed him into believing in their ideals.* **'brainwashing** *nu.*

'brainwave *nc* a sudden bright idea: *It was a brainwave to come here for our holidays.*

pick (someone's) brains *see* **pick**[2].

braise [breiz] *vti* to stew (meat *etc*) slowly in a closed dish.

braised *adj*: *braised beef; braised celery.*

brake [breik] *vti* to slow down or stop (the motion of a wheel or vehicle): *He braked (the car) suddenly.* – *nc* (*often in pl*) a device for doing this: *He put on the brake; His car brakes failed.*

bramble ['brambl] *nc* **1** (*usu in pl*) a blackberry bush: *The child was badly scratched when she fell into the brambles.* **2** in Scotland, its fruit: *We gathered brambles yesterday; (attrib) bramble jelly.*

bran [bran] *nu* the outer covering of grain separated from the flour: *Doctors often recommend bran as part of a healthy diet; (attrib) a bran loaf.*

branch [bra:ntʃ] *nc* **1** an arm-like part of a tree: *He cut some branches off the oak tree.* **2** an offshoot from the main part (of a family, business, railway *etc*): *There isn't a branch of that store in this town; (attrib) That train runs on the branch line.* – *vi* (*usu with* **out/off**: *usu fig*) to spread out like, or into, a branch or branches: *He's left the family business and branched out on his own; The line to Guildford branches off here.*

brand [brand] *nc* **1** a maker's name or trademark: *What brand of tea do you use?; (attrib) That is the firm's brand name.* **2** (*fig*) a variety: *He has his own brand of humour.* **3** a mark on cattle *etc* to show who owns them, made with a hot iron. **4** (*liter*) a burning piece of wood, often used as a torch: *They set the fire alight with brands.* **5** (*liter*) a sword: *a brand dripping with blood.* – *vt* **1** to mark with a hot iron: *He branded the cattle.* **2** (*fig*) to make a permanent impression on: *His name is branded on my memory for ever.* **3** (*fig*) to attach (permanent) disgrace to: *He was branded for life as a thief.*

,brand-'new *adj* completely new: *a brand-new dress; The car is not brand-new but it has only had one previous owner.*

brandish ['brandiʃ] *vt* (*formal*) to wave (*esp* a weapon) about: *He brandished the stick above his head.*

brandy ['brandi] **1** *ncu* a type of strong alcoholic spirit made from wine: *Brandy is usually drunk after dinner; This shop stocks a number of different brandies.* **2** *nc* a glass of brandy: *Two brandies, please.*

brash [braʃ] *adj* cheekily self-confident and impolite: *a brash young man; The new recruit was very brash.* **'brashness** *nu.*

brass [bra:s] **1** *nu, adj* (of) an alloy of copper and zinc: *This plate is (made of) brass; a brass door-knocker.* **2** *nc* (*usu in pl*) something made of brass: *Horse brasses were once used to decorate a horse's bridle.* **3** *nu* (in an orchestra, the group of people who play) wind musical instruments which are made of brass or other metal: *The brass is too loud; (attrib) the brass section.*

'brassy *adj* **1** like brass in appearance or like a brass musical instrument in sound. **2** (*derog inf*) bold and impudent: *a brassy barmaid; She looks rather brassy.*

brass band *nc* a band of players of (mainly) brass wind instruments: *My father plays the trumpet in a brass band.*

brass hat *nc* (*derog sl*) a high-ranking officer in the army *etc*: *All the brass hats were at the meeting, but none of the ordinary soldiers.*

brass neck *nu* shameless cheek or impudence: *After breaking off the engagement she had the brass neck to keep the ring.*

brass plate *nc* a nameplate on a door (*esp* of a doctor or other professional person).

get down to brass tacks (*inf*) to deal with basic principles or matters: *Let's stop arguing about nothing and get down to brass tacks.*

the top brass (*often derog*) people of the highest rank (in the army, a business *etc*): *He spends a lot of money on entertaining the top brass.*

brassière ['brasiə, (*Amer*) brə'ziər] (*usu abbrev* **bra** [bra:]) *nc* a woman's undergarment supporting the breasts: *What size of brassière does she take?*

brat [brat] *nc* (*derog*) a child: *That brat's howling again!*

bravado [brə'va:dou] *nu* (a show of) daring: *He's full of bravado, but really he's a coward.*

brave [breiv] *adj* without fear of danger, pain *etc*: *a brave soldier; a brave deed; You're very brave; It was brave of him to fight such an enemy.* – *vt* (*formal*) to meet or face boldly: *They braved the cold weather; Let us brave the dangers!* – *nc* a Red Indian warrior: *All the braves obeyed the Indian chief.*

'bravely *adv*: *He met his death bravely.*

'bravery *nu.*

bravo [bra:'vou, (*Amer*) 'bra:'vou] *interj* (when applauding a performer *etc*) well done!

brawl [bro:l] *nc* a noisy quarrel or physical fight: *The police were called out to a brawl in the pub.* – *vi* to fight noisily: *The men were brawling in the street after they came out of the pub.*

brawn [bro:n] *n nu* **1** (in men) muscle or physical strength: *Some women admire brawn more than brains.* **2** boiled and jellied meat from pig's flesh.

'brawny *adj* strong and muscular.

bray [brei] *ncu* the cry of an ass. – *vi* **1** to make such a cry. **2** (*derog*) (of people) to cry like an ass: *He brays like an ass when he laughs.*

brazen ['breizn] *adj* impudent or shameless: *a brazen young woman; Her behaviour seemed rather brazen.*

brazen it out to face a situation with impudent

boldness: *She knew her deception had been discovered but decided to brazen it out.*

brazier ['breiziə] *nc* a metal frame for holding a fire (*usu* used outdoors): *The night-watchman warmed himself at the brazier.*

Brazil, Brazilian *see* Appendix 2.

breach [bri:tʃ] *nc (formal)* **1** a breaking (of a law, promise *etc*). **2** a gap, break or hole: *There's a breach in the castle wall*; (*fig*) *There's a breach in our security.* – *vt* to make an opening in or break (someone's defence).

breach of the peace (*legal*) a riot, disturbance or public fight: *He was found guilty of breach of the peace.*

breach of promise (*legal*) breaking of a promise to marry someone: *She sued him for breach of promise.*

bread [bred] *nu* **1** a type of food made of flour or meal baked: *Would you like some bread and butter?*; *French bread*; *sliced bread.* **2** (*inf*) one's living: *This is how I earn my daily bread.* **3** (*sl*) money: *I don't make enough bread in this job.*

'bread-board *nc* a piece of wood used for cutting bread *etc* on.

'breadcrumbs *n pl* very tiny pieces of bread: *Dip the fish in egg and breadcrumbs.*

'breadfruit 1 *nc* a tropical tree with an edible starchy fruit. **2** *ncu* its fruit.

'bread-knife *nc* a large knife for cutting bread *etc.*

'breadwinner *nc* a person who earns money to keep a family: *When her husband died she had to become the breadwinner.*

bread and butter (a way of earning) one's living: *Writing novels is my bread and butter.*

on the 'breadline with barely enough to live on: *The widow and her children are living on the breadline.*

breadth [bredθ] **1** *nu* width; size from side to side: *The breadth of this table is one metre.* **2** *nu* (wideness of) scope or extent: *He is noted for his great breadth of outlook.* **3** *nc* a distance equal to the width (of a swimming-pool *etc*): *How many breadths of the pool can you swim?*
See also **broad**.

break [breik] – *pt* **broke** [brouk]: *ptp* **broken** ['broukən] – **1** *vti* to divide into two or more parts (by force): *The mirror broke*; *She broke her leg*; (*fig*) *He broke under the strain of all the worry.* **2** *vti* (*usu with* **off/away**) to separate (a part) from the whole (by force): *You've broken an arm off this chair.* **3** *vti* to make or become unusable or in need of repair: *The clock's broken*; *She's broken the toaster again.* **4** *vt* to go against, or not act according to (the law *etc*): *He breaks all the rules to get what he wants*; *She broke her promise to the child*; *He didn't know he was breaking the law by doing that*; *to do that would be to break one of the new laws that have just been passed*; *He broke his appointment with me at the last minute.* **5** *vt* to do better than (a sporting *etc* record): *He broke all the records for that course.* **6** *vt* to interrupt: *She broke her journey* (= she stopped travelling and stayed for a short time) *in London.* **7** *vt* to put an end to: *He finally broke the silence*; *She's broken all her bad habits.* **8** *vti* to make or become known: (*inf*) *The story broke in the Washington Post*; *They gently broke the news of his death to his wife.* **9** *vi* (of a boy's voice) to fall in pitch: *My voice broke when I was twelve.* **10** *vt* to soften the effect of (a fall, the force of the wind *etc*): *The dried leaves broke his fall from the ladder.* **11** *vt* (*inf*) to cause to collapse financially: *This expense will break me.* **12** *vt* (*often with* **in**) to tame or train (a horse or (*fig*) a person). **13** *vi* to begin: *Day will break soon*; *The storm broke before they reached shelter.* **14** *vi* (of a cricket ball) to change direction after hitting the ground. – *See also* **break** *in phrases below.* – *nc* **1** a pause: *a break in the conversation*; *The children have a break between classes at school.* **2** a change: *a break in the weather.* **3** an opening: *a break in the wall.* **4** (*inf*) a chance, opportunity or piece of (good or bad) luck: *This is your big break.* **5** (in billiards or snooker) a continuous series of scoring strokes.

'breakable *adj* (*neg* **un-**) able to be broken; likely to break: *Are these mugs breakable?*; *breakable toys* – *nc* (*usu in pl*) something able to be broken or likely to break: *Move all the breakables away from the baby!*

'breakage [-kidʒ] *ncu* the act of breaking, or its result(s): *Are you insured against breakage?*; *Who's going to pay for the breakages?*

'breaker *nc* **1** (*often in cmpds*) a person or thing that breaks (something): *a stone-breaker*; *a record-breaker.* **2** a (large) wave which breaks on rocks or the beach.

'breakdown *nc* **1** (*often* **nervous breakdown**) a mental collapse: *She couldn't stand all the stress, and eventually had a (nervous) breakdown.* **2** a mechanical failure causing a stop: *If that car has any more breakdowns I'd get rid of it.* – *See also* **break down**.

break-in *see* **break in (to)** (*def 1*).

'breakneck *adj* (*attrib*) (*usu* of speed) dangerous; reckless: *He drove at breakneck speed.*

breakout *see* **break out** (*def 2*).

'breakthrough *nc* a sudden solution of a problem leading to further advances, *esp* in science: *There's been a major breakthrough in cancer treatment.*

break-up *see* **break up** (*def 1*).

'breakwater *nc* a barrier to break the force of the waves.

break away *vi* to escape from control: *The dog broke away from its owner*; (*fig*) *Several of the states broke away and became independent.*

break camp (*formal*) to pack up tents *etc* when moving elsewhere.

break cover (*formal*) to come out of hiding: *He shot the tiger when it broke cover.*

break down 1 *vt sep* to use force on (a door *etc*) to cause it to open, sometimes resulting in breaking it: *We had to break the door down because we lost the key.* **2** *vi* to stop working properly: *My car has broken down.* **3** *vi* to fail; to be unsuccessful and so come to an end: *The talks have broken down.* **4** *vi* to be overcome with emotion: *She broke down and wept.* **5** *vi, vt sep* to divide into parts: *The results can be broken down in several ways*; *The chemist has broken the compound down into its parts.*

break even *vi* to make neither profit nor loss: *I spent £100 and made £100, so overall I broke even.*

break in(to) *vi, vt fus* **1** to enter (a house *etc*) by force or unexpectedly: *When the burglar broke in he was bitten by my dog*; *Someone tried to break into the house.* (*nc* **'break-in**: *The Smiths have had two break-ins since they moved to that house.*) **2** to interrupt (someone's conversation *etc*): *He broke in with a rude remark.*

break into song/a smile suddenly to begin singing, smiling *etc.*

break loose 1 to escape from control: *The dog has broken loose from its chain; Three prisoners have broken loose.* **2** to become detached: *A stone broke loose from the wall.*

break of day (*liter*) dawn: *He left at break of day.*

break off *vi, vt sep* **1** to stop: *He broke off communications with his family; She broke off in the middle of a sentence; They broke the engagement off yesterday.* **2** to (cause to) come off by breaking: *I've broken the handle off; The handle has broken off.*

break open to use force on (a box *etc*) to open it, sometimes resulting in breaking it: *We had to break open the lock; You'll have to break the box open.*

break out *vi* **1** to appear or happen suddenly: *War has broken out.* **2** to escape (from prison, restrictions *etc*): *A prisoner has broken out* (*nc* **'breakout**). **3** to become suddenly covered (in a rash *etc*): *Her face has broken out in a rash.*

break the back of (something) to complete the heaviest or most difficult part of (a task *etc*): *Now that you've broken the back of the job, have a rest.*

break the ice to overcome the first shyness *etc*: *Let's break the ice by inviting our new neighbours for a meal.*

break up *vi, vt sep* **1** to divide or break into pieces: *The sheet of ice is breaking up; He broke the old furniture up and sold the wood;* (*fig*) *The policeman broke up the crowd;* (*fig*) *John and Mary broke up* (= separated from each other) *last week;* (*fig*) *Their marriage has broken up.* (*nc* **'break-up**). **2** to finish or end: *The meeting broke up at 4.40; The schools break up for the holidays soon.*

'break with *vt fus* **1** to quarrel with and therefore stop being connected with: *He broke with the Labour Party in 1968; He broke with it some time ago.* **2** to depart from; to cease to follow: *He broke with tradition and married a girl of a different race.*

ˌmake a 'break for it to make an (attempt to) escape: *When the guard is not looking, make a break for it.*

breakfast ['brekfəst] *ncu* the first meal of the day: *What time do you serve breakfast?; I'll have* (= *eat*) *breakfast in my room; This hotel serves excellent breakfasts; I never eat breakfast; We had toast and coffee for breakfast.* – *vi* (*formal*) to have breakfast: *They breakfasted on the train; They breakfasted on eggs* (= ate eggs for breakfast) *this morning.*

'breakfast-time *nu* the time between about 7.30 am and 9.00 am, when people normally eat breakfast: *I'll deal with that at breakfast-time.*

breast [brest] *nc* **1** either of a woman's two milk-producing glands on the front of the upper body: *The baby was feeding from her left breast; She has cancer of the breast.* **2** the front of a human or animal body between the neck and belly: *He clutched the child to his breast; This recipe needs three chicken breasts.* **3** (*liter*) heart or feelings: *a much-troubled breast.* – *vt* **1** (*liter*) to face or oppose: *breast the waves.* **2** to come to the top of: *As we breasted the hill we saw the enemy in the distance.* **3** in running, to touch (the tape at the winning-post) with the chest.

'breastfeed *vti* to feed (a baby) with milk from the breast. **'breastfed** *adj.*

'breastplate *nc* a piece of armour for the chest.

breast pocket *n nc* a small pocket at the top of a jacket *etc*: *He always has a white handkerchief in his breast pocket.*

'breaststroke *nc* (*no pl*) a style of swimming in which the arms are pushed out in front and then sweep backwards: *She is good at the breaststroke; Her breaststroke is weak.*

breath [breθ] **1** *nu* the air drawn into, and then sent out from, the lungs: *My dog's breath smells terrible.* **2** *nc* an act of breathing: *Please take a deep breath.* **3** *nc* a faint breeze: *There's not a breath of wind today.* **4** *nu* (*liter*) life.

'breathless *adj* **1** having difficulty in breathing normally, either from illness or from hurrying *etc*: *His asthma makes him breathless; He was breathless after climbing the hill.* **2** (*attrib*) very eager or excited: *in breathless anticipation.*

'breathlessly *adv.* **'breathlessness** *nu.*

catch one's breath to stop breathing for an instant (often from fear, amazement *etc* or due to physical discomfort): *He caught his breath on seeing the view; The sharp pain made him catch his breath.*

get one's breath (back) to regain the ability to breathe properly (*eg* after exercise): *If you want me to climb the rest of the hill you'll have to give me time to get my breath back.*

hold one's breath to stop breathing (often because of anxiety or to avoid being heard): *He held his breath as he watched the daring acrobat; She held her breath and hoped that they wouldn't see her.*

out of breath breathless (through running *etc*): *I'm out of breath after climbing all these stairs.*

under one's breath in a whisper: *He swore under his breath.*

breathe [bri:ð] **1** *vti* to draw in and let out (air *etc*) from the lungs: *They came out of the tunnel and thankfully breathed the fresh air; He was unable to breathe because of the smoke; She breathed a sigh of relief; He breathed tobacco smoke into my face.* **2** *vt* (*inf*) to tell (a secret): *Don't breathe a word of this to anyone.* – *See also* **breathe in, out** *below.*

'breather *nc* (*inf*) a short rest or break from work *etc*: *I must have a breather before I walk any further.*

'breathing-space *nc* (*usu fig*) a short time allowed for rest: *I've only a ten-minute breathing-space before my next appointment.*

breathing down someone's neck 1 close behind someone: *I ran a fast race, but he was breathing down my neck all the way.* **2** extremely impatient: *He's breathing down my neck for this letter I'm typing.*

breathe in, out 1 *vi* to cause air to enter or leave the lungs by breathing: *He couldn't breathe in until he reached the surface.* **2** *vt sep* to cause (a gas, particles of dust *etc*) to enter or leave the lungs by breathing: *The workers had breathed in large quantities of poison gas.*

bred *see* **breed**.

breech [bri:tʃ] *nc* the back part of a gun, where it is loaded.

breeches ['britʃiz, (*Amer*) 'bri:-] *n pl* trousers, *esp* ones coming just below the knee: *riding breeches; a pair of breeches.*

breed [bri:d] – *pt, ptp* **bred** [bred] – **1** *vi* (*usu* of animals: *derog* of people) to produce young; to produce children: *Rabbits breed often; That family breeds like rabbits.* **2** *vt* to keep animals for the purpose of breeding young: *I breed dogs and sell them as pets.* **3** *vti* (*fig*) to cause, produce or be produced: *This sort of thing breeds trouble.* – *n nc* a type, variety or species (of animals): *a breed of* *dog*; *a breed of cattle*; (*fig*) *an entirely new breed of salesmen.*

bred [bred] *adj* (*often in cmpds*) **1** (of people) brought up in a certain way or place: *a well-bred young lady*; *She is British born and bred.* **2** (of animals) brought up or reared in a certain way or under certain conditions: *A pure-bred dog often has a long pedigree.*

'breeding *nu* **1** the act of producing, *usu* of animals kept by a breeder. **2** education and training; good manners: *He shows his breeding by always acting like a gentleman.*

breeze [bri:z] *nc* a gentle wind: *There's a lovely cool breeze today.* – *vi* (*inf*: *usu with* **in(to)**) to come (into a room *etc*) very cheerfully or without warning: *She breezed in as though nothing had happened.*

'breezy *adj* (*inf*) **1** windy: *a breezy day*; *It's breezy today.* **2** (of people *etc*) bright; lively: *She's always so bright and breezy*; *a breezy young man.*

brethren *see* **brother**.

breve [bri:v] *nc* (*music*) a note of a certain length. –*See also* Appendix 4.

breviary ['bri:viəri] *nc* (*relig*) a book containing the daily service of the Roman Catholic Church.

brevity *see* **brief**.

brew [bru:] **1** *vti* to make (beer, ale *etc*) by mixing, boiling and fermenting: *He brews beer at home.* **2** *vt* to make (tea *etc*) by mixing the leaves with boiling water: *She brewed another pot of tea.* **3** *vti* to prepare: to be prepared or formed: *There's something unpleasant brewing*; *There's a storm brewing.* – *nc* a batch or variety of beer *etc*: *This is an excellent brew.*

'brewer *nc*.

'brewery *nc* a place for brewing beer *etc*.

briar[1], **brier**[1] ['braiə] *nc* **1** a prickly shrub. **2** a wild rose bush.

briar[2], **brier**[2] ['braiə] **1** *nu, adj* (of) a hard wood from which some tobacco pipes are made. **2** *nc* a pipe made from this wood.

bribe [braib] *nc* a gift offered to persuade a person to do something, *usu* dishonest: *Policemen are not allowed to accept bribes.* – *vt* to give (someone) a bribe: *He bribed the guards to let him out of prison*; *Her bribed her into telling lies.*

'bribery *nu* the giving or taking of bribes.

bric-à-brac ['brikəbrak] *nu* (*often derog*) odds and ends, used as ornaments *etc*: *Her house is full of useless bric-à-brac.*

brick [brik] **1** *ncu* (a block of) baked clay used for building: *a pile of bricks*; *His new house is made of brick,* (= *built with bricks*) *not stone*; (*attrib*) *a brick wall.* **2** *nc* a child's (*usu* plastic or wooden) cube-shaped toy for building: *The child built a castle with her bricks.*

'brickbat *nc* an insult: *They hurled brickbats at the politician throughout his speech.*

'bricklayer *nc* a person who builds (houses *etc*) with bricks.

'brickwork *nu* something (*esp* the walls of a house) made of brick: *The brickwork is in need of repair.*

brick up *vt sep* **1** to close (a hole *etc*) with bricks: *They bricked up the fireplace*; *They bricked it up yesterday.* **2** to imprison (a person) behind a wall of bricks: *She was bricked up alive and died a horrible death.*

drop a brick *see* **drop**.

bride [braid] *nc* a woman about to be married, or newly married: *The bride wore a white dress.*

'bridal *adj* (*attrib*) **1** of a wedding: *the bridal suite/feast.* **2** of a bride: *bridal finery.*

'bridegroom *nc* a man about to be married, or newly married: *The bridegroom made a very amusing speech at the wedding reception.*

bridesmaid ['braidzmeid] *nc* an unmarried woman attending the bride at a wedding: *She had three bridesmaids.*

bridge[1] [bridʒ] *nc* **1** a structure carrying a road or railway over a river *etc*: *There's a road bridge and a railway bridge over the River Forth.* **2** the narrow raised platform for the captain of a ship. **3** the bony part (of the nose): *The bridge of her nose is slightly bent.* **4** the support of the strings of a violin *etc.* – *vt* **1** to build a bridge over: *The soldiers managed to bridge the stream.* **2** (*fig*) to make a connection: to close a gap, pause *etc*: *He bridged the awkward silence with a funny remark.*

'bridging loan *nc* a loan, *usu* from a bank, to cover the period between buying one house *etc* and selling another.

bridge[2] [bridʒ] *nu* a card game, played by two against two, the cards of one player all being shown before they are played: *Do you play bridge?*

bridle ['braidl] *nc* the harness on a horse's head, to which the reins are attached. – **1** *vt* to put a bridle on (a horse). **2** *vi* (*formal*) to react angrily: *He bridled at her insulting comments.*

'bridle path/road *nc* a path for riders and horses.

brief [bri:f] *adj* (*more formal than* **short**) not long; short: *a brief visit*; *a brief account of what happened*; *You'll have to be brief* (= say what you're going to say in a few words) *because I'm in a hurry.* – *nc* **1** (*formal or legal*) a short statement of facts (*esp* in a lawsuit, of a client's case): *a lawyer's brief.* **2** instructions about a job one is being asked to do: *Her brief was to find the right people for the job.* – *See also* **briefs**. – *vt* (*sometimes formal or legal*) to give detailed instructions to (*esp* a barrister, group of soldiers *etc*): *The astronauts were briefed before the space mission*; *We were well briefed before the meeting.*

'briefing *ncu* instructions and information: *The pilots were given a briefing before they left*; *Their briefing was inadequate.*

'briefly *adv*: *He told me briefly what had happened*; *Briefly, your work must improve.*

'briefness, (*formal*) **brevity** ['brevəti] *nus* shortness (of speech, writing, time *etc*): *The next speaker is well known for the brevity of his speeches*; *I was surprised at the briefness of his visit.*

briefs *n pl* (used *esp* in shops) women's pants or men's underpants: *a pair of briefs.*

'briefcase *nc* a light case for papers, made of leather *etc*: *a businessman's briefcase.*

in 'brief in a few words: *In brief, we have been successful.*

brier *see* **briar**.

brig [brig] *nc* a type of two-masted ship with square sails.

brigade [bri'geid] *nc* **1** a body of troops consisting of *usu* three battalions: *He was in charge of a brigade.* **2** a uniformed group of people organized for a particular purpose: *Call the fire brigade!*

brigadier [brigə'diə] *nc* (*with cap in titles*) in the British army, the commander of a brigade, an officer of the rank below major-general: *He is a brigadier*; *Brigadier Brown.* – *See also* Appendix 3.

brigand ['brigənd] *nc* (*old or liter*) a robber, *esp* one of a group in a remote part of a country: *They* *were attacked by brigands in the mountains.*

bright [brait] *adj* **1** shining with much light: *That lamp's very bright; in bright sunshine.* **2** (of a colour) strong and bold: *He drives a bright red car; That shade of red is too bright.* **3** cheerful: *She's always bright and happy; a bright smile.* **4** clever: *Judy teaches the bright children; He's extremely bright.* **'brightness** *nu.*

'brighten *vti* (*often with* **up**) to make or become bright or brighter: *The new wallpaper brightens up the room; They brightened up as soon as you arrived; A child will brighten your life.*

'brightly *adv*: *shining brightly; smiling brightly.*

brilliant ['briljənt] *adj* **1** very bright: *a brilliant jewel; The sea is a brilliant blue; the bird's brilliant feathers.* **2** very clever: *Your idea is brilliant!; a brilliant scholar.* **'brilliantly** *adv.*

'brilliance *nu* **1** brightness: *the brilliance of the moon.* **2** cleverness: *his brilliance as a surgeon.*

'brilliantine [-ti:n] *nu* a cosmetic used, *usu* by men, to make the hair glossy.

brim [brim] *nc* **1** the top edge of a cup, glass *etc*: *The jug was filled to the brim.* **2** the edge of a hat: *She pulled the brim of her hat down over her eyes.* – *v* – *pt, ptp* **brimmed** – *vi* (*formal*) to be, or become, full to the brim: *Her eyes were brimming with tears.*

ˌbrim'ful, ˌbrim-'full *adjs* (*pred*) full to the brim: *The bowl is brimful of roses; (fig) She's brimful of ideas.*

brim over *vi* (*with* **with**) to overflow: *The cup is brimming over with water; (fig) She is brimming over with excitement.*

brimstone ['brimstoun] *nu* (*old*) sulphur.

brine [brain] *nu* **1** very salty water: *a jar of olives in brine.* **2** (*liter*) the sea.

'briny *adj* (of water) very salty.

the briny (*liter or facet*) the sea.

bring [briŋ] – *pt, ptp* **brought** [bro:t] – *vt* **1** to make (something or someone) come (to or towards a place): *I'll bring plenty of food with me; Bring him to me!* **2** to cause or result in: *This medicine will bring you relief; His death brought sadness.* – *See also* **bring** *in phrases below.*

bring about *vt sep* to cause: *His disregard for danger brought about his death; What brought it about?*

bring a case against to take legal action against (someone) in court.

bring back *vt sep* to (cause to) return: *May I borrow your pen? I'll bring it back tomorrow; The government may bring back capital punishment; Her singing brings back memories of my mother; That brings it all back to me* (= reminds me of it).

bring down *vt sep* to cause to fall: *The storm brought all the trees down; (fig) That will bring down the dictator.*

bring forth *vt usu sep* (*formal*) (*esp* in the Bible) to give birth to or produce.

bring forward *see* **forward**.

bring home to to prove or show (something) clearly to (someone): *His illness brought home to her how much she depended on him.*

bring in *vt sep* **1** to introduce: *They will bring in a parliamentary bill.* **2** to produce as profit: *His books are bringing in thousands of pounds.* **3** (of a jury) to pronounce or give (a verdict): *They brought in a verdict of guilty.*

bring off *vt sep* (*inf*) to achieve (something attempted): *I never thought they'd bring it off!; They brought off an unexpected victory.*

bring on *vt sep* **1** (*sometimes facet*) to cause to come on: *Bring on the dancing girls!* **2** to help to develop: *His illness was brought on by not eating enough.*

'bring oneself to to persuade oneself with difficulty to (do something): *I can't bring myself to sack the old man.*

bring out *vt sep* **1** to make clear; to reveal: *He brought out the weaknesses of her theory.* **2** to publish: *He brings a new book out every year.*

bring round *vt usu sep* **1** to bring back from unconsciousness: *The smelling-salts brought him round.* **2** to persuade: *We'll bring him round to the idea.*

bring to *vt oblig sep* to bring (someone) back to consciousness: *These smelling-salts will bring him to.*

bring up *vt sep* to rear or educate: *She was brought up to behave herself; Her parents brought her up to be polite.* **2** to introduce (a matter) for discussion: *Bring the matter up at the next meeting.*

bring up the rear (*formal*) to come last: *One of the most experienced climbers brought up the rear.*

brink [briŋk] *nu* (*more formal than* **edge**) the edge or border of a steep, dangerous place or of a river: *She stood on the brink of the river; (fig) on the brink of disaster.*

briquette [bri'ket] *nc* a brick-shaped block of fuel made of coal dust.

brisk [brisk] *adj* active or fast moving: *a brisk walk; Business was brisk today.* **'briskly** *adv.* **'briskness** *nu.*

brisket ['briskit] *nu* the breast of an animal (*usu* bull or cow), when eaten as food: *She bought some brisket from the butcher.*

bristle ['brisl] *nc* a short, stiff hair on an animal or brush: *The dog's bristles rose when it was angry; The bristles of this paintbrush keep coming out.* – *vi* to stand straight up or stiffly as bristles do, indicating anger: *The dog's hair bristled; (fig) Mary bristled angrily; (fig) She bristled with anger.*

'bristly *adj* **1** having bristles; rough: *He had a bristly moustache; His chin was bristly as he hadn't shaved for two days.* **2** (*inf*) tending to be angry: *She's a bit bristly this morning.*

'bristle with *vt fus* (*formal*) to be full of: *The warship was bristling with guns; streets bristling with tourists.*

Britain, British, Briton *see* Appendix 2.

brittle ['britl] *adj* hard but easily broken: *brittle materials; Glass and dry twigs are brittle.* **'brittleness** *nu.*

broach ['broutʃ] *vt* (*formal*) to bring up; to begin to talk about (a subject): *I hate to broach the question of dismissal again.*

broad [bro:d] *adj* **1** wide; great (or greater than average) in size from side to side: *a broad street; The river is quite broad here.* **2** from side to side: *two metres broad.* **3** (*usu attrib*) general; not detailed: *We discussed the plans in broad outline.* **4** strongly or characteristically accented: *broad Scots; a broad dialect; His accent is very broad.* – *nc* (*Amer derog sl*) **1** a woman: *Who's that broad he's with?* **2** a prostitute.

'broaden *vti* to make or become broad or broader: *They have broadened the road; The path broadens further on; (fig) His experiences have broadened his mind.*

'broadly *adv* generally: *Broadly speaking, I'd say your chances are poor.*

'broadness *nu* **1** breadth (*def 2*): *She was amazed* *by the broadness of his shoulders.* **2** strongly accented quality: *The broadness of his Scots accent is very interesting.*

broad daylight *nu* full daylight: *The child was attacked in broad daylight.*

broad hint *nc* a clear, undisguised hint: *She kept making broad hints that she wanted a ring for her birthday.*

'broadloom *nu* carpet woven on a wide loom: *We bought five metres of broadloom*; (*attrib*) *broadloom carpet.*

ˌbroad-'minded *adj* ready to allow others to think or act as they choose without criticizing them: *a broad-minded headmaster*; *Her parents are broad-minded and allow her to come home very late.*

'broadside *nc* **1** (the firing of) all the guns on one side of a ship of war. **2** (*formal*) a strong verbal attack (on someone): *The prime minister delivered a broadside to the Opposition.*

'broadsword *nc* a heavy sword with a broad blade.

broadside on sideways: *The ships collided broadside on.*

the 'broad jump (*Amer*) the long jump.

See also **breadth**.

broadcast ['bro:dka:st] – *pt, ptp* **'broadcast** – **1** *vti* to send out (radio and TV programmes *etc*): *They broadcast a children's play*; *He broadcasts regularly.* **2** *vt* to make (something) widely known: *He broadcasts his views to everyone in the office.* **3** *vt* (*formal*) to scatter (seed) by hand. – *nc* a television or radio programme: *I heard his broadcast last night.*

'broadcaster *nc* a person who takes part in a broadcast.

'broadcasting *nu*.

brocade [brə'keid, (*Amer*) brou-] *nu, adj* (of) a (*usu* silk) material having a raised design on it: *curtains made of blue brocade*; *brocade curtains.*

broccoli ['brokəli] *nu* a variety of cauliflower, with branched green or purple heads.

brochure ['brouʃuə] *nc* a short booklet giving information about, or advertising, holidays, products *etc*: *Get some brochures from the travel agent.*

brogue [broug] *nc* **1** a type of strong shoe: *I want a pair of strong brogues for my walking holiday.* **2** a strong accent, *esp* Irish.

broil [broil] *vt* (*Amer*) to grill (food): *She broiled the chicken.*

broke [brouk] *v see* **break**. – *adj* (*inf*: *pred*) completely without money: *I'm broke till pay day.*

broken ['broukən] *adj* **1** *see* **break**: *a broken window*; *My watch is broken.* **2** (*esp attrib*) interrupted: *broken sleep.* **3** having an uneven surface: *a broken path*; *The surface was broken and uneven.* **4** (*attrib*) (of language) not fluent: *He speaks broken English.* **5** (*attrib*) ruined: *a broken marriage*; *The children come from a broken home* (= their parents are no longer living together).

'broken-down *adj* (*attrib*: *derog*) not in working order; not in good condition or good health: *a broken-down old ruin.*

ˌbroken-'hearted *adj* overcome by grief: *When the dog died she was broken-hearted*; *a broken-hearted mother.*

broker ['broukə] *nc* (*often in cmpds*) a person employed to buy and sell (*esp* shares *etc*) for others: *Did you consult an insurance broker?*; *He is a stockbroker*; *She took her jewellery to the pawnbroker.*

'brokerage [-ridʒ] *nu* (*formal*) the profit or commission charged by a broker.

brolly ['broli] *nc* (*inf*) an umbrella: *I'll take my brolly – I think it's going to rain.*

bromide ['broumaid] **1** *ncu* any of the compounds of the element **bromine** (symbol **Br**), *esp* one used to calm a person down. **2** *nc* a much-used statement or phrase, used to try to calm someone: *The customer was made even more angry by the bromides of the under-manager.*

bronchitis [broŋ'kaitis] *nu* inflammation of the **bronchi**, ['broŋkai] the air passages in the lungs, causing difficulty in breathing: *Wet weather makes his bronchitis worse.*

bronchial ['broŋkiəl] *adj* (*usu attrib*) of inflammation of the bronchi: *bronchial pneumonia.*

bronchitic [-'kitik] **1** *nc, adj* (a person who is) suffering from bronchitis: *a chronic bronchitic*; *a bronchitic patient.* **2** *adj* of, or caused by, bronchitis: *a bronchitis cough.*

bronze [bronz] **1** *nu* an alloy of copper and tin: *a medal made of bronze.* **2** *nu* its reddish brown colour. **3** *nc* a work of art made of bronze: *an exhibition of bronzes.* – *adj* **1** made of bronze: *a bronze medallion.* **2** of the colour of bronze: *bronze leaves.*

bronzed *adj* **1** coated with bronze. **2** (*formal or facet*) suntanned: *He came back from his holiday looking bronzed and healthy*; *a bronzed face.*

brooch [broutʃ] *nc* a decoration, *esp* for a woman's dress, fastened by a pin: *She wore a brooch on the collar of her dress.*

brood [bru:d] *vi* **1** (of birds) to sit on eggs to hatch them: *That hen is brooding.* **2** to think (about something) anxiously for some time: *She spent weeks brooding over what he had said*; *There's no point in brooding about what happened*; *Don't sit brooding all day!* **3** (*often with* **over**: *liter*) to hang threateningly over: *The dark clouds brooded over the horizon.* – *nc* **1** the number of young hatched at one time: *a brood of chickens.* **2** (*inf sometimes derog*) a (human) family of young children: *She took her brood to the cinema.*

'broody *adj* **1** (of birds) ready to brood: *broody hens.* **2** (*usu pred*) deep in anxious thought: *She looks a bit broody – I think she's worrying about something.* **3** (*inf*: *usu pred*) (of women) badly wanting to have children: *She always gets broody when she sees a new baby.*

brook[1] [bruk] *nc* (*liter*) a small stream.

brook[2] [bruk] *vt* (*formal*: *usu in neg*) to put up with: to tolerate: *He will not brook any interference.*

broom [bru:m] **1** *nu* a wild shrub of the pea family with (*usu* yellow) flowers: *The hillside was covered in broom.* **2** *nc* a long-handled sweeping brush: *Use a broom to sweep the leaves from the path!*

'broomstick *nc* the handle of a broom: *Witches are said to fly on broomsticks.*

broth [broθ] *nu* a type of soup containing vegetables and barley or rice: *Scotch broth.*

brother ['brʌðə] – *pls* **'brothers** (*all defs*), **brethren** ['breðrən] (*def 3*) – *nc* **1** the title given to a male child to describe his relationship to the other children of his parents: *He's my brother*; *my husband's brother.* **2** (*sometimes attrib*: *with cap in titles*) a fellow member of any group, *esp* a socialist society or trade union: *brother officers*; *We must fight for our rights, brothers!*; *Brother Wilson.* **3** (*with cap in names*) a member of a religious group: *Brother Matthew*; *The brothers of* *the order prayed together*; *The brethren met every week.*

'brotherhood 1 *nu* (*formal*) the state of being a brother; *the ties of brotherhood.* **2** *nc* an association of men for a certain purpose: *The outlaws formed a brotherhood.*

'brotherly *adj* like, or of, a brother; kind: *brotherly love*; *He is not in love with her – his attitude towards her is brotherly.*

'brother-in-law – *pl* **'brothers-in-law** – *nc* **1** the brother of one's husband or wife. **2** the husband of one's sister.

See also **fraternal**.

brought *see* **bring**.

brow [brau] *nc* **1** the eyebrow: *He has huge, bushy brows.* **2** the forehead: *His brow felt very hot, as if he had a fever.* **3** the top (of a hill): *I can't see over the brow of the hill.*

'browbeat – *pt* **'browbeat**: *ptp* **'browbeaten** – *vt* to bully, *usu* by words: *He browbeat me into going with him.*

knit one's brows *see* **knit**.

brown [braun] *adj* **1** of a colour similar to that of toasted bread, tanned skin, coffee *etc*: *brown paint*; *Her eyes are brown.* **2** suntanned: *She was very brown after her holiday in Greece.* – **1** *ncu* (any shade of) a colour similar to toasted bread, tanned skin, coffee *etc*: *That is a very attractive (shade of) brown.* **2** *ncu* something (*eg* paint, polish *etc*) brown in colour: *I prefer the brown to the green.* – *vti* to make or become brown: *He browned the steaks under the grill*; *You'll brown nicely in the sun today.*

'brownish *adj* rather brown; close to brown: *The carpet was a brownish colour*; *His eyes are brownish.*

'brownness *nu.*

a brown study (*formal*) deep thought: *She's in a brown study today* (= She pays no attention to what you say).

browned off (*inf*: *usu pred*) **1** bored: *I feel really browned off in this wet weather.* **2** annoyed: *I'm browned off with his behaviour.*

brownie ['brauni] *nc* **1** (*myth*) a friendly fairy. **2** (*with cap*: *short for* **Brownie Guide**) a junior Girl Guide. **3** (*Amer*) a sweet chocolate and nut cake.

browse [brauz] *vi* **1** (of people) to glance through a book *etc* reading bits and pieces in a casual way: *I don't want to buy a book – I'm just browsing.* **2** (of animals) to feed (on shoots or leaves of plants). – *nc* an act of browsing: *a browse through a magazine.*

bruise [bru:z] *nc* an injury caused by a blow to a person or a fruit, turning the skin a dark colour but not breaking it: *He has bruises all over his legs*; *These apples are covered in bruises.* – **1** *vt* to cause such a mark on the skin: *She bruised her forehead when she fell.* **2** *vi* to develop bruises as the result of a blow: *She bruises easily.*

brunette [bru:'net] *nc* a woman with brown or dark hair: *He prefers blondes to brunettes.*

brunt [brʌnt] : **bear the brunt of** (*formal*) to bear the worst of the effect of (a blow, attack *etc*): *I bore the brunt of his abuse/the storm.*

brush [brʌʃ] **1** *nc* (*often in cmpds*) an instrument with bristles, wire, hair *etc* for cleaning, scrubbing *etc*: *a hairbrush*; *a toothbrush*; *He sells brushes*; *Can I have some paint and a (paint)-brush?* **2** *nc* an act of brushing: *I'll have to give my shoes a brush.* **3** *nc* a bushy tail of a fox. **4** *nc* (*inf*) a short fight or disagreement: *He had a slight brush with the law.* **5** *nu* brushwood. – **1** *vt* to rub with a brush to remove dirt *etc*: *He brushed his jacket.* **2** *vt* to remove (dust *etc*) by sweeping with a brush or other object: *I'll brush the floor*; *Brush the dust off with this cloth!* **3** *vt* to make tidy by using a brush: *Brush your hair!* **4** *vti* to touch lightly in passing: *The leaves brushed her face*; *He brushed against me.* – *See also* **brush** *in phrases below.*

'brushwood *nu* **1** broken branches, twigs *etc*: *They collected brushwood to make a fire.* **2** undergrowth: *The small dog was hidden in the brushwood.*

brush aside *vt sep* to pay no attention to: *She brushed aside my objections*; *She brushed them aside rudely.*

brush away *vt sep* to wipe off: *She brushed away a tear*; *She brushed it away.*

brush on *vt sep* to put (paint *etc*) on with a brush.

brush up *vt sep, vi* (*with* **on**) (*inf*) to refresh one's knowledge of (*eg* a language): *He brushed up his Spanish before he went on holiday*; *I must brush up on British history.*

give, get the 'brush-off (*inf*) to reject or be rejected abruptly: *She gave me the brush-off when I asked her to go to the cinema.*

brusque [brusk, (*Amer*) brʌsk] *adj* blunt and abrupt in manner: *She's apt to be a bit brusque, but she's very kind*; *a brusque manner.* **'brusquely** *adv.* **'brusqueness** *nu.*

Brussels sprout [brʌsl'spraut] *nc* **1** (*in pl*) a variety of cabbage with sprouts on the stem like tiny cabbages. **2** (*usu in pl*) one of the sprouts: *We always eat Brussels sprouts with our Christmas turkey.*

brute [bru:t] *nc* **1** (*liter or inf*) an animal other than man: *My dog died yesterday, the poor brute*; (*attrib*) *I had to use brute force/strength to open the door.* **2** (*inf*: *sometimes facet*) a cruel person: *You're a brute not to take me to the party*; *He was an absolute brute to his wife.*

'brutal *adj* very cruel or severe: *She received a brutal beating*; *His treatment of her was brutal.* **bru'tality** [-'ta-] *ncu.*

'brutalize, -ise *vt* (*formal*) to make brutal: *His long years in prison brutalized him.*

'brutish *adj* of, or like, a brute: *He has such brutish manners that I wouldn't have him in my house*; *His manners are rather brutish.*

bubble ['bʌbl] *nc* (in air, liquids or solids) a floating ball of air or gas: *the bubbles in lemonade*; *Children love blowing bubbles.* – *vi* to form or rise in bubbles: *The champagne bubbled in the glass.* – *See* **bubble over** *below.*

'bubbly *adj* having bubbles. – *nu* (*inf*) champagne: *Let's celebrate with a bottle of bubbly.*

bubble over *vi* **1** to boil over: *The milk bubbled over.* **2** (*fig*) to be full (with happiness, excitement *etc*): *She was bubbling over with excitement at the news.*

buccaneer [bʌkə'niə] *nc* (*hist*) a type of pirate.

buck [bʌk] *nc* **1** the male of the deer, hare, rabbit *etc*: *a buck and a doe.* **2** (*Amer inf*) a dollar. – *vi* (of a horse or mule) to make a series of rapid jumps into the air, sometimes in an attempt to throw a rider: *That horse bucks so much that no-one can tame it.*

'buckshot *nu* a large size of rifle shot.

'buckskin *nu, adj* (of) a soft leather made of deerskin or sheepskin: *made of buckskin*; *a buckskin jacket.*

buck tooth *nc* (*esp inf*) a tooth which sticks out in front: *Her looks are spoiled by her buck teeth.*

buck up (*inf*) **1** *vi* to hurry: *You'd better buck up if you want to catch the bus.* **2** *vi, vt sep* to cheer up: *The good news will buck her up*; *She bucked up when she heard the news.* **3** *vi, vt sep* to improve (one's attitude *etc*): *Buck up your ideas or you'll be out of a job.*

pass the buck (*inf*) to pass on responsibility (to someone else): *Whenever he is blamed for anything, he tries to pass the buck.*

bucket ['bʌkit] *nc* **1** a container for holding water, milk *etc*: *We used buckets to carry water to the burning house.* **2** a bucketful: *Three buckets of water.*

'bucketful *nc* the amount contained in a bucket: *Bring a bucketful of coal.*

bucket seat *nc* (in a car *etc*) a seat with a rounded back, for one person.

buckle ['bʌkl] *nc* **1** a fastening for a strap or band consisting of a rim and *usu* a movable spike which goes through a hole in the belt: *I want a belt with a silver buckle.* **2** an ornamental version of this, which does not fasten (as on a shoe *etc*). – **1** *vti* to fasten with a buckle: *He buckled on his sword*; *The child could not buckle her shoes.* **2** *vti* (*usu* of something metal) to make or become bent or crushed: *The metal buckled in the great heat.*

buckle down *vi* (*inf*) (*often with* **to**) to begin (something) seriously: *You must just buckle down to the new job.*

buckle to *vi* (*inf*) to begin to work seriously: *You must buckle to or go.*

bud [bʌd] *nc* (*often in cmpds*) a shoot of a tree or plant, containing undeveloped leaves or flower(s) or both: *Are there buds on the trees yet?*; *a rosebud.* – *v* – *pt, ptp* **'budded** – *vi* to put out buds; to begin to grow: *The daffodils are budding early this year.*

'budding *adj* (*attrib*) just beginning to develop: *I think he is a budding poet.*

in 'bud producing buds: *The flowers will be in bud soon.*

nip (something) in the bud *see* **nip**.

Buddhism ['budizəm, (*Amer*) 'bu:-] *nu* the religion founded by Gautama or Buddha.

'Buddhist *nc* a believer in Buddhism. – *adj* of Buddhism: *a Buddhist monk.*

buddy ['bʌdi] *nc* (*inf*: *esp Amer*) a friend: *They've been buddies for years.*

budge [bʌdʒ] *vti* (*inf*) to (cause to) move, even slightly: *I can't budge it*; *It won't budge!*

budgerigar ['bʌdʒəriga:] (*inf abbrev* **'budgie** ['bʌdʒi] *nc* a type of small (*orig* Australian) brightly-coloured bird, often kept as a pet.

budget ['bʌdʒit] *nc* any plan showing how money is to be spent, *esp* (*with cap*) a statement put before parliament by the Chancellor of the Exchequer: *my budget for the month*; *the Chancellor's Budget.* – *v* – *pt, ptp* **'budgeted** – *vi* **1** to make a plan showing this: *We must try to budget or we shall be in debt.* **2** (*with* **for**) to allow for (something) in a budget: *I hadn't budgeted for a new car.*

'budgetary *adj* (*formal*): *the government's budgetary measures.*

budgie *see* **budgerigar**.

buff [bʌf] **1** *nu, adj* (of) a dull yellow colour: *This colour is midway between buff and grey*; *a buff envelope.* **2** *nu* a soft leather of this colour. – *vt* (*often with* **up**) to polish up: *The new electric polisher buffs up the floors well.*

the buff (*inf*) a person's skin: *stripped to the buff.*

buffalo ['bʌfəlou] – *pls* **'buffalo, 'buffalo(e)s** – *nc* **1** a large kind of ox, *esp* the Asian and African varieties: *two buffaloes*; *a herd of buffalo.* **2** the American variety of ox; the bison.

buffer ['bʌfə] *nc* **1** an apparatus, *esp* one using springs or padding, for lessening the force with which a moving object strikes something (*esp* used on railway engines *etc*). **2** a person, thing, country *etc* which lessens certain unpleasant effects: *My agent acts as a buffer between the newspaper reporters and me.*

old buffer (*derog and affectionately*) an old (incompetent) man: *He's a bit of an old buffer but I like him.*

buffet[1] ['bʌfit] *nc* (*formal*) a blow with the hand or fist: *He gave his son a buffet on the side of the head.* – *v* – *pt, ptp* **'buffeted** – *vt* **1** (*formal*) to strike with the fist. **2** to knock about: *The boat was buffeted by the waves.*

'buffeting *nc* (*formal*): *The waves gave the ship a buffeting.*

buffet[2] ['bufei, (*Amer*) bə'fei] *nc* **1** a refreshment bar, *esp* in a railway station or on a train *etc*: *We'll get some coffee at the buffet.* **2** a (*usu* cold) meal set out on tables from which people help themselves: *They had a buffet at the wedding*; (*attrib*) *a buffet supper.*

buffoon [bə'fu:n, (*Amer*) bʌ-] *nc* a clown; a fool.

buf'foonery *nu.*

bug [bʌg] *nc* **1** (*esp Brit*: *sometimes in cmpds*) an insect that lives in dirty houses and beds: *a bed-bug.* **2** (*esp Amer*: *sometimes in cmpds*) an insect: *There's a bug crawling up your arm*; *a harvest bug.* **3** (*inf*) a germ or infection: *There's a flu bug going around.* **4** (*inf*) a small hidden microphone. – *v* – *pt, ptp* **bugged** – *vt* **1** (*inf*) to place small hidden microphones in (a room *etc*): *The spy's bedroom was bugged.* **2** (*sl*) to annoy or worry: *She's always bugging me.*

get the bug (*inf*) to be taken with great enthusiasm (for): *He's got the travel/acting bug.*

bugbear ['bʌgbeə] *nc* something one fears or hates: *One of the biggest bugbears in modern industry is the threat of union disputes.*

bugger ['bʌgə] *nc* **1** (*Brit vulg*) used as a term of abuse: *That bugger spilled my drink*; *This problem's a real bugger!* **2** (*Amer*) used affectionately: *He's a nice little bugger.* – *interj* (*vulg*) used to show annoyance *etc*: *Oh bugger (it), I've dropped my cup!* – *vt* (*vulg*: *sometimes with* **up**) to spoil or ruin: *That's buggered (up) my chances of success!* – Also found in many vulgar verb phrases: *Stop buggering about* (= wasting time) *and get on with the work*; *Why don't you bugger off* (= go away) *?*

'buggered *adj* (*pred*: *vulg*) exhausted: *I'm buggered!*

buggy ['bʌgi] *nc* a light, open, one-horse vehicle. *See also* **baby buggy** *under* **baby**.

bugle ['bju:gl] *nc* a musical wind instrument *usu* made of brass, used chiefly for military signals: *He plays the bugle.* **'bugler** *nc.*

build [bild] – *pt, ptp* **built** [-t] – *vt* to form or construct from parts: *build a house/railway/bookcase.* – *See also* **build on, build up** *below.* – *nu* physical form: *a man of heavy build.*

'builder *nc* a person who builds houses *etc*: *The builder who built our house has gone bankrupt.*

'building **1** *nu* the art or business of putting up (houses *etc*). **2** *nc* anything built: *The new supermarket is a very ugly building.*

'building society *nc* a business firm that lends money for building or buying houses.

'build-up *nc* **1** an increase or piling up: *a build-up of pressure*; *a build-up of traffic.* **2** a piece of publicity: *a build-up for the next act.* – *See also* **build up** *below.*

,built-'in *adj* forming a permanent part of the building *etc*: *We've made built-in cupboards to save space.*

,built-'up *adj* covered with houses *etc*: *a built-up area.*

build on[1] *vt sep* to add on by building: *The hospital is bigger now – they built a new wing on in 1977.*

'build on[2] *vt fus* to use (something, *eg* a previous success) as a basis from which to develop: *You've had some success – you must build on it now.*

build (something) on (something) to base hopes, success *etc* on (something): *I've built all my hopes on this book being published.*

build up 1 *vi, vt sep* to increase (the size or extent of): *The traffic begins to build up around five o'clock*; *They built the wall up gradually*; (*fig*) *Don't build up the child's hopes – he may not get a present.* – *See also* **build**. **2** *vi, vt sep* to strengthen gradually (a business, one's health, reputation *etc*): *His father built up that grocery business from nothing*; *Good food and fresh air will help build the child up.* **3** *vt usu sep* (*inf*) to speak with great enthusiasm about (someone): *They built him up until I couldn't wait to meet him.*

bulb [bʌlb] *nc* **1** the ball-shaped part of the stem of certain plants, *eg* onions, tulips *etc*, from which their roots grow: *a bulb of garlic.* **2** (*also* **'light-bulb**) a pear-shaped glass globe surrounding the element of an electric light. **3** the pear-shaped end of various other objects, *eg* a thermometer.

'bulbous *adj* **1** like a bulb, *esp* in shape: *a bulbous nose.* **2** (*formal*: *esp attrib*) having or growing from a bulb: *a bulbous plant.*

Bulgaria, Bulgarian *see* Appendix 2.

bulge [bʌldʒ] *nc* **1** a swelling: *The dress was so tight that you could see the bulge of her hips*; *The glove made a bulge in his pocket.* **2** a sudden and temporary increase: *There was a bulge in the birthrate after the war.* – *vi* to swell out: *My stomach's bulging with all the food I've eaten*; *His muscles bulged.*

bulk [bʌlk] **1** *nu* the greater part: *The bulk of his money was spent on drink.* **2** *ncu* (great) size or mass: *It is the bulk of a parcel rather than the weight that decides whether it goes by parcel post or letter post*; *His huge bulk appeared round the corner.* – *adj* (*attrib*) in bulk: *bulk buying*; *bulk purchases.*

'bulky *adj* large in size, awkward to carry *etc*: *a bulky parcel*; *This is too bulky to send by post.*

bulk large (*formal*) to be important or prominent: *The coming court case bulked large in his thoughts.*

in 'bulk in large quantities: *Huge tankers now carry oil in bulk*; *They like to buy goods in bulk.*

bulkhead ['bʌlkhed] *nc* a division between one part of a ship's interior and another.

bull[1] [bul] *nc* **1** the male of the ox family and of the whale, walrus, elephant *etc*: *two cows and a bull.* **2** a bull's-eye: *He got five bulls in the shooting contest.*

'bullock [-lək] *nc* **1** a young bull. **2** a castrated bull.

'bulldog *nc* a small, fierce dog of heavy build.

'bullfight *nc* in Spain *etc* a fight between a bull and men on horseback and on foot, organized as public entertainment.

'bullring *nc* the enclosed area where a bullfight takes place.

'bull's-eye *nc* the centre of a target, *esp* in archery, darts *etc*: *He got three bull's-eyes one after the other*; (*fig*) *You hit the bull's-eye with that question!*

bull terrier *nc* a cross between a bulldog and a terrier.

a ,bull in a 'china shop (*inf*) a person who acts in a very clumsy way: *She came in like a bull in a china shop and knocked the vase of flowers off the shelf.*

take the bull by the horns to tackle a difficulty boldly: *If you want to improve the situation you must take the bull by the horns.*

bull[2] [bul] *nc* (*relig*) a formal letter, with seal attached, from the Pope: *a Papal bull.*

bull[3] [bul] *nu* (*Amer sl*) nonsense: *That's a load of bull!*

bull[4] [bul] *nu* (*mil sl*) the cleaning and polishing of equipment: *He hated army bull.*

bulldog *see* **bull**[1].

bulldozer ['buldouzə] *nc* a (*usu* large) tractor for clearing obstacles and levelling ground.

'bulldoze *vt* **1** (*formal*) to use a bulldozer on: *They bulldozed the building site.* **2** to force (someone to do something): *He bulldozed me into accepting his suggestion.*

bullet ['bulit] *nc* a piece of metal fired from certain types of hand gun, *eg* rifle, pistol *etc*: *He was killed by machine-gun bullets.*

'bullet-proof *adj* able to prevent bullets passing through it: *The president wore a bullet-proof vest*; *Is his shirt bullet-proof?*

bulletin ['bulətin] *nc* **1** an official (verbal) report of news: *They've issued another bulletin about the Queen's illness.* **2** a printed information-sheet or newspaper: *We produce a monthly bulletin of local news.*

'bulletin-board *nc* (*Amer*) a notice-board.

bullfight *see* **bull**[1].

bullion ['buliən] *nu* gold or silver in bulk, not made into coins.

bullock *see* **bull**[1].

bully ['buli] *nc* a person who hurts or frightens other, weaker people: *The fat boy was a bully at school.* – *vt* to act like a bully towards: *He's always bullying people* (*into doing things*).

bulrush ['bulrʌʃ] *nc* a tall strong water plant.

bulwark ['bulwək] *nc* **1** (*tech*) a wall built as a defence, often made of earth. **2** (*formal*) a thing or person that defends (a cause, way of life *etc*) and tries to prevent its destruction: *He thinks he's the last bulwark of upper-class society.* **3** the side of a ship projecting above the deck.

bum[1] [bʌm] *nc* (*inf*) the buttocks.

bum[2] [bʌm] *nc* (*inf*: *esp Amer*) a tramp or worthless person: *He doesn't work – he's just a bum.* – *adj* (*attrib*: *inf*) worthless or very bad: *This is a bum job.* *v* – *pt, ptp* **bummed** – *vt* (*Amer sl*) to try to borrow: *Can I bum a cigarette off you?*

bum around *vi* (*Amer sl*) to wander or travel around, *usu* without a (regular) job: *I spent last year bumming around in Europe.*

bumble-bee ['bʌmblbiː] *nc* a kind of large bee with a hairy body.

bump [bʌmp] **1** *vti* to knock or strike (something): *Another car bumped into ours*; *She bumped into me*; *I bumped my head against the ceiling*; *He bumped his* *elbow on the wall.* – *See also* **bump into** *below.* **2** *vi* to move unevenly: *We bumped along the rocky road.* – *nc* **1** (the sound of) a blow or knock: *We heard a loud bump.* **2** a swelling, sometimes caused by a blow: *I have a bump on my head.* **3** a raised, uneven part of a road *etc*: *This road is full of bumps.*

'bumper *nc* (*Amer* **'fender**) a bar on a motor vehicle to lessen the shock or damage when it collides with anything. – *adj* (*attrib*) excellent in some way, *esp* by being large: *a bumper crop.*

'bumpy *adj* uneven: *a bumpy road.*

bump into *vt fus* (*inf*) to meet (someone) by accident: *I bumped into him the other day in the street.* – *See also* **bump** (*def 1*).

bump off *vt sep* (*sl*) to kill: *The hero got bumped off halfway through the play.*

bumpkin ['bʌmpkin] *nc* (*derog*) a clumsy or stupid country person: *a country bumpkin.*

bumptious ['bʌmpʃəs] *adj* (*derog*) full of one's own importance: *He's so bumptious since his promotion!*; *a very bumptious young man.*

bun [bʌn] *nc* **1** a kind of sweet cake: *an iced bun*; *a currant bun.* **2** a rounded mass of hair on the head: *She always wears her hair in a bun.*

bunch [bʌntʃ] *nc* **1** a number of things fastened or growing together: *a bunch of keys*; *a bunch of bananas.* **2** (*in pl*) two pieces of hair tied separately and sticking out from each side of the back of the head: *The child wears her hair in bunches.* – *vti* (*often with* **up** *or* **together**) to come or put together in bunches, folds or groups: *The sewing-machine went wrong and started to bunch up the material*; *Traffic often bunches on a motorway.*

bundle ['bʌndl] *nc* a number of things bound together: *a bundle of rags*; *a bundle of firewood.* – **1** *vt* (*often with* **up** *or* **together**) to make into bundles: *Bundle up all your things and bring them with you.* **2** *vti* (*inf*) to send (off or out) hastily; to go or put (away) in a hurried or disorderly way: *They bundled him out of the room*; *We all bundled into his small car*; *He hastily bundled the papers into a drawer.*

bung [bʌŋ] *nc* the stopper of the hole in a barrel, in the bottom of a small boat *etc.* – *vt* **1** to block with such a stopper. **2** (*sl*) to throw: *Bung it over here.*

bunged up (*inf*: *with hyphen when attrib*) blocked (often of one's nose when one has a cold *etc*): *He's not speaking clearly because his nose is so bunged up*: *I hate having a bunged-up nose.*

bungalow ['bʌŋgəlou] *nc* a (*usu* small) house of one storey: *The old couple sold that large house and moved into a small bungalow.*

bungle ['bʌŋgl] *vti* (*derog*) to do (something) clumsily or badly: *He bungled the deal and lost thousands of pounds*; *Obviously someone has bungled.*

bunion ['bʌnjən] *nc* a swelling on the first joint of the big toe.

bunk[1] [bʌŋk] *nc* **1** (*also* **ˌbunk-'bed**) one of a pair of narrow beds one above the other: *The children sleep in bunk-beds.* **2** a sleeping-berth in a ship's cabin.

bunk[2] *see* **bunkum.**

bunker ['bʌŋkə] *nc* **1** a large container for storing coal. **2** a hollow containing sand on a golf course. **3** an underground shelter against bombs *etc.*

bunkum ['bʌŋkəm] *nu* (*also* **bunk**) nonsense: *His speech sounded convincing but it was all bunkum.*

bunsen ['bʌnsn] : **bunsen (burner)** *nc* a gas burner which produces a smokeless flame of great heating power: *Several of the bunsens in the chemistry laboratory are out of order.*

bunting ['bʌntiŋ] *nu* (*formal*) (a thin cloth for) flags for use in celebrations: *Bunting was hung in honour of the coronation.*

buoy [boi, (*Amer*) 'bu:i] *nc* a floating anchored mark, acting as a guide, as a warning, or as a mooring point for boats. – *See also* **lifebuoy.** – *vt* (*usu with* **up**) to keep afloat: *The boat has huge tanks full of air which buoy it up*; (*fig*) *It is cruel to buoy up his hopes if he's going to fail.*

'buoyancy *nu* **1** the ability to float on water or in the air: *the buoyancy of a balloon.* **2** the ability to keep up one's courage *etc*: *I admire her buoyancy.*

'buoyant *adj.*

bur, burr[1] [bə:] *nc* the prickly case round the seed(s) of certain plants, sticking readily to things it touches: *The sheep had burrs sticking to its wool.*

burble ['bə:bl] *vi* **1** (*inf*) to talk at length with little meaning, *esp* from excitement: *She's always burbling (on) about her visit to America.* **2** (*formal*) (of a stream *etc*) to make a similar sound.

burden[1] ['bə:dn] *nc* (*slightly formal*) **1** something to be carried: *The old man was carrying a heavy burden up the hill*; *The ox is sometimes a beast of burden* (= an animal that carries things). **2** sometimes difficult to carry, support or withstand: *the burden of taxation*; *Her aged mother is a burden to her.* – *vt* (*formal*) to put a load, responsibility *etc* on (someone): *I won't burden you with my troubles*; *She was burdened with cares.*

'burdensome *adj* (*formal*) difficult to carry, withstand *etc*: *burdensome chores.*

the burden of proof (*legal*) the responsibility for proving (something, *esp* a point in a court of law): *The burden of proof rests with you.*

See also **unburden.**

burden[2] ['bə:dn] *nc* **1** (*very formal*) the chief idea expressed: *the burden of his complaint.* **2** (*old*) part of a song repeated at the end of each verse: a refrain.

bureau ['bjuərou] – *pls* **'bureaux** [-z], **'bureaus** – *nc* **1** a writing-desk with drawers. **2** (*Amer*) a chest of drawers. **3** (*usu in cmpds*) an office for collecting and supplying information *etc*: *a travel bureau*; *an accommodation bureau.*

bureaucracy [bju'rokrəsi] **1** *nu* a system of government by officials working for a government: *Bureaucracy is preferable to dictatorship.* **2** *nc* these officials taken as a whole. **3** *nc* a country having a government which uses such officials: *Britain is a bureaucracy now.* **4** *nu* (*derog*) unnecessarily complicated ways of doing things officially: *It takes so long to get permission to build a house because of all the bureaucracy involved.*

bureaucrat ['bjuərəkrat] *nc* (*often derog*) one who practises or favours bureaucracy: *The bureaucrats at the town hall refused us permission to build houses.* **ˌbureau'cratic** *adj.*

burgh ['bʌrə] *nc* (*hist*) in Scotland, a town area of local government, electing local councillors.

See also **borough.**

burglar ['bə:glə] *nc* a person who enters a house *etc* illegally to steal: *The burglar climbed through the kitchen window.*

'burglary *ncu* (an act of) illegally entering a house *etc* to steal: *He has been charged with burglary.*

'burgle *vt*: *Our house has been burgled*; *We've been burgled twice.*

burial *see* **bury.**

burlesque [bə:'lesk] *ncu* (a) comic and exaggerated imitation in writing or acting.

burly ['bəːli] *adj* (of a person) big, strong and heavy: *a big burly labourer*; *He's not tall, but he's fairly burly.*

Burma, Burmese *see* Appendix 2.

burn [bəːn] – *pts, ptps* **burned, burnt** [-t] – **1** *vt* to destroy, damage or injure by fire, heat, acid *etc*: *Have you burnt (up) all the dead leaves yet?*; *The fire burned all my papers*; *His hand was badly burned by the acid*; *I've burnt the toast.* **2** *vt* to use as fuel: *Our heating system burns oil.* **3** *vt* to make (a hole *etc*) by fire, heat, acid *etc*: *The acid burned a hole in my dress*; *His cigarette burned a large hole in my coat.* **4** *vi* to catch fire; to be on fire or alight: *Paper burns easily*; *The fire/lamp has been burning all night.* **5** *vi* to feel great heat or passion: *She is burning with anger/shame.* – *See also* **burn down, burn out** *below.* – *nc* **1** an injury or mark caused by fire, heat, acid *etc*: *His burns will take a long time to heal*; *We could not repair the burn in the carpet.* **2** (*esp* of rocket-engines *etc*) an act of burning.

'**burner** *nc* **1** the part of a gas lamp, stove *etc* from which the flame rises. **2** (*loosely*) any device producing such a flame: *I'll have to use a burner to get this paint off.*

burn down *vi, vt sep* to destroy (completely) by fire: *Our house has burned down*; *If you smoke in bed you might burn the house down.*

burn one's boats (*fig*) to destroy one's means of retreat: *I've burnt my boats by resigning and I haven't got another job.*

burn out *vi* to become completely extinguished; to be no longer burning: *The flames have burned out now.*

burnish ['bəːniʃ] *vt* (*formal*) to make (metal) bright by polishing: *They burnished the silver.*

burnt *see* **burn**.

burr[1] *see* **bur**.

burr[2] [bəː] *nc* a feature, found in some accents and dialects, in which all the 'r' sounds are strongly pronounced at the back of the mouth.

burrow ['bʌrou, (*Amer*) 'bəː-] *nc* a hole dug by certain animals for shelter: *a rabbit burrow.* – *vi* **1** (*usu* of animals) to make or live in holes underground: *The mole burrows underground.* **2** (of people) to make a similar place for oneself to keep warm *etc* beneath blankets on a bed *etc*: *The child burrowed under the bedclothes to hide from his sister.*

bursar ['bəːsə] *nc* a person who controls (*esp* college) money; a treasurer.

burst [bəːst] – *pt, ptp* **burst** – **1** *vti* to break open or in pieces suddenly: *The bag burst and everything fell out*; *The bubble/balloon burst.* **2** *vi* (*with* **into, through** *etc*) to come or go suddenly or violently: *He burst into the room*; *The house burst into flames*; *She burst into tears/song*; *He burst through the door.* **3** *vi* (*formal*) (of buds) to open. **4** *vt* (of rivers) to overflow or flood (the banks): *The river has burst its banks.* – *nc* **1** a break or explosion: *There's a burst in the water pipes.* **2** an (often sudden and short) outbreak: *a burst of speed/applause.*

'**bursting** *adj* (*pred*: *inf*) very eager: *He was bursting to tell us the good news.*

burst open *vi, vt sep* to open suddenly or violently: *Suddenly the door burst open*; *He burst open the door and marched in.*

burst out laughing, crying *etc* suddenly and noisily to begin to laugh, cry *etc.*

bury ['beri] *vt* **1** to place (a dead body) in a grave, the sea *etc*: *They buried him in the graveyard by the church.* **2** (*often fig*: *sometimes facet*) to cover; to hide (under the ground *etc*): *My socks are buried somewhere in this drawer*; (*fig*) *He's buried himself in his work.* – *See also* **buried in** *below.*

'**burial** *ncu* (an instance of) burying (a dead body) in a grave *etc*: *my grandfather's burial*; (*attrib*) *a burial service.*

'**buried in** deeply involved in (one's work *etc*): *He was buried in a book.*

bury the hatchet to stop quarrelling: *The two families buried the hatchet when the young people married.*

bus [bʌs] *nc* a large road vehicle for carrying passengers: *the village bus*; *He came by bus*; *He got on the bus.* – *v* – *prp* '**bus(s)ing**: *pt, ptp* **bus(s)ed** – *vt* (*esp Amer*) to carry (*esp* school-children of one race to school in another district) by bus. – *See also* **bus it** *below.*

'**bus stop** *nc* a place where buses stop to let passengers on or off.

'**bus it** (*inf*) to go (somewhere) by bus: *'Are you going by car?' 'No, I think I'll bus it.'*

busman's holiday (*inf*) the free time spent in doing the same kind of work that one normally does for a living: *The joiner spent a busman's holiday putting up shelves for his wife.*

busby ['bʌzbi] *nc* a fur hat worn as part of the uniform of some British soldiers.

bush [buʃ] **1** *nc* a growing thing between a tree and a plant in size: *a rose bush.* **2** *nu* (in Australia, Africa *etc*) wild uncultivated country.

'**bushy** *adj* **1** covered in bushes: *a bushy area of country*; *It's rather bushy here.* **2** thick and spreading: *bushy eyebrows*; *The squirrel's tail is thick and bushy.*

(the) bush telegraph (*often facet*) the fast spreading of information, *usu* by word of mouth: *The bush telegraph in our office is the most effective way of spreading news*; *The news spread by bush telegraph.*

business ['biznis] **1** *nu* occupation; trade; buying and selling: *Selling china is my business*; *The shop does more business at Christmas than at any other time.* **2** *nc* a shop; a firm; a commercial company *etc*: *He has a greengrocer's business*; *He owns his own business.* **3** *nu* duty; concern: *Make it your business to see that the work is done properly*; *Mind your own business* (= Pay attention to what concerns you and not to what concerns others); *Let's get down to business* (= Let's start the work *etc* that must be done). **4** *nc* an affair; a matter: *This business is making me ill.* **5** *nu* right: *You've no business to be here!* – *See also* **on business** *below.*

'**businesslike** *adj* practical; methodical; alert and prompt: *a businesslike approach to the problem*; *She is always very businesslike in her dealings with other firms.*

'**businessman** *nc* a man who makes a living from some form of trade or commerce, not from one of the professions: *He used to be a teacher but he's a businessman now.*

on 'business in the process of doing business or something official: *No-one is admitted except on business*; *I am not here on holiday – I am here on business.*

busker ['bʌskə] *nc* a person who sings, plays music *etc* for money in the street *etc*: *a busker in a cinema queue.*

bust [bʌst] *nc* **1** (the measurement round) a woman's chest: *What bust is she?*; *She has a very* *small bust*; (*attrib*) *What is your bust measurement?* **2** a sculpture of a person's head and shoulders: *a bust of Julius Caesar.*

bustle[1] ['bʌsl] *vi* (*often with* **about**) to busy oneself (often noisily or fussily): *She bustled about doing things all day.* – *ncu* (a) hurry, fuss or (great amount of) activity. – *See also* **hustle**.

bustle[2] ['bʌsl] *nc* (*old*) a frame or pad making a skirt hang back from the hips.

busy ['bizi] *adj* **1** having a lot (of work *etc*) to do: *He's a busy man*; *I am very busy just now.* **2** full of traffic, people, activity *etc*: *The roads are busy*; *a busy office*; *a busy time of year.* **3** (*esp Amer*) (of a telephone line) engaged: *All the lines to New York are busy.* – *v refl* (*sometimes with* **with**) to occupy (oneself) with: *She busied herself preparing the meal.* **'busily** *adv.*

'busyness *nu* the state of being busy: *The busyness of the town confused the old lady.*

'busybody [-bodi] *nc* (*derog*) an interfering, nosey person: *She's just an old busybody.*

but [bʌt] *conj* **1** used to show a contrast between two or more things: *John was there but Peter was not*; *She's a pretty girl, but not very clever*; *It was a sunny but rather windy day*; *'It's time to go home.' 'But it's only nine o'clock!'* **2** in various formal uses: *You probably won't succeed – however, you can but try* (= trying is the only way to find out); *I couldn't but admit* (= I had to admit) *that he was right*; *It never rains but it pours* (= It never rains without pouring). – *prep* except (for): *no-one but me*; *the next road but one* (= the road after the next one).

'but for without: *But for your help we would have been late.*

but 'then however: *She is very beautiful – but then so are her sisters*; *I like living here – but then I've never lived anywhere else.*

butane ['bju:tein] *nu* a gas obtained from petroleum and used as fuel: *We use butane as fuel when we are camping*; (*attrib*) *butane gas.*

butch [butʃ] *adj* (*sl*) **1** (of a woman) mannish: *a butch hairstyle*; *butch clothes.* **2** (of a man) masculine; often tough and strong-looking.

butcher ['butʃə] *nc* **1** a person whose business is to kill cattle *etc* for food and/or sell their flesh. **2** a shop that sells mainly meat: *I'm going to the butcher.* **3** (*derog*) a person who enjoys cruel killing: *That general was a butcher who put many people to death.* – *vt* **1** to kill for food. **2** to kill cruelly: *All the prisoners were butchered by the dictator.*

'butcher's *nc* a butcher's shop: *There was a long queue at the butcher's.*

'butchery *nu* killing on a large scale.

butler ['bʌtlə] *nc* the head male servant of a household: *Very few households can afford a butler nowadays.*

butt[1] [bʌt] *vti* to strike (someone or something) with the head as a goat does: *He fell over when the goat butted him.* – *nc* such a blow.

butt in *vi* (*inf*) to interrupt or interfere: *Don't butt in while I'm speaking!*

butt into *vt fus* (*inf*) to interrupt (a conversation *etc*).

butt[2] [bʌt] *nc* a large barrel for beer, rainwater *etc.*

butt[3] [bʌt] *nc* someone whom others criticize or tell jokes about: *She's the butt of all his jokes.*

butt[4] [bʌt] *nc* **1** the thick and heavy end (*esp* of a rifle). **2** the end of a finished cigar, cigarette *etc*: *His cigarette butt was the cause of the fire.* **3** (*Amer inf*) the buttocks: *Get off your butt!*

butter ['bʌtə] *nu* a fatty substance made from cream by churning: *She spread butter on the bread.* – *vt* to spread with butter: *She buttered the bread.* – *See also* **butter up** *below.*

'buttery *adj*: *My fingers were buttery after I'd made the sandwiches*; *a buttery knife.*

'buttercup *nc* (a plant with) a cup-like yellow flower.

'butterfingers *nc* (*inf*) a person who often drops, or is likely to drop, things which he or she is carrying.

'buttermilk *nu* the milk left after butter has been churned.

'butterscotch [-skotʃ] *nu* a kind of hard toffee made with butter.

butter up *vt sep* (*inf*) to flatter (someone) *usu* because one wants him to do something for one: *He's always buttering up the boss because he wants promotion*; *He butters her up because she has a lot of money.*

butterfly ['bʌtəflai] *nc* a type of insect with large (often coloured) wings: *Some butterflies resemble moths.*

buttery *see* **butter**.

buttock ['bʌtək] *nc* **1** (*usu in pl*) either half of the part of the body on which one sits: *She smacked the child on the buttocks.* **2** the corresponding part of an animal; the rump: *the buttocks of the horse.*

button ['bʌtn] *nc* **1** a knob or disc of metal, bone, plastic *etc* used as a fastening, ornament or badge: *I lost a button off my coat.* **2** a small knob pressed to operate something: *This button turns the radio on.* – *vti* (*often with* **up**) to fasten by means of buttons: *This coat buttons up to the neck*; *Button your jacket (up)!*

'buttonhole *nc* **1** the hole or slit into which a button is put. **2** a flower or flowers worn in a buttonhole: *The bridegroom wore a carnation as a buttonhole.* – *vt* (*inf*) to catch someone's attention and hold him in conversation: *He buttonholed me and began telling me the story of his life.*

buttress ['bʌtris] *nc* (*tech*) a support built on to the outside of a wall. – *vt* (*tech or formal*) to support: *These massive planks of wood buttress the crumbling walls*; (*formal or fig*) *This loan will buttress my finances for a while.*

buxom ['bʌksəm] *adj* (of a woman) plump and *usu* attractive: *a buxom blonde*; *She is small and buxom.*

buy [bai] – *prp* **'buying**: *pt, ptp* **bought** [bo:t] – *vt* to get (something) by exchanging it for something else, *esp* money: *He has bought a car*; *He bought himself out of the army*; *You cannot buy freedom.*

buy in *vt sep* to buy a stock or supply of: *Have you bought in enough bread for the weekend?*

buy off *vt sep* (*inf*) to bribe: *The gangster's friends bought off the police witness.*

buy out *vt sep* to buy completely (a company's shares *etc*): *The large company expanded by buying out several smaller ones.*

buy up *vt sep* to buy (things) in large quantities: *I've bought up all the houses in this street.*

buzz [bʌz] **1** *vi* (of an insect) to make a noise by beating its wings *eg* when flying: *The bees buzzed angrily in the hive*; *The bluebottle buzzed around the room.* **2** *vi* to be filled with a similar noise: *My ears are buzzing*; *The crowd was buzzing with excitement*; *The whole firm was buzzing with the news of his promotion.* **3** *vi* (*inf*) to go quickly: *She's always buzzing around the place*; *Buzz off!* **4** *vt* (of aeroplanes) to fly very low over, or very close to. –

1 *nu* (*sometimes with* **a**) a buzzing sound: *a low buzz of conversation.* 2 *nc* (*no pl*: *inf*) a telephone call: *Give me a buzz sometime.*

'**buzzer** *nc* an electrical or other apparatus producing a buzzing sound: *The manager pressed the buzzer to ask his secretary to come in.*

buzzard ['bʌzəd] *nc* a large bird of prey.

by [bai] *prep* **1** next to; near; at the side of: *Stand by the door*; *He sat by his sister.* **2** past: *I saw him going by the house.* **3** through; along; across: *We came by the main road.* **4** used (in the passive voice) to show the person or thing which performs an action: *'Hamlet' was written by Shakespeare*; *He was struck by a stone.* **5** using: *He's going to contact us by letter*; *We're travelling to Glasgow by train*; *He gripped me by the throat.* **6** from; through the means of: *He earns his living by writing novels*; *I met her by chance*; *We met by accident.* **7** (of time) before; not later than: *Be here by 6 o'clock.* **8** during the time of: *We'll be travelling by day.* **9** to the extent of: *He's taller by ten centimetres.* **10** used to give measurements, compass directions *etc*: *4 metres by 2 metres*; *north-north-east by north.* **11** in quantities of: *We sell potatoes by the kilo*; *Can we pay by the week?* **12** with regard to; in respect of: *She is a teacher by profession*; *The house was sold to a doctor, Jones by name.* – *adv* **1** near: *A crowd stood by and watched.* **1** past: *A dog ran by.* **3** aside; away: *money put by for an emergency.*

'**by-election** *nc* an election during the sitting of parliament to fill a seat in one constituency where the sitting member has died or resigned.

'**bygone** *adj* (*liter*: *attrib*) past: *in bygone times.*

'**bygones: let bygones be bygones** to forgive and forget past causes of ill-feeling.

by-law *see* **bye-law**.

'**bypass** *nc* a road which avoids an obstruction or a busy area: *Take the bypass round the city.* – *vt* **1** to avoid (a place) by taking such a road. **2** to leave out (one person or step in a process): *I've bypassed my boss and gone straight to his boss.*

'**by-product** *nc* something obtained or formed during the making of something else: *Dyes and plastics can be made from coal tar, a by-product of the process of obtaining gas from coal.*

'**byroad, 'byway** *nc* (*formal*) a side road, path *etc* used by few people.

'**bystander** *nc* a spectator: a person who watches but does not take part: *There were several bystanders present when the accident happened but no-one would give a statement to the police.*

'**byword** *nc* a person or thing which is very well known and used as an example of something: *Her name is a byword for success.*

by and by after a short time: *By and by, everyone went home.*

by and large mostly; all things considered: *Things are going quite well, by and large.*

by oneself **1** alone: *He was standing by himself at the bus-stop.* **2** without anyone else's help: *He did the job (all) by himself.*

by the way incidentally: *By the way, have you a moment to spare?*

bye [bai] *nc* **1** a pass to the next round of a competition, not having drawn an opponent in the current round: *I got a bye into the third round of the tennis tournament.* **2** in cricket, a run made when the batsman has not hit the bowled ball.

'**bye-law, 'by-law** *nc* a law made by a local authority, not a national law: *There is a bye-law forbidding football games on Sunday in that village.*

Cc

cab [kab] *nc* **1** a carriage for hire, horse-drawn or now *usu* motor-driven ('**taxi-cab**): *Could you call a cab for me?* **2** the driver's compartment of a railway engine, lorry *etc.*

'**cabby** *nc* (*inf*) a taxi-driver.

cabaret ['kabərei] *ncu* (an) entertainment given in a restaurant *etc*: *She was a singer in a cabaret*; *She prefers cabaret to the stage.*

cabbage ['kabidʒ] **1** *nc* a type of vegetable with edible (*usu* green) leaves: *He bought a cabbage.* **2** *nu* the leaves as food: *Would you like some more cabbage?*

caber ['keibə] *nc* a long heavy pole tossed by Scottish Highland athletes.

cabin ['kabin] *nc* **1** a small house or hut (often made of logs *etc*): *They lived in a log cabin in a remote part of Canada.* **2** a (small) room, *esp* in a ship, aeroplane *etc*, for sitting or sleeping in: *We've booked a four-berth cabin on the ship*; *How many passengers does the cabin of this aircraft seat?*

'**cabin-boy** *nc* (*hist*) a boy who waits on the staff or passengers of a ship.

cabinet ['kabinit] *nc* **1** a piece of furniture with shelves and doors or drawers: *a filing cabinet.* **2** the casing round a television set, radio *etc*: *What wood is the cabinet of that television made of?*

the Cabinet in Britain and some other countries the group of chief ministers who govern a country: *The Prime Minister has chosen a new Cabinet.*

cable ['keibl] **1** *ncu* (a) strong rope or chain for hauling or tying anything, *esp* a ship. **2** *ncu* (a set of) wires for carrying electric current or signals: *They are laying (a) new cable.* **3** *ncu* (a rope made of) strands of metal wound together for supporting a bridge *etc.* **4** *nc* (*naut*) a measure of length or depth equal to 100 fathoms. **5** *nc* (*also* '**cablegram**) a telegram sent by cable. – *vti* to telegraph by cable: *I cabled news of my mother's death to our relations in Canada*; *I'll cable when I arrive.*

caboose [kə'buːs] *nc* (*Amer*) the van for the train crew on a freight train.

cacao [kə'kaːou, (*Amer*) kə'keiou] *nc* **1** (*also* **ca'cao tree**) the tropical tree from whose seeds cocoa and chocolate are made. **2** the seed.

cache [kaʃ] *nc* (*formal or facet*) **1** a hiding-place for treasures *etc.* **2** a quantity of such hidden things: *Despite being on a diet, she has a cache of chocolate in the cupboard.*

cackle ['kakl] *nc* **1** the sound made by a hen or goose. **2** (*derog*) a laugh which sounds like this: *an evil cackle.* – *vi* to make such a sound.

cacophony [kə'kofəni] *ncu* (*formal*) (an) unpleasant combination of loud noises: *These instruments make a cacophony of sounds.* **ca'cophonous** *adj.*

cactus ['kaktəs] – *pls* '**cacti** [-tai] , (*inf*) '**cactuses,** '**cactus** – *nc* a prickly plant whose stem stores water and does the work of leaves.

cad [kad] *nc* (*old*: *inf derog*) a dishonourable person: *I don't want that cad to marry my daughter.* '**caddish** *adj.*

cadaver [kə'davə] *nc* (*formal or tech*) a dead (*usu* human) body: *The police surgeon examined the cadaver.*

ca'daverous *adj* (*formal*) like a dead person; thin and pale: *pale, cadaverous cheeks*; *He looks cadaverous – I think he's going to die.*

caddie, caddy[1] ['kadi] *nc* a person who carries clubs for a golfer.

caddy[2] ['kadi] *nc* a small box for keeping tea leaves in: *The caddy is empty*; *a tea-caddy.*

cadence ['keidəns] (*formal*) **1** *ncu* the fall of the human voice; (a) falling intonation: *The cadence at the end of this sentence is quite marked.* **2** *nu* rhythm: *the cadence of poetry.* **3** *nc* a group of chords which end a piece of music: *These ten bars form the cadence.*

cadenza [kə'denzə] *nc* (*formal*) an ornamental passage for a solo instrument *usu* near the end of a piece of music.

cadet [kə'det] *nc* **1** a student in a military, naval or police school: *an army cadet*; *a police cadet.* **2** a schoolboy taking military training: *a school cadet*; (*attrib*) *He is in the school cadet force.*

café ['kafei, (*Amer*) ka'fei] *nc* a (*usu* small) shop where meals and drinks (in Britain, only non-alcoholic) are served: *We had coffee and sandwiches in a motorway café*; *We had delicious wine in that French café.*

cafeteria [kafə'tiəriə] *nc* a self-service restaurant: *This department store has a cafeteria.*

caffeine ['kafi:n, (*Amer*) ka'fi:n] *nu* a drug found in coffee and tea: *I drink lots of coffee when I'm working – the caffeine keeps me awake.*

caftan, kaftan ['kaftan] *nc* a type of long flowing dress or robe sometimes brightly-coloured.

cage [keidʒ] *nc* **1** (*sometimes in cmpds*) a box of wood, wire *etc* for holding birds or animals: *The lion has escaped from its cage*; *a bird-cage.* **2** a lift in a mine. – *vt* (*formal*) to put in a cage: *Some people think that it is cruel to cage wild animals.*

'**cagebird** *nc* a bird, *eg* a canary, suitable for keeping in a cage.

cagey ['keidʒi] *adj* (*inf*: *esp pred*) wary; cautious; secretive: *He's very cagey about telling people his plans.* '**caginess** *nu.*

cairn [keən] *nc* **1** a heap of stones set up to mark a place, *esp* a grave, hilltop, mountain pathway *etc.* **2** a type of small Scottish dog.

cairngorm [keən'go:m] *ncu* a (piece of) brown or yellow quartz often used as jewellery: *a necklace of cairngorms*; (*attrib*) *a cairngorm ring.*

cajole [kə'dʒoul] *vt* (*more formal than* **coax** *or* **persuade**) to coax (someone into doing something), often by flattery: *The little girl cajoled her father into buying her a new dress.*

cake [keik] **1** *nu* a food made by baking a mixture of flour, fat, eggs, sugar *etc*: *Have a piece of cake.* **2** *nc* a small or large shape of such a food: *a plate of cream cakes*; *a Christmas cake.* **3** *nc* (*often in cmpds*) a piece of other food pressed into shape: *fishcakes*; *oatcakes.* **4** *nc* a flattened hard mass: *a cake of soap/chocolate.* – *vti* to cover with a hard mass: *His shoes were caked with mud.*

a piece of cake *see* **piece**.

calamine lotion ['kaləmain] *nu* a pink lotion used to soothe inflamed or sore skin: *Put some calamine lotion on your sunburn.*

calamity [kə'laməti] *nc* (*sometimes facet*) a great misfortune or disaster: *It will be a calamity if he fails his exam.* **ca'lamitous** *adj.*

calcium ['kalsiəm] *nu* an element (symbol **Ca**) of which one compound (**calcium carbonate**) forms limestone, chalk *etc.*

calculate ['kalkjuleit] **1** *vti* (*more formal than* **count**) to count or estimate, using numbers: *Calculate the number of days in a century*; *I must calculate how much money I'll spend next week.* **2** *vi* (*formal*) (*with* **on**) to depend (on): *We can calculate on winning.* '**calculable** *adj.*

'**calculated** *adj* (*esp attrib*) deliberate: *a calculated attempt to kill someone.*

'**calculating** *adj* (*derog*: *usu attrib*) selfish; scheming: *a cold, calculating murderer*; *a calculating woman.*

ˌ**calcu'lation** (*formal*) **1** *ncu* (an act of) counting using numbers: *His calculations are never accurate*; *a fault of calculation.* **2** *nu* (*derog*) scheming *etc*: *His success was the result of his cunning and calculation.*

'**calculator** *nc* a machine for calculating: *Use a calculator for adding all those numbers.*

a calculated risk a possibility of failure that has been estimated and taken into consideration before a course of action is taken: *He took a calculated risk when he bought shares in that company.*

'**calculated to** designed or likely to: *His speech was calculated to cause trouble*; *I can think of nothing more calculated to cause trouble.*

See also **incalculable**.

calculus ['kalkjuləs] *nu* a mathematical system of calculation which studies variable quantities.

caldron *see* **cauldron**.

calendar ['kaləndə] *nc* **1** a table showing the months and days of the year: *Look at the calendar and tell me which day of the week November 22nd is.* **2** a list of important dates or events: *The football team's calendar is complete now.*

calf[1] [ka:f] – *pl* **calves** [ka:vz] – **1** *nc* the young of a cow, elephant, whale *etc.* **2** *nu* (*also* '**calfskin**) leather made from the skin of the young of a cow.

calve [ka:v] *vi* to give birth to a calf: *The cow calved last night.*

calf[2] [ka:f] – *pl* **calves** [ka:vz] – *nc* the thick fleshy back part of the leg below the knee: *She has slim ankles but fat calves.*

caliber *see* **calibre**.

calibrate ['kalibreit] *vt* (*tech*) **1** to mark out the scale on (a measuring instrument). **2** to correct or adjust (the scale or instrument): *He calibrated the weighing machine.*

calibre, (*Amer*) **caliber** ['kalibə] **1** *nc* the inner diameter of a gun barrel *etc.* **2** *nu* (*formal*) (of a person) quality of character; ability: *a salesman of extremely high calibre.*

calico ['kalikou] *nu, adj* (of) a type of cotton cloth: *two metres of calico*; *a calico skirt*; *My jacket is calico.*

calipers *see* **callipers**.

call [ko:l] **1** *vt* to give a name to: *My name is Andrew but my friends call me Drew*; *I'm called Sandy by my friends.* **2** *vt* to regard (something) as: *I call his behaviour abominable*; *I call that cheating.* **3** *vti* to speak loudly (to someone), often to attract attention: *Call everyone over here*; *She called aloud to attract attention.* **4** *vt* to summon; to ask (someone) to come (by letter, telephone *etc*): *They called him for interview*; *He called a doctor.* **5** *vi* to make a visit: *I shall call at your house this evening*; *You were out when I called.* – *See also* **call on**[1]. **6** *vt* to telephone: *I'll call you at 6 p.m.* – *See also* **call up**. **7** *vti* (in card games) to bid. – *See also* **call** *in phrases below*. – **1** *nc* an exclamation or shout: *a call for help.* **2** *nc* the song of a bird: *the call of the blackbird.* **3** *nc* a (*usu* short) visit: *The minister made calls on all the members of the congregation.* **4** *nc* the act of calling on the telephone: *I've just had a call from the police.* **5** *nc* (*usu with* **the**) attraction: *the call of the hills*; *the call of the sea.* **6** *nu* (*usu in neg*) a demand: *There's no call for shepherds nowadays.* **7** *nu* (*usu in neg*) a need or reason: *You've no call to say such things!* **'caller** *nc*.

'calling *nc* (*formal*) a trade or profession: *Teaching is a worthwhile calling.*

'call-box *nc* (*Brit*) a public telephone box.

'call-girl *nc* a prostitute.

call-up *see* **call up**.

'call for *vt fus* **1** to demand or require: *This calls for quick action*; *Was your rudeness really called for?* **2** to collect: *I'll call for you at eight o'clock.* – *See also* **uncalled-for**.

call in *vt sep* **1** to ask to come: *Call in the doctor!* **2** to request the return of: *The Bank of England has called in all the old ten-shilling notes.*

call off **1** *vi, vt sep* to cancel: *The party's been called off*; *She accepted the invitation to the party, but called off at the last minute*; *They called it off.* **2** *vt sep* to order a dog *etc* to stop attacking (someone): *He called off the dogs before they really injured their victims*; *Call your dog off – it's attacking mine.*

'call on[1] *vt fus* **1** to visit: *I'll call on our new neighbour tomorrow.* **2** (*formal*) to summon or gather together: *call on all one's resources.* **3** (*formal*) to appeal to: *They called on God for help.*

call on[2] *vt sep* to order to come forward: *I stopped my car at the halt-sign, but the policeman called me on.* – *See also* **call** (*def 5*).

call out *vt sep* **1** to instruct workers to come on strike: *The union has called out the electricity workers.* **2** to summon or bring into operation: *The army was called out to deal with the riot.*

call up *vt sep* **1** to call to service *esp* in the armed forces (*nc* **'call-up**). **2** to bring to memory; to recall: *Seeing the children playing called up memories of my own childhood.* **3** (*inf*) to telephone (someone): *He called his mother up from the airport.*

call in(to) question to challenge or cause to be doubted: *The new archaeological evidence called into question all previous historical accounts.*

call it a day *see* **day**.

call to account (*formal*) to demand an explanation from (someone): *The soldier was called to account for not saluting an officer.*

give (someone) a call (*inf*) to telephone (someone): *I'll give you a call around seven o'clock.*

on 'call keeping (oneself) ready to come out to an emergency: *Which of the doctors is on call tonight?*

calligraphy [kə'ligrəfi] *nu* (*tech*) (the art of) beautiful, decorative handwriting.

callipers, calipers ['kalipəz] *n pl* **1** compasses suitable for measuring the inside or outside diameter of objects. **2** metal leg supports for a disabled person: *Polio victims often wear callipers.*

callosity [kə'losəti] *nc* (*med*) (*also* **callus, callous**[1] ['kaləs]) a hard thickening of the skin.

callous[2] ['kaləs] *adj* (*derog*) unfeeling; cruel: *a callous person/attack*; *You are being rather callous.* **'callously** *adv*. **'callousness** *nu*.

callow ['kalou] *adj* (*formal derog*: *usu attrib*) young and inexperienced: *a callow youth.*

callus *see* **callosity**.

calm [ka:m] *adj* **1** still or quiet: *a calm sea*; *The weather was calm.* **2** not anxious or excited: *a calm person/expression*; *Please keep calm!* – **1** *ncu* (a period of) absence of wind and large waves. **2** *nu* peace and quiet: *He enjoyed the calm of the library.* – *vt* to make calm: *Calm yourself!* **'calmly** *adv*. **'calmness** *nu*.

calm down *vi, vt usu sep* to make or become calm: *He tried to calm her down by giving her some brandy*; *Calm down!*

See also **becalmed**.

Calor gas ® ['kalə] *nu* butane: *Our cooker uses Calor gas*; (*attrib*) *a Calor gas stove.*

calorie ['kaləri] *nc* (*tech*: *often abbrev* **cal** *when written*) **1** a unit of heat. **2** a unit of energy given by food: *My diet allows me 1200 calories per day.*

,calo'rific *adj* (*esp attrib*): *a calorific value of 200.*

,calo'rimeter [-'rimitə] *nc* (*tech*) an instrument for measuring heat.

calumny ['kaləmni] (*formal*) **1** *nc* a slanderous statement. **2** *nu* slander or lies: *He was found guilty of calumny.*

calve, calves *see* **calf**[1], **calf**[2].

calypso [kə'lipsou] –*pl* **ca'lypsos** – *nc* a West Indian folk-song, telling of a current event and sometimes made up as the singer goes along.

camaraderie [kamə'ra:dəri] *nu* (*formal*) the spirit of comradeship, friendliness: *He enjoyed the camaraderie of the army.*

camber ['kambə] *ncu* a slight curve across a surface (of a road *etc*).

Cambodia, Cambodian *see* Appendix 2.

cambric ['kambrik] *nu, adj* (of) a type of fine white linen or cotton: *white cambric*; *a cambric handkerchief.*

came *see* **come**.

camel ['kaməl] *nc* a desert animal with one (**dromedary** ['dromədəri]) or two (**bactrian (camel)** ['baktriən]) humps on its back, used for carrying goods and/or people.

camellia [kə'mi:liə] *nc* (the red or white flower of) an evergreen shrub from eastern Asia.

cameo ['kamiou] *nc* **1** an engraved stone in which the design is raised, used as jewellery: *Cameos were common in Victorian times*; (*attrib*) *a cameo brooch.* **2** (*formal*) a short play or piece of writing.

camera ['kamərə] *nc* **1** an apparatus for taking still or (**'movie-camera**) moving photographs. **2** in television, an apparatus which receives a picture and turns it into electrical impulses for transmitting.

in camera (of a law case) tried in secret.

camouflage ['kaməfla:ʒ] *ncu* something, *eg* protective colouring, that makes an animal, person, building *etc* difficult for enemies to see against the background: *The tiger's stripes are an effective camouflage in the jungle*; *The soldiers wound leaves and twigs round their helmets as camouflage.* – *vt* to hide (something) with camouflage: *The soldiers used tree-branches to camouflage the guns.*

camp[1] [kamp] *nc* **1** a piece of ground with tents pitched on it. **2** a collection of buildings, huts or tents in which people stay temporarily for a certain purpose: *a holiday camp.* **3** a military station, barracks *etc.* **4** a party or side: *They belong to different political camps.* – *vi* (*also* **go camping**) to set up, and live in, a tent/tents: *We camp there every summer; We go camping every year.*

'**camper** *nc* **1** a person who goes camping. **2** (*esp Amer*) a motor-caravan. '**camping** *nu.*

camp bed *nc* (*Amer* **cot**) a light folding bed (not only for camping): *The visitor will have to sleep on a camp bed.*

camp follower *nc* a person (not a soldier) who follows in the rear of an army: *Napoleon's camp followers;* (*fig: derog*) *She is not attached to the movement – she's only a camp follower.*

'**campsite** *nc* a piece of land on which tents may be pitched.

camp[2] [kamp] *adj* (*inf*) **1** (deliberately) effeminate: *camp behaviour/gestures; The way he walks is very camp.* **2** so absurdly old-fashioned, exaggerated *etc* as to be considered amusing: *That old film was rather camp; rather camp birthday cards.* – *nu* (*inf*) something, *eg* behaviour, acting *etc*, that is effeminate or absurdly affected, exaggerated or sentimental.

camp up *vt sep* (*inf*) to make (something) camp: *They camped up the original play so much that it was unrecognizable.*

campaign [kam'pein] *nc* **1** (*mil*) the operations of an army while fighting in one area or for one purpose: *the Burma campaign in the Second World War.* **2** (*formal*) a series of organized actions in support of a cause: *a campaign against smoking.* – *vi* (*formal*) to take part in a campaign: *He has campaigned against smoking for years.* **cam'paigner** *nc.*

campanology [kampə'nɔlədʒi] *nu* (*tech*) (the study of) bell-ringing. ˌ**campa'nologist** *nc.*

camphor ['kamfə] *nu* a strongly scented whitish substance, used for various medical and industrial purposes: *Moth balls contain camphor.*

'**camphorated** [-reitid] *adj* (*attrib*) treated or saturated with camphor: *camphorated oil.*

campus ['kampəs] *nc* college or university grounds: *The new library was built in the centre of the campus; That architect has designed several campuses.*

can[1] [kan] – *neg* **can't** [ka:nt], (*formal*) **cannot** ['kanət] – *modal aux* **1** to be able to: *You can do it if you try hard; He can be very charming when he likes.* **2** to know how to: *Can you drive a car?* **3** (*inf*) to have permission to: *You can go if you behave yourself; I can go, can't I?* **4** used in questions to indicate surprise, disbelief *etc*: *What can he be doing all this time?; How can she possibly marry him?*

See also **could**.

can[2] [kan] *nc* **1** (*often in cmpds*) a metal container for liquids and many types of food: *oil-can; beer-can.* **2** the amount contained in a can: *He drank six cans of beer.* – *v* – *pt, ptp* **canned** – *vt* to put (*esp* food) into cans, *usu* to preserve it: *They're canning raspberries.*

canned *adj* **1** put or contained in cans: *canned peas.* **2** (*inf: often derog*) recorded: *I hate canned music in restaurants.* **3** (*sl: pred*) drunk: *He was canned last night.*

'**cannery** *nc* a factory where goods are canned.

carry the can (*inf*) to take the blame: *I'm not going to carry the can for his mistakes.*

Canada, Canadian *see* Appendix 2.

canal [kə'nal] *nc* **1** (*often found with cap in place-names*) a (*usu* narrow) man-made waterway: *the barge on the canal; the Panama Canal.* **2** a passage in the body carrying fluids, food *etc*: *the alimentary canal.*

'**canalize, -ise** ['ka-] *vt* (*formal*) to direct into a regular channel; to make (a river) into a canal: (*fig*) *He canalized all his energies into making the old house habitable.*

canary [kə'neəri] *nc* a type of small, yellow, singing bird, kept as a pet: *two canaries in a cage.*

can-can ['kankan]: **the can-can** a type of high-kicking dance.

cancel ['kansəl] – *pt, ptp* '**cancelled**, (*Amer*) '**canceled** – **1** *vti* to decide or announce that (something already arranged, fixed *etc*) will not happen, be done *etc*: *He's cancelled his appointment; They cancelled after finding out how expensive the tickets were.* **2** *vt* to mark (stamps) with a postmark. **3** *vt* to stop payment of (a cheque, subscription *etc*): *I don't wish to be a member of the club any more – I've cancelled my subscription.* **4** *vt* to turn off (direction indicators on *eg* a car): *The driver of the car behind me thought I was turning right as I'd forgotten to cancel my indicator.* ˌ**cancel'lation** *ncu.*

cancel out *vt sep* **1** to strike out; to delete. **2** to make ineffective by having an exactly opposite effect; to neutralize: *These cancel each other out.*

cancer ['kansə] **1** *nc* a diseased growth in the body, often fatal: *The cancer has spread to her stomach.* **2** *nu* the (often fatal) condition caused by such diseased growth(s): *He is dying of cancer.* **3** *nc* (*fig formal*) an evil that gradually destroys: *Alcoholism is a cancer in our society.* **4** *n* (*with cap*) a sign of the zodiac, the Crab: *People born between June 21 and July 20 are said to be born under the sign of Cancer.*

'**cancerous** *adj.*

See also **carcinogenic**.

candelabra [kandə'la:brə] – *pl* ˌ**cande'labras** – *nc* (*also* (*rare*) ˌ**cande'labrum** [-brəm] – *pl* ˌ**cande'labra**) a branched and ornamented candlestick.

candid ['kandid] *adj* saying just what one thinks, without hiding anything: *a candid person; I was quite candid when she asked if I liked her new dress – I told her it was hideous.* '**candidly** *adv.* '**candour** [-də], '**candidness** *nus.*

candidate ['kandidət, (*Amer*) -deit] *nc* a person who enters for a competition or examination (for a job, prize *etc*): *He is a candidate for the job of manager; a parliamentary candidate;* (*fig*) *He's a candidate for the sack.*

'**candidacy** [-dəsi], '**candidature** [-dətʃə] (*formal*) **1** *nus* being a candidate. **2** *ncs* the position of a candidate.

candied *see* **candy**.

candle ['kandl] *nc* a moulded piece of wax with a wick in the centre, for giving light: *We had to use candles when the electric lights went out.*

'**candle-light** *nu* the light from a candle: *We had dinner by candle-light;* (*attrib*) *a candle-light supper.*

'**candlestick** *nc* a holder for a candle: *a pair of silver candlesticks.*

'**candlewick** [-wik] *nu* a cotton tufted material used for bedspreads *etc*: (*attrib*) *a candlewick bedspread.*

not worth the candle too difficult, troublesome *etc* for the advantages it would bring: *Working overtime isn't worth the candle because of the amount of tax I have to pay.*

candour *see* **candid**.

candy ['kandi] **1** *nu* sugar formed into a solid mass by boiling. **2** *ncu* (*Amer*) a sweet or sweets; (a piece of) confectionery: *That child eats too much candy*; *Have a candy!* – *vt* (*formal*) to coat (fruits *etc*) in sugar.

'**candied** *adj* (*attrib*) covered with sugar: *candied fruits.*

'**candy floss** *nu* (*Amer* **cotton candy**) flavoured sugar spun into a fluffy ball on the end of a stick.

'**candy-stripe(d)** *adj* striped with alternate bands of white and colour (often pink): *a candy-striped blouse.*

cane [kein] **1** *ncu* the stem of certain types of plant (*eg* a small palm, sugar plant, bamboo *etc*). **2** *nc* a stick used as an aid to walking or as an instrument of punishment: *He beat the child with a cane.* – *vt* to beat with a cane: *The schoolmaster caned the boy.*

'**caning** *nc* a beating with a cane: *He got a caning from the headmaster.*

cane sugar *nu* sugar obtained from the sugar cane.

canine ['keinain] *adj* (*attrib*: *formal*) like, or of, a dog or dogs: *canine characteristics.* – *nc* a canine tooth.

canine teeth *n pl* (*tech*) in man, the four sharp-pointed teeth.

canister ['kanistə] *nc* a box or case *usu* of metal, for holding tea, gas *etc*.

canker ['kaŋkə] *nc* (*formal*) a spreading sore: *a canker in a dog's ear*; (*fig*) *Drug addiction is a canker in the heart of society.*

cannabis ['kanəbis] *nu* a drug made from Indian hemp, whose use is illegal in many countries: *He is hooked on* (= addicted to) *cannabis.*

cannibal ['kanibəl] *nc* **1** a person who eats human flesh: *The missionary was eaten by cannibals.* **2** an animal *etc* which eats others of its own species: *Certain types of shark are cannibals.* '**cannibalism** *nu.* ˌ**canniba'listic** *adj.*

'**cannibalize, -ise** *vt* (*inf*) to take parts from (one or more machines) for use in repairing others: *I've cannibalized the first two TVs to get the third one working.*

cannon ['kanən] – *pls* '**cannons,** '**cannon** – *nc* **1** (*hist*) a type of large gun mounted on a carriage. **2** a stroke in billiards where the cue-ball hits both the other balls. – *vt* (*with* **into** *or* **off**) to hit or to hit and rebound from (something): *He came rushing round the corner and cannoned into me*; *The car cannoned off the lorry.*

'**cannonball** *nc* (*hist*) a ball, *usu* of iron, which is shot from a cannon.

cannot *see* **can**[1].

canoe [kə'nu:] *nc* a light narrow boat driven by a paddle or paddles: *He travelled by canoe.* – *vti* (*formal*) to travel by, paddle or carry in a canoe: *He canoed over the rapids.* **ca'noeist** *nc.*

canon ['kanən] *nc* **1** a law or rule (*esp* of the church). **2** (*with cap in titles*) a clergyman belonging to a cathedral: *He was made a canon*; *Canon Smith.* **3** a list of saints. **4** (*music*) a musical composition in which one part enters after another in imitation. **ca'nonical** [-'no-] *adj.*

'**canonize, -ise** *vt* to place in the list of saints: *Joan of Arc was canonized in 1920.* ˌ**canoni'zation, -s-** *ncu.*

canopy ['kanəpi] *nc* a covering hung over a throne, bed *etc* or (on poles) as a shelter: *a canopy to protect from strong sunlight.*

cant[1] [kant] *nu* **1** (*formal derog*) hypocritical and insincere speech: *He expects us to believe what he says but it's just politicians' cant.* **2** the special language or slang of a particular group of people: *thieves' cant.*

cant[2] [kant] *nc* (*formal*) an inclination; a slope: *This table has a definite cant.* – *vti* (*formal*) to tilt: *The ship began to cant.*

can't *see* **can**[1].

cantankerous [kan'taŋkərəs] *adj* (*formal*) quarrelsome, cross and unreasonable: *a cantankerous old man*; *He's feeling cantankerous.*

cantata [kan'ta:tə] *nc* a musical dramatic work sung (but not acted) by a chorus.

canteen [kan'ti:n] *nc* **1** a place where meals are sold in a factory, barracks *etc*: *It's cheaper to eat in the works canteen than to go out to a restaurant.* **2** a case for, or of, cutlery: *I gave them a canteen of cutlery as a wedding present.* **3** a small container used by soldiers for holding water *etc.*

canter ['kantə] *nc* (of a horse) an easy gallop: *He went off at a canter.* – *vti* to (cause to) gallop easily: *The horse cantered over the meadow.*

cantilever ['kantili:və] *nc* (*tech*) a large bracket for supporting balconies, stairs *etc.*

cantilever bridge *nc* a bridge composed of projecting arms built out from its supports and meeting in the middle of the span.

canto ['kantou] – *pl* '**cantos** – *nc* (*formal*) a division of a long poem.

canton ['kanton] *nc* in Switzerland, one of the federal states.

canvas ['kanvəs] **1** *nu, adj* (of) a coarse cloth made of hemp or flax *etc*, used for sails, tents *etc*, and for painting on: *canvas sails.* **2** *nc* (a piece of canvas for) a painting: *He painted twenty canvases, of which ten are in the art gallery.* **3** *nu* the sails of a ship.

under canvas in tents: *The children love living under canvas.*

canvass ['kanvəs] *vti* to go round (an area) asking (people) for (support, votes, custom *etc*): *We're canvassing for the Conservative Party candidate.* '**canvasser** *nc.*

canyon ['kanjən] *nc* (*often found with cap in place-names*) a deep valley between high steep banks, *usu* containing a river: *They looked down into the canyon*; *the Grand Canyon.*

cap [kap] *nc* **1** a soft hat *usu* with a peak: *a schoolboy's cap.* **2** a covering for the head, not with a peak: *a swimming cap*; *a nurse's cap.* **3** a cover or top (of a bottle, pen *etc*): *Replace the cap after you've finished with the pen.* – *v* – *pt, ptp* **capped** – *vt* **1** to cover (a bottle *etc*) with a cap. **2** to choose for a team: *He was capped for England at football.* **3** to do better than; to surpass: *He capped my joke with a better one*; *He was miserable enough before but to cap it all he's lost his job.*

capped *adj* (*usu in cmpds*: *usu fig*) having a cap (of a particular kind): *snow-capped mountains.*

cap in hand (*formal*) humbly: *You'll come back cap in hand when you've run out of money!*

capable ['keipəbl] *adj* **1** clever in practical ways; able: *a very capable person*; *She's so capable!* **2** (*pred*: *with* **of**) clever, skilful *etc* enough to; likely to; able to: *He is capable of doing better*; *He is quite capable of letting someone else take the blame*; *a car capable of doing 120 kilometres an hour.* '**capably** *adv.*

ˌ**capa'bility** *nu* (*formal*) the quality of being capable (of doing something): *He has the capability to complete this task.*

capacious [kə'peiʃəs] *adj* (*esp attrib*) roomy and

wide: *a capacious handbag.*

capacitor [kə'pasitə] *nc* (*tech*) an apparatus for collecting and storing electricity: *Capacitors are found in TVs and radios etc.*

capacity [kə'pasəti] **1** *nu* ability to hold, contain *etc*: *This tank has a capacity of 300 gallons*; *He has a great capacity for remembering facts.* **2** *nc* (*formal*) position: *in his capacity as a leader.*

to ca'pacity to the greatest possible extent: *filled to capacity*; *working to capacity.*

cape[1] [keip] *nc* a long, loose, sleeveless outer garment hanging from the shoulders and fastening at the neck: *She has a tweed cape*; *a waterproof cycling cape.*

cape[2] [keip] *nc* (*often found with cap in place-names*) a head or point of land sticking out into the sea: *The fishing-boat rounded the cape*; *Cape Breton.*

Cape Coloured *see* **coloured** *under* **colour**.

caper[1] ['keipə] *nc* the flower-bud of the caper shrub, pickled and used in sauces.

caper[2] ['keipə] *vi* (*formal*) to leap or jump about: *The child was capering about with excitement.* – *nc* **1** a leap or jump. **2** (*inf*) a prank; a piece of mischief: *That child's capers will get him into trouble.*

capillary [kə'piləri, (*Amer*) 'kapileri] *nc* (*tech*) a tube with a very small diameter, *esp* (*in pl*) the tiny vessels that join veins to arteries.

capita *see* **per capita** *under* **per**.

capital[1] ['kapitl] **1** *nc* the chief town or seat of government: *Paris is the capital of France*; (*attrib*) *the capital city.* **2** *nc* (*also* **capital letter**) any letter of the type found at the beginning of sentences, proper names *etc*: *THESE ARE CAPITAL LETTERS/CAPITALS.* – *See also* **block capitals** *under* **block**, **upper case** *under* **case**[2]. **3** *nu* money (for carrying on a business, investment *etc*): *You need plenty of capital to start a new business.* – *adj* **1** (*usu attrib*) involving punishment by death: *a capital offence.* **2** (*old inf*) excellent: *a capital idea*; *That's capital!*

'capitalism *nu* a system of economics in which money and business are controlled by capitalists.

'capitalist *nc* (*often derog*) a person who has much money in business concerns. **'capitalist, ˌcapita'listic** *adjs.*

'capitalize, -ise, on *vt fus* to take advantage of (a situation *etc*): *I'm capitalizing on being in bed ill by reading lots of books.*

make capital out of (*derog*) to capitalize on: *He made capital out of his ex-friend's difficult situation.*

capital[2] ['kapitl] *nc* in architecture, the top part of a column of a building *etc.*

capitulate [kə'pitjuleit] *vi* (*formal*) to surrender *usu* on agreed conditions: *We capitulated to the enemy.* **caˌpitu'lation** *nu.*

capon ['keipən, (*Amer*) -pon] *nc* a castrated cock bred for use as food: *We had a capon instead of a turkey at Christmas.*

caprice [kə'pri:s] (*formal*) **1** *ncu* an unreasonable sudden or impulsive change of mind, mood *etc*; a whim: *the caprices of a spoilt child*; (*liter fig*) *the caprice of the north wind.* **2** *nc* a fanciful and lively piece of music *etc.*

capricious [kə'priʃəs] *adj* changeable: (*liter fig*) *capricious winds*; *She's very capricious as she is constantly changing her mind.* **ca'priciously** *adv.* **ca'priciousness** *nu.*

Capricorn ['kapriko:n] *n* a sign of the zodiac, the Goat: *People born between December 21 and January 20 are said to be born under the sign of Capricorn.*

capsicum ['kapsikəm] *nc* any of various fruits of the family to which chillies and red and green peppers belong.

capsize [kap'saiz] *vti* (of a boat) to overturn, often sinking afterwards: *When the rowing-boat capsized the fishermen drowned.*

capstan ['kapstən] *nc* a drum-shaped machine, turned by levers or power-driven, used for winding *eg* a ship's anchor-cable.

capsule ['kapsju:l, (*Amer*) -sl] *nc* **1** a small gelatine case containing a dose of medicine *etc*: *Take two capsules after meals.* **2** a closed metal container: *a space capsule.* **3** the dry seedbox of a plant.

captain ['kaptən] *nc* (*with cap and often abbrev* **Capt.**, *when written in titles*) **1** in the British army, (a person of) the rank next below major: *Hasn't he been promoted yet? He's been a captain for years*; *Captain John Smith.* – *See also* Appendix 3. **2** in the British navy, (a person of) the rank next below commodore. – *See also* Appendix 3. **3** the leader of a team or club: *He is* (*the*) *captain of the football team.* – *vt* to be captain of (something non-military): *John captained the football team last year.*

'captaincy *nu* (*formal*) the job of captain: *He has given up the captaincy of the team.*

See also **group captain** *under* **group**.

caption ['kapʃən] *nc* a title or short note written on or beneath an illustration, cartoon, cinema or TV film *etc*: *The cartoon itself wasn't very funny but the caption was very witty.*

captious ['kapʃəs] *adj* (*very formal*) ready to find fault: *The old lady has become unbearably captious*; *He has a captious nature.*

captivate ['kaptiveit] *vt* (*formal*) to charm, fascinate, or hold the attention of: *He was completely captivated by her performance*; *He was captivated by her beauty.*

captive ['kaptiv] *nc* a prisoner: *Two of the captives escaped.* – *adj* **1** kept prisoner: *The captive soldiers tried to escape*; *The children were taken/held captive* (= taken/kept prisoner). **2** unable to (easily) get away: *a captive audience.*

cap'tivity *nu* a state of being a prisoner, caged *etc*: *animals in captivity in a zoo.*

'captor *nc* (*formal*) a person who captures someone: *He managed to escape from his captors.*

capture [-tʃə] *vt* **1** to take by force, skill *etc*: *The enemy captured the castle easily.* **2** to take possession of (*eg* a person's attention, imagination): *His brilliant performance captured the audience's imagination.* **3** (*formal*) to preserve; to succeed in keeping in a fixed or permanent form: *The photographer captured the happiness of the occasion*; *The painter captured the charm of the old lady.* – **1** *nu* the act of taking possession, *esp* by force: *the capture of the castle by the enemy.* **2** *nc* something caught: *A wild cat was his most recent capture.*

car [ka:] *nc* **1** (*Amer* **ˌautomo'bile**) a (*usu* privately-owned) motor vehicle on wheels for carrying people: *What kind of car do you have?*; *'Did you go by car?' 'No, we went by bus'*; *He was in his car at the time.* **2** a section for passengers in a train *etc*: *a dining-car*; *a restaurant car.* **3** (*Amer*) a railway carriage for goods or people: *a freight car.*

'car park *nc* (*Amer* **'parking lot**) a piece of land or a building where cars may be parked: *our office car park.*

'car port *nc* a shelter for a car, *esp* one with a roof and no walls built as an extension to a house: *Our* *house does not have a garage – it has a car port.*

carafe [kə'raf] *nc* **1** a glass bottle for serving water, wine *etc.* **2** the amount contained in a carafe: *He drank a whole carafe of red wine.*

caramel ['karəmel] **1** *nu* sugar melted and browned, used for colouring or flavouring: *This sauce is flavoured with caramel.* **2** *nc* a sweet made with sugar, butter *etc*: *Caramels are bad for one's teeth.*

carat ['karət] *nc* **1** a measure of weight for precious stones. **2** a unit for stating the purity of gold: *an eighteen carat gold ring.*

caravan ['karəvan] *nc* **1** (*Brit*) a vehicle on wheels for living in, able to be pulled by car, horse *etc*: *a holiday caravan*; *a gypsy caravan*; (*attrib*) *a caravan holiday.* **2** (*old*) a group of people travelling together for safety *esp* across a desert on camels: *a caravan of merchants.*

'**caravanning** *nu* taking holidays in a caravan: *We go caravanning every summer.*

ˌ**cara'vanserai** [-sərai] *nc* (*old*) an inn where desert caravans stop.

caraway ['karəwei] *nu* a plant with spicy-tasting seeds used as flavouring: *a cake flavoured with caraway.*

carbohydrate [ka:bə'haidreit] *ncu* (any of a group of) substances containing carbon, hydrogen and oxygen, *esp* the sugars and starches found in food: *Potatoes are full of carbohydrate.*

carbolic [ka:'bolik]: **carbolic acid** *nu* an acid from coal tar, used to kill germs.

carbon ['ka:bən] **1** *nu* an element (symbol **C**) occurring as diamond and graphite and also in coal *etc.* **2** *nc* a sheet of carbon paper: *Put a carbon in the typewriter – I want a copy of that letter.*

'**carbonate** [-nət] *ncu* (*tech*) a salt containing a certain combination of carbon, hydrogen, oxygen, and another element.

carbon copy *nc* **1** a copy of writing or typing made by means of carbon paper. **2** (*fig*) an exact copy: *He's a carbon copy of his brother.*

carbon dioxide [dai'oksaid] *nu* a gas present in the air, breathed out by man and other animals.

carbon monoxide [mə'noksaid] *nu* a colourless, very poisonous gas which has no smell: *There is carbon monoxide in the gases given off by a car engine*; (*attrib*) *carbon monoxide poisoning.*

carbon paper *nu* a type of paper coated with carbon *etc* which makes a copy when placed between the sheets being written or typed.

carbuncle ['ka:bʌŋkl] *nc* an inflamed swelling under the skin: *He had a carbuncle removed from his head.*

carburettor, (*Amer*) **carburetor** ['ka:bjuretə, (*Amer*) -bərei-] *nc* (*tech*) a part of an internal-combustion engine in which air is mixed with fuel: *If there is dirt in the carburettor the car will not start.*

carcase, (*esp Amer*) **carcass** ['ka:kəs] *nc* **1** a dead body, *usu* animal, not human: *They took the bull's carcase to the butcher's shop.* **2** (*derog or facet sl*) a live human body: *Shift your carcase!*

carcinogenic [ka:sinə'dʒenik] *adj* (*tech*) causing cancer: *Some chemicals are carcinogenic*; *carcinogenic substances.*

card [ka:d] **1** *nu* thick paper or thin board used for drawing *etc*: *The child painted his picture on card.* **2** *nc* (*also* '**playing-card**) a small piece of such paper *etc* with designs, used in playing certain games: *a pack of cards.* **3** *nc* a similar object used for *eg* sending greetings, showing membership of an organization, giving people a note of one's (*usu* business) address, storing information *etc*: *a Christmas card*; *a birthday card*; *a membership card*; *a business card*; *There's a card missing from the library's catalogue.*

cards *n sing* the game(s) played with playing-cards: *He cheats at cards.*

'**cardboard** *nu, adj* (of) a stiff kind of paper often made up of several layers: *Is your doll's house (made of) cardboard?*; *a cardboard box.*

'**card-carrying** *adj* (*attrib*) **1** openly showing support for or membership of an organization, point of view *etc*: *She's a card-carrying member of the women's liberation movement.* **2** (*orig*) holding a membership card of a political party *etc*: *He used to be a card-carrying member of the Communist party.*

card index *see* **index**.

'**card-sharp(er)** *nc* (*inf*: *derog*) a person who makes a business of cheating at cards played for money.

on the cards likely: *A February general election is very much on the cards.*

cardiac ['ka:diak] *adj* (*tech*: *attrib*) of the heart: *This patient has had a cardiac complaint for many years*; *cardiac failure* (= stopping of the heart).

cardigan ['ka:digən] *nc* a knitted woollen jacket which buttons up the front.

cardinal ['ka:dənl] *adj* (*formal*: *usu attrib*) of chief importance; principal: *cardinal sins/virtues.* – *nc* (*with cap in titles*) (the status of) one of the men next in rank to the Pope in the Roman Catholic Church: *He was made a cardinal*; *Cardinal Brown.*

cardinal numbers *n pl* (*formal or math*) numbers expressing quantity (1, 2, 3 *etc*) rather than order. – *See also* **ordinal numbers**.

cardinal points *n pl* the four chief points of the compass – north, east, south and west.

care [keə] **1** *nu* close attention: *Do it with care.* **2** *nu* keeping; protection: *Your belongings will be safe in my care*; *Her children have been taken into/are in care* (= into or in the keeping of welfare services, local authorities *etc*). **3** *ncu* (a cause for) worry: *I haven't a care in the world!*; *free from care*; *all the cares of the world.* – *vi* **1** to be anxious or concerned: *I couldn't care less about her* (= She is of no importance to me). **2** (*formal*) to wish or be willing (to): *Would you care to have dinner with me?* **3** *see* **care for** *below.*

'**careful** *adj* **1** taking care; being cautious: *Be careful when you cross the street*; *She is a careful driver.* **2** (*usu attrib*) thorough: *He has made a careful study of the problem.*

'**carefully** *adv*: *Please drive carefully*; *He studied the book carefully.* '**carefulness** *nu.*

'**careless** *adj* not careful (enough): *This work is careless*; *a careless worker.* '**carelessly** *adv.* '**carelessness** *nu.*

'**carefree** *adj* light-hearted: *a carefree attitude to life*; *She is carefree now.*

'**caretaker** *nc* a person who looks after something, *esp* a building.

'**careworn** *adj* aged or troubled by worry: *a careworn face*; *She looked careworn.*

'**care for** *vt fus* **1** to look after (someone): *The nurse will care for you from now on.* **2** to be fond of: *I don't care for him enough to marry him*; *I don't care for flowers very much.*

'**care of** (*usu written* **c/o**) at the house or address of: *Send the parcel to me care of Jones, 10 High Street.*

take care to be cautious, watchful, thorough *etc*: *Take care on the icy roads!*: *Do take care or you will fall!*

take care of to look after: *I will take care of you when your father dies*: *Take care of yourself while I am away.*

career [kə'riə] *nc* **1** a way of making a living (*usu* professional): *a career in publishing*; (*attrib*) *a career girl/woman* (= a woman who is very interested in her job and in getting promotion *etc*). **2** progress (through life): *The present government is nearly at the end of its career.* – *vi* to move rapidly (and often dangerously): *The runaway horse careered along the street.*

caress [kə'res] *vt* to touch gently and lovingly: *She fondly caressed the horse's neck.* – *nc* an act of touching in this way: *a loving caress.*

caret ['karit] *nc* in printing *etc*, a mark (∧ or ⋏) to show where to insert something.

cargo ['ka:gou] – *pl* **'cargoes** – *ncu* (a load of) goods carried by a ship, plane *etc*: *a cargo of cotton.*

caribou ['karibu:] – *pls* **'caribou, 'caribous** – *nc* the N American reindeer: *a herd of caribou*; *two caribou(s).*

caricature ['karikətjuə] **1** *nc* a drawing or imitation (of someone or something) which is so exaggerated as to appear ridiculous: *People often draw caricatures of politicians*; (*fig derog*) *Where's your caricature of a dog* (= your funny-looking dog) *?* **2** *nu* the art of making such drawings or imitations: *He is good at caricature.* – *vt* to ridicule (someone) by means of a caricature.

'caricaturist *nc* a person who makes caricatures.

caries ['keərii:z] – *nu* (*tech*) decay or rottenness of the bones or *esp* the teeth: *Cleaning your teeth regularly prevents caries.*

carnage ['ka:nidʒ] *nu* (*formal*) the slaughter of great numbers of people: *The carnage in the First World War was terrible.*

carnal ['ka:nl] *adj* (*formal*: *esp attrib*) sexual rather than spiritual: *carnal desires/pleasure.*

carnation [ka:'neiʃən] *nc* a type of garden flower, *usu* pink, red or white.

carnival ['ka:nivəl] *nc* **1** a public entertainment, often involving processions of people in fancy dress *etc*: *a winter carnival.* **2** a fair: *Children enjoy the merry-go-rounds at carnivals.*

carnivore ['ka:nivo:] *nc* (*tech*) a flesh-eating animal: *The lion is a carnivore.*

car'nivorous *adj* (*tech*): *Lions are carnivorous*; *A lion is a carnivorous animal.*

carol ['karəl] *nc* a song of joy or praise, *esp* for Christmas. – *v* – *pt, ptp* **carolled**, (*Amer*) **caroled** – *vi* (*liter*) to sing joyfully: *The children carolled happily.*

carouse [kə'rauz] *vi* (*formal*) to take part in a noisy drinking session: *They caroused all night.*

ca'rousal *nc.*

carousel [karə'sel] *nc* (*Amer*) a merry-go-round.

carp[1] [ka:p] – *pls* **carp**, (*sometimes*) **carps** – *nc* a freshwater fish which is common in ponds.

carp[2] [ka:p] *vi* (*derog*: *often with* **at**) to find fault with small errors *etc*: *He's always carping at/about unimportant details*; *She carps at her children constantly.*

carpenter ['ka:pəntə] *nc* a craftsman in wood, *esp* one who is employed in building houses *etc.*

'carpentry *nu* the work or trade of a carpenter.

carpet ['ka:pit] **1** *ncu* a woven covering for floors, stairs *etc*: *We have fitted carpets* (= carpets from wall to wall) *in our house*; *Our stair carpet is very badly worn*; *The floor was covered with some bits of old carpet.* **2** *nc* (*fig*: *formal or liter*) something which covers like a carpet: *a carpet of flowers.* – *vt* **1** to cover with, or as if with, a carpet: *They haven't carpeted the floor yet.* **2** (*inf*) to reprimand; to scold: *The teacher carpeted him for running away.*

carpet slippers *n pl* slippers with a covering of carpet-like material.

on the carpet (*inf*) summoned before someone in authority for (verbal) punishment: *You'll be on the carpet for that.*

carriage ['karidʒ] **1** *nu* the act or cost of carrying: *Does that price include carriage?*; *carriage free/paid.* **2** *nc* a vehicle for carrying (*esp* in Britain railway passengers): *I like to sit in the carriage nearest the engine*; *a railway carriage*; *a gun-carriage.* **3** *nc* (*esp hist*) a horse-drawn passenger vehicle. **4** *nc* the part of a typewriter which moves back and forwards, carrying the paper. **5** *nu* (*sometimes with* **a**: *formal*) bearing; way of walking: *She has a very dignified carriage*; *Good carriage is essential for a dancer.*

'carriageway *nc* (*tech*: *Brit*) the part of a road used by cars *etc*: *The overturned bus blocked the whole carriageway*; *the southbound carriageway.* – *See also* **dual carriageway**.

carrion ['kariən] *nu* dead animal flesh, eaten by other animals: *Vultures feed on carrion.*

carrot ['karət] **1** *nc* (a vegetable with) an edible, orange, pointed root. **2** *ncu* the root as food: *Would you like some more carrot(s)?*; (*attrib*) *carrot soup.*

carry ['kari] **1** *vt* to take from one place *etc* to another: *He carried the chairs out of the room*; *He carried the rubbish away*; *She carried the child over the river*; *You can't carry such a load*; *Telephone cables carry signals*; *Flies carry disease.* **2** *vi* to go from one place to another: *Sound carries better over water*; *His voice carries well.* **3** *vt* to support: *These stone columns carry the weight of the whole building.* **4** *vt* to have or hold: *He carries great responsibility*; *She carries all the information for her speeches in her head.* **5** *vt* (*usu in passive*) to approve (a bill, motion *etc*) by a majority of votes: *The parliamentary bill was carried by forty-two votes.* **6** *v refl* to hold (oneself in a certain way): *He carries himself like a soldier.* **7** *vt* (*inf*) to keep in stock or sell: *This shop doesn't carry cigarettes.* – *See also* **carry** *in phrases below.*

'carrier *nc* **1** a person or thing that carries. **2** a person who passes on a disease to other people: *There's been an outbreak of typhoid and they think he's a carrier.*

'carrier pigeon *nc* a pigeon that carries messages.

carry-on *see* **carry on.**

'carry-out *nc* (*Amer and Scottish*) a take-away.

be/get carried away to be overcome by one's feelings: *She was/got carried away by the excitement.*

carry forward *vt sep* to add on (a number from one column of figures to the next): *I forgot to carry the 2 forward.*

carry off *vt sep* **1** to take away by carrying: *She carried off the screaming child*; *She carried it off quickly.* **2** to succeed in (a difficult situation *etc*): *It was a difficult moment, but he carried it off well.*

carry on **1** *vi* to continue: *You must carry on*

working; *Carry on with your work.* **2** *vt sep* to manage (a business *etc*): *He carries on a business as a greengrocer.* **3** *vi* (*inf*) to behave badly: *The children always carry on when the teacher's out of the classroom* (*nc* ˌ**carry-ˈon**: *What a carry-on* (= fuss) *there was when the child didn't get a prize*). **4** *vi* (*inf derog*: *with* **with**) to have a love affair with: *She's been carrying on with the milkman* (*nc* ˌ**carry-ˈon**: *She's having a carry-on with the milkman*).

carry out *vt sep* to accomplish or successfully finish: *He carried out the plan successfully.* – *See also* **carry** (*def 1*), **carry-out** *above.*

carry over *vi, vt sep* to continue (into the following page, time *etc*): *We'll have to carry this discussion over into tomorrow*; *You must carry that word over into the next line.* – *See also* **carry** (*def 1*).

carry through *vt sep* (*formal*) **1** to help to continue: *Your support will carry me through.* **2** to complete or accomplish: *Now that you have begun the task you must carry it through to the end.*

carry the day to gain victory: *John's arguments carried the day for us.*

carry weight to have influence: *His opinion carries a lot of weight around here.*

cart [kaːt] *nc* **1** a two-wheeled (*usu* horse-drawn) vehicle for carrying loads: *a farm cart*; *Most farmers now use tractors instead of horses and carts.* **2** (*Amer*) a small wheeled vehicle pushed by hand, for carrying groceries, golf clubs *etc*: *a cart in a supermarket.* – *vt* to carry in a cart: *He carted the manure into the field.* – *See also* **cart around, cart off** *below.*

ˈ**cartwheel** *nc* **1** a wheel of a cart. **2** a sideways somersault. – *vi* to perform a sideways somersault.

cart around *vt sep* (*inf*) to carry around, often with difficulty: *She had to cart her luggage around all day.*

cart off *vt sep* (*inf*) to carry away, *usu* impolitely or abruptly: *They carted him off to jail.*

carte *see* **à la carte**.

carte blanche [kaːtˈblãnʃ] *nu* (*formal*) complete freedom to act as one thinks best: *I'm giving you carte blanche in this matter.*

cartel [kaːˈtel] *nc* (*formal*) a combination of business firms or political parties: *They formed a cartel in order to divide their costs.*

cartilage [ˈkaːtəlidʒ] (*tech*) **1** *ncu* a firm elastic substance found in the bodies of men and animals: *She thought she had broken her nose but she had just damaged the cartilage.* **2** *nc* a piece of this substance: *She had a cartilage removed from her leg.*

cartography [kaːˈtogrəfi] *nu* (*tech*) map-making. **carˈtographer** *nc.* ˌ**cartoˈgraphic** [-ˈgra-] *adj.*

carton [ˈkaːtən] *nc* **1** a (*usu* thin) cardboard or plastic container: *That orange juice is sold in cartons.* **2** the amount contained by a carton: *I bought six cartons of milk.*

cartoon [kaːˈtuːn] *nc* **1** a drawing making fun of someone or something: *There's a cartoon of the Prime Minister in the newspaper.* **2** a film consisting of a series of drawings in which the people and animals give the impression of movement: *a Walt Disney cartoon.* **3** (*formal*) a drawing to be used as a model for a painting *etc.*

carˈtoonist *nc* a person who draws cartoons, for a newspaper *etc.*

cartridge [ˈkaːtridʒ] *nc* **1** a metal case containing the explosive charge (and *usu* a bullet) for a gun: *We found the cartridges on the hillside where he had shot the deer.* **2** (of a record-player) a stylus and its holder. **3** a plastic container of photographic film or recording tape. **4** a tube containing ink for loading a fountain pen.

ˈ**cartridge paper** *nu* thick paper for drawing on.

carve [kaːv] *vt* **1** to make designs, shapes *etc* by cutting a piece of wood *etc*: *A figure carved out of wood*; *He carved her initials on a tree.* **2** to cut up (meat) into slices: *Father carved the joint.* ˈ**carver** *nc.*

ˈ**carving** *nc* a design, ornament *etc* carved from wood, stone *etc.*

carve-up *see* **carve up**.

carve out *vt sep* (*inf*) to achieve or gain (something): *He carved out a career for himself.*

carve up *vt sep* (*sl*) **1** to divide (money, business *etc*): *We're going to carve up the profits between ourselves* (*nc* ˈ**carve-up**). **2** to cut (a person) with a knife, *usu* badly: *The criminals really carved the old man up.*

cascade [kasˈkeid] *nc* (*formal*) a waterfall: *a magnificent cascade*; (*fig*) *a cascade of blonde hair.* – *vi* to fall in or like a waterfall: *Water cascaded over the rock*; *Her hair cascaded in waves down her back.*

case[1] [keis] *nc* **1** an instance or example: *It's a case of having to be careful*; *That's a bad case of measles*; *It's different in my case.* **2** a person under medical, psychiatric *etc* treatment: *The doctor has many cases to see today.* **3** a legal trial: *The judge in this case is very fair.* **4** a statement of facts and arguments or reasons: *They have a good case against him*; *There's a good case for thinking he's wrong.* **5** (*usu with* **the**) a fact: *I don't think that that's really the case.* **6** (*gram*) a form of a noun, pronoun or adjective showing its relation to other words in the sentence (*eg* **him** is the accusative case of **he**).

case history *nc* a record of the details of a person's past from a medical, social *etc* point of view: *The nurse has taken his case history*; *Because of his case history they did not give him drugs.*

a case in point a relevant example: *Talking of wasting money, my buying this car is a case in point.*

in any case *see* **any**.

in ˈcase in order to be safe; to guard against a possibility: *I'll take an umbrella (just) in case (it rains).*

in ˈcase of (*formal*) when (a particular thing) happens: *In case of fire, telephone the fire brigade.*

in ˈthat case if that should happen or should have happened: *You're leaving? In that case, I'm leaving too.*

case[2] [keis] *nc* **1** (*often in cmpds*) a container or outer covering: *The salesman carried a case of curtain samples*; *a suitcase*; *a seed-case.* **2** the quantity which such a container holds: *We bought six cases of whisky.* **3** a piece of furniture for displaying or containing things: *a glass case full of china*; *We have three bookcases.*

lower case *nu* small alphabetic letters such as those in which these words are printed.

upper case *nu* CAPITAL LETTERS LIKE THESE.

casement [ˈkeismənt] *nc* (*usu attrib*) **1** a window which opens on (*usu* vertical) hinges; opening outwards, not up and down: *a casement window.* **2** (*liter*) any type of window.

cash [kaʃ] *nu* **1** coins or paper money, not cheques

credit cards *etc*: *'Do you wish to pay cash?' 'No, by credit card'; I want to pay by cash.* 2 (*loosely*) payment by money or cheque as opposed to delayed payment by account: *'Cash or account, madam?' 'Oh, put it on my account, please.'*; (*attrib*) *The cash price is often lower than the price charged if you pay later.* 3 (*loosely*) money in any form: *He has plenty of cash.* – *vt* to turn into, or exchange for, money: *You may cash a traveller's cheque here; Can you cash a cheque for me?* – *See also* **cash in, cash in on** *below*.

cashier [ka'ʃiə] *nc* a person who receives and pays out money (*eg* in a bank), works at a cash register *etc*: *a bank cashier; a cashier in a supermarket.*

ˌcash-and-'carry *nc* a store (often wholesale) where goods are sold more cheaply for cash and taken away by the buyer.

'cash crop *nc* a crop grown for sale, not for use by the grower: *We grow tomatoes as a cash crop at the market garden.*

cash register *nc* a machine for holding money, which records the amount put in.

cash in *vt sep* to exchange for money: *I've cashed in all my shares; He had an insurance policy with our company but he has cashed it in.*

cash in on *vt fus* (*inf*) to make money or other types of profit by taking advantage of (a situation *etc*): *He is the sort of person who cashes in on other people's misfortunes.*

cashew ['kaʃu:] *nc* 1 a type of small nut: *Is that a cashew?*; (*attrib*) *a cashew nut.* 2 the tropical tree which bears it.

cashier[1] *see* **cash**.

cashier[2] [ka'ʃiə] *vt* (*mil*) to dismiss from a post in disgrace: *The officer was cashiered for deserting his men.*

cashmere [kaʃ'miə, (*Amer*) 'kaʒmiər] *nu, adj* (of) a type of material made from fine goats' hair: *a sweater made of cashmere; a cashmere sweater.*

casino [kə'si:nou] – *pl* **ca'sinos** – *nc* a building with gambling tables *etc*.

cask [ka:sk] *nc* 1 a barrel for holding liquids, *usu* wine. 2 the amount contained by a cask: *three casks of sherry.*

casket ['ka:skit] *nc* 1 a small case for holding jewels *etc*. 2 (*esp Amer*) a coffin.

casserole ['kasəroul] *nc* 1 a covered dish in which food is both cooked and served: *an earthenware casserole.* 2 the food cooked in a casserole: *I've made a casserole for dinner.*

cassette [kə'set] *nc* 1 a plastic container for photographic film or magnetic tape: *The tape in this cassette is twisted – it was damaged in the tape recorder.* 2 such a container including its contents: *I've put a new cassette in my camera; I bought a cassette of Scottish music*; (*attrib*) *a cassette recorder.*

cassock ['kasək] *nc* a long robe worn by clergymen and church choir-singers.

cast [ka:st] – *pt, ptp* **cast** – 1 *vt* (*more formal than* **throw**) to throw: *He cast a stone into the water*; (*fig*) *These facts cast a new light on the matter*; (*fig*) *He cast a glance of surprise at the untidy room*; (*fig*) *She cast him a look of hatred.* 2 *vt* to get rid of; to take off: *Some snakes cast their skins.* 3 *vti* to throw out (a fishing-line): *I'll cast (my line) into the river.* 4 *vt* to shape (metal, clay *etc*) by pouring into a mould: *Metal is melted before it is cast.* 5 *vt* to make (an object of metal, clay *etc*) by moulding: *The statue is cast in bronze.* 6 *vt* to give a part in a play *etc* to: *She was cast as Lady Macbeth.* 7 *vti* to select the actors for (a film *etc*): *The director is casting (the film) tomorrow.* 8 *vt* (*formal*) to give (a vote): *I cast my vote for the younger candidate; She cast her vote in favour of the Common Market.* – *See also* **cast** *in phrases below*. – *nc* 1 (*formal*) a throw: *a cast of the dice.* 2 an act of throwing out (a fishing-line): *At his third cast he caught a fish.* 3 something made by moulding: *The doctor put a plaster cast on his broken leg.* 4 a mould: *The hot metal is poured into a cast.* 5 the complete set of actors in a play, opera *etc*: *the whole cast of the play.* 6 (*formal*) a type: *He has a strange cast of mind.* 7 (*formal*) a squint of the eye: *He has a cast in his right eye.* 8 something that is ejected by certain animals, *eg* the earthworm: *There were worm casts all over the grass.*

'castaway *nc* a shipwrecked person.

casting vote *nc* the deciding vote of the chairman of a meeting when the other votes are equally divided.

cast iron *nu* unpurified iron melted and shaped in a mould.

'cast-iron *adj* (*esp attrib*) 1 made of cast iron: *a cast-iron frying-pan.* 2 (*fig*) very strong: *The police had a cast-iron case against him; a cast-iron will; He can eat anything – he has a cast-iron stomach.*

'cast-off *nc* (*inf*): *I don't want my sister's cast-offs.* – *adj* (*attrib*) (*esp* of clothes) laid aside or thrown away as unwanted.

cast aside *see* **cast off** (*def 2*).

cast an/one's eye over (*inf*) to look at or examine (something): *Would you cast an eye over this letter before I post it?*

cast lots *see* **draw lots** *under* **draw**.

cast off 1 *vi, vt sep* to untie (the mooring lines of a boat). 2 *vt sep* (*also* **cast aside**) (*often fig*) to throw away as unwanted: *He's cast off all his previous business connections; Her husband cast her aside for another woman.* 3 *vi, vt sep* in knitting, to finish (the final row of stitches).

cast on *vi, vt sep* in knitting, to make the first row of stitches.

cast up *vt sep* to raise as an unpleasant reminder: *She's always casting up my failures to me.*

castanets [kastə'nets] *n pl* two hollow pieces of ivory or hard wood struck together as a rhythm for (*esp* Spanish) dances.

caste [ka:st] 1 *nc* a social class *esp* in India: *She belongs to the lowest caste.* 2 *nu* the Indian system of social classes: *Caste does not matter so much nowadays*; (*attrib*) *the caste system.*

caster[1] ['ka:stə]: **caster sugar** *nu* fine sugar used in baking *etc*.

caster[2] *see* **castor**.

castigate ['kastigeit] *vt* (*formal*) to criticize or punish severely: *The soldier was castigated for leaving the camp without permission.* **ˌcasti'gation** *nu*.

castle ['ka:sl] *nc* 1 (*often found with cap in place-names*) a large building strengthened against attack, *usu* the home of an important person; *The duke lives in a castle; Edinburgh Castle.* 2 (*also* **rook**) a piece in chess.

castor, caster ['ka:stə] *nc* a small wheel on the legs of furniture to make it easier to move: *I can't move this wardrobe – it isn't on castors.*

castor oil [ka:stər'oil, (*Amer*) 'kastəroil] *nu* an oil from a tropical plant, used in medicine as a laxative, and in engineering: *Castor oil is used in the engines of racing-cars.*

castrate [kə'streit, (*Amer*) 'kastreit] *vt* to remove

the sexual organs of (a male animal): *The bull has been castrated.* **ca'stration** *nu.*

casual ['kaʒuəl] *adj* **1** (*sometimes derog*) not careful (enough): *I took a casual glance at the book; His attitude to work is rather casual.* **2** informal: *casual clothes; Her clothes were too casual for the occasion.* **3** (*esp attrib*) happening by chance: *I discovered it only because of a casual remark.* **4** (*attrib*) not regular or permanent: *He employs casual labour.* **'casually** *adv.* **'casualness** *nu.*

casualty ['kaʒuəlti] *nc* **1** a person who is wounded or killed in a battle, accident *etc*: *There were hundreds of casualties in that battle; Were there many casualties when the factory went on fire?* **2** (*no article*) the casualty department of a hospital: *The accident victims were rushed to casualty.* **3** (*often facet*) something that is lost, damaged *etc*: *His research project was one of the first casualties of the reduction in expenditure; That table was a casualty of our house removal.*

cat [kat] *nc* **1** a small, four-legged, fur-covered animal often kept as a pet: *We have a Siamese cat and two dogs;* (*attrib*) *cat food.* **2** a large wild animal of the same family (*eg* tiger, lion *etc*): *the big cats in the circus.* **3** (*derog*) an unpleasant, spiteful woman. **4** short for *cat-o'-nine-tails.*

'catty *adj* **1** (*usu* of women) fond of making unpleasant remarks about people; spiteful: *She's catty even about her best friend.* **2** spiteful; unpleasant and nasty: *catty remarks.*

'cat-burglar *nc* a burglar who breaks into houses *etc* by climbing walls, drainpipes *etc.*

'catcall *nc* a shrill whistle showing disagreement or disapproval: *The comedian left the stage because of the catcalls of the audience.*

'catgut *nu* a kind of cord made from the intestines of sheep and other animals, used for violin strings *etc.*

'cat-nap *nc* (*inf*) a short sleep: *I must have a cat-nap before the party.*

ˌcat-o'-'nine-tails *nc* a whip with nine lashes.

ˌcat's-'eye ® *nc* a small, thick piece of glass fixed in the surface of a road to reflect light and guide drivers at night.

'catsuit *nc* a woman's close-fitting one-piece trouser suit.

'catwalk *nc* a narrow footway, often high off the ground: *The engineer broke his back when he fell off the catwalk.*

let the cat out of the bag to let a secret become known unintentionally: *We tried to keep the party a surprise for my mother but my sister let the cat out of the bag.*

like a cat on hot bricks very nervous: *She was like a cat on hot bricks before her exam.*

like ˌsomething the 'cat brought in (*inf*) untidy, soaking wet, or otherwise unpleasant to look at: *He arrived looking like something the cat brought in.*

put the cat among the pigeons to cause a disturbance, *esp* suddenly: *If the workmen don't get a pay rise it will really put the cat among the pigeons.*

cataclysm ['katəklizəm] *nc* (*formal*) **1** a flood of water; a deluge. **2** a sudden and violent disaster or disturbance.

ˌcata'clysmic *adj* (*formal*): *World War I was cataclysmic for Europe.*

catacombs ['katəku:mz] *n pl* a series of tunnels containing underground burial places: *the catacombs of ancient Rome.*

catalogue, (*Amer*) **catalog** ['katəlog] *nc* (a book containing) an ordered list of names, goods *etc*: *The book is listed in the library catalogue but I can't find it on the shelves;* (*fig*) *He recited a catalogue of my faults;* (*attrib*) *a catalogue system.* – *vt* to put in an ordered list: *She catalogued all the books in the library in alphabetical order of author's name.*

catalyst ['katəlist] *nc* **1** (*tech*) a substance which causes or assists a chemical change in another substance without itself undergoing any permanent chemical change: *Manganese dioxide is used as a catalyst in the industrial production of oxygen.* **2** (*formal*) something or someone that causes a change in a situation *etc* or has a marked effect on the course of events *esp* without it or him being affected: *The minister for foreign affairs was said to be the catalyst in the revolution although he kept his post in the government.* **ˌcata'lytic** *adj.*

catamaran [katəmə'ran] *nc* a sailing-boat with two parallel hulls.

catapult ['katəpʌlt] *nc* **1** (*Amer* **'slingshot**) a small forked stick with an elastic string fixed to the two prongs for throwing small stones *etc, usu* used by children: *The cat was injured by a stone from a little boy's catapult.* **2** (*hist*) a war-machine for throwing large stones *etc.* – *vti* to throw or move suddenly and violently: *The driver was catapulted through the windscreen when his car hit the wall.*

cataract ['katərakt] *nc* **1** (*formal*) a waterfall. **2** (*med*) a clouding of the lens of the eye causing difficulty in seeing: *Cataracts can be cured by surgical operation.*

catarrh [kə'ta:] *nu* inflammation of the lining of the nose and throat causing a discharge of thick fluid: *She suffers from catarrh in the winter.*

catastrophe [kə'tastrəfi] *nc* a sudden great disaster: *The earthquake was a great catastrophe for the village; Her brother's death was a catastrophe for the family.* **catastrophic** [katə'strofik] *adj.* **ˌcata'strophically** *adv.*

catcall *see* **cat**.

catch [katʃ] – *pt, ptp* **caught** [ko:t] – (not used with **is, was** *etc* and **-ing** (*defs 3, 6*) **1** *vt* to stop and hold (something which is moving): *He can catch a cricket ball; The cat caught a mouse; Did you catch any fish?; I tried to catch his attention.* **2** *vt* to be in time for, or get on (a train, bus *etc*): *I'll have to catch the 9.45 (train) to London.* **3** *vt* to surprise (someone) in the act of: *I caught him stealing (my watch).* **4** *vt* to become infected with (a disease or illness): *You are more likely to catch (a) cold in the winter than in the summer; He caught flu.* **5** *vti* to (cause to) become accidentally attached or held: *My sleeve caught (on the door-handle); The child caught her fingers in the car door.* **6** *vt* to hit: *The punch caught him on the chin.* **7** *vt* to manage to hear: *Did you catch what she said?* **8** *vti* to start burning: *The fire caught immediately; When I dropped a match on the pile of wood it caught (fire) immediately.* – *See also* **catch** *in phrases below.* – *nc* **1** an act of catching: *He took a fine catch behind the wicket.* **2** a small device for holding (a door *etc*) in place: *The catch on my suitcase is broken.* **3** the total amount (of *eg* fish) caught: *the largest catch of herring this year.* **4** (*inf*) a trick, problem or disadvantage: *There must be a catch in this plan;* (*attrib*) *a catch question.* **5** (*inf*) something one is lucky to have obtained: *Your new girlfriend is quite a catch – she's both rich and beautiful.* **'catcher** *nc.*

'catching *adj* (*inf*: *usu pred*) infectious: *Is*

chicken-pox catching?; (*fig*) *I find his enthusiasm catching.*

'**catchy** *adj* (of a tune) attractive and easily remembered.

'**catchment area** *nc* **1** the area from which a river or a reservoir draws its water supply. **2** the area from which a school *etc* draws its pupils.

'**catch-phrase,** '**catch-word** *nc* a phrase or word in (often widespread) popular use for a time: *'Your country needs you' was a catch-phrase in World War I.*

catch one's breath *see* **breath**.

ˌ**catch** '**me,** '**him** *etc* **(doing something)!** (*inf*) You'll never get me *etc* (to do a certain thing): *Catch me washing dishes by hand! I have a machine to do it for me!*

catch the eye to attract (someone's) attention: *The advertisement caught my eye; I couldn't catch the waiter's eye and so we were last to be served.*

catch fire *see* **fire**.

catch hold of *see* **hold**.

'**catch it** (*inf*) to get a scolding: *You'll really catch it when I tell your mother what you have done.*

catch (someone) off guard *see* **guard**.

catch on *vi* (*inf*) **1** to become popular: *Long dresses have really caught on.* **2** to understand: *He's a bit slow to catch on; I suddenly caught on to what she was meaning.*

catch (someone) on the hop *see* **hop**.

catch out *vt sep* **1** to put out (a batsman) at cricket by catching the ball after it has been hit and before it touches the ground. **2** to cause (someone) to fail or to be unsuccessful by asking him to do something that is too difficult *etc*: *The last question in the exam caught them all out.*

catch (someone) out in to catch or detect (someone) in the act of (doing something wrong): *He thought he had a good alibi but the policeman caught him out in a lie.*

catch sight, a glimpse of to get a brief look at: *She caught sight of him as he turned the corner; He caught a glimpse of her in the crowd.*

catch up 1 *vi* (*with* **with, on**), *vt sep* to come level (with) and sometimes overtake: *We caught him up at the corner although he was walking very fast; Ask the taxi-driver if he can catch up with that lorry; We waited for him to catch up; I'll never catch up with my work now; She had a lot of schoolwork to catch up on after her illness.* **2** *vt sep* to take hastily: *I caught up my cases and dashed to the railway station but I missed the train.*

catechism ['katikizəm] *nc* **1** a book (*esp* religious) of instructions by means of question and answer. **2** (*formal*) a series of searching questions on any subject.

categorical [katə'gorikəl] *adj* (*formal*: *esp attrib*) absolute or definite and giving no possibility for doubt or argument: *a categorical refusal to help.*

ˌ**cate'gorically** *adv*: *She refused categorically to help.*

category ['katəgəri] *nc* (*more formal or tech than* **class**) a class or division of things (or people) of the same kind: *There are several different categories in the competition; What category does this come into?*

'**categorize, -ise** *vt* (*formal*) to put (things or people) into a category: *She categorized the books in my library; She tends to categorize people and not see them as individuals.*

cater ['keitə] *vi* **1** to provide food *etc*: *We cater for all types of functions.* **2** (*formal*) to supply what is needed: *We cater for all educational needs; We cater to the needs of the disabled.* '**caterer** *nc.* '**catering** *nu.*

caterpillar ['katəpilə] *nc* the larva of a butterfly or moth that feeds upon the leaves of plants: *There's a caterpillar on this lettuce.* – *adj* (*attrib*) moving on endless belts: *a caterpillar tractor.*

caterwaul ['katəwo:l] *vi* to shriek or cry like a cat. – *nc* such a cry.

'**caterwauling** *nu*: *I wish that child would stop his caterwauling.*

catgut *see* **cat**.

cathedral [kə'θi:drəl] *nc* the principal church of a district under a bishop.

cathode ['kaθoud] *nc* (*tech*) the conductor through which an electric current leaves a battery *etc*.

cathode ray tube (*often abbrev* **CRT**) *nc* (*tech*) a device in which a narrow beam of electrons strikes against a screen, as in a television set.
See also **anode**.

catholic ['kaθəlik] *adj* **1** comprehensive, wide-ranging and liberal in one's taste, point of view *etc*: *a catholic taste in books; Her interests are fairly catholic.* **2** (*with cap*) Roman Catholic: *the Catholic Church.* – *nc* (*with cap*) a Roman Catholic: *She is a Catholic.*

Catholicism [kə'θolisizəm] *nu* Roman Catholicism: *He believes in Catholicism.*

ˌ**catho'licity** [-səti] *nu* (*formal*) the state of being catholic in one's taste, point of view *etc*: *I admire the catholicity of his viewpoint.*

catsuit *see* **cat**.

cattle ['katl] *n pl* grass-eating animals, *esp* cows, bulls and oxen: *That farmer does not keep sheep but he keeps several breeds of cattle.*

catwalk *see* **cat**.

Caucasian [ko:'keiziən] *nc, adj* (a person who is) white-skinned.

caught *see* **catch**.

ca(u)ldron ['ko:ldrən] *nc* (*liter*) a large deep pot (used *esp* by witches) for boiling things in.

cauliflower ['koliflauə] **1** *nc* a vegetable of the cabbage family whose white flower-head is used as food: *He bought a cauliflower.* **2** *nu* the flower-head as food: *We're having cauliflower cheese* (= a dish made of cauliflower and cheese sauce) *for supper; Would you like some cauliflower?*

cause [ko:z] **1** *nc* something or someone that produces an effect or result: *Having no money is the cause of all my misery; He is the cause of his mother's nervous breakdown.* **2** *ncu* (a) reason for an action; a motive: *You had no cause to treat your wife so badly; You have plenty of cause for complaint.* **3** *nc* an aim for which an individual or group works: *I'm collecting money for the blind and other deserving causes; in the cause of peace.* – *vt* to make (something) happen; to bring about; to be the means of: *What caused the accident?; He caused me to drop my suitcase; He caused a lot of unhappiness.*

causeway ['ko:zwei] *nc* a raised pathway, road *etc* over wet ground or shallow water.

caustic ['ko:stik] *adj* **1** (*tech*: *esp attrib*) burning by chemical action: *caustic soda.* **2** (*formal*) (of remarks) bitter or severe; sarcastic: *He made several caustic comments about my work; He was very caustic about her success.*

'**caustically** *adv*: *He spoke caustically about the government's policies.*

cauterize, -ise ['ko:təraiz] *vt* (*tech*) to burn (a

wound) with a caustic substance or a hot iron (to destroy infection).

caution ['ko:ʃən] **1** *nu* carefulness (because of possible danger *etc*): *The accident was a result of his lack of caution*; *You must exercise extreme caution when crossing this road.* **2** *nc* (*legal*) a warning: *The policeman gave him a caution for speeding.* – *vt* (*legal*) to give a warning to: *He was cautioned for drunken driving.*

'**cautionary** *adj* (*formal*: *usu attrib*) giving a warning: *a cautionary tale.*

'**cautious** *adj* having or showing caution; careful: *She used to trust everyone but she's more cautious now*; *a cautious driver*; *Be very cautious when you're driving today.* '**cautiously** *adv.*

See also **incautious**.

cavalcade [kavəl'keid] *nc* (*formal*) a (*usu* ceremonial) procession of people or things: *A cavalcade of cars took the President to the White House.*

cavalier [kavə'liə] *nc* (*hist*) **1** a horseman or knight. **2** a supporter of the king in the time of Charles I: *Cavaliers and Roundheads.* – *adj* (*derog*: *esp attrib*) ill-mannered or off-hand: *cavalier treatment*; *He treats women in a very cavalier manner.*

cavalry ['kavəlri] *nc or n pl* (the part of an army consisting of) horse-soldiers: *cavalry and infantry*; *The cavalry were/was ordered to advance*; (*attrib*) *a cavalry officer.*

cave [keiv] *nc* a large natural hollow in rock or in the earth: *The children explored the caves.*

'**caveman** [-man] *nc* **1** (*hist*) a person who lives in a cave: *Cavemen dressed in skins of animals.* **2** (*inf fig*: *often attrib*) a man who acts in a rough, ill-mannered way towards women: *Some women like caveman treatment.*

cave in *vi* (of walls *etc*) to fall down; to collapse: *The ceiling caved in on them*; (*fig*) *My whole world is caving in on me*; (*fig*) *The opposition to his plan caved in.*

cavern ['kavən] *nc* (*formal or liter*) a large cave.

'**cavernous** *adj* (*formal*) **1** (*usu attrib*) huge and hollow: *a cavernous hole in the side of the ship.* **2** full of caverns: *The bottom of the sea is cavernous.*

caviar(e) ['kavia:, (*Amer*) kavi'a:] *nu* the pickled eggs (roe) of the sturgeon, used as food, considered a delicacy: *They served caviare and champagne at the wedding reception.*

cavil ['kavəl] – *pt, ptp* '**cavilled**, (*Amer*) '**caviled** – *vi* (*formal*) to make objections (about unimportant details): *He's always cavilling at silly little things.*

cavity ['kavəti] *nc* (*formal or tech*) a hollow place: a hole: *Your teeth are full of cavities*; *The dentist said she had three cavities*; *The thief hid the necklace in a cavity in the wall.*

cavort [kə'vo:t] *vi* (*formal*) to leap around excitedly: *He cavorted around the room when he heard the news of his success in the exam.*

caw [ko:] *vi* to make the call of a crow, rook *etc.* – *nc* such a call.

cayenne [kei'en, (*Amer*) kai-] *nu* a type of very hot red pepper: *Add some cayenne to the sauce*; (*attrib*) *cayenne pepper.*

cease [si:s] *vti* (*more formal than* **stop**) to stop or (bring to an) end: *They were ordered to cease firing*; *That department has ceased to exist*; *This foolishness must cease immediately!*; *Cease this noise!*

'**ceaseless** *adj.* '**ceaselessly** *adv.*

See also **cessation, incessant**.

cedar ['si:də] **1** *nc* a cone-bearing evergreen tree. **2** *nu, adj* (*also* '**cedarwood**) (of) its hard, sweet-smelling wood.

cede [si:d] *vt* (*formal*) to surrender or give up (something to someone else): *They ceded their lands to the Government.*

cession ['seʃən] *nu* (*formal*) the act of giving (something) up: *the cession of their lands.*

cedilla [si'dilə] *nc* (in some French *etc* words) a mark (¸) put under the letter *c* (**ç**) to show that it is to have the sound of *s.*

ceilidh ['keili] *nc* in Scotland and Ireland, an informal entertainment with songs, dances *etc.*

ceiling ['si:liŋ] *nc* **1** the inner roof (of a room *etc*): *Paint the ceiling before you paint the walls*; *The ballroom has a very decorative ceiling.* **2** the upper limit: *There is a 10% ceiling on wages and prices this year.*

celebrate ['seləbreit] *vti* to mark by giving a party, feast *etc* in honour of (a happy or important event): *I'm celebrating* (*my birthday*) *today.*

'**celebrated** *adj* famous: *a celebrated actress*; *He has become quite celebrated as a writer.*

ˌ**cele'bration** *ncu*: *the celebration of her birthday*; *birthday celebrations.*

ce'lebrity [-'le-] *nc* a well-known person: *celebrities from the world of entertainment.*

celery ['seləri] *nu* **1** the long juicy edible stalks of a type of vegetable, used raw in salads or as a cooked vegetable: *braised celery*; (*attrib*) *celery soup.* **2** the vegetable: *He is growing celery.*

celestial [sə'lestiəl, (*Amer*) sə'lestʃəl] *adj* (*formal*: *attrib*) of heaven or the skies: *celestial angels*; *Stars are celestial bodies.*

celibacy ['selibəsi] *nu* (*formal*) the state of being unmarried or not taking part in sexual intercourse, *esp* because of having taken a religious vow to this effect: *the celibacy of the Roman Catholic clergy.* '**celibate** [-bət] *adj.*

cell [sel] *nc* **1** a small room (*esp* in a prison or monastery). **2** a very small piece of the substance of which all living things are made; the smallest unit of living matter: *The human body is made up of cells.* **3** (the part containing the electrodes in) an electrical battery. **4** a small compartment in a larger structure *etc*: *the cells of a honeycomb.* **5** a small section of people within a larger organization: *a Communist cell.*

cellular ['seljulə] *adj* (*usu attrib*) **1** (*tech*) consisting of cells: *cellular tissue.* **2** containing tiny hollow spaces: *Foam rubber is a cellular substance*; *a cellular blanket.*

cellar ['selə] *nc* **1** a room, sometimes underground, *esp* one for stores of coal or wine. **2** a stock of wines: *The old duke has an excellent cellar.*

cello, 'cello ['tʃelou] *nc* (short for '**violoncello**) a stringed musical instrument similar to, but much larger than, a violin: *He plays the cello*; *He played the music on the cello.*

'**cellist, 'cellist** *nc* (short for '**violoncellist**) a person who plays the cello.

cellophane (® in the UK) ['seləfein] *nu* a type of clear wrapping material: *The bouquet of flowers was wrapped in cellophane*; (*attrib*) *cellophane wrapping.*

cellular *see* **cell**.

celluloid ['seljuloid] *nu* **1** a type of plastic used for making film, toys *etc.* **2** (*fig*) cinema film (in whose manufacture celluloid is used): *The actress's beauty was immortalized on celluloid.*

cellulose ['seljulous] *nu* the chief substance in the cell walls of plants, also found in wood, used in the making of plastic, paper *etc.*

Celsius ['selsiəs] *adj* (*often abbrev* **C** *when written*) centigrade: *twenty degrees Celsius*; *20°C.*

cement [sə'ment] *nu* **1** a mixture of clay and lime (*usu* with sand and water added) used for sticking things (*eg* bricks) together in building and to make concrete for making very hard surfaces: *The bricklayer has not mixed enough cement*; *Use cement to fill up the cracks in the stonework*; *Concrete is a mixture of cement, sand, water and very small stones.* **2** any of several types of glue for a similar purpose: *Plastic cement is for joining pieces of plastic*; (*formal fig*) *Concern for the children is the cement that holds many marriages together.* **3** a substance used to fill cavities in teeth: *The dentist's assistant mixed up some cement for the child's teeth.* – *vt* to join firmly with cement: *He cemented the bricks into place*; (*fig*) *This agreement has cemented our friendship.*

cemetery ['semətri, (*Amer*) -teri] *nc* a piece of ground, *usu* not round a church, where people are buried.
See also **churchyard**.

cenotaph ['senəta:f] *nc* (*formal*) a monument to a person or people buried elsewhere, *esp* a monument built in memory of soldiers *etc* killed in war.

censor ['sensə] *nc* **1** an official who examines books, films *etc* and has the power to remove any of the contents which are thought to be indecent, obscene or which might offend people: *His latest novel has been banned by the censor.* **2** a similar official (*eg* in the army, prison *etc*) who examines letters *etc* and removes any information which the authorities do not wish to be made known to the enemy, the public *etc* for political or other reasons: *The censor removed all the details about the battle from the soldier's letter.* – *vt* to deal with (material) as a censor does: *This film has been censored*; *The prisoners' letters are censored.*
cen'sorious [-'so:-] *adj* (*formal*) looking for mistakes or faults; harshly critical: *She is censorious about the behaviour of young people*; *a censorious person.*
'censorship *nu* **1** the work of a censor: *his censorship of films.* **2** the act of censoring: *Some people disapprove of censorship.*

censure ['senʃə] *vt* (*formal*) to criticize harshly or condemn as wrong; to blame: *He was censured for staying away from work.* – *nu* (*formal*) harsh criticism or condemnation: *a vote of censure against the board of directors.*

census ['sensəs] *nc* an official counting of a country's inhabitants *etc*: *When was the last census in Britain?*; *They're conducting a traffic census to find out how many cars use this road.*

cent [sent] *nc* a coin equal to the hundredth part of a dollar, rupee, rand *etc.*
See also **per cent**.

centaur ['sento:] *nc* (*myth*) a creature in Greek story, half man, half horse.

centenary [sen'ti:nəri, (*Amer*) 'sentəneri], (*formal*) **centennial** [sen'teniəl] *nc* a hundredth anniversary: *The firm is celebrating its centenary this year.*
centenarian [sentə'neəriən] *nc* a person who is a hundred or more years old: *My aunt is a centenarian.*

centi- [senti] (*in cmpds*) a hundredth part, as in **centimetre.**

centigrade ['sentigreid] *adj* (*often abbrev* **C** *when written*) as measured on a centigrade thermometer: *twenty degrees centigrade*; *20°C.*
centigrade thermometer *nc* a thermometer which shows the temperature at which water freezes as 0°, and that at which it boils as 100°.
See also **Celsius**.

centigram(me), centilitre, centimetre *see* Appendix 5.

centipede ['sentipi:d] *nc* a type of very small worm-like animal with many legs.

central ['sentrəl] *adj* **1** belonging to or near the centre (*eg* of a town): *His flat is very central*; *a central flat.* **2** principal or most important: *the central point of his argument*; *that is central to his argument.*
'centralize, -ise *vt* (*formal*) to bring (something) under one control: *plans to centralize the government in London.* **ˌcentrali'zation, -s-** *nu.*
'centrally *adv*: *centrally situated.*
central heating *nu* heating of a building by water, steam or air through pipes from one central boiler *etc*: *Do you have central heating?*; (*attrib*) *a central-heating system.*

centre, (*Amer*) **center** ['sentə] *nc* **1** the middle point, or middle of anything; the point or area farthest from the edge: *the centre of a circle*; *the centre of the city*; *the city centre.* **2** (*often in cmpds*) a place, area *etc* that is important for a particular activity, interest *etc*: *a centre of industry*; *a shopping-centre*; *a health-centre.* **3** an important point (of interest *etc*): *She's the centre of attention.* **4** a (political) position which is at neither extreme: *He is definitely to the left of centre*; (*attrib*) *There's a left-wing party and a right-wing party but is there a centre party?* – *vti* **1** to place, or to be, at the centre. **2** (*formal*) (*with* **on** *or* **round**) to collect or concentrate at, round *etc*: *Everyone's attention was centred on the speaker*; *Her plans always centre round her child.*

centri- [sentri] (*in cmpds*) centre, as in **centrifugal**.

centrifugal [sen'trifjugəl] *adj* (*tech*: *esp attrib*) tending to move away from a centre: *centrifugal force.*

centurion [sen'tjuəriən] *nc* (*hist*) a Roman officer in charge of a hundred soldiers.

century ['sentʃuri] *nc* **1** a (period of a) hundred years: *He was born in the 19th century*; *There has been a church on this site for more than a century.* **2** in cricket, a hundred runs: *He has just made his second century this year.*
this century *see* **this**.

ceramic [sə'ramik] *adj* (*formal*) (of the art) of pottery. – *nc* something made of pottery: *She sells ceramics and wood-carvings.*
ce'ramics *n sing* (*formal*) the art of pottery: *an expert in ceramics.*

cereal ['siəriəl] **1** *nc* a kind of grain used as food: *Wheat and barley are cereals*; (*attrib*) *cereal crops.* **2** *ncu* a type of (often breakfast) food prepared from such grain: *Pour milk over your cereal.*

cerebral ['serəbrəl, (*Amer*) sə'ri:brəl] *adj* **1** (*tech*: *esp attrib*) of the brain: *a cerebral haemorrhage.* **2** (*formal*: *esp pred*) intellectual rather than emotional: *His poetry is cerebral rather than passionate.*

ceremony ['serəməni, (*Amer*) -mouni] **1** *nc* (*often in cmpds*) a sacred or formal act, *eg* a wedding, funeral, official opening *etc*: *a marriage ceremony*; *The ceremony will take place today.* **2** *nu* (*formal*) solemn display and formality: *He always liked pomp and ceremony*; *Please do not stand on* *ceremony* (= Please do not behave in a very formal way) – *enjoy yourself.*

ˌ**cereˈmonial** [-ˈmou-] *adj* (*esp attrib*) formal or official: *a ceremonial occasion such as the opening of parliament.* ˌ**cereˈmonially** *adv.*

ˌ**cereˈmonious** [-ˈmou-] *adj* (*neg* **un-**: *formal*) carefully formal or polite. ˌ**cereˈmoniously** *adv.*

master of ceremonies *see* **master**.

cerise [səˈriːs] *nu, adj* (of) a light, clear red colour.

cert *see* **certainty** *under* **certain**.

certain [ˈsəːtn] **1** *adj* (*usu pred*) always true or without doubt: *It's certain that the world is round.* **2** *adj* (*pred*) free from doubt; absolutely sure: *I'm certain (that) he'll come*; *He is certain to forget.* **3** *adj* (*formal*: *attrib*) never failing in action or result: *Being constantly late is a certain way of losing one's job.* **4** *adj* (*attrib*), *pron* some (people or things) or a (person or thing) not definitely named, or not known to the listener(s): *Certain of the things he said were downright lies*; *certain Members of Parliament*; *a certain Mrs Smith.* **5** *adj* (*attrib*) slight; some: *There's a certain hostility in his manner*; *I have a certain amount of admiration for his work.*

ˈ**certainly** *adv* without doubt; definitely: *I can't come today, but I'll certainly come tomorrow*; *You may certainly* (= Of course you are allowed to) *have a chocolate.* – *interj* of course: *'Do you believe her?' 'Certainly!'*; *'May I borrow your typewriter?' 'Certainly (you may)!'*; *'May I drive your car?' 'Certainly not!'*

ˈ**certainty 1** *nc* (*inf abbrev* **cert** [səːt]) something which cannot be doubted or is sure to happen: *It's a certainty that he will win*; *That horse is a dead cert* (= is absolutely sure) *to win.* **2** *nu* freedom from doubt: *Is there any certainty of success?*

for ˈ**certain** definitely; having no doubt: *I know for certain that she is telling lies but I can't prove it*; *She may come but she can't say for certain.*

make certain to cause to be sure or to be without doubt: *I think he's dead but you'd better make certain*; *If you want to make certain of getting there in time, you'd better leave now.*

See also **uncertain.**

certificate [səˈtifikət] *nc* (*often in cmpds*) a written official declaration of some fact: *a marriage certificate*; *an exam certificate*; *a certificate of excellence.*

cerˈtificated [-kei-] *adj* (*attrib*) having been awarded a certificate; qualified: *a certificated teacher.*

certify [ˈsəːtifai] *vt* (*formal*) **1** to declare formally (*eg* that something is true): *I certify that I witnessed the signing of his will.* **2** to declare that someone is insane: *He was certified and sent to a mental hospital.* **cerˌtifiˈcation** *nu.*

certifiable [səːtiˈfaiəbl] *adj* able to be certified (*esp* as insane).

cessation [seˈseiʃən] *nu* (*formal*) stopping or ceasing: *the cessation of activities.*

cession *see* **cede**.

cesspit [ˈsespit], **cesspool** [ˈsespuːl] *nc* a pool or pit for collecting liquid waste or sewage.

Ceylon *see* Appendix 2.

chafe [tʃeif] **1** *vt* to make warm by rubbing *esp* with the hands: *She chafed the child's cold feet.* **2** *vti* to make or become sore by rubbing: *These tight shoes chafe my feet.* **3** *vi* (*formal*) to become angry or impatient: *Everyone's sitting chafing at the delay.*

chaff [tʃaf] *nu* **1** the husks of corn, removed by threshing. **2** something worthless. **3** good-humoured teasing. – *vt* to tease good-naturedly: *Her brothers all chaffed her about her shyness.*

chaffinch [ˈtʃafintʃ] *nc* a songbird of the finch family.

chagrin [ˈʃagrin, (*Amer*) ʃəˈgrin] *nu* (*formal*) disappointment and annoyance: *To his chagrin, his effort was a total failure.*

chain [tʃein] **1** *ncu* a series of (*esp* metal) links or rings passing through one another, used for fastening or binding, as a barrier, jewellery *etc*: *The dog was fastened to the kennel by a chain*; *Lock the door and put the chain on it*; *She wore a silver chain round her neck*; *a length of chain.* **2** *nc* a series: *a chain of events*; *a chain of shops*; *a mountain chain.* **3** *nc* (*rare*) a measure of length equal to 66 feet (about 20m). – *vt* to fasten or bind with chains: *The prisoner was chained to the wall*; (*fig*) *When her father became ill, she was chained to the house* (= she had to stay in the house most of the time).

ˈ**chain-gang** *nc* a gang of convicts chained together.

chain mail *nu* armour made of iron links.

chain reaction *nc* (*chem*: *often fig*) a process whose product starts off other similar processes: *This strike will start a chain reaction all over the country.*

ˌ**chain-ˈsmoker** *nc* a person who smokes (cigarettes *etc*) continuously. ˌ**chain-ˈsmoke** *vti*: *If you chain-smoke you may get lung cancer.*

ˈ**chain store** *nc* one of a series of shops (often department stores) under the same ownership: *There are so many chain stores around that the shops in one town are often exactly the same as the shops in another.*

chair [tʃeə] *nc* **1** a movable seat for one person, with a back to it: *a table and four chairs.* **2** the position of a person who is chairman at a meeting *etc*: *He takes the chair at every meeting*; *Who is in the chair?* **3** the office of a university professor: *He holds the chair of History at this university.* – *vt* to be chairman at (a meeting *etc*): *He chaired the meeting last night.*

ˈ**chairlift** *nc* a set of seats hanging from a cable, used to take skiers up a mountain.

ˈ**chairman, -person, -woman** *ncs* a person who takes charge of or directs a meeting. ˈ**chairmanship** *ncu.*

chalet [ˈʃalei, (*Amer*) ʃaˈlei] *nc* **1** in Switzerland, a summer hut in the mountains for shepherds *etc.* **2** a wooden house, sometimes attached to an hotel, used by holidaymakers *etc.*

chalice [ˈtʃalis] *nc* (*formal*) a wine-cup, *esp* one used in religious services.

chalk [tʃoːk] **1** *nu* a white rock; a type of limestone. **2** *ncu* (a piece of) a chalk-like substance used for writing (*esp* on blackboards): *I have chalk all over my clothes*; *This chalk is too short to write with*; *a box of chalks.*

ˈ**chalky** *adj* **1** of or like chalk: *a chalky substance.* **2** white and pale: *Her face looked chalky in the electric light.*

chalk up *vt sep* **1** to write (something) with chalk on a blackboard *etc*: *The teacher chalked up the answer on the blackboard.* **2** (*fig*) to score (a victory *etc*): *He chalked up three wins in a row.* **3** to note (the cost of something) as being owed by (someone): *Chalk up all these drinks to me.* **4** to think or say something has been caused by a particular thing; to ascribe: *You can't chalk his bad work up to lack of trying.*

chalk it up to experience to try not to regret that something unfortunate *etc* has happened but to try to make sure such a thing does not happen again: *There's no point in worrying about losing so much money – you'll just have to chalk it up to experience.*

not by a 'long chalk (*inf*) by no means: *You haven't finished yet by a long chalk.*

challenge ['tʃalindʒ] *vt* **1** to ask (someone) to take part in a contest: *He challenged his brother to a round of golf.* **2** (*formal*) to question (someone's right to do something *etc*): *Are you challenging the king's authority?* **3** (*legal*) to express an objection to (a juryman or jury, a decision *etc*). – **1** *nc* an invitation to a contest: *He accepted his brother's challenge to a fight.* **2** *nc* (*legal*) an objection: *The judge refused to allow the challenge.* **3** *nc* an order from a guard, sentry *etc* to give one's name, reason for calling *etc*: *'Who goes there?' was the challenge.* **4** *nu* the quality of demanding effort and a spirit of competition: *I don't get enough challenge in this job.*

'challenger *nc.*

'challenging *adj* (*esp attrib*) offering challenge; difficult: *a challenging job/idea.*

chamber ['tʃeimbə] *nc* **1** (*hist, liter or formal*) a room: *The king retired to his chamber.* **2** the place where an assembly (*eg* Parliament) meets: *There were few members left in the chamber.* **3** (*often with cap*) such an assembly: *the Upper and Lower Chambers.* **4** an enclosed space or cavity *eg* the part of a gun which holds the bullets: *Many pistols have chambers for six bullets.*

'chambermaid *nc* a female servant or hotel worker in charge of bedrooms.

'chamber music *nu* music for a small group of players, suitable for a room rather than a large hall.

'chamberpot *nc* a receptacle for urine *etc*, used (*esp* formerly) in a bedroom.

chameleon [kə'mi:liən] *nc* **1** a small lizard which is able to change colour. **2** (*fig*) a person who can easily change his personality, opinions, characteristics *etc* to suit a situation: *He could live anywhere in the world – he's a real chameleon*; (*attrib*) *a chameleon accent* (= an accent which changes according to where one is or to whom one is talking).

chamois ['ʃamwa:, (*Amer*) 'ʃami] – *pl* **'chamois** – **1** *nc* a small antelope living in mountainous country. **2** (*also* **shammy** ['ʃami]) *ncu* (a piece of) soft leather *orig* made from its skin and used *esp* for cleaning glass or polishing.

champ [tʃamp] *vti* (*esp* of horses) to chew noisily.

champing at the bit impatient: *By the time the bus arrived the man was champing at the bit.*

champagne [ʃam'pein] *nu* a type of white sparkling wine, *esp* from Champagne in France, often drunk at celebrations *etc*: *We all drank champagne at the wedding.*

champion ['tʃampiən] *nc* **1** in games, competitions *etc*, a competitor who has defeated all others: *a tennis champion*; *He is this year's golf champion*; (*attrib*) *a champion boxer.* **2** a person who defends a cause: *a champion of human rights.* – *vt* to defend or support: *He championed the cause of human rights for many years.*

'championship **1** *nc* a contest held to decide who is the champion (*def 1*): *The tennis championship will be decided this afternoon*; (*attrib*) *championship events.* **2** *nu* the act of defending or supporting: *He was famous for his championship of civil rights.*

chance [tʃa:ns] **1** *nu* luck or fortune: *You must leave nothing to chance – you must make all the arrangements carefully*; *It was by sheer chance that I found out the truth.* **2** *nc* an opportunity: *Now you have a chance to do well*; (*inf*) *This is your big chance.* **3** *nc* a possibility: *There's no chance of success*; *He has no chance of winning*; *Chances are* (= there is a good possibility) *that you will win*; *You stand a good chance of winning* (= you are likely to win); *Is there any chance of getting tickets for the opera?* **4** *ncu* (a) risk: *I'm taking a chance (by) going alone*; *There's an element of chance* (= an amount of risk) *in this business deal but you'll probably be successful.* – **1** *vt* to risk: *It is dangerous to try to escape but he'll just have to chance it.* **2** *vi* (*formal*) to happen accidentally or unexpectedly: *I chanced to see him last week.* – *adj* (*attrib*) happening accidentally or unexpectedly: *a chance meeting.*

'chancy *adj* (*inf*) risky or uncertain: *You might get a seat on the train but it's a bit chancy*; *a chancy arrangement.*

'chance on, (*formal*) **upon** *vt fus* **1** to meet by accident: *I chanced on a friend of yours in the library.* **2** to discover by accident: *I chanced upon some information that will interest you.*

by any chance used in questions to enquire about the possibility of something happening or having happened: *Did you by any chance meet my father on your way home?*; *Are you by any chance free to come to the theatre tonight?*

by 'chance by luck or by accident; without planning or arrangement: *They met quite by chance.*

chance one's arm (*inf*) to do something risky; to take a risk: *You're really chancing your arm by asking for an increase in salary just now – you'll probably get the sack.*

an even chance equal probability for and against: *We have an even chance of success.*

the ˌchances 'are it is likely (that): *The chances are he can't come tomorrow.*

not a chance (*inf*) certainly not: *'Are you going to marry her?' 'Not a chance!'* – *See also* **chance** *n* (*def 3*).

take (a) chance to do something risky: *You took quite a chance crossing the road without looking to see if there was a car coming*; *If you don't take chances you'll never be rich*; *She took a chance on the train's being late in leaving.*

take one's chance(s) to make the most of whatever opportunities occur: *You have to take your chance when it comes along*; *You'll just have to wait and take your chance(s)* (= take the risk of being unsuccessful, unlucky *etc*) *like everybody else.*

chancel ['tʃa:nsəl] *nc* the eastern part of a church, round the altar.

chancellor ['tʃa:nsələ] *nc* **1** a state or legal official of various kinds: *The Lord Chancellor is the head of the English legal system.* **2** the head of a university.

Chancellor of the Exchequer *n* the chief minister of finance in British government.

chandelier [ʃandə'liə] *nc* a frame with many-branched holders for lights, which hangs from the ceiling.

change [tʃeindʒ] **1** *vti* to make or become different: *They have changed the time of the train*; *He has changed a lot since I saw him last.* **2** *vt* to give or leave (one thing *etc* for another): *Has he changed his job?*; *I am going to change my hairdresser*; *She changed my library books for me.* **3** *vti* (*sometimes* *with* **into**) to remove (clothes *etc*) and replace them by clean or different ones: *I'm just going to change (my shirt); I'll change into an old pair of trousers; I must change the baby; Have you changed the sheets/bed yet?* **4** *vti* (*with* **into**) to make into or become (something different): *He's changed into a fine young man; The prince was changed into a frog.* **5** *vt* to give or receive (one kind of money for another): *Could you change a pound note for cash?; He changed francs into sterling.* – **1** *nu* the process of becoming or making different: *The town is constantly undergoing change.* **2** *nc* an instance of this: *There's a change in the programme; There may be a change in the weather.* **3** *nc* a substitution from one thing to another: *a change of train/clothes.* **4** *nu* coins rather than paper money: *I'll have to give you a pound note – I have no change.* **5** *nu* money left over or given back from the amount given in payment: *This costs 90p and I gave you £1, so I want 10p change.* **6** *nc* (*inf*) a holiday or change of job, house *etc*: *He has been ill – the change will do him good.*

'**changeable** *adj* changing often; liable to change often: *The weather is changeable; changeable moods.*

'**changeless** *adj* (*formal or liter*: *esp attrib*) not changing; remaining the same: *the changeless hills.*

change hands to pass into different ownership: *This car has changed hands three times.*

a change of heart a different attitude: *At first we refused to take them with us but we had a change of heart and took them.*

change of life (*inf*) the menopause: *The change of life makes some women very moody.*

change one's mind to alter one's intention or opinion (about something): *I used to think he was handsome but I've changed my mind; He was going to go to France but he changed his mind.*

change one's tune *see* **tune**.

for a 'change to be different; for variety: *We're tired of the cinema, so we're going to the theatre for a change.*

ring the changes *see* **ring**[2].

changeling ['tʃeindʒliŋ] *nc* (*myth or liter*) a child secretly taken or left in place of another, *esp* by the fairies.

channel ['tʃanl] *nc* **1** the bed of a stream or other way through which liquid can flow: *a sewage channel.* **2** a passage of deeper water in a river, through which ships can sail. **3** (*usu found in place-names with cap*) a narrow stretch of water joining two seas: *the English Channel.* **4** (*fig*) a means of sending or receiving information *etc*: *She doesn't get her information through the usual channels.* **5** (in television, radio *etc*) a band of frequencies for sending or receiving signals: *BBC Television now has two channels.* – *v* – *pt, ptp* '**channelled**, (*Amer*) '**channeled** – *vt* (*formal*) **1** to make a channel (through). **2** to direct into a particular course or channel: *He channelled all his energies into the project.*

chant [tʃa:nt] **1** *vt* to recite (religious songs, prayers *etc*) in a singing manner: *The monks were chanting their prayers.* **2** *vti* to repeat (a phrase, slogan *etc*) over and over out loud: *The crowd was chanting 'We want more!'* – *nc* **1** a kind of sacred song in which a number of syllables are sung on one note. **2** a phrase or slogan constantly repeated: *'Scotland forever' was the chant.*

chanty *see* **shanty**[2].

chaos ['keios] *nu* complete disorder or confusion: *The place was in utter chaos after the burglary.*

cha'otic [-tik] *adj*: *The traffic in Oxford Street is really chaotic; chaotic traffic conditions.* **cha'otically** *adv.*

chap [tʃap] *nc* (*Brit inf*) a man: *He's the sort of chap everyone likes.*

chapel ['tʃapəl] *nc* **1** a place of Christian worship not belonging to the established church of the country: *a Welsh chapel.* **2** a place of Christian worship attached to a house or institution: *a college chapel.* **3** a part of a larger church, with its own altar. **4** a local branch of certain trade unions: *He belongs to the printers' chapel.*

chaperone ['ʃapəroun] *nc* (*esp hist*) an older lady who accompanies a younger one when she goes out in public. – *vt*: *Their aunt chaperoned the two girls at the ball.*

chaplain ['tʃaplin] *nc* a clergyman attached to a ship, regiment *etc.*

'**chaplaincy** *ncu* the job or occupation of chaplain.

chapped [tʃapt] *adj* (*inf*) (of skin) cracked, *esp* by cold weather: *If you don't dry your hands thoroughly in winter they become chapped; chapped lips.*

chapter ['tʃaptə] *nc* **1** a main division of a book: *There are fifteen chapters in his new book.* **2** (*formal*) (an assembly of) the clergy of a cathedral.

chapter and verse (*formal*) (by) exact reference, quoting word for word: *The judge quoted the law chapter and verse.*

a chapter of accidents a whole series of disasters: *Let's forget the whole thing – it was just a chapter of accidents.*

char[1] [tʃa:] – *pt, ptp* **charred** – *vti* to burn or turn black by fire or heat: *The wood was charred by the intense heat.*

char[2] [tʃa:] – *pt, ptp* **charred** – *vi* (*Brit inf*) to do house cleaning in someone else's house *etc*: *She chars for my next-door neighbour; She goes out charring.* – *nc* (*Brit inf*: *also* '**charwoman**) a woman employed for this purpose.

character ['karəktə] **1** *ncu* the set of features or qualities (good and bad) that make someone or something different from others; nature; type: *Some people think they can tell a man's character from his handwriting; They changed the whole character of the house by adding an extra room; Publicity of this character is not good for the firm; Is he a man of good character?* **2** *nu* a set of qualities that are considered good or admirable in some way: *He showed great character in his handling of the awkward situation; a wine of great character; a house of character.* **3** *nu* reputation: *They tried to damage his character.* **4** *nc* a person in a play, novel *etc*: *Rosencranz is a minor character in Shakespeare's 'Hamlet'.* **5** *nc* an odd, eccentric or amusing person: *This fellow's quite a character!* **6** *nc* a letter or mark used in writing, typing *etc*: *Some characters on this typewriter are broken.*

ˌ**character'istic** *adj* (*neg* **un-**) typical (of a person *etc*): *He showed characteristic unwillingness to say what he thought; That kind of behaviour is characteristic of him.* – *nc* a typical quality: *It is one of his characteristics to be obstinate.*

ˌ**characte'ristically** *adv.*

'**characterize, -ise** *vt* **1** (*often passive*) to be part of the normal features of; to be typical of: *This type of scenery characterizes the whole region; This town is characterized by its steep streets.* **2** to describe (as): *She characterized him as fat, weak* *and indecisive.* ˌ**characteriˈzation, -s-** *ncu.*

charade [ʃəˈraːd, (*Amer*) ʃəˈreid] *nc* (*formal derog*) a piece of ridiculous pretence which is so obvious that it does not deceive anyone: *The choosing of a selection committee was just a charade because they had already appointed someone to the job.*

chaˈrades *n sing* a game in which each syllable of a word, and then the whole word, is acted and the audience has to guess the word.

charcoal [ˈtʃaːkoul] *nu* the black part of partly burned wood *etc*, used as fuel and for drawing: *a piece of charcoal*; (*attrib*) *a charcoal stove*; (*attrib*) *a charcoal drawing.*

charge [tʃaːdʒ] **1** *vti* to ask as the price (for something): *They charge 12p for a pint of milk, but they don't charge for delivery.* **2** *vt* to make a note of (a sum of money) as being owed: *Charge the bill to my account.* **3** *vt* (*with* **with**) to accuse (of something illegal): *He was charged with theft.* **4** *vti* to attack by moving quickly (towards): *We charged* (*towards*) *the enemy on horseback.* **5** *vi* to rush: *The children charged down the hill.* **6** *vti* to make or become filled with electricity: *Please charge my car battery.* **7** *vt* (*old or liter*) to load (a gun *etc*); to fill: *charge one's glass with wine.* **8** *vt* (*formal*) to make (a person) responsible for (a task *etc*): *He was charged with seeing that everything went well.* – *nc* **1** a price or fee: *What is the charge for a telephone call?*; *The bank charges for being overdrawn are very high.* **2** something with which a person is accused: *He faces three charges of murder.* **3** an attack made by moving quickly: *the charge of the Light Brigade.* **4** the amount of polarity of the electricity in something: *a positive or negative charge.* **5** (*formal*) something or someone (*esp* a child) which one takes care of: *These children are my charges.* **6** a quantity of ammunition or explosives: *Put the charge in place and light the fuse.* – *See also* **charge** *in phrases below.*

ˈchargeable *adj* **1** (*usu with* **to** *when pred*) liable to be paid by: *This expense is chargeable to the firm's account*; *chargeable expenses.* **2** liable to legal prosecution: *This is a chargeable offence.*

ˈcharger *nc* (*old*) a war-horse.

ˈcharge account *nc* (*esp Amer*) a credit account.

be in charge of to control and be responsible for: *I'm in charge of thirty men*; *He's in charge of the shop while I'm on holiday.*

be in someone's charge to be the responsibility of someone; to be in the care of someone: *These children are in my charge*; *You can leave the children in his charge.*

take charge 1 (*sometimes with* **of**) to begin to control, organize *etc* (something): *The department was in chaos until he took charge* (*of it*). **2** (*with* **of**) to look after or care for (a person thing *etc*); to take into one's possession: *The policeman said he would take charge of the gun.*

See also **discharge**.

chargé d'affaires [ʃaːʒeidaˈfeə] – *pl* **chargés d'affaires** [ʃaːʒei-] – *nc* an ambassador's deputy.

chariot [ˈtʃariət] *nc* (*hist*) a (*usu* two-wheeled) vehicle used in ancient warfare or racing.

ˌ**charioˈteer** *nc* a chariot driver.

charisma [kəˈrizmə] *nu* (*formal*) the ability to cause devotion, admiration *etc* in people: *President Kennedy had charisma.*

charismatic [karizˈmatik] *adj* (*formal*: *esp attrib*) (of someone's nature) having this ability: *Some politicians are charismatic figures.*

charity [ˈtʃarəti] **1** *nu* kindness (*esp* in giving money to poor people): *She gave clothes to the gypsies out of charity.* **2** *nc* an organization or fund set up to collect money for the poor or needy: *Many charities sent money to help the victims of the disaster.* **3** *nu* in the Bible, love for all people: *faith, hope and charity.*

ˈcharitable *adj* **1** (*neg* **un-**) kind: *That wasn't a very charitable remark*; *Try to be more charitable.* **2** of a charity: *a charitable organization.* **ˈcharitably** *adv.*

charlatan [ˈʃaːlətən] *nc* (*formal*) a person who claims to know more about something than he actually does know; a fraud: *He was not a real psychiatrist but a charlatan who got money out of wealthy women.*

charm [tʃaːm] **1** *ncu* (a) pleasant quality or attraction: *Her charm made up for her lack of beauty*; *The cottage has an air of old-world charm.* **2** *nc* a magical spell: *The witch recited a charm.* **3** *nc* something believed to have the power of magic or good luck: *Some women wear* (*lucky*) *charms on a bracelet.* – *vt* **1** to influence by charm; to attract and delight: *He can charm any woman.* **2** to influence or affect by magic or as if by magic: *He charmed the snake from its basket.*

charmed *adj* (*esp attrib*) protected, as if by a spell: *He leads a charmed life.*

ˈcharmer *nc* **1** (*inf*) a person who possesses great charm: *She's a real charmer!* **2** (*usu in cmpds*) a person who charms: *a snake-charmer.*

ˈcharming *adj* very attractive: *a charming child/smile*; *She's charming.* **ˈcharmingly** *adv.*

chart [tʃaːt] *nc* **1** a map of part of the sea, showing its coasts, sandbanks, depths *etc.* **2** (*often in cmpds*) a table or diagram giving information: *a weather chart*; *a sales chart.* – *vt* (*formal*) **1** to make a chart of (a part of the sea *etc*): *He charted the Black Sea.* **2** to make a table or diagram of information about: *I'm charting our progress.* **3** to plan (a course or direction): *We charted a course for India.*

charter [ˈtʃaːtə] *nc* (*formal*) a formal document giving titles, rights, or privileges, *esp* one granted by the sovereign or government: *a city charter*; *a civil rights charter.* – *vt* to let or hire (a ship, aircraft *etc*) on contract: *They chartered a sailing ship*; *They chartered a bus for the firm's outing.* – *adj* (*attrib*) **1** hired: *a charter plane.* **2** of an air journey made in a hired aircraft: *a charter flight.*

chartered accountant *nc* (*Brit*) an accountant qualified under the regulations of the Institute of Accountants.

charwoman *see* **char**[2].

chary [ˈtʃeəri] *adj* (*formal*: *with* **of** *or* **about**) cautious and careful: *Be chary of lending money to someone you don't know very well.*

chase [tʃeis] *vti* **1** (*sometimes with* **after**) to run after; to pursue: *He chased after them but did not catch them*; *We chased them by car for ten miles*; (*fig*) *He's always chasing after women* (= He is always trying to attract women). **2** (*with* **away, off** *etc*) to cause to run away: *I often have to chase the boys away from my fruit trees*; *The dog chased the cat out of the kitchen.* – **1** *nc* an act of chasing: *We caught him after a 70 mph chase.* **2** *nu* (*formal*: *with* **the**) hunting (of animals): *the pleasures of the chase.*

ˈchaser *nc* **1** a person or thing that chases. **2** (*inf*) a drink (*eg* beer) following another drink (*eg* whisky).

give chase (*formal*) to chase (someone): *The*

thieves ran off and the policeman gave chase.

chasm ['kazəm] *nc* a deep opening or drop between high rocks *etc*: *The climber could not cross the chasm*; (*formal fig*) *The two young people quarrelled and a chasm developed between their families.*

chassis ['ʃasi] – *pl* '**chassis** [-z] – *nc* the frame of a motor car, television set *etc*, to which all the smaller parts are fixed.

chaste [tʃeist] *adj* (*formal*) pure and virtuous sexually: *Brides were expected to be chaste before marriage*; *a chaste young girl.*

chastity ['tʃastəti], '**chasteness** *nus* sexual virtue or purity.

chasten ['tʃeisn] *vt* (*formal*) to correct or improve by punishment, suffering *etc*: *He was chastened by the thought that he had hurt his mother's feelings.*

chastise [tʃas'taiz] *vt* (*formal*) to punish (often by beating *etc*): *They chastised the child severely for his disobedience.* **chastisement** ['tʃastizmənt] *nu*.

chastity *see* **chaste**.

chat [tʃat] – *pt, ptp* '**chatted** – *vi* to talk in a friendly and informal way: *They chatted about the weather.* – *ncu* (a) friendly and informal talk: *We had a chat over coffee yesterday*; *He says women's chat bores him.*

'**chatty** *adj* (*inf*) **1** fond of chatting: *a chatty old lady.* **2** having a friendly, informal style: *a chatty letter*; *Her way of writing is chatty rather than elegant.*

chateau ['ʃatou, (*Amer*) ʃa'tou] – *pl* '**chateaux** [-z] – *nc* a (French) castle or large country house.

chattels ['tʃatlz]: **goods and chattels** *n pl* (*legal*) all movable property: *He left all his goods and chattels to his wife*; (*inf facet*) *Get all your goods and chattels out of here!*

chatter ['tʃatə] *vi* **1** to talk quickly (and *usu* noisily), often about unimportant things: *The children chattered when the teacher left the room.* **2** (of teeth) to knock together with the cold *etc*: *My teeth were chattering with/in terror.* **3** (of birds *etc*) to utter rapid short sounds: *The sparrows chattered in the trees.* – *nu* **1** rapid, noisy talk *usu* about unimportant things: *childish chatter.* **2** a similar sound: *the chatter of birds/the brook.*

'**chatterbox** *nc* (*inf*) a talkative person.

chauffeur ['ʃoufə, (*Amer*) ʃou'fəːr] *nc* a person employed as a car-driver for a rich or important person.

chauvinism ['ʃouvinizəm] *nu* unthinking enthusiasm for a particular country, group, point of view, cause *etc*: *The British are often accused of chauvinism*; *Men are accused of chauvinism if they dislike their wives working.* '**chauvinist** *nc*. ˌ**chauvi'nistic** *adj*.

male chauvinist *nc* (*inf derog*) a man who believes that women are inferior to men, and acts accordingly.

cheap [tʃiːp] *adj* **1** low in price or value: *This carpet is very cheap at £20*; *Eggs are cheap just now.* **2** of poor quality: *a cheap and nasty bottle of wine.* **3** (of people or their actions) of poor reputation; contemptible: *a cheap, common woman*; *That was a cheap trick to play on him.* – *adv* for a low price: *We're selling these books off cheap.*

'**cheapen** *vt* to make cheap, vulgar, worthy of contempt *etc*: *Her behaviour cheapened her in his eyes*; *The gold trimming cheapens the dress.*

'**cheaply** *adv*. '**cheapness** *nu*.

cheat [tʃiːt] *vti* to act dishonestly to gain an advantage or for profit: *He was cheated* (*out of £100*); *He cheats at cards.* – *nc* **1** a person who cheats: *He only wins because he is a cheat.* **2** a dishonest trick: *That was a cheat!*

check [tʃek] *vt* **1** to see if something (*eg* a sum) is correct or accurate: *Will you check my addition?* **2** to see if something (*eg* a machine) is in good condition or working properly: *Have you checked the tyres/engine?* **3** (*more formal than* **stop**) to hold back; to prevent; to stop: *We've checked the flow of water from the burst pipe*; *He was going to run away but was checked by the sight of the policeman.* – **1** *nc* an act of testing (a calculation *etc*). **2** *nc* an act of checking (a machine *etc*): *a tyre/engine check.* **3** *nc* something which prevents or holds back: *a check on imports.* **4** *nu* (*chess*) a position in which the king is attacked: *He put his opponent's king in check.* **5** *nu* a pattern of squares: *I like the red check on that material.* **6** *nc* a ticket received in return for checking in baggage *etc.* **7** *nc* (*esp Amer*) a bill: *The check please, waiter!* **8** *nc* (*Amer*) a cheque.

checked *adj* having a pattern of check: *She wore a checked skirt*; *Is the material checked or striped?*

'**checkbook** *nc* (*Amer*) a chequebook.

'**checkmate** *nu* **1** (*chess*: *also* **mate**) a position from which the king cannot escape. **2** (*fig*) a stoppage of progress: *The unions and bosses have refused to meet – they've reached checkmate.* – *vt* **1** (*chess*: *also* **mate**) to put (an opponent's king) in a position from which the king cannot escape. **2** to prevent from escaping or making any progress: *He's checkmated any chance of progress by his refusal to discuss the problem.*

'**checkout** *nc* a place where payment is made for goods bought in a supermarket: *Which is the checkout with the shortest queue?*

'**checkpoint** *nc* a place (*esp* at a barrier between countries) where cars, passports *etc* are inspected, or a place where contestants in a motor race must pass through: *How many cars have passed this checkpoint?*

'**check-up** *nc* a (*usu* regular) medical examination to discover the state of a person's health: *I've had my annual check-up and I'm completely healthy.*

check in 1 *vi* to arrive (at a hotel) and sign the register: *We checked in last night.* **2** *vt sep* to book a room (for someone at a hotel): *He checked us in at the George Hotel.* **3** *vt sep* to hand in (*eg* one's baggage at an airport terminal): *We'll check in our luggage and go and have a meal.*

check out 1 *vi* to leave (a hotel), paying one's bill *etc*: *You must check out before 12 o'clock.* **2** *vt sep* (*esp Amer*) to test or examine: *I'll check out your version of the events.*

check up on *vt fus* to investigate to see if (someone or something) is reliable, honest, true *etc*: *Have you been checking up on me?*

checkers *see* **chequers**.

cheek [tʃiːk] **1** *nc* the side of the face below the eye: *pink cheeks.* **2** *nu* impudence or disrespectful behaviour: *He had the cheek to refuse me entrance.* – *vt* (*inf*) to be cheeky to: *The child often cheeks his mother.*

'**cheeky** *adj* impudent or disrespectful: *a cheeky child/remark*; *Don't be so cheeky!* '**cheekiness** *nu*.

cheek by jowl side by side; close together: *The soldiers were packed cheek by jowl in the back of the lorry.*

cheep [tʃiːp] *vi* to make the shrill sound of a young bird. – *nc* **1** such a sound. **2** (*inf*: *in neg*) a single sound or word: *I have not heard a cheep from the baby since he went to bed*; *'Have you heard from her recently?' 'Not a cheep!'*

cheer [tʃiə] **1** *nc* a shout of approval, encouragement or welcome: *Three cheers for the Queen!* **2** *nu* (*old*) an optimistic or happy attitude: *Be of good cheer.* – *vti* to give a shout of approval *etc* to: *The crowd cheered the new champion.* – *See also* **cheer up** *below.*

'**cheerful** *adj* full of, or causing, happiness: *He is cheerful today; a cheerful smile; cheerful news; The kitchen curtains have a cheerful pattern.* '**cheerfully** *adv.* '**cheerfulness** *nu.*

'**cheerless** *adj* (*formal*) gloomy and without comfort: *a cheerless room; The day was dull and cheerless.*

cheers! *interj* (*inf*) **1** used as a toast when drinking. **2** cheerio!: *Cheers – see you tomorrow!*

'**cheery** *adj* (*inf*) lively and happy. '**cheerily** *adv.* '**cheeriness** *nu.*

'**cheer-leader** *nc* (*esp Amer*) a person who leads organized cheering at sports events *etc.*

cheer up *vi, vt sep* to make or become (more cheerful): *He cheered up when he saw her; The flowers will cheer her up; Do cheer up and try to smile.*

cheerio! [tʃiəri'ou] *interj* (*inf*) used when leaving someone *usu* whom one expects to see again.

cheese [tʃi:z] *ncu* (any type of) a food prepared from the curd of milk and *usu* pressed into a mass or shape: *Cheddar cheese; Cheese is full of protein; a selection of cheeses.*

'**cheesecake** *ncu* a type of sweet food made with cheese, eggs *etc.*

'**cheesecloth** *nu, adj* (of) a type of thin cloth used for covering cheese or making clothes *etc.*

'**cheese-paring** [-peəriŋ] *adj* (*formal derog*) very mean: *a cheese-paring old miser; She's rather cheese-paring in her house-keeping.* – *nu* meanness: *I'm tired of his cheese-paring.*

cheesed off (*sl*) bored or depressed: *He left his job because he was cheesed off; He was cheesed off with the job.*

cheetah ['tʃi:tə] *nc* a very swift-running animal of the cat family.

chef [ʃef] *nc* a head cook, *esp* in a hotel *etc*: *Chefs in large hotels are usually men.*

chef d'oeuvre [ʃei'də:vr] – *pl* **chefs d'oeuvre** [ʃei-] – *nc* (*very formal or facet*) a masterpiece: *Hemingway is considered to have written several of the chefs d'oeuvre of American literature.*

chemical, chemist *see* **chemistry**.

chemistry ['kemistri] *nu* (the science that deals with) the nature of substances and the ways in which they act on, or combine with, each other: *Chemistry was his favourite subject at school; (attrib) a chemistry lecture; the chemistry of the blood.*

'**chemical** *adj* (*attrib*) of chemistry or chemical(s): *a chemical reaction.* – *nc* a substance used in or obtained by a chemical process: *Some chemicals give off harmful fumes.*

'**chemist** *nc* **1** a scientist who studies or works in chemistry: *an industrial chemist.* **2** (*Amer* '**druggist**) a person who makes up and sells medicines and who sometimes sells soap, make-up *etc*: *If you can't find a doctor, the chemist will tell you what medicine to take for your headache.* **3** (*Amer* '**druggist**) a chemist's shop: *Where is the nearest chemist?*

'**chemist's** *nc* (*Amer* '**druggist's**) a chemist's shop: *I'm going to the chemist's to buy some cough mixture.*

cheque, (*Amer*) **check** [tʃek] *nc* a written order on a printed form telling a bank to pay money to the person named: *Will you cash this cheque?; I want to pay by cheque.*

'**cheque-book** *nc* a book of cheque forms: *I need a new cheque-book.*

cheque card *see* **banker's card**.

chequered ['tʃekəd] *adj* (*formal: esp attrib*) varied; partly good and partly bad: *a chequered career.*

chequers, (*Amer*) **checkers** ['tʃekəz] *n* **1** *sing* the game of draughts. **2** *pl* the pieces used in this game.

cherish ['tʃeriʃ] *vt* (*formal*) **1** (not *usu* used with **is, was** *etc* and **-ing**) to protect and love (a person): *She cherishes that child.* **2** to keep (a hope, idea *etc*) in the mind or heart: *She cherished the memory of his last visit; She cherishes the hope that he will return.*

cheroot [ʃə'ru:t] *nc* a cigar which is not pointed at either end.

cherry ['tʃeri] **1** *nc* a type of small *usu* red fruit with a stone: *He ate some cherries; (attrib) a cherry tree; (attrib) a cherry tart.* **2** *ncu* (the wood of) the tree which bears it: *That is made of cherry; (attrib) a cherry orchard.* – *adj* **1** (*also* ˌ**cherry-'red**) of the colour of ripe cherries: (*liter*) *cherry lips; a cherry-red dress.* **2** of the wood of the cherry tree: *a cherry veneer.*

cherub ['tʃerəb] *nc* **1** (*pl* '**cherubim** [-bim]) an angel *usu* in paintings shown with wings and the plump face and body of a child. **2** (*pl* '**cherubs**) a beautiful child: *sleeping cherubs.* **che'rubic** [-'ru:-] *adj.*

chess [tʃes] *nu* a game for two played with thirty-two (*usu* black and white) pieces ('**chessmen**) on a board ('**chessboard**) with sixty-four (*usu* black and white) squares: *Do you play chess?; Let's have a game of chess.*

chest[1] [tʃest] **1** *nc* the part of the body between the neck and the waist, containing the heart and the lungs: *'He has a severe pain in his chest.' 'Is it a heart attack?'; (attrib) chest disease.* **2** *nu* the measurement round this part of the body (*esp* of a man or child) or of a garment for this part of the body: *What chest is your husband?; (attrib) I want a sweater chest size 40.*

'**chesty** *adj* (*inf*) **1** (*esp pred*) likely to take colds or diseases of the chest: *The child's a bit chesty in the winter.* **2** (*derog*) (of a woman) have a large bust: *large, chesty ladies.*

get (something) off one's chest (*inf*) to tell the truth about something that is worrying one: *If you've got a problem you might as well get it off your chest.*

chest[2] [tʃest] *nc* a large, strong wooden or metal box: *The old lady stores linen in a wooden chest.*

chest of drawers *nc* a piece of furniture fitted with several drawers.

chestnut ['tʃesnʌt] **1** *nc* either of two types of reddish-brown nut (one type, the **sweet chestnut**, being edible; the other, the **horse chestnut**, not being edible): *(attrib) a chestnut tree.* **2** *ncu* (the wood of) either of the two types of tree that bear these. **3** *nc* a reddish-brown horse. – *adj* **1** of the colour of ripe chestnuts: *chestnut hair.* **2** of the wood of the chestnut tree.

an old chestnut an old joke, often repeated: *Not that old chestnut again!*

chevron ['ʃevrən] *nc* a V-shaped band (*eg* on the sleeve of a sergeant's uniform, a road-sign *etc*).

chew [tʃu:] *vti* to break (food *etc*) with the teeth before swallowing: *If you chew your food properly* *it is easier to digest*; *His broken jaw made it impossible for him to chew.* – *nc* **1** an act of chewing: *When he had toothache each chew was agony.* **2** (*inf*) something chewed, *esp* a kind of sweet: *cherry-flavoured chews*; *These chews are cherry-flavoured.*

'**chewing-gum** *nu* a type of sweet made from sweetened and flavoured gum.

chew over *vt sep* (*inf*) to think or talk about (a problem *etc*): *He chewed it over for a long time and then decided not to go*; *He chewed over the problem.*

chez [ʃei] *prep* (*usu* in names of shops *etc* or *facet*) at or to the house or home of: *Chez Pierre is a good restaurant*; *Are you going chez Smith tonight?*

chic [ʃi:k] *adj* (*formal*) stylish or fashionable: *a chic dress*; *She always looks very chic.* – *nu* fashionable elegance: *French women are known for their chic.*

chicanery [ʃi'keinəri] *nu* (*formal*) dishonest cleverness: *Politicians are sometimes accused of chicanery.*

chick [tʃik] *nc* a baby bird: *One of the chicks fell out of the blackbird's nest.*

chicken ['tʃikin] **1** *nc* a young bird, *esp* a young hen: *She keeps chickens.* **2** *nu* its flesh used as food: *a plate of fried chicken.* **3** *nc* (*Amer*) a hen of any age.

'**chickenfeed** *nu* (*fig*) something, *usu* a sum of money, very small and unimportant: *That may sound like a large salary to you but it's chickenfeed to him.*

ˌ**chicken-'hearted** *adj* (*derog*) cowardly.

'**chicken-pox** *nu* an infectious disease with fever and red itchy spots: *Have you ever had chicken-pox?*

'**chicken-run** *nc* an area of land surrounded by a wire fence for keeping chickens in.

chicken out *vi* (*sl*) to avoid doing something due to cowardice: *He chickened out of accepting the challenge*; *He chickened out at the last minute.*

chicory ['tʃikəri] *nu* **1** a plant whose edible leaves are used in salads. **2** its root (which is sometimes ground and mixed with coffee).

chide [tʃaid] *vti* (*formal*) to give a scolding (to): *The child was chided by his mother for eating too many sweets.*

chief [tʃi:f] *adj* (*attrib*) greatest in importance, rank, size *etc*: *the chief city of Germany*; *the chief police officer*; *the chief cause of disease.* – *nc* the head of a clan or tribe, or a department, business *etc*: *Chief of the Clan Graham*; *Mr Smith is the chief of my department.*

'**chiefly** *adv* mainly: *She became ill chiefly because she did not eat enough.*

'**chieftain** [-tən] *nc* (*formal*) the head of a clan, tribe *etc.*

chiffon ['ʃifon, (*Amer*) ʃi'fon] *nu, adj* (of) a thin, light material made from silk *etc*: *a dress of pink chiffon*; *a pink chiffon dress.*

chilblain ['tʃilblein] *nc* a painful swelling *esp* on hands or feet, caused by cold weather: *She suffers from chilblains every winter.*

child [tʃaild] – *pl* **children** ['tʃildrən] – *nc* **1** a young human being of either sex. **2** a son or daughter (of any age): *Her youngest child is five years old.*

'**childhood** *nu* the state or time of being a child: *She remembered her childhood as being a time of happiness*; (*attrib*) *childhood memories.*

'**childish** *adj* (*derog*) like a child; silly: *Stop being childish!*; *a childish attitude/remark.* '**childishly** *adv.* '**childishness** *nu.*

'**childlike** *adj* innocent; like a child: *She has a childlike faith in her husband's ability*; *Her personality was trustful and childlike.*

'**childbirth** *nu* (*formal*) the act of giving birth to a child: *She died in childbirth.*

'**child's play** *nu* (*inf*) something very easy: *Climbing that hill is child's play to an experienced mountaineer.*

with 'child (*arch or liter*) pregnant: *She is with child.*

Chile, Chilean *see* Appendix 2.

chili *see* **chilli.**

chill [tʃil] *nc* **1** (*no pl*) a coldness: *There's a chill in the air.* **2** an illness which causes shivering: *I think I've caught a chill.* **3** (*no pl*: *formal*) a depressing influence: *The bad news cast a chill over the proceedings.* – *adj* (*esp attrib*) cold: *a chill wind.* – *vt* **1** to make cold (without freezing): *Have you chilled the wine?* **2** (*formal*) to discourage: *The threat of rain chilled my enthusiasm for a swim.*

'**chilly** *adj* **1** cold: *a chilly day*; *It's chilly in here.* **2** (*inf*) hostile; unfriendly: *a chilly stare/reception.* '**chilliness** *nu.*

chilli, chili ['tʃili] – *pls* '**chilli(e)s,** '**chili(e)s** – *ncu* the hot-tasting pod of a type of pepper, often dried, powdered and used in sauces *etc*: *There is too much chilli in this curry*; *I've bought some chillies*; (*attrib*) *chilli peppers.*

See also **capsicum.**

chime [tʃaim] *nc* (the ringing of) a set of tuned bells: *the chime of the church bells*; *She listened for the chime of the grandfather clock.* – *vti* **1** to (cause to) ring: *The church bells chimed.* **2** (of a clock) to indicate the time by chiming: *The grandfather clock chimed 9 o'clock*; *The clock chimes every half-hour.*

chime in *vi* (*inf*) to break into a conversation: *He chimed in with a stupid remark.*

chimney ['tʃimni] *nc* **1** a passage for the escape of smoke *etc* from a fireplace or furnace: *a factory chimney*; *The chimney is on fire.* **2** a narrow opening up which one may climb on a rock face.

'**chimney-pot** *nc* a pipe made of earthenware, iron *etc* fitted at the top of a (house) chimney.

'**chimney-stack** *nc* a group of chimney-pots.

'**chimney-sweep** *nc* a person who cleans chimneys.

chimpanzee [tʃimpən'zi:] *nc* (*inf abbrev* **chimp**) a type of small African ape.

chin [tʃin] *nc* the part of the face below the mouth: *His beard completely covers his chin.*

china ['tʃainə] *nu* **1** a fine kind of baked and glazed clay; porcelain: *made of china*; (*attrib*) *a china vase.* **2** things (*esp* for drinking and eating from) made from this: *She used her best china for the tea-party.*

China, Chinese *see* Appendix 2.

chink[1] [tʃiŋk] *nc* **1** a narrow opening or crack: *a chink in the curtains.* **2** a narrow beam of light (showing through a chink): *There was no chink of light in the room.*

chink[2] [tʃiŋk] *nc* a sound like coins or glasses knocking together: *She could hear the chink of crockery coming from the kitchen.* – *vti* to (cause to) make such a noise.

chintz [tʃints] *nu, adj* (of) a type of cotton printed in several colours: *curtains of blue chintz*; *chintz chair-covers.*

chip [tʃip] – *pt, ptp* **chipped** – **1** *vti* to strike or chop small pieces off (wood, china *etc*): *This table/cup was chipped when we moved house*; *This glass chipped when I knocked it over.* **2** *vt* to kick or strike (a ball) a short distance in an upward direction: *He chipped the ball to the goalkeeper.* – *See also* **chip in** *below.* – *nc* **1** a small piece (often accidentally) knocked off a china, wood, stone *etc* object: *There's a chip of glass over there.* **2** a place from which such a piece is missing: *There's a chip in the edge of this saucer.* **3** (*Amer* **french fry**) (*usu in pl*) a cut piece of potato (fried): *We are having fish and chips/steak and chips.* **4** a counter representing a certain value, used in gambling.

chip in *vi* (*inf*) **1** to interrupt: *He chipped in with a remark.* **2** to give (money): *He'll chip in with a fiver.*

when the chips are down (*inf*) at a critical moment; at a point when an important decision must be made: *When the chips are down only your most loyal friends help you.*

See also **potato chip** *under* **potato**.

chiropodist [ki'ropədist] *nc* **1** a person who treats minor disorders of the feet. **2** the place where a chiropodist works: *Where is the nearest chiropodist?*

chi'ropodist's *nc* the place where a chiropodist works.

chi'ropody *nu* the work of, or treatment by, a chiropodist.

chirp [tʃə:p], **chirrup** ['tʃirəp] *nc* the sharp, shrill sound of certain birds and insects. – *vi* to make such a sound: *The crickets are chirruping.*

chirpy ['tʃə:pi] *adj* (*inf*) lively and happy: *The sun was shining and the postman was singing a chirpy tune*; *You seem to be feeling very chirpy today.*

chisel ['tʃizl] *nc* a tool with a cutting edge at the end. – *v* – *pt, ptp* **'chiselled**, (*Amer*) **'chiseled** – *vt* to cut or carve (wood *etc*) with a chisel: *He chiselled the wood into the shape of a horse*; *He chiselled a notch in the wood.*

chit[1] [tʃit] *nc* (*inf*) a brief note: *You must hand in a chit stating your expenses before you receive any money.*

chit[2] [tʃit] *nc* (*derog*) a young girl: *a mere chit of a girl.*

chivalry ['ʃivəlri] *nu* **1** (*formal*) kindness, *esp* towards women or to the weak: *Women like him for his chivalry.* **2** (*hist*) a standard of behaviour expected of medieval knights: *Sir Galahad was noted for his chivalry.*

'chivalrous *adj* (*formal*: *neg* **un-**) showing the qualities of an ideal knight; generous, courteous *etc*: *He is always very chivalrous*; *a chivalrous old gentleman.*

chive [tʃaiv] *nc* a herb of the same family as the leek and onion, used as a flavouring in food: *This cheese has chives in it.*

chivvy, chivy ['tʃivi] *vti* (*inf*: *often derog*) to keep urging (someone) *usu* in an irritating way to hurry, or to do something; *She chivvied him to mend the window*; *Do stop chivying – there's plenty of time.*

chlorine ['klo:ri:n] *nu* an element (symbol **Cl**), a yellowish-green gas with a suffocating smell, used as a disinfectant *etc*: *They put too much chlorine in the swimming-pool.*

'chloride [-raid] *ncu* any of certain compounds of chlorine.

chlorinate ['klorineit] *vt* (*formal*) to treat (*eg* water) with chlorine: *The water in the swimming-pool is being chlorinated.*

chloroform ['klorəfo:m] *nu* a liquid, the vapour of which, when breathed in, causes unconsciousness: *The kidnappers put a cloth soaked in chloroform over the child's face.*

chlorophyll ['klorəfil] *nu* (*tech*) the colouring matter of the green parts of plants.

chock-a-block [tʃokə'blok], **chock-full** [tʃok'ful] *adjs* (*inf*: *pred*) completely full: *Hotels in seaside resorts are chock-a-block* (*with tourists*) *during the summer*; *His pockets are chock-full of rubbish.*

chocolate ['tʃokələt] **1** *nu* a paste made from the seeds of the cacao tree. **2** *ncu* a sweet made from it: *Have a chocolate*; *Would you like some chocolate?* **3** *nu* a drink made from this: *a mug of hot chocolate.* – *adj* (*esp attrib*) **1** of, made from, covered with, chocolate: *a chocolate mouse*; *chocolate ice-cream*; *chocolate biscuits.* **2** dark brown in colour: *chocolate paint*; *The walls are chocolate.*

choice [tʃois] **1** *ncu* an act or the power of choosing: *He made a foolish choice*; *You have no choice – you must do it.* **2** *nc* a thing chosen: *Which car was your original choice?* **3** *nc* a variety of things which it is possible to choose; an alternative: *You have several choices available*; *This shop has the best choice of carpets available.* – *adj* (*often facet*) excellent; worthy of being chosen: *choice vegetables*; *He is a choice example of British manhood*; *Some of her remarks are really choice.*

See also **choose**.

choir ['kwaiə] *nc* **1** a group or band of singers: *He used to sing in the church choir*; (*attrib*) *the choir secretary*; (*in cmpds*) *a choirboy* (= a young boy who sings in a choir). **2** the part of a church where the singers stand: *The choir is the oldest part of that church.*

choke [tʃouk] **1** *vt* to interfere with, or stop, the breathing of: *The gas choked him*; *He choked her to death.* **2** *vi* to have the breathing interfered with or stopped: *I'm choking!* **3** *vt* to block; to cause an obstruction in: *This pipe was choked with dirt.* – *nc* **1** the action or sound of choking. **2** an apparatus in a car engine *etc* to prevent the passage of too much air when starting the engine: *If the car engine is cold, you must pull the choke out* (= pull out the knob which operates the choke).

'choker *nc* a tight-fitting decorative neckband or necklace: *She wore a black velvet choker.*

choler ['kolə] *nu* (*liter*) anger.

'choleric *adj* (*liter*): *a choleric old man.*

cholera ['kolərə] *nu* a highly infectious, often fatal disease occurring in hot countries: *He died of cholera.*

cholesterol [kə'lestərol] *nu* (*tech*) a substance, occurring naturally in the body, too much of which is thought to cause hardening of the arteries: *There is a lot of cholesterol in egg-yolks.*

choose [tʃu:z] – *pt* **chose** [tʃouz] : *ptp* **chosen** ['tʃouzn] – *vti* **1** to take (one thing rather than another from a number of things) according to what one wants: *Always choose* (*a book*) *carefully.* **2** to decide (on one course of action rather than another): *If he chooses to resign, let him do so.*

'choos(e)y *adj* (*inf*) difficult to please: *Don't be so choosy! Take what you're given!*

nothing/not much to choose between hardly any difference of quality *etc* between: *I don't know whether Jim or Jack will win – there's nothing to choose between them.*

pick and choose *see* **pick**.

See also **choice**.

chop[1] [tʃop] – *pt, ptp* **chopped** – *vt* (*sometimes with* **up**) to cut (into small pieces): *She chopped the meat into pieces*; *He chopped up the vegetables.* – *See also* **chop down** *below.* – *nc* **1** a slice of mutton, pork *etc* containing a rib. **2** a chopping movement: *He cut down the tree at one chop.* **3** a sharp downward blow: *He killed the rabbit by one chop on the back of its neck.*

'chopper *nc* **1** (*sometimes in cmpds*) a thing which chops: *The wood-chopper is blunt.* **2** (*inf*) a helicopter.

'choppy *adj* (of the sea) having irregular waves; rough. **'choppiness** *nu.*

chop and change to keep changing (*esp* one's mind): *I wish you'd stop chopping and changing your holiday plans.*

chop down *vt sep* to cause (*esp* a tree) to fall by cutting it with an axe: *He chopped down the fir tree.*

get the chop (*sl*) **1** to be sacked (from one's job *etc*). **2** to be discontinued, *usu* suddenly: *That research project will get the chop because it is too expensive.*

chop[2] [tʃop] *nc* (*in pl*: *sl* of people) the jaws or mouth, *esp* of an animal: *Blood was dripping from the wolf's chops.*

chopper, choppy *see* **chop**[1].

chopsticks ['tʃopstiks] *n pl* two small sticks of wood, ivory *etc* used by the Chinese *etc* instead of a knife and fork.

choral ['ko:rəl] *adj* of, for, or to be sung by, a choir: *a choral work.*

chord[1] [ko:d] *nc* (*music*) a number of notes played together.

chord[2] [ko:d] *nc* **1** the string of a harp *etc.* **2** *see* **cord** (*def 2*).

strike a chord to cause (someone) to remember (something): *Her name strikes a chord.*

touch a chord to cause emotion or sympathy (in someone): *The orphan's smile touched a chord in the stern old lady's heart.*

chord[3] [ko:d] *nc* (*geom*) a straight line joining any two points on a curve, or the ends of an arc: *the chord of a circle.*

chore [tʃo:] *nc* a piece of housework or other hard or dull job: *She always does her chores in the morning; Writing letters is a chore to him.*

choreography [kori'ogrəfi] *nu* (*formal*) the arrangement of dances (*esp* in ballet). **ˌchore'ographer** *nc.*

chorister ['koristə] *nc* (*formal*) a member of a (church) choir, *esp* a boy.

chortle ['tʃo:tl] *vi* to give a happy, satisfied laugh: *The baby chortled happily.* – *nc* such a laugh: *He gave a chortle of delight.*

chorus ['ko:rəs] *nc* **1** a group of singers: *the festival chorus.* **2** a group of singers and dancers in a musical show: *She was a member of the chorus but now she is the star of the show.* **3** part of a song repeated after each verse: *The audience joined in the chorus.* **4** a song sung by many people: *They sang choruses round the camp fire;* (*fig*) *a chorus of birds.* **5** something said or shouted by a number of people together: *He was greeted by a chorus of cheers.* **6** (*old*) a person or group that comments on the action of a play: *a Greek chorus.* – *vt* to sing or say together: *The children chorused 'Goodbye, Miss Smith'.*

in 'chorus all together: *They all spoke in chorus.*

See also **choral**.

chose, chosen *see* **choose**.

Christ [kraist] *n* Jesus.

christen ['krisn] *vt* **1** to baptize into the Christian church: *The priest christened three babies today.* **2** to give (a name) to: *She was christened Joanna.* **3** (*inf*: *often facet*) to use for the first time: *Let's have a drink to christen our new whisky glasses.*

Christendom ['krisndəm] *n* (*formal*) the part of the world in which Christianity is the recognized religion.

Christian ['kristʃən] *nc* a follower of or a believer in Christ. – *adj*: *He had a Christian upbringing.*

ˌChristi'anity [-'anəti] *nu* the religion of Christ.

'christian name (*Amer* **'given name**) *nc* the personal name given in addition to the surname: *Peter is his christian name.*

Christmas ['krisməs] *n* (*often written* **Xmas**) an annual festival in memory of the birth of Christ, held on December 25, Christmas Day.

'Christmas-box *nc* a Christmas gift (*esp* for tradesmen *etc*): *a Christmas-box for the milkman.*

Christmas Eve *n* (the evening of) December 24, the day before Christmas Day.

'Christmas-tree *nc* a (*usu* fir) tree on which decorations and Christmas gifts are hung.

chromatic [krə'matik, (*Amer*) krou-] *adj* (*tech*) of colours; coloured.

chromatic scale a series of musical notes, each separated from the next by a semitone.

chrome [kroum] *nu* **1** an alloy of chromium and steel: *The bumper of this car is made of chrome.* **2** something made of or covered with chrome: *He is polishing the chrome on his car.* – *nu, adj* (of) its steely colour.

chromium ['kroumiəm] *nu* a metallic element (symbol **Cr**) used in various metal alloys. – *nu, adj* (of) its steely colour.

chromosome ['krouməsoum] *nc* (*tech*) one of the rod-shaped bodies into which a cell nucleus divides, and in which the genes are found.

chrono- [krounou] (*in cmpds*) time, as in **chronometer**.

chronic ['kronik] *adj* **1** (*esp* of a disease) lasting a long time: *a chronic illness/invalid.* **2** (*sl*) very bad, boring *etc*: *That speech/speaker was chronic!* **'chronically** *adv.*

See also **acute**.

chronicle ['kronikl] **1** *nc* (*formal*: *esp in pl*) a record of (*esp* historical) events in order of time. **2** *n* (*with cap*) a word often used in the title of newspapers: *the Weekly Chronicle.* – *vt* (*formal*) to make (such a record). **'chronicler** *nc.*

chronology [krə'nolədʒi] *ncu* (*formal*) (a table or list illustrating) relative order (of events *etc*) in time.

chronological [kronə'lodʒikəl] *adj*: *He announced the dates of the meetings in chronological order.* **ˌchrono'logically** *adv.*

chronometer [krə'nomitə] *nc* a very accurate form of watch, clock *etc.*

chrysalis ['krisəlis] *nc* (the case enclosing) the form taken by some insects (*eg* butterflies) at an early stage in their development.

chrysanthemum [kri'sanθəməm] *nc* a type of autumn garden flower with a large, bushy head: *yellow, white and bronze chrysanthemums.*

chubby ['tʃʌbi] *adj* short and fat (in an attractive way); plump: *a baby's chubby face; He's becoming quite chubby.*

chuck [tʃʌk] *vt* **1** (*inf*) to throw: *I'm going to chuck this rubbish in the dustbin;* (*fig*) *He was chucked out of university for failing his exams.* **2** to pat (a child *etc*) gently (under the chin).

chuck up *vt sep* (*sl*) to abandon (an idea, project *etc*): *He chucked up his university course.*

chuckle ['tʃʌkl] *vi* to laugh quietly: *He sat chuckling over a funny book.* – *nc* such a laugh.

chug [tʃʌg] – *pt, ptp* **chugged** – *vi* **1** to make a dull, explosive sound like that of a small (*eg* boat) engine: *I could hear the boat chugging along the channel.* **2** (of a vehicle) to move along making such a noise: *The little car chugged up the steep hill.* – *nc* such a noise.

chum [tʃʌm] *nc* (*inf*) a close friend: *a school chum.*

'**chummy** *adj* (*inf*) friendly: *He is very chummy with the boy next door.*

chum up *vi* (*inf*) to become friends: *Her son has chummed up with some very badly-behaved children.*

chump [tʃʌmp] *nc* (*inf*) a foolish person: *He was a chump to lend money to a stranger.*

chunk [tʃʌŋk] *nc* (*inf*) a thick piece of anything, as wood, bread *etc*: *Put a chunk of coal on the fire*; *chunks of meat for the dog.*

'**chunky** *adj* **1** solid and strong: *chunky whisky glasses.* **2** containing chunks: *chunky marmalade.*

church [tʃə:tʃ] *nc* **1** a building for public Christian worship: *We have built a new church*; *Do you go to church every Sunday?*; *I shall see you after church*; (*attrib*) *a church service.* **2** (*with cap*) a group of (a type of) Christians considered as a whole: *the Catholic Church*; *the Church of England.*

'**churchgoer** *nc* a person who (regularly) attends church services: *My parents were churchgoers but I am not.*

ˌ**church'warden** *nc* a layman who looks after the interests of a parish or church.

'**churchyard** *nc* the burial ground round a church.

enter the Church (*formal*) to become a clergyman: *He entered the Church after graduating from university.*

churlish ['tʃə:liʃ] *adj* bad-mannered and bad-tempered: *He's such a churlish fellow that no-one likes him*; *His behaviour was extremely churlish.*

'**churlishly** *adv.* '**churlishness** *nu.*

churn [tʃə:n] *nc* **1** a machine for making butter. **2** a large milk can: *He collects the milk from the farm in churns.* – **1** *vt* to make (butter) in a churn: *We churn our own butter.* **2** *vi* to be disturbed or agitated: *My stomach's churning with anxiety.*

churn out *vt sep* (*inf often derog*) to produce continuously (*usu* similar things): *He's been churning out bad plays for ten years now*; *If he has to churn so much work out each day the quality will be poor.*

chute [ʃu:t] *nc* **1** a sloping channel for sending down water, rubbish *etc.* **2** a similar structure in a playground, for children to slide down. **3** (*inf abbrev*) a parachute.

chutney ['tʃʌtni] *nu* a sauce made from fruit, vegetables and spices: *tomato chutney.*

cider ['saidə] *ncu* an alcoholic drink made from apples: *a glass of cider*; *One can buy various different ciders here.*

cigar [si'ga:] *nc* a roll of tobacco leaves for smoking: *He smokes cigars after dinner.*

cigarette [sigə'ret, (*Amer*) 'sigəret] *nc* a tube of finely cut tobacco rolled in thin paper: *Have a cigarette*; (*attrib*) *a cigarette case.*

cinch [sintʃ] *nc* **1** (*Amer*) a band round a horse's belly, holding the saddle in place. **2** (*inf*) a certainty: *It's a cinch that he'll get the job.* **3** (*inf*) something easily done: *'Can he do the job?' 'Yes, it's a cinch.'*

cinder ['sində] *nc* a piece of burnt coal, wood *etc*: *She searched among the cinders in the fireplace for her missing ring.*

cine- [sini] (*in cmpds*) moving picture, as in **cine-camera**.

cine-camera ['sinikamərə] *nc* a camera for taking moving pictures.

cinema ['sinəmə] *nc* **1** a building in which films are shown: *They don't build many cinemas nowadays.* **2** (*with* **the**: *no pl*) films generally; any cinema: *He enjoys going to the cinema but he prefers the theatre*; *the decline of the cinema as a form of entertainment.*

cinnamon ['sinəmən] *nu* the bark of a tree of the laurel family, used as a spice: *Put some cinnamon on the baked apples.*

cipher ['saifə] **1** *nc* (*math*) the symbol **0**. **2** *nc* (*loosely*) any numeral. **3** *nc* a person or thing of no importance: *He's a mere cipher in this organization.* **4** *ncu* (a method of) secret writing; (a) code: *He could not read the message because it was written in cipher*; *He invented a new cipher.*

See also **decipher**.

circa ['sə:kə] *prep* (*liter*: *often abbrev* **c** *or* **ca** *when written*) about or around (a date): *circa 500 BC.*

circle ['sə:kl] *nc* **1** (*geom*) a figure (○) bounded by one line every point on which is equally distant from the centre: *I find it difficult to draw circles.* **2** something in the form of a circle: *She was surrounded by a circle of admirers.* **3** a company or group (of people): *She had a small circle of close friends*; *She moves in* (= lives her life among) *wealthy circles.* **4** a balcony in a theatre *etc*: *We sat in the circle at the opera.* – **1** *vti* to move in a circle or circles (round something): *The cows circled round the farmer who was bringing their food*; *The dancers were circling the floor energetically.* **2** *vt* to draw a circle round: *Please circle the word which you think is wrong.*

See also **circular, encircle**.

circlet ['sə:klit] *nc* (*formal*) an ornamental head-band: *The bridesmaid wore a circlet of flowers.*

circuit ['sə:kit] *nc* **1** a going round; a journey or course round something: *the earth's circuit round the sun*; *He ran three circuits of the race-track.* **2** a race-track, running-track *etc*: *The York circuit is very flat.* **3** the path of an electric current and the parts through which it passes. – *See also* **short circuit**. **4** a journey or tour made regularly and repeatedly *eg* by judges, salesmen, sportsmen *etc*: *Is that part of the chief judge's circuit?* **5** the route travelled and places visited on such a journey: *the American tennis circuit.*

circuitous [sə:'kjuitəs] *adj* (*formal*) roundabout; not direct: *a circuitous route.*

circular ['sə:kjulə] *adj* **1** having the form of a circle: *a circular piece of paper*; *The rug is not circular – it is oval.* **2** (*formal*) leading back to the point from which it started: *a circular tour of the area*; (*fig*) *Your argument seems to be rather circular.* – *nc* a notice *etc*, *esp* advertising something, sent to a number of persons: *We often get circulars advertising holidays.*

ˌ**circu'larity** [-'la-] *nu* (*formal*).

'**circularize, -ise** *vt* (*formal*) to send circular(s) to: *They circularized the whole department about the change in holiday arrangements.*

circulate ['sə:kjuleit] **1** *vti* to (cause to) go round in a fixed path (not usually a circle) coming back to a starting-point: *Blood circulates through the body*; *Water circulates in the pipes of some central heating systems.* **2** *vti* to (cause to) spread or pass around (news *etc*): *He circulates information about holidays*; *There's a rumour circulating that she is getting married.* **3** *vi* to pass from one person to another (at a party *etc*): *As hostess you are expected to circulate.*

ˌ**circuˈlation 1** *nu* the act of circulating: *There are several forged £5 notes in circulation; the circulation of information; She's been in hospital but she's back in circulation* (= getting out and meeting people *etc*) *now.* **2** *nu* (the efficiency of) the blood system: *She has very poor circulation.* **3** *nc* (*usu in sing*) the number of copies sold (of a magazine, newspaper *etc*): *What is the circulation of the local newspaper?*; (*attrib*) *circulation figures.*

ˈ**circulatory** [-lə-] *adj* (*formal*) of circulation, *esp* of the blood: *circulatory disease.*

circum- [səːkəm] (*in cmpds*) around, as in **circumlocution, circumnavigate**.

circumcise [ˈsəːkəmsaiz] *vt* to remove the foreskin of (a man) or (*now rarely*) the clitoris of (a woman).

ˌ**circumˈcision** [-ˈsiʒən] *nu*: *Circumcision is sometimes carried out for religious reasons, and sometimes for reasons of health or hygiene.*

circumference [səˈkʌmfərəns] *nc* (the length of) the boundary line of a circle or anything circular in shape: *the circumference of a circle/wheel.*

circumlocution [səːkəmləˈkjuːʃən] *ncu* (*formal*) (an example of) an indirect, unnecessarily long way of saying something: *He never says anything directly, but always speaks in circumlocutions.*

circumnavigate [səːkəmˈnavigeit] *vt* (*formal*) to sail round (*esp* the world). ˈ**circumˌnaviˈgation** *ncu.* ˌ**circumˈnavigator** *nc.*

circumscribe [ˈsəːkəmskraib] *vt* **1** (*math or formal*) to draw a line round: *circumscribe a circle.* **2** (*formal*) to prevent from going outside a certain area; to make limits for: *His activities have been circumscribed on his parents' orders.*

circumspect [ˈsəːkəmspekt] *adj* (*formal*: *esp pred*) taking all things into consideration and considering all circumstances before taking action; cautious: *He's being very circumspect before taking action.* ˈ**circumspectly** *adv.* ˌ**circumˈspection** [-ˈspekʃən] *nu.*

circumstance [ˈsəːkəmstans] *nc* **1** (*usu in pl*) a condition (time, place *etc*) relating to or connected with an act or event: *In/Under the circumstances, I don't see what I can do; Under no circumstances whatever must you lend her money* (= You must never lend her money). **2** (*in pl*) the state of one's affairs: *She's in very bad circumstances – she's almost penniless.*

circumstantial evidence *nu* (*legal*) details or facts that make something look like the truth, but do not prove it: *You cannot convict a man for murder on circumstantial evidence alone.*

pomp and circumstance *see* **pomp**.

circumvent [səːkəmˈvent] *vt* (*formal*) to find a way of overcoming or making ineffective (a law, rule) *etc* sometimes by trickery: *It is not difficult to circumvent the divorce law.* ˌ**circumˈvention** *ncu.*

circus [ˈsəːkəs] *nc* **1** a travelling show with performances by horsemen, acrobats, animals *etc*: *The children went to the circus.* **2** (*Brit*: *usu* used with *cap* in the names of streets) an open space in a town *etc* where several roads meet: *Piccadilly Circus.*

cissy *see* **sissy**.

cistern [ˈsistən] *nc* a tank *etc* for storing water or other liquid (*esp* for a lavatory).

citadel [ˈsitədl] *nc* a fortress, *esp* in or near a city.

cite [sait] *vt* **1** (*formal or legal*) to quote (something) as an example or proof: *He cited similar examples in his defence.* **2** to name (someone) *eg* in a divorce case: *She was cited as co-respondent* (= partner in adultery).

citation [saiˈteiʃən] **1** *nu* the act of citing. **2** *nc* something cited, *esp* an example of bravery in war, referred to in army records. **3** *nc* (*legal*) a summons to appear in court.

citizen [ˈsitizn] *nc* **1** an inhabitant of a city or town: *a citizen of London.* **2** a member of a state or country: *a British citizen; He is French by birth but he is now a citizen of the USA.*

ˈ**citizenship** *nu* the status, rights and duties of a citizen, *esp* of a particular country *etc*: *He has applied for British citizenship.*

See also **city, civic, civil**.

citric [ˈsitrik]: **citric acid** *nu* the acid which gives lemons and certain other fruits their sourness.

ˈ**citrus fruit** [ˈsitrəs] *ncu* a type of fruit including the lemon, orange, lime *etc.*

city [ˈsiti] *nc* **1** (*with cap in names*) a very large town: *London is a large city; the City of London.* **2** (*hist*) a town which has been granted rights of self-government.

city council *nc* in England and Wales, the council of a district or parish which has kept its historical title of 'city', whose chairman is called 'mayor'.

the City the business centre of a large town, *esp* of London: *He's a banker in the City.*

civic [ˈsivik] *adj* (*attrib*) of or belonging to a city or citizen: *Our offices are in the new civic centre; It is your civic duty to keep the city tidy.*

ˈ**civics** *n sing* the study of the duties of a citizen.

civil [ˈsivl] *adj* **1** polite: *a very civil person; He was not at all civil.* **2** (*attrib*) of the state or community: *civil rights; civil affairs.* **3** (*attrib*) ordinary; not military or religious: *civil life.* **4** (*legal*: *attrib*) concerned with cases which are not criminal: *Divorce cases are covered by civil law.*

civilian [siˈviljən] *nc* a person who has a civil job, not in the army or other armed forces: *He's left the army and become a civilian again*; (*attrib*) *a civilian job.*

civility [siˈviləti] *ncu* (an act of) politeness: *He always treated strangers with civility; She appreciates his civilities.*

ˈ**civilly** *adv* politely: *He answered me civilly enough.*

civil engineer *see* **engineer**.

civil liberties/rights *n pl* the rights of a citizen according to the law of the country.

civil list *nc* an allowance of money set aside by the government for the expenses of the British royal household.

civil marriage *ncu* (a) legal marriage with no religious ceremony.

civil servant *nc* a member of the civil service.

civil service *nu* the organization which runs the administration of a state: *He is with the British Civil Service.*

civil war *ncu* (a) war between citizens of the same state: *In Cromwell's time there was civil war in Britain; He lost his life in the American Civil War.*

civilize, -ise [ˈsivilaiz] *vt* **1** to change the ways of (a primitive people) to those found in a more advanced type of society: *The Romans tried to civilize the ancient Britons.* **2** (*formal or facet*) to make more polite: *Public schools claim to civilize their pupils.*

ˌ**civiliˈzation, -s- 1** *nu* the act of civilizing, or

process or state of being civilized: *The civilization of the savage tribes proved difficult.* **2** *nc* a civilized people and their way of life: *the ancient civilizations of Egypt and Greece.*

clad [klad] *adj* **1** (*liter or formal*: *pred or in cmpds*) clothed: *The man in the portrait was clad in silk*; *leather-clad motor-cyclists.* **2** (*usu in cmpds*) covered: *an ivy-clad wall*; *an armour-clad warship.* – *v see* **clothe**.

'cladding *nu* covering (*esp* for protecting pipes, boilers *etc* from cold): *We put cladding on the pipes before the winter started.*

claim [kleim] *vt* **1** to say that something is a fact: *She claims (that) this job is very easy*; *He claims to be the best runner in the class*; *She claims not to have met him before.* **2** to demand as a right: *You must claim compensation*; *You must claim your money back if the goods are damaged*; *He did not claim his right to see his children*; *His work claimed too much of his time.* **3** to state that one is the owner of: *Does anyone claim this book?* – *nc* **1** a statement (that something is a fact): *Her claim that she was the duke's daughter was disproved.* **2** (a demand for) a payment of compensation *etc*: *All industrial claims are dealt with by a tribunal*; *She has put forward a claim for damages against her employer.* **3** a demand for something or someone which (one says) one owns or has a right to: *He makes excessive claims on my time*; *You must assert your claim to your children.* **4** a piece of land allotted *eg* to a (gold) miner.

'claimant *nc* (*esp legal*) a person who makes a claim: *a claimant to the throne.*

clairvoyance [kleə'voiəns] *nu* (*formal*) the power of seeing things not able to be perceived by the normal senses (*eg* details about life after death).

clair'voyant *nc, adj* (*formal*): *She asked the clairvoyant to communicate with the spirit of her dead husband.*

clam [klam] *nc* **1** a shellfish with two shells joined together, used as food. **2** (*Amer inf*) a silent or secretive person.

clam up – *pt, ptp* **clammed** – *vi* (*inf*) to become silent suddenly: *She clammed up when she discovered he was a policeman*; *She was in the midst of a conversation when suddenly she clammed up on me.*

clamber ['klambə] *vi* to climb (often with difficulty) by holding on with hands and feet: *The children clambered over the rocks.*

clammy ['klami] *adj* damp and sticky: *clammy hands*; *clammy weather*; *It's clammy today.*

clamour, (*Amer*) **clamor** ['klamə] *ncu* (a) loud uproar, noise or shout (*esp* demanding something): *There was a clamour from the audience to have their money returned.* – *vi* to make such an uproar *etc*: *They're all clamouring for their money back.*

'clamorous *adj* (*formal*) noisy, *esp* when making loud demands: *clamorous children*; *The children were clamorous in their demands for refreshments.*

clamp [klamp] *nc* a piece of wood, iron *etc* used to fasten things together or to strengthen them. – *vt* to bind together with a clamp: *They clamped the iron rods together.*

clamp down *vi* (*with* **on**) to stop the activity of; to control strictly: *The government clamped down on public spending.* – (*nc* **'clampdown**: *There has been a clampdown on crime by the police*).

clan [klan] *nc* **1** a tribe or group of families (*esp* Scottish) under a single chief, *usu* all having one surname. **2** (*loosely*: *often derog*) a group of people (not necessarily of the same family) with similar interests, attitudes *etc*: *All the higher-grade engineers have formed a little clan of their own.*

'clannish *adj* (*derog*) closely united and showing little interest in people not of the group: *The people who belong to that club are so clannish that they won't speak to new members*; *a clannish set of people.*

'clansman ['klanz-] – *fem* **'clanswoman** – *nc* a member of a family clan.

clandestine [klan'destin] *adj* (*formal*: *usu attrib*) secret or hidden: *a clandestine marriage.* **clan'destinely** *adv.*

clang [klaŋ] *vti* to produce a loud, deep ringing sound, like that of a large bell: *The heavy gate clanged shut.* – *nc* such a sound: *the clang of the prison gates shutting.*

clanger ['klaŋə] *nc* (*inf*) a bad mistake or a very tactless remark: *That's a real clanger.*

drop a clanger *see* **drop**.

clank [klaŋk] *vi* to produce a sound like that made by heavy pieces of metal striking each other: *The chains clanked together.* – *nc* such a noise: *The clank of the gates closing made an eerie sound.*

clannish, clansman *see* **clan**.

clap [klap] – *pt, ptp* **clapped** – **1** *vti* to strike the palms of the hands together *eg* to show approval, to mark a rhythm, or to gain attention *etc*: *When the singer appeared, the audience started to clap loudly*; *They clapped him/the speech enthusiastically*; *Clap your hands in time to the music.* **2** *vt* to strike (someone) with the palm of the hand, often in a friendly way: *He clapped him on the back and congratulated him*; *He clapped his hands to his head in despair.* **3** *vt* to put suddenly (into prison, chains *etc*): *They clapped him in jail.* – *nc* **1** a sudden noise (of thunder). **2** an act of clapping: *They gave the performer a clap*; *He gave me a clap on the back.*

'clapper *nc* the part inside a bell which strikes against the side.

'clapping *nu* striking of the palms of the hands together to show approval *etc*: *the enthusiastic clapping of the audience.*

'claptrap *nu* (*derog*) insincere, empty words; rubbish: *Some people found his speech moving but it was just claptrap.*

claret ['klarət] **1** *ncu* a kind of French red wine. **2** *nu, adj* (of) its colour: *a dress of claret(-coloured) velvet.*

clarify ['klarəfai] *vti* **1** (*formal*) to make or become clear (in meaning *etc*): *Would you please clarify your last statement?* **2** (*esp* of butter) to make or become clear and pure: *Have you clarified the fat?*

ˌclarifi'cation [-fi-] *nu.*

clarinet [klarə'net] *nc* a type of musical wind instrument, *usu* made of wood, and played by means of keys and fingers covering combinations of holes: *He plays the clarinet*; *He played a tune on the clarinet.*

ˌclari'nettist (*Amer usu* **ˌclari'netist**) *nc* a person who plays the clarinet.

clarion ['klariən] *n* (*with cap*) a word often used in the title of newspapers: *the County Clarion.*

'clarion call *nc* (*usu fig*) a loud, rousing sound, often made (as if) by a trumpet: *a clarion call to action.*

clarity ['klarəti] *nu* (*formal*) **1** the state of being clear or easy to see through: *the clarity of water.* **2** the state of being easy to see, hear or understand: *the clarity of her speech/statement.*

clash [klaʃ] *nc* **1** a loud noise, like *eg* swords striking together: *the clash of metal on metal.* **2** a serious disagreement or difference: *a clash of points of view*; *a clash of personalities*; *a clash of colours.* **3** a battle: *a clash between opposing armies.* **4** (of two or more things) an act of interfering with each other because of happening at the same time: *a clash between two classes held at 3 p.m. on the same day.* – **1** *vti* to strike together noisily: *The cymbals clashed.* **2** *vi* to fight (in battle): *The two armies clashed at the mouth of the valley.* **3** *vi* to disagree violently: *They clashed over the question of whether to approve the plan.* **4** *vi* to interfere (with something or each other) because of happening at the same time: *My English lecture clashes with my Spanish lecture*; *The two lectures clash.* **5** *vi* (of colours) to appear unpleasant when placed together: *The (colour of the) jacket clashes with the (colour of the) skirt*; *The colours clash.*

clasp [kla:sp] *nc* **1** a fastening made of two parts which link together (*eg* on a necklace or brooch, or for keeping the hair in position): *The clasp of my necklace is broken.* – *vt* **1** to grasp or embrace: *She clasped the child in her arms.* **2** (*formal*) to fasten with a clasp: *He clasped the diamond necklace round her neck.*

class [kla:s] **1** *nc* a group of people or things that are alike in some way: *Plants can be divided into classes*; *an expensive class of house*; *The dog won first prize in its class in the dog show.* **2** *nu* the system according to which people are divided into social groups: *Class often prevents friendships between certain people*; (*attrib*) *the class system.* **3** *nc* one of these social groups: *the upper class*; *the middle class*; *the working class*; *To which class does he belong?* **4** *nc* a grade or rank (of merit): *a high class of degree.* **5** *nc* a number of students or scholars taught together: *John and I are in the same class.* **6** *nc* a school lesson or (*esp Amer*) college lecture *etc*: *a French class*; *I must go – I have a class at 3 o'clock.* **7** *nc* a year's intake or output of students: *the class of '79.* **8** *nu* (*inf*) style: *That woman really has class!* – *vt* to regard as being of a certain type: *I class her as one of the nicest people I know*; *He classes all women as stupid.*

'classy *adj* (*inf*) stylish: *That's a really classy dress.*

ˌclass-'conscious *adj* very much aware of (one's own or other people's) membership of a certain social class: *a class-conscious attitude to tradespeople*; *She's so class-conscious that she won't speak to workmen.*

'classmate *nc* (*formal*) a pupil in the same school class.

'class-room *nc* a room in a school were a class is taught.

class war *ncu* a struggle between different social classes in a community: *The struggle between management and workmen is part of the class war.*

See also **classify**.

classical ['klasikəl] *adj* (*esp attrib*) **1** (*esp* of literature, art *etc*) of ancient Greece or Rome, or both: *He lectures in classical studies at the university*; *a classical education.* **2** (of music or literature) having the traditional, established harmony and/or form: *He prefers classical music to popular music.* **3** (of literature) considered to be of the highest class: *Shakespeare's plays form an important part of Britain's classical drama.* **4** decorative without being ornate; simple: *a classical design.*

'classic (*esp attrib*) *adj* **1** standard or best: *the classic example*; *the classic authority.* **2** (of literature, art *etc*) of the highest quality (*esp* like that of ancient Greece and Rome). **3** (of dress *etc*) simple, elegant and traditional: *She always wears classic clothes.* – *nc* **1** an established work of art or literature of high quality: *I have read all the classics*; *'Wuthering Heights' is a classic.* **2** (*in pl*) the classical language and literature, *esp* of Greece and Rome: *He is studying classics.* **3** an article of clothing of simple and traditional style: *A short black dress is a classic.*

'classicist [-sist] *nc* a student of the classics of Greece and Rome.

classify ['klasifai] *vti* to put into, or be in, a particular class or group: *How are the books in the library classified?*; *I'd classify that as secret*; (*formal*) *That classifies as a failure.* **ˌclassifi'cation** [-fi-] *ncu.*

'classified *adj* (*attrib*: *neg* **un-**) **1** arranged in categories or classes: *All the classified books are on these shelves.* **2** (of information) secret: *I can't give you details about the battle – that's classified information.* **3** (of a road) entitled to receive a government grant to pay for its upkeep.

clatter ['klatə] *nu* a loud noise like hard objects falling, striking against each other *etc*: *the noisy clatter of children climbing the stairs.* – *vti* to (cause to) make such a noise: *The children clattered downstairs*; *They clattered the dishes in the sink.*

clause [klo:z] *nc* **1** (*gram*) a part of a sentence having its own subject and predicate, *eg* either of the two parts of the sentence: *John has a friend/who is rich.* **2** (*legal*) a paragraph in a contract, will, or act of parliament: *This clause means that you cannot receive the money until you are twenty-five.*

claustrophobia [klo:strə'foubiə] *nu* fear of narrow, small or enclosed places: *He gets claustrophobia working in that tiny office.* **ˌclaustro'phobic** *adj.*

clavicle ['klavikl] *nc* (*tech*) the collar-bone: *He has broken his clavicle.*

claw [klo:] *nc* **1** one of the hooked nails of an animal or bird: *The cat sharpened its claws on the tree-trunk.* **2** the foot of an animal or bird with hooked nails: *The owl held the mouse in its claw.* **3** (the pointed end of) the leg of a crab *etc.* **4** a mechanical instrument with a similar shape: *A large metal claw lifted the car on to the scrap-heap.* – *vti* to scratch or tear (at something) with claws or nails: *The two cats clawed at each other*; *The prisoner clawed desperately at the door*; *The cat clawed the mouse.*

clay [klei] *nu* a soft, sticky type of earth which is often baked into pottery, china, bricks *etc*: *My garden soil has a lot of clay in it*; *He likes to make things from clay*; *He works in clay*; (*attrib*) *a clay pot.*

'clayey *adj*: *The soil in his garden is very clayey*; *clayey soil.*

claymore ['kleimo:] *nc* (*hist*) a large double-edged sword used by Scottish Highlanders.

clean [kli:n] *adj* **1** free from dirt, smoke *etc*: *Your hands are clean now*; *a clean window*; *a clean dress.* **2** (*usu attrib*) neat and tidy in one's habits; hygienic: *Cats are very clean animals.* **3** (*usu attrib*) unused: *a clean sheet of paper.* **4** free from guilt or evil: *He leads a clean life*; *He has a clean record* (= He is not known to be a criminal); *His record is clean.* **5** (*usu attrib*) neat and even: *A blunt knife won't make a clean cut.* **6** (*usu attrib*) simple and attractive: *The ship has clean lines.* **7** not obscene; not indecent: *a clean joke*; *Keep your language clean!* – *adv* (*inf*) completely: *He got clean away.* – *vti* to (cause to) become free from dirt *etc*: *Will you clean the windows?*; *They cleaned this dress for me*; *I've cleaned the kitchen*; *This dress cleans well.* – *See also* **clean out, clean up** *below.* **'cleaner** *nc.*

'cleanly[1] *adv*: *The knife cut cleanly through the cheese.*

cleanly[2] ['klenli] *adj* (*formal*: *usu attrib*) clean in personal habits: *The cat is a cleanly animal.* **'cleanliness** ['klen-] *nu.*

clean-up *see* **clean up**.

clean out *vt sep* **1** to clean thoroughly, throwing out all rubbish *etc*: *We'll clean out the sitting-room tomorrow.* **2** (*sl*) to take all (someone's) money: *He was cleaned out by the huge expenses of moving house.*

clean up 1 *vi, vt sep* to clean (a place) thoroughly: *She cleaned (the room) up after they went home.* **2** *vi* (*sl*) to make a huge profit: *They cleaned up on their business deals.* – (*nc* **'clean-up**).

a clean bill of health a certificate saying that a person, the crew of a ship *etc* is entirely healthy (*esp* after being ill): *I've been off work but I've got a clean bill of health now.*

a clean slate a fresh start: *After being in prison he started his new job with a clean slate.*

come clean (*inf*) to tell the truth about something, often about something about which one has previously lied: *At first he lied to the police but he finally came clean.*

make a clean breast of to confess or admit to something, often something that one has previously denied: *At first he denied the offence, but he later decided to make a clean breast of it.*

make a clean sweep to get rid of everything unnecessary or unwanted: *The new manager made a clean sweep of all the lazy people in the department.*

cleanse [klenz] *vt* 2 (*formal*) to make clean or pure: *This cream will cleanse your skin*; *He felt that he had been cleansed of guilt.*

'cleanser *nc* something which cleans, *esp* a cosmetic used to clean the face: *I use soap and water – I don't use a cleanser.*

clear [kliə] *adj* **1** (*usu attrib*) easy to see through; transparent: *clear glass.* **2** free from mist or cloud: *a clear sky/day*; *Isn't the sky clear!* **3** easy to see, hear or understand: *He gave a very clear explanation*; *The details on that photograph are very clear.* **4** free from difficulty or obstacles: *a clear road ahead*; *The way is clear for you to do what you like.* **5** (*usu attrib*) after all charges, expenses *etc* have been taken off: *a clear profit/margin.* **6** free from guilt *etc*: *a clear conscience*; *My conscience is clear.* **7** free from doubt *etc*: *Are you quite clear about what I mean?*; *a clear understanding of the problems.* **8** (*pred*: *often with* **of**) without (risk of) being touched, caught *etc*: *Is the ship clear of the rocks?*; *We're clear of the police now.* **9** (*pred*: *often with* **of**) free (from debt *etc*): *clear of debt*; *clear of all infection.* **10** complete: *The bank needs three clear days to deal with a cheque.* – **1** *vt* to make or become free from obstacles, difficulties, or from anything that might prevent a thing being easily seen (through), understood, used *etc*: *He cleared the table*; *I cleared my throat*; *He cleared the path of snow*; *She cleared away the rubbish.* **2** *vt* (*often with* **of**) to prove the innocence of; to declare to be innocent: *He was cleared of all charges*; *'Was he found guilty?' 'No, he was cleared.'* **3** *vi* (of the sky *etc*) to become bright, free from cloud *etc*: *The sky cleared, leaving no cloud in sight.* **4** *vt* to get over or past something without touching it: *He cleared the jump easily.* **5** *vt* to make (a sum of money) as profit: *He cleared £100 on that deal.* **6** *vt* to allow (goods *etc*) to pass after examination: *This cargo has been cleared by Customs.* – *See also* **clear** *in phrases below.* – *adv* **1** so as to be easily heard, seen *etc*: *I hear you loud and clear.* **2** completely: *He got clear away.*

'clearance 1 *nu* the act of clearing, removing or tidying: *The clearance of these trees from the front of the window will give you more light*; *The clearance of the mess took some hours*; (*attrib*) *a clearance sale* (= a sale of all of the goods a shop has in stock). **2** *nc* the distance between two objects or between a moving and a stationary part of a machine: *You'll succeed in getting the lorry under the bridge – there's a clearance of half a metre.* **3** *ncu* (a certificate) giving permission for something to be done: *The ship obtained (a) clearance to sail*; *Have you had clearance of goods through customs?*; *He has been appointed ambassador but he is waiting for clearance from the Foreign Office*; (*loosely*) *Have you received clearance from the managing director for that project?*

'clearing 1 *nu* the act of making clear: *the clearing of weeds from the garden.* **2** *nc* a piece of land cleared of wood *etc* for cultivation: *a clearing in the forest.*

'clearly *adv.* **'clearness** *nu.*

,clear-'cut *adj* having a clear outline; plain and definite: *a clear-cut plan*; *Her features were clear-cut.*

'clearway *nc* a stretch of road on which motorists are forbidden to stop: *He would not have parked on the clearway but his car ran out of petrol.*

'clear of (*formal*) away from: *Stand clear of the doors!*

clear off 1 *vt sep* to get rid of; to pay (debts *etc*): *You must clear off your account before we give you any more credit.* **2** *vi* (*inf*) to go away; to leave: *He cleared off without saying a word.*

clear out 1 *vt sep* to get rid of: *He cleared the rubbish out of the attic.* **2** *vt sep* to make clear, tidy *etc* by emptying, throwing out rubbish *etc*: *He has cleared out the attic.* **3** *vi* (*inf*) to go away; to leave: *Clear out and leave me alone!*

clear up 1 *vt sep* to make clear, tidy *etc*: *Clear up this mess!*; (*fig*) *Have you cleared up the misunderstanding?* **2** *vi* to become better, healthier *etc*: *If the weather clears up, we'll go for a picnic*; *His infection has cleared up now.*

in the clear no longer under suspicion, in danger *etc*: *They've caught the real thief – you're in the clear now*; *He had tuberculosis but he's in the clear now.*

See also **clarify, clarity**.

cleave[1] [kli:v] – *pts* **cleft** [kleft], **cleaved, clove** [klouv]: *ptps* **cleft, cloven** ['klouvn] – (*formal or old*) **1** *vti* to split: *He can cleave a tree with one blow of his axe.* **2** *vt* to make (a way through): *They are cleaving a way through the jungle.*

'cleavage [-vidʒ] **1** *nc* (*formal*) a split: *a cleavage in the rock.* **2** *ncu* (the amount of) the space between a woman's breasts, *esp* as shown by a low-cut dress *etc*: *Men stared at her cleavage*; *She is showing a lot of cleavage in that dress!*

'cleaver *nc* a butcher's knife: *He murdered his wife with a cleaver.*

cloven hoof *nc* **1** a hoof, like those of cows, sheep

etc, which has a split up the centre. **2** (*fig*) a sign of the devil or of an evil nature.
See also **cleft**.

cleave[2] [kliːv]: **'cleave to** *vt fus* (*formal*) **1** to stick to: *Her wet dress cleaved to her body.* **2** (*fig*) to remain faithful to: *I cleave to the principles of honesty and truth.*

clef [klef] *nc* (*music*) a sign (*eg* 𝄞 or 𝄢) on the stave fixing the pitch of the notes.

cleft [kleft] *nc* (*formal or tech*) an opening made by splitting a crack: *a cleft in the rocks*; (*attrib*) *a cleft palate* (= a split in the roof of the mouth, present from birth).
in a cleft stick not being able to decide which of two possible courses of action to take: *We can't decide whether to sell our house before we've bought another or whether we should buy one and then try to sell this one – we're really in a cleft stick.*
See also **cleave**[1].

clement ['klemənt] *adj* (*formal*) **1** (of weather *etc*) mild: *a clement autumn day.* **2** merciful: *a clement ruler*; *The general was clement towards the enemy.*
'clemency *nu.*
See also **inclement**.

clench [klentʃ] *vt* **1** to close tightly together: *He clenched his teeth/fist.* **2** to grasp or grip firmly: *The dying man clenched the doctor's hand in agony.*

clergy ['kləːdʒi] *nu* the ministers, priests *etc* of the Christian religion: *the clergy of the Church of England.*
'clergyman *nc* one of the clergy; a priest, minister *etc*: *She asked for a clergyman when she was dying.*

cleric ['klerik] *nc* (*formal*) a clergyman.
'clerical[1] *adj* (*attrib*) of the clergy: *He is wearing a clerical collar.*

clerical[2] ['klerikəl] *adj* of a clerk or of his work: *The fact that the wrong bill was sent to you was the result of a clerical error*; *The errors were all clerical.*

clerk [klaːk, (*Amer*) kləːk] *nc* **1** a person who deals with letters, accounts *etc* in an office: *He is employed as a clerk in the Civil Service.* **2** a public official in charge of the business affairs of the town council *etc*: *the town clerk.* **3** a lay officer in the church: *the parish clerk.* **4** (*Amer*) a shop-assistant: *She is a clerk in the supermarket.*
'clerkess *nc* a female clerk: *She is a clerkess in the local bank.*
clerk of works *nc* (*Brit*) a person who superintends the putting up and maintenance of a building *etc*: *The clerk of works said that our roof was in need of repair.*

clever ['klevə] *adj* **1** quick to learn and understand: *a clever child*; *The child is clever.* **2** skilful: *He's clever with his hands*; *a clever carpenter.* **3** (of things) showing cleverness; well thought-out: *a clever idea*; *How clever his ideas are!* **'cleverly** *adv.* **'cleverness** *nu.*

cliché ['kliːʃei, (*Amer*) kliː'ʃei] *nc* a phrase which has been used too often, and has become meaningless: *'We're just good friends' has become a cliché among film stars.*

click [klik] *nc* a short, sharp sound, like that of a light-switch being turned on: *the click of a key turning in a lock*; *Did you take the photograph? I didn't hear the click of the camera*; *the click of her high-heeled shoes.* – **1** *vti* to (cause to) make such a sound: *The soldier clicked his heels together*; *The gate clicked shut*; *His jaws clicked as he chewed.* **2** *vi* (*inf*) to work properly; to become successful: *Things are suddenly beginning to click*; *The play clicked with the audience right away.* **3** *vi* (*inf*) to be understood: *It's just clicked what you meant me to do.* **4** *vi* (*sl*) to become friendly: *John and Mary have really clicked.*

client ['klaiənt] *nc* **1** a person who receives professional advice from a lawyer, accountant *etc*: *That bank-manager is very polite to all his clients.* **2** a customer: *That hairdresser is very popular with his clients.*
clientèle [kliːon'tel] *nu* (*formal or facet*) a group or type of clients: *We have a very high-class clientèle at this restaurant*; *a bank's clientèle.*

cliff [klif] *nc* a high steep rock, *esp* one facing the sea.
'cliff-hanger *nc* a story, situation *etc* where one is kept in suspense: *Last week's episode of the play was a real cliff-hanger*; (*attrib*) *We don't know whether the unions will go on strike or not – it's a cliff-hanger situation.*

climactic *see* **climax**.

climate ['klaimət] *nu* **1** the weather conditions of a region (temperature, moisture *etc*): *She left Africa because the climate did not agree with her*; *Britain has a temperate climate.* **2** (*fig*) the conditions in a country *etc*: *the economic/moral climate*; *climate of opinion* (= what people are thinking or feeling). **cli'matic** [-'ma-] *adj.*

climax ['klaimaks] *nc* the highest point; the most dramatic moment: *He has reached the climax of his career*; *the climax of the novel.*
cli'mactic [-'maktik] *adj* (*formal*: *attrib*): *the climactic moments of his career.*

climb [klaim] **1** *vti* (of a person *etc*) to go up or towards the top of (a mountain, wall, ladder *etc*) sometimes using the hands and feet: *He climbed to the top of the hill*; *He climbed up the ladder*; *The child climbed the tree*; *He climbed over the high wall.* – *See also* **climb down** *below.* **2** *vi* (of a mountain, rock face *etc*) to rise or slope upward: *The mountains climbed steeply from the floor of the valley*; *The plane began to climb.* – *nc* **1** an act of going up: *His climb to the top of his profession was very fast.* **2** a route or place to be climbed: *The guide showed us the best climb.*
'climber *nc.*
climb down 1 *vi, vt fus* to go down or towards the bottom of (a mountain, ladder *etc*) sometimes using the hands and feet: *It was difficult to climb down* (*the cliff*); *He climbed down* (*the ladder*) *carefully.* **2** *vi* to accept defeat; to take back what one has said: *He eventually climbed down and accepted our decision.*

clime [klaim] *nc* (*liter or facet*) a climatic region: *They moved to warmer climes.*

clinch [klintʃ] **1** *vt* (*inf*) to settle or come to an agreement about (an argument or a bargain): *The businessmen clinched the deal.* **2** *vti* (*formal*) (in boxing, wrestling *etc*) to grasp (one's opponent) tightly; to grapple: *The boxers clinched each other tightly*; *The lovers clinched passionately.* – *nc* **1** (in boxing *etc*) a tight grip: *in a tight clinch.* **2** (*inf*) a lovers' embrace: *The old lady was embarrassed when the boy and girl went into a clinch.*

cling [kliŋ] – *pt, ptp* **clung** [klʌŋ] – *vi* (*usu with* **to**) **1** to stick (to); to grip tightly: *The mud clung to her shoes*; *She clung to her husband as he said goodbye*; (*fig*) *He clings to a belief that she was faithful.* **2** to be fond of and too dependent on (a person): *He clings to his mother for support and affection.* **3** to stay close (to): *The boat clung to the coastline.*

clinic ['klinik] *nc* **1** a place or part of a hospital where a particular kind of medical treatment or advice is given: *a dental clinic*; *He is attending the skin clinic*; *He treats private patients at his clinic.* **2** a place where non-medical advice or instruction is given: *a car-testing clinic*; *a marriage guidance clinic.*

'clinical *adj* **1** of a clinic. **2** (*attrib*: *esp* of medical teaching) based on observation of the patient: *clinical medicine.* **3** (*usu attrib*) observing in a cool and unemotional way: *a clinical attitude to women*; *He cannot take a clinical view of the situation.*

clink[1] [kliŋk] *nc* a ringing sound (made by glasses, coins *etc* striking together): *the clink of coins in his pocket.* – *vti* to (cause to) make such a sound: *They clinked their glasses together and drank a toast to their absent friends*; *The coins clinked in his pocket.*

clink[2] [kliŋk] *nu* (*sl*) prison: *He's in clink again.*

clip[1] [klip] – *pt, ptp* **clipped** – *vt* **1** to cut (*esp eg* an animal's hair, wool *etc*) with scissors or shears: *The shepherd clipped the sheep*; *They clipped the dog before the dog show*; *The hedge was clipped.* **2** to shorten (words) by speaking indistinctly: *He clips his words when he speaks, especially when he's in a hurry.* **3** (*inf*) to strike sharply: *She clipped him on the ear.* – *nc* **1** an act of clipping: *One clip of the shears cut off the tangled wool.* **2** (*inf*) a sharp blow: *She gave him a clip on the ear.*

clipped *adj* (*usu attrib*) having or using shortened words: *He has rather a clipped way of speaking.*

'clipper *nc* **1** (*in pl*: *often in cmpds*) a tool for clipping: *hedge-clippers*; *nail-clippers.* **2** a type of fast sailing-ship.

'clipping 1 *nu* the act of cutting: *The clipping of the sheep took several hours.* **2** *nc* a thing clipped off or out of something, *esp* a newspaper: *She collects clippings about the royal family*; *Put the hedge clippings on the fire.*

clip someone's wings to take away from a person the power of doing something: *She used to go to a lot of parties but having to look after a baby has clipped her wings.*

clip[2] [klip] – *pt, ptp* **clipped** – *vt* to fasten with a clip: *Clip these papers together.* – *n nc* **1** (*often in cmpds*) something for holding things together *esp* a piece of bent metal for holding papers together: *a paper-clip.* **2** (*often in cmpds*) something for holding something in place: *a hair-clip*; *bicycle-clips* (= round pieces of metal *etc* for holding the bottom of trouser legs close to the leg); *a clip for holding two parts of a wound together.* **3** a kind of small brooch or ornamental pin: *a diamond clip.*

clique [kli:k] *nc* (*derog*) a group of people who are friendly with each other but exclude others: *the golf-club clique.*

'cliqu(e)y, 'cliquish *adjs*: *The members of that club are so cliquish that visitors feel unwelcome*; *a cliquey bunch of teenagers.*

clitoris ['klitəris] *nc* (*tech*) a part of the female external sexual organs equivalent to the male penis.

cloak [klouk] *nc* a (long) loose outer garment without sleeves, covering most of the body: *a woollen cloak*; (*fig*) *They arrived under cloak of darkness.* – *vt* (*formal*) to cover or hide: *Their discussions were cloaked in secrecy.*

'cloakroom *nc* **1** a room for coats, hats *etc.* **2** (*euph*) a lavatory: *the ladies' cloakroom.*

clobber ['klobə] *vt* (*Brit sl*) to hit (someone or something): *He clobbered me when I insulted him*; (*fig*) *The Tories were clobbered in the elections.* – *nu* (*Brit sl*) **1** clothing: *fashionable teenage clobber.* **2** bits and pieces; odds and ends: *The clobber he used to make his model aeroplanes took up a lot of space.*

clock [klok] *nc* **1** an instrument for measuring time, but not worn on the wrist like a watch: *We have five clocks in our house*; *an alarm-clock* (= a clock with a ringing device for waking one up in the morning); (*attrib*) *the clock face.* **2** (*inf*) an instrument for measuring speed of a vehicle or distance travelled by a vehicle; a speedometer or mileometer: *My car has 120 000 miles on the clock*; *The clock is registering 90 mph.* – *vt* to register (a time) on a stopwatch *etc*: *What time did he clock for the race?* – *See also* **clock in, out/on, off, clock up** *below.*

'clockwise *adv* in the direction of the movement of the hands of a clock: *The circle of children moved clockwise round the room, then anticlockwise.*

'clockwork *nu* machinery similar to that of a clock: *a toy which works by clockwork*; (*attrib*) *a clockwork train.*

clock in, out/on, off *vis* **1** register or record time of arriving at or leaving work. **2** (*loosely*) to begin or finish work: *We clock in at 8 o'clock.*

clock up *vt sep* to register on a mileometer *etc*: *I've clocked up eight thousand miles this year in my car.*

like 'clockwork very smoothly and without faults or problems: *Everything went like clockwork.*

round the clock the whole day and the whole night: *If we are to get this book published we'll have to work round the clock*; (*attrib*) *Doctors must provide a round-the-clock service.*

See also **anticlockwise**.

clod [klod] *nc* **1** a thick lump, *esp* of earth: *Clods of soil stuck to the spade.* **2** (*inf*) a stupid fellow.

'clodhopper *nc* (*sl*) **1** a clumsy person: *I hate dancing with that clodhopper.* **2** (*usu in pl*) a large, heavy boot or shoe: *He makes such a noise in those clodhoppers.*

clog[1] [klog] *nc* **1** a shoe made entirely of wood: *Dutch clogs.* **2** a shoe with a wooden sole: *Clogs are popular this summer*; *a pair of clogs.*

clog[2] [klog] – *pt, ptp* **clogged** – (*often with* **up**) **1** *vti* (of a pipe, drain *etc*) to make or become blocked: *The wastepipe of this sink clogs (up) easily*; *The drain is clogged (up) with hair.* **2** *vt* to hinder; to prevent from working smoothly: *Mud clogs (up) the wheels of a car*; (*fig*) *Too many laws can clog (up) the running of a country.*

cloister ['kloistə] *nc* **1** a covered walk forming part of a monastery, church or college. **2** (*formal*) a monastery or nunnery.

'cloistered *adj* (*formal*: *attrib*) living away from the ordinary busy life of the world: *a cloistered existence.*

close[1] [klous] *adv* **1** near in time, place *etc*: *These houses are very close together*; *Follow close behind*; *Their birthdays are very close together.* – *See also* **close to**[1] *below.* **2** tightly; neatly: *a close-fitting dress.* – *adj* **1** near in relationship; very friendly; well-liked: *a close friend*; *He has always been close to his father.* **2** having a narrow difference between (winning or losing): *That was a close contest*; *The result was close.* **3** (*usu attrib*) detailed or thorough: *a close examination of the facts*; *under close* (= heavily-guarded) *arrest*; *Keep a close watch on him.* **4** (*usu attrib*) tight: *a close fit.* **5** without fresh air; too warm for comfort: *a close atmosphere/room/day*; *The weather was close and* *thundery.* **6** (*usu attrib*) with little space in between the parts *etc*: *the close texture of the cloth.* **7** (*inf*: *usu pred*) mean: *He's very close (with his money).* **8** (*inf*: *usu pred*) secretive: *They're keeping very close about the whole business.*

'closely *adv*: *Look closely at him*; *She resembles her father closely.*

'closeness *nu.*

close call/shave *nc* a narrow (often lucky) escape: *That was a close call – the police nearly caught us*; *That was a close shave – that car nearly ran you over.*

close harmony *nu* harmony in which the parts are close together: *They sang in close harmony.*

'close season *nc* the time in a year when it is illegal to kill certain game or fish: *The close season for pheasant ends in October in Britain.*

,close-'set *adj* (of eyes *etc*) positioned very near each other: *She is quite pretty but her eyes are very close-set.*

close shave *see* **close call.**

'close-up *nc* a photograph or film taken near the subject and thus big in scale: *The close-up of the model showed her beautiful skin*; (*attrib*) *a close-up photograph.*

close at hand nearby; not far off: *Help is close at hand*; *My mother lives close at hand.*

close on (*inf*) almost; nearly: *It's close on 5 o'clock*; *She's close on sixty.*

'close to[1] **1** near in time, place, relationship *etc*: *close to 3 o'clock*; *close to the hospital*; *close to his mother.* **2** almost; nearly: *close to fifty years of age.*

,close 'to[2] near to a person *etc*; not far off: *Close to, he was older than I thought.*

close[2] [klous] **1** *nc esp* in Scotland, a narrow passage leading into a block of flats from the street. **2** *n* (*esp Brit*: *with cap*) a word used in the names of certain streets: *10 Sandpiper Close.* **3** *nc* the land, buildings *etc* surrounding and belonging to a cathedral.

close[3] [klouz] *vti* **1** to make or become shut, often by bringing together two parts so as to cover an opening: *The baby closed his eyes*; *The curtains are closed*; (*fig*) *The gap between the two runners gradually closed*; *Close the door*; *The door closed quietly*; *The shops close on Sundays.* **2** to finish; to come or bring to an end: *The meeting closed with everyone in agreement*; *They closed the discussion.* **3** to complete or settle (a business deal *etc*): *'Have you sold your house?' 'Yes, we closed the deal yesterday.'* – *See also* **close down, close in, close up** *below.* – *nc* (*no pl*) a stop, end or finish: *The meeting came to a close*; *the close of day*; *towards the close of the nineteenth century.*

closed circuit television *nu* a television system transmitting and showing films, which are not sent out to the general public, to a special audience: *The lecture-room is too small for the number of students and so some of them watch the lectures on closed circuit television.*

closed shop *nc* a factory *etc* in which only members of a (particular) trade union are employed: *There is a closed shop in the printing industry*; (*attrib*) *a closed-shop policy.*

close down 1 *vi, vt sep* (of a business) to close permanently: *High levels of taxation have caused many firms to close down*; *He closed down his firm when he retired.* **2** *vi* (of a TV or radio station *etc*) to stop broadcasting for the day (*nc* **'closedown**).

close in *vi* **1** to come nearer: *The enemy soldiers are closing in (on us).* **2** (of days) to become shorter, with fewer hours of daylight: *In th[e] autumn the days begin to close in.*

close ranks to come closer together: *The enem[y] closed ranks and marched in a solid mass*; (*fig*) *Th[e] staff have closed ranks and refused to discuss th[e] matter.*

close up *vi, vt sep* **1** to come or bring close[r] together: *He closed up the space between the lines o[f] print.* **2** to shut completely: *He closed up the hous[e] when he went on holiday*; *The seaside café closes u[p] in the winter.*

'close with *vt fus* (*liter*) to begin fighting with: *H[e] closed with the enemy.*

closet ['klozit] *nc* (*Amer*) a cupboard: *a clothe[s] closet.*

'closeted *adj* (*formal*: *pred*) engaged in a privat[e] conversation, often in a separate room from othe[r] people: *They're closeted in his office*; *He's closete[d] with the rest of the directors.*

See also **water-closet.**

closure ['klouʒə] *nc* **1** (*formal*) the end (of something); an act of closing: *the closure of a meeting/factory.* **2** something which close[s] (something): *Put a closure on the polythene ba[g] containing the sandwiches.*

clot [klot] *nc* **1** a mass of soft or fluid matter (*esp* blood) stuck together: *He died of a clot of blood o[n] the brain*; *Don't disturb the clot on the wound – it wil[l] start bleeding again.* **2** (*inf*) a fool or an idiot. – *v* – *pt, ptp* **'clotted** – *vti* to form into clots: *Mos[t] people's blood clots quite easily.*

clotted cream *nu* thick cream made by scalding milk.

cloth [kloθ] – *pl* **cloths** [kloθs, (*Amer*) klo:ðz] – *ncu* (*often in cmpds*) (a piece of) woven materia[l] from which clothes and many other items are made: *a tablecloth*; *a face-cloth*; *a floor-cloth*; *Woollen cloth is often expensive.*

clothe [klouð] – *pt, ptp* **clothed,** (*old or liter*) **clad** [klad] – *vt* (*more formal than* **dress**) **1** to provide with clothes: *The widow did not have enough money to clothe her children.* **2** (*sometimes refl*) to put clothes on: *She was clothed in silk*; *She clothe[d] herself in the most expensive materials.* **3** (*liter fig*) to cover (with or in): *The mountains were clothed/clad in snow.* – *See also* **clad.**

clothes [klouðz, (*Amer*) klouz] *n pl* **1** things wor[n] as coverings for various parts of the body: *She wears beautiful clothes*; *Wear warm clothes in winter*; (*in cmpds*) *a clothes-brush*; (*in cmpds*) *clothes-pegs.* **2** bedclothes: *The child pulled the clothes up tightly.*

'clothier *nc* (*formal*) a person who makes or sells clothes.

'clothing *nu* clothes: *warm clothing.*

'clothes-horse *nc* a frame on which clothes are hung to air or dry.

clothes-peg *see* **peg.**

cloud [klaud] **1** *ncu* a mass of tiny drops of water floating in the sky: *white clouds in a blue sky*; *The hills were hidden in cloud*; *There are usually grey clouds in the sky before it rains.* **2** *nc* a great number or quantity of anything small moving together: *a cloud of flies/smoke/dust.* **3** *nc* (*liter*) something causing fear, depression *etc*: *the gathering clouds of revolution*; *a cloud of sadness.* – **1** *vi* (*often with* **over**) to become cloudy: *The sky clouded over and it began to rain.* **2** *vti* (*liter or formal*) to (cause to) become blurred or not clear: *Tears clouded her eyes*; *Her eyes clouded with tears*; (*fig*) *Old age clouded his judgement.* **3** *vti* (*liter or formal*) to (cause to) become gloomy or troubled: *His face clouded at the unhappy news*; *The death of her dog clouded her happiness.*

'cloudless *adj* (*usu attrib*) free from clouds: *The sun shone in a cloudless sky.*

'cloudy *adj* **1** full of, having, or covered with clouds: *a cloudy sky*; *It is a bit cloudy today.* **2** not clear: *a cloudy photograph/memory*; *This mixture should be clear, not cloudy.*

'cloudburst *nc* a sudden heavy shower of rain: *A cloudburst spoiled their picnic.*

under a cloud under suspicion; in trouble or disgrace: *His business dealings are under a cloud*; *He wasn't expelled from school but he is certainly under a cloud.*

clout [klaut] (*inf*) **1** *nc* a blow: *His mother gave him a clout for being cheeky.* **2** *nu* influence or power: *He has a lot of clout in Parliament.* – *vt* (*inf*) to hit: *She clouted him with her umbrella.*

clove[1] [klouv] *nc* **1** a tropical tree. **2** its flower bud dried for use as a spice: *There are cloves in this fruit-cake.*

clove[2] [klouv] *nc* a section of a bulb: *a clove of garlic.*

clove[3], **cloven** *see* **cleave**[1].

clover ['klouvə] *nu* a plant with leaves in three parts, used as food for cattle *etc.*

in 'clover (*inf*) in great comfort and luxury: *When he married a wealthy woman he thought that he would live in clover for the rest of his life.*

clown [klaun] *nc* **1** a person who works in a circus, performing funny acts (*usu* while ridiculously dressed). **2** any person who behaves ridiculously and without dignity. – *vi* to behave ridiculously: *Stop clowning (around).*

'clownish *adj.*

cloy [kloi] *vi* (*formal*) to become unpleasant through too much sweetness, pleasure *etc*: *Too much sweet food eventually cloys*; *The pleasure of travelling abroad cloys after too many business trips.*

club [klʌb] *nc* **1** a heavy stick *etc* used as a weapon: *He used a club to defend himself against the fierce dog.* **2** a bat or stick used in certain games (*esp* golf): *Which club will you use?* **3** a number of people meeting for study, pleasure, games *etc*: *She's in the local tennis club.* **4** the place where these people meet: *He goes to the club every Friday night.* **5** one of the playing-cards of the suit clubs. – *v* – *pt, ptp* **clubbed** – *vt* to beat or strike with a club: *They clubbed him to death.* – *See* **club together** *below.*

clubs *n pl* (sometimes treated as *n sing*) one of the four card suits: *the six of clubs.*

club together *vi* to join together or put money together (as if) in a club for some purpose: *They clubbed together and bought her a present.*

cluck [klʌk] *nc* (a sound like) the call of a hen. – *vi* to make such a sound: *The hens clucked noisily*; *The old woman clucked disapprovingly at the children's behaviour.*

clue [klu:] *nc* anything that helps to solve a mystery, puzzle *etc*: *The car number was a clue to the identity of the murderer*; *I can't answer the second clue in this crossword.*

'clueless *adj* (*inf*) (of a person) stupid: *He's a clueless idiot!*; *He's quite clueless about art.*

clue up on *vt fus* (*inf*: *usu in passive*) to make or become well-informed on (a subject): *She's really clued up on politics.*

not to have a clue (*inf*) to be ignorant (about something); not to have any knowledge: *He doesn't have a clue about how to change the wheel of a car*; *'How does that work?' 'I haven't a clue.'*

clump[1] [klʌmp] *nc* a group (*eg* of trees, bushes or shrubs).

clump[2] [klʌmp] *vi* to walk heavily and noisily: *He clumps around in those heavy boots.*

clumsy ['klʌmzi] *adj* **1** awkward in shape, movement *etc*: *The wardrobe is a clumsy shape but it's very useful*; *He's very clumsy – he's always dropping things.* **2** (*usu attrib*) tactless; not skilfully made or carried out: *a clumsy apology.*

'clumsily *adv.* **'clumsiness** *nu.*

clung *see* **cling**.

cluster ['klʌstə] *nc* a closely-packed group (of people or things): *The children stood in a cluster round the injured dog*; *a cluster of berries.* – *vi* (*often with* **round**) to group together in clusters: *They clustered round the door to watch the arrival of the queen.*

clutch[1] [klʌtʃ] **1** *vi* (*with* **at**) to try to take hold of: *I clutched at a floating piece of wood to save myself from drowning.* **2** *vt* to hold tightly (in the hands): *She was clutching a pound note.* – *nc* **1** (*usu in pl*) control or power: *He fell into the clutches of the enemy.* **2** something by means of which two moving or revolving parts of an engine (*eg* of a car, bus *etc*) may be connected or disconnected: *He released the clutch and the car started to move.* **3** (in a car *etc*) the pedal operating the clutch mechanism: *He took his foot off the clutch.*

clutch at straws to hope that something may happen to help one in a difficult, dangerous situation *etc* when this is extremely unlikely: *They hoped the operation might save the child's life although they knew they were clutching at straws.*

clutch[2] [klʌtʃ] *nc* **1** a brood of chickens. **2** a number of eggs laid at one time.

clutter ['klʌtə] *ncu* (*derog*) (a) disorganized state of untidiness: *My desk is always full of clutter*; *The house is in a clutter.* – *vt* (*derog*) (*with* **with**) to make untidy: *The child cluttered the room with her toys.*

'cluttered *adj* (*usu pred*) untidy; too full of furniture *etc*: *Some people think it's a beautiful room but it's too cluttered for my taste.*

clutter up *vt sep* to fill or cover in an untidy way: *The drawer was cluttered up with scarves and odd gloves.*

co- [kou] (*in cmpds*) **1** joint or working *etc* together, as in **co-author**. **2** with or together, as in **co-exist**.

coach [koutʃ] *nc* **1** a railway carriage: *The last two coaches of the train were derailed.* **2** a (*usu* single-deck) bus for tourists *etc*: *The coach was full*; (*attrib*) *a coach trip.* **3** a trainer in athletics, sport *etc*: *He is the swimming-team's coach*; *the tennis coach.* **4** a private teacher: *They employed a coach to improve their son's knowledge of Latin.* **5** (*hist*) a four-wheeled horsedrawn vehicle. – *vt* to prepare (a person) for an examination, contest *etc*: *He coached his friend for the Latin exam.*

'coachbuilder *nc* a person or business concerned with building the bodies for modern vehicles.

'coachman *nc* the driver of an old horsedrawn carriage.

coagulate [kou'agjuleit] *vti* (*formal or tech*) to (cause to) become a thickened mass: *He suffers from a disease that makes his blood coagulate too quickly.* **co,agu'lation** *ncu.*

coal [koul] *ncu* a black mineral (formed from the wood of prehistoric trees), burned for fuel, heat, gas *etc*: *Put some coal on the fire*; *burning coals*; (*attrib*) *a coal fire.*

'**coal face** *nc* **1** the part of a mine from which coal is being dug. **2** in a mine, the surface of coal exposed by digging.

'**coalfield** *nc* an area where there is coal to be mined.

ˌ**coal-'fired** *adj* powered by coal: *a coal-fired boiler.*

coal gas *nu* the mixture of gases obtained from coal, used for cooking and heating: *Does your cooker use coal gas or natural gas?*

'**coalmine** *nc* a mine from which coal is dug.

'**coal-scuttle** *nc* a container for storing coal beside a domestic fire.

coal tar *nu* a thick, black liquid formed when gas is made from coal.

haul (someone) over the coals (*inf*) to reprimand; to scold: *The headmaster hauled the child over the coals for being absent without permission.*

See also **collier**.

coalesce [kouə'les] *vi* (*formal*) to grow together and unite: *In time the ideas of the group of politicians coalesced to form a policy.* ˌ**coa'lescence** *nu.*

coalition [kouə'liʃən] *nc* (*formal*) a *usu* temporary union or alliance, *esp* of states or political parties: *A coalition was formed to defeat the governing party*; (*attrib*) *a coalition government.*

coarse [ko:s] *adj* **1** rough in texture or to touch; not fine: *This coat is made of coarse material*; *Her skin is coarse*; *coarse salt.* **2** (*fig*) rude, vulgar or unrefined: *a coarse sense of humour*; *coarse jokes*; *Don't be so coarse.* '**coarsely** *adv.* '**coarseness** *nu.*

'**coarsen** *vti* (*formal*) to (cause to) become coarse; *The sea air coarsened her skin.*

coast [koust] *ncu* the side or border of land next to the sea: *The coast was very rocky.* – *vi* **1** to travel downhill (in a vehicle, on a bicycle *etc*) without the use of any power such as the engine or pedalling: *He coasted for two miles after the car ran out of petrol.* **2** (*fig*: *often with* **along**) to keep on doing something without making any effort: *He coasted along for four years before the manager realized that his work was being done by others.*

'**coastal** *adj* (*usu attrib*) of or near the coast: *a coastal town*; *coastal fishing.*

'**coaster** *nc* **1** a vessel that sails along near the coast. **2** a small mat for putting under a drinking-glass *etc*: *If you'd used coasters there would be no stains on the table.*

'**coastguard** *ncu* a man, or group of men, employed to watch the coast for smugglers, ships in distress *etc.*

coat [kout] *nc* **1** an item of outdoor clothing, with sleeves, that covers from the shoulders *usu* to roughly the knees: *I must buy a new winter coat.* **2** a jacket: *a man's coat and trousers.* **3** the hair or wool of an animal: *Some dogs have smooth coats.* **4** a covering (*eg* of paint): *This wall will need two coats of paint.* – *vt* (*with* **with**) to cover with a coat or layer of: *The wood was coated with a special paint*; *She coated the biscuits with chocolate.*

'**coating** *ncu* (a) covering: *a coating of snow*; *chocolate coating.*

coat-hanger *see* **hanger**.

coat of arms a family badge or crest: *Their coat of arms is above the door of their castle.*

coax [kouks] *vt* **1** to persuade (someone or something to do something) by flattery, by patient and gentle treatment *etc*: *He coaxed her to go to th dance by saying she was the best dancer he knew*; *H coaxed her into going.* **2** to succeed in gettin (something) by coaxing: *He finally coaxed som applause from the audience.*

cob [kob] *nc* **1** a short-legged strong horse. **2** a mal swan.

See also **corn on the cob**.

cobalt ['koubo:lt] *nu* a silver-white metal elemen (symbol **Co**), with compounds that give a blu colouring substance.

cobble[1] ['kobl], **cobblestone** ['koblstoun] *nc* rounded stone formerly used in paving streets *The coach rattled across the cobbles.*

cobble[2] ['kobl] *vt* **1** (*old*) to patch or mend (shoe *etc*): *He cobbles boots.* **2** (*inf*: *usu with* **together**) t put (things) together badly or roughly: *Sh quickly cobbled together a skirt for the dance.*

'**cobbler** *nc* **1** a person who mends shoes. **2** cobbler's shop.

cobbler's *nc* a cobbler's shop: *I'm taking this to th cobbler's.*

cobra ['koubrə] *nc* a poisonous snake found i India and Africa.

cobweb ['kobweb] *nc* a spider's web: *You can have cleaned this room – there are cobwebs in th corner*; *Her silk dress was as fine as a cobweb.*

blow away the cobwebs (*inf*) to get rid c feelings of dullness, tiredness *etc*: *He went o holiday for a few days after his exams to blow awa the cobwebs.*

cocaine [kə'kein] *nu* (*sl abbrev* **coke** [kouk]) a addictive drug formerly used as a loca anaesthetic.

cochineal ['kotʃini:l] *nu* a scarlet dye used i colouring food, made from the dried bodies c certain insects: *I've added cochineal to the icing f the birthday cake.*

cock [kok] *nc* **1** the male of birds, *esp* of th domestic fowl: *The old man kept a cock and thre hens*; (*attrib*) *a cock pheasant.* **2** a kind of tap fo controlling the flow of liquid, gas *etc.* **3** th hammer or lever of a gun. **4** (*vulg*) the penis. – *vt* to cause to stand upright or to lift: *The dog cocke its ears*; *The dog cocked its hind leg* (= in order t urinate). **2** to draw back the hammer of (a gun). to tilt up or sideways (*esp* the brim of a hat): *H cocked his hat.*

cockerel ['kokərəl] *nc* a young farmyard cock.

'**cocky** *adj* (*derog*) conceited; over-confident *He's so cocky that everyone hopes he fails*; *a cock attitude.*

ˌ**cock-and-'bull story** *nc* an absurd, unbelievab story: *The tramp told a cock-and-bull story abo finding the money hidden in a bottle behind a tree the park.*

'**cock-crow** *nu* (*liter*: *sometimes facet*) early morn ing: *He gets up at cock-crow.*

ˌ**cock-'eyed** *adj* (*inf*) ridiculous: *a cock-eyed idea The picture looks a bit cock-eyed.*

cockscomb ['kokskoum] *nc* a farmyard cock crest.

ˌ**cock'sure** *adj* very or too confident: *He was cocksure about passing the exam that he couldn believe that he had failed*; *a cocksure attitude.*

go 'off at ˌhalf-'cock not to be successful becaus of lack of preparation: *The government's ne schemes went off at half-cock.*

cockade [kə'keid] *nc* (*old*) a piece or knot of ribbo *usu* worn on one's hat as a badge: *The followers the prince wore white cockades.*

cockatoo [kokə'tu:] – *pl* **cocka'toos** – *nc* a parrot with a large crest.

cockerel *see* **cock**.

cocker spaniel ['kokə] *nc* a small type of spaniel dog: *Cocker spaniels have long ears.*

cockle ['kokl] *nc* a shellfish with a hinged, heart-shaped shell, used as food: *cockles and mussels.*

cockney ['kokni] **1** *nc* (*often with cap*) a native of the City of London. **2** *nu* the language of a Cockney: *He spoke cockney*; (*attrib*) *He had a cockney accent.*

cockpit ['kokpit] *nc* **1** a compartment in which the pilot of an aeroplane, driver of a racing-car *etc* sits: *He climbed into the cockpit and drove off.* **2** (*hist*) a pit where cock birds were placed to fight.

cockroach ['kokroutʃ] *nc* a beetle-like insect which is a household pest.

cockscomb, cocksure *see* **cock**.

cocktail ['kokteil] **1** *nc* an alcoholic drink mixed from different types of spirits and other drinks: *She makes her cocktails with gin.* **2** *ncu* a mixed dish of a number of things: *a prawn cocktail*; *a fruit cocktail.*

cocky *see* **cock**.

cocoa ['koukou] **1** *nu* (a powder made from) the crushed seeds of the cacao tree, used in making chocolate: *Cocoa has risen in price.* **2** *ncu* a drink made from the powder: *I'll have some cocoa tonight*; *a cup of cocoa*; *Two cocoas, please.*

coconut ['koukənʌt] **1** *nc* a large nut containing a white solid lining and a clear liquid: *We won a coconut at the funfair*; (*attrib*) *a coconut tree.* **2** *nu* its lining, used as food: *She put some coconut in the biscuits*; (*attrib*) *coconut icing.*

cocoon [kə'ku:n] *nc* a silk covering spun by many insect larvae, and in which they live while turning into butterflies: *The butterfly emerged from the cocoon*; (*fig*) *She keeps that child in a cocoon.* – *vt* to wrap in, or cover with, a cocoon: (*fig*) *She cocoons the child from the realities of life.*

cod [kod] – *pl* **cod** – **1** *nc* a type of edible fish found in northern seas: *They are fishing for cod.* **2** *nu* its flesh used as food: (*attrib*) *cod steaks.*

ˌcod-liver 'oil *nu* an oil obtained from cod's liver, rich in vitamins A and D.

coddle ['kodl] *vt* **1** to treat with great care like an invalid; to pamper: *She tended to coddle her youngest child.* **2** to cook (eggs) gently in hot water: *She coddled the eggs but I prefer them fried.*

code [koud] **1** *nc* a collection of (legal or moral) laws or rules: *the Highway Code*; *a code of behaviour.* **2** *ncu* a (secret) system of words, letters, or symbols: *the Morse Code*; *The message was in code*; *They failed to decipher the enemy's code*; *We have broken* (= deciphered) *the code at last.* **3** *ncu* a system of symbols *etc* for translating one type of language into another: *There are a number of codes for putting English into a form usable by a computer.* – *vt* to put into (secret, computer *etc*) code: *Have you coded the material for the computer?*

codify ['koudifai, (*Amer*) 'kodəfai] *vt* (*very formal*) to arrange (laws *etc*) into a code. **ˌcodifi'cation** [-fi-] *nu.*

See also **decode**.

codicil ['koudəsil, (*Amer*) 'ko-] *nc* (*legal*) a short addition to a will or treaty: *He added a codicil to his will just before he died.*

codify *see* **code**.

co-educational [kouedju'keiʃənl] (*abbrev* **co-ed** ['koued]) *adj* of the education of pupils or students of both sexes in the same school or college: *a co-educational school*; *Is the school co-educational?*

coerce [kou'ə:s] *vt* (*formal*) to force (a person into doing something): *He was coerced into helping the thieves.* **co'ercion** [-ʃən] *nu.*

co'ercive [-siv] *adj* (*very formal*) using force: *It was alleged that the police had used coercive methods to get a statement from the prisoner.*

co-exist [kouig'zist] *vi* (*formal*) (*esp* of nations *etc*) to exist at the same time (*esp* peacefully, in the same or nearly the same place): *After a few years the former enemies learned to co-exist quite happily side by side.* **ˌco-ex'istence** *nu.*

coffee ['kofi] **1** *nu* a kind of shrub whose ground beans are used to make a drink: *Coffee is grown in Brazil.* **2** *nu* the (ground) beans of the coffee shrub: *Half a pound of coffee, please.* **3** *nu* a drink made from the ground beans: *I'll have some coffee*; *a cup of coffee.* **4** *nc* a cup of this drink: *Two coffees please.* **5** *nu, adj* (of) its brown colour: *a brown dress with coffee*(*-coloured*) *lace.*

coffer ['kofə] *nc* (*formal*) a large chest for holding money or treasure, *esp* (*usu in pl*) in a bank: (*fig*) *The nation's coffers are empty.*

coffin ['kofin] *nc* (*Amer* **'casket**) a box for a dead body to be buried or cremated in: *The coffin was placed in the grave.*

cog [kog] *nc* **1** one of a series of teeth around the edge of a wheel which fits into one of a similar series in a similar wheel (or into a chain as in a bicycle) causing motion: *The chain came off the bicycle because some of the cogs were broken*; *The cogs in the gear-wheels of the car are so worn that the car broke down.* **2** (*fig*) a person or thing having a necessary but small part in an organization *etc*: *He's just a cog in the wheel of local government.*

cogent ['koudʒənt] *adj* (*formal*) convincing; to the point: *a cogent argument*; *His arguments were so cogent that they convinced everyone.* **'cogency** *nu.*

cogitate ['kodʒiteit] *vi* (*formal*) to think carefully (about something): *I spent a long time cogitating about my financial problems.* **ˌcogi'tation** *ncu.*

cognac ['konjak] **1** *nu* a kind of high-quality French brandy. **2** *nc* a glass of this: *Do have a cognac.*

cognate ['kogneit] *adj* (*gram*: *with* **with**) (*esp* of words) having the same origin or source: *English 'mother' is cognate with German 'Mutter'.* – *nc*: *'Mutter' and 'mother' are cognates.*

cognizance ['kognizəns]: **take cognizance of** (*very formal*) to acknowledge; to take into consideration: *When judging the standard of his work they took cognizance of the fact that he was not yet fully trained.*

cohabit [kou'habit] *vi* (*formal*) (of a man and woman) to live together as husband and wife, although not married: *They have been cohabiting for years although they have never married.* **coˌhabi'tation** *nu.*

cohere [kə'hiə] *vi* (*very formal*) to stick together: *The two surfaces cohered very well*; (*fig*) *I don't think the points in his argument cohered very well.* **co'hesion** [-ʒən] *nu.* **co'hesive** [-siv] *adj.*

coherent [kə'hiərənt] *adj* (*formal*) clear and logical: *He was able to give a coherent account of what had happened*; *She's not very coherent on the telephone.* **co'herently** *adv.* **co'herence** *nu.*

See also **incoherent**.

cohort ['kouho:t] *nc* **1** (*hist*) a tenth part of a Roman legion. **2** (*fig inf*) a group or band of people: *His supporters followed him round in cohorts.*

coiffure [kwa'fjuə] *nc* (*formal*: *sometimes facet*) a hairstyle: *She always has very elaborate coiffures.*

coil [koil] *vti* to wind into rings or loops: *The snake coiled (itself) round the tree.* – *nc* **1** a length (*eg* of rope) wound into rings or loops: *a coil of thick rope.* **2** one of these rings or loops: *The animal was held fast in the snake's coils.* **3** a wound length of wire for conducting electricity: *the coil in an electric fire.* **4** (*inf*) a type of contraceptive device for a woman: *She is using the coil instead of the pill.*

coin [koin] *ncu* (a piece of) metal used as money: *a handful of coins*; *What is the coin of that country?* – *vt* **1** to make metal into (money): *Do they still coin farthings?* **2** (*inf*) to gain (money) quickly in great quantity: *He's really coining the money these days.* **3** to invent (a word, phrase *etc*): *The scientist coined a word for the new process.*

'coinage [-nidʒ] **1** *nu* the process of coining (money from metal, a new word *etc*). **2** *nc* (*formal*) an example of a word which has been coined: *That word is a coinage based on the name of a politician.* **3** *nu* the money (system) used in a country: *Britain now uses decimal coinage.*

coincide [kouin'said] *vi* (*sometimes with* **with**) **1** to occupy (often by accident) the same space or time: *Her arrival coincided with his departure.* **2** to agree: *This coincides with what he told us*; *Their stories coincided*; *Their tastes in music coincide.*

coincidence [kou'insidəns] *ncu* (an) accidental happening of one event at the same time as another: *It was strange that you met her just after we had been talking about her but coincidences do happen*; *It was sheer coincidence that we were both on the same train.*

co,inci'dental [-'den-] *adj* (*usu pred*: *formal*): *Our arrival at the same time was quite coincidental.*

coitus ['kouitəs], **coition** [kou'iʃən] *nu* (*formal*) sexual intercourse.

coke[1] [kouk] *nu* a type of fuel obtained from coal.

coke[2] *see* **cocaine**.

colander, cullender ['kʌləndə] *nc* a bowl with small holes in it for draining water off vegetables *etc*: *Strain the cauliflower in the colander.*

cold [kould] *adj* **1** low in temperature: *That soup is cold*; *cold water*; *We'll have cold meat and salad.* **2** lower in temperature than is comfortable: *I feel cold*; *a cold day.* **3** unfriendly: *a cold welcome*; *His manner was cold.* **4** (*pred*: *inf*) not enthusiastic: *The whole idea leaves me cold.* – **1** *nu* the state of being cold or of feeling the coldness of one's surroundings: *She has gone to live in the South of France because she cannot bear the cold here*; *the bitter cold of the wind*; *He was blue with cold*; *Do come indoors out of the cold.* **2** *ncu* an illness with running nose, catarrh, coughing *etc*: *He has a bad cold*; *She has caught a cold*; *You might catch cold.*

'coldly *adv* **1** in an unfriendly way: *She looked at me coldly.* **2** without enthusiasm: *The committee listened to his suggestions coldly.*

'coldness *nu*: *the coldness of the soup/day/welcome.*

,cold-'blooded *adj* **1** having blood (like that of a fish) which takes the same temperature as the surroundings of the body: *Fish are cold-blooded (creatures).* **2** cruel and unfeeling: *cold-blooded murder*; *He was quite cold-blooded about it.*

cold comfort *nu* no consolation whatsoever: *I could tell you that he is as miserable as you are but that would be cold comfort.*

cold-shoulder *see* **give (someone) the cold shoulder**.

'cold snap *nc* (*inf*) a sudden period of cold weather: *All her plants died in that cold snap.*

cold war *nc* a major, *esp* political, struggle between nations which involves military threats but not military fighting.

get, have cold feet (*inf*) to lose or not to have courage: *I was going to apply for the job but I got cold feet.*

give (someone) the cold shoulder (*inf*) (*also* **,cold-'shoulder** *vt*) to show that one is unwilling to be friendly with (a person): *All the neighbours gave her the cold shoulder because she ill-treated her children*; *He cold-shouldered all his sister's friends.*

in cold blood deliberately and unemotionally: *He killed them in cold blood.*

(out) in the cold neglected, unwanted *etc*: *As he didn't like games he was left out in the cold every time his friends played football.*

pour/throw cold water on to discourage; to lessen enthusiasm for: *She often has good ideas but her boss throws cold water on all of them.*

cole-slaw ['koulslo:] *nu* a salad made with finely-cut raw cabbage.

colic ['kolik] *nu* severe pain in the abdomen: *The child is screaming because he is suffering from colic.*

collaborate [kə'labəreit] *vi* **1** to work together (with someone) on the same piece of work: *He and his brother collaborated on a book about aeroplanes.* **2** to work along (with someone) to betray secrets *etc*: *He was known to have collaborated with the enemy.* **col,labo'ration** *nu.* **col'laborator** *nc.*

collage [ko'la:ʒ] *nc* a design made by pasting pieces of paper, cloth, photographs *etc* on to a surface.

collapse [kə'laps] **1** *vi* to fall down and break into pieces: *The roof has collapsed!*; *The bridge collapsed under the weight of the traffic.* **2** *vi* (of a person) to fall down (often in a state of unconsciousness) because of illness, pain, shock *etc*: *She collapsed with a heart attack*; *He collapsed on hearing the news of the accident*; (*fig*) *The talks between the two countries have collapsed*; (*fig*) *The accused's defence collapsed under the careful questioning of the lawyer.* **3** *vti* to fold up or to (cause to) come to pieces (intentionally): *This table collapses and can be put in a cupboard when not in use*; *He collapsed the tent.*

col'lapsible *adj* able to be folded up *etc*: *These garden chairs are collapsible*; *a collapsible boat.*

collar ['kolə] **1** *nc* the part of a garment at the neck *esp* of a shirt, jacket *etc*: *This collar is too tight*; *What size (of) collar does he take?* **2** *nc* something worn round the neck: *The dog's name was on its collar*; *He wears a surgical collar to support his neck.* **3** *nu* a cut of meat from the neck of an animal: *collar of beef.* – *vt* (*inf*) to capture or seize: *They collared the entire market with their new product*; *He collared the speaker as he left the room.*

'collar-bone *nc* either of two bones joining breast-bone and shoulder-blade: *He has broken his collar-bone.*

collate [kə'leit] *vt* (*very formal*) to examine and compare (things which are similar): *The police collated the statements of the witnesses*; *He collated his bank statement with his own record of what he had spent.*

col'lation **1** *nu* (*very formal*) the act of collating. **2** *nc* (*formal or facet*) a light meal (often cold): *a cold collation at the wedding.*

collateral [kə'latərəl] *nu* (*formal*) financial securities: *What collateral can you offer against such a large loan?*

collation *see* **collate**.

colleague ['koli:g] *nc* a person with whom one is associated in a profession or occupation: *her teaching colleagues; He gets on well with his colleagues.*

collect [kə'lekt] **1** *vti* to bring or come together; to gather: *People are collecting in front of the house; She's collecting (clothes) for the jumble sale; I collect stamps as a hobby; (fig) He's trying to collect his thoughts.* **2** *vt* to call for and take away: *She collects the kids from school each day.* – *adv, adj (Amer)* **1** (of a telephone call) reverse-charge: *I'll call my parents collect; a collect call.* **2** (of a parcel *etc*) to be paid for by the addressee.

col'lected *adj* **1** (*usu attrib*) gathered together: *the collected poems of Robert Burns.* **2** (*pred*) composed; cool: *She appeared quite calm and collected as she entered the room.*

col'lection [-ʃən] **1** *ncu* (an) act of collecting: *This is a public holiday – there is no collection of rubbish today; Your letter won't get to London tomorrow – you've missed the last collection* (= of mail from a postbox) *for today.* **2** *nc* a set of objects *etc* collected: *a stamp collection; a strange collection of people.*

col'lective [-tiv] *adj* **1** (*formal*: *usu attrib*) of a number of people or states *etc* taken together as one group; combined: *The crowd gave a collective cheer; This was the result of a collective effort.* **2** (*gram*) of a noun which takes a singular verb but stands for many things taken as a whole: *Clergy is a collective noun, meaning all churchmen.* – *nc* a farm or organization run by a group of workers for the good of all of them: *Do you have collectives in your country?; (attrib) collective farming.*

col'lectively *adv*: *They were collectively responsible for the man's death.*

col'lector *nc* (*sometimes in cmpds*) a person who collects, as a job or as a hobby: *a ticket collector; a stamp collector; a collector of antiques.*

college ['kolidʒ] *nc* **1** (any or all of the buildings housing) a higher education institution: *The college is in the centre of town; He went to college in the autumn; He is at agricultural college; (attrib) a college tie.* **2** (*with cap in names*) an organization of people, joined together for scientific, literary or other specific purposes: *College of Surgeons; the electoral college.*

collegiate [kə'li:dʒət] *adj* (*formal*: *attrib*) of, containing, or belonging to a college or colleges: *collegiate life; the collegiate church of St Andrews; Is that a collegiate university?*

collide [kə'laid] *vi* to strike together (*usu* accidentally) with great force: *The cars collided in the fog; The van collided with a lorry; (fig) The views of the two politicians collide violently.*

collision [kə'liʒən] *nc* **1** a crash; a violent striking together (of *eg* two vehicles): *Ten people were injured in the collision between the bus and the car.* **2** (*fig*) a disagreement; a clash (of interests *etc*): *A collision between the opposing parties became inevitable.*

collie ['koli] *nc* a long-haired breed of sheepdog.

collier ['koliə] *nc* **1** a person who works in a coalmine: *Collier is another word for a coalminer.* **2** a ship that carries coal.

'colliery *nc* a coalmine: *There's been an accident at the local colliery.*

collision *see* **collide**.

colloquial [kə'loukwiəl] *adj* of or used in everyday informal, *esp* spoken, language: *a colloquial expression; His speech was very colloquial.* **col'loquially** *adv*.

col'loquialism *nc* an expression used in colloquial language: *I am going round the bend* (= becoming slightly mad) *is a colloquialism.*

collusion [kə'lu:ʒən] *nu* (*formal*) secret agreements to cooperate in being dishonest: *They acted in collusion to rob their employer; Their collusion was made public at the trial.*

cologne *see* **eau-de-cologne**.

colon[1] ['koulən] *nc* the punctuation mark (:), used *eg* to separate sentence-like units within a sentence, or before a list, a series of clauses *etc.*

colon[2] ['koulon] *nc* a part of the large intestine.

co'lonic *adj* (*formal*).

colonel ['kə:nl] *nc* (*with cap, and often abbrev* **Col.**, *when written in titles*) in the British army, (a person of) the rank next below brigadier: *He soon rose to the rank of colonel; Colonel Graham; He was promoted to colonel.* – *See also* Appendix 3.

colonial *etc see* **colony**.

colonnade [kolə'neid] *nc* a row of columns placed at regular intervals.

colony ['koləni] *nc* **1** (a group of people who form) a settlement in one country *etc* which is under the rule of another country: *France used to have many colonies in Africa.* **2** a group of people of one type or having the same interests, living *etc* together in a small area: *a colony of artists; a nudist colony.* **3** a collection of animals, birds *etc*, *usu* of one type, living together: *a colony of gulls; a colony of ants; whole colonies of seals.*

co'lonial [-'lou-] *adj* (*usu attrib*): *Britain was formerly a colonial power.*

'colonize, -ise *vt* to establish a colony in (a place): *The English colonized New England in 1620.*

'colonist *nc.* **ˌcoloni'zation, -s-** *nu.*

colossus [kə'losəs] *nc* **1** an enormous statue: *the Colossus at Rhodes.* **2** (*fig*) any thing or person that is very big, extremely powerful *etc*: *He is a colossus of a man.*

co'lossal *adj* (*inf*) very big; enormous: *There's been a colossal increase in the price of books; The meal was colossal.*

colour, (*Amer*) **color** ['kʌlə] **1** *ncu* a quality which objects have, and which can be seen, only when light falls on them: *What colour is her dress?; There's a lot of colour in the garden in spring; Red, blue and yellow are colours.* **2** *ncu* paint(s): *That artist uses water-colours; He paints in water-colour.* **3** *nu* a healthy redness (of the face): *This will bring (the) colour to your cheeks!* **4** *ncu* (a) skin-colour varying with race: *For some people colour is a sensitive subject of conversation; people of all colours.* **5** *nu* vividness; interesting qualities: *There's plenty of colour in his stories.* – **1** *vt* to put colour on; to stain or paint: *They coloured the walls yellow.* – *See also* **colour in**. **2** *vt* (*formal*) to give interesting qualities to (*eg* a story); to exaggerate: *The child's account of the accident was coloured by her vivid imagination; His lack of money coloured his attitude to rich people.* **3** *vi* to blush: *She coloured at his compliments.*

'coloured *adj* **1** (*usu attrib*) having colour: *She prefers white baths to coloured baths.* **2** (*loosely*: *often derog*) belonging to a dark-skinned race: *There are only two white families living in this street – the rest are coloured (people).* **3** (*S African*; *also* **Cape Coloured**) of mixed descent (*see* **coloured**

nc def 2). **4** (*S African*) of one of the official racial groups in South Africa (*see* **coloured** *nc def 3*). – *nc* **1** (*loosely*: *often derog*) a dark-skinned person, *esp* fully or partly of Negro origin: *Coloureds have moved into the house next door.* **2** (*S African*: *often with cap*: *also* **Cape Coloured**) a South African of mixed descent speaking either Afrikaans or English as his mother tongue. **3** (*S African*) a member of one of the official racial groups in South Africa; loosely, one who is neither white nor African.

'colourful *adj* **1** full of colour: *a colourful pattern*; *The material was very colourful.* **2** (*usu attrib*) vivid and interesting: *He gave a colourful account of his experiences in the jungle.*

'colouring *nu* **1** something used to give colour: *She put pink colouring in the icing.* **2** the putting on of colour: *The child wasn't good at colouring.* **3** the effect of putting on colour: *The colouring of the painting was very crude.* **4** complexion: *She had very high colouring* (= a very pink complexion).

'colourless *adj* **1** without colour: *Water is colourless*; *a colourless liquid.* **2** (*formal*: *usu attrib*) not vivid, lively or interesting: *She is rather a colourless young woman*; *He writes colourless short stories.*

'colours *n pl* **1** distinction awarded (for team placings) in some sports (*eg* rugby, cricket, rowing): *He won his cricket colours last season.* **2** a flag, ensign or standard: *Army regiments salute the colours when on parade.* **3** a tunic of certain colours worn by a jockey to show that his race-horse belongs to a certain person: *He had raced under the same colours for four years.*

'colour bar *nc* the making of a distinction between people so that they are treated differently according to whether they are white or coloured: *There's a colour bar in restaurants in some countries.*

'colour-blind *adj* unable to tell the difference between certain colours: *As he was colour-blind he could not distinguish between red and green.*

'colour code *nc* a code using colours to mean certain things, *esp* in electrical wiring.

'colour-scheme *nc* an arrangement or choice of colours in decorating a house *etc*: *The curtains don't match the colour-scheme.*

,off-'colour *adj* (*inf*: *usu pred*) not feeling very well: *He was a bit off-colour the morning after the party.*

colour in *vt sep* to put colour into (drawings *etc*): *He coloured in all the oblong shapes on the page.*

primary colours *see* **primary**.

show oneself in one's true colours to show or express one's real character, opinion *etc*: *He pretends to be very generous but he showed himself in his true colours when he refused to give money to charity.*

with flying colours with great success: *He passed his exam with flying colours.*

colt [koult] *nc* **1** a young horse. **2** a young male person (*esp* a player in a junior sports team): *He's not in the senior team – he plays for the colts.*

column ['koləm] *nc* **1** a stone or wooden pillar used to support or ornament a building: *the carved columns in the temple.* **2** something similar in shape: *a column of smoke.* **3** a vertical row (of numbers): *He added up the column (of figures) to find the answer.* **4** a vertical section of a page of print: *a newspaper column.* **5** a section in a newspaper, often written regularly by a particular person: *He writes a daily column about sport.* **6** a long file of soldiers marching in short rows: *a column of infantry.* **7** a long line of vehicles, ships *etc*, one behind the other.

columnist ['koləmnist] *nc* a person who writes regular articles for a newspaper.

See also **fifth column**.

coma ['koumə] *nc* a long-continuing unconscious state: *He was in a coma for several days after the accident.*

'comatose [-tous] *adj* (*formal*) **1** in a coma: *He was comatose for a week after the accident.* **2** (*fig*) drowsy or sluggish: *They lay around in a comatose state after eating their Christmas dinner.*

comb [koum] **1** *nc* a toothed instrument for separating, smoothing or cleaning hair, wool, flax *etc.* **2** *nc* an object (often decorative) of similar appearance worn by some women to keep a hair-style in place: *The Spanish lady wore a comb in her hair.* **3** *nu* the honey cells made by bees: *a comb of honey*; *a honeycomb.* **4** *nc* the crest of some birds. – *See also* **cockscomb** *under* **cock**. – *vt* **1** to arrange, smooth or clean with a comb: *Comb your hair!* **2** to search (a place) thoroughly (for something): *They combed the hills for the missing climber, but failed to find him.*

comb out *vt sep* **1** to remove (unwanted matter *etc* from hair) by combing: *She combed the mud out of his hair.* **2** (*fig*) to remove (unwanted things, people): *They combed out all except the fittest before setting out on the most difficult part of the expedition.* **3** to comb (hair) into a style after it has been set: *The new hairdresser is good at setting my hair but he doesn't comb it out very well.*

combat ['kombat, (*Amer*) kəm'bat] *ncu* (an act of) fighting: *The two knights met each other in single combat* (= they fought each other without anyone else taking part). – *vt* (*usu fig*: *formal*) to fight or struggle against; to oppose: *The residents of the town tried to combat the government's plans to build a motorway*; (*facet*) *She combated her cold with large doses of vitamin C.*

combatant ['kombətənt, (*Amer*) kəm'batənt] *nc* (*formal*) a person who is fighting: *They eventually separated the combatants*; (*attrib*) *a combatant attitude.*

combative ['kombətiv, (*Amer*) kəm'bativ] *adj* (*formal*) quarrelsome.

combine [kəm'bain] **1** *vti* to join together in one whole; to unite: *They combined (forces) to fight the enemy*; *The chemist combined calcium and carbon.* **2** *vt* to have or to do *etc* at the same time: *He combines stupidity with cunning*; *She combined watching television with writing to her parents.* – ['kombain] *nc* **1** an association of trading companies: *a large manufacturing combine.* **2** (*inf*) a combine harvester: *The farmer hired a combine.*

,combi'nation [-bi-] **1** *ncu* (the result of) combining or being combined: *The town was a combination of old and new architecture*; *He worked on the combination of the two elements.* **2** *nc* a set of numbers used to open certain types of lock: *He couldn't open the safe as he had forgotten the combination.* **3** *nc* a motorcycle and sidecar: *a motorcycle combination.*

,combi'nations *n pl* a one-piece undergarment combining a vest and underpants.

,combine 'harvester *nc* a machine that both harvests and threshes crops.

combustible [kəm'bʌstəbl] *adj* (*formal*) liable to catch fire and burn: *That material is highly combustible*; *combustible materials.* – *nc* (*usu in pl*:

formal) anything that will catch fire easily: *Paper and wood are common combustibles.*

combustion [kəm'bʌstʃən] *nu* (*tech*) burning: *the combustion of gases in the exhaust system. See also* **internal combustion**.

come [kʌm] – *pt* **came** [keim] *ptp* **come** – **1** *vi* to move *etc* towards the person speaking or writing, or towards the place being referred to by him: *Come here!*; *Come with me to the park*; *Come to my house tomorrow*; *Are you coming to the dance?*; *He has come to collect the children*; *She came running to welcome us*; *John has come to see me*; *Have any letters come for me?* **2** *vi* to become near or close to something in time or space: *Christmas is coming soon.* **3** *vi* to happen or be situated: *The letter 'd' comes between 'c' and 'e' in the alphabet*; *The number 4 comes before 5*; *The word 'comedy' comes later in the dictionary.* **4** *vi* (*often with* **to**) to happen (by accident): *How did you come to break your leg?*; *How did you come to be here today*; *Now that I come to think of it, he was late yesterday too.* **5** *vi* (*often with* **to**) to become or arrive at (a certain state *etc*): *My shoe has come off*; *What are things coming to? We have come to an agreement about my salary*; *We finally came to a decision*; *How did that plan come into being? It has come to my attention/notice that no work is being done*; *Suddenly the castle came into view.* **6** *vi* (*with* **to**) (of numbers, prices *etc*) to amount (to): *Your bill comes to £50.* **7** *vt* (*inf*) to play the part or rôle of: *She started to come the innocent little girl although she was obviously guilty.* **8** *vi* (*inf*) to reach sexual orgasm. – *See also* **come** *in verb phrases below.* – *interj* expressing disapproval, drawing attention *etc*: *Come, come! That was very rude of you!*

'comer *nc* (*usu in cmpds*) a person who comes: *a new-comer*; *a late-comer*; *all comers.*

'coming *ncu*: *They awaited his coming*; *They watched the comings and goings of the people in the street.*

'comeback **1** *nc* a return (*esp* to show business): *The actress tried to make a comeback after years of not appearing on the stage.* **2** *nu* way of getting compensation *etc*: *Unless you report the accident at once you'll have no comeback.*

'comedown *nc* (*inf*) a fall (*esp* in social rank, dignity *etc*) to a lower state: *The smaller car was a bit of a comedown after the Rolls Royce.*

come about *vi* to happen: *How did that come about?*

come across **1** *vi* to be understood or appreciated: *His speech came across well.* **2** *vt fus* to meet or find by chance: *He came across some old friends.*

come along *vi* **1** to come with or accompany the person speaking *etc*: *Come along with me!*; *Do come along – I'm in a hurry.* **2** (*inf*) to progress: *How are things coming along?*

come apart *see* **apart**.

come between *vt fus* to separate or make unfriendly: *We shouldn't let a little thing like this come between us.*

'come by *vt fus* to get or obtain: *He came by the books in London*; *How did you come by that black eye?*

come clean *see* **clean**.

come down *vi* to decrease; to become less: *The price of tea has come down*; *Tea has come down in price*; *He has come down in the world* (= He is less important, wealthy *etc* than he was).

come forward *vi* to present oneself or bring oneself to notice: *He came forward and gave us vital information*; *The police asked witnesses of the accident to come forward.*

'come from *vt fus* to have been born in, made in *etc*: *She comes from Italy*; *Where did this old book come from?*

come 'in for *vt fus* to receive; to be the target for: *She came in for a lot of criticism.*

come 'into *vt fus* to inherit: *She'll come into all her father's money when he dies.*

come into one's own to have the opportunity of showing what one can do *etc*: *He came into his own as a cook when his mother became ill*; *He has at last come into his own as a pop-singer.*

'come of *vt fus* to happen to or about: *Whatever came of her plans to go to Africa?*

come of age *see* **of age** *under* **age**.

come off *vi* **1** (*inf*) to happen (successfully): *The gamble didn't come off.* **2** to end by being treated in a good, bad *etc* way: *He was unsuccessful at first but he came off quite well in the end.*

come off it! don't be ridiculous (*esp* in trying to persuade someone of something they do not believe): *Come off it – stop pretending and tell me the truth!*

come on! **1** hurry up!: *Come on – we'll be late for the party!* **2** don't be ridiculous!: *Come on, you don't really expect me to believe that, do you?*

come out *vi* **1** to become known: *The truth finally came out.* **2** to be published: *This newspaper comes out once a week.* **3** (*inf*) to strike: *The men have come out* (*on strike*). **4** (of a photograph) to be developed: *This photograph has come out very well.* **5** to be shown (in a photograph): *You came out very well in the photos he took.* **6** to decide: *He came out in favour of the death penalty.* **7** to be removed: *This dirty mark won't come out.* **8** (*inf*) to be solved: *My calculations don't come out.* **9** (*old*) to make a first appearance in society: *The elder daughter came out last year.*

come 'out in *vt fus* to show or develop: *You've come out in spots!*

come out of something well, badly to benefit or not benefit from a situation *etc*: *He came out of the affair rather well, having gained £2000.*

come 'out with *vt fus* (*inf*) to say: *What will the child come out with next?*

come round *vi* **1** to visit: *Come round and see us soon.* **2** to regain consciousness: *He won't come round for twenty minutes at least.* **3** to be persuaded, or to persuade oneself, to accept (something): *He'll come round eventually* (*to your way of thinking*).

come through *vi, vt fus* (of people) to stay alive or survive (something): *Will he come through all right after the operation?*; *He came through the war uninjured.*

come to *vi* to regain consciousness: *When will he come to after the operation?* – *See also* **come** (*defs 4, 5 and 6*).

'come to (someone) *vt fus* (*only with* **it** *as subject*) to have the idea or thought (that): *It suddenly came to me that he was the murderer.*

come to a head *see* **head**.

come to be to reach the point of being: *He's come to be regarded as an expert.*

come to light (*formal*) to be discovered: *The theft only came to light when the owners returned from holiday.*

come to nothing *see* **nothing**.

come to pass (*liter*) (*esp in the Bible*) to happen:

It came to pass that there was a great flood.
'come upon *vt fus* (*liter or formal*) to meet, find or discover by chance: *I came upon a strange man in the park*; *She came upon a solution to the problem.*
come 'up to *vt fus* to reach: *This piece of work doesn't come up to your usual high standard.* – *See also* **up to scratch** *under* **scratch**.
come 'up with *vt fus* to think of; to produce: *He's come up with a great idea.*
come what may whatever happens: *I'll give you my support, come what may!*
have it coming *see* **have**.
to 'come (*formal*) (in the) future: *in days to come.*

comedy ['komədi] **1** *nc* a play of a pleasant or amusing kind: *We went to see a comedy last night.* **2** *nu* such plays generally: *As a rule, I don't enjoy comedy.* **3** *nu* humour or amusement: *They all saw the comedy of the situation.*
comedian [kə'mi:diən] – *fem* **comedienne** [kəmi:di'en, (*Amer*) kə'mi:diən] *nc* a performer who tells jokes or acts in comedies.

comely ['kʌmli] *adj* (*formal or liter*) (*usu* of women) pleasant to look at. **'comeliness** *nu.*

comet ['komit] *nc* a type of heavenly body which leaves a trail of light behind it as it moves.

comfort ['kʌmfət] **1** *nu* a pleasant condition of being physically or mentally relaxed, happy, warm *etc*: *They now live in comfort*; *She did it for his comfort.* **2** *ncu* anything that provides a little luxury, or makes one feel more relaxed, happier, or better able to bear misfortune: *He enjoyed the comforts of the four-star hotel*; *Her presence was a comfort to him in his grief*; *The minister said a few words of comfort to the widow.*
'comfortable *adj* (*inf abbrev* **'comfy**) **1** (*usu pred*) in comfort; pleasantly relaxed: *I don't feel comfortable at formal dinners*; *He looked very comfortable in his chair beside the fire.* **2** (*usu attrib*) producing a good physical feeling: *a very comfortable chair.* **3** (*inf*) financially secure without being rich: *We don't have a lot of money but we're comfortable*; *a comfortable standard of living.* **'comfortably** *adv.*
'comforter *nc* **1** a person who comforts. **2** (*old*) a woollen scarf. **3** a dummy teat for a baby to suck.
'comforting *adj* producing a pleasant or relaxed feeling: *That's a comforting thought*; *The boys found the hot tea very comforting after their ordeal on the mountain.*
'comfortingly *adv.*
be comfortably off (*inf*) to have enough money to live in comfort: *Our new neighbours seem to be very comfortably off, although they're not rich.*

comic ['komik] *adj* **1** (*attrib*) of comedy: *a comic actor*; *comic opera.* **2** causing amusement: *He made some comic remarks about the food*; *He looked very comic in his father's clothes.* – *nc* **1** an amusing person, *esp* a professional comedian: *That comic always tells old jokes.* **2** a children's periodical containing funny stories, adventures *etc*: *That child never reads books, only comics.*
'comical *adj* funny: *It was comical to see the chimpanzee pouring out a cup of tea*; *a comical expression.*
comic strip *nc* a (*usu* short) series of small pictures showing stages in an adventure.

comma ['komə] *nc* the punctuation mark (**,**) used to show a slight pause *etc.*

command [kə'ma:nd] *vt* (*formal*: not used with **is, was** *etc* and **-ing** (*defs 3, 4*)) **1** to order: *I command you to leave the room immediately!* **2** (*mil*) to have authority over: *He commands a regiment of soldiers.* **3** to have by right: *He commands great respect*; *He can command a high salary.* **4** to look over or down upon (a view *etc*): *My house commands a fine view over the bay.* – **1** *nc* an order: *They obeyed his commands.* **2** *nu* control: *He was in command of the whole situation.* **3** *nc* the thing over which one has authority: *Your command will be HMS Argosy.*
commandant [komən'dant, (*Amer*) 'koməndant] *nc* an officer who has the command of a place or of a body of troops. – *See also* Appendix 3.
com'mander *nc* **1** a person who commands: *He was the commander of the expedition.* **2** (*with cap, and often abbrev* **Com./Comdr**, *when written in titles*) in the British navy, (a person of) the rank next below captain: *He has been promoted to commander*; *Commander Smith.* – *See also* **wing commander** *under* **wing**, *and* Appendix 3.
com'manding *adj* (*formal*) **1** impressive: *He has a commanding appearance.* **2** with a wide view: *The house had a commanding position on the hill.*
com'mandment *nc* (*relig*) a command given by God, *esp* one of the ten given to Moses.
com,mander-in-'chief *nc* the officer in supreme command of an army, or of the entire forces of the state.

commandeer [komən'diə] *vt* to seize (private property) for use by the army *etc* during wartime: *They commandeered the castle for army billets*; (*fig*) *He commandeered his father's car to take his friends to the party.*

commando [kə'ma:ndou] – *pl* **com'mandos** – *nc* (a member of) a unit of troops specially trained for tasks requiring special courage and skill: *The commandos made a raid on the terrorists.*

commemorate [kə'meməreit] *vt* (*formal*) **1** (of people) to honour the memory of (someone) by a solemn celebration: *We always commemorate his birthday.* **2** (of things) to serve as a memorial to (someone or something): *This inscription commemorates those who died.* **com'memorative** [-tiv] *adj.*
com,memo'ration *ncu* (*formal*) (a solemn ceremony for) the preserving of the memory (of some person or thing): *They built a monument in commemoration of the soldiers' courage*; (*attrib*) *a commemoration service.*

commence [kə'mens] *vti* (*more formal than* **begin** *or* **start**) to begin: *The church service commenced with a hymn*; *The minister commenced the service with a hymn.*
com'mencement *ncu* **1** (*formal*) beginning. **2** graduation (ceremony) at some (*esp Amer*) universities.

commend [kə'mend] *vt* (*formal*) **1** to praise: *His ability was highly commended.* **2** to give (someone or something) to be looked after: *I commend him to your care.*
com'mendable *adj* (*formal*) praiseworthy: *His courage during the storm was commendable.*
,commen'dation [ko-] *nu* (*formal*) praise.

commensurate [kə'menʃərət] *adj* (*very formal*: *pred or placed immediately after noun*: *with* **with**) in proportion (to): *The salary is commensurate with the output.*

comment ['koment] *ncu* (a) spoken or written remark: *Did he make any comment on my statement?*; *He made several comments about her untidy appearance.* – *vi* to make such a remark: *'What did* *you say about his work?' 'I didn't comment.'* – *See also* **comment on** *below.*

'**commentary 1** *nu* (*also* **running commentary**) a series of (*esp* broadcast) comments by a spectator at a ceremony, sports event *etc.* **2** *nc* a book or notes in which the text of another book is explained.

'**commentate** [-teit] *vi* (*formal*) to give a commentary: *Who is commentating on the football match?* '**commentator** *nc.*

'**comment on** *vt fus* to make a remark *etc* about: *He commented on the disgusting mess in the house.*

commerce ['komə:s] *nu* the exchange of goods between nations or people; trade on a large scale: *He is engaged in commerce.*

commercial [kə'mə:ʃəl] *adj* **1** (*attrib*) of or like commerce: *Private cars are allowed to use this road but not commercial vehicles.* **2** (*often pred*) profit-making: *a commercial proposition*; *Is that suggestion commercial?* **3** (*attrib*) paid for by advertisements: *commercial television.* – *nc* a TV or radio advertisement: *I enjoyed the play but the commercials irritated me.*

commercialize, -ise [kə'mə:ʃəlaiz] *vt* (*often derog*) to try to make (something) a source of profit: *Christmas has become commercialized*; *The old village has become commercialized by the arrival of tourists.* **commercialism** [kə'mə:ʃəlizəm] *nu.*

commercial traveller *nc* a travelling representative of a business firm.

commiserate [kə'mizəreit] *vi* (*formal*) to feel or express sympathy (with): *She commiserated with him on the death of his mother.* **com,mise'ration** *ncu.*

commission [kə'miʃən] **1** *nu* money earned by a person who sells things for someone else, often based on the amount of sales and often in addition to a basic salary: *The insurance salesman doesn't earn a large salary but he gets a lot of commission*; *He is on commission.* **2** *nc* an order for a work of art: *She's had a commission to paint the president's portrait.* **3** *nc* an official paper giving authority, *esp* to an army officer *etc*: *My son got his commission last year.* **4** *nc* an official group appointed to report on a specific matter: *the Royal Commission on Education.* **5** *nu* (*very formal*) (an instance of) committing (a crime *etc*): *the commission of sins.* – *vt* **1** to give an order (*esp* for a work of art) to: *He was commissioned to paint the Lord Mayor's portrait*; *I was commissioned by the rest of the staff to tell the manager of our complaints*; *They commissioned me to buy her a present.* **2** to give a military commission to (*see* **commissioned officer** *below*).

com,missio'naire [-'neə] *nc* a doorkeeper in uniform: *the commissionaire at the cinema.*

com'missioner *nc* **1** a representative of the government in a district or department. **2** (*formal*) a member of a commission. **3** (*legal*) a person given a particular type of authority: *commissioner for oaths.*

commissioned officer *nc* an officer in the army, navy or air force above a certain rank. – *See also* Appendix 3.

in/out of commission (*inf*) in, or not in, a usable, working condition: *The car's out of commission just now*; *It'll be back in commission tomorrow.*

See also **commit, non-commissioned**.

commit [kə'mit] – *pt, ptp* **com'mitted** – **1** *vt* to perform; to do (*esp* something illegal): *He committed the murder when he was drunk.* **2** *vt* (*formal*) to give (a person or thing) to an institution *etc* for treatment, safekeeping *etc*: *He was committed (to the mental hospital) in July*; *They committed the criminal to the Tower of London.* **3** *v refl* to make a definite agreement (that one will do something): *'Are you going to join the club?' 'I don't want to commit myself yet'*; *She has committed herself to finishing her thesis this year.* **4** *vt* (*formal*: *with* **to**) to put (something) in or on: *He committed the story to paper*; *He committed the poem to memory.*

com'mitment (*formal*) **1** *ncu* (an act of) committing: *The commitment of the facts to paper helped him to understand them better.* **2** *nc* an arrangement, obligation or promise: *He could not go on holiday as he had a commitment to his employers*; *family commitments.*

com'mittal *ncu* (*formal*) the act of committing (*esp* to a mental hospital).

com'mitted *adj* pledged to do, or to support, something: *He was committed to looking after his uncle*; *He is a committed socialist.*

See also **commission**.

committee [kə'miti] *nc or n pl* a number of persons, selected from a larger body, to deal with some special business, *eg* the running of the larger body's affairs: *The committee meet(s) today*; *He is on several committees*; (*formal*) *He serves on several committees*; (*attrib*) *a committee meeting.*

commode [kə'moud] *nc* **1** a kind of chair with a chamber-pot fitted under the seat: *The nurse helped the old lady to sit on the commode as she could not walk to the toilet.* **2** (*old*) a chest of drawers.

commodious [kə'moudiəs] *adj* (*formal*) having a lot of room or space; spacious: *This is a commodious flat.*

commodity [kə'modəti] *nc* (*often in pl*: *formal*) an article which is bought or sold: *Household commodities include soap, washing-machines, brushes and cleaning fluids.*

commodore ['komədo:] *nc* **1** (*with cap, and often abbrev* **Com.**, *when written in titles*) in the British navy, (a person of) the rank next below rear admiral: *He is a commodore now*; *He has been promoted to commodore*; *Commodore Cairns.* – *See also* Appendix 3. **2** the president of a yacht club.

common ['komən] *adj* **1** seen or happening often; quite normal or usual: *a common occurrence*; *The sparrow is a common bird in Britain*; *a common expression*; *That is not so common nowadays.* **2** belonging equally to, or shared by, more than one: *This knowledge is common to all of us*; *We share a common language.* **3** (*attrib*) publicly owned: *common land*; *common property.* **4** coarse or impolite: *She uses some very common expressions*; *She looks very common with that dyed blonde hair and those tight clothes.* **5** of ordinary, not high, social rank: *the common people.* **6** (*gram*) of a noun, not beginning with a capital letter (except at the beginning of a sentence); the opposite of proper: *The house is empty.* **7** (*gram*) of the gender of a noun, either masculine or feminine: *The word 'cattle' has common gender.* – *nc* (a piece of) public land for everyone to use, with few or no buildings: *Cows used to graze on the village common.* – *See also* **commons** *below.*

'**commoner** *nc* a person who is not of high rank: *The royal princess married a commoner.*

'**commons** *n pl* **1** (*hist*) people of ordinary social rank. **2** (*with cap and* **the**) the House of Com-

mons: *The bill has been passed by the Commons.*
common knowledge *nu* something *usu* unpleasant *etc* known to everyone or to most people: *It is common knowledge that he is having an affair with another woman.*
common law *nu* in England, unwritten law based on custom: *They're married according to common law*; (*attrib*) *his common-law wife.*
'commonplace *adj* very ordinary and uninteresting: *I thought his speech would be interesting but it was very commonplace*; *He made some very commonplace remarks.*
'common-room *nc* in a college, school *etc* a sitting-room for the use of a particular group of people: *the senior common-room.*
common sense *nu* practical good sense: *If he has any common sense he'll change jobs.*
the Common Market an association of certain European countries to establish free trade (without duty, tariffs *etc*) among them. – *See also* **European Economic Community** *in* Appendix 2.
the House of Commons the lower house of the British parliament.
in 'common (of interests, attitudes, characteristics *etc*) shared or alike: *They had nothing in common.*
in 'common with in the same way as, like (some other person or persons): *In common with her friends, she has no idea of the cost of running a flat.*
See also **uncommon**.

commonwealth ['komənwelθ] **1** *nc* an association of states who have joined together for their common good: *the Commonwealth of Australia.* **2** *n* (*with cap and* **the**) the British Commonwealth.

commotion [kə'mouʃən] *ncu* (a) confused, noisy uproar: *They were awakened by the commotion in the street*; *There was great commotion outside.*

communal *see* **commune**[1].

commune[1] ['komju:n] *nc* **1** a group of people living together and sharing everything they own. **2** in France *etc* a small administrative division of the country.
'communal *adj* **1** of a community: *The communal life suited them.* **2** shared: *a communal television aerial.*

commune[2] [kə'mju:n] *vi* (*formal*: *usu with* **with**) **1** to feel close (to): *communing with Nature.* **2** to talk confidentially (with): *They communed together before taking any action.*

communicate [kə'mju:nikeit] **1** *vt* (*formal*) to make known or tell (information *etc*): *She reluctantly communicated the facts.* **2** *vt* (*formal*) to pass on or give (a disease *etc*): *He communicated his fear to her.* **3** *vi* to get in touch (with): *It's difficult to communicate with her now that she has left the country.* **4** *vi* (*formal*) to have something in common with someone: *She and I don't communicate any more.* **5** *vi* (*formal*) to be connected: *These two rooms communicate by this door.*
com'municable *adj* (*very formal*) able to be passed on: *a communicable disease.*
com,muni'cation **1** *ncu* (an act, or means, of) conveying information: *Communication is difficult in some remote parts of the country.* **2** *nc* (*formal*) something communicated, a piece of information, a letter *etc*: *I received your communication in this morning's post.*
com,muni'cations *n pl* means of sending messages or of transporting (*eg* troops and supplies).
com'municative [-tiv] *adj* (*neg* **un-**: *formal*: *esp pred*) inclined to give information; not reserved: *She's not very communicative this morning.*
com,muni'cation cord *nc* a chain *etc* in a railway carriage, to be pulled in an emergency.
See also **incommunicado**.

communion [kə'mju:njən] *nu* (*formal*) fellowship, *esp* religious; closeness in thoughts *etc*: *communion with God*; *communion with Nature.*
(Holy) Communion *n* in the Christian Church, the sacrament which commemorates the meal taken by Christ with His disciples before His crucifixion: *Did you go to Communion on Sunday?*

communiqué [kə'mju:nikei] *nc* an official announcement: *A communiqué about the King's health was posted on the palace gates.*

communism ['komjunizəm] *nu* (*often with cap*) a system of government under which there is no private industry and (in some forms) no private property, most things being state-owned.
'communist *nc* (*often with cap*) a person who believes in communism: *He is a Communist*; (*attrib*) *a Communist leader.*

community [kə'mju:nəti] *nc* **1** a group of people, *esp* having the same religion or nationality and living in the same general area: *the West Indian community in Manchester.* **2** the public in general: *He did it for the good of the community*; (*attrib*) *a community worker.*

commute [kə'mju:t] **1** *vi* to travel regularly between two places, *esp* between home in the suburbs and work in the city: *He commutes between Brighton and London.* **2** *vt* (*formal*) to change a criminal sentence for one less severe: *His death sentence was commuted to life imprisonment.*
com'muter *nc* a person who travels to work daily: *Most commuters to London travel by the early train*; (*attrib*) *a commuter train.*

compact[1] [kəm'pakt] *adj* closely packed or fitted neatly together: *She has a very compact kitchen*; *He wrote a very compact account of the meeting*; *Our new house is very compact.* – *vt* (*formal*) to press closely together; to make into a solid mass: *The snow on the road was quickly compacted by the heavy traffic.* – ['kompakt] *nc* a small container for women's face-powder: *Does your compact have a mirror?*

compact[2] ['kompakt] *nc* (*formal*) a contract or agreement: *The management and trade union leaders finally signed a compact agreeable to both parties.*

companion [kəm'panjən] *nc* **1** a person *etc* who (regularly) accompanies another person as a friend or associate: *His dog is his constant companion*; *The youth and his companions ran away when the police arrived.* **2** a person paid to accompany and help another: *Her companion does all her shopping.* **3** a helpful handbook on a particular subject: *The Gardening Companion.* – *adj* (*attrib*) accompanying; matching: *the companion volume to his earlier book.*
com'panionable *adj* (*usu attrib*) friendly; pleasant: *a companionable silence*; *a companionable evening.*
com'panionship *nu* state of being or of having companion(s): *She enjoys the companionship of young people.*
See also **company**.

companionway [kəm'panjənwei] *nc* on a ship *etc*, the ladder or stair from an upper to a lower deck or to a cabin.

company ['kʌmpəni] **1** *nc* a number of people

joined together for a certain (*esp* commercial) purpose: *a glass-manufacturing company*; *a theatre company*; *a company of merchants.* **2** *nu* guests; visitors: *I'm expecting company tonight.* **3** *nu* companionship: *My daughter is very good company*; *Her company was a great help*; *I was grateful for her company.* **4** *nc* a large group of soldiers, *esp* part of an infantry battalion.

keep company (with) (*old*) to be friendly (with), *esp* as a boy- or girl-friend: *They have kept company for more than two years*; *She has kept company with him for a long time.*

keep (someone) company to go, stay *etc* with (someone): *I'll come too, and keep you company.*

part company (with) (*formal*) to leave or separate: *The friends parted company at the bus stop*; (*facet*) *One leg of my chair has parted company with the rest of it.*

See also **accompany**.

comparable, comparative *see* **compare**.

compare [kəm'peə] **1** *vt* to put (things *etc*) side by side and examine their details, in order to see to what extent they are the same or different: *If you compare the two novels you will find that this one is much better than that*; *If you compare his work with hers you will find hers more accurate.* **2** *vt* to describe as being similar to: *She compared him to a monkey.* **3** *vi* (*usu in neg*) to be similar to (*esp* in quality): *He just can't compare with Mozart.*

comparable ['kompərəbl] *adj* (*formal*) of the same kind, on the same scale *etc*: *The houses were not at all comparable in size*; *Their salaries are not comparable.*

comparative [kəm'parətiv] *adj* **1** (*formal*) judged by comparing with something else: *When the children tired of playing express trains, we had comparative quiet* (= it seemed reasonably quiet because it was so noisy before); *The quiet was only comparative.* **2** (*gram*) (of a degree of comparison) between positive and superlative: *a comparative adjective.* – *ncu* (*gram*) (an adjective or adverb of) the comparative degree: *a bigger book*; *a better man*; *Try to be more careful*; *Do it more carefully*; *Blacker is the comparative of black*; *That adjective is in the comparative.*

com'paratively *adv*: *This house was comparatively cheap*; *We were comparatively comfortable in that hotel but I would have preferred a bit of luxury.*

comparison [kəm'parisn] *ncu* (an act of) comparing: *His comparison of the books was unfair*; *I think there's no comparison between Beethoven and pop music*; *Living here is cheap in comparison with London*; *She is quite pretty but she doesn't stand comparison with* (= she is not nearly as pretty as) *her beautiful elder sister.*

See also **incomparable**.

compartment [kəm'pa:tmənt] *nc* a separate part or division *eg* of a railway carriage, a box *etc*: *We couldn't find an empty compartment in the train*; *There was a special compartment for dangerous drugs in the medicine cupboard.*

compass ['kʌmpəs] **1** *nc* an instrument with a magnetized needle, used to find directions: *If he had carried a compass he would not have lost his way on the hills.* **2** *nc* (*usu in pl*) an instrument with two movable legs, for drawing circles *etc.* **3** *nu* (*formal*: *usu fig*) boundaries, reach or scope: *This matter is not within the compass of my department.* **4** *nu* (*music*) the range of pitch of a voice or instrument: *The high notes of the song were beyond the compass of her voice.*

compassion [kəm'paʃən] *nu* (*more formal than* **pity**) sorrow or pity for the sufferings of another person: *She was full of compassion for the orphans.*

com'passionate [-nət] *adj* (*more formal than* **sympathetic**) feeling compassion: *She was very compassionate towards the young refugees*; *a compassionate woman.*

compassionate leave *nu* special leave given to a soldier *etc* for personal reasons, *eg* when a close relative dies.

compatible [kəm'patəbl] *adj* (*usu pred*) **1** able to live, exist or associate happily together: *We share a flat together – we're quite compatible*; *Her taste in music is not compatible with mine*; *The two statements are not quite compatible*; (*formal*) *Riding a bike without lights is not compatible with safety.* **2** (*tech*) (of electrical goods *etc*) able to be used together: *Is your tape-recorder compatible with my amplifier?* **com,pati'bility** *nu.*

com'patibly *adv*: *They live together quite compatibly.*

See also **incompatible**.

compatriot [kəm'patriət, (*Amer*) -'pei-] *nc* (*formal*) a fellow-countryman: *Many of his compatriots were killed in the war.*

compel [kəm'pel] – *pt, ptp* **com'pelled** –*vt* to force: *I was compelled to resign*; *They compelled me to betray my country*; *Honesty compels me to say that I do not like him*; (*formal*) *Her beauty compels admiration.*

com'pelling *adj* (*formal*) **1** forcing (action *etc*): *I had no compelling reason to go.* **2** extremely interesting, admirable, worthy of attention *etc*: *a compelling novel*; *I find this book compelling.*

See also **compulsion**.

compendium [kəm'pendiəm] *nc* **1** a collection of games *etc*, all in one box: *The children got a compendium at Christmas.* **2** (*formal*) a summary: *He carried a compendium of the rules in his pocket.*

compensate ['kompənseit] *vti* **1** to give something (often money) (to someone) or do something (for someone), for loss or wrong they have experienced: *This payment will compensate (her) for the loss of her job.* **2** to undo or counteract the effect of a disadvantage, loss *etc*: *Her loyalty to the firm compensates for her lack of talent*; *The love the child received from his grandmother more than compensated for the cruelty of his parents.* **compensatory** [kəm'pensətəri] *adj* (*formal*).

,compen'sation *ncu* payment *etc* given for loss or injury: *He received a large sum of money as compensation when he was injured at work.*

compère ['kompə:] *nc* a person who introduces the different acts and items of an entertainment. –*vt*: *The comedian compèred the variety show.*

compete [kəm'pi:t] *vi* to try to beat others in a contest, fight *etc*; to be rivals: *Ten teams competed for the cup*; *The brothers competed for a place in the team*; *We are competing against them in the next round*; *Are you competing with her for the job?*

competition [kompə'tiʃən] **1** *nu* the process or act of competing; rivalry: *Competition makes children try harder.* **2** *nu* people competing for a prize *etc*: *Our team might not win – the competition is very strong*; *There's a lot of competition for this job.* **3** *nc* a contest for a prize: *Have you entered the tennis competition?*

competitive [kəm'petətiv] *adj* **1** (of a person) enjoying competition: *a very competitive child*; *He is not at all competitive.* **2** (of a price, product *etc*) able to compete successfully with the prices *etc* of rivals: *I always go to that shop – their prices are very competitive.* **3** (*attrib*) (of an examination, sports *etc*) in which a reward goes to the person or people who do best: *He doesn't like competitive sports.*

competitor [kəm'petitə] *nc* a person *etc* who takes part in a competition; an opponent; a rival: *All the competitors finished the race*; *They had been competitors for the directorship for a long time.*

competent ['kompətənt] *adj* (*formal*) capable; skilled: *She was a competent pianist*; *He is not competent to drive such a big car.*

'competence *nu* **1** (*formal*) capability, skill *etc*: *Her competence as a teacher is not in doubt*; *You must prove your competence to drive a car.* **2** (*legal*) powers, *esp* of a court: *It is not within the competence of this court to deal with this case.*

'competently *adv*.

See also **incompetent**.

compile [kəm'pail] *vt* (*formal*) to make (a book, table *etc*) from information collected from other books *etc*: *He compiled a list of all known chemical elements.* **compilation** [kompi'leiʃən] *ncu*. **com'piler** *nc*.

complacent [kəm'pleisnt] *adj* showing satisfaction with one's own situation (and often, lack of care about anything else): *He was so complacent that he irritated everyone*; *He is not at all complacent about his future career*; *a complacent attitude.*

com'placence, com'placency *nus*.

com'placently *adv*: *The cat sat complacently by the fire.*

complain [kəm'plein] *vi* **1** to state one's displeasure, dissatisfaction *etc* (to someone) (about something): *I'm going to complain to the police*; *He complained about the noise.* **2** (*with* **of**) to state that one has (pain, discomfort *etc*): *He's complaining of difficulty in breathing.*

com'plainant *nc* (*legal*) a person who complains.

com'plaint **1** *ncu* (a statement of one's) dissatisfaction or sorrow: *The customer made a complaint about the lack of hygiene in the food shop.* **2** *nc* a sickness, disease, disorder *etc*: *He's always suffering from some complaint or other*; *He has a heart complaint.*

complement ['kompləmənt] *nc* **1** (something which makes) a complete number or quantity: *A ship's complement is the full number of officers and crew.* **2** (*gram*) the words of the predicate, not including the verb. **3** (*geom*) the angle that must be added to a given angle to make it 90°.

,comple'mentary [-'men-] *adj* **1** making up a whole: *a complementary amount*; *These notes are complementary to the ones I gave you last week.* **2** making up a right angle: *An angle of 20° is complementary to an angle of 70°*; *a complementary angle.*

complete [kəm'pli:t] *adj* **1** whole; with nothing missing: *He has a complete set of Shakespeare's plays*; *My collection of stamps is complete now.* **2** thorough: *My car needs a complete overhaul*; *It was a complete surprise to me when he walked in*; (*formal*) *My happiness is now complete*; *He is always the complete gentleman* (= he has all the qualities that a gentleman has); *'Which sport does he play?' 'Oh, he's a complete all-rounder'* (= he plays all or most sports). **3** (*pred*) finished: *My picture will soon be complete.* – **1** *vt* (*more formal than* **finish**) to finish: *When will he complete the job?*; *This stamp completes my collection.* **2** to make perfect: *The news of his success completed her happiness.*

com'pletely *adv*: *I am not completely satisfied*; *He is completely unaware of the situation.*

com'pleteness *nu* (*formal*) state of being whole, perfect or thorough: *The teacher was surprised at the completeness of the child's answer.*

com'pletion [-ʃən] *nu* (*formal*) finishing or state of being finished: *He'll bring the book to completion*; *You will be paid on completion of the work.*

See also **incomplete**.

complex ['kompleks, (*Amer*) kəm'pleks] *adj* **1** composed of many parts: *This is a complex piece of machinery.* **2** (*more formal than* **difficult**) complicated or difficult: *a complex problem*; *You must make the instructions more simple – they are too complex for children.* – ['kompleks] *nc* **1** something made up of many different pieces: *a housing complex*; *The leisure complex will include a swimming-pool, tennis courts, a library etc.* **2** (*often used loosely*) a mental illness caused by experiences in one's past which affect one's behaviour: *She has an inferiority complex*; *He has an Oedipus complex* (= he is unnaturally over-fond of his mother); (*inf*) *She has a complex about her feet being too big* (= she is worried and self-conscious about having big feet).

complexity [kəm'pleksəti] *nu* (*formal*): *She was worried about the complexity of the arrangements.*

complexion [kəm'plekʃən] *ncu* **1** the colour or appearance of the skin *esp* of the face: *Her complexion is rather dark*; *She has a beautiful complexion.* **2** (*fig*) general appearance: *This puts a new complexion on the whole theory.*

complexity *see* **complex**.

compliance, compliant *see* **comply**.

complicate ['komplikeit] *vt* to make difficult: *This will complicate matters even more*; *My problem is complicated by the fact that he is being so unhelpful.*

'complicated *adj* (*neg* **un-**) (*more formal than* **difficult**) difficult to understand; involved: *These are complicated instructions*; *a complicated system of roads*; *That puzzle is too complicated for the children.*

,compli'cation **1** *ncu* (something) making a situation *etc* more difficult: *Taking the dog on holiday with them was an added complication.* **2** *nc* a development (in an illness *etc*) which makes things worse: *The old lady's broken leg healed well, but she died of the pneumonia which followed as a complication.*

complicity [kəm'plisəti] *nu* (*very formal*) the state of having a share in the committing (of a crime *etc*): *He denied complicity in his brother's crime.*

compliment ['kompləmənt] *nc* an expression of praise or flattery: *She accepted his compliment about her dress with a smile*; *He's always paying her compliments.* – *See also* **compliments**. – [kompli'ment] *vt* to praise or flatter; to congratulate (on): *He complimented her on her cooking*; *He complimented her on winning.*

,compli'mentary [-'men-] *adj* (*neg* **un-**) **1** flattering or praising: *complimentary remarks*; *His remarks were very complimentary.* **2** (*usu attrib*) given free: *a complimentary ticket.*

'compliments *n pl* (*formal*) greetings: *My compliments to your father!*; (*attrib*) *Don't bother sending a letter with that book – a compliments slip will do.*

with 'compliments used when sending a gift *etc*

as a sign of greeting or respect: *'With compliments from a secret admirer'.*

comply [kəm'plai] *vi* (*formal*) to act in the way that someone else has commanded or wished: *You must comply* (*with her wishes*). **com'pliance** *nu.* **com'pliant** *adj* (*formal*) willing to comply: *You must not be too compliant – you must take your own wishes into consideration*; *a compliant person.*

component [kəm'pounənt] *nc* (*more formal or tech than* **bit**) a part of a machine (*eg* a car), instrument (*eg* a radio) *etc*: *He bought components for the television set he was repairing*; (*attrib*) *component parts.*

compose [kəm'pouz] **1** *vt* (*formal*: not used with **is, was** *etc* and **-ing**) to form by putting parts together: *A word is composed of several letters put together*; *Our group is composed of older people.* **2** *vti* to write (*esp* music, poetry or (*formal*) a letter): *Mozart began to compose when he was six years old*; *He composed a letter to his solicitor.* **3** *vt* (*formal*: *often v refl*) to get control over or to calm emotions, thoughts *etc*: *Stop crying and compose yourself!*

com'posed *adj* (of people) quiet, calm or unemotional: *She was quite composed at her sister's funeral*; *in a composed state of mind.*

com'poser *nc* a writer, *esp* of a piece of music.

composition [kompə'ziʃən] **1** *nc* something composed, *esp* in literature, music or painting: *His latest composition is too modern for my taste.* **2** *nu* (*formal*) the act of composing: *He spent six months on the composition of the symphony.* **3** *nc* an essay written as a school *etc* exercise: *The children had to write a composition about their holiday.* **4** *nu* the parts of which a thing is made: *Have you studied the composition of the chemical?*

compositor [kəm'pozitə] *nc* a person who puts together type for printing: *How many compositors does the printer employ?*

com'posure [-ʒə] *nu* (*formal*) (*usu* of people) calmness: *I admired her composure during all the trouble*; *She kept her composure.*

See also **component**.

composite ['kompəzit, (*Amer*) kəm'pozit] *adj* (*formal*: *usu attrib*) made up of two or more distinct parts: *The mural was a composite effort of all the children in the class.* – *nc*: *Her novel is a composite of several styles.*

composition, compositor *see* **compose**.

compost ['kompost, (*Amer*) -poust] *nu* rotting vegetable matter *etc* used as fertilizer: *He uses compost instead of chemicals on his garden*; (*attrib*) *a compost heap.*

composure *see* **compose**.

compound[1] ['kompaund] *adj* (*usu attrib*) composed of a number of parts: *a compound substance.* – *nc* a substance, word *etc* formed from two or more elements: *Baking powder is a compound of sodium bicarbonate and cream of tartar*; *The word racetrack is a compound.* – [kəm'paund] *vt* (*formal*) **1** to increase (*esp* difficulties) greatly: *The shortage of food was compounded by the arrival of six motorists stranded by the snowstorms*; *He compounded the crime.* **2** to mix or combine (pieces or ingredients) to make a whole: *The pain-killing drug was compounded of two different chemicals.*

compound fracture *nc* (*tech*) a break in a bone accompanied by a break in the skin over or near it: *He has a compound fracture of the femur*; *He sustained a compound fracture in the motor accident.*

compound[2] ['kompaund] *nc* a fenced or walled-in area containing a house or factory, or in a prison *etc.*

comprehend [kompri'hend] *vt* (not used with **is, was** *etc* and **-ing**) **1** (*formal*) to understand: *It is difficult to comprehend the behaviour of such a man.* **2** (*very formal*) to include: *His lecture comprehended several aspects of the topic.*

ˌcompre'hensible *adj* (*formal*: *usu pred*) capable of being understood: *We did not find his lecture at all comprehensible*; *This is comprehensible only to him.*

ˌcompre'hension [-ʃən] *nu* (*formal*) the act or power of understanding: *How he manages to live on his salary is beyond my comprehension.*

ˌcompre'hensive [-siv] *adj* **1** (*formal*) taking in or including many things: *He gave a comprehensive account of the meeting*; *His account of the meeting was most comprehensive.* **2** (of education, schools *etc*) providing teaching for children over the entire range of abilities. – *nc* a comprehensive school: *He goes to the local comprehensive.*

ˌcompre'hensively *adv.* **ˌcompre'hensiveness** *nu.*

See also **incomprehensible**.

compress [kəm'pres] *vt* (*formal*) to press together; to force into a narrower space: *All his belongings were compressed into a very small suitcase*; (*fig*) *As there was so little time left, he compressed his lecture into ten minutes.* – ['kompres] *nc* a (wet) pad or folded cloth used to apply pressure to a part of the body, *esp* to prevent swelling: *Apply a cold compress to your injured ankle.*

com'pressible *adj.* **com'pression** [-ʃən] *nu.*

compressed air *nu* air which is at a pressure higher than atmospheric pressure: *Deep-sea divers breathe compressed air.*

comprise [kəm'praiz] *vt* (*formal*: not used with **is, was** *etc* and **-ing**) to contain, include or consist of: *Her family comprises two sons and a daughter*; *The house comprises four bedrooms.*

compromise ['komprəmaiz] *ncu* (a) settlement of differences in which each side gives up or concedes something it has previously demanded: *Their holiday with his parents was a compromise between going abroad and having no holiday at all*; *We argued for a long time but finally reached/arrived at a compromise.* – **1** *vi* to make a compromise: *They compromised by going to the cinema although she wanted to go to the theatre and he wanted to go to the pub.* **2** *vt* to put into a dangerous or scandalous situation by an indiscreet act *etc*: *His position was compromised by the discovery of his associations with criminals*; *He refused to compromise her by staying alone in the house with her overnight before they were married.*

'compromising *adj* (*usu attrib*) exposing to danger, suspicion or scandal: *a compromising situation.*

See also **uncompromising**.

compulsion [kəm'pʌlʃən] **1** *nu* (*formal*) compelling or being compelled: *As there was no compulsion to go, he decided to stay at home*; *You are under no compulsion to go.* **2** *nc* a force driving a person (to do something unreasonable or not sensible): *He had a sudden compulsion to run naked through the streets.*

com'pulsive [-siv] *adj* (*formal*: *attrib*) of or arising from an impulse (as if one is forced): *He's a compulsive eater.* **com'pulsively** *adv.*

com'pulsory *adj* (*formal*) which must be done or carried out: *Is it compulsory for me to attend the* *meeting?*; *Attendance at the meeting is compulsory*; *a compulsory examination.* **com'pulsorily** *adv.* *See also* **compel**.

compunction [kəm'pʌŋkʃən] *nu* (*formal*) uneasiness of conscience: *He had no compunction about keeping the money as the old man already owed him quite a lot.*

compute [kəm'pju:t] *vt* (*very formal*) to calculate or estimate: *He computed that the project would take four years to complete.*

ˌcompu'tation [kom-] *ncu* (*very formal*): *Are your computations accurate?*

computer [kəm'pju:tə] *nc* a *usu* large electronic machine capable of storing and processing large amounts of information and of performing calculations.

com'puterize, -ise *vt* (*formal*) to put (information *etc*) into a form suitable for use by a computer: *Are you intending to computerize your book-ordering system?*

comrade ['komrid, (*Amer*) -rad] *nc* **1** (*formal*) a close companion: *his comrades in battle.* **2** a fellow communist or socialist: *Comrades, we must join forces against the bosses.*

'comradely *adj*: *He acted in a comradely way.*

'comradeship *nu*: *I miss the comradeship of the office now that I am working at home.*

con [kon] – *pt, ptp* **conned** – *vt* (*inf*) **1** to perform a confidence trick on: *He certainly conned me.* **2** to trick or persuade dishonestly: *He was conned into buying a gadget which he would never use*; *He conned her into giving him money.* – *nc* (*inf*) a confidence trick.

'con-man [-man] *nc.* **'con-trick** *nc.*

concave [kon'keiv] *adj* (of an object or surface) curved inwards: *Spoons are concave*; *a concave dish.* **con'cavity** [-'ka-] *ncu* (*formal*).
See also **convex**.

conceal [kən'si:l] *vt* (*more formal than* **hide**) to hide or keep secret: *He concealed his disappointment from his friends*; *The child was reading a book which was concealed under his desk.*

con'cealment 1 *nu* (*formal*) the act of hiding: *The concealment of the stolen money was difficult.* **2** *nc* a disguise or hiding-place: *His bookshop acted as a concealment for his illegal activities.*

concede [kən'si:d] *vt* (*formal*) **1** to admit (the truth of something): *He conceded that he had been wrong.* **2** to grant (*eg* a right): *He has conceded the right of way across his land.*
See also **concession**.

conceit [kən'si:t] **1** *nu* too much pride in oneself: *He's full of conceit about his good looks.* **2** *nc* (*liter*) an example of fanciful style: *His writings are full of conceits.*

con'ceited *adj* having too much pride in oneself: *She is a very conceited young lady*; *He's so conceited!*

conceive [kən'si:v] (*formal*: not used with **is, was** *etc* and **-ing**) **1** *vt* to form (an idea *etc*) in the mind: *Who conceived the idea of coming here for a holiday?* **2** *vt* to imagine or believe: *I can't conceive why you did that.* **3** *vi* (of a woman) to become pregnant: *She has conceived at last.*

con'ceivable *adj* (*usu attrib*) able to be imagined or thought of: *for no conceivable reason.*

con'ceivably *adv*: *He is conceivably the best writer we have today.*
See also **concept, conception, inconceivable**.

concentrate ['konsəntreit] **1** *vi* (*often with* **on**) to give all one's energies, attention *etc* (to one purpose): *I wish you'd concentrate* (*on what I'm saying*). **2** *vt* (*formal*) to bring together in one place: *He's concentrated his soldiers at the gateway*; *He has concentrated all his resources on that one project.* **3** *vt* to make (something, *esp* a liquid) stronger by reducing its volume: *They concentrated the sea water by boiling off some of the water.* – *ncu* something concentrated, *esp* a liquid: *concentrate of clove oil.*

'concentrated *adj* (of a liquid *etc*) made stronger; not diluted: *This orange squash is too concentrated for me – I'll add some water to it*; *concentrated orange juice.*

ˌconcen'tration *ncu*: *She lacks concentration – she will never pass the exam*; (*formal*) *the concentration of our resources.*

concentric [kən'sentrik] *adj* (*tech*) (of circles) having a common centre.

concept ['konsept] *nc* (*formal*) an idea or theory: *His design was a new concept in town-planning*; *His concept of a woman's place in society is out of date.*

conception [kən'sepʃən] (*formal*) **1** *nu* the act of conceiving. **2** *nc* something (*eg* an idea) conceived or imagined: *You have no conception of how stupid she is!*
See also **conceive**.

concern [kən'sə:n] **1** *vt* (not used with **is, was** *etc* and **-ing**) to have to do with: *This order doesn't concern us*; *So far as I'm concerned, you can do what you like.* **2** *vt* (*formal*: *with* **for** *or* **about**) to make (*usu* oneself) uneasy or worried: *Don't concern yourself about his future*; *I am concerned for her happiness.* **3** *v refl* (*with* **with** *or* **in**) to interest (oneself) in; to pass one's time in: *He doesn't concern himself with unimportant details*; *You mustn't concern yourself in other people's affairs.* – **1** *nc* something that concerns or belongs to one: *His problems are not my concern.* **2** *nu* (*formal*) anxiety: *Concern for the child's safety is growing – she has not been seen all day*; *The condition of the patient is giving rise to concern.* **3** *nc* (*formal*) a business: *There are two manufacturing concerns in this town.*

con'cerning *prep* (*formal*) about, regarding or on the part of: *I'm a little worried concerning your business affairs*; *He wrote to me concerning a business arrangement.*

concert ['konsət] *nc* a musical entertainment: *Are you going to the school concert?*; *an orchestral concert.*

in 'concert (*formal*) together; simultaneous(ly): *They acted in concert to defeat the enemy.*

concerted [kən'sə:tid] *adj* (*attrib*) arranged beforehand and carried out by people acting together: *a concerted attack*; *a concerted effort.*
See also **disconcert**.

concertina [konsə'ti:nə] *nc* a portable musical wind instrument with bellows and a keyboard: *He plays the concertina*; *He played a tune on his concertina.*

concerto [kən'tʃə:tou] – *pl* **con'certos** – *nc* a piece of music written for one or more solo instruments and orchestra: *a piano concerto*; *a concerto for violin and cello.*

concession [kən'seʃən] **1** *nc* (*formal*) something admitted or granted: *As a concession we were given a day off work to go to the wedding.* **2** *nu* (*very formal*) the act of conceding or granting: *The government's concession of land to the Indians prevented further war.*

con'cessionary *adj* (*very formal*) granted as a

right: *a concessionary bus pass for elderly people.* *See also* **concede**.

conciliate [kən'silieit] *vt* (*formal*) to win over or gain the support, friendship *etc* of (someone previously hostile or angry): *My mother is very angry with me because I did not send her a birthday card and I have been unable to conciliate her.*

con,cili'ation *nu* (*formal*): *My attempts at conciliation failed*; (*attrib*) *The government has set up a conciliation board to deal with the union dispute.*

con'ciliatory *adj* (*usu attrib*: *formal*) intended or showing desire to conciliate: *a conciliatory manner.*

See also **reconcile, reconciliation**.

concise [kən'sais] *adj* brief but comprehensive: *He gave a clear concise report.* **con'cisely** *adv.* **con'ciseness** *nu.*

conclave ['konkleiv] *nc* (*formal*) a private, secret meeting: *a conclave of cardinals*; *They had met in conclave to discuss the current problems.*

conclude [kən'klu:d] *vti* **1** (*more formal than* **end**) to come or bring to an end: *We concluded (the meeting) with a vote of thanks*; *He concluded by thanking everyone.* **2** *vt* (*more formal than* **decide**: not used with **is, was** *etc* and **-ing**) to come to believe: *We concluded that you weren't coming.*

con'clusion [-ʒən] *nc* **1** an end: *There was applause at the conclusion of his speech.* **2** a judgement: *His conclusion was that the thief had cut his hand on the broken window*; *I came to the conclusion that the house was empty.*

con'clusive [-siv] *adj* (*formal*) convincing or giving proof: *The evidence of the blood-stained knife was quite conclusive*; *conclusive proof.* **con'clusively** *adv.* **con'clusiveness** *nu.*

in conclusion (*formal*) finally: *In conclusion, I'd like to thank Mr Smith.*

See also **inconclusive**.

concoct [kən'kokt, (*Amer*) kon-] *vt* (*formal*) **1** to mix (*eg* a dish in cookery, a drink): *I've concocted a new dessert for you to try.* **2** to make up or invent (an untrue story): *The child concocted a story about having been attacked.*

con'coction [-ʃən] *ncu* (*facet*: *sometimes derog*): *This concoction tastes most peculiar.*

concomitant [kən'komitənt] *adj* (*very formal*) accompanying; going together with: *The socialist MP's great wealth is not concomitant with his political views*; *poverty and its concomitant misery.*

concord ['koŋko:d] *nu* (*formal*) agreement; state of peace: *The lack of concord affected the work in the office*; *There seemed very little concord among the committee members.*

con'cordance [-'ko:-] *nc* an index of the words of a book or author, with references to where they are used: *a concordance to the Bible*; *a Shakespeare concordance.*

concourse ['koŋko:s] *nc* **1** (*formal*) a large open space for people, *eg* in a railway station, airport *etc*: *They arranged to meet under the clock in the concourse.* **2** (*very formal*) a crowding together: *a concourse of people.*

concrete ['koŋkri:t] *adj* **1** made of concrete: *a concrete pillar*; *The walls are concrete.* **2** (*attrib*: *formal*) able to be felt by the senses; not abstract: *A wooden table is a concrete object.* **3** (*attrib*: *gram*) (of nouns) not abstract: *Cocoa is a concrete noun.* **4** (*formal*) definite; real: *concrete proof/evidence*; *Our plans are not yet concrete.* – *nu* a mixture of cement with sand, very small stones *etc* used in building: *The workmen mixed the concrete for our new garden path.* – *vt* to spread with concrete: *We'll have to concrete the garden path.* **'concreteness** *nu.*

See also **abstract**.

concubine ['koŋkjubain] *nc* **1** (*old*) a woman who lives with a man but is not his wife: *King Charles II of Britain was said to have many concubines.* **2** (in societies where more than one wife is acceptable) a second or later wife.

concubinage [kon'kju:binidʒ] *nu* (*old or formal*) the state of being a concubine.

concur [kən'kə:] – *pt, ptp* **con'curred** – *vi* (*formal*) **1** to agree: *I cannot concur with you in this matter.* **2** to happen or act together: *Circumstances concurred to make the conference a great success.*

con'currence [-'kʌ-, (*Amer*) -'kə:-] *nu* (*formal*): *the concurrence of our views*; *the concurrence of events.*

concurrent [kən'kʌrənt, (*Amer*) -'kə:-] *adj* (*formal*) coming or existing together: *Are his two prison sentences to be concurrent?*; *Fortunately, the dates of their holidays were concurrent.*

con'currently *adv* at the same time; not consecutively: *The criminal received three sentences of six months, to run concurrently.*

concuss [kən'kʌs] *vt* (*formal*: *used in passive*) to suffer from concussion: *He was concussed for several hours but he is all right now.*

con'cussion [-ʃən] *nu* temporary harm to the brain caused by a heavy blow on the head: *He is suffering from concussion.*

condemn [kən'dem] *vt* **1** to say that (something) is morally wrong or evil: *Everyone condemned her for being cruel to her child*; *Murder is condemned by all reasonable people.* **2** to sentence to (a punishment): *She was condemned to death.* **3** to declare (a building) to be unfit to use: *These houses have been condemned.* **condemnation** [kondem'neiʃən] *ncu.*

con'demned cell *nc* a cell for a prisoner under sentence of death.

condense [kən'dens] **1** *vt* (*formal*) to make smaller: *They condensed the book for children by taking out all the difficult passages.* **2** *vt* to make (a liquid) thicker, stronger or more concentrated: *condensed milk*; *condensed soups.* **3** *vi* (of vapour) to turn to liquid: *Steam condensed on the kitchen windows.*

,conden'sation [konden-] *nu* **1** (*formal*) the act of condensing. **2** liquid formed from vapour (*esp* water vapour): *I can't see because of the condensation on the window.*

con'denser *nc* (*old tech*) a capacitor.

condescend [kondi'send] *vi* **1** to act graciously (to do something): *The Queen condescended to open our factory.* **2** (*often ironic*) to act in a condescending manner: *Will you kindly condescend to remove your feet from my desk?*

,conde'scending *adj* having or giving the impression (to someone) that one is superior: *She is very condescending to her poor relations*; *a condescending manner.* **,conde'scendingly** *adv.*

,conde'scension [-ʃən] *ncu.*

condiment ['kondimənt] *ncu* (*formal*) a seasoning (*usu* salt or pepper) used at table to give flavour to food.

condition [kən'diʃən] **1** *ncu* state or circumstances in which a person or thing is: *The house is not in very good condition*; *He is in no condition* (= he is not well *etc* enough) *to leave hospital*; *The experiment must be carried out under ideal conditions*; *The books are in poor condition*; *living* *conditions*; *good housing conditions.* **2** *nc* something that must happen or be done before some other thing happens or is done; a term or requirement in an agreement: *It was a condition of his going that he should pay his own expenses*; *That is a condition of sale*; *That is one of the conditions in the agreement.* – *vt* **1** (*formal*) to affect or control: *His behaviour was conditioned by his circumstances*; *He was conditioned to believe that women are inferior to men.* **2** (*usu in cmpds*) to put into the required state: *Some buildings are air-conditioned to cool them down in summer*; *Well-conditioned hair is shiny.*

con'ditional *adj* (*formal*) depending on certain conditions: *This order is conditional on your being able to supply the goods next week*; *a conditional offer.* **con'ditionally** *adv.*

con'ditioner *ncu* (*usu in cmpds*) something which helps in conditioning: (*a*) *hair conditioner.*

con'ditioning *nu* (*formal*) the bringing into a good or the required state: *Much of our behaviour is the result of conditioning by our parents.*

on con'dition that (*more formal than* **if**) if, and only if (something is done): *You will be paid tomorrow on condition that the work is finished by then.*

See also **unconditional.**

condolence [kən'douləns] *ncu* (*formal*: *usu in pl*) sympathy: *a letter of condolence*; *He sent her his condolences on the death of her husband.*

condom ['kondom] *nc* a covering or sheath which is sometimes worn on the penis during sexual intercourse as a contraceptive.

condone [kən'doun] *vt* (*formal*) to excuse or forgive (an offence or wrong): *He could not condone his wife's infidelity.*

conducive [kən'dju:siv] *adj* (*formal*: *pred with* **to**) tending or helping towards: *Going to bed late is not conducive to good health.*

conduct [kən'dʌkt] **1** *vt* (*formal*) to lead or guide: *We were conducted down a narrow path by the guide*; *We went on a conducted tour.* **2** *vti* to carry or allow to flow: *The hot water is conducted through these pipes*; *Most metals conduct electricity.* **3** *vti* to direct (an orchestra, choir *etc*). **4** *v refl* (*formal*) to behave (oneself): *He conducted himself well at the reception.* **5** *vt* (*formal*) to manage or carry on (a business): *You cannot conduct a successful business in such a manner.* – ['kondʌkt] *nu* **1** behaviour: *His conduct at school was disgraceful.* **2** the way in which something is managed, done *etc*: *The government's conduct of the affair was not satisfactory.*

con'duction [-ʃən] *nu* (*tech*) transmission, carrying (*eg* of heat) by a conductor: *the conduction of electricity.*

ˌconduc'tivity *nu* (*tech*) (the measure of) the ability to conduct (heat, electricity *etc*).

con'ductor *nc* **1** (*tech*) a thing that conducts (electricity *etc*): *Copper is a good conductor of heat.* **2** a director of an orchestra, choir *etc.* **3** (*fem* **con'ductress**) a person who collects fares on a bus *etc*: *That bus had no conductor – the driver collected the fares.* **4** (*Amer*) a guard (*def 3*).

conduit ['kondit, (*Amer*) -duit] *nc* (*tech*) a channel or pipe for carrying water, electric cables *etc* (*esp* in the walls of a building).

cone [koun] *nc* **1** a solid figure with a point and a base in the shape of a circle or an ellipse. **2** the fruit of the pine, fir *etc*: *fir-cones.* **3** something similar to a cone in shape, *esp* a pointed holder for ice-cream, or a warning sign placed next to roadworks *etc* or where parking is not allowed: *an ice-cream cone*; *The parking wardens put those cones there after I had parked my car.*

conical ['konikəl] *adj* (*formal*) cone-shaped: *a conical mountain.*

confectioner [kən'fekʃənə] *nc* **1** a person who makes or sells sweets or cakes. **2** (*formal*) a confectioner's shop.

con'fectioner's *nc* a confectioner's shop.

con'fectionery *nu* **1** sweets, chocolates *etc.* **2** the shop or business of a confectioner.

confederate [kən'fedərət] **1** *nc* (*often derog*) a person who has agreed to work with others (often to commit a crime *etc*): *He and his confederates were found with stolen money in their possession.* **2** *n* (*Amer hist*: *with cap*) a supporter or follower of the Confederacy. – *adj* (*attrib*: *formal or hist*) allied: *a confederate state.*

con'federacy [-rəsi] **1** *nc* a league or alliance (of states *etc*). **2** *n* (*Amer hist*: *with cap and* **the**) in the Civil War, the league of eleven states which separated from the rest of America.

conˌfede'ration *nc* (*formal*) (the forming of) a league or alliance, *esp* of states *etc*: *the Confederation of British Industry.*

confer [kən'fə:] – *pt, ptp* **con'ferred** – (*formal*) **1** *vi* (*often with* **with**) to consult each other: *The staff conferred* (*with the headmaster*) *about the new plans for the school.* **2** *vt* (*with* **on**) to give (an honour) to someone: *The university conferred honorary degrees on two world-famous scientists.*

conference ['konfərəns] *ncu* a meeting for discussion: *The conference of heart specialists was held in New York*; *Our managing director is in conference just now.*

con'ferment *nu* (*formal*) the giving (of honours): *the conferment of an honorary degree.*

confess [kən'fes] *vti* **1** to make known that one is guilty, wrong *etc*; to admit: *He confessed* (*to the crime*); *He confessed that he had broken the vase*; (*fig formal*) *I must confess to being amazed at his ability.* **2** to make (one's wrongs *etc*) known to a priest: *He confessed his evil thoughts about his father.*

con'fession [-ʃən] *ncu* **1** acknowledgement of a crime or fault: *The youth made several confessions to the police officer*; *He signed his written confession of guilt.* **2** (an) act of confessing one's sins to a priest: *She went to confession every Friday*; *Father Smith heard her confession.*

con'fessional [-ʃə-] *nc* (*relig*) the seat *etc* where a priest sits when hearing confessions.

con'fessor *nc* (*relig*) a priest who hears confessions.

confetti [kən'feti] *nu* small pieces of coloured paper thrown in celebration at weddings: *Confetti is usually thrown as the bride and groom leave the church.*

confide [kən'faid] **1** *vi* (*with* **in**) to tell secrets or private thoughts: *He confided in his brother.* **2** *vt* to tell (secrets, plans, thoughts *etc*) to someone: *He confided his fears to his brother.*

confidant [konfi'dant] – *fem* **ˌconfi'dante** – *nc* (*old or formal*) a person whom one trusts with secrets *etc.*

confidence ['konfidəns] **1** *nu* trust or belief in someone's ability: *I have great confidence in you.* **2** *nu* belief and faith in one's own ability: *She shows a great deal of* (*self-*)*confidence for her age.* **3** *nc* (*formal*) a piece of information given in the belief that it will not be passed on.

confident ['konfidənt] *adj* having a great deal of trust (*esp* in oneself): *I'm confident of winning*; *She is confident that she will win*; *He was a confident competitor.*

confidential [konfi'denʃəl] *adj* **1** secret; not to be told to others: *This is completely confidential*; *confidential information.* **2** (*attrib*) trusted to keep secrets: *a confidential secretary.* **confidentiality** ['konfidenʃi'aləti] *nu.*

ˌ**confi'dentially** *adv* secretly; not wishing to have the information passed on to anyone else: *Confidentially, I think he will get the job*; *She could not tell me what he said – he was speaking confidentially.*

con'fiding *adj* trustful or unsuspicious: *She is bound to get hurt – she is too confiding*; *her confiding nature.* **con'fidingly** *adv.*

'**confidence trick** (*abbrev* '**con-trick**) *nc* (*Amer* '**confidence game**) the trick of a swindler who first gains a person's trust and then persuades him to hand over money: *He plays confidence tricks on rich old ladies.* – *See also* **con.**

in 'confidence as a secret; confidentially: *He told me the story in (strictest) confidence.*

take (someone) into one's confidence to tell one's private thoughts, plans, secrets *etc* to someone: *He decided to take her into his confidence.*

vote of confidence *see* **vote.**

confine [kən'fain] *vt* **1** to limit or keep (something) within limits; to stop from spreading *etc* too far: *They succeeded in confining the fire to a small area*; *Confine your attention to your own affairs*; *The politician confined his remarks to matters of local interest.* **2** to shut up or imprison: *The prince was confined in the castle for three years.*

con'fined *adj* **1** (*pred*: *formal*: *with* **to**) kept in or shut up in: *confined to bed with a cold*; *confined to barracks.* **2** (*pred*: *old*) (of a woman) being in bed for the birth of a child. **3** having limits: *a confined space*; *This space is too confined.*

con'finement (*formal*) **1** *nu* state of being shut up or imprisoned: *He was sentenced to two years' solitary confinement.* **2** *ncu* (the time of) the birth of a child: *This was her third confinement*; *Was there a doctor present at the confinement?*

'**confines** ['kon-] *n pl* (*formal*) limits or boundaries: *within the confines of the city*; (*fig*) *She did as much as she could within the confines of her income.*

confirm [kən'fəːm] *vt* **1** to establish or make (something) quite certain by repeating it in writing *etc*: *This letter is to confirm your appointment*; *They confirmed their hotel booking by phone.* **2** to make (a person) more firm (*eg* in a belief, an attitude *etc*): *Her remarks confirmed (me in) my opinion that she was a very rude young lady.* **3** to admit to full membership of certain Christian churches: *She goes to church every Sunday but she has not yet been confirmed.* ˌ**confir'mation** [kon-] *nu.*

con'firmed *adj* **1** (*attrib*) settled in a habit or way of life: *a confirmed bachelor/drunkard.* **2** shown to be true: *There have been no confirmed reports of the incident.*

confiscate ['konfiskeit] *vt* to seize or take (something) away, *esp* when one has the authority to do so, *usu* as a punishment or penalty: *The teacher confiscated the boy's comic which he had been reading during the history lesson.* ˌ**confi'scation** *nu.*

conflagration [konflə'greiʃən] *nc* (*very formal*) a great fire: *Ten people perished in the conflagration.*

conflict ['konflikt] **1** *ncu* (*formal*) (a) disagreement; (a) quarrel: *There was considerable conflict about which plan should be accepted*; *The two sides have been in conflict for years*; *The conflict between the two politicians took place in public.* **2** *nc* (*formal* or *liter*) a struggle or contest; a fight: *After the conflict there were many dead on both sides.* – [kən'flikt] *vi* to contradict each other; to disagree: *The two accounts of what had happened conflicted (with each other).*

con'flicting *adj* opposing; not in agreement: *The two brothers had conflicting political views*; *They gave conflicting accounts of what had happened.*

confluence ['konfluəns] *ncu* (*very formal*) a flowing together or the meeting-place of two rivers. '**confluent** *adj.*

conform [kən'foːm] *vi* **1** to behave, dress, worship *etc* in the way that most other people do: *If you are to be accepted as a member of the club you must conform.* **2** (*with* **to**) to act according to; to be in agreement with: *You must conform to the rules*; *He eventually conformed to the standards of society.* **3** (*formal*: *with* **to**) to be similar (in style, character *etc*): *The two scientists stopped working together because their theories did not conform.*

con'formist, con'former *ncs* a person who conforms, *esp* to the worship of the established church. **con'formist** *adj.*

con'formity *nu* **1** (*formal*) behaviour *etc* which is the same as most people's: *Young people today do not care so much about conformity – they do what they like.* **2** (*with* **with**) obedience (to), agreement (with): *in conformity with her wishes.*

See also **non-conformist.**

confound [kən'faund] *vt* (*formal*) **1** to puzzle and surprise greatly: *Her attitude completely confounded me.* **2** (*old*) to defeat (one's enemies *etc*).

con'founded *adj* (*inf*: *attrib*) damned; very annoying: *Where is that confounded man?*

con'found it! *interj* damn!

confront [kən'frʌnt] *vt* (*formal*) **1** to bring (a person) face to face with (accusers, evidence, something unpleasant *etc*): *I'll confront him with the evidence*; *I've just been confronted with a new problem.* **2** to face in a hostile manner; to oppose: *They confronted the enemy at dawn.* ˌ**confron'tation** [kon-] *ncu.*

confuse [kən'fjuːz] *vt* **1** to put in disorder; to mix up: *He confused the arrangements by arriving late*; *He confused the issue with unnecessary details.* **2** to fail to realize the difference between; to mix up in one's mind: *I always confuse John and his twin brother.* **3** to make puzzled or mixed up (in the mind): *He completely confused me by his questions.*

con'fused *adj* **1** (*often formal*) in disorder; mixed up: *a confused mass of information*; *The message I received was rather confused.* **2** mixed up in the mind; not able to think clearly: *in a confused state of mind*; *Since her fall, the old lady has been very confused.* **con'fusedly** [-zidli] *adv.*

con'fusion [-ʒən] *nu* **1** disorder: *The books lay about in confusion.* **2** mixing up: *He apologized for his confusion of their names.* **3** puzzlement or bewilderment: *The old man looked in confusion at his new surroundings.* **4** embarrassment: *When she realized her mistake, she was covered in confusion.*

congeal [kən'dʒiːl] *vti* (*esp* of blood, grease *etc*) to solidify when cooled: *The fat congealed on the cold plates.*

congenial [kən'dʒiːniəl] *adj* (*formal*) **1** (of people) having the same tastes, interests *etc*: *Our neighbours are very congenial*; *very congenial people.* **2**

(of things) pleasant, suited to one's taste *etc*: *a congenial task*; *congenial company*. **con,geni'ality** [-ni'a-] *nu*.

congenital [kən'dʒenitl] *adj* (*tech*) of diseases or deformities existing at or before birth: *congenital paralysis*; *The child's brain disorder was congenital.* **con'genitally** *adv*.

congested [kən'dʒestid] *adj* **1** (*formal*) overcrowded: *The shopping precinct is always congested on Saturday mornings.* **2** (*tech*) (of a part of the body) too full of blood: *congested lungs.*

con'gestion [-tʃən] *nu* **1** (*formal*) overcrowding (*eg* of traffic in a street). **2** (*tech*) a gathering of too much blood in a part of the body: *She suffers from congestion of the lungs.*

conglomerate [kən'glomərət] *nc* **1** (*very formal*) a mass formed from parts of different kinds: *The house was a conglomerate of architectural styles*; (*geol*) *This rock is a conglomerate*; (*attrib*) *a conglomerate rock.* **2** a business group formed of firms of different kinds.

con,glome'ration *nc* (*sometimes facet*) a collection (of things of mixed kinds): *What a conglomeration of old clothes!*

congratulate [kən'gratjuleit] *vt* (*often with* **on**) to express pleasure and joy to (a person) at a happy event, a success he has had *etc*: *Did you win a prize? Let me be the first to congratulate you*; *She congratulated him on passing his driving test*; *He congratulated himself on his escape.*

con,gratu'lation *ncu* (*usu in pl*): *Congratulations on the birth of your baby*; *I send you my warmest congratulations*; *a message of congratulation.*

con'gratulatory [-lə-] *adj* (*very formal*): *a congratulatory telegram.*

congregate ['koŋgrigeit] *vti* to come or bring together: *A large crowd congregated in the street.*

,congre'gation **1** *nc* a group gathered together, *esp* people in a church for a service, or belonging to a church: *The minister visited all the members of his congregation.* **2** *nu* (*formal*) a gathering together of people.

congress ['koŋgres, (*Amer*) -gris] **1** *nc* (*sometimes with cap*) a formal meeting, *esp* an assembly of diplomats or delegates *etc*: *the third World Congress of Botanists.* **2** a law-making body or parliament, *esp* (*with cap*) that of the United States: *He has been elected to Congress.* **con'gressional** [-ʃənl] *adj*. **'congressman, 'congresswoman** *ncs*.

congruent ['koŋgruənt] *adj* (*geom*) of two or more figures, touching at all points when one is fitted on top of the other: *These triangles are congruent.* **con'gruity** [-'gru:-] *nu*.

conical *see* **cone**.

conifer ['konifə, (*Amer*) 'kou-] *nc* (*tech*) a cone-bearing tree, *eg* the fir: *The larch tree is a conifer.* **co'niferous** *adj* (*tech*) cone-bearing. – *See also* **deciduous**.

conjecture [kən'dʒektʃə] *ncu* (*formal*) (an) opinion formed on slight evidence; a guess or guessing: *He made several conjectures about where his son might be*; *I could be wrong – that's pure conjecture.* – *vt* (*formal*) to form an opinion on slight evidence; to guess. **con'jectural** *adj*.

conjugal ['kondʒugəl] *adj* (*formal*) of marriage and married life: *conjugal rights*; *conjugal bliss.*

conjugate ['kondʒugeit] *vt* (*gram*) to give the different parts of (a verb).

,conju'gation (*gram*) **1** *nc* a group of verbs which follow the same grammatical pattern when indicating tense, number *etc*. **2** *nu* (the act of giving) the various forms of a certain verb.

See also **declension, decline**.

conjunction [kən'dʒʌŋkʃən] *nc* (*gram*) a word that connects sentences, clauses or words: *John sang and Mary danced*; *I'll do it if you want.*

in con'junction (with) (*formal*) (acting) together (with): *They work in conjunction with two other groups*; *These groups always work in conjunction.*

conjure ['kʌndʒə, (*Amer*) 'kon-] *vi* to perform tricks (**'conjuring tricks**) that seem magical, *esp* as an entertainment. **'conjuror, 'conjurer** *ncs*.

conjure up *vt sep* (*formal*) **1** to bring up in the mind (a picture *etc*): *His description of the holiday conjured up a picture of long, hot days by the sea.* **2** (*formal*) to make appear (as if) from nothing (*esp* the spirits of dead people, devils *etc*): *He conjured up the spirit of her dead mother*; (*facet*) *When we arrived unexpectedly she conjured up a meal from some vegetables and a piece of ham.*

conker ['koŋkə] *nc* (*inf*) a horse-chestnut.

'conkers *n sing* (*Brit*) a game played by children in which a chestnut on a string is used to destroy, if not first destroyed by, one's opponent's chestnut on a string.

connect [kə'nekt] **1** *vti* to join or be joined in some way; to tie or fasten or link together: *He connected the radio to the mains*; *This road connects the two farms*; (*fig*) *He is connected with royalty*; (*fig*) *This telephone line connects with the President.* **2** *vt* to associate in the mind: *I'd never have connected you with the George Parsons I used to know.*

con'nection [-ʃən] **1** *nc* something that connects or is connected: *The connection to the lamp is faulty.* **2** *ncu* (a) state of being connected or related: *His connection with the family is very slight*; *family connections*; *My journey to London is in connection with my work*; *I wish to talk to you in connection with my daughter's career.* **3** *nc* a useful person whom one can contact, *esp* in business: *He has a lot of connections in the clothing trade.* **4** *nc* a train, bus *etc* on to which one changes from another in the course of a journey: *As the local train was late, I missed the connection to London.*

con'nective [-tiv] *adj* (*tech*) joining: *connective tissue in the body.*

in con'nection with (*formal*) about; concerning: *The police are making inquiries in connection with a bank-robbery.*

in this connection when we are considering this matter.

connive [kə'naiv] *vi* (*formal derog*: *with* **at**) to make no attempt to hinder (something wrong or illegal): *Her mother connived at the child's truancy*; *He connived at the attack on the security guard.*

con'nivance *nu* (*formal*): *The crime was committed with the connivance of his parents.*

connoisseur [konə'sə:] *nc* an expert judge (of the finer things of life, *eg* art, music, wine *etc*): *Let him choose the wine – he's the connoisseur*; *a connoisseur of beauty.*

connotation [konə'teiʃən] *nc* (*formal*) what is suggested by a word in addition to its simple meaning: *The word 'intercourse' has come to have strong sexual connotations.*

conquer ['koŋkə] *vti* (*more formal than* **defeat**) to overcome or defeat: *The Normans conquered England in the eleventh century*; *You must conquer your fear of the dark*; *They vowed to fight and to conquer.* **'conqueror** *nc*.

conquest ['koŋkwest] **1** *ncu* (an) act of conquering: *The Norman Conquest of England*; (*facet*) *He's very impressed with you – you've made quite a conquest there.* **2** *nc* something won by force or effort, *esp* (*facet*) a person's (current) lover: *Her new boyfriend is quite a conquest – he's both rich and handsome.*

conscience ['konʃəns] *ncu* (that part of one's mind which holds one's) knowledge or sense of right and wrong: *The injured man was on her conscience* (= She felt guilty about him) *because she was responsible for the accident*; *She had a bad conscience* (= She felt guilty) *about the injured man*; *He had no conscience* (= He did not feel guilty) *about dismissing the men.*

in all conscience (*formal*) being fair and reasonable: *In all conscience, I can't bring myself to do it.*

conscientious [konʃi'enʃəs] *adj* **1** careful and hard-working: *She is very conscientious*; *a conscientious pupil.* **2** (*formal*) guided by conscience: *a conscientious objector.* **ˌconsci'entiousness** *nu.* **ˌconsci'entiously** *adv*: *She always works conscientiously.*

conscientious objector *nc* a person who objects on grounds of conscience, *esp* to military service.

conscious ['konʃəs] *adj* **1** aware of oneself and one's surroundings; not asleep or in a coma or under the influence of drugs *etc*: *The patient was conscious*; *in a conscious state.* **2** (*pred*: *sometimes with* **of**) aware or having knowledge (of): *He was conscious that they disapproved*; *They were conscious of his disapproval.* **3** (*attrib*) deliberate or intentional: *He made a conscious effort to please.* **'consciously** *adv.*

'consciousness *nu* **1** the state of being conscious: *The patient soon regained consciousness.* **2** (*formal*) awareness (of *eg* what one is doing); feelings, thoughts *etc*: *His consciousness of the urgency of the situation encouraged him to hurry*; *He has reached political consciousness.*

conscript ['konskript] *nc* a person legally ordered by the state to serve in the armed forces *etc*: *He is a conscript – not an army volunteer.* – [kən'skript] *vt* legally to order (someone) to serve in the armed forces *etc*: *He was conscripted into the army.*

con'scription [-ʃən] *nu* the act or system of conscripting: *Conscription has been abolished in many countries.*

consecrate ['konsikreit] *vt* **1** (*relig*) to set apart for a holy use; to make sacred: *The bishop consecrated the new church.* **2** (*formal*) to devote or dedicate: *He consecrated himself to the cause of peace.*

ˌconse'cration *ncu* (*relig*): *the consecration of the new church.*

consecutive [kən'sekjutiv] *adj* following one after the other in regular order: *He visited us on two consecutive days, Thursday and Friday*; *These two pages are consecutive.* **con'secutively** *adv.*

consensus [kən'sensəs] *nc* (*formal*: *pl rare*) **1** (*with* **the**) the general feeling or trend: *The consensus of opinion is that we should do this.* **2** (*with* **a**) an agreement: *Can we stop arguing and reach a consensus?*

consent [kən'sent] *vi* (*formal*) to give permission or agree (to): *I refuse to consent to that plan*; *He refused to consent to my going abroad.* – *nu* agreement; permission: *You have my consent to sell the shares.*

age of consent (*formal or legal*) the age which a girl must be before a boy or man may legally have sexual intercourse with her: *If you have sexual intercourse with a girl before she reaches the age of consent you can be prosecuted.*

consequence ['konsikwəns, (*Amer*) -kwens] **1** *nc* (*more formal than* **result**) (*usu in pl*) a result: *This decision will have important consequences*; *One consequence of the stormy meeting was the resignation of the chairman.* **2** *nu* (*formal*) importance: *A small error is of no consequence.* **3** *nu* (*old*) social status: *He's a man of consequence.*

'consequent *adj* (*with* **on** *or* **upon**: *very formal*) following, *esp* as a natural result: *There will be a general election consequent upon the defeat of the government.*

'consequently *adv* (*formal*) so; therefore: *She didn't explain it clearly – consequently, he didn't understand.*

ˌconse'quential [-'kwen-] *adj* (*formal*) **1** important; (of people) self-important. **2** following as a result.

See also **inconsequential**.

conservatism, conservative *see* **conserve**.

conservatory [kən'sə:vətri, (*Amer*) -to:ri] *nc* **1** a (*usu* heated) kind of greenhouse, or a glass-walled part of a building, in which plants are grown: *We sit in the conservatory on summer evenings.* **2** a school of music, art *etc.*

conserve [kən'sə:v] *vt* (*slightly formal*) to keep from changing, being damaged or lost: *We must conserve the country's natural resources*; *We must conserve the character of old buildings*; *Conserve your energy – you'll need it for climbing the hill tomorrow.* – *nc* (*formal*) something preserved, *eg* fruits in sugar, jam *etc.*

con'servancy **1** *nc* a group or organization who control a port, river, or protect trees, wildlife *etc*: *the Nature Conservancy.* **2** *nu* (*formal*) the act or policy of conserving.

ˌconser'vation [kon-] *nu* the act of conserving *esp* wildlife, the countryside, the environment, old buildings *etc.*

ˌconser'vationist [kon-] *nc* a person who is interested in conservation: *The conservationists are going to try to prevent the town council from pulling down those old buildings.*

con'servatism [-vətizəm] *nu* dislike of (*esp* sudden or extreme) change.

con'servative [-tiv] *adj* **1** disliking change: *Older people tend to be conservative in their attitudes*; *conservative opinions.* **2** (*usu attrib*) moderate or understated: *£100 is a conservative estimate for the repair of your car.* **3** (*with cap*) of the Conservative Party: *a Conservative politician.* – *nc* (*with cap*) a person belonging to the **Conservative Party**, one of the main political parties in the UK.

consider [kən'sidə] **1** *vt* to think about (carefully): *He considered our comments carefully*; *We're considering going.* **2** *vi* (*formal*) to think: *Consider carefully before doing anything.* **3** *vt* to take into account; to make allowance for: *You must consider other people's feelings/points of view.* **4** *vt* (*formal*: not used with **is, was** *etc* and **-ing**) to regard as being: *I consider you very foolish*; *They consider him unfit for that job.*

con'siderable *adj* fairly large in number; great in quantity or importance: *a man of considerable wealth/influence*; *a considerable number of people*; *The increase has been considerable.*

con'siderably *adv*: *Considerably fewer people came than I expected.*

See also **inconsiderable**.

considerate [kən'sidərət] *adj* thoughtful about

others: *He is always considerate to elderly people; considerate behaviour.*

con,side'ration 1 *nu* (the act of) thinking about something, *esp* the needs or feelings of other people: *He stayed at home out of consideration for his mother.* – *See also* **take into consideration**. 2 *nc* a fact to be taken into account in making a decision *etc*: *The cost of the journey is our main consideration.* 3 *nc* (*euph*) a payment or reward: *I'll do what you ask for a small consideration.*

con'sidering *prep* taking into account; despite: *Considering his deafness he manages to understand very well; Considering that she is supposed to be ill, she looks quite healthy.*

take into consideration to allow for (in considering a situation or problem): *You must take his illness into consideration before dismissing him.*

See also **inconsiderate**.

consign [kən'sain] *vt* (*formal*) 1 (*sometimes facet*) to put into or deliver to: *The body was consigned with reverence to the grave; Consign this to the fire!* 2 to send (goods) by rail *etc*.

con'signment 1 *nc* a load (of goods): *the latest consignment of books.* 2 *nu* (*formal*) the act of consigning: *the consignment of the body to the grave.*

consist [kən'sist] *vi* (*with* **of**: not used with **is, was** *etc* and **-ing**) to be composed or made up: *The house consists of six rooms.*

con'sistency[1] *nu* the degree of thickness or firmness: *the consistency of treacle; of the consistency of dough.* – *See also* **consistent**.

consistent [kən'sistənt] *adj* (*formal*) 1 (*pred*: *often with* **with**) not contradictory; in agreement (with): *The two statements are not consistent; The second statement is not consistent with the first.* 2 always (acting, thinking or happening) according to the same rules or principles; the same or regular: *He was consistent in his attitudes; He has a consistent style of writing.*

con'sistency[2] *nu* (*formal*) the state of being consistent: *You have to admire the consistency of his work.* – *See also* **consist**.

con'sistently *adv* (*formal*) regularly or habitually: *He is consistently late for appointments; His work is consistently good.*

See also **inconsistent**.

console[1] [kən'soul] *vt* (*more formal than* **comfort**) to give comfort to; to lessen the grief or disappointment of: *She could not console the weeping child; (facet) Console yourself with the thought that you don't have to work tomorrow.*

,conso'lation [kon-] 1 *nu* the act of consoling. 2 *nc* something or someone that consoles: *His great wealth was no consolation for the loss of his reputation; (attrib) a consolation prize* (= a prize for someone who just failed to win).

console[2] ['konsoul] *nc* 1 (*music*) the part of an organ containing the keyboards, pedals *etc*. 2 (*tech*) a panel with dials, switches *etc* on an electronic machine *etc*.

consolidate [kən'solideit] *vti* (*formal*) 1 to make or become solid; to strengthen: *You must consolidate your present position before taking on more work; The business is consolidating nicely.* 2 to unite or combine: *They consolidated four small firms into one large one.* **con,soli'dation** *ncu*.

consonant ['konsənənt] *nc* (*gram*) 1 any letter of the alphabet except *a, e, i, o, u*. 2 any of the sounds represented by the letters of the alphabet excluding *a, e, i, o, u*, and also *y* as in *my*.

'consonant with (*very formal*) in agreement with: *His behaviour is not consonant with his government's policy.*

consort ['konso:t] *nc* (*formal*) 1 a (*usu* royal) wife or husband: *prince/king consort* (= the husband of a reigning queen); *queen consort* (= the wife of a reigning king). 2 an accompanying ship: *a naval consort.* – [kən'so:t] *vi* (*formal*: *with* **with**) to have dealings or associations (with, *usu* in a bad sense): *He's been consorting with thieves for some time.*

consortium [kən'so:tiəm, (*Amer*) -ʃiəm] *nc* (*formal*) an association, union, *esp* of bankers or businessmen: *a consortium of merchant bankers.*

conspicuous [kən'spikjuəs] *adj* (*usu pred*) catching the attention; very noticeable: *Her red hat was very conspicuous in church; She always makes herself conspicuous by wearing very colourful clothes; (facet) He was conspicuous by his absence* (= It was noticeable that he was not present).

con'spicuously *adv.* **con'spicuousness** *nu*.

See also **inconspicuous**.

conspire [kən'spaiə] *vi* (*formal*) 1 to plot or secretly make plans together: *They conspired with the terrorists to overthrow the government.* 2 (of *eg* events) to work together (to bring about a result): *Events conspired to make him a rich man.*

con'spiracy [-'spi-] *ncu* (a plan made by) conspiring: *The government discovered the conspiracy in time; They were arrested for conspiracy.*

con'spirator [-'spi-] *nc* a person who conspires: *The conspirators met secretly under the bridge.*

constable ['kʌnstəbl, (*Amer*) 'kon-] *nc* 1 (*Brit*: *with cap in titles*) a policeman, *esp* one not of high rank: *He has been promoted from constable to sergeant; If you've been robbed tell that police constable over there; Constable Hunter.* 2 (*hist*) the chief officer of a king's household. 3 (*hist*) the keeper of a royal castle.

con'stabulary [-'stabju-] *nc* a police force.

constant ['konstənt] *adj* 1 (*usu attrib*) never stopping; ceaseless: *There's a constant noise in this place!* 2 unchanging: *The force of gravity is constant at ground level; It must be kept at a constant temperature.* 3 (*liter*) faithful: *a constant friend; He alone remained constant.*

'constancy *nu* (*formal*) 1 the state of being unchanging: *Constancy of temperature is essential for newborn babies.* 2 faithfulness: *He was amazed at her constancy in spite of his long absence.*

'constantly *adv* 1 (*inf*) very often; frequently: *I'm constantly telling him to behave himself.* 2 always; without stopping: *The light in the lighthouse has to be kept burning constantly.*

See also **inconstant**.

constellation [konstə'leiʃən] *nc* a named group of stars: *The Plough and Orion are constellations.*

consternation [konstə'neiʃən] *nu* (*formal*) astonishment or dismay: *She stared at the policeman in consternation; She was filled with consternation at the news; To my consternation, when I reached home I found I had lost the key of the house.*

constipated ['konstipeitid] *adj* (*usu pred*) having difficulty in passing waste matter (as regularly as normal) from the bowels: *The child is a bit constipated this morning.*

,consti'pation *nu*: *She suffers from constipation.*

constituent [kən'stitjuənt] *nc* 1 (*formal*) a necessary part: *Hydrogen is a constituent of water.* 2 a voter from a particular MP's constituency: *He deals with all his constituents' problems.* – *adj* (*attrib*) helping to make up: *He broke it down into its constituent parts.*

con'stituency *nc* the group of voters, or the area in which they live, represented by a member of parliament: *His constituency covers a large part of Edinburgh.*

constitute ['konstitju:t] *vt* (*formal*: not used with **is, was** *etc* and **-ing**) to form; to make up; to be: *Eighty years constitute a longer-than-average lifetime*; *This disease constitutes a serious risk to life.*

ˌconsti'tution 1 *nc* a set of rules governing an organization; the supreme laws and rights of a country's people *etc*: *The Constitution of the United States was written in 1787.* 2 *nc* the way in which something is formed or made up; physical characteristics, health *etc*: *He has a strong constitution* (= He is very healthy). 3 *nu* (*formal*) the act of forming or constituting: *He was responsible for the constitution of a new committee.*

ˌconsti'tutional *adj* 1 legal according to a given constitution: *It was pointed out that the proposed solution would not be constitutional*; *constitutional matters.* 2 (*usu attrib*: *formal*) of health or a person's constitution: *He suffers from a constitutional weakness of the chest.* 3 (*usu attrib*) controlled by the law of the land: *a constitutional monarch.* – *nc* (*old or facet*) a walk for the good of one's health.

ˌconsti'tutionally *adv.*

constrain [kən'strein] *vt* (*formal*: *usu in passive*) to force (a person to do something): *You must not feel constrained to go.* **con'strained** *adj.*

con'straint *nu* (*formal*) compulsion: *He agreed to go only under constraint.*

constrict [kən'strikt] *vt* (*formal*) to press together tightly; to make narrow: *He felt as though the tight collar was constricting his neck*; (*fig*) *He felt constricted by the constant presence of his superiors.*

construct [kən'strʌkt] *vt* (*more formal than* **build**) to build; to put together: *They are planning to construct a new supermarket near our house*; *Constructing a bridge over that wide river will need careful planning*; *He is good at constructing theories but not good at putting them into practice*; *She is incapable of constructing a grammatical sentence*; (*geom*) *Construct* (= Draw) *a triangle inside the circle.*

con'struction [-ʃən] 1 *nu* (*formal*) (a way of) constructing or putting together: *The construction of that factory will take several months*; *The bridge is still under construction* (= still being built); *He knows a lot of English vocabulary but finds the construction of sentences difficult.* 2 *nc* something built, put together *etc*: *That construction won't last long.* 3 *nc* (*formal*) meaning: *She always puts a wrong construction on what I say.*

con'structional *adj* (*formal*): *constructional methods*; *constructional toys.*

con'structive [-tiv] *adj* (*formal*) helpful; having to do with making, not with destroying: *Constructive criticism tells you both what is wrong and also what to do about it.* **con'structively** *adv.*

con'structor *nc* (*formal*) a person who constructs: *a constructor of bridges.*

construe [kən'stru:] *vt* (*formal*: *often in passive*) to interpret or explain: *My silence was construed as* (*meaning*) *approval.*

consul ['konsəl] *nc* an agent who looks after his country's residents in (part of) a foreign country: *the British Consul in Berlin.* 2 (*hist*) either of the two chief magistrates in ancient Rome. **'consular** [-sju-] *adj.*

consulate ['konsjulət, (*Amer*) -sələt] *nc* the office or residence of a consul (*def 1*).

consult [kən'sʌlt] 1 *vt* to ask for advice or information from: *You should consult your lawyer*; *Consult your doctor*; *Consult the map*; *He consulted his watch*; (*formal*) *He consulted with me about what we should do next.* 2 *vi* (of a doctor *etc*) to give professional advice: *He consults on Mondays and Fridays.*

con'sultant *nc* 1 a person who gives professional advice: *He is a management consultant*; *He is consultant to a firm of engineers*; (*attrib*) *a consultant engineer.* 2 (*Brit*) a senior hospital doctor specializing in a particular branch of medicine: *His condition is so serious that they have sent for the consultant*; (*attrib*) *a consultant physician.*

ˌconsul'tation [kon-] *ncu*: *How much does he charge for a consultation?*

con'sultative [-tiv] *adj* (*formal*) (of a committee *etc*) set up to provide consultation only: *He was a member of the local amenities consultative committee*; *His position in the firm is purely consultative.*

consume [kən'sju:m] *vt* (*formal*) 1 to eat or drink: *The average person consumes many kilos of food per week*; *He consumes a huge amount of alcohol.* 2 to use: *How much electricity do you consume?*; *We consume less energy than before.* 3 (*esp fig*) to destroy, *eg* by fire: *He was consumed with jealousy*; *The entire building was consumed by fire.*

con'sumer *nc* a person who eats, uses, buys things *etc*: *The average consumer spends £x per year on toothpaste*; *The consumer must be protected against the sale of poor-quality goods*; (*attrib*) *consumer protection.*

con'suming *adj* (*attrib except in cmpds*) taking up or using a great deal of (time, energy, interest *etc*): *His consuming interest in life was his garden*; *His interest in gardening is all-consuming*; *a time-consuming process.*

consumption [kən'sʌmpʃən] *nu* 1 (*formal*) the act of consuming: *The consumption of coffee has increased.* 2 (*formal*) the amount consumed: *Last year's consumption was 3000 tonnes.* 3 (*old*) tuberculosis of the lungs.

consumptive [kən'sʌmptiv] *nc, adj* (*old*) (a person) suffering from consumption.

con'sumer goods *n pl* goods which can be used immediately to satisfy human needs, *eg* clothing, food, TV sets *etc*, not machines for manufacturing things.

consummate ['konsəmeit] *vt* (*formal*) to complete (*esp* a marriage by sexual intercourse between the husband and wife): *She obtained a divorce on the grounds that the marriage had never been consummated.* – [-mət] *adj* (*attrib*: *formal*) complete; perfect: *We did it with consummate ease.*

ˌconsum'mation *ncu* (*formal*) (an) act of consummating.

consumption *etc see* **consume**.

contact ['kontakt] 1 *nu* physical touch or nearness: *Her hands came into contact with acid*; *This child has spots. Has she been in contact with measles?*; *We don't come into contact with many foreigners here.* – *See* **come, get in(to) contact (with)**. 2 *nu* communication; the sharing or exchanging of news, information *etc*: *Do you keep in contact with your old schoolfriends?*; *I've lost contact with all my old friends*; *We have succeeded in making* (*radio*) *contact with the ship*; *How can I get in contact with him?* **3** *nc* a person with influence, knowledge *etc* which might be useful: *I made several good contacts in London.* **4** *nc* (a place where) a wire *etc* carrying electric current (may be attached): *Clean the contacts on the car's battery.* **5** *nc* a person who has been near someone with an infectious disease: *We must trace all known contacts of the cholera victim.* **6** *nc* a person or thing that provides a means of communicating with someone: *His radio is his only contact with the outside world*; *When I was ill she was my sole contact with life outside the hospital.* – *vt* (*formal*) to communicate; to get in touch with in order to give or share information *etc*: *I'll contact you by telephone*; *Have you contacted the relatives of the dead man?*

contact lens *nc* a small plastic lens on the eyeball worn, instead of spectacles, to improve sight.

come, get in(to) contact (with) *vti* (*formal*) **1** to touch (physically): *The crane came into contact with the overhead electric cable.* **2** (of people) to meet or communicate with: *I got in contact with him about the new arrangements.*

contagious [kənˈteidʒəs] *adj* (*tech*) spreading from one person to another by physical contact: *Is that skin disease contagious?*; *a contagious disease*; (*fig*) *Excitement is contagious.*

conˈtagion *nu* (*very formal*): *The contagion is spreading.*

contain [kənˈtein] *vt* (not used with **is, was** *etc* and **-ing** (*defs 1, 3*)) **1** to keep or have inside: *All his possessions are contained in that box*; *This box contains a pair of shoes*; *How much wine does a magnum contain?* **2** (*formal*) to control: *He could hardly contain his excitement*; *They have succeeded in containing the epidemic.* **3** (*formal*) to enclose; to form the boundary of: *an angle contained by two lines.*

conˈtainer *nc* **1** something made to contain things: *You can buy special containers for storing food in a freezer*; *They bring the food for school lunches in large containers.* **2** a very large sealed metal box for carrying freight or goods on a lorry, ship *etc*: *The ship carried twenty containers*; *We are sending the books by special container*; (*attrib*) *a container ship*; (*attrib*) *a container lorry.*

conˈtainerize, -ise *vt* (*formal*) to put (*esp* freight) into containers.

contaminate [kənˈtamineit] *vt* to make impure, diseased *etc*: *The cook has typhoid – she will have contaminated the food*; *The town's water-supply has been contaminated by chemicals from the factory*; (*fig*) *Her attitude to life has been contaminated by the wicked people she associates with*; (*facet*) *Don't contaminate whisky with water!* **conˌtamiˈnation** *nu.*

contemplate [ˈkontəmpleit] *vt* **1** to think seriously (about): *I was contemplating having a holiday*; *She contemplated her future gloomily.* **2** (*liter*) to look thoughtfully at: *When I contemplate the sea I feel calm.* **ˌcontemˈplation** *nu.*

contemplative [kənˈtemplətiv, (*Amer*) ˈkontəmpleitiv] *adj* (*usu attrib*): *in contemplative mood.* **conˈtemplatively** *adv.*

contemporary [kənˈtempərəri] *adj* **1** living at, happening at or belonging to the same period: *That chair and the painting are contemporary – they both date from the seventeenth century*; *Marlowe was contemporary with Shakespeare.* **2** of the present time; modern: *I much prefer the paintings of the sixteenth and seventeenth centuries to contemporary painting*; *The old lady detests the contemporary fashion for casual clothes.* – *nc* a person living at the same time: *Shakespeare's contemporaries include Marlowe and Jonson*; *She was one of my contemporaries at university.*

contempt [kənˈtempt] *nu* **1** lack of respect; very low opinion: *She spoke with utter contempt (of the people around her)*; (*formal*) *He holds them in contempt.* **2** (*legal*) disregard (*esp* for the rules of a court of law): *He was charged with contempt (of court) after disobeying the court's rules.*

conˈtemptible *adj* deserving contempt: *His behaviour was contemptible*; *a contemptible liar.* **conˈtemptibly** *adv.*

conˈtemptuous [-tʃuəs] *adj* (*usu attrib*) showing contempt: *She gave a contemptuous sneer.* **conˈtemptuously** *adv.*

contend [kənˈtend] (*formal*) **1** *vi* (*usu with* **with**) to struggle (against): *He's contending with problems of all kinds.* **2** *vt* (*with* **that**) to say or maintain (that): *He contends that your plan is still faulty.*

conˈtender *nc* a person who has entered a competition (for a title *etc*): *He's the new contender for the heavy-weight boxing championships*; (*fig*) *He's one of the contenders for the chairmanship.*

conˈtention (*formal*) **1** *nc* an opinion supported in debate: *My contention is that we should have done something before now.* **2** *nu* argument or debate: *There's great contention in the town over the idea of a new motorway.*

conˈtentious [-ʃəs] *adj* (*very formal*) **1** (*usu attrib*) likely to cause argument or quarrelling: *That was a contentious decision by the government.* **2** quarrelsome: *They are a very contentious couple – they are always arguing*; *Try to be less contentious.*

content[1] [kənˈtent] *adj* (*pred*) satisfied; quietly happy: *I am very content with my life at present*; *He doesn't want more money – he's content with what he has*; *She's quite content to sit and read a book.* – *nu* the state of being satisfied or quietly happy: *She smiled with content*; *You're on holiday – you can lie in the sun to your heart's content* (= as long as you want). – *vt* to satisfy: *As the TV's broken, you'll have to content yourself with listening to the radio*; *That baby will not be contented until he gets enough milk.*

conˈtented *adj* satisfied; quietly happy: *a contented cow/sigh*; *She looks very contented now.* **conˈtentedly** *adv.* **conˈtentment** *nu.*

See also **discontent**.

content[2] [ˈkontent] *nu* (*formal*) **1** the subject-matter (of a book, speech etc): *The content of his speech was interesting but he spoke uninterestingly.* **2** the amount or proportion of something which is contained in (another thing): *What is the carbon content of this substance?*; *Oranges have a high vitamin C content.*

ˈcontents *n pl* **1** the things contained in something: *the contents of a box*; *He drank the contents of the bottle thinking it was lemonade.* **2** a list of the things contained *esp* in a book: *Look up the contents at the beginning of the book.*

contention, contentious *see* **contend**.

contest [ˈkontest] *nc* a struggle, competition *etc* to gain an advantage or victory: *a sporting contest.* – [kənˈtest] *vt* **1** to try to win, *esp* in (political) competition: *He's contesting the election next week*; *He's contesting the seat for the first time.* **2** (*formal*) to argue over; to dispute: *He's contesting your ability to complete the book.*

conˈtestant *nc* a person who takes part in a

contest: *He is the youngest contestant in the swimming competition.*

context ['kontekst] *nu* the parts directly before or after a word or phrase (written or spoken) which affect its meaning: *This statement, taken out of its context, gives a wrong impression of the speaker's opinions; That speech is from 'Hamlet' but I do not know the exact context; (fig) We must look at this incident in the broader context of the whole war.*

continence *see* **continent**[2].

continent[1] ['kontinənt] *nc* **1** one of the great divisions of the land surface of the world – Europe, America, Australia, Asia or Africa. **2** (*Brit*: *with* **the**) Europe excluding Britain: *We are going to the continent for our holidays.*

ˌconti'nental [-'nen-] *adj* **1** (*Brit*) (typical) of the mainland of the continent of Europe: *After spending a year in Paris she became quite continental in her outlook; continental food; a continental holiday.* **2** of a continent or the continents: *Continental drift is the measure of how the continents move.* – *nc* (*Brit*) an inhabitant of the continent of Europe: *He is a true continental.*

continental breakfast a light breakfast of rolls and coffee.

continental quilt *see* **duvet**.

continent[2] ['kontinənt] *adj* (*tech*: *usu pred*) able to control *esp* the bladder and/or bowel: *The old lady is no longer continent.* '**continence** *nu.*

See also **incontinent**.

contingent [kən'tindʒənt] *adj* (*pred*: *very formal*) of a happening *etc*, dependent (on some other happening or circumstances): *Our ability to go is contingent on our fare being paid by the company.* – *nc* a number or group, *esp* of soldiers.

con'tingency *nc* a chance happening: *We're prepared for all future contingencies; (attrib) We've made contingency plans* (= alternative plans in case something happens).

continue [kən'tinju:] **1** *vi* to go on being, doing *etc*; to last or keep on: *She continued to run; They continued running; He will continue in his present job; The noise continued for several hours; The road continues for a hundred and fifty kilometres.* **2** *vti* to go on (with) often after a break or pause: *He continued his talk after the interval; This story is continued on p. 53.*

con'tinual *adj* (*usu attrib*) very frequent; repeated many times: *I've had continual interruptions throughout the day.* **con'tinually** *adv.*

con'tinuance *nu* (*very formal*) the state of going on; continuing: *The continuance of the drought may cause a water shortage.*

conˌtinu'ation **1** *nu* the act of continuing, often after a break or pause: *The continuation of his studies is vital to him.* **2** *nc* something which carries on, *esp* a further part of a story *etc*: *This is just a continuation of what he said last week.*

con'tinued *adj* (*attrib*) without stopping; without interruption: *His continued interest in aeroplanes; a long period of continued silence.*

ˌconti'nuity [kon-] *nu* **1** the state of being continuous or logically related: *These irrelevant sections destroy the book's continuity; It is important to children to have some continuity in their education.* **2** (*tech*) the detailed arrangement of the parts of a story *etc* for a film script *etc*: *He is responsible for the continuity of the new film; (attrib) continuity girl.*

con'tinuous *adj* (*usu attrib*) joined together, or going on, without interruption: *a continuous series; continuous rain.*

con'tinuously *adv*: *It rained continuously all day.*

continuous tense *nc* a tense which shows that an action *etc* is in progress: *He is going; He hit me while I was talking to him.*

See also **discontinue**.

contort [kən'to:t] *vti* (*formal*) to twist or turn violently: *His face was contorted with pain; His face contorted in agony.* **con'tortion** [-ʃən] *nc.*

con'tortionist *nc* an entertainer who contorts his body: *The contortionist at the circus twisted himself into incredible shapes.*

contour ['kontuə] *nc* **1** (*formal*) an outline: *the contours of the coastline; the contours of her figure.* **2** (*tech*) (*also* '**contour line**) on a map, a line joining points at the same height or depth.

contraband ['kontrəband] *nu* (*formal*) goods which are legally forbidden to be brought into a country; smuggled goods: *The customs officer discovered the contraband; (attrib) contraband cigarettes.*

contraception [kontrə'sepʃən] *nu* the prevention of conceiving children; birth-control: *Fewer unwanted children are being born since the introduction of more reliable methods of contraception.*

ˌcontra'ceptive [-tiv] *nc* a means of contraception: *The pill is a modern contraceptive; (attrib) contraceptive pills; (attrib) contraceptive methods.*

contract [kən'trakt, (*def 2 Amer*) 'kontrakt] **1** *vti* to make or become smaller, less, shorter, tighter *etc*: *Metals expand when heated and contract when cooled; 'I am' is often contracted to 'I'm'; As the muscles contracted the pain grew worse.* **2** *vi* (*formal*) to promise legally in writing: *They contracted to supply us with 1000 metres of cable.* **3** *vt* (*formal*) to become infected with (a disease): *He contracted malaria when he was in India; (fig) He's contracted the habit of talking to himself.* **4** *vt* (*formal*) to come to owe (a debt): *She contracted debts of £5000.* **5** *vt* (*very formal*: *usu in passive*) to promise (in marriage): *She was contracted (in marriage) to a wealthy doctor.* – ['kontrakt] *nc* a legal written agreement: *He has a four-year contract (of employment) with us; The firm won a contract for three new aircraft; a marriage contract.*

con'traction [-ʃən] **1** *ncu* an act of contracting: *the contraction of metals; painful contraction of the stomach muscles; contractions (of the muscles of the womb) in childbirth.* **2** *nc* a word shortened in speech or spelling: *'I'm' is a contraction of 'I am'; 'Fred' is a contraction of 'Frederick'.*

con'tractor *nc* a person or firm that promises to do work or supply goods at a fixed rate: *a building contractor; Get estimates from several contractors.*

contradict [kontrə'dikt] *vt* to say the opposite of; to argue or disagree with: *His second statement contradicts his first; It's unwise to contradict your boss; His behaviour contradicts his religious beliefs.*

ˌcontra'diction [-ʃən] *ncu.* **ˌcontra'dictory** *adj.*

a contradiction in terms a statement, idea *etc* which contains a contradiction: *Is a poor landowner a contradiction in terms?*

contralto *see* **alto**.

contraption [kən'trapʃən] *nc* (*derog*) a strange machine or apparatus: *He tried to fly over the Atlantic in a home-made contraption.*

contrary[1] ['kontrəri] *adj* (*pred*: *often with* **to**) opposite (to) or in disagreement (with): *The second statement is contrary to the first; That decision was contrary to my wishes; Contrary to* *popular belief he is an able politician.* – *nc* (*with* **the**) the opposite.

on the contrary the very opposite (is true): *'Are you busy?' 'No, on the contrary, I'm out of work.'*

to the 'contrary (*formal*) giving an opposite or contradictory statement or point of view: *It may be true – there is no evidence to the contrary*; *If you do not hear to the contrary, I shall visit you on Tuesday.*

contrary[2] [kən'treəri] *adj* obstinate in deciding to do the opposite of what is reasonable, expected, or decided by the majority; perverse: *She's so contrary that you never know what she will do*; *a contrary child.* **con'trariness** *nu.*

contrast [kən'tra:st] **1** *vi* to show marked difference from: *His words contrast with his actions.* **2** *vt* to compare so as to show differences: *Contrast fresh and frozen vegetables and you'll find the fresh ones taste better.* – ['kontra:st] **1** *ncu* difference(s) in things or people that are compared: *The contrast between these books is very marked.* **2** *nc* a thing or person that shows a marked difference (to another): *She's a complete contrast to her sister.*

contravene [kontrə'vi:n] *vt* (*formal or legal*) to go against or break (a law, principle *etc*): *By parking there you are contravening the traffic regulations.* **ˌcontra'vention** [-'venʃən] *ncu.*

contretemps ['kontrətã] *nc* (*formal*) an embarrassing event at an awkward moment: *There was a slight contretemps when his ex-wife walked in.*

contribute [kən'tribjut] *vti* **1** (*more formal or tech than* **give**) to give (money, help *etc*) along with others: *Have you contributed* (*any money*) *to this charity?*; *I've been contributing* (*written articles*) *to this paper for many years.* **2** *vi* (*formal*: *with* **to**) to help to cause to happen: *His gambling contributed to his downfall.*

ˌcontri'bution [kon-] **1** *nu* (*formal*) the act of contributing: *His contribution to literature was very great.* **2** *nc* something contributed, *esp* money: *Would you like to make a contribution to this charity?* **con'tributor** *nc.*

con'tributory *adj* (*formal*: *attrib*) helping to bring about: *His poor health was a contributory factor in his decision to retire.*

contrite ['kontrait] *adj* (*formal*) deeply sorry for something one has done: *He was very contrite when he realized how much he had offended you*; *a contrite expression.* **'contriteness** *nu.*

contrition [kən'triʃən] *nu* (*formal*) contriteness: *She was filled with contrition on hearing of the death of her divorced husband.*

contrive [kən'traiv] *vt* **1** (*more formal than* **try**) to manage (to do something); to succeed (in doing something) with difficulty: *He contrived to make me feel very unhappy*; *He contrived to remove the money from her bag.* **2** to cause (something) to happen with difficulty: *They contrived a secret meeting between the lovers.*

con'trivance (*formal*) **1** *nu* the act of contriving. **2** *nc* something contrived (*esp* something mechanical): *I've invented a contrivance for making the door open automatically.* **3** *nc* a plan, scheme or excuse: *This is purely a contrivance to get me to go with him.*

con'trived *adj* artificially complicated: *a long, contrived explanation of his behaviour*; *I did not like the ending of the play – it was a bit contrived.*

control [kən'troul] **1** *nu* the right of directing or of giving orders; power or authority: *She has control over all the decisions in that department*; *She has no control over that dog.* **2** *nu* the act of holding back or restraining: *control over the number of immigrants*; *control of prices*; *I know you're angry but you must not lose control* (*of yourself*); *She regained control of herself.* **3** *nc* (*often in pl*) a lever, button *etc* which operates (a machine *etc*): *The clutch, brake and accelerator are all foot controls*; *The new pilot is at the controls.* **4** *ncu* (*often in cmpds*) a point or place at which an inspection takes place: *a border control*; *passport control*; (*attrib*) *a control point.* – *See also* **in, out of, under control** *below.* – *v* – *pt, ptp* **con'trolled** – *vt* **1** to direct or guide; to have power or authority over: *The captain controls the whole ship*; *She controls the whole department*; *There are many factors which control my decision*; *Control your dog, before he bites me!* **2** to hold back; to restrain (oneself or one's emotions *etc*): *I know you're upset but you must control yourself*; *Control your rage!* **3** to regulate; to cause to keep to a fixed standard: *The government is controlling prices and wages.*

con'troller *nc* a person or thing that controls: *an air-traffic controller.*

con'trol-tower *nc* a building at an airport from which take-off and landing instructions are given.

in control (of) having power or authority (over); in charge (of): *There is a new government in control*; *He is in control of the whole project*; (*fig*) *She is very much in control of the situation.*

out of control not under the authority or power of someone: *The driver has had a heart attack – the car is out of control!*; *Those children are completely out of control since their father left.*

under control **1** restrained or held back: *Is your temper under control yet?*; *Keep your dog under control!* **2** in good order; working smoothly (*esp* after a state of panic or chaos): *Everything's under control now, and back to normal.*

controversy [kən'trovəsi, 'kontrəvə:si] *ncu* (*formal*) (an) argument between opposing points of view: *His decision to publish the book gave rise to much controversy*; *The controversy over the appointment of the new chairman lasted for several weeks.*

controversial [kontrə'və:ʃəl] *adj* causing controversy: *a controversial decision*; *His new book is very controversial.* **ˌcontro'versially** *adv.*

conundrum [kə'nʌndrəm] *nc* a riddle or puzzling question.

conurbation [konə'beiʃən] *nc* (*formal*) a group of towns forming a single built-up area: *London, Manchester and other large conurbations.*

convalesce [konvə'les] *vi* to recover health and strength after an illness, often a long or severe illness: *He's left hospital and is convalescing in the country.*

ˌconva'lescent *nc* a person who is recovering from an illness: *Convalescents often need a special diet.* – *adj* **1** (*usu pred*) recovering health and strength after illness: *He is convalescent now.* **2** (*usu attrib*) for convalescents: *a convalescent home/hospital.* **ˌconva'lescence** *nu.*

convection [kən'vekʃən] *nu* (*tech*) the passing of heat through liquids or gases by means of currents which are due to the movement of the heated particles: *heated by convection*; (*attrib*) *convection currents.*

con'vector (heater) *nc* a heater which works by this method.

convene [kən'vi:n] *vti* (*formal*) to (cause to) assemble or come together: *We'll convene a*

meeting of all the people concerned; *The committee will convene next month.*
con'vener *nc* a person who convenes a meeting or meetings.

convenient [kən'vi:njənt] *adj* **1** suitable; not causing trouble or difficulty: *When would it be convenient for me to come?*; *It was very convenient that you called just as we were starting to eat*; *a convenient moment.* **2** (*usu attrib*) easy to use *etc*: *a modern, convenient kitchen*; *a convenient size of house.* **3** easy to reach *etc*; accessible: *This house is convenient for the children's school*; *Keep this in a convenient place.*
con'venience 1 *nu* the state or quality of being convenient; freedom from trouble or difficulty: *The shops are open late on Thursday for the convenience of the customers*; *I appreciate the convenience of living near the office.* **2** *nc* (*formal*) any means of giving ease or comfort: *We enjoy the conveniences of modern life.* **3** *nc* (*also* **public convenience**: *formal euph*) a public lavatory.
con'veniently *adv*: *a conveniently placed shelf.*
at your convenience (*formal*) when it suits you: *Come and see me at your convenience.*
See also **inconvenient**.

convent ['konvənt, (*Amer*) -vent] *nc* a building in which nuns live: *The Convent of the Sacred Heart*; (*attrib*) *She went to a convent school.*

convention [kən'venʃən] **1** *ncu* a way of behaving that has become usual; (an) established custom: *Shaking hands when meeting people is a normal convention in many countries*; *He always does exactly what he wants to do and does not care about convention*; *You must observe local conventions when visiting a foreign country.* **2** *nc* in the US, a meeting of delegates from a political party for nominating a presidential candidate: *the Democratic Party convention.* **3** *nc* an assembly, *esp* of representatives for some common purpose: *a businessmen's convention.*
con'ventional *adj* (*neg* **un-**) **1** according to the accepted standards of conduct, manners or taste: *conventional dress*; *He's not very conventional in his behaviour.* **2** (*attrib*) not original or unusual; traditional: *This gallery only exhibits the more conventional forms of art.*
con,ventio'nality [-'na-] *ncu* (*formal*) (a) conventional quality: *the rather boring conventionality of his art*; *He always observed the conventionalities of behaviour.*

converge [kən'və:dʒ] *vti* (*formal*) to (cause to) move towards or meet at one point: *The roads converge in the centre of town*; *The crowd converged on the town hall.* **con'vergence** *nu.* **con'vergent** *adj.*
See also **diverge**.

conversant [kən'ʌə:sənt] *adj* (*formal*: *pred with* **with**) familiar or acquainted with; having a thorough knowledge of: *Are you fully conversant with the plays of George Bernard Shaw?*

conversation [konvə'seiʃən] *ncu* talk: *It's difficult to have/hold/carry on a conversation with all this noise going on*; *They were deep in conversation.*
,conver'sational *adj* (*usu attrib*) **1** informal or colloquial: *Conversational English is different in form and structure from the English used when writing for a job.* **2** (*formal*) fond of talking: *He's in a conversational mood today.*
conver'sationalist *nc* a person who is fond of or good at conversation.

converse[1] [kən'və:s] *vi* (*formal*) to talk: *It is difficult to converse with people who do not speak your language.*

converse[2] ['konvə:s] *nc* (*formal*) the opposite: *I think that the converse of your argument is true.*
conversely [kon'və:sli] *adv.*

conversion [kən'və:ʃən, (*Amer*) -ʒən] **1** *nu* (*formal*) the act of converting: *his conversion to Christianity*; *the conversion of the mansion house into a hotel.* **2** *nc* something converted to another use: *That building firm specializes in conversions* (= in converting houses *etc*).

convert [kən'və:t] *vti* (*formal*) **1** to change from one thing into another: *He has converted his large house into four separate flats*; *He's converted the van into a motor caravan*; *This sofa converts into a bed.* **2** to change from one religion *etc* to another: *He was converted to Christianity*; (*fig*) *You've converted me to your way of thinking.* – ['konvə:t] *nc* a person who has been converted to a particular religion *etc*: *a convert to Buddhism*; (*fig*) *I'm a convert to this new system of yours.*
con'vertible *adj* that may or can be converted: *a convertible sofa.* – *nc* a car with a folding or detachable top. **con,verti'bility** *nu* (*formal*).

convex ['konveks] *adj* (of an object or surface) curved outwards, like the surface of the eye: *a convex lens.* **con'vexity** *ncu*(*formal*). **'convexness** *nu.*
See also **concave**.

convey [kən'vei] *vt* **1** (*formal*) to carry: *Huge ships convey oil from the Middle East*; (*fig*) *Convey my regards to your brother*; *This book conveys his ideas rather well.* **2** (*legal*) to transfer the ownership of (property by legal means): *He conveyed the estate to his son before his retirement.*
con'veyance 1 *nu* (*formal*) the act of conveying: *the conveyance of goods from place to place.* **2** *nc* (*formal*) a vehicle of any kind: *A bus is a public conveyance.* **3** *nu* (*legal*) the act of transferring property: *The conveyance of his property took a long time.*
con'veyancing *nu* (*legal*) the branch of the law dealing with transfer of property.
con'veyor *nc* (*formal*) a person or thing that conveys: *He was the conveyor of bad news.*
con'veyor belt *nc* an endless, moving belt of rubber, metal *etc* carrying articles from one place to another, in a factory *etc*: *She put nuts on the chocolates as they went down the conveyor belt.*

convict [kən'vikt] *vt* (*formal*) to prove or declare (someone) guilty: *The evidence convicted him*; *She was convicted of theft.* – ['konvikt] *nc* a person serving a sentence for a crime: *Two of the convicts have escaped from prison.*
con'viction [-ʃən] *ncu* **1** (*legal*) (an) act of convicting or being convicted: *She has had two convictions for drunken driving.* **2** (a) strong belief: *It's my conviction that he's right*; *She said it with complete conviction.*

convince [kən'vins] *vt* to persuade (a person) that something is true: *You've convinced me that you can do it*; *I am convinced that he is innocent*; *Her smile convinced me that she was happy*; *She is convinced of his innocence.*
con'vincing *adj* (*neg* **un-**) having the power to convince: *a convincing argument*; *She is very convincing.*

convivial [kən'viviəl] *adj* (*formal*) pleasantly sociable and friendly: *We spent a convivial evening with them*; *in convivial company*; *The wine made* the party very convivial. **con'vivially** *adv.* **con-ˌvivi'ality** [-'a-], *nu.*

convoy ['konvoi] *nc* **1** a group of ships, lorries, cars *etc* travelling together: *an army convoy*; *a police convoy*. **2** a fleet of merchant ships escorted for safety by warships.

convulse [kən'vʌls] *vt* (*formal*) to shake violently: *I was convulsed with laughter.* **con'vulsive** [-siv] *adj.* **con'vulsively** *adv.*

con'vulsion [-ʃən] *nc* (*often in pl*) a sudden stiffening or jerking of the muscles of the body: *The child had convulsions during his illness*; (*fig*) *Her jokes had us all in convulsions* (*of laughter*).

coo [ku:] – *3rd pers sing prt* **coos**: *pt, ptp* **cooed** – *vi* to make a sound like a dove, *esp* (of people) when speaking soothingly to a baby *etc*: *I could hear the doves cooing*; *The women cooed over the new baby.* – *nc* such a sound.

cook [kuk] **1** *vti* to prepare (food) by heating: *One cooks a chicken, but makes or prepares a salad*; *This kind of rice cooks more quickly than that kind.* **2** *vt* (*inf*) to alter or make false (accounts *etc*): *The accountant was found to have cooked the books.* – *See also* **cook up**. – *nc* a person who cooks, *esp* for a living: *She was employed as a cook at the manor house.*

'cooker *nc* **1** an apparatus on which food is cooked: *She has an electric cooker but would prefer a gas one.* **2** (*inf*) an apple *etc* used in cooking, not for eating raw: *'Do you grow apples?' 'Only cookers.'*

'cookery *nu* the art or practice of cooking food: *She was taught cookery at school*; (*attrib*) *cookery classes.*

'cookery-book *nc* (*Amer* **'cook-book**) a book of instructions on how to prepare and cook various dishes.

cook one's goose (*inf*) to ruin (one's chances of success *etc*): *That's cooked his goose!*

cook up *vt sep* (*inf*) to invent or make up a false story *etc*: *I cooked up a story about my car having broken down*; *How long did it take you to cook it up?*

cookie ['kuki] *nc* (*Amer*) a biscuit.

cool [ku:l] *adj* **1** slightly cold: *cool weather*; *It's cool today.* **2** (*usu pred*) calm or not excitable: *He's very cool in a crisis.* **3** indifferent; not very friendly: *He was very cool towards his ex-wife*; *He gave her a cool look.* **4** (*inf*) impudent: *That's cool – he's just asked me to lend him £5000!*; *He's a cool fellow!*; **5** (*inf*) used for emphasis: *She spent a cool million* (*pounds*) *in three years.* **6** (*sl*) excellent: *He looked cool in his new clothes.* – **1** *vti* to make or become less warm: *The jelly will cool better in the refrigerator*; *Let the child's food cool a bit*; *She cooled her hands in the stream.* **2** *vi* to become less excited, less emotional *etc*: *His affection for her has cooled recently.* – *See also* **cool** *in phrases below.* – *nu* (*with* **the**) cool air or atmosphere: *in the cool of the evening.*

cooler *nc* **1** something which cools or in which things are cooled: *a wine cooler.* **2** (*sl*: *usu with* **the**) jail.

'coolly *adv.* **'coolness** *nu.*

cool-'headed *adj* not easily excited, and so able to act calmly: *She's always cool-headed in a crisis*; *a cool-headed approach to the problem.*

cool down *vi, vt sep* **1** to make or become less warm: *Let your food cool down a bit!*; *Put it in the fridge to cool it down.* **2** to make or become less excited or less emotional: *He was very angry but he's cooled down a bit now*; *Her apology cooled him down a bit.*

cool off **1** *vi, vt sep* to make or become less warm: *I'm going to have a cold shower and cool off*; *A cold shower will cool me off.* **2** *vi* to become less enthusiastic, less emotional *etc*: *He used to love her very much but he has cooled off now.*

cool one's heels (*inf*) to be kept waiting: *I've left him to cool his heels for a while.*

keep one's cool (*inf*) not to become over-excited or confused: *If you keep your cool you won't fail.*

lose one's cool (*inf*) not to keep one's cool.

play it cool (*inf*) to deal with a situation, problem *etc* in a calm way: *If you play it cool you'll probably get the job.*

coop [ku:p] *nc* (*often in cmpds*) a box or cage for keeping fowls or small animals in: *a chicken-coop.*

coop up *vt sep* to shut into a small place: *We've been cooped up in this tiny room for hours*; *If you coop children up they become naughty.*

co-operate [kou'opəreit] *vi* to work together: *They have promised to co-operate* (*with us*) *in the planning of the exhibition.*

co-ˌope'ration *nu* **1** the act of working together. **2** willingness to act or work together: *I would be grateful for your co-operation.*

co-'operative [-tiv] *adj*: *I have always found her very co-operative* (= willing to be helpful *etc*); *a co-operative attitude.*

co-operative society (*inf abbrev* **co-op** ['kouop]) *nc* a profit-sharing association for the cheaper purchase of goods or for other trading purposes.

co-opt [kou'opt] *vt* (*formal*) to choose (someone) to join a committee or other body of people: *She was co-opted on to the committee.*

co-ordinate [kou'o:dineit] *vt* to adjust (a movement or action) so that it fits in or works smoothly (with other movement or actions): *In swimming the movement of one's arms and legs must be co-ordinated*; *He co-ordinates the activities of all the organizations.* – [-nət] *nc* (*geog*) a number *etc* by which the position of a fixed point within a grid can be referred to: *The town's co-ordinates on this map are 965037.*

co-'ordinated [-nei-] *adj* (*neg* **un-**) able to co-ordinate one's physical movements: *Athletes are usually well co-ordinated.*

cop[1] [kop] *nc* (*sl*) a policeman: *The cops are after me*; *A New York cop.*

See also **copper**[2].

cop[2] *vt* (*sl*) to catch: *Cop* (*hold of*) *this cup of coffee, will you?*

'cop it (*sl*) to be punished: *You'll really cop it when your dad sees the mess you've made.*

cope [koup] *vi* to manage; to deal with successfully: *I can't cope with all this work*; *The widowed mother had a nervous breakdown because she couldn't cope.*

coping ['koupiŋ] *nu* the top row of stones in a wall.

'coping-stone *nc* one of the stones at the top of a wall.

copious ['koupiəs] *adj* (*formal*: *usu attrib*) plentiful: *a copious supply of paper*; *copious information on the subject.* **'copiously** *adv.* **'copiousness** *nu.*

copper[1] ['kopə] **1** *nu* an element (symbol **Cu**), a metal of a brownish-red colour: *This pipe is made of copper.* **2** *nc* (*inf*) (a piece of) money made of copper or a substitute: *Have you any coppers in your change?* **3** *nc* (*old*) a container made of copper, often one to boil water in: *a copper to boil* *clothes in.* – *adj* **1** made of copper (*def 1*): *The pipes are all copper*; *a copper pipe.* **2** (*also* '**copper-coloured**) of the colour of copper (*def 1*).

'**copper-plate** *nu* very fine and regular hand-writing: *written in copper-plate*; (*attrib*) *copper-plate hand-writing.*

copper[2] ['kopə] *nc* (*Brit inf*) a policeman: *Run – there's a copper after you!*
See also **cop**[1].

coppice ['kopis] (*also* **copse** [kops]) *nc* (*formal*) a wood of small trees which are cut from time to time.

copra ['koprə, (*Amer*) 'kou-] *nu* the dried kernel of the coconut which gives coconut oil.

copse *see* **coppice**.

copulate ['kopjuleit] *vi* (*formal* of animals: *derog* of people) to have sexual intercourse (with): *The child saw the cow and bull copulating*; *'You can't walk through the park in the evening without seeing couples copulating,' she said in disgust.* ˌ**copu'lation** *nu.*

copy ['kopi] **1** *nc* an imitation or reproduction: *This painting isn't by Van Dyck – it's a copy by someone else*; *That dress is a copy of one I saw at a Paris fashion show.* **2** *nc* a single book, newspaper *etc*: *Can I have six copies of this dictionary, please?* **3** *nu* written or typed material to be sent to a printer: *Has the copy gone to the printer yet?* **4** *nu* (*inf*) material worth including in a newspaper: *Your story will make good copy.* **5** *nu* material written for advertising or publicity purposes: *He is very good at writing copy for television advertisements.* – *vti* to make an imitation or reproduction (of something): *Copy the way I speak*; *Copy this passage into your notebook*; *The designs are copied by machine*; *This pale writing doesn't copy* (= photocopy) *very well.*

'**copybook** *nc* a writing or drawing book with models for imitation: *Schoolchildren used to have copybooks*; (*attrib*) *a copybook* (= perfect) *example of how it should be done.*

'**copy-cat** *nc* (*inf derog*) a person who imitates or copies: *She's such a copy-cat that she always has the same style of clothes as I do.*

'**copyright** *nu* (*usu abbrev* ©) the sole right to reproduce a literary, dramatic, musical or artistic work, and also to perform, translate, film, or record such a work: *This book is our copyright*; (*attrib*) *copyright regulations.* – *adj* protected by copyright: *His work is still copyright.*

'**copywriter** *nc* a person who writes advertising copy.

coquettish [kə'ketiʃ] *adj* (*formal*) fond of flirting: *a coquettish young girl*; *a coquettish smile.* **co'quettishly** *adv.* **co'quettishness** *nu.*

coral ['korəl] **1** *nu* a hard substance of various colours, made up of skeletons of a kind of tiny animal: *Coral may be used for making attractive souvenirs*; (*attrib*) *a coral reef/island*; (*attrib*) *a coral necklace.* **2** *nu, adj* (of) an orange-pink colour.

cord [ko:d] **1** *ncu* (a piece of) thin rope or thick string: *The burglars tied up the nightwatchman with thick cord.* **2** *nc* (*formerly sometimes* **chord**) a part of the body resembling this: *the spinal cord*; *the vocal cords.* **3** *ncu* a length of electric cable or flex attached to an electrical appliance: *the cord of his electric razor.* **4** *nu, adj* (*inf*) (of) a kind of fabric with a ribbed appearance: *a dress of brown cord*; *a cord dress.*

cords *n pl* trousers made of cord (*def 4*): *a pair of cords.*

corded velvet *nu, adj* (of) a kind of velvet with a ribbed appearance: *a dress of blue corded velvet*; *a corded velvet dress.*

cordial ['ko:diəl, (*Amer*) 'ko:rdʒl] *adj* (*formal*) (of greetings *etc*) warm and affectionate: *a cordial welcome*; *a cordial smile.* – *nu* a refreshing drink: *lime juice cordial.*

ˌ**cordi'ality** [-'a-] *nu* (*formal*). '**cordially** *adv.*

cordon ['ko:dn] *nc* a line of sentries or policemen to prevent people from entering an area: *They've put a cordon round the house where the bomb is planted.*

cordon off *vt sep* to enclose with a cordon: *The police cordoned off the area where the gunman was last seen*; *They have cordoned it off.*

cordon bleu [ko:dõ'blə:] *nu, adj* (of) a first class cook: *She's a cordon bleu cook*; *His cooking is cordon bleu.*

corduroy [ko:də'roi] *nu, adj* (of) a thick ribbed cotton fabric: *a dress made of corduroy*; *a corduroy dress.*

core [ko:] *nc* the innermost part of something, *esp* fruit: *an apple-core*; *the core of the earth*; (*fig*) *We must get to the core of the problem.* – *vt* to take out the core of (fruit): *Core the apples.*

cork [ko:k] **1** *nu* the outer bark of the cork tree (an oak of S Europe, N Africa *etc*): *Cork floats very well*; (*attrib*) *cork floor-tiles.* **2** *nc* a stopper for a bottle *etc*, often made of cork: *Put the cork back in the wine-bottle.* – *vt* to put a cork or stopper in: *He has corked the bottles of his home-made wine.*

corked *adj* **1** having a cork. **2** (*pred*) (of wine) smelling or tasting bad because of having had a faulty cork: *This port is corked.*

'**corkscrew** *nc* a tool with a screw-like spike, used for drawing corks from bottles. – *adj* (*attrib*) like a corkscrew in shape: *corkscrew curls.*

corm [ko:m] *nc* (*tech*) the bulb-like underground stem of certain plants: *the corm of a crocus.*

corn[1] [ko:n] **1** *nu* the seeds of cereal plants, *esp* (in Britain) wheat, or (in N America) maize. **2** *nu* (*Amer* **grain**) the plants themselves: *a field of corn.* **3** *nc* a single grain or seed (*esp* of pepper; *see also* **peppercorn**).

corned beef *nu* salted beef (*usu* cooked and canned).

'**cornflour** *nu* finely ground (*esp* maize) flour: *She used cornflour to thicken the sauce.*

'**cornflower** *nc* a blue-flowered plant which grows in cornfields.

ˌ**corn-on-the-'cob** *nu* maize which is still attached to the ear on which it grows: *We'll have corn-on-the-cob for the first course of the meal.*

corn[2] [ko:n] *nc* a little bump of hard skin found chiefly on the foot: *My foot is sore – I have a corn on my little toe.*

cornea ['ko:niə] *nc* the transparent covering of the eyeball.

corner ['ko:nə] *nc* **1** a point where two lines, walls, roads *etc* meet: *the corners of a triangle/cube*; *the corner of the street*; *There's a dangerous corner on this road*; *There's a pub just round the corner from our house.* **2** (*inf*) a place, *usu* a small quiet place: *Let's find a quiet corner and sit down.* **3** (*inf*) an awkward or difficult situation: *I'm in a bit of a corner just now regarding money.* **4** in football, a free kick from the corner of the field: *We've been awarded a corner.* – **1** *vt* to force (a person or animal) into a place from which it is difficult to escape: *The thief was cornered in an alley.* **2** *vt* to put (a person) into an awkward or difficult situation: *He cornered the witness by clever questioning.* **3** *vi* (of a vehicle) to turn a corner or corners: *He cornered on only three wheels; This car corners very well.* **4** *vt* (*inf*) to gain control of: *They've cornered the market/all the business by clever advertising.*

'cornered *adj* **1** (*esp in cmpds*) having (a given number of) corners: *a three-cornered hat.* **2** forced into a position from which it is difficult to escape: *A cornered animal can be very dangerous.*

'cornerstone *nc* **1** the stone that joins the two walls of a building at a corner, *esp* one built into the corner of the foundation: *The mayor laid the cornerstone of the new town hall.* **2** (*fig*) something upon which something depends or is based; basis; foundation: *Our laws are the cornerstone of our society.*

cut corners to use less money, effort, time *etc* when doing something than was thought necessary, often giving a poorer result: *You can't cut corners if you want the building to be of good quality.*

take a corner *see* **take**.

turn the corner 1 to go round a corner: *He's turned the corner of the street.* **2** (*fig*) to get past a difficulty or danger: *We've turned the financial corner, and business is improving steadily; He was very ill but he's turned the corner now.*

cornet ['ko:nit, (*Amer*) ko:r'net] *nc* **1** a brass musical instrument with three valves similar to the trumpet: *He plays the cornet; He played a tune on his cornet.* **2** a cone-shaped object, made of wafer biscuit, for holding ice-cream: *an ice-cream cornet.*

cornflour, cornflower *see* **corn**[1].

cornice ['ko:nis] *nc* a decorative border made of moulded plaster round a ceiling: *We painted the cornice a different colour from the ceiling.*

Cornish pasty ['ko:niʃ] *nc* a kind of small pie containing meat and vegetables.

corny ['ko:ni] *adj* (*inf*) not original or interesting: *a corny joke; All his jokes are corny.*

corollary [kə'roləri] *nc* (*formal*) something that follows when one thing has been proved; a consequence: *If you know that the animals grow a thick winter coat, the corollary is that they come from a cold country.*

coronary ['korənəri] *adj* (*attrib*: *tech*) (of arteries) supplying blood to the heart: *coronary arteries.* – *nc* (*inf*) an attack of coronary thrombosis: *He's had a coronary.*

coronary thrombosis *nu* a heart disease caused by blockage of one of the coronary arteries: *Coronary thrombosis is common in middle-aged men.*

coronation [korə'neiʃən] *nc* the act or ceremony of crowning a king or queen: *We watched the queen's coronation on television.*

coroner ['korənə] *nc* an official who inquires into the causes of accidental or sudden, unexpected deaths.

coronet ['korənit] *nc* **1** a small crown: *The baronet wore a gold coronet.* **2** an ornamental headdress: *The bridesmaid wore a coronet of flowers.*

corporal[1] ['ko:pərəl] *nc* (*with cap, and often abbrev* **Corp.**, *when written in titles*) in the British army, (a person of) the rank below sergeant: *He is a corporal; He has been promoted to corporal; Corporal Jones.* – *See also* Appendix 3.

corporal[2] ['ko:pərəl] *adj* (*formal*) of the body: *Corporal punishment involves the beating or birching of the offender.*

corporate ['ko:pərət] *adj* (*formal*: *usu attrib*) **1** united: *The success was due not to one man but to corporate effort.* **2** legally joined to form a body or corporation: *a corporate business.*

ˌcorpo'ration *nc* **1** a body of people acting as one individual *eg* for administration or business purposes: *the British Steel Corporation; The corporation* (=The town council) *have ordered that trees are to be planted here;* (*attrib*) *a corporation bus.* **2** (*inf*) a (person's) large stomach: *You're getting a huge corporation!*

corps [ko:] – *pl* **corps** [ko:z] – *nc* **1** a division of an army: *The Royal Armoured Corps.* **2** (*formal*) a group or company: *the diplomatic corps; the corps de ballet.*

corpse [ko:ps] *nc* a dead body, *esp* of a human being: *Don't move the corpse before you send for the police.*

corpulent ['ko:pjulənt] *adj* (*formal*) fat: *a corpulent old man.* **'corpulence** *nu.*

corpuscle ['ko:pʌsl] *nc* (*tech*) one of the red or white cells in the blood.

correct [kə'rekt] *vt* **1** to remove faults and errors from: *He has corrected the proofs of his novel; These spectacles will correct his eye defect; Please correct me if I'm wrong.* **2** (of a teacher *etc*) to mark errors in: *I have fourteen exercise books to correct this evening.* – *adj* **1** (*usu pred*) free from faults or errors: *This page is correct.* **2** right; not wrong: *You are correct in thinking he is a fool; Did I get the correct idea from what you said?*

cor'rection [-ʃən] *ncu* (an) act of making something correct: *The correction of his work took a long time; He made several corrections.*

cor'rective [-tiv] *adj* (*very formal*) intended or having the power to set right: *The government is taking corrective measures on these unfair regulations.*

cor'rectly *adv*: *Did I hear you correctly?; He spelt it correctly.*

cor'rectness *nu*: *He was complimented on the correctness of his behaviour/work.*

See also **incorrect**.

correlate ['korəleit] (*very formal*) **1** *vt* to cause or show a relationship between (two or more things): *I can't correlate these two sets of figures.* **2** *vi* to have a relationship: *The figures don't correlate* (*with the figures previously mentioned*).

ˌcorre'lation *ncu.*

correspond [korə'spond] *vi* **1** (*with* **to**) to be similar in some way: *A university professor in America corresponds to a university lecturer in Britain.* **2** (*formal*) (*with* **with**) to be in agreement with; to match: *His treatment of his staff does not correspond with his political ideas.* **3** (*formal*) to communicate by letter (with): *Do they often correspond* (*with each other*)?

ˌcorre'spondence *nu* (*formal*) **1** agreement: *There is a lack of correspondence between his promises and his actions.* **2** similarity or likeness: *There is a marked correspondence between these two murders.* **3** (communication by) letters: *The job involves a large amount of correspondence; There's a big pile of correspondence for you today.*

ˌcorre'spondent *nc* **1** (*formal*) a person with whom one exchanges letters: *He has correspondents all over the world.* **2** a person who contributes letters or news to a newspaper *etc*: *He's foreign correspondent for 'The Times'.*

ˌcorre'sponding *adj* (*attrib*) **1** similar in some way or able to be compared in some way: *The* *unemployment figures are high this month but they are not as high as those for the corresponding month last year.* 2 accompanying; related; matching; in agreement: *You will have a higher salary in this job but you'll have a corresponding increase in responsibility.*

ˌcorreˈspondence course *nc* a course of lessons by post: *He took a correspondence course in accountancy.*

corridor [ˈkoridoː] *nc* a passageway, *esp* one off which rooms open: *Go along the corridor and up the stairs*; (*attrib*) *a corridor carriage/train.*

corrigendum [koriˈdʒendəm] – *pl* **ˌcorriˈgenda** [-də] – *nc* (*very formal*) a mistake requiring correction, *esp* in a book *etc*: *There is a list of corrigenda at the beginning of that book.*

corroborate [kəˈrobəreit] *vt* (*formal*) to support or confirm (evidence *etc* already given): *She corroborated her sister's story*; *The witness's statement was corroborated by other evidence.* **corˌroboˈration** *nu.*

corˈroborative [-rətiv] *adj* (*very formal*) tending to confirm or support: *corroborative evidence.*

corrode [kəˈroud] 1 *vt* to destroy or eat away (as rust, chemicals *etc* do): *Salt corrodes car bodies*; (*formal fig*) *Moral standards are gradually being corroded.* 2 *vi* to be destroyed; to be eaten away: *Many metals corrode in water.* **corˈrosion** [-ʒən] *nu.*

corˈrosive [-siv] *adj* (*tech*) tending to corrode: *A corrosive substance damages the skin.* – *nc* a substance which corrodes: *Acids are corrosives.*

corrugated [ˈkorəgeitid] *adj* (*usu attrib*) folded or shaped into ridges: *corrugated iron*; *Use corrugated paper to wrap round the books.*

corrupt [kəˈrʌpt] *vt* 1 to make or become evil or morally bad: *He was corrupted by the bad influence of two friends.* 2 (*formal*) to make or become impure: *These expressions merely corrupt your good English.* – *adj* 1 morally bad or evil: *Their government is corrupt*; *corrupt ideas.* 2 (*usu attrib*) impure: *She speaks a corrupt form of English.*

corˈruptible *adj* (*formal*) that may be corrupted: *Offer the official a bribe – he is obviously corruptible*; *a corruptible organization.* **corˌruptiˈbility** *nu.*

corˈruption [-ʃən] 1 *nu* the act of corrupting or state of being corrupt: *the corruption of a child's mind*; *That country is noted for the corruption of its government.* 2 *nc* an impure (or *orig* impure) form of a word: *Caterpillar is probably a corruption of the Old French word meaning 'hairy cat'.*

See also **incorruptible**.

corsage [koːˈsaːʒ] *nc* (*formal*) a small bouquet for pinning on to a dress.

corset [ˈkoːsit] *nc* a close-fitting stiff undergarment to support the body: *She wears a corset to make her appear slimmer*; *He wears a corset to support his sore back.*

cortège [koːˈteʒ] *nc* (*formal*) a procession, *esp* at a funeral: *The cortège followed the president's coffin.*

cosh [koʃ] *nc* (*Brit*) a short, heavy length of rubber *etc* filled with metal, used as a weapon. – *vt* to hit with a cosh or something heavy: *The thieves coshed the night-watchman*; *They coshed him on the head.*

cosily, cosiness *see* **cosy**.

cosmetic [kozˈmetik] *adj* designed to increase the beauty and hide the defects of something, *esp* the face: *She had cosmetic surgery to improve the shape of her nose*; (*fig*) *The improvements in this book are purely cosmetic* (= superficial, not real or basic). – *nc* a preparation for this purpose: *She's quite pretty – she does not need to wear/use so many cosmetics* (= lipstick, eye-shadow, face-cream *etc*).

cosmic [ˈkozmik] *adj* having to do with the universe or outer space: *cosmic rays.*

ˈcosmonaut [-noːt] *nc* a person who travels in space; an astronaut.

the cosmos [ˈkozmos, (*Amer*) -məs] (*formal*) the universe: *all the stars in the cosmos.*

cosmopolitan [kozməˈpolitən] *adj* 1 belonging to all parts of the world: *There was a cosmopolitan group of people at the congress*; *The population of London is very cosmopolitan.* 2 not prejudiced on grounds of one's own nationality: *He has a cosmopolitan attitude to politics/food*; *His ideas are quite cosmopolitan.* – *nc* a person who is not prejudiced in this way.

cosmos *see* **cosmic**.

cosset [ˈkosit] – *pt, ptp* **ˈcosseted** – *vt* (*formal*) to treat with too much kindness; to pamper: *They cosset their children with all this luxury*; *I feel cosseted having breakfast in bed.*

cost [kost] – *pt, ptp* **cost** (*def 1*), **ˈcosted** (*def 2*) – *vt* 1 (not *usu* used with **is, was** *etc* and **-ing**) to be obtainable at a certain price: *This jacket costs £40*; (*fig*) *The victory cost two thousand lives*; (*fig*) *That mistake will cost you your job.* 2 to estimate the cost of: *It will take some complicated calculations to cost this project.* – *ncu* the price to be paid (for something): *What is the cost of this coat?*; *I'll compare costs and buy the cheapest*; (*fig*) *the cost of human life.* – *See also* **costs** *below.*

ˈcostly *adj* (*formal*) costing much: *a costly wedding reception*; (*fig*) *a costly victory.* **ˈcostliness** *nu.*

costs *n pl* the expenses of a legal case: *He won his case and was awarded costs of £200.*

at all costs no matter what the cost or outcome may be: *We must prevent disaster at all costs.*

to one's ˈcost to one's disadvantage, discomfort *etc*: *The new boss seems very kind and friendly but I have discovered to my cost that he is not* (= he has been very unkind to me); *The sea looks warm but I know to my cost that it is not* (= I have felt it and it's very cold).

costume [ˈkostjuːm] *ncu* (an outfit of) dress *esp* that of a particular, often historical, period worn in a play, at a fancy-dress party *etc*: *She needs a new swimming-costume*; *We're going to the party in eighteenth-century costume*; (*attrib*) *a costume party/play* (= one in which the dress of a particular period in the past is worn).

costumier [koˈstjuːmiə], **ˈcostumer** *ncs* (*formal*) a person who makes or deals in costumes.

costume jewellery *nu* jewellery made of inexpensive materials, not genuine precious stones: *She always wears costume jewellery and keeps her diamonds in the bank.*

cosy, (*Amer*) **cozy** [ˈkouzi] *adj* warm and comfortable: *We had a cosy chat*; *a cosy armchair*; *This jacket will keep you cosy.* – *nc* a covering for a teapot (**ˈtea-cosy**) or for an egg (**ˈegg-cosy**), used to keep the contents warm.

ˈcosily *adv.* **ˈcosiness** *nu.*

cot [kot] *nc* 1 (*Amer* **crib**) a small bed with high sides for a child *etc*: *One of the wooden rails of the cot is broken.* 2 (*Amer*) a camp bed.

coterie [ˈkoutəri] *nc* (*formal*) a number of people interested in the same things who know each other very well and who tend to exclude other people: *It is difficult to get an article published in that magazine*

– *it is run by a coterie of poets.*

cottage ['kotidʒ] *nc* a small house, *esp* in the country or in a village: *miners' cottages*; *We have a holiday cottage in Devon.*

'**cottager** *nc* (*old*) a person who lives in a cottage.

cottage cheese *nu* a type of soft white cheese made from curds.

cottage hospital *nc* (*Brit*) a small hospital in a small town *etc.*

cottage industry *nc* (a system of) production and manufacture of goods in workers' own houses, *eg* knitting, weaving *etc*: *The tweed industry used to be largely a cottage industry.*

cottage loaf *nc* a loaf with a small lump on top of the main loaf.

cotton[1] ['kotn] **1** *nu* a soft substance like fine wool got from the seeds of the cotton plant, used in making thread or cloth. **2** *nu, adj* (of) the yarn or cloth made from this: *The buttons are sewn on with cotton*; *This shirt is* (*made of*) *cotton*; *a cotton shirt.* **3** *nu* the cotton plant or plants: *a field of cotton*; (*attrib*) *a cotton plantation.*

cotton candy *nu* (*Amer*) candy floss.

,**cotton'wool** *nu* (*Brit*) loose cotton pressed into a mass or sheet used for absorbing liquids, wiping or protecting an injury *etc*: *She bathed the wound with cottonwool*; (*fig*) *She's been wrapped in cottonwool all her life, and never had to face the realities of the world*; (*attrib*) *a cottonwool existence.*

cotton[2] ['kotn] : **cotton on** *vi* (*inf*) to begin to understand: *He'll soon cotton on* (*to what you mean*).

couch[1] [kautʃ] *nc* a type of sofa for sitting or lying on: *There's room for four of us on the couch*; *A psychiatrist's couch has a raised end for supporting one's head.*

couch[2] [kautʃ] *vt* (*formal*) to express (in words): *He couched his reply in deliberately vague terms.*

cougar ['ku:gə] *nc* (*esp Amer*) a puma.

cough [kof] *vti* to make a harsh sound when bringing air or harmful matter from the lungs or throat: *He's coughing badly because he has a cold*; (*fig*) *My car's coughing smoke all over the place.* – *See also* **cough up** *below.* – *nc* **1** an act of coughing: *He gave a short cough of embarrassment.* **2** an illness causing coughing: *I've had a smoker's cough for years.*

'**cough-mixture** *nu* a preparation used for relieving coughing: *Give the child some cough-mixture.*

cough up 1 *vt sep* to produce by coughing; to remove from the throat, chest *etc* by coughing: *He must be very ill – he's coughing up blood*; *Try and cough up the mucus*; *I can't cough it up.* **2** *vi, vt sep* (*sl*) to pay (money): *I can't afford that dress – perhaps mother will cough up* (*the money*) *for it.*

could [kud] – *neg short form* **couldn't** ['kudnt] – *modal aux* **1** *pt of* **can**: *They asked if I could drive a car*; *She asked if she could go.* **2** used to express an alternative (*esp* an unlikely one) or possibility in the present or future: *I could go but I'm not going to*; *I could do it next week if you helped me.*

'**could have** used to express an alternative (*esp* an unlikely one) or possibility in the past: *We could have gone, but we didn't.*

council ['kaunsəl] *nc* **1** a group of people formed in order to advise, organize, make decisions *etc*: *The King formed a council of wise men to advise him*; *He is a member of the Central Council for Physical Recreation.* **2** in the UK, a body of people elected to control the workings of local government in a county, region, district *etc*: *The council have voted to increase the rates this year*; (*attrib*) *a council meeting.*

'**councillor** *nc* a person who is elected to serve on a council.

counsel ['kaunsəl] **1** *nu* (*formal*) advice: *He'll give you good counsel on your problems.* **2** *nc* a barrister or advocate: *counsel for the defence.* – *v* – *pt, ptp* – '**counselled**, (*Amer*) '**counseled** – *vt* (*very formal*) to advise; to recommend: *He counselled me to go to university.*

'**counsellor**, (*Amer*) **counselor** *nc* a person who gives advice: *a marriage guidance counsellor.*

keep (one's own) counsel (*formal*) to keep something secret: *She considered sharing her problem with her friend but decided to keep her own counsel.*

count[1] [kaunt] *nc* (*with cap in titles*) (the status of) a foreign nobleman equal in rank to a British earl: *She is married to a German count*; *the Count of Monte Cristo.*

'**countess** *nc* (*with cap in titles*) **1** (the status of) the wife or widow of an earl or count. **2** (the status of) a woman of the same rank as an earl or count in her own right.

count[2] [kaunt] **1** *vi* to name the numbers (up to): *Count up to ten.* **2** *vti* to calculate using numbers: *Count* (*up*) *the number of pages*; *Count how many people there are*; *There were six people present, not counting the chairman*; *I've never been able to count very well.* **3** *vi* (not *usu* used with **is, was** *etc* and **-ing**) to be important or have an effect or value: *He used to be important but nowadays what he says doesn't count*; *All these essays count towards my exam results.* **4** *vt* (*formal*: not used with **is, was** *etc* and **-ing**) to consider or think of: *I count him among my best friends*; *I count you as my dearest friend*; *Count yourself lucky to be here.* – *See also* **count** *in phrases below.* – *nc* **1** an act of numbering: *They took a count of how many people attended.* **2** the number counted: *What was the count at the meeting last night?* **3** (*formal*) a charge brought against a prisoner *etc*: *She faces three counts of assault and one of theft*; *He is guilty on all counts.* – *adj see* **countable** (*def 2*).

'**countable** *adj* **1** (*usu pred*: *formal*) capable of being numbered: *Millionths of a second are countable only on very complicated instruments.* **2** (*neg* **un-**: *also* (*attrib*) **count**) (of a noun) capable of forming a plural and using the definite or indefinite article: *Table is a count*(*able*) *noun, but milk is an uncountable noun.*

'**counter**[1] *nc* **1** a person or thing that counts: *a counter of votes*; *This machine has a counter on the side to tell you how many photocopies it will make.* **2** a token used in numbering or playing certain games: *counters for playing ludo etc.*

'**countless** *adj* very many: *Countless visitors come here every summer.*

'**countdown** *nc* (used *orig* of a rocket) a counting backwards to check the time remaining until the beginning of an event, regarded as zero: *It's five minutes to countdown.*

count against 1 *vt fus* to be a disadvantage to (someone): *Your previous criminal record will count against you in this trial.* **2** (*vt oblig sep*: *usu in neg*) to take (a disadvantage) into consideration: *I don't like him but I won't count that against him when I'm considering him for the job.*

count for much (*usu in neg*), **count for little** to be important, unimportant *etc*: *My small contribu-*

tion doesn't count for much when you consider the total cost.

count in *vt usu sep* to include: *Have you counted John in?*; *If you're going to the cinema, count me in.*

ˈ**count on** *vt fus* to rely on (a person or happening): *I'm counting on you to persuade her*; *I'm counting on the train's being empty so that I can get a seat.*

count out 1 *vt usu sep* not to include: *If you're going to the cinema, you can count me out.* **2** *vt sep* to say that (a boxer) is the loser because he cannot get up, within a count of ten seconds: *He was counted out in the fourth round.*

out for the count 1 (of a boxer) still unconscious or not standing after the count of ten: *He was out for the count in the third round.* **2** (*fig*) exhausted, asleep or unconscious: *As soon as he came home from his exhausting walk, he sat down and was out for the count.*

countenance [ˈkauntinəns] *nc* (*formal*) the face: *a gloomy countenance*; (*fig*) *The whole countenance of the countryside has changed.* – *vt* (*formal*) to favour or encourage; to approve of or accept: *We can't possibly countenance these widespread changes.*

give countenance to (*formal*) to countenance: *You must not give countenance to these rumours.*

counter[1] *see* **count**[2].

counter[2] [ˈkauntə] *adv* (*formal*) in the opposite direction or manner: *The election is running counter to all the forecasts*; *This wheel turns counter to all the others.* – *adj* (*pred*: *formal*) contrary or opposite: *This result is counter to what we expected.* – *vti* (*formal*) to meet or answer (a stroke or move *etc* by another): *He countered (the awkward question) with a clever reply*; *He successfully countered all attempts to defeat him.*

counter- (*in cmpds*) **1** against; in opposition to: *counter-revolution.* **2** opposite: *counter-clockwise.*

counter[3] [ˈkauntə] *nc* a kind of table or surface on which goods are laid: *Can you get me some sweets from the confectionery counter?*

counteract [kauntərˈakt] *vt* to undo or prevent the effect of: *the government's efforts to counteract inflation*; *Antibiotics will counteract the infection.*

ˌ**counterˈaction** *ncu.*

counter-attack [ˈkauntərətak] *nc* an attack in reply to an attack: *The enemy made a counter-attack at dawn.* – *vti* to make such an attack (on): *As soon as they withdraw, our troops must counter-attack.*

counter-attraction [ˈkauntərətrakʃən] *ncu* (*formal*) something which is more attractive or popular than something else: *Cinema can't compete with the counter-attractions of television.*

counter-charge [ˈkauntətʃa:dʒ] *nc* an accusation made in opposition to another: *She brought counter-charges against the man who accused her of spying.*

counterfeit [ˈkauntəfit] *adj* **1** copied or made in imitation *esp* with a dishonest purpose: *counterfeit money*; *These £1 notes are counterfeit.* **2** not genuine or not real: *counterfeit tears/emotion.* – *vt* **1** to make a copy of for dishonest purposes: *to counterfeit £1 notes.* **2** (*formal*) to pretend: *She counterfeited tears.*

counterfoil [ˈkauntəfoil] *nc* a section able to be detached or removed from a cheque or postal order *etc* and kept by the giver as a receipt: *Mark the amount paid on the counterfoil in your cheque book.*

countermand [kauntəˈma:nd, (*Amer*) ˈkauntərmand] *vt* (*formal*) to give an order contradicting one already given: *The captain's order was countermanded by his superiors.*

counter-measure [ˈkauntəmeʒə] *nc* (*often in pl*) an action taken to prevent, or try to undo the effect of, another action: *The police have developed new counter-measures against terrorists.*

counterpane [ˈkauntəpein] *nc* a top cover for a bed: *Remove the counterpane before getting into bed.*

counterpart [ˈkauntəpa:t] *nc* (*formal*) a person or thing having the same qualities, characteristics, jobs *etc* as another: *I'm managing director of Smith's, and he's my counterpart at Brown and Co.*

countersign [ˈkauntəsain] *vt* to sign (something) as additional proof of its accuracy, genuineness *etc*: *He had to countersign the cheque in the presence of the bank-manager.*

countess *see* **count**[1].

country [ˈkʌntri] **1** *nc* any of the nations of the world; the land occupied by a nation: *Canada is a larger country than Spain.* **2** *nc* the people of a country: *The whole country is in agreement with your views.* **3** *nu* (*usu with* **the**) districts where there are fields, moors *etc* as opposed to towns and areas with many buildings: *We're having a quiet holiday in the country*; *She prefers living in the country to being in the town*; (*attrib*) *country districts.* **4** *nu* an area or stretch of land: *hilly country.* **5** *nu* (*fig*) areas of knowledge, experience *etc*: *We're going into completely new country, since no-one has ever used this process before.*

ˌ**country-and-ˈwestern (music), country music** *nus* songs written in the style of old rural American or cowboy ballads, *usu* accompanied by the guitar.

country dance *ncu* a (style of) dance in which partners are arranged in parallel lines: (*attrib*) *country-dance music.*

country house/country seat *ncs* a landowner's large house in the country: *They have a large country house.*

ˈ**countryman** – *fem* ˈ**countrywoman** – *nc* **1** a person who lives in the country: *Countrymen usually like walking.* **2** a person born in the same country as another: *Churchill and Chamberlain were fellow countrymen.*

ˈ**countryside** *nu* country areas: *He paints pictures of the English countryside*; *The countryside is beautiful at this time of year.*

county [ˈkaunti] *nc* **1** the larger of the two main administrative units of local government in England and Wales: *There are fifty-three counties in England and Wales*; (*attrib*) *a county council.* **2** in the US, the largest of the units of local government within a state: *Marin County*; (*attrib*) *the county sheriff.*

See also **district, region.**

coup [ku:] *nc* **1** (*formal*) a sudden successful action: *He pulled off* (= made) *a real coup by completing this deal.* **2** a coup d'état: *There's been a coup in one of the African republics.*

coup d'état [ku:deiˈta:] – *pl* **coups d'état** [ku:dei-] – *nc* a sudden and violent change in government: *The president was killed during the coup d'état.*

coupé [ˈku:pei, (*Amer*) ku:ˈpei] *nc* a two-door car with a fixed roof.

couple [ˈkʌpl] *nc* **1** (*no pl*: *inf*: *usu with* **a**) two; (*loosely*) a few: *Can I borrow a couple of chairs?*; *Lend me a couple of cigarettes*; *I knew a couple of people at the party – but not many.* **2** a man and wife, or a boyfriend and girlfriend: *a married* couple; *The party was full of couples, with no unattached or single people.* – **1** *vt* (*often with* **together**) to join together: *The coaches were coupled (together), and the train set off.* **2** *vt* (*often with* **together**) to associate (people or things) in one's mind: *I always couple Hemingway and Steinback together as being typically American writers.* **3** *vi* (*usu derog or liter*) to have sexual intercourse (with).

'**couplet** [-lit] *nc* two lines of verse, one following the other, which rhyme with each other.

'**coupling 1** *nc* a link for joining things together: *The railway carriage was damaged when the coupling broke.* **2** *nu* (*usu derog or liter*) the act of having sexual intercourse.

coupon ['ku:pon] *nc* **1** a piece of paper *etc* giving one the right to something, *eg* a gift or discount price: *During the war when many goods were rationed each person received coupons to be exchanged for food, clothes etc; This coupon gives 5p off your next purchase.* **2** a betting form for the football pools: *I can't win a prize – I forgot to send in my (football) coupon.*

courage ['kʌridʒ, (*Amer*) 'kə:-] *nu* the quality that makes a person able to meet dangers without fear; bravery: *It took courage to sail the Atlantic singlehanded; The soldier showed great courage in the battle; He didn't have the courage to tell his mother that he had failed.*

courageous [kə'reidʒəs] *adj* having courage: *a courageous soldier; He was courageous in battle.*

cou'rageously *adv.*

the courage of one's convictions the courage to do what one believes to be right: *People will try to make you change your decision but you must have the courage of your convictions.*

courgette [kuə'ʒet] *nc* (*esp Brit*: *Amer usu* **zuc'chini**) a type of small green vegetable similar to the marrow.

courier ['kuriə] **1** *nc* a guide who travels with, and looks after, parties of tourists: *a courier on a coach trip.* **2** *nc* (*formal*) a messenger: *He's a courier for the government spy agency.* **3** *n* (*with cap*) a word often used in the title of newspapers: *the Southern Courier.*

course [ko:s] *nc* **1** a series (of lectures, medicines *etc*): *I'm taking a course (of lectures) in sociology; He's having a course of treatment for his leg.* **2** a division or part of a meal: *Now we've had the soup, what's (for) the next course?* **3** (*often in cmpds*) the ground over which a race is run or a game (*esp* golf) is played: *a racecourse; a golf-course; The course is flooded.* **4** the path or direction in which something moves: *Which course do we take when flying to Paris?; What course does the road take from here to Berlin?; We followed the course of the Nile for fifty miles.* **5** (*no pl*) the usual progress or development (of events): *Things will follow/run/take their normal course (of events) despite the strike.* **6** a way (of action): *What's the best course (of action) in the circumstances?* – *vi* **1** (*liter or formal*) to run swiftly: *Tears were coursing down her cheeks.* **2** to hunt (*esp* hares) with dogs.

'**coursing** *nu* the hunting of animals in this way: *hare coursing.*

in the 'course of (*formal*) during: *In the course of our talk, he told me he was going on holiday soon.*

in due course at the appropriate or normal time: *In due course, this acorn will grow into a tree.*

a matter of course *see* **matter**.

of 'course naturally or obviously: *Of course, he didn't tell me any secrets.*

off course not (going) in the right direction or path: *We've drifted off course.*

on course (going) in the right direction or path: *We're on course for Jamaica.*

court [ko:t] *nc* **1** a place where legal cases are heard: *a magistrates' court; the High Court.* **2** the judges and officials of a legal court: *The accused is to appear before the court on Friday.* **3** (*often in cmpds*) a marked-out space for certain games: *a tennis-court; a squash court; We want to play badminton but there isn't a vacant court.* **4** the officials, councillors *etc* of a king or queen: *the court of King James.* **5** the palace of a king or queen: *Hampton Court.* **6** an open space surrounded by houses or by the parts of one house: *The children can play safely in the back court.* – **1** *vti* (*old*) to try to win the love of (someone); to woo: *John's been courting Mary for three months; John and Mary are courting.* **2** *vt* (*formal*) to try to gain: *He courted the audience's affection.* **3** *vt* (*formal*) to act in a way which is likely to bring about (something unpleasant): *He's courting disaster by trying to sail the Atlantic in such a small boat.*

'**courtier** [-tiə] *nc* a member of the court of a king or queen: *He was one of King James' courtiers.*

'**courtly** *adj* (*old*) having fine manners: *a courtly knight; courtly behaviour.* '**courtliness** *nu.*

'**courtship** *ncu* (*old*) (a period of) courting or being courted (*usu* in the romantic sense): *John's courtship of Mary was unsuccessful.*

'**courthouse** *nc* a building where legal cases are held.

ˌ**court-'martial** – *pl* ˌ**courts-'martial** – *nc* a court held by officers of the armed forces to try offences against service discipline.

'**courtyard** *nc* a court or enclosed ground beside, or surrounded by, a building: *the courtyard of the castle.*

pay court to (*old or formal*) to try to win the affection or love of (someone): *He paid court to the duke's daughter.*

courteous ['kə:tiəs] *adj* polite; considerate and respectful: *a courteous young man; It was courteous of him to write a letter of thanks.* '**courteously** *adv.*

'**courteousness** *nu.*

courtesan [ko:ti'zan, (*Amer*) 'ko:rtizn] *nc* (*formal or old*) a prostitute, *esp* one with wealthy clients.

courtesy ['kə:təsi] **1** *nu* politeness; considerate and respectful behaviour: *Even a small amount of courtesy is greatly appreciated.* **2** *nc* (*formal*) a courteous act: *He's always paying her little courtesies.*

courtier *see* **court**.

cousin ['kʌzn] *nc* **1** a son or daughter of one's uncle or aunt. **2** a son or daughter of any of the descendants of one's uncle or aunt: *a distant cousin.*

first/full cousin *nc* a son or daughter of one's uncle or aunt.

second cousin *nc* a child of one's parent's first cousin.

cove [kouv] *nc* a small bay or inlet of the sea: *They bathed in a quiet cove.*

coven ['kʌvən] *nc* a gathering or society of witches: *She is head of the coven; The coven met in the churchyard.*

covenant ['kʌvənənt] *nc* (*legal*) an agreement between two people or two parties to do, or not to do, something: *She signed a covenant to give money to the school fund.*

Coventry ['kovəntri]: **send (someone) to Coventry** to refuse to speak to (someone), *usu* because of something he has done: *His workmates sent him to Coventry because he worked during the strike.*

cover ['kʌvə] *vt* **1** to put or spread something on, over or in front of: *They covered (up) the body with a sheet; The table was covered with food; This book is covered with leather; Cover the hole with boards in case anyone falls down it; My shoes are covered in paint; (fig) He was covered in confusion.* **2** to be enough to pay for: *Will £5 cover your expenses?* **3** to travel: *We covered forty miles in one day.* **4** to include: *Does this definition cover the figurative meaning?* **5** to stretch over a length of time *etc*: *His diary covered three years.* **6** (*often with* **up**) to hide: *He's bluffing to cover (up) his lack of knowledge.* **7** to protect: *Are we covered by your car insurance?* **8** to report on: *I'm covering the race for the local newspaper.* **9** to point a gun at: *Cover the prisoners to stop them from escaping!; I have them covered.* – *See also* **cover up** *below.* – **1** *nc* (*sometimes in cmpds*) something which covers, *esp* a cloth over a table, bed *etc*: *Put the cover on the manhole in case someone falls down it; a table-cover; Put the cover on the bed.* **2** *nu* something that gives protection or shelter: *The animal sought cover when the dogs were chasing him; The soldiers took cover to hide from the enemy gunfire; She has £10 000-worth of insurance cover.* **3** *ncu* (*inf*) something that hides: *His business trips abroad are a cover for his smuggling; He escaped under cover of darkness.*

'**coverage** [-ridʒ] *nu* **1** the covering of items by an insurance policy: *I have very little insurance coverage.* **2** the extent of the inclusion of items in a news report *etc*: *The TV coverage of the Queen's Silver Jubilee was extensive; The coverage of technical vocabulary is poor in that dictionary.*

'**covering** *ncu* something which covers: *My car has a thick covering of dirt; a slight covering of snow.*

'**cover charge** *nc* a charge per person for service in a restaurant: *Is the cover charge included in the price?*

'**cover-girl** *nc* a girl pictured on a magazine cover.

covering letter *nc* a letter to explain documents *etc* enclosed with it: *I received a cheque from the firm but no covering letter.*

cover ground *see* **ground**.

cover up 1 *vt sep* to put a cover on (something): *Cover up the soup so that the flies don't get at it; The child covered up her dirty dress with her coat.* **2** *vt sep, vi* to hide or conceal (something illegal or dishonest): *Did you think you'd succeeded in covering up all your mistakes?* (*nc* '**cover-up**). **3** *vi* (*with* **for**) to try to prevent the dishonest, illegal *etc* deeds of someone from being discovered by concealing the truth, lying *etc*: *He's been covering up for his friend by telling lies.* (*nc* '**cover-up**: *His story was a cover-up for his friend.*)

take cover to find (a place of) protection or shelter: *The soldiers took cover from the gunfire; The travellers took cover in an old barn as the storm started.*

under cover of protected or hidden by (something): *under cover of darkness.*

See also **uncover, undercover**.

coverlet ['kʌvəlit] *nc* (*old or formal*) a top cover for a bed.

covert ['kʌvət] *adj* (*attrib*: *formal*) secret or concealed: *covert activities; She gave a covert glance at the policeman.*

covet ['kʌvit] – *v* – *pt, ptp* '**coveted** – *vt* (*formal*) to desire or wish for eagerly (*esp* something belonging to someone else): *I covet her fur coat; The farmer covets his neighbour's prize herd.* '**covetous** *adj.* '**covetously** *adv.* '**covetousness** *nu.*

covey ['kʌvi] *nc* a brood or small flock (of partridges).

cow[1] [kau] *nc* **1** the female of cattle used for giving milk: *He has ten cows and a bull; dairy cows.* **2** the female of certain other animals *eg* the elk, elephant, whale. **3** (*sl derog*) an unpleasant or objectionable woman: *Silly cow!*

'**cowboy** *nc* in the US, a man who looks after cattle on a ranch: (*attrib*) *a cowboy hat.*

'**cowherd** *nc* (*old*) a person who looks after cows.

'**cowhide** *nu, adj* (of) the skin of a cow made into leather: *a bag made of cowhide; a cowhide bag.*

till the '**cows come home** (*inf*) for a very long time: *We could cheerfully sit here talking till the cows come home.*

cow[2] [kau] *vt* (*formal*) to subdue or frighten with threats: *She looked slightly cowed after her interview with the headmaster; Her stern father cowed her into doing what he asked.*

coward ['kauəd] *nc* a person who shows fear easily or is easily frightened: *The cowards ran away when they saw the enemy approaching; I am such a coward that I rarely visit the dentist.* '**cowardly** *adj.*

'**cowardice** [-dis], '**cowardliness** *nus* lack of courage: *cowardice in battle; He was surprised at the cowardliness of the bully.*

cower ['kauə] *vi* to crouch down or draw back because of fear: *He was cowering away from the fierce dog; cowering in fear.*

cowl [kaul] *nc* **1** (a cap or hood like) a monk's hood. **2** a cover for a chimney-pot *etc.*

coxswain ['koksn] *nc* **1** (*often abbrev* **cox** [koks] a person who steers a (small, *usu* racing) boat. **2** a petty officer in charge of a boat and crew.

coy [koi] *adj* (pretending to be) shy: *She gave her brother's friend a coy smile; She seemed rather coy in his presence.*

'**coyly** *adv*: *The little girl peeped coyly round the door.* '**coyness** *nu.*

cozy *see* **cosy**.

crab[1] [krab] **1** *nc* an edible sea animal with a shell and five pairs of legs, the first pair having claws. **2** *nu* its flesh used as food: *crab in mayonnaise.*

crab[2] [krab] *nc* (*also* '**crab apple**) a kind of wild bitter apple: *People don't usually eat crab apples;* (*attrib*) *crab-apple jelly;* (*attrib*) *a crab-apple tree.*

crabbed ['krabid] *adj* bad-tempered: *a crabbed old man; She's very crabbed today – she has a hang-over.*

crack [krak] **1** *vti* to (cause to) break partly without falling to pieces: *The window cracked down the middle; Her bone isn't broken – it's just cracked.* **2** *vti* to break (open): *He cracked the peanuts between his finger and thumb.* **3** *vti* to (cause to) make a sudden sharp sound, like a nut splitting: *My knees cracked when I knelt down.* **4** *vt* (*inf*) to make (a joke): *He's always cracking jokes.* **5** *vt* (*inf*) to open (a safe) by illegal means. **6** *vt* to solve (a code): *People were employed to crack enemy codes during the war.* **7** *vti* to (cause to) give in to persuasion, torture or similar pressures: *The spy finally cracked under their questioning and told them everything he knew;* (*formal*) *They cracked his composure by telling him* that his friend had died. – *See also* **crack down on, crack up** *below.* – *nc* **1** a split or break: *a crack in the wall*; *There's a crack in this cup.* **2** a narrow opening: *The door opened a crack.* **3** a sudden sharp sound: *the crack of a whip*; *the crack of a pistol.* **4** a blow: *I got a nasty crack on the jaw.* **5** (*inf*) a joke: *He made a crack about my big feet.* – *See also* **have a crack (at)** *below.* – *adj* (*attrib*) expert: *She's a crack racing-driver.*

cracked *adj* **1** damaged by cracks: *a cracked cup*; *The glass was cracked.* **2** (*usu pred*: *sl*) crazy: *She must be cracked to suggest such a ridiculous scheme!*

'**cracker** *nc* **1** a thin crisp biscuit: *crackers and cheese.* **2** a small exploding firework. **3** (*esp* **Christmas cracker**) a decorated paper tube, containing paper hats *etc*, which gives a loud crack when pulled apart.

'**crackers** *adj* (*pred*: *inf*) crazy: *You must be crackers to believe that!*

'**crackpot** *nc* (*inf*) a crazy person: *This place is full of crackpots!*; (*attrib*) *a crackpot scheme.*

crack down on *vt fus* to take strong action against: *The police are cracking down on vandals in this area.*

crack up *vi* (*usu fig inf*) to break into pieces; to become unable to continue: *If he works as hard as this all the time he'll eventually crack up*; *He has cracked up under the strain of over-working*; *His health is slowly cracking up.*

get cracking (*inf*) to get moving quickly; to get busy: *We'll have to get cracking if we want to catch that train!*

have a crack (at) (*inf*) to have a try at; to make an attempt to: *I've never driven a lorry that size before but I'll have a crack at (driving) it.*

not all it's *etc* **cracked up to be** (*inf*) not as good as it *etc* is said to be: *That film is not all it's cracked up to be*; *He's not as good a driver as he's cracked up to be.*

crackle ['krakl] *vi* to make a continuous cracking noise: *The dry branches crackled under my feet.* – *nu* slight cracking sounds: *the crackle of burning wood.*

'**crackling** *nu* **1** the crisp rind of roast pork. **2** the sound of something which crackles: *The crackling of the twigs frightened the deer.*

'**crackly** *adj* tending to crackle: *The radio reception is very crackly here*; *a crackly noise.*

cradle ['kreidl] *nc* **1** a child's bed *esp* one in which it can be rocked. **2** a frame of similar shape, *eg* one under a ship that is being built or repaired. – *vt* to hold or rock as if in a cradle: *She cradled the child in her arms.*

craft [kra:ft] – *pl* **craft** (*def 2*), **crafts** – **1** *nc* an art or skill: *the craft of wood-carving.* **2** *nc* (*formal*) a boat or ship: *Craft of all types are taking part in the race*; *sailing craft.* **3** *nu* (*formal*) cunning or trickery: *Craft and deceit are often used by confidence tricksters.*

'**crafty** *adj* cunning and sly. '**craftily** *adv.* '**craftiness** *nu.*

'**craftsman** ['kra:ftsmən] *nc* a person who is skilled at making things (*esp* by hand): *The joiner who made our windows was a real craftsman.*

'**craftsmanship** ['kra:fts-] *nu* skill in making things.

crag [krag] *nc* (*often found with cap in place-names*) a rough, steep mountain or piece of rock: *Salisbury Crags.*

'**craggy** *adj* **1** rocky. **2** (*usu* of people's faces) with strong or rough features: *the shepherd's craggy face.*

cram [kram] – *pt, ptp* **crammed** – **1** *vt* to fill very full: *He crammed himself with food*; *The drawer was crammed with papers.* **2** *vt* to push or force: *He crammed food into his mouth.* **3** *vti* (*inf*) to prepare (someone) in a short time for an examination: *The child is being crammed for Eton*; *He crammed through the summer holidays.*

cramp [kramp] *ncu* (a) painful stiffening of the muscles: *The swimmer got cramp and drowned*; *I have cramp in my leg*; *He suffered from cramps.* – *vt* to put into too narrow or too small a space: *We were all cramped into a tiny room*; (*fig*) *Lack of money cramped our efforts* (= prevented them from being as successful as they might have been).

cramped *adj* **1** without enough room: *We have a very cramped dining-room.* **2** (of handwriting) small and closely written.

cramp one's style to prevent one from showing one's ability to the full: *Working as a commercial artist tends to cramp his style as a creative artist*; (*ironic*) *Having a wife and child has certainly cramped his style* (= prevented him from having such a carefree life as before).

crampon ['krampən] *nc* an iron plate with spikes, attached to the foot when hill-climbing, walking on ice *etc.*

crane [krein] *nc* a machine with a long arm and a chain, for raising heavy weights. – *vt* to stretch out (the neck, to see round or over something): *He craned his neck in order to see over the wall*; *He craned forward to see if there was a bus coming.*

crank [kraŋk] *nc* (*derog*) a person with strange or odd ideas. '**cranky** *adj.* '**crankiness** *nu.*

cranny *see* **nook**.

crap [krap] *nu* **1** (*vulg*: *esp Amer*) solid waste matter discharged from the bowels; faeces. **2** (*sl*) nonsense or rubbish: *Clear all that crap off your desk!* – *v* – *pt, ptp* **crapped** – *vi* (*vulg*: *esp Amer*) to discharge faeces from the bowels.

crash [kraʃ] *nc* **1** a noise as of heavy things breaking or falling on something hard: *I heard a crash, and looked round to see that he'd dropped all the plates.* **2** a collision; a violent meeting: *There was a crash involving three cars.* **3** (*inf*) a failure of a business *etc*: *the Wall Street crash.* – **1** *vti* to (cause to) fall with a loud noise: *The glass crashed to the floor*; *He crashed his fist down on my desk.* **2** *vti* to drive or be driven violently (against, into): *He crashed (his car)*; *His car crashed into a wall.* **3** *vti* (of aircraft) to land or be landed in such a way as to be damaged or destroyed: *He crashed (the plane)*; *His plane crashed in the mountains.* **4** *vi* (*inf*) (of a business) to fail: *The firm crashed soon after his death.* **5** *vi* to force one's way noisily (through, into): *He crashed through the undergrowth.* **6** *vt* (*inf*) to attend (a party *etc*) uninvited. – *adj* (*attrib*) rapid and concentrated: *a crash course in shorthand and typing.*

ˌ**crash-'dive** *vi* (of a submarine) to dive very fast.

'**crash-helmet** *nc* a covering for the head worn for protection by racing-motorists, motor cyclists *etc.*

ˌ**crash-'land** *vti* to land (an aircraft), *usu* in an emergency, with the under-carriage up: *He crash-landed (the plane) a mile from the houses.*

crass [kras] *adj* (*formal*: *usu attrib*) very obvious or very great: *a crass insult*; *a crass mistake.*

crate [kreit] *nc* **1** a container *usu* made of wooden slats for carrying goods, fruit *etc*, sometimes with compartments for bottles. **2** the amount contained by a crate: *We've ordered three crates of bananas.* – *vt* (*formal*) to pack (things) in a crate: *The furniture removers crated the china before doing anything else.*

crater ['kreitə] *nc* **1** the bowl-shaped mouth of a volcano. **2** a hollow made in the ground by the explosion of a shell, a falling meteor *etc.*

cravat [krə'vat] *nc* a kind of scarf worn instead of a tie round the neck: *He wore a silk cravat tucked inside his shirt.*

crave [kreiv] *vt* **1** (*old*) to beg earnestly for: *I crave forgiveness.* **2** (*formal*) to long for: *I crave the freedom to travel abroad*; (*facet*) *I crave a cigarette.*

'**craving** *nc* a desire or longing: *She had a craving for oranges during her pregnancy.*

craven ['kreivən] *adj* (*old*) cowardly: *a craven bully.*

craving *see* **crave**.

crawfish *see* **crayfish**.

crawl [kro:l] *vi* **1** to move slowly along the ground: *The injured dog crawled away.* **2** (of people) to move on hands and knees or with the front of the body on the ground: *The baby can't walk yet, but she crawls everywhere.* **3** to move very slowly: *Because of the roadworks, the traffic could only crawl along at ten kilometres per hour.* **4** (always with **is, was** *etc* and **-ing**) to be covered with crawling things: *His hair was crawling with lice*; (*fig inf*) *The town's always crawling with people on a Saturday.* **5** (*inf*) to act very humbly, usually trying to put oneself into favour with someone: *She's always crawling to the boss because she wants more money.* – *nc* (*no pl*) **1** a very slow movement or speed: *We were very careful, and only drove along at a crawl.* **2** a style of swimming in which the arms make alternative overarm movements: *She's better at the crawl than she is at the breaststroke.*

crayfish ['kreifiʃ] – *pl* '**crayfish** – (*also, esp Amer,* **crawfish** ['kro:fiʃ] – *pl* '**crawfish**) **1** *nc* either of two different varieties of shellfish. **2** *nu* their flesh as food.

crayon ['kreiən] *nc* a coloured pencil or stick of chalk *etc* for drawing with. – *vti* to use crayons to draw a picture *etc.*

craze [kreiz] *nc* a (*usu* temporary) fashion; great (but temporary) enthusiasm: *the current craze for cutting one's hair extremely short.*

'**crazy** *adj* **1** (*often inf*) insane: *You don't have to be crazy to work here, but it helps*; *a crazy idea.* **2** (*pred*: *inf*) very enthusiastic: *She's crazy about her current boyfriend.* '**crazily** *adv.* '**craziness** *nu.*

crazy paving *nu* paving for paths *etc*, made of irregular pieces fitted together.

creak [kri:k] *vi* to make a sharp grating sound like a hinge which needs oil: *That chair is creaking beneath your weight.* – *nc* such a sound: *The strange creaks in the old house kept the girl awake.*

'**creaky** *adj.* '**creakiness** *nu.*

cream [kri:m] **1** *nu* the yellowish-white oily substance that forms on the top of milk, and from which butter and cheese are made. **2** *ncu* any of many substances made of, or similar in texture to, cream: *Ice-cream is very refreshing*; *Cold cream helps to keep one's skin in good condition*; (*attrib*) *cream cheese.* **3** *nu* (*fig*) the best part: *the cream of the medical profession.* **4** *nu* a yellowish-white colour. **5** *nu* something (*eg* paint) cream in colour. – *vt* **1** to make into a cream-like mixture: *Cream the eggs, butter and sugar together to form a smooth paste.* **2** (*sometimes with* **off**) to take the cream off: *She creamed the milk*; (*fig*) *The new school creamed off the best pupils in the district.* – *adj* **1** (*attrib*) made with or containing cream: *a cream cake.* **2** (*also* '**cream-coloured**) yellowish-white: *cream wallpaper*; *Her dress was cream.* **3** (*attrib*) (of sherry) sweet.

'**creamery** *nc* a place where butter and cheese are made.

'**creamy** *adj* **1** full of, or like, cream: *creamy milk*; *It tasted very creamy.* **2** smooth and cream-coloured: *a creamy complexion*; *Her skin was soft and creamy.* '**creaminess** *nu.*

cream of tartar *nu* an ingredient in baking powder.

crease [kri:s] *nc* **1** a mark made by folding or doubling something: *He always has a smart crease in his trousers*; *My dress is full of creases after being in my suitcase*; *This material is meant to be crease-resistant* (= should not crease easily). **2** in cricket, a line showing the position of the batsman or bowler. – *vti* to make or become creased: *You've creased my newspaper badly*; *Your dress will crease unless you hang it in the wardrobe.*

create [kri'eit] **1** *vt* (*sometimes formal*) to cause to exist; to make: *How was the earth created?*; *The circus created great excitement.* **2** *vt* to give (a rank *etc* to): *Sir John was created a knight in 1958.* **3** *vi* (*inf*) to make a fuss: *She created until all the rubbish was cleared away.*

cre'ation **1** *nu* the act of creating: *The creation of the Roman Empire took many years.* **2** *nc* something created: *artistic creations*; *The dress designer is showing his latest creations*; (*facet and usu derog*) *Where did she get that creation?* (= a hat or dress *etc*). **3** *nu* (*formal*) the universe: *the Lord of all creation*; (*facet*) *He's the meanest person in all creation.*

cre'ative [-tiv] *adj* having or showing the power and imagination to create: *a creative writer*; *a creative dress-designer*; *His work is creative but not practical.* **cre'atively** *adv.* **cre'ativeness,** **ˌcrea'tivity** [kri:ə-] *nus.*

cre'ator *nc* a person who creates.

the Creator God.

creature ['kri:tʃə] *nc* **1** an animal or human being: *We are all God's creatures.* **2** a term of contempt or pity: *Don't let that filthy creature into the house!*; *Look at that poor creature sitting in the doorway.*

crèche [kreʃ] *nc* a nursery for babies whose mothers are at work, in church *etc*: *Some factories have crèches for the children of their workers.*

credence ['kri:dəns] *nu* (*formal*) the quality of being believed: *His statements no longer have any credence.*

credentials [kri'denʃəlz] *n pl* (*formal*) (*esp* written) evidence of trustworthiness or authority: *She asked the policeman to show her his credentials.*

credible ['kredəbl] *adj* (*usu pred*) that may be believed: *The story he told was barely credible.*

'**credibly** *adv.*

ˌcredi'bility *nu* (*formal*): *His statements no longer have any credibility*; *She lost all credibility for her failure to do the work.*

See also **incredible**.

credit ['kredit] **1** *nu* time allowed for payment of goods *etc* after they have been received: *We don't give credit at this shop*; (*attrib*) *I have a credit limit of £100.* **2** *nu* money loaned (by a bank): *The bank will not give you any more credit until you repay the previous loan.* **3** *nu* trustworthiness regarding ability to pay for goods *etc*: *Your credit is good at the moment.* **4** *nc* (an entry on) the side of an account on which payments received are entered: *Our credits are greater than our debits*; (*attrib*) *on the credit side*; (*attrib*) *We have a credit balance of £3500.* **5** *nu* the sum of money which someone has in an account at a bank: *Your credit amounts to £243.53.* **6** *nu* (*formal*) belief or trust: *His story lends credit to what the child told us.* **7** *nc* (*Amer*) a certificate or other record to show that a student has completed a course which counts towards his degree. – *See also* **credits, be a credit to, give credit for, take the credit, to one's credit** *below.* – *vt* **1** to enter (a sum of money) on the credit side (of an account): *This cheque was credited to your account last month.* **2** (*formal*: *with* **with**) to think of (a person or thing) as having: *I don't credit her with much intelligence*; *Very ordinary objects were sometimes credited with magical powers.* **3** (*inf*: not used with **is, was** *etc* and **-ing**) to believe (something) to be possible: *Well, would you credit that!*

'creditable *adj* (*usu attrib*: *formal*) bringing honour or respect: *He made a very creditable attempt.* **'creditably** *adv.*

'creditor *nc* a person to whom a debt is owed: *Luckily, I have few creditors and plenty of money.*

'credits *n pl* the list of names of the actors, producer, director *etc* given at the beginning or end of a film.

'credit card *nc* a card which allows the holder to buy goods or services on credit: *I should like to pay by credit card.*

'credit-worthy *adj* worthy of being given financial credit: *The bank doesn't regard you as credit-worthy, and will not lend you any money*; *a credit-worthy customer.* **'credit-worthiness** *nu.*

be a 'credit to (someone), do (someone) credit to bring honour or respect to (someone or something): *Your son is a credit to you*; *Your son is a credit to his school*; *Your honesty does you credit.*

give (someone) credit (for something) (*often in passive*) to acknowledge and praise (someone for a good piece of work *etc*): *He was given all the credit for completing the work although she had done most of it.*

on 'credit payment being made after the date of sale: *Do you sell goods on credit?*

take (the) credit (for something) to accept the praise given (for something): *I did all the work, and he took all the credit.*

to one's 'credit (*formal*) worthy of praise: *It's to your credit that you were so honest.*

credulous ['kredjuləs, (*Amer*) -dʒu-] *adj* (*formal*) believing too easily: *a credulous young woman*; *He's credulous enough to believe anything you tell him.* **'credulousness, cre'dulity** [-'dju:-] *nus. See also* **incredulous**.

creed [kri:d] *nc* **1** a short statement of one's (*esp* religious) beliefs. **2** one's (religious) beliefs: *Wearing a turban is part of his religious creed.*

creek [kri:k] *nc* **1** (*Brit*) a small inlet, *esp* off a river. **2** (*Amer*) a small river.

up the creek (*inf*) in a difficult or impossible situation: *We're really up the creek now – here we are, in a foreign country, with no money.*

creel [kri:l] *nc* a basket, *esp* for carrying fish: *a creel of herring.*

creep [kri:p] – *pt, ptp* **crept** [krept] – *vi* **1** to move slowly, quietly or secretly: *They arrived late and crept into the church*; *The traffic was creeping along very slowly.* **2** to move on hands or knees or with the body close to the ground: *The dog crept under the hedge.* **3** (*often formal or liter*) (of plants) to grow along the ground, up a wall, or on supports: *Ivy crept over the wall until it covered the whole house.* – *See also* **creep up** *below.* – **1** *nu* an act of creeping. **2** *nc* (*inf*) a highly unpleasant person: *That fellow is a real creep!*

'creeper *nc* a creeping plant.

'creepy *adj* causing feelings of fear and disgust *etc*: *That was a creepy film we saw last night*; *The house is rather creepy at night.* **'creepily** *adv.* **'creepiness** *nu.*

,creepy-'crawly *nc, adj* (*inf*) (of) a small creeping insect.

creep up *vi* (*sometimes with* **on**) to approach slowly and stealthily (often from behind and unseen): *The cat crept up* (*on the pigeon*); (*fig*) *Old age crept up on her before she had done many of the things she hoped to do.*

give (someone) the creeps (*inf*) to make a person feel fear and disgust: *Spiders in the bath give me the creeps.*

make one's flesh creep to cause one to feel as if horrible creatures are crawling all over one: *That science fiction story really made my flesh creep.*

cremate [kri'meit] *vt* to burn dead (human) bodies: *He wanted to be cremated, not buried, when he died.* **cre'mation** *ncu.*

crematorium [kremə'to:riəm] *nc* a place where cremation is carried out: *The funeral service took place at the crematorium.*

creosote ['kriəsout] *nu* an oily liquid obtained from coal tar, used in preserving wood. – *vt* to treat with creosote: *He creosoted the fence.*

crêpe [kreip] *nu, adj* (of) a thin silk-like fabric with a wrinkled surface, sometimes used in dress-making: *a dress made of crêpe*; *a crêpe dress.*

crêpe paper *nu* paper with a similar surface.

crept *see* **creep**.

crescendo [kri'ʃendou] *nc* a gradual and continuous increase in loudness: *The shouting of the crowd grew to a crescendo*; (*music*) *There is a crescendo in the last four bars of the piece of music.* – *adv* (*music*) gradually increasing in loudness: *The conductor asked the orchestra to play the last four bars crescendo.*

crescent ['kresnt] *adj* (*attrib*) curved in shape like the moon in the first or last quarter: *the crescent moon*; *crescent-shaped bread rolls.* – **1** *nc* something of this shape, *esp* a curved street: *a handsome crescent of Georgian houses.* **2** *n* (*esp* in Britain: *with cap*: *often abbrev* **Cres.** *when written*) a word often used in the names of such streets: *He lives at 4 Park Crescent.*

cress [kres] *nu* any of several edible plants including **'watercress**, with sharp-tasting leaves used in salads.

crest [krest] *nc* **1** the comb or tuft on the head of a cock or other bird. **2** the summit or highest part: *the crest of a wave.* **3** feathers on the top of a helmet. **4** a badge or emblem: *the crest of the Clan Graham*; *the family crest.*

'crested *adj* (*attrib*) having a tuft on the head: *a crested tit.*

crestfallen ['krestfo:lən] *adj* (*usu pred*) very disappointed: *He was crestfallen when he heard that his holiday had been cancelled.*

cretin ['kretin] *nc* **1** (*med*) a person who is mentally subnormal and physically deformed. **2** (*inf derog*) used as a term of contempt and abuse: *He is an* *absolute cretin, and can't be trusted to do anything properly.* **'cretinous** *adj.*

crevasse [kri'vas] *nc* a very deep crack or split in a glacier: *The skier fell into a hidden crevasse.*

crevice ['krevis] *nc* a crack or narrow opening (in a wall, rock-face *etc*): *Many kinds of rock plants grew in the crevices of the wall.*

crew[1] [kru:] *nc* **1** the group of people who work or operate a ship or boat, an aeroplane, a bus, train *etc.* **2** (*inf: often derog*) a group or gang of people: *What an ill-assorted crew!* – *vi* (*usu with* **for**) to act as a crew member (for someone): *Will you crew for me this weekend?*

'crewcut *nu* a hairstyle in which the hair is extremely short: *His crewcut showed off his big ears.*

crew[2] *see* **crow**.

crib [krib] *nc* **1** (*Brit*) a very small bed with sides, often on rockers, for a very young baby; a cradle. **2** (*Amer*) a child's cot. **3** a key or translation used when studying a text in a foreign language. **4** something copied from such a translation, or from someone else's work: *This essay is full of cribs from well-known textbooks.* **5** a manger. – *v* – *pt, ptp* **cribbed** – *vt* to copy (another person's work): *She cribbed the answers from her friend's exercise-book.*

crick [krik] *nc* a painful stiffening of the muscles, *esp* in the neck. – *vt* to produce a crick in: *He cricked his neck playing bowls.*

cricket[1] ['krikit] *nu* an outdoor game played with bats, a ball and wickets, between two sides of eleven each: *We play cricket in the summer*; (*attrib*) *a cricket match*; *a game of cricket.*

'cricketer *nc* a person who plays cricket.

not cricket (*fig*) unfair or not sportsmanlike: *It's definitely not cricket to cheat in exams.*

cricket[2] ['krikit] *nc* an insect related to the grasshopper, the male of which makes a chirping noise by beating its wing covers.

crier *see* **cry**.

crime [kraim] **1** *ncu* act(s) punishable by law: *Murder is a crime*; *Crime is on the increase*; (*attrib*) *The crime rate is rising steadily.* **2** *nc* something not actually illegal, but morally wrong: *The widespread destruction of wooded areas is a crime against nature.*

criminal ['kriminl] *adj* **1** (*attrib*) concerned with crime: *criminal law*; *a criminal lawyer.* **2** (*attrib*) against the law: *Theft is a criminal offence.* **3** (*inf*) very wrong; wicked: *That is a criminal waste of food*; *It was criminal to cut that tree down.* – *nc* a person who has been found guilty of a crime.

'criminally *adv*: *He was criminally involved in the incident.*

crimson ['krimzn] **1** *nu, adj* (of) a deep red colour: *He was* (= his face was) *crimson with embarrassment*; *a crimson dress.* **2** *nu* something (*eg* material, paint *etc*) crimson in colour.

cringe [krindʒ] *vi* to shrink back in fear, terror *etc*: *The dog cringed when his cruel master raised his hand to strike him*; *The way he treats foreigners makes me cringe* (*with embarrassment*).

crinkle ['kriŋkl] *vti* to (cause to) wrinkle up: *The paper crinkled in the heat of the sun*; *She crinkled her nose in disapproval.* – *nc* a wrinkle.

'crinkly *adj* having a wrinkled appearance: *He has thick grey crinkly hair.*

crinoline ['krinəli:n] *nc* (*hist*) (a dress worn over) an undergarment consisting of a stiff fabric covering wire hoops used to make skirts stick out.

cripple ['kripl] *vt* **1** to make lame or disabled: *He was crippled when the horse threw him off.* **2** to make less strong, less efficient *etc*: *The cost of the war has crippled the country's economy.* – *nc* a lame or disabled person: *He's been a cripple since the car accident.*

crisis ['kraisis] – *pl* **'crises** [-si:z] – *nc* **1** a deciding moment or turning-point (*esp* of an illness): *Although she is still very ill, she has passed the crisis*; (*attrib*) *the crisis point.* **2** a time of great danger or suspense: *A crisis such as the recent flooding can result in many tragic situations*; (*attrib*) *a crisis situation.*

See also **critical** *under* **critic**.

crisp [krisp] *adj* **1** stiff and dry enough to break easily: *These biscuits are deliciously crisp*; *a crisp cracker.* **2** (of some vegetables) firm and fresh: *a crisp lettuce*; *The vegetables are fresh and crisp.* **3** (of air) cold and refreshing: *a crisp winter's morning*; *The air was crisp and sharp.* **4** (*usu attrib*) (of a style of speech *etc*) exact; firm and decided: *This speaker has a crisp style of delivery.* – *nc* short for **potato crisp**.

'crisply *adv.* **'crispness** *nu.* **'crispy** *adj.* **'crispiness** *nu.*

criss-cross ['kriskros] *adj* (*usu attrib*) made of lines which cross each other repeatedly: *a criss-cross pattern.* – *vti* to cross (something) in forming such a pattern: *The roads around here criss-cross all over the place*; *Lines of footprints criss-crossed the snow.*

criterion [krai'tiəriən] – *pl* **cri'teria** [-ə] – *nc* (*formal*) a standard used or referred to in judging something: *What are your criteria for deciding which words to include in this dictionary?*

critic ['kritik] *nc* **1** a person who judges or comments on literary or artistic work: *He has been the literary critic of the local newspaper for twenty years.* **2** a person who finds fault: *His critics would say that he is unsuitable for the job.*

'critical *adj* **1** (*attrib*) judging good and bad points: *He has written several critical works on Shakespeare.* **2** fault-finding: *He's very critical about/of people who drive badly*; *a critical attitude.* **3** of, at or having the nature of, a crisis; very serious: *The situation has become critical*; *There's a critical shortage of food*; (*esp med*) *After the accident, his condition was said to be critical.* **4** of great(est) importance: *Help arrived at the critical moment*; *The amount of sugar in the recipe is critical.*

'critically *adv*: *He is critically ill*; *She looked critically at the newly decorated room.*

'criticize, -ise [-saiz] **1** *vti* to find fault (with): *He's always criticizing her, and never pays her a compliment.* **2** *vt* to give an opinion of or judgement on (something): *Would you criticize my essay and tell me if it's any good?* **'criticism** *ncu.*

critique [kri'ti:k] *nc* (*very formal*) a critical piece of writing; a review: *He's written a critique of your play.*

croak [krouk] *vti* to utter a low hoarse sound like that of a frog or raven: *I could hear the frogs croaking*; *'I've got a sore throat,' she croaked.* – *nc* such a sound.

crochet ['krouʃei, (*Amer*) krou'ʃei] – *ptp* **'crocheting**: *pt, ptp* **'crocheted** – *vti* to knit using a single small needle with a hooked end (a **'crochet hook**). – *nu* a kind of knitting done or made in this way: *The old lady enjoys doing crochet*; *She put her crochet into her work-basket.*

crock [krok] *nc* **1** an earthenware pot or jar: *a crock* *of cooking salt.* **2** (*inf*) a worthless, old and decrepit person or thing: *He is a bit of an old crock*; *That car's an old crock.*

crockery ['krokəri] *nu* earthenware and china dishes, *eg* plates, cups, saucers *etc*: *I've washed the crockery but the cutlery is still dirty.*

crocodile ['krokədail] *nc* a large reptile found in the rivers of Asia, Africa, South America and northern Australia.

crocodile tears *n pl* pretended tears of grief: *They're only crocodile tears, because he's not really sorry at all.*

crocus ['kroukəs] *nc* a plant growing from a bulb and having brilliant yellow, purple or white flowers.

croft [kroft] *nc* a small piece of enclosed farm land, *usu* with a house, found in the Scottish Highlands.

'**crofter** *nc* a person who lives on and works a croft.

crone [kroun] *nc* (*derog*: *usu old*) an ugly old woman.

crony ['krouni] *nc* (*inf*: *often derog*) a close companion: *He spent the evening drinking with his cronies.*

crook [kruk] *nc* **1** a (shepherd's or bishop's) stick, bent at the end. **2** a cheat or criminal: *The two crooks stole the old woman's jewels.* **3** (*in sing with* **the**) the inside of the bend (of one's arm at the elbow): *She held the puppy cradled in the crook of her arm.* – *vt* to bend (*esp* one's finger) into the shape of a hook: *She crooked her finger to beckon to him to come to her.*

'**crooked** [-kid] *adj* **1** (*usu attrib*) badly shaped: *a crooked little man.* **2** not straight: *That picture is crooked* (= not horizontal); *crooked lines.* **3** dishonest: *He's certainly crooked, but we can't prove that he's broken the law.* – *adv* not horizontally: *The picture is hanging crooked.*

'**crookedly** [-kid-] *adv* **1** not horizontally: *He put the hat crookedly on the scarecrow.* **2** dishonestly: *He had always acted crookedly in his commercial dealings.* '**crookedness** [-kid-] *nu.*

croon [kru:n] *vti* **1** to sing or hum in a low voice: *She crooned a lullaby to the baby.* **2** to sing quietly in a very sentimental manner: *Bing Crosby used to croon romantic songs.* '**crooner** *nc.*

crop [krop] *nc* **1** a plant which is farmed and harvested: *There's a fine crop of potatoes this year*; *We grow a variety of crops, including cabbages, wheat and barley*; (*fig*) *He's produced a whole new crop of theories.* **2** a short whip used when horse-riding. **3** a (short) haircut: *a crop of red hair.* **4** (of certain birds) the first stomach, which hangs like a bag from the neck. – *v* – *pt, ptp* **cropped** – *vt* to cut (short): *The sheep crop the grass very short*; *She's had her hair cropped.*

cropped *adj*: *a field of cropped grass.*

crop up *vi* (*inf*) to happen unexpectedly: *I'm sorry I'm late, but something important cropped up.*

cropper ['kropə]: **come a cropper** (*inf*) to meet with misfortune: *His boat came a cropper on the rocks*; *That child's so cheeky that he's bound to come a cropper soon.*

croquet ['kroukei, (*Amer*) krou'kei] *nu* a game in which wooden balls are driven by mallets through a series of hoops stuck in the ground: *Let's have a game of croquet*; *Do you play croquet?*; (*attrib*) *a croquet match.*

crosier, crozier ['krouziə] *nc* (*formal*) a bishop's crook.

cross[1] [kros] *adj* angry: *He gets very cross when he loses*; *a cross old man.* '**crossly** *adv.*

cross[2] [kros] *nc* **1** a symbol formed by two (or in certain cases, more) lines placed across each other, *eg* + or ×. **2** (*hist*) two wooden beams placed thus, on which Christ and criminals were nailed. **3** (*with cap*) the symbol of the Christian religion (†). **4** (*fig*) a lasting cause of suffering *etc*: *I'm afraid that is a cross you will have to bear.* **5** the result of breeding two varieties of animal or plant: *This dog is a cross between an alsatian and a labrador*; (*fig*) *That cake is a cross between a biscuit and a loaf of bread!* **6** (*hist*) a monument in the shape of a cross, often found in market-places or at crossroads. **7** (*with cap*) any of several types of medal given for bravery *etc*: *the Victoria Cross/George Cross/Military Cross.* – **1** *vti* to go from one side to the other (of): *Let's cross* (*the street*); *This road crosses the desert.* **2** *vt* (*neg* **un-**) to place (two things) across each other: *He sat down and crossed his legs.* **3** *vti* to go or be placed across (each other): *The roads cross in the centre of town.* **4** *vi* to meet and/or pass: *John and I crossed in the street yesterday*; *Our letters must have crossed in the post.* **5** *v refl* to make the sign of the Cross (as a blessing *etc*) across one's chest: *He prayed and crossed himself.* **6** *vt* to put a line across: *Please cross your 't's' carefully.* **7** *vt* to make (a cheque or postal order) payable only through a bank by drawing two parallel lines across it enclosing the words '& Co.'. **8** *vt* to breed (something) from two different varieties: *I've crossed two varieties of rose.* **9** *vt* (*inf*) to go against the wishes of; to annoy: *If you cross me, you'll regret it!* – *See also* **cross out**.

cross- (*in cmpds*) **1** going or placed across: *cross-winds*; *cross-pieces.* **2** of mixed variety: *a cross-breed.*

'**crossing 1** *nc* a place where a road *etc* may be crossed: *It's safer to use the pedestrian crossing*; (*also in cmpds*) *a level-crossing.* **2** *nc* a journey over the sea: *I was seasick as it was a very rough crossing.* **3** *nu* an act of crossing: *Crossing the road here can be dangerous.*

crossbones *see* **skull**.

'**crossbow** *nc* (*hist*) a bow fixed to a stand with a mechanism for pulling back and releasing the string.

'**cross-breed** *nc* an animal bred from two different breeds. '**cross-bred** *adj.*

cross-'country *adj* (*attrib*) across fields *etc*, not on roads: *a cross-country run.*

ˌ**cross-ex'amine** *vt* (*legal*) to test or check the previous evidence of (a witness) by questioning him: *The defence lawyer cross-examined the prosecution witnesses.* '**cross-exˌami'nation** *ncu.*

ˌ**cross-'eyed** *adj* having a squint: *Before treatment the child had been very cross-eyed.*

'**cross-fire** *nu* the crossing of lines of gunfire from two or more points.

at ˌcross-'purposes of two or more people, confused about what they are saying or doing because of thinking of different things or misunderstanding one another: *I think we're talking at cross-purposes.*

ˌ**cross-re'fer 1** *vti* to give or be a cross-reference (to): *In this dictionary went is cross-referred to go/went cross-refers to go.* **2** *vt* (*formal*) to refer (the reader) to another entry for more information: *The user of this dictionary is cross-referred from went to go.*

ˌ**cross-'reference** *nc* a reference from one part of a

book, list *etc* to another, *eg* **crawfish** *see* **crayfish**.

'crossroads *n sing* **1** a place where two or more roads cross or meet: *At the crossroads we'll have to decide which road to take.* **2** (*fig*) a point where an important choice of action has to be made: *We have come to a crossroads in our lives.*

ˌcross-'section *nc* **1** (a drawing *etc* of) the area or surface made visible by cutting through something, *eg* across a pipe at right angles to the length. **2** a sample or quantity taken as representative of the whole: *He interviewed a cross-section of the audience to get their opinion of the play.*

'crossword ('puzzle) *nc* a square word-puzzle in which the blanks in a pattern of blank and solid checks are to be filled with words reading across and down, the words being found from clues.

cross one's fingers to place a finger across the one next to it, for good luck: *I am crossing my fingers that I get the job*; *He's going for an interview for a job – keep your fingers crossed for him.*

cross one's heart *see* **heart**.

cross out *vt sep* to draw a line through: *He crossed out all her mistakes.*

See also **crucify**.

crotch [krotʃ], **crutch** [krʌtʃ] *nc* **1** in humans, the place where the legs meet together and join the body: *These trousers are tight round the crotch.* **2** the area of a pair of trousers *etc* which covers this part of the body: *The crotch of these trousers is very tight.*

crotchet ['krotʃit] *nc* (*music*) a note of a certain length. – *See also* Appendix 4.

crotchety ['krotʃəti] *adj* (*inf*) bad-tempered: *a crotchety old man*; *You're very crochety today.*

crouch [krautʃ] *vi* **1** to stand with the knees well bent; to squat: *He crouched behind the bush.* **2** (of animals) to lie close to the ground, in fear, readiness for action *etc*: *The tiger was crouching ready to spring on its prey.*

croupier ['kru:piei] *nc* a person who takes and pays bets at a gambling table in a casino *etc.*

croûton ['kru:ton] *nc* a small piece of fried or toasted bread, served in soup *etc*: *Add some croûtons to the salad.*

crow [krou] *nc* **1** the name given to a number of large birds, generally black, including the rook, hooded crow and carrion crow. **2** the cry of a cock. – *v* – *pt* **crowed** (*defs 1–3*), **crew** [kru:] (*def 1*): *ptp* **crowed** – *vi* **1** to utter the cry of a cock. **2** to utter a cry of delight *etc*: *The baby crowed with happiness.* **3** (*derog*) to boast: *He's always crowing about how well they're progressing.*

ˌcrow's-'feet *n pl* the wrinkles at the outer corner of the eye, often considered a sign of age.

ˌcrow's-'nest *nc* a shelter at the masthead of a ship, used as a lookout post.

as the crow flies in a straight line: *We're fifty miles from London as the crow flies.*

crowbar ['krouba:] *nc* a large iron lever with a bend at the end: *He used a crowbar to lift up the paving-stone.*

crowd [kraud] *nc* **1** a number of persons or things closely pressed together without order or arrangement: *A crowd of people gathered in the street.* **2** (*inf*) a group of friends, *usu* known to one another: *Over the last few weeks, I have met most of John's crowd.* – **1** *vti* to gather in a large group: *The people crowded together in the square*; *They crowded round the injured motorcyclist*; *The police crowded everyone into a corner of the square.* **2** *vt* to fill too full by coming together in: *Demonstrators crowded the building.* **3** *vt* (*inf*) to give too little space to: *Please move away a little and don't crowd me!*

'crowded *adj* having or containing a lot of people or things: *The train is very crowded this evening*; *crowded buses*; *The pages of that dictionary are too crowded* (= with type).

crown [kraun] *nc* **1** a circular, often jewelled, head-dress, *esp* one worn as a mark of royalty or honour: *the queen's crown*; *a crown of victory.* **2** (*with cap*) the king or queen or governing power in a monarchy: *How much authority does the Crown carry in Britain?* **3** the top *eg* of a head, hat, hill *etc*: *He hit him on the crown of the head*; *We reached the crown of the hill*; *He has dented the crown of his hat.* **4** (*usu formerly*) a five-shilling coin, or its value (now 25p). **5** used to mean different kinds of non-British currency *eg* krone. **6** a bird's crest. **7** (an artificial replacement for) the part of a tooth which can be seen. – *vt* **1** to place a crown on the head of (someone): *The archbishop crowned the queen.* **2** to make (someone) king or queen: *Succeeding to the throne in 1837, Victoria was crowned in 1838.* **3** to form the top part of (something): *A gold star crowned the Christmas tree.* **4** (*fig*) to reward or complete happily: *Success crowned her efforts.* **5** to put an artificial crown on (a tooth). **6** (*inf*) to hit (someone) on the head: *If you do that again, I'll crown you!*

crowned head *nc* (*formal*: *usu in pl*) a king or queen: *the crowned heads of Europe.*

crown land *nu* land belonging to the king or queen *etc.*

crown prince *nc* (*with cap in titles*) in some countries, (the status of) the heir to the throne.

crown princess *nc* (*with cap in titles*) **1** (the status of) the wife of a crown prince. **2** in some countries, (the status of) the female heir to the throne.

crozier *see* **crosier**.

crucial ['kru:ʃəl] *adj* (*formal*) involving making a decision; of the greatest importance: *He finally took the crucial step of asking her to marry him*; *He arrived at the crucial moment*; *The next game is crucial – if we lose it we lose the match.*

See also **crux**.

crucible ['kru:sibl] *nc* a pot in which metals *etc* may be melted: *He heated the chemicals in a crucible in the laboratory.*

crucify ['kru:sifai] *vt* **1** to put to death by fixing the hands and feet to a cross: *Christ was crucified.* **2** (*fig*) to treat in a cruel way: *The politician was crucified by his party members when he lost the election.*

'crucifix [-fiks] *nc* a figure or picture of Christ fixed to the cross.

ˌcruci'fixion [-'fikʃən] *ncu* (a) death on the cross, *esp* (*with cap*) that of Christ.

crude [kru:d] *adj* **1** (*usu attrib*) unrefined: *crude oil.* **2** (*usu attrib*) rough or primitive: *crude methods of birth-control*; *a crude shelter.* **3** vulgar: *a crude joke/suggestion*; *Don't be crude!* **'crudeness** *nu.* **'crudity** *ncu.*

cruel ['kru:əl] *adj* **1** pleased at causing pain; merciless: *He was a cruel man who beat his wife*; *He was cruel to his dog.* **2** causing pain or severe distress: *Fate dealt him a cruel blow*; *The disappointment was cruel.* **'cruelly** *adv.* **'cruelty** *ncu.*

cruet ['kru:it] *nc* **1** a small jar or bottle for salt, pepper, vinegar *etc.* 2 (*also* **'cruet-stand**) a holder for such jars *etc*, often with them on it: *Pass me the cruet, please!*

cruise [kru:z] *vi* **1** (*also* **go cruising**) to sail for pleasure: *We cruised in the Mediterranean last year*; *We're going cruising for our holidays.* **2** to go at a steady, comfortable speed: *We were cruising along the road when we met a flock of sheep*; *This car cruises at roughly eighty kilometres per hour*; *The plane is cruising at an altitude of 10 000 metres.* – *nc* a voyage from place to place made for pleasure and relaxation: *They went on a cruise (on a liner).*

'cruiser *nc* **1** a high-speed battleship. **2** (*also* **'cabin-cruiser**) a motor yacht with living quarters.

crumb [krʌm] *nc* a fragment or tiny piece, *esp* of bread: *She puts crumbs for the birds on her window-sill*; (*fig*) *a crumb of comfort.*

crumble ['krʌmbl] *vti* to break into crumbs or small pieces: *She crumbled the bread for the birds*; *The building had crumbled into ruins*; (*fig*) *Her hopes of success finally crumbled.*

'crumbly *adj* tending to crumble: *crumbly pastry*; *These biscuits are rather crumbly.*

crummy ['krʌmi] *adj* (*sl*) inferior or of poor quality: *We had a crummy room at the back of the hotel*; *Don't bother going to see that film – it's crummy!*

crumpet ['krʌmpit] **1** *nc* a type of soft round cake: *toasted crumpets.* **2** *nu* (*sl*: *derog*) attractive womanhood: *She's a nice bit of crumpet.*

crumple ['krʌmpl] *vti* (*more formal than* **crease**) to make or become wrinkled or creased: *This material crumples easily*; (*fig*) *Her face crumpled and she began to cry*; *She crumpled up the piece of paper and threw it away.*

crunch [krʌntʃ] **1** *vt* to crush something hard, *usu* using the teeth, the feet *etc*: *She crunched sweets all through the film*; *He crunched the nut under his heel.* **2** *vi* to make a harsh sound by crushing something in this way: *Was that you crunching during the film?*; *He crunched all the way up the gravel path.* – **1** *nu* such a sound: *the crunch of snow under the car wheels.* **2** *nc* (*with* **the**: *no pl*) the actual moment of testing or trial: *When it came to the crunch she decided to stay with her mother rather than with her father*; *When the crunch came the firm went bankrupt.*

'crunchy *adj* hard or crisp, but able to be crunched: *Hard snow is crunchy*; *crunchy biscuits.*

crusade [kru:'seid] *nc* **1** (*hist*: *often with cap*) a military expedition of Christians to win back the Holy Land from the Turks. **2** (*formal*) a continued effort to help a (good) cause: *He's leading a crusade against dishonest advertising.* – *vi* to take part in a crusade. **cru'sader** *nc.*

crush [krʌʃ] **1** *vt* to break or squash by squeezing together *etc*: *The car was crushed between the two lorries*; *He accidentally crushed the lady's hat by sitting on it.* **2** *vti* to crumple or crease: *She crushed the dress by packing it badly*; *That material crushes easily.* **3** *vt* to overcome; to defeat: *He crushed the rebellion*; (*fig*) *He was crushed by her refusal to marry him.* **4** *vti* to push, press *etc* together: *We (were) all crushed into the tiny room.* – **1** *nu* violent squeezing or pushing together: *He was killed by the crush of the bear's great paws.* **2** *nc* (*usu in sing*) a tightly packed crowd: *I was delayed in the crush at the shops.* **3** *nu* a drink made from the juice of crushed fruit: *lemon crush.*

'crushing *adj* (*usu attrib*) overwhelming; completely defeating: *a crushing defeat of the enemy*; *a crushing refusal to his proposal of marriage.*

'crush-barrier *nc* a barrier put up (*eg* at football matches) to keep back a crowd.

have a 'crush on (*inf*) (*usu* of a young girl or boy) to have a great (sexual) liking for (someone); to be in love with (someone): *She has a crush on John Smith*; *She has a crush on the new gym mistress.*

crust [krʌst] **1** *ncu* (a piece of) the hard outside coating of bread: *The crust of the bread is burnt*; *The child would not eat the crusts.* **2** *nu* (*Amer*) pastry: *The crust of this apple-pie is delicious*; *She makes excellent crust.* **3** *nu* a hard surface *esp* the outer layer of the planet Earth: *the Earth's crust*; *the crust over the wound.*

'crusty *adj* **1** having a crust: *crusty bread*; *I like my rolls crusty.* **2** (*usu attrib*) surly or irritable: *a crusty old man.* **'crustily** *adv.* **'crustiness** *nu.*

crustacean [krʌ'steiʃən] *nc, adj* (*formal or tech*) (of) any of a large group of animals, including crabs, lobsters, shrimps *etc*, whose bodies are *usu* covered with a hard shell.

crusty *see* **crust**.

crutch[1] *see* **crotch**.

crutch[2] [krʌtʃ] *nc* **1** a stick with a bar at the top to support a lame person: *He's been badly injured, and can walk only by using crutches.* **2** (*fig*) a support; a help: *She uses religion as a crutch for her insecurity.*

crux [krʌks] *nc* (*formal*) a difficult or essential point: *That is the crux of the matter/problem.* *See also* **crucial**.

cry [krai] **1** *vti* to let tears come from the eyes; to weep: *She cried when she heard of the old man's death*; *The child cried himself to sleep* (= went to sleep while crying). **2** *vti* (*often with* **out**) to shout out (a loud sound): *As she fell, she cried out 'Help!'*; *She cried out for help.* **3** *vt* (*old*) to announce in public, *esp* for sale: *The traders cried their wares in the market.* – *nc* **1** a shout or exclamation: *He gave a cry of triumph.* **2** a (short) time of weeping: *The baby had a cry after every feed.* **3** the sound made by some animals: *the cry of a wolf.*

'crier *nc* (*also* **town crier**: *hist*) an official who announces news by shouting it out in public.

a crying need something requiring notice or attention: *There is a crying need for more hospitals.*

a far cry (*fig*) a long way (from): *This place is still a far cry from being properly organized.*

cry off *vi, vt sep* (*inf*) to cancel (an engagement or agreement): *After promising to come to the party she cried off at the last minute*; *They cried off the engagement.*

cry wolf to give a false alarm: *She's cried wolf so often now that no-one believes her any longer.*

in full cry enthusiastically chasing something: *The dogs were in full cry after the fox*; (*fig*) *The women rushed into the sale in full cry after the bargains.*

crypt [kript] *nc* an underground cell or chapel, *esp* beneath a church: *The duke is buried in the crypt.*

cryptic ['kriptik] *adj* intentionally very difficult to understand or make sense of: *a set of cryptic clues for a crossword*; *a cryptic message*; *The letter you sent was very cryptic.*

crystal ['kristl] **1** *nc* a small part of a solid substance (*eg* salt or ice) which has a regular shape. **2** *nu* a special kind of very clear glass often used for cut glass ornaments *etc*: *This bowl is made of crystal*;

(*attrib*) *a crystal necklace.* **3** *nu* things made of cut glass: *My aunt has a large collection of crystal.* – *adj* like crystal in clearness: *crystal water.*

'crystalline [-lain] *adj* **1** (*tech*) (of minerals *etc*) formed into crystals: *Salt is a crystalline substance.* **2** (*liter*) like crystal in clearness: *the crystalline depths of the lake.*

'crystallize, -ise 1 *vti* to form (into) crystals: *Salt crystallized from the solution; He crystallized the salt from the sea water.* **2** *vt* to cover with a coating of sugar crystals: *crystallized fruits.* **3** *vti* (*formal*) to make or become definite or clear: *His thoughts about the matter had not had time to crystallize; He tried to crystallize his ideas by writing them down on paper.* **ˌcrystalliˈzation, -s-** *nu.*

crystal ball *nc* a glass ball used in fortune-telling.

'crystal-gazing *nu* **1** gazing into a crystal ball in order to concentrate while fortune-telling. **2** (*derog*: *fig*) attempting to predict what will happen when in fact one has no way of knowing: *The government was accused of crystal-gazing when it produced its budget plans.*

cub [kʌb] *nc* **1** the young of certain animals such as foxes, lions *etc*: *a bear and her cub; a bear cub; a tiger cub.* **2** (*with cap*: *short for* **Cub Scout**) a member of the junior branch of the Scouts. – *v* – *pt, ptp* **cubbed** – *vi* (*formal*) to produce cubs: *A vixen cubbed in the barn last night.* – *adj* (*attrib*) young and inexperienced: *He's a cub reporter on the newspaper.*

Cuba, Cuban *see* Appendix 2.

cubby-hole ['kʌbihoul] *nc* (*inf*) a very small room, cupboard *etc*: *I'm going to go and work in my cubby-hole; The little girl hid all her favourite toys in a cubby-hole in her bedroom.*

cube [kju:b] *nc* **1** a solid body having six equal square faces. **2** the result of multiplying a number by itself twice: *The cube of* $4=4\times4\times4=4^3=64$. – *vt* **1** to calculate the cube of (a number): *If you cube 2, you will get the answer 8.* **2** to make into a cube or cubes: *She cubed the carrots for the soup.*

'cubic *adj* shaped like a cube: *a cubic shape.*

cube root *nc* the number of which a given number is the cube: *The cube root of 64 is 4.*

cubic centimetre (*often abbrev* **cc**), **metre** *etc nc* the volume of, or the volume equivalent to, a cube whose sides measure one centimetre, metre *etc*: *The volume of a solid 2 metres by 2 metres by 3 metres is 12 cubic metres; This jug holds 500 cubic centimetres.*

cubicle ['kju:bikl] *nc* a small room *etc* closed off in some way from a larger one: *Please use the (changing-)cubicle to change into your swimming trunks.*

cubit ['kju:bit] *nc* (*hist*) a measure equal to the length of the arm from the elbow to the tip of the middle finger (45 to 56 centimetres).

cuckoo ['kuku:] – *pl* **'cuckoos** – *nc* a bird, named after its call, which lays its eggs in the nests of other birds. – *adj* (*pred*: *sl*) stupid or crazy: *He's completely cuckoo!*

cucumber ['kju:kʌmbə] **1** *nc* a type of creeping plant. **2** *ncu* its long green edible fruit, often used in salads *etc*: *cucumber, lettuce and tomato*; (*attrib*) *cucumber sandwiches.*

cud [kʌd] *nu* food brought from the first stomach of certain animals (*eg* the cow) back into the mouth and chewed again.

chew the cud 1 (of cows *etc*) to bring food from the first stomach back into the mouth and chew it again. **2** (*inf fig*) to think deeply to oneself: *He sat chewing the cud for hours, but never wrote anything down.*

cuddle ['kʌdl] *vti* to hug or embrace affectionately (*usu* a person): *The child cuddled its teddy-bear; The mother cuddled the child until he fell asleep.* – *nc* a hug or affectionate embrace.

'cuddly *adj* (*inf*) looking as though one would like to give it *etc* a cuddle: *a cuddly teddy-bear; He's not handsome – he's small and cuddly.*

cudgel ['kʌdʒəl] *nc* (*formal*) heavy stick or club. – *v* – *pt, ptp* **'cudgelled**, (*Amer*) **'cudgeled** – *vt* (*formal*) to beat with a cudgel.

take up the cudgels on behalf of (someone or something) to defend (a person, cause *etc*) vigorously: *She's taken up the cudgels on behalf of women's rights.*

cue[1] [kju:] *nc* **1** the last words of another actor's speech, or a noise or movement *etc*, serving as a sign to an actor to speak *etc*: *Your cue is '– whatever the vicar says!'.* **2** a hint about how to act or behave: *I've never been in this situation before, so I'll take my cue from you.*

cue[2] [kju:] *nc* a stick which gets thinner towards one end and the point of which is used to strike the ball in playing billiards.

cuff[1] [kʌf] *nc* **1** the end of the sleeve (of a shirt, coat *etc*) near the wrist: *Does your shirt have buttons on the cuffs?* **2** (*esp Amer*) the turned-up part of a trouser leg: *Are cuffs in fashion this year?* **3** (*in pl*: *sl*) short for **handcuffs**: *The cop put the cuffs on the thief.*

'cufflinks *n pl* two ornamental buttons *etc* joined by a small bar, chain *etc* used to fasten a shirt cuff.

off the cuff without planning; unprepared: *He spoke entirely off the cuff, with no notes; His speech was entirely off the cuff*; (*attrib*) *an off-the-cuff remark.*

cuff[2] [kʌf] *nc* (*inf*) a blow with the open hand: *I'll give you a cuff on the ear, you rascal!* – *vt* (*inf*) to give such a blow: *He cuffed the side of the child's head; He cuffed him on the head.*

cuisine [kwi'zi:n] *nu* (*formal*) style of cookery: *I'm very fond of French cuisine; This restaurant is famous for its cuisine.*

cul-de-sac ['kʌldəsak] *nc* a street closed at one end.

culinary ['kʌlinəri] *adj* (*formal*: *usu attrib*) of or used in the kitchen or in cookery: *culinary herbs; She learned her culinary skills in France.*

cull [kʌl] *vt* **1** (*formal or liter*) to gather: *His knowledge is culled from a huge number of sources.* **2** to select and kill (surplus animals in a population): *They are culling the seals.* – *nc* an act of killing surplus animals: *Every so often there is a seal cull to reduce the population; a cull of seals.*

cullender *see* **colander**.

culminate ['kʌlmineit] *vi* (*formal*: *with* **in**) to reach the highest or most important point: *The town's bicentenary celebrations culminated in a firework display in the local park.*

ˌculmiˈnation *nu*: *His book was the culmination of many years research.*

culotte [kju:'lot] *nc* (*usu in pl*) women's knee-length trousers cut so as to look like a skirt.

culpable ['kʌlpəbl] *adj* (*formal or legal*) deserving blame; guilty: *He was found guilty of culpable homicide; She was the one who committed the crime but he was culpable also.*

ˌculpaˈbility *nu.*

culprit ['kʌlprit] *nc* **1** (*formal*) a person responsible for something wrong, unpleasant *etc*: *As soon as he saw the broken window he began to look for the* *culprit.* **2** (in English and US law) a prisoner accused but not yet tried: *The culprit is in custody.*

cult [kʌlt] **1** *nc* a particular, often temporarily fashionable, system of (religious) belief or worship: *Meditation and yoga have increased interest in the Indian religious cults*; (*attrib*) *He's now a cult figure, and his books sell millions of copies every year*; *Physical fitness has become a cult with him.* **2** *nu* the followers of such a system: *He belongs to a strange religious cult.*

cultivate [ˈkʌltiveit] *vt* **1** to prepare (land) for crops. **2** (*formal*) to grow (a crop in a garden, field *etc*): *He cultivates mushrooms in the cellar.* **3** (*formal*) to develop, or improve, by care or study: *She cultivates good manners.* **4** (*formal*) actively to seek (the company of a person, *usu* to use them to one's own advantage): *She cultivates her next-door-neighbours because they know a lot of important people.*

ˈcultivated *adj* **1** (of fields *etc*) prepared for crops; used for growing crops: *cultivated land*; *This field has not been cultivated for years.* **2** (*attrib*) grown in a garden *etc*; not wild: *a cultivated variety of raspberries.* **3** (*formal*) having good manners; educated and well-informed: *a very cultivated young lady*; *He has extremely cultivated tastes in literature and music.*

ˌcultiˈvation *nu* **1** the art or practice of cultivating: *By careful cultivation, we'll produce a fine crop.* **2** (*formal*) sophistication; good manners *etc*: *a woman of cultivation.*

ˈcultivator *nc* a tool or machine for breaking up ground and removing weeds.

culture [ˈkʌltʃə] **1** *nc* a form or type of civilization of a certain race or nation and the customs associated with it: *the Jewish culture*; *He was a product of two cultures – German and French.* **2** *nu* improvement or development of the mind *etc* by education, training *etc*: *He was an enthusiastic seeker of culture.* **3** *nu* educated taste in art, literature, music *etc*: *He thinks that anyone who dislikes Bach is totally lacking in culture.* **4** *ncu* (*tech*) (a) cultivated growth of bacteria *etc*: *The culture of bacteria from the urine specimen showed the presence of an infection.* **5** *nu* the commercial rearing of oysters, fish, certain plants *etc*.

ˈcultural *adj* (*usu attrib*) of or having to do with (a) culture: *the Greek cultural influence*; *He regarded the concert as the cultural experience of his holiday.*

ˈcultured *adj* (*usu attrib*: *neg* **un-**) well-educated and refined: *a cultured gentleman.*

cultured pearl *nc* a pearl which is naturally grown in commercially reared oysters and is of less value than one grown in the wild: *He gave her a necklace of cultured pearls as a wedding present.*

culvert [ˈkʌlvət] *nc* (*esp tech*) an arched channel carrying water under a road *etc*.

cumbersome [ˈkʌmbəsəm] *adj* (of things) heavy and clumsy: *a cumbersome piece of furniture*; *That sweater is very cumbersome.*

cumulative [ˈkjuːmjulətiv] *adj* (*formal*) becoming greater by stages or additions: *Frequent small doses of this drug have a cumulative effect.*

cunning [ˈkʌniŋ] *adj* **1** sly; clever in a deceitful way: *Don't be fooled by any of her cunning tricks*; *The thief was very cunning.* **2** clever: *a cunning device for opening the high window*; *He was very cunning about it.* **3** (*attrib*: *Amer*) pretty, appealing *etc*: *What a cunning dress/baby!* – *nu* slyness or deceitful cleverness: *full of cunning.*

ˈcunningly *adv*: *He was cunningly disguised as a fisherman.*

cunt [kʌnt] *nc* (*vulg*) **1** the female sexual organs. **2** used as a term of abuse: *You stupid cunt!*

cup [kʌp] *nc* **1** (*sometimes in cmpds*) a (*usu* round) hollow container to hold liquid for drinking, often with a handle: *a teacup*; *He dropped the cup and broke it.* **2** the amount contained in a cup: *I've already had two cups of tea.* **3** something shaped like a cup: *the cup of an acorn*; *a brassière cup.* **4** (*also* **ˈcupful**) in cooking, a measure of volume equal to half a pint; in Britain 0·3 litre (10 fluid ounces), in America 0·28 litre (8 fluid ounces). **5** an ornamental vessel, *usu* of silver or other metal, given as a prize in sports events *etc*: *They won the Football League Cup.* **6** a competition for which the prize is a cup: *We played in the cup last year.* – *v* – *pt*, *ptp* **cupped** – *vt* **1** to form (one's hands) into the shape of a cup: *He cupped his hands to catch the ball.* **2** to hold (something) in one's cupped hands: *He cupped the mug of hot tea in his hands to warm them.*

ˈcupful *nc* **1** the amount contained by a cup: *three cupfuls of water.* **2** a cup (*def 4*).

cupboard [ˈkʌbəd] *nc* (*Amer* **ˈcloset**) a cabinet of any size up to that of a small room for storing anything: *Put the food in the cupboard, please*; *a broom cupboard.*

cupboard love *nu* love and affection shown to a person with the intention of getting something one wants from him or her: *The little girl cuddled her mother but it was cupboard love – she wanted a chocolate biscuit.*

cup final *nc* the final match in a football competition in which the prize is a cup (*def 5*).

ˈcup-tie *nc* one of a series of games in a football competition in which the prize is a cup.

one's cup of tea (*inf*: *usu in neg*) the sort of thing one likes or prefers: *Classical music is not really my cup of tea.*

cupidity [kjuˈpidəti] *nu* (*formal*) desire for wealth; greed: *His cupidity led him to do more overtime than he was fit to do.*

cupola [ˈkjuːpələ] *nc* (*formal*) **1** a small dome on the top of a building. **2** the internal part of a dome. **3** a curved ceiling.

cuppa [ˈkʌpə] *nc* (*inf*) a cup of something, *esp* tea: *Would anybody like a cuppa?*

cur [kəː] *nc* (*derog*) **1** a dog of mixed breed. **2** (*old*) a surly, rude or cowardly person.

curable *see* **cure**.

curate [ˈkjuərət] *nc* a clergyman in the Church of England assisting a rector or vicar.

curative *see* **cure**.

curator [kjuəˈreitə] *nc* a person in charge of something, *eg* a place where things are shown, such as a museum.

curb [kəːb] *nc* **1** something which holds back, restrains or controls: *We'll have to put a curb on his wild enthusiasm.* **2** a chain or strap attached to the bit for holding back a horse. **3** (*Amer*) a kerb. – *vt* (*formal*) to hold back, restrain or control: *You must curb your spending*; *Curb your enthusiasm!*

ˈcurbstone *nc* (*Amer*) a kerbstone.

curd [kəːd] *nu* **1** (*also* **curds**) the solid substance formed when milk turns sour, used in making cheese. **2** anything of a similar texture: *lemon curd.*

See also **whey**.

curdle [ˈkəːdl] *vti* to turn into curd: *The heat has*

curdled the milk; This milk has curdled.

curdle (someone's) blood/make (someone's) blood curdle to shock or terrify someone: *That shriek curdled my blood; It made by blood curdle.*

cure [kjuə] **1** *vt* to make better: *That medicine cured me; It cured him of his headaches; (fig) That will cure him of his bad habits.* **2** *vt* get rid of (an illness, bad habit *etc*): *That pill cured my headache; The ointment quickly cured the burn on her leg; This treatment should cure your alcoholism.* **3** *vt* to preserve (bacon *etc*) by drying, salting *etc.* **4** *vi* to be preserved in this way. – *nc* something which cures: *They're trying to find a cure for cancer.*

'curable *adj* able to be cured: *Is that disease curable?; a curable form of cancer.* – *See also* **incurable**.

curative ['kjuərətiv] *adj* (*attrib*: *formal*) intended to, or likely to, cure: *the curative powers of this medicine.*

curfew ['kə:fju:] **1** *nc* an order forbidding people to be in the streets after a certain hour: *There's a curfew in force from ten o'clock tonight.* **2** *ncu* (the start of) the period of time during which such an order applies: *You can't go out after/during curfew.* **3** *nc* (*hist*) the ringing of a bell as a signal to put out fires and lights.

curio ['kjuəriou] – *pl* **'curios** – *nc* an article valued for its oddness or its rareness: *The antique shops are full of curios.*

curious ['kjuəriəs] *adj* **1** strange; odd: *a curious habit of staring at people; He has a curious scar on his cheek.* **2** anxious or interested (to learn): *I'm curious (to find out) whether he passed his exams; He's too curious about other people's affairs.*

,curi'osity [-'o-] **1** *nu* eagerness to learn: *She shows great curiosity about how things work; She was very unpopular because of her curiosity about other people's affairs.* **2** *nc* something strange and rare: *That old chair is quite a curiosity.*

'curiously *adv*: *The house was very curiously furnished; She looked curiously at the unusual flower.*

curl[1] [kə:l] **1** *vti* to twist or turn (*esp* hair) into small coils or rolls: *My hair curls easily.* **2** *vi* (*sometimes with* **up**) to move in curves: *The smoke curled into the evening air.* **3** *vi* (*sometimes with* **up**) to bend or roll: *The paper curled (up) at the edges.* – **1** *nc* a coil of hair *etc.* **2** *nu* the state or quality of being curled: *My hair has very little curl in it.*

'curler *nc* an object round which hair is curled to give it curl, fastened in the hair.

'curly *adj*: *curly hair; Is her hair curly?* **'curliness** *nu.*

curl up *vi, v refl* to go, move or roll into a position or shape: *She curled (herself) up in the chair; The hedgehog curled up into a ball; The child curled up on the sofa and went to sleep.*

See also **curling**.

curling ['kə:liŋ] *nu* a game played by sliding heavy smooth stones (**'curling stones**) over ice towards a fixed mark: (*attrib*) *a curling match.*

curl[2] *vi* to play the game of curling.

curly *see* **curl**.

currant ['kʌrənt, (*Amer*) 'kə:-] *nc* **1** a small black raisin or dried seedless grape: *This cake has currants in it.* **2** (*in cmpds*) any of several types of small, soft fruit: *a redcurrant/blackcurrant.*

currency[1] ['kʌrənsi, (*Amer*) 'kə:-] *ncu* the money (notes and coins) of a country: *the currencies of the world; I have £100 in travellers' cheques and £20 in foreign currency.*

See also **current**.

current ['kʌrənt, (*Amer*) 'kə:-] *adj* (*formal*: *usu pred*) **1** passing from person to person; generally accepted: *This story is current.* **2** (*attrib*) of or belonging to the present: *current affairs; the current month; the current temperature.* – **1** *nc* (the direction of) a stream of water or air: *the current of a river; a cold current of air; (fig) the current of events.* **2** *ncu* (a) flow of electricity: *This circuit uses a high current; The supply of current here is 240 volts AC.*

'currency[2] *nu* (*formal*) the state or time of being current or accepted: *His promises have lost all currency among his supporters.*

'currently *adv* at the present time: *John is currently working as a bus-driver.*

current account *nc* an account with a bank on which one is not paid interest and from which money may be withdrawn by cheque: *We paid so many bills by cheque last month that we have very little money left in our current account.*

curriculum [kə'rikjuləm] – *pl* **cur'ricula** [-lə] – *nc* a course, *esp* of study at school or university: *They are changing the curriculum.*

curriculum vitae ['vi:tai] *nc* a written record of the main events of one's life, including personal details and a summary of one's career: *Please send your curriculum vitae with your application form.*

curry[1] ['kʌri, (*Amer*) 'kə:ri] *ncu* (an *orig* Indian dish of) meat, fish, eggs or vegetables cooked with spices and herbs: *chicken curry; Curries take a long time to prepare.* – *vt* to cook in this way: *Are you going to curry this meat?*

'curried *adj* (*usu attrib*): *a curried chicken.*

'curry powder *ncu* a selection of spices ground together and used in making a curry.

curry[2] ['kʌri, (*Amer*) 'kə:ri] *vt* to rub down or comb and clean (a horse).

curry favour (*derog*) (*often with* **with**) to seek (a) favour by flattery: *She wants a rise in her pay, so she's currying favour with the boss.*

curse [kə:s] **1** *vt* to wish that evil may fall upon (someone or something): *I curse the day that I was born!; The witch cursed him with strange and frightening words.* **2** *vi* to use violent language; to swear: *He cursed (at his own stupidity) when he dropped the hammer on his toe.* – *nc* **1** an act of cursing, or the words used: *He suddenly remembered the witch's curse.* **2** a thing or person which is cursed: *Having to work is the curse of his entire life.*

cursed *adj* **1** (*pred*) under a curse: *Some people believe that certain types of animal are cursed; She is cursed with* (= she has the misfortune to have) *a cruel husband.* – ['kə:sid] *adj* (*attrib*: *old or liter*) damned, annoying, hated *etc*: *That woman is a cursed idiot!*

cursory ['kə:səri] *adj* (*attrib*: *formal*) hurried and not at all thorough: *He gave it only a cursory glance.* **'cursorily** *adv.*

curt [kə:t] *adj* rudely brief: *He gave me a curt reply and told me to leave; He is always very curt in his replies.* **'curtly** *adv.* **'curtness** *nu.*

curtail [kə:'teil] *vt* (*formal*) to make less; often to make less, shorter *etc* than was originally intended: *His powers/activities have been severely curtailed by the new law; I've had to curtail my visit.* **cur'tailment** *nu.*

curtain ['kə:tn] *nc* a piece of material hung up to act as a screen at a window, on a theatre stage, round a bed *etc*: *I can't see in because the curtains are closed; The maid drew the curtains* (= pulled them across the window); *The curtain came down at the end of the play*; (*fig*) *The soldiers were hidden behind a curtain of smoke.* – *See also* **curtains**. – *vt* (*formal*) to put curtains in or on: *We still have to curtain this room*; *She curtained the windows in red velvet.* – *See also* **curtain off**.

'curtains *n pl* (*inf*) the end: *If you are late once more, it'll be curtains for you* (= you will get the sack).

'curtain call *nc* an appearance by actors, singers *etc* after a performance for the purpose of receiving applause: *After the play the actors took ten curtain calls.*

curtain off *vt sep* to separate or enclose with a curtain: *She curtained off the alcove.*

curtsy, curtsey ['kə:tsi] – *pl* **'curtsies** – *nc* a bow made by women by bending the knees. – *vi* to make a curtsy: *She curtsied to the queen.*

curvaceous [kə:'veiʃəs] *adj* (*facet*) (of women) having attractive curves of the body: *a curvaceous blonde.*

curvature ['kə:vətʃə, (*Amer*) -tʃuər] (*formal*) **1** *nu* the condition of being curved, *esp* abnormally: *He has curvature of the spine.* **2** *nu* the extent to which something is curved: *the curvature of the earth.* **3** *nc* a curved part: *The curvatures on the legs of this table are quite distinctive.*

curve [kə:v] *nc* **1** a line which is not straight at any point, like part of the edge of a circle. **2** anything shaped like this: *a curve in the road*; *the curves of her body.* – *vti* to bend in a curve: *The road curves gently towards the east*; *He curved the metal to form a horse-shoe.*

curved *adj*: *This knife has a curved handle*; *The road is curved.*

'curving *adj* (*usu attrib*): *The curving road went over the hills into the next valley.*

'curvy *adj.*

cushion ['kuʃən] *nc* **1** a bag of cloth *etc* filled with soft material, *eg* foam, feathers *etc*, used to support or to make something more comfortable, softer *etc*: *The sofa has four cushions*; *I'll sit on a cushion on the floor*; *Put this cushion under you as the bench is very hard*; (*fig*) *His savings are a cushion against inflation.* **2** any such support: *A hovercraft travels on a cushion of air.* – *vt* to lessen the force of a blow *etc*: *The soft snow cushioned his fall*; (*fig*) *This loan will cushion the effect of all the money you have spent on your house.*

cushy ['kuʃi] *adj* (*inf*: *derog*) easy and comfortable: *a cushy job.*

cuss [kʌs] *nc* (*inf*) **1** (*esp Amer*) a swear word or act of swearing: *The cusses he knows would fill a book!* **2** an obstinate or unpleasant person: *He's a bad-tempered old cuss!*

'cussed [-sid] *adj* (*usu attrib*) obstinate: *That cussed old fool just refuses to move!*

'cussedness [-sid-] *nu*: *He refused to do it out of pure cussedness.*

custard ['kʌstəd] *nu* milk, eggs *etc* cooked together and sweetened, used as a sauce for sweet dishes such as fruit *etc*: *Pour some custard over the pudding.*

custody ['kʌstədi] *nu* (*formal*) **1** care or keeping: *in the custody of her mother.* **2** the care or guard of the police or prison authorities: *The accused is in custody.*

cu'stodian [-'stou-] *nc* a person who guards or takes care of something: *the custodian of an art collection*; (*fig formal*) *the custodian of public morals.*

put into custody (*formal*) to imprison: *The accused was put into custody until his case was heard.*

take into custody (*formal*) to arrest: *The policeman took the three drunks into custody.*

custom ['kʌstəm] **1** *nc* what a person *etc* is in the habit of doing or does regularly: *Bathing in the River Ganges is a religious custom among the Hindus*; *It's my custom to go for a walk on Saturday mornings.* **2** *nu* the regular buying of goods at the same shop *etc*; trade or business: *The new supermarket has taken away all my custom*; (*formal*) *The woman was so annoyed at the shopkeeper that she took her custom elsewhere.* **3** *nu* (*formal*) social habit or a convention: *Custom demands that we get married before having children.* – *See also* **customs** *below.*

'customary *adj* (*formal*) habitual; usually done *etc*: *He makes his customary visit every week*; *It is customary to eat turkey for Christmas dinner.*

'customarily *adv.*

'customer *nc* **1** a person who buys from a shop *etc*: *In this shop, most of my customers are old age pensioners.* **2** (*inf*: *usu derog*) a person: *He's a funny* (= strange) *customer.*

'customs *n pl* **1** taxes paid on goods coming into a country: *Did you have to pay customs on those cigarettes?* **2** the government department which collects these taxes: *He works for the customs*; (*attrib*) *customs duty.* **3** the place at a port *etc* where these taxes are collected: *I was searched when I came through customs at the airport.*

,custom-'built, ,custom-'made *adjs* made or built to an individual customer's order or requirements: *He had his boat custom-built*; *custom-built kitchen cupboards*; (*fig*) *This job is custom-built for you*; *He wore elegant custom-made suits.*

cut [kʌt] – *prp* **'cutting**: *pt, ptp* **cut** – **1** *vti* to make an opening (in something) *usu* with something with a sharp edge: *He cut the paper with a pair of scissors*; *He had to cut the envelope open*; *I'll hold the wood in place while you cut it with the saw*; *This saw cuts well.* **2** *vt* to break off or divide by cutting: *She cut the bread (into slices)*; *She cut a slice of bread*; *The child cut the pictures out of the magazine*; *She cut the meat up into small pieces*; *The doctor cut away the clothing from her injured chest*; (*fig*) *He's cut all his ties with the rest of the family.* **3** *vi* to be able to be cut: *This cheese doesn't cut very easily.* **4** *vt* to make (something) by cutting: *She cut a little man out of a piece of cardboard*; *She cut a hole in the cloth.* **5** *vt* to shorten by cutting; to trim: *He's going to cut my hair today*; *I'll cut the grass tomorrow.* **6** *vt* to reduce; to make less: *They cut my wages by ten per cent*; *I've cut the essay from five thousand words to three thousand*; *All our prices have been cut drastically.* **7** *vt* to remove: *They cut several passages from the film.* **8** *vt* to wound or hurt by breaking the skin (of): *I cut my hand on a piece of glass.* **9** *vti* to divide (a pack of cards): *Cut (the cards) to decide who deals.* **10** *vi* to stop filming: *When the actress said the wrong words, the director ordered 'Cut!'.* **11** *vti* (*inf*) to switch off: *He cut the engine and turned off the lights*; *The engines suddenly cut for no apparent reason.* **12** *vt* (*sl*) to stop: *Cut the talking at once!* **13** *vi* (*usu with* **through**) to move or go (through), *usu* to shorten one's journey: *He cut through the park on his way to the office.* **14** *vt* to meet and cross (a line or geometrical figure): *An axis cuts a circle in two places.* **15** *vt* (*inf*) to stay away from (a class, lecture *etc*): *He cut school and went to the cinema.* **16** *vt* (*inf*) to record (a gramophone record): *The pop star cut a new disc.* **17** *vt* (*inf*) to ignore completely; to pretend not to recognize: *She cut me in the High Street after our children quarrelled.* – *See also* **cut** *in phrases below.* – **1** *nc* (*sometimes in cmpds*) the result of an act of cutting: *a six-inch cut in the material*; *a cut on the head*; *a power-cut*; *He made a cut in the piece of wood/film/book*; *a haircut*; *a cut in prices.* **2** *nu* the way in which something is tailored, fashioned *etc*: *the cut of his clothes.* **3** *nc* a piece of meat cut from an animal: *What cut of beef did you use for that stew?*; *a very tasty cut of beef.* **4** *nc* a share (of profits *etc*): *Your cut will be £150.* **5** *nc* a cutting for a railway *etc*: *The kids are playing in the cut.*

'**cutter** *nc* **1** (*often in cmpds*) a person or thing that cuts or is used for cutting: *a wood-cutter*; *a glass-cutter.* **2** a type of small sailing ship.

'**cutting** *nc* **1** a piece of a plant cut off and replanted to form another plant: *She grew those geraniums from cuttings which her mother gave her.* **2** an article cut out from a newspaper *etc*: *She collects cuttings about the Royal Family.* **3** a trench or hollow made by digging a piece out of a hillside or other high ground, in which a railway, road *etc* is built. – *adj* **1** insulting or offending: *a cutting remark*; *She was very cutting about it.* **2** (*usu attrib*) bitterly cold: *a cutting wind.*

cutback *see* **cut back**.

cut glass *nu* glass with ornamental patterns cut on the surface, used for vases, drinking glasses *etc*: *I prefer plain glass to cut glass*; (*attrib*) *a cut-glass vase.*

'**cut-out** *nc* a safety device for breaking an electrical circuit when voltage through it reaches too high a level: *Most modern machines have safety cut-outs.* – *See also* **cut out**.

ˌ**cut-'price, 'cut-'rate** *adjs* (*usu attrib*) (offering a price) cheaper than normal: *cut-price goods*; *a cut-price store.*

'**cut-throat** *nc* (*old*) a wicked and dangerous person; a murderer. – *adj* **1** (*usu attrib*) fierce; ruthless: *cut-throat business competition.* **2** (*Brit*: *attrib*) (of a razor) having a long blade which is completely uncovered when in use: *Cut-throat razors are rare nowadays.*

ˌ**cut-'up** *adj* (*inf*: *pred*): *He was very cut-up when his girl-friend married someone else.*

a cut above (obviously) better than: *He's a cut above the average engineer*; *She thinks she's a cut above her neighbours.*

cut across *vt fus* **1** to pass in front of, *usu* interfering with the progress of: *The lorry cut across* (*the path of*) *the little car.* **2** to interfere with or disagree with: *His ideas cut across my own on this subject.* **3** to take a shorter route by way of: *He cut across the grass so as not to be late.*

cut and dried fixed and definite: *Her views on this are very cut and dried*; *cut-and-dried opinions.*

cut and thrust (*formal*) competition: *the cut and thrust of big business.*

cut back *vi, vt sep* to reduce considerably: *The government cut back on public spending*; *Spending was cut back by £10 million* (*nc* '**cutback**: *a cutback in public spending*).

cut both ways (*inf*) to affect both parts of a question, both people involved, good and bad points *etc*: *That argument cuts both ways!*

cut corners *see* **corner**.

cut a dash/figure to have an impressive (*usu* smart or fashionable) appearance: *He cuts quite a dash in his purple suit*; *He cuts a handsome figure in that jacket.*

cut (someone) dead to ignore completely someone whom one knows: *She cut me dead when I spoke to her.*

cut down 1 *vt sep* to cause to fall by cutting: *He has cut down the apple tree.* **2** *vi* to reduce (an amount taken *etc*): *I haven't given up smoking but I'm cutting down*; *You must cut down on sugar to lose weight.*

cut (someone) down to size (*inf*) to reduce someone's sense of their own importance: *I'll cut this cheeky young rascal down to size!*

cut in *vi* **1** to interrupt: *She cut in with a remark.* **2** to move sharply in front of one and so interfere with one's progress: *I had to swerve when a lorry cut in in front of me.*

cut it fine (*inf*) to allow barely enough time, money *etc* for something that must be done: *Don't cut it too fine or you'll miss the train*; *I meant to keep enough money for my bus fare but I cut it a bit fine.*

cut no ice to have no effect: *This sort of flattery cuts no ice with me.*

cut off *vt sep* **1** to interrupt or break a telephone connection: *I was cut off in the middle of the telephone call*; *They cut me off.* **2** to separate: *They were cut off from the rest of the army* (*by the enemy forces*); *They have cut us off.* **3** to stop or prevent delivery of: *They've cut off our supplies of coal*; *They have cut them off.* **4** to leave (someone) nothing in a will: *He cut his daughters off without a penny*; *He cut them off without a penny.* **5** (*fig*) to kill or cause to die sooner than is usual or natural: *He was cut off in his prime.*

cut one's losses to decide to spend no more money, effort *etc* on something which is proving unprofitable: *I have invested a lot of money in that firm and I cannot get it back but I have decided to cut my losses and resign.*

cut one's teeth 1 to grow one's first teeth: *The baby's cutting his first tooth.* **2** (*sl*) to gain one's first experiences: *I cut my teeth on Spitfires in the war, and now I'm flying passenger aircraft.*

cut open *see* **cut** (*def 1*).

cut out 1 *vt sep see* **cut** (*defs 2 and 4*). **2** *vi* to stop working, sometimes because of a safety device: *The engines slowed down and finally cut out*; *My hair-drier cuts out if it gets over-heated.* – *See also* **cut-out**. **3** *vt sep* (*inf*) to stop or put an end to: *Cut out all the noise! Cut it out!* **4** *vt sep* to stop (*esp* eating or drinking): *I've cut out smoking*; *He's cut out cigarettes – I've cut them out too.*

ˌ**cut 'out for,** ˌ**cut 'out to be** (*usu in neg*) suited to or able for: *I'm not cut out to be an athlete*; *I'm not cut out for athletics.*

cut short 1 to make shorter than intended: *He cut short his holiday to deal with the crisis*; *He had to cut short his speech because the audience were threatening him.* **2** to cause (someone) to stop talking by interrupting them: *I tried to apologize but he cut me short.*

cut up 1 *see* **cut** (*def 2*). **2** (*usu with* **rough**: *sl*) to become very angry and violent: *He'll cut up rough when he finds out what you've done.*

cut (someone) to the quick (*formal*) to hurt or offend someone greatly: *His unkind remarks cut me to the quick.*

have one's work cut out *see* **work**.

See also **uncut**.

cute [kju:t] *adj* **1** (*esp Amer*) attractive or pleasing in any way: *a cute baby/dress/way of speaking*; *He's cute!* **2** (*inf*: *often derog*) cunningly clever: *You think you're pretty cute, don't you!*

cuticle ['kju:tikl] *nc* the dead skin at the inner edge of a fingernail or toenail: *She removed the cuticles when manicuring her nails.*

cutlass ['kʌtləs] *nc* (*old*) a short, broad, slightly curved sword with one cutting edge: *The pirates fought with cutlasses.*

cutlery ['kʌtləri] *nu* knives, forks and spoons: *The waitress laid the cutlery on the table.*

cutlet ['kʌtlit] *nc* **1** a small slice of meat (mutton, veal, pork) with rib or other bone attached, *usu* cooked by frying or grilling: *We had lamb cutlets for dinner.* **2** a piece of other food made up into a similar shape: *The vegetarian had a nut cutlet for dinner.*

cutter, cutting *see* **cut**.

cyanide ['saiənaid] *nu* a deadly type of poison: *He poisoned his wife with cyanide.*

cycle[1] ['saikl] *vi* to go by bicycle: *He cycles to work every day*; *He cycled uphill slowly.* – *nc* (*usu attrib*) shortened form of **bicycle**: *They bought the child a cycle for Christmas*; (*attrib*) *a cycle shop.*

'**cyclist** *nc* a person who rides a bicycle: *Because of the price of petrol more people are becoming cyclists.*

cycle[2] ['saikl] *nc* **1** (*formal or tech*) (a period of time with) a number or round of events happening one after the other in a certain order, over and over again: *the cycle of the seasons*; *the life-cycle of the butterfly.* **2** a series of poems, songs *etc* written about one main event *etc*: *a cycle of mystery plays based of the life of Christ*; *a song cycle.* **3** (*tech*) (of alternating current, radio waves *etc*) one complete series of changes in a regularly varying supply, signal *etc*: *The mains electricity supply here is fifty cycles per second* (sometimes *abbrev* **c.p.s.** when written: now more commonly **hertz**).

'**cyclic** *adj* (*very formal*) of or in cycles: *the cyclic movement of the earth round the sun.* '**cyclically** *adv.*

cyclist *see* **cycle**[1].

cyclone ['saikloun] *nc* a violent wind-storm: *Th cyclone ripped the roofs off houses and tore up trees*

cygnet ['signit] *nc* a young swan: *a swan with thr cygnets.*

cylinder ['silində] *nc* **1** a solid shape or object wit a circular base and top and straight sides. **2** any several pieces of machinery of this shape, solid c hollow: *The brake cylinder of his car is leaking.* **3** container in the shape of a cylinder: *two cylinde of oxygen.*

cy'**lindrical** *adj* (*formal or tech*) shaped like cylinder: *A beer-can is cylindrical.*

'**cylinder head** *nc* the closed end of the cylinder an engine in a car *etc.*

cymbal ['simbəl] *nc* (*usu in pl*) a brass music instrument like a plate with a hollow in the centr two of which are struck together to produce noise: *She plays the cymbals*; *The cymbals clashed*

cynical ['sinikəl] *adj* **1** having a low opinion human nature and unwilling to believe th happiness is possible *etc*: *He has a cynical attitu to life*; *She's very cynical about life.* **2** (*usu prec loosely*) tending to expect failure or disappoin ment: *He remained cynical about our chances success.* '**cynically** *adv.*

'**cynic** *nc* a person who has a low opinion of huma nature and believes the worst about everyone: *H is a cynic – he thinks that everyone who works in th charity is a crook.*

'**cynicism** [-sizəm] *nu* the attitude to life taken b a cynic.

cypress ['saipris] **1** *nc* a type of evergreen tree. **2** *n adj* (of) its wood.

Cyprian, Cypriot, Cyprus *see* Appendix 2.

cyst [sist] *nc* a kind of liquid-filled blister on a internal part of the body or just under the ski *The surgeon removed a cyst from her scalp.*

czar, czarina *see* **tsar, tsarina**.

Czech, Czechoslovak, Czechoslovakia *s* Appendix 2.

Dd

'd *see* **have, would**.

dab[1] [dab] – *pt, ptp* **dabbed** – *vti* (*sometimes with* **at**) to touch gently with something soft or moist: *He dabbed the wound gently with cottonwool*; *She dabbed at the bloodstain to try and remove it.* – *nc* **1** a small lump of anything soft or moist: *a dab of butter.* **2** a gentle touch: *She gave the stain a dab with her wet cloth.*

dab[2] [dab]: **a dab hand at** (*inf*) an expert at: *He's a dab hand at carpentry.*

dabble ['dabl] **1** *vt* to play with water by moving (one's hands and feet *etc*) about in it: *He dabbled his feet in the river.* **2** *vi* to do anything in a half-serious way or as a hobby: *He dabbles in witchcraft.* '**dabbler** *nc.*

dachshund ['dakshund, (*Amer*) 'da:ks-] *nc* a type of small dog with a long body and very short legs.

dad [dad], **daddy** ['dadi] *nc* (*with cap when used as a name*: *inf*) children's words for father: *Where is your daddy?*; *What are you doing, Daddy?*

daffodil ['dafədil] *nc* a kind of yellow spring flower which grows from a bulb.

daft [da:ft] *adj* (*inf*) silly or foolish: *a daft idea*; *That idea is daft!*; *That's a daft way to do it!*

dagger ['dagə] *nc* (*usu hist*) a knife or short swor for stabbing.

at daggers drawn (*formal*) ready to sta fighting or quarrelling at any moment: *They' been at daggers drawn for years.*

dago ['deigou] – *pl* '**dagoes** – *nc* (*offensive*) a ma of Spanish, Portuguese or Italian origin.

dahlia ['deiljə, (*Amer*) 'daljə] *nc* a kind of garde plant with large, colourful flowers, often wi spiky petals.

daily ['deili] *adj* (*attrib*) happening *etc* every day: *daily walk*; *a daily newspaper*; *This is a dai occurrence.* – *adv* every day: *Our cream is fre daily.* – *nc* **1** a newspaper published every day: *W take three dailies and a weekly.* **2** (*inf*: *also* **dail help**) a person who is paid to come regularly a help with housework: *Our daily (help) comes on on Mondays, Wednesdays and Fridays.*

dainty ['deinti] *adj* small or fragile and attractive *The little girl is so dainty*; *a dainty nightdress*; *dainty little girl.* – *nc* (*formal*: *usu in pl*) somethin special to eat: *the dainties at a child's birthd party.*

'**daintily** *adv.* '**daintiness** *nu.*

dairy ['deəri] *nc* **1** a shop supplying milk, butter, cheese *etc*: *We bought milk at the dairy.* **2** the place on a farm *etc* where milk is kept and butter and cheese are made: *The milkman collected the milk from the farm dairy.*

dairy cow – *pl* **dairy cows/cattle** – *nc* a cow kept for its milk.

'**dairy farm** *nc* a farm specializing in producing milk and milk products.

'**dairymaid,** '**dairyman** *ncs* a woman or man who works in a farm dairy.

dais ['deiis] *nc* a raised floor in a hall *etc*: *I couldn't see the speaker although he was standing on a dais.*

daisy ['deizi] *nc* a type of small common flower with a yellow centre and *usu* white petals: *The field was full of daisies*; (*in cmpds*) *a daisy-chain* (= a necklace *etc* made (*eg* by children) from daisies).

dale [deil] *nc* (*usu liter* or in N England: *sometimes found in place-names*) an area of low ground between hills; a valley: (*fig*) *up hill and down dale* (= everywhere); *the Yorkshire Dales.*

dally ['dali] *vi* **1** (*old or liter*: *with* **with**) to play with or think about in an idle manner: *He dallied with the idea of asking her to marry him.* **2** to go *etc* slowly: *Don't dally – do hurry up!*

'**dalliance** *nu* (*old*) flirting.

See also **dilly-dally**.

dam[1] [dam] *nc* **1** a bank or wall of earth, concrete *etc* to keep back water: *A new dam was being built at the mouth of the valley.* **2** the water kept back in this way: *The water-level in the dam was low today.* – *v* – *pt, ptp* **dammed** – *vt* **1** (*sometimes with* **up**) to hold back by means of a dam: *The river has been dammed up.* **2** (*formal or liter*) (*with* **up** *or* **back**) to control or hold back: *She tried bravely to dam back her tears.*

dam[2] [dam] *nc* (of certain animals) a female parent: *Is that the foal's dam?*

damage ['damidʒ] **1** *nu* injury or hurt, *esp* to a thing: *The storm did/caused a lot of damage*; *Her foolish action did her (reputation) a lot of damage*; *She suffered brain-damage as a result of the accident.* **2** *nc* (*legal*: *in pl*) payment due to one person for loss or injury suffered through the fault of another: *The court awarded him £300 damages.* **3** *nu* (*inf facet*) cost: *'What's the damage?' he asked the waiter.* – *vt* to make less effective or less usable *etc*; to spoil: *The bomb destroyed two buildings and damaged several others*; *The book was damaged in the post.*

'**damaged** *adj* (*neg* **un-**): *The car is slightly damaged*; *a damaged table.*

damask ['daməsk] *nu, adj* (of) a kind of silk or *usu* linen cloth with a design woven into it, often used for tablecloths *etc*: *a damask tablecloth.*

dame [deim] *nc* **1** (*with cap in titles*) (the status of) a lady of the same rank as a knight: *There were several dames at the society wedding*: *Dame Margot Fonteyn is a famous ballerina.* **2** (*Amer sl*) a woman. **3** a comic woman in a pantomime, *usu* played by a man.

dammed *see* **dam**[1].

damn [dam] *vt* **1** (*relig*) to sentence to unending punishment in hell: *His soul is damned.* **2** (*loosely*) to cause (someone or something) to be condemned as bad, unacceptable *etc*: *His old-fashioned ideas damn him from the start*; *That film is very popular although it was damned by the critics.* – *interj* expressing anger, irritation *etc*: *Damn! I've forgotten my purse.* – *nc* (*inf*) something unimportant or of no value: *It's not worth a damn*; *I don't give a damn!* (= I don't care in the least).

damnable ['damnəbl] *adj* (*formal*) hateful or deserving to be condemned: *I think their actions are damnable*; *What damnable impertinence!*; (*loosely*) *What damnable weather!*

damnation [dam'neiʃən] *nu* (*relig*) unending punishment in hell: *condemned to eternal damnation.* – *interj* a less emphatic form of **damn**: *Oh damnation! I've dropped it!*

damned *adj* **1** (*relig*: *pred*) sentenced to unending punishment in hell: *His soul is damned.* **2** (*inf*: *attrib*) annoying, irritating, greatly disliked *etc*: *Get that damned dog out of here!*

'**damning** *adj* (*formal*) causing someone to be condemned by showing faults, sins *etc*: *a damning remark*; *The evidence was damning.*

damp [damp] *adj* slightly wet: *damp weather*; *This towel is still damp.* – *nu* slight wetness, *esp* in the air: *The walls were brown with (the) damp*; *Wear a coat if you're going out in the damp.* – *vt* (*usu* '**dampen**) to make slightly wet: *Damp the shirt before you iron it.* – *See also* **damp down** *below.*

'**dampen** *vt* **1** to make damp: *I must dampen this dress before I iron it.* **2** (*fig*) to make or become less fierce or strong (interest *etc*): *The rain dampened everyone's enthusiasm considerably.*

'**damper** *nc* **1** (*fig*) something which lessens the strength of enthusiasm, interest *etc*: *Her presence cast a damper on the proceedings.* **2** a movable plate for controlling the draught *eg* in a stove: *I don't know how to adjust the damper.*

'**dampness** *nu* slight wetness: *the dampness of the weather.*

damp down *vt sep* to make (a fire) less strong so that it burns slowly (*eg* overnight): *There was little firelight, as I had damped down the fire for the night*; (*fig*) *I had the impression he was trying to damp down their enthusiasm.*

damsel ['damzəl] *nc* (*arch or liter*) a young girl: *a damsel in distress.*

damson ['damzən] *nc* a small dark-coloured type of plum or the tree that bears it: (*attrib*) *damson jelly.*

dance [da:ns] *vti* **1** to move in time to music by making a series of rhythmic steps: *She began to dance as soon as she heard the music*; *Can you dance the waltz?* **2** to move quickly up and down: *The child danced up and down in rage*; *The father was dancing the baby on his knee*; (*fig*: *liter*) *The daffodils were dancing in the breeze.* – *nc* **1** a series of fixed steps made in time to music: *Have you done this dance before?*; *Will you have the next dance with me?*; (*attrib*) *dance music*; (*attrib*) *dance steps.* **2** a social gathering at which people dance: *We're going to a dance next Saturday*; *They're giving a dance for their daughter's birthday.*

'**dancer** *nc*: *a ballet dancer.*

'**dancing** *nu* (*often in cmpds*): *She likes dancing*: *ballet dancing*; *country dancing*: (*attrib*) *dancing shoes*; (*attrib*) *dancing partner.*

dance attendance on (*derog*) to wait near (someone) ready to carry out his or her wishes: *She expects everyone to dance attendance on her.*

dandelion ['dandilaiən] *nc* a kind of common wild plant with jagged leaves and a yellow flower.

dander ['dandə]: **get one's dander up** (*inf*) to become angry: *Rudeness really gets his dander up.*

dandruff ['dandrʌf] *nu* dead skin which collects on the head under the hair and falls off in small pieces: *The shoulders of his dark suit were white with dandruff.*

dandy ['dandi] *nc* (*old*) a man who pays a lot of attention to his dress.

Dane *see* Appendix 2.

danger ['deindʒə] **1** *nc* something that may cause harm or injury: *The canal is a danger to children*; *Such men are a danger to us all.* **2** *nu* a state or situation in which harm may come to a person or thing: *He is in danger*; *The bridge is in danger of collapse*; *There is no danger of the murderer getting out of prison*; *He is out of danger now.*

'**dangerous** *adj* very unsafe and likely to be the cause of danger: *a dangerous road*; *a dangerous enemy*; *It is dangerous to cross the road here.*

See also **endanger**.

dangle ['daŋgl] **1** *vti* to (cause to) hang loosely: *She dangled her scarf out of the car window*; *The belt of her coat dangled in the mud.* **2** *vt* (*fig*) to keep before a person's mind (*usu* with the intention of persuading): *He dangled the prospect of higher wages in front of me.*

Danish *see* Appendix 2.

dank [daŋk] *adj* (*formal*) wet and airless: *a dank atmosphere in the forest*; *The cellar is always dank.*

dapper ['dapə] *adj* (*formal*) small, neat and smart: *The bank-manager was a dapper little man in a pin-striped suit*; *You look very dapper.*

dappled ['dapld] *adj* marked with rounded spots of a darker shade.

dapple-'grey *adj* (of a horse) of a pale grey colour with darker spots.

dare [deə] – *neg short form* **daren't** – **1** *modal aux, vt* (*vt usu with* **to**) to be brave enough (to do something): *I daren't go*; *I don't dare* (*to*) *go*; *He wouldn't dare do a thing like that*; *Don't you dare say such a thing again!* **2** *vt* to challenge: *I dare you to do it.* **3** *vt* (*formal*) to be bold enough to take the risk of: *I am not brave enough to dare her anger.* – *nc* a challenge: *He said that he had gone into the lion's cage for a dare.*

'**daring** *adj* bold; courageous: *He was a reckless and daring pilot*; *He's young and daring*; *They made a daring attempt to rescue the climber.* – *nu* boldness: *We thought he was stupid to do it, but we couldn't help admiring his daring.*

'**dare-devil** *nc* a bold or reckless person: *That motorcyclist is a real dare-devil*; (*attrib*) *a dare-devil motorcyclist.*

I dare say (*also* **I ˌdare'say**: *inf*) I suppose (so): *I dare say you're right*; *'Will you be there?' 'Oh, I daresay.'*

dark [da:k] *adj* **1** without light: *a dark room*; *It's getting dark*; (*fig*) *Don't look on the dark* (= not cheerful) *side.* **2** blackish or closer to black than white: *a dark red colour*; *a dark dress*; *dark* (*brown*) *eyes*; *She has rather a dark* (= not very white or fair) *complexion*; *Her hair is dark.* **3** evil and *usu* secret: *dark deeds*; *a dark secret.* – *See also* **keep it dark** *below.* – *nu* absence of light: *I can't find anything in the dark*; *He is afraid of the dark*; *He never goes out after dark*; (*fig*) *We are totally in the dark* (= we have no knowledge) *about what is happening.*

'**darken** *vti* to make or become dark or darker: *The sun had darkened her complexion*; *Night was approaching, and the sky was already darkening.*

'**darkly** *adv* (*formal*) in a secretive manner or tone of voice: *He hinted darkly that we would learn something to our advantage if we went.*

'**darkness** *nu* the state of being dark: *The house was in darkness*: *Darkness is falling* (= It is getting dark).

a dark horse (*fig*) a person about whose abilitie *etc* little is known: *We knew how three of the fou competitors would perform, but the fourth was a dar horse.*

keep it dark (*inf*) to keep something a secret *They're engaged to be married but they want to kee it dark.*

darling ['da:liŋ] *nc* **1** a dearly loved person (ofte used as a term of endearment): *Is that you darling?*; *Jane is her father's darling.* **2** (*inf*) lovable person: *Mary really is a darling!* – *adj* (*attrib*) much loved: *My darling child!* **2** (*inf*: *us attrib*) lovable; pretty and appealing: *What darling little girl!*

darn[1] [da:n] *vt* to mend (clothes *etc*) with rows o stitches crossing one another: *Use a darning needle to darn that sock.* – *nc* the place mended i this way: *Can you see the darn in my stocking?*

darn[2] [da:n] *interj* (*euph*: *also* **darn it**) a much les emphatic form of **damn**: *Darn that cat – scratched me!*

darned *adj* (*attrib*: *euph*) irritating or dislike (used as a mild form of **damned**): *I fall over tha darned rug every time I come into this house!*

dart [da:t] *nc* **1** a pointed arrow-like weapon fo throwing or shooting: *a poisoned dart.* – *See als* **darts** *below.* **2** a sudden and quick movement *The mouse made a sudden dart and disappeared.* – *vi* to move suddenly and quickly: *The mous darted into a hole.* **2** *vt* (*formal*) to send quickly *She darted a look at him across the table.*

darts *n sing* a game in which darts are thrown at board ('**dart-board**) which has a series of num bers on it by which one scores: *a game of darts They're playing darts*; (*attrib*) *a darts match.*

dart-board *see* **darts**.

dash [daʃ] **1** *vi* to move with speed and violence: *man leapt out of the car and dashed into a shop.* **2** *v* (*formal*) to knock, throw *etc* violently, *esp* so as t break: *He dashed the bottle to pieces against the wal* **3** *vt* (*fig formal*) to bring down suddenly an violently or to make very depressed: *Our hope were dashed when she came back empty-handed Her spirits were dashed by the incident.* – *See als* **dash off** *below.* – **1** *nc* a sudden rush o movement: *The child made a dash for the door.* **2** *n* a small amount of something, *esp* liquid: *whisk with a dash of soda.* **3** *nc* (in writing) a short lin (–) to show a break in a sentence *etc.* **4** *nu* energ and enthusiasm: *All his activities showed the sam dash and spirit.* – *interj* (*euph*: *also* '**dash it**) much less emphatic form of **damn**: *Dash! I'v broken the cup.*

dashed *adj* (*attrib*: *euph*) irritating or dislike (used as a mild form of **damned**): *I've got to go t that dashed meeting.*

'**dashing** *adj* smart and lively: *a dashing youn man*; *She looks very dashing in her riding-clothes.*

dash off **1** *vt sep* (*formal*) to write *etc* hurriedl and without much care: *I dashed off a letter or tw while I was waiting.* **2** *vi* (*inf*) to leave or mov away in a hurry: *I must dash off to the shops befor they shut.*

dashboard ['daʃbo:d] *nc* a board *etc* with dials switches *etc* in front of the driver's seat in a car.

dastardly ['dastədli] *adj* (*old*) (of conduct or person) cowardly and mean: *dastardly behaviour*

data ['deitə] *nu* (*orig n pl* and still sometime formally used as such) facts or information give from which other facts may be worked out (*es* the information given to a computer): *I'm afraid* *had insufficient data to work out all the statistics you wanted; All the data has/have been fed into the computer.*

ˈdata-bank *nc* a large amount of information which is stored in a computer and from which particular pieces of information can be acquired when needed.

ˌdata-ˈprocessing *nu* the handling and processing of information by computer.

date[1] [deit] *nc* **1** a statement on a letter, document *etc* giving the day of the month and *usu* the month and year when it was written, sent *etc*: *I can't read the date on this letter.* **2** the day and month and/or the year in which something happened or is going to happen: *The date of our party will be December 12; What is your date of birth?* (= the day, month and year when you were born); *Wasn't 1815 the date of the battle of Waterloo?* **3** (*inf*) an appointment or engagement, *esp* a social one with a member of the opposite sex: *She was sad because he had never asked her for a date.* **4** (*inf*) a person with whom one has an appointment of this kind: *Who's your date for tonight?* – **1** *vt* to have or put a date on: *This letter isn't dated; Why didn't you date the letter?* **2** *vi* (*with* **from** *or* **back**) to belong to; to have been made, written *etc* at (a certain time): *Their quarrel dates back to last year; Our house dates from the seventeenth century.* **3** *vt* (*formal*) to guess at or find out the date of: *We have been unable to date the piece of pottery we dug up.* **4** *vti* (*inf*) to go out with (a member of the opposite sex) *esp* regularly: *I date her occasionally; They have been dating for years.* **5** *vi* to become obviously old-fashioned: *His books haven't dated much.*

ˈdated *adj* (*usu pred*: *formal*) obviously old-fashioned: *Her clothes looked very dated; His attitudes are rather dated now.*

ˈdateline *nc* the line drawn on the map of the W Pacific, east and west of which the date is different.

out of date 1 old-fashioned: *This coat is out of date/very out-of-date; That has gone out of date; an out-of-date coat.* **2** no longer able to be (legally) used; no longer valid: *Your ticket is out of date/very out-of-date; an out-of-date ticket; an out-of-date telephone directory.*

to ˈdate (*formal*) up to the present time: *This is the best entry we've received to date.*

up to date 1 completed *etc* up to the present time: *I try to keep my correspondence up to date/fully up-to-date; an up-to-date catalogue.* **2** modern and in touch with the latest ideas: *This method is up to date/very up-to-date; an up-to-date method;* (*inf*) *I've been away – you'll have to bring me up to date with the news* (= tell me the latest news).

See also **update**.

date[2] [deit] *nc* the brown, sticky fruit of the **ˈdate palm**, a kind of tree growing in the tropics.

daub [do:b] **1** *vt* to cover (something) with (*eg* paint) roughly and unevenly; to smear: *The wall had been daubed with blood.* **2** *vti* (*derog*) to paint roughly or without skill: *He's just daubing paint on that canvas; He can't paint – he just daubs.* – *nc* **1** (*inf or derog*) a roughly-made or unskilful painting: *He tried to sell us a couple of his daubs.* **2** a piece of soft, sticky material such as clay *etc*: *daubs of glue.*

daughter [ˈdo:tə] *nc* a female child (when spoken of in relation to her parents): *That is Mary's daughter; She has two daughters and a son.*

ˈdaughter-in-law – *pl* **ˈdaughters-in-law** – *nc* a son's wife.

daunt [do:nt] *vt* (*formal*) to frighten; to make less brave or eager: *She was somewhat daunted by the size of the job.*

ˈdaunting *adj* (*formal*) difficult; requiring courage: *a daunting task.*

nothing daunted (*formal often facet*) not at all discouraged; not frightened or made less enthusiastic *etc*: *She was an old lady but nothing daunted she hit her attacker with her umbrella.*

See also **undaunted**.

dawdle [ˈdo:dl] *vt* to waste time *esp* by moving slowly: *Hurry up, and don't dawdle!* **ˈdawdler** *nc*. **ˈdawdling** *nu*.

dawn [do:n] *vi* (*formal*) (*esp* of daylight) to begin to appear: *A new day has dawned.* – *See also* **dawn on** *below*. – *ncu* **1** the very beginning of a day; very early morning: *We must get up at dawn; The birds began to sing at dawn; the dawn of a new day.* **2** (*fig formal*) the very beginning of (something): *the dawn of civilization.*

ˈdawning *nu* the act of beginning: *the dawning of a new day; We have watched the dawning of a new age.*

ˈdawn on/(*formal*) **upon** *vt fus* to become suddenly clear to (a person): *It suddenly dawned on me what he had meant.*

day [dei] **1** *ncu* the period from sunrise to sunset: *She sat by his bedside day and night; She worked all day; He works by night and sleeps by day; The days are warmer, but the nights are very cold.* **2** *nc* a part of this period *eg* that part spent at work: *How long is your working day?; The school day ends at 3 o'clock; I see him every day;* (*attrib*) *a day nursery* (= a nursery where children are looked after during most of the day *eg* when their mothers are at work). **3** *nc* the period of twenty-four hours from one midnight to the next: *How many days are in the month of September?* (*loosely*) *She was ill for three days* (= She was ill for approximately this length of time *eg* for Monday, Tuesday and Wednesday). **4** *nc* (*formal*: *often in pl*) the period of, or of the greatest activity, influence, strength *etc* of (something or someone): *in my grandfather's day; in the days of steam-power.*

ˈdaybreak *ncu* (*formal*) dawn; the first appearance of light: *We left at daybreak.*

day-by-day *see* **day by day** *below*.

ˈday-dream *nc* a dreaming or imagining of pleasant events; the making of unreal plans *etc* while awake: *In her day-dreams she imagined herself as rich and famous.* – *vi*: *She often day-dreams.*

ˈdaylight *nu* **1** the light given by the sun: *We wanted to get the car repairs done while daylight lasted;* (*attrib*) *daylight hours.* **2** dawn: *To get there on time we must leave before daylight.*

ˌday-reˈlease *nu* a system by which employees are given time off work to attend classes at college *etc*: *He goes to the technical college on day-release;* (*attrib*) *a day-release scheme.*

ˈday school *nc* a school whose pupils attend only during the day and live at home.

ˈday shift 1 *ncu* (a period of) work during the day: *She's on* (*the*) *day shift this week.* **2** *n pl* the people who work during this period: *The day shift finish at six o'clock.*

ˈday-time *nu* the time when it is day.

call it a day (*inf*) to bring (something) to an end; to stop (*eg* working): *I haven't finished this piece of* *work but I'm so tired that I'll have to call it a day; They were engaged to be married but they quarrelled so often that they decided to call it a day* (= to end their engagement).

carry the day *see* **carry.**

day by day every day: *He's getting better day by day*; (*attrib*) *day-by-day improvements.*

day in, day out *see* **in.**

have had one's day (*inf*) to be past the most successful *etc* period of one's life: *Steam trains have had their day; He used to be a very able businessman but he's had his day.*

make someone's day (*inf*) to make (someone) very happy: *It made the old lady's day when she received a bunch of flowers; That baby's smile made my day.*

name the day *see* **name.**

one day 1 at some time in the future: *He hopes to go to America one day.* **2** on a day in the past: *I saw him one day last week; I saw him one day with a girl.*

some day at some time in the future: *She hopes to get married some day.*

the other day not long ago: *I saw Mr Smith the other day.*

win the day *see* **win.**

daze [deiz] *vti* to make or feel confused (*eg* by a blow or a shock): *Banging his head on the bookcase dazed him for a moment; She was dazed by the news.* – *nc* a bewildered or absent-minded state: *She's been going around in a daze all day.*

dazed *adj* confused (by a blow *etc*): *He came in looking dazed and white with shock; in a dazed condition.*

dazzle ['dazl] *vt* **1** (of a strong light) to prevent one from seeing properly: *I was dazzled by the car's headlights.* **2** (*fig formal*) (of great beauty, cleverness *etc*) to affect one's ability to make correct judgements: *She was dazzled by his charm.*

'**dazzling** *adj* **1** so bright as to prevent one from seeing properly: *The car's headlights were dazzling; a dazzling light;* (*fig*) *dazzling white teeth.* **2** (*fig*) colourful; impressive; very remarkable: *a dazzling display of wit.*

'**dazzlingly** *adv*: *Her washing was dazzlingly white; She was dazzlingly beautiful.*

deacon ['di:kən] *nc* **1** the lowest rank of clergyman in the Church of England. **2** a church officer in other churches.

dead [ded] *adj* **1** without life; not living: *His heart was still beating when they found him, but he was dead on arrival in hospital; a dead body; Throw out those dead flowers; Sweep up the dead leaves.* **2** (*fig: pred*) not working and not giving any sign of being about to work: *The phone/engine is dead.* **3** (*attrib*) absolute or complete: *There was dead silence at his words; He came to a dead stop; dead centre.* – *adv* (*inf* in some usages) completely: *dead certain; dead drunk.*

'**deaden** *vt* to lessen, weaken or make less sharp, strong *etc*: *That will deaden the pain; His feelings were deadened; The soft grass deadened the sounds of his footsteps.*

'**deadly** *adj* **1** causing death: *a deadly poison; That poison is deadly.* **2** (*attrib*) very great: *He is in deadly earnest* (= He is completely serious); *deadly earnestness.* **3** (*inf*) very dull or uninteresting: *What a deadly job this is; That film is deadly.* – *adv* (*inf*) extremely: *deadly dull; deadly serious.*

dead cert *see* **certain.**

dead end *nc* a road closed off at one end: *There's no good going along that road – it's a dead end.*

'**dead-end** *adj* (*inf fig: attrib*) leading nowhere: *dead-end job.*

dead heat *nc* a race, or a situation happening in race, in which two or more competitors cross th finishing line together: *There was a dead heat fo first place; That race was a dead heat.*

dead language *nc* a language no longer spoke by ordinary people, *eg* Latin.

'**deadline** *nc* a time by which something must b done or finished: *Monday is the deadline fo handing in this essay.*

'**deadlock** *nu* a situation in which no furthe progress towards an agreement (in discussion *etc*) is possible: *Talks between the two sides ended i deadlock tonight.*

dead loss *nc* (*inf*) someone or something which i completely useless (*esp* for a particular purpose) *He's a dead loss as far as mending things concerned; This pencil-sharpener is a dead loss.*

ˌ**dead-'pan** *adj* (*usu attrib*) (of an expression *etc* showing no emotion at all, *esp* pretending to b serious: *He tells jokes with such a dead-pa expression.*

dead shot *nc* a person who can shoot ver accurately (*usu* with a gun).

dead spit *nc* (*inf*) someone who looks exactly lik (someone else): *He is the dead spit of his father.*

dead weight *nc* something or someone that i heavy to lift or carry: *This bag of cement is a dea weight.*

dead beat (*inf*) exhausted or very tired: *She wa dead beat after doing her spring-cleaning.*

ˌ**dead 'set on** (*inf*) determined or very anxious (t do or obtain something): *My wife is dead set o that house; I'm dead set on getting to America.*

dead to the world (*inf*) fast asleep: *When h arrived home at midnight his wife was dead to th world.*

See also **death, die.**

deaf [def] *adj* **1** unable to hear: *She has been dea since birth; a deaf old man.* **2** (*formal*) (*pred wit* **to**) refusing to understand or to listen: *He wa deaf to all arguments.* '**deafness** *n nu.*

'**deafen** *vt* to make hearing difficult: to have a unpleasant effect on the hearing: *I was deafened b the noise in there!*

'**deaf aid** *nc* (*inf*) a hearing-aid: *She has to wear deaf aid now that her hearing is so bad.*

ˌ**deaf-'mute** *nc* a person who is deaf and dumb

turn a deaf ear to deliberately to ignore; t refuse to take any notice of: *They tried to persuad her not to go but she turned a deaf ear to their advice.*

deal [di:l] *nc* **1** a bargain or arrangement: *a busines deal;* (*inf*) *Will you do a deal with me?* **2** the act o dividing cards among players in a card game. *See also* **a good deal/a great deal** *below.* – *v* – *p ptp* **dealt** [delt] – **1** *vi* to do business, *esp* to bu and sell: *I've dealt with your firm for years; I thin he deals in stocks and shares.* **2** *vt* (*formal*) to give (blow): *He dealt the boy a blow on the ear.* **3** *vt* t distribute (cards): *Will you deal the cards?* – *Se also* **deal with** *below.*

'**dealer** *nc* **1** a person who buys and sells: *a deale in antiques; a used-car dealer.* **2** the person wh distributes the cards in a card game: *You're deale this time.*

'**dealing** *nu, nc* (*usu in pl*) contact (often i business), bargaining, argreement *etc* mad (between two or more people or groups *fair/honest dealing; There has been no dealing on th Stock Market today; I have no dealings with hi* *now*; *We have not mentioned money in all our dealings.*

'**deal with** *vt fus* **1** to be concerned with; to discuss: *This book deals with methods of teaching English.* **2** to take action about, *esp* in order to solve a problem, get rid of a person, complete a piece of business *etc*: *I want to deal with this letter before I do anything else*; *She deals with all the inquiries.*

a good deal/a great deal much or a lot: *They made a good deal of noise*; *She spent a great deal of money on it.*

dean [di:n] *nc* **1** the chief clergyman in a cathedral church. **2** an important official in a university.

dear [diə] *adj* **1** (*usu pred*) high in price: *Cabbages are very dear this week*; *The dear houses are selling better than the cheaper ones.* **2** (*attrib*) very lovable: *He is such a dear little boy.* **3** (*pred with* **to**) much loved: *She is very dear to me.* **4** used as a polite way of addressing someone, *esp* in a letter: *Dear Sir*; *My dear Mrs Smith.* – *nc* **1** a person who is lovable or charming: *He is such a dear!* **2** (*also* (*inf*) '**dearie** *or* '**deary**) a person who is loved or liked (*esp* used to address someone): *Come in, dear*; *Mary, my dear, is that you?* – *adv* (*formal or old*: *often fig*) at a high price: *His decision to ignore her cost him dear.*

'**dearly** *adv* **1** very much or very strongly: *I would dearly like to see you*; *She loved him dearly.* **2** (*formal*) at a high cost: *The battle was dearly won* (= many men were killed).

dear, dear!/oh dear! *interjs* mild expressions of regret, sorrow, pity *etc*: *Oh dear! I've forgotten my key.*

dear me! *interj* a mild expression of various emotions, *esp* surprise and sympathy: *Dear me! I'm sorry to hear that.*

dearth [də:θ] *nc* (*formal*) a scarcity or shortage: *There is a dearth of talent in the theatre here.*

death [deθ] **1** *ncu* the act of dying: *There have been several deaths in the town recently*; *Most people fear death.* **2** *ncu* something which causes one to die: *Smoking too much was the death of him*; (*fig*) *Living outside London was death to him*; (*facet*) *His temper will be the death of him one day!* **3** *nu* the state of being dead: *eyes closed in death.*

'**deathly** (*formal*) *adj* (*usu attrib*), *adv* as if caused by death: *a deathly silence*; *It was deathly quiet.*

'**death-bed** *nc* (*formal*) the bed in which a person dies: *He repented on his death-bed*; (*attrib*) *a death-bed repentance.*

'**death blow** *nc* (*fig*) the final happening, decision *etc* which puts an end to something: *The plan received its death blow when the leader was killed*; *The proposal to build an opera house received its death blow when the Government refused to give money.*

'**death certificate** *nc* an official piece of paper signed by a doctor stating the cause of someone's death.

'**death rattle** *nc* a rattling in the throat which is sometimes heard before a person's death.

'**death-trap** *nc* (*inf*) a place, building *etc* in which one is in danger of being killed: *Old buildings without fire-escapes are real death-traps!*

'**death warrant** *nc* an order for the execution of a criminal.

at death's door (*inf*) on the point of dying: *It's remarkable that she's still alive, because when I last saw her, I thought she was at death's door.*

be in at the death to be present during the final stages of a course of events, *esp* a hunt of some kind.

catch one's death (of cold) (*inf*) to get a very bad cold: *If you go out in that rain without a coat you'll catch your death* (*of cold*).

'**death to** (*formal or facet*) active in killing; fatal to; bad for: *Our cat is death to mice*; (*fig*) *Detergent is death to my skin.*

put to death (*formal*) to cause to be killed: *The criminal was put to death by hanging.*

to 'death (*inf*) very greatly: *I'm sick to death of the rain*; *I've been worried to death about you.*

See also **dead, die.**

deb [deb] short for **debutante**.

debar [di'ba:] – *pt, ptp* **de'barred** – *vt* (*formal*) to shut out or prevent (from doing something): *People under eighteen are debarred from voting.*

debase [di'beis] *vt* (*formal*) to make of less value or of less high quality: *Our coinage is now debased*; (*fig*) *His ideals seemed debased by his obvious interest in money.*

See also base[2].

debate [di'beit] *ncu* a discussion or argument, *esp* a formal one in front of an audience: *There will be a debate on whether or not the club should admit women members*; *a Parliamentary debate*; *After some debate, they decided not to take part.* – **1** *vti* to hold a formal discussion (about): *Parliament will debate the question tomorrow*; *Parliament debated until after midnight.* **2** *vt* to think about or talk about something before coming to a decision: *We debated whether to go by bus or train.*

de'batable *adj* (*formal*) doubtful; able to be argued about: *a debatable point*; *That is debatable.*

debauched [di'bo:tʃt] *adj* (*formal*) inclined to debauchery: *a debauched medical student.*

de'bauchery *ncu* (*formal*) too much indulgence in pleasures *usu* considered immoral, *esp* sexual activity and excessive drinking: *a life of debauchery*; *the debaucheries of his youth.*

debilitate [di'biliteit] *vt* (*formal*) to make weak: *He was greatly debilitated by lack of food.*

de'bility *nu* (*formal*) bodily weakness: *Despite his debility, he leads a normal life.*

debit ['debit] *nc* (*formal or tech*) an entry on the side of an account which records what is owed: *His debits outnumbered his credits*; (*attrib*) *the debit side.* – *v* – *pt, ptp* '**debited** – *vt* to enter or record on this side of an account: *His account was debited with the money he paid for the car.*

debonair [debə'neə] *adj* (*formal*) of pleasant and elegant appearance and manners: *He was young and debonair*; *a debonair appearance.*

debris ['deibri:, (*Amer*) də'bri:] *nu* (*more formal than* **rubbish**) **1** the remains of something broken, destroyed *etc*: *The fireman found a corpse among the debris.* **2** (*loosely*) rubbish: *There was a lot of debris in the garden of the new house after the builder had left.*

debt [det] *nc* what one person owes to another: *He will never pay all his debts*; *His debts amount to over £1000*; (*fig*) *a debt of gratitude.*

'**debtor** *nc* a person who owes a debt.

in 'debt owing money: *Because he was so deeply in debt, he was declared to be bankrupt.*

in someone's debt (*formal*) under an obligation to someone; owing someone a favour *etc*: *After your kindness, I shall always be in your debt.*

debunk [di:'bʌŋk] *vt* (*inf*) to take away an undeserved good reputation from (a person or thing): *He wrote an article debunking the much-*

admired theories of his main opponent.

debut, début ['deibju:, (*Amer*) dei'bju:] *nc* (*formal*) a first public appearance on the stage, in society *etc*: *She made her stage debut at the age of eight*; *She made her debut as a singer.*

debutante ['debjuta:nt] *nc* a girl making her first formal appearance as an adult in upper-class society: *In Britain debutantes used to be presented to the king or queen.*

decade ['dekeid, di'keid] *nc* **1** (*slightly formal*) a period of ten years: *the first decade of this century* (= 1900–09 inclusive). **2** (*loosely*: *inf*) a very long time: *She's been in that job for decades.*

decadence ['dekədəns] *nu* (*formal*) **1** a falling from high to low standards in morals or the arts: *the decadence of the late Roman empire.* **2** the state of having low or incorrect standards of behaviour; immorality: *He lived a life of decadence*; *She considered having breakfast in bed the height of decadence.*

'decadent *adj*: *a decadent young man*; *That hat makes you look rather decadent.*

decagram(me), decalitre, decametre *see* Appendix 5.

decamp [di'kamp] *vi* (*facet or formal*) to go away, *esp* secretly: *Meanwhile, the treasurer of the society had decamped with the money.*

decant [di'kant] *vt* (*formal*) to pour (wine) from one bottle to another, leaving the sediment behind: *The butler decanted the claret several hours before dinner.*

de'canter *nc* an ornamental bottle for holding wine, sherry, whisky *etc*: *a whisky decanter.*

decapitate [di'kapiteit] *vt* (*formal*) to cut the head from (*esp* a person): *He was decapitated in the accident*; (*facet*) *She decapitated all the withered roses.* **de,capi'tation** *ncu.*

decay [di'kei] (*more formal or tech than* **rot**) *vti* to (cause to) become rotten or ruined: *Sugar decays your teeth*; *Sugar makes your teeth decay.* – *nu* the act or process of decaying: *tooth decay*; *in a state of decay*; *At that time, the Roman Empire was already in decay.*

deceased [di'si:st] *adj* (*legal*) dead: *his deceased wife*; *His parents, now deceased, were very wealthy.*

the deceased (*legal*) the dead person already mentioned, *esp* one who has recently died: *Were you a friend of the deceased?.*

deceit [di'si:t] *ncu* (an act of) deceiving: *She was too honest to be capable of deceit.*

de'ceitful *adj* deceiving or insincere: *She's such a deceitful child!*; *a deceitful trick.* **de'ceitfully** *adv.* **de'ceitfulness** *nu.*

deceive [di'si:v] *vt* to mislead or cause to make mistakes, *usu* by giving or suggesting false information: *The lights deceived him into thinking he was near a village*; *He was deceived by her innocent appearance*; *She deceived herself into believing that she would win.*

de'ceiver *nc* (*old*) a person who deceives, *esp* a man who tricks women into thinking he will marry them.

See also **deception.**

decelerate [di:'seləreit] *vti* (*formal*) to slow down, *esp* in a car *etc*: *You must decelerate before a crossroads.* **de,cele'ration** *nu.*

See also **accelerate.**

December [di'sembə] *n* the twelfth month of the year, the month following November: *He visited me in December*; *I am going there on December 22* (said as 'on December (the) twenty-second' or 'on the twenty-second of December'): *He is coming on the 22nd/twenty-second of December*; *She died last December.*

decent ['di:snt] *adj* **1** (*inf*: *usu attrib*) fairly good; of fairly good quality: *a decent standard of living*; *Where can I get a decent meal in this town?*; *a decent bottle of wine*; *If I'm going to the wedding I'll have to get a decent dress – all my clothes are old-fashioned.* **2** (*inf*) kindly, tolerant or likeable: *He's a decent enough fellow*; *She's being very decent about the whole affair*; *It was decent of you to look after the children yesterday.* **3** (*usu pred*) not vulgar or immoral; modest: *Keep your language decent!*; *I don't think that low-cut dress is exactly decent!* **4** (*formal*) fitting; suitable; showing respect: *They did not consider it decent that his widow married again so soon after his death.*

'decency *ncu* (the general idea of) what is proper, fitting, moral *etc*; the quality or act of being decent: *In the interests of decency, we have banned nude bathing*; (*formal*) *She observed the decencies demanded by the occasion* (= She acted in a manner suitable to the occasion); *He had the decency to admit that it was his fault.*

'decently *adv* in a manner acceptable to the general idea of what is proper or suitable: *You're not going out unless you're decently dressed.*

See also **indecent.**

deception [di'sepʃən] *ncu* (an act of) deceiving: *Deception is difficult in these circumstances*; *Only a minor deception was necessary to achieve our aim.*

de'ceptive [-tiv] *adj* (*formal*) deceiving; misleading: *Appearances may be deceptive*; *a deceptive bend in the road.*

de'ceptively *adj* (*formal*): *She is deceptively shy.*

See also **deceive.**

decibel ['desibel] *nc* (*formal*: *often abbrev* **db** *when written*) the main unit of measurement of the loudness of a sound: *Traffic noise is measured in decibels.*

decide [di'said] **1** *vti* to (cause to) make up one's mind: *I have decided to retire*; *She decided not to go*; *He decided against leaving*; *What decided you against going?* **2** *vt* to settle or make the result (of something) *etc* certain: *The last goal decided the match.*

de'cided *adj* (*attrib*: *formal*) **1** clear and definite: *His height was a decided advantage.* **2** determined: *She spoke in a very decided manner, as if her mind was made up.*

de'cidedly *adv* (*formal*) certainly; definitely: *I am most decidedly not going.*

See also **decision, decisive, undecided.**

deciduous [di'sidjuəs, (*Amer*) -dʒuəs] *adj* (*tech*) (of trees) having leaves that fall in autumn: *Oaks are deciduous trees.*

See also **coniferous.**

decigram(me), decilitre *see* Appendix 5.

decimal ['desiməl] *adj* numbered by tens: *the decimal system.* – *nc* a decimal fraction: *Convert these fractions to decimals.*

'decimalize, -ise *vt* to convert (figures or a country's currency) from a non-decimal to a decimal form: *When did Britain decimalize its currency?* **,decimali'zation, -s-** *nu.*

decimal currency *nu* a system of money in which each coin or note is either a tenth of or ten times another in value.

decimal fraction *nc* a fraction expressed as so many tenths, hundredths, thousandths *etc* and

written with a decimal point, like this: 0·1 (= 1/10), 2·33 (= 2 33/100).
See also **vulgar fraction** *under* **vulgar**.

decimate ['desimeit] *vt* (*formal*) (of disease, battle *etc*) to reduce greatly in number: *The population was decimated by the 'plague.* ˌ**deci'mation** *nu.*

decimetre *see* Appendix 5.

decipher [di'saifə] *vt* **1** to translate (writing in code) into ordinary, understandable language: *The enemy could not decipher the spy's letter.* **2** (*formal*) to make out the meaning of (something which is difficult to read): *It took me some time to decipher his handwriting.*
See also **indecipherable**.

decision [di'siʒən] **1** *ncu* the act of deciding; a judgement: *a time/moment of decision*; *I think you made the wrong decision*; *They have finally come to a decision about the child's future*; *He takes all the decisions.* **2** *nu* (*formal*) firmness: *You must act with decision.*
See also **decide, decisive, indecision**.

decisive [di'saisiv] *adj* (*formal*) **1** final; putting an end to a contest, dispute *etc*: *The battle was decisive*; *That was a decisive factor in his decision to emigrate.* **2** showing decision and firmness: *He has a decisive manner*; *He's very decisive.* **de'cisiveness** *nu.*
de'cisively *adj*: *He acted very decisively.*
See also **decide, decision, indecisive**.

deck[1] [dek] *vt* (*usu old*) to put decorations *etc* on: *They decked the house with holly*; (*facet*) *They decked themselves out in their Sunday clothes.*

deck[2] [dek] *nc* **1** a platform extending from one side of a ship *etc* to the other and forming the floor: *The cars are in the lower deck.* **2** a floor in a bus: *Let's go on the top deck.* **3** a pack of playing-cards: *The gambler used his own deck of cards.*
-decker (*in cmpds*) (of a bus *etc*) having (a certain number of) decks: *a single-decker bus.*
'**deck-chair** *nc* a light collapsible chair made of wood and canvas or other heavy fabric: *They were sitting in deck-chairs on the beach.*

declaim [di'kleim] *vti* (*formal*) to make (a speech) in an impressive and dramatic manner: *The politician declaimed his views on immigration to his audience*; *She declaimed against immorality.*

declare [di'kleə] **1** *vt* to announce publicly or formally: *War was declared this morning*; *He declared his intentions to leave the country in a long, boring speech.* **2** *vt* to say firmly: *'I don't like him at all,' she declared.* **3** *vt* to make known (goods on which duty must be paid, income on which tax should be paid *etc*): *He did not declare the wine*; *He decided to declare his untaxed earnings to the tax-office.* **4** *vti* (in cricket) to end (an innings) before ten wickets have fallen: *They declared before tea.* – *See also* **declare** *in phrases below.*
declaration [deklə'reiʃən] *nc* a formal announcement: *a declaration of marriage/war.*
de'clared *adj* (*attrib*: *formal*: *neg* **un-**) clearly and firmly stated: *It was his declared intention to go to Australia.*
declare for, against *vt fus* (*formal*) to say that one supports or opposes (an opinion, group *etc*): *He always declares for the losing side.*
de'clare oneself (*formal*) to say which side one is on, or what one is going to do: *He finally declared himself a member of the Labour Party.*

declassify [di:'klasifai] *vt* to take (a document *etc*) off the list of secret documents and allow the public *etc* to read it: *These reports have just been declassified.*
See also **classified** *under* **classify**.

declension [di'klenʃən] (*gram*) **1** *nc* a group of nouns *etc* which follow the same grammatical pattern when indicating case, number *etc.* **2** *nu* (the act of giving) the various forms of a certain noun *etc.*
See also **decline, conjugate**.

decline [di'klain] **1** *vt* (*formal*) to say 'no' to (an invitation *etc*); to refuse: *We declined his offer of a lift as we wanted to walk.* **2** *vi* (*formal*) to become less strong or less good *etc*: *His health has declined recently*; *Our profits have temporarily declined.* **3** *vt* (*gram*) to give the various cases of (a noun or adjective). – *ncu* (*formal*) a gradual loss of strength, worsening (of health, standards, quantity *etc*): *From then on, his fortunes were in decline*; *There has been a gradual decline in the birthrate.*
See also **declension**.

decode [di:'koud] *vt* to translate (a coded message) into ordinary understandable language.

decompose [di:kəm'pouz] *vti* (*formal*) **1** (of vegetable or animal matter) to (cause to) decay or rot: *Grass cuttings decompose in a compost heap*; *The heat helped to decompose the grass cuttings*; *Corpses decompose quickly in heat.* **2** to separate into parts or elements: *to decompose a compound into its elements.* **decomposition** [di:kompə'ziʃən] *nu.*

decompress [di:kəm'pres] *vt* (*tech*) to decrease the pressure (of the air *etc*) on, *esp* gradually: *Deep-sea divers must be decompressed gradually.*
ˌ**decom'pression** [-ʃən] *nu* (*tech*) the act of decompressing: *the decompression of divers*; (*attrib*) *a decompression chamber.*

décor ['deiko:, (*Amer*) dei'ko:r] *ncu* (*formal or facet*) the decoration of a room *etc* and the arrangement of the objects in it: *It was a comfortable room, but I didn't like the décor.*

decorate ['dekəreit] *vt* **1** to add some kind of ornament *etc* to (something) to make more beautiful, striking *etc*: *We decorated the Christmas tree with glass balls and lights.* **2** to put paint, paper *etc* on the walls, ceiling and woodwork of (a room): *He spent a week decorating the living-room.* **3** (*formal*) to give a medal or badge to (someone) as a mark of honour: *He was decorated for his war-work.*
ˌ**deco'ration** **1** *ncu* something used to decorate: *Christmas decorations*; *I added a piece of holly to the Christmas pudding for decoration.* **2** *nu* the act of decorating: *The decoration of the house will be a long job.*
'**decorative** [-rətiv] *adj* ornamental or beautiful (*esp* if not useful): *a decorative arrangement of flowers*; (*facet*) *The new secretary is not very good at typing but she's at least decorative.*
'**decorator** *nc* a person who decorates rooms, houses *etc*: *He was a painter and decorator by trade.*

decorous ['dekərəs] *adj* (*formal*: *usu attrib*) (behaving in a manner which is) acceptable, *esp* quiet and dignified: *In Victorian times girls were expected to behave in a decorous manner.* '**decorously** *adv.*
decorum [di'ko:rəm] *nu* (*formal*) quiet, dignified and proper behaviour: *The man behaved with decorum in the old lady's presence.*
See also **indecorous**.

decoy [di'koi] *vt* (*formal*) to lead (a person or animal) into a trap: *They decoyed him away from* the house by telling him his mother was in hospital. – ['di:koi] *nc* anything intended to lead someone or something into a trap: *The policewoman acted as a decoy when the police were trying to catch the rapist.*

decrease [di'kri:s] *vti* to make or become less: *Their numbers had decreased over the previous year; The university has gradually decreased the number of students.* – ['di:kri:s] *ncu* a growing less: *a decrease of fifty per cent; There has been a gradual decrease in unemployment.*
See also **increase**.

decree [di'kri:] *nc* (*formal*) **1** an order, edict or law: *The king issued a decree forbidding hunting on royal land.* **2** (*legal*) a ruling of a court of civil law. – *v* – *pt, ptp* **de'creed** – *vt* (*formal*) to order, command or decide (something): *The court decreed that he should pay the fine in full.*
decree nisi ['naisai] (*legal*: *not in Scotland*) a decree of divorce which becomes effective after a certain period of time unless anyone who has a right to object to it does so: *She was granted a decree nisi.*

decrepit [di'krepit] *adj* **1** (*derog*) not strong or healthy because of old age: *decrepit old men; He has become very decrepit.* **2** (*formal*) broken-down; almost in ruins: *a decrepit old chair.* **de'crepitude** [-tju:d] *nu* (*very formal*).

decry [di'krai] *vt* (*very formal*) to express disapproval of, *esp* by trying to make appear worthless: *He decried his country's attempts to make peace.*

dedicate ['dedikeit] *vt* **1** (*formal*) to give up wholly to; to devote to: *He dedicated his life to good works; He dedicates his Saturdays to football.* **2** (*formal*) to set apart, *esp* for a holy or sacred purpose: *He decided to dedicate a chapel to his wife's memory.* **3** to name a person *eg* in the front page of (a book): *He dedicated the book to his father; He dedicated that song to her.*
'dedicated *adj* spending a great deal of one's time and energy on a subject, one's job *etc*: *She's a dedicated teacher; He is dedicated to music.*
,dedi'cation **1** *nu* (*formal*) the quality of being dedicated; the act of dedicating: *He was given a medal for dedication to duty; We were present at the dedication of the church.* **2** *nc* the words dedicating a book to someone: *We can put the dedication at the top of the page.*

deduce [di'dju:s] *vt* (*formal*: not *usu* used with **is, was** *etc* and **-ing**) to work out from facts one knows or guesses: *From the height of the sun I deduced that it was about ten o'clock.*
deduction[1] [di'dʌkʃən] (*formal*) **1** *nu* the act of deducing: *I did a quick deduction and decided I had come about thirty miles.* **2** *nc* something that has been deduced: *Is this deduction accurate?* – *See also* **deduct**.

deduct [di'dʌkt] *vt* (*formal*) to subtract; to take away: *They deducted the expenses from his salary.*
de'duction[2] [-ʃən] *nc* something that has been deducted: *I made a small deduction from the price of the car because I was selling it to a friend; There were a lot of deductions from my salary this month.* – *See also* **deduce**.

deed [di:d] *nc* **1** (*usu formal or liter*) something done; an act: *a good deed.* **2** (*legal*) a signed statement or agreement *eg* about the ownership of a house: *He has lost the deeds of his house.*

deem [di:m] *vt* (*very formal or facet*: not used with **is, was** *etc* and **-ing**) to judge or think: *He deemed it unwise to tell her about his plans for the future.*

deep [di:p] *adj* **1** going or being far down or far into: *That water is too deep for the children to swim in; a deep lake; a deep wound.* **2** going or being far down by a named amount: *a hole six feet deep.* **3** (*fig*) occupied or involved to a great extent: *She was deep in a book; He is deep in debt.* **4** intense; strong: *The sea is a deep blue colour; Her feelings for her children are very deep; They are in a deep sleep.* **5** low in pitch: *a deep, musical sound; His voice is very deep.* **6** hard to understand: *thoughts too deep for me; a deep scientific work;* (*inf*) *She is very deep – you never know what she is thinking.* – *adv* far down or into: *He went deep into the wood.* – *nu* (*liter*: *with* **the**) the sea.
'deepen *vti* **1** to make or become deeper: *The flood water was deepening all the time: He deepened the hole.* **2** (*fig*) to increase: *His troubles were deepening.*
'deeply *adv* (*formal*) very greatly: *He felt her betrayal deeply.*
'deepness *nu* the quality of being deep.
,deep-'freeze *nc* a type of refrigerator which freezes food quickly and can keep it for a long time. – *vt* to freeze and keep (food) in this.
'deep-sea *adj* (*attrib*) of, for, or in the deeper parts of the sea: *deep-sea diving; deep-sea fishing.*
,deep-'seated, ,deep-'rooted *adj* (*formal*) firmly fixed and not easily removed: *She had a deep-seated dislike of crowds.*
in deep water in difficulties or trouble: *He found himself in deep water when he took over the management of the firm.*
See also **depth**.

deer [diə] – *pl* **deer** – *nc* a kind of large, grass-eating animal, the male of which has antlers: *a herd of deer.*

deface [di'feis] *vt* (*formal*) to spoil the appearance of: *The statue had been defaced with red paint.*
de'facement *nu*.

defamation [defə'meiʃən] *nu* (*formal*: *usu legal*) the act of trying to harm the reputation of someone: *defamation of character.*
defamatory [di'famətəri] *adj* (*formal*) tending to damage someone's reputation: *He was said to have made certain defamatory remarks about her.*

default [di'fo:lt] *vi* (*formal*: *usu legal*) to fail to do something one ought to do, *eg* to pay a debt: *He was supposed to pay his wife alimony but he defaulted.* – *nu* the act of defaulting: *He lost the match by default* (= by not turning up to play).

defeat [di'fi:t] *vt* to win a victory over: *They defeated our team by three goals; We will defeat the enemy eventually; The motion* (= subject which has been debated) *was defeated by sixty votes to thirty.* – *ncu* the loss of a game, battle, race *etc*: *His defeat in the last race depressed him; Another defeat will mean the end of the war; We suffered yet another defeat;* (*fig*) *the defeat of all our hopes.*
de'feated *adj* (*neg* **un-**): *a defeated enemy; He looks completely defeated.*
de'featism *nu* a state of mind in which one expects and accepts defeat too easily: *The defeatism of the captain affects the rest of the players.*
de'featist *nc, adj* (of) a person who gives up too easily and is too easily discouraged: *She was very upset when she could not get a job and she is such a defeatist that she did not try again; She has a defeatist attitude to life.*

defecate ['defəkeit] *vi* (*formal*) to empty the bowels. **,defe'cation** *nu*.
See also **faeces**.

defect ['di:fekt] *nc* (*formal*) a fault or flaw: *It was a* *basic defect in her character; There was a defect in the china.* – [di'fekt] *vt* to leave a country, political party *etc* to go and join another; to desert: *He defected to the West.*

de'fection [-ʃən] *ncu* (*formal*) (an act of) desertion or failure in duty: *His defection was totally unexpected.*

de'fective [-tiv] *adj* (*formal*) having a fault or flaw: *a defective machine; This machine is defective; He is mentally defective.* – *nc* (*formal*) a person who does not have normal mental ability.

See also **deficient, deficiency**.

defence, (*Amer*) **defense** [di'fens] **1** *ncu* the act or action of defending against attack: *during the defence of Rome*; (*fig*) *He spoke in defence of the government's plans.* **2** *nc* the method or equipment used to guard or protect: *The walls will act as a defence against flooding*; (*fig*) *She has no defence against his charm.* **3** *nc* a person's answer to an accusation made against him, *esp* in a law-court: *What is your defence?* – *See also* **the defence** *below.*

de'fenceless *adj* helpless or without protection: *a defenceless animal; She is a defenceless child.*

the defence (*legal*) the case on behalf of a person who is accused in a law court: *The defence rests* (= That is the end of the evidence for the defence); *the counsel for the defence.*

See also **defend**.

defend [di'fend] *vt* **1** to guard or protect against attack: *The soldiers defended the castle; When attacked he defended himself with an umbrella*; (*fig*) *I am prepared to defend my opinions.* **2** (*legal*) to conduct the defence of (a person) in a law-court: *He was too inexperienced to defend the suspected murderer adequately.*

de'fendant *nc* (*legal*) a person accused or sued in a law-court.

de'fender *nc* a person who defends (someone or something): *the defenders of the castle; the defender of (religious) faith.*

de'fensible *adj* (*formal*) able to be defended: *Do you consider his actions defensible?*

de'fensive [-siv] *adj* (*formal*: *usu attrib*) protective or resisting attack: *a defensive attitude; defensive action.*

on the defensive prepared and expecting to defend oneself against attack or criticism: *He can't relax because he is always on the defensive.*

See also **defence, indefensible, plaintiff**.

defer[1] [di'fəː] – *pt, ptp* **de'ferred** – *vt* (*formal*) to put off to another time: *We shall defer judgement in the meantime; They cannot defer their departure any longer.*

defer[2] [di'fəː] – *pt, ptp* **de'ferred** – *vi* (*formal*: *with* **to**) to act according to the wishes or opinions of another or the orders of authority instead of one's own wishes or opinions: *I defer to your greater knowledge of the matter.*

deference ['defərəns] *nu* (*formal*) **1** willingness to consider the wishes *etc* of others: *The young man always treats his grandmother with deference.* **2** the act of deferring.

deferential [defə'renʃəl] *adj* (*formal*) showing deference or respect: *He is always deferential to the manager; a deferential salute/attitude.* **ˌdefe'rentially** *adv.*

in 'deference to (*formal*) deferring to; showing recognition or respect for: *I let him speak first, in deference to his greater knowledge and experience.*

defiance [di'faiəns] *nu* (*formal*) open disobedience; challenging or opposition: *He went in defiance of my orders.*

de'fiant *adj* (*formal*) hostile; showing or feeling defiance: *a defiant attitude; a defiant child; He was defiant about it.* **de'fiantly** *adv.*

See also **defy**.

deficient [di'fiʃənt] *adj* (*formal*) lacking in what is needed: *Their food is deficient in vitamins.*

de'ficiency *ncu* (*formal*) (a) shortage or absence of what is needed: *Her deficiencies as an organizer were soon discovered; He suffers from a deficiency of vitamin B.*

See also **defect**.

deficit ['defisit] *nu* (*formal*) the amount by which an amount (of money *etc*) is less than the amount required: *The yearly accounts showed a deficit of several hundred pounds.*

defile [di'fail] *vt* (*old or formal*) **1** to make dirty: *I wouldn't defile my hands with his money!* **2** to corrupt or make bad or evil: *They defiled the minds of the children.* **de'filed** *adj* (*neg* **un-**).

de'filement *nu* (*old or formal*) the act of making dirty or bad: *Defilement of this membership card makes it invalid.*

define [di'fain] *vt* **1** to fix or state the exact meaning of: *Words are defined in a dictionary; Can you define the word 'deer' for me?* **2** (*formal*) to fix the limits of: *The powers of a judge are defined by law.* **de'finable** *adj.*

definition [defi'niʃən] **1** *nc* an explanation of the exact meaning of a word or phrase: *Is that definition accurate?* **2** *nu* (*formal*) sharpness of outline: *The definition in this photograph is excellent.*

See also **indefinable**.

definite ['definit] *adj* clear; fixed or certain: *I think I can come, but I'll give you a definite answer later; She was very definite about having seen him; Is it definite that he is not coming?*

'definitely *adv* clearly or certainly: *She definitely said I wasn't to wait; Her dress is definitely not red.*

definite article (*gram*) the name given to the word **the**.

See also **indefinite**.

definition *see* **define**.

definitive [də'finətiv] *adj* (*formal*) decisive; final and settling things once and for all: *the definitive version of a story; He thinks that he has written the definitive book on Ben Jonson.*

deflate [di'fleit] *vt* (*formal*) **1** to let gas out of (a tyre *etc*): *You'll have to deflate the air-bed to get it into the car.* **2** (*fig*) to reduce (a person's) importance, self-confidence *etc*: *He was completely deflated by his failure.* **de'flation** *nu.*

See also **inflate**.

deflect [di'flekt] *vt* (*formal*) to turn aside (from a fixed course or direction): *He deflected the blow with his arm*; (*fig*) *Don't try to deflect me from my intention!* **de'flection** [-ʃən] *nu.*

deform [di'foːm] *vt* (*formal*) to spoil the shape of: *Heat deforms plastic.*

de'formed *adj* twisted out of the correct shape: *The cripple was self-conscious about his deformed foot; His foot was deformed.*

de'formity (*formal*) **1** *nu* the state of being badly shaped or formed: *Drugs taken by the mother caused deformity of the foetus.* **2** *nc* a part which is not the correct shape: *A twisted foot is a deformity.*

defraud [di'froːd] *vt* (*formal*: *with* **of**) to prevent (someone), by cheating, fraud *etc*, from having something to which they have a right: *He* *defrauded a number of his clients of money and property.*

defray [di'frei] *vt* (*formal*) to pay for: *The firm defrayed the cost of his meal*; *We shall defray all expenses.*

defrost [di:'frost] **1** *vt* to remove frost or ice from (*eg* a refrigerator): *I keep forgetting to defrost the freezer.* **2** *vti* (of frozen food *etc*) to (cause to) be no longer frozen; to thaw (out): *Make sure you defrost the chicken thoroughly*; *I left a packet of sausages defrosting on the kitchen table.*

deft [deft] *adj* (*formal*) skilful, quick and neat: *deft fingers*; *He was admired for his deft handling of the situation*; *He is very deft with his fingers.* **'deftly** *adv.* **'deftness** *nu.*

defunct [di'fʌŋkt] *adj* (*facet or formal*) no longer active, usable or in use: *a defunct system*; *I'm afraid your car is defunct.*

defuse [di:'fju:z] *vt* **1** (*tech*) to remove the fuse from (a bomb *etc*): *The army train men specially to defuse bombs.* **2** (*fig*) to make harmless or less dangerous: *He succeeded in defusing the situation before any real trouble started.*

defy [di'fai] *vt* **1** to dare (someone to act); to challenge: *I defy you to try and stop me!* **2** to resist boldly or openly: *Are you defying my authority?* **3** (*formal*) to make impossible: *Her beauty defies description.*

See also **defiance**.

degenerate [di'dʒenərət] *adj* (*formal*) having become immoral or inferior: *the degenerate son of well-respected parents*; *The empire became very degenerate.* – *nc* (*formal*) a person, plant *etc* that is degenerate. – [-reit] *vi* to become much less good or admirable: *The discussion soon degenerated into an exchange of insults.*

de'generacy *nu* (*formal*) the state of being degenerate: *the degeneracy of modern youth.*

de,gene'ration *nu* (*formal*) the process or act of degenerating: *the degeneration of moral standards.*

degrade [di'greid] *vt* to disgrace or make contemptible: *She won't degrade herself by asking for money*; *He felt degraded by having to ask for money.*

de'grading *adj* tending to make lower in rank *etc* or to disgrace: *a degrading occupation*; *I find it degrading to travel in these filthy buses.*

degradation [degrə'deiʃən] *ncu* (*formal*): *The old man was horrified by the degradation of his son*; *Prisoners have to suffer many degradations.*

degree [di'gri:] **1** *ncu* (*formal*) (an) amount or extent: *There is still a degree of uncertainty*; *What degree of proof do you need?*; *The degree of skill varies considerably from person to person*: *He is not in the slightest degree concerned about her.* – *See also* **to a degree** *below.* **2** *nc* a unit of temperature: *20°* (= 20 degrees) *Centigrade.* **3** *nc* a unit by which angles are measured, one 360th part of a complete revolution: *at an angle of 90°* (= 90 degrees). **4** *nc* a title or certificate given by a university *etc*: *He was awarded an honorary degree*; (*attrib*) *a degree course*; *He took a degree in chemistry.*

by de'grees (*formal*) gradually: *We reached the desired standard of efficiency by degrees.*

third degree *see* **third**.

to a de'gree 1 to a small extent: *I agree with you to a degree, but I have serious doubts about some of your conclusions.* **2** (*formal*) to a great extent: *She is economical to a degree – she can make a meal from almost nothing.*

dehydrate [di:hai'dreit] *vt* (*formal or tech*) to remove water from or dry out (*esp* foodstuffs): *Vegetables take up less space if they have been dehydrated*; *People can become dehydrated from not drinking enough fluid.* **,dehy'dration** *nu.*

deign [dein] *vti* (*formal*) to act or give (something) as if one is giving a favour: *She did not deign to reply*; *She eventually deigned a reply.*

deity ['deiəti, (*Amer*) 'di:əti] *nc* (*formal*) a god or goddess: *Bacchus was one of the Roman deities.*

dejected [di'dʒektid] *adj* gloomy or miserable: *He looked rather dejected when the rest of the class received prizes*; *in rather a dejected mood.* **de'jectedly** *adv.* **de'jection** [-ʃən] *nu.*

dekagram(me), dekalitre, dekametre *see* Appendix 5.

delay [di'lei] **1** *vt* to put off to another time: *We have delayed publication of the book till the spring.* **2** *vti* to keep or stay back or slow down: *I was delayed by traffic*; *She delayed a few hours in order to see me.* – *ncu* (something which causes) keeping back or slowing down: *He came without delay*; *My work is subject to delays of all sorts.*

delectable [di'lektəbl] *adj* (*formal*) delightful or pleasing: *She always makes the most delectable sweets*; *She looks most delectable in that hat.*

delectation [di:lek'teiʃən] *nu* (*very formal*) delight: *This concert is for your delectation.*

delegate ['deləgeit] *vt* **1** to give (a piece of work, power *etc*) to someone else: *He delegates a great deal of work to his assistant.* **2** (*formal or facet*) to send or name (a person) as a representative, as the person to do a job *etc*: *I was delegated to collect the money for her present*; *I was delegated to do the washing-up.* – [-gət, (*Amer*) -geit] *nc* an elected representative (to a conference, Parliament, committee *etc*): *The delegates met in the conference room*; *He is one of the British delegates to the European Parliament.*

,dele'gation *nc* (*formal*) a body of delegates: *The British delegation arrived late at the conference.*

delete [di'li:t] *vt* (*formal*) to rub or strike out (*eg* a piece of writing): *Delete his name from the list of applicants*; *Please delete all reference to that matter.*

de'letion *ncu* (*formal*).

deliberate [di'libərət] *adj* **1** intentional and not by accident: *That was a deliberate insult*; *It wasn't an accident – it was deliberate!*; *deliberate rudeness.* **2** cautious and not hurried: *He had a very deliberate way of walking.* – [-reit] *vti* (*formal*) to think carefully and seriously (about): *He deliberated whether to go or stay*; *He deliberated on the problems of youth.*

de'liberately [-rət-] *adv* **1** on purpose: *You did that deliberately to upset him!* **2** slowly, carefully and without hurrying: *He spoke quietly and deliberately.*

de,libe'ration (*formal*) *nu* **1** careful thought: *After some deliberation, he decided not to go.* **2** carefulness; lack of hurry: *speaking with deliberation*; *moving with deliberation.*

de,libe'rations *n pl* formal discussions: *The committee's deliberations were held in secret.*

delicate ['delikət] *adj* **1** requiring special treatment or careful handling (*esp* because easily damaged, made ill *etc*): *delicate china*: *My wife has always been delicate*; (*fig*) *a delicate situation/problem.* **2** of fine texture *etc*; dainty: *The plate had a delicate pattern of leaves*; *the delicate skin of a child.* **3** able to do fine, difficult work or to deal with subjects, objects *etc* requiring careful handling: *delicate movements of the fingers*; *a delicate instrument*; *delicate handling of a subject*; *You will have to be* *very delicate in your handling of the situation.* **4** subtle and light in flavour, appearance *etc*: *a delicate wine*; *a delicate shade of blue.* **'delicately** *adv.*

'delicacy 1 *nu* the state or quality of being delicate: *the delicacy of the china/situation.* **2** *nc* something delicious and special to eat: *Caviare is considered to be a delicacy.* – *See also* **delicious**.

See also **indelicate**.

delicatessen [delikə'tesn] *ncu* (a shop selling) foods prepared ready for the table, *esp* cooked meats and *usu* unusual and foreign foods: *I bought some smoked sausage at the delicatessen.*

delicious [di'liʃəs] *adj* giving great pleasure, *esp* highly pleasing to the taste: *a delicious meal*; *There are delicious smells coming from the kitchen*; *That smells delicious!* **de'liciously** *adv.* **de'liciousness** *nu.*

See also **delicacy** *under* **delicate**.

delight [di'lait] **1** *vt* to please greatly: *I was delighted by/at the news*; *She was delighted to hear of his success*; *They were delighted to accept the invitation.* **2** *vi* (*formal*) to have or take great pleasure (from): *He delights in teasing me*; *She delights in the beauty of her home.* – *ncu* (something which causes) great pleasure: *Peacefulness is one of the delights of country life*; *She takes delight in simple things.*

de'lightful *adj* causing delight: *a delightful person/party.* **de'lightfully** *adv.*

delineate [di'linieit] *vt* (*very formal*) to show by drawing or by describing what something is like: *He delineated his plans for us.* **de,line'ation** *nu.*

delinquent [di'liŋkwənt] *adj* (*usu attrib*: *formal or legal*) guilty of an offence or misdeed. – *nc* a person who is delinquent, *esp* a young person (**juvenile delinquent**): *The police arrested the delinquent responsible for the damage which had been done.*

de'linquency *nu* (*formal or legal*) the act of being delinquent, *esp* minor law-breaking among young people: *Delinquency becomes more common during periods of high unemployment.*

delirious [di'liriəs] *adj* (*usu pred*) **1** wandering in the mind and talking complete nonsense (*usu* as a result of fever): *We tried to get information from the sick man, but he was delirious and nothing he said made sense.* **2** (*fig*) wild with excitement: *She was delirious with happiness at the news.*

de'liriously *adv*: *deliriously happy.*

de'lirium [-əm] *nu* (*formal*) the state of being delirious: *In his delirium the man talked nonsense.*

deliver [di'livə] *vt* **1** to give or hand over (something) to the person for whom it is intended: *The postman delivers letters*; *Did he deliver my message?* **2** (*formal*) to give: *He delivered a long speech*; *He delivered a blow to his attacker.* **3** to assist (a woman) at the birth of (a child): *The doctor delivered the twins safely*; *The nurse delivered her of a healthy baby.* **4** (*old*) to set free or rescue: *He was delivered from prison eventually.*

de'liverance *nu* (*old*) rescue; freeing: *deliverance from prison/slavery.*

de'livery *ncu* **1** (an act of) handing over (letters, parcels *etc*): *There are two parcel deliveries a week*; *Delivery of your order might be a bit difficult.* **2** the process of the birth of a child: *There was no doctor present at the delivery of the twins.*

deliver the goods *see* **good**.

dell [del] *nc* (*liter*) a small valley or hollow, *usu* with trees.

delta ['deltə] **1** *nc* a roughly triangular area of land formed at the mouth of a river which reaches the sea in two or more branches: *the delta of the Nile.* **2** *n* the fourth letter of the Greek alphabet (Δ, δ).

delude [di'lu:d] *vt* (*formal*) to deceive or mislead (*usu* without actually telling lies): *She deluded herself into thinking he cared for her*; *She deluded him into believing that she was wealthy.*

de'lusion [-ʒən] **1** *nc* a false belief, *esp* as a symptom of mental illness: *The doctor did not realize that the young man was suffering from delusions*; *He is under the delusion that he is Napoleon.* **2** *nu* (*formal*) the act of deluding.

See also **illusion**.

deluge ['delju:dʒ] *nc* (*formal*) a great quantity of water: *Few people survived the deluge*; (*fig*) *We've had a deluge of letters on that subject.* – *vt* (*fig*) to fill or overwhelm with a great quantity: *We've been deluged with orders for our new book.*

delusion *see* **delude**.

de luxe [də'luks] *adj* (*attrib*: *used esp in shops etc*) very luxurious or elegant; special (*esp* with extra qualities not found in an ordinary version of something): *a de luxe model of a car*; *Would you like a de luxe edition of that dictionary?*

delve [delv] *vi* (*formal or facet*) to search, often patiently and carefully, for something (an object, information *etc*) which is hidden or difficult to find: *She was delving in a cupboard looking for old clothes*; *I've been delving into my family history.*

demand [di'ma:nd] *vt* **1** to ask or ask for firmly and sharply: *He demanded to know what we were doing*; *I demanded an explanation.* **2** (*formal*) to require or need: *This demands careful thought.* – **1** *nc* a request made so that it sounds like a command: *They refused to meet the workers' demands for more money*; *The landlord has just sent us a demand for last month's rent.* **2** *nc* an urgent claim: *The children make demands on my time.* **3** *nu* willingness or desire to buy or obtain (certain goods *etc*); a need for (certain goods *etc*): *There's no demand for books of this kind*; *Those books are always in great demand*; *She is in great demand as a babysitter.*

de'manding *adj* requiring a lot of effort, ability *etc*: *a demanding job*; *This job is very demanding.*

on demand when asked for: *I'm expected to supply meals on demand*; *Do you feed the baby every four hours or on demand?*

demarcation [di:ma:'keiʃən] *nu* (*formal*) the strict marking off of work to be done by one kind of craftsman *etc* from that to be done by craftsmen of other trades *etc*: *The firm has suffered in the past from arguments over demarcation*; (*attrib*) *demarcation disputes.*

demean [di'mi:n] *v refl* (*formal*) to lower one's dignity or become less respected: *I wouldn't demean myself by arguing with him.*

demeanour, (*Amer*) **demeanor** [di'mi:nə] *nu* (*formal*) manner; bearing; the way one behaves: *I could tell from her demeanour that she had done something wrong.*

demented [di'mentid] *adj* **1** (*often loosely*) out of one's mind; insane: *That noise is enough to drive me demented!*; *She was nearly demented with the pain in her ear.* **2** (*inf*) very worried: *I was nearly demented when my child did not arrive home from school at the usual time.*

demerara [demə'reərə] *nu* (*also* **demerara sugar**) a form of brown sugar in large crystals: *I'll have some demerara sugar in my coffee.*

demise [di'maiz] *nc* (*formal*) a death: *His great work was cut short by his sudden demise*; (*fig*) *the demise of Roman civilization.*

demo ['demou] short for **demonstration** (*def 2*).

demob [di:'mob] (*Brit*) short for **1 demobilize** (*def 1*): *He was demobbed shortly after the war.* **2 demobilization**: *What are you going to do after your demob?*

demobilize, -ise [di:'moubilaiz] **1** *vt* (*usu abbrev* **demob**) to free (a soldier) from army service at the end of a war. **2** *vi* to break up an army after the end of a war. **de͵mobili'zation, -s-** *nu.*

democracy [di'mokrəsi] *ncu* (a country having) a form of government in which the people freely elect representatives to govern them: *Which is the world's largest democracy?*; *He believes in democracy and insists that everyone should have a part in making major decisions.*

democrat ['deməkrat] *nc* **1** one who believes in democracy as a principle: *She likes to pretend she's a democrat but she really regards the working classes as being inferior*; *He is politically a social democrat.* **2** (*with cap*) a member of the **Democratic Party**, one of the two chief political parties in the US: *He is a Democrat, not a Republican.*

democratic [demə'kratik] *adj* **1** (*neg* **un-**) belonging to, governed by or typical of democracy: *a democratic country.* **2** (*neg* **un-**) believing in equal rights and privileges for all: *The boss is very democratic and treats all his employees alike*; *He has a very democratic attitude towards his fellow workers.* **3** (*with cap*) of or belonging to the **Democratic Party**, one of the two chief political parties of the US.

democratically [demə'kratikəli] *adv* (*neg* **un-**) following democratic principles: *The issue was decided democratically by taking a general vote*; *He was democratically elected.*

demolish [di'moliʃ] *vt* (*more formal than* **pull down**) to pull or tear down: *They're demolishing the old buildings in the centre of town*; (*fig facet*) *The children at the party demolished the food in record time.* **͵demo'lition** [demə-] *nu.*

demon ['di:mən] *nc* **1** an evil spirit; a devil: *demons from Hell.* **2** (*fig*) a person who is very energetic, efficient *etc*: *She will finish the job in time – she's a real demon for work.* **de'monic** [-'mo-] *adj* (*formal*).

demonstrate ['demənstreit] **1** *vt* (*formal*) to show or point out clearly: *This demonstrates his ignorance of the situation.* **2** *vt* to show how (something) works: *He demonstrated the new vacuum cleaner.* **3** *vi* to express an opinion (*usu* political) by marching, showing banners *etc* in public: *A crowd collected to demonstrate against the new taxes.*

͵demon'stration *nc* **1** a display or exhibition (of how something works *etc*): *I'd like a demonstration of this dishwasher*; *a demonstration of bad temper.* **2** a public expression of opinion by holding meetings and processions, showing placards *etc*: *The police were present at the demonstration.*

demonstrative [di'monstrətiv] *adj* **1** (*neg* **un-**) in the habit of showing one's feelings: *She loves her children dearly but she is not demonstrative and does not often cuddle or kiss them.* **2** (*formal*) pointing out or proving: *These figures are demonstrative of our progress.*

'demonstrator *nc* **1** a person who takes part in a public demonstration: *Some of the demonstrators were imprisoned.* **2** a teacher or assistant who helps students with practical work: *He has got a job as demonstrator in the chemistry laboratory.*

demonstrative adjective/pronoun *nc* (*gram*) any one of the words **this, that, these** or **those**.

demoralize, -ise [di'morəlaiz] *vt* to take away the confidence and courage of: *The army was demoralized by the completeness of their defeat.* **de͵morali'zation, -s-** *nu.*

See also **morale**.

demote [di'mout] *vt* (*formal*) to reduce to a lower rank or grade: *The officer was demoted for misconduct.*

de'motion *nu* (*formal*): *The demotion of the manager pleased the rest of the staff.*

demur [di'mə:] – *pt, ptp* **de'murred** – *vi* (*formal*: *with* **at**) to object mildly to: *She demurred at having to leave so early.* – *nu* mild objection (*formal*): *She accepted his criticism without demur*; *She accepted the criticism with no demur.*

demure [di'mjuə] *adj* quiet, shy, modest and well behaved (sometimes deceptively): *She looked too demure ever to do such a bold thing*; *a demure smile.* **de'murely** *adv.* **de'mureness** *nu.*

demurred *see* **demur**.

den [den] *nc* **1** the home of a wild beast: *a lion's den*; (*fig*) *a den of thieves.* **2** (*inf*) a private room for working in *etc*: *You could hear the sound of typing from the author's den.*

denial *see* **deny**.

denier ['deniə] *nu* a unit of weight of silk, rayon and nylon thread: *30 denier tights*; *These tights are 30 denier – I wanted 15.*

denigrate ['denigreit] *vt* (*formal*) to attack the reputation *etc* of: *I'm not trying to denigrate her achievement.* **͵deni'gration** *nu.*

denim ['denim] *nu, adj* (of) a kind of cotton cloth, often blue, used for making jeans, overalls *etc*: *I bought some blue denim*; *blue denim trousers.*

'denims *n pl* clothes, *esp* jeans, made of denim: *She was wearing blue denims and a leather jacket*; *a pair of denims.*

denizen ['denizn] *nc* (*liter or formal facet*) an inhabitant (human or animal): *the denizens of the deep.*

Denmark *see* Appendix 2.

denomination [dinomi'neiʃən] *nc* **1** a value (of a stamp, coin *etc*): *banknotes of all denominations.* **2** a group of people with the same religious beliefs: *This service is open to people of all denominations.* **3** (*formal*) a name or title: *The firm is still operating under another denomination.*

denote [di'nout] *vt* (*formal*) to be the sign of or to mean: *Do you think his silence denotes guilt?* **͵deno'tation** [di:nou-] *nu.*

dénouement [dei'nu:mã, (*Amer*) deinu:'mã] *nc* (*formal*) the last part of a story or plot in which everything is explained and settled: *The start of the story was exciting but I was disappointed by the dénouement*; *I was away that weekend and so missed the dénouement of the whole affair.*

denounce [di'nauns] *vt* (*formal*) to inform against or accuse publicly (of a crime *etc*): *He was denounced by the press as a murderer.* **denunciation** [dinʌnsi'eiʃən] *ncu.*

dense [dens] *adj* **1** thick and close: *We made our way with difficulty through dense forest*; *A bear has dense fur*; *The fog was so dense that we could not see anything.* **2** (*usu pred*: *inf*) very stupid: *He's so dense I have to tell him everything twice.*

'densely *adv* very closely together: *The crowd was densely packed.*

'denseness *nu* the quality which a thing or person

has when dense: *the denseness of the forest*; (*fig*) *The denseness of my pupils is unbelievable.*

'density *nu* **1** the number of items, people *etc* found in a given area compared with other areas *esp* if large: *the density of the population*; *The density of the forest made it very dark.* **2** (*tech*) the quantity of matter in each unit of volume: *the density of a gas.*

dent [dent] *nc* a small hollow made by pressure or a blow: *My car has a dent where it hit a lamp-post.* – *vt* to make such a hollow in: *The side of the car was dented when it ran into a wall*; (*fig*) *Nothing will dent his self-composure.*

dental ['dentl] *adj* (*attrib*) of or for the teeth: *Regular dental care is essential for healthy teeth.*

dental plate *see* **plate**.

dental surgeon *nc* (*formal*) a dentist.

dentist ['dentist] *nc* **1** a person who cares for diseases *etc* of the teeth, by filling or removing them, making false ones *etc*: *Our dentist is very slow but very careful.* **2** a dentist's practice: *I hate going to the dentist.*

'dentistry *nu* (*formal*) a dentist's work: *preventive dentistry* (= the work of a dentist which prevents tooth decay).

'dentist's *nc* a dentist's practice: *I've got toothache – I must go to the dentist's.*

denture ['dentʃə] *nc* (*formal*: *usu in pl*) a set of artificial teeth: *Do you wear dentures?*

denude [di'nju:d] *vt* (*formal*) to make bare or strip (something) of a covering of any kind: *The land was denuded of vegetation.*

denunciation *see* **denounce**.

deny [di'nai] *vt* **1** to declare not to be true: *He denied having written to me*; *He denied the charge of theft*; *He denied that he had spoken*; *It cannot be denied that he is guilty.* **2** (*formal*) to refuse (to give or grant someone something); to say 'no' to: *He was denied admission to the house*; *She denies that child nothing* (= She gives that child everything he wants). – *See also* **deny oneself**.

de'nial *ncu* **1** (an act of) declaring that something is not true: *Do you accept her denial?*; *To do that would be a denial of my religious faith.* **2** (*formal*) (an act of) refusing someone something: *a denial of his request*; *a denial of privileges.*

deny oneself (*formal*) to do without (things that one desires or needs): *You must deny yourself sweet things if you're dieting.*

there is no denying (the fact) that it must be admitted that: *There is no denying that he is a brilliant scientist but he sometimes behaves very stupidly.*

See also **undeniable**.

deodorant [di:'oudərənt] *ncu* a substance that destroys or conceals unpleasant (body) smells: *She perspires a lot – she should use (a) deodorant.*

depart [di'pa:t] *vi* (*formal*) **1** to go away: *The tour departed from the station at nine a.m.* **2** (*with* **from**) to cease to follow (a course of action); to behave in an unusual manner: *We decided to depart from our original plan.*

de'parture [-tʃə] *nc* an act of departing: *The departure of the train was delayed*; *His behaviour was a departure from the normal.*

depart this life (*formal or liter euph*) to die: *He departed this life June 20, 1850.*

a new departure a change of purpose or method in doing something: *The release of a jazz record represents a new departure for a folk-singer.*

the departed (*euph*) a person who is or people who are dead: *You mustn't speak ill of the departed.*

department [di'pa:tmənt] *nc* (*often with cap*) a part or section of a government, university, office or shop: *The Department of Justice*; *the Department of French*; *the sales department*; *the menswear department.*

departmental [di:pa:t'mentl] *adj* (*usu attrib*) of or concerning a department or departments: *a departmental manager/dispute.*

de'partment store *nc* a large shop with many different departments selling a wide variety of goods: *I do all my shopping at that department store.*

departure *see* **depart**.

depend [di'pend] *vi* (*with* **on**, (*formal*) **upon**) **1** to rely on: *You can't depend on his arriving on time*; *You can't depend on the weather being fine.* **2** to rely on receiving necessary (financial) support from: *The school depends for its survival on money from the Church*; *He depends on his parents for his university fees.* **3** (not *usu* used with **is, was** *etc* and **-ing**) (of a future happening *etc*) to be decided by: *Whether I come on Tuesday or not depends on the amount of work I get through before then*; *Our success depends on everyone working hard.*

de'pendable *adj* (*neg* **un-**) trustworthy or reliable: *I know he'll remember to get the wine – he's very dependable.*

de'pendant, (*esp Amer*) **de'pendent** *nc* a person who is kept or supported by another: *He has five dependants to support – a wife and four children.*

de'pendence *nu* **1** the state of being dependent. **2** (*formal*) reliance or trust: *I wouldn't place much dependence on what he says.*

de'pendency *nc* a country governed or controlled by another: *Britain used to have many dependencies.*

de'pendent *adj* (*usu pred with* **on**) **1** relying on (someone *etc*) for (financial) support: *He is totally dependent on his parents.* **2** (of a future happening *etc*) to be decided by: *Whether we go or not is dependent on whether we have enough money.* – *nc* (*esp Amer*) a dependant.

it/that depends, it all depends what happens, is decided *etc* will be affected by something else: *It depends whether you want a really good job or not*; *I don't know if I'll go to the party – it all depends.*

See also **independent**.

depict [di'pikt] *vt* (*formal*) **1** to paint, draw *etc*: *The artist depicts him as a tall, imposing-looking man.* **2** (*fig*) to describe: *Her novel depicts the life of country people in the late nineteenth century.*

depilatory [di'pilətəri] *nc* (*tech*) a substance able to remove unwanted hair: *She uses a depilatory to remove the hair from under her arms.*

deplete [di'pli:t] *vt* (*formal*) to make smaller in amount, number *etc*: *Our numbers at the garden party were depleted because of the rain*; *Our supplies of food are rather depleted.* **de'pletion** *nu.*

deplore [di'plo:] *vt* (*formal*) to express disapproval and regret about (something): *We all deplore the actions of murderers and thieves*; *I deplore his inefficiency.*

de'plorable *adj* (*formal*) very bad or regrettable: *Her conduct on that occasion was deplorable*; *such deplorable behaviour.*

de'plorably *adv*: *I'm afraid he behaved deplorably.*

deploy [di'ploi] *vt* (*mil*) to spread out (troops) so as to cover a large area, *esp* in order to prepare for battle: *He deployed his men along the ridge*; (*formal* *fig) You should deploy your resources as efficiently as possible.*

de'ployment *nu* (*mil*) the spreading out and organization of forces *etc*: *the deployment of troops*; (*formal*) *We have spent a great deal of time deciding on the deployment of our workers.*

depopulate [di:'popjuleit] *vt* (*formal*) to reduce greatly the population of (a region): *That area of the country is becoming depopulated because it is so remote.* **de,popu'lation** *nu.*

deport [di'po:t] *vt* (of a government *etc*) to send (a person) out of the country *eg* because he has committed a crime or because he is not officially supposed to be there: *He is being deported because he has no passport*; *He has been deported on a charge of murder.* **,depor'tation** [di:po:-] *nu.*

deportment [di'po:tmənt] *nu* (*formal*) the way one holds or carries oneself, *esp* the correct way: *She was praised for her deportment.*

depose [di'pouz] *vt* to remove from a high position (*eg* from that of a king): *They have deposed the emperor.*

deposit [di'pozit] *vt* **1** (*formal*) to put or set down: *She deposited her shopping in the kitchen*; (*facet*) *She deposited herself on the most comfortable chair.* **2** to put in for safe keeping: *He deposited the money in the bank.* – *nc* **1** an act of putting money in a bank *etc*: *She made several large deposits at the bank during that month.* **2** an act of paying money as a guarantee that money which is or will be owed will be paid: *We have put down a deposit on a house in the country*; *Our landlord asked for a deposit to cover damage which we might cause during our stay.* **3** the money put into a bank or paid as a guarantee in this way: *He went to the bank to draw out his deposit*; *We decided we could not afford to go on holiday and managed to get back the deposit which we had paid.* **4** a quantity of solid matter that has settled at the bottom of a liquid, or is left behind by a liquid: *The flood-water left a yellow deposit over everything.* **5** a layer (of coal, iron *etc*) occurring naturally in rock: *rich deposits of iron ore.*

de'posit account *nc* an account with a bank on which one is paid interest and from which money can be taken only by the person who deposited it: *I don't have a cheque book because I don't have a current account – I have a deposit account.*

depot ['depou, (*Amer*) 'di:-] *nc* **1** the place where railway engines, buses *etc* are kept and repaired: *a bus depot*; *The driver had to return to the depot.* **2** a storehouse or warehouse. **3** a military station or headquarters.

depraved [di'preivd] *adj* (*formal*) evil or corrupt; wicked: *By the time he was fifteen he was so depraved that he raped his sister*; *a depraved mind.*

de'pravity [-'pra-] *ncu* (*formal*) (an act of) great wickedness: *The judge described the murder as an act of unbelievable depravity.*

deprecate ['deprikeit] *vt* (*formal*: not *usu* used with **is, was** *etc* and **-ing**) to show disapproval of (an action or a condition): *They issued a statement deprecating the soldiers' actions.* **,depre'cation** *nu.*

depreciate [di'pri:ʃieit] *vi* (*formal*) to fall in value: *Shares have depreciated recently.*

de,preci'ation *nu* (*formal*) fall in value: *the depreciation of the pound.*

See also **appreciate**.

depress [di'pres] *vt* **1** to make sad or gloomy: *I am always depressed by rainy weather.* **2** (*formal*) to make less active: *This drug depresses the action of the heart*; *Trade was depressed by the rise in oil-prices.* **3** (*formal*) to press down: *If you depress this lever, all the lights will go out.*

de'pressed *adj* **1** sad or unhappy; in low spirits: *The news made me very depressed*; *She's in a very depressed state.* **2** made less active: *The stock-market is depressed at present*; *the depressed state of the stock-market.*

de'pressing *adj* tending to make one sad or gloomy: *What a depressing piece of news!*; *I find that news depressing.*

de'pression [-ʃən] **1** *nu* a state of sadness and low spirits: *She was treated by the doctor for depression.* **2** *nc* lack of activity in trade: *He was unemployed for many years during the depression of the 1930s.* **3** *nc* an area of low pressure in the atmosphere: *The bad weather is being caused by a depression over the Atlantic.* **4** *nc* (*formal*) a hollow: *a depression in the Earth's surface.*

deprive [di'praiv] *vt* (*formal*: *with* **of**) to take something away from: *This move deprived the prisoner of his means of escape*; *They deprived him of food and drink.*

deprivation [depri'veiʃən] *ncu* (*very formal*) **1** (a condition of) loss, hardship *etc* caused by being deprived of necessities, rights *etc*: *He considered that he lived in a state of deprivation because he had no bathroom*; *They suffered many deprivations during the long siege.* **2** (an) act of depriving: *She held him responsible for the deprivation of her rights as a mother.*

de'prived *adj* suffering from hardship *etc*, under-privileged: *deprived areas of the city*; *a deprived childhood.*

depth [depθ] *nu* **1** the distance from the top downwards or from the surface inwards *esp* if great: *The bottom of the river cannot be seen because of its depth*; *Coal is mined at a depth of 1 000 m*; *The bullet penetrated the wall to a depth of 5 cm.* **2** intensity or strength *esp* if great: *The depth of colour was astonishing*; *The depth of his feeling prevented him from speaking*; *The depth of her knowledge of philosophy surprised him.* – *See also* **depths**.

depths *n pl* a part far under the surface or in the middle of something: *She was in the depths of despair*; *the depths of the sea*; *the depths of winter*; *the depths of one's memory.*

'in-depth *adj* (*attrib*) (of a survey *etc*) deep and thorough: *an in-depth report on alcoholism.*

in 'depth deeply and thoroughly: *I have studied the subject in depth.*

out of one's depth 1 in water deeper than one can stand up in: *The child is out of her depth in that part of the swimming-pool.* **2** (*fig*) in a situation with which one cannot deal: *I felt rather out of my depth during the discussions as I didn't understand a word.*

See also **deep**.

depute [di'pju:t] *vt* (*formal or facet*) **1** to appoint a person to take over a task *etc*: *She was deputed to do the shopping for the party.* **2** to hand over (a task *etc*) to someone else to do for one: *They deputed the job of collecting money for the present to his secretary.*

,depu'tation [depju-] *nc* a group of people appointed to represent and speak on behalf of others: *The miners sent a deputation to present a petition to the Prime Minister.*

,deputize, -ise ['depju-] *vi* (*formal*) to act as a deputy: *She deputized for her father at the meeting.*

deputy ['depjuti] *nc* someone appointed to help a

person and take over some of his jobs if necessary: *While the manager was ill, his deputy ran the office very successfully.*

derail [di'reil] *vt* (*tech*) to cause (a railway train) to leave the rails: *The train was derailed by a piece of iron on the railway line.*

de'railment *nu* (*tech*): *Our train was delayed because of the derailment of the express train further along the line.*

deranged [di'reindʒd] *adj* (*formal*) insane: *His mind had become deranged as a result of his ordeal*; *mentally deranged*; *a deranged mind*; (*facet*) *I think your sister must have been deranged when she wrote this.* **de'rangement** *nu.*

derelict ['derilikt] *adj* abandoned and left to fall to pieces: *a derelict airfield*; *All these cottages are derelict now.*

ˌdere'liction [-ʃən] *nu* (*formal*) neglect (of duty): *The officer was accused of dereliction of duty.*

deride [di'raid] *vt* (*formal*) to laugh at; to mock: *His efforts to write poetry were derided by his friends.*

derision [di'riʒən] *nu* (*formal*) mockery or laughter which shows scorn and contempt: *His remarks were greeted with shouts of derision from the audience.*

de'risive [-siv] *adj* (*formal*) **1** mocking; showing scorn: *derisive laughter.* **2** causing or deserving scorn: *The salary they offered me was derisive.*

de'risory [-səri] *adj* (*formal*) **1** ridiculous and arousing derision: *His attempts to put things right were derisory.* **2** mocking and showing scorn: *Several newspapers published derisory articles on the new Government proposals.*

derive [di'raiv] (*formal*: *with* **from**) **1** *vi* to come or arise from: *The word derives from an old French word.* **2** *vt* to draw or take from (a source or origin): *He derives his authority from an Act of Parliament*; *We derive a lot of comfort from his presence.*

ˌderi'vation [deri-] *ncu* **1** the source or origin (of a word *etc*): *What is the derivation of that word?* **2** (*formal*) the process of deriving.

derivative [di'rivətiv] *adj* (*formal*) derived from something else (*eg* the work of someone else) and not original: *His work seems very derivative.* – *nc* a word, substance *etc* formed from another word, substance *etc*: *'Reader' is a derivative of 'read'.*

dermatitis [dəːmə'taitis] *nu* inflammation of the skin: *He has dermatitis on his hands.*

ˌderma'tology [-'tolədʒi] *nu* the branch of science concerned with the skin and its diseases. **ˌderma'tologist** *nc.*

derogatory [di'rogətəri] *adj* (*formal*) harmful to one's dignity, reputation *etc* or indicating disapproval and scorn: *a derogatory remark*; *Did you think his remarks derogatory?*; *'Quack' is a derogatory word for doctor.*

derrick ['derik] *nc* an apparatus like a mechanical crane for lifting weights: *The ship was unloaded, using the large derricks on the quay.*

descant ['deskant] *nc* (*music*) a part played or sung above the main tune: *Six of the choir sang the descant.*

descend [di'send] (*formal*) **1** *vti* to go or climb down from a higher place or position: *He descended the staircase with dignity*; (*fig*) *He would never descend to begging.* **2** *vi* to slope downwards: *The hills descend to the sea just beyond the town.* **3** *vi* (*with* **on**) to make a sudden attack on: *The soldiers descended on the helpless inhabitants of the village*; (*fig derog*) *Visitors descend on us* (= come to stay with us) *every summer*; (*fig*) *The children descended on the food as soon as they arrived.*

de'scendant *nc* the child, grandchild, great-grandchild *etc* of a person: *This is a photograph of my grandmother with all her descendants.*

de'scent [-t] (*formal*) **1** *nc* the act of descending: *The descent of the hill was quickly completed.* **2** *nc* a slope: *That is a steep descent.* **3** *nu* family; ancestry: *She is of royal descent.*

be de'scended from to be a descendant of: *I am descended from William the Conqueror.*

See also **ascend**.

describe [di'skraib] **1** *vt* to give an account of in words: to tell in words what something or someone is like: *He described what had happened*; *Would you describe her as beautiful?*; *Could you describe the man to me?* **2** *v refl* to say that one is something: *He describes himself as a travelling salesman*; *She describes herself as a personal assistant.* **3** *vt* (*geom or fig*) to trace the line of or draw: *He described a circle in the air with his arm.*

de'scription [-'skrip-] **1** *ncu* (an) act of describing: *The description of his appearance is not easy*; *I recognized him from your description.* **2** *nc* an account of anything in words: *He gave a description of his holiday.* **3** *nc* (*inf*) a sort or kind: *He carried a gun of some description.*

de'scriptive [di'skriptiv] *adj*: *a descriptive passage in a book*; *His novels are very descriptive.*

See also **indescribable**.

desecrate ['desikreit] *vt* (*formal*) to treat (a holy place *etc*) without reverence: *The church had been desecrated by being used as a stable by a regiment of cavalry.* **ˌdese'cration** *nu.*

desert[1] [di'zəːt] **1** *vt* to go away from and leave without help *etc*; to leave or abandon: *Why did you desert us just when we needed you?*; (*fig*) *My courage deserted me*; (*fig*) *His sense of humour has deserted him.* **2** *vi* to run away, *usu* from the army: *He was shot for trying to desert from the front line.*

de'serted *adj* **1** with no people *etc*: *The streets are completely deserted – everyone is watching the football match on television*; *He looked miserably at the deserted streets.* **2** (*attrib*) having been left without help *etc*; abandoned: *his deserted wife and children.*

de'serter *nc* a man who deserts from the army *etc.*

de'sertion [-ʃən] *ncu* (an) act of deserting (*esp* one's husband or wife or from the army *etc*): *He was granted a divorce on the grounds of desertion*; *It was decided that his actions amounted to desertion.*

desert[2] ['dezət] *nc* an area of barren country, *usu* hot, dry and sandy, where there is very little rain: *Parts of the country are so dry as to be almost desert*; (*attrib*) *desert plants.*

deserts [di'zəːts]: **get one's (just) deserts** to suffer the fate or results *etc* which one deserves (*esp* if bad): *He'll get his just deserts one day!*

deserve [di'zəːv] *vt* (not used with **is, was** *etc* and **-ing**) to have earned as a right by one's actions; to be worthy of: *She deserves better than to be married to him*; *She deserved first prize*; *He deserves recognition of his achievements.*

de'serving *adj* (*neg* **un-**) **1** (*attrib*) worthy or suitable (to be given charity *etc*): *I only give money to deserving causes.* **2** (*pred with* **of**: *formal*) worthy of: *He is deserving of better treatment than this.*

de'servedly [-vidli] *adv* (*formal*: *neg* **un-**) justly: *He was deservedly punished.*

desiccated ['desikeitid] *adj* (*attrib*) completely dried out, *esp* as a means of preserving: *desiccated coconut.* ˌ**desic'cation** *nu.*

design [di'zain] *vt* **1** to invent and prepare a plan of (something) before it is built or made: *A famous architect designed this building; Who designs the clothes for that firm?* **2** (*formal*) to intend: *This was not what was designed to happen; This part of the garden was designed for vegetables.* – **1** *ncu* a sketch or plan produced before something is made: *a design for a dress.* **2** *nu* style; the way in which something has been made or put together: *It is very modern in design; I don't like the design of that building.* **3** *nc* a painted, printed, embroidered *etc* picture, pattern *etc*: *The curtains have a flower design on them.* **4** *ncu* a plan formed in the mind; (an) intention: *Our holidays coincided by design and not by accident.* – *See also* **have designs on** *below.*

de'signer *nc* a person who makes designs or patterns: *He is a designer for a famous dressmaker; She was introduced to the designer of the yacht.*

de'signing *adj* (*derog*) cunning: *She is a designing young woman who wants to marry a rich man.* – *nu* the art of making designs or patterns: *The designing of the bridge was difficult; dress-designing.*

have de'signs on (*inf*) to be trying to get (*usu* something belonging to someone else): *He has designs on my job.*

designate ['dezigneit] *vt* (*formal*) **1** to call or name: *It was designated a conservation area.* **2** to point out or identify: *He designated our table with a wave of the hand; He has been designated our next Prime Minister; The sign '⚔' designates the site of a battle.* – *adj* (*very formal: placed immediately after noun*) appointed to an office *etc* but not yet having begun it: *the ambassador designate.*

ˌ**desig'nation** *nc* (*formal*) a name or title: *His designation has been changed recently from Area Manager to District Organizer.*

designer *etc see* **design**.

desire [di'zaiə] **1** *nc* a wish or longing: *I have a sudden desire for a bar of chocolate; He felt a desire to find somewhere quiet to sit.* **2** *nu* strong sexual interest and attraction: *He claimed that she was the only woman who had ever aroused his desire.* **3** *nu* (*usu in neg*) great longing in general: *I have no desire ever to see him again.* – *vt* (not used with **is, was** *etc* and **-ing**) **1** (*formal*) to long for or feel desire for: *After a day's shopping, all I desire is a hot bath and a cup of tea.* **2** (*old or very formal*) to ask: *Her Majesty desires you to enter.*

de'sirable *adj* **1** (*usu attrib*) pleasing or worth having: *a desirable residence.* **2** (*usu* sexually) attractive: *He finds her very desirable; a very desirable young lady.*

deˌsira'bility *nu* (*formal*) the extent to which something is desirable: *He spent some time looking into the desirability of changing to a different system.*

de'sirous *adj* (*very formal: sometimes with* **of**) wanting strongly: *His Excellency is desirous of your company; He is desirous that no one else should learn of this.*

See also **undesirable**.

desist [di'zist] *vi* (*formal: often with* **from**) to stop: *You must desist from this irresponsible behaviour at once!*

desk [desk] *nc* a piece of furniture, often like a table, for sitting at while writing, reading *etc*: *She kept the pile of letters in a drawer in her desk.*

desolate ['desələt] *adj* **1** (of landscapes, areas *etc*) very lonely or barren: *a stretch of desolate moorland; That countryside is very desolate.* **2** (of people) very sad, lonely and unhappy: *When her husband died, she was left desolate.*

'**desolated** [-lei-] *adj* (*formal*) **1** made desolate: *The houses are desolated now; a desolated area.* **2** (*usu pred*) made very sad: *She was desolated by the news.*

ˌ**deso'lation** *nu* **1** (*formal*) the state of being desolate: *the desolation of the countryside.* **2** loneliness, grief or sadness: *When everyone had gone, she was overcome by a feeling of desolation.* **3** (*liter*) lonely and barren land: *There was a single house in the middle of miles of desolation.*

despair [di'speə] *vi* to lose hope (of): *I despair of ever teaching my son anything; Whatever happens to her, she never despairs.* – **1** *nu* the state of having given up hope: *He was sunk in despair; He was filled with despair at the news.* **2** *nc* (*no pl: with* **the**: *formal*) something which causes someone to despair: *He is the despair of his mother.*

de'spairing *adj* (*attrib*) showing or revealing despair: *a despairing cry for help.* **de'spairingly** *adv.*

despatch *see* **dispatch**.

desperado [despə'ra:dou] – *pl* ˌ**despe'rado(e)s** – *nc* (*old or liter*) a bold or violent criminal.

desperate ['despərət] *adj* **1** (*sometimes used loosely*) despairingly reckless or violent: *He was desperate to get away; She was desperate to get into university; a desperate criminal.* **2** very bad or almost hopeless: *We are in a desperate situation; The situation is desperate.* **3** (*usu attrib*) urgent and despairing: *He made a desperate appeal for help; Desperate remedies are called for in such a very serious situation.*

'**desperately** *adv* **1** in a despairing or desperate manner: *I heard her calling desperately for help.* **2** (*loosely*) extremely: *That hill is desperately steep; She is desperately anxious to help.*

ˌ**despe'ration** *nu*: *In desperation we asked the police for help; Sheer desperation made her try to escape.*

despise [di'spaiz] *vt* **1** to look upon with scorn and contempt: *I know he despises me for being stupid.* **2** to refuse to have, use *etc*; to scorn: *She despises such luxuries as fur boots.*

despicable [di'spikəbl] *adj* (*formal*) contemptible, worthless and deserving to be despised: *She is a despicable person!; His behaviour was despicable.* **de'spicably** *adv.* **de'spicableness** *nu.*

despite [di'spait] *prep* in spite of: *He didn't get the job despite all his qualifications; Despite the fact that we tried our best we didn't win.*

despoil [di'spoil] *vt* (*old or formal*) to rob or steal everything valuable from (a place): *The king's soldiers despoiled the monastery.*

despondent [di'spondənt] *adj* (*formal*) feeling miserable, unhappy, gloomy *etc*: *She was utterly despondent at her failure.* **de'spondently** *adv.* **de'spondency** *nu.*

despot ['despot, (*Amer*) -pət] *nc* a person (*usu* the king or ruler of a country) with absolute power, often a tyrant. **de'spotic** *adj.* **de'spotically** *adv.*

'**despotism** [-pə-] *nu* absolute power or tyranny: *The age of despotism is over.*

dessert [di'zə:t] **1** *nu* the sweet course in a meal; pudding: *We had strawberries and cream for dessert.* **2** *nc* fruits, sweets *etc* served at the end of dinner.

des'sertspoon *nc* **1** a spoon twice the size of a teaspoon, used as a measure in cooking. **2** a

dessertspoonful: *Add two dessertspoons of sugar.*
des'sertspoonful *nc* the amount held by such a spoon: *a dessertspoonful of sugar.*

destination [desti'neiʃən] *nc* (*formal*) the place to which someone or something is going: *I think we've arrived at our destination at last.*

destined ['destind] *adj* **1** (*formal*) (having a future) organized or arranged beforehand (by a person or by fate): *This was destined to happen*; *He was destined to enter the church*; *She was destined for success*; *his destined rôle in life.* **2** (*formal or facet*: *pred*) bound or heading (for a place): *destined for London*; *Where are you destined?*

destiny ['destəni] (*formal*) **1** *nu* the power which appears or is thought to control events; fate: *We are all subject to the tricks played by destiny.* **2** *nc* what happens to a person or what is destined to happen: *I wonder what his destiny will be?*

destitute ['destitju:t] *adj* **1** in great need of food, shelter *etc*: *The widow is completely destitute*; *destitute people*; *They were left destitute when he died.* **2** (*formal*: *pred with* **of**) completely lacking in: *destitute of common sense*; *destitute of ideas.*
ˌdesti'tution *nu* (*formal*) the state of being in need of food and shelter: *The rich woman was horrified by the destitution of the poor family.*

destroy [di'stroi] *vt* **1** to put an end to or make useless; to ruin: *Vandals had destroyed the painting*; *His continual selfishness finally destroyed our relationship.* **2** to kill (animals): *This poison destroys rats.*
de'stroyer *nc* a type of small fast warship: *naval destroyers.*

destruction [di'strʌkʃən] *nu* **1** the act or process of destroying or being destroyed: *They planned the destruction of the city in detail.* **2** the state of being destroyed; ruin: *a scene of destruction after the battle.*
des'tructive [-tiv] *adj* **1** causing or able to cause destruction: *Small children can be very destructive*; *Deer can be very destructive to trees*; (*formal*) *His greed was destructive of happiness.* **2** (of criticism *etc*) pointing out faults *etc* without suggesting improvements: *I appreciate constructive comments but not destructive ones.* **de'structively** *adv.* **de'structiveness** *nu.*
See also **indestructible, constructive**.

desultory ['desəltəri] *adj* (*formal*) moving from one subject to another without a fixed plan: *The discussion was desultory and nothing was decided.*

detach [di'tatʃ] *vt* to unfasten or remove (from): *I detached the bottom part of the form and sent it back.*
de'tachable *adj* able to be detached: *That coat has a detachable lining*; *The handle is detachable.*
de'tached *adj* **1** standing *etc* apart or by itself: *a detached house*; *The houses in that street are all detached.* **2** (*formal*) not personally involved or showing no emotion or prejudice: *a detached attitude to the problem*; *I used to care a great deal about what happened to him but now I feel completely detached.*
de'tachment **1** *nu* (*formal*) the state of not being influenced by emotion or prejudice: *She watched events from a position of complete detachment.* **2** *nu* (*formal*) the act of detaching: *The detachment of the broken part proved difficult.* **3** *nc* a group (*esp* of soldiers) detached from a larger group for a special purpose: *A detachment was sent to guard the supplies.*
See also **attach**.

detail ['di:teil, (*Amer also*) di'teil] **1** *nc* a small part or an item: *She paid close attention to the small details.* **2** *nu* all the small features and parts considered as a whole: *Look at the amazing detail in this drawing!* – *See also* **in detail** *below.* – *vt* (*formal*) **1** to set (a person) to do a particular job: *She was detailed to feed the hens each night.* **2** to tell fully, giving all the facts of: *He detailed the arrangements for the party.*
'detailed *adj* giving many details with nothing left out: *He gave us a detailed account of their conversation*; *His instructions were very detailed.*
in 'detail item by item, giving attention to the details: *If you come to my office, I'll tell you the story in detail.*

detain [di'tein] *vt* (*formal*) **1** to hold back and delay: *He was detained by a woman who wanted to speak to him*; *I won't detain you just now – I can see you're in a hurry.* **2** (of the police *etc*) to keep under guard: *Three suspects were detained at the police station.*
ˌdetai'nee *nc* (*formal*) a person who is detained (by the police *etc*): *Several political detainees were released in exchange for the hostage.*
de'tention [-'ten-] **1** *nu* (*formal*) the state of being imprisoned: *The criminals are in detention.* **2** *ncu* a forced stay (*eg* a punishment at school at the end of the day): *He was given* (*a*) *detention for being late for school.*

detect [di'tekt] *vt* (*formal*: not *usu* used with **is, was** *etc* and **-ing**) to notice or discover (*usu* something which should not be there or was not meant to be obvious): *She thought she could detect a smell of gas*; *I detected his presence by the sound of his voice*; *Do I detect a note* (= a sound) *of sarcasm in your voice?*
de'tection [-ʃən] *nu* (*formal*) the act or practice of detecting.
de'tective [-tiv] *nc* a person (often a policeman) who tries to find criminals or watches suspected persons: *She employed a private detective* (= not a policeman) *to keep a watch on her husband.*
de'tector *nc* (*often in cmpds*) a machine that detects something: *a metal-detector.*

detention *see* **detain**.

deter [di'tə:] – *pt, ptp* **de'terred** – *vt* (*formal*) to make less willing or prevent (from doing something) by frightening: *She was not in the least deterred by his threats.*
de'terrent [-'te-, (*Amer*) -'tə:-] *nc* (*formal*) something (*esp* a weapon) which deters: *The heavy sentences for this crime are intended to act as a deterrent to criminals*; *The nuclear deterrent* (= the threat of nuclear warfare) *is more powerful than any weapon.* – *adj* (*formal*) deterring or intended to deter: *deterrent methods*; *Our forms of punishment do not seem to be sufficiently deterrent.*

detergent [di'tə:dʒənt] *ncu* a (soapless) substance used for cleaning: *She recommended a new dish-washing detergent to me*; *She poured half a packet of detergent into the washing-machine*; (*attrib*) *a detergent powder.*

deteriorate [di'tiəriəreit] *vt* (*formal*) to grow worse: *I'm afraid the condition of the patient is deteriorating rapidly*; *His work has deteriorated recently.* **deˌterio'ration** *nu.*

determine [di'tə:min] *vt* (*formal*) **1** to fix or settle; decide: *He determined his course of action*; *His course of action has been determined by circumstances.* **2** to find out exactly: *He tried to determine what had gone wrong*; *Have they determined the cause of death?*

ˌ**de termi'nation** *nu* **1** the state of being determined, *esp* firmness of character or stubbornness: *She showed her determination by refusing to give way.* **2** (*formal*) the act of determining: *The determination of his exact position proved difficult*; *The determination of the cause of death proved impossible.*

de'termined *adj* **1** (*pred*) having one's mind made up; decided: *She is determined to succeed this time.* **2** usually stubborn and not easily made to give in or change one's mind: *He's very determined*; *She has a very determined look.* **3** (*formal*) fixed or settled: *Our route has already been determined.*

deterrent *see* **deter**.

detest [di'test] *vt* (not used with **is, was** *etc* and **-ing**) to hate intensely: *Cruelty is something I detest.*

de'testable *adj* (*formal*) extremely hateful: *He is a detestable man!*; *I think he is detestable.* **de'testably** *adv.*

ˌ**dete'station** [diːtes-] *nu* (*very formal*) great hatred: *He has a detestation of unpunctuality.*

dethrone [diː'θroun] *vt* (*formal*) to remove (a king *etc*) from a position of power: *The emperor has been dethroned.* **de'thronement** *nu.*

detonate ['detəneit] *vti* (*tech*) to (cause to) explode violently: *This device is used to detonate a charge of explosive*; *It detonates at the slightest touch.*

ˌ**deto'nation** *nc* an explosion.

'**detonator** *nc* something (*esp* a piece of equipment) that sets off an explosion.

detour ['diːtuə] *nc* a wandering from the direct way (from one place to another): *We made a detour through the mountains in order to look at the scenery.*

detract [di'trakt] *vi* (*formal*: *with* **from**: not *usu* used with **is, was** *etc* and **-ing**) to take away from or lessen, *esp* reputation or value: *The crack detracted from the value of the plate*; *His recent behaviour detracted from my high opinion of him.* **de'traction** [-ʃən] *nu.*

detriment ['detrimənt] *nu* (*formal*) harm, damage or disadvantage: *without detriment to his reputation*; *to the detriment of his health.*

ˌ**detri'mental** [-'men-] *adj* (*very formal*) causing harm or damage: *I think this development may be detrimental to our long-term plans*; *a detrimental decision.*

deuce[1] [djuːs] *n* (in lawn tennis) forty points each.

deuce[2] [djuːs] *nc, interj* (*old*) the devil: *I had the deuce of a time getting here*; *What the deuce do you mean?*

Deutsche Mark, Deutschmark *see* **mark**[1].

devalue [diː'valjuː] *vt* to reduce the value of (*esp* a currency): *The government devalued the pound.*

ˌ**devalu'ation** [diːval-] *nu* the act of devaluing: *the devaluation of sterling.*

devastate ['devəsteit] *vt* (*formal*) **1** to leave in ruins: *The fire devastated the countryside.* **2** to overwhelm (a person) with grief: *She was devastated by the terrible news.*

'**devastating** *adj* (*formal*) overwhelming: *a devastating flood*; (*fig*) *The news was devastating.*

'**devastatingly** *adv* (*formal*: *usu fig*): *She is devastatingly beautiful.*

ˌ**deva'station** *nu* (*formal*) **1** the act of devastating. **2** the result of devastating: *They surveyed the devastation caused by the bomb.*

develop [di'veləp] – *pt, ptp* **de'veloped** – **1** *vti* to (cause to) grow bigger or to a more advanced state: *The plan developed slowly in his mind*; *She has developed into a very beautiful girl*; *It has developed into a very large city.* **2** *vt* (*formal*) to acquire gradually: *He developed the habit of getting up early.* **3** *vi* to become active, visible *etc*; *Spots developed on her face.* **4** *vt* to use chemicals to make (a photograph) visible: *My brother develops all his own films.* **5** *vt* to begin to use (an area of land) for building factories, shops, houses *etc*: *They're at last thinking about developing that stretch of waste land.*

de'velopment 1 *nu* the process or act of developing: *a crucial stage in the development of a child*; *The development of these films will not take long.* **2** *nc* something new which is the result of developing: *There have been several developments since this morning*; *important new developments in the scientific field.*

deviate ['diːvieit] *vi* (*formal*) to turn aside, *esp* from a right, normal or standard course: *He never deviates from his high moral standards*; *She will not deviate from her routine.*

ˌ**devi'ation** *ncu*: *sexual deviations*; *There has been a slight deviation from our original plan.*

device [di'vais] *nc* **1** something made for a purpose, *eg* a tool or instrument: *This penknife has a device for getting stones out of horses' hooves.* **2** (*formal*) a plan or system of doing something, sometimes involving trickery: *This is a device for avoiding income-tax*; *She thought of a cunning device to avoid staying at home.* **3** (*formal rare*) a sign or pattern: *a device on a shield.*

devil ['devl] *nc* **1** (*no pl*: *with* **the** *and cap*) the spirit of evil; Satan: *He does not worship God – he worships the Devil.* **2** any evil or wicked spirit or person: *That woman is a devil!* **3** (*loosely inf*) a person who is bad or disapproved of: *She's a lazy devil*; *He's a bit of a devil with women.* **4** (*loosely*: *inf*) an unfortunate person for whom one feels pity: *Poor devils! I feel really sorry for them.*

'**devilish** *adj* **1** of or like a devil, *esp* very **wicked**: *That child can be really devilish when he doesn't get his own way.* **2** (*inf*) very great: *That's a devilish problem.* – *adv* (*old inf*): *That's devilish cunning.*

'**devilment** *nu* (*formal or facet*) mischief: *That child is full of devilment but he's not really bad.*

ˌ**devil-may-'care** *adj* (*attrib*) reckless and not caring what happens: *She envied his devil-may-care attitude to life.*

See also **diabolic**.

devious ['diːviəs] *adj* (*formal*) not direct; not straightforward: *We climbed the hill by a devious route*; (*fig derog*) *He used devious methods to get what he wanted*; (*fig derog*) *a devious mind*; *He's always so devious.* '**deviously** *adv.* '**deviousness** *nu.*

devise [di'vaiz] *vt* (*formal*) to invent; to make up or put (quickly) together: *A new scheme was hurriedly devised*; *The system was devised by an engineer working for the firm.*

devoid [di'void] *adj* (*formal*: *pred with* **of**) free from or lacking: *He is totally devoid of fear*; *That is devoid of any meaning.*

devolve [di'volv] *vti* (*formal*) to (cause to) fall as a duty (upon someone, an organization *etc*): *The duty of disposing of the dead man's possessions devolved on him*; *The national government devolved all responsibility for education to local government.*

devolution [diːvə'luːʃən, (*esp Amer*) de-] *nu* the act of devolving, *esp* of certain powers to a regional government by a central government:

Did Scotland demand devolution?; (*attrib*) *the Devolution Bill.*

devote [di'vout] *vt* (*with* **to**) to give up wholly to or use entirely for: *She devotes her life to music*; *He devoted his energies to the cause of peace.*

de'voted *adj* (*formal*) **1** (*with* **to** *when pred*) loving and loyal: *a devoted friend*; *I am devoted to him.* **2** (*pred*: *with* **to**) given up (to): *He is devoted to his work.*

devotee [devə'ti:] *nc* (*formal*) a keen follower; an enthusiast: *a devotee of football*; *a devotee of Beethoven.*

de'votion *nu* (*formal*) **1** great love: *her undying devotion for her children.* **2** the act of devoting or of being devoted: *His devotion to duty was admired by all*; *the devotion of his energies to the cause of peace.*

de'votions *n pl* (*formal*) prayers: *The monks were at their devotions.*

devour [di'vauə] *vt* (*formal or facet*) to eat up greedily: *He was devoured by a lion*; *She devoured a whole box of chocolates*; (*fig*) *The fire devoured half the forest*; (*fig*) *He devours* (= reads) *books of all sorts.*

devout [di'vaut] *adj* **1** (*attrib*: *formal*) earnest or sincere: *Please accept my devout thanks.* **2** religious: *a devout Christian*; *She is very devout.* **de'voutness** *nu.*

de'voutly *adv* (*formal*) earnestly; sincerely: *It is devoutly to be hoped that the goods will arrive on time.*

dew [dju:] *nu* tiny drops of moisture coming from the air as it cools, *esp* at night: *The grass is wet with early morning dew.*

'dewy *adj* (*usu liter*) covered in dew: *dewy grass*; (*fig*) *a dewy freshness.* **'dewiness** *nu.*

dexterity [dek'sterəti] *nu* (*formal*) skill and/or quickness, *esp* with the hands: *She showed her dexterity with a needle and thread*; *the child's dexterity in making things.*

'dext(e)rous *adj* (*usu attrib*: *formal*) skilful, *esp* with the hands: *He is a very dexterous surgeon.*

diabetes [daiə'bi:ti:z] *nu* a disease in which there is usually too much sugar in the blood: *He suffers from diabetes and so has to take insulin.*

ˌdia'betic [-'be-] *nc* a person who suffers from diabetes: *He is a diabetic.* – *adj* **1** relating to or suffering from diabetes: *a diabetic condition*; *a diabetic patient*; *She's diabetic.* **2** (*attrib*) specially made *etc* for people who have diabetes: *diabetic chocolate.*

diabolic(al) [daiə'bolik(əl)] *adj* devilish or very wicked: *His treatment of her is diabolical*; (*loosely*) *Our working conditions are diabolical.* **ˌdia'bolically** *adv.*

diaeresis, (*Amer*) **dieresis** [dai'erəsis] – *pls* **di'aereses**, (*Amer*) **di'ereses** [-si:z] – *nc* a mark (¨) placed over a vowel to show that it is to be pronounced separately, as in naïve.

diagnose [daiəg'nouz, (*Amer*) -'nous] *vt* to say what is wrong (with a sick person *etc*) after making an examination: *The doctor diagnosed her illness as flu*; (*fig*) *The mechanic examined the car and diagnosed a faulty gearbox.*

ˌdiag'nosis [-sis] – *pl* **ˌdiag'noses** [-si:z] – *nc* a conclusion reached by diagnosing: *What diagnosis did the doctor make?*; *Has his diagnosis been confirmed?*

ˌdiag'nostic [-'nos-] *adj* (*attrib*): *a diagnostic test*; *He is a diagnostic radiologist* (= He X-rays people to find out what's wrong with them).

diagonal [dai'agənl] *nc* a line going from one corner to the opposite corner: *The two diagonals of a rectangle cross at the centre*; (*attrib*) *There was a diagonal path across the square.*

di'agonally *adv* in a diagonal line: *He walked diagonally across the field.*

diagram ['daiəgram] *nc* a drawing used to explain something that is difficult to understand: *This book has diagrams showing the parts of a car engine.*

ˌdiagram'matic [-'ma-] *adj* (*formal or tech*: *esp attrib*) of or like a diagram: *diagrammatic detail.*

dial ['daiəl] *nc* **1** the face of a watch or clock: *My watch has a luminous dial so you can see it in the dark.* **2** the turning disc over the numbers on a telephone. **3** any disc *etc* bearing numbers *etc* and a pointer and used to give information: *The cabin of the aircraft was lined with panels full of mysterious dials*; *the dial on a transistor radio.* – *v* – *pt, ptp* **'dialled** – *vt* to turn a telephone dial to get a number: *She dialled the wrong number.*

dialect ['daiəlekt] *nc* a way of speaking found only in a certain area or among a certain group or class of people: *a Scottish dialect*; *They were speaking in dialect.*

ˌdia'lectal [-'lek-] *adj* (*formal*): *Her speech is dialectal, not ungrammatical.*

dialogue, (*Amer*) **dialog(ue)** ['daiəlog] *ncu* (a) talk between two or more people, *esp* in a play or novel: *The whole play consists of a dialogue between two old men in a mental hospital*; *That novelist is very good at writing dialogue but poor at writing descriptive passages.*

diameter [dai'amitə] *nc* (the length of) a straight line drawn from side to side of a circle, passing through its centre: *Could you measure the diameter of that circle?*; *How wide is it in diameter?*

ˌdia'metrically [-'metri-]: **diametrically opposed** (*formal*) completely opposed: *His views on education are diametrically opposed to mine*; *We hold diametrically opposed views.*

diamond ['daiəmənd] **1** *ncu* a very hard, colourless precious stone: *Her brooch had three diamonds in it*; (*attrib*) *a diamond ring.* **2** *nc* a piece of diamond (often artificial) used as a tip on *eg* a record-player stylus: *The diamond on my stylus is getting worn and the sound reproduction is now rather poor.* **3** *nc* a kind of four-sided figure or shape; ◊ : *There was a pattern of red and yellow diamonds on the bedcover*; *diamond-shaped.* **4** *nc* one of the playing-cards of the suit diamonds, which have red symbols of this shape on them. – *See also* **diamonds** *below.* – *adj* (*attrib*) (of a wedding anniversary, jubilee *etc*) sixtieth: *They celebrated their diamond wedding (anniversary) last Wednesday*; *Queen Victoria's diamond jubilee was in 1897.*

'diamonds *n pl* (sometimes treated as *n sing*) one of the four card suits: *the five of diamonds.*

diaper ['daiəpə] *nc* (*Amer*) a baby's napkin: *The baby's diaper needs changing.*

diaphanous [dai'afənəs] *adj* (*formal*) (of cloth) so fine as to be transparent: *a diaphanous nightdress.*

diaphragm ['daiəfram] *nc* **1** a thin layer of muscle separating the chest from the abdomen: *He has strained a muscle in his diaphragm.* **2** (*formal*) any thin dividing layer *eg* in the earpiece of a telephone.

diarist *see* **diary**.

diarrhoea, (*Amer*) **diarrhea** [daiə'riə] *nu* (*med*) too much liquid in and too frequent emptying of the bowels: *He is suffering from sickness and diarrhoea*; *He has diarrhoea.*

diary ['daiəri] *nc* a (small book containing a) record

of daily happenings: *The explorer kept a diary of his adventures.*

'diarist *nc* (*formal*) a person who keeps a diary, *esp* one which is published: *Samuel Pepys was a famous diarist.*

diatribe ['daiətraib] *nc* (*formal*) an angry attack in speech or writing (against someone or something): *Her fierce diatribe against scientific experiments on animals won her many supporters.*

dice [dais] – *pl* **dice** – *nc* (*old or Amer* **die** [dai]) a small cube, *usu* with numbered sides or faces, used in certain games: *It is your turn to throw the dice.* – **1** *vt* to cut (vegetables *etc*) into small cubes: *She diced the carrots for the soup.* **2** *vi* (*formal*) to compete (with someone) at throwing dice; to gamble.

'dicey *adj* (*inf*) uncertain; risky: *You may catch the train if you hurry but it's a bit dicey*; *She may not die but her condition's a bit dicey*; *a dicey situation.*

dice with death to do something very risky (and dangerous): *He diced with death every time he took a short cut across the main railway line.*

dichotomy [dai'kotəmi] *nc* (*formal*) a division into two (*esp* contrasting) parts or groups: *the political dichotomy between the Right and the Left.*

dicky ['diki] *adj* (*inf*: *attrib*) shaky or not working *etc* very well: *He has a dicky heart.*

dictate [dik'teit, (*Amer*) 'dikteit] **1** *vti* to say or read out (something) for someone else to write down: *He always dictates his letters (to his secretary).* **2** *vt* (*formal*) to state officially or with authority: *He dictated the terms of our offer.* **3** *vti* (*often derog*) to give orders to; to command: *I certainly won't be dictated to by you* (= I won't do as you say); *She spends most of her time dictating to her unfortunate staff*; (*fig*) *He decided to act as circumstances dictated.*

dictates ['dikteits] *n pl* (*formal*) an order or instruction as to what should be done *etc*: *She always obeys the dictates of fashion.*

dic'tation **1** *nc* something read for another to write down: *The new secretary types very well but she is hopeless at taking dictation.* **2** *nu* the act of dictating: *The dictation of the notes took hours.*

dic'tator *nc* an all-powerful ruler: *As soon as he became dictator, he made all political parties illegal and governed the country as he liked.*

dic'tatorship **1** *nu* the authority of a dictator: *His dictatorship is threatened by the terrorists.* **2** *nc* a state ruled by a dictator: *That country is a dictatorship now.*

dictatorial [diktə'to:riəl] *adj* (*formal*) like or suggesting a dictator; fond of showing authority or giving orders to people: *He is very unpopular with his staff because he is so dictatorial*; *I dislike his dictatorial manner.* **ˌdicta'torially** *adv.*

diction ['dikʃən] *nu* (*more formal than speech*) the manner of speaking: *Her diction is always very clear*; *clear diction.*

dictionary ['dikʃənəri] *nc* **1** a book containing the words of a language alphabetically arranged, with their meanings *etc*: *This is an English dictionary.* **2** book containing other information alphabetically arranged: *a dictionary of place-names.*

did *see* **do**[1].

didactic [di'daktik] *adj* (*formal*) intended to teach: *The new minister's sermons are always very didactic*; (*derog*) *His speeches are too didactic.*

diddle ['didl] *vt* (*inf*) to obtain money from (a person) by cheating: *She diddled me out of quite a lot of money.*

didn't *see* **do**[1].

die[1] [dai] – *prp* **dying** ['daiiŋ] : *pt, ptp* **died** – *vi* **1** to lose life; to stop living and become dead: *Those flowers are dying*; *She just died of old age.* **2** to cease (gradually) to exist: *The daylight was dying fast*; *The music suddenly died as the radio was switched off.* **3** (*inf*) to have a strong desire (for something or to do something): *I'm dying for a drink*; *I'm dying to see her again.* – *See also* **die** *in phrases below.*

'diehard *nc* a person with very old-fashioned ideas who resists change very strongly. – *See also* **die hard**.

die away *vi* to fade from sight or hearing: *The sound died away into the distance.*

die down *vi* to lose strength or power: *I think the wind has died down a bit.*

die hard *vi* to die or disappear only after a long struggle: *Old habits die hard.*

die off *vi* to die quickly or in large numbers: *Herds of cattle were dying off because of the drought.*

die out *vi* to cease to exist anywhere: *The custom died out during the last century.*

See also **death, dead**.

die[2] [dai] *nc* a stamp or punch for making raised designs on money, paper *etc*: *He makes dies for stamping addresses on notepaper.*

the die is cast a step has been taken which makes the future inevitable: *I am not sure that I want to leave this job after all but the die is cast – I've handed in my resignation.*

die[3] *see* **dice**.

dieresis *see* **diaeresis**.

diesel engine ['di:zəl] *nc* an internal-combustion engine, used in lorries *etc*, in which a heavy form of oil is set on fire by heat produced by pressure.

'diesel fuel/oil heavy oil used as fuel for a diesel engine: *These lorries use diesel oil, not petrol.*

diet ['daiət] *nc* food, *esp* a course of recommended foods, for losing weight or as treatment for an illness *etc*: *In these islands they live on a diet of fish and oatmeal*; *He is on a salt-free diet because he has a heart condition*; *She went on a diet to lose weight.* – *vi* to eat certain kinds of food to lose weight: *She has to diet to stay as slim as that.*

dietetics [daiə'tetiks] *n sing* (*tech*) the science of regulating what people eat: *She is studying dietetics*; (*attrib*) *the dietetics department.*

differ ['difə] *vi* **1** (*more formal than* **be different**) (*often with* **from**) to be not like or alike: *Our views differ in several ways*; *Her house differs from mine in having the staircase at the front.* **2** (*more formal than* **disagree**) to disagree (with): *I think we will have to agree to differ*; *She differed with me over the choice of menu for the dinner.*

difference ['difrəns] **1** *nc* what makes one thing unlike another: *I can't see any difference between these two pictures*; *It doesn't make any difference* (=It does not matter) *to me whether you go or stay*; *Earning more money will make a difference to your standard of living*; *There's not much difference between them*; *What is the difference between your room and mine?* **2** *nc* (*formal*) an act of differing, *esp* a disagreement: *We had a difference of opinion*; *Have they settled their differences?* (= Have they stopped arguing?). **3** *nu* the amount by which one quantity or number is greater than another: *If you buy it for me I'll give you £5 now and make up the difference later*; *The difference in their weight is about five kilos.*

'different *adj* (*often with* **from**) not the same:

These gloves are not a pair – they're different; I saw him with three different women; My ideas are different from his; Her ideas are no different from mine.

ˌ**diffe'rential** [-'renʃəl] *nc* (*formal*) a difference in prices or wages: *The union did not wish to preserve the differential between office workers and factory workers.*

ˌ**diffe'rentiate** [-'renʃieit] *vti* (*formal*) **1** to see or be able to tell a difference or distinction (between): *I cannot even differentiate a blackbird and a starling.* **2** to treat differently: *She does not differentiate between her two children although one is adopted.* **'diffeˌrenti'ation** *nu.*

difficult ['difikəlt] *adj* **1** hard to do or understand; not easy: *He can't do difficult sums; It is a difficult task; It is difficult to know what is the best thing to do.* **2** hard to deal with or needing to be treated *etc* in a special way: *a difficult child; I think your mother is going to be difficult about it.*

'difficulty 1 *nu* the state or quality of being hard (to do) or not easy: *I have difficulty in understanding him.* **2** *nc* an obstacle or objection: *I see no difficulty in our supplying the goods on time; He is suitable otherwise but his age presents a difficulty; He has a habit of foreseeing difficulties.* **3** *nc* (*usu in pl*) troubles, *esp* money troubles: *Because of his lack of business experience, his firm was soon in difficulties.*

diffident ['difidənt] *adj* (*usu pred*: *formal*) not confident; not showing pride (in one's ability *etc*): *He is diffident about his achievements.* **'diffidently** *adv.* **'diffidence** *nu.*

diffuse [di'fju:z] *vti* (*formal*) to (cause to) spread in all directions: *The poison gradually diffused through her system.* – [di'fju:s] *adj* (*formal*) **1** widely spread: *diffuse light.* **2** (of a style of writing *etc*) using many words: *I like his novels but his style is so diffuse that it irritates some people.* **dif'fusion** [-ʒən] *nu.*

dig [dig] – *prp* **'digging**: *pt, ptp* **dug** [dʌg] – **1** *vti* to turn up (earth) with a spade *etc*: *He hates digging (the garden).* **2** *vt* to make (a hole) in this way: *The child dug a tunnel in the sand; He is digging a grave; They are digging up the road.* **3** *vti* to poke or thrust: *She dug (her spoon) into the pudding; He dug his brother in the ribs with his elbow.* – *See also* **dig** *in phrases below.* – *nc* **1** a thrust or a poke: *a dig in the ribs*; (*fig*) *I knew that his remarks about women drivers were a dig at me* (= that he thought that I had the faults which he referred to). **2** a digging up, or the place dug up, by archaeologists: *She is taking part in a dig – they hope to find the remains of a Roman camp; Where is the dig?*

'digger *nc* a machine for digging: *The workmen used a digger to make a trench for the cables.*

dig in 1 *vi* (*inf*) to make an energetic start on something, *esp* eating a meal: *She put a pot of stew on the table and we all dug in.* **2** *vt sep* to put into the soil by digging: *I dug in a whole sackful of peat.*

dig in one's heels *see* **heel**.

dig oneself in (*inf*) to become settled or established: *They quickly dug themselves in at their holiday cottage; We'll never get rid of her now – she's dug herself in.*

dig out *vt sep* **1** to get (something or someone) out (of somewhere) by digging: *We had to dig the car out of the snow; When we got stuck in the snowdrift we had to dig ourselves out.* **2** (*inf*) to find by searching: *I have that newspaper somewhere – I'll have to dig it out.*

dig up *vt sep* **1** *see* **dig** (*def 2*). **2** to remove by digging: *We dug up that old tree; They dug up a skeleton.* **3** (*inf*) to find or reveal: *I dug up some old magazines you might like.*

digest [dai'dʒest] *vt* **1** to break up (food) in the stomach *etc* and turn (it) into a form which the body can use: *The invalid had to have food that was easy to digest.* **2** (*fig formal*) to take in and think over (information *etc*): *It took me five minutes to digest what he had said.* – ['daidʒest] *nc* (*formal*) a summary of something written: *This book contains a digest of several articles on nuclear physics which were published this year.*

di'gestible *adj* able to be digested: *That pudding was not very digestible; digestible food.*

di'gestion [-tʃən] **1** *nu* the act of digesting food. **2** *nc* the power of digesting food: *She has a very poor digestion.*

di'gestive [-tiv] *adj* (*formal or tech*: *esp attrib*) digesting of food: *That illness has affected his digestive system.*

See also **indigestion**.

digit ['didʒit] *nc* **1** any of the figures 0 to 9: *105 is a number with three digits.* **2** (*formal or facet*) a finger or toe: *She has a fracture of the third digit of her left foot.*

'digital *adj* (*usu attrib*) (of a computer *etc*) using the numbers 0–9.

digital clock/watch *nc* a clock or watch which shows the time in numbers instead of on a dial.

dignified ['dignifaid] *adj* (*neg* **un-**) stately, serious or showing dignity: *She decided that it would not be dignified to run for the bus; She is a very dignified young lady.*

dignitary ['dignitəri] *nc* (*formal*) a person who has a high rank or office: *He is one of the town's dignitaries.*

dignity ['dignəti] **1** *nu* stateliness or seriousness of manner: *Holding her head high, she retreated with dignity.* **2** *nu* importance or seriousness: *She was conscious of the dignity of the occasion; Her dignity had been offended.* **3** *nc* (*often facet*) high rank, *esp* with its privileges: *He had risen to the dignity of an office of his own.*

be/stand on one's dignity to be ready to take offence very easily: *She tended to stand on her dignity and did not like being made fun of; She's always so much on her dignity that she never enjoys herself.*

See also **indignity**.

digress [dai'gres] *vi* (*formal*) to wander from the point, or from the main subject in speaking or writing: *His speech was too long because he kept digressing to tell funny stories; He keeps digressing from the main topic of his speech.*

di'gression [-ʃən] (*formal*) **1** *nc* a piece of writing or speaking which wanders from the main subject: *He mentions his visit to Africa in one of the digressions in Chapter 8.* **2** *nu* the act of digressing: *his constant digression from the subject under discussion.*

dike *see* **dyke**.

dilapidated [di'lapideitid] *adj* falling to pieces and needing repair: *All the houses in that street are dilapidated; a dilapidated old building.* **diˌlapi'dation** *nu.*

dilate [dai'leit] *vti* (*formal*) to make or become larger; to swell out: *The sudden darkness made the pupils of his eyes dilate; His pupils dilated under the* *influence of the drug.* **di'lation** *nu.*

dilatory ['dilətəri] *adj* (*formal*) slow (in doing things) or inclined to delay. **'dilatoriness** *nu.*

dilemma [di'lemə] *nc* a position or situation giving a choice of two courses of action, *usu* both equally unpleasant: *His dilemma was whether to leave the party early and get a lift in his friend's car or to stay and walk five miles home.*

dilettante [dili'tanti] *nc* (*formal*) a person who has a slight but not serious interest in several subjects.

diligent ['dilidʒənt] *adj* (*formal*) earnest and hardworking: *He's not very clever, but he is very diligent*; *a diligent student.* **diligently** *adv.* **'diligence** *nu.*

dilly-dally [dili'dali] *vi* (*inf*) to waste time, *esp* by stopping often (while one is doing something, going somewhere *etc*): *She's always dilly-dallying on the way to school.*

See also **dally**.

dilute [dai'lju:t] *vt* to lessen the strength *etc* of by mixing *esp* with water: *You are supposed to dilute that lime juice with water*; *This dye must be diluted in a bowl of water*; (*fig*) *I diluted her statement a little when I told him what she had said.* – *adj* (*usu attrib*: *formal*) reduced in strength; weak: *He filled his car battery with dilute acid.* **di'lution** *nu.*

dim [dim] *adj* **1** not bright or distinct: *We saw a dim light in the distance*; (*fig*) *I have only a dim memory of last night's events*; *The light is growing dim.* **2** (*inf*) (of a person) not understanding clearly: *She's a bit dim!*; *He's rather a dim child.* – *v* – *pt, ptp* **dimmed** – *vti* to make or become dim: *Tears dimmed her eyes*; *He dimmed the lights in the theatre.*

'dimly *adv*: *The light shone dimly*; *I dimly remember him.*

'dimness *nu.*

take a dim view of (*inf*) to disapprove of: *I take a dim view of his attitude towards his parents.*

dime [daim] *nc* the tenth part of an American dollar; 10 cents: *I haven't a dime in the world*; *This isn't worth a dime* (= This isn't worth anything).

dimension [di'menʃən] *nc* (*formal or tech*) a measurement in length, breadth, or thickness: *The dimensions of the box are 20 cm by 10 cm by 4 cm*; *Objects have three dimensions – length, breadth and depth.*

-dimensional (*in cmpds*) of (a certain number of) dimensions: *a three-dimensional figure.*

diminish [di'miniʃ] *vti* (*formal*) to make or become less: *Our supplies are diminishing rapidly*; *His reputation had been diminished by his failure to deal with the crisis.*

di'minished *adj* (*neg* **un-**).

diminution [dimi'nju:ʃən] *nu* (*very formal*) lessening: *Although the wind had dropped, there was no diminution of the rain.*

diminutive [di'minjutiv] *adj* (*formal*) very small: *The girl looked diminutive beside her six-foot boyfriend*; *a diminutive child.* – *nc* a word formed from another to express a little one, or used as a nickname: *'Droplet' is a diminutive of 'drop' and 'Sue' of 'Susan'.*

See also **diminish**.

dimple ['dimpl] *nc* a small hollow *esp* on the surface of the skin: *She has a dimple in her cheek when she smiles.* – *vti* (*usu liter*) to (cause to) show or form dimples: *Rain dimpled the surface of the water*; *She dimpled prettily at his compliment.*

din [din] *nc* a loud continuous noise: *What a terrible din that machine makes!* – *v* – *pt, ptp* **dinned** – *vi* (*inf*) to make such a noise: *The noise of the machine dinned in my ears.*

din (something) into (someone) to repeat (something) loudly and continually to try to make (someone) remember it: *She had had the rules of grammar dinned into her at school.*

dinar ['di:na:] *nc* the standard unit of currency in Yugoslavia and several Arab countries, *eg* Algeria, Libya and Iraq.

dine [dain] *vi* (*formal*) to have dinner: *We shall dine at half-past eight.*

'diner *nc* **1** (*formal*) a person who dines: *The diners ran from the restaurant when the fire started.* **2** a restaurant car on a train.

'dining-room *nc* a room used mainly for eating in: *When we have guests we eat in the dining-room – otherwise we eat in the kitchen.*

'dine on *vt fus* (*formal*) to have for one's dinner: *They dined on lobster and champagne.*

dine out *vi* (*formal*) to have dinner somewhere other than one's own house *eg* in a restaurant or at the house of friends *etc*: *We are dining out this evening.*

See also **dinner**.

ding-dong ['diŋdoŋ] *adj* (*inf*: *attrib*) (of an argument, contest *etc*) very closely fought with first one and then the other side seeming about to win: *They had a ding-dong argument about which of them should go.* – *nc* (*inf*) a noisy argument: *They had a ding-dong when he discovered she was being unfaithful to him.*

dinghy ['diŋgi] *nc* **1** a small boat carried on a larger boat to take passengers ashore. **2** a small sailing or rowing boat: *He has a sailing dinghy on the lake*; *He was in his dinghy.*

dingo ['diŋgou] – *pl* **'dingoes** – *nc* a type of wild dog found in Australia.

dingy ['dindʒi] *adj* dull; faded and dirty-looking: *The old lady's room is so dingy*; *We must get rid of that dingy wallpaper.* **'dinginess** *nu.*

dinner ['dinə] *ncu* the main meal of the day; a formal party or gathering, *esp* in the evening, when such a meal is eaten: *They had dinner at the airport*; *Do you have dinner in the evening or in the middle of the day?*; *Is it time for dinner yet?*; *What did you have for dinner?*; *They asked me to dinner*; *They serve excellent dinners here*; (*attrib*) *She gave a dinner-party*; *He was the guest of honour at the dinner.*

'dinner-jacket *nc* a man's formal jacket for wear in the evening: *All the men were in dinner-jackets at the dinner given in honour of the president.*

'dinner-time *nu* the time in the middle of the day or in the evening at which dinner is eaten: *I'll speak to him about it at dinner-time.*

See also **dine**.

dinosaur ['dainəso:] *nc* any of several types of extinct giant reptile.

dint [dint] *nc* a hollow made by a blow; a dent.

by 'dint of (*formal*) by means of: *He succeeded by dint of sheer hard work.*

diocese ['daiəsis] *nc* the district over which a bishop has authority.

diocesan [dai'osisn] *adj* (*formal*) relating to or concerning a diocese.

dip [dip] – *pt, ptp* **dipped** – **1** *vt* to lower into any liquid for a moment: *He dipped his bread in the soup*; *He dipped his spoon into the soup.* **2** *vi* to slope downwards: *The road dipped gently just beyond the crossroads.* **3** *vt* to lower the beam of (car headlights): *He dipped his lights as the other car* *approached.* **4** *vt* to lower (a flag) and raise again: *The soldiers dipped their flags as they marched past the Queen.* – *See also* **dip into** *below.* – *nc* **1** a hollow (in a road *etc*): *The car was hidden by a dip in the road.* **2** a liquid or semi-liquid substance into which something is dipped, *esp* as a kind of party food: *a cheese dip.* **3** (*inf*) a short swim or bathe: *We all went for a dip in the sea.*

dip into *vt fus* **1** to take something (*esp* money) from: *I've been dipping into my savings quite a lot recently.* **2** to look briefly at (a book) or to study (a subject) in a casual manner: *I've dipped into his book on Shakespeare, but I haven't read it right through; I dipped into Chinese history while I worked in a library.*

diphtheria [dif'θiəriə] *nu* an infectious disease of the throat.

diphthong ['difθoŋ] *nc* (*gram*) two vowel sounds pronounced as one syllable: *The vowel sound in 'out' is a diphthong.*

diploma [di'ploumə] *nc* a written statement saying that one has passed a certain examination *etc*: *She has a diploma in Social Studies*; (*attrib*) *a diploma course* (= a course of study for which one is given a diploma).

diplomacy [di'plouməsi] *nu* **1** the business of making agreements, treaties *etc* between countries; the business of looking after the affairs of one's country *etc* in a foreign country: *He had a brilliant career in diplomacy.* **2** (*formal*) skill or cleverness in dealing with people or making them agree: *The agreement was brought about largely through her diplomacy.*

diplomat ['dipləmat] *nc* **1** a person engaged in diplomacy: *He is a diplomat at the American embassy in Britain.* **2** a very tactful person: *She's good at settling quarrels – she's a real diplomat.*

diplomatic [diplə'matik] *adj* **1** concerning diplomacy: *He was on a diplomatic mission*; *When he was charged with the crime he claimed diplomatic immunity* (= freedom from being charged with an offence because of being a foreign diplomat). **2** (*formal*) tactful: *She made diplomatic enquiries about his health.* **ˌdiplo'matically** *adv.*

dire ['daiə] *adj* (*formal or facet*) dreadful: *He said there would be dire consequences if she left.*

direct [di'rekt] *adj* **1** (*usu attrib*) straight; following the quickest and shortest path from beginning to end: *Is this the most direct route?*; *He has a direct telephone link with the President.* **2** (of manner *etc*) straightforward and honest: *She did not give me a direct answer*; *She was very direct about it.* **3** occurring as an immediate result of, with no other circumstances or reason coming between: *His dismissal was a direct result of his lack of ability*; *That was a direct result of the accident.* **4** exact; complete: *Her opinions are the direct opposite of his.* **5** in an unbroken line of descent from father to son *etc*: *He is a direct descendant of George Washington.* – *vt* **1** (*formal*) to point, aim or turn in a particular direction: *He directed my attention towards the notice*; *My remarks were directed at the younger members of the audience.* **2** to show the way: *She directed him to the station.* **3** (*formal*) to order or instruct: *We will do as you direct.* **4** to control or organize: *A policeman was directing the traffic*; *to direct a play/film.* **5** (*formal*) to put a name and address on (a letter).

di'rection [-ʃən] **1** *ncu* (the) place or point to which one moves, looks *etc*: *What direction did he go in?*; *They were heading in my direction* (= towards me); *I looked in the direction of the door*; *I have very little sense of direction* (= I am not good at finding my way unless I know a place well). **2** *nu* (*formal*) guidance or advice: *They are under your direction*; *We are under the direction of the government.* **3** *nc* (*often in pl*) information or instructions as to what one should do, how one should use something *etc*: *We asked the policeman for directions* (= how we get to where we want to go); *I have lost the directions for this washing-machine* (= instructions on how to use it). **4** *nu* (*formal*) the act of aiming or turning (something or someone) towards a certain point. **di'rectional** *adj.*

di'rective [-tiv] *nc* (*formal*) a general instruction as to what is to be done *etc*, issued by a higher authority (*eg* a government): *We have received a directive from our head office that we are to close the bank early.*

di'rectly *adv* **1** in a direct manner: *I went directly to the office.* **2** almost at once: *He will be here directly.* **di'rectness** *nu.*

di'rector *nc* a person or thing that directs, *eg* one of a group of persons who manage the affairs of a business or a person who is in charge of the making of a film, play *etc*: *He is on the board of directors of our firm*; *The producer and the director quarrelled about the film.*

di'rectory *nc* a type of book giving names and addresses *etc*: *a telephone directory.*

direct object [di'rekt] *nc* (*gram*) the word in a sentence which stands for the person or thing on which the action of the verb is done: *In 'She stroked the cat', the cat is the direct object.*

direct speech ['dairekt] *nu* (*gram*) speech reported in the exact words of the speaker: *She said 'He is lazy' is the form in direct speech of She said that he was lazy.*

direct taxation *nu* taxation of income or property.

See also **indirect**.

dirge [dəːdʒ] *nc* (*formal*) **1** a funeral song or hymn. **2** (*loosely*) a sad song.

dirt [dəːt] *nu* any unclean substance, such as mud, dust, dung *etc*: *I think you'll have to wash that to get the dirt off*; *His shoes are covered in dirt.*

'dirty *adj* **1** not clean: *dirty washing*; *His feet are dirty.* **2** (*usu attrib*) not morally acceptable: *dirty books.* **3** (*usu attrib*) mean or unfair: *a dirty trick.* **4** (of weather) stormy. – *vti* to soil; to make or become dirty: *He dirtied his hands/shoes*; *That carpet dirties very easily.* **'dirtiness** *nu.*

ˌdirt-'cheap *adj, adv* (*inf*) very cheap: *She got that car dirt-cheap.*

'dirt track *nc* an earth-track for motor-racing.

dirty word *nc* **1** a word generally considered to be obscene. **2** (*fig*) the word for a feeling, opinion, idea *etc* not in favour at a certain time: *Imperialism is a dirty word nowadays.*

dirty work *nu* **1** work which makes one dirty: *Mining is dirty work.* **2** (*fig*) an unpleasant task or morally wrong action, *esp* one done for someone else: *He wanted me to do his dirty work for him.*

disable [dis'eibl] *vt* (*formal*) to take away (wholly or partly) the ability or strength of; to cripple: *He was disabled during the war*; *It took them a few minutes to disable the guns.*

disability [disə'biləti] *nc* (*formal*) something which disables: *He has a disability which prevents him from walking*; *It is certainly a disability in this job to have no phone*; (*attrib*) *a disability allowance.*

dis'abled *adj* (*formal*) (partly) without ability or strength; crippled: *a disabled soldier*; *I would have helped him if I had realized that he was disabled.*

dis'ablement *nu* **1** (*formal*) the act of disabling. **2** the state of being disabled: *His disablement does not prevent him from travelling.*

See also **enable, unable.**

disabuse [disə'bju:z] *vt* (*very formal or facet*) to make the truth known to (someone) about a wrong belief or opinion: *Disabuse him of that idea!*

disadvantage [disəd'va:ntidʒ] *nc* something which makes a difficulty or which is an unfavourable circumstance: *There are several disadvantages to this plan*; *The steep path up to the house is its only disadvantage.* – *See also* **at a disadvantage** *below.*

ˌ**disad'vantaged** *adj* (*usu attrib*: *very formal*) having a disadvantage of some kind, *esp* poverty, homelessness *etc*: *disadvantaged families.*

disadvantageous [disadvən'teidʒəs] *adj* (*formal*) unfavourable: *a disadvantageous arrangement*; *It would be disadvantageous to you to change your plans now.*

at a disadvantage in an unfavourable position: *His power was strengthened by the fact that he had us all at a disadvantage.*

disaffected [disə'fektid] *adj* (*formal*: *usu attrib*) discontented, disloyal and rebellious: *disaffected soldiers.* ˌ**disaf'fection** [-ʃən] *nu* (*formal*).

disagree [disə'gri:] *vi* **1** (*sometimes with* **with**) to hold different opinions *etc* (from someone else): *We disagree about almost everything*; *I disagree with you on that point.* **2** to quarrel: *We never meet without disagreeing.* **3** (*with* **with**) (of food) to be unsuitable (to someone) and cause pain: *Onions disagree with me.*

ˌ**disa'greeable** *adj* unpleasant: *a disagreeable task*; *He is a most disagreeable person*; *She is often rather disagreeable in the morning.* ˌ**disa'greeably** *adv.*

ˌ**disa'greement 1** *nu* the act of disagreeing: *There seemed to be considerable disagreement between the two accounts of the accident.* **2** *nc* a quarrel: *We had a violent disagreement last time we met.*

disallow [disə'lau] *vt* (*usu formal*) to refuse to allow or admit a claim *etc*: *His appeal was disallowed by the judges.*

disappear [disə'piə] *vi* **1** to vanish from sight: *The sun disappeared slowly below the horizon.* **2** to fade out of existence: *This kind of idea had disappeared by the end of the century.* **3** to go away so that other people do not know where one is: *A search is being carried out for the small boy who disappeared from his home on Monday.*

ˌ**disap'pearance** *nc* the act of disappearing: *His disappearance caused a great deal of concern.*

disappoint [disə'point] *vt* **1** to not succeed in fulfilling the hopes or expectations of: *Her lack of success disappointed Mary.* **2** (*formal*) to fail to fulfil: *This disappointed her hopes.*

ˌ**disap'pointed** *adj* unhappy or dissatisfied by having one's hopes, plans *etc* unfulfilled: *I was disappointed to hear that the party had been cancelled*; *She was disappointed by his attitude to work*; *When they found that the swimming-pool was closed, the disappointed children went home.*

ˌ**disap'pointment 1** *nu* the state of being disappointed: *Her disappointment was obvious from her face.* **2** *nc* something which disappoints: *His failure was a great disappointment to his wife.*

disapprove [disə'pru:v] *vti* to have an unfavourable opinion (of): *Her mother disapproved wholeheartedly of her behaviour*; (*formal*) *She disapproved the arrangements for the wedding.*

ˌ**disap'proval** *nu* the state of disapproving: *His disapproval of her behaviour was obvious from his expression.*

ˌ**disap'proving** *adj* (*usu attrib*) showing disapproval: *a disapproving look.* ˌ**disap'provingly** *adv.*

disarm [dis'a:m] **1** *vt* to take away weapons from: *He crept up from behind and managed to disarm the man with the gun.* **2** *vi* to get rid of weapons of war: *When peace was made, the victors began gradually to disarm.* **3** *vt* (*formal*) to make (a person) less angry; to charm: *She disarmed me at once by admitting that she had been at fault.*

dis'armament *nu* the act of doing away with war-weapons.

dis'arming *adj* gaining friendliness; charming: *a disarming smile*; *Her manner was frank and disarming.* **dis'armingly** *adv.*

See also **unarmed.**

disarrange [disə'reindʒ] *vt* (*formal*) to throw out of order; to make untidy: *The strong wind had disarranged her hair.* ˌ**disar'rangement** *nu.*

disarray [disə'rei] *nu* (*formal*) disorder: *By the third day of fighting, the army was in complete disarray.*

disassociate *see* **dissociate.**

disaster [di'za:stə] *nc* an extremely unfortunate event or happening, *esp* one that causes great damage, loss *etc*: *The earthquake was the greatest disaster the country had ever experienced*; (*fig facet*) *That dress I made was a disaster!*

di'sastrous *adj* causing or involving disasters: *a disastrous decision*; *a disastrous journey*; (*facet*) *a disastrous dinner-party.* **di'sastrously** *adv.*

disband [dis'band] *vti* (*formal*) to (cause to) break up or cease to act as a group (*esp* an army): *The regiment disbanded at the end of the war*; *They disbanded the local Guide company because of lack of support.*

disbelieve [disbi'li:v] *vt* (*formal or old*: not *usu* used with **is, was** *etc* and **-ing**) not to believe: *He was inclined to disbelieve her story.*

ˌ**disbe'lief** [-f] *nu* (*formal*) the state of not believing: *She stared at him in disbelief.*

See also **unbelief.**

disc, disk [disk] *nc* **1** a flat, thin, circular object: *From the earth, the full moon looks like a silver disc*; *The name and address of the injured dog's owner was on a disc on its collar.* **2** (*inf*) a gramophone record.

'**disc jockey** *nc* a person employed to present a programme of music (*usu* pop-music) on the radio *etc*, from gramophone records.

slipped disc *see* **slip.**

discard [di'ska:d] *vt* (*formal*) to throw away as useless: *She decided to discard the piece of sewing she had already done and start again*; *They discarded the empty bottles.*

discern [di'sə:n] *vt* (*formal*: not *usu* used with **is, was** *etc* and **-ing**) to see or realize: *We could discern from his appearance that he was upset.*

di'scernible *adj* (*formal*) able to be seen and understood: *I could see no discernible difference between them*; *The ship was still discernible on the horizon.* **di'scernibly** *adv.*

di'scerning *adj* (*formal*) quick or clever at noticing or understanding: *We hope that discerning people will realize the quality of what we are selling*; *She's very discerning.*

di'scernment *nu.*

discharge [dis'tʃa:dʒ] **1** *vt* to allow to leave; to send away or dismiss: *The prisoner was at last discharged; She was discharged from hospital; I'm going to discharge my servants.* **2** *vti* (*formal*) to fire (a gun): *He discharged his gun at the policeman; The gamekeeper's gun discharged as he climbed over the wall.* **3** *vt* (*formal*) to perform (a task *etc*): *He discharges his duties conscientiously.* **4** *vt* (*formal*) to pay (a debt): *He discharged all his debts before committing suicide.* **5** *vti* (*formal*) to (cause to) let or send out: *The chimney was discharging clouds of smoke; The drain discharged into the street.* **6** *vti* to unload (a cargo): *The ship discharged (bananas) at the Jubilee Dock.* – ['distʃa:dʒ] (*formal*) **1** *nu* (an) act of discharging: *He was given his discharge from the army; She is efficient in the discharge of her duties.* **2** *nc* something which is given or let out: *a discharge from a wound; The discharge from the chemical works killed hundreds of fish in the river.*

disciple [di'saipl] *nc* a person who believes in the teaching of another, *esp* one of the original followers of Christ: *Jesus and his twelve disciples; Jung was a disciple of Freud.*

discipline ['disiplin] *nu* **1** training in an orderly way of life: *All children need discipline.* **2** order kept by means of control: *During the fire, their remarkable discipline was noticeable.* – *vt* **1** to bring under control: *You must discipline yourself so that you do not waste time.* **2** to punish: *The students who caused the disturbance have been disciplined.*

ˌdiscipli'narian *nc* a person who keeps strict discipline: *Our Latin master was a poor disciplinarian – we all read comics in his class.* – *adj* (*usu attrib*: *formal*) (of methods *etc*) involving strict discipline: *He runs the school according to disciplinarian principles.*

'disciplinary *adj* (*usu attrib*: *formal*) **1** of discipline: *disciplinary aims.* **2** punishing and intended to keep control: *They took disciplinary action against the demonstrators.*

disclaim [dis'kleim] *vt* (*formal*) to refuse to have anything to do with; to deny: *I disclaimed all reponsibility.*

dis'claimer *nc* (*formal*) a denial: *The Government issued a disclaimer stating that no such promise had ever been made.*

disclose [dis'klouz] *vt* (*formal*) to uncover, reveal or make known: *He refused to disclose his identity; Please do not disclose his name to the newspaper reporter.*

dis'closure [-ʒə] (*formal*) **1** *nc* something that is disclosed: *He was distressed by the newspapers' disclosures about his private life.* **2** *nu* the act of disclosing: *She was sure that disclosure would mean ruin.*

disco ['diskou] short for **discotheque**.

discolour, (*Amer*) **discolor** [dis'kʌlə] *vti* (*formal*) to (cause to) change colour or become stained: *The wallpaper had discoloured with the damp.*

disˌcolou'ration (*formal*) *nu* **1** the state of being discoloured: *The room had to be repainted due to the discolouration of the walls by cigarette smoke.* **2** the act of discolouring.

discomfit [dis'kʌmfit] *vt* (*formal*) **1** to make uncomfortable; to embarrass: *He realized that his remarks had succeeded in discomfiting her.* **2** to defeat: *Our surprise attack discomfited the enemy.* **dis'comfiture** [-tʃə] *nu.*

discomfort [dis'kʌmfət] (*formal*) **1** *nu* lack of comfort; the state of being uncomfortable: *Her broken leg caused her great discomfort.* **2** *nc* something that causes lack of comfort: *She came home early as she did not like the discomforts of a camping holiday.*

disconcert [diskən'sə:t] *vt* (*formal*) to embarrass or take aback: *He was a little disconcerted by the amount he had to pay.*

ˌdiscon'certed *adj*: *She was disconcerted by his frankness; a disconcerted look.*

disconnect [diskə'nekt] *vt* to separate or break the connection (*esp* electrical) with: *Our phone has been disconnected; I disconnected two wires from the battery.*

ˌdiscon'nected *adj* **1** separated and no longer connected: *a disconnected wire.* **2** (of speech, writing) not well joined together: *All he had written was a few disconnected sentences.* **ˌdiscon'nection** [-ʃən] *ncu.*

disconsolate [dis'konsələt] *adj* (*formal*) sad or unhappy: *She was disconsolate over the death of her cat; The disconsolate tourists looked at the rain.* **dis'consolately** *adv.*

discontent [diskən'tent] *nu* the state of not being contented; dissatisfaction: *There is a lot of discontent among young people.*

ˌdiscon'tented *adj* dissatisfied or not happy: *She's discontented with her life; a discontented sigh.* **ˌdiscon'tentedly** *adv.* **ˌdiscon'tentment** *nu.*

discontinue [diskən'tinju] *vt* (*formal*) to stop or put an end to: *I have discontinued my visits there.* **'disconˌtinu'ation** *nu.*

discord ['disko:d] **1** *nu* (*formal*) disagreement or quarrelling: *Their house was full of discord.* **2** *nc* (*music*) a group of notes played together which give an unpleasant sound: *a series of discords.*

dis'cordant *adj* (*formal*) disagreeing; not fitting in or not in harmony (with): *They were a discordant family – they were always having rows; His remark introduced a discordant note into the meeting; Some modern music sounds very discordant to me.*

discotheque ['diskətek] *nc* (*usu abbrev* **disco** ['diskou]) **1** a place, or a type of entertainment, at which recorded music is played for dancing: *We're going to a disco on Saturday.* **2** the equipment for playing records and *usu* providing special lighting effects; *esp* a complete unit, with an operator, hired to provide music for parties: *Which disco have you got for next Friday's party?*

discount ['diskaunt] *nc* a (small) sum taken off the price of something: *He gave me a discount of 20%.* – [dis'kaunt] *vt* (*formal*) to leave aside and not consider: *I have discounted most of what he said as being the words of a lunatic!*

discourage [dis'kʌridʒ, (*Amer*) -'kə:-] *vt* **1** to take away the confidence, hope *etc* of: *His lack of success discouraged him.* **2** (*formal*) to try to prevent (by showing disapproval *etc*): *She discouraged all his attempts to find where she lived.* **3** (*with* **from**) to persuade against: *The rain discouraged him from going camping.* **dis'couragement** *ncu.*

See also **encourage**.

discourse ['disko:s] *nc* (*formal*) a speech, lecture or conversation. – [dis'ko:s] *vi* (*formal with* **on/upon**) to talk (about).

discourteous [dis'kə:tiəs] (*formal*) *adj* not polite; rude: *It was very discourteous of him not to reply to my letter; a discourteous remark.* **dis'courtesy** [-təsi] *nu.*

discover [dis'kʌvə] *vt* **1** to find by chance, *esp* for the first time: *Columbus discovered America*; *I discovered a really nice place to have lunch.* 2 to find out: *Try to discover what's going on!*

dis'covery 1 *nu* the act of finding out: *a voyage of discovery.* 2 *nc* something which is discovered: *She made several startling discoveries.*

discredit [dis'kredit] (*formal*) **1** *nu* loss of good reputation: *I know something to his discredit.* **2** *nc* something that causes loss of good reputation; a disgrace: *Her untidy garden is a discredit to the whole street.* – *vt* (*formal*) **1** to make unbelievable or disbelieved: *They have discredited his story at last.* **2** to disgrace: *He was discredited by the details which now came to light.*

dis'creditable *adj* (*formal*) bringing discredit or disgrace: *The football fans' behaviour was discreditable to their team*; *a discreditable action.* **dis'creditably** *adv.*

discreet [di'skri:t] *adj* wise, cautious and not saying anything which might cause trouble: *My secretary won't let the secret out – she's very discreet*; *discreet behaviour.* **di'screetness** *nu.*

di'scretion [-'skre-] *nu* (*formal*) **1** discreetness: *I admired your secretary's discretion in not saying where you had been on business.* **2** wise and tactful judgement: *I leave the arrangements entirely to your discretion.*

at the di'scretion of according to the judgement of: *Money will be given at the discretion of the management.*

See also **indiscreet**.

discrepancy [di'skrepənsi] *ncu* (*formal*) (an act of) disagreement or difference (between two stories, amounts of money *etc*): *There is some discrepancy between the two accounts of what happened*; *There are several discrepancies in the two accounts of what happened*; *The auditors found discrepancies in the firm's books.*

discretion *see* **discreet**.

discriminate [di'skrimineit] *vi* **1** (*formal*: *with* **between**) to make or see a difference between (two people or things): *It is sometimes difficult to discriminate between real and pretended cases of need.* **2** to treat (a certain kind of people) differently: *He was accused of discriminating against women employees.*

dis'criminating *adj* (*formal*) **1** showing good judgement: *He was most discriminating in his choice of furniture*; *a discriminating theatre-goer.* **2** (*attrib*) making distinctions: *One discriminating feature is the colour of the bird's head.*

dis,crimi'nation *nu* **1** the act of discriminating: *His action in appointing a man to the job led him to be accused of sex discrimination* (= making distinctions based on sex). **2** (*formal*) the ability to recognize small differences; good judgement: *He showed fine discrimination in picking out the genuine paintings*; *I leave the choice entirely to your discrimination.*

See also **indiscriminate**.

discursive [dis'kə:siv] *adj* (*very formal*) (of speaking, writing *etc*) not keeping to the main point or subject: *in discursive prose*; *His treatment of the subject is rather discursive.*

discus ['diskəs] *nc* a heavy disc of metal *etc* thrown in a type of athletic competition.

discuss [di'skʌs] *vt* (*more formal than* **talk about**) to talk about: *We had a meeting to discuss our plans for the future.*

di'scussion [-ʃən] *ncu* (an act of) talking about something: *I think there has been too much discussion of this subject*; *Discussions between the heads of state took place in an atmosphere of strict security.*

disdain [dis'dein] *nu* (*formal*) scorn or pride: *He turned away with a look of disdain.* – *vt* (*old or formal*) **1** to be too proud (to do something): *She disdained to save herself by telling lies.* **2** to look down on (something): *She disdains our company.*

dis'dainful *adj* (*formal*) showing pride and scorn: *a disdainful glance*; *Don't be so disdainful!* **dis'dainfully** *adv.*

disease [di'zi:z] *ncu* (an) illness: *She's suffering from a disease of the kidneys*; (*fig*) *Violent crime is one of the most serious diseases of modern society.*

di'seased *adj* not healthy: *The doctor discovered that her liver was diseased*; *a diseased spleen.*

disembark [disim'ba:k] *vti* (*formal*) to (cause to) go from a ship on to land: *We disembarked soon after breakfast.* **,disembar'kation** *nu.*

disembodied [disim'bodid] *adj* (*formal*: *attrib*) (*esp* of a spirit, soul *etc*) separated from the body: *A disembodied voice came from the loudspeaker.*

disenchanted [disin'tʃa:ntid] *adj* (*formal*: *often with* **with**) (of a person) having lost all one's pleasant but false beliefs (about something): *a disenchanted attitude to life*; *I am completely disenchanted with politics.* **,disen'chantment** *nu.*

disengage [disin'geidʒ] **1** *vt* (*tech*) to separate or free (one thing from another): *He disengaged the clutch and the driving-wheel stopped turning.* **2** *vi* (*formal*) (of opponents in a battle *etc*) to stop fighting: *The armies disengaged at nightfall.*

disentangle [disin'taŋgl] *vt* (*formal*) to free from being tangled; to unravel: *He disentangled himself from the brambles*; *She disentangled a piece of string from the heap in the drawer.* **,disen'tanglement** *nu.*

disfavour, (*Amer*) **disfavor** [dis'feivə] *nu* (*formal*) **1** the state of being out of favour: *He was in disfavour because he had stayed out late.* **2** displeasure or disapproval: *He regarded the shop with disfavour because they had refused to exchange a pair of gloves.*

disfigure [dis'figə, (*Amer*) -'figjər] *vt* (*formal*) to spoil the beauty of; to deface: *That scar will disfigure her for life*; *The town is being disfigured by a lot of new building.* **dis'figurement** *nu.*

disgorge [dis'go:dʒ] *vt* (*formal*) to produce, vomit or throw out or up violently: *The chimney was disgorging clouds of black smoke*; *Wild dogs disgorge half-digested food for their puppies*; (*fig*) *She reluctantly disgorged the missing papers.*

disgrace [dis'greis] **1** *nu* the state of being out of favour: *He is in disgrace because of his behaviour.* **2** *nu* a state of being without honour and regarded without respect: *There seemed to be nothing ahead of him but disgrace and shame.* **3** *nc* (*no pl*) something which causes or ought to cause one to be regarded in this way: *Your clothes are a disgrace!* – *vt* **1** to bring shame upon: *Did you have to disgrace me by appearing like that?* **2** (*very formal*) to dismiss (someone) from a position of importance or influence.

dis'graceful *adj* very bad or shameful: *disgraceful behaviour*: *The service in that hotel was disgraceful.* **dis'gracefully** *adv.*

disgruntled [dis'grʌntld] *adj* dissatisfied and sulky: *He is very disgruntled at the way things are going*; *The disgruntled child refused to smile at her aunt.*

disguise [dis'gaiz] *vt* **1** to hide the identity (of

someone or something) by changing his, its *etc* appearance: *He disguised himself as a pirate*; *She disguised her voice with a strong Birmingham accent.* **2** to hide (*eg* one's intentions *etc*): *He tried hard to disguise his feelings.* – **1** *nu* a disguised state: *I can't help feeling that his attitude is just racism in disguise.* **2** *nc* something, *esp* a set of clothes, make-up *etc* which disguises or is intended to disguise: *He was wearing a false beard and a long grey raincoat as a disguise.*

disgust [dis'gʌst] *vt* (not used with **is, was** *etc* and **-ing**) to cause feelings of dislike and sickness in: *The smell of that soup disgusts me*; (*fig*) *Your attitude disgusts me*; (*fig*) *She was disgusted by your behaviour.* – *nu* the state or feeling of being disgusted: *She left the room in disgust*; *My disgust at what he had said grew stronger all the time.*

dis'gusting *adj* causing disgust, *esp* feelings of sickness: *What a disgusting smell!*; *That picture is disgusting*; *Her house is in a disgusting mess* (= very unpleasantly untidy). **dis'gustingly** *adv.*

dish [diʃ] *nc* **1** a plate, bowl *etc* in which food is brought to the table: *a large shallow dish.* **2** food mixed and prepared for the table: *She served us an interesting dish containing chicken and almonds.*

dish out *vt sep* (*inf*) to distribute or give to people: *He dished out the potatoes*; (*fig*) *They dished out jobs all round.*

dish up *vi, vt sep* (*inf*) to place (food) on plates, dishes *etc* ready to be brought to the table: *I'll dish up while you have another drink.*

dishearten [dis'ha:tn] *vt* (*formal*) to take courage or hope away from: *The failure of her first attempt disheartened her.*

dis'heartening *adj* (*formal*) discouraging or depressing: *The news that the factory was to close was very disheartening to the workers*; *a disheartening report.* **dis'hearteningly** *adv.*

dishevel [di'ʃevəl] – *pt, ptp* **di'shevelled**, (*Amer*) **di'sheveled** – *vt* (*formal*) to make untidy: *Her hair was dishevelled by the wind.*

di'shevelled *adj* (*pred*): *She arrived home from the hike, wet and dishevelled.*

dishonest [dis'onist] *adj* not honest; deceitful: *You got that money in a thoroughly dishonest manner*; *She was dishonest about her qualifications when she applied for the job.* **dis'honestly** *adv.*

dis'honesty *nu* the state or quality of being dishonest: *I would not have expected such dishonesty from him.*

dishonour [dis'onə] *nu* (*formal*) disgrace; shame. – *vt* (*formal*) to cause shame to: *You have dishonoured your family by your actions!*

dis'honourable *adj* disgraceful; having no (sense of) honour: *a dishonourable action*; *It was dishonourable to steal the blind man's money.* **dis'honourably** *adv.*

disillusion [disi'lu:ʒən] *vt* (*formal*) to destroy the false but pleasant beliefs held by (a person): *I thought his job sounded interesting, but he soon disillusioned me.*

ˌdisil'lusioned *adj* without illusions, *esp* having a low opinion of the world: *He had become thoroughly disillusioned as a result of his involvement in local politics.* **ˌdisil'lusionment** *nu.*

disinclination [disinkli'neiʃən] *nu* (*formal*) unwillingness: *He suffers from a serious disinclination to do any work.*

ˌdisin'clined [-'klaind] *adj* (*pred*: *formal*) unwilling (to do something): *I am disinclined to make any further statement on the situation.*

See also **incline**.

disinfect [disin'fekt] *vt* to destroy disease-causing germs in: *This sink should be disinfected regularly.*

ˌdisin'fectant *ncu* a substance that destroys germs: *She wiped the walls with hot soapy water containing* (*a*) *disinfectant.*

See also **infect**.

disinherit [disin'herit] *vt* to prevent (a person) from inheriting something: *He was disinherited by his father and wasn't left any money.*

disintegrate [dis'intigreit] *vti* (*formal or facet*) to (cause to) fall to pieces: *The paper bag was so wet that the bottom disintegrated and all the groceries fell out*; (*fig*) *He is of the opinion that the values of society are disintegrating.*

disˌinte'gration *nu*: *The complete disintegration of the aircraft proved that there had been an explosion*; (*fig*) *the gradual disintegration of his way of life.*

disinter [disin'tə:] – *pt, ptp* **ˌdisin'terred** – *vt* (*formal*) to take out of a grave: *The body was disinterred at dead of night*; (*fig*) *The subject was disinterred yet again.*

disinterested [dis'intristid] *adj* not influenced by private feelings or selfish motives: *Would you give us your opinion, as a disinterested observer?*; *To give a fair judgement, you must be entirely disinterested.* *See also* **interest, uninterested**.

disjointed [dis'dʒointid] *adj* (*formal*) not properly connected: *some disjointed remarks.* **dis'jointedly** *adv.* **dis'jointedness** *nu.*

disk *see* **disc**.

dislike [dis'laik] *vt* (not used with **is, was** *etc* and **-ing**) not to like; to have strong feelings against: *I know he dislikes me*; *She disliked the idea.* – **1** *nu* strong feeling directed against a thing, person or idea: *He doesn't go to football matches because of his dislike of crowds.* **2** *nc* a thing against which one has strong feelings: *He has few real dislikes.*

take a dislike to to begin to dislike (someone or something): *The boss was friendly at first, but he has taken a dislike to me now.*

dislocate ['disləkeit, (*Amer*) -lou-] *vt* (*formal or tech*) to put (a bone) out of joint; to displace: *She dislocated her hip when she fell.* **ˌdislo'cation** *nu.*

dislodge [dis'lodʒ] (*formal*) *vt* **1** to drive from a place of rest, hiding or defence: *The enemy troops were finally dislodged from the town.* **2** to knock accidentally out of place: *He dislodged a stone from the wall while climbing over.*

disloyal [dis'loiəl] (*formal*) *adj* unfaithful or not loyal: *I didn't expect him to be so disloyal to his friends*; *disloyal feelings.* **dis'loyally** *adv.* **dis'loyalty** *nu.*

dismal ['dizməl] *adj* gloomy and not cheerful: *I've never seen anyone look as dismal as she did about such a small problem*; *Isn't it a dismal day?* **'dismally** *adv.*

dismantle [dis'mantl] *vt* (*formal*) to pull down or take to pieces: *The wardrobe was so large we had to dismantle it to get it down the stairs.*

dismay [dis'mei] *vt* to make (a person) anxious, discouraged and afraid: *We were dismayed by the violence of his reaction.* – *nu* the state of being anxious, discouraged and afraid: *We watched his actions with horrified dismay.*

dismember [dis'membə] *vt* (*rare*) to tear to pieces, *esp* to tear the limbs from: *The hungry lion dismembered the antelope*; *The murderer dismembered his victim and threw the pieces into the ravine.*

dismiss [dis'mis] *vt* **1** (*formal*) to send or put away: *She dismissed him with a wave of the hand*; *Dismiss* *the idea from your mind!* **2** (*more formal than* **sack**) to remove from office or employment: *He was dismissed from his post for being lazy.* **3** to stop or close (a law-suit *etc*): *Case dismissed!*

dis'missal *ncu* the act of dismissing or being dismissed: *His dismissal was very unexpected as he always worked hard.*

dismount [dis'maunt] *vi* (*formal*) get off a horse, bicycle *etc*: *He dismounted and pushed his bicycle up the hill.*

disobey [disə'bei] *vt* to fail or refuse to do what is commanded: *He disobeyed my orders not to go into the road; He disobeyed his mother.*

ˌdiso'bedience [-'bi:djəns] *nu* the act of failing or refusing to obey: *You must be punished for your disobedience!*

ˌdiso'bedient [-'bi:djənt] *adj* failing or refusing to obey: *a disobedient child; I shall be angry if you are disobedient.* **ˌdiso'bediently** *adv.*

disobliging [disə'blaidʒiŋ] *adj* (*formal*) unwilling to consider or to carry out the wishes of other people: *I asked her to help, but she was in her most disobliging mood and refused; She can be very disobliging at times.*

See also **oblige**.

disorder [dis'o:də] **1** *nu* (*formal*) lack of order; confusion or disturbance: *The strike threw the whole country into disorder; The demonstration was accompanied by scenes of disorder and rioting.* **2** *nc* (*formal or tech*) a disease: *disorders of the lungs.* – *vt* (*formal*) to throw out of order: *She disordered the whole system by making several mistakes.*

dis'orderly *adj* (*formal*) **1** (*attrib*) not neatly arranged; in confusion: *Clothes lay about the floor in a disorderly fashion.* **2** lawless; causing trouble: *a disorderly group of people; He was charged with being drunk and disorderly.*

disorganized, -s- [dis'o:gənaizd] *adj* in confusion or not organized: *She's the most disorganized person I know; The meeting was very disorganized.* **disˌorgani'zation, -s-** *nu.*

See also **organize**.

disown [dis'oun] *vt* (*formal*) to refuse to acknowledge as belonging to oneself: *She disowned her son when he was sent to prison.*

disparage [di'sparidʒ] *vt* (*formal*) to speak of as being of little value or importance: *He disparaged his wife's skill as a gardener; Do not disparage his achievements.*

di'sparagement *nu* (*formal*) the act of disparaging: *She spoke of his work with disparagement.* **di'sparagingly** *adv.*

disparity [dis'parəti] *ncu* (*formal*) inequality or difference (in age, amount *etc*): *There is some disparity between their ages.*

dispassionate [dis'paʃənət] *adj* (*formal*) **1** (*usu attrib*) favouring no-one: *a dispassionate observer.* **2** showing coolness and calm judgement: *a dispassionate statement of the difficulties; He was quite dispassionate about the whole affair.* **dis'passionately** *adv.*

dispatch, despatch [di'spatʃ] *vt* **1** (*formal*) to send off (a messenger *etc*): *He dispatched several letters asking for financial help.* **2** (*formal*) to finish off or deal with quickly: *She dispatched several pieces of business in quick succession.* **3** (*old*) to kill: *The musketeer dispatched the scoundrel with his sword.* – **1** *nc* a written official report: *a dispatch from the front line; a dispatch sent to a newspaper from its correspondent.* **2** *nc* (*formal*) an act of sending away: *the dispatch of a letter.* **3** *nu* (*formal*) haste: *They acted with dispatch.* **4** *n* (with cap) a word often used in the titles of newspapers: *the Baberton Dispatch.*

di'spatches *n pl* (*formal*) official papers, *esp military or diplomatic: He was mentioned in dispatches.*

di'spatch box *nc* a box for holding dispatches or valuable papers.

di'spatch rider *nc* a carrier of military dispatches by motor-cycle.

dispel [di'spel] – *pt, ptp* **di'spelled** – *vt* (*formal*) to drive away or make disappear: *His words dispelled her fears.*

dispense [di'spens] **1** *vt* (*formal*) to give or deal out: *He dispensed money to the poor; The judge had dispensed justice in the same court for over twenty years;* (*facet*) *The hostess dispensed cakes with her usual charm.* **2** *vti* to prepare (medicines, *esp* prescriptions) for giving out: *The pharmacist dispensed the prescription with great care.* – *See also* **dispense with** *below.*

di'spensary *nc* a place *esp* in a hospital where medicines are given out: *In this hospital, the dispensary is on the ground floor.*

ˌdispen'sation [dispen-] *ncu* (*formal*) (a licence *etc* giving) special leave to break a rule *etc*, *esp* of the Church: *by dispensation of the bishop; Dispensations were freely granted at that time.*

di'spenser *nc* **1** a person who dispenses, *esp* medicines. **2** a machine which dispenses: *a soap-dispenser.*

di'spense with *vt fus* (*formal*) to get rid of or do without: *We could economize by dispensing with two assistants; As our deep-freeze was uneconomical, we dispensed with it.*

disperse [di'spə:s] *vti* (*formal*) **1** to (cause to) scatter in all directions: *The seeds of this tree are dispersed by the wind.* **2** to (cause to) spread (news *etc*): *Information is dispersed by volunteers who distribute leaflets.* **3** to (cause to) vanish: *By this time the crowd had dispersed; We used electric fans to disperse the smoke.*

di'spersal *nu* (*formal*) the act or result of dispersing: *Strong winds caused the widespread dispersal of dandelion seeds last year; Mounted police helped in the dispersal of the crowd.*

dispirited [di'spiritid] *adj* (*formal*) sad and discouraged: *He looked tired and dispirited; She gave a dispirited sigh.*

displace [dis'pleis] *vt* (*formal*) **1** to disarrange or put out of place: *Some of the objects on the table had been displaced by the thief.* **2** to take the place of: *The dog had displaced her doll in the little girl's affections.*

dis'placement *nu* **1** the quantity of water, gas *etc*, moved out of a place by an object, *esp* a ship *etc* when floating: *a liner with a displacement of 2 000 tonnes.* **2** (*formal*) a putting or being out of place: *She suffered a great deal of pain from the displacement of a joint.*

ˌdisplaced 'person *nc* a person forced to leave his own country as a result of war, his political opinions *etc.*

display [di'splei] *vt* **1** to set out for show: *The china was displayed in a special cabinet.* **2** (*formal*) to show: *He displayed remarkable tact when his mother-in-law came to visit; She displayed a talent for mimicry.* – **1** *ncu* (an) act of showing or making clear: *a display of power/strength.* **2** *nc* an entertainment *etc* intended to show the ability *etc* of those taking part: *a dancing display; a military* *display.* **3** *nc* something which shows or sets out something else: *an advertising display.*

displease [dis'pli:z] *vt* (*formal*) to offend or annoy: *The children's behaviour displeased their father.*

dis'pleased *adj* (*formal*) annoyed: *She was displeased with him for being late; I was displeased at her rudeness; She gave the noisy child a displeased look.*

displeasure [dis'pleʒə] *nu* (*formal*) annoyance or disapproval: *She showed her displeasure by leaving at once.*

dispose [di'spouz] *vt* (*formal*) **1** to make inclined: *I am not disposed to help him.* **2** to arrange or settle: *He refused to rest until things were disposed as he wanted them.*

di'sposable *adj* intended to be thrown away or destroyed after use: *We used disposable cups so as to reduce the amount of washing-up we had to do; Are the plates disposable?*

di'sposal *nu* (*formal*) the act of getting rid of something: *We shall have to make arrangements for the disposal of waste paper.* – *See also* **at one's disposal** *below.*

di'sposed *adj* (*pred*: *formal*) inclined: *I'm not disposed to believe you.* – *See* **well-, ill-disposed** *below.*

at one's disposal available for one's use: *They put a car at his disposal during his stay; It's terrible that with all the facilities at his disposal he can't find anything to do.*

di'spose of *vt fus* (*formal or facet*) to get rid of: *He disposed of the arguments against his plan in two sentences; I've disposed of your old coat by giving it to a jumble sale.*

ˌwell-, ˌill-di'sposed (*formal*) having kind or unkind feelings (towards): *He is well-/ill-disposed towards his neighbours.*

See also **indisposed, indisposition.**

disposition [dispə'ziʃən] **1** *nc* nature; personality: *The child has a naturally placid disposition.* **2** *ncu* (*formal*) (an) arrangement: *He studies the disposition of the firm's warehouses across the country; the disposition of the battalions on the field of battle.* **3** *nc* (*legal*) a giving over of (property *etc*) to another: *He made a disposition in favour of his brother.*

dispossess [dispə'zes] *vt* (*formal*) to take (property) away from: *He was dispossessed of all his lands after the uprising.*

disproportionate [disprə'po:ʃənət] *adj* (*formal*: *often with* **to**) too large or too small in relation to something else: *The amount of money spent on the machine was disproportionate to its usefulness; A disproportionate part of our holiday was spent on travelling.*

ˌdispro'portionately *adv*: *Dinosaurs were enormous, with disproportionately small brains.*

See also **proportion.**

disprove [dis'pru:v] *vt* (*formal*) to prove to be false or wrong: *His arguments have been disproved by modern scientific research.*

dispute [di'spju:t] **1** *vt* to argue against or deny: *I'm not disputing the truth of what you say.* **2** *vti* (*more formal than* **argue**) to argue (about): *They disputed the ownership of the land for years.* – *ncu* (an) argument or quarrel: *Nothing is ever arranged here without dispute; Pay disputes upset production schedules.*

di'sputable *adj* (*formal*) able to be argued about: *Whether this change was an improvement is disputable; That is a disputable point.*

ˌdispu'tation *nc* (*formal*) an argument, *esp* a formal one.

See also **indisputable.**

disqualify [dis'kwolifai] *vt* **1** to put out of a competition *etc* for breaking rules: *She was disqualified for being too young.* **2** to make unfit for some purpose: *His colour-blindness disqualified him from joining the Air Force.*

disˌqualifi'cation [-fi-] **1** *nu* an instance of being disqualified: *He disputed the reason for his disqualification from the competition.* **2** *nc* something which disqualifies: *Her age was a disqualification to membership of the club.*

disquiet [dis'kwaiət] *nu* (*formal*) uneasiness or anxiety: *She could sense a feeling of disquiet in the crowd.* – *vt* (*formal*) to worry or make uneasy: *Her unusual silence disquieted him.*

disregard [disrə'ga:d] *vt* (*formal*) to ignore or pay no attention to: *He consistently disregards my warnings.* – *nu* (*formal*) lack of attention or neglect: *He has a complete disregard for my feelings; His disregard for the rules led to his disqualification.*

disrepair [disrə'peə] *nu* (*formal*) the state of needing repair: *I'm afraid the old family house has fallen into disrepair.*

disrepute [disrə'pju:t] *nu* (*formal*) bad reputation: *He has brought the family into disrepute.*

dis'reputable [-'repju-] *adj* **1** not respectable, *esp* in appearance: *a disreputable old coat; He always looks rather disreputable.* **2** (*usu attrib*) of bad reputation: *He's rather a disreputable character, I'm afraid.*

disrespect [disrə'spekt] *nu* (*formal*) rudeness or lack of respect: *He spoke of his parents with surprising disrespect.*

ˌdisre'spectful *adj* (*formal*) showing disrespect: *He gave his father a disrespectful look; She has always been disrespectful to older people.*

ˌdisre'spectfully *adv.*

disrupt [dis'rʌpt] *vt* (*formal*) to break up or put into a state of disorder: *He disrupted the meeting by shouting abuse; Traffic was disrupted by floods.*

dis'ruption [-ʃən] *nu.*

dis'ruptive [-tiv] *adj* (*formal*) breaking up or causing disorder: *He has a disruptive influence on the class; His appearance at the meeting was disruptive.*

dissatisfy [di'satisfai] *vt* to fail to satisfy or to displease: *The teacher was dissatisfied with the pupil's behaviour.* **disˌsatis'faction** [-'fakʃən] *nu.*

dissect [di'sekt] *vt* **1** (*tech*) to cut into parts for (scientific) examination: *This morning the anatomy class dissected an arm.* **2** (*fig formal*) to study and criticize (*eg* a man's character or motives): *He dissected our handling of the situation point by point, indicating where we had made mistakes.* **dis'section** [-ʃən] *nu.*

dissemble [di'sembl] *vti* (*formal*) to act so as to disguise (one's true feelings): *She dissembled when asked her opinion on the subject.*

disseminate [di'semineit] *vt* (*very formal*) to scatter or spread around: *The agency's main function was to disseminate information.* **disˌsemi'nation** *nu.*

dissent [di'sent] *nu* (*formal*) disagreement: *There was a murmur of dissent.* – *vi* (*formal*) **1** to have a different opinion (*esp* from those of the church established by law): *I'm afraid this is where I dissent from the general opinion.* **2** to refuse to agree: *Only three members of the committee dissented.*

dis'sension [-ʃən] *nu* (*formal*) disagreement: *The proposal caused a great deal of dissension among the committee.*

dis'senter *nc* (*relig*) a member of a sect which has broken away from an established church.

See also **assent**.

dissertation [disə'teiʃən] *nc* a long formal talk or piece of writing (for a university degree *etc*): *She gave a long dissertation on the evils of smoking*; *The dissertation he wrote was long enough to be called a thesis.*

disservice [dis'sə:vis] *nc* (*formal*) an injury; an action which is not helpful: *She did her son a disservice by doing his homework for him.*

dissident ['disidənt] *nc* (*formal*) a person who disagrees, *esp* with a ruling group or form of government: *a demonstration by a large number of dissidents*; (*attrib*) *dissident voices.* **'dissidence** *nu.*

dissimilar [di'similə] *adj* (*formal*: *often in neg*) unlike or unalike: *The two cases are not dissimilar*; *The sisters have very dissimilar characters.* **dis,simi'larity** [-'la-] *ncu.*

dissimulate [di'simjuleit] *vti* (*formal*) to conceal or disguise (one's feelings *etc*): *He suspected that she was dissimulating so as not to shock him by revealing her real opinions.* **dis,simu'lation** *nu.*

dissipate ['disipeit] *vt* (*formal*) **1** to cause (fog, fears *etc*) to disappear: *The sun gradually dissipated the mist*; *Her doubts were dissipated by his confidence in her.* **2** to use up carelessly or waste: *He had dissipated his fortune by the age of twenty-five.*

'dissipated *adj* (*formal*) having wasted one's energy on too much drinking and other pleasures: *a dissipated young man*; *Their son returned from London, dissipated and penniless.*

,dissi'pation *nu* (*formal*) **1** the act of causing to disappear or of disappearing: *the dissipation of our fears.* **2** wasteful spending (of money, energy *etc*): *dissipation of valuable resources.* **3** the act of becoming, or the state of being, dissipated: *a life of dissipation.*

dissociate [di'sousieit] (*formal*) **1** *vt* to separate, *esp* in thought: *I can never dissociate him in my mind from the circumstances in which we met.* **2** *v refl* (*also* **,disas'sociate** [disə'sousieit]: *with* **from**) not to be associated with or to give one's support to: *I'm dissociating/disassociating myself completely from their actions.*

dissolute ['disəlu:t] *adj* (*formal*) bad or immoral: *dissolute behaviour*; *He has become dissolute and quite irresponsible.* **'dissoluteness** *nu.*

dissolution *see* **dissolve**.

dissolve [di'zolv] **1** *vti* to (cause to) melt or break up, *esp* by putting in a liquid: *He dissolved the pills in water*; *The pills dissolved easily in water.* **2** *vt* (*formal*) to put an end to (a parliament, a marriage *etc*).

dissolution [disə'lu:ʃən] *nu* (*formal*) an act or instance of dissolving: *the dissolution of Parliament.*

dissonance ['disənəns] **1** *ncu* (*music*) (a) discord, *esp* used in music deliberately: *That composer uses dissonance extensively*; *The dissonances in his music were very effective.* **2** *nu* (*formal*) disagreement: *Dissonance marred the discussions.*

'dissonant *adj* (*usu attrib*) not harmonious; forming a discord; not in agreement: *a dissonant chord*; (*formal*) *a dissonant meeting.*

dissuade [di'sweid] *vt* (*formal*) to stop (from doing something) by advice or persuasion: *I tried to dissuade him from what I felt to be a foolish course of action.* **dis'suasion** [-ʒən] *nu.*

See also **persuade**.

distance ['distəns] **1** *ncu* the space between things, places *etc*, *esp* if large: *Some of the children have quite long distances to walk on their way to school*; *We have quite a distance to walk to the bus stop*; *It is sometimes difficult to judge distance when driving at night*; *What's the distance from here to London?* **2** *nu* a far-off place or point: *We could just see the town in the distance*; *He disappeared into the distance*; *Your dress looks all right at a distance* (= when not too near). **3** *nu* (*formal*) coldness of manner: *There was more distance in his manner than before.*

'distant *adj* **1** far away or far apart, in place or time: *the distant past*; *a distant country*; (*formal*) *We live many miles distant from one another.* **2** (*attrib*) not close: *a distant relation.* **3** cold in manner and not friendly: *Her manner was rather distant*; *She replied in a rather distant voice.*

distaste [dis'teist] *nu* (*formal*) dislike (of something unpleasant or unattractive): *She looked at the untidy room with distaste.*

dis'tasteful *adj* (*formal*) disagreeable and unpleasant: *The whole subject is distasteful to me*; *a distasteful job.* **dis'tastefully** *adv.* **dis'tastefulness** *nu.*

See also **tasteful**.

distemper[1] [di'stempə] *nu* a disease affecting young dogs.

distemper[2] [di'stempə] *nu* a kind of paint *usu* used on walls. – *vt* to paint with distemper.

distend [di'stend] *vti* (*formal or tech*) to stretch outwards: *The animal's stomach was distended*; *Her cheeks distended with the effort of blowing.*

distil, (*Amer*) **distill** [di'stil] – *pt*, *ptp* **di'stilled** – *vt* **1** to get (a liquid) in a pure state by heating to steam or a vapour and cooling again. **2** to obtain alcoholic spirit from anything by this method: *Whisky is distilled from barley.* **,distil'lation** *nu.*

di'stiller *nc* a person or firm that distils and makes spirits: *a firm of whisky-distillers.*

di'stillery *nc* a place where distilling (of whisky, brandy *etc*) is carried on.

distinct [di'stiŋkt] *adj* **1** easily seen, heard or noticed: *There are distinct differences between the two*; *distinct handwriting*; *Her voice is very distinct*; *There was a distinct coldness in her reply.* **2** separate or different: *We employ three distinct types of people*; *Those two birds are quite distinct – you couldn't confuse them.*

di'stinctly *adv* **1** clearly or in a distinct manner: *He pronounces his words very distinctly.* **2** certainly or without doubt: *I distinctly heard him tell you to wait!*; *She looked distinctly ill.* **di'stinctness** *nu.*

di'stinction [-ʃən] **1** *ncu* (*formal*) (the making of) a difference: *He makes no distinction between professional and manual workers*; *What is the distinction between the two cases?*; *He chose children to act in the play without distinction of sex or age.* **2** *nu* outstanding ability or achievement: *She passed her exams with distinction*; (*formal*) *His books are quite without distinction.* **3** *nc* a mark of honour: *As a special distinction he was allowed to go first*; *military/academic distinctions.*

di'stinctive [-tiv] *adj* (*formal*) different and easily identified: *I recognized her from a long way*

off – she has a very distinctive walk; *Her appearance is certainly distinctive!* **di'stinctively** *adv*.
See also **indistinct**.

distinguish [di'stiŋgwiʃ] 1 *vt* (*formal*: *often with* **from**) to mark as different: *What distinguishes this café from all the others?* 2 *vt* (*formal*) to identify, make out or recognize: *He could just distinguish the figure of a man running away.* 3 *vi* (*formal*: *usu with* **between**) to recognize a difference between: *I can't distinguish between the two types – they both look the same to me.* 4 *v refl* (*formal or facet*) to gain distinction: *He distinguished himself at school by winning a prize in every subject.* **di'stinguishable** *adj*.
di'stinguished *adj* famous or outstanding: *He is a very distinguished scientist*; *She is very distinguished.*
See also **undistinguished, indistinguishable**.

distort [di'sto:t] (*formal*) 1 *vti* to make or become twisted out of shape: *Her face was distorted with pain*; *Metal distorts under stress*; (*fig*) *He had a habit of distorting the truth.* 2 *vt* to make (sound) indistinct and unnatural: *There's something wrong with my radio – it distorts the sound very badly.*
di'stortion [-ʃən] (*formal*) 1 *nu* the act or result of distorting: *The distortion of the trees was caused by the strong wind.* 2 *nc* something which distorts: *What she told you was a distortion of the truth.*

distract [di'strakt] *vt* to draw aside (the mind or attention of): *He was constantly being distracted from his work by what was happening outside.*
di'stracted *adj* 1 (*pred*) turned aside (from what one is doing or thinking): *He had slipped out while her attention was distracted.* 2 (*formal*) out of one's mind; mad: *The noise of those machines is driving me distracted!*; *a distracted old woman.* 3 (*formal*) troubled or confused; distressed: *She sounded a bit distracted on the phone so I thought she might need some help*; *The distracted mother couldn't reach her child in the burning house.*
di'straction [-ʃən] 1 *nc* something that takes the mind off other *esp* more serious affairs: *There are too many distractions here to allow one to work properly*; *Knitting and playing the piano were the old lady's only distractions.* 2 *nu* (*formal*) anxiety and confusion: *She phoned in some distraction to ask what she should do.*

distraught [di'stro:t] *adj* (*formal*) very agitated or worried: *I'm concerned about her – she looked distraught when I saw her*; *The distraught mother ran out of the burning house with the child in her arms.*

distress [di'stres] (*formal*) 1 *nu* great sorrow, trouble or pain: *She was in great distress over his disappearance*; *Is your leg causing you any distress?*; *The loss of all their money left the family in acute distress.* 2 *nc* a cause of sorrow: *My inability to draw has always been a distress to me.* – *vt* to cause pain or sorrow to: *I'm distressed by your lack of interest.* **di'stressing** *adj*. **di'stressingly** *adv*.

distribute [di'stribjut] *vt* 1 to divide (something) among several (people); to deal out: *He distributed sweets to all the children in the class*; *She was there to distribute leaflets to the crowd.* 2 to spread out widely: *Our shops are distributed all over the city.*
ˌdistri'bution [-'bju:-] *nu* (*formal*) 1 the process of being distributed: *the distribution of mail.* 2 the situation or location of objects *etc*: *He asked about the distribution of hospitals in that town.*

district ['distrikt] *nc* 1 an area of a country, town *etc*: *He lives in a poor district of London*; *Public transport is often infrequent in country districts*; (*attrib*) *a district nurse.* 2 in the UK, the smaller of the two main administrative units of local government: *Edinburgh District*; *There are several districts in a county or region*; (*attrib*) *a district council.*
See also **county, region**.

distrust [dis'trʌst] *nu* (*formal*) suspicion; lack of trust or faith: *He has always had a distrust of aeroplanes*; *How did he earn your distrust?* – *vt* (*formal*) to have no trust in: *He distrusts his own judgement.* **dis'trustful** *adj*. **dis'trustfully** *adv*. **dis'trustfulness** *nu*.

disturb [di'stə:b] *vt* 1 to interrupt or take attention away from: *I'm sorry, am I disturbing you?* 2 to worry or make anxious: *This news has disturbed me very much.* 3 to stir up or throw into confusion: *A violent storm disturbed the surface of the lake.*
di'sturbance 1 *nc* a noisy or disorderly happening: *He was thrown out of the meeting for causing a disturbance.* 2 *nc* an interruption: *I've done quite a lot of work, despite several disturbances.* 3 *nu* (*formal*) an act of disturbing: *He was complaining about the disturbance of his papers*; (*legal*) *He was arrested for disturbance of the peace.*

disuse [dis'ju:s] *nu* (*formal*: *usu with* **into**) the state of not being used: *The canal gradually fell into disuse.*
dis'used [-'ju:zd] *adj* no longer used: *a disused warehouse*; *Those old buildings are now disused.*
See also **abuse, misuse**.

ditch [ditʃ] *nc* a long narrow hollow dug in the ground *esp* one to drain water from a field, road *etc*: *He climbed over the fence and fell into a ditch.* – *vt* (*sl*) to get rid of: *The stolen car had been ditched by the thieves several miles away*; *He ditched the girl after going out with her for only three months.*
dull as ditchwater *see* **dull**.

dither ['diðə] *vi* (*inf*) 1 to hesitate or be uncertain: *I'm still dithering about what to do.* 2 (*usu derog*) to act in a nervous, uncertain manner: *I wish you'd stop dithering (about)!* – *nu* (*fig inf*) a state of indecision or nervousness: *She's all in/of a dither about her visitors coming.*

ditto ['ditou] (*often abbrev* **do** *when written*) *pron* the same thing: *Three pencils at 5p, ditto at 6p = 33p.* – *adv* (*inf*) likewise; the same: *Mrs Jones has had three days off this month – Mrs Brown ditto*; *Mrs Jones is sick – ditto Mrs Brown.*

ditty ['diti] *nc* (*often facet*) a simple little song: *He never imagined that his simple ditty would become a popular song.*

divan [di'van, (*Amer*) 'daivan] *nc* a long, low couch without back or arms, *usu* able to be used as a bed.
divan bed *nc* a type of bed without a fixed board at the head or foot.

dive [daiv] – *pt, ptp* **dived**, (*Amer*) **dove** [douv] – *vi* 1 to plunge headfirst into water or down through the air: *He dived off a rock into the sea*; *The eagle dived on its victim.* 2 (*loosely*) to go quickly and suddenly out of sight: *She dived down a back street and into a shop.* – *nc* 1 an act of diving: *She made/did a beautiful dive into the deep end of the pool.* 2 (*sl*) a place for drinking *etc*, *usu* not respectable and often underground.
'diver *nc* a person who dives, *esp* one who works under water using special breathing equipment.

diverge [dai'və:dʒ] *vi* (*formal*) 1 to separate and go in different directions: *The roads diverge three kilometres further on.* 2 to differ (from someone or something else); to go away (from a standard): *This is where our opinions on the subject begin to* *diverge*; *On this matter he diverged from the views of his colleagues.* **di'vergence** *nu.*

di'vergent *adj* (*formal*) differing (from one another or from a standard): *divergent opinions*; *Their ideas are somewhat divergent.*

See also **converge**.

diverse [dai'və:s] *adj* (*formal*) different; of various kinds: *We have received help from diverse sources*; *The firm's interests are diverse.* **di'versely** *adv.* **di'verseness** *nu.*

di'versify [-fai] *vti* to make or become varied or different: *The firm has recently diversified* (*the range of goods which it sells*).

di'versity *nu* (*formal*) the state of being of various kinds: *an amazing diversity of detail.*

diversion [dai'və:ʃən, (*Amer*) -ʒən] **1** *nc* an alteration to a traffic route: *There's a diversion at the end of the road.* **2** *ncu* (an act of) diverting: *He created a diversion while I slipped out, so that no-one noticed me.* **3** *ncu* (*formal*) (an) amusement: *They organized many picnics and similar diversions.*

diversity *see* **diverse**.

divert [dai'və:t] *vt* **1** to cause to turn aside or change direction: *Traffic had to be diverted because of the accident*; (*fig*) *She diverted her energies to organizing the move.* **2** (*formal*) to amuse: *The child was diverted by the antics of the clown.*

di'verting *adj* (*formal*) amusing.

divest [dai'vest] *vt* (*formal*) to strip or deprive (of anything): *He was divested of all his titles and positions.*

divide [di'vaid] **1** *vti* to separate into parts or groups: *The wall divided the garden in two*; *The group divided into three when we got off the bus*; (*fig*) *We are divided* (= We do not agree) *as to where to spend our holidays.* **2** *vt* (*with* **between** *or* **among**) to share: *We divided the sweets between us*; *He gave the job his undivided attention* (= He concentrated on what he was doing). **3** *vti* (*math*) to find out how many times one number contains another: *I worked out the answer by dividing X by Y*; *6 divided by 2 equals 3*; *Although she is good at adding she always divides wrongly.* – *nc* (*formal*) a split or division: *There is now a great divide between the two parties.*

di'viders *n pl* a measuring instrument used in geometry.

divisible [di'vizəbl] *adj* (*usu pred*: *formal*) able to be divided: *100 is divisible by 4.*

division [di'viʒən] **1** *ncu* (an) act of dividing: *We made a division of the profits.* **2** *nc* a barrier; something that divides or separates: *a division between two parts of the garden.* **3** *nc* a part or section (of an army *etc*): *He belongs to B division of the local police force*; *Contact our electrical goods division – I'll give you their telephone number.* **4** *ncu* (a) separation: *a division of responsibility/interests.* **5** *nu* (*math*) the finding of how many times one number is contained in another: *I hated division when I was at school.*

divisional [di'viʒənl] *adj* (*attrib*) of or making a division: (*formal*) *a divisional line*; *The soldier contacted divisional headquarters.*

di'visive [-siv] *adj* (*formal*) tending to divide (people or things): *divisive policies*; *Such a decision would be very divisive in its effect.*

See also **indivisible**.

dividend ['dividend] *nc* the interest paid on shares *etc*: *a dividend of 2%* (= two per cent).

divine [di'vain] *adj* **1** of or belonging to God or a god: *divine wisdom.* **2** (*inf*) very good or excellent: *What divine weather!* – *nc* (*old*) a clergyman. – *vt* (*very formal*) to notice or find out by keen understanding or insight: *I divined the truth by a combination of guesswork and inside information.*

ˌdivi'nation [divi-] *nu.*

di'viner *nc* a person who has or claims a special ability to find hidden water or metals.

di'vining *nu* (*usu in cmpds*) discovering the presence of underground water, metal *etc* by holding a device (a **di'vining-rod**) which moves when held directly above the water *etc*: *water-divining.*

di'vinity [-'vi-] **1** *nu* the study of the nature of God; religious studies in general. **2** *nc* a god or goddess: *The Ancient Greeks worshipped many divinities.* **3** *nu* the state of being divine: *the divinity of God.*

divisible, division *etc see* **divide**.

divorce [di'vo:s] **1** *ncu* the legal ending of a marriage: *Divorce is becoming more common nowadays*; *There have been several divorces in that family.* **2** *nc* (*formal*) a complete separation: *A divorce of the musical from the dramatic activities of the club would be very unwise.* – *vt* **1** to end one's marriage (with): *He's divorcing her for desertion*; *They were divorced two years ago.* **2** (*formal*) to separate: *I am unable to divorce the two concepts in my mind.*

di'vorced *adj* **1** having ended one's marriage: *Are you single, married or divorced?*; *a divorced person.* **2** (*formal*: *with* **from**) completely cut off from: *divorced from reality.*

diˌvor'cee *nc* a divorced person: *He/She is going to marry a divorcee.*

divulge [dai'vʌldʒ] *vt* (*formal*) to let out or make known (a secret *etc*): *She divulged her fears about the future to him.*

dizzy ['dizi] *adj* **1** (*usu pred*) giddy or confused: *If you spin round and round like that, you'll make yourself dizzy.* **2** (*usu attrib*: *inf*) silly; unreliable: *a dizzy young girl.* **3** (*attrib*) causing dizziness: *dizzy heights.* **'dizzily** *adv.* **'dizziness** *nu.*

do[1] [du:] – *3rd pers sing prt* **does** [dʌz]: *pt* **did** [did]: *ptp* **done** [dʌn]: *neg short forms* **don't** [dount], **doesn't** ['dʌznt], **didn't** ['didnt] – *aux* **1** used with a more important verb in questions and negative statements: *Do you smoke?*; *I don't know him*; **2** used with a more important verb for emphasis: *I do think you should let him know where you are*; *I did see him, although for a time I thought I wasn't going to.* **3** used to avoid repeating a verb which comes immediately before: *I thought she wouldn't come, but she did*; *'Did you tell him?' 'Yes, I did.'* **4** (*formal*) used with a more important verb in inverted grammatical constructions after **seldom, rarely** and **little**: *Seldom/Rarely do we meet without quarrelling*; *Little did he know what was in store for him.* – **1** *vt* to carry out or perform: *Go on – do something!*; *What shall I do?*; *That was a terrible thing to do to her.* **2** *vt* to manage to finish or complete: *When you've done that, you can start on something else*; *I can only do half of this crossword*; *We did a hundred kilometres in just under an hour.* **3** *vt* to perform some obvious action concerning: *to do the washing/the cooking*; *to do the garden/the windows/the silver.* **4** *vti* (*inf*) to be (just) enough for (a purpose): *Will this piece of fish do two of us?*; *Shall I make some more or will that do?*; *If you drop me at the corner, it'll do nicely.* **5** *vti* to be suitable or able to be used (for a purpose): *Do you want me to look for a blue one or will a pink one do?*; *Will next*

Saturday do for our next meeting? **6** *vt* to work at or study: *She's doing sums; He's at university doing science; I'm doing some research on General de Gaulle.* **7** *vi* to manage or prosper: *How's your wife doing?; She was very ill, but she's doing better now; Umbrella makers are doing badly because of the lack of rain.* **8** *vt* to put in order or arrange in an attractive and desirable form: *She's doing her hair; Who did the flowers?* **9** *vi* to act or behave: *Why don't you do as we do?* **10** *vt* (*often formal*) to give or show (*usu* publicly) by one's actions *etc*: *The whole town gathered to do him honour; His sentiments do him no credit at all.* **11** *vt* to cause: *What damage did the storm do?; It won't do him any harm.* **12** *vt* (*inf*) to swindle or cheat: *I had the uneasy feeling that I was being done; That butcher did me – the meat was underweight.* **13** *vt* (*inf*) to spend (time) in prison: *He's done six years for assault.* **14** *vt* (*inf*) to see everything and visit everything in: *They tried to do London in four days.* – *n* – *pl* **do's** – *nc* (*inf*) an affair or a festivity, *esp* a party: *The firm is having some sort of a do for Christmas; Was their wedding a big do?* – *See also* **do's and don'ts** *below.*

'**doer** *nc* (*rare*) a person who does something: *an evildoer; a doer of good deeds; He is a doer rather than a thinker.*

'**doing** *nc* (*sl*) a beating or other unkind treatment: *to give someone a doing.*

'**doings** *n* **1** *pl* the things which a person does: *He tells me about all your doings.* **2** *sing* (*inf*) the thing which is wanted or needed and whose name one cannot remember: *Where's the doings to open this with?*

done [dʌn] *adj* **1** (*pred*) finished or complete: *That's that job done at last.* **2** (*pred*) (of food) completely cooked and ready to eat: *I don't think the meat is quite done yet.* **3** (*pred*: *inf*) exhausted: *Sit down – you look absolutely done!* **4** (*inf*: *esp in neg*) accepted behaviour: *My dear, such things are just not done!; That is not the done thing!*

ˌ**do-'gooder** *nc* (*derog*) a person who is over-anxious to help people through social reform *etc*: *Poor areas are always full of do-gooders being a nuisance.*

ˌ**do-it-your'self** *nu* the art or practice of doing one's own decorating, the repair of one's house *etc*: *I've just bought a book on do-it-yourself so I can try to tile the bathroom;* (*attrib*) *a do-it-yourself job.*

to-'do (*Brit inf*: *no pl*) a fuss: *There was a tremendous to-do about the missing papers.* – *See also* **to do** *below.*

I, he *etc* **could be doing with/could do with** it would be better if I, he *etc* had or did (something): *I could do with a cup of coffee; This house could be doing with a coat of paint; You could do with a wash.*

do away with *vt fus* **1** to get rid of, *esp* to abolish officially: *They did away with uniforms at that school years ago.* **2** (*fig inf*) to kill, *esp* secretly: *He's afraid someone might try to do away with him.*

do down *vt sep* (*Brit inf*) to cheat or overcome in some way: *He enjoys doing other people down.*

'**do for** *vt fus* **1** (*inf*) to kill or cause the end of: *The coming of television did for the cheap cinemas.* **2** (*inf*) to do housework for: *Mrs Brown comes in twice a week to do for us.* – *See also* **done for** *below.*

do in *vt sep* (*inf*) to kill: *The general opinion about the missing woman was that someone had done her in.* – *See also* **done in** *below.*

'**done for** (*inf*) ruined or about to be killed *etc* without there being any hope of rescue or recovery: *We're done for if we stay here and the bomb goes off; I'm afraid he's done for – she reported him to the police.* – *See also* **do for** *above.*

done in (*inf*) exhausted. – *See also* **do in** *above.*

done with *see* **over and done with** *under* **over**.

do out *vt sep* (*inf*) to clean thoroughly: *I spent the morning doing out the living-room; The room's tidy – I did it out yesterday.*

do out of *vt oblig sep* (*inf*) to prevent from getting, *esp* by using dishonest methods: *He feels that he has been done out of a rise in salary; It's all a plot to do me out of a day's holiday.*

do's and don'ts [dounts] rules or advice for action (*usu* in special circumstances): *If you want to lose weight, I can give you a list of do's and don'ts.*

do well by *vt fus* to act justly or generously towards: *He did well by his son in giving him so much money.*

do to death (*often facet*) to kill: *That kind of play has been done to death!*

do well out of *vt fus* to get profit or advantage from: *I think he did well out of the change of job – he's bought a new car.*

do without **1** *vt fus, vi* to manage without and accept the lack of (something one wants): *We'll just have to do without a phone; A lot of people have to do without in other ways in order to buy a house; If you don't want to come and get one, you can just do without.* **2** *vt fus* (*facet*) to manage better without having: *I can do without your opinion, if you don't mind; We could have done without this little problem!*

make do *see* **make**.

now you've *etc* **done it, that's done it** (*inf*) what you, I *etc* have done will cause something bad or unpleasant to happen: *That's done it! He is bound to realize we were playing a trick on him now.*

to 'do not yet done: *Half of the work is still to do.* – *See also* **to-do** *above.*

to 'do with **1** (*with* **have**) to have social or business dealings with: *I never had anything to do with the neighbours; Our firm has quite a lot to do with yours.* **2** (*with* **have**) to be involved in, *esp* to be (partly) responsible for: *Did you have anything to do with her death?; He had quite a lot to do with the arrangements for the royal visit.* **3** (*with* **have**) to be connected with, *esp* to be caused by: *Has this decision anything to do with what I said yesterday?* **4** (*with* **be** *or* **have**) to be about or concerned with: *This letter is/has to do with Bill's plans for the summer.* **5** (*with* **have**) to be the concern of (*usu in negatives and questions*): *I'm sorry, but that question has nothing to do with me; What has that (got) to do with him?* (= Why is that his concern).

what are you *etc* **doing with** **1** why or how have you *etc* got: *What is she doing with your umbrella – don't you need it?* **2** what action are you *etc* taking about: *What are they doing with the children during the day if they're both working?*

See also **undo**.

do[2] *see* **ditto**.

docile ['dousail, (*Amer*) 'dosl] *adj* (of a person or animal) quiet and easy to manage: *She's a docile child and doesn't argue; That old pony is very docile.*

'**docilely** *adv.* **do'cility** [də'si-] *nu.*

dock[1] [dok] **1** *ncu* a deepened part of a harbour *etc* where ships go for loading, unloading, repair *etc*: *The ship was in dock for three weeks.* **2** *nc* (*usu in pl*) the area surrounding this: *He works down at the docks.* **3** *nc* the box in a law court where the accused person sits or stands. – *vti* to (cause to) enter the deepened part of a harbour and tie up alongside a quay: *The liner docked in Southampton this morning.*

'**docker** *nc* a person who works in the docks.

'**dockyard** *nc* a naval harbour with docks, stores *etc.*

dock[2] [dok] *vt* to cut short or remove part from: *The dog's tail had been docked*; (*inf*) *His wages were docked to pay for the window he had broken.*

docket ['dokit] *nc* a label or note giving the contents of something. – *vt* to attach such a label to: *to docket a consignment of goods.*

dockyard *see* **dock**[1].

doctor ['doktə] *nc* **1** (*with cap, and often abbrev* **Dr** *when written in titles*) (the title of) a person who is trained to treat ill people: *Doctor Davidson*; *You should call the doctor if you are ill.* **2** a doctor's practice: *I'll have to go to the doctor.* **3** (*with cap*: *often abbrev* **Dr** *when written in titles*) (the title of) a person who has gained the highest university degree in any subject. – *vt* **1** to interfere with, *esp* by adding something (harmful) to: *Someone had doctored her drink and she was very ill.* **2** (*often facet*) to treat by giving or taking medicine *etc*: *I'm doctoring my cold with aspirin.*

'**doctorate** [-rət] *nc* the degree of Doctor.

'**doctored** *adj* (*usu pred*) **1** interfered with: *The drink was doctored.* **2** (*esp* of an animal) neutered: *His cat is doctored.*

doctor's *nc* a doctor's practice: *I've got a sore throat so I'm going to the doctor's.*

doctrine ['doktrin] *ncu* (*formal*) a belief or set of beliefs which is taught: *church doctrine*; *It was one of my father's doctrines that pain was good for you.*

doctrinal [dok'trainl] *adj* (*usu attrib*) of or concerning doctrine: *There are doctrinal differences between those two church denominations.*

See also **indoctrinate**.

document ['dokjumənt] *nc* a written statement giving information, proof, evidence *etc*: *She signed several legal documents relating to the sale of her house.* – [dokju'ment] (*formal*) *vt* **1** to supply or provide with documents: *This period of history is remarkably well documented.* **2** to prove by documents: *In this book, the author documents the reaction of various politicians to one crisis.*

ˌ**docu'mentary** [-'men-] *adj* (*attrib*: *formal*) of or found in documents: *documentary evidence.* – *nc* a film, programme *etc* giving information on a certain subject: *a documentary on the political situation in Argentina*; *a documentary about pottery-making.*

dodder ['dodə] *vi* (*inf*) to shake or tremble, *esp* as a result of old age: *The old man doddered down the steps.*

'**doddery** *adj* inclined to tremble and to be unsteady on one's feet: *a doddery old man*; *He has been very doddery since his accident.*

dodge [dodʒ] *vti* to avoid (something) by a sudden and/or clever movement: *She dodged the blow*; *He dodged round the corner out of sight*; (*fig*) *She always manages to dodge the washing-up*; (*fig*) *Politicians are very good at dodging difficult questions.* – *nc* **1** an act of dodging: *He made a quick dodge to avoid the blow.* **2** (*fig inf*) a trick: *You'll never catch him – he knows every dodge there is.*

'**dodgy** *adj* (*sl*) **1** difficult or risky to do or carry out: *I think he's involved in some dodgy business deals*; *Catching the 5.15 train after the meeting will be rather dodgy.* **2** (of a person, organization *etc*) not trustworthy or safe, financially or otherwise: *I think their whole business is a bit dodgy*; *rather a dodgy business.*

doe [dou] *nc* the female of the fallow deer, rabbit, hare *etc.*

doer, does, doesn't *see* **do**[1].

doff [dof] *vt* (*old formal*) to take off (one's hat *etc*): *He doffed his hat to the lady.*

See also **don**[2].

dog [dog] *nc* **1** a domestic, meat-eating animal related to the wolf and fox: (*attrib*) *a dog basket.* **2** (*inf*) a general term for a person: *You lucky dog!*; *He's a bit of a dirty dog.* – *See also* **dog** *in phrases below.* – *adj* (*in cmpds*) (*usu* of members of the dog family) male: *a dog-fox.* – *v* – *pt, ptp* **dogged** – *vt* to follow closely as a dog does: *She dogged his footsteps.*

dogged ['dogid] *adj* (*usu attrib*: *formal*) keeping on at what one is doing in a determined and persistent manner: *I admire him for his dogged, if rather unimaginative, attention to duty.*

'**doggedly** [-gid-] *adv* (*formal*): *He went doggedly on with his work despite the interruptions.* '**doggedness** [-gid-] *nu.*

'**doggy** *adj* **1** (*attrib*) of or concerning dogs: *a doggy smell.* **2** (*attrib*: *inf*) fond of dogs: *a doggy person.* – *nc* a child's word for a dog.

'**dog collar** *nc* (*fig inf*) a close-fitting collar worn by a clergyman.

'**dog-eared** *adj* **1** (of a book) having the pages turned down at the corner: *I discovered several dirty and dog-eared volumes in a cupboard.* **2** (of the pages of a book) turned down at the corner: *Several pages were dog-eared.*

dog-in-the-manger *see* **dog in the manger** *below.*

'**dog-paddle** *nc* (*no pl*) a kind of swimming resembling the way a dog swims.

'**dogsbody** ['dogz-] *nc* someone who is given odd jobs, *esp* unpleasant ones, to do: *She acts as secretary and general dogsbody to the firm.*

ˌ**dog-'tired** *adj* (*pred*) very tired: *I'm dog-tired this morning after sitting up all night in the train.*

dog in the manger someone who tries to prevent another person from having or doing something which he himself does not want or cannot use or do: *He's a real dog in the manger – even though he doesn't have a car he won't let anyone else use his garage*; (*attrib*) *a dog-in-the-manger attitude.*

a dog's breakfast/dinner (*inf*) an untidy mess: *What a dog's breakfast you've made of your homework!*

a 'dog's life (*inf*) a life of misery: *She led a dog's life with her alcoholic husband*; *He led her a dog's life.*

go to the dogs (*inf*) to be ruined, *esp* to ruin oneself: *His business has just gone to the dogs*; *He seems to have gone completely to the dogs and spends all his time in the pub.*

in the 'doghouse (*inf*) in disgrace: *He forgot his wife's birthday, so he's in the doghouse.*

ˌ**not a 'dog's chance** (*inf*) no chance at all: *He hasn't a dog's chance of getting a ticket at this late date.*

the dogs (*inf*) greyhound racing.

dogged *see* **dog**.

doggerel ['dogərəl] *nu* bad poetry: *A lot of his work is just doggerel.*

doggo ['dogou]: **to lie doggo** (*inf often fig*) to

remain in hiding without giving any sign of one's presence.

doggy *see* **dog**.

dogma ['dogmə] *nu* (*formal*) opinions settled or fixed by an authority, *eg* the Church.

dogmatic [dog'matik] *adj* (*formal*) tending to force one's own opinions on other people: *He's very dogmatic on this subject*; *a dogmatic personality*. **dog'matically** *adv*.

'**dogmatism** ['dog-] *nu* (*very formal*) dogmatic manner or attitude.

'**dogmatize, -ise** ['dog-] *vi* (*very formal*) to state one's opinion dogmatically.

doily, doyley ['doili] *nc* a small ornamented mat: *It was a very elegant tea-party and all the cakes had lace doilies under them.*

doing, doings *see* **do**[1].

doldrums ['doldrəmz]: **the doldrums** *n pl* **1** those parts of the ocean near the equator where there is frequently little or no wind. **2** (*fig*) low spirits: *There's no need to get into the doldrums about such an unimportant problem.*

dole [doul] *vt* (*inf*) (*usu with* **out**) to hand or give out shares (of): *She doled him out a plateful of stew*; *He doled out the money.* – *nu* (*inf*) (*with* **the**) payment made by the state to an unemployed person: *He's been on the dole for years.*

doleful ['doulful] *adj* (*formal*) sorrowful or sad: *There was a doleful expression on his face*; *Don't be so doleful – you're going on holiday tomorrow!* '**dolefully** *adv*. '**dolefulness** *nu*.

doll [dol] *nc* **1** a toy in the shape of a small human being: *a china doll.* **2** (*sl*: *esp Amer*) an attractive and fashionable young woman.

dollar ['dolə] *nc* (*usu abbrev* **$** *when written*) the standard unit of currency in several countries, *eg* the US, Canada and Australia: *It costs ten dollars/$10.*

dollop ['doləp] *nc* (*inf*) a lump, *esp* of something soft or semi-liquid: *He put a dollop of jam on the slice of bread.*

dolly ['doli] *nc* a child's word for a doll.

'**dolly-bird** *nc* (*sl*) a fashionable and attractive young girl.

dolphin ['dolfin] *nc* a type of sea-animal about two and a half to three metres long, closely related to the porpoise: *The children watched the dolphins playing in the pool at the zoo.*

dolt [doult] *nc* (*rare*) a dull or stupid person: *Don't be such a dolt – you won't be able to lift that stone yourself.*

domain [də'mein] *nc* **1** (*old*) the lands, large or small, which belong to a person: *He spent some time looking over his whole domain*; *the domain of a king.* **2** (*formal fig*) an area of interest or of knowledge: *That question falls a little outside my domain.*

dome [doum] *nc* a roof shaped like half a ball: *the dome of the cathedral*; (*fig*) *the smooth, pink dome of his bald head.*

domed *adj* (*usu attrib*) having or resembling a dome: *a domed forehead.*

domestic [də'mestik] *adj* **1** (*usu attrib*) of or in the house or home: *a domestic servant*; *This carpet is designed for domestic use.* **2** (*usu attrib*) concerning one's private life, *esp* one's home: *He has his domestic problems, but he doesn't let them interfere with his work.* **3** (of animals) tame and living with or used by people. **4** (*usu attrib*) not foreign: *the Government's domestic policy.* **5** (*loosely*: *pred*) interested in and good at cooking, housework *etc*: *I'm afraid I'm not very domestic – I hate housework.* – *nc* (*old or formal*) a servant in the house.

do'mesticate [-keit] *vt* (*formal*) to make (animals) domestic.

do'mesticated [-keitid] *adj* **1** (of animals) accustomed to living near and being used by people: *Cows and sheep have been domesticated for many thousands of years.* **2** (*formal or facet*) fond of and/or good at doing jobs associated with running a house: *My husband has become very domesticated since I've been ill*; *a domesticated husband.*

do,mesti'cation *nu* (*formal*) (*usu* of animals) the state or process of being domesticated: *The domestication of that breed of cat took hundreds of years.*

domesticity [doume'stisəti] *nu* (*formal*) **1** home life: *The family, as they sat round the fire, made a picture of happy domesticity.* **2** the state or quality of being fond of and good at running a home.

domestic help *ncu* (a person paid to give) assistance with housework *etc*: *She needs some/a domestic help.*

dominant ['dominənt] *adj* ruling; most important or most influential: *the dominant group in society*; *the dominant theme of a speech*; *The theme of nationalism was dominant in his speech.* '**dominance** *nu*.

'**dominate** [-neit] *vti* **1** to have command or influence (over): *The stronger man dominates the weaker.* **2** (*often liter*) to be most strong or most noticeable *etc* (in): *He dominates the history of modern political thought*; *The castle on its rock dominates the town*; *Although the cathedral and the castle are both noticeable, the cathedral dominates.*

,**domi'nation** *nu*.

domineering [domi'niəriŋ] *adj* (*derog*) tending to order people about: *The children suffer from having a domineering mother*; *She can be very domineering.*

dominion [də'minjən] *nu* (*formal*) **1** rule or power: *There was no-one left to challenge his dominion.* **2** (*sometimes with cap*) a self-governing country of the British Commonwealth, *esp* the official title of Canada and New Zealand: *the Dominion of Canada.*

domino ['dominou] – *pl* '**dominoes** – *nc* an oblong piece of wood *etc* marked with spots with which the game of '**dominoes** is played.

don[1] [don] *nc* a lecturer at a university (*usu* Oxford or Cambridge): *The dons were sympathetic to the students' requests.*

don[2] [don] – *pt*, *ptp* **donned** – *vt* (*old or formal*) to put on (a coat *etc*): *He donned his coat before leaving the house.*

See also **doff**.

donate [də'neit, (*Amer*) 'douneit] *vt* to give to a fund *etc*: *He donated £50 to the memorial fund.*

do'nation *nc* a gift of money or goods to a fund or collection: *I've been collecting donations for our annual party for poor children.*

donor ['dounə] *nc* a giver of a gift or (*esp in cmpds*) of a part of the body *etc* used to replace a diseased *etc* part of someone else's body: *The new piano in the hall is the gift of an anonymous donor*; *I would like to be a kidney-donor*; *He is a blood-donor.*

done *see* **do**[1].

donkey ['doŋki] *nc* **1** a domesticated ass, a type of animal with long ears related to the horse but smaller. **2** (*fig*) a stupid person: *Don't be such a donkey!*

'donkey-work *nu* (*inf*) hard, uninteresting work: *We have a computer now, which saves us a lot of donkey-work.*

'donkey's years/ages (*inf*) a very long time: *I haven't seen him in donkey's ages*; *It's donkey's years since I was last there.*

donor *see* **donate**.

don't *see* **do**[1].

doodle ['du:dl] *vi* to make meaningless drawings and scribbles, *usu* while thinking, talking on the telephone *etc*: *I have a habit of doodling on my blotting-paper when I'm thinking.* – *nc* a drawing of this sort: *She has drawn doodles all over my notebook.*

doom [du:m] *nu* fate, *esp* something terrible and final which is about to happen (to one): *The whole place had an atmosphere of doom*; *Once he had decided to stay where he was his doom was inevitable.* – *vt* to condemn; to make certain to come to harm, fail *etc*: *His crippled leg doomed him to long periods of unemployment*; *The plan was doomed by their refusal to give it any financial support.*

doomed *adj* (*usu pred*) destined or certain to fail, die, be destroyed or ruined *etc*: *The project was doomed to failure*; *He was doomed from the moment he first took drugs.*

'doomsday ['du:mz-]: **till 'doomsday** (*inf*: *often with cap*) for an exceedingly long time: *You can sit there till doomsday for all I care!*

door [do:] *nc* **1** the *usu* hinged barrier, *usu* of wood, which closes the entrance of a room, house *etc*: *He knocked loudly on the door*; (*fig*) *The door to success stood open at last.* **2** the entrance itself: *She stood watching them, blocking the door.*

'doorknob *nc* a knob-shaped handle for opening and closing a door.

'doormat *nc* **1** a mat kept in front of the door for people to wipe their feet on. **2** (*fig*) a person whom other people constantly treat without consideration and who never complains about it: *She's been a doormat for so long now I doubt if she'll ever stand up for herself.*

'doorstep *nc* a raised step just outside the door of a house: *She stood on the doorstep and talked for an hour.*

ˌdoor-to-'door *adj* (*usu attrib*), *adv* (of selling, collecting money *etc*) going from one house to another in an area in turn: *a door-to-door salesman*; *We did most of our canvassing for the election door-to-door.*

'doorway *nc* the space usually filled by a door: *The door flew open and there he was, standing in the doorway.*

next door *see* **next**.

on one's doorstep very close to where one lives: *The Welsh mountains are on our doorstep.*

out of doors *see* **out**.

dope [doup] *nu* (*inf*) **1** any drug or drugs: *He was accused of stealing dope from the chemist.* **2** information, *esp* written and *esp* given in advance: *I got a lot of dope on washing-machines when I was thinking of buying one.* – *vt* (*inf*) to drug: *They discovered that the racehorse had been doped.*

'dopey *adj* (*inf*) made stupid (as if) by drugs: *I was still dopey from lack of sleep*; *He's rather a dopey little boy.*

dormant ['do:mənt] *adj* (*formal or tech*) not dead but not active: *a dormant volcano*; *Seeds remain dormant in the earth during winter.*

dormer ['do:mə] *nc* (*also* **dormer window**) a small window sticking out from a sloping roof: *We built two dormers so that we could use the attics as bedrooms.*

dormitory ['do:mitri] *nc* a room used for sleeping in, with many beds.

dorsal ['do:səl] *adj* (*attrib*: *tech*) of the back: *a dorsal fin.*

dose [dous] *nc* **1** the quantity of medicine *etc* to be taken at one time: *It's time you had a dose of cough-mixture.* **2** (*fig*) any unpleasant thing (*esp* an illness) which one is forced to suffer: *He had a nasty dose of flu earlier this month.* – *vt* to give medicine to: *She dosed him with cough-mixture.*

'dosage [-sidʒ] *ncu* (*formal*) the size of, or method of giving, a dose of medicine *etc*: *The dosage of this drug for a child of five is very small.*

doss [dos]: **doss down** *vi* (*sl*) to lie down to sleep in an unusual or temporary place: *I dossed down on his sofa for the night.*

'doss-house *nc* (*inf*) a cheap lodging-house.

dossier ['dosiei] *nc* (*formal*) a set of papers containing information *etc* about one person or subject: *He had made a secret dossier on the whole affair.*

dot [dot] *nc* a small, round mark: *She marked the paper with a dot*; (*fig*) *a dot of butter.* – *v* – *pt*, *ptp* **'dotted** – *vt* to place dots on or scatter (small objects *etc*) over: *He dotted the page with tiny pictures of flowers*; *The lawn was dotted with daisies.*

'dotted *adj* **1** (*attrib*) consisting of dots: *a dotted line.* **2** having a dot or dots: *a dotted tie*; *That curtain material is too dotted – it dazzles me.*

dotage ['doutidʒ] : **be in one's dotage** to have become foolish and childish because of old age: *Don't pay any attention to what the old man says – he's in his dotage.*

dote [dout]: **'dote on** *vt fus* to be fond of to an extent which is foolish: *He just dotes on that child!*

dotted *see* **dot**.

dotty ['doti] *adj* (*inf*) tending to behave strangely; slightly mad: *My aunt is a dear old lady, but a bit dotty.*

double ['dʌbl] *adj* **1** (*attrib*) of twice the (usual) weight, size *etc*: *A double whisky, please*; *a double helping of peas.* **2** (*usu attrib*) two of a sort together or occurring in pairs: *a double window overlooking the lawn*; *He gave a double knock on the door.* **3** (*usu attrib*) consisting of two parts or layers: *a double thickness of paper*; (*fig*) *a double meaning/purpose.* **4** (*attrib*) for two people: *a double bed*; *a double ticket to a dance.* – *adv* **1** twice: *I gave her double the usual quantity.* **2** in two: *The coat had been folded double and laid on a chair.* – **1** *nu* a double quantity: *He got quite a lot of money but she got double.* **2** *nc* someone who is exactly like another: *He is my father's double.* – **1** *vti* to (cause to) become twice as large or numerous: *He doubled his income in three years*; *The number of such accidents happening every year has doubled recently.* **2** *vi* to have two jobs or uses or a second job: *This sofa doubles as a bed*; *The history teacher doubled as a hockey coach.*

double- (*in cmpds*) twice or once again: *These figures must be double-checked.*

'doubles *ncu* in tennis *etc*, a kind of match with two players on each side: *I enjoy playing doubles*; (*attrib*) *a doubles match.*

double agent *nc* a spy paid by each of two countries hostile to each other: *Our man in Berlin appears to have been a double agent.*

ˌdouble-'barrelled *adj* **1** (of a gun) having two

barrels. **2** (*fig*) (of a name) made up of two names: *He had a double-barrelled name like Ponsonby-Smythe.*

double bass [beis] *nc* a type of large stringed instrument, the largest and deepest in sound of the violin family: *He plays the double bass*; *Can you play that on the double bass?*

ˌ**double-ˈbedded** *adj* (*usu attrib*) containing a double bed: *a double-bedded room.*

ˌ**double-ˈbreasted** *adj* (of a coat or jacket) overlapping at the front, *usu* with two sets of buttons: *He prefers double-breasted suits*; *I'd like the jacket double-breasted.*

ˌ**double-ˈcross** *vt* to betray (someone for whom one has already arranged to do something deceitful): *I paid him to lose the fight but he double-crossed me and tried to win.* – *nc* the act of doing this: *He was himself cheated by his colleague's double-cross.*

ˌ**double-ˈdealing** *nu* cheating and deceitfulness. – (*adj attrib*) cheating: *You double-dealing liar!*

ˌ**double-ˈdecker** *nc* a bus *etc* having two decks or levels: *Here comes a double-decker!*; (*attrib*) *a double-decker bus.*

ˌ**double-ˈDutch** *nu* (*inf*) nonsense: *I couldn't understand what he was saying – it was double-Dutch to me.*

double figures *n pl* the numbers between 10 and 99 inclusive, *esp* (*loosely*) the lower ones: *The number of times you have been late for work is now well into double figures.*

ˌ**double-ˈglazing** *nu* the system of having two thicknesses of glass in a window to keep in heat and keep out noise.

ˌ**double-ˈjointed** *adj* (*usu pred*) (of a person) having joints which can be bent in the opposite direction from normal: *If she can bend herself into that shape she must be double-jointed.*

ˌ**double-ˈquick** *adj, adv* (*inf*) very quick(ly): *Please get those files up here double-quick/in double-quick time!*

ˈ**double-talk** *nu* talk which sounds good but which means something different from what it seems to mean: *A lot of what is said by politicians is just double-talk.*

at the ˈdouble very quickly: *He came up the road at the double and rushed into the house.*

double back *vi* to turn and go back the way one came: *The fox doubled back and went down a hole near to where it had started.*

double up 1 *vi, vt sep* to (cause to) fold over suddenly at the waist: *Everyone doubled up with laughter*; *He received a blow in the stomach which doubled him up.* **2** *vi* to share a bedroom (with someone else): *The house was so full some of the guests had to double up.*

see double to see two images of everything instead of only one: *When I first met the twins, I thought I was seeing double, they were so alike.*

double entendre [du:blã'tãdr] *ncu* (*formal*) (the practice of making) a remark which has two possible meanings, one of them *usu* indecent: *There was an element of double entendre in his last remark that he hoped to see a lot more of her!*

doublet ['dʌblit] *nc* (*hist*) a kind of close-fitting jacket once worn by men.

doubt [daut] (not used with **is, was** *etc* and **-ing**) **1** *vti* to feel uncertain (about), but inclined not to believe (that something is the case): *I doubt if he'll come now*; *I doubt that she was invited*; *He might have a screwdriver, but I doubt it*; *She is always very suspicious and ready to doubt.* **2** *vt* not to be sure of the quality *etc* of: *Sometimes I doubt your intelligence!* – *ncu* a feeling of not being sure and sometimes of being suspicious: *There is some doubt as to what happened*; *I have doubts about that place.*

ˈ**doubtful** *adj* **1** (*usu pred*) feeling doubt; uncertain what to think, expect *etc*: *He is doubtful about the value of your suggestions.* **2** able to be doubted; not clear: *The meaning is doubtful*; *a doubtful result.* **3** uncertain but probably bad, not true, not trustworthy *etc*: *The wisdom of this action is doubtful*; *It is doubtful whether this will work*; *a doubtful improvement.* **4** (*attrib*: *inf*) suspicious: *There's a doubtful character looking in the windows of their house.* ˈ**doubtfully** *adv.* ˈ**doubtfulness** *nu.*

ˈ**doubtless** *adv* (*formal*) probably: *John has doubtless told you about me.*

beyond doubt (*formal*) certain(ly): *Beyond doubt, they will arrive tomorrow*; *His honesty is quite beyond doubt.*

in ˈdoubt (*formal*) uncertain: *The result of the dispute is still in doubt.*

no doubt (*formal*) surely; probably: *No doubt you would like to see your bedroom*; *He will come back again tomorrow, no doubt.*

See also **indubitably, dubious, undoubted**.

dough [dou] *nu* **1** a mass of flour moistened and kneaded but not baked. **2** (*sl*) money: *He must have a lot of dough to buy such a big house!*

ˈ**doughnut** [-nʌt, (*Amer*) -nət] *nc* a ring-shaped cake, with a hole in the middle, fried in fat.

douse [daus] *vt* (*formal*) to put out (lights, a fire *etc*) *esp* with water: *He brought a bucket of water to douse the fire.*

dove[1] [dʌv] *nc* a kind of pigeon.

ˈ**dovecot** [-kot], ˈ**dovecote** [-kout] *nc* a building designed for housing pigeons: *There is a dovecot in the grounds of the castle.*

ˈ**dovetail** *nc* (*tech*) a method of joining wood *etc* by fitting wedge-shaped pieces into wedge-shaped slots. – *vti* (*usu fig*) to fit (one thing exactly into another): *The two families dovetailed their holidays so that one could move into the caravan as soon as the other left it*; *Their holidays dovetailed exactly.*

dove[2] *see* **dive**.

dowdy ['daudi] *adj* (*derog*) not smart; (*esp* of dress) unfashionable: *She looks so dowdy in that old-fashioned hat!*; *That's a very dowdy suit you are wearing!*

down[1] [daun] *adv, adj* **1** towards or in a low or lower position, level or state: *He climbed down to the bottom of the ladder*; *She could see him standing further down*; (*fig*) *I met everyone, from the managing director down.* **2** on or to the ground: *The little boy fell down and cut his knee.* **3** from earlier to later times: *The recipe has been handed down in our family for years.* **4** from a greater to a smaller size, amount *etc*: *Prices have been going down steadily*; *I've cut the list down quite a bit.* **5** towards or in a place thought of as being lower, *esp* southward or away from a centre: *We went down from Edinburgh to London*; *He doesn't live in London – he lives down in Hampshire.* **6** in writing *etc*: *I have your number down in my address book.* **7** in cash at the time of buying: *I paid him half the money down and I'll give him the rest over three months.* – *prep* **1** in a lower position on: *Their house is halfway down the hill*; *The ice-cream van was parked down the street.* **2** to a lower position on, by, through or along: *The boat moved slowly* *down the river*; *Water poured down the drain.* **3** along: *The teacher's gaze travelled slowly down the line of children.* – *adj* **1** (*attrib*) going or reaching towards a lower or more distant position: *We had a blockage in the down pipe from the roof*; *We caught the down train* (= the train going away from the main station). **2** (*inf*: *pred*) depressed or in low spirits: *We felt very down after the party was over.* – *vt* (*inf*) to finish (a drink) very quickly, *esp* in one gulp: *He downed what was left of his coffee and ran after the others*; *She can down several pints of beer in half-an-hour.* – *See also* **down tools** *below.*

ˈ**downward** *adj* (*usu attrib*) leading, moving *etc* down: *a downward curve*; *a downward movement.*

ˈ**downward(s)** *adv* towards a lower position or state: *The path led downward(s) towards the sea*; (*fig*) *After losing his job, he moved steadily downward(s) in society.*

ˌ**down-and-ˈout** *nc, adj* (*derog*) (a person) having no money, no means of earning a living and no hope of ever doing so: *They are volunteer workers in a hostel for down-and-outs*; *a down-and-out old man.*

ˌ**down-at-ˈheel** *adj* (*fig*) shabby, untidy and not well looked after or well-dressed: *The hotel looked rather down-at-heel and had obviously seen better days* (= once been much more prosperous).

ˈ**downcast** *adj* (*formal*) **1** (of a person) depressed or in low spirits: *He was downcast over the failure of his plans*; *a downcast expression.* **2** (of eyes) looking downwards: *Her eyes were downcast*; *a downcast gaze.*

ˈ**downfall** *nc* (*usu fig*) a disastrous fall, *esp* a final failure or ruin: *This last mistake caused the downfall of the entire firm*; *the downfall of our hopes.*

ˌ**downˈgrade** *vt* (*formal*) to reduce to a lower level, *esp* of importance: *His job was downgraded to that of an assistant.* – ˈ**downgrade** *nc* a slope going downwards.

ˌ**downˈhearted** *adj* (*usu pred*) depressed and in low spirits, *esp* lacking the inclination to carry on with something: *We were very downhearted about the poor results of the first part of our plans.*

ˌ**downˈhill** *adv* **1** down a slope: *The road goes downhill all the way from our house to yours.* **2** (*fig*: *with* **go**) towards a worse and worse state: *We expected him to die, I suppose, because he's been going steadily downhill for months.* – *adj* going downwards: *The way is all downhill*; *His fortunes took a downhill turn suddenly.*

ˌ**down-in-the-ˈmouth** *adj* (*usu pred*) miserable or in low spirits: *Don't look so down-in-the-mouth – you're not dead yet* (= there is still hope).

down payment *nc* a payment in cash, *esp* to begin the purchase of something for which further payments will be made over a period of time: *We've just made a down payment on a house.*

ˈ**downpour** *nc* a very heavy fall of rain.

ˈ**downright** *adv* completely or absolutely: *I think he was downright rude!* – *adj* (*attrib*) absolute and complete: *I think it would be a downright advantage to us!*; *He is a downright nuisance!*

ˈ**downstairs** *adj* (*attrib*), ˌ**downˈstairs** *adv* on or towards a lower floor of a building: *He walked slowly downstairs*; *I left my book downstairs*; *a downstairs flat.*

ˌ**downˈstream** *adv* further along a river towards the sea: *We found the boat several miles downstream.*

ˌ**down-to-ˈearth** *adj* practical and not concerned with theories, ideals or possibilities: *He has a very down-to-earth approach to the subject*; *She is always down-to-earth about these problems.*

ˈ**downtown** *adj* (*attrib*: *Amer*) the part (of a city) containing the main centres for business and shopping: *downtown Manhattan.* – ˌ**downˈtown** *adv* (*Amer*) towards this area: *to go downtown.* – *See also* **down town** *below.*

ˈ**down-trodden** *adj* (*usu attrib*: *fig*) oppressed or treated without respect by other people: *She is consistently unkind to her down-trodden secretary.*

ˌ**downˈwind** *adv* in or towards the direction in which the wind is blowing: *The deer could not smell us as we were downwind from it.*

be ˈdown on/have a ˈdown on (*inf*) to be hostile or opposed to: *The headmaster is very down on the wearing of make-up at school*; *He has a down on university students and won't rent his flat to them.*

down on one's luck (*inf*) having bad luck: *He's been down on his luck since his wife died.*

down town (*inf*) in or towards the centre of a town, *usu* from the outskirts: *I was down town yesterday shopping*; *I'm going down town – do you want anything there?* – *See also* **downtown** *above.*

down under (*often facet or derog*) in or to Australia and New Zealand.

be/go ˈdown with (*inf*) to be or become ill with: *I was down with flu for a week last winter*; *The children all went down with measles one after the other.*

down tools (*inf*) to stop working: *When the man was sacked his fellow workers downed tools and walked out*; *They downed tools because it was so cold in the factory.*

ˈ**down with** (*interj*) get rid of: *Down with injustice!*

get ˈdown to *vt fus* to begin working seriously at or on: *I must get down to writing some letters!*

suit (someone) down to the ground (*inf*) to suit completely or perfectly: *That arrangement will suit me down to the ground.*

down[2] [daun] *nu* small, soft feathers: *a quilt filled with down.*

downie Ⓡ *see* **duvet**.

ˈ**downy** *adj* soft, like feathers: *She had fair, downy hair.*

downs [daunz] *n pl* an area of low, grassy hills, *esp* (*with cap*) two such areas in the south-east of England: *the North and South Downs.*

dowry [ˈdauəri] *nc* (*old*) money and property brought by a woman to her husband when they marry: *She had a dowry of £20 000.*

doyley *see* **doily**.

doze [douz] *vi* to sleep lightly or for short periods: *The old lady dozed in her armchair.* – *nc* a short sleep.

doze off *vi* to go into a light sleep: *I dozed off in front of the fire.*

dozen [ˈdʌzn] – *pls* ˈ**dozens**, (after a number or a word signifying a quantity) ˈ**dozen** – *nc* a group of twelve: *a dozen eggs*; *two/several dozen handkerchiefs*; *These eggs are 60p a dozen*; *Half-a-dozen eggs, please*; *We sell eggs in dozens.*

ˈ**dozens (of)** (*loosely*) very many: *I've been there dozens of times*; *'Have you got many records?' 'Yes. Dozens.'*

drab [drab] *adj* dull and uninteresting, *esp* in colour: *She always wears such drab clothes*; *a drab brown*; *His existence is so drab that I thought I would try to brighten it up.* ˈ**drably** *adv.* ˈ**drabness** *nu.*

drachma ['drakmə] – *pls* '**drachmas,** '**drachmae** [-mi:], '**drachmai** [-mai] – *nc* the standard unit of Greek currency.

draft [dra:ft] **1** *nc* a rough sketch or outline of something, *esp* written: *This is a rough draft of my speech.* **2** *nc* a group (of soldiers *etc*) taken from a larger group: *The first draft for the new camp went off today.* **3** *nc* an order (to a bank *etc*) for the payment of money: *He gave me a bank draft for £40.* **4** *nc* (*Amer*) conscription: *He emigrated to avoid the draft.* **5** *ncu* (*Amer*) (a) draught. – *vt* **1** to make in the form of a rough plan: *I've drafted a list of topics we might discuss; Could you draft some sort of report on this?* **2** to pick out (*esp* soldiers) for a special purpose: *Four men were drafted to do guard-duty.* **3** (*Amer*) to conscript into the army *etc*: *He was drafted into the Navy.*

draftsman *see* **draughtsman**.

drag [drag] – *pt, ptp* **dragged** – **1** *vt* to pull, *esp* by force or roughly: *She was dragged screaming from her car.* **2** *vt* to pull (something) slowly (*usu* because heavy): *He dragged a heavy table across the doorway.* **3** *vti* to (cause to) move along the ground: *The child was tired and dragged his feet as he walked; His coat was so long it dragged on the ground at the back.* **4** *vt* to search (the bed of a lake *etc*) by using a net or hook: *Police are dragging the canal to try to find the body.* **5** *vi* (*inf*) to appear to be very slow-moving and boring: *The evening wasn't very exciting and dragged a bit.* – **1** *nc* something which slows something down: *He felt that his lack of education was a drag on his progress.* **2** *ncu* (an act of) dragging or keeping back. **3** *nc* (*sl*) an act of drawing in smoke from a cigarette *etc*: *He took a long drag at his cigarette.* **4** *nc* (*sl*) something or someone that is dull and boring: *He's nice but his wife is a drag; Washing-up is a drag.* **5** *nu* (*sl*) women's clothes when worn by men: *She looked like a prize-fighter in drag;* (*attrib*) *a drag act* (= a theatrical act in which a man dresses as a woman).

dragon ['dragən] *nc* **1** (*myth*) a *usu* large, winged, fire-breathing reptile: *St George and the dragon.* **2** (*fig inf*) a fierce or rather frightening person, *esp* a woman: *Her mother is a real dragon.*

dragonfly ['dragənflai] *nc* a kind of insect with a long body and double wings.

dragoon [drə'gu:n] *nc* a heavily-armed horse-soldier. – *vt* (*fig*) to force or bully (a person into doing something): *Several people were dragooned into agreeing to help with the concert.*

drain [drein] **1** *vt* to clear (land) of water by the use of ditches and pipes: *If this wet land was drained it would be good farmland.* **2** *vi* (of water) to run away: *The water drains out of the flower-pot through the holes in the bottom.* **3** *vti* to pour off the water *etc* from or allow the water *etc* to run off from: *Would you drain the potatoes while I serve out the meat; He drained the petrol tank; The blood drained from her face when she heard the news of her husband's death.* **4** *vt* to drink everything contained in: *He drained his glass.* **5** *vt* to use up completely (the money, strength *etc* of): *The effort drained all his energy; The expense drained us of all the money we had.* – *See also* **drain away/off** *below.* – *nc* **1** something (a ditch, trench, waterpipe *etc*) designed to carry away water: *Last night's heavy rain has caused several drains to overflow.* **2** (*fig*) something which slowly exhausts a supply, *esp* of one's money or strength: *His car is a constant drain on his money.*

'**drainage** [-nidʒ] *nu* the process, method or system of carrying away extra water: *Drainage is our main problem; The town's drainage is very efficient;* (*attrib*) *He is a drainage expert.*

'**draining-board** *nc* the area at the side of a sink which is divided into slightly sloping hollows to allow water from dishes to drain away: *She left the dishes to drain on the draining-board.*

'**drainpipe** *nc* a pipe which carries water from the roof of a building to the ground.

drain away/off **1** *vt sep* to allow (water *etc*) to run away completely: *We drain off the hot-water system when we leave our holiday cottage for the winter.* **2** *vi* (of water *etc*) to run away completely: *The flood on the road eventually drained off into the ditch.*

down the drain (*inf*) wasted: *We had to scrap everything and start again – six months' work down the drain!*

drake [dreik] *nc* a male duck: *A drake, a duck and their four ducklings swam round the bend in the river.*

drama ['dra:mə] **1** *nc* a play for acting on the stage: *He has just produced a new drama;* (*fig*) *Did I tell you the end of our little drama* (= succession of happenings as in a play) *at the office?* **2** *nu* plays for the stage in general: *the drama of Shakespeare.* **3** *nu* the art of acting in plays: *He studied drama at college.* **4** *nu* exciting events: *Life here is full of drama.*

dramatic [drə'matik] *adj* **1** (*usu attrib*) of or in the form of a drama: *a dramatic entertainment.* **2** vivid or striking: *There has been a dramatic improvement in his condition; Her entrance in a white mink coat was dramatic.* **3** (*usu pred*: *derog*) (of a person) showing (too) much feeling or emotion: *She tends to be very dramatic about everything.* **dra'matically** *adv.*

'**dramatist** ['dra-] *nc* a writer of plays: *Arthur Miller is a famous American dramatist.*

ˌ**dramati'zation, -s-** [dra-] **1** *nc* a play *etc* adapted from a real story or another kind of literature: *a dramatization of the life of Joan of Arc.* **2** *nu* (*derog*) the act of dramatizing (*def 2*): *I think he's guilty of dramatization.*

'**dramatize, -ise** ['dra-] *vt* **1** to turn (something) into the form of a play: *She dramatized the novel for television.* **2** (*derog*) to make real events seem like things that happen in a play: *She dramatizes everything so!*

dramatis personae ['dramətis pə:'souni:] *n* (*formal*) **1** *pl* the characters of a play: *The list of dramatis personae often appears at the beginning of the written version of a play.* **2** *sing* the list of these characters.

drank *see* **drink**.

drape [dreip] *vt* **1** to hang cloth in folds (about): *We draped the sofa in red velvet;* (*fig*) *She arrived draped with parcels and plastic bags.* **2** to hang in folds: *We draped sheets over the boxes to hide them;* (*fig*) *She draped herself across the arm of his chair.*

'**draper** *nc* a person who sells cloth, clothing *etc.*

'**drapery** **1** *nc* a draper's business. **2** *nu* cloth used for draping: *The walls were hung with blue drapery.*

drapes *n pl* (*Amer*) curtains.

drastic ['drastik] *adj* (*formal*) violent, severe and covering a wide area: *At this point they decided to take drastic action; Unless there is a drastic improvement in efficiency, we will go out of business; The effects of the financial cuts were drastic.* '**drastically** *adv.*

draught, (*Amer*) **draft** [dra:ft] **1** *nc* a movement of air, *esp* one which causes discomfort in a room or which helps a fire to burn: *We increase the heat in the furnace by increasing the draught*; *There's a dreadful draught in this room!* **2** *nc* a quantity of liquid drunk at once without stopping: *He took a long draught of beer.* **3** *nu* the amount of water a ship requires to float it: *This boat has a shallow draught/a draught of half a metre.*

draughts, (*Amer* '**checkers**) *n* **1** *sing* a game for two people, played on a board (a '**draught-board**, (*Amer*) '**checkerboard**) exactly like a chessboard, with twenty-four discs. **2** *pl* the discs.

'**draughty** *adj* full of draughts of air: *This room is terribly draughty with the window open.*

draught beer *nu* beer sold from the barrel, not in bottles or cans.

draughtsman, (*esp Amer*) **draftsman** ['dra:ftsmən] – *pl* '**draughtsmen**, '**draftsmen** – *nc* a person who is good at or employed in making drawings: *My son is a draughtsman in a firm of civil engineers.*

draw [dro:] – *pt* **drew** [dru:]: *ptp* **drawn** – **1** *vti* to make a picture or pictures (of), *usu* with a pencil, crayons *etc*: *During his stay in hospital he drew a great deal*; *He was drawing on the windows of the bus with his finger*; *Shall I draw a cow?*; **2** *vt* to pull along, out or towards oneself: *She drew the chair towards her*; *He drew a gun suddenly and fired*; *All water had to be drawn from a well*; *The cart was drawn by a fat, brown pony.* **3** *vi* to move (towards or away from someone or something): *The car drew away from the kerb*; *The demonstrators drew nearer*; (*fig*) *Christmas is drawing closer.* **4** *vti* to play (a game) in which neither side wins: *We always draw when we play them*; *The match was drawn at 1-1.* **5** *vt* to obtain (money) from a fund, bank *etc*: *to draw a pension/an allowance.* **6** *vt* to open or close (curtains): *We draw the curtains early to shut out the rainy weather*; *She drew the curtains and let the sunshine into the room.* **7** *vt* to attract: *She was trying to draw my attention to something*; (*formal*) *His appearance drew all eyes.* **8** *vt* (*tech*) (of a ship) to require (a certain depth of water) to float in: *This canal can take ships which draw up to six metres.* – *See also* **draw** *in phrases below.* – *nc* **1** a drawn game: *The match ended in a draw.* **2** (*inf*) an attraction: *I think our new bargain-counter should be a real draw.* **3** the selecting of winning tickets in a raffle, lottery *etc*: *a prize draw.* **4** (*inf*) an act of drawing, *esp* a gun: *He's quick on the draw.*

'**drawing** *ncu* (the art of making) a picture made with a pencil, crayon *etc* by the use of lines and shading: *the drawings of Leonardo da Vinci*; *I am not good at drawing.*

drawn *adj* **1** (of curtains) pulled together or closed: *All the curtains were drawn, although it was still daylight*; *behind drawn curtains.* **2** (of a game *etc*) neither won nor lost: *a drawn match*; *The game was drawn.* **3** (of a blade *etc*) pulled out of its sheath: *a drawn sword.* **4** (of a person) tense, strained and tired: *His face was pale and drawn with pain.* **5** (*pred*: *hist*) (*of a criminal*) having (had) one's stomach and intestines *etc* cut out: *The rebels were sentenced to be hanged, drawn and quartered.*

'**drawback** *nu* a disadvantage: *There are several drawbacks to this method of dealing with the problem.*

'**drawbridge** *nc* (*usu hist*) a bridge (at the entrance to a castle) which can be pulled up or let down.

'**drawing-pin** *nc* (*Amer* '**thumbtack**) a pin with a broad, flat head used for fastening paper to a board *etc*: *A notice was fixed on the door with a drawing-pin.*

'**drawstring** *nc* a cord threaded through the top of a bag *etc* and used for closing it: *He kept his money in a leather bag with a drawstring.*

the days, nights are drawing in the days are getting shorter and the nights longer (as happens in autumn): *Now that the days are drawing in, I like to leave work early and get home before dark.*

draw a blank (*inf*) to be unsuccessful in a search, inquiry *etc*: *He looked for a red fur coat all over town but drew a blank.*

draw breath to breathe, *esp* deeply when one is out of breath: *We stopped at the top of the hill to draw breath*; (*fig*) *Before we could draw breath, we had to start on the next task.*

draw a conclusion from to come to a conclusion after thinking about (what one has learned): *Don't draw any hasty conclusions from what I've said!*

draw in *vi* (of a car *etc*) to come to a halt at the side of the road: *Just draw in beyond that yellow car while I post a letter.*

draw the line to fix a limit *esp* for what one is prepared to do: *No, there I draw the line – I will not invite him to my party!*; *She draws the line at doing his washing.*

draw/cast lots to decide who is to do *etc* something by drawing names out of a box *etc*: *Five of us drew lots for the two pop-concert tickets.*

draw off *vt sep* to pour out (liquid) from a large container: *He drew off a pint of water from the tank to examine its purity*; *The barman drew off a pint of beer.*

'**draw on**[1] *vt fus* to use (money, strength, memory *etc*) as a source: *He drew on his imagination for a lot of the details*; *She's been drawing on her capital for years*; *He draws on her strength a lot.*

draw on[2] **1** *vt sep* to pull on: *He drew on his gloves.* **2** *vi* (*often liter*) to come nearer: *Night drew on and it was soon quite dark.*

draw out 1 *vt sep* to take (money) from a bank: *I drew out twenty pounds yesterday.* **2** *vt sep* to make long or longer than necessary: *We drew out the journey as much as we could but we still arrived early.* **3** *vi* (of a car *etc*) to move away from the kerb: *A car drew out in front of us as we were overtaking.* **4** *vt sep* to encourage to become less shy, *esp* to speak: *He sits silently in a corner unless someone takes the trouble to draw him out.*

draw up 1 *vi* (of a car *etc*) to stop: *We drew up outside their house.* **2** *vt sep* to arrange in an acceptable form or order: *They drew up the soldiers in line*; *The solicitor drew up a contract for them to sign.* **3** *vt sep* to move closer: *Draw up a chair!* **4** *v refl* to stand upright: *He drew himself up to his full height.*

long drawn out *adj* going on for a long time: *The meeting was so long drawn out that we missed our train*; (*attrib*) *a long-drawn-out meeting/scream.*

drawer [dro:] *nc* a sliding box without a lid, for clothes *etc*, which fits into a chest, table *etc*: *I think there's some paper in the bottom drawer of my desk.*

drawing *see* **draw**.

drawing-room ['dro:iŋrum] *nc* a sitting-room, *esp* a large one or one used mainly for formal occasions.

drawl [dro:l] *vti* to speak or say in a slow, lazy manner: *He drawled his words in an irritating manner.* – *nc* a slow, lazy manner of speaking: *She had a fascinating Southern drawl.*

drawn, drawstring *see* **draw**.

dread [dred] *ncu* (*usu formal or liter*) great fear: *She lives in dread of her child being drowned in the canal; I have a dread of finding a caterpillar in my cabbage; a dread of heights; His voice was husky with dread.* – *vt* to fear greatly: *We were dreading his arrival.*

'**dreadful** *adj* **1** terrible: *a dreadful accident.* **2** (*loosely*) very bad or annoying: *What dreadful children!; Her paintings are dreadful.* '**dreadfulness** *nu.*

'**dreadfully** *adv* (*inf*) very: *She's dreadfully clever.*

dream [dri:m] *nc* **1** thoughts and pictures in the mind that come mostly during sleep: *I had a terrible dream last night.* **2** a state of being completely occupied by one's own thoughts: *Don't sit there in a dream!* **3** (*inf*) something perfect or very beautiful: *a dream of a dress; Your apricot soufflé was a dream!* **4** an ambition or hope: *It's my dream to win a Nobel Prize.* – *v* – *pts, ptps* **dreamed, dreamt** [dremt] – *vti* (*sometimes with* **of**) to see visions and pictures in the mind, *esp* when asleep: *She was dreaming peacefully; I dreamed I was King Kong; For years I dreamed of being a great artist; I dreamt last night that the house had burnt down.*

'**dreamer** *nc* a person who is often occupied by dreams, *esp* of ambitions which he will never carry out: *I'm afraid my son is a bit of a dreamer and not very practical.*

'**dreamless** *adj* (*usu attrib*) (of sleep) sound; not disturbed by dreams: *She awoke refreshed after a dreamless sleep.*

'**dreamy** *adj* **1** as if of a person who is not quite awake: *She had a vague, dreamy smile on her face; She is too dreamy.* **2** (*inf*) very beautiful or attractive: *I met the most dreamy man on the bus this evening!* '**dreamily** *adv.* '**dreaminess** *nu.*

dream up *vt sep* (*derog*) to invent (often taking too much trouble to do so): *He's dreamed up some sort of special recipe for fish; I'm sure she'll dream up some silly plan.*

See also **undreamed-of**.

dreary ['driəri] *adj* **1** gloomy: *What dreary weather!; Their old house is very dreary.* **2** (*inf*) very dull: *I've got to go to another dreary meeting tomorrow; She's a dreary companion.* '**drearily** *adv.* '**dreariness** *nu.*

dredge[1] [dredʒ] *vti* to use a system of buckets, pumps *etc* to deepen or clear the bed of (a river *etc*) by bringing up mud: *The channel is dredged regularly to keep it open; The boat has been dredging for months.* – *nc* an apparatus for doing this.

'**dredger**[1] *nc* a boat specially fitted with apparatus for dredging.

dredge[2] [dredʒ] *vt* to sprinkle (*usu* food with sugar *etc*): *The pancakes were dredged with sugar.*

'**dredger**[2] *nc* (*often in cmpds*): *a sugar-dredger.*

dregs [dregz] *n pl* **1** the solid matter which is left at the bottom of a container when the liquid is all used up: *the dregs of the wine.* **2** (*fig*) anything worthless: *the dregs of society.*

drench [drentʃ] *vt* to soak (something or someone) completely (with a liquid): *They went out in the rain and were drenched to the skin; The hosepipe burst and drenched everyone with cold water.*

dress [dres] **1** *vti* to put clothes or a covering on: *We dressed in a hurry and my wife dressed the children.* **2** *vi* (*esp old*) to put on formal clothes for an evening meal *etc*: *They made a habit of dressing for dinner in the evening.* **3** *vt* to prepare (food *etc*) to be eaten: *She dressed a salad.* **4** *vt* to treat and bandage (wounds): *He was sent home from hospital after his burns had been dressed.* – **1** *nu* what one is wearing or dressed in: *He was in formal dress; Her dress was always a little peculiar.* **2** *nc* a piece of women's clothing with a top and skirt in one piece: *Shall I wear a dress or a blouse and skirt?*

dressed *adj* (*pred*: *often with* **in**: *sometimes in cmpds*) wearing (clothes): *Don't come in – I'm not dressed!; She was dressed in black; You must get dressed* (= put on your clothes) *immediately; What is the well-dressed man wearing this autumn?*

'**dresser** *nc* a kitchen sideboard for holding dishes *etc.*

'**dressing** **1** *ncu* something put on as a covering: *We gave the rose-bed a dressing of manure.* **2** *ncu* a sauce added *esp* to salads: *oil and vinegar dressing.* **3** *nc* a bandage *etc* used to dress a wound: *He changed the patient's dressing.*

'**dressy** *adj* (*inf*) **1** (of a person) fond of smart and fashionable clothes: *She was always a very dressy woman; She's too dressy for me!* **2** (of a piece of clothing) for formal rather than casual wear: *This coat is a bit dressy to wear to work; She's wearing a very dressy suit today.*

dress circle *nc* the first gallery in a theatre, *orig* intended for people in evening dress.

ˌ**dressing-'down** *nc* (*inf*) a scolding: *His boss gave him a dressing-down for being late so often.*

'**dressing-gown** *nc* a garment like a loose coat worn indoors when not fully dressed, over pyjamas *etc.*

'**dressing-room** *nc* a room (in a theatre *etc*) for people to dress in, *esp* in special clothes.

'**dressing-table** *nc* a table in a bedroom *etc*, with a mirror and *usu* drawers, at which women sit to put on make-up *etc.*

'**dressmaker** *nc* a person who makes clothes for women.

dress rehearsal *nc* a full rehearsal (often the last rehearsal) of a play *etc* with all costumes *etc* as they will be for the performance.

dress shirt, suit, uniform *nc* a shirt *etc* for wearing on formal occasions.

dress up **1** *vi* to put on fancy-dress: *He dressed up as a pirate for the party.* **2** *vi, vt sep* to dress in formal, not casual, clothes: *Don't dress up specially for the party – just come as you are.* **3** *vt sep* (*inf*) to make (something) appear better, more pleasant *etc* than it is by adding to it *etc*: *We dressed it up when we told him, of course, but the plain fact is that he's useless; You can dress that blouse up with a necklace.*

See also **undress**.

drew *see* **draw**.

dribble ['dribl] **1** *vi* to fall in small drops: *Water dribbled out of the tap.* **2** *vi* to allow saliva to run from the mouth: *Does that baby always dribble like that?* **3** *vti* in football, hockey *etc* to kick or hit (the ball) along little by little: *He dribbled expertly up the field.* – *nc* a small quantity of liquid, *esp* of saliva: *There was only a dribble of water in the pipe; A dribble ran down his chin.*

dribs and drabs [dribzən'drabz] (*inf*) very small quantities: *I'm doing the spring-cleaning in dribs and drabs as I feel like it.*

drift [drift] *nc* **1** a heap of something driven together, *esp* snow: *His car stuck in a drift during the snowstorm*; *a drift of sand/leaves.* **2** (*no pl*: *usu fig*) the direction in which something is going; the general meaning or subject: *I saw the drift of his argument quite clearly*; *I couldn't hear you clearly, but I did catch the drift of what you said.* – **1** *vti* to (cause to) float or be blown along: *Snow drifted across the road*; *The boat drifted slowly down the river*; *The wind drifted the snow against the door.* **2** *vi* (of people) to wander or live aimlessly: *She drifted around, taking casual jobs from time to time*; *He drifts in to see us now and again.*

'**drifter** *nc* **1** a fishing-boat that uses a net (a '**drift-net**) which floats near the surface of the water. **2** a person who drifts: *Don't expect him to keep that job – he's just a drifter.*

'**driftwood** *nu* wood floating on or cast up on the shore by water, *esp* the sea: *We made a fire with driftwood we found on the beach.*

drill [dril] **1** *vti* to make (a hole) with a drill: *He drilled four holes in the piece of wood to take the screws*; *By this time the geologists were drilling into solid rock*; *They have drilled for oil here.* **2** *vt* to make a hole in: *The soldiers drilled the door with bullets.* **3** *vti* (of soldiers *etc*) to exercise or be exercised: *The soldiers were rigorously drilled every morning*; *The recruits drilled regularly.* – **1** *nc* a tool for making holes: *a hand-drill*; *an electric drill*; *An enormous drill was being used to look for oil in the sea-bed.* **2** *nu* exercise or practice, *esp* of soldiers: *We do half-an-hour of drill after tea.* **3** *nc* a long hollow with seeds *etc* sown in it: *Beetroot is sown thinly in shallow drills.*

drily *see* **dry**.

drink [driŋk] – *pt* **drank** [draŋk]: *ptp* **drunk** [drʌŋk] – **1** *vti* to swallow (a liquid): *She drank a pint of water*; *He drank thirstily from a green bottle.* **2** *vi* to take alcoholic liquids, *esp* in too great a quantity: *I've got orange juice for those who don't drink*; *I'm afraid her husband drinks.* – *See also* **drink** *in phrases below.* – **1** *nc* (an act of drinking) a liquid suitable for swallowing: *He had/took a drink of water*; *Would you like a drink of milk?*; *Lemonade is a refreshing drink when you're thirsty.* **2** *ncu* (a glassful *etc* of) alcoholic liquor: *He likes a drink when he returns home from work*; *Have we any drink in the house?*; (*attrib*) *He has a drink problem* (= He is addicted to alcohol).

drink in *vt sep* (*usu fig*) to take in rapidly or eagerly: *The audience were fascinated, drinking in every expression of his voice.*

'**drink to** *vt fus*/**drink (to) the health of** to offer good wishes to, or wish well to, while drinking: *Let's drink to that!*; *He gave us some money to drink his health*; *Raise your glasses and drink to (the health of) the bride and groom.*

drink up *vt sep* to finish by drinking: *Drink up your milk!*; *We had guests last night and they've drunk up all the beer.*

take to drink (*inf*) to begin drinking large quantities of alcohol frequently or regularly: *He took to drink after his wife died.*

drip [drip] – *pt, ptp* **dripped** – *vti* to (cause to) fall in single drops: *Rain dripped slowly off the roof*; *Her coat dripped water into a puddle on the floor.* – **1** *nc* a small quantity (of liquid) falling in drops: *A drip of water ran down her arm.* **2** *nu* the noise made by dripping: *The only noise was the steady drip of rain falling from the trees.* **3** *nc* (*med*) an apparatus for passing a liquid slowly and continuously into a vein of the body. **4** *nc* (*inf*) a person without spirit, originality or strength of character: *Oh, come with us – don't be such a drip!*

'**dripping** *nu* fat obtained from meat while it is roasting *etc.*

ˌ**drip-'dry** *adj* (of a garment *etc*) requiring no, or little, ironing if allowed to dry by hanging up while soaking wet. – *vti* to dry in this manner: *This shirt can be drip-dried*; *The blouse drip-dries quickly.*

drive [draiv] – *pt* **drove** [drouv]: *ptp* **driven** ['drivn] – **1** *vti* to control or guide (a car *etc*): *She can drive a tractor*; *Do you want to drive, or shall I?* **2** *vi* to go in a vehicle: *I've driven with him often and he hasn't crashed yet.* **3** *vt* to take, bring *etc* in a car: *My mother is driving me to the airport.* **4** *vt* to force or urge along: *Two men and a dog were driving a herd of cattle across the road.* **5** *vt* to hit hard: *He drove a nail into the door*; *He drove a golf-ball from the tee.* **6** *vt* to cause to work by providing the necessary power: *This mill is driven by water.* – *See also* **drive on, drive off** *below.* – **1** *nc* a journey in a car, *esp* for pleasure: *She didn't speak during the short drive to the hotel*; *Since it was such a nice day we decided to go for a drive.* **2** *nc* a private road leading from a gate to a house *etc*: *The drive is lined with trees.* **3** *nu* energy and enthusiasm: *I think he has just the drive we need for this job.* **4** *nc* a campaign or special effort: *We're having a drive to increase our efficiency at present.* **5** *nc* a piece of machinery for operating something: *I think there's something wrong with the drive of my sewing-machine.* **6** *ncu* a method for operating something: *This car has front-wheel drive* (= its engine turns the front wheels rather than the back wheels). **7** *nc* in sport, a hard stroke (with a golf-club, a cricket bat *etc*).

'**driver** *nc* a person who drives a car *etc.*

'**drive-in** *adj* (*attrib*) (of a cinema, café *etc*, *esp* in North America) catering for people who remain in their cars while watching a film, eating *etc*: *a drive-in movie.* – *nc* a drive-in cinema or restaurant.

be 'driving at (*inf*) to be trying to say or suggest: *I don't know what he was driving at, but it sounded rude.*

drive a hard bargain to make an agreement with someone which is very much in one's own favour.

drive off **1** *vi* to leave or go away in a car *etc*: *He got into a van and drove off.* **2** *vt sep* to keep away: *The place where we picnicked was swarming with wasps and we spent most of the time driving them off.* **3** *vi* in golf, to make the first stroke of a hole from the tee.

drive on **1** *vi* to carry on driving (a car *etc*): *Drive on – we haven't time to stop!* **2** *vt oblig sep* to urge strongly forward: *He drove his horse on towards the fence*; (*fig*) *It was ambition which drove him on.*

drivel ['drivl] *nu* (*inf*) nonsense: *He talks a lot of drivel!* – *v* – *pt, ptp* '**drivelled,** (*Amer*) '**driveled** – *vi* to talk nonsense: *Oh, don't drivel – you know perfectly well that's not the case!*

drizzle ['drizl] *vi* (*only with* **it** *as subject*) to rain in small drops. – *nu* fine, light rain: *The rain has almost stopped – it's just drizzle now.*

'**drizzly** *adj*: *a drizzly day*; *It's cold and drizzly today.*

droll [droul] *adj* (*old or formal*) amusing, often because odd: *a droll child*; *a droll story*; *His way of speaking is very droll.*

dromedary *see* **camel**.

drone [droun] **1** *nc* the male of the bee. **2** *nc* (*fig*) a person who is lazy and idle as the drone bee is thought to be: *Society is divided into useful workers and useless drones.* **3** *nu* a deep, humming sound: *There was no sound but the distant drone of traffic on the motorway.* – *vi* **1** to make a low, humming sound: *An aeroplane droned overhead.* **2** (*fig*) to speak in a dull, boring voice: *Time passed, and the lecturer droned on and on.*

drool [dru:l] *vi* (*inf*) **1** to let saliva flow from or in the mouth in anticipation of food: *The delicious smells from the kitchen had us all drooling.* **2** (*fig*) to anticipate anything in an obvious manner: *He sat there drooling over the prospect of promotion.*

droop [dru:p] **1** *vti* (*formal*) to (cause to) hang down: *Several willows drooped over the pond.* **2** *vi* (*fig inf*) to grow weak or faint: *It had been a hard day and we were all drooping visibly.*

drop [drop] *nc* **1** a small round or pear-shaped blob of liquid, *usu* falling: *a drop of rain.* **2** a small quantity (of liquid): *If you want more wine, there's a drop left.* **3** an act of falling: *a drop in temperature.* **4** a vertical descent: *From the top of the mountain there was a sheer drop of a thousand feet.* **5** (*fig*) something shaped like a drop of water: *She had a pair of diamond drops in her ears.* – *v* – *pt, ptp* **dropped** – **1** *vt* to let fall, *usu* accidentally: *She dropped a whole box of pins all over the floor.* **2** *vi* to fall: *The penny dropped through the grating; The cat dropped* (= jumped down) *on to its paws;* (*fig*) *He finally dropped into a restless sleep.* **3** *vt* (*sometimes inf*) to give up (a friend, a habit *etc*): *I think she's dropped the idea of going to London.* **4** *vt* (*inf*) to set down from a car *etc*: *The bus dropped me at the end of the road.* **5** *vt* to say or write in an informal and casual manner: *I'll just drop a note to my sister while I'm waiting; I'll drop her a note; He dropped one or two general remarks about the weather.* – *See also* **drop** *in phrases below.*

'**droplet** [-lit] *nc* (*often liter*) a tiny drop: *Droplets of rain shone on her hair.*

'**dropper** *nc* an instrument for making liquid fall in drops: *She measured the liquid out of the bottle with a dropper.*

'**droppings** *n pl* excrement (of animals or birds): *mouse droppings.*

'**drop-out** *nc* (*inf*) a person who withdraws, *esp* from a course at a university *etc* or the normal life of society: *She was worried because her son had given up his job and become a drop-out.* – *See also* **drop out** *below.*

at the drop of a hat immediately and needing only the slightest reason or excuse: *Watch her – she'd report you to the police at the drop of a hat; He expects me to dash off to Paris at the drop of a hat, whether it's convenient or not.*

drop a brick/drop a clanger to mention a subject or communicate a piece of information to a person or persons to whom one should not have mentioned it, *esp* to do so in such a way that the mistake cannot be covered up: *You certainly dropped a brick when you mentioned Jack to her – they were divorced two years ago.*

drop back *vi* to slow down while walking *etc* so that one ceases to be in the group in which one originally was: *I was tired of being at the front of the crowd so I dropped back to speak to Bill.*

drop by *vi* to visit someone casually and without being invited: *I'll drop by on my way home if I've time.*

drop in 1 *vi* to arrive informally to visit someone: *Do drop in if you happen to be passing!* **2** *vt oblig sep* to leave (something) for someone: *Just drop the book in at my house sometime, when you've finished it!*

a drop in the bucket/ocean a tiny part of the quantity which is needed: *The work we can do in this area is, of course, just a drop in the ocean.*

drop off 1 *vi, vt fus* to become separated or fall off: *I was trying to open the door when the door-handle dropped off; I think this button has just dropped off your coat.* **2** *vi* (*inf*) to fall asleep: *I was so tired I dropped off in front of the television.* **3** *vi* (*inf*) to become less: *Sales have dropped off during the last three months.*

drop out *vi* (*often with* **of**) to withdraw, *esp* from a course at university *etc* or from the normal life of society: *There are only two of us going to the theatre now Mary has dropped out; She's dropped out of college.* – *See also* **drop-out** *above.*

dross [dros] *nu* small or waste pieces of coal: *There's nothing but dross left in the coal-cellar;* (*derog inf*) *All the best students have found jobs – there's just the dross left.*

drought [draut] *ncu* (a period of) lack of rain or of water: *The land was in a state of drought for six months; The reservoir dried up completely during the drought.*

drove [drouv] *v see* **drive**. – *nc* a number of moving cattle or other animals: *A drove of cattle was moving across the hill;* (*fig*) *I battled my way along the High Street through droves of shoppers.*

'**drover** *nc* (*hist*) a man employed to drive cattle.

drown [draun] **1** *vti* to (cause to) sink in water and so suffocate and die: *He drowned in the river; Somebody had drowned her in her bath.* **2** *vt* (*fig often liter*) to flood or soak in a liquid: *The river had overflowed its banks and drowned the low-lying farmland;* (*facet*) *She drowned her steam-pudding in custard.* **3** *vt* (*sometimes with* **out**) to cause (a sound) not to be heard by making a louder sound: *His voice was drowned* (*out*) by the roar of the traffic.

drowsy ['drauzi] *adj* **1** sleepy: *drowsy children; The warmth of the fire made him feel drowsy.* **2** causing sleepiness: *a drowsy day.* '**drowsily** *adv.* '**drowsiness** *nu.*

drudge [drʌdʒ] *vi* to do dull, very hard or humble work: *You should leave your job – you just drudge all day for poor wages!* – *nc* a person who does such work: *His wife is treated as a mere drudge.*

'**drudgery** *nu* hard or humble work.

drug [drʌg] *nc* **1** any substance used in medicine: *She has been prescribed a new kind of drug for her stomach-pains.* **2** a substance, sometimes one used in medicine, taken by some people to achieve a certain effect, *eg* great happiness or excitement: *I think she takes drugs; He behaves as though he is on drugs.* – *v* – *pt, ptp* **drugged** – *vt* to make to lose consciousness by giving a drug: *She drugged him and tied him up.*

'**druggist** *nc* **1** (*old or Amer*) a person who sells medicines *etc*; a chemist (*def 2*). **2** (*Amer*) a pharmacist. **3** a druggist's shop: *Where is the nearest druggist?*

'**druggist's** *nc* (*Amer*) a druggist's shop: *I'm going to the druggist's.*

'**drug-ˌaddict** *nc* a person who has formed the habit of taking drugs.

'**drugstore** *nc* (*Amer*) a shop which sells various articles (*eg* cosmetics, newspapers and soft drinks) as well as medicines.

drum [drʌm] *nc* **1** a musical instrument constructed of skin *etc* stretched on a round frame of wood or metal and beaten with a stick: *He plays the drums.* **2** something shaped like a drum, *esp* a container: *an oil-drum.* **3** an eardrum. – *v* – *pt, ptp* **drummed** – **1** *vi* to beat a drum: *He bought himself a drum-kit and spent the evenings drumming in the attic.* **2** *vti* to tap continuously *esp* with the fingers: *Stop drumming (your fingers) on the table!* **3** *vi* to make a sound like someone beating a drum: *The rain drummed loudly on the metal roof.* **4** *vt* (*with* **into**) to force (someone) to remember (something) by constantly repeating it: *My mother kept drumming it into me that I was to remember to thank you.*

'drummer *nc* a person who plays the drums.

'drum-kit *nc* a set of three or more drums used for playing in a band *etc.*

,drum-'major *nc* the marching leader of a military band.

'drumstick *nc* **1** a stick used for beating a drum. **2** the lower part of the leg of a cooked chicken *etc.*

drum in *vt sep* to force someone to remember (something) by repeating it constantly: *You never remember anything unless I drum it in.* – *See also* **drum** (*def 4*).

drunk [drʌŋk] *v see* **drink** – *adj* overcome by having too much alcohol: *He was arrested for causing a nuisance while drunk; A drunk man fell off the bus; (fig) She was too drunk with unexpected success to listen.* – *nc* a drunk person, *esp* one who is often drunk: *I was befriended by a drunk at the bus-stop who was difficult to get rid of.*

'drunkard [-kəd] *nc* (*formal*) a person who is often drunk: *I'm afraid he's turning into a drunkard.*

'drunken *adj* (*attrib*) **1** drunk: *She was approached by several drunken soldiers who were in the pub.* **2** caused by being drunk: *a drunken stupor.*

'drunkenness *nu.*

dry [drai] *adj* **1** having little, or no, moisture, sap, rain *etc*: *The ground is quite dry – it hasn't rained for ages; The leaves of this plant have become dry and withered; Can I have milk with my pudding – it's very dry; I'll need to find dry socks for the children – their feet are soaking after their walk in the rain.* **2** (*usu pred*) uninteresting and not lively: *This book is so dry it's difficult to read.* **3** (of humour or manner) quiet, restrained and unemotional: *He has such a dry sense of humour that a lot of people miss his jokes altogether; His sense of humour is very dry.* **4** (of wine) not sweet: *a dry white wine; That wine is too dry for my taste.* – *vti* to (cause to) become dry: *I washed the dishes and he dried them; The roads dried quickly in the sunshine.* – *See also* **dry** *in phrases below.*

'drier, 'dryer *nc* (*often in cmpds*) a machine *etc* that dries: *a spin-drier; a hair-dryer.*

'drily, 'dryly *adv* in a quiet, unrestrained and unemotional, but often humorous, manner: *He commented drily on the untidiness of the room.*

'dryness *nu.*

,dry-'clean *vt* to clean (clothes *etc*) with chemicals, not with water.

dry land *nu* the land as opposed to the sea *etc.*

dry rot *nu* the decay of timber caused by fungi which make it dry and brittle: *The timbers of the roof are full of dry rot.*

cut and dried *see* **cut**.

dry off *vi, vt sep* to make or become completely dry (*esp* something which is not very wet or only wet on the surface): *She climbed out of the bath and dried herself off.*

dry out 1 *vi, vt sep* to make or become completely dry (*esp* something which is soaked through): *It'll take ages to dry out your gloves!* **2** *vt sep* (*fig inf*) to cure or make better (an alcoholic): *He went to a nursing-home to be dried out.*

dry up 1 *vi* (of a liquid or of a source of liquid) to cease completely to be or provide liquid: *All the rivers dried up in the heat; (fig) All my normal sources of news have dried up; Supplies of bandages for the refugees have dried up sooner than expected.* **2** *vt sep* to make dry: *The sun dried up the puddles in the road.* **3** *vi* (*inf*) (of a speaker) to forget what to say, *eg* in a play: *He dried up in the middle of the scene.*

high and dry *see* **high**.

dual ['djuəl] *adj* (*attrib*) **1** consisting of two separate parts: *As an employee and a shareholder, he had a dual interest in the firm.* **2** in the hands of two people: *My sister and I have dual ownership of the flat; The driving instructor's car has dual controls.*

dual carriageway *nc* a road divided by a central strip of land *etc* with each side used by traffic moving in one direction.

,dual-'purpose *adj* serving two purposes: *a dual-purpose tool.*

dub[1] [dʌb] – *pt, ptp* **dubbed** – *vt* **1** to give (a film) a new sound-track (*eg* in a different language): *This film has been dubbed – the characters don't look as if they're speaking English.* **2** to add sound effects or music to (a film *etc*): *The battle scene was dubbed with suitable noises later.* **'dubbing** *nu.*

dub[2] [dʌb] – *pt, ptp* **dubbed** – *vt* (*formal*) **1** to give a nickname to: *He was dubbed Shorty because of his size.* **2** to give a knighthood to, by touching each shoulder with a sword: *He was dubbed a knight by the Queen.*

dubious ['dju:biəs] *adj* (*formal*) **1** (*usu pred*) doubtful: *I am dubious about the wisdom of this action.* **2** (*derog*) probably not honest: *dubious behaviour; His reasons for coming seem rather dubious.*

dubiety [dju'baiəti], **'dubiousness** *nus* (*formal*) the state or quality of being dubious: *The dubiety of his dealings gave cause for concern.*

ducal *see* **duke**.

duchess ['dʌtʃis] *nc* (*with cap in titles*) **1** the wife or widow of a duke: *the Duchess of Buckingham.* **2** a woman of the same rank as a duke: *When did she become a duchess?*

duchy ['dʌtʃi] *nc* (*with cap in names*) the territory ruled or owned by a duke: *the Duchy of Parma.*

duck[1] [dʌk] **1** *vti* to go, or push (someone), briefly under water: *They splashed about, shouting and ducking each other like a lot of children.* **2** *vi* to lower the head suddenly as if to avoid a blow: *He ducked as the ball shot over his head.*

duck[2] [dʌk] – *pls* **ducks**, (*rare*) **duck** – **1** *nc* a kind of wild or domesticated water-bird with short legs and a broad flat beak. **2** *nu* its flesh used as food: *roast duck.* **3** *nc* a female duck. – *See also* **drake**. **4** *nc* in cricket, a score by a batsman of nil: *He was out for a duck.*

'duckling [-liŋ] *nc* a baby duck.

duct [dʌkt] *nc* a tube or pipe for fluids, electric cable *etc*: *a ventilation duct; a tear duct.*

ductile ['dʌktail] *adj* (*tech*) capable of being drawn out into wire or threads: *Silver is a ductile metal.*

dud [dʌd] *nc* (*inf*) something which is useless, does

not work or is broken *etc* before being used: *This light-bulb is a dud; I think your washing-machine is a dud.* – *adj* useless or not working: *a dud battery; This penknife is dud – the blades are blunt.*

dudgeon ['dʌdʒən] : **in high dudgeon** in a state of great resentment or anger: *She stalked off in high dudgeon.*

due [dju:] *adj* **1** (*pred*) owed: *I think I'm due several pounds in expenses*; (*formal*) *Our thanks are due to the doctor.* **2** (*pred*) expected according to timetable, promise *etc*: *The bus is due in three minutes.* **3** (*attrib*) proper: *Take due care; We paid due attention to the problem.* – *adv* directly: *sailing due east.* – *nc* **1** what is owed, *esp* what one has a right to: *I'm only taking what is my due.* **2** (*in pl*) charge, fee or toll: *He paid the dues on the cargo.*

'**duly** *adv* properly, *esp* at the proper time or as expected: *The bus duly arrived; He duly asked her as he had been told to.*

'**due to 1** brought about by: *His success was due to hard work.* **2** (*loosely*) because of: *The game has been cancelled due to frost.*

give (someone) his due to be fair to someone (*usu* by mentioning a point in his favour when he is being criticized): *To give him his due, he did try to warn me.*

See also **undue**.

duel ['djuəl] *nc* **1** (*hist*) a fight (with swords or pistols) between two people over a matter of honour *etc.* **2** (*fig*) any contest between two people or two sides: *The two teams are locked in a duel for first place.* – *v* – *pt, ptp* '**duelled** – *vi* (*hist*) to fight a duel: *They duelled on the common at daybreak.*

'**duellist** *nc* (*hist*) a person who fights in a duel.

duet [dju'et] *nc* a musical piece for two singers or players: *The two sisters played a piano duet; a duet for soprano and alto.*

duffel-coat, duffle-coat ['dʌfəlkout] *nc* a coat of coarse woollen cloth *usu* with a hood attached, and toggles instead of buttons.

'**duffel bag** *nc* a large bag with a round bottom, straight sides and a drawstring at the top: *She had her swimming things in a duffel bag over her shoulder.*

duffer ['dʌfə] *nc* (*slightly old*) a stupid person, *esp* one who cannot do something: *He's a duffer when it comes to schoolwork.*

dug *see* **dig**.

duke [dju:k] *nc* (*with cap in titles*) a nobleman of the highest rank: *Her daughter has married a duke; the Duke of Gloucester.*

ducal ['dju:kəl] *adj* (*formal*) of a duke.

'**dukedom** *nc* the title, rank or territories of a duke.

See also **duchess, duchy**.

dulcet ['dʌlsit] *adj* (*liter*: *attrib*) sweet to the ear: *the dulcet tones of a flute.*

dull [dʌl] *adj* **1** slow to learn or to understand: *I'm afraid this book is too advanced for the dull children in the class; Their eldest child is very dull.* **2** not bright or clear: *a dull day; The day was dull but dry.* **3** not exciting or interesting: *a very dull book/party; The play we saw last night was very dull.* **4** blunt: *The edge of this knife is quite dull.* – *vt* to make or become less sharp, clear or aware: *Her senses were dulled by the amount she had drunk; The drugs dulled the pain of his injury.*

'**dully** *adv.* '**dullness** *nu.*

ˌ**dull as** '**ditchwater** (*inf*) extremely dull and uninteresting: *She is very lively but her husband is as dull as ditchwater.*

duly *see* **due**.

dumb [dʌm] *adj* **1** without the power of speech: *She was born dumb*; (*fig*) *Not unnaturally, this remark struck us dumb; You mustn't hurt poor dumb animals.* **2** (*liter*) silent: *On this point, the great writers are dumb.* **3** (*inf*: *esp Amer*) very stupid: *Well, that was a dumb thing to do!; She's what is known as a dumb blonde; Don't be so dumb!*

'**dumbness** *nu.*

'**dumbly** *adv* without saying anything *esp* because unable to think of anything to say: *Dumbly, we did as we were told.*

dum(b)found [dʌm'faund] *vt* to make speechless with amazement: *His peculiar behaviour has frequently dumbfounded me!*

dummy ['dʌmi] *nc* **1** something which seems real but is not: *All the packets of cigarettes on display were dummies*; (*attrib*) *How was I to know that that was a dummy bottle of wine?* **2** a model of a human used for displaying clothes *etc*: *a dressmaker's dummy.* **3** an artificial teat put in a baby's mouth to comfort it.

dummy run *nc* a practice to try out or test something: *To make sure that the ceremony would go smoothly, the organizers arranged a dummy run the day before.*

dump [dʌmp] *vt* **1** (*inf*) to set (down) heavily: *She dumped the heavy shopping-bag on the table.* **2** to unload and leave (rubbish *etc*): *People come and dump things over our wall.* – *nc* a place for leaving or storing unwanted things: *a rubbish dump.*

dumpiness *see* **dumpy**.

dumpling ['dʌmpliŋ] *ncu* (a) thick pudding or ball of cooked dough: *We had dumpling and custard; stewed beef and dumplings.*

dumps [dʌmps]: **(ˌdown) in the** '**dumps** in a state of depression or low spirits: *He's in the dumps today.*

dumpy ['dʌmpi] *adj* (*derog*) short and thick or fat: *She was a plain, dumpy little woman; I had forgotten that she was so dumpy.* '**dumpiness** *nu.*

dun[1] [dʌn] *adj* (*attrib*) of a pale yellowish or greyish brown colour: *a dun horse.*

dun[2] [dʌn] – *pt, ptp* **dunned** – *vt* (*old or formal*) to demand payment from: *The servants were all dunning him for their wages.*

dunce [dʌns] *nc* a person who is slow at learning or stupid: *I was an absolute dunce at school.*

dunderhead ['dʌndəhed] *nc* (*inf*) a stupid person.

dune [dju:n] *nc* (*also* '**sand-dune**) a low hill of sand: *Between the beach and the road were many sand-dunes.*

dung [dʌŋ] *nu* the waste matter passed out of an animal's body, *esp* when used as manure: *I was given a load of dung to put on my roses.*

'**dunghill** *nc* a heap of dung.

dungarees [dʌŋgə'ri:z] *n pl* trousers made of coarse, hard-wearing material with a bib: *a pair of dungarees.*

dungeon ['dʌndʒən] *nc* a dark underground prison.

dunk [dʌŋk] *vt* (*inf*) to dip (cake *etc* which one is eating) into coffee, tea *etc*: *I wish you wouldn't dunk your doughnut in your coffee in that disgusting way!*

duodenum [dju:ə'di:nəm] *nc* (*tech*) part of the digestive system of a person or animal, the first part of the small intestine below the stomach.

ˌ**duo'denal** *adj* (*attrib*): *a duodenal ulcer.*

dupe [dju:p] *nc* a person who is cheated or

deceived: *She has been making you her dupe for much too long.* – *vt* to deceive or trick: *He duped me into thinking he had gone home.*

duplicate ['dju:plikət] *adj* (*attrib*) exactly the same (as something else): *a duplicate copy*; *a duplicate key.* – *nc* **1** another thing of exactly the same kind: *He managed to find a perfect duplicate of the ring she had lost.* **2** an exact copy, *usu* written: *She gave everyone a duplicate of her report.* – [-keit] *vt* to make an exact copy or copies of: *It occurred to me that I was just duplicating his work*; *He duplicated the letter so that we could all have a copy.*
ˌ**dupli'cation** *nu.*
'**duplicator** [-kei-] *nc* a machine for making exact copies of documents *etc.*
in 'duplicate [-kət] (*formal*) in two copies: *All applications have to be submitted in duplicate.*

duplicity [dju'plisəti] *nu* (*formal*) deceit and trickery: *I wouldn't have thought him capable of such duplicity!*

durable ['djuərəbl] *adj* (*formal*) **1** lasting or able to last: *There is no hope of a durable peace between the two countries.* **2** wearing well: *This coat is durable enough to wear every day*; *His trousers are of very durable material.* ˌ**dura'bility** *nu.*

duration [dju'reiʃən] *nu* (*formal*) the length of time anything continues: *We all had to stay indoors for the duration of the crisis.*

duress [dju'res]: **under duress** (*formal*) under the influence of force, threats *etc*: *The defendant claimed to have signed the paper under duress.*

during ['djuəriŋ] *prep* throughout all or part of the time of: *We couldn't get cigarettes during the war.* **2** at a particular point within (a period of time): *He died during the war.*

dusk [dʌsk] *ncu* (*slightly liter*) (the time of) partial darkness after the sun sets; twilight: *Dusk sets in early in winter*; *I remember sitting on the verandah during summer dusks, drinking wine.*
'**dusky** *adj* (*liter*) dark-coloured. '**duskiness** *nu.*

dust [dʌst] *nu* **1** fine grains of earth, sand *etc*: *In midsummer the road was covered in dust*; *My mother was cleaning the room and the air was full of dust.* **2** (*often in cmpds*) anything in the form of fine powder: *gold-dust*; *sawdust*; *The cloth was so ancient that it fell to dust as he touched it.* – **1** *vti* to free (furniture *etc*) from dust: *She dusted the ornaments carefully*; *She dusts once a week.* **2** *vt* to cover with a powdery substance: *She dusted the sweets with icing sugar.*
'**duster** *nc* a cloth for removing dust.
'**dusty** *adj* covered with, or containing, dust: *She looked disapprovingly at the dusty floor*; *The furniture was dusty and the house looked untidy.* '**dustiness** *nu.*
dustbin ['dʌsbin] *nc* (*Amer* '**garbage-can** *or* '**trash-can**) a container for household rubbish: *She put the potato-peelings in the dustbin outside the back door.*
dust-jacket ['dʌsdʒakit] *nc* the loose paper cover of a book.
dustman ['dʌsmən] *nc* a person employed to remove household rubbish: *The rubbish piled up when the dustmen were on strike.*
dustpan ['dʌspan] *nc* a type of flat container with a handle, used for holding dust swept from the floor.
'**dust-sheet** *nc* a cloth used to protect furniture *etc* from dust: *When the room was not in use they covered the furniture with dust-sheets.*
'**dust-up** *nc* (*inf*) an argument or quarrel: *I'm afraid there was a bit of a dust-up when they found out.*
bite the dust *see* **bite**.
dust down *vt sep* **1** to brush in order to remove the dust from: *She picked herself up and dusted herself down.* **2** (*fig inf*) to reprimand or scold: *He dusted his staff down about the drop in their efficiency.*
throw dust in someone's eyes to (attempt to) deceive: *She only mentioned the possibility in order to throw dust in my eyes.*

Dutch [dʌtʃ]: **Dutch comfort** *nu* telling a person to whom something unpleasant has happened that they have been spared something worse.
Dutch courage *nu* an artificial courage gained by drinking alcohol: *He needed some Dutch courage before asking her to marry him.*
Dutchman, Dutchwoman *see* Appendix 2.
double-Dutch *see* **double**.
go Dutch (*inf*) to pay each for oneself (at a restaurant, the cinema *etc*): *Since neither had much money, they always went Dutch when they were out together.*
See also Appendix 2.

duty ['dju:ti] **1** *nu* what one ought morally or legally to do: *He acts for the most part out of duty*; *I do my duty as a responsible citizen.* **2** *nc* (*often in pl*) an action or task requiring to be done, *esp* one attached to a job: *I had a few duties to perform in connection with my position as warden.* **3** *ncu* (a) tax on goods: *You must pay duty when you bring wine into the country.*
'**dutiable** *adj* (*formal*) (of goods) on which tax is to be paid: *I didn't bring any dutiable goods home from holiday with me*; *These things are not dutiable.*
'**dutiful** *adj* (*neg* **un-**) careful to do what one should: *I went to visit my mother like a dutiful daughter*; *He's usually so dutiful and obedient.*
ˌ**duty-'free** *adj* free from tax: *You are allowed to buy a certain number of cigarettes duty-free on the plane*; *duty-free wines.*
off duty not actually working and not liable to be asked to do so: *I'm off duty this weekend so I'm going out*; (*attrib*) *She spent her off-duty hours at home.*
on duty carrying out one's duties or liable to be asked to do so during a certain period: *I'm on duty again for four hours this evening.*

duvet ['du:vei] *nc* (*also* **continental quilt, downie** ® ['dauni]) a type of quilt stuffed with feathers, down or a man-made material and used instead of blankets on a bed.

dwarf [dwo:f] – *pls* **dwarfs**, (*rare*) **dwarves** [dwo:vz] – *nc* **1** an animal, plant or person much smaller than normal: (*attrib*) *a dwarf tree.* **2** in fairy tales *etc*, a creature like a tiny man, with magic powers: *the story of Snow White and the seven dwarfs.* – *vt* **1** to make to appear small: *The cathedral was dwarfed by the skyscrapers which rose all around it.* **2** to stop from growing: *The plants had been dwarfed by the lack of warmth.*

dwell [dwel] – *pts, ptps* **dwelt** [-t], **dwelled** – *vi* (*arch or liter*) to live (in a place): *She dwelt in the middle of a dark forest.*
'**dwelling** *nc* (*old*) a house, flat *etc* where people live.
'**dwelling-house** *nc* (*formal*) a house used for living in, not as an office, shop *etc.*
'**dwell on** *vt fus* to think or speak about something for a long time: *It doesn't help to dwell on your problems for too long*; *He dwelt at length in his*

speech on various approaches to the subject.

dwindle ['dwindl] *vi* to grow less in size; to waste away: *His fortune/hopes dwindled.*

dye [dai] – *pt, ptp* **dyed**: *prp* '**dyeing** – *vt* to give a permanent colour to (clothes, cloth *etc*): *I've just dyed my coat green; I'm sure she dyes her hair.* – *nu* a powder or liquid for colouring: *I bought a bottle of dye to use on my curtains.*

ˌ**dyed-in-the-'wool** *adj* (*derog*: *usu attrib*) of firmly fixed opinions: *He's a dyed-in-the-wool Tory.*

dying *see* **die**[1].

dyke, dike [daik] *nc* (*dial*) **1** a ditch. **2** an embankment or wall.

dynamic [dai'namik] *adj* **1** (*tech*) concerned with force. **2** (of a person) forceful and very energetic: *She was such a dynamic person she could make everyone enthusiastic.* **dy'namically** *adv*.

dy'namics *n sing* the science that deals with movement and force.

dynamite ['dainəmait] *nu* a type of powerful explosive.

dynamo ['dainəmou] – *pl* '**dynamos** – *nc* a machine that produces electric currents by means of the movement of conductors and magnets.

dynasty ['dinəsti, (*Amer*) 'dai-] *nc* (*formal*) a succession or series of rulers of the same family: *the Tudor and Stuart dynasties.* **dy'nastic** [-'nas-] *adj*.

dysentery ['disəntri] *nu* an infectious disease with severe diarrhoea.

dyslexia [dis'leksiə] *nu* (*tech*) great difficulty in reading and spelling, caused by an inability to see words as meaningful shapes: *She teaches children who suffer from dyslexia.*

dys'lexic *nc, adj* (*tech*) (a person) suffering from dyslexia: *The child is a dyslexic; a dyslexic child.*

dyspepsia [dis'pepsiə] *nu* (*formal or tech*) indigestion: *The doctor said the pains in her chest were caused by dyspepsia.*

dys'peptic [-tik] *adj* (*formal or tech*) **1** suffering from dyspepsia: *He is a bit dyspeptic after meals.* **2** of, or caused by, dyspepsia: *a dyspeptic condition.* **3** (*inf*) bad-tempered: *a dyspeptic old man.*

Ee

each [iːtʃ] *adj* (*attrib*) every (thing, person, group *etc*) of two or more, considered separately: *each house in this street; He has an apple in each hand.* – *pron* every single one, of two or more: *Each of the boys was eager to go; Each of them has 5p; They each have 5p.* – *adv* to or for each one; apiece: *I gave them an apple each; The apples are 10p each.*

each other used as the object when an action takes place between two (loosely, more than two) people *etc*: *They wounded each other; She and her mother talk to each other on the phone every day; The members of that family are very attached to each other.* – *See also* **one another**.

eager ['iːgə] *adj* full of desire, interest *etc*; keen; enthusiastic: *He is always eager to win; I am eager for her to win; They were eager for victory; He is an eager collector of stamps.* '**eagerness** *nu*.

'**eagerly** *adv*: *He listened eagerly to what she was saying; He watched eagerly for the postman.*

eagle ['iːgl] *nc* a kind of large bird of prey noted for its good eyesight.

eaglet ['iːglit] *nc* a young eagle.

ear[1] [iə] *nc* **1** the part of the head by means of which we hear, or its external part only: *Doctors need special instruments to examine the inner parts of ears; Her new hair-style covers her ears; The dog lost an ear in the fight;* (*attrib*) *She has an ear infection.* **2** the sense or power of hearing *esp* the ability to hear the difference between sounds: *She has sharp ears; He has a good ear for music.* **3** (*formal fig*) (favourable) attention: *He succeeded in getting the chairman's ear; He has the king's ear and influences all his decisions.*

'**earache** *nu* pain in the inner part of the ear: *That child often has earache in the winter; He suffers from earache.*

'**eardrum** *nc* the layer of tissue separating the inner from the outer ear.

'**earmark** *vt* to set aside (for a particular purpose): *This money is earmarked for our holiday.*

earphones *see* **headphones**.

'**earring** *nc* an ornament worn attached to the ear: *She wore silver earrings.*

'**earshot** *nu* the distance at which sound can be heard: *He did not hear her last remark as he was out of earshot; Are the children within earshot?*

be all ears (*inf*) to listen with keen attention: *The children were all ears when their father was describing the car crash.*

be out on one's ear (*inf*) to be dismissed; to be asked to leave suddenly: *If the manager finds out you're always late for work, you'll be out on your ear.*

go in one ear and out the other (*inf*) not to make any lasting impression: *I keep telling that child to work harder but my words go in one ear and out the other.*

have one's ear to the ground to pay attention to, and keep oneself well informed about, all that is happening around one: *If you keep your ear to the ground you'll soon find a new job.*

play/learn by ear to play *etc* (a piece of music) without looking at and without having memorized printed music: *They asked him to play the piano at the party but he could not play by ear and he had no music with him.*

play it by ear *see* **play**.

turn a deaf ear *see* **turn**.

up to one's ears (in) deeply involved (in): *I'm up to my ears in work; He is up to his ears in trouble/debt.*

See also **aural**.

ear[2] [iə] *nc* the part of a cereal plant which contains the seed: *ears of corn/barley.*

earl [əːl] *nc* (*with cap in titles*) (the status of) a British nobleman between a marquis and a viscount in rank: *He was made an earl; the Earl of Baberton.*

'**earldom** *nc* the title, rank or territories of an earl.

See also **countess** *under* **count**[1].

early ['əːli] *adv* **1** near the beginning (of a period of time, course, series *etc*): *early in my life; She arrived early in the afternoon; early in the development of television.* – *See also* **early on** *below*. **2** sooner than others; sooner than usual; sooner than expected or than the appointed time: *He* *arrived early*; *She came an hour early to avoid the crowd*; *He was too early for his interview.* – *adj* (*usu attrib*) **1** belonging to, or happening, near the beginning of a period of time *etc*: *The birds sing in the early morning*; *in the early part of the century.* **2** belonging to the first stages of development: *early musical instruments.* **3** happening *etc* sooner than usual or than expected: *He grows early potatoes*; *They were unprepared for the baby's early arrival*; *It's too early to get up yet.* **4** happening in, or belonging to, the near future; prompt: *I hope for an early reply to my letter.* '**earliness** *nu.*

early bird *nc* (*inf*) **1** an early riser: *People with young children are usually early birds.* **2** a person who gains advantage by acting more promptly than others: *You have to be an early bird if you want to get a bargain at an auction sale.*

early on at or near the beginning of a period of time, series *etc*: *He became famous early on in his career*; *We realized early on that the child was brilliant.*

earmark *see* **ear**[1].

earn [əːn] *vti* **1** to gain (money, wages, one's living) by working: *He earns £50 a week*; *She earns a high salary*; *He earns his living by playing the piano*; *You can afford a car now that you're earning.* **2** to gain: *My quick action earned me his praise.* **3** to deserve: *I've earned a rest.*

'**earnings** *n pl* money *etc* earned: *His earnings are not sufficient to support his family.*

See also **well-earned**.

earnest ['əːnist] *adj* **1** (*sometimes derog*) serious or over-serious: *He is an earnest student of theology*; *She wore an earnest expression*; *She is very amusing but her fiancé is rather earnest.* **2** (*often formal*) showing determination, sincerity or strong feeling: *He made an earnest attempt to improve his work*; *The father could not refuse the child's earnest request.* '**earnestness** *nu.*

'**earnestly** *adv*: *He earnestly believes that he is right*; *He spoke earnestly about his religious beliefs.*

in 'earnest 1 serious; not joking: *I am in earnest when I say this.* **2** seriously; with energy and determination: *He set to work in earnest.*

earring, earshot *see* **ear**[1].

earth [əːθ] **1** *n* (*with cap and/or* **the**) the third planet in order of distance from the Sun; the planet on which we live: *Is Earth nearer the Sun than Mars is?*; *the geography of the earth.* **2** *n* the world as opposed to heaven: *heaven and earth.* **3** *nu* soil: *Fill a plant pot with earth and plant the seeds.* **4** *nu* dry land or the land surface; the ground: *the earth, sea and sky.* **5** *nc* a burrow or hole of an animal, *esp* of a fox. **6** *nc* (a wire that provides) an electrical connection with the earth. – *vt* to connect to earth electrically: *Is your washing-machine properly earthed?* – *See also* **earth** *in phrases below.*

'**earthen** *adj* (*formal*: *esp attrib*) **1** (of a floor *etc*) made of earth. **2** (of pottery) made of baked clay: *an old earthen jar.*

'**earthly** *adj* (*usu attrib*) **1** (*liter*) of or belonging to this world; not heavenly or spiritual: *In this earthly life nothing is perfect.* **2** (*inf*: *used in neg*) possible: *You have no earthly chance of winning*; *This car is of no earthly use.* – *See also* **not have an earthly** *below.*

'**earthy** *adj* **1** (*inf*) of, like or covered in soil: *These potatoes are very earthy.* **2** (*fig*) without gentleness or refinement; coarse: *He has a very earthy sense of humour.* '**earthiness** *nu.*

'**earthenware** *nu, adj* (of) a kind of pottery coarser than china: *She collects earthenware*; *an earthenware dish.*

'**earthquake** *nc* a shaking of the earth's surface: *Most of the houses in the village were destroyed in the earthquake*; *The village was destroyed by an earthquake.*

'**earth-tremor** *nc* a slight earthquake.

'**earthwork** *nc* (*often in pl*: *hist*) a wall, defensive bank *etc* built of earth: *Archaeologists have uncovered some ancient earthworks.*

'**earthworm** *nc* (*usu* **worm**) a kind of small animal with a ringed body and no backbone, living in damp earth.

come back/down to earth to start being aware of the practical details of life after a period of dreaming, great happiness *etc*: *They were thrilled when the baby arrived but came back to earth suddenly when he cried all night*; *She was madly in love with him for several weeks but came down to earth (with a bang) when she discovered he was married.*

go to earth (of a fox *etc*) to go into its hole or hiding-place: *The huntsman could not catch the fox before it went to earth*; (*fig*) *The police could not find the thief – he had gone to earth.*

like nothing on earth *see* **nothing**.

move heaven and earth *see* **move**.

not have an earthly (*inf*) **1** to have not the slightest chance of success: *He has entered the tennis competition but he hasn't an earthly.* **2** to have no knowledge or information about: *'Do you know where he is now?' 'No, I haven't an earthly.'*

on 'earth used for emphasis: *What on earth are you doing?*; *He is the stupidest man on earth*; *Where on earth did you get that?*

run to earth 1 to chase or hunt a fox to its hole or hiding-place. **2** to find (something or someone) after a long search: *He has been looking for a copy of that book for a long time. He finally ran one to earth in Edinburgh.*

See also **unearthly**.

earwig ['iəwig] *nc* a kind of insect with pincers at the end of its body.

ease [iːz] *nu* **1** (*often formal*) freedom from pain or from worry or hard work: *The medicine brought him some ease*; *He led a lifetime of ease.* – *See also* **take one's ease** *below.* **2** freedom from difficulty: *The horse jumped the stream with ease*; *He passed his exam with ease.* **3** naturalness: *Other actors admire his ease of manner.* – *See also* **at ease** *below.* – **1** *vt* (*formal*) to free from pain, trouble or anxiety: *The news that her child was safe eased her mind*; *A hot bath eased his tired limbs.* **2** *vti* (*often with* **off**) to make or become less strong, less severe, less tight, less fast *etc*: *The pain has eased (off)*; *The driver eased off as he approached the town.* **3** *vt* to move (something heavy or awkward) gently or gradually in or out of position: *You will have to ease the wardrobe carefully up the narrow staircase*; *You will have to ease that dress over the hips.*

'**easily** *adv* **1** without difficulty; with ease: *She won the race easily*; *He can do that job easily.* **2** clearly; beyond doubt; by far: *He is easily the best worker we have*; *This is easily the best book I've read this year.* **3** very probably; very likely: *The train may easily be late*; *It may easily rain tomorrow.*

'**easiness** *nu* the state or quality of being easy.

'**easy** *adj* **1** not difficult: *This is an easy job (to do)*; *Those sums were easy.* **2** free from pain, trouble, anxiety *etc*: *He had an easy day at the office.* **3** not stiff or formal; friendly: *an easy manner/smile*; *She is very easy to work with.* **4** relaxed; not strained; leisurely: *The farmer walked with an easy stride.* **5** (*inf*: *pred*) having no strong preference: *'Do you want this one or that one?' 'I don't mind – I'm easy.'* – *interj* a command to go or act gently: *Easy! You'll fall if you run too fast.*

easy chair *nc* a chair that is soft and comfortable, *eg* an armchair: *two easy chairs by the fire.*

ˌ**easy-'going** *adj* not inclined to worry: *The new teacher is so easy-going that the children are becoming very noisy*; *an easy-going young man.*

ill-at-ease *see under* **ill**.

at 'ease 1 free from anxiety or embarrassment: *He is completely at ease among strangers.* **2** (*mil*) (standing) with legs apart and hands clasped behind the back.

easier said than done more difficult than it at first seems: *Getting seats for the theatre is easier said than done.*

go easy on (*inf*) to be careful with: *Go easy on the wine – there won't be enough for the rest of the guests.*

stand at ease (*mil*) to stand with legs apart and hands clasped behind the back.

stand easy (*mil*) to stand in a more relaxed position than standing at ease.

take it easy 1 not to work *etc* hard or energetically; to avoid using much effort: *Take it easy – you don't have to finish the job until tomorrow*; *The doctor told him to take it easy.* **2** (*usu in imperative*) not to get upset, angry *etc*: *Take it easy! There's no need to lose your temper.*

take one's ease (*formal or facet*) to make oneself comfortable; to relax: *There he was – taking his ease in his father's armchair!*

See also **uneasy**.

easel ['i:zl] *nc* a (hinged) stand for supporting a blackboard, an artist's picture *etc*.

east [i:st] *nu* **1** the direction from which the sun rises, or any part of the earth lying in that direction: *We looked towards the east*; *The wind is blowing from the east*; *He lives in a small town to the east of* (= further east than) *Glasgow*; *He lives in the east of England.* **2** (*often with cap*: *also* **E**) one of the four main points of the compass: *He took a direction 10° E of N* (= ten degrees east of north). – *See also* **the East** *below*. – *adj* (*attrib*) **1** in the east: *He lives on the east coast.* **2** from the direction of the east: *That is an east wind.* – *adv* towards the east: *The house faces east.*

'**easterly** *adj* (*usu attrib*) **1** (of a wind, breeze *etc*) coming from the east: *an easterly wind.* **2** looking, lying *etc* towards the east: *We are travelling in an easterly direction.*

'**eastern** *adj* of the east or the East: *That is an eastern custom*; *That custom is eastern in origin.*

'**easternmost** *adj* being furthest east: *Which is the easternmost city in America?*; *the easternmost of the islands.*

'**eastward** *adj* (*usu attrib*) towards the east: *in an eastward direction.*

'**eastward(s)** *adv* towards the east: *They are travelling eastwards.*

the East 1 the countries east of Europe: *the Middle/Far East.* **2** (*polit*: *sometimes without* **the**) the USSR, the countries of Eastern Europe, and the People's Republic of China: *the different political systems of* (*the*) *East and* (*the*) *West.*

Easter ['i:stə] *n* a Christian festival held in the spring, to celebrate Christ's coming back to life after the Crucifixion: *Christians celebrate Easter*; (*attrib*) *the Easter holidays.*

'**Easter egg** *nc* a decorated egg, *esp* one made of chocolate, eaten at Easter.

easy *see* **ease**.

eat [i:t] – *pt* **ate** [et, eit; (*Amer*) eit]: *ptp* '**eaten** – **1** *vt* to (chew and) swallow: *They are forbidden to eat meat*; *They ate up* (= ate all of) *the cakes as soon as they appeared.* **2** *vi* to take food: *We must eat to live*; *What time are we eating?*; *We are eating out* (= not at home but in a restaurant *etc*). – *See also* **eat into** *below*.

'**eatable** (*neg* **un-**) *adj* (*usu pred*) fit to be eaten: *The meal was scarcely eatable.* – *nc* (*in pl*: *inf*) food: *Cover all eatables to keep mice away.*

eats *n pl* (*inf*) food: *What kind of eats did you have at the party?*

'**eating apple** *nc* an apple for eating raw.

'**eating house** *nc* (*old*) a restaurant.

eat humble pie to humble oneself *eg* by admitting a mistake: *You'll have to eat humble pie if he's proved right.*

eat into *vt fus* to destroy or waste gradually: *Acid eats into metal*; *The school fees have eaten into our savings.*

eat one's words to admit humbly that one was mistaken in saying something: *I'll make him eat his words!*

See also **edible, inedible**.

eau-de-cologne [oudəkə'loun] (*also* **co'logne**) *nu* a type of perfume first made at Cologne.

eaves [i:vz] *n pl* the edge of the roof sticking out beyond the wall: *There are birds nesting under the eaves.*

eavesdrop ['i:vzdrop] – *pt, ptp* '**eavesdropped** – *vi* (*with* **on**) to listen in order to overhear a private conversation: *Were you eavesdropping?*; *The child eavesdropped on her parents' discussion.* '**eavesdropper** *nc*.

ebb [eb] *vi* **1** (of the tide) to go out from the land: *They swam till the tide began to ebb.* **2** (*fig*: *often liter*) to become less or worse: *His strength was ebbing fast*; (*formal*) *The greatness of Rome was ebbing.* – *nu* the act of ebbing: *the ebb of the tide.*

ebb tide *nc* the ebbing tide: *They sailed on the ebb tide.*

at a low ebb in a poor or depressed state: *She was at a low ebb after the operation.*

on the ebb ebbing or getting less or worse: *His power is on the ebb.*

ebony ['ebəni] **1** *nu, adj* (of) a type of wood, *usu* black and almost as heavy and hard as stone: *ebony ornaments.* **2** *adj* (*liter*) black as ebony.

ebullient [i'bʌljənt] *adj* (*formal*) high-spirited; very cheerful: *The fine weather made her feel quite ebullient*; *He's in an ebullient mood.* **e'bullience** *nu*.

eccentric [ik'sentrik] *adj* (of a person, his behaviour *etc*) odd; unusual: *He is growing more eccentric every day*; *an eccentric old man*; *He had an eccentric habit of collecting stray cats.* – *nc* an eccentric person: *Children often laugh at eccentrics.*

ec'centrically *adj*: *She was dressed very eccentrically.*

eccentricity [eksen'trisəti] *ncu* oddness of behaviour or an example of this: *His eccentricities annoyed the others*; *Eccentricity is often thought to be commonest among academic people.*

ecclesiastic [ikli:zi'astik] *nc* (*old formal*) a priest or clergyman.

ecˌclesi'astic(al) *adj* of the church or clergy.

echelon ['eʃəlon] *nc* (*formal*) a group of people at a certain level, or of a certain grade, in a particular organization: *the upper/lower echelons of society.*

echo ['ekou] – *pl* '**echoes** – *nc* the repeating of a sound caused by its striking a surface and coming back: *The children shouted loudly in the cave so that they could hear the echoes of their voices.* **2** (*formal fig*) an imitator or imitation (sometimes accidental): *She has no ideas of her own – she is just her husband's echo; Echoes of Tennyson are to be found in her poems.* – *v* – *pt* '**echoed** – **1** *vi* to sound loudly with an echo: *The cave was echoing with shouts.* **2** *vt* (*formal*) to send back an echo of: *The hills echoed his shout.* **3** *vt* (*fig*) to repeat (a sound or a statement): *She always echoes her husband's opinion.* **4** *vt* (*fig*) to imitate or to resemble in some way: *The colour scheme echoed the taste of the 1930s.*

eclair [i'kleə] *nc* a long iced cake *usu* with cream filling and chocolate icing.

eclipse [i'klips] *nc* **1** the disappearance of the whole or part of the sun when the moon comes between it and the earth or of the moon when the earth's shadow falls across it: *When was the last total eclipse of the sun?* **2** (*formal fig*) a loss of brilliance or a decline: *His reputation is in eclipse; His reputation is suffering an eclipse.* – *vt* (*formal*) **1** to obscure or cut off the light or sight of (the sun or moon): *The sun was partially eclipsed at 9 a.m.* **2** to be much better than: *His great success eclipsed his brother's achievements.*

eco- [i:kou] (*in cmpds*) concerned with living things in relation to their environment: *the* '*eco-system.*

ecology [i'kolədʒi] *ncu* (*tech*) (the study of) living things considered in relation to their environment: *Pollution has a disastrous effect on the ecology of a region.* **e'cologist** *nc.*

ˌ**eco'logical** [i:-] *adj* (*tech*: *esp attrib*) of ecology: *The students were told to make an ecological study of a woodland area; the ecological effects of motorways.* ˌ**eco'logically** *adv.*

economy [i'konəmi] *ncu* **1** (*formal*) the thrifty, careful management of money *etc* to avoid waste: *Please use the water with economy; We must make economies in household spending.* **2** organization of money and resources: *In Britain the Chancellor of the Exchequer is in charge of the country's economy; She is responsible for the household economy; The economy of the island is dependent on the fishing industry.*

economic [i:kə'nomik] *adj* **1** (*attrib*) of or concerned with (an) economy: *the country's economic future.* **2** likely to bring a profit: *You must charge an economic rent/price; It is not economic to rent our house for any less money because we have to pay very high rates.*

economical [i:kə'nomikəl] *adj* thrifty; not extravagant: *economical use of supplies; This car is very economical on petrol; It is more economical to take our own car across on the ferry than to hire a car there.* ˌ**eco'nomically** *adv.*

economics [i:kə'nomiks] *n sing* the study of production and distribution of money and goods: *He is studying economics at University; They are considering the economics of replacing the old machines.*

e'conomist *nc* a person who is an expert in economics: *He is one of the government's economists.*

e'conomize, -ise *vi* to spend money or goods carefully: *We must economize to avoid debt; They now have to economize on fuel/holidays/clothes.*

ecstasy ['ekstəsi] *ncu* (*formal*) (a feeling of) very great joy or other overwhelming emotion: *She is in a state of religious ecstasy;* (*fig inf*) *She went into ecstasies over that television programme.*

ec'static [-'sta-] *adj* (*formal*) of, showing, or causing ecstasy: *She was ecstatic at her team's victory; an ecstatic mood.* **ec'statically** *adv.*

ecumenical [i:kju'menikəl, (*Amer*) ek-] *adj* (*formal*) bringing together branches of the whole Christian church: *The Catholics and Protestants held a joint religious service as part of the local ecumenical weekend.*

eczema ['eksimə] *nu* a type of skin disease in which there is an itchy rash: *That child has very bad eczema; She suffers from eczema.*

eddy ['edi] *nc* a current of water or air running back against the main stream or current. – *vi* (*formal*) to move round and round: *The water eddied round the pier;* (*fig*) *The crowds eddied to and fro in the square.*

edge [edʒ] *nc* **1** the part farthest from the middle of something; a border: *Don't put that cup so near the edge of the table – it will fall off; She stood by the edge of the lake; Flowers were growing at the water's edge; The edges of the lawn need trimming;* (*fig*) *He had reached the edge of exhaustion.* **2** the cutting side of something sharp, *eg* a knife or weapon: *He felt the edge of the sword with his finger; The edge of this razor blade is very sharp; The blade has lost its edge* (= is no longer sharp). **3** (*no pl*) keenness; sharpness: *His wit/voice had an edge to it; This cheese has quite an edge to it* (= it has a sharp taste); *The chocolate took the edge off his hunger.* – **1** *vt* (*often passive*) to form a border to: *The handkerchief was edged with lace; The lawn is edged with flowers.* **2** *vti* to move or push little by little: *He edged his chair nearer to her; She edged her way through the crowd; They edged forward gradually so as to avoid being seen.*

'**edging** *ncu* a border or fringe round a garment: *The king has gold edging round his robe.*

'**edgy** *adj* (*inf*) irritable: *He's in an edgy mood; That actress is always edgy before a performance.* '**edgily** *adv.* '**edginess** *nu.*

'**edgeways,** '**edgewise** *adv* sideways: *Move the table edgeways slightly.*

have the edge on/over to have an advantage over: *In his tennis match he had the edge on his opponent at the start, but was beaten in the end.*

on '**edge** uneasy; nervous; irritable: *She was on edge when waiting for her exam results.*

set someone's teeth on edge to cause an unpleasant feeling of discomfort *etc* to someone: *These sour grapes set my teeth on edge;* (*fig*) *That shrill bell set everyone's teeth on edge.*

edible ['edəbl] *adj* (*formal*) fit to be eaten: *These are edible plants; Are these berries edible?* ˌ**edi'bility** *nu.*

See also **inedible**.

edict ['i:dikt] *nc* (*formal*) order or command from someone in authority; a decree: *by edict of the emperor.*

edification *see* **edify**.

edifice ['edifis] *nc* (*formal*) a large building: *The new cathedral is a magnificent edifice.*

edify ['edifai] *vt* (*formal*) to improve the mind or morals of.

ˌ**edifi'cation** [-fi-] *nu* (*formal or facet*): *I told you that piece of news for your edification.*

'**edifying** *adj* (*formal or facet*) instructive; morally improving: *an edifying lecture.*

edit ['edit] *vt* to prepare (a book, manuscript, newspaper, programme, film *etc*) for publication, or for broadcasting *etc*, *esp* by correcting, altering *etc*: *He edited her novel carefully*; *You will have to edit that tape – it's too long*; *It took him a long time to edit the film.*

edition [i'diʃən] *nc* a number of copies of a book *etc* printed at a time, or the form in which they are produced: *the third edition of the book*; *Is there a paperback edition of his book?*; *the evening edition of the newspaper.*

'editor *nc* **1** a person who edits books *etc*: *a dictionary editor.* **2** a person who is in charge of (part of) a newspaper, journal *etc*: *She has been appointed fashion editor*; *He is news editor.*

ˌedi'torial [-'to:-] *adj* (*usu attrib*) of or belonging to editors: *editorial work/staff.* – *nc* the leading article in a newspaper: *The editorials in all the national newspapers criticized the government's actions.*

educate ['edjukeit] *vt* to train and teach: *He was educated at a public school.*

ˌedu'cation *nu* instruction and teaching, *esp* of children and young people in schools, universities *etc*: *His lack of education prevented him from being promoted*; *He is willing to pay for his children's education.*

ˌedu'cational *adj* **1** of education: *educational studies/methods.* **2** providing information: *Our visit to the zoo was educational as well as enjoyable*; *educational books.*

ˌedu'cation(al)ist *nc* (*formal*) an expert in methods of educating.

eel [i:l] *nc* a kind of fish with a long smooth cylindrical or ribbon-shaped body.

eerie ['iəri] *adj* causing fear; weird: *There was an eerie silence in the dark woods*; *It was eerie seeing a faint light in the deserted old house.* **'eerily** *adv.* **'eeriness** *nu.*

efface [i'feis] **1** *vt* (*formal*) to rub out; to remove: *Wind and rain had effaced the name on the tombstone*; (*fig*) *You must try to efface the event from your memory.* **2** *v refl* to avoid drawing attention to (oneself): *She did her best to efface herself at parties.* – *See also* **self-effacing**.

effect [i'fekt] *ncu* **1** a result or consequence: *She is recovering from the effects of her illness*; *He is suffering from the effects of over-eating*; *His discovery had little effect at first.* **2** an impression given or produced: *The speech did not have much effect on them*; *The colours of the flowers blended together to produce a pleasing effect.* – *See also* **effect** *in phrases below.* – *vt* (*formal*) to make happen; to bring about: *He tried to effect a reconciliation between his parents.*

ef'fective [-tiv] *adj* **1** having power to produce, or producing, a desired result: *This new washing-powder is very effective*; *Is that an effective pain-killer?*; *These new teaching methods have proved very effective*; *The government must adopt effective economic measures.* **2** striking or pleasing: *That is an effective display of flowers*; *That display is very effective.* **3** (*pred*) in operation; working; active: *The new laws become effective next week.*

ef'fectively [-tivli] *adv* **1** in an effective way: *He knows how to speak effectively.* **2** more or less; in effect: *His work was effectively finished.*

ef'fects *n pl* **1** (*formal*) property; goods: *She left few personal effects when she died.* **2** in drama *etc*, devices for producing suitable sounds, lighting *etc* to accompany a play *etc*: *sound effects*; *lighting effects*; *Who is in charge of effects?*

ef'fectual [-tʃuəl] *adj* (*formal*: *often with a negative*) successful in producing the desired results: *There was no effectual opposition to the government's economic plans*; *This drug is effectual only in some cases.*

come into effect (of a law *etc*) to begin to operate, be valid *etc*: *The law came into effect last month.*

for ef'fect for the sake of making an impression or in order to impress others: *The politician made that speech just for effect.*

give effect to (*formal*) to act in accordance with (a decision): *He gave effect to his promise and allowed them to have a barbecue on the beach.*

in ef'fect 1 (of a rule *etc*) in operation: *That law is no longer in effect.* **2** in truth or in practical terms: *In effect our opinions differed very little.*

put into effect to put (a law *etc*) into operation: *He has begun to put his theories into effect.*

take effect to begin to work; to come into force: *This regulation does not take effect until June 9*; *When will the drug take effect?*

to that effect, to the ef'fect that (*formal*) with that meaning or with the meaning that: *He said he was dissatisfied with our standards of work, or words to that effect*; *He left a message to the effect that* (= saying that) *he was resigning.*

See also **ineffective, ineffectual**.

effeminate [i'feminət] *adj* (*formal*) (of a man) unmanly or womanish: *He walks in a very effeminate way*; *He speaks in an effeminate manner*; *He is very effeminate.*

effervesce [efə'ves] *vi* **1** (*formal*) to give off bubbles of gas; to fizz: *The champagne effervesced in the glasses.* **2** to act in a lively way: *She effervesced gaily at the party.* **ˌeffer'vescence** *nu.* **ˌeffer'vescent** *adj.*

effete [i'fi:t] *adj* (*derog*) **1** (of institutions, organizations *etc*) old and no longer effective: *effete organizations*; *Often, young people regard the established political parties as being effete.* **2** (of a person) lacking all energy and vitality: *an effete young man*; *He is rather effete.*

efficacious [efi'keiʃəs] *adj* (*formal*) producing the result intended: *an efficacious cure*; *The medicine was most efficacious.* **efficacy** ['efikəsi] *nu.*

efficient [i'fiʃənt] *adj* **1** (of a person) capable; skilful: *That nurse looks most efficient*; *a very efficient secretary.* **2** (of an action, tool *etc*) producing (quick and) satisfactory results: *The new bread knife is much more efficient than the old one*; *the most efficient method*; *a very efficient lawnmower.* **ef'ficiently** *adv.* **ef'ficiency** *nu.* *See also* **inefficient**.

effigy ['efidʒi] *nc* a likeness of a person, animal *etc* (in wood, stone *etc*): *effigies of Buddha.*

effluent ['efluənt] *ncu* (*formal*) (a flowing out of) waste matter from a factory *etc*: *The effluent from the factory affected the town's water supply*; *Effluent is a cause of pollution.*

effort ['efət] **1** *nu* hard work; energy: *Learning a foreign language requires effort*; *Put some effort into your work*; *The effort of climbing the hill made the old man very tired.* **2** *nc* a trying hard; a struggle: *With an effort he managed not to laugh*; *The government's efforts to improve the economy were unsuccessful*; *It was an effort to get up this morning*; *Please make every effort* (= try your best) *to be punctual.* **3** *nc* the result of an attempt: *Your drawing was a good effort.*

'**effortless** *adj* done without (apparent) effort: *a dancer's effortless movements; Her movements looked effortless.*

'**effortlessly** *adv*: *The dancer moved effortlessly across the stage.*

effrontery [i'frʌntəri] *nu* (*formal*) impudence: *He had the effrontery to call me a liar.*

effusive [i'fju:siv] *adj* (*often derog*) showing too much feeling; emotional: *She wrote an effusive letter of thanks; I find my elderly aunt rather effusive.* **ef'fusively** *adv.*

egg[1] [eg] *nc* **1** an oval object *usu* covered with shell, laid by a bird, reptile *etc*, from which a young one is hatched: *The female bird is sitting on the eggs in the nest.* **2** such an object laid by a hen, used as food: *I bought a dozen eggs last week; Did you use eggs in the cake?; Would you rather have boiled, fried or scrambled eggs?* **3** in the female mammal, the cell from which the young one is formed; the ovum: *The egg is fertilized by the male sperm.* **4** (*inf fig*) something resembling an egg, *eg* a lump *etc*: *The child had quite an egg on his forehead after the accident.*

'**egg-cup** *nc* a small cup-shaped container for holding a boiled egg while it is being eaten.

'**egghead** *nc* (*inf derog*) a very clever person; an intellectual: *That child's such an egghead that he doesn't like pop music.*

'**eggplant** *ncu* (*esp Amer*) (an) aubergine.

put all one's eggs in one basket to depend entirely on the success of one scheme, plan *etc*: *You should apply for more than one job – don't put all your eggs in one basket; He put all his eggs in one basket when he invested all his money in one firm.*

teach one's grandmother to suck eggs (*inf*) to try to show someone more experienced than oneself how to do something: *It was a case of him teaching his grandmother to suck eggs when he told me how to pitch a tent – I had been going camping for years.*

egg[2] [eg]: **egg on** *vt sep* (*inf*) to urge (somebody) on (to do something): *He egged on his friend to steal the radio; She egged him on to apply for a better job.*

ego ['i:gou] *nc* (*formal*) **1** personal pride: *His criticism wounded my ego.* **2** (*psych*) the part of a person that is conscious and thinks; the self.

egocentric [egə'sentrik, (*Amer*) i:gou-] *adj* (*formal derog*) interested in oneself only.

'**egoism** ['e-, (*Amer*) 'i:-] *nu* (*derog*) the consideration of oneself before others; selfishness.

'**egoist** ['e-, (*Amer*) 'i:-] *nc* (*derog*) a person who thinks and speaks too much about himself. ˌ**ego'istic,** ˌ**ego'istical** *adjs.*

'**egotism** ['e-, (*Amer*) 'i:-] *nu* (*derog*) a frequent use of the pronoun I; speaking much of oneself. '**egotist** *nc.* ˌ**ego'tistic,** ˌ**ego'tistical** *adjs.*

egregious [i'gri:dʒəs] *adj* (*very formal*: *usu attrib*) outrageous; very bad: *an egregious lie; an egregious mistake.*

Egypt, Egyptian *see* Appendix 2.

eiderdown ['aidədaun] **1** *nu* the down or soft feathers of the '**eider duck** (a northern sea duck). **2** *nc* a bedcover filled with this or other material; a quilt: *In winter we put an eiderdown over the blankets for extra warmth.*

eight [eit] **1** *nc* the number or figure 8: *Four and four are/is/make eight; There were eight of us present; He drew a neat row of eights.* **2** *nu* the age of 8: *children of eight and over; Children under eight/8 will not be admitted.* **3** *nc* the crew of an eight-oared racing boat: *Did the Cambridge eight defeat the Oxford eight?* – *adj* **1** (*usu attrib*) 8 in number: *eight people; He is eight years old.* **2** (*pred*) aged 8: *He is eight today.*

eight- (*in cmpds*) having eight (of something): *an* ˌ*eight-page* '*document; an* ˌ*eight-sided* '*figure.*

eighth [eitθ] **1** *nc* one of eight equal parts: *They each received an eighth of the money.* **2** *nc, adj* (the) last of eight (people, things *etc*); (the) next after the seventh: *His horse was eighth in the race; Are you having another cup of coffee? That's your eighth this morning; Henry VIII* (said and rarely written as 'Henry the Eighth').

'**eight-year-old** *nc* a person or animal that is eight years old: *Is this game suitable for an eight-year-old?* – *adj* (*attrib*) (of a person, animal or thing) that is eight years old: *an eight-year-old child.*

figure of eight a pattern, movement *etc* in the shape of the figure 8: *The skater did a series of figures of eight.*

See also Appendix 1.

eighteen [ei'ti:n] **1** *nc* the number or figure 18: *There were eighteen at the party.* **2** *nu* the age of 18: *a girl of eighteen; people over/under eighteen/18.* – *adj* **1** (*usu attrib*) 18 in number: *eighteen horses; He is eighteen years old.* **2** (*pred*) aged 18: *He is eighteen now.*

eighteen- (*in cmpds*) having eighteen (of something): *an* ˌ*eighteen-page* '*booklet.*

ˌ**eigh'teenth** **1** *nc* one of eighteen equal parts: *seventeen eighteenths.* **2** *nc, adj* (the) last of eighteen (people, things *etc*); (the) next after the seventeenth: *He was eighteenth in the competition; the eighteenth storey; Louis XVIII* (said and rarely written as 'Louis the Eighteenth').

ˌ**eigh'teen-year-old** *nc* a person or animal that is eighteen years old: *He is married to an eighteen-year-old.* – *adj* (*attrib*) (of a person, animal or thing) that is eighteen years old: *an eighteen-year-old girl; an eighteen-year-old film.*

See also Appendix 1.

eighty ['eiti] **1** *nc* the number or figure 80: *There were eighty of us in the choir.* **2** *nu* the age of 80: *a woman of eighty; men over/under eighty/80.* – *adj* **1** (*usu attrib*) 80 in number: *eighty books; She is eighty years old.* **2** (*pred*) aged 80: *He was eighty yesterday.*

'**eighties** *n pl* **1** the period of time between one's eightieth and ninetieth birthdays: *He is in his eighties.* **2** the range of temperatures between eighty and ninety degrees: *It was in the eighties in London yesterday.* **3** the period of time between the eightieth and ninetieth years of a century: *He was a famous artist in the 'eighties/'80s; life in the nineteen-eighties/1980s.*

'**eightieth** **1** *nc* one of eighty equal parts: *eleven eightieths.* **2** *nc, adj* (the) last of eighty (people, things *etc*); (the) next after the seventy-ninth: *His name was eightieth on the list; 'How many people have you invited?' 'You are the eightieth.'*

eighty- (*in cmpds*) having eighty (of something): *an* ˌ*eighty-page* '*book.*

'**eighty-year-old** *nc* a person or animal that is eighty years old: *a lively eighty-year-old.* – *adj* (*attrib*) (of a person, animal or thing) that is eighty years old: *an eighty-year-old widow; an eighty-year-old house.*

See also Appendix 1.

either [(*esp Brit*) 'aiðə, (*esp Amer*) 'i:ðə(r)] *pron* the one or the other of two: *Either of them is capable of doing this; You may borrow either of these books; I offered him coffee or tea, but he didn't want either.* –

adj (*attrib*) **1** the one or the other (of two things, people *etc*): *He can write with either hand*; *You can borrow either book.* **2** (*formal*) the one and the other (of two things, people *etc*); both: *on either bank of the river*; *at either side of the garden.* – *adv* **1** used after negative statements for emphasis: *I don't want this one, and I don't want that one either*; *She hasn't finished her work and he hasn't either*; *If you don't go, I won't either.* **2** (*inf*) (used after a negative sentence or phrase) moreover; besides: *I used to sing, and I hadn't a bad voice, either.*

either ... or introducing alternatives: *You must either go now or stay*; *Either you must go to see him or send an apology*; *You can send either John or his brother to the shop.*

either way in the one case or the other: *Either way he wins*; *You can tell him whether you're innocent or not – but either way he'll think you're guilty.*

See also **neither**.

ejaculate [i'dʒakjuleit] *vti* **1** (*liter*) to utter or exclaim suddenly: *'What is that?' he ejaculated in surprise.* **2** (of a male human being or other animal) to eject or discharge semen. **eˌjacu'lation** *ncu.*

eject [i'dʒekt] **1** *vt* (*formal*) to throw out with force: *They ejected the bomb from the aircraft*; (*fig*) *They were ejected from their house for not paying the rent*; (*fig*) *They were ejected from the club for misbehaviour.* **2** *vi* to leave an aircraft in an emergency by causing one's seat to be ejected: *The pilot had to eject when his plane caught fire.* **e'jection** [-ʃən] *nu.*

eke [i:k]: **eke out** *vt sep* **1** to make (a supply of something) last longer *eg* by adding something else to it: *You could eke out the meat with potatoes.* **2** to manage with difficulty to make (a living, livelihood *etc*): *The artist could scarcely eke out a living from his painting.*

elaborate [i'labəreit] **1** *vt* (*formal*) to work out or describe (a plan *etc*) in detail: *He elaborated his theory.* **2** *vi* (*esp with* **on**/(*formal*) **upon**) to discuss details: *She elaborated on the next day's menu*; *The headmaster elaborated upon the idea for a new school uniform*; *I know already what you think about it – you needn't elaborate.* – [-rət] *adj* **1** very detailed or complicated: *This is one of her more elaborate designs*; *Her designs are always very elaborate.* **2** (*attrib*) carefully planned: *They have made elaborate plans for their escape.* **e'laborately** *adv.* **eˌlabo'ration** *nu.*

elapse [i'laps] *vi* (*formal*) (of time) to pass: *A month had elapsed since our last meeting.*

elastic [i'lastik] *adj* **1** (*usu attrib*) (of a material or substance) able to return to its original shape or size after being pulled or pressed out of shape: *The doctor put an elastic bandage on her sore leg*; *Rubber is an elastic substance.* **2** (*fig*) able to be changed or adapted: *My holiday plans are elastic*; *This is a fairly elastic arrangement.* – *nu* a type of cord containing strands of rubber: *Put elastic round the tops of the child's socks to stop them from falling down.* **elasticity** [i:la'stisəti, (*Amer*) ilas-] *nu* (*formal*).

elastic band *nc* (*also* **rubber band**) a small thin piece of rubber for holding things together or in place: *Put an elastic band round those papers.*

elated [i'leitid] *adj* very cheerful; in high spirits: *She felt elated after her victory in the tennis match*; *an elated group of prize-winners.* **e'lation** *nu.*

elbow ['elbou] *nc* **1** the joint where the arm bends: *He leant forward on his elbows.* **2** the part of a coat, jacket *etc* which covers this: *I've torn the elbow of my blouse.* – *vt* to push with the elbow: *He elbowed his way through the crowd*; *He elbowed the others out of the way.*

'elbow-grease *nu* (*inf facet*) hard work; energy: *If you use a bit of elbow-grease you'll get that floor clean.*

'elbow-room *nu* space enough for moving or doing something: *Get out of my way and give me some elbow-room!*

at one's elbow close to one: *The journalist always works with a dictionary at his elbow.*

out at elbow (*formal liter*) ragged; shabby; worn out: *He always wears that old jacket although it is out at elbow.*

elder[1] ['eldə] *adj* **1** (often of members of a family) older; senior: *He has three elder sisters*; *He is the elder of the two children.* **2** used before or after a person's name to distinguish between him and another person of the same name: *the elder Pliny*; *Pliny the elder.* – *nc* **1** a person who is older: *Take the advice of your elders*; *He is her elder* (= He is older than she is) *by four years.* **2** an office-bearer in Presbyterian churches: *The elders distribute the bread and the wine at Communion services.*

'elderly *adj* (rather) old; a more polite way of saying 'old': *an elderly unmarried lady*; *He is elderly now but still very active.*

'eldest *adj* oldest: *He is the eldest child in the school*; *She is the eldest of the three children.*

elder statesman *nc* an important senior or retired member of a group, institution *etc*: *He has become the elder statesman of British politics.*

the elderly people who are (rather) old; a more polite way of saying 'the old': *It is important for the elderly to keep warm in winter.*

elder[2] ['eldə] *ncu* a kind of shrub or tree with purple-black fruit (**'elderberries**).

elect [i'lekt] *vt* **1** to choose by vote: *He was elected (to be) chairman*; *She was elected (on) to the committee.* **2** (*formal*) to choose (to do something): *They elected to go by taxi.* – *adj* (*placed immediately after noun*) chosen for office but not yet in it: *the president elect.* – *n pl* (*usu with* **the**: *relig old*) the people chosen (by God for salvation after death): *one of the elect of God.*

e'lection [-ʃən] *ncu* the choosing, or choice, (*usu* by vote) of person(s) for office: *When do the elections take place?*; *He is standing for election again.* – *See also* **general election** *under* **general**.

eˌlectio'neer [-ʃə-] *vi* to work to bring about the election of a candidate: *They were electioneering on behalf of the socialist candidate.*

e'lector *nc* a person who has the right to vote at an election: *Not all the electors bothered to vote.*

e'lectoral *adj* (*attrib*) of elections or electors: *The names of all electors are listed in the electoral roll.*

e'lectorate [-rət] *nc* all electors taken together: *Half of the electorate did not vote.*

electricity [elek'trisəti] *nu* a form of energy used to give heat, light, power *etc*: *These machines are all worked by electricity*; *Don't switch on all the lights – you are wasting electricity.*

electric [ə'lektrik] *adj* **1** of, produced by, or worked by, electricity: *an electric motor/iron*; *electric light*; *Is this cooker electric?* **2** (*fig*) full of excitement: *The atmosphere in the theatre was electric*; *There was an electric silence.*

e'lectrical *adj* (*esp attrib*) related to electricity: *electrical engineering*; *electrical goods on sale in a* *shop; The machine broke because of an electrical fault.*

e'lectrically *adv*: *Is this machine electrically operated?*

ˌelec'trician [-ʃən] *nc* a person whose job is to make, install, repair *etc* electrical equipment: *The electrician mended the electric heater.*

e'lectrified [-faid] *adj* supplied or charged with electricity: *an electrified wire fence; Is the fence electrified?*

e'lectrify [-fai] *vt* **1** to convert (a railway *etc*) to the use of electricity as the moving power: *They are electrifying this section of the line.* **2** (*fig*) to excite or astonish: *The news electrified us.* **eˌlectrifi'cation** [-fi-] *nu.*

e'lectrifying *adj* exciting: *an electrifying speech.*

electric chair *nc* a chair used to execute criminals by sending a powerful electric current through them.

electro- [ilektrou] (*in cmpds*) of or caused by electricity, as in **electromagnetic.**

electrocute [i'lektrəkju:t] *vt* **1** to kill (a person *etc*) accidentally by electricity: *The child was electrocuted when he touched an uncovered electric wire.* **2** to put (a person) to death by means of electricity: *He was not hanged – he was electrocuted.*

electrode [i'lektroud] *nc* (*tech*) a conductor through which a current of electricity enters or leaves a battery *etc.*

electromagnetic waves [ilektrəməg'netik] *n pl* (*tech*) waves of energy travelling through space *etc, eg* light waves, X-rays, radio waves.

electron [i'lektron] *nc* (*tech*) a very small particle within the atom, having the smallest possible charge of electricity.

electronic [elək'tronik] *adj* (*attrib*) **1** worked or produced by devices built or made according to the principles of electronics: *an electronic calculator; electronic music.* **2** concerned or working with such machines: *an electronic engineer.* **3** of electronics: *an electronic code.*

electronics [elək'troniks] *n sing* the branch of science that deals with the study of the movement and effects of electrons and with their application to machines *etc*: *Electronics is one of the more modern sciences.*

elegant ['eligənt] *adj* having or showing good taste and stylishness: *She always wears elegant clothes; She is an elegant woman; You do look elegant today; He has an elegant style of writing.* **'elegance** *nu. See also* **inelegant.**

elegy ['elidʒi] *nc* song or poem of mourning: *The poet wrote an elegy for his dead friend.*

element ['eləmənt] *nc* **1** an essential part of anything: *Sound teaching of grammar is one of the elements of a good education.* **2** (*chem*) a substance that cannot be split by chemical means into simpler substances: *Hydrogen, chlorine, iron and uranium are elements.* **3** surroundings necessary for life: *Water is a fish's natural element.* **4** (*hist*) any one of the four substances, earth, air, fire and water, of which the Earth *etc* was once supposed to be made. **5** a slight amount; a trace: *an element of doubt.* **6** the heating part in an electric kettle, heater *etc*: *The kettle needs a new element; The element of the electric fire has burnt out.*

ˌele'mental [-'men-] *adj* (*formal*: *esp attrib*) of or like the powers or the spirits of nature: *the elemental forces of nature.*

ˌele'mentary [-'men-] *adj* very simple; not advanced: *elementary mathematics; My knowledge of mathematics is very elementary.*

'elements *n pl* **1** the first things to be learned in any subject: *He has not yet learned the elements of musical theory.* **2** (*formal*) the forces of nature, as wind and rain: *Your skin should not be exposed to the elements for too long.*

in one's element in the surroundings that are most natural or pleasing to one: *He is in his element when he is organizing something.*

elephant ['elifənt] *nc* a very large type of animal with very thick skin, a trunk and two tusks: *African elephants have large ears.*

ˌele'phantine [-'fantain, (*Amer*) -tin] *adj* (*derog*) like an elephant; large and awkward; clumsy: *That new supermarket is an elephantine construction; Her daughter is absolutely elephantine!*

white elephant *see* **white.**

elevate ['eliveit] *vt* (*formal*: *sometimes facet*) **1** to raise to a higher position or to a higher rank *etc*: *He has been elevated to the peerage.* **2** to improve (a person's mind *etc*); to uplift: *The teacher thought that reading stories about saints would elevate the child's mind.* **3** to make more cheerful: *These drugs can elevate a person's mood.*

ˌele'vation (*formal*) **1** *nu* the act of elevating, or state of being elevated, *eg* in position, rank or standard: *his elevation to the peerage.* **2** *nc* (*no pl*) height, *eg* of a place above sea-level: *The town is at an elevation of 1500 metres.* **3** *nc* (*old*) a high place; a hill. **4** *nc* an architect's drawing of one side of a building: *On this plan the front elevation looks out of proportion.*

'elevating *adj* (*formal*) improving the mind *etc*; uplifting: *an elevating talk; I found his sermon elevating.*

'elevator *nc* **1** (*esp Amer*) a lift or machine for raising persons, goods, grain *etc* to a higher floor: *There is no elevator in this shop – you will have to climb the stairs.* **2** a tall storehouse for grain: *The corn is stored in an elevator at the docks after it has been unloaded from the ship.*

eleven [i'levn] **1** *nc* the number or figure 11. **2** *nu* the age of 11. **3** *nc* in hockey, football *etc*, a team of eleven players: *He plays for his school's first eleven* (= best football, hockey *etc* team). – *adj* **1** (*usu attrib*) 11 in number. **2** (*pred*) aged 11. – *See* **eight** *for constructions.*

eleven- (*in cmpds*) having eleven (of something): *an eleven-page booklet.*

e'leventh 1 *nc* one of eleven equal parts. **2** *nc, adj* (the) last of eleven (people, things *etc*); (the) next after the tenth. – *See* **eighth** *under* **eight** *for constructions.*

e'leven-year-old *nc* a person or animal that is eleven years old. – *adj* (*attrib*) (of a person, animal or thing) that is eleven years old. – *See* **eight-year-old** *under* **eight** *for constructions.*

at the eleventh hour at the last possible moment; only just in time: *The child was saved from the kidnappers at the eleventh hour;* (*attrib*) *an eleventh-hour attempt to rescue the child.*

See also Appendix 1.

elf [elf] – *pl* **elves** [elvz] – *nc* a tiny and mischievous fairy.

'elfin *adj* (*liter*) of or like an elf: *The little girl has elfin features.*

'elfish *adj* like an elf; mischievous: *an elfish grin.*

elicit [i'lisit] *vt* (*formal*) to succeed in getting (information *etc*) from a person, *usu* with difficulty: *She elicited his address from his secretary; The police elicited a confession from him.*

eligible ['elidʒəbl] *adj* **1** suitable or worthy to be chosen (for a job, as a husband *etc*): *He is London's most eligible bachelor*; *She is eligible for promotion.* **2** (legally) qualified or entitled to be chosen: *He is eligible for unemployment benefit*; *Is he eligible to join the Boy Scouts?* ˌ**eligi'bility** *nu.* *See also* **ineligible**.

eliminate [i'limineit] *vt* (*formal*) to get rid of; to omit or exclude: *We must eliminate any possibility of error*; *We can eliminate most of the suspects*; *He was eliminated from the tennis match in the first round.* **eˌlimi'nation** *nu.*

élite [ei'li:t, (*Amer*) i-] *nc* the best or most important people *esp* within society: *She considers herself to be one of the élite because she has a university degree.*

é'litism *nu* (*derog*) (the belief in) the use of a system (*eg* of education) that develops an élite: *English public schools are sometimes accused of encouraging élitism.* **é'litist** *nc, adj.*

elixir [i'liksə] *ncu* (*hist*) a liquid that would supposedly make people able to go on living for ever, or a substance that would turn the cheaper metals into gold: *the elixir of life.*

Elizabethan [ilizə'bi:θən] *adj* of (the time of) Queen Elizabeth of England (reigned 1558–1603): *Elizabethan drama.* – *nc* a person living during that time: *Drake and Raleigh were both famous Elizabethans.*

elk [elk] – *pls* **elks, elk** – *nc* the largest of all deer, found in the north of Europe and Asia.

ellipse [i'lips] *nc* (*esp geom*) a figure that is a regular oval.

el'liptical[1] *adj*: *an elliptical shape.*

ellipsis [i'lipsis] – *pl* **el'lipses** [-si:z] – *ncu* (*gram*) a figure of speech in which a word or words needed for the sense or grammar are omitted but understood: *The sentence 'He was delighted at the idea, and I very bored', contains an ellipsis.*

el'liptical[2] *adj*: *an elliptical style of speaking.*

elm [elm] **1** *nc* (*also* '**elm tree**) a kind of tall tree with tough wood and corrugated bark: *Many elms in Britain have been killed by disease*; (*attrib*) *an elm wood.* **2** *nu, adj* (of) its wood: *This garden seat is made of elm.*

elocution [elə'kju:ʃən] *nu* the art of speaking clearly and effectively: *Actors study elocution.*

elongated ['i:loŋgeitid, (*Amer*) i'lo:ŋgeitid] *adj* (made) long and narrow; stretched out: *An oval looks like an elongated circle.* ˌ**elon'gation** *nu.*

elope [i'loup] *vi* to run away secretly, *esp* with a lover: *They eloped because her parents refused to give them permission to marry.* **e'lopement** *ncu.*

eloquence ['eləkwəns] *nu* (*formal*) **1** the power of expressing feelings or thoughts in words that impress or move other people: *a speaker of wit and eloquence.* **2** words that have this effect: *They were moved by his eloquence.*

'**eloquent** *adj* having or showing eloquence: *an eloquent speaker/speech*; *Her enthusiasm made her quite eloquent.* '**eloquently** *adv.*

else [els] *adj, adv* (used after interrogative, indefinite or negative pronouns or adverbs) besides; other than that already mentioned: *What else can I do?*; *What else is there for me to do?*; *Can we go anywhere else?*; *He took someone else's pencil*; *'Do you want anything else to eat?' 'Nothing else, thank you.'*

ˌ**else'where** *adv* in, or to, another place; somewhere or anywhere else: *You must look elsewhere if you want a less tiring job.*

or 'else otherwise: *You must hurry or else you will be too late*; (*inf*) *Do what I say – or else!* (= otherwise you'll suffer in some way).

elucidate [i'lu:sideit] *vti* (*formal*) to make clear or explain (*eg* something difficult or mysterious): *He was unable to elucidate the situation further.* **eˌluci'dation** *nu* (*formal*).

elude [i'lu:d] *vt* (*formal*) **1** to escape or avoid (someone or something) by a trick, quickness or cleverness: *He eluded capture/his pursuers.* **2** to be too difficult *etc* for (a person) to understand or remember: *The meaning of this poem eludes me*; *I know her face but her name eludes me.*

e'lusive [-siv] *adj* (*formal*) **1** escaping or vanishing, often or cleverly: *He is a most elusive criminal*; *I wanted to speak to the manager but he seems to be very elusive.* **2** hard to understand or to express: *He can understand the most elusive mathematical problems.*

elves *see* **elf**.

emaciated [i'meisieitid] *adj* (*formal*) having become very thin (through illness, starvation *etc*): *The dying woman was emaciated*; *an emaciated old woman.* **eˌmaci'ation** *nu.*

emanate ['eməneit] *vi* (*formal*) to flow out; to come out (from some source): *This information emanates from his family*; *Certain poisonous gases emanate from these chemicals.* ˌ**ema'nation** *ncu.*

emancipate [i'mansipeit] *vt* (*formal*) to set free from slavery or other strict or unfair control: *William Wilberforce helped to emancipate slaves*; *Women are being emancipated* (= set free from unfair social conditions *etc*) *little by little.*

eˌmanci'pation *nu* (*formal*) the act of emancipating or the state of being emancipated: *Women are still struggling for emancipation from unfair domination by men.*

emasculate [i'maskjuleit] *vt* (*formal*) **1** to remove the sexual organs of (a male animal). **2** (*fig*) to deprive of force and strength: *The author's work was considerably emasculated by the alterations of his editors.* **eˌmascu'lation** *nu.*

embalm [im'ba:m] *vt* to preserve (a dead body) from decay by treatment with spices or drugs: *The Egyptians embalmed the corpses of their kings.*

embankment [im'baŋkmənt] *nc* a bank or ridge made *eg* to keep back water or to carry a railway over low-lying places *etc*: *The child ran down the embankment on to the railway line.*

embargo [im'ba:gou] – *pl* **em'bargoes** – *ncu* an official order forbidding, or the official forbidding of, something, *esp* trade with another country: *They put an embargo on certain goods*; *The government placed certain goods under* (*an*) *embargo*; *They have lifted the embargo on trade* (= They are now allowing trade) *with that country.*

embark [im'ba:k] *vti* (*formal*) to go, or put, on board ship: *Passengers should embark early*; *They embarked the troops at dawn.* ˌ**embar'kation** [em-] *nu.*

em'bark on/(*formal*) **upon** *vt fus* to start or engage in: *They embarked on a war against the French*; *She embarked on a new career.*

See also **disembark**.

embarrass [im'barəs] *vt* **1** to cause to feel uneasy or self-conscious: *She was embarrassed by his praise*; *They embarrassed her by complimenting her on her beauty.* **2** (*formal*: *usu passive*) to involve in (*esp* financial) difficulties: *He was frequently embarrasssed by debts.* **em'barrassment** *ncu.*

em'barrassed *adj*: *He looked very embarrassed*

when the teacher asked him to read his essay to the class; He gave her an embarrassed smile.

em'barrassing *adj* causing embarrassment: *He asked an embarrassing question; I found the question embarrassing.*

embassy ['embəsi] *nc* (the official residence of) an ambassador and his staff: *the American embassy in London*; (*attrib*) *an embassy official.*

embed [im'bed] – *pt, ptp* **em'bedded** – *vt* to fix deeply (in something): *The bullet was embedded in the wall*; (*formal fig*) *The idea that men are superior to women is embedded in tradition.*

embellish [im'beliʃ] *vt* (*formal*) **1** to increase the interest of (a story *etc*) by adding (untrue) details: *The soldier embellished the story of his escape.* **2** to make beautiful with ornaments *etc*: *His uniform was embellished with gold braid.* **em'bellishment** *ncu.*

ember ['embə] *nc* (*formal*) a piece of burning or glowing coal or wood: *An ember fell out of the fire on to the rug.*

'embers *n pl* the sparking or glowing remains of a fire: *She stared into the embers of the fire*; (*fig*) *the embers of their love affair.*

embezzle [im'bezl] *vt* to take dishonestly (money that has been entrusted to oneself): *As the firm's accountant, he embezzled £4 000 in two years.* **em'bezzlement** *ncu.* **em'bezzler** *nc.*

embitter [im'bitə] *vt* (*formal*) to make bitter and resentful: *He was embittered by poverty and failure.*

em'bittered *adj*: *She is an embittered old woman; He returned from the war, embittered and resentful.*

emblazon [im'bleizən] *vt* (*formal*) **1** to adorn with heraldic devices or some other bright design: *The herald's tunic was emblazoned with the family arms.* **2** to display in a very obvious or noticeable way: *The firm's name was emblazoned on all their vans.*

emblem ['embləm] *nc* an object chosen to represent an idea, a quality, a country *etc*: *The thistle is the emblem of Scotland; The dove is the emblem of peace.*

,emble'matic [-'matik] *adj* (*formal*: *usu pred*) serving as an emblem: *The dove is emblematic of peace.*

embody [im'bodi] *vt* (*formal*: not *usu* used with **is, was** *etc* and **-ing**) **1** to include: *The new machine embodies many new safety features.* **2** to express or represent in words, in actions, in (living) form *etc*; to give form (to an idea *etc*): *His opinions are embodied in this essay; That building embodies my idea of ugliness.*

em'bodiment *nc* (*formal*: *often with* **the**) a thing or person that embodies something: *He was the embodiment of cruelty.*

embolden [im'bouldən] *vt* (*old or formal*: *usu passive*) to make bold; to give someone courage (to do something): *He was emboldened to ask her to marry him.*

embossed [im'bost] *adj* (*esp attrib*) (of metal, leather *etc*) ornamented with a raised design: *The seats of the chairs are covered in embossed leather.*

embrace [im'breis] **1** *vti* (*more formal than* **hug**) to take (a person *etc*) in the arms with affection; to hug: *The two sisters embraced; She embraced her brother warmly.* **2** *vt* (*formal*) to take (*eg* an opportunity) eagerly, or accept (*eg* a religion) wholeheartedly: *She has embraced Christianity/socialism.* **3** *vt* (*formal*: not used with **is, was** *etc* and **-ing**) to include: *The term 'man' often embraces men, women and children.* – *nc* a clasping in the arms; a hug: *The child tried to avoid the kisses and embraces of his aunts; a loving embrace; The lovers were in a tight embrace.*

embroider [im'broidə] *vti* **1** to ornament with designs in needlework: *The child embroidered her name on her handkerchief; She embroiders beautifully.* **2** to add (untrue) details to (a story *etc*): *His story was basically true but he had embroidered it a bit to impress his readers.*

em'broidery *nu*: *Embroidery is one of her hobbies; What a beautiful piece of embroidery!*

embroil [im'broil] *vt* (*formal*) to involve (a person) in a quarrel or in a difficult situation: *I do not wish to become embroiled in their family quarrels.*

embryo ['embriou] – *pl* **'embryos** – *nc* **1** (*tech*) a young animal or plant in its earliest stages in seed, egg or womb: *An egg contains the embryo of a chicken*; (*attrib*) *A seed contains an embryo plant*; (*attrib*) *an embryo child.* **2** (*fig*) the beginning stage of anything: *This science is still in* (*its*) *embryo*; (*attrib*) *The project is still at the embryo stage.*

,embry'ology [-'olədʒi] *nu* the science of the formation and development of the embryo. **,embryo'logical** [-'lo-] *adj.* **,embry'ologist** *nc.*

,embry'onic [-'onik] *adj* (*formal*: *usu attrib*) in an early stage of development: *The cold weather killed the embryonic plant*; (*fig*) *Our plans are still in the embryonic stage.*

emend [iː'mend] *vt* to correct errors in (a book, a statement *etc*): *The editor emended the manuscript slightly.*

,emen'dation *ncu*: *He made many emendations to the text; The emendation of the manuscript took a long time.*

See also **amend**.

emerald ['emərəld] **1** *ncu* a type of precious stone, green in colour: *Her engagement ring has a huge emerald in it*; (*attrib*) *She has an emerald ring.* **2** *nu, adj* (*also* **emerald green**) (having) its colour: *She has an emerald green coat; a patch of emerald green.*

emerge [i'məːdʒ] *vi* (*more formal than* **come out**) **1** to rise out (from water *etc*); to come out; to come into view: *The swimmer emerged from the water; His head emerged from the blankets*; (*fig*) *He was already thirty before his artistic talent emerged.* **2** to become known: *It emerged that they had had a disagreement; The true facts began to emerge.*

e'mergence *nu* (*formal*) the act of coming out, becoming known *etc*: *his emergence as a poet; the emergence of the facts.*

e'mergent *adj* (*formal*: *usu attrib*) being in the process of emerging or developing: *the emergent nations* (= countries becoming culturally and politically independent).

emergency [i'məːdʒənsi] *nc* an unexpected happening or situation: *Call the doctor – it's an emergency; Call this telephone number only in an emergency; You must save some money for emergencies*; (*attrib*) *an emergency exit*; (*attrib*) *This patient is an emergency case.*

emergent *see* **emerge**.

emeritus [i'meritəs] *adj* (*sometimes placed after the noun*: *with cap in titles*) (*usu* of a professor) retired: *a professor emeritus; He is the emeritus professor of English; Emeritus Professor Brown.*

emery ['eməri] *nu* a very hard kind of mineral, used as a powder *etc* for polishing.

'emery board *nc* a small flat strip of wood or card coated with emery powder and used for filing the fingernails: *I never use a metal nail-file on my nails*

– *I always use an emery board.*

'**emery paper, cloth** *nu* paper or cloth covered with emery for polishing, grinding *etc*: *He cleaned the parts of the machine with emery paper.*

emetic [i'metik] *ncu, adj* (*attrib*: *tech*) (a medicine) causing vomiting: *He was given an emetic after he swallowed the poison*; *an emetic medicine.*

emigrate ['emigreit] *vi* to leave one's country and settle in another: *Many doctors have emigrated from Britain to America.*

'**emigrant** *nc, adj* (*attrib*) (a person) emigrating or having emigrated: *The numbers of emigrants are increasing*; *emigrant doctors.* ˌ**emi'gration** *ncu.*

See also **immigrant, migrate**.

eminent ['eminənt] *adj* (*formal*) outstanding; distinguished; famous: *He is an eminent lawyer*; *He is eminent both as a teacher and writer.*

'**eminence 1** (*formal*) *nu* distinction; fame: *his eminence as a poet*; *The politician rose to eminence immediately after the war.* **2** *nc* (*very formal*) an area of rising ground; a hill: *from an eminence above the town.* **3** *n* (*with cap*: *with* **His, Your** *etc*) a title of honour used to or of a cardinal: *His Eminence Cardinal Kelly.*

'**eminently** *adv* very; obviously: *He is eminently suitable for the job.*

emissary ['emisəri] *nc* (*formal*) a person sent to give a message or enter negotiations *etc* (sometimes secret or underhand): *He was sent to Spain as the French king's emissary.*

emission *see* **emit**.

emit [i'mit] – *pt, ptp* **e'mitted** – *vt* (*formal*) to give out (light, heat, a sound, a smell *etc*): *She emitted a cry of horror*; *The fire emitted a great heat*; *The mixture emitted a curious smell.* **e'mission** [-ʃən] *ncu.*

emolument [i'moljumənt] *ncu* (*formal*: *often in pl*) profit made from employment, salary, fees *etc*: *His emoluments as a part-time lecturer amounted to £3 000 a year.*

emotion [i'mouʃən] **1** *nc* a (strong) feeling of any kind: *Fear, joy, anger, love, jealousy are all emotions.* **2** *nu* the moving or upsetting of the mind or feelings: *Emotion overcame her as she remembered the sad day*; *He was overcome by/with emotion.*

e'motional *adj* **1** of the emotions: *Emotional problems are affecting her work*; *Her problems are mainly emotional.* **2** (*neg* **un-**) causing or showing emotion: *an emotional farewell*; *The president's speech to the crowds was very emotional.* **3** (*neg* **un-**) (of a person) easily affected by joy, anger, grief *etc*: *She is a very emotional person*; *She is very emotional.*

e'motionally *adv*: *She spoke emotionally of her dead husband*; *She is emotionally upset just now.*

e'motive [-tiv] *adj* (*formal*) (of words *etc*) tending to affect the emotions: *The politician made an emotive speech about the rights of women*; *Race is an emotive subject*; *His speech was emotive and sincere.*

empathy ['empəθi] *nu* (*formal*) the ability to understand and share the feelings, experience *etc* of someone else: *A certain empathy must exist between an author and the readers of his book.*

emperor ['empərə] – *fem* '**empress** – *nc* (*with cap in titles*) (the status of) the head of an empire: *Charlemagne was emperor of a large part of the world*; *the Emperor Napoleon.*

emphasis ['emfəsis] – *pl* '**emphases** [-si:z] – **1** *ncu* stress put on certain words in speaking *etc*; greater force of voice used in words or parts of words to make them more noticeable: *In writing we sometimes underline words to show emphasis*; *In the word 'dictionary' the emphasis is on the first part of the word.* **2** *nu* force; firmness: *'I do not intend to go,' he said with emphasis.* **3** *ncu* importance given to something: *The emphasis of the talk was on the need to work hard*; *The emphasis must be on hard work*; *He placed great emphasis on this point.*

'**emphasize, -ise** *vt* to lay or put emphasis on: *You should emphasize this word*; *Which part of the word does one emphasize?*; *He emphasized the importance of working hard.*

em'phatic [-'fa-] *adj* (*neg* **un-**) expressed with emphasis; firm and definite: *an emphatic denial*; *He was most emphatic about the importance of arriving on time.*

em'phatically *adv*: *He spoke emphatically about the need to improve production*; *'Please re-consider your decision to resign.' 'Emphatically no!'*

empire ['empaiə] *nc* **1** (*sometimes with cap*) a group of states *etc* under a single ruler or ruling power: *the British Empire*; *the Roman empire.* **2** a large industrial organization controlling many firms: *He owns a washing-machine empire.*

See also **emperor, imperial**.

empiric(al) [im'pirik(əl)] *adj* (*esp philos*) depending on, or known by, experiment, observation or experience: *Our knowledge of the colour and shape of things is empirical*; *Chemistry is an empirical branch of science.*

employ [im'ploi] *vt* **1** to give (*esp* paid) work to: *He employs three typists*; *She is employed as a teacher.* **2** to occupy the time or attention of: *She was busily employed (in) writing letters.* **3** (*formal*) to make use of: *You should employ your time better*; *It is necessary to employ a little tact.* – *nu* (*formal*) employment or service: *He was in my employ for three years*; *When did he leave your employ?*

em'ployed *adj* having a job; working: *an employed person*; *He is employed now, but he was unemployed for several months.*

em'ployee, ˌ**employ'ee** [em-] *nc* a person employed for wages, a salary *etc*: *That firm has fifty employees.*

em'ployer *nc* a person who employs others: *His employer dismissed him.*

em'ployment *nu* **1** the act of employing or state of being employed: *He is in employment now*; *She was in my employment*; (*attrib*) *an employment agency.* **2** occupation, *esp* regular paid work: *This will give employment to more men.*

See also **unemployed, unemployment**.

empower [im'pauə] *vt* (*very formal or legal*) to authorize; to give official permission to: *I was empowered by the committee to use the society's money.*

empty ['empti] *adj* **1** having nothing inside: *an empty box*; *an empty cup*; *My glass is empty*; (*fig*) *My life is empty now that the children have left home.* **2** unoccupied: *an empty house*; *an empty room*; *That house is empty.* **3** (*formal*: *pred*: *with* **of**) completely without: *This sentence is empty of meaning.* **4** (*usu attrib*) having no practical result; (likely to be) unfulfilled: *empty threats*; *empty dreams.* – *vti* to make or become empty: *He emptied the jug*; *The cinema emptied quickly at 10.30*; *He emptied out* (= completely) *his pockets*; (*formal*) *Empty the drawer of its contents.* – *vti* to tip, pour, or fall out of a container: *She emptied the milk into a pan*; *The rubbish emptied on to the* *ground.* – *nc* (*inf*) an empty bottle *etc*: *The milkman collects the empties.*

'emptiness *nu.*

ˌempty-'handed *adj* (*pred*) carrying nothing: *I went to collect my wages but returned empty-handed.*

ˌempty-'headed *adj* (*derog*) stupid; brainless: *an empty-headed young girl*; *She is foolish and empty-headed.*

emu ['iːmjuː] *nc* a type of Australian bird which cannot fly: *Emus can run very fast*; *The emu is related to the ostrich.*

emulate ['emjuleit] *vt* (*formal*) to try hard to equal or be better than: *He knew he could never emulate his brother at sport*; *It is impossible to emulate his achievements.* **ˌemu'lation** *nu.*

emulsion [i'mʌlʃən] *ncu* (*tech*) a milky liquid prepared by mixing *eg* oil and water.

emulsion paint *nu* a paint mixed with water rather than oil: *We used emulsion paint on the walls and gloss paint on the doors.*

enable [i'neibl] *vt* (*formal*) to make able by giving means, power or authority (to do something): *The money I inherited enabled me to go on a world cruise.*

enact [i'nakt] *vt* (*formal*) to act (a rôle, scene *etc*) not necessarily on stage: *A strange scene was enacted before his eyes.*

e'nactment (*formal*) **1** *nu* the passing of a bill (or the act of passing a bill) into law: *the enactment of the new divorce bill.* **2** *nc* a law: *The enactment dated from February 1974.*

enamel [i'naməl] *nu* **1** a variety of glass applied as coating to a metal or other surface and made hard by heating: *This pan is covered with enamel*; (*attrib*) *an enamel plate.* **2** the coating of the teeth: *The enamel of her teeth is very white.* **3** a glossy paint: *He painted the model train with enamel*; (*attrib*) *enamel paint.* – *v* – *pt*, *ptp* **e'namelled,** (*Amer*) **e'nameled** – *vt* to cover or ornament (metal *etc*) with enamel: *This brooch has been enamelled.*

enamoured [i'naməd]: **e'namoured of/with** (*formal or facet*) in love with or delighted with: *I am not enamoured of the idea of going abroad.*

encampment [in'kampmənt] *nc* (*formal*) a place where troops *etc* are settled in or camp: *a Roman encampment.*

encase [in'keis] *vt* (*formal*) **1** (not used with **is, was** *etc* and **-ing**) to enclose (as if) in a case: *The nuts were encased in hard outer coverings.* **2** to surround, cover or (*facet*) clothe: *She was encased in a sheepskin jacket.*

enchant [in'tʃaːnt] *vt* **1** (*formal*) to delight: *I was enchanted by the children's concert.* **2** (*old*) to put a magic spell or charm on: *A wizard had enchanted her.*

en'chanted *adj*: *an enchanted castle.*

en'chanter – *fem* **en'chantress** – *nc* a person who enchants.

en'chantment **1** *nu* (*formal*) the act of enchanting or state of being enchanted: *There was a look of enchantment on the children's faces.* **2** *nc* (*old*) a magic spell: *The witch's enchantment lasted for three years.* **3** *ncu* (*formal*) charm; attraction: *the enchantment(s) of a big city*; *Working as an actress has lost all enchantment for her.*

See also **disenchant**.

encircle [in'səːkl] *vt* (*formal*) to surround; to form a circle around (something): *Enemies encircled him*; *The railway line encircled the hill.*

enclave ['enkleiv] *nc* (*formal*) a piece of territory entirely enclosed within foreign territory: *a British enclave in the middle of Africa*; (*fig*) *Your room is an enclave of peace in this noisy school.*

enclose [in'klouz] *vt* **1** to put inside a letter or its envelope: *I enclose a cheque for £2.00.* **2** (*formal*) to shut in; to surround: *He enclosed the garden with a high wall.*

en'closure [-ʒə] **1** *nu* (*formal*) the act of enclosing. **2** *nc* land surrounded by a fence or wall: *He keeps a donkey in that enclosure.* **3** *nc* (*formal*) something put in along with a letter: *I received your enclosure with gratitude.*

encompass [in'kʌmpəs] *vt* **1** (*formal*) to include: *The teachers, pupils, lessons and buildings are encompassed by the word 'school'.* **2** (*old*) to surround: *Water encompasses the castle.*

encore ['oŋkoː] *nc, interj* (a call from an audience for) a repetition of a performance, or (for) a further performance: *The audience cried 'Encore!'*; *The singer gave two encores.*

encounter [in'kauntə] *vt* (*formal*) **1** to meet *esp* unexpectedly: *She encountered the manager in the hall.* **2** to meet with (difficulties *etc*): *I expect to encounter many difficulties in the course of this job.* – *nc* (*formal*) **1** a meeting: *I feel that I know him quite well, even after a brief encounter.* **2** a fight: *The encounter between the armies was fierce.*

encourage [in'kʌridʒ, (*Amer*) -'kəː-] *vt* **1** to give support, confidence or hope to (someone): *The general tried to encourage the troops*; *You should not encourage him in his extravagance*; *I felt encouraged by his praise.* **2** to urge (a person) to do something: *You must encourage him to try again.* **en'couraging** *adj.* **en'couragingly** *adv.*

en'couragement *ncu*: *Do give the child a few words of encouragement*; *He must be given some/every encouragement*; *Your success may act as an encouragement to your brother.*

See also **discourage**.

encroach [in'kroutʃ]: **en'croach on/upon** *vt fus* (*formal*) **1** to advance into (someone else's land *etc*): *In making his garden larger, he encroached on Mr Brown's wood.* **2** to remove part of (someone's right, privilege *etc*) unjustly: *Is the Government slowly encroaching on the liberty of the individual?*

en'croachment *ncu.*

encumber [in'kʌmbə] *vt* (*formal*) to prevent (a person *etc*) from moving easily and freely; to burden: *She was encumbered by two suitcases*; (*fig*) *It's difficult to do the shopping when you're encumbered by three small children.*

en'cumbrance *nc* (*formal*) something which acts as a burden or which prevents a person *etc* from moving easily: *the encumbrance of two suitcases and a bag*; (*fig*) *She regarded the children as encumbrances.*

encyclop(a)edia [insaiklə'piːdiə] *nc* a reference work containing information on every branch of knowledge, or on one particular branch: *an encyclopaedia of jazz*; *If you do not know the capital city of Hungary, look it up in an encyclopaedia.*

enˌcyclo'p(a)edic *adj* **1** having a large amount of information on a great variety of subjects: *an encyclopaedic memory*; *His knowledge is encyclopaedic.* **2** of, belonging to, or like, an encyclopaedia: *That is an encyclopaedic dictionary – it gives biographical and geographical information as well as meanings of words.*

end [end] *nc* **1** the last or farthest part of the length of something: *He lives in the house at the end of the road*; *The man sat at the end of the table*; *There are* *doors at both ends of the room*; *Put the tables end to end* (= with the end of one touching the end of another); (*attrib*) *We live in the end house over there.* **2** the finish or conclusion: *She is coming home at the end of the week*; *The talks have come to an end*; *That was the end of the affair*; *The affair is at an end*; *The old man is at the end of his strength*; *They fought bravely to the end*; *If she wins the prize we'll never hear the end of it* (= she will often talk about it). **3** (*formal*: *no pl*) death: *The soldiers met their end bravely*; *The end came suddenly for the old man.* **4** (*formal*) an aim: *What end have you in view?*; *To what end are you working so hard?* **5** a small piece left over; a fragment; an odd piece: *The ash-tray was full of cigarette ends.* – *vti* to bring or come to an end: *The scheme ended in disaster*; *How does the play end?*; *How should I end* (*off*) *this letter?*; *The play ends with the hero's death.* – *See also* **end** *in phrases below.*

'ending *nc* **1** the end, *esp* of a story, poem *etc*: *Fairy stories have happy endings.* **2** (*gram*) the end part of a word; a suffix: *'-ing' is the ending of 'buying'.*

'endless *adj* **1** (*derog*) going on for ever or for a very long time: *The discussion seemed endless*; *They had endless discussions.* **2** (*attrib*) continuous, because of having the two ends joined: *an endless chain.*

'endways *adv* (*sometimes with* **on**) with the end forward: *You will have to turn the table endways* (*on*) *to get it through the door.*

at a loose end (*inf*) with nothing to do: *He went to the cinema because he was at a loose end.*

end up *vi* **1** to reach or come to an end, *usu* unpleasant: *I knew that he would end up in prison*; *He ended up in hospital*; *We ended up without enough money to pay our bus fare home.* **2** to end; to finish; to do something in the end: *He said he would not go but he ended up by going*; *He refused to believe her but he ended up apologizing.*

in the 'end finally; after a long time; after a series of events or after much discussion, work *etc*: *We could not decide what to do but we went to the cinema in the end*; *He had to work very hard but he passed his exam in the end.*

make (both) ends meet to live within one's income; not to get into debt: *The widow and her four children found it difficult to make ends meet.*

no 'end (of) (*inf*) very much: *I feel no end of a fool*; (*sl*) *I liked it no end.*

on 'end 1 upright; erect: *Stand the table on end or you won't get it through the door*; *The cat's fur stood on end.* **2** continuously; without a pause: *For days on end we had hardly anything to eat.*

put an end to (*formal*) to cause to finish; to stop: *You must put an end to this quarrelling*; *The government put an end to public execution.*

the end (*inf*) the limit (of what can be borne or tolerated): *His behaviour is the end*; *That child really is the end!*

See also **unending**.

endanger [in'deindʒə] *vt* (*formal*) to put in danger: *Drunk drivers endanger the lives of others.*

endear [in'diə] *vt* (*formal*) to make (someone or something) dear or more dear (to someone): *He endeared himself to me by his kindness*; *His loyalty endeared him to me.*

en'dearing *adj* arousing feelings of affection: *his endearing truthfulness*; *I find her loyalty most endearing.*

en'dearment *nc* (*formal*) a word of love: *He whispered endearments in her ear.*

endeavour [in'devə] *vi* (*formal*) to attempt; to try (to do something): *He endeavoured to attract the waiter's attention.* – *nc* an effort; an attempt: *He succeeded in his endeavour to climb Everest*; *All his endeavours proved unsuccessful.*

endemic [en'demik] *adj* (*formal*) (of a disease *etc*) regularly found in people or a district owing to local conditions: *Malaria is endemic in/to certain tropical countries.*

endive ['endiv, (*Amer*) -daiv] *nc* a type of salad plant related to chicory.

endorse [in'do:s] *vt* **1** to write one's signature on the back of (a cheque): *The bank refused to cash the cheque as it was not endorsed.* **2** to make a note of an offence on (a driving licence): *The magistrate endorsed his licence because of his dangerous driving.* **3** (*formal*) to give one's approval to; to support (a decision, statement *etc*): *The court endorsed the judge's decision.*

en'dorsement *ncu*: *After three endorsements he was banned from driving*; *the endorsement of the cheque*; *the endorsement of his decision.*

endow [in'dau] *vt* **1** to give a permanent income to (*esp* an institution or part of one): *That Oxford college was endowed by him*; *She endowed a bed in the local hospital in memory of her husband.* **2** (*formal*: *usu passive*) to give (a talent, quality *etc*) to: *She was endowed with great beauty.* **en'dowment** *ncu.*

endure [in'djuə] **1** *vt* to bear patiently; to undergo; to tolerate: *She has to endure great pain*; *She endures her troubles bravely*; *I can endure her rudeness no longer.* **2** *vi* (*formal*) to remain firm; to last: *You must endure to the end*; *The memory of her great acting has endured.*

en'durable *adj* (*formal*) (*neg* **un-**) able to be borne or tolerated: *This pain is scarcely endurable.*

en'durance *nu* the power or ability to bear or to last: *He has amazing* (*power of*) *endurance*; *His endurance amazes me*; *Her rudeness is beyond endurance*; (*attrib*) *One of the endurance tests that the soldiers had to perform was to spend a night on the mountain.*

enema ['enəmə] *nc* (*med*) the injection of a liquid into the rectum: *He was given an enema to clean out the bowels before his operation.*

enemy ['enəmi] **1** *nc* a person who hates or wishes to harm one: *She is so good and kind that she has no enemies*; (*fig*) *He is an enemy of progress.* **2** *nc or n pl* troops, forces, a nation *etc* opposed to oneself in war *etc*: *He's one of the enemy*; *The enemy attacked them unexpectedly*; *Napoleon met the enemy outside the city*; *The enemy was/were encamped on the hillside*; (*attrib*) *enemy forces*; (*attrib*) *enemy attack.*

See also **enmity**.

energy ['enədʒi] **1** *ncu* the ability to act, or the habit of acting, strongly and vigorously; force: *He has amazing energy for his age*; *That child has too much energy*; *I must devote my energies to gardening today.* **2** *nu* (*phys etc*) the power, *eg* of electricity, of doing work: *electrical energy*; *nuclear energy.*

ˌener'getic [-'dʒetik] *adj* **1** vigorous; very active: *Her child is very energetic*; *an energetic child.* **2** requiring energy: *an energetic walk.* **ˌener'getically** *adv.*

enervating ['enəveitiŋ] *adj* (*formal*) taking away strength or energy from (a person): *I find this climate very enervating*; *an enervating climate.*

enforce [in'fo:s] *vt* (*formal*) **1** to cause (a law, a command, one's own will *etc*) to be carried out: *There is a law against dropping litter but it is rarely enforced.* **2** to force (an action or way of acting): *He will now try to enforce payment of the money.* **en'forcement** *nu.*

en'forceable *adj* (*formal*: *usu pred*) able to be enforced: *That law is not easily enforceable.*

engage [in'geidʒ] **1** *vt* to begin to employ (a workman *etc*): *He has engaged three new assistants*; *He engaged him as his assistant.* **2** *vt* (*formal*) to book; to reserve: *He has engaged an entertainer for the children's party.* **3** *vt* (*formal*) to take hold of or hold fast; to occupy: *That book engaged his attention for hours*; *The poor child engaged his sympathy.* **4** *vti* (*formal*) to join battle with: *The two armies were fiercely engaged.* **5** *vti* to (cause part of a machine *etc* to) fit into and lock with another part: *The driver engaged second gear.*

en'gaged *adj* **1** bound by promise (*esp* to marry): *She became engaged to John.* **2** (*formal*: *pred*: *with* **in**) employed or occupied: *She is engaged in social work*; *She is engaged in writing her memoirs.* **3** (*formal*) busy; not free; occupied: *Please come if you are not already engaged for that evening*; *The room/telephone line is engaged*; *There is an engaged sign* (= a notice saying 'engaged') *on the door.*

en'gagement 1 *nu* (*formal*) the act of engaging or state of being engaged: *He gave permission for the engagement of three new assistants.* **2** *nc* an agreement between two people to marry: *When shall we announce our engagement?*; (*attrib*) *an engagement ring.* **3** *nc* (*formal*) an arrangement (to do something *etc*) made in advance; a commitment; an appointment: *Have you any engagements tomorrow?*; *She cannot have dinner with us – she has another engagement.* **4** *nc* a fight, battle *etc*: *a naval engagement.*

en'gaging *adj* attractive: *an engaging smile*; *Her manner is most engaging.*

See also **disengage**.

engine ['endʒin] *nc* **1** a machine in which heat or other energy is used to produce motion: *The car has a new engine.* **2** a railway engine: *He likes to sit in a seat facing the engine.*

'engine-driver *nc* (*esp Brit*) a person who drives a railway engine.

ˌengi'neer *nc* **1** a person who designs, makes, or works with, machinery: *a mechanical engineer*; *an electrical engineer.* **2** (*usu* **civil engineer**) a person who designs, constructs, or manages public works such as roads, railways, bridges, sewers *etc.* **3** an officer who manages a ship's engines: *He is first engineer.* **4** (*Amer*) an engine-driver. – *vt* (*often derog*) to arrange or bring about, by skill or by cunning means: *He engineered my promotion.*

ˌengi'neering *nu* the art or profession of an engineer: *He is studying engineering at university*; (*attrib*) *an engineering course.*

English ['iŋgliʃ] **1** *adj* of England or its inhabitants: *three English people*; *He is English, not Scottish.* **2** *adj* (*loosely*: *sometimes offensive to Scots, Welsh or Irish*) of Great Britain or its inhabitants. **3** *adj, n* (of) the main language of Britain, North America, a great part of the British Commonwealth and some other countries: *He speaks English*; *the English language.*

England *see* Appendix 2.

'Englishman – *fem* **'Englishwoman** – *nc* **1** a person born in England. **2** (*loosely*: *sometimes offensive to Scots, Welsh or Irish*) a person born in Britain and/or having British citizenship.

See also Appendix 2.

engrave [in'greiv] *vt* **1** to cut (letters or designs) on stone, wood, metal *etc*: *He engraved her initials on the tree-trunk*; *They engraved his initials on the silver cup.* **2** to ornament (metal *etc*) in this way: *He engraved the silver cup.* **3** (*fig*) to impress deeply (on the mind *etc*): *The scene would always be engraved on his memory.* **en'graver** *nc.*

en'graving 1 *nu* the art or act of an engraver. **2** *nc* a picture taken from an engraved plate or print: *He hung the engraving on the wall.*

engrossed [in'groust] *adj* **1** (*pred*: *often with* **in**) having one's attention and interest completely taken up: *He is completely engrossed in his work*; *She started to read the book, and quickly became engrossed (in it).* **2** (*formal*: *attrib*) showing that a person is engrossed: *an engrossed look.*

en'grossing *adj* (*formal*) completely taking up the attention and interest of: *This is an engrossing book*; *I find this book engrossing.*

engulf [in'gʌlf] *vt* (*formal*) (of waves, flames *etc*) to swallow up completely: *Flames engulfed him*; (*fig*) *Grief engulfed him.*

enhance [in'ha:ns] *vt* (*formal*) to make to appear greater or better; to increase: *The soft evening light enhanced her beauty*; *Your improvements will enhance the value of the house.*

enigma [i'nigmə] *nc* (*formal*) anything or anyone difficult to understand; a mystery: *Why he goes on working here is a complete enigma*; *She has worked here for years but she is still an enigma to all of us.*

enigmatic [enig'matik] *adj* (*formal*) puzzling; mysterious: *an enigmatic smile*; *I found his personality rather enigmatic.* **ˌenig'matically** *adv.*

enjoy [in'dʒoi] *vt* **1** to find pleasure in: *I enjoy skating*; *He enjoyed the book*; *He enjoyed the meal.* **2** to experience; to be in the habit of having (*esp* a benefit): *He enjoyed good health all his life.* – *See also* **enjoy oneself** *below.*

en'joyable *adj* (*neg* **un-**): *This is an enjoyable book*; *We had an enjoyable game of tennis*; *We spent an enjoyable afternoon at the zoo*; *That was most enjoyable.*

en'joyment *nu*: *He finds enjoyment in simple things.*

en'joy oneself to experience pleasure or happiness: *She enjoyed herself at the party.*

enlarge [in'la:dʒ] *vt* **1** (*formal*) to make larger: *He enlarged the rose garden.* **2** to reproduce on a larger scale (a photograph *etc*): *We had the photograph enlarged.* – *See also* **enlarge on/upon** *below.*

en'largement 1 *nc* something enlarged, *esp* a photograph: *There is an enlargement of that photograph on her mantelpiece.* **2** *nu* (*formal*) the act of enlarging or state of being enlarged: *Enlargement of the glands in the neck is usually a sign of illness.*

en'large on/upon *vt fus* (*formal*) to speak, write *etc* in more detail: *Would you like to enlarge on your original statement?*; *He enlarged upon his holiday plans.*

enlighten [in'laitn] *vt* (*formal*) to give more information to (a person): *Will someone please enlighten me as to what is happening?*

en'lightened *adj* wise through knowledge; free from prejudice: *an enlightened headmaster*; *an enlightened decision*; *We call ourselves enlightened, but we still do not treat our disabled citizens very well.* **en'lightenment** *nu.*

enlist [in'list] **1** *vi* to join an army *etc*: *My father* *enlisted on the day after war was declared.* **2** *vt* to obtain the support and help of: *He has enlisted George to help him organize the party.* **3** *vt* to obtain (support and help) from someone: *I've enlisted George's help to raise the money; They enlisted the support of five hundred people for their campaign.*

enliven [in'laivn] *vt* (*formal*) to make (more) active, lively or cheerful: *I tried to think of something that might enliven the party.*

en masse [ã'mas, (*Amer*) on-] *adv* (*formal*) all together in a body: *I'd rather talk to them separately than en masse.*

enmity ['enməti] *nu* unfriendliness; ill-will; hatred: *The enmity between the two families lasted for many years; I cannot understand his enmity towards her.*
See also **enemy**.

enormous [i'no:məs] *adj* very large: *The new building is enormous; We had an enormous lunch.*
e'normousness *nu*.
e'normity **1** *ncu* (*formal*) wickedness; great crime: *the enormity of his assault on the little girl; the enormities committed during the war.* **2** *nu* (*loosely*) great size: *The enormity of the task discouraged him.*

enough [i'nʌf] *adj* in the number or quantity *etc* needed: *Have you enough money to pay for the books?; We haven't enough food to feed everyone;* (*formal*) *There is food enough.* – *pron* the amount needed: *He has had enough to eat; We haven't found enough of these; I've had enough of her rudeness.* – *adv* (following the adjective *etc* that it qualifies) **1** to the degree needed: *Is it hot enough (for him) to go swimming?; I was idiot enough/idiotic enough to believe her; He swam quickly enough to pass the test.* **2** fairly: *The news is bad enough but I had thought it would be worse; She's pretty enough, I suppose, but I don't admire her.* **3** rather: *Stupidly enough, I forgot my umbrella; Oddly enough, it isn't raining.*

enquire, enquiry *see* **inquire**.

enrage [in'reidʒ] *vt* (*formal*) to make very angry: *His son's rudeness enraged him; He was enraged at/by the rude remarks.*

enrapture [in'raptʃə] *vt* (*formal*) to give great pleasure or delight to: *The child was enraptured by the sight of the Christmas tree.*

enrich [in'ritʃ] *vt* (*formal*) to improve the quality of: *Fertilizers enrich the soil; Some cream will enrich the sauce;* (*fig formal*) *Reading enriches the mind.*

enrol, (*Amer usu or Brit rare*) **enroll** [in'roul] – *pt, ptp* **en'rolled** – *vt* to add (someone), or have oneself added, to a list or roll (as a pupil at a school, a member of a club *etc*): *Can we still enrol for this class?; You must enrol your child before the start of the school term.* **en'rolment** *ncu*.

en route [ã'ru:t, (*Amer*) on-] *adv* (*sometimes with* **to** *or* **for**) on the way (to): *I'm en route for my office; We are en route from London to Edinburgh; En route to the theatre we stopped for a drink.*

ensconce [in'skons] *vt* (*liter or facet*) to settle (oneself *etc*) comfortably (in): *The cat was ensconced in the armchair; He ensconced himself in the best chair.*

ensemble [ãn'sãblə, (*Amer*) on'sombl] *nc* **1** (*formal*) a woman's complete outfit of clothes: *She wore a matching ensemble.* **2** in opera *etc*, a passage performed by all the singers, musicians *etc* together. **3** a group of musicians performing regularly together. **4** (*formal*) all the parts of a thing taken as a whole: *The costumes and scenery were combined in an effective ensemble.*

enshroud [in'ʃraud] *vt* (*liter or formal*) to cover completely: *Mist enshrouded the hilltops; The affair is enshrouded in mystery.*

ensign ['ensain] *nc* **1** the flag of a nation, regiment *etc.* **2** (*hist: with cap in titles*) in the British army, the lowest commissioned rank, or an officer of this rank (one of whose duties was to carry the flag).

ensnare [in'sneə] *vt* (*liter: usu fig*) to catch in a snare; to trap: *He was ensnared by her beauty.*

ensue [in'sju:] *vi* (*formal*) to come after; to result (from): *It was too late to stop the panic that ensued from the false news report.*
en'suing *adj* (*formal: attrib*) coming after; happening as a result: *She was killed in the ensuing riots.*

ensure [in'ʃuə] *vt* (*formal*) to make sure; to make certain: *You must ensure that your television set is switched off at night.*
See also **insure, sure**.

entail [in'teil] *vt* **1** (*formal*) to bring as a result; to require: *These alterations will entail great expense.* **2** (*legal hist*) to leave (land) to a series of heirs, so that none may sell it *etc* as he wishes. – (*legal*) **1** *nu* the practice of entailing (land). **2** *nc* an entailed estate.

entangle [in'taŋgl] *vt* (*often passive*) to cause (something) to become twisted or tangled with something else: *His long scarf entangled itself in a thorn bush;* (*formal fig*) *He was entangled in an unhappy love affair.*
en'tanglement *ncu*: *His frequent entanglements with women/the police.*
See also **disentangle**.

enter ['entə] (*more formal than* **go/come in**) **1** *vi* to go or come in: *You may enter now; Enter by this door.* **2** *vt* to come or go into (a place): *He slowly entered the room.* **3** *vti* to give the name of (another person or oneself) for a competition *etc*: *He entered for the race; I entered my pupils for the examination.* **4** *vt* to write (one's name *etc*) in a book *etc*: *Did you enter your name in the visitors' book?* **5** *vt* (*formal*) to join or start in (a school, a job *etc*): *She entered his employment last week.* **6** *vt* to begin: *They are entering a new stage in their lives.*
enter into *vt fus* **1** to take part in: *He entered into an agreement with the film director.* **2** to take part enthusiastically in: *They entered into the Christmas party spirit.* **3** to begin to discuss: *We cannot enter into the question of salaries yet.* **4** to be a part of: *The price did not enter into the discussion.*
'enter on/upon *vt fus* (*formal*) to begin: *We have entered upon the new term.*
See also **entrance, entry**.

enterprise ['entəpraiz] **1** *nc* something that is attempted or undertaken (*esp* if it requires boldness or courage): *He started several business enterprises; The gala day, which they hope to hold annually, is a completely new enterprise for the village.* **2** *nu* willingness to try new lines of action: *We need someone with enterprise and enthusiasm to lead the expedition; He showed great enterprise in taking that job.*
'enterprising *adj* (*neg* **un-**) full of enterprise; adventurous: *It was enterprising of you to try to swim the English Channel; He is full of enterprising schemes.*
private enterprise *see* **private**.

entertain [entə'tein] **1** *vti* to receive, and give food *etc* to (guests): *They entertained us to dinner*; *We don't entertain very much.* **2** *vt* to amuse: *His stories entertained us for hours.* **3** *vt* (*formal or liter*: not used with **is, was** *etc* and **-ing**) to hold in the mind or feelings: *He entertained a belief that his wife would return one day.*

ˌenter'taining *adj* amusing: *I find him most entertaining*; *He tells entertaining stories.*

ˌenter'tainment 1 *nc* something that entertains, *eg* a theatrical show *etc*: *The entertainment at the new theatre changes nightly.* **2** *nu* the act of entertaining: *The entertainment of the children exhausted him.* **3** *nu* amusement: *The children complained of lack of entertainment.*

enthral, (*Amer usu or Brit rare*) **enthrall** [in'θro:l] – *pt, ptp* **en'thralled** – *vt* (*liter*) to delight greatly: *He was completely enthralled by her beauty*; *His stories enthralled the children.* **en'thralling** *adj.* **en'thralment** *nu.*

enthrone [in'θroun] *vt* (*formal*) to place on a throne; to crown (as a king, queen, bishop *etc*): *The queen was enthroned with great pomp and ceremony.* **en'thronement** *ncu.*

enthuse [in'θju:z] *vi* (*inf*: *often with* **over** *or* **about**) to be enthusiastic: *I couldn't enthuse over the new baby*; *He is constantly enthusing about his new job.*

enthusiasm [in'θju:ziazəm] *ncu* strong or passionate interest: *He has a great enthusiasm for sport*; *His enthusiasm for travelling makes him go abroad every year*; *He did not show any enthusiasm for our new plans.*

en'thusiast *nc* a person filled with enthusiasm: *an opera enthusiast.*

enˌthusi'astic *adj* (*neg* **un-**) full of enthusiasm or approval: *He is an enthusiastic mountaineer*; *I'm enthusiastic about the new teaching methods.* **enˌthusi'astically** *adv.*

entice [in'tais] *vt* to attract (someone into doing something) by arousing hope and desire: *He enticed the child into his house by promising her sweets*; *Goods are displayed in shop windows to entice people into going into the shop.* **en'ticement** *ncu.*

en'ticing *adj* attractive or tempting: *An enticing smell came from the kitchen*; *That meal looks most enticing.*

entire [in'taiə] *adj* (*attrib*) whole: *I spent the entire day on the beach*; *The entire job was completed in a week.*

en'tirely *adv* completely: *The house was almost entirely hidden by the trees*; *His work is not entirely satisfactory*; *The two books are entirely different.*

en'tirety [-rəti] *nu* (*formal*) completeness; wholeness: *Until we know all the facts we cannot study the problem in its entirety.*

entitle [in'taitl] *vt* **1** to give (a person) a right (to, or to do, something): *You are not entitled to free school lunches*; *He was not entitled to borrow money from the cash box*; *You are entitled to think what you like.* **2** (*formal*) to give to (a book *etc*) as a title or name: *a story entitled 'The White Horse'.* **en'titlement** *nu.*

entity ['entəti] *nc* (*formal*) a thing *etc* that exists: *gases and other entities*; *a separate entity.*

entomology [entə'molədʒi] *nu* the science or study of insects. **ˌentomo'logical** [-'lo-] *adj* (*tech*). **ˌento'mologist** *nc.*

entourage [ontu'ra:ʒ] *nc* (*formal or facet*) a group of followers, *esp* of a person of high rank: *the nobleman and his entourage.*

entrails ['entreilz] *n pl* the internal parts of the body, *esp* the intestines: *a chicken's entrails.*

entrance[1] ['entrəns] **1** *nc* a place of entering, *eg* an opening, a door *etc*: *A fall of rock had blocked the entrance to the tunnel*; *The church has an impressive entrance.* **2** *ncu* (*formal*) (an) act of entering: *Hamlet now makes his second entrance.* **3** *nu* the right to enter: *He has applied for entrance to university*; (*attrib*) *a university entrance exam*; *They had not bought tickets, so they were refused entrance.*

'entrant *nc* one who enters (*esp* a competition, a profession *etc*): *There were sixty entrants for the musical competition.*

See also **enter, entry**.

entrance[2] [in'tra:ns] *vt* to fill with great delight; to enchant: *The audience were entranced by her singing*; *They stood entranced at the beauty of the scene.*

entrant *see* **entrance**[1].

entreat [in'tri:t] *vt* (*formal*) to ask (a person) earnestly and seriously (to do something): *I entreat you to help me*; *Don't leave me, I entreat you.*

en'treaty *ncu* (*formal*) (an) earnest request or plea: *I begged her not to go, but she would not listen to my entreaties*; *No amount of entreaty would persuade her to go.*

entrée ['ontrei] (*formal*) **1** *nc* a (meat) dish served at dinner between chief courses: *What shall we serve as the entrée?*; (*attrib*) *entrée dishes.* **2** *ncu* (the right of) admission or entry (*esp* to a certain group or circle of people): *His reputation as an amusing talker gave him (an) entrée to the houses of the wealthy.*

entrench [in'trentʃ] *vt* (*fig formal*) to establish firmly or in a strong position: *He was entrenched in his old-fashioned opinions.* **en'trenchment** *ncu.*

entrepreneur [ontrəprə'nə:] *nc* (*formal*: *sometimes derog*) a person who starts or organizes a business company, *esp* one involving risk: *The new book shop is owned by an entrepreneur who is only interested in making a lot of money – he is not interested in books.*

entrust [in'trʌst] *vt* (*formal*) to give into the care of another; to trust (somebody with something): *I entrusted my jewellery to her*; *I entrusted this secret to her*; *I entrusted her with the duty of locking up.*

entry ['entri] **1** *ncu* (an) act of coming in or going in: *They were silenced by the entry of the headmaster*; *Britain's entry into the European Common Market.* **2** *ncu* the right to enter: *We at last gained (an) entry to the private library*; *We can't go in – the sign says 'No Entry'.* **3** *nc* place of entrance, *esp* a passage or small entrance hall: *Don't bring your bike in here – leave it in the entry.* **4** *nc* a person or thing, or the total number of persons *etc*, entered for a competition *etc*: *There are forty-five entries for the painting competition*; *Only twenty-one people are taking part in the competition – rather a small entry.* **5** *nc* something written in a list in a book *etc*: *inaccurate entries in your account book*; *She made three entries in her diary*; *How many entries are there in that dictionary?*

entwine [in'twain] *vt* (*formal*) (*sometimes with* **around**) to wind round: *They walked with arms entwined*; *a snake entwined round a pole.*

enumerate [i'nju:məreit] *vt* (*formal*) to give a list of: *He enumerated my faults – laziness, vanity etc.* **eˌnume'ration** *ncu.*

enunciate [i'nʌnsieit] *vti* (*formal*) to pronounce clearly and distinctly: *He carefully enunciated each*

syllable of the word; *He always enunciates clearly.*
eˌnunci'ation *ncu.*

envelop [in'veləp] – *pt, ptp* **en'veloped** – *vt* to cover by wrapping; to surround completely: *She enveloped herself in a thick cloak*; (*fig*) *Mist enveloped the hilltops.*

envelope ['envəloup] *nc* a thin, flat wrapper or cover, *esp* for a letter: *The letter arrived in a long envelope.*

enviable, envious *see* **envy**.

environment [in'vaiərənmənt] *ncu* (a set of) surrounding conditions, *esp* those influencing development or growth: *An unhappy home environment may drive a teenager to crime* (= cause him to become a criminal); *Many people think that we should protect the environment* (= the natural conditions in which we live) *from destruction by modern chemicals etc.*
enˌviron'mental [-'men-] *adj*: *environmental influences/conditions.*
enˌviron'mentalism [-'men-] *nu* concern about the natural environment and its protection from pollution and other things likely to harm it: *He believes in environmentalism and so does not use chemicals on his garden.* **enˌviron'mentalist** *nc.*

environs [in'vaiərənz] *n pl* (*formal*) outskirts; outlying districts (of a town *etc*): *Paris and its environs.*

envisage [in'vizidʒ] *vt* (*formal*) to picture in one's mind and consider: *I tried to envisage her as a young woman*; *This was the plan that we envisaged.*

envoy ['envoi] *nc* (*formal*) a messenger, *esp* one sent to deal with foreign government: *He was sent to France as the king's envoy.*

envy ['envi] *nu* a feeling of discontent at another's good fortune or success: *She could not conceal her envy of me*; *Their envy at my new dress was obvious.* – *vt* **1** to feel envy towards (someone): *He envied me*; *She envied him his money.* **2** to feel envy because of: *We envy his success*; *I've always envied that dress.*
'enviable *adj* (*neg* **un-**) that is to be envied: *She spoke in public with enviable ease.*
'envious *adj* feeling or showing envy: *They are envious of her beauty*; *She is a spiteful, envious person.*
the 'envy of something envied by: *Her piano-playing was the envy of her sisters.*

enzyme ['enzaim] *nc* (*tech*) a substance, produced by living cells, that affects the speed of chemical changes without itself permanently changing: *Washing powders containing enzymes are claimed to remove dirt more effectively.*

eon *see* **aeon**.

epaulet(te) ['epəlet] *nc* a shoulder ornament on a uniform *etc*: *That soldier has epaulettes.*

ephemeral [i'femərəl] *adj* (*formal*) lasting a very short time: *ephemeral pleasures*; *Beauty is ephemeral.*

epic ['epik] *nc* **1** a long poem telling a story of great deeds: *an epic about a hero killed in battle*; (*attrib*) *an epic poem.* **2** a long story, film *etc* telling of great deeds and adventure: *That film producer has made many Biblical epics*; (*attrib*) *an epic film.*

epicurean [epikju'ri:ən] *adj* (*formal*) having pleasure, *esp* of eating, as the chief aim: *His epicurean tastes led him into extravagance.*

epidemic [epi'demik] *nc* an outbreak of a disease that spreads rapidly and attacks large numbers at one time: *an epidemic of measles*; (*attrib*) *Doctors expect that influenza will reach epidemic proportions this winter.*

epigram ['epigram] *nc* a short, neat saying in prose or verse: *'Brevity is the soul of wit' is an epigram.*
ˌepigram'matic [-'matik] *adj.*

epilepsy ['epilepsi] *nu* a disease of the nervous system causing attacks of unconsciousness, *usu* with violent movements of the body: *She suffers from epilepsy.*
ˌepi'leptic [-tik] **1** *nc, adj* (a person who is) suffering from epilepsy: *Doctors have discovered that she is (an) epileptic.* **2** *adj* of, or caused by, epilepsy: *She often has epileptic fits.*

epilogue, (*Amer*) **epilog** ['epilog] *nc* **1** the closing section of a book, programme *etc*: *Some radio and television companies end the day's broadcasting with an epilogue.* **2** a speech at the end of a play: *Some of Shakespeare's plays end with an epilogue.*
See also **prologue**.

epinephrine [epi'nefri:n] *nu* (*Amer*) adrenalin.

episcopal [i'piskəpəl] *adj* (*attrib*) (of a church) governed by bishops: *an episcopal church.*
eˌpisco'palian [-'peiliən] **1** *adj* of (government by) bishops: *The established church in England is episcopalian.* **2** *adj, nc* (*with cap*) a member of an episcopal church: *Is she a Roman Catholic or an Episcopalian?*

episode ['episoud] *nc* **1** an incident, or series of events, occurring in a longer story *etc*: *The episode of/about the donkeys is in Chapter 3*; *That is an episode in her life that she wishes to forget.* **2** a part of a radio or television serial that is broadcast at one time: *This is the last episode of the serial.*
ˌepi'sodic [-'sodik] *adj* (of *eg* a novel or story) containing or consisting of a series of incidents: *Episodic novels can be easily adapted as serials in magazines*; *His style is episodic.*

epistle [i'pisl] *nc* **1** in the Bible, a letter from an apostle: *The epistles of St Paul.* **2** (*facet*) a letter: *I received a long epistle from him yesterday.*

epitaph ['epita:f] *nc* something written or said about a dead person, *esp* something written on a tombstone: *The simple epitaph on her tombstone was 'She died a friend of all'.*

epithet ['epiθet] *nc* (*formal*) an adjective or descriptive phrase that shows a familiar or important quality of the noun it describes: *The blue sky*; *Alexander the Great.*

epitome [i'pitəmi] *nc* **1** (*formal*) something that in a small way perfectly represents a larger or wider idea, issue *etc*: *The story of the Jones family's hardships is an epitome of the social evils of Victorian times.* **2** (*loosely*) something, a person *etc* that is a perfect example of a quality *etc*: *He is the epitome of selfishness.*
e'pitomize, -ise *vt* (*formal*) to make or be an epitome of: *His treatment of his wife epitomizes his attitude to women.*

epoch ['i:pok, (*Amer*) 'epək] *nc* (the start of) a particular period of history, development *etc*: *The invention of printing marked an epoch in the history of education.*
'epoch-making *adj* (*formal or facet*) great and important enough to affect the course of history and begin a new epoch; (*loosely*) very important: *The scientist made a epoch-making discovery*; *I don't regard his new theory as epoch-making.*

equable ['ekwəbl] *adj* (*formal*) **1** (of climate *etc*) never extremely hot, cold, stormy *etc*: *Britain has an equable climate.* **2** (of a person) not easily annoyed or upset: *That child would annoy the most* *equable person*; *She is very equable.*

equal ['i:kwəl] *adj* the same in size, amount, value *etc*: *Cut the cake into four equal slices*; *These coins are of equal value*; *Are these pieces equal in size?*; *Women want their wages to be equal with men's wages.* – *nc* one of the same age, rank, ability *etc*: *He was among his equals in the competition*; *I am not his equal at running*; *You will not see his equal again.* – *See also* **equal to** *below.* – *v* – *pt, ptp* **'equalled**, (*Amer*) **'equaled** – *vt* (not *usu* used with **is, was** *etc* and **-ing**) to be the same in amount, value, size *etc*: *I cannot hope to equal him*; *She equalled his score of twenty points*; *Five and five equals ten.*

equality [i'kwoləti] *nu* the state of being equal: *Women want equality of opportunity with men.*

'equalize, -ise *vti* to make or become equal: *Our team were winning by one goal – but the other side soon equalized* (= got another goal and so the score was equal).

'equally *adv*: *All are equally good*; *He divided his chocolate equally between us.*

'equal to fit or able for: *Is he equal to this heavy task?*; *I do not feel equal to telling him the truth.*

See also **equate, inequality, unequal**.

equanimity [ekwə'niməti] *nu* (*formal*) calmness of temper: *Throughout the unpleasant row he did not lose his equanimity*; *I find it difficult to regard his behaviour with any degree of equanimity.*

equate [i'kweit] *vt* to regard as the same in some way: *He equates money with happiness.*

e'quation [-ʒən] **1** *nc* (*math*) a statement that two things are equal or the same: $xy+xy=2xy$ *is an equation.* **2** *nc* (*chem*) a formula expressing the action of certain substances on others: $2H_2+O_2=2H_2O$ *is an equation.* **3** *ncu* (*formal*) (an) act of making, or regarding as, the same or equal: *His equation of money with happiness led to his wife divorcing him.*

equator [i'kweitə] *n* (*with* **the**) an imaginary line (or one drawn on a map *etc*) passing round the globe, at an equal distance from the North and South poles: *It is very hot at the equator.*

equatorial [ekwə'to:riəl] *adj* of or near the equator: *That country has an equatorial climate.*

equerry ['ekwəri] *nc* an official attending a member of a royal family *etc*: *the king's equerry.*

equestrian [i'kwestriən] *adj* (*formal*: *usu attrib*) of the art of horse-riding: *There will be equestrian events at the sports meeting.*

equi- [i:kwi] (*in cmpds*) equal, as in **equidistant**.

equidistant [i:kwi'distənt] *adj* (*formal*: *pred with* **from**) equally distant: *Points A and B are equidistant from C*; *The cottage is equidistant from the two villages.*

equilateral [i:kwi'latərəl] *adj* (*geom*) having all sides equal: *an equilateral triangle.*

equilibrium [i:kwi'libriəm] *nu* **1** a state of equal balance between weights, forces *etc*: *The scales are in equilibrium when the weights in the pans are equal.* **2** a balanced state of mind, feelings or emotions: *Nothing disturbs his equilibrium.*

equine ['ekwain] *adj* (*very formal*) of or like a horse or horses: *The saddle is an item of equine equipment*; (*fig derog*) *She has rather equine features.*

equinox ['ekwinoks] *nc* the time when the sun crosses the equator, making night and day equal in length, about March 21 and September 23.

ˌequi'noctial [-'nokʃəl] *adj* (*tech*: *attrib*) of the equinoxes, or the time of these: *equinoctial gales.*

equip [i'kwip] – *pt, ptp* **e'quipped** – *vt* to fit out or provide (someone or something) with everything needed: *He was fully equipped for the journey*; *Her kitchen is equipped with labour-saving devices*; *Please equip yourself with a rifle*; *The speaker was well equipped* (= well able) *to answer the audience's questions.*

e'quipment *nu* **1** the clothes, machines, tools *etc* necessary for a particular kind of work, activity *etc*: *The mechanic could not repair the car because he did not have the right equipment*; *The boy could not afford the equipment necessary for mountaineering.* **2** (*formal*) the act of equipping: *The equipment of his studio cost him a great deal of money.*

equitable ['ekwitəbl] *adj* (*formal*) fair and just: *Distribute the money in an equitable manner.* **'equitably** *adv.*

equity ['ekwəti] *nu* (*formal*) fairness; justice: *Magistrates are not always noted for the equity of their decisions.*

equivalent [i'kwivələnt] *adj* equal in value, power, meaning *etc*: *A metre is not quite equivalent to a yard*; *Would you say that 'bravery' and 'courage' are exactly equivalent?*; *For this recipe, you need about 100 grams of butter, or an equivalent amount of margarine.* – *nc* something or someone that is equivalent to something or someone else: *Six yards is the equivalent of slightly less than two metres*; *In that firm, he is the equivalent of our manager*; *This word has no equivalent in French.*

equivocal [i'kwivəkəl] *adj* (*formal*: *neg* **un-**) **1** capable of meaning two or more things: *Lawyers try to avoid using equivocal terms.* **2** of an uncertain nature: *He found himself in a somewhat equivocal situation.*

equivocate [i'kwivəkeit] *vi* (*formal*) to use words of double meaning in order to mislead or to avoid giving a direct answer: *Politicians often equivocate when asked about their policies.* **eˌquivo'cation** *ncu.*

er [ə:] *interj* an expression of doubt or uncertainty: *'Where are my gloves?' 'Er, I don't know.'*

era ['iərə] *nc* **1** a number of years counting from an important point in history: *the Elizabethan era*; *the Victorian era.* **2** a period of time marked by an important event or events: *The era of the steam engine is over*; *an era of social reform.*

eradicate [i'radikeit] *vt* (*formal*) to get rid of completely: *Smallpox has almost been eradicated.* **eˌradi'cation** *nu* (*formal*).

erase [i'reiz, (*Amer*) i'reis] *vt* (*formal*) to rub out (pencil marks *etc*): *The typist tried to erase the error*; (*fig*) *He couldn't erase the event from his memory.*

e'raser *nc* (*esp Amer*) something that erases, *esp* a piece of india-rubber *etc* for erasing pencil, ink *etc.*

erasure [i'reiʒə, (*Amer*) -ʃər] *ncu* (*very formal*) (a place of) rubbing out: *The erasures in that letter are obvious*; *the erasure of the incident from his memory.*

ere [eə] *prep, conj* (*liter*) before: *He will be here ere long.*

erect [i'rekt] *adj* upright: *He held his head erect*; *She walks in a very erect way*; *She has an erect manner of walking.* – *vt* (*formal*) **1** to set up; to put up or to build: *They erected a statue in memory of the dead soldier*; *The soldiers erected their tents behind the hill*; *They plan to erect an office block there.* **2** to set upright (a mast *etc*).

e'rection [-ʃən] **1** *nu* the act of erecting: *the erection of a statue.* **2** *nc* (*sometimes derog*) a building or structure: *What a peculiar erection!* **3**

ncu the enlarging and hardening of the penis: *to have an erection.*

e'rectly *adv.* **e'rectness** *nu.*

ermine ['ə:min] **1** *nu, adj* (of) the white winter fur of the stoat, used as trimming for robes of judges *etc*: *robes trimmed with ermine*; *ermine robes.* **2** *nc* the stoat in its white winter fur.

erode [i'roud] *vt* (*formal or tech*) to eat or wear away (metals *etc*); to destroy gradually: *Acids erode certain metals*; *Water has eroded the rock*; (*fig*) *The individual's freedom and right to privacy is being eroded.*

e'rosion [-ʒən] *nu*: *the erosion of the rock*; (*fig*) *the erosion of moral standards.*

erotic [i'rotik] *adj* of, or arousing, sexual love or desire: *erotic pictures of nude women*; *the erotic dancing of the strip-tease artiste.*

err [ə:] *vi* (*formal*) to make a mistake; to be wrong; to do wrong: *You erred in not obeying your parents*; *To err is human – to forgive divine.*

err on the side of to be guilty of a fault or of what might be seen as a fault in order to avoid an opposite and greater fault: *It is better to err on the side of leniency when punishing a child.*

See also **erratic, erratum, erroneous, error**.

errand ['erənd] *nc* **1** a short journey made in order to get something or do something *esp* for someone else: *He has sent the child on an errand*; *The child will run errands for you*; *He has gone on an errand.* **2** the purpose of such a journey: *She accomplished her errand.*

errant ['erənt] *adj* (*old or liter*: *attrib*) straying; doing wrong: *an errant husband/wife.*

errata *see* **erratum**.

erratic [i'ratik] *adj* inclined to be irregular or unpredictable; not dependable: *His behaviour/work is erratic*; *The learner-driver steered an erratic course down the road.* **er'ratically** *adv.*

erratum [i'ra:təm] – *pl* **er'rata** [-tə] – *nc* (*formal*) an error in writing or printing: *The errata are listed at the beginning of the book.*

erroneous [i'rouniəs] *adj* (*formal*) (not used of a person) wrong or mistaken; incorrect: *an erroneous statement*; *Your conclusions are erroneous.*

er'roneously *adv.* **er'roneousness** *nu.*

error ['erə] **1** *nc* a mistake: *That child's exercise is full of errors.* **2** *ncu* (*old*) wrong-doing: *He has seen the error of his ways.* **3** *nu* (*formal*) the state of being mistaken: *I did it in error*; *You are in error if you think that.*

ersatz ['eəsats] *adj* (*derog*) used instead of something else; substitute: *ersatz coffee.*

erudite ['erudait] *adj* (*formal*) scholarly and learned: *erudite remarks*; *an erudite professor*; *He is extremely erudite.* **ˌeru'dition** [-'diʃən] *nu.*

erupt [i'rʌpt] *vi* (*often fig*) (of a volcano) to throw out lava *etc*: *When did Mount Etna last erupt?*; *The demonstration started quietly but suddenly violence erupted*; *The rash on her face has erupted* (= appeared) *again.* **e'ruption** [-ʃən] *ncu.*

escalate ['eskəleit] *vi* to increase or enlarge rapidly: *How can we stop the war from escalating?*; (*formal*) *Prices are escalating.* **ˌesca'lation** *nu.*

escalator ['eskəleitə] *nc* a moving staircase in a shop, underground railway *etc*: *I don't like escalators – I'll climb the stairs.*

escapade [eskə'peid] *nc* a daring or adventurous act, often one that is disapproved of by others: *a newspaper story about the latest escapades of the film actress.*

escape [i'skeip] **1** *vi* (*often with* **from**) to gain freedom: *He escaped from prison*; *He was recaptured after he escaped.* **2** *vt* to manage to avoid (punishment, disease *etc*): *He escaped having to join the army*; *She escaped the infection.* **3** *vt* to avoid being noticed or remembered by; to avoid (the observation of): *The fact escaped me/my notice*; *His name escapes me/my memory.* **4** *vi* (of a gas, liquid *etc*) to leak; to find a way out from where it is supposed to be kept: *The gas escaped from the hole in the pipe*; *Heat escapes from a room if windows and doors do not fit properly.* – *ncu* (act of) escaping; state of having escaped: *His escape from prison was soon discovered*; *Make your escape while the guard is away*; *There have been several escapes from that prison*; *He was involved in a situation from which escape was impossible*; *The explosion was caused by an escape of gas.*

e'scapism *nu* (*often derog*) the tendency to escape from unpleasant reality into day-dreams *etc*: *She was unhappily married and her liking for romantic novels and films was a form of escapism.* **e'scapist** *nc, adj.*

escarpment [i'ska:pmənt] *nc* (*formal*) the steep side of a hill or rock.

eschew [is'tʃu:] *vt* (*liter or very formal*) to avoid; to keep away from: *You must eschew his company – he is an evil man*; (*facet*) *If you wish to remain slim you must eschew biscuits and sweets.*

escort ['esko:t] *nc* person(s), ship(s) *etc* accompanying for protection, guidance, courtesy *etc*: *He offered to be my escort round the city*; *The transport supplies were under military/police escort*; (*attrib*) *an escort vessel.* – [i'sko:t] – *vt* to accompany or attend as escort: *He offered to escort her to the dance*; *Four police motorcyclists escorted the president's car along the route.*

esoteric [esə'terik] *adj* (*formal*) known by, or revealed to, only a few people; secret; mysterious; obscure: *I don't understand his poetry – it is too esoteric for me*; *esoteric literature.*

especial [i'speʃəl] *adj* (*formal*) more than the ordinary; particular: *You must treat this with especial care*; *This book is an especial favourite of mine.*

e'specially *adv* particularly: *These insects are quite common, especially in hot countries*; *Please telephone soon, especially as we're leaving next week.* *See also* **special**.

Esperanto [espə'rantou] *nu* the name of an invented language intended for international use.

espionage ['espiəna:ʒ] *nu* (*formal*) **1** the activity of spying: *He has never been involved in espionage.* **2** the using of spies: *Rival manufacturers discovered his design through industrial espionage.*

esplanade [esplə'neid] *nc* a level space for walking or driving *esp* at the seaside: *Our hotel is on the esplanade and overlooks the sea.*

espouse [i'spauz] *vt* (*formal*) to give one's support to (a cause *etc*): *He enthusiastically espoused Marxism in his student days.* **e'spousal** *nu* (*formal*).

espy [i'spai] *vt* (*liter or facet*) to catch sight of: *He espied a human figure moving on the hillside*; *I espy a cream cake on your plate – I thought you were slimming!*

Esquire [i'skwaiə, (*Amer*) 'eskwaiər] *n* (*usu abbrev* **Esq** *when written*) in Great Britain, a title of respect used after a man's name in addressing letters: *H Jones Esq.*

essay ['esei] *nc* a written composition; a piece of written prose: *The examination consists of four* *essays*; *Have you read his essay on Shakespeare?* – [e'sei] *vt* (*old*) to attempt (a job *etc*): *You would be foolish to essay this task.*

'essayist *nc* a writer of literary essays: *Charles Lamb was a well-known English essayist.*

essence ['esns] **1** *nu* (*formal*) the most important part or quality: *Tolerance is the essence of friendship*; *Time is of the essence* (= very important) *in this project.* **2** *ncu* a substance obtained from a plant, drug *etc* in concentrated form: *essence of peppermint*; *vanilla essence.*

in 'essence (*formal*) essentially: *The various problems are in essence the same.*

essential [i'senʃəl] *adj* **1** absolutely necessary: *Strong boots are essential for mountaineering*; *It is essential that you come home early*; *It is essential to arrive early.* **2** (*attrib*) of the basic or inner nature of something: *There is no essential difference between our two opinions*; *His essential kindliness is obvious to everyone.* – *nc* a thing that is fundamental or necessary: *Everyone should learn the essentials of first aid*; *Is a television set an essential?*

es'sentially *adv* **1** basically: *She is an essentially selfish person.* **2** in fact; in reality: *Her job, essentially, is to act as an interpreter for Dutch visitors.*

See also **inessential**.

establish [i'stabliʃ] *vt* **1** to settle firmly in a position (*eg* a job, business *etc*): *He established himself* (*in business*) *as a jeweller.* **2** to found; to set up (*eg* a university, a business): *How long has the firm been established?* **3** to show to be true; to prove: *The police established that he was guilty*; *The police established his guilt.* **4** to cause people to accept (a custom, claim *etc*): *He established his claim to the estate when his father died.*

e'stablished *adj* (*attrib*) **1** settled or accepted: *established customs.* **2** (of a church) recognized as the official church of a country: *Which is the established church in England?*

e'stablishment 1 *nu* the act of establishing: *The establishment of such an organization would be difficult.* **2** *nc* (*formal*) a permanent civil or military force or business staff: *All employees of this establishment get a bonus at New Year.* **3** *nc* (*formal or facet*) a person's residence, household, and style of living: *a bachelor's establishment.*

the Establishment (*Brit*) the people holding important positions in a country, society or community: *Young people often distrust the Establishment.*

estate [i'steit] **1** *nc* a large piece of land owned by one person or a group of people *etc*: *They have an estate in Ireland.* **2** *nc* a piece of land developed for building *etc*: *a housing/industrial estate.* **3** *ncu* (*legal*) a person's total possessions (property, money *etc*): *His estate was divided among his sons.* **4** *nu* (*old*) condition or rank: *The family is of high estate.*

e'state agent *nc* (*Amer* **'realtor**) a person whose job is to sell houses and land: *We bought our house through an estate agent.*

e'state-car *nc* (*Amer* **'station wagon**) a car with a large area behind the seats for luggage *etc*, and a rear door: *We prefer an estate car to an ordinary car with a boot because it holds more luggage.*

See also **real estate**.

esteem [i'sti:m] *vt* (*formal*: not used with **is, was** *etc* and **-ing**) **1** to value or respect: *I esteem honesty/his work very highly.* **2** to consider (something) to be: *I should esteem it a favour if you would go.* – *nu* favourable opinion; respect: *His foolish behaviour lowered him in my esteem*; *I held him in great esteem.*

esthetic *see* **aesthetic**.

estimate ['estimeit] *vt* **1** to judge size, amount, value *etc*, *esp* roughly or without measuring: *He estimated that the journey would take two hours.* **2** (not used with **is, was** *etc* and **-ing**) to form an idea or judgement of how good *etc* something is: *I did not estimate my chances of escape very highly.* – [-mət] *nc* a calculation (*eg* of the probable cost *etc* of something): *He gave us an estimate of the cost of repairing the stonework*; *I don't know how long this book will be. I can give you only a rough estimate* (= a length based on guessing).

ˌesti'mation *nu* judgement; opinion: *In our estimation, he is the more gifted artist.*

See also **inestimable**.

estranged [i'streindʒd] *adj* (*with* **from** *when pred*) no longer friendly or loving (towards): *After her second marriage, her daughter became estranged from her*; *He does not communicate with his estranged wife.* **e'strangement** *ncu.*

estuary ['estjuəri] *nc* the wide lower part of a river up which the tide flows: *the Thames estuary*; *the estuary of the Thames.*

et cetera [it'setrə, (*Amer*) et-] (*usu abbrev* **etc** *or* **&c** *when written*) a Latin phrase meaning 'and the rest', 'and so on': *The refugees need food, clothes, blankets etc.*

etch [etʃ] *vti* to make (designs) on metal, glass *etc* using an acid to eat out the lines: *He made a drawing and then etched it on copper*; (*fig*) *The scene remained etched on his mind for years.*

'etching 1 *nu* the act or art of etching. **2** *nc* the picture from an etched plate: *He has a fine collection of etchings.*

eternal [i'tə:nl] *adj* **1** (*formal*) without end; lasting for ever; unchanging: *God is eternal*; *eternal life.* **2** (*inf*: *attrib*) never ceasing: *I am tired of your eternal complaints.*

e'ternally *adv*: *I shall be eternally* (= always) *grateful to you.*

e'ternity 1 *nc* an endless, or seemingly endless, time: *He waited for* (*what seemed like*) *an eternity.* **2** *nu* (*formal*) the state or time after death: *Do you believe in eternity?*

ether ['i:θə] *nu* a colourless liquid used to dissolve fats *etc*, and, medically, as an anaesthetic: *Ether was one of the earliest anaesthetics but it is rarely used now.*

ethereal [i'θiəriəl] *adj* (*formal*) delicate and fairy-like: *Her face had an ethereal beauty.*

ethics ['eθiks] *n* **1** *sing* the study or the science of morals: *Students of philosophy usually study ethics as one of their subjects* **2** *pl* rules or principles of behaviour: *We should consider very carefully the ethics of protecting terrorists from the law*; *The ethics of this matter are very complicated.*

'ethical *adj* (*neg* **un-**) **1** (*attrib*) of or concerning morals, justice or duty: *an ethical problem.* **2** morally right: *The doctor's behaviour was perfectly ethical.* **'ethically** *adv.*

Ethiopia, Ethiopian *see* Appendix 2.

ethnic ['eθnik] *adj* of nations or races of mankind or their customs, dress, food *etc*: *ethnic groups/dances.*

ethnology [eθ'nolədʒi] *nu* the study of the different races of mankind. **ˌethno'logical** [-'lo-] *adj.* **eth'nologist** *nc.*

etiquette ['etiket] *nu* rules for correct or polite

behaviour between people, or within certain professions: *Etiquette was more important in the last century than it is now*; *medical/legal etiquette.*

etymology [eti'molədʒi] **1** *nu* the study of the origin and development of words and their meanings: *He is interested in etymology.* **2** *nc* an explanation of the history of a particular word: *Some dictionaries give etymologies.*

ˌetymo'logical [-'lo-] *adj*: *Is there an etymological connection between these words?* **ˌetymo'logically** *adv.*

ˌety'mologist *nc.*

eucalyptus [ju:kə'liptəs] – *pls* **ˌeuca'lyptuses, ˌeuca'lypti** [-tai] – **1** *nc* (*also* **ˌeuca'lyptus tree**) a type of large Australian evergreen tree, giving timber, gum and an oil that is used in the treatment of colds. **2** *nu, adj* (of) its timber.

eulogy ['ju:lədʒi] *ncu* (*formal or facet*) (a speech or piece of writing containing) high praise: *He addressed a long poem of eulogy to the king*; *His novel earned the eulogies of the critics.*

'eulogize, -ise *vt* (*very formal*) to praise highly: *This politician was formerly much eulogized by the press.*

euphemism ['ju:fəmizəm] *ncu* (*formal*) a pleasant name for something that is unpleasant: *'Pass on' is a euphemism for 'die'.* **ˌeuphe'mistic** *adj.*

euphony ['ju:fəni] *nu* (*very formal*) pleasing sound: *He admired the euphony of her voice.* **eu'phonious** [-'fou-] *adj.*

euphoria [ju'fo:riə] *nu* (*formal*) a strong feeling of well-being and cheerfulness: *Her bouts of euphoria were followed by fits of depression.*

eu'phoric [-'fo-] *adj* having, or produced by, such a feeling: *She was quite euphoric after hearing that she had won*; *She's in a euphoric mood.*

Euro- [juərou] (*in cmpds*) of Europe: *'Euro-currency.*

Europe, European, European Economic Community *see* Appendix 2.

euthanasia [ju:θə'neiziə] *nu* the painless killing of someone who is suffering from a painful and incurable illness: *Many old people would prefer euthanasia to the suffering they have to endure*; *Doctors are not allowed to practise euthanasia* (= to kill people to prevent suffering).

evacuate [i'vakjueit] *vt* **1** to leave or withdraw from (a place), *esp* because of danger: *The troops evacuated their position because of the enemy's advance.* **2** to cause (inhabitants *etc*) to leave a place, *esp* because of danger: *Children were evacuated from London to the country during the war.* **eˌvacu'ation** *ncu.*

eˌvacu'ee *nc* a person removed from danger in an evacuation: *She was one of the many evacuees who were separated from their parents during the war.*

evade [i'veid] *vt* (*formal*) **1** to escape or avoid by trickery or skill: *The prisoner evaded capture for several days*; *He managed to evade his pursuers* (= those who were chasing him); *He tries to evade paying income tax.* **2** to avoid answering (a question): *He evaded my questions about his future plans.*

e'vasion [-ʒən] **1** *nu* the act of evading: *He has been accused of income tax evasion.* **2** *nc* a trick or excuse used to evade: *We asked him direct questions and he answered with evasions.*

e'vasive [-siv] *adj* **1** having the purpose of evading: *He took evasive action.* **2** not frank and direct: *He gave evasive answers*; *His answers were deliberately evasive.* **e'vasively** *adv.* **e'vasiveness** *nu.*

evaluate [i'valjueit] *vt* **1** (*formal*) to form an idea or judgement of (the worth of) something: *It is difficult to evaluate him as a writer.* **2** (*math*) to work out the numerical value of: *If $x=1$ and $y=2$ we can evaluate x^2+y^2.* **eˌvalu'ation** *ncu.*

evangelical [i:van'dʒelikəl] *adj* (*attrib*) seeking to convert people, *esp* to Christianity: *an evangelical preacher.*

e'vangelist [i-] *nc* a person who preaches Christianity *esp* at large public meetings. **eˌvange'listic** *adj.*

evaporate [i'vapəreit] *vti* to (cause to) change into vapour and disappear: *The small pool of water evaporated in the sunshine*; *Heat evaporates water*; (*fig formal*) *His enthusiasm soon evaporated.*

e'vaporated *adj* (*attrib*) having had some moisture removed by evaporation: *evaporated milk.*

eˌvapo'ration *nu.*

evasion, evasive *see* **evade**.

eve [i:v] *nc* (*pl rare*) **1** the day or evening before a festival: *Christmas Eve*; *New Year's Eve.* **2** the time just before an event: *on the eve of (the) battle.* **3** (*liter*) evening.

even[1] ['i:vən] *adj* **1** level; the same in height, amount *etc*: *Are the table-legs even?*; *Keep the room at an even temperature.* **2** smooth: *Make the path more even.* **3** regular: *He is not very ill – he has a strong, even pulse.* **4** divisible by 2 *with no remainder: 2, 4, 6, 8, 10 etc are even numbers.* **5** equal (in number, amount *etc*): *Their examination marks were even*; *The teams have scored one goal each and so they are even now.* **6** (*attrib*) (of temper, temperament *etc*) calm: *She has a very even temper.* – *v* – *pt, ptp* **'evened** – *vt* **1** to make equal: *Smith's goal evened the score.* **2** (*formal*) to make smooth or level: *The ground needs to be evened.* – *See also* **even out, even up** *below.*

'evenly *adv.* **'evenness** *nu.*

be/get 'even with (*inf*) to be revenged on: *He tricked me, but I'll get even with him.*

break even *see* **break**.

an even chance *see* **chance**.

even out 1 *vi* to become level or regular: *The road rose steeply and then evened out*; *His irregular heartbeats began to even out.* **2** *vt sep* to make smooth or equal: *He raked the soil to even it out.* **3** *vt sep* to make equal: *If Jane would do some of Mary's typing, that would even the work out.*

even up *vt sep* to make equal: *John did better in the maths exam than Jim and that evened up their marks.*

See also **uneven**.

even[2] ['i:vən] *adv* **1** used to point out something unexpected in what one is saying: *'Have you finished yet?' 'No, I haven't even started.'*; *Even the winner got no prize*; *They take even the cat on holiday with them.* **2** (*used with a comparative*) yet; still: *My boots were dirty, but his were even dirtier.*

'even as 1 (*formal*) just at the time when: *He walked in even as I mentioned his name.* **2** (*old*) exactly as; just as: *It turned out even as we expected.*

'even if no matter whether: *Even if I leave now, I'll be too late.*

even so in spite of that: *It rained, but even so we enjoyed the day.*

even though in spite of the fact that: *I like the job even though it's badly paid.*

evening ['i:vniŋ] *ncu* **1** the part of the day between the afternoon and the night: *He leaves the house in the morning and returns in the evening*; *On summer* *evenings we often have supper in the garden; tomorrow evening; There will be a meeting on Tuesday evening; The early evening would be a suitable time;* (*attrib*) *the evening performance.* **2** (*fig formal*) the last part (of one's life *etc*): *in the evening of her life.*

'evening dress 1 *nu* clothes worn for formal occasions in the evening: *You will have to wear evening dress to that dinner.* **2** *nc* a formal dress worn by a woman in the evening: *She bought a short black evening dress.*

this evening *see* **this**.

event [i'vent] *nc* **1** something that happens; an incident or occurrence: *That night a terrible event occurred; I prefer to forget the events of the past few days.* **2** an item in a programme of sports *etc*: *The long-jump was to be the third event.*

e'ventful *adj* (*neg* **un-**) full of events; exciting: *We had an eventful day; The rest of the holiday was not very eventful.*

at 'all events/in 'any event in any case: *At all events, we can't make things worse than they already are.*

in 'that event if that happens: *In that event you must do as he says.*

in the event (*inf*) in the end, as it happened/happens/may happen: *In the event, I did not need to go to hospital.*

in the e'vent of (*formal*) if (something) occurs: *In the event of his death, you will inherit his money.* *See also* **non-event**.

eventide ['i:vəntaid] *nu* (*liter*) evening.

eventide home *nc* a home for elderly people: *My aunt is in an eventide home.*

eventual [i'ventʃuəl] *adj* (*formal*: *attrib*) happening as a result; final: *their quarrel and eventual reconciliation.*

e,ventu'ality [-'a-] *nc* (*formal*) a possible happening: *We are ready for all eventualities.*

e'ventually *adv* finally; at length: *I thought he would never ask her to marry him, but he did eventually; He will probably be late but he'll come eventually.*

ever ['evə] *adv* **1** (used in negative sentences, questions, and sentences with 'if', or with comparatives and superlatives) at any time: *Nobody ever visits us; She hardly ever writes to us; Have you ever ridden on an elephant?; If I ever see him again I shall get my revenge; If ever I see him again I'll ask him for the money he owes me; Your work is better than ever; It was the brightest star they had ever seen.* **2** always; continually: *They lived happily ever after; I've known her ever since she was a baby;* (*old or formal*) *She was growing ever weaker;* (*old or formal*) *He was ever a keen reader.* **3** (*inf*) used for emphasis: *Come as quickly as ever you can; The new doctor is ever so gentle; Her mother was ever such a good person; What ever shall I do?; However did you manage to do that?*

ever- (*in cmpds*) always; continually: *the 'ever-in,creasing 'traffic.*

'evergreen *adj* (of trees *etc*) having green leaves all the year round: *Holly is evergreen; We planted an evergreen tree.* – *nc* an evergreen tree: *Firs and pines are evergreens.*

,ever'lasting *adj* endless; continual; unchanging: (*inf derog*) *I'm tired of your everlasting grumbles; everlasting life/flowers;* (*inf*) *That concert seemed everlasting!*

,ever'lastingly *adv*: (*inf*) *She complains everlastingly about her health.*

,ever'more *adv* for all time: *He said that he would love her (for) evermore.*

for 'ever/for'ever *adv* **1** continually: *He was forever looking at his watch.* **2** for all time: *I'll love you for ever (and ever).*

See also **however, never, whatever, whatsoever, whenever, wherever, whichever**.

every ['evri] *adj* (*attrib*) **1** each one of or all (of a certain number): *Every room is* (= All the rooms are) *painted white; Not every family has* (= Not all families have) *a car.* **2** each (of an indefinite number or series): *Every hour brought the two countries nearer war; He attends to her every want.* **3** the most absolute or complete possible: *We have every reason to believe that she will get better.* **4** used with numbers, and with **other** and **few** to show continual repetition (of an action *etc*) after certain intervals of time or space: *I go to the supermarket every four or five days; Every second house in the row was bright pink; 'Every other day' means 'every two days' or 'on alternate days'.*

'everybody, 'everyone *pron* every person: *Everyone thinks I'm mad; Everybody in this street has a car.*

'everyday *adj* (*attrib*) **1** happening, done, used *etc* daily: *Her everyday duties include cooking meals for old people.* **2** common or usual: *Train delays are an everyday event.*

everyone *see* **everybody**.

'everything *pron* all things; all: *Have you everything you want?; His child is/means everything to him.*

'everywhere *adv* (in or to) every place: *The flies are everywhere; Everywhere is covered with dust; Everywhere I go, he follows me.*

every 'bit as just as: *You're every bit as clever as he is; He is every bit as good a pianist as his brother.*

every man jack *see* **jack**.

every now and then/every now and again/every so often occasionally: *We get a letter from him every now and then; Every now and again we hear news of him.*

every time 1 always; invariably: *We use this method every time.* **2** whenever: *Every time he comes, we quarrel.*

evict [i'vikt] *vt* (*formal*) to put out from house or land *esp* by force of law: *As they hadn't paid their rent for months, they were evicted.* **e'viction** [-ʃən] *ncu*.

evidence ['evidəns] **1** *nu* information *etc* that gives reason for believing something; proof (*eg* in a law case): *Have you enough evidence (of his guilt) to arrest him?; Anything you say may be used in evidence against you; He was convicted on the evidence of his fellow-workers.* **2** *ncu* (an) indication; a sign: *Her bag on the table was the only evidence of her presence;* (*formal*) *The room bore evidence of a struggle.*

in 'evidence easily seen; clearly displayed: *Copies of her new novel are much in evidence everywhere.* – *See also* **evidence** (*def 1*).

on the 'evidence of if one can use (something) as evidence: *On the evidence of his work so far, he'll do well.* – *See also* **evidence** (*def 1*).

turn King's/Queen's 'evidence (of an accomplice in a crime) to give evidence against his partner(s) with the result that his own sentence is less severe: *He was sentenced to two years' imprisonment for his part in the crime because he turned Queen's evidence. His accomplices were sentenced to five years.*

evident ['evidənt] *adj* clearly to be seen or understood: *He signed his name with evident satisfaction*; *It is evident (to everyone) that you have misunderstood me.*

'evidently *adv* **1** as far as can be seen: *Evidently he disagrees.* **2** clearly or obviously: *He was quite evidently furious.*

evil ['i:vl] *adj* very bad; wicked; sinful: *He has no evil intentions*; *He is an evil man*; *He looks evil*; *His evil deeds will be remembered*; *She has an evil tongue* (= She says wicked things about people). – **1** *nu* wrong-doing, harm or wickedness: *He tries to ignore all the evil in the world*; *He can do a lot of evil*; *Do not speak evil of anyone.* **2** *nc* anything evil, *eg* crime, misfortune etc: *London in the eighteenth century was a place of crime, filth, poverty and other evils*; *I can't decide whether to write to him or telephone him – it is a question of which is the lesser of the two evils* (=the least unpleasant of two choices).

evil- (*in cmpds*) bad, wicked or horrible: *ˌevil-'minded*; *ˌevil-'smelling.*

'evilly *adv* (*liter*) in an evil way: *He leered evilly at his unsuspecting victim.*

'evilness *nu.*

ˌevil-'doer *nc* (*formal*) a wicked or sinful person.

the evil eye the supposed power of causing harm by a look: *I have had bad luck since I met him – I think he put the evil eye on me.*

evince [i'vins] *vt* (*formal*) to show (a quality *etc* that one has): *The child evinced remarkable powers of reasoning.*

evocation, evocative *see* **evoke**.

evoke [i'vouk] *vt* (*formal*) **1** to cause or produce (*esp* a response, reaction *etc*): *The child's tears evoked sympathy*; *His letter in the newspaper evoked a storm of protest.* **2** to bring into the mind: *A piece of music can sometimes evoke (memories of) the past.*

ˌevo'cation [evə-] *ncu.*

evocative [i'vokətiv] *adj* (*with* **of** *when pred*) tending to evoke memories *etc*: *evocative smells*; *Her dress was evocative of the 1920s.*

evolution, evolutionary *see* **evolve**.

evolve [i'volv] *vti* (*formal*) to (cause to) develop gradually: *Man evolved from the apes*; *A difficult situation has evolved*; *He evolved a system for making money quickly.*

evolution [i:və'lu:ʃən, (*Amer*) e-] *nu* **1** gradual working out or development: *the evolution of our form of government.* **2** (the teaching that explains) the development of the higher kinds of animals (*eg* man), plants *etc*, from the lower kinds: *Darwin's theory of evolution.*

evolutionary [i:və'lu:ʃənəri, (*Amer*) e-] *adj* (*formal*) of development or (the theory of) evolution.

ewe [ju:] *nc* a female sheep: *The ewe had two lambs.*

ewer ['juə] *nc* (*hist or formal*) a large water jug with a wide spout: *She poured water from the ewer into the basin.*

exacerbate [ig'zasəbeit] *vt* (*formal*) to make worse (a bad situation, anger, pain *etc*): *An attempt to hide one's grief may only exacerbate it*; *Heat seems to exacerbate the rash on my face.* **exˌacer'bation** *nu.*

exact [ig'zakt] *adj* **1** absolutely accurate or correct in every detail; the same in every detail; precise: *What are the exact measurements of the room?*; *For this recipe the measurement of the quantities must be absolutely exact*; *This vase is an exact copy of an ancient Egyptian vase*; *What is the exact time?*; *He walked in at the exact moment that I decided to leave.* **2** (of a person, his mind *etc*) capable of being accurate over small details: *Accountants have to be very exact*; *Scientists usually have very exact minds.* – *vt* (*formal*) **1** to force the payment of or giving of: *We should exact fines from everyone who drops litter on the streets.* **2** to insist upon having; to demand: *He exacted obedience from his children.*

ex'acting *adj* requiring much effort or work from a person: *His boss is very exacting*; *She has a very exacting job.*

ex'actitude [-titju:d] *nu* (*very formal*) correctness: *He spoke with great exactitude.*

ex'actly *adv* **1** just; quite; absolutely: *He's exactly the right man for the job.* **2** in accurate detail; precisely: *Work out the prices exactly*; *What exactly did you say?* **3** (as a reply) you are quite right: *'If we don't go now, we'll be too late.' 'Exactly.'* **ex'actness** *nu.*

See also **inexact**.

exaggerate [ig'zadʒəreit] **1** *vt* to make (something) appear to be, or describe it as, greater *etc* than it really is: *You seem to be exaggerating his faults*; *That dress exaggerates her thinness.* **2** *vi* to go beyond the truth in describing something *etc*: *You can't trust her. She always exaggerates.*

ex'aggerated *adj* (*usu attrib*) **1** going beyond the truth: *The prime minister made exaggerated statements about the improvements in the country's economy*; *She had an exaggerated idea of the jewel's value.* **2** (intended to be) very obvious; overdone: *She gave an exaggerated frown at her child's behaviour although she was really amused by it.*

exˌagge'ration **1** *nu* the act of exaggerating. **2** *nc* an exaggerated description, term *etc*: *To say she is beautiful is an exaggeration, but she does have nice eyes.*

exalted [ig'zo:ltid] *adj* (*often facet*) high in rank, position *etc*; noble; important: *He holds a very exalted position in the government.*

exam *see* **examine**.

examine [ig'zamin] *vt* **1** to look at closely; to inspect closely: *They examined the animal tracks and decided that they were those of a fox.* **2** (of a doctor) to inspect (a person's body) thoroughly to check for disease *etc*: *The doctor examined the child and said she was healthy.* **3** to consider carefully: *The police must examine the facts.* **4** (*formal*) to test the knowledge or ability of (students *etc*): *She examines pupils in mathematics.* **5** (*legal*) to question: *The lawyer examined the witness in the court case.*

exˌami'nation **1** *ncu* (a) close inspection: *Make a thorough examination of the area where the crime took place*; *After his medical examination he had to go into hospital*; *On* (= As a result of) *examination the patient was discovered to have appendicitis.* **2** *nc* (*also* **ex'am**) a test of knowledge or ability: *school examinations*; *a French/dancing exam*; *When does she sit her degree examinations?*; (*attrib*) *examination/exam papers*; *He failed* (=He was unsuccessful in) *the English exam*; *She passed* (=She was successful in) *the French exam*; *He had to take the Spanish exam again.* **3** *ncu* (*formal*) (a) formal questioning (*eg* of a witness): *The examination of the witnesses lasted two hours.*

exˌami'nee *nc* (*very formal*) a person who is examined, *esp* a person who takes part in a school, university *etc* examination: *How many of the examinees passed?*

ex'aminer *nc* a person who examines students, goods before sale *etc*: *He is an English examiner for* *the London area*; *The examiner's initials are often on the back of new furniture.*

example [ig'za:mpl] *nc* **1** something that represents other things of the same kind; a specimen: *an example of his handwriting*; *This vase is an example of early Greek sculpture.* **2** something that shows clearly or illustrates a fact *etc*: *His recent behaviour is yet another example of his selfishness*; *Can you give me an example of how this word is used?* **3** a person or thing that is a pattern to be copied: *She was an example to the rest of the class*; *Her courage was an example to us all.* **4** a warning to be heeded: *Let this be an example to you, and never do it again!*

for ex'ample (*often abbrev* **eg** [i:'dʒi:]) for instance; as an example: *Several European countries have no sea-coast – for example, Switzerland and Austria.*

make an example of to punish as a warning to others: *The judge decided to make an example of the young thief and sent him to prison for five years.*

set (someone) an example to act in such a way that other people will copy one's behaviour: *Teachers must set a good example to their pupils*; *Their father set a bad example to the family by being drunk every night.*

See also **exemplary, exemplify**.

exasperate [ig'za:spəreit] *vt* to irritate (someone) very much indeed: *He was exasperated by continual interruptions*; *She was exasperated by the lateness of the train.*

ex,aspe'ration *ncu*: *She hit the child in exasperation at his stupidity.*

excavate ['ekskəveit] *vt* **1** (*formal*) to dig up (a piece of ground *etc*) or to dig out (a hole) by doing this: *They excavated a pit*; *The workmen excavated the building site.* **2** in archaeology, to uncover or open up (a structure *etc* remaining from earlier times) by digging: *The archaeologist excavated a Stone-Age tomb.* **,exca'vation** *nu*.

,exca'vations *n pl* a place that is being excavated: *excavations of a Roman camp.*

'excavator *nc* (*formal*) **1** a machine used for excavating: *They used an excavator to dig a hole in the road.* **2** a person, *esp* an archaeologist, who excavates: *She was the excavator of the ancient city of Jericho.*

exceed [ik'si:d] *vt* to go beyond; to be greater than: *His expenditure exceeds his income*; *He exceeded the speed limit on the motorway*; *His success exceeded his hopes.*

ex'ceedingly *adv* very; extremely: *exceedingly nervous.*

excel [ik'sel] – *pt, ptp* **ex'celled** – **1** *vi* (*formal*: *with* **in** *or* **at**) to stand out beyond others (in some quality *etc*); to do very well (in or at some activity): *He excelled in mathematics/at football.* **2** *vt* (*formal*) to be better than: *She excels them all at swimming.*

'excellence ['ek-] *nu* unusual goodness or worth: *The excellence of his suggestion was recognized by everyone*; *this man's excellence as a teacher.*

'Excellency ['ek-] *n* (*with* **His, Your** *etc*) a title of honour, used *eg* for ambassadors: *His/Your Excellency*; *Their Excellencies have arrived.*

'excellent ['ek-] *adj* unusually good: *an excellent plan*; *It is excellent that you succeeded in getting such a good job.* **'excellently** *adv*.

except [ik'sept] *prep* leaving out; not including: *They're all here except him*; *You've done everything except what I asked you (to do)*; *Your essay was good except that* (=apart from the fact that) *it was too long.* – *vt* (*formal*) to leave out or exclude: *To be fair, I must except Mary from my criticism of the girls.*

ex'cepted *adj* (*placed immediately after the noun*) excluded; left out: *all European countries, Denmark excepted* (=except Denmark).

ex'cepting *prep* (*formal*: *sometimes with* **always** *or* **not**) leaving out or excluding: *A good memory is important in most school subjects not excepting mathematics*; *Those cars are all reliable, always excepting the old red one.*

ex'ception [-ʃən] *nc* **1** something or someone not included: *They all work hard, without exception*; *With the exception of Jim we all went home early.* **2** something not according to the rule: *We normally eat nothing at lunchtime, but Sunday is an exception.* **3** an act of excluding: *Everyone must begin work punctually – the firm makes no exceptions.*

ex'ceptional *adj* (*neg* **un-**) unusual; remarkable: *She showed exceptional loyalty*; *His ability is quite exceptional.*

ex'ceptionally *adv* unusually: *That was an exceptionally stupid action*; *Exceptionally, she was late for school.*

ex'cept for 1 apart from; leaving aside considerations of: *We enjoyed the holiday except for the expense.* **2** except: *Except for John, they all arrived punctually.*

take exception to/at to object to or take offence at: *The old lady took exception to the rudeness of the children.*

excerpt ['eksə:pt] *nc* a part taken from a book *etc*; an extract: *I heard an excerpt from his latest novel on the radio*; *musical excerpts from Strauss.*

excess [ik'ses] **1** *nu* (*formal*) the (act of) going beyond normal or suitable limits: *He ate well, but not to excess.* **2** *nu* (*formal*: *often with* **an**) an abnormally large amount: *An excess of generosity embarrasses people*; *an excess of alcohol.* **3** *nc* (*old or formal*: *usu in pl*) an outrageous act: *I continually forgave his excesses including his drunkenness.* **4** *nu* (*formal*: *often with* **an**) an amount by which something is greater than something else: *He found he had paid an excess of £2.50 over what was actually on the bill.* – *adj* (*attrib*) extra; additional (to the amount needed, allowed or usual): *The firm were accused of making excess profits*; *He had to pay extra for his excess baggage on the aircraft.*

ex'cessive [-siv] *adj* beyond what is right and proper: *The manager expects them to do an excessive amount of work*; *I find his attention to detail rather excessive.* **ex'cessively** *adv*. **ex'cessiveness** *nu*.

in ex'cess of (*formal*) going beyond; more than: *Their pay claim is in excess of the agreed limits*; *His salary is in excess of £10 000 a year.*

exchange [iks'tʃeindʒ] *vt* **1** to give, or give up, in return for something else: *Can you exchange a £1 note for two 50p pieces?* **2** to give and receive in return: (*formal*) *They exchanged rings when they promised to marry each other*; *They exchanged amused glances.* – **1** *ncu* the giving and taking of one thing for another: *He gave me a pencil in exchange for the marble*; *An exchange of opinions is helpful.* **2** *nc* (*formal*) a conversation or dispute: *An angry exchange took place between the two brothers when their father's will was read*; *a friendly exchange of views*; *There were angry exchanges between the two MPs in the House of Commons.* **3** *nu* the act of exchanging the money of one country for that of another: *the exchange of American dollars for German marks.* **4** *nu* the difference between the value of money in different countries: *What is the rate of exchange between the pound and the mark?* **5** *nc* a place where business shares are bought and sold or international financial dealings carried on: *news from the foreign exchanges.* **6** *nc* (*also* '**telephone exchange**) a central telephone system where lines are connected: *the telephone operators at the exchange.*

ex'changeable *adj.*

exchequer [iks'tʃekə]: **the Exchequer 1** the government department in charge of the nation's finances. **2** (*no cap*: *formal*) the national or public money supply, or (*often facet*) one's personal finances: *There is not much left in the exchequer.*

excise[1] ['eksaiz] *nu* the tax on goods *etc* made and sold within a country and on certain licences *etc*: *the excise on whisky*; (*attrib*) *Excise duty must be paid on whisky.*

'**exciseman** [-man] *nc* an officer collecting excise.

excise[2] [ik'saiz] *vt* (*formal*: *esp med*) to cut out or off: *The surgeon excised one of her kidneys.*

excision [ik'siʒən] *nu* (*formal*: *esp med*) the act of cutting out: *the excision of her appendix.*

excite [ik'sait] *vt* **1** to cause or rouse strong feelings of expectation, happiness *etc* in: *They were all excited by the good news*; *The children were excited at the thought of the party.* **2** (*formal*) to cause or rouse (feelings, emotions *etc*): *His letter did not excite my interest.*

ex'citable *adj* easily becoming excited or upset: *She was very excitable after the birth of her baby*; *a very excitable dog.* **ex,cita'bility** *nu.*

ex'cited *adj*: *The excited children hurried to the party*; *The boy, excited by his success, forgot to collect his prize.* **ex'citedly** *adv.*

ex'citement *nu* **1** the state of being excited: *His arrival caused great excitement.* **2** the quality of being exciting: *He enjoys the excitement of travel.*

exclaim [ik'skleim] *vti* (*formal or liter*) to call out, or say, suddenly and loudly: *'Good!' he exclaimed*; *She exclaimed in astonishment at the sight of the presents.*

exclamation [ekskla'meiʃən] *nc* (*formal*) an expression of surprise or other sudden feeling: *He gave an exclamation of anger.*

,**excla'mation mark** *nc* the mark (**!**) following and showing an exclamation.

exclude [ik'sklu:d] *vt* (*formal*) **1** to prevent (someone) from sharing or taking part in something: *They excluded her from the meeting.* **2** to shut out; to keep out: *Fill the bottle to the top so as to exclude all air.* **3** to leave out of consideration: *We cannot exclude the possibility that he was lying.*

ex'clusion [-ʒən] *nu.*

ex'cluding *prep* not counting; without including: *The club's expenses, excluding the cost of stationery, amounted to £140.*

to the ex'clusion of (*formal*) so as to exclude: *He painted continuously, to the exclusion of all other hobbies*; *He loves her to the exclusion of all others.*

exclusive [ik'sklu:siv] *adj* **1** (*pred*) leaving out; shutting out: *'These two statements are mutually exclusive' means that they cannot both be true.* **2** (of a group *etc*) not easily or readily mixing with others (*esp* if they are considered inferior) or allowing others in: *He belongs to a very exclusive club.* **3** limited to, or given to, only one individual or group *etc*: *They have exclusive rights to sell our books in that country*; *The story is exclusive to this newspaper.* **4** fashionable and expensive: *exclusive shops/restaurants.* **ex'clusively** *adv.* **ex'clusiveness** *nu.*

ex'clusive of excluding: *That is the price of the meal exclusive of service charge.*

excrement ['ekskrəmənt] *nu* (*formal*) matter, *esp* solid, discharged from the body; faeces; dung: *The streets are filthy with dogs' excrement.*

excrete [ik'skri:t] *vt* (*formal*) to discharge (waste matter) from the body: *The sweat glands excrete sweat.*

ex'cretion [-ʃən] **1** *nu* (*formal*: *tech*) the act of excreting: *the excretion of sweat.* **2** *ncu* that which is excreted: *bodily excretions.*

excruciating [ik'skru:ʃieitiŋ] *adj* causing extreme bodily or mental pain: *I have an excruciating headache*; (*facet*) *Listening to that child playing the violin is excruciating.*

ex'cruciatingly *adv*: *excruciatingly painful.*

excursion [ik'skə:ʃən, (*Amer*) -ʒən] *nc* (*formal*) a trip; an outing, *usu* for pleasure: *The parents and children made an excursion to the seaside.*

excuse [ik'skju:z] *vt* **1** to forgive or pardon: *Excuse me – can you tell me the time?*; *I'll excuse your carelessness this time*; *You must excuse him for being so late.* **2** to free (someone) from a task, duty *etc*: *May I be excused from writing this essay?* – [ik'skju:s] *nc* a reason (given by oneself) for being excused, or a reason for excusing: *Have you any excuse for your lateness?*; *He has no excuse for being so late.*

excusable [ik'skju:zəbl] *adj* pardonable: *Her rudeness is excusable as she is rather deaf.*

See also **inexcusable**.

execrable ['eksikrəbl] *adj* (*very formal*) very bad; disgraceful: *This essay is an execrable piece of work.*

execute ['eksikju:t] *vt* **1** to put to death by order of the law: *After the war many traitors were executed.* **2** (*formal*) to perform; to carry out (instructions *etc*): *See that my orders are fully executed.* **3** (*formal*) to perform (a movement/music *etc usu* requiring skill): *She executed a difficult turn on her skis.*

,**exe'cution** [-ʃən] **1** *ncu* (an act of) killing by law: *The judge ordered the execution of the murderer*; *The executions were held the day after the trial.* **2** *nu* (*formal*) the act of executing (orders or skilled movements *etc*) or state of being executed: *The plan is already in execution*; *His execution of the flute sonata was excellent.*

,**exe'cutioner** *nc* a person whose duty is to put to death condemned persons.

executive [ig'zekjutiv] *adj* (*usu attrib*) **1** (in a business organization *etc*) concerned with management: *He has executive status*; *Has he the necessary executive skills?* **2** concerned with the carrying out of laws *etc*: *executive powers/authority.* – *nc* **1** (*usu with* **the**) the branch of the government that puts the laws into effect. **2** a person or body of people in an organization *etc* that has power to direct or manage: *He is an executive in an insurance company*; *He is on the executive that is organizing the conference.*

executor [ig'zekjutə] *nc* (*legal*) a person appointed to see to the carrying out of what is stated in a will: *His two brothers are his executors.*

exemplary [ig'zempləri] *adj* (*formal*) worth following as an example: *His behaviour is always exemplary*; *exemplary behaviour.*

exemplify [ig'zemplifai] *vt* (*formal*) to be an example of; to show by means of an example: *This* castle exemplifies the architectural style of the period; His originality as a composer is exemplified by the following group of songs.

exempt [ig'zempt] *vt* (*formal*) to free (a person) from a duty that other people have to carry out: *He was exempted from military service; They exempted her from paying tax.* – *adj* (*pred: formal*) free (from a duty *etc*): *Children under 16 are exempt from the usual charges for dental treatment.*
ex'emption [-ʃən] *ncu*: *exemption from paying tax; exemption from military service.*

exercise ['eksəsaiz] **1** *nu* training or use (*esp* of the body) through action or effort: *Swimming is one of the healthiest forms of exercise; Take more exercise; Exercise of the mind is essential to keep housewives from getting bored.* **2** *nc* an activity intended as training: *ballet exercises; exercises in spelling; These exercises are intended to strengthen the ankles.* **3** *nc* (*mil*) a series of tasks, movements *etc* for training troops *etc*: *His battalion is on an exercise in the mountains.* – **1** *vti* to train or to give exercise to: *Dogs should be exercised frequently; I exercise every morning.* **2** *vt* (*formal*) to use; to make use of: *She was given the opportunity to exercise her skill as a pianist; I can exercise my right to refuse.*

exert [ig'zə:t] *vt* (*formal*) **1** to bring forcefully into use or action: *We must exert all our strength; He likes to exert his authority.* **2** to force (oneself) to make an effort: *Please exert yourselves and try to finish this job.*
ex'ertion [-ʃən] (*formal*) **1** *nu* the act of bringing forcefully into use: *the exertion of one's influence.* **2** *ncu* (an) effort: *They failed in spite of their exertions; You should have a rest after any period of exertion.*

exeunt ['eksiunt] *vi* (used as a stage direction to more than one person) (they) go off the stage: *Exeunt all.* – *See also* **exit**.

exhale [eks'heil] *vti* (*formal*) to breathe out: *Asthma sufferers have difficulty in exhaling; He exhaled a cloud of smoke.* **exhalation** [eksə'leiʃən] *ncu.*
See also **inhale**.

exhaust [ig'zo:st] *vt* **1** to make very tired: *She was completely exhausted by her long walk; Don't exhaust yourself unnecessarily.* **2** (*formal*) to use all of; to use completely: *We have exhausted our supplies; Our supplies are exhausted; You're exhausting my patience.* **3** (*formal*) to say all that can be said about (a subject *etc*): *We've exhausted that topic of discussion.* – *ncu* (an outlet from the engine of a car, motorcycle *etc* for) fumes and other waste: *Where is the exhaust fitted in this machine?*; (*attrib*) *exhaust fumes/system/pipe.*
ex'hausted *adj* extremely tired: *An exhausted climber arrived at the police station with news of the accident; You look exhausted.*
ex'haustion *nu* **1** extreme tiredness: *He collapsed from exhaustion.* **2** (*formal*) the act of exhausting: *the exhaustion of our supplies.*
ex'haustive [-tiv] *adj* (*formal*) complete; very thorough: *We made an exhaustive search; The police enquiries into the murder were exhaustive.*

exhibit [ig'zibit] *vt* **1** to show; to display to the public: *My picture is to be exhibited in the art gallery.* **2** (*formal*) to show (a quality *etc*): *He exhibited a complete lack of concern for others.* – *nc* **1** an object displayed publicly (*eg* in a museum): *One of the exhibits is missing.* **2** (*legal*) an object or document produced in court as part of the evidence: *The blood-stained scarf was exhibit number one in the murder trial.*
exhibition [eksi'biʃən] **1** *nc* a public display (*eg* of works of art, industrial goods *etc*): *We attended an exhibition of her drawings; an exhibition of children's books.* **2** *nu* an act of showing (*eg* a quality): *That was a disgraceful exhibition of bad temper.*
ˌexhi'bitionism [eksi-] *nu* (*derog*) the tendency to behave deliberately in such a way as to attract attention to oneself: *His exhibitionism embarrasses his wife.*
ˌexhi'bitionist [eksi-] *nc* (*derog*) a person who behaves in this way: *She is an exhibitionist and always wears low-cut, brightly-coloured dresses.*
ex'hibitor *nc* a person who provides an exhibit for a display *etc*: *He is one of the exhibitors at the flower show.*
make an exhibition of oneself (*derog*) to behave foolishly in public: *The little girl made an exhibition of herself by screaming loudly at her mother; The drunk man made an exhibition of himself and embarrassed everyone.*

exhilarate [ig'ziləreit] *vt* (*formal*) to make (a person) feel happy and lively: *He was exhilarated by the walk.* **exˌhila'ration** *nu.*
ex'hilarating *adj*: *They had an exhilarating discussion.*

exhort [ig'zo:t] *vt* (*old or formal*) to urge strongly and earnestly: *I exhorted him to give up gambling.*
ˌexhor'tation [egzo:-] *ncu.*

exhume [ig'zju:m] *vt* (*formal*) to dig out (*esp* a body from a grave): *The police exhumed the body for further investigation.* **exhumation** [eksju'meiʃən] *ncu.*

exigency [ig'zidʒənsi] *ncu* (*often in pl: very formal*) (an) urgent need: *He was forced by the exigencies of the situation to sell his house.*

exile ['eksail] **1** *nc* a person who lives outside his own country either from choice or because he is forced to do so: *He has been an exile from his native land for many years.* **2** *nu* a (*usu* long) stay in a foreign land (*orig* as a punishment): *He was sent into exile.* – *vt* to send away or banish (a person) from his own country: *The king's friends were exiled by his enemies after his death.*

exist [ig'zist] *vi* **1** to be something real or actual: *Do ghosts really exist?; No difficulties ever existed for him.* **2** to stay alive; to continue to live: *He cannot exist on such low wages; It is possible to exist on bread and water.*
ex'istence **1** *nu* the state of existing: *He does not believe in the existence of God; How long has this rule been in existence?* **2** *ncu* (a way of) life: *He leads an uneventful existence.*
See also **non-existent**.

exit ['egzit] *nc* **1** a way out of a building *etc*: *The exit was blocked; Where is the emergency exit?* **2** an actor's departure from the stage: *Macbeth's exit.* **3** an act of going out or departing: *She made a noisy exit.* – *vi* (used as a stage direction to one person) (he/she) goes off the stage: *Exit Hamlet.* – *See also* **exeunt**.

exodus ['eksədəs] *nc* (*usu only in sing: formal sometimes facet*) a going away of many people: *There was a general exodus from the room.*

exonerate [ig'zonəreit] *vt* (*formal*) to free from blame: *He was exonerated from responsibility for the accident.* **exˌone'ration** *nu.*

exorbitant [ig'zo:bitənt] *adj* (*formal*) (of prices or demands) very high or unreasonable: *That shop charges exorbitant prices; The war continued be-*

cause the enemy's demands were exorbitant. **ex'orbitantly** *adv.* **ex'orbitance** *nu.*

exorcize, -ise ['ekso:saiz] *vt* (*esp relig*) **1** to drive away or get rid of (an evil spirit): *The priest exorcized the evil spirits from the haunted house.* **2** to free (someone or something) from an evil spirit that is inside him or it: *They asked the priest to exorcize the haunted house* (*of evil spirits*).

'exorcism *ncu* (*esp relig*) (an) act of exorcizing.

'exorcist *nc* (*esp relig*) a person who exorcizes: *They asked the priest to act as exorcist.*

exotic [ig'zotik] *adj* **1** unusual or colourful: *She always wears rather exotic clothes*; *the exotic feathers of these birds.* **2** brought or introduced from a foreign country: *exotic plants*; *She uses exotic vegetables in her cooking.*

expand [ik'spand] **1** *vti* to make or grow larger; to spread out wider: *Metals expand when heated*; *He does exercises to expand his chest*; (*fig*) *The school's activities have expanded to include climbing and mountaineering.* **2** *vi* (*esp liter*) to become more good-humoured or talkative: *He began to expand a little after he had had a glass of wine.*

ex'panse [-s] *nc* a wide area or extent: *He noticed an expanse of water on his left*; *the broad expanse of the sky.*

ex'pansion [-ʃən] *nu* the act or state of expanding: *In planning bridges, one must allow for expansion in hot weather.*

ex'pansive [-siv] *adv* **1** (of a person or his personality *etc*) expressing feelings freely; good-humoured and talkative: *He was in an expansive mood, and chatted till midnight.* **2** (of an arm movement or gesture) stretching wide: *He included the whole audience in his expansive gesture of farewell.*

expatiate [ik'speiʃieit] *vi* (*very formal*) (*with* **on**) to talk or write at length about: *He expatiated on his state of health.*

expatriate [eks'peitriət] *nc* a person living outside his own country: *There are many Polish expatriates in America*; (*attrib*) *an expatriate community of Poles.*

expect [ik'spekt] *vt* **1** to think of as likely to happen or come: *I'm expecting a letter today*; *We expect her on tomorrow's train.* **2** to think or believe (that something will happen): *He expects to be home tomorrow*; *I expect that he will be there tomorrow*; *I expect there to be* (= that there will be) *a delay*; *'Will she go too?' 'I expect so'/'I don't expect so'/'I expect not.'* **3** to require *eg* as one's right: *They expect high wages for skilled work*; *You are expected to tidy your own room.* **4** to suppose or assume: *I expect* (*that*) *you're tired.* – *See also* **be expecting** *below.*

ex'pectancy *nu* (*formal*) the state of expecting or hoping: *a feeling/look/air of expectancy.*

ex'pectant *adj* **1** (*formal*) full of hope or expectation: *the expectant faces of the audience.* **2** (*attrib*) expecting (a baby): *She is an expectant mother – the baby's due next month.* **ex'pectantly** *adv.*

ˌexpec'tation [ekspek-] **1** *nu* the state of expecting: *In expectation of a wage increase, he bought a washing-machine.* **2** *ncu* (*often pl*) what is expected: *He failed his exam, contrary to expectation(s)*; *Did the concert come up to your expectations?*

ˌexpec'tations [ekspek-] *n pl* (*old*) money, property *etc* that one expects to gain, *esp* by inheritance.

expectation of life/life expectancy *nu* the length of time that one can expect to live: *The expectation of life is greater for women than men.*

be ex'pecting (*inf*) to be pregnant: *She is expecting* (*a baby*) *and does not feel very well.*

expedient [ik'spi:diənt] *adj* (*formal*: *usu pred*) (sometimes of an unjust act *etc*) convenient or advisable: *It would not be expedient to pay him what he asks*; *It is more expensive but expedient to pay by instalments*; *A change of policy may be expedient in this case.* – *nc* (*formal*) a plan, idea *etc* that may solve or solves a problem: *Borrowing the money from his mother was an expedient he had not considered.*

ex'pedience, ex'pediency *nus* (*formal*) **1** fitness or advisability; convenience; suitability: *I have doubts about the expedience of your plan.* **2** the consideration of one's own advantage: *In running a business we must act from expediency, not generosity.*

expedite ['ekspidait] *vt* (*formal*) to hasten or speed up (a work process *etc*): *Can the government expedite their plans for improvement of the railway system?*

ˌexpe'ditious [-'diʃəs] *adj* (*formal*) quick (and efficient): *He was very expeditious in his reply to my letter.* **ˌexpe'ditiously** *adv.*

expedition [ekspi'diʃən] *nc* **1** an organized journey with a purpose: *He took part in an expedition to the South Pole.* **2** a group making such a journey: *He was a member of the expedition which climbed Mount Everest.*

ˌexpe'ditionary *adj* (*attrib*) (*esp* of troops) forming, or sent on, an expedition *eg* to fight abroad: *An expeditionary force was sent to Africa.*

expel [ik'spel] – *pt, ptp* **ex'pelled** – *vt* **1** to send away in disgrace (a person from a school *etc*): *The child was expelled for stealing.* **2** (*formal*) to get rid of; to drive out: *an electric fan for expelling kitchen smells.*

expulsion [ik'spʌlʃən] *ncu*: *His expulsion from school shocked his parents.*

expend [ik'spend] *vt* (*formal*) to use or spend (time, supplies *etc*): *He has expended all his energy on the scheme.*

ex'pendable *adj* (*formal*) that may be sacrificed for some purpose or cause: *Generals sometimes regard soldiers as expendable.*

ex'penditure [-tʃə] **1** *nu* the act of spending: *the expenditure of money and resources.* **2** *ncu* (an) amount of money spent: *His expenditure(s) amounted to £1500.*

ex'pense [-s] **1** *nu* the spending of money *etc*; cost: *I've gone to a lot of expense to educate you well*; *She was put to* (= had to bear) *the expense of providing meals for them.* **2** *nc* a cause of spending: *What an expense clothes are!* – *See also* **at the expense of** *below.*

ex'penses [-siz] *n pl* money spent in carrying out a job *etc*: *His firm paid his travelling expenses.*

ex'pensive [-siv] *adj* costing a great deal: *She always buys expensive clothes.*

at the ex'pense of **1** being paid for by; at the cost of: *He equipped the expedition at his own expense*; *He did not go to London at his own expense – he went at the expense of the firm*; *at the firm's expense*; (*fig*) *His successful career was at the expense of his social life.* **2** (*fig*) making (a person) appear ridiculous: *He told a joke at his wife's expense.*

See also **inexpensive**.

experience [ik'spiəriəns] **1** *nu* (knowledge, skill or wisdom gained through) practice in some activity, or the doing of something: *Learn by experience – don't make the same mistake again*; *Has she had much driving experience?*; *Has she had experience in teaching?*; *my experience of life at sea.* **2** *nc* an event that affects or involves a person *etc*: *The earthquake was a terrible experience.* – *vt* (*formal*) to have experience of; to feel: *I have never before experienced such rudeness!*; *For the first time in her life the child experienced real affection.*

ex'perienced *adj* having gained knowledge from experience; skilled: *an experienced taxi-driver*; *an experienced mountaineer*; *He is experienced in legal matters.*

See also **inexperience**.

experiment [ik'sperimənt] *ncu* a test done in order to find out something, *eg* if an idea is correct, or if a machine works *etc*: *He performs chemical experiments in the laboratory*; *They are conducting experiments in traffic control*; *We shall have to find out by experiment.* – *vi* (*with* **on** *or* **with**) to try to find out something by making tests: *He experimented for years with various medicines to find the safest cure*; *The doctor experiments on animals.*

ex,peri'mental [-'mentl] *adj* (*esp attrib*) of, or used for, an experiment: *experimental teaching methods*; *an experimental farm attached to the agricultural department of the university*; *His new scheme is at an experimental stage.* **ex,peri'mentally** *adv.*

ex,perimen'tation *nu* (*formal*) the carrying out of experiments: *He was criticized for his experimentation on dogs*; (*attrib*) *experimentation techniques.*

expert ['ekspə:t] *adj* (*with* **at** *or* **on** *when pred*) skilled through training or practice: *an expert car-designer*; *I'm expert at map-reading*; *Get expert advice on plumbing.* – *nc* a person who is an expert: *He is an expert in political history*; *She is an expert on the Bronze Age.* **'expertly** *adv.* **'expertness** *nu.*

,exper'tise [-'ti:z] *nu* special skill or knowledge: *a lawyer's expertise*; *We admired the expertise of the racing-driver.*

See also **inexpert**.

expiate ['ekspieit] *vt* (*liter or very formal*) to make up for (wrong one has done); to make amends for: *How can a murderer expiate his crime?*; *The soldiers wanted to expiate the bombing of the church by building a new one.* **,expi'ation** *nu.*

expire [ik'spaiə] *vi* **1** (*formal*) (of a limited period of time) to come to an end: *His three weeks' leave expires tomorrow.* **2** (*formal*) (of a ticket, licence *etc*) to go out of date: *My driving licence expired last month.* **3** (*liter or very formal*) to die: *The old man expired after a long illness.*

expiration [ekspi'reiʃən] *nu* (*formal*): *They had to leave the flat on the expiration of their lease.*

ex'piry *nu* (*formal*) the end of a period of time or of an agreement *etc* with a time limit: *the date of expiry of my driving licence*; (*attrib*) *What was the expiry date of our television licence?*

explain [ik'splein] *vt* **1** to make (something) clear or easy to understand: *Can you explain the railway timetable to me?*; *He explained what he was making*; *Did she explain why she was late?* **2** to give, or be, a reason for (something): *I cannot explain his failure*; *That explains his silence.* – *See also* **explain away** *below.*

explanation [eksplə'neiʃən] **1** *nu* the act or process of explaining: *Let me give a few words of explanation.* **2** *nc* a statement or fact that explains: *There are several possible explanations for the sudden cold weather.*

ex'planatory [-'splanə-] *adj* (*formal*: *usu attrib*) giving an explanation: *There are explanatory notes in this book.*

explain away *vt sep* to get rid of (difficulties *etc*) by clever explaining: *She tried to explain away the fact that the money was missing by saying it had been stolen*; *How did she explain it away?*

See also **explicable**.

expletive [ek'spli:tiv] *nc* (*formal or facet*) an exclamation, *esp* a swear-word: *He uttered several expletives when he realized he had missed the train.*

explicable [ek'splikəbl] *adj* (*formal*: *pred*) capable of being explained: *His bad temper is explicable only if he is in pain.*

See also **explain, inexplicable**.

explicit [ik'splisit] *adj* (*formal*) stated, or stating, fully and clearly: *He gave me explicit instructions on how to use the machine*; *Can you be more explicit about your reasons for leaving?*; *The old lady does not like novels which give explicit details about sexual relationships.* **ex'plicitly** *adv.* **ex'plicitness** *nu.*

See also **implicit**.

explode [ik'sploud] **1** *vti* to (cause to) blow up with a loud noise: *The bomb exploded and caused great damage*; *The police exploded the bomb where it could cause no damage.* **2** *vi* (*fig*) suddenly to show a strong or violent emotion: *The teacher exploded with anger*; *The children exploded into laughter.* **3** *vt* to prove (a theory *etc*) wrong: *The idea that babies should be fat was exploded years ago.*

ex'plosion [-ʒən] **1** *nc* a blowing up, or the noise caused by this: *a gas explosion*; *The explosions which damaged the building could be heard a long way off.* **2** *nu* the action of exploding: *the explosion of the atom bomb*; *the explosion of his theory.* **3** *nc* (*fig*) a sudden showing of strong feelings *etc*: *an explosion of laughter.* **4** *nc* (*fig*) a sudden great increase: *Wage increases led to an explosion in food prices.*

ex'plosive [-siv] *adj* (*esp attrib*) **1** likely to explode: *Hydrogen is a dangerously explosive gas*; (*fig*) *Don't mention wages to the manager – it's an explosive subject.* **2** bursting like an explosion: *an explosive noise.* – *ncu* (a) material that is likely to explode: *gelignite and other high explosives*; *We need some explosive to make a hole in the rock.*

exploit ['eksploit] *nc* a (daring) deed or action: *I was amazed at his military exploits*; *His children's latest exploits amused their father.* – [ik'sploit] *vt* **1** (*formal*) to make good or advantageous use of: *We must exploit fully the country's natural resources*; *We must exploit our own abilities.* **2** to use (*eg* a person) unfairly for one's own advantage: *Many children were exploited as cheap labour in factories.*

,exploi'tation *nu.*

explore [ik'splo:] **1** *vti* to search or travel through (a place) for the purpose of discovery: *Has that continent been fully explored yet?*; *Let's go exploring in the caves.* **2** *vt* (*formal*) to examine carefully: *I'll explore the possibilities of getting a job here.*

exploration [eksplə'reiʃən] *nu*: *the exploration of unknown parts of the Amazon*; *the exploration of all possibilities*; *a journey of exploration.*

ex'ploratory [-'splorə-] *adj* (*formal*) for the purpose of exploration or investigation: *The surgeon needs to perform an exploratory operation to see what is causing you pain*; *That expedition up the river was mainly exploratory.*

ex'plorer *nc* a person who explores unknown

regions: *The early explorers were searching for new trade-routes*; *explorers in space.*

explosion, explosive *see* **explode**.

expo *see* **exposition**.

exponent [ik'spounənt] *nc* (*formal*) **1** a person able to demonstrate skilfully a particular art or activity: *an able exponent of the art of fly-fishing*; *She was an accomplished exponent of Bach's flute sonatas.* **2** a person who explains and supports (a theory or belief *etc*): *He was one of the early exponents of Marxism.*

export [ek'spo:t] *vt* to send or take (goods *etc*) to another country (for sale): *Jamaica exports bananas to Britain.* – ['ekspo:t] **1** *nu* the act or business of exporting: *the export of whisky to America.* **2** *nc* something which is exported: *Paper is an important Swedish export.*

ˌexpor'tation [ek-] *nu.*

ex'porter *nc* a person who exports goods: *His father was a tobacco exporter.*

expose [ik'spouz] *vt* **1** to uncover; to leave unprotected from (*eg* weather, danger, observation *etc*): *Paintings should not be exposed to direct sunlight*; *Don't expose children to unnecessary dangers*; *Her jewels lay exposed on the table.* **2** (*formal*) to discover and make known (*eg* criminals or their activities): *You must expose the plot to assassinate the king*; *It was a newspaper that exposed the murderer of the child.* **3** by releasing the camera shutter, to allow light to fall on (a photographic film).

ex'posure [-ʒə] **1** *ncu* (an) act of exposing or state of being exposed: *Prolonged exposure of the skin to hot sun can cause sunstroke*; *His reputation was harmed by the constant exposures in the newspapers of details of his private life*; *The criminals dared not risk exposure* (= being discovered and made known to the police *etc*); *A child lost in these hills can easily die of exposure* (= from the effects of cold *etc*). **2** *nc* an exposing of one frame of a photographic film *etc*: *I have two exposures left.*

exposé [ek'spouzei, (*Amer*) ekspou'zei] *nc* (*formal or facet*) an account (sometimes outspoken): *Could you give a brief exposé of the firm's aims?*; *She gave a frank exposé of her past life.*

exposition [ekspə'ziʃən] (*formal*) **1** *ncu* a detailed explanation or account (of a subject): *He gave a very clear exposition of the facts.* **2** *nc* (*inf abbrev* **'expo**) an exhibition: *a trade exposition.*

See also expound.

exposure *see* **expose**.

expound [ik'spaund] *vt* (*formal*) to explain in detail; to give an exposition of: *He expounded his theory to his colleagues.*

express [ik'spres] *vt* **1** to put into words: *He expressed his ideas very clearly*; *She expressed her thanks for the present.* **2** *v refl* to put one's own thoughts into words: *You haven't expressed yourself clearly.* **3** (*formal*) to show (thoughts, feelings *etc*) by looks, actions *etc*: *She smiled to express her agreement.* **4** (*formal*) to press or squeeze out: *She expressed milk from her breast.* **5** to send by fast (postal) delivery: *Will you express this letter, please?* – *adj* (*attrib*) **1** travelling, carrying goods *etc*, especially fast: *an express train* (= a fast train that stops at very few stations); *Send the parcels by express delivery.* **2** (*formal*) clearly stated: *You have disobeyed my express wishes.* – *adv* by express train or fast delivery service: *Send your letter express*; *He travelled express.* – **1** *nc* an express train: *the London to Cardiff express.* **2** *nu* the service provided *eg* by the post office for carrying goods *etc* quickly: *The parcel was sent by express.* **3** *n* (*with cap*) a word often used in the titles of newspapers: *the Glasgow Express.*

ex'pressly *adv* (*formal*) **1** in clear, definite words: *I expressly forbade you to do that.* **2** with a certain definite purpose: *I came expressly to tell you the good news.*

ex'pression [-ʃən] **1** *nc* (*usu in sing*) a look on one's face that shows one's feelings: *He always has a bored expression/an expression of dissatisfaction.* **2** *nc* a word or phrase: *'Dough' is a slang expression for 'money'*; *'Flitting' is the Scottish expression for 'moving house'.* **3** *ncu* (*often formal or liter*) (a) showing of thoughts or feelings by words, actions *etc*: *This poem is an expression of his grief*; *He gave expression to* (= expressed) *his anger by swearing*; *He wrote to the king with many expressions of loyalty.* **4** *nu* the showing of feeling when *eg* reciting, reading aloud or playing a musical instrument: *Put more expression into your playing!*

ex'pressionless *adj* (of a face or voice) showing no feeling: *He spoke in a cold, expressionless tone*; *She remained expressionless as the judge pronounced her guilty.*

ex'pressive [-siv] *adj* **1** showing meaning or feeling clearly: *She has an expressive face*; *Her voice is very expressive.* **2** (*pred*: *with* **of**: *liter or formal*) expressing: *a gesture expressive of weariness.* **ex'pressiveness** *nu.*

ex'pressively *adv* in a way that shows meaning or feeling clearly: *She uses her hands expressively when speaking.*

expropriate [iks'prouprieit] *vt* (*legal or formal*) to take (property *etc*) away from the owner, *esp* for one's own use: *Has the government the right to expropriate private gardens for public use?* **exˌpropri'ation** *ncu.*

expulsion *see* **expel**.

expunge [ik'spʌndʒ] *vt* (*old or very formal*) to cross out or remove (*eg* words from a book): *You must try to expunge the tragedy from your memory*; *He expunged all references to the political situation from his speech.*

expurgate ['ekspəgeit] *vt* (*formal*) to remove any words or passages supposed to be offensive or harmful from (a book *etc*): *The teacher thinks Shakespeare's plays should be expurgated before his pupils read them.* **ˌexpur'gation** *ncu.*

exquisite ['ekskwizit] *adj* very beautiful or skilful: *exquisite embroidery*; *exquisite flute-playing*; *Her portrait of the child was exquisite.* **'exquisitely** *adv.*

extant [ek'stant, (*Amer*) 'ekstənt] *adj* (*formal*) still existing: *Queen Mary's last letter, of 1587, is still extant*; *extant remains of Roman encampments.*

extempore [ik'stempəri] *adv* (*formal*) without previous thought or preparation: *He had no time to make notes for his speech, so had to speak extempore.* – *adj* (*formal*) (made up and) spoken or performed without preparation: *extempore verses*; *an extempore performance*; *His speech was quite extempore.*

ex'temporize, -ise *vi* (*formal*) to speak or perform extempore: *He forgot his speech and had to extemporize.*

extend [ik'stend] **1** *vt* to make longer or larger: *extend a building*; *He extended his vegetable garden*; *Can you extend your holiday by a few days?* **2** *vi* to reach or stretch: *The school grounds extend as far as this fence.* **3** *vt* (*formal*) to hold out or stretch out (a limb *etc*): *Extend your right arm*; *He extended his hand to her.* **4** *vt* (*formal*) to offer (kindness *etc*): *May I extend a welcome to you all?*

ex'tension [-ʃən] **1** *nc* an added part: *He built an extension to his house*; *They arranged a two-day extension to their holiday*; *He has telephone extensions* (= telephones) *in every bedroom.* **2** *nu* the process of extending: *His main aim was the extension of his territory.*

ex'tensive [-siv] *adj* large in area or amount: *extensive tree plantations*; *His knowledge of the subject is quite extensive*; *He suffered extensive injuries in the accident.*

ex'tent [-t] *ncu* (*usu in sing*) **1** the area or length to which something extends: *The bird's wings measured 20 centimetres at their fullest extent*; *The garden is nearly a mile in extent*; *A vast extent of grassland was damaged by the fire*; (*fig*) *I admired the (great) extent of his knowledge.* **2** amount; degree: *What is the extent of the damage?*; *To what extent can we trust him?*

to a certain extent/to some extent partly but not completely: *I trust him to some extent*; *To a certain extent you are correct.*

extenuating [ik'stenjueitiŋ] *adj* (*formal*) making (a crime *etc*) seem less serious by showing that there was some excuse for it: *Because of the extenuating circumstances, the judge ordered him to pay a fine rather than go to prison.*

exterior [ik'stiəriə] *adj* (*usu attrib*) on or from the outside; outer: *an exterior wall of a house*; (*formal*) *The inhabitants of the village were not affected by exterior influences.* – *nc* (*formal*) the outside (of something or someone): *The exterior of the house is in need of painting*; *He's a kind person in spite of his unattractive exterior*; *On the exterior she was charming, but she was known to have a very violent temper.*

exterminate [ik'stə:mineit] *vt* (*formal*) to get rid of or destroy completely: *Rats must be exterminated from a building or they will cause disease*; *Whales must be protected or they will soon be exterminated.* **exˌtermi'nation** *nu*.

external [ik'stə:nl] *adj* (*usu formal*) of, for, from, or on, the outside: *Chemists often label skin creams 'For external use only'*; *Don't let external considerations affect your decision.* **ex'ternally** *adv*.

extinct [ik'stiŋkt] *adj* **1** (of a type of animal *etc*) no longer in existence: *Mammoths became extinct in prehistoric times.* **2** (of a volcano) no longer active: *That volcano was thought to be extinct until it suddenly erupted ten years ago.*

extinction [ik'stiŋkʃən] *nu* (*formal*) **1** making or becoming extinct: *Efforts have been made to avoid the extinction of the species.* **2** the act of putting out or extinguishing or the state of being put out or extinguished: *Complete extinction of the fire was difficult because of the strong wind*; *The children were frightened by the sudden extinction of the lights because of the electricity failure.*

extinguish [ik'stiŋgwiʃ] *vt* (*formal*) to put out (a fire *etc*): *The firemen could not extinguish the flames*; *Please extinguish your cigarettes*; (*formal fig*) *All hope was extinguished.*

ex'tinguisher *nc* a spraying apparatus containing chemicals for putting out fire: *There are fire extinguishers on every floor of the building.*

See also **extinction**.

extol [ik'stoul] – *pt, ptp* **ex'tolled** – *vt* (*formal*) to praise highly: *Her virtues have so often been extolled.*

extort [ik'sto:t] *vt* to obtain (from a person) by threats or violence: *He extorts money by blackmail*; *She extorted a confession from the child by torture.*

ex'tortion [-ʃən] *ncu*.

ex'tortionate [-nət] *adj* (of a price) much too high: *That restaurant's prices are extortionate!*; *He paid an extortionate price for that rickety old chair at an auction – it certainly isn't an antique.*

extra ['ekstrə] *adj* additional; more than usual or necessary: *They demand an extra £5 a week*; *We need extra men for this job*; *The basic price of the car is £3 000 – the radio is extra.* – *adv* unusually: *an extra large box of chocolates.* – *pron* an additional amount: *The book costs £4.00 but we charge extra for postage.* – *nc* **1** something extra, or something for which an extra price is charged: *The college fees cover teaching only – stationery and other equipment are extras.* **2** in cinema or television, an actor employed in a small part, *eg* as a person in a crowd: *The star had begun her acting career as an extra in a television documentary.* **3** a special edition of a newspaper containing later or special news: *Extras were rushed out with the news of the king's death.*

extra- [ekstrə] (*in cmpds*) outside or beyond, as in **extramural**; ˌ*extra-*'*large.*

extract [ik'strakt] *vt* **1** (*formal*) to pull out, or draw out, *esp* by force or with effort: *I have to have a tooth extracted*; (*fig*) *How did you manage to extract the information/promise from her?* **2** to select (passages from a book *etc*): *He showed me two paragraphs that had been extracted from the report.* **3** to take out (a substance forming part of something else) by *eg* crushing, or by chemical means: *Vanilla essence is extracted from vanilla beans.* – ['ekstrakt] **1** *nc* a passage selected from a book *etc*: *Let me read you a short extract from his novel.* **2** *nu* a substance obtained by an extracting process: *beef/yeast extract*; *extract of malt.*

ex'traction [-ʃən] **1** *nu* (*formal*) race or parentage: *He is of Greek extraction.* **2** *ncu* (*formal or tech*) (an) act of extracting *esp* a tooth: *He had to have three extractions*; *The extraction of the tooth was painful*; (*attrib*) *an extraction process at the chemical works.*

extradite ['ekstrədait] *vt* (*formal*) to give (someone) up to the police of another country (for a crime committed there): *The French police have agreed to extradite the man wanted for murder in Britain.* ˌ**extra'dition** [-'di-] *nu*.

extramural [ekstrə'mjuərəl] *adj* (*usu attrib*) **1** (of teaching, lectures *etc*) for people who are not full-time students at a college *etc*: *The college has a programme of extramural lectures for the local people.* **2** separate from or outside the area of one's studies (in a university *etc*): *The students have many extramural activities.*

extraneous [ik'streiniəs] *adj* (*formal*) not belonging to something, or having nothing to do with a subject: *The book is too long – the author should cut out the extraneous information*; *There were several extraneous pieces that didn't seem to fit in anywhere.*

extraordinary [ik'stro:dənəri] *adj* **1** surprising; unusual: *What an extraordinary thing to say!*; *She is behaving in a most extraordinary way*; *Her behaviour is extraordinary.* **2** (*formal*: *placed immediately after noun*) special or with particular work to do: *ambassador extraordinary.*

extraordinarily [ik'stro:dənərəli, (*Amer*) ikstro:rdə'nerəli] *adv*: *He has extraordinarily big feet*; *She is extraordinarily beautiful.*

extra-terrestrial [ekstrətə'restriəl] *nc, adj* (*formal*) (people *etc*) not living on or coming from the planet Earth.

extravagant [ik'stravəgənt] *adj* (*usu derog*) **1** using or spending too much; wasteful: *You are too extravagant with my money!*; *an extravagant use of materials/energy/money.* **2** (of ideas, emotions *etc*) exaggerated or too great: *the extravagant praise of the critics for his new novel.* **ex'travagantly** *adv.*
ex'travagance *ncu* (*usu derog*): *His wife's extravagance is the reason why they have no money*; *Food is a necessity, but wine is an extravagance*; *She was irritated by the extravagance of his praise.*

extravert *see* **extrovert**.

extreme [ik'stri:m] *adj* **1** (*usu attrib*) very great, *esp* much more than usual: *The meeting gave her extreme pleasure*; *He is in extreme pain.* **2** (*attrib*) very far or furthest in any direction, *esp* out from the centre: *the extreme south-western tip of England*; *the extreme edge of the town/the cliff*; (*fig*) *He is a member of the extreme left/right.* **3** very violent or strong; not ordinary or usual: *This crisis calls for extreme measures*; *He holds extreme views on education*; *He is always very extreme (in his views).* – *nc* **1** something as far, or as different, as possible from something else: *the extremes of sadness and joy.* **2** the greatest degree of any state, *esp* if unpleasant: *The extremes of heat in the desert make life uncomfortable.* – *See also* **in the extreme, to extremes** *below.*
ex'tremely *adv* very: *It would be extremely kind of you to do that for me.*
ex'tremism *nu* (*derog*) the holding of views which are as far from being moderate as possible: *The politician's extremism made him unpopular with the more moderate members of his party.*
ex'tremist *nc* (*derog*) a person who holds such views, *usu* in politics: *He was considered an extremist who was trying to bring about revolution*; (*attrib*) *extremist policies.*
ex'tremity [-'stre-] **1** *nc* (*formal*) the farthest point or place: *the extremities of the earth.* **2** *ncu* (*old or liter*) an extreme degree; the quality of being extreme: *Their suffering reached such extremities that many died*; *in the extremity of his distress.* **3** *nc* (*formal*) a situation of great danger or distress: *They need help in this extremity.* **4** *n pl* (*formal*) the farthest parts of the body *eg* the hands and feet: *He had poor circulation in his extremities.*
in the ex'treme (*formal*) to the highest degree; very: *It was dangerous in the extreme.*
to ex'tremes (*fig*) very far, *esp* further than is thought to be reasonable: *She can never express an opinion without going to extremes*; *He thought that calling in the police was taking the matter to extremes.*

extricate ['ekstrikeit] *vt* (*formal*: *usu fig*) to set free: *She managed to extricate herself from the crowd of excited children*; *He extricated her from her difficulties.* **ˌextri'cation** *nu.*
See also **inextricably**.

extrovert, extravert ['ekstrəvə:t] *nc, adj* (of) a person who is more interested in what happens around him than his own ideas and emotions: *He is such an extrovert that he is a wonderful person to have at a party*; *She is so extrovert that she is always very good company* (=good fun to be with).
See also **introvert**.

exuberant [ig'zju:bərənt] *adj* (*formal*) **1** happy and excited or in high spirits: *She was exuberant about passing her exams*; *He was in an exuberant mood.* **2** (*fig*) strong or full of life: *exuberant colours*; *an exuberant growth (of plants etc).*
ex'uberance *nu.*

exude [ig'zju:d] *vt* (*formal*) to give off or out in great amounts: *The hard work made him exude sweat*; (*fig*) *She exuded happiness.*

exult [ig'zʌlt] *vi* **1** (*formal*: *with* **in** *or* **at**) to be very happy; to rejoice: *They exulted in their victory/at the news of their victory.* **2** (*formal*: *with* **over**) to triumph over; to be happy because one has defeated someone: *She exulted over her rival.*
ex'ultant *adj* (*formal*) very happy (at a victory or success *etc*): *They were exultant at the news of their victory*; *an exultant crowd.*
ˌexul'tation [eg-] *ncu.*

eye [ai] *nc* **1** the part of the body with which one sees: *Open your eyes*; *She has blue eyes.* **2** anything like or suggesting an eye, *eg* the hole in a needle, the loop or ring into which a hook connects *etc*: *The eye of this needle is very small – I can't get the thread through it.* **3** the ability to see and appreciate small differences in something and to make good choices: *She has an eye for detail/colour/beauty.* – *See also* **eye** *in phrases below.* – *vt* to look at (carefully): *The boys were eyeing the girls at the dance up and down*; *The thief eyed the policeman warily.*
'eyeful *nc* (*no pl*) **1** (*inf*) an interesting or beautiful sight: *She is quite an eyeful!* **2** (*sl*) a look or view: *Get an eyeful of* (=Have a good look at) *that!*
'eyeball *nc* **1** the round part of the eye: *The surgeon removed the lead shot from the back of the boy's eyeball.* **2** the eye itself (the part between the eyelids): *Her eyeballs were inflamed.*
'eyebrow *nc* the line of hair (*usu* curved) above each eye: *She darkens her eyebrows with eyebrow pencil.* – *See also* **raise one's eyebrows** *below.*
'eye-catching *adj* striking or noticeable, *esp* if attractive: *an eye-catching hat*; *That advertisement is very eye-catching.*
'eyelash *nc* one of the (rows of) hairs that grow on the edge of the eyelids: *She looked coyly at him through her eyelashes.*
'eyelet [-lit] *nc* a small hole in fabric, leather *etc* for a thread, string, rope *etc.*
'eyelid *nc* the movable piece of skin that covers or uncovers the eye: *She coloured her eyelids with eyeshadow.*
'eye-opener *nc* (*inf*) something that reveals an unexpected fact *etc*: *Our visit to their office was a real eye-opener – they are so inefficient!*
'eye-piece *nc* the part of a telescope, microscope *etc* to which one puts one's eye.
'eyeshadow *ncu* a kind of coloured make-up worn around the eyes: *She wears too much eyeshadow.*
'eyesight *nu* the ability to see: *I have good eyesight*; *Her eyesight is faulty.*
'eyesore *nc* (*inf*) something (*esp* a building) that is ugly to look at: *That new skyscraper is a real eyesore!*
'eye-witness *nc* a person who sees something (*esp* a crime) happen: *Several eye-witnesses to the murder were questioned by the police*; (*attrib*) *an eye-witness report.*
before/under one's very eyes in front of one, *usu* with no attempt at concealment: *It happened before my very eyes*; *The watch was stolen from under my very eyes.*
be up to the eyes in/with to be very busy or

deeply involved in or with: *She's up to the eyes in work.*

close one's eyes to to ignore (*esp* something blameworthy): *She closed her eyes to the children's misbehaviour.*

in the eyes of in the opinion or estimation of: *He was discredited in the eyes of his friends as a result of the scandal.*

in the mind's eye *see* **mind**.

keep an eye on 1 to watch closely: *You must keep an eye on the price of bread.* **2** to look after: *Keep an eye on the baby while I am out!*

lay/set eyes on (*inf*) to see, *esp* for the first time: *I wish I'd never laid eyes on her!*; *I recognized it as soon as I set eyes on it.*

make eyes at to look at (someone) with sexual interest or admiration: *Stop making eyes at that blonde!*

not (be able to) take one's eyes off (something) not to be able to stop watching something: *I didn't dare take my eyes off the sick baby for an instant*; *He couldn't take his eyes off the blonde girl.*

one in the eye (*inf*) a hard or unkind refusal or rejection: *It was one in the eye for him when she refused to go out with him.*

raise one's eyebrows to (lift one's eyebrows in order to) show surprise: *She raised her eyebrows a little when I told her, but she didn't say anything*; *Her behaviour when her husband is away causes the neighbours to raise their eyebrows.*

see eye to eye (*usu in neg*) to be in agreement: *We've never seen eye to eye about this matter.*

turn a blind eye *see* **turn**.

with an 'eye to (something) with something as an aim: *He always worked with an eye to promotion.*

with one's eyes open with full awareness of what one is doing: *I knew what the job would involve – I went into it with my eyes open.*

eyrie, aerie ['aiəri] *nc* the nesting-place of eagles or other birds of prey, *usu* in a high, rocky place.

Ff

fable ['feibl] **1** *nc* a story (*usu* about animals) that teaches a lesson about human behaviour: *Aesop's fables.* **2** *ncu* (*loosely*) a legend or untrue story: *We could not decide if it was fact or fable.*

fabulous ['fabjuləs] *adj* **1** (*inf*) wonderful; marvellous: *That's a fabulous idea!*; *You look fabulous in that dress.* **2** (*formal*: *attrib*) existing (only) in a fable: *The phoenix is a fabulous bird.*

'fabulously *adv*: *He's fabulously wealthy.*

fabric ['fabrik] *ncu* **1** (*more formal than* **cloth**) (a type of) cloth or material: *I have enough fabric left over from my coat to make a skirt*; *Nylon is a man-made fabric.* **2** (*formal*) the outside part (walls *etc*) of a building: *The fabric of their house is in good condition, although the inside is badly in need of repair*; (*fig*) *The fabric of society is crumbling away.*

fabricate ['fabrikeit] *vt* (*formal*) to make up something that is not true (a story, accusation *etc*): *I don't want to attend the meeting tonight – I shall fabricate some excuse or other.*

ˌfabri'cation (*formal*) **1** *nc* something that is not true; a lie: *Her account of the accident was a complete fabrication.* **2** *nu* the act of fabricating: *The lonely child was given to fabrication.*

fabulous *see* **fable**.

façade, facade [fə'sa:d] *nc* **1** (*formal or archit*) the front of a building: *an eighteenth-century façade.* **2** (*fig formal*) a false appearance: *In spite of his brave facade, he was afraid.*

face [feis] **1** *nc* the front part of the head, from forehead to chin: *She has a beautiful face.* **2** *nc* a surface *esp* the front surface: *a rock face*; *the face of the earth.* **3** *nu* (*inf*) impudence: *I don't know how he had the face to come!* **4** *nc* (*sometimes in cmpds*) in mining, the end of a tunnel *etc* where work is being done: *a coal face*; *a face-worker.* – **1** *vt* to be opposite to: *My house faces the park.* **2** *vti* to turn, stand *etc* in the direction of: *She faced him across the desk*; *The house faces north.* **3** *vt* to meet or accept boldly: *I'm afraid you'll just have to face the fact that you've failed*; *When faced with the evidence he had to admit he was guilty.* **4** *vt* to cover (a building *etc*) with a surface of different material: *The walls are brick faced with marble.* – *See also* **face** *in phrases below.*

-faced *adj* (*in cmpds*) having a face of a certain kind: *a baby-faced man.*

facial ['feiʃəl] *adj* (*usu attrib*) of the face: *facial expressions.* – *nc* a beauty treatment for the face: *She would look much older if she didn't have regular facials.*

facing *ncu* (material for making) a surface or covering over something: *The walls had a facing of marble*; *I need some more facing for this dress I'm making.* – *prep* opposite: *The hotel is on the left, facing the church.*

face card *nc* in playing-cards, the king, queen or jack.

'face-cloth *nc* a small piece of soft cloth used for washing the face *etc*: *Have you packed soap and a face-cloth?*

'facelift *nc* **1** an operation to smooth and firm the face: *She had a facelift last year.* **2** (*fig*) a process intended to make a building *etc* look better: *Several million pounds will be spent on giving this mining village a facelift.*

'face-powder *nu* a type of make-up in the form of a fine powder: *She put on face-powder to stop her nose shining.*

'face-saving *adj* (*inf*) of something which helps a person not to look stupid or not to appear to be giving in: *He agreed to everything we asked and as a face-saving exercise we offered to consult him occasionally.* – *See also* **save one's face** *below.*

face value *nc* the value stated on the face of a coin *etc*: *A gold sovereign is now worth a great deal more than its face value.*

at face value as being as valuable *etc* as it appears: *You must take this offer at face value.*

face the music (*inf*) to accept punishment or responsibility for something one has done: *The child had to face the music after playing truant from school.*

face to face both or all people concerned actually being present: *They finally met face to face to discuss the problem*; (*attrib*) *a face-to-face encounter.*

face up to *vt fus* to meet or accept boldly: *He faced up to his difficult situation.*
in the 'face of having to deal with and in spite of: *He succeeded in the face of great difficulties.* – *See also* **fly in the face of** *under* **fly**[2].
lose face to suffer a loss of respect or reputation: *You will really lose face if you are defeated in the tennis match against a younger player.*
make/pull a face to twist one's face into a strange expression: *That rude child is making faces at me*; *He pulled faces at the baby to make it laugh.*
on the 'face of it as it appears at first glance, *usu* deceptively: *On the face of it, the problem was quite easy, but it actually turned out to be very difficult.*
put a good face on it to give the appearance of being satisfied *etc* with something when one is not: *Now it's done we'll have to put a good face on it, but I am not pleased with it.*
save one's face to avoid appearing stupid or wrong: *I refuse to accept the responsibility for that error just to save your face – it's your fault.*
show one's face (*usu in neg*) to be sufficiently confident or unashamed to be able to go to a particular place: *After making such a fool of myself I'll never be able to show my face in there again!*
to one's 'face while one is present: *You wouldn't be brave enough to say that to his face!*

facet ['fasit] *nc* **1** (*tech*) a side of a many-sided object, *esp* a cut jewel: *the facets of a diamond.* **2** (*formal*) an aspect or view of a subject: *There are several facets to this question*; *Many facets of this problem must be taken into consideration.*
'faceted *adj* (*usu in cmpds*) (*esp* of a jewel) with several sides: *a many-faceted diamond.*

facetious [fə'si:ʃəs] *adj* (*more formal than* **funny**) not serious; intended to be funny or humorous: *a facetious remark*; *You must not be facetious about serious matters.* **fa'cetiously** *adv.* **fa'cetiousness** *nu.*

facial *see* **face**.

facile ['fasail] *adj* (*formal*) **1** too easily done or said to have any importance: *Such a facile victory was no credit to him*; *facile words.* **2** (*derog*) (of a person) speaking or behaving in this manner: *Don't be so facile! Think a little before you speak.*
facilitate [fə'siliteit] *vt* (*formal*) to make (something) easier: *It would facilitate matters if fewer people had to be consulted.*
facilities [fə'silətiz] *n pl* the means to do something: *There are facilities for cooking*; *There are cooking facilities.*
facility [fə'siləti] (*formal*) **1** *nu* ease or quickness: *He showed great facility in learning languages.* **2** *nc* a skill: *He has a great facility for always being right.*

facing *see* **face**.

facsimile [fak'siməli] *nc* (*formal*) an exact copy: *A facsimile of the medal was put on show at the museum*; (*attrib*) *a facsimile edition of an eighteenth-century book.*

fact [fakt] **1** *nc* something known or believed to be true: *Give me the facts, and I shall make my own conclusions*; *It is a fact that smoking is a danger to health.* **2** *nu* reality: *fact or fiction*; *It is difficult to work out how much of what she says is fact.*
factual ['faktʃuəl] *adj* of or containing facts: *He tried to give a factual account of what had happened*; *His account was factual.* **'factually** *adv.*
after, before the fact *see* **accessory**.
as a matter of fact, in 'fact, (*formal*) **in point of fact** actually or really: *I didn't see him – as a matter of fact I didn't try*; *She doesn't like him much – in fact I think she hates him!*; *He hoped to finish the work last week but in point of fact he did not.*
the 'fact of the matter the basic truth: *The fact of the matter is that he does not like work.*

faction ['fakʃən] *nc* a group of people (within a larger group) who have the same opinions, intentions *etc*: *There were various factions within the (political) party.*

factor ['faktə] *nc* **1** something, *eg* a fact, which has to be taken into account or which affects the course of events: *There are various factors to be considered before you change your job*; *An increase in salary was the major factor in his decision not to leave.* **2** (*math*) a number which exactly divides into another: *3 is a factor of 6.*

factory ['faktəri] *nc* a workshop where manufactured articles are made in large numbers: *There is a huge car factory employing thousands of men just outside the town*; (*attrib*) *a factory worker.*

factotum [fak'toutəm] *nc* (*formal*: *often facet*) a person employed to do all kinds of work: *The new girl in the office is treated as a general factotum.*

factual *see* **fact**.

faculty ['fakəlti] *nc* **1** (*formal*) a power of the mind: *the faculty of reason.* **2** a natural power of the body: *the faculty of hearing*; *She is a very old lady but she still has all her faculties.* **3** (*formal*) ability or skill: *He has a faculty for saying the right thing at the right time.* **4** (*often with cap*) a section of a university: *the Faculty of Arts/Science.* **5** (*esp Amer*: *often with cap*) all the teachers within these departments: *a meeting of the Faculty and students.*

fad [fad] *nc* (*derog*) an (unimportant) like or dislike which is not strong or long lasting: *His interest in motorbikes is not permanent – it's only a fad.*
'faddy *adj* (*inf or derog*) having fads; fussy: *That child is very faddy about what he eats*; *a faddy child.*

fade [feid] *vti* to (make something) lose strength, colour, loudness *etc*: *The flowers fade in autumn*; *The sun will fade the curtains*; *The noise gradually faded* (*away*); *Hope of finding the child alive is fading rapidly.*
fade out *vt sep, vi* (of sound, a film picture *etc*) to (cause to) grow faint and disappear: *The last scene of the film faded out and the lights came on*; *The radio engineer faded out the sound too early.*

faeces, (*Amer*) **feces** ['fi:si:z] *n pl* solid waste matter passed out from the body: *Dogs' faeces in parks may cause disease.*
See also **defecate**.

fag [fag] *nc* **1** (*no pl*: *inf*) hard or boring work: *What a fag!*; *It was a real fag to clean the whole house.* **2** (*sl*: *esp Brit*) a cigarette: *I'm dying for a fag – have you got one?* **3** (*Brit inf*) in certain schools, a junior schoolboy who acts as a servant for a senior one. **4** (*Amer sl*) a homosexual. – *v* – *pt, ptp* **fagged** – *vi* **1** (*inf*: *often with* **away**) to work hard: *He fagged* (*away*) *at it for hours.* **2** (*Brit inf*) to be a fag (*def 3*): *He fagged for the head boy.*
fag-end *nc* (*inf*) the small, useless piece of a cigarette that remains after it has been smoked: *The ashtray was full of 'fag-ends*; (*fig*) *He only managed to hear the ˌfag-'end of the conversation.*
fagged out (*inf*) very tired: *I'm completely fagged out after that long walk.*

faggot, (*Amer*) **fagot** ['fagət] *nc* (*old*) a bundle of sticks for burning.

Fahrenheit ['farənhait] *adj* (*often abbrev* **F** *when written*) as measured on a Fahrenheit thermometer: *fifty degrees Fahrenheit* (*50° F*).

Fahrenheit thermometer *nc* a thermometer which shows the temperature at which water freezes as 32° and the temperature at which it boils as 212°.

fail [feil] **1** *vti* to be unsuccessful (in): *They failed in their attempt to climb the mountain; She failed to win the prize; I failed my examination.* **2** *vi* to break down or cease to work: *The brakes failed and the car crashed into a wall.* **3** *vti* to be insufficient or not enough: *His courage failed (him).* **4** *vt* (in a test, examination *etc*) to reject (a candidate); to declare that he or she is not good enough: *The examiner failed half the class.* **5** *vt* to disappoint: *They did not fail him in their support; She felt she had failed her parents by not getting into University.* **6** *vi* (*inf*) to lose strength: *She has been failing since her eightieth birthday.*

'failing *nc* a fault or weakness: *He may have his failings, but he has always treated his children well.* – *prep* if (something) fails or is lacking: *Failing his help, we shall have to try something else.*

'failure [-jə] **1** *nu* the state or act of failing: *She was upset by her failure in the exam; He died of heart failure caused by too much exertion; failure of the electricity supply.* **2** *nc* an unsuccessful person or thing: *He felt he was a failure as his first novel had been badly reviewed; The party was a failure – only ten people came to it.* **3** *ncu* inability, refusal *etc* to do something: *His failure to reply was very worrying.*

without fail definitely or certainly: *I shall do it tomorrow without fail.*

See also **fallible, unfailing.**

faint [feint] *adj* **1** lacking in strength, brightness, courage *etc*: *The sound of shouting grew faint; A faint light shone in the distance;* (*liter*) *A faint heart will never succeed.* **2** (*usu pred*) physically weak and about to lose consciousness: *Suddenly he felt faint.* – *vi* to lose consciousness: *She fainted from lack of blood; She fainted on hearing the news of his death.* – *nc* loss of consciousness: *Her faint gave everybody a fright.*

'faintly *adv* **1** in a faint manner: *A light shone faintly in the distance; She spoke faintly.* **2** slightly; rather: *She looked faintly surprised.*

'faintness *nu.*

,faint-'hearted *adj* (*formal or liter*) lacking in courage; not brave: *He was too faint-hearted to rescue the princess; a faint-hearted youth.*

fair[1] [feə] *adj* **1** light-coloured; with light-coloured hair and skin: *She has fair hair; Scandinavian people are often fair; She's a very fair child.* **2** just; not favouring one side: *a fair judgement; a fair judge; You must be fair to both sides; It is not fair to give more to him than to me.* **3** (of weather) fine; without rain: *I hope it will be fair tomorrow for the garden party; a fair afternoon.* **4** quite good; neither bad nor good: *His work is only fair; He made a fair attempt at the task.* **5** (*inf*: *attrib*) quite big, long *etc*: *Their house is a fair size; It's a fair journey to the nearest town.* **6** (*liter*) beautiful: *a fair maiden.* **'fairness** *nu.*

'fairly *adv* **1** justly; honestly: *He was fairly judged.* **2** quite or rather: *The work was fairly hard.*

'fairway *nc* **1** (on a golf-course) the broad path of short grass which stretches from the tee to the green. **2** the channel of deep water used by ships along a river into a harbour *etc.*

by fair means or foul in any possible way, just or unjust: *I intend to win by fair means or foul!*

fair and square (*inf*) **1** straight or directly: *He hit him fair and square on the chin.* **2** honest and open: *The deal was completely fair and square.*

fair enough *interj* (*inf*) expressing agreement or approval, or admitting that someone has acted or spoken reasonably *etc*: *Fair enough, you're probably right.*

fair play honest treatment; an absence of cheating, biased actions *etc*: *He's not involved in the contest – he's only here to see fair play.*

the fair sex (*usu facet*) women.

See also **unfair.**

fair[2] [feə] *nc* **1** a collection of entertainments (roundabouts, sideshows *etc*) that travels from town to town: *She won a large doll at the fair.* **2** (*usu old*) a large market held at fixed times: *A fair used to be held here every spring.* **3** an exhibition of goods from different countries, firms *etc*: *a trade fair.* **4** a sale of goods for charities *etc*: *They held a Christmas fair in aid of charity.*

fairy ['feəri] *nc* **1** (*myth*) an imaginary creature in the form of a very small (often winged) human, with magical powers: *Small children often believe in fairies;* (*attrib*) *the fairy people.* **2** (*Brit sl*) a homosexual.

'fairy light *nc* a small coloured light used for decoration: *the fairy lights on the Christmas tree.*

'fairy-story *nc* **1** an old, or children's, story of fairies, magic *etc*: *The child was given a book of fairy-stories.* **2** (*fig*) an untrue statement; a lie: *I don't want to hear any fairy-stories about where you've been!*

'fairy-tale *nc* a fairy-story: *He was a collector of fairy-tales; The child used to tell fairy-tales about her family;* (*attrib*) *the fairy-tale appearance of the countryside covered in snow.*

faith [feiθ] **1** *nu* trust or belief: *He had faith in his ability to mend things.* **2** *ncu* religious belief: *Years of hardship had not caused him to lose his faith.* **3** *nu* loyalty to one's promise: *to keep/break faith with someone.*

'faithful *adj* **1** loyal and true; not changing: *His wife remained faithful to him throughout his years in prison; a faithful friend; He will be faithful to his promise.* **2** true or exact: *He gave me a faithful account of what had happened.* **'faithfully** *adv.* **'faithfulness** *nu.*

'faithless *adj* (*liter*) **1** without faith: *a faithless nation.* **2** unfaithful; disloyal: *a faithless wife.* **'faithlessness** *nu.*

in (all) good faith sincerely: *She made the offer in good faith.*

yours faithfully *see* **yours.**

See also **fidelity, unfaithful.**

fake [feik] *nc* (*inf*) **1** a worthless imitation (*esp* intended to deceive); a forgery: *That picture is not a Picasso – it's only a fake.* **2** a person who pretends to be something he is not: *He pretended to be a doctor, but he was a fake.* – *adj* **1** made in imitation of something more valuable, *esp* with the intention of deceiving: *fake diamonds; These diamonds are fake.* **2** (*usu attrib*) pretending to be something one is not: *a fake clergyman.* – *vt* to pretend or imitate in order to deceive: *Could you fake your brother's signature?*

falcon ['foːlkən, (*Amer*) 'fal-] *nc* a kind of bird of prey sometimes used for hunting.

'falconry *nu* the training and use of falcons for hunting.

fall [foːl] – *pt* **fell** [fel]: *ptp* **'fallen** – *vi* **1** to go down from a higher level *usu* unintentionally:

The apple fell from the tree; The rain was falling steadily; (fig) Her eye fell on an old book. **2** (*often with* **over**) to go down to the ground *etc* from an upright position, *usu* by accident: *He fell into the stream; She fell (over) and hurt her knee; A tree has fallen across the road.* **3** to become lower or less: *The temperature is falling; The wind fell; Prices have fallen recently.* **4** to happen or occur: *Easter falls early this year.* **5** to enter a certain state or condition: *He fell asleep; She fell silent; He fell ill; They fell in love.* **6** to hang down: *Her hair fell to her waist.* **7** to be captured, defeated, or suddenly lose (political) domination: *Rome finally fell to* (= was captured by) *the Goths; The Conservative Government fell in 1974; When did Khrushchev/Nkrumah fall (from power)?* **8** (*liter euph*) to die in battle: *Hugh fell on Flanders Field.* **9** (*formal: only with* **it** *as subject*) to come as one's duty *etc*: *It falls to me to take care of the children.* – *See also* **fall** *in phrases below.* – **1** *nc* the act of falling from a higher or upright position *etc*: *He had a fall and broke his leg; There has been a fall in temperature.* **2** *nc* (a quantity of) something that has fallen: *a fall of snow; The entrance to the cave was blocked by a fall of rock.* **3** *nu* capture or (political) defeat: *the fall of Rome; the fall of Hitler.* **4** *ncu* (*Amer*) the autumn: *Leaves change colour in the fall; We are going to Canada in the fall* (= the fall of this year); *in the fall of 1951; We visited him last fall* (= in the fall of last year); (*attrib*) *fall colours* (= the colours of leaves in fall); *Fall is my favourite season; We have had a number of very cold falls recently.*

falls *n pl* (*often found with cap in place-names*) a waterfall: *Niagara Falls; the Falls of Clyde; These falls are used to provide electric power.*

'**fallout** *nu* radioactive dust from a nuclear explosion *etc.*

his, her *etc* **face fell** he, she *etc* looked suddenly disappointed: *When she heard she had lost the game her face fell.*

fall apart *vi* to break into pieces: *My bicycle is falling apart.*

fall away *vi* **1** to become less in number: *The crowd began to fall away.* **2** to slope downwards: *The ground fell away steeply.*

fall back *vi* to move back or stop coming forward: *The men following him fell back as he turned to face them.*

fall back on *vt fus* (*inf*) to use, or to go to for help, finally when everything else has been tried: *Whatever happens you have your father's money to fall back on.*

fall behind **1** *vi, vt fus* to be slower than (someone else): *Hurry up! You're falling behind (the others); (fig) He is falling behind in his schoolwork.* **2** *vi* (*with* **with**) to become late in regular payment, letter-writing *etc*: *Don't fall behind with the rent!*

fall down *vi* (*sometimes with* **on**) (*inf*) to fail (in): *That's the point where his plans fall down – he hasn't said what we're to do if he's out; He's falling down on his job.*

fall flat **1** (of a person) to fall completely to the ground *eg* so that one is lying horizontally. **2** (*inf*) (*esp* of jokes *etc*) to fail completely or to have no effect: *His booby trap fell flat; His attempt at humour fell flat.*

'**fall for** *vt fus* (*inf*) **1** to be deceived by (something): *I made up a story to explain why I had not been at work and he fell for it.* **2** to fall in love with (someone): *He has fallen for your sister.*

fall in with *vt fus* **1** to join with (someone) for company: *On the way home we fell in with some friends.* **2** to agree with (a plan, idea *etc*): *They fell in with our suggestion.*

fall off *vi* to become smaller in number or amount: *Theatre audiences often fall off during the summer.*

'**fall on**/(*formal*) **upon** *vt fus* to attack: *He fell on the old man and beat him; (fig) They fell hungrily upon the food.*

fall on one's feet *see* **foot**.

fall out *vi* (*sometimes with* **with**) (*inf*) to quarrel: *I have fallen out with my brother; She and her friends are always falling out.*

fall over oneself to be very eager to go to a lot of trouble (to do something): *All the men fell over themselves to find her a chair.*

fall short (*often with* **of**) to be not enough or not good enough *etc*: *The money we have falls short of what we need; He was always trying to be as capable as she thought he was, and always falling short.*

fall through *vi* (of plans *etc*) to fail or come to nothing: *We had planned to go to Paris, but the plans fell through.*

fall to *vi* (*old*) to begin enthusiastically, *esp* eating: *The food was put on the table and they fell to eagerly.*

fallacy ['faləsi] *ncu* (*formal*) a wrong idea or belief, *usu* one that is generally believed to be true; false reasoning: *The belief that women are always weaker than men is just a fallacy; Did you notice the fallacy in his argument?*

fallacious [fə'leiʃəs] *adj* (*formal*) wrong, mistaken or showing false reasoning: *a fallacious argument; It is fallacious to believe that all women want to have children.*

fallen *see* **fall**.

fallible ['faləbl] *adj* (*formal: usu pred*) able or likely to make mistakes: *Human beings are fallible.* *See also* **fail, infallible**.

fallout *see* **fall**.

fallow ['falou] *adj* (of land) left to its own natural growth and not planted with seeds: *We will let this field lie fallow for a year; fallow fields.*

false [fo:ls] *adj* **1** not true; not correct: *He made a false statement to the police; Do you think his story is false or true?; When I first met him I got a totally false impression of the sort of man he is; He got the job under false pretences* (= by telling lies and deceit). **2** not genuine; intended to deceive: *He has a false passport; I think his documents are false.* **3** (*usu attrib*) artificial: *false teeth.* **4** (*formal*) not loyal: *false friends; His wife has never been false to him.*

'**falsehood** *ncu* (*formal*) (the telling of) a lie: *I refuse to believe that he is lying – he is incapable of (uttering a) falsehood.*

'**falsify** [-fai] *vt* (*formal*) to make false: *He falsified the accounts.* ˌ**falsifi'cation** [-fi-] *ncu.*

'**falsity** *ncu* (*formal*): *The police discovered the falsity of his statement.*

false alarm *nc* a warning of something which does not in fact happen: *We were told that there was a bomb in that parcel but it was a false alarm; The expectant mother thought that she had gone into labour but it was a false alarm – it was another month before the baby was born.*

false start *nc* **1** in a race, a start which is declared not valid and has to be repeated *eg* because a runner has left the starting-point before the correct signal has been given: *The runner was disqualified after three false starts.* **2** a beginning in some activity which is unsuccessful and so has to be repeated: *After several false starts he eventually made a success of his business.*

falsetto [foːl'setou] – *pl* **fal'settos** – *ncu* an unnaturally high (singing) voice in men, or a man with such a voice: *He was singing in falsetto; He is a falsetto;* (*attrib*) *a falsetto voice;* (*attrib*) *He spoke in high falsetto tones which irritated everyone.* – *adv* with a falsetto voice: *He sings falsetto.*

falsification, falsify, falsity *see* **false**.

falter ['foːltə] **1** *vi* to stumble or hesitate: *She walked the whole length of the top of the wall without faltering.* **2** *vti* to speak with hesitation: *His voice faltered several times while he was reading aloud the letter about his mother's death; He managed to falter out a few words of thanks although he was obviously embarrassed.* **'faltering** *adj.* **'falteringly** *adv.*

fame [feim] *nu* the quality of being well-known: *His novels about country life brought him fame.*

'famous *adj* well-known (for good or worthy reasons): *He is famous for his strength; She is a famous author.*

'famously *adv* (*old inf*) very well: *She is getting on famously with her new job; The two children got on famously together.*

See also **infamous**.

familiar [fə'miljə] *adj* **1** (*neg* **un-**) well-known: *The house was familiar to him; I don't really remember where I have seen him before but he looks very familiar (to me); The old lady was a familiar sight in the village.* **2** (*pred: with* **with**) knowing about: *Are you familiar with the plays of Shakespeare?* **3** (*formal often derog*) too friendly: *You are much too familiar with my wife!; His familiar behaviour annoys me – I don't know him at all well.*

fa'miliarly *adv* (*often derog*) in a familiar, *esp* too friendly, manner: *She thought he treated her rather familiarly.*

fa,mili'arity [-li'a-] **1** *nu* the state of being familiar: *I was surprised by his familiarity with our way of life.* **2** *nc* (*often derog*) an act of (too) friendly behaviour: *You must not allow such familiarities from junior members of staff.*

fa'miliarize, -ise *vt* (*with* **with**: *formal*) to make something well known to (someone): *You must familiarize yourself with the Highway Code before you take your driving test; Have they familiarized you with the rules of our club?* **fa,miliari'zation, -s-** *nu.*

family ['faməli] **1** *nc or n pl* a man, his wife and their children: *These houses were built for families; That family is unpopular in the district; The (members of the) Smith family are all very athletic;* (*attrib*) *a family holiday.* **2** *nc* a group of people related to each other, including cousins, grandchildren *etc*: *He comes from a wealthy family; His family disapprove of her;* (*attrib*) *the family home.* **3** *ncu* the children of a man and his wife: *When I get married I should like a large family; Have you got any family?* **4** *nc* a group of plants, animals, languages *etc* that are connected in some way: *The ash is a tree of the olive family.*

family man *nc* **1** a man with a wife and children. **2** a man who likes very much being at home with his family.

family planning *nu* controlling or limiting the number of children that people have *esp* by using a means of contraception: *Some religions used to disapprove of family planning;* (*attrib*) *She went to a family planning clinic for advice on contraceptives.*

family tree *nc* (a plan showing) a person's ancestors (and sometimes his descendants): *If you want to know the relationship of the present Queen of Britain to the Stewart kings you must consult her family tree.*

famine ['famin] *ncu* (a) great lack or shortage *esp* of food: *Many people died during the wheat famine; Some parts of the world suffer regularly from famine.*

famished ['famiʃt] *adj* (*inf: usu pred*) very hungry: *I was famished after my long walk.*

famous, famously *see* **fame**.

fan[1] [fan] *nc* **1** a flat instrument held in the hand and waved to direct a current of air across the face in hot weather, *esp* one made of flat sticks (of wood, ivory *etc*) joined at one end, that can be spread out into a shape like a half circle: *Ladies used to carry fans to keep themselves cool.* **2** a mechanical instrument causing a current of air: *She has had a fan fitted in the kitchen for extracting smells;* (*attrib*) *a fan heater.* – *v* – *pt, ptp* **fanned** – *vt* **1** to cool with a fan or as if with a fan: *She sat in the corner, fanning herself (with a folded newspaper).* **2** to increase or strengthen (as if by blowing on a fire): *They fanned the fire until it burst into flames;* (*liter*) *His remark fanned her anger.* – *See also* **fan out** *below.*

'fanlight *nc* a window above a door, *esp* one shaped like a half circle.

fan out *vi, vt sep* to spread out in the shape of a fan: *He fanned out the photographs in his hand; The crowd fanned out across the square.*

fan[2] [fan] *nc* an enthusiastic admirer of a sport, hobby or well-known person: *I'm a great fan of his; The train was full of football fans;* (*attrib*) *The filmstar replies personally to all her fan mail/letters* (= letters *etc* sent by admirers).

fanatic [fə'natik] *nc* (*often derog*) a person who is (too) enthusiastic about something: *a religious fanatic; a fanatic about health-foods.*

fa'natic(al) *adj* (*often derog*) (too) enthusiastic: *He is quite fanatical about physical exercise; a fanatical follower of football.* **fa'natically** *adv.*

fa'naticism [-sizəm] *nu* (*formal: derog*) (too) great enthusiasm, *esp* about religion: *Fanaticism is the cause of most religious hatred.*

fancy ['fansi] **1** *nc* (*inf*) a sudden (often unexpected) liking or desire: *The pregnant woman had many peculiar fancies.* – *See also* **take a fancy to, take one's fancy** *below.* **2** *nu* (*usu liter*) the power of the mind to imagine things: *She had a tendency to indulge in flights of fancy.* **3** *nc* (*esp liter*) something imagined: *He had a sudden fancy that he could see Spring approaching.* – *adj* (*inf*) decorated; not plain: *fancy cakes; fancy wallpaper; That pattern is too fancy for me.* – *vt* (not used with **is, was** *etc* and **-ing**) **1** (*inf*) to like the idea of having or doing something: *I fancy a cup of tea; I don't fancy living in that cold house!* **2** (*formal*) to think or have a certain feeling or impression (that): *I fancied that you were angry; I fancy I know the man you mean.* **3** (*sl*) to have a strong sexual interest in (a person): *He fancies her a lot.* – *See also* **fancy oneself** *below.*

'fancier *nc* (*in cmpds*) a person whose hobby is keeping animals, birds *etc* of a particular kind: *a pigeon-fancier.*

'fanciful *adj* **1** inclined to have fancies, *esp* strange, unreal ideas: *She's a very fanciful girl;*

She is very fanciful. **2** imaginary or unreal: *He has a very fanciful idea of the way we live; That idea is rather fanciful.* **'fancifully** *adv.*

fancy dress *ncu* clothes representing a particular character, nationality, historical period *etc*: *He went to the party in fancy dress;* (*attrib*) *a fancy-dress party.*

'fancy oneself *v refl* **1** to think of oneself (as being, or as being likely to be, good at a particular thing): *She always fancied herself as an actress; He fancied himself in the rôle of organizer.* **2** (*derog sl*) to have an (unjustifiably) high opinion of oneself *esp* of one's attractiveness: *He's good-looking, but he fancies himself.*

take a fancy to to become fond of, often suddenly or unexpectedly: *He bought that house because his wife took a fancy to it; That child has certainly taken a fancy to you!*

take one's fancy to be liked or wanted by (someone): *When my wife goes shopping she just buys anything that takes her fancy.*

fanfare ['fanfeə] *nc* a short piece of music played by trumpets *etc* at the entry of a king or queen during a ceremony *etc.*

fang [faŋ] *nc* **1** a long pointed tooth *esp* of a fierce animal: *The wolf bared its fangs.* **2** the poison-tooth of a snake.

fanlight *see* **fan**.

fantasy ['fantəsi], (*old*) **'phantasy 1** *nc* an imaginary (*esp* not realistic) scene, story *etc*: *She was always having fantasies about becoming rich and famous;* (*attrib*) *She lived in a fantasy world.* **2** *nu* ideas not based on reality: *She was unable to make plans without indulging in fantasy.*

fantastic [fan'tastik] *adj* **1** (*esp attrib*) unbelievable and like a fantasy: *She told me some fantastic story about her father being a Grand Duke!* **2** (*inf*) wonderful; very good: *You look fantastic in those clothes!; He gave me a fantastic present.*

fan'tastically *adv* very; to an unbelievable extent: *She's fantastically beautiful; He earns a fantastically high salary.*

far [fa:] *adv* **1** (*usu in questions or in negative sentences*) indicating distance, progress *etc*: *How far is it from here to his house?; How far did you walk today?; We had not gone very far when he passed us; We cannot get very far in this project without some help.* **2** (*usu with adv or prep*) at or to a long way away: *He went far away/off; far into the distance; far above in the sky.* **3** very much: *He was a far better swimmer than his friend was; She is far more beautiful than her sister.* – *adj* **1** distant; a long way away: *a far country; His house is not far from here.* – *See also* **far from** *below.* **2** (*attrib*) more distant (*usu* of two things): *the far side of the moon; He lives on the far side of the lake.*

farther, farthest *see* **further**.

'faraway *adj* (*attrib*) **1** (*liter*) distant: *faraway countries.* **2** not paying attention; dreamy: *She had a faraway look in her eyes.*

ˌfar-'fetched *adj* (*sometimes derog*) very unlikely: *a far-fetched story; I find his account of what happened somewhat far-fetched.*

ˌfar-'flung *adj* (*liter*) extending over a great distance: *the far-flung empire.*

ˌfar-'reaching *adj* having, or likely to have, an effect on a lot of other things: *The government have made many far-reaching decisions; His new plans for the future of the company are more far-reaching than was at first realized.*

ˌfar-'sighted *adj* **1** being aware of what is likely to happen in the future and being prepared for it: *She was far-sighted and had arranged to leave the country should war break out.* **2** showing this quality: *a far-sighted plan.* **3** able to see things that are (quite) far away more easily than things that are near: *Both his children are near-sighted although he is far-sighted.*

as 'far as 1 to the place or point mentioned: *We walked as far as the lake.* **2** (*also* **so 'far as**) as great a distance as: *He did not walk as far as his friends.* **3** (*also* **so 'far as**) to the extent that: *As far as I know he is well but I haven't seen him for a long time; As far as we can judge she is quite efficient but she hasn't worked here very long.*

by 'far by a large amount: *She is the best teacher we have by far; They have by far the largest family in the village.*

far and away by a very great amount: *He is far and away the cleverest boy in the class!*

ˌfar ˌbe it from 'me (to) (*inf: usu facet*) I do not like (to): *Far be it from me to ask embarrassing questions, but I must find out the facts.*

a far cry (from) a long way from; very different from: *The conditions he's living in are a far cry from what he is used to.*

'far from 1 not only not but; instead of: *Far from liking him, I detest him; Far from being best friends, they are bitter enemies.* **2** not at all: *His work is far from* (*being*) satisfactory.

go as/so far as, go too far *see* **go**.

in so far as *see* **in**.

so far 1 until now: *So far we have been quite successful but I am not sure about the future.* **2** up to a certain point: *We can get so far but no further on this project without more help; Without more information we can progress only so far.*

so far as *see* **as far as** *above.*

farce [fa:s] **1** *ncu* a (kind of) comic play in which both the characters and the events shown are improbable and ridiculous: *He is well known as a writer of farce; The play is a classic farce.* **2** *nc* (*fig*) any funny or stupid situation in real life: *The meeting was an absolute farce – nobody knew what we were supposed to be discussing.*

farcical ['fa:sikəl] *adj* completely ridiculous, and therefore *usu* humorous: *The whole idea was farcical; It is farcical to think of trying to get into university with so few qualifications.*

fare [feə] **1** *nc* the price of a journey on a train, bus, ship *etc*: *He climbed on the bus, paid his fare and sat down.* **2** *nc* (*formal*) a paying passenger in a hired vehicle, *esp* in a taxi: *The taxi-driver was asked by the police where his last fare got out.* **3** *nu* (*formal or liter*) food: *simple fare.* – *vi* (*formal*) to do or get on (well, badly *etc*): *How did you fare in the examination?*

farewell [feə'wel] *nc* an act of saying goodbye: *They said their farewells at the station;* (*attrib*) *a farewell dinner.* – *interj* (*old or liter*) goodbye: *'Farewell for ever!' she cried.*

farm [fa:m] *nc* **1** an area of land, including buildings, used for growing crops, breeding and keeping cows, sheep, pigs *etc*: *Much of England is good agricultural land and there are many farms.* **2** the farmer's house and the buildings near it in such a place: *At the farm they gave us bed and breakfast;* (*attrib*) *a farm kitchen.* **3** a place where particular animals are bred and kept: *a fish farm; a mink farm.* – *vti* to cultivate (the land) in order to grow crops, breed and keep animals *etc*: *He* *farms (5 000 acres) in Yorkshire.* – *See also* **farm out** *below.*

'farmer *nc* the owner or tenant of a farm who works on the land *etc*: *How many farmworkers does that farmer employ?*

'farming *nu* the business of owning or running a farm: *There is a lot of money involved in farming*; (*attrib*) *the farming communities of Wales.*

'farmhouse *nc* the house in which a farmer lives.

'farmstead [-sted] *nc* (*formal*) a farmhouse and the other buildings near it on a farm: *We could see the farmstead at the bottom of the valley.*

'farmyard *nc* the open area surrounded by the farm buildings: *There were several hens loose in the farmyard*; (*attrib*) *farmyard animals.*

farm out *vt sep* (*inf*) to give (work for which one is responsible) to others to do: *If the firm has a lot of extra orders, we usually farm them out to other companies*; *He farms out work to other people.*

farrier ['fariə] *nc* **1** a man who shoes horses. **2** (*old*) a man who does this and also treats horses' illnesses.

farther, farthest *see* **further**.

farthing ['fa:ðiŋ] *nc* (*hist*) **1** one quarter of an old penny (¼d). **2** a coin of this value.

fascinate ['fasineit] *vt* to charm; to attract or interest very strongly: *She was fascinated by the strange clothes and customs of the country people.*

'fascinating *adj* very charming, attractive or interesting: *a fascinating story*; *a fascinating young lady*; *I found his story fascinating.*

ˌfasci'nation 1 *nu* the act of fascinating or state of being fascinated: *You should have seen the look of fascination on the children's faces as they watched the conjuror.* **2** *ncu* the power of fascinating or something that has this: *Old books have/hold a fascination for him*; *the fascination of a crossword puzzle*; *the fascinations of the fairground.*

Fascism ['faʃizəm] *nu* a nationalistic and anti-Communist system of government like that of Italy 1922–43, where all aspects of society are controlled by the state and all criticism or opposition is suppressed.

'fascist *adj* (*often with cap*: *sometimes derog loosely*) of or supporting Fascism: *a Fascist government.* – *nc* (*often with cap*: *sometimes derog loosely*) a member or supporter of a Fascist government or philosophy: *He is a Fascist*; *The managing director is a real fascist!*

fashion ['faʃən] **1** *ncu* the style and design of clothes: *Are you interested in fashion?*; (*attrib*) *She is the fashion correspondent for an important newspaper.* **2** *nc* the way of behaving, dressing *etc* which is popular at a certain time: *Fashions in music and art are always changing.* **3** *nc* (*formal*) a way of doing something: *She spoke in a very strange fashion.* – *vt* (*liter*) to make or form: *He fashioned a toy from/out of a piece of wood*; *She fashioned the clay into a bowl.*

'fashionable *adj* (*neg* **un-**) following, or in keeping with, the newest style of dress, way of living *etc*: *a fashionable woman*; *a fashionable part of town*; *a fashionable dress*; *That style of dress is no longer fashionable.* **'fashionably** *adv.*

after a fashion in a way, but not very well: *He can speak French after a fashion.*

after the fashion (*formal*) in the style of or in imitation (of): *lines written after the fashion of the Romantic poets.*

all the fashion very fashionable: *Long skirts were all the fashion that year.*

be in, come into fashion to be or become fashionable: *Tweed jackets are in fashion again*; *They have come into fashion again.*

be, go out of fashion to be or become not fashionable: *Long skirts are out of fashion at present*; *When did they go out of fashion?*

See also **old-fashioned**.

fast[1] [fa:st] *adj* **1** quick-moving: *a fast car*; *The pace is too fast for me.* **2** quick: *a fast worker*; *Our new workers are very fast.* **3** (*inf usu derog*) inclined to start sexual relations after only a short acquaintance with a person: *He has a reputation for being rather fast*; *fast women.* **4** (*pred*) (of a clock, watch *etc*) showing a time in advance of the correct time: *My watch is five minutes fast.* – *adv* quickly: *She speaks so fast I can't understand her.*

'fastness *nu* quickness; speed. – *See also* **fast**[3].

fast[2] [fa:st] *vi* to go without food, *esp* for religious or medical reasons: *Muslims fast during the festival of Ramadan*; *She had to fast for twelve hours before her operation.* – *nc* a time or act of fasting: *He has just finished two days' fast.* **'fasting** *nu.*

fast[3] [fa:st] *adj* **1** (of a colour) fixed; that does not disappear when washed: *If the colours are fast, you can wash the shirt in hot water*; *clothes of fast colours.* **2** (*formal or liter*: *usu pred*) made firm; fixed: *He made fast* (= tied) *the end of the rope to a tree*; *Is the window fast?* (= closed firmly or locked). – *adv* (*liter*) firmly: *He stood fast against the enemy.*

'fastness 1 *nu* (of a colour) the quality of being fixed: *I can't guarantee the fastness of the blue in this dress.* **2** *nc* (*arch*) a castle or fortress. – *See also* **fast**[1].

fast and loose *see* **play fast and loose** *under* **play**.

fast asleep completely asleep: *The baby fell fast asleep in my arms.*

hard-and-fast *see* **hard**.

fasten ['fa:sn] *vt* to fix or join (together): *Fasten the gate!*; *She could not fasten the zip of her dress*; *She fastened a flower to the front of her dress*; (*fig*) *He fastened his eyes intently upon her face.*

'fastener *nc* something that fastens things (together): *The dress has a zip-fastener*; *The fasteners on this bag are very stiff.*

'fasten on/(*formal*) **upon** *vt fus* to seize on or fix one's attention on: *He fastened (up)on her last remark.*

See also **unfasten**.

fastidious [fə'stidiəs, (*Amer*) fa-] *adj* (*sometimes derog*) very critical and difficult to please: *She is so fastidious about her food that she will not eat in a restaurant*; *a fastidious old lady.* **fa'stidiously** *adv.* **fa'stidiousness** *nu.*

fat [fat] **1** *nu* an oily substance made by the bodies of animals and by some plants: *This meat has got a lot of fat on it.* **2** *ncu* a kind of such substance, used *esp* for cooking: *There are several good cooking fats on the market.* – *adj* **1** having a lot of fat on one's body; large, heavy and round in shape: *He was a very fat child*; *He is too fat.* **2** (*inf facet*) large or abundant: *His business made a fat profit*; (*ironic*) *A fat lot of good that is* (= That is no good at all).

'fatness *nu*: *His fatness made him unhealthy.*

'fatted *adj* (*formal or liter*) made fat: *the fatted calf* (*see* **kill the fatted calf** *below*).

'fatten *vti* (*often with* **up**) to make or become fat: *They are fattening up a chicken to eat at Christmas*; *That pig is fattening up well.*

'fatty *adj* containing, or like, fat: *This meat is very fatty; a fatty substance.* **'fattiness** *nu.*

'fat-head *nc* (*derog sl*) a stupid person.

kill the fatted calf to have a great celebration to welcome someone, *esp* someone whom one has not seen for a long time.

the fat of the land the best and richest part of anything: *He lives off the fat of the land* (= luxuriously).

the fat's in the fire trouble has been started off (by something happening): *The fat's in the fire now that he's found out about his wife's affair with a neighbour.*

fatal ['feitl] *adj* **1** causing death: *a fatal accident; His injuries proved fatal.* **2** (*sometimes facet*) disastrous: *She made the fatal mistake of forgetting to invite him to her party.* **'fatally** *adv.*

fatality [fə'taləti] *nc* (an accident causing) death: *There are always a great many fatalities on the roads during bad weather.*

See also **fate**.

fate [feit] **1** *nu* (*sometimes with cap*) the supposed power that controls events: *Fate prevented us from ever meeting again; By a strange stroke of fate we met again at Milan airport; Who knows what fate has in store* (= waiting for us in the future)? **2** *nc* a destiny or doom, *eg* death: *Is it my fate to remain in the same office for the rest of my life?; A terrible fate awaited her; He went out bravely to meet his fate.* **3** *nc* (*often with cap: myth*) one of the divine beings who control man's birth, life and death: *He thought that his last hour had come, but fortunately the Fates had decreed otherwise.*

'fatalism *nu* the belief that fate controls everything, and man cannot change it.

'fatalist *nc* a person who believes in fatalism: *He is a complete fatalist – he just accepts everything that happens to him.* **,fata'listic** *adj.*

'fated *adj* (*usu pred*) controlled or intended by fate: *He seemed fated to arrive late wherever he went.*

'fateful *adj* (*formal: attrib*) involving important decisions, results *etc*: *At last the fateful day arrived; a fateful decision.*

a fate worse than death (*inf: often facet*) a dreadful happening: *Having to eat her cooking for a whole week would be a fate worse than death!*

father ['fa:ðə] *nc* **1** a male parent, *esp* human: *Mr Smith is her father; She does not know who the father of her child is.* **2** (*with cap*) the title of a (*usu* Roman Catholic) priest: *I met Father Sullivan this morning.* **3** (*fig*) a person who begins, invents or first makes something: *King Alfred was the father of the English navy.* – *vt* (*formal*) to be the father of: *King Charles II fathered a great number of children.*

'fatherhood *nu* (*formal*) the state or condition of being a father: *Now that the children are older I am enjoying fatherhood.*

'fatherly *adj* like a father: *He showed a fatherly interest in his friend's child; Is his interest in her entirely fatherly?*

'father-in-law *nc* the father of one's wife or husband.

See also **paternal**.

fathom ['faðəm] *nc* (*naut*) a measure of depth of water (6 feet or 1·8 metres): *The water is 8 fathoms deep.* – *vt* (*formal or facet: fig*) to understand (a mystery *etc*): *I cannot fathom why she should have left home; I just cannot fathom it.*

See also **unfathomable**.

fatigue [fə'ti:g] **1** *nu* (*more formal than* **tiredness**) great tiredness (caused *esp* by hard work or effort): *The mountaineer was suffering from fatigue when he was rescued.* **2** *nu* (*tech*) (*esp* in metals) weakness caused by continual use: *This aircraft is showing signs of metal fatigue.* **3** *nc* (*mil: usu in pl*) a hard task given as punishment to soldiers *etc*: *The major put them all on fatigues.*

fa'tigued *adj* (*usu pred: more formal than* **tired**) made very tired: *He was fatigued by the constant questioning; If you get too fatigued your heart disease will get worse.*

fatted, fatten, fatty *see* **fat**.

fatuous ['fatjuəs] *adj* (*formal*) stupid: *He is always making fatuous remarks; That remark was utterly fatuous.*

'fatuously *adv*: *He smiled fatuously.*

faucet ['fo:sit] *nc* (*Amer*) a tap^2.

fault [fo:lt] *nc* **1** a mistake; something for which one is to blame: *I'm sorry – that was entirely my fault; The accident was your fault.* **2** an imperfection; something wrong: *There is a fault in this machine; a fault in his character.* **3** (*tech*) a crack in the rock surface of the earth: *A rift valley is a piece of land that has sunk between two faults in the earth's crust.* – *vt* (*formal: usu with neg*) to find fault with: *I couldn't fault him/his piano-playing.*

'faultless *adj* (*more formal than* **perfect**) without fault; perfect: *The dancer gave a faultless performance; Her performance was faultless.* **'faultlessly** *adv.*

'faulty *adj* (*usu* of something mechanical) not made or working correctly: *This watch is faulty; a faulty piece of machinery.*

at 'fault (*formal*) wrong or to blame: *She was at fault for letting him in to the house.*

find fault with (*more formal than* **criticize**) to criticize or complain of: *She is always finding fault with the way he eats.*

to a 'fault (*formal*) excessively; to too great an extent: *He was generous to a fault and embarrassed his friends by his lavish gifts.*

faun [fo:n] *nc* (*myth*) an imaginary creature, half man and half goat.

fauna ['fo:nə] *nu* (*tech*) the animals of a district or country as a whole: *He is very interested in South American fauna.*

See also **flora**.

faux pas [fou'pa:] – *pl* **,faux 'pas** [-z] – *nc* (*formal*) an embarrassing mistake: *I made a terrible faux pas when I asked about her husband – apparently he had just divorced her.*

favour, (*Amer*) **favor** ['feivə] **1** *nc* a kind action: *Will you do me a favour and lend me your car?* **2** *nu* (*formal*) kindness or approval: *She looked on him with great favour.* **3** *nu* (*formal*) preference or too much kindness: *By doing that he showed favour to the other side.* **4** *nu* (*formal*) a state of being approved of: *He was very much in favour with the Prime Minister.* **5** *nc* a gift, token, badge *etc*: *The favours of the team's supporters were red and white ribbons.* – *See also* **in favour of, in one's favour** *below.* – *vt* **1** to support or show preference for: *Which side do you favour?*; (*fig*) *Darkness favoured his escape.* **2** (*formal*) to give (someone) something as a favour: *The Duke favoured them with a short speech.* **3** (*inf*) to look like: *The baby favours his father.*

'favourable *adj* (*neg* **un-**) **1** showing approval: *a favourable reaction to his request; Was his reaction favourable or unfavourable?* **2** helpful or advantageous: *a favourable wind*; *Are conditions favourable?* **'favourably** *adv.*

'favourite [-rit] *adj* (*attrib*) best-liked; preferred: *my favourite teacher*; *his favourite city.* – *nc* **1** a person or thing that one likes best: *Of all his paintings that is my favourite*; *That song is one of my favourites*; *She was a great favourite of the King's.* **2** someone or something, *esp* a horse, expected to win: *It was a disappointing race – the favourite came in last.*

'favouritism [-ri-] *nu* (*formal*: *usu derog*) preferring or supporting one person *etc* more than another: *I can't be accused of favouritism – I voted for everyone!*

in 'favour of in support of: *I am in favour of higher pay.*

in one's favour to one's benefit or advantage: *The wind was in our favour.*

fawn[1] [fo:n] **1** *nc* a young deer. **2** *nu, adj* (of) its colour, a light yellowish brown: *a fawn sweater*; *Her sweater is light fawn.*

fawn[2] [fo:n] *vi* **1** (of dogs) to show affection (by wagging the tail, pawing, rolling over *etc*). **2** (*liter*: *derog*: *with* **upon**) to be too humble or to flatter (someone) in a servile way: *The courtiers fawned upon the king.*

fear [fiə] *ncu* (a) feeling of great worry or anxiety caused by the knowledge of danger: *The soldier tried not to show his fear when he saw the enemy*; *I can understand the mother's fears about her child's health*; *The child has no fear of water.* – *See also* **for fear of, in fear of** *below.* – (*more formal than* **to be afraid (of)**: *usu liter*) **1** *vti* to feel fear because of (something): *She feared her father when he was angry*; *I fear for my father's safety* (= I am worried because I think he is in danger). **2** *vt* to regret; to be sorry to say that: *I fear you will not be able to see him today*; *'Is the old man dying?' 'I fear so.'*

'fearful *adj* **1** (*more formal than* **frightened**) afraid: *She gave a fearful look towards the thunderclouds*; *She looked rather fearful as she walked through the dark wood.* **2** (*inf*) terrible: *The lion gave a fearful roar.* **3** (*inf*) very bad: *She made a fearful mistake*; *Her work is fearful!* **'fearfully** *adv.*

'fearless *adj* (*formal*) without fear; brave: *He is quite fearless about going to the dentist*; *a fearless soldier.* **'fearlessly** *adv.*

for 'fear of so as not to; so that he *etc* should not: *She would not go swimming for fear of catching a cold.*

in 'fear of in a state of being afraid of: *He lived in fear of his father finding out about the dent in the car.*

no fear *interj* (*inf*) not likely: *'Are you thinking of getting married?' 'No fear, I like being a bachelor.'*

there is not much fear of (*inf*) it is not likely that: *There's not much fear of him leaving the firm – he is too well paid to do that.*

feasible ['fi:zəbl] *adj* (*more formal than* **possible**) able to be done: *Is it feasible to do that?*; *That's a good idea but is it really feasible?*; *There is only one feasible solution to the problem.*

,feasi'bility *nu* (*formal*) possibility: *We must study the feasibility of building a new town in that area*; (*attrib*) *Have any feasibility studies been done?*

feast [fi:st] *nc* **1** a large and rich meal, *usu* eaten to celebrate some occasion: *The king invited them to a feast in the palace*; (*fig*) *The scene was a feast for the eyes.* **2** (*sometimes with cap*) a particular day on which some (*esp* religious) person or event is remembered and celebrated: *Today is the feast of St Stephen.* – **1** *vi* to eat (as if) at a feast: *We feasted all day on the best food and drink.* **2** *vt* (*formal*) to give (someone) a feast: *He feasted his friends generously.*

feat [fi:t] *nc* (*formal*) a very difficult thing to do: *feats of gymnastics*; *Arranging that business successfully was quite a feat.*

feather ['feðə] *nc* one of the things that grow from a bird's skin that form the covering of its body: *They cleaned the oil off the seagull's feathers.* – *vt* (*formal*) to line, cover or decorate with feathers: *The eagle feathers its nest with down from its own breast.*

'feathered *adj* (*attrib*): *a feathered hat.*

'feathery *adj* **1** (*usu attrib*) of, like, or covered in, a feather or feathers: *a feathery hat.* **2** (*fig*) soft and light: *a feathery touch*; *a feathery sponge cake*; *This sponge cake is really feathery.*

,feather'bed *nc* a *usu* soft bed the mattress of which is stuffed with feathers. – *v* – *pt, ptp* **,feather'bedded** –*vt* (*fig*) to pamper; to spoil by doing too much for: *He had featherbedded her for so long that she became absolutely dependent on him*; *The government featherbedded some industries for a time.*

'feather-brained *adj* (*inf*: *derog*) silly and foolish; frivolous: *a feather-brained young girl*; *She is feather-brained.*

a feather in one's cap (*fig*) something one can be proud of: *Winning the race was quite a feather in his cap.*

feather one's (own) nest (*derog*) to gain money for oneself or to make oneself rich while serving others in a position of trust: *All the time he has been a member of that committee he has been feathering his own nest.*

feature ['fi:tʃə] *nc* **1** a mark by which anything is known; a quality: *The use of bright colours is one of the features of his painting.* **2** (*often in pl*) one of the parts of one's face (eyes, nose *etc*): *She has very regular features.* **3** a special article in a newspaper: *'The Times' is doing a feature on holidays.* **4** the main film in a cinema programme *etc*: *The feature begins at 7.30*; (*attrib*) *a feature film.* – *vti* to give or have a part (*esp* an important one): *The economic problem featured in our last discussion*; *The Prime Minister featured among the politicians who attended the meeting*; *That film features the best of the British actresses.*

'featureless *adj* (*formal*) with no points of interest: *a dull, featureless landscape*; *It is totally featureless.*

February ['februəri] *n* the second month of the year, the month following January: *It sometimes snows here in February*; *He was born on February 24* (said as 'on February (the) twenty-fourth' or 'on the twenty-fourth of February'); *He was born on the 24th/twenty-fourth of February*; *He died last February.*

feces *see* **faeces**.

feckless ['feklis] *adj* (*derog*) careless or inefficient: *He was so feckless that he couldn't even boil an egg*; *a feckless young woman.*

fecund ['fi:kənd] *adj* (*liter or very formal*) fertile: *miles of fecund fields*; (*fig*) *a fecund imagination.*

fe'cundity [-'kʌn-] *nu.*

fed *see* **feed**.

federal ['fedərəl] *adj* (*attrib*) (of a government or group of states) joined together, *usu* for national and external affairs only: *the federal government of* *the United States of America.*

ˈ**federated** [-rei-] *adj* (*attrib*) joined by a treaty, agreement *etc*.

ˌ**fedeˈration** *nc* people, societies, unions, states *etc* joined together for a common purpose: *the International Federation of Actors.*

fee [fi:] *nc* the price paid for work done by a doctor, lawyer *etc* or for some special service or right: *The lawyer's fee was very high*; *We paid the entrance fee*; *He can't pay his university fees.*

feeble [ˈfi:bl] *adj* weak: *The old lady has been rather feeble since her illness*; *She heard a feeble cry*; *That is a feeble excuse.*

ˈ**feebly** *adv* in a feeble manner; weakly: *A light glowed feebly from the window.*

feed [fi:d] – *pt, ptp* **fed** [fed] – **1** *vt* to give food to: *He fed the child with a spoon*; *She feeds the baby every four hours.* **2** *vi* (*with* **on**) to eat: *Cows feed on grass.* **3** *vt* (*formal*) to give (something) what is necessary: *She fed the fire with logs.* **4** *vt* to supply (material *etc*) to: *She fed the questions into the computer.* **5** *vt* (*formal*) to satisfy or encourage: *to feed someone's vanity.* – **1** *nc* food *esp* for a baby: *Have you given the baby his feed?* **2** *nu* food for animals: *cattle feed.* **3** *nc* (*esp* of babies) a time of eating: *She has four feeds a day.* **4** *nc* (*inf*: *usu in sing*) a meal: *What a feed she gave us!*

fed up (*sl*) tired; bored and annoyed: *I'm fed up with all this work!*

See also **food**.

feel [fi:l] – *pt, ptp* **felt** [felt] – **1** *vt* to become aware of (something) by the sense of touch: *She felt a cold wind on her face*; *She felt his hand on her shoulder.* **2** *vt* to find out the shape, size, texture *etc* of something by touching, *usu* with the hands: *The doctor felt the bump on her head*; *She felt the parcel carefully.* **3** *vt* to experience or be aware of (an emotion, sensation *etc*): *He felt a sudden anger*; *She feels the cold very much.* **4** *vi* to think (oneself) to be: *I feel angry*; *She feels sick*; *They are beginning to feel hungry*; *Do you feel better now?*; *The child feels cold*; *I felt extremely foolish*; *I felt a complete fool*; *How does she feel about leaving Edinburgh?* **5** *vt* (not used with **is, was** *etc* and **-ing**) to believe or consider: *They feel that they must try again*; *She feels that the firm treated her badly.* – *See also* **feel** *in phrases below.*

ˈ**feeler** *nc* **1** (in certain animals, insects *etc*) an organ for touching, *esp* one of the two thread-like parts on an insect's head. **2** (*fig inf*) an attempt to find out other people's opinions: *I think we should put out some feelers before we make a final decision.*

ˈ**feeling 1** *nu* power and ability to feel: *I have no feeling in my little finger.* **2** *nc* something that one feels physically: *a feeling of great pain.* **3** *nc* (*usu in pl*) something that one feels in one's mind: *Her feelings were confused*; *His angry words hurt my feelings*; *a feeling of happiness.* **4** *nc* an impression or belief: *I have a feeling that the work is too hard.* **5** *nc* a natural ability: *He has a feeling for languages.* **6** *nu* affection: *He has no feeling for her now.* **7** *nu* emotion: *He spoke with great feeling.*

feel as if/as though to have the sensation (physical or mental) or feeling that: *I feel as if I am going to be sick*; *She feels as though she has known him for years.*

ˈ**feel for** *vt fus* **1** (*formal*) to be sympathetic with: *She felt for him in his sorrow.* **2** to try to find by feeling: *She felt for a pencil in her handbag.*

ˈ**feel like 1** to have the feelings that one would have if one were: *I feel like a princess in this beautiful dress*; *He felt like an idiot* (= He felt very foolish). **2** (*inf*) to feel that one would like to (have, do *etc*): *I feel like a drink*; *Do you feel like going to the cinema?*

feel one's way to make one's way by feeling: *I could not see in the dark – I had to feel my way to the door.*

get the feel of (*inf*) to become accustomed to: *Once I got the feel of my new job I enjoyed it.*

See also **unfeeling**.

feet *see* **foot**.

feign [fein] *vt* (*liter or formal*) to pretend to feel: *He feigned illness.*

feigned *adj* (*formal*) pretended: *feigned happiness*; *His illness is feigned.*

See also **unfeigned**.

feint [feint] *nc* (*formal*) a movement intended to deceive: *He made a feint in my direction, then ran towards the house.*

felicity [fəˈlisəti] *nu* (*liter or very formal*) happiness.

feˈlicitate [-teit] *vt* (*very formal*) to congratulate: *May I felicitate you on your safe arrival.*

feˌlicitaˈtions *n pl* (*very formal*) congratulations.

feˈlicitous *adj* (*liter or very formal*) happy: *on this felicitous occasion.*

feline [ˈfi:lain] *adj* of or like a cat: *She had a feline appearance*; *Her movements are rather feline.*

fell[1] *see* **fall**.

fell[2] [fel] *vt* to cut or knock down to the ground: *They are felling all the trees in this area*; (*liter*) *He felled his opponent with a single blow.*

fell[3] [fel] *nc* a moorland hill, *esp* in northern England.

fellow [ˈfelou] *nc* **1** (*inf often derog*) a man: *He's quite a nice fellow but I don't like him*; *He's rather a strange fellow.* **2** (*often in cmpds*) a companion and equal: *She is playing with her schoolfellows*; *Her fellows share her interest in music.* **3** a distinguished member of a learned *usu* academic society: *a fellow of the college.* **4** (*formal*) one of a pair: *I can't find the fellow to this glove.* – *adj* (*attrib*) belonging to the same group, country *etc*: *a fellow Scotsman*; *a fellow citizen*; *a fellow music-lover.*

ˈ**fellowship 1** *nc* an association (of people with common interests): *a youth fellowship* (= a club for young people). **2** *nc* an award to a university graduate: *He has just been given a fellowship.* **3** *nu* (*old*) friendliness.

ˌ**fellow-ˈfeeling** *nu* sympathy (*esp* for someone in a similar situation, of similar tastes *etc*): *I had a fellow-feeling for the other patient with the broken leg.*

felon [ˈfelən] *nc* (*liter or legal*) a person who is guilty of a serious crime.

feˈlonious [-ˈlou-] *adj* (*liter or legal*) criminal: *with felonious intent.*

ˈ**felony** *nc* (*legal*) a serious crime: *He committed a felony.*

felt[1] *see* **feel**.

felt[2] [felt] *nu, adj* (of) a type of cloth made of wool that has been pressed together not woven: *She bought a metre of felt to re-cover the card table* (= table for playing cards on); *a felt hat.*

female [ˈfi:meil] **1** *nc, adj* (a person, animal *etc*) of the sex that gives birth to children, produces eggs *etc*: *a female blackbird*; *the female of the species.* **2** *nc, adj* (a plant) that produces seeds. **3** *nc* (*derog*) a woman: *Just look at that female over there!*

See also **male**.

feminine [ˈfeminin] *adj* **1** (*usu attrib*) of a woman:

a feminine voice. **2** with all the essential qualities of a woman: *She was a very feminine person*; *She is so feminine.* **3** (*gram*) in certain languages, of one of *usu* two or three genders of nouns *etc*.

ˌ**femi'ninity** *nu* the quality of being feminine: *She used her femininity to win the argument.*

'**feminism** *nu* the thought and actions of people who want to make woman's (legal, political, social *etc*) rights equal to those of men.

'**feminist** *nc* a supporter of feminism: *Although she is a feminist she still expects her husband to attend to all financial matters.*

femur ['fi:mə] *nc* (*tech*) the thigh bone: *He broke his femur playing rugby.*

fen [fen] *ncu* an area of low marshy land often covered with water, *esp* (*in pl with cap*) such an area in South-East England: *He lives in the Fens.*

fence[1] [fens] *nc* a line of wooden or metal posts joined by wood, wire *etc* to stop people, animals *etc* moving on to or off a piece of land: *They put a fence round the field to keep the cows out*; *The garden was surrounded by a wooden fence.* – *vt* to enclose (an area of land) with a fence *eg* to prevent people, animals *etc* from getting in: *We are going to fence (in) the garden to prevent schoolchildren from stealing the apples*; *We fenced off the lake in case the children fell in.*

'**fencing**[1] *nu* (the material used for) a fence: *We will need a hundred metres of fencing*; *The fencing round the garden is defective.*

fence[2] [fens] *vi* **1** to fight with (blunted) swords as a sport. **2** (*fig*) to avoid answering questions: *He fenced with me for half an hour before I got the truth.*

'**fencing**[2] *nu* the sport of fighting with (blunted) swords: *I used to be very good at fencing when I was at school.*

fence[3] [fens] *nc* (*sl*) a person who buys things knowing that they have been stolen: *The owner of the second-hand shop was known to be a fence.*

fend [fend] : **fend for oneself** to look after oneself: *He is old enough to fend for himself.*

fender ['fendə] *nc* **1** (*naut*) anything used to protect a boat from touching another, a pier *etc*: *He hung some old car tyres over the side of the boat to act as fenders.* **2** a low guard around a fireplace to prevent coal *etc* from falling out. **3** (*Amer*) the bumper of a car.

fennel ['fenl] *nu* a type of herb with yellow flowers, used for flavouring food.

ferment [fə'ment] *vti* **1** to (make something) go through a particular chemical change (as when yeast is added to dough in the making of bread): *Grape juice must be fermented for some time before it becomes wine*; *If you leave fruit juice in a warm place it will ferment.* **2** (*fig formal*) to excite or be excited: *He is the kind of person to ferment trouble.* – ['fə:ment] *nc* (*fig*) a state of excitement: *The whole city was in a ferment.*

ˌ**fermen'tation** [fə:men-] *nu* the chemical change which occurs when something ferments or is fermented.

fern [fə:n] *nc* a kind of plant with no flowers and delicate feather-like leaves.

ferocious [fə'rouʃəs] *adj* fierce or savage: *A lion is a ferocious animal*; *Wolves are thought to be more ferocious than they actually are.* **fe'rociously** *adv*.

ferocity [fə'rosəti] *nu*.

See also **fierce**.

ferret ['ferit] *nc* a type of small, weasel-like animal used to chase rabbits out of their holes.

ferret (about) *vi* (*inf*) to search busily and persistently: *He ferreted about in the cupboard*; *What are you ferreting in that drawer for?*

ferret out *vt sep* (*inf*) to find out after a search: *He managed to ferret out a very interesting piece of news*; *He ferreted it out after a very long search.*

ferro- [ferou] (*tech*: *in cmpds*) of or containing iron: ˌ*ferro-'concrete.*

ferrule ['feru:l] *nc* a ring or cap (*usu* metal) to strengthen or protect the tip of a walking-stick, umbrella *etc*.

ferry ['feri] *vt* to carry (people, cars *etc*) from one place to another by boat (or plane): *He ferried us across the river in a small boat.* – *nc* **1** a boat which ferries people, cars *etc* from one place to another: *We took the cross-channel ferry from Dover to Calais*; *We came across on the ferry.* **2** a place where a boat regularly operates as a ferry: *We had lunch when we arrived at the ferry.*

fertile ['fə:tail] *adj* **1** producing a lot: *fertile fields*; *fertile land*; *This land is very fertile*; (*fig*) *a fertile mind/imagination.* **2** able to produce fruit, children, young animals *etc*: *fertile seeds*; *fertile eggs*; *a fertile animal*; *a woman no longer fertile.*

fer'tility [-'ti-] *nu* the state or condition of being fertile.

'**fertilize, -ise** [-ti-] *vt* to make fertile: *He fertilized his fields with manure*; *An egg must be fertilized before it can develop.* ˌ**fertili'zation, -s-** *nu*.

'**fertilizer, -s-** [-ti-] *ncu* a substance (manure, chemicals *etc*) used to make land (more) fertile.

See also **infertile**.

fervent ['fə:vənt] *adj* (*formal*) enthusiastic and very sincere: *fervent hope*; *a fervent reply*; *He is a fervent supporter of the Liberal party.* '**fervently** *adv*.

fervid ['fə:vid] *adj* (*usu attrib*: *liter or formal*) intense and almost too enthusiastic: *a fervid desire.*

fervour (*Amer* **fervor**) ['fə:və], **fervency** ['fə:vənsi] *nus* (*formal*) enthusiasm and strength of emotion: *He spoke with great fervour*; *His religious fervour makes him try to convert others to his faith.*

fester ['festə] *vi* (of an open injury *eg* a cut or sore) to become infected: *The wound on his leg began to fester.*

festival ['festəvəl] *nc* **1** an occasion of public celebration: *In Italy, each village holds a festival once a year.* **2** a season of musical, theatrical *etc* performances: *Every three years the city holds a drama festival*; (*attrib*) *a festival programme.*

festive ['festiv] *adj* (*formal*) happy and (as if) celebrating: *The Christmas decorations looked very festive*; *There was a festive atmosphere.*

fe'stivity [-'sti-] (*formal*) **1** *nu* happiness: *There was great festivity in the village.* **2** *nc* a celebration: *Come and join in the festivities.*

festoon [fə'stu:n] *vt* (*formal*) to decorate with ribbons, strings of flowers *etc*: *The streets were festooned with flags.*

fetal *see* **foetus**.

fetch [fetʃ] *vt* **1** to go and get (something or someone) and bring it: *My sister would like to meet you – I'll fetch her*; *Fetch me some bread from the shop.* **2** to be sold for (a certain price): *The picture fetched £100 at the auction.*

'**fetching** *adj* (*old*) charming or attractive: *You look very fetching in that hat*; *a fetching smile.*

'**fetchingly** *adv* (*old*): *She smiled fetchingly at the young man.*

fête [feit] *nc* an entertainment, *esp* in the open air, with competitions, displays, the selling of goods *etc usu* to raise money, *esp* for charity: *We are holding a summer fête in aid of charity.* – *vt* (*formal*) to entertain richly or to fuss over (someone): *When he returned home after his triumph, he was fêted by the whole town.*

fetid, (*old*) **foetid** ['fi:tid] *adj* (*formal*) having a bad smell; stinking: *a fetid pool of water*; *That marsh is fetid.*

fetish ['fetiʃ] *nc* **1** an object worshipped, *esp* because a spirit is supposed to lodge in it. **2** (*fig*) something which is regarded with too much reverence or given too much attention: *It is good to dress well, but there is no need to make a fetish of it.*

fetlock ['fetlok] *nc* the part of a horse's leg just above the hoof: *The horse has an injured fetlock.*

fetter ['fetə] *nc* (*formal*: *usu in pl*) a chain that holds the foot or feet of a prisoner, animal *etc* to prevent running away: *The prisoner was in fetters.* – *vt* **1** to fasten with a fetter: *He fettered the horse.* **2** (*fig formal*) to keep (someone) from advancing; to restrain: *He was fettered by memories of the past.*

fettle ['fetl]: **in fine/good fettle** in good health or good spirits: *He was ill when I saw him last but he seems in fine fettle now.*

fetus *see* **foetus**.

feud [fju:d] *nc* a long-lasting quarrel or war between families, tribes *etc*: *There has been a feud between our two families for two hundred years.*

feudal ['fju:dl] *adj* (*hist*) of the system by which people gave certain services *eg* military support to a more powerful man in return for lands, protection *etc.*

'**feudalism** *nu* the feudal system.

fever ['fi:və] *ncu* (an illness causing) high body temperature and quick heart-beat: *She is in bed with a fever*; *Fever and constant coughing weakened the old lady*: (*fig*) *a fever of excitement.*

'**feverish** *adj* **1** (*also* '**fevered**) having a slight fever: *She seems a bit feverish tonight*; *a feverish child*; *He is a bit fevered*; (*formal*) *She stroked his fevered brow.* **2** (*fig*) restlessly excited: *There's a feverish air about the town tonight as the Queen is coming tomorrow.*

'**feverishly** *adv* (*fig*) quickly and excitedly: *He wrote feverishly for three hours but did not finish his essay.*

at 'fever pitch at a level of great excitement: *The crowd's excitement was at fever pitch as they waited for the filmstar to appear.*

few [fju:] *adj, pron* not many (emphasizing the smallness of the number): *Few people visit me nowadays*; *Few things interest him nowadays*; *Buses pass here every few minutes* (= very frequently); *Such opportunities are few*; *Few are as clever as he is*; *Very few of them came to last night's meeting.*

a few a small number (emphasizing that there are indeed some): *There are a few books in this library about geology*; *We have only a few left.*

few and far between (*inf*) very few: *Interesting jobs are few and far between.*

no fewer than as many as; not less than.

a good few/quite a few a considerable number: *A good few/quite a few people came to the concert even though it was a stormy night.*

the few a small number (emphasizing that there are not many): *The few that were left enjoyed themselves.*

fez [fez] *nc* a type of brimless hat with a tassel, *usu* red and worn by some Muslims.

fiancé [fi'ãsei, (*Amer*) fi:ɔn'sei] – *fem* **fi'ancée** – *nc* a person to whom one is engaged to be married: *her fiancé*; *his fiancée*; *The fiancé of the injured girl died later in hospital.*

fiasco [fi'askou] – *pl* **fi'ascos** – *nc* a complete failure: *The party was a fiasco.*

fib [fib] *nc* (*inf*) an unimportant lie: *That child is always telling fibs.* – *v* – *pt, ptp* **fibbed** – *vi* to tell a fib: *She fibbed about her age.*

fibre, (*Amer*) **fiber** ['faibə] **1** *nc* a fine thread or something like a thread: *a fibre of wool*; *a nerve fibre.* **2** *nu* a material made up of fibres: *The mats were made of coconut fibre.* **3** *nu* (*fig*) character: *A man of strong moral fibre.*

'**fibrous** *adj* (*formal*) made of or like fibres: *This meat is very fibrous.*

'**fibreglass** *nu, adj* **1** (of) very fine threadlike pieces of glass, used for insulation, in materials *etc*: *We've insulated the loft with fibreglass*; *fibreglass curtains.* **2** (of) a plastic material reinforced with such glass, used for many purposes *eg* building boats: *Fibreglass is a very light material*; *a fibreglass boat.*

fickle ['fikl] *adj* (*formal*) (*usu* of persons) always changing (one's mind, one's likes and dislikes *etc*): *It is a popular belief that women are fickle*; *a fickle lover.* '**fickleness** *nu.*

fiction ['fikʃən] *nu* stories *etc* which tell of imagined, not real, characters and events: *I prefer reading fiction to hearing about real events.*

'**fictional** *adj* (of novels, stories *etc*) imagined: *a fictional account of life in the fourteenth century*; *The events in this play are mostly fictional.*

fictitious [fik'tiʃəs] *adj* **1** (*formal*) not true: *a fictitious account of what had happened.* **2** not real or based on fact: *All the characters in the book are fictitious.*

See also **non-fiction**.

fiddle ['fidl] *nc* **1** (*inf*) a violin: *He played a tune on the fiddle.* **2** (*sl*) a dishonest business arrangement: *He's working a fiddle over his taxes.* – **1** *vi* (*inf*) to play a violin: *He fiddled while they danced.* **2** *vi* (*with* **with**) to make restless, aimless movements: *Stop fiddling with your pencil!* **3** *vt* (*inf derog*) to manage (money, accounts *etc*) dishonestly: *He has been fiddling the accounts for years.*

'**fiddler** *nc* (*inf*) a person who fiddles (*usu only def 1*).

on the fiddle (*sl derog*) dishonest: *He's always on the fiddle.*

fidelity [fi'deləti] *nu* **1** (*formal*) faithfulness or loyalty: *his fidelity to his wife*; *fidelity to a promise.* **2** (*very formal*) (of a copy, reproduction *etc*) exactness or accuracy: *They were amazed by the fidelity of the colours of the painting.*

See **high-fidelity**.

fidget ['fidʒit] – *pt, ptp* '**fidgeted** – *vi* to move (the hands, feet *etc*) restlessly: *Stop fidgeting while I'm talking to you!* – *nc* (*inf*) a person who fidgets: *She's a terrible fidget!*

the 'fidgets (*inf*) nervous restlessness: *I've got the fidgets – I can't sit still.*

field [fi:ld] **1** *nc* a piece of land enclosed for growing crops, keeping animals *etc*: *Our house is in the country surrounded by fields.* **2** *nc* (*usu in cmpds*) a wide area: *an ice-field*; *playing fields* (= an area for games, sports *etc*). **3** *nc* (*usu in cmpds*) a piece of land *etc* where minerals or other natural resources are found: *a North Sea oil-field*; *a coalfield.* **4** *nc* (*formal*) an area of knowledge, interest, study *etc*: *in the fields of literature/economic development*; *That is completely outside my field*; *What are his main fields of interest?* **5** *nc* an area affected, covered or included by something: *a magnetic field*; *in his field of vision.* **6** *nc* (*liter or mil*) an area of battle: *Her brother fell on the field of Waterloo*; (*attrib*) *a field-gun*; (*attrib*) *field artillery.* **7** *nu* the people, horses *etc* taking part in a race and certain games *esp* cricket: *Three of her horses were among the field of nineteen.* – *vti* (in cricket, basketball *etc*) to catch (the ball) and return it: *Our team are fielding, while our opponents bat*; *He fielded the ball and threw it back.*

'fielder, 'fieldsman ['fi:ldz-] *ncs* a person who fields in cricket *etc.*

'field-day *nc* (*usu facet*) a day of great activity or success: *She had a field-day in the shops when she went out to spend her year's clothes allowance all at once*; *The reporters had a field-day when the princess got married.*

'field-glasses *n pl* binoculars.

field marshal *nc* (*with cap in titles*) (a person of) the highest rank in the British army: *Her brother is a field marshal*; *He was promoted to field marshal*; *Field Marshal Brown.* – *See also* Appendix 3.

'fieldwork *nu* work done outside the laboratory, office *etc* (*eg* collecting information): *The geologist spends two months every summer doing fieldwork.*

fiend [fi:nd] *nc* **1** (*esp liter*) a devil: *the fiends of hell.* **2** a wicked or cruel person: *She's an absolute fiend when she's angry.* **3** (*inf*) a person who is very enthusiastic about something: *She's always opening windows – she's a fresh air fiend*; *a fiend for work.*

'fiendish *adj* **1** (*usu attrib*) wicked or devilish: *a fiendish temper.* **2** (*inf*) very difficult, clever *etc*: *The last question in the exam was fiendish*; *a fiendish plan.*

'fiendishly *adv* **1** wickedly: *The villain in the play was fiendishly clever.* **2** (*inf*) very: *a fiendishly difficult problem.*

fierce [fiəs] *adj* **1** very angry and likely to attack: *a fierce dog*; *That dog looks fierce*; *The old man looks fierce but he is very gentle*; *He has a fierce expression – he must be very angry.* **2** intense or strong: *They were fierce rivals*; *They were driven back by the fierce heat of the fire*; *It won't be easy to win the race – the competition is very fierce.* **'fiercely** *adv.*

See also **ferocious.**

fiery ['faiəri] *adj* **1** (*attrib*) like fire: *There was a fiery light in the sky*; *fiery red hair.* **2** (*usu attrib*) angry: *He had a fiery temper.* **3** (*esp* of a horse) high-spirited: *The horse was almost too fiery for the child to control*; *a fiery horse.*

fiesta [fi'estə] *nc* **1** a (religious) holiday, *esp* in Roman Catholic countries. **2** a festival or celebration.

fife [faif] *nc* (*chiefly mil music*) a type of small flute: *The fifes and drums played a marching tune.*

fifteen [fif'ti:n] **1** *nc* the number or figure 15. **2** *nu* the age of 15. **3** *nc* a team containing fifteen members: *a rugby fifteen.* – *adj* **1** (*usu attrib*) 15 in number. **2** (*pred*) aged 15. – *See* **eighteen** *for constructions.*

fifteen- (*in cmpds*) having fifteen (of something): *a 'fifteen-ˌpage re'port.*

ˌfif'teenth 1 *nc* one of fifteen equal parts. **2** *nc, adj* (the) last of fifteen (people, things *etc*); (the) next after the fourteenth. – *See* **eighteenth** *under* **eighteen** *for constructions.*

ˌfif'teen-year-old *nc* a person or animal that is fifteen years old. – *adj* (*attrib*) (of a person, animal or thing) that is fifteen years old. – *See* **eighteen-year-old** *under* **eighteen** *for constructions.*

See also Appendix 1.

fifth [fifθ] **1** *nc* one of five equal parts. **2** *nc, adj* (the) last of five (people, things *etc*); (the) next after the fourth. – *See* **eighth** *under* **eight** *for constructions.*

fifth column *nc* people in a town, country *etc* who try to help an enemy with whom the town, country *etc* is at war. **fifth columnist** *nc.*

See also Appendix 1.

fifty ['fifti] **1** *nc* the number or figure 50. **2** *nu* the age of 50. – *adj* **1** (*usu attrib*) 50 in number. **2** (*pred*) aged 50. – *See* **eighty** *for constructions.*

'fifties *n pl* **1** the period of time between one's fiftieth and sixtieth birthdays. **2** the range of temperatures between fifty and sixty degrees. **3** the period of time between the fiftieth and sixtieth years of a century. – *See* **eighties** *under* **eighty** *for constructions.*

'fiftieth 1 *nc* one of fifty equal parts. **2** *nc, adj* (the) last of fifty (people, things *etc*); (the) next after the forty-ninth. – *See* **eightieth** *under* **eighty** *for constructions.*

fifty- (*in cmpds*) having fifty (of something): *a ˌfifty-page 'book.*

'fifty-year-old *nc* a person or animal that is fifty years old. – *adj* (*attrib*) (of a person, animal or thing) that is fifty years old. – *See* **eighty-year-old** *under* **eighty** *for constructions.*

ˌfifty-'fifty *adv* half and half: *We'll divide the money fifty-fifty.* – *adj* equal: *His chances of survival must be about fifty-fifty*; *a fifty-fifty chance of survival.*

See also Appendix 1.

fig [fig] *nc* a type of soft pear-shaped fruit, often eaten dried: *Figs are full of seeds*; (*attrib*) *a fig tree.*

'fig leaf *nc* a leaf of a fig tree, traditionally used as a covering for the male genital organs in otherwise nude statues *etc.*

not to give a fig for (*old*) not to care about at all: *I don't give a fig for what he thinks.*

fight [fait] – *pt, ptp* **fought** [fo:t] – **1** *vti* to act against (someone or something) with physical violence: *The two countries have been fighting each other for years*; *The two boys are fighting over* (=because of; so that one of them might get possession of) *some money they found*; *The two dogs began to fight*; (*fig*) *He is fighting for his life.* **2** *vti* to resist strongly; to take strong action to prevent: *We shall fight the council's decision to build a motorway*; *The firemen are fighting the fire*; *We must fight against any attempt to deprive us of our freedom*; *He fought increasing ill health for the last five years of his life.* **3** *vi* to quarrel: *His parents were always fighting.* – *See* **fight back, fight off** *below.* – **1** *nc* an act of physical violence between people, countries *etc*: *There was a fight going on in the street*; *The two children have been in a fight.* **2** *nc* a struggle; action involving effort: *the fight for freedom of speech*; *the fight against disease*; *the fight against the government's economic plans.* **3** *nu* the will or strength to resist: *There was no fight left in him.* **4** *nc* a boxing-match.

'fighter *nc* **1** a person who fights, *eg* a person who takes part in a boxing-match. **2** a small fast aircraft designed to shoot down other aircraft.

fight back to use (physical) violence against someone who is using (physical) violence against one: *If he hits you, fight back.*

fight it out to fight on to a decisive end: *Although they were both exhausted the armies fought it out until the attackers were victorious at dawn*: (*fig*) *Fight it out among yourselves which of you is to go.*

fight off *vt sep* to drive (someone or something) away by using (physical) violence: *They fought off the enemy with machine-guns*; (*fig*) *I'll fight this cold off by going to bed early.*

fight one's way to make one's way with difficulty and effort: *He fought his way through the thick smoke*; (*fig*) *He fought his way to the top of his profession.*

fight shy of to avoid: *He fought shy of introducing her to his wife.*

put up a good fight (*often fig*) to fight well or bravely: *He put up a good fight but he was thrown to the ground by his opponent*; (*fig*) *She put up a good fight in the finals of the tennis competition but was defeated*; *That candidate did not win the parliamentary seat but he put up a good fight.*

figment ['figmənt]: **a figment of the/one's imagination** (*formal*) something one has imagined and which has no reality: *That rich uncle in America that he talks about is just a figment of his imagination.*

figure ['figə, (*Amer*) 'figjər] *nc* **1** the form or shape of a person: *I could see three figures in the painting*; *A mysterious figure came towards me*; *That girl has got a good figure*; *He is a fine figure of a man* (= He looks strong and muscular). **2** a (geometrical) shape: *The page was covered with a series of triangles, squares and other geometrical figures.* **3** a symbol representing a number: *Could you add up this line of figures*; *a six-figure telephone number*; *double figures* (= 10–99); *Her present salary is into five figures* (= between 10 000 and 99 999). – *See also* **figures** *below.* **4** (*inf*) a price: *They were asking a high figure for the house*; *The figure they asked for was £35 000.* **5** a well-known person: *He is a popular figure in our city.* **6** (*sometimes abbrev* **fig**) a diagram or drawing to explain something: *The parts of a flower are shown in figure 3.* – *vi* **1** to appear (in a story *etc*): *He figures largely in the story.* **2** (*inf esp Amer*) to think, estimate or consider: *I figured that you would arrive before half-past eight.* – *See also* **figure out** *below.*

'**figurative** [-rətiv] *adj* (*formal*) of or using figures of speech: *In his poetry he uses very figurative language*; *That use of the word is figurative.*

'**figuratively** *adv* (*formal*): *Can you use that word figuratively or only literally?*

'**figured** *adj* (*usu attrib*) marked with a design: *figured silk.*

'**figures** *n pl* counting; arithmetic: *I'm hopeless at figures – will you add this column for me?*

'**figurehead** *nc* **1** a person who is officially a leader but who does little or has little power: *She is the real leader of the party – he is only a figurehead.* **2** (*hist*) an ornamental figure (*usu* of carved wood) attached to the front of a ship: *the figurehead of a Viking ship.*

figure of eight *see* **eight**.

figure of speech one of several devices (*eg* metaphor, simile) for using words not with their ordinary meanings but to make a striking effect.

figure out *vt sep* (*inf*) to understand: *I can't figure out why he said that*; *I just can't figure it out.*

that 'figures (*inf*) that is what I would expect: *He has gone away? That figures – he always disappears without warning.*

figurine ['figjəri:n] *nc* (*formal*) a small statue of a person: *china figurines of Spanish ladies.*

filament ['filəmənt] *nc* something very thin shaped like a thread, *esp* the thin wire in an electric light bulb.

filch [filtʃ] *vt* (*inf*) to steal (something small): *He used to filch paper-clips from the office.*

file[1] [fail] *nc* a line of soldiers *etc* walking one behind the other; *esp in the phrase* **in single file** (*see below*). – *vi* to walk in a file: *They filed across the road in an orderly fashion.*

in single file (moving along) singly, one behind the other: *They went downstairs in single file.*

file[2] [fail] *nc* **1** a folder, loose-leaf book *etc* to hold papers: *Ask the secretary to get some more files from the stationer's.* **2** a collection of papers on a particular subject (kept in such a folder): *Where is my file on pronunciation schemes?* – **1** *vt* to put (papers *etc*) in a file: *He filed the letter under P*; *Shall I file these letters in alphabetical order?* **2** *vti* (*legal*) to bring (a suit) before a law court: *She was filing* (*a suit*) *for divorce.*

'**filing cabinet** *nc* a piece of furniture with drawers *etc* for holding papers: *We need a new filing cabinet in this office.*

on file in a file: *We have no vacancies for secretaries at the moment but I shall keep your name on file.*

file[3] [fail] *nc* a steel tool with a rough surface for smoothing or rubbing away wood, metal *etc.* – *vti* to cut or smooth with a file: *He managed to file through the bars on the window*; *She sat there filing her nails.*

'**filings** *n pl* pieces of wood, metal *etc* rubbed off with a file: *iron filings.*

filial ['filiəl] *adj* (*very formal or facet*) of or suitable to a son or daughter: *filial behaviour*; *filial respect* (= respect for parents); *His behaviour is far from filial.*

filibuster ['filibʌstə] *nc* a very long speech in order to delay the passing of a (parliamentary) law *etc.* – *vi* to make such a speech for this purpose.

filigree ['filigri:] *nu, adj* (of) ornamental work made of threads of gold, silver *etc*: *a brooch of silver filigree*; *a filigree brooch.*

Filipino *see* Appendix 2.

fill [fil] **1** *vt* to put (something) into (until there is no room for more); to make full: *She filled the cupboard with books*; *Will you fill my cup, please?*; (*fig*) *The sight of the dead man filled me with horror*; (*fig*) *The news filled him with joy.* – *See also* **fill up** *below.* **2** *vi* to become full: *Her eyes filled with tears*; *The room filled quickly*; (*fig*) *Her heart filled with joy.* – *See also* **fill up** *below.* **3** *vt* (*formal*: not used with **is, was** *etc* and **-ing**) to satisfy (a condition, requirement *etc*): *Does he fill all our requirements?* **4** *vt* to occupy (time) completely: *He filled the day with activity.* **5** *vt* to appoint someone to (a job): *Has the post been filled yet?* **6** *vt* to put something in a hole (in a tooth *etc*) to stop it up: *The dentist filled two of my teeth yesterday.* – *See also* **fill in, fill out** *below.* – *nu* (*often facet*) as much as fills or satisfies someone: *He ate his fill of the excellent food*; *I've had my fill of his rudeness* (= I've had as much of his rudeness as I can put up with).

filled *adj* (*neg* **un-**) having been filled (*esp defs 3–6*).

'**filling** *ncu* anything used to fill: *The filling has come out of my tooth*; *She put an orange filling in the cake*; *What kind of filling shall I put in the biscuits?*

'**filling-station** *nc* a place where petrol is sold.

fill in 1 *vt sep* to add or put in (whatever is needed to make something complete): *The teacher drew outlines of animals and the children filled them in*; *I've got a general idea of what happened – could you fill in the details?* 2 *vt sep* to complete (forms, applications *etc*) by putting in the information required: *Have you filled in your tax form yet?*; *You must fill in this form if you want a new passport*; *Have you filled it in correctly?* 3 *vt oblig sep* to give (someone) all the necessary information: *I've been away – can you fill me in on what has happened?* 4 *vt sep* to occupy (time): *He had several drinks in the bar to fill in time until the train left*; *Now that I'm not working I have a lot of spare time – I don't know how to fill it in!* 5 *vi* (*inf*) to do another person's job temporarily: *I'm filling in for his secretary while she's in hospital*; *He doesn't usually work here – he's just filling in.*

fill out 1 *vi, vt sep* to (cause to) become rounder or fatter: *She used to be very thin but she has filled out a bit now*; *Her face has filled out since I last saw her*; *Eating all that food will certainly fill her out.* 2 *vt sep* to fill in (*def 2*): *I'm tired of filling out forms.*

fill up *vi, vt sep* to make or become completely full: *Fill up the petrol tank please*; *Fill it up*; *The hall filled up quickly.*

fillet ['filit] *ncu* a piece of meat or fish without bones: *fillet of veal*; *cod fillet*; (*attrib*) *fillet steak.* – *v* – *pt, ptp* **'filleted** – *vt* to remove the bones from (meat or fish): *Ask the fishmonger to fillet it for you.*

filly ['fili] *nc* a young female horse.

film [film] 1 *ncu* (a thin strip of) celluloid made sensitive to light on which photographs are taken: *Is there a film in your camera?*; *I use colour film.* 2 *nc* (*esp Brit*) a story, play *etc* shown as a motion picture in a cinema, on television *etc*: *They are going to make a film on her life-story*; *Did you see the cowboy film on television last night?*; (*attrib*) *a film addict*; (*attrib*) *Have you seen the film version of 'Jane Eyre'?* 3 *nc* a thin skin or covering: *a film of dust*; *She could not see properly through a film of tears.* – 1 *vti* to make a motion picture (of): *They are going to film the race*; *We shall be filming in Scotland for a month.* 2 *vi* (*formal*: *usu with* **over**) to cover with a film: *Her eyes gradually filmed (over) with tears.*

'filmy *adj* (*usu attrib*) very light and thin: *She was wearing a dress of filmy material.*

'filmstar *nc* a famous actor or actress in films.

filter ['filtə] *nc* 1 a strainer or other device through which liquid, gas, smoke *etc* can pass, but not solid material: *A filter is used to make sure that the oil is clean and does not contain any dirt*; *The filter on a cigarette traps the nicotine etc*; (*attrib*) *filter paper.* 2 (*tech*) a kind of screening plate used to change or correct certain colours: *If you are taking photographs in sun and snow, you should use a blue filter.* 3 a green arrow on a traffic light which allows one line of traffic to move while the main stream is stopped: *You can go now – the filter's on*; (*attrib*) *a filter light.* – 1 *vti* (of liquids) to (become) clean by passing through a filter: *At this stage the wine must be filtered*; *The rain-water filtered into a tank.* 2 *vi* (*fig*) to come bit by bit or gradually: *Light filtered through the dirty window*; *People began to filter into the room*; *The news filtered out.* 3 *vi* (of cars *etc*) to move gradually into a stream of traffic: *The traffic filtered into the main road*; *When the green arrow lights up you can filter (to the) left.*

'filter-bed *nc* (*tech*) a layer of sand, gravel *etc* used for filtering water or sewage.

ˌfilter-'tip *nc* (a cigarette with) a filter (*def 1*).

filth [filθ] *nu* 1 anything very dirty or foul: *Look at all that disgusting filth on your boots!* 2 something obscene or immoral: *That firm publishes nothing but filth.*

'filthy *adj* 1 very dirty: *The whole house is absolutely filthy*; *a filthy tea-towel.* 2 obscene: *That is a filthy story.*

fin [fin] *nc* 1 a thin movable part on a fish's body by which it balances, moves, changes direction *etc.* 2 anything that looks or is used like a fin: *the tail-fin of an aeroplane.*

final ['fainl] *adj* 1 (*attrib*) the very last: *the final chapter of the book.* 2 (*usu pred*) (of a decision *etc*) definite; decided and not to be changed: *The judge's decision is final.* – *nc* the last part of a competition: *The first parts of the competition will take place throughout the country, but the final will be in London.* – *See also* **finals** *below.*

'finally *adv* 1 the last (of many): *The soldiers rode past, then came the Royal visitors, and finally the Queen.* 2 at last, after a long time: *We waited and waited, and the train finally arrived.*

'finalist *nc* a person who reaches the final stage in a competition: *It was difficult to decide which of the two finalists was the better tennis player.*

fi'nality [-'na-] *nu* (*formal*) (*usu* of a decision *etc*) the state or condition of being final: *The finality of his decision was unquestioned*; *She shut the door with an air of finality.*

'finalize, -ise *vt* (*formal*) to make a final decision about plans, arrangements *etc*: *We must finalize the arrangements by Friday.* **ˌfinali'zation, -s-** *nu.*

'finals *n pl* the last examinations for a university degree *etc*: *I am sitting/taking my finals in June.*

finale [fi'naːli] *nc* the last part of anything, *esp* a concert, opera, musical show *etc*: *The whole cast of the concert appeared in the finale.*

finalist *see* **final**.

finance [fai'nans] 1 *nu* (the study or management of) money affairs: *He had been minister of finance for several years before he resigned*; *He is an expert in finance.* 2 *nc* (*often in pl*) the money one has to spend: *The government is worried about the state of the country's finances.* – *vt* to give money for (a plan, business *etc*): *Will the company finance your trip to Germany?*

fi'nancial [-ʃəl] *adj* concerning money: *our financial affairs*; *They have a financial commitment to us*; *His interest in the business is purely financial.*

fi'nancially *adv*: *The business is financially insecure.*

fi'nancier [-siə, (*Amer*) fainan'siər] *nc* (*formal*) a person who manages (large sums of money): *As a financier he was knowledgeable about the stock market.*

financial year *nc* (*often with* **the**) a period of twelve months at the end of which accounts are balanced: *In Britain, the government's financial year runs from April 1 or 6 to March 31 or April 5, and in the USA it runs from July 1 to June 30.*

finch [fintʃ] *nc* (*often in cmpds*) one of several kinds of small bird: *a greenfinch.*

find [faind] – *pt, ptp* **found** [faund] – (not used with **is, was** *etc* and **-ing** (*defs 1, 5*)) 1 *vt* to come upon or meet with accidentally or after searching: *Look what I've found in my pocket!*; *The child found a £5 note in the street*; *I looked everywhere for my book, and finally found it under the bed.* 2 *vt* to discover: *I found that I couldn't do the work*; *I* *found that I had missed the train; You don't find much water in a desert.* **3** *vt* to succeed in getting (time, courage, money *etc*) for: *I managed to find the courage to ask for more money; She found (the) time to talk to me.* **4** *vt* to consider; to think (something) to be: *I found the weather very cold in Norway; He found it rather difficult to answer their questions.* **5** *v refl* to discover oneself to be in a situation *etc*: *I found myself without money; They found themselves in a dark wood.* **6** *v refl* (*formal*) to discover a career *etc* one enjoys and that suits one's abilities: *He has finally found himself as a musician.* – *See also* **find out** *below.* – *nc* something found, *esp* something of value or interest: *That old book is quite a find!*

find one's feet to become able to cope with a new situation: *She found the new job difficult at first but she soon found her feet.*

find out 1 *vt sep* to discover: *I found out what was troubling her; When did you find it out?* **2** *vt oblig sep* to discover the truth (about someone), *usu* that he has done wrong: *He had been stealing for years, but eventually they found him out.*

fine[1] [fain] *adj* **1** (*usu attrib*) (*usu* of art *etc*) very good; of excellent quality: *There are many fine paintings in the Louvre; She gave a fine performance.* **2** (of weather) bright; not raining: *It's a fine day; I'm glad it was fine on the day of the picnic.* **3** (*usu pred*) well; healthy: *I was ill yesterday but I am feeling fine today!* **4** thin or delicate: *Her evening dress was made of a very fine material; That thread is very fine.* **5** (*usu attrib*) careful; detailed: *Fine workmanship is required for such delicate embroidery.* **6** (*usu attrib*) made of small pieces, grains *etc*: *fine sand; fine rain.* **7** (*formal*) slight: *There is a fine distinction between the meanings of joy and happiness; The balance between genius and madness is very fine.* **8** (*ironic*) wonderful: *You've made a fine mess of everything!; We've no money left – this is a fine state of affairs!* **9** perfectly satisfactory: *There's nothing wrong with your work – it's fine.* – *adv* satisfactorily: *This arrangement suits me fine; My pen's missing, but this ballpoint will do fine.* – *interj* good; well done *etc*: *You've finished already – fine!*

'**finely** *adv.*

'**finery** *nu* (*often facet*) beautiful clothes, jewellery *etc*: *She arrived in all her finery when the rest of us were in casual clothes.*

fine art *ncu* art that appeals immediately to the senses, *eg* painting, sculpture, music *etc*: *She is studying fine art; Painting is one of the fine arts.*

fine[2] [fain] *nc* money which must be paid as a punishment: *I was given a fine of £5 for parking my car in the wrong place; I had to pay a fine.* – *vt* to make (someone) pay a fine: *He was fined £10 for leaving rubbish on the road.*

finesse [fi'nes] *nu* (*formal or facet*) cleverness and skill in dealing with a situation *etc*: *She managed that situation with great finesse.*

finger ['fiŋgə] *nc* **1** one of the five end parts of the hand, sometimes excluding the thumb: *the forefinger; She pointed a finger at the thief; She has injured her thumb and one of her fingers.* **2** the part of a glove into which a finger is put: *There's a hole in the finger of this glove.* **3** anything made, shaped, cut *etc* like a finger: *She ate a finger of toast; The children ate fish-fingers and chips.* – *vt* to touch or feel with the fingers: *She fingered the keyboard of the piano absentmindedly; She fingered the beautiful material with admiration.*

'**finger bowl** *nc* a small bowl of water for cleaning one's fingers during or just after a meal: *Finger bowls are not common in Britain now except at very formal meals.*

'**fingernail** *nc* the nail at the tip of the finger: *I broke my fingernail while opening that box; She painted her fingernails scarlet.*

'**fingerprint** *nc* (*usu in pl*) the mark made by the tip of the finger, often used by the police *etc* as a means of identification: *The thief wiped his fingerprints off the safe; Who put the dirty fingerprint on this book?*

'**fingertip** *nc* the very end of a finger: *She burnt her fingertips on the stove.* – *See also* **have (something) at one's fingertips** *below.*

be all fingers and thumbs/my *etc* **fingers are all thumbs** (*inf*) to be very awkward or clumsy in handling or holding things: *He was so excited that his fingers were all thumbs and he dropped the cup; She could not undo the string of the parcel – she was all fingers and thumbs.*

have (something) at one's fingertips to know all the details (of a subject) thoroughly: *He has the history of the firm at his fingertips.*

have a finger in the pie/in every pie (*inf: often derog*) **1** to have an interest or share in a plan, business *etc* or in several plans, businesses *etc*: *He was so anxious for the scheme to do well that I knew he had a finger in the pie; He's a millionaire already but he likes to have a finger in every pie.* **2** to be involved in everything that happens: *Mrs Jones likes to have a finger in every pie in the village.*

put one's finger on (*inf*) to point out or describe exactly; to identify: *You've put your finger on what's wrong with their marriage; He put his finger on the cause of our financial trouble; You put your finger on it when you told him he was a lazy good-for-nothing.*

finicky ['finiki] *adj* (*inf derog*) too much concerned with detail: *She is a very finicky person; There is too much finicky detail in the picture; That pattern is very finicky.*

finish ['finiʃ] **1** *vti* to bring or come to an end: *She's finished her work; The music finished; She finished (her speech) by thanking everybody.* **2** *vt* to use, eat, drink *etc* the last of: *Have you finished your tea?; She's finished the cake!* **3** *vt* (*formal*) to complete the (social) education of a girl at a finishing-school: *She was finished at a school in Switzerland.* – *See also* **finish** *in phrases below.* – **1** *nu* the last touch (of paint, polish *etc*) that makes the work perfect: *The wood has a beautiful finish.* **2** *nc* (*no pl*) the last part (of a race *etc*): *They were almost together at the finish; It was a close finish.*

'**finished** *adj* **1** (*pred*) ended: *Her chances of success are finished.* **2** (*neg* **un-**) done; completed: *The work is finished; The finished painting is beautiful.* **3** (*pred*) having been completely used, eaten *etc*: *The ice-cream is finished – there's none left.* **4** (of a performance or performer) excellent; perfect: *She gave a very finished performance at the piano; That performance was very finished.* **5** (*pred usu derog*) (of a person) no longer able to continue in a career *etc*: *She used to be a wonderful actress, but she's finished now.*

'**finishing-school** *ncu* a private, *usu* expensive, school in which girls are taught subjects which will improve their social behaviour rather than prepare them for a career or job: *He has sent his daughter to finishing-school in Switzerland.*

finish off *vt sep* **1** to complete: *He finished off the* job yesterday. 2 to use, eat *etc* the last of: *We've finished off the pudding.* 3 (*inf usu facet*) to kill (a person): *His last illness nearly finished him off.*

finish up 1 *vt sep* to use, eat *etc* the last of; to finish: *Finish up your meal as quickly as possible; I have finished it up; We've finished up all the red paint.* 2 *vi* to end: *It was no surprise to me when he finished up in jail; The car finished up in the dump.*

'**finish with** *vt fus* to stop being fond of: *They used to be friendly but they're finished with each other now; He used to collect stamps but he's finished with that hobby now.*

finite ['fainait] *adj* 1 having an end or limit: *Human knowledge is finite, divine knowledge infinite. – See also* **infinite**. 2 (*gram*) (of a verb) having a subject: *He speaks; I ran; She fell. – See also* **infinitive**.

Finland, Finn, Finnish *see* Appendix 2.

fiord, fjord [fjo:d] *nc* a long narrow inlet of the sea between mountains (*esp* in Norway).

fir [fə:] 1 *nc* (also '**fir tree**) a kind of evergreen tree that bears cones ('**fir-cones**) and is often grown for its wood. 2 *nu, adj* (of) its wood.

fire ['faiə] 1 *nc* anything that is burning, whether accidentally or not: *There was a warm fire in the sitting-room; Several houses were destroyed in a fire in the town centre.* 2 *nc* an apparatus for heating: *a gas fire; an electric fire.* 3 *nu* the heat and light produced by burning: *Fire is one of man's greatest benefits.* 4 *nu* (*formal or liter*) enthusiasm: *with fire in his heart; patriotic fire.* 5 *nu* (*liter*) (of jewels *etc*) a glowing light: *The rubies shone with a sparkling fire.* 6 *nu* attack by gunfire: *The soldiers were continually under fire.* – 1 *vt* (*formal*) to set on fire: *They believe the house was fired on purpose.* 2 *vt* (of china, pottery *etc*) to heat in an oven, or kiln, in order to harden and strengthen: *The pots must be fired before they can be decorated.* 3 *vt* (*formal*) to make (someone) enthusiastic; to inspire: *The story fired his imagination.* 4 *vti* to operate (a gun *etc*) by discharging a bullet *etc* from it: *He fired his revolver three times; The man fired once and killed the deer. – See also* **fire away** *below.* 5 *vt* to send out or discharge (a bullet *etc*) from a gun *etc*: *He fired three bullets at the target.* 6 *vi* (*often with* **at** *or* **on**) to aim and operate a gun at; to shoot at: *The soldier fired at the approaching enemy; They suddenly fired on us; He fired at the target.* 7 *vt* (*inf*) to send away someone from his/her job; to dismiss: *He was fired from his last job for being late.*

'**fire alarm** *nc* an apparatus (*eg* a bell) to give warning of a fire: *Everyone had to leave the building when the fire alarm rang.*

'**firearm** *nc* (*formal*) any type of gun: *In certain countries you need a licence to keep firearms.*

'**fire-bomb** *nc* a bomb that causes fire: *It was a fire-bomb that caused the explosion in the factory.*

'**firebrand** *nc* (*fig*) a person who causes political or social trouble or excitement: *He was a real firebrand in his youth but he has lost his political enthusiasm now.*

'**fire-brigade** *nc* a company of firemen: *Call the fire-brigade!*

'**fire-engine** *nc* a vehicle carrying firemen and their equipment.

'**fire-escape** *nc* a means of escape from a building in case of fire, *usu* in the form of a metal staircase on the outside of the building: *In Britain hotels must have fire-escapes.*

'**fire-extinguisher** *nc* an apparatus (*usu* containing chemicals) for putting out fires: *There must be fire-extinguishers in every room.*

'**fire-guard** *nc* a metal framework placed in front of a fireplace for safety: *The child was burnt by a spark from the fire because the fire-guard was not in place.*

'**fireman** *nc* a man whose job is to put out accidental fires or those caused deliberately as a criminal act: *The firemen failed to put out the forest fire.*

'**fireplace** *nc* a space in a room (*usu* in a wall) with a chimney above, for a fire: *There was a wide stone fireplace in which a coal fire burned brightly.*

'**fire-raising** *nu* the crime of causing a fire deliberately; arson.

'**fireside** *nc* 1 a place beside a fireplace: *The old man slept by the fireside;* (*attrib*) *a fireside chair.* 2 (*fig*) home: *I prefer my own fireside to visiting other people.*

'**fire station** *nc* the building or buildings where fire-engines and other pieces of equipment used by firemen are kept.

'**firewood** *nu* wood that is suitable for burning as fuel: *He went into the garden to cut firewood.*

'**firework** *nc* a small exploding device which gives off a colourful display of lights: *The child's face was burned when the firework he was holding exploded; The children were saving money to buy fireworks for the party;* (*attrib*) *We always have a firework display on November 5.*

'**fireworks** *n pl* (*fig inf*) a show of anger or bad temper: *If I am late home again there will be fireworks!*

'**firing-squad** *nc* a group of soldiers with guns, to execute a prisoner: *He must face the firing-squad at dawn.*

catch fire to begin to burn: *Dry wood catches fire easily.*

fire away *vi* 1 to begin to fire guns *etc*: *'Fire away!' called the sergeant-major to the young soldiers.* 2 (*inf*) to begin doing something; to go ahead: *I'm ready to start writing down what you're going to say – fire away!* 3 (*often with* **at**) to continue shooting at for some time: *They fired away at the target for several minutes.*

hang fire *see* **hang**.

on 'fire 1 burning: *Leave the building – it's on fire!* 2 (*formal*) full of emotion or enthusiasm: *hearts on fire.*

open fire (*usu with* **on**) to begin shooting at: *The enemy opened fire (on us) before we reached safety.*

play with fire (*fig*) to do something dangerous or risky: *She knew she was playing with fire by having an affair with a married man.*

set fire to (something)/set (something) on fire to cause (something) to begin burning *usu* accidentally or deliberately as a criminal act: *His cigarette set fire to the bedclothes; The terrorists set fire to the ambassador's house; He has set the house on fire.*

under fire 1 being shot at: *We have been under fire from the enemy all day.* 2 (*inf*) being criticized or blamed: *The government is under fire for its economic policy.*

firm[1] [fə:m] *adj* 1 (fixed) strong and steady: *Is the table firm?; His hand felt firm on her shoulder; a firm handshake.* 2 decided; not changing one's mind: *He was quite firm about travelling by train; She gave a firm refusal.*

'**firmly** *adv*: *The picture is firmly fixed to the wall; She refused politely but firmly.*

firm[2] [fə:m] *nc* a business company: *I work for an*

engineering firm; *His firm is closing down.*

firmament ['fəːməmənt] *nc* (*liter*) the sky; the heavens: *The stars shine in the endless firmament.*

first [fəːst] **1** *adj, adv* before all others in place, time or rank: *She was the first person to arrive*; *That was the first time that I met him*; *The American President's wife is called the First Lady*; *The boy spoke first*; *He came in first in the race.* **2** *adv* before doing anything else: *'Shall we eat now?' 'Wash your hands first!'* – *nc* **1** the person, animal *etc* that does something before any other person, animal *etc*: *She was the first to arrive.* **2** the highest class of university or college degree: *He got a first in English.*

'**firstly** *adv* in the first place: *I have three reasons for not going – firstly, it's cold, secondly, I'm tired, and thirdly, I don't want to!*

first aid *nu* treatment of a wounded or sick person before the doctor's arrival: *Everybody should have some knowledge of first aid*; (*attrib*) *first-aid treatment.*

'**first-born** *nc, adj* (*attrib*) (*formal*) one's eldest child: *our first-born* (*child*).

ˌ**first-'class** *adj* **1** of the best quality: *This programme is first-class!*; *a first-class hotel.* **2** (for) travelling in the best and most expensive part of the train, plane, ship *etc*: *a first-class passenger*; *His ticket is first-class.* – *adv*: *He always travels first-class.* – *See also* **second-class** *under* **second**[1].

first floor *nc* (*with* **the**) the floor above the ground floor; (*Amer*) the ground floor: *Our office is on the first floor*; (*attrib*) *a first-floor flat.*

ˌ**first-'hand** *adj, adv* (of a story, description *etc*) obtained directly, not through various other people: *He gave me a first-hand account of what had happened*; *I heard the story first-hand – it must be true.*

first night *nc* **1** the evening on which the first public performance of a production of a play *etc* takes place: *This is the first night of the new opera.* **2** such a performance: *She loves going to first nights*; (*attrib*) *a first-night performance*; (*attrib*) *first-night nerves.*

first person (*gram*) *see* **person**.

ˌ**first-'rate** *adj* of the best quality: *He is a first-rate architect*; *She is first-rate at her job.*

at 'first at the beginning: *At first I didn't like him, but I soon changed my mind.*

at first hand obtained *etc* directly: *I was able to acquire information about the accident at first hand.*

first and foremost (*formal*) first of all; before anything else: *First and foremost, we must thank you for your help.*

first of all **1** as the first thing (to be) done, said *etc*: *First of all, we had better clear all this rubbish away.* **2** in the first place: *I have two objections to this – first of all, I don't think it's possible, and secondly we can't afford it.*

in the first place *see* **place**.

See also **one** *and* Appendix 1.

fiscal ['fiskəl] *adj* (*formal*: *attrib*) of financial matters, *esp* public money: *the end of the fiscal year*; *fiscal affairs.*

See also **financial year**.

fish [fiʃ] – *pls* **fish**, (*rare*) '**fishes** – **1** *nc* a kind of creature that lives in water and breathes through gills: *There are plenty of fish around the coast of Britain.* **2** *nu* its flesh eaten as food: *Do you prefer meat or fish?*; *fish and chips*; (*attrib*) fish-cakes. – **1** *vti* to (try to) catch fish (in): *He likes fishing*; *He is fishing for salmon*; *He fished the river all day and caught nothing.* **2** *vi* (*inf*: *usu with* **for**) search for: *She fished around in her handbag for a handkerchief.* **3** *vi* (*inf*: *usu with* **for**) to try to get by indirect means: *She is always fishing for compliments*; *He is fishing for an invitation to our party.* – *See also* **fish out** *below.*

'**fishery** **1** *nc* an area of sea where a lot of fishing is done: *deep-sea fisheries.* **2** *ncu* the business of fishing: *The Ministry of Agriculture and Fisheries.*

'**fishy** *adj* **1** (*usu attrib*) of or like a fish: *a fishy smell.* **2** (*inf*) odd or suspicious: *There's something fishy about that man*; *It all seems very fishy to me*; *That's a fishy excuse.*

'**fisherman** *nc* a man who fishes either as a job or as a hobby: *There are two fishermen at the end of the pier*; *The fishermen were mending their nets as the weather was too stormy to go out to the fishing-grounds.*

'**fishing-line** *ncu* a fine strong thread, now *usu* made of nylon, used with a rod, hooks *etc* for catching fish.

'**fishing-rod** *nc* a long thin flexible rod used with a fishing-line and hooks *etc* for catching fish.

'**fishmonger** *nc* **1** a person who sells fish: *Our fishmonger goes to the market early every morning.* **2** a shop that sells mainly fish: *I must go down to the fishmonger – I need to buy salmon for dinner.*

'**fishwife** *nc* **1** (*old*) a woman who prepares and sometimes sells fish. **2** (*derog*) a woman with a loud voice and who uses vulgar language.

fish out *vt sep* (*inf*) to pull something out with some difficulty: *At last he fished out the letter he was looking for.*

like a fish out of water in an uncomfortable or unaccustomed situation; ill at ease: *The middle-aged woman felt like a fish out of water at her daughter's party.*

fission ['fiʃən]: **nuclear fission** *nu* (*tech*) the splitting of the nuclei of atoms.

fissure ['fiʃə] *nc* (*formal*) a crack: *There was a fissure in the rock along which he was able to climb*; (*tech*) *She has a fissure in her lip and it is taking a long time to heal.*

fist [fist] *nc* a tightly closed hand: *Boxers fight with their fists*; *He shook his fist at me in anger*; *He clenched his fists in agony as the doctor cleaned the wound.*

fit[1] [fit] *adj* **1** in good health: *He has been ill and he's not completely fit yet*; *I am feeling very fit*; *Exercise makes people fit.* **2** suitable; correct for a particular purpose or person: *You are not fit* (= you are too dirty, untidy *etc*) *to be seen!*; *a dinner fit for a king*; *Do you think this man is fit for the job?* – *nu* the right size or shape for a particular person, purpose *etc*: *Your dress is a very good fit.* – *v* – *pt, ptp* '**fitted** – (not used with **is, was** *etc* and **-ing** (*defs 1, 2*)) **1** *vti* to be the right size or shape (for someone or something): *The coats fits* (*you*) *very well*; *That cover fits the armchair perfectly.* **2** *vt* to make suitable (for): *He always tried to make the punishment fit the crime*; *His speech fitted the occasion well.* **3** *vt* to put (something) in position: *Who fitted this cooker?*; *You must fit a new lock on the door*; *They began to fit the pieces of the machine together.* **4** *vt* to supply with; to equip with: *He fitted the cupboard with shelves.* – *See also* **fit in, fit out** *below.*

'**fitment** *nc* (*formal*) a fitting (*n def 1*).

'**fitter** *nc* **1** a person who puts the parts of a

machine together. **2** a person who makes clothes fit properly.

'fitting *adj* suitable: *This is a fitting occasion to wish you good luck*; *It is fitting that you should attend the ceremony.* – *nc* **1** something, *eg* a piece of furniture, which is fixed, *esp* in a house *etc*: *The bathroom fittings are all pale blue.* **2** the trying-on of a dress *etc* and altering to make it fit: *I am having a fitting for my wedding-dress tomorrow.*

fit in *vi* (*often with* **with**) to be able to live, exist *etc* in agreement or harmony: *The girl is unhappy at school – she just doesn't fit in* (*with the rest of the children*); *My holiday plans must fit in with my colleague's plans.*

fit out *vt sep* to provide with everything necessary (clothes, equipment *etc*): *They were fitted out for their expedition by the best shop in London*; *The shop fitted them out at very short notice*; *The ship left dock after it was fitted out.*

'fit to (*inf*) ready to: *I was fit to scream with anger.*

fit (someone) up with (something) (*inf*) to supply (someone) with (something); to give (someone) what is needed: *I think I can fit you up with a good pair of shoes.*

see/think fit to consider that some action is right, suitable *etc*: *I won't tell you what to do – you may do as you see fit* (*to do*).

See also **misfit, unfit**.

fit[2] [fit] *nc* **1** a sudden attack of illness, *esp* epilepsy: *She suffers from fits.* **2** something which happens as suddenly as this: *a fit of laughter/coughing.*

'fitful *adj* (*formal*) irregular; stopping and starting: *a fitful breeze*; *fitful sleep.*

'fitfully *adv* (*formal*): *He slept fitfully.*

by fits and starts (*inf*) irregularly; often stopping and starting again: *He did his work by fits and starts.*

five [faiv] **1** *nc* the number or figure 5. **2** *nu* the age of 5. – *adj* **1** (*usu attrib*) 5 in number. **2** (*pred*) aged 5. – *See* **eight** *for constructions.*

five- (*in cmpds*) having five (of something): *a 'five-a,partment 'house.*

'fiver *nc* (*inf*) (a banknote worth) £5 or $5: *It cost me a fiver*; *Have you got change of/for a fiver?*

'five-year-old *nc* a person or animal that is five years old. – *adj* (*attrib*) (of a person, animal or thing) that is five years old. – *See* **eight-year-old** *under* **eight** *for constructions.*

See also **fifth** *and* Appendix 1.

fives [faivz] *n sing* a ball-game played in a court with high walls.

fix [fiks] *vt* **1** to make firm or steady: *He fixed the post firmly in the ground*; (*fig*) *He fixed his eyes on the door.* **2** to attach; to join: *He fixed the shelf to the wall.* **3** to mend or repair: *He has succeeded in fixing my watch.* **4** to direct (attention, a look *etc*) at: *She fixed all her attention on me*; *She fixed me with an angry stare.* **5** (*often with* **up**) to arrange; to settle: *to fix a price*; *We fixed* (*up*) *a meeting for next week.* **6** (*inf*) to arrange dishonestly: *You fixed it so that I would be blamed.* **7** (*inf*) to deal with (somebody) in revenge *etc*: *I'll fix him!* **8** to make (something) permanent by the use of certain chemicals: *After printing the photograph you must fix it so that it doesn't fade*; *He has not succeeded in fixing the dye.* **9** (*esp Amer*) to prepare; to get ready: *I'll fix dinner tonight.* – *See also* **fix on** *below.* – *nc* **1** (*inf*) trouble; a difficulty: *I'm in a terrible fix!* **2** (*sl*) an injection of a drug: *He's just had a fix.* **3** (*inf*) something arranged dishonestly or illegally: *His appointment as manager was a fix.*

fix'ation *nc* a strong idea or opinion for or against something that one does not or cannot change: *She has a fixation about travelling alone and always takes someone with her.*

fixed *adj* **1** arranged in advance; settled: *There's a fixed price for the meal at that restaurant*; *Gas prices are fixed for the next two years.* **2** (*usu attrib*) steady; not moving: *a fixed gaze/stare.* **3** (*pred*) arranged illegally or dishonestly: *The result of that race was fixed.*

fixedly ['fiksidli] *adv* steadily: *He stared fixedly at the picture.*

fixture ['fikstʃə] *nc* **1** a fixed piece of furniture *etc*: *We can't move the cupboard – it's a fixture.* **2** an event, *esp* sporting, arranged for a certain time: *The football team has a fixture on Saturday.*

'fix on *vt fus* (*inf*) to decide or to choose: *Have you fixed on a date for your party yet?*

fix (someone) up with (something) (*inf*) to provide (someone) with (something): *Can you fix me up with a car for tomorrow?*

fizz [fiz] *vi* (of a liquid) to release or give off many small bubbles, as a result of fermentation *etc*: *I like the way champagne fizzes.* – *nu* **1** the sound made or the feeling in the mouth produced by this: *This lemonade has lost its fizz.* **2** (*inf*) champagne.

'fizzy *adj* (of drinks, *usu* non-alcoholic) in which small bubbles, *usu* of carbon dioxide, are released: *fizzy lemonade*; *Children like fizzy drinks*; *My drink is too fizzy.*

fizzle ['fizl]: **fizzle out** *vi* (*inf*) to fail; to come to nothing: *The fire eventually fizzled out*; *Their plans to go abroad fizzled out when they realized how expensive the trip would be.*

fjord *see* **fiord**.

flabbergasted ['flabəga:stid] *adj* (*inf*: *usu pred*) very surprised: *She was quite flabbergasted when we told her that her friend was in jail.*

flabby ['flabi] *adj* (*inf*) loose and fat; not firm: *flabby cheeks*; *She used to be very slim but she's flabby now.*

flaccid ['flaksid] *adj* (*formal*) (of a person's flesh) hanging in loose folds; not firm: *He used to be very athletic but his flesh is rather flaccid now*; *flaccid cheeks.*

flag[1] [flag] *nc* **1** a piece of cloth with a particular design representing a country, party, association *etc*: *The ship was flying the French flag from the mast.* **2** a small paper badge bought in aid of charity: *She was selling flags in aid of the blind.*

'flag-pole/'flagstaff *ncs* the pole on which a flag is hung: *The youth climbed the flag-pole and stole the club's flag.*

flag down – *v* – *pt, ptp* **flagged** – *vt sep* to wave at (a car *etc*) in order to make it stop: *We flagged down a taxi in the High Street*; *You might be able to flag a taxi down.*

flag[2] [flag] – *pt, ptp* **flagged** – *vi* to become tired or weak: *Halfway through the race he began to flag.* *See also* **unflagging**.

flag[3] *see* **flagstone**.

flagellate ['fladʒəleit] *vt* (*formal*) to whip. **,flagel'lation** *nu*.

flagon ['flagən] *nc* a large container for liquids: *Bring me a flagon of wine*; *They bought eight flagons of cider for the party.*

flagrant ['fleigrənt] *adj* (*formal*: *usu attrib*) (*usu* of something bad) very obvious; easily seen: *flagrant injustice*; *a flagrant breaking of the rules.*

'flagrantly *adv*. **'flagrancy** *nu*.

flagstone ['flagstoun] *nc* (*also* **flag**) a flat stone used for a floor or path.

flair [fleə] *nc* a natural ability or cleverness for (doing) something: *She has a flair for (learning) languages.*

flake [fleik] *nc* a very small piece: *a snowflake*; *flakes of skin.* – *vi* (*usu with* **off**) to come off in flakes: *Her skin is flaking. The paint is flaking off that door.*

'**flaky** *adj* coming off in flakes: *flaky paintwork*; *The walls are rather flaky.*

flamboyant [flam'boiənt] *adj* (*formal*) intended to attract notice: *She wore flamboyant clothes because she liked people to look at her*; *He was too flamboyant to be popular*; *His flamboyant behaviour attracted a lot of attention.* **flam'boyance** *nu.*

flame [fleim] *nc* **1** the bright light of something burning: *A small flame burned in the lamp*; *Flames leaped high in the fireplace.* **2** (*liter*) passion; strong feeling: *the flame of love.* – *vi* **1** to burn with flames: *The fire flamed brightly*; (*fig*) *His eyes flamed with anger.* **2** to become very hot, red *etc*: *Her cheeks flamed with embarrassment.*

'**flaming** *adj* (*attrib*) **1** burning with flames: *a flaming fire.* **2** (of colours, *esp* red) very bright: *She had flaming red hair.* **3** (*inf*) (of anger, temper *etc*) violent: *He was in a flaming temper.*

flammable ['flaməbl] *adj* (*esp Amer or tech*) able or likely to burn: *The child's nightdress caught fire because it was made of flammable material*; *That material is highly flammable.*

See also **inflammable, non-flammable**.

flamingo [flə'miŋgou] – *pl* **fla'mingo(e)s** – *nc* a type of long-legged wading bird, pink or bright red in colour: *We saw flamingoes at the zoo yesterday.*

flammable *see* **flame**.

flan [flan] *ncu* a flat open tart of pastry and fruit *etc*: *a cheese and onion flan*; *a strawberry flan*; *Would you like some flan?*

flange [flandʒ] *nc* (*tech*) a raised edge on the rim of a wheel *etc.*

flank [flaŋk] *nc* the side of anything *esp* an animal's body or an army: *He stroked the horse's flank*; *They marched around the enemy's flank.* – *vt* **1** to be at the side of: *The prisoner appeared, flanked by two policemen.* **2** (*usu mil*) to come around the side of: *The troops flanked the enemy forces.*

flannel ['flanl] **1** *nu, adj* (of) loosely woven woollen cloth: *blankets made of flannel*; *My grandmother used to wear a flannel petticoat.* **2** *nc* a small piece of material used for washing the face *etc*; a face-cloth: *soap and a face flannel.*

ˌ**flanne'lette** [-'let] *nu, adj* (of) a cotton cloth made in imitation of flannel: *sheets made of flannelette*; *flannelette sheets.*

'**flannels** *n pl* trousers made of flannel or similar material: *He wears white flannels to play cricket*; *a pair of flannels.*

flap [flap] *nc* **1** anything broad or wide that hangs loosely: *A flap of canvas formed the door of the tent.* **2** the sound made when such a thing moves: *We could hear the flap of the flag blowing in the wind.* **3** (*inf*) great confusion or panic: *They are all in a terrible flap over the robbery.* – *v* – *pt, ptp* **flapped** – **1** *vti* to (make something) move with the sound of a flap: *The leaves were flapping in the breeze*; *The bird flapped its wings and flew away.* **2** *vi* (*inf*) to become confused; to get into a panic: *There is no need to flap – you'll be ready in time.*

See also **unflappable**.

flare [fleə] *vi* **1** to burn with a bright unsteady light: *The firelight flared across the room.* **2** (of a skirt, trousers *etc*) to become wider at the bottom edge: *Her new skirt is not straight – it flares slightly.*

flare up *vi* suddenly to burn brightly: *A sudden wind made the fire flare up*; (*fig*) *A quarrel flared up between them*; (*fig*) *The spots on his face flared up again* (*nc* '**flare-up**).

flash [flaʃ] *nc* **1** a quick showing of a bright light: *a flash of lightning*; (*fig*) *a flash of understanding.* **2** a moment; a very short time: *He was with her in a flash.* **3** a flashlight (*def 2*). **4** (*often* '**newsflash**) a brief news report sent by radio, television *etc*: *Did you hear the flash about the king's death?* **5** a distinctive mark in a uniform: *I could tell his rank from the flashes he wore.* – **1** *vti* (of a light) to (cause to) shine quickly: *He flashed a torch*; *A light flashed out from the window*; (*fig*) *She flashed a smile at him.* **2** *vi* (*usu with* **by** *or* **past**) to pass quickly: *The days flashed by*; *The cars flashed past.* **3** *vt* (*inf*) to show; to display: *He flashed a card and was allowed to pass*; *She flashed her diamonds to impress all her friends.* **4** *vt* to send (a message) *usu* by radio *etc*: *We flashed a message to the ship.*

'**flashy** *adj* (*derog sl*) big, bright *etc* but cheap and of poor quality: *a flashy car*; *flashy clothes.* '**flashily** *adv.*

'**flash-back** *nc* (in a play, film *etc*) a scene from the past: *As the hero is sleeping, there is a flash-back to his childhood.*

'**flashlight** *nc* **1** a (battery) torch: *He took a small flashlight out of his pocket.* **2** (*often abbrev* **flash**) an instrument which produces a sudden bright light for taking photographs.

a flash in the pan (*inf*) a sudden, brief success which is not likely to happen again: *She did pass one exam but it was just a flash in the pan.*

flask [fla:sk] *nc* **1** a container in which drinks can be carried: *a flask of whisky*; *a brandy flask.* **2** a vacuum flask: *The workmen carried flasks of tea.* **3** (*chem*) a bottle, *usu* with a narrow neck. **4** the amount contained in a flask: *He drank the whole flask of tea.*

flat [flat] **1** *adj* level; without rise or fall: *I need a flat surface to work on*; *The countryside was quite flat.* **2** *adj* (*inf*) dull; without interest: *She spent a very flat weekend after her friends left*; *After the excitement was over, she felt rather flat.* **3** *adj* (of something said, decided *etc*) definite; emphatic: *a flat denial*; *I am not going and that's flat.* **4** *adj* (of a tyre) not inflated, having lost most of its air; not blown up: *He could not drive his car as it had a flat tyre.* **5** *adj, adv* (of drinks) no longer fizzy: *My beer has gone flat*; *flat lemonade.* **6** *adj, adv* (*music*) slightly lower than a note should be; under the true pitch: *That last note was flat*; *The choir went very flat.* **7** *adv* stretched out: *She was lying flat on her back.* – *nc* **1** (*Amer* **a'partment**) a set of rooms in a larger building: *Do you live in a house or a flat?* **2** (in musical notation) a sign (♭) which makes a note a semitone lower. **3** a level, even part: *the flat of her hand*; *the flat of a sword.* **4** (*inf*) a flat tyre: *We got a flat on the way home.* **5** (*usu in pl*) an area of flat land, *esp* beside the sea, a river *etc*: *mud flats.*

'**flatly** *adv* definitely; emphatically: *She flatly denied it.*

'**flatten** **1** *vti* (*often with* **out**) to make or become flat: *He flattened (out) the bent metal*; *The countryside flattened out as they came near the sea.* **2** *vt* (*often with* **down**) to make (something) flat:

The wind had flattened (down) the farmer's wheat.
'**flat race** *nc* a race over level ground without jumps: *Her child won the flat race at the school sports*; (*attrib*) *The jockey was training for the flat-race season.*
flat rate *nc* a fixed amount, *esp* one that is the same in all cases: *He charged a flat rate for the work*; (*attrib*) *flat-rate contributions.*
fall flat *see* **fall**.
flat out (*inf*) as fast, energetically *etc* as possible: *He ran flat out down the road*; *She worked flat out to get it finished.*

flatter ['flatə] **1** *vt* to praise too much or insincerely: *If you want to please him, flatter him by complimenting him on his singing.* **2** *vt* to show, describe *etc* someone or something as being better than someone *etc* really is: *The photograph flatters him.* **3** *v refl* to be pleased to admit (that one can do something): *I flatter myself that I can speak French perfectly.* '**flatterer** *nc.*
'**flattery** *ncu* insincere praise: *His flattery made her feel very angry as she knew that in fact she was looking very untidy.*

flatulence ['flatjuləns, (*Amer*) -tʃu-] *nu* (*formal or med*) gas in the stomach: *He often suffers from flatulence.* '**flatulent** *adj.*

flaunt [flo:nt] *vt* (*formal derog*) to show off in order to attract attention to oneself: *She always flaunts her expensive clothes in front of her poor relations.*

flautist ['flo:tist] *nc* a flute-player.

flavour, (*Amer*) **flavor** ['fleivə] **1** *ncu* taste: *The tea has a wonderful flavour*; *There are many different flavours of ice-cream.* **2** *nu* atmosphere; quality: *The celebrations had an Eastern flavour.* – *vt* to give flavour to: *She flavoured the cake with lemon.*
'**flavouring** *nc* anything used to give a particular taste: *lemon flavouring.*

flaw [flo:] *nc* a fault; something which makes something not perfect: *There is a flaw in the material*; *There must be a flaw in that argument but I can't think what it is.*
flawed *adj* (*formal*) having a flaw: *flawed beauty*; *This china is flawed.*
'**flawless** *adj* (*formal*) perfect: *her flawless beauty*; *Her reasoning is not flawless.*

flax [flaks] *nu* a type of plant whose fibres are woven into linen cloth.
'**flaxen** *adj* (*liter*) (of hair) very fair or blonde: *She had flaxen hair and blue eyes.*

flea [fli:] *nc* a type of small blood-sucking insect that jumps instead of flying and lives on the bodies of animals or people: *The dirty old tramp had fleas on him*; *That stray dog has fleas.*

fleck [flek] *nc* a spot: *not a fleck of dust to be seen*; *There were flecks of blood in her urine.*
paper; *a flecked pattern*; *flecked with blood.*
paper; *a flecked pattern*; *flecked with blood.*

fled *see* **flee**.

fledg(e)ling ['fledʒliŋ] *nc* a young bird ready to fly.

flee [fli:] – *pt, ptp* **fled** [fled] – *vti* (*formal or liter*) to run away (from danger): *She screamed and fled*; *He has fled the danger.*
See also **flight**[2].

fleece [fli:s] *nc* a sheep's coat of wool: *The farmer sold two hundred fleeces last year.* – *vt* **1** to cut wool from (sheep). **2** (*sl*) to rob (of money): *He fleeced the tourists of several hundred pounds.*
'**fleecy** *adj* soft and woolly: *a fleecy blanket.*

fleet[1] [fli:t] *nc* **1** a number of ships or boats under one command or sailing together: *the Sixth fleet*; *a fleet of fishing boats.* **2** the entire navy of a country: *the British fleet.* **3** a group of buses, taxis *etc* owned by one person or travelling together: *He runs a fleet of taxis in London*; *A fleet of buses arrived to collect the school-children.*

fleet[2] [fli:t] *adj* (*liter*) quick and agile: *fleet-footed*; *fleet of foot.*
'**fleeting** *adj* (*formal or liter*) passing quickly: *For a fleeting moment she looked sad but then she smiled again*; *the fleeting joys of youth*; *Some pleasures are only fleeting.*

Flemish *see* Appendix 2.

flesh [fleʃ] *nu* **1** the soft substance (muscles *etc*) that covers the bones of animals: *We can eat the flesh of most animals.* **2** (*liter*) the body: *The spirit is willing, but the flesh is weak.* **3** fatness: *He used to be very slim but he has a great deal of flesh now.* **4** the soft part of fruit: *the golden flesh of a peach.*
'**fleshly** *adj* (*old*) of the body; not spiritual: *fleshly desires.*
'**fleshy** *adj* (*derog*) fat: *a fleshy face.*
'**flesh-coloured** *adj* of the colour of Caucasian skin; pinkish white: *flesh-coloured tights.*
flesh and blood **1** relations; family: *She is my own flesh and blood.* **2** human nature: *It is more than flesh and blood can tolerate.*
in the 'flesh actually present: *I have seen him on television, but never in the flesh.*

flew *see* **fly**[2].

flex [fleks] *vt* to bend, *esp* in order to test: *He flexed his muscles*; *She slowly flexed her arm to find out if it was less painful.* – *ncu* (a piece of) thin insulated wire for carrying electricity: *That lamp has a long flex.*
'**flexible** *adj* **1** that can be bent easily: *flexible metal*; *This material is not very flexible.* **2** (*fig*) able or willing to change according to circumstances *etc*: *She won't mind the change of plan – she's a very flexible person*; *My holiday plans are very flexible.*
ˌ**flexi'bility** *nu.*
See also **inflexible**.

flick[1] [flik] *nc* a quick, sharp movement: *With a flick of the wrist the tennis player hit the ball over the net.* – *vti* to make this kind of movement (to or with something): *He flicked open a packet of cigarettes*; *She flicked a duster over the furniture*; *He flicked through the pile of photographs.*
'**flick-knife** *nc* a kind of knife with a blade which springs out when a button in the handle is pressed: *The teenager attacked the old man with a flick-knife.*

flick[2] [flik]: **the flicks** (*Brit inf*) the cinema: *I'm going to the flicks tonight.*

flicker ['flikə] *vi* **1** to burn unsteadily: *The candle flickered.* **2** (*fig*) to move quickly and unsteadily: *A smile flickered across her face.* – *nc* an unsteady light or flame: *I saw the flicker of an oil lamp*; (*fig*) *There was a flicker of interest in his plan at first but then people forgot about it.*

flier *see* **fly**[2].

flight[1] [flait] **1** *ncu* act of flying: *the flight of a bird*; (*fig*) *a flight of fancy.* **2** *nc* a journey in a plane: *How long is the flight to New York?* **3** *nc* a number of steps or stairs: *A flight of steps led up to the front door.* **4** *nc* a number of birds *etc* flying or moving through the air: *a flight of geese*; *a flight of arrows.*
'**flightless** *adj* (*formal*) (of birds) unable to fly: *The emu is a flightless bird.*
'**flighty** *adj* (*usu* of girls and women) with easily changed ideas; not thinking deeply; always looking for amusement: *Young girls are so flighty nowadays.*

'**flight deck** *nc* **1** the upper deck of an aircraft carrier where planes take off or land. **2** the forward part of an aeroplane where the pilot and crew sit.

ˌ**flight lieu'tenant** *nc* (*with caps in titles*) in the British air force, (a person of) the rank next below squadron leader: *He is a flight lieutenant*; *He was promoted to flight lieutenant*; *Flight Lieutenant Smith*. – *See also* Appendix 3.

in 'flight flying: *Have you seen the geese in flight?*

See also **fly**[2].

flight[2] [flait] *ncu* (*formal*) the act of fleeing or running away from an enemy, danger *etc*: *The general regarded the flight of his army as a disgrace.*

put to flight to cause (someone) to flee or run away: *The army put the rebels to flight.*

See also **flee**.

flimsy ['flimzi] *adj* (*often derog*) **1** thin and light: *You'll be cold in those flimsy clothes.* **2** not very well made; likely to break: *He's attempting to sail across the Atlantic in that flimsy boat*; *That box is very flimsy*; (*fig*) *They'll never believe that flimsy excuse.*

flinch [flintʃ] *vi* to make a sudden movement back or away in fear, pain *etc*: *She flinched as he raised his hand as if to strike her*; *He flinched away from the sudden heat.* – *nc* such a movement: *a flinch of pain.*

See also **unflinching**.

fling [fliŋ] – *pt*, *ptp* **flung** [flʌŋ] – **1** *vt* to throw with great force: *He flung a brick through the window*; *She flung herself into a chair.* **2** *vi* to rush: *He flung out of the house and never returned*; *She flung off without a word.* – *nc* **1** (*inf*) an enjoyable time: *He regarded the party the night before he was married as his last fling*; *You must let young people have their fling while they have no responsibilities.* **2** a lively Scottish dance: *They danced a Highland fling.*

flint [flint] **1** *nu*, *adj* (of) a kind of very hard stone: *There's a lot of flint in the rock round here*; *Prehistoric man used flint knives.* **2** *nc* a piece of hard mineral from which sparks can be struck: *I must buy a new flint for my cigarette-lighter.*

flip [flip] – *pt*, *ptp* **flipped** – *vt* **1** to throw (something) in the air (so that it turns): *They flipped a coin to see which side it landed on.* **2** (*sometimes with* **over**) to turn over quickly: *He flipped over the record*; *She flipped over the pages of the book.* – *nc* an act of flipping: *a quick flip of a coin.*

'**flip side** *nc* (*also* '**B-side**) the side of a gramophone record which is thought to be going to be less popular: *I actually prefer the flip side of their latest hit.*

flippant ['flipənt] *adj* not serious, *esp* about something that other people regard as being serious: *She made a flippant reply to her father's questions*; *Young people often seem flippant to their parents.* '**flippantly** *adv*. '**flippancy** *nu*.

flipper ['flipə] *nc* **1** a limb for swimming, *esp* of a seal, walrus *etc*. **2** a kind of rubber or plastic shoe, worn when swimming, which is shaped like the flipper of a seal *etc*: *I can swim much faster with these new flippers.*

flirt [flə:t] *vi* (*often with* **with**) to behave (towards someone) as though one were in love but without serious intentions: *She flirts with every man she meets*; (*fig formal*) *She flirts with the idea of going to America.* – *nc* a person, *esp* a woman, who behaves in this way: *She is a terrible flirt!*

flir'tation *ncu* act of flirting: *Her many flirtations made her husband angry*; (*formal*) *Her flirtation with the idea of going to America did not last long.*

flir'tatious [-ʃəs] *adj* (*formal*). **flir'tatiously** *adv*.

flit [flit] – *pt*, *ptp* '**flitted** – *vi* **1** to move quickly and lightly from place to place: *Butterflies were flitting around the garden.* **2** (*Scottish*) to move one's possessions from one house to another; to move house.

'**flitting** *ncu*: *Their flitting must be taking place today – I see the removal lorry at their door*; *the flitting of the butterflies from flower to flower.*

float [flout] **1** *vti* to (make something) stay on the surface of a liquid: *There was grease floating on the soup*; *The children often float their toys in the bath*; *A piece of wood was floating in the stream*; (*fig*) *The sound of bells floated* (*away*) *on the wind.* **2** *vt* (*formal*) to start or set going (a company, scheme *etc*): *They've floated a fund to aid developing countries.* **3** *vt* to allow (a currency) to vary or change in value according to the value of other international currencies rather than have a fixed, permanent value: *The government decided to float the pound to try to improve exports.* – *nc* **1** something that floats on a fishing-line: *If the float moves, there is probably a fish on the hook.* **2** (*usu in cmpds*) a vehicle for transporting certain things: *a milk-float*; *The cattle were taken to market in a cattle-float.* **3** a vehicle decorated and used in a procession: *A prize is given to the best float in the procession.* **4** an amount of money set aside for giving change *etc*: *Before the shop opened, each cashier was given a float of £20.*

floating currency *nc* a currency whose value is allowed to change or vary according to the value of other international currencies.

floating voter *nc* a person who does not regularly vote for any particular party: *The party that attracts the floating voters will win the election.*

flock [flok] *nc* **1** a number of certain animals or birds together: *a flock of sheep*; *a flock of starlings.* **2** (*fig*: *often facet*) a Christian congregation: *the priest and his flock.* – *vi* (*with* **to, into** *etc*) to gather or go somewhere together in a group or crowd: *We all flocked into the dining-room*; *People flocked to the football match.*

flog [flog] – *pt*, *ptp* **flogged** – **1** *vt* to beat; to whip: *You will be flogged for stealing the money*; *The drunken sailor was flogged.* **2** *vi* (*sl*: *often with* **away**) to work very hard: *He flogged away at his homework.* **3** *vt* (*Brit sl*) to sell: *He tried to flog me a stolen car.*

'**flogging** *ncu* (a) beating: *I gave the boy a good flogging.*

flog a dead horse (*inf*) to go on doing something after there is clearly no chance of success: *You'll be flogging a dead horse if you try to find a hotel room in London in August – they've been booked up for months.*

flood [flʌd] *nc* **1** a great overflow of water: *If it continues to rain like this, we shall have floods*; (*fig*) *a flood of tears.* **2** any great quantity: *a flood of letters*; *a flood of light.* – *vti* to (cause something to) overflow with water: *The river has flooded*; *She left the water running and flooded the kitchen*; (*fig*) *They flooded the market with cheap products.*

'**floodlight** *ncu* a kind of very strong light often used to light up football pitches, the outside of buildings *etc*: *There were floodlights all round the castle*; *They've installed floodlights in the sports stadium*; *Tonight's match is being played under floodlight.* – *v* – *pt*, *ptp* '**floodlit** [-lit] – *vt* to light with floodlights: *They floodlight the football pitch for evening matches.* '**floodlighting** *nu.*

'**floodlit** *adj*: *The castle is floodlit tonight*; *a floodlit football match.*

flood-'tide *nc* the rising tide.

floor [flo:] *nc* **1** the surface in a room *etc* on which one stands or walks. **2** all the rooms on the same level in a building: *The library has seven floors*; *My office is on the third floor.* **3** the part of a hall where ordinary members of a (law-making) assembly *etc* sit: *The Member of Parliament spoke from the floor.* – *vt* **1** to make or cover a floor: *We've floored the kitchen with plastic tiles.* **2** (*inf*) to knock down: *He floored him with a powerful blow*; (*fig*) *The question completely floored her* (= She could not answer the question at all).

-floored (*in cmpds*) having a floor or floors (of a particular kind): *a stone-floored kitchen.*

'**flooring** *nu* material for making or covering floors.

take the floor (*formal*) **1** to rise to speak to a group of people: *The chairman asked Mr Smith to take the floor.* **2** to begin to dance: *The young couple took the floor and waltzed round the room.*

flop [flop] – *pt, ptp* **flopped** – *vi* **1** to fall or sit down suddenly and heavily: *She flopped into an armchair.* **2** to hang or swing about loosely: *Her hair flopped over her face as she ran.* **3** to move about in a heavy, clumsy way: *She flopped around the house in her old slippers.* **4** (*fig*) (of a theatrical production) to fail; to be unsuccessful: *It was a surprise to us when his latest play flopped in London.* – **1** *ncu* (a) flopping movement. **2** *nc* (*fig*) a failure: *The show was a complete flop.*

'**floppy** *adj* (*usu attrib*) tending to flop; flopping: *a floppy hat.*

flora ['flo:rə] *nu* (*tech*) the plants of a district or country as a whole.

See also **fauna**.

floral ['flo:rəl] *adj* (*attrib*) **1** (*formal*) made of flowers: *floral decorations.* **2** having a pattern consisting of flowers: *a floral dress.*

florid ['florid] *adj* **1** (*formal or derog*) too richly decorated or ornamented: *florid architecture*; *florid handwriting.* **2** (of a complexion) highly coloured: *His florid complexion is a result of drinking too much alcohol.*

florin ['florin] *nc* (*hist*) a silver coin worth 10 old pence (10d).

florist ['florist] *nc* **1** a person who (grows and) sells flowers. **2** a florist's shop: *I bought some roses at the florist.*

'**florist's** *nc* a florist's shop.

flotilla [flə'tilə] *nc* a fleet of small ships: *A flotilla of yachts entered the harbour.*

flotsam ['flotsəm] *nu* goods lost by shipwreck and found floating on the sea.

See also **jetsam**.

flounce[1] [flauns] *vi* (*usu with* **out, away** *etc*) to move (away) in anger, impatience *etc*: *She flounced out of the room.*

flounce[2] [flauns] *nc* a decorative strip of material, *usu* frilled, sewn to the skirt of a dress, covers for furniture *etc*: *There are flounces at the bottom of her evening skirt.*

flounced *adj* decorated with a flounce: *a flounced skirt*; *The bedspread was flounced at the hem.*

flounder ['flaundə] *vi* **1** to move one's legs and arms violently and with difficulty (in water, mud *etc*): *She floundered helplessly in the mud.* **2** to think or speak with difficulty or confusion: *His question surprised her, and she floundered for a moment before answering.*

flour ['flauə] *nu* wheat, or other cereal, ground into a powder and used for cooking, baking *etc*: *You need flour, sugar and eggs to make this cake.*

'**floury** *adj* (*usu attrib*) **1** like flour: *floury potatoes.* **2** covered in flour: *She wiped her floury hands on her apron.*

flourish ['flʌriʃ, (*Amer*) 'flə:-] **1** *vi* to be healthy; to grow well; to thrive: *The children are flourishing*; *My plants are flourishing*; *The garden has been flourishing this year.* **2** *vi* to be successful or active: *His business is flourishing*; *Painting flourished in Italy in the fifteenth century.* **3** *vt* (*formal*) to hold or wave something as a show, threat *etc*: *He flourished his sword angrily.* – **1** *nc* an ornamental stroke of the pen in writing: *His writing was full of flourishes.* **2** *nc* an impressive, sweeping movement (with the hand or something held in it): *He bowed and made a flourish with his hat.* **3** *nu* grand, impressive behaviour: *The king and his courtiers entered the hall with great flourish.* **4** *nc* an ornamental passage of music: *There was a flourish on the trumpets.*

'**flourishing** *adj* **1** successful: *a flourishing business.* **2** growing well; healthy: *flourishing crops.*

flout [flaut] *vt* (*formal*) to treat with contempt; openly to refuse to obey: *He flouted his mother's wishes*; *You must not flout authority.*

flow [flou] *vi* **1** to move along in the way that water does: *The river flowed into the sea*; *Oil flows along the pipe*; *Blood flowed from the wound*; (*fig*) *Money flowed into Britain when the value of the pound was low*; (*fig*) *The traffic began to flow normally again.* **2** (of the tide) to rise: *The boat left the harbour when the tide began to flow.* **3** (*formal*) (of hair) to hang loosely and smoothly: *Her hair flowed down to her waist.* – *nu* the act of flowing: *The doctor could not stop the flow of blood*; (*fig*) *The flow of traffic was interrupted for several hours*; *the ebb and flow of the tide.*

flower ['flauə] *nc* **1** the part of a plant or tree from which fruit or seed grows, often brightly coloured and sometimes including the stem on which it grows: *flowers from the rose bushes*; *He gave her a bunch of flowers.* **2** a plant which is grown for its flowers: *Her garden has many flowers but no vegetables*; (*attrib*) *a flower-garden.* **3** (*liter*: *no pl*) the best of anything: *The flower of the nation died on the battlefield*; *the flower of one's achievements.* –*vi* (of plants *etc*) to produce flowers: *This plant flowers in early May.*

'**flowered** *adj* (*usu attrib*) having a pattern of flowers: *flowered curtain material.*

'**flowery** *adj* **1** (*usu attrib*) having, or decorated with, flowers: *a flowery hat.* **2** (of language) using ornamental words and phrases; poetic: *He made a very flowery speech*; *His style of writing is too flowery for me.*

'**flower-bed** *nc* a piece of earth prepared and used for the growing of plants.

'**flower-pot** *nc* a container made of earthenware, plastic *etc* in which a plant is grown.

in 'flower (of a plant) having flowers in bloom: *The cherry trees are in flower in May*; *When will the roses be in flower?*

See also **floral**.

flown *see* **fly**.

flu [flu:] short for **influenza**.

fluctuate ['flʌktjueit] *vi* (*formal*) to change or vary frequently (in number, price, level *etc*): *The cost of living continually fluctuates; He fluctuates between loving and hating her.*

'**fluctuating** *adj* (*attrib*): *a fluctuating economy.*

ˌ**fluctu'ation** *ncu* change or variation: *the fluctuation of the economy; fluctuations in the price of gold.*

flue [flu:] *nc* a passage for air and smoke in a stove or chimney: *The fire would not burn because the flue needed cleaning.*

fluent ['fluənt] *adj* **1** (of a language *etc*) smoothly and skilfully spoken: *He spoke fluent French; His German is not so fluent.* **2** (of a person) able to express oneself easily: *He is a fluent speaker of several European languages; He is fluent in French.*

'**fluency** *nu* ease in speaking or expressing: *The fluency of her French surprised her colleagues.*

'**fluently** *adv*: *He speaks Spanish fluently.*

fluff [flʌf] *nu* small pieces of soft, wool-like material from blankets *etc*: *My coat is covered with fluff because it was lying on the bedcover; There's a lot of fluff under the bed.* – *vt* **1** (*often with* **out** *or* **up**) to make full and soft like fluff: *The bird fluffed out its feathers; Fluff up the pillows and make the invalid more comfortable.* **2** (*inf*) to make a mistake in doing (something): *The actress fluffed her lines; The golfer fluffed his stroke.*

'**fluffy** *adj* **1** soft and woolly: *a fluffy kitten; Her gloves were warm and fluffy.* **2** (*usu attrib*) soft, light and full of air: *She cooked a fluffy omelette.*

fluid ['fluid] *nc* **1** (*tech*) a substance (liquid or gas) whose particles can move about freely. **2** any liquid substance: *cleaning fluid.* – *adj* **1** able to flow like a liquid: *a fluid substance; As it became warmer, the substance became more fluid.* **2** smooth and graceful: *fluid movements of a dancer; Her movements are very fluid.* **3** (*usu pred*) (of arrangements, plans *etc*) able to be changed easily: *My holiday plans are fluid.* **flu'idity** *nu.*

fluke [flu:k] *nc* (*inf*) a chance success: *Passing the exam was a fluke – I had done no work.*

flung *see* **fling**.

flunk [flʌŋk] *vt* (*inf*) **1** to fail or be unsuccessful in a test, examination *etc*: *He has flunked his French exam three times; I was going to ask her to marry me but I flunked it at the last minute.* **2** to declare (someone) to have failed an exam *etc*: *They flunked half of the applicants for the university course.*

flunkey ['flʌŋki] *nc* **1** (*old*) a male servant wearing uniform; a footman. **2** (*derog*) someone who treats someone else with too much respect and humility: *The millionaire is always surrounded by flunkeys.*

fluorescent [fluə'resnt] *adj* giving off a certain kind of light: *fluorescent light; fluorescent colours; I used paint which is fluorescent.* ˌ**fluo'rescence** *nu.*

fluoride ['fluəraid] *ncu* any of several substances containing fluorine, *esp* one which helps to prevent tooth decay: *This toothpaste contains fluoride; Which fluoride does it contain?*

'**fluoridate** [-rideit], '**fluoridize, -ise** [-ri-] *vti* (*tech*) to add fluoride to (drinking water): *The council have decided to fluoridate the town's water supply.* ˌ**fluori'dation,** ˌ**fluoridi'zation, -s-** *nus.*

fluorine ['fluəri:n] *nu* an element (symbol **F**), a pale greenish-yellow gas.

flurry ['flʌri, (*Amer*) 'flə:ri] *nc* **1** a sudden rush (of wind *etc*): *A flurry of wind made the door bang.* **2** a confusion: *She was in a flurry when the visitors arrived.* – *vt* (*inf*) to cause to be nervous or confused; to agitate: *She was flurried by the early arrival of her guests.*

flush[1] [flʌʃ] *nc* **1** a flow of blood to the face, making it red: *A slow flush covered her face.* **2** (the device that works) a rush of water which cleans a toilet: *The flush isn't working very well/is broken;* (*attrib*) *a flush toilet.* – *See also* **(in) the first flush of** *below.* – **1** *vi* to become red in the face: *She flushed with embarrassment;* (*fig*) *He was flushed with success.* **2** *vt* to clean by a rush of water: *to flush a toilet.* **3** *vt* (*usu with* **out**) to cause (an animal *etc*) to leave a hiding place: *The hounds flushed out the fox from the woods; The police soon flushed out the criminal.* – *adj* (*inf*: *usu pred*) having a lot of money: *I'm always flush after I receive my salary.*

flushed *adj* red in the face: *You look very flushed; She arrived with untidy hair and a flushed face.*

(in) the first flush of (in) the early stages of (something) when a person is feeling fresh, strong, enthusiastic *etc*: *in the first flush of youth; In the first flush of their victory they thought they had won the war but there were more battles to come.*

flush[2] [flʌʃ] *adj* level (with another surface): *The door is flush with the wall.*

fluster ['flʌstə] *nu* excitement and confusion caused by hurry: *She was in a terrible fluster when unexpected guests arrived.* – *vt* to (cause to) be worried or nervous; to agitate: *Don't fluster me!*

flute [flu:t] *nc* a type of high-pitched woodwind musical instrument: *He plays the flute; He played a tune on the flute.*
See also **flautist**.

fluted ['flu:tid] *adj* (*usu attrib*: *tech*) decorated with long carved lines: *a fluted pillar.*

'**fluting** *nu* decoration of this kind.

flutter ['flʌtə] *vti* **1** to (cause to) move quickly: *The bird fluttered its wings wildly but it could not get off the ground; She fluttered her eyelashes at him; A leaf fluttered to the ground.* **2** (of a bird, insect *etc*) to move the wings rapidly and lightly: *The moth fluttered round the light.* – *nc* **1** a quick irregular movement (of the pulse *etc*): *She felt a flutter in her chest.* **2** (*no pl*: *inf*) nervous excitement: *She was in a great flutter about travelling by aeroplane.* **3** (*inf*) a bet; a gamble: *I had a flutter on a horse and won £10.*

flux [flʌks] *nu* (*formal*) continual change: *Events are in a state of flux.*

fly[1] [flai] *nc* **1** a type of small winged insect: *The dead rabbit was covered in flies.* **2** a fish-hook made to look like a fly so that a fish will take it in its mouth: *Which fly should I use to catch a trout?* **3** (*often in pl*) a piece of material with buttons or a zip, *esp* at the front of trousers: *He was embarrassed when he discovered that his fly was undone; He buttoned his flies.*

(a) fly in the ointment something that spoils something or makes something less perfect, less valuable *etc*: *I enjoy my job – the fly in the ointment is that I start early in the morning.*

fly[2] [flai] – *pt* **flew** [flu:]: *ptp* **flown** [floun] – **1** *vti* to (make something) go through the air on wings *etc* or in an aeroplane: *The pilot flew (the plane) across the North Sea; The birds are flying south for the winter; The child wanted to fly his kite.* **2** *vti* (*liter*) to run away (from): *He flew (the country).* **3** *vi* (of time) to pass quickly: *The days flew past.* **4** *vi* to burst or break (into many small pieces): *The glass flew into pieces.* – *See also* **fly** *in phrases below.* – *adj* (*inf derog*) clever; knowing: *a fly person; a fly look; He is too fly to be caught by the police.*

'**flyer,** '**flier** *nc* a person who flies an aeroplane *etc*: *the flier of a model aeroplane.*

'**flying officer** *nc* (*with caps in titles*) in the British air force, (a person of) the rank next below flight lieutenant: *He is a flying officer*; *He was promoted to flying officer*; *Flying Officer Stewart.* – *See also* Appendix 3.

flying saucer *nc* a strange flying object thought possibly to come from another planet.

'**flying squad** *nc* a section of the police force using fast cars: *The flying squad was called to the scene of the murder.*

flying visit *nc* a very short, often unexpected, visit: *She paid her mother a flying visit before she went back to university.*

'**flyleaf** *nc* a blank page at the beginning or end of a book: *Would you sign your name on the flyleaf of this book?*

'**flyover** *nc* a road *etc* which is built up so as to cross above another: *Several flyovers were built across the motorway.*

'**flywheel** *nc* a heavy wheel which makes a machine able to run at a steady speed: *Washing machines have flywheels.*

fly in the face of (*fig*) to oppose or defy; to treat with contempt: *She always flew in the face of public opinion*; *He flew in the face of danger.*

fly into (a rage, temper *etc*) suddenly to become very angry *etc*: *The child flew into a rage when she was told that she could not watch television.*

fly off the handle (*inf*) to lose one's temper: *He flew off the handle when he heard that the boys had raided his garden again.*

get off to a flying start (*fig*) to have a very successful beginning: *Our new shop has got off to a flying start.*

let fly (*often with* **at**) to throw, shoot or send out violently: *He aimed carefully and let fly* (*an arrow*) *at the target*; *She let fly all her anger and frustration*; (*inf*) *She let fly at him for being late.*

send (someone/something) flying to hit or knock someone or something so that he or it falls down or falls backwards: *His father punched him and sent him flying*; *The children rushed through the shop and sent all the goods flying.*

with flying colours *see* **colour**.

See also **flight**.

foal [foul] *nc* a young horse. – *vi* to give birth to a foal: *The mare should foal this week.*

foam [foum] *nu* a mass of small bubbles on the surface of liquids *etc*: *the foam on the sea*; *the foam on a glass of beer.* – *vi* to produce foam: *The beer foamed in the glass*; *The mad dog foamed at the mouth.*

foam rubber *nu* a form of rubber which has a sponge-like appearance, used for stuffing chairs, mattresses *etc*.

fob[1] [fob]: **fob (someone) off with (something)** (*inf*) to get (someone) to accept (something worthless): *He tried to fob me off with worthless furniture*; *He fobbed me off with promises.*

fob[2] [fob] *nc* (*old*) **1** a small pocket for a watch. **2** a chain hanging from it.

focal *see* **focus**.

focus ['foukəs] – *pls* '**focuses, foci** ['fousai] – *nc* **1** (*tech*) the point at which rays of light meet after passing through a lens. – *See also* **in, out of focus** *below.* **2** a point to which light, a look, attention *etc* is directed: *She was the focus of everyone's attention.* – *v* – *pt, ptp* '**focus(s)ed** – *vt* **1** to adjust (a camera, binoculars *etc*) in order to get a clear picture: *Remember to focus the camera/the picture before taking the photograph.* **2** to direct (attention *etc*) to one point: *The accident focussed public attention on the danger.*

'**focal** *adj* (*attrib*: *tech*) of the focus: *focal length.* – *See also* **bifocal**.

in, out of focus giving or not giving a clear picture: *You'll have to get her in focus before you take the photo*; *These photographs are out of focus.*

fodder ['fodə] *nu* food for farm animals (hay, oats *etc*).

foe [fou] *nc* (*old or liter*) an enemy: *a deadly foe*; *He fought bravely against the foe.*

foetid *see* **fetid**.

foetus, (*Amer*) **fetus** ['fi:təs] *nc* (*tech*) a young human being, animal, bird *etc* in the early stages of development before it is born or hatched: *They X-rayed the mother to see if the foetus was normal.*

'**foetal,** (*Amer*) '**fetal** *adj* (*attrib*: *tech*) of a foetus: *in a foetal position*; *foetal abnormalities.*

fog [fog] *ncu* a thick cloud of moisture or water vapour in the air which makes it difficult to see: *I had to drive very slowly because of the fog.* – *v* – *pt, ptp* **fogged** – *vti* (*usu with* **up**) to cover with fog: *Her glasses were fogged up with steam.*

'**foggy** *adj* full of, or covered with, fog: *It is very foggy tonight*; *a foggy night.*

'**fog-bank** *nc* a thick cloud of fog: *The fog-bank resulted in many accidents on the motorway.*

'**fog-bound** *adj* unable to move or function because of fog: *The plane is fog-bound at the airport*; *The airport is fog-bound*; *hundreds of fog-bound passengers.*

'**fog-horn** *nc* a horn used as a warning to or by ships in fog: *The captain gave the order to sound the fog-horn.*

ˌ**not to have the** '**foggiest (idea)** (*inf*) to have no knowledge or ideas about something: *I haven't the foggiest* (*idea*) *why he left so suddenly.*

fogey, fogy ['fougi] *nc* (*inf*: *derog*) a dull or old-fashioned person: *Her father was such an old fogey that he wouldn't let her stay out after midnight.*

foible ['foibl] *nc* (*formal*) a slight weakness, or peculiarity in one's character; an eccentricity: *Old people often develop strange foibles.*

foil[1] [foil] *vt* (*formal*) to defeat; to disappoint: *She was foiled in her attempt to become President.*

foil[2] [foil] **1** *nu* extremely thin sheets of metal that resemble paper: *silver foil*; *Roast the chicken in cooking foil.* **2** *nc* (*formal*) a dull person or thing against which someone or something else seems brighter: *She acted as a foil to her beautiful sister.*

foil[3] [foil] *nc* a blunt sword with a button at the end, used in the sport of fencing.

foist [foist]: **foist (something) on to (someone)** to try to get someone to accept something worthless or unwanted: *He foisted a load of machinery on to a foreign dealer*; *The shopkeeper tried to foist his broken biscuits on to the old lady.*

fold[1] [fould] *vt* **1** to double over (material, paper *etc*); to lay one part on top of another: *She folded the paper in half and put it in the envelope*; *She folded the sheets and put them in the airing-cupboard.* **2** to lay one on top of another: *She folded her hands in her lap.* **3** to bring in (wings) close to the body: *The eagle folded its wings and settled on the branch.* **4** to hold or cross (one's arms) across one's chest: *He folded his arms and waited.* – *nc* **1** a doubling of one layer of material, paper *etc* over another: *Her dress hung in folds.* **2** a mark made *esp* on paper *etc* by doing this; a crease: *There was a fold in the page.*

'folder *nc* a cover for keeping loose papers together: *The speaker kept the notes for his speech in a folder.*

'folding *adj* (*attrib*) that can be folded: *a folding chair.*

See also **unfold**.

fold[2] [fould] *nc* a place surrounded by a fence or wall, in which sheep are kept: *a sheep fold.*

foliage ['fouliidʒ] *nu* (*formal*) leaves: *This plant has very beautiful foliage.*

folio ['fouliou] – *pl* **'folios** – (*tech*) **1** *nc* a sheet of paper folded once. **2** *ncu* a book in which the pages are made of sheets of paper folded once: *Shakespeare's plays were first printed in folio.*

folk [fouk] *n pl* (*inf*: *esp Amer* **folks**) people: *The folk in this town are very friendly.* – *adj* (*attrib*) (of the traditions) of the common people of a country: *folk customs*; *folk dance*; *folk music*; *folk song*; *folk tale.*

folks *n pl* (*inf*) one's family: *My folks all live in this part of the country.*

'folklore *nu* the study of the customs, beliefs, stories, traditions *etc* of a particular people: *the folklore of the American Indians.*

follow ['folou] **1** *vti* to go or come after: *I will follow (you)*; *The storm was followed by beautiful weather.* **2** *vt* to go along (a road, river *etc*): *Follow this road until you get to the station.* **3** *vti* to understand: *Do you follow (my argument)?* **4** *vt* to act according to: *I followed his advice.* **5** *vi* (*usu with* **it** *as subject*) to happen as a result: *He has been to Italy, but it does not follow that he understands the Italians.* **6** *vt* to have an interest in (sports *etc*): *He follows football regularly.* – *See also* **follow up** *below.*

'follower *nc* **1** a person who follows, *esp* the philosophy, ideas *etc* of another person: *He is a follower of Plato* (= Plato's theories). **2** (*hist*) an admirer, *usu* a boyfriend: *Kitchen maids were forbidden to have followers.*

'following *nu* supporters: *He has a great following among the poorer people.* – *adj* (*attrib*) **1** coming after: *The following day they went home.* **2** about to be mentioned: *You will need the following things – a pen, a notebook and a ruler.* – *prep* after; as a result of: *Following his illness, his hair turned white.* – *pron* things about to be mentioned: *You must bring the following – pen, pencil, paper and rubber.*

'follow-up *nu* (*inf*) something following and depending on something else: (*inf*) *Did you get any follow-up to the meeting on Friday?*; (*attrib*) *The doctor did some tests on me today and I have to go back next week for a follow-up examination.*

follow up *vt sep* **1** to go further in doing something: *I liked painting, so I decided to follow it up*; *He has never followed up his original interest in the subject*; *The police are following up a clue.* **2** to find out more about (something): *I heard the news about him, and decided to follow it up.*

folly ['foli] **1** *ncu* (*formal*) foolishness: *It would be folly to light a fire near that wood*; *She regretted the follies of her youth.* **2** *nc* (*hist*) a *usu* useless but often costly building, intended to be seen from a distance: *In the grounds of the estate they found the ruins of a huge eighteenth-century folly.*

fond [fond] *adj* (*attrib*) **1** loving: *fond looks*; *a fond husband.* – *See also* **fond of** *below.* **2** (of wishes, hopes *etc*) wanted but unlikely to happen: *His fond ambition was to be a film star.*

'fondly *adv* **1** lovingly: *She smiled fondly at the baby.* **2** in a foolishly hopeful way: *He fondly imagined that his father would lend him the money for a new bike.*

'fondness *nu* (*esp with* **for**) affection; liking: *her fondness for children.*

'fond of having a liking for: *He is very fond of dogs*; *She seems (to be) fond of him.*

fondle ['fondl] *vt* to touch, stroke *etc* affectionately: *He fondled the dog's ears.*

font [font] *nc* the basin (in a church) holding water for baptism: *There is a beautifully carved stone font in our church.*

food [fu:d] *nu* what living things eat: *Horses and cows eat different food from dogs*; *I like German food*; *This liquid is the best food for your plants*; (*fig*) *That's food for thought* (= something to think about).

'foodstuff *nc* (*formal*) a material used for food: *frozen foodstuffs.*

See also **feed**.

fool [fu:l] *nc* **1** a person without sense or intelligence: *He is such a fool he never knows what to do*; *If she is fool enough to* (= such a fool as to) *spend all her money at once, let her!* **2** (*hist*) a person employed by kings, nobles *etc* to amuse them; a court jester. – **1** *vt* to deceive: *She completely fooled me with her story.* **2** *vi* (*often with* **about** *or* **around**) to act like a fool or playfully: *Every time I see him he seems to be fooling*; *Stop fooling about with that knife!*

'foolery *nu* (*formal*) foolish or ridiculous behaviour: *The rest of the children laughed at his foolery on the roundabout.*

'foolish *adj* **1** having no sense: *He is a foolish young man*; *It is foolish to run away from home*; *She is being very foolish about it.* **2** ridiculous: *He made a foolish attempt to sing*; *He looked very foolish.*

'foolishly *adv.*

'foolishness *nu* behaviour which is not sensible: *They were amazed at the foolishness of some of the drivers in the fog.*

'foolhardy *adj* (*formal*) taking foolish risks; rash: *It was foolhardy of you to drive on such icy roads*; *He made a foolhardy attempt to climb the mountain in winter.* **'foolhardiness** *nu.*

'foolproof *adj* unable to go wrong: *His new plan seems completely foolproof*; *He finally thought of a foolproof way of doing it.*

make a fool of to make (someone) appear ridiculous or stupid: *The schoolchildren made a fool of their new schoolfellow because his clothes seemed strange to them*; *He made a real fool of her by promising to marry her and then leaving her when he had spent all her money.*

make a fool of oneself to act in such a way that people consider one ridiculous or stupid: *She made a fool of herself in the pub last night when she was drunk*; *He didn't want to make a fool of himself by asking her to the party when he knew that she would refuse to go.*

play the fool to act in a foolish manner, *esp* with the intention of amusing other people: *He always played the fool when the teacher left the classroom.*

foolscap ['fu:lskap] *nu* a large size of paper for writing or printing: *The schoolchildren are writing their essays on foolscap.*

foot [fut] – *pl* **feet** [fi:t] (*defs 1–3*), **foot** (*def 3*) – *nc* **1** the part of the leg on which a person or animal stands or walks: *My feet are very sore from walking* *so far*; *Each human foot has five toes.* **2** the lower part of anything: *Her cottage stands at the foot of the hill*; *There are notes at the foot of the page*; *the foot of the bed.* **3** (*often abbrev* **ft** *when written*) a measure of length equal to twelve inches (30·48 cm): *He is five feet/foot six inches tall*; *a four-foot wall.*

'footing *nu* **1** balance: *It was difficult for him to keep his footing on the narrow path*; *He missed his footing* (= stumbled) *and fell over.* **2** foundation: *The business is now on a firm footing.* **3** relationship: *We are on a friendly footing with all our neighbours.*

'football 1 *nu* a game played by kicking a large ball: *The children played football in the back garden.* **2** *nu* (*Brit*) soccer: *He plays football at school, not rugby*; *He plays football professionally*; (*attrib*) *a football fan*; (*attrib*) *football pools.* **3** *nc* the ball used in this game: *The child's football burst.*

'foothill *nc* (*usu in pl*) a small hill at the foot of a mountain: *the foothills of the Alps.*

'foothold *nc* a place to put one's feet when climbing: *It was difficult to find footholds on the slippery rock*; (*fig*) *Once you have gained a foothold in the industry, you can start to work your way up.*

'footlight *nc* (*usu in pl*) (in a theatre) a light which shines on the actors *etc* from the front of the stage: *Coloured footlights varied the white costumes of the dancers.*

'footman – *pl* **'footmen** – *nc* a male servant wearing a uniform: *The footman opened the door of the queen's carriage.*

'footmark *nc* a footprint: *He made dirty footmarks on her clean floor.*

'footnote *nc* a note at the bottom of a page: *There were several footnotes referring to other chapters of the book.*

'footpath *nc* a path or way for walking, not for cars, bicycles *etc*: *You can go by the road or by the footpath through the wood.*

'footprint *nc* the mark or impression of a foot: *She followed his footprints through the snow.*

'footsore *adj* (*pred*) with painful feet from too much walking: *He arrived, tired and footsore.*

'footstep *nc* the sound of a foot: *She heard his footsteps on the stairs.*

'footwear *nu* (*formal*) boots, shoes, slippers *etc*: *He always buys expensive footwear.*

fall on one's feet to have some unexpected good luck, *esp* after or because of something bad or unpleasant: *He was dismissed from his job last year, but he really fell on his feet – he is now doing the same job for someone else at a higher salary.*

find one's feet *see* **find**.

follow in someone's footsteps to do the same as someone has done before one: *When he joined the police force he was following in his father's footsteps.*

foot the bill (*inf*) to pay the bill: *My brother footed the bill for the party.*

get off on the wrong foot to make a bad beginning: *She got off on the wrong foot by being half an hour late for her interview.*

on 'foot walking: *She arrived at the house on foot.*

put one's best foot forward *see* **best**.

put one's feet up *see* **put**.

put one's foot down (*inf*) to be firm about something: *He wanted to go to Spain, but I put my foot down and refused to let him go.*

put one's 'foot in it (*inf*) to say or do something stupid: *I really put my foot in it when I asked about his wife – she has just run away with his friend!*

set foot in, on to arrive at or on: *As soon as he set foot in the hotel he knew it would be unsuitable for his mother's holiday.*

See also **afoot, underfoot**.

fop [fop] *nc* (*derog*) a man who is vain about his dress: *He's such a fop that he changes his shirt three times a day.* **'foppish** *adj.*

for [foː] *prep* **1** to be given or sent to: *This letter is for you*; *Will you make some tea for us?* **2** towards; in the direction of: *We set off for London*; *He is aiming for a much better job than the one he has at present*; *Is this the train for London?* **3** through a certain time or distance: *They waited for three hours*; *They walked for three miles.* **4** in order to have, get, be *etc*: *He asked me for some money*; *He was fishing for trout*; *Go for a walk*; *He is studying for a degree.* **5** in return; as payment: *He paid £2 for his ticket*; *He got a reward for his bravery.* **6** in order to be prepared: *He's getting ready for the journey*; *We must buy some more coal soon for the cold weather*; *He's working for an exam.* **7** representing: *He is the member of parliament for Hull*; *G stands for George.* **8** on behalf of: *Will you do it for me?*; *I can only speak for myself.* **9** in favour of: *Are you for or against the plan?* **10** because of: *for this reason*; *She wept for shame*; *The town is famous for its beautiful churches.* **11** having a particular purpose: *a cupboard for the toys*; *He gave her money for her bus fare*; *He went to France for a holiday.* **12** indicating an ability or an attitude to: *a liking for peace*; *a hatred for everything violent*; *an ear for music*; *It's good for you.* **13** as being: *Don't take me for a fool* (= Don't think that I'm a fool); *They mistook him for someone they knew.* **14** considering: *It is quite warm for January* (= considering that it is January when it is *usu* cold). **15** in spite of: *For all his money, he didn't seem happy.* – *conj* (*not used at the beginning of a sentence*) because: *It must be late, for I have been here a long time.*

if it hadn't been/wasn't for if someone had not done something; if something had not happened: *If it hadn't been for you, we would have finished much sooner*; *If it wasn't for your stupidity, this would not have happened.*

forage ['foridʒ] *vi* (*inf*: *often with* **about**) to search thoroughly: *He foraged about in the cupboard*; *He foraged for food in the cupboard.* – *nu* food for horses and cattle.

foray ['forei] *nc* (*formal or mil*) a sudden raid for plunder: *They made a successful foray into enemy country under cover of darkness.*

forbade *see* **forbid**.

forbear [fə'beə] – *pt* **forbore** [fə'boː] : *ptp* **forborne** [fə'boːn] – *vi* **1** (*formal*: *with* **from** *or infinitive*) to keep oneself from doing something: *We must forbear from talking about it*; *We must forbear to discuss it.* **2** (*old or liter*) to be patient: *We must forbear.*

for'bearance *nu* (*formal*) patience; control of temper: *She showed great forbearance in answering his rude questions.*

for'bearing *adj* (*formal*) patient: *She is very forbearing towards her demanding children*; *a patient and forbearing friend.*

forbears *see* **forebears**.

forbid [fə'bid] – *pt* **forbade** [fə'bad] : *ptp* **for'bidden** – *vt* (*old or formal*) to tell (someone) not to do something: *She forbade him to go.*

for'bidden *adj* not allowed: *forbidden customs*; *customs forbidden by law*; *Smoking is forbidden*; *It* *is forbidden to smoke in the theatre.*

for'bidding *adj* (*formal*) rather frightening: *The castle had a forbidding appearance*; *The new headmaster seemed stern and forbidding.*

forbore, forborne *see* **forbear**.

force [fo:s] *nc* **1** strength or power that can be felt: *the force of the wind*; (*fig*) *the force of his argument.* **2** a person or thing that has great power: *the forces of Nature*; *He is a great force in the Labour Party.* **3** (*sometimes with cap*) a group of men prepared for action: *the police force*; *the Royal Air Force*; *a military force.* – *See also* **forces** *below.* – *vt* **1** to make (someone or something) do something, go somewhere *etc*, often against his *etc* will: *He forced me to give him money*; *He forced the key into the lock*; *Don't try to force that child's foot into a slipper that's too small for it.* **2** to get something by strength or effort: *He forced his way through the crowd*; *He forced an entry*; *He forced a smile despite his grief*; *The police forced a confession from him.* **3** to cause (a plant) to grow quickly: *He forced the plants by keeping them in the dark.*

forced *adj* done with great effort: *a forced march*; *a forced smile*; *His smile was rather forced.*

'forceful *adj* powerful: *a forceful argument*; *a forceful personality*; *His speech was so forceful that it convinced everyone.* **'forcefully** *adv.*

'forcible *adj* (*very formal*: *esp legal*) done *etc* with great force or violence: *a forcible entry.*

'forcibly *adv* (*formal*: *esp legal*): *The house had been forcibly entered*; *He was forcibly impressed by her knowledge of the subject.*

'forces *n pl* (*with* **the** *and often with cap*) the army, navy and air force considered together: *The Forces played a large part in the parade.*

ˌforce'feed – *pt, ptp* **ˌforce'fed** – *vt* to feed (a person) by making him swallow (liquid) food: *They forcefed the prisoners.*

in, into 'force (*formal*) in or into operation; working or effective: *That rule has never been put into force*; *The new law is now in force.*

forceps ['fo:seps] *n pl* a medical instrument used for holding things firmly: *Forceps are sometimes used to deliver babies*; *a pair of forceps.*

ford [fo:d] *nc* a shallow crossing-place in a river. – *vt* to cross (water) on foot *etc*: *They forded the river on horseback.*

fore [fo:] : **to the 'fore** (*formal*) in the front; easily seen: *She is always to the fore at important social occasions*; (*fig*) *He has recently come to the fore in local politics.*

fore- [fo:] (*in cmpds*) before or in front, as in **foreground, foreleg**.

forearm[1] ['fo:ra:m] *nc* the lower part of the arm (between wrist and elbow): *Tennis players usually have strong forearms.*

forearm[2] [fo:r'a:m] *vt* (*formal*) to prepare before: *He knew they would ask him questions so he was forearmed with the answers*; *Forewarned is forearmed* (= If you know beforehand what difficulties, dangers *etc* are likely to arise, you can prepare for them).
See also **forewarn**.

forebears, forbears ['fo:beəz] *n pl* (*formal*) ancestors: *My forebears lived in that castle*; *One of her forebears murdered someone in a church.*

foreboding [fo:'boudiŋ] *nc* (*formal*) a feeling that something bad is going to happen: *He has a strange foreboding that he will die young*; *He thinks of lonely old age with foreboding.*

forecast ['fo:ka:st] – *pt, ptp* **'forecast** *or* **'forecasted** – *vti* to tell about (something) before it happens: *He forecast good weather for the next three days*; *The government find it difficult to forecast what will happen to the country's economic future.* – *nc* a statement about what is going to happen; a prediction: *a weather-forecast*; *His forecasts about the economy proved correct.*

forecourt ['fo:ko:t] *nc* a court or space in front of, and belonging to, a building *etc*: *There is a fountain in the forecourt of the castle*; *The petrol pumps are in the garage forecourt.*

forefathers ['fo:fa:ðəz] *n pl* ancestors: *Several of his forefathers emigrated to America.*

forefinger ['fo:fiŋgə] *nc* the finger next to the thumb: *He pointed out the route on the map with his forefinger.*

forefront ['fo:frʌnt] : **in the 'forefront** (*formal*) at or in the very front: *in the forefront of the battle*; (*fig*) *She is in the forefront of the anti-litter campaign.*

foregone ['fo:gon]: **a foregone conclusion** a result that is so obvious that it can be seen before it happens: *If an Olympic runner races against schoolboys, it is a foregone conclusion who will win.*

foreground ['fo:graund] *nc* (*usu in sing*) the part of a view or picture nearest to the person looking at it: *The photograph was of a landscape, with two horses in the foreground.*
See also **background**.

forehand ['fo:hand] *nc* in tennis *etc*, (the ability to make) a stroke or shot with the palm of one's hand turned towards the ball: *His forehand always confuses his opponents*; *A clever forehand won her the match point*; (*attrib*) *a forehand stroke.*

forehead ['forid] *nc* the part of the face above the eyebrows and below the hairline; the brow: *Her fringe completely covers her forehead – I wish she would get her hair cut.*

foreign ['forən] *adj* **1** belonging to a country other than one's own: *a foreign passport*; *foreign visitors to Britain*; *Most of my friends are foreign.* **2** (*attrib*) concerned with all countries other than one's own: *the Foreign Office*; *foreign exchange.* **3** (*attrib*: *formal*) not belonging naturally in a particular place: *The foreign object/body in the milk was found to be a piece of plastic.* **4** (*fig*: *pred*: *with* **to**) not naturally part of: *Anger was foreign to her nature.*

'foreigner *nc* **1** a person from another country: *There are always a lot of foreigners in London.* **2** (*fig facet*) an unfamiliar person: *There's a foreigner among us!*

'Foreign Office *n* (*with* **the**) the department of the government which is concerned with foreign affairs.

foreleg ['fo:leg] *nc* an animal's front leg: *The horse was black with white patches on its forelegs.*
See also **hind**[2].

forelock ['fo:lok] *nc* (*esp* of animals: *facet* of people) the piece of hair that hangs over the forehead: *The horse had a black mane and forelock*; *He touched his forelock as a sign of respect.*

foreman ['fo:mən] – *pl* **'foremen** – *nc* the supervisor or leader of a group, *esp* of workmen or members of a jury: *The foreman here is in charge of twenty workmen*; *The foreman of the jury gave the verdict.*

foremost ['fo:moust] *adj* (*attrib*), *pron* (the) most famous or important: *He is considered the foremost British artist of this century*; *He is certainly among the foremost.*

first and foremost *see* **first**.

forenoon [foːˈnuːn] *nc* (*esp* in Scotland) the morning: *My train leaves in the forenoon and arrives late afternoon.*

forensic [fəˈrensik] *adj* (*attrib*: *formal*) of or concerning courts of law: *forensic medicine.*

forerunner [ˈfoːrʌnə] *nc* a person or thing which is a sign of what is to follow: *Penicillin was the forerunner of modern antibiotics.*

foresee [foːˈsiː] – *pt* **foreˈsaw** [-ˈsoː]: *ptp* **foreˈseen** – *vt* to see or know about before or in advance: *He could always foresee the difficulties the government would meet; You could not possibly foresee that he would kill himself; Due to unforeseen circumstances, tonight's performance of the play has had to be cancelled.*

foreˈseeable *adj* (*usu attrib*: *formal*: *neg* **un-**) able to be foreseen: *He may recover but at the moment there is no foreseeable chance of his walking again; I shall not be able to give you back the money I owe you in the foreseeable future* (= soon; within a reasonably short space of time).

ˈforesight [-sait] *nu* the ability to see in advance what may happen and to plan for it: *Fortunately she had had the foresight to drive carefully in case the roads were icy, or the accident might have been worse; He admired her foresight in storing up fuel for the winter.*

foreshadow [foːˈʃadou] *vt* (*formal*) to give an indication in advance of something that is going to happen: *The rise in prices foreshadowed great economic difficulties; His masterpiece was foreshadowed by his earlier work.*

foresight *see* **foresee**.

foreskin [ˈfoːskin] *nc* the skin that covers the end of the penis.

forest [ˈforist] *ncu* **1** (a large piece of) land covered with trees: *Forest stretched into the distance as far as they could see; Every day they went exploring in the nearby pine forest.* **2** an area of land in which animals, *esp* deer, are kept: *a deer forest.*

ˈforester *nc* a person who works in a forest or is involved in forestry.

ˈforestry *nu* (the science of) growing and looking after forests: *Forestry is very important in Scotland*; (*attrib*) *a forestry worker.*

forestall [foːˈstoːl] *vt* (*formal*) to do something before someone else: *She was about to speak but he forestalled her.*

foretaste [ˈfoːteist] *nc* (*fig*) a small sample or experience of something before it happens: *This cold weather is just a foretaste of winter.*

foretell [foːˈtel] – *pt*, *ptp* **foreˈtold** [-ˈtould] – *vt* (*more formal than* **predict**) to tell (about something) before it has happened: *Astrologers say that they can foretell the future from the stars.*

forethought [ˈfoːθoːt] *nu* (*formal*) thought about, or concern for, the future: *They acted without sufficient forethought.*

foretold *see* **foretell**.

forever, for ever *see* **ever**.

forewarn [foːˈwoːn] *vt* (*liter*) to warn (someone) before something happens: *She was forewarned about his attitude to women.*

See also **forearm**[2].

foreword [ˈfoːwəːd] *nc* a piece of writing as an introduction at the beginning of a book; a preface: *The foreword was written by a famous scholar.*

forfeit [ˈfoːfit] *nc* something that must be given up because one has done something wrong, *esp* in games: *If you lose the game you will have to pay a forfeit.* – *vt* (*formal*) to lose (something) because one has done something wrong: *He has forfeited his rights to the money by ignoring the lawyer's letters; He forfeited our respect by telling lies about his wife.* – *adj* (*formal*: *pred*) forfeited: *His former rights are forfeit now.*

forgave *see* **forgive**.

forge[1] [foːdʒ] *nc* **1** a very hot oven in which metals are melted *etc*; a furnace: *Steel is manufactured in a forge.* **2** a blacksmith's shop, where he shoes horses, mends tools *etc*: *The blacksmith in his forge used to be a common sight in villages.* – *vt* to shape metal by heating and hammering: *He forged a horse-shoe out of an iron bar*; (*fig formal*) *His strong personality was forged by the pride and ambition of his family.*

forge[2] [foːdʒ] *vt* to copy (*eg* a letter or a signature) and pretend that it is genuine, *usu* for illegal purposes: *He forged my signature on cheques.*

ˈforgery **1** *nu* (the crime of) copying pictures, documents, signatures *etc* and pretending they are genuine: *He was sent to prison for forgery.* **2** *nc* a picture, document *etc* copied for this reason: *The painting for which he had paid £2 500 was discovered to be a forgery.*

forge[3] [foːdʒ] *vi* to move steadily: *They forged ahead with their plans; He forged through the crowd to get to the front.*

forget [fəˈget] – *pt* **forgot** [fəˈgot]: *ptp* **forgotten** [fəˈgotn] – **1** *vti* to fail to remember: *He has forgotten my name; She forgot to meet him at the station; They forgot (that) she was coming to dinner; I shan't forget; I did not go to the meeting because I forgot all about it.* **2** *vt* to leave behind accidentally: *She has forgotten her handbag again.* **3** *v refl* (*formal*) to lose one's dignity, self-control or good sense: *She forgot herself so far as to criticize her boss to his face.*

forˈgetful *adj* often forgetting: *She is a very forgetful person; It was very forgetful of me to leave my notes in the office.* **forˈgetfully** *adv.*

forˈget-me-not *nc* a small plant with blue flowers.

See also **unforgettable**.

forgive [fəˈgiv] – *pt* **forgave** [fəˈgeiv]: *ptp* **forˈgiven** – (not *usu* used with **is, was** *etc* and **-ing**) **1** *vti* to stop being angry with (someone who has done something wrong): *He forgave her for stealing his watch.* **2** *vt* (*formal*) to stop being angry about (something that someone has done): *He forgave her angry words.*

forgiveness [fəˈgivnis] *nu* **1** the act of forgiving: *He asked for forgiveness.* **2** readiness to forgive: *He showed great forgiveness towards those who treated him badly.*

forˈgiving *adj* (*neg* **un-**) ready to forgive (often): *She is a forgiving person.*

forgo [foːˈgou] – *pt* **forwent** [foːˈwent]: *ptp* **forgone** [foːˈgon] – *vt* (*formal*) to give up or do without: *Are you prepared to forgo your holiday?*

See also **foregone**.

forgot, forgotten *see* **forget**.

fork [foːk] *nc* **1** an instrument with two or more pointed pieces for piercing and lifting things: *We usually eat with a knife, fork and spoon; He was digging the vegetable plot with a garden(ing) fork.* **2** the point at which a road, river *etc* divides into two or more branches or divisions: *You will see a fork in the river.* **3** one of the branches or divisions of a road, river *etc* into which the road, river *etc* divides: *Take the left fork (of the road).* – **1** *vi* (of a road, river *etc*) to divide into (*usu* two) branches or divisions: *The main road forks here – I don't know whether to go left or right.* **2** *vi* (of a person or vehicle) to follow one of the branches or divisions into which a road has divided: *Fork right at the school!*; *The car forked left.* **3** *vt* to lift or move with a fork: *The farmer forked the hay*; *He forked the manure on to the field.* – *See also* **fork out** *below.*

forked *adj* (*usu attrib*) divided into two branches or divisions: *A snake has a forked tongue*; *forked lightning.*

ˌfork-lift 'truck *nc* a small power-driven machine with an arrangement of steel prongs which can lift, raise up high and carry heavy packages and stack them where required.

fork out *vt sep* (*inf*) to pay *usu* unwillingly; to hand over (*usu* money): *I'll have to fork out the cost of the meal*; *I've forked out enough money on this holiday already but I suppose I'll have to fork more out.*

forlorn [fə'loːn] *adj* pitiful; unhappy because left alone: *She looked like a forlorn child*; *She seems rather forlorn since he left.*

for'lornly *adv*: *She stood forlornly in the empty room.*

a forlorn hope a vain or faint hope which is unlikely to be fulfilled: *We may see you next week but it's rather a forlorn hope.*

form[1] [foːm] **1** *ncu* (a) shape; outward appearance: *He saw a strange form in the darkness*; *Squares and circles are geometric forms*; *What form does his madness take?* (= What are the outward signs of his madness); *Is air without shape or form?* – *See also* **take form** *below.* **2** *nc* a kind, type or variety: *What form of ceremony usually takes place?*; *Great politeness can sometimes be a form of insult.* **3** *nc* a document containing certain questions, the answers to which must be written on it: *an application form*; *Fill in this form.* **4** *ncu* (*formal*) a fixed way of doing things: *What is the correct form of address for a bishop?*; *the forms and ceremonies of church ritual*; *It's a matter of form to say 'How are you?' when one meets a friend.* **5** *nc* a school class: *He is in the sixth form.* **6** *nu* the ability and performance of an athlete or racehorse: *I always study the form of a horse before I bet on it.* – *See also* **form** *in phrases below.* – **1** *vt* to make; to cause to take shape: *He formed a circle with the matches*; *How do you form the feminine of the word 'mayor'?*; *They decided to form a drama group*; (*fig*) *I somehow formed the impression that he was mad.* **2** *vi* to come into existence; to take shape: *Icicles have formed on the edge of the roof*; *An idea slowly formed in his mind.* **3** *vti* (*formal*) to organize or arrange (oneself or other people) into a particular order: *He formed the children into three lines*; *The women formed* (*themselves*) *into three groups.* **4** *vt* (*formal*) to be; to make up: *These anatomy lectures form part of the medical course*; *These ideas will form the basis of our five-year plan*; *This office block forms the centre section of the new building complex.*

-form (*in cmpds*) having a particular shape or form, as in **waveform**.

for'mation 1 *nu* the act of forming or making: *He agreed to the formation of a music society.* **2** *ncu* (a) particular arrangement or order: *The planes flew in formation*; *We were amazed at the strange rock formations that we saw on our journey*; (*attrib*) *formation dancing.*

'formative [-mətiv] *adj* making something or someone have a certain form or develop in a certain way: *A child's first five years are the most formative*; *during a child's formative years.*

be in good form to be in a good mood: *She's in good form after her holiday.*

good, bad form (*formal*) according to or not according to custom: *It is bad form to laugh at a funeral.*

in the 'form of having the shape, character, style *etc* of: *He wrote a novel in the form of a diary.*

take form (*formal*) to come into existence; to begin to have a visible shape: *At first his painting did not mean anything to me but as it took form I recognized the local church*; *His ideas slowly took form until he was able to present the director with his plans for the company.*

form[2] [foːm] *nc* a long, *usu* wooden seat: *The children were sitting on forms.*

formal ['foːməl] *adj* **1** done *etc* according to a fixed and accepted way: *a formal letter of thanks*; *Is his visit formal?*; *a formal request for a grant*; *a formal dance* (= one at which special evening clothes, not casual clothes, are worn). **2** suitable or correct for occasions when things are done according to a fixed and accepted way: *You must wear formal dress to the Queen's garden party – you cannot wear jeans and a sweater.* **3** (of behaviour, attitude *etc*) not relaxed and friendly: *She was very formal with him*; *formal behaviour.* **4** (of language) exactly correct by grammatical *etc* rules but not conversational: *Her French was very formal*; *'To alight from a bus' is a formal way of saying 'to get off a bus'.* **5** (*usu attrib*) (of designs *etc*) precise and following a fixed pattern rather than occurring naturally: *formal gardens.* **'formally** *adv.*

for'mality [-'ma-] **1** *nc* something which is done for appearance but has little meaning: *The chairman's speech was only a formality.* **2** *nu* unrelaxed correctness of behaviour: *His formality made him appear unfriendly.*

See also **informal**.

format ['foːmat] *nc* (*tech*) **1** (of books, magazines *etc*) the size and shape in which they are issued: *That novel is being reissued in a new format.* **2** the design or arrangement of an event *etc* (*eg* a television programme): *Have they decided on the format of the new current affairs programme?*

former ['foːmə] *adj* (*attrib*) of an earlier time: *He is a former president of that company*; *In former times people did not travel so much*; *his former dislike of her.*

'formerly *adv* in earlier times: *He formerly worked in a factory*; *Formerly this large town was a small village.*

the former the first of two things mentioned: *We visited Venice and Florence, staying longer in the former than in the latter*; *She wears blue dresses and green dresses, but she suits only the former.*

See also **latter**.

Formica ® [foː'maikə] *nu, adj* (of) a plastic material which resists heat, used for covering tables *etc.*

formidable ['foːmidəbl] *adj* (*formal*) **1** rather frightening: *He had a formidable appearance*; *He looked very formidable in his uniform.* **2** very difficult to overcome: *They were faced with formidable difficulties*; *The difficulties were more formidable than we had anticipated.* **'formidably** *adv.*

formula ['foːmjulə] – *pls* **'formulae** [-liː], **'formulas** – *nc* **1** an arrangement of signs or letters used in chemistry, arithmetic *etc* to express an idea briefly: *The formula for water is H_2O.* **2** a recipe or set of instructions for making something: *The shampoo was made to a new formula*; (*fig*) *the formula for success.*

formulate ['fo:mjuleit] *vt* (*formal*) to express clearly and in a definite form: *The interest shown by the class encouraged him to formulate his ideas into a theory.*

forsake [fə'seik] – *pt* **forsook** [fə'suk]: *ptp* **for'saken** – *vt* (*liter*) to leave alone; to abandon: *He was forsaken by his friends*; *She forsook all her high principles and stole some money.*

forswear [fo:'sweə] – *pt* **forswore** [fo:'swo:]: *ptp* **forsworn** [fo:'swo:n] – *vt* (*old*) to give up; to stop: *He has forsworn all his bad habits.*

fort [fo:t] *nc* a building which is built so that it can be defended against an enemy: *The crusaders built stone forts in the desert.*
See also **fortify, fortress**.

forte ['fo:tei, (*Amer*) fo:rt] *nc* (*no pl*: *formal*) something one is particularly good at: *Making pastry is not her forte.*

forth [fo:θ] *adv* (*old*: *liter*) forward; onward: *He came forth from the tomb*; *They went forth into the desert*; *from this day forth.*
and so forth *see* **so**.
back and forth first in one direction and then in the other; backwards and forwards: *We had to go back and forth many times before we moved all our furniture to the new house.*
hold forth *see* **hold**.

forthcoming [fo:θ'kʌmiŋ] *adj* (*formal*) **1** happening or appearing soon: *forthcoming events*; *No reply seems to be forthcoming.* **2** (*neg* **un-**) (of a person) open and willing to talk: *She wasn't very forthcoming about her work*; *not a very forthcoming personality.*

forthright ['fo:θrait] *adj* honest and straightforward: *He is a very forthright young man*; *Politicians' answers are not usually very forthright.*

forthwith [fo:θ'wiθ] *adv* (*formal*) immediately: *You are to leave the country forthwith!*

fortieth *see* **forty**.

fortify ['fo:tifai] *vt* (*formal*) **1** to prepare (a building, city *etc*) for an attack by strengthening and arming it: *The king fortified the castle against the attacking armies*; (*fig*) *He fortified himself against the cold with a heavy coat.* **2** to strengthen or enrich (*eg* food, drink): *The breakfast cereal is fortified with vitamins.*
'fortified *adj* (*usu attrib*) strengthened; enriched: *Sherry is a fortified wine* (= a wine strengthened by the addition of alcohol).
,fortifi'cation [-fi-] **1** *nc* walls *etc* built to strengthen an army, city, nation *etc* against attack: *The fortifications of Florence were designed by Michelangelo.* **2** the act of fortifying.
See also **fort, fortress**.

fortitude ['fo:titju:d] *nu* (*formal*) courage and endurance: *He showed great fortitude during his long illness.*

fortnight ['fo:tnait] *nc* (*Brit*) two weeks: *a fortnight's holiday*; *It's a fortnight since I last saw her.*
'fortnightly *adj, adv* every fortnight: *a fortnightly visit*; *He is paid fortnightly.*

fortress ['fo:tris] *nc* a (*usu* large) fort or fortified building: *The Tower of London is a huge fortress beside the River Thames.*

fortuitous [fə'tju:itəs] *adj* (*very formal*) happening by chance: *I didn't plan our meeting – it was quite fortuitous*; *a fortuitous meeting.* **for'tuitously** *adv.*

fortune ['fo:tʃən] **1** *nu* whatever happens by chance or (good or bad) luck: *He had the good fortune to marry a beautiful girl*; *He accepts whatever fortune may bring.* **2** *nc* a large amount of money: *That ring must be worth a fortune!*; *He went to London to make his fortune.* – *See also* **tell (someone's) fortune** *below.*
'fortunate [-nət] *adj* having good fortune; lucky: *He is a very fortunate man to have such a beautiful house*; *It was fortunate that no-one was killed in the accident.* **'fortunately** *adv.*
'fortune-teller *nc* someone who tells fortunes: *the fortune-teller at the local fair.*
tell (someone's) fortune to foretell what will happen to someone in the future: *The gypsy told my fortune.*
See also **misfortune, unfortunate**.

forty ['fo:ti] **1** *nc* the number or figure 40. **2** *nu* the age of 40. – *adj* **1** (*usu attrib*) 40 in number. **2** (*pred*) aged 40. – *See* **eighty** *for constructions.*
'forties *n pl* **1** the period of time between one's fortieth and fiftieth birthdays. **2** the range of temperatures between forty and fifty degrees. **3** the period of time between the fortieth and fiftieth years of a century. – *See* **eighties** *under* **eighty** *for constructions.*
'fortieth **1** *nc* one of forty equal parts. **2** *nc, adj* (the) last of forty (people, things *etc*); (the) next after the thirty-ninth. – *See* **eightieth** *under* **eighty** *for constructions.*
forty- (*in cmpds*) having forty (of something): *a ,forty-page 'index.*
'forty-year-old *nc* a person or animal that is forty years old. – *adj* (*attrib*) (of a person, animal or thing) that is forty years old. – *See* **eighty-year-old** *under* **eighty** *for constructions.*
forty winks (*inf*) a short sleep: *He always has forty winks after dinner.*
See also Appendix 1.

forum ['fo:rəm] *nc* **1** any public place in which discussions take place, speeches are made *etc*: *In modern times the television studio is as much a forum for public opinion as the market-places of ancient Rome used to be.* **2** a meeting to talk about a particular subject: *They are holding a forum on local politics.* **3** (*hist*) a market-place in ancient Roman cities and towns.

forward ['fo:wəd] *adj* **1** (*usu attrib*) moving on; advancing: *a forward movement.* **2** (*attrib*) at or near the front: *The forward part of a ship is called the 'bows'.* **3** (*pred*) (of plants *etc*) developing more quickly than usual: *These crops are well forward this year.* **4** (*derog*) (of people) putting oneself forward into people's attention: *She is a very forward young lady*; *She is too forward.* – *adv* **1** (*also* **'forwards**) moving towards the front: *A pendulum swings backward(s) and forward(s)*; *She swung her bag backwards and forwards*; *He moved forward to the front of the stage*; *She stepped forward to receive her prize.* **2** to a later time: *from this time forward*; *Put the clock forward tonight* (= Adjust the clock so that the time shown on it is an hour in advance of the previous time). – *nc* (in certain team games, *eg* football, hockey) a player in a forward position. – *vt* **1** to send (letters *etc*) on to another address: *I have asked the post office to forward my mail.* **2** (*formal*) to send: *We shall forward the goods on receipt of your cheque.* **3** (*formal*) to help to make successful: *He agreed to forward our plans in any way he could.*
bring forward *vt sep* **1** (*formal*: *also* **put**

forward) to bring to people's attention; to cause to be discussed *etc*: *They will consider the suggestions which you have brought/put forward*; *If you want us to consider your proposal bring it forward at the next meeting.* 2 to make to happen at an earlier date; to advance in time: *They have brought forward the date of their wedding*; *They have brought it forward by one week.*

come forward *see* **come**.

look forward to *see* **look**.

put forward *see* **bring forward** *above.*

forwent *see* **forgo**.

fossil ['fosl] *nc* 1 the hardened remains of an animal or vegetable found in rock: *Fossils have been found here which may be a million years old.* 2 (*inf*) an old-fashioned person: *He is just an old fossil who will not accept new ideas.*

'**fossilize, -ise** *vti* (*formal*) to change into a fossil: *Time had fossilized the animal remains in the river-bed*; *The leaves had fossilized very rapidly*; (*fig*) *He seemed to fossilize when he went to live in the country.*

foster ['fostə] *vt* 1 to look after for a period of time; to bring up a child that is not one's own: *She fostered the children for several months.* 2 (*fig formal*) to encourage or give help to (ideas *etc*): *She fostered the child's talents*; *He fostered her ambition to be an actress.*

'**foster-brother,** '**foster-sister** *nc* a child that has been fostered in another child's family: *He lives with us as he is my foster-brother.*

'**foster-child** *nc* a child that has been fostered by a family.

'**foster-parent ('foster-father, 'foster-mother)** *nc* a person who looks after a child that is not his or her own.

fought *see* **fight**.

foul [faul] *adj* 1 (*esp* of smell or taste) causing disgust: *There's a foul smell in the kitchen!* 2 (*often inf*) very unpleasant; nasty: *His bedroom is in a foul mess*; *He was absolutely foul to his young sister.* 3 (*usu attrib*) wicked or obscene: *foul language.* 4 (of weather) stormy; very bad: *They are having foul weather on the east coast*; *The weather last week was foul.* – *nc* an action *etc* which breaks the rules of a game: *The other team committed a foul.* – 1 *vti* to break the rules of a game (against): *He fouled his opponent*; *He has fouled three times already in this game.* 2 *vt* (*formal*) to make dirty, *esp* with faeces: *Dogs often foul the pavement.* 3 *vti* to become tangled up (with): *The rope fouled the anchor*; *The anchor fouled on the rope.* 4 *vt* (*inf*: *often with* **up**) to spoil or ruin; to throw into disorder: *You have really fouled up our holiday plans*; *He's always fouling things up.*

foul play *nu* (*formal*) a criminal act, *esp* involving murder: *A man has been found dead and the police suspect foul play.*

fall foul of (*formal*) to get into trouble with: *At an early age he fell foul of the law.*

found[1] *see* **find**.

found[2] [faund] 1 *vt* to start or establish: *The school was founded by Henry VI*; *That publishing company was founded in 1800*; *The Romans founded many cities.* 2 *vi* (*with* **on**/(*formal*) **upon**: *usu in passive*) to base on: *a town founded on rock*; *The story was founded upon fact.*

foun'dation 1 *nu* the act of founding: *the foundation of a new university.* 2 *nc* the base on which something is built: *First they laid the foundations, then they built the walls*; (*fig*) *His story has no foundation in fact.* 3 *nc* an amount of money to be used for a special purpose or the organization that manages it: *The British Foundation for Cancer Research.*

'**founder** *nc* a person who founds a school, college, organization *etc*: *Founder's Day is held every February to commemorate the founder of the school.*

See also **unfounded**.

founder ['faundə] *vi* (*formal or liter*) (of a ship) to sink: *Many of the Spanish ships foundered off the Scottish coast.*

foundling ['faundliŋ] *nc* (*liter*) a child abandoned by its parents.

foundry ['faundri] *nc* a place where metal or glass is formed by melting and pouring into moulds.

fount [faunt] *nc* (*liter*) a source: *God is the fount of all wisdom.*

fountain ['fauntin] *nc* 1 an often ornamental structure which produces a spring of water that rises into the air: *Rome is famous for its beautifully carved stone fountains*; *a drinking fountain.* 2 the water coming from such a structure: *It was so hot that he stood under the fountain to get cool.* 3 (*liter*) a source; a fount: *God is the fountain of all goodness.*

fountain pen *nc* a kind of pen with a nib and containing a supply of ink which is released as one writes: *She uses a fountain pen, not a ballpoint pen.*

four [fo:] 1 *nc* the number or figure 4. 2 *nu* the age of 4. – *adj* 1 (*usu attrib*) 4 in number. 2 (*pred*) aged 4. – *See* **eight** *for constructions.*

four- (*in cmpds*) having four (of something): *a ˌfour-man 'team.*

fourth 1 *nc* (*more formal than* **quarter**) one of four equal parts. 2 *nc, adj* (the) last of four (people, things *etc*); (the) next after the third. – *See* **eighth** *under* **eight** *for constructions.*

'**fourfold** *adj, adv* (*formal or liter*) four times as much or as great: *a fourfold increase*; *Output has increased fourfold.*

ˌ**four-'poster** ('**bed**) *nc* (*esp hist*) a large bed with four posts on which to hang curtains.

'**fourscore** *adj* (*attrib*), *nc* (*old or liter*) eighty: *fourscore* (*years*) *and ten.*

'**foursome** *nc* a group of four people, *esp* for playing games, *eg* golf: *We'll play in a foursome*; *Will you two join us to make up a foursome at the dance?*

'**four-year-old** *nc* a person or animal that is four years old. – *adj* (*attrib*) (of a person, animal or thing) that is four years old. – *See* **eight-year-old** *under* **eight** *for constructions.*

on all fours on hands and knees: *He went up the steep path on all fours.*

See also Appendix 1.

fourteen [fo:'ti:n] 1 *nc* the number or figure 14. 2 *nu* the age of 14. – *adj* 1 (*usu attrib*) 14 in number. 2 (*pred*) aged 14. – *See* **eighteen** *for constructions.*

fourteen- (*in cmpds*) having fourteen (of something): *a 'fourteen-ˌvolume enˌcyclo'paedia.*

ˌ**four'teenth** 1 *nc* one of fourteen equal parts. 2 *nc, adj* (the) last of fourteen (people, things *etc*); (the) next after the thirteenth. – *See* **eighteenth** *under* **eighteen** *for constructions.*

ˌ**four'teen-year-old** *nc* a person or animal that is fourteen years old. – *adj* (*attrib*) (of a person, animal or thing) that is fourteen years old. – *See* **eighteen-year-old** *under* **eighteen** *for constructions.*

See also Appendix 1.

fowl [faul] – *pls* **fowl, fowls** – *nc* (*often in cmpds*) a bird, *esp* the farmyard kind, *eg* hens, ducks, geese *etc*: *He keeps fowls and a few pigs*; *He shoots wildfowl on the marshes.*

fox [foks] *nc* a type of reddish-brown wild animal which looks like a dog: *They are hunting foxes*; (*attrib*) *fox-fur.* – *vt* to puzzle or confuse: *She was completely foxed.*

'foxy *adj* **1** (*formal*) clever in a deceitful way: *He's a foxy fellow*; *You'll have to be very foxy to persuade him.* **2** like a fox: *She had rather foxy features.*

'foxglove *nc* a kind of tall wild flower.

'foxhound *nc* a kind of dog trained to chase foxes.

fox terrier *nc* a kind of dog *orig* trained to drive foxes out of their holes in the ground.

'foxtrot *nc* a kind of dance: *To be a champion ballroom dancer you and your partner will have to be good at the foxtrot.*

See also **vixen**.

foyer ['foiei, (*Amer*) 'foiər] *nc* an entrance hall to a theatre, hotel *etc*: *I'll meet you in the foyer.*

fracas ['fraka:, (*Amer*) 'freikəs] – *pl* **fracas** ['fraka:z], (*Amer*) **fracases** ['freikəsiz] – *nc* (*formal*) a noisy quarrel: *There was a fracas in the kitchen when the guest said that the food was badly cooked.*

fraction ['frakʃən] *nc* **1** a part; not a whole number *eg* $^1/_2$, $^3/_5$, $^7/_8$ *etc.* **2** a small part: *She has only a fraction of her brother's intelligence.*

'fractional *adj* (*formal*) very small: *The difference between bus and rail fares is fractional*; *a fractional amount.*

fractious ['frakʃəs] *adj* (*formal*) cross; bad-tempered: *a fractious child*; *The baby is fractious because he is teething.*

fracture ['fraktʃə] *nc* a break of anything hard, *esp* a bone: *a fracture of the left thigh-bone*; *There must be a fracture in the water-pipe.* – *vti* (*formal or tech*) to break: *She fractured her arm*; *Under great pressure the metal pipes fractured.*

compound fracture *see* **compound**.

simple fracture *see* **simple**.

fragile ['fradʒail] *adj* easily broken: *a fragile glass vase*; *That china seems very fragile*; (*fig*) *She looked pale and fragile* (= weak); (*fig*) *After last night's party I feel rather fragile* (= rather ill).

fra'gility [-'dʒi-] *nu* (*formal*).

fragment ['fragmənt] *nc* **1** a piece broken off: *The floor was covered with fragments of glass.* **2** something which is not complete: *a fragment of poetry.* – [frag'ment, (*Amer*) 'fragmənt] *vi* (*formal*) to break into pieces: *The special glass is very strong but will fragment if hit by something sharp.*

'fragmentary *adj* (*formal*) made of pieces; incomplete: *a fragmentary account of what happened*; *The evidence against him is rather fragmentary.*

fragrant ['freigrənt] *adj* (*formal*) having a sweet smell: *fragrant flowers*; *The air was fragrant with the scent of flowers.*

'fragrance *ncu* (a) sweet smell: *all the fragrance(s) of the East.*

frail [freil] *adj* weak, *esp* in health: *a frail old lady*; *She became very frail after her accident.*

'frailty *ncu* (*formal*) physical or moral weakness: *As he grew older his frailty increased*; *She loved him in spite of his frailties.*

frame [freim] *nc* **1** a hard main structure round which something is built or made: *the wooden frame of a canoe*; *the steel frame of the aircraft*; *The frame of the building is now complete*; *the iron frame of the bed.* **2** something made to enclose something: *a picture-frame*; *a window-frame*; *The lenses of my spectacles are in good condition but I need new frames.* **3** a box-like object made of wood, steel *etc* and glass or plastic in which young plants are grown: *He grew his tomatoes from seed in a cold frame* (= a frame which was not heated) *before planting them in the garden.* **4** (*formal*) the human body: *He has a slight frame.* – *vt* **1** to put a frame around: *to frame a picture.* **2** to act as a frame for: *Her hair framed her face.* **3** (*fig formal*) to put together; to form: *He managed to frame a reply to the question.* **4** (*sl*) to make (someone) seem guilty of a crime: *I did not do it – I have been framed!*

'frame-up *nc* (*sl*) an arrangement or plan which makes someone seem guilty of a crime: *I did not do it – it's a frame-up!*

'framework *nc* the basic supporting structure of anything: *The building will be made of concrete on a steel framework.*

frame of mind (*formal*) mental state: *He is in a strange frame of mind.*

franc [fraŋk] *nc* the standard unit of currency in France, Belgium, Switzerland and several other countries, *eg* in some parts of Africa where French is spoken.

France *see* Appendix 2.

franchise ['frantʃaiz] *nu* (*formal*) the right to vote (*esp* in a general election): *Women did not get the franchise until the twentieth century.*

Franco- [fraŋkou] (*in cmpds*) French: *ˌFranco-'Scottish.*

frank [fraŋk] *adj* saying or showing openly what is in one's mind; honest: *He is a very frank, outspoken person*; *a frank reply*; *a frank face/expression*; *He is frank and honest.* – *vt* to mark a letter by machine to show that postage has been paid.

'frankly *adv.*

frankfurter ['fraŋkfə:tə] *nc* a kind of smoked sausage.

frantic ['frantik] *adj* **1** anxious or very worried: *She became quite frantic when her son did not arrive home*; *The frantic mother looked everywhere for her child.* **2** wildly excited: *the frantic pace of modern life*; *She joined in the frantic gaiety.* **'frantically** *adv.*

fraternal [frə'tə:nl] *adj* (*formal*: *attrib*) of or like a brother: *a fraternal greeting.* **fra'ternally** *adv.*

fra'ternity *nc* **1** (*formal*) a company of people who regard each other as equals, *eg* monks. **2** (*often facet*) a company of people with the same interest, job *etc*: *the banking fraternity.*

'fraternize, -ise ['fra-] *vi* (*formal*) to meet together as friends with: *The soldiers were ordered not to fraternize with the people in the town.*

fratricide ['fratrisaid] (*formal or legal*) **1** *nu* the murder of a brother: *He was found guilty of fratricide.* **2** *nc* a person who murders his or her brother.

ˌfratri'cidal *adj* (*formal or legal*): *He has fratricidal tendencies.*

fraud [fro:d] **1** *ncu* (an act of) dishonesty: *He was sent to prison for fraud*; *The whole affair was a fraud.* **2** *nc* a person who pretends to be something that he isn't: *Don't do any business with that man – he's a fraud*; *Father is not really angry with us – he's just an old fraud!*

'fraudulent [-djulənt, (*Amer*) -dʒulənt] *adj* (*formal*) dishonest or intending to deceive: *fraudulent behaviour*; *The way he obtained the car* *was definitely fraudulent.* **'fraudulently** *adv.* **'fraudulence** *nu* (*formal*).

fraught [fro:t] *adj* (*formal*) **1** anxious; tense or worried: *You look very fraught; She wore rather a fraught expression.* **2** (*pred: inf*) causing anxiety or worry: *The situation grew more and more fraught.* **3** (*formal or liter: pred with* **with**) full of: *fraught with danger.*

fray[1] [frei] *vti* (of cloth, rope *etc*) to make or become worn at the ends or edges, so that the threads or fibres come loose: *This material frays easily; My dress has frayed at the hem; Constant rubbing against the rock has frayed the rope;* (*fig*) *Everyone's temper was frayed* (= everyone was becoming angry) *by having to wait so long.*

fray[2] [frei] *nc* (*old*) a fight: *They all entered the fray.*

freak [fri:k] *nc* **1** an unusual or abnormal event, person or thing: *A storm as bad as that one is a freak of nature; The doctor made a study of dwarfs and other freaks;* (*facet*) *You do look a freak in those clothes!;* (*attrib*) *Rain is not usual here at this time of year – this is a freak storm;* (*attrib*) *a freak result.* **2** (*inf: usu in cmpds*) a person who is wildly enthusiastic about something: *a film-freak.*

'freakish *adj* **1** apt to change the mind suddenly: *She is very freakish and unreliable; a freakish individual.* **2** like a freak; odd or unusual: *That result is a bit freakish; freakish results.*

freak out *vi* (*sl*) to become very excited, *esp* because of having taken drugs (*nc* **'freak-out**).

freckle ['frekl] *nc* a small brown spot on the skin: *In summer her face was always covered with freckles.* – *vt* to cover with small brown spots: *Her face was freckled by exposure to the sun.* **'freckled, 'freckly** *adjs.*

free [fri:] *adj* **1** allowed to move where one wants; not shut in, tied, fastened *etc*: *The prisoners have been set free; The prison door opened, and he was a free man; The animals were free to wander over the hills;* (*fig*) *Her hair hung free.* **2** not forced or persuaded to act, think, speak *etc* in a particular way: *Every man has a right to free speech; She was allowed to give free expression to her artistic talent; You are quite free to think what you like;* (*fig*) *a free translation* (= a translation of the sense of the book rather than of each word). **3** (*pred: with* **with**) generous: *He is always free with his money/advice.* **4** frank, open and ready to speak: *a free manner; He is frank and free towards everyone.* **5** costing nothing: *It didn't cost me anything – I got it free!; a free gift; I have some free tickets for tonight's concert; Do you send books post free?* **6** not working or having another appointment; not busy: *I shall be free at five o'clock; Are you free to come for a drink this evening?; Saturday is a free day for me.* **7** (*usu pred*) not occupied; not in use: *Is this table free?; Are these seats free?; We have one table free.* **8** (*pred: with* **of** *or* **from**) without or no longer having (*esp* something or someone unpleasant *etc*): *She is free from pain now; Keep the wound free from dirt; The roads are free of heavy traffic now; He is glad to be free of his wife; We shall do this free of charge.* – *v* – *pt, ptp* **freed** – *vt* **1** to make or set (someone) free: *He freed all the prisoners.* **2** (*with* **from** *or* **of**) to rid or relieve (someone) of something: *The government intended to free the people from their terrible poverty; She was able to free herself of her debts by working very hard.*

'freedom *nu* the state of not being under control and being able to do whatever one wishes: *The prisoner was given his freedom; All people must be allowed complete freedom of thought; He managed to get freedom from taxation.*

'freely *adv* **1** in a free manner: *She always gives freely* (= generously) *to charity; I feel that I can speak freely* (= without hiding anything; openly) *to you.* **2** willingly; readily: *I freely admit that the accident was my fault.*

,free-for-'all *nc* (*inf*) an argument, discussion *etc* in which everybody is allowed to express their opinions: *The discussion opened quietly but soon became a free-for-all about education in general.*

'freehand *adj, adv* (of drawing *etc*) (done) without using any drawing instruments except a pencil or pen: *He took a pencil and made a quick freehand sketch of the house; He drew it freehand.* – *See also* **a free hand** *below.*

'freehold *adj* (*legal*) (of land, property *etc*) belonging completely to the owner, not just for a certain time.

'freelance *nc, adj* (of or done by) a person who is working on his own, not for any one employer: *He is not employed by a newspaper – he is a freelance journalist; He does freelance work; He is freelance now.* – *vi* to work in this way: *He is freelancing now.*

'Freemason *nc* a member of a secret society for men which encourages friendship and helping one another.

,free-'range *adj* **1** (of chickens, ducks *etc*) allowed to move about freely; not kept indoors: *This farm has only free-range chickens; These hens are free-range.* **2** (of eggs) laid by chickens, ducks *etc* of this kind: *I always buy free-range eggs; These eggs are free-range.* – *See also* **battery** (*def 2*).

free speech *nu* the right to express any opinion freely: *I believe in free speech.*

free trade *nu* trade with foreign countries without customs duties, taxes *etc.*

free verse *nu* verse written in lines of irregular length.

'freeway *nc* (*Amer*) a motorway.

,free'wheel *vi* to travel (downhill) on a bicycle, in a car *etc* without using mechanical power: *I'm not going to pedal downhill – I'll freewheel; The car's engine is switched off – the driver is freewheeling.*

free will *nc* the ability to choose and act freely: *He did it of his own free will.*

a free hand freedom to do whatever one likes: *He gave her a free hand with the servants.* – *See also* **freehand** *above.*

set free to make (someone) free: *The soldiers set the terrorists' prisoners free.*

freeze [fri:z] – *pt* **froze** [frouz]: *ptp* **frozen** ['frouzn] – **1** *vti* to make into or become ice: *The low temperature froze the pond; The pond is freezing; The liquid has frozen solid; It's so cold that the river has frozen over.* **2** *vi* (of weather) to be at or below **'freezing-point** (*see below*): *If it freezes again tonight all my tomato plants will die.* **3** *vti* (*sometimes inf*) to make or be very cold: *If you had stayed out all night in the snow you might have frozen to death* (= died of exposure to cold); (*inf*) *This room is freezing – why don't you put the heating on?;* (*inf*) *My feet are freezing.* **4** *vt* to make (food) very cold in order to preserve it: *You can freeze the rest of that food and eat it later.* **5** *vti* to make or become stiff, still or unable to move (with fear *etc*): *She froze when she heard the strange thumping sound downstairs; If you hear anyone coming, freeze!; The rabbit froze in the headlights of the car; My blood froze* (= I was very scared) *when I saw* *the ghost*; *When he was about to speak she froze him with a warning look*; *The teacher's stern expression was enough to freeze the boldest of the pupils.* **6** *vt* to fix prices, wages *etc* at a certain level: *If the situation does not improve, wages will be frozen again.* – *nc* **1** (*no pl*) a period of very cold weather when temperatures are below freezing-point: *How long do you think the freeze will last?* **2** (*usu in cmpds*) (a period of) government control of wages, prices *etc*: *During the pay-freeze some people found it difficult to live on their salaries*; *The unions are not happy about having another wage-freeze.*

'**freezer** *nc* a cabinet for keeping food at, or bringing it down to, a temperature below freezing-point.

'**frozen** *adj*: *frozen foods*; *My hands are frozen.*

'**freezing-point** *nc* the temperature at which a liquid becomes solid: *The freezing-point of water is 0° centigrade.*

freeze up *vi, vt sep* to stop moving or functioning because of extreme cold: *The car engine froze up and wouldn't start*; (*fig*) *The actor was so nervous that he froze up* (= could not speak or remember his lines); *The cold weather has frozen up the gate – it won't open!*

freight [freit] *nu* (*tech*) **1** goods being carried from place to place: *air-freight*; (*attrib*) *a freight train.* **2** the money charged for carrying such goods: *He charged me £100 freight.*

'**freighter** *nc* a ship (or aircraft) that carries freight rather than passengers: *There were several freighters in the harbour.*

French [frentʃ]: **French bean** *nc* a kind of green bean of which the pod and its contents are eaten.

French fries [fraiz] *n pl* (*Amer*) chips (*def 3*): *steak and French fries.*

French horn *see* **horn**.

French leave *nu* absence or holiday from work or military duty without permission: *The soldier took French leave because he wanted to see his girlfriend.*

Frenchman, Frenchwoman *see* Appendix 2.

French polish *nu* a kind of varnish for furniture.

ˌ**French-'polish** *vt*: *I had the chairs French-polished.*

French window *nc* a long window also used as a door: *The burglar escaped through the French window.*

See also Appendix 2.

frenetic [frə'netik] *adj* (*formal*) very excited; frantic or frenzied: *the frenetic pace of modern life.*

frenzy ['frenzi] *nu* a state of great excitement, fear *etc*: *She waited in a frenzy of anxiety*; *The pop-group's fans worked themselves up into a state of frenzy.*

'**frenzied** *adj* (*attrib*) very excited: *in frenzied haste.* '**frenziedly** *adv.*

frequent ['fri:kwənt] *adj* (*slightly formal*) happening often: *He made frequent journeys to France*; *His trips to France are less frequent now.* – [fri'kwent] *vt* (*very formal or facet*) to visit often: *He used to frequent the bar of the George Hotel.*

'**frequency** **1** *nu* the state of happening often: *The frequency of her visits surprised him*; *His holidays seemed to increase in frequency.* **2** *nc* (*tech*) (in electricity, radio *etc*) the number of waves, vibrations *etc* per second: *At what frequency does the sound occur?* **3** *nc* a set wavelength on which radio stations regularly broadcast: *All the BBC radio stations changed their frequencies at the same time.*

'**frequently** *adv* (*more formal that* **often**) often: *He frequently arrived late*; *Frequently he forgot to come at all.*

See also **infrequent, unfrequented**.

fresco ['freskou] – *pl* '**fresco(e)s** – *nc* a picture painted on a wall while the plaster is still wet: *The tourists admired the frescoes on the walls of the old cathedral.*

fresh [freʃ] *adj* **1** newly made, gathered, arrived *etc*: *fresh fruit* (= fruit that is not tinned, frozen *etc*); *fresh flowers*; *fresh eggs*; *He is fresh from the city.* **2** (of people *etc*) healthy; not tired: *You are looking very fresh this morning even although you were at a party last night*; *a fresh look/complexion.* **3** (*attrib*) another; different; not already used, begun, worn, heard *etc*: *He started reading a fresh chapter*; *Give me a fresh piece of paper*; *Is there any fresh news?*; *After her divorce she tried to make a fresh start* (= forget her past life and try to begin a new way of life). **4** (of weather *etc*) cool; refreshing: *a fresh breeze from the sea*; *Let some fresh air into the room – open the door*; *The wind is fresh.* **5** (*usu attrib*) (of water) without salt: *The indoor swimming-pool has fresh water in it, not sea water.* **6** (*sl*) impertinent or cheeky *esp* towards someone of the opposite sex: *He tried to get fresh with the new secretary*; *rather a fresh young man.*

'**freshen** **1** *vi* to become fresh or cool: *The wind began to freshen.* **2** *vti* (*often with* **up**) to (cause to) become less tired or untidy looking: *I must freshen up before dinner*; *A wash and a rest will freshen me up.*

'**freshly** *adv* (*before ptps of verbs*) newly; recently: *freshly gathered plums*; *freshly arrived from the country.*

'**freshman, 'fresher** *ncs* (*sl*) a first-year college or university student.

'**fresh-water** *adj* (*attrib*) of inland rivers or lakes; not of the sea: *fresh-water fish.*

fret [fret] – *pt, ptp* '**fretted** – *vi* to worry or show anxiety or discontentment: *She was always fretting about something or other*; *The children fret when their mother is away.*

'**fretful** *adj* cross; discontented: *When children are tired they often get fretful*; *fretful children crying all night.*

fretwork ['fretwə:k] *nu* decorated cut-out work in wood.

'**fretsaw** *nc* a saw specially designed for doing fretwork.

friar ['fraiə] *nc* a member of certain religious orders in the Christian (*usu* Roman Catholic) Church, *esp* one who has made a vow to live in poverty.

'**friary** *nc* a house in which friars live.

friction ['frikʃən] *nu* **1** (*formal or tech*) the rubbing together of two things: *The friction between the head of the match and the matchbox causes a spark*; *Constant friction caused the rope to break.* **2** (*tech*) the resistance felt when one object is moved against another (or through liquid or gas): *There is little friction between the wheels of a car and icy roads and so it is difficult to drive a car on such roads.* **3** (*fig*) quarrelling; disagreement: *There seems to be some friction between the workmen and the manager about rates of pay.*

Friday ['fraidei] *n* the sixth day of the week, the day following Thursday: *She arrived on Friday*; *She will visit her mother next Friday*; *She visits her mother on Fridays* (= every Friday, or only on a Friday but not necessarily every Friday); (*attrib*) *Friday evening.*

fridge [fridʒ] short for **refrigerator**.

friend [frend] *nc* **1** someone who knows and likes another person very well: *They are good friends; He is my best friend; That is her latest boyfriend.* **2** a person who acts in a friendly and generous way to people *etc* he or she does not know: *She is a friend to everyone who is in need; a friend to animals.* – *See also* **make friends with** *below.*

'friendless *adj* (*formal*) without friends: *He was alone and friendless in a foreign country; friendless old people.*

'friendly *adj* **1** (*neg* **un-**) kind and willing to make friends: *She is very friendly to everybody; There are a great many friendly people in our street.* **2** (*pred*) knowing and liking another person very well: *They have been friendly (with each other) for many years.* **3** (*attrib*) (of a sports match, game *etc*) not played with the aim of winning a prize or points in a competition *etc*: *The two football teams played a friendly match.*

'friendship **1** *nu* the state of being friends: *Friendship is a wonderful thing.* **2** *nc* a particular relationship between two friends: *Our friendship grew through the years.*

make friends (with) to start a friendly relationship; to become friends with someone: *The child tried to make friends with the dog.*

See also **befriend**.

frieze [fri:z] *nc* a narrow strip around the walls of a room, building *etc* near the top, *usu* decorated with pictures, carving *etc*: *The walls were decorated with a frieze of horses.*

frigate ['frigət] *nc* a small warship: *Frigates escorted the aircraft carrier up the English Channel.*

fright [frait] **1** *ncu* a sudden fear: *The noise gave me a terrible fright; She got a fright when she heard footsteps behind her; She took fright at the idea of travelling in an aeroplane; You gave me a fright by coming into the room so quietly.* **2** *nc* (*inf*) a person who looks ridiculous: *She looks a fright in those clothes.*

'frighten *vt* to make (someone) afraid: *The crowds of people frightened her; She was frightened by a large dog.*

'frightened *adj*: *a frightened child; There is nothing to be frightened about; She is frightened of spiders.*

'frightful *adj* **1** (*usu attrib*) terrible or frightening: *I had a frightful experience when my car skidded on the ice.* **2** (*inf*) very bad: *He is a frightful liar – he never tells the truth; We saw a frightful play last night; It was frightful.*

'frightfully *adv* (*inf*) very: *He's frightfully clever.*

take fright to become frightened *usu* suddenly and quickly: *She knocked on the door, but took fright and ran away when the man opened it.*

frigid ['fridʒid] *adj* **1** (*formal*) cold and unemotional: *The actor received a frigid reception from the audience; He behaves in a frigid manner even to his own family; He was rather frigid towards the rest of the staff.* **2** (*usu* of a woman) having no sexual desire: *He has affairs with other women because his wife is frigid; a frigid woman.* **3** (*formal*: *attrib*) frozen: *the frigid zones of the world* (= the Arctic and Antarctic). **'frigidly** *adv.* **fri'gidity** *nu.*

frill [fril] *nc* **1** a decorative edging to a piece of cloth, made of a strip of cloth gathered along one side and sewn on: *She sewed a frill along the bottom of the skirt.* **2** (*fig*: *often in pl*) something unnecessary added as decoration: *He likes being successful in business, but he doesn't enjoy all the frills* (= having expensive dinners, travelling a lot, going to parties *etc*).

frilled, 'frilly *adjs* decorated with frills: *a frilled curtain; a frilly dress; That dress is too frilly for my taste.*

fringe [frindʒ] *nc* **1** a border of loose threads on a carpet, shawl *etc*: *Her red shawl has a black fringe.* **2** hair cut to hang over the forehead: *You should have your fringe cut before it covers your eyes.* **3** (*usu in sing*: *often fig*) the outer area; the edge; the part farthest from the main part or centre of something: *the fringes of the forest; on the fringe of the city; on the fringe of Labour politics;* (*attrib*) *fringe medicine.* – *vt* (*liter*) to make or be a border around: *Trees fringed the pond.*

fringe benefits *n pl* things that one gets from one's employer for a job in addition to wages or a salary, *eg* a house, a car: *He is not very well paid but has a lot of fringe benefits.*

frisk [frisk] **1** *vi* (*usu liter*) to jump about playfully: *The lambs are frisking in the fields.* **2** *vt* (*sl*) to search (a person) for something he might be carrying *eg* a gun: *All the passengers were frisked as they entered the aeroplane.*

'frisky *adj* lively; playful: *a frisky puppy; You're looking very frisky this morning.* **'friskily** *adv.*

fritter[1] ['fritə] *nc* a piece of fruit, vegetable, meat *etc* fried in batter: *banana fritters.*

fritter[2] ['fritə] *vt* (*often with* **away**) to throw away or waste gradually: *He frittered (away) all his money on gambling; She frittered away her time in going to the cinema instead of studying.*

frivolous ['frivələs] *adj* (*often derog*) not serious; playful: *He wasted his time on frivolous pleasures; In a serious world it's sometimes a good thing to be frivolous.* **'frivolously** *adv.* **'frivolousness** *nu.*

fri'volity [-'vo-] (*often derog*) **1** *nu* frivolousness: *The frivolity of his behaviour displeased his mother.* **2** *nc* a frivolous action or thought: *I have no time for such frivolities as parties because I have to work too hard.*

frizz [friz] *vti* (*sometimes with* **out**) to (cause hair to) form a mass of tight curls: *Her hair tends to frizz; The hairdresser frizzed (out) her hair.*

'frizzy *adj* (of hair) in very small curls: *He had frizzy red hair; Her hair is too frizzy.*

fro [frou]: **to and fro** *see* **to**.

frock [frok] *nc* **1** (*formal or old*) a woman's or girl's dress: *She was wearing a summer frock.* **2** a monk's wide-sleeved garment.

,frock-'coat *nc* (in old or ceremonial dress) a man's knee-length coat.

frog [frog] *nc* a small jumping animal, without a tail, that lives on land and in water: *I find it difficult to tell the difference between a frog and a toad.*

'frogman *nc* an underwater swimmer who uses breathing apparatus and flippers: *The frogmen looked for treasure in the ship at the bottom of the sea.*

frolic ['frolik] – *pt, ptp* **'frolicked** – *vi* (*formal*) (of children, young animals *etc*) to play happily: *The puppies frolicked in the garden.*

'frolicsome *adj* (*usu attrib*: *formal or liter*) gay; lively: *frolicsome children.*

from [from] *prep* **1** used before the place, thing, person, time *etc* that is the point at which an action, journey, period of time *etc* begins: *He travelled from France to Scotland; They work from Monday to Friday; He will be on holiday from December 20 (onwards); She has been like that from her childhood; The letter was from her father; The* *prices range from £10 to £20; It has been translated from Italian.* **2** used to indicate that from which something or someone comes: *a quotation from the Bible; I painted it from memory; He comes from a wealthy family; The curtain was made from an old blanket.* **3** used to indicate separation: *Take it from him; He stayed away from work; I can't tell one child from another.* **4** used to indicate a cause or reason: *He is tired from overwork; He is suffering from a cold.*

from now, then *etc* **on** starting from now, then *etc*: *I'll be more careful from now on; From that time on/from then on, he never again drank alcohol.*

frond [frond] *nc* (*formal or liter*) a leaf, *esp* of a fern or palm.

front [frʌnt] *nc* **1** the part of anything (intended to be) nearest the person who sees it; *usu* the most important part of anything: *There are roses at the front of the house; the front of the picture;* (*attrib*) *the front door;* (*attrib*) *the front page of the newspaper;* (*attrib*) *a front seat in the theatre.* **2** the part of anything that faces the direction in which it moves: *the front of the ship; He sat in the front of the bus;* (*attrib*) *He sat in the front seat of the bus.* **3** the part of a city or town that faces the sea: *We walked along the (sea) front.* **4** (in war) the line of soldiers nearest the enemy: *They are sending more soldiers to the front; A front has been established near the border;* (*fig*) *They presented a united front against all opposition.* **5** (*tech*) a boundary separating two masses of air of different temperatures: *A cold front is approaching from the Atlantic.* **6** an outward appearance: *He put on a brave front although he was really scared.* **7** a name sometimes given to a political movement: *the Popular Front for Liberation.* **8** (*sl*) a business, organization *etc* to hide illegal activity: *His café is a front for smuggling.* – *vt* (*formal*) (*usu with* **on, on to, towards**) to stand opposite to: *Their house fronts on to the park.*

'frontage [-tidʒ] *nc* (*formal*) the front part of a building: *They decided to paint the frontage of the building.*

'frontal *adj* (*formal*: *attrib*) from the front: *a frontal attack.*

ˌfront-'bencher *nc* in Britain, a government minister or a member of an opposition party of similar status.

at the 'front of (standing *etc*) in the front part of something: *There is a door at the front of the house; They stood at the front of the crowd, listening to the speaker.*

in 'front of (placed, standing, moving *etc*) outside something on its front or forward-facing side: *There is a garden in front of the house; The speaker stood in front of the crowd; He ran in front of the car and was knocked down.*

frontier ['frʌntiə, (*Amer*) frʌn'tiər] **1** *nc* (*formal or hist*) a boundary between countries: *We crossed the frontier;* (*attrib*) *a frontier town.* **2** *nu* (*hist Amer*) the farthest area of land on which people live and work, before the country becomes wild and deserted: *Many families went to make a new life on the frontier.* **3** *nc* (*formal fig*) the limits or boundaries (of knowledge *etc*): *He pushed back the frontiers of scientific knowledge.*

frontispiece ['frʌntispi:s] *nc* a picture at the very beginning of a book.

frost [frost] **1** *nu* frozen dew, vapour *etc*: *The ground was covered with frost this morning; There is frost on the windows.* **2** *ncu* the coldness of weather needed to form ice: *There'll be (a) frost tomorrow.* – **1** *vi* (*often with* **over** *or* **up**) to become covered with frost: *The fields frosted (over) during the night; The windscreen of my car frosted up last night.* **2** *vt* to make something look as though it is covered with frost: *The glasses for the dessert were frosted with sugar.*

'frosty *adj* **1** covered with frost: *the frosty countryside; It's going to be frosty tonight.* **2** (*fig*) of behaviour, very unfriendly: *a frosty manner; She was rather frosty to me today.* **'frostily** *adv.*

'frostbite *nu* injury caused to the body by very great cold: *He was suffering from frostbite in his feet.*

'frostbitten *adj* affected by frostbite: *His feet were frostbitten; frostbitten fingers.*

See also **defrost**.

froth [froθ] *nu* a mass of small bubbles on the top of a liquid *etc*: *Some beer has more froth than others.* – *vi* to have or produce froth: *Mad dogs usually froth at the mouth;* (*fig*) *He was frothing at the mouth with anger.*

'frothy *adj* **1** containing froth: *frothy beer; The beer is not frothy enough.* **2** (*usu liter*) light, like froth: *frothy silk dresses.*

frown [fraun] *vi* to make the forehead wrinkle and the eyebrows move down (as a sign of worry, disapproval, deep thought *etc*): *He frowned at her bad behaviour.* – *nc* such a movement of the forehead and eyebrows: *He gave her a frown of disapproval.*

'frown on/(*formal*) **upon** *vt fus* to disapprove of (something): *My family frowns (up)on smoking and drinking.*

froze, frozen *see* **freeze**.

frugal ['fru:gəl] *adj* (*formal*) **1** careful about spending money; thrifty: *a frugal wife; frugal habits; He is frugal in his habits.* **2** costing little: *a frugal meal; That meal was rather frugal.* **fru'gality** [-'ga-] *nu.* **'frugally** *adv.*

fruit [fru:t] **1** *ncu* the part of a plant that produces the seed, *esp* when eaten as food: *The fruit of the vine is the grape; an arrangement of flowers and fruits; We don't eat much fruit; What fruit shall I take to my mother in hospital?* **2** *nc* (*fig*) a result; something gained as a result of hard work *etc*: *the fruit of his hard work; the fruits of prosperity.* – *vi* (*formal or tech*) to produce fruit: *This tree fruits early.*

'fruiterer *nc* **1** a person who sells fruit: *There is a fruiterer's (shop) down the road.* **2** a fruiterer's shop: *I bought these apples at the fruiterer this morning.*

'fruitful *adj* (*fig formal*) producing (good) results: *a fruitful meeting; fruitful discussions; The discussions were most fruitful.* – *See also* **unfruitful**.

fruition [fru'iʃən] *nu* (*formal*) an actual result; the happening of something that was thought of, hoped for *etc*: *Her dreams came to fruition; His ideas were finally brought to fruition.*

'fruitless *adj* (*fig formal*) useless; with no results: *a fruitless attempt to prevent a strike; It is fruitless to try again.* **'fruitlessly** *adv.*

'fruity *adj* **1** of or like fruit: *a fruity taste; a fruity drink.* **2** (*sometimes derog*) (of a voice *etc*) deep: *the fruity voice of the telephone operator.* **'fruitily** *adv.*

bear fruit *see* **bear**.

fruit salad *see* **salad**.

frump [frʌmp] *nc* (*inf*) a plain woman who is badly or unfashionably dressed: *She's such a frump and* *her husband is so well-dressed.*

frustrate [frʌ'streit, (*Amer*) 'frʌstreit] *vt* **1** to make (someone) feel disappointed, useless *etc*: *Staying at home all day frustrated her because she had been a brilliant scientist before her marriage.* **2** to make useless: *His efforts to be friendly were frustrated by her rudeness.* **fru'stration** *ncu.*

fru'strated *adj* **1** (*pred*) disappointed; unhappy; not satisfied: *She is very unhappy and frustrated as a teacher.* **2** (*attrib*) unable to have the kind of job, career *etc* that one would like: *Literary critics are often frustrated writers.* **3** not sexually satisfied: *a frustrated unmarried woman*; *She is bad-tempered because she is frustrated.*

fry[1] [frai] *vti* to cook in hot oil or fat: *Shall I fry the eggs or boil them?*; *The sausages won't take long to fry.*

'frying-pan, (*Amer*) **'fry-pan** *nc* a shallow pan, *usu* with a long handle, for frying food in.

out of the frying-pan into the fire from a difficult or dangerous situation into a worse one: *His first marriage was unhappy but his second was even more unhappy – it was a real case of out of the frying-pan into the fire.*

fry[2] [frai] : **'small fry** *n pl* (*inf derog*) unimportant people or things: *The local politicians are just small fry – we must convince the people in power.*

fuchsia ['fju:ʃə] *nc* a type of bush with long hanging flowers.

fuck [fʌk] *vti* (*vulg*) to have sexual intercourse (with someone). – *interj* (*vulg*) used to express annoyance, disapproval *etc.*

'fucking *adj* (*attrib*: *vulg*) used to express extreme disapproval, annoyance *etc* or for emphasis: *He is a fucking idiot*; *That fucking thing fell on my foot.*

fuck off *vi* (*usu as a command*: *vulg*) to go away.

fuddy-duddy ['fʌdidʌdi] *nc* (*inf derog*) a person with very old-fashioned ideas: *Fuddy-duddies don't like young people to enjoy themselves*; (*attrib*) *fuddy-duddy ideas.*

fudge [fʌdʒ] *nu* a type of soft, sugary sweet: *chocolate fudge*; *Would you like a piece of fudge?*

fuel ['fjuəl] *ncu* any substance by which a fire, engine *etc* is made to work (*eg* coal, oil, petrol): *Have you enough fuel for the winter?*; *The machine ran out of fuel*; (*fig*) *His rudeness added fuel to her anger.* – *v* – *pt, ptp* **'fuelled,** (*Amer*) **fueled** – *vti* to give or take fuel: *The tanker will leave when it has finished fuelling*; *Have they fuelled the tanker yet?*

fug [fʌg] *nc* (*inf*) a warm, heavy atmosphere: *The room was filled with a terrible fug of cigarette smoke.*

fugitive ['fju:dʒətiv] *nc* a person who is running away (from the police *etc*): *a fugitive from justice*; (*attrib*) *fugitive soldiers.*

fugue [fju:g] *nc* a piece of music in which a tune is repeated by different parts or voices: *Bach wrote many fugues.*

fulcrum ['fulkrəm] *nc* (*tech*) the point on which a lever turns or on which it is supported: *Use this stone as a fulcrum to lever out the tree-stump.*

fulfil, (*Amer*) **fulfill** [ful'fil] – *pt, ptp* **ful'filled** – *vt* (*formal*) **1** to carry out or perform (a task, promise *etc*): *He always fulfils his promises.* **2** to satisfy (requirements): *They made a list of all their requirements, and looked for a man who could fulfil them.*

ful'filled *adj* (*neg* **un-**) (of a person) satisfied, having achieved everything he or she needs to have and to do: *With her family and her career, she is a very fulfilled person*; *She didn't feel fulfilled till she had children.* **ful'filment** *nu.*

full [ful] *adj* **1** holding or containing as much as possible: *My basket is so full that I cannot carry it*; *three full glasses of wine*; *My cup is too full.* **2** (*attrib*) complete: *She was abroad for a full year*; *The flowers are in full bloom*; *He gave the police a full account of what happened.* **3** plump and rounded: *She is very pretty but has rather a full face*; *She has become quite full in the face*; *a full figure.* **4** (of clothes) containing a large amount of material: *a full skirt*; *That skirt is too full for me – I prefer a straight skirt. The dress has full sleeves.* – *adv* **1** (*sometimes in cmpds*) completely: *Fill the petrol tank full*; *a full-grown dog*; *a full-face photograph*; *a full-length novel.* **2** exactly; directly: *She hit him full in the face.*

'fully *adv* **1** (*sometimes in cmpds*) completely: *He was fully aware of what was happening*; *fully-grown dogs.* **2** quite; at least: *It will take fully three days to reach there.*

,full-'blown *adj* (*formal*) (of a flower) completely open, blooming: *a full-blown rose.*

,full-'length *adj* (*usu attrib*) **1** complete; of the usual or standard length: *a full-length novel.* **2** down to the feet: *a full-length coat*; *a full-length portrait.*

full moon *nc* (the time of) the moon when it appears at its most complete: *There is a full moon tonight*; *It is an old belief that some people go mad at/during the full moon.*

,full-'scale *adj* (*attrib*) **1** (of a drawing *etc*) of the same size as the subject: *a full-scale drawing of a flower.* **2** (*usu attrib*) using all equipment *etc*: *a full-scale military operation.*

full stop *nc* a written or printed point (.) marking the end of a sentence; a period.

,full-'time *adj, adv* occupying one's working time completely: *She was a part-time teacher for several years, but now she is full-time again*; *a full-time job*; *She works full-time now.*

'fully-fledged *adj* **1** (*attrib*: *fig*) completely trained and qualified: *She is no longer at college – she is a fully-fledged teacher now.* **2** (of birds) old enough to have grown feathers.

'full of 1 filled with; containing or holding very much or very many: *The bus was full of people when it crashed*; *The bag which she dropped was full of eggs.* **2** (*inf*) completely concerned with: *She rushed into the room full of the news about her engagement.*

'full of oneself (*derog*) having a good opinion of oneself; conceited: *She is so full of herself that people dislike her.*

full well (*formal or liter*) very well; completely: *She knows full well that she won't win the race.*

in 'full (*formal*) completely: *Write your name in full*; *He paid his bill in full.*

in the fullness of time (*formal or liter*) when the proper time (has) arrived; eventually: *In the fullness of time her son was born*; *In the fullness of time he will be promoted to manager.*

to the 'full (*formal*) as much as possible: *They all enjoyed themselves to the full.*

fulsome ['fulsəm] *adj* (*formal*: *derog*) praising too much: *I was embarrassed by his fulsome words about me*; *His compliments were fulsome.*

fumble ['fʌmbl] **1** *vi* to use one's hands awkwardly and with difficulty: *He fumbled with the key*; *She fumbled about in her bag for her key.* **2** *vt* to handle awkwardly and *usu* drop (a ball *etc*): *He fumbled* *the catch and dropped the ball.*

fume [fjuːm] *nc* (*usu in pl*) smoke or vapour which can be seen or smelled: *They could see fumes rising from the rubbish dump*: *He smelled the petrol fumes.* – *vi* (*inf*) to be very angry whilst trying not to show it: *He was fuming* (*with rage*).

fumigate [ˈfjuːmigeit] *vt* (*tech*) to destroy germs, infection *etc* by using certain kinds of smoke or vapour: *They fumigated the room after the child died of an infectious fever.* ˌ**fumiˈgation** *nu.*

fun [fʌn] *nu* enjoyment; a good time: *They had a lot of fun at the party*; *Isn't this fun!*; (*attrib*: *inf*) *having a fun time*; (*attrib*: *inf*) *fun clothes.*

ˈ**funny** *adj* **1** amusing; making one laugh: *a funny story*; *That comedian is very funny*; *That joke is not funny.* **2** strange; peculiar: *What a funny idea!*; *I heard a funny noise*; *That's funny – I thought I locked the door but now it's open.* ˈ**funnily** *adv.*

ˈ**funny-bone** *nc* a bone in the elbow: *When I hit my funny-bone on the edge of the door it was very painful.*

for ˈ**fun** as a joke; for amusement: *The children threw stones at the dog for fun – they didn't mean to hurt it.*

in ˈ**fun** as a joke; not seriously: *I said it in fun – I didn't mean to offend her.*

make fun of to laugh at (someone, *usu* unkindly): *They made fun of her because she wore such old-fashioned clothes.*

function [ˈfʌŋkʃən] *nc* (*formal*) **1** a special job, use or duty (of a machine, part of the body, person *etc*): *The function of the brake is to stop the car*; *The heart's function is to pump blood around the body*; *His function is to welcome the guests at the door.* **2** a party, dinner, meeting *etc*; a social gathering: *They often attend functions in the town.* – *vi* (*formal*) (of a machine *etc*) to work; to operate: *This typewriter isn't functioning very well*; *The office is functioning as normal although it is a public holiday*; (*facet*) *My brain does not function very well early in the morning.*

ˈ**functional** *adj* (*formal*) **1** designed to be useful rather than to look beautiful: *She wears functional clothes*; *a functional building*; *Her clothes are functional rather than fashionable.* **2** (*pred*) able to operate: *It's an old car, but it's still functional.*

fund [fʌnd] *nc* **1** a sum of money for a special purpose: *Have you given money to the fund for the repair of the local church?* **2** a store or supply: *He has a fund of funny stories.*

funds *n pl* (*inf*) money ready to spend: *Have you enough funds for your journey?*; *I'd like to go to Italy but I don't have enough funds.*

fundamental [fʌndəˈmentl] *adj* (*formal*) of great importance; essential; basic: *There is a fundamental difference in political beliefs between the two parties*; *There has been a fundamental change in his beliefs*; *Respect for law and order is fundamental to a peaceful society.* – *nc* (*usu in pl*: *formal*) a basic or essential part of anything: *Learning to read is one of the fundamentals of education.*

ˌ**fundaˈmentally** *adv*: *His plans for the future are fundamentally different from mine*; *He was fundamentally honest.*

funeral [ˈfjuːnərəl] *nc* the ceremony before the burying or cremation of a dead body: *His funeral was held at the local church*; *A large number of people attended the president's funeral*; (*attrib*) *a funeral procession.*

ˈ**funeral director**, (*Amer*) **mortician** *nc* (*more formal than* **undertaker**) a person who prepares dead bodies for burial and makes arrangements for the funeral.

funereal [fjuˈniəriəl] *adj* (*formal*) mournful; suitable for a funeral: *She was dressed in funereal black*; *That music is too funereal for my taste.*

fungus [ˈfʌŋgəs] – *pls* ˈ**fungi** [-gai], ˈ**funguses** – **1** *ncu* any of several kinds of soft spongy plants without any leaves or green part, including mushrooms, toadstools and yeast and also several disease-causing plants or organisms: *It is sometimes difficult to tell which fungi are edible and which are poisonous*; *That tree has a fungus growing on it.* **2** *nu* a disease caused by the growth of a fungus: *The fish died of fungus*; (*attrib*) *She has a fungus infection in her mouth.*

ˈ**fungicide** [-gisaid] *ncu* (*tech*) a substance used to kill fungus.

ˈ**fungoid** [-goid] *adj* (*tech*: *usu attrib*) like or of fungus: (*a*) *fungoid growth on a tree.*

funicular [fjuˈnikjulə]: **funicular (railway)** *nc* a kind of railway in which carriages are pulled uphill by cable *etc.*

funk [fʌŋk] *ncu* (*no pl*: *inf*) (a state of) fear: *He was in a funk over his exam results*; *She refused to go to the party out of funk.* – *vt* (*inf*) not to do (something) because one is afraid: *She funked the appointment with her bank-manager because she knew she had no money in her account.*

a blue funk (*sl*) a state of terror or extreme fear: *She was in a blue funk about going to the dentist.*

funnel [ˈfʌnl] *nc* **1** a wide-mouthed tube through which liquid can be poured into a narrow bottle *etc*: *You will need a funnel if you are going to pour petrol into that can.* **2** a chimney on a ship *etc* through which smoke escapes.

funnily, funny *etc see* **fun**.

fur [fəː] **1** *nu* the thick, short, fine hair of certain animals: *Bears have thick fur.* **2** *ncu, adj* (of) the skin(s) of these animals, often used to make or decorate clothes *etc* for people: *a hat made of fur*; *a fur coat.* **3** *nc* a coat, cape *etc* made of fur: *She was wearing her fur.* **4** *ncu* (*fig*) a thick layer of a substance *eg* on the tongue or the inside of kettles: *Hard water causes fur on kettles.*

furrier [ˈfʌriə, (*Amer*) ˈfəː-] *nc* a person who (makes and) sells furs.

ˈ**furry** *adj* **1** covered with fur: *a furry animal.* **2** like fur: *furry material.*

furious, furiously *see* **fury**.

furl [fəːl] *vti* (*old or liter*) (*usu* of flags, sails or umbrellas) to roll up: *They furled the sails*; *My umbrella won't furl properly.*

See also **unfurl**.

furlong [ˈfəːloŋ] *nc* a measure of length equal to one-eighth of a mile (201·2 metres): *a six-furlong race.*

furlough [ˈfəːlou] *ncu* (*formal*: *often mil*) a period of absence from one's work, *esp* for people working abroad: *Next year he will have six weeks' furlough*; *The missionary is home on furlough.*

furnace [ˈfəːnis] *nc* a very hot oven or closed-in fireplace for melting iron ore, making steam for heating *etc.*

furnish [ˈfəːniʃ] *vt* **1** to provide (a house *etc*) with furniture: *We spent a lot of money on furnishing our house.* **2** (*formal*) to give (what is necessary); to supply: *They furnished the library with new books*; *He told me the story, but his wife furnished the details.*

'**furnished** *adj* (*neg* **un-**): *a furnished flat; We rent this flat furnished – our previous one was unfurnished.*

'**furnishings** *n pl* furniture, equipment *etc*: *The office had very expensive furnishings.*

'**furniture** [-tʃə] *nu* things in a house *etc* such as tables, chairs, beds *etc*: *We prefer modern furniture; Our office furniture is very old-fashioned.*

furrier *see* **fur**.

furrow ['fʌrou, (*Amer*) 'fə:-] *nc* **1** a line cut into the earth by a plough: *The farmer planted potatoes in the furrows.* **2** (*formal*) a line in the skin of the face; a wrinkle: *The furrows in her forehead made her look older.* – *vt* (*formal*) to make furrows in: *Her face was furrowed with worry and anxiety.*

'**furrowed** *adj* (*formal*: *usu attrib*: *neg* **un-**): *a furrowed brow/field.*

furry *see* **fur**.

further ['fə:ðə] **1** *adv* (*sometimes* '**farther** ['fa:-]) at or to a great distance or degree: *I cannot go any further; He moved further away.* **2** *adv, adj* more; in addition: *He spoke further on the subject; There is no further news;* (*formal*) *The school is closed until further notice.* – *vt* (*formal*) to help (something) to proceed or go forward quickly: *He furthered our plans by obtaining official permission for us; Arriving at work late will certainly not further his prospect of promotion.*

ˌ**further'more** [-'mo:] *adv* in addition (to what has been said): *Furthermore, I should like to point out . . .*

'**furthest** *adv* (*also* '**farthest** ['fa:-]) at or to the greatest distance or degree: *Who lives furthest away?; She lives furthest from the school.*

further education *nu* (*often attrib*) education beyond the usual school leaving age in a college *etc*: *More money must be spent on further education;* (*attrib*) *further education courses.*

See also **far**.

furtive ['fə:tiv] *adj* (*formal*) secretive; trying to hide one's action or intentions *usu* with the intention of deceiving someone: *He threw a furtive glance in her direction; He looked very furtive with the parcel under his arm.* '**furtively** *adv.* '**furtiveness** *nu.*

fury ['fjuəri] *ncu* very great anger; rage: *full of rage and fury; She was in a terrible fury; She flew into a fury* (= She became very angry).

'**furious** *adj* **1** very angry: *She was furious with him about it; in a furious mood.* **2** (*often formal or liter*) violent: *a furious argument; a furious storm; The motorcyclist drove at a furious speed.*

like fury (*inf*) with great effort, enthusiasm *etc*: *She got into the car and drove like fury in order to be there on time.*

fuse[1] [fju:z] **1** *vti* (*tech*: *sometimes with* **together**) to melt (together) as a result of great heat: *Copper and tin fuse together to make bronze; They fused zinc and copper to make brass;* (*formal fig*) *They disagreed at first but eventually their ideas fused.* **2** *vi* (of an electric circuit or appliance) to stop working because of the melting of a fuse: *Suddenly all the lights fused.* **3** *vt* to cause an electric circuit or appliance to stop working because of the melting of a fuse: *She fused all the lights by switching on too many electrical appliances at once.* – *nc* a piece of easily-melted wire included in an electric circuit so that a dangerously high electric current will break the circuit and switch itself off: *She had to send for the electrician because she could not mend the fuse.*

fusion ['fju:ʒən] *nu* **1** (*tech*) the act of melting together: *the fusion of the metal pieces.* **2** (*formal fig*) a very close joining of things: *the fusion of his ideas into a complete plan.*

fuse[2] [fju:z] *nc* a piece of material, a mechanical device *etc* which makes a bomb *etc* explode at a particular time: *He set the fuse for 10 o'clock and left the bomb under a table; He lit the fuse and waited for the explosion.*

fuselage ['fju:zəla:ʒ, (*Amer*) -sə-] *nc* (*tech*) the body of an aeroplane: *Several repairs were needed to the fuselage before the plane could take off.*

fusillade [fju:zi'leid] *nc* (*formal*) a shooting of several guns together: *The soldiers fired a fusillade;* (*fig*) *a fusillade of questions.*

fusion *see* **fuse**[1].

fuss [fʌs] *nu* (*sometimes with* **a**) unnecessary excitement, worry or activity, often about something unimportant: *There was so much fuss and bother over the president's visit that we were glad when it was over; Don't make such a fuss about that small cut on your finger.* – *vi* to be too concerned with or pay too much attention to (unimportant) details: *Stop fussing! – You're not going to be late; He's always fussing about his health although he's never really ill; She fusses over those children.*

'**fussy** *adj* **1** too concerned with details; too particular; difficult to satisfy: *She is very fussy about her food; We can go to the cinema or the theatre – I'm not fussy which* (= I don't mind which we go to). **2** (of clothes *etc*) with too much decoration: *She wore a very fussy hat; That hat is much too fussy for the occasion.* '**fussily** *adv.*

make/cause a fuss (*inf*) to complain: *She called for the manager and made a fuss about the bad service; You will have to cause a fuss if you want your money back in place of these damaged goods.*

make a fuss of (*inf*) to pay a lot of attention to: *He always makes a fuss of his grandchildren.*

fusty ['fʌsti] *adj* smelling stale and old: *a dark and fusty corridor; This smells rather fusty.*

futile ['fju:tail] *adj* (*formal*) useless; having no effect: *He made a futile attempt to lift the heavy box; His attempt to stop the war was futile.*

fu'tility [-'ti-] *nu* (*formal*) uselessness: *He realized the futility of trying to continue his journey when the storm grew worse.*

future ['fju:tʃə] *ncu* **1** (what is going to happen in) the time to come: *He was afraid of what the future might bring; Fortune-tellers claim to be able to tell the future; That young couple will have a happy future together;* (*attrib*) *I wish you good luck in your future life;* (*attrib*) *his future wife.* **2** (*gram*) (a verb in) the future tense. – *adj* (*gram*) (of a tense of a verb) indicating an action which will take place at a later time: *In the sentence 'He will come', the verb is in the future tense.*

in 'future *adv* after this; from now on: *Don't do that in future; In future I shall be more careful about whom I trust.*

fuzz [fʌz] **1** *nu* a mass of soft, light material such as fine light hair *etc*: *The peaches were covered with fuzz.* **2** *nu or n pl* (*sl*) the police: *Watch out for the fuzz!*

'**fuzzy** *adj* **1** (*usu attrib*) covered with fuzz: *The child loved her fuzzy teddy bear.* **2** indistinct; blurred; not clear: *The television picture was fuzzy.* **fuzzily** *adv.* '**fuzziness** *nu.*

Gg

gab *see* **gift of the gab**.

gabardine, gaberdine [gabə'di:n] **1** *nu, adj* (of) a fabric, *usu* wool or cotton: *The coat is (made of) gabardine; a gabardine coat.* **2** *nc* a coat made from this material.

gabble ['gabl] *vti* (*derog*) to talk, or say (something), very quickly and not very clearly: *The lady was obviously upset as she gabbled (out) her story to the policeman; She was so upset, she was just gabbling.*

gaberdine *see* **gabardine**.

gable ['geibl] *nc* the triangular part of the side wall of a building between the sloping parts of the roof.

'**gabled** *adj* having or forming a gable or gables: *a gabled house/roof; Is the roof gabled?*

gad [gad] – *pt, ptp* '**gadded** – **gad about/around** *vi* (*inf derog*) to go around to one place after another (*usu* in order to amuse oneself): *She's forever gadding about now that the children are at school.*

'**gadabout** *nc* (*derog*) a person who likes to go around to one place after another (*usu* for amusement): *She's become a real gadabout since her divorce.*

gadget ['gadʒit] *nc* (*sometimes derog*) a *usu* small tool, machine *etc*: *Her kitchen was full of gadgets; I find this a most useful gadget for loosening bottle lids.*

Gael [geil] *nc* a person from the Scottish Highlands or Ireland who speaks Gaelic.

Gaelic ['geilik, 'galik] *nu* **1** a language spoken in parts of the Scottish Highlands. **2** (*usu* **Irish** ['aiəriʃ] : *also* **Irish Gaelic**) a similar language spoken in parts of Ireland.

See also Appendix 2.

gaff [gaf] *nc* a hook for pulling large fish, such as salmon, out of a river *etc.*

blow the gaff (*sl*) to tell (something secret) to someone: *When the police arrived, the thieves realized that someone had blown the gaff.*

gaffe [gaf] *nc* (*inf*) a mistake or blunder; something which ought not to have been said, done *etc*: *When I'm at a party, I'm always scared of making a gaffe.*

gaffer ['gafə] *nc* (*Brit inf*: *sometimes facet*) the person in charge of a group of workmen: *Tell the gaffer that the machine has broken down.*

gag [gag] – *pt, ptp* **gagged** – **1** *vt* to prevent (a person) talking or making a noise, by putting something in or over his mouth: *The prisoners were tied up and gagged; (fig) The government tried in vain to gag the newspapers.* **2** *vi* to choke and almost be sick: *He gagged when the doctor examined his throat.* – *nc* **1** something which is put in or over a person's mouth to prevent him talking or making a noise. **2** (*inf*) a joke or amusing story: *That comedian always tells the same gags.*

gaga ['ga:ga:] *adj* (*sl*: *usu pred*) silly; foolish; not completely sane: *She makes so many silly suggestions that I'm beginning to think she's a bit gaga.*

gage *see* **gauge**.

gaiety, gaily *see* **gay**.

gain [gein] **1** *vt* (*formal*) to get or obtain (something): *The new teacher quickly gained experience; He gained a bad reputation; He gained possession of the house.* **2** *vti* (*often with* **by** *or* **from**) to get (something good, *eg* money) by doing something: *What have I to gain by staying here?* **3** *vt* to have an increase in, or a greater amount of, (something): *He soon gained strength again after his illness; She gained (three pounds in) weight.* **4** *vti* (of a clock or watch) to go too fast: *This clock gains (four minutes a day).* **5** *vt* (*formal*) to reach or arrive at (a place): *With some difficulty, he at last gained the shore.* – *ncu* **1** an increase (in weight *etc*): *a gain of one pound; Has there been any gain in weight?* **2** (the getting of) profits, advantage, wealth *etc*: *His loss was my gain; He'd do anything for gain.* – *See also* **gains** *below.*

'**gainful** *adj* (*formal*: *usu attrib*) producing something good or useful: *gainful employment.*

'**gainfully** *adv.*

gains *n pl* profits; money *etc* that has been got in some (*usu* bad) way: *ill-gotten gains.*

gain ground 1 to make progress: *The younger runner is still ahead but the older one is gaining ground.* **2** to become more generally accepted or influential: *His views were once unacceptable but are now gaining ground rapidly.*

'**gain on**/(*formal*) **upon** *vt fus* to get or come closer to (a person, thing *etc* that one is chasing): *Drive faster – the police car is gaining on us.*

gain time to cause (something) to be delayed in order to give oneself more time to do (something else): *He knew that his work would not be ready for the meeting so he pretended to be ill in order to gain time.*

gainsay [gein'sei] *vt* (*very formal*: *usu* found only in the form **gain'saying** in negative sentences) to deny: *There is no gainsaying that the country is in difficulties.*

gait [geit] *nc* (*pl rare*) the way in which a person or animal walks: *The old man walked with a shuffling gait.*

gaiter ['geitə] *nc* a covering for the leg and ankle, *usu* of cloth or leather, which fits over the shoe.

gala ['ga:lə, 'geilə; (*Amer*) 'geilə] *nc* **1** an occasion of entertainment and enjoyment out of doors: *a miners' gala.* **2** a meeting for certain sports: *a swimming gala.*

galaxy ['galəksi] *nc* **1** a very large group of stars. **2** (*fig*) a large group of famous, beautiful, well-dressed, impressive *etc* people, things *etc*: *a galaxy of well-known entertainers at a show; a galaxy of new cars at the Motor Show.*

galactic [gə'laktik] *adj* (*tech*: *esp pred*) of a galaxy or the Galaxy.

the Galaxy *see* **the Milky Way** *under* **milk**.

gale [geil] *nc* a strong wind: *A great many trees were blown down in the gale; There's quite a gale blowing.*

'**gale force** the speed or strength of a gale: *The winds reached gale force; (attrib) gale-force winds.*

gall[1] [go:l] *nu* **1** (*formal*) a bitter liquid which is produced in the liver and which is stored in the gall bladder. **2** (*inf*) impudence: *I don't know how you have the gall to say you're my friend after being so rude to me yesterday.* **3** (*liter*) hate; bitter feelings. – *vt* to annoy or irritate (a person) very much: *It really galls me to think that he is earning more money than me.*

'**galling** *adj* (*usu pred*) very annoying: *She found it galling that her young sister was married before her.*

'**gall bladder** *nc* an organ of the body attached to the liver, in which gall is stored: *She had an* *operation to have her gall bladder removed.*

'**gallstone** *nc* a small hard object that is sometimes formed in the gall bladder, often needing to be removed by surgery.

gall[2] [go:l] *nc* a small round growth on trees and plants, *esp* oak trees, caused by insects.

gallant ['galənt, (*def 3 also*) gə'lant] 1 *adj* (*formal*) brave: *a gallant leader*; *The soldier was very gallant.* 2 *adj* (*old or liter*) which looks splendid or fine: *a gallant ship.* 3 *nc, adj* (*esp old*) (a man who is) very polite and attentive to ladies: *That young man is so gallant*; *Such a gallant young man*; *Gallants and their ladies attended the ball.*

'**gallantly, gal'lantly** *advs.*

'**gallantry** *nu* 1 (*formal*) bravery: *He won a medal for gallantry.* 2 (*esp old*) (an act of) politeness and attention to ladies: *The young man was noted for gallantry.*

galleon ['galiən] *nc* (*hist*) a large, *usu* Spanish, sailing-ship.

gallery ['galəri] *nc* 1 a large room or building in which paintings, statues *etc* are on show: *an art gallery.* 2 an upper floor of seats in a church, hall, theatre *etc, esp* (in a theatre) the top floor: *We had a good view of the stage from the front row of the gallery.* 3 (*often in cmpds*) a long passage or a long narrow room: *a shooting-gallery.* 4 an underground passage *eg* in a mine.

play to the gallery to try to become popular by doing, saying *etc* what would appeal to the less educated, less sophisticated section of the population.

galley ['gali] *nc* 1 (*hist*) a long low ship with one deck, moved by oars (and often sails). 2 a ship's kitchen.

galling *see* **gall**[1].

gallivant [gali'vant] *vi* (*inf*: *usu derog*: *usu* found only in the form ˌ**galli'vanting**) to go, or travel around, to one place after another (*usu* in order to amuse oneself): *I wish you would stop gallivanting around.*

gallon ['galən] *nc* (*often abbrev* **gal(l)**. *when written*) a measure for liquids, eight pints (in Britain, 4·546 litres; in the US, 3·785 litres): *five gallons of petrol.*

'**gallons (of)** (*loosely*) a large amount (of something liquid): *The children drank gallons of orange juice*; *'Have you enough beer?' 'Yes, we've got gallons.'*

gallop ['galəp] *ncu* (a period of riding at) the fastest pace of a horse: *The horse broke into a gallop* (= began to gallop); *He took the horse out of the stables for a gallop*; *The horse went off at a gallop* (= at its fastest pace). – *vi* 1 (of a horse) to move at a gallop: *The horse galloped round the field.* 2 (*inf*: *with* **through**) to do, say *etc* (something) very quickly: *He galloped through his homework so that he could watch television.*

'**galloping** *adj* (*fig*: *usu attrib*) increasing, or making progress, very quickly: *The country is suffering from galloping inflation.*

gallows ['galouz] *n sing* (*esp hist*) a wooden frame on which criminals are hanged: *The murderer was sent to the gallows.*

gallstone *see* **gall**[1].

Gallup poll ['galəp] *nc* a method of finding out the feelings, opinions *etc* of the public by asking a sample of people for their feelings, opinions *etc.*

galore [gə'lo:] *adj* (*inf*: *placed immediately after noun*) in large amounts; in large numbers: *There are book-shops galore in this town.*

galosh, (*also, esp Brit*) **golosh** [gə'loʃ] *nc* (*usu in pl*) a rubber shoe worn over an ordinary shoe in wet weather: *Put on your galoshes*; *a pair of goloshes. See also* **overshoe**.

galvanize, -ise ['galvənaiz] *vt* 1 (*tech*) to cover (iron or steel) with a thin layer of zinc to prevent it rusting. 2 (*formal or facet*) (*fig*: *with* **into**) to cause or move (a person) to do something: *The threat of losing their jobs galvanized the men into action.*

gambit ['gambit] *nc* 1 a first move in a game, *esp* chess, in which something is given away or lost in order to make one's position stronger. 2 (*fig*: *usu* **opening gambit**) a starting move, action, remark *etc* in a piece of business, conversation *etc*: *As an opening gambit, he accused his opponents of lying.*

gamble ['gambl] 1 *vi* to risk (losing) money on the result of a card game, horse-race *etc*: *He gambled and drank all night and in the morning had no money left.* 2 *vi* (*fig*: *with* **on**) to take a chance or risk: *I'm gambling on having enough money to pay for the car by the time the account arrives.* 3 *vt* to risk losing (money *etc*) on the result of something: *He gambled a great deal of money on the result of the final race.* – *nc* (something which involves) a risk: *The whole business was a bit of a gamble.* '**gambler** *nc.*

'**gambling** *nu* the act of trying to win (*usu* money) by playing cards *etc*: *He is too fond of gambling.*

gamble away *vt sep* to lose (a sum of money) by gambling unsuccessfully: *He got £5 000 from his father, but gambled it all away.*

take a gamble to do something which has a certain amount of risk or chance about it, in the hope that it will be successful: *I don't know if I can rely on him, but I'm willing to take a gamble*; *I'll take a gamble on it.*

gambol ['gambl] – *pt, ptp* '**gambolled**, (*Amer*) '**gamboled** – *vi* (*liter or formal*) (*usu* only of lambs) to jump around playfully.

game [geim] 1 *nc* an enjoyable activity, sometimes with rules, which *eg* children play: *Young children often play a game of pretending to be mothers and fathers.* 2 *nc* a form of activity, with rules, in which one person, team *etc* tries to beat another person, team *etc*: *Football, tennis and chess are games.* 3 *nc* a particular case of two people, teams *etc* meeting for such an activity; a match; (in some sports or games) one part of a match: *Let's have a game of tennis!*; *I'm winning (by) three games to one.* 4 *nc* the apparatus or things which a person needs to play a particular game: *My aunt bought me a game of ludo for Christmas.* 5 *nc* (*no pl*: *inf*: *usu derog*) a scheme, plan or trick: *I wonder what his game is.* 6 *nu* (*sometimes in cmpds*) (the flesh of) certain birds and animals which are killed for sport: *He's very fond of game*; (*attrib*) *game laws*; (*attrib*) *game-birds.* – *adj* (*inf*: *often pred with* **for**) brave; willing; ready for anything: *He's a game old guy*; *He's game for anything/game to do anything, no matter how dangerous it is.*

'**gamely** *adv*: *Gamely, he carried on to the end.*

games *n pl* (*with cap in names*) an athletic competition, sometimes with other sports: *the Olympic Games*; *Highland games.*

'**gaming** *nu* (*esp attrib*) gambling: *a gaming table.*

'**gamekeeper** *nc* a person who looks after game-birds *etc, usu* for the owner of the land on which they live: *The gamekeeper was looking for the poacher who had been shooting the young pheasants*;

The gamekeeper shot the fox which was carrying a pheasant in its mouth.

game point *nc* the winning point in certain games.

'**game reserve** *nc* an area of land set aside for the protection of animals, in which hunting is *usu* not allowed: *The tourists wanted to visit a game reserve in Africa.*

'**game warden** *nc* **1** a person who guards a game reserve. **2** in the US, a person whose job it is to make sure that the laws regarding the shooting *etc* of game in a particular area are kept.

big game *see* **big**.

the game is up (*inf*) our, your *etc* plan or trick has failed or has been found out: *The thief knew the game was up when he saw the policeman.*

game of chance a game in which winning or losing depends on chance rather than on a person's skill, *eg* cards, roulette.

give the game away *see* **give**.

play the game *see* **play**.

gamma ['gamə] *n* the third letter of the Greek alphabet (Γ, γ)

gamma rays *n pl* (*tech*) a powerful form of radiation given off by radium and other radioactive substances.

gammon ['gamən] *nu* the meat of the leg of a pig, salted and smoked: *He had a slice of gammon and two eggs for breakfast*; (*attrib*) *a gammon steak.*

gamut ['gamət] *nc* **1** the whole range of sound which a voice or instrument can make. **2** (*no pl*) the full range (of anything, *eg* of a person's emotions): *Her reactions ranged through the whole gamut of emotions from intense fear to great anger.*

gander ['gandə] *nc* a male goose.

gang [gaŋ] *nc* **1** a number (of workmen *etc*) working together: *a gang of men working on the railway.* **2** a group (of people), *usu* formed for a bad purpose: *a gang of jewel thieves*; *The children in our street have formed two gangs and they're always fighting each other.*

'**gangster** *nc* a member of a gang of criminals: *I am tired of seeing films about American police and gangsters.*

'**gangplank** *nc* a gangway (*def 1*).

'**gangway** *nc* **1** a movable bridge by means of which people *etc* can get on or off a boat. **2** a passage between rows of seats, *eg* in a theatre. – *interj* give me *etc* room to pass; make way!: *Gangway for members of the committee!*

gang up on *vt fus* (*inf*) to join or act with a person *etc* against (some other person *etc*): *The manager felt that the younger members of staff were ganging up on him.*

gang up with *vt fus* (*inf*) to join or act with (a person *etc*) for some purpose, *eg* amusement: *The girls ganged up with the boys they met on the beach.*

ganglion ['gaŋgliən] – *pls* '**ganglia** [-ə], '**ganglions** – *nc* (*tech*) **1** a group of nerve-cells. **2** a growth or swelling in the covering of a tendon.

gangling ['gaŋgliŋ], **gangly** ['gaŋgli] *adj* (*derog*) tall, very thin and *usu* awkward: *a gangly red-haired youth*; *She is small and dainty and he is tall and gangling.*

gangplank *see* **gang**.

gangrene ['gaŋgri:n] *nu* the decay of a part of the body of a living person, animal *etc*, because the blood supply to that part of the body has stopped: *They have amputated his right foot because it has gangrene in it.*

'**gangrenous** [-grə-] *adj* (*tech*) suffering from or having gangrene: *a gangrenous wound*; *The wound may be gangrenous.*

gangster, gangway *see* **gang**.

gannet ['ganit] *nc* **1** a type of large white sea bird. **2** (*inf derog*) a greedy person: *You little gannet! You've eaten six cakes!*

gantry ['gantri] *nc* a bridge-like structure which supports a crane, railway signals *etc.*

gaol, gaoler *see* **jail, jailer**.

gap [gap] *nc* a break or open space: *a gap between two blocks of flats*; *a gap in conversation*; *a gap in his knowledge.*

gape [geip] *vi* **1** (*often derog*: *often with* **at**) to stare with open mouth, *eg* in surprise: *The crowd of tourists gaped at the King and Queen.* **2** (*formal*) to be wide open: *A great hole in the ground gaped in front of them.* – *nc* an open-mouthed stare: *a gape of amazement.*

'**gaping** *adj* (*usu attrib*) wide open: *a gaping hole in the wall*; *a gaping wound.*

garage ['gara:dʒ, (*Amer*) gə'ra:ʒ] *nc* **1** a small building *usu* beside a house, in which a car is kept: *We are looking for a house with a garage.* **2** a building where cars are repaired and *usu* petrol, oil *etc* is sold: *He has taken his car to the garage to have the engine repaired.*

garb [ga:b] *nu* (*old or liter*) clothes: *He wore the garb of a monk.*

garbed *adj* (*old or liter*: *pred*) dressed: *He came to the party garbed as a monk.*

garbage ['ga:bidʒ] *nu* **1** (*esp Amer*) waste substances from kitchens *etc*; rubbish: *Where do you put the garbage in this kitchen?*; (*attrib*) *There is a garbage chute at the end of the corridor.* **2** (*fig*: *sl*) anything which is of little or no value: *If you read his report, you will realize that it's just garbage.*

'**garbage can** *nc* (*Amer*) a dustbin.

garbled ['ga:bld] *adj* (*derog*) (of a statement, story *etc*) mixed up and muddled: *He was so upset that his statement ot the police was rather garbled*; *The child gave a very garbled account of the accident because she was still very frightened.*

garden ['ga:dn] *nc* **1** a piece of ground, *usu* beside a house, on which flowers, vegetables *etc* are grown: *We have a small garden at the front of the house and a large one at the back*; (*attrib*) *garden flowers.* **2** (*fig*) a fertile area in a country: *This region is known as the garden of France.* – *vi* to work in a garden, *usu* as a hobby: *She does not garden very much nowadays – she tires easily.*

'**gardener** *nc* a person who works in, and looks after, a garden, either as a job or as a hobby: *Both he and his wife are enthusiastic gardeners*; *They have to employ two gardeners to look after that huge garden.*

'**gardening** *nu* the work of looking after a garden: *Gardening is his favourite hobby*; *Gardening is the only job he is trained to do*; (*attrib*) *gardening clothes/tools.*

'**gardens** **1** *n sing or pl* a park, *esp* one where animals are kept or special trees or flowers are grown: *zoological/botanical gardens*; *The botanical gardens is a very interesting place/are beautiful at this time of year.* **2** *n* (*with cap*: *sometimes abbrev* **Gdns** *when written*) a word used in the names of certain roads or streets: *His address is 21 Sunnyside Gardens.*

'**garden party** *nc* a large (*usu* formal) party, held in the garden of a house *etc*: *The Queen held a garden party in the palace grounds.*

gargle ['ga:gl] *vi* to wash the throat with a soothing

or germkilling liquid, without swallowing the liquid: *If you gargle every morning when you have a sore throat it will ease the pain.* – *ncu* the liquid used in this way.

gargoyle ['ga:goil] *nc* a carved figure, *usu* of an odd or horrible person, animal or demon, sticking out from the gutter on the roof of a church *etc*, through which rain-water pours from the roof.

garish ['geəriʃ] *adj* (*derog*) unpleasantly bright or showy: *garish shirts*; *His shirts are very garish.* **'garishly** *adv.* **'garishness** *nu.*

garland ['ga:lənd] *nc* flowers or leaves tied or woven into a circle: *The islanders wore garlands of flowers round their heads.*

garlic ['ga:lik] *nu* a plant with a bulb shaped like an onion, which has a strong taste and smell and which is used in cooking: *This sauce is tasteless – you should have flavoured it with garlic and herbs.*

garment ['ga:mənt] *nc* (*formal*) an article of clothing: *This shop sells ladies' garments.*

garnet ['ga:nit] *ncu* a *usu* red semi-precious stone: *She has garnets in her necklace*; (*attrib*) *a garnet ring.*

garnish ['ga:niʃ] *vt* (*formal*) to decorate (a dish of food): *Parsley is often used to garnish salads.* – *ncu* (*formal*) something which is used to decorate a dish of food: *She used fresh mint leaves as a garnish for the soup.*

garret ['garət] *nc* (*formal or liter*) a *usu* small and sometimes dark and unpleasant room just under the roof of a house: *He used to be very poor and lived in a garret but now he is a famous artist.*

garrison ['garisn] *nc* a number of soldiers, for guarding a fortress, town *etc*: *Call out the garrison!*; (*attrib*) *a garrison town.* – *vt* (*formal*) to supply (a town *etc*) with troops to guard it: *They have garrisoned the city.*

garrulous ['garələs] *adj* (*formal derog*) fond of talking; talking a great deal: *a garrulous old man*; *He is old and garrulous.* **'garrulously** *adv.* **gar'rulity** [-'ru:-], **'garrulousness** *nus.*

garter ['ga:tə] *nc* a band, *eg* of elastic, used to hold up a stocking or sock: *The child's stocking keeps falling down – he has lost a garter.*

the Garter (the badge of) the highest order of knighthood in Britain.

gas [gas] **1** *ncu* a substance like air: *Oxygen is a gas.* **2** *nu* any gas, *eg* coal gas, which is used for heating, cooking *etc*: *Do you cook by gas or electricity?*; *Does your cooker use natural gas or coal gas?* **3** *nu* (*inf*) a gas, *usu* nitrous oxide, which is used by dentists as an anaesthetic: *I was given gas when I went to have my teeth taken out.* **4** *nu* a poisonous or irritating gas used in war *etc*: *The police used tear gas to control the riot.* **5** (*inf*) short for **gasoline**. – *v* – *pt, ptp* **gassed** – **1** *vt* to poison or kill (a person or animal) with gas: *He was gassed during World War I.* **2** *vi* (*sl derog*) to talk for a long time without saying anything of importance: *He gasses on the phone for hours.*

gaseous ['gasiəs] *adj* (*tech*) of or like (a) gas: *a gaseous substance*; *It is gaseous in nature.*

'gassy *adj* full of gas: *This lemonade is rather gassy.* **'gassiness** *nu.*

'gas-bag *nc* (*derog sl*) a person who talks a great deal: *She's just an old gas-bag.*

'gas chamber *nc* a room in which people are killed by means of gas: *Many people were sent to the gas chamber in World War II*; *In some countries the means of execution is the gas chamber.*

'gas-fitter *nc* a person whose job it is to supply a building *etc* with the pipes *etc* used for heating, cooking *etc* by means of gas.

'gas mask *nc* something which is used to cover the face to prevent a person breathing poisonous gas: *Many people in Britain were given gas masks during World War II.*

'gas meter *nc* an instrument which measures the amount of gas which is used *eg* in a house for cooking, heating *etc*: *You will receive a bill from the Gas Board after your gas meter has been read.*

gasoline, gasolene ['gasəli:n] *nu* (*Amer*: *also* (*inf*) **gas**) petrol.

gasometer [ga'somitə] *nc* a large, round tank for storing gas.

'gas station *nc* (*Amer*) a petrol station.

'gasworks *n sing* a place where gas is made: *The gasworks is rather an ugly building.*

gash [gaʃ] *nc* a deep, open cut or wound: *He had a nasty gash on his cheek.* – *vt* to make a gash in (something): *The vandals gashed the seats in the cinema.*

gasolene *etc see* **gas**.

gasp [ga:sp] *nc* the sound made by suddenly breathing in, *eg* because of surprise or sudden pain: *She gave a gasp of fear when she saw the gun.* – **1** *vi* to make a gasp: *He gasped as he stepped into the cold water.* **2** *vi* to breathe with difficulty and with frequent gasps: *By the time he reached the top of the hill, he was gasping and panting.* **3** *vt* (*usu with* **out**) to say (something) while out of breath: *The boy ran up and gasped out his story to the policeman.*

be 'gasping for (*sl*) to want (something) very much: *I'm gasping for a drink/cigarette.*

gassy *see* **gas**.

gastric ['gastrik] *adj* (*tech*: *attrib*) of the stomach: *a gastric ulcer*; *gastric 'flu.*

gastritis [ga'straitis] *nu* (*tech*) inflammation of the stomach: *He is suffering from gastritis.*

gastro-enteritis ['gastrouentə'raitis] *nu* (*tech*) inflammation of the inner surface of the stomach and the intestines: *He is suffering from gastro-enteritis.*

gastronomic [gastrə'nomik] *adj* (*formal*) of good food: *the gastronomic delights of France.*

gasworks *see* **gas**.

gate [geit] *nc* **1** (the metal, wooden *etc* doorlike object which closes) the opening in a wall, fence *etc* through which people *etc* pass into or out of a garden, park, city *etc*: *Shut the garden gate to stop the dog getting out*; *I'll meet you at the park gate(s)*; *There were many beggars at the city gates.* **2** (the money paid by) the total number of people who go to a football match *etc*: *Less important football teams have small gates.*

'gate-crash *vti* (*inf*) to enter or go to (a party, meeting *etc*) without being invited or without paying: *She only invited a few friends but some other people gate-crashed (the party).*

'gate-crasher *nc* (*inf*): *If you don't want any gate-crashers ask your guests to bring their invitation cards.*

'gate-house *nc* a house above or beside the gate into a city, park *etc*, often occupied by a gate-keeper.

'gate-keeper *nc* a person who is in charge of a gate into a city, park *etc*.

'gate-post *nc* a post to which a gate (*def 1*) is fixed.

'gateway *nc* **1** an opening or entrance into a city *etc*, which contains a gate. **2** (*fig*) a way or path to (something): *A university degree is not necessarily a gateway to a good job.*

between you (and) me and the gate-post (*inf*) said when the speaker does not want the person or people to whom he is speaking to tell anyone else what is said: *Between you, me and the gate-post, I don't think much of her suggestions.*

gâteau, gateau ['gatou, (*Amer*) ga:'tou] – *pls* '**gateaux** [-z], **gateaus** – *ncu* (*formal*) a rich cake *usu* with cream: *Do have a (piece of) gateau*; *a selection of cream gâteaux.*

gather ['gaðə] **1** *vti* to (cause to) come together in one place: *A crowd of people gathered near the accident*; *Gather (together) as many people as possible to listen to his speech.* **2** *vt* (*formal*) to learn or come to a conclusion (from what has been seen, heard *etc*): *I gather you are leaving tomorrow.* **3** *vt* to collect or get: *She gathered information/flowers.* **4** *vt* to increase (speed): *The car slowly gathered speed/momentum as it ran down the hill.* **5** *vt* to pull (material, part of a piece of clothing) into small folds and stitch together: *She gathered the skirt at the waist.* **6** *vt* to pull (a cloak *etc*) closely round oneself: *She gathered her cardigan around her.* – *nc* a fold in material, a piece of clothing *etc.*

'**gathering** *nc* (*formal*) a meeting or a crowd of people: *a family gathering.*

gather round *vi* to come together around a person, thing *etc*: *Will everyone please gather round?*

gather together *vi, vt sep* to come or bring together, in a group: *The lecturer gathered his books and papers together*; *He gathered them together*; (*fig*) *I had no time to gather my thoughts together before I was asked to speak.*

gather up *vt sep* to collect together by picking up: *He gathered up his books and walked out*; *He gathered them up.*

gauche [gouʃ] *adj* (*formal*) awkward and clumsy when with other people: *Some of the girls at the party were a bit gauche*; *a gauche young woman.* '**gauchely** *adv.* '**gaucheness** *nu.*

gaudy ['go:di] *adj* (*often derog*) very bright in colour; often too bright to be in good taste: *a bird's gaudy plumage*; *That dress is too gaudy for a funeral*; *She always wears gaudy clothes.* '**gaudily** *adv.* '**gaudiness** *nu.*

gauge, (*also, esp Amer*) **gage** [geidʒ] *vt* **1** (*formal or tech*) to measure (something) very accurately: *They gauged the January rainfall.* **2** to estimate, guess or judge: *He tried to gauge her height from looking at her*; *Can you gauge her willingness to help?* – *nc* **1** (*often in cmpds*) an instrument for measuring the amount of rain which is falling, the speed of wind *etc*: *a rain-gauge.* **2** (*tech*) the standard size or one of the standard sizes (of wire, bullets *etc*): *This transformer is wired with 38 gauge wire*; *What gauge of wire do you require?* **3** (*tech*) the distance between the rails of a railway line: *standard gauge*; (*attrib*) *a narrow-gauge railway.*

gaunt [go:nt] *adj* (of a person) thin or thin-faced: *a gaunt old woman*; *She is growing more and more gaunt as her illness gets worse.* '**gauntness** *nu.*

gauntlet ['go:ntlit] *nc* **1** a heavy glove which covers the wrist, worn when fencing, riding a motorcycle *etc.* **2** (*hist*) a heavy glove covered in or made of metal, worn by knights and soldiers in the Middle Ages.

run the gauntlet (*fig*) to suffer or be exposed to criticism, blame, danger *etc*: *The government always has to run the gauntlet of the trade unions*; *She had to run the gauntlet of her neighbours' disapproval.*

throw down, pick up the gauntlet (*fig*) to make, or accept, a challenge: *He threw down the gauntlet by calling his opponent a liar.*

gauze [go:z] *nu* a thin cloth that can be seen through, used *eg* to cover wounds or to protect food from flies: *She used a length of gauze to bandage his leg*; (*attrib*) *a gauze bandage.*

gave *see* **give**.

gawky ['go:ki] *adj* (of a person) looking clumsy or awkward: *gawky teenagers*; *She is tall and gawky.* '**gawkiness** *nu.*

gay [gei] *adj* **1** happy or full of fun; making people happy or produced when people are happy: *The children were gay and cheerful*; *gay music/voices.* **2** (*usu attrib*) bright: *gay colours.* **3** (*sl*) homosexual, or of homosexuals: *a gay club*; *Is he gay?* '**gayness** *nu.*

gaiety ['geiəti] **1** *ncu* (an occasion of) fun or happiness: *They joined in the gaiety.* **2** *nu* the state of being gay (*defs 1, 2*): *the gaiety of the music*; *the gaiety of the flags*; *the gaiety of the streets decorated with flags.*

'**gaily** *adv* **1** in a gay (*defs 1, 2*) manner: *She was singing gaily*; *gaily-coloured flags.* **2** (*fig*) not aware of problems *etc*: *She gaily went on believing she had no enemies.*

gaze [geiz] *vi* (*often with* **at**) to look steadily (at something or someone) for some time, *usu* in surprise, out of interest *etc*: *The child gazed in wonderment at the Christmas tree*; *She gazed dreamily into the distance.* – *nc* a long, steady look.

gazelle [gə'zel] – *pls* **ga'zelles, ga'zelle** – *nc* a type of small antelope: *three gazelles*; *a herd of gazelle.*

gazette [gə'zet] **1** *nc* a type of newspaper which has lists of government notices. **2** *n* (*with cap*) a word often used in the titles of newspapers: *the Evening Gazette.*

gazetteer [gazə'tiə] *nc* a dictionary of geographical names: *Look up a gazetteer to find which river that city stands on.*

gear [giə] **1** *nc* (*usu in pl*) a set of toothed wheels (gear-wheels), levers *etc* which act together to carry motion *eg* from the engine of a car *etc* to its wheels: *He is not used to driving a car with automatic gears.* **2** *nu* a particular combination of these wheels, *eg* in a car: *He changed gear*; *The car is in first gear.* – *See also* **gear** *in phrases below.* **3** *nu* (*often in cmpds*) an apparatus or mechanism used for a particular purpose: *an aeroplane's landing-gear.* **4** *nu* (*inf*) the things (*eg* tools) needed for a particular job, sport *etc*: *The workman gathered all his gear together*; *That shop sells sports gear.* **5** *nu* (*inf*) clothes: *Young people always want to wear the latest gear.* – *vt* (*fig*: *with* **to**) to adapt or design (something) to suit a particular need: *This book has been geared to adult students.*

'**gearbox** *nc* the part of a car *etc* which has the gears in it.

'**gear lever/change/stick** (*Brit*), '**gear shift** (*Amer*) *ncs* the apparatus in a car *etc* which is used to change gear.

bottom/first, second, third, top/fourth gear the gears by means of which a car *etc* is made to move increasingly quickly by its motor: *You'll have to go into second gear to get the car up this hill.*

in(to) 'gear with the motor connected to what it is providing the power to (*eg* the wheels of a car): *If the car is not in gear, it won't move*; *First you need to put it into gear.*

high/low gear a gear which makes something turn, move *etc* relatively quickly or slowly when driven *eg* by a motor.

geese *see* **goose**.

geisha ['geiʃə] *nc* (*often* **'geisha girl**) a Japanese girl trained to entertain (men) by her conversation, dancing *etc*.

gelatine ['dʒelətiːn, (*Amer*) -tin] *nu* a jelly-like substance made from hooves, animal bones *etc* and used in food: *The jelly wouldn't set as she hadn't used enough gelatine.*

gelatinous [dʒə'latənəs] *adj* (*formal or tech*: *usu attrib*) like (a) jelly or gelatine: *a gelatinous substance.*

gelding ['geldiŋ] *nc* a castrated horse.

gelignite ['dʒelignait] *nu* an explosive: *The bandits blew up the bridge with gelignite.*

gem [dʒem] *nc* **1** (*formal*) a precious stone *esp* when cut into a particular shape, *eg* for a ring or necklace. **2** (*fig inf*) anything or anyone that is thought to be especially good: *The jokes he tells are absolute gems*; *My landlady is a gem*; *This picture is the gem of my collection.*

'gemstone *nc* (*formal*) a precious or semi-precious stone *esp* before it is cut into shape for a ring *etc*.

Gemini ['dʒemini, (*Amer*) -nai] *n* a sign of the zodiac, the Twins: *People born between May 21 and June 20 are said to be born under the sign of Gemini.*

gen [dʒen] – *pt, ptp* **genned** – **gen up** *vi, vt sep* (*Brit sl*) to study (something) or get the information one needs on (some subject): *I'll have to gen up on the rules of debating if I'm to be the chairman*; *Will you gen me up on the situation?*

the gen (*Brit sl*) information, often about something which is not generally known: *He gave me the gen on the office scandal.*

gender ['dʒendə] (*gram*) **1** *nc* any of a number of classes (*usu* two or three in European languages) into which nouns and pronouns can be divided (*eg* masculine, feminine, neuter). **2** *nu* the grouping of nouns and pronouns into such classes: *Is there gender in English?*

gene [dʒiːn] *nc* (*biol*) any of the basic elements of heredity, passed from parents to their offspring, which cause the offspring to have certain features that the parents have: *If the children are red-haired, one of their parents must have a gene for red hair.*

genetic [dʒə'netik] *adj* of genes of genetics: *That baby has a genetic abnormality*; *His abnormality is genetic in origin.*

genetics [dʒə'netiks] *n sing* the science of heredity: *Genetics is a modern science*; (*attrib*) *genetics lectures.*

genealogy [dʒiːni'alədʒi] **1** *nu* (*tech*) the history of families from generation to generation: *He is studying the genealogy of the royal house of Tudor.* **2** *nc* (*more formal than* **family tree**) a plan, list *etc* of the ancestors of a person or family: *The book was illustrated by genealogies of the families involved in the plot.* **,genea'logical** [-'lo-] *adj*.

,gene'alogist *nc* a person who studies or makes genealogies.

genera *see* **genus**.

general ['dʒenərəl] *adj* **1** (*usu attrib*) of, involving *etc* all, most or very many people, places, things *etc*: *The general feeling is that you have made a serious mistake*; *This stormy weather is general throughout Britain*; *His general knowledge is good although he is not good at English or mathematics*; *At the minute, there is a general interest in education*; *His interest in the subject is general rather than particular.* **2** (*usu attrib*) covering a large number of cases or examples: *a general rule*; *Is this rule general?* **3** (*usu attrib*) without details: *I'll just give you a general idea of the plan*; *You must supply more details – your description is too general.* **4** (*attrib or placed immediately after noun*) (as part of an official title) chief: *the Postmaster General*; *the General Secretary of the Trades Union Congress.* – *nc* (*with cap, and often abbrev* **Gen.**, *when written in titles*) in the British army, (a person of) the rank next below field marshal: *He is a general*; *When was he promoted to general? General Smith.* – *See also* Appendix 3.

,gene'rality [-'ra-] (*very formal*) **1** *nu* the quality of being general: *the generality of a person's remarks.* **2** *nc* a general rule; a general statement without details: *He always talks in generalities.* **3** *nu* the majority (of some group of people, things *etc*): *The generality of students are honest and hard-working.*

'generalize, -ise *vt* (*formal*) **1** to make a general rule, statement *etc* that can be applied to many cases, based on a certain number of cases: *He's trying to generalize from only two examples.* **2** to talk (about something) in general terms and without details: *I think it is time we stopped generalizing and discussed each problem separately.*

,generali'zation, -s- *ncu* (the act of making) a general statement, rule *etc*: *I wish you wouldn't make such sweeping generalizations.*

'generally *adv* usually; in most cases; by most people; on the whole: *He is generally disliked*; *He generally gets good marks for French.*

general election *nc* in Britain, an election in which the voters of every constituency in the country elect a Member of Parliament.

general post office (*often abbrev* **GPO** [dʒiːpiː'ou]) *nc* the main post office in a town or district.

general practitioner (*often abbrev* **GP** [dʒiː'piː]) *nc* a doctor who treats the general illnesses of the people in a district, not specializing in any particular branch of medicine: *My GP transferred me to a heart specialist.*

general store *nc* a shop that sells a wide range of goods.

as a general rule usually; in most cases: *As a general rule, we don't employ unskilled workers.*

in 'general usually; in most cases; most of (a group of people *etc*): *People in general were not very sympathetic*; *People were in general not very sympathetic.*

the general public the people of a town, state, country *etc*: *These facts must not become known to the general public.*

generate ['dʒenəreit] *vt* (*formal or tech*) to cause or produce: *This machine generates electricity/heat*; *His suggestions generated a lot of ill-feeling.*

,gene'ration **1** *nu* (*formal*) the act of producing (electricity, heat *etc*). **2** *nc* one stage in the descent of a family: *All three generations – children, parents and grandparents – lived together quite happily.* **3** *nc* people born at about the same time: *People of my generation all think the same way about this.* **4** *nc* the supposed average time between the birth of one generation and the birth of the next, *usu* considered to be about thirty years: *This happened a generation ago.*

'**generator** *nc* a machine which produces electricity, gas *etc*: *The hospital has an emergency generator in case the public electricity supply breaks down.*

generic *see* **genus**.

generous ['dʒenərəs] *adj* (*neg* **un-**) **1** willing to give a lot of money, time *etc* for some purpose: *She was always a generous giver of her money and time to charity*; *It is very generous of you to pay for our holiday.* **2** large; larger than necessary: *a very generous sum of money*; *a very generous piece of cake*; *That salary is more than generous.* **3** kind, willing to forgive, ready to admit other people's good qualities *etc*: *Try to be generous and forgive*; *a person's generous nature/remarks.* ˌ**gene'rosity** [-'rosəti] *ncu.*

'**generously** *adv*: *Please give generously to this charity*; *Generously, she forgave him.*

genetic, genetics *see* **gene**.

genial ['dʒiːniəl] *adj* (*formal*) **1** kindly; friendly; good-natured: *a genial person*; *Our new neighbours seem very genial.* **2** pleasant to live in: *a genial climate*; *The climate seems genial.* '**genially** *adv.* ˌ**geni'ality** [-'a-] *nu.*

genitals ['dʒenitlz] *n pl* (*formal*: *often with* **the**) the organs of sexual reproduction in man and animals.

'**genital** *adj* (*attrib*: *formal*) of the genitals or of sexual reproduction: *the genital organs.*

genitive ['dʒenitiv] *ncu* (*gram*) (the case or form of) a noun, pronoun *etc* which shows possession: *In John's hat, 'John's' is in the genitive/is a genitive*; (*attrib*) *the genitive case.*

genius ['dʒiːnjəs] – *pl* '**geniuses** – **1** *nc* a person who is very clever: *The new professor of mathematics has been described as a genius.* **2** *nu* very great cleverness: *The child showed genius from an early age.* **3** *nc* (*no pl*) a natural ability: *You seem to have a genius for saying the wrong thing.*

genocide ['dʒenəsaid] *nu* (*formal*) the deliberate killing of a race of people: *The dictator was accused of genocide.*

gent, gents *see* **gentleman**.

genteel [dʒən'tiːl] *adj* (*often derog*) acting, talking *etc* with a very great (often too great) attention to the rules of polite behaviour: *She was laughed at for being too genteel*; *genteel table manners.* **gen'teelly** *adv.* **gen'teelness** *nu.*

See also **gentility**, **gentle**.

gentile [(*Brit and Amer*) 'dʒentail] *nc, adj* (*also with cap*: *esp* in the Bible) (of) anyone who is not a Jew.

gentility [dʒən'tiləti] *nu* (*formal*) **1** good manners, often to too great an extent: *She was laughed at for her gentility.* **2** (*old*) noble birth; the state of belonging to the upper class or aristocracy: *She kept a butler and a maid, just to give an appearance of gentility.*

See also **genteel, gentle**.

gentle ['dʒentl] *adj* **1** (of people) behaving, talking *etc* in a mild, kindly, pleasant way: *a gentle old lady*; *The doctor was very gentle when bathing her wound*; *Mothers are usually gentle with their babies.* **2** not strong or rough: *a gentle breeze*; *gentle heat*; *This soap is gentle enough for your sensitive skin.* **3** (of hills) rising gradually: *a gentle slope*; *This slope is gentle enough for you to walk up.* **4** (*old*: *attrib*) belonging to the upper classes: *a lady of gentle birth.* '**gently** *adv.* '**gentleness** *nu.*

See also **gentility, genteel**.

gentleman ['dʒentlmən] – *pl* '**gentlemen** – *nc* (*sl abbrev* **gent**) **1** a polite word for a man: *Two gentlemen came to see you this morning*; *He's a typical city gent.* **2** a polite, well-mannered man: *He's a real gentleman.*

'**gentlemanly** *adj* (*formal or old*) (of men) polite; well-mannered: *gentlemanly behaviour*; *That was very gentlemanly of you.* '**gentlemanliness** *nu.*

gents *nc* (*inf*: *usu with* **the**) a public toilet for men: *Where's the nearest gents?*

gentleman's/gentlemen's agreement an agreement which is not written down, and which the people who have made the agreement have to keep only because they have promised to do so, not because they are forced to do so by law: *You cannot force the company to supply the goods – you have no written contract but only a gentleman's agreement.*

gently *see* **gentle**.

gentry ['dʒentri]: **the gentry** (*formal*) the rich, *usu* land-owning class of people, next below the aristocracy.

gents *see* **gentleman**.

genuine ['dʒenjuin] *adj* **1** real; not fake or artificial: *This is a genuine pearl*; *Is this old table a genuine antique?*; *It seems genuine.* **2** honest; sincere: *He shows a genuine desire to improve*; *His wish to help seems genuine.* '**genuineness** *nu.*

'**genuinely** *adv*: *He was genuinely pleased to see her.*

genus ['dʒiːnəs] – *pl* **genera** ['dʒenərə] – *nc* (*tech*) a group of animals, plants *etc* which is made up of a number of related species: *To what genus does this tree belong?*

generic [dʒə'nerik] *adj* (*attrib*) **1** of a genus: *'Rosa' is the Latin generic name for roses.* **2** (of a name, term *etc*) referring to several similar objects *etc*: *'Furniture' is a generic term for chairs, tables etc.*

geography [dʒi'ogrəfi] *nu* the science that describes the surface of the Earth and its inhabitants: *He is studying geography*; (*attrib*) *geography lessons.*

ge'ographer *nc* a person who studies geography.

geographic(al) [dʒiə'grafik(əl)] *adj* (*usu attrib*): *He is making a geographical study of the area.* ˌ**geo'graphically** *adv.*

geology [dʒi'olədʒi] *nu* the science of the history and development of the Earth as shown by rocks *etc*: *He is studying geology*; (*attrib*) *geology lectures.*

geological [dʒiə'lodʒikəl] *adj* (*usu attrib*): *a geological survey.* ˌ**geo'logically** *adv.*

ge'ologist *nc.*

geometry [dʒi'omətri] *nu* a branch of mathematics dealing with the study of lines, angles *etc*: *He is studying geometry*; (*attrib*) *geometry books.*

geometric(al) [dʒiə'metrik(əl)] *adj* **1** of geometry: *geometric problems.* **2** made up of lines, circles *etc* and with a regular shape: *a geometrical design on wallpaper.* ˌ**geo'metrically** *adv.*

geranium [dʒə'reiniəm] *nc* a kind of plant, often with bright red flowers.

geriatrics [dʒeri'atriks] *n sing* the branch of medicine concerned with the diseases of old age: *Geriatrics is a particular interest of our new doctor.*

ˌ**geri'atric** *adj* (*usu attrib*: *formal or tech*) for the very old (and ill): *a geriatric hospital*; *He looks after the geriatric cases.*

ˌ**geria'trician** [-ʃən] *nc* a doctor who specializes in treating the diseases of old age.

germ [dʒəːm] *nc* **1** a very tiny animal or plant that causes disease: *Disinfectant kills germs.* **2** (*fig*) the

small beginning (of anything): *the germ of an idea.*
germicide ['dʒə:misaid] *ncu* (*tech*) a substance that destroys the germs which cause disease.

German ['dʒə:mən] : **German measles** *n sing* an infectious disease which causes a person's skin to be covered in pink spots: *German measles is not a serious disease but it should be avoided by pregnant women as it can affect unborn babies.*
German, Germany *see* Appendix 2.

germane [dʒə:'mein] *adj* (*very formal*: *usu pred with* **to**) relevant; of importance: *That fact is not germane to the present argument.*

germicide *see* **germ**.

germinate ['dʒə:mineit] *vti* (*tech*) to (cause *eg* a seed to) begin to grow.
ˌgermi'nation *nu*: *The children are studying the germination of the bean at school.*

gesticulate [dʒe'stikjuleit] *vi* (*formal*) to wave one's hands and arms about, *eg* when speaking or to express excitement, emotion *etc*: *He has a very irritating habit of gesticulating wildly when he talks.*
geˌsticu'lation *ncu*.

gesture ['dʒestʃə] *nc* **1** a movement of the head, hand *etc* to express an idea, feeling, emotion *etc*: *The speaker emphasized his words with violent gestures.* **2** (*fig*) an action which is intended to show a person's feelings: *Refusing to answer John when he spoke to you was a rather unfriendly gesture.* – *vi* to make a gesture or gestures: *He gestured to her to keep quiet.*

get [get] – *pt* **got** [got]: *ptp* **got**, (*Amer*) **gotten** ['gotn] – (not *usu* used in formal speech: not used with **is, was** *etc* and **-ing** (*defs 13, 15, 16*)) **1** *vt* (*sometimes with* **back**) to be given, receive or obtain (something): *I got a letter this morning; I'll get that book back from you at the end of the week; What do we get if we add three and five?; After a great deal of thought, I finally got the answer; You'll get the answers at the back of the book; You can't get French television stations in Scotland.* **2** *vti* (*with* **about, across, in, on, out, through** *etc*) to (manage to) move, come, go, take, put *etc*; to cause to do this: *There's too much traffic on this road – I'll never get across; He needs a car to get around; Can you get that dictionary down for me please?; The rain gets in through that hole in the roof; Get out your books and turn to page three; You'll never get that bag through the window; How did you get up that tree?* **3** *vt* (*often with* **back, in, off** *etc*) to send, fetch, bring, buy *etc* (something) for or to someone: *Will you get me some sandwiches while you are out?; I'll get that book (back) to you by five o'clock; We must get a letter off to John today; Do you want me to get the washing in before it rains?* **4** *vt* to cause (something) to be done, to be in a certain condition *etc*: *I'll get everything ready; I couldn't get the car started/the car to start this morning; Go and get your hair cut!; Go and get a haircut!; You'll get me into trouble.* **5** *vi* to become: *You're getting old; You'll get wet if you don't take an umbrella; You'll soon get used to our system.* **6** *vt* to persuade or tell (a person to do something): *I'll try to get John to go to the meeting.* **7** *vti* (*usu with* **back, in** *or* **to**) to (manage to) go to, reach, or arrive at (a place); to help (a person) to do this: *You can have a drink when we get home; I won't see him till I get to Glasgow; I'll get you* (= I will take you) *(back) home; When does the train get in?; I'm sorry I didn't get to the meeting; I didn't get to bed last night.* **8** *vi* (*inf*) to be allowed (to do something): *I get to stay up till eleven o'clock on Fridays.* **9** *vti* (*inf*) to do (something): *I suppose I'd better get this book read* (= I'd better read this book); *We'll get started* (= We'll start) *on this tomorrow.* **10** *vti* to succeed (in doing or obtaining something); to happen (to do something): *I'll soon get to know what you are planning; He got a glimpse of the Queen as she drove past.* **11** *vt* to catch (a disease *etc*): *If you stay out in the rain, you'll get a cold.* **12** *vt* (*inf*) to prepare (a meal): *I'll get dinner.* **13** *vt* (*inf*) to suffer (something which happens to oneself, *usu* by accident): *John got his arm broken/a broken arm while playing rugby last Saturday.* **14** *vt* (*inf*) to receive as a punishment: *You can get three years (in prison) for stealing a car.* **15** *vt* (*inf*) to catch or attack (someone): *If anyone breaks into the factory, the guard-dog will get him.* **16** *vt* (*inf*) (of things) to kill, injure or harm (a person *etc*): *A bullet got him and he died instantly.* **17** *vt* (*inf*) to annoy or irritate (a person): *What gets me is his stupid smile.* **18** *vt* (*inf*) to understand: *I don't get the joke/your point; I don't get it.* **19** *vt* (*inf*) to hear: *I didn't quite get your name.* – *See also* **get** *in phrases below.*

'getaway *nc* (*inf*) an escape: *The thieves made their getaway in a stolen car;* (*attrib*) *The getaway car was found later on by the police.* – *See also* **get away** *below.*

'get-together *nc* (*inf*) an informal meeting: *I don't want to have an organized meeting, just a get-together with a few of our colleagues.* – *See also* **get together** *below.*

'get-up *nc* (*inf derog*) clothes, *usu* odd or unattractive: *You should have seen some of the get-ups the women were wearing.* – *See also* **got up** *below.*

ˌget-up-and-'go *nu* (*inf*) energy: *She's got a lot of get-up-and-go.*

be ˌgetting 'on for (*inf*) to be close to (a particular age, time *etc*): *It's getting on for three o'clock; He must be getting on for sixty at least.*

get about *vi* **1** (of stories, rumours *etc*) to become well known: *I don't know how the story got about that she was leaving.* **2** to be able to move or travel about, often of people who have been ill: *She didn't get about much after her operation; Now that they have sold their car, they don't get about a lot.*

ˌget a'bove oneself to think that, or behave as if, one is more important than one actually is: *Don't get above yourself. Remember you are only a typist, not the director of the firm.*

get across *vi, vt usu sep* (*inf*) to be or make (something) understood: *This is something which rarely gets across to the general public; The plan seems quite clear to me, but I just can't get it across (to anyone else).*

get 'after *vt fus* to follow or chase (a person, thing *etc*): *If you want to catch him, you had better get after him at once.*

get ahead *vi* **1** to make progress; to be successful: *If you want to get ahead, you must work hard.* **2** (*with* **of**) to make more progress than (someone or something else): *This company intends to get ahead of all its rivals.*

get along *vi* (*inf*) **1** to manage or make progress: *I can't get along without some help; How are things getting along?* **2** (*often with* **with**) to be friendly or on good terms (with someone): *I get along very well with him; The children just cannot get along together.* **3** to move or go away (often to some other place): *I must be getting along now or I'll miss the bus.*

ˌget a'long/a'way with you!, ˌgo a'long/a'way

with you! (*inf*) I don't believe what you are telling me.

get anywhere *see* **get somewhere**.

get around 1 *vi* (of stories, rumours *etc*) to become well known: *I don't know how the story got around that she was leaving.* **2** *vi* (*inf*) (of people) to be active or involved in many activities: *He really gets around, doesn't he!* **3** *vt fus* to avoid or solve (a problem *etc*): *I don't see any way of getting around these difficulties.*

get around to *see* **get round to**.

'get at *vt fus* **1** to reach (a place, thing *etc*): *The farm is very difficult to get at; The hole is too deep for me to get at the ring I dropped;* (*fig*) *Somehow or other, I will get at the truth; Whatever you say, I must get at the books in your room.* **2** (*inf*) to suggest or imply (something): *What are you getting at?* **3** (*inf*) to point out (a person's faults) or make fun of (a person): *He's always getting at me.* **4** (*inf: usu in passive*) to persuade (a person) by money, threats *etc* to tell lies *etc*: *The witnesses have been got at.*

get away 1 *vi* (*often with* **from**) to (be able to) leave: *I usually get away (from the office) at four-thirty.* **2** *vi* to escape: *The thieves got away in a stolen car. – See also* **getaway**. **3** *vt sep, vi* (*inf*) (of a letter *etc*) to post or be posted: *I must get this letter away tonight; This letter must get away tonight.* **4** *vt sep* (*inf: with* **from**) to take (something) away (from a person *etc*): *I must get that letter away from her before she reads what I said about her.* **5** *vi* (*with* **from**: *usu in neg*) to deny (something) or avoid taking (something) into consideration: *There is no getting away from the fact that John is not the right man for the job; He's a clever man – there's no getting away from it/that.*

get a'way from it all to go away somewhere, or have a holiday somewhere, where one does not need to think about one's job, one's family, one's problems *etc*.

get away with *vt fus* to do (something bad) without being punished for it: *Murder is a serious crime and one rarely gets away with it.*

get away with you! *see* **get along/away with you!** *above*.

get back *vi, vt oblig sep* to move away: *The policeman told the crowd to get back; He managed to get the sheep back from the edge of the cliff.*

get 'back at *vt fus* (*inf*) to have revenge on (a person *etc*): *You can laugh now, but I'll get back at you somehow.*

get 'by *vi* (*inf*) **1** to manage: *I can't get by on £20 a week.* **2** (*inf*) to be acceptable: *This definition isn't very good but it will probably get by.*

get 'down 1 *vi* (*sometimes with* **from**) to leave (a bus, train *etc*): *The platform is so low that it is difficult to get down (from the train).* **2** *vt oblig sep* (*inf*) to make (a person) sad: *Working in this place really gets me down.* **3** *vt usu sep* to swallow (*usu* with difficulty or unwillingly): *I feel sick, but I'll try to get some food down.* **4** *vt sep* to write (something) down: *Did you get down everything he said?*

get 'down to *vt fus* to begin to work (hard) at (something): *I must get down to work tonight, as I've got exams next week.*

get 'in *vt sep* **1** to send for (a person): *The television is broken – we'll need to get a man in to repair it.* **2** to manage to give, have *etc*: *I'm hoping to get in a couple of hours' study before dinner; The boxer only managed to get a couple of punches in before the referee stopped the fight.*

get 'into *vt fus* **1** to put on (clothes *etc*): *I find it very difficult to get into these tight trousers; How on earth did she get into that dress – it's much too tight!; Get into your pyjamas.* **2** to (begin to) be in a particular state or behave in a particular way: *He gets into a temper if you argue with him; You'll get into trouble if you break that vase; I don't know what has got into him* (= I don't know why he is behaving the way he is). **3** (*inf*) to begin to enjoy, understand *etc* (a book): *I just can't get into that book.*

get 'in with *vt fus* (*inf*) to become friendly or on good terms with (a person), *usu* for one's own benefit or advantage: *He's trying to get in with the boss in order to get a pay rise.*

get it together (*sl*) to arrange something; to manage to do something properly: *I tried to work hard for my exams, but I just couldn't seem to get it together.*

get lost *see* **lose**.

get nowhere (*inf*) to make no progress; to get or produce no results: *You'll get nowhere if you follow his instructions; Flattering me will get you nowhere. – See also* **get somewhere/anywhere, get there**.

get 'off 1 *vi, vt fus* to leave (a bus, train *etc*): *I get off at the next stop; We all got off the bus.* **2** *vi* (*inf*) to leave (a place): *I must be getting off now; It's time you got off to school.* **3** *vt oblig sep* to take off or remove (clothes, marks *etc*): *I can't get my boots off; I'll never get these stains off (my dress).* **4** *vi, vt oblig sep* (*inf: usu with* **with**) to (cause or help someone to) receive little or no punishment (after doing wrong): *The thief got off with a small fine; The thief's lawyer got him off with a small fine. – See also* **let off**. **5** *vt fus* (*inf*) to manage not to do (something that one doesn't want to do): *I got off digging the garden this week by pretending to feel ill.* **6** *vt fus* to stop talking, writing *etc* about (something); to change (the subject which one is talking, writing *etc* about): *Can we get off this subject, please?; We've rather got off the subject. – See also* **tell (someone) where to get off** *below*.

get off on the wrong foot *see* **foot**.

get off to a flying start *see* **fly**[2].

get off to a good/bad start *see* **start**.

get off to sleep *see* **sleep**.

get 'off with *vt fus* (*sl*) to form a close, often sexual, relationship with (someone), *eg* at a dance, party: *I'm hoping to get off with Mary tonight.*

get 'on 1 *vi* (*often with* **in**) to make progress or be successful: *How are you getting on in your new job?; It takes intelligence and hard work to get on in life.* **2** *vi* (*inf: sometimes with* **with**) to work, live *etc* in a friendly way: *We get on very well together; I get on well with him.* **3** *vi* (*inf*) to grow old: *Our doctor is getting on a bit now.* **4** *vt oblig sep* to put (clothes *etc*) on: *Go and get your coat on – we're just about to leave.* **5** *vi* (*inf*) to leave (somewhere) to go somewhere else: *Well, I must be getting on now.* **6** *vi* (*often with* **with**) to continue doing (something): *I must get on, so please don't interrupt me; I must get on with my work.*

get on at (*inf*) to criticize (a person) continually or frequently: *My wife is always getting on at me to clean my shoes/for not cleaning my shoes.*

get on for *see* **be getting on for** *above*.

get 'on to *vt fus* **1** (*inf Brit*) to make contact with (a person *etc*) *eg* by telephone (often because one is displeased with something or to get information about something): *This is the third time this week that my television has broken down – I'll need to get on to the manager about it*; *You must get on to the airline at once to see if your flight has been delayed.* **2** (*inf Brit*) to deal with (a problem *etc*): *I'll get on to the matter of your television at once.*

get 'on with you! (*inf*) I don't believe what you are saying!

get 'out 1 *vi* to leave or escape: *I'm not interested in your nonsense, so just get out!*; *No-one knows how the lion got out.* **2** *vi* (of information) to become known: *I've no idea how word got out that you were leaving.* **3** *vt sep* to manage to say (something) *usu* with some difficulty: *I wanted to say I loved her, but I couldn't get the words out.* **4** *vt sep* to prepare and publish (a report, book *etc*): *We'll have to get this pamphlet out before next week.* **5** *vt sep* to borrow (books *etc*) from a library *etc*: *Will you get two books out for me when you go to the library?*

get 'out of 1 *vt* to leave (a car *etc*); to escape (from somewhere): *He got out of the car*; *The lion got out of its cage.* **2** *vt fus, vt oblig sep* to (help a person *etc* to) avoid doing something: *I wonder how I can get out of washing the dishes*; *I wonder how I can get him out of going to the party?*; *How can I get him out of it?* **3** *vt oblig sep* (*inf*) to persuade or force (a person *etc*) to give someone something: *I'll get the money/facts out of him.* **4** *vt fus, vt oblig sep* (*inf*) to (persuade a person *etc* to) stop doing something which is usually done by that person: *I wish I could get out of the habit of kicking the table*; *I wish I could get that child out of the habit of sucking his thumb.*

get out of the way to move to a position where one is not blocking (a person's *etc*) path or progress: *Get out of my way – I'm in a hurry!*; *Get that car out of the way!*; (*fig*) *Let's get these complaints out of the way first* (= let's deal with them first), *then go on to other matters.*

get 'over 1 *vt fus* to recover from (an illness, disappointment *etc*): *I've got over my cold now.* **2** *vt fus* (*inf*) to no longer feel sad when thinking about (a person, *usu* of the opposite sex, with whom one was once very friendly): *It took me a long time to get over my first girl-friend.* **3** *vt oblig sep* to manage to make (oneself or something) understood: *We must get our message over to the general public.* **4** *vt fus* (*inf*: *with* **can/could**: *only in neg*) to stop being surprised at or troubled by (something that has happened): *I just can't get over her leaving so suddenly.* **5** *vt oblig sep* (*also with* **with**) to do (something one does not want to do): *I'm not looking forward to this meeting, but let's get it over (with).*

get 'round 1 *vt fus* (*inf*) to persuade (a person *etc*) to do something he, she *etc* would not wish to do: *She can always get round her grandfather by giving him a big smile.* **2** *vt fus* to solve (a problem *etc*): *We can easily get round these few difficulties.*

get (a)'round to *vt fus* (*inf*) to manage to (do something); to find enough time to (do something): *I don't know when I'll get round to (painting) the door.*

get somewhere/anywhere (*inf*) to make progress: *We don't seem to be getting anywhere in this discussion.* – *See also* **get nowhere, get there**.

'get there (*inf*) to succeed or make progress: *There have been a lot of problems but we're getting there now.* – *See also* **get nowhere, get somewhere/anywhere**.

get 'through 1 *vt fus* to finish (work *etc*): *We've got to get through a lot of work today*; (*inf*) *We got through a lot of whisky at the party.* **2** *vi* to make contact (with another person *etc*) by telephone: *I couldn't get through (to my mother) yesterday.* **3** *vi, vt fus* (*inf*) to pass (an examination): *I'll never get through (my French exam).* **4** *vt oblig sep* to help (a person *etc*) to pass an examination: *He's a good teacher, but even he couldn't get her through (her French exam).* **5** *vi* to arrive (somewhere), *usu* with some difficulty: *The food got through to the fort despite the enemy's attempts to stop it.* **6** *vi, vt fus, vt oblig sep* (*esp* of a bill in Parliament) to (cause to) be agreed or accepted: *The new bill will never get through*; *The abortion bill has got through Parliament*; *The government succeeded in getting the bill through.* **7** *vi* (*with* **to**) to make oneself understood (by someone): *I just can't seem to get through to her any more.* **8** *vt* (*with* **to**) to make (someone) understand (something): *We can't get it through to him that smoking is bad for his health.*

get together 1 *vt oblig sep* to bring (people, things *etc*) together: *I'd like you to get the staff together, please.* **2** *vi* (*inf*) to meet: *We usually get together once a week.* – *See also* **get-together, get it together**.

get to sleep *see* **sleep**.

get 'up 1 *vi, vt oblig sep* to (cause to) get out of bed: *I got up at seven o'clock*; *Get me up at seven o'clock*; *You'll never get John up on time.* **2** *vi* to stand up: *Please don't get up on my account.* **3** *vt sep* to increase (*usu* speed): *The car got up speed as it ran down the hill.* **4** *vi* (of a wind *etc*) to begin to be strong, fierce or rough: *There's quite a wind getting up outside.* **5** *vt fus* (*inf*) to arrange, organize or prepare (something): *We must get up some sort of celebration for him when he leaves.* **6** *vt sep* (*inf*) to cause oneself to feel (an emotion *etc*): *I just can't get up any enthusiasm for this project.* – *See also* **got up**.

get 'up to *vt fus* **1** to reach: *So far I've got up to page sixty.* **2** (*inf*) to do (something bad): *He's always getting up to mischief*; *What will he get up to next?*

got up (*inf*: *sometimes derog*) dressed (as someone or something); dressed for a particular occasion or to attract attention: *She was got up as a clown*; *She was all got up for the party.* – *See also* **get-up, get up**.

have got, have got on, have got to *etc see* **have, have on, have to** *etc under* **have**.

tell (someone) where to get off/where he *etc* **gets off** (*Brit inf*) to tell (someone) that his bad, arrogant *etc* behaviour will not be tolerated: *He was trying to tell me how to do my job, but I soon told him where to get off.*

geyser ['gi:zə] *nc* **1** an underground spring that produces and sends out hot water and steam: *There are geysers in Iceland and New Zealand.* **2** a small gas or electric water heater in a bathroom, kitchen *etc*.

Ghana, Ghanaian *see* Appendix 2.

ghastly ['ga:stli] *adj* **1** (*inf*) very bad, ugly *etc*: *a ghastly mistake*; *That picture is ghastly.* **2** (*usu attrib*) horrible; terrible: *a ghastly murder*; *a ghastly experience.* **3** (*inf*: *usu pred*) ill; upset: *I felt ghastly after last night's party*; *I feel ghastly about causing all that trouble.* **4** (*formal or liter*) very pale, *esp* of a person's face: *He stood there, his face ghastly with fear*; *He collapsed, his face a ghastly white.* **'ghastliness** *nu*.

gherkin ['gə:kin] *nc* a small cucumber, *usu* pickled.

ghetto ['getou] – *pl* '**ghetto(e)s** – *nc* (*derog*) a (poor) part of a city *etc* in which a certain group of people (*esp* immigrants) lives: *Large cities like New York have many ghettoes.*

ghost [goust] *nc* **1** a spirit, *usu* of a dead person: *Do you believe in ghosts?*; *Hamlet thought he saw his father's ghost.* **2** (*fig*) a slight suggestion (of anything): *a ghost of an idea/a smile.*

'**ghostly** *adj* of or like a ghost or ghosts: *He could see a ghostly figure in the darkened room.* '**ghostliness** *nu.*

'**ghost-town** *nc* a town which has once been busy but which all or most of the inhabitants have left for some reason: *When the local coal-mine closed, Kilarden almost became a ghost-town.*

'**ghost-writer** *nc* a person who writes books, speeches *etc* for another person who pretends to have written them himself. '**ghost-write** *vti.*

give up the ghost (*formal or facet*) to die.

ghoul [gu:l] *nc* **1** a person who takes an unusually great interest in death, disaster and other horrible things: *Whenever there is a train crash or traffic accident, the ghouls will gather round to look.* **2** (*myth*) an evil spirit which eats dead bodies.

'**ghoulish** *adj*: *She takes a ghoulish interest in descriptions of traffic accidents*; *Don't be so ghoulish (about it)!* '**ghoulishly** *adv.* '**ghoulishness** *nu.*

GI [dʒi:'ai] *nc* (*inf*) a soldier in the army of the United States of America, *esp* during World War II.

giant ['dʒaiənt] – *fem* '**giantess** – *nc* **1** (in fairy stories *etc*) a huge person: *Jack met a giant when he climbed the beanstalk.* **2** a person of unusually great height and size: *His bodyguard was an absolute giant.* **3** (*fig*) a person of very great ability or importance: *Einstein is one of the giants of twentieth-century science.* – *adj* (*usu attrib*) of unusually great height or size: *a giant cod*; *a giant fern.*

gibber ['dʒibə] *vi* to make meaningless noises: *He was gibbering with fear*; *monkeys gibbering at each other in a cage*; (*derog*) *The politician gibbered away for an hour but he said nothing of importance.*

'**gibberish** [-riʃ] *nu* nonsense; meaningless words: *His explanations are just gibberish to me.*

gibbering idiot *nc* (*inf*) a fool: *That gibbering idiot has broken the tape-recorder again.*

gibbet ['dʒibit] *nc* (*hist*) a gallows in the shape ˥ on which criminals used to be executed or hung up after execution.

gibbon ['gibən] *nc* a type of ape with very long arms.

gibe *see* **jibe**.

giblets ['dʒiblits] *n pl* the eatable parts from the inside of a chicken *etc*, *eg* the heart and the liver: *She used the giblets to make sauce for the roast chicken.*

giddy ['gidi] *adj* **1** having a feeling of unsteadiness; feeling that one is going to fall over, or that everything is spinning round: *I was dancing round so fast that I felt quite giddy*; *a giddy feeling.* **2** (*usu attrib*) causing such a feeling: *I looked down to the valley from the giddy height of the cliff*; (*fig*) *She was exhausted after her giddy round of parties and dances.* **3** (*derog*: *usu attrib*) not having good or sensible rules of behaviour: *Will these giddy young fools ever settle down?* '**giddily** *adv.* '**giddiness** *nu.*

gift [gift] *nc* **1** something given willingly, *eg* as a present: *He gives gifts of money to the poor.* **2** a natural ability: *My daughter has a gift for music.* **3** (*inf*) something which is easily done *etc*: *The examination paper was a gift.* – *vt* (*formal*: *usu in passive*) to give or present (something) as a gift: *This painting was gifted by our former chairman.*

'**gifted** *adj* having very great natural ability: *a gifted musician/child*; *She is very gifted both as a writer and as a musician.*

gift of the gab [gab] (*inf derog*) the ability to persuade (a person *etc*) to do, believe *etc* whatever one wishes: *Politicians need to have the gift of the gab.*

See also **give**.

gigantic [dʒai'gantik] *adj* very large: *a gigantic wave*; *The waves were really gigantic.* **gi'gantically** *adv.*

giggle ['gigl] *vi* to laugh in a nervous or silly way: *The girl giggled when the boy asked her if she would like to dance.* – *nc* a laugh of this kind: *'Yes, please,' she answered with a giggle.* '**giggler** *nc.*

'**giggly** *adj* giggling often: *Young girls are often said to be giggly.*

gild [gild] *vt* **1** to cover with gold or something like gold: *We could gild the frame of that picture*; (*liter fig*) *The morning sun gilds the sky.*

'**gilding** *nu* **1** the gold or gold-like substance with which ornaments *etc* are sometimes covered. **2** the act of gilding.

gild the lily to try to improve something which is already beautiful enough: *If she wore make-up it would just be gilding the lily.*

See also **gilt**.

gill[1] [gil] *nc* one of the openings on the side of a fish's head through which it breathes.

gill[2] [dʒil] *nc* a measure of liquids, a quarter of a pint (in Britain, 142 cc; in the US, 118 cc).

gillie ['gili] *nc* (*esp* in Scotland) a man who helps and guides a sportsman who is fishing or shooting: *That landowner employs four gillies on his Highland estate.*

gilt [gilt] *nu* the gold or gold-like substance with which ornaments *etc* are sometimes covered: *a tiny vase covered with gilt*; (*attrib*) *a gilt brooch.*

ˌ**gilt-'edged** *adj* (of financial matters) not risky; safe to invest in and certain to produce interest: *gilt-edged stocks/securities.*

See also **gild**.

gimcrack ['dʒimkrak] *adj* (*derog*: *usu attrib*) cheap and badly made: *gimcrack furniture*; *gimcrack houses.*

gimlet ['gimlit] *nc* a T-shaped tool for boring holes in wood *etc* by hand by being screwed into the wood *etc.*

gimmick ['gimik] *nc* (*usu derog*) something which is used to attract attention to (something or someone) or to make (something or someone) more popular *etc*: *The politician visited hospitals and old people's homes as a gimmick to gain popularity*; *Advertising agencies often try to find gimmicks to promote a firm's products.* '**gimmicky** *adj.*

'**gimmickry** *nu* (*usu derog*) (the use of) gimmicks.

gin[1] [dʒin] **1** *nu* a type of alcoholic drink made from grain and flavoured with juniper berries: *a bottle of gin.* **2** *nc* a glass of gin: *a gin and tonic.*

gin[2] [dʒin] *nc* a trap, snare or net for catching animals *etc.*

'**gintrap** *nc* a powerful type of trap fitted with teeth: *The hare was in agony as its leg was caught in a gintrap.*

ginger ['dʒindʒə] *nu* a hot-tasting root which is

used as a spice: *Ginger is widely used in Chinese cookery.* – *adj* **1** (*usu attrib*) flavoured with ginger: *ginger cake.* **2** (*usu* of hair) reddish-brown in colour: *bright ginger hair*; *Her hair is ginger, not blonde.*

ginger ale, ginger beer 1 *nus* a type of non-alcoholic drink flavoured with ginger: *The child likes ginger beer.* **2** *ncs* a glass of this: *Two ginger ales, please.*

'gingerbread *ncu* (a) cake flavoured with treacle and ginger: *She made (a) gingerbread for tea*; (*attrib*) *a gingerbread man* (= a cake or biscuit made of gingerbread and shaped like a man).

'ginger group *nc* (*Brit*) a small group of people within a larger group, *eg* a political party, which tries to make the rest of the group more active and enthusiastic.

ginger up *vt sep* (*inf*) to make (a person *etc*) more active and lively: *The leaders of the political party decided they would need to ginger up some of their local branches.*

gingerly ['dʒindʒəli] *adv* very gently and carefully: *He gingerly lifted the lid of the box, not knowing what was inside.*

gingham ['giŋəm] *nu, adj* (of) a striped or checked cotton cloth: *The dress is (made of) gingham*; *a gingham dress.*

gintrap *see* **gin**[2].

gipsy *see* **gypsy**.

giraffe [dʒi'ra:f] – *pls* **gi'raffes, gi'raffe** – *nc* an African animal with a very long neck, long legs and spots: *two giraffes*; *a herd of giraffe.*

gird [gə:d] – *pts, ptps* **'girded, girt** [gə:t] – *vt* (*arch or liter*) to fasten a belt, or something like a belt, round something *eg* the waist.

gird on *vt sep* (*arch or liter*) to fasten (*eg* a sword) round *eg* one's waist with a belt.

gird up one's loins *see* **loin**.

girder ['gə:də] *nc* a large beam of wood, iron or steel, *eg* to support a floor, wall, road or bridge: *The steel girders of the bridge have collapsed.*

girdle[1] ['gə:dl] *nc* **1** a close-fitting woman's under-garment *usu* made of an elastic material, worn round the waist, hips and buttocks: *This girdle will make you look much slimmer.* **2** a belt or cord worn round the waist: *The girl wore a girdle round her gym tunic.*

girdle[2] *see* **griddle**.

girl [gə:l] *nc* **1** a female child: *What a pretty little girl!*; *How old are your girls* (= daughters) *now?* **2** a young *usu* unmarried woman: *The young men whistled at the girls as they walked past them.* **3** (*inf*) a girl-friend: *She is John's girl.* **4** (*usu in cmpds*) a woman of any age who works in a shop, factory *etc*: *a shop-girl.* **5** a (*usu* young) female servant: *She employs a girl to look after the children.*

'girlhood *nu* (*formal*) the state or time of being a girl: *She spent her girlhood in London*; (*attrib*) *a girlhood friend.*

'girlish *adj* of or like a girl: *Although over forty, she still had a look of girlish innocence*; *That hairstyle is too girlish for her.* **'girlishly** *adv.* **'girlishness** *nu.*

'girl-friend *nc* (*inf*) a girl or woman who is often in the company of a particular man or boy who likes her but may not be in love with her: *He's taking his girl-friend to the cinema tonight.*

Girl Guide (*also* **Guide**), (*Amer*) **Girl Scout** *ncs* (*also no caps*) a member of an organization for girls which is aimed at developing character *etc.*

giro ['dʒairou] *nu* (*also with cap*) a system by which payment may be made through banks, post offices *etc* directly to people's accounts, rather than to the people themselves: *I'll pay this account by giro*; (*attrib*) *a giro account.*

girt *see* **gird**.

girth [gə:θ] *nc* **1** (*formal*) the measurement round a tree, a person's waist *etc*: *They put a piece of string round the tree to measure its girth.* **2** the strap that holds a saddle on a horse.

gist [dʒist]: **the gist** the main points (of an argument, story *etc*): *Just give me the gist of what he said.*

give [giv] – *pt* **gave** [geiv]: *ptp* **'given** – **1** *vt* to cause (a person *etc*) to have, receive *etc*: *My aunt gave me a book for Christmas*; *I was given a book for Christmas*; *I give books to all my friends*; *If you buy the tickets, I'll give you the money for mine later*; *Can you give me his telephone number?*; *I'll give you £5 for that book*; *We're giving the first prize to a French architect*; *Give my regards to your wife*; *You've given me your cold*; *The furniture gave the room an old-fashioned look*; *Working in the garden gives me a lot of pleasure*; *I can only give you half an hour to finish this job*; *This ticket gives you the right to travel free on our buses*; *Who gave you permission to be here?*; *Can you give me an opinion on this?*; *Give me your attention, please*; *I'll give the problem some thought*; (*formal*) *I'm given to understand* (= Someone has told me) *that you are leaving soon.* **2** *vt* to produce (something): *Cows give milk but horses do not*; *He gave a sigh/smile* (= He sighed/smiled); *He gave no sign of having heard her*; *He gave a talk on his travels in Asia.* **3** *vt* to do *etc* (something) to a person, thing *etc*: *He gave her a push* (= He pushed her); *He gave the door a kick* (= He kicked the door). **4** *vt* (*often with* **to**) to devote (oneself, one's time *etc*) to doing something: *She gives herself completely to her work for charity*; *She gives all her time to her work for charity.* **5** *vi* to yield, bend, break *etc*: *This door looks solid, but it will give under the slightest pressure.* **6** *vt* to organize (some event *etc*): *We're giving a show in aid of charity*; *We're giving a party next week.* **7** *vt* to have as a result: *Four into twenty gives five.* – *nu* the ability to move, yield or bend under pressure: *This chair has a lot of give in it.*

'given *adj* **1** (*attrib*) fixed; stated: *to do a job at a given time for a given sum of money.* **2** (*formal*: *pred*: *with* **to**) in the habit of (doing) something: *He's a nice fellow, but rather given to making stupid remarks.* **3** (*formal*) taking (something) as a fact; assuming (something) as a basis for discussion *etc*: *Given that x equals three, x plus two equals five.*

'give-away *nc* (*inf*) **1** (*no pl*) something which causes or allows (plans, secrets *etc*) to become known *usu* accidentally: *He pretended to be poor but his clothes were a (dead) give-away – everyone could see he was wealthy.* **2** something which is so easy to do that it is almost a present: *That last question in the maths paper was a real give-away.* – *See also* **give away**.

'given name *nc* (*Amer*) a person's first name or personal name; a Christian name: *His given name is John.*

give and take a willingness to grant or allow a person *etc* something in return for being granted something: *There must be some give and take in discussions between trade unions and management.*

give away *vt sep* **1** to give, send, present *etc* (something) to someone (*eg* because one no longer wants it): *I'm going to give all my money away.* **2** to cause or allow (information, one's plans *etc*) to become known *usu* accidentally: *Don't give me away*; *He gave away our hiding-place.* – *See also* **give-away**.

give back *vt sep* to give to someone something that he or she gave to one earlier: *She gave me back the book that she borrowed last week*; *Girls who break their engagements usually give back their engagement rings.*

give birth, give chase *see* **birth, chase**.

give the game/show away to let a secret, trick *etc* become known (*usu* accidentally): *Don't laugh or you'll give the game away.*

give ground *see* **ground**.

give in 1 *vi* (*often with* **to**) to stop fighting and admit that one has been defeated: *The only way to win a war is to keep fighting and never think about giving in (to the enemy).* **2** *vt sep* to hand, bring or present (something) to someone (often a person in authority): *Do we have to give in our books at the end of the lesson?*

give one's life (*formal*) to be killed *eg* in war: *He gave his life for his country.*

give off *vt fus* to produce (something): *That fire is giving off a lot of smoke.*

give or take adding or taking away (something) within certain limits: *I weigh sixty-five kilos, give or take a little* (= I weigh approximately sixty-five kilos).

give out 1 *vt sep* to give (something) *usu* to several people: *The mayor is giving out the school prizes this year.* **2** *vi* (*inf*) to come to an end or be used up: *My patience/money gave out.* **3** *vt fus* to send out or produce (something): *The fire burned fiercely, giving out a lot of heat.* **4** *vi* (*inf*: *often with* **on**) to break down, stop working *etc*: *My car engine gave out (on me).* **5** *vt sep* to make (something) known: *It was given out that there would be another wage freeze.*

give over 1 *vt usu sep* to give (a person, thing *etc*) to someone: *He gave his prisoners/the jewels over to the police.* **2** *vi, vt fus* (*sl*) to stop (doing something): *Give over whistling!*; *Do give over!* **3** *vt usu sep* (*formal*: *usu in passive*) to be devoted to or used for (some purpose): *This evening will be given over to discussion of this paper.*

give 'rise to (*formal*) to cause: *This gives rise to a large number of problems.*

give the show away *see* **give the game/show away** *above*.

give up 1 *vi, vt sep* to stop doing (something) or trying to do (something): *I can't understand this problem – I think I'll give up (trying to solve it)*; *I must give up smoking*; *We'll have to give up the search until tomorrow.* **2** *vt sep* to stop using, eating, seeing *etc* (a person, thing *etc*): *You'll have to give up cigarettes*; *He gave them up last year*; *I won't give up all my hobbies for you.* **3** *vt sep* to give (a person, thing *etc*) to (a person *etc*) or allow (a person *etc*) to have (a person, thing *etc*): *Children should give up their seats on the bus if other people are standing*; *The police called on the thief to give himself up*; *He gave himself up to the police.* **4** *vt sep* to devote (one's life, time *etc*) to doing something: *I have given up so much of my time to this job that I won't stop now.* **5** *vt usu sep* (*often with* **as** *or* **for**) to consider (a person, thing *etc*) to be: *You took so long to arrive that we had almost given you up (for lost/as dead).* **6** *v refl sep* (*with* **to**: *formal*) to do or feel (something) without trying to control (oneself) any longer: *She gave herself up to despair/grief.*

give (a person, thing *etc*) **up as a bad job** to stop trying to do (something) because it is too difficult *etc*; to stop trying to help, teach, improve *etc* (someone) because he is too bad, stupid *etc*: *I've been trying to solve this problem for hours – I think I'll give it up as a bad job*; *The girl showed so little progress after having piano lessons for three years that the teacher gave her up as a bad job.*

give way (*often with* **to**) **1** to stop in order to allow (someone or something) to pass: *Give way to traffic coming from the right.* **2** to break and fall down under pressure: *The bridge will give way any day now.* **3** (*formal*) to be replaced or followed by (something): *His fear gave way to anger.* **4** (*formal*) to agree to (something) or allow (a person) to do (something) against one's will (*eg* because of threats): *I have no intention of giving way to demands like that.* **5** (*formal*) to feel or do (something) without trying to control (oneself) any longer: *He gave way to despair/grief.*

'give (someone) ˌwhat 'for (*inf*) to scold or punish (a person): *Your father will give you what for if you go home late.*

give one's word *see* **word** (*def 4*).

what gives? (*sl*) what is happening?; what is the matter?: *Everyone seems to be in a bad mood – what gives?*

See also **gift**.

glacé ['glasei, (*Amer*) gla'sei] *adj* (*attrib*) iced or sugared: *glacé cherries.*

glacier ['glasiə, (*Amer*) 'gleiʃər] *nc* a mass of ice, formed from the snow on mountains, which moves slowly downhill.

glacial ['gleisiəl, (*Amer*) -ʃəl] *adj* **1** (*tech*) of or caused by ice or glaciers. **2** (*inf*) very cold: *glacial winds.*

glad [glad] *adj* **1** (*usu pred*) pleased or happy (about something): *I'm very glad of your help*; *I'll be only too glad* (= very glad) *to help you*; (*formal*) *the glad smiles of the children.* **2** (*attrib*) which makes people glad: *Have you heard the glad news?*

'gladden *vt* (*formal*) to make (a person *etc*) glad: *The news gladdened his heart* (= made him glad).

'gladly *adv*: *I'd gladly help but I have too many other things to do*; (*formal*) *smiling gladly.* **'gladness** *nu*.

glad rags (*inf*) a person's best clothes, worn for special occasions: *I'll get my glad rags on for the party.*

glade [gleid] *nc* (*old or liter*) an open space in a wood.

gladiator ['gladieitə] *nc* (*hist*) in ancient Rome, a man trained to fight with other men or with animals for the amusement of spectators.

glamour, (*Amer*) **glamor** ['glamə] *nu* **1** the often false or superficial beauty or charm which attracts people to a place, thing *etc*: *Many girls were attracted to Hollywood by the glamour of a career in films.* **2** great beauty or sexual charm, achieved with the aid of make-up, beautiful clothes *etc*: *the glamour of film stars.*

'glamorize, -ise *vt* to make (something) attractive or glamorous: *This film attempts to glamorize war.*

'glamorous *adj* having glamour: *a glamorous film star*; *You're looking very glamorous today.* **'glamorously** *adv*.

glance [gla:ns] *vi* to look very quickly (at a person, thing *etc*): *He glanced at the book*; *I glanced through the newspaper*; *He glanced over the accounts.* – *See also* **glance off** *below*. – *nc* a brief or quick look: *Would you take a glance at these accounts?; I had a glance at them last night; Her father threw a disapproving glance at her* (= glanced at her in disapproval). – *See also* **at a glance** *below.*

'glancing *adj* (*attrib*) which hits (something) and glances off: *a glancing blow.*

at a 'glance at once: *I could tell at a glance that something was wrong.*

glance off *vi, vt fus* to hit (something) and bounce off to one side: *The ball glanced off the edge of his bat.*

gland [gland] *nc* a part of the body that takes substances from the blood and stores them for use or in order that the body may get rid of them: *a sweat gland; He has a sore throat and swollen glands (in his neck).*

'glandular [-djulə, (*Amer*) -dʒulər] *adj* (*usu attrib*) of the glands: *glandular fever; Her fatness is caused by glandular trouble.*

glare [gleə] *vi* 1 (*usu with* **at**) to stare fiercely and angrily (at someone): *She glared at the little boy.* 2 to shine very brightly, *usu* to an unpleasant extent: *The sun glared down on us as we crossed the desert.* – 1 *nc* a fierce or angry look: *She gave me an angry glare and walked past; She shot him a glare of displeasure* (= She glared at him with displeasure). 2 *nu* unpleasantly bright light: *the glare of the sun.*

'glaring *adj* unpleasantly bright; too bright: *the glaring sun; glaring colours; These colours are too glaring for me.* 2 (*usu attrib*) obvious; easily noticed: *a glaring error.*

'glaringly *adv*: *a glaringly obvious mistake.*

glass [gla:s] 1 *nu, adj* (of) a hard *usu* breakable substance which can be seen through and which is used for windows *etc*: *The bottle is (made of) glass; a glass bottle.* 2 *nc* (*sometimes in cmpds*) a *usu* tall hollow object made of glass, used for drinking: *We have sherry-glasses and wine-glasses but no whisky-glasses.* 3 *nc* a glassful: *He drank a large glass of milk.* 4 *nc* a mirror: *You only have to look in the glass to see you're getting older.* – *See also* **looking-glass**. 5 *nc* a barometer, or the atmospheric pressure shown by one: *The glass is falling.* 6 *nu* glassware: *People often give glass as wedding presents.*

'glasses *n pl* two round pieces of glass in some sort of frame, worn in front of the eyes for reading *etc*; spectacles: *I need glasses when I watch television; a pair of glasses.*

'glassful *nc* the amount that a drinking-glass will hold: *Pour in two glassfuls of water.*

'glassily *adv* without showing any expression: *He stared at her glassily.*

'glassy *adj* 1 (*usu attrib*) (of people's faces or eyes) not showing any expression: *a glassy stare.* 2 like glass: *a glassy sea; The sea was smooth and glassy.* **'glassiness** *nu.*

'glasshouse *nc* 1 a greenhouse: *He grows tomatoes in a glasshouse.* 2 (*sl*) an army prison.

'glassware *nu* ornaments *etc* made of glass: *We got a lot of glassware as wedding presents.*

glaze [gleiz] 1 *vt* to fit glass into (a frame, *eg* the windows of a building): *Do you know how to glaze a window?* 2 *vt* to cover (a thing) with glass or something like glass: *The potter glazed the vase.* 3 *vi* (of eyes) to become blank or dull; to stop showing any expression: *When the doctor gave her an injection, her eyes glazed and she became unconscious.* 4 *vt* to put a shiny coating, *eg* of sugar, on fruit *etc*: *We sometimes glaze pears and grapes for dessert at Christmas.* – *ncu* 1 a glassy coating put on pottery *etc*: *He put a pink glaze on the grey vase.* 2 a shiny coating *eg* of sugar on fruit *etc*: *an apricot glaze on an apple tart.*

'glazier [-ziə, (*Amer*) -ʒər] *nc* a person who puts glass in window frames *etc*: *The glazier put a new window in the shop.*

See also **double-glazing** *under* **double**.

gleam [gli:m] *vi* to shine faintly or very briefly: *I saw a light gleaming in the distance; The girl's eyes gleamed in the candlelight.* – *nc* 1 a brief or faint glow: *the gleam of her eyes.* 2 (*fig*) a slight sign or amount (of something): *a gleam of hope.*

glean [gli:n] *vt* (*formal*) to collect (news, facts *etc*) together: *I have gleaned all the information I can but I still do not know all the facts.*

glee [gli:] *nu* great delight *eg* at one's own success *etc* or at another person's failure, difficulty *etc*: *The children laughed with glee when their teacher fell off his chair.*

'gleeful *adj* (*usu attrib*) feeling or showing glee. **'gleefully** *adv.*

glen [glen] *nc* (*often found with cap in place-names*) *esp* in Scotland, a long narrow valley: *We walked up to the head of the glen to see the deer; Glen Affric.*

glib [glib] *adj* (*derog*) 1 speaking easily and persuasively but *usu* without real feeling or sincerity: *The carpet salesman was a very glib talker; I never believe him – he is too glib.* 2 (of a reply *etc*) quick and ready, but showing little thought or sincerity: *glib excuses; His explanation for the mistake was a bit too glib.* **'glibly** *adv.* **'glibness** *nu.*

glide [glaid] *vi* 1 to move smoothly and easily: *The dancers glided across the floor; The seagulls glided across the sky;* (*fig*) *The months glided quickly by.* 2 to travel by or fly a glider *eg* as a hobby. – *nc* a gliding movement: *The dancers crossed the floor in a series of glides.*

'glider *nc* a small, light aeroplane which has no engine.

'gliding *nu* the flying of gliders *eg* as a hobby: *I'm very keen on gliding.*

glimmer ['glimə] *vi* (*formal or liter*) to burn or shine faintly: *A single candle glimmered in the hall.* – *nc* 1 (*formal or liter*) a faint light: *the glimmer of a candle.* 2 (*fig*) a slight sign or amount of (something): *a glimmer of hope.*

glimpse [glimps] *nc* a very brief look: *You might catch a glimpse of the Queen; I got a brief glimpse of her.* – *vt* (*formal*) to get a brief look at (something): *He thought he glimpsed her in the crowd.*

glint [glint] *vi* to gleam or sparkle: *In the distance, we could see the cottage windows glinting in the sunlight.* – *ncu* a gleam or sparkle; gleaming or sparkling quality: *the glint of steel;* (*fig*) *There was a glint of anger in her eyes; He had a glint* (= a look of pleasure) *in his eye as he watched the girls in their summer dresses.*

glisten ['glisn] *vi* (*formal*) (*esp* of things that are wet or polished) to shine faintly or sparkle: *His skin glistened with sweat; The tears were glistening on her cheeks.*

glitter ['glitə] *vi* to sparkle or shine faintly with flashes of light: *Her diamonds glittered in the light.* – *nu* the quality of glittering: *the glitter of her diamonds.*

'glittering *adj* 1 which glitters: *glittering jewels.* 2 (*fig*) excellent; splendid: *The singer gave a* *glittering performance; Her last performance was the most glittering of her career.*

gloat [glout] *vi* (*usu with* **over**) to look at or think about (something good of one's own or something bad or unpleasant which has happened to someone else) with wicked pleasure: *He gloated over his own success and his rival's failure; He gloated over his treasure.*

'**gloatingly** *adv*: *He gazed gloatingly at the gold coins.*

globe [gloub] *nc* **1** (*usu with* **the**) the Earth: *I've travelled to all parts of the globe.* **2** a large ball, *usu* on a stand, which has a map of the Earth on it: *If you want to know where Moscow is, look on the globe.* **3** a large ball or object shaped like a globe, *eg* a glass cover on a lamp: *This paraffin lamp needs a new globe; The chemicals were crushed to a powder in a large metal globe.*

'**global** *adj* (*usu attrib*) **1** affecting the whole world: *War is now a global problem.* **2** affecting, or taking into consideration, the whole of a group of people, things *etc*: *We can perhaps make a global rule that will cover all these problems.* '**globally** *adv.*

globular ['globjulə] *adj* (*tech*) shaped like a globe or globule.

globule ['globju:l] *nc* (*esp tech*) a very small drop of liquid: *globules of sweat.*

'**globe-trotter** *nc* (*inf*) a person who goes sightseeing all over the world.

'**globe-trotting** *nu*: *Now that he has retired he spends all his time globe-trotting.*

gloom [glu:m] **1** *nu* (*formal*) a state of not quite complete darkness, *eg* just before night falls: *I could not tell the colour of the car in the gloom.* **2** *ncu* (*pl rare*) sadness, often with a feeling of despair: *The king's death cast a gloom over the whole country.*

'**gloomy** *adj* **1** (which makes people) sad or depressed: *gloomy news about the country's financial state; Don't look so gloomy.* **2** dim; dark: *the gloomy rooms of a castle; Their new house is small, dark and gloomy.* '**gloominess** *nu.*

glory ['glo:ri] **1** *nu* fame or honour: *The soldiers hoped to win glory on the field of battle; He took part in the competition for the glory of the school.* **2** *nc* something which is a source of pride, fame *etc*: *These churches are the glory of this city; This building is one of the many glories of Venice.* **3** *nu* (of things) the quality of being very beautiful or magnificent: *The sun rose in all its glory.* **4** *nu* (*relig*) praise and thanks given to God: *The angel said 'Glory to God in the highest, and on Earth, peace'.* – *vi* (*with* **in**) to take (too) great pleasure in or be (too) proud of (something): *He glories in his work as a tax inspector.*

'**glorify** [-fai] *vt* (*formal*) **1** to make (something) seem better, more beautiful *etc* than it is: *That book glorified war.* **2** to praise or worship (God).

ˌ**glorifi'cation** [-fi-] *nu.*

'**glorious** *adj* **1** (*attrib*) splendid; deserving great praise: *a glorious career/victory.* **2** (*inf*) very pleasant; delightful: *glorious weather; Isn't the sunshine glorious?* '**gloriously** *adv.*

See also **inglorious**.

gloss [glos] **1** *nu* (*sometimes with* **a**) brightness or shininess on the surface of something: *Her hair has a lovely gloss; Hot plates sometimes damage the gloss on a table;* (*attrib*) *Use gloss paint* (= paint which has a glossy surface when it dries) *on the woodwork of your house if you want it to be shiny* (*see also* **emulsion**). **2** *nc* an explanation of a difficult word, phrase *etc* in a book *etc*, *usu* in the margin or at the foot of the page. – *vt* **1** to add explanations of (difficult words, phrases *etc*) in a book *etc*: *You will have to gloss that phrase – it is so idiomatic that people will not understand it.* – *See also* **gloss over** *below.*

'**glossary** [-səri] *nc* a list of words *etc* with their meanings: *There is a glossary of technical terms at the back of that book; They have published a Shakespeare glossary.*

'**glossy** *adj* smooth and shining: *The dog has a glossy coat; This polish will make your table glossy; There was a pile of glossy magazines* (= magazines dealing with fashion *etc*, printed on thick, shiny paper) *on the table.* '**glossiness** *nu.*

gloss over *vt fus* to try to hide, or to try to prevent anyone noticing (a mistake *etc*): *The chairman tends to gloss over any information that would prove him wrong.*

glove [glʌv] *nc* a covering for the hand, *usu* with a separate covering for each finger: *a pair of gloves.*

fit like a glove to fit perfectly: *This suit fits like a glove.*

glow [glou] *vi* **1** to give out heat or light without any flame: *The coal was glowing in the fire.* **2** (*often fig*) to have red cheeks because of heat, cold, emotion *etc*: *Her cheeks were glowing with health; The little boy glowed with pride.* **3** (*formal or liter*) to have or produce a bright *usu* red, brown or golden colour: *The autumn leaves glowed in the evening sun.* – *nu* the state of glowing: *the glow of the coal in the fire;* (*liter*) *the sun's evening glow.*

'**glowing** *adj* (*usu attrib*) **1** that glows: *glowing colours.* **2** full of praise: *I hear glowing accounts of his bravery; glowing reviews of his new book.*

'**glow-worm** *nc* a kind of beetle whose tail glows in the dark.

glower ['glauə] *vi* (*often with* **at**) to stare angrily (at someone): *When she asked the speaker to justify his remarks, he just glowered at her.*

'**glowering** *adj* (*usu attrib*) angry; threatening: *a glowering look.* '**gloweringly** *adv.*

glucose ['glu:kous] *nu* a kind of sugar found in the juice of fruit.

glue [glu:] *ncu* a substance used for sticking or joining things together: *What kind of glue should I use to stick plastic to wood?; There are various glues on the market.* – *vt* to join (things) with glue: *The first thing to do is to glue these two bits together.*

'**gluey** *adj* sticky, like glue: *a gluey substance; Something gluey has been spilt on the table.*

See also **glutinous**.

glum [glʌm] *adj* gloomy and sad: *Don't look so glum – the sun is shining!; Her face wore a glum expression.* '**glumly** *adv.* '**glumness** *nu.*

glut [glʌt] *nc* too great a supply (of something); more (of something) than people wish to buy: *There has been a glut of apples this year.* – *v* – *pt, ptp* '**glutted** – *vt* to supply (something) with too much (of something): *They glutted the market with apples.*

glutinous ['glu:tinəs] *adj* (*formal or tech*) gluey; sticky: *Something went wrong with the dough and the bread ended up as a rather glutinous mass.*

glutton ['glʌtən] *nc* **1** (*derog*) a person who eats too much: *That child is fat because he is such a glutton.* **2** (*with* **for**: *often facet*) a person who is always eager for more of something *usu* difficult or unpleasant: *She must be a glutton for punishment* (= hardship) *to go on teaching at that terrible school; He's a glutton for work.*

ˈ**gluttonous** *adj* very greedy. ˈ**gluttonously** *adv.* ˈ**gluttony** *nu* greediness in eating; the habit of eating too much.

glycerin(e) [ˈglisəriːn, (*Amer*) -rin] *nu* a sweet, sticky, colourless liquid: *Add glycerine to the icing for the cake – it will prevent it becoming too hard.*

gnarled [naːld] *adj* (*formal or liter*) (of trees, branches *etc*) twisted; with knots (*def 2*): *a gnarled tree*; *wood gnarled with age*; (*fig*) *gnarled fingers*; (*fig*) *fingers gnarled with age.*

gnash [naʃ] *vt* (*usu fig*) to rub (the teeth) together in anger *etc*: *He was gnashing his teeth in fury as he watched the burglar run away.*

gnat [nat] *nc* a very small, *usu* blood-sucking, fly.

gnaw [noː] **1** *vti* (*often with* **at**) to bite or chew (something) with a scraping movement: *The dog was gnawing (at) a large bone.* **2** *vt* to make (a hole *etc*) by gnawing at something: *The mice have gnawed holes in the walls of this room.* **3** *vti* (*formal*: *often with* **at**) to cause physical or mental pain: *Guilt gnawed at her all day long*; *She was gnawed by a sense of guilt*; *Unbearable pain gnawed at her constantly before her death.*

gnome [noum] *nc* (*myth*) a small, ugly, man-like creature who lives underground, often guarding treasure.

gnu [nuː] – *pls* **gnus, gnu** – *nc* a type of large African antelope: *two gnus*; *a herd of gnu.*

go [gou] – *3rd pers sing prt* **goes**: *pt* **went** [went]: *ptp* **gone** [gon] – **1** *vti* (*often with* **about, across, by, down, for** *etc*) to walk, travel, move *etc*: *I'm going (back/down) to London*; *He is going across the field*; *I'm going by bus*; *Are you going my way?* (= in the same direction as I am); *Are we going across (the river) or not?*; *Go straight ahead*; *When did he go out?* **2** *vi* to be sent, passed on *etc*: *This book must go (off) by tonight's post*; *Complaints have to go through the proper channels.* **3** *vi* (*with* **to** *or* **for**) to be given, sold *etc* (to a person *etc*): *The prize goes to John Smith*; *When I die, this house will go to you*; *The table went for £50.* **4** *vi* to lead to, extend to, stretch to *etc*: *Where does this road go?*; *This road goes all the way to London*; *This stair goes to the attic*; *My property only goes as far back as those trees*; *My family goes back to the 15th century* (= There are records of my family from the 15th century onwards). **5** *vi* (*with* **to**) to visit (a place), often regularly, for some purpose; to attend (an event): *He goes to school every day*; *He goes to church*; *I have to go to hospital for an operation*; *I decided not to go to the movie*; *Did you go to his lecture?* **6** *vi* to be destroyed, taken down *etc*: *This wall will have to go.* **7** *vi* to proceed, be done or carried out *etc* (in a particular way): *The meeting went very well*; *Things are going badly at the moment.* **8** *vi* to leave or move away: *I think it is time you were going*; *Will you please go away?*; *Don't go away with that book* (= Don't take that book away). **9** *vi* to be lost, used up or finished; to disappear: *All my money is/has gone*; *My purse has gone!* **10** *vi* (*with* **for, on** *or a verb ending in* **-ing**) to do (some action or activity): *I'm going for a walk*; *I am going on a hike*; *I'm going hiking next week-end.* **11** *vi* to break, break down, fail *etc*: *My hearing has gone*; *The clock-spring has gone*; *I think the clutch on this car is going.* **12** *vi* to be in motion, working *etc*: *I've managed to get the car going again*; *I don't think that clock is going.* **13** *vi* to become; to begin to be in a certain state or condition: *The milk has gone off*; *These apples have gone bad*; *The fire has gone out*; *He's going blind*; *The patient went into a coma*; *Long skirts have gone out of fashion.* **14** *vi* to be (in a state or condition): *There are many people in the world who regularly go hungry.* **15** *vi* to be placed or put; to belong in a particular place: *Where does this book go?*; *Spoons go in that drawer.* **16** *vi* to fit or be put (in or into something): *That pile of books will never go into these two boxes.* **17** *vi* (of time) to pass: *Time goes quickly when you are enjoying yourself.* **18** *vi* (*sometimes with* **on**) to be used (for something or for some purpose): *This money will go to build a new church*; *All her pocket-money goes on sweets.* **19** *vi* (*usu with negative adj*) to manage to be (something) when one ought not to; to fail to be (something) which one ought to be: *The thieves must not go unpunished*; *His talents went unrecognized.* **20** *vi* (*inf*) to be acceptable, valid, applicable *etc*: *Anything goes in this office*; *They'll have to work a lot harder and that goes for you too*; *He thinks it's a crazy idea, and that goes for me too* (= I think so too); *What I say, goes* (= must be followed or obeyed). **21** *vi* to have a particular result *eg* after a contest, discussion *etc*: *The voting went against him*; *The voting went in his favour.* **22** *vi* (*inf*) to make a particular noise: *Dogs go woof, not miaow.* **23** *vi* to have particular words, a particular tune *etc*: *How does that song go?*; *We'll need to put our noses to the grindstone* (= work very hard), *as the saying goes.* **24** *vi* to lead (to a conclusion): *That just goes to show/prove that you're a liar.* **25** *vi* (*with* **to**) to contribute, or act together, towards (making or producing something): *Honesty, courage, sympathy – these are the qualities that go to make a policeman.* **26** *vi* (*with* **to**) to give oneself (trouble, expense *etc*): *You shouldn't have gone to all this trouble for me.* **27** *vi* (*inf*: *with* **and**) to act in such a way as to do something: *Why did you have to go and spoil my picture?* **28** *vt* to be willing to pay (a certain sum of money) (for something): *I'm willing to go as high as fifty pounds for that table*; *He'll go to a hundred pounds*; *I'll go halves/fifty-fifty with you on the cost of the bike.* **29** *vi* (*inf*) to become lively, successful *etc*: *I'll have to do something to make this party go*; *I'll have to do something to get this party going.* **30** *vti* (of a number) to be able to divide a number: *Five into three won't go*; *Five into ten goes two.* **31** *vt* (*inf*: *with* **could**) to want (something): *I could really go a large glass of beer.* **32** *vt* (*inf*) to take part in (a round of boxing *etc*): *He'll never go ten rounds against the champion.* **33** *vi* to die: *I'm afraid he's gone – he has stopped breathing.* – *n* – *pl* **goes** – (*inf*) **1** *nc* an attempt: *I'm not sure how to do it, but I'll have a go*; *He managed to cut five planks of wood at one go.* **2** *nc* a chance (to do something): *I want a go on the swings.* **3** *nu* energy: *She's got a lot of go for a woman of her age*; *She's full of go.*

-goer (*in cmpds*) a person who goes (to a certain place) regularly: *a cinema-goer*; *a theatre-goer.*

ˈ**going** *nu* **1** the act of leaving (somewhere): *We'll have a party to celebrate your going*; *We watched the comings and goings of the people in the street.* **2** the conditions under which something is done: *It was very heavy going because of all the mud*; (*inf*) *I find talking to him very heavy going.* **3** the speed with which something is done: *To type ten pages an hour is very good going.* – *adj* **1** (*attrib*) successful: *The shop is very much a going concern now.* **2** (*attrib*) in existence or valid at present: *What is the going rate for typing manuscripts these days?* **3** (*pred*: *inf*) available: *Is there any coffee going?*

'go-ahead *adj* (*inf*) which makes progress and is successful, *usu* because of a willingness to try out new ideas: *a go-ahead firm with go-ahead directors*; *His firm is very go-ahead.* – *nc* permission (to do something): *We'll start as soon as we get the go-ahead from you*; *We've been given the go-ahead for our new plans.* – *See also* **go ahead** *below.*

'go-between *nc* a person who carries messages between two people *etc*, *eg* who are in love or who refuse to speak to each other.

go-by *see* **give the go-by** *below.*

,go-'getter *nc* (*inf*) a person with a great deal of energy, ability *etc* who gets what he wants.

,going-'over *nc* (*no pl*) **1** a study or examination: *The treasurer gave the accounts a thorough going-over.* **2** the act of cleaning *etc* (something): *She gave the room a good going-over.*

,goings-'on *n pl* (*usu* strange) happenings or behaviour: *There have been a lot of strange goings-on here in the past few months.* – *See also* **go on.**

'go-kart [-ka:t] *nc* (*also* **kart**) a small low-powered racing car.

go-slow *see* **go slow**.

,no-'go *adj* (*attrib*) (of a district *etc*) which a person *etc* is not allowed to enter: *a no-go area.* – *See also* **no go** *below.*

all go (*inf*) very busy; causing or having a great deal of activity: *It's all go in this office today.*

as far as it goes within certain limits: *What you say is correct as far as it goes, but I'm sure there must be more to the story than that*; *His reports aren't bad as far as they go, but there's not enough detail in them.*

as (people, things *etc*) **go** when compared to (people, things *etc*) in general: *This new girl is quite good, as secretaries go.*

be ,going 'on (for) (*inf*) to be near or close to (a time, age *etc*): *It must be going on (for) six o'clock*; *He must be going on (for) eighty.*

be going strong to be successful, healthy *etc*: *Our business/grandfather is still going strong.*

be 'going to (do something) to intend to, or be about to (do something) in the (near) future: *I think I'm going to be sick in a minute*; *After I've finished this job I'm going to relax.*

be 'gone on (*sl*) to be filled with foolish love for: *My brother is really gone on that actress*; *She's quite gone on that silly little dog.*

from the word go from the very beginning: *I want accuracy right from the word go.*

get going (*inf*) to get started; to leave: *If you want to finish that job you'd better get going*; *If you want to reach Glasgow tonight you'd better get going.*

,give (a person, thing *etc*) **the 'go-by** (*sl*) to ignore (a person) in an unfriendly way; to ignore (something) or not deal with it: *It was very rude of you to give her the go-by like that*; *I think we'll give all his stupid suggestions the go-by.*

go about 1 *vi* (*also* **go around**) (of rumours *etc*) to be passed from one person to another: *There's a story going about that you are in debt.* **2** *vt fus* to (begin to) work at (a job, problem *etc*): *I don't know the best way to go about the job!*; *When the Director comes in, just go about your work as normal.* **3** *vi* (of a ship) to change direction or turn around.

go about with *vt fus* (*inf*) to be friendly with and often seen in the company of (a person *usu* of the other sex): *She goes about with Tom.*

,go after *vt fus* **1** (*inf*) to try to get or win (something): *He's going after that prize/job.* **2** to follow or chase (a person *etc*): *Go after him and apologize.*

go against *vt fus* **1** to resist, oppose or refuse to act on (a person's suggestions, wishes *etc*): *A child should never go against his parents' wishes.* **2** to be unacceptable to (a person *etc*) because of his beliefs *etc*: *This goes against my conscience, but I'll have to do it.* **3** to be unfavourable to (a person, thing *etc*): *A gambler should stop gambling when luck is going agaisnt him.* – *See also* **go** (*def 21*).

go against the grain *see* **grain**.

go ahead *vi* (*often with* **and** *or* **with**) to (start to) do (something): *I warned him not to touch it but he went ahead and did it*; *'Can I borrow this book?' 'Yes, go ahead'*; *Can I go ahead with this job now?* – *See also* **go-ahead** *above.*

go along *vi* **1** (*often with* **to**) to go (to a meeting, party *etc*): *I'll go along (to the meeting) with you.* **2** to be in the process of doing (something): *I never check my work after I've finished it – I prefer to do the checking as I go along.*

go along with *vt fus* (*inf*) to agree with (a person, suggestion *etc*): *I'm afraid I can't go along with you on that.*

go along with you! *see* **get along/away with you!** *under* **get**.

go around *vi* (of stories, rumours *etc*) to be passed from one person to another: *There's a rumour going around that you are leaving.*

go around with *vt fus* (*inf*) to be friendly with and often in the company of (a person): *I don't like the group of friends you're going around with.*

go as/so far as to be willing to say, do *etc* (something): *I won't/wouldn't go so far as to say that he's a fool, but he does make stupid mistakes*; *I wouldn't go as far as resigning but I am not happy with my present job.*

'go at *vt fus* (*inf*) **1** to attack (a person *etc*): *The little boys went at each other with their fists.* **2** to do (something) or deal with (a job *etc*) with enthusiasm: *He really went at the job of painting the living room.*

go away with you! *see* **get along/away with you!** *under* **get**.

go back *vi* **1** to return or take (a person's or one's own) mind back to an earlier time, topic of conversation *etc*: *Let us go back to the time of Queen Victoria*; *My memory doesn't go back as far as that*; *Let's go back for a minute to what we were talking about earlier.* **2** to begin to do something one had stopped doing: *He has gone back to smoking cigars again.* – *See also* **go** (*def 4*).

go 'back on *vt fus* to fail to do (something one has promised to do): *I never go back on my promises.*

go below *vi* (*naut*) to go below the deck (in a ship).

'go by *vt fus* **1** (*inf*) to base an opinion or a judgement on (something): *We can't go by what he says.* **2** (*inf*) to be guided by (something): *When I'm not sure what to do, I always go by the instructions you gave me.* **3** to be known as (something): *His name is Charles but he always goes by the name of Plug.*

go by the board *see* **board**.

go down *vi* **1** (*inf*) (of food) to be swallowed: *Yoghurt goes down easily.* **2** to become smaller (because of the loss of air *etc*): *My tyres have gone down*; *The swelling on my arm has gone down a bit.* **3** (*inf*) (*with* **well/badly**) to be approved or disapproved of: *The story went down well (with them)*; *His jokes went down badly (with the* *audience*). **4** (*naut*) (of a ship) to sink: *They were lost at sea when the ship went down.* **5** (of the sun or moon) to go below the horizon. **6** (*with* **in**) to be remembered: *Your bravery will go down in history.* **7** to be written down: *This will all go down in my report.* **8** (of a book) to deal with events as far as (a certain date): *This history book only goes down to the First World War.* **9** (*inf*) (of places) to become less pleasant or desirable: *This part of town has gone down in the last twenty years.*

go 'down with *vt fus* (*inf*) to catch (a disease): *He has gone down with flu.*

go easy on/with *see* **easy**.

go far (*inf*) **1** to be successful: *If you keep on working as hard as this, I'm sure you'll go far.* **2** (of money) to buy much: *£5 doesn't go far nowadays.*

'go for *vt fus* (*inf*) **1** to attack (a person, animal *etc*) physically or in words: *The two dogs went for each other as soon as they met*; *The newspapers went for the Prime Minister over the Government's tax proposals.* **2** to be attracted by (a person, thing *etc*): *I go for redheads in short skirts. – See also* **go** (*def 10*).

go forth (*arch or liter*) *vi* to be sent out or announced: *The news went forth that Saint George had killed the dragon.*

go in *vi* **1** (of the sun or moon) to become covered by cloud. **2** to begin work: *What time does school go in?*

go 'in for *vt fus* **1** to take part in (an examination, competition *etc*): *I'm not going in for the 1 000 metres race.* **2** to do (something) as a hobby, job, habit *etc*; *to study (something) at university etc*: *My son is going in for medicine*; *My son goes in for collecting postcards*; *We don't go in for using people's surnames in this office.*

go 'into *vt fus* **1** to make a careful study (of something) or inquiry (into something): *We'll need to go into this plan in more detail before we make any decision.* **2** to discuss or describe (something) in detail: *I don't want to go into the problems at the moment as there isn't any time before my next appointment.* **3** to begin to do (something) as a job: *My son hopes to go into politics.*

go a long way *see* **way**.

gone on *see* **be gone on** *above.*

go 'off **1** *vi* (of a gun) to fire; (of a bomb *etc*) to explode: *The little boy was injured when the rifle/firework went off in his hand.* **2** *vi* (*often with* **with**: *often in a bad sense*) to leave: *He went off yesterday*; *He has gone off with* (=He has stolen) *our money*; *His wife had gone off with the postman.* **3** *vt fus* (*inf*) to begin to dislike (someone or something once liked): *I've gone off Shakespeare/whisky*; *I went off that girl when I met her friends.* **4** *vi* to take place and be successful: *Did the party go off all right last night?* **5** *vi* (of an alarm) to ring, make a noise *etc*: *The thieves ran away as soon as the alarm went off.*

go on[1] *vi* **1** (*often with* **to**) to continue going; to go as far as (a place): *There's no room in this hotel – let's go on to the next town.* **2** (*often with* **with**) to continue doing (something): *Go on with what you're doing.* **3** to continue (by doing something) after doing something: *The pianist played a piece by Bach, and then went on to play one of Beethoven's sonatas.* **4** to talk a great deal, *usu* too much, (about something): *She goes on and on about the time she met the Queen.* **5** (*inf*) to happen: *What is going on here? – See also* **goings-on**. **6** to pass by: *Things will get better as time goes on.* **7** to behave, *esp* badly: *If you go on like that much longer, someone will slap your face.*

'go on[2] *vt fus* to (be able to) base one's investigations *etc* on (information *etc*): *The police began a search for the murderer, but they had very few clues to go on.*

go 'on (with you)! (*inf*) you're joking!; stop teasing!; I don't believe you!

go 'on at *vt fus* (*inf*) to speak (to someone) in an angry or criticizing way, *usu* for some time: *Her mother went on at her for coming home late after the dance.*

go on for *see* **be going on for** *above.*

go out *vi* **1** (*with* **to**) to go to a distant country, sometimes to stay: *I can't find a job here, so I'm going out to Canada to try there.* **2** to go to parties, meetings *etc*: *We don't go out as much as we did when we were younger.* **3** (*often with* **with**) to be seen frequently in the company of (a person, *usu* of the opposite sex): *My girl-friend and I have been going out (together) for eighteen months now*; *I've been going out with her for months.* **4** no longer to be part (of a competition *etc*) because one has been beaten: *The local team went out in the first round.*

go out like a light (*inf*) to fall quickly and deeply asleep.

go out to work to have a job: *My mother stayed at home while we were young, but now she goes out to work.*

go over **1** *vt fus* to study or look at (something) carefully: *I want to go over the work you have done before you do any more*; *The police went over the whole room for clues. – See also* **going-over**. **2** *vt fus* to repeat (a story *etc*); to practise (part of a play, music *etc*): *Some of you haven't understood this lesson, so I'll go over the whole thing again*; *Act III is not very good yet, so we'll go over it again tomorrow*; *Act III is not very good, so I'll go over it again with you tomorrow.* **3** *vt fus* to list, discuss or consider: *I have no intention of going over all your faults.* **4** *vi* (*with* **to**) to change to another religion, political party, type of food *etc*: *He's gone over to the Liberals*; *I don't eat butter now – I've gone over to margarine.* **5** *vi* (of plays, behaviour *etc*) to be received (well or badly): *The play didn't go over at all well the first night.*

go 'round to be enough for everyone: *Is there enough food to go round?*

go slow (*Brit*) (of workers in a factory *etc*) to work less quickly than usual, *eg* as a form of protest: *All our mail is being delayed as the postal workers are going slow* (*nc* **,go-'slow**).

go so far as *see* **go as far as**.

go steady (with someone) (*inf*) to have a close friendly relationship (with someone of the opposite sex) and be seen frequently in his or her company: *My girl-friend and I have been going steady for a year – we're going to get engaged next month.*

go 'through[1], **'go through** **1** *vt fus* to make a close study or examination of (something); to search for something in (something): *The treasurer went through the society's accounts*; *I've gone through all my pockets but I still can't find my key.* **2** *vt fus* to suffer: *You have no idea what I went through to get this finished in time.* **3** *vt fus* to use up (something): *He's gone through a lot of paper since he started.* **4** *vt fus* to do or complete (some action, ceremony *etc*): *You have to go through certain formalities before you can emigrate.*

go 'through[2] *vi* to be agreed to or completed: *The*

Bill went through (= was passed by parliament) *yesterday*; *After long hours of negotiations, the deal went through.*

go 'through with *vt fus* to do (something) or finish doing (something): *I'm going to go through with this in spite of what you say*; *She went through with the wedding despite her parents' disapproval.*

go together *vi* **1** to look well together: *The carpet and curtains go together very well.* **2** (*inf*) to go steady (*see* **go steady** *above*).

go too far to do something which is so bad as to be unacceptable: *No-one objects to an occasional joke, but one day you'll go too far.*

'go towards *vt fus* to help to buy *etc* (something): *The money we collect will go towards a new roof for the church.*

go 'under *vi* to be ruined: *He has no idea how to run a shop – he/his business is bound to go under eventually.*

go 'up *vi* **1** to increase in size, value *etc*: *The temperature has gone up*; *The price of bread is going up tomorrow*; *He has gone up in my estimation* (= I think more highly of him than before). **2** to be built: *There are office blocks going up all over town.*

go up in smoke/flames to catch fire; to be destroyed or damaged by fire *etc*: *The building across the street went up in flames.*

'go with *vt fus* **1** to be given or sold with (something): *The carpets will go with the house.* **2** to look, taste *etc* well (with something): *The carpet goes with the wallpaper*; *Whisky doesn't go very well with tea.* **3** to be found in the same place (as something): *Illness often goes with poverty.* **4** (*inf*) to go steady (*see* **go steady** *above*) with (someone): *I've been going with Mary for six months.*

go without *vt fus, vi* to manage without (something): *If you can't afford a new dress, you'll have to go without (one).*

go without saying (*only with* **it** *as subject*) to be quite obvious without anyone saying it: *It goes without saying that he's an excellent artist.*

have a go *see* **go** (*n def 1*).

one's heart/sympathy goes out to (a person) one feels great sympathy or pity for (a person): *Her heart went out to the little orphan.*

keep going to continue doing what one is doing; to continue to walk *etc*; to survive: *The snow was falling heavily, but we had to keep going*; *Business is bad at the moment, but we'll manage to keep going.*

let go (of) *see* **let**.

let oneself go (*inf*) **1** to cease to take a pride in oneself, one's appearance *etc*: *She used to be very well-dressed, but since her husband died she has just let herself go.* **2** to cease to feel bound by rules (*eg* of correct behaviour): *I like John's parties – I feel I can let myself go for once.*

make a go (of something) (*inf*) to make a success (of something): *He has never owned a shop before, but I think he'll make a go of it.*

no go (*inf*) unsuccessful; useless; not getting agreement or approval: *I asked if he would agree to our plans, but it's no go, I'm afraid.* – *See also* **no-go** *above.*

one's sympathy goes out to *see* **one's heart goes out to** *above.*

on the go very busy or active: *He's always on the go, from morning to night.*

to 'go remaining; to be done, finished *etc*: *There's only one more page to go after this one.*

goad [goud] *vt* to urge or force (a person *etc*) to do something by annoying (him *etc*): *His wife goaded him into digging the garden*; *I was goaded into being rude to him.* – *nc* **1** (*fig*) something that urges or forces (a person *etc*) to do something. **2** a sharp-pointed stick used for driving cattle *etc.*

goal [goul] *nc* **1** (the space enclosed by) the two upright posts between which players attempt to kick, hit *etc* a ball in football, rugby, hockey *etc*: *The ball just missed the goal.* **2** in such games, the act of kicking, hitting *etc* a ball between these posts; the point gained by doing this: *He scored six goals.* **3** an aim or purpose: *My goal in life is to be Prime Minister.*

'goal-keeper *nc* (*also inf* **'goalie** [-li]) a player, *eg* in hockey or football, whose job is to prevent members of the other team from scoring goals, *eg* by catching the ball.

'goalpost *nc* one of the two upright posts which form the goal in football, rugby, hockey *etc.*

goat [gout] *nc* an animal of the sheep family, with horns and a long-haired coat: *Some people drink goats' milk.*

act the goat (*inf*) to behave intentionally in a silly way; to play the fool: *Do stop acting the goat and try to be serious.*

get someone's goat (*inf*) to annoy or irritate (a person): *What got my goat was the way she kept laughing at my mistakes.*

gobble ['gobl] **1** *vti* (*sometimes with* **up**) to swallow food *etc* quickly: *You'll be sick if you keep gobbling your meals like that*; (*fig*) *That duplicating machine just gobbles up the ink.* **2** *vi* (of turkeys) to make a noise in the throat: *We could hear the turkeys gobbling in the farmyard.*

goblet ['goblit] *nc* **1** a drinking-cup with a thin stem: *He served the wine in goblets.* **2** (*hist*) a large cup without handles.

goblin ['goblin] *nc* (*myth*) a mischievous, ugly spirit: *a frightening fairy-story about goblins.*

god [god] – *fem* **'goddess** (*def 2*) – **1** *n* (*relig*: *with cap*) the creator and ruler of the world (in the Christian, Jewish *etc* religions). **2** *nc* (*myth or relig*) a supernatural being who is worshipped: *the gods of Greece and Rome*; (*fig*) *Money is his god.*

'godless *adj* (*formal or liter*: *usu attrib*) **1** not religious; not believing in God. **2** (*loosely*) wicked: *a godless life.*

'godly *adj* (*formal*) religious; following God's laws: *a godly man/life*; *He is the most godly of men.*

'godliness *nu.* – *See also* **ungodly**.

,god-'awful *adj* (*sl*: *usu attrib*) very bad: *What god-awful weather this is!*; *a god-awful book.*

'godchild, 'goddaughter, 'godson *ncs* a child who has a godparent or godparents.

'godfather, 'godmother, 'godparent *ncs* a person who, at a child's baptism, promises to make sure that the child is brought up according to the beliefs of the Christian church.

'God-fearing *adj* (*also without cap*: *formal*) religious; following God's laws: *a God-fearing man*; *He is too God-fearing to tell lies.*

'god-forsaken *adj* (*attrib*: *also with cap*) (of places) terrible; unpleasant: *This is a god-forsaken spot you have brought me to.*

'godsend *nc* a very welcome piece of unexpected good luck: *Your cheque was an absolute godsend.*

'bid/'wish (someone) ,god'speed (*old*) to wish (a person who is leaving) success, a safe journey *etc*: *They stood at the harbour and wished/bade the captain godspeed.*

for ,God's 'sake **1** an expression used when

urgently begging a person to do something: *For God's sake, will you come at once!* 2 (*offensive to some people*) an exclamation of disgust, annoyance *etc*: *'He says he wants to see you this evening.' 'Oh, for God's sake, why?'*

'**God knows** (*inf*: *offensive to some people*) 1 I don't know; it is impossible to understand: *'Why did he do that?' 'Oh, God knows.'* 2 used for emphasis: *I don't know why you're angry with me – God knows, it wasn't my fault.*

the gods (*inf*) (the people in) the top balcony in a theatre: *We had to sit in the gods – we couldn't get any better seats.*

thank God an expression used to show that a person is glad that something has, or has not, happened: *Thank God you're here!*; *Thank God for that!*

goggle ['gogl] *vi* to have wide, staring eyes (*eg* because of surprise): *He goggled when he saw the chest of gold coins*; *He goggled at the amount of money he received.*

ˌ**goggle-'eyed** *adj* (*usu pred*) with wide, staring eyes: *She stared goggle-eyed at the film star.*

goggles ['goglz] *n pl* a type of spectacles used to protect the eyes from dust, water *etc*: *Many swimmers wear goggles in the water*; *Can you lend me a pair of goggles?*

gogo ['gougou]: '**gogo dancer** *nc* a girl who entertains people *eg* in a public house, by dancing *usu* while wearing very little clothing.

go-kart *see* **go**.

gold [gould] 1 *nu* an element (symbol **Au**), a precious yellow metal used for making jewellery *etc*: *This watch is made of gold.* 2 *nu* coins, jewellery *etc* made of gold. 3 *ncu* the colour of the metal: *the browns and golds of autumn leaves.* 4 *nu* (loosely) wealth. – *adj* 1 made of gold (*def 1*): *This watch is gold*; *a gold watch.* 2 of the colour of gold (*def 1*): *They bought a gold carpet*; *Their curtains are gold.*

'**golden** *adj* of gold or the colour of gold: *golden hair*; *Her hair is golden.* 2 (*attrib*) (of a wedding anniversary, jubilee *etc*) fiftieth: *They will celebrate their golden wedding (anniversary) next month*; *Queen Victoria's golden jubilee was in 1887.*

'**gold-digger** *nc* 1 (*sl derog*) a woman who is friendly towards men merely for the sake of the presents they give her: *She married him because he is wealthy – she's a real gold-digger.* 2 a person who digs for gold.

'**gold-field** *nc* an area where gold is found and mined.

'**goldfish** – *pl* '**goldfish** – *nc* a small golden-yellow fish often kept as a pet: *The child kept a goldfish in a small bowl.*

ˌ**gold-'leaf** *nu* gold beaten into a very thin sheet: *a brooch made of gold-leaf.*

'**gold-mine** *nc* 1 a place where gold is mined. 2 (*fig*) a source of wealth or profit: *That clothes shop is an absolute gold-mine.*

'**gold-rush** *nc* a rush of people to a part of a country where gold has been discovered.

'**goldsmith** *nc* a person who makes jewellery, ornaments *etc* of gold.

as good as gold (*inf*) (*usu* of children) very well-behaved: *The new baby is as good as gold – he very rarely cries.*

golden opportunity a very good or favourable chance: *When you were speaking to the boss you should have asked for a higher salary – you missed a golden opportunity.*

golf [golf] *nu* a game in which a small white ball is hit across open ground and into small holes by means of long, thin clubs: *He plays golf every Sunday*; (*attrib*) *a golf match.* – *vi* to play golf: *Do you golf?*

'**golfer** *nc* a person who plays golf: *He is a keen golfer.*

'**golfing** *nu* the playing of golf: *I'm keen on golfing*; (*attrib*) *a golfing holiday.*

'**golf-club** *nc* the long thin stick used to hit the ball in golf: *He bought a new set of golf-clubs.*

'**golf club** *nc* 1 a society of people who play golf: *He belongs to the local golf club.* 2 the building where they meet: *Let's have a drink in the golf club.*

'**golf course** *nc*, '**golf links** *n sing or pl* the place where golf is played.

golosh *see* **galosh**.

gondola ['gondələ] *nc* 1 a long narrow boat used on the canals of Venice. 2 the car which hangs under an airship, cable railway *etc*.

ˌ**gondo'lier** [-'liə] *nc* a person who rows a gondola.

gone *see* **go**.

gong [goŋ] *nc* a metal plate (*usu* hanging in a frame) which, when struck, gives a ringing sound, used *eg* to call people to meals in a hotel *etc*: *Did you hear the dinner gong?*

good [gud] – *compar* **better** ['betə]: *superl* **best** [best] – *adj* 1 well-behaved; not causing trouble *etc*: *The little boy's mother told him to be good while she was away*; *She's such a good baby.* 2 (living, behaving *etc* in a way which is) generally considered to be correct, desirable *etc*: *Everyone agreed that the man had a good wife*; *It is not considered good manners to spit in the street*; *His table manners are not very good*; *Is this sentence good English?* 3 of a high standard; of high quality: *good food/literature*; *His piano-playing is very good*; *He made a good job of the repairs* (= did the repairs well); *That's a good picture of you* (= it resembles you). 4 (*with* **at** *or* **with** *when pred*) skilful; able to do something well: *He's a good doctor/artist*; *He's good at tennis*; *He's good with children/horses.* 5 (*often with* **to** *when pred*) kind: *You've been very good to him*; *a good deed*; *He's a good father*; *Give him my good wishes*; (*formal*) *Would you be good enough to come into my office* (= please come into my office) *for a minute?* 6 (*often with* **for** *when pred*) helpful; beneficial; likely to make people *etc* healthy; able to cure or prevent something: *What you need is a good night's sleep*; *Do you know of anything that is good for warts?*; *Cheese is good for you*; *These berries aren't good to eat.* 7 (causing a person to feel) pleased, happy *etc*: *He's in a good mood today*; *It's good to see you again*; *good news.* 8 pleasant; enjoyable; desirable: *Did you have a good time* (= Did you enjoy yourself) *at the party?*; *I like to read a good book before I go to sleep*; *The weather wasn't very good last week*; *Editing dictionaries is a good job*; *Ice-cream is good to eat*; *a good joke.* 9 (*attrib*: *often used to emphasize other words*) (fairly) large, long *etc*; enough: *a good salary*; *Leave a good margin at the side of the page*; *A good deal of what he said was nonsense*; *I've lived here a good many* (= very many) *years*; *What he needs is a good (hard) kick in the pants*; *Don't hide your grief – have a good cry.* 10 (*attrib*: *with* **for**) useful; suitable; able to do (something): *Smith would be a good man for that job*; *Wet weather is good weather for fishing.* 11 free from illness, injury *etc*; not rotten, broken *etc*: *He is in good health*; *His eyesight is good*; *He only has one good* *eye – the other was damaged in a car crash*; *This car has good brakes.* **12** (*usu attrib*) sensible; acceptable; based on, or showing, reason: *Can you think of one good reason for doing that?*; *We'll have to rely on his good judgement.* **13** (*inf*: *attrib*) (of clothes *etc*) only used, worn *etc* on special occasions: *I'd better put on my good suit if we're going out to dinner.* **14** attractive, nice to look at *etc*: *She has a good figure*; *She looks good in that hat.* **15** (*attrib*) proper; careful: *Take good care of my bike*; *Take a good look at that diagram*; *I didn't get a good look at him as he ran off.* **16** (*attrib*) showing approval (of a person, thing *etc*): *He didn't have a good word to say for the plan*; *We've had very good reports about you.* **17** (*attrib*) having or deserving respect: *Nothing must damage the good name* (= good reputation) *of this firm.* **18** (*attrib*) very friendly: *We're good friends.* **19** (*attrib*) bringing a desirable result; suggesting that something will have a desirable result: *good luck/fortune*; *a good omen.* **20** (*attrib*) loyal; correct; thinking, behaving *etc* as is expected: *a good Catholic/communist.* **21** (*inf*: *attrib*) thorough; complete: *I'll give this room a good clean tomorrow.* **22** likely to bring profits: *a good investment.* **23** (*usu attrib*) of a high social class: *He comes from a good family.* **24** (*inf*: *pred*) well; healthy: *I don't feel very good this morning.* – *nu* **1** advantage or benefit: *He devoted his whole life to working for the good of the poor*; *I'm punishing you for your own good*; *Does spanking children ever do (them) any good?*; *This behaviour will do his reputation no good*; *What's the good of buying a car if you can't drive?*; *What good is a dictionary that's full of mistakes?* – *See also* **no good** *in phrases below.* **2** goodness: *I always try to see the good in people.* – *interj* an expression of approval, gladness *etc*: *'John says he can come.' 'Good!'* – *adv* (*Amer inf*) well: *I don't hear too good* (= very well) *now.*

'goodly *adj* (*arch*) quite large: *a goodly sum of money.*

'goodness *nu* the state of being good. – *interj* (*also* **my goodness**) an expression of surprise *etc.*

goods *n pl* **1** objects *etc* for sale: *leather goods.* **2** (*esp Brit*) articles sent by rail, not road, sea or air: *This station is for passengers and goods*; (*attrib*) *a goods train/station.* **3** (*old*) personal property: *When I die, I shall leave all my worldly goods to you.* – *See also* **deliver the goods** *below.*

'goody (*inf*) *nc* (*usu in pl*) **1** a good, honest *etc* person in a war or in a crime story *etc* (*eg* the police as opposed to criminals, the army of one's own country as opposed to the enemy): *The goodies always beat the baddies in the end.* **2** (*usu in pl*: *facet*) any food (*eg* cake, ice-cream) which is particularly enjoyable to eat: *all the goodies at a children's party.* – *interj* (used *esp* by children) an expression of pleasure: *'We're going to the beach this afternoon.' 'Oh, goody!'* – *See also* **goody-goody** *below.*

good afternoon *see* **good morning**.

good'bye [-'bai] *interj, nc* an expression used when leaving someone or when someone is leaving: *Goodbye – it was good of you to visit us*; *They said their goodbyes at the station.*

good-day, good evening *see* **good morning**.

ˌgood-for-'nothing *adj, nc* (*derog*) (a person who is) useless or lazy: *That boy's a lazy good-for-nothing (rascal).*

good humour *nu* kindliness and cheerfulness.

ˌgood-'humoured *adj*: *a good-humoured smile*; *He's very good-humoured.* **ˌgood-'humouredly** *adv.*

ˌgood-'looking *adj* handsome; beautiful; attractive: *a good-looking girl/man*; *He is very good-looking.*

good 'morning, good ˌafter'noon, good-'day (*formal*)**, good 'evening, good 'night** *interjs, ncs* words used (depending on the time of day) when meeting or leaving someone or when someone is leaving: *Good morning, Mrs Brown*; *Good night, everyone – I'm going to bed.*

ˌgood-'natured *adj* kind; pleasant; not easily made angry: *He is very good-natured – he never loses his temper*; *a good-natured fellow.*

ˌgood'will, good will *nu* **1** the good reputation and trade with customers that a business firm has: *We are, of course, selling the goodwill of the business along with the shop.* **2** (*with* **toward(s)**) kind thoughts; friendliness: *He has always shown a good deal of goodwill towards us.*

good works *n pl* acts of charity: *He is known throughout the city for his good works.*

ˌgoody-'goody *adj* (*usu pred*), *nc* (*inf*) (a person who takes too great pleasure in being, and showing people that he is) very moral, virtuous, well-behaved *etc*: *The other children don't like that boy – he's too goody-goody.*

a good (*inf*) (in expressions of size, quantity *etc*) at least; fully: *They live a good five miles from here*; *That wrestler must weigh a good hundred kilos.*

a good thing (*inf*) something which is desirable: *I think private schools are a good thing*; *I think it would be a good thing if you wrote to her yourself.* – *See also* **be on to a good thing** *below.*

all in good time *see* **time**.

all to the good *see* **to the good** *below.*

as 'good as almost; virtually: *He as good as called me a thief*; *The job's as good as done.*

as good as gold *see* **gold**.

be as good as one's word to keep one's promises; to do what one has promised to do: *He said he would lend me the money if I needed it, and he was as good as his word.*

be in someone's good books *see* **book**.

be 'on to a ˌgood 'thing (*inf*) to be in a situation, job *etc* which is particularly good, pleasant, desirable *etc*: *He sits in that office and does almost nothing all day, and gets paid for it – he's really on to a good thing there!*

be up to no good (*inf*) to be doing, or about to do, something wrong or illegal: *There's something odd about the way that fellow is behaving – I'm sure he's up to no good.*

come to no good (of a person) to get into disgrace or an immoral, dishonest *etc* state: *When he started drinking heavily and gambling, we knew he would come to no good.*

deliver the goods (*inf*) to do what one has promised to do or what one is expected to do: *He said he could easily arrange the loan for us, but I don't think he can deliver the goods.*

do good to do good, kind acts: *Jesus went about doing good.* – *See also* **do-gooder** *under* **do**.

for 'good (*sometimes* **for good and all**) for ever; permanently: *He's not going to France for a holiday – he's going for good.*

for goodness' sake an expression of annoyance: *For goodness' sake, will you stop that noise!*

give as good as one gets (in an argument, fight *etc*) to be as successful as one's opponent; to do as much harm as one's opponent does; to give as

good arguments or replies as one's opponent does: *I didn't think he would have the courage to argue with the boss, but he certainly gave as good as he got.*
'good and (*inf*) very: *He kicked him good and hard.*
'good for 1 certain to last (a period of time): *These houses are good for another hundred years at least.* **2** certain to pay (a sum of money): *He's good for £50.* **3** certain to cause (something): *That story is always good for a laugh.* – *See also* **good** (*defs 10, 12*).
good for you, him *etc* an expression of approval: *You've passed your exam – good for you!*
Good Friday the Friday before Easter Sunday: *Christ was crucified on Good Friday.*
good gracious an expression of surprise.
good heavens an expression of surprise, dismay *etc*: *Oh, good heavens! I've left the tickets at home*; *Good heavens! What are you doing here?*
goodness gracious, goodness me expressions of surprise: *Goodness me! I didn't know you were coming too.*
goodness knows an expression used to show that a person does not know (something), often showing worry, irritation *etc*: *If she loses that job, goodness knows what she'll do*; *'Why did he do that?' 'Oh, goodness knows!'*
'good old (Bill, Smith *etc***)** (*inf*) an expression used to show approval *etc*: *Good old Fred! I knew he would help us out.*
goods and chattels *see* **chattels**.
have a good mind (to do something) *see* **mind**.
hold good *see* **hold**.
in good time *see* **time**.
make good (*inf*) to be successful: *He had very little money when he arrived, but through hard work and ability, he soon made good.*
make (something) good (*formal*) **1** to get or give money *etc* which compensates or makes up for loss, damages *etc* one has suffered; to repair (something) one has damaged: *This year's profits will make good last year's losses*; *The damage you caused to my car must be made good.* **2** to prove (a claim, accusation *etc*): *He made good his claim to be the strongest man in the country.*
make good time *see* **time**.
my goodness *see* **goodness** *above*.
no good useless; pointless; worthless: *It's no good crying for help – no-one will hear you*; *This penknife is no good (to me) – the blades are blunt*; *My watch is no good any more* (= is now useless) *– the minute hand is broken*; *I tried several times to start the car, but it was no good – the battery was flat.* – *See also* **good** (*n def 1*), **be up to no good** *and* **come to no good** *above*.
not much good/(*inf*) **not a lot of good** rather useless; rather pointless; almost worthless: *He's not much good as a lecturer*; *That washing-machine is not much good*; *I'm not a lot of good at making speeches.*
put in a good word for (someone) to praise or recommend (someone): *Put in a good word for me when you see the boss.*
take (something) in good part not to be upset, offended or annoyed (*eg* by a joke, remark *etc*): *Several jokes were made about John's unfortunate accident with the pot of paint, but he took it all in good part.*
thank goodness an expression used to show that a person is glad that something has, or has not, happened: *Thank goodness you've come!*; *Thank goodness it isn't raining*; *Thank goodness for that!*
to the 'good 1 (*also* **all to the good**) to (someone's) benefit: *'John said he was bringing a friend.' 'That's all to the good – we need all the help we can get!'* **2** (*inf*) richer; with gain or profit of: *After buying and selling some of these paintings, we finished up £100 to the good.*
the good (*formal*) good people: *The good are said to die young.*
the Good Book the Bible.
See also **well**.

goose [gu:s] – *pl* **geese** [gi:s] – **1** *nc* a web-footed animal like a duck, but larger: *The farmer's wife keeps geese.* **2** *nu* its flesh used as food: *We had roast goose for Christmas dinner.* **3** *nc* (*inf, esp old*: *also* **silly goose**) a silly person.
'goose-flesh *nu*, **'goosepimples** *n pl* small bumps on the skin caused by cold or fear.
'goose(-)step *nu* a way of marching without bending one's knees. – *v* – *pt, ptp* **'goose(-)stepped** – *vi* to march in this way.
he *etc* **can't/couldn't/wouldn't say boo to a goose** he *etc* is very timid: *She ought to have complained about it but she's so quiet, she wouldn't say boo to a goose.*
See also **gander, gosling**.

gooseberry ['guzbəri, (*Amer*) 'gu:s-] *nc* **1** a round, eatable, *usu* green berry: *I don't like gooseberries*; (*attrib*) *gooseberry jelly*; (*attrib*) *a gooseberry bush.* **2** (*inf*) a person who is with two other people (*usu* people who are in love) who wish that the person was not there: *I'm certainly not coming with you and your fiancée – I hate playing gooseberry*; *I'm not coming with you – I don't want to be a gooseberry.*

gore[1] [go:] *nu* (*liter or facet*) blood from a dead or wounded person *etc* (*esp* when it is thick and solid): *After the battle, the knight was covered in gore.* – *vt* (of an animal) to pierce (someone) with its horns, tusks *etc*: *The bull gored the farmer to death.*
'gory *adj* (*usu attrib*) with a lot of blood or bloodshed: *a gory battle*; *a gory tale.*

gore[2] [go:] *nc* a triangular piece of material put into a garment to widen it.
gored *adj* (*usu attrib*) having a gore or gores: *a gored skirt.*

gorge [go:dʒ] *nc* (*often found with cap in place-names*) a deep narrow valley: *the Cheddar Gorge.* – *vi, v refl* (*often with* **on**) to eat (food) greedily until one is full: *He gorged himself (on fruit) at the party.*

gorgeous ['go:dʒəs] *adj* **1** beautiful; showy; splendid: *a gorgeous dress*; *a bird's gorgeous plumage*; *These colours are gorgeous.* **2** (*loosely*) very pleasant or enjoyable: *We had a gorgeous trip to the seaside/a gorgeous day at the seaside*; *That meal was gorgeous.* **'gorgeously** *adv*. **'gorgeousness** *nu*.

gorilla [gə'rilə] *nc* the largest type of ape: *Two gorillas have escaped from the zoo.*

gorse [go:s] *nu* a prickly bush with yellow flowers: *The hillside was covered in gorse*; (*attrib*) *a gorse bush.*

gosh [goʃ] *interj* an expression or surprise.

gosling ['gozliŋ] *nc* a young goose.

gospel ['gospəl] **1** *nc* (*often with cap*) (one of the four descriptions in the Bible of) the life and teaching of Christ: *the Gospel according to St Luke*; *In which gospel is the parable of the sower?* **2** *nu* (*inf*) the absolute truth: *What I'm saying is gospel*; (*attrib*) *the gospel truth.*

gossamer ['gosəmə] *nu* the fine threads made by a

spider which float in the air or lie on bushes. – *adj* (*attrib*) like gossamer or as if made of gossamer: *a blouse of a gossamer material.*

gossip ['gosip] **1** *nu* (*derog*) talk about other people's affairs, not always true and often spiteful: *I never pay any attention to gossip.* **2** *nc* a casual and friendly chat: *She dropped in for a cup of coffee and a gossip.* **3** *nc* (*derog*) a person who listens to and passes on gossip: *She's a dreadful gossip.* – *vi* **1** to pass on gossip: *I don't like people who gossip* (*about their neighbours*). **2** to chat: *She spends the whole day gossiping with her neighbours.*

'**gossipy** *adj* (*derog*) fond of gossiping: *We've got very gossipy neighbours.*

'**gossip column** an article in a newspaper *etc* containing gossip about famous people (*eg* film-stars).

got, gotten *see* **get**.

gouge [gaudʒ] *nc* (*tech*) a chisel with a rounded, hollow blade, for cutting grooves or holes in wood *etc.* – *vt* (*sometimes with* **out**) **1** to make (a groove or hole) in something with a gouge or some other tool: *He gouged* (*out*) *a hole in the wood.* **2** to take, force or cut (a thing) out of something: *The sharp rock gouged a piece of flesh from his leg*; *The tyrant gouged out the prisoner's eyes.*

goulash ['gu:laʃ] *ncu* a spicy stew of meat and vegetables: *We had* (*a*) *Hungarian goulash for supper.*

gourd [guəd, (*Amer*) go:rd] *nc* **1** a type of large fruit, or the plant on which it grows. **2** the skin of such a fruit used as a bottle, cup *etc.*

gourmet ['guəmei] *nc* (*formal*) a person who enjoys, and knows a great deal about, good food and wines: *A gourmet like him always eats in expensive restaurants.*

gout [gaut] *nu* a painful swelling of the smaller joints in the bones *esp* those of the big toe: *The old man is suffering from gout.*

govern ['gʌvən] **1** *vti* to rule (a country or state): *Britain is governed by Parliament, not by the Queen*; *The emperor governed wisely and well.* **2** *vt* (*formal*) to guide or influence (a person, decision *etc*): *Our policy is governed by three factors.* **3** *vt* (*gram*) to require a noun *etc* to be in a particular case.

'**governess** *nc* a woman who teaches children in their home.

government ['gʌvəmənt] **1** *nc* (*often with cap*) the people who (are *usu* elected to) rule (a country or state): *the British Government*; (*attrib*) *government papers.* **2** *nu* the way in which a country or state is ruled: *Democracy is one form of government.* **3** *nu* the ruling of a country or state: *We have entrusted the politicians with the government of this country.* **4** *nu* (*gram*) the state of requiring a noun *etc* to be in a particular case.

governmental [gʌvn'mentl] *adj* (*attrib*) of (a) government: *governmental interference.*

'**governor** *nc* **1** (*sometimes with cap*) in the US, a person who is elected as the head of a state: *the Governor of Ohio.* **2** a member of the committee of people who govern a school, hospital *etc*: *He is on the board of governors.* **3** (*hist*) a person who governs a province or colony. **4** (*usu* ˌ**Governor-'General** – *pl* ˌ**Governors-'General**) the representative of the British monarch in a country of the British Commonwealth. '**governorship** *ncu.*

gown [gaun] *nc* **1** (*formal*) a woman's dress, *esp* one of high quality for dances, parties *etc*: *The princess wore a satin gown.* **2** a loose robe worn by clergymen, lawyers, teachers *etc*: *The students had to wear gowns at the graduation ceremony.*

grab [grab] – *pt, ptp* **grabbed** – **1** *vti* to seize or grasp (a person, thing *etc*) suddenly: *He grabbed a biscuit*; *His mother told him it was rude to grab.* **2** *vt* (*inf*) to get or take (something) quickly: *I'll just grab a sandwich and a cup of coffee*; *Grab a taxi* (= Get into a taxi) *and come round to my house.* **3** *vt* (*inf*) to get (something) by rough or illegal means: *Many people tried to grab land when oil was discovered in the district.* – *See also* **grab at** *below.* – *nc* a sudden attempt to grasp or seize (a person, thing *etc*): *He made a grab at the boy.*

'**grab at** *vt fus* **1** to try to grasp or seize (a person, thing *etc*), not necessarily successfully: *He grabbed at the boy.* **2** (*fig*) to seize or take: *He grabbed at the chance to leave.*

grace [greis] **1** *nu* (*usu* of people) beauty of form or movement: *The dancer's movements had very little grace.* **2** *nu* (*formal*) a sense of what is right or decent: *At least he had the grace to leave after his dreadful behaviour.* **3** *ncu* a short prayer of thanks before or after a meal: *The minister said* (*the*) *grace.* **4** *nu* a delay allowed to (a person *etc*) as a favour: *You should have paid me today but I'll give you a week's grace.* **5** *n* (*with cap*: *with* **his, your** *etc*) a title used in talking to or about a duke, duchess or archbishop: *Your/His Grace.* **6** *nu* (*arch or relig*) mercy: *by the grace of God.* – *vt* (*formal*) **1** (*often facet or ironic*) to honour (*eg* a social event) by being present at it: *We are grateful to you for gracing our dinner with your presence.* **2** to adorn or decorate (a person, thing *etc*): *Beautiful flowers graced the tables.*

'**graceful** *adj* **1** having or showing beauty of form or movement: *a graceful dancer/bow*; *The ballet dancer is so graceful.* **2** showing a sense of what is correct or decent: *a graceful apology*; *Her apology was so graceful that we forgave her.* '**gracefully** *adv.* '**gracefulness** *nu.*

'**gracious** [-ʃəs] *adj* **1** kind or polite: *The Queen gave a gracious smile*; *Her reply was gracious but firm.* **2** (*formal*: *pred*) (of God) merciful. – *interj* an exclamation of surprise: *Gracious! – I didn't hear you come in.*

'**graciously** *adv* in a gracious manner: *The Queen smiled graciously.* '**graciousness** *nu.*

airs and graces *see* **air**.

good(ness) gracious, gracious me exclamations of surprise.

with (a) good/bad grace (un)willingly: *He did what I told him, but with* (*a*) *very bad grace*; *She accepted his apology with good grace.*

grade [greid] *nc* **1** one level in a scale of qualities, sizes *etc*: *Eggs are sorted into seven grades now*; *a high-grade ore.* **2** (*Amer*) (the pupils in) a class or year at school: *We're in the fifth grade now.* **3** (*Amer*) a mark for an essay, examination *etc*: *I always got good grades at school.* **4** (*esp Amer*) the slope of a railway *etc*; gradient. – **1** *vt* to sort (people, things *etc*) into different grades: *to grade eggs.* **2** *vi* to pass or change from one thing to another through a series of slightly different intermediate stages: *Blues and reds grade into purple.*

gradation [grə'deiʃən] (*formal*) **1** *nc* (one stage or degree in) a series of gradual and successive stages: *There are various gradations of colour between red and purple.* **2** *ncu* the act or process of grading. **3** *nu* the gradual change or movement from one state, note, colour *etc* to another: *The background in the picture shows a gradation from light to dark blue.*

'**grade school** *nc* (*Amer*) a primary school.

make the grade (*inf*) to do as well as necessary (in an examination, job *etc*): *We'll have to wait until we get the results of the exam before we know whether you have made the grade or not.*

gradient ['greidiənt] *nc* **1** the amount of slope (*eg* of a railway): *a gradient of 1 in 4.* **2** (*formal*) a slope: *The car slid down the steep gradient into the river.*

gradual ['gradjuəl] *adj* advancing or happening gently and slowly: *a gradual rise in temperature*; *a gradual slope*; *The improvement in our sales figures has been gradual.*

'**gradually** *adv*: *His health is gradually improving.*

graduate ['gradjueit] **1** *vi* (*with* **in** (a subject), **from** (a place)) to receive a university degree (in Britain) or a degree, diploma *etc* of any educational institution (in the US): *He graduated in German and French from Oxford.* **2** *vt* (*formal*) to mark out (*eg* a thermometer, a ruler) with regular divisions: *A thermometer is graduated in degrees.* **3** *vt* (*formal*) to arrange (something) in regular steps or stages, according to size *etc*: *This tax scheme is graduated so that people who earn more money pay more tax.* – [-ət] *nc* (*with* **in** (a subject), **of** (a place)) a person who has been awarded a university degree (in Britain) or a degree or diploma of any educational institution (in the US): *a graduate in French*; (*attrib*) *a graduate course in French*; *a graduate of Oxford university.*

,**gradu'ation 1** *nu* the act of graduating from a college, university *etc.* **2** *nc* the ceremony at which this takes place: *The graduation will be held in the large hall*; (*attrib*) *a graduation ceremony.* **3** *nu* (*formal*) the marking of regular divisions (on a ruler, thermometer *etc*). **4** *nc* (*formal*) one of the divisions so marked: *the graduations on a thermometer.*

'**graduate school** (*Amer*) a section of a university which offers instruction beyond the level of a bachelor's degree.

See also **post-graduate, undergraduate**.

graffiti [grə'fi:ti:] *n sing or pl* words or drawings scratched or painted on a wall *etc*: *the graffiti on the walls of a public lavatory.*

graft[1] [gra:ft] *vti* (*with* **in, into, on, together** *etc*) **1** to fix a shoot of one plant on to, or into, another, so that it will grow there: *Cultivated roses are often grown by being grafted on to the roots of wild roses.* **2** to fix (skin, bone *etc*) from one part of the body on to or into another part of that body: *The doctor treated her burns by grafting skin from her leg on to her back.* **3** to transfer (an organ of the body) from one person to another: *The surgeon grafted the dead man's kidneys into his patient.* – *nc* **1** a piece of skin, bone *etc* which is grafted: *a skin graft.* **2** a shoot or twig which is grafted.

graft[2] [gra:ft] (*sl*) **1** *ncu* (an example of) the use of illegal or unfair means to gain profit, *esp* in public life: *He was accused of graft by his opponents.* **2** *nu* the profit gained in this way. **3** *nu* (hard) work: *I got where I am today by sheer hard graft.*

grain [grein] **1** *nc* a seed of wheat, oats *etc.* **2** *nu* corn (*def 1*) in general: *Grain is ground into flour.* **3** *nc* a very small, hard particle: *a grain of sand.* **4** *ncu* the way in which the lines of fibre run in wood, leather *etc* or the pattern formed by these lines. **5** *nc* (*fig*) a very small amount: *There isn't a grain of truth in that story.* **6** *nu* (*Amer*) corn (*def 2*): *a field of grain.*

go against the grain to be against a person's wishes, feelings *etc*: *It goes against the grain for me to tell lies.*

See also **granary, granule**.

gram *see* **gram(me)**.

grammar ['gramə] **1** *nu* (the study of) the rules for forming words and for combining words to form sentences: *He's an expert on French grammar*; *He has a good understanding of grammar.* **2** *nc* a description of the rules of grammar of a particular language *etc*, or a book containing this: *I'm writing a grammar of French*; *Could you lend me your Latin grammar?*; (*attrib*) *a grammar book.* **3** *nu* a person's wrong or correct use of the grammatical rules of a language: *His grammar is bad*; *This essay is full of bad grammar.*

gram'marian [-'meə-] *nc* (*formal*) an expert on grammar.

gram'matical [-'ma-] *adj* **1** (*neg* **un-**) correct according to the rules of grammar: *This is a grammatical sentence*; *It would not be grammatical to say that.* **2** of (a) grammar: *a grammatical rule.*

gram'matically *adv.*

'**grammar school** *nc* **1** a type of secondary school giving an education specially suitable for pupils who intend to go on to a university. **2** (*Amer*) a primary school.

gram(me) [gram] *nc* (*often abbrev* **gm** *when written*) the basic unit of weight in the metric system.

See also Appendix 5.

gramophone ['graməfoun] *nc* (*Amer* '**phonograph**: *old*) a record-player.

gran [gran] *nc* (*inf*: *with cap when used as a name*) a grandmother.

granary ['granəri] *nc* a storehouse for grain.

grand [grand] *adj* **1** splendid; magnificent: *The soldiers looked very grand in their white and red uniforms*; *a grand procession.* **2** proud; looking as if one thinks oneself important: *I don't know why she gives herself grand airs like that*; *She looks so grand and arrogant.* **3** (*inf*) very pleasant: *We had a grand day at the seaside.* **4** (*attrib*) wonderful; highly respected: *a grand old man.* **5** very dignified: *to write in the grand style*; *His style is too grand for his subject.* **6** (*often in titles*) of a high rank or great importance: *a grand vizier* (= formerly a chief minister in some Muslim countries). – *n* – *pl* **grand** – *nc* (*sl*) $1 000 or £1 000: *I paid five grand for that car.*

grand duchess *nc* (*with cap in titles*) **1** (the status of), the wife or widow of a grand duke. **2** (the status of) a lady who rules a grand duchy.

grand duchy *nc* (*with cap in names*) a small country, state *etc* ruled by a grand duke or grand duchess: *the Grand Duchy of Luxembourg.*

grand duke *nc* (*with cap in titles*) (the status of) a high-ranking nobleman who rules a grand duchy.

grand finale *nc* the final act or scene in a show *etc*, *usu* with all the actors, singers *etc* on the stage.

grand jury *nc* in the US, a jury which decides whether there is enough evidence for a person to be brought to trial.

grand master/grand'master *nc* a chess-player of the highest ability.

grand opera *nu* a form of opera in which all the dialogue is sung: *Wagner wrote grand opera.*

grand piano *nc* a type of piano with a large flat top shaped like a harp, used *esp* in concerts of classical music: *She has bought a grand piano.*

'grandstand *nc* rows of raised seats at a sports ground *etc* which give a good view of the events: *We watched the sports meeting from the grandstand*; (*attrib*) *grandstand seats*; (*fig*: *attrib*) *As the parade went right past our house, we had a grandstand view of everything.*

grand total *nc* the final total; the total of several smaller totals: *If we add your expenses to mine and his, that will give us the grand total for our expenses.*

grand- [grand] (*in cmpds*) separated by one generation, as in **grandson, grandfather**.

grandchild ['grantʃaild], **grand-daughter** ['grando:tə], **grandson** ['gransʌn] *ncs* the child, daughter or son, of one's son or daughter: *She has three grandchildren.*

grandad ['grandad] *nc* (*inf*: *with cap when used as a name*) a grandfather.

grand-daughter *see* **grandchild**.

grandeur ['grandʒə] *nu* (*formal*) **1** great and impressive beauty: *the grandeur of snow-covered mountains.* **2** importance: *He suffers from delusions of grandeur* (= He thinks that he is important but he is not).

grandfather ['granfa:ðə], **grandmother** ['granmʌðə], **grandparent** ['granpeərənt] *ncs* the father or mother of one's father or mother: *I have two grandfathers – my father's father and my mother's father.*

grandfather clock *nc* a clock with a tall *usu* wooden case which stands on the floor: *The grandfather clock ticks very loudly.*

grandiloquent [gran'diləkwənt] *adj* (*formal*: *usu derog*) (of speeches *etc*) spoken or written in a style which is too formal **gran'diloquence** *nu*.

grandiose ['grandious] *adj* **1** (*derog*) attempting or intended to appear impressive to an excessive or foolish degree: *He produced several grandiose schemes for a holiday resort in the North of Scotland, but no resort was ever built.* **2** (*formal*) splendid; magnificent; impressive: *a palace built in a grandiose style.*

grandma ['granma:] *nc* (*inf*: *with cap when used as a name*) a grandmother.

grandmother *see* **grandfather**.

grandpa ['granpa:] *nc* (*inf*: *with caps when used as a name*) a grandfather.

grandparent *see* **grandfather**.

grandson *see* **grandchild**.

granite ['granit] *nu, adj* (of) a type of hard *usu* grey or red rock used for building: *buildings built of granite*; *an old granite building.*

granny/grannie ['grani] *nc* (*inf*: *with cap when used as a name*) a grandmother.

grant [gra:nt] *vt* **1** (*formal*) to agree to (a request); to give a person (something asked for): *Would you grant me one favour*; *He granted the man permission to leave.* **2** (not *usu* used with **is, was** *etc* and **-ing**) to agree or admit (that something is true): *I grant (you) that it was a stupid thing to do.* – *nc* something, *usu* money, given for a particular purpose: *In Britain many students receive a grant in order to be able to study at university*; *a grant of land.*

'granted, *also* **'granting** (*often with* **that**) (even) if; assuming: *Granted that you are right, we will have to move fast.*

take for granted 1 to assume (that something is true, will happen *etc*) without checking: *I just took it for granted that you had been told about this.* **2** to treat (a person, thing *etc*) casually, without giving (him, it *etc*) much thought, attention or kindness: *I wish people would stop taking me for granted*; *People take electricity for granted until their supply is cut off.*

granule ['granju:l] *nc* (*formal*) a very small particle or grain (of something): *a granule of sugar.*

'granular *adj* (*tech*) made of tiny particles: *a granular substance*; *The substance is hard and granular.*

'granulated [-lei-] *adj* (*attrib*) broken into tiny particles: *granulated sugar.*

grape [greip] *nc* a green or black smooth-skinned eatable berry from which wine is made: *a bunch of grapes*; (*attrib*) *grape juice.*

'grapevine *nc* **1** (*fig*) an informal means of passing news, rumours *etc* from person to person *eg* in an office: *This isn't official but I did hear through the grapevine that he is leaving.* **2** a vine.

sour grapes saying or pretending that something is not worth having because one cannot obtain it: *He said he didn't want to be made the manager but it was just sour grapes.*

grapefruit ['greipfru:t] – *pls* **'grapefruit, 'grapefruits** – *ncu* (the flesh of) a large yellow-skinned fruit similar to an orange: *She had half a grapefruit for breakfast. Could you buy me four grapefruit?*; *Grapefruit is delicious for breakfast*; (*attrib*) *grapefruit juice.*

grapeshot ['greipʃot] *nu* small bullets which scatter when fired (*eg* from a cannon).

graph [graf] *nc* a diagram consisting of a line or lines drawn to show changes in some quantity (*eg* changes in temperature through the day, changes in prices over a year): *He has made a graph of this year's sales figures.*

'graphic *adj* (*formal*) **1** vivid; told with many details: *a graphic description of an accident*; *His description was most graphic.* **2** (*usu attrib*) of painting, drawing *etc*: *the graphic arts.* **'graphically** *adv.*

'graph paper *nu* paper covered in small squares, used for drawing graphs on.

graphite ['grafait] *nu* a form of carbon used in the leads of pencils.

grapple ['grapl] *vi* (*often with* **with**) **1** to grasp and fight (with a person *etc*): *The policeman grappled with the thief.* **2** (*fig*) to (try to) deal with (a problem *etc*) *usu* with some difficulty: *He enjoys grappling with mathematical problems.*

grasp [gra:sp] *vt* **1** to take hold of (a person, thing *etc*) by putting one's fingers or arm(s) round (him, it *etc*): *He grasped the thief firmly to stop him running away*; *He grasped the rope as it swung past him*; (*fig*) *He grasped the opportunity to ask for a higher salary.* **2** to understand: *I can't grasp what he's getting at.* – *See also* **grasp at** *below.* – *nc* (*no pl*) **1** a grip with one's hand *etc*: *Have you got a good grasp on that rope?*; (*fig*) *The country is in the grasp of a dictator.* **2** (*fig*) the power or ability to do (something): *The changing of that law is within his grasp.* **3** the ability to understand: *His ideas are quite beyond my grasp.*

'grasping *adj* greedy (*esp* for money): *He's just a grasping old man*; *He's mean and grasping.*

'grasp at *vt fus* **1** to attempt to take hold of (a person, thing *etc*): *The drowning man grasped at a branch.* **2** (*fig*) to accept (an opportunity *etc*) eagerly: *I'd grasp at any opportunity to see France again.*

grass [gra:s] **1** *nu* the green plant which covers fields, garden lawns *etc*: *This grass is in need of* *cutting.* **2** *nc* (*tech*) any species of grass, including also corn, reeds and bamboo: *He studies grasses.*

'**grassy** *adj* (*usu attrib*) covered with grass: *a grassy bank/slope.*

'**grasshopper** *nc* a type of insect which jumps and which makes a noise by rubbing its wings.

grass roots *n pl* (*inf*) the ordinary people in an association, trade union, country *etc* as opposed to those who take decisions: *There is some dissatisfaction at the grass roots about our union's policies*; (*attrib*) *a grass-roots movement.*

'**grass-snake** *nc* a harmless type of snake.

ˌ**grass-'widow** *nc* a wife whose husband is temporarily not living with her.

let the grass grow under one's feet to delay or waste time: *The Managing Director is not a man who lets the grass grow under his feet when there are decisions to be made.*

grate[1] [greit] *nc* a framework of iron bars for holding a fire in a fireplace.

grate[2] [greit] **1** *vt* to rub (cheese, vegetables *etc*) into small pieces by means of a grater. **2** *vi* (*often with* **on** (*formal*) **upon**) to irritate or annoy (someone): *His voice really grates on me.* **3** *vti* to make an unpleasant, grinding sound by rubbing against something else: *He grated his teeth together*; *The knife grated on the plate.*

'**grater** *nc* an instrument with a rough surface on which cheese, vegetables *etc* can be rubbed into small pieces.

'**grating**[1] *adj* (of sounds) unpleasant and grinding: *the grating noise of a knife scraping against metal*; *I find that noise grating.*

grateful ['greitful] *adj* (*usu pred with* **to** (someone), **for** (something)) feeling thankful; showing or giving thanks: *I am grateful to you for your help.*

'**gratefully** *adv*: *She accepted his offer of help gratefully.*

See also **gratitude, ingratitude, ungrateful**.

gratified ['gratifaid] *adj* (*formal*: *usu pred*) pleased: *I was very gratified at the way my suggestions were received*; *I was gratified to see my suggestions received so well.*

ˌ**gratifi'cation** [-fi-] (*formal*) **1** *nu* the state of feeling pleased or satisfied: *At least I have the gratification of knowing he was wrong.* **2** *nu* the act of pleasing or satisfying (a person, a person's desires *etc*). **3** *nc* something which gratifies (a person, a person's desires *etc*): *The feeling of doing something useful is one of the main gratifications of this job.*

'**gratify** ['gratifai] *vt* (*formal*) **1** (*with* **at** *or* **with**) to please (a person). **2** to satisfy (a person's desires *etc*).

'**gratifying** *adj* causing (a person) to feel pleasure or satisfaction: *a gratifying result*; *The response was most gratifying.*

grating[1] *see* **grate**[2].

grating[2] ['greitiŋ] *nc* a framework of iron, wooden *etc* bars, lying parallel to or across each other, which is placed over *eg* a window in order to prevent people climbing through it: *She caught the heel of her shoe in a grating in the road.*

gratis ['gratis] *adv* (*formal*) for nothing; without payment: *That's such a small job, I'll do it gratis.*

gratitude ['gratitju:d] *nu* the state of feeling grateful: *I wish there was some way of showing my gratitude for all you have done for me.*

See also **ingratitude**.

gratuity [grə'tjuəti] *nc* **1** (*formal*) a small sum of money given to *eg* a waiter or waitress as a reward for good service; a tip. **2** a sum of money given to a soldier, an employee *etc* when he retires or leaves his employment: *He hopes to start a bookshop with his gratuity.*

gra'tuitous *adj* (*formal*: *usu attrib*) **1** (*derog*) done, said *etc* without good reason or excuse or when not wanted: *gratuitous insults.* **2** done, given *etc* without payment: *gratuitous advice.* **gra'tuitously** *adv.* **gra'tuitousness** *nu.*

grave[1] [greiv] *nc* a plot of ground, or the hole dug in it, in which a dead person or animal is buried: *He laid flowers on the grave*; *The coffin was lowered into the grave.*

'**gravedigger** *nc* a person whose job is digging graves.

'**gravestone** *nc* a stone placed at a grave on which the dead person's name *etc* is written.

'**graveyard** *nc* a place where the dead are buried.

at the 'graveside beside (a person's) grave: *There was a man in black standing at the graveside.*

have one foot in the grave (*facet*) to be very old or near to death: *That young woman thinks anyone over forty years old has one foot in the grave.*

turn in one's grave (*fig*) (of someone who is dead) to be disturbed in one's rest by displeasing events in the world of living people: *Your grandfather would turn in his grave if he could see you acting like that.*

grave[2] [greiv] *adj* **1** (*attrib*) important: *A grave responsibility rests on your shoulders*; *There are grave decisions to be made.* **2** serious, worrying or dangerous: *grave news*; *a grave situation*; *The news from the battlefront is grave indeed.* **3** serious or sad: *He always looks so very grave*; *He wore a grave expression.*

'**gravely** *adv*: *The doctor looked gravely at the badly injured child.*

'**graveness** *nu*: *The graveness of his expression made us aware of how bad the situation was.*

'**gravity** ['gra-] *nu*: *The gravity of the situation was clear to us all.*

grave[3] [gra:v] *nc* (*also* **grave accent**) a mark (`) over a vowel in some languages to show its pronunciation (*eg* **è** in French).

gravel ['gravəl] *nu* very small stones: *We bought six bags of gravel for the garden path.*

graven ['greivən] *adj* (*old*) carved: *a graven image* (= an idol).

gravity[1] *see* **grave**[2].

gravity[2] ['gravəti] *nu* the force which attracts things towards the Earth and causes them to fall to the ground.

'**gravitate** [-teit] *vi* (*formal*) to move towards (a person, place *etc*) as if attracted by some force: *The crowds gravitated to*(*wards*) *the scene of the accident.*

ˌ**gravi'tation** *nu* (*formal*) **1** the act or process of gravitating: *the gravitation of people from the country to the towns.* **2** the force of attraction between two objects *eg* gravity.

gravy ['greivi] *ncu* (a sauce made from) the juices from meat that is cooking: *She made some gravy to pour over the roast beef*; *Add some wine to the gravy.*

gray *see* **grey**.

graze[1] [greiz] *vi* (of animals) to eat grass *etc* which is growing: *The sheep were grazing quietly in the field*; *The cows were grazing on the clover.*

'**grazing** *nu* the act of feeding (animals) on grass which is growing: *This field of grass will be kept for grazing, the others will be ploughed for crops.*

graze[2] [greiz] *vt* **1** to scrape the skin from (a part of the body): *I've grazed my hand/myself on that stone wall.* **2** to touch (something) lightly in passing: *The bullet grazed the car.* – *nc* the mark or slight wound caused by grazing a part of the body: *That's a nasty graze you've got on your hand.*

grease [gri:s] *nu* **1** soft, thick, animal fat: *A lot of grease comes out of a duck when it is being cooked.* **2** any thick, oily substance: *Put some grease on the hinge of that door to stop it squeaking.* – *vt* to cover (something) with grease; to put some grease on or in (something): *The mechanic greased the car's axle.*

'**greasy** *adj* **1** of or like grease: *a greasy substance*; *This food is rather greasy.* **2** covered in grease: *Oily hands are greasy*; *Don't wipe your greasy hands on that towel.* **3** slippery, as if covered in grease: *greasy roads*; *The roads are greasy.* **4** (*inf*) insincerely friendly or flattering: *a greasy character*; *He's too greasy for me.* '**greasiness** *nu.*

'**greasepaint** *nu* a kind of make-up used by actors *etc.*

great [greit] *adj* **1** (*usu attrib*) of a better quality, ability *etc* than average; worthy of respect; important or of high rank; (having) more (of anything) than average: *a great writer*; *They are great friends*; *a great wine*; *Churchill was a great man.* **2** (*attrib*) very large, loud *etc*: larger, louder *etc* than average: *There was a great crowd of people at the football match*; *There was a great noise of mooing coming from the cowshed.* **3** (*usu attrib*) of a high degree; to a great extent: *He's in great pain*; *The pain is too great to bear*; *a great deal of trouble*; *Take great care of that book.* **4** (*inf*: *attrib*) used to emphasize other words describing size: *a great big stick*; *A great many people believe in astrology.* **5** (*attrib*) describing something which is done often and which the speaker *usu* approves of: *He's a great reader* (= He reads a lot). **6** (*inf*) very good, very pleasant *etc*: *We had a great time at the party*; *That's great!* **7** (*inf*: *sometimes with* **at** *when pred*) clever and expert: *John's great at football*; *He's a great footballer.* **8** (*attrib*) most important: *The great attraction in this museum is their model Roman fort.*

'**greater** *adj* (*attrib*) (used with the names of certain cities) consisting of the city and its suburbs: *Greater London.*

'**greatly** *adv*: *I was greatly impressed by the nursing at the hospital.*

'**greatness** *nu*: *How do you explain Shakespeare's greatness as a dramatist?*

'**greatcoat** *nc* (*esp Brit*) a heavy overcoat: *The soldier wore a khaki greatcoat.*

Great Britain *see* Appendix 2.

the Great War World War I (1914–1918).

great- [greit] (*in cmpds*: *with* **uncle, aunt, nephew, niece,** and relatives in **grand-**) separated (from a person) by one generation more than (an uncle, grandfather *etc*): *A great-uncle is one's father's or mother's uncle*; *a great-grandchild.*

Greece *see* Appendix 2.

greed [gri:d] *nu* a (too) great desire for food, money *etc*: *You have already eaten enough. Taking another cake is just sheer greed*; *greed for money.*

'**greedy** *adj.* '**greedily** *adv.* '**greediness** *nu.*

Greek [gri:k]: **it is (all) Greek to me** (*inf*) I don't understand: *The doctors were discussing my illness, but what they were saying was Greek to me.*

See also Appendix 2.

green [gri:n] *adj* **1** of the colour of growing grass or the leaves of most plants: *a green hat*; *Our new car is green.* **2** covered with grass *etc*: *green fields.* **3** not ripe: *green bananas*; *Those tomatoes are too green to eat.* **4** (*inf*) without training or experience; easily fooled: *He's green but he'll soon learn what to do*; *a green apprentice*; *Only someone as green as you would believe a story like that.* **5** (of a person's face) pale; looking as if one is about to be sick (*eg* because of seasickness): *The boat was rocking so violently that half the passengers turned green*; (*fig*) *He was green with envy* (= very jealous). **6** not dried: *green tobacco.* – **1** *ncu* (any shade of) the colour of grass or the leaves of plants: *the green of the trees in summer*; *This material comes in a variety of greens.* **2** *ncu* something (*eg* material, paint *etc*) green in colour: *I've used up all my green.* **3** *nc* (*often in cmpds*) an area of grass: *a village green*; *a drying-green* (= a piece of ground where clothes are hung out to dry). **4** *nc* one of *usu* eighteen flat areas of grass on a golf course each with a small hole in the centre into which golfers try to hit a ball.

ˌ**greenery** *nu* (the leaves of) green plants: *Add some greenery to that vase of flowers.*

'**greenish** *adj* fairly green; close to green: *She was wearing a greenish dress*; *Her hat was greenish in colour, not blue.*

'**greenness** *nu.*

greens *n pl* green vegetables: *Children are often told that they must eat their greens.*

'**green belt** *nc* open land surrounding a town or city: *You will not get permission to build houses in that area – it is a green belt.*

'**greenfly** – *pl* '**greenfly** – *nc* (*Brit*) a type of small, green insect; the aphis: *The leaves of this rose tree have been eaten by greenfly.* – *See also* **aphid**.

'**greengage** [-geidʒ] *nc* a greenish-yellow type of plum: (*attrib*) *greengage jam.*

'**greengrocer** *nc* **1** a person who sells fruit and vegetables: *Her father is a greengrocer.* **2** a greengrocer's shop: *I'm going to the greengrocer to buy some onions.*

'**greengrocer's** *nc* a greengrocer's shop: *I'm going to the greengrocer's.*

'**greenhouse** *nc* a building *usu* of glass, in which plants are grown: *In most parts of Britain you can grow peaches only in a greenhouse.*

have green fingers, (*Amer*) **a green thumb** (*inf*) to be skilled at gardening: *My mother's garden is beautiful – she has green fingers.*

the green light (*inf*) permission to begin (doing) something: *We can't start until we get the green light*; *We can't start until he gives us the green light.*

greet [gri:t] *vt* **1** to welcome or say 'Hello', 'How do you do' *etc* to (a person): *She was waiting at the door to greet me when I arrived.* **2** (*formal*) to react to (a suggestion *etc*): *His proposals were greeted with cheers/dismay.* **3** to meet the eyes, ears *etc* of (a person): *When he opened the door, he could hardly believe the sight that greeted him*; *A smell of frying bacon greeted him when he went into the kitchen.*

'**greeting** *ncu* friendly words or actions used to welcome someone or when meeting someone: *One should always say some polite greeting to someone one has just met*; *a few words of greeting.*

'**greetings** *n pl* a friendly message: *We send Christmas greetings to our friends.*

gregarious [gri'geəriəs] *adj* **1** liking the company of other people: *a gregarious person*; *She is very gregarious and hates to be alone.* **2** (of animals, birds

etc) living in groups: *Geese are gregarious (birds)*.
gre'gariousness *nu*.

grenade [grə'neid] *nc* a small bomb, *esp* one thrown by hand (a **'handgrenade**).

grew *see* **grow**.

grey, (*esp Amer*) **gray** [grei] *adj* **1** of a mixture of colour between black and white: *grey eyes*; *a grey dress*; *Her dress is grey and red.* **2** dull; dismal: *a grey day*; *It's very grey outside – I think it's going to rain.* **3** grey-haired: *He's turning/going grey.* – **1** *ncu* (any shade of) a colour between black and white: *The pattern was printed in a variety of greys*; *Grey is rather a dull colour.* **2** *ncu* something (*eg* material, paint *etc*) grey in colour: *I never wear grey.* **3** *nu* dull light: *the grey of a rainy winter's morning.* – *vi* to become grey or grey-haired: *He used to have very black hair but he is greying a bit now.*
'greyish *adj* fairly grey; close to grey: *Is he ill? His face looks greyish*; *a greyish dress.*
'greyness *nu*.

greyhound ['greihaund] *nc* a breed of dog which can run very fast: *Does he keep greyhounds as pets or does he breed them for racing?*; (*attrib*) *He likes going to the greyhound racing.*

grid [grid] *nc* **1** a set of vertical and horizontal lines drawn on a map (*eg* to help a person find a place on that map). **2** (*often with cap*) a system of wires that carry electricity throughout Britain: *the National Grid.* **3** (*often in cmpds*) a framework of iron bars: *a cattle-grid* (= a grid set over a hole at the entrance to a field *etc* to prevent cattle leaving the field).

griddle ['gridl], (*also, esp Scottish*) **girdle** ['gəːdl] *nc* a flat iron plate for baking cakes on over a fire or on top of a stove.

gridiron ['gridaiən] *nc* a frame of iron bars for cooking (*eg* meat) over a fire.

grief [griːf] *ncu* (*formal*) (something or someone that causes a person to feel) great sorrow or unhappiness: *She was filled with grief at the news of her sister's death*; *Your wickedness is a great (source of) grief to me.*
'grief-stricken *adj* (*liter or formal*) overcome by a feeling of very great grief: *He was grief-stricken at the death of his wife*; *the grief-stricken widow.*
come to grief (*inf*) to be unsuccessful, suffer some bad luck *etc*: *The project came to grief*; *You'll come to grief if you go on like that.*
See also **grieve**.

grievance ['griːvəns] *nc* a cause or reason for complaint: *The workers gave the directors a list of their grievances.*

grieve [griːv] **1** *vt* (*formal*) to cause (a person) to feel great sorrow: *Your wickedness grieves me deeply.* **2** *vi* (*sometimes with* **for**) to feel sorrow (*eg* because a person has died or gone away): *He was still grieving for his wife five years after she died.*
'grievous *adj* (*formal*: *attrib*) severe or very bad; causing a lot of suffering: *grievous pain*; (*legal*) *He was found guilty of inflicting grievous bodily harm* (= very serious injuries) *on the old man.*
See also **grief**.

grill[1] [gril] *vt* **1** (*Brit*) to cook (*eg* meat) directly under heat (on a gas or electric cooker): *Shall I grill the chops or fry them?* **2** (*inf*) to question (a person) closely, *usu* for a long time: *The police grilled the man they thought was the murderer.* – *nc* **1** the part of a cooker used for grilling: *Put the meat under the grill.* **2** a frame of metal bars for grilling food on. **3** (*Brit*) (a dish of) grilled food: *a mixed grill* (= a plate of grilled steak, bacon, liver, tomato, sausage *etc*). **4** (*also* **'grill-room**) a restaurant in a hotel *etc* which specializes in grilled food.

grille, grill[2] [gril] *nc* a framework of metal bars over a window, door *etc*: *a grille on the door of a prison cell.*

grim [grim] *adj* **1** (*usu attrib*) terrible; horrible; very unpleasant: *The soldiers had a grim task looking for bodies in the wrecked houses*; (*fig*) *a grim necessity.* **2** cruel; without mercy: *He is grim and ruthless*; *The pirate captain was a grim man to work for.* **3** angry; fierce-looking: *The boss looks a bit grim this morning*; *The headmaster wore a grim expression.* **4** (*attrib*) unwilling to stop or give in: *He held on with grim determination.* **5** (*inf*: *pred*) slightly unwell: *I feel a bit grim this morning – I shouldn't have drunk so much wine last night.*
'grimness *nu*.
'grimly *adv*: *He held on grimly to the steering-wheel/to his opinion.*
like grim death (*inf*) firmly; with great determination: *He held on to the rope like grim death.*

grimace [gri'meis, (*Amer*) 'griməs] *nc* a twisting of the face: *The child made a grimace behind the teacher's back.* – *vi* to make a grimace: *He grimaced with pain as the doctor touched his wound.*

grime [graim] *nu* dirt (*esp* sooty dirt) which is difficult to remove: *The chimney-sweep was covered in grime.*
'grimy *adj* covered in grime: *grimy buildings*; *buildings grimy from the smoke of the factories.*

grin [grin] – *pt, ptp* **grinned** – **1** *vi* to smile broadly: *The children grinned happily as the photographer took their photograph.* **2** *vt* to express (pleasure *etc*) by grinning: *She grinned her satisfaction at the result.* – *nc* a broad smile: *a grin of happiness.*
grin and bear it to put up with something unpleasant without complaining: *He doesn't like his present job but he'll just have to grin and bear it till he finds another.*

grind [graind] – *pt, ptp* **ground** [graund] – **1** *vt* to crush (something) into powder or small pieces, or to produce (something) in this way: *This machine grinds coffee*; *This machine grinds wheat into flour*; *This machine grinds flour.* **2** *vt* to sharpen (knives, scissors *etc*) by rubbing (*eg* on a grindstone). **3** *vti* to (cause something to) rub together, *usu* producing an unpleasant noise: *He grinds his teeth*; *You can hear the machine's gears grinding.* **4** *vt* to rub (something) into or against something else, or to crush (something) in this way: *He ground his heel into the earth*; *He ground the flowers into the earth with his heel*; (*fig*) *The tyrant ground the faces of his people into the dirt* (= He treated them cruelly). – *See also* **grind down, grind out, grind up** *below.* – *nu* (*inf*) boring hard work: *Learning vocabulary is a bit of a grind.*
'grinder *nc* (*usu in cmpds*) a person or machine that grinds: *a coffee-grinder*; *a knife-grinder.*
'grinding *adj* (*usu attrib*) **1** making a noise like or because of something grinding: *The train came to a grinding stop.* **2** severe: *grinding poverty.*
'grindstone *nc* a wheel-shaped stone that turns, used for sharpening knives *etc.* – *See also* **keep (some)one's nose to the grindstone** *below.*
back to the grindstone (*inf facet*) back to work: *Lunchtime is over – now it's back to the grindstone.*
grind down *vt sep* (*usu fig*) to crush: *In spite of their brave resistance, the dictator finally ground*

them down by his constant tyranny; The people were ground down by heavy taxes; She was ground down by poverty.

grind out *vt sep* (*inf*) to (continue to) produce (something) over a period of time, often badly: *He was grinding out a tune; He was grinding out statements of his party's political doctrine.*

grind up *vt sep* to grind (something) into powder or small pieces: *This machine grinds up these rocks into powder; It grinds them up quickly.*

keep (some)one's nose to the grindstone to (force someone to) work hard, without stopping: *The new boss does hardly any work although he keeps his workers' noses to the grindstone.*

grip [grip] – *pt, ptp* **gripped** – *vti* to take a firm hold (of or on something): *He gripped his stick; The car's tyres didn't grip on the wet road and it skidded; (fig) The speaker gripped (the attention of) his audience.* – *nc* **1** a firm hold; the power or way of holding: *He had a firm grip on his stick; That wrestler is using a rather odd grip; He has a very strong grip; (fig) The ship was in the grip of the storm.* **2** a bag used by travellers for carrying clothes *etc*: *He carried his sports equipment in a large grip.* **3** (*inf*) understanding: *He has a good grip of the details of this project.*

'**gripping** *adj* which holds the attention: *a gripping story; I found his accounts of the war gripping.*

get a 'grip (on oneself) to stop being foolish, afraid *etc*: *She started to panic but managed to get a grip on herself.*

get/come to grips with to deal with (a problem, difficulty *etc*): *You must get to grips with your financial problems or you will go bankrupt.*

lose one's grip to lose control or understanding (of something): *It's time the manager retired – he's losing his grip.*

gripe [graip] *vi* (*inf*) to complain: *Don't listen to his complaints – he's always griping (about being badly paid).* – *nc* (*inf*) a complaint.

grisly ['grizli] *adj* horrible: *A grisly sight met their eyes; The sight of the murdered body was too grisly for words.*

grist [grist]: **grist to the mill** something which brings profit or advantage (to a person *etc*): *Selling these matches only brings in a little profit, but it's all grist to the mill.*

gristle ['grisl] *nu* a tough, rubbery substance found in meat: *There's too much gristle in this steak.*

'**gristly** *adj* like or full of gristle: *This meat is too gristly; tough, gristly meat.*

grit [grit] *nu* **1** very small pieces of stone: *She's got a piece of grit in her eye; Grit is spread on icy roads to prevent cars skidding.* **2** (*inf*) courage: *He's got a lot of grit.* – *v* – *pt, ptp* '**gritted** – *vt* **1** to spread grit on (roads *etc*): *They are gritting the icy roads.* **2** to keep (the teeth) tightly closed together: *He gritted his teeth to stop himself crying out in pain.*

'**gritty** *adj* like, covered with, or containing, grit: *a gritty substance; The surface of the road is gritty.* '**grittiness** *nu.*

grizzly ['grizli] *nc* (*usu* **grizzly bear**) a large fierce N American bear.

groan [groun] *vi* **1** (of people) to produce a deep sound (because of pain, unhappiness *etc*): *He groaned when he heard that he had failed his exam; The injured man groaned with pain all night.* **2** (of things) to make a similar noise: *The hut groaned in the strong wind; (fig) The table was groaning with food* (= there was a great deal of food on it). – *nc* a deep sound produced because of pain, unhappiness *etc*: *He gave a groan of despair on hearing of his failure.*

grocer ['grousə] *nc* **1** a person who sells certain kinds of food and household supplies (*eg* tea, sugar, soap): *Our grocer has just died.* **2** a grocer's shop: *Our local grocer has closed.*

'**grocer's** *nc* a grocer's shop: *Could you get me a kilo of sugar at the grocer's?*

'**groceries** *n pl* food *etc* sold in a grocer's shop.

'**grocery** *nc* (*usu attrib*) a grocer's shop: *a grocery store; the grocery business.*

groggy ['grogi] *adj* (*inf*: *pred*) weak and walking unsteadily (because of a blow on the head, illness, drugs *etc*): *I'm not seriously hurt – I just feel a bit groggy.* '**grogginess** *nu.*

groin [groin] *nc* the part of the front of the body where the inner part of the thigh joins the rest of the body.

groom [gru:m] *nc* **1** a person who looks after horses: *He is employed as a groom at the stables.* **2** a bridegroom: *The bride and groom walked down the aisle.* – *vt* **1** to clean, brush *etc* a horse's coat: *The horses were being groomed for the horse show.* **2** to make (a person or animal) clean and neat: *The monkeys sat in the trees grooming each other.* **3** to prepare (a person) for some task, purpose *etc*: *He's being groomed as a possible successor to our head of department.*

well-groomed *see* **well**.

groove [gru:v] *nc* a long, narrow cut made in the surface of something: *The needle of a record-player moves along the groove in the record.*

grooved *adj* having grooves: *The glass dish has grooved edges.*

grope [group] *vti* (*often with* **for**) to search for something by feeling with one's hands, *eg* when blind or in the dark: *He groped his way through the smoke-filled room; He groped for the door in the dark; (fig) He groped for the word he wanted.*

gross[1] [grous] *adj* **1** (*attrib*) very bad; obvious: *gross errors/indecency.* **2** (*usu attrib*) rude or vulgar: *gross behaviour/language.* **3** too fat: *a large, gross woman; She is so gross!* **4** (*attrib*) entire or total: *My gross salary is the total salary I receive before tax etc is taken away; The gross weight of a parcel is the total weight of the contents, the box, the wrapping etc.* – *vt* to make a gross profit of (a sum of money): *We gross £50 000 a year* (= We make a profit of £50 000 before we take off costs). – *nc* the total amount (of several things added together).

'**grossly** *adv* **1** very (of things one considers to be bad or undesirable): *I'm grossly underpaid in this job.* **2** (*formal*) in a rude or vulgar way: *He behaved grossly at the party.*

'**grossness** *nu* rudeness (of behaviour, language *etc*).

gross[2] [grous] – *pls* '**grosses**, (after a number or word signifying a quantity) **gross** – *nc* (*old*) twelve dozen; 144: *a gross/two gross of pencils; We sell pencils in dozens and grosses.*

grotesque [grə'tesk] *adj* (*formal*) very odd or strange-looking: *The sculptor carved a grotesque figure; You look grotesque in those clothes.* **gro'tesquely** *adv.* **gro'tesqueness** *nu.*

grotto ['grotou] – *pl* '**grotto(e)s** – *nc* a cave, *usu* an artificial one in a park *etc.*

grouch [grautʃ] *vi* (*inf*) to grumble or complain (about something): *He's quite happy in his job although he's always grouching (about it).* – *nc* (*inf*) **1** a person who grumbles or complains: *He's just* *an old grouch.* **2** a complaint: *I'm tired of his grouches.* ˈ**grouchy** *adj.*

ground[1] *see* **grind**.

ground[2] [graund] **1** *nu* (any part of) the solid surface of the Earth: *The dead man was lying on the ground*; *Seeds are planted in the ground*; *high ground*; *marshy ground.* **2** *nc* (*often in cmpds*) a piece of land used for some purpose: *a sports-ground*; *a football ground.* – **1** *vt* (*formal*: *usu in passive*: *with* **on**) to base (an argument, complaint *etc*) on (something): *His argument is grounded on a series of wrong assumptions.* **2** *vt* (*usu in passive*: *with* **in**) to teach (a person) the basic facts of a subject: *He has been well grounded in mathematics.* **3** *vti* to (cause a ship to) hit the seabed or shore and remain stuck. **4** *vt* to prevent (an aeroplane, pilot) from flying: *He was a pilot in the air force but was grounded because of an eye injury*; *All planes have been grounded because of the fog.*

ˈ**grounding** *ncu* (*no pl*) the teaching of the basic facts of a subject: *We give our pupils a good grounding in mathematics*; *He hasn't had any grounding in Latin grammar.*

ˈ**groundless** *adj* (*formal*: *usu pred*) without reason: *Your fears are groundless.*

grounds *n pl* **1** the garden or land round a large house *etc*: *They walked round the castle grounds.* **2** good reasons: *Have you any grounds for calling him a liar?*; *His wife divorced him on the grounds of his cruelty.* **3** the powder which remains in a cup (*eg* of coffee) which one has drunk: *coffee grounds.*

ground floor *nc* the rooms of a building which are at street level: *My office is on the ground floor*; (*attrib*) *He lives in a ground-floor flat.*

groundnut *see* **peanut**.

ˈ**groundsheet** *nc* a waterproof sheet spread on the ground *eg* in a tent by campers *etc.*

ˈ**groundsman** [ˈgraundz-] *nc* a man who takes care of *eg* a sports field: *He is a groundsman at Lord's cricket ground.*

ˈ**groundwork** *nu* the first stages of work on anything before the main work is started: *Producing a dictionary needs a great deal of groundwork.*

break new/fresh ground to deal with a new subject for the first time: *Our firm is breaking new ground with this project.*

cover ground **1** to travel (some distance): *We have a lot of ground to cover today.* **2** to do or deal with (a piece of work, a subject of discussion *etc*): *We've covered a lot of ground at this morning's meeting.*

gain ground *see* **gain**.

get (something) off the ground to get (a project *etc*) started: *We must try to get the campaign off the ground by the middle of next week.*

give ground to lose ground (*def 1*).

hold/stand one's ground to refuse to move back or retreat when attacked: *Although many were killed, the soldiers held their ground*; (*fig*) *Although many people criticized his theories, he held his ground.*

lose ground **1** to (be forced to) move back or retreat: *The general sent in reinforcements when he saw that his troops were losing ground.* **2** To lose one's advantage; to lose one's good, strong or leading position: *The leader of the political party said that he was worried because his party was losing ground.*

shift one's ground (*fig*) to change one's opinions, arguments *etc*: *It's impossible to prove him wrong because he keeps shifting his ground.*

suit down to the ground *see* **suit**.

group [gru:p] *nc* **1** (*with a pl verb when used with* **all**) a number of persons or things together: *There was a group of boys standing at the corner of the street*; *This group of chemicals all behave in the same way.* **2** a group of people who play or sing together: *a jazz/pop group*; *a folk group* (= people who play folk music); *Did the British group win the song contest?* – *vti* to form into a group or groups: *The pupils were grouped according to their ability in French*; *The children grouped round the teacher.* – *See also* **group together** *below.*

group captain *nc* (*with cap, and often abbrev* **Gp. Capt.**, *when written in titles*) in the British air force, (a person of) the rank next above wing commander: *He is now a group captain*; *He was promoted to group captain*; *Group Captain Andrews.* – *See also* Appendix 3.

group together *vi, vt sep* to form into a group or groups: *We should group together all the books by the same author*; *Group these books together*; *Dictionaries and encyclopedias can be grouped together under the heading of reference books.*

grouse[1] [graus] – *pl* **grouse** – *nc* a kind of game bird hunted on moors and hills, *esp* in Scotland: *He shoots grouse and pheasants.*

grouse[2] [graus] *vi* (*inf*) to complain: *He's grousing about his job again.* – *nc* (*inf*) a complaint: *If you have any grouses tell the boss about them.*

grove [grouv] **1** *nc* (*liter*) a small group of trees. **2** *n* (*with cap*) a word used in the names of certain roads or streets: *His address is 21 Aspen Grove.*

grovel [ˈgrovl] – *pt, ptp* ˈ**grovelled**, (*Amer*) ˈ**groveled** – *vi* to make oneself (too) humble, *usu* because one wants (something, or someone to do something); to ask or beg (for something) with (too) great humility, respect or fear: *If you want an increase in salary, you'll have to grovel (for it).*

ˈ**groveller** *nc.*

grow [grou] – *pt* **grew** [gru:] : *ptp* **grown** – **1** *vi* (of plants) to have life; to develop: *Carrots grow well in this soil*; *There are mushrooms growing in the middle of the lawn.* **2** *vi* to become bigger, longer *etc*: *Hasn't your little girl grown!*; *My hair has grown too long – I must get it cut*; *Our friendship grew as time went on*; *Their influence has grown considerably.* **3** *vt* to cause or allow (plants, hair *etc*) to grow: *I intend to grow carrots in this part of the garden*; *He has grown a beard.* **4** *vi* (*often with* **into**) (of people *etc*) to develop into or become (something) while becoming older: *Your daughter has grown into a beautiful woman*; *She has grown to be a beautiful woman*; *He has grown to be a horrible little boy.* **5** *vi* to become: *It's growing dark – I think we ought to go home*; *The wind grew stronger*; *She's growing old.* **6** *vi* gradually to reach a state where one does, feels, thinks *etc* (something): *She grew to hate her husband*; *You'll grow to like this work eventually.* – *See also* **grow** *in phrases below.*

ˈ**grower** *nc* **1** (*often in cmpds*) a person who grows (plants *etc*): *a tomato-grower.* **2** a plant that grows (well): *These tomatoes are good growers.*

grown *adj* adult: *a grown man*; *He is fully grown now.*

-grown (*in cmpds*) developed: *A full-grown Alsatian is a large dog.*

growth [-θ] **1** *nu* the act or process of growing, increasing, developing *etc*: *the growth of trade unionism.* **2** *nu* the state of being developed *etc*: *When will your dog reach full growth?* **3** *nc* (*no pl*) something that has grown: *The first thing he did when he was rescued was shave off his week's growth of beard.* **4** *ncu* the amount by which something grows: *We use this stick to measure the growth of these plants.* **5** *nc* something unwanted (*esp* a cancer) which grows in or on the body: *a cancerous growth*; *The surgeon removed a growth from her neck.*

'**grown-'up** *nc* an adult; a person who is fully grown: *The little girl said she wasn't allowed to cross the street unless there was a grown-up with her.* – *See also* **grown up, grow up** *below.*

grow into *vt fus* to become big enough to wear (clothes *etc*): *These shoes are a little too big for him, but he'll grow into them.* – *See also* **grow** (*def 4*).

grown up mature; (like an) adult; fully grown: *Her children are grown up now*; (*attrib*) *a grown-up daughter.* – *See also* **grown-up, grow up**.

'**grow on** (*formal*) **upon** *vt fus* to gradually become liked by (someone): *I didn't like the painting at first, but it has grown on me.*

grow out of *vt fus* **1** to become too big to wear (clothes *etc*): *He has grown out of that coat.* **2** to stop doing (something) as one grows older and becomes an adult: *He'll eventually grow out of sucking his thumb.*

grow up *vi* **1** to become an adult: *I'm going to be an engine-driver when I grow up.* **2** to behave the way an adult ought to behave: *I do wish he would grow up and stop behaving like a five-year old.* – *See also* **grown-up, grown up** *above.*

growl [graul] **1** *vi* (of dogs) to make a deep, rough sound: *The dog growled angrily (at the postman).* **2** *vi* (of people) to make a similar sound in order to show or showing anger *etc*: *He has a headache because he drank too much whisky last night – that's why he's growling at everyone today.* **3** *vt* to say or show (something) with a growl: *He growled his displeasure*; *He growled out a command.* – *nc* a deep, rough sound: *The dog looked up with a growl*; *The old man gave an angry growl.*

grown, growth *see* **grow**.

grub [grʌb] **1** *nc* the form of an insect after it hatches from its egg: *A caterpillar is a grub.* **2** *nu* (*sl*) food: *Have we enough grub to eat?* – *v* – *pt, ptp* **grubbed** – *vi* (*often with* **around, away** *etc*) to search (for something) by digging: *The pigs were grubbing around for roots*; (*fig*) *He was grubbing around among the old books in the library.*

grub out/up *vt sep* to find or remove (something) by digging.

grubby ['grʌbi] *adj* (*inf*) dirty: *a grubby little boy*; *Wash your hands – they're grubby!* '**grubbiness** *nu.*

grudge [grʌdʒ] *vt* **1** to be unwilling to do, give *etc* (something); to do give *etc* (something) unwillingly: *I grudge wasting time on this, but I suppose I'll have to do it*; *She grudges the dog even the little food she gives it.* **2** to be annoyed with someone who has done, got *etc* (something) which one feels is not deserved: *I grudge him his success.* – *nc* a feeling of anger, dislike *etc*: *He has a grudge against me*; *He bears me a grudge because I got the job he wanted.*

'**grudging** *adj* (*usu attrib*) said, done *etc* unwillingly: *a grudging admission*; *grudging admiration.* '**grudgingly** *adv.*

gruel ['gruəl] *nu* a thin mixture of oatmeal boiled in water.

gruelling, (*Amer*) **grueling** ['gruəliŋ] *adj* exhausting: *a gruelling race*; *I find this heat gruelling.*

gruesome ['gru:səm] *adj* horrible: *a gruesome sight*; *I find the sight of blood gruesome.*

gruff [grʌf] *adj* **1** (of a person's voice) deep and rough: *His voice is low and gruff*; *a gruff voice.* **2** (of a person's manner) rough; (seeming to be) unfriendly: *a gruff old man*; *He's a bit gruff, but really very kind.* '**gruffly** *adv.* '**gruffness** *nu.*

grumble ['grʌmbl] *vi* **1** to complain in a bad-tempered way: *He's grumbling about his wages again*; *He grumbled at the way he had been treated.* **2** to make a low and deep sound: *Thunder grumbled in the distance.* – **1** *nc* a complaint made in a bad-tempered way: *I have to listen to all their grumbles.* **2** *nu* a low, deep sound: *the grumble of thunder.*

grumpy ['grʌmpi] *adj* (*inf*) cross; bad-tempered: *The boss is a bit grumpy today*; *a grumpy old man.* '**grumpily** *adv.* '**grumpiness** *nu.*

grunt [grʌnt] **1** *vi* (of pigs) to make a low, rough sound. **2** *vi* (of people) to make a sound like a pig. **3** *vt* (of people) to say (something) in a way that sounds like grunting: *He grunted that he was too busy to talk to me*; *He grunted his agreement.* – *nc* **1** a low, rough sound made by pigs. **2** a similar sound made by people: *He gave a grunt to show his disapproval.*

guarantee [garən'ti:] **1** *ncu* a (*usu* written) statement by the maker (of a car, watch, camera *etc*) that something will work for a certain period of time and that it will be repaired or replaced free of charge if it breaks down within that time: *This guarantee is valid for one year*; *The manufacturers will have to repair that watch free of charge – it's still under guarantee.* **2** *nc* (*fig*) a thing that makes something likely or certain: *There is no guarantee that I'll be able to come*; *Ability is no guarantee of success*; *It is no guarantee against failure.* **3** *nc* something valuable, *eg* money, which will be handed over if a promise, contract *etc* is broken: *£500 would be sufficient guarantee.* **4** *nc* a promise to pay money on behalf of another person if that person fails to pay money he has promised to pay. **5** *nc* a person who gives such a promise; a guarantor: *I'll act as guarantee for you buying that car.* – *vt* **1** (*often with* **against**) to act as, or give, a guarantee: *This watch is guaranteed for six months.* **2** (*fig*) to promise something; to state that something is true, definite *etc*: *I can't guarantee that what he told me is correct.*

ˌ**guaran'tor** *nc* a person who gives a guarantee (*def 4*): *His father is acting as his guarantor.*

guard [ga:d] **1** *vt* to protect (a person, thing *etc*) from danger or attack: *The soldiers were guarding the king/palace.* **2** *vt* to prevent (a person) escaping: *The soldiers guarded their prisoners.* **3** *vi* (*formal*: *with* **against**) to try to prevent (something) by being careful: *Check your work thoroughly in order to guard against mistakes.* – **1** *nc* a person or number of people whose job is to protect (a person, thing *etc*) from danger or attack: *There was a guard round the king/palace.* **2** *nc* a person or number of people whose job is to prevent (a person) escaping: *There was a guard with the prisoner every hour of the day.* **3** *nc* (*Amer* **conductor**) a person in change of a train who *usu* travels at the back of the train. **4** *nu* the state or duty of protecting (a person, thing *etc*) from danger, attack, escape *etc*: *There were six soldiers on guard round the tent.* **5** *nu* (in boxing, cricket *etc*) a position of defence. **6** *nc* something which serves to protect a person *etc* from heat, flames, injury *etc*: *Put a guard* (= fire-guard) *in front of the fire in case a bit of coal falls out.*

'**guarded** *adj* cautious: *He gave guarded replies to their questions*; *His replies were rather guarded.* '**guardedly** *adv.* '**guardedness** *nu.* – *See also* **unguarded**.

'**guardsman** ['ga:dz-] *nc* a soldier of the Guards.

catch (someone) off guard to do (something) to a person or cause (a person) to do something when he is surprised or not prepared to prevent it: *I didn't mean to tell him our secret but he caught me off guard.* – *See also* **off (one's) guard** *below.*

guard of honour soldiers or other people who are lined up, *eg* at an airport, at a wedding *etc* as an honour to someone important: *The Guides acted as a guard of honour to their captain at her wedding.*

keep guard (on) to guard (a person, thing *etc*): *The soldiers kept a close guard on their prisoners.*

mount guard to begin to act as a guard round *eg* a building: *The police mounted guard on the embassy.*

off (one's) guard unprepared for something to happen: *He hit me while I was off my guard.* – *See also* **catch (someone) off guard** *above.*

on one's guard (*often with* **against**) prepared for something to happen and ready to prevent it: *He was trying to trick me but I was on my guard all the time*; *Be on your guard against his tricks.*

stand guard to be on duty as a guard: *There were soldiers standing guard round the general's tent.*

the Guards (*also no cap*) certain regiments of soldiers whose duty is to protect the king or queen: *the Scots Guards*; *the Life Guards.*

guardian ['ga:diən] *nc* **1** a person who has the legal right to take care of a child (*usu* an orphan): *He became the child's guardian when her parents were killed in a car crash.* **2** a person who looks after (a person, thing *etc*): *the guardian of a castle*; (*attrib*) *a guardian angel.*

'**guardianship** *nu* the state or duty of being a guardian.

guava ['gwa:və] *nc* **1** the yellow pear-shaped fruit of a type of tropical American tree. **2** the tree.

guer(r)illa [gə'rilə] *nc* a member of a *usu* small group of fighters (*usu* not belonging to an army) who make sudden attacks on an enemy, a town *etc*: *The soldiers attacked the guerrillas' camp*; (*attrib*) *guerrilla warfare.*

guess [ges] *vti* **1** to say what is likely to be the case on the basis of little or no information: *I'm trying to guess the height of this building*; *If you don't know the answer, just guess.* **2** (*esp Amer*: not used with **is, was** *etc* and **-ing**) to think or suppose: *I guess I'll have to leave now.* – *nc* an opinion, answer *etc* got by guessing: *I would say, at a guess* (= by guessing), *that the building is about thirty metres high*; *My guess is that he's not coming.*

'**guesswork** *nu* the process or result of guessing: *I got the answer by guesswork.*

anybody's guess (*inf*) something that no-one can be certain about: *What the result of our negotiations will be is anybody's guess at present.*

guest [gest] *nc* a visitor received and offered food, a bed *etc* in a person's house, in a hotel *etc*: *We are having guests for dinner*; *That hotel has room for fifty guests*; (*attrib*) *Do you have a guest bedroom?*

'**guesthouse** *nc* a small hotel.

ˌ**be my 'guest** (*inf*: *only in the imperative*) please do (the thing you are wanting to do): *'May I have a look at these books?' 'Be my guest.'*

guest artist a singer, comedian *etc* who appears on another person's show, *eg* on television.

guffaw [gə'fo:] *vi* to laugh loudly: *He guffawed loudly at the antics of the monkeys.* – *nc* a loud laugh: *He gave a loud guffaw at the comedian's joke.*

guide [gaid] *vt* **1** to lead, direct or show the way to (a person *etc*): *I don't know how to get to your house – I'll need someone to guide me*; (*fig*) *The Government guided the country through its difficulties*; (*fig*) *Your comments guided me in my final choice.* **2** to control the movement of (a person, thing *etc*): *The teacher guided the child's hand as she wrote.* – *nc* **1** a person who shows a person the way to go *esp* one who takes tourists *etc* round a building, city *etc* and points out interesting things to them: *A guide will show you round the castle.* **2** (*also* '**guidebook**) a book which contains information for tourists *etc* about a building, city *etc*: *We have bought a guide to Edinburgh.* **3** (*usu with cap*) a Girl Guide: *My daughter is in the Guides.* **4** someone or something which influences a person's decisions, behaviour *etc* or that leads a person to some opinion *etc*: *A person's clothes are not a guide to his intelligence.*

'**guidance** *nu* help or advice towards doing something: *This project has been prepared under the guidance of Professor Smith.*

guidebook *see* **guide** *n* (*def 2*).

'**guideline** *nc* (*usu in pl*) a rule or indication as to how something should be done: *We'll need a few guidelines before we start this project.*

guided missile an explosive rocket which after being fired can be guided to its target by radio waves.

guild [gild] *nc* **1** (*hist*) in the Middle Ages, an association of merchants or craftsmen of a particular trade. **2** a name used by some societies or clubs: *the Church Ladies' Guild.*

guilder ['gildə] *nc* the standard unit of Dutch currency.

guile [gail] *nu* (*formal*) the ability to deceive or trick people: *She used guile to get him to propose to her.*

'**guileless** *adj* (*formal*) honest; sincere; without trickery: *She is completely guileless*; *a guileless person/smile.* '**guilelessly** *adv.* '**guilelessness** *nc.*

guillotine ['gilətiːn] *nc* **1** an instrument (used in France) for cutting criminals' heads off: *During the French Revolution many of the French nobles were sent to the guillotine.* **2** a machine for cutting paper. – *vt* **1** to cut a person's head off with a guillotine. **2** to cut paper with a guillotine.

guilt [gilt] *nu* **1** a sense of shame because one knows one has done wrong: *a feeling of guilt.* **2** the state of having done wrong or having broken a law: *Fingerprints left in the room proved the murderer's guilt.* **3** the blame for having done wrong: *It's easy to see where the guilt lies.*

'**guilty** *adj* having, feeling, or causing guilt: *I feel guilty about not having written to you sooner*; *The jury found the prisoner guilty*; *a guilty conscience.* '**guiltiness** *nu.*

'**guiltily** *adv* in a way that suggests that a person feels guilt: *He looked at his mother guiltily.*

guinea ['gini] *nc* **1** (*hist*) a British gold coin. **2** a word for £1.05p, sometimes used in stating prices (*esp* of horses, works of art), fees, or prizes (*esp* in horse-racing).

guinea-pig ['ginipig] *nc* **1** a small animal, like a rabbit, with short ears and often kept as a pet. **2** (*sometimes derog*) a person used as the subject of an experiment: *We'd like to use you as a guinea-pig to test some of our theories.*

guise [gaiz] *nc (formal or liter: usu in sing)* dress or appearance, *esp* a disguised or false appearance: *The thieves entered the house in the guise of gas-fitters*; *(fig) He did his evil deeds under the guise of friendship.*

guitar [gi'ta:] *nc* a type of musical instrument with *usu* six strings: *He plays the guitar*; *He played a tune on his guitar.*

gui'tarist *nc* a person who plays the guitar.

gulch [gʌltʃ] *nc (Amer)* a narrow, rocky valley.

gulf [gʌlf] *nc* **1** *(often found with cap in place-names)* a part of the sea with land round a large part of it: *the Gulf of Mexico.* **2** *(fig)* a wide division or difference between people, opinions *etc*: *They used to be friends but a great gulf has developed between them.*

gull [gʌl] *nc (often* **'seagull**) a type of web-footed sea bird, *usu* black and white or grey and white.

gullet ['gʌlit] *nc* the tube by which food passes from the mouth to the stomach: *The dog choked because it had something stuck in its gullet.*

gullible ['gʌləbl] *adj* easily tricked or fooled: *He persuaded a large number of gullible people to buy totally worthless land supposedly to build cottages on*; *He is so gullible that he believes everything you tell him.* **ˌgulli'bility, 'gullibleness** *nus.*

gully ['gʌli] *nc* a channel worn by running water *eg* on a mountain side.

gulp [gʌlp] **1** *vti* to swallow (food *etc*) eagerly or in large mouthfuls: *Children are often told not to gulp (their food)*: *He gulped down a sandwich and ran out of the house.* **2** *vi* to make a swallowing movement *eg* because of fear: *She gulped as she saw the policeman coming.* – *nc* **1** a swallowing movement: *'There's a ghost out there,' he said with a gulp*; *He ate the whole slice of bread at/in one gulp.* **2** the amount of food *etc* taken at one time: *He took a gulp of his coffee and dashed out of the room.*

gum[1] [gʌm] *nc (usu in pl)* the firm flesh in which the teeth grow: *His gums are bleeding*; *(attrib) a gum infection.*

'gumboil *nc* a painful swelling in the gum: *I don't have toothache – I've got a gumboil.*

gum[2] [gʌm] **1** *ncu* a sticky juice got from some trees and plants. **2** *nu* such a juice, or a similar substance, used as a glue: *We can stick these pictures into the book with gum.* **3** *nc* a type of sweet: *a fruit gum.* **4** *nu* chewing-gum: *He chews gum when he is working.* – *v* – *pt, ptp* **gummed** – *vt* to glue (something) with gum: *These two pieces of paper have to be gummed together*; *I'll gum this bit on to the other one.*

'gummy *adj (inf)* of, like, or covered with, gum: *a gummy substance.* **'gumminess** *nu.*

'gumboot *nc* a rubber boot. – *See also* **wellingtons**.

gum up the works *(inf)* to cause a machine, a system of working *etc* to break down: *He produced so many rules and regulations for the office that he gummed up the works completely.*

gumption ['gʌmpʃən] *nu (inf)* common sense; good judgement: *My new secretary keeps asking me how this or that should be done – she doesn't seem to have enough gumption to think of the answers on her own.*

gun [gʌn] *nc* any weapon which fires bullets or shells from a long metal tube: *He fired a gun at the burglar*; *Do the police carry guns here?*

'gunboat *nc* a small warship with large guns.

'gun dog *nc* a dog trained to fetch birds *etc* after they have been shot by sportsmen, hunters *etc*: *Spaniels are excellent gun dogs.*

'gunfire *nu* the firing of gun(s): *I could hear the sound of gunfire in the distance.*

'gunman *nc* a criminal who uses a gun to kill or rob people: *Three gunmen robbed the bank.*

'gunpowder *nu* an explosive in the form of a powder.

'gun-running *nu* the act of bringing guns illegally into a country: *The terrorists were found guilty of gun-running.* **'gun-runner** *nc.*

'gunshot 1 *nc* the sound of a gun firing: *I heard a gunshot and a man dropped dead.* **2** *nu* the distance over which a gun can fire a bullet *etc.* – *adj (attrib)* caused by the bullet from a gun: *a gunshot wound.*

gun down – *v* – *pt, ptp* **gunned** – *vt sep* to shoot or kill (a person) with a gun in a cruel or ruthless manner: *The bandits gunned down the villagers.*

'gun for – *v* – *pt, ptp* **gunned** – *vt fus (usu with* **is/was** *etc) (fig)* to attack or criticize (a person): *He has been gunning for me ever since I criticized his new book.*

jump the gun *see* **jump**.

stick to one's guns to hold to one's position in an argument *etc*: *No-one believed her story but she stuck to her guns.*

gurgle ['gə:gl] **1** *vi* (of water) to make a bubbling noise while flowing: *The brook gurgled*; *The water gurgled from the tap.* **2** *vti* (of people *etc*) to make a noise like this, or say something by or as if gurgling: *The baby lay cooing and gurgling*; *The baby gurgled its pleasure.* – *nc* a gurgling sound: *a gurgle of delight.*

guru ['guru:] *nc* **1** a religious teacher in India and in certain religious groups. **2** a greatly-respected person whose opinions have a lot of influence among some groups of people: *He is one of the gurus of modern socialism.*

gush [gʌʃ] **1** *vi* (of liquids) to flow out suddenly and in large amounts: *Blood gushed from his wound.* **2** *vi (derog)* to exaggerate one's enthusiasm, emotions *etc* while talking (about something): *The lady kept gushing about her husband's success.* – *nc* a sudden flowing (of a liquid): *a gush of water*; *(fig) a gush of enthusiasm.*

'gushing *adj* **1** *(formal: attrib)* pouring out (something liquid): *a gushing wound.* **2** *(derog)* speaking or spoken in an exaggerated manner: *gushing women/remarks*; *She's a bit too gushing for me.*

'gushingly *adv* in an exaggerated manner: *She spoke gushingly of her husband's success.*

gust [gʌst] *nc* a sudden blast (of wind): *There were gusts of wind of up to eighty kilometres an hour last night.*

'gusty *adj* with the wind blowing in gusts: *a gusty day*; *It is a bit gusty today.* **'gustily** *adv.* **'gustiness** *nu.*

gusto ['gʌstou] *nu (inf)* enthusiasm or enjoyment: *The boy was blowing his trumpet with great gusto.*

gusty *see* **gust**.

gut [gʌt] **1** *ncu* the tube in the lower part of the body through which food passes. **2** *nu* a strong thread made from the gut of an animal, used for violin strings *etc.* – *v* – *pt, ptp* **'gutted** – *vt* **1** to take the guts out of (something): *Her job was to gut fish.* **2** to destroy (something) completely, except for the outer frame: *The fire gutted the house.*

guts *n pl* **1** the gut, liver, kidneys *etc.* **2** *(inf)* courage: *He's got a lot of guts.*

hate someone's guts (*sl*) to hate (someone) very much.

gutter ['gʌtə] *nc* **1** a channel for carrying away water, *esp* at the edge of a road or roof: *The gutters are flooded with water.* **2** (*fig*) poverty; very unpleasant living conditions: *He picked her up out of the gutter.*

the gutter press (*derog*) such newspapers as give a great deal of space to scandals and gossip: *The gutter press was full of stories of the princess's divorce today.*

guttural ['gʌtərəl] *adj* **1** (of sounds) formed in the throat. **2** (of a language or a person's speech) having or using such sounds; harsh: *He has a very guttural accent*; *His voice is rather guttural.* – *nc* a guttural sound. **'gutturally** *adv*. **'gutturalness** *nu*.

guy [gai] *nc* **1** (*inf*) a man: *I don't know the guy you're talking about.* **2** in Great Britain, a figure in the form of a man, made from old clothes *etc*, which is burned on November 5, Guy Fawkes Day: *The children are collecting old clothes for their guy.* **3** (*also* **'guy-rope**) a rope which keeps a tent *etc* steady: *Could you loosen the guys, please?*

guzzle ['gʌzl] *vti* (*inf*) to swallow (food or drink) greedily: *No wonder he's fat – he's always guzzling (chocolate).* **'guzzler** *nc*.

gym [dʒim] (*inf*) short for **gymnasium** and **gymnastics**: *The children have gym on Thursdays*; (*attrib*) *a gym teacher*; (*attrib*) *a gym lesson.*

'gym shoe *nc* a light, canvas *usu* rubber-soled shoe worn for gymnastics.

gymkhana [dʒim'ka:nə] *nc* a meeting for sports competitions *usu* for horse-riders: *She was first in the horse-jumping at the gymkhana.*

gymnasium [dʒim'neiziəm] – *pls* **gym'nasiums, gym'nasia** [-ə] – *nc* a building or room (*eg* in a school) with equipment for physical exercise.

gymnast ['dʒimnast] *nc* a person who does gymnastics: *She was one of the gymnasts who competed in the Olympic Games.*

gym'nastic [-'nas-] *adj* of gymnastics.

gym'nastics [-'nas-] *n sing* physical exercises *usu* done in a gymnasium with certain types of equipment.

gynaecology, (*Amer*) **gynecology** [gainə'kolədʒi] *nu* the branch of medicine which deals with the diseases of women: *He specializes in gynaecology*; (*attrib*) *the gynaecology department.* **,gynaeco'logical** [-'lo-] *adj* (*tech or formal*). **,gynae'cologist** *nc*.

gypsum ['dʒipsəm] *nu* a soft mineral like chalk, used to make plaster of Paris *etc*.

gypsy, gipsy ['dʒipsi] *nc* a member of a race of people who formerly used to wander from place to place round Europe, living in caravans: *A gypsy told her fortune at the fair*; (*attrib*) *a gypsy caravan.*

gyrate [dʒai'reit, (*Amer*) 'dʒaireit] *vi* (*formal*) to spin round: *A spinning-top gyrates.* **gy'ration** *ncu*.

gyroscope ['dʒairəskoup] *nc* (*tech*) an apparatus in which a rapidly turning wheel is used to keep steady the object in which it is fixed.

Hh

ha! [ha, ha:] *interj* an expression of surprise, triumph *etc*: *Ha! I've found it!*
See also **ha! ha!**

haberdashery ['habədaʃəri] **1** *nu* ribbons, needles, thread, buttons and other similar small articles: *She sells dress material and haberdashery*; (*attrib*) *the haberdashery department.* **2** *nu* (*Amer*) men's clothes such as hats, shirts, ties and socks. **3** *nc* a shop which sells haberdashery: *I bought this ribbon at the haberdashery in the next street.*

'haberdasher *nc* **1** a person who sells haberdashery. **2** a haberdashery.

'haberdasher's *nc* a haberdashery.

habit ['habit] **1** *nc* something which a person does usually or regularly, *esp* something difficult to stop doing: *I am in the habit of going for a walk before I go to bed*; *He has an irritating habit of interrupting you when you talk to him.* **2** *nu* (*formal*) a tendency to do the same things that one has always done: *He's a creature of habit.* **3** *nc* (*formal*: *often in cmpds*) clothes: *a monk's habit*; (*old*) *a woman's riding-habit.*

habitual [hə'bitjuəl] *adj* (*formal*: *usu attrib*) **1** having a habit of doing, being *etc* (something): *He's a habitual drunkard.* **2** seen, done *etc* regularly: *He took his habitual glass of wine before going to bed.*

habitually [hə'bitjuəli] *adv* (*formal*) usually or regularly: *He's habitually late for our meetings.*

habituate [hə'bitjueit] *vt* (*formal*) to cause (a person *etc*) to become used to (something): *If one goes to live in a foreign country, one has to habituate oneself to new ways of doing things.*

'habit-forming *adj* (of a drug) which a person will find it difficult or impossible to stop using: *Some barbiturates are habit-forming*; *habit-forming sleeping-pills.*

from force of habit because one is used to doing (something): *I didn't mean to smoke that cigarette – I just took it from force of habit.*

get (someone) into, out of the habit of to make (a person) start or stop doing (something) as a habit: *I wish I could get him out of the habit of biting his nails*; *I wish I could get out of the habit of biting my nails*; *You must get your children into the habit of cleaning their teeth.*

habitable ['habitəbl] *adj* (*formal*: *neg* **un-**) (*usu* of buildings) fit to be lived in: *That cottage would be quite habitable if someone spent some money on repairing it*; *The council are demolishing perfectly habitable houses.*

'habitat [-tat] *nc* (*esp tech*) the natural home of an animal or plant: *The Antarctic is the penguin's natural habitat.*

,habi'tation *nu* the act of living in (a building *etc*): *These houses are not fit for human habitation.*
See also **inhabitable** *under* **inhabit**.

habitual, habituate *see* **habit**.

hack [hak] **1** *vt* (*sometimes with* **up**) to cut or chop up (*eg* meat) roughly: *The butcher hacked the side of beef into large pieces*; *He hacked the large tree up into smaller pieces.* **2** *vt* (*sometimes with* **out**) to cut (a path *etc*) roughly: *The explorer hacked his way through the jungle*; *He hacked (out) a path through the jungle.* **3** *vti* to kick (a person's leg) in football *etc*. **4** *vi* (*sl*) to cough: *He hacked away all night.* – *See also* **hack at, hack down** *below.* – *nc* **1** a rough cut made in something: *He marked the tree* *by making a few hacks on the trunk.* **2** the act of making a cut (in a tree *etc*): *He took a hack at the tree.* **3** a horse, or in the US a car, for hire. **4** a kick on the leg in football *etc.* **5** a person, *usu* a writer, who does hard and boring work, often for low wages: *He's employed as a hack on the local newspaper*; (*attrib*) *a hack writer*; (*attrib*) *Some people think that writing dictionaries is hack work* (= boring, uninteresting work).

'hacking *adj* (*attrib*) (of a cough) rough and dry: *He has had a hacking cough for weeks.*

'hacking jacket *nc* a kind of jacket, *usu* made of tweed, worn *esp* when riding a horse.

'hacksaw *nc* a saw for cutting metals.

'hack at *vt fus* to hit (a tree *etc*) with something sharp (*eg* an axe): *He hacked at the trunk of the tree.*

hack down *vt sep* to cut (a tree *etc*) down with rough blows (*eg* of an axe).

hackles ['haklz] *n pl* the hair on a dog's neck or the feathers on the neck of a farmyard cock.

make someone's hackles rise (*fig*) to make someone angry: *Her unnecessary rudeness really made my hackles rise.*

hackney ['hakni]: **'hackney carriage/cab** *nc* (*formal or old*) a taxi.

hackneyed ['haknid] *adj* (*usu* of things said or written) used too often: *Writers should always try to avoid hackneyed phrases*; *That politician's speeches are so hackneyed.*

hacksaw *see* **hack**.

had *see* **have**.

haddock ['hadək] – *pls* **'haddock, 'haddocks** – **1** *nc* a kind of small sea fish: *two haddock(s)*; *a shoal of haddock.* **2** *nu* its flesh used as food: *We had haddock and chips for supper.*

hadn't *see* **have**.

haemoglobin, (*Amer*) **hemoglobin** [hiːmə'gloubin] *nu* (*tech*) the oxygen-carrying substance in red blood cells.

haemorrhage, (*Amer*) **hemorrhage** ['hemərid͡ʒ] *nc* (*tech*) bleeding in large amounts, from damaged blood-vessels: *He had a haemorrhage after his operation.* – *vi* (*tech*) to bleed in this way: *She haemorrhaged after the birth of her baby.*

haemorrhoid, (*Amer*) **hemorrhoid** ['heməroid] *nc* (*tech*: *usu in pl*) a *usu* painful or irritating swollen vein around the anus: *He suffers from haemorrhoids.*

See also **piles**.

haft [haft] *nc* (*formal or liter*) a handle (of a knife, sword, axe *etc*).

hag [hag] *nc* (*usu derog*) an ugly old woman: *She was beautiful when she was young but she's an old hag now.*

haggard ['hagəd] *adj* (of a person) looking very tired and thin-faced, because of pain, worry *etc*: *She looked haggard after a sleepless night*; *a thin, haggard old woman.*

haggis ['hagis] *ncu* a Scottish food made from the chopped-up heart, lungs and liver of a sheep, mixed with oatmeal, and cooked in a sheep's stomach or something similar.

haggle ['hagl] *vi* to argue about the price of something, or about the terms of an agreement: *In some parts of the world, people are expected to haggle with the merchants over the (price of) goods they are selling*; *Don't haggle about the price – it seems reasonable to me.*

ha! ha! [haː'haː] *interj* an expression of laughter, sometimes used as a sneer: *Ha! ha! That's a good joke!*

hail[1] [heil] **1** *nu* small balls of ice falling from the clouds: *There was rain last night and hail the night before.* **2** *nc* (*fig*) a shower (of things): *a hail of arrows*; *a hail of abuse.* – *vi* (*only with* **it** *as subject*) to shower hail: *It was hailing as I drove home.*

'hailstone *nc* (*usu in pl*) a single ball of hail: *Hailstones battered against the windows.*

hail[2] [heil] *vt* **1** to shout to (a person, boat *etc*) in order to attract attention: *We hailed a taxi*; *The captain hailed the passing ship.* **2** (*formal*) to greet or welcome (a person, thing *etc*) as something: *His discoveries were hailed as a great step forward in medicine.* – *See also* **hail from** *below.* – *nc* a shout (to attract attention): *Give that ship a hail.* – *interj* (*arch*) a word of greeting: *Hail, Caesar!*

'hail from *vt fus* (*inf*) to come from or belong to (a place): *He hails from Texas.*

hair [heə] **1** *nc* one of the mass of thread-like objects that grow from the skin: *He brushed the dog's hairs off his jacket.* **2** *nu* the mass of these, *esp* on a person's head: *He's got brown hair.* **3** *nc* (*fig*) a hair's-breadth: *That knife missed me by a hair.*

-haired (*in cmpds*) having (a certain kind of) hair: *a fair-haired girl.*

'hairy *adj* covered in hair or having a lot of hair: *a hairy chest*; *Her dog is very hairy.* **'hairiness** *nu.*

hair-brained *see* **hare-brained**.

'hair('s)-breadth *nc* a very small distance: *That knife missed me by a hair's-breadth*; (*attrib*) *a hair-breadth escape.*

'haircut *nc* the act or style of cutting a person's hair: *Go and get a haircut*; *That's a good haircut.*

'hair-do – *pls* **'hair-dos, 'hair-do's** – *nc* (*inf*) the act or result of cutting and styling (a person's, *usu* a woman's) hair: *I like her new hair-do*; *That hair-do cost a lot of money.*

'hairdresser *nc* **1** a person who cuts, washes, styles *etc* a person's hair. **2** a hairdresser's shop or salon: *I'm going to the hairdresser on Friday.*

'hairdresser's *nc* a hairdresser's shop or salon.

'hair-drier *nc* an electrical apparatus which dries a person's hair by blowing a current of hot air over it.

'hairline *nc* the line along the forehead where the hair begins to grow: *She has a low hairline.* – *adj* (*fig*: *attrib*) having a very narrow width: *a hairline space*; *a hairline fracture.*

'hairpin *nc* a bent wire for keeping (*usu* a woman's) hair in place. – *adj* (*attrib*) (of a bend) sharp and U-shaped, *esp* on a mountain or a hill.

'hair-raising *adj* terrifying: *The explorer told some hair-raising stories about his adventures*; *The bus journey through the mountains was hair-raising.*

'hair-splitting *nu* the act of making small, unnecessary distinctions: *To say there's any difference between these two shades of blue is hair-splitting – to me they're identical.* – *See also* **split hairs** *below.*

get in (someone's) hair (*inf*) to annoy (a person): *During the school holidays the children keep getting in my hair.*

keep one's hair on (*inf*) to remain calm and not become angry: *Keep your hair on – I'm working as fast as I can.*

let one's hair down (*inf*) to behave in a free and relaxed manner: *I've had enough of formal meetings – tonight I'm going to a party to let my hair down.*

make (someone's) hair stand on end to terrify (a person): *That horror film really made my hair stand on end.*

(not to) turn a hair to remain calm: *He didn't turn a hair when the madman ran towards him waving a knife*; *He did it without turning a hair.*

split hairs to make small, unnecessary distinctions; to worry about unimportant details. – *See also* **hair-splitting** *above.*

tear one's hair (*inf*) to show great irritation or despair: *He was tearing his hair by the time he'd finished marking the exam papers.*

hake [heik] – *pls* **hake, hakes** – **1** *nc* a kind of sea fish like a cod: *two hakes*; *a shoal of hake.* **2** *nu* its flesh used as food: *They had hake for supper.*

halcyon ['halsiən]: **halcyon days** (*formal or liter*) a time of peace and happiness: *The old lady often talked about the halcyon days of her youth.*

hale [heil]: **hale and hearty** healthy: *He's over ninety but still hale and hearty.*

half [ha:f] – *pl* **halves** [ha:vz] – *nc* **1** one of two equal parts of anything which together form the whole thing: *He tried to stick the two halves together again*; *Half (of) the students failed their exams*; *half a kilo of sugar*; *a kilo and a half of sugar*; *one and a half kilos of sugar.* **2** one of two equal parts of a game (*eg* in football, hockey) *usu* with a break between them: *Rangers scored three goals in the first half.* – *adj* **1** being (equal to) one of two equal parts (of something): *a half bottle of wine.* **2** being made up of two things in (approximately) equal parts: *A centaur is a mythical creature, half man and half horse.* **3** not full or complete: *a half smile.* – *adv* **1** to the extent of one half: *This cup is only half full*; *It's half empty.* **2** almost; partly; to some extent: *I'm half hoping he won't come*; *He was half dead from cold and hunger.*

half- (*in cmpds*) being (equal to) one of two equal parts forming a whole: *a half-dozen*; *a half-pound of tea.*

halve [ha:v] *vt* **1** to divide (something) into two equal parts: *He halved the apple.* **2** to make (costs, problems *etc*) half as great as they were or might be: *By going away early in the year, we nearly halved the cost of our holiday.*

ˌhalf-and-'half *adv, adj* in equal parts: *We can split the costs between us half-and-half*; *a half-and-half mixture.*

'half-back *ncu* in football, hockey *etc*, (a player in) a position directly behind the forwards.

ˌhalf-'baked *adj* (*sl*: *usu attrib*) stupid: *She is full of half-baked ideas.*

'half-breed (*derog*), **'half-caste** *ncs* a person whose father and mother are of different races, *esp* white and black.

'half-brother, 'half-sister *ncs* a brother or sister by one parent only: *My father has been married twice, and I have two half-brothers.*

half-caste *see* **half-breed**.

ˌhalf(-)'crown (*also* **half a crown**) *nc* (*hist*) a coin in British money, worth two shillings and sixpence ($12\frac{1}{2}$ pence).

ˌhalf-'hearted *adj* not eager; (done) without enthusiasm: *a half-hearted cheer/attempt*; *Her attempts were rather half-hearted.* **ˌhalf-'heartedly** *adv.* **ˌhalf-'heartedness** *nu.*

ˌhalf-'holiday *nc* part of a day (*usu* the afternoon) during which no work is done: *The school-children were given a half-holiday to celebrate the queen's birthday.*

ˌhalf-'hourly *adj* (*attrib*), *adv* done *etc* every half-hour: *at half-hourly intervals*; *The buses to town run half-hourly during the day.*

halfpenny ['heipni, (*Amer*) 'hafpeni] – *pls* **halfpence** ['heipəns, (*Amer*) 'hafpens] (*defs 3, 4*), **halfpennies** ['heipniz, (*Amer*) 'hafpeniz] (*defs 2, 5*) – *nc* **1** (*no pl*: *also* (*not formal*) **ˌhalf'p** [-'pi:], **ˌhalf'pence**) half a penny (*def 1*): *Each of these is worth a halfpenny*; (*attrib*) *a halfpence piece.* **2** (*also* (*formal*) **new halfpenny**) a coin of this value: *I need a penny but I only have two halfpennies.* **3** (*hist*) half a penny (*def 3*): *These sweets cost three halfpence each.* **4** half a penny (*def 7*). **5** a coin of the value of a halfpenny (*defs 3, 4*).

half-sister *see* **half-brother**.

ˌhalf-'term *ncu* (the period when students are given) a holiday about the middle of a school, college *etc* term: *We get a week's holiday at half-term*; (*attrib*) *a half-term holiday.*

ˌhalf-'time *ncu* a short rest between two halves of a game (of football *etc*): *The players ate oranges at half-time*; (*attrib*) *the half-time score.*

ˌhalf-'truth *nc* a statement which has some true facts in it, but which does not give the whole truth.

ˌhalf-'way *adj, adv* of or at a point equally far from the beginning and the end (of a distance, journey, period of time *etc*): *We are half-way through the work now*; *We have reached the half-way point*; *The two teams started from different places and met halfway.* – *See also* **meet (someone) halfway** *below.*

'half-wit *nc* (*derog*) a fool or idiot.

ˌhalf-'witted *adj* foolish or idiotic.

ˌhalf-'yearly *adj* (*attrib*), *adv* done *etc* every six months: *a half-yearly report*; *We balance our accounts half-yearly.*

at half mast (of flags) flying at a position half-way up a mast or flag-pole to show that someone of importance has died: *The president is dead – the flags are flying at half mast.*

one's better half (*inf facet*) a person's wife or husband: *I don't know where we're going on holiday – ask my better half.*

by 'half (*inf*) to too great an extent: *He's too clever by half.*

do things by halves (*inf*: *usu in neg*) to do things in an incomplete, careless *etc* way: *He never does things by halves.*

go halves (*inf*: *usu with* **with**) to share the cost (of something) with someone: *I'll go halves with you in a bottle of lemonade* (= in buying a bottle of lemonade).

go off at half-cock *see* **cock**.

half measures actions which are not sufficient to deal with (a problem, source of trouble *etc*): *We must take definite action against these criminals – half measures will not do* (= will not be sufficient).

half past three, four, seven *etc*, (*Amer*) **half after three** *etc* at thirty minutes past the hour stated: *I'm leaving at half past six.*

in 'half in(to) two (approximately) equal parts: *He cut the cake in half*; *The pencil broke in half.*

meet (someone) halfway (*fig*) to reach an agreement (with someone) by meeting some of his demands in return for his meeting some of yours: *You'll have to be prepared to meet each other halfway if you're ever to reach an agreement.*

not half *interj* (*inf*) very much so: *'Are you enjoying yourself?' 'Not half!'* – *adv* (*inf*) **1** very much: *He wasn't half annoyed.* **2** not nearly: *That isn't half good enough.* **3** not at all: *That wine is not half bad* (= quite good).

halibut ['halibət] – *pls* **'halibut, 'halibuts** – **1** *nc* a kind of large flatfish: *two halibut(s)*; *a shoal of* *halibut.* **2** *nu* its flesh used as food: *We had halibut in oyster sauce for dinner.*

halitosis [hali'tousis] *nu* (*tech*) (the state of having) breath which smells bad: *He suffers from halitosis.*

hall [ho:l] *nc* **1** a room or passage at the entrance to a house: *We left our coats in the hall.* **2** (a building with) a large public room, used for concerts, meetings *etc*: *a church hall.* **3** a building with offices where the administration of a town *etc* is carried out: *a town hall*; (*Amer*) *the city hall.* **4** (*Amer*) a passageway through a building; a corridor. **5** a building of a university, college *etc*, *esp* one in which students *etc* live: *a hall of residence.* **6** (*Brit*: *with cap*: *usu in names*) a large country-house; the house of a landowner: *He lives at the Hall/Crumpy Hall.*

'**hallmark** *nc* **1** a mark put on gold and silver articles to show the quality of the gold or silver: *You can find out how valuable your ring might be by looking at the hallmark.* **2** (*fig*) anything which shows the quality of a person, thing *etc*: *Politeness is the hallmark of good manners.*

'**hallstand** *nc* a piece of furniture, *usu* in a hall (*def 1*) on which coats, hats *etc* are hung.

'**hallway** *nc* a hall (*defs 1 and 4*).

hallo *see* **hello**.

hallowed ['haloud] *adj* (*relig or formal*: *usu attrib*) holy: *hallowed ground.*

Hallowe'en [halou'i:n] *n* the evening of October 31, when witches and ghosts are said to appear: *We always have a party at Hallowe'en*; (*attrib*) *a Hallowe'en party/cake.*

hallstand *see* **hall**.

hallucination [həlu:si'neiʃən] *nc* the seeing of something that is not really there: *He had hallucinations after he took drugs.*

hallway *see* **hall**.

halo ['heilou] – *pls* '**halo(e)s** – *nc* **1** a ring of light round the sun or moon. **2** a similar ring of light round a person's head (*eg* in pictures of saints *etc*): *He painted St Joan with a halo round her head*; (*fig*) *I've worked so hard today my halo's shining* (= I've been very good).

halt [ho:lt] *vti* (*more formal than* **stop**) to (cause to) stop walking, marching, running *etc*: *The driver halted the train*; *The train halted at the signals.* – *nc* **1** (*more formal than* **stop**) a complete stop: *The train came to a halt.* **2** (*more formal than* **stop**) a short stop (on a march *etc*). **3** a small railway station.

'**halting** *adj* (*formal*) showing or having hesitation, uncertainty *etc*: *He spoke in a halting voice*; *His voice was rather halting.* '**haltingly** *adv.*

call a halt (to) (*fig*) to stop; to put an end (to): *It's time to call a halt to these stupid arguments*; *I've had enough of this – let's call a halt.*

halter ['ho:ltə] *nc* a rope for holding and leading a horse by its head.

halter neck *nc* the neck of a dress *etc* formed by a strap which goes round the wearer's neck, leaving the shoulders bare: *This dress has a halter neck*; (*attrib*) *a halter-neck dress.*

halve, halves *see* **half**.

halyard ['haljəd] *nc* (*naut*) a rope for raising or lowering a sail or flag.

ham [ham] **1** *nc* the top of the back leg of a pig, salted and dried: *There were two hams hanging in the butcher's shop.* **2** *nu* the meat of a pig's ham: *a slice of ham.* **3** *nc* (*inf*) a bad actor, *esp* one who exaggerates emotions *etc* on stage: *He's not a good actor – he's just a ham*; (*attrib*) *a ham actor.* **4** *nc* (*inf*) an amateur radio operator: *a radio ham.* – *v* – *pt, ptp* **hammed** – *vti* (*sometimes with* **up**) (of actors) to act badly by exaggerating emotions *etc*: *I wish he wouldn't ham all the time*; *He hammed (up) the part of Othello.*

,**ham-'fisted** *adj* (*inf derog*) clumsy: *He can't tie a knot in that rope – he's too ham-fisted*; *a ham-fisted idiot.*

hamburger ['hambə:gə] *nc* **1** a round cake of minced beef, *usu* fried: *I'm frying hamburgers for supper.* **2** a bread roll containing one of these: *He ate a hamburger as he walked along the street.*

hamlet ['hamlit] *nc* (*often liter*) a small village.

hammer ['hamə] *nc* **1** a tool with a heavy *usu* metal head, used for driving nails into wood, breaking hard substances *etc*: *a joiner's hammer*; *a coal-hammer.* **2** the part of a bell, piano, clock *etc* that hits against some other part, so making a noise. **3** the part of a gun that strikes the explosive. **4** in sport, a metal ball on a long steel handle for throwing: *He throws the hammer as a hobby.* – **1** *vti* to hit, beat, break *etc* (something) with a hammer: *He hammered the nail into the wood*; *He hammered it in*; *I could hear him hammering all afternoon.* **2** *vt* (*fig inf*) to beat (someone) severely (physically, in a game *etc*): *Our local football team hammered their opponents last Saturday*; *The bully hammered the little boy.* **3** *vt* (*fig*) to teach a person (something) with difficulty, by repetition: *The only way to teach him French verbs is to hammer them into his head.* – *See also* **hammer away at, hammer out** *below.*

give (someone) a hammering (*sl*) to hammer (*def 2*) (a person): *His father gave him a hammering for stealing.*

go/be 'at it ,hammer and 'tongs to fight or argue violently.

hammer away at *vt fus* (*inf*) to keep working on (a problem *etc*): *We'll hammer away at this until we get it solved.*

hammer (something) home to make great efforts to make a person realize or understand (something): *We'll have to hammer home to them the problems we face with this project.*

hammer out *vt sep* to produce (an agreement *etc*) with a great deal of effort and discussion: *The two political parties finally hammered out a solution which was acceptable to both of them.*

hammock ['hamək] *nc* a long piece of netting, canvas *etc* hung up by the corners and used as a bed, *eg* in a ship: *She lay in the sun in a hammock tied between two apple trees.*

hamper ['hampə] *vt* (*formal*) to make it difficult (for someone) to do something: *I tried to run away but I was hampered by my long coat.* – *nc* a large basket with a lid: *a picnic hamper.*

hamster ['hamstə] *nc* a small animal, rather like a fat rat without a tail, often kept as a pet.

hamstring ['hamstriŋ] *nc* the tendon at the back of the knee: *The runner has strained a hamstring and will miss the next race.* – *v* – *pt, ptp* '**hamstrung** [-strʌŋ] – *vt* (*fig*) to make (a person) powerless in some way: *We've been hamstrung by our lack of information.*

hand [hand] *nc* **1** the part of the body at the end of the arm: *He had a knife in his hand*; *Each hand has five fingers.* **2** a pointer on a clock, watch *etc*: *Clocks usually have an hour hand and a minute hand.* **3** (*often in cmpds*) a person who works in certain places, *esp* on a farm or on a ship: *a farm hand*; *All hands on deck!* **4** (*no pl*: *inf*) help;

assistance: *Can I lend a hand?* (= Can I help?); *Do you need a hand?*; *Give me a hand with this box, please.* **5** (*no pl*: *inf*) clapping; applause: *Give the little girl a big hand, ladies and gentlemen.* **6** a set of playing-cards dealt to a person: *I was holding/had a very good hand so I thought I had a chance of winning the game.* **7** a game (of cards): *Let's play a couple of hands of poker.* **8** a measure (= 4 inches, approx 10 centimetres) used for measuring the height of horses: *a horse of 14 hands (high).* – *See also* **hand** *in phrases below.* – *vt* (*often with* **back, down, up** *etc*) **1** to give (something) to someone by hand: *He handed me the book*; *He took the book from me, then handed it back to me*; *I'll go up the ladder, and you can hand the tools up to me.* **2** (*fig*) to pass, send *etc* (a person, thing *etc*) to a person, place *etc*: *That is the end of my report from Paris. I'll now hand you back to Fred Smith in the television studio in London.* – *See also* **hand** *in phrases below.*

hand- (*in cmpds*) **1** done by a person with his hands, or with tools held in the hand: *ˌhand-ˈknitted.* **2** for holding in the hand, as in **handbag**. **3** made for a person to hold with his hand: *a ˈhandrail.* **4** worked by hand, as in **handbrake**.

ˈhandful *nc* **1** as much as can be held in one hand: *He took a handful of sweets*; *handfuls of peanuts.* **2** (*inf*) a small amount or a small number: *Only a handful of people came to the meeting.* **3** (*inf*: *pl rare*) a person or people who cause trouble or are difficult to control: *Her three children are a bit of a handful.*

ˈhandless *adj* (*derog*) clumsy: *I wouldn't let him carry the vase – he's a bit handless*; *a handless creature.*

ˈhandbag *nc* (*Amer usu* **purse**) a small bag carried by women, for personal belongings such as their money, lipstick *etc.*

ˈhand-ball *nu* a game in which a ball is hit with the palm of the hand.

ˈhandbill *nc* a small printed notice.

ˈhandbook *nc* a small book giving information about (how to do) something: *a handbook of European birds*; *Is there a handbook that tells me how to mend my car?*

ˈhandbrake *nc* (in a car, bus *etc*) a brake which is operated by a lever which is moved by the driver's hand: *He forgot to put the handbrake on and the car rolled down the hill.*

ˈhandcuff *vt* to put handcuffs on (a person): *The police handcuffed the criminal.*

ˈhandcuffs *n pl* steel rings, joined by a short chain, put round the wrists of prisoners: *a pair of handcuffs.*

ˈhand-grenade *see* **grenade**.

ˌhandˈmade *adj* made with a person's hands or with tools held in the hands, rather than by machines: *This furniture is all handmade*; *handmade sweaters.*

ˈhand-out *nc* **1** a leaflet of information given *eg* to students before a lecture, to newspaper reporters *etc.* **2** (*inf*: *usu derog*) money *etc* given to someone who needs it: *You needn't come to me looking for a hand-out.* – *See also* **hand out** *below.*

ˌhand-ˈpicked *adj* chosen very carefully: *Employees of the Foreign Office are hand-picked*; *I have a hand-picked team of men.*

ˈhandshake *nc* **1** the act of grasping (a person's) hand *eg* as a greeting: *After finally agreeing on the price of the horse, the two men sealed the bargain with a handshake.* **2** the grasp itself: *He has a very strong handshake.* – *See also* **shake hands** *below.*

ˈhandstand *nc* the act of balancing one's body upright in the air with one's hands on the floor or ground: *The children always do a handstand at the beginning of their gym lesson.*

hand-to-hand *see* **hand to hand** *below.*

ˈhandwriting *nu* **1** writing with a pen or pencil: *Today we will practise handwriting.* **2** the way in which a person writes: *Your handwriting is terrible!*

first-hand, left-hand, right-hand, second-hand *see* **first, left, right, second**.

at first, second hand *see* **first, second**.

at ˈhand 1 (*with* **close** *or* **near**) near: *The bus station is close at hand.* **2** (*formal*) available; able to be used; ready for use when needed: *Help is at hand.*

at the ˈhand(s) of (someone) from, or by the action of, (someone): *He received very rough treatment at the hands of the terrorists.*

be hand in glove (with someone) to be very closely associated with someone, *usu* in a bad sense, for a bad purpose: *Some well-known politicians have been found to be hand in glove with leading gangsters.*

by ˈhand 1 with a person's hand or tools held in the hands, rather than with machinery: *This furniture was all made by hand*; *I want this letter written by hand, not typed.* **2** not by post but by a messenger *etc*: *This parcel was delivered by hand.*

change hands *see* **change**.

fall into the hands (of someone) to be caught, found, captured *etc* by someone: *He fell into the hands of bandits*; *The documents fell into the wrong hands* (= were found, captured *etc* by someone who was not supposed to see them).

force someone's hand to force someone to do something either which he does not want to do or sooner than he wants to do it: *I did not want to sack him – but he forced my hand by always being late.*

a free hand *see* **free**.

get one's hands on (*inf*) **1** to catch (someone who has *usu* done something bad): *If I ever get my hands on him, I'll make him sorry for what he did!* **2** to get or obtain (the use of something): *I'd love to get my hands on a car like that.*

give/lend a helping hand (*inf*) to help or assist: *I'm always ready to give/lend a helping hand.*

hand down *vt sep* to pass on (a precious object, a belief, a tradition *etc*) from one generation to the next: *These customs have been handed down from father to son since the Middle Ages*; *One generation handed them down to another.*

hand in *vt sep* **1** to give or bring (something) to a person, place *etc*: *The teacher told the children to hand in their exercise-books*; *They handed them in.* **2** to give or bring (something) to a person, place *etc* by coming or going into a place: *I'll hand this letter in to his office as I go past tonight*; *I'll also hand in the parcel.*

hand in hand with one person holding the hand of another: *The boy and girl were walking along hand in hand*; (*fig*) *Poverty and crime go hand in hand.*

ˈhand it to someone (*inf*: *usu with* **have (got) to**) to show or feel admiration for (a person); to give (a person) the praise that he deserves: *You've got to hand it to him – he said he'd be a millionaire one day and he's done it.*

hand on *vt sep* to give (something) to someone: *When you have finished reading these notes, hand them on to the person after you on this list*; *The secret* has been handed on from father to son.

hand out *vt sep* **1** to give (a number of things) by hand (to several people): *The teacher handed out books to all the pupils; They were handing out leaflets in the street.* **2** (*fig*) to give (something to someone): *It's very easy to hand out criticism, but could you do the job any better?* – *See also* **hand-out** *above.*

hand over *vt sep* to give, send *etc* (a person, thing *etc* to someone): *We know you have the jewels, so hand them over; They handed the thief over to the police;* (*fig*) *The reporter handed the viewers over to Fred Smith in the television studio.*

hand over fist (*inf*) in large amounts; very quickly: *He's making money hand over fist in that shop.*

hands down (*inf*) very easily: *He's not very good at chess – you'll win hands down.*

hands off! (*inf*) do not touch or take (something): *Hands off (those cakes)!*

hands up! raise your hands above your head: *'Hands up!' shouted the bank-robbers as they pulled out their guns.*

hand to hand while being beside the person one is fighting *etc*: *The soldiers fought the enemy hand to hand;* (*attrib*) *hand-to-hand fighting.*

have a hand in (something) (*formal*) to be one of the people who have caused, done *etc* (something): *Did you have a hand in the building of this boat/in the success of the project?*

have (got) one's hands full (*inf*) to be very busy: *She must have her hands full with those four children to look after.*

have/get/gain the upper hand (*formal*) to (begin to) win, beat the enemy *etc*: *The enemy made a fierce attack but failed to get the upper hand.*

hold hands (with someone) to be hand in hand with someone, *usu* as a sign of affection: *The boy and girl walked along the street holding hands; He was seen holding hands with a girl.*

in good hands receiving care and attention: *Your husband will soon be well again. He's in good hands here.*

in 'hand 1 not used *etc*; remaining: *We've spent £50, so we still have £10 in hand; These two football teams have won the same number of points but one of them has a game in hand* (= has played one game less than the other). **2** (*formal*) being dealt with; being done *etc*: *We have received your complaint about the smell and the matter is now in hand.* – *See also* **take in hand** *below.*

in the 'hands of (someone) (*formal*) being dealt with, done *etc* by someone: *This matter is now in the hands of my solicitor.*

keep one's hand in (*inf*) to remain good or skilful at doing something by doing it occasionally: *I still sometimes play a game of billiards, just to keep my hand in.*

keep one's hands off (*inf*) not to take or touch (something): *Keep your hands off those cakes!*

lay (one's) hands on (*inf*) **1** to reach or find (something one is looking for): *Your report is on my desk, but I can't just lay (my) hands on it at the moment.* **2** to catch (someone who has *usu* done something bad): *If I ever lay (my) hands on the person who stole my car, he'll wish he hadn't.*

lend a helping hand *see* **give a helping hand** *above.*

off someone's hands (*inf*) no longer needing to be looked after *etc*: *You'll be glad to get the children off your hands for a couple of weeks.*

on 'hand near; present; ready for use *etc*: *We always keep some candles on hand in case there's a power failure; You'd better be on hand in case you are needed.*

on someone's hands (*inf*) left over; remaining; not sold *etc*: *We were left with a lot of rubbish on our hands at the end of the sale.*

(on the 'one hand) . . . on the 'other hand an expression used to introduce two opposing parts of an argument *etc*: *(On the one hand) we could stay and help you, but on the other hand, it might be better if we went to help him instead.*

out of hand 1 unable to be controlled: *The angry crowd was getting out of hand.* **2** (*formal*) quickly; without thinking, waiting *etc*: *The soldiers shot the bandits out of hand* (= without a trial).

set/put one's hand to (something) to try or begin to do (something): *He's very clever – he can do anything he sets his hand to.*

shake hands with (someone)/shake someone's hand to grasp a person's (*usu* right) hand, in one's own (*usu* right) hand, as a form of greeting, as a sign of agreement *etc*: *The leaders of the two sides shook hands to show that the dispute was over.* – *See also* **handshake** *above.*

a show of hands at a meeting, debate *etc*, a vote expressed by people raising their hands: *The union leaders called for a show of hands to decide whether or not to come out on strike.*

take in hand to look after, discipline or train (someone): *These young hooligans need to be taken in hand.*

to 'hand (*formal*) here; easily reached: *All the tools you need are to hand;* (*very formal*) *We have your letter to hand.*

try one's hand (at something) *see* **try**.

turn one's hand to (something) *see* **turn**.

wash one's hands of (a person, thing *etc***)** to say that one is no longer willing to be involved in (a project *etc*) or be responsible for (a project, a person *etc*): *He told them that if they wouldn't listen to his advice, he would wash his hands of them/their scheme.*

handicap ['handikap] **1** *nc* something that makes doing something more difficult: *The loss of a finger would be a handicap for a pianist.* **2** *nc* (in a race, competition *etc*) a disadvantage of some sort (*eg* having to run a greater distance in a race) given to the best competitors so that others have a better chance of winning. **3** *nc* a race, competition *etc* in which some people *etc* have a handicap (*def 2*). **4** *ncu* (a form of) physical or mental disability: *This school has been built for children with all forms of physical handicap.* – *v* – *pt, ptp* **'handicapped** – *vt* **1** to make something (more) difficult for (a person): *He wanted to be a pianist, but was handicapped by his deafness.* **2** (in a race, competition *etc*) to give (a person *etc*) a handicap: *Are there any rules on how to handicap horses for a race?*

'handicapped *adj* physically or mentally disabled: *He is physically handicapped and cannot walk; a handicapped child.*

handicraft ['handikra:ft] *nu* skilled work done by hand, not machine, *eg* knitting, pottery, model-making *etc.*

handiwork ['handiwə:k] *nu* **1** thing(s) made by hand: *Examples of the pupils' handiwork were on show.* **2** (*ironic*) something bad done by or caused by a particular person: *This destruction looks like a child's handiwork.*

handkerchief ['haŋkətʃif] – *pls* **'handkerchiefs,**

'**handkerchieves** [-tʃi:vz] – *nc* (*inf abbrev* **hankie, hanky** ['haŋki]) a small *usu* square piece of cloth or paper tissue used for wiping or blowing one's nose into.

handle ['handl] *nc* the part of an object (*eg* a cup, spoon, door) by which it may be held or grasped: *I've broken the handle off this cup*; *You've got to turn the handle in order to open the door.* – *vt* **1** to touch or hold with the hand: *Please wash your hands before handling food.* **2** to control, manage or deal with (a person, situation *etc*): *He'll never make a good teacher – he doesn't know how to handle children.* **3** (*formal*) to buy or sell (goods); to deal in: *I'm afraid we do not handle such goods in this shop.* **4** to treat (a person, animal *etc*) in a particular way: *You should never handle animals roughly.*

-handled (*in cmpds*) having a (certain kind of) handle: *a long-handled knife.*

'**handler** *nc* a person who trains and controls an animal (*esp* a dog): *a police dog and its handler.*

'**handling** *nu* (*formal*) the way in which a person, situation, thing *etc* is handled: *We were very impressed by your handling of this affair.*

'**handlebars** *n pl* the *usu* bent bar at the front of a bicycle *etc* which is held by the rider and by which the bicycle *etc* is steered: *The cyclist was thrown over the handlebars when the bike crashed.*

handlebar moustache *nc* a wide, thick moustache with curved ends thought to resemble the handlebars of a bicycle in shape.

fly off the handle *see* **fly**.

handless, handmade, handshake *see* **hand**.

handsome ['hansəm] *adj* **1** (*usu* of men) good-looking: *a handsome prince*; *She likes men who are tall, dark and handsome.* **2** (*formal*) very large; generous: *He gave a handsome sum of money to charity*; *It was handsome of you to forgive him.*

'**handsomely** *adv.* '**handsomeness** *nu.*

handstand, handwriting *see* **hand**.

handy ['handi] *adj* **1** (*pred*) ready (to use); in a convenient place: *I like to keep my tools handy*; *This house is handy for the shops.* **2** easy to use; useful: *This is a very handy tool*; *This new kitchen gadget is very handy.* **3** (*usu pred*: *inf*) clever with one's hands: *My husband is very handy round the house.* '**handiness** *nu.*

'**handyman** [-man] *nc* a man who does jobs, for himself or other people, *esp* around the house.

come in handy (*inf*) to be useful: *I'll put these bottles in the cupboard – they might come in handy some day.*

hang [haŋ] – *pt, ptp* **hung** [hʌŋ] (*defs 1, 2, 4, 5, 6, 7*), **hanged** (*def 3*) – **1** *vti* to put or fix (something), or to be put or fixed, at some point above the ground *eg* by a hook: *We'll hang the picture on that wall*; *The picture is hanging on the wall.* **2** *vti* to fasten (something), or to be fastened, at the top or side so that it can move freely but cannot fall: *We'll hang the curtains tonight*; *A door hangs by its hinges*; *Hang your coat in the cupboard.* **3** *vti* to kill (a criminal, oneself *etc*), or to be killed, by having a rope put round the neck and being allowed to drop: *Murderers used to be hanged in the United Kingdom, but no-one hangs for murder now*; *He committed suicide by hanging himself.* **4** *vi* (*often with* **down** *or* **out**) to be bending, drooping or falling downwards: *The dog's tongue was hanging out*; *The wallpaper was hanging off the wall*; *Her hair was hanging down.* **5** *vt* to fix (wallpaper) to a wall: *You've hung that paper with the pattern upside down.* **6** *vi* (of birds *etc*) to remain more or less still in the air. **7** *vt* to bow (one's head): *He hung his head in shame.* – *See also* **hang** *in phrases below.* – *nc* (*no pl*) the way in which something hangs: *the hang of a dress.* – *See also* **get the hang of** *below.*

'**hanger** *nc* (*usu* '**coat-hanger**) a metal, wooden or plastic object on which jackets, dresses *etc* are hung up: *There aren't enough hangers for my clothes in that hotel wardrobe.*

'**hanging** *ncu* the (act of) killing a criminal by hanging: *He was put to death by hanging*; *There have been no hangings in this country recently.*

'**hangings** *n pl* (*formal*) curtains or material hung on walls for decoration: *All the hangings are included in the price of the house.*

ˌ**hanger-'on** – *pl* ˌ**hangers-'on** – *nc* (*derog*) a person who stays near someone in the hope of gaining some advantage: *Rich men always have a lot of hangers-on.*

'**hangman** *nc* the man who hangs criminals.

'**hangover** *nc* **1** the unpleasant effects of having had too much alcohol: *He woke up with a dreadful hangover.* – *See also* **hung over** *below.* **2** something which remains from an earlier time: *This may not be the best way of doing things – it's just a hangover from the old system.*

'**hang-up** *nc* (*sl*) something about which a person is obsessed: *She's got a real hang-up about her husband's promotion prospects.* – *See also* **hang up** *below.*

hung-over *see* **hung over** *below.*

get the hang of (*inf*) to learn or begin to understand how to do (something): *It may seem difficult at first, but you'll get the hang of it after a few weeks.*

hang about/around (*derog*) **1** *vi, vt fus* to stand around, doing nothing: *I don't like to see all these youths hanging about (street-corners).* **2** *vt fus* to be close to (a person) frequently: *I don't want you hanging about my daughter.*

hang back *vi* to hesitate or be unwilling to do (something): *The soldiers all hung back when the sergeant asked for volunteers for the mission.*

a '**hangdog** '**look** a sly, ashamed or guilty look: *I know the child has done wrong – he's got that hangdog look.*

hang fire to delay or be delayed: *Our plans for the new factory are hanging fire at the moment.*

hang in the balance (*formal*) to be in doubt: *The success of this project is hanging in the balance.*

hang on *vi* **1** (*inf*) to wait: *Will you hang on a minute – I'm not quite ready.* **2** (*often with* **to**) to hold (something): *Hang on to that rope.*

hang out 1 *vi* (*sl*) to live: *Where does he hang out nowadays?* **2** *vt sep* to hang (wet clothes *etc*) on a rope outside to dry: *I'll go and hang out the washing.*

hang together *vi* (*fig*) to agree or be consistent: *His statements just do not hang together – he must be lying.*

hang up 1 *vt sep* to hang (something) on something: *Hang up your coat in the cupboard*; *I'll hang the washing up in the bathroom.* **2** *vi* (*often with* **on**) to put the receiver back after a telephone conversation: *I tried to talk to her, but she hung up (on me).* – *See also* **hang-up** *above.*

hung over (*inf*) having a hangover (*def 1*): *You look a bit hung over this morning*; (*attrib*) *a hung-over look.*

I'll *etc* **be** '**hanged if I'll** (*etc*) (**do something**) (*old inf*) I am *etc* determined not to: *I'll be hanged if I'll put up with her rudeness!*; *She said she'd be hanged if she would agree to such a stupid idea.*

hangar ['haŋə] *nc* a shed for aeroplanes.

hank [haŋk] *nc* a coil or loop of rope, wool, string *etc*: *I wanted balls of knitting-wool but I could only buy it in hanks.*

hanker ['haŋkə] *vi* (*with* **after** *or* **for**: *inf*) to want (something): *I rather hanker after going to America*; *She was obviously hankering for an invitation.*

have a 'hankering for (something) (*inf*) to want (something): *I have a hankering for a strawberry ice-cream.*

hankie, hanky ['haŋki] short for **handkerchief**.

haphazard [hap'hazəd] *adj, adv* depending on chance; without planning or system: *a haphazard arrangement*; *Their plans for the holiday seem rather haphazard.* **hap'hazardly** *adv.*

hapless ['haplis] *adj* (*arch or liter*: *attrib*) unlucky; unfortunate: *the hapless youth.*

happen ['hapən] *vi* **1** to take place or occur; to occur by chance: *What happened next?*; *It just so happens that I have the key in my pocket*; *As it happens, I have the key in my pocket*; *Strange things are happening in this place.* **2** (*usu with* **to**) to be done to (a person, thing *etc*): *What happened to you yesterday?*; *What has happened to my salary this month? – it's less than it usually is*; *She's late – something must have happened to her.* **3** to do or be (something) by chance: *I happened to find him*; *He happens to be my friend.*

'happening *nc* (*often in pl*) an event or occurrence: *strange happenings in the middle of the night.*

'happen (up)on *vt fus* (*formal*) to find (a person, thing) by chance: *He happened upon the perfect solution to the problem just as he was about to give up his research.*

happy ['hapi] *adj* **1** having a feeling of pleasure or contentment or showing that one has such a feeling: *a happy person*; *a happy smile*; *I feel happy today*; *I am so happy to hear of your engagement.* **2** (*pred*) willing: *I'd be happy to help you.* **3** (*formal*: *attrib*) lucky: *By a happy chance I have the key with me.* **4** (*attrib*) well-chosen; appropriate: *a happy choice of words.* **'happiness** *nu.*

'happily *adv*: *The child smiled happily*; *I'll happily help you all I can*; *Happily* (= Fortunately) *she arrived home safely in the end.*

ˌhappy-go-'lucky *adj* not worrying about what might happen: *a happy-go-lucky person*; *She is always cheerful and happy-go-lucky.*

happy medium a sensible middle course between two extreme positions: *You can surely find some happy medium between starving yourself and over-eating*; *I'm a great believer in finding happy mediums.*

See also **unhappy**.

hara-kiri [harə'ki:ri:] *nu* a form of suicide once common in Japan: *He committed hara-kiri.*

harangue [hə'raŋ] *nc* (*formal*) a loud, rousing speech (to a crowd): *The children listened in silence to the headmaster's harangue on good behaviour.* – *vti* (*formal*) to give a harangue (to a crowd): *The politician harangued his audience.*

harass ['harəs, (*esp Amer*) hə'ras] *vt* **1** to annoy or trouble (a person) constantly or frequently: *The children have been harassing me all morning*; *He said that the police had been harassing him since he came out of prison.* **2** (*formal*) to make frequent sudden attacks on (an enemy): *The army was constantly harassed by groups of terrorists.*

'harassed *adj*: *a harassed mother*; *She always looks so harassed.*

'harassment *nu* (*formal*) the harassing (of a person): *He accused the police of harassment*; *Her children are a constant source of harassment to her.*

harbinger ['ha:bindʒə] *nc* (*liter*) a sign of something that is to come: *Swallows and cuckoos are harbingers of summer.*

harbour, (*Amer*) **harbor** ['ha:bə] *nc* **1** a place of shelter for ships: *All the ships stayed in the harbour during the storm*; (*fig formal*) *This part of town has been a harbour for criminals for years.* – *vt* (*formal*) **1** to give shelter or refuge to (a person): *It is against the law to harbour criminals.* **2** to have (*usu* bad) thoughts in one's head: *He harbours a grudge against me.*

'harbour-master *nc* the official in charge of a harbour.

hard [ha:d] *adj* **1** firm; solid; not easy to break, scratch *etc*: *The ground is too hard to dig*; *Granite is a very hard stone.* **2** not easy to do, learn, solve *etc*: *Is English a hard language to learn?*; *This is a hard sum*; *He is a hard man to please*; *It is hard to know what is the best course of action.* **3** not feeling or showing pity, sympathy or kindness: *a hard master*; *He has a hard look on his face*; *He is hard and unfeeling towards his children.* **4** (*attrib*) doing (something) with a great deal of effort: *He is a hard worker.* **5** (*attrib*) (of weather) severe: *a hard winter/frost.* **6** having or causing suffering: *She's had a hard life*; *These are hard times*; *Times are hard.* **7** (of water) containing many chemical salts and so not easily forming bubbles when soap is added: *I prefer soft water to hard water*; *The water in that part of England is very hard.* **8** (of the letters *c* and *g*) pronounced as in *cat* and *got*: *Is the 'g' in 'get' hard or soft?* – *See also* **be hard on** *below.* – *adv* **1** with great effort: *He works very hard*; *You'll have to pull harder than that*; *You must know the answer – think hard.* **2** with great force; heavily: *Don't hit him too hard*; *It was raining hard when I left*; (*fig*) *She was hard hit* (= very upset) *by the news of her father's death*; (*fig*) *She took her father's death very hard* (= she was very upset). **3** with great attention: *He stared hard at the man.* **4** to the full extent; completely: *'Hard aport,' shouted the captain, and the ship slowly turned to the left*; *The car turned hard right.*

'harden *vti* to make or become hard: *Don't touch the toffee till it hardens*; (*fig*) *You must try to harden your heart against him – he is just trying to make you feel sorry for him and lend him money.* – *See also* **be, become hardened to** *below.*

'hardness *ncu.*

'hardship *ncu* (something which causes) pain, suffering *etc*: *She's seen a lot of hardship in her life, but things are better now*; *Hardships came one after another.*

'hard-and-fast *adj* (*attrib*) (of rules) that can never be changed or ignored: *There are no hard-and-fast rules about the use of hyphens in English.*

'hard-back *ncu* a book or edition with a hard cover: *I always buy hard-backs – paperbacks bend too easily*; *Is this book appearing in hard-back?*; (*attrib*) *a hard-back edition.*

ˌhard-'bitten *adj* (*inf*) (of people) tough; toughened by experience; stubborn: *a hard-bitten* *soldier; She's become really hard-bitten since her divorce.*

ˌ**hard-'boiled** *adj* (of eggs) boiled until the white and the yolk are solid: *Put some hard-boiled eggs in the salad; Do you like your eggs hard-boiled?*

'**hard case** *nc* (*inf*) a person who is difficult to deal with or reform: *Some of the criminals in this prison are real hard cases.*

hard cash *nu* (*inf*) coins and bank-notes, as opposed to cheques *etc*: *I prefer to be paid in hard cash for a job like this.*

'**hard-earned** *adj* (*attrib*) earned by hard work or with difficulty: *I deserve every penny of my hard-earned wages.*

hardened criminal *nc* a criminal who is or would be difficult to reform.

hard facts *n pl* facts that cannot be denied: *I don't care what he says – the hard facts are that the mistakes were mainly caused by him.*

ˌ**hard-'headed** *adj* clever; practical; not influenced by emotion: *a hard-headed businessman; Successful businessmen must be shrewd and hard-headed.*

ˌ**hard-'hearted** *adj* not feeling or showing pity or kindness: *a cruel, hard-hearted attitude to the poor; She is beautiful to look at but she is hard-hearted.*

hard labour *nu* a sentence of imprisonment during which a prisoner is given hard physical work to do, *eg* breaking rocks: *He was sentenced to five years hard labour.*

hard line *nc* a policy of taking strong action on something, or of holding firmly to decisions, policies *etc* that have been made: *The Government is adopting a hard line over its new pay policy;* (*attrib*) *hard-line policies.*

ˌ**hard-'liner** *nc* a person who believes in following a hard line on some matter, *esp* one who believes in holding strictly to the beliefs and policies of a particular political party: *The hard-liners of the Liberal party will never agree to a coalition with the Labour party.*

hard shoulder *nc* the hard surface at the side of a motorway *etc*, on which cars *etc* may stop in an emergency: *He stopped on the hard shoulder to change a wheel.*

'**hardware** *nu* metal goods such as pots, tools *etc*: *This shop sells hardware;* (*attrib*) *a hardware department.*

ˌ**hard-'wearing** *adj* that will not wear out easily: *a suit made from a hard-wearing material; That tweed is very hard-wearing.*

be, become 'hardened to to be or become used to doing something unpleasant: *When I started teaching, I didn't like punishing children, but I soon became hardened to it.*

be 'hard on 1 to punish or criticize (a person) severely: *Don't be too hard on the boy – he's too young to know that he was doing wrong.* **2** to be unfair to (a person): *I know we can't make exceptions to our rules, but it's a bit hard on those who did nothing wrong.*

be ˌhard 'put to it to have difficulty (in doing something): *I'd be hard put to it to finish making this dress by this evening.*

drive a hard bargain *see* **drive**.

go hard with (*formal*) to be unpleasant for (a person); to cause (a person) trouble or suffering: *It will go hard with him if he tries to bully me.*

ˌ**hard 'at it** (*inf*) busy doing (something): *I've been hard at it all day, trying to get this report finished.*

hard by (*old*) close or near: *Hard by the tower, there was a large gate; There was a gate hard by.*

ˌ**hard 'done by** (*inf*) unfairly treated: *We gave him a fair share of the money but he still says he has been hard done by.*

harden one's heart to refuse to show sympathy or kindness: *It is very difficult to harden your heart when a beggar comes to your door.*

hard hit badly hurt or troubled by (something): *Our firm has been hard hit by rising prices.*

hard lines/luck (*inf*) bad luck: *Hard lines/luck! I'm afraid you haven't won this time; It's hard lines that you didn't win; It's hard luck that he broke his leg.*

ˌ**hard-'luck story** the story of a person's bad luck and suffering, *usu* intended to gain sympathy for the person concerned: *I'm tired of listening to his hard-luck stories – he brought all his misfortunes on himself.*

hard of hearing (*pred*) rather deaf: *He is a bit hard of hearing now.*

hard on (someone's) heels close behind: *The thief ran off, with two policemen hard on his heels.*

a hard time (of it) trouble, difficulty, worry *etc*: *The audience gave the speaker a hard time of it at the meeting; The speaker had a hard time (of it) trying to make himself heard.*

hard up (*inf*: *usu pred*) not having much *esp* money: *I'm a bit hard up at the moment;* (*fig*) *You must be hard up for boyfriends* (= You must have difficulty in finding boyfriends) *if you are going out with him.*

hardly ['ha:dli] *adv* **1** almost no, none, ever *etc*: *Hardly anyone says that nowadays; Hardly any small businesses are successful nowadays; I hardly ever go out now.* **2** only just; almost not: *You can't marry the girl – you hardly know her; My feet are so sore, I can hardly walk; I had hardly got my coat off before they wanted to know when I was leaving again.* **3** probably not: *He's hardly likely to forgive you after what you said about him.*

hardship, hardware *see* **hard**.

hardy ['ha:di] *adj* **1** tough; strong; able to bear cold, tiredness *etc*: *You must be very hardy to sleep out of doors in winter, and wash with icy water; hardy young men climbing hills in winter.* **2** (*old or liter*) brave: *a hardy warrior.* '**hardiness** *nu*.

hare [heə] *nc* an animal with long ears, like a rabbit but slightly larger.

'**hare-brained** *adj* (*also* '**hair-brained**) (of people, actions *etc*) done or acting in a foolish manner, often without thought for the consequences of what is done: *This is a hare-brained scheme; All his plans are so hare-brained.*

harem ['heərəm] *nc* **1** the part of a Muslim house occupied by the women. **2** the women themselves.

haricot ['harikou] *nc* (*usu attrib*) a type of bean: *a haricot bean.*

hark [ha:k] *vi* (*usu in imperative*: *liter or facet*) to listen (to someone or something): *Just hark at him!; Hark! The church bells are ringing.*

hark back *vi* (*with* **to**) (*formal*) to refer to something that has been said or done earlier: *Harking back to what you said last night, I think a decision will need to be made soon; To hark back to what you said, I think we should make a decision soon.*

harken *see* **hearken**.

harm [ha:m] *nu* damage; injury; distress: *I'll make sure you come to no harm; He meant no harm; It'll do you no harm to go.* – *vt* to cause (a person) harm: *There's no need to be frightened – he won't harm you; It wouldn't harm you to eat some of the pudding.*

'harmful *adj* doing harm: *Some medicines are harmful if you take too much of them*; *the harmful effects of some drugs.*

'harmless *adj* not dangerous or liable to cause harm: *Don't be frightened of that snake – it's harmless*; *He's just a harmless old man.* **'harmlessly** *adv.* **'harmlessness** *nu.*

out of harm's way in a safe place: *I'll put this glass vase out of harm's way, in case it gets broken.*

harmonic *see* **harmony**.

harmonica [ha:'monikə] *nc* a kind of small musical instrument played with the mouth: *He plays the harmonica*; *He played a tune on the harmonica.*

harmonium [ha:'mouniəm] *nc* a musical instrument like a small organ: *She plays the harmonium*; *Can you play that sort of music on the harmonium?*

harmony ['ha:məni] **1** *ncu* (of musical sounds, colours *etc*) (the state of forming) a pleasing combination: *The singers sang in harmony*; *There are some beautiful harmonies in that song.* **2** *nu* (*formal*) the agreement of people's feelings, opinions *etc*: *They lived as husband and wife, in perfect harmony*; *Your ideas are in harmony with ours.*

har'monic [-'mo-] *adj* of, or concerned with, harmony.

har'monious [-'mou-] *adj* **1** (*usu attrib*) pleasant-sounding: *a harmonious melody*; *That line is so harmonious.* **2** (*formal*) pleasant to the eye: *harmonious combinations of colours*; *I like colour schemes to be harmonious.* **3** (*formal*) without disagreement or bad feeling: *a harmonious relationship*; *Their relationship is no longer harmonious.* **har'moniously** *adv.* **har'moniousness** *nu.*

'harmonize, -ise **1** *vi* to sing or play musical instruments in harmony. **2** *vt* (*music*) to add different parts to (a melody) to form harmonies. **3** *vti* (*formal*) to (cause to) be in harmony or agreement: *The colours in this room harmonize nicely.* **ˌharmoni'zation, -s-** *ncu.*

harness ['ha:nis] *ncu* the leather straps *etc* by which a horse is attached to a cart *etc* which it is pulling and by means of which it is controlled. – *vt* **1** to put the harness on (a horse). **2** (*fig*) to make use of (a source of power, *eg* a river) for some purpose, *eg* to produce electricity or to drive machinery: *Attempts are now being made to harness the sun as a source of heat and power.*

harp [ha:p] *nc* a *usu* large musical instrument which is held upright, and which has many strings which are plucked with the fingers: *Angels are said to play the harp*; *She can play almost any sort of music on her harp.*

'harpist *nc* a person who plays a harp.

'harp on *vt fus*, **ˌharp 'on (about)** *vi, vt fus* (*inf*) to keep on talking or to talk too much (about something): *He's forever harping on* (*about his low wages*); *She keeps harping on his faults.*

harpoon [ha:'pu:n] *nc* a spear fastened to a rope, used *esp* for killing whales. – *vt* to strike with the harpoon: *He has harpooned the whale.*

harpsichord ['ha:psiko:d] *nc* a type of early keyboard musical instrument: *She played the harpsichord at the concert*; *He played a tune on the harpsichord.*

harrowing ['harouiŋ] *adj* (*formal*) extremely distressing: *a harrowing story/experience*; *It was harrowing to see the child die.*

harry ['hari] *vt* (*formal or liter*) **1** to torment or worry (a person) frequently: *He never pays his debts unless you harry him.* **2** to destroy or plunder (a country, district *etc*); to attack (a country, district *etc*) frequently: *The English army harried the Borders of Scotland.*

harsh [ha:ʃ] *adj* **1** (of people, discipline *etc*) very strict; cruel: *That is a very harsh punishment to give a young child*; *The punishment is too harsh.* **2** rough and unpleasant to hear, see, taste *etc*: *a harsh voice*; *harsh colours*; *I don't like the colour of that dress – it's too harsh.*

'harshly *adv*: *The judge dealt harshly with the prisoner*; *She spoke sternly and harshly.*

'harshness *nu*: *the harshness of the prison sentence*; *the harshness of her voice*; *the harshness of the weather.*

harum-scarum [heərəm'skeərəm] *nc, adj* (*inf*) (a person) who behaves in a foolish and thoughtless way: *a silly harum-scarum girl*; *She's such a harum-scarum.*

harvest ['ha:vist] **1** *ncu* the gathering in of ripened corn and other crops, *usu* in late summer or early autumn: *The farmer says he can't go on holiday until after* (*the*) *harvest*; (*attrib*) *a harvest festival.* **2** *nc* the corn and crops so gathered in: *There's been a good harvest this year.* **3** *nc* (*formal*) the amount of any natural product: *the harvest of pearls*; *the harvest of the sea.* **4** *nc* (*formal fig*) the consequences or results of some action: *We're now reaping the harvest of our wrong decisions.* – *vti* to gather in (crops *etc*): *We harvested the apples yesterday.*

'harvester *nc* a person or machine that harvests corn. – *See also* **combine harvester**.

has, has-been *see* **have**.

hash [haʃ] **1** *nc* a dish of chopped meat, vegetables, *etc*: *We had corned beef hash for lunch.* **2** *nu* (*sl*) hashish.

make a hash of (something) (*inf*) to spoil (something) completely; to do (something) badly: *I made a complete hash of that translation.*

settle someone's hash (*sl*) to deal with a person in such a way that he ceases to be a nuisance, or is unable to do what he intended to do: *He thinks he's going to marry my daughter but I'll soon settle his hash!*

hashish ['haʃi:ʃ] *nu* (a drug made from) the dried leaves, flowers *etc* of the hemp plant, *usu* smoked or chewed; cannabis.

hasn't *see* **have**.

hassle ['hasl] (*inf*) **1** *ncu* trouble or fuss: *It's such a hassle to get to work on time*; *Travelling with children is such a hassle.* **2** *nc* a fight or argument: *I got into a bit of a hassle with a couple of thugs.* – (*inf*) **1** *vi* to argue or fight: *It seemed pointless to hassle over such a small matter.* **2** *vt* to annoy (a person): *I don't like people hassling me.*

hassock ['hasək] *nc* a stuffed cushion or stool for putting one's feet on or for kneeling on: *He knelt on a hassock while he prayed.*

haste [heist] *nu* (*more formal than* **hurry**) (too much) speed: *Your work shows signs of haste – there are too many mistakes in it*; *It was done with great haste.*

hasten ['heisn] **1** (*more formal than* **hurry**) *vti* to (cause to) move with speed: *I saw the old man hastening towards me.* **2** *vt* to do (something) at once: *He hastened to add an explanation.*

'hasty *adj* **1** (*more formal than* **quick**: *attrib*) done in a hurry: *You will have time for a hasty snack before the train leaves.* **2** acting or done with too much speed and without thought: *She is too hasty – she should think carefully before making such an* *important decision*; *a hasty decision.* **3** (*attrib*) easily made angry: *a hasty temper.* **'hastily** *adv.* **'hastiness** *nu.*

in 'haste 1 (*formal*) in a hurry; quickly: *I am writing in haste before I go away on holiday tonight.* **2** (*old or liter*) with too much speed; rashly: *Act in haste, repent at leisure.*

make haste (*old or liter*) to hurry: *You must make haste if you are to reach your destination by nightfall.*

hat [hat] *nc* (*sometimes in cmpds*) a covering for the head, *usu* worn out of doors: *Women used always to wear hats in church*; *He raised his hat as the lady approached*; *a bowler-hat*; *a cowboy-hat.*

'hatter *nc* (*formal*) a person who makes or sells hats.

'hatstand *nc* a piece of furniture with hooks or pegs on which one hangs hats, coats *etc.*

'hat trick *nc* **1** (in cricket) the putting out of three batsmen by three balls in a row. **2** (in football) three goals scored by one player in a match: *He scored a hat trick.* **3** any action done three times in a row: *I've got a hat trick – that's the third car I've sold today.*

keep (something) under one's hat (*inf*) to keep (something) secret: *Keep it under your hat but I'm getting married next week.*

mad as a hatter *see* **mad**.

pass/send round the hat to ask for or collect money on someone's behalf: *When Tom had an accident and was out of work, his colleagues passed round the hat for him.*

,take one's 'hat off to (*inf*) to admire (someone) for doing something: *I take my hat off to that woman for bringing up five children on her own.*

talk through one's hat (*inf*) to talk nonsense: *Don't believe what he says – he always talks through his hat.*

hatch[1] [hatʃ] *nc* (the door or cover of) an opening in a wall, floor, ship's deck *etc*: *There's a hatch between the kitchen and dining-room for serving food from.*

'hatchway *nc* an opening, *esp* in a ship's deck; also in a floor, wall *etc.*

hatch[2] [hatʃ] **1** *vt* to produce young birds *etc* from eggs: *My hens have hatched ten chicks.* **2** *vi* to break out of the egg: *These chicks hatched this morning.* **3** *vi* to become young birds: *Four of the eggs have hatched already.* **4** *vt* (*fig*) to plan (something, *usu* bad) in secret: *The thieves hatched their wicked scheme while in prison together.*

hatchet ['hatʃit] *nc* a small axe held in one hand: *The police searched for the hatchet used by the murderer.*

bury the hatchet *see* **bury**.

hatchway *see* **hatch**[1].

hate [heit] *vt* (not used with **is, was** *etc* and **-ing**) to dislike (someone or something) very much: *I hate them for what they did to my father*; *The child hates eggs*; *I hate getting up in the morning.* **1** *nu* great dislike: *a look of hate.* **2** *nc* (*often with* **pet**) something which is greatly disliked: *Getting up in the morning is one of my pet hates* (= one of the things I hate most).

'hateful *adj* **1** very bad; very unpleasant: *That was a hateful thing to do to her*; *It is hateful of you to treat people in that way.* **2** (*pred*) causing great dislike: *Such behaviour is hateful to me.* **'hatefully** *adv.* **'hatefulness** *nu.*

hatred ['heitrid] *nu* (*formal*) great dislike: *There was a look of hatred in his eyes*; *I have a deep-seated hatred of liars.*

hatstand, hatter *see* **hat**.

haughty ['ho:ti] *adj* (showing that one thinks that one is) very proud or very important: *a haughty look*; *a haughty young woman*; *She looks rather haughty.* **'haughtily** *adv.* **'haughtiness** *nu.*

haul [ho:l] **1** *vti* to pull with great effort or difficulty: *Horses are used to haul barges along canals*; *He was hauling on the rope.* **2** *vt* to carry by some form of transport: *Coal is hauled by road and rail.* – *nc* **1** a strong pull: *He gave the rope a haul*; *He gave a haul on the rope.* **2** the amount of anything, *esp* fish, which is caught at one time: *The fisherman had a good haul*; (*fig*) *The thieves got away from the jeweller's with a good haul.* – *See also* **a long haul** *below.*

'haulage [-lidʒ] *nu* (money charged for) the carrying of goods by road, rail *etc.*

'haulier [-liə] *nc* a person who owns lorries which carry goods for other people.

haul (someone) over the coals *see* **coal**.

a long haul (*inf fig*) a long or tiring job *etc*: *Writing dictionaries can be a long haul*; *The journey from Edinburgh to London is rather a long haul.*

haunch [ho:ntʃ] *nc* **1** (*usu in pl*) the fleshy part of the hip: *The children were squatting on their haunches.* **2** the leg and lower part of the body of a deer *etc*, as meat: *a haunch of venison.*

haunt [ho:nt] *vt* **1** (of a ghost) to stay in (a place): *A ghost is said to haunt this room.* **2** (*fig*) (of something unpleasant) to keep coming back to a person's mind: *Her look of misery haunts me.* **3** (*inf*) to visit (a place or person) very often: *He haunts that café.* – *nc* (*inf*) a place one often visits: *This is one of my favourite haunts.*

'haunted *adj* inhabited by ghosts: *a haunted castle*; *The old house is said to be haunted.*

haute couture [(h)outku'tjuə] *nu* (*formal*) (the products of) the most important fashion designers and dress-making firms: *Not many women can afford haute couture nowadays*; (*attrib*) *haute couture garments.*

haute cuisine [(h)outkwi:'zi:n] *nu* (*formal*) cookery of a very high standard or the fine food so prepared: *The restaurant is noted for its haute cuisine.*

have [hav] – *3rd pers sing prt* **has** [haz]: *pt, ptp* **had** [had]: *short forms* **I've** [aiv] **(I have)**, **you've** [ju:v] **(you have)**, **he's** [hi:z] **(he has)**, **she's** [ʃi:z] **(she has)**, **it's** [its] **(it has)**, **we've** [wi:v] **(we have)**, **they've** [ðeiv] **(they have)**, **I'd** [aid] **(I had)**, **you'd** [ju:d] **(you had)**, **he'd** [hi:d] **(he had)**, **she'd** [ʃi:d] **(she had)**, **it'd** ['itəd] **(it had)**, **we'd** [wi:d] **(we had)**, **they'd** [ðeid] **(they had)**: *neg short forms* **ain't** [eint] **(have/has not)** (*only aux*: *inf or facet*), **hadn't** ['hadnt] **(had not)**, **hasn't** ['haznt] **(has not)**, **haven't** ['havnt] **(have not)** – *aux* (not used with **is, was** *etc* and **-ing**) used with *ptp* of other verbs to show that an action is in the past and has been completed: *I've bought a new dictionary*; *Has he gone yet?* – *vt* (not used with **is, was** *etc* and **-ing** (*defs 1–3, 8, 10, 12–14*)) **1** (*also, esp Brit,* **have got**) to hold or possess (something which belongs to oneself or to someone else): *I have a book of yours at home*; *He's got your book*; *I don't have any books by Sir Walter Scott*; *He had a knife in his hand.* **2** (*also, esp Brit,* **have got**) to possess something as part of oneself or in some way connected with oneself: *She has blue eyes*; *She has (got) two sons*; *Our house has six rooms*; *I've got a pain in my stomach.* **3** (*sometimes with* **back**) to receive or get (something): *Have you had any news of your brother?*; *Thank you for lending me the book – you can have it back next week.* **4** to produce (something): *He does have some good ideas*; *She has had a baby.* **5** to cause (something) to be done: *I'm having a tooth (taken) out*; *Have Smith come and see me.* **6** to enjoy or suffer (something): *We had a lovely/terrible holiday.* **7** to do (something): *I'll have a talk with him* (= I'll talk to him); *Let me have a try* (= Let me try). **8** to allow, accept or tolerate (something): *I will not have you wearing clothes like that!* **9** (*with* **back, in, round** *etc*) to ask (a person) to one's house as a guest or to do a job: *We're having friends round for dinner*; *We're having someone in to paint this room.* **10** to state (something): *Rumour has it* (= People are saying) *that you are leaving*; *God made the country and men made the town, as the poet Cowper has it.* **11** to think or feel (something): *I have some doubts about this project*; *I'm having second thoughts about it.* **12** (*inf*) (*also, esp Brit,* **have got**) to have an advantage over (someone): *You have me there*; *You've got me there.* **13** (*inf*: *usu in past tense and passive*) to trick (someone): *You've been had!* **14** (*inf*) to take revenge on (someone): *I'll have him for what he did to me.*

'has-been *nc* (*inf derog*) a person who no longer has the position of importance or influence that he once had: *She still appears in some films but she's really a has-been now.*

have, ˌhave-'not *ncs* (*usu in pl*) a person who has, or does not have, wealth: *Society consists of the haves and have-nots.*

had better, best, rather *see* **better, best, rather**.

have 'done with (something) to stop or put an end to (something): *Let's have done with all this quarrelling.*

have 'had it (*inf*) to be dead, ruined *etc*: *The bullet went into his brain – he's had it, I'm afraid.*

have ˌhad 'that (*inf*) not to be going to get (something): *She wants a new bike, but she's had that* (= she won't get one).

'have it to win: *The ayes have it* (= The people who voted in favour (of something) have won).

ˌhave it 'coming, (*also, esp Brit,* **have got it coming**) (*inf*) to deserve the bad luck, punishment *etc* that one has got: *Don't feel sorry for him – he had it coming/he's got it coming (to him).*

ˌhave it 'in for (someone), (*also, esp Brit,* **have got it in for**) (*inf*) to dislike (someone); to be unpleasant to (someone); to try to cause trouble for (someone): *I don't know why he has it in for me – I've always been nice to him.*

ˌhave it 'in oneself *etc* to have the courage or ability to do something: *I hear she told her boss to stop shouting at her – I didn't think she had it in her.*

ˌhave it 'off (*sl*: *often with* **with**) to have sexual intercourse (with someone); to have an affair with: *There's a rumour that he's having it off with his secretary.*

ˌhave it 'out (*often with* **with**) to argue with (a person) in order to put an end to some disagreement: *This argument has been going on for weeks, so I'm going to have it out with her once and for all.*

have on 1 *vt sep* (*also, esp Brit,* **have got on**) to wear: *That's a nice suit you have on.* **2** *vt oblig sep* (*Brit inf*) to fool (someone): *You're having me on – that's not really true, is it?* **3** *vt oblig sep* (*also, esp Brit,* **have got on**: *inf*) to be busy with (something): *Have you (got) anything on this afternoon?*

'have to (*also, esp Brit,* **have 'got to**) to be obliged to (do something): *I don't want to do this, but I have to*; *Do you have to go so soon?*; *I've got to leave soon*; *You didn't have to do that* (= It was not necessary for you to do it); *You hadn't to do that* (= You should not have done it).

have to do with (a person or thing), (*also, esp Brit,* **have got to do with**) to be of importance, relevance or concern to (a person or thing): *What have these letters to do with you?*; *Your remarks have (got) nothing to do with the subject we are discussing.*

have up *vt sep* (*inf Brit*: *often in passive*: *usu with* **for**) to make (a person) appear in court to answer some charge: *He was had up for drunken driving.*

have what it takes, (*also, esp Brit,* **have got what it takes**: *inf*) to have the qualities or ability that one needs to do something: *He has what it takes to make a good officer*; *He would like to be a doctor but he hasn't got what it takes.*

I have it!, (*also, esp Brit,* **I've got it!**) I have found the answer (to a problem *etc*).

ˌlet (someone) 'have it (*inf*) to attack (someone) with words or blows: *We'll wait till he comes out, then we'll let him have it.*

haven ['heivn] *nc* **1** (*formal*) a place of safety or rest: *This hostel is a haven for tramps.* **2** (*liter*) a harbour.

haven't *see* **have**.

haversack ['havəsak] *nc* a bag worn over one shoulder for carrying food *etc*: *The hiker sat down beside a stream and took his sandwiches out of his haversack.*

havoc ['havək] *nu* (*formal*) great destruction or damage: *The hurricane created havoc over a wide area.*

play havoc (with) *see* **play**.

hawk[1] [ho:k] *nc* a type of bird of prey.

ˌhawk-'eyed *adj* having very good eye-sight.

hawk[2] [ho:k] *vt* (*formal*) to carry goods round for sale: *He hawked the carpets from door to door*; (*fig*) *He's been hawking that idea around for months but no-one is interested.*

'hawker *nc* a person who goes about from door to door offering goods for sale: *She never buys anything from hawkers.*

hawser ['ho:zə] *nc* a thick rope or a steel cable for towing ships or tying them to a dock *etc.*

hawthorn ['ho:θo:n] *ncu* (*also* **'hawthorn tree/bush**) a small tree with thorns and white or pink blossom.

hay [hei] *nu* grass, cut and dried, used as food for cattle *etc*: *There is enough hay in the barn for the cows in the winter*; (*attrib*) *a hay-field.*

ˌhay-'fever *nu* an illness like a bad cold, caused by the pollen of flowers *etc*: *Whenever my father mows the lawn he gets hay-fever – he is allergic to grass seeds.*

'hayrick [-rik], **'hay-stack** *ncs* hay built up into a large pile.

'haywire *adj* (*inf*) out of order; in a state of disorder; crazy: *Our computer has gone haywire – we can't get any sensible answers from it.*

hazard ['hazəd] *nc* (something which causes) a risk of harm or danger: *the hazards of mountain-climbing*; *Fog can be a hazard on the motorways in winter.* – *vt* **1** (*very formal*) to risk (something); to be prepared to do (something, the result of which is uncertain): *Are you prepared to hazard your life* for the success of this mission? 2 (*formal*) to put forward (a guess *etc*) which one knows may be wrong: *I don't know what they will do, but I'm prepared to hazard a guess.*

'**hazardous** *adj* (*formal*: *usu attrib*) dangerous: *a hazardous journey.* '**hazardousness** *nu.*

haze [heiz] *nc* a thin mist: *a haze lay over the sea*; *The mountains were covered in haze.*

'**hazy** *adj* **1** misty: *a hazy view*; *You won't get a good view of the mountains today – it's too hazy.* **2** (*inf*: *usu with* **about**) not clear or certain: *I have only a hazy idea about what happened*; *I'm a bit hazy about what happened.* '**haziness** *nu.*

hazel ['heizl] *nc* a kind of small tree on which nuts grow. – *adj* of a light-brown colour: *hazel eyes.*

'**hazel-nut** *nc* the nut of the hazel, which can be eaten.

H-bomb ['eitʃbom] short for **hydrogen bomb**.

he [hi:] *pron* (used only as the subject of a verb) **1** a male person or animal already spoken about: *When I spoke to John, he told me he had seen you.* **2** (*formal*) any (male) person: *He who hesitates is lost.* – *nc* a male person or animal: *Is a cow a he or a she?*

he- (*in cmpds*) (*inf*) male: *a he-goat.*

'**he-man** [-man] – *pl* '**he-men** – *nc* (*inf*) a very strong, powerful man, *esp* one who likes to show how strong he is.

See also **him, himself, his**.

head [hed] *nc* **1** the top part of the human body, containing the eyes, mouth brain *etc*; the same part of an animal's body: *The rock fell and hit him on the head*; *The child patted the horse's head*; *He scratched his head in amazement*; (*attrib*) *He died of head injuries.* **2** a person's mind: *An idea came into my head last night that might be of interest to you*; *He's got a good head on his shoulders.* **3** (*no pl*) the height or length of a head: *He is a head taller than his brother*; *The horse won by a head.* **4** the chief or most important person (of an organization, country *etc*): *Our head of department is a hard man to please*; *Kings and presidents are heads of state*; (*attrib*) *a head waiter*; *The firm's head* (= most important) *office is in London.* **5** anything that is like a head in shape or position: *the head of a pin/axe*; *One hits the head of a nail with the head of a hammer*; *a head of cabbage*; *The boy went round the garden knocking the heads off the flowers.* **6** the place where a river, lake *etc* begins: *the head of the Nile*; *The head of Lake Naru is the point at which the River Naru flows into it.* **7** the top, or the top part, of anything: *Write your address at the head of this letter/page*; *the head of a bed*; *The father sat at the head of the table.* **8** the front part of (a procession *etc*): *Several Members of Parliament were to be seen at the head of the procession.* **9** the ability to do (something), go (somewhere) *etc*: *He has no head for heights* (= He feels uncomfortable, unwell or unhappy when he is at the top *eg* of a high building, and can see how high up he is); *She has a good head for figures.* **10** (*inf*) a headmaster or headmistress: *I'm taking these boys to the head for punishment.* **11** (*no pl*) (for) one person: *This dinner costs £5 a head.* **12** (*usu found with cap in place-names*) a headland: *Beachy Head.* **13** (*inf*) the foam on the top of a glass of beer *etc*. – *See* **head** *in various phrases below.* – **1** *vt* to go at the front of or at the top of (something): *The procession was headed by several Members of Parliament*; *Whose name headed the list?* **2** *vt* to be in charge of (something); to be the leader or chief person: *He heads a team of scientists investigating cancer.* **3** *vti* (*often with* **for**) to (cause to) move in a certain direction: *The explorers headed south*; *The boys headed for home*; *The ship headed out to sea*; (*fig*) *I told him he was heading for disaster.* **4** *vt* to put or write (something) at the beginning of a chapter, top of a letter *etc*: *His report was headed 'Ways of Preventing Industrial Accidents'.* **5** *vt* (in football) to hit the ball with the head: *He headed the ball into the goal.* – *See also* **head** *in phrases below.*

-headed (*in cmpds*) having (a certain number or type of) head(s): *The old lady assured the policeman that she had seen a two-headed man*; *a bald-headed old man.*

'**header** *nc* (*inf*) **1** a fall or dive forwards: *He slipped and took a header into the mud.* **2** (in football) the act of hitting the ball with the head: *He scored with a great header into the corner of the goal.*

'**heading** *nc* what is written at the top of a page, letter, report *etc*: *The teacher said that he wouldn't accept essays that didn't have a proper heading.*

heads *n, adv* (on) the side of a coin with the head of a king, president *etc* on it: *He tossed the penny and it came down heads.* – *interj* a call showing that a person has chosen that side of the coin when tossing a coin to make a decision *etc*. – *See also* **heads or tails** *below.*

'**heady** *adj* (*formal*) which makes a person (behave as if) drunk or excited: *a heady wine/success*; *He was heady with success.*

'**headache** *nc* **1** a pain in the head: *I have a headache*; *She suffers from headaches.* **2** (*fig*) someone or something that worries or annoys (a person): *Lack of money is a real headache for some charities.*

'**headband** *nc* a strip of material worn round the head *esp* of a woman or girl: *The tennis player wore a headband to keep the hair out of her eyes.*

'**headboard** *nc* a board at the top end of a bed: *Some modern beds do not have headboards.*

'**head-dress** *nc* something, *usu* ornamental, which is worn on, and covers, the head, *esp* those worn by North American Indians and tribesmen of other parts of the world: *The natives were wearing magnificent head-dresses of fur and feathers.*

ˌ**head'first** *adv* **1** while moving forwards, upwards or downwards, often quickly, with one's head in front or bent forward: *I ran headfirst into him as I turned the corner*; *He fell headfirst into a pool of water.* **2** without thought or delay, often foolishly: *He runs headfirst into trouble.*

'**headgear** *nu* anything that is worn on the head: *Hats, caps and helmets are headgear.*

'**head-hunter** *nc* a person, *usu* a primitive tribesman who kills other people (*eg* enemies) and keeps their heads as a sign of his victory, courage *etc*. '**head-hunting** *nu.*

'**headlamp** *nc* a headlight.

'**headland** *nc* a point of land which sticks out into the sea.

'**headlight** *nc* a powerful light at or on the front of a car, lorry, train, ship, aeroplane *etc*: *As it was getting dark, the driver switched on his headlights to light up the road ahead.*

'**headline** *nc* the words written in large letters at the top of newspaper articles stating the most important points of the articles: *I never read a paper in detail – I just glance at the headlines*; *I saw* *a headline about the murder.* – *See also* **hit the headlines** *under* **hit**.

ˈ**headlines** *n pl* a brief statement of the most important details of the main items of news read out on the television or the radio: *the news headlines.*

ˈ**headlong** *adj* (*attrib*), *adv* **1** (while) moving forwards, upwards or downwards, often quickly, with one's head in front or bent forward: *a headlong dive into the pool of water*; *He fell headlong into a pool of water.* **2** (done) without thought or delay, often foolishly: *a headlong rush to disaster*; *He rushes headlong into every job he does without stopping to plan what he's doing.*

ˌ**head**ˈ**master** – *fem* ˌ**head**ˈ**mistress** – *nc* the person in charge of a school.

ˌ**head-**ˈ**on** *adv, adj* (*usu attrib*) (*usu* of cars *etc*) with the front of one car *etc* hitting the front of another car *etc*: *a head-on collision*; *The two cars crashed into each other head-on*; (*fig*) *I prefer to meet criticism head-on.*

ˈ**headphones** *n pl* (*also* ˈ**earphones**) a pair of electronic instruments which are held over a person's ears, *usu* by a metal band over the head, and which are connected to a radio, record-player *etc* allowing the person wearing them to listen to the radio, a record *etc* without the sound being heard by others: *While I was in hospital, I used headphones to listen to the radio so as not to disturb the other patients*; *a set of headphones.*

ˌ**head**ˈ**quarters** *n sing or pl* (*often abbrev* **HQ** [eitʃˈkjuː] *nc*) the place from which the chief officers or leaders of an organization (*esp* an army) direct and control the activities of that organization: *During the election, his house was used as the campaign headquarters.*

ˈ**headrest** *nc* a sort of small cushion which supports a person's head, *eg* as fitted to a dentist's chair, a car seat: *Our new car has a headrest on the back of the driver's seat.*

ˈ**headroom** [-ruːm] *nu* space between a person's head and the top of a door, the ceiling of a room, the roof of a car *etc*: *There isn't much headroom in this car.*

ˈ**headscarf** *nc* (*Brit*) a *usu* square scarf worn by women over or round the head: *This shop has a beautiful selection of headscarves.*

ˈ**headsquare** *nc* (*Brit*) a headscarf.

ˈ**headstone** *nc* a stone put at the top of a grave, *usu* with the name of the dead person on it, the date of his birth and death *etc.*

ˈ**headstrong** *adj* (of people) difficult to persuade or control; always doing or wanting to do what they themselves want: *He always was a headstrong child – his parents couldn't control him, nor could his teachers*; *He is obstinate and headstrong.*

headway *see* **make headway** *below.*

ˈ**headwind** *nc* a wind which is blowing towards one.

above someone's head (*inf*) too difficult (for someone) to understand: *What he said was well above their heads – he should have made his talk much simpler.*

bring (something) to a head, come to a head to (cause to) come to a state of climax or crisis when urgent action is needed: *The government's difficulties were brought to a head by the miners' strike*; *The government's difficulties came to a head when the miners went on strike.*

get (something) into someone's head (*inf*) to make someone realize that something is true, necessary *etc*: *I can't get it into his head that he will never be an artist*; *Will you get it into your head that you must get to work on time?*

give (a person *etc***) his head** (*inf*) to allow (a person *etc*) to do what he *etc* wants with regard to something: *His idea may sound a bit odd but I think we should still give him his head.*

go over someone's head to ignore (someone) and talk to someone more senior: *The workman went over the head of the foreman and complained to the manager.* – *See also* **over someone's head** *below.*

go to someone's head 1 (of alcoholic drinks) to make (someone) slightly drunk: *Champagne always goes to my head.* **2** (of praise, success *etc*) to make (someone) arrogant, foolish, careless *etc*: *All the publicity he has had because of his book has gone to his head.*

head and shoulders above (other people) (*inf fig*) very much better, cleverer *etc* (than other people): *He is head and shoulders above all his colleagues.*

head off 1 *vt sep* to make (a person, animal *etc*) change his, its *etc* direction of movement by getting in front of him, it *etc*: *One group of the soldiers rode across the valley to head the bandits off.* **2** *vi* (*inf*) to go in some direction: *He headed off towards the river.*

head over heels 1 (*fig*) completely: *He fell head over heels in love.* **2** turning over completely; headfirst: *He fell head over heels into a pond.*

heads or tails? used when tossing a coin, *eg* to decide which of two people does, gets *etc* (something): *Heads or tails? Heads you do the dishes, tails I do them.* – *See also* **heads, tails**.

keep one's head to remain calm and sensible *eg* in a crisis or sudden difficulty: *She kept her head when she found the flats were on fire. If she had panicked, many people might have died.*

keep one's head above water (*inf*) to get or earn enough money, profits *etc* to remain out of debt: *We're not making a lot of money in the shop, but we are keeping our heads above water.*

lose one's head to become angry or excited, or to act foolishly, *eg* in a crisis or sudden difficulty, or when someone does something wrong *etc*: *I must apologize – I rather lost my head when I thought that you had lost the only copy of my manuscript.*

make head or tail of (something) (*inf*: *usu in neg with* **can** *or* **could**) to understand (something): *I can't make head or tail of these instructions.*

ˈ**make** ˈ**headway** to make progress: *We're not making much headway with this new scheme*; *The ship made very little headway in the storm.*

off one's head (*inf*) mad: *You must be off your head to go for a picnic on such a cold day.*

off the top of one's head (*inf*) without much thought; without making sure that what is said *etc* is correct: *When asked what the company's profits were, he said he could only give them some figures off the top of his head.*

on your, his *etc* ˌ**own head** ˈ**be it** (*inf*) you, he *etc* will bear the responsibility for any harm *etc* caused by your, his *etc* actions or wishes: *He insists on going to the football match even though he has a bad cold, so on his own head be it if he catches pneumonia.*

over someone's head 1 (in a way which is) too difficult (for someone) to understand: *He talked over the heads of the children in the audience*; *What* *he said was/went over their heads.* 2 when others (seem to) have a better right (to something): *He was promoted over the heads of three people who were senior to him.* – *See also* **go over someone's head** *above.*

take it into one's head 1 to come to believe, *usu* wrongly, that something is true *etc*: *He's taken it into his head that everyone hates him.* 2 to decide to do something *usu* foolish: *He's taken it into his head to have a cold shower every morning.*

turn someone's head *see* **turn**.

heal [hi:l] *vti* (*often with* **up**) (*esp* of cuts, wounds *etc*) to make or become healthy; to (cause to) return to a normal state or condition: *That scratch will heal (up) in a couple of days; This ointment will soon heal your cuts.*

'healer *nc* (*relig, arch or fig*) a person or thing that heals: *Time is a great healer* (=Feelings of anger, sorrow *etc* are forgotten in time).

health [helθ] *nu* **1** the state of being well or ill: *He seemed to be in good/poor health; (fig) the health of the nation's economy.* **2** the state of being well: *I may be getting old, but so long as I keep my health, I'll be happy.*

'healthy *adj* **1** (generally) having good health: *I don't feel very well today, but I'm really a very healthy person; He seems very healthy; (fig) My bank account looks very healthy at the moment.* **2** causing or helping (a person) to have good health: *a healthy climate; This heat isn't very healthy.* **3** as good *etc* as that of a healthy person: *He may be ill but he still has a healthy appetite.* **4** (*fig*) wise; showing good sense; good (for a person): *He shows a healthy respect for the law; He shows a healthy scepticism about the promises made by politicians.* **'healthiness** *nu.*

'health centre *nc* a building in which the doctors, nurses *etc* who serve a particular area work and hold clinics *etc.*

'health farm *nc* a place, *usu* in the country, to which people go in order to improve their health by dieting, exercise *etc.*

'health food *nu* food which is eaten because it is (thought to be) particularly good for one's health, and which is *usu* grown without the use of artificial fertilizers *etc*: (*attrib*) *a health food shop.*

'health service *nu* (*often with caps*) (the organization which runs) all the medical services of a country which are available to the public: *Most hospitals in Britain are run by the (National) Health Service but some are run by private organizations.*

'health visitor *nc* (*Brit*) a nurse who visits people (*eg* old people, mothers with young children) at home.

drink (to) someone's health to drink a toast (to someone), wishing him good health, often using the words 'Your health!'.

See also **unhealthy**.

heap [hi:p] *nc* **1** a large amount (of something), or a large number (of things), in a pile: *a heap of sand/apples.* **2** (*inf fig*: *usu in pl usu with* **of**) a large amount; many, much or plenty (of something): *We've got heaps of bread/time; I've done that heaps of times; Have you got enough time? Yes, I've got heaps.* – *vt* **1** to put, throw *etc* (something) in a heap: *I'll heap these stones (up) in a corner of the garden; (fig) In just ten days, he's managed to heap up a lot of trouble for himself.* **2** to fill or cover (something or someone) with a heap of, or large amount of, something: *He heaped his plate with vegetables; (fig) He heaped abuse on his opponent.*

heaped *adj* having enough (of something) on it to form a heap: *A heaped spoonful of sugar is more than a level spoonful.*

heaps *adv* (*inf*) very much: *I'm feeling heaps better now.*

hear [hiə] – *pt, ptp* **heard** [hə:d] – **1** *vti* (not *usu* used with **is, was** *etc* and **-ing**) to (be able to) receive (sounds, news *etc*) by ear: *I'm afraid I don't hear very well; Will you speak louder – I can't hear you; I hear (that) you are leaving; I've heard that story before; I didn't hear you come in.* **2** *vt* to listen (to something) for some purpose: *People go to church to hear Mass; A judge hears court cases; Part of a manager's job is to hear workers' complaints.* **3** *vti* (*usu with* **about, from** *or* **of**) to know (someone or something); to receive (news *etc*) about or from (someone or something): *'Have you heard from your sister?' 'Yes, I got a letter from her this morning'; I've never heard of him. Who is he?; This is the first I've heard about moving to London.*

'hearing 1 *nu* the ability to hear: *My hearing is not very good.* **2** *nu* the distance within which something can be heard: *I don't want to tell you when so many people are within hearing; I think we're out of hearing now.* **3** *nc* (*formal*) an act of listening to (someone or something): *The new boss is strict but he'll give you a fair hearing* (= he'll listen to what you have to say). **4** *nc* a court case: *The hearing is tomorrow.*

'hearing-aid *nc* a *usu* small electronic instrument which helps some deaf people to hear by making sounds louder by means of an amplifier.

'hearsay [-sei] *nu* something that one has been told about, but which one cannot be certain is true because one has not seen or experienced it for oneself: *I never trust anything that I learn by hearsay; (attrib) Hearsay evidence is not accepted in court cases.*

be hearing things *see* **things**.

hard of hearing *see* **hard**.

hear! hear! (*esp Brit*) a shout to show that one agrees with what a speaker has said (*eg* in Parliament or at a meeting).

hear out *vt oblig sep* (*formal*) to allow (someone) to finish saying what he wants to say: *Please hear me out before you come to a decision.*

hear tell of (something) (*old*) to hear of or about (someone or something): *I have heard tell of his courageous actions.*

I, he *etc* **will, would not hear of (something)** I, he *etc* will or would not allow (someone) to do something: *He would not hear of her going home alone, and insisted on going with her.*

See also **unheard (-of)**.

hearken, (*also Amer*) **harken** ['ha:kən] *vi* (*arch or liter*: *with* **to**) to listen to or pay attention to (something that is said).

hearsay *see* **hear**.

hearse [hə:s] *nc* a car used for carrying a dead body in a coffin to a cemetery *etc*: *The hearse led the procession of cars to the graveyard.*

heart [ha:t] **1** *nc* the organ which pumps blood through the body: *How fast does a person's heart beat?; The students cut up a sheep's heart in the biology class; (attrib) He suffers from heart disease; (attrib) He is a heart specialist* (= He is a doctor who specializes in diseases of the heart). **2** *nc* the central part of a town, wood *etc*, or of certain plants: *I prefer to live in the heart of the city; deep in* *the heart of the forest; Use the heart of the lettuce in the salad; (fig) Let's get straight to the heart of the matter/problem.* **3** *nc* the part of the body where a person's emotions (*esp* love), feelings, conscience *etc* are imagined to arise: *She has a kind heart* (= She is kind); *Whatever reasons you have for not going, you know in your heart that you ought to go; She has no heart* (= She has no sympathy or feelings for others). **4** *nu* courage and enthusiasm: *The soldiers were beginning to lose heart; The soldier said he had no heart for all the killing.* **5** *nc* a symbol supposed to represent the shape of the heart; ♡: *a white cardigan with little pink hearts on it; heart-shaped.* **6** *nc* one of the playing-cards of the suit hearts, which have red symbols of this shape on them. – *See also* **hearts** *below.*

-hearted (*in cmpds*) having emotions, feelings *etc* of a particular kind or in a particular state, as in **kind-hearted, hard-hearted, broken-hearted**.

'hearten *vt* (*formal*) to encourage or cheer up (a person *etc*): *We were greatly heartened by your news.*

'heartless *adj* cruel; very unkind: *She is cruel and heartless; a heartless person; heartless remarks.* **'heartlessly** *adv.* **'heartlessness** *nu.*

hearts *n pl* (sometimes treated as *n sing*) one of the four card suits: *the two of hearts.*

'hearty *adj* **1** (*usu attrib*) very friendly: *a hearty welcome.* **2** (*usu attrib*: *more formal than* **strong**) enthusiastic: *hearty support for a project; He gave the door a hearty push.* **3** very cheerful; sometimes too cheerful: *a hearty person/laugh; He is too hearty.* **4** (*attrib*) (of meals) large: *He ate a hearty breakfast.* **5** (*usu attrib*) (of a person's appetite) needing a great deal of food: *He has a hearty appetite.* – *See also* **hale**. **'heartily** *adv.* **'heartiness** *nu.*

'heartache *ncu* (a feeling of) great sadness, *eg* as caused by the loss of, or the failure to get, a person's love.

'heart attack *nc* a sudden failure of the heart to function correctly, often causing death: *My father has had a slight heart attack.*

'heartbreak *ncu* (something which causes) great sorrow: *I have suffered many heartbreaks in my life; the heartbreak of the mother when her child died.*

'heartbroken *adj* feeling very great sorrow: *She's absolutely heartbroken over the death of her pet cat; a heartbroken widow.*

'heartburn *nu* a burning feeling in the chest caused by indigestion: *She suffers from heartburn after meals.*

'heart failure *nu* (death caused by) the sudden stopping of the heart's beating: *The old man died of heart failure.*

'heartfelt *adj* (*attrib*: *formal*) sincere: *I offer you my heartfelt thanks for your help.*

'heart-searching *nu* (*formal*) the close examination of one's feelings, conscience *etc*: *After a great deal of heart-searching she decided to break off her engagement.*

ˌheart-to-'heart *adj* (*attrib*) open and sincere, *usu* in private: *I'm going to have a heart-to-heart talk with him.* – *nc* (*inf*) an open and sincere talk, *usu* in private: *After our heart-to-heart I felt more cheerful.*

'heart-warming *adj* causing a person to feel pleasure: *Seeing the old lady's happiness was a heart-warming experience; It was heart-warming to see the happiness of the children.*

after one's own heart (of people) of exactly the type one likes: *You're a man after my own heart.*

at 'heart (*formal*) really; basically: *He seems rather stern but he is at heart a very kind man.*

break someone's heart to cause (someone) great sorrow: *If you leave her, it'll break her heart.*

cross my, your heart (*inf*) said *esp* by children to emphasize the truth of what is being said, (sometimes accompanied by a movement of the hand making an X over the heart): *I promise I'll do it, cross my heart (and hope to die).*

do one's heart good (*old or liter*) to give one a feeling of pleasure: *It does my heart good to see you again.*

find it in one's heart (to do something) (*formal*) to manage or persuade (oneself) to do something: *Can you find it in your heart to forgive me?*

from the bottom of one's heart very much; very sincerely: *She thanked him from the bottom of her heart for all his help.*

have a change of heart to change a decision *etc*, *usu* to a better, kinder one: *He's had a change of heart – he's going to help us after all.*

have a heart! (*inf*) show some pity or kindness: *Have a heart! He'll never be able to do all that unless we help him.*

have (something) at heart (*formal*) to have or feel a kind concern for or interest in (something): *He never shows it, but he has the interest of his workers at heart.*

have one's heart set on *see* **set one's heart on** *below.*

heart and soul completely; with all one's attention and energy: *She devoted herself heart and soul to working for the church.*

learn, know (something) (off) by heart to learn, or have learned (a poem, a set of facts *etc*) so that one has it accurately and completely in one's memory: *He has to learn all the kings and queens of England (off) by heart by next week.*

lose heart to become discouraged: *After more than fifty unsuccessful attempts to get a job, he began to lose heart.*

not have the heart (to do something) not to want or be unkind enough (to do something unpleasant): *I don't have the heart to tell him that everyone laughed at his suggestions.*

set one's heart on (something)/have one's heart set on (something) to want (something) very much: *He had set his heart on winning the prize; He had his heart set on winning.*

take heart (*formal*) to become encouraged or more confident: *The soldiers took heart when they heard that reinforcements were coming.*

take (something) to heart 1 to be made very sad or upset (by something): *You mustn't take his unkind remarks to heart.* **2** to pay great attention to (something): *He seems to have taken my criticisms to heart – his work has improved a lot since I spoke to him.*

take (someone) to one's heart (*formal*) to show a strong liking or affection for (someone): *The child took her new stepmother to her heart.*

to one's heart's content (*inf*) as much as one wants: *During the summer, she can play in the garden to her heart's content.*

with all one's heart very willingly or sincerely: *I hope with all my heart that you will be happy.*

hearth [haːθ] *nc* **1** (the part of a room beside) the fireplace: *a chair by the hearth*; *She was cleaning the hearth.* 2 (*liter fig*) home: one's house.

heartily *etc see* **heart**.

heat [hi:t] 1 *nu* the amount of hotness (of something), *esp* of things which are very hot: *Would you test the heat of the water before I bath the baby.* 2 *nu* the (feeling of) warmth a person *etc* gets from something which is hot: *The heat from the fire will soon dry your coat*; *What is the effect of heat on this metal?*; *the heat of the sun.* 3 *nc* (*no pl*) the hottest time (of the day): *the heat of the day.* 4 *nu* (*fig*) anger or excitement: *He didn't mean to be rude – he just said these things in the heat of the moment/debate.* 5 *nc* in a sports competition *etc*, one of two or more races or contests from which the winners or best competitors go on to take part in later stages of the contest, *eg* the finals or semifinals: *Having won his heat he is going through to the final.* – *vti* (*sometimes with* **up**) to make or become hot or warm: *The soup is cold now – we'll have to heat it* (*up*) *again*; *We'll heat* (*up*) *the soup*; *That small fire won't heat a large room*; *That small room will soon heat up.*

'**heated** *adj* 1 having been made hot: *a heated swimming-pool*; *Is the swimming-pool heated?* 2 (*fig*) having or showing great anger, excitement *etc*: *a heated argument*; *He gets very heated in an argument.* '**heatedly** *adv.* '**heatedness** *nu.*

'**heater** *nc* (*often in cmpds*) an apparatus which gives out heat in order to warm a room *etc*, or which heats water *etc eg* in a water-tank: *a paraffin heater* (= a heater which burns paraffin); *a water-heater* (= a heater which heats water).

'**heating** *nu* the system of heaters *etc* which heat a room, building *etc*: *We turn the heating off in the summer*; *Do you have gas or electric heating?*; (*attrib*) *heating engineers.*

heatspot *nc* a kind of a spot on the skin.

'**heat wave** *nc* a period of very hot weather.

in/on heat (of female animals) sexually aroused in the breeding season: *They are planning to mate their spaniel bitch when she is in heat.*

See also **hot**.

heath [hi:θ] *ncu* 1 an area of uncultivated, open, flat country with poor soil and often covered with plants like heather: *I'll go and take the dog for a walk over the heath.* 2 any of several plants like heather: *I'm going to plant heath*(*s*) *in this part of the garden.*

heathen ['hi:ðən] *nc, adj* (of) a person who believes in a less advanced form of religion, *esp* one with many gods: *Missionaries tried to convert the heathens to Christianity*; *heathen ideas.*

the heathen (*formal*) heathens: *He has made it his aim to convert the heathen to Christianity.*

heather ['heðə] *ncu* a plant with small purple or white flowers which grows on moorland: *purple heather*; (*attrib*) *heather honey.*

heave [hi:v] 1 *vti* to (try to) lift or to pull, with great effort: *The sailors heaved* (*on*) *the rope*; *They heaved with all their strength, but could not move the rock*; *They heaved the wardrobe* (*up*) *into the lorry*; *The gate was jammed, but he heaved at it until it opened.* 2 *vt* (*inf*) to throw (something, *usu* heavy): *Someone heaved a stone through my window.* 3 *vi* to rise, or rise and fall again several times: *The earthquake made the ground heave*; *His chest was heaving because he was out of breath.* – *ncu* the act of heaving: *He gave a great heave on the rope*; *the heave* (= rising and falling) *of the waves.*

heave a sigh/groan (*often liter*) to sigh or groan: *He heaved a sigh of relief when he reached safety.*

heave to – *pt, ptp* **hove** [houv] – *vi, vt oblig sep* (*naut*) (of a ship) to (cause to) stop while at sea: *The ship hove to*; *The captain told the crew to heave to*; *The crew hove the ship to.*

heaven ['hevn] 1 *nc* (*no pl*: *often with cap*) in some religions, the place where God or the gods live, and where good people go when they die: *The little girl said she would like to be one of the angels in Heaven.* 2 *nc* the sky: *He raised his eyes to heaven/the heavens.* 3 *nu* (*fig inf*) (something which brings) great happiness: *'This is heaven', she said, lying on the beach in the sunshine.*

'**heavenly** *adj* 1 (*inf*) very pleasant; delightful; beautiful: *What heavenly weather!*; *Isn't that dress heavenly?* 2 of or from Heaven. '**heavenliness** *nu.*

'**heavens** (*also* **good heavens**) (*interj*) an expression of surprise, dismay *etc*: *Heavens! I forgot to buy your birthday present.*

heavenly bodies *n pl* (*formal*) the sun, moon, planets, stars *etc.*

ˌ**heaven-'sent** *adj* (*usu attrib*) very lucky or convenient; coming at a good time: *That was a heaven-sent opportunity to ask for a pay-rise*; *That opportunity was heaven-sent.*

for heaven's sake an expression used to show anger, surprise *etc*: *For heaven's sake, will you stop making that noise!*; *What did you do that for, for heaven's sake?*

heaven knows 1 I don't know: *Heaven knows what he's trying to do.* 2 certainly: *Heaven knows, I ought to have known I couldn't trust him.*

move heaven and earth *see* **move**.

thank heavens an expression used to show that a person is glad something has (not) happened: *Thank heavens he isn't coming!*; *Thank heavens for that!*

heavy ['hevi] *adj* 1 having great weight; difficult to lift or carry: *The postman was carrying a heavy parcel*; *This parcel is too heavy for me to carry.* 2 (*pred*) having a particular weight, but not necessarily a great weight: *I wonder how heavy our little baby is.* 3 (*usu attrib*) of very or unusually great size, amount, force, power *etc*: *a heavy fall of snow*; *heavy artillery*; *a heavy blow on the head*; *Our expenses were heavier than we expected*; *The ship capsized in the heavy seas*; *heavy taxes.* 4 doing (something) to a very great, an unusually great, or too great an extent: *He's a very heavy smoker.* 5 dark and cloudy: *a heavy sky*; *The sky was heavy just before the rain.* 6 difficult to read, do, understand *etc*: *This report is/makes very heavy reading*; *Books on philosophy are too heavy for me – I prefer fiction.* 7 (of food) solid; hard to digest: *This cake is very heavy*; *a heavy sponge cake.* 8 (*usu attrib*) (of breathing) loud, because of excitement, difficulty *etc*: *The lady complained to the police that every time she answered the phone, all she heard was heavy breathing.* 9 (of ground) difficult to dig; solid: *heavy soil*; *The soil is very heavy in this part of the world.* 10 (of people, their movements *etc*) slow and rather clumsy: *heavy footsteps.* 11 (of people's faces *etc*) having a lot of flesh: *heavy features*; *His features are rather heavy.* 12 (of the atmosphere *etc*) making a person feel sleepy: *a heavy, smoky atmosphere*; *The atmosphere is heavy today.* – 1 *nu* (*esp* in Scotland) a type of beer: *a pint of heavy.* 2 *nc* (*sl*) a large, strong, often not very intelligent, man used by someone (often a criminal) as a bodyguard *etc*:

The gangster always had a couple of heavies with him.

'heavily *adv.*

'heaviness *nu.*

,heavy-'duty *adj* (*usu attrib*) made to stand up to very hard wear or use: *heavy-duty tyres.*

,heavy-'handed *adj* not showing good judgement or good taste; made in too dramatic, shocking, lengthy, emphatic *etc* a way: *heavy-handed compliments*; *The film shows a very heavy-handed treatment of its theme*; *The dramatic effects were rather heavy-handed.*

,heavy-'hearted *adj* (*liter*) sad. – *See also* **a heavy heart** *below.*

heavy industry *nu* industries such as coal-mining, ship-building *etc* which involve the use of large or heavy machines or which produce large or heavy products.

,heavy-'laden *adj* (*liter*) carrying a heavy load: *a heavy-laden cart*; (*fig*) *heavy-laden with the cares of the world.*

'heavyweight 1 *adj* (*attrib*), *nc* (a person) in the heaviest of the various classes into which competitors in certain sports (*eg* boxing, wrestling) are divided according to their weight: *These two boxers are heavyweights*; *a heavyweight boxer.* **2** *adj* (*attrib*) of such people, competitions between such people *etc*: *a heavy-weight competition/champion.*

heavy going (*inf*) causing difficulty in doing, understanding or making progress with (something): *I found his book very heavy going*; *It's heavy going but we'll finish the job eventually.*

a heavy heart (*liter*) a feeling of sadness: *I say this with a heavy heart.* – *See also* **heavy-hearted**.

make heavy weather of (something) (*inf*) to find great difficulty in doing (something which *usu* should be easy to do): *He said he'd finish the job in half an hour, but he seems to be making rather heavy weather of it.*

Hebrew *see* Appendix 2.

heckle ['hekl] *vti* to ask difficult questions or to shout comments while someone is making a speech (*eg* in an election campaign): *The politician was heckled at the meeting*; *Several people started heckling.* **'heckler** *nc.*

hectare ['hekta:, (*Amer*) -teər] *nc* a metric unit of area, 10 000 square metres.

hectic ['hektik] *adj* very busy; quick; rushed: *Life is pretty hectic these days*; *a hectic rush.* **'hecticness** *nu.*

hectogram(me), hectolitre, hectometre *see* Appendix 5.

hector ['hektə] *vti* (*formal*) to (try to) bully or frighten (someone) into doing what one wants by shouting at him: *The new teacher is disliked by the children because he is always hectoring them.*

he'd *see* **have, would**.

hedge [hedʒ] *nc* **1** a line of bushes *etc* planted so closely together that their branches form a solid mass, grown round the edges of gardens, fields *etc*: *Our garden is separated from our neighbour's by a high hedge*; *a yew hedge* (= a hedge consisting of yew trees). **2** (*fig*) something which protects (a person) from possible loss, damage, criticism *etc*: *He bought some jewels as a hedge against inflation.* – **1** *vi* (*formal*) to avoid giving a clear answer to a question: *There's no point in asking him – he always hedges.* **2** *vt* to enclose (an area of land) with a hedge: *We can hedge the garden (in)*; *We have hedged off part of the garden for the children to play in.*

'hedgehog *nc* a small brown prickly-backed animal.

'hedgerow [-rou] *nc* a row of bushes forming a hedge, *esp* in the country.

hedge one's bets (*inf fig*) to do (something) in order to protect oneself from possible loss, criticism *etc*: *We don't know which of them is going to be in charge of this department, so we'd better hedge our bets and be nice to both of them.*

heed [hi:d] *vt* (*formal*) to pay attention to (someone or something, *usu* advice or a warning): *You had better heed my warning*; *You had better heed what I say!*

'heedful *adj* (*formal*: *usu pred with* **of**) careful; paying attention to (someone or something): *Heedful of my warning, he stayed at home.*

'heedless *adj* (*formal*: *usu pred with* **of**) careless; not paying attention to (someone or something): *Heedless of the danger, he ran into the burning building to rescue the girl.* **'heedlessly** *adv.*

pay/give heed to, take heed of (*formal*) to pay attention to (someone or something): *I warned him not to go, but he never takes any heed of what I say*; *He never gives any heed to what I say.*

heel [hi:l] *nc* **1** the back part of the foot: *I have a blister on my heel because my shoe is too tight.* **2** the part of a sock, stocking *etc* that covers this part of the foot: *I have a hole in the heel of my sock.* **3** the part of a shoe, boot *etc* under or round the heel of the foot: *The heel has come off this shoe – I'll need to nail it on again.* – *See also* **heel** *in phrases below.* – **1** *vt* to put a heel on (a shoe *etc*): *Ask the cobbler to heel my shoes, please.* **2** *vt* (in football *etc*) to hit (the ball) backwards with the heel: *He heeled the ball to the goal-keeper.* **3** *vi* (*usu with* **over**) (of ships) to lean to one side: *The boat heeled over in the strong wind.*

-heeled (*in cmpds*) having (a certain kind, size *etc* of) heel(s): *high-heeled shoes.*

at/on a person's heels close behind: *The thief ran off with the policeman close on his heels.*

cool one's heels *see* **kick one's heels** *below.*

,dig ,in one's 'heels (*inf*) to refuse to do, allow *etc* (something): *I'm going to dig in my heels over this – it must be done the way I say.*

down-at-heel *see* **down**.

head over heels *see* **head**.

kick/cool one's heels (*inf*) to be kept waiting for some time: *Although I arrived on time for the meeting, I was left kicking my heels for half an hour.*

show (someone) a clean pair of heels (*sl*) to run away (from someone).

take to one's heels (*inf*) to run away: *The thief took to his heels when the policeman arrived.*

to 'heel 1 (of dogs *etc*) at a person's heel: *The street was busy, so he made his dog walk to heel.* **2** (*fig inf*) under control: *That boy thinks he is tough, but his teachers will soon bring him to heel.*

turn on one's heel to turn round or away suddenly, *usu* with the intention of moving in the opposite direction: *When he finished talking, he turned on his heel and walked away.*

hefty ['hefti] *adj* (*inf*) **1** (*sometimes derog*) (of people) big and strong: *Her husband is pretty hefty – he plays rugby*; *rather a hefty young woman.* **2** (*usu attrib*) (of punches *etc*) powerful: *a hefty kick.*

heifer ['hefə] *nc* a young cow.

height [hait] **1** *ncu* the distance from the bottom to the top (of something): *What is the height of this building?*; *He is 1·75 metres in height.* **2** *nc* (*usu fig*) the highest, greatest, strongest *etc* point (of something): *He is at the height of his career*; *The storm was at its height.* **3** *nu* a very good, bad or serious example (of something): *Only someone with a lot of money can afford to be dressed in the height of fashion* (= in the most up-to-date clothes); *His actions were the height of folly.* **4** *nc* (*formal: often in pl*) a high place: *We looked down from the heights at the valley beneath us*; *The climber fell from a great height.*

'**heighten** *vti* **1** to make or become higher: *I am going to heighten the garden wall.* **2** to make or become greater, stronger, brighter *etc*: *We'll use old pictures to heighten the effect of this display.*

See also **high**.

heinous ['heinəs] *adj* (*very formal: usu attrib*) very wicked: *a heinous crime.*

heir [eə] – *fem* '**heiress** – *nc* a person who by law receives wealth, property, a title *etc* when the owner dies (**heiress** applies *esp* to someone who has received or will receive great wealth when some person dies): *A person's eldest son is usually his heir*; *A king's eldest son is the heir to the throne*; *Many men dream of marrying a rich heiress.* – *See also* **fall heir to** *below.*

'**heirloom** [-luːm] *nc* something valuable that has been handed down in a family from generation to generation: *These rings are family heirlooms.*

fall heir to (*formal*) to receive or inherit (something that has belonged to someone else): *He fell heir to a large fortune*; (*fig*) *We fell heir to all their problems when they left.*

See also **heritage, inherit**.

held *see* **hold**.

helicopter ['helikoptə] *nc* a flying-machine kept in the air by large propellors fixed on top of it which go round very fast: *A helicopter was sent to pick up the injured man from the sea.*

helium ['hiːliəm] *nu* an element (symbol **He**), a very light gas which does not burn and which it used *eg* in balloons.

hell [hel] **1** *n* (*often with cap*) (according to some religions) the place or state of punishment of the wicked after death. **2** *nu* (*inf*) any place or state of wickedness or misery or pain: *It was absolute hell trying to get this report finished on time*; *Drug-addicts go through hell when they try to give up drugs.* – *interj* (*vulg*) used to express anger, annoyance *etc*: *Oh, hell! I've lost my keys.*

'**hellish** *adj* (*vulg*) causing great pain or misery; very bad; very unpleasant: *There's a hellish atmosphere in this office*; *I'm in hellish pain*; *That film was hellish*; *That was a hellish thing to do to her.* – *adv* (*vulg*) very: *It was hellish difficult.*

'**hellishly** *adv* (*vulg*) **1** very: *The plan was hellishly complicated.* **2** very badly or unpleasantly: *He treated his wife hellishly.*

for the 'hell of it (*inf*) for no particular reason; just for fun: *The boys said they had set fire to the house just for the hell of it.*

ˌ**hell'bent on** (*inf*) determined (to do something): *I've told him it will be dangerous, but he's hellbent on going.*

(a) 'hell of a (*inf*) very good; very bad; very (much): *He's a hell of a (nice) fellow*; *That's a hell of a big parcel.*

he'll *see* **will**.

hello, hallo, hullo [hə'lou] *interjs, ncus* a word used as a greeting, to attract attention, or to express surprise: *Say hello to your aunt*; *'Hullo,' I said to myself, 'What's going on here?'*

helm [helm] *nc* the wheel or handle by which a ship is steered: *He asked me to take the helm* (= steer the ship); (*formal fig*) *There's a new man at the helm of* (= in charge of) *the company.*

'**helmsman** ['helmz-] *nc* a person who steers a ship.

helmet ['helmit] *nc* a metal, leather *etc* covering to protect the head: *Soldiers wear helmets when fighting*; *English policemen wear helmets.*

help [help] **1** *vti* to do (something) with or for another person that he cannot do alone; to do (something) which another person will find useful: *Will someone please help me with this translation?*: *Will you please help me (to) translate this poem?*; *Can I help?*; *Would it help if I left the room?*; *Will you help me up?* (= help me to stand up, climb up *etc*); *Will you help me up with this box?* (= help me to carry or put this box up). **2** *vti* to make (a disease *etc*) less bad: *An aspirin will help (your headache).* **3** *vt* to serve (a person) in a shop: *Can I help you, sir?* **4** *vt* (*formal: with* **to**) to offer (someone) food: *Can I help you to another slice of cake?* **5** *vt* (*with* **can(not), could(not)**) to be able not to do (something) or to prevent (something): *He looked so funny that I couldn't help laughing*; *Can I help it if it rains?* **6** *vti* to play a part in making (something) successful: *Henry's sensible suggestions helped the negotiations immensely.* – *See also* **help out** *below.* – **1** *ncu* (*no pl*) the act of helping, or the result of this: *Can you give me some help?*; *I need your help*; *Your digging the garden was a big help*; *Can I be of help to you?*; *He is beyond help* (= He cannot be helped). **2** *nc* (*no pl*) someone or something that is useful to (a person): *You're a great help to me*; *I find this tool is a great help when I dig the garden.* **3** *ncu* (*esp Amer*) a servant, farmworker *etc* or all of a person's servants *etc* as a group: *She has hired a new help.* – *See also* **home help** *under* **home**. **4** *nc* (*no pl: usu with* **no**) a way of preventing (something) or of making good some damage that has been done: *Even if you don't want to do it, the decision has been made – there's no help for it now.*

'**helper** *nc* someone who helps; an assistant: *We need several helpers for this job.*

'**helpful** *adj* that gives help to or is useful to (a person): *He's a very helpful boy*; *You may find this book helpful*; *These instructions aren't helpful.* '**helpfully** *adv.* '**helpfulness** *nu.*

'**helping** *nc* the amount (of food) one has on one's plate: *a large helping of pudding.*

'**helpless** *adj* needing the help of other people; unable to do anything for oneself: *A baby is almost completely helpless*; *a helpless child*; *The thieves left the man tied up and helpless*; *I was helpless to assist*; *Without these guns, I'd be helpless against thieves.* '**helplessly** *adv.* '**helplessness** *nu.*

a helping hand *see* **hand**.

help oneself 1 (*with* **to**) to give oneself or take (food *etc*): *Help yourself to another cake*; *'Can I have a pencil?' 'Certainly – help yourself.'* **2** (*inf: with* **to**) to steal: *He just helped himself to my jewellery.* **3** (*inf: with* **cannot, could not**) to be able to stop (oneself): *I burst out laughing when he told me – I just couldn't help myself.*

help out *vi, vt usu sep* (*inf*) to help (a person), *usu* for a short time because the person is in some difficulty: *I don't mind helping out in the shop from time to time, but not every day*; *Could you help me* *out by looking after the baby for an hour?*

helter-skelter [heltə'skeltə] *adv* (*inf*) in great hurry and confusion. – *nc* a small tower in a park or fairground which has a slide going down round the outside of it.

hem [hem] *nc* the border of a piece of clothing, folded over and sewn: *That skirt is too short for the child but you can make it longer by undoing the hem.* – *v* – *pt, ptp* **hemmed** – *vt* to make a hem on (a piece of clothing): *I hemmed the skirt last night.*

hem in *vt sep* **1** to surround (someone): *The soldiers were hemmed in on all sides by the enemy.* **2** (*fig*) to make unable to move freely: *I feel hemmed in in the city.*

hemi- [hemi] (*in cmpds*) half, as in **hemisphere**.

hemisphere ['hemisfiə] *nc* (*also with cap*) one half of the Earth: *The British Isles are in the northern hemisphere.*

ˌ**hemi'spherical** [-'sfe-] *adj* (*tech*) like half a ball in shape.

hemoglobin *see* **haemoglobin**.

hemorrhage *see* **haemorrhage**.

hemorrhoid *see* **haemorrhoid**.

hemp [hemp] *nu* **1** a coarse fibre used to make rope, bags, sails *etc*. **2** a drug. – *See also* **cannabis, hashish, marijuana**. **3** the plant from which the fibre and the drug are obtained.

hen [hen] *nc* **1** the female farmyard fowl: *Hens lay eggs.* **2** the female of any bird: *The hen is sitting on the nest*; (*attrib*) *a hen blackbird.*

'**henpecked** [-pekt] *adj* (*inf*) (of a man) ruled by his wife: *He never does anything without asking his wife first – he's completely henpecked*; *a henpecked husband.*

hence [hens] *adv* **1** (*formal*) for this reason: *Hence, I shall have to stay.* **2** (*very formal*) from this time: *a year hence.* **3** (*old or very formal*) from this place: *Get you hence!* (= Go away).

hence'forth *adv* (*formal*) from now on: *Henceforth I shall refuse to work with him.*

henchman ['hentʃmən] – *pl* '**henchmen** – *nc* (*often derog*) someone who works for, supports, and *usu* obeys without question (a political leader, a gangster *etc*): *The army was controlled by the dictator's henchmen.*

henpecked *see* **hen**.

her [hə:] *pron* (used as the object of an actual or implied verb or preposition or (*inf*) as the subject of an implied verb) a female person or animal already spoken about: *I'll ask my mother when I see her*; *Give her the book*; *He came with her*; (*inf*) *'Who did it?' 'Her.'* (= She did it); *'Who was he with?' 'Her.'* – *adj* (*attrib*) belonging to such a person or animal: *My mother bought this car, so it's her car*; *a cat and her kittens.*

hers [hə:z] *pron* something which belongs to a female person or animal already spoken about: *It's not your car – it's hers*; *Hers is on that shelf.*

her'self *pron* **1** used as the object of a verb or preposition when a female person or animal is the object of an action she performs: *She kicked herself*; *The cat licked herself*; *She looked at herself in the mirror.* **2** used to emphasize **she, her,** or the name of a female person or animal: *She herself played no part in this*; *Mary answered the letter herself.* **3** without help *etc*: *She did it all herself.*

by herself *see* **by oneself** *under* **by**.

she is not herself *see* **not be oneself** *under* **one**.

See also **she**.

herald ['herəld] **1** *nc* (*liter*) something that is a sign of something to come: *The swallow is a herald of summer.* **2** *nc* (*hist*) a person who carries and reads important messages and notices (*eg* from a king): *The king sent out heralds to announce the new law.* **3** *n* (*with cap*) a word often used in the titles of newspapers: *the Edinburgh Herald.* – *vt* (*formal or liter*) to announce or be a sign of (something which is about to happen): *Swallows herald the beginning of summer.*

he'raldic [-'ral-] *adj* (*formal*: *attrib*) of heraldry: *heraldic devices.*

'**heraldry** *nu* the study of coats of arms, crests *etc* and of the history of the *usu* important families who have the right to use them: *She is interested in heraldry.*

herb [hə:b] *nc* a *usu* small plant used to flavour food or to make medicines: *Parsley and thyme are herbs*; (*attrib*) *a herb garden.*

'**herbal** *adj* (*usu attrib*) of herbs, *esp* herbs used to make medicines: *a herbal remedy.*

'**herbalist** *nc* a person who deals in herbs, *esp* those used to make medicines: *He refuses to go to a doctor – he insists on consulting a herbalist about his cough.*

herbaceous border [hə:'beiʃəs] *nc* the part of a garden where plants which grow again and flower each year are planted.

herculean [hə:kju'li:ən] *adj* (*formal*: *also with cap*) having, or requiring, very great strength: *a herculean task.*

herd [hə:d] *nc* a group of animals of one kind that stay, or are kept, together: *a herd of cattle*; *a herd of elephant(s).* – **1** *vti* (*with* **in(to), together** *etc*) to gather together, or be brought together, in a group: *The dogs herded the sheep together*; (*fig*) *The tourists were herded into a tiny room.* **2** *vt* to look after (a herd of sheep *etc*).

-herd (*in cmpds*) a person who looks after a herd of certain kinds of animals: *a goat-herd.*

'**herdsman** ['hə:dz-] *nc* a person who looks after a herd of animals.

the (common) herd (*derog*) the mass of ordinary people who (it is supposed) all accept the same views and act in the same way: *The new typist refused to be like the common herd and would not call her boss 'sir'.*

the herd instinct the tendency to behave, think *etc* like everyone else.

See also **shepherd**.

here [hiə] *adv* **1** (at, in or to) this place: *He's here*; *Come here*; *He lives not far from here.* **2** at this time; at this point in an argument: *Here the speaker had to wait until the audience stopped cheering*; *Here is where I disagree with you.* **3** (used for emphasis, or to point out or indicate someone or something) beside one: *It's this book here you need*; *My colleague here will deal with the matter.* – *See also* **here** *in phrases below.* – *interj* **1** a shout of surprise, disapproval *etc*: *Here! what do you think you're doing?* **2** a shout used to show that one is present: *Shout 'Here!' when I call your name.*

here- (*in cmpds*) **1** at this place, as in **hereabouts**. **2** now, as in **hereafter**. **3** this, as in **herein**.

ˌ**herea'bout(s)** *adv* near this place: *He lives somewhere hereabouts.*

here'after *adv* (*legal or formal*) after this; from now on: *This concerns the will of John Smith, hereafter referred to as 'the deceased'.* – *See also* **the hereafter** *below.*

ˌ**here'by** *adv* (*legal or formal*) now, by means of (*eg* this statement): *I hereby declare that I will not be responsible for any of her debts.*

ˌhere'in *adv* (*legal or formal*) in this (letter *etc*): *Please complete the form enclosed herein and return it to us.*

here and there in, or to, various places: *'Where did you go for your holiday?' 'Oh, here and there.'*

here are *see* **here is** *below*.

here (he, it *etc*) **comes/here comes** (a person, thing *etc*) I can see, hear *etc* (a person, thing *etc*) coming: *Here they come now*; *Here comes the bus.*

here goes (*inf*) I'm starting or going to do (something) now: *I've never tried diving before, but here goes!*

'here (he, it, they *etc*) **is/are, here is/are (someone or something)** I have got, found *etc* what you, he *etc* are looking for, wanting *etc*: *Here is the book you need*; *Here it is.* – *See also* **here you are** *below*.

'here's to (someone or something) *interj* used as a toast to the health, success *etc* of (someone or something): *Here's to the success of the new company.*

here, there and everywhere (*inf*) in, or to, a larger number of places; in all directions: *People were running around here, there and everywhere.*

here you are I have got, found *etc* what you want, are looking for *etc*: *Here you are. This is the book you were looking for.*

look here! *see* **look**.

neither here nor there not important: *His opinion of us is neither here nor there.*

see here! *see* **see**.

the hereafter (*formal*) life after death.

heredity [hiˈredəti] *nu* the passing on of qualities (*eg* appearance, intelligence) from parents to children: *Does a child's musical talent depend on heredity?*

heˈreditary *adj* (*formal*) (able to be) passed on in this way: *Is musical ability hereditary?*; *a hereditary defect.*

herein *see* **here**.

heresy [ˈherəsi] *ncu* (the holding or teaching of) a (*usu* religious) opinion or belief which does not agree with the official opinion or belief of a group: *He is making a study of early Christian heresies*; (*fig*) *His suggestion that the government should nationalize the building industry was heresy to the other members of his party.*

'heretic [-tik] *nc* a person who holds or teaches such an opinion: *The Protestants were burned as heretics by the Catholic king.*

heretical [həˈretikl] *adj* (*formal*) (holding or teaching an opinion) which is a heresy: *heretical beliefs*; *The king considered her views heretical.*

heritage [ˈheritidʒ] *nc* (*formal*) things (*esp* valuable things such as buildings, literature *etc*) which are passed on from one generation to another: *We must all take care to preserve our national heritage.*

hermetically [həˈmetikəli]: **hermetically sealed** (*tech*) completely closed and airtight: *This medicine is stored in a hermetically sealed container.*

hermit [ˈhəːmit] *nc* a person who lives alone, *esp* for religious reasons.

'hermitage [-tidʒ] *nc* the place where a hermit lives.

hernia [ˈhəːniə] *ncu* a medical condition caused by one of the organs of the body (*esp* in the part of the body between the chest and the hips) sticking out through an opening or weak spot in the surrounding tissue: *He had a hernia*; *He had to have an operation for hernia.*

hero [ˈhiərou] – *pl* **'heroes**: *fem* **heroine** [ˈherouin] – *nc* **1** a man or boy admired (by many people) for his brave deeds: *The young soldier was regarded as a hero for saving his friend's life.* **2** the chief male person in a story, play *etc*: *The hero of this book is a young American boy called Tom Sawyer.*

heroic [hiˈrouik] *adj* **1** very brave: *heroic deeds*; *His behaviour was indeed heroic.* **2** (*formal*: *usu attrib*) of heroes: *heroic tales.* **he'roically** *adv*.

heroism [ˈherouizm] *nu* great bravery: *The policeman was given a medal in recognition of his heroism.*

'hero-worship *nu* very great, sometimes too great, admiration for a person: *the boy's hero-worship of the famous footballer.* – *vt* to show such admiration for (someone): *The boy hero-worshipped the footballer.*

heroin [ˈherouin] *nu* a habit-forming drug, obtained from opium.

heroine, heroism *see* **hero**.

heron [ˈherən] *nc* a type of large water-bird, with long legs and a long neck.

herring [ˈheriŋ] – *pls* **'herring, 'herrings** – **1** *nc* a kind of small sea fish: *two herring(s)*; *a shoal of herring.* **2** *nu* its flesh used as food: *They had fried herring for tea.*

red herring *see* **red**.

hers, herself *see* **her**.

hertz [həːts] – *pl* **hertz** – *nc* (*tech*: *often abbrev* **Hz** *when written*) a unit of frequency used of radio waves *etc* and corresponding to one cycle per second.

he's *see* **be, have**.

hesitate [ˈheziteit] **1** *vi* to pause briefly in speaking or acting *eg* because of uncertainty: *He hesitated before answering*; *The diver hesitated for a minute on the diving-board.* **2** *vt* to be unwilling (to do something) *eg* because one is not sure it is right: *I hesitate to say he lied but he certainly misled me*; *Don't hesitate to tell me if you have any complaints.*

'hesitancy *nu* the state of making or having frequent hesitations.

'hesitant *adj* making or having frequent hesitations: *a hesitant speaker*; *hesitant speech*; *He was rather hesitant about offering her advice.* **'hesitantly** *adv*.

ˌhesi'tation **1** *ncu* (an) act of hesitating: *The footballer's hesitation cost his team a goal.* **2** *nu* unwillingness or uncertainty: *I have little hesitation in agreeing to this proposal.*

hessian [ˈhesiən, (*Amer*) ˈheʃən] *nu, adj* (of) a type of coarse cloth made of jute: *This wallpaper is (made of) hessian*; *a hessian bag.*

het [het]: **het up** (*inf*) over-anxious and excited: *She's getting all het up about the money she lost.*

hetero- [hetərou] (*in cmpds*) other or different, as in **heterosexual**.

heterogeneous [hetərəˈdʒiːniəs] *adj* (*formal*) made up of parts, people, things *etc* of very different kinds: *a heterogeneous mixture/crowd.*

heterosexual [hetərəˈsekʃuəl] *adj* (*usu pred*) sexually attracted to people of the opposite sex: *He is completely heterosexual – he has no homosexual tendencies.*

hew [hjuː] – *pt* **hewed**; *ptp* **hewed, hewn** [hjuːn] – (*liter*) **1** *vti* to cut or hit (a person or thing) with an axe, sword *etc*: *He hewed down the great oak tree.* **2** *vt* to cut out or shape (something) with an axe, sword *etc*: *He hewed a path through the forest.*

hexagon [ˈheksəgən] *nc* a six-sided figure.

hey [hei] *interj* a shout expressing joy, or a

question, or used to attract attention: *Hey! What are you doing there?*

heyday ['heidei] *nc* (*no pl*) a time when (someone or something) has great power, importance *etc*: *The fifties were the heyday of rock and roll*; *In her heyday she was the best actress in Hollywood.*

hi [hai] *interj* **1** (*inf*) a word of greeting: *Hi! How are you?* **2** (*esp Brit*) a word used to express surprise or to attract attention: *Hi! I didn't know you were back in town.*

hibernate ['haibəneit] *vi* (of certain animals) to pass the winter in a condition like sleep: *Hedgehogs hibernate.*

ˌ**hiber'nation** *nu*: *The squirrels have gone into hibernation for the winter.*

hiccup, hiccough ['hikʌp] *nc* **1** (the sound caused by) a sudden brief stopping of the breath caused by laughing, or by eating or drinking too much, too quickly *etc.* **2** (*in pl*) the frequent repetition of this, at intervals of a few seconds: *I had an attack of hiccoughs*; *He's got the hiccups.* – *v* – *pt, ptp* '**hiccuped** (*Amer also* '**hiccupped**) – *vi* to make a hiccup or hiccups.

hide[1] [haid] – *pt* **hid** [hid]: *ptp* **hidden** ['hidn] – **1** *vti* to put (a person, thing *etc*) in a place where it cannot be seen or easily found: *I'll hide the children's presents under the bed*; *You go and hide, and I'll come and look for you*; (*fig*) *He is in love with her but he tries to hide his feelings.* **2** *vi* to be in a place where one cannot be seen or easily found: *She's hiding (from you) because she thinks you are angry with her.* – *nc* a small, often hidden, hut *etc* from which birds *etc* can be watched, photographed *etc.*

'**hidden** *adj* (made in such a way as to be) difficult to see or find: *a hidden door*; *There's a hidden meaning to this letter*; *Try to keep this hidden.*

hide-and-seek *nu* a children's game in which one person searches for other people who have hidden themselves.

'**hide-out** *nc* a place where one can hide or is hiding: *The police searched for the bandits' hide-out.*

'**hiding-place** *nc* a place where a person or thing can be or is hidden: *We'll have to find a safe hiding-place for our jewels.*

be in, go into hiding to have hidden or hide oneself: *He has gone into hiding because he knows the police are looking for him*; *He is still in hiding – he does not realize that the police are no longer looking for him.*

come out of hiding to come out of the place where one was hiding: *The burglar came out of hiding when the police car drove off.*

hide[2] [haid] *ncu* (*often in cmpds*) the skin of an animal: *He makes coats out of animal hides*; *Her coat is made of cow-hide.*

'**hiding** *nc* (*inf*) a beating on the back or buttocks (*usu* of a child as punishment): *What that child needs is a good hiding.*

hidebound ['haidbaund] *adj* (*derog*) narrow-minded; not willing to accept new ideas or opinions: *It's a great idea, but the manager is far too hidebound to agree to it*; *hidebound ideas.*

hideous ['hidiəs] *adj* extremely ugly: *a hideous vase*; *She looks hideous in that dress.* '**hideously** *adv.* '**hideousness** *nu.*

hierarchy ['haiəra:ki] *ncu* **1** (an) arrangement (of *usu* people in a group, also things *etc*) in order of rank, importance *etc*: *He rapidly climbed up the hierarchy to become a director of the firm*; *You will find some system of hierarchy in nearly all organizations.* **2** the group of people in any organization who control that organization: *the hierarchy of a political party.*

hie'rarchical [-'ra:-] *adj* (*formal*) forming a hierarchy: *the hierarchical structure of an organization.*

hieroglyphics [haiərə'glifiks] *n pl* **1** a form of writing used *eg* in ancient Egypt, in which pictures represent words and sounds. **2** (*fig inf*) writing that is difficult to read: *I can't read his hieroglyphics.*

hi-fi ['haifai] (*inf*) **1** *nu* (*usu attrib*) high quality and great accuracy (in the reproduction of sound): *hi-fi equipment.* **2** *ncu* (the use of) any electronic apparatus (*eg* a record-player) which gives such good reproduction: *He put the record on his hi-fi*; *He's very interested in hi-fi.* – *See also* **high fidelity** *under* **high**.

higgledy-piggledy [higldi'pigldi] *adv, adj* (*usu pred*: *inf*) in great disorder: *His clothes were lying higgledy-piggledy in piles all over the room.*

high [hai] *adj* **1** (of things) at, from, or reaching up to, a great distance from ground-level, sea-level *etc*: *Mount Everest is a very high mountain*; *That shelf is too high for me to put anything on it*; *a high dive*; *a dive from the high diving-board.* **2** (*pred*: *usu* of things; also of people who are abnormally small *eg* dwarfs, and sometimes of horses) having a particular height: *This building is about forty foot/feet high*; *My neighbour is only three foot/feet high*; *My horse is fifteen hands high.* **3** great; (with) very much (of something): *The car was travelling at high speed*; *He has a high opinion of her work* (= He thinks her work is very good); *This job requires a high degree of intelligence*; *They charge high prices*; *Their prices are too high*; *He has high hopes of becoming a director*; *The child has a high temperature*; *The child's temperature is quite high.* **4** (*usu attrib*) most important; very important: *the high altar in a church*; *Important criminal trials are held at the High Court*; *The king called together the high officials of the land*; *Going to university was a high point in his life*; *Seeing the queen was one of the high spots of her life.* **5** noble; good: *high ideals.* **6** (of a wind) strong: *a high wind*; *The wind is high tonight.* **7** (of sounds) at or towards the top of a musical scale: *a high note.* **8** (of voices) like a child's voice (rather than like a man's): *He spoke in a high voice*; *His voice is very high for a teenage boy.* **9** (*inf*: *usu pred*: *often with* **on**) drunk or affected by drugs: *He was high on marijuana.* **10** (*inf*: *pred*) (of food, *esp* meat) beginning to go bad: *Some game birds are not cooked until they are high.* **11** having great value: *Aces and kings are high cards*; *high numbers*; *high stakes.* – *See also* **high** *in phrases below.* – *adv* **1** at, or to, a great distance from ground-level, sea-level *etc*: *The plane was flying high in the sky*; (*fig*) *He'll rise high in his profession.* – *nc* (*inf*) a high point: *Prices have reached a new high this month.*

'**highly** *adv* **1** very; very much: *He was highly delighted at the news*; *She is one of our most highly paid workers.* **2** with approval: *He thinks/speaks very highly of you.*

'**highness** **1** *nu* the state or quality of being high: *The highness of that shop's prices will lose it a lot of custom.* **2** *n* (*with cap*) a title of a prince, princess *etc*: *Your Highness*; *Her Highness.*

ˌ**high-'born** *adj* (*formal or liter*) of noble birth.

'**highboy** *nc* (*Amer*) a tallboy.

'**highbrow** (*inf often derog*) *nc* a person who is

interested in things such as classical music, great literature *etc*: *I am not a highbrow – I enjoy popular music.* – *adj* of things such as classical music, great literature *etc*: *The books he reads are too highbrow for me – I prefer a good cowboy story.*

ˈ**high-chair** *nc* a chair with long legs, used by a baby or young child at mealtimes.

ˌ**high-ˈclass** *adj* (*usu attrib*) of high quality: *This is a high-class hotel.*

higher education *nu* education beyond the level of secondary school education, *eg* at a university: *She is not interested in higher education – she wants to leave school and start working*; (*attrib*) *higher education establishments such as universities.*

high explosive *ncu* a very powerful explosive *eg* TNT: *The lorry was carrying high explosives.*

ˌ**high-exˈplosive** *adj* (*usu attrib*) containing a high explosive: *high-explosive shells.*

high-falutin', ˌ**high-faˈluting** [-fəˈluːtn] *adj* (*inf*) very, *usu* too, showy or grand: *high-falutin' ideas*; *She is too high-falutin' to speak to her workers when she meets them in the street.*

high fidelity *nu* high quality and great accuracy (in the reproduction of sound): *This record-player reproduces music with high fidelity*; (*attrib*) *high-fidelity equipment.* – *See also* **hi-fi**.

ˌ**high-ˈhanded** *adj* (*derog*) **1** (of people) acting without thought or consideration for others: *He is so high-handed – he never consults anyone else before acting*; *a very high-handed young man.* **2** (of actions *etc*) done without thought or consideration for others: *People dislike his high-handed attitude*; *His treatment of other people is very high-handed.* ˌ**high-ˈhandedly** *adv.* ˌ**high-ˈhandedness** *nu.*

high jump *see* **the high jump** *below.*

ˈ**Highland** *adj* **1** of or from the Highlands: *Highland cattle.* **2** of or from the highlands of a country.

ˈ**Highlander** *nc* a person who comes from the Highlands.

Highland games *n pl* a meeting for people to compete in certain sports, Scottish dancing *etc*, *esp* in Scotland, the US, and Canada.

ˈ**highlands** *n pl* a mountainous part of certain countries, *esp* (*with cap*) of Scotland: *The sheep are brought down from the highlands in winter*; *We always go to the Highlands for our holidays.*

ˈ**high-level** *adj* (*attrib*) involving important people: *high-level talks between the Prime Ministers of two countries.*

ˈ**highlight** *nc* the best or most memorable event, experience, part of something *etc*: *The highlight of our holiday was a trip to a brewery.* – *vt* to draw particular attention to (a person, thing *etc*): *Is there any way we can highlight the major features of this scheme?*

ˌ**highly-ˈstrung** *adj* very nervous; very easily upset or excited: *The child was so highly-strung that he jumped at the slightest noise*; *delicate and highly-strung children.*

ˌ**high-ˈminded** *adj* having or showing good or noble ideals, principles *etc*: *Our minister is so high-minded that he does not realize when he is being cheated*; *The high-minded young man was horrified by the corruption in politics.* ˌ**high-ˈmindedness** *nu.*

high-octane *see* **octane**.

ˌ**high-ˈpitched** *adj* (of sounds, voices *etc*) high (*def 7*); sharp: *The only sound they could get out of the radio was a high-pitched whine*; *Her voice is high-pitched and rather unpleasant.*

ˌ**high-ˈpowered** *adj* **1** (*usu attrib*) (with an engine which is) very powerful: *a high-powered motor-boat/engine.* **2** (*fig*) strong and forceful; aggressive; very efficient: *I dislike high-powered salesmen*; *I don't like working for him – he is too high-powered*; *a high-powered political campaign.*

ˌ**high-ˈpressure** *adj* (*attrib*) **1** having, using *etc* air, water *etc* at a high pressure. **2** (*fig*) very forceful and persuasive: *a high-pressure salesman.*

ˈ**high-rise** *adj* (*attrib*) with many storeys: *She does not like living in a high-rise flat as the children cannot get out to play easily.*

ˈ**highroad** *nc* (*esp old*) a main road.

ˈ**high school** *nc* a secondary school: *She goes to high school next year*; *He was a pupil of the High School of Glasgow.*

ˌ**high-ˈsounding** *adj* (*usu attrib*) (of style, language *etc*) sounding or seeming very important, often more important than is in fact the case: *The dictator awarded himself a number of high-sounding titles.*

ˌ**high-ˈspirited** *adj* showing high spirits: *a high-spirited horse*; *Her new mare is very high-spirited.*

high spirits *n pl* (the state of having) a sense of fun, enjoyment *etc*: *He's in high spirits today.*

ˈ**high street** *nc* (*with cap when used as a name*) the main street of a town *etc*, *usu* with shops *etc*: *The procession wended its way down the High Street*; (*attrib*) *high-street prices.*

high tea *nc* (*Brit*) a meal with cooked food (*eg* meat, fish *etc*) in the late afternoon: *We have dinner at eight o'clock – the children have high tea at five o'clock.*

high tide *nc* the time when the tide is farthest up the shore: *High tide today is at 15.46*; *They set sail at high tide yesterday.*

high treason *see* **treason**.

high water *nc* **1** the time at which the tide or other water (*eg* a river) is at its highest point: *Last night at high water the river burst its banks.* **2** (*often attrib*) this point itself: *high-water mark.*

ˈ**highway** *nc* (*esp legal*) a road, *esp* a large or main road.

Highway Code *nc* (*Brit*) (a booklet containing) a set of official rules for road users in Britain: *If you want to pass your driving test, you must learn the Highway Code.*

ˈ**highwayman** – *pl* ˈ**highwaymen** – *nc* (*hist*) a man *usu* on horseback, who attacked and robbed people travelling in coaches *etc* on public roads.

high wire *see* **wire**.

for the ˈhigh jump (*sl*) about to be punished *etc* because one has done something wrong: *If the boss finds out that you broke that machine, you'll be for the high jump.* – *See also* **the high jump** *below.*

high and dry (of boats) on the shore; out of the water: *The boat was left high and dry on the beach*; (*fig inf*) *Her husband has left her high and dry without any money.*

high and low (*inf*) everywhere: *I've searched high and low for that book.*

high and mighty (*inf*) thinking, or behaving as if one thinks, that one is very important: *There's no reason for you to be so high and mighty – you're no-one special.*

high gear *see* **gear**.

the ˈhigh jump a sports contest in which people jump over a bar which is raised until no-one can jump over it: *She has entered for the high jump and the long jump in the school sports.* – *See also* **for the high jump** *above.*

the high seas (*esp formal or liter*) the open seas; far from land.

it is *etc* **high time** (*inf*) something ought to be or have been done *etc* by this, or that, time: *It is high time that this job was finished*; *It's high time someone told him to stop being stupid.*

on high (*liter*) **1** at or to a high place or position; in or to the sky: *birds flying on high.* **2** in or to heaven: *the angels on high.*

on one's high horse difficult to argue with *etc, eg* because one thinks oneself to be very important or that one has not been shown enough respect *etc*: *As soon as anyone criticizes him, he gets on his high horse.*

run high (*formal*) (of feelings, tempers *etc*) to be excited, angry *etc*: *Feelings ran high at the meeting held to protest against the new motorway.*

See also **height, tall**.

hijack ['haidʒak] *vt* **1** to take control of (an aeroplane *etc*) while it is moving and force the pilot *etc* to fly *etc* to a place chosen by the hijacker: *A young man tried to hijack the plane and force the pilot to fly to North Africa.* **2** to stop and rob (a vehicle): *Thieves hijacked a lorry carrying £2 000 worth of whisky.* **3** to steal (something) from (a vehicle) *eg* by stopping the vehicle: *Thieves hijacked £2 000 worth of whisky from a lorry.* – *nc* the act of hijacking (something). '**hijacker** *nc.*

hike [haik] *nc* a long walk, *usu* in the country, often carrying equipment on one's back: *I'm going on a twenty-mile hike at the weekend.* – *vi* to go on a hike or hikes: *He has hiked all over Britain.* '**hiker** *nc.*

go hiking to go on a hike or hikes: *I often go hiking at the weekend.*

hilarious [hi'leəriəs] *adj* (*formal*) very funny; very amusing: *The play was hilarious*; *a hilarious comedy.* **hi'lariously** *adv.*

hi'larity [-'la-] *nu* (*formal*): *The speaker's remarks caused a lot of hilarity*; *the hilarity of his remarks.*

hill [hil] **1** *nc* (*often found with cap in place-names*) a piece of high land, smaller than a mountain: *We went for a walk in the hills yesterday*; (*attrib*) *hill-walking*; *He lives in a little village called Saxby Hill.* **2** *nc* a slope on a road: *This car has a lot of difficulty going up steep hills.* **3** *n* (*with cap*) a word used in the names of certain roads or streets: *His address is 24 Holly Hill.*

'**hillock** [-lək] *nc* (*formal or liter*) a small hill.

'**hilly** *adj* having many hills: *hilly country*; *The countryside around here is very hilly.*

'**hillside** *nc* the side or slope of a hill: *Heather covers the Scottish hillsides in August.*

over the hill (*inf*) past one's best; (too) old: *Although thirty-eight is old for a footballer, Smith is certainly not over the hill.*

hilt [hilt] *nc* (*formal or liter*) the handle, *esp* of a sword.

(up) to the hilt completely: *If you decide to do this, I'll back you to the hilt.*

him [him] *pron* (used as the object of an actual or implied verb or preposition or (*inf*) as the subject of an implied verb) a male person or animal already spoken about: *I saw him yesterday*; *I gave him a book*; *I came with him*; *'Who did it?' 'Him.'* (= He did it); *'Who was she with?' 'Him.'*

him'self *pron* **1** used as the object of a verb or preposition when a male person or animal is the object of an action he performs: *He kicked himself*; *He looked at himself in the mirror.* **2** used to emphasize **he, him** or the name of a male person or animal: *John himself played no part in this.* **3** without help *etc*: *He did it himself.*

by himself *see* **by oneself** *under* **by**.

he is not himself *see* **not be oneself** *under* **one**.

See also **he, his**.

hind[1] [haind] *nc* a female deer, *esp* of the red deer: *The two stags fought over the hind.*

hind[2] [haind] *adj* (*attrib*) at the back (*usu* of an animal): *a hind leg.*

hind- (*in cmpds*) at the back (*usu* of an animal), as in **hindquarters**.

hinder ['hində] *vt* to delay or prevent (someone or something); to make (something) difficult: *All these interruptions hinder my work*; *All the interruptions hinder me from working.*

'**hindrance** [-drəns] *nc* a person, thing *etc* that hinders (someone or something): *I know you are trying to help me but you're really just being a hindrance.*

Hindi *see* Appendix 2.

hindmost ['haindmoust] *adj* (*old or liter*) last; farthest behind: *The farmer caught the hindmost child as the children ran from the orchard.*

hindquarters ['haindkwo:təz] *n pl* (of an animal) the back legs and the part of the body above them: *I think our dog has injured its hindquarters – it is walking in a peculiar way.*

hindrance *see* **hinder**.

hindsight ['haindsait] *nu* (*formal*) wisdom or knowledge got only after something (*usu* bad) has happened: *I thought I was doing the right thing, but with hindsight I can see that I made the wrong decision.*

Hindu [hin'du:] *nc, adj* (of) a person who believes in, and lives according to the rules of, the religion of **Hinduism**.

hinge [hindʒ] *nc* the joint by means of which a door is fastened to a door-frame, a lid is fastened to a box *etc* and on which the door, lid *etc* turns when it opens or closes: *I must oil the hinges on that door.*

'**hinge on** (*formal*) **upon** *vt fus* to depend on: *The result of the whole competition hinges on the last match*; *Whether we go to France or not hinges on the cost of transport.*

hint [hint] *nc* **1** a statement that passes on information without giving it openly or directly: *He didn't actually say he wanted more money, but he dropped* (= said) *a few hints.* **2** a helpful suggestion (about how to do something): *Have you a copy of the book called 'Gardening Hints'?* **3** a very small amount (of something); a slight impression or suggestion (of something): *There was a hint of fear in his voice.* – *vti* to (try to) pass on information without stating it openly or directly: *He hinted (to me) that he would like more money*; *He refused to say what was going to happen, but he hinted at major changes.*

take a/the hint (*inf*) to understand what (a person) is hinting at, and do what (the person) wants: *I keep making jokes to my secretary about her coming to work late every day, but she never takes the hint.*

hinterland ['hintəland] *nc* the district lying inland from the coast.

hip [hip] (*often in pl*) **1** *nc* (the bones in) either of the two sides of the body just below the waist: *She fell and broke her left hip.* **2** *ncu* (the measurement round) the body at the level of the hips and buttocks: *This exercise is good for the hips*; *She's rather large round the hips*; *These trousers are too tight at the hip*; *What (size of) hip are you?*;

(*attrib*) *What's her hip measurement?*

hippie, hippy ['hipi] *nc, adj* (*inf*: *slightly old*) (of) a *usu* young person who does not wish to live by the normal rules of society and who shows his rejection of these rules by his unusual clothes, habits *etc*: *The farm cottage was bought by a group of young hippies*; (*attrib*) *hippy clothes.*

hippopotamus [hipə'potəməs] – *pls* ˌ**hippo'potamuses,** ˌ**hippo'potami** [-mai] – *nc* a large African animal with very thick skin living in or near rivers.

hippy *see* **hippie**.

hire ['haiə] *vt* **1** (*often with* **from**) to get the use (of something which belongs to someone else) by paying money: *He's hiring a car* (*from us*) *for the week.* **2** (*often with* **out**) to give (someone) the use of (something which belongs to someone else) in exchange for money: *Will you hire me your boat for the week-end?*; *Does this firm hire out cars, or just sell them?* **3** (*esp Amer*) to employ (a servant, workman *etc*): *They have hired a team of labourers to dig the road.* – *nu* (money paid for) the hiring (of something or someone): *Is this hall for hire?*; *How much is the hire of the hall?*; *We don't own this crane – it's on hire from another firm.* '**hirer** *nc.*

'**hireling** [-liŋ] *nc* (*formal*: *usu derog*) a person who works for another person: *He never does unpleasant jobs himself – he always gets one of his hirelings to do it.*

ˌ**hire-'purchase** *nu* (*also abbrev* **HP** [eitʃ'pi:]) a way of buying an article by paying the price in several weekly or monthly parts: *I got this television on hire-purchase*; (*attrib*) *a hire-purchase agreement.*

hirsute ['hə:sju:t] *adj* (*formal*: of a woman, *offensive*) having hair on the face; hairy; shaggy: *She is rather a hirsute young woman*; *He is small, dark and hirsute.*

his [hiz] *adj* (*attrib*), *pron* belonging to a male person already spoken about: *John says it's his book*; *He says the book is his*; *'Is this John's book?' 'No, his is on the table'.*

hiss [his] **1** *vti* (of snakes, geese, people *etc*) to make a sound like that of the letter *s* [s], *eg* to show anger or displeasure: *The children hissed* (*at*) *the witch when she came on stage*; *The geese hissed at the dog.* **2** *vt* (*formal*) to say (something) with a hissing sound: *The children hissed their displeasure at the witch's actions on stage.* – *nc* such a sound: *The speaker ignored the hisses of the angry crowd.*

'**hissing** *adj* (*attrib*) sounding like the letter *s* [s]: *The gas-fire burned with a hissing sound.*

history ['histəri] **1** *nu* the study of events *etc* that happened in the past: *She lectures in British history at the university*; *He studies history*; (*attrib*) *a history student*; (*attrib*) *a history lesson.* **2** *nc* a description *usu* in writing of past events, ways of life *etc*: *I'm writing a history of Scotland*; (*attrib*) *a history book.* **3** *nc* (*usu in sing*) the frequent occurrence (of something) in a person's past life, his parents' lives *etc*: *The man denied that there was any history of madness in his family.* **4** *nc* (the description of) the *usu* interesting events *etc* associated with (something): *This desk/project has a very interesting history.*

hi'**storian** [-'sto:-] *nc* a person who studies (and writes about) history: *His brother is a mathematician and his sister is a well-known historian.*

hi'**storic** [-'sto-] *adj* (*usu attrib*) famous or important in history: *a historic battle*; *On this historic spot, a battle was fought which changed the history of the world.*

hi'**storical** [-'sto-] *adj* (*usu attrib*) **1** of or about history; of or about people or events from history: *He is engaged in historical research*; *She likes reading historical novels.* **2** that actually happened or existed (not in legend *etc*): *Is Macbeth a historical person?*; *Is the murder of Duncan in Shakespeare's 'Macbeth' a historical event/fact?*

hi'**storically** [-'sto-] *adv*: *Is this play historically accurate?*

make history to do something very important, *esp* to be the first person or people to do something: *The Wright brothers made history when they were the first to fly an aeroplane.*

histrionic [histri'onik] *adj* (*formal derog*: *usu attrib*) (of behaviour *etc*) exaggerated; showing too much emotion: *Her histrionic behaviour in a crisis embarrasses her family.*

ˌ**histri'onics** *n pl* (*formal*) behaviour which shows exaggerated or too great emotion: *I'm tired of her histrionics.*

hit [hit] – *prp* '**hitting**: *pt, ptp* **hit** – **1** *vti* to (cause or allow to) come into hard contact with (someone or something): *The ball hit him on the head*; *He hit his head on/against a low branch*; *The car hit a lamp-post*; *He hit me on the head with a bottle*; *There was a terrible noise when the two buses hit each other*; *His next arrow hit the target*; *He was hit by a bullet from a rifle*; *That boxer can certainly hit hard!* **2** *vt* to (cause to) come into hard contact with (something), and force or cause it to move in some direction: *The batsman hit the ball* (*over the wall*). **3** *vt* (*usu with* **hard**) to cause to suffer: *The farmers were badly/hard hit by the lack of rain*; *The lack of rain hit the farmers hard*; *Her husband's death hit her hard.* **4** *vt* (*inf*) to find (something) by chance: *If we keep going in this direction, we're bound to hit the road eventually.* **5** *vt* to succeed in reaching, obtaining *etc*: *She used to be a famous soprano but she cannot hit the high notes now*; (*inf*) *We were completely lost but we finally hit the right road by chance.* – *See also* **hit** *in phrases below.* – *nc* **1** the act of hitting (someone or something): *That was a good hit.* **2** a point scored by hitting a target *etc*: *He scored five hits.* **3** (*inf*) something which is popular or successful: *The play/record is a hit*; *He sang all his hits*; (*attrib*) *a hit song.*

ˌ**hit-and-'run** *adj* (*attrib*) **1** (of a driver) causing injury to a person and driving away without stopping or reporting the accident. **2** (of an accident) caused by such a driver.

ˌ**hit-or-'miss** *adj* (*usu attrib*) without any system or planning; careless: *hit-or-miss methods.*

'**hit parade** *nc* the (*usu* weekly) list of best-selling records: *His record is number five in the hit parade this week.*

hit back 1 *vt oblig sep* to hit (someone by whom one has been hit): *He hit me, so I hit him back.* **2** *vi* (*often with* **at**) to criticize or attack in words (someone by whom one has been criticized or attacked): *He hit back at those who sneered at his plan.*

hit (someone) below the belt (*esp fig*) to hit in an unfair way: *It was hitting below the belt to tell him he was to blame for his child's death.*

hit it off (*inf*) to become friendly: *We hit it off as soon as we met*; *I hit it off with him.*

'**hit on** (*formal*) **upon** *vt fus* to find (an answer *etc*) by chance: *We've hit on the solution at last.*

hit out *vi* (*often with* **against** *or* **at**) **1** to attempt to hit (someone): *The injured man hit out blindly at his attackers.* 2 to criticize or attack in words (someone with whom one does not agree): *The Prime Minister hit out at his opponents.*

hit the headlines (*inf*) (of a person or something he has done) to be printed as one of the main news items in a newspaper, *usu* under large headlines (*eg* because the news is important, shocking, sensational *etc*): *You really hit the headlines by marrying that blonde actress.*

hit the nail on the head *see* **nail**.

hit the roof *see* **roof**.

make a hit with (someone) (*inf*) to make oneself liked or approved of (by someone): *That young man seems to have made quite a hit with your daughter.*

hitch [hitʃ] 1 *vt* to fasten (something) to something: *He hitched his horse to the fence-post; He hitched his car to his caravan.* 2 *vi* (*inf*) to hitch-hike: *I can't afford the train-fare to London – I'll have to hitch.* – *See also* **hitch up** *below.* – *nc* 1 an unexpected problem or delay: *The job was completed without a hitch; The demonstration had to be cancelled because of a technical hitch.* 2 a kind of knot. 3 a sudden, short pull (up): *She gave her skirt a hitch.*

'**hitch-hike** *vi* to travel by means of free rides in other people's cars: *He has hitch-hiked all over Britain.* '**hitch-hiker** *nc.*

hitch a lift/ride (*inf*) to get a free ride in someone else's car: *I've no money, so I'll try to hitch a lift to Edinburgh.*

hitch up *vt sep* to pull up or raise (something) with a sudden short pull: *He hitched up his trousers.*

hither ['hiðə] *adv* (*old*) to this place: *Come hither, child!*

ˌ**hither'to** *adv* (*formal*) up to this or that time: *Hitherto, he had been living in France; Hitherto, this information has been confidential.*

hither and thither (*old or liter*) in various directions: *The villagers ran hither and thither trying to escape their attackers.*

hive [haiv] *nc* 1 a box *etc* where bees live and store up honey: *He's building a hive so that he can keep bees.* 2 the bees that live in such a place: *The whole hive flew after the queen bee.* 3 (*fig*) a place in which people are working very busily: *The shop was a hive of activity.*

hive off *vt sep* (*inf*) 1 (*often derog*) to give (some work, part of a job *etc*) to some other person, firm *etc*: *If we can't meet the schedule, we can hive off some of the work to another firm.* 2 to make (part of an organization) independent: *We can hive off part of the company and make it a separate firm.*

h'm, h'mm [m] *interj* the conventional spelling of a sound used to show uncertainty, disbelief *etc*: *H'mm – I wonder what he means by that.*

hoard [ho:d] *nc* a (sometimes hidden) store (of treasure, food *etc*): *When she was supposed to be on a diet she secretly kept a hoard of potato crisps in a cupboard.* – *vti* to store up or keep large quantities of (something), often in secret: *His mother told him to stop hoarding old newspapers.* '**hoarder** *nc.*

hoarding ['ho:diŋ] *nc* 1 a *usu* temporary fence of boards, *eg* round a place where a building is being knocked down or built: *They have erected a hoarding round the building-site.* 2 a *usu* large, *usu* wooden, flat object on which advertisements, posters *etc* are stuck: *All the hoardings have advertisements for beer.*

hoar-frost ['ho:frost] *nu* the white frost seen on grass, leaves *etc.*

hoarse [ho:s] *adj* 1 (of voices, shouts *etc*) rough; harsh: *He gave a hoarse cry; His voice sounds rather hoarse.* 2 (of people) having a hoarse voice, *usu* because one has a cold or cough, or because one has been shouting: *She sounded rather hoarse on the telephone; The spectators shouted themselves hoarse in support of the teams.* '**hoarseness** *nu.*

hoary ['ho:ri] *adj* (*liter*) 1 white or grey with age: *his hoary head.* 2 (*formal*) very old: *hoary traditions/ruins.* '**hoariness** *nu.*

hoax [houks] *nc* a trick played to deceive people: *The firemen said that some of the emergencies had been hoaxes; There was not a bomb in the school at all – it was just a hoax;* (*attrib*) *They had answered several hoax calls.*

play a hoax on to carry out such a trick on (someone).

hob [hob] *nc* 1 the flat framework on top of a gas *etc* cooker, on which pots are placed to be heated: *A pan of stew was simmering on the hob.* 2 (*esp old*) a small shelf next to a fireplace on which pots *etc* may be kept hot.

hobble ['hobl] *vi* to walk with difficulty, *usu* taking short steps (*eg* because one is lame or because one's feet are sore): *By the end of the twenty-mile hike, many of the walkers could only hobble along very slowly.*

hobby ['hobi] *nc* something a person enjoys doing (*usu* frequently) in his spare time: *Stamp-collecting is a popular hobby; He did not know what to do when he retired from work as he had no hobbies.*

hobby-horse ['hobiho:s] *nc* (*fig*) a subject which a person talks about frequently: *The falling standards in education is one of his hobby-horses.*

hobnailed, hobnail ['hobneil(d)] *adj* (*usu attrib*) having large-headed nails hammered into the soles: *hobnailed boots.*

hobnob ['hobnob] – *pt, ptp* '**hobnobbed** – *vi* (*inf*: *usu with* **with**) to be friendly with (*usu* someone who is richer, more important *etc* than oneself): *He hobnobs with the nobility.*

hobo ['houbou] – *pl* '**hobo(e)s** – *nc* (*Amer sl*) a tramp.

hock[1] [hok] *ncu* a type of white wine: *He had a glass of hock with the fish course; We had a very good hock last night.*

hock[2] [hok] *nc* a joint on the hind leg of an animal, below the knee: *The horse has an injured hock.*

hock[3] [hok]: **in 'hock** (*sl*) having been pawned: *My watch is in hock at the moment.*

hockey ['hoki] *nu* a game for two teams of eleven players, played with clubs which are bent at one end ('**hockey-sticks**) and a ball, or in '**ice hockey**, a round flat disc called a puck: *They play hockey and netball at her school; We played hockey against a team from Canada;* (*attrib*) *a hockey match.*

hocus-pocus [houkəs'poukəs] *nu* (*formal*) trickery; words, actions *etc* which are intended to deceive or mislead (someone): *The people were not deceived by the political hocus-pocus of the prospective candidate.*

hod [hod] *nc* 1 a V-shaped, *usu* wooden, box on a pole, used for carrying bricks and mortar: *a hod of bricks.* 2 a coal scuttle.

hoe [hou] *nc* a *usu* long-handled tool with a *usu* metal blade used for removing or destroying weeds *etc*: *The gardener used a hoe to remove weeds from the rows of tomato plants.* – *v* – *prp* '**hoeing** –

vti to use a hoe *eg* to remove or destroy weeds: *This morning I hoed the garden/weeds.*

hog [hog] *nc* **1** (*esp Amer*) a pig. **2** (*inf derog*) a selfish, greedy, bad-mannered or dirty person: *He's such a hog he ate all the food before some people had sat down.* – *v* – *pt, ptp* **hogged** – *vt* (*inf*) to take or use more of (something) than one ought to; to keep or use (something) longer than one ought to: *She's hogging the mirror and no-one else can use it.*

'**hogwash** *nu* (*inf*: *esp Amer*) nonsense: *That's hogwash – I don't believe a word of it.*

road-hog *see* **road**.

go the whole hog (*inf*) to do (something) completely: *I've bought a new dress – I think I'll go the whole hog and buy shoes and a handbag.*

Hogmanay ['hogmənei] *n* in Scotland, (the evening of) the last day of the year (December 31) when many parties are held and people visit each other.

ho! ho! [hou'hou] *interj* an expression used to show amusement or (ironic) disbelief.

hoist [hoist] *vt* **1** to lift (someone or something that *usu* is heavy): *He hoisted the sack on to his back*; *He hoisted the child up on to his shoulders.* **2** to raise or lift (something) by means of some apparatus, a rope *etc*: *The cargo was hoisted on to the ship*: *They hoisted the flag.* – *nc* **1** an apparatus for lifting *usu* heavy objects: *We have had to instal a hoist for my mother – she is now disabled and cannot walk.* **2** (*inf*) a lift or push up: *Give me a hoist over this wall, will you!*

be hoist with one's own petard [pi'ta:d] (*very formal*) to be the victim of, or ruined by, one's own trick which one intended to ruin or harm someone else.

hoity-toity [hoiti'toiti] *adj* (*inf derog*) too proud or haughty: *There's no reason for you to be so hoity-toity – you're no-one special*; *a very hoity-toity young woman.*

hold[1] [hould] – *pt, ptp* **held** [held] – (not used with **is, was** *etc* and **-ing** (*defs 6, 9–11, 17, 22*)) **1** *vt* to have (a thing *etc*) in one's hand(s) or between one's hands: *He was holding a knife (in his hand)*; *Hold that dish in/with two hands*; *He held the little boy's hand*; *He held the bag by the handle.* **2** *vt* to have (a person, thing *etc*) in a part, or between parts, of the body, or between parts of a tool *etc*: *The artist held the paintbrush between his teeth*; *She was holding a pile of books in her arms*; *She held a beautiful baby in her arms*; *He held the postage stamp with tweezers.* **3** *vt* (*often with* **down, up** *etc*) to support or keep (a person, thing *etc*) from moving, running away, falling *etc*: *What holds that shelf up?*; *We'll have to use very large screws to hold that shelf in place*; *He held the door closed by leaning against it*; *Hold your hands above your head*; *Hold his arms so that he can't struggle.* **4** *vi* to remain in position, fixed *etc* (*eg* when under pressure): *I've tied the two pieces of string together, but I'm not sure the knot will hold*; *Will the anchor hold in a storm?* **5** *vt* to keep (a person) in some place or in one's power: *The police are holding a man for questioning in connection with the murder*; *He was held captive.* **6** *vt* to (be able to) contain (a substance, a quantity of a substance *etc*): *This jug holds two pints*; *You can't hold water in a handkerchief*; *This drawer holds all my shirts.* **7** *vt* to cause to take place: *The meeting will be held next week*; *We'll hold the meeting in the hall.* **8** *v refl* (*formal*) to keep (oneself), or to be, in a particular state or condition: *We'll hold ourselves in readiness in case you send for us*; *She holds herself very erect when she walks.* **9** *vt* to have or be in (an official position, job *etc*): *He held the position of company secretary for five years.* **10** *vt* (*often formal*) to think strongly; to consider (a person *etc*) to be (something or worthy of something): *I hold that this was the right decision*; *He holds me (to be) responsible for everyone's mistakes*; *He is held in great respect*; *He holds certain very odd beliefs.* **11** *vi* (*formal*) to continue (to be valid or apply): *Our offer will hold until next week*; *These rules hold under all circumstances.* **12** *vt* (*with* **to**) to force (a person) to do something he has promised to do: *I intend to hold him to his promises*; *You promised to take me out to dinner and I shall hold you to that.* **13** *vt* to defend (something): *They held the castle against the enemy.* **14** *vt* not to be beaten by (an enemy who is attacking): *The general realized that the soldiers could not hold the enemy for long.* **15** *vt* to keep (a person's attention). **16** *vt* (*formal*) to celebrate: *Not everyone holds Christmas.* **17** *vt* to be the owner of (something): *He holds shares in this company.* **18** *vi* (of good weather) to continue: *I hope the weather holds until after the school sports.* **19** *vi* (*also* **hold the line**) (of a person who is making a telephone call) to wait while the person one is calling comes to the telephone, finishes what he is doing *etc*: *Mr Brown is busy at the moment – will you hold or would you like him to call you back?* **20** *vt* to continue to sing (a musical note): *Please hold that note for four whole beats.* **21** *vt* to keep (something): *We'll hold a few of these in reserve in case we need them later*; *They'll hold your luggage at the station until you collect it.* **22** *vt* (of the future) to be going to produce: *I wonder what the future holds for me?* – *See also* **hold** *in phrases below.* – **1** *nu* the act of holding: *He caught/got/laid/took hold of the rope* (= He grasped the rope) *and pulled*; *Keep hold of that rope*; *Keep a hold on the dog.* – *See also* **get hold of** *below.* **2** *nu* (*sometimes with* **a**) power; influence: *He has a strange hold over that girl.* **3** *nc* (in wrestling *etc*) a manner of holding (someone): *The wrestler invented a new hold.* **4** *nc* (in mountain-climbing *etc*) something a person can grasp or hold: *There aren't many holds on that part of the cliff.*

-holder (*in cmpds*) a person or thing that holds (something): *a pen-holder*; *a ticket-holder* (= a person who has a ticket for something).

'**holding** *nc* the amount (of land, shares in a company *etc*) which a person *etc* has: *He has a large holding in this firm.* – *See also* **smallholding**.

'**hold-all** *nc* a (*usu* large) bag with a zip, used for clothes *etc, eg* when travelling: *He carried his sports equipment in a hold-all.*

hold-up *see* **hold up** *below.*

get 'hold of (*inf*) **1** to manage to speak to (someone): *I've been trying to get hold of you by phone all morning.* **2** to get, buy or obtain (something): *I've been looking for a copy of that book for years, but I've never managed to get hold of one.*

hold (something) against (someone) to dislike, have a bad opinion of *etc* (a person *etc*) because one knows that that person has done something bad, wrong *etc*: *I won't hold it against you if you don't support me*; *I don't hold his foolish remarks against him.*

hold back 1 *vt sep* to refuse to tell someone (something): *The police were convinced the man* *was holding something back.* **2** *vt sep* to prevent (something) from happening, being seen *etc*, *usu* with some effort: *The little girl succeeded in holding back her tears.* **3** *vt usu sep* to prevent (a person *etc*) from making progress or to make his progress slower: *I meant to finish cleaning the house but the children have held me back all morning.*

hold one's breath *see* **breath**.

hold (a person, thing *etc*) **dear** (*old or liter*) to like (a person, thing *etc*) very much: *He holds Britain dear.*

hold down *vt sep* to keep or be allowed to stay in (a job): *He is incapable of holding down a job.*

hold everything (*inf*: *usu in imperative*) to stop what one is doing: *Hold everything! There's something else we've forgotten to do.*

hold forth *vi* (*usu derog*) to talk or give one's opinions, often loudly, at great length and forcefully or dogmatically: *The prime minister held forth for hours on the success of his government.*

hold good to be true or valid; to apply: *Does that rule hold good in every case?*

'hold it (*inf*: *usu in imperative*) to stop or wait: *Hold it! Don't start till I tell you to.*

hold one's nose to block the nostrils by pressing one's nose between one's thumb and first finger, *eg* because of a bad smell, or to stop oneself sneezing.

hold off 1 *vi* (of weather) to stay away: *I hope the rain holds off.* **2** *vt sep* to keep (someone) away; to fight successfully against (an enemy attack): *The soldiers were greatly outnumbered but still managed to hold off the enemy.*

hold on *vi* **1** (*often with* **to**) to keep (a grip on) (something): *She held on to me to stop herself slipping*; *Hold on to that rope and we'll pull you out*; *I couldn't hold on any longer, so I let go of the rope*; *Can I hold on to this book for another week?* **2** (*inf*: *usu in imperative*) to stop or wait: *Hold on – I'm not quite ready yet*; *The telephonist asked the caller to hold on while she connected him with the manager's office.* – *See also* **hold** *v def 19*.

hold out 1 *vi* to continue to survive, or resist difficulties, dangers *etc* until help *etc* arrives: *The rescue team hoped the men in the boat could hold out till they arrived.* **2** *vi* to continue to fight against an enemy attack: *The soldiers held out for eight days.* **3** *vi* to be enough to last: *Will our supplies hold out till the end of the month?* **4** *vt sep* to offer: *The doctor said he could hold out little hope for the patient.* **5** *vi* (*with* **for**) to continue to demand or fight for (something): *The management offered the workers a rise of eight per cent, but the unions said they would hold out for fifteen per cent.*

hold out on *vt fus* (*inf*) to keep back money, information *etc* from (someone): *He says he knows nothing about it, but I think he's holding out on us.*

hold one's own to be as successful in a fight, argument *etc* as one's opponent: *His opponents tried to prove his arguments wrong but he managed to hold his own.*

hold the line *see* **hold** (*def 19*).

'hold to *vt fus* (*formal*) to continue to believe, follow *etc* (opinions, decisions *etc*): *I've tried to tell him he's wrong, but he still holds to his original opinion.*

hold one's tongue (*inf*) to remain silent or stop talking: *There were a lot of things I wanted to say, but I thought I'd better just hold my tongue.*

hold up *vt sep* **1** to stop or slow (the progress of something): *I'm sorry I'm late – I got held up at the office* (*nc* **'hold-up**). **2** to stop and rob (someone): *The bandits held up the stagecoach* (*nc* **'hold-up**). **3** (*with* **as**) to show or mention (someone): *He was held up as an example to everyone.*

'hold with *vt fus* (*formal*) to approve of (something): *He doesn't hold with smoking.*

hold[2] [hould] *nc* (in ships) the place, below the deck, where cargo is stored.

hole [houl] *nc* an opening or gap in or through something: *The dog got out through a hole in the fence*; *I must mend the holes in my socks.* **2** a hollow space in something solid (but which does not go through to the other side of it): *There's a hole in my tooth*; *Many animals live in holes in the ground*; *a hole in the road.* **3** (*inf*: *no pl*) an unpleasant place: *The room we work in is a bit of a hole.* **4** (*sl*) a difficulty: *I'm in a hole and need your help.* **5** (in golf) (the point scored by the player who takes the fewest strokes to hit his ball over) any one of the *usu* eighteen sections of the golf course between the tees and the holes in the middle of the greens: *He won by two holes*; *We played nine holes.* – *vt* **1** to make a hole in (something): *The ship was badly holed when it hit the rock.* **2** to hit (a ball *etc*) into a hole: *The golfer holed his ball from twelve metres away.*

hole out *vi* to hit a golfball into a hole: *He holed out in one at the fourth hole* (= He hit the golfball from the tee into the hole with one stroke).

make a hole in (something) (*fig inf*) to use a lot of (something): *Buying a car made a large hole in my savings.*

pick holes in (something) *see* **pick**[1].

holiday ['holədi] *nc* **1** a day when one does not have to work: *Next Monday is a holiday.* **2** (*esp Brit*: *often in pl*) a period of time when one does not have to work: *The summer holidays will soon be here*; *We're going to Brighton for our holiday(s)*; *I'm taking two weeks' holiday in June*; (*attrib*) *holiday clothes.*

'holiday camp *nc* (*Brit*) a place, *usu* near the sea, where people go for their holidays, and where there are games, activities, shows *etc* for their amusement.

'holidaymaker *nc* a person who has gone *eg* to the seaside for a holiday.

on 'holiday not working; having a holiday: *Mr Smith has gone on holiday*; *She is on holiday in France.*

Holland *see* Appendix 2.

holler ['holə] *vti* (*inf*: *often with* **about, at** *or* **to**) to shout: *He hollered at the boy to go away*; (*fig*) *He's hollering about the cost of petrol again.*

holiness *see* **holy**.

hollow ['holou] *adj* **1** having an empty space in it: *a hollow tree*; *Bottles, pipes and tubes are hollow*; (*fig*) *hollow cheeks* (= cheeks which curve in); (*fig*) *hollow promises* (= insincere promises which will not be carried out); (*fig*) *a hollow victory* (= a victory which gives no benefit to the winner). **2** (*esp attrib*) sounding as if made by, or in, something hollow: *a hollow sound.* – *nc* **1** something hollow: *hollows in her cheeks.* **2** a small valley; a piece of ground that is lower than the ground round it: *You can't see the farm from here because it's in a hollow.* **'hollowness** *nu.*

ˌhollow-'eyed *adj* having the skin surrounding the eyes curving in, because of tiredness *etc*: *The student was hollow-eyed from studying all night*; *a pale hollow-eyed young man with a book in his hand.*

beat (someone) hollow (*inf*) to beat (someone)

thoroughly at a game *etc*: *The local team were beaten hollow by eight goals to one on Saturday.*

hollow out *vt sep* **1** to make (something) hollow: *They hollowed out a tree-trunk to make a boat.* **2** to make (something) by making something hollow: *They hollowed out a boat.*

holly ['holi] *nu* a type of evergreen tree or bush (**'holly tree/bush**) with prickly leaves and red berries: *At Christmas we decorate the house with holly*; (*attrib*) *holly berries.*

holocaust ['holəkoːst] *nc* (*formal*) great destruction, *usu* by fire, *esp* of people's lives: *When the hotel burned down, fifty-six people died in the holocaust.*

holster ['houlstə] *nc* the *usu* leather case for a pistol, *usu* worn on a person's hips.

holy ['houli] *adj* **1** (*usu attrib*) (worthy of worship or respect because) associated with God, Jesus, a saint *etc*; sacred: *holy relics*; *the Holy Bible*; *holy ground*; *This ground is holy.* **2** good; pure; following the rules of a religion: *a holy man/life*; *He is very holy.*

'holiness **1** *nu* the state of being holy. **2** *n* (*with cap*: *with* **His, Your** *etc*) a title of the Pope.

holy orders *see* **order**.

holy terror (*inf*) **1** a person who is feared: *The boss is a holy terror when he's angry.* **2** a badly-behaved child: *Her little boy is a right holy terror.*

'Holy Week the week before Easter.

the Holy Father the Pope.

the 'Holy Land Palestine.

See also **unholy**.

homage ['homidʒ] *nu* (*formal*) (a sign of) great respect shown to a person: *We should pay homage to this great man*; *The soldiers paid homage to the courage of the general.*

home [houm] *nc* **1** the house, town, country *etc* where a person *etc usu* lives: *At present I live in Glasgow, but my home is in Edinburgh*; *He invited me round to his home*; *He says he intends to make his home* (= live) *in France*; *Africa is the home of the lion*; *We'll have to find a home for these dictionaries. How about that shelf?* **2** the place from which a person, thing *etc* comes originally: *America is the home of jazz.* **3** a place where children without parents, old people, people who are ill *etc* live and are looked after: *an old folk's home*; *a nursing home.* **4** a place where people stay while they are working: *a nurses' home.* **5** (*formal or facet*) a house: *Crumpy Construction build fine homes for fine people.* – *adj* (*attrib*) **1** of a person's home or family: *home comforts.* **2** of the town, country *etc* where a person lives, where a thing is made *etc*: *These products are aimed at the home market.* **3** in football *etc*, of a team which is playing at its own ground or of the game which that team is playing in: *the home team*; *a home game.* – *adv* **1** at or to a person's home: *I'm going home now*; *I'll wait till he is home.* **2** completely; to the place, position *etc* a thing is intended to be: *He drove the nail home* (= right into the wood *etc*); *Very few of his punches went home*; (*fig*) *He tried to drive home* (= make people realize) *the terrible conditions of the refugees by showing photographs of them*; (*fig*) *Your critical remarks certainly hit home* (= were understood) – *his behaviour has improved since then*; (*fig*) *These photographs of the war brought home to me* (= made me aware of) *the suffering of the soldiers*; (*fig*) *It has finally come home to me* (= I have finally realized) *that he is wicked.*

'homeless *n pl* (*with* **the**), *adj* (people) without a place to live in: *This charity was set up to help the homeless*; *aid for homeless people*; *Since her husband died she has been homeless.*

'homely *adj* **1** simple but pleasant: *homely food*; *a homely person*; *She is homely and motherly.* **2** making a person feel he is at home: *a homely atmosphere.* **3** (*Amer*) (of a person) not attractive; ugly. **'homeliness** *nu.*

'homing *adj* (*attrib*) **1** (of pigeons *etc*) which (can) fly home when set free a long way from home. **2** able to take a missile *etc* to its target: *These torpedoes have homing devices in their noses.*

'home-brew *ncu* beer *etc* which is brewed in a person's home. **ˌhome-'brewed** *adj.*

'home-coming *nc* the return home of a person (who has *usu* been away from home for some time): *We had a party to celebrate the home-coming of my brother from the army.*

Home Counties (*Brit*) *n pl* the counties round London.

ˌhome-'grown *adj* (of vegetables *etc*) grown in one's own garden or in one's own country: *These tomatoes are home-grown*; *home-grown potatoes.*

home help *nc* (*Brit*) a woman who is paid, *usu* by the local authority, to help people who are old, ill *etc* by cleaning their houses *etc*: *For some time after she came out of hospital, she had to have a home help five days a week to clean her house.*

'homeland *nc* (*liter*) a person's native land: *Immigrants often weep for their homeland.*

ˌhome-'made *adj* made, often not very well, by a person at home: *All this furniture is home-made*; *This dress looks home-made.*

'Home Office *n* the department of the British government which deals with matters relating to law and order, immigration *etc* in England and Wales.

home rule *nu* the government of a country or part of a country by its own citizens in its own parliament: *Their party wants home rule for Scotland.*

Home Secretary *n* the government minister in charge of the Home Office.

'homesick *adj* wanting to go home (*eg* when in a foreign country): *When the boy first went to boarding-school he was very homesick*; *homesick children separated from their parents.* **'homesickness** *nu.*

'homestead [-sted] *nc* a house, *esp* a farm, with the land and other buildings (*eg* barns) which belong to it, *esp* in the US, Australia *etc.*

home truth *nc* (*usu in pl*) a plain statement of something which is unpleasant but true (about a person, his behaviour *etc*) said directly to the person: *I'm not putting up with his bad behaviour any longer – it's time someone told him a few home truths about how to behave in public.*

'homeward *adj* (*attrib*) going home: *his homeward journey.*

'homeward(s) *adv* towards home: *his journey homeward*; *He journeyed homewards.*

'homework *nu* work or study done at home, *esp* by a school pupil: *maths homework*; *She always does her homework before dinner.*

at 'home **1** in one's home: *I'm afraid he's not at home.* **2** (in football *etc*) in one's own ground: *The team is playing at home today.* **3** (*formal*: *often with* **to**) willing to allow people to visit: *Mother is at home on Wednesday afternoons*; *She is not at home to newspaper reporters.* – *See also* **be/feel at home** *below.*

be/feel at home (with) to feel as relaxed as one does in one's own home or in a place or situation one knows well: *I always feel at home in France when I go there on holiday*; *He's quite at home with cows – he used to live on a farm*; *My secretary is quite at home* (= she is used to dealing) *with matters as complicated as this.*

a home from home (*inf*) a place where a person feels as relaxed, happy *etc* as when he is at home.

home in on *vt fus* to move towards (a target *etc*): *The missile is designed to home in on things which produce heat, such as aeroplane engines*; (*fig*) *The discussion was too general – we should have homed in on individual problems.*

leave home 1 to leave one's house: *When I go to work, I usually leave home at a quarter to eight.* **2** to leave one's home and family to go and live somewhere else: *He left home at the age of fifteen and went to live in London.*

make oneself at home to make oneself as comfortable, or to behave in as relaxed a way, as one would at home: *Make yourself at home!*

nothing to write home about (*inf*) not very exciting, important *etc*: *The concert was nothing to write home about.*

homicide ['homisaid] (*esp legal*) **1** *ncu* the killing of one person by another: *He has been found guilty of homicide.* **2** *nc* a person who has killed another person: *He is a convicted homicide.*

ˌhomi'cidal *adj*: *a homicidal maniac.*

homily ['homəli] *nc* (*formal*) **1** a sermon. **2** (*derog*) a long, boring talk, *usu* about good or correct behaviour: *The headmaster delivered a homily to the children on their behaviour in the school bus.*

homo- [homou, houmou] (*in cmpds*) the same, as in **homosexual**.

homogeneous [homə'dʒiːniəs] *adj* (*formal*) (made up of parts that are) all of the same kind.

homogenize, -ise [hə'modʒənaiz] *vt* to treat (milk) so that the cream does not separate itself and rise to the surface.

homonym ['homənim] *nc* (*usu in pl*) a word having the same sound as another word, but a different meaning: *The words 'there' and 'their' are homonyms.*

homosexual [homə'sekʃuəl] **1** *adj, nc* (a person, *esp* a man, who is) sexually attracted to people of the same sex: *He's* (*a*) *homosexual.* **2** *adj* of or concerning a homosexual or homosexuals: *a homosexual relationship*; *I do not believe that there is anything homosexual about their friendship.*

'homoˌsexu'ality [-'a-] *nu.*

See also **lesbian**.

hone [houn] *vt* (*formal*) to sharpen (a knife *etc*).

honest ['onist] *adj* **1** (of people or their behaviour, statements *etc*) truthful; not cheating, stealing *etc*: *My secretary is absolutely honest*; *To be perfectly honest, I don't like your hat at all*; *This is an honest business – we don't cheat our customers*; *Give me an honest opinion.* **2** (of a person's appearance) suggesting that a person is honest: *He has an honest face.* **3** (*attrib*) (of wealth *etc*) not gained by cheating, stealing *etc*: *The man said he was going to try to earn an honest living when he got out of jail.* – *adv, interj* (*inf*) used to stress that a person is not lying: *I didn't eat that cake, Mummy, honest* (*I didn't*).

'honestly *adv* **1** in an honest way: *He gained his wealth honestly.* **2** used to stress the truth of what a person is saying: *Honestly, that's exactly what he said*; *I honestly don't believe that he will be able to do that job.* – *interj* used to express mild anger, disbelief *etc*: *Honestly! That was a stupid thing to do!*

'honesty *nu*: *The child showed his honesty by giving the money he found to the police*; *I admired his honesty in saying that he was not able to do the job.*

in all honesty if I am *etc* completely honest: *I could not in all honesty say that I knew nothing about this.*

See also **dishonest**.

honey ['hʌni] **1** *nu* a sweet, thick fluid made by bees from the nectar of flowers: *She spread a piece of bread with butter and honey*; (*attrib*) *a honey cake*; (*in cmpds*) *a honeybee.* **2** *nc* (*inf*: *esp Amer*) darling; a word used when speaking to someone one loves.

'honeycomb 1 *ncu* the mass formed by rows of wax cells in which bees store their honey. **2** *nc* anything which is like a honeycomb: *They explored the honeycomb of cellars beneath the old house.*

'honeymoon *nc* a holiday spent immediately after one's marriage: *These two are obviously on their honeymoon*; *We went to London for our honeymoon*; (*attrib*) *a honeymoon couple* (= two people having a honeymoon). – *vi* (*formal*) to spend one's honeymoon in a place: *We honeymooned in London.*

Hong Kong *see* Appendix 2.

honk [hoŋk] *nc* (a sound like) the cry of a goose or the sound of a motor-car horn. – *vti* to make such a noise: *Don't honk that horn any more – you'll disturb the neighbours.*

honor *see* **honour**.

honorarium [onə'reəriəm] *nc* (*formal*) a gift, *eg* money, given to someone in return for something he has done which is not paid for by wages or a salary: *He is given a small honorarium for acting as secretary to our club.*

honorary *see* **honour**.

honour, (*Amer*) **honor** ['onə] **1** *nu* respect for truth, honesty *etc*: *a man of honour.* **2** *nu* (the keeping or increasing of) a person's country's *etc* good reputation: *We must fight for the honour of our country*; *The honour of the regiment must be protected.* **3** *nu* fame; glory: *He won honour on the field of battle.* **4** *nu* respect: *This ceremony is being held in honour of those who died in the war*; *We hold him in great honour.* **5** *nc* (*no pl*: *formal*: used in certain polite forms of speech) something which a person feels to be a reason for pride, satisfaction *etc*: *It is a great honour to be asked to address this meeting*; *We would be grateful if you would do us the honour of joining us for dinner*; *I have the honour to be president of this association.* **6** *nc* (*often in pl*) a title, degree *etc* given to a person as a mark of respect for his services, work, ability *etc*: *He has received many honours for his research into cancer.* **7** *n* (*with cap*: *with* **His, Your** *etc*) a title of respect used when talking to or about judges, mayors *etc*: *My client wishes to plead guilty, Your Honour.* – *See also* **honour, honours** *in phrases below.* – *vt* **1** to show great respect to (a person, thing *etc*): *We should honour the Queen*; *Honour the flag!* **2** (*formal*) to do, say *etc* (something) which another person feels is a reason for pride, satisfaction *etc*: *I feel very honoured to have been asked to address this meeting*; *Will you honour us with your presence at the meeting?* **3** to give (someone) a title, degree *etc* as a mark of respect for his ability *etc*: *He was honoured for his work with the mentally handicap-*

ped. **4** (*formal*) to do, pay *etc* (what one has promised to do, pay *etc*): *We'll honour our agreement*; *He honoured his debts before committing suicide.*

'honorary *adj* **1** (*often with cap*: *often abbrev* **Hon.** *in writing*) (of an official position) not having any payment: *the Honorary Secretary of an association*; *He was appointed Honorary Vice-President to the society to mark his fifty years of membership.* **2** given to a person as a mark of respect for his ability *etc*: *an honorary degree.*

'honourable *adj* **1** having, showing, bringing or deserving honour: *an honourable man*; *He is the most honourable of men.* **2** (*attrib*: *with cap*: *often abbrev* **Hon.** *when written*) in Great Britain, a word used as a title for the children of certain nobles, for Members of Parliament *etc*: *the Hon. Mrs Smythe*; *the Honourable Member for West Cheshire* (*see also* **Right Honourable** *under* **right**).

'honours *n pl* **1** (*sometimes with cap*: *sometimes abbrev* **Hons** *when written*) (one of *usu* three grades of) a *usu* Bachelor's degree awarded by universities, colleges *etc* to students who achieve good results in their final degree examinations, or who carry out advanced or specialized study or, *esp* in the US, some research; the course of study leading to the awarding of such a degree: *He got First Class Honours in French*; *a degree with honours*; (*attrib*) *an honours degree*; (*attrib*: *Amer*) *an honors course*; (*attrib*) *He's studying for an honours English degree*; *BA* (*Hons*) *in French.* **2** ceremony, when given as a mark of respect: *The dead soldiers were buried with full military honours*; *The visiting president was received with full honours.*

do the honours (*formal or facet*) to do what is expected of a person who has guests, *esp* serve food *etc* to them: *The wine is over there – will you do the honours?*

guard of honour *see* **guard**.

(in) honour bound forced (to do something) not by law, but because one knows it is right: *I said I would go if he sent for me, and I feel honour bound to do as I promised.*

the birthday/New Year honours (list) in Great Britain, (the list of) people who have been awarded titles *etc*, either on the Queen's or King's official birthday or on New Year's Day, as a mark of respect for their services to the country *etc*.

on/(*formal*) **upon one's honour** an expression used to emphasize the truth and solemnity of something which is said: *On my honour, I swear it is true*; *Do you swear, on your honour, never to reveal what you see here?*

word of honour a promise which cannot be broken without loss of honour: *I give you my word of honour that I'll do it.*

See also **dishonour**.

hood [hud] *nc* **1** a *usu* loose covering for the whole head, often attached to a coat, cloak *etc*: *The monk pulled his hood over his head.* **2** a folding cover on a car, pram, carriage *etc*: *He drives his sports car with the hood down even when it is raining*; *Put the hood of the pram up – the baby is getting wet.* **3** (*Amer*) the bonnet of a car: *He raised the hood to look at the engine.* **4** a fold of cloth worn by university graduates over their gowns on ceremonial occasions: *The professors and lecturers all wore their gowns and hoods for the graduation ceremony.*

'hooded *adj* wearing a hood (*def 1*): *The lady said she was attacked by a hooded man.*

hoodlum ['hu:dləm] *nc* **1** a (*usu* young) violent, destructive or badly-behaved person: *The shop windows were smashed by a gang of hoodlums.* **2** (*esp Amer*) a criminal.

hoodwink ['hudwiŋk] *vt* to trick or deceive (someone): *She hoodwinked her mother into believing that she was on holiday with a girlfriend but she was really with her boyfriend.*

hoof [hu:f, (*Amer*) huf] – *pls* **hooves** [hu:vz, (*Amer*) huvz] , **hoofs** – *nc* the horny part of the feet of horses, cows *etc*: *That horse cannot take part in the race – it has an injured hoof.*

hook [huk] *nc* **1** a small piece of *usu* metal shaped like a J, used for catching fish *etc*: *He carefully removed the trout from the hook of his fishing-line*; (*in cmpds*) *a fish-hook.* **2** a bent piece of metal *etc* used for hanging coats, cups *etc* on: *Hang your jacket on that hook behind the door*; (*in cmpds*) *a coat-hook.* **3** something which is shaped like a hook: *Do you write f, g, j, and y with hooks or loops at the bottom?* **4** in boxing, a kind of punch with the elbow bent: *a left hook.* – **1** *vt* to catch (a fish *etc*) with a hook: *He hooked a large salmon.* **2** *vti* to fasten or to be fastened to a hook or hooks, or to something else by means of a hook or hooks: *Is there some way in which these two parts hook together?*; *He hooked the ladder on* (*to the branch*). **3** *vti* to fasten (a piece of clothing), or to be fastened, by means of small hooks: *The dress hooks/is hooked* (*up*) *at the back*; *Would you hook me up, please?* (= Would you hook up the back of my dress, please?). **4** *vt* in golf, to hit (the ball) far to the left of where it should be (or to the right if one is left-handed).

hooked *adj* **1** curved like a hook: *a hooked nose.* **2** (*sl*: *often with* **on**) very interested in, or showing a great liking for (something); addicted to: *He's hooked on modern art*; *I took one mouthful of avocado pear, and that was me hooked*; *He's hooked on marijuana.*

by hook or by crook (*inf*) by some means or another; in any way possible: *I'll get her to marry me, by hook or by crook.*

hook, line and sinker (*inf*) completely; in all details: *He fell for the story, hook, line and sinker* (= He believed all the lies he was told).

off the hook (*sl*) free from some difficulty or problem: *If he couldn't keep the terms of the contract, he shouldn't have signed it – I don't see how we can get him off the hook now.*

hook(e)y ['huki]: **play hook(e)y** (*Amer sl*) to be absent from school *etc* without permission.

hooligan ['hu:ligən] *nc* a young violent, destructive or badly-behaved person: *The old lady told the police that a group of young hooligans had been throwing stones at her dog.*

'hooliganism *nu* violent or destructive behaviour by young people: *The judge said that there was too much hooliganism at football matches.*

hoop [hu:p] *nc* a thin ring of metal, wood *etc*: *At the circus we saw a dog jumping through a hoop.*

hoop-la ['hu:pla:] *nu* a game played at fairs *etc* in which small rings are thrown at objects, any object which a ring falls over being given as a prize to the person who threw the ring: *He won the ashtray at hoop-la*; (*attrib*) *a hoop-la stall.*

hooping-cough *see* **whooping-cough**.

hoorah, hooray *see* **hurrah**.

hoot [hu:t] **1** *vti* to sound the horn of a car *etc*: *The driver hooted* (*his horn*) *at the old lady.* **2** *vi* (of car *etc* horns, sirens *etc*) to make a loud noise, as a warning, signal *etc*: *You can't leave the factory till the siren hoots.* **3** *vi* (of owls) to call out: *An owl hooted in the wood.* **4** *vti* (of people) to make a loud noise of laughter or disapproval: *They hooted with laughter at the old tramp who claimed to be a friend of the Queen; The crowd hooted their disapproval of what the speaker was saying.* – *nc* **1** the sound of a car *etc* horn, a siren *etc.* **2** the call of an owl. **3** a loud shout of laughter or disapproval.

'**hooter** *nc* **1** an instrument which makes a hooting sound: *The workers leave the factory when they hear the hooter.* **2** (*sl derog*) a nose: *What a hooter that man has got!*

not care a hoot/two hoots (*inf*) not to care in the least: *He doesn't care two hoots what anyone thinks of him.*

Hoover ® ['huːvə] *nc* a kind of vacuum cleaner. – *vti* (*no cap*) to clean (a carpet *etc*) with a vacuum cleaner: *She hoovered the carpets and the chairs; I'll hoover tomorrow.*

hooves *see* **hoof**.

hop[1] [hop] – *pt, ptp* **hopped** – **1** *vi* (of people) to jump on one leg: *The children had a competition to see who could hop the farthest; He hopped about in agony when the hammer fell on his foot.* **2** *vi* (of certain small birds, animals and insects) to jump on both or all legs: *The sparrow/frog hopped across the lawn.* **3** *vti* to jump: *He hopped (over) the fence and ran away;* (*fig*) *The old man hopped out of bed like someone half his age.* **4** *vi* (*inf*: *with* **in(to), out (of)**) to get into or out of a car *etc*: *The car stopped and the driver told the hikers to hop in; She hopped into the car and drove to town.* **5** *vi* (*inf*: *with* **over**) to make a short journey, *esp* by air: *He hopped over to France for a couple of days.* **6** *vt* (*Amer inf*) to get on to or into a train, plane *etc*: *When he feels like taking a trip to Europe, he just hops a plane.* – *nc* **1** (of people) a short jump on one leg. **2** (of certain small birds, animals and insects) a short jump on both or all legs: *The sparrow crossed the lawn in a series of hops.* **3** (*inf*) any part of a *usu* long journey by air which the aeroplane travels without landing: *The plane completed the journey to Australia in three hops.* **4** (*inf*) an informal dance or party with modern popular music: *I'm taking Jenny to the hop in the church hall.*

'**hopper** *nc* a large funnel or other container in which corn *etc* is put and later passed down through a hole in the bottom of the container to grinding *etc* machinery.

'**hopscotch** [-skotʃ] *nu* a game played *usu* by children in which they hop into a series of squares drawn on the ground: *The children are playing hopscotch on the pavement.*

catch (someone) on the hop (*inf*) to do something to (someone) when they are not prepared: *He wasn't expecting to be asked such detailed questions – we rather caught him on the hop.*

hopping mad (*inf*) very angry: *I was hopping mad when he told me he'd crashed the car.*

'**hop it** (*Brit sl*) to go away: *You'd better hop it before someone finds you here.*

keep (someone) on the hop to keep (someone) busy, active, alert *etc*: *The boss never tells us when he is going to inspect our work – he likes to keep us on the hop all the time.*

hop[2] [hop] *nc* a climbing plant, the bitter fruits of which (**hops**) are used in brewing beer: *Beer is flavoured with hops.*

hope [houp] *vti* (*sometimes with* **for**) to want something to happen and have some reason to believe that it will or might happen: *He's very late, but we are still hoping he will come; I hope to be in London next month; We're hoping for some help from other people; It's unlikely that he'll come now, but we keep on hoping; 'Do you think it will snow?' 'I hope so/not'* (= I hope it will/will not). – **1** *ncu* (any reason or encouragement for) the state of feeling that what one wants will or might happen: *He has lost all hope of becoming the president; He is poor now, but he lives in hope (of becoming rich and famous); He came to see me in the hope that I would help him; He went abroad in the hope of earning more money; He has hopes of becoming president; The rescuers said there was no hope of finding anyone alive in the mine; They held out little hope of finding survivors; His hopes of becoming president are based on three things – his ability, his background and his friends; They are trying to cure him of his drug addiction but he is beyond hope* (= there is no hope of curing him). **2** *nc* a person, thing *etc* that one is relying on for help *etc*: *He's my last hope – if he doesn't help me, there is no-one else I can ask.* **3** *nc* something hoped for: *My hope is that he will get married and settle down soon.*

'**hopeful** *adj* **1** (*neg* **un-**) full of hope: *The police are hopeful that they will soon find the killer; hopeful young people;* (*formal*) *He is hopeful of success in his new job.* **2** giving a reason or encouragement for hope: *That's a hopeful sign – perhaps he is going to change his mind after all.* **3** (*pred*) likely to be pleasant, successful *etc*: *The future looks quite hopeful for him* (= He is likely to be successful *etc*). '**hopefulness** *nu*.

'**hopefully** *adv* **1** in a hopeful way: *The dog looked hopefully at the joint of meat.* **2** it is to be hoped that (something will happen *etc*): *Hopefully, that will never happen.*

'**hopeless** *adj* **1** not likely to be successful: *It's hopeless to try to persuade him to help you; a hopeless attempt; The future looks hopeless.* **2** (*inf*: *with* **at** *when pred*) not good: *I'm a hopeless housewife; He's hopeless at French.* **3** unable to be stopped, cured *etc*: *The doctors considered the patient's case hopeless; He's a hopeless liar/idiot.* '**hopelessly** *adv*. '**hopelessness** *nu*.

hope against hope to continue hoping (that something will *etc* (not) happen *etc*) when there is no reason or no longer any reason for this hope: *Their cat had been missing for six weeks but they were still hoping against hope that it would come back to them.*

hope for the best to hope that something will succeed, that nothing bad will happen *etc*: *We don't really have enough money for this scheme yet, but we'll start it in any case, and hope for the best.*

not have a hope (of something) (*inf*) to be certainly not going to do, be, have *etc* (something): *He hasn't a hope of getting this done by the end of the week.*

raise someone's hopes to give (someone) good reason to believe that something will (not) happen, has (not) happened *etc*: *I don't want to raise your hopes too much, but I've heard that you are being considered for the manager's job.*

horde [hoːd] *nc* (*often derog*) a crowd or large number (of people *etc*): *Hordes of tourists visit Scotland during the summer; His plants were eaten by a horde of insects.*

horizon [həˈraizn] *nc* **1** the line at which the earth and the sky seem to meet: *The sun went down* *below the horizon; A ship could be seen on the horizon.* 2 (*formal fig*: *usu in pl*) the limit of a person's knowledge, interests, experience *etc*: *He is a man of very limited horizons.*

horizontal [hori'zontl] *adj* (*usu attrib*) at right angles to vertical; parallel to the horizon; lying level or flat: *a horizontal line*; *This game must be played on a horizontal surface.*

ˌhori'zontally *adv*: *That must lie horizontally.*

hormone ['ho:moun] *nc* a substance produced by certain glands of the body, which makes some organ of the body active: *Adrenalin is a hormone.*

hor'monal [-'mou-] *adj* (*esp tech*) of a hormone or hormones: *She is not well – she has been suffering from a hormonal disturbance since the birth of her child.*

horn [ho:n] 1 *nc* a hard object which grows (*usu* in pairs) on the head of a cow, sheep *etc*: *A ram has horns.* 2 *nu, adj* (of) the material of which this is made: *These spoons are (made of) horn*; (*attrib*) *horn spoons.* 3 *nc* something which is made of horn: *a shoehorn.* 4 *nc* something which looks like a horn in shape: *a snail's horns.* 5 *nc* the apparatus in a car *etc* which gives a warning sound: *The driver blew his horn when a child ran in front of his car.* 6 *nc* an instrument, *orig* an animal's horn but now made of brass, that is blown to produce a musical sound: *a hunting-horn.* 7 *nc* (*also* **French horn**) the type of coiled brass horn with valves that is played in orchestras *etc*: *He plays the horn*; (*attrib*) *a horn solo*; *He played the tune on the horn.*

horned *adj* (*attrib*) having a horn or horns: *A buffalo is a horned animal.*

-horned (*in cmpds*) having (a certain number or type of) horns: *a ˌlong-horned 'antelope.*

'horny *adj* 1 (*attrib*) like horn: *The ornaments were made of a horny substance.* 2 as hard as horn: *horny hands*; *The labourer's hands are rough and horny.*

hornet ['ho:nit] *nc* a kind of large wasp: *Our picnic was spoiled by hornets buzzing around the jam.*

hornpipe ['ho:npaip] *nc* 1 a lively sailor's dance, *usu* danced by one person: *The little girl danced the hornpipe.* 2 a tune for it: *The fiddler played a hornpipe.*

horoscope ['horəskoup] *nc* the prediction of a person's future based on the position of the stars and planets at the time of his birth: *My horoscope says that I will become rich and famous one day*; *I always look up my horoscope for the month in that magazine.*

horrible, horrid *etc see* **horror**.

horror ['horə] 1 *ncu* (something which causes) great fear or dislike: *She has an absolute horror of spiders*; *She looked at me in horror when I told her I'd shot the dog.* 2 *nc* (*inf*) a disagreeable person or thing: *Her little boy is an absolute horror.*

'horrible *adj* 1 causing horror; dreadful: *A horrible sight met her eyes.* 2 (*inf*) unpleasant: *What a horrible day!*; *How horrible of him to behave like that.* **'horribleness** *nu*. **'horribly** *adv*.

'horrid [-rid] *adj* 1 (*inf*) unpleasant: *a horrid child*; *That was a horrid thing to say*; *She was horrid to me yesterday.* 2 (*formal*) horrifying.

horrific [hə'rifik] *adj* 1 (*inf*) horrifying: *a horrific accident.* 2 terrifying: *We had a horrific car journey through torrential rain with faulty windscreen wipers*; *Sailing on that stormy sea was horrific.*

'horrify [-fai] *vt* to shock (someone) greatly: *Mrs Smith was horrified to find that her son had grown a beard.* **'horrifying** *adj*.

hors d'oeuvre [o:'də:vr, (*Amer*) o:r'də:rv] – *pl* **hors d'oeuvre(s)** [o:'də:vr, (*Amer*) o:r'də:rv(z)] – *ncu* food *eg* olives, sardines *etc* served before or at the beginning of a meal in order to increase the appetite.

horse [ho:s] 1 *nc* a large four-footed animal which is used to pull carts *etc* or to carry people *etc.* 2 *nu* the flesh of a horse, as meat: *This isn't beef, it's horse.* 3 *nu* (*formal*) cavalry: *a regiment of horse.* 4 *nc* a piece of apparatus used for jumping, vaulting *etc* in a gymnasium. 5 *nc* (*also* **'clothes-horse**) a frame on which clothes *etc* are hung to dry: *When it started to rain she brought in the washing from the garden and hung it on the clothes-horse.*

'horsy *adj* (*inf*) 1 horse-like: *She has a rather horsy face.* 2 (*sometimes derog*) very interested in horses and horse-racing *etc*: *a horsy young woman*; *She is going through a horsy stage*; *She is very horsy – she wants to be a vet.*

'horse-box *nc* an enclosed vehicle *etc* used for carrying horses.

horse chestnut *see* **chestnut**.

'horseflesh *nu* 1 the meat of a horse. 2 (*inf*) horses for riding, racing *etc.*

'horsefly *nc* a large fly that bites horses *etc.*

'Horse Guards *n pl* the cavalry brigade of the British army who act as a guard for the king and queen and their family *eg* on ceremonial occasions.

'horsehair *nu, adj* (of) the hair from a horse's mane or tail: *The mattress is stuffed with horsehair*; (*attrib*) *a horsehair mattress.*

'horse laugh *nu* a loud, harsh laugh: *His horse laugh could be heard throughout the hotel lounge.*

'horseman – *fem* **'horsewoman** – *nc* a rider, *esp* a skilled one: *She is a very competent horsewoman.*

'horsemanship *nu* the art of riding and of training and managing horses: *His horsemanship is remarkable.*

'horseplay *nu* rough and noisy play: *It's harmless for children to indulge in horseplay.*

'horsepower (*usu abbrev* **h.p.** *when written*) *nc* (*often attrib*) a standard unit used to measure the power of engines, cars *etc*: *a twenty-horsepower engine.*

'horseradish *nc* a plant with a sharp-tasting root which is used in making **horseradish sauce**: *We always have roast beef with horseradish sauce for lunch on Sunday.*

'horse sense *nu* plain good sense: *It's sometimes safer to rely on horse sense than on the advice of one's colleagues.*

horseshoe ['ho:ʃʃu:] *nc* 1 a curved iron shoe for a horse. 2 something in the shape of a horseshoe: *The bride was presented with a lucky silver horseshoe*; (*attrib*) *a horseshoe bend in a river.*

horsewoman *see* **horseman**.

(straight) from the horse's mouth from a well-informed and reliable source: *I got that story straight from the horse's mouth.*

on 'horseback riding on a horse: *The soldiers rode through the town on horseback.*

See also **equine**.

horticulture ['ho:tikʌltʃə] *nu* (*formal*) the science and art of gardening: *He studied horticulture at college*; *He has always been interested in horticulture – he has a beautiful garden.*

ˌhorti'cultural *adj*: *His onions won first prize at the horticultural show.*

ˌhorti'culturist *nc* an expert gardener.

hose [houz] 1 *nc* (*also* **'hosepipe**) a rubber, plastic *etc* tube which bends and which is used to carry water *etc*: *a garden hose*; *a fireman's hose.* **2** *nu* (*formal or old*) stockings or socks: *woollen hose.* – *vt* to apply water to (something) by means of a hose: *I'll go and hose the garden/car.*

hosiery ['houziəri] *nu* knitted goods, *esp* stockings, socks and tights.

hose down *vt sep* to clean (*eg* a car) by means of water brought by a hose: *I'll go and hose down the car.*

hospice ['hospis] *nc* **1** (*arch*) a house for travellers, *esp* one kept by monks. **2** (*esp in titles*) a hospital, *esp* for sufferers from incurable diseases: *St Columba's Hospice.*

hospitable [hə'spitəbl] *adj* showing kindness to guests: *She is one of the most hospitable people I know*; *He is always very hospitable.* **ho'spitably** *adv.* **ho'spitableness** *nu.*

hospitality [hospi'taləti] *nu* a friendly welcome for guests or strangers, which often includes offering them food, drink *etc*: *He thanked the ladies for their hospitality.*

See also **inhospitable**.

hospital ['hospitl] *nc* a building or group of buildings where people who are ill or injured are given treatment: *After the train crash, the injured people were taken to hospital.*

'hospitalize, -ise *vt* (*esp Amer*) to take (a person) to hospital for treatment: *After the crash, six people had to be hospitalized.* **ˌhospitali'zation, -s-** *ncu.*

host[1] [houst] – *fem* **'hostess** (*def 1*) – *nc* **1** a person who entertains someone else as his guest, *usu* in his own house: *While we were in Germany, our host was a fellow I met at last year's conference*; *Our hostess introduced us at the party.* **2** (*tech*) an animal or plant on which another lives as a parasite: *Apple-trees sometimes act as hosts to mistletoe.*

See also **air hostess**.

host[2] [houst] *nc* (*inf*) a very large number: *I have a whole host of things to do today*; *Hosts of people gatecrashed the party.*

hostage ['hostidʒ] *nc* a person who is held prisoner as a guarantee that demands, the conditions of an agreement *etc* will be carried out: *The terrorists took three people with them as hostages.*

take, hold (someone) hostage to take or keep (someone) as a hostage: *The police were unable to attack the terrorists because they were holding three people hostage.*

hostel ['hostəl] *nc* **1** a building with simple accommodation, *esp* for young people, hikers *etc*: *It is much cheaper to stay in a youth hostel than in a hotel.* **2** a building where students *etc* may live: *a university hostel*; *a nurses' hostel*; (*attrib*) *hostel accommodation.*

'hostelry *nc* (*arch or liter*) an inn; a guest-house.

hostess *see* **host**.

hostile ['hostail] *adj* **1** unfriendly; warlike: *Explorers in Africa often met hostile tribesmen*; *The tribesmen were often hostile.* **2** (*attrib*: *formal*) belonging to an enemy: *a hostile army.* **3** showing dislike or opposition to something: *His suggestions met with a very hostile reception*; *His colleagues were hostile to his suggestions.*

ho'stilities [-'sti-] *n pl* (*formal*) acts of war; battles: *The two armies were engaged in hostilities.*

ho'stility [-'sti-] *nu* unfriendliness; opposition: *His suggestions met with some hostility.*

hot [hot] *adj* **1** having or causing a great deal of heat: *a hot oven*; *a hot fire*; *That water is very hot.* **2** very warm: *a hot day*; *Running makes me feel hot.* **3** (of food) having a sharp, burning taste: *Too much pepper makes food too hot to eat*; *a hot curry.* **4** easily made angry: *He has a very hot temper.* **5** (*usu pred*) (of news) recent; fresh: *This story is hot from the press.* **6** (*sl*) stolen: *These jewels are hot*; *This is hot property.*

'hotly *adv* **1** eagerly; quickly: *The thieves were hotly pursued by the police.* **2** angrily; passionately: *The Government's proposals were hotly debated in Parliament.*

hot air *nu* (*inf*) boastful words, promises that will not be kept *etc*: *Most of what he said was just hot air*; *He's just talking hot air.*

'hotbed *nc* (*fig*) a place of rapid growth, *esp* of something bad: *a hotbed of disease/revolution.*

ˌhot-'blooded *adj* **1** passionate; having strong sexual feelings: *He is a normal hot-blooded male but she is rather frigid*; *He is too hot-blooded to keep away from women for long.* **2** easily made angry; excitable.

hot dog *nc* a hot sausage sandwich.

'hotfoot *adv* (*inf*) in a great hurry: *He arrived hotfoot from the meeting.*

'hothead *nc* a hotheaded person: *Don't be such a hothead – if you rush off and say that to the boss he'll sack you at once!*

ˌhot'headed *adj* easily made angry; inclined to act suddenly and without sufficient thought for the consequences: *a hotheaded youth*; *He was too hotheaded and kept quarrelling with the rest of the staff.*

'hothouse *nc* a glass-house kept warm for growing plants in: *He grows orchids in his hothouse*; (*attrib*) *hothouse plants.*

'hot line *nc* (*inf*) a line of quick communication between two (*usu* important) people *etc* for use in emergencies: *The American president has a hot line to Moscow*; (*fig*) *That man claims to have a hot line to God.*

'hot-plate *nc* **1** the part of a cooker on which food is heated for cooking. **2** a portable heated plate of metal *etc* for keeping plates of food *etc* hot.

'hot seat *nc* (*inf*) an uncomfortable or difficult position: *The Prime Minister is really in the hot seat over this problem.*

hot stuff *nu* (*sl*) **1** a person *etc* of a high quality, ability *etc*: *He is hot stuff with a trumpet.* **2** a person who has strong sexual passions: *She's really hot stuff.*

be in, get into hot water (*inf*) to be in or get into trouble: *You will be in/get into hot water if you're late again.*

hot up – *pt, ptp* **'hotted** – *vi* to increase; to become more exciting, dangerous, intense *etc*: *Competition between our two companies is hotting up.*

in hot pursuit chasing (a person) as fast as one can: *The thief ran off, with the shopkeeper in hot pursuit.*

like 'hot cakes (*inf*) very quickly: *These old books are going/selling like hot cakes.*

See also **heat**.

hotchpotch ['hotʃpotʃ] *nc* a confused mass of things: *His report was a hotchpotch of facts and figures.*

hotel [hə'tel] *nc* a *usu* large house or building where travellers, holidaymakers *etc* may receive food, lodging *etc* in return for payment: *The new luxury hotel has over five hundred bedrooms.*

ho'telier [-liə] *nc* a person who owns, and sometimes manages, a hotel.

hotfoot *etc see* **hot**.

hound [haund] *nc* a hunting-dog: *The fox threw the hounds off the scent and escaped.* – *vt* to pursue or hunt (someone), *esp* to force (someone) to go away: *They hounded the gypsies from town to town.*

hour ['auə] *nc* (*sometimes abbrev* **hr** *when written*) **1** sixty minutes, the twenty-fourth part of a day: *He spent an hour trying to start the car this morning; She'll be home in half an hour; a five-hour delay.* **2** the time at which something is usually done: *the hour of prayer; business hours.* – *See also* **hour** *in phrases below.*

'**hourly** *adj, adv* (happening or done) every hour: *Take his temperature hourly; Take hourly readings of his temperature; hourly reports.*

after-hours *see* **after hours** *below.*

'**hour-glass** *nc* a device that measures time in hours by passing sand from one glass container through a narrow tube into a lower container. – *adj* (*attrib*) shaped like an hour-glass: *That girl has an hour-glass figure.*

'**hour hand** *nc* the smaller of the two hands of a watch or clock, which shows the time in hours: *All clocks have an hour hand and a minute hand.*

after hours after the end of a working day or after the time during which a shop *etc* is normally open: *People are not allowed to buy beer in public houses after hours;* (*attrib*) *after-hours drinking.*

at all hours at irregular times, *esp* late at night: *He comes home at all hours.*

for 'hours for a very long time: *We waited for hours for the train – there had been an accident further up the line; She sat at the window for hours every day.*

in my, his *etc* **hour of need** (*formal or facet*) at a time when I am, he is *etc* in need of help: *I knew you would help me in my hour of need.*

on the hour at exactly one, two, three *etc* o'clock: *Buses leave here for London on the hour until 10 o'clock in the evening.*

house [haus] – *pl* **houses** ['hauziz] – *nc* **1** a building in which people, *usu* a single family, live: *Houses have been built on the outskirts of the town for the workers in the new industrial estate.* **2** (*usu in cmpds*) a place or building used for a particular purpose: *a hen-house; a public house; a picture-house* (= a cinema). **3** (*usu with cap*) the body of people who govern a country, make laws, *etc* or the place where they meet: *the House of Representatives; the House of Commons.* **4** (*usu with cap*) a business firm: *These shops are now owned by the House of Archer.* **5** a theatre, or the audience in a theatre: *The actors were playing to full/empty houses.* **6** a family, *usu* important or noble, including its ancestors and descendants: *the house of David.* **7** (*Brit*) a section of the pupils at a school: *Baird House beat Lynne House at rugby this term.* – [hauz] *vt* (*often formal*) **1** to provide with a house or similar shelter: *All these people will have to be housed; The animals are housed in the barn.* **2** to store or keep (something) somewhere: *The generator for the electricity is housed in the garage.*

'**housing** [-ziŋ] **1** *nu* houses: *These flats will provide housing for the immigrants.* **2** *nu* the act of providing housing: *The housing of the immigrants was very efficiently done.* **3** *nc* the hard cover round a machine *etc*: *The housing on this machine is designed to protect the operator.*

'**house agent** (*Amer* '**real-estate agent**) *nc* a person who arranges the sale or letting of houses.

house arrest *ncu* a type of arrest in which a person is not allowed to leave his own house: *The government put the leaders of the opposition parties under house arrest.*

'**houseboat** *nc* a type of boat, *usu* with a flat bottom, which is built to be lived in.

'**housebreaker** *nc* a person who breaks into a house in order to steal. '**housebreaking** *nu.*

'**household** *nc* the people who live together in a house, including their servants: *How many people are there in this household?;* (*attrib*) *household expenses.*

'**householder** *nc* **1** the person who owns a house or pays the rent for it. **2** the head of a family.

household cavalry *n sing or pl* (*often with caps*) regiments of cavalry who act as guards to the king or queen, *eg* on special occasions: *The Queen's coach was preceded by members of the Household Cavalry.*

household word *nc* something which is well-known to everyone: *His name is a household word throughout the country.*

'**housekeeper** *nc* a person, *usu* a woman, who is paid to look after the management of a *usu* large house.

'**housekeeping** *nu* **1** (*usu attrib*) the management of a house: *housekeeping expenses.* **2** (*inf*) money set aside, *eg* by a husband and wife, to pay for the expenses of running a house: *How much housekeeping do you get?; We pay the electricity bill out of the housekeeping.*

'**houseman** *nc* a recently qualified doctor who is living in a hospital while working there to complete his training.

'**housemaster** – *fem* '**housemistress** – *nc* (*Brit*) the teacher in charge of a house (*def 7*).

'**housetrain** *vt* to train (a dog, cat *etc*) to defecate and urinate only in places where it is allowed to do so.

'**house-warming** *nc* a party given after moving into a new house: *I hope you can come to our house-warming;* (*attrib*) *a house-warming party.*

'**housewife** – *pl* '**housewives** – *nc* a woman who looks after her house, her husband and her family, and who *usu* does not have a job outside the home.

'**housework** *nu* the work of keeping a house clean and tidy: *My mother has a woman to help her with the housework.*

like a house on fire (*inf*) **1** very well: *The two children got on like a house on fire* (= played *etc* together in a happy, friendly way). **2** very quickly: *I'm getting through this job like a house on fire.*

hovel ['hovəl, (*Amer*) 'hʌ-] *nc* (*derog*) a small, dirty house: *The widow kept her home clean and shining – even though from the outside it seemed only a hovel.*

hover ['hovə, (*Amer*) 'hʌ-] *vi* **1** to remain in the air without moving in any direction: *A hawk hovered in the sky above them.* **2** to move around while still remaining near a person *etc*: *That girl is always hovering (a)round me; I wish she'd stop hovering about and go away.* **3** (*formal*) (*with* **between**) to be undecided: *She hovered between leaving and staying.*

'**hovercraft** *nc* a vehicle which is able to move over land or water, supported by a cushion of air: *We crossed the Channel by hovercraft; I've never been in a hovercraft.*

how [hau] *adv, conj* **1** in what way: *How do you make bread?; Do you know how to make bread?* **2** to what extent: *How do you like my new hat?; How far is Paris from London?; Do you know how far Paris is from London?* **3** by what means: *How did* *you get here?*; *I've no idea how he came here.* **4** in what condition: *How are you today?*; *How do I look?* **5** for what reason: *How is it that I am the last to know about this?*

how'ever *adv* **1** in spite of that: *I don't like your suggestion. However, you may do as you please*; *It would be nice if we had more money. However, I suppose we'll manage with what we have*; (*formal*) *I shall remain here. You, however, are free to leave if you wish.* **2** (*also* **how ever**) (*inf*: used *esp* to show surprise) in what way; by what means: *However did you get here?*; *However did you do that?* **3** (*formal*) to no matter what extent: *However hard I try, I still can't do it.* – *conj* in no matter what way: *This painting still looks wrong however you look at it.*

ˌ**and 'how** (*sl*) yes indeed; very much so: *'That was a terrific party last night.' 'And how!'*

'**how about** (*inf*) **1** I would like to suggest: *'Where shall we go tonight?' 'How about the cinema?'* **2** what is he, are you *etc* going to do?; what does he, do you *etc* think?: *We're going to the cinema tonight. How about you?*; *I rather like that picture. How about you?*

how come (*inf*) for what reason: *How come I didn't get any cake?*

ˌ**how do you 'do?** words that are said by a person to someone he is being introduced to: *'How do you do? My name is Smith,' he said, shaking her hand.*

however *see* **how**.

howl [haul] **1** *vi* to make a long, loud cry: *The wolves howled*; *That child is always howling*; *He howled with pain/fear/scorn*; (*fig*) *We howled with laughter.* **2** *vi* (of wind) to make a similar sound: *The wind howled through the trees.* **3** *vt* to shout (words *etc*): *The sergeant howled his orders at the soldiers.* – *nc* such a cry: *He gave a howl of pain*; *the howls of the wolves*; (*fig*) *howls of laughter.*

'**howler** *nc* (*sl*: *slightly old*) a bad mistake: *This history essay is full of howlers.*

hoy [hoi] *interj* a word used to attract attention: *Hoy! You leave those apples alone!*

hub [hʌb] *nc* **1** the centre of a wheel. **2** the main point of activity, interest *etc*: *the hub of society/the universe.*

'**hubcap** *nc* the metal cover over the centre of the wheel of a car *etc.*

hubbub ['hʌbʌb] *nc* (*no pl*) **1** a confused noise of many sounds *esp* voices: *The speaker's voice couldn't be heard because of the hubbub in the room.* **2** uproar; protest: *The decision to close the museum caused a great hubbub.*

huddle ['hʌdl] **1** *vti* (*often with* **together**) to (cause to) crowd closely together: *The cows huddled together in the corner of the field*; *The police arrested more than twenty demonstrators and huddled them all into one police van.* **2** *vi* to sit curled up: *The old man huddled near the fire to keep warm.* – *nc* (*inf*) a number of people, things *etc* crowded together: *There was a huddle of people round the injured man.*

huddle up *vi* (*often with* **together**) to huddle: *The cows huddled up together to keep warm.*

hue[1] [hju:] *nc* (*formal or liter*) colour: *There were flowers of many hues in the garden.*

hue[2] [hju:]: **a hue and cry** a loud protest: *There will be a great hue and cry about this decision.*

huff [hʌf]: **in(to) a/the huff** (*inf*) being or becoming silent because one is angry, displeased *etc*: *He is in the huff*; *He went into a huff.*

'**huffy** *adj* (*inf*) **1** in a huff. **2** easily offended, and likely to go into a huff: *Don't be so huffy – I was only joking when I said you had a big nose.* '**huffily** *adv.* '**huffiness** *nu.*

hug [hʌg] – *pt, ptp* **hugged** – *vt* **1** to hold (someone or something) close to oneself with the arms, *esp* to show love: *The old lady hugged her son when he returned from the war.* **2** (*formal or liter*) to keep close to (something): *During the storm, the ships all hugged the shore.* **3** to hold (a belief *etc*) very firmly. – *nc* a tight grasp with the arms, *esp* to show love: *As they said good-bye, she kissed her son and gave him a hug.*

huge [hju:dʒ] *adj* very large: *a huge dog*; *a huge sum of money*; *Their new house is huge.* '**hugeness** *nu.*

'**hugely** *adv* (*rare*) very much: *They enjoyed themselves hugely.*

hulk [hʌlk] *nc* **1** the body of an old ship from which everything has been taken away: *There were four hulks lying in the harbour.* **2** (*derog*) a ship which is or looks difficult to steer or control: *You won't get to Africa in that old hulk.*

'**hulking** *adj* (*inf*: *attrib*) large and clumsy: *Her husband is a hulking* (*great*) *brute of a man.*

hull [hʌl] *nc* the frame or body of a ship: *The hull of the ship was painted black.*

hullo *see* **hello**.

hullabaloo [hʌləbə'lu:] *nc* (*inf*) **1** an uproar: *The teacher told the pupils to stop making such a hullabaloo.* **2** loud public protest: *There will be a great hullabaloo over the decision to close down the railway line.*

hum [hʌm] – *pt, ptp* **hummed** – **1** *vti* to make a musical sound with closed lips: *He was humming a tune to himself.* **2** *vi* to make a similar sound: *The bees were humming round the hive*; *The machines hummed all around us in the factory.* **3** *vi* (*inf*) to be active: *Things are really humming round here.* **4** *vi* (*sl*) to give off a bad smell: *We left the cheese so long that it began to hum.* – *ncu* (*no pl*) **1** a humming sound: *I could hear the quiet hum of the machines*; *There was a hum of conversation coming from the next room.* **2** (*sl*) a bad smell: *What a hum! That cheese has definitely gone off.*

'**humming-bird** *nc* a small brightly-coloured American bird which makes a humming sound with its wings.

hum and haw [ho:] to make sounds which express doubt, uncertainty *etc*: *He obviously didn't know the answer to my question – he just stood there humming and hawing.*

human ['hju:mən] *adj* of, natural to, concerning, or belonging to, mankind: *human nature*; *The use of computers reduces the possibility of human error*; *Don't be ashamed – bursting into tears like that was a very human* (= understandable in a human being) *reaction*; *human affairs*; *The dog was so clever that he seemed almost human*; (*facet*) *Don't be afraid of the boss – he can be quite human* (= kindly). – *nc* a person: *Humans are not as different from animals as people often think.*

'**humanism** *nu* a non-religious system of thought which holds that man alone can decide what is or is not correct moral behaviour *etc.* '**humanist** *nc, adj.*

humanize, -ise *see* **humane**.

'**humanly** *adv* within human power: *If it is humanly possible, he will do it.*

human being *nc* a person: *Animals may behave like that, but human beings shouldn't.*

See also **inhuman**.

humane [hju'mein] *adj* kind; not cruel: *a humane man*; *a humane way to kill rats and mice*; *Is that* *method of killing mice humane?* **hu'manely** *adv.* **hu'maneness** *nu.*

'humanize, -ise ['hjuːmə-] *vti* (*formal*) to make or become (more) humane or civilized: *There is no way one can humanize war.*

See also **humanity, inhumane**.

humanity [hjuˈmanəti] *nu* **1** kindness: *He is a man of great humanity.* **2** people in general: *I feel a great love for all of humanity.*

hu,mani'tarian 1 *nc, adj* (a person) wishing or trying to increase the welfare of human beings by means of reform *etc*: *a humanitarian person.* **2** *adj* intended to increase the welfare of human beings: *a humanitarian action*; *His action was truly humanitarian.* **hu,mani'tarianism** *nu.*

the Humanities language, literature, philosophy *etc, esp* Latin and Greek language and literature: *My son is studying the Humanities at university.*

See also **humane**.

humble ['hʌmbl] *adj* **1** not having a good opinion of oneself, one's abilities *etc*: *He's certainly not humble – he has confidence in his own ability and lets everyone know it*; *a humble attitude.* **2** (*usu attrib*) unimportant; having a low position in society *etc*: *a man of humble origins.* – *vt* (*formal*) to make (someone) humble: *The king tried to humble the proud barons.*

'humbly *adv.* **'humbleness** *nu.*

eat humble pie *see* **eat**.

See also **humility**.

humbug ['hʌmbʌg] **1** *nc* (*inf derog*) a person who pretends to be something he is not: *What a humbug that man is! He said he knew all about Greece, but he hasn't been able to answer any of our questions about it.* **2** *nu* (*inf derog*) nonsense; insincere talk: *What he said was just humbug.* **3** *nc* (*inf derog*) a trick; something done to deceive a person: *We believed he was trying to help us, but the whole thing was just a humbug.* **4** *nc* (*Brit*) a hard sweet, *usu* flavoured with peppermint. – *interj* (*old*) nonsense: *Humbug! That is certainly not the case.*

humdrum ['hʌmdrʌm] *adj* dull; without variety: *a humdrum life*; *Our holiday this year was rather humdrum.*

humid ['hjuːmid] *adj* damp: *a humid climate*; *The atmosphere was very humid yesterday.* **hu'midity** *nu.*

humiliate [hjuˈmilieit] *vt* to make (someone) feel ashamed or look foolish in front of another person: *Mrs Jones felt humiliated by her son's bad behaviour in front of the vicar.* **hu'miliating** *adj.* **hu,mili'ation** *ncu*: *He had rarely experienced the humiliation of defeat*; *the humiliations of prison life.*

humility [hjuˈmiləti] *nu* modesty; humbleness: *Despite his powerful position in the government, he was still a man of great humility.*

See also **humble**.

humour, (*Amer*) **humor** ['hjuːmə] *nu* **1** the ability to amuse people or to be easily amused by people *etc*: *His humour is very clever – sometimes I don't understand it!*; *He has a very good sense of humour.* **2** the quality of being amusing: *I do see the humour in this situation.* – *vt* to please (someone) by agreeing with him or doing as he wishes: *There is no point in telling him he is wrong – just humour him instead.*

'humorist *nc* a person who writes or tells amusing stories, jokes *etc*: *James Thurber was a famous American humorist.*

'humorous *adj* (*more formal than* **funny**) funny; amusing: *I suppose this is a rather humorous situation*; *I suppose his remark was intended to be humorous.* **'humorously** *adv.* **'humorousness** *nu.*

-humoured (*in cmpds*) having, or showing, feelings or a personality of a particular sort: *He was cheerful and good-humoured*; *What an ill-humoured remark!*

good humour *see* **good**.

hump [hʌmp] *nc* **1** a large lump on the back of an animal, person *etc*: *a camel's hump.* **2** part of a road *etc* which rises and falls in the shape of a hump: *There is a hump in the road just round this corner.*

'humpback *nc* **1** a back with a hump. **2** (*rare*) a hunchback. – *adj* (*attrib*) rising and falling in the shape of a hump: *a humpback bridge.*

'humpbacked *adj* having a hump on the back.

humus ['hjuːməs] *nu* (*formal*) a substance like earth, made of decayed plants, leaves *etc*: *The gardener dug some humus into the soil before sowing the seeds.*

hunch [hʌntʃ] *nc* (*inf*) an idea or belief based on one's feelings or suspicions rather than on clear evidence: *I have a hunch he won't arrive on time.*

'hunchback *nc* a person with a hump on his back.

'hunchbacked *adj* having a hump on one's back.

hunched up with one's back and shoulders bent forward: *He sat hunched up near the fire.*

hundred ['hʌndrəd] – *pls* **'hundred** (*defs 1, 4*), **'hundreds** (*defs 2, 4*) **1** *nc* (preceded by **a**, a number, or a word signifying a quantity) the number 100: *Ten times ten is a hundred*; *There were more than one/a hundred of them*; *There must be at least six hundred of them here.* **2** *nc* the figure 100. **3** *nu* (*usu with* **a**) the age of 100: *Aunt Susan was a hundred yesterday*; *Three residents of the old people's home are over a hundred.* **4** *nc* a hundred pounds or dollars: *I lost several hundred at the casino last night.* **5** (*rare*: *loosely*) very many. – *See also* **hundreds of** *below.* – *adj* **1** (preceded by **a**, a number, or a word signifying a quantity: *usu attrib*) 100 in number: *There are at least six hundred people here*; *a few hundred pounds.* **2** (*usu with* **a**: *pred*) aged 100: *He is a hundred today.*

'hundred- (*in cmpds*) having a hundred (of something): *a hundred-dollar bill.*

'hundredfold *adj, adv* (*usu with* **a**: *formal or liter*) one hundred times as much or as great: *Output has increased a hundredfold*; *a hundredfold increase in output.*

'hundredth 1 *nc* one of a hundred equal parts. **2** *nc, adj* (the) last of a hundred (people, things *etc*) or (the person, thing *etc*) in an equivalent position.

'hundredweight (*usu abbrev* **cwt** *when written*) – *pl* (*def 1*) **'hundredweight**, (*def 2*) **'hundredweights** – **1** *nu* (*Brit*) 112 pounds (50·8 kilogrammes), (*Amer*) 100 pounds (45·4 kilogrammes). **2** *nc* a quantity of something weighing one hundredweight: *I had to buy my coal in three separate hundredweights.*

'hundreds of 1 several hundred: *He has hundreds of pounds in the bank.* **2** (*loosely*) very many: *There were hundreds of people at the party.*

,one, ,two *etc* **'hundred hours** (*usu written* **01 00, 02 00** *etc* **hours**; said as 'oh one, two *etc* hundred hours' with numbers up to nine; used *esp* in the armed forces and in timetables *etc*): *He arrived at 08 00 hours this morning*; *The plane is due to arrive at fourteen hundred (14 00) hours* (= two o'clock in the afternoon).

See also Appendix 1.

hung *see* **hang**.

Hungarian, Hungary *see* Appendix 2.

hunger ['hʌŋgə] *nu* **1** the desire for food: *A cheese roll won't satisfy my hunger.* **2** the state of not having enough food: *Poor people in many parts of the world suffer from constant hunger.* **3** (*fig*) any strong desire: *a hunger for love.* – *vi* (*liter*: *usu with* **for**) to have a strong desire for something (not food): *I hunger for her touch.*

'**hungry** *adj* wanting or needing food *etc*: *a hungry baby*; *He's hungry – he hasn't eaten all day*; (*fig*) *He's hungry for adventure.* '**hungrily** *adv.* '**hungriness** *nu.*

'**hunger strike** a refusal to eat, as a form of protest or to force (someone) to agree to certain demands *etc*: *The prisoners went on hunger strike as a protest against prison discipline.*

hunk [hʌŋk] *nc* (*inf*) a lump of something (*usu* food) broken or cut off from a larger piece: *a hunk of cheese/bread*; *He was carving something from a hunk of wood.*

hunt [hʌnt] **1** *vti* to chase (animals *etc*) for food or for sport: *He spent the whole day hunting (deer).* **2** *vi* (*Brit*) to hunt foxes: *Do you hunt?* **3** *vt* to pursue (someone) or drive (someone) out: *The murderer was hunted from town to town.* – *See also* **hunt** *in phrases below.* – **1** *nu* the act of hunting animals *etc*: *a tiger hunt.* **2** *nc* (*inf*) a search: *I'll have a hunt for that lost necklace this afternoon.* **3** *nc* a group of people who hunt (foxes *etc*): *The local hunt meets here once a month.*

'**hunter** – *fem* '**huntress** (*def 1*) – *nc* **1** a person who hunts. **2** a horse used in hunting, *esp* fox-hunting.

'**hunting** *nu* the act of chasing animals *etc* for food or for sport: *He loves hunting*; (*attrib*) *hunting clothes.*

'**huntsman** ['hʌnts-] *nc* **1** a hunter (*def 1*). **2** (*Brit*) a man who manages the hounds during a fox-hunt.

hunt down *vt sep* to search for (someone or something) until found: *The police hunted down the escaped prisoner.*

'**hunt for** *vt fus* (*inf*) to search for: *I've been hunting for that shoe all morning.*

hunt high and low to search everywhere (for something).

hunt out *vt sep* (*inf*) to search for (something that has been put away) until it is found: *I haven't got all the information you need with me, but I'll hunt it out for you*; *We should hunt out all our old clothes and give them to charity.*

hunt up *vt sep* (*inf*) to find or get (information *etc*) by study or research: *I'll hunt up the details for you in our library.*

hurdle ['həːdl] *nc* **1** a frame to be jumped in a race. **2** (*fig*) a problem or difficulty: *There are several hurdles to be got over in this project.* – *vi* to run in a race in which hurdles are used: *He has hurdled since he was twelve.* '**hurdler** *nc.* '**hurdling** *nu.*

hurl [həːl] *vt* to throw violently: *He hurled himself to the ground*; *They hurled rocks at their attackers*; (*fig*) *The boys hurled* (= shouted) *abuse at each other.*

hurly-burly [həːli'bəːli] *nu* the noisy activity of crowds of people: *the hurly-burly of town life.*

hurrah, hurray, hoorah, hooray [hu'rei] *nc, interj* a shout of joy, enthusiasm *etc*: *Hurrah! We're getting an extra day's holiday*; *the hurrahs of the crowd.*

hurricane ['hʌrikən, (*Amer*) 'həːrikein] *nc* a violent storm with winds blowing at over 120 kilometres (75 miles) per hour.

'**hurricane-lamp** *nc* a kind of lamp which has the light sheltered from the wind.

hurry ['hʌri, (*Amer*) 'həːri] **1** *vti* to (cause to) move or act quickly, often too quickly: *You'd better hurry if you want to catch that bus*; *If you try to hurry me, I'll start to make mistakes.* **2** *vt* to move (someone or something) quickly: *After the accident, the injured man was hurried to the hospital.* – *See also* **hurry up** *below.* – *nu* **1** the act of doing (something) quickly, often too quickly: *In his hurry to leave, he fell and broke his arm.* **2** the need to do (something) quickly: *Is there any hurry for this job?*

'**hurried** *adj* **1** done quickly, often too quickly: *This was a very hurried piece of work.* **2** (*neg* **un-**) forced to do something quickly, often too quickly: *I hate feeling hurried.* '**hurriedness** *nu.*

'**hurriedly** *adv*: *This was done rather hurriedly.*

in a '**hurry** **1** acting quickly: *I did this in a bit of a hurry.* **2** wishing or needing to act quickly: *I'm in a hurry.* **3** (*in neg*: *ironic*) soon; easily: *You won't untie this knot in a hurry.* **4** (*in neg*: *ironic*) soon; willingly: *I won't have that man in my house again in a hurry.* **5** eager: *I'm in a hurry to see my new house.*

hurry up **1** *vi, vt usu sep* to (cause to) move quickly: *Hurry him up, will you*; *Do hurry up!* **2** *vi* (*often with* **to**) to come near quickly: *The woman hurried up to her husband.*

hurt [həːt] – *pt, ptp* **hurt** – **1** *vt* to injure or cause pain to: *I hurt my hand on that broken glass.* **2** *vt* to upset (someone) or cause (someone) mental or emotional pain: *He hurt the girl's feelings by ignoring her when she spoke to him.* **3** *vi* to be painful: *My tooth hurts.* **4** *vti* to do harm (to) or have a bad effect (on): *It won't hurt if we don't go after all*; *It wouldn't hurt you to work late just once.* – (*formal*) **1** *nc* an injury: *No-one suffered any hurt in the accident.* **2** *ncu* harm: *It will do you no hurt to eat this one little cake.* – *adj* **1** (*often with* **at** *or* **by** *when pred*) upset; distressed: *She gave him a hurt look*; *She felt hurt at not being asked to the party*; *She felt very hurt by his behaviour*; *her hurt feelings.* **2** injured: *his hurt hand*; *Are you badly hurt?*

'**hurtful** *adj* causing mental pain: *a hurtful remark*; *She can be very hurtful at times – she doesn't think of other people's feelings.* '**hurtfully** *adv.* '**hurtfulness** *nu.*

hurtle ['həːtl] *vti* to (cause to) move very quickly and violently: *The car hurtled down the hill at top speed*; *The waves hurtled the little boat on to the beach.*

husband ['hʌzbənd] *nc* a man to whom a woman is married. – *vt* (*formal*) to spend or use carefully, a little at a time: *He'll need to husband his resources/strength.*

'**husbandry** *nu* (*formal*) **1** farming: *animal husbandry.* **2** the management of what a person possesses: *good husbandry.*

hush [hʌʃ] *interj* be quiet; silence: *Hush! Don't wake the baby.* – *ncu* (*no pl*) silence: *A hush came over the room*; (*inf*) *Can we have some hush, please?* – *vti* to (cause to) become silent: *Will everyone please hush!* – *See also* **hush up** *below.*

ˌ**hush-**'**hush** *adj* (*inf*) secret: *The plans are very hush-hush*; *a hush-hush affair.*

'**hush money** *nu* (*inf*) money which is paid to a person to persuade him not to make certain facts known to someone else: *The criminals gave the boy hush money when they realized that he had overheard their plans for the robbery.*

hush up *vt sep* to prevent (something) becoming known to the general public: *Their affair was hushed up to prevent a scandal.*

husk [hʌsk] *nc* the dry thin covering of certain fruits and seeds. – *vt* to remove the husk from (a fruit or seed).

husky[1] ['hʌski] *adj* **1** (of a voice) rough in sound: *a husky voice*; *You sound rather husky today.* **2** (*inf*) big and strong: *a large, husky man*; *He is tall and husky.* **'huskiness** *nu.*

'huskily *adv*: *'I have a sore throat,' she replied huskily.*

husky[2] ['hʌski] *nc* a N American dog used for pulling sledges: *The Eskimo harnessed the team of six huskies to his sledge and set off to hunt seals.*

hussar [hə'za:] *nc* a lightly armed cavalry soldier.

hussy ['hʌsi] *nc* (*derog*) **1** a badly-behaved or mischievous girl: *How dare you say that, you little hussy!* **2** a sexually immoral woman: *You brazen hussy!*

hustings ['hʌstiŋz] *n sing* **1** the platform *etc* from which speeches are made during a political election campaign. **2** the speeches *etc* which form a political campaign.

hustle ['hʌsl] *vt* **1** to push (someone) quickly and roughly: *The man was hustled out of the office.* **2** (*inf*) to make (someone) act quickly: *Don't try to hustle me into making a sudden decision.* – *nu* quick and busy activity of crowds of people: *There was a great deal of hustle and bustle in the town.*

hut [hʌt] *nc* a small house or shelter, *usu* made of wood: *During the storm, the climbers sheltered in a little hut.*

hutch [hʌtʃ] *nc* a box with a wire front in which rabbits are kept: *The children kept their pet rabbit in a hutch in the garden.*

hyacinth ['haiəsinθ] *nc* a plant, a member of the lily family, growing from a bulb and having a sweet-smelling flower.

hyaena *see* **hyena**.

hybrid ['haibrid] *nc* **1** the offspring of animals or of plants of two different breeds *etc*: *A mule is a hybrid of a horse and a donkey.* **2** a word formed of parts from different languages: *'Television' is a hybrid made from Greek 'tele' and Latin 'visio'*; (*attrib*) *'Television' is a hybrid word.*

hydrant ['haidrənt] *nc* a pipe connected to the main water supply *esp* in a street, to which a hose can be attached in order to draw water off *eg* to put out a fire.

hydraulic [hai'dro:lik] *adj* (*tech*) **1** worked by the pressure of water or some other liquid: *hydraulic brakes.* **2** (*esp attrib*) relating to hydraulics: *Her brother is a hydraulic engineer.* **hy'draulically** *adv.*

hy'draulics *n sing* the study of the behaviour of moving liquids (*eg* of water in pipes) and of how to deal with them.

hydro ['haidrou] *nc* a type of hotel (*orig* with swimming-baths *etc* to which people came to improve their health).

hydro- [haidrou] (*in cmpds*) of or by means of water, as in **hydroelectricity**.

hydroelectricity ['haidrouelek'trisəti] *nu* electricity produced by means of water-power.

ˌhydroe'lectric [-'lek-] *adj*: *There are several large hydroelectric power stations in the Scottish Highlands.*

hydrogen ['haidrədʒən] *nu* an element (symbol **H**), the lightest gas, which burns and which, when combined with oxygen, produces water.

'hydrogen bomb *nc* (*also* **H-bomb** ['eitʃbom]) a very powerful bomb in which the explosion is caused by turning hydrogen into helium at a very high temperature.

hydrophobia [haidrə'foubiə] *nu* **1** the fear of water: *Hydrophobia is a symptom of rabies.* **2** the inability to swallow water. **3** rabies: *That dog has hydrophobia.* **ˌhydro'phobic** *adj.*

hydroplane ['haidrəplein] *nc* a light, flat-bottomed motorboat which, at high speed, skims along the surface of the water.

hyena, hyaena [hai'i:nə] *nc* a dog-like animal with a howl which sounds like human laughter.

hygiene ['haidʒi:n] *nu* (*more formal or tech than* **cleanliness**) (the rules or science of) cleanliness whose aim is to preserve health and prevent the spread of disease.

hy'gienic [-'dʒi:-, (*Amer*) -'dʒe-] *adj* (*neg* **un-**) free from germs or dirt: *hygienic conditions in a hospital*; *This kitchen is not very hygienic.*

hy'gienically [-'dʒi:-, (*Amer*) -'dʒe-] *adv*: *These biscuits are hygienically produced in our modern factory.*

hymen ['haimən] *nc* (*tech*) a thin membrane that partially closes the vagina of a virgin.

hymn [him] *nc* a (*usu* religious) song of praise: *Let us sing Hymn 434*; *We sang four hymns in church this morning.*

hymnal ['himnəl], **hymnary** ['himnəri] *ncs* a book of hymns.

hyper- [haipə] (*in cmpds*) more than normal; over; beyond: *hyperactive.*

hyperbole [hai'pə:bəli] *ncu* (the use of) exaggeration in speech or writing in order to produce a particular effect: *'I saw mice as big as elephants' is (a) hyperbole.* **hyperbolic** [haipə'bolik] *adj.*

hypercritical [haipə'kritikl] *adj* (*formal*) too critical.

hypermarket ['haipəma:kit] *nc* a very large supermarket.

hypersensitive [haipə'sensətiv] *adj* (*formal*) very sensitive: *You'll have to be very careful what you say to him – he's hypersensitive to criticism/about his big ears.*

hypertension [haipə'tenʃən] *nu* (*tech*) high blood pressure: *He suffers from hypertension*; *These pills are to cure his hypertension.*

hyphen ['haifən] *nc* a short stroke (-) which is used to join two parts of a word or phrase: *co-exist*; *a sleeping-bag*; *a well-thought-out plan.*

'hyphenate [-neit] *vt* to put a hyphen in: *Is 'co-operate' hyphenated or not?*

ˌhyphe'nation *nu*: *There are no fixed rules for hyphenation in English.*

hypnosis [hip'nousis] *nu* a sleep-like state caused by the action of another person who can then make the sleeper obey his commands.

hyp'notic [-'no-] *adj* **1** of, causing, or caused by, hypnosis: *a hypnotic stare/state.* **2** causing sleepiness: *a hypnotic drug.* – *nc* a hypnotic drug.

'hypnotize, -ise *vt* to put (someone) in a state of hypnosis: *The hypnotist hypnotized three people from the audience*; (*fig*) *He is absolutely hypnotized by the flashing lights.*

'hypnotism *nu* the art of producing hypnosis. **'hypnotist** *nc.*

hypochondria [haipə'kondriə] *nu* (*formal or facet*)

the state of worrying too much about one's health: *She was annoyed by her husband's constant hypochondria.*

ˌ**hypo'chondriac** [-ak] *nc, adj (formal or facet)* (a person) who suffers from hypochondria: *She is such a hypochondriac that she thinks she has appendicitis every time she has a pain in her stomach; a hypochondriac old man.* ˌ**hypochon'driacal** [-'drai-] *adj.*

hypocrisy [hi'pokrəsi] *nu* the act or state of pretending to be better than one is or to have feelings or beliefs which one does not actually have.

hypocrite ['hipəkrit] *nc* a person who pretends to be good or to have feelings or beliefs that he does not actually have: *He is a real hypocrite – he goes to church on Sundays and ill-treats his wife during the week.*

ˌ**hypo'critical** [hipə'kri-] *adj*: *It would be hypocritical of me to say that I enjoyed his latest novel – I found it extremely boring; He is very hypocritical in his attitude to betting – he pretends to disapprove of it, but secretly asks a neighbour to place his bets; a hypocritical person.* ˌ**hypo'critically** *adv.*

hypodermic [haipə'də:mik] *adj* used for injecting a drug under the skin: *a hypodermic syringe.* – *nc* an instrument with a thin hollow needle which is used to give injections under the skin; a hypodermic syringe.

hypothesis [hai'poθəsis] – *pl* **hy'potheses** [-si:z] – *nc (formal)* **1** something which is assumed to be true and on which an argument *etc* may be based: *His argument is correct but the hypothesis on which it is based is nonsense.* **2** a theory: *On the basis of the facts, one can form a hypothesis.*

hy'pothesize, -ise *vti (very formal)* to form or give a hypothesis: *On the basis of these facts, we can hypothesize that a great battle took place on this site over two thousand years ago.*

hypothetical [haipə'θetikəl] *adj (more formal than* **imaginary***)* assumed; imaginary: *I don't see the point in discussing hypothetical situations; That situation is completely hypothetical.*

hypothetically [haipə'θetikəli] *adv*: *We could assume hypothetically that we already have the money and go on to discussing how to spend it.*

hysteria [hi'stiəriə] *nu* **1** *(tech)* a severe nervous upset which causes unnatural behaviour *etc* such as uncontrolled crying, imaginary illnesses *etc.* **2** *(loosely)* a fit of uncontrolled laughing and crying. **3** uncontrolled excitement, *eg* of a crowd of people: *mass hysteria.*

hy'steric [-'ste-] *nc (tech)* a person who suffers from hysteria (*def 1*).

hy'sterical [-'ste-] *adj* **1** of or suffering from hysteria: *a hysterical girl/illness; Her illness is hysterical.* **2** *(inf)* very amusing: *The situation was absolutely hysterical; a hysterical situation.*

hy'sterically [-'ste-] *adv* **1** in a hysterical way. **2** *(inf)* very (amusing): *The situation was hysterically funny.*

hy'sterics [-'ste-] *n pl* **1** a fit of hysteria. **2** *(loosely)* a fit of laughing and crying: *Her mother is always having hysterics about something.*

Ii

I [ai] *pron* (only as the subject of a verb) the word used by a speaker or writer in talking about himself or herself: *I can't find my book; John and I have always been friends.*

See also **me, mine, my, myself.**

Iberian Peninsula *see* Appendix 2.

ice [ais] **1** *nu* frozen water: *The pond is covered with ice.* **2** *nc* an ice-cream: *Have an ice!; Three ices, please.* – *vt* to cover with icing: *She iced the cake.* – *See also* **ice over.**

'**icily** *adv* in an icy way: *She was icily polite.*

'**iciness** *nu.*

'**icing** *nu* **1** a mixture of sugar, white of egg, water *etc* used to cover or decorate cakes.

'**icy** *adj* **1** very cold: *icy winds; That wind is icy.* **2** covered with ice: *icy roads; Don't run – the path is icy.* **3** *(fig)* unfriendly: *an icy tone of voice; She sounded rather icy.* – *adv* as ice: *The wind was icy cold.*

'**ice age** *nc* a time when a great part of the earth's surface was covered with ice.

'**ice axe** *nc* a type of axe used by mountain climbers to cut holes in ice for their hands and feet to grip.

'**iceberg** *nc* a huge mass of ice floating in the sea.

'**ice box** *nc* **1** *(Amer)* a refrigerator. **2** the part of a refrigerator in which food may be (kept) frozen: *Put the frozen peas in the ice box and the butter in the lower part of the fridge.* **3** a box in which food is kept cool by means of ice: *You will need an ice box if you are camping in hot countries.*

ˌ**ice-'cream 1** *nu* cream or a mixture of creamy substances, flavoured and frozen: *He makes ice-cream.* **2** *nc* a portion of ice-cream: *two ice-creams with pears.* **3** *nc* an ice-cream cone *etc*: *Two ice-creams, please.*

ˌ**ice-'cream cone** *nc* (an ice-cream served in) a thin cone-shaped biscuit.

'**ice field** *nc* a large area, *usu* of water, covered with ice.

ice lolly *nc (Brit inf)* flavoured water or ice-cream *etc*, frozen on a lollipop stick.

'**ice rink** *nc* a large room or building with a floor of ice for skating: *The children go skating at the ice rink every Saturday.*

cut no ice *see* **cut.**

ice over/up *vi* to become covered with ice: *The garden pond iced over during the night; The car windows have iced up.*

on 'ice 1 of wine *etc*, kept cold by being placed in a bucket of ice: *champagne on ice.* **2** *(fig)* put aside for use, attention *etc* at a later date: *We'll put these plans on ice for the time being.*

Iceland, Icelander, Icelandic *see* Appendix 2.

ichthyology [ikθi'olədʒi] *nu (tech)* the study of fish: *He is interested in ichthyology.* ˌ**ichthy'ologist** *nc.*

icicle ['aisikl] *nc* a long hanging piece of ice formed by the freezing of dripping water: *icicles hanging from the roof of the garage.*

icing *see* **ice**.

icon, ikon ['aikon] *nc esp* in the Eastern Orthodox Churches, a painting *etc* of Christ or a saint.

iconoclasm [ai'konəklazəm] *nu* (*formal*) the attacking of beliefs or customs which have been held for a long time: *The new manager's iconoclasm caused a lot of resentment among the staff.* **i'conoclast** *nc.* **iˌcono'clastic** *adj.*

icy *see* **ice**.

I'd *see* **have, would**.

idea [ai'diə] *nc* **1** opinion; belief: *I have an idea that it won't work.* **2** a plan: *I've an idea for solving this problem.* **3** mental picture: *This will give you an idea of what I mean.*

ideal [ai'diəl] *adj* perfect: *In an ideal world everyone would be well-fed; This tool is ideal for the job I have in mind.* – *nc* **1** a person, thing *etc* that is looked on as being perfect: *She was clever and beautiful – in fact she was his ideal of what a wife should be.* **2** a person's standard of behaviour *etc*: *a man of high ideals.*

i'dealist *nc* a person having (too) high ideals of behaviour *etc*: *He is such an idealist that he does not understand that most people are not as kind and generous as he is.* **i'dealism** *nu.* **ˌidea'listic** [aidiə-] *adj.*

i'dealize, -ise *vt* (*formal*) to regard or treat (a person *etc*) as perfect: *She idealized her mother.* **iˌdeali'zation, -s-** *ncu.*

i'deally *adv* **1** perfectly: *This tool is ideally suited for this job.* **2** under perfect conditions: *Ideally, we should look at this more carefully, but we haven't enough time.*

identical [ai'dentikəl] *adj* **1** the same in every detail: *They wore identical dresses; Their dresses were identical.* **2** (*attrib*) the very same: *That is the identical car that I saw outside the bank just before the robbery.* **i'dentically** *adv.* **i'denticalness** *nu.*

identify [ai'dentifai] *vt* **1** to (claim to) recognize (someone *etc*) as being a certain person *etc*: *Would you be able to identify the man who robbed you?; He identified the coat as his brother's.* **2** (*formal*) to think of as being the same: *He identifies beauty with goodness.* **iˌdentifi'cation** [-fi-] *nu.*

i'dentify with *vt fus* to feel sympathy for someone *eg* because he appears to have the same problems, feelings *etc* as one has: *When reading a novel, we very often identify with the main character in it.*

i'dentify oneself with/be i'dentified with to be associated with or give one's full support or interest to (a political party *etc*): *He said that he did not wish to identify himself with the new proposals; He had always been closely identified with the Liberal party.*

identity [ai'dentəti] **1** *ncu* who or what a person is: *The police are still uncertain of the murderer's identity.* **2** *nu* (*formal*) the state of being exactly the same.

i'dentity card *nc* a named card (often with a photograph) which is carried by a person to show or prove who he is: *The old lady asked to see the telephone engineer's identity card before she let him into the house.*

identikit picture [ai'dentikit] *nc* a rough picture of a person the police wish to catch, based on people's descriptions of the person: *The police issued an identikit picture of the murderer of the little girl.*

ideology [aidi'olədʒi] *nc* the beliefs or way of thinking of a large group, *esp* of a political party or group: *Communist ideology.* **ˌideo'logical** [-'lo-] *adj.*

idiocy *see* **idiot**.

idiom ['idiəm] **1** *nc* (*gram*) an expression with a meaning that cannot be guessed from the meanings of the individual words: *His mother passed away* (= died) *this morning.* **2** *nu* the expressions of a language in general: *the English idiom.* **3** *nu* an individual style in music *etc*: *the early jazz idiom.*

ˌidio'matic [-'matik] *adj* (*neg* **un-**) using many idioms: *His friends in Paris admired Mr Smith's idiomatic French.* **ˌidio'matically** *adv.*

idiosyncrasy [idiə'siŋkrəsi] *nc* (*formal or facet*) a feature, *usu* odd, of a person's way of behaving *etc*: *His one idiosyncrasy was eating breakfast with his hat on.* **ˌidiosyn'cratic** [-'kratik] *adj.*

idiot ['idiət] *nc* **1** a foolish person: *She was an idiot to give up such a good job.* **2** (*tech*) a person with very low intelligence.

'idiocy **1** *nc* a foolish action: *The idiocies of some drivers in the fog were the cause of several accidents.* **2** *nu* the state of being an idiot.

ˌidi'otic [-'otik] *adj*: *an idiotic action; an idiotic young man; It was idiotic of you to drive a car without a driving licence.* **ˌidi'otically** *adv.*

idle ['aidl] *adj* **1** not working; not in use: *These men are idle because there is no work for them; There are ships lying idle in the harbour.* **2** lazy: *He has work to do, but he's idle and just sits around; idle young men laughing at the old man working.* **3** (*attrib*) having no effect or result: *idle threats.* **4** (*attrib*) unnecessary; without good reason or foundation: *idle fears; idle gossip.* – *vi* **1** (*formal*) to be idle or do nothing: *On holiday they just idled from morning till night.* **2** (*tech*) of an engine *etc*, to run gently without doing any work: *They kept the car engine idling while they checked their position with the map.* **'idler** *nc.* **'idleness** *nu.* **'idly** *adv.*

idle away *vt sep* to spend (time) doing nothing: *He is just idling the hours away.*

idol ['aidl] *nc* **1** an image of a god, which is worshipped: *The heathens bowed down before the idol.* **2** a greatly loved person, thing *etc*: *Popular singers are sometimes known as teenage idols.*

idolatry [ai'dolətri] *nu* (*formal*) **1** the worship of idols: *The missionary tried to persuade the tribesmen to become Christians and give up idolatry.* **2** too great or too much love or admiration: *The parents were worried by their daughter's idolatry of the pop-star.* **i'dolatrous** *adj.* **i'dolatrously** *adv.*

'idolize, -ise *vt* to love or admire a person *etc* (too) greatly or too much: *She idolized her older brother.*

idyll ['idil, (*Amer*) 'ai-] *nc* a short poem or story describing a simple scene *usu* of country life.

i'dyllic *adj* simple and delightful: *an idyllic setting for a country cottage; The setting is idyllic for a country cottage.*

i'dyllically *adv*: *They were idyllically happy.*

if [if] *conj* **1** in the event that; on condition that: *If it snows tomorrow, we will build a snowman; He will have to go into hospital if his illness gets any worse; I'll only stay if you can stay too; He will take the job only if you give him a large salary.* **2** supposing that: *If he were to come along now, we would be in trouble.* **3** whenever: *If I sneeze, my nose bleeds.* **4** although: *He is a very kindly man, if a bit frightening in appearance; They are happy, if poor.* **5** whether: *I don't know if I can come or not; She* did not say if she knew him or not.

if 'only (*in interjs*) I wish that: *If only I could be the Queen!*

igloo ['iglu:] – *pl* **'igloos** – *nc* an Eskimo hut, *usu* built of blocks of snow: *The Eskimo family of six all lived in one igloo.*

igneous ['igniəs] *adj* (*tech*: *attrib*) produced by the action of great heat within the earth: *igneous rocks.*

ignite [ig'nait] *vti* (*formal or tech*) to (cause to) catch fire: *Petrol is easily ignited.*

ignition [ig'niʃən] **1** *nc* the instrument in a car *etc* which ignites the petrol in the engine: *He switched on the car's ignition.* **2** *nu* (*formal*) the act of igniting. **3** *nu* (*formal*) the setting on fire of an explosive mixture of gases *etc* by means of an electric spark *etc.*

ignoble [ig'noubl] *adj* **1** (*formal or liter*) shameful: *an ignoble action.* **2** (*old*) of low birth. **ig'nobleness** *nu.* **ig'nobly** *adv.*

ignominy ['ignəmini] *nu* (*formal*) the loss of a person's good name; public disgrace: *He had to suffer the ignominy of being publicly dismissed.*

ˌigno'minious *adj* (*formal*: *usu attrib*) shameful: *an ignominious defeat.* **ˌigno'miniously** *adv.* **ˌigno'miniousness** *nu.*

ignoramus [ignə'reiməs] *nc* (*often facet*) an ignorant person: *She was a complete ignoramus about cooking.*

ignorant ['ignərənt] *adj* **1** knowing very little: *He's really very ignorant – he ought to read more*; *He's very ignorant about money matters.* **2** (*with* **of**) unaware: *He continued on his way, ignorant of the dangers which lay ahead*; *He was totally ignorant of what was happening in the firm.* **'ignorantly** *adv.* **'ignorance** *nu.*

ignore [ig'no:] *vt* to take no notice of: *He ignored all my warnings*; *Try to ignore her – she is just trying to make you angry.*

See also **ignorant**.

ikon *see* **icon**.

ill [il] – *compar* **worse** [wə:s]: *superl* **worst** [wə:st] – *adj* **1** (*usu pred*) not in good health; not well: *She was ill for a long time*; *a very ill old lady.* **2** (*attrib*) bad: *ill health*; *These pills have no ill effects.* **3** (*attrib*) evil or unlucky: *ill luck*; *an ill omen.* – *adv* (*formal*) not easily: *We could ill afford to lose that money.* – (*formal*) **1** *nu* evil: *I'm not the kind of person to wish anyone ill.* **2** *nc* trouble: *He seems to carry all the ills of this world.*

ill- (*in cmpds*) badly: *ˌill-e'quipped*; *ˌill-'used.* – *See also* **ill-** *in cmpds below.*

'illness *ncu* a state or occasion of being unwell: *There has not been a lot of illness this winter*; *I've had one illness after another this winter.*

ˌill-ad'vised *adj* foolish or not wise: *You would be ill-advised to do that*; *an ill-advised action.*

ˌill-at-'ease *adj* uncomfortable; embarrassed: *She is very quiet and feels ill-at-ease at parties.*

ill-bred *see* **ill-mannered**.

ˌill-di'sposed *adj* (*pred*: *formal*) unfriendly (towards): *He is not ill-disposed towards all his neighbours.*

ˌill-'fated *adj* ending in, or bringing, disaster: *an ill-fated expedition*; *The expedition was ill-fated.*

ˌill-'feeling *ncu* (an) unkind feeling (towards another person): *The two men parted without any ill-feeling(s).*

ˌill-'mannered/ˌill-'bred *adjs* having or showing bad manners: *He's an ill-mannered young man*; *rough and ill-mannered.*

ill-natured *see* **ill-tempered**.

ˌill-'starred *adj* (*formal or liter*) unlucky.

ˌill-'tempered/ˌill-'natured *adjs* having or showing bad temper: *He's an ill-natured baby – he's always crying*; *Don't be so ill-natured just because you're tired*; *an ill-natured old woman.*

ˌill-'timed *adj* done *etc* at an unsuitable time: *an ill-timed remark*; *Your action was ill-timed.*

ˌill-'treat *vt* to treat badly or cruelly: *She often ill-treated her children.* **ˌill-'treatment** *nu.*

ˌill-'use [-'ju:z] *vt* (*formal*) to ill-treat.

ˌill-'will *nu* unkind feeling (towards someone): *I bear you no ill-will.*

be taken ill to become ill: *He was suddenly taken ill at the party and was rushed to hospital.*

ˌill-gotten 'gains [-gotn] (*formal or facet*) money got in a bad or unlawful way: *He's living in South America on the ill-gotten gains from the bank-robbery*; *He spent all the ill-gotten gains he won playing cards.*

take it ill (*formal*) to be offended (that): *She will take it ill if you refuse her invitation.*

I'll *see* **will**.

illegal [i'li:gəl] *adj* not allowed by the law; not legal: *It is illegal to park a car here*; *illegal actions.* **il'legally** *adv.*

illegality [ili'galəti] *ncu*: *the illegality of his actions.*

illegible [i'ledʒəbl] *adj* (almost) impossible to read; not legible: *His writing is illegible*; *faint, illegible handwriting.* **il'legibly** *adv.* **ilˌlegi'bility** *nu.*

illegitimate [ili'dʒitəmət] *adj* **1** born of parents not married to each other; not legitimate: *illegitimate children*; *Her daughter is illegitimate.* **2** (*formal*: *usu attrib*) unacceptable or not allowed (*esp* by law): *an illegitimate use of a word*; *the illegitimate use of someone else's property.* **ˌille'gitimately** *adv.* **ˌille'gitimacy** *nu.*

illiberal [i'libərəl] *adj* (*formal*) having strict opinions about morality, behaviour *etc*; not liberal: *a person of illiberal views.* **ilˌlibe'rality** [-'ra-] *nu.*

illicit [i'lisit] *adj* (*usu attrib*) unlawful or not permitted: *the illicit sale of alcohol.* **il'licitly** *adv.* **il'licitness** *nu.*

illiterate [i'litərət] *adj* **1** unable to read and write; not literate: *He cannot read that letter – he is illiterate*; *backward, illiterate children.* **2** (*loosely*) having little or no education: *He hasn't heard of Shakespeare? He must be illiterate.*

il'literacy *nu*: *The government is worried about illiteracy among adults*; *adult illiteracy.*

illness *see* **ill**.

illogical [i'lodʒikəl] *adj* not logical; not based on, or showing, sound reasoning: *It is quite illogical to assume that everyone thinks the same way as you do*; *illogical reasoning.* **il'logically** *adv.* **ilˌlogi'cality** [-'ka-] *nu.*

illuminate [i'lu:mineit] *vt* **1** (*formal*) to light up: *The gardens were illuminated by hundreds of small lamps.* **2** (*formal*) to make (something) clear or explain (something): *If you do not understand this, I'll try to illuminate it for you.*

il'luminated *adj* (of a manuscript) decorated with ornamental lettering or illustrations: *In early times, monks worked for years on illuminated manuscripts.*

il'luminating *adj* helping to make (something) clear: *I found his talk very illuminating*; *a most illuminating account of life in Britain.*

ilˌlumi'nation *ncu* the act or result of illuminating.

il͵lumi'nations *n pl* the decorative lights in a town *etc*: *People go to Blackpool to see the illuminations.*

illusion [i'lu:ʒən] *nc* (something that produces) a false impression, idea or belief: *an optical illusion*; *an illusion of grandeur.* – *See also* **be under the illusion (that)** *below.*

il'lusive [-siv], **il'lusory** [-səri] *adjs* (*formal*) unreal or based on a false impression *etc*; deceptive: *All our gains are really illusory*; *an illusory victory.*

il'lusionist *nc* (*formal*) a conjuror.

be under an/the illusion (that) to have a false impression or belief (about): *She is under the illusion that he is honest although he is cheating her.*

illustrate ['iləstreit] *vt* **1** to provide (a book, lecture *etc*) with pictures, diagrams *etc*: *If you illustrate the book it will be more expensive.* **2** to make (a statement *etc*) clearer by providing examples *etc*: *I'll illustrate my point by referring to the behaviour of rabbits*; *This diagram will illustrate what I mean*; *His behaviour today illustrates what I was telling you about him yesterday.*

'illustrated *adj* having pictures *etc*: *They sent out an illustrated catalogue of his works.*

͵illu'stration **1** *nc* a picture or example: *The coloured illustrations in that book are most attractive.* **2** *nu* the act of adding pictures or giving examples: *By way of illustration, I'll refer to the behaviour of rabbits.*

'illustrative [-strətiv, (*Amer*) i'lʌstrətiv] *adj* (*formal*: *usu attrib*) being or acting as an example in order to make (a statement *etc*) clearer: *an illustrative phrase.*

'illustrator *nc* a person who draws pictures *etc* for books *etc*: *He is both author and illustrator of these children's books.*

illustrious [i'lʌstriəs] *adj* (*formal*) of a very high quality, ability *etc*; famous: *an illustrious career*; *He is the most illustrious of a famous family.*

il'lustriousness *nu.*

I'm *see* **be**.

image ['imidʒ] *nc* **1** (*formal*) a likeness or copy of a person *etc* made of wood, stone *etc*: *images of the saints.* **2** (*inf*) a close likeness: *She's the very image of her sister.* **3** (*formal*) reflection: *She looked at her image in the mirror.* **4** mental picture: *I have an image of the place in my mind.* **5** the general opinion that people have about a person, company *etc*: *We must not do anything that would harm our image.*

'imagery *nu* (the use of) figures of speech *etc* in a poem, story *etc*: *He studied D. H. Lawrence's use of imagery in his novels.*

imagine [i'madʒin] *vti* **1** to form a mental picture of (something): *I can imagine how you felt.* **2** to see or hear *etc* (something which is not true or does not exist): *Children often imagine that there are wolves under their beds.* **3** (not used with **is, was** *etc* and **-ing**) to think; to suppose: *I imagine (that) he will be late.*

i'maginable *adj* (*neg* **un-**: *attrib*) able to be thought of: *for no imaginable reason*; *unimaginable squalor.*

i'maginary *adj* (*esp attrib*) existing only in the mind or imagination; not real: *The child had an imaginary friend*; *Her illnesses are usually imaginary.*

i͵magi'nation **1** *ncu* (the part of the mind which has) the ability to form mental pictures: *I can see it all in my imagination.* **2** *nu* the creative ability of a writer *etc*: *This book shows a lot of imagination.* **3** *nu* the seeing *etc* of things which do not exist: *There was no-one there – it was just your imagination.*

i'maginative [-nətiv, (*Amer*) -neitiv] *adj* (*neg* **un-**) having or created with imagination: *an imaginative writer*; *an imaginative book*; *This essay is interesting and imaginative.*

imbalance [im'baləns] *nc* (*formal*) lack of balance; inequality: *There is a serious imbalance between what this country exports and what it has to import.*

imbecile ['imbəsi:l, (*Amer*) -sl] *nc* **1** a stupid person; a fool: *You must be an imbecile to go swimming in this weather!* **2** (*tech*) a person of very low intelligence who is not able to manage his own affairs. – *adj* (*usu attrib*) stupid; foolish: *He made some very imbecile comments.* **͵imbe'cility** [-'si-] *ncu.*

imbibe [im'baib] *vti* (*formal or facet*) to drink (in).

imbue [im'bju:] *vt* (*formal*) to fill or inspire (someone) with feelings, ideas *etc*: *He had been imbued with feelings of patriotism.*

imitate ['imiteit] *vt* to (try to) be, behave or look the same as (a person *etc*): *Children imitate their friends rather than their parents*; *He could imitate the song of most common birds.*

͵imi'tation **1** *nu* the act of imitating: *Young children learn how to speak by imitation.* **2** *nc* a copy: *This isn't really a sixteenth-century chair – it's an imitation.* – *adj* made to look like (something else): *imitation wood*; *They say the fireplace is marble – but it's only imitation.*

'imitative [-tətiv] *adj* trying to behave, look or sound like a person *etc*: *Monkeys are imitative animals*; *Children are very imitative*; *Words like 'moo' and 'bow-wow' are imitative words because they sound like the noises that cows and dogs make.*

'imitativeness *nu.*

'imitator *nc* a person who imitates: *Like all great artists, Michelangelo had his imitators.*

immaculate [i'makjulət] *adj* (*formal*) perfectly clean and neat; spotless: *an immaculate suit*; *She looked immaculate in her white dress*; *an immaculate appearance*; (*fig*) *The pianist gave an immaculate performance.*

immaterial [imə'tiəriəl] *adj* (*formal*: *usu pred*) not important: *It is immaterial to us what you do.*

immature [imə'tjuə] *adj* **1** childish and behaving like someone much younger; not mature: *She is very immature for her age*; *a shy, immature woman.* **2** (*formal*) not fully grown or fully developed; not ripe or mature: *The vine was covered in bunches of tiny, immature grapes*; *The fruit is still immature.*

͵imma'turity *nu.*

immeasurable [i'meʒərəbl] *adj* (*formal*) **1** (*attrib*) very great: *There has been an immeasurable improvement in his work recently.* **2** not able to be measured: *The universe is immeasurable*; *immeasurable distance.* **im'measurably** *adv.*

immediate [i'mi:diət] *adj* **1** happening at once and without delay: *There was an immediate response to his request*; *The response was immediate.* **2** (*attrib*) without anyone *etc* coming between: *His immediate successor was Bill Jones.* **3** (*attrib*) close: *She was not aware of anything beyond her immediate surroundings.*

im'mediately *adv* at once: *He answered immediately.* – *conj* as soon as: *You may leave immediately you finish your work*; *Immediately she heard his voice, she trembled with fear.*

immemorial [imi'mo:riəl]: **from time immemorial** from a time beyond anyone's memory or written records; for a very long time: *That family has lived in the village from time immemorial.*

immense [i'mens] *adj* very large or very great: *He gets immense satisfaction from his job; immense stretches of grassland; an immense expanse of desert; immense amounts of money; The profits on that transaction were immense.* **im'mensely** *adv.*

im'mensity *nu* (*formal*): *He was discouraged by the immensity of the task.*

immerse [i'mə:s] *vt* **1** (*formal*) to put completely under the surface of a liquid: *She immersed the vegetables in boiling water.* **2** to give one's whole attention to: *He immersed himself in his work; He was immersed in thought.* **im'mersion** [-ʃən, (*Amer*) -ʒən] *nu.*

immersion heater *nc* an electric water-heater which is immersed in water which is to be heated, *usu* inside a hot-water tank: *If you want hot water for a bath, you will have to switch on the immersion heater.*

immigrant ['imigrənt] *nc* a person who has come into a foreign country to live there permanently, not as a tourist or visitor: *The eastern part of the city is inhabited by immigrants;* (*attrib*) *the immigrant population.*

ˌimmi'gration *ncu*: *The population was increased by immigration; The family came to this country in the immigration of 1937;* (*attrib*) *the immigration rate/authorities.*

See also **emigrate**.

imminent ['iminənt] *adj* (*esp* of something unpleasant) likely to happen *etc* very soon: *imminent danger; According to the radio, a storm is imminent in the North Sea.* **'imminence** *nu.*

immobile [i'moubail] *adj* (*formal*) **1** not able to move or be moved; not mobile: *His leg was put in plaster and he was immobile for several weeks; a large immobile rock.* **2** not moving or mobile: *He lay there immobile until they had gone; They saw an immobile figure lying on the rocks at the foot of the cliff.* **ˌimmo'bility** [-'bi-] *nu.*

im'mobilize, -ise [-bi-] *vt* (*formal*) to make (someone or something) immobile: *He immobilized the car by removing part of the engine.*

immoderate [i'modərət] *adj* (*formal*) going much beyond normal or reasonable limits; not moderate: *He made immoderate demands; She was disturbed by his immoderate drinking; She considered his demands immoderate.* **im'moderately** *adv.*

immodest [i'modist] *adj* (*formal*) **1** shameless or indecent; not modest: *an immodest dress; Her behaviour was very immodest.* **2** rude or lacking in humility or modesty: *immodest boasting; It is immodest to tell everyone of your success.* **im'modestly** *adv.* **im'modesty** *nu.*

immoral [i'morəl] *adj* wrong or wicked; not moral: *He considered cheating to be immoral; immoral conduct.* **im'morally** *adv.* **ˌimmo'rality** [-'ra-] *ncu.*

See also **amoral**.

immortal [i'mo:tl] *adj* living for ever and never dying; not mortal: *A person's soul is said to be immortal;* (*fig*) *the immortal poems of Milton.* – *nc* **1** (*usu with cap*) a Greek or Roman god. **2** a person who will always be remembered: *He was one of the immortals of the theatre.* **ˌimmor'tality** [-'ta-] *nu.*

im'mortalize, -ise *vt* (*formal*) to make (a person *etc*) famous for ever: *He wrote a song immortalizing the battle.*

immovable [i'mu:vəbl] *adj* **1** impossible to move; not movable: *an immovable object;* (*fig*) *Once he gets an idea in his head, he's quite immovable* (= he will not change his opinions). **2** (*fig*) not showing or feeling sorrow, pity *etc*: *Someone as immovable as he is will hardly be affected by your tears; stern, immovable men.*

immune [i'mju:n] *adj* **1** (*usu pred*: *often with* **to**) protected against, or naturally resistant to, *eg* a disease: *immune to measles; I've never had measles – I think I must be immune;* (*fig*) *She's quite immune to criticism.* **2** (*usu pred*: *often with* **from**) free from or protected from: *immune from danger; immune from taxes.*

im'munity *nu*: *Babies have a natural immunity to disease; Some foreign diplomats enjoy immunity from taxation.*

'immunize, -ise ['imju-] *vt* (*tech*) to make a person *etc* immune to a disease, *eg* by an injection of a weak form of the disease. **ˌimmuni'zation, -s-** *nu.*

immutable [i'mju:təbl] *adj* (*formal*) that cannot be changed: *immutable laws; laws which are quite immutable.* **imˌmuta'bility** *nu.*

imp [imp] *nc* **1** (*myth*) a small devil or wicked spirit. **2** (*inf fig*) a mischievous child: *Her grandson is a little imp.* **'impish** *adj.*

impact ['impakt] *ncu* **1** (the force of) one object *etc* hitting against another: *He was thrown out by the impact of the car crashing into a wall; The cars disintegrated on impact.* **2** a strong effect or impression: *We want this book to make a strong impact; The news did not make much impact on me.* – [im'pakt] *vt* (*formal*) to press closely or firmly together: *The ground had been impacted by many people walking across it.*

im'pacted *adj* (*tech*) (of a tooth) pressed between the jawbone and another tooth in such a way that it is unable to grow: *The dentist removed the impacted tooth; The tooth had become impacted.*

impair [im'peə] *vt* (*formal*) to damage, weaken or make less good: *He was told that continual smoking would impair his health; She wrote a good essay impaired by spelling mistakes.* **im'pairment** *ncu.*

impale [im'peil] *vt* (*formal*) to fix on, or pierce with, a long pointed object such as a spear *etc*: *He fell out of the window and was impaled on the railings below.*

impart [im'pa:t] *vt* (*formal*) **1** to make (something) known to someone: *She said she had vital information to impart.* **2** to give (a quality *etc*) to something: *These curtains will impart an air of luxury to your bedroom.*

impartial [im'pa:ʃəl] *adj* not favouring one person *etc* more than another: *an impartial witness/judge; It is difficult for you to be impartial when judging the singing competition if one of the singers is your daughter.* **im'partially** *adv.* **imˌparti'ality** [-ʃi'a-] *nu.*

impassable [im'pa:səbl] *adj* not able to be passed through or travelled along: *The road is impassable because of flooding; totally impassable mountain roads.*

impasse ['ampa:s, (*Amer*) im'pas] *nc* (*formal*: *esp fig*) a situation from which there is no way out: *We seem to have reached an impasse in our discussions.*

impassioned [im'paʃənd] *adj* (*formal*: *usu attrib*) moved by, or showing, very strong feelings: *He made such an impassioned plea for the release of the prisoners that they were freed on the spot.*

impassive [im'pasiv] *adj* (*formal*) not feeling or showing emotion: *His impassive expression gave no* *clue to his thoughts*; *The prisoner remained impassive throughout the trial.* **im'passively** *adv.*

impatient [im'peiʃənt] *adj* **1** not willing to wait or delay; not patient: *Don't be so impatient – it will soon be your turn.* **2** (*pred with* **of**) not willing to tolerate (argument, restraint *etc*): *He is impatient of all opposition*; *impatient of delay.*

im'patience *nu*: *He showed his impatience by walking up and down.*

im'patiently *adv*: *He sat at the table impatiently tapping his fingers.*

impeach [im'pi:tʃ] *vt* (*legal*) to accuse (a person) of a crime, *esp* to accuse a person who works for or belongs to the government of a crime against the State: *Several politicians were impeached for accepting bribes.* **im'peachment** *ncu.*

See also **unimpeachable**.

impeccable [im'pekəbl] *adj* (*formal*) without a fault or flaw: *He is a man of impeccable character*; *His behaviour was impeccable.*

im'peccably *adv*: *He is always impeccably dressed.*

impecunious [impi'kju:niəs] *adj* (*formal*) having little or no money: *impecunious students*; *He is too impecunious to buy books.*

impede [im'pi:d] *vt* (*formal*) to prevent or delay the start or progress of (an activity *etc*): *Progress on the building was impeded by a heavy fall of snow.*

impediment [im'pedimənt] *nc* **1** (*formal*) a thing or person that delays or prevents the start or progress of (an activity *etc*): *His illness was an impediment to his holiday plans.* **2** (*tech*) a small fault in a person's speech: *A stammer is a speech impediment.*

impel [im'pel] – *pt, ptp* **im'pelled** – *vt* (*formal*) to urge or force (someone) (to do something): *Hunger impelled the boy to steal.*

See also **impulse**.

impending [im'pendiŋ] *adj* (*formal*) about to happen: *the impending elections*; *I assume that an election is impending.*

impenetrable [im'penitrəbl] *adj* (*formal*) **1** that cannot be penetrated, entered or passed through: *an impenetrable jungle*; *Those forests are completely impenetrable.* **2** (*fig*) impossible to understand: *an impenetrable mystery.*

impenitent [im'penitənt] *adj* (*formal*) not sorry for having done something wrong; not penitent: *Even when sent to prison, the thief remained impenitent*; *an impenitent criminal.* **im'penitently** *adv.*

imperative [im'perətiv] *adj* **1** (*usu pred*: *formal*) absolutely necessary; urgent: *It is imperative that this is finished by Friday*; *These orders are imperative.* **2** (*gram*) of the mood of a verb which is used to express commands: *'Come here!' is in the imperative mood.* – (*gram*) **1** *nu* the imperative mood: *a verb in the imperative.* **2** *nc* a verb in this mood: *'Sing!' is an imperative.*

imperceptible [impə'septəbl] *adj* (*formal*) too small to be seen, heard, noticed *etc*: *The scratch on the painting was almost imperceptible*; *There's an imperceptible difference between these two paintings.* **ˌimper'ceptibly** *adv.*

imperfect [im'pə:fikt] *adj* **1** (*usu pred*) having a fault or defect; not perfect: *This coat is being sold at half-price because it is imperfect.* **2** (*gram*) of the tense expressing an action or state in the past which is in progress and not completed: *the imperfect tense.* – (*gram*) **1** *nu* the imperfect tense: *a verb in the imperfect.* **2** *nc* a verb in this tense. **im'perfectly** *adv.*

ˌimper'fection [-'fekʃən] *ncu* (the state of having) a fault or defect: *He noted several imperfections in the painting*; *We do not tolerate imperfection in this firm.*

imperial [im'piəriəl] *adj* (*attrib*) **1** of an empire or an emperor: *the imperial crown.* **2** (of weights and measures) according to the standard legal in the United Kingdom: *an imperial gallon/pound.*

im'perialism *nu* (belief in) the policy of having or extending control over the territory of other nations: *Imperialism resulted in many injustices.* **im'perialist** *nc, adj.*

imperil [im'perəl] – *pt, ptp* **im'perilled**, (*Amer*) **im'periled** – *vt* (*formal*) to put (a person *etc*) in danger: *The village was imperilled by the rapid erosion of the coast*; (*fig*) *The strike imperilled the success of the conference.*

See also **peril**.

imperious [im'piəriəs] *adj* (*formal*) proud and overbearing, as if expecting to be, or in the habit of being, obeyed: *She disliked his imperious manner*; *She is proud and imperious.* **im'periousness** *nu.*

imperishable [im'periʃəbl] *adj* (*formal*) which will last for ever; not perishable: *imperishable fame.*

impermeable [im'pə:miəbl] *adj* (*tech*: *with* **by** *when pred*) not allowing liquids *etc* to pass through; not permeable: *Clay is impermeable by water.* **imˌpermea'bility** *nu.*

impersonal [im'pə:sənl] *adj* **1** not showing, or being affected by, personal feelings: *Her letters are always formal and impersonal*; *Hospitals are very impersonal places.* **2** (*gram*: *attrib*) having a subject which does not refer to a person, thing *etc*: *'It is raining' is an example of an impersonal verb.* **im'personally** *adv.* **imˌperso'nality** [-'na-] *nu.*

impersonate [im'pə:səneit] *vt* to copy the behaviour *etc* of or pretend to be (another person), sometimes in order to deceive: *The comedian impersonated the prime minister.* **im'personator** *nc.*

imˌperso'nation *ncu*: *He was known for his impersonations of politicians*; *He was good at impersonation.*

impertinent [im'pə:tinənt] *adj* impudent or rude: *an impertinent child*; *impertinent remarks*; *She was impertinent to her teacher.* **im'pertinently** *adv.*

im'pertinence *ncu*: *The child was scolded for her impertinence.*

imperturbable [impə'tə:bəbl] *adj* (*formal*) not easily worried or perturbed; always calm: *Despite all her problems, she remained imperturbable*; *She had a completely imperturbable personality.* **ˌimper'turbably** *adv.* **ˌimperturba'bility** *nu.*

impervious [im'pə:viəs] *adj* (*formal*: *usu pred with* **to**) **1** not easily influenced or affected by: *impervious to criticism.* **2** not allowing (liquids *etc*) to pass through: *impervious to damp.*

impetuous [im'petjuəs] *adj* (*more formal than* **hasty**) acting in a hasty manner and without thinking: *an impetuous child/action*; *Don't be so impetuous!* **im'petuously** *adv.* **imˌpetu'osity** [-'o-] *ncu.*

impetus ['impətəs] **1** *nu* (*formal or tech*) the force or energy with which something moves: *The impetus was so great that the ball smashed through the plate-glass window.* **2** *nc* stimulus or encouragement: *This discovery gave a fresh impetus to the* *development of the industry.*

impiety *see* **impious**.

impinge [im'pindʒ] *vi* (*formal*) (*with* **(up)on**) **1** to interfere with (a person's freedom, rights *etc*): *The shade from the tree impinged on the adjoining garden.* **2** to come into contact with or make an impression on (a person's mind *etc*): *The sound impinged upon her ears.*

impious ['impiəs] *adj* (*formal*) not showing respect for God or for what is sacred; not pious. **'impiously** *adv.*

impiety [im'paiəti] *nu* (*formal*) lack of respect for God, sacred things *etc.*

implacable [im'plakəbl] *adj* (*formal*) not able to be calmed or satisfied: *an implacable enemy*; *implacable hatred*; *She is so angry that she is completely implacable.* **im'placably** *adv.*

implant [im'pla:nt] *vt* **1** (*formal*) to put (ideas *etc*) into a person's mind: *He implanted a hatred of killing in the minds of the children.* **2** (*tech*) to put (something) permanently into a part of the body: *The surgeon implanted a piece of bone.* – ['impla:nt] *nc* (*tech*) something which is implanted in the body. **ˌimplan'tation** [implan-] *nu.*

implausible [im'plo:zəbl] *adj* not easy to believe or likely to be true; not plausible: *In order to conceal his guilt, he made up a rather implausible story about being robbed by three masked men.* **im'plausibly** *adv.* **imˌplausi'bility** *nu.*

implement ['implimənt] *nc* (*more formal than* **tool**) a tool or instrument: *kitchen/garden implements.* – [impli'ment] *vt* (*formal*) to fulfil or carry out: *implement an agreement.* **ˌimplemen'tation** *nu.*

implicate ['implikeit] *vt* (*formal*) to show or suggest that a person has taken part in something bad, *eg* a crime: *The criminals' statements implicated a local politician in the crime.*

ˌimpli'cation[1] *nu* **1** the act of implicating: *By their implication of him in the crime they cleared the other suspect.* **2** the state of being implicated: *His implication in the crime was obvious to all.* – *See also* **imply**.

implicit [im'plisit] *adj* (*formal*) **1** meant but not put into actual words; understood: *Her disapproval was implicit in what she was saying*; *the implicit meaning.* **2** (*usu attrib*) unquestioning; complete: *implicit obedience/trust.* **im'plicitly** *adv.*

implore [im'plo:] *vt* (*formal*) to ask (someone) earnestly to do something or for something: *She implored her husband to give up his life of crime*; *She implored his forgiveness.* **im'ploringly** *adv.*

imply [im'plai] *vt* to suggest or hint at (something) without actually stating it: *Are you implying that I am a liar?*

implication[2] [impli'keiʃən] *ncu*: *He did not actually say that she was a liar but that was the implication.* – *See also* **implicate**.

impolite [impə'lait] *adj* (*formal*) not polite; rude: *It was impolite of them to ignore our invitation*; *That child becomes more and more impolite.* **ˌimpo'litely** *adv.* **ˌimpo'liteness** *nu.*

imponderable [im'pondərəbl] *adj* (*formal*) having an influence, importance *etc* which is difficult or impossible to measure or estimate: *Public opinion is an imponderable factor in a political campaign*; *What the effect of the strike will be on the firm is imponderable.* – *nc* (*formal*: *often in pl*) something which has an influence, importance *etc* which is difficult or impossible to measure or estimate: *The future rate of inflation is one of the great imponderables of economic planning.*
See also **ponder**.

import[1] [im'po:t] *vt* to bring in (goods *etc*) from abroad *usu* for sale: *We import wine from France.* – ['impo:t] **1** *nc* something which is imported from abroad: *Our imports are greater than our exports.* **2** *nu* the act of bringing in goods from abroad: *the import of wine from France.*

ˌimpor'tation *ncu.* **im'porter** *nc.*

import[2] ['impo:t] *nu* (*very formal*) **1** importance: *matters of great import.* **2** meaning: *the import of his words.*

important [im'po:tənt] *adj* (*neg* **un-**) having great value, influence or effect: *an important book/person/occasion*; *It is important that you arrive here on time*; *It is very important to her that she gets the job.* **im'portantly** *adv.*

im'portance *nu*: *They discussed matters of great importance.*

importune [impə'tju:n, (*Amer*) impo:r-] *vt* (*formal*) to make repeated, often annoying, requests to: *The child importuned his parents for money.*

importunate [im'po:tjunət, (*Amer*) -tʃu-] *adj* (*formal*) troublesomely or annoyingly persistent: *an importunate beggar*; *importunate in their demands.*

impose [im'pouz] (*formal*) **1** *vt* to place (a tax, fine *etc*) on someone or something: *The government have imposed a new tax on cigarettes.* **2** *vt* to force (oneself, one's opinions *etc*) on a person: *He liked to impose his authority on the teachers who had newly arrived at the school.* **3** *vi* (*often with* **on**) to ask someone to do something which he should not be asked to do or which he will find difficult to do: *I hope I'm not imposing on you by asking you to help*; *I don't want to impose.*

imposition [impə'ziʃən] (*formal*) **1** *ncu* (an) act of imposing: *The imposition of taxes is unpopular.* **2** *nc* an unfair demand; a burden: *I don't regard helping him as an imposition.* **3** *nc* a written exercise given as a punishment: *The teacher gave the children impositions because they were talking in class.*

imposing [im'pouziŋ] *adj* (*formal*) making a great impression because of large size, handsome appearance *etc*: *an imposing building*; *Their new butler is a very imposing person*; *The new office block looks most imposing.*

impossible [im'posəbl] *adj* **1** that cannot be or be done; not possible: *It is impossible to sing and drink at the same time*; *That answer to the sum is impossible*; *She set me an impossible task.* **2** (*inf*) hopelessly unsuitable; unacceptable: *an impossible hat/suggestion*; *That child's behaviour is quite impossible.* **im'possibly** *adv.* **imˌpossi'bility** *ncu.*

impostor [im'postə] *nc* a person who pretends to be someone else, or to be something he is not, in order to deceive another person: *That soldier is obviously an impostor as he doesn't know how to use a gun.*

im'posture [-stʃə] *ncu* (*very formal*) (an act of) deceiving someone in this way: *His imposture as a soldier was soon discovered*; *His habit of imposture led to his dismissal.*

impotent ['impətənt] *adj* **1** (*formal*) not able to do (something) because of lack of strength *etc*: *As the thief drove off in his car the women shook their fists in impotent rage*; *We are impotent against the power of* *the dictator.* 2 (of men) lacking in sexual power. **'impotence** *nu.*

See also **potent.**

impound [im'paund] *vt* (*formal*) 1 to take legal possession of (a thing *etc*): *The police impounded the car; They impounded his furniture as he had not paid his rent.* 2 to shut up (a stray animal), *esp* until it is claimed: *They impounded the dog in the cat and dog home.*

impoverish [im'povəriʃ] *vt* (*formal*) 1 to make (a person *etc*) poor: *He was impoverished by his habits of drinking and betting; His wife's extravagances gradually impoverished him.* 2 to make (something, *usu* soil) poor in quality: *Over-cultivation has impoverished the soil.* **im'poverishment** *nu.*

impracticable [im'praktikəbl] *adj* not able to be put into practice, or used; not practicable: *That is a completely impracticable idea; That scheme is all very well in theory but it is totally impracticable.* **im,practica'bility** *nu.*

impractical [im'praktikəl] *adj* lacking common sense; not practical: *an impractical person; She is very artistic but thoroughly impractical; It is impractical to think that two people can live as cheaply as one; an impractical idea/suggestion.*

imprecation [impri'keiʃən] *nc* (*very formal or facet*) a curse: *The old woman was muttering imprecations under her breath.*

imprecise [impri'sais] *adj* (*formal*) not clear; vague: *an imprecise description/definition; Her directions were so imprecise that we lost our way.* **,impre'ciseness** *nu.*

impregnable [im'pregnəbl] *adj* (*formal*) not able to be captured or overcome by force: *an impregnable fortress; (fig) The football team is in an impregnable position at the top of the league.*

impregnate ['impregneit, (*Amer*) im'pregneit] *vt* (*tech*) to mix one substance with another; to cause one substance to take in a great deal of another substance: *The water was impregnated with chemical salts.*

impresario [impre'sa:riou] – *pl* **,impre'sarios** – *nc* the organizer or manager of a play, concert *etc*: *The impresario had assembled many famous artistes for the charity concert.*

impress [im'pres] 1 *vti* to cause feelings of admiration *etc* in (a person): *I was most impressed by his good behaviour; He tries very hard to impress (people).* 2 *vt* (*with* **on** *or* **upon**) to stress (something to someone): *I must impress upon you the need for silence.* 3 *vt* (*formal*) to fix (a fact *etc*) in the mind: *She re-read the plans in order to impress the details on her memory.* 4 *vt* (*formal*) to make (a mark) in or on something by pressing another object against it: *She impressed the shape of a thistle on the shortbread.*

im'pression [-ʃən] 1 *ncu* the idea or effect produced in someone's mind by a person, experience *etc*: *That made a great impression on me; His book did not make much impression (on the public) at first.* 2 *nc* a vague idea: *I have the impression that he isn't coming.* – *See also* **be under the impression (that)** *below.* 3 *nc* (*formal*) the mark left by an object on another object: *The dog left the impression of its paws in the wet cement.* 4 *nc* a single printing of a book *etc*: *This is the third impression of this edition of the book.*

im'pressionism *nu* a method of painting or writing which attempts to reproduce the effect something makes on the artist or writer without paying much attention to detail. **im'pressionist** *nc.*

im'pressive [-siv] *adj* (*neg* **un-**) making a great impression on a person's mind, feelings *etc*: *an impressive ceremony; I found the pianist's performance most impressive.* **im'pressively** *adv.* **im'pressiveness** *nu.*

be under the impression (that) to have the (often wrong) feeling or idea that: *I was under the impression that you were paying for this meal.*

imprint ['imprint] *nc* (*formal*) 1 a mark made by pressure: *She saw the imprint of a foot in the sand.* 2 a permanent effect produced on a person by someone else or by an experience: *His face showed the imprint of years of pain.* – [im'print] *vt* (*formal*) to fix (an idea *etc*) in a person's mind: *That day will always be imprinted on my memory.*

imprison [im'prizn] *vt* to put (someone) in prison: *Because of the seriousness of his crime he was imprisoned for twenty years; (fig) She imprisoned the boy in his room for the afternoon because he wouldn't eat his lunch.* **im'prisonment** *nu.*

improbable [im'probəbl] *adj* 1 not likely to happen or exist; not probable: *It is improbable that she will come to the party; Although death at his age was improbable, he had already made his will.* 2 (*formal*) hard to believe: *improbable excuses.* **im'probably** *adv.*

im,proba'bility (*formal*) 1 *nu* the state of being unlikely: *You must accept the improbability of having a sunny day for your wedding in February.* 2 *nc* something which is unlikely to happen or exist: *It is unlikely that he will get the job but improbabilities do happen.*

impromptu [im'promptju:] *adj, adv* (made or done) without preparation beforehand: *an impromptu speech; His speech was impromptu but very informative; He spoke impromptu for ten minutes.*

improper [im'propə] *adj* 1 not fitting in with acceptable standards (often of sexual morality); not proper: *improper suggestions; improper behaviour; I find her style of dress most improper.* 2 (*usu attrib*) not correct; wrong: *That was an improper use of the word.*

impropriety [imprə'praiəti] (*formal*) 1 *nc* something which is improper: *He seemed to be unaware of the improprieties in his behaviour.* 2 *nu* the state of being improper: *The impropriety of her dress attracted the attention of all.*

improper fraction *nc* a fraction which is larger than 1: $^7/_5$ *is an improper fraction.*

improve [im'pru:v] *vti* to (cause to) become better, of higher quality *etc*: *His work has greatly improved; They recently improved the design of that car.* – *See also* **improve on** *below.*

im'provement 1 *ncu* the state or act of improving or being improved: *There has been a marked improvement in her work; The patient's condition shows some improvement.* 2 *nc* something which improves, or adds to, the beauty, value *etc* of something: *I've made several improvements to the house.*

im'prove on/(*formal*) **upon** *vt fus* to produce something which is better, more useful *etc* than something else: *I think I can improve on that suggestion.*

improvident [im'providənt] *adj* (*very formal*) taking no thought for future needs; not provident; wasteful: *Spending half your wages in a public house is most improvident behaviour; It was improvident of you to spend all your money.*

improvise ['imprəvaiz] *vti* **1** to compose and perform (a poem, tune *etc*) without preparation: *The pianist forgot his music and had to improvise.* **2** to make (something) from materials that happen to be available, often materials that are not normally used for that purpose: *They improvised a shelter from branches and blankets.* **ˌimproviˈsation** *ncu.*

imprudent [im'pru:dənt] *adj* (*formal*) not having or showing good sense; unwise; not prudent: *an imprudent action/person*; *It was imprudent of you to tell her your secret.* **imˈprudently** *adv.* **imˈprudence** *nu.*

impudent ['impjudənt] *adj* rude and lacking in respect: *an impudent child/suggestion*; *She is bold and impudent.* **ˈimpudently** *adv.* **ˈimpudence** *nu.*

impulse ['impʌls] **1** *ncu* (the cause of) a sudden desire to do something without thinking about the consequences: *I had an impulse to steal the chicken*; *I stole the chicken on impulse*; (*attrib*) *an impulse buy* (= something bought because of a sudden desire). **2** *nc* (*tech*) (the effect of) a sudden force or stimulation: *an electrical impulse.*

imˈpulsive [-siv] *adj* **1** likely to act suddenly without careful thought: *an impulsive person*; *She is so impulsive that she decided to take a day off work just because the sun was shining.* **2** done without thought: *an impulsive action*; *Her action was too impulsive.* **imˈpulsively** *adv.* **imˈpulsiveness** *nu.*

See also **impel**.

impunity [im'pju:nəti] *nu* (*formal*) freedom from punishment, injury *etc*: *You cannot expect to break the law with impunity.*

impure [im'pjuə] *adj* (*formal*) **1** (*usu attrib*) not moral; bad; wrong: *impure thoughts.* **2** dirty, with other substances mixed in; not pure: *impure air*; *The air in there is impure.*

imˈpurity **1** *nc* (*usu in pl*) something which is mixed into another substance, but which should not be: *There are too many impurities in this steel.* **2** *nu* (*formal*) the state of being impure: *Complaints were made about the impurity of the milk from that farm.*

impute [im'pju:t] *vt* (*formal*: *with* **to**) to consider (something bad) as having been done, thought *etc* by someone *etc*: *I impute the failure of this project to your poor leadership.*

imputation [impju'teiʃən] *ncu*: *He was angered by the imputations of negligence in the report.*

in [in] *prep* **1** describing the position of a thing *etc* which is surrounded by something else: *My mother is in the house*; *in London.* **2** showing the direction of movement: *He put his hand in his pocket*; *He went in the direction of your house.* **3** describing the time at, after or within which something happens: *in the morning*; *I'll be back in a week*; *I'll be finished in five or ten minutes.* **4** indicating amount or relative number: *in large numbers*; *There are seven days in a week*; *At this bank, money earns interest of 10p in the pound.* **5** expressing circumstances, state, manner *etc* of an event, person *etc*: *dressed in a brown coat*; *walking in the rain*; *in a hurry*; *written in English*; *He is in the army*; *books tied up in bundles*; *She is in her sixties* (= between sixty and sixty-nine years old). – **1** *adv, adj* (*pred*) expressing the position of a person *etc, usu* at or to a place where the person *etc* is expected to be, *eg* home, office, station: *Is Mr Smith in?*; *Is the train in yet?*; *Is he coming in today?* **2** *adv, adj* (*pred*) describing something which is fashionable or popular: *Short skirts are in at the moment.* **3** *adv, adj* (*pred*) describing a person *etc* who occupies a position of power *etc*: *The Conservatives are in.* **4** *adj* (*pred*) burning: *Is the fire still in?* **5** *adj* (*pred*) describing a cricket *etc* team who are batting: *Yorkshire are in at the moment.* **6** *adv, adj* (*pred*) (of the tide) with the water at, or moving to, its highest level: *The tide is in*; *The tide is coming in.* **7** *adj* (*attrib*) describing direction of movement: *the in door* (= the door by which people should enter a building).

in- (*in cmpds*) **1** expressing popularity: *the ˌin-ˈthing*; *an ˌin-ˈword.* **2** forming or belonging to a particular group of people: *an ˌin-ˈjoke.*

-in (*in cmpds*) describing an activity *usu* carried out by groups of people as a form of protest *etc*: *a ˈsit-in*; *a ˈwork-in.*

ˈinmost *adj* (*attrib*) **1** most private or secret: *my inmost thoughts.* **2** farthest in; most central: *the inmost circle*; *the inmost room.*

in-depth *see* **depth**.

ˈin-service *adj* (*attrib*) carried on while a person is employed: *in-service training.*

insofar as, in so far as to the degree or extent that: *I gave him the details insofar as I knew them.*

ˈin-tray *nc* a container, *eg* on an office desk, for letters *etc* which have not yet been dealt with: *Miss Smith is on holiday – leave her mail in the in-tray.*

day *etc* **in, day** *etc* **out** day *etc* after day *etc* without a break: *I do the same boring job day in, day out*; *Last summer it rained week in, week out.*

inasmuch as, in as much as (*formal*) because; in consideration of the fact that: *It would not be completely true to say he had retired from this firm, inasmuch as he still does a certain amount of work for us.*

ˈin for (*inf*) likely to experience (something, *usu* something bad): *We're in for some bad weather*; *You're letting yourself in for trouble.*

ˈin for it (*inf*) in for trouble; likely to be punished: *You're in for it now that you've broken the window again!*

ˈin on (*inf*) to know; to have a share in (something): *I'm in on the secret.*

ins and outs (*inf*) the complex details of a plan *etc*: *He alone knows all the ins and outs of this scheme.*

ˈin that because; from the fact that: *This is not a good plant for your garden in that its seeds are poisonous.*

(ˌwell) ˈin with (*inf*) very friendly with (someone).

inability [inə'biləti] *nu* the lack of power, means, ability *etc* (to do something): *I was surprised at his inability to understand the lecture.*

See also **unable, disability** *under* **disable**.

inaccessible [inək'sesəbl] *adj* (*formal*) not able to be (easily) approached, reached or obtained; not (easily) accessible: *Our farm is inaccessible by road in winter.* **ˈinacˌcessiˈbility** [-sesə-] *nu.*

inaccurate [in'akjurət] *adj* **1** containing errors; not correct or accurate: *inaccurate translation*; *The addition of this column of figures is inaccurate.*

inˈaccuracy **1** *nu* the state of not being correct or exact: *I was surprised at the inaccuracy of the translation.* **2** *nc* a mistake: *There are many inaccuracies in this account.*

inactive [in'aktiv] *adj* (*formal*) **1** not taking much exercise: *You're fat because you're so inactive*;

Inactive people tend to become fat. **2** no longer working or functioning: *an inactive company/volcano*; *The volcano has been inactive for some years.* **3** (*usu attrib*) not taking part in the activities of a group to which a person belongs: *an inactive member of a political party.* **in'action, ˌinac'tivity** *nus.*
See also **active.**

inadequate [in'adikwət] *adj* **1** not sufficient; not adequate: *inadequate salary/supplies*; *Our resources are inadequate for what we have to do.* **2** (of a person) not able to deal with (a task, situation *etc*): *There are so many problems in this job that I am beginning to feel quite inadequate*; *People with inadequate personalities find it difficult to find jobs.*
in'adequacy *ncu*: *His inadequacy in the job depressed him*; *There are inadequacies in every system of government.*

inadmissible [inəd'misəbl] *adj* (*formal or legal*: *usu attrib*) not allowable; not admissible: *inadmissible evidence.* **'inadˌmissi'bility** *nu.*

inadvertent [inəd'vəːtənt] *adj* (*formal*: *usu attrib*) not done on purpose: *an inadvertent insult*; *an inadvertent result of his action.* **ˌinad'vertently** *adv.*

inadvisable [inəd'vaizəbl] *adj* (*formal*) unwise; not advisable: *It would be inadvisable for you to go alone*; *inadvisable conduct.* **'inadˌvisa'bility** [-vai-] *nu.*

inalienable [in'eiliənəbl] *adj* (*formal*: *attrib*) not capable of being taken or given away: *a mother's inalienable right to take care of her child.*

inane [i'nein] *adj* silly or meaningless: *inane remarks/behaviour*; *Her comments were rather inane.*
i'nanity [i'na-] (*formal*) **1** *nu* silliness. **2** *nc* a silly remark, action *etc*: *His speech was nothing but a collection of inanities.*

inanimate [in'animət] *adj* (*formal*) not living or animate: *A rock is an inanimate object*; *Is it animate or inanimate?*

inapplicable [in'aplikəbl] *adj* not applicable: *I think these rules are inapplicable in this case.*

inappropriate [inə'proupriət] *adj* (*sometimes with* **to** *or* **for** *when pred*) not appropriate or suitable: *inappropriate remarks*; *His speech was inappropriate to the occasion.* **ˌinap'propriateness** *nu.*

inarticulate [inaː'tikjulət] *adj* (*formal*) **1** unable to express oneself clearly and fluently: *He becomes inarticulate when he is anxious*; *an inarticulate teenager.* **2** badly expressed; spoken indistinctly: *inarticulate remarks*; *His speech was dull and inarticulate.* **ˌinar'ticulateness** *nu.*
See also **articulate.**

inasmuch as *see* **in.**

inattentive [inə'tentiv] *adj* not paying attention; not attentive: *This pupil is very inattentive in class*; *an inattentive audience.* **ˌinat'tention, ˌinat'tentiveness** *nus.*

inaudible [in'oːdəbl] *adj* (*formal*) not loud or clear enough to be heard; not audible: *Her voice was quite inaudible because of the noise in the background*; *inaudible whispers.* **in'audibly** *adv.* **inˌaudi'bility** *nu.*

inaugurate [i'noːgjureit] *vt* (*formal*) **1** to place (a person) in an official position with great ceremony: *to inaugurate a president.* **2** to make a start to (some activity) with great ceremony: *This meeting is to inaugurate our new Social Work scheme.* **3** to open (a building, exhibition *etc*) formally to the public: *The Queen inaugurated the new university buildings.* **iˌnaugu'ration** *ncu.*
i'naugural *nc, adj* (*attrib*) (of) a speech, lecture *etc* officially made by a person on taking office: *The professor's inaugural (lecture) was exceptionally well attended.*

inauspicious [inoː'spiʃəs] *adj* (*formal*) unlucky, suggesting that an activity *etc* will be unlikely to end in success; not auspicious: *His accident was an inauspicious start to the project.* **ˌinau'spiciousness** *nu.*

inborn ['in'boːn] *adj* natural; (apparently) possessed by a person from birth: *an inborn ability to paint*; *His love of painting was inborn.*

inbred ['in'bred] *adj* **1** (*usu attrib*) natural; possessed by a person from birth: *a natural, inbred talent.* **2** (*usu pred*) resulting from inbreeding; having closely related ancestors: *Many of the villagers are inbred*; *inbred deformities.*
inbreeding ['in'briːdiŋ, (*Amer*) 'inbriːdiŋ] *nu* (the result of) the process of repeatedly mating closely related animals *etc.*

incalculable [in'kalkjuləbl] *adj* (*formal*) not able to be estimated; not calculable: *incalculable risks*; *The degree of risk is incalculable*; *a jewel of incalculable value.*
See also **calculate.**

in camera *see* **camera.**

incandescent [inkan'desnt] *adj* **1** (*tech*) glowing or white (when heated): *incandescent heat.* **2** of or containing a material which glows white when heated: *an incandescent lamp.*

incantation [inkan'teiʃən] (*formal*) *nc* words said or sung as a spell: *The witches sang their incantations by candlelight.*

incapable [in'keipəbl] *adj* **1** (*pred with* **of**) not able (to do something): *incapable of lying.* **2** (*usu pred*) unable to do anything; helpless and unfit: *He was found to be drunk and incapable.* **inˌcapa'bility** *nu.*
See also **capable.**

incapacitate [inkə'pasiteit] *vt* (*formal*) to take away a person's strength, ability, right *etc* to work *etc*: *My uncle was a coal-miner but he was incapacitated by an accident five years ago.*
ˌinca'pacity *nu* (*formal*) the state of not having the physical or mental ability to do something: *His incapacity for work dated from his accident.*

incarcerate [in'kaːsəreit] *vt* (*formal often fig*) to imprison: *As it rained non-stop for three days they were incarcerated in the caravan.* **inˌcarce'ration** *nu.*

incarnate [in'kaːnət] *adj* (*formal*: *placed immediately after noun*) in human form: *a devil incarnate.*
incarnation [inkaː'neiʃən] **1** *nc* the human form taken by a divine being *etc*: *Most Christians believe that Christ was the incarnation of God.* **2** *nc* a person representing a quality *etc* in a very marked way: *He is the very incarnation of stupidity.* **3** *nu* the taking of human form by a divine being *etc.*

incautious [in'koːʃəs] *adj* (*formal*) acting or done without thinking; not cautious: *an incautious action/remark/person*; *That was a rather incautious statement to make.* **in'cautiousness** *nu.*

incendiary [in'sendiəri] *adj* (*attrib*) used for setting (a building *etc*) on fire: *an incendiary bomb.* – *nc* **1** a person who sets fire to buildings *etc* unlawfully. **2** an incendiary bomb.

incense[1] [in'sens] *vt* (*formal*) to make (someone) very angry: *He was incensed by her casual attitude to his mother's death.*

incense[2] ['insens] *nu* a substance which is burned

esp in religious services, and which gives off a pleasant smell.

incentive [in'sentiv] *ncu* (*formal*) something that encourages an action *etc*: *Hope of promotion was an incentive to hard work*; *He had no incentive to work after his wife died.*

inception [in'sepʃən] *nc* (*formal*) a beginning: *He was a member of the club from its inception.*

incessant [in'sesnt] *adj* (*formal*) going on without stopping: *incessant noise*; *The noise from the party was loud and incessant.* **in'cessantly** *adv.*

incest ['insest] *nu* sexual relations between members of the same family other than husband and wife: *He was found guilty of incest with his daughter.*

incestuous [in'sestjuəs] *adj* involving incest: *an incestuous relationship*; *I am sure that their relationship is not incestuous.*

inch [intʃ] *nc* **1** (*often abbrev* **in** *when written*) a measure of length, the twelfth part of a foot (2·54 centimetres): *He is six inches taller than me*; *a twelve-inch ruler.* **2** (*loosely*) a small amount: *There is not an inch of room to spare.* – *vti* to move slowly and carefully: *He inched (his way) along the narrow ledge.*

every inch completely; entirely; in every way: *He is every inch a nobleman.*

within an inch of almost; very near(ly): *He came within an inch of failing the exam.*

incident ['insidənt] *nc* (*formal*) an event or happening: *There was a strange incident in the supermarket today.* – *adj* (*tech*) (of a ray of light) falling or striking (on something): *The beam from the light was incident on the mirror.*

'incidence *nu* **1** the frequency, extent *etc* of an occurrence *etc*: *In that year the incidence of influenza in the United Kingdom was high.* **2** (*tech*) the way in which a ray of light *etc* falls on an object.

ˌinci'dental [-'den-] *adj* **1** occurring *etc* by chance in connection with something else: *incidental benefits*; *an incidental remark*; (*formal*) *Such advantages are entirely incidental to the new job.* **2** (*usu attrib*) accompanying (something) but not forming part of it: *He wrote the incidental music for the play.*

ˌinci'dentally [-'den-] *adv* **1** by the way: *Incidentally, where were you last night?* **2** in an incidental manner: *The firm will pay you a basic salary and any expenses that you may incur incidentally.*

incinerate [in'sinəreit] *vt* (*formal*) to burn (paper, dead leaves *etc*) to ashes: *The mass murderer incinerated the bodies of his victims.* **inˌcine'ration** *nu.*

in'cinerator *nc* a furnace or other container for burning rubbish *etc*: *The gardener burned the leaves in the incinerator.*

incipient [in'sipiənt] *adj* (*formal*: *attrib*) beginning to exist: *an incipient cold*; *The soldiers quelled the incipient rebellion.*

incision [in'siʒən] (*esp formal or tech*) **1** *nc* a cut, *esp* one made in a person's body by a surgeon: *The surgeon made a deep incision to remove the appendix*; *The incision healed very quickly.* **2** *nu* the act of cutting *esp* by a surgeon: *the moment of incision.*

incisive [in'saisiv] *adj* (*formal*) clear and sharp; to the point: *He has a brilliant, incisive mind*; *His style is concise and incisive.*

incisor [in'saizə] *nc* (*tech*) one of the four front cutting teeth in the upper or lower jaw.

incite [in'sait] *vt* (*formal*) **1** to urge (someone) to do something: *The leader of the revolt incited the people to rise against the king.* **2** to stir up or cause: *They incited violence in the crowd.*

in'citement *ncu*: *They were encouraged by the incitement of their leader*; *His enthusiasm about the island was an incitement to others to go there.*

incivility [insi'viləti] *ncu* (*formal*) (an act of) impoliteness: *The incivility of his remarks angered her.*

inclement [in'klemənt] *adj* (*formal or facet*: *attrib*) (of weather) stormy or very cold; very unpleasant: *We enjoyed our holiday in spite of the inclement weather.* **in'clemency** *nu.*

incline [in'klain] *vt* to bow (one's head *etc*): *The queen acknowledged their cheers by graciously inclining her head.* – *See also* **be inclined to** *below.* – ['inklain] *nc* a slope: *There was a gentle incline up to the hotel from the beach.*

inclination [inklə'neiʃən] **1** *ncu* a tendency or slight desire to do something: *Has he any inclinations towards engineering?*; *She has artistic inclinations*; *I have no inclination to go to the party*; *I felt an inclination to hit him*; *I'd like to be free to follow my own inclinations.* **2** *ncu* (*formal*) (an act of) bowing (the head *etc*): *He acknowledged her presence with an inclination of his head.* **3** *nc* (*formal*) a slope: *a steep inclination.*

be in'clined to 1 to have a tendency to (do something): *He is inclined to be a bit lazy.* **2** to have a slight desire to (do something): *I am inclined to accept their invitation.*

include [iŋ'klu:d] *vt* to take in or consider along with (other people, things *etc*) as part of a group, set *etc*: *Am I included in the team?*; *Your duties include making the tea.* **in'clusion** [-ʒən] *nu.*

in'clusive [-siv] *adj* including everything mentioned or understood: *an inclusive charge*; *The price is inclusive*; *May 7 to May 9 inclusive is three days.*

in'clusive of including: *The meal cost £6, inclusive of wines.*

incognito [iŋkog'ni:tou] *adv, adj* (*pred*) without letting people know who one is, *eg* by using a false name: *He travelled incognito to Paris.*

incoherent [inkə'hiərənt] *adj* **1** (*formal*) not arranged, said *etc* in any logical order; not easy to follow or understand: *incoherent remarks*; *He gave a very incoherent explanation*; *She was so upset that her account of the accident was incoherent.* **2** talking, writing *etc* in a way which is not easy to follow: *He was quite incoherent with rage*; *a dull and incoherent speaker.* **ˌinco'herently** *adv.* **ˌinco'herence** *nu.* *See also* **coherent**.

incombustible [inkəm'bʌstəbl] *adj* (*formal*) not able to be burned; not combustible: *That new building material is quite incombustible*; *an incombustible substance.*

income ['iŋkəm] *ncu* money received by a person as wages *etc*: *He cannot support his family on his income*: *The government rely on the income from exports.*

'income tax *nu* a tax paid on income over a certain amount.

incoming ['inkʌmiŋ] *adj* (*attrib*) **1** which is coming in; approaching: *the incoming tide*; *incoming telephone calls.* **2** next or following: *the incoming chairman.*

See also **outgoing**.

incommode [inkə'moud] *vt* (*formal or facet*) to cause inconvenience or discomfort to (a person):

I hope that it will not incommode you if we change the date of our meeting.

incommunicado ['inkəmju:ni'ka:dou] *adv, adj* (*pred*) not allowed to communicate with other people: *The prisoner was held incommunicado.*

incomparable [in'kompərəbl] *adj* without equal; not comparable: *incomparable beauty*; *Her beauty is quite incomparable.*

in'comparably *adv* **1** beyond comparison: *She is incomparably lovely.* **2** (*loosely*) very much: *She is incomparably better than my last secretary.*

incompatible [inkəm'patəbl] *adj* **1** (of people) certain to disagree, fight *etc*: *Although they are married, they are quite incompatible*; *They are an incompatible couple.* **2** (of statements *etc*) not in agreement with one another: *The reports of the two witnesses were incompatible*; *incompatible statements.* **'incom,pati'bility** *nu.*

See also **compatible**.

incompetent [in'kompitənt] *adj* not good enough at doing a job *etc*; not competent: *He was a very incompetent mechanic*; *He is totally incompetent.*

in'competence *nu*: *He was dismissed for incompetence.*

incomplete [inkəm'pli:t] *adj* not complete or finished; with some part missing: *His novel was incomplete when he died*; *an incomplete pack of cards.*

incomprehensible [inkompri'hensəbl] *adj* impossible to understand; not comprehensible: *He gave a quite incomprehensible explanation*; *I find his attitude quite incomprehensible.*

inconceivable [inkən'si:vəbl] *adj* not able to be imagined or believed: *I find it inconceivable that he would do such a wicked thing*; *inconceivable happenings.*

inconclusive [inkən'klu:siv] *adj* (*formal*) not leading to a definite decision, result *etc*; not conclusive: *inconclusive evidence/argument*; *We found the evidence inconclusive.* **,incon'clusiveness** *nu.*

incongruous [iŋ'koŋgruəs] *adj* unsuitable or out of place; odd: *Boots look incongruous with evening dress*; *an incongruous mixture.* **in'congruousness** *nu.*

,incon'gruity [-'gru:-] (*formal*) **1** *nu* the state of being incongruous: *The incongruity of the situation amused them all.* **2** *nc* something which is incongruous: *There were some strange incongruities in her style of dress.*

inconsequential [inkonsi'kwenʃəl] *adj* (*formal*) of no importance: *All her actions were quite inconsequential*; *inconsequential remarks.*

See also **consequential** *under* **consequence**.

inconsiderable [inkən'sidərəbl] *adj* (*usu with* **not**: *formal*) small in amount, value *etc*: *These are not inconsiderable* (= quite large) *difficulties.*

See also **considerable** *under* **consider**.

inconsiderate [inkən'sidərət] *adj* not showing thought for the feelings, rights *etc* of other people; thoughtless; not considerate: *He's a most inconsiderate person*; *It was inconsiderate of you to arrive unexpectedly.* **,incon'siderateness** *nu.*

inconsistent [inkən'sistənt] *adj* **1** (*often with* **with**) (having parts that are) contradictory in some way; not in agreement: *His cruel method of hunting was inconsistent with his teaching about kindness to animals*; *The style of the book was inconsistent.* **2** (of people) not always speaking, acting *etc* according to the same principles etc: *His attitude to his wife was quite inconsistent and she could not foretell his reactions to anything.*

,incon'sistency *ncu*: *His account of the occasion was full of inconsistencies*; *inconsistency of style.*

See also **consistent**.

inconsolable [inkən'souləbl] *adj* (*formal*) not able to be comforted: *After his wife's death he was quite inconsolable*; *the inconsolable widow.*

inconspicuous [inkən'spikjuəs] *adj* (*formal*) not noticeable or conspicuous: *The detective tried to be as inconspicuous as possible*; *ordinary inconspicuous people.* **,incon'spicuousness** *nu.*

inconstant [in'konstənt] *adj* (*formal or liter*) (of people) having feelings, intentions *etc* which change frequently: *an inconstant lover.*

incontinent [in'kontinənt] *adj* (*formal*) unable to control one's bladder and/or bowels: *Old people often become incontinent*; *incontinent old people.*

in'continence *nu.*

incontrovertible [inkontrə'və:təbl] *adj* (*formal*) too clear and certain to be questioned: *incontrovertible evidence*; *The evidence is incontrovertible.* **in,contro'vertibly** *adv.*

inconvenient [inkən'vi:njənt] *adj* causing trouble or difficulty; awkward; not convenient: *Will it be inconvenient for him to attend that meeting?*; *This has come at a very inconvenient time.*

,incon'venience *ncu* (something which causes) trouble or difficulty: *That stone in the middle of the path is a great inconvenience*; *He apologized for the inconvenience caused by his late arrival*; *Until it can be repaired, you will just have to put up with the inconvenience of not having a car.* – *vt* (*formal*) to cause trouble or difficulty to (someone): *I hope I haven't inconvenienced you.*

incorporate [in'ko:pəreit] *vt* (*formal*) **1** (not used with **is, was** *etc* and **-ing**) to contain as part of the whole: *The shopping centre also incorporates a library and a bank.* **2** to include (something) so that it forms part of the whole: *We have incorporated all your suggestions into the plan.*

in'corporated *adj* (*Amer* as used in company titles, or legal: *often with cap*: *often abbrev* **Inc.**, **inc.**) formed into a company, corporation *etc*: *The name of our company is 'Field Services, Incorporated'.*

incorrect [inkə'rekt] *adj* **1** not accurate or correct; wrong: *incorrect translation of a word*; *These answers are incorrect.* **2** not according to the best or accepted standards: *incorrect behaviour*; *It would be incorrect to offer to pay him for the book that he brought – it was obviously a present.* **,incor'rectness** *nu.*

incorrigible [in'koridʒəbl] *adj* (*formal*) too bad to be corrected or improved: *He's an incorrigible liar*; *incorrigible behaviour*; *That child is incorrigible.*

incorruptible [inkə'rʌptəbl] *adj* (*formal*) not able to be bribed or corrupted; honest: *an incorruptible judge*; *The police should be incorruptible.* **'incor,rupti'bility** *nu.*

increase [in'kri:s] *vti* to (cause to) grow in size, number *etc*: *The number of tourists has increased greatly in recent years*; *They had to increase the size of the classes to accommodate all the children.* – ['inkri:s] *ncu* (the amount, number *etc* added by) growth: *an increase in population*; *There has been a marked increase in the value of property recently*; *Some increase in productivity will be necessary.*

in'creasingly *adv* more and more: *It became increasingly difficult to find helpers.*

on the increase becoming more frequent or becoming greater (in number, value *etc*): *Acts of violence are on the increase.*

incredible [in'kredəbl] *adj* 1 (*loosely*) hard to believe: *He does an incredible amount of work*; *It is incredible to think that he got the job without any qualifications.* 2 impossible to believe; not credible: *I found his story incredible.* **in'credibly** *adv.* **in,credi'bility** *nu.*

incredulous [in'kredjuləs, (*Amer*) -dʒu-] *adj* 1 (*usu attrib*) showing that a person does not believe something: *an incredulous look on a person's face.* 2 (*formal*: *pred*) not believing what is said, seen *etc*: *She was incredulous about his experiences in the Himalayas.* **,incre'dulity** [-'dju:-] *nu.*
See also **credulous**.

increment ['iŋkrəmənt] *nc* (*formal*) an increase, *esp* in salary: *His salary will rise by ten annual increments.*

incriminate [in'krimineit] *vt* to show that a person has committed, or taken part in, a crime or some other act of wrong-doing: *The thief was incriminated by a letter he had written to a friend.* **in'criminating** *adj.* **in,crimi'nation** *nu.*

incubate ['iŋkjubeit] 1 *vti* to produce (young birds) from eggs by sitting on them or by keeping them warm by some other means. 2 *vi* (of germs or disease) to develop until signs of the disease appear: *How long does chickenpox take to incubate?* 3 *vt* (*tech*) to cause (germs) to develop *eg* in a laboratory.
,incu'bation *nu* (*often attrib*): *The incubation period for mumps is three weeks.*
'incubator *nc* a heated box-like apparatus for hatching eggs or a similar one for rearing premature babies *etc.*

inculcate ['inkʌlkeit, (*Amer*) in'kʌlkeit] *vt* (*formal*) 1 to fix (ideas, standards of behaviour *etc*) in a person's mind by frequent repetition: *She inculcates good manners in all her children.* 2 to cause a person to have (an idea, standard of behaviour *etc*) by frequent repetition: *He inculcated the child with a love of wisdom.* **,incul'cation** *nu.*

incumbent [in'kʌmbənt] *adj* (*pred with* **on/upon**: *formal*) resting as a duty on (someone): *It is incumbent on us to support our leader now.* – *nc* (*formal*) a person who holds some office, *esp* in the church.

incur [in'kə:] – *pt, ptp* **in'curred** – *vt* (*formal*) 1 to bring (something unpleasant) upon oneself: *He incurred her displeasure.* 2 to become liable to pay (a debt): *During his stay in London he incurred debts of over two hundred pounds.*

incurable [in'kjuərəbl] *adj* not able to be cured or corrected; not curable: *an incurable disease/habit*; *The cancer is incurable.* – *nc* (*old*) a person who has an incurable illness.

incursion [in'kə:ʃən, (*Amer*) -ʒən] *nc* (*formal*) a brief invasion; a raid: *In the morning they made an incursion into enemy territory*; (*fig*) *All this extra work makes incursions on my free time.*

indebted [in'detid] *adj* (*pred with* **to**: *formal*) having reason to be grateful to (a person *etc*): *I am indebted to you for your help.* **in'debtedness** *nu.*

indecent [in'di:snt] *adj* 1 offending against accepted sexual or moral standards; not decent: *Her clothes are positively indecent*; *indecent behaviour.* 2 (*usu attrib*) not in good taste: *The widow remarried in indecent haste.* **in'decency** *ncu.*

indecipherable [indi'saifərəbl] *adj* (*formal*) impossible to read; not decipherable: *He sent an indecipherable message in code*; *indecipherable handwriting*; *This code is indecipherable.*

indecision [indi'siʒən] *nu* the state of not being able to decide; hesitation: *Because of her indecision about holidays she was eventually too late to book.*
,inde'cisive [-'saisiv] *adj* 1 not producing a clear decision or a definite result: *an indecisive argument/battle*; *The battle proved indecisive.* 2 frequently unable to make firm decisions: *an indecisive person*; *She is so indecisive that her husband has to make all the decisions*; *an indecisive manner.*

indecorous [in'dekərəs] *adj* not decorous; not acceptable or dignified: *Her behaviour was rather indecorous.*

indeed [in'di:d] *adv* 1 really; in fact; as you say; of course *etc*: *The picture was indeed where you said it would be*; *He is indeed a man of great talent*; *'Do you remember your grandmother?' 'Indeed I do!'* 2 used for emphasis: *Thank you very much indeed*; *He is very clever indeed.* – *interj* used to show surprise, interest *etc*: *'John said your idea was stupid.' 'Indeed!'*

indefatigable [indi'fatigəbl] *adj* (*formal*) untiring in effort: *She was indefatigable in her attempts to raise money for charity*; *indefatigable Liberal party workers.*

indefensible [indi'fensəbl] *adj* (*esp fig*) not able to be defended: *Indefensible behaviour*; *Her action was quite indefensible.*

indefinable [indi'fainəbl] *adj* (*formal*: *usu attrib*) not able to be clearly defined, described or put into words: *She had an indefinable air of mystery.*

indefinite [in'definit] *adj* 1 (*usu attrib*) not fixed or exact; without clearly marked outlines or limits: *an indefinite area*; *She invited her mother to stay for an indefinite time.* 2 vague; uncertain: *indefinite opinions/replies*; *His ideas are indefinite at the moment.* **in'definiteness** *nu.*
in'definitely *adv* for an indefinite period of time: *The match was postponed indefinitely.*
indefinite article the name given to the words **a** and **an**.
See also **definite**.

indelible [in'deləbl] *adj* (*formal*) (making a mark) that cannot be removed: *indelible ink*; *an indelible stain*; *This stain seems indelible*; (*fig*) *The events of that day have left an indelible impression on my mind.*

indelicate [in'delikət] *adj* (*formal*) 1 slightly indecent; rude; not delicate: *indelicate language*; *Her remarks were rather indelicate for a lady.* 2 lacking in tact: *an indelicate question*; *It would be indelicate to ask if she is pregnant – she is not married.* **in'delicacy** *ncu.*
See also **delicate**.

indemnity [in'demnəti] *ncu* (*legal*) (something which gives) protection from, insurance against, or compensation for loss of property, injury *etc*: *His insurance policy gave him no indemnity against flood damage*; (*attrib*) *an indemnity policy.*

indent [in'dent] 1 *vi* (*with* **for**: *formal*) to make out a written order (for equipment *etc*): *The soldier had to indent for a new uniform.* 2 *vt* to begin (a line of writing) farther in from the margin than the other lines: *Many people indent the first line of a paragraph.* – ['indent] *nc* 1 (*formal*) a written order for equipment *etc*: *The headmaster put in an indent for fifty new desks.* 2 (*also* **,inden'tation**) the space left at the beginning of the first line of a paragraph.

ˌinden'tation [inden-] *nc* **1** a V-shaped cut (in the edge or outline of an object): *an indentation on a piece of paper.* **2** a deep inward curve in a coastline. – *See also* **indent** *nc* (*def 2*).

in'dented *adj* **1** having an edge, outline *etc* that has V-shaped cuts in it. **2** having deep inward curves: *an indented coastline*; *The coastline is much indented there.*

in'denture [-tʃə] *nc* (*formal*) a written agreement, *esp* a contract by which an apprentice is bound to work for a master for a given period.

independent [indi'pendənt] *adj* **1** not controlled by other people, countries *etc*: *an independent country*; *Our company has remained independent despite attempts by larger companies to buy it*; *That country is independent of Britain now.* **2** not willing, or needing, to accept help from (a person *etc*); not relying on, or influenced by (a person, thing *etc*): *an independent old lady*; *She is completely independent and receives no money from her family*; *She is now independent of her parents*; *an independent observer*; *to arrive at an independent conclusion*; *By winning £100 000, he became completely independent.* **3** not related to, or affected by, each other: *Three separate and quite independent factors have to be taken into account.* – *nc* (*often with cap*) a politician who does not belong to a political party: *I am standing as an Independent in the next election.*

ˌinde'pendence *nu.*

ˌinde'pendently *adv.*

independent means an income which is not gained by working: *She is a lady of independent means, living on money she has inherited.*

See also **dependent**.

indescribable [indi'skraibəbl] *adj* (often of something bad) not able to be described: *The mess was indescribable*; *a scene of indescribable beauty.*

indestructible [indi'strʌktəbl] *adj* (*formal*) not able to be destroyed: *an indestructible toy*; *That country is small but indestructible because the people are so brave.*

indeterminate [indi'tə:minət] *adj* (*formal*) not fixed; not settled: *an indeterminate quantity/value*; *My plans for the future are rather indeterminate at the moment.*

index ['indeks] – *pls* **'indexes** (*defs 1, 2, 4*), **indices** ['indisi:z] (*def 3*) – *nc* **1** an alphabetical list of names, subjects *etc* at the end of a book, or on cards (**card index**) *etc.* **2** (*fig*) something which indicates or points to (opinions *etc*): *The result of an election is one index of public opinion on the government's policies.* **3** (*math*) the figure which indicates the number of times a figure *etc* must be multiplied by itself *etc*: *In* $\sqrt[3]{9}$ *and* 7^5, *the figures 3 and 5 are the indices.* **4** a pointer on a dial, scale *etc* (not used to refer to the hands of clocks or watches).

'index finger *nc* the finger next to the thumb: *She pointed at the map with her index finger.*

Indian ['indiən] *nc* **1** (*also* **American Indian, Mexican Indian** *etc*) one of the native inhabitants of North, Central or South America. – *See also* **Red Indian** *under* **red**. **2** a person born in India and/or having Indian citizenships. – *adj* **1** of India. **2** of Indians (*def 1*).

Indian corn *nu* maize.

Indian ink *nu* a black ink used by artists.

Indian summer *nc* a period of warm, dry, calm weather in late autumn: *We had very hot, sunny weather last October – it was a real Indian summer.*

See also Appendix 2.

india-rubber [indiə'rʌbə] *ncu* rubber, *esp* a piece for rubbing out pencil marks *etc.*

indicate ['indikeit] *vt* **1** (*formal*) to point out or show: *We can paint an arrow here to indicate the right path*; (*fig*) *I'll just indicate the main points of the plan now.* **2** (*formal*) to be a sign of: *A sneeze doesn't always indicate a cold.* **3** (*med, formal or facet*) (*usu in passive*) to show (a particular treatment *etc*) to be necessary or desirable: *I think surgery is indicated for this patient's condition*; *Drastic action is indicated if we are to save the company from bankruptcy.*

ˌindi'cation *ncu* (*formal*): *There are clear indications that the war will soon be over*; *He had previously given no indication that he was intending to resign.*

indicative [in'dikətiv] *adj* **1** (*formal*: *pred with* **of**) showing or suggesting the existence of: *The change in her manner was indicative of a new attitude towards us.* **2** (*gram*) describing verbs which occur as parts of statements and questions: *In 'I ran home' and 'Are you going?'* ran *and* are going *are in the indicative mood.* – (*gram*) **1** *nu* the indicative mood. **2** *nc* a verb in this mood.

'indicator *nc* a pointer, sign, instrument *etc* which indicates something or gives information about something: *the indicator on the petrol gauge of a car*; (*attrib*) *the arrivals and departures indicator board in a railway station.*

indices *see* **index**.

indict [in'dait] *vt* (*legal*) to accuse (someone) of a crime, *esp* formally or in writing: *He was indicted on a charge of murder.*

in'dictment **1** *nc* (*legal*) a written accusation. **2** *nu* (*legal*) the act of accusing a person, *esp* formally or in writing, of having committed a crime. **3** *nc* (*loosely*) something which criticizes or points to the inadequacy of (plans *etc*): *This is a severe indictment of government policy.*

indifferent [in'difrənt] *adj* **1** (*pred*: *often with* **to**) showing no interest in or not caring about (opinions, events *etc*): *She is quite indifferent to other people's suffering.* **2** (*attrib*) not very good: *He is a rather indifferent card-player.*

in'differently *adv.*

in'difference *nu* **1** the state of showing no interest in or not caring about (opinions, events *etc*): *She showed complete indifference to the cries of the baby.* **2** the state of being of little or no importance to (a person): *Your leaving is a matter of complete indifference to me.*

indigenous [in'didʒinəs] *adj* (*formal*) belonging naturally to a country: *These plants are indigenous to northern Europe*; *indigenous plants.*

indigent ['indidʒənt] *adj* (*very formal*) poor; in need: *He spoke of the indigent peoples in many parts of the world*; *That family used to be wealthy but extravagance has made them indigent.*

indigestion [indi'dʒestʃən] *nu* (discomfort or pain which is caused by) difficulty in digesting food: *She suffers from indigestion after eating fatty food.*

ˌindi'gestible *adj* not easily digested: *tough, indigestible meat*; *The old lady finds those vegetables indigestible.* **'indiˌgesti'bility** *nu*.

indignant [in'dignənt] *adj* (*more formal than* **angry**) angry, *usu* because of some wrong that has been done to oneself or others: *I feel most indignant at the way I've been treated*; *The indignant customer complained to the manager*; *She*

was indignant at being spoken to so rudely. **in'dignantly** *adv.*
ˌindig'nation *nu.*

indignity [in'dignəti] (*formal*) **1** *nc* treatment *etc* which causes a person to feel shame: *The soldiers who were captured suffered many indignities at the hands of the enemy.* **2** *nu* the state of feeling shame: *She blushed at the indignity of falling off her horse in front of so many people.*
See also **dignity**.

indirect [indi'rekt] *adj* **1** not leading straight to the destination; not direct: *We arrived late because we took rather an indirect route*; *If you go along this road you will reach your destination but it's rather indirect*; (*fig*) *In order to find out exactly what happened I asked her several questions but she kept giving me indirect answers.* **2** (*attrib*) not intended; not directly aimed at: *an indirect result.* **ˌindi'rectness** *nu.*
indirect object *nc* (*gram*) the word in a sentence which stands for the person or thing to or for whom something is given, done *etc*: *In 'Give me the book', me is the indirect object.*
indirect speech *nu* (*gram*) a person's words as they are reported rather than in the form in which they were said: *He said that he would come is the form in indirect speech of He said 'I will come'.*
indirect tax *nc* a tax which is not paid directly by the taxpayer as income tax is, but which is added to the price of goods and which is paid by the customer in the form of higher prices. **indirect taxation** *nu.*

indiscipline [in'disəplin] *nu* (*formal*) bad behaviour; unwillingness to obey orders: *Indiscipline had spread throughout the school.*
See also **discipline**.

indiscreet [indi'skri:t] *adj* **1** giving too much information away; not discreet: *Do not tell her your secret – she is so indiscreet that she will tell everyone*; *The details of our plans were given to another company by an indiscreet secretary.* **2** not wise or cautious: *The chairman was asked to resign because of his indiscreet action*; *His love affair with his secretary was rather indiscreet.*
ˌindi'scretion [-'skreʃən] **1** *nu* the state of being indiscreet: *She is well-known for her indiscretion – don't tell her anything confidential.* **2** *nc* an indiscreet act: *He committed several indiscretions during his term of office.*

indiscriminate [indi'skriminət] *adj* (*formal*) making little or no distinction in value *etc* between one person, thing *etc* and another: *indiscriminate praise*; *There was indiscriminate killing of civilians and soldiers alike*; *The teacher's punishment of the children was totally indiscriminate – both the innocent and guilty were punished.*

indispensable [indi'spensəbl] *adj* (*formal*) necessary; that cannot be done without; not dispensable: *This book is quite indispensable*; *indispensable medical assistance.*

indisposed [indi'spouzd] *adj* (*formal*: *pred*) **1** (slightly) ill: *She apologized that she could not come as she was indisposed.*
'inˌdispo'sition *ncu* (*formal*): *She has a slight indisposition.*

indisputable [indi'spju:təbl] *adj* (*formal*) not able to be denied; certainly true: *indisputable facts*; *The evidence is indisputable.*

indistinct [indi'stiŋkt] *adj* not clear to a person's eye, ear or mind; not distinct: *an indistinct outline of a ship*; *His speech is rather indistinct.* **ˌindi'stinctly** *adv.* **ˌindi'stinctness** *nu.*

indistinguishable [indi'stiŋgwiʃəbl] *adj* (*formal*: *usu pred*) not able to be seen as different or separate; not distinguishable: *This copy is indistinguishable from the original.*
See also **undistinguished**.

individual [indi'vidjuəl] *adj* **1** (*attrib*) single; separate: *Put price labels on each individual item.* **2** (*attrib*) intended for, used by *etc* one person *etc*: *Customers in shops should be given individual attention.* **3** special to one person *etc*, showing or having special qualities: *He has a very individual style of painting*; *Her style of dress is very individual.* – *nc* **1** a single person, animal *etc* in contrast to the group to which it belongs: *the rights of the individual in society.* **2** (*inf*) a person: *He's an untidy individual.*
ˌindi'vidualist *nc* a person who shows great independence in thought, action *etc.* **ˌindi'vidualism** *nu.*
'indiˌvidu'ality [-'a-] *nu* the qualities that distinguish one person *etc* from others: *The individuality of his painting is very noticeable.*
ˌindi'vidually *adv* each separately: *I'll deal with each question individually.*

indivisible [indi'vizəbl] *adj* (*formal*) not able to be divided or separated. **'indiˌvisi'bility** *nu.*

Indo- [indou] (*in cmpds*) of India: *an ˌIndo-ˌChinese 'friendship pact.*

indoctrinate [in'doktrineit] *vt* (*formal*: *often derog*) to fill with a certain teaching or set of opinions, beliefs *etc*: *The dictator tried to indoctrinate schoolchildren with the ideals of his party.* **inˌdoctri'nation** *nu.*
See also **doctrine**.

indolent ['indələnt] *adj* (*formal*) lazy; avoiding work or exercise: *She was an indolent woman who spent her days sitting on a sofa eating chocolates*; *She is too indolent to look for a job.* **'indolence** *nu.*

indomitable [in'domitəbl] *adj* (*formal*) that cannot be overcome or defeated: *He was a man of indomitable courage*; *He is truly indomitable.*

Indonesia, Indonesian *see* Appendix 2.

indoor ['indo:] *adj* (*attrib*) used, done *etc* inside a building: *indoor games*; *an indoor swimming-pool.*
ˌin'doors *adv* in or into a building: *He stays indoors all winter*; *The child has gone indoors as it is too cold to play outside.*
See also **outdoor** *and* **out of doors** *under* **out**.

indubitably [in'dju:bitəbli] *adv* (*formal*) without doubt; certainly: *He is indubitably the best candidate for the job.* **in'dubitable** *adj.*

induce [in'dju:s] *vt* **1** to persuade or cause (a person to do something): *Nothing would induce me to visit that place again!* **2** to cause or bring about (a feeling *etc*): *a feeling of contentment induced by good food and wine.* **in'ducement** *ncu.*

induction [in'dʌkʃən] *ncu* (*formal*) the act or process of introducing (a person) into a new job *etc*: *He learned a great deal about building during his three-week induction into the firm*; (*attrib*) *an induction course.*

indulge [in'dʌldʒ] (*formal*) **1** *vt* to allow (a person) to do or have what he wishes: *You shouldn't indulge that child.* **2** *vt* to allow (a person) to follow (a wish, interest *etc*): *He indulged his love of foreign food by dining at an expensive Italian restaurant.* – *See also* **indulge in** *below.*
in'dulgence (*formal*) **1** *nu* the quality of allowing a person to do or have what they wish: *The judge was known for his indulgence to young offenders.* **2**

(*often facet*) *nc* something in which a person indulges: *Cigarettes are my only indulgence.*

in'dulgent *adj* willing to allow people to do or have what they wish (often to too great an extent): *an indulgent parent*; *She is too indulgent towards that child.*

in'dulge in *vt fus* to allow oneself to do (something) or to express (an emotion) not because one should but because one wishes to: *She indulged in a fit of temper*; *He tends to indulge in pessimism.*

industry ['indəstri] **1** *ncu* (any part of) the business of producing or making goods: *the ship-building industry*; *The government should invest more money in industry.* **2** *nu* (*formal*) hard work or effort: *He owed his success to both ability and industry.*

in'dustrial [-'dʌs-] *adj* having, concerning *etc* industries or the making of goods: *That area of the country is industrial rather than agricultural.*

in'dustrialist [-'dʌs-] *nc* a person who takes part in the running of a large industrial organization: *He is a wealthy industrialist.*

in'dustrialize, -ise [-'dʌs-] *adj* (of a country) having a large number of industries. **in,dustriali'zation, -s-** *nu.*

in'dustrious [-'dʌs-] *adj* (*more formal than* **hard-working**) busy and hard-working: *The truth has been discovered by an industrious researcher*; *The child is intelligent and industrious.*

industrial action *nu* strikes or other actions which are intended to slow down or stop production in a factory *etc*, *eg* in order to force the management to increase wages: *The leaders of the trade union said they were forced to take industrial action in order to get a fair wage for their men.*

industrial estate *nc* an area of a town *etc* set aside for (the building of) factories: *They are building a new electronics factory on the industrial estate.*

industrial relations *n sing or pl* the relationship between the management and the workers in a factory *etc*: *Industrial relations in this firm are very good – we hardly ever have strikes*; *Industrial relations is a subject that causes a lot of discussion.*

inebriated [i'ni:brieitid] *adj* (*formal or facet*) drunk: *The witness told the court that he had been slightly inebriated at the time*; *inebriated guests at the party.* **i,nebri'ation** *nu.*

inedible [in'edibl] *adj* (*formal*) not fit or suitable to be eaten; not edible: *The food was so awful it was inedible*; *completely inedible food.*

ineffective [ini'fektiv] *adj* (*formal*) (*usu* of courses of action *etc*) useless; not producing any result or the result desired; not effective: *ineffective methods*; *These methods are ineffective.* **,inef'fectiveness** *nu.*

ineffectual [ini'fektʃuəl] *adj* (*formal*) **1** not producing any result or the desired result: *His attempts to swim were quite ineffectual*; *ineffectual efforts to make her happy.* **2** (of a person) not confident or able to lead people; not able to get things done: *an ineffectual officer/teacher*; *He is too ineffectual ever to get a responsible job.* **,inef'fectualness** *nu.*

inefficient [ini'fiʃənt] *adj* not working or producing results *etc* in the best way and so wasting time, energy *etc*; not efficient: *These workmen are most inefficient*; *They use very inefficient machinery in that factory.* **,inef'ficiently** *adv.* **,inef'ficiency** *nu.*

inelegant [in'eligənt] *adj* (*formal*) not graceful; not elegant: *She was sprawled in a chair in a most inelegant fashion*; *She looks most inelegant in those clothes.* **in'elegantly** *adv.* **in'elegance** *nu.*

ineligible [in'elidʒəbl] *adj* (*formal*: *pred*) not eligible: *Children under eighteen years of age are ineligible to vote in elections.* **in,eligi'bility** *nu.*

inept [i'nept] *adj* (*formal*) foolish; said, done *etc* at the wrong time, in the wrong way, in the wrong place *etc*: *inept remarks/behaviour*; *His behaviour at the funeral was very inept.* **i'neptitude** *nu.*

inequality [ini'kwoləti] *ncu* (a case of) the existence of differences in size, value *etc* between two or more objects *etc*: *There is always some inequality between a manager's salary and a workman's wages*; *inequality of opportunity.*

See also **unequal**.

inert [i'nə:t] *adj* (*formal*) **1** without the power to move: *A stone is inert*; *inert objects.* **2** (of people) not wanting to move, act or think: *She is completely inert and likes to sit in a chair reading books all day*; *lazy, inert people.* **i'nertness** *nu.*

i'nertia [-ʃiə] *nu* the tendency of people, things *etc* to remain in the state, position *etc* they are in and not to change: *It was difficult to overcome the inertia of the heavy roller and start it moving.*

inescapable [ini'skeipəbl] *adj* (*formal*) that cannot be avoided: *The unfortunate but inescapable conclusion is that he is a liar*; *That result is quite inescapable.*

See also **escape**.

inessential [inə'senʃəl] *nc*, *adj* (*formal*) (of) something which is not essential: *We have no money for inessentials*; *inessential luxuries.*

inestimable [in'estiməbl] *adj* (*formal*) too great or of too great value to be estimated: *inestimable kindness*; *Our debt to him is inestimable.* **in'estimably** *adv.*

inevitable [in'evitəbl] *adj* that cannot be avoided; certain to happen, be done, said, used *etc*: *The Prime Minister said that war was inevitable*; *The Prime Minister's speech was accompanied by the inevitable jokes about members of other parties.*

in,evita'bility *nu*: *the inevitability of death.*

in'evitably *adv*: *Inevitably the train was late.*

inexact [inig'zakt] *adj* (*formal*) not quite correct, exact or true: *The figures my colleague gave you last week were inexact*; *a rather inexact description of what happened.* **,inex'actness** *nu.*

inexcusable [inik'skju:zəbl] *adj* too bad *etc* to be excused or justified; not excusable: *Her behaviour was inexcusable*; *inexcusable rudeness.* **,inex'cusably** *adv.*

inexhaustible [inig'zo:stəbl] *adj* very large; not likely to be used up: *He seems to have an inexhaustible supply of bad jokes*; *Her energy seems inexhaustible.* **,inex'haustibly** *adv.* **'inex,hausti'bility** *nu.*

inexorable [in'eksərəbl] *adj* (*formal*: *usu attrib*) not yielding or able to be persuaded: *The inexorable process of ageing.*

in'exorably *adv* (*formal*): *The day of the examination drew inexorably nearer.*

inexpensive [inik'spensiv] *adj* (*more formal than* **cheap**) not costly; not expensive: *It is so difficult to find good, inexpensive clothes in the shops*; *Those shoes seem very inexpensive.* **,inex'pensively** *adv.*

inexperience [inik'spiəriəns] *nu* lack of experience or skilled knowledge: *He seems good at the job in spite of his youth and inexperience.*

,inex'perienced *adj* lacking knowledge, skill and experience: *Inexperienced climbers should not at-*

tempt to climb high mountains during winter; The new teacher is too inexperienced to cope with the older children.

inexpert [in'ekspəːt] *adj* (*formal*) unskilled or clumsy; not expert: *She laughed at my inexpert attempts at dressmaking; I am hopelessly inexpert at baking.* **in'expertly** *adv.*

inexplicable [inik'splikəbl] *adj* (*formal*) impossible to explain or understand: *His inexplicable absence worried all of us; His sudden illness was inexplicable.*

ˌinex'plicably *adv* in a way impossible to explain: *She felt inexplicably uneasy, although everything appeared to be going well.*

inexplicit [inik'splisit] *adj* (*formal*) not clearly and exactly stated; not explicit: *The instructions for using the machine were rather inexplicit.*

inexpressible [inik'spresəbl] *adj* (*formal*: *usu attrib*) that cannot be expressed or described: *inexpressible delight.* **ˌinex'pressibly** *adv.*

inextricably [inik'strikəbli] *adv* (*formal*: *esp fig*) in such a manner or to such a degree as to be unable to be freed: *Her skirt was inextricably caught up in the brambles;* (*fig*) *He is inextricably involved in an unhappy love affair.* **ˌinex'tricable** *adj.*
See also **extricate**.

infallible [in'faləbl] *adj* **1** (of a person or his judgement *etc*) never making a mistake: not fallible: *You should take his advice – his judgement is infallible; He is an infallible authority on Shakespeare.* **2** (of a remedy *etc*) always successful: *To cure a cold, drink a glass of hot whisky before bedtime – it's infallible; infallible cures.* **inˌfalli'bility** *nu.* **in'fallibly** *adv.*
See also **fail, unfailing**.

infamous ['infəməs] *adj* (*formal*) having a bad reputation: *the infamous Dr Goebbels; He is infamous for his dishonesty and laziness.*

'infamy *nu* (*formal*) **1** bad reputation: *His infamy had spread through the country.* **2** shame or disgrace: *the infamy of defeat.*
See also **fame, famous**.

infant ['infənt] *nc* (*sometimes formal*) a baby or very young child: *the service for the baptism of infants; She is trained to look after infants;* (*attrib*) *An infant school takes children up to the age of 7;* (*attrib*) *Infant mortality means the death of children under a year old.*

'infancy *nu* the state or time of being a baby: *They had two children who died in infancy;* (*fig*) *This research is still in its infancy.*

infanticide [in'fantisaid] **1** *nu* the murder of a child: *The mother pleaded guilty to the charge of infanticide.* **2** *nc* (*formal*) a person who murders a child.

'infantile [-tail] *adj* **1** (*formal*) of babies: *infantile diseases.* **2** (*derog*) very childish: *I'm tired of that man's infantile behaviour!; His attitude is infantile.*

infantile paralysis *nu* (*esp old*) polio.

infantry ['infəntri] *nc or n pl* (the part of an army consisting of) foot-soldiers: *The infantry was/were sent on ahead, with the artillery following in the rear.*

infatuated [in'fatjueitid] *adj* (*derog*: *usu pred with* **with**) having foolish and unreasoning love (for): *He is infatuated with her, and doesn't see her faults.*

inˌfatu'ation *ncu* (*derog*) (a) state of being infatuated: *She developed an infatuation for him; Infatuation usually does not last long.*

infect [in'fekt] *vt* **1** to fill with germs that cause disease; to give a disease to: *You must wash that cut on your knee in case it becomes infected; She had a bad cold last week and must have infected me* (*with it*). **2** to pass on or spread (a feeling *etc*) to: *Her enthusiasm infected us all.*

in'fection [-ʃən] **1** *nu* the process of infecting or state of being infected: *You should wash your hands after handling raw meat to avoid infection; A person in a weak state is liable to infection.* **2** *nc* a disease: *He caught an infection from the swimming-pool; His throat infection is getting worse.*

in'fectious [-ʃəs] *adj* (of a disease or an emotion) likely to spread to others: *Is his cough infectious?; Measles is an infectious disease; infectious laughter; Her happiness was infectious.* **in'fectiously** *adv.*

infer [in'fəː] – *pt, ptp* **in'ferred** – *vt* **1** (*formal*) to form an opinion or judge (from facts or reasoning): *I inferred from your silence that you were angry.* **2** (*loosely*) to imply: *Are you inferring that I tell lies?*

inference ['infərəns] (*formal*) **1** *nu* the act of inferring: *You seemed to know about this book, and by inference I thought you had read it.* **2** *nc* something that is inferred: *What inference are we to draw from her absence?*

inferior [in'fiəriə] *adj* (*sometimes with* **to** *when pred*) **1** of poor, or poorer, quality *etc*: *Her brother's successes made her feel* (*very*) *inferior* (*to him*)*; This carpet is inferior to that; a rather inferior bit of work.* **2** (*formal*) lower in rank: *Is a colonel inferior to a brigadier?* – *nc* someone who is inferior: *We no longer speak of those in a lower social class as inferiors.*

inˌferi'ority [-'o-] *nu*: *The inferiority of the cheap furniture was obvious.*

inˌferi'ority complex *nc* a constant feeling that one is not as good as others in some way: *She had an inferiority complex about her appearance.*
See also **superior**.

infernal [in'fəːnl] *adj* (*attrib*) **1** (*inf*) damned: *Who let that infernal dog in?; She is an infernal nuisance.* **2** (*liter*) of hell: *the infernal regions.*

in'fernally *adv* (*inf*) extremely; very: *He is infernally clever; That job was infernally difficult.*

in'ferno [-nou] – *pl* **in'fernos** – *nc* (*formal*) a place full of horror and confusion, *esp* because of fire: *The house was a blazing inferno.*

infertile [in'fəːtail] *adj* **1** (of soil *etc*) not fertile or producing good crops: *The land was stony and infertile; infertile ground.* **2** (of persons or animals) unable to have young: *An attack of mumps had made him infertile; Infertile women often adopt children.*

ˌinfer'tility [-'ti-] *nu*: *The doctor is trying to cure her infertility;* (*attrib*) *an infertility clinic.*

infest [in'fest] *vt* (*formal*) (of something bad) to swarm over and cover or fill: *The dog was infested with fleas.*

ˌinfe'station [infe-] *nu*: *an infestation of mice.*

infidelity [infi'deləti] *ncu* (*formal*) (an act of) disloyalty or unfaithfulness (*eg* to a marriage partner); lack of fidelity: *Her husband's infidelity towards her was well-known; She forgave his occasional infidelities.*

in-fighting ['infaitiŋ] *nu* rivalry or quarrelling among members of the same group: *The organization was weakened by constant in-fighting.*

infiltrate ['infiltreit, (*Amer*) in'filtreit] *vti* **1** (of soldiers) to get through the enemy lines a few at a time: *Some troops managed to infiltrate* (*into*) *enemy territory.* **2** (of a group of persons) to enter (an organization) gradually and *usu* secretly in numbers large enough to influence its decisions: *Men who want to destroy the government are gradually infiltrating the trade unions.* **ˌinfil'tration** *nu.*

infinite ['infinit] *adj* 1 without end or limits; not finite: *We believe that space is infinite; infinite space.* 2 (*loosely*) immeasurable; very great: *Infinite damage could be caused by such a mistake; The scope for improvement is infinite.*

'infinitely *adv* (*often inf*) extremely; to a very great degree: *an infinitely boring book; He is infinitely kinder than she is; The time at which our sun will finally cease to burn is infinitely far away.*

'infiniteness *nu.*

ˌinfini'tesimal [-'tesiməl] *adj* (*formal or facet*) infinitely or extremely small: *The amount of inconvenience this plan will cause is infinitesimal compared with the good it will do; infinitesimal differences.* **ˌinfini'tesimally** *adv.*

in'finity [-'fi-] *nu* 1 space, time or quantity that is without limit, or is immeasurably great or small: *The night sky seemed to stretch away to infinity.* 2 (*math*: often represented by the symbol ∞) an indefinitely large number, quantity or distance: *Parallel lines meet at infinity.*

infinitive [in'finətiv] *ncu* (*gram*) the part of the verb used in English with or without *to*, that expresses an action but has no subject: *The sentence 'You need not stay if you want to go' contains two infinitives, stay and go.*

infinity *see* **infinite**.

infirm [in'fə:m] *adj* (*formal*) (of a person) weak or ill: *We should do more to help elderly and infirm people; She is too infirm to live alone.*

in'firmary *nc* a name given to some hospitals: *The Royal Infirmary is one of the city's bigger hospitals.*

in'firmity *ncu* (*formal*) (something which causes) weakness or illness: *Old age usually brings infirmity; He suffered from an infirmity which prevented him travelling.*

inflame [in'fleim] *vt* (*often formal or liter*) to cause (feelings *etc*) to become violent: *The manager's words inflamed (the anger of) the men even more.*

in'flamed *adj* hot and red *esp* because of infection: *Her throat was very inflamed when she was ill; His face became inflamed with anger.*

inflammable [in'flaməbl] *adj* easily set on fire: *Paper is highly inflammable; It is dangerous to make children's clothes out of inflammable materials;* (*fig*) *An inflammable situation is developing in the pay dispute.* **inˌflamma'bility** *nu.*

inflammation [inflə'meiʃən] *ncu* (a place in the body where there is) development of heat with pain, redness and swelling: *Inflammation of the tonsils is called tonsillitis; He has had an inflammation in the knee joint.*

in'flammatory *adj* (*derog*) likely to inflame angry feelings: *inflammatory speeches; The manager's remarks to the workers were inflammatory.*

See also **flammable, non-inflammable**.

inflate [in'fleit] *vti* (*formal*) to blow up or expand (*esp* a balloon, tyre or lungs with air): *He used a bicycle pump to inflate the ball;* (*fig*) *Her recent success will inflate her sense of her own importance.*

in'flatable *adj* (of *eg* a cushion, ball *etc*) that can be filled with air for use: *an inflatable beach ball; Is that rubber boat inflatable?*

in'flation *nu* 1 (*formal*) the process of inflating or being inflated: *The inflation of the air-bed took several minutes.* 2 a situation in a country's economy where prices and wages keep forcing each other to increase: *Inflation usually affects many countries at the same time.*

in'flationary *adj* (*formal*) of, or causing, inflation in the economy: *The government avoided taking inflationary action; Any increase in salaries at this time would be considered inflationary.*

inflect [in'flekt] *vt* (*formal*) to vary the pitch or tone of (the voice): *Try to inflect your voice more – it sounds very dull.*

in'flected *adj* (*neg* **un-**: *gram*) (of a language) changing the endings or forms of words to show their grammatical relations: *Chinese is not an inflected language.*

in'flection, in'flexion [-ʃən] 1 *ncu* (an act of) inflecting: *There was a strange inflection in her voice as she spoke; Correct inflection of the voice is essential in speaking Chinese.* 2 *nc* a change in the ending or form of a word to show its grammatical function: *She found it a difficult language to learn because of its many inflections.*

inflexible [in'fleksəbl] *adj* 1 (of a person or a personal quality) never yielding or giving way: *They pleaded with him to change his mind, but he was inflexible; The father's inflexible will dominated the family.* 2 (*formal*) not able to bend: *If we do not take plenty of exercise, our joints become stiff and inflexible; tough, inflexible substances.* **in'flexibly** *adv.* **inˌflexi'bility** *nu.*

See also **flexible**.

inflexion *see* **inflection** *under* **inflect**.

inflict [in'flikt] *vt* (*with* **on**: *formal or facet*) to give or impose (something unpleasant and unwanted): *He inflicted a heavy blow on the back of her head; Was it necessary to inflict such a punishment on him?; She is always inflicting her company on me.*

in'fliction [-ʃən] *ncu.*

influence ['influəns] 1 *nu* the power to affect people, actions or events, *esp* by using one's personality or position of importance: *It was through his influence that she became interested in sociology; He used his influence to get her the job; She won't obey me – I have no influence over her; I believe she has some influence with the headmaster – she might persuade him; He should not have driven the car while under the influence of alcohol.* 2 *nc* a person or thing that has this power: *His mother was the strongest influence in his early life; She is a bad influence on him.* – *vt* to have an effect on: *The weather seems to influence her moods; Try not to be influenced by what he says; He influenced my decision to leave.*

ˌinflu'ential [-'enʃəl] *adj* 1 having much influence: *an influential person; He is now in quite an influential job; Mr Smith is head of that department and is very influential.* 2 (*pred with* **in**) playing an important part in: *He was influential in getting the plan accepted.* **ˌinflu'entially** *adv.*

influenza [influ'enzə] (*usu abbrev* **flu** *or* **'flu** [flu:]) *nu* a type of infectious illness *usu* causing headache, fever, a cold *etc*: *Influenza is common during the winter months;* (*attrib*) *a flu epidemic.*

influx ['inflʌks] *nc* (*formal*) a coming in or arrival (of something) in great quantities or numbers: *We are to have yet another influx of visitors next week.*

inform [in'fo:m] 1 *vt* (*esp formal*) to tell; to give knowledge to: *Please inform me of your intentions in this matter; I was informed that you were absent from the office.* 2 *vi* (*formal*: *with* **against** *or* **on**) to tell facts to *eg* the police about (a criminal *etc*):

He informed against his fellow thieves.
in'formant *nc* (*formal*) someone who tells or informs: *My informant tells me that a statement will be made tomorrow.*
ˌinfor'mation *nu* facts told or knowledge gained or given: *Can you give me any information about this writer?*; *My information is that the train will be late*; *What is the latest information on the progress of the war?*; *He is full of interesting bits of information*; (*attrib*) *You can get a timetable at the information desk*; (*attrib*) *Ask at the tourist information office.*
in'formative [-mətiv] *adj* giving useful or interesting information: *an informative book/speaker*; *His account of the war was most informative.*
in'formed *adj* (*formal*: *usu attrib*) having or showing knowledge: *He would be able to give you an informed opinion on any legal matter.*
in'former *nc* (*often derog*) a person who informs against a criminal *etc*: *The police informer was found murdered.*
informal [in'foːml] *adj* **1** not formal or official; friendly and relaxed: *The two prime ministers will meet for informal discussions today*; *We are having an informal dance tonight*; *Will the party be formal or informal?*; *Her office had a pleasant, informal atmosphere*; *friendly, informal manners.* **2** (of speech or vocabulary) used in conversation but not *usu* when writing formally, speaking in public *etc*: *'Won't' and 'can't' are informal forms of 'will not' and 'cannot'.*
ˌinfor'mality [-'ma-] *nu*: *We appreciated the informality of the occasion.*
in'formally *adv*: *She was informally dressed although she was a guest at a formal ball.*
infra- [infrə] (*in cmpds*) below or beneath, as in **infra-red**.
infra-red [infrə'red] *adj* (*attrib*) (of rays) below the red end of the spectrum: *Infra-red rays have a heating effect and can be used in cooking.*
infrequent [in'friːkwənt] *adj* not frequent: *His visits became more and more infrequent*; *On his infrequent visits to his children he usually managed to upset them.* **in'frequency** *nu.*
infringe [in'frindʒ] *vt* (*formal*) to break (a law *etc*) or interfere with (a person's freedom or rights): *You have infringed the regulations by parking here!*
in'fringement *ncu* (*formal*) (an act of) infringing: *Infringement of this regulation may lead to prosecution*; *Keeping such records is an infringement of personal liberty.*
infuriate [in'fjuərieit] *vt* (*formal*) to make very angry: *I was infuriated by his words*; *You have infuriated him by being late.*
in'furiating *adj* likely to cause great anger: *his infuriating behaviour*; *I find his silly jokes infuriating.* **in'furiatingly** *adv.*
infuse [in'fjuːz] (*formal*) **1** *vt* to put (a quality *etc*) into (a person *etc*): *We must infuse some enthusiasm into the team*; *He was infused with the spirit of adventure.* **2** *vti* to (cause herbs *etc* to) soak in hot water *etc*; to prepare (tea or other hot liquid) or be prepared in this way: *She infused the herbs*; *The tea is still infusing*; *I'll infuse the tea while you make the toast.* **in'fusion** [-ʒən] *ncu.*
ingenious [in'dʒiːnjəs] *adj* (*more formal than* **clever**) **1** (of a person or his personality *etc*) clever at inventing: *He was ingenious at making up new games for the children*; *an ingenious liar.* **2** (of an object or idea) cleverly made or thought out: *an ingenious plan/machine/lie*; *That plan is the most ingenious that the government have ever thought of.*
in'geniously *adv.* **in'geniousness, ingenuity** [indʒə'njuəti] *nus.*
ingenuous [in'dʒenjuəs] *adj* (*formal*: *sometimes derog*) frank, trusting and lacking cunning or deceitfulness: *Her face had a sweet, ingenuous expression*; *I might have believed him if I were still young and ingenuous*; *It was rather ingenuous of you to believe such a liar.* **in'genuously** *adv.* **in'genuousness** *nu* (*formal*).
inglorious [in'gloːriəs] *adj* (*formal*: *often liter*) **1** humble or ordinary: *From his inglorious beginnings he rose to be the greatest actor of the century.* **2** shameful: *He met an inglorious death in a drunken street-fight*; *His last defeat was the most inglorious.*
in'gloriously *adv.*
See also **glorious**.
ingot ['iŋgət] *nc* (*tech*) a mass of metal (*eg* gold or silver) cast in a mould: *The gold was transported as ingots.*
ingrained [in'greind] *adj* fixed firmly: *ingrained selfishness*; *Caution was ingrained in his character*; *It is difficult to get this child clean – the dirt is ingrained in him*; *ingrained stains.*
ingratiate [in'greiʃieit] *v refl* (*formal derog*) to get (oneself) liked or approved of (by a person): *He tried to ingratiate himself with the manager.*
ingratitude [in'gratitjuːd] *nu* lack of gratitude or thankfulness: *I felt hurt by his ingratitude.*
See also **ungrateful**.
ingredient [in'griːdiənt] *nc* one of the things that goes into a mixture: *Could you give me a list of the ingredients of the cake?*; (*fig*) *Sympathy and understanding are two basic ingredients of a happy marriage.*
inhabit [in'habit] *vt* (*formal*: not *usu* used with **is, was** *etc* and **-ing**) (of people, animals *etc*) to live in (a region *etc*): *Polar bears inhabit the Arctic region*; *That house is now inhabited by a Polish family.*
in'habitable *adj* (*neg* **un-**) fit to be lived in: *The area was no longer inhabitable.*
in'habitant *nc* a person or animal that lives permanently in a place: *the inhabitants of the village*; *tigers, leopards and other inhabitants of the jungle.*
See also **habitable**.
inhale [in'heil] *vti* (*usu formal*) to breathe in: *He inhaled deeply*; *It is very unpleasant to have to inhale the smoke from other people's cigarettes.*
inhalation [in(h)ə'leiʃən] *ncu.*
in'haler *nc* **1** (*med*) a *usu* small apparatus by means of which people inhale certain medicines. **2** (*formal*) a person who inhales.
inherent [in'hiərənt] *adj* (*with* **in** *when pred*: *formal*) (of a quality *etc*) belonging naturally (to a person or thing): *Her inherent dignity was admired by all*; *The instinct for survival is inherent in everyone.*
in'herently *adv* (*formal*) basically; having a certain quality *etc* in one's nature: *He may be mischievous but he is not inherently wicked.*
inherit [in'herit] **1** *vti* to receive (property *etc* belonging to someone who has died): *He inherited the house from his father*; *She inherited four thousand pounds from her father*; (*fig*) *She inherited all her predecessor's problems when she started this job.* **2** *vt* (not used with **is, was** *etc* and **-ing**) to have the same qualities as one's parents *etc*: *She inherits her quick temper from her mother*; *She inherits her good teeth from her mother.*

in'heritance 1 *nc* something inherited: *He spent most of his inheritance on drink.* 2 *nu* (*formal*) the act of inheriting: *Quite a lot of money came to him by inheritance.*
See also **heir, heritage**.

inhibit [in'hibit] *vt* (*formal*) to stop or hinder (*eg* someone from doing something): *She was inhibited from taking the decision to emigrate by the thought of her mother's loneliness*; *The size of the audience inhibited her and she did not sing very well.*
in'hibited *adj* unable to relax and express one's feelings in an open and natural way: *She was a bit inhibited about speaking in public*; *Very inhibited people do not usually enjoy parties.*
inhibition [ini'biʃən] 1 *nc* a feeling that hinders one from doing something: *She had no inhibitions about walking down the street in a swimsuit.* 2 *nu* (*formal*) the act of inhibiting: *Inhibition of a child's natural impulses can lead to problems.*
See also **uninhibited**.

inhospitable [inhə'spitəbl] *adj* not welcoming guests; not friendly towards strangers; not hospitable: (*fig*) *Greenland is a bleak and inhospitable country*; *She could not refuse to invite them in without seeming inhospitable.*

inhuman [in'hjuːmən] *adj* extremely cruel or brutal; not seeming to be human: *He was horrified by their inhuman cruelty*; *His treatment of his children was inhuman.*
ˌinhu'manity [-'ma-] *nu* cruelty or lack of pity: *They were shocked by his inhumanity in refusing to visit her before she died.*
See also **human, humane**.

inhumane [inhju'mein] *adj* unkind or cruel; not humane: *They were accused of inhumane treatment of prisoners*; *It is inhumane to keep that dog alive – it is old and blind.* **ˌinhu'manely** *adv*.

inimical [i'nimikəl] *adj* (*very formal*: *pred*) (of conditions *etc*) hostile or not favourable: *The soil conditions here are inimical to the growth of raspberries.*

inimitable [i'nimitəbl] *adj* (*formal*: *usu attrib*) (of a quality *etc*) belonging only to one person and impossible to imitate: *The book is written in his inimitable style.* **i'nimitably** *adv*.

iniquitous [i'nikwətəs] *adj* (*formal*) extremely wicked and unjust: *Imprisoning debtors was an iniquitous practice.*
i'niquity *ncu* (*old formal or facet*) (an act of) wickedness: *It would be an act of iniquity to burn that old chair – it's a genuine antique*; *She forgave her son's iniquities.*

initial [i'niʃəl] *adj* (*formal*: *attrib*) of, or at, the beginning: *There were difficulties during the initial stages of building the house.* – *nc* the letter that begins a word, *esp* a name: *The picture was signed with the initials JJB, standing for John James Brown*; *I know his surname but I don't know his initials.* – *v* – *pt, ptp* **i'nitialled** – *vt* to mark or sign with the initials of one's name: *Any alteration on a cheque should be initialled.*
i'nitially *adv* (*formal*) at the beginning; at first: *Initially, she was unwilling to go, but she changed her mind and went*; *This project will cost a lot of money initially but will eventually make a great deal of profit.*
i'nitiate[1] [-ʃieit] *vt* (*formal*) 1 to start (*eg* a plan, scheme, changes, reforms *etc*): *He initiated a scheme for helping old people with their shopping and housework.* 2 to take (a person) into a society *etc*, *esp* with secret ceremonies: *No-one who had been initiated into the society ever revealed the details of the ceremony*; *On her first day at the office, she was initiated into their methods of working.*
i'nitiate[2] [-ʃiət] *nc* (*formal*) a person who has been initiated (into a society *etc*): *Each year there are more initiates into black magic societies.*
iˌniti'ation [-ʃi'ei-] *nu* (*formal*) the act of initiating or process of being initiated: *She was responsible for the initiation of the reforms*; *the initiation of Red Indian braves*; (*attrib*) *an initiation ceremony.*
i'nitiative [-ʃətiv] 1 *nc* a first step or move that leads the way: *Acting on his initiative, they reported the matter to the police*; *He took the initiative in organizing a search party to look for the girl*; *A move to start peace talks is sometimes called a peace initiative.* 2 *nu* the ability to lead or make decisions for oneself: *He is quite good at his job, but lacks initiative*; *She hasn't the initiative to start such a project*; *My son actually went to the hairdresser's on his own initiative without being dragged there!*
See also **uninitiated**.

inject [in'dʒekt] *vt* to force (a liquid *etc*) into the body of (a person) by means of a needle and syringe: *The doctor injected the sedative into her arm*; *He has to be injected twice daily with an antibiotic*; (*fig*) *I wish I could inject some life into this class!*
in'jection [-ʃən] *ncu* (an act of) injecting or process of being injected: *One method of giving a patient medicine is by injection*; *She should have daily injections of penicillin.*

injudicious [indʒu'diʃəs] *adj* (*formal*) unwise; not judicious: *That was a rather injudicious remark to make*; *It was somewhat injudicious to give up your job without first finding another one.*

injunction [in'dʒʌŋkʃən] *nc* (*legal or formal*) an order forbidding an action or commanding that something should be done: *A court injunction has been issued preventing him from taking the child from its mother.*

injure ['indʒə] *vt* to harm or damage: *He injured his arm when he fell*; *They were not badly injured when the car crashed*; (*fig*) *A story like that could injure his reputation*; (*fig*) *He is not really upset that she refused his proposal of marriage but his pride has been injured.*
'injured *adj* wounded or harmed: *The injured people were all taken to hospital after the accident*; (*fig*) *injured pride/feelings*; (*fig*) *'Why didn't you tell me before?' he said in an injured voice.*
injurious [in'dʒuəriəs] *adj* (*formal*: *usu pred with* **to**) harmful: *Smoking is injurious to one's health*; *Marriage to such a woman will be injurious to his career.*
'injury *ncu* (an instance of) harm or damage: *Badly designed chairs can cause injury to the spine*; *The motor cyclist sustained* (= received) *severe injuries in the crash*; *The injury to his head proved fatal – he died yesterday.*
do (someone) an injury (*often inf or facet*) to hurt or harm (someone): *You could do yourself an injury trying to lift that box!*

injustice [in'dʒʌstis] *ncu* (an act of) unfairness or the lack of justice: *He complained of injustice in the way he had been treated*; *They agreed that an injustice had been committed*; *You must try to forget past injustices.*
do (someone) an injustice (*formal*) to treat (someone) unfairly and without justice: *You do me an injustice if you think I could tell such a lie.*
See also **unjust**.

ink [iŋk] *nu* a black or coloured liquid used in writing, printing *etc*: *Please sign your name in ink rather than pencil*; *You have spilt red ink all over my dress.*

'inky *adj* **1** covered with ink: *inky fingers*; *Don't touch that wall – your hands are inky.* **2** (*formal or liter*: *usu attrib*) like ink; black or very dark: *the inky darkness of the night.*

'inkpot, 'inkwell *ncs* a small pot or container for ink.

inkling ['iŋkliŋ] *nc* (*usu with neg*) a slight idea or suspicion held or given (about something that is happening): *I had no inkling of what was going on until she told me all about it.*

inky *see* **ink**.

inlaid *see* **inlay**.

inland ['inlənd] *adj* (*attrib*) **1** not beside the sea: *inland areas.* **2** done *etc* inside a country: *inland trade.* – [in'land] *adv* in, or towards, the parts of the land away from the sea: *They travelled inland for several miles*; *These flowers grow better inland.*

the Inland Revenue (*Brit*) the Government department concerned with the collecting of money within the country from taxes, excise *etc*: *We should be quite rich if the Inland Revenue did not take so much of our money in taxation.*

inlay ['inlei] *ncu* material set into the surface of *eg* a table to form a design: *The top of the table had an elaborate inlay of ivory.*

ˌin'laid *adj* decorated in this way: *an inlaid table*; *The box is beautifully inlaid.*

inlet ['inlit] *nc* a small bay in the coastline of a sea, lake *etc*: *There are several pretty inlets suitable for bathing.*

inmate ['inmeit] *nc* one of the people living in an institution, *esp* a prison or mental hospital: *He had been an inmate of the mental hospital for twelve years.*

inmost *see* **innermost** *under* **inner**.

inn [in] *nc* **1** a name given to some small hotels or public houses *esp* in villages or the countryside: *We didn't stay at a large hotel – we stayed at a charming country inn*; *We had a drink at the Downberry Inn.* **2** (*arch*) a house providing food and lodging for travellers.

'innkeeper *nc* a person who owned or ran an inn (*def 2*).

innate [i'neit] *adj* (*formal*: *attrib*) (of a quality *etc*) belonging to a person as part of his nature: *his innate gentleness.* **in'nately** *adv.*

inner ['inə] *adj* (*attrib*) **1** placed *etc* on the inside or further in: *The inner tube of his tyre was punctured.* **2** (*formal*) (of feelings *etc*) secret or hidden: *I could not guess what his inner thoughts might be.*

'innermost *adj* (*attrib*: *often liter*) **1** placed *etc* furthest from the edge or outside: *the innermost parts of the castle.* **2** (*also* **inmost**) most secret or hidden: *his innermost feelings*; *in the inmost corners of his heart.*

innings ['iniŋz] – *pl* **'innings** – *nc* **1** in a game of cricket, a team's turn at batting: *At the end of their second innings, the West Indian team was 279 runs ahead.* **2** (*fig*) a period during which a person has something, *esp* the chance to act: *The members of this government have had their innings and should make way for younger politicians*; *He had a good innings before they discovered his inefficiency and dismissed him.*

'inning *nc* in a game of baseball, any of the nine periods in which each team bats.

innocent ['inəsnt] *adj* **1** not guilty (of a crime, misdeed *etc*): *A man should be presumed innocent of a crime until he is proved guilty*; *They have hanged an innocent man – they have now found the real murderer.* **2** (of an action *etc*) harmless or without harmful or hidden intentions: *innocent games and amusements*; *an innocent remark*; *His remarks seemed innocent but he was really trying to cause trouble.* **3** free from, or knowing nothing about, evil *etc*: *an innocent child*; *You can't be so innocent as to believe what advertisements say! – See also* **innocent of** *below.* **'innocently** *adv.*

'innocence *nu* the quality of being innocent: *He at last managed to prove his innocence*; *She had the innocence of a child.*

in all innocence without harmful or hidden intentions: *I told her in all innocence that I admired him, not knowing that she hated him/that he was her brother.*

'innocent of 1 *see* **innocent** (*def 1*). **2** (*formal*) not having; lacking: *Her face was innocent of make-up.*

innocuous [i'nokjuəs] *adj* (*formal*) harmless: *This drug was at first thought to be innocuous*; *The children are afraid of that innocuous old lady because she is ugly and fierce-looking.*

innovation [inə'veiʃən] *ncu* (the act of making) a change or a new arrangement *etc*: *He hates innovation – he likes everything to remain the same*; *The new system for giving out the wages was a welcome innovation*; *Innovations in factories often cause industrial trouble.*

'innovative [-tiv] *adj.* **'innovator** *nc.*

innuendo [inju'endou] – *pl* **ˌinnu'endoes** – *nc* (*formal*) (a remark containing) a (hidden) insult or disagreeable suggestion: *I'm sure he thinks I stole the money – he kept making innuendoes about my 'new-found wealth'.*

innumerable [i'nju:mərəbl] *adj* (*formal*: *esp attrib*) too many to be counted; a great many: *innumerable difficulties.*

innumerate [i'nju:mərət] *adj* (*formal*) not having a basic understanding of mathematics and science; not numerate: *I am not exactly innumerate – but I am not very good at counting*; *She is not illiterate but she is innumerate*; *innumerate children.*

inoculate [i'nokjuleit] *vt* to give (a person *etc*) a mild form of a disease, *usu* by injecting germs into his body, so as to prevent him from catching a more serious form: *Has he been inoculated against diphtheria?*

iˌnocu'lation *ncu*: *As a result of widespread inoculation many diseases are now rare*; *How many inoculations will the baby need?*

inoffensive [inə'fensiv] *adj* harmless; not likely to offend: *an inoffensive remark*; *He seems a very inoffensive young man but I don't like him*; *His comments seemed inoffensive.*

inoperable [in'opərəbl] *adj* (*tech*) not suitable for a surgical operation: *an inoperable cancer*; *The cancer was diagnosed so late that it is now inoperable.*

inoperative [in'opərətiv] *adj* (*formal*) not operative (*def 2*).

inopportune [in'opətju:n] *adj* (*formal*) not suitable; not convenient or opportune: *He called at a rather inopportune moment*; *My arrival was rather inopportune – they were having dinner.*

inordinate [i'no:dinət] *adj* (*formal*) unreasonably great: *He makes inordinate demands on my time*; *I consider your demands inordinate.*

i'nordinately *adv* (*formal*) extremely: *He is inordinately proud of her.*

inorganic [ino:'ganik] *adj* (*tech*) not having the

special characteristics of living bodies; not organic: *Stone, metal and other minerals are inorganic (substances).*

in-patient ['inpeiʃənt] *nc* a patient living in, as well as receiving treatment in, a hospital: *At first she was attending the out-patients department of the local hospital but she is now an in-patient in the Royal Infirmary.*

input ['input] *nu* **1** something, *eg* an amount of electrical energy, that is supplied to a machine *etc.* **2** information put into a computer for processing.

inquest ['inkwest] *nc* a legal inquiry into a case of sudden and unexpected death: *When the apparently healthy baby died while asleep there had to be an inquest.*

inquire, enquire [in'kwaiə] (*more formal than* **ask**) **1** *vt* to ask: *He inquired the way to the art gallery; She inquired what time the bus left; He inquired whether she was warm enough.* **2** *vi* (*with* **about**) to ask for information about (something): *They inquired about trains to London.* **3** *vi* (*with* **after**) to ask for information about the state of (*eg* a person's health): *He inquired after her mother.* **4** *vi* (*with* **for**) to ask to see or talk to (a person): *Someone rang up inquiring for you, but you were out.* **5** *vi* (*with* **for**) to ask for (goods in a shop *etc*): *Several people have been inquiring for the new catalogue.* **6** *vi* (*with* **into**) to try to discover the facts of: *The police are inquiring into the matter.*

in'quirer *nc* (*formal or liter*) a person who inquires: *All inquirers were told that he was taking a week's holiday.*

in'quiring *adj* (*attrib*) (*eg* of a person's mind) showing eagerness to find out or learn: *Any child with an inquiring mind enjoys a visit to a museum.*

in'quiringly *adv* (*formal*) as if asking a question: *He looked up inquiringly as I called his name.*

in'quiry [*Amer also* 'inkwəri], **en'quiry** [*Amer also* 'enkwəri] (*slightly formal*) **1** *ncu* (an act of) asking or investigating: *His inquiries finally led him to her hotel; After a lot of searching and inquiry, he discovered the hotel;* (*attrib*) *All questions will be dealt with at the inquiry desk.* **2** *nc* a question: *My inquiry remained unanswered.* **3** *nc* an investigation: *An inquiry is being held into her disappearance.*

make inquiries to ask for information: *I shall make inquiries about the air fare; I do not know if your lost handbag has been found but I shall make inquiries.*

inquisition [inkwi'ziʃən] *nc* (*formal*: *often derog*) a careful questioning or investigation: *He was subjected to an inquisition about his apparent expenses in London.*

inquisitive [in'kwizətiv] *adj* (*derog*) eager to find out about other people's affairs: *He was rather inquisitive about the cost of our house; We have very inquisitive neighbours.* **in'quisitively** *adv.* **in'quisitiveness** *nu.*

inroads ['inroudz]: **make inroads into/on/** (*formal*) **upon 1** to use up large amounts of (time, money *etc*): *While unemployed, he made inroads into the money he had saved.* **2** to finish part of (a task *etc*): *I didn't manage to finish the job, but I did make some inroads into it last night.*

insane [in'sein] *adj* **1** mad; mentally ill; not sane: *After examination, he was found to be insane; Insane people are sometimes dangerous.* **2** (*inf*) extremely foolish: *What an insane thing to do!; It was insane to try to drive on these icy roads.* **in'sanity** [-'sa-] *nu.*

insanitary [in'sanətəri] *adj* (*formal*) so dirty as to be a danger to health; not sanitary: *The family was living in crowded, insanitary conditions; Insanitary habits can spread disease; Conditions are so insanitary on that campsite.* **in'sanitariness** *nu.*

insatiable [in'seiʃəbl] *adj* (*formal or facet*) not able to be satisfied: *He had an insatiable desire for adventure; His greed for money was insatiable.* **in'satiably** *adv.* **in'satiableness** *nu.*

inscribe [in'skraib] *vt* (*formal*) to carve (words) or write: *The date of her death was inscribed on the gravestone; The monument was inscribed with the names of the men who died in the war; He carefully inscribed his name in his new book;* (*fig*) *His name was inscribed on her heart.*

inscription [in'skripʃən] *nc* something written, *eg* on a gravestone or on a coin: *The coin was so worn that the inscription could scarcely be read; What inscription should I write in the inside cover of the book which I am giving her as a present?*

inscrutable [in'skru:təbl] *adj* (*formal*) (of a person, his personality *etc*) that cannot be searched into and understood; mysterious: *He glanced at her to see what she thought, but she remained inscrutable; Throughout the trial her face remained inscrutable; an inscrutable expression.* **in'scrutably** *adv.* **in,scruta'bility, in'scrutableness** *nus.*

insect ['insekt] *nc* **1** any of many kinds of small six-legged creatures with wings and a body divided into sections: *We were troubled by flies, wasps and other insects.* **2** (*loosely*) any similar creature *eg* a spider.

insecticide [in'sektisaid] *ncu* a substance (*usu* in powder or liquid form) for killing insects: *This is a very effective insecticide – look at all the dead flies!; She does not like eating fruit and vegetables which have been sprayed with insecticide(s).*

,insec'tivorous [-'tivərəs] *adj* (*tech*) (of plants or animals) feeding (mainly) on insects: *Hedgehogs are insectivorous (animals).*

insecure [insi'kjuə] *adj* **1** (of a person) unsure of oneself or lacking confidence: *Whenever he was in a crowd of people he was/felt anxious and insecure; He is rather an insecure child.* **2** (*formal*) not safe or firmly fixed: *This chair-leg is insecure; My suitcase has rather an insecure lock.*

,inse'curely *adv* not firmly or safely: *The parcel burst open as it had been insecurely wrapped.*

,inse'curity *nu* **1** the quality of being unsafe: *He feared the insecurity of a job without a good pension.* **2** lack of confidence: *The child's (feeling/sense of) insecurity was caused by his mother's early death.*

See also **secure**.

insensible [in'sensəbl] *adj* (*old*: *usu pred*) unconscious: *He lay on the floor bleeding and insensible.*

insensitive [in'sensətiv] *adj* (*with* **to** *when pred*) **1** not noticing or not sympathetic towards (*eg* others' feelings): *He was insensitive to her grief; His behaviour was cruel and insensitive.* **2** (*formal*: *usu pred with* **to**) not feeling or not reacting to (touch, light *etc*): *The dentist's injection numbed the nerves and made the tooth insensitive to the drill.* **in,sensi'tivity** *nu.*

See also **sensitive**.

inseparable [in'sepərəbl] *adj* not to be separated or parted: (*fig*) *The two friends were inseparable;* (*fig*) *inseparable companions;* (*formal*) *This question is inseparable from the main problem.*

insert [in'sə:t] *vt* (*formal*: *with* **in** *or* **into**) to put or place (something) in: *He inserted the money in the parking meter; An extra chapter has been inserted* *into the book; They inserted the announcement in the newspaper.* – ['insə:t] *nc* (*formal*) something that has been inserted (*esp* an extra sheet or leaflet in a book or magazine): *There's a special insert in that magazine about holidays abroad.*

in'sertion [-ʃən] *ncu* (*formal*): *The medical examination involved the insertion of a needle into her spine; This paragraph was a last-minute insertion.*

inset ['inset] *nc* (*formal*) a small map, picture *etc* that has been put in the corner of a larger one: *In a map of a coastline, there may be an inset to show any offshore islands.*

inshore [in'ʃo:] *adv* near the shore: *The small boat was blown inshore.* – ['inʃo:] *adj* (*attrib*) near the shore: *inshore fishing.*

inside [in'said] *nc* **1** the inner side, or the part or space within: *The inside of our house has been recently painted but not the outside; The door-handle is broken on the inside; The inside of this apple is quite rotten.* **2** (*often pl*: *inf euph*) the stomach and bowels: *He ate too much and got a pain in his inside(s).* – ['insaid] *adj* (*attrib*) **1** being on or in the inside: *The story is on the inside pages of the newspaper; On a road divided into traffic lanes, the inside lane is the one nearest to the edge or kerb.* **2** (*inf*) coming from, or done by, someone within an organization: *He was given some inside information about the firm's plans.* – [in'said] *adv* **1** to, in, or on, the inside: *The door was open and he went inside; She shut the door but left her key inside by mistake.* **2** in a house or building: *You should stay inside in such bad weather.* **3** (*sl*) in jail: *He is inside for four years for armed robbery.* – [in'said] *prep* **1** (*sometimes* (*Amer inf*) *with* **of**) within; to or on the inside of: *She is inside the house; He went inside the shop.* **2** (*inf*: *sometimes with* **of**) in less than, or within, a certain time: *He finished the work inside* (*of*) *two days.*

ˌinside 'out 1 with the inner side out: *Haven't you got your shirt on inside out?* **2** (*inf*) very thoroughly: *He knows the plays of Shakespeare inside out.* – *See also* **outside in**.

insidious [in'sidiəs] *adj* (*formal derog*) (of something unpleasant) developing gradually without being noticed; causing unseen harm: *The king was the victim of an insidious plot; Her insidious jealousy eventually spoiled their friendship; Cancer is often an insidious disease.* **in'sidiously** *adv.* **in'sidiousness** *nu.*

insight ['insait] *ncu* (*sometimes with* **into**) (the quality of having) a realization or understanding of something: *He shows remarkable insight for such a young man; His job as a salesman gave him an insight into the toughness of the business world.*

insignia [in'signiə] *n pl* badges or other symbols worn or carried, showing that one holds an office or an award *etc*: *The crown and sceptre are the insignia of a king.*

insignificant [insig'nifikənt] *adj* (*often derog*) of little value or importance; not significant: *They paid me an insignificant sum of money; She is a small, insignificant person; His contribution to our project was insignificant.* **ˌinsig'nificance** *nu.*

insincere [insin'siə] *adj* not sincere; not genuine: *His praise of me was obviously insincere; insincere promises.* **ˌinsin'cerely** *adv.* **ˌinsin'cerity** [-'se-] *nu.*

insinuate [in'sinjueit] (*derog*) **1** *vt* (*formal*) to hint in an unpleasant way: *He insinuated that I was careless at my job.* **2** *v refl* (*very formal*: *with* **into**) to make a way for (oneself) gradually and cunningly (*eg* into a person's favour): *He insinuated himself into his aunt's affections in order to inherit her money.*

inˌsinu'ation (*derog*) **1** *nc* (*formal*) an unpleasant hint: *I ignored his insinuations about my friendship with the manager.* **2** *nu* (*very formal*) the act of insinuating: *If you have some criticism to make, please make it – I don't like your habit of insinuation; his gradual insinuation of himself into her affections.*

insipid [in'sipid] *adj* (*derog*) **1** (of *eg* a person, book, conversation *etc*) without interest or liveliness: *I don't know why he married such an insipid person!; She looks so insipid in that shade of pink.* **2** (of food *etc*) tasteless: *I like highly spiced food – this food seems insipid to me.*

insist [in'sist] **1** *vti* (*with* **that** *or* **on**) to state, emphasize, or hold firmly to (an opinion, plan *etc*): *He insists that I was to blame for the accident; I insisted on driving him home.* **2** *vti* (*often with* **on** *or* **that**) to demand or urge: *He insists on punctuality/obedience; They insisted on my coming with them; She insisted on coming with me; He insisted that I should go; She insisted on the necessity of changing this law; I didn't want her to come but he insisted* (*on it*).

in'sistence *nu* (*formal*) the act of insisting: *She went to see the doctor at her husband's insistence.*

in'sistent *adj* (*formal*) insisting; forcing action or attention: *He was insistent that we should go/that he was right; an insistent ring at the doorbell; insistent demands for money.*

insofar as *see* **in**.

insolent ['insələnt] *adj* (of a person or his behaviour) insulting or offensive: *He gave her a long and insolent stare; That child is lazy and insolent.* **'insolently** *adv.* **'insolence** *nu.*

insoluble [in'soljubl] *adj* **1** (*tech*) (of a substance) impossible to dissolve: *This chemical is insoluble* (*in water*). **2** (of a problem or difficulty) impossible to solve: *The mystery of his disappearance remained insoluble; an insoluble problem.*

inˌsolu'bility *nu.*

See also **soluble**.

insolvent [in'solvənt] *adj* (*formal*) not able to pay one's debts; not solvent: *He had to sell his business – he was insolvent; I am in a temporarily insolvent state.* **in'solvency** *nu.*

insomnia [in'somniə] *nu* inability to sleep: *She takes sleeping-pills as she suffers from insomnia.*

in'somniac [-ak] *nc, adj* (*formal*) (of) a person who suffers from insomnia: *My husband is an insomniac but I sleep very well; insomniac tendencies.*

inspect [in'spekt] *vt* **1** to look at, or examine, carefully or formally: *He inspected the bloodstains; The new building was inspected as soon as it was completed.* **2** to visit (*eg* a restaurant or school) officially, to make sure that it is properly run: *Cafés must be regularly inspected to find out if they are kept clean.* **3** to look at (troops *etc*) ceremonially: *The Queen will inspect the Household Cavalry.*

in'spection [-ʃən] *ncu* (an) act of inspecting: *On inspection, the coin turned out to be a rare Roman one; This school has not had an inspection for years.*

in'spector *nc* **1** a person appointed to inspect: *a school inspector.* **2** a police officer below a superintendent and above a sergeant in rank: *He has been promoted to inspector; Inspector Smith of the Liverpool police.*

inspire [in'spaiə] *vt* **1** to encourage (a person) by filling him with *eg* confidence, enthusiasm *etc*: *His friend's words inspired him to try again*; *The players were inspired by the loyalty of their supporters and played better football than ever before.* **2** (*formal*) to be the origin or source of a poetic or artistic idea: *An incident in his childhood inspired the poem.*

inspiration [inspə'reiʃən] **1** *nu* (the arousing of) feelings that inspire, or ideas that help, artistic creation: *Conversations with Coleridge were a source of inspiration to the poet Wordsworth.* **2** *nc* a person or thing that inspires: *His hard work is a constant inspiration to us all*; *Their father was an inspiration to the whole family.* **3** *nc* (*inf*) a very good idea: *Whose inspiration was it to paint the door blue?*

in'spired *adj* **1** extremely good: *He gave an inspired talk on early music*; *That was an inspired suggestion*; *His latest idea for saving money isn't exactly inspired.* **2** (*formal*) filled with artistic or creative ability; as though helped by higher or divine powers: *He spoke as if inspired*; *Although no longer inspired, he was determined to finish the novel.*

in'spiring *adj*: *His inspiring words encouraged the new recruits*; *I find my father's religious faith inspiring.*

See also **uninspired, uninspiring**.

instability [instə'biləti] *nu* lack of stability or steadiness *esp* of personality: *Because of his instability he could not be trusted with any responsible job.*

install [in'sto:l] *vt* (*often with* **in**) **1** (*more formal than* **put in**) to put (something) in (a place) ready for use: *When was the telephone/electricity installed (in this house)?*; *We have installed gas central heating.* **2** to put (a thing, oneself or another person) in a place or position: *He was installed as president yesterday*; *They soon installed themselves in the new house*; (*facet*) *The cat always installs itself in a comfortable armchair.*

installation [instə'leiʃən] **1** *nu* the act of installing: *The installation of the central heating system will take two weeks.* **2** *nc* a piece of equipment that has been installed: *The cooker, heaters, and other electrical installations are all in perfect working order.*

in'stalment, (*Amer*) **in'stallment** *nc* **1** one payment out of a number of payments into which an amount of money, *esp* a debt, is divided: *The new carpet is being paid for by monthly instalments.* **2** a part of a story that is printed one part at a time *eg* in a weekly magazine, or read in parts on the radio: *Did you hear the final instalment last week?*

instance ['instəns] *nc* an example, *esp* of a condition or circumstance: *As a social worker, he saw many instances of extreme poverty.* – *vt* (*formal*) to give or quote as an example: *He instanced vandalism as one of the features of modern life.*

for 'instance for example: *Some birds, penguins for instance, cannot fly at all.*

in that, this instance in that or this case: *You have done wrong, but in this instance you were not to blame.*

in the first instance (*formal*) as the first step in an action: *If you wish to join the club, you should apply to the secretary in the first instance.*

instant ['instənt] *adj* **1** (*usu attrib*) immediate: *Anyone disobeying these rules will face instant dismissal*; *His latest play was an instant success.* **2** (*attrib*) (of food *etc*) able to be prepared *etc* almost immediately: *instant coffee/potato.* – *nc* **1** a point in time: *He climbed into bed and at that instant the telephone rang*; *He came the instant* (*that*) (=as soon as) *he heard the news.* – *See also* **this instant** *below.* **2** a moment or very short time: *It all happened in an instant*; *I'll be there in an instant.*

'instantly *adv* immediately: *He went to bed and instantly fell asleep.*

this instant straight away; at this very moment: *Give it back this instant!*

instantaneous [instən'teiniəs] *adj* (*formal*) done, happening or acting in an instant or very quickly: *The effect of this poison is instantaneous*; *Death was instantaneous*; *Her instantaneous reaction to his suggestion annoyed him because he thought she should have considered it carefully.* **ˌinstan'taneously** *adv.*

instead [in'sted] *adv* as a substitute; in place of something or someone: *I don't like coffee. Could I please have tea instead?*; *His mother was too tired to go, so he took his aunt instead.*

in'stead of in place of: *He was told to use a pencil instead of his pen*; *Please take me instead of him*; *You should have been working instead of watching television*; *Could we go by car instead of by train?* *See also* **stead**.

instep ['instep] *nc* the arched upper part of the foot: *The strap of that shoe is too tight across the child's instep.*

instigate ['instigeit] *vt* (*formal*: *usu derog*) to suggest and encourage (*usu* a wrong action): *The boy committed the theft, but it was instigated by his father.*

ˌinsti'gation *nu* (*formal*): *He stole the money at the instigation of his friends.*

'instigator *nc* (*formal*): *He was the instigator of the plot against the king.*

instil, (*Amer*) **instill** [in'stil] – *pt, ptp* **in'stilled** – *vt* (*formal*: *often with* **into**) to put (ideas *etc*) gradually into the mind of (a person): *The habit of punctuality was instilled into me early in my life.*

ˌinstil'lation *nu.*

instinct ['instiŋkt] *ncu* a natural tendency to behave or react in a particular way, without thinking and without having been taught: *As winter approaches, swallows fly south by instinct*; *He has an instinct for choosing the right clothes*; *Her instincts warned her of the danger.*

in'stinctive [-tiv] *adj* arising from instinct or from a natural ability: *Blinking our eyes is an instinctive reaction when something suddenly comes close to them*; *He has an instinctive flair for design*; *I couldn't help putting my foot on the brake when I saw the other car coming towards me – it was instinctive.*

in'stinctively *adv.*

institute ['institju:t] *nc* (*often with cap*) a society or organization, or the building it uses: *There is a lecture at the Philosophical Institute tonight*; *She is a member of the Women's Rural Institute.* – *vt* (*formal*) to start or establish: *When was the Red Cross instituted?*; *He is instituting legal proceedings against her.*

ˌinsti'tution **1** *nu* (*formal*) the act of instituting or process of being instituted: *The public demanded the institution of a public inquiry.* **2** *nc* (the building used by) an organization *etc* founded for a particular purpose, *esp* care of people, or education: *schools, hospitals, prisons and other institutions.* **3** *nc* (*formal or facet*) a custom or tradition: *His monthly lectures at the museum have become an institution.*

ˌ**insti'tutional** *adj*: *institutional life*; *The food in this hospital is typically institutional.*

instruct [in'strʌkt] *vt* (*formal*) **1** to teach or train (a person in a subject or skill): *Girls as well as boys should be instructed in woodwork.* **2** to order or direct (a person *esp* to do something): *He was instructed to come here at nine o'clock*; *I have already instructed you how to cook the meat.*

in'struction [-ʃən] **1** *nu* (*formal*) the act of instructing (*esp* in a school subject or a skill) or the process of being instructed: *She sometimes gives instruction in skating.* **2** *nc* (*often in pl*) an order or direction: *You must learn to obey instructions.* **3** *nc* (*often in pl*) (a book *etc* giving) directions, *eg* about the use of a machine *etc*: *Could I look at the instructions, please?*

in'structive [-tiv] *adj* (*formal*) giving knowledge or information: *He gave an instructive talk about electrical repair work*; *I thought the lecture on archaeology was most instructive.* **in'structively** *adv.* **in'structiveness** *nu.*

in'structor – *fem* **in'structress** – *nc* a person who gives instruction (in a skill *etc*): *a ski-instructor*; *He is an instructor at the local swimming-pool.*

instrument ['instrəmənt] *nc* **1** a tool, *esp* if used for delicate scientific or medical work: *medical/surgical/mathematical instruments.* **2** (*also* **musical instrument**) an apparatus for producing musical sounds: *He can play the piano, violin and several other instruments.*

ˌ**instru'mental** [-'men-] *adj* **1** performed on, or written for, musical instrument(s) rather than voices: *She likes instrumental music*; *Most of the music in the concert was instrumental.* **2** (*formal*: *pred with* **in**) chiefly responsible for the doing of something: *He was instrumental in finding me a job in this country.*

ˌ**instru'mentalist** [-'men-] *nc* a person who plays a musical instrument: *There are three instrumentalists and one singer in the group.*

insubordinate [insə'bo:dənət] *adj* (*formal*) (of a person or his behaviour) disobedient or rebellious: *an insubordinate employee.*

'insuˌbordi'nation [-bo:-] *nu*: *He was dismissed for insubordination.*

insufferable [in'sʌfərəbl] *adj* (*formal*) unbearable or detestable: *insufferable rudeness*; *I find him insufferable.*

in'sufferably *adj*: *insufferably rude.*

insufficient [insə'fiʃənt] *adj* (*formal*) not enough; not sufficient: *The prisoner was released because the police had insufficient proof of his guilt*; *The salary is insufficient for my requirements.* ˌ**insuf'ficiently** *adv.* ˌ**insuf'ficiency** *nu.*

insular ['insjulə] *adj* **1** (*derog*) (of a person or his opinions *etc*) narrow-minded or full of prejudice: *He is very insular and old-fashioned in his ideas*; *He has an insular outlook on life.* **2** (*formal*: *esp attrib*) of, or belonging to, an island or islands: *There are some plants that grow only in an insular climate.*

ˌ**insu'larity** [-'la-] *nu.*

insulate ['insjuleit] *vt* **1** to cover, protect or separate (something) with a material that does not let *esp* electrical currents or heat *etc* pass through it: *Rubber and plastic are used for insulating electric wires and cables*; *Double-glazing of windows helps to insulate the house from the cold weather.* **2** (*fig formal*) to protect (*eg* a person) from unpleasant or worrying experiences: *All her life she has been insulated from the harsh realities of the world.*

ˌ**insu'lation** *nu* **1** the process of insulating or being insulated: *The insulation of their attic saved money on heating bills*; *her insulation from the troubles of the world.* **2** material used for insulating: *fibreglass insulation.*

insulin ['insjulin] *nu* a substance obtained from the pancreas of animals (*eg* cows), used in the treatment of the disease diabetes: *He treated her with insulin*; (*attrib*) *insulin injections.*

insult [in'sʌlt] *vt* to treat (a person) rudely or contemptuously: *He insulted her by telling her she was not only ugly but stupid too*; *She was insulted when the art teacher thought that her painting had been done by a child.* – ['insʌlt] *ncu* (a) comment or action that insults: *She was upset by his insult in refusing to shake hands with her*; *Such simple instructions were an insult to our intelligence*; *He failed to persuade her by flattery, so next he tried insult.*

in'sulting *adj* contemptuous or offensive: *insulting words/behaviour*; *I consider that remark insulting*; *He did not mean to be insulting.*

insuperable [in'sju:pərəbl] *adj* (*formal*) (of a problem *etc*) that cannot be overcome: *insuperable difficulties*; *The problems are difficult but not insuperable.*

insure [in'ʃuə] *vt* to arrange for the payment of a sum of money in the case of the loss of (something) or accident or injury to (someone): *Is your car insured?*; *He insured his life for twenty thousand pounds*; *Employers have to insure employees against accident.*

in'surance **1** *nu* the promise of a sum of money in case of loss *eg* by fire or other disaster, given in compensation by a company *etc* in return for regular payments: *Have you paid the insurance on your jewellery?*; *The insurance of his house costs forty pounds a year*; (*attrib*) *insurance companies*; (*attrib*) *an insurance premium.* **2** *nc* (*no pl*) anything done to try to prevent possible loss, disappointment *etc*: *He is teaching himself carpentry as an insurance against boredom after he retires.*

in'surance policy *nc* (a document setting out) an agreement with an insurance company: *My insurance policy matures next year.*

take out insurance on to arrange for the insurance of: *He has taken out (an) insurance on his life.*

See also **assure, ensure**.

insurgent [in'sə:dʒənt] *adj* (*formal*) (*esp attrib*) rising up in rebellion: *an insurgent nation.* – *nc* (*formal*) a rebel: *The king ordered the death of the leading insurgents.*

insurmountable [insə'mauntəbl] *adj* (*formal*) that cannot be surmounted, overcome or solved: *insurmountable difficulties*; *The difficulties are not insurmountable.*

insurrection [insə'rekʃən] *ncu* (*formal*) (a) rebellion or revolt: *The king was killed during the insurrection*; *The nobles feared peasant insurrection.*

intact [in'takt] *adj* (*usu pred*) undamaged or whole: *The stolen china was recovered intact*; *The box was washed up on the beach with its contents still intact*; (*fig*) *Her self-confidence remained intact although she had been dismissed from her job.*

intake ['inteik] *nc* **1** the thing or quantity taken in: *This year's intake of students is smaller than last year's.* **2** (*tech*) a place at which *eg* water is taken into a channel *etc*: *The ventilation system broke down when something blocked the main air intake.* **3** the act of taking in: *an intake of breath.*

intangible [in'tandʒəbl] *adj* (*formal*) **1** not able to be clearly defined or understood; not tangible: *There was an intangible difference in their relationship after the quarrel.* **2** not able to be felt by touch: *Air is intangible.* **in'tangibly** *adv.*

integral ['intigrəl]: **integral part** a part necessary to make something complete: *This course is an integral part of your training.*

integrate ['intigreit] **1** *vti* to (cause to) mix freely with other groups in society *etc*: *The immigrants are not finding it easy to integrate into the life of our cities.* **2** *vt* (*formal*) to fit parts together to form a whole: *I am trying to integrate the different sections of my work into a single report.* ˌ**inte'gration** *nu.* *See also* **disintegrate**.

integrity [in'tegrəti] *nu* **1** (*more formal than* **honesty**) honesty: *He is a man of absolute integrity.* **2** (*formal*) the state of being a single whole: *These arguments are threatening the integrity of the group.*

intellect ['intilekt] **1** *nu* the thinking power of the mind: *He was a person of great intellect.* **2** *nc* (a person having) great mental ability: *She felt that she had come into contact with a great intellect.*

ˌ**intel'lectual** [-'lektʃuəl] *adj* of, or appealing to, the intellect: *He has a great deal of intellectual ability*; *He does not play football – his interests are mainly intellectual*; *He is an intellectual person* (= one having intellectual interests). – *nc* (*sometimes derog*) a person whose interests are in literature, art, thinking about life *etc*, *usu* considered to have no practical sense: *In the train, two intellectuals were discussing philosophy*; *He was an intellectual who understood Greek but could not look up a bus timetable correctly.*

intelligent [in'telidʒənt] *adj* (*neg* **un-**) **1** clever and quick at understanding: *She's an intelligent child*; *That dog is so intelligent.* **2** showing these qualities: *an intelligent question*; *Her replies to my questions were intelligent and interesting.* **in'telligently** *adv.*

in'telligence *nu* **1** the quality of being intelligent: *It requires a high degree of intelligence to do this job well.* **2** (*formal*) news or information given: *We have received intelligence to the effect that the enemy is retreating.* **3** (*with cap*) a department of state or of the army *etc* which deals with secret information: *He works in Intelligence.*

intelligible [in'telidʒəbl] *adj* (*neg* **un-**) able to be understood: *His answer was barely intelligible because he was speaking through a mouthful of food*; *She left me a scarcely intelligible message about where she had gone.* **in**ˌ**telligi'bility** *nu.* **in'telligibly** *adv.*

intemperate [in'tempərət] *adj* (*formal*) not temperate; going beyond reasonable limits; uncontrolled: *intemperate language*; *She considered his behaviour intemperate.* **in'temperately** *adv.* **in'temperance** *nu.*

intend [in'tend] *vt* **1** to mean or plan (to do something or that someone else should do something): *Do you still intend going/to go?*; (*formal*) *Do you intend them to go?*; (*formal*) *Do you intend that they should go too?* **2** (*often with* **as**: *usu in passive*) to mean (something) to be understood in a particular way: *His remarks were intended to be a compliment*; *Was that remark intended as an insult?* **3** (*often in passive*: *with* **for**) to send to, say to, aim at *etc* (a particular person): *That letter/bullet was intended for me*; *He is intended for a career in the diplomatic service.*

in'tended *adj* (*formal*) meant or planned: *This apparatus should only be used for its intended purpose.* – *nc* (*old or facet*) a fiancé(e): *He introduced me to his intended.*

in'tent [-t] *adj* **1** (*pred with* **on**/(*formal*) **upon**) meaning, planning or wanting to do (something): *He's intent on going*; *He's intent on marrying the girl*; *He is intent upon revenge.* **2** (*with* **on**/(*formal*) **upon** *when pred*) (showing that a person is) paying a great deal of attention to (something) or doing (something) with great care: *He was intent on the job he was doing*; *with an intent expression on his face.* – *nu* (*legal*) purpose; what a person means to do: *He entered the building with criminal intent*; *he broke into the house with intent to steal.*

in'tention [-ʃən] *ncu* what a person plans or intends to do: *He has no intention of leaving*; *He went to see the boss with the intention of asking for a pay rise*; *His intentions are good*; *If I have offended you, it was quite without intention.*

in'tentional [-ʃənl] *adj* (*neg* **un-**) (*more formal than* **deliberate**) done, said *etc* deliberately and not by accident: *I'm sorry I offended you – it wasn't intentional*; (*formal*) *She was horrified by his acts of intentional cruelty towards the children.* **in'tentionally** *adv.*

in'tently *adv* in an intent (*def 2*) manner: *He was watching her intently.*

to all intents (and purposes) (*formal*) almost exactly; in all important aspects: *There are small differences between the two plans, but to all intents (and purposes), they are the same.*

intense [in'tens] *adj* **1** very great: *the intense heat of the furnace*; *a feeling of intense bitterness*; *Her hatred of him was too intense for her ever to forgive him.* **2** (*sometimes derog*) being too strong, eager or serious in one's opinions *etc*: *He was approached by an intense young man who asked him if he accepted Jesus as his Saviour*; *I always avoid her company – she is too intense.*

in'tensely *adv* very much: *I dislike that sort of behaviour intensely.*

in'tenseness *nu* the state of being intense (*usu def 2*).

in'tensify [-sifai] *vti* (*formal*) to make or become greater, stronger, more intense *etc*: *His efforts intensified*; *He intensified his efforts.* **in**ˌ**tensifi'cation** [-fi-] *nu.*

in'tensity *nu* the quality of being intense: *the intensity of the heat from the furnace*; *the intensity of their love*; *the intensity of the young poet.*

in'tensive [-siv] *adj* very great; showing or having great care *etc*: *The police began an intensive search for the murderer*; *The hospital has just opened a new intensive care unit*; *His investigations were intensive and thorough but revealed nothing.* **in'tensively** *adv.* **in'tensiveness** *nu.*

intent, intention *etc see* **intend**.

inter [in'tə:] – *pt, ptp* **in'terred** – *vt* (*formal or liter*) to bury (a person *etc*): *The two lovers were interred together.*

in'terment *ncu* (*formal*) the act of burying (a person *etc*: *the interment of the corpse.*

inter- [intə] (*in cmpds*) between, among or together, as in **intermarry**.

interact [intər'akt] *vi* (of two or more people, things *etc*) to act, or have some effect, on each other.

ˌ**inter'action** [-ʃən] *nu*: *The interaction of the two groups produced many good ideas*; *Her illness was caused by the interaction of the two drugs.*

intercede [intə'si:d] *vi* (*formal*) **1** to try to put an end to a fight, argument *etc* between two people, countries *etc*: *All attempts to intercede between the two warring nations failed.* **2** to try to persuade someone not to do something to someone else: *The condemned murderer's family interceded (with the President) on his behalf.* ˌ**inter'cession** [-'seʃən] *ncu.*

intercept [intə'sept] *vt* to stop or catch (a person, thing *etc*) before he, it *etc* arrives at the place to which he, it *etc* is going, being sent *etc*: *The rebels intercepted the message before it reached the king; The messenger was intercepted on his way to the king.* ˌ**inter'ception** *nu.*

intercession *see* **intercede**.

interchange ['intətʃeindʒ] **1** *nc* a place where two or more main roads or motorways at different levels are joined by means of several small roads, so allowing cars *etc* to move from one road to another. **2** *ncu* (*formal*) (an) exchange; (an) act of putting each of two things *etc* in the place of the other: *At conferences the interchange of ideas can be beneficial.*

ˌ**inter'changeable** *adj* able to be used, put *etc* in the place of each other without a difference in effect, meaning *etc*: *'Great' and 'big' are not interchangeable; We have bought interchangeable bedcovers.*

intercom ['intəkom] *nc* a system of communication within an aeroplane, factory *etc usu* by means of microphones and loudspeakers: *The pilot spoke to the passengers over the intercom; Have you an intercom in the office?*; (*attrib*) *an intercom system.*

intercourse ['intəko:s] *nu* **1** sexual intercourse: *He was accused of having had intercourse with a young girl without her consent.* **2** (*formal*) conversation, business dealings, trade *etc* between two or more people, countries *etc*: *There has been no intercourse between the two countries for several years.*

interdict ['intədikt] *nc* (*legal*) an official order forbidding (someone to do something): *He was prevented from building a new garden wall by a court interdict.*

interest ['intrəst] **1** *nu* curiosity; attention: *A good teacher will always find some way of arousing his pupils' interest; That newspaper story is bound to attract interest.* **2** *ncu* (something that has) the power to arouse a person's curiosity and attention: *Gardening is one of my main interests; This book will be of interest to you; A few photographs will add interest to this book; What you decide to do is of no interest to me.* **3** *nu* money paid in return for borrowing a *usu* large sum of money: *The (rate of) interest on this loan is eight per cent*; (*attrib*) *the interest rate.* **4** *nc* (a share in the ownership of) a business firm *etc*: *He bought an interest in the night-club.* **5** *nc* a group of people, businesses *etc* who are all involved in the same sort of activity *etc* and who often act together to their own advantage: *I suspect that the scheme will be opposed by the banking interest* (=all the banks acting together). – *See also* **vested interest**. – *vt* **1** to arouse the curiosity and attention of (someone *etc*); to be of importance or concern to (someone): *Political arguments don't interest me at all; This matter interests all of us who are concerned about pollution.* **2** (*with* **in**) to persuade (someone) to do, buy *etc* (something): *Can I interest you in (buying) this dictionary?; We'll try to interest him in the project.*

'**interested** *adj* **1** (*often pred with* **in**) showing attention or having curiosity: *He's not interested in politics; Don't tell me any more – I'm not interested; I'll be interested to see what happens next week; Only the really interested students attended his lectures.* **2** (*often pred with* **in**) willing, or wanting, to do, buy *etc* (something): *Are you interested in (buying) a second-hand car?* **3** (*esp attrib*) involved in (some project, disagreement *etc*), *esp* likely to gain or lose because of some piece of business *etc*, and therefore having opinions about it that may be influenced by selfish motives: *Before we can come to a decision, we'll have to have a talk with all the interested parties* (= people, groups).

'**interesting** (*neg* **un-**) *adj* arousing interest: *an interesting book; This work is not at all interesting.*

'**interestingly** *adv* **1** in an interesting way: *He writes very interestingly about his travels in Africa.* **2** it is of interest that (something is true *etc*): *Interestingly (enough), I met him only last week.*

in one's *etc* **(own) (best) interest(s)** bringing, or in order to bring, advantage, benefit, help *etc* to oneself *etc*: *It would be in our own interest to help him, as he may be able to help us later; It is not in your interests to be so rude to the owner of the firm; It is in my best interest to invest in this firm.*

in the 'interest(s) of (*formal*) in order to get, achieve, increase *etc*: *The political march was banned in the interests of public safety.*

lose interest to stop being interested: *He used to be very active in politics, but he's lost interest now.*

take an interest to be interested: *I take a great interest in everything they do.*

See also **disinterested, self-interest, uninterested**.

interfere [intə'fiə] *vi* **1** (*derog*: *often with* **in, with**) to (try to) become involved in (something), give advice to (someone) *etc* when one's help *etc* is not wanted: *I wish you would stop interfering (with my plans); Don't interfere in other people's business!* **2** (*with* **with**) to prevent, stop or slow down the progress of, (something): *He doesn't let anything interfere with his game of golf on Saturday mornings.*

ˌ**inter'ference** *nu* **1** (*often derog*) the act of interfering: *Thanks to your interference, we'll have to start all over again; She resented his mother's interference in their holiday arrangements.* **2** (the spoiling of radio or television reception by) the noise caused by programmes from another station, bad weather *etc*: *This television set picks up a lot of interference.*

ˌ**inter'fering** *adj* (*derog*): *She's an interfering busybody; My mother-in-law is so interfering that she tries to help us make all our decisions.*

interim ['intərim] *adj* (*attrib*: *formal*) temporary; not intended to be final or to last: *an interim report; We'll need to find a better solution eventually, but as an interim measure, we'll ban all political meetings.*

in the 'interim (*formal*) in the meantime; from a given time till a given time: *Our new secretary is joining us next week, but in the interim we will have to type our own letters.*

interior [in'tiəriə] *adj* (*attrib*) on, of *etc*, the inside of (something): *the interior walls of a building.* – *nc* **1** (*formal*) the inside of a building *etc*: *The interior of the house was very attractive.* **2** (*usu in sing*) the part of a country away from the coast, borders *etc*: *The explorers landed on the coast, and then travelled into the interior.*

interior decoration *nu* the art and process of designing, decorating, furnishing *etc* the insides of houses, offices *etc.*

interior decorator *nc* a person who does interior decoration.

interjection [intə'dʒekʃən] 1 *nc (gram)* a word or words, or some noise, used to express surprise, dismay, pain or other feelings and emotions: *Oh dear! I think I've lost my key; Ouch! That hurts!* 2 *nu (formal)* the act of interjecting (something).
ˌ**inter'ject** *vti (formal)* to say (something) which interrupts what someone else is saying or what one is saying oneself: *He told the story while she interjected a comment at intervals.*

interlock [intə'lok] *vti (formal or tech)* (of two or more pieces of machinery *etc*) to fit or fasten, or be fitted or fastened, together, so as to work together or form something larger *etc*: *The pieces of a jigsaw puzzle interlock.*
ˌ**inter'locking** *adj* which interlock: *the interlocking pieces of a jigsaw puzzle; These pipes are interlocking.*

interloper ['intəloupə, *(Amer)* intər'loupər] *nc (formal)* a person who goes into a place *etc* where he has no right to go, *usu* to do something wrong: *The police removed an interloper from the official enclosure; (fig) He was treated as an interloper by the rest of the staff.*

interlude ['intəlu:d] *nc* **1** *(formal)* a *usu* short period between the acts of a play in which something of a different type takes place: *During the interlude between the first and second rounds of the competition, we were entertained by a singer; (fig) interludes of sunshine between showers.* **2** something which happens during an interlude, *eg* a short piece of music played at this time.

intermarry [intə'mari] *vi* **1** *(usu with* **with***)* (of one group or race of people) to marry people of a different group or race: *The invaders intermarried with the native population.* **2** (of people belonging to one group or family) to marry each other: *In isolated areas, members of the same family tend to intermarry.* ˌ**inter'marriage** [-ridʒ] *nu.*

intermediary [intə'mi:diəri] *nc (formal)* a person who takes messages from one person or group of people to another in a negotiation, dispute *etc*, *esp* a person who does so in order to settle the dispute: *He offered to act as an intermediary in the disagreement between management and work-force.*

intermediate [intə'mi:diət] *adj (esp attrib)* in the middle; placed between two things, stages *etc*: *An intermediate English course is more advanced than a beginners' course, but not as difficult as an advanced course; This country is now at an intermediate stage of development between a primitive agricultural community and an advanced industrialized nation.*

interment *see* **inter**.

interminable [in'tə:minəbl] *adj (formal derog)* going on for a very long, *usu* too long, time: *I'm tired of this interminable discussion about what colour the carpet should be; His talk was very boring and seemed interminable.*
in'terminably *adv*: *He spoke interminably about the brilliance of his scheme.*
See also **terminate**.

intermission [intə'miʃən] *nc* a *usu* short pause or gap between two (television or radio) programmes, parts of a programme, play *etc*: *We had a drink at the bar during the intermission.*

intermittent [intə'mitənt] *adj* happening occasionally; stopping for a while and then starting again: *intermittent rain; an intermittent pain; The pain is intermittent but severe.*
ˌ**inter'mittently** *adv*: *The pain occurs intermittently.*

intern[1] [in'tə:n] *vt (formal)* during a war, to keep (someone who belongs to an enemy nation but who is living in one's own country) a prisoner, or to make (him or her) stay within a particular area.
ˌ**inter'nee** *nc (formal)* a person who is interned.
in'ternment *ncu (formal)* the act of interning or state of being interned.

intern[2] ['intə:n] *nc (Amer) (also* **interne***)* a houseman (= a junior doctor) in a hospital.

internal [in'tə:nl] *adj* **1** *(formal or tech)* of, on or in the inside of something *(esp* a person's body*)*: *The man suffered internal injuries in the accident; The patient's injuries are mainly internal; (fig) There is internal evidence, such as the style of the handwriting, to show that this document is his work.* **2** concerning what happens within a country *etc*, rather than its relationship with other countries *etc*: *The prime ministers agreed that no country should interfere in another country's internal affairs; The government's problems are internal rather than international in nature.*
in'ternally *adv*: *He is bleeding internally; These political problems can only be settled internally.*
internal combustion *nu* a means of producing power *eg* in the engine of a motor car (an **inˌternal-com'bustion engine**) by the burning of a fuel gas (*eg* petrol vapour) inside the cylinder(s) of the engine.

international [intə'naʃənl] *adj* involving, or done by, two or more nations: *international trade; an international football match; an international conference; The drug problem is international.* – *nc (esp Brit)* **1** a football *etc* match played between teams from two countries: *Have you got a ticket for the international?* **2** *(also* ˌ**inter'nationalist***)* a player in such a match.
ˌ**inter'nationally** *adv* in or by two or *usu* more nations: *an internationally famous singer.*

interne *see* **intern**[2].

internee, internment *see* **intern**[1].

interplay ['intəplei] *nu (formal)* the action of two or more things on each other: *They admired the interplay of light and shade in his paintings.*

interpose [intə'pouz] *(very formal or liter)* **1** *vti* to interrupt or add (a remark, comment *etc*) to (a conversation, quarrel *etc*): *He interposed a few well-chosen words; He tried to interpose in their dispute.* **2** *vt* to put forward (an objection *etc*) that prevents or interferes with some action: *A judge can interpose his authority to prevent certain questions being asked of witnesses.*

interpret [in'tə:prit] **1** *vti* to translate a speaker's words, while he is speaking, into the language of his hearers: *He spoke to the audience in French and she interpreted (it) into English for them.* **2** *vt (formal)* to explain the meaning of: *How do you interpret these lines of the poem?* **3** *vt (formal)* to understand the meaning of (a remark, action *etc*) to be: *I interpret your remark as a threat.* **4** *vt (formal)* to show or bring out the meaning of (*eg* a rôle in a play or a piece of music) in one's performance of it: *The sonata was skilfully interpreted by the pianist.*
inˌterpre'tation *ncu*: *What is your interpretation of these words?; She was good at interpretation into German.*
in'terpreter *nc* a person who translates the words of a speaker into the language of his hearers: *He acted as interpreter at the international conference.*

interrogate [in'terəgeit] *vt* to question (a person) thoroughly: *The police spent five hours interro-*

gating the prisoner. **in,terro'gation** *ncu.* **in'terrogator** *nc.*

interrogative [intə'rogətiv] *adj* (*esp gram*) asking a question: *'Who?' is an interrogative pronoun.* – *nc* (*gram*) an interrogative word: *'How?' and 'Why?' are interrogatives.*

interrupt [intə'rʌpt] **1** *vti* to stop a person while he is saying or doing something, *esp* by saying *etc* something oneself: *He interrupted her while she was speaking; He interrupted her speech by shouting abuse; Listen to me and don't interrupt!* **2** *vt* to stop or make a break in (an activity *etc*): *He interrupted his work to eat his lunch; You interrupted my thoughts; Our friendship was interrupted by his departure for India.* **3** *vt* (*formal*) to cut off (a view *etc*): *A block of flats interrupted their view of the sea.*

,inter'ruption [-ʃən] **1** *nu* the act of interrupting or state of being interrupted: *His failure to complete the job was due to constant interruption.* **2** *nc* something that interrupts: *I get too many interruptions in my work.*

intersect [intə'sekt] *vti* (*formal or math*) to divide (*eg* lines or roads) by cutting or crossing: *The line AB intersects the line CD at X; Where do the two roads intersect?*

,inter'section [-ʃən] **1** *nu* (*formal or math*) the act of intersecting: *Point X is found by the intersection of line CD by line AB.* **2** *nc* a place where lines, roads *etc* intersect: *The crash occurred at the intersection between/of the three roads.*

intersperse [intə'spə:s] *vt* (*formal*) to scatter something between or among other things: *His talk was interspersed with jokes.*

interval ['intəvəl] *nc* **1** a time or space between happenings, activities *etc*: *He went out and I got some work done in the interval before he returned; Short skirts returned to fashion after an interval of fifteen years.* **2** a short break in a play, concert *etc*: *We had ice-cream in the interval between the second and third acts of the play.*

at 'intervals here and there; now and then: *He yawned at intervals during the performance; Trees grew at intervals along the road.*

intervene [intə'vi:n] *vi* **1** (*formal*) to interfere in a quarrel: *He tried to intervene between the two angry men; He intervened in the dispute.* **2** (*liter*) to be or come between, in place or time: *We could meet more often if the sea did not intervene.*

,inter'vening *adj* coming between: *His piano exam was to be in June, and he practised hard during the intervening weeks.*

,inter'vention [-'venʃən] *ncu* (an) act of intervening (in a quarrel *etc*): *His intervention was not welcomed by either side.* – *See also* **non-intervention**.

interview ['intəvju:] *nc* a formal meeting and discussion with someone, *eg* a person applying for a job, or a person with information to broadcast on radio or television: *My interview for the job is next week; In the interview that he gave on television last night, the Prime Minister seemed optimistic.* – *vt* to question (a person) in an interview: *They interviewed seven people for the job; He was interviewed by reporters about his policies.*

'interviewer *nc.*

intestate [in'testeit] *adj* (*legal*: *pred*) without having made a will: *He died intestate.*

intestine [in'testin] *ncu* (*esp tech*: *often in pl*) the lower part of the food passage in man and animals: *the small/large intestine; She had a blockage in her intestines.*

intestinal [intes'tainl, (*esp Amer*) in'testinl] *adj* (*tech*: *esp attrib*) of the intestines: *an intestinal infection.*

intimate ['intimət] *adj* (*formal*) **1** close and affectionate: *They have been intimate friends for years; They had been intimate for a long time.* – *See also* **be intimate with** *below.* **2** private or personal: *He would not discuss the intimate details of his marriage; an intimate discussion; The discussion was too intimate for my liking.* **3** (of knowledge *etc*) deep and thorough: *He has an intimate knowledge of French grammar.* – *nc* (*liter or facet*) a close friend: *his circle of intimates.* – [-meit] *vt* (*formal*) to give information or announce: *He intimated that he would soon be resigning as club secretary.*

'intimacy [-məsi] *nu* **1** (*formal*) the quality of being intimate: *the intimacy of their talk.* **2** (*old*) close friendship: *Intimacy grew between them over the years.* **3** (*formal or legal euph*) sexual intercourse *esp* if not lawful.

'intimately [-mət-] *adv*: *They were not intimately acquainted.*

,inti'mation [-'mei-] (*formal*) **1** *nu* a hint: *He gave us no intimation of his intentions.* **2** *nc* an announcement: *birth intimations.*

be 'intimate with (*formal or legal euph*) to have sexual intercourse with, *esp* unlawfully: *He was accused of having been intimate with a young girl.*

intimidate [in'timideit] *vt* (*formal*) to frighten (a person) *eg* by threatening violence *esp* in order to make him do what one wants: *They were intimidated into giving him the money; He intimidates the children by shouting at them.* **in,timi'dation** *nu.*

into ['intu] *prep* **1** to or towards the inside of; to within: *The eggs were put into the box; They disappeared into the mist.* **2** against: *The car ran into the wall.* **3** to the state or condition of: *A tadpole turns into a frog; I've sorted the books into piles; He terrified her into silence; He terrified her into doing what he wanted.* **4** (*math*) expressing the idea of division: *Two into four goes twice.*

intolerable [in'tolərəbl] *adj* (*formal*) that cannot be endured or borne: *intolerable pain; It is intolerable to have to wait so long for a bus.* **in'tolerably** *adv.*

in'tolerant *adj* (*often with* **of** *when pred*) unwilling to endure or accept *eg* people whose ideas *etc* are different from one's own, members of a different race or religion *etc*: *She's narrow-minded and intolerant; an intolerant, bad-tempered old woman; He is always intolerant of new ideas.* **in'tolerance** *nu.*

See also **tolerate**.

intonation [intə'neiʃən] *nu* the rise and fall of the voice in speech: *He spoke very monotonously, with very little change in intonation.*

intoxicate [in'toksikeit] *vt* (*formal or liter*) to make drunk: *Three pints of beer were enough to intoxicate him;* (*fig*) *He was intoxicated by her beauty.* **in,toxi'cation** *nu.* **in'toxicating** *adj.*

in'toxicant *nc* (*formal*) an intoxicating drink: *The judge accused him of having taken intoxicants.*

intra- [intrə] (*in cmpds*) within or inside, as in **intravenous**.

intractable [in'traktəbl] *adj* (*formal*: *derog if of a person*) difficult to control or manage: *an intractable child; He has an intractable temper; That child is completely intractable.*

intransigent [in'transidʒənt] *adj* (*formal derog*) refusing to come to any agreement: *In the frontier dispute, both countries remained intransigent; stub-*

born, intransigent people. **in'transigence** *nu.*

intransitive [in'transitiv] *adj* (*gram*) (of a verb) that does not have an object: *The baby lay on the floor and kicked; Go and fetch the book!* **in'transitively** *adv.*
See also **transitive**.

intravenous [intrə'vi:nəs] *adj* in or into a vein or veins: *an intravenous injection.*

intrepid [in'trepid] *adj* (*formal*) bold and fearless: *an intrepid explorer; We value his intrepid support of our cause; Are you intrepid enough to climb that mountain?* **in'trepidly** *adv.* **ˌintre'pidity** [-'pi-] *nu.*

intricate ['intrikət] *adj* (*formal*) complicated: *This is a very intricate knitting pattern; This pattern is very intricate; He told me the story but I couldn't understand all the intricate details.* **'intricately** *adv.*
'intricacy (*formal*) **1** *nu* the quality of being intricate: *They admired the intricacy of the embroidery.* **2** *nc* (*usu pl*) something that is intricate: *I could never master the intricacies of German grammar.*

intrigue [in'tri:g, 'intri:g] **1** *nu* (*derog*) the activity of plotting or scheming: *Amongst the members of any profession there is a certain amount of intrigue.* **2** *nc* (*derog*) a plot or scheme: *He was made king as a result of various intrigues.* **3** *nc* (*formal*) a secret love affair: *He suspected an intrigue between his wife and the doctor.* – [in'tri:g] **1** *vt* to fascinate, arouse the curiosity of or amuse: *The book intrigued me.* **2** *vi* (*formal*) to plot: *The rival political groups constantly intrigued against each other.*
in'triguing *adj* curious or amusing: *What an intriguing idea!; It is intriguing to think that we might never have met each other if we had not gone to that party.*

intrinsic [in'trinsik] *adj* (*formal: esp attrib*) (of value, worth *etc*) belonging to a thing as part of its nature: *The necklace was made of glass, not diamonds, so it had little intrinsic worth.* **in'trinsically** *adv.*

introduce [intrə'dju:s] *vt* **1** (*often with* **to**) to make (people) known by name to each other: *He introduced the guests (to each other); Let me introduce you to my mother; May I introduce myself? I'm John Brown; I know your name, although we have never been introduced.* **2** (*often with* **into**) to bring in (something new, *eg* to a country): *Grey squirrels were introduced into Britain from Canada; Why did you introduce such a boring subject (into the conversation)?* **3** (*formal*) to propose or put forward: *He introduced a bill in Parliament for the abolition of income tax; She introduced a suggestion that the committee should meet every week.* **4** (*with* **to**: *formal*) to cause (a person) to get to know (a subject, a writer's works *etc*): *Children are introduced to algebra at about the age of eleven.*
ˌintro'duction [-'dʌkʃən] **1** *nu* the act of introducing, or the process of being introduced: *He encouraged the introduction of new medical treatments.* **2** *nc* an act of introducing one person to another: *The hostess made the introductions and everyone shook hands.* **3** *nc* something written at the beginning of a book explaining the contents, or said at the beginning of a speech *etc*: *The author says in his introduction that the novel is based on his own childhood.*
ˌintro'ductory [-'dʌktəri] *adj* (*esp attrib*) giving an introduction: *He made a few introductory remarks about the film before showing it; This brand of cigarettes will not always be so cheap – it is a new brand and this is an introductory offer* (= a special cheap price to introduce them into the market).

introspection [intrə'spekʃən] *nu* (*formal*) the examination of one's own thoughts, feelings *etc.*
ˌintro'spective [-tiv] *adj* (*formal*) showing introspection: *poetry of an introspective nature; She is always unhappy because she is so introspective.*

introvert ['intrəvə:t] *nc* (*formal*) a person who is more concerned with his own thoughts and feelings than with other people or happenings outside him: *He is such an introvert that he hardly ever talks to anyone.*
See also **extrovert**.

intrude [in'tru:d] *vti* (*sometimes with* **on**) to enter, or cause (something) to enter, when unwelcome or unwanted: *He opened her door and said 'I'm sorry to intrude'; I'm sorry to intrude on your time;* (*formal*) *He was always intruding his company on her;* (*formal*) *The memory kept intruding itself into her mind.*
in'truder *nc* a person who intrudes, *eg* a burglar: *Fit a good lock to your front door, to keep out possible intruders.*
in'trusion [-ʒən] *ncu* (*formal*) (an) act of intruding or process of being intruded: *Please forgive this intrusion.*
in'trusive [-siv] *adj* (*formal*) tending to intrude: *She means to help, but she does it in rather an intrusive way; I find her rather intrusive.* **in'trusiveness** *nu.*

intuition [intju'iʃən] **1** *nu* the power of understanding or realizing something without thinking it out: *She knew by intuition that he was telling her the truth.* **2** *nc* something understood or realized by this power: *Her intuitions are always right.*
intuitive [in'tju:ətiv] *adj* (*formal: esp attrib*) having or showing intuition: *an intuitive mind.*

inundate ['inəndeit] *vt* (*formal*) to flood (a place, building *etc*): *The river burst its banks and all the fields were inundated;* (*fig*) *She is inundated with work this week.* **ˌinun'dation** *ncu.*

inure [i'njuə] *vt* (*formal*) (*usu in passive: with* **to**) to make (a person) accustomed (to something unpleasant): *He was inured to pain/insults.*

invade [in'veid] *vt* **1** (of an enemy) to enter (a country *etc*) with an army: *Britain was twice invaded by the Romans;* (*formal fig*) *These unpleasant thoughts kept invading his mind.* **2** (*formal*) to interfere with (a person's rights *etc*): *He claimed that the newspaper reporters were invading his privacy.*
in'vader *nc* a person, or (*sometimes in sing with* **the**) an armed force *etc*, that invades: *Our armies fought bravely against the invader(s).*
in'vasion [-ʒən] *ncu* (an) act of invading or process of being invaded: *The army succeeded in fighting off the foreign invasion;* (*fig*) *This town always has an invasion of tourists in the summer.*

invalid[1] [in'valid] *adj* (*esp pred*) **1** (*legal*) (of a document or agreement *etc*) having no legal force; not valid: *Your passport is out of date and therefore invalid.* **2** (*formal*) (of reasoning *etc*) not valid; incorrect or unreliable: *His whole argument is invalid.*
in'validate [-deit] *vt* (*formal*) to make invalid: *The lack of a signature invalidates this document.*
invalidity [invə'lidəti] *nu.*

invalid[2] ['invəlid] *nc* a person who is ill or disabled: *During his last few years, he was a permanent* *invalid*; (*attrib*) *an* ˈ*invalid chair*. – [-li:d] *vt* **1** (*usu with* **out**) to remove (*esp* a soldier) from service, because of illness: *He was invalided out of the army.* **2** to cause (*esp* a soldier) to be ill or disabled: *He was invalided in the last war.*

invaluable [inˈvaljuəbl] *adj* (*formal*) of value too great to be estimated: *Thank you for your invaluable help*; *This information was invaluable to him.*

invariable [inˈveəriəbl] *adj* unchanging; not variable: *His invariable habit of running in the park before breakfast kept him fit.*

inˈvariably *adv* always: *They invariably quarrel when he comes home.*

invasion *see* **invade**.

invective [inˈvektiv] *nu* (*liter or formal*) words of hate or scorn: *bitter invective.*

inveigle [inˈvi:gl, (*esp Amer*) -ˈvei-] *vt* (*formal*: *often derog*) to trap or coax (a person) into doing something: *He was inveigled into lending them ten pounds.*

invent [inˈvent] *vt* **1** to be the first person to make or use (*eg* a machine, method *etc*): *Who invented the microscope?*; *When was printing invented?* **2** to make up or think of (*eg* an excuse or story): *I'll have to invent some excuse for not going with him.*

inˈvention [-ʃən] **1** *nu* the act of inventing or the ability to invent: *He had great* (*powers of*) *invention.* **2** *nc* something invented: *What a marvellous invention the sewing-machine was!*; *He told the teacher that he felt ill, but it was obviously just an invention.*

inˈventive [-tiv] *adj* good at inventing: *an inventive mind*; *She is very inventive.* **inˈventiveness** *nu.*

inˈventor *nc* a person who invents: *Alexander Graham Bell was the inventor of the telephone.*

inventory [ˈinvəntri] *nc* a formal and detailed list of goods *eg* house furniture or business stock: *The house agent made an inventory before letting the house.*

invert [inˈvə:t] *vt* (*very formal*) to turn (something) upside down or reverse the order of: *He trapped the wasp by inverting a glass over it.*

inˈverse [-s] *adj* (*esp math*: *usu attrib*) opposite or reverse: *inverse proportion/ratio.* – *nu* (*with* **the**) opposite: $^2/_3$ *is the inverse of* $^3/_2$; *The inverse of the statement is also true.*

inˈversion [-ʃən] *ncu.*

inverted commas *n pl* single or double commas, the first (set) of which is turned upside down (" ", ' '), or similar marks used in writing to show where direct speech begins and ends: *"It is a lovely day," she said.*

invertebrate [inˈvə:tibrət] *adj* (*tech*) (of an animal *eg* a worm) not having a backbone: *Insects are invertebrate*; *invertebrate creatures.* – *nc* a creature without a backbone: *worms and other invertebrates.*

invest[1] [inˈvest] *vti* (*with* **in**) **1** to put (money) into a firm or business, *usu* by buying shares in it, in order to make a profit: *He invested* (*two hundred pounds*) *in a building firm.* **2** (*formal*) to spend (*eg* time, money, energy *etc*) on something: *They've invested a lot of time and money in modernizing their house*; *It's time that we invested in a new car.*

inˈvestment **1** *nu* the act of investing. **2** *nc* a sum of money invested: *She has a few small investments.* **3** *nc* something on which money has been spent in the hope of future advantage or profit: *A good house is considered an investment.*

inˈvestor *nc* a person who invests money in a business *etc.*

invest[2] [inˈvest] *vt* **1** (*formal*) to establish (a person) officially in a position of power: *The governor will be invested next week.* **2** (*liter*) to give (a place, person *etc*) a certain quality: *The ruined castle had been invested with mystery for years.*

inˈvestiture [-titʃə] *ncu* (a ceremony of) giving (the robes *etc* of) high rank or office to someone: *They attended the investiture of the Prince of Wales at Caernarvon Castle.*

investigate [inˈvestigeit] *vt* to examine or inquire into (something) carefully: *The police are investigating the mystery*; *They are investigating ways of increasing their profits.*

inˌvestiˈgation *ncu*: *methods of investigation*; *The police have finished their investigations into the crime.*

inˈvestigator *nc* a person, *eg* a detective, who investigates.

investment *see* **invest**[1].

inveterate [inˈvetərət] *adj* (*formal*: *attrib*) **1** firmly fixed in a habit by long practice: *an inveterate liar.* **2** (of a habit, feeling *etc*) firmly established: *I have an inveterate dislike of football crowds.*

invidious [inˈvidiəs] *adj* (*formal*: *esp attrib*) likely to cause ill-will or envy: *She had the invidious task of judging the baby competition.* **inˈvidiously** *adv.* **inˈvidiousness** *nu.*

invigilate [inˈvidʒileit] *vti* (*formal*) to supervise students while they are doing an examination: *I am going to invigilate* (*at*) *the English exam*; *The candidates were not properly invigilated.* **inˌvigiˈlation** *nu.* **inˈvigilator** *nc.*

invigorate [inˈvigəreit] *vt* (*formal*) to strengthen or refresh: *The bath invigorated her*; *I was invigorated by my walk in the cold air.* **inˈvigorating** *adj.*

invincible [inˈvinsəbl] *adj* (*formal*) that cannot be overcome or defeated: *That general thinks that his army is invincible*; *the invincible enemy troops.* **inˈvincibly** *adv.* **inˌvinciˈbility** *nu.*

inviolable [inˈvaiələbl] *adj* (*formal*) (of *eg* a law or right) that must not be broken or interfered with; not violable: *Freedom of speech should be an inviolable right*; *He regards the ten commandments as being inviolable.*

inˈviolate [-lət] *adj* (*formal or liter*) (of *eg* a promise *etc*) not violated.

invisible [inˈvizəbl] *adj* not able to be seen; not visible: *Only in stories can people make themselves invisible*; *The air is full of millions of invisible particles*; *Our invisible exports include money spent by tourists from abroad.* **inˈvisibly** *adv.* **inˌvisiˈbility** *nu.*

invite [inˈvait] *vt* **1** to ask (a person) politely to come (*eg* to one's house, to a party *etc*): *They have invited us to dinner tomorrow.* **2** to ask (a person) politely to do something: *He was invited to speak at the meeting.* **3** (*formal*) to ask for (another person's suggestions *etc*): *He invited proposals from members of the society.* **4** to behave as if asking for (something unpleasant): *To go mountain-climbing in winter weather is just inviting trouble.*

invitation [inviˈteiʃən] **1** *nc* a (written) request to come or go somewhere: *Have you received an invitation to their party?*; *We have had to refuse the invitation to the wedding.* **2** *nu* the act of inviting: *He attended the committee meeting on the invitation of the chairman.*

inˈviting *adj* (*neg* **un-**) attractive or tempting: *A* *walk in the rain is not an inviting prospect; I don't find the suggestion of a walk in the rain very inviting.*

invocation *see* **invoke**.

invoice ['invois] *nc* a list sent with goods giving details of price and quantity: *You must send an invoice with the books we ordered.* – *vt* to make such a list of (goods) or send such a list to (a customer): *The two sets of books were separately invoiced; Have you been invoiced for the goods?*

invoke [in'vouk] *vt* (*formal*) **1** to appeal to (some power, *eg* God, the law *etc*): *Any woman who is ill-treated and beaten by her husband should be able to invoke the law for her protection.* **2** to appeal for (help *etc*): *He invoked the support of his trade union.* **3** to summon or bring (*eg* a spirit) into the mind: *His music invokes the spirit of nature.*

invocation [invə'keiʃən] *ncu*.

involuntary [in'voləntəri] *adj* (of an action *etc*) not done intentionally: *He gave an involuntary cry; His reaction to the news of her death was obviously completely involuntary.* **in'voluntarily** *adv*.

involve [in'volv] *vt* **1** (not used with **is, was** *etc* and **-ing**) to require; to bring as a result: *His job involves a lot of travelling; I shall not accept that job until I know exactly what it involves.* **2** (*often with* **in**) to cause (a person) to take part (in an activity *etc*) or to be mixed up (in trouble *etc*): *He has always been involved in acting; They tried to involve me in their quarrel; Don't ask my advice – I don't want to be/get involved.*

in'volved *adj* complicated; mixed up: *His account of the affair was so involved that no-one could understand what had happened; Her business affairs seem to have become very involved.*

in'volvement *nu*.

invulnerable [in'vʌlnərəbl] *adj* (*formal*: *usu fig*) that cannot be wounded, damaged or successfully attacked; not vulnerable: *He is invulnerable to criticism; She looks stern and invulnerable but she is actually quite sensitive; As a friend of the manager, he is in an invulnerable position.*

inward ['inwəd] *adj* (*attrib*) **1** being within, *esp* in the mind: *his inward thoughts.* **2** moving towards the inside: *an inward curve in the coastline.*

'inward, 'inwards *advs* towards the inside or the centre: *When one of the eyes turns inwards, we call the effect a squint.*

'inwardly *adv* in one's thoughts; secretly: *He was inwardly pleased when she failed; She was laughing/groaning inwardly.*

iodine ['aiədiːn, (*Amer*) -dain] *nu* **1** an element (symbol **I**) used in medicine and photography, forming black crystals which give off a violet-coloured vapour when heated. **2** (*also* **tincture of iodine**) a liquid form of the element used as an antiseptic: *She put some iodine on the scratch on the child's finger.*

ion ['aion] *nc* (*tech*) an electrically charged atom or group of atoms that has become so charged by losing or gaining electrons.

iota [ai'outə] *nc* (*usu with neg*) a very small quantity: *There isn't an iota of truth in what he says.*

IOU [aiou'juː] *nc* short for **I owe you**, a signed note given as a receipt for borrowed money *etc*: *When I discovered I had forgotten my wallet and cheque book I had to give the hotel an IOU.*

Iran, Iranian *see* Appendix 2.

Iraq, Iraqi *see* Appendix 2.

irascible [i'rasibl] *adj* (*formal*) irritable or easily made angry: *He became more irascible as he got older; an irascible old man.* **i'rascibly** *adv*.

iˌrasci'bility *nu*.

irate [ai'reit] *adj* (*formal or facet*) angry: *The irate butcher chased the thieving dog out of the shop; I became more and more irate as I waited for my friend who was very late in arriving.*

ire ['aiə] *nu* (*liter*) anger: *The nobles dreaded the ire of the king.*

Ireland *see* Appendix 2.

iridescent [iri'desnt] *adj* (*formal*) shining or glittering with the colours of the rainbow: *Soap bubbles, mother-of-pearl and patches of oil are iridescent; iridescent colours.* **ˌiri'descence** *nu*.

iris ['aiəris] *nc* **1** (*tech*) the coloured part of the eye: *Her irises are very unusual – they are almost black.* **2** a kind of brightly-coloured flower with sword-shaped leaves: *a bunch of blue and yellow irises.*

Irish ['airiʃ] **1** *adj* of, or belonging to, Ireland or its inhabitants: *Irish whiskey; four Irish golfers.* **2** *adj, n* (of) a language spoken in parts of Ireland. – *See also* **Gaelic** *under* **Gael**. **3** *adj* (*pred*) comically illogical: *It sounds a bit Irish to say you're tired but not sleepy.*

Irishman, Irishwoman *see* Appendix 2.

See also Appendix 2.

irk [əːk] *vt* (*formal*) to annoy or weary: *It irks me to have to write letters.*

'irksome *adj* (*formal*) annoying or irritating: *Bed-making is an irksome job; I find waiting for people irksome.*

iron ['aiən] **1** *nu, adj* (*usu attrib*) (of) an element (symbol **Fe**) that is the most common metal, is very hard, and is widely used for making tools *etc*: *Steel is made from iron; The ground is as hard as iron; iron railings;* (*fig*) *an iron will* (= a very strong will); (*fig*) *iron determination* (= very strong determination). **2** *nc* a flat-bottomed instrument that is heated up and used for smoothing clothes *etc*: *I borrowed an iron from the hotel kitchen; a steam-iron.* **3** *nc* a type of golf-club: *He took his number three iron out of his golf-bag.* – *See also* **irons** *below*. – *vti* to smooth (clothes *etc*) with an iron: *This dress needs to be ironed; I've been ironing all afternoon.* – *See also* **iron out** *below*.

'ironing *nu* clothes *etc* waiting to be ironed, or just ironed: *What a huge pile of ironing!*

'irons *n pl* (*hist*) a prisoner's chains: *They put him in irons.*

Iron Curtain *n* the barrier, considered to exist between Communist countries and other countries, that prevents free communication and trading: *I have a nephew living behind the Iron Curtain;* (*attrib*) *Iron Curtain countries.*

'iron foundry *nc* a foundry where cast iron is made.

'ironing-board *nc* a padded board on which to iron clothes.

iron lung *nc* an apparatus used in hospitals *etc* to perform the breathing action for a patient whose lungs fail to work.

'ironmonger *nc* **1** a dealer in articles of metal *eg* tools, locks *etc* and other goods. **2** an ironmonger's shop: *Where is the nearest ironmonger?*

'ironmonger's *nc* an ironmonger's shop: *You can buy things like that at an ironmonger's.*

'ironmongery *nu* the business or goods of an ironmonger.

'ironworks *n sing or pl* a place where iron is smelted or made into heavy goods.

have several, too many *etc* **irons in the fire** to be involved in, or doing, several *etc* things at the same time: *Even if this project fails, he has several other irons in the fire.*

iron out *vt sep* **1** to get rid of (creases *etc*) by ironing: *I shall have to iron out the creases in this dress*; *Look at the creases in that skirt! Have you time to iron them out?* **2** (*fig*) to get rid of (difficulties *etc*) so that progress becomes easier: *They ironed out all the obvious problems at the first committee meeting*; *A few difficulties remain but I think that we can iron them all out.*

strike while the iron is hot to act *etc* while the situation is favourable: *On hearing of his inheritance she struck while the iron was hot and asked him to repay the money he owed her.*

irony ['aiərəni] **1** *nu* a form of deliberate mockery in which one says the opposite of what is obviously true: *'That was clever,' he said with irony, looking at the burnt pan.* **2** *nu* seeming mockery in a situation, words *etc*: *The irony of the situation was that he stole the money which she had already planned to give him.* **3** *nc* an ironical situation: *It was just one of life's little ironies.*

ironic(al) [ai'ronik(l)] *adj* containing, showing or expressing irony: *An ironic(al) situation/remark*; *It is ironic that you killed a man who was about to die of a heart attack.* **i'ronically** *adv.*

irrational [i'raʃənl] *adj* (*formal*) not reasonable or rational: *He had a terror of spiders and several other irrational fears*; *Even sensible people can be quite irrational in their attitude to their own children.* **ir,ratio'nality** *ncu.* **ir'rationally** *adv.*

irreconcilable [irekən'sailəbl] *adj* **1** (*with* **with**) (of ideas, opinions *etc*) not agreeing or fitting together: *We believe that the policy of domination by white men over black is irreconcilable with a belief in human rights.* **2** (*formal*) (of people) not willing to be reconciled: *Long after the quarrel they were still irreconcilable.* **ir,recon'cilably** *adv.*

irrefutable [iri'fju:təbl] *adj* (*formal*) (of a statement *etc*) not able to be rejected or proved false: *His argument is completely irrefutable*; *irrefutable evidence.*

irregular [i'regjulə] *adj* **1** not happening *etc* regularly: *His attendance at classes was irregular*; *She's a very irregular church-attender.* **2** not formed smoothly or evenly: *irregular handwriting*; *The road has an irregular surface*; *The surface of the table is very irregular.* **3** (*formal*) contrary to rules: *It is extremely irregular for police officers to drink alcohol while on duty.* **4** (*gram*) not formed *etc* in the normal way: *irregular verbs*; *The plural of 'woman' is irregular.* **ir'regularly** *adv.*

ir,regu'larity [-'la-] *ncu*: *The irregularity of English pronunciation causes trouble for beginners*; *He sandpapered the irregularities in the wood.*

irrelevant [i'relivənt] *adj* **1** not connected with the subject that is being discussed *etc*: *Your remark is irrelevant to the present problem*; *Please do not make such irrelevant comments.* **2** (*esp pred*) unimportant; not relevant: *When they heard about the disaster, their own troubles seemed irrelevant.* **ir'relevantly** *adv.*

ir'relevance, ir'relevancy *ncus*: *the irrelevance of your suggestion*; *We're wasting time on irrelevancies.*

irremovable [iri'mu:vəbl] *adj* (*formal*) (*eg* of a stain) that cannot be removed.

irreparable [i'repərəbl] *adj* (*formal*) (of injury, loss *etc*) that cannot be restored or put right: *The art gallery suffered irreparable losses in the fire*; *The damage to the house is quite irreparable.*

ir'reparably *adv*: *The building was irreparably damaged.*

See also **repair**.

irreplaceable [iri'pleisəbl] *adj* too good, rare *etc* to be able to be replaced if lost or damaged: *Don't drop that precious vase – it's irreplaceable*; *irreplaceable family heirlooms.*

irrepressible [iri'presəbl] *adj* (of a person or his cheerful spirits *etc*) not able to be subdued or repressed: *an irrepressible little boy*; *his irrepressible cheerfulness*; *That child is irrepressible – I have never seen him quiet or unhappy.* **,irre'pressibly** *adv.*

irreproachable [iri'proutʃəbl] *adj* (*formal*) (of behaviour *etc*) free from faults: *His conduct was irreproachable*; *His irreproachable behaviour tended to annoy his wife.*

irresistible [iri'zistəbl] *adj* too strong, delightful, tempting *etc* to be resisted: *He had an irresistible desire to hit her*; *She looked irresistible in the hat.* **,irre'sistibly** *adv.* **'irre,sisti'bility** *nu.*

irresolute [i'rezəlu:t] *adj* (*formal*) (of a person or his behaviour) full of hesitation and doubts; not resolute: *He was too weak and irresolute to make a good leader*; *She stood irresolute, not knowing whether to go forward or turn back*; *The irresolute captain was responsible for the defeat of his troops.*

ir'resolutely *adv.* **ir'resoluteness, ir,reso'lution** [-ʃən] *nus.*

See also **resolve** *under* **resolution**.

irrespective [iri'spektiv]: **irrespective of** (*formal*) without consideration of: *The pupils are all taught together, irrespective of age or ability*; *I shall come tomorrow, irrespective of whether it is raining or not.*

irresponsible [iri'sponsəbl] *adj* (of a person or his behaviour) not reliable, trustworthy or sensible; not responsible: *It is irresponsible to leave a small child alone in the house*; *irresponsible parents/conduct.* **'irre,sponsi'bility** *nu.* **,irre'sponsibly** *adv.*

irretrievable [iri'tri:vəbl] *adj* (*formal*) (of *eg* a loss or mistake) that cannot be recovered or put right; not retrievable: *Her lies did irretrievable damage to the trust that was between them*; *She obtained a divorce on the grounds of the irretrievable breakdown of their marriage*; *The damage done to the firm by that scandal proved irretrievable.* **,irre'trievably** *adv.*

irreverent [i'revərənt] *adj* showing no respect or reverence (*eg* for holy things, or people and things generally considered important): *It is irreverent to talk noisily in a church*; (*formal*) *He wrote an irreverent poem about his university professor.*

ir'reverently *adv.* **ir'reverence** *nu.*

irrevocable [i'revəkəbl] *adj* (*formal*) that cannot be altered: *an irrevocable decision*; *That course of action will be quite irrevocable.* **ir'revocably** *adv.* **ir,revoca'bility, ir'revocableness** *nus.*

See also **revoke**.

irrigate ['irigeit] *vt* to supply water to (land), *esp* by canals or other artificial means: *The paddy-fields were irrigated by a network of canals*; (*formal or liter*) *A broad river irrigated the plain.* **,irri'gation** *nu.*

irritate ['iriteit] *vt* **1** to annoy or make angry: *The children's chatter irritated him*; *I was feeling irritated with her.* **2** to make (a part of the body) sore, red, itchy *etc*: *Wool can irritate a baby's skin.*

'irritable *adj* easily annoyed: *He was in an irritable mood*; *The old man grows more irritable as* *his pain increases.* **'irritably** *adv.* **ˌirrita'bility, 'irritableness** *nus.*

'irritant *nc, adj* (*tech or formal*) (something) that causes irritation: *Nettles contain an irritant (substance).*

'irritating *adj* tending to annoy or irritate: *She has an irritating voice; I find her manner extremely irritating.*

ˌirri'tation 1 *nu* the process of irritating or condition of being irritated: *A peeled onion causes irritation to the eyes and nose.* **2** *nc* something that is irritating: *The neighbours' radio is a constant irritation to me.*

is *see* **be**.

Islam ['izla:m] *nu* the Muslim religion.

Is'lamic [-'la-] *adj* of Islam: *Islamic festivals; I think that custom is Islamic in origin.*

island ['ailənd] *nc* **1** a piece of land surrounded by water: *The island lay a mile off the coast*; (*fig*) *An oasis is an island of vegetation in the middle of the desert*; (*attrib*) *island scenery/life.* **2** (*also* **'traffic island**) a traffic-free area, built in the middle of a street, for pedestrians to stand on.

'islander *nc.*

See also **insular**.

isle [ail] (*liter or found with cap in place-names*) an island: *a tropical isle; the Isle of Man.*

isn't *see* **be**.

isolate ['aisəleit] *vt* to separate or keep apart from others: *Several cottages have been isolated by the flood water*; (*formal*) *A child with an infectious disease should be isolated.*

'isolated *adj* **1** (of a place) lonely or remote: *isolated country districts; His cottage is rather isolated.* **2** solitary; without companions: *As a child he had an isolated life; He keeps himself isolated in the country.* **3** (*usu attrib*) not part of a group or trend: *It was an isolated instance of rape.*

ˌiso'lation *ncu.*

isotope ['aisətoup] *nc* (*tech*) one of two or more kinds of atom of the same element, some being heavier than others.

Israel, Israeli *see* Appendix 2.

issue ['iʃu:] **1** *vt* to give or send out, or to distribute, *esp* officially: *The police issued a description of the criminal; The general issued fresh instructions; Rifles were issued to the troops; When were decimal coins first issued in Britain?* **2** *vi* (*formal*) to flow or come out (from something): *A strange noise issued from the room.* – **1** *nu* the act of issuing or process of being issued: *Stamp collectors like to buy new stamps on the day of issue.* **2** *nc* something which is issued: *A recent issue of £5 notes was discovered to be wrongly printed.* **3** *nc* one number in the series of a newspaper, magazine *etc*: *Have you seen the latest issue of that magazine?; Where is today's issue of the Times?* **4** *nc* a subject for discussion and argument: *The question of pay is not an important issue at the moment; The issue of independence for Scotland was debated in Parliament today.* **5** *nu* (*legal*) children: *He died without issue.*

make an issue of (something) to make (something) the subject of an argument: *I don't agree with you, but I don't want to make an issue of it.*

the point at issue (*formal*) the question that is being discussed: *The point at issue is not whether we would like a holiday, but whether we could afford one.*

take issue with (*formal*) to disagree with (a person): *I take issue with you on the question of education.*

isthmus ['isməs] *nc* (*sometimes found with cap in place-names*) a narrow strip of land joining two larger pieces: *the Isthmus of Panama.*

it [it] *pron* **1** (used as the subject of a verb or object of a verb or preposition) the thing spoken of, used *esp* of lifeless things, but also of animals and babies, when the sex is unknown or not important: *If you find my pencil, please give it to me; The dog is in the garden, isn't it?; I picked up the baby because it was crying; I bought a new pen, but I can't write very well with it.* **2** used as a subject in certain kinds of sentences, and *esp* in talking about the weather, distance or time: *Is it raining very hard?; It's cold today; It is five o'clock; Is it the fifth of March?; It's only two miles to the village; It looks as if we can't have our holiday; Is it your turn to make the tea?; I'd never have succeeded if it hadn't been for you; It isn't that I don't want to help you – it's just that I haven't time.* **3** used as the grammatical subject of a sentence when the real subject comes later: *It was difficult finding your house* (= Finding your house was difficult); *Will it be necessary to come back?; It is impossible for him to finish the work* (= For him to finish the work is impossible); *It was nice of you to come; Is it likely that he would go without us?* **4** (*usu* as the object of a verb or preposition) used to refer to a general situation or to some fact *etc* already mentioned or understood: *He decided to do exercises every morning, but couldn't keep it up; My mother is ill and the worst of it is that our doctor is on holiday; 'Could I speak to you for a moment?' 'Yes, what is it?'; I'm leaving – I can't endure it any longer.* **5** (*usu* as the subject of the verb **be**) used to give emphasis to a certain word or phrase in a sentence: *It was you (that) I wanted to see, not Mary; It was the bad weather that caused his illness; Who is it that keeps borrowing my umbrella?; It was this chair I put my book on, not that one.* **6** (*often inf*) used with some verbs as a direct object with little meaning: *The car broke down and we had to walk it; Oh, bother it!; He was inclined to lord it over us.*

its *adj* (*attrib*), *pron* (something) which belongs to it: *The bird has hurt its wing; The table was standing in the rain and its surface is spoilt.*

itself *pron* **1** used as the object of a verb or preposition when an object, animal *etc* is the object of an action it performs: *The cat looked at itself in the mirror; The cat stretched itself by the fire.* **2** used to emphasize **it** or the name of an object, animal *etc*: *The house itself is quite small, but the garden attached to it is big.* **3** without help *etc*: *It did it itself.*

by itself *see* **by oneself** *under* **by**.

it is not itself *see* **not be oneself** *under* **one**.

Italian *see* Appendix 2.

italic [i'talik] *adj* (of print) of the sloping kind used *esp* to show emphasis and for the examples in this dictionary: *This example is printed in italic type.*

i'talicize, -ise [-saiz] *vti* to put (words) in italics: *We italicize the examples in this dictionary; He italicizes too much.*

i'talics *n pl* italic print: *This example is printed in italics.*

Italy *see* Appendix 2.

itch [itʃ] *nc* **1** an irritating feeling in the skin which makes one want to scratch: *He had an itch in the middle of his back and could not scratch it easily.* **2** (*fig inf*) a strong desire: *I have an itch to go to*

Malta. – *vi* **1** to have an itch: *Some pills and medicines can cause the skin to itch.* **2** (*fig inf*: *usu with* **is, was** *etc*) to have a strong desire (for something, or to be something): *I was itching to slap the child*; *They were itching for the post to arrive.*

'itchy *adj* itching: *His rash was itchy*; *I feel itchy all over – do you think that I have chickenpox?*

'itchiness *nu*.

it'd *see* **have, would**.

item ['aitəm] *nc* **1** a separate object, article *etc*, *esp* one of a number named in a list: *He ticked the items as he read through the list.* **2** a separate piece of information or news: *Did you see the item about dogs in the newspaper?*

itinerant [i'tinərənt] *adj* (*formal*: *esp attrib*) travelling from place to place, *eg* on business: *an itinerant preacher.*

itinerary [ai'tinərəri] *nc* (*formal*) a route for a journey: *Have you planned your itinerary yet?*; *I have just received my itinerary from the travel agent's office.*

it'll *see* **will**.

it's, itself *see* **it**.

it's *see* **be, have**.

I've *see* **have**.

ivory ['aivəri] **1** *nu*, *adj* (of) the hard white substance forming the tusks of an elephant, walrus *etc*: *Ivory was formerly used to make piano keys*; (*attrib*) *ivory chessmen.* **2** *nc* a figure *etc* carved out of ivory: *This museum has a collection of Japanese ivories.*

ivy ['aivi] *nu* a type of climbing evergreen plant with small shiny leaves that grows up trees and walls: *The walls of the cottage are covered in ivy.*

Jj

jab [dʒab] – *pt, ptp* **jabbed** – *vt* to poke or prod: *He jabbed me in the ribs with his elbow*; *She jabbed the needle into her finger by mistake.* – *See also* **jab at** *below.* – *nc* **1** a sudden hard poke or prod: *He gave me a jab with his finger*; (*fig*) *I felt a jab of pain.* **2** (*inf*) an injection: *Has the baby had all his jabs yet?*

'jab at *vt fus* to poke or prod: *He jabbed at the tree angrily with his stick.*

jabber ['dʒabə] *vti* (*inf*: *usu derog*) to talk idly, rapidly and indistinctly: *The women are always jabbering at one another*; *He jabbered a hasty apology.*

jack [dʒak] *nc* **1** an instrument for lifting up a motor car or other heavy weight: *You should always keep a jack in the car in case you need to change a wheel.* – *See also* **jack up** *below.* **2** the playing-card between the ten and queen, sometimes called the **knave**: *The jack, queen and king are the three face cards.*

every man jack (*inf*) everybody: *Every man jack of us must help.*

jack up *vt sep* to raise (a motor car *etc*) and keep it supported, with a jack: *You need to jack up the car before you try to remove the wheel.*

jackal ['dʒako:l, (*Amer*) -kl] *nc* a type of wild animal similar to a dog or wolf.

jackass ['dʒakas] *nc* **1** a male ass. **2** (*inf*) a stupid person: *the silly jackass!*

laughing jackass *nc* a type of Australian bird that sounds as if it is laughing.

jackboot ['dʒakbu:t] *nc* a type of tall *esp* military boot that reaches above the knee: *a pair of jackboots.*

jackdaw ['dʒakdo:] *nc* a type of bird of the crow family that sometimes steals bright objects.

jacket ['dʒakit] *nc* **1** a short coat: *When he took his suit out of the cupboard, he found that the jacket was dirty*; *He wore brown trousers and a blue jacket.* **2** (*sometimes in cmpds*) a covering, *esp* a loose paper cover for a book: *I like the design on this book-jacket*; *She removed the jacket of the book before I could admire the design.*

'jacketed *adj* (*usu in cmpds*) wearing, or in, a jacket: *leather-jacketed teenagers.*

jack-in-the-box ['dʒakinðəboks] *nc* a toy consisting of a figure, fixed to a spring inside a box, which comes out suddenly when the lid is opened: *She was given a jack-in-the-box as a birthday present*; *The child was jumping up and down with excitement like a jack-in-the-box.*

jack-knife ['dʒaknaif] *nc* a large folding knife. – *vi* (of *eg* a lorry and its trailer) to swing together so that the trailer is at a sharp angle to the cab: *The lorry skidded on the ice and jack-knifed, blocking the road.*

jackpot ['dʒakpot] *nc* in playing cards, some competitions *etc*, a fund of prize-money that goes on increasing until it is won: *The jackpot now amounts to £1 750.*

hit the jackpot (*inf*) to win or obtain a lot of money or success: *He must have hit the jackpot with the sales of his last gramophone record.*

jade [dʒeid] **1** *nu*, *adj* (of) a type of hard stone, *usu* green in colour: *a piece of jade*; *jade ornaments.* **2** *nu* jade ornaments *etc*: *He collects jade.*

jaded ['dʒeidid] *adj* (of *eg* a person or his interest, appetite *etc*) worn out and made tired and dull: *She looked a bit jaded after the party*; *He thought a walk would revive his jaded spirits.*

jagged ['dʒagid] *adj* (*usu attrib*) having rough or sharp and uneven edges: *jagged rocks*; *a jagged tear in his jacket.* **'jaggedly** *adv.* **'jaggedness** *nu.*

jaguar ['dʒagjuə, (*Amer*) 'dʒagwa:r] *nc* a South American beast of prey of the cat family, resembling the leopard.

jail, gaol [dʒeil] *ncu* (a) prison: *There are bad conditions in some jails*; *You could be sent to jail for doing that.* – *vt* to put in prison: *He was jailed for two years.*

'jailer, 'jailor, 'gaoler *nc* a person who has charge of a jail or of prisoner(s): *The jailer was knocked unconscious in the riot.*

'jailbird, 'gaolbird *nc* (*derog inf*) a person who is or has often been in jail: *Her father and both her uncles are jailbirds.*

jam[1] [dʒam] *nu* a thick sticky substance made of fruit *etc* preserved by being boiled with sugar: *Have some raspberry jam on your bread*; (*attrib*) *a jam sandwich.*

jammy *adj* **1** covered, or filled, with jam: *jammy fingers*; *Don't let that child touch me! His fingers are jammy*; (*inf*) *a jammy biscuit.* **2** (*Brit inf*) lucky; very good; easy: *a jammy job*; *Your new job sounds too jammy to be true.*

jam[2] [dʒam] – *pt, ptp* **jammed** – **1** *vt* to crowd full: *The gateway was jammed with angry people.* **2** *vt* to squeeze, press or wedge tightly or firmly: *He jammed his foot in the doorway; He jammed his hat on his head.* **3** *vti* to stick and (cause to) be unable to move: *The door/steering-wheel has jammed; He jammed the door open with his foot.* **4** *vt* (of a radio station) to cause interference with (another radio station's broadcast) by sending out signals on a similar wavelength. – *nc* **1** (*sometimes in cmpds*) a crowding together of vehicles, people *etc* so that movement is difficult or impossible: *traffic-jams*; (*inf*) *There's a terrible jam at the car park exit.* **2** (*fig inf*) a difficult situation: *I'm in a bit of a jam – I haven't got enough money to pay for this meal.*

jam on *vt sep* to put (brakes *etc*) on with force and haste: *When the dog ran in front of his car he jammed on his brakes and skidded; He jammed them on suddenly.*

jamb [dʒam] *nc* (*sometimes in cmpds*) the side post of a door or fireplace *etc*: *He leaned lazily on the jamb of the door; the door-jamb.*

jamboree [dʒambə'riː] *nc* **1** (*inf*) a large and lively gathering: *Our neighbours have a noisy jamboree every Saturday night.* **2** a rally of Boy Scouts, Girl Guides *etc.*

jammed *see* **jam**[2].

jammy *see* **jam**[1].

jangle ['dʒaŋgl] **1** *vti* to (cause to) give a harsh (ringing) sound: *The bell jangled noisily.* **2** *vt* (*inf*) to upset or irritate: *The baby's constant crying jangled her nerves.*

janitor ['dʒanitə] – *fem* **'janitress** – *nc* a caretaker or a doorkeeper.

January ['dʒanjuəri] *n* the first month of the year, the month following December: *He is coming next January; He will be here in January; He will arrive on January 16* (said as 'on January (the) sixteenth' or 'on the sixteenth of January'); *He is coming on the 16th/sixteenth of January.*

Japan, Japanese *see* Appendix 2.

jar[1] [dʒaː] *nc* (*sometimes in cmpds*) a kind of bottle made of glass or pottery, with a wide mouth: *She poured the jam into large jars; jam-jars.*

jar[2] [dʒaː] – *pt, ptp* **jarred** – **1** *vi* (*with* **on**) to have a harsh and startling effect (on): *Her sharp tone jarred on my ears.* **2** *vt* to give a shock to the nerves of: *The violent quarrel with her husband had jarred her badly.* – *nc* a shock to the feelings or nerves: *To be reminded of his foolishness gave him an unpleasant jar.*

'jarring *adj* startling or harsh: *The orange curtains with the purple carpet had a jarring effect; I think that her voice is very jarring.*

jargon ['dʒaːgən] *nu* **1** (*usu derog*) special words or phrases used within a trade or profession *etc, esp* if used unnecessarily: *legal jargon; A broken thigh is a 'fractured femur' in medical jargon; Can't you explain the matter clearly, without all that sociological jargon?* **2** (*old*) something said or written, which is difficult to understand: *Thieves use a special jargon in order to confuse anyone who overhears.*

jarred, jarring *see* **jar**[2].

jaundice ['dʒoːndis] *nu* a diseased state of the body in which the skin and whites of the eyes become yellow: *He is suffering from jaundice.*

'jaundiced *adj* **1** suffering from jaundice: *The baby was very jaundiced.* **2** (*fig*) (of a person or his judgement) affected by envy, disappointment *etc*: *He had a jaundiced view of life; His attitude to women has been rather jaundiced since his wife left him.*

jaunt [dʒoːnt] *nc* (*inf*) a brief trip or journey made for pleasure: *Did you enjoy your jaunt to Paris?*

jaunty ['dʒoːnti] *adj* gay and cheerful: *a jaunty mood/hat; You do seem jaunty today.* **'jauntily** *adv.* **'jauntiness** *nu.*

javelin ['dʒavəlin] *nc* a light spear for throwing: *Throwing the javelin was the most popular event in the local athletic competition.*

jaw [dʒoː] *nc* either of the two bones of the mouth in which the teeth are set: *the upper/lower jaw; His jaw was broken in the fight.*

jaws *n pl* **1** the mouth (*esp* of an animal): *The crocodile's jaws opened wide*; (*fig*) *He was saved from the jaws of death.* **2** the parts of a tool (*eg* a vice) that can hold things tightly: *He held the cable in the jaws of the insulated pliers.*

jay [dʒei] *nc* a brightly-coloured bird of the crow family.

jaywalker ['dʒeiwoːkə] *nc* (*derog*) a person who walks carelessly among traffic: *She never looks to see if there's a car coming before she crosses the road – she's a jaywalker.*

'jaywalking *nu*: *The police were concerned about the number of accidents involving jaywalking.*

jazz [dʒaz] *nu* popular music of American Negro origin: *He plays jazz as a hobby; She prefers jazz to classical music*; (*attrib*) *a jazz musician.*

'jazzy *adj* (*inf*) **1** bright or bold in colour or design: *a jazzy shirt; Her clothes are too jazzy for my taste.* **2** (*usu attrib*) of or like jazz: *I don't like such jazzy music.*

jazz up *vt sep* (*inf*) to make (something, *orig* music) more lively or interesting: *He jazzed up the folk tune; I'll jazz up the stew with some courgettes; This party is boring – let's try and jazz it up a bit.*

jealous ['dʒeləs] *adj* **1** (*pred with* **of**) feeling or showing envy: *She is jealous of her sister; She was jealous of her friend's good looks.* **2** having feelings of dislike for any possible rivals (*esp* in love): *a jealous husband; Don't ask her to dance with you – her husband is very jealous.* **3** (*formal*) anxiously looking after something that one has: *They are jealous of their rights/privileges.* **'jealously** *adv.*

'jealousy *ncu*: *In a fit of jealousy he tore up his friend's drawing*; (*formal*) *the jealousies and rivalries of school life.*

jeans [dʒiːnz] *n pl* trousers, *usu* tight-fitting, made of denim: *She wore a white sweater and blue jeans; a pair of jeans.*

jeep [dʒiːp] *nc* a kind of small motor vehicle used *esp* by the armed forces.

jeer [dʒiə] **1** *vt* to shout at or laugh at rudely or mockingly: *He was jeered as he tried to speak to the crowds.* **2** *vi* (*with* **at**) to make fun of (someone) rudely: *He's always jeering at her stupidity.* – *nc* a rude or mocking shout: *the jeers and boos of the audience.*

'jeering *adj* (*usu attrib*) mocking or scornful: *a jeering comment; He spoke in a jeering voice.* **'jeeringly** *adv.*

jelly ['dʒeli] **1** *nu* the juice of fruit boiled with sugar until it is firm: *The child spread butter and blackcurrant jelly on her bread; gooseberry jelly.* **2** *ncu* (a portion of) a transparent, smooth and rather soft food, *usu* fruit flavoured: *I've made ten raspberry jellies for the party.* **3** *nu* any jelly-like substance: *Frogs' eggs are enclosed in a kind of jelly.*

'jellyfish – *pls* **'jellyfish, 'jellyfishes** – *nc* a kind of sea animal with a jelly-like body: *The beach was* *covered with dead jellyfish; The child was stung by a jellyfish.*

jemmy ['dʒemi] *nc* (*inf*) a kind of short crowbar, used *esp* by burglars: *When the police arrested the suspect, he had a jemmy in his pocket.*

jeopardy ['dʒepədi] *nu* (*formal*) danger: *This strike has put many men's jobs in jeopardy.*

'jeopardize, -ise *vt* (*formal*) to put in danger: *Always being late could jeopardize your chances of promotion.*

jerk [dʒə:k] *nc* a short, sudden movement: *We felt a jerk as the train started; He sat up with a jerk.* – *vti* to move with a jerk or jerks: *He grasped my arm and jerked me round; The car jerked to a halt.*

'jerky *adj* jerking; full of jerks: *a jerky movement; a jerky way of speaking; She has some disease which makes all her movements rather jerky.* **'jerkily** *adv.* **'jerkiness** *nu.*

jerkin ['dʒə:kin] *nc* a type of short jacket: *The motor-cyclist wore a black leather jerkin.*

jerry-built [dʒeri'bilt] *adj* (*derog*) built hastily, cheaply and badly: *a street of modern jerry-built houses; I don't like that office building – it looks jerry-built.*

jersey ['dʒə:zi] *nc* a sweater or pullover: *I think that I'll put a jersey on over my blouse – it's a bit cold today.*

Jerusalem artichoke *see* **artichoke**.

jest [dʒest] *nc* (*arch or facet*) a joke; something done or said to cause amusement: *He started his speech with a jest about the weather.* – *vi* (*arch or facet*) to joke: *This is not a matter to jest about.*

'jester *nc* (*hist*) a man employed in the courts of kings, nobles *etc* to amuse them with jokes *etc.*

in 'jest (*arch, facet or formal*) as a joke; not seriously: *I was speaking in jest when I suggested a swim before going to bed.*

jet[1] [dʒet] *nu, adj* (of) a hard black mineral substance, used for ornaments *etc*: *The beads are* (*made of*) *jet; a jet brooch.*

,jet-'black *adj* very black: *jet-black hair; Her hair is jet-black.*

jet[2] [dʒet] *nc* **1** a sudden, strong stream or flow (of liquid, gas, flame or steam), forced through a narrow opening: *Firemen have to be trained to direct the jets from their hoses accurately.* **2** a narrow opening in an apparatus through which a jet comes: *This gas jet is blocked.* **3** an aeroplane driven by jet propulsion: *We flew by jet to America.* – *v* – *pt, ptp* **'jetted** – *vti* (*inf*) to (cause to) go by jet aeroplane: *They jetted over to the United States at least once a year; The avocadoes have been jetted from Israel.*

'jet-lag *nu* the unpleasant or undesirable symptoms such as tiredness and lack of concentration shown by a person whose normal patterns of working and sleeping have been upset by travelling a long distance across several time zones in a short period of time: *He was obviously suffering from jet-lag – what he was saying did not make sense.*

,jet-pro'pelled *adj* driven by jet propulsion: *He is driving one of the latest jet-propelled racing-cars; Concorde is jet-propelled.*

jet propulsion *nu* a method of producing very fast forward motion (for aircraft, missiles *etc*) by sucking air or liquid *etc* into a **jet engine** and forcing it out from behind.

the 'jet set (*often derog*) very wealthy people who enjoy a life of frequent travel (by jet) and expensive holidays: *I don't like that part of France since the jet set started going there.*

jetsam ['dʒetsəm] *nu* goods thrown overboard from a ship (and washed up on the shore). *See also* **flotsam**.

jetted *see* **jet**[2].

jettison ['dʒetisn] *vt* **1** (*formal*) to throw (cargo *etc*) overboard to lighten a ship, aircraft *etc* in times of danger: *When one of the engines failed the crew of the aeroplane jettisoned the luggage.* **2** (*formal fig*) to abandon (*eg* a plan) in times of difficulty *etc*: *Because of the shortage of money, they had to jettison their plans to travel to Greece.*

jetty ['dʒeti] *nc* a small pier for use as a landing-place: *There were two fishing-boats tied up at the jetty.*

Jew [dʒu:] – *fem* **'Jewess** [-es, (*Amer*) -is] – *nc* **1** a person of the Jewish race or religion. **2** (*offensive*) a person who is mean about, or very anxious to make more, money.

'Jewish *adj* of the race or religion of a people originally living in the territory around Jerusalem but now found in most countries of the world. *See also* Appendix 2.

jewel ['dʒu:əl] *nc* **1** a precious stone: *rubies, emeralds and other jewels.* **2** (*fig*) something that is highly valued: *This painting by Manet is the jewel of his art collection.*

'jewelled, (*Amer*) **'jeweled** *adj* (*attrib*) ornamented with jewels: *a jewelled crown.*

'jeweller, (*Amer*) **'jeweler** *nc* **1** a person who makes, or deals in, ornaments and other articles made of precious stones and metals. **2** a jeweller's shop: *Is there a jeweller near here?*

'jeweller's, (*Amer*) **'jeweler's** *nc* a jeweller's shop: *I must take my watch to the jeweller's to be mended.*

'jewellery, (*Amer*) **'jewelry** *nu* articles made or sold by a jeweller, *esp* those worn for personal adornment, *eg* bracelets, necklaces, brooches, rings *etc*: *Which jewellery will you wear with that dress?; All her jewellery was stolen by the thieves.*

jib[1] [dʒib] *nc* **1** a three-cornered sail in front of a ship's foremast. **2** the jutting-out arm of a crane.

jib[2] [dʒib]: **'jib at** – *pt, ptp* **jibbed** *vt fus* to refuse (to do something) or to object (to something, or to doing something): *The horse jibbed at the water jump; I jibbed at having to wash all the dishes myself.*

jibe, gibe [dʒaib] *nc* a cruel or unkind remark or taunt: *cruel jibes.* – *vi* (*with* **at**) to make fun (of), cruelly or unkindly: *His friends jibed at his love of poetry.*

jiffy ['dʒifi] *nc* (*inf*) a moment: *I'll be back in a jiffy.*

jig [dʒig] *nc* (a piece of music for) a type of lively dance: *Can you dance an Irish jig?; The band played a lively jig.* – *v* – *pt, ptp* **jigged** – *vi* (*inf*) to jump (about) or move jerkily: *Stop jigging about and stand still!*

jiggle ['dʒigl] *vti* (*inf*) to (cause to) jump (about) or move jerkily: *He jiggled his keys about on his key-ring; I can't comb your hair if you jiggle up and down.*

jigsaw (puzzle) ['dʒigso:] *nc* a puzzle made up of many differently-shaped pieces that fit together to form a picture: *While she was ill in bed, the child spent her time doing jigsaws.*

jilt [dʒilt] *vt* to reject or send away (someone with whom one has been in love): *After being her boyfriend for two years, he suddenly jilted her.*

jingle ['dʒiŋgl] **1** *ncu* a slight metallic ringing sound (made *eg* by coins or by small bells): *The dog pricked up its ears at the jingle of its master's keys.* **2**

nc a simple rhyming verse or tune: *nursery rhymes and other little jingles*; *advertising jingles.* – *vti* to (cause to) make a clinking or ringing sound: *He jingled the coins in his hand*; *The bells on the horse's harness jingled merrily.*

jinx [dʒiŋks] *nc* (*inf*) an evil spell or influence: *Something always goes wrong with our holiday plans – there seems to be a jinx on them.*

jitters ['dʒitəz] *n pl* (*with* **the**: *inf*) great nervousness: *Being alone in the house at night gives me the jitters.*

'jittery *adj* very nervous and easily upset: *She has become very jittery since her accident*; *She gets jittery if she is alone in the house at night*; *in rather a jittery state.*

job [dʒob] *nc* **1** a person's daily work or employment: *She has a job as a bank-clerk*; *Many men may lose their jobs*; *Some of the unemployed men have been out of a job for four years.* **2** a piece of work or a task: *I have several jobs to do before going to bed*; *The car has to be repaired, and I don't know what the job will cost*; *His firm sent him off on a job in the Middle East.*

'jobbing *adj* (*attrib*) doing various kinds of jobs for different people for payment: *a jobbing gardener.*

give (something) up as a bad job (*inf*) to decide that something is not worth doing, or impossible to do, and so stop doing it: *I could not persuade him to practise the piano, and finally gave it up as a bad job.*

a good job (*inf*) a lucky or satisfactory state of affairs: *It's a good job that she can't hear what you're saying*; *He has lost his trumpet, and a good job too!*

have a 'job (*inf*) to have difficulty (doing something, to do something, with something): *I've had quite a job with this essay*; *He has a hard job to pay all the bills*; *You'll have a job finishing all this work tonight.*

a job lot a mixed collection (*eg* of goods) *esp* if of poor quality: *I bought this clock in a job lot at an auction and I'm surprised that it works.*

just the job (*inf*) entirely suitable: *These gloves are just the job for gardening.*

make the best of a bad job (*inf*) to do one's best in difficult circumstances: *We haven't the right tools or materials, but we must just make the best of a bad job.*

jockey ['dʒoki] *nc* a person employed to ride horses in races.

jockey for position to try to push one's way into a favourable position: *The senior staff in this firm are all jockeying for position.*

jocose [dʒə'kous] *adj* (*very formal or facet*) (of a person, his personality *etc*) humorous; inclined to joke: *a jocose old gentleman*; *He seems very jocose today – I think he's been drinking wine.* **jo'cosely** *adj.* **jo'coseness** *nu.*

jocular ['dʒokjulə] *adj* (*formal*) intended to be humorous: *some jocular comments about schoolteachers*; *His remarks were meant to be jocular but she was upset by them.* **ˌjocu'larity** [-'la-] *nu.*

'jocularly *adj*: *He jocularly referred to his father as the Old Miser.*

jodhpurs ['dʒodpəz] *n pl* riding breeches that fit tightly from the knee to the ankle: *a pair of jodhpurs*; *Where are my jodhpurs?*

jog [dʒog] – *pt, ptp* **jogged** – **1** *vt* to push, shake or knock gently: *He jogged my arm and I spilt my coffee*; (*fig*) *I have forgotten, but something may jog my memory later on.* **2** *vi* to travel slowly: *The cart jogged along the rough track.* **3** *vi* to run at a gentle pace, *esp* for the sake of exercise: *She jogs round the park for half an hour every morning.*

at a 'jog-trot at a gentle running pace: *Every morning he goes down the road at a jog-trot.*

joggle ['dʒogl] *vti* (*inf*) to (cause to) shake or move slightly from side to side: *Don't joggle the table!*

join [dʒoin] **1** *vt* (*often with* **up, on** *etc*) to put together or connect: *The electrician joined the wires (up) wrongly*; *You must join this piece (on) to that piece*; *He joined the two stories together to make a play*; *The island is joined to the mainland by a sandbank at low tide.* **2** *vt* to connect (two points) *eg* by a line, as in geometry: *Join point A to point B.* **3** *vt* to become a member of (a group): *He joined the team a year ago*; *Join our club!* **4** *vti* (*sometimes with* **up**) to meet and come together (with): *This lane joins the main road*; *Do you know where the two rivers join?*; *They joined up with us for the remainder of the holiday.* **5** *vt* (*inf*) to come into the company of: *I'll join you later in the restaurant*; *Who'll join me in a drink?* (= Who will have a drink with me?) – *See also* **join in, join on, join up** *below.* – *nc* a place where two things are joined: *You can hardly see the joins in the wallpaper.*

join battle (*liter*) to begin fighting: *The two armies joined battle at about midday.*

join forces (with) to come together for united work or action: *We would do better if we joined forces (with each other).*

join hands to clasp one another's hands (*eg* for dancing): *Join hands with your partner*; *They joined hands in a ring* (= forming a circle).

join in 1 *vi* to take part: *We're playing a game – do join in!* **2** *vt fus* to take part in: *He would not join in the game/the conversation.*

join on *vi* to add oneself to a group: *They were going for a walk and we joined on.*

join up *vi* to become a member of an armed force: *He joined up in 1940.*

See also **joint, junction.**

joiner ['dʒoinə] *nc* **1** a skilled worker in wood who puts doors, stairs *etc* into buildings: *He is a joiner by trade.* **2** a joiner's workshop: *Is there a joiner near here?*

'joiner's *nc* a joiner's workshop: *Go round to the joiner's and ask him to come as soon as possible.*

'joinery *nu* the work of a joiner: *The joinery in his house has been very well done*; (*attrib*) *joinery work.*

joint [dʒoint] *nc* **1** the place where two or more things join: *The plumber tightened up all the joints in the pipes.* **2** a part of the body where two bones meet but are able to move in the manner of *eg* a hinge: *The shoulders, elbows, wrists, hips, knees and ankles are joints.* **3** a piece of meat for cooking containing a bone: *A leg of mutton is a fairly large joint.* **4** (*derog sl*) a cheap club, café or other meeting-place, *esp* one for gambling, drinking, drug-taking etc: *We went to some joint or other down near the docks.* **5** (*sl*) a cigarette containing cannabis: *They were all having a joint when the police raided the party.* – *adj* (*attrib*) **1** united; done together: *The two climbers reached the summit only through the joint efforts of the whole team.* **2** shared by, or belonging to, two or more: *She and her husband have a joint bank account*; *They have a joint responsibility to keep the road repaired.* – *vt* to divide (an animal *etc* for cooking) at the, or into, joints: *Joint the chicken before cooking it.*

'jointed *adj* **1** (*attrib*) having (*esp* movable)

joints: *a jointed doll.* **2** (of an animal *etc* for cooking) divided into joints or pieces: *a jointed chicken*; *I bought the chicken already jointed.* – *See also* **double-jointed**.

'jointly *adv* together: *They worked jointly on this book.*

out of joint (of a limb *etc*) not in the correct place; dislocated: *He put his shoulder out of joint when he moved the wardrobe.*

See also **disjointed, join, junction**.

joist [dʒoist] *nc* a beam to which the boards of a floor or the laths of a ceiling are fastened: *The joists of the old house were infested with woodworm.*

joke [dʒouk] *nc* **1** anything said or done to cause laughter: *He told/made the old joke about the Englishman and the Irishman*; *He dressed up as a ghost for a joke*; (*attrib*) *a joke-book.* **2** something that causes laughter or amusement: *The children thought it a huge joke when the cat stole our fish.* – *See also* **play a joke on** *below.* – *vi* **1** to make a joke or jokes: *They joked about my mistake for a long time afterwards.* **2** to talk playfully and not seriously: *Don't be upset by what he said – he was only joking.*

'joker *nc* **1** in a pack of playing-cards, an extra card (*usu* having a picture of a jester) used in some games. **2** a person who enjoys telling jokes, playing tricks *etc*: *He's such a joker, you can't believe a word he says.*

'jokingly *adv* in a joking or playful way: *He looked out at the rain and jokingly suggested a walk.*

it's ˌno 'joke (*inf*) it is a serious or worrying matter: *It's no joke when water gets into the petrol tank.*

joking apart/aside let us stop joking and talk seriously: *I feel like going to Timbuctoo for the weekend – but, joking apart, I do need a rest!*

play a joke (on somebody) to do something (to somebody) as a joke: *We played a joke on him and pretended to be out when he telephoned.*

take a joke to be able to accept or laugh at a joke played on oneself: *The trouble with him is that he can't take a joke.*

See also **jocose, jocular**.

jolly ['dʒoli] *adj* merry and cheerful: *They had a jolly time at the party*; *She seems very jolly today.* – *adv* (*inf*) very: *Taste this – it's jolly good!* **'jolliness** *nu.*

ˌjollifi'cation [-fi-] (*very formal or facet*) **1** *nu* merriment: *a cause for jollification.* **2** *nc* (*often pl*) a cheerful celebration: *We all enjoyed the end-of-term jollifications.*

'jollity *nu* (*formal*) merriment: *an evening of great jollity.*

jolly along *vt usu sep* (*inf*) to keep (someone) in a good temper in order to gain his goodwill or co-operation: *He might help you, if you jolly him along a bit.*

jolt [dʒoult] **1** *vi* to go forward with sudden, short movements: *The bus jolted along the road.* **2** *vt* to shake or move suddenly: *I was violently jolted as the train stopped.* – *nc* **1** a sudden movement or shake: *The car gave a jolt and started.* **2** (*fig*) a shock: *He got a bit of a jolt when he heard the bad news.*

Jordan, Jordanian *see* Appendix 2.

joss stick ['dʒosstik] *nc* a stick of incense used *eg* to give a sweet smell to a room.

jostle ['dʒosl] *vti* to push roughly: *We were jostled by the crowd of onlookers*; *I felt people jostling against me in the dark.*

jot [dʒot] *nc* (*usu with a negative*) a small amount: *I haven't a jot of sympathy for him.* – *v* – *pt, ptp* **'jotted** – *vt* (*usu with* **down**) to write briefly or quickly: *He jotted (down) the telephone number in his notebook*; *He jotted it down.*

'jotter *nc* a notebook or notepad, *esp* in Scotland, as used in school.

'jotting *nc* (*usu in pl*) something jotted down: *random jottings.*

joule [dʒu:l] *nc* (*tech*: *often abbrev* **J** *when written*) a unit of energy or heat equal to 0·2390 calories.

journal ['dʒə:nl] *nc* **1** (*with cap in titles*) a magazine or other regularly published paper (*eg* of a society): *He writes for the 'Historical Review' and other learned journals*; *the British Medical Journal*; *The Baberton Weekly Journal is a newspaper which is published once a week.* **2** a diary giving an account of each day's activities: *Young girls of the nineteenth century were encouraged to keep journals.*

'journalism *nu* the business of running, or writing for, newspapers or magazines: *Writing for a women's magazine and for a daily newspaper are two very different types of journalism.*

'journalist *nc* an editor, manager of or writer for a newspaper, magazine *etc.*

ˌjourna'listic *adj* (*often derog*) of or like journalists: *He writes in a racy, journalistic style*; *His style of writing is very journalistic.*

journey ['dʒə:ni] *nc* a distance travelled, *esp* over land; an act of travelling: *By train, it is only a two-hour journey from here to London*; *He made a second journey to the station to fetch her luggage*; *He went on the journey with them.* – *vi* (*often old or liter*) to travel: *They journeyed to the city on foot.*

joust [dʒaust] *nc* (*hist*) an armed contest between two knights on horseback at a tournament. – *vi* to fight on horseback at a tournament.

jovial ['dʒouviəl] *adj* (*formal*) full of good humour: *He seems to be in a very jovial mood this morning*; *The old man is kind and jovial.* **ˌjovi'ality** [-'a-] *nu.* **'jovially** *adv.*

jowl [dʒaul] *nc* (*often in pl*) the jaw or lower part of the cheek: *He has a large face, with heavy jowls.*

-jowled (*in cmpds*) having (a certain kind of) jowls: *ˌlean-'jowled*; *ˌheavy-'jowled.*

See also **cheek by jowl** *under* **cheek**.

joy [dʒoi] (*more formal than* **happiness**) **1** *nu* great happiness: *He could find no words to express his joy at the news*; *The children jumped for joy when they saw the new toys.* **2** *nc* a cause of great happiness: *Our son is a great joy to us.*

'joyful *adj* (*esp attrib*) (*more formal than* **happy**) filled with, showing or causing joy: *The sun shone and he walked along in a joyful mood*; *joyful faces/news.* **'joyfully** *adv.* **'joyfulness** *nu.*

'joyless *adj* (*formal*) gloomy or dismal: *Brought up by a strict, elderly aunt, he had a rather joyless childhood*; *His life is rather joyless.*

'joyous *adj* (*liter*: *esp attrib*) joyful: *the joyous song of the blackbird.* **'joyously** *adv.*

jubilant ['dʒu:bilənt] *adj* (*formal*) showing and expressing triumphant joy: *Jubilant crowds welcomed the victorious team home*; *They were jubilant at the news of their victory.* **'jubilantly** *adv.*

ˌjubi'lation [-'lei-] (*formal*) **1** *nu* (triumphant) rejoicing: *There was great jubilation over the victory.* **2** *nc* (*usu in pl*) an act of rejoicing or celebration: *The jubilations went on till midnight.*

jubilee ['dʒu:bili:] *nc* a celebration of a special anniversary (*esp* the 25th, 50th or 60th) of some event, *eg* the succession of a king or queen: *The firm celebrated its golden jubilee* (= fiftieth anniversary) *last year*; (*attrib*) *a jubilee mug.*

judder ['dʒʌdə] *vi* (*inf*) (*esp* of a vehicle) to shake or jerk: *The old bus juddered to a halt.* – *nc* (*inf*): *The car gave a judder and stopped.*

judge [dʒʌdʒ] **1** *vt* to hear and try (cases) in a court of law: *Who will be judging this murder case?* **2** *vti* to decide which is the best in a competition *etc*: *Is she going to judge the singing competition again?*; *Who will be judging the vegetables at the flower show?*; *Who is judging at the horse show?* **3** *vti* to consider and form an idea (of): *You can't judge a man by his appearance*; *Watch how a cat judges the distance before it jumps*; *She couldn't judge whether/if he was telling the truth*; (*formal*) *I judge it (to be) better to tell him*; *It looks as if it's about five metres long, but I can't judge accurately from here.* **4** *vt* (*formal*) to criticize (someone) for doing wrong: *We have no right to judge him – we might have done the same thing ourselves.* – *nc* **1** a public officer who hears and decides cases in a law court: *The judge asked if the jury had reached a verdict.* **2** a person who decides which is the best in a competition *etc*: *Before you enter the crossword competition you must realize that the judge's decision is final* (= you cannot argue with the judge's decision); *He was asked to be on the panel of judges at the beauty contest.* **3** a person who is skilled at deciding how good *etc* something is: *He says she's honest, and he's a good judge of character*; *He seems a very fine pianist to me, but I'm no judge*; *He considers himself a good judge of wines.*

'judg(e)ment **1** *nc* the decision of a judge in a court of law: *It looked as if he might be acquitted but the judgement went against him.* **2** *nu* the act of judging (*def 3*): *Faulty judgement in overtaking is a common cause of traffic accidents.* **3** *nu* the ability to make right or sensible decisions: *The manager seems to lack judgement in his dealings with employees*; *You showed good judgement in choosing this restaurant.* **4** *ncu* (an) opinion: *His judgements of his colleagues are very valuable*; *In my judgement, he is a very good actor.* **5** *nc* a punishment thought to have been sent by God: *They thought that his illness was a judgement on him for his wickedness.*

the Day of Judgement (*relig or fig*) the day on which God decides which people deserve to go to heaven and which to hell; *The Day of Judgement is at hand*; *Now you have sat your exams – when is the day of judgement?* (= when do you get your results?)

'judging from/to 'judge from if one can use (something) as an indication: *Judging from the sky, there'll be a storm soon.*

the Last Judgement *see* **last**[1].

pass judgement (on) to criticize or condemn: *Do not pass judgement (on others) unless you are perfect yourself.*

sit in judgement on to take upon oneself the responsibility of criticizing others: *The old man was always sitting in judgement on his neighbour's gardening abilities.*

judicature *see* **judiciary**.

judicial [dʒu'diʃəl] *adj* (*formal or legal*: *esp attrib*) of a judge or court of law: *In a police court, the magistrate has judicial powers*; *He could bring judicial proceedings against you.* **ju'dicially** *adv.*

judiciary [dʒu'diʃiəri] *nc* (*formal*) (*also* **judicature** ['dʒu:dikətʃə]) a country's body of judges, or its courts of justice.
See also **jurisdiction**.

judicious [dʒu'diʃəs] *adj* (*formal*) showing wisdom and good sense: *With a judicious choice of words, he made a reply that pleased them both*; *His choice of words was far from judicious.* **ju'diciously** *adv.* **ju'diciousness** *nu.*
See also **injudicious**.

judo ['dʒu:dou] *nu* a Japanese form of wrestling: *He learns judo at the sports centre.*

jug [dʒʌg] **1** *nc* (*sometimes in cmpds*) a deep container for liquids, *usu* with a handle and a shaped lip for pouring: *She put the milk into a jug*; *a milk-jug.* **2** *nu* (*sl*) jail: *He's been in jug three times in the last five years.*

juggernaut ['dʒʌgəno:t] *nc* **1** (*inf*) a very large lorry: *These juggernauts should not be allowed to drive through small villages.* **2** (*formal*) a large and destructive force which is an object of devotion and sacrifice: *the juggernaut of industrialization.*

juggle ['dʒʌgl] **1** *vi* to keep throwing in the air and catching a number of objects (*eg* balls or clubs): *He entertained the audience by juggling with four balls and four plates at once.* **2** *vti* (*sometimes derog*: *sometimes with* **with**) to arrange (something, *eg* facts, figures or statistics) so as to give a false impression: *Any business company can juggle (with) the figures and appear to be doing better than it really is.*

'juggler *nc* a person who juggles (*eg* at a circus).

jugular (vein) ['dʒʌgjulə] *nc* one of the large veins on either side of the neck bringing the blood back from the head: *He died very quickly as the knife had pierced his jugular (vein).*

juice [dʒu:s] **1** *nu* the liquid part of fruits or vegetables or of animal bodies: *She squeezed the juice out of the orange*; *tomato juice.* **2** *nc* (*often in pl*) the fluid contained in meat: *Roasting meat in tin foil helps to preserve the juices.* **3** *nu* (*sl*) electricity: *That fan heater uses a lot of juice.* **4** *nu* (*sl*) petrol: *The car ran out of juice just before we reached our destination.* **'juicy** *adj.* **'juiciness** *nu.*

'juices *n pl* fluid contained in the organs of the body, *eg* to help digestion: *digestive/gastric juices.*

juke-box ['dʒu:kboks] *nc* a machine that plays selected records automatically when coins are put into it: *The juke-box in the café was often out of order.*

July [dʒu'lai] *n* the seventh month of the year, the month following June: *She left in July*; *She left last July*; *She left on July 16* (said as 'on July (the) sixteenth' or 'on the sixteenth of July'); *She left on the 16th/sixteenth of July.*

jumble ['dʒʌmbl] *vt* (*often with* **up** *or* **together**) to mix or throw together without order: *In this puzzle, the letters of all the words have been jumbled (up)*; *His shoes and clothes were all jumbled (together) in the cupboard.* – **1** *nc* a confused mixture: *He found an untidy jumble of things in the drawer.* **2** *nu* (*inf*) unwanted possessions suitable for a jumble sale: *Have you any jumble to spare?*

'jumble sale *nc* a sale of unwanted possessions, *eg* used clothing, *usu* to make money for a charity *etc*: *We are holding a jumble sale in aid of a children's charity.*

jump [dʒʌmp] **1** *vti* to (cause to) go quickly off the ground with a springing movement: *He jumped off the wall/across the puddle/over the fallen tree/into the swimming-pool*; *Don't jump the horse over that fence!* **2** *vi* to rise; to move quickly (upwards): *She jumped to her feet*; *He jumped into the car*; (*fig*) *The price of coffee shares jumped today.* **3** *vi* to make a startled movement: *The noise made me jump.* **4** *vt* to pass over (a gap *etc*) by bounding:

He jumped the stream easily. **5** *vt* (*esp Amer: sl*) to make a sudden attack on: *The boys jumped the old man as he came round the corner.* – *See also* **jump** *in phrases below* – *nc* **1** an act of jumping: *She got to her feet with a jump.* **2** the height or distance jumped: *a jump of two metres.* **3** an obstacle to be jumped over: *Her horse fell at the third jump.* **4** (*usu in sing*) a jumping competition: *the high jump.* **5** a startled movement: *She gave a jump when the door suddenly banged shut.* **6** a sudden rise, *eg* in prices: *There has been a jump in the price of potatoes.*

'jumpy *adj* (*inf*) nervous; easily upset: *He has been very jumpy and irritable lately*; *in a jumpy mood.*

'jump at *vt fus* (*inf*) to take or accept eagerly: *He jumped at the chance to go to Germany for a fortnight.*

jump down (someone's) throat (*inf*) to attack (someone) verbally in a violent way before they can explain themselves: *She jumped down my throat before I had a chance to apologize.*

jump for joy (*inf*) to show great pleasure: *She jumped for joy when she heard the good news.*

,jumping-'off place/point a place from which to start: *If you want to get to Finland, Newcastle is the best jumping-off place.*

'jump on *vt fus* **1** to make a sudden attack on: *He was waiting round the corner and jumped on me in the dark.* **2** (*inf fig*) to criticize unfairly: *She's always jumping on me for my bad spelling.*

jump on the bandwagon *see* **bandwagon**.

jump the gun (*inf*) to start before the proper time: *We shouldn't be going on holiday till tomorrow, but we jumped the gun and caught today's last flight.*

jump the queue (*often fig*) to move ahead of others in a queue without waiting for one's proper turn: *Many wealthy or important people try to jump the queue for hospital beds.*

jump the rails/track (of a train or tram) to go off the rails suddenly.

jump to conclusions/jump to the conclusion that to form an idea without making sure of the facts: *He saw my case in the hall and jumped to the conclusion that I was leaving*; *Stop jumping to conclusions! Just because I asked for a small loan you think I'm bankrupt!*

'jump to it (*inf*) to hurry up: *Jump to it and wash the dishes before you go out for the evening!*; *If you don't jump to it you will miss the train.*

jumper ['dʒʌmpə] *nc* **1** (*Brit*) a sweater or jersey: *I'm going to wear a jumper today – it's too cold for a blouse.* **2** (*Amer*) a pinafore dress: *She wore a blue jumper over her red sweater.*

junction ['dʒʌŋkʃən] *nc* **1** a place at which things (*eg* railway lines) join: *Our train waited for a long time in a siding at a junction*; *There was an accident at the junction of Park Road and School Lane*; (*attrib*) *The place where electrical circuits join is usually covered by a junction box.* **2** (*formal*) an act of joining: *The junction between the two armies is to take place here tomorrow.*

See also **join, joint**.

juncture ['dʒʌŋktʃə]: **at this/that juncture** (*formal*) at this or that moment or point: *At this juncture the chairman declared the meeting closed.*

June [dʒu:n] *n* the sixth month of the year, the month following May: *She will be leaving in June*; *She left last June*; *He will arrive on June 24* (said as 'on June (the) twenty-fourth' or 'on the twenty-fourth of June'); *He will be here on the 24th/twenty-fourth of June.*

jungle ['dʒʌŋgl] *ncu* a thick growth of trees and plants in tropical areas: *Great areas of jungle surround the River Amazon*; *Tigers are found in the jungles of Asia*; (*attrib*) *These soldiers are already trained in jungle warfare.*

junior ['dʒu:njə] **1** *nc, adj* (a person who is) younger in years or lower in rank or authority: *He is two years my junior*; *She is the office junior*; *The school sent two juniors and one senior to take part*; *junior army officers*; *junior pupils in the school*; *He is junior to me in the firm*; *She is still in the junior school.* **2** *adj* (*with cap*: *placed immediately after a name*: *often abbrev* **Jnr, Jr** *or* **Jun.** *when written*) used to indicate the son (*rare* the daughter) of a person who is still alive and who has the same name: *I'm referring to John Jones Junior, not John Jones Senior.* **3** *n* (*with cap*: *inf esp Amer*) a name for the child (*usu* a son) of a family: *Do bring Junior with you!*

See also **senior**.

juniper ['dʒu:nipə] *nc* a type of evergreen shrub with berries and prickly leaves.

junk[1] [dʒʌŋk] *nu* (*inf*) worthless articles or rubbish: *That cupboard is full of junk*; *There's nothing but junk in this magazine*; (*attrib*) *This vase was bought in a 'junk shop* (= a shop which sells junk).

junk[2] [dʒʌŋk] *nc* a Chinese flat-bottomed sailing ship, high in the bow and stern.

junket ['dʒʌŋkit] *ncu* milk curdled by adding a kind of acid, and *usu* sweetened and flavoured.

junketing ['dʒʌŋkitiŋ] *nu*, **'junketings** *n pl* (*inf*) feasting and merry-making: *I can't stand all this junketing every evening*; *The junketings went on until after midnight.*

junkie ['dʒʌŋki] *nc* (*sl*) a person who is addicted to drugs, *esp* heroin.

junta ['dʒʌntə] *nc* a group of army officers that has taken over the administration of a country by force: *The country had suffered a succession of military juntas.*

Jupiter *see* Appendix 6.

jurisdiction [dʒuəris'dikʃən] *nu* (*formal*) **1** legal power or authority: *Many driving offences come under the jurisdiction of the police courts.* **2** the district *etc* over which power is held: *That school does not fall within the jurisdiction of this education authority.*

jurisprudence [dʒuəris'pru:dəns] *nu* (*tech*) the science of law: *Law students must study jurisprudence as part of their syllabus.*

jury ['dʒuəri] *nc* **1** a group of men and/or women legally selected to hear a case and to decide what are the facts, *eg* whether or not a prisoner accused of crime is guilty: *The verdict of the jury was that the prisoner was guilty of the crime.* **2** a group of judges for a competition, contest *etc*: *The jury recorded their votes for the song contest.*

'juror, 'juryman *nc* a member of a jury (*def 1*): *She was called to be a juror.*

just[1] [dʒʌst] *adj* **1** right and fair; not favouring one more than another: *The head teacher was not being just when he punished only one of the boys*; *It was a fair and just decision.* **2** reasonable; based on one's rights: *He certainly has a just claim to the money*; *Do you think his claim is just?* **3** (*formal*: *attrib*) deserved: *He got his just reward when he crashed the stolen car and broke his leg.*

'justly *adv* in a fair or reasonable manner: *He was quite justly blamed for the accident.*

ˈ**justness** *nu* rightness or fairness: *The justness of his criticism is clear to everyone.*
See also **justify, unjust**.

just[2] [dʒʌst] *adv* **1** (*often with* **as**) exactly or precisely: *This penknife is just what I needed*; *That's just what I said*; *He was behaving just as he always did/just as if nothing had happened.* **2** (*with* **as**) quite: *This dress is just as nice as that one.* **3** very lately or recently: *He has just gone out of the house*; *She has just left the firm.* **4** on the point of; in the process of: *She is just coming through the door*; *At seven o'clock I was just starting to cook the supper.* **5** at the particular moment: *Why do you bother me just when I'm busy?* **6** (*often with* **only**) barely: *We have only just enough milk to last till Friday*; *I just managed to escape*; *You came just in time – a minute later would have been too late.* **7** only or merely: *Don't be angry with him – he's just a child*; *They waited for six hours just to get a glimpse of the Queen*; *'Where are you going?' 'Just to the post office'*; *'Are you tired?' 'Just a little'*; *Could you wait just a minute, please?* **8** (*inf*) used for emphasis, *eg* with commands: *Now, just listen to me!*; *Just look at that mess!*; *That just isn't true!*; *I just don't know what to do.* **9** (*inf*) absolutely: *The weather is just marvellous.*
just about more or less: *We shall have just about enough time if we go now*; *Is your watch just about right?*
ˈ**just as 1** at the very moment when: *She was putting on her coat just as I came in.* **2** in exactly the same state as: *The tree lay just as it fell.*
just ˈ**now 1** at this particular moment: *I can't do it just now.* **2** a short while ago: *She fell and banged her head just now, but she feels better again.*
just then 1 at that particular moment: *He was feeling rather hungry just then.* **2** in the next minute: *She opened the letter and read it. Just then the door bell rang.*
only just *see* **just**[2] (*def 6*).

justice [ˈdʒʌstis] **1** *nu* fairness or rightness in the treatment of other people: *Everyone has a right to justice*; *The boy does not deserve to be punished – I appeal to your sense of justice*; *The wrong girl was given the prize, but justice was done in the end.* **2** *nu* the law or the administration of it: *Their dispute had to be settled in a court of justice.* **3** *nc* (*esp with cap in titles*) a judge: *the Lord Chief Justice.*
Justice of the Peace – *pl* **Justices of the Peace** – *nc* (*often abbrev* **JP** – *pl* **JPs**) a citizen who has the authority to act as a judge in certain cases: *He has just been made a Justice of the Peace.*
bring to justice (*formal or legal*) to arrest, try and sentence (a criminal): *The murderer escaped but was finally brought to justice.*
do (someone/something) justice/do justice to (someone/something) 1 to treat fairly or properly: *It would not be doing him justice to call him lazy when he's so ill.* **2** to fulfil the highest possibilities of; to get the best results from; to show fully or fairly: *I was so tired that I didn't do myself justice in the exam*; *The portrait is good, but doesn't do justice to her beauty.* **3** (*facet*) to consume (a meal *etc*) with a good appetite: *You've certainly done justice to the pie!*
in ˈ**justice to (him, her** *etc***)/to do (him, her** *etc***) justice** if one must be fair (to him, her *etc*): *In justice to him, we only have ourselves to blame*; *To do her justice, I must admit that she was only trying to help when she broke the cup.*
See also **injustice**.

justify [ˈdʒʌstifai] *vt* **1** to prove or show (a person, action, opinion *etc*) to be just, right, desirable or reasonable: *How can the government justify the spending of millions of pounds on weapons?*; *Such behaviour cannot be justified*; *I don't think spending a lot of money on new equipment would justify itself – it won't increase the output from the factory.* **2** to be a good excuse for: *Your state of anxiety does not justify your being so rude to me.*
ˌ**justiˈfiable** *adj* (*neg* **un-**) able to be justified: *Such conduct is never justifiable*; (*legal*) *Justifiable homicide is the killing of someone in self-defence.*
ˌ**justifiˈcation** [-fi-] *nu* **1** (the act of) justifying or excusing: *There is a great deal to be said in justification of old-fashioned teaching methods*; *She has behaved badly, but her unhappiness should be mentioned in justification of her behaviour.* **2** something that justifies: *You have no justification for criticizing him in that way.*

jut [dʒʌt] – *pt, ptp* ˈ**jutted** – *vi* (*usu with* **out**) to stick out or project: *In many older houses the top storey jutted out over the bottom one.*

jute [dʒu:t] *nu, adj* (of) the fibre of certain plants found in Pakistan and India, used for making sacks *etc.*

jutted *see* **jut**.

juvenile [ˈdʒu:vənail] **1** *nc, adj* (*often legal*) (a person who is) young or youthful: *She will not be sent to prison – she is still a juvenile*; *Children or young people who break the law are referred to as juvenile offenders.* **2** *adj* (*usu derog*) childish or typical of young people: *juvenile behaviour*; *His attitude to girls is so juvenile.* **3** *adj* (*attrib*) intended or suitable for young people: *Formerly, such an offence would have been dealt with in the juvenile courts.*

juxtapose [dʒʌkstəˈpouz] *vt* (*formal or liter*) to place (*eg* words) side by side: *He juxtaposed the words 'red' and 'rosy' for effect in the phrase 'her red rosy lips'.*
ˌ**juxtapoˈsition** [-ˈziʃən] (*formal*) **1** *nu* the act of juxtaposing: *two phrases placed in juxtaposition.* **2** *nc* an example of this.

Kk

kaftan *see* **caftan**.

kale [keil] *nu* a type of cabbage with open curled leaves: *The sheep were eating kale in the field.*

kaleidoscope [kəˈlaidəskoup] *nc* a tube-shaped toy in which loose coloured pieces of glass *etc* reflected in two mirrors form changing patterns.
kaˌleidoˈscopic [-ˈsko-] *adj* (*usu attrib*) **1** with many changing colours: *the kaleidoscopic effect of the flashing lights.* **2** (of effects, impressions *etc*) changing constantly: *My impressions of the city were of a kaleidoscopic range of sights, sounds and smells.*

kangaroo [kaŋgəˈru:] – *pl* ˌ**kangaˈroos** – *nc* a type of large Australian animal with very long hind legs and great power of leaping, the female of which carries her young in a pouch on the front of her body.

kapok ['keipok] *nu* a very light waterproof fibre fluff obtained from a type of tropical tree and used to stuff toys *etc.*

kaput [kə'put] *adj* (*sl*: *usu pred*) broken or finally out of action: *I'm afraid our television is kaput and we're having to get a new one.*

karate [kə'ra:ti] *nu* a Japanese form of unarmed fighting, using blows and kicks: *He is an expert in karate.*

kart *see* **go-kart** *under* **go**.

kayak ['kaiak] *nc* an open canoe, *esp* an Eskimo canoe made of sealskins stretched over a frame.

kebab [ki'bab] *nc* small pieces of meat *etc, usu* cooked on a skewer: *They ate kebabs and rice in the Indian restaurant.*

kedgeree [kedʒə'ri:] *ncu* a dish made with rice, fish and other ingredients: *She made a kedgeree for supper*; *Kedgeree is not one of my favourite dishes.*

keel [ki:l] *nc* the long supporting piece of a ship's frame that lies lengthways along the bottom: *The boat's keel stuck in the mud near the shore.*

keel over 1 *vt oblig sep* to turn (*esp* a boat) over: *He keeled the boat over to examine the hole made by the rock.* **2** *vi* (*inf*) to fall over (*usu* suddenly or unexpectedly): *She seemed to be perfectly well, and then she just keeled over in the middle of the kitchen.*

be/keep on an even keel to be, keep or remain in a calm and untroubled state: *He kept the business on an even keel in spite of the many changes in staff*; *I think that we are on an even keel at last.*

keen [ki:n] *adj* **1** eager or enthusiastic: *He is a keen golfer*; *She is keen to get the job.* **2** (*formal*) sharp: *That knife has a keen edge*; *Her eyesight is as keen as ever.* **3** (*formal or liter*) very cold and biting: *There was a keen frost last night*; *The north wind is keen and biting.* – *See also* **keen on** *below.* **'keenly** *adv.*

'keenness *nu*: *The young man got the job because of his keenness*; *the keenness of the frost.*

'keen on (*inf*) very enthusiastic about, interested in or fond of: *I don't think he's very keen on the idea*; *She's keen on sailing*; *She's been keen on him for years.*

keep[1] [ki:p] – *pt, ptp* **kept** [kept] – **1** *vt* to have for a very long or indefinite period of time: *He gave me the picture to keep*; *She kept her sense of humour until the day she died.* **2** *vt* not to give or throw away; to preserve: *I kept the books that seemed to be the most interesting*; (*fig*) *Can you keep a secret?* **3** *vti* to (cause to) remain in a certain state or position: *I keep this gun loaded*; *She kept the light burning*; *He kept inside the house*; *How do you keep cool in this heat?*; *Will you keep me informed of what happens?* **4** *vi* to go on (performing or repeating a certain action): *He kept walking*; *She kept coming back again and again.* – *See also* **keep on** *below.* **5** *vt* to have in store or in stock: *This shop doesn't keep sausages*; *I always keep a tin of baked beans for emergencies.* **6** *vt* to look after or care for: *She keeps the garden beautifully*; *I think they keep hens*; *Would you keep my watch for me while I go swimming?* **7** *vi* (*inf*) to remain in good condition: *You'd better finish the cream – it won't keep*; *That meat won't keep till tomorrow in this heat unless you put it in the fridge.* **8** *vt* to make entries in (a diary, accounts *etc*): *She keeps a diary to remind her of her appointments*; *He kept the accounts for the club.* **9** *vt* to hold back or delay: *Sorry to keep you*; *What could be keeping her?* **10** *vt* to provide food, clothes, housing for (someone): *He has a wife and child to keep*; *Her money keeps all of us.* **11** *vt* to act in the way demanded by: *She kept her promise*; *He kept the law and reported the accident.* **12** *vt* to celebrate: *to keep Christmas.* – *See also* **keep** *in phrases below.* – *nu* (*inf*) food and lodging: *She gives her mother money every week for her keep*; *Our cat really earns her keep – she kills all the mice in the house.*

'keeper *nc* a person who looks after something, *esp* a gamekeeper or a person who looks after animals in a zoo: *The lion has killed its keeper.*

'keeping *nu* care or charge: *The money had been given into his keeping.*

ˌkeep-'fit *nu* a series or system of exercises, *usu* simple, intended to improve the physical condition of ordinary people, *esp* women: *She's very keen on keep-fit but it doesn't do her much good*; (*attrib*) *keep-fit exercises.*

'keepsake [-seik] *nc* something given or taken to be kept in memory of the giver or of the previous owner: *She gave him a piece of her hair as a keepsake.*

for 'keeps (*inf*) permanently: *Do you mean I can have it for keeps?*; *She's coming home tomorrow for keeps.*

in 'keeping with (*formal*) suited to: *He has moved to a house more in keeping with his position as an MP.*

keep an eye on *see* **eye**.

keep at arm's length *see* **arm**[1].

ˌkeep 'at it (*inf*) to go on doing something, *esp* to continue to work at something until one succeeds or finishes: *You'll get through all that work by tomorrow if you keep at it.*

keep away *vi, vt sep* to (make something) remain at a distance: *Keep away – it's dangerous!*; *She kept her children away until he had left.*

keep back 1 *vi, vt sep* not to (allow to) move forward: *She kept the child back on the edge of the crowd*; *Everybody keep back from the door!*; (*fig*) *While his friends went up into the next class, John was kept back* (= was made to remain in his previous class). **2** *vt sep* not to tell or make known: *I feel he's keeping the real story back for some reason.* **3** *vt sep* not to give or pay out: *Part of my allowance is kept back to pay for my meals*; *Will they keep it back every week?*

keep one's distance to stay quite far away (from): *The deer did not trust us and kept their distance*; (*fig*) *I should like to be friends with her but she is inclined to keep her distance.*

keep down 1 *vi, vt sep* not to (allow to) rise up: *Keep down – they're shooting at us!*; (*fig*) *He won't let his mother keep him down any longer.* **2** *vt sep* to control or put a limit on: *They are taking steps to keep down the rabbit population*; *They won't keep it down for long.* **3** *vt sep* to digest without vomiting: *The patient is unable to keep down anything but water*; *He has eaten some food but he won't be able to keep it down.*

ˌkeep one's 'end up (*inf*) to perform one's part in something equally as well as all the others who are involved: *Everyone else is so good at what they are doing that he has a hard job keeping his end up.*

'keep from *vt fus* to stop oneself from (doing something): *I could hardly keep from hitting him.*

keep going 1 to go on doing something despite difficulties: *I think we'll get it done if we can just keep going.* **2** (*inf*) to make (a person) able to continue doing something *etc*: *Can you lend me a pound to keep me going until tomorrow?*; *I think she* *has enough work to keep her going.*

keep hold of not to let go of: *Keep hold of that bag, because it would be awful if we lost it!*

keep house for to do the cooking, housework *etc* for: *She keeps house for her brother.*

keep in *vt oblig sep* not to allow to go or come out or outside: *He's not well, so his mother has kept him in until he's better.*

keep (a person, thing *etc***) in mind** to remember (a person, thing *etc*) and take him, it *etc* into consideration when making decisions later: *I'll keep her offer in mind in case we are able to accept it sometime*; *We cannot offer you a job just now but we shall keep you in mind for any future vacancies.*

ˌ**keep 'in with** *vt fus* (*inf*) to remain friendly with, *usu* for a special reason: *It's a good idea to keep in with the police in case you need their help one day.*

keep it dark *see* **dark**.

ˌ**keep it 'up** (*inf*) to carry on doing something at the same speed or as well as one is doing it at present: *Your work is good – keep it up!*

keep late/early hours (*formal*) to go to bed late or early: *If you keep such late hours you will not be able to work properly.*

keep off 1 *vi, vt fus* to stay away (from): *There are notices everywhere warning people to keep off*; (*fig*) *The rain kept off and we had sunshine for the wedding*; (*fig*) *We kept off* (= we did not speak about) *the subject of money.* **2** *vt sep* to prevent from getting to or on to (something): *This umbrella isn't pretty, but it keeps off the rain*; *She tried in vain to keep the children off the rose-bed*; *She could not keep them off it.*

keep on 1 *vi* to continue (doing something or moving): *She kept on until it was finished*; *He didn't answer, but just kept on writing*; *They kept on until they came to a petrol station.* **2** *vt sep* to continue to use or to employ: *We kept on the housekeeper after Grandfather died.*

ˌ**keep 'on at** *vt fus* (*inf*) to urge constantly (to do something): *She kept on at me to write to him.*

keep oneself to oneself (*inf*) to tell others very little about oneself, and not to be very friendly or sociable: *Our new neighbours keep themselves to themselves.*

keep one's hair on *see* **hair**.

keep one's hand in *see* **hand**.

keep one's head *see* **head**.

keep one's head above water *see* **head**.

keep out *vt sep* not to allow to enter: *This coat keeps out the wind*; *It does not keep it out completely.*

keep out of *vt fus* (*fig*) not to become involved in: *I tried to keep out of the argument as it was none of my business*; *Do try to keep out of trouble!*

keep tabs on *see* **tab**.

keep the peace *see* **peace**.

keep time 1 (of a clock *etc*) to show the time accurately: *Does this watch keep* (*good*) *time?* **2** (*with* **with**) to perform an action in the same rhythm (as someone else): *She doesn't keep time with her partner when she dances.*

'**keep to** *vt fus* not to leave or go away from: *Keep to this side of the park!*; *We kept to the roads we knew.*

keep (something) to oneself not to tell anyone (something): *He kept his conclusions to himself.*

keep up 1 *vt sep* to continue, or cause to remain, in operation: *I enjoy our friendship and try to keep it up*; *We try to keep up our family's reputation for hospitality*; *We do not always succeed in keeping it up.* **2** *vi, vt sep* to (cause to) remain in good condition *etc*: *He was finding it difficult to keep up the garden*; *He cannot keep it up properly*; *The weather has kept up well, hasn't it?* **3** *vi* (*often with* **with**) to move fast enough not to be left behind (by): *Even the children managed to keep up*; *Don't run – I can't keep up with you*; (*fig*) *Everyone in the class was so clever that I couldn't keep up with them.*

keep up appearances *see* **appear**.

keep up with the Joneses ['dʒounziz] (*inf*) to have everything one's neighbours have: *She didn't need a new cooker – she just bought one to keep up with the Joneses.*

keep watch to remain awake and looking out (for something or someone): *We put someone outside the door to keep watch* (*for the police*) *while we held our secret meeting.*

keep[2] [ki:p] *nc* the strongest part of a medieval castle: *The ruined keep was all that remained of the old castle.*

keg [keg] *nc* a type of small barrel: *a keg of brandy.*

kelp [kelp] *nu* a type of large brown seaweed.

ken [ken]: **beyond one's ken** outside the extent of one's knowledge or understanding: *Such things are beyond my ken, I'm afraid.*

kennel ['kenl] *nc* **1** a type of small hut for a dog: *Their dog lives in a kennel in the garden.* **2** (*usu in pl*) a place where dogs can be looked after: *Our dog was in kennels while we were on holiday.*

Kenya, Kenyan *see* Appendix 2.

kept *see* **keep**[1].

kerb [kə:b] *nc* (*esp Amer* **curb**) an edging, *usu* of stone, round a raised area, *esp* a pavement: *The old lady stepped off the kerb right in front of a car.*

'**kerbstone** *nc* a stone used as part of a kerb.

kerchief ['kə:tʃif] *nc* (*old*) a square piece of cloth used as a piece of clothing to cover the head, neck *etc*: *The women working in the fields wore kerchiefs to protect their heads from the hot sun.*

kernel ['kə:nl] *nc* **1** the softer substance inside the shell of a nut, or the stone of a fruit such as a plum, peach *etc.* **2** (*fig formal*) the important part of anything: *The account of his visit to Germany formed the kernel of his report*; *the kernel of his argument.*

kerosene ['kerəsi:n] *nu* paraffin oil, obtained from petroleum or from coal: *The jet plane refuelled with kerosene*; *We bought some kerosene for the camping-stove*; (*attrib*) *a kerosene lamp.*

kestrel ['kestrəl] *nc* a kind of small falcon: *The kestrel swooped down on its prey.*

ketch [ketʃ] *nc* a type of two-masted sailing boat.

ketchup ['ketʃəp] *nu* a flavouring sauce made from tomatoes or mushrooms *etc*: *The child poured tomato ketchup over his sausages.*

kettle ['ketl] *nc* **1** a metal pot, *usu* with a special part for pouring and a lid, for heating liquids: *a kettle full of boiling water*; *Pour some hot water from the kettle into the teapot.* **2** the amount of liquid *etc* contained in a kettle: *a kettle of water.*

'**kettledrum** *nc* a type of drum made of a brass or copper bowl covered with a stretched skin *etc.*

a 'pretty kettle of fish (*inf*) a mess or awkward situation: *Oh dear, this is a pretty kettle of fish!*

key [ki:] *nc* **1** an instrument or tool by which something (*eg* a lock or a nut) is turned or screwed: *Have you the key for this door?*; *Is there a key to turn off the central heating?* **2** in musical instruments, one of the small parts pressed to sound the notes: *the keys of a clarinet*; *piano keys.* **3** in a typewriter, calculator *etc*, one of the parts which one presses to cause a letter *etc* to be printed, displayed *etc*: *I wish that she would not hit the keys of the typewriter so hard.* **4** the chief note of a piece of music: *What key are you singing in?*; *the key of F.* **5** (*fig*) a general tone or style of expression or emotion: *Let's treat this whole affair in a very low* (= not dramatic *etc*) *key.* **6** something that explains a mystery or gives an answer to a mystery, a code *etc*: *I think she's just provided the key to the whole problem*; *This is the key to the maths exercises.* – *adj* (*attrib*: *formal*) most important or controlling: *key industries*; *He is a key man in the firm.*

'**keyboard** *nc* the keys in a piano, typewriter *etc* arranged along or on a flat board: *The pianist sat down at the keyboard and immediately began to play*; *The computer keyboard was very complicated*; (*attrib*) *A harpsichord is an early keyboard instrument.*

'**keyhole** *nc* the hole in which a key of a door *etc* is placed: *The child looked through the keyhole to see if his teacher was still with his parents.*

'**keynote** *nc* **1** the chief note of a piece of music. **2** (*fig*: *often liter*) the chief point or theme (of a meeting, lecture *etc*): *The keynote of his speech was 'Let us prepare!'*; *The keynote of the discussions is the desire to preserve peace.*

key-signature *see* **signature**.

'**keystone** *nc* **1** the stone at the highest point of an arch, which holds the rest in position: *a carved keystone.* **2** (*fig*) (of an argument, theory *etc*) the most important part, on which the rest depends: *The basic honesty of the individual was the keystone of his argument.*

(all) keyed up (*inf*) excited; tense: *The actress always gets keyed up before a performance*; *The child is all keyed up about the party.*

khaki ['ka:ki] **1** *nu*, *adj* (of) a dull brownish or greenish yellow: *a khaki uniform*; *He disliked the khaki of the uniform.* **2** *nu* cloth of this colour used for soldiers' uniforms: *The café was full of men in khaki*; *soldiers' uniforms made of khaki.*

Khmer *see* Appendix 2.

kick [kik] **1** *vti* to hit or strike out with the foot: *The child kicked his brother*; *He kicked the ball into the next garden*; *The child kicked crossly at his mother's ankles*; *He tried to kick the door down* (= open the door by kicking it); *He kicked open the gate* (= opened the gate by kicking it). **2** *vi* (of a gun) to jerk or spring back violently when fired. **3** *vi* (*sl*) to resist or object: *He's kicking a bit, but I think he'll do as I asked.* – *See also* **kick** *in phrases below.* *nc* **1** a blow with the foot: *The boy gave him a kick on the ankle*; *His leg was injured by a kick from a horse.* **2** the springing back of a gun after it has been fired. **3** (*sl*) a pleasant thrill: *She gets a kick out of making people miserable.*

kick-off *see* **kick off**.

for a 'kick-off (*sl*) in the first place or to start (an argument or complaint *etc*): *You can forget about having lunch early for a kick-off – there's too much to be done.*

for 'kicks (*sl*) in order to get a thrill; for fun: *These young criminals beat people up for kicks.*

kick about/around (*inf*) **1** *vt oblig sep* to treat badly or bully: *The bigger boys are always kicking him around.* **2** *vi*, *vt fus* to be lying *etc* without being used or dealt with: *That letter has been kicking around for weeks and no-one's answered it yet.* **3** *vi*, *vt fus* to wander about without having anything to do: *There was nothing going on, so we kicked about a bit and then went home.*

kick off *vi* to start a football game by kicking the ball: *We kick off at 2.30*; (*fig inf*) *I'll speak last at today's meeting if you kick off* (= begin). (*nc* '**kick-off**: *The kick-off is at 2.30 this afternoon.*)

kick up (*inf*) *vt fus* to cause or start off: *to kick up a row*; *He kicked up a fuss about the mess in the garden.*

kid[1] [kid] **1** *nc* (*inf*) a child: *They've got three kids now, two boys and a girl*; *There's a crowd of kids playing football in the park.* **2** *nc* (*inf*) a young person; a teenager: *More than a hundred kids went to the disco last night.* **3** *nc* a young goat. **4** *nu*, *adj* (of) the leather made from its skin: *slippers made of white kid*; *kid gloves.*

kid brother, sister (*inf*) a younger brother or sister: *He has two kid sisters and an older brother.*

with kid gloves (*fig*) in a delicate and tactful manner: *She has a terrible temper and has to be handled with kid gloves.*

kid[2] [kid] – *pt*, *ptp* '**kidded** – *vti* (*inf*: *also* **kid on** *vt oblig sep*) to deceive or tease (someone), *esp* for amusement, in a gentle and harmless manner: *We were kidding him on about the girl who keeps sending him love-letters*; *He tried to kid me into thinking he'd forgotten my birthday*; *He didn't mean that – he was only kidding!*

kidnap ['kidnap] – *pt*, *ptp* '**kidnapped**, (*Amer*) '**kidnaped** – *vt* to carry off (a person) by force, often demanding money in exchange for them: *He is very wealthy and lives in fear of his children being kidnapped.*

'**kidnapper** *nc*: *The child's kidnappers demanded a ransom of £50 000.*

kidney ['kidni] *nc* one of two organs in the body which remove waste matter from the blood and produce urine: *The kidneys of some animals are used as food*; *The surgeon had to remove one of her kidneys, as it was diseased*; *We had lamb's kidneys for breakfast*; (*attrib*) *steak and kidney pie.*

kill [kil] *vt* to cause the death of: *He killed the rats with poison*; *The outbreak of typhoid killed many people*; (*fig*) *The sudden fog killed any hopes we had of getting home before midnight.* – *See also* **kill off** *below.* – *nc* **1** an act of killing: *The hunter was determined to make a kill before returning to the camp.* **2** an animal *etc* killed: *The lioness took her kill back to the cubs.*

'**killer** *nc* a person, animal or (*inf*) a thing which kills: *There was a killer somewhere in the village*; *That road is a killer* (= so dangerous that there are many accidents on it)*!*; (*attrib*) *a killer disease.*

'**killing** *adj* **1** (*inf*) exhausting: *That hill up to your house is killing!*; *The runner set off at a killing pace.* **2** (*inf*: *usu pred*) very funny: *The whole situation was really killing.*

'**killingly** *adv* (*inf*) very: *That story was killingly funny.*

'**kill-joy** *nc* (*derog*) someone who prevents other people from enjoying themselves: *The park-keeper is such a killjoy that he doesn't let the children make any noise in the park.*

be ˌin at the 'kill **1** to be present when a hunted animal, *eg* a fox, is killed: *Most of the huntsmen were in at the kill.* **2** (*fig*) to be present at the most exciting or advantageous moment: *All the neighbours were in at the kill when the old lady's furniture was being sold.*

kill off *vt sep* to destroy completely: *So many deer have been shot that the species has almost been killed off*; *We have killed them all off*; (*fig*) *I think that plan's been killed off.*

kill time (*inf*) to find something to do to use up spare time, such as a period of waiting: *I'm just killing time until I hear whether I've got a job or not.*

kiln [kiln] *nc* a type of large oven for baking pottery or bricks, drying grain *etc*.

kilo ['ki:lou] short for **kilogramme**.

kilogram(me), kilometre *see* Appendix 5.

kilowatt ['kiləwot] *nc* (*often abbrev* **kW** *when written*) a measure of power, 1000 watts.

kilt [kilt] *nc* an item of Scottish national dress, a pleated tartan skirt reaching to the knees and traditionally worn by men: *The kilts of the soldiers swung as they marched.*

'**kilted** *adj* (*usu attrib*): *a kilted soldier.*

kimono [ki'mounou, (*Amer*) -nə] – *pl* **ki'monos** – *nc* a loose Japanese robe, fastened with a sash.

kin [kin] *n pl* (*formal*) persons of the same family; relations: *I hate her and all her kin.*

'**kinsfolk** ['kinz-] *n pl* (*formal*) people of the same family as oneself: *All his kinsfolk were at his mother's funeral.*

'**kinsman** ['kinz-], '**kinswoman** ['kinz-] – *pls* '**kinsmen,** '**kinswomen** – *ncs* (*old*) a man or a woman of the same family as oneself: *He was accompanied by several of his kinsmen.*

kith and kin *see* **kith**.

next of kin (*legal*) one's nearest relative(s): *When he was killed in a car accident they didn't know who was his next of kin; You must inform his next of kin of the accident.*

See also **kindred**.

kind[1] [kaind] *nc* a sort or type: *What kind of car is it?; The child doesn't like that kind of chocolate; He is not the kind of man who would be cruel to children.*

in 'kind (*formal*) **1** (of payment) in goods and not money: *He paid in kind with a sack of potatoes.* **2** in the same way or with the same treatment: *He spoke rudely to her and she replied in kind.*

of a 'kind 1 of the same sort: *They are two of a kind – both unreliable.* **2** scarcely deserving the name: *We received hospitality of a kind at their house but we had to have a meal at a restaurant on the way home.*

kind[2] [kaind] *adj* ready or anxious to do good to others; friendly: *She has been very kind about letting us use her house; He's such a kind man; It was such a kind gesture; It would be very kind of you to look after the children today.*

'**kindly** *adv* **1** in a kind manner: *She kindly lent me a handkerchief.* **2** (*often facet or ironic*) please: *Would you kindly sit down; Would you kindly stop talking!* – *adj* (*usu attrib*) having or showing a gentle and friendly nature: *a kindly smile; a kindly old lady; It was a kindly gesture to offer to look after the children.* '**kindliness** *nu*.

'**kindness 1** *nu* the quality of being kind: *I'll never forget her kindness.* **2** *nc* a kind act: *It would be a kindness to tell him; I appreciate her many kindnesses to me.*

ˌ**kind-'hearted** *adj* having or showing kindness: *a kind-hearted old lady; a kind-hearted gesture; She is too kind-hearted to hurt an animal.*

See also **unkind**.

kindergarten ['kindəga:tn] *nc* a school for very young children: *He started at kindergarten when he was three years old.*

kindle ['kindl] *vti* to (cause to) catch fire: *I was so cold that I kindled a fire as soon as I reached home; The fire kindled easily;* (*fig*) *His eyes kindled with excitement; His speech kindled the anger of the crowd.*

'**kindling** *nu* dry wood *etc* for starting a fire: *She came in with a bundle of kindling and some matches.*

kindliness, kindly, kindness *see* **kind**.

kindred ['kindrid] *n pl* (*old*) one's relatives. – *adj* (*attrib*: *formal*) of the same sort: *He enjoys climbing and other kindred sports like camping and hiking.*

See also **kin**.

kinetic [ki'netik] *adj* (*tech*: *esp attrib*) of motion: *kinetic energy.*

king [kiŋ] *nc* **1** (*with cap in titles*) (the status of) a male ruler of a nation, who inherits his position by right of birth: *He became king when his father died; King Charles III.* **2** the playing-card with the picture of a king: *I have two cards – the ten of spades and the king of diamonds.* **3** the most important piece in chess.

'**kingdom** *nc* **1** (*with cap in names*) a state having a king (or queen) as its head: *The United Kingdom of Great Britain and Northern Ireland; He rules over a large kingdom.* **2** (*fig*) any of the three great divisions of natural objects: *the animal, plant/vegetable and mineral kingdoms.*

'**kingly** *adj* (*formal*) **1** of royal rank: *kingly dignity; He is kingly and dignified.* **2** (*attrib*) suitable for a king: *a kingly feast.* '**kingliness** *nu*.

'**kingfisher** *nc* a type of bird with brilliant blue feathers which feeds on fish.

'**kingpin** *nc* the most important person in an organization *etc*: *As the kingpin of the brewing industry his opinion was highly valued.*

'**king-size(d)** *adj* (*esp attrib*) of a large size; larger than normal: *a king-size(d) bed; king-size cigarettes.*

turn king's/queen's evidence (*legal*) to become a witness against an accomplice: *He received a shorter prison sentence than the other two thieves because he turned queen's evidence.*

See also **queen**.

kink [kiŋk] *nc* **1** a twist in a string, rope *etc*: *There's a kink in that rope – let me straighten it out!* **2** (*inf*) a twist or oddness of the mind: *That's only one of his kinks!*

'**kinky** *adj* (*Brit inf*) deliberately strange or not normal, and *usu* not according to ordinary standards of (sexual) behaviour: *He has some very kinky ideas like having a glass wall in his bathroom; He thought she looked rather kinky in a short satin skirt and black leather boots.* '**kinkiness** *nu*.

kinsman, kinswoman *etc see* **kin**.

kiosk ['ki:osk] *nc* (*sometimes in cmpds*) **1** a small roofed stall, either out-of-doors or in a public building *etc*, for the sale of newspapers, confectionery *etc*: *I bought a magazine at the kiosk at the station.* **2** a public telephone box: *She phoned from the kiosk outside the post-office; a telephone-kiosk.*

kipper ['kipə] *nc* a herring split down the back and smoked, used as food: *He had two kippers for breakfast.*

kiss [kis] *vti* **1** to touch with the lips, *esp* as a sign of affection: *She kissed him warmly when he arrived; The child kissed his parents goodnight; The lovers kissed passionately.* **2** (*liter fig*) to touch gently: *The sun kissed the flowers.* – *nc* an act of kissing: *He gave her an affectionate kiss; They exchanged kisses* (= They kissed each other).

kiss of life a mouth-to-mouth method of restoring breathing: *When the body was carried unconscious from the sea we thought he was dead, but he began to breathe after he was given the kiss of life by the life-saver.*

kit [kit] **1** *ncu* (*inf*) (an outfit of) tools, clothes *etc* (necessary for a particular job *etc*): *He carried his tennis kit in a bag*; *a repair kit for mending punctures in bicycle tyres*; *I think I've left some of my kit in the changing-room.* **2** *nc* a collection of the materials *etc* required to make something: *He bought a kit to make a model aeroplane*; (*attrib*) *These kitchen units are sold in kit form.* – *See also* **kit out** *below.*

'**kitbag** *nc* a strong bag for holding (*usu* a soldier's) kit.

kit out – *pt, ptp* '**kitted** – *vt sep* (*inf*) to provide with all the clothes, tools *etc* necessary for a particular purpose: *He spent a lot of money kitting himself out to go climbing in the Antarctic*; *The old man kitted out the entire school football team.*

kitchen ['kitʃin] *nc* a room where food is cooked: *Our kitchen has too few cupboards*; *We have breakfast in the kitchen but dinner in the dining-room*; (*attrib*) *a kitchen table.*

ˌ**kitche'nette** [-'net] *nc* a small kitchen: *They live in a small modern house with a kitchenette. I prefer a big, old-fashioned kitchen.*

kitchen garden *nc* a vegetable garden: *The mansion has a large kitchen garden.*

kite [kait] *nc* a light frame covered with paper or other material, and with string attached, for flying in the air: *The children were flying their kites in the park.*

kith [kiθ]: **kith and kin** (*formal*) relatives: *Surely he wouldn't refuse to see his own kith and kin?*

kitted *see* **kit**.

kitten ['kitn] *nc* a young cat: *The cat had five kittens last week.*

'**kittenish** *adj* (*usu derog*) (of a woman) acting in a playfully coy way: *a kittenish blonde*; *She was being ridiculously kittenish.*

kitty ['kiti] *nc* (*inf*) a sum of money put aside for a purpose, or the box *etc* containing it: *We kept a kitty for buying food when we were camping.*

kiwi ['kiːwiː] *nc* **1** a type of bird which is unable to fly, found in New Zealand. **2** (*sl*: *sometimes derog*) a person who was born or lives in New Zealand.

kleptomania [kleptə'meiniə] *nu* (*formal or tech*) an uncontrollable desire to steal: *He was prosecuted for shoplifting – but the charges were dropped when it was learned he was suffering from kleptomania.*

ˌ**klepto'maniac** [-ak] *nc, adj* (*formal or tech*) (of) a person who suffers from kleptomania: *She is a kleptomaniac*; *She has kleptomaniac tendencies.*

knack [nak] *nc* (*usu in sing*) the ability to do something skilfully and easily: *It took me some time to acquire the knack of making pancakes.*

knackered ['nakəd] *adj* (*Brit sl*: *usu pred*) worn out or exhausted: *I've been rushing about all day, and I'm knackered!*

knapsack ['napsak] *nc* (*esp old*) a small bag for food, clothes *etc* slung on the back: *The walkers wore knapsacks on their backs.*

knave [neiv] *nc* **1** (*old or formal*) a jack in a pack of playing-cards: *the knave of diamonds.* **2** (*arch*) a dishonest person: *The knave stole all the old man's money.*

'**knavery** *nu* (*old*) dishonesty.

knead [niːd] *vti* to press together and work (dough *etc*) with the fingers: *His mother was kneading (dough) in the kitchen.*

knee [niː] *nc* **1** the joint at the bend of the leg: *The child fell down and cut his knee*; *The child climbed on to her father's knee as he sat in the chair*; *She was on her knees weeding the garden*; *He went down on his knees* (= he knelt) *to pray.* **2** the part of an article of clothing covering this joint: *He has a hole in the knee of his trousers.*

'**kneecap** *nc* the flat, round bone on the front of the knee joint.

ˌ**knee-'deep** *adj* so deep as to reach one's knees; *knee-deep water*; *He is knee-deep in water.*

bring (someone) to his *etc* **knees** to make (someone) humble; to make (someone) realize that he has been defeated: *Napoleon brought his enemy to his knees*; (*fig*) *Poverty brought him to his knees.*

kneel [niːl] – *pt, ptp* **knelt** [nelt] – *vi* to be in, or move into, a position in which both the foot and the knee of one or both legs are on the floor, ground *etc*: *She was kneeling in front of an open cupboard, searching for something*; *He came forward and knelt in front of her.*

kneel down *vi* to go into a kneeling position: *She knelt down to look under the table.*

knell [nel] *nc* (*formal*: *usu fig*: *usu in sing*) the sound of a bell giving warning of a death or funeral: *the funeral knell*; (*fig*) *His words were the knell of all our hopes.*

knelt *see* **kneel**.

knew *see* **know**.

knickers ['nikəz] *n pl* (*Brit*) women's and girls' underwear for the lower part of the body, *esp* if long enough to cover the thigh: *The schoolgirls all wore blue woollen knickers*; *There were three pairs of knickers hanging on the washing-line.*

knick-knack ['niknak] *nc* (*sometimes derog*) a small (*usu* inexpensive) ornament: *The mantelpiece was covered with knick-knacks.*

knife [naif] – *pl* **knives** [naivz] – *nc* **1** an instrument for cutting: *He carved the meat with a large knife*; *I need a knife to spread butter on the bread.* **2** a weapon with a blade: *She pulled out a knife and stabbed him with it.* – *vt* (*inf*) to stab with a knife: *Before she realized what was happening, he knifed her.*

have one's knife in (someone) (*inf*) to be continually hostile or unfair towards (someone): *He would love to get me into trouble – he's had his knife in me for years.*

knight [nait] *nc* **1** (*hist*) a man of noble birth who is trained to fight, *esp* on horseback: *King Arthur and his knights.* **2** a man of the rank next below a baronet, having the title 'Sir', which cannot be passed on automatically to his descendants: *The Queen has made him a knight in recognition of his political work.* **3** a piece used in chess, *usu* shaped like a horse's head. – *vt* to make (a person) a knight: *He was knighted for his services to industry.*

'**knighthood** *nc* the rank or title of a knight: *He was rewarded with a knighthood*; *He received a knighthood from the Queen.*

'**knightly** *adj* of, suited to, or involving a knight or knights: *knightly conduct*; *His behaviour was far from knightly*; *a knightly procession.*

knit [nit] – *pt, ptp* '**knitted**, (*esp fig*: *not def 1*) **knit** – **1** *vti* to form (material, a garment) from yarn (of wool *etc*) by making and connecting loops, using knitting-needles: *She is teaching children to knit and sew*; *She knitted him a sweater for Christmas*; *She used to spend the evenings knitting and watching television.* **2** *vi* (of broken bones) to grow together: *The bone in his arm took a long time to knit.* **3** *vt* (*fig*) (of common interests *etc*) to draw (people) together: *Their dependence on one another knit them into a close group.* – *See* **knit one's brows** *below.*

'**knitter** *nc*: *She's a very good knitter.*

'knitting *nu* **1** the work of a knitter: *She was occupied with her knitting.* **2** the material made by knitting: *a piece of knitting.*

'knitting-needle *nc* a thin rod of steel or plastic *etc*, used in knitting.

knit one's brows (*formal*) to draw together or wrinkle the brows; to frown: *He knit his brows as he read the closely-written letter.*

knives *see* **knife**.

knob [nob] *nc* **1** a hard rounded part standing out from the main part: *The glass vase had knobs all round the bottom for decoration.* **2** a rounded handle on or for a door or drawer: *There were brass knobs on all the doors in the old house.*

'knobbly *adj* having knobs or lumps: *a knobbly walking-stick*; *a knobbly type of wool*; *knobbly knees* (= bony knees); *the material is rough and knobbly.*

knock [nok] **1** *vi* to make a sharp noise by hitting or tapping, *esp* on a door *etc* to attract attention: *Just then, someone knocked at the door*; *She knocked on the window and told the children to stop fighting.* **2** *vt* to cause to move, *esp* to fall, by hitting (often accidentally): *She knocked a vase on to the floor while she was dusting.* **3** *vt* to put into a certain state or position by hitting: *He knocked the other man senseless.* **4** *vti* (*often with* **against, on**) to strike against or bump into: *She knocked against the table as she passed and spilled his cup of coffee*; *I knocked my head on the car door as I got out.* **5** *vt* (*inf*) to find fault with or criticize, *esp* unfairly: *Stop knocking his work – it's really very good!* – *See also* **knock** *in phrases below.* – *nc* **1** an act of knocking or striking: *She gave two knocks on the door*; *He had a nasty bruise from a knock he had received playing football.* **2** the sound made by a knock, *esp* on a door *etc*: *Suddenly they heard a loud knock.* **3** (*inf*) an unfortunate experience: *She's had a few knocks recently – first her husband was ill and then she lost her job.*

'knocker *nc* a piece of metal *etc* fixed to a door and used for knocking: *The postman banged the knocker until the door was opened.*

'knockers *n pl* (*Brit vulg*) a woman's breasts: *She has a fantastic pair of knockers!*

'knock-about *adj* (*usu attrib*) (of comedy *etc*) rough and containing a lot of physical activity: *a knock-about farce.*

'knock-down *adj* (*attrib*) **1** (*inf*) (of prices) very low: *I picked it up for a knock-down price in a sale.* **2** able to be taken to pieces easily: *a knock-down wardrobe.* – *See also* **knock down** *below.*

ˌknock-'kneed *adj* having knees (**ˌknock-'knees**) which touch when one is walking: *That child is knock-kneed*; *a knock-kneed child.*

'knock-out *nc* **1** an act of knocking out: *The boxer won his match by a knock-out*; (*attrib*) *a knock-out blow.* **2** (*inf*) something which causes a great impression because it is very attractive: *Their new secretary is a knock-out!* – *See also* **knock out** *below.*

'knock-up *nc* (in tennis *etc*) a period of practice immediately before beginning a match, or of playing for practice without scoring: *She was playing well in the knock-up but played badly in the actual match.*

knock about/around (*inf*) **1** *vt oblig sep* to treat in a rough and unkind manner, *esp* to hit repeatedly: *I've heard that her husband knocks her about.* **2** *vi, vt fus* to move about (in) in a casual manner without a definite destination or purpose: *He spent six months knocking around (in) Europe seeing the sights and living as cheaply as possible.* **3** *vi* to be present without doing anything in particular: *Three youths were knocking around outside the cinema when the incident occurred.*

knock around with/about with *vt fus* (*inf*) to be friendly with or form part of the same group for social activities as: *I don't like the people she knocks around with and I wish she'd make some more friends of her own age.*

knock back *vt sep* (*inf*) to eat or drink, *esp* quickly and/or in large quantities: *He knocked back three pints of beer in the space of ten minutes.*

knock (someone) cold (*inf*) to make (a person) unconscious by a blow: *The beam swung round, hit him on the back of the head and knocked him cold.*

knock down *vt sep* **1** (*esp* of a person or a vehicle) to cause to fall by striking: *He was so angry with the man that he knocked him down*; *The old lady was knocked down as she crossed the street.* **2** (*inf*) to reduce the price of (goods): *She bought a coat that had been knocked down to half-price.* **3** (*with* **to**) to sell goods at an auction: *The clock was finally knocked down to a London dealer for £1 000.* – *See also* **knock-down** *above.*

knock off **1** *vt sep* to cause to fall off by striking: *He knocked her hat off with his umbrella.* **2** *vi, vt fus* (*inf*) to stop (working): *I knocked off (studying) at six o'clock after I had been working for four hours*; *What time do you knock off in this factory?* **3** *vt sep* (*sl*) to steal: *He was caught trying to get rid of a lot of cigarettes he had knocked off from a local tobacconist's*; *Where did you get that car? Did you knock it off?* **4** *vt sep* (*inf*) to reduce the price of something by a certain amount: *Since it was damaged, the shopkeeper knocked £1 off the price*; *He refused to knock off any more.* **5** *vt sep* (*inf*) to complete or do hurriedly: *The typist knocked off all the letters before lunch*; *She knocked them all off.* **6** *vt sep* (*sl*) to kill: *The boys boasted that they had knocked off the old man*; *Run – I think you've knocked him off!*

knock out *vt sep* **1** to remove from position by striking: *He took a hammer and knocked out the peg*; *He knocked it out.* **2** to empty by a blow: *He knocked his pipe out on the ashtray.* **3** to make unconscious by a blow, or (in boxing) unable to recover within the required time: *The boxer knocked his opponent out in the third round*; (*fig*) *Those sleeping pills really knock you out*; (*fig*) *A bottle of these pills would knock out the whole family.* **4** to defeat and cause to retire from a competition: *That team knocked us out of the contest in the semi-finals*; *They knocked out our other team as well.* – *See also* **knock-out** *above.*

knock over *vt sep* to (cause to) fall from an upright position: *The dog knocked over a chair as it rushed past*; *He knocked it over.*

knock spots off (*inf*) to do something much better, faster *etc* than: *That little girl can knock spots off her elder brother at tennis.*

knock up *vt sep* **1** to put together or make hurriedly: *We had to have somewhere to put the books, so my husband knocked up a couple of shelves*; *He knocked it up in two hours.* **2** (*Brit inf*) to awaken by knocking: *He asked the hotel porter to knock him up at six o'clock as he had a train to catch*; *Will he knock up the whole family?* **3** (*sl*: *usu refl*) to exhaust or make very tired: *Don't work so hard or you'll knock yourself up!* **4** (*vulg sl*: *esp Amer*) to make pregnant.

knot [not] *nc* **1** a lump or join made in string, rope *etc* by twisting the ends together and drawing tight the loops formed: *She fastened the string round the parcel, tying it with a knot.* **2** a lump in wood at the join between a branch and the trunk: *The wood was full of knots, which made it unsuitable for making furniture.* **3** a (small) collection, group or gathering: *a small knot of people*; (*liter*) *a knot of flowers.* **4** a measure of speed for ships (1 nautical mile (about 1·85 km) per hour). – *v* – *pt, ptp* **'knotted** – *vt* to tie (a piece of string *etc*) in a knot: *He knotted the rope around the gate-post*; *He knotted the sheets together to make a rope and climbed down from the window.*

'knotty *adj* **1** containing knots (*defs 1, 2*): *a knotty piece of string*; *These logs are all knotty.* **2** (of a problem *etc*) difficult: *She was occupied with the knotty problem of getting rid of him without hurting his feelings*; *That problem is rather knotty.*

know [nou] – *pt* **knew** [nju:] : *ptp* **known** – *vt* (not used with **is, was** *etc* and **-ing**) **1** to be aware of or to have been informed about: *He knows everything*; *I know that you are telling lies*; *I know he is at home because his car is in the drive*; *He knows all about it because I told him*; *I know of no reason why you cannot go.* **2** to have learned and remember: *I know a lot of interesting stories about him*; *I know a poem about the lives of fishermen.* **3** to be aware of the identity of; to be friendly with: *I know Mrs Smith – she lives up the road from me*; *He knows my father.* **4** to (be able to) recognize or identify: *You would hardly know her now – she has become very thin*; *He knows a good car when he sees one.* **5** (*liter*) to experience: *He has known many sorrows.* – *See also* **know** *in phrases below.*

'knowing *adj* showing secret understanding: *She gave him a knowing look*; *The look she gave him was knowing and sly.*

'knowingly *adv* **1** in a knowing manner: *She smiled knowingly.* **2** (*formal*) deliberately or on purpose: *He would not knowingly insult her.*

'know-all *nc* (*inf derog*) a person who thinks he knows everything: *I hate it when that know-all watches me mending my car – he always offers me advice.*

'know-how *nu* (*inf*) the practical knowledge and skill to deal with something: *I didn't have the know-how to be able to benefit from the situation*; *She acquired a lot of know-how about cars.*

in the know (*inf*) having information possessed by a small group of people and not by those outside it: *Several people asked me for information because they thought I was in the know*; *People in the know tell me that she has got the job.*

I wouldn't know (*inf*) I am not in a position to know: *'Is that the new hotel?' 'I wouldn't know, as I'm a visitor here myself.'*

know backwards to know extremely well or perfectly: *He knows the road to London backwards*; *He knows the publishing business backwards.*

know better to be too wise or well-taught (to do something): *She should know better at her age!*; *He should have known better than to trust them.*

know how to to have learned the way to: *I don't know how to use her washing-machine*; *She knew how to read when she went to school.*

know the ropes to understand the detail and procedure (of a job *etc*): *He'll be very good once he knows the ropes a bit better.*

know (on) which side one's bread is buttered to know which action will be more profitable to oneself: *He won't take action against you because you're useful to him, and he knows (on) which side his bread is buttered.*

what do you know? (*inf*: *esp Amer*) an expression of surprise: *What do you know? I thought that man over there had died last year.*

knowledge ['nolidʒ] *nu* **1** the fact of knowing: *The knowledge that she had won first prize in the competition cheered up the lonely old lady*; (*formal*) *It has come to my knowledge* (= I have found out) *that you stole from me.* **2** information or what is known: *He had a vast store of knowledge about boats.* **3** the whole of what can be learned or found out: *Science is a branch of knowledge about which I am completely ignorant.*

'knowledgeable *adj* (*formal*) having a great deal of information: *He is very knowledgeable about the history of the city*; *Knowledgeable children are often to be found in the library.*

common knowledge *see* **common**.

general knowledge knowledge about a wide range of subjects: *The child is bad at mathematics but his general knowledge is excellent.*

known *see* **know**.

knuckle ['nʌkl] **1** *nc* a joint of a finger: *She hit her hand against the wall as she fell and grazed her knuckles.* **2** *ncu* in a calf, pig *etc*, the joint of the knee, *esp* as used as food: (*a*) *knuckle of beef.*

'knuckle-duster *nc* a metal covering for the knuckles, used for attack.

knuckle down *vi* (*inf*: *often with* **to**) to start working seriously (at): *I don't really want to start studying for my exams but I'll just have to knuckle down (to it).*

knuckle under *vi* (*inf*) to give in (to someone else): *When we have disagreements, it's always me who has to knuckle under and do what I'm told.*

koala (bear) [kou'a:lə] *nc* a type of Australian tree-climbing animal like a small bear, the female of which carries her baby in a pouch.

Koran [ko'ra:n, (*Amer*) kou-] *n* the holy book of the Muslims.

Korea, Korean *see* Appendix 2.

kosher ['kouʃə] *adj* (*esp* of food) pure and clean, according to Jewish law: *a kosher butcher*; *kosher meat.*

kowtow [kau'tau] *vi* (*inf derog*: *with* **to**) to show too much respect for the wishes and views of: *I left the club because I couldn't stand the way everyone had to kowtow to the president.*

krona ['krounə] – *pl* **'kronor** – *nc* the standard unit of Swedish currency.

krone ['krounə] – *pl* **'kroner** – *nc* the standard unit of Danish and Norwegian currency.

kudos ['kju:dos] *nu* (*inf*) credit, fame or glory: *His new appointment was not particularly well-paid, but there was a lot of kudos attached to the position.*

Kuwait, Kuwaiti *see* Appendix 2.

L1

lab [lab] short for **laboratory**: *The doctor sent samples of her blood to the lab*; (*attrib*) *She has got a job as a lab assistant.*

label ['leibl] *nc* a small written note fixed on or near anything to tell its contents, owner *etc*: *The parcel had an orange label tied to it*; *The label on the blouse said 'Do not iron'.* – *v* – *pt, ptp* **'labelled**, *Amer* **'labeled** – *vt* **1** to attach a label to: *She labelled all the boxes of books carefully.* **2** (*fig*: *sometimes derog*) to call by a certain name or describe in a certain way: *She found it difficult to get work because she had been labelled* (*as*) *a troublemaker.*

laboratory [lə'borətəri, (*Amer*) 'labrəto:ri] *nc* (*inf abbrev* **lab** [lab]) a place where scientific experiments are carried on or where drugs *etc* are prepared: *The new product has been developed in the firm's research laboratory*; (*attrib*) *a laboratory experiment.*

labour, (*Amer*) **labor** ['leibə] **1** *ncu* hard work: *The labour involved in building the cathedral was considerable*; *People engaged in manual labour are often badly paid*; (*formal*) *After the labours of the past few years she is now able to take a holiday.* – *See also* **labour of love** *below.* **2** *nu* workmen on a job: *The firm is having difficulty hiring labour*; (*attrib*) *labour problems.* **3** *nu* (in a pregnant woman *etc*) the process of childbirth: *She was in labour for several hours before the baby was born.* **4** *n* (*with cap*) the Labour Party, one of the main political parties in the UK, whose aims and policies are Socialist: *'Forward with Labour!' is our new slogan.* – *vi* **1** to work hard or with difficulty: *They could hear the car engine labouring a bit as it came up the steep hill.* **2** to be employed to do hard and unskilled work: *He spends the summer labouring on a building site.* **3** (*formal*) to move slowly: *The children laboured through the snow towards the park.* **4** (*formal*: *with* **under**) to suffer through (something which makes a task, decision *etc* more difficult): *I think you're labouring under a misunderstanding.* – *adj* (*usu pred*: *with cap*) of, or supporting, the Labour Party: *We're all Labour in this house.*

laborious [lə'bo:riəs] *adj* (*formal*) requiring hard work: *To carry the coal up to the bedroom fires required several laborious journeys*; *I hate this job – it is so laborious and boring.* **la'boriously** *adv.* **la'boriousness** *nu.*

'laboured *adj* (*formal*) showing signs of effort: *The patient's laboured breathing worried the doctors*; *Her breathing seemed rather laboured after she had climbed the hill.*

'labourer *nc* a workman who is employed to do heavy work requiring little skill: *the labourers on a building site*; *The bricklayers have a team of labourers to help them build the houses*; *He is working as a labourer although he is a university graduate.*

'labour-saving *adj* intended to lessen work: *a labour-saving device for the kitchen*; *Her kitchen is modern and labour-saving but I prefer a more homely atmosphere.*

hard labour *see* **hard**.

labour of love a job *etc* which one does for one's own satisfaction or pleasure (or for that of someone whom one loves) and for which one is usually not paid: *It took her a long time to make her daughter's wedding dress – but it was a real labour of love.*

labour a point (*formal*) to emphasize a point too greatly and repeat it too often: *You have referred to your dissatisfaction with the job often enough – there is no need to labour the point.*

labrador ['labrədo:] *nc* a breed of large black- or yellow-coated dog often used as a gun-dog.

laburnum [lə'bə:nəm] *ncu* (*also* **la'burnum tree** *nc*) a type of small tree of the pea family with hanging yellow flowers, grown in gardens.

labyrinth ['labərinθ] *nc* (*formal*) a place full of long, winding passages or paths, through which it is difficult to find the way; a maze: *There was a labyrinth in the grounds of the Greek temple*; *She made her way through a labyrinth of corridors to the other end of the building*; (*fig*) *the labyrinth of questions on the income tax form.* **ˌlaby'rinthine** [-θain, (*Amer*) -θin] *adj.*

lace [leis] **1** *nc* a string or cord for fastening shoes *etc*: *I had to buy a new pair of laces for my tennis shoes*; *My lace is broken.* **2** *nu* delicate net-like decorative fabric made with fine thread: *Her dress was decorated with yards of beautiful lace*; (*attrib*) *a lace shawl.* – **1** *vti* to fasten or be fastened with a lace which is threaded through holes: *She wore a leather waistcoat which laced up the front*; *Lace* (*up*) *your boots firmly or the lace will come undone.* **2** *vt* to add something extra (*esp* alcohol) to (coffee *etc*): *She laced his coffee with rum/arsenic.*

See also **unlace**.

lacerate ['lasəreit] *vt* (*formal*) to tear or wound: *The sharp metal edge lacerated his leg*; (*fig*) *Her feelings were lacerated by his cruel words.*

ˌlace'ration *ncu*: *She had several deep lacerations on her arm.*

lack [lak] *vt* (*formal*: not used with **is, was** *etc* and **-ing**) to have too little or none of: *We lacked the experience to succeed*; *He lacked the courage to join the army.* – *nu* (*sometimes with* **a**) the state of not having any or enough: *There was a general lack of interest among the staff*; *our lack of information.*

be 'lacking (*formal*: *often with* **in**) **1** to be without or not to have enough: *I think he is lacking in intelligence.* **2** to be absent; to be present in too little an amount: *Before we had a child we felt that there was something lacking in our lives*; *Money for the project is not lacking but enthusiasm is.*

'lack for *vt fus* (*formal*: *usu in neg*) not to have enough: *In any case, they don't lack for money*; *The children lack for nothing although the parents are poorly dressed.*

lackadaisical [lakə'deizikəl] *adj* (*formal*) without energy or interest: *He has a lackadaisical approach to his schoolwork and rarely bothers to study properly*; *She is quite clever but she is far too lackadaisical to be in charge of a department.*

lackey ['laki] *nc* **1** (*old*) a manservant. **2** (*derog*) a person who does what he is told; a person who fetches and carries *etc* like a servant: *The Prime Minister was accused of being the lackey of the upper classes*; *I did not speak to the manager – it was one of his lackeys who answered the phone.*

laconic [lə'konik] *adj* (*formal*) using few words to express a meaning: *He had a laconic way of speaking and rarely said much*; *She is so laconic and uninteresting.* **la'conically** *adv.*

lacquer ['lakə] *nu* **1** a type of varnish: *He painted the iron table with black lacquer.* **2** a substance used to keep hair tidy: *She doesn't use lacquer on her hair – it makes it sticky.* – *vt* to cover with lacquer: *He lacquered the vase*; *She lacquers her hair to keep it in place.*

lacrosse [lə'kros] *nu* a team game played with a small ball and a long stick with a shallow net at one end.

lactic ['laktik] *adj* (*tech*: *esp attrib*) of or from milk: *lactic acid.*

lad [lad] *nc* (*inf or dial*) a boy or a youth: *He's quite a pleasant lad*; *I knew him when he was a lad.*

quite a lad (*inf*) (of a male person) a remarkable, often slightly shocking, person: *He's quite a lad, your brother – he seems to know everyone in town!*

See also **lass**.

ladder ['ladə] *nc* **1** a set of rungs or steps between two long supports, for climbing up or down: *She was standing on a ladder painting the ceiling*; (*fig formal*) *The young actor is well up the ladder of success*; (*fig formal*) *She is certainly climbing the social ladder* (= being accepted by the members of a social class higher than her own) *by marrying him.* **2** a long, narrow flaw caused by the breaking of a stitch in a stocking or other knitted fabric. – *vti* to (cause to) develop such a flaw: *I laddered my best pair of tights today*; *These stockings are very fine and ladder very easily.*

laden ['leidn] *adj* carrying a lot (of); heavily loaded (with): *People left the shops laden with purchases*; *Several laden lorries turned out of the yard.*

See also **load**.

ladle ['leidl] *nc* a large spoon with a long handle, for lifting out liquid, *etc* from a container: *a soup ladle.* – *vt* to lift and deal out with a ladle or in large quantities: *He ladled soup into the plates*; (*inf*) *She was ladling syrup on to her steamed pudding*; (*inf*) *The new teacher ladles out the homework!*

'ladleful *nc* as much as fills a ladle: *I'll have two ladlefuls of soup.*

lady ['leidi] *nc* **1** a more polite form of **woman**: *Tell that child to stand up and let that lady sit down*; *The lady in the flower shop said that roses are expensive just now*; *She is a sweet old lady*; (*attrib*) *She would prefer to be examined by a lady doctor*; *The police found a lady's shoe by the dead body*; *The children's department is upstairs – where is the ladies' department?* **2** a woman of good manners and refined behaviour: *She is a real lady!*; *She is too much of a lady to swear*; *Ladies do not shout in public.* **3** (*with cap*) in the UK, the title of a peeress, the wife of a lord, baronet or knight and the daughter of a duke, marquis or earl: *Lady Smith is a baroness*; *Sir James and Lady Brown*; *The Duke's eldest daughter is Lady Anne.* **4** (*sometimes with cap*) in the UK *etc*, any noblewoman or woman of rank: *The lords and ladies were dressed in their robes.* **5** (*with cap*) in the UK, used as part of several official titles: *the Lady Mayoress.*

the 'ladies' *nc* (*inf*) a women's lavatory: *The ladies' in the restaurant was difficult to find*; *Ask the waitress where the ladies' is.*

'ladylike *adj* like a lady in manners: *She was a gentle, ladylike girl who never used bad language*; *She is too ladylike to swear.*

'Ladyship *n* (*with* **Her**, **Your** *etc*) a word used in speaking to, or about, a woman with the title 'Lady': *I shall do that right away, Your Ladyship*; *Her Ladyship the Countess of Carrick.*

'ladybird *nc* (*Amer* **'ladybug**) a type of little round beetle, usually red with black spots.

'lady-killer *nc* (*inf*: *usu derog*) a man who is said to be very popular with women: *He thinks he's a lady-killer but most women find him boring.*

lag[1] [lag] – *pt*, *ptp* **lagged** – *vi* to move too slowly and become left behind: *Several times we had to wait for the children, who were lagging behind the rest.* – *nu* an act of lagging or the amount by which one thing is later than another: *There is a time-lag of several minutes between our hearing the train and our actually seeing it*; *a lag of several seconds.*

See also **jet-lag** *under* **jet**.

lag[2] [lag] – *pt*, *ptp* **lagged** – *vt* to cover a boiler, hot-water pipes *etc* with a thick covering to keep the heat in: *Our hot water costs less since we had the boiler lagged.*

'lagging *nu* thick material for covering pipes *etc*: *The lagging is coming off our pipes.*

lager ['la:gə] **1** *ncu* (any type of) a light-coloured beer: *I don't like lager.* **2** *nc* a glass of lager: *He went to the bar and bought three lagers and a whisky and soda.*

lagoon [lə'gu:n] *nc* a shallow stretch of water separated from the sea by sandbanks, coral reefs *etc.*

laid *see* **lay**[1].

lain *see* **lie**[2].

lair [leə] *nc* the den of a wild beast: *It was said that a bear had its lair among the rocks at the top of the valley.*

laird [leəd] *nc* in Scotland, a landowner: *The laird visits all his tenants once a year.*

laity *see* **lay**[3].

lake [leik] *nc* (*often found with cap in place-names*) a large area of water surrounded by land: *They have a house near a large lake where they sail*; *They live near Lake Michigan.*

lamb [lam] **1** *nc* a young sheep: *The ewe has had three lambs.* **2** *nu* its flesh eaten as food: *We had roast lamb for lunch*; *a leg of lamb.* **3** *nc* (*fig inf*) a kind, lovable or gentle person, *usu* a child: *Isn't she a lamb!*

'lambskin *nu* the skin of a lamb, *usu* with the wool left on it: (*attrib*) *a lambskin coat.*

'lambswool ['lamz-] *nu* a fine type of wool obtained from a lamb: *a sweater made of lambswool*; (*attrib*) *a lambswool sweater.*

lame [leim] *adj* **1** unable to walk properly: *He was lame for weeks after his fall*; *The lame child cannot run with his friends.* **2** (*fig*) not satisfactory; unacceptable: *a lame excuse*; *I don't believe his story – it sounds a bit lame.* – *vt* to make unable to walk properly: *He was lamed by a bullet in the ankle.* **'lamely** *adv.* **'lameness** *nu.*

lame duck *nc* (*fig*: *sometimes derog*) a helpless, injured or inefficient person: *Her house is always full of lame ducks who need help.*

lament [lə'ment] *vti* (*formal*) to feel or express regret (for): *She lamented that she had never been to Paris*; *He lamented his carelessness*; *I lament my lack of musical talent*; *We all lament his death*; *They sat lamenting* (*over*) *their lack of money.* – *nc* **1** a poem or piece of music which laments something: *This piece of poetry is a lament for the writer's lost youth*; *This tune is a lament for those killed in battle.* **2** (*inf*) a show of grief, regret *etc*: *She started a long lament about the weather.*

la'mented *adj* (*neg* **un-**).

lamentable ['laməntəbl] *adj* (*formal derog*) disappointing or regrettable: *a lamentable state of affairs; a lamentable performance; The government's attempt at improving the economy is lamentable.*

ˌ**lamen'tation** [lamən-] *ncu (formal or liter)* (an) act of lamenting: *the lamentations of the widows.*

laminated ['lamineitid] *adj (tech)* made in thin layers: *This table is made of laminated plywood; The top of this table is laminated.* ˌ**lami'nation** *ncu.*

lamp [lamp] *nc (often in cmpds)* a (glass-covered) light: *an oil-lamp; a table lamp; a street-lamp.*

'**lamp-post** *nc* the pillar supporting a street-lamp.

'**lampshade** *nc* a structure, *usu* of cloth, paper or metal, covering a lamp, which lessens, softens or directs the light coming from it: *The lampshades in her sitting room match the curtains; That lampshade is too dark – it does not let out enough light.*

lampoon [lam'puːn] *nc (formal)* an abusive piece of writing ridiculing a particular person violently, and often cruelly: *a political lampoon.* – *vt (formal)* **1** to write lampoons about. **2** (of a piece of writing) to ridicule violently: *His latest essay lampoons the Prime Minister.*

lance [laːns] *nc (hist)* a weapon with a long shaft or handle of wood, a spearhead and often a small flag: *The knight carried a lance and shield as he rode into battle.* – *vt* to cut open (a boil *etc*) with a knife: *The doctor lanced the boil on my neck.*

lance corporal *nc (with cap in titles)* in the British army, (a person of) the rank next below corporal: *He is a lance corporal; He was promoted to lance corporal; Lance Corporal Foster.* – *See also* Appendix 3.

land [land] **1** *nu* the solid part of the surface of the Earth which is not covered by the sea: *We had been at sea a week before we saw land; The sailor's wife wants him to get a job on land.* **2** *nc (formal or liter)* a country: *foreign lands.* **3** *nu* the ground or soil: *He never made any money at farming as his land was poor and stony.* **4** *ncu (sometimes in pl)* an estate: *He owns land/lands in Scotland; This river forms the boundary of his land.* – **1** *vti* to come or bring (an aircraft) down from the air upon the land or the sea: *The plane landed in the sea; They managed to land the helicopter safely; She fell twenty feet, but landed without injury.* **2** *vti* to come or bring (something) from the sea on to the land: *After being at sea for three months, they finally landed at Plymouth; He landed the big fish with some help.* **3** *vti (loosely: fig)* to (cause to) finish or to (be) put in the end (in a certain, *usu* the wrong, place or a certain, *usu* bad, condition): *They had a serious accident which landed them in hospital; When we tried to do it ourselves, we landed (ourselves) in more trouble.* **4** *vt (inf)* to succeed in obtaining: *He landed the job/the prize.* **5** *vt (inf)* to give (a blow): *She landed him one* (= she hit him) *with the book she was holding.* – *See also* **land up, land with** *below.*

'**landed** *adj (attrib: formal)* owning land or estates: *the landed gentry.*

'**landing 1** *ncu* (an act of) coming to shore or to ground: *The spaceship made a successful landing in the Pacific; The landing of the fishing-boat's catch was achieved without difficulty; (attrib) a landing place.* **2** *nc* the level part of a staircase between flights of steps: *Her room was on the first floor, across the landing from mine.* **3** *nc* a place for coming ashore: *There were several people waiting at the ferry landing.*

'**landward** *adj (attrib)* lying *etc* toward the land: *The ship was anchored on the landward side of the harbour-wall.*

'**landfall** *nc (formal or tech)* **1** an approach to land after a journey by sea or air: *The ship/plane made a landfall at Hawaii.* **2** the land approached in this way: *The coast of Ireland was our first landfall for ten days.*

'**landing-gear** *nu* the parts of an aircraft that carry the load when it lands: *The accident was caused by the failure of the plane's landing-gear.*

'**landing-stage** *nc* a platform, fixed or floating, on which to land passengers or goods from a boat.

landlady *see* **landlord** *below.*

'**landlocked** *adj* enclosed by land: *a landlocked bay; That area is completely landlocked.*

'**landlord** – *fem* '**landlady** – *nc* **1** a person who has tenants or lodgers: *My landlady has just put up my rent.* **2** a person who keeps a public house: *The landlord of the 'Swan' is Mr Smith.*

'**landmark** *nc* **1** an object on land that serves as a guide to seamen or others: *The church-tower has been a landmark for sailors for centuries because it stands on the top of a cliff.* **2** *(formal fig)* an event of great importance: *This meeting is a landmark in the history of democracy.*

'**land mine** *nc* a mine laid on or near the surface of the ground, which is set off by something passing over it.

'**landowner** *nc* a person who owns land, *esp* a lot of land: *The local landowners don't like having gipsies camping on their land.*

'**Landrover** ® [-rouvə] *nc* a type of strong motor vehicle used for driving over rough ground: *The shepherd drove his Landrover up the mountain road.*

'**landslide** *nc* **1** a piece of land that falls down from the side of a hill: *His car was buried in the landslide.* **2** *(fig)* in an election, a great majority of votes for one side: *(attrib) a landslide victory.*

land up *vi (inf)* to finish or come eventually to be (in a certain, *usu* the wrong, place or a certain, *usu* bad, condition): *He wanted to go to London, but got on the wrong train and landed up in Bristol; If you go on like that, you'll land up in jail.*

land (someone) with (something) *(inf)* to give or pass (a job, an object *etc* which is unpleasant or unwanted) to (someone else): *She was landed with the job of telling him; They landed me with the things no-one else wanted.*

see how the land lies to look at the conditions, state of affairs *etc* which exist before taking an action or making a decision: *I can't say what I'll do until I get there – I shall have to see how the land lies.*

landscape ['landskeip] *nc* **1** the area of land that a person can look at all at the same time: *He stood on the hill surveying the landscape.* **2** a picture showing a view of the countryside: *eighteenth-century landscapes; He paints landscapes but his wife paints portraits.* – *vt* to have landscape gardening done on: *We are having our back garden landscaped.*

landscape gardening *nu* the art of planning and laying out gardens, parks *etc*: *He is studying landscape gardening.* **landscape gardener** *nc.*

landslide, landward *see* **land**.

lane [lein] **1** *nc* a narrow road or street: *A winding lane led down towards the river.* **2** *n (with cap)* a word used in the names of certain roads or streets: *His address is 12 Penny Lane.* **3** *nc* a division of a road for one line of traffic: *The new motorway has three lanes in each direction.* **3** *nc* a regular course across the sea taken by ships: *The shipwrecked* *man saw few ships as he was not on a regular shipping lane.*

language ['laŋgwidʒ] **1** *nu* human speech: *They were studying the development of language in children*; (*attrib*) *language teaching.* **2** *nc* the speech of a particular nation: *She is very good at languages* (= at learning, speaking *etc* foreign languages); *Russian is a difficult language to learn.* **3** *nc* the words and way of speaking, writing *etc* usually connected with a particular group of people *etc*: *the language of journalism.* **4** *nu* any manner of expressing thought, *esp* a style of writing or speaking: *sign language*; *The language in this poem is very difficult.*

bad language *nu* (*inf*) swearing: *He uses too much bad language.*

'language laboratory *nc* (*inf abbrev* **'language lab**) a room in which pupils are taught languages by means of pre-recorded tapes.

speak the same language *see* **speak**.

languid ['laŋgwid] *adj* (*formal*) without liveliness, energy or spirit: *She had a languid manner and seemed rarely to move from her sofa*; *She is pale and languid.* **'languidly** *adv.*

languor ['laŋgə] *nu* (*formal*) the state of being languid: *She roused herself from her languor long enough to order tea to be brought.* **'languorous** *adj.*

languish ['laŋgwiʃ] *vi* (*formal or liter*) to grow weak: *The business is languishing for want of new ideas.*

lank [laŋk] *adj* long, straight and not springy: *She had lank, greasy hair which never looked clean*; *Her hair is lank and dull.*

'lanky *adj* thin, tall and not elegant: *a lanky youth*; *He is tall and lanky.* **'lankiness** *nu.*

lanolin(e) ['lanəlin] *nu* fat obtained from wool: *This face-cream contains lanolin.*

lantern ['lantən] *nc* a case for holding or carrying a light.

lap[1] [lap] – *pt, ptp* **lapped** – *vti* **1** to drink by licking with the tongue: *The cat lapped milk from a saucer.* **2** (*formal*) (of a liquid) to wash or flow (against): *Water lapped the side of the boat*; *The waves lapped against the shore.*

lap up *vt sep* **1** to drink by lapping: *The dog lapped up the water.* **2** (*fig derog*) to accept eagerly, uncritically and in large quantities: *He was unbelievably insincere in his flattery, but she just lapped it up.*

lap[2] [lap] *nc* **1** the part from waist to knees of a person when he/she is sitting: *The baby was lying in its mother's lap.* **2** one round of a racecourse or other competition track: *The runners have completed five laps, with three still to run.* – *v* – *pt, ptp* **lapped** – *vt* in a race, to get a lap ahead of (another competitor): *The leader has already lapped the man who is in fourth place.*

'lap dog *nc* a small pet dog.

the lap of luxury very luxurious conditions: *We lived in the lap of luxury and didn't have to pay a penny!*

lapel [lə'pel] *nc* the part of a coat joined to the collar and folded back across the chest: *a coat with very wide lapels.*

lapse [laps] *vi* (*formal*) **1** to cease to exist, often because of lack of effort: *His insurance policy had lapsed and was not renewed*; *Conversation lapsed for lack of anything to say.* **2** to pass, *esp* gradually, into a different, often bad or worse, state: *After several efforts to speak, he lapsed into silence*; *I'm afraid our standards have lapsed over the holidays.* – *nc* (*formal*) **1** a mistake or failure (in goodness, memory *etc*): *He's been guilty of several lapses recently*; *a lapse of memory.* **2** a passing away (of time): *I saw him again recently after a lapse of some five years.*

lapsed *adj* (*usu attrib*) **1** having fallen into disuse: *a lapsed insurance policy.* **2** having fallen into wickedness or error: *a lapsed Christian.*

larceny ['la:səni] *ncu* (*legal*) the term in England, Ireland and Wales for stealing: *He has been found guilty of larceny.*

larch [la:tʃ] *nc* (*also* **'larch tree**) a type of cone-bearing, deciduous tree related to pines and firs.

lard [la:d] *nu* the melted fat of the pig, used in cooking: *She uses lard and butter in making pastry*; *Melt some lard in a pan – I'm going to fry some potatoes.* – *vt* **1** to put lard on; to cover with lard: *He larded the lean meat.* **2** (*tech*) to stuff (meat) with bacon or pork. **3** (*fig inf*) to fill as full as possible with (something): *He larded his remarks with quotations.*

larder ['la:də] *nc* a room or place where food is kept: *We don't have a fridge but the larder is a cool place.*

large [la:dʒ] *adj* (*more formal than* **big**) great in size, amount *etc*; not small: *a large number of people*; *a large box*; *They live in a large house with many bedrooms*; *He has a large family*; *This house is too large for two people.*

'largely *adv* (*formal*) **1** mainly or chiefly: *This success was largely due to her efforts.* **2** to a great extent: *Our attempts to do better have been largely successful.* **'largeness** *nu.*

at 'large (*formal*) **1** (of prisoners *etc*) free: *Despite the efforts of the police, the escaped prisoner is still at large.* **2** in general: *the country at large* (= the people of the country as a whole).

largess(e) [la:'dʒes] *nu* (*very formal or facet*: *sometimes derog*) money *etc* given generously: *They went around distributing largesse to the poor.*

lark[1] [la:k] *nc* a general name for several types of singing-bird, *esp* the skylark, which flies high into the air as it sings: *They could hear a lark singing*; *She gets up with the lark* (= She rises early in the morning).

lark[2] [la:k] *nc* (*inf*) a piece of fun or mischief: *He only did it for a lark!*

lark about/around *vi* (*inf*) to play about in a rough and *usu* noisy manner: *Several teenagers were larking about in the hall.*

larva ['la:və] – *pl* **'larvae** [-vi:] – *nc* (*tech*) a developing insect in a state very different from the adult, *eg* the caterpillar of a butterfly.

'larval *adj* (*tech*: *attrib*): *in the larval stage of development.*

larynx ['lariŋks] *nc* (*tech*) the upper end of the windpipe containing the cords which produce the voice.

laryngitis [larin'dʒaitis] *nu* inflammation of the larynx: *She couldn't talk because she was suffering from laryngitis.*

lasagne [la'sanjə] *nu* an Italian dish made of flat pieces of pasta baked with tomatoes, cheese and meat.

laser ['leizə] *nc* (*tech*) (an instrument that produces) a narrow and very intense beam of light: *The men were cutting sheet metal with a laser*; (*attrib*) *a laser beam.*

lash [laʃ] *nc* **1** an eyelash: *She looked at him secretly through her lashes.* **2** a stroke with a whip *etc*: *The* *sailor was sentenced to receive twenty lashes.* **3** a thin piece of rope or cord, *esp* of a whip: *The coachman had a whip with a long, thin lash.* – **1** *vt* to strike with a lash: *He lashed the horse with his whip*; (*fig*) *She lashed him with her tongue for ten minutes*; (*formal fig*) *He lashed himself into a rage.* **2** *vt* to fasten with a rope or cord: *All the equipment had to be lashed to the deck of the ship.* **3** *vti* to make a sudden or restless movement (with) (a tail): *The cat crouched in the grass, its tail lashing from side to side.* **4** *vi* (*inf*) (of rain *etc*, *usu in progressive tenses*) to come down very heavily: *The rain is lashing down outside*; *It was lashing when we left.* – *See also* **lash out** below.

'lashing 1 *nc* an act of whipping: *The lashing of soldiers was a common punishment in the army during the last century.* **2** *nc* (*formal*) a rope or cord for tying things to something else: *He untied the lashings holding the box to the deck of the ship.*

'lashings *n pl* (*inf*) a large amount (*esp* of something to eat): *We had three sausages each and lashings of chips.*

lash out *vi* **1** (*often with* **at**) to kick or hit out violently: *He lashed out with his foot and kicked his attacker on the ankle*; (*fig*) *In his speech the Prime Minister lashed out at his opponents.* **2** (*inf*) to spend money in large quantities: *For our anniversary, we decided to lash out and have a really big party.*

lass [las] *nc* (*liter or dial*) a girl.
See also **lad**.

lassitude ['lasitju:d] *nu* (*formal*) tiredness or lack of energy: *Such lassitude often follows severe illness.*

lasso [la'su:] – *pl* **las'so(e)s** – *nc* a long rope with a loop which tightens when the rope is pulled, used for catching wild horses *etc.* – *v* – *prt* **las'soes**: *pt, ptp* **las'soed** – *vt* to catch with a lasso: *The cowboy lassoed the horse that headed the stampede.*

last[1] [la:st] *adj* **1** coming at the end of a series: *We set out on the last day of November*; *He was last in the race*; *He caught the last bus home in the evening.* **2** (*attrib*) most recent; next before the present: *Our last house was much smaller than this one*; *He went to Greece for his holidays last year.* **3** coming or remaining after all the others: *The last guest did not leave until six o'clock*; *He was the last to leave*; *It was March before the last snows melted.* – *See also* **last** *in phrases below.* – *adv* at the end of or after all the others: *He took his turn last.*

'lastly *adv* finally or at the end: *Lastly, I would like to thank you all for listening so patiently to what I have been saying*; *Having checked everything else, I look lastly at the windows to make sure they're shut.*

at (long) last in the end, *esp* after a long delay: *At long last she arrived, about half an hour late*; *Oh, there he is at last!*

breathe one's last (*liter euph*) to die.

hear, see *etc* **the last of** to hear of or see something for the last time: *I think we've seen the last of him!*; *You haven't heard the last of this!*

the Last Judgement in some religions, God's judgement of good and bad people on the Day of Judgement.

last of all lastly: *And last of all, I would like to thank Mr Smith for all his help.*

the 'last person a person who is very unlikely, unwilling or unsuitable to do something or who is dangerous, unsuitable *etc* to do something to: *He's the last person you should offend*; *She's the last person you would suspect of such a thing*; *I would be the last person to complain.*

the last straw a fact, happening *etc* which, when added to all other facts or happenings, makes a situation finally impossible to bear: *Everything was going wrong, and his message was the last straw – she just burst into tears.*

the Last Supper (*relig*) in the Bible, the meal eaten by Christ and his disciples on the day before the Crucifixion.

the 'last thing something very unlikely, unwanted, not intended *etc*: *It's the last thing you would think of looking for*; *The last thing I want is to hurt anyone.*

the last word 1 the final remark in an argument *etc*: *She always must have the last word!* **2** the final decision: *The last word on the project rests with the manager.* **3** (*inf*) something very fashionable or up-to-date: *Her hat was the last word in elegance.*

on one's last legs very near to falling down or collapsing with exhaustion, old age *etc*: *By the time we arrived we'd walked twenty miles and were on our last legs*; *My washing-machine is on its last legs – I've had it twenty-five years.*

to the 'last (*formal*) until the very end, or until the last possible moment: *A fighter to the last, he was still firing his gun as he died.*

last[2] [la:st] **1** *vi* to continue to exist: *This situation lasted until she got married*; *I hope this fine weather lasts until the weekend.* **2** *vti* to remain in good condition: *This carpet has lasted well – it's forty years old and as good as new*; *The bread won't last another two days – we'll need more*; *This coat will last me until I die.*

last out *vti* to be or have enough to survive or continue to exist (until the end of): *I hope the petrol lasts out until we reach a garage*; *They could only last out another week on the little food they had*; *The sick man was not expected to last out the night.*

last[3] [la:st] *nc* a foot-like shape on which a shoemaker makes and repairs shoes.

latch [latʃ] *nc* a catch of wood or metal used to fasten a door *etc*: *She lifted the latch and walked in.* – *vt* to fasten with a latch: *She latched the gate behind her.*

'latchkey *nc* a small front-door key: *She put her latchkey in the lock.*

on the latch shut but not locked: *She had left the door on the latch so that she could get back in.*

late [leit] *adj* **1** (*esp pred*) coming *etc* after the expected or usual time: *The train is late tonight*; *She was late getting to work*; *I try to be punctual but I am always late.* **2** (*esp pred*) far on in the day or night: *late in the day*; *late at night*; *It was very late when I finally got to bed*; *You have missed the late bus – try to get a taxi.* **3** (*attrib*: *formal*) dead, *esp* recently: *the late king*; *Mrs Smith is the widow of the late Mr John Smith.* **4** (*attrib*: *formal*) recently, but no longer, holding an office or position: *Mr Allan, the late chairman, made a speech.* – *adv* **1** after the expected or usual time: *He arrived late for his interview.* **2** far on in the day or night: *They always go to bed late.* **'lateness** *nu.*

'lately *adv* in the recent past or not long ago: *Have you seen her lately?*

'latish *adj, adv* (*inf*) rather late: *He arrived back latish after the office party.*

later on at a later time: *He hasn't arrived yet but no doubt he'll be here later on.*

of 'late (*formal*) lately: *He thought she had been less friendly of late.*

See also **belated**.

latent ['leitənt] *adj* (*esp attrib*: *formal*) hidden or undeveloped but capable of becoming developed or active: *latent talent*; *a latent suspicion*; *The hostility remained latent.*

lateral ['latərəl] *adj* (*formal or tech*: *esp attrib*) of, at, to or from the side: *lateral movement*; *a lateral position.* '**laterally** *adv.*

latex ['leiteks] *nu* the milky juice of some plants *esp* rubber trees: *Rubber is manufactured from latex*; (*attrib*) *latex foam.*

lath [la:θ] *nc* a thin narrow strip of wood: *The inside walls of houses used to be made of laths covered with plaster.*

lathe [leið] *nc* a machine for shaping wood, metal *etc*, which turns the piece of wood *etc* which is to be shaped round and round against a tool held steady by the operator.

lather ['la:ðə] *nu* **1** a mixture of water and soap *etc* producing bubbles: *She added detergent to the washing-machine until it formed a lather.* **2** (of animals) a mixture of similar appearance made by sweat: *The horse's neck was covered in lather.* – **1** *vt* to cover with lather: *She sat in the bath and lathered herself carefully.* **2** *vi* to form a lather: *Soap doesn't lather well in water from our area – the water is too hard.*

in a lather (*fig inf*) very excited or upset: *She was all in a lather over the preparations for the party.*

Latin ['latin] **1** *n, adj* (of) the language spoken in ancient Rome: *We studied Latin at school*; *a Latin lesson.* **2** *adj* (*attrib*) (of a language) derived from Latin: *Italian, French and Spanish are Latin languages.* **3** *nc, adj* (*attrib*) (a person) who speaks a Latin language: *All the people present were Latins*; (*attrib*) *the Latin peoples.*

Latin America *n* the countries of Central and South America, where the official language is usually a form of Spanish or Portuguese. **Latin American** *nc, adj.*

See also Appendix 2.

latitude ['latitju:d] **1** *nu* the distance, measured in degrees on the map, that a place is north or south of the Equator: *What is the latitude of London?* **2** *nu* freedom of action or choice: *His new job allows him far more latitude than his old one.* **3** *nc* (*in pl*) areas of the world which are all a similar distance from the equator: *In these latitudes the summer is very short/the sun sets very quickly.*

See also **longitude**.

latrine [lə'tri:n] *nc* (*formal*) a lavatory, *esp* one used by soldiers *etc.*

latter ['latə] *adj* (*formal*: *attrib*) towards the end: *He mentioned it in the latter part of his speech.*

'**latterly** *adv* recently or in the last part of a period of time: *He remained in good health until he died, although latterly* (= at the end of his life) *he became rather deaf.*

'**latter-day** *adj* (*attrib*: *formal*) recent or modern: *latter-day writers.*

the latter the second of two things mentioned: *John and Mary arrived, the latter wearing a green wool dress*; *She enjoys embroidery and knitting, but is not very good at the latter.*

See also **former**.

lattice ['latis] **1** *ncu* (*usu* '**lattice-work**) a network of crossed bars of wood *etc*: *He is building some lattice-work for his rose bushes to climb up.* **2** *nc* (*esp attrib*) a window with small diamond-shaped panels: *a lattice window.*

laudable ['lo:dəbl] *adj* (*formal*) worthy of being praised: *This pupil has made a laudable attempt to help his less fortunate classmates with their work*; *His conduct is not at all laudable.* '**laudably** *adv.*

laugh [la:f] *vi* to make sounds with the voice in showing happiness, amusement, scorn *etc*: *We laughed at the funny photographs*; *Children were laughing in the garden as they played.* – *See also* **laugh at** *below.* – *nc* an act or sound of laughing: *Suddenly she heard a laugh from outside*; *He gave a scornful laugh.*

'**laughable** *adj* **1** ridiculous or deserving scorn: *Her attempts at drawing were laughable*; *laughable attempts at dancing.* **2** amusing: *It seems laughable now, but it wasn't funny at the time*; *The children were amused by the laughable antics of the clown.*

'**laughably** *adv.*

'**laughingly** *adv* **1** (*formal*) with a laugh; with laughter: *The adults looked on laughingly as the children played.* **2** as a joke: *She suggested laughingly that he should try it himself.*

'**laughter** *nu* the act or sound of laughing: *We could hear laughter/the sound of laughter from the next room.*

'**laughing-stock** *nc* someone who is laughed at: *If I wear that hat, I'll be the laughing-stock of the village.*

'**laugh at** *vt fus* to make it obvious that one regards something or someone as humorous, ridiculous or deserving scorn: *Everyone will laugh at me if I wear that dress!*; *He was not sure that it was a good idea, but the others laughed at his fears.* – *See also* **laugh** *above.*

laugh up one's sleeve to laugh secretly: *I had the feeling she was laughing up her sleeve at something I didn't understand/at me.*

launch[1] [lo:ntʃ] *vt* **1** to make (a boat or ship) slide into the water or (a rocket) leave the ground: *As soon as the alarm was given, the lifeboat was launched*; *The Russians have launched a rocket.* **2** (*fig*) to start (a person, project *etc*) off on a course: *His success launched him on a brilliant career*; *We held a party to launch our new product.* **3** (*formal*) to throw: *The natives launched spears in our direction across the river.* – *See also* **launch out** *below.* – *ncu* (an) act of launching: *A party was held for the launch of the firm's new venture.*

'**launching-pad** *nc* a platform from which a rocket can be launched.

launch forth *vi* (*formal or liter*) to begin something in a colourful or dramatic manner: *She launched forth into a long tale about what she had been doing.*

launch out *vi* to throw oneself freely into some new activity (often involving spending money): *The firm has recently launched out into the field of fashion.*

launch[2] [lo:ntʃ] *nc* a large, power-driven boat, *usu* used for short trips or for pleasure: *We cruised round the bay in a motor launch*; *He came by launch.*

launder ['lo:ndə] *vt* (*formal*) to wash and iron: *I pay a woman to launder my clothes.*

laund(e)rette [lo:n'dret] *nc* a shop where customers may wash clothes in washing-machines: *She cannot afford to buy a washing-machine – she has to go to a launderette.*

'**laundress** *nc* (*formal*) a woman who launders: *She is employed as a laundress at the hospital.*

'**laundry** **1** *nc* a place where clothes *etc* are washed, *esp* in return for payment: *She works in the hospital laundry*; *I always take my tablecloths to the laundry.* **2** *nu* clothes *etc* which have been, or are to be, washed: *a bundle of laundry.*

laurel ['lorəl] *nc* (*also* '**laurel tree**) a type of tree, once used for making wreaths to crown winners of races or competitions *etc.*

look to one's laurels to be careful not to lose a position or reputation due to better performances *etc* by others: *If you want to win the race you had better look to your laurels and start training.*

rest on one's laurels to keep a position or reputation because of past successes without actually doing anything more: *I think the school used to be good, but they've been resting on their laurels for twenty years or so.*

lava ['la:və] *nu* liquid, melted rock *etc* thrown out from a volcano and becoming solid as it cools.

lavatory ['lavətəri] *nc* **1** (*more formal than* **toilet**) a (small) room containing equipment for receiving and getting rid of waste matter from the body: *In their house the lavatory is separate from the bathroom; The child wants to go to the lavatory.* **2** (*usu attrib*) the piece of equipment itself: *a lavatory brush* (= a brush, with a handle, for cleaning the inside of a lavatory).

lavender ['lavində] **1** *nu* a type of plant with sweet-smelling pale bluish-purple flowers: *The sheets were scented with lavender.* **2** *nu, adj* (*also* **lavender blue**) (of) the colour of the flowers: *Her dress was of the palest lavender; a lavender blue dress.*

'lavender water *nu* a perfume containing oil of lavender.

lavish ['laviʃ] *vt* (*formal*) to spend or give very freely: *She lavishes both care and money on her appearance; She lavishes so much attention on that child.* – *adj* (*formal*) **1** (of a person) spending or giving generously and sometimes too freely: *a lavish host; a lavish cook; She spread icing on the cake with a lavish hand; You have been too lavish with the brandy in this cake.* **2** given generously or too freely: *lavish gifts; Her Christmas gifts are always lavish and expensive.* **'lavishly** *adv.* **'lavishness** *nu.*

law [lo:] **1** *nu* the collection of rules according to which people live or a country *etc* is governed: *Such an action is against the law; The police are concerned with keeping law and order.* **2** *nc* any one of such rules: *A new law has been passed by Parliament; You must read all the laws of the club before you are allowed to join.* **3** *nc* (in science) a rule that says that under certain conditions certain things always happen: *the law of gravity; the laws governing motion.* – *See also* **the law** *below.*

'lawful *adj* (*formal or legal*) **1** (*neg* **un-**) allowed by law: *He was attacked while going about his lawful business; Such behaviour is not lawful.* **2** (*esp attrib*) just or rightful: *She is the lawful owner of the property.* **'lawfully** *adv.*

'lawless *adj* (*formal*) paying no attention to and not keeping the law: *In its early days, the American West was full of lawless men; The bandits were wild and lawless.* **'lawlessly** *adv.* **'lawlessness** *nu.*

lawyer ['lo:jə] *nc* a person whose work it is to know about and give advice and help to others concerning the law: *If you want to divorce your husband you must consult a lawyer.*

'law-abiding *adj* (*formal*) obeying the law: *I have always tried to be a law-abiding citizen; He would like to be law-abiding but he cannot help stealing.*

'law court *nc* (*also* **court of law**) a place where people accused of crimes are tried and legal disagreements between people are judged.

'lawsuit *nc* a quarrel or disagreement taken to a court of law to be settled: *This incident caused a famous lawsuit in the House of Lords.*

be a law unto oneself not to obey rules or orders: *I can't say that she will agree to do it – she's a law unto herself.*

break a/the law *see* **break** (*def 4*).

common law *see* **common**.

have the law on (*inf*) (*usu* used as a threat) to make sure that legal action is taken against (someone who is breaking the law): *I'll have the law on you, you thief!*

the law (*inf*) the police: *The thief was still in the building when the law arrived.*

the law of the land the established law of a country: *If you do not obey the law of the land you deserve to go to prison.*

lay down the law to state something in a way that indicates that one expects one's opinion and orders to be accepted without argument: *He tried to lay down the law to us when he first arrived, but soon discovered that we didn't do as we were told.*

take the law into one's own hands to obtain justice in a way not involving the law, the police *etc*: *The riotous mob took the law into their own hands and hanged the murderer.*

See also **illegal, legal**.

lawn[1] [lo:n] *nc* an area of smooth, short grass, *esp* as part of a garden: *During the summer we have tea on the lawn in front of the house; He is mowing the lawn.*

lawn tennis *see* **tennis**.

lawn[2] [lo:n] *nu* a type of fine linen: *This handkerchief is made of lawn;* (*attrib*) *a lawn handkerchief.*

lax [laks] *adj* (*formal*) careless or not strict in discipline or morals: *His running of the office had become rather lax in recent months; She was disturbed by the lax state of the morals of society as a whole.* **'laxly** *adv.* **'laxity, 'laxness** *nus.*

laxative ['laksətiv] *ncu* a medicine which makes it easier to pass waste matter from the bowels: *If you are constipated, take a laxative.*

lay[1] [lei] – *pt, ptp* **laid** [leid] – **1** *vt* to place, set or put (down), often carefully: *She laid the clothes in a drawer/on a chair; He laid down his pencil; Lay it down over there;* (*fig formal*) *He laid the burden of organizing the meeting on his secretary;* (*fig formal*) *The case was laid before the court.* **2** *vt* to make (something or someone) lie down: *She laid the baby on his back.* **3** *vt* to put in order or arrange: *She went to lay the table for dinner; They laid a trap for the thief; He laid his plans so that nothing would go wrong.* **4** *vt* to put in a particular condition or position: *The animal laid back its ears; The wind laid the corn flat.* **5** *vt* (*formal*) to cause to disappear or become quiet or more quiet: *to lay a ghost; The news laid any doubts he might have had.* **6** *vt* (of a bird) to produce (eggs): *The hen blackbird laid four eggs.* **7** *vi* (*usu* of a hen) to produce eggs: *My hens are laying well.* **8** *vt* (*inf*) to place (a bet): *I'll lay five pounds that you don't succeed.* **9** *vt* (*sl*) (of a man) to have sexual intercourse with (a woman): *He's been trying to lay his secretary for months.* – *See also* **lay** *in phrases below.* – *nc* (*sl*) a partner (*usu* female) in sexual intercourse: *She's a good lay.*

'layer *nc* **1** a thickness or covering: *When it became colder, we put on more layers of clothing; The cake was covered with a layer of icing; There was a layer of clay a few feet under the ground.* **2** something which lays, *esp* a hen: *a good layer.* – *vt* to put, cut or arrange in layers: *She had her hair layered at the hairdressers.*

'layabout *nc* (*derog*) a lazy, idle person: *He's a layabout who hasn't done a day's work in his life!*

'lay-by – *pl* **'lay-bys** – *nc* (*Brit inf*) a short extra part at the side of a road for people to stop their cars in out of the way of the traffic: *Let's stop the car in a lay-by while we have lunch.*

lay-off *see* **lay off**.

'layout *nc* **1** the manner in which something is displayed or laid out: *He showed us the layout of the building.* **2** something which is or is intended to be spread out or arranged in a careful manner: *a model train layout.* – *See also* **lay out**.

laid up (*inf*) ill in bed: *When I caught flu, I was laid up for a fortnight.*

,lay a'bout one to strike blows in all directions: *He seized a long piece of wood and laid about him with it.*

lay aside *vt sep* to put away or to one side, *esp* to be used or dealt with at a later time: *She laid aside several boxes that might be of use, and threw the rest out*; *She laid them aside for later use.*

lay bare (*formal*) to show clearly or cause to be seen: *After digging for an hour, the workmen laid bare the water-main*; (*fig*) *In his speech, he laid his heart bare so that his feelings were clear to everyone.*

lay by *vt sep* to put away for future use: *She laid by a store of tinned vegetables to be used in emergencies.*

lay down *vt sep* **1** to give up; to cease by one's own actions to have: *They laid down their arms*; (*fig*) *After losing the battle, the general laid down his command*; (*fig*) *The soldiers laid down their lives in the cause of peace.* **2** to order or instruct: *The rule book lays down what should be done in such a case*; *The correct procedure has been laid down by the manager.* **3** to store: *My father laid down a good stock of wine which I am now drinking.* – *See also* **lay** (*def 1*).

lay (one's) hands on (*inf*) **1** to find or be able to obtain: *I wish I could lay (my) hands on that book!*; *I can't lay my hands on the brand of coffee I want.* **2** to catch: *The police had been trying to lay hands on the criminal for months.*

lay in *vt sep* to get and store a supply of: *I've laid in an extra stock of drinks for Christmas*; *You've laid it in too early.*

lay into *vt fus* (*inf*) to beat thoroughly: *He laid into his attacker with his walking-stick.*

,lay it 'on (*inf*) to do anything, *esp* to flatter, in an extravagant manner: *I thought that to say I was one of the most marvellous people in the world was laying it on a bit.*

lay low (*usu in passive*) (of an illness) to make (someone) ill: *I was laid low by pneumonia just before my exams*; *Pneumonia laid him low for weeks.*

lay off 1 *vt sep* to dismiss (employees) temporarily: *Because of a shortage of orders, the firm has laid off a quarter of its workforce*; *His employer laid him off last week* (*nc* **'lay-off**). **2** *vt fus, vi* (*inf*) to stop doing something: *I told him to lay off following me or he'd be sorry!*; *I'm fed up with hearing about it and I wish you'd lay off!* **3** *vt fus* (*inf*) to leave alone and not annoy, attack, mention *etc*: *Lay off the subject of money while he's here*; *Oh, will you lay off him for just a moment!*

lay on *vt sep* to provide (a supply of): *The dinner was laid on by the firm*; *They laid on huge quantities of drink for the party.*

lay out *vt sep* **1** to arrange over a wide area (*esp* according to a plan): *He was the architect who laid out the public gardens*; *He laid them out at the request of the council.* **2** to spread so as to be easily seen: *He laid out the contents of the box on the table.* **3** (*inf*) to knock unconscious: *The branch struck him on the head and laid him out*; *Such a blow would have laid out anyone.* **4** (*inf*) to spend (money): *They laid out a lot of money on their daughter's wedding.* **5** (*formal*) to prepare (a dead body) to be buried: *The undertaker has laid out the old lady.* – *See also* **layout**.

lay siege to *see* **siege**.

lay to rest (*euph*) to bury (a dead body): *She was laid to rest in the local churchyard.*

lay up *vt sep* **1** to keep or store: *We laid up a good supply of apples this year from our own trees*; (*fig*) *She's laying up problems for the future by her behaviour.* **2** to put (a ship) out of use in a dock: *The ship is laid up at Portsmouth being refitted.*

lay waste (*formal*) to make (a piece of land) into barren country by burning and plundering: *The invaders laid waste the whole country.*

lay[2] *see* **lie**[2].

lay[3] [lei] *adj* (*attrib*) **1** not a member of the clergy: *The church has a number of lay preachers.* **2** (*fig*) not an expert or a professional (in a particular subject): *The lay public has no idea of the meaning of most medical terms.*

laity ['leiəti] *nu* (*with* **the**: *very formal*) ordinary people, not the members of a particular profession, *esp* the clergy: *It is proposed to allow the laity a larger part in the management of the church.*

'layman *nc* (*usu fig*) a lay person: *This book is a handbook of legal procedure for the layman, not the professional lawyer.*

layer *see* **lay**[1].

layette [lei'et] *nc* a complete outfit for a baby: *She knitted most of the baby's layette herself.*

layman *see* **lay**[3].

layout *see* **lay**[1].

lazy ['leizi] *adj* not wanting to do anything or very much, to take exercise *etc*: *I take the bus to work as I'm too lazy to walk*; *He's lazy and lets other people do his work for him*; *Lazy people tend to become fat.* **'lazily** *adv.* **'laziness** *nu.*

'lazy-bones *nc* (*inf*) a lazy person.

lead[1] [li:d] – *pt, ptp* **led** [led] – **1** *vt* to guide or direct (something or someone) or cause to go in a certain direction, *esp* by going first or by holding by the hand, a rope *etc*: *We followed a car which led us to the motorway*; *She took the child by the hand and led him across the road*; *He was already leading the horse into the stable when she arrived*; *The sound of hammering led us to the garage*; *We followed his car and he led us to the motorway*; (*fig*) *The firm's financial policies led it to bankruptcy*; (*fig*) *You led us to believe that we would be paid!* **2** *vti* to go or carry to a particular place or along a particular course: *A small path leads through the woods*; *The road led traffic away from the centre of the town.* **3** *vi* (*fig*: *with* **to**) to cause or bring about a certain situation or state of affairs: *The heavy rain led to serious floods*; *Eating too many sweets leads to rotten teeth*; *This course of action might lead to difficulties.* **4** *vti* to be first (in): *He leads the world in scientific experiment*; *An official car led the procession*; *The world champion is leading in the competition at present.* **5** *vt* to live (a certain kind of life): *She leads a pleasant existence on the Greek island which she owns.* – *See also* **lead** *in phrases below.* – **1** *nu* (*with* **the**) the front place or position: *He has taken over the lead in the last* *competition!* **2** *nc* the state of being first: *We have a lead over the rest of the world in this kind of research.* **3** *nu* the act of leading: *We all followed his lead.* **4** *nc* the amount by which one is ahead of others: *He has a lead of twenty metres over the man in second place.* **5** *nc* a leather strap or chain for leading a dog *etc*: *All dogs must be kept on a lead.* **6** *nc* (*inf*) a piece of information which will help to solve a mystery *etc*: *The police have several leads concerning the identity of the thief.* **7** *nc* a leading part in a play *etc*: *Who plays the lead in that film?*

'**leader** *nc* **1** a person who is in front or goes first: *The fourth runner is several miles behind the leaders.* **2** a person who is the head of, organizes or is in charge (of something): *The leader of the party is a scientist*; *He has always been a leader.* **3** (*also* **leading article**) an article in a newspaper *etc* written to express the opinions of the editor.

'**leadership** *nu* **1** the state of being a leader: *He took over the leadership of the Labour party two years later.* **2** the quality of being able to be a leader: *The post requires a person who combines leadership and energy.*

leading article *see* **leader** (*def 3*).

leading light *nc* (*sometimes facet*) a very important and influential person (in a certain field): *She is one of the leading lights of the new movement in education*; *He is one of the leading lights in the golf club.*

leading question *nc* a question asked in such a way as to suggest the desired answer: *It was a leading question to ask the witness if the man he saw was bald.*

lead astray *see* **astray**.

lead off *vi, vt sep* to begin: *The band led (the dance) off with a waltz.*

lead on 1 *vt oblig sep* to deceive by causing to have false hopes: *She led us on to believe that we would be paid for our work.* **2** *vi* to go forward first: *Lead on, then!*

lead (someone) up the garden path to deceive someone into believing something quite untrue.

lead up to *vt fus* to prepare (to do something, for something to happen *etc*) by steps or stages: *He talked for a long time and seemed to be leading up to something*; *We studied the events leading up to the First World War.*

lead the way to go first (*esp* to show the way): *She led the way upstairs*; (*fig*) *Our country has led the way in the field of electronics for years.*

lead[2] [led] **1** *nu, adj* (of) an element (symbol **Pb**), a soft, heavy, bluish-grey metal: *lead pipes*; *Are these pipes (made of) lead or copper?* **2** *nc* the part of a pencil that leaves a mark, actually made of graphite, not lead: *The lead of my pencil has broken.* **3** *nc* a weight for measuring the depth of the water at sea *etc*.

'**leaden** *adj* **1** (*liter*) lead-coloured: *The sea was leaden*; *leaden skies.* **2** (*usu liter*) heavy: *a leaden weight.* **3** (*old*: *attrib*) made of lead: *a leaden statue.*

leaf [li:f] – *pl* **leaves** [li:vz] – *nc* **1** a part of a plant growing from the side of a stem, *usu* green, flat and thin, but of various shapes depending on the plant: *Many trees lose their leaves in autumn.* **2** something thin like a leaf, *esp* the page of a book: *Several leaves had been torn out of the novel.* **3** an extra part of a table, either attached to one side with a hinge or added to the centre when the two ends are apart: *He had put another leaf in the table to make room for ten people.*

'**leaflet** [-lit] *nc* a small, printed sheet containing information *etc*: *The society publishes a leaflet telling you all about the scheme.*

'**leafy** *adj* (*often liter*) having many leaves: *a leafy plant*; *a leafy wood*; *These plants are very leafy.*

take a leaf out of someone's book to use someone as an example: *It would be better if you took a leaf out of Mary's book and arrived early.*

turn over a new leaf to begin a new and better way of behaving, working *etc*: *He has been in jail several times, but recently he seems to have turned over a new leaf.*

league[1] [li:g] *nc* (*often with cap*) **1** a union of persons, nations *etc* for the benefit of each other: *They formed the League for the Protection of Shopkeepers.* **2** a grouping of sports clubs for games: *They are top of the Junior League.*

league[2] [li:g] *nc* (*old*) a measure of distance, *usu* 3 miles (about 4·8 km).

leak [li:k] *nc* **1** a crack or hole which should not be there and through which liquid or gas passes: *Water was escaping through a leak in the pipe.* **2** (of gas, electric current *etc*) an act of passing by accident through a crack or hole which should not be there: *a gas-leak*; (*fig*) *Government officials are investigating a reported leak of top-secret information.* – *vti* **1** to have a leak (of): *This bucket leaks – I can't use it!*; *The boiler leaked hot water all over the kitchen floor.* **2** to (cause something) to pass through a leak: *Gas was leaking out of the cracked gas-main*; (*fig*) *He was accused of leaking vital secrets to the enemy.*

'**leakage** [-kidʒ] (*formal*) **1** *ncu* (an act of) leaking: *Leakages in several water-mains had been reported*; (*fig*) *There has been a leakage of information somewhere.* **2** *nu* something that enters or escapes by leaking: *She got a cloth and mopped up the leakage from the tank.*

'**leaky** *adj* having leaks: *a leaky boat*; *His boat is old and leaky.*

lean[1] [li:n] – *pts, ptps* **leant** [lent], **leaned** – **1** *vi* to slope over to one side; not to be upright: *The lamp-post was leaning across the road at an angle of thirty degrees.* **2** *vti* to rest (something) (against): *She leaned the ladder against the wall*; *Don't lean your elbows on the table*; *He leant on the table*; *He leant wearily on the gate.* – *See also* **lean on** *below.*

'**leaning** *nc* (*fig formal*) a liking or preference (for something): *She has a leaning towards the arts.*

'**lean-to** *nc* a shed *etc* built up against another building or wall: *She kept her bicycle in a lean-to at the back of the house*; (*attrib*) *a lean-to greenhouse.*

'**lean on** *vt fus* **1** to use as a support: *The lame man leant on a stick*; (*fig*) *She leans on her husband for advice.* **2** (*fig*: *sl*) to use slight force to persuade (someone) to do something *etc*: *I'll have to lean on her a bit – I don't think she's working hard enough.* – *See also* **lean**[1] (*def 2*).

lean[2] [li:n] *adj* **1** thin; not fat: *a lean man*; *He is tall and lean and she is small and fat.* **2** not containing much fat: *lean meat*; *This beef is deliciously lean.* **3** (*esp attrib*) poor; not producing much (money *etc*): *a lean year.* – *nu* meat without fat: *She cuts all the fat off her meat and only eats the lean.* '**leanness** *nu.*

leant *see* **lean**[1].

leap [li:p] – *pts, ptps* **leapt** [lept], (*esp Amer*) **leaped** – **1** *vi* to jump: *He leapt into the boat.* **2** *vt* to jump over: *The dog leapt the wall.* **3** *vi* (*fig*) to rush eagerly: *She leaped over to see them.* – *nc* **1** an act of leaping: *The cat jumped from the roof and* *reached the ground in two leaps.* **2** the distance leaped: *It was a three-metre leap across the river.*

'leap-frog *nu* a game in which one player leaps over another's bent back. – *v* – *pt, ptp* **'leap-frogged** – *vt* (*fig*) to go forward by passing each other one after the other.

'leap year *nc* every fourth year, which consists of 366 days, February having 29, *ie* 1976, 1980, 1984 *etc.*

a leap in the dark an action, decision *etc* whose results cannot be foreseen: *Since he was quite unknown as an artist, employing him to paint such an important picture was a leap in the dark.*

by leaps and bounds extremely rapidly and successfully: *The building of the new sports complex is going ahead by leaps and bounds.*

learn [lə:n] – *pts, ptps* **learned, learnt** – **1** *vt* to get to know: *It was then that I learned that she was dead.* **2** *vti* to gain knowledge or skill (in): *A child is always learning; I have decided to learn French; She is learning how to swim; She is learning to knit.*

'learned [-nid] *adj* (*formal*) having or showing great learning: *a learned professor; a learned publication; a learned speech; He is the most learned of the professors.*

'learner *nc* a person who is in process of learning: *I'm no good at this – I'm only a learner;* (*attrib*) *a learner driver.*

'learning *nu* (*formal*) knowledge which has been gained by learning: *The professor was a man of great learning.*

lease [li:s] *nc* (the period of) an agreement giving the use of a house *etc* on payment of rent: *We signed the lease yesterday; a twenty-year lease.* – *vti* to give or acquire a house *etc* in this way: *He leases the land from the local council.*

leash [li:ʃ] *nc* (*formal*) a strip of leather or piece of chain attached to a collar round its neck by which a dog *etc* is held. – *vt* (*formal*) to put on a leash. *See also* **unleash**.

least [li:st] *adj* (*attrib*), *pron* (something) which is the smallest or the smallest amount that exists, is possible *etc*: *I think the least you can do is to apologize!; None of my friends has much money but he has least of all; Please don't worry about owing me money – that's the least of my troubles; Have you the least idea of the trouble you've caused?; She wanted to know how to do it with the least amount of bother.* – *adv* (*sometimes with* **the**) to the smallest or lowest degree (of all, that is possible *etc*): *I like her* (*the*) *least of all the girls; Least of all do I want to hurt anyone; That is the least important of our problems.*

at 'least at any rate; anyway: *I think she's well – at least she was when I saw her last.*

not in the least not at all: *You're not disturbing me in the least!*

See also **little, less**.

leather ['leðə] *nu, adj* (of) the skin of an animal prepared (by tanning) for use as clothes *etc*: *Her shoes were made of genuine leather; a leather jacket.*

'leathery *adj* like leather, *esp* tough: *a leathery piece of meat; The plant had broad, leathery leaves; This meat is hard and leathery.*

leave[1] [li:v] – *pt, ptp* **left** [left] **1** *vti* to go away or depart (from), often without intending to return: *He left the room for a moment to fetch something; They left at about six o'clock; I have left that job now; He has left his wife and is living with another woman.* **2** *vt* (*often with* **behind**) to go without taking: *She left her gloves in the car; He left his children behind when he went to France.* **3** *vt* to allow to remain in a particular state or condition: *He has left his wife and children penniless; She left the job half-finished.* **4** *vt* to let (a person or a thing) do something without being helped or attended to: *I think I'll leave my husband to dig the garden; I'll just leave the meat to cook for a while.* **5** *vt* to allow to remain for someone to do, make *etc*: *We left the decision to him; Leave that job to the experts!* **6** *vt* to make a gift of (something) in one's will: *She left all her property to her son; My grandmother is leaving me all her jewellery.* – *See also* **leave** *in phrases below.*

'leavings *n pl* (*inf often derog*) things which are left: *I don't want your leavings.*

'leftovers *n pl* pieces of food that have not been eaten up at a meal: *If we have a leg of mutton on Sunday, we can live on the leftovers until Wednesday.* – *See also* **left over** *below.*

leave (someone) alone not to disturb, upset or tease (someone): *Why can't you leave your little brother alone?; I do wish you'd leave that book alone – stop fiddling with it.*

leave off *vi, vt fus* (*inf*) to stop (doing something): *You can leave off looking for the book – I've found it; I wish you would leave off!*

leave out *vt sep* not to include or put in: *You've left out a word in that sentence; We'll have to invite her because we can hardly leave her out.*

left over not used up, eaten *etc*: *We had a lot of food left over from the party; When everyone took a partner there was one person left over.*

leave[2] [li:v] **1** *nu* (*formal*) permission to do something, *eg* to be absent: *Have I your leave to go?* **2** *ncu* (*esp* of soldiers, sailors *etc*) a holiday: *He is home on leave at the moment.*

take one's leave (of) (*formal*) to say goodbye (to): *I took my leave* (*of the others*) *and went out.*

leaven ['levn] *nu* (*old*) a substance which makes dough rise.

'leavened *adj* (*neg* **un-**) containing leaven: *leavened bread.*

leaves *see* **leaf**.

Lebanese, Lebanon *see* Appendix 2.

lecherous ['letʃərəs] *adj* (*derog*) having or showing sexual desire: *a lecherous old man; a lecherous glance; Be careful of that man – he is really lecherous.* **'lecherously** *adv.*

'lechery *nu.*

lectern ['lektən] *nc* a stand for holding a book *etc* to be read from, *esp* for a lecture or in a church.

lecture ['lektʃə] *nc* **1** a formal talk given to an audience to give information: *The professor gave a lecture to his students on Shakespeare; a history lecture.* **2** (*fig*) a long and boring or irritating speech, warning or scolding: *The teacher gave the children a lecture for running in the corridor.* – *vti* to give a lecture or lectures (to): *He lectures on Roman Art; She lectured him on good behaviour.*

'lecturer *nc* a person who lectures, *esp* to students: *He is a lecturer in the English department.*

'lectureship *nc* (*formal*) the position of a lecturer in a college or university.

led *see* **lead**[1].

ledge [ledʒ] *nc* a shelf or an object that sticks out like a shelf: *He grew plants on the window-ledge outside the kitchen window; They stopped on a ledge halfway up the mountain; The ship was caught on a ledge of rock under the surface of the sea.*

ledger ['ledʒə] *nc* the chief book of accounts of an office or shop, in which entries from other books are recorded.

lee [liː] *nc* (*no pl*: *more formal or tech than* **shelter**) the sheltered side, away from the wind: *We sheltered from the gale in the lee of a group of trees.*

'leeward *adj*, *adv* (*naut*) in the direction towards which the wind blows.

'leeway *nu* **1** (*naut*) the drifting of a ship *etc* to leeward away from its true course, or the amount of this: *The boat had a flat bottom and made a lot of leeway*; (*fig*) *He has a lot of leeway to make up at school* (= a lot of work to do to catch up on his classmates) *after his illness.* **2** (*fig*) extra space, time *etc* allowed more than is necessary: *If you buy more curtain material than you think you will need, it will allow us a bit of leeway to make the curtains longer.*

leech [liːtʃ] *nc* a kind of blood-sucking worm, once used by doctors to take blood from patients.

leek [liːk] *nc* a type of vegetable closely related to the onion, but long and thin instead of ball-shaped: *Shall I use the green parts as well as the white parts of the leeks?*; (*attrib*) *leek soup.*

leer [liə] *nc* (*derog*) a secret, sideways look, *esp* one expressing sexual desire: *She tried to ignore the sailor's leers.* – *vi* to look in this way: *His wife said he only sat on the beach in order to leer at all the girls sunbathing.*

lees [liːz] *n pl* (*formal or liter*) the dregs that settle at the bottom of wine.

left[1] *see* **leave**.

left[2] [left] *adj* (*attrib*) on, for, or belonging to the side of the body that in most people has the less skilful hand or the side of a person or thing which is toward the west when that person or thing is facing north (opposite to **right**): *She wore an engagement-ring on her left hand*; *Do they drive on the left side of the road?* – *adv* to or towards this side: *He turned left at the end of the road.* – *nu* **1** the left side, part *etc*: *The doctor was sitting on her left*; *She turned to her left*; *Take the first road on the left.* **2** (*sometimes with cap*) the most radical, socialist or communist party or parties in a Parliament *etc*, or the most radical, socialist or communist members of a party *etc*: *the policies of the Left*; *He is on the left of his party.*

'leftist *adj* (*often derog*) having radical, socialist or communist views.

'lefty *nc* (*inf derog*) a person having views of this kind.

'left-hand *adj* (*attrib*) **1** at the left; to the left of something else: *the bottom left-hand drawer of the desk*; *the left-hand side of the road.* **2** towards the left: *a left-hand bend in the road.*

ˌleft-'handed *adj* **1** having the left hand more skilful than the right: *He is left-handed and can't write with his right hand*; *Left-handed children should not be forced to write with their right hands.* **2** for use by people of this kind: *left-handed scissors.*

ˌleft-'handedness *nu.*

ˌleft-'wing *adj* (having opinions which are) extremely radical, socialist or communist: *He is very left-wing in his views on taxation*; *His left-wing views have made him unpopular with his colleagues.*

ˌleft-'winger *nc* a person who has left-wing opinions, or who supports a left-wing political party or the left wing of a party.

left wing the members of a political party who hold more radical, socialist or communist opinions: *He is on the left wing of the party.*

leg [leg] *nc* **1** one of the limbs by which animals and man walk: *The horse injured a front leg*; *She stood on one leg and took one of her shoes off.* **2** the part of an article of clothing that covers one of these limbs closely: *He has torn the leg of his trousers.* **3** a long, narrow support of a table *etc*: *One of the legs of the chair was broken and it would not stand upright.* **4** one stage in a journey, competition *etc*: *We were very tired as we boarded the plane for the last leg of the trip*; *He gained several places in the second leg of the contest.*

-legged [legid] *adj* (*in cmpds*) having (a certain number or type of) leg(s): *a long-legged girl*; *a four-legged animal.*

'leggings *n pl* outer coverings for the lower legs: *The farmer wore canvas leggings to keep his legs clean.*

'leggy *adj* (*inf*: *often derog*) having long thin legs: *She was a thin, leggy child*; *The young horse is thin and rather leggy.*

'leg-pull *nc* (*inf*) a joking attempt to make someone believe something which is not true. – *See also* **pull someone's leg** *below.*

a leg up (*inf*) a help in climbing up *etc*: *I can climb in this window if someone gives me a leg up.*

he *etc* **ˌhasn't got a ˌleg to 'stand on** he *etc* has no way of excusing his behaviour, justifying his requests *etc*: *She hasn't got a leg to stand on if she's forgotten to write, because I reminded her every day for a week.*

on one's last legs *see* **last**[1].

pull someone's leg (*inf*) to try as a joke to make someone believe something which is not true: *You haven't really got a black mark on your face – he's only pulling your leg.* – *See also* **leg-pull** *above.*

legacy ['legəsi] *nc* **1** something left in a will by someone who has died: *He was left a legacy by his great-aunt.* **2** (*fig*: *facet or formal*) something left behind by the person who previously had one's job, owned one's house *etc* or by past experiences: *The filing-system is a legacy from the previous secretary*; *His rheumatism is a legacy from his years as a fisherman.*

ˌlega'tee [-'tiː] *nc* (*legal*) a person to whom a legacy (*def 1*) is left.

legal ['liːgəl] *adj* **1** lawful; allowed by the law: *Is it legal to bring watches into the country?*; *a legal contract.* **2** (*attrib*) concerned with or used in the law: *a legal term*; *the legal profession.* **'legally** *adv.*

le'gality [-'ga-] *nu.*

'legalize, -ise *vt* (*formal*) to make legal or lawful: *This practice was legalized last year.*

See also **illegal**.

legatee *see* **legacy**.

legation [li'geiʃən] *nc* (*formal*) (the headquarters of) an official group of people acting on behalf of the government of their own country *etc* in another country: *Which street is the Chinese legation in?*; *He is a member of a legation visiting this country to discuss trade between China and Britain.*

legend ['ledʒənd] *nc* **1** a story handed down from one generation to another but probably not true: *There is a legend in our family that Queen Elizabeth I once visited this house*; *the legend of St George.* **2** (*formal or tech*) words accompanying an illustration or picture: *The legend below the photograph reads 'April 1948'.*

'legendary *adj* **1** (*formal*) mentioned *etc* in legend: *a legendary character*; *King Arthur may never have existed – he may be legendary.* **2** very famous because very great, good *etc*: *She is best known for her legendary beauty*; *His generosity is legendary*; (*fig*) *There are many legendary* (= not to be believed) *accounts of the meeting.*

legible ['ledʒəbl] *adj* (*more formal than* **readable**) clear enough to be read: *The writing was faded but still legible; The note had been written so hurriedly it was hardly legible; She left me a scarcely legible note.* **'legibly** *adv.* **ˌlegi'bility** *nu.*
See also **illegible**.

legion ['liːdʒən] *nc* **1** (*hist*) in ancient Rome, a body of from three to six thousand soldiers. **2** (*formal fig*) a great many or a very large number: *I had to try to get rid of the legions of people who had come in answer to the advertisement*; (*no pl: not used with* **a** *or* **the**) *Unemployed university graduates are legion these days.*
'legionary *nc* (*hist*) a soldier of a legion.

legislate ['ledʒisleit] *vi* (*formal*) to make laws: *The government plan to legislate against the import of foreign cars; We have tried to legislate for every possible situation.*
ˌlegi'slation *nu* (*formal*) **1** the act of legislating. **2** a law or group of laws: *The government intend to bring in new legislation regarding the sale of alcohol.*
'legislative [-lətiv] *adj* (*esp attrib: formal*) law-making: *a legislative assembly; Does the assembly have legislative powers?*
'legislator *nc* (*formal*) a person who makes laws.
'legislature [-lətʃə] *nu* the part of the government which has the power of making laws.

legitimate [li'dʒitimət] *adj* **1** (*formal*) lawful: *The thief has a perfectly legitimate business as a car-salesman; Is his business legitimate?* **2** born to parents who are married to each other: *a legitimate child; Their second child is legitimate although their first child was illegitimate.* **3** (*very formal*) (of an argument or deduction *etc*) reasonable or logical: *The conclusion he came to was quite legitimate; legitimate conclusions.* **le'gitimately** *adv.*
le'gitimacy *nu.*
See also **illegitimate**.

leisure ['leʒə, (*Amer*) 'liːʒər] *nu* time which one can spend as one likes, *esp* when one does not have to work: *She leads a life of leisure; I seldom have leisure to consider the problem*; (*attrib*) *leisure occupations.*
'leisured *adj* (*formal or facet: attrib*) not occupied in work or business: *the leisured upper classes.*
'leisurely *adj, adv* not hurrying; taking plenty of time: *She had a leisurely bath and got dressed slowly; He strolled leisurely into town.*

lemon ['lemən] **1** *nc* a type of oval, juicy, citrus fruit with pale yellow skin and very sour juice: *She added the juice of a lemon to the pudding*; (*attrib*) *a lemon tree.* **2** *nu* (*also* **lemon yellow**) the colour of this fruit. – *adj* **1** (*also* **lemon yellow**) of this colour: *The kitchen was painted lemon and white; a pale lemon dress.* **2** (*usu attrib*) with the taste of lemon juice: *a lemon drink.*
ˌlemo'nade [-'neid] *nc* a (fizzy) drink flavoured with lemons.

lend [lend] – *pt, ptp* **lent** [lent] – *vt* **1** to give (someone) the use of (something) for a time: *She had forgotten her umbrella so I lent her mine to go home with.* **2** (*formal or liter*) to give or add (interest, beauty *etc*) to (something or someone): *Desperation lent him strength; Her presence lent an air of respectability to the occasion.*
'lend itself to (*formal*) to be suitable for or adapt easily to: *This room lends itself to formal occasions; The play lends itself to performance by children.*
lend a hand *see* **hand** (*def 4*).
See also **loan**.

length [leŋθ] **1** *nu* the distance from one end to the other of an object, period of time *etc, esp* if great: *It was a journey of some length; What is the length of your car?; Please note down the length of time it takes you to do this.* **2** *nc* (*sometimes in cmpds*) a piece of something, *esp* cloth, which is long or of a known length: *She took several lengths of string out of a drawer; I bought a skirt-length of tweed* (= a piece long enough to make a skirt). **3** *nc* in racing, the measurement from end to end of a horse, boat *etc*: *He won by a length; The other boat is several lengths in front.*
'lengthen *vti* to make or become longer: *I'll have to lengthen this skirt; The days are lengthening now that the Spring has come.*
'lengthways/'lengthwise *advs* in the direction of the length: *She folded the towels lengthways and hung them on the towel-rail.*
'lengthy *adj* (*often derog*) of great, often too great, length: *He gave a lengthy summary of the meeting; This essay is interesting but lengthy.*
at 'length 1 in detail; taking a long time: *She told us at length what had been decided.* **2** at last: *At length, we began to understand what he wanted.*
go to any lengths to do anything, no matter how extreme, dishonest, wicked *etc* to get what one wants: *I'm not surprised that she's having an affair with the boss – she'll go to any lengths to get promotion.*

lenient ['liːniənt] *adj* (*formal*) merciful or punishing only lightly: *They received a lenient sentence; You are much too lenient with wrongdoers.*
'leniently *adv.*
'lenience, 'leniency *nus.*

lens [lenz] *nc* **1** a piece of glass *etc* curved on one or both sides and used to make spectacles, microscopes, cameras *etc*: *I need new lenses in my spectacles; The camera lens is dirty.* **2** a similar part of the eye: *The disease has affected the lens of his left eye.*
contact lens *see* **contact**.

Lent[1] [lent] *n* (in the Christian religion) the six and a half weeks before Easter during which a forty days' fast is kept.

lent[2] *see* **lend**.

lentil ['lentil] *nc* the small orange seed of a pod-bearing plant, used in soups *etc*: *half a kilo of lentils*; (*attrib*) *lentil soup.*

Leo ['liːou] *n* a sign of the zodiac, the Lion: *People born between July 21 and August 22 are said to be born under the sign of Leo.*

leopard ['lepəd] *nc* a type of large spotted animal of the cat family.

leotard ['liətaːd] *nc* a kind of tight-fitting garment worn (*esp* by women) for dancing, gymnastics *etc*: *The ballet dancer wore a black leotard during rehearsals but a short white dress for the actual performance.*

leper ['lepə] *nc* a person who has leprosy: *Lepers used to be sent away from the communities in which they lived because people were afraid of catching the disease; When he refused to join the trade union he was treated like a leper* (= outcast) *by the rest of the staff.*
'leprosy [-rəsi] *nu* a contagious skin disease, causing serious and permanent damage to the body, including loss of fingers, nose *etc.* **'leprous** [-rəs] *adj.*

lesbian ['lezbiən] **1** *nc, adj* (of) a woman who is sexually attracted to other women: *She's* (*a*) *lesbian.* **2** *adj* of or concerning a lesbian or lesbians: *a lesbian relationship.* **'lesbianism** *nu.*

lesion ['li:ʒən] *nc* (*tech*) an injury or wound: *His illness was caused by a brain lesion; The lesions on the child's back made the doctor think that he'd been beaten by his parents.*

less [les] *adj* (*often with* **than**) **1** not as much (as): *We had less time than I had hoped; Think of a number less than forty; He drank his tea and wished he had put less sugar in it; The firm has less money and fewer staff than last year; The salary for that job will be not less than £10 000.* **2** (*in neg*) not as important: *I had dinner with no less a person than the Queen.* – *adv* not as much or to a smaller extent: *I like her less every time I see her; He had never met anyone less attractive; You should eat less if you want to lose weight;* (*formal*) *I do not think that he is very efficient – still less do I think that his assistant is efficient.* – *pron* a smaller part or amount: *He has less than I have.* – *prep* minus: *He earns £90 a week less £30 income tax.*

'lessen *vti* to make or become less: *Opening the windows lessened the heat a little; When the children left, the noise lessened considerably.*

'lesser *adj* smaller or not as important: *He was a lesser figure in the town than his brother; one of the lesser mountains in the area.* – *adv* less: *the lesser-known streets of London.*

none the less *see* **nonetheless** *under* **none**.

the less . . . because/if to a greater degree or extent . . . because or if: *He'll be (all) the less inclined to help if you are rude to him.*

the less . . . the less/more in proportion to the amount that one thing happens less, another thing happens less or more: *The less I see of it, the less easy it is for me to form an opinion about it.*

See also **little, least, few**.

lesson ['lesn] *nc* **1** something which is learned or taught: *The lesson which we learned from the experience was never to trust anyone.* **2** a period of teaching: *She became ill during the French lesson.* **3** a part of the Bible read in church: *He was asked to read the lesson on Sunday morning.*

lest [lest] *conj* (*old or formal*) for fear that; in case: *He wouldn't put the letter in his pocket lest he forgot about it.*

let[1] [let] – *prp* **'letting**: *pt, ptp* **let** – *vt* **1** to allow or permit (to go or become): *She refused to let her children go out in the rain; He let the dog out.* **2** to cause to: *I will let you know how much it costs; She let him see what he had done.* **3** (*formal* except **let's**: not used with **you**) used in the imperative to give orders or suggestions: *Let the people sing!; If they will not work, let them starve; Let's* (= let us) *leave right away!*

'let-down *nc* (*inf*) a disappointment: *It was a terrible let-down for the children when the party was cancelled.* – *See also* **let down** *below.*

'let-up *nc* a stopping of something by making less violent *etc*: *There was no sign of a let-up in the storm.* – *See also* **let up** *below.*

let alone (someone or something) not to mention (someone *etc*); without taking (someone *etc*) into consideration: *It will cost us a fortune for the food, let alone the wine!; There's no room for her, let alone the children.*

let (someone or something) alone/be to leave (someone *etc*) alone; not to disturb or worry (someone *etc*): *Why don't you let him be when he's not feeling well!; Do let the child alone – he can't help not being good at arithmetic; Do let those curtains alone* (=stop touching the curtains).

let down *vt sep* **1** to lower: *She let down the blind; She let it down slowly.* **2** to disappoint or fail to help when necessary *etc*: *You must give a film show at the party – you can't let the children down; She felt he had let her down by not coming.* **3** to make flat by allowing the air to escape: *When he came back, he found that some children had let his car tyres down; They had been let down some hours before.* **4** to make longer: *She had to let down the child's skirt.* – *See also* **let-down** *above.*

let fall to drop: *She was so startled she let fall everything she was carrying.*

let fly *see* **fly**[2].

let go (of) to stop holding (something): *Will you let go of my coat!; When he was nearly at the top of the rope he suddenly let go and fell.*

let in *vi* to allow water *etc* to pass in: *This pair of boots is letting in badly.*

let (someone) in for (something) (*inf*) to involve (someone) in (something difficult or unpleasant): *The trip let me in for more expense than I intended; I didn't know what I was letting myself in for when I agreed to do that job.*

let (someone) in on (something) (*inf*) to share (a secret *etc*) with (someone): *I think we'll have to let your mother in on our plans.*

let off *vt sep* **1** to fire (a gun) or cause (a firework *etc*) to explode: *He let the gun off in error; He let it off accidentally.* **2** to allow to go without punishment *etc*: *The policeman let him off with a warning; The police let off all the young offenders; I'll let you off doing the washing up; The taxman let us off with half what we expected to pay.*

let up *vi* to become less strong or violent; to stop: *I do wish the rain would let up; He never lets up, does he?* – *See also* **let-up** *above.*

let well alone to allow things to remain as they are, in order not to make them worse: *The old lady didn't know her son had been killed and it was easier to let well alone and not tell her because it would have broken her heart.*

let[2] [let] – *prp* **'letting**: *pt, ptp* **let** – *vt* to give the use of (a house, farm *etc*) in return for payment: *He lets his house to holiday-makers in the summer and goes abroad.*

to 'let for letting: *house to let.*

lethal ['li:θəl] *adj* (*formal*) causing death: *a lethal blow; a lethal dose of poison; The overdose of drugs proved lethal.*

lethargy ['leθədʒi] *nu* (*formal*) lack of interest or energy: *The heat made her sleepy, but she roused herself from her lethargy and went indoors to make dinner.* **le'thargic** [-'θa:-] *adj.*

letter ['letə] *nc* **1** a mark expressing a sound: *the letters of the alphabet.* **2** a written message *usu* sent by post, sometimes including the envelope: *She slowly took the letter from its envelope; The postman came early, bringing her a letter from her mother; Did you post my letter?*

'lettering **1** *nu* the way in which letters are formed: *She was interested in the art of lettering.* **2** *nc* (*no pl*) letters which have been drawn, painted *etc*: *A man was repainting the lettering over the shop window.*

'letterbox *nc* (*esp Brit*) **1** a slit in a door (sometimes with a box behind it) through which mail from the post is put: *The front door was locked so he put the card through the letterbox.* **2** a postbox. – *See also* **mailbox**.

'letterhead *nc* a printed heading on notepaper *etc.*

the letter of the law an interpretation of the law

which follows exactly what it says (as opposed to what the writer meant): *What he did was illegal according to the letter of the law, but he would never be convicted for it.*

to the 'letter exactly; according to every detail: *He followed his father's instructions to the letter.*

lettuce ['letis] **1** *nc* a type of green plant with large leaves used as a salad: *Go and buy a couple of lettuces*; (*attrib*) *lettuce leaves.* **2** *nu* the leaves: *a dish of lettuce and tomatoes*; (*attrib*) *lettuce sandwiches.*

leukaemia, (*Amer*) **leukemia** [lu:'ki:miə] *nu* a very serious disease which causes an abnormal number of white cells in the blood: *Their youngest child died of leukaemia when he was sixteen years old.*

level ['levl] *nc* **1** height, position, strength, rank *etc* in comparison with some standard: *The level of the river rose*; *a conference at national level*; *a high level of intelligence.* **2** a horizontal division or floor in a house *etc*: *Their house is built on two levels*; *the upper level of the multi-storey car park.* **3** a kind of instrument for showing whether a surface is level: *a spirit level.* **4** (*no pl*) a flat, smooth surface or piece of land: *It was difficult running uphill but he could run fast on the level.* – *adj* **1** flat, even, smooth or horizontal: *a level surface*; *The road was fairly level*; *a level spoonful* (= an amount which just fills the spoon to the top of the sides). **2** (*pred*) of the same height, standard *etc*: *The sink in the kitchen is level with the window-sill*; *The scores of the two teams are level*; (*fig*) *The twins are about level in their schoolwork.* **3** steady, even and not rising or falling much: *Despite her excitement, she spoke in a calm, level voice*; *Her tone was calm and level.* – *v* – *pt, ptp* **'levelled**, (*Amer*) **'leveled** – *vt* **1** to make flat, smooth or horizontal: *He levelled the earth in the flower-bed.* **2** to make equal: *His goal levelled the scores of the two teams.* **3** (*usu with* **at**) to aim (a gun *etc*): *He levelled his pistol at the target.* **4** to pull down: *The bulldozer levelled the block of flats.* – *See also* **level off, level out** *below.*

'levelness *nu.*

level crossing *nc* a place where a road crosses a railway without a bridge: *When there is a train coming the gates of the level crossing are closed to prevent cars crossing the railway line.*

ˌlevel-'headed *adj* having good sense: *He is very level-headed and can think quickly in an emergency*; *a level-headed young woman.*

do one's level best (*inf*) to do one's very best: *She did her level best to get it finished, but couldn't quite manage it.*

find one's/its (own) level to find the place, rank *etc* to which one/it naturally belongs: *She felt she had found her own level as an assistant and had no ambition to become the manager of the firm*; *The government let the pound find its own level against foreign currencies.*

level off *vi, vt sep* to make or become flat, even, steady *etc*: *She levelled off the icing on the cake with a knife*; (*fig*) *After rising for so long, prices have now levelled off.*

level out *vi, vt sep* to make or become level: *The road levels out as it comes down to the plain*; *We have been trying to level out differences in the price of our goods in various shops*; *We did not succeed in levelling them all out.*

level pegging *see* **peg**.

on the level (*sl*) fair; honest: *Is his offer on the level?*

lever ['li:və, (*Amer*) 'levər] *nc* **1** (*tech*) a bar of wood, metal *etc* used to lift heavy weights by resting the middle on something and lifting the weight on one end by pressing down on the other. **2** a bar used to help move or remove something that is stiff or difficult to move: *You must use a coin as a lever to get the lid of that tin off*; *a tyre lever.* **3** a bar or handle for operating a machine *etc*: *This is the lever that switches on the power.* **4** (*fig*) anything that can be used to gain an advantage: *He used his wealth as a lever to get what he wanted.* – *vt* to move with or as if with a lever: *He levered the heavy box into position.*

'leverage [-ridʒ] *nu* the power gained by the use of a lever: *The longer the lever you use, the more leverage you get*; (*fig*) *I think we'll get you the job, with a bit of leverage.*

leveret ['levərit] *nc* a young hare.

levitation [levi'teiʃən] *nu* (*formal*) (the illusion of) raising a heavy body in the air without support: *The magician gave us an amazing example of levitation by making his assistant float in the air.*

'levitate *vti* (*formal*) to (make something or someone) float in the air.

levity ['levəti] *nu* (*formal or facet*) lack of seriousness: *A funeral is not an occasion for levity.*

levy ['levi] *vt* (*formal*) to raise or collect (*esp* an army or a tax): *A tax was levied on tobacco.* – *nc* (*formal*) **1** soldiers or money collected by order: *a levy on imports.* **2** the act of levying: *The levy produced an army of 30 000 men.*

lewd [lu:d] *adj* (*formal*) taking pleasure in indecent thoughts or acts; lustful; indecent: *He has lewd dreams about naked women*; *The smile he gave the young girl was lecherous and lewd.*

'lewdness *nu.*

lexicon ['leksikən, (*Amer*) -kon] *nc* (*formal*) a dictionary.

ˌlexi'cographer [-'kogrəfə] *nc* a person who writes a dictionary. **ˌlexi'cography** *nu.*

liable ['laiəbl] *adj* **1** (*pred with* **to**: *formal*) tending to have, get, suffer from *etc*: *This road is liable to flooding.* **2** (*pred with* **to**) possibly or probably about to do something or to happen: *Watch the milk – it's liable to boil over.* **3** (*usu pred*: *legal*) responsible (for) or bound to do something: *He is liable for this debt* (= He must pay the money which is owed); *I shall not pay my wife's debts – I do not hold myself liable.*

ˌlia'bility **1** *nu* (*formal*) the state of being legally liable: *He accepted liability for the damage done to the car.* **2** *nc* (*formal*) a debt or obligation *etc*: *He has many liabilities.* **3** *nc* (*loosely*: *inf*) something which is a nuisance or more of a disadvantage than an advantage: *That old car of yours is a liability!*

liaison [li:'eizon, (*Amer*) 'li:eizon] **1** *ncu* a contact or communication: *There is very little liaison between the two branches of that firm*; *We kept up a liaison with the teachers in primary schools*; (*attrib*) *a liaison officer.* **2** *nc* (*formal*) an unlawful sexual relationship between a man and a woman: *He had a liaison with a married woman that lasted for years.*

liaise [(*Brit and Amer*) li:'eiz] *vi* to make or have a close relationship (with someone else): *As sales manager, she is responsible for liaising with our foreign representatives.*

liar *see* **lie**[1].

libel ['laibəl] *ncu* (*legal*) something written which is harmful to a person's reputation: *I think what* *you wrote about her amounts to libel.* – *v* – *pt, ptp* **'libelled**, (*Amer*) **'libeled** – *vt* (*legal*) to damage the reputation of (someone) by libel.

'libellous *adj*: *I think certain parts of his book about my father are libellous*; *a libellous book about a great man.* **'libellously** *adv.*

liberal ['libərəl] *adj* **1** (*formal*) generous: *She gave me a liberal helping of apple pie*; *She was very liberal with her money.* **2** tolerant; not criticizing or disapproving: *He has a very liberal approach to other people's opinions*; *He is very liberal in his attitude to other people's religious views.* **3** (*with cap*) of the **Liberal party**, one of the main political parties in the UK: *Liberal policies.* **4** (of an education) not specialized or technical, aiming at general culture: *a liberal education*; *His education was liberal and wide-ranging.* – *nc* (*with cap*) a person supporting or belonging to the Liberal Party.

ˌlibe'rality [-'ra-] *nu.* **'liberally** *adv.*

See also **illiberal**.

liberate ['libəreit] *vt* (*formal*) to set free: *The prisoners were liberated by the new Government*; *After spending many years as a housewife she felt liberated when she got a job as a secretary.*

ˌlibe'ration *nu.* **'liberator** *nc.*

liberty ['libəti] **1** *nu* (*formal*) freedom from captivity or from slavery: *He ordered that all prisoners should be given their liberty*; *I value my liberty too much to risk going to prison.* **2** *nu* freedom to do as one pleases: *Children have a lot more liberty now than they used to.* **3** *nc* (*usu with* **take**) too great freedom of speech or action: *I think it was (taking) a liberty to ask such a question!*; *The director of this play has taken terrible liberties with Shakespeare's writing.* – *See also* **take the liberty of** *below.*

'liberties *n pl* (*formal*) privileges, rights *etc*: *civil liberties.*

'libertine [-tiːn] *nc* (*old or liter*) a person who leads an immoral life.

take the liberty of (doing something) (*formal*) to do (something), *usu* without permission: *I took the liberty of moving the papers from your desk – I hope you don't mind.*

Libra ['liːbrə, 'li-, (*esp Amer*) 'lai-] *n* a sign of the zodiac, the Scales: *People born between September 23 and October 22 are said to be born under the sign of Libra.*

library ['laibrəri] *nc* (a building or room containing) a collection of books or some other collection, *eg* of gramophone records: *He works in the public library*; *She has a fine library of books on art.*

li'brarian [-'breə-] *nc* a person who is employed in a library.

libretto [li'bretou] – *pl* **li'bretti** [-tiː], (*inf*) **li'brettos** – *nc* (a book of) the words of an opera, musical show *etc*: *He wrote the libretto for the opera and his friend wrote the music.*

Libya, Libyan *see* Appendix 2.

lice *see* **louse**.

licence, (*Amer*) **license** ['laisəns] **1** *nc* a (printed) form giving permission to do something (*eg* to keep a dog, television set *etc*, drive a car, sell alcohol *etc*): *Have you a licence for that television?*; *a dog licence*; *a driving licence.* **2** *nu* (*formal*) too great freedom of action *etc*: *He allows his daughter too much licence.* – *See also* **poetic licence** *under* **poet**.

'license *vt* to give a licence to or permit: *He is licensed to sell our books abroad.*

'licensed *adj* (of a shop, hotel *etc*) legally allowed to sell alcohol to customers: *Is this hotel licensed?*; *a licensed grocer.*

ˌlicen'see *nc* a person to whom a licence (*esp* to keep a licensed hotel or public house) has been given.

licentious [lai'senʃəs] *adj* (*formal or liter*) in the habit of behaving immorally or improperly; indecent: *The court of King Charles II was immoral and licentious*; *licentious conduct.* **li'centiousness** *nu.*

off-licence *see* **off**.

licence number *see* **registration number** *under* **register**.

lichen ['laikən] *ncu* any of a large group of simple plants which grow on stones, trees *etc*: *The roof was covered in lichen.*

lichgate *see* **lychgate**.

lick [lik] *vt* to pass the tongue over: *The dog licked her hand*; (*fig formal*) *Flames licked the walls.* – *nc* **1** an act of licking: *The child gave the ice-cream a lick.* **2** (*inf*) a very small amount: *a lick of paint.*

a lick and a promise (*inf*) a short and not very thorough wash or clean: *Since it was late she only gave the children a lick and a promise before bed.*

lick into shape (*inf*) to put into more perfect form or make more efficient: *It only took him half an hour to lick the rough draft of the letter into shape and send it.*

licorice *see* **liquorice**.

lid [lid] *nc* **1** a cover for a pot, box *etc*: *He lifted the lid of the box and looked inside*; *She put a lid on the pot with the potatoes in it.* **2** an eyelid: *The infection has not affected the eye itself although the lid is swollen.*

lie[1] [lai] *nc* a false statement made with the intention of deceiving: *It would be a lie to say I knew, because I didn't.* – *v* – *prp* **'lying**: *pt, ptp* **lied** – *vi* to say *etc* something which is not true with the intention of deceiving: *There's no point in asking her – she'll just lie about it.*

liar ['laiə] *nc* a person who tells lies, *esp* as a habit: *If she says I did that, she is a liar, because I certainly did not do it*; *You can't believe a word she says – she's such a liar.*

give the lie to (*formal*) to show (a statement *etc*) to be false: *Her pale face gave the lie to her statement that she felt quite well.*

white lie *see* **white**.

lie[2] [lai] – *prp* **'lying**: *pt* **lay** [lei]: *ptp* **lain** [lein] – *vi* **1** to be in or take a more or less flat or horizontal position: *She went into the bedroom and lay on the bed*; *The book/The piece of string was lying in the hall.* **2** (*formal*) (*esp* of a house, a town, a piece of land *etc*) to be situated: *The farm lay three miles from the sea*; *His estate lay along the banks of the river*; (*fig*) *His interest lies in farming.* **3** to remain in a certain state: *The shop is lying empty now*; *He decided to lie hidden for a few days longer.* **4** (*with* **in**) (of feelings, impressions *etc*) to be caused by or contained in: *The difficulty lies in our lack of money*; *His charm lies in his honesty.* – *See also* **lie** *in phrases below.*

lie back *vi* **1** to lean back on a support: *He lay back against the pillows and went to sleep.* **2** (*fig*) to rest, *esp* after a period of hard work: *I thought I'd just lie back and enjoy myself.*

lie down *vi* to take a flat or horizontal position: *The dog/The man lay down*; *I've just washed my hair, and I can't get it to lie down.*

lie in *vi* **1** to stay in bed late in the morning: *I like to lie in until nine on a Saturday.* **2** (*old*) to be in bed before and after giving birth to a child.
lie in wait (for) to be waiting to catch or attack (someone or something): *As he left the building, she was lying in wait for him because she wanted to speak to him; They lay in wait at the corner of the street and attacked him on his way home.*
lie low to stay quiet or hidden: *The criminal lay low until the police stopped looking for him.*
the lie of the land the way in which the land slopes *etc*: *He went up the hill to look at the lie of the land*; (*fig*) *I'll write you a report as soon as I've studied the lie of the land in the department.*
'lie with *vt fus* (*formal*) (of a choice, duty *etc*) to be the responsibility of: *The decision lies with you.*
see how the land lies to (wait and) find out all the facts *etc* about a situation which will affect one's decisions before deciding on a course of action: *I won't promise to ask him for everything you want – I'll have to see how the land lies.*
take (something) lying down (*usu in neg*) to accept or suffer (something) without arguing, complaining or trying to avoid it: *I do not intend to take this insult lying down, and will write to my lawyer!*
See also **lay**[1].

lieu [luː] : **in 'lieu of** (*formal*) in place of or instead of: *He gave me this radio in lieu of the money he owes me.*

lieutenant [ləf'tenənt, (*Amer*) luː-] *nc* (*with cap, and often abbrev* **Lt., Lieut.,** *when written in titles*) **1** in the British army, (a person of) the rank next below captain: *He is a lieutenant now; He was promoted to lieutenant; Lieutenant Seaton.* **2** in the British navy, (a person of) the rank next below lieutenant-commander. – *See also* Appendix 3.

life [laif] – *pl* **lives** [laivz] – **1** *nu* the quality belonging to plants and animals which distinguishes them from rocks, minerals *etc* and things which are dead: *Doctors are fighting to save the child's life; Although the plant looked dead, she was sure that there was still some life in it.* **2** *nc* the period between birth and death: *He had a long and happy life*; (*attrib*) *He is a life member of several clubs*; (*attrib*) *life imprisonment.* **3** *nu* liveliness: *She was full of life and energy.* **4** *nc* a manner of living: *He did not enjoy married life* (= being married); *She lived a life of ease and idleness; What exciting lives kings and queens seem to have led!* **5** *ncu* the period during which any particular state of affairs exists: *He had many different jobs during his working life.* **6** *nu* living things: *There is now considered to be no life on Mars; animal life.* **7** *nc* the story of a life: *He has written a life of Churchill; His life was the subject of an excellent film.* **8** *nu* (*inf*) life imprisonment: *he was given life for murder.*
'lifeless *adj* **1** (*formal*) dead: *a lifeless corpse; Is he dead? He certainly looks lifeless.* **2** not lively and often uninteresting because of this: *The actress was not well and gave a lifeless performance; She is usually very sociable but she seems rather lifeless today.*
'lifelike *adj* like a living person, animal *etc*: *The statue was very lifelike; a lifelike portrait.*
ˌlife-and-'death *adj* (*often fig*: *attrib*) serious and deciding between life and death: *a life-and-death struggle/decision.* – *See also* **matter of life and death** *under* **matter**.
'lifebelt *nc* a ring or belt filled with air or made of a material which floats, for keeping a person afloat: *He threw a lifebelt to the child who had fallen into the sea.*
'lifeblood *nu* (*fig*: *usu liter*) something necessary to the operation of something: *Oil is the lifeblood of modern society.*
'lifeboat *nc* a boat for saving shipwrecked people: *The lifeboat rescued the crew of the sinking ship.*
'lifebuoy *nc* a buoy intended to support a person in the water till he can be rescued: *When the boat sank there were not enough lifebuoys for all the members of the crew and five of them drowned.*
'life-cycle *nc* the various stages through which a living thing passes: *He is studying the life-cycle of the snail.*
life expectancy *nu* the (average) length of time a person can expect to live: *Thanks to improvements in medical science, life expectancy has increased a great deal.*
'lifeguard *nc* **1** a person employed in the US *etc* to protect and rescue swimmers at a swimming-pool, beach *etc.* **2** (*with cap*) a member of one of the British cavalry regiments which provides the Queen's bodyguard.
'life-jacket *nc* a sleeveless jacket filled with material that will float, for keeping a person afloat: *The child survived when he fell out of the boat because he was wearing a life-jacket.*
'lifeline *nc* **1** a rope for support in dangerous operations or thrown to rescue a drowning person. **2** (*formal*: *fig*) a very important line of communication: *We kept open a lifeline to the area of the disaster; The people who visit her in hospital are a lifeline to her/her lifeline.*
'lifelong *adj* (*attrib*) lasting the whole length of a life: *a lifelong friendship.*
life peer – *fem* **life peeress** – *nc* a person who is made a baron or baroness but whose title is not passed to anyone on his or her death: *He has been made a life peer for his service to politics.*
'life-saving *nu* the act or skill of rescuing people from drowning: *The boy is being taught life-saving*; (*attrib*) *a life-saving certificate.*
'life-size(d) *adj, adv* (of a copy, drawing *etc*) as large as the original: *a life-sized statue of a man; The statue is more than life-size.*
'lifetime *nc* the period of a person's life: *He saw many changes in his lifetime.*
as large as life in person; actually: *I went to the party and there was John as large as life.*
bring to life to make lively or interesting: *His lectures on the subject really brought it to life.*
come to life to become lively or interesting: *The play did not come to life until the last act.*
for 'life until death: *They became friends for life.*
the life and soul of the party a person who is very active, enthusuastic, amusing *etc* at a party: *He sings, tells jokes and dances with all the girls – he's the life and soul of the party.*
a matter of life and death *see* **matter**.
ˌnot for the 'life of me, him *etc* (*inf*) not even if it was necessary in order to save my, his *etc* life: *I couldn't for the life of me remember his name!*
not on your life! (*inf*) certainly not!: *'Will you get married?' 'Not on your life!'*
take (one's) life (*formal*) to kill: *In despair at his failure, he took his own life; It is a sin to take life.*
take one's life in one's hands to take the risk of being killed: *He took his life in his hands when he entered the burning building to try to rescue the child*; (*fig inf*) *I took my life in my hands and asked for a rise in salary.*

to the 'life exactly (like): *When he put on that uniform, he was Napoleon to the life; She can imitate her mother to the life!*

See also **live**[1], **live**[2].

lift [lift] **1** *vt* to raise or bring to a higher position: *The box was so heavy I couldn't lift it.* **2** *vt* to take and carry away: *He lifted the table through into the kitchen.* **3** *vi* (of mist *etc*) to disappear: *By noon, the fog was beginning to lift; (fig) In the morning, she discovered that her depression had lifted a little.* **4** *vi* (*formal or liter*) to rise: *The aeroplane lifted into the air.* **5** *vt* (*formal or liter: often with* **up**) to make (the voice) loud or easily heard: *They lifted (up) their voices and sang.* – *nc* **1** the act of lifting: *a lift of the eyebrows; The weight-lifter made a lift of several hundred kilos.* **2** (*Amer* **'elevator**) a small enclosed platform *etc* that moves up and down (between floors) carrying goods or people: *Since she was too tired to climb the stairs, she went up in the lift.* **3** a ride in someone's car *etc*: *Can I give you a lift into town?; We got a lift part of the way in a lorry.* **4** (*inf: in sing*) a raising of the spirits or an act of helping (someone) to become happier: *It gave her a lift to speak to him.*

lift off *vi* (of a rocket *etc*) to leave the ground (*nc* **'lift-off**).

ligament ['ligəmənt] *nc* a piece of tough substance that joins together the bones of the body: *She pulled a ligament in her knee when she fell.*

light[1] [lait] **1** *nu* (*sometimes in cmpds*) the brightness given by the sun, a flame, lamps *etc* that makes things able to be seen: *It was nearly dawn and the light was getting stronger; The candle did not give a good enough light to read by; She opened the curtains and light came into the room; The snow glistened in the moonlight; Sunlight streamed into the room.* **2** *nc* something which gives light (*eg* a lamp): *There was a light outside their house; Suddenly all the lights went out.* **3** *nc* (*inf*) something which can be used to set fire to something else; a flame: *Have you got a light (= a match etc) for my cigarette?* **4** *nu* (*fig*) a way of viewing or regarding: *He looked at his action in a favourable/different light; Viewed in this light, the problem seemed less important.* **5** *nc* (*fig*) a gleam or sparkle, indicating excitement: *There was a strange light in his eyes as he spoke.* – *adj* **1** having light; not dark: *The studio was a large, light room; By the time we had finished, the sky was already light.* **2** (of a colour) pale; closer to white than black: *light green.* – *v* – *pt, ptp* **lit** [lit], **'lighted** – **1** *vt* to give light to: *The room was lit only by candles.* **2** *vti* to (make something) catch fire: *She lit the gas and put a pot of soup on the cooker; I think this match is wet, because it won't light.* – *See also* **light up** *below.*

'lightness[1] *nu.*

'lighten[1] *vti* to make or become brighter: *The white ceiling lightened the room; It was nearly dawn, and the sky was lightening.*

'lighter *nc* something used for lighting (a cigarette *etc*): *She gave him a silver lighter for Christmas.*

'lighting *nu* a means of providing light: *The lighting was so bad in the restaurant that we could hardly see.*

light-bulb *see* **bulb**.

'lighthouse *nc* a building built on rocks, coastline *etc* with a (flashing) light to guide or warn ships.

'light-year *nc* the distance light travels in a year (nearly 9·5 million million kilometres).

according to one's lights (*formal*) following one's own standards: *He was a good father according to his lights, but very strict.*

bring to light (*formal*) to reveal or cause to be noticed: *The scandal was brought to light by the investigations of a journalist.*

come to light (*formal*) to be revealed or discovered: *The manuscript came to light in a box of books at an auction.*

go out like a light *see* **go**.

in the 'light of (*formal*) taking into consideration (information acquired *etc*): *The theory has been abandoned in the light of modern discoveries.*

light up **1** *vi* to begin to give out light: *As we watched, the streetlights lit up.* **2** *vi, vt sep* to make, be or become full of light: *The powerful searchlight lit up the building; It lit them all up; She watched the house light up as everyone awoke.* **3** *vi, vt sep* (*fig*) to make or become happy: *Her face lit up when saw him; When she smiles, it lights up her whole face; It lights it up completely.* **4** *vi* (*inf*) to light a cigarette *etc*: *He produced a cigar and lit up.*

Northern/Southern lights *see* **aurora**.

see the light **1** (*often* **see the light of day**) (*usu fig*) to be born, discovered, produced *etc*: *That was one of our projects which never saw the light (of day) at all.* **2** (*often facet*) to be converted to someone else's point of view *etc*: *She finally saw the light and agreed to follow our suggestions.*

set light to to cause to begin burning: *He set light to the pile of rubbish in his garden.*

shed light on *see* **shed**[2].

See also **alight**[2].

light[2] [lait] *adj* **1** easy to lift or carry; of little weight: *I bought a light suitcase for plane journeys; This table is light enough for one person to move.* **2** easy to bear, suffer or do: *You must look for light work after you leave hospital; Next time the punishment will not be so light.* **3** (of food) easy to digest: *a light meal; The meal was light but filling.* **4** (*pred*) of less weight than it should be: *The load of grain was several kilos light.* **5** of little weight, or less weight than the average, for its size: *Aluminium is a light metal; The dress was made in a light wool; This dress is light but warm.* **6** (*pred*) lively or agile: *She was very light on her feet.* **7** (*esp attrib*) cheerful; not serious: *light opera; light entertainment; light music.* **8** (*esp attrib*) little in quantity; not intense, heavy, strong *etc*: *light rain.* **9** (of soil) containing a lot of sand: *The soil in our garden is rather light; light, sandy soil.* **'lightly** *adv.* **'lightness**[2] *nu.*

'lighten[2] *vti* (*formal*) to make or become less heavy or of less weight: *She lightened her suitcase by taking out several pairs of shoes; The postman's bag of parcels lightened as he went from house to house.*

lights *n pl* the lungs of an animal, used for food.

,light-'fingered *adj* likely to steal: *Don't leave your handbag for a moment – this place is full of light-fingered people!; Watch him – he's light-fingered.*

,light-'headed *adj* dizzy or giddy: *After five glasses of champagne, she began to feel light-headed; in rather a light-headed state.*

,light-'hearted *adj* happy and free from anxiety; not grave or serious: *She was light-hearted at the prospect of going on holiday the following day; in a light-hearted mood; This film takes a light-hearted look at tourism.*

'lightweight *adj* **1** (*esp attrib*) light in weight: *a lightweight raincoat; This coat is a bit lightweight for this climate.* **2** (*sometimes derog*) not serious or grave: *a lightweight comedy*; *His latest novel is rather lightweight.* – *nc* (*usu fig*) a person who weighs little: (*fig*) *an intellectual lightweight* (= a person who is not very clever).

get off lightly to escape or be allowed to go without severe punishment *etc*: *The thief was lucky to get off so lightly!*

make light of to treat as unimportant: *He had a bad fall, but made light of his cuts and carried on.*

travel light to travel with little luggage.

light[3] [lait]: '**light on** – *pt, ptp* **lit** [lit] – *vt fus* to find by chance: *While wandering round the town, we lit on a very cheap restaurant.*

lighten *see* **light**[1], **light**[2].

lighter *see* **light**[1].

lightning ['laitniŋ] *nu* a flash of electricity between clouds or from a cloud to earth during a storm, *usu* followed by thunder: *She is afraid of thunder and lightning*; *The house was struck by lightning.*

'**lightning-conductor** *nc* a metal rod that protects buildings *etc* from the electricity of lightning by leading it down to earth.

like[1] [laik] *adj* the same as or similar to: *They're as like as two peas.* – *prep* the same as or similar to; in the same or a similar way as: *He climbs like a cat*; *My house is like yours*; *She is a bit like her mother.* – *nc* (*no pl*) someone or something which is the same or as good *etc* as another: *You won't see his like/their like again.* – *conj* in the same or a similar way as: *No-one does it like he does.*

'**likely** *adj* **1** probable: *One likely result of the train strike is that people will take their cars to work*; *It's likely that she knows him.* **2** looking *etc* as if it might be good, useful, suitable *etc*: *She was looking for a likely spot for a picnic*; *'Have you found a suitable person for the job?' 'No, but she's the most likely so far.'* – *See also* **he** *etc* **is likely to** *below.*

'**likelihood** *nu* probability: *I'll go home if there's any likelihood of her coming.*

'**liken** *vt* (*formal*) to think or speak of as being similar; to compare: *He likened our firm to a huge tree.*

'**likeness 1** *ncu* (a) similarity or resemblance: *The likeness between them is amazing.* **2** *nc* something which is like or resembles (someone or something): *That photo of Mary is a good likeness.* **3** *nc* (*formal*) a painting or photograph of someone: *He paid an artist to paint a likeness of his wife.*

'**likewise** *adv* **1** in the same or a similar manner: *He ignored her, and she ignored him likewise.* **2** also: *Mrs. Brown came, likewise Mrs. Smith.*

ˌ**like-'minded** *adj* having a similar opinion or purpose: *He got together with several like-minded people and formed a club.*

a 'likely story! I don't believe you, him *etc*: *She says she spent the whole evening working? A likely story – she was probably watching TV!*

as likely as not probably: *As likely as not, he won't remember to come.*

be like someone (*usu with* **it, that** *or* **this** *as subject*) to be typical of someone: *It isn't like him to be late*; *I'm sure she'll forget to come – that would be just like her.*

'**feel like 1** to be inclined, willing or anxious to (do or have something): *I don't feel like going out in that rain*; *I expect he feels like a cup of tea.* **2** to feel as if one was: *I feel like a queen in this outfit!*

he *etc* **is 'likely to** it is probable that he *etc* will: *He is not likely to come*; *I felt that it was likely to rain*; *Would you be likely to be in on Sunday?*

'**look like 1** to appear similar to: *She looks very like her mother.* **2** to show the effects, signs or possibility of: *It looks like rain.* – *See also* **what . . . like?** *under* **what**.

not likely! (*inf*) certainly not!: *'Would you be willing to put your head in a lion's mouth?' 'Me? Not likely!'*

what is it *etc* **like?** *see* **what . . . like?** *under* **what**.

See also **unlike, unlikely**.

like[2] [laik] *vt* (not *usu* used with **is, was** *etc* and **-ing**) **1** to be pleased with; to find pleasant or agreeable: *I like him very much*; *I like the way you've decorated this room*; *She likes children.* **2** to enjoy: *I like gardening*; *She likes going to the cinema.*

'**lik(e)able** *adj* lovable or attractive: *Of course I like her – she's a very likeable person*; *She is so sweet and likeable that I cannot understand his dislike of her.*

'**liking** (*formal*) **1** *nc* a taste or fondness (for): *He has a particular liking for chocolate.* **2** *nu* satisfaction: *I have had the office decorated to my liking* (= as I like it).

I/we should/would like (to), you *etc* **would like (to)** I *etc* want (to): *I would just like to say how pleased I am to be here*; *Would you like a cup of tea?*

take a liking to to begin to like: *I've taken a liking to him/chocolate.*

See also **dislike**.

lilac ['lailək] **1** *ncu* (*also* '**lilac tree** *nc*) a type of small tree with bunches of white or pale purple flowers. **2** *nu, adj* (of) a pale, *usu* pinkish, purple colour: *She wore a dress of pale lilac*; *lilac sheets.*

lilt [lilt] *nc* (a tune *etc* with) a strong rhythm: *He had a lilt in his way of speaking that made it clear he was Welsh.*

lily ['lili] *nc* a type of tall plant grown from a bulb, with white or coloured flowers.

'**lily-livered** *adj* (*liter*) cowardly.

ˌ**lily-of-the-'valley** *ncu* a type of plant with small, white bell-shaped flowers.

limb [lim] *nc* (*formal*) **1** an arm or leg: *He broke several limbs in his fall.* **2** a branch: *She sat on a limb of the tree and looked down.*

out on a limb having ideas or opinions not shared by others; in a dangerous or disadvantageous position: *In making his views on the subject known, he had put himself out on a limb.*

limber ['limbə]: **limber up** *vi* to exercise so as to become able to move easily: *The hall was full of dancers limbering up before the performance.*

limbo ['limbou]: **in 'limbo** (*formal*) forgotten, neglected or cast aside: *Plans were completed last year, but the whole project has been in limbo since then.*

lime[1] [laim] *nu* the white substance left after heating limestone and used in making cement.

'**limestone** *nu* a kind of rock made mainly of calcium carbonate.

lime[2] [laim] **1** *nc* a type of small, very sour, yellowish-green citrus fruit related to the lemon: *Limes are not easy to find in this country*; (*attrib*) *a lime tree*; (*attrib*) *lime juice.* **2** *nu* (*also* **lime green**) the colour of this fruit. **3** *ncu* (a drink flavoured with) lime juice: *She ordered a gin and lime.* – *adj* **1** (*also* **lime green**) of the colour of a lime. **2** (*usu attrib*) with the taste of lime juice: *a lime jelly.*

lime[3] [laim] **1** *nc* (*also* **lime tree**) a type of tree with rough bark and small, heart-shaped leaves, often planted to form avenues *etc*: *We planted an avenue* *of limes.* 2 *nu, adj* (of) its wood.

limerick ['limərik] *nc* a type of humorous poem with five lines, the third and fourth lines being shorter than the others.

limit ['limit] *nc* 1 (*esp in pl*: *formal*) the farthest point or place; the boundary: *the limits of the earth/of his estate*; (*fig*) *He had reached the limits of his patience*; *There was no limit to his ambition.* 2 the largest (or smallest) extent, degree *etc*: *I intend to press this claim to the limit* (= as much as possible). 3 a restriction: *We must put a limit on our spending.* – *vt* to set or keep to a limit or restriction: *We must limit the amount of time we spend on this work.*

,limi'tation 1 *ncu* (*formal*) an act of limiting: *We shall do our best within the limitations imposed by lack of time.* 2 *nc* weakness about a person or thing which sets a limit on what he, it *etc* can do: *We all have our limitations.*

'limited *adj* 1 (*neg* **un-**) not very great, large or wide-ranging *etc*; restricted: *My experience of this subject is rather limited*; *He is of limited intelligence*; *She is rather limited in the amount of work she can do as she has three small children.* 2 (*with cap, and often abbrev* **Ltd.**, *when written*) a word used in the titles of limited companies: *W. and R. Chambers Ltd.*

'limitless *adj.*

limited company a business company whose shareholders are responsible for its debts only to the extent of the money they have invested.

limousine ['liməzi:n] *nc* a kind of large motor car *esp* one with a screen separating the front seat from the back: *The guest of honour arrived in a large black limousine.*

limp[1] [limp] *adj* lacking stiffness or drooping: *She had forgotten to water the plant and all the leaves were limp*; *He gave her a limp, cold handshake.*

limp[2] [limp] *vi* to walk in an uneven manner (*usu* because one has hurt one's foot or leg): *Despite having twisted his ankle, he got up and limped away*; (*fig*) *The ship limped into port with only one engine operating.* – *nc* the act of limping: *He walks with a limp*; *His limp became more noticeable as he grew more tired.*

limpet ['limpit] *nc* 1 a type of small, cone-shaped shellfish that fastens itself very firmly to rocks. 2 (*fig derog*) a person who is difficult to get rid of: *That boring man is such a limpet – he tries to join me for lunch every day.*

limpid ['limpid] *adj* (*liter*) (of water, the air, eyes *etc*) clear or transparent: *a limpid pool*; *Her eyes were large and limpid.*

linchpin ['lintʃpin] *nc* 1 a pin-shaped rod used to keep a wheel on an axle. 2 (*fig*) a person who is very important to a business *etc*: *She is the linchpin of the whole organization*; *Since the death of her mother the eldest daughter has become the linchpin of her family.*

line[1] [lain] 1 *ncu* (a piece of) thread, cord, rope *etc*, *esp* one for fishing, hanging clothes *etc*: *The washing was drying quickly on the line*; *The boat carried a lifebelt attached to a hundred metres of line*; *a fishing-rod and line.* 2 *nc* a long, narrow mark, streak or stripe: *His car was painted black with a gold line along the side*; *She drew straight lines across the page*; *a dotted/wavy line*; (*attrib*) *a line-drawing.* 3 *nc* (*math*) the path which a moving object is considered to leave behind it, having length but no breadth. 4 *nc* (*usu in pl*) outline or shape: *The ship had very graceful lines*; *The dress designer was often praised for the line of his clothes.* 5 *nu* (*formal or tech*) the use in painting, design *etc* of long, narrow marks or outlines: *The ship was famous for its beauty of line*; (*attrib*) *a line drawing.* 6 *nc* a groove like a long narrow stripe drawn on the skin; a wrinkle: *The old woman had many lines on her face.* 7 *nc* a row or group of objects or persons arranged side by side or one behind the other: *The children stood in a line*; *A line of fine houses faced the park*; *a line of trees.* 8 *nc* (*inf*) a short letter: *I suppose I should drop him a line.* 9 *nc* a series or group of persons which come one after the other *esp* in the same family: *a line of kings*; *It's no surprise he's in jail – he comes from a long line of criminals.* 10 *nc* a route, track or direction: *He pointed out the line of the new road*; (*fig*) *I couldn't see the aim of this new line of questioning.* 11 *nc* the railway or a single track of the railway: *Passengers must cross the line by the bridge only.* 12 *nc* (*often in cmpds*) a continuous system (*esp* of pipes, electrical or telephone cables *etc*) connecting one place with another: *a pipeline*; *a line of communication*; *All lines* (= telephone lines) *out of Manchester are engaged.* 13 *nc* a row of letters written or printed on a page or a separate part of a poem: *The letter contained only three lines*; *a poem of sixteen lines*; *a four-line verse.* 14 *nc* a regular service of ships, aircraft *etc*: *a shipping line.* 15 *nc* (*inf*) a group or class (of goods for sale) or a field of activity, interest *etc*: *This has been a very popular new line*; *I'm afraid such decisions are not really in my line*; (*fig*) *He has a good line in compliments.* 16 *nc* (*often in pl*) an arrangement of troops, *esp* when ready to fight: *the front line* (= the position nearest the enemy); *This photograph shows the Prime Minister visiting the lines.* – *See also* **lines** *below.* – *vt* 1 to form lines along (a street *etc*): *Trees lined the river bank*; *Crowds lined the pavement to see the queen.* 2 to mark with lines: *Age had lined her face.*

lineage ['liniidʒ] *nu* (*old or formal*) ancestry or family: *He was of aristocratic lineage.*

lineal ['liniəl] *adj* (*formal*: *esp attrib*) (of ancestry or family) in a direct line: *a lineal descendant of the poet.*

linear ['liniə] *adj* (*formal or tech*: *esp attrib*) of, consisting of or like a line or lines: *a linear diagram.*

lined[1] *adj* having lines: *lined paper*; *a lined face*; *The paper is lined.*

'liner[1] *nc* a ship or aircraft of a regular line or company: *They sailed to America in a large liner.*

lines *n pl* 1 a written punishment task, *usu* consisting of a sentence written out a given number of times: *The boy was given a hundred lines for talking in class.* 2 the words an actor has to say: *He had difficulty remembering his lines.* 3 (*inf*: *also* **marriage lines**) a marriage licence.

'linesman ['lainz-] *nc* in sport, a judge or umpire at a boundary line: *The linesman said that the ball had gone over the line.*

line-up *see* **line up** *below.*

draw the line *see* **draw**.

hard lines! (*inf*) bad luck!: *You didn't get the job? Hard lines!*

hot line *see* **hot**.

in 'line for likely to get or to be given something: *He is in line for promotion.*

in, out of line with (*formal*) in or out of agreement or harmony with: *His statement is in line with his previous attitude to the subject*; *His* *views are out of line with those of his colleagues.*

line up 1 *vi, vt sep* to form a line: *The children lined up ready to leave the classroom*; *She lined up the chairs in front of the stage.* **2** *vt sep* (*inf*) to collect, prepare and arrange: *I have lined up several important people for you to meet*; *There are a lot of interesting programmes lined up to be shown on television this autumn* (*nc* **'line-up**).

party line *see* **party**.

read between the lines to understand something from a piece of writing *etc* which is not actually stated: *She said she was managing all right, but reading between the lines I could see she was tired.*

toe the line *see* **toe**.

line[2] [lain] *vt* **1** to cover on the inside: *She lined the box with newspaper.* **2** to put a lining (*def 2*) in: *She lined the dress with silk.*

lined[2] *adj* (*neg* **un-**) having a lining: *Is this skirt lined?*; *I prefer a lined skirt.*

'liner[2] *nc* something used for lining: *a dustbin liner*; *Could I have a liner for the baby's nappy?*

'lining 1 *ncu* (a) covering on the inside: *The basket had a padded lining.* **2** *nc* a fairly exact copy (of a piece of clothing) attached to the inside to help it keep its shape *etc*: *I've put a lining in this dress as it's made of a very thin fabric*; (*attrib*) *lining material.*

linen ['linin] **1** *nu, adj* (of) cloth made of flax used to make sheets, tablecloths, tea-towels *etc*: *This handkerchief is* (*made of*) *linen* ; (*attrib*) *linen sheets.* **2** *nu* (*often in cmpds*) articles made of, or *orig* made of, linen: *table-linen*; *bed-linen.*

liner *see* **line**[1], **line**[2].

linger ['liŋgə] *vi* **1** (*formal*) to remain, last or continue for a long time or after the expected time: *We should have left before supper, but were persuaded to linger*; *The smell of burning lingered for days.* **2** to proceed slowly or delay: *We lingered in the hall, looking at the pictures.*

lingerie ['lãʒəri:] *nu* (*usu* used in shops) women's underwear: *Nightdresses are among the lingerie, on the first floor of the shop*; (*attrib*) *the lingerie department.*

lingo ['liŋgou] – *pl* **'lingoes** – *nc* (*old derog*) language: *I don't understand a word of their damned lingo!*

lingua franca [liŋgwə'fraŋkə] *nc* (*no pl*) any (often simplified) language used by people from different nations *etc* so that they can talk to one another.

linguist ['liŋgwist] *nc* a person who studies language and/or is good at languages: *He is not studying English literature – he is a linguist*; *He is no linguist – he speaks only English.*

lin'guistic *adj* of languages.

lin'guistics *n sing* the science of languages.

lining *see* **line**[2].

liniment ['linimənt] *nu* a kind of thin, *usu* oily, ointment for rubbing into the skin to ease muscular pain *etc*: *The athlete rubbed some liniment on his aching limbs.*

link [liŋk] *nc* **1** a ring of a chain: *There was a worn link in the chain and it broke*; (*fig*) *The discovery of the fingerprints was an important link in the evidence collected by the police.* **2** anything connecting two things: *His job was to act as a link between the government and the press*; (*attrib*) *He was a link-man between the workers and the management*; (*attrib*) *a link-road to the motorway.* – *vt* to connect as by a link: *The new train service links the suburbs with the heart of the city.*

link up *vt sep, vi* to join or be joined closely or by a link: *This exercise links up with the work you were doing last week*; *An electrician called to link up our house to the mains electricity supply* (*nc* **'link-up**).

links [liŋks] *n pl* **1** a stretch of more or less flat ground along a seashore. **2** (*often with sing verb*) a golf course.

linoleum [li'nouliəm] *nu* (*abbrev* **lino** ['lainou]) a type of smooth, hard-wearing covering for floors: *We had to remove the old linoleum from the kitchen floor before we laid the tiles*; *She slipped on the wet lino and broke her leg.*

linseed ['linsi:d]: **linseed oil** *nu* oil made from flax seed.

lint [lint] *nu* **1** linen in the form of a soft woolly material for putting over wounds. **2** fine, very small pieces of wool, cotton *etc*: *Everything in the cotton mill was covered in a fine layer of lint.*

lintel ['lintl] *nc* a piece of wood or stone placed over a doorway or window: *There was an inscription carved on the lintel above the door.*

lion ['laiən] – *fem* **'lioness** – *nc* a type of large, flesh-eating animal of the cat family, the male of which has a long, coarse mane: *She could hear the lions roaring in the jungle.*

'lionize, -ise *vt* (*formal*) to treat (a person) as a celebrity: *He was lionized in New York after the success of his film.*

the lion's share the largest share: *When his money was divided, his wife got the lion's share.*

lip [lip] *nc* **1** either of the folds of flesh which form the edge of the mouth: *The child fell and cut his lip*; *She bit her lip.* **2** (*fig formal*) the edge of something: *the lip of a cup.*

-lipped (*in cmpds*) having (a certain kind of) lip(s): *She was pale and tight-lipped with anger.*

'lip-read *vi* to understand what a person is saying by watching the movement of his lips: *The deaf woman trained herself to lip-read and so knew what people were saying.*

'lipstick *nu* (a stick of) colouring for the lips: *She was wearing bright red lipstick.*

ˌpay 'lip-service to (*formal*) to pretend to agree with and approve of (an idea, way of thinking *etc*) without really doing so: *She has stopped even paying lip-service to the rules.*

liquefy *see* **liquid**.

liqueur [li'kjuə, (*Amer*) -'kə:r] *ncu* a strong alcoholic drink, strongly flavoured and *usu* sweet, drunk at the end of a meal: *They drank liqueurs out of tiny glasses with their coffee.*

liquid ['likwid] *adj* **1** able to flow; not solid, but not a gas: *The tanker was carrying liquid nitrogen*; *Would you like the medicine in liquid form?*; *The ice-cream is melting – it has become liquid.* **2** (*fig*: *usu liter*) clear in appearance, sound *etc*: *the liquid song of a blackbird*; *The child has large liquid eyes*; *Her eyes are black and liquid.* **3** (*attrib*) in cash, or able to be converted into cash: *a firm's liquid assets.* – *ncu* a substance which flows, like water: *a clear liquid.*

liquefy ['likwifai] *vti* (*formal*) to make or become liquid: *The butter had liquefied in the heat.*

'liquidate [-deit] *vt* **1** to close, and finish the affairs of (a business, person *etc* that has no money to continue): *The company was liquidated last year.* **2** (*inf*) to get rid of by violence: *All the dictator's opponents had been liquidated.* **ˌliqui'dation** *nu.* **'liquidator** *nc.*

'liquidize, -ise *vt* to make (food *etc*) into a liquid or semi-liquid substance by grinding it up in a liquidizer: *She made a sauce by liquidizing fresh raspberries.*

'**liquidizer, -s-** *nc* an electrical device used in cookery to grind up food: *A liquidizer is useful for making soups.*

liquor ['likə] *nu* **1** strong alcoholic drink: *His breath smelt of liquor*; (*attrib*) *the liquor laws in America.* **2** (*formal*) a liquid containing a strong solution of something: *She made a sauce with the liquor in which the ham had been boiled.*

liquorice, (*Amer*) **licorice** ['likəris, (*Amer*) -riʃ] *nu* a plant with a sweet root, or a black, sticky type of sweet made from it.

lira ['liərə] – *pl* **lire** ['liərei] – *nc* the standard unit of Italian currency.

lisp [lisp] *vi* **1** to say *th* for *s* or *z* because of being unable to pronounce these sounds correctly. **2** (*liter*) to speak as a small child does: *The child lisped happily in its cot.* – *nc* the act or habit of lisping: *She has a slight lisp.*

list[1] [list] *nc* a series *eg* of names, numbers, prices *etc* written down or said one after the other: *a shopping-list*; *We have a long list of people who are willing to help*; *We had to listen to a long list of complaints.* – *vt* to place in a list: *He listed on a piece of paper the things he still had to do*; *Could you list all the people whom you consider to be suitable?*

list[2] [list] *vi* to lean over to one side: *The ship is listing.* – *nc* an act or amount of listing: *The ship had a heavy list to one side.*

listen ['lisn] *vi* **1** (*often with* **to**) to give attention so as to hear (what someone is saying *etc*): *I don't think you've listened to a word I said!*; *I told her three times, but she wasn't listening*; *We listened to the radio last night*; *Do stop talking and listen to the music!* **2** (*with* **to**) to follow the advice of: *If she'd listened to me, she wouldn't have got into trouble.*

listen in *vi* **1** (*old*: *often with* **to**) to listen to a radio broadcast: *If you listen in tonight you'll hear my brother talking about his new play.* **2** (*often with* **on**) to listen intentionally to a telephone conversation, a message intended for someone else *etc*: *It was impossible to discuss anything private over the telephone, as the operator was in the habit of listening in (on our conversations).*

listless ['listlis] *adj* tired and without energy or interest: *The heat made us listless*; *The teacher tried to interest the listless children in what she was saying.* '**listlessly** *adv.* '**listlessness** *nu.*

lit *see* **light**[1], **light**[3].

litany ['litəni] *nc* (*relig*) a set group of prayers following one another in a set order.

liter *see* **litre**.

literacy *see* **literate**.

literal ['litərəl] *adj* **1** (*esp attrib*) following the exact meaning with no exaggeration and nothing added by the imagination: *He did not believe that what she said was the literal truth.* **2** understanding the meaning by taking one word at a time: *a literal translation*; *That translation is not quite literal.* **3** (of a person) unimaginative: *He has a very literal mind*; *He is too literal for my liking – I prefer someone with more imagination.* '**literalness** *nu.*

'**literally** *adv* (*often used loosely*): *We had literally a minute to catch the train – we arrived at 11.59 and it left at 12 noon*; (*loosely*) *When we got home, I was literally dead with exhaustion.*

literary ['litərəri] *adj* **1** (*attrib*) concerning literature or the writing of books: *a literary magazine.* **2** (of a person) knowledgeable about books: *He is one of my literary friends*; *His tastes are rather literary.*

literate ['litərət] *adj* **1** able to read and write: *Many people leaving school today are only just literate*; *Literate people do not appreciate the problems of those who cannot read and write.* **2** (*formal*) clever and having read a great deal: *He is one of the most literate people I know*; *He is the most literate of the whole family.* '**literacy** *nu.*

See also **illiterate**.

literature ['litrətʃə] *nu* **1** poems, novels, plays *etc* in verse or prose, *esp* if of fine quality: *She studies literature as well as language*; *French literature.* **2** (*sometimes facet*) something written on a subject, *esp* catalogues, leaflets *etc* advertising something: *He doesn't have time to read all the literature on the latest medical research*; *I've written away for some literature about student grants/a holiday on the Mediterranean.*

lithe [laið] *adj* (*formal*) (used *esp* of the human body) bending easily; flexible: *He was young, strong and as lithe as a cat*; *In one lithe movement, she jumped on to the wall.* '**litheness** *nu.*

litigation [liti'geiʃən] *nu* (*formal or legal*) a private law-suit: *He is always involved in litigation with his neighbours over who is responsible for repairing the fence.*

'**litigant** *nc* (*formal or legal*) a person involved in a lawsuit.

litre, (*Amer*) **liter** ['li:tə] *nc* a measure of (*usu* liquid) capacity: *a litre of wine*; (*attrib*) *Is that a litre bottle?* – *See also* Appendix 5.

litter[1] ['litə] **1** *nu* an untidy mess of paper, rubbish *etc*: *It is against the law to leave litter lying about in this park*; *Put all your litter in that litter-bin over there.* **2** *nu* a heap of straw *etc* for animals to lie on *etc.* **3** *nc* a number of animals born to the same mother at the same time: *a litter of kittens.* – **1** *vt* to cover (the ground *etc*) with scattered objects: *Papers littered the table.* **2** *vi* (*formal*) (of animals) to produce a number of young: *How many times a year do rabbits litter?*

litter[2] ['litə] *nc* (*hist*) a kind of bed for carrying sick people, important people, women *etc* on journeys.

little ['litl] *adj* **1** small in size: *He is only a little boy*; *a little room*; *She was beautiful when she was little* (= a child) *but she is now rather a plain young woman.* **2** small in amount; not much (emphasizing the smallness of the amount): *He has little knowledge of the difficulties involved.* – *See also* **a little** *below.* **3** (*fig*: *attrib*) not important: *I did not expect her to make such a fuss about such a little thing.* – *pron* a small quantity (of something): *Nearly all the wine had been drunk, but we finished the little that was left*; *We see little of them* (= We don't see them very often). – *See also* **a little** *below.* – *adv* (*often formal*) **1** not much: *I go out little nowadays.* **2** (*often in cmpds*) only to a small degree: *a little-known fact*; *She is little liked.* **3** not at all: *He little knows how ill he is*; *Little does he know what is going to happen.*

a little **1** a short time or distance: *Why don't you lie down for a little?*; *Move a little to the right!* **2** a small quantity of something (emphasizing that there is some): *He has a little money to spare*; *'Is there any soup left?' 'Yes, a little.'* **3** slightly or to a small degree: *She was a little frightened*; *He was teased a little about his mistake.*

little by little gradually or by degrees: *Little by little, over the months, we began to get to know him.*

make little of **1** to treat (something) as unimportant, not serious *etc*: *He made little of his injuries.* **2** not to be able to understand (much of)

(something): *I could make little of his instructions.*
think little of *see* **think**.
See also **few, less, least, small**.

liturgy ['litədʒi] *nc* (*relig*) the standard form of service of a church. **li'turgical** [-'tə:-] *adj*. **li'turgically** [-'tə:-] *adv*.

live[1] [liv] **1** *vi* (*formal*) to have life; to be alive and not lifeless or dead: *This poison is dangerous to everything that lives*; (*fig*) *It was the acting of the principal characters which made the play live.* **2** *vi* to continue to be alive; to survive: *The doctors say he is very ill, but they think he will live*; *It was difficult to believe that she had lived through such an experience.* **3** *vi* to have one's home or dwelling (in a particular place): *She lives next to the church*; *They went to live in Bristol*; *He is living in a huge house.* **4** *vti* to pass (one's life): *He lived a life of luxury*; *She lives in fear of being attacked.* **5** *vi* (*with* **by**) to make enough money *etc* to feed and house oneself: *He lives by fishing and keeping sheep.* – *See also* **live** *in phrases below.*

-lived *adj* (*in cmpds*) having (a certain type of) life: *ˌlong-'lived.*

'living *adj* **1** having life; being alive and not lifeless: *a living creature*; *The aim of the project was to discover if there was anything living on Mars.* **2** now alive: *He is considered to be our greatest living artist*; *He is the greatest artist living.* – *nc* (*no pl*) the money *etc* needed to feed and house oneself and keep oneself alive: *He earns his living driving a taxi*; *She makes a good living as an author.*

'living-room *nc* the room of a house *etc* in which the occupants of the house usually sit during their leisure time: *Our television set is in the living-room.*

living wage *nc* a wage on which a man and his family can live comfortably: *Some men cannot make a living wage even when they work overtime.*

live and let live to tolerate other people's actions and expect them to tolerate one's own: *They thought differently about most things, but worked together on a principle of live and let live.*

live by *see* **live** (*def 5*) *above.*

live down *vt sep* to continue living in a normal way until a wrong action, mistake *etc* is forgotten: *It took her a long time to live down the scandal caused by her arrest*; *She never really lived it down.*

live in, out *vi* to have one's home at or away from the place where one works: *All the hotel staff live in*; *She chose to live out and to be paid extra.*

live it up (*sl*) to live in a rather too active and expensive manner: *When he went to Paris on business he wasted the firm's money by living it up in the night clubs.*

'live on *vt fus* **1** to keep oneself alive by eating: *He lives on fish and potatoes.* **2** to be supported (financially) by: *He lives on £20 a week*; (*derog*) *She and her children live on the State.*

live out *see* **live in** *above.*

live up to *vt fus* to behave in a manner worthy of: *He found it difficult to live up to the reputation of being a hero.*

(with)in living memory within a period recent enough to be remembered by someone still alive: *It was the coldest winter in living memory.*

See also **life**.

live[2] [laiv] *adj* **1** (*attrib*) having life; not dead: *a live mouse.* **2** (of a radio or television broadcast, performance in the theatre *etc*) heard or seen as the event takes place; not recorded: *I went to see a live performance of my favourite opera*; *We watched a live current affairs programme on television*; *Was the performance live or recorded?* **3** full of energy, *esp* of electricity, and capable of becoming active: *live (telephone) wire*; *A bomb was dug up and found to be still live.* **4** (*attrib*) burning: *a live coal.* – *adv* (of a radio or television broadcast *etc*) as the event takes place: *The final stages of the competition will be broadcast live later tonight.*

'lively *adj* active and full of life, high spirits or movement: *She took a lively interest in us*; *a lively piece of music*; *a lively child*; *The music is bright and lively*; *The child is healthy and lively.* **'liveliness** *nu.*

'livestock *nu* domestic animals, *esp* horses, cattle, sheep, and pigs: *He was employed to look after the livestock on the farm.*

live wire *nc* **1** *see* **live** (*def 3*) *above.* **2** (*fig inf*) a person who is full of energy and enthusiasm: *He is very quiet, but his sister is a real live wire.*

See also **alive**.

livelihood ['laivlihud] *nc* (*usu in sing*) a means of living, *esp* of earning enough money to feed oneself *etc*: *Any change in the fishing laws will affect the livelihood of thousands of fishermen.*

liveliness, lively *see* **live**[2].

liver ['livə] *nc* **1** a large organ in the body which carries out several important functions, including purifying the blood: *He had damaged his liver through drinking too much.* **2** this organ in certain animals used as food: *We had lamb's liver for lunch.*

livery ['livəri] *nc* (*formal*) a *usu* distinctive uniform worn by menservants *etc.*

'liveried *adj* (*formal*: *esp attrib*) wearing livery: *liveried servants.*

lives *see* **life**.

livestock *see* **live**[2].

livid ['livid] *adj* **1** (*usu pred*: *formal*) white or very pale: *Her hands were livid with cold.* **2** of a bluish, lead-like colour: *There were livid bruises on her body.* **3** (*Brit inf*) very angry: *She was livid when she found it was broken!*; *in a really livid mood.* **'lividness** *nu.*

living *see* **live**[1].

lizard ['lizəd] *nc* any of several types of *usu* small, four-footed reptile.

'll *see* **will**.

lo! [lou] *interj* (*old liter*) look!: *Lo! an angel appeared.*

lo and behold (*inf*: *old or liter*) an expression indicating surprise *etc* at seeing or finding something: *We'd just started when, lo and behold, Anne appeared.*

load [loud] *nc* **1** something which is being carried: *The lorry had to stop because its load had fallen off*; *She climbed the hill slowly because she was carrying a load of groceries*; (*fig*) *She has taken on a heavy load of work this year.* **2** (*often in cmpds*) as much as can be carried at one time: *He ordered two lorry-loads of earth for his garden.* **3** (*inf*) a large amount: *Her furniture is just a load of junk*; *He talked a load of rubbish*; *We were given loads of ice-cream.* **4** the power carried by an electric circuit: *The wires were designed for a load of 15 amps.* – **1** *vti* to take or put on what is to be carried (*esp* if heavy): *They loaded the luggage into the car*; *She loaded herself with parcels*; *The lorry was still loading when they arrived.* **2** *vt* to put ammunition into (a gun): *He loaded the revolver and fired.* **3** *vt* to put film into (a camera): *The animal moved before I could load my camera to take a picture of it.*

'loaded *adj* **1** carrying a load: *a loaded van*; *Was* *the van fully loaded?* **2** (of a gun) containing ammunition: *a loaded pistol*; *Is the rifle loaded?* **3** (of a camera) containing film. **4** (*sl*: *pred*) very wealthy: *He can afford it – he's loaded!*

a loaded question *nc* a question intended to lead someone into saying, admitting or agreeing to something which he is unwilling to do: *The police kept asking him loaded questions.*

load the dice against (someone) to take away any chance a person has of succeeding at something: *The dice were loaded against him.*

See also **unload**.

loaf[1] [louf] – *pl* **loaves** [louvz] – *nc* a regularly shaped mass of bread: *They ate half a loaf between them at every meal*; *She went to the baker's for a brown loaf.*

loaf[2] [louf] *vi* (*often with* **about** *or* **around**) to pass time without doing anything in particular: *He spent the evening loafing about (the street) looking for something to do.*

'loafer *nc* **1** a person who loafs: *He is an idle loafer.* **2** (*Amer*) a lightweight shoe: *I didn't hear him coming – he was wearing loafers.*

loan [loun] *nc* **1** anything lent, *esp* money: *I shall have to ask the bank for a large loan.* **2** the act of lending: *I gave him the loan of my bicycle until tomorrow.* – *vt* (*inf*: *esp Amer*) to lend: *Can you loan me a pen?*

See also **lend**.

loath, loth [louθ] *adj* (*formal*) unwilling (to): *I am loth to spend money on such an old car.*

nothing lo(a)th (*often facet*) willing or willingly: *We had just finished tea when he arrived, but, nothing loath, we had another cup.*

loathe [louð] *vt* (*formal*) to dislike greatly; to hate very much: *I loathe that old man*; *I loathe cold rice-pudding!*

'loathing *nu* (*formal*) great dislike and disgust: *He had a loathing for deceit of any kind*; *He looked at his enemy with loathing.*

'loathsome *adj* (*liter or facet*) arousing loathing; horrible: *a loathsome insect*; *He is fat, ugly and loathsome.*

loaves *see* **loaf**[1].

lob [lob] *nc* a slow, high throw *etc* of a ball *etc.* – *v* – *pt, ptp* **lobbed** – *vt* to throw or strike (a ball *etc*) so that it moves high and slowly: *He took an apple for himself and lobbed one across the room to his brother.*

lobby ['lobi] *nc* **1** a (small) entrance-hall or passage from which several rooms open: *a hotel lobby.* **2** a group of people who try to influence the Government *etc* in a certain way or for a certain purpose: *Several MPs were approached by members of the anti-nuclear lobby.* – *vt* to try to influence (the Government *etc*): *A group of people have been lobbying Members of Parliament to draw their attention to these problems.*

lobe [loub] *nc* **1** the soft lower part of the ear: *She wore gold rings in the lobes of her ears.* **2** (*tech*) a division of the lungs, brain *etc*: *The pneumonia has affected both lobes of the lungs.*

lobster ['lobstə] **1** *nc* a type of shellfish with large claws: *He caught several lobsters.* **2** *nu* its flesh as food: *We had lobster for dinner*; (*attrib*) *lobster salad.*

local ['loukəl] *adj* (*esp attrib*) of, coming from or confined to a certain place or district: *The local shops are very good*; *local problems*; *The town is so full of visitors that local people find it difficult to park their cars.* – *nc* (*Brit inf*) **1** the local or nearest public house: *Come and have a drink in my local!* **2** (*usu in pl*) a person who lives in a certain place or district: *One of the locals showed me the way to the post office.*

locale [lə'ka:l] *nc* (*formal*) the scene (of an event): *The film-producer's choice of locale was unfortunate.*

locality [lə'kaləti] *nc* (*formal*) a district: *Public transport is a problem in this locality*; *After the scandal they moved to a locality where they were not known.*

'localize, -ise *vt* (*formal*) to restrict to a place or area: *The firemen succeeded in localizing the fire to one part of the building.*

'localized *adj*: *a localized reaction to the drug.*

'locally *adv* **1** near the place mentioned: *We can't buy bottled gas locally – we have to get it in town.* **2** in (a) certain place(s): *This development may cause problems locally, but nationally it will be an improvement.*

locate [lə'keit, (*Amer*) 'loukeit] *vt* (*formal*) **1** to set in a particular place or position: *The kitchen is located in the basement.* **2** (not *usu* used with **is, was** *etc* and **-ing**) to find the place or position of: *He located the street he was looking for on the map.*

lo'cation [-'keiʃən] (*formal*) **1** *nc* position or situation: *She asked about the location of the house.* **2** *nu* the act of locating: *His job involves the location of people in need of help.* – *See also* **on location** *below.*

local authority *nc* (*often in pl*) a group of people elected to be the local government in an area.

local colour *nu* details in a story *etc* which are characteristic of the time or place in which it is set: *His description of the harbour added a bit of local colour to an otherwise boring book.*

local government *ncu* administration of local affairs of towns, counties *etc*, as opposed to national or central government: *He is giving up local government to become a Member of Parliament.*

on location (of filming) in natural surroundings outside the studio.

loch [lox] *nc* (*often found with cap in place-names*) in Scotland, a lake, or a long narrow part of the sea closed at one end: *He fished for trout in the loch*; *They live near Loch Ness.*

lock[1] [lok] *nc* **1** a mechanism for fastening doors *etc*: *The front door has two locks on it*; *He put the key in the lock.* **2** a closed part of a canal for raising or lowering boats to a higher or lower part of the canal. **3** the part of a gun by which it is fired. **4** a tight hold (in wrestling *etc*). – *vt* **1** to fasten or become fastened with a lock: *She locked the drawer*; *This door doesn't lock.* **2** to make or become impossible to move: *The wheels locked and the car skidded*; *She locked the paper into the machine with a special bar.* – *See* **lock in, lock out, lock up** *below.*

'locker *nc* a small cupboard, *esp* for sports equipment: *His golfclubs were stolen from his locker.*

'locket [-kit] *nc* a little ornamental case hung round the neck: *She wore a gold locket containing a piece of his hair.*

'lockjaw *nu* a form of the disease tetanus which makes the muscles of the jaw stiff.

'lockout *nc* the act of locking out, *esp* used of the closing of factories *etc* by employers during a dispute with their employees. – *See also* **lock out** (*def 2*) *below.*

'locksmith *nc* a person who makes and mends locks.

'lockup *nc* a place for locking up prisoners, motor cars *etc*: *He spent the night in the lockup at the police station*; *We don't have a garage attached to our house but we rent a lockup*; (*attrib*) *a lockup garage*. – *See also* **lock up** *below*.

lock in *vt usu sep* to prevent from getting out of a building *etc* by using a lock: *She found someone had locked her in, and had to climb out of the window.*

lock out *vt usu sep* **1** to prevent from getting into a building *etc* by using a lock: *It is easy to lock yourself out (of the house) if you forget your key.* **2** to prevent (employees) from entering a factory *etc* during an industrial dispute: *The steelworkers have been locked out.*

lock, stock and barrel completely or with all the various parts included: *They moved the business lock, stock and barrel to a new office.*

lock up 1 *vt sep* to confine or prevent from leaving or being taken away by using a lock: *She locks up the silver in a safe after using it*; *She locked it up.* **2** *vi* to lock whatever should be locked: *He always locks up before leaving the shop in the evening.* **3** *vt sep* to lock very securely: *He locked up the front door and went to bed*; *He locked it up every night.*

See also **unlock**.

lock[2] [lok] *nc* (*old or formal*) a section of hair: *She cut off a lock of his hair.*

locomotive [loukə'moutiv] *nc* (*formal or tech*) a railway engine – *adj* (*formal*) capable of, or helping in, movement from place to place.

ˌloco'motion [-'mouʃən] *nu* (*formal*) the act of moving from place to place.

locum ['loukəm] *nc* a person who takes the place of another (*esp* a doctor, dentist *etc*) for a time: *My own doctor is on holiday but his locum treated my sore hand.*

locust ['loukəst] *nc* a type of large insect of the grasshopper family, found in Africa and Asia, which moves in very large groups and destroys growing crops by eating them.

lode [loud] *nc* a thin band or strip of rock which contains metal, running through other rock.

lodge [lodʒ] *nc* **1** a small house, *esp* one at a gate to the grounds of a large house: *They live in the lodge at the West Gate.* **2** (*sometimes in cmpds*) a house occupied during the shooting or hunting season: *a shooting-lodge.* **3** a room at a college gate *etc* for an attendant: *the porter's lodge.* **4** (the meeting-place of) a branch of some societies: *He belonged to the local lodge of the Orange Order.* – **1** *vi* to live in rooms for which one pays, in someone else's house: *He lodges with the Smiths.* **2** *vti* (*formal*) (*usu with* **in**) to make or become fixed (in): *The bullet lodged in his spine*; *It was too firmly lodged to be moved.* **3** *vt* (*formal*) to make formally or officially: *He lodged an appeal against the sentence*; *It is too late to lodge any objections.*

'lodger *nc* a person who lives in a room or rooms, for which he pays, in someone else's house: *She rented a room to a lodger to make a little extra money.*

'lodging 1 *nc* (*often in pl*) a room or rooms hired in someone else's house: *She lives in lodgings in the town.* **2** *nu* a place to stay: *He paid the landlady for board and lodging.*

See also **dislodge**.

loft [loft] *nc* **1** a room or space under a roof: *They keep a lot of spare furniture in the loft.* **2** *a gallery in a hall or church*: *the organ-loft.*

'lofty *adj* **1** (*attrib*: *liter or formal*) very high: *a lofty building*; (*fig*) *He has a lofty position in the firm.* **2** (*formal*) very impressive and admirable (because very good): *lofty phrases*; *lofty sentiments*; *Those sentiments are lofty but not very realistic.* **3** (*derog*: *attrib*) haughty or proud: *She had a lofty disregard for other people's feelings.* **'loftily** *adv.* **'loftiness** *nu.*

log [log] *nc* **1** a thick piece of unshaped wood: *The trees were sawn into logs and taken to the sawmill.* **2** a logbook: *The captain of the ship entered the details in the log.* – *v* – *pt, ptp* logged – *vt* to write down or record in a logbook (*esp* the distance covered during a journey): *He logged 800 miles in the first ten days at sea.*

'logbook *nc* an official record of the journey of a ship or aeroplane: *All the details of the flight were entered in the logbook.*

sleep like a log *see* **sleep**.

logarithm ['logəriðəm] *nc* (*sometimes abbrev* **log** [log]) the number of times a base (*usu* 10) must be multiplied by itself to produce a particular number (*eg* 3 is the logarithm of 1000 to the base 10 because 10^3 or $10\times10\times10=1000$): *Logarithms are used to make complicated mathematical calculations easier.*

loggerheads ['logəhedz]: **at 'loggerheads** (*formal*) quarrelling: *We have been at loggerheads with the neighbours for years.*

logic ['lodʒik] *nu* **1** the study and art of reasoning correctly: *She studies philosophy and logic at University.* **2** correctness of reasoning: *I found it difficult to follow the logic of his argument.*

'logical *adj* (thinking or acting) according to the rules of logic or correct reasoning: *The logical result of her action would be an increase in sales*; *It is logical to assume that you will get a higher salary if you are promoted*; *He is not a logical person*; *She is always very logical in her thinking.* **'logically** *adv.*

See also **illogical**.

loin [loin] *ncu* the back of an animal when cut into pieces for food: *loin of lamb.*

loins *n pl* (*usu old*: *liter or facet*) the lower part of the back.

'loincloth *nc* a piece of cloth worn round the hips, *esp* in India and south-east Asia.

gird up one's loins (*arch or facet*) to prepare for energetic action.

loiter ['loitə] *vi* (*formal*) to proceed, work *etc* slowly or to stand doing nothing in particular: *They were loitering outside the shop as if waiting for someone*; *He was accused of loitering beside the car with intent to steal it.*

loll [lol] *vi* **1** (*often with* **about**) to lie lazily (about): *Several bored-looking people were lolling in chairs*; *In this heat all I want to do is loll about all day.* **2** (of the tongue) to hang down or out: *The dog lay down, his tongue lolling to one side.*

lollipop ['lolipop] *nc* a large, *usu* round, flat sweet on a stick: *The little girl was sucking an orange lollipop.*

lolly ['loli] **1** *nc* (*inf*) a lollipop, or a similar type of sweet made of ice-cream etc: *an ice-lolly.* **2** *nu* (*facet sl*) money: *It's an awful job, but it gives me lots of lovely lolly!*

lone [loun] *adj* (*attrib*: *formal or liter*) solitary, without companions, by itself *etc*: *She could see a lone figure on the deserted beach.*

'lonely *adj* **1** lacking or wanting companionship: *Aren't you lonely, living by yourself?*; *She was a lonely child, without friends.* **2** (of a place) far away from busy places, having few people: *a lonely island*; *Their country cottage is a bit lonely.* 'loneliness *nu.*

'**loner** *nc* (*inf*) a person who prefers to be alone and do things by himself: *She's always been a bit of a loner.*

'**lonesome** *adj* (*esp Amer*) (causing one to be) sad or miserable because of being by oneself: *The child feels rather lonesome when her brothers are at school*; *rather a lonesome feeling.* '**lonesomeness** *nu.*

lone wolf *nc* a person who prefers to be by himself, without companions: *I am rather a lone wolf – I like to go on holiday by myself.*

See also **alone**.

long[1] [loŋ] *adj* **1** not short; measuring a great distance from one end to the other: *I am going on a long journey*; *a long road*; *She has very long legs*; *The arms of this sweater are too long*; *This coat is not long enough for me.* **2** having a great period of time from the first moment to the last: *The book took a long time to read*; *We had a long conversation*; *His speech was long and boring*; *There was a long delay before the plane took off.* **3** measuring a certain amount in distance or time: *The wire is two centimetres long*; *The television programme was just over an hour long.* **4** (*fig*: *esp attrib*) seeming to measure a greater distance (in space or time) from one end to the other than usual: *Due to the bad weather, it was a very long three miles into town*; *It's been a very long day.* **5** (*pred*) away, doing or using something *etc* for a great period of time: *Will you be long?* **6** (*usu attrib*) reaching to a great distance in space or time: *She has a long memory* (= She can remember events that happened a long time ago). **7** (*formal or tech*: *esp attrib*) greater in value, amount *etc* than the usual: *a long ton.* – *adv* **1** a great period of time: *This happened long before you were born.* **2** (*formal*, except when placed at or near the end of a sentence after a verb like **wait, stand** *etc*) for a great period of time: *Have you been waiting long?*; *He had long wanted to write a book.*

'**longways** *adv* in the direction of the length: *The planks had to go into the lorry longways.*

ˌ**long-'distance** *adj* (*attrib*) covering, travelling *etc* a long distance of time: *He runs in long-distance races*; *He is a long-distance lorry-driver.*

ˌ**long-drawn-'out** *adj* taking a needlessly long time: *They are always having long-drawn-out discussions about simple problems*; *These talks seem rather long-drawn-out.*

'**longhand** *nu* ordinary writing as opposed to shorthand: *She writes longhand but she writes very quickly.*

long haul *nc* **1** (*formal or tech*) the carrying of cargo over a long distance. **2** (*fig*) any difficult or heavy work which goes on for a long time: *It was a long haul to build up our business again after the loss of so much money.*

long johns *n pl* (*inf*) long, warm underwear for the lower part of the body, *usu* for men.

long jump *see* **the long jump** *below.*

long odds *n pl* (in betting) odds showing that the person betting is not expected to win: *The bookie gave me such long odds that I'm sure the horse I bet on will come in last.*

ˌ**long-playing 'record** *nc* (*usu abbrev* **LP**) a gramophone record which plays for a long time.

ˌ**long-'range** *adj* (*attrib*) **1** able to reach a great distance: *long-range rockets.* **2** taking into consideration a long period of time: *a long-range weather forecast.*

'**long shot** *nc* (*inf*) a guess, attempt *etc* unlikely to be right or succeed, but worth trying: *Guessing he would stay at home was a long shot, but it paid off!*

ˌ**long-'sighted** *adj* **1** (*esp pred*) able to see things far away, but not things close at hand: *She is long-sighted and wears glasses for reading.* **2** having or showing the ability to guess what is going to happen in the future: *a long-sighted decision*; *It was long-sighted of you to buy a house for your retirement so soon.* ˌ**long-'sightedness** *nu.*

'**long-standing** *adj* (*attrib*) having existed or continued for a long time: *We had a long-standing invitation to visit his house, but had never gone*; *a long-standing argument.*

ˌ**long-'suffering** *adj* patiently enduring a great deal of trouble: *It was yet another problem which his long-suffering wife had to accept*; *She is so long-suffering that she never scolds those naughty children.*

ˌ**long-'term** *adj* (*esp attrib*) (of a plan *etc*) concerned with the future, not just with the present: *long-term plans.*

long wave *see* **wave(band)** *under* **wave.**

ˌ**long-'winded** *adj* (*derog*) (of a speaker or his speech) tiresomely long: *I haven't time to listen to long-winded explanations!*; *The speaker was so long-winded.*

as 'long as/so 'long as 1 provided only that: *You'll get there in time, so long as you don't miss the bus*; *As long as you're happy, it doesn't matter what you do.* **2** while; during the time that: *As long as he's here I'll have more work to do.*

before (very) long soon: *Come in and wait – he'll be here before long!*; *Before (very) long, they could see that the approaching car was green, not blue.*

in the 'long run in the end: *We thought we would save money, but in the long run our spending was about the same as usual.*

the 'long jump a sports contest in which people jump as great a distance as possible across *usu* a stretch of sand: *He entered for the high jump and the long jump.*

the ˌlong and the 'short of it (*inf*) the story, *etc* told in a few words: *I made a mistake, and that's the long and the short of it!*

no longer not now as in the past: *This cinema is no longer used to show films – it is now a bingo hall.*

so long! (*inf*) goodbye!

so long as *see* **as long as** *above.*

See also **short**.

long[2] [loŋ] *vti* (*often with* **for**) to wish very much: *He longed to go home*; *I am just longing to hear from you*; *She longed for it to be time for lunch*; *I am longing for a drink*; *They longed for a chance to speak.*

'**longing** *ncu* a great desire or wish (for something): *He could not express his longing for peace*; *She looked at the cream cakes with longing, but did not eat any.*

'**longingly** *adv*: *She looked at the cream cakes longingly.*

longevity [lon'dʒevəti] *nu* (*formal*) great length of life: *That whole family are noted for their longevity.*

longitude ['loŋgitju:d] *nu* the distance, measured in degrees on the map, that a place is east or west of a standard north-south line, *usu* that which passes through Greenwich: *What is the latitude and longitude of that town?* ˌ**longi'tudinal** *adj.* ˌ**longi'tudinally** *adv.*

See also **latitude**.

loo [lu:] *nc* (*Brit: inf euph*) a lavatory: *She's gone to the loo.*

look [luk] *vi* **1** to turn the eyes in a certain direction so as to see or to try to find something: *Look over there!*; *He looked out of the window*; *I've looked everywhere, but he's disappeared*; *She looked at me and smiled*; *He looked carefully at the book.* **2** to seem *esp* because having a certain appearance to the eyes: *It looks as if it's going to rain*; *The car looks all right, but it doesn't work*; *She looks sad today*; *She doesn't want to look stupid*; *Things don't look too good – business is bad.* **3** (*fig*) to face: *The house looks west.* – **1** *nc* the act of looking or seeing: *Let me have a look!*; *Take a look at that!* **2** *nc* a glance: *a look of surprise.* **3** *nu* appearance: *The house had a look of neglect.* – *See also* **looks, by the look(s) of, have a look of** *below.*

-looking (*in cmpds*) having a (certain kind of) appearance: *good-looking*; *strange-looking.*

looks *n pl* (*inf*) (attractive) appearance: *She used to be very beautiful but she completely lost her looks as she grew older*; *She was noted for her good looks at school.* – *See also* **by the look(s) of** *below.*

ˌlooker-ˈon *nc* a person who is watching something but not taking part: *After the accident the lookers-on were sent away by the police.* – *See also* **look on** *below, and* **onlooker**.

look-in *see* **not to get/have a look-in** *below.*

ˈlooking-glass *nc* (*old or formal*) a mirror.

ˈlookout *nc* **1** (*no pl*) a careful watch: *She kept a sharp lookout from the window to make sure no-one was coming*; (*attrib*) *a lookout post.* **2** a place from which such a watch can be kept: *They used the tower as a lookout.* **3** a person who has been given the job of watching: *There was a shout from the lookout at the top of the hill.* **4** (*fig inf*) a concern or a subject to be dealt with (by a particular person *etc*): *If he catches you leaving, I'm afraid that's your lookout!* – *See also* **look out** *below.*

by the look(s) of judging from the appearance of (someone or something) it seems likely or probable: *By the looks of him, he won't live much longer*; *By the looks of that house it is no longer occupied*; *We won't get there on time by the look of it*; *It's going to rain by the look of it.*

have a look of (*inf*) to look like; to resemble: *She has a look of her mother.*

look after *vt fus* to attend to or take care of: *She is paid to look after the children*; *The secretary looks after all the complaints we receive.*

look ahead *vi* (*often with* **to**) to consider what will happen at some time in the future: *Let's look ahead to next month and consider what to do then.*

look at *see* **look** (*def 1*).

look down one's nose at (*inf*) to think of with contempt: *She looks down her nose at my cooking*; *His mother looks down her nose at his wife.*

look down on *vt fus* to think of (someone or something) as being inferior: *She has always looked down on us for not having a car.*

ˈlook for *vt fus* **1** to search for: *She lost her handbag and wasted ten minutes looking for it.* **2** to expect: *He is always looking for praise.*

look forward to *vt fus* to wait with pleasure for (something which is going to happen): *I am looking forward to seeing you*; *She is looking forward to the Christmas holidays.*

look here! (*inf*) give your attention to this (*esp* to what I am saying): *Look here! Isn't that what you wanted?*; *Look here, Mary, I won't have you saying things like that!*

ˌlook ˈin on *vt fus* to visit briefly and without invitation: *I decided to look in on Paul and Carol on my way home.*

ˈlook into *vt fus* to inspect or investigate closely: *I shall look into the possibility of buying a house*; *The manager is going to look into your complaint.*

look like *see* **like**.

look on[1] *vi* to watch something without taking part: *No, I don't want to play – I'd rather look on.*

ˈlook on[2] *vt fus* (*with* **as**) to think of or consider: *I have lived with my aunt since I was a baby, and I look on her as my mother*; *She looked on his behaviour as a grave mistake.*

look out 1 *vi* (*usu with* **for**) to watch: *She was looking out for him and saw him long before he saw her.* **2** *vt sep* to find by searching or choose: *I've looked out a couple of books I think might be useful to you*; *I must look out my winter clothes if the weather's going to be cold.* – *See also* **lookout** *above.*

look out! (*interj*) beware! take care!

look over *vt sep* to examine, but not with great care: *We have been looking over the new house*; *You have looked over it already.*

look sharp *see* **sharp**.

look through *vt fus* to look at or study (a book, papers *etc*) *usu* briefly: *I've looked through your report and made some notes on it.*

look up 1 *vi* (*inf*) to improve or become better: *Things have been looking up lately and most of my worries have disappeared.* **2** *vt sep* (*inf*) to pay a visit to (a person): *I hadn't seen them for months so I thought it was time I looked them up*; *We looked up several old friends.* **3** *vt sep* to search for in a book of reference: *You should look the word up* (*in a dictionary*). **4** *vt sep* to consult (a reference book): *I looked up the encyclopedia and it doesn't mention him*; *I looked it up twice.*

look up to *vt fus* to respect the conduct, opinions *etc* of: *He has always looked up to his father.*

not to ˌget/ˌhave a ˈlook-in (*inf*) not to have any attention paid to one: *As soon as the blonde appeared none of the other girls got a look-in*; *She is so beautiful that no-one else has a look-in when she's here.*

See also **outlook, overlook, unlooked-for**.

loom[1] [lu:m] *nc* a machine in which thread is woven into a fabric.

loom[2] [lu:m] *vi* (*often with* **up**) to appear indistinctly, often threateningly: *The shape of a huge ship loomed* (*up*) *through the fog*; (*fig*) *The date for my exams is looming.*

loony [ˈlu:ni] (*offensive*) short for **lunatic**.

loop [lu:p] *nc* **1** a doubled-over part of a piece of rope, chain *etc*: *She made a loop in the string and put it over the door-handle.* **2** a U-shaped bend in a river *etc.* – *vt* to fasten with, or form into, a loop or loops: *He looped the rope round a post.*

loop the loop (of aeroplanes *etc*) to move in a complete vertical loop or circle: *At the air display the pilots kept looping the loop.*

loophole [ˈlu:phoul] *nc* (*fig*) a means of escape or of avoiding obeying the law *etc*: *The new Act of Parliament is badly drawn-up and full of loopholes.*

loose [lu:s] *adj* **1** not tight; not firmly stretched: *She wore a long, loose coat*; *This belt is rather loose.* **2** not firmly fixed: *a loose knot*; *The buttons on my coat are loose.* **3** not tied; free: *He left the end of the rope hanging loose*; *He told us that the horses were loose in the field*; *the loose end of the rope.* **4** not (closely) packed: *He refused to sell us loose nails and we had to buy a box of 100; I don't want the sweets in a box – I want them loose.* **5** vague or not exact: *There had been a loose agreement about who should pay for what; The contract was rather loose.* **6** (*attrib*) careless, bad or not approved of; immoral: *a loose woman; loose morals.* – *vt* (*formal*) to unfasten or untie.

'loosely *adv.* **'looseness** *nu.*

'loosen *vti* **1** to make or become loose: *She loosened the ribbon round the box; The screw had loosened and fallen out.* **2** to relax (*eg* a hold): *He loosened his grip; His grip on the rope loosened.*

ˌloose-'leaf *adj* (*esp attrib*) having a cover made in such a way that pages can be easily added or removed: *a loose-leaf notebook.*

at a loose end *see* **end**.

break loose to escape: *The prisoner broke loose from his guards and ran away.*

let loose to make free from control: *Don't let the dogs loose; The circus trainer has let the lions loose.*

See also **unloose**.

loot [lu:t] *nu* something which is stolen: *The thieves got away with a lot of loot.* – *vti* to rob or steal from (a place), often in a violent and destructive manner: *The soldiers looted the shops of the captured town.*

lop [lop] – *pt, ptp* **lopped** – *vt* to cut off parts from *eg* the top or ends of a tree: *We lopped several branches from the tree;* (*fig inf*) *Could you lop a few pounds off the price?*

lope [loup] *vi* (*formal*) to run with long steps: *The big dog loped across the garden and out of the gate.*

loquacious [lə'kweiʃəs] *adj* (*formal*) talking a lot: *a loquacious old lady; She is so loquacious that she bores everyone.* **lo'quaciousness, loquacity** [-'kwa-] *nus.*

lord [lo:d] *nc* **1** a master; a man or animal that has power over others or over an area: *The Lord of the Manor; The lion is lord of the jungle.* **2** (*sometimes with cap*) in the UK *etc* a nobleman or man of rank: *He has just been made a lord; the House of Lords.* **3** (*with cap*) in the UK *etc* the title of all noblemen up to the rank of marquis: *Lord Jones is a baron, but Lord Ashworth is an earl.* **4** (*with cap*) in the UK, used as part of several official titles: *the Lord Mayor.*

'lordly *adj* (*often derog*) like a lord, *esp* dignified, grand or proud: *He is so proud and lordly that he does not speak to his employees; He has a lordly attitude to his wife and family.* **'lordliness** *nu.*

'Lordship *n* (*with* **His, Your** *etc*) a word used in speaking to, or about, a man with the title 'Lord' and also certain judges who do not have this title: *I would be grateful if your Lordship would accept the invitation; His Lordship the Earl of Carrick.*

the Lord God; Christ.

the Lord's Day (*formal or old*) Sunday.

the (House of) Lords the upper (non-elected) house of the British parliament: *The Lords has not passed the House of Commons' latest bill.*

'lord it over (*inf*) to act like a lord, or like a master, towards: *He thinks he knows enough to lord it over everyone else here.*

lore [lo:] *nu* (*formal or old*) the whole body of knowledge (*esp* knowledge handed down by word of mouth) on a subject: *the lore of the sea;* (*in cmpds*) *folklore.*

lorry ['lori] *nc* (*Amer* **truck**) a motor vehicle for carrying heavy loads: *He has a licence to drive a lorry; a coal-lorry;* (*attrib*) *a lorry-driver; We could deliver it by lorry.*

lose [lu:z] – *pt, ptp* **lost** [lost] – **1** *vt* to stop having; to have no longer: *She has lost interest in her work; I have lost my watch; He lost hold of the rope and vanished.* **2** *vt* to have taken away from one (by death, accident *etc*): *She lost her father last year; The ship was lost in the storm; He has lost his job.* **3** *vt* to put (something) where it cannot be found: *My secretary has lost your letter.* **4** *vti* not to win (a game, competition *etc*): *I always lose at cards; She lost the race.* **5** *vt* to waste or use more (time) than is necessary: *He lost no time in informing the police of the crime.* **6** *vi* to be in a worse position as the result of an event *etc*: *Whatever happens, you can't lose.* **7** *vt* to cause (someone) to no longer have (something) or not to get (something): *His stupidity lost him his job.*

'loser *nc* a person who loses: *The losers congratulated the winners.* – *See also* **a bad/good loser** *below.*

loss [los] **1** *ncu* the act or fact of losing: *She was upset at the loss of her memory/job; The loss* (= death) *of our friend was a great blow to us.* **2** *nc* something which is lost: *It was only after he was dead that we realized what a loss he was.* **3** *nc* the amount (*esp* of money) which is lost: *a loss of £500; Their losses were enormous.*

lost *adj* **1** missing; no longer to be found: *a lost ticket; I think the book is lost.* **2** not won: *a lost game; The game is lost.* **3** wasted; not used properly: *a lost opportunity; Once an opportunity is lost it will not occur again.* **4** (*attrib*) ruined or destroyed: *a lost soul.* **5** (*pred*) no longer knowing where one is, or in which direction to go: *I don't know whether to turn left or right – I'm lost.*

lost cause *nc* an aim, ideal *etc* that cannot be achieved: *Trying to ban violence on television is a lost cause nowadays.*

at a 'loss not knowing what to do, say *etc*: *He was at a loss for words to express his disappointment.*

a bad, good loser someone who behaves badly or well when they lose a game *etc.*

cut one's losses *see* **cut**.

get lost 1 to become lost (*defs 1 and 5*). **2** *interj* (*inf*) a rude way of saying 'go away!'.

lose one's cool *see* **cool**.

lose face *see* **face**.

lose ground *see* **ground**.

lose one's head *see* **head**.

lose oneself in to have all one's attention taken up by: *to lose oneself in a book.*

lose one's memory to stop being able to remember things.

lose out *vi* to suffer loss or be at a disadvantage: *She lost out by being ill and missing the party.*

lose one's rag *see* **rag**[3].

lose one's temper *see* **temper**.

lose one's voice *see* **voice**.

lose one's way *see* **way**.

'lost in having one's attention wholly taken up by: *She was lost in thought.*

'lost on wasted, or having no effect, on (a person): *She has no sense of humour and his jokes are lost on her.*

'lost to (*formal*) **1** no longer, or not, feeling in a certain way *etc*: *She was lost to all sense of shame.* **2** no longer belonging to, or (of *eg* opportunity) open to (a person): *He saw that the children were lost to him.*

lot [lot] *nc* **1** (*formal*) a person's fortune or fate: *It* *seemed to be her lot to be unhappy.* 2 a separate part: *She gave one lot of clothes to a jumble sale and sold another lot to a rag merchant.* 3 one article or several, sold as a single item at an auction: *Are you going to bid for lot 28?*

lots *n pl* (*more informal than* **many** *or* **much**) a large quantity or number: *There were lots of people there*; *She had lots and lots of food left over from the party*; *I've got very little money, but he has lots.*

a lot (*more informal than* **many** *or* **much**) a large quantity or number: *What a lot of letters!*; *There was a lot of dust in the air.*

draw/cast lots *see* **draw**.

loth *see* **loath**.

lotion ['louʃən] *ncu* a liquid for soothing or cleaning the skin: *hand-lotion*; *The doctor gave me some lotion to put on the child's rash.*

lottery ['lotəri] *nc* the sharing out of money or prizes won by chance, through drawing lots: *They held a public lottery in aid of charity.*

loud [laud] *adj* 1 making a great sound; not quiet: *She has a loud voice*; *loud music*; *a loud cry*; *That music is too loud*; *The cry was loud enough for all to hear.* 2 (*inf*) showy and too brightly coloured: *He was wearing a very loud shirt*; *That dress is too loud to wear to work.* – *adv* in such a way as to make a great sound: *He plays his record-player unbearably loud.*

'loudly *adv*. **'loudness** *nu*.

,loud-'hailer *nc* a simple type of loudspeaker: *The police used a loud-hailer to tell the crowd to get back.*

,loud-'mouthed *adj* (*derog*) talking loudly, and *usu* boasting, in an irritating or unpleasant manner: *He is nothing but a loud-mouthed bully*; *He's hated in the office – he's so loud-mouthed.*

,loud'speaker *nc* 1 an instrument for increasing the loudness of sounds so that they can be heard further away: *The politician addressed the crowds from his car through a loudspeaker.* 2 a speaker (*def 3*).

lounge [laundʒ] *vi* 1 to lie back in a casual manner: *He was found lounging on a sofa looking bored.* 2 to move about lazily; to be inactive: *I spent the day lounging about the house.* – *nc* (*more formal than* **sitting-room**) a room in a house, hotel *etc* where the occupants sit in their leisure hours: *We'll have coffee in the lounge*; (*attrib*) *We'll have some sherry in the lounge bar* (= a bar in a hotel *etc* with comfortable seats *etc*); *They watched television in the hotel lounge.*

lounge suit *nc* (*Brit*) a man's suit for ordinary, everyday (but not casual) wear: *There is no need to wear a dinner jacket this evening – a lounge suit will do.*

lour *see* **lower**[1].

louse [laus] – *pl* **lice** [lais] – *nc* a type of wingless, blood-sucking insect, sometimes found on the bodies of animals and people: *That child has lice in her hair.*

See also **lousy**.

lousy ['lauzi] *adj* 1 (*sl*) of very poor quality; worthy of contempt: *What lousy weather!*; *I told him I didn't want his lousy job!*; *It was a nice hotel, but the food was lousy.* 2 (*inf*) having lice: *That child is lousy.*

'lousiness *nu*.

lout [laut] *nc* (*derog*) a clumsy, often ill-mannered boy or man: *My brother is a lout – he smashed my spectacles by sitting on them.*

'loutish *adj*.

love [lʌv] 1 *nu* great fondness or feeling caused by a person or thing that gives one delight: *She has a great love of music*; *Her love for her children made her stay with her husband.* 2 *nu* strong attachment with sexual attraction: *They have been in love with one another for months.* 3 *nc* a person or thing that is thought of with (great) fondness (used also as a term of affection): *Climbing is one of the loves of his life*; *Mary, my love, are you ready to leave?*; *Are you ready, love?* 4 *nu* a score of nothing in tennis: *The present score is fifteen love* (written 15–0). – *vt* (not *usu* used with **is, was** *etc* and **-ing**) 1 to be (very) fond of: *She loves her children dearly*; *She no longer loves her husband.* 2 to take pleasure in: *They both love dancing.*

'lovable *adj* (*neg* **un-**) making a person (want to) love him, it *etc*; attractive: *a lovable child*; *The new baby is so lovable.*

'loveless *adj* (*esp attrib*) without love: *a loveless marriage.*

'lovely *adj* 1 (*neg* **un-**) causing love or admiration; beautiful: *She is a lovely girl*; *She looked lovely in that dress.* 2 (*loosely*: *inf*) delightful in any way: *Someone told me a lovely joke last night, but I can't remember it*; *That was a lovely meal*; *I didn't like the meat but the dessert was lovely.* **'loveliness** *nu*.

'lover *nc* 1 (*often in cmpds*) a person who enjoys (doing something) or admires (something): *She is an art-lover*; *He is a lover of sport.* 2 (*often in cmpds*) a person who loves (someone or something): *a home-lover*; *a lover of children/animals.* 3 (*in sing usu* a man) a person who has a close sexual relationship with another, *usu* (except *liter* or *old*) a partner in sexual intercourse: *They became lovers while on holiday in France*; *He was generally believed to be her lover.*

'loving *adj*. **'lovingly** *adv*.

'love affair *nc* a (temporary and often sexual) relationship between two people who are in love but not married: *He is having a love affair with his secretary.*

'love-letter *nc* a letter expressing love: *When he was in the army she wrote love-letters to him every day.*

'lovelorn [-lo:n] *adj* (*formal or liter*) having been abandoned by a person with whom one was in love: *a lovelorn young girl*; *She is sad and lovelorn.*

'love-match *nc* a marriage for love: *Her parents tried to make her marry a wealthy old man but in the end she married a handsome young man whom she loved dearly – it was a real love match.*

'lovesick *adj* (*formal*) sad because of being in love: *He kept giving her lovesick glances*; *The office boy is sad and lovesick because he is in love with one of the typists who never looks at him.*

fall in love (with) to develop feelings of love and sexual attraction (for): *They met at a party and immediately fell in love*; *He fell in love with the manager's daughter.*

for love or money (*in neg*) in any way at all: *We couldn't get a taxi for love or money.*

in 'love (with) feeling love and desire (for): *She has been in love with him for years.*

make love 1 (*euph*) to have sexual intercourse: *She became pregnant after making love with her boyfriend.* 2 (*liter or old*) to kiss and embrace as if in love; to show affection for: *He made love to her frequently but did not wish to marry her.*

there's no love lost between them they dislike one another.

low[1] [lou] *adj* 1 not at or reaching up to a great distance from the ground, sea-level *etc*: *low hills*;

This cottage has rather a low roof; This chair is too low for the child – she cannot reach the table. **2** making little sound; not loud: *She said something to the child in a low voice; Her voice was low and rather indistinct.* **3** at the bottom of the range of musical sounds: *the low notes of a tuba; That note is too low for a female voice.* **4** small: *a low price; These prices seem rather low.* **5** not strong; weak or feeble: *She cooked the soup over a low heat; The fire is too low now – it's not giving out any heat.* **6** not important in society: *a man of low rank/birth.* **7** depressed or unhappy: *After they had gone she felt very low and discouraged; in rather a low mood.* **8** morally bad, indecent or vulgar: *He thinks her taste is very low; low humour; low tastes. – See also* **be low on** *below.* – *adv* in or to a low position, manner or state: *The ball flew low over the net; He turned the music down low.* – *nc* (*inf*) a low point: *Our firm's morale has reached a new low.*

'lower 1 *vti* to make or become less high: *She lowered her voice.* **2** *vt* to let down: *He lowered the blinds.*

'lowly *adj* **1** (*formal or facet*) having little rank: *He had a lowly position in the firm; I am too lowly in this firm for anyone to ask my opinion.* **2** (*liter*) modest and not proud: *She is modest and lowly; a lowly manner.* **'lowliness** *nu.*

'low-down *adj* (*inf: attrib*) mean and worthy of contempt: *He is a dirty, low-down thief! – See also* **the low-down on** *below.*

lower case *see* **case**.

lower class *nc* (*usu with* **the**: *sometimes in pl*), *adj* (*sometimes derog*) the least skilled and educated and *usu* the poorest part of a community: *members of the lower class; His tastes are rather lower-class; lower-class housing.*

lower house *nc* (*sometimes with caps*) the larger and more representative part of a parliament that has two parts: *The House of Commons is the lower house of the British parliament.*

'lowland *adj* (*attrib*) of or concerning lowlands: *lowland districts.*

'lowlander *nc* a person who lives in the lowlands.

'lowlands *n pl* land which is low compared with other, higher land: *There is much good farming land in the lowlands beyond the hills.*

ˌlow-'pressure *adj* (of steam, steam-engine) using or creating little pressure.

ˌlow-'spirited *adj* sad; not lively.

low tide/water time when the sea is lowest at a particular place during ebb-tide: *There is three feet of water in the harbour, even at low water.*

be 'low on (*inf*) not to have much or enough of: *I'll have to go to the supermarket – we're low on coffee and sugar; We have enough salesmen but we're low on secretaries in this firm.*

lay/lie low *see* **lay**[1], **lie**[2].

the 'Low Countries Holland and Belgium.

the 'low-down on (*sl: esp Amer*) information, *esp* damaging, about (a person, organization or activity).

low gear *see* **gear**.

low[2] [lou] *vi* (*formal or liter*) to make the noise of cattle: to moo: *The cows were lowing in the field.*

lower[1], **lour** ['lauə] *vi* (*liter*) (of the sky *etc*) to become dark or threatening. **'lowering** *adj.*

lower[2] *see* **low**[1].

loyal ['loiəl] *adj* faithful: *She was a loyal friend; She has remained loyal to him throughout his misfortune.* **'loyally** *adv.* **'loyalty** *ncu.*

'loyalist *nc* (*esp hist*) a person who is loyal to his king or queen.

See also **disloyal**.

lozenge ['lozindʒ] *nc* a small sweet for sucking: *peppermint lozenges.*

lubricate ['lu:brikeit] *vt* (*formal or tech*) to oil (a machine *etc*) to make it move more easily and smoothly. **ˌlubri'cation** *nu.*

'lubricant *nc* (*formal*) something (oil *etc*) which lubricates.

lucid ['lu:sid] *adj* (*more formal than* **clear**) **1** easily understood: *He had a lucid style of writing; Her prose is clear and lucid.* **2** (of a person's mind) clear and not confused: *He was still ill in the morning, but his mind was lucid and he was able to talk; a remarkably lucid old lady.* **'lucidly** *adv.* **lu'cidity** *nu.*

luck [lʌk] *nu* **1** the state of happening by chance: *Whether you win or not is just luck – there's no skill involved.* **2** something good which happens by chance: *She has all the luck!*

'luckless *adj* (*liter: attrib*) unfortunate: *luckless children.*

'lucky *adj* **1** having good luck: *He was very lucky to escape from the accident alive; She is a lucky child to have such kind parents.* **2** bringing good luck (to the owner *etc*): *a lucky number; a lucky charm; This was not my lucky day; That number wasn't lucky for me.* **'luckily** *adv.* **'luckiness** *nu.*

lucky dip *nc* a form of amusement at a fair *etc* in which prizes are drawn from a container without one seeing what one is getting: *They made a lot of money from the lucky dip at the jumble sale.*

bad luck! an expression of sympathy for someone who has failed in something or has been unlucky: *Bad luck! You tried very hard!*

down on one's luck (*formal or liter*) experiencing misfortune: *He used to be wealthy but he's down on his luck now.*

good luck! an expression of encouragement made to someone who is about to take part in a competition, sit an exam *etc*: *He came round the night before her exam to say good luck; She wished him good luck.*

push one's luck (*inf*) to risk complete failure by trying to gain too much when one has already been reasonably successful: *I think he's pushing his luck to ask for another day off this week.*

strike lucky *see* **strike**.

worse luck! (*inf*) most unfortunately!: *He's allowing me to go, but he's coming too, worse luck!*

See also **unlucky**.

lucrative ['lu:krətiv] *adj* (*formal*) producing a large amount of money: *Dealing in scrap-metal is a very lucrative occupation; Selling second-hand cars can be very lucrative.* **'lucratively** *adv.*

ludicrous ['lu:dikrəs] *adj* (*formal*) completely ridiculous: *It is ludicrous to suggest that we can finish in time; What a ludicrous idea!* **'ludicrously** *adv.* **'ludicrousness** *nu.*

ludo ['lu:dou] *nu* a game played (*usu* by children) with counters on a board: *The children are playing ludo; Let's have a game of ludo.*

lug [lʌg] – *pt, ptp* **lugged** – *vt* (*often inf*) to pull or drag with difficulty: *She lugged the heavy trunk out of the cupboard.*

luggage ['lʌgidʒ] *nu* the suitcases, trunks *etc* of a traveller: *He carried her luggage to the train; (attrib) a luggage compartment.*

lugubrious [lə'gu:briəs] *adj* (*very formal: sometimes facet*) mournful or sad: *a lugubrious expres-*

sion; *The mourners looked sad and lugubrious.* **lu'gubriously** *adv.* **lu'gubriousness** *nu.*

lukewarm ['lu:kwo:m] *adj* **1** slightly warm: *Several people complained that the soup served in the cafe was only lukewarm*; *I hate lukewarm soup.* **2** (*fig*) (of *eg* interest, supporters *etc*) not enthusiastic: *There was only lukewarm support for his proposals*; *I found the response to our request rather lukewarm.* **'lukewarmly** *adv.*

lull [lʌl] *vt* to make calm or quiet: *The sound of the waves lulled him to sleep*; *She had been lulled into a false sense of security.* – *nc* a time of calm (during a storm *etc*): *We were very busy in the shop this morning but there's a bit of a lull now.*

lullaby ['lʌləbai] *nc* a song sung to make children go to sleep.

lumbago [lʌm'beigou] *nu* pain in the lower part of the back: *He suffers from lumbago.*

lumbar ['lʌmbə] *adj* (*tech*: *attrib*) of the lower part of the back: *He was complaining of lumbar pain.*

lumber[1] ['lʌmbə] *nu* **1** anything no longer of use, *esp* if large and heavy (*eg* furniture): *We must get rid of some of this lumber*; (*attrib*) *We have trunks of old clothes in the lumber room.* **2** (*tech*) timber sawn up. – *vt* (*inf derog*: *often in passive with* **with**) to give (someone) an unpleasant unwanted responsibility or task: *I've been lumbered with her kids for the weekend*; *I got lumbered with driving her home.*

'lumberjack [-dʒak] *nc* a person employed to cut down, saw up and move trees.

lumber[2] ['lʌmbə] *vi* (*formal*) to move about heavily and clumsily: *The rhinoceros lumbered across the grass towards him.*

luminous ['lu:minəs] *adj* giving out light: *a luminous clock-face*; *Is your watch luminous?* **'luminously** *adv.* **ˌlumi'nosity** [-'no-] *nu.*

lump [lʌmp] *nc* **1** a small solid mass of no particular shape: *The custard was full of lumps and no-one would eat it.* **2** a swelling: *She had a lump on her head where she had hit it on a door.* **3** a small, *usu* cube-shaped, mass (of sugar). **4** (*inf*: *usu in sing*) the whole (of something) taken together: *You'll have to accept it in a lump.* – *vt* (*inf*) (*usu with* **together**) to treat or think of as (all) alike: *She lumped the whole family together in her mind as a group of idiots*; *He was annoyed to find that he had been lumped with the children and had to eat in the kitchen.* – *See also* **lump it** *below.*

'lumpish *adj* (of a person) heavy or dull: *She was a lumpish, unattractive girl who seldom spoke*; *She is rather lumpish.*

'lumpy *adj* containing lumps: *This custard is lumpy*; *lumpy custard.* **'lumpiness** *nu.*

lump sum *nc* an amount of money given all at once, not in parts over a period of time: *I would prefer to have the money in a lump sum rather than in instalments.*

'lump it (*inf*) to endure a situation: *I'm afraid that complaining will do no good – we'll just have to lump it.*

if you don't like it, you can lump it whether you like the situation or not, you will have to endure it: *I know working here is not very pleasant but, if you don't like it, you can lump it.*

lunacy ['lu:nəsi] *nu* (*usu fig*: *more formal than* **madness**) insanity: *It was sheer lunacy to lend him money – he'll never repay it.*

'lunatic [-tik] *adj, nc* (*esp fig*) (*offensive sl abbrev* **loony** ['lu:ni]) (a person who is) insane or crazy: *Only a lunatic would do such a thing!*

lunar *adj* (*formal or tech*) of the moon: *a lunar eclipse.*

lunatic *see* **lunacy**.

lunch [lʌntʃ], *also* (*formal*) **luncheon** ['lʌntʃən] *ncu* a meal eaten in the middle of the day between breakfast and dinner: *We had* (= ate) *lunch in a small restaurant*; *They serve excellent lunches here*; *We had steak and chips for lunch.* – *vi* (*formal*) to eat this meal: *We lunched on the train*; *We lunched on steak* (= had steak for lunch) *at Romano's*; *We usually lunch at one o'clock.*

'luncheon-meat *nu* a type of pre-cooked (often canned) meat, *usu* served cold: *We had luncheon meat and salad for supper.*

'luncheon voucher *nc* a ticket or other piece of paper given by firms to employees to pay for lunches *etc.*

'lunchtime *nu* the time between 12.00 p.m. and 2.00 p.m., when people normally eat lunch: *I'll be back about lunchtime.*

lung [lʌŋ] *nc* one of the pair of organs of breathing, in man and other animals: *The disease affected both lungs.*

lunge [lʌndʒ] *vi* to make a sudden strong or violent forward movement: *The attacker lunged towards his victim.* – *nc* a movement of this sort: *He made a lunge at her.*

lurch [lə:tʃ] *vi* to move suddenly or unevenly forward; to roll to one side: *The drunken man lurched towards the bar.* – *nc* such a movement: *The train gave a lurch and started off.*

leave in the lurch (*inf*) to leave (a person *etc*) in a difficult situation and without help: *Soon after their child was born he went off and left her in the lurch.*

lure [luə] *ncu* (*formal*) attraction; something very attractive or tempting: *The lure of the hills drew him back to Scotland*; *He married her because he could not resist the lure of her money.* – *vt* to tempt or attract: *They lured him away from the firm by offering him a much larger salary.*

lurid ['luərid] *adj* (*formal*) **1** (too) brightly coloured or vivid: *a lurid dress/painting/sky.* **2** unpleasantly shocking: *He gave us all the lurid details of his accident/divorce*; *I think he could have omitted some of the details – his account of the accident was rather lurid.* **'luridly** *adv.* **'luridness** *nu.*

lurk [lə:k] *vi* to wait in hiding *esp* with a dishonest or criminal purpose: *She saw someone lurking in the shadows.*

luscious ['lʌʃəs] *adj* (*formal*) very sweet, juicy and delicious: *a luscious pear*; (*fig*) *a luscious blonde*; *The fruit looked ripe and luscious.* **'lusciousness** *nu.*

lush [lʌʃ] *adj* (*formal or liter*) green and plentiful in growth: *lush meadows*; *The grass in that field is very fresh and lush.*

lust [lʌst] *ncu* (*sometimes in cmpds*) (a) very strong (often sexual) desire: *The dictator has a lust for power*; *His eyes were full of lust as he gazed at her*; *wanderlust.* **'lustful** *adj.* **'lustfully** *adv.*

'lusty *adj* **1** (*formal*) strong or loud: *The baby gave a lusty yell*; *The baby's cry was strong and lusty.* **2** (*liter*) strong and healthy: *a lusty young man/woman*; *He is strong and lusty.* **'lustily** *adv.* **'lustiness** *nu.*

'lust after/for *vt fus* (*esp liter or facet*) to desire greatly: *He's always lusting after some woman*; *They lusted for revenge.*

lustre, (*Amer*) **luster** ['lʌstə] *nu* (*formal*) shininess

or brightness: *Her hair had a brilliant lustre*; (*fig*) *Her presence gave added lustre to the occasion.*
'lustrous [-trəs] *adj* (*formal*) bright and shining: *lustrous eyes*; *Her eyes are large and lustrous.*

lusty *see* **lust**.

lute [luːt] *nc* an old stringed instrument, shaped like a half pear, played like a guitar: *He sang a love song, accompanying himself on the lute.*

Luxemb(o)urg, Luxemb(o)urger *see* Appendix 2.

luxuriant [lʌg'zjuəriənt] *adj* (*formal*: *esp attrib*) (of plants *etc*) abundant and healthy in growth: *the luxuriant growth of the vegetation*; *a luxuriant moustache.* **lu'xuriantly** *adv.*
lu'xuriance, lu'xuriancy *nus* (*formal*) the state of being luxuriant.

luxuriate [lʌg'zjuərieit] *vi* (*formal or facet*) to enjoy a situation of pleasure and comfort: *She luxuriated in a hot bath.*

luxury ['lʌkʃəri] **1** *nu* great comfort *usu* among expensive things: *They live in luxury*; (*attrib*) *fur coats and other luxury goods.* **2** *nc* something pleasant but not necessary, and often rare and expensive: *It's a real luxury to be able to have a holiday nowadays*; *We're going to give up all those luxuries and only spend money on essentials.*
luxurious [lʌg'zjuəriəs] *adj* supplied with luxuries: *a really luxurious flat/life.* **lu'xuriously** *adv.* **lu'xuriousness** *nu.*

lychgate, lichgate ['litʃgeit] *nc* a gate with a roof over it in a churchyard wall.

lying *see* **lie**[1], **lie**[2].

lynch [lintʃ] *vt* to condemn and put to death (*usu* by hanging) without a legal trial: *The crowd dragged him from the prison and lynched him*; *Some politicians deserve to be lynched!*

lyre ['laiə] *nc* a musical instrument similar to a harp: *The ancient Greeks sang their songs to (the accompaniment of) the lyre.*

lyric ['lirik] *adj* (of poetry) expressing the poet's personal feeling and *orig* intended for singing: *Greek lyric poetry.* – *nc* **1** (*formal*) a lyric poem or a song: *These lyrics were inspired by his love for a young girl.* **2** (*in pl*: *esp with* **the**) the words of a song: *I like the lyrics, but the tune is awful.*
'lyrical *adj* **1** (*formal*) lyric; song-like: *the lyrical quality of his poetry/writing.* **2** (of a person *etc*) full of enthusiastic praise: *He became quite lyrical about the delights of country life.* **'lyrically** *adv.*

Mm

'm *see* **be**.

mac [mak] short for **mackintosh**: *I should take your mac – it's going to rain.*

macabre [mə'kaːbr] *adj* (*formal*) weird, unearthly or horrible: *Edgar Allan Poe wrote some macabre horror stories*; *I find his stories rather macabre.*

macaroni [makə'rouni] *nu* a form of pasta, pressed out to form tubes, and dried: *a packet of macaroni*; *the macaroni is over-cooked*; *macaroni cheese* (= a dish of macaroni and cheese sauce).

macaroon [makə'ruːn] *nc* a sweet cake or biscuit made with almonds or coconut.

mace[1] [meis] *nc* **1** (*hist*) a metal or metal-headed war club, often with spikes. **2** an ornamental rod used as a mark of authority, *eg* by a mayor, on ceremonial occasions.

mace[2] [meis] *nu* a type of spice obtained from the same fruit as nutmeg: *She added some powdered mace to the Christmas cake.*

Macedonian *see* Appendix 2.

Mach [maːx]: **'Mach number** *nc* the ratio of the speed of an aircraft to the speed of sound: *Mach 5 means a speed five times the speed of sound.*

machinations [maki'neiʃənz] *n pl* (*formal*: *derog*) (the making of) a crafty scheme or plot, *usu* with an evil or unpleasant purpose: *Their machinations to remove him from the directorship were finally successful.*

machine [mə'ʃiːn] *nc* **1** (*often in cmpds*) a working arrangement of wheels, levers or other parts, driven *eg* by human power, electricity *etc*, or operating electronically, producing power and/or motion for a particular purpose: *a sewing-machine*; *a printing-machine*; *Computers and tape-recorders are machines, but TVs and radios are not.* **2** an organization, *esp* political: *The party machine is going into action to get him elected.* **3** (*inf*) a vehicle, *esp* a motorbike: *That's a fine machine you have!* – *vt* **1** (*formal or tech*) to shape, make or finish with a power-driven tool: *The articles are machined to a smooth finish.* **2** to sew with a sewing-machine: *You should machine the seams before sewing the hem.*
ma'chinery *nu* **1** machines in general: *Many products are made by machinery rather than by hand.* **2** (*fig*) the workings or processes: *the machinery of government.*
ma'chinist *nc* a person skilled in the use of machines, *eg* a sewing-machine, or electrical tools: *She's a machinist in a clothes factory.*
ma'chine-gun *nc* an automatic gun that fires very rapidly. – *vt* to fire a machine-gun at (someone or something): *He machine-gunned a crowd of defenceless villagers.*
machine tool *nc* a power-driven machine that shapes metal, wood, or plastics by cutting, pressing, or drilling.
See also **mechanic**.

macintosh *see* **mackintosh**.

mackerel ['makrəl] – *pls* **'mackerel, 'mackerels** – **1** *nc* a type of edible sea-fish, bluish green with wavy markings: *They are fishing for mackerel*; *two mackerels.* **2** *nu* its flesh as food: *We had fried mackerel for supper.*

mackintosh, macintosh ['makintoʃ] *nc* (*often abbrev* **mac** [mak]) a waterproof overcoat, *esp* made of plastic material.

mad [mad] *adj* **1** (*often loosely or fig*) mentally disturbed or insane: *Insanity runs in the family – they're all mad*; *Ophelia went mad after her father's death*; *You must be mad if you think you can lift that car all by yourself*; *He was mad with rage*; *The pain was driving him nearly mad*; *We were chased by a mad bull.* **2** (*inf*: *pred*: *sometimes with* **at** *or* **with**) very angry: *His untidiness makes me mad*; *She was mad at me for losing my keys.* **3** (*inf*: *pred with* **about**) having a great liking or desire for: *I'm just mad about Harry.* **4** (of dogs) infected with rabies: *She was bitten by a mad dog*; *If that dog was mad* *when it bit you, you might get rabies.* '**madly** *adv.* '**madness** *nu.*

'**madden** *vt* to make mad or very angry: *The animal was maddened by the pain.*

'**maddening** *adj* likely to cause anger: *maddening delays*; *These delays are absolutely maddening.* '**maddeningly** *adv.*

'**madcap** *nc, adj* (*attrib*) (a person who is) foolish or reckless: *What a madcap that child is!*; *a madcap plan.*

'**madhouse** *nc* **1** (*old or derog*) a mental hospital. **2** (*inf*) a place of great confusion and noise: *This place has been a madhouse since the kids came home from school!*

'**madman** – *pl* '**madmen**: *fem* '**madwoman** – *nc* a person who is insane: *He drove/fought like a madman.*

(as) mad as a hatter (*usu fig*) utterly crazy; completely insane: *He's very clever but as mad as a hatter.*

like 'mad wildly, desperately, very quickly *etc*: *struggling/trying/running like mad.*

madam ['madəm] – *pls* **mesdames** [mei'dam] (*def 1*), '**madams** – **1** *n* (*formal*) a polite form of address (spoken or written) to a woman. **2** *nc* an unpleasant or selfish woman or girl: *She's a real little madam!*

madcap, madden, maddening, maddeningly *see* **mad**.

made *see* **make**.

madhouse, madman *see* **mad**.

Madonna [mə'donə] *n* (*with* **the**) the Virgin Mary, mother of Christ, *esp* as shown in works of art: *a painting of the Madonna and Child.*

madrigal ['madrigəl] *nc* a type of song for several voices singing in harmony without accompaniment.

maelstrom ['meilstrəm] *nc* **1** a place or state of confusion and struggle: *the maelstrom of city life.* **2** (*liter*) a whirlpool.

maestro ['maistrou] – *pl* '**maestros** – *nc* (*sometimes formal*) (a title given to) a master in one of the arts, *esp* a musical composer or conductor: *The audience clapped wildly as the maestro arrived on the platform.*

magazine [magə'zi:n, (*Amer*) 'magəzi:n] (*inf abbrev* **mag** [mag]) *nc* **1** a publication issued regularly containing articles, stories, *etc* by various writers: *women's magazines*; (*attrib*) *I've been reading a magazine article* (= a piece of writing in a magazine) *about children's teeth.* **2** a compartment in or on a gun that holds cartridges. **3** a storeroom for ammunition, explosives *etc*: *He stole the gunpowder from the army magazine.*

maggot ['magət] *nc* the worm-like grub or larva of a fly, *esp* a bluebottle: *There are maggots crawling over the cheese.*

magic ['madʒik] *nu* **1** (the charms, spells *etc* used in) the art or practice of using supernatural forces: *The prince was turned by magic into a frog.* **2** the art of producing illusions by tricks or sleight-of-hand: *The conjuror's magic delighted the children.* **3** fascination or great charm: *the magic of Turner's paintings.* – *adj* (*attrib*) **1** used in magic: *a magic wand.* **2** using magic: *a magic spell.*

'**magical** *adj* (*formal*: *attrib*) **1** produced by, or as if by, the art of magic: *She has some kind of magical power.* **2** fascinating; charming or very beautiful: *Going to the theatre was a magical experience for the children.* '**magically** *adv.*

ma'gician [-ʃən] *nc* a person skilled in the art of magic: *They hired a magician to entertain the children at the Christmas party.*

black magic, white magic *see* **black, white.**

magistrate ['madʒistreit] *nc* a person who has power to put the laws into force and sentence those guilty of lesser crimes, *esp* a justice of the peace in one of the lower courts: *He was fined by the magistrate for driving while drunk.*

'**magistracy** [-strəsi] *nc* (*formal*) the position of a magistrate.

magnanimous [mag'naniməs] *adj* (*formal*) noble and generous: *a magnanimous person*; *It was a magnanimous gesture to offer to pay her fare to America*; *It was magnanimous of you to lend her so much money.* **mag'nanimously** *adv.*

magnanimity [magnə'niməti] *nu*: *He showed great magnanimity in ignoring my stupid mistake.*

magnate ['magneit] *nc* a man of wealth or power: *He is a rich shipping magnate.*

magnesia [məg'ni:ʒə] *nu* (*also* **milk of magnesia**) a white compound of magnesium and oxygen, used in liquid form as a cure for indigestion *etc.*

mag'nesium [-ziəm] *nu* a silver-white metallic element (symbol **Mg**) that burns with a bright, white light.

magnet ['magnit] *nc* a piece of iron, or of certain other materials, that attracts or repels other pieces of iron *etc*, either naturally or because of an electric current passed through it: *He picked all the pins up with a magnet*; *His personality draws women like a magnet.*

mag'netic [-'ne-] *adj* **1** of, or having the powers of, or operating by means of, a magnet or magnetism: *magnetic force/ore*; *Is this metal magnetic?* **2** strongly attractive: *He has a magnetic personality*; *To be a successful businessman you must be enthusiastic and magnetic.* **mag'netically** *adv.*

'**magnetism** *nu* **1** power of attraction: *his personal magnetism.* **2** (the science of) magnets and their power of attraction: *the magnetism of the earth.*

'**magnetize, -ise** *vt* **1** to make magnetic: *You can magnetize a piece of iron.* **2** to attract or to influence strongly: *She's the kind of person who can magnetize others.*

magnetic field *nc* the area in which the pull of a magnet, or thing acting like a magnet, is felt: *the earth's magnetic field.*

magnetic needle *nc* any slender bar of magnetized steel, *esp* that in a compass which always points to the magnetic north.

magnetic north *nu* the direction, either east or west of the true north, in which a magnetized needle points.

magnetic tape *nu* a type of tape, coated with magnetic material, that records sound or other information.

magneto [mag'ni:tou] – *pl* **mag'netos** – *nc* a device producing electric sparks, *esp* for lighting the fuel in a motor car engine.

magnificent [məg'nifisnt] *adj* great and splendid: *The king wore a magnificent costume*; *The actor gave a magnificent performance*; *The view over the valley is magnificent.* **mag'nificently** *adv.* **mag'nificence** *nu.*

magnify ['magnifai] *vt* (*formal or tech*) to cause to appear greater: *A telescope magnifies the image of anything that one looks at through it*; (*fig*) *She is inclined to magnify all her troubles.*

ˌ**magnifi'cation** [-fi-] *nu* (*formal or tech*) **1** the act of magnifying (something). **2** the power of magnifying: *the magnification of a pair of binoculars.* **3** the extent to which something (*eg* a photograph) has been magnified: *The magnification of (this photograph of) this spider is ten times (10×).*

'magnifying-glass *nc* a piece of glass with curved surfaces that makes an object looked at through it appear larger: *This print is so small that I need a magnifying-glass to read it.*

magnitude ['magnitju:d] *nu* (*formal*) **1** importance: *a decision of great magnitude.* **2** size: *a star of great magnitude.*

magnum ['magnəm] *nc* a two-quart bottle, *eg* of champagne.

magpie ['magpai] *nc* a black-and-white bird of the crow family, known for its habit of collecting shiny objects.

maharaja(h) [ma:hə'ra:dʒə] *nc* (*esp hist: with cap in titles*) (the status of) an Indian (*def 2*) prince of high rank.

ˌmaha'rani, ˌmaha'ranee [-ni:] *nc* (*esp hist: with cap in titles*) **1** (the status of) the wife or widow of a maharajah. **2** (the status of) a woman of the same rank as a maharajah in her own right.

mahogany [mə'hogəni] **1** *nu, adj* (of) the wood of a tropical American tree, much used for making furniture: *This table is made of mahogany; a mahogany table.* **2** *nu, adj* (of) its dark brown colour. **3** *nc* (*also* **ma'hogany tree**) the tree.

maid [meid] *nc* **1** (*liter*) an unmarried woman, *esp* a young one: *a pretty young maid.* **2** a female servant: *The maid answered the door; a lady's/kitchen maid.*

maiden ['meidən] *nc* (*liter*) a (young) unmarried woman: *a maiden of seventeen; All the village maidens were in love with him.*

maiden lady *nc* (*formal*) a middle-aged or elderly unmarried woman.

maiden name *nc* a woman's surname before her marriage: *Mrs Johnson's maiden name was Scott.*

maiden speech *nc* (*esp Brit*) a Member of Parliament's first speech: *He made a memorable maiden speech to the House of Commons.*

maiden voyage *nc* a ship's first voyage.

mail[1] [meil] **1** *nu* letters, parcels *etc* by post: *Is there any mail for me this morning?; His secretary opens his mail in his absence.* **2** *n* (*with cap*) a word often used in the titles of newspapers: *the Morning Mail.* – *vt* (*esp Amer*) to send by post: *They keep mailing things to me that I don't want.*

'mailbag *nc* a bag for letters *etc*: *The letters and parcels are put into mailbags and sent to London by train.*

'mailbox *nc* (*esp Amer*) a postbox.

'mailman [-man] *nc* (*Amer*) a postman: *Has the mailman been yet?*

mail order *nu* the system of ordering or selling goods by post: *He runs a firm which deals only by mail order; (attrib) a mail-order firm/catalogue.*

mail[2] [meil] *nu* (*hist*) armour for the body, *esp* when made of steel rings: *The knight wore a suit of heavy mail.*

maim [meim] *vt* (*formal: usu in passive*) to injure (a person or animal) badly, *esp* with permanent effects: *The hunter was maimed for life* (= permanently) *after the attack by the lion.*

main[1] [mein] *adj* (*attrib*) chief, principal or most important: *What is the main purpose of this expedition?; He is the main character in the story; the main street of a village/town.* – *nc* (*also* **mains**) the chief pipe or cable in a branching system of pipes or cables: *The water's been turned off at the main(s); (attrib) the mains electricity supply.*

'mainly *adv* more (of) the thing mentioned than anything else; mostly or largely: *This skirt is mainly dark grey; The crowd was made up mainly of children.*

main clause *nc* (*gram*) a clause which can function as an independent sentence: *I will do it if he asks me to; I am sorry that you can't come.*

'maindeck, 'mainmast, 'mainsail *etc ncs* the principal deck, mast, sail *etc* of a ship.

'mainland *nc* (*usu in sing*) a large piece of land as compared with neighbouring islands: *The Shetland Islands are off the Scottish mainland; Britain is not part of the mainland of Europe.*

'mainspring *nc* the chief spring, *esp* the spring that causes the wheels to move in a watch or clock: *The mainspring has broken; (fig formal) His love for his wife was the mainspring* (= chief moving force) *of his life.*

'mainstay *nc* (*fig formal*) the chief support: *He's one of the mainstays of the English aristocracy.*

'mainstream *nc* (*formal: no pl*) the chief direction or trend of a system of theories, developments *etc*: *His paintings depart greatly from the mainstream of traditional art; He is not in the mainstream of socialist politics.*

in the 'main (*formal*) mostly: *In the main, I find this composer's music pleasant to listen to.*

might and main *see* **might**[2].

main[2] [mein] *nc* (*liter: no pl*) the high sea: *They sailed across the Spanish main.*

maintain [mein'tein] *vt* **1** (*formal*) to continue: *How long can you maintain this silence?* **2** (*formal*) to keep in good condition: *He maintains his car very well.* **3** (*formal*) to pay the expenses of: *How can you maintain a wife and three children on your small salary?* **4** (not *usu* used with **is, was** *etc* and **-ing**) to continue to argue or believe (that): *I maintain that the Labour Party will lose the next election.*

'maintenance [-tənəns] *nu* **1** the process of keeping something in good condition: *I'm learning about motorcycle maintenance.* **2** (money supplied, *eg* by a husband to his wife after they are divorced *etc*, for) the process of supporting life: *How much maintenance does he pay his ex-wife?; His wife married again, but he has to pay a sum towards the maintenance of the children.* **3** (*formal*) the act of maintaining (a point of view *etc*).

maisonette [meizə'net] *nc* (used *esp* by estate agents *etc*) a flat or apartment sometimes on two floors or stories.

maize [meiz] *nu* (*Amer* **corn, Indian corn**) an important cereal, grown *esp* in America: *Maize is grown in many parts of the world; (attrib) maize flour.*

majesty ['madʒəsti] **1** *nu* (*formal*) greatness; impressive dignity: *the majesty of God; mountain peaks of breathtaking majesty.* **2** *n* (*with cap: with* **His, Your** *etc*) a title used when speaking to or of a king or queen: *Her Majesty the Queen; Their Majesties are leaving now; Thank you, Your Majesty.*

ma'jestic [-'dʒes-] *adj* having great dignity: *The king looked a majestic sight in his ceremonial robes; He looked truly majestic.* **ma'jestically** *adv.*

major ['meidʒə] *adj* (*attrib: more formal than* **great** *or* **greater**) great, or greater, in size, importance *etc*: *major and minor roads; That was a major discovery in the field of space travel; He played a* *major rôle in a play*; *The major part of the audience was laughing.* – *nc* **1** (*with cap, and often abbrev* **Maj.**, *when written in titles*) in the British army, (a person of) the rank next below lieutenant-colonel: *He is a major*; *He was promoted to major*; *Major Burns.* – *See also* Appendix 3. **2** (*Amer*) a student specializing in a particular subject: *He's a psychology major.* – *vi* (*Amer*) to specialize (in a particular subject): *She majored in history.*

ma'jority [mə'dʒo-] **1** *nu* (*more formal than* **most**) the greater number: *The majority of people in Britain live in towns or cities.* **2** *nc* the difference between a greater and a smaller number: *The Democratic Party won by/with a majority of six hundred votes.*

ˌmajor-'general *nc* (*with cap, and often abbrev* **Maj.-Gen.**, *when written in titles*) in the British army, (a person of) the rank next below lieutenant-general: *He is a major-general*; *He was promoted to major-general*; *Major-General Hunter.*

the age of majority legal adulthood (in Britain, eighteen years of age): *He has not yet reached the age of majority.*

See also **minor**.

make [meik] – *pt, ptp* **made** [meid] – **1** *vt* to create, form or produce: *God made the Earth*; *She makes all her own clothes*; *He made an aeroplane out of a piece of paper*; *Many shoes nowadays are made of plastic*; (*inf*) *We'll show the other team what we're made of!* (= how strong, skilful *etc* we are); *We'll soon make a footballer of him!*; *He's always making a nuisance of himself* (= causing trouble); *He has made a muddle/mess of the job* (= done the job badly); *Our kitchen is being made into* (= converted, or turned, into) *a dining-room*; *Will they make the book into a film?*; *I'm just going to make* (= prepare) *lunch/coffee*; *She made a cake for tea*; *The dog has made a big hole in the garden*; *We made an arrangement/agreement/deal/bargain*; *She made several changes/new rules when she became headmistress*; *He'll make trouble* (= cause difficulties) *for you if you don't do what he wants*; *Stop making such a noise/mess!* **2** *vt* to compel, force or cause (a person or thing to do something): *She didn't want to do it, but they made her* (*do it*); *The children must be made to tidy their room*; *His appearance made me laugh*; *What makes the world go round?* **3** *vt* to cause to be: *She made her feelings obvious*; *I made it clear that I disapproved of the decision*; *You've made me very unhappy*; *When will the news be made public?* (= announced to the public). **4** *vt* to gain or earn: *He makes £45 a week*; *He makes a good living*; *Our business has only just started, so we won't be making a profit for a while.* **5** *vt* (of numbers *etc*) to add up to; to amount to: *2 and 2 make(s) 4.* **6** *vt* to become, turn into, or be: *He'll make an excellent teacher*; *This barrel makes a good seat*; *His adventures make a good story*; *This material will make me* (= for me) *a nice dress.* **7** *vt* to estimate as: *I make the total 483.* **8** *vt* to appoint, or choose, as: *He was made manager at the age of thirty*; *We made this our aim.* **9** *vt* (*inf*) to reach: *We'll make Edinburgh by seven o'clock tonight*; *I can come to the party, but my husband can't make it* (= manage to come); *Will he make* (= manage to be chosen for) *the team?* **10** *vi* (*esp formal or liter*) to go, *esp* quickly: *He made towards the door*; *We made after the thieves in a fast car.* **11** *vi* (*formal*) to attempt, or start, to do something: *He made to stand up, but sat down again.* **12** *vt* to score, in a game *etc*: *He made only 10 runs in the cricket match.* **13** *vt* (*old*) to eat (a meal): *They made a hasty breakfast.* **14** *vt* (*vulg*) to have sexual intercourse with: *He tries to make every woman he meets.* **15** *vt* used with many nouns to give a similar meaning to that of the verb from which the noun is formed: *He made several attempts* (= attempted several times) *to reach her*; *They made a left turn* (= turned left); *What time shall we make a start?*; *He made* (= offered) *a suggestion/proposal/bid*; *Have you any comments to make?* – *See also* **make** *in phrases below.* – *nc* a (*usu* manufacturer's) brand: *What make is your new car?*; *Which make of washing-powder do you use?*

made *adj* (*inf*) certain of success: *If this part of the plan works, we're made!*; *You'll be a made man if this succeeds!*

'maker **1** *nc* (*usu in cmpds*) a person who makes: *He is a tool-maker*; *She is such a good dressmaker that she makes all her own clothes.* **2** *n* (*with cap*) God: *He has gone to meet his Maker* (= He has died).

'making *nu* (*esp in cmpds*) the process of producing or forming something: *The making of a new town takes a long time*; *He is employed in glass-making*; (*attrib*) *bread-making techniques*; (*attrib*) *the road-making industry.*

ˌmake-be'lieve *nu* the act or art of pretending and imagining: *This child lives in a world of make-believe*; (*attrib*) *a make-believe world.* – *See also* **make believe** *below.*

'makeshift *adj* temporary and *usu* of poor quality: *We have constructed a makeshift garden shed*; *The greenhouse is a bit makeshift but it will do.*

'make-up *nu* **1** cosmetics applied to the face *etc*: *She never wears any make-up.* **2** (*formal*) the set, or combination, of characteristics or ingredients that together form something, *eg* a personality; composition: *Violence is just not part of his make-up.* – *See also* **made up, make up** *below.*

be 'made for (*inf*) to be ideally suitable for: *John and Mary were made for each other.*

be of one's own making to be made or caused by one's own actions: *You can't blame me – this trouble is entirely of your own making.*

be the 'making of (someone) to be the thing or person that ensures the success or improvement of (*usu* a person): *The discovery of this new process will be the making of us!*; *Two years in the navy will probably be the making of him!*

have the 'makings of (*formal*) to have the clear ability for becoming: *Your son has the makings of an excellent engineer.*

in the 'making (*formal*) being made or formed at this very moment: *A revolution is already in the making – we must take care.*

made up **1** invented: *I don't believe her account of the accident – I think it's made up*; (*attrib*) *a made-up story.* **2** having a covering of cosmetics: *She is always well made up*; (*attrib*) *heavily made-up eyes.*

'make as if to (*formal*) to behave as if one were about to: *He made as if to hit me, but he was only pretending.*

make away with *see* **make off with** *below.*

make a/one's bed to tidy and straighten the sheets, blankets *etc* on a bed after it has been used: *The children must make their own beds every morning.*

make believe to pretend (that): *The children made believe they were cowboys and Indians.* – *See* *also* **make-believe** *above.*

make certain *see* **certain**.

make do (*with* **with**) to use something as a poor-quality or temporary alternative to the real thing: *There's no meat in the house, so we'll just have to make do with potatoes*; *We couldn't find what we wanted, but we made do somehow.*

make eyes at *see* **eye**.

ˈ**make for** *vt fus* **1** to go towards: *We're making for Glasgow, via York.* **2** (*formal*) to have as a result; to cause: *All these arguments make for bad feeling among the people involved.*

make good *see* **good**.

ˈ**make it** (*inf*) to be successful: *After twenty years, we've finally made it (to the United States for a holiday)!*; *We've made it at last – our products are selling all over the world.*

ˌ**make it ˈup 1** to become friends again after a quarrel: *It's time you two made it up (with each other).* **2** to give compensation or make amends for something: *I couldn't take Jackie to the circus as I promised, but I'll make it up to him somehow.* – *See also* **make up** *below.*

make light of *see* **light**[2].

make little of *see* **little**.

make much of *see* **much**.

make nothing of *see* **nothing**.

make (something) of (something) to understand (something) by or from (something): *What do you make of all this?*

make off *vi* (*formal*) to go away, *esp* hurriedly or secretly: *They made off in the middle of the night.*

make off/(*formal*) **away with** to run away with or steal: *Thieves made off with all her jewellery.*

make or break (someone/something) to be the thing that causes either the success or failure of (a person or thing): *This new scheme of his is likely to make or break him.*

make out 1 *vt sep* to see, hear or understand: *Can you make out what he's trying to say?*; *He could make out a ship in the distance*; *I cannot make it out.* **2** *vt fus* to make it seem that: *He made out that he was earning a huge amount of money.* **3** *vt sep* to write or fill in: *The doctor made out a prescription*; *He made it out yesterday.* **4** *vi* (*inf*) to manage or succeed: *We'll make out, despite all these problems*; *How are you making out these days?*

make over *vt sep* (*formal*) to transfer (*esp* ownership): *The property was made over to the son before his father died.*

make up 1 *vt sep* to invent: *He made up the whole story – it's all lies*; *She's very good at making up stories to tell the children at bedtime*; *She made the whole thing up.* **2** *vt sep* to put together: *I'll make up a parcel and send it to you*; *She will help me make it up.* **3** *vt sep* to compose or be part(s) of: *Ten poems make up the entire book*; *The group was made up of doctors and lawyers.* **4** *vt sep* to complete: *We need one more player – will you make up the number(s)?* **5** *vi, vt sep* to apply cosmetics to (the face): *I don't like to see women making up (their faces) in public.* **6** *vi, vt sep* to become friends again (after a quarrel *etc*): *They've finally made up (their disagreement).* – *See also* **make it up** *above.* **7** *vt sep* to arrange (a bed): *I'll make up a bed for you in the spare room.* – *See also* **made up, make-up** *above.*

ˌ**make ˈup for** *vt fus* to supply a reward, substitute *etc* for disappointment, damage, loss (of money or time) *etc*: *This will make up for all the occasions when you've lost*; *Next week we'll try to make up for lost time.*

ˌ**make ˈup to** *vt fus* (*inf*) to try to gain the favour or love of by flattery *etc*: *She's always making up to the teacher by bringing him presents.*

on the ˈmake (*sl*) trying to make a profit (often unfairly large or illegal): *I don't trust him to give me a bargain – I think he's on the make.*

See also **unmade**.

mal- [mal] (*in cmpds*) bad(ly), as in **maladjusted**.

maladjusted [maləˈdʒʌstid] *adj* unable to be happy in one's home life, work *etc*: *He works in a home for maladjusted children*; *The child is quite happy now but he was rather maladjusted for a time when his parents divorced.*

ˌ**maladˈjustment** *nu.*

malady [ˈmalədi] *nc* (*old or formal*) an illness or disease: *He is suffering from some strange malady.*

malaria [məˈleəriə] *nu* a fever caused by the bite of a certain type of mosquito: *He has had another attack of malaria.*

Malawi, Malawian *see* Appendix 2.

Malay, Malaysia, Malaysian *see* Appendix 2.

malcontent [ˈmalkəntent] *nc, adj* (*formal derog*) (a person who is) dissatisfied and inclined to rebel: *The people are being encouraged to revolt by a few malcontents.*

male [meil] *nc, adj* **1** (a person, animal *etc*) of the sex having testes or an organ or organs performing a similar function; not (of) the sex which carries the young until birth *etc*: *Males are said to be stronger than females*; *The male of the species is sometimes not any stronger than the female*; *The male bird is black and the female is brown*; *the male rabbit.* **2** (a plant) having flowers with stamens which can fertilize female flowers.

male chauvinist *see* **chauvinism**.

See also **female**.

malediction [maliˈdikʃən] *nc* (*very formal*) a curse.

malefactor [ˈmalifaktə] *nc* (*old or formal*) a person who does evil *esp* a criminal.

malevolent [məˈlevələnt] *adj* (*formal*) wishing evil to others: *The wicked old woman gave a malevolent smile*; *She is wicked and malevolent.*

maˈlevolently *adv.* **maˈlevolence** *nu.*

malformation [malfoːˈmeiʃən] *ncu* (*formal or tech*) (a part that has a) faulty or bad shape: *He has a (degree of) malformation of the hip.*

malˈformed [-ˈfoːmd] *adj.*

malfunction [malˈfʌŋkʃən] *ncu* (*formal or tech*) faulty performance or a faulty process: *There's a malfunction in the main engine*; *The men have had to stop work because of the malfunction of the machinery.*

malice [ˈmalis] *nu* (*formal*) the wish to harm other people *etc*: *There was no malice intended in what she said.*

malˈicious [-ʃəs] *adj* (*formal*): *She took a malicious pleasure in hurting others*; *She is cruel and malicious.* **maˈliciously** *adv.*

malice aforethought [əˈfoːθoːt] (*legal*) deliberate intention to commit an illegal act.

malign [məˈlain] *vt* (*formal*) to say unpleasant things about (someone or something), *esp* without reason: *He's always maligning his wife when she isn't there.*

malignant [məˈlignənt] *adj* **1** (*formal*: *esp attrib*) (of people, their actions *etc*) intending, or intended, to do harm: *She has a malignant nature*; *a malignant remark.* **2** (*tech*) (of a tumour, disease *etc*) likely to become worse and cause death: *The lump in her breast is not malignant; She died of a malignant tumour.* **ma'lignantly** *adv.*

malinger [mə'liŋgə] *vi* (*formal*) to pretend to be unwell *eg* in order to avoid work: *He says he's ill, but I think he's just malingering.* **ma'lingerer** *nc.*

mallard ['mala:d] – *pls* **'mallards, mallard** – *nc* a type of common wild duck: *a flock of mallard; a couple of mallards.*

malleable ['maliəbl] *adj* (*formal*) **1** (*esp* of metal) able to be beaten, rolled *etc* into shape: *Gold is a malleable substance; It is malleable.* **2** (of a person) easy to influence or persuade: *Young children are usually malleable; She is rather a malleable young woman.* **ˌmallea'bility** *nu.*

mallet ['malit] *nc* **1** a type of small wooden hammer: *We hammered the tent pegs into the ground with a mallet.* **2** a long-handled wooden hammer for playing croquet or polo.

malnutrition [malnju'triʃən] *nu* (*esp tech*) (a medical condition resulting from) eating too little or getting too little nourishing food: *About half of the population is suffering from malnutrition.*

malodorous [mal'oudərəs] *adj* (*formal or liter*) foul-smelling: *a malodorous pile of rubbish; That chemical is rather malodorous.*

malpractice [mal'praktis] *ncu* (*formal*) (an act of) behaving improperly and illegally in one's business affairs: *The lawyer was accused of malpractice by two of his clients; He was dismissed from the firm for certain malpractices.*

malt [mo:lt] **1** *nu* (*usu attrib*) barley or other grain soaked in water, allowed to sprout, and dried in a kiln, used in brewing beer, whisky *etc*: *We bought some malt to make our own beer;* (*attrib*) *malt liquor.* **2** *nc* a variety of malt whisky: *This pub sells fifteen different malts.* – *vt* to make into, or mix with, malt.

'malted *adj* (*attrib*): *malted barley; malted milk.*

maltreat [mal'tri:t] *vt* (*formal*) to treat (a person, animal or thing) unkindly, roughly or without care: *The dog had been maltreated and had become very thin and weak.* **ˌmal'treatment** *nu.*

mamma, mama [mə'ma:] *nc* (*old*) a (name for one's) mother.

mammal ['maməl] *nc* any member of the class of animals (including man) in which the females feed the young with their own milk: *Monkeys are mammals.*

mam'malian [-'mei-] *adj* (*tech*).

mammary ['maməri] *adj* (*tech: attrib*) of the breasts or milk glands: *the mammary glands.*

mammoth ['maməθ] *nc* (*hist*) a large hairy elephant of a kind no longer found living. – *adj* (*inf: attrib*) very large (and often very difficult): *a mammoth project/task.*

man [man] – *pl* **men** [men] – **1** *nc* an adult male human being: *Hundreds of men, women and children crowded into the building; The police found a man's shoe by the body; I know where the boys' department is in the store but where is the men's department?; a four-man bobsleigh team.* **2** *nu* (*no article*) human beings taken as a whole; the human race: *Man's curiosity has led to some fascinating discoveries.* **3** *nc* obviously masculine male person: *He's independent, tough, strong, brave – a real man!* **4** *nc* (*old*) a male servant or (*usu* domestic) employee: *I'll get my man to call a taxi for you.* **5** *n* (*inf*) a word sometimes used in speaking informally or giving commands to someone: *Get on with your work, man, and stop complaining!* **6** *nc* an ordinary soldier, who is not an officer: *officers and men of the second battalion.* **7** *nc* a piece used in playing chess or draughts: *I took three of his men in one move.* **8** *nc* (*inf or dial*) a husband or boyfriend: *Her man is away at sea; She's found herself a man at last!* – *v* – *pt, ptp* **manned** – *vt* to supply with men (*esp* soldiers): *We manned the barricades all night; The colonel manned the guns with soldiers from our regiment.*

-man [-mən, -man] (*in cmpds*) a person (formerly *usu* used for either sex; currently, often replaced by **-person** when the person referred to can be of either sex) who performs a particular activity, as in **postman, milkman, chairman** *etc.*

'manful *adj* (*usu attrib*) brave and courageous: *He made a manful effort to win the race, but he only came second.* **'manfully** *adv.* **'manfulness** *nu.*

'manhood *nu* **1** (of a male) the state of being adult, physically (and mentally) mature *etc*: *He died before he reached manhood.* **2** manly qualities: *He took her refusal to marry him as an insult to his manhood.*

man'kind *nu* (*no article*) the human race as a whole: *He thought that some day his invention would be of use to all mankind.*

'manly *adj* having the qualities thought desirable in a man, *ie* strength, determination, courage *etc*: *a manly bearing/figure; He is strong and manly.* **'manliness** *nu.*

manned *adj* supplied with men: *a manned spacecraft; Was the boat manned when it sank?*

'mannish *adj* (*derog*) (*usu* of women) having masculine, rather than feminine, features or personality: *She is big and mannish; He doesn't like mannish women.* **'mannishness** *nu.*

ˌman-about-'town *nc* a man who lives and acts fashionably and in a sophisticated way: *He was born in the country but he has become a man-about-town since he went to live in London.*

'man-eating *adj* (*usu attrib*) which will eat people: *a man-eating tiger.* **'man-eater** *nc.*

man'handle *vt* **1** (*formal*) to move, carry *etc* (something) by hand: *When the crane broke down, they had to manhandle the crates on to the boat.* **2** to treat (someone or something) roughly: *You'll break all the china if you manhandle it like that!*

'manhole *nc* a hole (*usu* in the middle of a road or pavement) through which someone may go to inspect sewers *etc*: *The workmen left the cover of the manhole off and the child fell down it.*

'man-hour *nc* a unit used in measuring the amount of work done by one man in one hour: *The company lost three thousand man-hours last year because of strikes.*

'manhunt *nc* an organized (*usu* large-scale) search for someone, *esp* a criminal or someone who is lost: *The men of the village organized a manhunt to look for the child's murderer.*

ˌman-'made *adj* made, happening or formed by man, not by natural means: *man-made fibres; a man-made lake; Is that fabric man-made?*

ˌman-of-'war – *pl* **ˌmen-of-'war** – *nc* (*hist*) a type of sailing ship used by the navy as a warship.

'manpower *nu* the number of people available for employment *etc*: *There's a shortage of manpower in the building industry.*

'manservant – *pl* **'menservants** – *nc* (*old*) a male servant (*esp* one employed as a valet): *His butler is his only manservant.*

'mansize(d) *adj* (*esp attrib*) of a size suitable for a man; large: *a mansized breakfast*; *mansize paper tissues.*

'**manslaughter** *nu* (*legal*) the crime of killing someone, without intending to do so: *Murder is intentional, but manslaughter is accidental*; *He was found guilty of manslaughter.*

man-to-man *see* **man to man** *below.*

'**mantrap** *nc* a metal trap with jaws, formerly used for catching poachers, trespassers *etc*, but now illegal.

'**menfolk** *n pl* (*often inf*) male people, *esp* male relatives: *All the menfolk in his family are little, thin people.*

menservants *see* **manservant**.

'**men's (room)** *nc* (*often with* **the**) a gentlemen's lavatory.

'**menswear** ['menz-] *nu* clothing for men: *Do you sell menswear?*; (*attrib*) *the menswear department.*

as one man (*liter*) simultaneously; together: *They rose as one man to applaud his speech.*

be one's own man to be independent, not relying on, or controlled by, anyone else: *He's not his own man since his mother-in-law came to stay!*

be your, my *etc* **man** to be the most suitable person (for a particular job, enquiry *etc*): *If you want a good electrician, Paul's your man.*

best man *see* **best**.

every man jack *see* **jack**.

man and boy from childhood to adulthood: *He lived in this town, man and boy, for fifty years.*

man and wife (*formal*) husband and wife: *The priest pronounced them man and wife.*

the man in the street the ordinary, typical, average man: *The man in the street often has little interest in politics.*

man of God (*liter*) a minister, vicar, priest *etc.*

man of letters (*formal*) a writer and/or scholar: *Shakespeare was perhaps Britain's greatest man of letters.*

man of the world a sophisticated man who is not likely to be shocked or surprised by most things: *You can speak freely in front of John – he's a man of the world.*

man to man as one man to another; openly or frankly: *They talked man to man about their problems*; (*attrib*) *a man-to-man discussion.*

old man *see* **old**.

to a 'man every one, without exception: *They voted to a man to accept the proposal.*

manacle ['manəkl] *nc* (*hist*: *usu in pl*) a handcuff; shackles for hands or feet. – *vt* to put manacles on (someone).

manage ['manidʒ] **1** *vt* to be in control or charge of: *My son is a lawyer, so he manages all my legal affairs/money.* **2** *vt* to be manager of: *James manages the local football team.* **3** *vt* to deal with, or control: *That horse is difficult to manage*; *She's good at managing people.* **4** *vti* (*more inf than* **succeed**) to be able to do something; to succeed or cope: *Will you manage to repair your bicycle?*; *Don't worry – we'll manage quite well by ourselves*; *How will they manage without her?*; *Can you manage with £10 till I get some more money?*; *I don't think the old lady will manage (to climb) the stairs*; *Can you manage (to eat) some more meat?*

'**manageable** *adj* (*neg* **un-**: *usu pred*) **1** that can be controlled: *How manageable are your children?* **2** that can be done: *Are you finding this task manageable?* ˌ**managea'bility** *nu.*

'**management** **1** *nu* the art of managing: *The management of this company is a difficult task.* **2** *nc or n pl* the managers of a firm *etc* as a group: *The management has/have agreed to pay the workers more*; *The managements of all the other firms will do the same.*

'**manager** – *fem* ˌ**manage'ress** – *nc* a person who is in charge of *eg* a business, football team *etc*: *the manager of the new store.*

ˌ**mana'gerial** [-'dʒiə-] *adj* (*esp attrib*) of a manager or (a) management: *managerial skills.*

mandarin ['mandərin] *nc* **1** (*also* **mandarin orange**) a type of small orange. **2** (*hist*) an official of high rank in the Chinese Empire.

mandate ['mandeit] *nc* (*formal*) **1** a power given to a nation, person, or political party to act in the name of others: *By voting for this party at the election, the people of this country gave it a mandate to put its policies into action.* **2** an order given by a superior: *The land was divided up according to royal mandate.*

'**mandatory** [-də-] *adj* (*formal*) not allowing any choice; compulsory: *This offence carries a mandatory sentence of at least two years*; *It is preferable but not mandatory to have a university degree in this job.*

mandible ['mandibl] *nc* (*tech*) **1** a jaw or jawbone, *esp* the lower one. **2** a part of the beak of a bird, *esp* the lower.

mandolin, mandoline ['mandəlin] *nc* a musical instrument similar to a guitar: *He plays the mandolin*; *He played a tune on the mandolin.*

mane [mein] *nc* the long hair on the back of the neck of a horse, lion *etc*: *The male of the lion has a mane*; (*facet or liter*) *The girl has an absolute mane of red hair.*

maneuver *see* **manoeuvre**.

manful, manfully, manfulness *see* **man**.

mange [meindʒ] *nu* a skin disease of furry animals, *eg* dogs, cats *etc*: *Our cat is suffering from mange.*

'**mangy** *adj* suffering from mange: *a mangy dog*; *That dog is mangy*; *She was wearing a mangy old fur coat.* '**manginess** *nu.*

manger ['meindʒə] *nc* (*esp old*) a box or trough in which food for horses and cattle is placed.

dog in the manger *see* **dog**.

mangle ['maŋgl] *vt* **1** to crush to pieces: *The car was badly mangled in the accident.* **2** (*inf*) to spoil (*eg* a piece of music) by bad mistakes *etc*: *He mangled the music by his terrible playing.* **3** to put (clothing *etc*) through a mangle. – *nc* a machine with rollers for squeezing the water out of, and smoothing, wet clothes *etc.*

mango ['maŋgou] – *pl* '**mango(e)s** – *nc* **1** the yellowish fruit of an Indian tropical tree: *We had mangoes for dessert.* **2** (*also* '**mango tree**) the tree.

mangy *see* **mange**.

manhandle, manhole, manhood, manhunt *see* **man**.

mania ['meiniə] **1** *nu* (*med*) a form of mental illness in which the sufferer is over-active, over-excited, and unreasonably happy: *He is in a state of acute mania.* **2** *nc* an unreasonable enthusiasm for something: *He has a mania for fast cars*; *He has a mania for collecting teapots.*

'**maniac** [-ak] *nc* an insane (and dangerous) person; a madman: *A maniac has escaped from the psychiatric hospital*; (*fig*) *A maniac driving at 160 kph passed me on the motorway.*

manic ['manik] *adj* **1** (*med*) of, or suffering from, mania: *He's severely manic*; *She's in a manic state.* **2** (*loosely*) extremely energetic, active and excited: *The new manager is one of those manic people* *who can't rest even for a minute; He's really manic – he never sits still.*

ˌ**manic-de'pressive** [manik-] *nc, adj* (a person) suffering from an illness in which fits of acute excitement and severe depression alternate.

manicure ['manikjuə] *vt* to care for (the hands and nails): *She manicures her nails every night.* – *nc* a treatment for the hands and nails: *I'm going for a manicure.* **'manicurist** *nc.*

manifest ['manifest] *vt* (*formal*) to show (clearly): *He manifested in his behaviour a strong dislike of his younger sister.* – *adj* easily seen by the eye or understood by the mind; obvious: *It was manifest to all of us that he would fail; his manifest stupidity.* **'manifestly** *adv.*

ˌ**manife'station** (*formal*) **1** *nc* an obvious or clear example: *This is yet another manifestation of his ignorance.* **2** *nu* the act of showing clearly.

manifesto [mani'festou] – *pl* ˌ**mani'festo(e)s** – *nc* a public *usu* written announcement of policies and intentions, *esp* by a political party: *Political parties rarely fulfil the promises made in their manifestos.*

manifold ['manifould] *adj* (*formal*) many and various: *The reasons for not smoking are manifold; his manifold talents.* – *nc* (*tech*) a pipe, *eg* in a car's exhaust system, with several openings for connections to other pipes.

manil(l)a [mə'nilə] *nu, adj* (of) a type of thick, strong brown paper: *a manil(l)a envelope; These envelopes are white, not manilla.*

manipulate [mə'nipjuleit] *vt* (*formal*) **1** to handle *esp* skilfully: *I watched him manipulating the controls of the aircraft.* **2** to manage or influence cleverly (and dishonestly): *A clever lawyer can manipulate a jury.* **maˌnipu'lation** *ncu.* **ma'nipulator** *nc.*

mankind, manliness, manly, manned *see* **man**.

mannequin ['manikin] *nc* a person, *usu* a woman, employed to wear clothes in order to display them to possible buyers; a model.

manner ['manə] *nc* **1** a way in which anything is done *etc*: *She greeted me in a friendly manner; The manner in which elections are held is considered unsatisfactory by many people.* **2** the way in which a person behaves, speaks *etc*: *He has an easy, frank manner; I don't like her manner.* **3** (*in pl*) (polite) behaviour, *usu* towards others: *Why doesn't she teach her children (good) manners?; It is bad manners to talk with your mouth full of food; He has no manners; table manners* (= behaviour at mealtimes).

-'mannered (*in cmpds*) having, or showing, manners of a certain kind: *a well-/bad-mannered person; His remark was very ill-mannered* (= rude).

'mannered *adj* (*formal derog*) (of a style *etc*) unnatural and artificial: *a mannered style of writing/speaking; His style of prose is rather mannered.*

'mannerism *nc* an odd and obvious habit in a person's behaviour, speech *etc*: *He scratches his ear when he talks and has other noticeable mannerisms.*

'mannerly *adj* (*old formal*) polite: *Children should be taught to behave in a mannerly way; All her children have been taught to be mannerly.*

all 'manner of (*formal*) all kinds of: *He has all manner of problems.*

(as if) to the ˌmanner 'born (*facet*) (as though) accustomed since birth to a particular occupation, rôle *etc*: *He speaks in public (as if) to the manner born.*

by no manner of means/not by any manner of means *see* **means**[1].

in a manner of speaking (*more formal than* **in a way**) in a certain way: *I suppose, in a manner of speaking, you could call me an engineer.*

mannish, mannishness *see* **man**.

manoeuvre, (*Amer*) **maneuver** [mə'nu:və] *nc* **1** (*formal or tech*) a planned movement (of troops, ships, aircraft, vehicles *etc*): *The soldiers were out on the hill, practising manoeuvres; Can you perform all the manoeuvres required by the driving test?* **2** a skilful or cunning plan or action: *His appointment was the result of many cunning manoeuvres.* – *vti* (*formal*) to (cause to) perform manoeuvres: *I watched the tanks manoeuvring into position; She had difficulty manoeuvring her car into the narrow space; (fig) She manoeuvred me into a position where I had to agree.*

manor ['manə] *nc* **1** (*also* **'manor-house**) the house belonging to a country estate. **2** (*hist*) the land belonging to a nobleman or gentleman: *the lord of the manor.* **ma'norial** [-'no:-] *adj* (*formal*).

manpower *see* **man**.

manse [mans] *nc* (*esp* in Scotland) the house of a clergyman.

mansion ['manʃən] *nc* a large (luxurious) house: *They own a country mansion.*

'Mansions *n* a word often used in the names of blocks of (luxury) flats: *She lives in Curzon Mansions.*

manservant, mansize(d), manslaughter *see* **man**.

mantelpiece ['mantlpi:s], **mantelshelf** ['mantlʃelf], **mantel** ['mantl], *nc* the shelf above a fireplace: *She has a large collection of glass ornaments on her mantelpiece.*

mantle ['mantl] *nc* **1** a thin piece of net round a gas or oil lamp that glows when it is lit: *If we are going camping we'll have to get a new mantle for the gas lamp.* **2** (*liter*) a cloak or loose outer garment: *He put her mantle round her shoulders for her; (fig) The hills were covered with a mantle of snow.*

manual ['manjuəl] *adj* (*esp attrib*) **1** of the hand or hands: *manual skills/labour.* **2** working with the hands: *He is a manual worker.* **3** worked or operated by the hand: *a car with a manual gearbox.* – *nc* **1** a handbook *eg* of technical information about a machine *etc*: *an instruction manual.* **2** a keyboard of an organ *etc.*

'manually *adv* by hand: *You have to operate this sewing-machine manually – it is not electric.*

manufacture [manju'faktʃə] *vt* (*more formal than* **make**) **1** to make, *orig* by hand but now *usu* by machinery and in large quantities: *This firm manufactures cars at the rate of two hundred per day.* **2** to invent (something false): *He manufactured an excuse for being late.* – **1** *nu* the process of manufacturing: *This town is famous for the manufacture of glass.* **2** *nc* (*esp in pl*) something manufactured: *Is this country importing too many foreign manufactures?*

ˌ**manu'facturer** *nc* a person or firm that manufactures goods: *He is a carpet manufacturer.*

manure [mə'njuə] *nu* a mixture containing animal dung, spread on soil to help produce better crops *etc*: *The farmer is putting manure on his fields.* – *vt* (*formal*) to treat (soil or plants) with manure: *The farmer has been manuring the fields.*

manuscript ['manjuskript] *nc* **1** the handwritten or

typed material for a book *etc*, *usu* prepared for printing: *The publishers have lost the manuscript of my book.* **2** (*tech*) a book or document written by hand: *His library contains a good collection of manuscripts as well as of printed books.*

many ['meni] – *compar* **more** [mo:]: *superl* **most** [moust] – *adj* (*used with ncs*) a great number of: *Many languages are spoken in Africa*; *Very many adults cannot read*; *'Were there a lot of people there?' 'Not very many'*; *Children eat too many sweets*; *We have one too many* (= one more than the necessary number of) *chairs here*; *You've made a great/good many mistakes.* – *See also* **many a** *below.* – *pron* a great number: *A few people survived, but many died*; *Many of them died.*

many- (*in cmpds*) having a great number of (something): *ˌmany-'coloured*; *ˌmany-'sided.*

'many a (*with a sing noun*: *liter and used for emphasis*) a great number of: *Many a fine man* (= Many fine men) *died in that battle*; *I've told him many a time to be more polite.*

many's the thing *etc* **(that)** there are a great many things *etc* that: *Many's the time* (*that*) *I've thought of leaving*; *Many's the job I've left unfinished.*

See also **more, most, much**.

map [map] *nc* **1** a drawing or plan, in outline, of (any part of) the surface of the earth, with various features shown (*usu* roads, rivers, seas, towns *etc*): *a map of the world/Spain/London*; *He bought a road map of France*; *This village is not shown/marked on the map.* **2** a similar type of drawing showing *eg* the surface of the moon, the position of the stars in the sky *etc.* – *v* – *pt, ptp* **mapped** – *vt* (*formal or tech*) to make a map of (an area): *Africa was mapped by many different explorers.*

map out *vt sep* to plan (a route, course of action *etc*) in detail: *We started to map out a possible route for our journey*; *We did not have time to map it out in detail.*

put on the map (*inf*) to cause (a place) to be important: *The recent events in that town have certainly put it on the map.*

maple ['meipl] *nc* (*also* **'maple tree**) one of several kinds of tree, some of which yield a type of sugar that is often used for syrup: *We have several maples in our garden*; (*attrib*) *We poured maple syrup over the pancakes.*

mar [ma:] – *pt, ptp* **marred** – *vt* (*formal*) to spoil or damage (enjoyment, beauty *etc*): *Her beauty was marred by a scar on her cheek*; *The death of the old man marred their happiness.*

marathon ['marəθən, (*Amer*) -θon] *nc* a long-distance footrace, *usu* 42 km 195 m (26 miles 385 yd): *He came third in the marathon*; (*fig*) *There's so much to discuss that this meeting could turn out to be a real marathon*; (*attrib*) *a marathon race/discussion.*

marauder [mə'ro:də] *nc* (*liter*) a person who attacks places and steals things from them.

ma'rauding *adj* (*attrib*): *We were attacked by marauding tribesmen.*

marble ['ma:bl] **1** *nu, adj* (of) a kind of hard, *usu* highly polished stone, cold to the touch: *This table is* (*made of*) *marble*; *a marble statue.* **2** *nc* a small hard ball of glass used in children's games: *The little boy rolled a marble along the ground.* – *See also* **marbles** *below.*

'marbled *adj* (*formal*) having irregular streaks of different colours, like some types of marble: *We admired the marbled stonework of the fireplace.*

'marbles *n sing* any of several games played with marbles: *The boys were playing marbles on the pavement.*

March [ma:tʃ] *n* the third month of the year, the month following February: *She is leaving in March*; *She is leaving on March 23* (said as 'on March (the) twenty-third' or 'on the twenty-third of March'); *He is coming on the 23rd/twenty-third of March*; *He died last March.*

march [ma:tʃ] **1** *vti* to (cause to) walk at a constant rhythm, and often in step with others: *Soldiers were marching along the street.* **2** *vi* (*often fig*) to go on steadily: *Time marches on.* – **1** *ncu* (the) act of marching: *We took part in a long march today*; *a thirty-mile march*; (*fig*) *the march of time/progress.* **2** *nc* a piece of music for marching to: *Sousa wrote several famous marches*; (*attrib*) *This music should be played in march time.*

ˌget one's 'marching orders 1 to get the order to march: *The troops were waiting for their marching orders.* **2** (*inf*) to be dismissed (from a job *etc*): *She got her marching orders and was told never to come back.*

on the march marching or progressing: *The soldiers are on the march*; (*fig*) *The forces of change are on the march.*

marchioness *see* **marquis**.

mare [meə] *nc* a female horse: *The mare has just had a foal.*

margarine ['ma:dʒəri:n] *nu* (*inf abbrev* **marge** [ma:dʒ]) a butter-like substance made mainly from vegetable fats: *We don't use margarine because it is cheaper than butter but because we think it is better for our health.*

margin ['ma:dʒin] *nc* **1** the blank edge round a page of writing or print: *Please write your comments in the margin.* **2** (*formal or liter*) an edge or border: *Reeds were growing round the margin of the lake.* **3** (*often fig*) something extra, beyond what should be needed: *Leave a wide margin for error in your calculations!*; *In the cosmetics business, the profit margin* (= the difference between cost price and selling price) *seems to be enormous.*

'marginal *adj* **1** (*formal*) small and almost non-existent or unimportant: *There has been a marginal improvement in the firm's sales*; *The improvement in his work is marginal.* **2** (*very formal*: *attrib*) of or in a margin or margins: *I glanced at the editor's marginal comments in the typescript.* **3** (*esp attrib*) (of a political seat, constituency *etc*) having no clear majority or preference for one particular party or candidate: *All the parties will be trying hard to capture the marginal seats at the next election.*

marigold ['marigould] *nc* **1** a plant of the daisy type. **2** its yellow or orange flower.

marijuana, marihuana [mari'wa:nə] *nu* a type of drug (illegal in many countries) made from the dried flowers and leaves of the hemp plant, and often smoked in cigarettes.

marina [mə'ri:nə] – *pl* **ma'rinas** – *nc* a harbour or area of sheltered water for the mooring of private pleasure boats.

marine [mə'ri:n] *adj* (*attrib*) of the sea: *marine animals*; *marine law.* – *nc* a soldier serving on board a ship: *He has joined the marines.*

mariner ['marinə] *nc* (*formal or liter*) a sailor: *a master mariner.*

marionette [mariə'net] *nc* (*formal*) a type of puppet moved by strings.

marital ['maritl] *adj* (*formal*: *esp attrib*) of mar-

riage: *They're having marital problems*; *Their marital relations* (= the relationship between them as a married couple) *are very bad*.
See also **marriage, marry**.

maritime ['maritaim] *adj* (*formal*: *esp attrib*) **1** of the sea, shipping *etc*: *maritime law*. **2** lying near the sea, and therefore having a navy, merchant shipping *etc*: *Britain was once a great maritime nation*.

marjoram ['ma:dʒərəm] *nu* a type of sweet-smelling herb used as a seasoning.

mark[1] [ma:k] *nc* **1** (*also* **Deutsche Mark, Deutschmark** ['doitʃma:k]) the standard unit of currency in the Federal Republic of Germany. **2** the standard unit of currency in the German Democratic Republic.

mark[2] [ma:k] *nc* **1** a sign or spot that can be seen, *eg* on a person's or animal's body: *My dog has a white mark on his nose*. **2** a point given as a reward for good work *etc*: *She got good marks in the exam*. **3** a stain: *That spilt coffee has left a mark on the carpet*. **4** a sign used as a guide to position *etc*: *There's a mark on the map showing where the church is*. **5** a cross or other sign used instead of a signature: *He couldn't sign his name, so he made his mark instead*. **6** (*formal*) an indication or sign of a particular thing: *Some men still raise their hats as a mark of respect in greeting a woman*; *Carefulness in the use of words is the mark of an accurate mind*. **7** the position from which a competitor starts in a race: *On your marks!* – **1** *vti* to put a mark or stain on, or to become marked or stained: *Every pupil's coat must be marked with his name*; *That tomato sauce has marked the tablecloth*; *This white material marks easily*. **2** *vt* to give marks to (a piece of work): *I have forty exam-papers to mark tonight*. **3** *vt* to show; to be a sign of: *The moon landings marked the beginning of a new era*; *X marks the spot where the treasure is buried*. **4** *vt* to note: *Mark it down in your notebook*. **5** *vt* (*old or formal*) to watch closely or give one's attention to: *He'll be late again – mark my words!* (= you'll see that I'm right.) **6** *vt* (in football *etc*) to keep close to (an opponent) so as to prevent his getting the ball: *Your job is to mark the centre-forward*.

marked *adj* (*esp attrib*) obvious or easily noticeable: *There has been a marked improvement in her work*. – *See also* **be a marked man** *below*.

'**markedly** [-kid-] *adv* (*formal*) noticeably: *It's markedly easier to do it by this method*.

'**marker** *nc* **1** a person who marks *eg* the score at games. **2** something used for marking, *eg* in scoring, showing the position of something *etc*: *The area is indicated by large green markers*. **3** a type of pen, *usu* with a thick point.

marked man *see* **be a marked man** *below*.

'**marksman** ['ma:ks-] *nc* a person who shoots well: *The police marksman did not kill the criminal – he wounded him in the leg to prevent him escaping*.

'**marksmanship** *nu* a person's skill as a marksman.

mark-up *see* **mark down/up** *below*.

beside/off/wide of the mark (*formal*) off the target or subject: *His guess was rather wide of the mark*.

be a marked man (*often fig*) to be in danger because enemies are trying to kill or harm one: *He is a marked man – the criminals whom he reported to the police are looking for him*; *You are a marked man – your boss is trying to find a reason to sack you*.

be up to the mark to reach the required or normal standard: *His work hasn't been up to the mark for some time*.

leave/make one's mark to make a permanent or strong impression: *The horrors of the war have left their mark on the children*; *Many great statesmen have left their mark on the literary scene*; *He is beginning to make his mark as an actor*.

mark down, up *vt sep* to bring down or increase the price of (an article for sale in a shop): *This jacket has been marked down from £10 to £8* (*nc* '**mark-up**: *The retailers must be making very large profits – there's a huge mark-up on these goods*).

mark off *vt sep* to put marks on (something) indicating divisions *etc*: *The artist marked off his canvas in squares before starting to paint*; *He marked it off neatly*.

mark out *vt sep* **1** to mark the boundary of (*eg* a football pitch) by making lines *etc*: *The pitch was marked out with white lines*; *They marked it out yesterday*. **2** to select or choose for some particular purpose *etc* in the future: *He had been marked out for an army career from early childhood*.

mark time to move the feet up and down as if marching, but without going forward: *The soldiers marked time for a few seconds, and then moved towards the lorries*; (*fig*) *He's only marking time in this job till he gets one more suited to his qualifications*.

market ['ma:kit] *nc* **1** a public place where people meet to buy and sell or the public event at which this happens: *He has a clothes stall in the market*; *Markets are held in the square every Wednesday*. **2** (a place where there is) a demand for certain things: *There is a market for cotton goods in hot countries*; *The Arctic is not a very good market for refrigerators*. – *vt* to (attempt to) sell: *I produce the goods and my brother markets them all over Europe*.

'**marketable** *adj* (*formal*) wanted by the public and therefore able to be sold: *I don't think your new product is marketable*; *If you have a marketable product they will sell it for you*.

'**marketing** *nu* (*often in cmpds*) (the study of) the processes by which anything may be sold: *He is in charge of marketing*; *egg-/potato-marketing*; (*attrib*) *marketing methods*; (*attrib*) *marketing director*.

ˌ**market-'garden** *nc* a garden where fruit and vegetables are grown for sale.

'**market-place,** ˌ**market-'square** *nc* the open space or square in a town in which the market is held.

market price/value *nc* the price at which a thing is being sold at a particular time: *What's the current market price of gold?*; *Pictures of this sort have a high market value*.

market research *nu* investigation of the habits and preferences of the public in choosing what goods to buy: *She does market research for a cosmetics firm*.

be in the 'market for (*inf*) wishing to buy: *Are you in the market for second-hand furniture these days?*

be on the market to be for sale: *Her house has been on the market for months*.

marksman, marksmanship *see* **mark**[2].

marmalade ['ma:məleid] *nu* a type of jam made from oranges, lemons or grapefruit: *She spread marmalade on her toast at breakfast*; *Could I have some jam? I don't like marmalade*.

maroon[1] [mə'ru:n] *nu, adj* (of) a dark brownish-red colour: *a large maroon car*; *His new car is maroon.*

maroon[2] [mə'ru:n] *vt* **1** (*formal or old*) to put (someone) on shore on a lonely island from which he cannot escape. **2** to leave (someone) in a helpless, lonely or uncomfortable position: *He found himself marooned in the middle of enemy territory*; *When the wheel fell off my car, I was marooned on a lonely country road.*

marquee [ma:'ki:] *nc* a very large tent used for circuses, parties *etc*: *There were too many guests at the wedding to hold the reception in the house so we hired a marquee.*

marquis, marquess ['ma:kwis] – *nc* (*with cap in titles*) (the status of) a nobleman next in rank below a duke: *She is going to marry a marquis*; *The Marquis of Rutherglen.*

marchioness ['ma:ʃənis] *nc* (*with cap in titles*) **1** (the status of) the wife or widow of a marquis. **2** (the status of) a woman of the same rank as a marquis in her own right.

marriage ['maridʒ] **1** *nc* the ceremony by which a man and woman become husband and wife: *Our marriage was a very quiet event*; (*attrib*) *the marriage ceremony.* **2** *ncu* the state of being married; married life: *Marriage is not the ideal state for everyone*; *Their marriage lasted for thirty happy years.* **3** *nc* (*formal*) a close joining together: *the marriage of his skill and her judgement.*

'**marriageable** *adj* suitable, or at a proper age, for marriage: *He has four marriageable daughters*; *Is she of marriageable age?*; *As she grows older she becomes less marriageable.*

'**marriage licence** *nc* a paper giving official permission for a marriage to take place.

marriage of convenience (*formal*) a marriage entered into for the advantages it will bring rather than for love: *It was just a marriage of convenience when their father married the housekeeper after their mother's death.*

See also **marry, marital**.

marrow 1 *nu* the soft substance in the hollow parts of bones: *Beef marrow is needed for this dish*; (*fig*) *I forgot my coat and came home chilled to the marrow* (= very cold). **2** *nc* (*Amer* **squash**) a large, green, thick-skinned vegetable: *They grow cucumbers and marrows.* **3** *nu* (*Amer* **squash**) its flesh as food: *We had stuffed marrow for supper.*

marry ['mari] **1** *vti* to take (a person) as one's husband or wife: *John married my sister*; *They married in church.* **2** *vt* (of a clergyman *etc*) to perform the ceremony of marriage between (two people): *The vicar of the village church married them.* **3** *vt* (*formal*) to give (a son or daughter) as a husband or wife: *He married his son to a rich princess.*

'**married** *adj* (*neg* **un-**): *She has two married daughters*; *Is her younger daughter married?*

marry off *vt sep* (*inf*) to find a husband or wife for (one's son or daughter): *He managed to marry off all his daughters to wealthy or aristocratic young men*; *He has finally married her off.*

See also **marriage, marital**.

Mars *see* Appendix 6.

marsh [ma:ʃ] *ncu* (an area of) soft wet land: *As he walked across the hills he fell into a marsh and could not get out.* '**marshy** *adj.* '**marshiness** *nu.*

marshal ['ma:ʃəl] *nc* **1** (*formal or tech*) an official who arranges ceremonies, processions *etc.* **2** (*Amer*) an official with certain duties in the lawcourts. **3** (*Amer*) the head of a police or fire department. – *v* – *pt, ptp* '**marshalled**, (*Amer*) '**marshaled** – *vt* (*formal*) **1** to arrange (forces, facts, arguments *etc*) in order: *Give me a minute to marshal my thoughts.* **2** to lead or show the way to: *We marshalled the whole group into a large room.*

'**marshalling-yard** *nc* a place where railway wagons are sorted out and made up into trains.

See also **field marshal** *and* Appendix 3.

marshmallow ['ma:ʃmalou] *nc* a type of very soft sweet with a spongy texture.

marsupial [ma:'sju:piəl] *nc, adj* (*tech*) (an animal) having a pouch in which to carry its young: *The kangaroo is a marsupial.*

mart [ma:t] *nc* (*esp in cmpds*) a place where things are sold: *a used-car mart*; *a cattle-mart.*

martial ['ma:ʃəl] *adj* (*formal*: *usu attrib*) **1** warlike or fond of fighting: *a martial nation.* **2** belonging to or suitable for war: *martial music.*

martial law *nu* (*formal*) the ruling of a country by the army in time of war or great national emergency, when ordinary law does not apply: *The country is now under martial law.*

Martian *see* Appendix 6.

martinet [ma:ti'net] *nc* (*formal*) a person whose discipline of others is very strict: *The new teacher is a real martinet.*

martyr ['ma:tə] *nc* **1** a person who suffers death or hardship for what he or she believes: *St Joan is said to have been a martyr.* **2** a person who continually suffers from a disease, difficulty *etc*: *She is a martyr to rheumatism*; *She makes a martyr of herself by doing all the cooking and cleaning herself – she should get her daughters to help.* – *vt* to put (someone) to death or cause (him) to suffer greatly for his beliefs: *Saint Joan was martyred by the English.*

'**martyrdom** *nu* the suffering or death of a martyr.

marvel ['ma:vəl] *nc* something or someone astonishing or wonderful: *the marvels of the circus*; *She's a marvel at producing delicious meals.* – *v* – *pt, ptp* '**marvelled**, (*Amer*) '**marveled** – *vi* (*formal*: *often with* **at**) to feel astonishment or wonder (at): *They marvelled at the fantastic sight.*

'**marvellous**, (*Amer*) '**marvelous** *adj* **1** wonderful: *The Alps are a marvellous sight.* **2** (*loosely*: *inf*) very good in some way; excellent: *I've had a marvellous idea*; *You're coming to the party? How marvellous!* '**marvellously** *adv.*

marzipan [ma:zi'pan, (*Amer*) 'ma:rzəpan] *nu, adj* (of) a sweet paste made of crushed almonds and sugar, used in decorating cakes, making sweets *etc*: *I put marzipan on the Christmas cake before the icing*; *I've made some marzipan decorations for the cake.*

mascara [ma'ska:rə] *nu* colouring for the eyelashes: *She uses brown mascara.*

mascot ['maskət] *nc* a person, animal or thing supposed to bring good luck: *She takes a little toy mouse into exams as a mascot.*

masculine ['maskjulin] *adj* **1** of the male sex: *masculine qualities.* **2** (of a woman or her appearance *etc*: *usu offensive*) mannish: *a tall, rather masculine woman*; *Some women athletes are rather masculine.* **3** (*gram*) in certain languages, of one of *usu* two or three genders of nouns *etc*: *Is the French word for 'door' masculine or feminine?* ˌ**mascu'linity** *nu.*

mash [maʃ] *vt* to crush into small pieces or a soft mass: *Put in some butter when you mash the potatoes.* – *nu* **1** (*inf*) mashed potato: *sausage and mash.* **2** a mixture of bran with meal or turnips, used as food for animals: *Have the hens had their mash yet?*

mask [maːsk] *nc* **1** something, *eg* a covering resembling a face, used for hiding or protecting the whole or part of the face: *The thief wore a black mask over the upper part of his face, so that he could not be recognized*; (*fig formal*) *Her face was a mask* (= showing no feelings) *so I couldn't tell her thoughts*; (*fig formal*) *He often came to our house under the mask of friendship* (= pretending to be a friend). – *vt* (*formal*) to hide or disguise: *The shadow masked her face*; *He managed to mask his feelings rather well.*
See also **unmask**.

masochism ['masəkizm] *nu* (*tech*) unnatural (*esp* sexual) pleasure obtained from receiving cruel or painful physical or (*loosely*) mental treatment.
'masochist *nc* a person who obtains pleasure in this way: *She likes being beaten by her husband – she's a masochist.* **ˌmaso'chistic** *adj.*

mason ['meisn] *nc* **1** (*usu* **'stonemason**) a skilled worker or builder in stone. **2** short for **'Freemason**: *He has been a keen mason all his life.*
masonic [mə'sonik] *adj* (*attrib*) of Freemasons or Freemasonry: *a masonic lodge.*
'masonry *nu* stone(work): *He was killed by falling masonry.*

masquerade [maskə'reid] **1** *ncu* (a) pretence or disguise: *His trial/Her show of friendship was* (*a*) *mere masquerade.* **2** *nc* (*old*) a dance where people wear masks: *They met at the New Year masquerade.* – *vi* (*formal*) (*with* **as**) to pretend to be, *usu* intending to deceive: *The criminal was masquerading as a respectable businessman.*

mass[1] [mas] **1** *nc* a large lump or quantity, gathered together: *a mass of concrete*; *The people were marching in a huge mass*; *The picture was painted in broad masses of colour.* **2** *nc* (*esp in pl*: *inf*) a large quantity: *I've masses of work/things to do*; *'Is there any bread?' 'Yes, masses'*; *There's a mass of good reasons why you should come.* **3** *nc* (*no pl*) the bulk, principal part or main body: *The mass of people are in favour of peace.* **4** *ncu* (*formal or tech*) (a) measure of the quantity of matter in an object: *The mass of the rock is 500 kilos.* – *vti* (*formal*) to bring or come together in large numbers or quantities: *He massed the troops/The troops massed for an attack.* – *adj* (*attrib*) of large quantities or numbers: *mass murder*; *a mass meeting.*
ˌmass-pro'duced *adj* (*sometimes derog*) (of goods) all exactly the same and produced in great numbers or quantity: *mass-produced plastic toys*; *Don't buy that – it's cheap and mass-produced.* **ˌmass-pro'duce** *vt.* **ˌmass-pro'duction** *nu.*
be a 'mass of to be covered with, full of *etc*: *The battlefield was a mass of bodies*; *His face was a mass of pimples.*
the masses (*derog*) the ordinary people, *esp* of the working class: *I think we should have a new opera house – I don't care what the masses think.*
the mass media (*sometimes derog*) those channels of communication (TV, radio, newspapers *etc*) that reach large numbers of people.
See also **massive**.

mass[2] [mas] **1** *ncu* (*esp with cap*) (a) celebration, *esp* in the Roman Catholic church, of Christ's last meal (**Last Supper**) with his disciples: *What time do you go to Mass?* **2** *nc* a setting to music of some of the words used in this service.

massacre ['masəkə] *nc* **1** the killing of a large number of *usu* people, *esp* with great cruelty: *There was a terrible massacre of villagers here during the war.* **2** (*inf fig*) a very bad defeat: *That last game was a complete massacre.* – *vt* to kill (large numbers) cruelly: *The school children were brutally massacred*; (*inf fig*) *Our team was massacred on Saturday.*

massage ['masaːʒ, (*Amer*) mə'saːʒ] *vt* to treat (a person's body or part of it) by rubbing, kneading *etc* to ease and remove pain or stiffness: *She massaged my sore back.* – *ncu* (a) treatment by massaging: *I'm going to have a massage*; *His ankle was treated by massage.*
masseur [ma'səː] – *fem* **masseuse** [ma'səːz, (*Amer also*) mə'suːz] – *nc* (*formal or tech*) a person who gives massage professionally.

massive ['masiv] *adj* (*esp attrib*) huge or heavy: *The new library is a massive building*; *During the last century there was a massive expansion of industry*; *a massive burden of taxation.* **'massively** *adv.* **'massiveness** *nu.*

mast [maːst] *nc* a long upright pole *esp* for carrying the sails of a ship, an aerial, flag *etc*: *The sailor climbed the mast.*
-masted (*in cmpds*) having (a certain number of) masts: *ˌsingle-'masted*; *ˌfour-'masted.*
'masthead *nc* the top of a mast.

master ['maːstə] – *fem* **mistress** ['mistris] (*defs 1–3*) – **1** *nc* a person or thing that commands or controls: *I'm master in this house!* **2** *nc* an owner (of a slave, dog *etc*): *The dog ran to its master.* **3** *nc* a male teacher: *the Maths master.* **4** *nc* the commander of a merchant ship: *He got his master's ticket* (= licence) *ten years ago.* **5** *nc* (*formal*) a person very skilled in an art, science *etc*: *He's a real master at carving animals.* **6** *n* (*with cap*) a polite title for a boy, in writing or in speaking: *Master John Smith.* **7** *nc* (*usu* **master copy**) something from which duplicates are made: *Photograph this, keep the photocopy and give me back the master.* – *adj* (*attrib*) (of a person in a job) fully qualified, skilled and experienced: *a master builder/mariner/plumber.* – *vt* **1** to overcome (an opponent, handicap *etc*): *She has mastered her fear of heights.* **2** to become skilful in: *I don't think I'll ever master arithmetic.*
'masterful *adj* showing the power, authority or determination of a master: *Many women like their husbands to be masterful*; *He's rather a masterful man.* **'masterfully** *adv.* **'masterfulness** *nu.*
'masterly *adj* showing the skill of a master: *a masterly handling of a sword*; *His handling of the situation was indeed masterly.* **'masterliness** *nu.*
'mastery *nu* (*usu with* **over** *or* **of**) control, great skill or knowledge: *This boy seems to have complete mastery of the basic principles of chemistry*; *We have gained mastery over the enemy.*
'master key *nc* a key which opens a number of locks: *The policeman had a master key and so could open all the doors in the office.*
'mastermind *nc* the person planning and controlling an undertaking or scheme: *He was the mastermind behind the scheme.* – *vt* to plan (such a scheme): *Who masterminded the robbery?*
'masterpiece *nc* a piece of work or art worthy (to be called the greatest achievement) of a master: *He considers this picture his masterpiece*; *The book is a masterpiece!*
'master stroke *nc* a very clever thing to do: *This sudden, unexpected attack was a master stroke.*
'master switch *nc* a switch for controlling a

number of other switches: *There is a master switch in the basement of the building that controls all the electricity.*

Master of Arts, Science *etc* a person who has passed examinations (*usu* at a higher level than those for a Bachelor's degree) or who has written a thesis, in Arts, Science *etc* at a university.

master of ceremonies (*inf abbrev* **MC**) a person who announces the various stages of an entertainment, formal social gathering, series of speakers at a dinner *etc*: *The master of ceremonies introduced the speaker*; *The MC announced the next dance*; *He acted as MC at the wedding reception.*

See also **mistress**.

masthead *see* **mast**.

masticate ['mastikeit] *vti* (*tech or formal*) to chew. **ˌmastiˈcation** *nu.*

mastiff ['mastif] *nc* a type of powerful dog, formerly used in hunting.

mat [mat] *nc* **1** (*often in cmpds*) a flat piece of material (rushes, rubber, carpet, cork *etc*) for wiping shoes on, covering a floor, or various other purposes: *Wipe your shoes on the doormat*; *Put a table-mat under that hot dish.* **2** a covering or tangle of vegetation, hair *etc*: *He had a thick mat of hair on his chest.*

ˈmatted *adj* in a thick untidy mess: *matted hair*; *His hair is matted with blood.*

ˈmatting *nu* material used for making mats: *coconut matting.*

matador ['matədo:] *nc* the man who kills the bull in a bullfight.

match[1] [matʃ] *nc* a short piece of wood or other material tipped with a substance that catches fire when rubbed against a rough or specially-prepared substance: *He struck* (= lit by rubbing) *a match and lit his cigarette*; *a box of matches.*

ˈmatchbox *nc* a box for holding matches: *an empty matchbox.*

ˈmatchstick *nc* a match that has been used or that has no head: *He taught me a trick using six matchsticks.*

ˈmatchwood *nu* (*formal*) tiny pieces of wood: *The force of the blow reduced the box to matchwood.*

match[2] [matʃ] *nc* **1** a contest or game: *a football/rugby/chess match*; *What time does the match start?* **2** a thing that is similar to or the same as another in some way(s) *eg* in colour or pattern: *These trousers are not an exact match for my jacket.* **3** a person who is able to equal another: *At running, Jack is no match for Jim*; *She has finally met her match at arguing* (= met a person who argues as persistently as she does). **4** (*formal*) a marriage or an act of marrying: *She hoped to arrange a match between her daughter and some rich young man.* **5** (*formal*) a person to be gained in marriage: *She'll make a fine match for my son.* – **1** *vti* to be equal or similar to something or someone in some way *eg* in colour or pattern: *That dress matches her red hair*; *The two pieces of wallpaper don't match exactly.* **2** *vt* to set (two things, people *etc*) to compete: *John and Bill will be matched in the final*; *He's going to try and match his skill against the champion's.*

matched *adj* (*often in cmpds*) paired or joined together, *eg* in marriage, or as contestants in a competition *etc*: *Jack and Mary are a well-matched couple*; *The two boxers were evenly matched.*

ˈmatchless *adj* (*liter*) having no equal: *a woman of matchless beauty.*

ˈmatchmaker *nc* a person who tries to arrange marriages between people: *The old lady is a real matchmaker – she's always introducing her nephew to girls.*

mate [meit] *vti* **1** to come, or bring (animals *etc*), together for breeding: *The bears have mated and produced a cub*; *Our puppy will not be old enough to be mated for a year or two.* **2** (*chess*) to checkmate (someone). – **1** *nc* an animal *etc* with which another is paired for breeding: *Some birds sing in order to attract a mate.* **2** *nc* (*facet*) a husband or wife: *Be careful – she's looking for a mate, not just a friend.* **3** *nc* (*esp Brit*: *inf*) a companion or friend: *We've been mates for years.* **4** *nc* a fellow workman or assistant: *a carpenter's mate.* **5** *nc* a merchant ship's officer under the master or captain: *the first mate.* **6** *ncu* (*chess*) checkmate.

the ˈmating season spring, the time of year when birds build their nests.

material [məˈtiəriəl] **1** *ncu* anything out of which something is, or may be, made: *Tables are usually made from solid material such as wood*; *Have you all the materials you need for doing the job?*; (*fig*) *She's excellent teacher material* (= could be an excellent teacher). **2** *nu* cloth: *I'd like three metres of blue woollen material.* – *adj* **1** (*formal or tech*) consisting of solid(s), liquid(s), gas(es) or any combination of these: *the material world.* **2** (*formal often derog*) belonging to the world; not spiritual: *He wanted material things like money, possessions and power*; *His interest in the job is purely material.* **3** (*formal*: *esp pred with* **to**) essential or important: *evidence that is material to his defence.*

maˈterially *adv* (*formal*) to a great or important extent: *Circumstances have changed materially since yesterday.*

maˈterialism *nu* (*formal often derog*) a tendency to attach too much importance to bodily comfort, money, success *etc.* **maˈterialist** *nc.* **maˌteriaˈlistic** *adj.*

maˈterialize, -ise *vi* (*formal*) **1** to take solid or bodily form: *The figure materialized as we watched with astonishment*; (*inf*) *He promised to come, but so far he hasn't materialized* (= arrived). **2** (of something expected or hoped for) to happen: *I don't think her plans will ever materialize.* **maˌterialiˈzation, -s-** *nus.*

raw material *see* **raw**.

See also **immaterial**.

maternal [məˈtə:nl] *adj* (*formal*) **1** of or like a mother: *His wife is very maternal in her attitude towards him*; *maternal feelings.* **2** (*attrib*) related on the mother's side of the family: *my maternal grandfather.* **maˈternally** *adv.*

maternity [məˈtə:nəti] *nu* (*usu attrib*) the state of being or becoming a mother: *She had her first baby at a maternity hospital*; *maternity clothes* (= clothes for a pregnant woman); *maternity benefit* (= money supplied to a woman when she has a baby).

mathematics [maθəˈmatiks] *n sing* (*inf abbrev* **maths** [maθs], (*Amer*) **math** [maθ]) the science or branch of knowledge dealing with measurements, numbers and quantities: *He is studying mathematics*; (*attrib*) *a mathematics lecture.*

ˌmatheˈmatical *adj* (*esp attrib*) **1** of or done by mathematics: *mathematical tables.* **2** very exact or accurate: *She landed the plane with mathematical precision.* **ˌmatheˈmatically** *adv.*

ˌmathemaˈtician [-ˈtiʃən] *nc* **1** a person who is good at mathematics: *For a young boy, he's quite a mathematician!* **2** someone who works in mathematics: *He is a mathematician with a local engineering firm.*

matinée ['matinei, (*Amer*) matə'nei] *nc* a performance at a theatre, circus, cinema *etc* held in the afternoon or morning: *They do six evening performances and three matinées every week*; (*attrib*) *a matinée performance.*

matins, mattins ['matinz] *n pl* morning prayers or service in certain churches.

matriarch ['meitria:k] *nc* (*formal*) a woman who is head and ruler of her family or of a tribe.

ˌmatri'archal *adj* (*formal*: *often used loosely*) of, like, ruled by *etc* a matriarch or matriarchs: *Is the United States a good example of a matriarchal society?* (= a society dominated by women); *Few early civilizations were matriarchal in nature.* *See also* **patriarch**.

matric *see* **matriculation**.

matricide ['matrisaid] (*formal or tech*) **1** *nu* the killing of a mother by her own child: *He was guilty of matricide.* **2** *nc* a person who kills his or her own mother.

matriculate [mə'trikjuleit] *vti* to (cause to) become a member of a university *etc* by being enrolled: *You have to matriculate before you can get a university union card.* **maˌtricu'lation** *nu* (*inf abbrev* **matric** [mə'trik]).

matrimony ['matriməni, (*Amer*) -mouni] *nu* (*formal*) the state of being married: *You have been joined in holy matrimony*; *He wishes to remain a bachelor – he is not interested in matrimony.*

ˌmatri'monial [-'mou-] *adj* (*esp attrib*): *matrimonial difficulties.*

matrix ['meitriks] – *pl* **'matrices** [-si:z], **'matrixes** – *nc* **1** (*math*) a rectangular arrangement of (often related) items or symbols: *Put all the prime numbers into the same matrix.* **2** (*tech*) something in which something else is embedded (*eg* the rock in which a gem *etc* lies). **3** (*tech*) a mould in which metals *etc* are shaped.

matron ['meitrən] *nc* **1** a senior nurse in charge of a hospital: *In Britain now a matron is officially called a senior nursing officer.* **2** a woman in charge of nursing and domestic arrangements in a school *etc*: *The matron bandaged the boy's knee.* **3** (*formal*: *sometimes derog*) a dignified married woman: *Her behaviour shocked all the middle-class matrons in the neighbourhood.*

'matronly *adj* **1** dignified and calm. **2** (*euph*) rather fat: *She has a matronly figure*; *She was looking almost matronly.*

matt(e) [mat] *adj* (of paint *etc*) having a dull surface without gloss or shine: *I prefer photographic prints with a matt rather than shiny surface*; *Is this paint matt?*

matted *see* **mat**.

matter ['matə] **1** *nu* (*formal or tech*) solids, liquids and/or gases in any form, from which everything physical is made: *The entire universe is made up of different kinds of matter.* **2** *nc* (*often in pl*) a subject or topic (of discussion *etc*): *We were discussing a private matter*; *He is an expert on money matters.* **3** *nu* pus: *The wound was infected and full of matter.* – *vi* (not used with **is, was** *etc* and **-ing**) to be important: *That car matters a great deal to him*; *It doesn't matter what you say.*

ˌmatter-of-'fact *adj* keeping to the actual facts; not fanciful, emotional or imaginative: *a matter-of-fact account/statement/opinion/attitude*; *She was very matter-of-fact about the whole terrible affair*; *He's a calm, matter-of-fact person.*

as a matter of fact *see* **fact**.

be the 'matter (*often with* **with**) to be the/a trouble, difficulty or thing that is wrong: *Is anything the matter?*; *What's the matter with you?*; *He would not tell me what the matter was.*

for 'that matter (used *eg* when referring to some alternative or additional possibility) as far as that is concerned: *I could go this afternoon, or, for that matter, I could go tomorrow.*

a 'matter of **1** used in giving quantity, time *etc* approximately: *This job will only take a matter of minutes.* **2** used in saying what is involved or necessary: *It's a matter of asking her to do it.*

a matter of course something that one expects to happen, be done *etc*: *You don't have to ask her – she'll do it as a matter of course.*

a matter of life and death something of great urgency, sometimes involving the possibility that someone will lose their life: *Get the doctor to come quickly and tell him it's a matter of life and death.*

a matter of opinion something about which different people have different opinions or views: *Whether she's clever or not is a matter of opinion.*

no matter *interj* (*formal*) it is not important: *'He's not here.' 'No matter, I'll see him later.'*

no matter who, what, where *etc* whoever, whatever, wherever *etc*: *Don't open the door, no matter who calls!*; *No matter what happens, I'll still go.*

matting *see* **mat**.

mattins *see* **matins**.

mattress ['matris] *nc* a thick, firm layer of *eg* horsehair, rubber, or other form of padding, covered in cloth *etc*, for lying on, *usu* as part of a bed: *I am uncomfortable in this bed – the mattress is too soft for me.*

mature [mə'tjuə] *adj* **1** (having the qualities of someone who, or something that, is) fully grown or developed: *She's both physically and mentally mature for her age* (= more fully developed than is usual at her age); *A mature pine tree can be hundreds of feet tall*; *Is that plant fully mature?* **2** (of cheese, wine *etc*) ready for eating or drinking: *Is the wine mature yet?*; *a mature claret.* – **1** *vti* (*formal*) to make or become mature: *This experience matured him greatly*; *She matured early.* **2** *vi* (of an insurance policy) to become due to be paid: *My insurance policy matures when I reach sixty-five.* **ma'turely** *adv*.

ˌmatu'ration [matju-] *nu* (*formal*) the process of becoming mature.

ma'turity, ma'tureness *nus* the state of being mature: *He's rather a silly young man – he lacks maturity*; *This tree has not reached full maturity yet.* *See also* **immature**.

maudlin ['mo:dlin] *adj* (*formal*) stupidly sentimental, *esp* as a result of drunkenness: *Gin often makes her maudlin*; *He told maudlin stories about his childhood.*

maul [mo:l] *vt* (*esp* of an animal) to injure (a person or animal) *usu* badly: *He was badly mauled by an angry lion.*

mausoleum [mo:sə'liəm] *nc* a very fine tomb, often with a monument: *They buried the duke in the mausoleum.*

mauve [mouv] *nu, adj* (of) a pale purple colour.

maxim ['maksim] *nc* a saying, general truth or rule giving a guide to good behaviour: *'He who hesitates is lost' is a well-known maxim.*

maximum ['maksiməm] *adj* (*attrib*: *formal*) greatest: *This requires maximum effort/the maximum* *amount of effort.* – *n* – *pls* 'maximums, 'maxima [-mə] – *nc* the greatest number or quantity or the highest point or degree: *Has the level of water in the tank reached maximum yet?*; *Two hundred an hour is the maximum we can produce.*

'**maximize, -ise** *vt* (*formal*) to make as great as possible in size, quality *etc*: *We must try to maximize profits and minimize costs.*

may [mei] – *neg short form* **mayn't** ['meiənt] – *modal aux* **1** to have the permission to: *It's four o'clock – you may go home now.* **2** used to express a possibility in the present or future: *If I feel ill, I may not go*; *He may be here today but it is unlikely*; *He may be here at the moment, I just don't know.* **3** (*formal*) used to express a wish: *May you live a long and happy life.*

may as well might as well.

'**may have** used to express a possibility in the past: *He may have been here, but we cannot be sure.* *See also* **might**.

May [mei] *n* the fifth month of the year, the month following April: *She is leaving in May*; *He is coming on May 22* (said as 'on May (the) twenty-second' or 'on the twenty-second of May'); *He is coming on the 22nd/twenty-second of May*; *He died last May.*

'**May Day** *n* the first day of May, an *esp* socialist holiday or festival in many countries.

'**maypole** *nc* (*esp hist*) a decorated pole for dancing round on May Day.

maybe ['meibi:] *adv* it is possible (that); perhaps: *Maybe he'll come, and maybe he won't*; *'Is he coming?' 'Maybe.'*

mayday ['meidei] *nc* the international distress signal sent out by ships and aircraft: *The ship sent out a mayday (signal) before it sank.*

mayhem ['meihem] *nu* (*formal or facet*) a state of violence, great confusion and disorder *etc*: *If they don't get what they want, they'll create mayhem.*

mayn't *see* **may**.

mayonnaise [meiə'neiz, (*Amer*) 'meiəneiz] *nu* a thick sauce made of egg yolk, oil, vinegar or lemon and seasoning, and often used on salads: *Pour some mayonnaise over the lettuce*; *egg mayonnaise* (= a dish of hard-boiled eggs with mayonnaise).

mayor [meə, (*Amer*) 'meiər] *nc* (*esp* in England, Ireland and the United States: *sometimes with cap*) (the title or status of) the chief public official of a city, town or borough. – *See also* **provost**.

'**mayoress** *nc* **1** (the title or status of) a mayor's wife: *The mayor and mayoress attended the dinner.* **2** (the title or status of) a female mayor: *She has just been elected mayoress.*

lord mayor (*often with caps*) *nc* in Britain (the title or status of) the mayor of some capital and other cities: *the Lord Mayor of London.*

maypole *see* **May**.

maze [meiz] *nc* a deliberately confusing series of paths, often surrounded by walls or hedges, from which it's difficult to find the way out: *There is a maze at Hampton Court in London*; (*fig*) *I'm lost in a maze of rules and regulations.*

me [mi:] *pron* (used as the object of an actual or implied verb or preposition or (*inf*) as the subject of an implied verb) the word used by a speaker or writer when referring to himself: *He hit me*; *Give that to me*; *'Who's there?' 'It's only me'*; *'Who did that?' 'Me.'* (= I did it); *'Who did he come with?' 'Me.'*; *He took John and me to the circus*; *He can go with John and me.*

See also **I, mine, my, myself**.

meadow ['medou] *nc* (*often in pl*) a field of grass, *usu* on low ground: *There were cows in the meadow*; *a walk through the meadows.*

meagre, (*Amer*) **meager** ['mi:gə] *adj* (*formal*) poor or not enough: *a meagre portion of food*; *his meagre strength*; *His present salary is rather meagre.* '**meagrely** *adv.* '**meagreness** *nu.*

meal[1] [mi:l] *nc* the food taken at one time: *She eats three meals a day – breakfast, lunch and dinner*; *This cafe serves about two hundred meals every lunchtime*; *He had* (= ate) *a good meal before he left.*

make a meal of (something) (*inf*) to take more than the necessary amount of time or trouble over (something) or make (it) seem more complicated than it really is: *He really made a meal of that job – it took him four hours!*

meal[2] [mi:l] *nu* (*esp in cmpds*) the edible parts of grain ground to a coarse powder: *Sacks of meal were waiting ready at the mill*; *I need a kilo of oatmeal.*

'**mealy** *adj* like, or containing, meal.

ˌ**mealy-'mouthed** [-'mauðd] *adj* (*derog*) not frank or sincere in what one says: *Many politicians are too mealy-mouthed to tell the plain truth*; *mealy-mouthed politicians.*

mean[1] [mi:n] *adj* **1** not generous (with money *etc*): *He's very mean (with his money/over pay)*; *a mean old man*; *He is too mean to give his daughter a present.* **2** likely or intending to cause harm or annoyance: *It is mean to tell lies about people*; *That was a mean thing to do.* **3** of little value: *He only gives mean little presents.* **4** (*esp Amer*: *inf*) bad-tempered, vicious or cruel: *He's feeling really mean today because he had an argument with his wife*; *in a mean mood.* **5** (*liter*) (of a house *etc*) of poor quality; humble: *a mean dwelling.* **6** (*formal or liter*) not noble (in rank or birth): *He married a woman of mean birth*; *mean and lowly.* '**meanly** *adv.* '**meanness** *nu.*

'**no mean** (*formal*) an important or good (thing or person of a particular kind): *He is no mean actor.*

mean[2] [mi:n] *adj* (*attrib*) **1** (of a statistic) having the middle position between two points, quantities *etc*: *the mean value on a graph.* **2** average: *the mean annual rainfall in Bombay.* – *nc* (*formal or tech*) something that is midway between two opposite ends or extremes: *Three is the mean of the series one to five.*

mean[3] [mi:n] – *pt, ptp* **meant** [ment] – *vt* **1** (not used with **is, was** *etc* and **-ing**) to (intend to) express, show or indicate: *'Vacation' means 'holiday'*; *What does his silence mean?*; *A dictionary tells you what words mean*; *What do you mean by (saying/doing) that?* **2** to intend: *I meant to go to the exhibition but forgot*; *I didn't mean her to find out*; *He meant this present for me*; *He meant this box for keeping nails in*; *For whom was that letter meant?*; *John and Mary were obviously meant for each other – it'll be a very suitable marriage*; *He meant no harm*; *He means mischief*; *He means* (= is determined) *to be a rich man some day.*

'**meaning** *ncu* the sense in which a statement, action, word *etc* is (intended to be) understood: *What is the meaning of this phrase?*; *What is the meaning of his behaviour?*; *This word can have several meanings*; *That picture doesn't seem to have much meaning*; *She glanced at him with a look that was full of meaning.* – *adj* (*esp attrib*) (of a look, glance *etc*) showing a certain feeling or giving a certain message: *The teacher gave the boy a* *meaning look when he arrived late.*

'**meaningful** *adj* (often used loosely) important in some way: *a meaningful statement/relationship*; *I did not find his remarks at all meaningful.*

'**meaningless** *adj* without meaning or reason; of no importance: *meaningless arguments*; *meaningless chatter*; *His comments were quite meaningless.*

be meant to (*inf*) to be required or supposed; to have to: *Why is that child out of bed? He's meant to be asleep!*; *I'm meant to practise the piano for an hour every day.*

mean much/little/a great deal to (someone) to have much, little, a great deal of *etc* importance to (someone): *This gift means a lot to your grandmother.*

mean well to have good intentions: *He meant well by what he said.*

meander [mi'andə] *vi* (*formal*) **1** (of a river) to flow slowly along with many bends and curves: *The stream meandered through the meadows.* **2** (*fig*) (of people *etc*) to wander about in various directions: *This farmer objects to people meandering about in his fields*; *His writing meanders all over the page.* – *nc* a winding loop or curve in a river.

meaning, meant *see* **mean**[3].

means[1] [mi:nz] *n sing or pl* the instrument(s), method(s) *etc* by which a thing is, or may be, done or made to happen: *Is there any means of finding out?*; *By what means can we find out where she went?*; *We'll get there by some means or other* (= somehow); *He used unfair means to win the competition*; *He won the race by unfair means.*

by all means (*formal*) yes, of course: *If you want to use the telephone, by all means do.*

by 'means of using: *We escaped by means of a secret tunnel.*

by no manner of means/not by any manner of means (*formal*) not at all; by no means: *You haven't finished the work by any manner of means.*

by 'no means 1 (*formal*) definitely not: *'Can I go home now?' 'By no means!'* **2** (*also* **not by any means**) not at all: *I'm by no means certain to win*; *He's not the best person for the job by any means.*

means[2] [mi:nz] *n pl* (*formal*) money available or necessary for living *etc*: *Our means are small*; *She hasn't the means to give up work*; *She's a person of considerable means* (= She has plenty of money).

a man of means (*esp old*) a wealthy or rich man.

meantime ['mi:ntaim] *adv, nu* (in the) time or period between: *I shan't see her till tomorrow, so please give her the message if you meet her in the meantime*; *I'll hear her account of the matter later – meantime, I'd like to hear yours.*

meanwhile ['mi:nwail] *adv* during this time; at the same time: *The child had gone into the park. Meanwhile, his mother was searching for him in the street.*

measles ['mi:zlz] *n sing* an infectious disease with red spots on the skin: *Measles is a disease that people usually get in childhood.*

measly ['mi:zli] *adj* (*inf derog*: *esp attrib*) poor or mean: *a measly little piece of bread.*

measure ['meʒə] **1** *nc* (*sometimes in cmpds*) an instrument for finding the size, amount *etc* of something: *a glass measure for holding liquids*; *a tape-measure.* **2** *nc* a unit: *The metre is a measure of length.* **3** *nu* a system of measuring: *dry/liquid/square measure.* **4** *nc* (*usu in pl*) a plan of action or something done: *We must take* (= use, or put into action) *certain measures to stop the increase in crime*; (*formal*) *What measures do you suggest?* **5** *ncu* (*no pl*: *formal*) a certain amount: *I feel a measure of sympathy for her*; *You must feel some measure of excitement.* **6** *nc* (*formal*) musical time or rhythm: *The measure of this piece is three beats to the bar.* **7** *nc* (*old*) a slow and dignified dance: *a stately measure.* – *See also* **measure** *in phrases below.* – **1** *vti* to find the size, amount *etc* of (something): *He measured the table to see if it was large enough*; *Can you wait until I've finished measuring?* **2** *vt* to show the size, amount *etc* of: *A thermometer measures temperature.* **3** *vt* (*with* **against, besides** *etc*) to judge in comparison with: *She measured her skill in cooking against her friend's.* **4** *vi* (not used with **is, was** *etc* and **-ing**) to be a certain size: *This table measures two metres by one metre.*

'**measured** *adj* (*formal*) slow and steady in rhythm: *He walked with measured steps*; *The pace was slow and measured.*

'**measureless** *adj* (*liter*: *attrib*) huge or vast, therefore not able to be measured: *We looked across the measureless expanse of desert.*

'**measurement 1** *nc* (*often in pl*) size, amount *etc* found by measuring: *What are the measurements of this room?*; *What's your waist measurement?* **2** *nc* (*in pl*) the sizes of various parts of the body, *usu* the distance round the chest, waist and hips: *What are your measurements, madam?* **3** *nu* the act of measuring: *We can find the size of something by means of measurement.*

made-to-measure *see* **made to measure** *below.*

measuring-tape *see* **tape-measure**.

be a 'measure of (something) (*formal*) to be a way of showing (something abstract): *Giving you this job is a measure of how much I trust you.*

beyond measure (*formal or liter*) very great: *I'm offering you riches beyond measure!*

for good measure as something extra or above the minimum necessary: *The shopkeeper weighed out the sweets for the child and put in a few more for good measure.* – *See also* **measure out, measure up** *below.*

full measure (no less than) the correct amount: *Scales in shops should be checked regularly, to ensure that customers get full measure.*

get/have someone's measure/the measure of someone to form an idea or judgement of someone: *He was not a man to be trusted, and she soon had his measure.*

made to measure (of clothing) made to fit the measurements of a particular person: *Was your jacket made to measure?*; (*attrib*) *a made-to-measure suit.*

measure out *vt sep* to give (to someone) a measured amount of (something): *He measured (me) out a kilo of sugar*; *Is that the correct weight of sugar? Did he measure it out?*

measure up *vi* (*often with* **to**) to reach a certain required standard: *John's performance doesn't measure up (to the others).*

short measure less than the correct or stated amount: *She complained when the shopkeeper gave her short measure.*

See also **immeasurable**.

meat [mi:t] *nu* **1** the flesh of animals or birds used as food: *She does not eat meat*; *Did you have meat or fish for dinner?*; (*attrib*) *What did you have for the meat course?* **2** (*fig*) the important part: *the meat of the argument.*

'**meaty** *adj* **1** full of (animal) meat: *a meaty soup/stew*; *This tastes meaty.* **2** (tasting, smelling *etc*) like meat: *a meaty smell*; *This smells meaty.* 3 full of information *etc*: *a meaty lecture*; *His talk was interesting and meaty.*

mechanic [mi'kanik] *nc* a skilled worker who repairs or mountains machinery: *That's the mechanic who repairs my car.*

me'chanical *adj* 1 (*attrib*) having to do with machines: *mechanical engineering.* 2 (*esp attrib*) worked or done by machinery: *a mechanical doll.* 3 done *etc* without thinking, from force of habit: *You do these things so often that your actions become mechanical*; *a completely mechanical action.* **me'chanically** *adv.*

me'chanics 1 *n sing* the science of the action of forces on objects: *He is studying mechanics.* 2 *n sing* the art of building machines: *He applied his knowledge of mechanics to designing a new type of wheelchair.* 3 *n pl* the ways in which something works or is applied: *The mechanics of the legal system are very complicated.*

'mechanism ['me-] *nc* (*formal*) a (*usu* small) piece of machinery: *a watch mechanism*; (*fig*) *the complicated mechanism of local government.*

'mechanize, -ise ['me-] *vt* (*formal*) 1 to introduce machinery into (an industry *etc*): *We've mechanized the entire bottling process.* 2 to supply (troops) with motor vehicles. **,mechani'zation, -s-** *nu.*

medal ['medl] *nc* a piece of metal with a design, inscription *etc* stamped on it, given as a reward for bravery, long service, excellence *etc*, or made to celebrate a special occasion: *He won many medals in the War*; *A commemorative medal was made in memory of the Queen's Silver Jubilee.*

medallion [mi'daljən] *nc* a large (*usu* commemorative) medal.

'medallist, (*Amer*) **'medalist** *nc* a person who has won a medal in a competition *etc*: *He was a gold medallist in the Olympic Games.*

meddle ['medl] *vi* (*derog*) to interfere: *She was always trying to meddle (with things she knew nothing about or which were none of her business).* **'meddler** *nc.*

'meddlesome *adj* (*derog*) fond of meddling: *a meddlesome old woman*; *She is interfering and meddlesome.*

media *see* **medium**.

mediaeval *see* **medieval**.

mediate ['mi:dieit] *vi* (*formal*) to try to settle a dispute between people who are disagreeing: *The United States is trying to mediate (in the dispute) between these two countries.* **,medi'ation** *nu.* **'mediator** *nc.*

medical ['medikəl] *adj* (*attrib*) 1 of healing, medicine or doctors: *He is receiving excellent medical care*; *Does he have medical insurance?* 2 concerned with medicine rather than surgery: *Is he in a medical ward or a surgical ward?* – *nc* (*inf*) a medical examination. **'medically** *adv.*

medicament [mi'dikəmənt] *nc* (*very formal*) a medicine.

medicated ['medikeitid] *adj* having a healing or health-giving substance mixed in: *Medicated shampoo keeps your hair healthy*; *Is this shampoo medicated?*

,medi'cation *nu* 1 the mixing in of healing or health-giving substances: *I think that the medication of shampoo is a good idea.* 2 (*formal or tech*) (treatment by) medicine: *Has she been receiving any medication for this illness?*

medicine ['medsin] 1 *ncu* a substance, *esp* a liquid for swallowing, that is used to treat or keep away disease or illness: *Have you taken your medicine yet?*; *He must have a dose of medicine after each meal*; *She has a cupboard full of different medicines.* 2 *nu* the science of curing people who are ill, or making their suffering less (*esp* by means other than surgery): *advances in the field of medicine*; *He has studied both medicine and surgery.*

medicinal [mə'disinl] *adj* (*esp attrib*) 1 having the power to heal and used as a medicine: *medicinal substances.* 2 of healing: *alcohol for medicinal purposes.*

me'dicinally *adv* for the purpose, or with the effect, of curing an illness *etc*: *alcohol taken medicinally.*

medieval, mediaeval [medi'i:vəl, (*Amer*) mi:-] *adj* 1 (*esp attrib*) of, or belonging to, the Middle Ages: *in medieval times*; *medieval plays/music.* 2 (*fig derog*) primitive or uncivilized: *Some of their methods of punishment are absolutely medieval!*; *rather medieval methods of contraception.*

mediocre [mi:di'oukə] *adj* (*derog*) not very good or great; ordinary: *a mediocre performance/effort*; *His drawings are rather mediocre.* **,medi'ocrity** [-'o-] *nu.*

meditate ['mediteit] *vi* 1 (*formal*) to think deeply: *He was meditating on his troubles.* 2 to spend short, regular periods in deep (*esp* religious) thought: *He meditates twice a day.*

,medi'tation *ncu*: *He is deep in meditation*; *I'm sorry to interrupt your meditations.*

'meditative [-tətiv, (*Amer*) -teitiv] *adj* (*formal*) thoughtful: *She was in a meditative mood that afternoon*; *He seemed rather sad and meditative.* **'meditatively** *adv.*

medium ['mi:diəm] – *pls* **media** [-diə] (*defs 1, 2 and 4*), **mediums** (*defs 1–4*) – *nc* 1 (*formal*) something by or through which an effect is produced: *Air is the medium through which sound is carried.* 2 (*esp in pl*) a means (*esp* radio, television and newspapers) by which news *etc* is made known: *The facts were incorrectly reported through the news media*; *There'll be a fuss when the media get hold of the story*; *Radio and television are both mediums of communication/news media.* 3 a person through whom spirits of dead people are said to speak: *I know a medium who says she can communicate with Napoleon and Abraham Lincoln.* 4 (*tech*) a substance in which specimens are preserved, bacteria are grown *etc.* – *adj* middle or average in size, quality *etc*: *Would you like the small, medium or large packet?*; *Her hair is medium brown*; *'Is she tall or short?' 'She's medium.'*

a/the happy medium a middle way between alternatives, opposites or extremes: *Sometimes it's difficult to find a happy medium between extravagance and meanness.*

the mass media *see* **mass**.

medley ['medli] *nc* 1 a piece of music put together from a number of other pieces: *She sang a medley of Noel Coward songs.* 2 (*formal or liter*) a mixture: *The island contains a medley of different nationalities.*

meek [mi:k] *adj* humble and not likely to complain, argue, react strongly *etc*: *his meek little wife*; *She looks so meek but she has a very quick temper.*

'meekly *adv*: *She meekly accepted her mother's decision on the matter.* **'meekness** *nu.*

meet[1] [mi:t] – *pt, ptp* **met** [met] – 1 *vti* to come face to face with (*eg* a person whom one knows), by chance: *I met Mrs Smith in the street today*; *She met a man on the train who told her about his travels*; *Jill and I quite often meet in the supermarket.* **2** *vti* (*sometimes, esp Amer, with* **with**) to come together with (a person *etc*), by arrangement: *We arranged to meet (each other) again next day*; *The committee meets every Monday*; *The class tutor meets with his students once a week.* **3** *vti* to be introduced to (someone) for the first time: *Come over here and meet my wife*; *Goodbye – I enjoyed meeting you.* **4** *vti* to join with (an opponent) to fight a contest *etc*: *These boxers last met (each other) in the world title match last year.* **5** *vti* to join: *This lane meets the main road in two miles*; *Where do the two roads meet?* **6** *vt* to be equal to or satisfy (*eg* a person's needs, requirements *etc*): *Will there be sufficient stocks to meet the public demand?* **7** *vt* to pay fully: *Even £200 won't meet my debts.* **8** *vt* to come into the view, experience or presence of: *Clouds of smoke met her as she went into the kitchen*; *A terrible sight met him/her eyes when he opened the door.* **9** *vt* to come to or be faced with: *He met his death in a car accident*; (*liter*) *He met his end in a plane crash*; *She has met her match* (= a person who can challenge or equal her) *at last.* **10** *vi* (*formal*: *with* **with**) to experience or suffer; to receive a particular response: *She met with an accident*; *The scheme met with their approval.* **11** *vt* to answer or oppose: *We will meet force with greater force.* – *nc* a gathering, *esp* of sportsmen: *The local huntsmen are holding a meet this week.*

'meeting *nc* **1** an act of meeting: *I wanted to avoid a meeting with her*; *The meeting between my mother and my husband was not friendly.* **2** a gathering of people for discussion or another purpose: *I have to attend a committee meeting in five minutes' time.*

ˌmeet (someone) ˌhalf'way to respond to (someone) by making an equal effort or a compromise: *I'll invest £5 000 in this idea if you meet me halfway and do the same.*

meet[2] [miːt] *adj* (*old*: *pred*) proper or suitable: *It is not meet that you should associate with such people.*

mega- [megə] (*in cmpds*) **1** a million, as in **megaton**. **2** (*also* **megalo-** [megəlou]) large or great, as in **megaphone, megalomania**.

megalomania [megələ'meiniə] *nu* (*formal or tech*) the idea, *usu* false, that one is great or powerful, combined with a passion for more greatness or power: *He shows signs of megalomania.*

ˌmegalo'maniac [-ak] *adj, nc* (of) a person having megalomania: *That country is under the power of a dangerous megalomaniac.*

megaphone ['megəfoun] *nc* a funnel-shaped device for speaking through, that causes sounds to be made louder and/or sent in a given direction: *He shouted instructions to the crowd through a megaphone.*

megaton ['megətʌn] *adj* (*usu with a number*) (of a bomb) giving an explosion as great as that of a million tons of TNT: *a five-megaton bomb.*

melancholy ['melənkəli] *nu* (*formal or liter*) depression or sadness: *He was overcome by a feeling of melancholy.* – *adj* (*formal or liter*) sad; showing or causing sadness: *huge, dark, melancholy eyes*; *the melancholy call of a lone bird*; *She seems rather melancholy now that he has gone away.*

mêlée ['melei, (*Amer*) 'mei-] *nc* (*formal or facet*) a confused struggle, *usu* involving large numbers of people: *Everyone was rushing to catch the train, and he was hurt in the mêlée.*

mellow ['melou] *adj* (*formal*) **1** (*esp pred*) (of character) made softer and more mature, relaxed *etc* by age and/or experience: *Her personality became more mellow as middle age approached.* **2** (of sound, colour, light *etc*) soft, not strong or unpleasant: *the mellow glow from a small light in the corner*; *The light from the lamp was soft and mellow.* **3** (of wine, cheese *etc*) kept until the flavour has developed fully: *a mellow burgundy*; *This claret is mellow and full-bodied.* – *vti* (*formal*) to make or become softer or more mature: *Old age has mellowed him*; *He has mellowed with old age.*

'mellowness *nu.*

melodic, melodious, melodiousness *see* **melody**.

melodrama ['melədraːmə] *ncu* **1** a (type of) play in which emotions and the goodness or wickedness of the characters are exaggerated greatly: *Melodramas were popular in Britain in the last century*; *He loves Victorian melodrama.* **2** (*derog*) (an example of) behaviour similar to a play of this sort: *He makes a melodrama out of every little thing that happens*; *All this melodrama is very tiring.*

ˌmelodra'matic [-drə'ma-] *adj*: *Some newspapers tell their stories in a very melodramatic style*; *Don't be so melodramatic!* **ˌmelodra'matically** *adv.*

melody ['melədi] *nc* **1** a tune: *He played three beautiful Irish melodies on the harp.* **2** (*music*) the principal part in a piece of harmonized music: *The sopranos sang the melody, and all the other voices added the harmony very effectively.*

me'lodic [-'lo-] *adj* (*formal*) of melody: *This composer has a very individual melodic style.*

me'lodious [-'lou-] *adj* (*formal*) pleasing to the ear; tuneful: *Most birdsong is melodious*; *I like sweet, melodious tunes.* **me'lodiously** *adv.* **me'lodiousness** *nu.*

melon ['melən] **1** *nc* a large, sweet fruit with many seeds. **2** *nu* its firm yellow or red flesh as food: *We started the meal with melon.*

melt [melt] **1** *vti* to (cause to) become soft or liquid, *usu* by heating/being heated: *The heat melted the wax*; *All the ice has melted*; (*fig*) *I was very angry with him, but I/my heart melted a little when I saw how sorry he was*; *The snow melted away* (= disappeared by melting); (*fig*) *The crowd melted away into the sidestreets when the police arrived.* – *See also* **melt down** *below.*

'melting-point *nc* the temperature at which a given solid melts: *The melting-point of ice is 0° centigrade.*

be ˌin the 'melting-pot to be in the process of changing and forming something new: *This whole area of man's thinking is in the melting-pot.*

melt away *see* **melt** *above.*

melt down *vt sep* to melt (a metal object) so that it loses its shape: *He melted down the stolen silver articles into lumps of metal.*

See also **molten**.

member ['membə] *nc* **1** a person who belongs to a group, club, society, trade union *etc*: *The association has three thousand members*; *Are you a member of the local golf club?* **2** (*usu with cap*: *esp Brit*) short for **Member of Parliament**: *the Member for Glasgow West.* **3** (*old or liter*) a part of the body, *esp* an arm or leg.

'membership **1** *nu* the state of being a member: *His membership of the Communist Party was something we knew nothing about.* **2** *nc* a group of members: *a society with a large membership.* **3** *nc* the amount of money paid to a society *etc* in order to become a member: *The membership has increased to £5 this year.*

membrane ['membrein] *ncu* (*tech*) a thin film or layer of tissue that covers or lines parts of the body, forms the outside of cells *etc*: *The eyeballs are covered with a thin membrane.*

memento [mə'mentou] – *pl* **me'mento(e)s** – *nc* (*formal*) something kept or given as a reminder or souvenir: *They gave her a small gift as a memento of the occasion.*

memo ['memou] short for **memorandum**.

memoir ['memwa:] *nc* **1** (*formal*) a written statement about events or people in the past: *a memoir of the Crimean War/about his grandfather.* **2** (*in pl*) a person's written account of his own life; an autobiography: *When I retire, I'm going to write my memoirs.*

memorable ['memərəbl] *adj* worthy of being remembered: *That was a memorable event*; *The occasion was memorable for its splendour and grandeur.*

See also **immemorial, memorial, memory**.

memorandum [memə'randəm] – *pls* **ˌmemo'randums, ˌmemo'randa** [-də] *nc* (*often abbrev* **memo** ['memou] – *pl* **'memos** –) **1** a note to help one to remember: *He wrote a memo about the date of the next meeting on the pad of paper beside the telephone*; (*attrib*) *a memo pad.* **2** a (brief) written statement about a particular matter, often passed around between colleagues: *a brief memorandum on Thursday's meeting.*

memorial [mi'mo:riəl] *nc* something (*eg* a monument) that honours or commemorates people or events of the past: *This statue is a memorial to Sir Winston Churchill*; *a war memorial* (= a monument commemorating the soldiers who died); (*attrib*) *There's a memorial sculpture at the entrance to her house.*

See also **immemorial, memorable, memory**.

memory ['meməri] **1** *ncu* the power to remember things: *My memory is very bad nowadays!*; *Old peoples' memories often fail*; *She has a good memory for details of that sort.* **2** *nc* the mind's store of remembered things: *Her memory is filled with stories about interesting people.* **3** *nc* something remembered: *I have an early memory of seeing a comet*; *She told us her memories of her childhood in China.* **4** *nu* the time as far back as can be remembered: *the greatest fire in memory.* – *See also* **memory** *in phrases below.*

'memorize, -ise *vt* to learn (something) so well that one can remember all of it without looking at it: *The actress memorized five hundred lines of Shakespeare.*

from 'memory by remembering; without using a book *etc* for reference: *He said the whole poem from memory.*

in 'memory of/to the 'memory of as a reminder or memorial of: *They built a monument in memory of their dead leader.*

lose one's memory *see* **lose**.

(with)in living memory *see* **live**[1].

See also **immemorial, memorable, memorial, remember**.

men *see* **man**.

menace ['menəs] **1** *nc* something likely to cause injury, damage *etc*: *Large lorries are a menace on narrow roads*; (*loosely*) *That child is a menace!* (= a nuisance.) **2** *ncu* (*legal or liter*) a threat or show of hostility: (*legal*) *He was accused of demanding money with menaces*; (*liter*) *His voice was full of menace.* – *vt* (*formal*) to threaten: *The whole country is being menaced by this new and terrible danger.*

'menacing *adj* (*formal*) **1** threatening to harm: *a menacing weapon*; *The burglar looked menacing.* **2** threatening-looking: *a menacing sky*; *The sky was dark and menacing.* **'menacingly** *adv.*

menagerie [mi'nadʒəri] *nc* (a place for keeping) a collection of wild animals.

mend [mend] **1** *vt* to put (something broken, torn *etc*) into good condition again; to repair: *Can you mend this broken chair?*; *Try to mend this hole in my shirt.* **2** *vi* (*inf*) to grow better, *esp* in health: *My broken leg is mending very well.* – *nc* a repaired place: *This shirt has a mend in the sleeve.*

'mending *nu* **1** the act of repairing: *The mending of the chair took longer than he thought.* **2** things needing to be mended, *esp* by sewing: *Put your torn shirt with my pile of mending!*

be on the mend (*inf*) to be getting better: *My broken leg is already on the mend*; *He has been ill, but he's on the mend now.*

mend one's manners/ways (*formal*) to improve one's behaviour: *A good beating will soon make him mend his manners.*

menfolk *see* **man**.

menial ['mi:niəl] *adj* (*formal*) (of work) mean, humble or unskilled: *a menial task*; *She considered such a job too menial.* – *nc* (*formal derog*) a person who does such work: *I don't expect my wife to clean the house – she employs a menial to do that.*

meningitis [menin'dʒaitis] *nu* a serious disease in which there is inflammation of the membranes round the brain or spinal cord: *The child died of meningitis.*

menopause ['menəpo:z] *nu* (*formal*) the ending of menstruation and the ability to bear children: *During the menopause many women feel rather emotional and nervous.*

'menopausal *adj*: *She keeps bursting into tears – I think she must be menopausal*; *menopausal symptoms.*

menstruate ['menstrueit] *vi* (*formal*) to discharge blood monthly from the uterus: *Many girls begin to menstruate at the age of 12 or 13.* **ˌmenstru'ation** *nu.*

menswear *see* **man**.

mental ['mentl] *adj* **1** (*attrib*) of the mind: *His mental development was slow*; *mental illnesses/disorders.* **2** (*attrib*) done or made by the mind: *mental arithmetic*; *a mental picture.* **3** (*attrib*) for those who are ill in mind: *a mental hospital.* **4** (*attrib*) suffering from an illness of the mind: *a mental patient.*

men'tality [-'ta-] *ncu* (*formal*) **1** (a level of) mental power: *He is a man of very low mentality.* **2** (a person with) a certain way of thinking or outlook: *What type of mentality actually enjoys beating up old ladies?*

'mentally *adv* in the mind: *She's mentally incapable of understanding*; *Picture the scene mentally*; *He is mentally ill.*

menthol ['menθəl] *nu* a sharp-smelling substance got from peppermint oil used to help give relief from colds *etc*: *If you have a cold put some menthol in boiling water and breathe in the steam*; *Some cigarettes contain menthol.*

'mentholated [-leitid] *adj* (*formal*) containing menthol: *mentholated cigarettes*; *Are these cigarettes mentholated?*

mention ['menʃən] *vt* **1** to speak of or refer to: *He* *mentioned the plan, but gave no details; Mention my name at the receptionist's desk, and they'll let you in.* **2** to remark or say *usu* briefly or indirectly: *She mentioned (that) she might be leaving.* – **1** *ncu* (*often with* **of**) a (*usu* brief) remark (about): *Did he make any mention of having seen me?; No mention was made of this matter at our last meeting; Our society got a short mention in the newspaper.* **2** *nc* (in the army *etc*) a personal reference, made because of bravery *etc*: *The hero was given an honourable mention in the report.*

not to mention used to emphasize something important or to excuse oneself for mentioning something relatively unimportant: *It's far too late for you to go out and play football, not to mention the fact that it's raining.*

See also **unmentionable**.

mentor ['mento:] *nc* (*formal or liter*) a (wise) person who gives (good) advice: *He was my mentor throughout my university career.*

menu ['menju:] *nc* (a card with) a list of dishes that may be ordered at a meal: *He sat down in the café, picked up the menu and read through it; What's on the menu today?*

mercantile ['mə:kəntail, (*Amer*) -ti:l] *adj* (*formal*: *attrib*) of commerce or trade: *mercantile law.*

mercantile marine *nu* the merchant marine.

mercenary ['mə:sinəri] *adj* (*derog*) too strongly influenced by desire for money: *a mercenary attitude; She is so mercenary that she would not marry a poor man.* – *nc* a soldier from one country who hires his services to another country: *Mercenaries have gone from Britain to fight in Africa.*

merchandise ['mə:tʃəndaiz] *nu* (*formal*) goods to be bought and sold: *This store sells merchandise from all over the world.*

merchant ['mə:tʃənt] *nc* **1** a trader, *esp* wholesale, in goods of a particular kind: *Mr Smith is a wool merchant; timber/tea/wine merchants.* **2** (*sl*) a person who has an excessive fondness for a particular activity *etc*: *One of those stupid speed merchants* (= people who like driving dangerously fast) *tried to pass me on a corner.*

merchant marine, navy, service *nu* the ships of a country that are employed in trading, and their crews: *His son has joined the merchant navy.*

merchant ship *nc* a ship involved in trade.

merciful, mercifulness, merciless *see* **mercy**.

mercury ['mə:kjuri] *nu* an element (symbol **Hg**), a poisonous, silvery, liquid metal used *esp* in thermometers *etc.*

mer'curial [-'kju:-] *adj* (*formal*) (of a person) lively or showing quick changes of mood: *He is such a mercurial child; I never know what kind of mood she will be in – she is so mercurial.*

Mercury *see* Appendix 6.

mercy ['mə:si] **1** *nu* kindness towards a person, *esp* an enemy, who is in one's power: *He showed his enemies no mercy whatsoever.* **2** *nc* (*inf*) a piece of good luck or something for which one should be grateful: *It was a mercy that it didn't rain; Her death was a mercy because her disease was incurable.*

'merciful *adj* willing to forgive or to punish only lightly: *He's a very merciful judge; God is kind and merciful.* **'mercifully** *adv.*

'merciless *adj* without mercy; cruel: *merciless criticism; The tyrant was utterly merciless.* **'mercilessly** *adv.*

'mercy-killing *nu* (*more informal than* **euthanasia**) the act of killing, by a painless method, a person who is dying of a painful disease, in order to stop his sufferings.

at the 'mercy of wholly in the power of or liable to be harmed by: *A sailor is at the mercy of the weather; At last he had his enemies at his mercy.*

have 'mercy on to give kindness to (an enemy *etc* who is in one's power): *Have mercy on a poor beggar, sir!; The general had no mercy on the captured enemy.*

mere [miə] *adj* (*attrib*: *no compar*) no more than or no better than: *She's a mere child; That's mere nonsense!; She became annoyed at the merest suggestion of criticism.*

'merely *adv* (*formal*) simply or only: *She was merely a child; I was merely turning the door-handle when it broke off.*

merge [mə:dʒ] **1** *vti* to (cause to) combine or join: (*formal*) *The sea and sky appear to merge at the horizon; The two firms have been merged.* **2** *vi* (*with* **into**) to change gradually into something else: *Summer slowly merged into autumn.* **3** *vi* (*with* **into** *etc*) to disappear into (*eg* a crowd, background *etc*): *He merged into the crowd and disappeared from view; Some animals' colouring helps them to merge into the background.*

'merger *nc* a joining together of business firms: *There's been a merger between two large investment companies.*

meridian [mə'ridiən] *nc* (*tech*) an imaginary line on the earth's surface passing through the poles and any given place; any line of longitude.

meringue [mə'raŋ] *ncu* (a cake made from) a crisp cooked mixture of sugar and white of eggs: *They had meringues filled with cream for tea.*

merit ['merit] **1** *nu* the quality of worth, excellence or praiseworthiness: *He reached his present senior position through sheer merit; If he is not promoted then the management must be incapable of recognizing merit.* **2** *nc* a good point or quality: *Her plan has its merits; His speech had at least the merit of being short.* – *vt* (*formal*) to deserve as reward or punishment: *Your case merits careful consideration.*

ˌmeri'torious [-'to:-] *adj* (*formal*) deserving reward or praise: *a meritorious performance; His performance was certainly meritorious.*

according to its merits, on its merits according to the degree of rightness or wrongness, or its good or bad points: *Each case/application will be considered on its merits.*

mermaid ['mə:meid] – *masc* **'merman** [-man] – *nc* an imaginary sea creature with a human body down to the waist and a fish's tail.

merry ['meri] *adj* **1** cheerful; noisily or laughingly lively *etc*: *The merry children ran to the party; They had a merry time at the party; Christmas is a time to be bright and merry.* **2** (*inf*: *esp pred*) slightly drunk: *He's been getting merry on a half-bottle of whisky.* **'merrily** *adv.* **'merriness** *nu.*

'merriment *nu* fun and laughter: *There was a great deal of merriment at the party.*

'merry-go-round *nc* (*Amer* **ˌcarou'sel**) a revolving ring of toy horses *etc* on which children ride at a fair.

'merrymaking *nu* cheerful celebration: *After all the merrymaking at Christmas he felt slightly ill.* **'merrymaker** *nc.*

mesdames *see* **madam**.

mesh [meʃ] **1** *ncu* (one of) the openings between the threads of a net: *a net of (a) very fine* (= small) *mesh.* **2** *nc* (*often in pl*) a network: *A fly was struggling in the meshes of the spider's web*; (*fig*) *She* *has been caught up in a mesh of political spying.* – *vi* (*tech*) (of teeth on *eg* gear wheels) to become engaged with each other: *The teeth on these two cogwheels mesh when they go round.*

mesmerize, -ise ['mezməraiz] *vt* (*often loosely*) to hypnotize: *He mesmerized the woman by getting her to watch an object swinging in front of her*; *A weasel is able to mesmerize a rabbit so that it cannot run away*; *The child was mesmerized* (= fascinated) *by the television screen.* '**mesmerism** *nu.*

mess[1] [mes] *ncu* (*usu in sing*) a state of disorder or confusion; an untidy, dirty or unpleasant sight or muddle: *This room is in a terrible mess!*; *His business affairs are in a mess*; *There was an untidy mess in the children's room*; *Our house is always such a mess!*; (*offensive*) *She looked a mess in that dress*; *The spilt food made a horrible mess on the carpet*; *I hate any job that involves a lot of mess*; *The new government will have to clear up the mess left by the previous one.* – *vi* (*with* **with**: *inf esp Amer*) to meddle, or to have something to do with: *Don't mess with things that you don't understand*; *She's always messing with the television set.*

'**messy** *adj* dirty: *a messy job*; *Don't let the children play with paint – it's so messy.* '**messily** *adv.* '**messiness** *nu.*

'**mess-up** *nc* (*inf*) a muddle or state of confusion: *There has been a mess-up in the timetable.* – *See also* **mess up** *below.*

make a mess of **1** to make dirty, untidy or confused: *The heavy rain has made a real mess of the garden.* **2** to do (something) badly: *He made a mess of his essay, and received very low marks.* **3** to spoil or ruin (*eg* one's life): *He made a mess of his life by drinking too much.*

mess about/around (*inf*) **1** *vi* to behave in a foolish or annoying way: *The children were shouting and messing about in the classroom when the teacher arrived.* **2** *vi* to work with no particular plan in a situation that involves mess: *I love messing about in the kitchen.* **3** *vi* (*with* **with**) to meddle or interfere with: *Who's been messing about with my papers?* **4** *vt usu sep* to upset or put into a state of disorder or confusion: *The travel agents have really messed me about*; *The wind messed her hairstyle about a bit.*

mess up *vt sep* to spoil; to make a mess of: *My husband's broken leg has really messed up our holiday plans*; *Don't mess the room up!*; *You've messed it up already.* – *See also* **mess-up**.

mess[2] [mes] *nc* a place where a number of people in the armed services eat together: *the officers' mess.*

message ['mesidʒ] *nc* **1** a piece of information spoken or written, passed from one person to another: *I have a message for you from Mr Johnston*; *Could you leave a message for Mr Smith asking him to phone me back?* **2** (*formal*: *usu in sing*) the instruction or teaching of a moral story, religion, prophet *etc*: *What message is this story trying to give us?*

'**messenger** [-sindʒə] *nc* a person who carries letters, information *etc* from place to place: *The king's messenger brought news of the army's defeat.*

Messiah [mə'saiə] *n* (*with* **the**) Jesus Christ.

messily, messiness *see* **mess**[1].

Messrs ['mesəz] *n pl* a polite (written or spoken) way of addressing a firm, or more than one man: *Have you written that letter to Messrs Brown and Smith?*

See also **mister, madam**.

messy *see* **mess**[1].

met *see* **meet**.

metabolism [mi'tabəlizəm] *nc* (*tech*) the system of chemical changes in the cells of a living body which provide energy for bodily processes and activities, or which build up material into living matter: *His fatness is not caused by overeating but by a disorder of his metabolism.*

metabolic [metə'bolik] *adj* (*tech*: *esp attrib*): *He has a high metabolic rate and therefore needs to eat large quantities of food*; *a metabolic disorder.*

metal ['metl] *ncu, adj* **1** (of) any of a group of substances, *usu* shiny, that can conduct heat and electricity and can be hammered into shape, or drawn out in sheets, bars *etc*: *Gold, silver and iron are all metals*; *a piece of metal*; *a metal window-frame.* **2** (of) a combination of more than one of such substances: *Brass is a metal made from copper and zinc.*

me'tallic [-'ta-] *adj* (*esp attrib*) **1** made of metal: *a metallic element.* **2** like a metal (*eg* in appearance or sound): *His new car is painted metallic blue*; *The prison gate closed with a metallic clank.*

metallurgy [mi'talədʒi, (*Amer*) 'metələrdʒi] *nu* (*tech*) the study of metals, *esp* the art of getting metals from the ore in rock *etc* and preparing them for use. **metallurgic(al)** [metə'lə:dʒik(əl)] *adj.* **metallurgist** [mi'talədʒist, (*Amer*) 'metələrdʒist] *nc.*

metamorphosis [metə'mo:fəsis] – *pl* ˌ**meta'morphoses** [-si:z] – *ncu* (*formal or tech*) (a) marked change of form, appearance, character *etc*: *a caterpillar's metamorphosis into a butterfly*; *her sudden metamorphosis from a schoolgirl into an elegant woman.*

ˌ**meta'morphose** [-fouz] *vti* (*formal, tech or facet*) to (cause to) undergo this type of change: *The tadpole metamorphosed into a frog*; *The witch metamorphosed the prince into a rabbit.*

metaphor ['metəfə] *ncu* a form of expression (not using 'like' or 'as') in which a quality or characteristic is given to a person or thing by using a name, image, adjective *etc* normally used of something else which has greatly similar qualities *etc*: *'He's a tiger when he's angry' is an example of (a) metaphor, as are 'His hair was a flaming red colour', 'My aunt sailed into the room', and 'He produced a rather lame excuse for being late'.*

ˌ**meta'phoric(al)** [-'fo-] *adj* of, like or using metaphors: *metaphorical language*; *His poetry is rather metaphorical.* ˌ**meta'phorically** *adv.*

mixed metaphor *ncu* an expression that is a confusion of two or more metaphors: *An example of (a) mixed metaphor is 'A black cloud was gnawing at his peace of mind'.*

mete [mi:t]: **mete out** *vt sep* (*formal*) to give (punishment *etc*): *The judge meted out severe sentences to all the criminals.*

meteor ['mi:tiə] *nc* (*also* ˌ**shooting** '**star**) a small mass or body travelling very quickly through space which appears very bright after entering the earth's atmosphere.

ˌ**mete'oric** [-'o-] *adj* (*usu attrib*) (of success *etc*) rapid and often only lasting for a short time: *a meteoric rise to fame*; *Her promotion was certainly meteoric.*

'**meteorite** [-rait] *nc* a small meteor that has fallen to earth.

meteorology [mi:tiə'rolədʒi] *nu* the study of weather and climate. ˌ**meteo'rologist** *nc.* ˌ**meteoro'logical** [-'lo-] *adj*: *meteorological charts.*

meter ['mi:tə] *nc* **1** an instrument for measuring,

esp quantities of electricity, gas, water *etc*: *Where is the gas meter in this house?*; *If you want to know how much electricity you have used you will have to look at the meter.* 2 (*Amer*) *see* **metre**[1], **metre**[2]. – *vt* (*formal*) to measure (*esp* electricity *etc*) by using a meter: *This instrument meters rainfall*; (*fig*) *He carefully metered their progress day by day.*

method ['meθəd] 1 *nc* the way in which one does something: *I don't much like his methods of training workers.* 2 *nc* an orderly or fixed series of actions for doing something: *Follow the method set down in the instruction book.* 3 *nu* good sense and a definite plan: *Her work seems to lack method*; *There is method in his madness* (= Although he seems to be doing things in the wrong way, he is in fact following a logical plan).

me'thodical [-'θo-] *adj* (*neg* **un-**) 1 arranged or done in an orderly manner or according to a plan: *He made a methodical search for the missing documents*; *This office needs a more methodical filing system*; *The filing system is far from methodical.* 2 (in the habit of) acting in a planned, orderly way: *a methodical person/nature*; *He is careful and methodical but not very clever.* **me'thodically** *adv.*

methylated spirit(s) ['meθileitid] *nu* (*inf abbrev* **meths** [meθs]) a type of alcohol which is unsuitable for drinking, used in some forms of heating and lighting: *We have a camping stove which uses methylated spirits*; *He is so dependent on alcohol that he will drink methylated spirits if he can't get whisky or beer although he knows it is dangerous to health*; (*attrib*) *a meths drinker.*

meticulous [mi'tikjuləs] *adj* (*sometimes derog*) very careful, almost too careful (about small details): *He paid meticulous attention to detail*; *He is not very clever but he is useful in the office because he is so meticulous*; *He is so meticulous that he can never do anything in a hurry.* **me'ticulously** *adv.*

metre[1], (*Amer*) **meter** ['mi:tə] *nc* (*often abbrev* **m** *when written*) the chief unit of length in the metric system, equal to 39·37 inches: *This table is one metre broad*; *The wavelength of this radio station's broadcasts is 1500 metres*; *a two-metre wall.*

metric ['metrik] *adj* of the metre or metric system: *Could you give the metric equivalents of these weights?*; *Are these scales metric?*

metricate ['metrikeit] *vti* (*formal*) to change (something) to the metric system: *Britain metricated her currency in 1971.* **,metri'cation** *nu.*

go metric to metricate: *Britain's currency went metric in 1971.*

the metric system a system of weights and measures based on tens (*eg* 1 metre = 100 centimetres, 1 centimetre = 100 millimetres *etc*). *See also* Appendix 5.

metre[2], (*Amer*) **meter** ['mi:tə] *nu* (in poetry) the regular arrangement of syllables that are stressed or unstressed, long or short: *The metre of this passage is typical of Shakespeare.*

'metrical ['me-] *adj* (*formal or tech*) of or in poetry: *a metrical translation of Chaucer*; *metrical psalms*; *The translation is not metrical – it is in prose.*

metronome ['metrənoum] *nc* an instrument that can be set to make a ticking noise at different speeds to mark musical time.

metropolis [mə'tropəlis] *nc* (*formal or facet*) a large city, *esp* the chief city of a country: *London is England's metropolis*; *Overcrowding is a problem in our metropolises*; *Since he comes from a small village he thinks every small town is a metropolis.*

metropolitan [metrə'politən] *adj* (*esp attrib*) of or in a capital city: *the metropolitan area/police.*

mettle ['metl] *nu* (*formal or liter*) courage, determination *etc*: *He is obviously a man of mettle.*

put (someone) on his mettle (*formal*) to rouse or stimulate someone to his best efforts: *Everyone else's fine performances put her on her mettle.*

mew [mju:] *vi* to make the cry of a (young) cat: *The kittens mewed when they were hungry.* – *nc* such a cry.

mews [mju:z] 1 *nc* a street or yard with, or *orig* with, stables: *I live in the mews round the corner*; (*attrib*) *a mews flat.* 2 *n* (*with cap*) a word used in the names of certain roads or streets: *Her address is 6 Wellington Mews.*

Mexican, Mexico *see* Appendix 2.

mezzo ['metsou], **mezzo-soprano** [metsousə'pra:nou] – *pls* **'mezzos, ,mezzo-so'pranos** – *nc* 1 (a person having) a singing voice between soprano and alto: *Janet Baker is a fine mezzo.* 2 in music, a part written for a voice at this pitch: *The mezzo-soprano is not easy*; (*attrib*) *the mezzo-soprano part.* – *adv* with a mezzo-soprano voice: *She sings mezzo-soprano.*

miaow [mi'au] *vi* to make the cry of a cat: *The cat miaowed all night and kept me awake.* – *nc* such a cry.

mice *see* **mouse**.

mick(ey) ['mik(i)]: **take the mick(ey) (out of)** (*Brit inf*) to make fun (of) or ridicule (someone or something): *He's always taking the mickey out of his little brother.*

micro- [maikrou] (*in cmpds*) 1 very small: *'microprint*; *,micro-'organism.* 2 one millionth part: *'microvolt* (= one millionth of a volt); *'microsecond.*

microbe ['maikroub] *nc* (*tech*) a very tiny living thing invisible to the naked eye, *esp* a germ causing disease.

microfilm ['maikrəfilm] *nu* film on which documents, books *etc* are recorded very much smaller than actual size: *The library keeps previous copies of national newspapers on microfilm.*

microphone ['maikrəfoun] *nc* (*inf abbrev* **mike** [maik]) an electronic instrument for picking up sound waves to be broadcast, recorded or amplified as in radio, the telephone, a tape-recorder, a Tannoy *etc*: *If you speak into the microphone when I switch on the tape-recorder, your voice will be recorded on the tape*; *Performers use microphones to make themselves heard better in large halls etc.*

microscope ['maikrəskoup] *nc* an instrument which makes very small objects able to be seen by the naked eye by magnifying them greatly: *Germs are very small, and can only be seen with the aid of a microscope.*

,micro'scopic [-'sko-] *adj* 1 (*tech*) seen only by the aid of a microscope: *microscopic bacteria.* 2 (*facet*) very tiny: *They charged us a huge amount for an absolutely microscopic steak*; *The amount of money they spend on food is microscopic.* **,micro'scopically** *adv.*

mid [mid] *adj* (*often in cmpds*) at, or in, the middle of: *at mid term*; *in mid-ocean*; *a midweek football match*; *He jumped up and caught the ball while he was still in mid air* (= with his feet off the ground); (*attrib*) *a mid-air collision between two jet aircraft.*

,halt/,stop/,pause etc in ,mid'stream (*formal*) to pause while doing something busily, *esp* talking: *He stopped speaking in midstream at the sound of the telephone.*

See also **amid(st), midst**.

midday [mid'dei] *nu* the middle of the day; twelve o'clock: *We'll meet you at midday*; (*attrib*) *a midday meal.*

midden ['midn] *nc* (*inf or dial*) a rubbish-heap or compost-heap: *We put all the rotten vegetables on the midden at the bottom of the garden*; (*fig*) *His room is a complete midden.*

middle ['midl] *nc* **1** (*usu in sing*) the middle point or part: *the middle of a circle.* **2** (*inf*) the central area of the body; the waist: *You're getting rather fat round your middle.* – *adj* (*attrib*) equally distant from both ends: *the middle seat in a row.*

'middling *adj* average: *He is a man of only middling ability*; *He's neither tall nor short, but of middling height*; *'Is he tall or small?' 'He's middling'.*

middle age *nu* the years between youth and old age: *When she was well into middle age she decided to study medicine.*

,middle-'aged *adj* between youth and old age: *I may still be young, but I feel middle-aged*; *a middle-aged woman.*

Middle Ages *n* (*with* **the**) the time between the end of the Roman Empire and the Renaissance.

middle class *nc* (*with* **the**: *sometimes in pl*), *adj* (*sometimes derog*) (of) people (including professional people, bankers, shop-owners *etc*) who come between the working class and the aristocratic or the very wealthy: *Her father belonged to the middle class*; *His attitudes are very middle-class*; *middle-class attitudes.*

Middle East *n* (*with* **the**) Egypt and the countries of Asia west of Pakistan.

'middleman [-man] *nc* a dealer who buys goods from the person who makes or grows them, and sells them to shopkeepers or to the public; a wholesaler: *You can save money by buying direct from the factory and cutting out the middleman.*

,middle-of-the-'road *adj* midway between extremes; moderate: *His political beliefs are very middle-of-the-road*; *His middle-of-the-road views do not appeal to the extremists in the party.*

be in the 'middle of (doing) something to be busily occupied doing something: *Please excuse my appearance. I was in the middle of washing my hair.*

midge [midʒ] *nc* any of several kinds of small fly some of which bite: *We were badly bitten by midges yesterday evening*; (*attrib*) *a midge bite.*

midget ['midʒit] *nc* a person who is fully developed but has not grown to normal height.

midland ['midlənd] *adj* (*attrib*) of the central part of a country: *the midland counties of England.*

the Midlands the counties in the centre of England.

midnight ['midnait] *nu* twelve o'clock at night: *I'll go to bed at midnight*; (*attrib*) *a midnight raid on the post-office.*

midriff ['midrif] *nc* the middle of the body just below the ribs: *She was wearing a very short blouse which left her midriff bare.*

midst [midst] : **in the 'midst of 1** among or in the centre of: *in the midst of a crowd of people.* **2** at the same time as: *In the midst of all these troubles, his father suddenly became ill.*

in our, your, their midst among, or in the same place as, us, you or them: *Large office blocks keep rising in our midst.*

See also **amid(st), mid**.

midsummer [mid'sʌmə] *nu* the middle of summer, the period around June 21: *It happened in midsummer/on a midsummer's day*; (*attrib*) *A Midsummer Night's Dream.*

midway [mid'wei] *adj, adv* in the middle of the distance or time between two points; halfway: *the midway point*; *He was standing midway across the bridge.*

midwife ['midwaif] – *pl* **'midwives** [-waivz] – *nc* a woman (*usu* a trained nurse) who helps at the birth of children: *The midwife had to send for a doctor as she was having difficulty in delivering the child.*

mid'wifery [mid'wi-, (*Amer*) 'midwai-] *nu* the art or practice of helping at the birth of children: *The nurse is specializing in midwifery.*

midwinter [mid'wintə] *nu* the middle of winter: *He arrived in midwinter/on a midwinter's day*; (*attrib*) *Christmas is a midwinter festival.*

might[1] [mait] – *neg short form* **mightn't** ['maitnt] – *modal aux* **1** *pt* of **may**: *I thought I might find you here*; *I telephoned her to ask if I might* (= if she would allow me to) *borrow her book*; *He might come if you offered him a meal.* **2** used instead of 'may' *eg* to make a possibility seem less likely, or a request for permission more polite: *He might win if he tries hard*; *'Are you going to the party?' 'I might.'*; *Might I speak to you for a few minutes, please?* **3** used in suggesting that a person is not doing what he should: *You might help me wash the dishes.*

might as well used to suggest that there is no good reason for not doing something: *Since I am already checking some of these definitions, I might as well check them all at the one time.*

'might have 1 used to suggest that something would have been possible if something else had been the case: *You might have caught the bus if you had run.* **2** used to suggest that a person has not done what he should: *You might have told me you were bringing an extra person to supper.* **3** used to show that something was a possible action *etc* but was in fact not carried out or done: *I might have gone to the meeting, but in the end I decided not to.* **4** used when a person does not want to admit to having done something: *'Have you seen this man?' 'I might have. Why do you want to know?'*

I *etc* **might have known** (often used in annoyance) I *etc* ought to have known, thought, guessed *etc* that something was or would be the case: *I might have known you would lose the key!*

might[2] [mait] *nu* (*liter*) power or strength: *The might of the opposing army was too great for us.*

'mighty *adj* (*liter*) **1** having great power: *a mighty nation*; *The dictator is not so mighty now.* **2** (*esp attrib*) very large: *They came to a mighty oak door.* – *adv* (*inf*: *esp Amer*) very: *She's a mighty clever woman!*

'mightily *adv*. **'mightiness** *nu*.

with might and main [mein] (*liter*) with all the strength and power that one has: *He struggled with might and main to move the stone.*

mightn't *see* **might**[1].

migraine ['mi:grein, (*Amer*) 'mai-] *ncu* (an attack of) a type of very severe headache, often accompanied by vomiting and difficulty in seeing: *She suffers from migraine*; (*inf*) *She has gone to bed – she's got a migraine.*

migrate [mai'greit, (*Amer*) 'maigreit] *vi* **1** (of certain birds and animals) to travel from one region to another at certain times of the year: *Many geese rest in Scotland when they are migrating* *in the early winter.* **2** (of people) to change one's home to another country or (regularly) from place to place: *The Gothic peoples who overwhelmed the Roman Empire migrated from the East.* **mi'gration** [(*Brit and Amer*) -'grei-] *ncu.*

'migrant [(*Brit and Amer*) 'mai-] *nc* a person, bird or animal that migrates or has migrated: *The swallow is a summer migrant to Britain*; (*attrib*) *Germany employs many migrant workers from Turkey.*

'migratory [(*Brit and Amer*) 'maigrə-] *adj* (*formal*) migrating or wandering: *a migratory race of people*; *migratory birds*; *Are those birds migratory?*

mike *see* **microphone**.

mild [maild] *adj* **1** (of a person or his personality) gentle in temper or behaviour: *I can't understand why you are afraid of the new headmaster – he's such a mild man*; *He is so mild and yet his wife is so bad-tempered.* **2** (of beer) not sharp or bitter to the taste. **3** (of punishment *etc*) not severe: *a mild rebuke*; *a mild sentence*; *The sentence was mild.* **4** (of weather *esp* if not in summer) not cold; rather warm: *a mild spring day*; *It is very mild today.* **5** (of spices, spiced foods *etc*) not hot: *This curry is very mild*; *a mild curry.* – *nu* mild beer: *Tom will have a pint of mild.*

'mildly *adv.* **'mildness** *nu.*

mildew ['mildju:] *nu* a disease on plants *etc* caused by the growth and spread of very tiny fungi: *There is mildew on our roses.*

mile [mail] *nc* (*sometimes abbrev* **m** *when written*) a measure of length equal to 1760 yards (1·61 km): *We walked ten miles today*; *This car cannot go any faster than 70 miles per hour* (sometimes written **mph**); *The nearest village is five miles away*; *a ten-mile hike.*

'mileage, 'milage [-lidʒ] *nu* the number of miles travelled: *What's the mileage on your car?*; (*attrib*) *a mileage allowance in one's travel expenses*; *What mileage does your motorbike do per gallon?*

'milestone *nc* **1** a stone set up to show distances in miles to various places. **2** a very important event: *The discovery of penicillin was a milestone in medical history.*

milieu ['mi:ljə:, (*Amer*) mi:l'jə:] – *pls* **'milieus, 'milieux** [-z] – *nc* (*formal*) a particular social setting or environment: *A peasant worker, a banker and a duchess each come from a different milieu.*

militant ['militənt] *adj* wishing to take, or taking, strong or violent action: *The demonstrators are becoming more militant as time goes on*; *The more militant workers prevented the others from working normally.* **'militantly** *adv.*

'militancy *nu.*

'militate [-teit] *vi* (*formal*: *with* **against**) to exert force or strong influence (against): *This evidence of his bad behaviour militated against his being chosen for the team.*

military ['militəri] *adj* (*esp attrib*) of soldiers or (*loosely*) armed forces generally, or war: *military supplies/discipline/power.* – *nu* (*with* **the**: *formal*) the army: *We'll have to get the military to deal with this.*

militate *see* **militant**.

militia [mi'liʃə] *nc* a body of men trained to fight as soldiers but only used in the home country, if and when it is attacked.

mi'litiaman – *pl* **mi'litiamen** – *nc* a member of a militia.

milk [milk] *nu* a white liquid produced by female mammals as food for their young: *It is thought that babies are healthiest if fed on their mothers' milk*; *The commonest source of milk is the cow*; (*attrib*) *milk chocolate* (= chocolate (*def 2*) containing milk). – *vt* **1** to obtain milk from: *The farmer milks his cows each day.* **2** (*inf*) to force, or take, money over a period of time from (a person): *The blackmailer milked his victims of huge amounts of money.*

'milky *adj* **1** containing milk: *He likes his tea very milky*; *milky coffee.* **2** like milk in appearance: *A milky substance can be obtained from this plant*; *The liquid in the bottle was not transparent – it was milky.* **3** (*liter*) white or pale: *She had dark hair and a milky complexion*; *Her skin is milky.* **'milkiness** *nu.*

'milk-float *nc* a vehicle (*usu* electrically-powered) used for delivering milk: *Our milkman used to deliver the milk by horse and cart but now he drives a milk-float.*

'milkmaid *nc* (*old*) a woman employed to milk cows by hand before it was done by machine.

'milkman *nc* a man who delivers milk: *What time does the milkman come in the morning?*

'milkshake *nc* a drink made by shaking up milk and a particular flavouring: *I'd like a chocolate/strawberry milkshake.*

milk tooth *nc* one of the first set of a baby's teeth: *The child's milk teeth started to come out when he was six years old.*

milk and honey comfort, luxury, plenty *etc*: *This is no longer the land of milk and honey.*

milk of magnesia *see* **magnesia**.

the Milky Way (*also* **the Galaxy**) a huge collection of stars stretching across the sky.

mill [mil] *nc* **1** (*often in cmpds*) a machine, sometimes now electrical, for grinding coffee, pepper *etc* by crushing it between rough, hard surfaces: *a coffee-mill*; *a pepper-mill.* **2** a building where grain is ground: *The farmer took his corn to the mill.* **3** (*often in cmpds*) a building where certain types of things are manufactured: *a woollen-mill*; *a steel-mill.* – **1** *vt* to grind or press: *This flour was milled locally.* **2** *vt* to put ridges and grooves on the rim of (coins). **3** *vi* (*usu with* **about** *or* **around**) (of crowds) to move about in a disorganized way: *There's a huge crowd of people milling around in front of the theatre.*

milled *adj* (of the edges of coins) having grooves.

'miller *nc* a person who works a grain mill.

'millpond *nc* (*old*) a pond holding water for driving a grain mill: *The sea was as calm as a millpond.*

'millstone *nc* **1** one of the two large, heavy stones used in an old-fashioned mill for grinding grain. **2** (*fig*: *usu with* **round one's/the neck**) something that is a heavy burden or responsibility, and prevents easy progress: *He regarded his mother-in-law as nothing but a millstone round his neck.*

'millwheel *nc* a wheel, *esp* a waterwheel, used for driving an old-fashioned grain mill.

put (someone) through, go through the mill to put (someone) through, or to go through, a series of difficult tests or troublesome experiences: *They really put her through the mill during the inquiry, asking lots of difficult questions.*

run-of-the-mill *see* **run**.

millennium [mi'leniəm] – *pl* **mil'lennia** [-niə] – *nc* (*formal*) a period of a thousand years: *Almost two millennia have passed since the birth of Christ.*

millet ['milit] *nu* a type of grain used as food: *The peasant farmer grows millet*; (*attrib*) *The budgie eats millet seed.*

milligram(me), millilitre, millimetre *see* Appendix 5.

milliner ['milinə] *nc* a person who makes and/or sells women's hats.

'**millinery** *nu* (*a term used esp in shops*) the goods made or sold by milliners: *We sell more millinery in the summer than in the winter*; (*attrib*) *the millinery department.*

million ['miljən] – *pls* '**million** (*defs 1, 3*), '**millions** (*defs 2, 3, 4*) – *nc* **1** (preceded by **a**, a number, or a word signifying a quantity) the number 1 000 000: *a million*; *one million*; *five million*; *several million*; *a few million.* **2** the figure 1 000 000. **3** a million pounds or dollars: *He made five million on the Stock Exchange*; *Her fortune amounts to several million(s).* **4** (*rare*: *loosely*) a lot (of). – *See also* **millions of** *below.* – *adj* (preceded by **a**, a number, or a word signifying a quantity: *usu attrib*) 1 000 000 in number: *six million people.*

'**million-** (*in cmpds*) having a million (of something): *Is there such a thing as a million-pound banknote?*

ˌ**millio'naire** [-'neə] – *fem* ˌ**millio'nairess** – *nc* a person having a million pounds, dollars *etc* or more.

'**millionth 1** *nc* one of a million equal parts. **2** *nc, adj* (the) last of a million (people, things *etc*) or (the person, thing *etc*) in an equivalent position: *the millionth car across the Forth Road Bridge.*

'**millions of 1** several million: *He won millions of pounds while gambling.* **2** (*loosely*) lots of: *I had to read millions of books for my exams.*

See also Appendix 1.

millpond, millstone, millwheel *see* **mill**.

mime [maim] **1** *nu* the art of using movement to perform the function of speech, *esp* in drama: *She is studying mime at the local college of drama.* **2** *nc* a play in which no words are spoken and the actions tell the story: *I enjoyed the mime that the children performed.* **3** *nc* an actor in such a play; someone who practises this art: *Marcel Marceau is a famous mime.* – *vti* to act, *eg* in such a play, using movements rather than words: *He mimed his love for her by holding his hands over his heart.*

mimic ['mimik] – *pt, ptp* '**mimicked** – *vt* to imitate (someone or something), *esp* with the intention of making him or it appear ridiculous or funny: *The comedian mimicked the Prime Minister's way of speaking.* – *nc* a person who mimics: *Children are often good mimics.*

'**mimicry** *nu* (*formal*) the art of mimicking.

minaret [minə'ret] *nc* a tower on a mosque from which the call to prayer is sounded.

mince [mins] **1** *vt* to cut into small pieces or chop finely: *Would you like me to mince the meat for you?* **2** *vi* (*derog*) to walk with short steps, in an unpleasantly dainty or delicate way: *She minced over to him with an unpleasant smile on her face.* – *nu* meat (*usu* beef) chopped up into small pieces: *We had mince and potatoes for lunch.*

'**mincer** *nc* a machine for mincing meat *etc*: *Could you put the meat in the electric mincer?*

'**mincing** *adj* (*attrib*: *derog*) too dainty or prim: *He walked with little mincing steps.* '**mincingly** *adv.*

'**mincemeat** *nu* a mixture of raisins, other fruits *etc, usu* with suet (used in baking ˌ**mince-'pies**).

make 'mincemeat of (someone) (*inf*) to defeat or destroy (someone) completely, or punish him severely: *If I catch you stealing my apples again, I'll make mincemeat of you!*

not to mince matters/words (*formal*) to be entirely frank and open, not trying to make one's words have less effect than they should: *He didn't mince matters – he just told her she was useless.*

mind [maind] *nc* **1** the power by which one thinks *etc*; the intelligence or understanding: *You're not using your mind, staying at home looking after the children*; *Her ten-year-old daughter already has the mind of an adult.* **2** a person who has great mental ability *etc*: *Some of our best minds are emigrating to better-paid jobs abroad.* – *vt* **1** to look after or supervise (*eg* a child): *She asked her daughter to stay at home and mind the baby.* **2** (not used with **is, was** *etc* and **-ing**) to be upset by; to object to: *You must try not to mind when he criticizes your work.* **3** to be careful of: *Mind* (= be careful not to trip over) *the stone step!* **4** to pay attention to or obey: *You should mind your parents' words/advice.* – *interj* be careful!: *Mind! There's a car coming!*

-minded (*in cmpds*) having a (certain type of) mind, as in **narrow-minded, like-minded**.

'**mindless** *adj* stupid and senseless: *mindless violence*; *These teenagers must be completely mindless to damage property in that way.* '**mindlessly** *adv.* '**mindlessness** *nu.*

'**mindreader** *nc* a person who claims to know other people's thoughts.

bear/keep in mind to remember or take into consideration: *Bear in mind that you'll have to save some money if you want a holiday.*

be out of one's mind (*inf*) to be mad: *He must be out of his mind to think he can sail round the world in that boat.*

change one's mind *see* **change**.

do you mind! used to show annoyance, stop someone doing something *etc*: *Do you mind! That's my best shirt you're using as a floor-cloth!*

give (someone) a piece of one's mind (*inf*) to scold or blame (a person) angrily: *If he does that again, she's going to give him a piece of her mind.*

go out of one's mind (*inf*) to go mad: *Stop making that irritating noise before I go out of my mind!*

have a good mind to (*inf*) to feel very much inclined to (do something): *I've a good mind to tell your father what a naughty girl you are!*

have (ˌhalf) a 'mind to to feel (slightly) inclined to (do something): *I've half a mind to take my holidays in winter this year.*

ˌ**have it in 'mind to** (*formal*) to intend to: *I have it in mind to promote Mr Davidson next month.*

in one's mind's eye in one's imagination: *If you try hard, you can see the room in your mind's eye.*

in one's right mind (*usu in neg*) sane: *No-one in his right mind would behave like that.*

in two minds undecided: *He's in two minds about going/whether to go.*

keep one's mind on to give all one's attention to: *Keep your mind on what you're doing!*

know one's own mind (*usu in neg*) to know what one really thinks, wants to do *etc*: *She doesn't know her own mind yet about abortion.*

make up one's mind to decide: *They've made up their minds to stay in Africa*; *Don't try to argue with her – her mind's made up.*

'**mindful of** (*formal*) remembering or taking into consideration: *She was always mindful of her mother's advice.*

mind one's own business to attend to one's own affairs, not interfering in other people's: *Why do you keep asking all these questions? Go away and mind your own business!*

mind one's p's and q's (*inf*) to be very careful: *Mind your p's and q's if you don't want to annoy him!*

never mind don't bother; it's all right: *Never mind, I'll do it myself.*

of one mind (*formal*) in agreement: *They are all of one mind as to what action they should take.*

on one's mind making one anxious, worried *etc*: *She has a lot on her mind.*

an open mind *see* **open**.

peace of mind *see* **peace**.

presence of mind *see* **presence**.

put (someone) in mind of to remind (someone) of: *This place puts me in mind of a book I once read.*

speak one's mind to say frankly what one means or thinks: *If you'll allow me to speak my mind, I think your plan is quite unsuitable.*

take/keep one's mind off to turn one's attention from; to prevent one from thinking about: *A good holiday will take your mind off all the unhappiness of the past few months; Try to keep his mind off his operation.*

time out of mind *see* **time**.

to 'my mind in my opinion: *To my mind, you're better off working here than in most other places.*

mine[1] [main] *pron* something which belongs to me: *Are these pencils yours or mine?*; *This is your pen – mine is in the box*; *Some of his books were saved from the fire, but most of mine are missing*; *He is a friend of mine* (= one of my friends).

See also **I, me, my, myself**.

mine[2] [main] *nc* **1** (*often in cmpds*) a place (*usu* underground) from which metals, coal, salt *etc* are dug: *a coalmine*; *My father worked in the mines for ten years.* **2** a type of bomb used underwater or placed just beneath the surface of the ground: *The ship has been blown up by a mine.* – **1** *vti* to dig (for metals *etc*) in a mine: *Coal is mined in South Wales.* **2** *vt* to dig mines in: *This whole area was extensively mined.* **3** *vt* to place explosive mines in: *They've mined the mouth of the river.* **4** *vt* to blow up with mines: *His ship was mined in mid-Atlantic.*

'miner *nc* (*sometimes in cmpds*) a person who works in a mine, in Britain *usu* a coalminer: *The miners are asking for higher wages.*

'minefield *nc* an area of ground or water which is full of explosive mines.

'minehunter, 'minelayer, 'minesweeper *ncs* types of ships used for finding, placing or removing mines in the sea.

'mineshaft *nc* a vertical shaft or sloping tunnel into a mine.

a mine of information a plentiful source of information: *He's a mine of information about insects.*

See also **undermine**.

mineral ['minərəl] *nc* a substance (metals, gems, coal, salt *etc*) found naturally in the earth and mined: *What minerals are mined in that country?*; (*attrib*) *a country's mineral wealth*; (*attrib*) *mineral ores.*

ˌmine'ralogy [-'ralədʒi] *nu* the study of minerals: *He is studying mineralogy*; (*attrib*) *a mineralogy lecture.* **ˌminera'logical** [-'lo-] *adj.* **ˌminer-a'logically** [-'lo-] *adv.* **ˌmine'ralogist** [-'ra-] *nc.*

'mineral water 1 *nu* a type of water containing small quantities of health-giving minerals. **2** *nc* (*esp in pl*: *formal*) a fizzy, non-alcoholic drink such as lemonade: *I don't want whisky or wine – have you any mineral waters?*

mingle ['miŋgl] *vti* (*often liter*) to mix: *The spy mingled with the crowd*; *The various sounds mingled pleasantly.* **'mingled** *adj.*

mingy ['mindʒi] *adj* (*inf*) mean or ungenerous: *a mingy person*; *That's a mingy little piece of meat*; *He's so mingy that he never gives presents at Christmas.*

mini ['mini] **1** (*in cmpds*) small, as in **minibus**. **2** short for **miniskirt**. **3** *nc* (*with cap*: ®) a type of small car. – *adj* (*inf attrib*) small: *a mini dictionary.*

miniature ['minitʃə] *adj* (*attrib*) smaller than normal, often very small: *a miniature radio.* – *nc* **1** a very small painting of a person. **2** a copy or model of something, made on a small scale.

in 'miniature on a small scale: *The station in the child's model train set is King's Cross Station in miniature*; *That boy is his father in miniature.*

minibus ['minibʌs] *nc* a small bus, *usu* with only a dozen seats or so: *The school hired a minibus to take the football team to the match.*

minim ['minim] *nc* (*music*) a note of a certain length. – *See also* Appendix 4.

minimum ['miniməm] *adj* (*attrib*: *formal*) smallest or lowest (possible, obtained, recorded *etc*): *the minimum temperature at which water remains liquid*; *the minimum temperature last night.* – *n* – *pls* **'minimums, 'minima** [-mə] – *nc* the smallest possible number, quantity *etc* or the lowest level: *He always did the very minimum of work*; *Costs must be kept to a minimum*; *Tickets will cost a minimum of £1* (= at least £1).

'minimal *adj* (*formal*) very small indeed: *The amount of difference it makes is minimal*; *The new scheme will involve us in only minimal expense.*

'minimize, -ise *vt* (*formal*) **1** to make as little as possible: *He took steps to minimize the dangers.* **2** to cause to seem little or unimportant: *He spoke as if he had achieved it all on his own, minimizing the help he had received.*

minion ['minjən] *nc* (*derog or facet*) a slave-like follower or employee: *He won't do that job himself – he'll probably get one of his minions to do it for him.*

miniskirt ['miniskə:t] *nc* (*inf abbrev* **mini** ['mini]) a short skirt the hem of which is well above the knees: *Miniskirts were popular in Britain in the nineteen-sixties.*

minister ['ministə] *nc* **1** a clergyman in certain branches of the Christian Church: *He is the minister of the local Presbyterian church*; *He is studying to be a minister.* **2** (*often with cap*) (the title of) the head of any of the divisions or departments of a government: *the Minister for Education.* – *vi* (*formal*: *with* **to**) to give help (to): *She ministered to her husband's needs.*

ministerial [mini'stiəriəl] *adj* (*formal*) of or concerning ministers (*esp def 2*): *ministerial duties.*

ˌmini'strations *n pl* (*formal*) the act of giving help, care *etc*: *She quickly recovered, thanks to the nurse's ministrations.*

'ministry 1 *ncu* the profession, duties or period of service of a minister of religion: *He's decided to enter the ministry*; *His ministry lasted for fifteen years.* **2** *nc* (*often with cap*) a department of government or the building where its employees work: *the Transport Ministry.*

mink [miŋk] **1** *nc* a small weasel-like kind of

animal. **2** *nu, adj* (of) its fur: *a hat made of mink; a mink coat.* **3** *nc* (*inf*) a mink coat: *She went to the theatre mainly to show off her new mink.*

minor ['mainə] *adj* (*esp attrib: more formal or tech than* **lesser** *or* **unimportant**) less, or little, in importance, size *etc*: *Always halt when driving from a minor road on to a major road; He has a minor post in the Swedish embassy; She has to go into hospital for a minor operation; The part he played was relatively minor.* – *nc* a person who is not yet legally an adult (in Britain, 18 years of age): *Do they send minors to prison?*

mi'nority [mi'no-, mai'no-] **1** *nc* a small number; less than half: *Only a minority of people live in the countryside; a racial/political minority;* (*attrib*) *She's a member of one of the political minority groups.* **2** *nu* (*legal*) the state of being a minor: *He was her guardian during her minority.*

be in the minority to be in the smaller of two groups: *Women were very much in the minority* (= There were far more men than women) *at the meeting.*

See also **major**.

minster ['minstə] *nc* (*arch: now only in titles*) **1** the church of a monastery: *York Minster.* **2** (*loosely*) a large church or cathedral.

minstrel ['minstrəl] *nc* (*hist*) a musician who went about the country in medieval times, reciting or singing poems: *A band of minstrels entertained the king by reciting ballads.*

mint[1] [mint] *nc* **1** (*often with cap*) a place where money is made by the government: *Whereabouts in Britain is the Mint?* **2** (*inf: no pl*) a large sum (of money): *He made an absolute mint (of money) by dealing in stocks and shares.* – *vt* (*formal or tech*) to manufacture (money): *When were decimal coins first minted in Britain?*

in mint condition **1** unused: *a stamp in mint condition.* **2** (*loosely*) used, but in extremely good condition: *My car is two years old, but it's still in mint condition.*

mint[2] [mint] **1** *nu* a plant with strong-smelling leaves, used as a flavouring: *We grow mint in the garden;* (*attrib*) *roast lamb and mint sauce.* **2** *nc* (*also* '**peppermint**) a sweet flavoured by means of these leaves or by a synthetic preparation tasting like this: *a box of mints;* (*attrib*) *mint chocolate.* **3** *nu* (*also* '**peppermint**) the flavouring.

minuet [minju'et] *nc* **1** (*hist*) a slow, graceful dance with short steps. **2** a piece of music to accompany such a dance.

minus ['mainəs] *prep* **1** (*esp math*) used to show subtraction: *Ten minus two equals eight* (10−2=8). **2** (*inf*) without: *I'm minus my umbrella today.* – *nc* (*math: also* '**minus sign**) a sign (−) used to show subtraction or negative quality. – *adj* (*attrib*) negative or less than zero: *a minus number; The temperature was minus four (degrees) today; Twelve from ten equals minus two* (10−12=−2).

See also **plus**.

minuscule ['miniskju:l] *adj* (*formal or facet*) very small: *minuscule handwriting; This piece of meat is minuscule.*

minute[1] ['minit] *nc* **1** (*sometimes abbrev* **min.** *when written*) the sixtieth part of an hour; sixty seconds: *It is twenty minutes to eight; They talked on the telephone for at least thirty minutes; a ten-minute delay.* **2** (*geog or geom*) in measuring an angle, the sixtieth part of a degree; sixty seconds: *an angle of 47° 50′* (= forty-seven degrees, fifty minutes). **3** (*inf*) a very short time: *Wait a minute while I finish writing this sentence; I never thought so for a minute* (= at all); *It will be done in a minute* (= very quickly or very soon). **4** a particular point in time: *At that minute, the telephone rang; At any minute* (= Very soon, or without warning) *he may come through the door.* **5** (*usu in pl*) the notes taken at a meeting recording what was said: *The chairman asked for this decision to be recorded in the minutes; Would you get your secretary to do a short minute on this afternoon's meeting?*

'**minute hand** *nc* the larger of the two pointers on a clock or watch, which shows the time in minutes past the hour: *The minute hand on my watch is broken although the hour hand is working normally.*

the 'minute (that) as soon as: *Telephone me the minute he arrives!*

to the 'minute (of time) exactly; precisely: *The cooking time must be correct to the minute.*

up to the minute most modern or recent: *Her clothes are always right up to the minute* (= very fashionable); (*attrib*) *an up-to-the-minute report/dress.*

minute[2] [mai'nju:t] *adj* (*formal*) **1** very small: *minute details; The diamonds in the brooch were minute.* **2** paying attention to the smallest details: *minute care; A minute examination revealed small flecks of blood on the coat.* **mi'nutely** *adv.* **mi'nuteness** *nu.*

minutiae [mi'nju:ʃii:] *n pl* (*formal and often derog*) very small details: *Concentrate on the major points and forget about the minutiae.*

miracle ['mirəkl] *nc* **1** something which man is not normally capable of making happen and which is therefore thought to be done by a god or God: *Christ's turning of water into wine was a miracle.* **2** (*loosely*) a fortunate happening that has no obvious natural cause or explanation: *It's a miracle he wasn't killed in the plane crash.*

mi'raculous [-'rakju-] *adj*: *a miraculous recovery from an illness; His recovery has been quite miraculous.* **mi'raculously** *adv.*

mirage ['mira:ʒ, (*esp Amer*) mi'ra:ʒ] *nc* (*formal*) something that one imagines one sees, that is not really there, *esp* the appearance of an area of water seen by travellers in a desert.

mire ['maiə] *nu* (*formal or liter*) deep mud: *Pigs like rolling about in the mire.*

mirror ['mirə] **1** *nc* a piece of glass or metal having a surface that reflects an image: *She always uses a mirror while she's putting on her hat; She seems to spend a lot of time looking in the mirror.* **2** *nc* (*fig*) something that gives a true picture or reflection: *The election results in this town will probably be a mirror of voting in the country as a whole.* **3** *n* (*with cap*) a word often used in the titles of newspapers: *the Evening Mirror.* – *vt* (*formal*) to reflect as a mirror does: *The smooth surface of the lake mirrored the surrounding mountains;* (*fig*) *He saw his own horror mirrored in her face.*

mirror image *nc* (*formal*) an image with the right and left sides reversed as in a mirror: *The twins are not absolutely identical, as one is a mirror image of the other.*

mirth [mə:θ] *nu* (*formal*) laughter or amusement: *His jokes caused great mirth among his companions.* '**mirthless** *adj.*

mis- [mis] (*in cmpds*) **1** wrong(ly), as in **miscalculate**. **2** bad(ly), as in **misbehave**.

misadventure [misəd'ventʃə] *ncu* (*formal or legal*)

an unlucky happening or accident: *A verdict of death by misadventure was brought in by the jury.*

misanthrope ['mizənθroup], **misanthropist** [mi'zanθrəpist] *nc* (*formal*) a person who hates all mankind: *He has been a misanthrope since his wife and family were killed in a car accident.* **ˌmisan'thropic** [-'θro-] *adj.*
mi'santhropy *nu* (*formal*) hatred or distrust of all mankind.
See also **philanthropy**.

misapply [misə'plai] *vt* (*very formal*) to use for a wrong purpose: *His skill as an engineer was misapplied to burgling safes.*
ˌmisappli'cation [-apli'keiʃən] *ncu* (*formal*) (a) wrong use: *a misapplication of the rules.*

misapprehension [misapri'henʃən] *nc* (*formal*) a misunderstanding of meaning or facts, or a wrong belief: *He's under a misapprehension about his brother's intentions.*
See also **apprehend**.

misappropriate [misə'prouprieit] *vt* (*formal or legal*) to put to a wrong use, *esp* to use someone else's money for oneself: *He was sacked for misappropriating company funds.* **ˌmis-apˌpropri'ation** *ncu.*

misbehave [misbi'heiv] *vi* to behave badly: *If you misbehave, I'll send you to bed.* **ˌmisbe'haviour** [-'heivjə] *nu.*

miscalculate [mis'kalkjuleit] *vti* (*formal*) to calculate or estimate wrongly: *I miscalculated the bill*; *If a racing driver miscalculates when turning a corner, he could be in serious trouble.* **misˌcalcu'lation** *ncu.*

miscarriage ['miskaridʒ] **1** *nc* in pregnancy, the loss of the baby from the womb before it is able to survive: *She had a miscarriage last week*; *She has had several miscarriages.* **2** *ncu* (*formal or legal*) (a) failure, *eg* of a plan *etc*: *This led to the miscarriage of all his schemes*; *By a miscarriage of justice* (= a wrong judgement) *the wrong man was condemned*; *Miscarriages of justice are rare.*
mis'carry (*formal*) *vi* **1** to be unsuccessful or obtain the wrong result: *Their plan miscarried and they suffered a defeat.* **2** (of a female) to have a miscarriage: *She miscarried in the second month of her pregnancy.*

miscellaneous [misə'leiniəs] *adj* (*attrib*: *formal*) composed of several kinds; mixed: *a miscellaneous collection of pictures.*
miscellany [mi'seləni, (*Amer*) 'misəleini] *nc* (*formal*) a collection or mixture of things *eg* writings on different subjects, of different kinds, or by different authors: *a Dylan Thomas miscellany*; *a miscellany of objects.*

mischance [mis'tʃa:ns] *ncu* (*formal*) (a piece of) bad luck: *It was by sheer mischance that the firm went bankrupt*; *Mischances are unavoidable.*

mischief ['mistʃif] *nu* **1** (*usu* of children) action or behaviour that causes small troubles or annoyance to others: *That boy is always up to some mischief, such as pulling little girl's hair.* **2** (*formal*) evil, damage or harm: *Bombs from the enemy planes did a lot of mischief in the crowded city.*
'mischievous [-vəs] *adj* **1** tending, or inclined, to cause trouble or annoyance: *a mischievous child*; *That little boy is so mischievous*; (*formal*) *a mischievous remark.* **2** (fond of) teasing *etc* in a playful manner: *a mischievous smile.* **'mischievously** *adv.*
do (someone) a mischief (*inf*) to hurt someone: *I almost did myself a mischief when I tried to climb the wall.*
make mischief (*formal*) to cause trouble *etc*: *He tries to make mischief by telling the manager about the other employees' mistakes.*

misconception [miskən'sepʃən] *nc* (*formal*) a wrong idea or impression: *There has been some misconception about the terms of agreement.*
See also **conceive**.

misconduct [mis'kondʌkt] *nu* (*formal*) bad behaviour: *The doctor was found guilty of professional misconduct.*

misconstrue [miskən'stru:] *vt* (*formal*) to misunderstand; to misinterpret: *You have misconstrued my words.* **ˌmiscon'struction** [-'strʌk-] *nc.*

miscount [mis'kaunt] *vt* (*formal*) to count wrongly: *I'm sorry, I miscounted the number of seats.* – *nc* (*formal*) a wrong count: *He doesn't believe the result, and says there must have been a miscount.*

miscreant ['miskriənt] *nc* (*formal or liter*) a criminal or wicked person: *The miscreants were jailed for six months.*

misdeed [mis'di:d] *nc* (*formal*) an instance of bad or criminal behaviour: *You'll suffer for your misdeeds!*

misdemeanour, (*Amer*) **misdemeanor** [misdi'mi:nə] *nc* **1** (*formal*) an act of misbehaviour: *The child was punished for his misdemeanours.* **2** (*legal*) a petty crime.

misdirect [misdi'rekt, -dai-] *vt* (*formal*) to direct wrongly: *She was misdirected, and ended up in the wrong room.*

miser ['maizə] *nc* a mean and ungenerous person who lives very poorly in order to store up wealth: *That old miser wouldn't give you a penny!*; (*fig*) *He's a real miser with his favours.* **'miserly** *adj.* **'miserliness** *nu.*

miserable ['mizərəbl] *adj* **1** very unhappy; *She's been miserable since he went away*; *The miserable little girl wept quietly in the corner.* **2** (*formal*: *esp attrib*) very poor in quantity or quality: *miserable payment*; *a miserable house*; *The house was in a miserable condition.* **3** (*liter*: *attrib*) shameful: *his miserable cowardice.* **'miserably** *adv.*

misery ['mizəri] **1** *nu* (*sometimes with* **a**) great unhappiness: *the poverty and misery of the fatherless children*; *She tried to be cheerful but her misery at the death of her child was too great*; (*inf*) *They've made my life a misery.* **2** *nc* (*inf*) a depressing, cheerless person: *He's a real misery today!*

misfire [mis'faiə] *vi* **1** (of a gun, bomb *etc*) to fail to explode or catch fire. **2** (of a motor engine) to fail to ignite properly. **3** (of a plan *etc*) to produce the wrong effect; to have no success: *Their plan to get rid of the prime minister misfired.*

misfit ['misfit] *nc* a person who is not able to live or work happily in the situation in which he finds himself: *The social work department tries to help all kinds of misfits.*

misfortune [mis'fo:tʃən] *ncu* (*formal*) (a piece of) bad luck: *I had the misfortune to break my leg yesterday*; *Misfortunes rarely come singly.*

misgiving [mis'giviŋ] *ncu* (*formal*: *often in pl*) (a feeling of) fear or doubt: *They have serious misgivings about the wisdom of continuing to spend money on your ideas*; *It was with a good deal of misgiving that I appointed him to the job – but he was the only candidate.*

misguided [mis'gaidid] *adj* (*formal*) acting from, or showing, mistaken beliefs or motives: *His misguided attempts to help only made things worse*;

His attempts to help were done with the best of intentions but they were rather misguided.

mishandle [mis'handl] *vt* (*formal*) to handle without skill: *She mishandled the whole affair.*

mishap ['mishap] *nc* an unlucky accident (often not serious): *She had a small mishap with her cup of tea.*

misinform [misin'foːm] *vt* (*formal*) to give wrong information to: *We were misinformed about the date of the meeting.*

misinterpret [misin'təːprit] *vt* to understand wrongly: *He misinterpreted my action as a sign of hostility.* **'misin,terpre'tation** *ncu.*

misjudge [mis'dʒʌdʒ] *vt* to have an unfairly low opinion of (a person): *You misjudge me if you think I'd do something awful like that.*

mislay [mis'lei] – *pt, ptp* **mis'laid** – *vt* to lose (something) *usu* temporarily, often through not being able to remember where it was put: *I seem to have mislaid my wallet somewhere.*

mislead [mis'liːd] – *pt, ptp* **mis'led** [-'led] – *vti* to give a wrong idea to (a person): *Her friendly attitude misled me into thinking I could trust her; Advertisements of that kind are apt to mislead.*
mis'leading *adj*: *a very misleading remark; His comments were rather misleading.*

mismanage [mis'manidʒ] *vt* (*formal*) to manage badly and without skill: *He badly mismanaged the company's financial affairs.* **,mis'management** *nu.*

misnomer [mis'noumə] *nc* (*formal or facet*) a wrong or unsuitable name: *'Road' was a misnomer for the rough track along which we had to drive.*

misogynist [mi'sodʒənist] *nc* (*formal*) a person who hates women: *He will never marry – he is a misogynist.* **mi'sogyny** *nu.*

misplace [mis'pleis] *vt* (*formal*) **1** to lose temporarily: *I'm afraid I've misplaced your letter, but I'll try hard to find it.* **2** to give (*eg* trust, affection) to an unworthy person *etc*: *Your trust in him was misplaced.*

misprint ['misprint] *nc* a mistake in printing: *This newspaper is full of misprints.*

mispronounce [misprə'nauns] *vt* to pronounce (words *etc*) wrongly: *She has a Polish name – I always mispronounce it.* **'mispro,nunci'ation** [-nʌnsi-] *ncu.*

misquote [mis'kwout] *vt* to make a mistake or a deliberate error in repeating what someone has written or said: *His speech was misquoted in many of the newspapers.*

misread [mis'riːd] –*pt, ptp* **,mis'read** [-'red] – *vt* (*formal*) **1** to read wrongly: *He misread the sentence twice before getting it right.* **2** to understand wrongly; to misinterpret: *He misread her remark as an insult.*

misrepresent [misrepri'zent] *vt* (*formal*) to give intentionally a false idea of (a person or what he does or says): *He was misrepresented by his critics as an enemy of Britain, whereas he was really one of its greatest friends.*
'mis,represen'tation *ncu*: *a gross misrepresentation of the facts.*

Miss [mis] **1** *n* (sometimes *no cap* when not followed by a name) a polite title given to an unmarried female, either in writing or in speech: *Miss Wilson; the Misses Wilson; Could you ask Miss Smith to type this letter?; Miss Morris, would you open the window please?*; (used when talking to a young woman) *Excuse me, miss. Could you tell me how to get to Princess Road?* **2** *n* (*often no cap*) a term often used when addressing a female school teacher, whether married or not: *Please, miss, may I sharpen my pencil?* **3** *nc* (*no cap*: *derog or facet*) a girl or young woman: *She's a cheeky little miss!* *See also* **Madam, Mrs, Ms**.

miss [mis] **1** *vti* to fail to hit, catch *etc*: *The arrow missed the target; You missed!* **2** *vt* to fail to arrive in time for: *He missed the 8 o'clock train/the first ten minutes of the film.* **3** *vt* to fail to take advantage of: *You've missed your big opportunity/chance.* **4** *vt* to feel sad because of the absence of: *You'll miss all your friends when you go to live abroad.* **5** *vt* to notice the absence of: *I didn't miss my umbrella until after I got off the bus.* **6** *vt* to fail to hear or see: *He missed what you said because he wasn't listening; She missed (seeing) him because she wasn't looking.* **7** *vt* to fail to go to: *I'll have to miss my lesson next week, as I'm going to the dentist.* **8** *vt* to fail to meet: *We missed you in the crowd.* **9** *vt* to avoid: *The thief only just missed being caught by the police.* **10** *vi* (of an engine) to misfire: *The engine kept missing.* – *nc* a failure to hit, catch *etc*: *He scored two hits and two misses.* – *See also* **give (something) a miss** *below.*
missing *adj* not in the usual place or not able to be found: *One of my earrings is missing from the box; The child has been missing since Tuesday; A search was made for the missing papers.*
be missing (something or someone) (*inf*) to lack: *My bicycle is missing a pedal; Our team is missing a goalkeeper.*
give (something) a miss to leave (something) out, not go to (something) *etc*: *I think I'll give the party a miss.*
go missing to be lost: *A group of climbers went missing in Scotland last week.*
miss one's footing *see* **footing** *under* **foot**.
miss out 1 *vt sep* to omit or fail to include: *Don't miss out your brother when you send round the invitations.* **2** *vi* (*inf*: *often with* **on**) to be left out (of something) or unable to take part (in) or enjoy (something): *George missed out (on all the fun) because of his broken leg.*
miss the boat (*inf*) to be left behind, miss an opportunity *etc*: *I meant to send her a birthday card but I missed the boat – her birthday was last week.*
miss the point (of something) to fail to see or understand the purpose (of a remark, argument, action *etc*): *You've completely missed the point (of what I was saying)!*

misshapen [miʃ'ʃeipən] *adj* (*formal or liter*) badly formed: *a bent, misshapen tree; The tree is rather misshapen.*

missile ['misail] *nc* **1** (*formal*) a weapon or object which is thrown or fired from a gun, bow *etc.* **2** a rocket-powered weapon carrying an explosive charge: *a ground-to-air missile.*
guided missile *nc* a rocket-powered missile which is directed to its target by a built-in device or by radio waves *etc.*

missing *see* **miss**.

mission ['miʃən] *nc* **1** (*formal*) a purpose for which a person or group of people is sent: *His mission was to seek help.* **2** (*formal*) the purpose for which (one feels) one was born: *He regards it as his mission to help the cause of world peace.* **3** a group of people sent to have political and/or business discussions: *a Chinese trade mission.* **4** a place where missionaries live: *You'll find Father Jones at the mission.* **5** a group of missionaries: *She went to that country as part of a Catholic mission.*

ˈ**missionary** *nc* a person who tries to spread (a particular) religion among people who do not believe in (that) religion: *At the beginning of the century he went to Africa as a missionary.*

missive [ˈmisiv] *nc* (*facet or arch*) a letter, *esp* a long or serious-looking one: *I hope you received my last missive in February.*

misspell [misˈspel] – *pts, ptps* ˌ**misˈspelt,** ˌ**misˈspelled** – *vt* to spell (a word) wrongly: *She always misspells the word 'correspondence' – she spells it 'correspondance'.*

misspent [misˈspent] *adj* (*formal or liter: usu in the phrase* **misspent youth**) used or spent in the wrong way: *His skills as a criminal are the results of a misspent youth.*

mist [mist] *ncu* a cloud of moisture in the air but very close to the ground, which makes it difficult to see any distance: *The hills are covered in thick mist*; (*fig*) *The origin of this custom has been lost in the mists of time.* – *v see* **mist over, mist up** *below.*

ˈ**mistily** *adv* (as if) through a mist: *He gazed mistily out of the window as tears came to his eyes.*

ˈ**misty** *adj.* ˈ**mistiness** *nu.*

mist over *vi* to become covered (as if) with mist: *The hills/The mirror misted over.*

mist up 1 *vi* (of a surface) to mist over: *The mirror/windscreen misted up.* **2** *vt sep* to cause (a surface) to mist over: *Their breath misted up the windows.*

mistake [miˈsteik] – *pt* **miˈstook** [-ˈstuk] : *ptp* **miˈstaken** – *vt* **1** (*with* **for**) to think that (one person or thing) is another: *I mistook you for my brother in this bad light.* **2** to make an error about: *They mistook the date, and arrived two days early.* – *ncu* a wrong act or judgement: *a spelling mistake*; *It was a mistake to trust him*; *You made several mistakes in this French essay*; *I made a bad mistake in spending all the money at once*; *I took your umbrella by mistake – it looks like mine.*

miˈstaken *adj* (*formal*) wrong: *You are mistaken in thinking that he's dishonest*; *a mistaken impression.* **miˈstakenly** *adv.*

See also **unmistakable.**

Mister [ˈmistə] *n* (*usu abbrev* **Mr** *when written*) a polite title given to a particular male adult, either in writing or in speech: *Mr Smith*; *Mr Jones and Mr Black started work on the same day.*

See also **Esquire, Messrs, Sir.**

mistime [misˈtaim] *vt* (*formal*) **1** to time badly: *The cricketer mistimed his stroke and missed the ball.* **2** to do or say (something) at an unsuitable time: *He badly mistimed his remarks on immigration.*

mistletoe [ˈmisltou] *nu* a plant with white berries, growing on trees, which is used in Christmas decorations: *At Christmas she decorated the room with holly and mistletoe.*

mistress [ˈmistris] *nc* **1** a woman who is the lover of a man to whom she is not married: *He has a wife in London and a mistress in Paris.* **2** a female teacher: *the games mistress.* **3** a woman who commands, controls or owns: *mistress of the household*; *a dog and his mistress.* **4** a female employer (of a servant): *The servant stole her mistress's jewellery.*

See also **Mrs.**

mistrust [misˈtrʌst] *vt* (*formal*) to suspect or have no trust in (someone): *She seems honest enough but I mistrust her.* – *nu* lack of trust. ˌ**misˈtrustful** *adj.* ˌ**misˈtrustfully** *adv.*

See also **distrust.**

misty *see* **mist.**

misunderstand [misʌndəˈstand] – *pt, ptp* ˌ**misunderˈstood** [-ˈstud] – *vt* to take a wrong meaning from (*eg* a statement or a person or his words or actions): *She misunderstood what I said, and took it as an insult.*

ˌ**misunderˈstanding 1** *ncu* (a) confusion or mistake as to meaning: *There's been a (certain amount of) misunderstanding about the date for which we booked.* **2** *nc* (*euph*) a slight disagreement: *They had a misunderstanding, but they've become friendly again recently.*

ˌ**misunderˈstood** *adj* (of a person) not understood or appreciated: *As a child he often felt hurt and misunderstood*; *a much misunderstood person.*

misuse [misˈju:s] *ncu* (a) wrong or bad use: *the misuse of company money*; *The machine was damaged by misuse.*

ˌ**misˈuse** [-ˈju:z] *vt* **1** to use wrongly: *He misused the society's money to buy himself a car.* **2** (*formal*) to treat badly: *If you misuse these things and they get broken, you won't be given any more.*

See also **abuse, disuse.**

mite [mait] *nc* **1** a tiny person or child: *Look at that poor little mite!* **2** a type of very small insect related to the spider.

miter *see* **mitre.**

mitigate [ˈmitigeit] *vt* **1** (*legal*) to excuse (a wrong action) to some extent: *The judge declared that the circumstances mitigated his offence.* **2** (*very formal*) to make (pain, anger, punishment *etc*) less great or severe: *Nothing seemed able to mitigate his rage.*

ˈ**mitigating** *adj* (*formal: attrib*): *mitigating circumstances*; *pain-mitigating drugs.* ˌ**mitiˈgation** *nu.*

See also **unmitigated.**

mitre[1], (*Amer*) **miter**[1] [ˈmaitə] *nc* a type of headdress worn by archbishops and bishops.

mitre[2], (*Amer*) **miter**[2] [ˈmaitə] *nc* (*tech: also* ˈ**mitre-joint**) a joint made between two pieces that form an angle (*usu* a right angle, the end of each piece being cut at 45°). – *vt* (*tech*) join by means of a mitre: *He mitred the pieces of wood to make a picture-frame.*

mitt [mit] *nc* short for **mitten**: *The child has lost a mitt*; *She was wearing mitts – not gloves.*

mitten [ˈmitn] *nc* (*also* **mitt** [mit]) a kind of glove with two sections, one for the thumb and the other for the fingers: *a pair of mittens.* **2** a type of glove with separate sections for each finger, reaching only to halfway down the fingers: *golf mittens.*

mix [miks] **1** *vt* to put or blend (different things) together to form one mass: *She mixed the butter and sugar together*; *He mixed the blue paint with yellow paint to make green paint*; (*fig*) *In Britain, many different races of people are mixed together.* **2** *vt* to prepare or make (something) by doing this: *She mixed the cement in a bucket*; *I'm mixing a cake.* **3** *vi* to go together or blend successfully to form one mass: *Oil and water don't mix.* **4** *vi* to go together socially: *At the party, everybody mixed (in) together happily*; *People from different classes used to mix very little.* – **1** *nc* the result of mixing things or people together: *London has a particularly interesting racial mix.* **2** (*in cmpds*) a collection of ingredients used to make something: (*a*) *cake-mix.*

mixed *adj* **1** consisting of different kinds: *I have mixed feelings* (= doubts and gladness) *about leaving home*; *My feelings about him are rather mixed.* **2** done, used *etc* by people of different sexes: *mixed tennis*; *a mixed swimming-pool*; *Is* *your child's primary school mixed?*

'mixer *nc* **1** (*often in cmpds*) a person or thing that mixes; a thing which is used for mixing: *an electric food-mixer.* **2** (*inf*: *with* **good, bad** *etc*) a person who mixes (*def 4*) easily/with difficulty with others: *He's a very good mixer at a party.*

mixture ['mikstʃə] **1** *ncu* the result of mixing things or people together: *a mixture of eggs, flour and milk*; *I'll have to adjust the mixture* (*ie* of petrol vapour and air) *to get the car engine running properly.* **2** *ncu* a number of things mixed together and used for a given purpose: *Put some milk into the cake mixture if it's too thick*; *The doctor gave the baby some cough mixture to cure his cough.* **3** *nu* (*formal*) the act of mixing: *The mixture of green, red and blue light creates white light.*

mixed blessing *nc* something which has both advantages and disadvantages: *My mother often looks after my children for me, but it's a mixed blessing, because she gives them too many sweets.*

mixed marriage *ncu* (a) marriage between people of different races or religions: *They married without their parents' consent. She is a Roman Catholic and he is a Protestant and both sets of parents disapprove of mixed marriages*; *the mixed marriage between an Indian girl and an Englishman.*

mixed metaphor *see* **metaphor**.

'mix-up *nc* (*inf*) a confused situation *etc*: *How did we get into this mix-up?*; *There was a bit of a mix-up over tickets and too many people arrived for last night's concert.*

be mixed up (in something *or* **with someone)** to be involved (*esp* in something illegal): *He was mixed up in an attempt at revolution*; *He was mixed up with some revolutionaries.*

mixed up (*inf*) confused or upset: *The teenage girl has been rather mixed up since her mother died*; (*attrib*) *The mixed-up teenagers of today cause a lot of trouble.*

mix up *vt sep* **1** to blend (different things) together: *Put the eggs and sugar in the bowl and mix them up together*; *I'll need to mix up another tin of paint.* **2** to confuse or muddle (different things): *I mixed the dates up and arrived on the wrong day*; *I'm always mixing the twins up*; *She put the lottery tickets in the hat and mixed them up thoroughly.* **3** to confuse or upset (a person): *You've mixed me up completely with all this information.*

mnemonic [ni'monik] *nc* something (often a rhyme) that helps the memory: *'Thirty days have September, April, June and November' is a mnemonic.*

moan [moun] *vi* **1** to make a low sound of grief, pain *etc*: *The wounded soldier moaned in his sleep.* **2** (*inf*) to complain: *She's always moaning about how hard she has to work.* – *nc* a sound of grief, pain *etc*: *He gave a long moan of pain*; (*fig*) *the continuous moan of the wind.* **2** (*inf*) a complaint: *That's one of his frequent moans.*

moat [mout] *nc* a deep ditch, dug round a castle *etc*, *usu* filled with water.

mob [mob] *nc* (*derog*) a noisy, violent or disorderly crowd of people: *He was attacked by an angry mob of youths*; (*attrib*) *mob violence.* – *v* – *pt, ptp* **mobbed** – *vt* (of a crowd) to surround, push or attack (a person) in a disorderly way: *The singer was mobbed by a huge crowd of his fans*; *The fans mobbed the singer as he left the theatre.*

mobile ['moubail] *adj* **1** able to move: *The van supplying country districts with library books is called a mobile library*; *The old lady is no longer mobile – she has to stay in bed all day.* **2** able to move or be moved quickly or easily: *Most of the furniture is very light and mobile*; (*inf or facet*) *I can't visit you today – I won't be mobile till tomorrow when I get my car back.* **3** (of someone's features or face) changing easily in expression: *That actress has very mobile features*; *Her face is so mobile!* – *nc* a group of ornamental objects hung so that they move slightly in the air: *The baby was fascinated by the mobile of plastic butterflies.*

mo'bility [-'bi-] *nu*.

'mobilize, -ise [-bi-] *vti* (*formal or tech*) to make (*esp* troops, an army *etc*), or become, ready for use or action: *The general ordered his officers to mobilize their men.* **ˌmobili'zation, -s-** [-bi-] *nu*.

See also **move, demobilize, immobile**.

moccasin ['mokəsin] *nc* a type of shoe, made of soft leather, worn by American Indians; an imitation of it.

mock [mok] *vt* to laugh at or cause to seem ridiculous: *They mocked my efforts at riding a bike*; *The children mocked the little boy because he wore thick spectacles*; (*formal fig*) *The mountains mocked our attempts to climb them.* – *adj* (*attrib*) pretended or not real: *a mock battle*; *He looked at me in mock horror.*

'mockery *nu* an act of making fun of something: *She became the target of a great deal of mockery*; *She could not tolerate their mockery any longer.*

'mocking *adj*: *a mocking laugh/smile*; *His laugh was mocking and cruel.* **'mockingly** *adv*.

'mock-up *nc* a full-size non-working model: *We were shown round a mock-up of the new plane.*

make a mockery of (something) (*formal*) to make (something) appear ridiculous: *The ease with which they got past us made a mockery of our attempts to stop them.*

modal *see* **mode**.

mod cons [mod'konz]: **all mod cons** (*inf*) short for **all modern conveniences**: *This house has all mod cons, such as central heating, a garage, a deep freeze and so on.*

mode [moud] *nc* (*formal*) **1** a manner of doing something: *He has some strange modes of expression*; *He has a strange mode of expressing himself.* **2** a kind or type: *Which mode of writing do you prefer to read?* **3** a fashion: *Large hats are the latest mode.*

'modish *adj* (*formal*) fashionable and smart: *a modish young lady*; *Her hats are always very modish.* **'modishly** *adv*.

modal auxiliary *nc* a modal verb used as an auxiliary verb: *I might come*; *He could do it.*

modal verb *nc* a verb used, *usu* as an auxiliary, to express possibility, ability, permission, conditionality, compulsion, duty *etc* (*eg* **can, may, should, will, must, used to** *etc*).

model ['modl] *nc* **1** a copy or representation of something *usu* on a much smaller scale: *They made a model of the Houses of Parliament out of matchsticks*; (*attrib*) *a model aeroplane.* **2** (one example of) a particular type or design of something, *eg* a car, that is manufactured in large numbers: *Our Renault car is a 1976 model*; *This refrigerator is the latest model.* **3** a person who wears clothes *etc* so that possible buyers can see them being worn: *He has a job as a male fashion model.* **4** a person who is painted, sculpted, photographed *etc* by an artist, photographer *etc*: *I work as an artist's model.* **5** something which is to be copied: *Use this statue as your model*; *Hemingway's writings will be my model.* **6** a person or thing which is an excellent example: *She is a model of politeness*; (*attrib*) *a model example of what is worst in modern architecture*; (*attrib*) *model behaviour*. – *v* – *pt, ptp* **'modelled**, (*Amer usu*) **'modeled** – **1** *vti* to wear (clothes *etc*) to show them to possible buyers: *They model* (*underwear*) *for a living*. **2** *vi* to work or pose as a model for an artist, photographer *etc*: *She models at the local art school*. **3** vti to make models (of things or people): *We model* (*the heads of famous people*) *in clay*. **4** *vt* to form (something) into a (particular) shape: *She modelled the clay into a long, thin roll*; (*fig*) *She models her behaviour on her brother's* (= She tries to behave like her brother); (*fig*) *She models herself on her older sister*.

'modelling, (*Amer*) **'modeling** *nu* **1** the art of making models: *He's very keen on aircraft modelling*; (*attrib*) *modelling glue*. **2** the occupation of a fashion model: *She learnt modelling in Paris*.

moderate ['modəreit] *vti* (*formal*) to make or become less extreme: *He was forced to moderate his demands*; *Gradually the pain moderated*. – [-rət] *adj* **1** keeping within reasonable limits; not extreme: *The prices were moderate*; *a man of moderate views/opinions*. **2** (*sometimes derog*) medium or average; not particularly good: *workmanship of moderate quality*; *a man of* (*only*) *moderate ability*. – *nc* a person whose views, aims, are not extreme: *Politically, she's a moderate*.

'moderately *adv*.

'moderateness [-rət-] *nu* the quality of being moderate: *the moderateness of his views*.

,mode'ration **1** *nu* the quality of being moderate: *Moderation in all things is thought to be a virtue*; *Alcohol isn't harmful if it's taken in moderation*. **2** *ncu* (an) act of moderating: *There has been a slight moderation in the rate of inflation*.

See also **immoderate**.

modern ['modən] *adj* belonging to the present or to recent times; not old or ancient: *modern furniture/literature/clothes*; *The furniture in this office is very modern*. – *nc* (*formal*) a person living in modern times.

'modernly *adv*. **mo'dernity** [-'də:-], **'modernness** *nus*.

'modernize, -ise *vt* to bring up to date: *We've modernized the house by putting in central heating and new electrical wiring*. **,moderni'zation, -s-** *ncu*.

modern language *nc* (*often in pl*) a language spoken nowadays, contrasted with ancient Greek and Latin: *He learns Latin and two modern languages at school*.

modest ['modist] *adj* **1** not having, or showing, too high an opinion of one's abilities *etc*: *a modest young man*; *He's very modest about his achievements*. **2** decent, or showing good taste; not shocking: *She is too modest to wear a dress with such a low neckline*; *a dress with a modest neckline*. **3** not very large; moderate: *There's been a modest increase in our sales this month*; *She's a person of modest ambitions*; *The increase in sales is modest but steady*. **'modestly** *adv*. **'modesty** *nu*.

See also **immodest**.

modicum ['modikəm] *nc* (*esp in negative sentences, questions etc*: *no pl*: *formal or facet*) a small quantity: *He hasn't even a modicum of tact*.

modify ['modifai] *vt* **1** (*formal*) to change the form or quality of, *usu* slightly: *We had to modify the original design slightly*; *He was forced to modify his rather extreme views*; *They have since modified the plans for the new building*. **2** (*gram*) (of an adverb) to change slightly, or give information about, (the action of a verb, the quality of an adjective, or an adverb): *'Loudly' modifies 'shouted' in the sentence 'He shouted loudly'*; *'Very' modifies 'small' and 'loudly' in the sentence 'The very small boy shouted very loudly.'* **'modifier** *nc*.

,modifi'cation [-fi-] (*formal*) **1** *nu* (the) act of modifying or process of being modified: *The modification of the design will take a long time*. **2** *nc* a change or alteration: *We want to make a few minor modifications to this machine*.

'modified *adj* (*neg* **un-**): *a modified version*.

modish *see* **mode**.

modulate ['modjuleit] *vt* (*formal*) to vary the tone, pitch, frequency *etc* of (a sound *etc*): *She will never be a good actress – she finds it difficult to modulate her voice*. **,modu'lation** *ncu*.

module ['modju:l] *nc* (*tech*) a self-contained unit forming part of a spacecraft: *a lunar module*.

mohair ['mouheə] **1** *nu* the long silken hair of a type of goat. **2** *nu, adj* (of) a type of cloth or wool made from it: *This jersey is* (*made of*) *mohair*; (*attrib*) *a mohair jersey*.

Mohammedan [mə'hamidən] *adj* (*offensive to many Muslims*) of Islam; Muslim. – *nc* (*offensive to many Muslims*) a person whose religion is Islam.

Mo'hammedanism *nu* (*offensive to many Muslims*) Islam.

moiety ['moiəti] *nc* (*formal or liter*) a half.

moist [moist] *adj* damp; slightly wet: *This earth is moist owing to the recent rain*; *Her eyes were moist with tears*; *The fruit cake was rich and moist*; *moist, fertile soil*; *large, moist eyes*. **'moistly** *adv*. **'moistness** *nu*.

moisten ['moisn] *vt* (*formal*) to wet slightly: *Moisten this cake mixture with some milk*.

moisture ['moistʃə] *nu* something that is slightly wet: *There's a great deal of moisture in the ground*; *This soil is in need of moisture*.

'moisturize, -ise [-stʃə-] *vt* to keep the moisture in (skin): *This cream is used to moisturize the skin*.

'moisturizer, -s- *ncu*.

molar ['moulə] *nc* (*tech*) a back tooth which is used for grinding food: *The dentist had to extract one of my molars*.

molasses [mə'lasiz] *nu* (*Amer*) treacle.

mold *see* **mould**.

mole[1] [moul] *nc* a small, *usu* dark, spot on the skin: *They were able to identify the corpse as their son because he had a large mole on the back of his left hand*.

mole[2] [moul] *nc* a small burrowing animal with very small eyes and soft fur: *Moles stay underground most of the time*.

'molehill *nc* a little heap of earth dug up by a mole while tunnelling: *Our garden is full of molehills*.

'moleskin *nu, adj* **1** (of) mole's fur. **2** (of) a type of smooth, hardwearing fabric used for making clothes: *trousers made of moleskin*; *moleskin trousers*.

make a mountain out of a molehill to exaggerate the importance of a problem *etc*: *You don't have to assume that the child has had an accident just because he's late – you're always making mountains out of molehills*.

molecule ['molikju:l] *nc* (*tech*) the group of atoms that is the smallest unit into which a substance can be divided without losing its basic nature or identity: *A molecule of water is made up of two atoms of hydrogen and one atom of oxygen*.

mo'lecular [-'le-] *adj* (*tech*: *esp attrib*): *the molecular structure of a given substance.*

molehill, moleskin *see* **mole**[2].

molest [mə'lest] *vt* (*formal or legal*) to annoy or interfere with (*eg* sexually): *The woman complained that she had been molested in the park.* ˌ**mole'station** [mou-, mo-] *ncu.*

mollify ['molifai] *vt* (*formal*) to calm, soothe or lessen the anger of: *He was greatly mollified by their offer of compensation.* ˌ**mollifi'cation** [-fi-] *nu.*

mollusc, (*Amer*) **mollusk** ['moləsk] *nc* (*tech*) any of a family of animals having no backbone, and *usu* with a hard shell *eg* the shellfish, snail *etc.*

mollycoddle ['molikodl] *vt* to take excessive care of (a person, animal *etc*): *Don't mollycoddle your children, or they'll never learn to be independent!*

molten ['moultən] *adj* (*formal or tech*: *attrib*) (of a solid) in a liquid state, having been melted: *molten rock.*
See also **melt**.

moment ['moumənt] *nc* **1** a very short space of time: *I'll be ready in a moment*; *after a few moments' silence*; *I never for a moment* (= at all) *thought he'd win.* **2** a particular point in time: *At that moment, the man he was looking for was in Germany*; *They'll be arriving at any moment* (= almost immediately). – *See also* **moment** *in phrases below.*
'**momentary** *adj* (*formal*) lasting for only a moment: *a momentary feeling of fear*; *Their hesitation was momentary.* '**momentarily** [(*Amer*) moumən'te-] *adv.*
mo'mentous [-'men-] *adj* (*formal*: *esp attrib*) of great importance: *The discovery of radio waves was a momentous event.* **mo'mentously** *adv.* **mo'mentousness** *nu.*
at the 'moment at this particular time; now: *She's rather busy at the moment.*
the 'moment (that) exactly when: *I want to see him the moment he arrives.*
of 'moment (*formal*) important: *a matter of great moment*; *Nothing of moment occurred.*

momentum [mə'mentəm] *nu* (*formal or tech*) the amount or force of motion in a moving body: *He tried to stop, but his momentum carried him over the cliff edge*; *The car gathered momentum* (= moved increasingly fast) *down the hill.*

monarch ['monək] *nc* (*esp liter*) a king, queen, emperor, or empress.
mo'narchic(al) [-'na:-] *adjs* (*liter*) of or like a monarch or (a) monarchy.
'**monarchist** *nc* a person who supports monarchy: *He does not believe in republics – he is a monarchist.*
'**monarchy** *ncu* (a country *etc* that has) government by a monarch: *Britain is a monarchy*; *Monarchy is becoming a less popular form of government.*

monastery ['monəstəri] *nc* a house in which a community of monks lives: *King Henry VIII of England destroyed many of the monasteries when he made himself head of the church.*
mo'nastic [-'na-] *adj* (*formal*: *esp attrib*) of, or like, monks or monasteries: *monastic orders/vows*; *the monastic way of life.*
monasticism [mə'nastisizəm] *nu* (*formal*) the way of life in a monastery, *usu* involving a certain amount of personal hardship.

Monday ['mʌndi] *n* the second day of the week, the day following Sunday: *He will go on Monday*; *She will go next Monday*; *They come on Mondays* (= every Monday, or only on a Monday but not necessarily every Monday); (*attrib*) *Monday morning.*

monetary ['mʌnitəri] *adj* (*formal*: *esp attrib*) of, or consisting of, money: *The country is having monetary problems*; *He doesn't want any monetary rewards.*

money ['mʌni] *nu* coins or banknotes used in trading: *Have you any money in your purse?*; *The desire for money is a cause of much unhappiness.*
'**moneyed** *adj* (*formal*) wealthy: *the moneyed classes*; *His parents are moneyed but hers are poor.*
'**moneys,** '**monies** *n pl* (*old or legal*) amounts of money: *The bank has various moneys which it can use for this purpose.*
'**money-box** *nc* a box for saving money in: *She gave little Johnny some pennies for his money-box.*
'**moneylender** *nc* a person whose business is lending money: *She borrowed some money from a moneylender and then she could not pay his high rates of interest.*
'**money order** *nc* an order for the transfer of money from one person to another through post offices: *My mother sent me a money order for £20 on my birthday.*
'**money-spinner** *nc* (*inf*) something which makes a great deal of profit: *His latest recording has been a real money-spinner.*
be in the money (*inf*) to be wealthy: *He's in the money now, since his rich uncle died.*
for 'my money in my opinion; if I were to choose: *For my money, I'd rather have an amusing friend than an honest one.*
ˌ**get one's 'money's worth** to get full value for one's money: *He didn't get his money's worth at the cinema because the film broke down in the middle.*
lose, make money to make a loss or a profit: *This film is making a lot of money in America.*
ready money *see* **ready**.

-monger [mʌŋgə] (*in cmpds*) a trader or dealer, as in **fishmonger, ironmonger**.

mongol ['moŋgəl] *nc, adj* (a person) suffering from mongolism: *Their youngest child is a mongol.*
'**mongolism** *nu* a type of disease, also called **Down's syndrome**, with which a child can be born, that causes mental deficiency and a broadening and flattening of the features: *Mongolism is commoner in the children of older mothers.*
'**mongoloid** [-loid] *adj* (*tech*).

Mongol, Mongolia, Mongolian *see* Appendix 2.

mongrel ['mʌŋgrəl] *nc, adj* (*sometimes derog*) (an animal, *esp* a dog) bred from different types: *My dog is a mongrel*; *a mongrel dog.*

monies *see* **money**.

monitor ['monitə] *nc* **1** a senior pupil who helps to see that school rules are kept. **2** (*tech*) any of several kinds of instrument or arrangement for checking levels, events *etc*, *esp* a small screen in a television studio showing the picture which is being transmitted at any given time: *Watch the monitor and tell me if the level goes above forty decibels.* – *vt* to act as, or to use, a monitor (*def 2*); to keep a careful check on: *These machines/These men monitor the results constantly*; *The nurse monitored the patient's condition carefully.*

monk [mʌŋk] *nc* a member of a male religious group, who lives in a monastery, away from the rest of society.

monkey ['mʌŋki] *nc* **1** an animal of the type most like man, *esp* those which are small and have long tails (*ie* not the apes): *The children were amused by* *the behaviour of the monkeys in the zoo.* 2 (*inf*) a mischievous child: *Their son is a cheeky little monkey!* – *vi* (*inf*: *esp with* **with**) to meddle or interfere: *Who's been monkeying with the television set?*

'**monkey business** *nu* (*inf*) mischievous or illegal happenings *etc*: *He seems to be involved in some monkey business or other.*

monkey-nut *see* **peanut**.

'**monkey-wrench** *nc* a type of adjustable tool used for gripping and turning bolts *etc.*

monkey about/around *vi* (*often with* **with**: *inf*) to act foolishly; to interfere: *Stop monkeying around (with my papers)!*

monkey with *see* **monkey** *above.*

mono- [monou] (*in cmpds*) one or single, as in **monosyllable**.

mono ['monou] *adj* (of records, record-playing equipment *etc*) using one channel only; not stereo: *a mono tape-recorder*; *Is this record mono?*

monochrome ['monəkroum] *adj* (*tech*) 1 (of a television set, photograph *etc*) having or producing no colours except black, white and shades of grey: *Fewer monochrome television sets are now being sold*; *Is that television set monochrome?* 2 of one colour only: *a monochrome design.*

monocle ['monəkl] *nc* a lens or eyeglass for one eye only, having a similar purpose to a pair of spectacles: *The old colonel always wears a monocle – he refuses to wear spectacles.*

monogamy [mə'nogəmi] *nu* (*formal*) marriage to one wife or husband only: *Monogamy is the only legal form of marriage in most countries.* **mo'nogamous** *adj.*

monogram ['monəgram] *nc* (*formal*) a single design made up of several letters (often a person's initials): *These sheets of paper carry his monogram.*

monograph ['monəgra:f] *nc* (*formal*) a research paper on one particular subject: *He has written a monograph on the Hundred Years' War.*

monolith ['monəliθ] *nc* (*tech*) a single block of stone forming a vertical monument of some kind.

ˌ**mono'lithic** *adj* 1 (*tech*) of, or like, a monolith. 2 (*derog*) huge and difficult to deal with: *a monolithic organization*; *That political party is positively monolithic.*

monologue ['monəlog] *nc* a long speech by one person *eg* in a film, play *etc*: *the monologues in Christopher Marlowe's plays*; (*fig*) *At lunch today he delivered a boring monologue on the behaviour of today's young people.*

monoplane ['monəplein] *nc* an aeroplane (*usu* small) with one set of wings.

monopoly [mə'nopəli] *nc* 1 the sole right of making, selling or doing something: *This firm has a local monopoly of soap-manufacturing*; (*fig inf*) *Surely we are allowed to feel sad too – you don't have a monopoly of sadness.* 2 something controlled in this way: *a soap-making monopoly*; *You mustn't think you have a monopoly of the good sense in this family.*

mo'nopolize, -ise *vt* 1 (*tech*) to have a monopoly of or over: *They've monopolized the fruit-canning industry.* 2 (*formal*) to take up the whole of (a conversation, someone's attention *etc*): *She monopolized their time/attention.*

monorail ['monəreil] *nc* a system of railways with trains which run hanging from, or along the top of, one rail.

monosyllable ['monəsiləbl] *nc* (*formal*) a word of one syllable: *'Hit' is a monosyllable*; *He always speaks in monosyllables.*

ˌ**monosyl'labic** [-'la-] *adj* (*formal*) 1 having one syllable: *a monosyllabic word*; *'Word' is monosyllabic.* 2 using one-syllable words: *a monosyllabic reply*; *His reply was short and monosyllabic.*

monotone ['monətoun] *nc* (*formal*) a single, unchanging tone of voice: *He spoke in a monotone.*

monotonous [mə'notənəs] *adj* lacking in variety; dull: *She makes bad jokes with monotonous regularity*; *a monotonous piece of music.* **mo'notonously** *adv.*

mo'notony *nu.*

monsoon [mon'su:n] *nc* 1 a wind that blows in the Indian Ocean, from the SW in summer, from the NE in winter. 2 (*also* **mon'soon season**) the rainy season caused by the SW monsoon.

monster ['monstə] *nc* 1 (*esp attrib*) something of unusual size, form or appearance: *That is a monster turnip* (= That turnip is very large); *a monster tomato.* 2 a huge and/or horrible creature: *prehistoric monsters*; *Small children often like books about dragons and other monsters.* 3 a very evil person: *The man must be a monster to treat his children so badly!*

mon'strosity [-'strosə-] *nc* (*often facet*) something, *usu* large, that is horrible to look at: *That new building in the High Street is a monstrosity!*

'**monstrous** *adj* 1 huge and often unpleasant. 2 shocking or horrible: *That's a monstrous lie!*; *It's monstrous to charge such prices!* '**monstrously** *adv.*

month [mʌnθ] *nc* one of the twelve divisions of the year (January, February *etc*), varying in length between 28 and 31 days.

'**monthly** *adj* happening, being published *etc* once a month: *a monthly magazine/event*; *Will this event be monthly?* – *nc* something which is published once a month: *This magazine is a monthly.* – *adv* once a month: *The magazine is published monthly.*

month in, month out *see* **in**.

a month of Sundays (*inf*) an extremely long time: *You'll never finish that job in a month of Sundays.*

monument ['monjumənt] *nc* 1 something built in memory of a person or event, *eg* a building, tomb *etc*: *They erected a monument in his honour.* 2 (*formal*: *with* **to**) a tribute to, or reminder of: *The graveyards of France are a monument to the tragedy of man's folly in fighting two World Wars.*

ˌ**monu'mental** [-'men-] *adj* (*formal or facet*) of great size or scale: *a monumental achievement/book*; *This task is monumental.*

ˌ**monu'mentally** [-'men-] *adv* (*inf*) extremely: *monumentally stupid/bored.*

ancient monument *nc* any structure, *eg* a dwelling-place, grave *etc* remaining from ancient times.

moo [mu:] – *3rd pers sing prt* **moos**: *pt, ptp* **mooed** – *vi* to make the sound of a cow. – *nc* such a sound.

mood[1] [mu:d] *nc* any of the set of forms of the verb used to indicate whether the action of the verb is fact, command or possibility *etc*: *the indicative/imperative/subjunctive mood.*

See also **modal auxiliary, modal verb** *under* **mode**.

mood[2] [mu:d] *nc* 1 the state of a person's feelings, temper, mind *etc* at a particular time: *What kind of mood is she in?*; *She's in a terrible mood!* 2 a state of bad temper, depression *etc*: *He's been in a mood all morning.*

'**moody** *adj* often changing one's mood; often bad-tempered or depressed: *He is a very moody child*; *He seems very moody today.* '**moodily** *adv.* '**moodiness** *nu.*

moon [mu:n] **1** *n* (*with* **the** *and sometimes with cap*) the heavenly body that moves once round the earth in a month and reflects light from the sun: *The moon was shining brightly*; *Spacemen landed on the moon.* **2** *nc* any of the similar bodies moving round the other planets: *the moons of Jupiter.*

'**moonless** *adj* (*esp attrib*) (of a night) dark and having no moonlight: *a dark and moonless night.*

'**moonbeam** *nc* a beam of light reflected from the moon.

'**moonlight** *nu* (*often attrib*) the light reflected by the moon: *The sea looked silver in the moonlight*; (*attrib*) *a moonlight raid.* – *vi* (*Brit inf*) to work at a second job that is unofficial and done outside normal working hours: *He's a plumber during the day, but moonlights as an electrician in the evenings.*

'**moonlit** *adj* lit by the moon: *a moonlit hillside*; *The countryside looks even more beautiful when it is moonlit.*

do a moonlight (flit/flitting) (*Brit sl*) to move away suddenly, *esp* at night (*usu* to avoid people to whom one owes money).

moon about/around *vi* to wander around as if dazed, *eg* because one is in love: *Ever since she met that boy, she spends her time mooning around waiting for him to telephone.*

See also **lunar**.

moor[1] [muə] *ncu* a large stretch of open, unfarmed land with poor soil often covered with heather, coarse grass *etc*: *They are shooting game-birds on the moor near our house*; *We walked for miles over the moors.*

'**moorland** *nu* a stretch of moor.

moor[2] [muə] *vti* to fasten (a ship *etc*) by a rope, cable or anchor: *He moored his boat alongside ours*; *We/The launch moored in the bay for the night.*

'**mooring** *ncu* the act, or a means, of fastening a ship: *The mooring broke.*

'**moorings** *n pl* the place where a ship is anchored or fastened.

moose [mu:s] – *pl* **moose** – *nc* a type of large deer found in North America, and also in northern Europe where it is known as the elk.

moot [mu:t] : **a moot point** (*formal*) *nc* an undecided point or a matter of opinion: *It's a moot point whether he deserved to lose his job.*

mop [mop] *nc* **1** a pad of sponge, or a bunch of pieces of coarse string or yarn *etc*, fixed on a handle, for washing floors, dishes *etc.* **2** a thick mass of hair: *She combed her curly mop*; *a mop of red hair.* **3** an act of mopping: *He gave the floor a quick mop.* – *v* – *pt, ptp* **mopped** – *vt* **1** to rub or wipe with a mop: *She mopped the kitchen floor.* **2** to wipe or clean (*eg* a face covered with sweat): *He mopped his brow.*

mop up *vi, vt sep* to clean (something) away using a mop, cloth, piece of paper *etc*: *He mopped up the mess with his handkerchief*; (*inf fig*) *The troops mopped up the remains of the enemy forces within a week.*

mope [moup] *vi* (*sometimes with* **around**) to be depressed and mournful: *Come out for a walk instead of moping (around) in the house!*

moped ['mouped] *nc* a pedal-cycle which has a small motor.

moral ['morəl] *adj* **1** of, or relating to, character or behaviour *esp* right behaviour: *a woman of high moral standards*; *We must make our own moral decisions*; *He leads a very moral* (= virtuous and good) *life*; *His attitude to life is very moral.* **2** (*esp attrib*) teaching correct behaviour: *a moral tale/story.* – *nc* the lesson to be learned from something that happens, or from a story: *The moral of this story is that crime doesn't pay.* – *See also* **morals** *below.*

mo'rality [-'ra-] *nu* **1** quality of being morally right or wrong: *He questioned the morality of the government's actions.* **2** virtuous conduct: *Different people's ideas of morality vary greatly.*

'**moralize, -ise** *vi* (*derog*) to write or speak about morals and lessons to be learned from events: *He's always moralizing about the behaviour of today's young people.*

'**morally** *adv* **1** from the point of view of morals: *Her action wasn't criminal, but I think it was morally wrong.* **2** in a moral manner: *They always behave terribly morally.*

morals *n pl* one's principles and behaviour: *He has no morals and will do anything for money.*

moral support *nu* encouragement, but not actual or physical help: *You don't have to do or say anything, but just come with me for moral support.*

See also **amoral, immoral**.

morale [mə'ra:l] *nu* the level of courage and confidence in *eg* an army: *In spite of the defeat, morale was still high*; *They need something to raise their morale.*

See also **demoralize**.

morass [mə'ras] *nc* (*esp fig*) a bog or swamp: *We seem to be stuck in a morass of rules and regulations.*

morbid ['mo:bid] *adj* **1** (of a person, his thoughts *etc*) not healthy, because too much concerned with horrible or gloomy things: *Is it morbid curiosity that leads people to go in crowds to the scene of a major accident?*; *I find his interest in death rather morbid.* **2** (*tech*) (of a growth, tumour *etc*) diseased. '**morbidly** *adv.* **mor'bidity,** '**morbidness** *nus.*

more [mo:] – *compar of* **many, much** – *adj* **1** a greater number or quantity of: *I've more pencils than he has*; *This packet of washing-powder gives more value for money.* **2** an additional number or quantity of: *We need some more milk*; *There's no more cake*; *Aren't there any more biscuits?*; *There are only two more weeks till the exam.* – *adv* **1** used to form the comparative of many adjectives and adverbs, *esp* those of more than two syllables: *She can do it more easily than I can*; *He is much more intelligent than they are*; *She's no more attractive than you are*; *He isn't any more capable of it than I am.* **2** to a greater degree or extent: *I'm exercising a little more now than I used to*; *I don't like it any more than you do*; *The building had more the look of a prison than a school.* **3** again: *We'll play it twice more and then stop.* – *pron* **1** a greater number or quantity: *'Are there a lot of people?' 'There are far more than we expected.'* **2** an additional number or amount: *We've run out of paint. Will you go and get some more?*; *I have only two cans. I need three more*; *There's a bit more of that pudding left*; *'I've done my best – what more can you expect?' 'Nothing more.'*

more'over *adv* also; what is more important: *I don't like the idea, and moreover, I think it's illegal.*

any more any longer; nowadays: *He doesn't go any more, but he used to go twice a week.* – *See also*

more *adj* (*def 2*), *adv* (*defs 1, 2*).

more and more increasingly: *It's becoming more and more difficult to see.*

more fool you (*inf*) you are/were foolish: *More fool you if you believe(d) him; More fool you for believing him.*

'more of to a greater degree or extent: *She's more of a singer than a guitarist.*

more or less approximately or almost: *They've more or less finished the job; The distance is ten kilometres, more or less.*

'more so to a greater degree or extent: *He is very skilled as a pianist, but she is even more so.*

more's the pity it's a great shame: *They've torn down many of the old buildings, more's the pity.*

no 'more (*formal*) neither: *'I really can't decide what to do.' 'No more can I.'*

the more ... because/if to a greater degree or extent ... because or if: *He'll be the more inclined to help you if you're polite to him.*

the more ... the more/less in proportion to the amount that one thing happens more, another thing happens more or less: *The more I see her, the more/less I like her.*

what is/what's more moreover: *He came home after midnight, and what's more, he was drunk.*

See also **many, most, much**.

morgue [mo:g] *nc* a building where people who have been found dead are laid until they are identified *etc*: *The police took the corpse to the morgue.*

moribund ['moribʌnd] *adj* (*fig formal*) in the process of dying: *This industry has been moribund for some time now; in a moribund state.*

morn [mo:n] *ncu* (*liter*) morning.

morning ['mo:niŋ] *ncu* the first part of the day, approximately up to noon: *He works for us three mornings a week; It is peaceful in (the) early morning; I'll be seeing him tomorrow morning; He arrived in the morning; He was here on Monday morning;* (*attrib*) *the morning sky;* (*fig liter*) *in the morning of his life.*

'morning dress *nu* a man's formal wear for use during the early part of the day: *All the men wore morning dress at the wedding.*

morning sickness *nu* (a feeling of) sickness occurring in the mornings during the early stages of pregnancy.

morning star *nc* a planet, *usu* Venus, seen in the eastern sky before sunrise.

this morning *see* **this**.

Moroccan, Morocco *see* Appendix 2.

moron ['mo:ron] *nc* **1** a person of very low mental ability. **2** (*inf derog*) a very stupid person: *The girl who answered the telephone was a real moron.* **mo'ronic** [-'ro-] *adj*.

morose [mə'rous] *adj* angry and silent: *He is so morose that he will not speak to any of his colleagues; in rather a morose mood.* **mo'rosely** *adv.* **mo'roseness** *nu.*

morphia ['mo:fiə] , **morphine** ['mo:fi:n] *nu* a drug used to cause sleep or deaden pain, addictive if taken in large quantities.

morrow ['morou] *nc* (*no pl*: *with* **the**: *old liter*) tomorrow: *We shall go there on the morrow; We shall see what the morrow brings.*

Morse (code) [mo:s] *nu* (*also without cap*) a code for signalling and telegraphy in which each letter is made up of dots and dashes, or short and long sounds or flashes of light.

morsel ['mo:səl] *nc* (*formal*) a small piece of something, *esp* food: *She kept a tasty morsel of fish for the cat; We have not a morsel of bread left in the house.*

mortal ['mo:tl] *adj* **1** liable to die; unable to live for ever: *Man is mortal; mortal creatures.* **2** (*esp liter: esp attrib*) of or causing death: *mortal agony; a mortal illness; mortal enemies* (= enemies willing to fight each other till death); *mortal combat; a mortal* (= punishable by death) *crime.* **3** (*old inf: esp attrib*) very great: *He lived in mortal fear of his father's anger.* – *nc* a human being: *All mortals must die sometime.*

mor'tality [-'ta-] *nu* **1** the state of being mortal: *One of the few certain things in life is mortality.* **2** (*also* **mor'tality rate**) the number of deaths in proportion to the population; the death rate: *Infant mortality is decreasing every year.*

'mortally *adv* **1** in such a way as to cause death: *He has been mortally wounded.* **2** very greatly: *He was mortally afraid.*

mortal sin *nc* (*esp* in Roman Catholicism) a very serious sin, as a result of which the soul is damned for ever.

See also **immortal**.

mortar[1] ['mo:tə] *nu* a mixture of cement, sand and water, used in building *eg* to hold bricks in place.

mortar[2] ['mo:tə] *nc* a type of small dish in which substances are ground with a pestle: *I grind spices in an electric grinder – I do not use a mortar and pestle.*

mortar[3] ['mo:tə] *nc* a type of short gun for firing shells upwards, in close-range attacks.

mortar-board ['mo:təbo:d] *nc* a type of cap with a square flat top, worn on formal occasions at universities.

mortgage ['mo:gidʒ] *nc* a legal agreement by which a sum of money is lent for the purpose of buying buildings, land *etc* (the borrower promising to give up the buildings *etc* to the lender if he fails to repay the loan): *A 90% mortgage is one in which the buyer of a house is lent 90% of its cost.* – *vt* to offer (buildings *etc*) as security for a loan: *He mortgaged his house to finance his company's new product.*

mortician [mo:'tiʃən] *nc* (*Amer*) an undertaker.

mortify ['mo:tifai] *vt* (*often in passive*: *formal*) to make (someone) feel greatly ashamed or hurt by wounding his pride: *I was mortified when the teacher complained to me about my child's naughtiness.* **ˌmortifi'cation** [-fi-] *nu.*

mortise, mortice ['mo:tis] *nc* **1** (*tech*) a hole cut into a piece of wood to hold a **tenon** (= the shaped end of another piece of wood). **2** (*also* **'mortise lock**) a type of lock which is built into a door frame.

mortise and tenon (joint) ['tenən] (*tech*) a joint made in this way between two pieces of wood.

mortuary ['mo:tʃuəri] *nc* a building or room *eg* in a hospital, where dead bodies are kept before burial or cremation.

mosaic [mə'zeiik] **1** *ncu* (the art of making) a design formed by fitting together small pieces of coloured marble, glass *etc*: *a huge multicoloured mosaic;* (*attrib*) *a mosaic pavement.* **2** *nc* something made by piecing different things together: *a mosaic of flowers.*

Moslem *see* **Muslim**.

mosque [mosk] *nc* a Muslim place of worship.

mosquito [mə'ski:tou] – *pl* **mo'squito(e)s** – *nc* any of several types of small insect, which suck blood from animals and people and in this way transmit diseases such as malaria: *He was badly bitten by mosquitoes*; (*attrib*) *a mosquito bite.*

moss [mos] *ncu* (any variety of) a type of small flowerless plant, found in damp places, forming a soft green covering on tree trunks *etc*: *The bank of the river was covered in moss.*

'mossy *adj* (*esp attrib*): *a mossy bank.*

'moss-grown *adj* (*liter*) covered with moss.

most [moust] – *superl of* **many, much** (*often with* **the**) – *adj* **1** (the) greatest number or quantity of: *Which of the students has read the most books?*; *Reading is what gives me most enjoyment.* **2** the majority or greater part of: *Most boys like playing football*; *Most modern music is difficult to understand.* – *adv* **1** used to form the superlative of many adjectives and adverbs, *esp* those of more than two syllables: *Of all the women I know, she's by far the most beautiful*; *This tool is the most useful of all*; *This is the most delicious cake I've ever tasted*; *We see her mother or father sometimes, but we see her grandmother most frequently.* **2** to the greatest degree or extent: *They like sweets and biscuits but they like ice-cream most of all*; *What annoyed me* (*the*) *most was his late arrival.* **3** (*esp formal*) very or extremely: *I'm most grateful to you for everything you've done*; *He really is a/the most annoying child!* **4** (*Amer inf*) almost: *Most everyone I know has read that book.* – *pron* **1** the greatest number or quantity: *I ate two cakes, but Mary ate more, and John ate* (*the*) *most.* **2** the greatest part; the majority: *He'll be at home for most of the day*; *Most of these students speak English*; *Everyone is going to vote, but most have not yet decided whom to vote for.*

'mostly *adv* to the greatest degree or extent, or for most of the time; mainly: *The air we breathe is mostly nitrogen and oxygen*; *Mostly, I go to the library rather than buy books.*

at (the) 'most taking the greatest estimate: *There can be no more than fifty people in the audience at* (*the*) *most*; *There are at most three weeks of summer remaining.*

for the 'most part mostly: *For the most part, the passengers on the ship were Swedes.*

make the most of (something) to take advantage of (an opportunity *etc*) to the greatest possible extent: *You'll only get one chance, so you'd better make the most of it!*

See also **many, more, much**.

motel [mou'tel] *nc* a hotel which caters particularly for motorists.

moth [moθ] – *pl* **moths** [moθs, (*Amer*) moːðz] – *nc* **1** any of a large number of insects, rather like butterflies but with wider bodies, seen mostly at night and attracted by light: *Is that a butterfly or a moth?* **2** a clothes moth: *The moths have been at my evening dress.*

'clothes moth *nc* a type of moth whose larva feeds on cloth and makes holes.

'mothball *nc* a small ball of a chemical used to protect clothes from clothes moths.

'moth-eaten *adj* **1** (of cloth) eaten or cut by moths: *a moth-eaten blanket*; *This sweater is moth-eaten.* **2** (*loosely or fig*) old and worn: *moth-eaten ideas.*

mother ['mʌðə] *nc* **1** a female parent, *esp* human: *John's mother lives in Manchester*; (*attrib*) *The mother bird feeds her young.* **2** (*often with cap*: *also* **Mother Superior**) the female leader of a group of nuns. **3** (*formal*) the cause or origin: *Necessity is the mother of invention.* – *vt* to care for as a mother does; to protect (sometimes too much): *His wife mothered him for twenty years, never letting him be independent.*

'motherhood *nu* the state of being a mother: *She is not really suited to motherhood*; *Motherhood has made her even more beautiful.*

motherland *see* **mother-country**.

'motherless *adj* having no mother: *motherless children*; *The children were left motherless by the accident.*

'motherly *adj* like a mother; of, or suitable to, a mother: *a motherly type of woman*; *motherly love*; *She is very motherly.* **'motherliness** *nu.*

'mother-country/'motherland [-land] *ncs* (*formal*) the country where one was born: *He has lived in America for years but he still has a deep love for his motherland.*

'mother-in-law – *pl* **'mothers-in-law** – *nc* the mother of one's husband or wife.

ˌmother-of-'pearl *nu, adj* (of) the shining, hard, smooth substance on the inside of certain shells. – *See also* **pearl**.

'mother-tongue *nc* (*formal*) a person's native language: *My mother-tongue is Hindi.*

See also **maternal**.

motif [mou'tiːf] *nc* (*formal*) an often-repeated pattern, or important feature in a design, play or musical work: *This motif is repeated throughout the opera whenever a certain character comes on stage.*

motion ['mouʃən] **1** *nu* (*formal or tech*) the act or state of moving: *the motion of the stars*; *He lost the power of motion*; *sideways motion.* **2** *nc* a single movement or gesture: *He summoned the waiter with a motion of the hand.* **3** *nc* a proposal put before a meeting: *She was asked to speak against the motion in the debate.* **4** *nc* (*formal or tech*) an act of emptying the bowels, or the waste matter expelled in this way. – *See also* **in motion** *below.* – **1** *vti* to make a movement or sign *eg* directing a person or telling him to do something: *I approached him, but he motioned me away*; *He motioned* (*to*) *her to come nearer.*

'motionless *adj* (*formal*) not moving: *He stood motionless*; *a motionless figure.*

motion picture *nc* (*formal or tech*) a cinema film.

in 'motion moving: *Don't jump on the bus while it is in motion*; (*fig*) *The whole organization has been put in motion.*

ˌgo through the 'motions to pretend, or make an unenthusiastic attempt, to do something: *I don't really want to do this, but I suppose I'd better go through the motions* (*of doing it*).

See also **mobile, move**.

motive ['moutiv] *nc* something that makes a person choose to act in a particular way; a reason: *His motive for asking me was not clear*; *He always has some motive when he is generous to people.*

'motivate [-veit] *vt* (*formal*) (*usu in passive*) to be a reason for the actions of (a person): *He was motivated by jealousy.*

motley ['motli] *adj* (*attrib*) **1** (*old or facet*) made up of many different kinds: *a motley crowd of people.* **2** (*arch*) of many different colours: *a motley coat.* – *nu* (*arch*) the dress of a court fool or jester: *dressed in motley.*

motor ['moutə] *nc* (*often attrib and in cmpds*) a machine, *usu* a petrol engine or an electrical device, that gives motion or power: *The motor of a lawn-mower uses petrol or diesel fuel*; *a washing-machine has an electric motor*; *a motor* (= driven by a motor) *vehicle*; *a motor boat*; *a motor-mower.* –

adj (*tech*) giving or transmitting motion: *a motor nerve.* – *vi* to travel by car: *We motored down to Cardiff at the weekend.*

'**motorist** *nc* a person who drives a motor car: *The motorist could not avoid hitting the dog.*

'**motorize, -ise** (*formal or tech*) *vt* **1** to fit a motor to (*eg* a bicycle). **2** to supply (*eg* troops) with motor vehicles: *Many army units have been motorized.*

'**motorcade** [-keid] *nc* (*formal*) a procession in which everyone goes by car: *a Presidential motorcade through Washington.*

'**motorway** *nc* a road (*usu* specially made) for fast traffic: *They are building a new motorway linking the two cities*; (*inf*) *You will be able to drive to London very quickly – it's motorway all the way.*

'**motorbike,** '**motorcycle**, (*formal*) '**motor bicycle** *ncs* any of several types of *usu* heavy bicycle moved by a motor: *Can you ride a motorbike?*; *He was run over by a motorcycle*; *He was on his motorbike at the time.*

'**motor car** *nc* (*usu* **car**) a vehicle on four wheels, moved by a motor, but not a lorry or van; an automobile.

'**motorcyclist** *nc* a person who rides a motorbike: *The motorcyclist was injured in the road accident.*

mottled ['motld] *adj* marked with spots or patches of many colours or shades: *mottled leaves*; *His face is red and mottled.*

motto ['motou] – *pl* '**mottoes** – *nc* **1** (a short sentence or phrase which expresses) a principle of behaviour *etc*: *'Honesty is the best policy' is my motto*; *'Be prepared' is the motto of the Scout Movement*; *a school/family motto.* **2** a printed saying *etc*, often found inside a Christmas cracker.

mould[1], (*Amer*) **mold**[1] [mould] *nu* **1** (soil which is full of) rotted leaves *etc*: *leaf mould.* **2** a growth on stale food, trees *etc*: *This bread is covered with mould.*

'**moulder** *vti* (*liter*) to crumble away gradually: *The papers lay mouldering in an old cupboard.*

'**mouldy** *adj* **1** (of food *etc*) overgrown or covered with mould: *mouldy cheese*; *The cheese is mouldy.* **2** (*inf derog*: *esp attrib*) old, worn, of poor quality *etc*: *I don't want to wear your mouldy old hat.* '**mouldiness** *nu.*

go mouldy (of food *etc*) to become covered with mould: *If you don't put the bread into the tin, it will go mouldy.*

mould[2], (*Amer*) **mold**[2] [mould] *nc* **1** a shape into which a substance in liquid form is poured so that it may take on that shape when it cools and/or hardens: *a jelly mould.* **2** something, *esp* a food, formed in a mould: *We had banana cream mould for lunch.* – *vt* **1** to form in a mould: *The metal is moulded into long bars.* **2** to work into a shape: *He moulded the clay into a ball.* **3** to make the shape of (something): *She moulded the figure out of/in clay.* **4** (*formal*) to shape or influence (*eg* character, opinions) in a particular way: *Their characters were moulded by their early childhood experiences.*

'**moulding** *nu* a decorative border of moulded plaster, *eg* for, or on, a picture frame, wall *etc.*

cast in the same mould (as) very similar (to): *He's cast in the same mould as his father.*

moult, (*Amer*) **molt** [moult] *vi* (of birds, dogs or cats, snakes *etc*) to shed feathers, hair, a skin *etc*: *The parrot is moulting – there are feathers all over its cage.*

mound [maund] *nc* a small hill or heap of earth *etc*, either man-made or natural: *an ancient burial-mound*; *a grassy mound*; *a mound of rubbish.*

mount [maunt] **1** *vti* (*often formal*) to get or climb up (on or on to): *He mounted the platform and began to speak*; *She mounted* (*the horse*) *and rode off.* **2** *vi* (*formal*) to rise in level or amount: *Prices are mounting steeply.* **3** *vt* to put into a frame, on a backing *etc*: *The picture was mounted in a simple wooden frame*; *He mounted the photograph* (*on a piece of stiff cardboard*). **4** *vt* to hang or put up on a stand, support *etc*: *He mounted the tiger's head on the wall*; *The soldier mounted his gun on its stand.* **5** *vt* (*formal*) to organize or stage: *The army mounted an attack*; *The museum has mounted an exhibition of nineteenth century dresses.* – *nc* **1** (*liter or formal*) a thing or animal that one rides, *esp* a horse: *Her mount was a beautiful black stallion.* **2** a support or backing on which anything is placed for display: *Would this picture look better on a red mount or a black one?*

'**mounted** *adj* **1** (*esp attrib*) on horseback: *mounted soldiers*; *mounted policemen.* **2** hung on a wall, fastened in a frame or to a backing *etc*: *a mounted photograph*; *Would you like the photograph mounted?*

'**mountie** [-ti] *nc* (*usu with cap*) a member of the Royal Canadian Mounted Police.

mount guard *see* **guard**.

Mount [maunt] *n* (*in place-names*) a mountain: *Mount Everest.*

mountain ['mauntən] *nc* (*often found, esp in pl, with cap in place-names*) a high hill: *Scafell Pike is the highest mountain in England*; (*attrib*) *mountain people*; *a mountain stream*; (*fig*) *I have a mountain* (= a great deal) *of work to do this week.*

ˌ**mountai'neer** *nc* a person who climbs mountains, *esp* with skill, or as his occupation: *He is one of the mountaineers who climbed Everest.*

ˌ**mountai'neering** *nu* mountain-climbing: *Mountaineering is his favourite hobby.*

'**mountainous** *adj* full of mountains: *mountainous country*; *The country is very mountainous.*

'**mountain-side** *nc* the slope of a mountain: *The avalanche swept the climbers down the mountain-side.*

'**mountain-top** *nc* the summit of a mountain: *Clouds hid the mountain-tops.*

mourn [mo:n] *vti* to have or show great sorrow *eg* for a person who has died: *The relatives of the dead man will mourn for a week*; *She still mourns her husband*('*s death*).

'**mourner** *nc*: *The mourners stood round the graveside.*

'**mournful** *adj* feeling or showing sorrow: *a mournful expression*; *Don't look so mournful.* '**mournfully** *adv.*

'**mourning** *nu* **1** grief shown *eg* because of someone's death: *the mourning of the woman for her dead husband.* **2** black or dark-coloured clothes suitable for a mourner: *She was wearing mourning.*

be in/go into mourning to (wear such clothes in order to) show grief: *The whole court went into mourning when the king died.*

mouse [maus] – *pl* **mice** [mais] – *nc* any of several types of small furry gnawing animal with a long tail, found in houses and in fields: *A mouse ate some cheese in our kitchen*; *The mouse ran into a hole in the kitchen wall*; *a fieldmouse.*

'**mouser** *nc* a cat used for hunting mice: *The cat is a good mouser.*

'**mousy** *adj* (*often derog*) like a mouse, *esp* in colour: *mousy* (= dull brown) *hair*; *a mousy little* *woman*; *Her hair is dull and mousy.*

'**mousehole** *nc* a hole made or used by mice.

'**mousetrap 1** *nc* a mechanical trap for a mouse: *They put some cheese in the mousetrap as bait for the mouse.* **2** *nu* (*Brit inf*) ordinary cheese: *We haven't any blue cheese – we only have mousetrap.*

mousse [mu:s] *ncu* (a portion of) a dish made from flavoured cream *etc*, whipped and eaten cold: *She made (a) chocolate mousse*; *They had lemon mousse for dessert*; *Could we have three strawberry mousses, please?*

moustache, (*esp Amer*) **mustache** [mə'sta:ʃ, (*Amer*) 'mʌstaʃ] *nc* the hair on the upper lip of a man: *The young man has grown a moustache*; *He has a black, bushy moustache.*

mouth [mauθ] – *pl* **mouths** [mauðz] – *nc* **1** the opening in the head by which a human or animal eats and speaks or makes noises: *Open your mouth so that I can look at your teeth*; *What has the baby got in its mouth?* **2** the opening or entrance *eg* of a bottle, river *etc*: *the mouth of the harbour*; *the mouth of the jam-jar.* – [mauð] *vti* to move the lips as if forming (words), but without making any sound: *He mouthed the words to me so that no-one could overhear.*

'**mouthful** *nc* **1** as much as fills the mouth: *She took a mouthful of the soup*; *He ate the cake in two mouthfuls*; (*facet*) *His name is rather a mouthful!* (= long, or difficult to pronounce.) **2** (*esp with* **just** *or* **only**) a small quantity: *Well, all right, I'll just have a mouthful of dessert.*

'**mouth-organ** *nc* a small musical instrument played by blowing or sucking air through its metal pipes: *He plays the mouth-organ*; *He played a tune on the mouth-organ.*

'**mouthpiece** *nc* **1** the piece of a musical instrument *etc* which is held in the mouth: *the mouthpiece of a horn.* **2** the part of a telephone *etc* into which one speaks: *The mouthpiece of our telephone is broken.* **3** (*formal*) a person who acts as a spokesman: *He is a mouthpiece for thousands of refugees who are living in poverty.*

'**mouthwash** *nu* an antiseptic liquid used for cleaning out the mouth: *The dentist gave me some mouthwash after he filled my tooth.*

by word of mouth *see* **word**.

down in the mouth *see* **down**[1].

See also **oral**.

move [mu:v] **1** *vti* to (cause to) change position or go from one place to another: *He moved his arm/car*; *The trees moved in the wind*; *At that point in the chess game John moved (his bishop) and put me into check.* **2** *vi* to change houses: *We're moving on Saturday.* **3** *vt* to affect the feelings or emotions of (a person): *I was deeply moved by your speech.* **4** *vt* (*formal*) to cause (someone) to act in a given way: *His question moved me to look at the whole problem once again.* **5** *vt* (*formal*) to propose or suggest formally: *I move that we adjourn*; *He moved an adjournment.* – *See also* **move** *in phrases below.* – *nc* **1** (in board games) an act of moving (a piece): *You can win this game in three moves.* **2** an act of changing homes: *How did your move go?*

'**movable, 'moveable** *adjs.*

'**movement 1** *ncu* (an act of) changing position or going from one point to another: *The animal turned sideways with a swift movement*; *It was a calm day with little movement in the air.* **2** *nu* activity: *In Shaw's plays there is a lot of discussion but not much movement.* **3** *nu* (*formal*) the art of moving gracefully or expressively: *She teaches movement and drama.* **4** *nc* an organization or association: *the trade union movement*; *the Scout movement.* **5** *nc* (*tech*) the moving parts of a watch, clock *etc*: *Your watch will need a complete new movement.* **6** *nc* a section of a large-scale piece of music: *the third movement of Beethoven's Fifth Symphony.* **7** *nc* a general tendency towards a habit, point of view *etc*: *There's a movement towards simple designs in clothing these days.* **8** *nc* (*formal or tech*) the act of emptying one's bowels or the waste matter expelled in this way.

movie [-vi] *nc* (*esp Amer*) **1** a cinema film: *I went to see a horror movie last night.* **2** (*in pl*: *with* **the**) films and the film industry in general: *I have not been to the movies for a long time.*

'**moving** *adj* having an effect on the emotions *etc*: *a very moving speech*; *His speech was very moving.*

'**movingly** *adv.*

movable feast *nc* (*relig*: *sometimes facet*) a religious festival that occurs on different dates in different years: *Easter is a movable feast*; (*facet*) *Dinner in this house is rather a movable feast.*

prime mover *see* **prime**[1].

get a move on (*inf*) to hurry or move quickly: *Get a move on, or you'll be late!*

make a move 1 to move at all: *If you make a move, I'll shoot you!* **2** (*with* **for** *or* **towards**) to move (in the direction of): *He made a move for the door.*

move along *vi, vt sep* to keep moving, not staying in one place: *The police told the crowd that had gathered to move along*; *They moved us along.*

move heaven and earth to do everything that one possibly can: *He moved heaven and earth to get them to agree to his plan.*

move house to change one's home or place of residence: *They're moving house next week.*

move in *vi* to go into and occupy a house *etc*: *We can move in on Saturday*; (*fig*) *When his business collapsed, we moved in and took over all his old customers.*

move off *vi* (of vehicles *etc*) to begin moving away: *The bus moved off just as I got to the bus stop.*

move on *vi, vt sep* to (cause to) move to another place, situation *etc*: *The policeman moved the drunk man on*; *He tried to move him on*; *I feel like moving on and doing something different.*

move out *vi* to leave, and cease to live in, a house *etc*: *She has to move out before the new tenants arrive.*

move up *vi* to move in any given direction so as to make more space: *Move up and let me sit down, please.*

on the move 1 moving from place to place: *With his kind of job, he's always on the move.* **2** advancing or making progress: *The frontiers of scientific knowledge are always on the move.*

See also **mobile, motion**.

movie *see* **move**.

mow [mou] – *pt* **mowed**: *ptps* **mowed, mown** – *vt* to cut (grass *etc*) with a scythe or mower: *He mowed the grass/lawn.*

'**mower** *nc* a machine for cutting grass.

mow down *vt sep* to kill (soldiers *etc*) in large numbers: *Our troops were mown down by machine-gun fire*; *The enemy troops mowed them down.*

Mozambique, Mozambiquean *see* Appendix 2.

Mr *see* **Mister**.

Mrs ['misiz] *n* (short for **Mistress**) a polite title given to a married woman, in writing or in speaking: *Please come in, Mrs Anderson*; *Mrs*

Smith and Mrs Jones both attended the meeting.

Ms [miz] *n* a polite title given to a married or unmarried woman, either in writing or in speaking, to avoid distinguishing between a married and an unmarried woman or because one does not know whether the woman is married or unmarried: *Ms Johnson.*

much [mʌtʃ] – *compar* **more** [mo:]: *superl* **most** [moust] (*often formal in simple affirmative statements; used esp with negatives, in questions, and in special phrases*) – *adj* (*only with uncountable nouns*) a great amount or quantity of: (*formal*) *Much effort will be required; This job won't take much time; Did you have much trouble finding the house?; I found it without much difficulty; How much* (= How large a quantity of) *sugar is there left?; There's far too much* (= too large a quantity of) *salt in my soup; He ate so much ice-cream that he was sick; Take as much money as you need; After much discussion they decided to go.* – *pron* a large amount; a great deal: (*formal*) *He has much to learn; He didn't say much about it; Much of this trouble could have been prevented; Did you eat much at suppertime?; No, not much; Yes, too much; Yes, as much as I wanted; How much did you eat?; Only this/that/so much; How much is* (= What is the price of) *that fish?; Please tidy your room – it isn't much to ask.* – *adv* **1** (*used to qualify comparatives and superlatives*) (by) a great deal; (by) far: *She's much prettier than I am; He isn't much older than you; How much further must we walk?; You can do it much more easily than I can; He's much the best person to consult; This doll is much the most expensive.* **2** to a great extent or degree: (*formal*) *He will be much missed; We don't see her much* (= often); *I thanked her very much; He doesn't like her much and she doesn't much like him; You're much too late; I've much too much to do; The accident was as much my fault as his; It isn't so much my opinion as hers that matters; Much to my dismay, she began to cry.*

as/this/that much the facts, information *etc* mentioned: *'I've quarrelled with my husband.' 'I guessed as much.'; 'That much I had guessed.'; I don't know what disease she has, but this much I do know, that she's very ill.*

be much of a muchness (*inf*: *usu derog*) (of several things) to be not very different: *The candidates were all much of a muchness – none of them would be suitable for the job.*

be not much of a to be not a very good or great thing of a particular kind: *I'm not much of a photographer; That wasn't much of a lecture.*

be not up to much (*inf*) to be not very good: *The dinner wasn't up to much.*

be too much to be unreasonable: *I can't believe that – it's too much!*

be too much for to overwhelm: to be too difficult *etc* for: *Is the job too much for you?*

in as much as *see* **in**.

make much of to make a fuss of (a person) or about (a thing): *He made much of his nephew; She makes much of the fact that you lied to her.*

'much as although: *Much as I should like to come, I can't.*

much the same not very different: *The patient's condition is still much the same.*

nothing/not anything much nothing important, impressive *etc*: *'What are you doing?' 'Nothing much.'*

not much nothing important, impressive *etc*: *My car isn't much to look at* (= isn't beautiful) *but it's fast.*

so much for that's all that can be said about: *So much for that – let's talk about something else;* (*derog*) *He arrived half an hour late – so much for his punctuality!*

think too much of to have too high an opinion of: *He thinks too much of himself.*

with,out so 'much as without even: *He took my umbrella without so much as asking.*

See also **many, more, most.**

muck [mʌk] *nu* (*inf*: *usu derog*) dung, filth, rubbish *etc*: *farmyard muck; The food in this place is terrible muck!*

'mucky *adj* (*inf*) very dirty; like muck: *Your face and hands are mucky.*

'muck-raking *nu* (*derog*) the activity of searching for and making public scandalous information about a person or people.

make a muck of (*inf*: *esp fig*) to make a mess of (something): *You've made a muck of this clean floor;* (*fig*) *I made a muck of the interview for that job* (= I didn't do very well at it).

muck about/around (*esp Brit inf*) **1** to do things without a definite plan: *muck about in the garden.* **2** to act foolishly: *Stop mucking about!*

muck in *vi* (*inf*) to share *eg* accommodation, work *etc*: *I mucked in with Jim till I found a flat of my own; We all mucked in and finished the job in two days.*

muck out *vi, vt sep* (*inf*) to clean (*esp* stables): *It's her turn to muck out (the stable).*

muck up *vt sep* (*inf*: *esp fig*) to make a mess of: *You've mucked up the whole house with your dirty boots!;* (*fig*) *You've mucked up my plans for the evening; You mucked them up by asking him to join us.*

mucus ['mju:kəs] *nu* (*formal or tech*) the slimy fluid from the nose *etc*.

mud [mʌd] *nu* wet soft earth.

'muddy *adj* covered with or containing mud: *muddy boots/water; Those shoes are so muddy.* – *vt* (*inf*) to make muddy: *Don't you dare muddy my nice clean floor!; You've muddied the floor!*

'mudflat *nc* (*often in pl*) an area of muddy seaside land which is covered with water at high tide.

'mudguard *nc* a shield or guard over the wheel of a car, bicycle *etc* to keep mud, rainwater *etc* from splashing upwards.

'mud-slinging *nu* (*inf*) the activity of exchanging vicious insults *etc*: *The politician accused the members of the opposition of mud-slinging.*

'my, his *etc* **name is mud** (*inf*) I am, he is *etc* considered to have misbehaved; I am, he is *etc* disapproved of: *I smacked her daughter, so my name is mud.*

muddle ['mʌdl] *vt* to confuse or mix up together: *Don't talk while I'm counting, or you'll muddle me; He has muddled all the different types together in one box.* – *See also* **muddle along/through, muddle up** *below.* – *nc* a state of confusion: *All these papers keep getting in a muddle; She's good at sorting out muddles.*

'muddled *adj*: *She gave me a muddled answer; Her thinking is so muddled.*

'muddle-headed *adj* (*derog*) incapable of clear thinking: *Men seem to think that all women are muddle-headed; a muddle-headed apprentice.*

muddle along/through *vi* to progress in spite of one's unsatisfactory methods and foolish mistakes: *She is a very disorganized person but she*

always seems to muddle through.
muddle up *vt usu sep* to confuse (*eg* two different things): *I'm always muddling the twins up.*

muff[1] [mʌf] *nc* a tube-shaped cover often made of fur, for keeping the hands warm: *The princess wore a black velvet cape and a white fur muff.*

muff[2] [mʌf] *vt* (*inf*) **1** in some games, to fail to hold (a catch) *etc*: *He is hopeless at cricket – he keeps muffing catches.* **2** to miss (a chance, opportunity *etc*): *You were given the opportunity of earning some more money but you muffed it.*

muffin ['mʌfin] *nc* a type of round, flat cake eaten hot with butter.

muffle ['mʌfl] *vt* to deaden the sound of: *They used a gag to muffle his cries.*
'muffler *nc* **1** a scarf worn round the neck: *The old man wore a red muffler.* **2** (*Amer*) a silencer: *The muffler is broken – the car is making a loud noise.*

mug[1] [mʌg] *nc* **1** a type of cup with *usu* tall, more or less vertical sides: *Pour the cocoa into this mug.* **2** a mugful: *He drank three mugs of coffee.*
'mugful *nc* the amount contained in a mug: *a mugful of coffee.*

mug[2] [mʌg] *nc* (*sl*) the face: *What an ugly mug!*

mug[3] [mʌg] *nc* (*Brit sl*) a stupid person: *You must be a complete mug to believe that story!*

mug[4] [mʌg] – *pt, ptp* **mugged** – **mug up** *vi, vt sep* (*sometimes with* **on**) to study (a subject) hard for an exam *etc*: *She's mugging up her history*; *She has already mugged it up*; *She's mugging up on her French for the exam.*

mug[5] [mʌg] – *pt, ptp* **mugged** – *vt* to attack and *usu* rob (someone): *He was mugged when coming home late at night.*
'mugger *nc* a person who attacks others in this way: *The police have arrested the muggers.*

muggy ['mʌgi] *adj* (*inf derog*) (of weather) warm, stuffy and damp: *It's rather muggy today – I think there's going to be a storm*; *a muggy day.*

mulberry ['mʌlbəri] **1** *nc* (*also* **mulberry tree**) a type of tree on whose leaves silkworms feed. **2** *nu, adj* (of) its wood: *a table inlaid with mulberry*; *an oak and mulberry wardrobe.* **3** *nu* its (*usu* purple) edible fruit: *I don't like mulberries*; (*attrib*) *mulberry pie/jam.*

mulch [mʌltʃ] *ncu* compost, peat, straw *etc* laid on the soil around plants in order to keep the soil moist, to protect the plants' roots, to prevent weeds growing *etc.* – *vti* to put (a) mulch round plants: *He mulched (the roots of) the blackcurrant bushes*; *He mulched the rose-bed.*

mule[1] [mju:l] *nc* an animal whose parents are a horse and an ass, known for its habit of being stubborn.
'mulish *adj* (*derog*) like a mule, *esp* in being stubborn: *a stupid, mulish young man*; *He is being obstinate and mulish.*

mule[2] [mju:l] *nc* a loose, backless slipper: *She wore a dressing-gown and mules.*

mull[1] [mʌl]: **mull over** *vt sep* to think about carefully: *She mulled the problem over for a few days.*

mull[2] [mʌl] *vt* to warm, spice and sweeten (wine, ale *etc*): *We mulled some wine for the party.*
mulled *adj*: *mulled wine.*

multi- [mʌlti] (*in cmpds*) many, as in **multi-coloured**.

multicoloured, (*Amer*) **multicolored** [mʌlti-'kʌləd] *adj* (*esp attrib*) having many colours: *a multicoloured shirt.*

multifarious [mʌlti'feəriəs] *adj* (*formal or facet*) of many kinds: *multifarious activities*; *His hobbies are varied and multifarious.*

multimillionaire [mʌltimiljə'neə] *nc* a person who has wealth valued at several million pounds, dollars *etc.*

multinational [mʌlti'naʃənəl] *nc, adj* (a company or business) having branches in several different countries: *He works for a huge multinational*; *a multinational steel company.*

multiple ['mʌltipl] *adj* (*esp attrib*) **1** having, or affecting, many parts: *She suffered multiple injuries when she fell out of the window.* **2** involving many things of the same sort: *Fifteen vehicles were involved in the multiple crash on the motorway.* – *nc* (*math*) a number that contains another number an exact number of times: *65 is a multiple of 5.*

multiply ['mʌltiplai] **1** *vti* to add a number to itself a given number of times and find the total: *4+4+4 or 4 multiplied by 3 or 4×3=12.* **2** *vti* to (cause to) increase in number, *esp* by breeding: *Rabbits multiply very rapidly*; *Her fortune was multiplied as the years passed.*
ˌmultipli'cation [-pli-] *nu* the act of multiplying (numbers).
ˌmulti'plicity [-'plisə-] *ncu* (*no pl*: *formal*) a great number and variety: *This tool has a multiplicity of uses.*

multiracial [mʌlti'reiʃəl] *adj* including, for, or of, people of many races: *The island of Trinidad has a multiracial society*; *Britain is becoming more and more multiracial.*

multi-storey, multi-story [mʌlti'sto:ri] *adj* (*attrib*) having many floors or storeys: *a multi-storey car park.*

multitude ['mʌltitju:d] *nc* **1** (*formal*) a great number or crowd: *a multitude of reasons*; *multitudes of birds/people.* **2** (*arch*) a huge crowd of people: *A great multitude gathered in the city.*

mum[1], **mummy**[1] ['mʌm(i)] *nc* (*with cap when used as a name*: *inf*) a child's name for his or her mother: *Goodbye, Mum(my)!*; *Where's your mum(my), John?*

mum[2] [mʌm] *adj* (*esp old inf*: *pred*) silent; not speaking: *Stay/Keep mum!*

mumble ['mʌmbl] *vti* to speak (words) in such a way that they are difficult to hear: *The old man mumbled (a few words) quietly to himself.*

mummy[1] *see* **mum**[1].

mummy[2] ['mʌmi] *nc* a dead human body preserved *eg* by the ancient Egyptians by wrapping in bandages and treating with spice, wax *etc.*
'mummify [-fai] *vt* (*formal*) to preserve (a dead body) in this or a similar way: *The ancient Egyptians mummified their kings.*

mumps [mʌmps] *n sing* a contagious disease affecting the saliva-producing glands, and causing painful swelling at the sides of the neck and face: *Mumps is a painful disease*; *The child has mumps.*

munch [mʌntʃ] *vti* to chew (something) with the lips closed: *He was munching (his breakfast) noisily.*

mundane [mʌn'dein] *adj* (*formal*) ordinary or dull: *a very mundane existence*; *My life seems very mundane compared with hers.*

municipal [mju'nisipəl] *adj* (*attrib*) of, or controlled or owned by, the government of a city or town: *the municipal buildings.* **mu'nicipally** *adv.*
muˌnici'pality [-'pa-] *nc* a self-governing city or town, or a larger area which is governed like a city: *Peking is a municipality.*

munificence [mju'nifisns] *nu* (*formal*) great

generosity: *the munificence of the emperor.* **mu'nificent** *adj.*

munitions [mju'niʃənz] *n pl* weapons and ammunition used in war: *This factory makes munitions*; (*attrib*) *a munitions factory.*

mural ['mjuərəl] *nc* a painting that is painted directly on to a wall: *He painted a mural of the three wise men giving gifts to the baby Jesus.*

murder ['mə:də] **1** *ncu* (an) act of killing a person on purpose and illegally: *The police are treating his death as a case of murder*; *an increase in the number of murders*; (*attrib*) *the murder victim*; (*attrib*) *a murder hunt* (= a hunt for a murderer). **2** *nu* any killing or causing of death that is considered morally the same as this: *the murder of innocent people by terrorists*; *We regard the imprisonment of these sick old men as nothing but legalized murder.* **3** *nu* (*inf*) something that is extremely difficult to do or endure: *This arithmetic is murder!*; *His piano-playing is murder (to listen to)!* – *vt* **1** to kill (a person) on purpose and illegally: *They murdered two innocent children.* **2** (*inf*) to spoil or ruin (*eg* a piece of music) by performing it very badly: *She's murdering a perfectly good song!*

'murderer – *fem* **'murderess** – *nc*: *Murderers are no longer hanged in Britain.*

'murderous *adj* (*esp attrib*) intending, intended for, or capable of, murder: *There was a murderous look in his eye*; *That's a murderous-looking knife.*

'murderously *adv.*

murk [mə:k] *nu* (*with* **the**: *liter*) darkness: *The ship disappeared into the murk.*

'murky *adj* dark and gloomy: *a murky night*; *The night was dark and murky*; (*fig*) *I don't know much about him but I think he has rather a murky* (= suspicious) *past.*

murmur ['mə:mə] *nc* a quiet, often peaceful sound, *eg* that of running water or low voices: *the murmur of the sea*; *There was a low murmur among the crowd.* – *vti* to make such a sound: *The child murmured (something) in his sleep.* **'murmuring** *adj.*

muscle ['mʌsl] **1** *ncu* (any of the bundles of) fibres in the body which, by contracting or relaxing, cause movement of the body: *He has well-developed muscles in his arms*; *He strained a muscle in his leg.* **2** *nu* strength: *He's all muscle and no brain*; (*fig inf*) *Those large companies carry a great deal of political muscle.*

muscular ['mʌskjulə] *adj* **1** of, or relating to, muscle(s): *great muscular strength*; *The pain is mainly muscular.* **2** having well-developed muscles; strong: *a large, muscular woman*; *She is tall and muscular.*

muscle in *vi* (*often with* **on**: *inf derog*) to gain entry, or gain a share of something by force: *The large firms have muscled in on all the important contracts.*

muse[1] [mju:z] *vi* (*formal*) to think about a matter *usu* without serious concentration: *She gazed out the window, musing quietly to herself*; *He mused on the beauty of the countryside.*

muse[2] [mju:z] *nc* (*often with cap*: *myth*) any one of the nine goddesses of poetry, music and the arts.

museum [mju'ziəm] *nc* a place where collections of things of artistic, scientific or historic interest are set out for show: *The children admired the stone-age tools and the skeletons of the dinosaurs in the museum.*

mush [mʌʃ] *nu* (*inf*) something pulpy: *The potatoes have turned to mush after being boiled for so long.*

'mushy *adj* soft and pulpy: *mushy peas*; *These vegetables are mushy.*

mushroom ['mʌʃrum] *nc* a type of fungus, *usu* shaped like an umbrella, many varieties of which are edible: *She was very ill because she ate a poisonous toadstool in mistake for a mushroom*; (*attrib*) *mushroom soup.* – *vi* to grow in size very rapidly: *The town has mushroomed since all the new industry was brought in.*

music ['mju:zik] *nu* **1** the art of arranging and combining tones or sounds in order and often together to make a complete unit which has beauty of form and which is *usu* intended to communicate some emotion: *Mozart wrote a great deal of music*; *She prefers classical music to popular music*; *She is studying music*; (*attrib*) *a music lesson*; (*attrib*) *a music room.* **2** the written form in which such tones *etc* are set down: *The pianist has forgotten her music – she will have to go home for it.*

'musical *adj* **1** (*attrib*) of or producing music: *a musical instrument.* **2** like music, *esp* in being pleasant to hear: *a musical sound/voice*; *Her voice is sweet and musical.* **3** (of a person) having a talent for music: *Their children are all musical*; *a musical family.* – *nc* a film or play that includes a large amount of singing, dancing *etc*: *musicals such as 'My Fair Lady' and 'West Side Story'.*

'musically *adv.*

musician [mju'ziʃən] *nc* **1** a person who is skilled in music: *The conductor of this orchestra is a fine musician.* **2** a person who plays a musical instrument: *This show has ten singers, twenty dancers and fifty musicians.*

'music-hall *ncu* (a theatre for) variety entertainment: *The Victorians were very fond of music halls*; *The actress had previously made one or two appearances in music hall as a singer and dancer*; (*attrib*) *a music-hall artist.*

musk [mʌsk] *nu* a substance with a strong scent, obtained from the male of a type of deer and used in perfumes.

'musky *adj* (*attrib*): *a musky perfume.*

musket ['mʌskit] *nc* an old type of gun once carried by foot-soldiers.

ˌmuske'teer *nc* a soldier armed with a musket.

Muslim ['muzlim], **Moslem** ['mozləm] *nc, adj* (a person) of the religion known as Islam.
See also **Mohammedan**.

muslin ['mʌzlin] *nu, adj* (of) a type of fine soft cotton cloth: *She strained the jelly through a piece of muslin*; *a muslin bonnet.*

musquash ['mʌskwoʃ] **1** *nu, adj* (of) the fur of a type of large N American water-rat: *Her coat is (made of) musquash*; *a musquash coat.* **2** *nc* a musquash coat.

mussel ['mʌsl] *nc* a variety of edible shellfish with a shell in two parts: *They started the meal with fresh mussels.*

must [mʌst] – *neg short form* **'mustn't** [-snt] – *modal aux* **1** (*no neg*) used with another verb to express need: *We must go to the shops to get milk.* **2** (*neg rare*) used, *usu* with another verb, to suggest a probability: *'They must be finding it very difficult to live in such a small house.' 'Yes, they must.'*; *She must have been very young when she got married.* **3** used, *usu* with another verb, to express duty or obligation: *'You must come home before midnight.' 'Must I?'*; *Policemen must be over five feet eight inches. They must not be under this height.* – *nc* (*inf*) something necessary, essential, or not to be missed: *This new tent is a must for the serious*

camper; *Matthew Foster's new play is a must!*
'must have used to state that there is no doubt that something has happened in the past: *He must have been here already.*
See also **have to**.
mustache *see* **moustache**.
mustang ['mʌstaŋ] *nc* a type of wild horse found on the American prairies.
mustard ['mʌstəd] *nu* a type of seasoning with a hot taste made from the seeds of the mustard plant: *Will you have some mustard on your roast beef?*
muster ['mʌstə] (*formal*) **1** *vti* to gather together (*esp* soldiers for duty or inspection): *The troops were mustered for an attack.* **2** *vt* to gather (courage, energy *etc*): *He mustered his energy for a final effort.* – *nc* (*formal*) an assembly or gathering, *usu* of soldiers.
pass muster (*formal*) to be accepted as satisfactory after being examined: *Your work here just won't pass muster unless it improves greatly.*
mustn't *see* **must**.
musty ['mʌsti] *adj* damp or stale in smell or taste: *the musty smell of very old books*; *This room is musty – open a window.*
mutation [mju'teiʃən] (*formal or tech*) **1** *ncu* an act or the process of changing: *New kinds of plant can sometimes occur by mutation.* **2** *nc* (*also* **mutant**) (a plant or animal showing) a change in form or make-up from that of its parents, which can be passed on to later generations: *In the science fiction story an increase in radio-activity in the atmosphere led to many mutants (mutations) being born.*
mu'tate *vi* (*tech*) to change *usu* in a biological way.
mute [mju:t] *adj* **1** (*formal*: *esp pred*) unable to speak; dumb: *The child has been mute since birth.* **2** silent: *He remained completely mute for several minutes*; *She gazed at him in mute horror.* **3** (of a letter of the alphabet) not sounded in certain words: *The word 'dumb' has a mute 'b' at the end.* – *nc* a dumb person: *She was born a deaf mute.*
'muted *adj* (*formal*: *esp attrib*) **1** (of sound) made quieter; hushed: *in muted tones.* **2** (of colours) not bright: *in muted shades of blue.*
'mutely *adv.*
mutilate ['mju:tileit] *vt* (*formal*) to remove an important part of or damage badly: *The body had been badly mutilated.* **ˌmuti'lation** *nu.*
'mutilated *adj*: *a mutilated copy of a book.*
mutiny ['mju:tini] *ncu* (a) refusal to obey one's superiors, *esp* in the navy or other armed services: *There has been a mutiny on HMS Tigress*; *The sailors were found guilty of mutiny.* – *vi* (*esp* of sailors *etc*) to refuse to obey commands from those in authority: *The sailors mutinied because they did not have enough food.*
ˌmuti'neer *nc* a person who mutinies.
'mutinous *adj* **1** (*formal*) having mutinied or likely to mutiny: *mutinous sailors*; *The hungry sailors soon became mutinous.* **2** obstinate and sulky as if going to disobey; rebellious: *The child looked mutinous*; *a mutinous stare.*
mutter ['mʌtə] *vti* to utter words in a quiet voice *esp* when grumbling, insulting someone *etc*: *They won't be able to hear what you're saying if you mutter.* – *nc* such a sound: *He spoke in a mutter.*
mutton ['mʌtn] *nu* the flesh of sheep, used as food: *They had boiled mutton for dinner*; (*attrib*) *mutton stew.*
mutual ['mju:tʃuəl] *adj* **1** given *etc* by each of two or more to the other(s): *mutual help/dislike*; *Their dislike was mutual.* **2** (*attrib*) common to, or shared by, two or more: *a mutual friend.*
'mutually *adv.*
muzzle ['mʌzl] *nc* **1** the jaws and nose of an animal such as a dog. **2** an arrangement of straps *etc* round the muzzle of an animal to prevent it from biting: *The dog wore a muzzle to prevent it biting people.* **3** the open end of the barrel of a gun *etc.* – *vt* **1** to put a muzzle on (a dog *etc*): *She muzzled the dog to prevent it biting.* **2** to silence (a person *etc*): *Many of the newspapers have been muzzled by the new censorship laws.*
muzzy ['mʌzi] *adj* dazed, confused, hazy *etc*: *My head feels muzzy in this heat*; *a muzzy feeling.*
'muzziness *nu.*
my [mai] *adj* (*attrib*) of or belonging to me: *That is my book*; *I hurt my leg*; *She borrowed my pen.* – *interj* used to express surprise: *My, how you've grown!*
my'self *pron* **1** used as the object of a verb or preposition when the speaker or writer is the object of an action he or she performs: *I cut myself while shaving*; *I looked at myself in the mirror.* **2** used to emphasize **I, me** or the name of the speaker or writer: *I myself can't tell you, but my friend will*; *I don't intend to go myself.*
by myself *see* **by oneself** *under* **by**.
I am not myself *see* **not be oneself** *under* **one**.
See also **I, me, mine**[1].
myopia [mai'oupiə] *nu* (*tech*) short-sightedness: *She suffers from myopia.*
my'opic [-'o-] *adj*: *a myopic old lady*; *a myopic condition*; *She's slightly myopic.*
myriad ['miriəd] *nc* (*esp liter*) a very great number: *myriads of islands.* – *adj* (*esp liter*) countless and of infinite variety: *myriad plants and animals.*
myself *see* **my**.
mystery ['mistəri] **1** *nc* something that cannot be, or has not been, explained: *the mystery of how the universe was formed*; *How she got here so early is a mystery to me*; *The mystery of his disappearance was never solved.* **2** *nu* (things which have) the quality of being impossible to explain, understand *etc*: *His whole background seemed to be full of mystery*; *Her death was surrounded by mystery.*
my'sterious [-'stiəriəs] *adj* difficult to understand or explain, or full of mystery: *a mysterious gentleman dressed in black*; *mysterious happenings*; *He's being very mysterious* (= refuses to explain fully) *about what his work is.* **my'steriously** *adv.*
'mystery tour *nc* an outing on which the travellers are not told in advance where they are going: *The old age pensioners were delighted to find that their mystery tour had taken them to Brighton.*
mystic ['mistik] *adj* (*also* **'mystical**) (*esp attrib*) of or relating to (*esp* religious or spiritual) mysteries: *mystic rites.* – *nc* a person who attempts or claims direct and complete communication with God.
'mysticism [-sizəm] *nu* the beliefs, actions *etc* of a mystic.
mystify ['mistifai] *vt* (*formal*) to be impossible for (someone) to explain or understand: *These problems mystify me*; *I was completely mystified by his behaviour.*
mystique [mi'sti:k] *nu* (*formal*) the quality of being mysterious (*esp* to an outsider): *The art of writing books has a definite mystique for those who have never written.*

myth [miθ] **1** *nc* an ancient, fictional story, *esp* one dealing with gods, heroes *etc*: *The Greeks had many myths.* **2** *ncu* (an example of) things which are often thought to be true, but which are in fact untrue: *He thinks that this idea of men being stronger than women is a myth.* **3** *ncu* (an) invention; a lie or lies: *His story about being tremendously wealthy was (a) complete myth.* **'mythical** *adj.* **'mythically** *adv.*

mythology [mi'θolədʒi] *ncu* (a collection of) myths: *the mythology of the Romans.* **,mytho'logical** [-'lo-] *adj.*

Nn

nab [nab] – *pt, ptp* **nabbed** – *vt* (*inf*) to take, catch or get hold of: *The police nabbed the thief.*

nadir ['neidiə] *nc* (*formal or liter*) the lowest point (of hope, despair *etc*): *The standard of honesty in this country has reached its nadir.*

nag[1] [nag] *nc* (*derog*) an old, weak or small horse: *This old nag cost me a huge amount of money!*

nag[2] [nag] – *pt, ptp* **nagged** – *vti* **1** (*often with* **at**) to complain or criticize continually: *She nags (at) her husband about their lack of money*; *Stop nagging!* **2** to hurt or worry continually: *This headache's been nagging me all day*; *That unpleasant thought has been nagging him for weeks.*

nail [neil] *nc* **1** (*often in cmpds*) a piece of horn-like substance which grows over the ends of the fingers and toes to protect them: *When I injured my finger, I broke my nail*; *toe-nails*; *finger-nails*; *You must stop biting your finger-nails if you want them to grow!*; (*attrib*) *nail scissors.* **2** a thin pointed piece of metal used to fasten pieces of wood *etc* together: *Do you prefer using nails or screws when you make furniture?*; *He hammered a nail into the wall and hung a picture on it.* – *vt* **1** to fasten with nails: *He nailed the picture to the wall.* **2** (*sl*) to catch or trap: *I tried to avoid him, but he finally nailed me in the corridor.* – *See also* **nail up** *below.*

'nail-brush *nc* a (*usu* small) brush used for cleaning nails (*def 1*).

'nail-file *nc* a small instrument with a rough surface, used for smoothing or shaping the edges of one's finger-nails.

'nail-polish, 'nail-varnish *nu* a substance used to colour and/or varnish the nails (*def 1*).

as hard as nails (*usu fig*) very hard, tough, strong *etc*: *Don't ask for sympathy from him – he is as hard as nails.*

hit the nail on the head to be absolutely accurate (in one's description of something or someone, in an estimate of something *etc*): *You hit the nail (right) on the head when you described her as being naïve.*

nail up *vt sep* to fasten or close completely with nails: *He tried to open the door, but it was nailed up.*

on the 'nail (*inf*) immediately: *He paid cash on the nail and took the car away with him.*

naïve, naive [nai'i:v] *adj* **1** simple and straightforward in one's way of thinking, speaking or acting: *the naïve manner of a child*; *a naïve young girl.* **2** (*derog*) ignorantly simple: *Don't be so naïve!*; *You can't be so naïve as to believe that!* **na'ïvely** *adv.* **naïveté** [nai'i:vtei], **naïvety, naivety** [nai'i:vəti] *nus.*

naked ['neikid] *adj* **1** without clothes: *a naked woman*; *She was completely naked.* **2** (*fig*: *attrib*) openly shown or seen, not hidden (and therefore often shocking): *the naked truth.* **3** (*attrib*) (of a light or flame) uncovered or unprotected: *Naked lights are dangerous.* **'nakedly** *adv.* **'nakedness** *nu.*

the naked eye the eye unaided by any artificial means such as spectacles, a microscope *etc*: *Germs are too small to be seen by the naked eye.*

namby-pamby [nambi'pambi] *nc, adj* (*derog inf*) (*usu* of men and boys) (a person who is) childish, weak, without strength of personality *etc*: *He is a terrible namby-pamby. He cries as soon as any other children come near him.*

name [neim] *nc* **1** a word by which a person, place or thing is called: *My name is Rachel*; *What is the name of the village?*; *She knows all the flowers by name.* **2** (*no pl*) reputation; fame: *He has a name for honesty.* – *See also* **make a name for oneself** *below.* **3** a (famous) person: *Several famous names were invited to the party.* – *vt* **1** (*more formal than* **call**) to give a name to: *They named the child Thomas.* **2** to speak of or list by name: *He could name all the kings of England.* **3** (*formal*) to appoint: *They named my father president of the club.* – *See also* **name after** *below.*

named *adj* (*neg* **un-**) whose name is stated *etc*: *He got his information from an unnamed source.*

'nameless *adj* **1** (*esp attrib*) not having a name: *a nameless fear.* **2** (*esp pred*) not spoken of by name: *The author of the book shall be nameless.*

'namely *adv* that is: *Only one student passed the exam, namely John.*

'name-dropping *nu* trying to impress people by the mentioning of famous people's names as if they were one's friends: *Her name-dropping annoys me – but no one believes she knows half the people she says she does.* **'name-dropper** *nc.*

'nameplate *nc* a piece of metal, plastic *etc* with a name on it: *You will know his office by the nameplate on the door.*

'namesake *nc* a person with the same name as another: *Your famous namesake is on television tonight, Arthur.*

name-tab *see* **tab**.

call (someone) names to insult someone by applying rude names to them: *They keep calling her names, shouting things like 'Bighead!' and 'Foureyes!'* (= someone who wears spectacles).

christian name *see* **Christian**.

in the 'name of (*formal*) by the authority of: *I arrest you in the name of the Queen.*

in name only only by title, not really in practice: *He's the boss in name only, because I issue all the orders*; *They're married in name only, since they have been living apart for years.*

,make a 'name for oneself to become famous, get a (*usu* good) reputation *etc*: *He made a name for himself as the first man to step on to the moon*; *He really made a name for himself when he went to London.*

'name after, (Amer) 'name for to give (a child or a thing) the name of another person in order to honour the latter: *Peter was named after his father*; *'Stedman' is a method of bell-ringing which was named after its inventor, Fabian Stedman.*

name the day (*facet*) to announce a date for something, *esp* the date on which one is to be married.

proper name *see* **proper**.

take someone's name in vain *see* **vain**.

See also **surname**.

nanny ['nani] *nc* (*with cap when used as a name*) a children's nurse: *She worked as a nanny for a rich family*; *May I go out, Nanny?*

nanny-goat ['nanigout] *nc* a female (*usu* adult) goat.

See also **billy-goat**.

nap[1] [nap] *nc* (*slightly inf*) a short sleep: *She always takes/has a nap after lunch.*

catch (someone) napping (*inf*) to meet or find (someone) when they are not prepared: *He was caught napping in the garden when he should have been working*; *The first heavy snowfall of the winter caught the roads department napping – they had no grit.*

nap[2] [nap] *ncu* a rough, woolly surface on cloth *etc*: *Make sure that the nap is the same on both pieces of velvet.*

napalm ['neipa:m] *nu* petrol in a jelly-like form, used in bombs to cause fire.

nape [neip] *nc* (*no pl*) the back of the neck: *His hair curled over the nape of his neck.*

napkin ['napkin] *nc* **1** (*formal* '**table napkin**) a small piece of cloth or paper for protecting the clothes from drips *etc* and for wiping the lips at meals: *Put the table-mats, napkins and cutlery on the table.* **2** (*formal*) full form of **nappy**.

nappy ['napi] *nc* (*Amer* '**diaper**) a piece of cloth or paper put between a baby's legs to soak up urine *etc*: *Is the child still wearing a nappy at his age?*

narcotic [na:'kotik] *nc* (*esp tech*) a type of drug that stops pain or makes one sleep, often addictive when taken in large doses: *Opium is a narcotic*; (*attrib*) *the narcotic effects of opium*; (*attrib*) *the narcotics division of the police force.*

narrate [nə'reit] *vt* (*formal*) to tell (a story): *He narrated the events of the afternoon to the judge.*

nar'ration *ncu* (*very formal*) the telling of a story: *She interrupted his narration to say that tea was ready.*

narrative ['narətiv] *nc* (*formal*) a story: *an exciting narrative.* – *adj* (*usu attrib*: *formal*) telling a story: *a narrative poem.*

nar'rator *nc* a person who tells a story, often as an accompaniment to filmed, acted, written *etc* events, to connect them: *In this novel, the narrator is the heroine's sister*; *In her play, the narrator has several speeches which are used to join one scene to the next.*

narrow ['narou] *adj* **1** having or being only a small distance from side to side: *There is a narrow road leading to their house*; *a narrow strip of carpet*; *This ribbon is too narrow*; *The bridge is too narrow for large lorries to cross.* **2** (*attrib*) only just successful: *a narrow escape*; *a narrow victory.* **3** (of interests or experience) not wide, great or extensive: *He lived a narrow life*; *His experience in business has so far been very narrow.* – *vti* to make or become narrow: *The road suddenly narrowed*; (*formal fig*) *Living in a convent narrowed her views.*

'**narrowly** *adv* closely; only just: *The ball narrowly missed his head.*

'**narrows** *n pl* a narrow sea-passage: *The ship entered the narrows at the mouth of the river.*

ˌ**narrow-'minded** *adj* (*derog*) unwilling to accept ideas different from one's own: *He is a very narrow-minded person*; *He is so narrow-minded that he disapproves of all young people.*

nasal ['neizəl] *adj* **1** (*formal or tech*) of the nose: *a nasal infection.* **2** sounding through the nose: *You sound very nasal today – do you have a cold?*; *a nasal accent.*

nasty ['na:sti] *adj* **1** unpleasant to the senses: *a nasty smell*; *The smell coming from that chemical is rather nasty.* **2** unfriendly or unpleasant in manner: *The man was very nasty to me*; *a nasty old man*; *The thieves turned* (= became) *nasty and hit me.* **3** (*usu attrib*) wicked or dirty; obscene: *You have a nasty mind.* **4** (of weather) very poor, cold, rainy *etc*: *nasty weather*; *In November the weather is usually rather nasty.* **5** (of a wound, cut *etc*) serious: *That dog gave her a nasty bite*; *That cut looks nasty.* **6** (*attrib*) awkward or very difficult: *We found ourselves in a very nasty situation.*

'**nastily** *adv.* '**nastiness** *nu.*

turn nasty *vi* (*inf*) to become nasty (*defs 2–6*).

nation ['neiʃən] *nc* **1** a group of people living in a particular country, forming a single political and economic unit: *In Anglo-Saxon times the many tribes and small kingdoms in England came together to form a nation.* **2** a large number of people who share the same history, ancestors, culture *etc* (whether or not they all live in the same country): *the Jewish nation.*

national ['naʃənəl] *adj* (*usu attrib*) of or belonging to a particular nation: *national government*; *national pride.* – *nc* (*formal*) a person belonging to a particular nation: *He is a British national.*

'**nationally** *adv.*

'**nationalism** ['na-] *nu* **1** a sense of pride in the history, culture, achievements *etc* of one's nation: *International football matches bring out a sense of nationalism in the football supporters.* **2** the desire to bring the people of a nation together under their own government: *the politics of Scottish nationalism.*

'**nationalist** ['na-] *nc* a person who believes in nationalism. ˌ**nationa'listic** *adj.*

nationality [naʃə'naləti] **1** *nu* the state of belonging to a particular nation: *He has British nationality*; *He is of British nationality.* **2** *nc* a person or group belonging to a particular nation: *You can see (people of) many nationalities in London.*

'**nationalize, -ise** ['na-] *vt* to make (something *esp* an industry) the property of the nation as a whole rather than the property of an individual: *The railways in Britain were nationalized in 1947.*

ˌ**nationali'zation, -s-** *nu.*

'**nationalized, -s-** ['na-] *adj*: *Coal-mining is a nationalized industry in Britain.*

national anthem *nc* a nation's official song or hymn: *As the King arrived we sang the national anthem.*

national park *nc* an area whose natural beauty, wildlife *etc* is preserved by the nation.

national service *nu* in some countries (formerly including Britain), a period of compulsory service in the armed forces.

ˌ**nation-'wide** *adj, adv* (happening *etc*) throughout the whole nation: *a nation-wide broadcast*; *They travelled nation-wide.*

native ['neitiv] *adj* (*attrib*) **1** (of the place) where one was born: *my native land*; *my native language.*

2 belonging by race to a country: *a native Englishman.* **3** belonging to a person naturally: *native intelligence.* – *See also* **native to** *below.* – *nc* **1** a person born in a certain place: *a native of Scotland; a native of London.* **2** (*sometimes offensive when applied to a coloured or black person*) one of the original inhabitants of a country *eg* before the arrival of explorers, immigrants *etc*: *Columbus thought the natives of America were Indians.* **3** (*in S Africa now offensive, previously acceptable*) a black person: (*attrib*) *the native workers.*

native speaker *nc* (*formal*) a person who has spoken (a particular language) ever since he was able to speak at all: *I am a native speaker of English.*

'native to (*formal*) (of plants and animals) *orig* belonging to a particular place: *The Shetland pony is native to the Shetland Islands.*

the Nativity [nə'tivəti] the birth of Christ: *Christians celebrate the Nativity at Christmas time.*

natter ['natə] *vi* (*inf*) to chatter or talk continuously, *usu* about unimportant things: *They were nattering in the kitchen.* – *nc* (*inf*: *no pl*): *They were having a good natter.*

natty ['nati] *adj* (*inf*) tidy; smart; neat: *He wore a natty suit; He looks very natty today.*

'nattily *adv* (*inf*): *nattily dressed.*

natural ['natʃərəl] *adj* **1** (*esp attrib*) of or produced by nature, not made by men: *the natural world; Coal, oil etc are natural resources; Wild animals are happier in their natural state than in a zoo.* **2** (*attrib*) born in a person: *A girl with natural beauty does not need to use cosmetics; He had a natural ability for playing the piano.* **3** (of manner) simple, direct and not artificial: *Children are usually more natural in their manner than adults; a sweet, natural smile.* **4** normal; as one would expect: *It's quite natural for a boy of his age to be interested in girls; a natural reaction.* **5** (*music*) not sharp or flat: *G natural is lower in pitch than G sharp.* – *nc* **1** (*inf*) a person who is naturally good at something: *She would be a natural for Lady Macbeth* (= to play the part of Lady Macbeth). **2** in music (a sign (♮) indicating) a note which is not to be played sharp or flat.

'naturalist *nc* a person who studies animal and plant life.

ˌnatura'listic *adj* (*esp pred*) (of a picture *etc*) very like the subject: *The way he paints trees makes them look very naturalistic.*

'naturally *adv* **1** of course; as one would expect: *Naturally I didn't want to risk being ill.* **2** by nature; as a natural characteristic: *She is naturally kind.* **3** normally; in an unselfconscious or relaxed way: *She spoke very naturally; Although he was very nervous, he behaved quite naturally.*

natural gas *nu* gas suitable for burning, found underground or under the sea: *Our gas cooker uses natural gas, not coal gas.*

natural history *nu* the study of plants and animals.

natural philosophy *see* **philosophy**.

natural resources *n pl* sources of energy, wealth *etc* which occur naturally and are not made by man, *eg* coal, oil, forests *etc.*

See also **unnatural**.

nature ['neitʃə] **1** *nu* the physical world, *eg* trees, plants, animals, mountains, rivers *etc*, or the power which made them: *Many poets write about the beauty of nature; the mighty forces of nature;* (*attrib*) *a nature-study course.* **2** *nc* (*no pl*) the qualities born in a person; personality: *She has a generous nature.* **3** *nc* (*formal*: *no pl*: *with* **the**) quality; what something is or consists of: *He will explain to you the nature of your work.* **4** *nc* (*no pl*) a kind, type *etc*: *bankers and other people of that nature.*

-natured (*in cmpds*) having certain qualities *etc*: *good-natured; ill-natured.*

in the 'nature of (*formal*) having the qualities of: *His words were in the nature of a threat.*

naught [no:t] *nu* (*liter or old*) nothing: *His plans were brought/came to naught; She cared naught for him.*

See also **nought**.

naughty ['no:ti] *adj* (*usu* of children) badly-behaved: *You're a very naughty boy (to do that)!; It is naughty to kick other children.* **'naughtily** *adv.* **'naughtiness** *nu.*

nausea ['no:ziə, (*Amer*) -ʃə] *nu* (*formal*) a feeling of sickness or disgust: *As the boat crossed the Channel he was affected by nausea; She was filled with nausea at the thought of killing a chicken.*

nauseate ['no:zieit, (*Amer*) -ʒi-] *vt* (*formal*) to make (someone) feel nausea: *The smell of oil nauseates me; His behaviour nauseated me.*

nauseous ['no:ziəs, (*Amer*) -ʃəs] *adj* **1** (*formal*) sickening or disgusting: *The doctor gave me a nauseous mixture to drink; That medicine is nauseous.* **2** (*pred*: *Amer*) affected by nausea: *I often feel nauseous on the bus.*

nautical ['no:tikəl] *adj* of ships or sailors: *nautical information; The blue hat made her look very nautical.*

nautical mile *nc* 1·85 kilometres (6 080 ft).

See also **knot**.

naval *see* **navy**.

nave [neiv] *nc* the middle or main part of a church: *St Peter's Basilica has the longest nave of any church in Europe.*

navel ['neivəl] *nc* the small hollow in the centre of the stomach, caused by the cutting of the umbilical cord: *In some countries, women wear a jewel in the navel for decoration.*

navigate ['navigeit] **1** *vt* to direct, guide or move a ship, aircraft *etc* in a particular direction: *He navigated the ship through the dangerous rocks outside the harbour.* **2** *vi* to find or follow one's route when in a ship, aircraft, car *etc*: *If I work the engine, will you navigate?*

'navigable *adj* (*formal*: *neg* **un-**) able to be travelled along: *a navigable river; a navigable road; Are the roads navigable?*

ˌnavi'gation *nu* the art or skill of navigating: *He is studying navigation; Your navigation isn't very good, is it? We're lost.*

'navigator *nc* a person who navigates a ship, aircraft, car *etc*: *The plane is carrying two pilots and a navigator.*

navvy ['navi] *nc* (*sometimes derog*) a general labourer who works *esp* on road-building *etc*: *He is one of the navvies on the nearby building site.*

navy ['neivi] **1** *nc* a country's warships and the people who work in and with them: *Russia has one of the largest navies in the world; I joined the navy fifteen years ago.* **2** *see* **merchant navy** *under* **merchant**. **3** *nu, adj* (*also* **navy blue**) (of) a dark blue colour: *a navy (blue) jersey.*

'naval *adj* (*attrib*) of the navy: *naval uniform; a naval officer.*

nay [nei] *interj* (*old*: *liter*) **1** no: *Nay, I will not.* **2** indeed: *I think, nay, I am certain (that) we will succeed.*

near [niə] *adj* **1** not far away in place or time: *The station is near; Christmas is getting near; The car did not hit me but it was a near miss* (= it almost hit me). **2** (*attrib*) not far away in relationship: *He is a near relation.* **3** (*attrib*) (of vehicles *etc*) nearside: *The near front wheel is loose.* – *adv* (*also* ˌ**near'by**) to or at a short distance: *He lives quite near(by).* – *prep* (*sometimes with* **to**) not far away; at a very small distance from (in place, time *etc*): *She lives near the church; It was near midnight when they arrived; She sat near (to) the door.* – *vti* (*formal*) to come near (to): *The roads became busier as they neared the town; as evening was nearing.*

'**nearly** *adv* not far from; almost: *It's nearly one o'clock; He has nearly finished.* '**nearness** *nu.*

'**nearside** *adj* (*Brit*: *attrib*) (of the side of a vehicle *etc*) furthest from the centre of the road (in Britain the left): *The nearside headlamp is broken.*

ˌ**near-'sighted** *adj* (*usu pred*) short-sighted: *I cannot see the time on that clock – I am near-sighted.*

a near miss *see* **near** (*adj def 1*).

a near thing *see* **thing**.

neat [ni:t] *adj* **1** tidy; well-ordered, with everything in the right place: *a neat house; She had a neat appearance; She is very neat and tidy.* **2** (*inf*) skilfully done: *He has made a neat job of the repair; a neat phrase; That's neat!* **3** (of drink, *esp* alcoholic) without added water: *neat whisky; I drink my whisky neat.*

'**neatly** *adv* tidily or skilfully: *Please write neatly.* '**neatness** *nu.*

nebulous ['nebjuləs] *adj* (*formal*) vague; indistinct or not clear: *a nebulous shape; a nebulous idea; My plans are still rather nebulous.*

necessary ['nesisəri] *adj* (*formal when attrib*) needed; essential: *Unfortunately, money is necessary in life; Is it necessary to give one's name?; Do you have the necessary skills for this job?; I shall do all that is necessary.*

ˌ**neces'sarily** [-'se-] *adv* by need; unavoidably: *That isn't necessarily true; Because he exports goods, he necessarily has to travel abroad a great deal.*

necessitate [ni'sesiteit] *vt* (*formal*) to make necessary: *Re-building the castle would necessitate spending a lot of money.*

necessity [ni'sesəti] **1** *nc* something needed or essential: *For this job, a knowledge of Italian is a necessity; the necessities of life.* **2** *nu* (*formal*) great need: *It was necessity that made him steal.*

of ne'cessity (*formal*) logically, unavoidably and necessarily: *His story must, of necessity, be true.*

See also **unnecessary**.

neck [nek] *nc* **1** the part of the body between the head and chest: *She wore a scarf around her neck; The horse broke its neck when it fell.* **2** the part of an article of clothing that covers that part of the body: *The neck of that shirt is dirty; I want a blue shirt – neck size 16 inches.* **3** anything like a neck in shape or position: *the neck of a bottle.* – *vi* (*sl*) (of people) to kiss and embrace: *They were necking on the sofa.*

'**necklace** [-ləs] *nc* a string of jewels, beads *etc* worn around the neck: *She wore a diamond necklace.*

'**neckline** *nc* the edge of a piece of clothing at or around a person's neck: *The dress has a very low neckline.*

'**necktie** *nc* (*Amer*) a man's tie.

get it in the neck (*sl*) to be given the blame and be severely scolded or punished (for something one has done *etc*): *Clear up this mess before your father gets home, or you'll really get it in the neck!*

neck and neck (in a race) exactly equal: *The horses were neck and neck as they came up to the finish;* (*attrib*) *a neck-and-neck finish.*

stick one's neck out *see* **stick**[1].

nectar ['nektə] *nu* **1** the sweet liquid collected by bees to make honey. **2** (*formal or facet*) a delicious drink: *Nectar was the drink of the gods; A cup of tea is nectar when one is very tired.*

née [nei] *adj* born; used to state what a woman's name was before she married: *Mrs Jane Brown, née Black.*

need [ni:d] – *neg short form* **needn't** ['ni:dnt] – **1** *vt* to require: *This page needs to be checked again; This page needs checking again; You'll need some money if you're going shopping; 'Do you need any help?' 'No, I don't need any, thanks.'* **2** *vt, modal aux* (*vt with* **to**) to be obliged: *You'll need to work hard if you want to succeed; They needn't come/don't need to come until six o'clock; She needn't have given me such an expensive present.* – **1** *nc* (*formal*) something essential, that one must have: *Food is one of our basic needs.* **2** *nu* (*formal*) poverty or other difficulty: *Many people are in great need.* **3** *nc* (*no pl*) a reason: *What is the need for all this hurry?; There's no need to be so unpleasant; There is no need for panic.*

'**needful** *adj* (*formal or facet*) necessary: *Do whatever is needful.* – *nu* (*inf*) **1** whatever is necessary: *Can I leave it to you to do the needful?* **2** (*facet*) money: *I'm a bit short of the needful at the moment.*

'**needless** *adj* (*usu attrib*), *adv* (*formal*) unnecessary: *the needless killing of innocent children; You are doing a lot of needless work; Needless to say, he couldn't do it.*

'**needlessly** *adv* (*formal*): *Do not disturb him needlessly.*

'**needy** *adj* (*formal*) poor: *You must help needy people.*

in 'need of requiring; having a lack of (something) which must be corrected: *We're in need of more money to finance our plans; These roses are badly in need of pruning/of being pruned.*

a 'need for a state in which there is a lack of or requirement for: *There's an urgent need for more teachers in this city.*

the needy needy people: *The government should help the needy.*

needle ['ni:dl] *nc* **1** a small, sharp piece of steel with a hole (called an eye) at one end for thread, used in sewing *etc*: *a sewing needle; I can't get the thread to go through the eye of my needle.* **2** a longer piece of steel *etc*, used for various purposes, *eg* knitting, giving injections *etc*: *a knitting needle; A hypodermic needle is hollow, so that the substance injected can flow through it.* **3** (in a compass) the moving pointer which always points to the north. **4** the thin, sharp-pointed leaf of a pine, fir *etc.* – *vt* to irritate or annoy *usu* by saying unpleasant things: *She was continually needling me about how slow I was.*

'**needling** *adj* (*usu attrib*) worrying or irritating: *a needling doubt.*

'**needlework** *nu* work done with a needle (*def 1*) *ie* sewing, embroidery *etc*: *She was very good at needlework.*

needn't *see* **need**.

ne'er [neə] *adv* (*liter*) never: *I fear he will ne'er return.*

'**ne'er-do-well** *nc, adj* (*attrib*) (*derog old*) (a

person who is) lazy or worthless: *her ne'er-do-well brother*; *He's nothing but a ne'er-do-well.*

nefarious [ni'feəriəs] *adj* (*very formal*: *attrib*) very wicked: *nefarious crimes.*

negative ['negətiv] *adj* **1** (*formal or tech*) meaning or saying 'no': *a negative answer*; *'Un-' is a negative prefix*; *Was the response purely negative?* **2** (*formal*) expecting to fail: *He has a negative attitude to everything*; *His attitude is rather negative.* **3** (*math*: *attrib*) less than zero: *−4 is a negative or minus number*; *a negative quantity.* **4** (*tech*: *esp attrib*) having more electrons than normal: *The battery has a negative and a positive terminal.* – *nc* **1** a word, statement or grammatical form by which something is denied: *'No' and 'never' are negatives.* **2** the photographic film, from which prints are made, on which light and dark are reversed: *I gave away the prints, but I still have the negative.* '**negatively** *adv.*

in the 'negative (*formal*) in a way meaning or saying 'no': *He answered my question in the negative.*

See also **affirmative** *under* **affirm**, *and* **positive**.

neglect [ni'glekt] *vt* **1** to treat carelessly or not give enough attention to: *He neglected his wife/his work.* **2** (*formal*: *with* **to**) not to do something: *He neglected to answer the letter.* – *nu* lack of care and attention: *The garden is suffering from neglect.*

See also **negligence**.

négligée ['negliʒei, (*Amer*) negli'ʒei] *nc* (*a term used esp in shops*) a woman's very thin, light dressing-gown for wearing over a nightdress.

negligence ['neglidʒəns] *nu* (*formal*) carelessness: *The accident was caused by the driver's negligence*; *She does not look after those children properly – she was found guilty of negligence.* '**negligent** *adj.* '**negligently** *adv.*

See also **neglect**.

negligible ['neglidʒəbl] *adj* (*formal*) too small, few or unimportant to be considered or worthwhile: *The amount of rainfall was negligible*; *We got negligible results from all our hard work.*

negotiate [ni'gouʃieit] (*formal*) **1** *vi* to bargain or discuss a subject in order to agree: *The two countries negotiated* (*with each other*) *for several weeks.* **2** *vt* to arrange (a treaty, payment *etc*), *usu* after a long discussion: *They negotiated a peace treaty*; *He negotiated a loan from the bank.* **3** *vt* to get past (an obstacle or difficulty): *They managed to negotiate the rough path.*

ne'gotiable [-ʃəbl] *adj* (*formal*: *usu pred*) **1** (of a document concerned with the payment of money) that can be transferred from one person to another: *Is this cheque negotiable?* **2** able to be negotiated: *Because of snow and ice, these roads are scarcely negotiable.*

neˌgoti'ation *ncu* discussion in order to reach agreement: *Negotiations ended without any settlement being agreed*; *The dispute was settled by negotiation.* **ne'gotiator** *nc.*

Negro ['ni:grou] – *fem* '**Negress**: *pl* '**Negroes** – *nc, adj* (*sometimes offensive*) (of) a person or the people belonging to or descended from the black-skinned race from the area of Africa south of the Sahara.

'**negroid** [-groid] *adj* like a Negro in appearance: *negroid features* (*of the face*); *Her features are rather negroid.*

neigh [nei] *vi* to utter the cry of a horse: *They could hear the horses neighing*; (*fig*) *He neighed with laughter.* – *nc* such a cry: *The horse gave a neigh.*

neighbour, (*Amer*) **neighbor** ['neibə] *nc* a person who lives near another: *My cousin and I are neighbours*; *This is my next-door neighbour.*

'**neighbourhood** *nc* **1** a district or area, *esp* in a town or city: *a poor neighbourhood.* **2** a district or area surrounding a particular place: *He lives somewhere in the neighbourhood of the station.* – *See also* **in the neighbourhood of** *below.*

'**neighbouring** *adj* (*attrib*) near or next in place: *France and Belgium are neighbouring countries.*

'**neighbourly** *adj* (*neg* **un-**) friendly: *a very neighbourly person*; *She is kind and neighbourly.*

in the 'neighbourhood of (*formal*) approximately: *There must have been in the neighbourhood of five hundred people there.*

neither ['naiðə, (*esp Amer*) 'ni:ðə(r)] *adj, pron* not the one nor the other (of two things or people): *Neither window faces the sea*; *Neither of them could understand Italian.* – *conj* (*formal*: with the following subject and verb inverted) and not (also): *He could not dance, neither could he sing.*

neither ... nor introducing alternatives which are both impossible, forbidden, untrue *etc*: *Neither John nor David could come*; *He can neither read nor write*; *That's neither right nor wrong.*

See also **either**.

nemesis ['nemisis] *nc* (*formal*: *no pl*) fate; punishment that must follow a sin or crime.

neo- [ni:ou] (*in cmpds*) new: ˌ*neo-'natal* (= of new-born babies).

neon ['ni:on] *nu* an element (symbol **Ne**), a colourless gas used in certain forms of electric lighting, *eg* advertising signs: *These tubes are filled with neon*; (*attrib*) *neon lighting.*

Nepal, Nepalese, Nepali *see* Appendix 2.

nephew ['nefju:] – *fem* **niece** [ni:s] – *nc* the son or daughter of a brother or sister: *My sister's two sons are my nephews, and I am their uncle.*

nepotism ['nepətizəm] *nu* (*formal*: *derog*) the giving of good jobs *etc* by a person in authority to his relatives: *He only got his job because he's the boss's son. It's downright nepotism!*

Neptune *see* Appendix 6.

nerve [nə:v] **1** *nc* one of the cords which carry messages between all parts of the body and the brain: *He has damaged a nerve in his back*; *The nerves in my fingers are tingling.* – *See also* **nerves** *below.* **2** *nu* courage: *He must have needed a lot of nerve to do that*; *He lost his nerve.* **3** *nu* (*inf*) rudeness: *What a nerve!*; *You've got a nerve to come here uninvited!* – *vt* (*formal*) to give courage to: *He nerved himself to climb the high tower.*

nerves *n pl* the condition of being too easily excited or upset: *She suffers from nerves*; *The doctor gave her a sedative to calm her nerves.*

'**nervous** *adj* **1** (*attrib*) of the nerves: *the nervous system*; *nervous tension.* **2** rather afraid: *She was nervous about travelling by air*; *She is rather a nervous old lady.* '**nervously** *adv.* '**nervousness** *nu.*

'**nervy** *adj* (*inf*) excitable: *She is a very nervy person*; *The horse is rather nervy.* '**nerviness** *nu.*

'**nerve centre** *nc* (*fig*) the most important part of a system or organization, from which everything is controlled: *the nerve centre of the government.*

'**nerve-racking** *adj* causing great anxiety or nervousness: *a nerve-racking experience*; *Driving on those icy roads was rather nerve-racking.*

nervous breakdown *nc* (*not a tech term*) a period of mental illness caused by a time of great mental or physical strain: *The school-teacher had a nervous breakdown.*

nervous system *nc* the brain, spinal cord and nerves of a person or animal: *This drug is very dangerous, because it acts on the central nervous system.*

get on one's nerves (*inf*) to irritate: *Her behaviour really gets on my nerves.*

nest [nest] *nc* **1** a structure or place in which birds (and some animals and insects) hatch or give birth to and look after their young: *The swallows are building a nest under the roof of our house*; *We found the nest of a harvest-mouse in the field*; *a wasp's nest.* **2** a warm and comfortable place: *a nest of cushions.* **3** a set of things that fit one inside another: *a nest of tables.* – *vi* to build a nest and live in it: *A pair of robins are nesting in that bush.*

'nestling [-liŋ] *nc* a young bird (still in the nest): *The nestlings will soon be learning to fly.*

'nest-egg *nc* (*inf*) something saved up for the future, *usu* money: *I have a nest-egg in the bank.*

feather one's (own) nest *see* **feather**.

nestle ['nesl] *vi* **1** to lie close together as if in a nest: *The children nestled together*; *She nestled up to him.* **2** (*usu with* **down**) to settle comfortably: *She nestled down in front of the fire*; *She nestled sleepily on the sofa.*

nestling *see* **nest**.

net[1] [net] (*often in cmpds*) **1** *nc* a loose open fabric made of string, thread *etc* knotted together and used for catching fish, birds, insects *etc*: *The fishermen are mending their nets*; *a fishing-net*; *a butterfly-net.* **2** *ncu* any fabric made like this: *A hair-net is sometimes used to keep one's hair in place*; *The tennis-ball hit the net before it dropped over*; *curtain-net*; (*attrib*) *a net curtain.* – *v* – *pt, ptp* **'netted** – *vt* to catch in a net: *They netted several tons of fish.*

'netting *nu* material made in the form of a net: *The wire netting is there to keep the chickens in the yard.*

'netball *nu* a team-game in which a ball is thrown into a net hanging high up on a pole.

'network *nc* **1** (*fig*) anything in the form of a net, *ie* with many lines crossing each other: *A network of roads covered the countryside.* **2** a widespread organization: *a radio network.*

net[2], **nett** [net] *adj* **1** (of a profit *etc*) remaining after all expenses *etc* have been paid: *The net profit from the sale was £100.* **2** (of the weight of something) not including the packaging or container: *The sugar has a net weight of 1 kilo*; *The sugar weighs one kilo net.* – *v* – *pt, ptp* **'netted** – *vt* to gain as profit: *They netted £100 from the sale.*

netball *see* **net**[1].

nether ['neðə] *adj* (*old or liter*: *attrib*) lower: *nether garments* (= trousers); *the nether regions of the house.*

'nethermost *adj* (*old or liter*) lowest: *the nethermost regions of Hell.*

the Netherlands *see* Appendix 2.

nett *see* **net**[2].

netting *see* **net**[1].

nettle ['netl] *nc* a type of plant covered with hairs that cause pain if touched: *Nettles grow wild in a great variety of places*; (*attrib*) *a nettle sting/rash.*

'nettled *adj* (*pred*) annoyed or irritated: *She was nettled by what he said.*

network *see* **net**[1].

neuro- [njuərou] (*in cmpds*) of the nerve(s): *a 'neuro-surgeon.*

neurosis [nju'rousis] – *pl* **neu'roses** [-si:z] – *nc* (*tech*) a type of mental illness in which a person suffers from great anxiety and fear: *She is suffering from several neuroses.*

neurotic [-'ro-] **1** *nc, adj* (a person who is) suffering from a neurosis: *He has a neurotic personality*; *Her mother was in a mental hospital for some time – she is a neurotic.* **2** *adj* (*loosely*) in a nervous state: *She is a very neurotic woman*; *Their pet dog is neurotic*; *I hate working with him – he is so neurotic.*

neuter ['nju:tə] *adj* **1** (*gram*) in certain languages, of the gender which is neither masculine nor feminine: *a neuter noun.* **2** without sex: *Worker bees are neuter, being neither male nor female.* – *vt* to make (an animal) unable to bear or father young: *The cat has been neutered.*

neutral ['nju:trəl] *adj* **1** not taking sides in a quarrel or war: *Sweden was neutral in the Second World War*; *A neutral country was asked to help settle the dispute.* **2** (of colour) not strong or definite: *Grey is a neutral colour*; *I don't want bright red curtains – I want something more neutral.* **3** (*tech*) neither positively nor negatively charged. – **1** *nc* (*formal*) (a person belonging to) a nation that takes no part in a war or quarrel: *Neutrals were allowed to return to their own countries.* **2** *nu* the position of the gear of an engine in which no power passes (to the wheels *etc*): *I put the car into neutral.*

neu'trality [-'tra-] *nu* the state of being neutral: *Sweden has kept its neutrality for many years.*

'neutralize, -ise *vt* (*tech or formal*) to make useless or harmless *usu* by having an opposite effect.

neutron ['nju:tron] *nc* (*tech*) one of the particles (without electrical charge) which, with protons, make up the nucleus of an atom.

never ['nevə] *adv* (*sometimes in cmpds*) not ever; at no time: *I shall never go there again*; *I have never seen a house as beautiful as this*; (*formal*) *Never have I been so angry*; *The discussions were never-ending* (= very long); *his never-failing kindness.*

,never'more *adv* (*liter*) never again.

,neverthe'less [-ðə'les] *adv* (*formal*) in spite of that: *I am feeling ill, but I shall come with you nevertheless.*

never ever (*inf or liter*) an emphatic form of **never**: *I shall never ever speak to you again.*

See also **ever**.

new [nju:] *adj* **1** only just happened, built, made, bought *etc*: *She has a new hair style*; *She is wearing a new dress*; *We are building a new house*; *Is that dress new?* **2** (*esp attrib*) only just discovered, experienced *etc*: *a new country*; *The police have got some new information*: *Flying in an aeroplane was a new experience for her.* **3** (*attrib*) changed: *He is a new man*; *She is beginning a new life.* **4** just arrived *etc*: *a new student*; *The schoolchildren teased the new boy*; *Is your teacher new?* – *See also* **new to** *below.* – *adv* (*in cmpds*) freshly: *new-laid eggs.*

'newly *adv* only just (happened *etc*); recently: *She is newly married*; *Her hair is newly cut.*

'newcomer *nc* a person who has just arrived: *He is a newcomer to this district.*

,new'fangled [-'faŋgld] *adj* (*inf derog*) (of things, ideas *etc*) new but not very good: *He has too many newfangled ideas*; *This machine is too newfangled for that old man to operate.*

'new to having no previous experience of: *He's new to this kind of work.*

news [nju:z] **1** *nu* a report of, or information

about, recent events: *You can hear the news on the radio at 9 o'clock*; *Is there any news about your friend?*; (*attrib*) *a news broadcast.* **2** *n* (*with cap*) a word often used in the titles of newspapers: *the Rutherglen Evening News.*

'newsy *adj* (*inf*) full of news: *a newsy letter*; *Her letters are always so newsy.*

'newsagent *nc* (*Amer* **'news dealer**) **1** a person who has a shop selling newspapers (and *usu* other goods). **2** a newsagent's shop: *Is there a newsagent near here?*

'newsagent's *nc* (*Amer* **'news dealer's**) a newsagent's shop: *I got it at the newsagent's.*

'newscast *nc* (*formal*) a broadcast of news in a radio or television programme: *We listened to the newscast about the duke's death.*

'newscaster *nc* a person who presents a news broadcast.

'news dealer('s) *nc* (*Amer*) a newsagent('s).

'newsletter *nc* a sheet containing news issued to members of a group, organization *etc*: *We received last month's newsletter from the football association.*

'newspaper *nc* a paper, printed daily or weekly, containing news *etc*: *We buy two Sunday newspapers*; *Do you buy a daily newspaper?*

'newsprint *nu* the paper on which newspapers are printed: *There's a shortage of newsprint, so the papers have not been published today.*

newt [nju:t] *nc* a type of small animal which lives on land and in water.

New Zealand, New Zealander *see* Appendix 2.

next [nekst] *adj* nearest in place, time *etc*: *When you have called at one house, go on to the next one*; *I'd only just put the phone down when it rang again the next moment*; *The next person to arrive late will be sent away*; *Who is next on the list?* – *adv* immediately after in place or time: *John arrived first and Jane came next*; *Read this book next.* – *pron* the person or thing nearest in place, time *etc*: *Finish one question before you begin to answer the next*; *One minute he was sitting beside me – the next he was lying on the ground*; *The first five people arrived on time but the next were all late.*

next best, biggest, oldest *etc* the one immediately after the best, biggest, oldest *etc*: *I can't go to Paris so London is the next best place.*

next door *adv* in the next house: *I live next door* (*to Mrs Smith*).

next of kin (*formal or legal*) a person's closest relative(s): *Who is your next of kin?*; *He has no next of kin.*

'next to beside: *She sat next to me*; *He lives in the house next to mine.*

next to nothing *see* **nothing**.

nib [nib] *nc* (*also* **'pen-nib**) the pointed, metal part of a fountain-pen or other pen from which the ink flows: *This pen has a gold nib*; *Do you have any spare nibs?*

-nibbed (*in cmpds*) having a (certain kind of) nib: *a fine-nibbed pen.*

nibble ['nibl] *vti* (*sometimes with* **at**) to take very small bites (of): *She was nibbling (at) a biscuit.* – *nc* (*inf*) a small bite: *Have a nibble of this cake.*

nice [nais] *adj* **1** (*sometimes ironic*) pleasant; agreeable: *It's really nice weather*; *The old lady is such a nice person*; (*ironic*) *We're in a nice mess now*; *She seems very nice*; *Was the weather nice?* **2** (*formal*: *esp attrib*) exact; precise: *a nice sense of timing*; *That's a nice distinction.*

'nicely *adv* very well: *The weather has turned out nicely*; *This pair will suit me nicely, thanks.*

nicety ['naisəti] *nc* (*formal*) a precise or delicate detail: *the niceties of dealing with angry customers.*

to a 'nicety (*formal*) exactly: *He judged the distance to a nicety.*

niche [nitʃ, ni:ʃ] *nc* (*formal*) **1** a hollow in a wall for a statue, ornament *etc*: *She placed a bowl of roses in the niche beside the fireplace.* **2** a suitable place in life: *He found his niche in engineering.*

nick [nik] *nc* **1** (*inf*) a small cut: *There was a nick in the doorpost.* **2** (*Brit sl*) a prison or police-station: *Take him down to the nick.* – *vt* **1** (*inf*) to make a small cut in something: *He nicked his chin while he was shaving.* **2** (*Brit sl*) to arrest (a criminal): *The police nicked him for robbery.* **3** (*Brit sl*) to steal: *He nicked a bottle of whisky.*

in good/reasonable nick (*Brit sl*) in good (*esp* physical or working) condition: *He's in very good nick just now – he's been taking a lot of exercise*; *This car's in very good nick.*

in the nick of time at the last possible moment; just in time: *He arrived in the nick of time.*

nickel ['nikl] **1** *nu* an element (symbol **Ni**), a greyish-white metal used *esp* for mixing with other metals and for plating: *Nickel is sometimes added to steel to make it resistant to rust.* **2** *nc* (*Amer*) a five-cent coin.

nickname ['nikneim] *nc* an informal, unofficial name given in affection, admiration, dislike *etc*: *Wellington's nickname was 'the Iron Duke'*; *John Smith's nickname is 'Smithy'.* – *vt* to give a nickname to (someone or something): *We nicknamed him 'Foureyes' because he wore spectacles.*

nicotine ['nikəti:n] *nu* a harmful substance contained in tobacco: *Doctors believe that nicotine is dangerous to health*; *His fingers are stained with nicotine.*

niece *see* **nephew**.

nifty ['nifti] *adj* (*inf*) smart, clever, very good *etc*: *He's done some very nifty work on the car*; *He has a nifty turn of speed.*

Nigeria, Nigerian *see* Appendix 2.

niggardly ['nigədli] *adj* (*formal*) **1** not generous; unwilling to give or spend money: *a very niggardly person*; *He's niggardly with his money.* **2** of very small value or importance: *a niggardly gift.*

nigger ['nigə] *nc* (*offensive*) a Negro: (*attrib*) *a nigger minstrel*; (*attrib*) *nigger brown* (= (a) dark brown (colour)).

niggle ['nigl] *vi* (*sometimes with* **about**) to complain (about unimportant details): *She's always niggling.*

'niggling *adj* (*attrib*) **1** unimportant: *Don't bother with these niggling details.* **2** worrying or irritating: *She has niggling doubts about marrying him*; *a niggling fear.*

nigh [nai] *adv* (*arch*) near: *They came nigh.*

nigh on, well nigh (*old or dial*) nearly; almost: *It's nigh on ten o'clock*; *He is well nigh eighty years old.*

night [nait] **1** *nc* the period from sunset to sunrise: *We sleep at night*; *They talked all night (long)*; *He travelled by night and rested during the day*; *The days were warm and the nights were cool*; (*attrib*) *He is doing night work.* **2** *nu* the time of darkness: *In the Arctic in winter, night lasts for twenty-four hours out of twenty-four.*

'nightly *adj* (*attrib*), *adv* every night: *a nightly news programme*; *He goes there nightly.*

'nightcap *nc* **1** a cap worn in bed at night: *People rarely wear nightcaps nowadays.* **2** a drink (often

alcoholic taken just before going to bed at night: *Will you have a glass of whisky as a nightcap?*
'night-club *nc* a club open at night for drinking, dancing, entertainment *etc*: *They had dinner, and then went on to a night-club.*
'nightdress, 'nightgown *nc* a garment, *esp* for wearing in bed: *She wore a short, nylon nightdress.*
'nightfall *nu* (*liter*) the beginning of night; dusk: *They arrived at nightfall.*
'night life *nu* entertainment in the evenings and at night: *What is the night life like in this city?*
'night-light *nc* a lamp *etc* which gives a dim light, and is left on all night: *The child is scared of the dark – he has to have a night-light in his room.*
'nightmare *nc* a frightening dream: *I had a nightmare about being strangled*; *I had a nightmare about a plane crashing.* **'nightmarish** *adj.*
'night-school *nc* (*no pl*) a place where educational classes are held in the evenings for people who are at work during the day: *She goes to night-school to learn French.*
'night shift 1 *ncu* (a period of) work during the night: *He's on* (*the*) *night shift this week.* **2** *n pl* the people who work during this period: *We met the night shift leaving the factory.*
'night-time *nu* the time when it is night: *Owls are usually seen at night-time.*
ˌnight-'watchman *nc* a person who looks after a building *etc* during the night: *The thieves killed the night-watchman before stealing the gold.*
See also **nocturnal**.

nightingale ['naitiŋgeil, (*Amer*) -tən-] *nc* a type of small bird with a beautiful song.

nil [nil] *nu* (*esp Brit*: often used when stating the score in games) nothing; zero: *Leeds United won two-nil/2–0/by two goals to nil*; (*attrib*) *There was a nil response* (= no-one replied) *to our questionnaire.*

nimble ['nimbl] *adj* quick and light in movement: *a nimble jump*; *The young tennis player is very nimble*; (*fig*) *a nimble mind.* **'nimbly** *adv.*

nincompoop ['niŋkəmpu:p] *nc* (*old derog*) a foolish person: *He was a nincompoop to lend his friend money.*

nine [nain] **1** *nc* the number or figure 9. **2** *nu* the age of 9. – *adj* **1** (*usu attrib*) 9 in number. **2** (*pred*) aged 9. – *See* **eight** *for constructions.*
nine- (*in cmpds*) having nine (of something): *a ˌnine-page 'booklet.*
ninth 1 *nc* one of nine equal parts. **2** *nc, adj* the last of nine (people, things *etc*); (the) next after the eighth. – *See* **eighth** *under* **eight** *for constructions.*
'nine-year-old *nc* a person or animal that is nine years old. – *adj* (*attrib*) (of a person, animal or thing) that is nine years old. – *See* **eight-year-old** *under* **eight** *for constructions.*
See also Appendix 1.

ninepins ['nainpinz] *n sing* a game in which nine bottle-shaped objects are knocked over with a ball: *a game of ninepins*; *Ninepins is a very good game.*

nineteen [nain'ti:n] **1** *nc* the number or figure 19. **2** *nu* the age of 19. – *adj* **1** (*usu attrib*) 19 in number. **2** (*pred*) aged 19. – *See* **eighteen** *for constructions.*
nineteen- (*in cmpds*) having nineteen (of something): *a ˌnineteen-page 'document.*
ˌnine'teenth 1 *nc* one of nineteen equal parts. **2** *nc, adj* (the) last of nineteen (people, things *etc*); (the) next after the eighteenth. – *See* **eighteenth** *under* **eighteen** *for constructions.*
ˌnine'teen-year-old *nc* a person or animal that is nineteen years old. – *adj* (*attrib*) (of a person, animal or thing) that is nineteen years old. – *See* **eighteen-year-old** *under* **eighteen** *for constructions.*
(talk) nineteen to the dozen (*inf*) (to talk) continually or for a long time.
See also Appendix 1.

ninety ['nainti] **1** *nc* the number or figure 90. **2** *nu* the age of 90. – *adj* **1** (*usu attrib*) 90 in number. **2** (*pred*) aged 90. – *See* **eighty** *for constructions.*
'nineties *n pl* **1** the period of time between one's ninetieth and one hundredth birthdays. **2** the range of temperatures between ninety and one hundred degrees. **3** the period of time between the ninetieth and one hundredth years of a century. – *See* **eighties** *under* **eighty** *for constructions.*
'ninetieth 1 *nc* one of ninety equal parts. **2** *nc, adj* (the) last of ninety (people, things *etc*); (the) next after the eighty-ninth. – *See* **eightieth** *under* **eighty** *for constructions.*
ninety- (*in cmpds*) having ninety (of something): *a ˌninety-pound 'fine.*
'ninety-year-old *nc* a person or animal that is ninety years old. – *adj* (*attrib*) (of a person, animal or thing) that is ninety years old. – *See* **eighty-year-old** *under* **eighty** *for constructions.*
See also Appendix 1.

ninny ['nini] *nc* (*derog*) a foolish person: *Don't be such a ninny – that dog won't bite you.*

nip [nip] – *pt, ptp* **nipped** – **1** *vti* to press between the thumb and a finger, or between claws, causing pain: *He nipped her ear*; *He nipped her on the arm*; *A crab nipped her.* **2** *vti* (of a dog *etc*) to bite; to press painfully between the teeth: *The dog nipped her ankle.* **3** *vi* (of ointment *etc*) to be stingingly painful: *Iodine nips when it is put on a cut.* **4** *vi* (*inf*) (*with* **along, in, out, over** *etc*) to move quickly; to make a quick, *usu* short, journey: *Why don't you nip along the road to the shops for a paper?*; *I'll just nip into this shop for cigarettes*; *He nipped over to Paris for the week-end.* **5** *vt* to cut by pressing between the cutting edges of a small tool or the finger and thumb: *He nipped the wire with a pair of pliers*; *The little boy nipped off the heads of the flowers.* **6** *vt* (*formal*) to stop the growth of (plants *etc*): *The frost has nipped the roses.* – *nc* **1** the act of pressing painfully between the thumb and a finger or between claws: *He gave me a nip on the arm.* **2** (of a dog *etc*) a slight bite: *His dog gave her a nip on the ankle.* **3** (*inf*: *no pl*) a sharp coldness in the weather: *There's a nip in the air.* **4** (*inf*) a small drink, *esp* of spirits: *a nip of whisky.*
'nippy *adj* **1** (*Brit inf*: *usu pred*) very cold: *It's a bit nippy this morning.* **2** (*inf*) quick-moving; nimble: *She's nippy on her feet although she's eighty years old*; *a nippy little car.*
nip (something) in the bud to stop (something) as soon as it starts: *The managers nipped the strike in the bud.*

nipple ['nipl] *nc* **1** the darker, pointed part of a woman's breast from which a baby sucks milk. **2** (*Amer*) the rubber mouth-piece of a baby's feeding-bottle; a teat. **3** anything shaped like this, *esp* the parts of a machine through which oil or grease is passed: *greasing nipples.*

nippy *see* **nip**.

nisi *see* **decree nisi** *under* **decree**.

nit [nit] *nc* **1** the egg of a louse or other small insect (*eg* found in a person's hair): *There are nits in that* *child's hair.* 2 (*inf*: *esp Brit*) a stupid or foolish person: *Silly nit!*

'**nit-picking** *nu* (*inf*: *derog*) the act of finding unimportant faults in something: *His constant nit-picking irritates me.*

'**nitwit** *nc* (*inf*) a stupid or foolish person: *He is rather a nitwit.*

nitrate *see* **nitrogen**.

nitrogen ['naitrədʒən] *nu* an element (symbol **N**), a type of gas making up nearly four-fifths of the air we breathe.

'**nitrate** *ncu* (*tech*) any of several substances containing nitrogen, often used as soil fertilizers: *He put some potassium nitrate on the soil*; *Various nitrates are used as fertilizers.*

nitro-glycerine [naitrə'glisəri:n, (*Amer*) -rin] *nu* a powerful type of explosive.

nitwit *see* **nit**.

no [nou] *adj* (*attrib*) 1 not any: *We have no food*; *No two people ever agree about this*; *No other person could have done it.* 2 not allowed: *No smoking.* 3 (*formal*: *used for emphasis*) not a: *She is no beauty*; *He is no friend of mine*; *It's no easy thing to say this to you.* – *adv* not (any): *He is no better at golf than swimming*; *He went no further than the door*; *You can go as far as the shop and no further.* – *interj* a word used to show disagreement, a refusal, that something is not true *etc*: *'Do you like travelling?' 'No, (I don't).'*; *'Are you Scottish?' No, (I'm not,) I'm English.'*; *No, I don't agree*; *'Will you help me?' 'No, I won't.'* – *pl* **noes** – *nc* 1 a refusal: *She answered with a definite no.* 2 a vote against (something). –*See also* **the noes** *below*.

'**nobody** *pron* no person; no-one: *Nobody likes him*; *He is afraid of nobody* – *nc* (*derog*) a very unimportant person: *She's just a nobody.*

no-go *see* **go**.

'**no-one** *pron* no person; nobody: *No-one came*; *She will see no-one*; *No-one is to blame.*

the noes the people voting against (something): *The noes have it* (= The people voting 'no' have won).

no go *see* **go**.

there's no saying, knowing *etc* (*inf*) it is impossible to say, know *etc*: *There's no denying it*; *There's no knowing what she will say.*

See also **no-man's-land**.

nobility *see* **noble**.

noble ['noubl] *adj* (*formal*: *usu attrib*) 1 honourable; unselfish: *a noble mind*; *a noble deed.* 2 of high birth or rank: *a noble family*; *of noble birth.* – *nc* (*esp hist*) a person of high birth or rank: *The nobles planned to murder the king.*

no'bility [-'bi-] *nu* 1 (*formal*) the state of being noble: *the nobility of his mind/birth.* 2 nobles *ie* dukes, earls *etc*: *The nobility supported the king during the revolution.*

'**nobly** *adv* (*formal*): *He worked nobly for the cause of peace.*

'**nobleman** – *fem* '**noblewoman** – *nc* (*esp hist*) a noble: *The king was murdered by a nobleman at his court.*

See also **ignoble**.

nobody *see* **no**.

nocturnal [nok'tə:nl] *adj* 1 (*formal or tech*) active at night: *The owl is a nocturnal bird*; *The bat is nocturnal.* 2 (*formal or liter*: *attrib*) happening at night: *a nocturnal encounter.*

nocturne ['noktə:n] *nc* (*tech*) a piece of music or a painting describing, or giving an impression of, night-time: *Chopin composed several nocturnes.*

nod [nod] – *pt, ptp* '**nodded** – 1 *vti* to make a quick forward and downward movement of the head to show agreement, as a greeting *etc*: *I asked him if he agreed and he nodded (his head)*; *He nodded to the man as he passed him in the street*; *I asked if he would help and he nodded.* 2 *vi* to let the head fall forward and downward when sleepy: *Grandmother sat nodding by the fire.* – *See also* **nod off** *below*. 3 *vt* to show by nodding: *He nodded his agreement.* – *nc* a nodding movement of the head: *He gave the woman a nod as he passed her in the street*; *He answered with a nod.*

have a nodding acquaintance (with someone) to know (someone) slightly: *I only have a nodding acquaintance with some of the staff here*; (*fig*) *I have a nodding acquaintance with Greek literature*; *He and I have a nodding acquaintance.*

nod off *vi* (*inf*) to fall asleep: *He nodded off while she was speaking to him.*

Noel, Nowell, Noël [nou'el] *n* (*old or liter*) Christmas.

noes *see* **no**.

noise [noiz] 1 *nc* a sound: *I heard a strange noise outside*; *the noise of gunfire.* 2 *ncu* an unpleasantly loud sound: *I hate noise*; *Somebody is making a noise.*

'**noiseless** *adj* (*formal*: *usu attrib*) without any sound: *noiseless footsteps.* '**noiselessly** *adv*.

'**noisy** *adj* making a (loud) noise: *noisy children*; *a noisy engine*: *That music is so noisy.* '**noisily** *adv*.

noise abroad *vt sep* (*very formal or old*) to be made generally known *esp* by rumour: *It was noised abroad that there would be an election soon.*

nomad ['noumad] *nc* one of a group of people with no permanent home who travel about with their sheep, cattle *etc*: *Many of the people of central Asia are nomads*; (*fig*) *He doesn't like living in one place for long – he's a bit of a nomad.*

no'madic *adj* living as nomads: *nomadic tribes*; *In former times many people living in the desert were nomadic.* **no'madically** *adv*.

no-man's-land ['noumanzland] *nu* land which no-one owns or controls, *esp* between opposing armies: *It was extremely dangerous to go into no-man's-land*; *He was killed while trying to drag a wounded soldier back from no-man's-land to the British trenches.*

nom-de-plume [nomdə'plu:m] – *pl* **noms-de-'plume** [nom-] – *nc* (*formal*) a name used by a writer who does not wish to use his own name: *'Currer Bell' was Charlotte Brontë's nom-de-plume.*

nomenclature [nə'menklətʃə] (*very formal*) 1 *ncu* a system, *esp* a scientific one, of naming things: *according to zoological nomenclature.* 2 *nu* the names themselves: *The flowers have all been given their botanical nomenclature in this list.*

nominal ['nominl] *adj* 1 in name only; not actually: *He was the nominal head of the organization, but his brother did all the work*; *His position as head of the firm is purely nominal.* 2 very small; unimportant: *He had to pay a nominal amount of money*; *The salary we pay him is purely nominal.* 3 (*gram*: *attrib*) of nouns: *nominal compounds.*

'**nominally** *adv*: *He is nominally in charge of the firm but actually he has no power at all.*

nominate ['nomineit] *vt* 1 (*usu with* **for**) to name (someone) for possible election to a particular job *etc*: *They nominated four people for president*; *They nominated him as captain.* 2 (*usu with* **to**) to appoint (someone) to a post or job: *He was* *nominated to the presidency.*

ˌ**nomiˈnation 1** *nu* the act of nominating: *We must discuss the nomination of a president.* **2** *nc* the act of nominating a particular person or the person nominated: *They asked for nominations for the post of secretary; We've had four nominations for the job.*

ˌ**nomiˈnee** *nc* (*formal*) a person who is nominated for a job *etc.*

nominative [ˈnominətiv] (*gram*) **1** *nu, adj* (of) the case showing the subject of a verb in certain languages *eg* Latin: *The Latin word 'mensa' is in the nominative (case).* **2** *nc* a word in the nominative case.

non- [non] (*in cmpds*) (used with many words to change their meanings to the opposite) not, as in **non-commissioned, nonconformist**.

nonagenarian [nonədʒiˈneəriən] *nc* (*formal*) a person who is between ninety and ninety-nine years old: *My grandfather is a nonagenarian.*

non-alcoholic [ˈnonalkəˈholik] *adj* (of a drink) not containing any alcohol: *Is this non-alcoholic?; a non-alcoholic drink.*

non-aligned [nonəˈlaind] *adj* (*formal*) not attached to either of the two main groups in world politics, *usu* thought of as being headed by the USA and the USSR respectively: *There are still some non-aligned nations in the world.*

ˌ**non-aˈlignment** *nu* (*formal*) the state of being non-aligned: *Our government follows a policy of non-alignment.*

nonchalant [ˈnonʃələnt, (*Amer*) nonʃəˈlont] *adj* (*formal*) not having or showing much interest or enthusiasm: *He's always so nonchalant, it's difficult to know what he likes or doesn't like; nonchalant behaviour.* ˈ**nonchalantly** *adv.* ˈ**nonchalance** *nu.*

non-commissioned [nonkəˈmiʃənd] *adj* (*mil*) not holding a commission (*ie* in the army, below the rank of second lieutenant): *Corporals and sergeants are non-commissioned officers.*

non-committal [nonkəˈmitl] *adj* (*formal*) not expressing, or not willing to express, an opinion: *a non-committal reply; You're being very non-committal about it.*

nonconformist [nonkənˈfoːmist] *nc, adj* (a person) that does not agree with those in authority, *esp* in religious matters: *In the nineteenth century, nonconformists built their own churches; nonconformist beliefs.*

nondescript [ˈnondiskript] *adj* (*formal*) having no noticeable, interesting or memorable characteristics: *a nondescript appearance; I can hardly remember him – he was quite nondescript.*

none [nʌn] *pron* not one; not any: *'How many tickets have you got?' 'None'; He asked me for some food but there was none in the house; None of us have/has seen him.* – *adv* not at all: *He is none the worse for his accident.*

ˈ**none but** (*formal*) only: *None but the brave deserve our respect.*

ˈ**none of (something)** an expression used to tell a person not to do something or to stop doing something (*usu* something bad): (*I'll have*) *none of your impertinence* (= Don't be impertinent); *None of that!* (= Stop doing that.)

none other (than) *see* **other**.

ˌ**nonetheˈless, none the less** nevertheless; in spite of this: *He hadn't bought a ticket – nonetheless he wanted to come with us.*

none the wiser *see* **wise**.

nonentity [nonˈentəti] *nc* (*formal*) a person of no importance: *I do not know why he married her – she is an absolute nonentity.*

nonetheless *see* **none**.

non-event [noniˈvent] *nc* something that was planned to be an important event, but loses importance, interest *etc* when it happens: *The celebrations were quite a non-event – only eight people came.*

non-existent [nonigˈzistənt] *adj* (*formal*) not existing; not real: *He is afraid of some non-existent monster; He thinks he has problems but they are non-existent compared to mine.* ˌ**non-exˈistence** *nu.*

non-fiction [nonˈfikʃən] *nu* books, magazines *etc* that deal with facts, information *etc, ie* not stories, novels, plays, poetry: *I read a lot of non-fiction.*

non-flammable [nonˈflaməbl] *adj* (*formal*) non-inflammable: *Children should wear non-flammable nightdresses; Babies' clothes should be non-flammable.*

non-inflammable [noninˈflaməbl] *adj* (*formal*) not able to burn or be set alight: *This dress is made of non-inflammable material; Asbestos is non-inflammable.*

non-intervention [nonintəˈvenʃən] *nu* (*formal*) the state of not taking part in, or interfering with, the affairs of another country: *Our government follows a policy of non-intervention.*

non-payment [nonˈpeimənt] *nu* (*formal*) the act or state of not paying (bills, debts *etc*): *Non-payment of bills may result in repossession of goods* (= the taking back of goods by the shop that sold them).

nonplussed [nonˈplʌst] *adj* (*pred*) completely puzzled; bewildered: *He was nonplussed by her strange behaviour.*

ˌ**nonˈplus** – *pt, ptp* ˌ**nonˈplussed** – *vt* to puzzle or confuse (someone): *Her behaviour completely nonplussed me.*

non-resident [nonˈrezidənt] *adj* not living in (a school *etc*): *We have several non-resident members of staff.*

nonsense [ˈnonsəns, (*Amer*) -sens] *ncu* (*no pl*) foolishness; foolish words, actions *etc*; something that is ridiculous: *He's talking nonsense; I think the whole thing is a lot of nonsense; It is nonsense to say that; What a nonsense!*

ˌ**nonˈsensical** [-ˈsen-] *adj*: *It is nonsensical to behave like that; nonsensical behaviour.*

non sequitur [nonˈsekwitə] *nc* (*formal*) (in an argument, discussion *etc*) something that does not follow logically what has just been said: *You cannot discuss anything with her, she is always making non sequiturs; Her arguments are full of non sequiturs.*

non-starter [nonˈstaːtə] *nc* (*inf*) a person, thing, idea *etc* that has no chance of success: *This whole project is a non-starter.*

non-stick [nonˈstik] *adj* (of a pan *etc*) treated, *usu* by covering with a special substance, so that food *etc* will not stick to it: *a non-stick frying-pan; Is this frying-pan non-stick?*

non-stop [nonˈstop] *adj* continuing without a stop: *non-stop entertainment; This is a non-stop train; Is this train non-stop?*

non-violence [nonˈvaiələns] *nu* the refusal to use any violent means in order to gain political, social *etc* aims: *They followed a policy of non-violence.* ˌ**non-ˈviolent** *adj.*

noodle [ˈnuːdl] *nc* a strip of paste *usu* made with water, flour and egg: *chicken soup with noodles;* (*attrib*) *chicken noodle soup.*

nook [nuk] *nc* **1** (*rare*) a small area in a room

formed by the angle of walls *etc*: *She kept the brushes in a nook in the kitchen.* 2 (*liter*) a shaded, quiet place *eg* in a wood.

every nook and cranny (*inf*) everywhere: *They searched in every nook and cranny* (*of the house*).

noon [nu:n] *nu* twelve o'clock midday: *They arrived at noon.*

noose [nu:s] *nc* 1 a loop in rope, wire *etc* that becomes tighter when pulled. 2 such a loop in a rope used for hanging a person: *The hangman tightened the noose round the murderer's neck.*

nor [no:] *conj* (with the subject following the verb: used after a negative statement) and not: *He did not know then what had happened, nor did he ever find out* (= and he never found out); *I'm not going, nor is John* (= and John isn't going either); *I have never done that, nor do I intend to start now.*

neither . . . nor *see* **neither**.

norm [no:m] *nc* (*formal*) an expected or normal pattern or standard to judge other things by: *A person ought to conform to the norms of behaviour*; *This boy's reading ability is below the norm for children of his age.*

normal ['no:məl] *adj* usual; without any special characteristics or circumstances: *How much work do you do on a normal day?*; *normal people*; *His behaviour is far from normal.*

nor'mality [-'ma-] *nu* (*formal*).

'normally *adv* 1 in a usual, ordinary way: *He was behaving quite normally yesterday.* 2 usually; most often: *I normally go home at 4 o'clock.*

See also **abnormal**.

north [no:θ] *nu* 1 the direction to the left of a person facing the rising sun, or any part of the earth lying in that direction: *He faced towards the north*; *The wind is blowing from the north*; *They live to the north of* (= further north than) *Lyons*; *I used to live in the north of Scotland.* 2 (*often with cap*: *also* **N**) one of the four main points of the compass: *Steer 3° E of N* (= three degrees east of north). – *See also* **the North** *below.* – *adj* (*attrib*) 1 in the north: *on the north bank of the river* (= on the side nearest the north). 2 from the direction of the north: *a north wind.* – *adv* towards the north: *The stream flows north.*

'northerly [-ðə-] *adj* (*usu attrib*) 1 (of a wind *etc*) coming from the north: *a northerly breeze.* 2 looking, lying *etc* towards the north: *in a northerly direction.*

'northern [-ðən] *adj* of the north or the North: *His way of speaking is northern English*; *Her accent is northern.*

'northerner [-ðə-] *nc* a person who lives, or was born, in a northern region or country.

'northernmost [-ðən-] *adj* being furthest north: *the northernmost border of the country*; *the northernmost of the cliffs.*

'northward *adj* (*usu attrib*) towards the north: *in a northward direction.*

'northward(s) *adv* towards the north: *They were travelling northwards.*

'northbound *adj* (*usu attrib*) travelling northwards: *the northbound railway-line.*

ˌnorth-'east/ˌnorth-'west *nus* the direction midway between north and east or north and west, or any part of the earth lying in that direction. – *adjs* (*attrib*) 1 in the north-east or north-west: *the north-east counties.* 2 from the direction of the north-east or north-west: *a north-east wind.* – *advs* towards the north-east or north-west: *The building faces north-west.*

ˌnorth-'easterly/ˌnorth-'westerly *adjs* (*usu attrib*) 1 (of a wind *etc*) coming from the north-east or north-west: *a north-easterly wind.* 2 looking, lying *etc* towards the north-east or north-west: *a north-westerly direction.*

ˌnorth-'eastern/ˌnorth-'western *adjs* of the north-east or north-west: *a north-western accent*; *Is your accent north-eastern?*

the North (in Britain) the northern part of England, and sometimes including Scotland also.

the Northern Lights *see* **aurora**.

the North Pole the northern end of the imaginary line through the earth, round which it turns.

Norway, Norwegian *see* Appendix 2.

nose [nouz] *nc* 1 the part of the face by which people and animals smell and *usu* breathe: *She held the flower to her nose*; *He punched the man on the nose.* 2 the sense of smell: *Police dogs have good noses and can follow criminals' trails*; (*fig inf*) *The newspaper reporter had a good nose for a news story.* 3 the part of anything which is like a nose in shape or position: *the nose of an aeroplane.* – 1 *vti* to make a way by pushing carefully forward: *The ship nosed* (*its way*) *through the ice.* 2 *vti* (*inf*: *with* **around** *or* **about**) to look or search around (in something) as if by smelling: *He nosed about* (*in*) *the cupboard.*

-nosed (*in cmpds*) having a (particular type of) nose: *a long-nosed dog.*

'nos(e)y *adj* (*derog inf*) taking too much interest in other people and what they are doing: *She is a very nos(e)y person*; *I would not employ her – she's too nosey.* **'nosily** *adv.* **'nosiness** *nu.*

'nose-bag *nc* a food-bag for horses, hung over the head: *The horse ate oats hungrily from its nose-bag.*

'nosedive *nc* a dive or fall with the head or nose first: *The aeroplane did a nosedive into the sea.* – *vi* to make such a dive: *Suddenly the plane nosedived.*

blow one's nose *see* **blow**.

follow one's nose (*inf*) to go straight forward: *When you get to the corner just follow your nose.*

keep (a person's) nose to the grindstone *see* **grindstone**.

lead (someone) by the nose to make (a person) do whatever one wants: *She leads her husband by the nose.*

look down one's nose (at someone) *see* **look**.

nose out *vt sep* (*inf*) to find (something) by smelling: *The dog nosed out its master's glove*; (*fig*) *The detective nosed out a plot to rob the bank*; *They nosed it out quickly.*

pay through the nose (*sl*) to pay a lot for something: *If you want a really good car you have to pay through the nose for it.*

poke one's nose in *see* **poke**.

turn up one's nose (at) to treat with contempt: *They turned their noses up at their poor relations*; *The child turned up his nose at the school dinner.*

under (a person's) (very) nose 1 right in front of (a person); clearly to be seen: *The book I was looking for was right under my very nose.* 2 while (a person) is there: *He stole my jewels from under my very nose.*

See also **nasal**.

nosegay ['nouzgei] *nc* (*old*) a bunch of sweet-smelling flowers: *She wore a white dress and carried a nosegay.*

nosh [noʃ] *nu* (*sl*: *esp Brit*) food.

nostalgia [no'staldʒə] *nu* (*formal*) a longing for past times: *She felt a great nostalgia for her childhood.* **no'stalgic** *adj.* **no'stalgically** *adv.*

nostril ['nostril] *nc* one of the two openings in the nose through which one breathes, smells *etc.*

not [not] *adv* **1** (not used after a verb except old or liter: often abbrev **n't** after aux, modal aux and parts of the verbs **have** and **be**) a word used to state that something is wrong, a lie *etc,* to forbid someone to do something, to express the opposite of something or to express a refusal: *I did not see him; I didn't see him; He isn't here; Isn't he coming?; They told me not to go; Not a single person came to the party; We're going to Glasgow, not Edinburgh; That's not true!; I didn't think he would come* (= I thought he wouldn't come). **2** (*with certain verbs such as* **hope, seem, believe, expect** *and also with* **be afraid**) used to replace a clause containing **not**: *'Have you got much money?' 'I'm afraid not'* (= I'm afraid I haven't); *'Is he going to fail his exam?' 'I hope not'* (= I hope he isn't going to).

ˌ**not at 'all** it does not matter; it is not important *etc*: *'Thank you for helping me.' 'Not at all.'* – *See also* **at all** *under* **all**.

'**not that** (although) it is not the case that: *If you don't pay us, we could take you to court – not that we would do such a thing, of course.*

notable *etc see* **note**.

notary (public) ['noutəri] – *pl* '**notaries ('public)** – *nc* a person who makes sure that official documents are correctly written.

notation [nə'teiʃən] *ncu* (*formal*) (the use of) a system of signs representing numbers, musical sounds *etc*: *musical/mathematical notation*: (*attrib*) *a notation system.*

notch [notʃ] *nc* a small V-shaped cut: *He cut a notch in his walking-stick.* – *vt* to make a notch in (something).

notch up *vt sep* (*inf*) to achieve or score (something): *He has notched up more goals than anyone else this season; He notched them up in four matches.*

note [nout] *nc* **1** a piece of writing to call attention to something: *He left me a note about the meeting; He made a note in the margin of the book.* **2** (*usu in pl*) ideas for a speech, details from a lecture *etc* written down in short form: *He made notes for his speech on a piece of paper; The students took notes on the professor's lecture.* **3** a written or mental record (of something): *We'll make a note of your suggestions; Have you kept a note of which books have been stolen?* **4** a short explanation: *There is a note in your book about that difficult word.* – *See also* **footnote**. **5** a short letter: *She wrote a note to her friend.* **6** (*Amer* **bill**) a piece of paper used as money; a bank-note: *a five-pound note; a thousand-lire note; I don't have any change – I have only notes.* **7** a musical sound: *The song ended on a high note.* **8** a written or printed symbol representing a musical note. **9** (*no pl*) a sign or state (of something): *There was a note of hysteria in her voice; The conference ended on a note of hope and confidence.* – *vt* **1** (*often with* **down**) to write down: *He noted her telephone number in his diary; He noted down what she said.* **2** (*more formal than* **notice**) to notice; to be aware of: *He noted a change in her behaviour.*

'**notable** *adj* (*formal*) worth taking notice of; important: *There is a notable book on that subject by Professor Brown; There were several notable people at the meeting; He is notable for his work on hormones.* – *nc* (*formal or facet*) an important person: *The Prime Minister and other notables were there.* ˌ**nota'bility** *nu.*

'**notably** *adv* **1** in particular: *Several people arrived late, notably Mrs Brown.* **2** in a notable or noticeable way: *Her behaviour was notably different from usual.*

'**noted** *adj* (*formal*: *with* **as** *or* **for** *when pred*) well-known: *a noted author; This town is noted for its cathedral; He is noted as an expert on flies.*

'**notelet** [-lit] *nc* a small piece of notepaper, often folded like a card and with a picture on it, used for short letters: *She sent me a notelet thanking me for the birthday present.*

'**notebook** *nc* a small book in which to write notes: *The policeman wrote their names and addresses in his notebook.*

'**notecase** *nc* a case for bank-notes, carried in the pocket.

'**notepaper** *nu* paper for writing letters: *I have plenty of notepaper but no envelopes.*

'**noteworthy** *adj* (*usu pred*) worthy of notice; remarkable: *Nothing particularly noteworthy happened.* '**noteworthiness** *nu.*

of 'note (*formal*) famous, distinguished or important: *No-one of note was there.*

strike the right note (*inf*) to say, do *etc* (something suitable or pleasing to someone): *The Prime Minister's speech struck just the right note.*

take note of (*formal*) to notice and remember: *He took note of the change in her appearance.*

nothing ['nʌθiŋ] *pron* no thing; not anything: *There was nothing in the cupboard; I have nothing to say; He says nothing new in that report.* – **1** *nc* the number 0; nought: *I don't remember his telephone number, but it did have three nothings in it.* **2** *nu* used in measurements to show that *usu* a person is an exact number of feet *etc* in height: *She is four foot nothing.* – *adv* not at all: *He's nothing like his father.*

'**nothingness** *nu* (*formal*) the state of being nothing or of not existing; emptiness: *When a person dies, does he just become nothingness?; All her dreams melted into nothingness.*

be nothing to *see* **mean nothing to** *below.*

be 'nothing (compared) to to be much less than: *Your problems are nothing (compared) to mine.*

be/have nothing to do with to be something which a person should not be interested in: *That letter is/has nothing to do with you.*

come to nothing to fail: *His plans came to nothing.*

for 'nothing 1 free; without payment: *I'll do that for you for nothing; We bought these six chairs, and they gave us the other one for nothing.* **2** (*usu with* **all**) without result; in vain: *I've been working on this book for six years, and all for nothing!*

go for nothing (*usu as ptp*) to have no result; to be wasted: *All his notes were destroyed in the fire – three years of research gone for nothing.* – *See also* **go for little/nothing** *under* **go**.

have nothing to do with to avoid completely: *I will have nothing to do with anything illegal; After he came out of prison, many of his former friends would have nothing to do with him.*

like nothing on earth (*inf*) rather ill, ugly, untidy *etc*: *You look like nothing on earth this morning – are you ill?; You look like nothing on earth in that dress; If I drink too much wine, I feel like nothing on earth the next morning.*

make nothing of (*formal*) not to understand: *I*

can make nothing of this letter.
mean/be nothing to to be a person, thing *etc* which someone is not interested in: *She means nothing to me now, although I used to be very fond of her.*
mean nothing to not to be (able to be) understood (by someone): *These mathematical formulae mean nothing to me.*
next to nothing (*inf*) almost nothing: *We had a lot of cakes to sell when the sale began, but there's next to nothing left now.*
'nothing but just; only: *The fellow's nothing but a fool!; He drinks nothing but the best wines*; (*inf*) *'Does he drink whisky?' ',Nothing 'but!'*
nothing doing! (*inf*) an expression used to show a strong or emphatic refusal: *'Would you like to go to the meeting instead of me?' 'Nothing doing!'*
nothing if not an expression used to emphasize something: *His life has been nothing if not exciting* (= His life has really been exciting).
there is *etc* **,nothing 'for it but (to do something)** the only possible thing to do is, was *etc* (something): *When the boat hit a rock and sank, there was nothing for it but to swim for the shore.*
there is *etc* **nothing to choose between** *see* **choose**.
there is *etc* **,nothing 'to it** (*inf*) it is *etc* easy: *You'll soon see how to do this job – there's nothing to it!*
think nothing of not to consider it difficult, unusual *etc* (to do something): *My father thought nothing of walking five miles to school every day when he was a boy.*
'think ,nothing 'of it it doesn't matter; it is not important: *'Thank you so much for your help.' 'Think nothing of it!'; 'I'm sorry my dog tore your trousers.' 'Oh, think nothing of it.'*
to say 'nothing of as well as; and in addition: *When her mother comes to stay with us, she brings all her jewellery with her, to say nothing of her three fur coats.*

notice ['noutis] **1** *nc* a written or printed statement to announce something publicly: *He stuck a notice on the door, saying that he had gone home; They put a notice in the paper announcing the birth of their daughter.* **2** *nu* attention: *His skill attracted their notice; I'll bring that to his notice as soon as possible; It has come to our notice that certain members of staff are not happy.* **3** *nu* warning given *esp* before leaving a job or dismissing someone: *Her employer gave her a month's notice; The cook gave in her notice.* – *See also* **notice** *in phrases below.* – *vti* to see, observe, or keep in one's mind: *I noticed a book on the table; He noticed her leave the room; He noticed that you weren't there; Did he say that? I didn't notice.*
'noticeable *adj* (*usu formal when attrib*) (likely to be) easily noticed: *There's no noticeable difference between these two dresses; There's a slight stain on this dress but it's not really noticeable.*
'noticeably *adv*: *This ball of wool is noticeably darker than these others.*
'noticed *adj* (*neg* **un-**).
'notice-board (*Amer* **'bulletin board**) *nc* a *usu* large board (*def 2*) *eg* in a hall, school *etc* on which notices are put: *There is a list of football matches pinned to the notice-board.*
at short notice without much warning time for preparation *etc*: *He had to make the speech at very short notice when his boss suddenly fell ill.*
give notice of (*formal*) to warn about something: *She gave notice of her intention to leave the country.*
take notice (of) (*often in neg*) to pay attention to a person's warnings, unpleasant remarks *etc*: *He never takes any notice of what his father says; Take no notice of what people say about you – they don't understand why you did what you did.*

notify ['noutifai] *vt* (*formal*: *often with* **of**) to inform or warn about something: *He notified the teacher that he was going away; He notified her of his intentions; The theft was notified to the police.*
'notifiable *adj* (*esp Brit*: *formal or tech*: *esp attrib*) (of certain diseases) that must be reported to public health authorities: *Typhoid is a notifiable disease.*
,notifi'cation [-fi-] *ncu* (*formal*) information; warning: *We have received notification of their departure.*

notion ['nouʃən] **1** *nu* understanding: *I've no notion what he's talking about.* **2** *nc* an uncertain belief; an idea: *He had a notion that she wouldn't like it; He has some very odd notions.* **3** *nc* (*often with* **for**) a desire for something or to do something: *He took a sudden notion to visit his aunt; When my wife was pregnant, she had a notion for coal – she used to eat large lumps of it.*

notorious [nə'to:riəs] *adj* (*formal*: *with* **as** *or* **for** *when pred*) well-known for badness or wickedness: *a notorious thief; He was notorious for his evil deeds; He was notorious as a murderer.* **notoriety** [noutə'raiəti] *nu.*
no'toriously *adv* (*formal*) in a way or to an extent that is very well-known: *It is notoriously difficult to find a needle in a haystack.*

notwithstanding [notwið'standiŋ] *prep* (*formal*) in spite of: *Notwithstanding the bad weather* (= although the weather was bad), *the ship arrived on schedule.* – *adv* (*formal*) nevertheless; in spite of this/that: *Notwithstanding, they finished the work.*

nougat ['nʌgət] *nu* a sticky kind of sweet containing nuts *etc.*

nought [no:t] **1** *nu* naught; nothing. **2** *nc* (*math*) the figure 0: *The number contained five noughts.*
noughts and crosses a game in which the players try to make a line of three noughts or crosses between vertical and horizontal lines: *We usually play noughts and crosses on the train.*

noun [naun] *nc* (*gram*) a word used as the name of a person, animal, place, state or thing: *The words 'boy', 'James' and 'happiness' are all nouns.*
See also **nominal**.

nourish ['nʌriʃ, (*Amer*) 'nə:-] *vt* **1** (*formal*: *esp fig*) to cause or help (someone or something) to grow, *usu* by feeding: *Good food nourishes people*; (*fig*) *to nourish feelings of anger and envy.* **2** to make (land, soil *etc*) rich and good for growing things in: *Fertilizer nourishes the earth.*
'nourishing *adj* giving the body what is necessary for health and growth: *nourishing food; Milk is nourishing.*
'nourishment *nu* something that nourishes; food: *Plants draw nourishment from the earth; Young babies get nourishment from their mothers' milk.*
See also **nutritious, undernourished**.

novel[1] ['novəl] *nc* a book telling a long story in prose: *the novels of Charles Dickens.*
'novelist *nc* the writer of a novel: *Dickens was a great novelist.*
novella [nə'velə] *nc* (*formal or tech*) a short story or short novel.

novel[2] ['novəl] *adj* new and strange: *What a novel idea!*; *Snow is novel to people from hot countries.*

'novelty 1 *nu* newness and strangeness: *It took her a long time to get used to the novelty of her surroundings.* **2** *nc* (*no pl*) something new and strange: *It was a novelty to work in the theatre.* **3** *nc* a small, cheap manufactured thing sold as a toy or souvenir: *Most stations have a shop nearby that sells novelties.*

novella *see* **novel**[1].

November [nə'vembə] *n* the eleventh month of the year, the month following October: *My birthday is in November*; *He is coming on November 23* (said as 'on November (the) twenty-third' or 'on the twenty-third of November'); *He is coming on the 23rd/twenty-third of November*; *He died last November.*

novice ['novis] *nc* **1** a beginner: *He can't ski very well yet – he's only a novice.* **2** a monk or nun who has not yet taken all his or her vows.

now [nau] *adv* **1** (at) the present period of time: *I am living in England now*; *Now would be a good time to go to France.* **2** at once; immediately: *I can't do it now – you'll have to wait.* **3** (at) this moment: *No doubt he'll be at home now*; *Now is the time to ask him for more money*; *He ought to have reached Glasgow by now*; *From now on, I shall be more careful about what I say to her.* **4** (in stories) then; at that time: *We were now very close to the city.* **5** because of what has happened *etc*: *She lied to me once – now I could never trust her again.* **6** a word used in explanations, warnings, commands, or to show disbelief: *Now this is what happened*; *Now this is what I think we should do*; *Stop that, now!*; *Do be careful, now – the pavement is covered in ice*; *You don't mean that, now, do you?* – *conj* (*often with* **that**) because or since something has happened, is now true *etc*: *Now that you are here, I can leave*; *Now you have left university, you will have to find a job.*

'nowadays *adv* at the present period of time: *Food is very expensive nowadays.*

,as of 'now from this time on: *These new rules apply as of now.*

for 'now until a later time: *That will be enough for now – we'll continue our conversation tomorrow.*

just 'now a moment ago: *I saw him just now in the street.*

(every) now and then/again sometimes; occasionally: *We go to the theatre every now and then*; *I see him at the club now and again.*

now ... now/then (*formal*) at one time ... at another time: *Now we could see him, now/then he disappeared behind a tree.*

now, now! an expression used when warning or telling someone, *esp* a child, not to do something or to stop doing something: *Now, now! That's not a nice thing to say to your brother.*

'now then an expression used to attract attention, when warning or telling someone not to do something, to comfort someone *etc*: *'Now then,' said the policeman, 'what's going on here?'*; *Now then, that's not a very nice thing to say*; *Now then, don't worry about it.*

Nowell *see* **Noel**.

nowhere ['nouweə] *adv* in or to no place; not anywhere: *It was nowhere to be found*; (*liter*) *Nowhere could I see him*; *'Where have you been?' 'Nowhere in particular.'*

get nowhere *see* **get**.

nowhere near (*inf*) not nearly: *We've nowhere near enough money to buy a car.*

noxious ['nokʃəs] *adj* (*formal*) harmful; poisonous: *noxious fumes*; *That chemical is noxious.*

nozzle ['nozl] *nc* a narrow end-piece fitted to a pipe, tube *etc*: *The fireman pointed the nozzle of the hose-pipe at the fire.*

-n't *see* **not**.

nuance ['nju:ãs, (*Amer*) -a:ns] *nc* (*formal*) a slight difference in meaning, opinion, colour *etc*: *These words are not exactly the same although the nuance in meaning is slight*; *Even a colour like white can have a number of nuances.*

nucleus ['nju:kliəs] – *pl* **'nuclei** [-kliai] – *nc* **1** (*tech*) the central part of an atom: *The nucleus of an atom consists of neutrons, protons and other particles.* **2** (*formal*) the central part around which something grows: *The encyclopaedia formed the nucleus of his collection of books.* **3** (*tech*) the part of a plant or animal cell that controls its development.

nuclear ['nju:kliə] *adj* **1** (*usu attrib*) using atomic or nuclear energy: *a nuclear power station.* **2** (*formal*) of a nucleus.

nuclear disarmament *nu* the act of ceasing to use atomic weapons.

nuclear energy *nu* atomic energy.

nuclear fission *see* **fission**.

nuclear reactor *nc* an apparatus for producing nuclear energy.

nude [nju:d] *adj* without clothes: *a picture of a nude woman*; *Artists' models sometimes have to pose nude.* – *nc* **1** an unclothed human figure: *There was a photograph of a nude on the cover of the magazine.* **2** a picture or statue of an unclothed human figure: *The gallery has several of Michelangelo's nudes.*

'nudism *nu* the practice of not wearing clothes *usu* because it is thought to be healthy.

'nudist *nc* a person who believes in or practises nudism: *There's a beach near here reserved for nudists*; (*attrib*) *a nudist camp.*

'nudity *nu* the state of not wearing clothes: *There is nothing shameful about nudity.*

in the 'nude without clothes: *She always sunbathes in the nude.*

nudge [nʌdʒ] *nc* (*slightly inf*) a gentle push *usu* with the elbow: *He gave her a nudge.* – *vt* (*slightly inf*) to hit (someone) gently, *usu* with the elbow: *She nudged him in the ribs.*

nudism *etc see* **nude**.

nugget ['nʌgit] *nc* a lump, *esp* of gold: *a gold nugget.*

nuisance ['nju:sns] *nc* a person or thing that is annoying or troublesome: *The child is a terrible nuisance*; *It's a nuisance to have to go out in bad weather*; *He's always making a nuisance of himself* (= being a nuisance).

null *see* **void**.

numb [nʌm] *adj* not able to feel or move: *My arm has gone numb*; *She was numb with cold*; *numb fingers.* – *vt* to make numb: *The cold numbed her fingers*; (*fig formal*) *She was numbed by his death.* **'numbly** *adv.* **'numbness** *nu.*

number ['nʌmbə] **1** *nc* (*sometimes abbrev* **no** – *pl* **nos** – *when written in front of a figure*) a word or figure showing *eg* how many of something there is, or the position of something in a series, row *etc*: *Seven was often considered a magic number*; *There are thirty houses in our street*; *Their house is number four*; *Answer nos 1–10 of exercise 2.* **2** *nc* a (large) quantity or group (of people or things): *He has a number of records*; *There was/were a* *large number of people in the room.* **3** *nc* one issue of a (*usu* monthly) magazine: *the autumn number*; *last month's number.* **4** *nc* (*inf*) a popular song or piece of music: *Give us another number on the piano!* **5** *nu* (*gram*) in words, the property of expressing singular, plural *etc*. – *vt* **1** to put a number on: *He numbered the pages in the bottom corner.* **2** (*with* **among**) to include: *He numbered her among his closest friends.*

'**numbered** *adj* with a number on: *The pages are all numbered*; *the numbered pages.*

'**numberless** *adj* (*formal or liter*) more than can be counted; very many.

'**number-plate** *nc* one of the metal plates carried on the front and back of a motor vehicle showing the registration number of the vehicle.

his *etc* **days are numbered** he *etc* is about to die, to be dismissed from his *etc* job *etc*: *If she continues to behave like that, her days in this firm are numbered.*

in 'number (*formal*) forming a group of (a certain number of people, things *etc*): *They were ten in number* (= There were ten of them).

his *etc* **number is up** (*inf*) he *etc* is about to die, to suffer something unpleasant *etc*: *When the police arrived, the thieves knew their number was up.*

without number (*formal or liter*) more than can be counted; very many: *I've told him times without number* (= very often) *not to do that.*

numeral ['nju:mərəl] *nc* a figure used to express a number: *1, 2, 73 are Arabic numerals*; *I, X, C are Roman numerals.*

nu'merical [-'me-] *adj* (*usu attrib*) of, using or consisting of numbers: *a numerical code.*

nu'merically *adv* (*formal or tech*) **1** in, or by means of, numbers: *It's easier to express our results numerically than in words.* **2** in size or amount: *The enemy forces were numerically superior, but we had better weapons.*

in numerical order following the order one, two, three, four *etc*: *Answer the questions in numerical order.*

numerate ['nju:mərət] *adj* (*very formal*) having some understanding of mathematics and science: *The child is scarcely numerate*; *The more numerate pupils are studying mathematics.*

See also **innumerate**.

numerical *etc see* **numeral**.

numerous ['nju:mərəs] *adj* (*more formal than* **many**) very many: *There are numerous people waiting for you*; *His faults are too numerous to mention.*

nun [nʌn] *nc* a member of a female religious community.

'**nunnery** *nc* a house in which a group of nuns live; a convent.

nuptial ['nʌpʃəl] *adj* (*attrib*: *formal or liter*) of marriage: *the nuptial day*; *nuptial bliss.*

'**nuptials** *n pl* (*formal or liter*) a marriage (ceremony): *the celebration of the King's nuptials.*

nurse [nə:s] *nc* **1** a person who looks after sick or injured people in hospital: *She wants to be a nurse.* **2** a person, *usu* a woman, who looks after small children: *The children have gone out with their nurse.* – *vt* **1** to look after sick or injured people, *esp* in a hospital: *He was nursed back to health.* **2** to give (a baby) milk from the breast; to suckle: *I don't know how she manages to knit while nursing the baby.* **3** to hold with care: *She was nursing a kitten.* **4** to look after with care: *He nurses his tomato plants.* **5** (*fig*) to have or encourage (feelings *eg* of anger or hope) in oneself: *He nursed a hope that he would succeed.*

'**nursery** *nc* **1** a room for young children: *The children spend most of the day in the nursery.* **2** a place where young plants are grown: *You can buy tomato plants at the nursery.*

'**nursing** *nu* **1** the profession of being a nurse (*def 1*): *Nursing is a hard but satisfying job.* **2** the act of nursing (*defs 1 and 4*).

'**nursemaid** *nc* a nurse (*def 2*).

'**nurseryman** *nc* a person who runs or works in a nursery (*def 2*).

'**nursery rhyme** *nc* a short, *usu* simple and often silly poem for children.

'**nursery school** *nc* a school for very young children: *He went to the nursery school till he was five.*

'**nursing-home** *nc* a small private hospital: *The old lady preferred to go into a nursing-home rather than live with her daughter.*

nurture ['nə:tʃə] *vt* (*formal*) to encourage the growth and development of (a child, plant *etc*): *The child has been carefully nurtured*; (*fig*) *He nurtured a desire for revenge.* – *nu* (*formal*) care; help in growing or developing.

nut [nʌt] *nc* **1** (*often in cmpds*) a fruit consisting of a single seed in a hard shell: *a hazel-nut*; *a walnut*; *Squirrels eat nuts.* **2** a small round piece of metal with a hole through it, for screwing on the end of a bolt to hold pieces of wood, metal *etc* together: *He fixed the handle to the door with a nut and bolt.* **3** (*Brit sl*) a person's head: *It hit him on the nut.*

nuts *adj* (*pred*: *sl*) **1** mad: *He's quite nuts.* **2** (*with* **about**) very enthusiastic or keen, often to a ridiculous extent: *He's nuts about her/cars/football.*

'**nutty** *adj* **1** containing, or tasting of, nuts: *nutty chocolate*; *a nutty flavour.* **2** (*sl*) mad: *He's quite nutty*; *a nutty old man.* **3** (*pred*: *sl*: *with* **about**) very enthusiastic or keen, often to a ridiculous extent: *He's nutty about her/cars.*

'**nutcase** *nc* (*sl*) a person who is mad: *Anyone who could do a thing like that must be a complete nutcase.*

'**nutcracker** *nc* (*usu in pl*) an instrument for cracking nuts open: *a pair of nutcrackers.*

'**nutshell** *nc* the hard covering of a nut.

in a 'nutshell expressed, described *etc* very briefly: *I'll tell you the story in a nutshell.*

nutmeg ['nʌtmeg] *ncu* a hard seed ground into a powder and used as a spice in food: *Add a pinch of nutmeg.*

nutritious [nju'triʃəs] *adj* (*formal or tech*) valuable as food; nourishing: *Fruit is very nutritious*; *a nutritious substance.*

nutrient ['nju:triənt] *nc* (*formal or tech*) a substance which gives nourishment: *This food contains important nutrients*; (*attrib*) *a nutrient solution.*

'**nutriment** *ncu* (*formal or tech*) nourishment; food: *This soil contains all the nutriment(s) a plant needs.*

nu'trition *nu* (*formal or tech*) (the act of giving or getting) nourishment, or the scientific study of this: *She's an expert in nutrition.*

nu'tritional *adj* (*esp attrib*) of nutrition or nourishment: *the nutritional value of milk.*

nutshell, nutty *see* **nut**.

nuzzle ['nʌzl] *vti* to press, rub or caress with the nose: *The horse nuzzled* (*against*) *her cheek.*

nylon ['nailən] *nu*, *adj* (of) a type of material made from chemicals and used for clothes, ropes, brushes *etc*: *My shirt is (made of) nylon; a nylon shirt.*

'nylons *n pl* stockings made of nylon: *She's torn her nylons; I bought three pairs of black nylons.*

nymph [nimf] *nc* (*myth*) a goddess or spirit of the rivers, trees *etc*.

nymphomania [nimfə'meiniə] *nu* (*formal*) abnormally great sexual desire in women: *She seems to be suffering from nymphomania.*

ˌnympho'maniac [-ak] *nc* (*inf abbrev* **'nympho** [-fou] – *pl* **'nymphos** –) a woman suffering from nymphomania. – *adj* (*usu attrib*) of, or suffering from, nymphomania: *She has nymphomaniac tendencies.*

Oo

o [ou] *interj* (*liter*) an expression used when speaking to a person, thing *etc*: *O Skylark, bird of heavenly joy!*

See also **oh**.

oaf [ouf] *nc* (*derog*) a stupid or clumsy person: *That stupid oaf is always knocking things over.*

'oafish *adj* (*derog*): *oafish behaviour; He is so oafish!*

oak [ouk] **1** *nc* (*also* **'oak tree**) a type of large tree with hard wood: *That tree is an oak*; (*attrib*) *an oak wood.* **2** *nu, adj* (of) its wood: *Ships used to be made of oak; oak panelling.*

oar [o:] *nc* a long piece of wood with a flat end for rowing a boat: *He pulled on the oars to make the boat go faster.*

put/stick one's oar in (*inf derog*) to interfere in what another person is saying, doing *etc* by offering opinions *etc* when they are not wanted: *We were quite capable of coming to an agreement without your help – no-one asked you to put your oar in.*

oasis [ou'eisis] – *pl* **o'ases** [-si:z] – *nc* an area in a desert where water is found and plants grow: *The travellers stopped at an oasis*; (*fig formal*) *Her house is an oasis of peace after our noisy house.*

oatmeal *see* **oats**.

oath [ouθ] – *pl* **oaths** [ouθs, ouðz] – *nc* **1** a solemn promise to tell the truth, be loyal, do something particular *etc*: *He swore an oath to support the king.* **2** a word or phrase *usu* with the name of God or of some other holy person or thing, used when swearing *eg* because of anger or surprise: *He could hear curses and oaths from the men outside as they tried to break open the door.*

on/under oath (*legal*) having sworn an oath (*def 1*) to tell the truth in a court of law: *The witness is on/under oath.*

take an oath to swear an oath (*def 12*).

oats [outs] *n pl or sing* a type of cereal plant or its grain (seeds): *The oats are ready for harvesting; a field of oats; Horses eat oats; Oats is a crop grown mainly in cool climates.*

'oatcake *nc* a thin hard dry biscuit made with oat meal.

'oatmeal *nu* meal made by grinding the grain of oats: *These biscuits are made of oatmeal; Porridge is made with oatmeal.*

sow one's wild oats (*usu* of young men) to live a life of wild enjoyment before settling down to a quieter, more serious and respectable life: *The students sowed their wild oats before leaving university to become teachers, doctors etc.*

obdurate ['obdjurət] *adj* (*liter or formal*) stubborn; impossible to persuade to change: *an obdurate sinner; I tried to persuade him to come but he remained obdurate.* **'obdurately** *adv.* **'obduracy** *nu.*

obedience, obedient *see* **obey**.

obelisk ['obəlisk] *nc* a tall four-sided pillar with a pointed top: *That obelisk is a memorial to a historic British victory.*

obese [ə'bi:s] *adj* (*formal*) (of people) very fat: *an obese man; The doctor says that he is obese.*

o'besity *nu*: *Obesity is a danger to health.*

obey [ə'bei, (*Amer*) ou-] *vti* to do what one is told to do (by someone or in a command): *He told me to go home and I obeyed (him); I obeyed the order*; (*fig*) *I must obey my conscience.*

obedience [ə'bi:djəns] *nu* **1** the act of obeying: *obedience to an order.* **2** willingness to obey orders: *She showed great obedience.*

o'bedient *adj*: *She is a very obedient child; The little boy was well-behaved and obedient.* **o'bediently** *adv.*

See also **disobey**.

obituary [ə'bitjuəri] *nc* a notice (*eg* in a newspaper) or an announcement of a person's death, often with an account of his life and work: *I read his obituary in the local newspaper.*

object[1] ['obdʒikt] *nc* **1** a thing that can be seen or felt: *There were various objects on the table; I could see a dark object in the distance but I could not see what it was.* **2** an aim; a purpose or intention: *His main object in life was to become rich.* **3** (*formal*) the person to whom, or thing to which, something is done: *The object of her study was the history of Venice; She was the object of his attention.* **4** (*gram*) the word or words in a sentence or phrase which represent(s) the person/people or thing(s) affected by the action of the verb: *He hit me; He likes my work; He gave me the book; You can eat what you like.*

direct object, indirect object *see* **direct, indirect**.

object[2] [əb'dʒekt] *vi* (*often with* **to**) to feel or express dislike or disapproval of: *He wanted us to travel on foot but I objected (to that); I object to people smoking in theatres.*

objection [əb'dʒekʃən] *nc* **1** an expression of disapproval: *He made/raised no objection (to the idea).* **2** (*often with* **against** *or* **to**) a reason for disapproving: *My objection (to/against the candidate) is that he is too young.*

ob'jectionable [-'dʒekʃə-] *adj* disagreeable; unpleasant: *He is a very objectionable person; I agree with what he said but the way he said it was thoroughly objectionable.* **ob'jectionably** *adv.*

conscientious objector *see* **conscientious**.

objective [əb'dʒektiv] *nc* (*formal*) a thing aimed at or wished for: *Our objective is freedom for all; The travellers' objective was the next town.* – *adj* not depending on, or influenced by, personal opinions, advantages *etc*: *He tried to take an objective view of the situation and make an objective decision; You are too emotionally involved in that situation to be objective about it.*

ob'jectively *adv* looking at facts without prejudice, personal interest *etc*: *He considered the problem objectively and decided that he had been wrong.*

ˌobjec'tivity [ob-] *nu*: *A scientist should always strive for objectivity in his experiments; I find it difficult to think about that subject with any degree of objectivity.*

oblige [ə'blaidʒ] *vt* (*formal*) **1** (*usu in passive*: not *usu* used with **is, was** *etc* and **-ing**) to force (someone) to do something: *She was obliged to go out to work when her husband died; The police obliged him to leave; Poverty obliged her to live a hard life.* **2** (*usu with* **by** *or* **with**) to do (someone) a favour or service: *He obliged me with a loan of £5; Could you oblige me by taking this to the post office, please?*

obligation [obli'geiʃən] *ncu* a promise or duty which one must keep or do: *We are all under an obligation to help other people; You are under no obligation to buy this.*

obligatory [ə'bligətəri] *adj* (*formal*: *usu pred*) that must be done *etc*; compulsory: *Military service is obligatory in some countries; Attendance at tonight's meeting is obligatory.* **o'bligatorily** *adv.* **o'ligatoriness** *nu.*

'obliged *adj* (*formal*: *with* **to**) forced (to do something): *I don't really want to do this, but I'm obliged to; I shall be obliged to report you if you are late again.*

o'bliging *adj* willing to help other people: *a very obliging person; He'll help you – he's always very obliging.* **o'bligingly** *adv.*

I'm/I'd be (much) obliged (*formal*) I am/I would be (very) grateful: *Can you give me a match? Thank you – I'm (much) obliged (to you); I'd be obliged if you'd make less noise.*

oblique [ə'bli:k] *adj* (*formal*) **1** sloping; not vertical or horizontal: *He drew an oblique line from one corner of the paper to the other.* **2** (*usu attrib*) not straight or direct: *He steered an oblique course towards the shore;* (*fig*) *He made an oblique reference to his work.* **o'bliquely** *adv.* **o'bliqueness** *nu.*

obliterate [ə'blitəreit] *vt* (*formal*) **1** to cover (something); to prevent (something) being visible: *The snow obliterated his footprints.* **2** to destroy (something) completely: *The whole town was obliterated by the bombs.* **oˌblite'ration** *nu.*

oblivion [ə'bliviən] *nu* (*formal*) **1** the state of being unaware of (something) or of having forgotten (something): *He lived in complete oblivion of his surroundings/of his wicked deeds.* **2** the state of being forgotten: *After his death, his name quickly fell/sank into oblivion* (= became forgotten).

o'blivious *adj* (*formal*: *pred usu with* **of** *or* **to**) unaware of or not paying attention to (something): *He did not realize that his wife was having an affair with another man – he was completely oblivious of what was happening; He was oblivious to our warnings; He was so drunk that he was completely oblivious to his surroundings.* **o'bliviously** *adv.* **o'bliviousness** *nu.*

oblong ['obloŋ] *nc* (*geom*) a two-dimensional, rectangular figure, but with one pair of opposite sides longer than the other pair. – *adj* shaped like this: *an oblong table; This cake is oblong – I wanted a round one.*

obnoxious [əb'nokʃəs] *adj* causing dislike; offensive: *He is such an obnoxious man; The smell of that mixture is really obnoxious.* **ob'noxiously** *adv.* **ob'noxiousness** *nu.*

oboe ['oubou] *nc* a type of high-pitched woodwind musical instrument: *He plays the oboe; He played a tune on his oboe.*

'oboist *nc* a person who plays an oboe.

obscene [əb'si:n] *adj* disgusting, *esp* sexually: *The photographs of naked women in this book are positively obscene; The censor has removed most of the obscene passages from that book.* **ob'scenely** *adv.*

obscenity [-'se-] **1** *nu* obscene behaviour or language: *There are laws against obscenity in films.* **2** *nc* an obscene act or word(s): *He shouted obscenities at the police.*

obscure [əb'skjuə] *adj* **1** (*usu attrib*) not clear; hidden; difficult to see: *The book was hidden in an obscure corner of the library.* **2** not well-known: *an obscure author; You may not have heard of the painter of this portrait – he is rather obscure.* **3** difficult to understand: *an obscure poem; He made an obscure reference to that book; I find his comments on my essay rather obscure.* – *vt* to make (something) obscure: *A large tree obscured the view from the kitchen window.* **ob'scurely** *adv.*

ob'scurity **1** *nu* the state of being obscure: *He prefers to live in obscurity.* **2** *nc* (*formal*) something that is obscure: *The poem is full of obscurities.*

obsequious [əb'si:kwiəs] *adj* (*formal*) too humble or too ready to agree with someone, *usu* in order to flatter him or get a favour from him: *He bowed in an obsequious manner; The rest of the workers hate him – he is so obsequious to the manager.* **ob'sequiously** *adv.* **ob'sequiousness** *nu.*

observe [əb'zə:v] (*formal*) **1** *vt* to notice: *I observed a letter on the table; He observed that she arrived late but he did not comment on it.* **2** *vt* to watch carefully: *She observed his actions with interest.* **3** *vt* to obey (laws *etc*): *We must observe the rules.* **4** *vt* to perform certain polite, traditional *etc* actions or ceremonies: *They observed a minute's silence in memory of the dead; They still observe the old traditions here; They observed Easter in the usual way.* **5** *vti* to make a remark: *'It's a lovely day,' he observed; He observed that it was a lovely day.*

ob'servance (*formal*) **1** *nu* the act of obeying rules *etc*: *the observance of the law.* **2** *ncu* the act of observing (a tradition *etc*): *the observance of religious holidays; religious observances.*

ob'servant *adj* (*neg* **un-**) quick to notice: *A scientist must be observant; An observant young man remembered the car's registration number.*

ˌobser'vation [ob-] **1** *nu* (*more formal than* **watching**) the act of noticing or watching: *She is in hospital for observation; The police/doctors kept the man under observation.* **2** *nc* (*formal*) a remark: *He made a polite observation about her new dress.*

ob'servatory *nc* a place for observing and studying the stars, weather *etc.*

ob'server *nc* **1** a person who observes (someone or something). **2** a person who goes to meetings *etc* to watch and listen but not take part: *He attended the discussions as an observer.*

obsess [əb'ses] *vt* (*usu in passive*) to occupy (someone's mind) completely or too much: *He is obsessed by the fear of death; She is obsessed by what she looks like.*

ob'session [-ʃən] *ncu*: *an obsession about motorbikes; His obsession with motorbikes infuriates his wife; That is just another of his many obsessions.*

ob'sessional [-ʃə-] *adj* (*often derog*) of, related

to, or having, an obsession or obsessions: *I am tired of his obsessional behaviour*; *He's obsessional about arriving at work on time.*

ob'sessive [-siv] *adj* (*tech or derog*) of, relating to, or having an obsession or obsessions: *It's good to want one's work to be tidy but he's really obsessive about it*; *an obsessive personality*; *He is so obsessive about cleanliness that he washes his hands about twenty times a day.* – *nc* (*tech*) a person who has an obsession or obsessions: *The psychiatrist thinks that she is an obsessive.*

ob'sessively *adv.* **ob'sessiveness** *nu.*

obsolescent [obsə'lesnt] *adj* (*formal*) going out of use: *That kind of engine is obsolescent*; *obsolescent slang.* **ˌobso'lescence** *nu.*

obsolete ['obsəliːt, (*Amer also*) obsə'liːt] *adj* no longer in use; out of date: *The steam engine is almost totally obsolete nowadays*; *The enemy soldiers are using obsolete weapons*; (*fig*) *obsolete ideas.* **'obsoleteness** *nu.*

obstacle ['obstəkl] *nc* (*usu fig*) something which stands in a person's way or prevents progress: *His inability to learn foreign languages was an obstacle to his career*; *Her parents tried to put obstacles in the way of her marriage* (= they tried to prevent her marriage).

'obstacle race *nc* a race in which runners have to climb over, crawl through *etc* obstacles such as tyres, nets *etc.*

obstetrics [ob'stetriks] *n sing* the science of helping women before, during, and after, the birth of babies: *He specializes in obstetrics*; (*attrib*) *the obstetrics department.*

ob'stetric(al) *adj* (*tech*: *usu attrib*) of obstetrics: *obstetrical instruments*; *She has had good obstetrical care.*

obstetrician [obstə'triʃən] *nc* a doctor who specializes in obstetrics: *There was no obstetrician present at the birth – only a midwife.*

obstinate ['obstinət] *adj* refusing to change one's opinion, do what someone else asks *etc*: *She won't change her mind – she's very obstinate*; *an obstinate child*; (*formal*) *obstinate resistance.*

'obstinacy [-nəsi] *nu*: *She was annoyed at the child's obstinacy.*

'obstinately *adv*: *She was obstinately refusing to go.*

obstreperous [əb'strepərəs] *adj* (*formal*) noisy and uncontrolled: *He becomes very obstreperous when he is drunk*; *He was asked to leave the bar because of his obstreperous behaviour.*

obstruct [əb'strʌkt] (*formal*) *vt* **1** to block or close (something): *The road was obstructed by a fallen tree.* **2** to stop (someone or something) moving past or through: *The crashed lorry obstructed the traffic*; (*fig*) *A thick curtain obstructed the light.* **3** to make it difficult or impossible for a decision to be made, an act of parliament to be passed *etc*: *A group of workers obstructed the union committee's attempt to stop the strike.*

ob'struction [-ʃən] (*formal or tech*) **1** *nc* something that obstructs: *There was an obstruction in the water-pipe*; *She choked to death because of an obstruction in her throat.* **2** *nu* the act of obstructing (someone or something): *The strike caused obstruction of food supplies*; *the obstruction of an amendment to a bill in Parliament.*

obtain [əb'tein] *vt* (*more formal than* **get**) to get (something); to become the owner or possessor of (something): *He obtained a large sum of money by buying and selling houses.*

ob'tainable *adj* (*pred*: *neg* **un-**) able to be obtained: *That book is no longer obtainable.*

obtrusive [əb'truːsiv] *adj* (*formal*: *neg* **un-**) very noticeable; very obvious: *She always wears such obtrusive clothes*; *I find that loud music very obtrusive*; *She was not at all obtrusive in her efforts to help them.* **ob'trusively** *adv.* **ob'trusiveness** *nu.*

obtuse [əb'tjuːs] *adj* **1** (*geom*) (of an angle) greater than a right-angle. **2** (*formal*) stupid; slow to understand: *Don't be so obtuse!*; *rather an obtuse young man.* **ob'tusely** *adv.* **ob'tuseness** *nu.*

obvious ['obviəs] *adj* easily seen or understood; evident: *It was obvious (to everyone) that we would have to help them*; *There has been no obvious improvement in the condition of the patient.*

'obviousness *nu.*

'obviously *adv* it is obvious (that something is the case): *Obviously, I'll need some help with this.*

occasion [ə'keiʒən] *nc* **1** a particular time: *I'll say nothing more about your behaviour on this occasion, but don't do it again*; *I've heard him speak on several occasions.* **2** a special event: *The wedding was a great occasion.* **3** (*no pl*: *formal*) an opportunity: *You should change your job if the occasion arises.* **4** (*no pl*: *formal*) reason: *You've no occasion to do that.* – *vt* (*very formal*) to cause: *What occasioned his remark?*

oc'casional *adj* (*usu attrib*) happening, done *etc* now and then: *I take an occasional trip to London*; *I do read an occasional book.*

oc'casionally *adv* sometimes; now and then: *I occasionally go to the theatre*; *She sees him occasionally.*

rise to the occasion *see* **rise**.

occult [ə'kʌlt]: **the occult** supernatural practices, ceremonies *etc*: *He has made a study of witches, magic and the occult.*

occupy ['okjupai] *vt* **1** (*more formal than* **fill**) to be in or fill (time, space *etc*): *The job will occupy very little of your time*; *A table occupied the centre of the room*; *He occupies an important position in the steel industry.* **2** to live in (a house *etc*): *The family occupied a two-roomed flat.* **3** to seize or capture: *The soldiers occupied the town.* **4** to employ or use (one's energy *etc*): *The baby occupied herself playing with her toy*; *She occupied herself with various small jobs.*

'occupancy (*formal*) **1** *nu* the act of occupying (a house *etc*): *the occupancy of a large house.* **2** *nc* a period of time during which a house *etc* is occupied: *an occupancy of five years.*

'occupant *nc* (*formal*) a person who occupies (a house *etc*), not necessarily the owner of the house: *He is the occupant of the top flat.*

ˌoccu'pation **1** *nc* a person's job or work: *'What is your occupation?' 'I am a teacher.'* **2** *nc* an activity that occupies a person's attention, free time *etc*: *I have various occupations that keep me busy on wet winter evenings.* **3** *nu* the act of occupying or state of being occupied (*defs 2, 3*): *He agreed to the family's occupation of his brother's house*; *The people resented the occupation of their country by a foreign power.* **4** *nc* the period of time during which a town, house *etc* is occupied: *During the occupation, the people kept away from the enemy soldiers.*

ˌoccu'pational *adj* (*usu attrib*) of, or caused by, a person's job: *Bronchitis used to be an occupational disease of coalminers.*

'**occupier** *nc* an occupant: *He rents the house – he is not an owner-occupier.*

occupational therapy *nu* the treatment of a mental or physical illness or injury by giving the patient some *usu* simple work to do *eg* basket-making: *He was given occupational therapy after the operation on his legs.* **occupational therapist** *nc.*

occur [ə'kə:] – *pt, ptp* **oc'curred** – *vi* **1** (*more formal than* **happen**) to happen or take place: *The accident occurred yesterday morning.* **2** (*with* **to**) to come into one's mind: *An idea occurred to him; It occurred to me to visit my parents.* **3** (*more formal than* **be found**) to appear or be found: *Oil occurs under the North Sea.*

oc'currence [-'kʌ-, (*Amer*) -'kə:-] *ncu What a strange occurrence!; strange occurrences; Climbing in these hills can be dangerous due to the occurrence of sudden snow-storms;* (*formal*) *He is studying the occurrence of these flowers in the Alps.*

ocean ['ouʃən] **1** *nu* the salt water that covers most of the earth's surface. **2** *nc* (*often found with cap in place-names*) one of its five main divisions: *the Atlantic Ocean.*

ˌ**oce'anic** [ouʃi'a-] *adj* (*formal*: *esp attrib*) of, or found in, the ocean: *oceanic currents.*

ochre, (*Amer usu*) **ocher** ['oukə] **1** *nu* a type of fine pale-yellow or red clay, used for colouring. **2** *nu, adj* (of) its colour: *yellow ochre.*

o'clock [ə'klok] *adv* used, in stating the time, to refer to a particular hour: *It's five o'clock; It happened between two and three o'clock in the morning; She will arrive at six o'clock;* (*attrib*) *She is coming by the three o'clock train.*

octagon ['oktəgən, (*Amer*) -gon] *nc* (*geom*) a two-dimensional figure with eight sides.

oc'tagonal [-'ta-] *adj* (*formal or geom*) having eight sides: *an octagonal figure; It is octagonal in shape.*

octane ['oktein]: ˌ**high-'octane** *adj* (*tech*) (of petrol) of a high quality and efficiency.

octave ['oktiv] *nc* (*music*) **1** a series of eight notes *eg* on a piano from one note up to and including the next note of the same name, *eg* from C to the C above. **2** an equivalent range of notes *eg* in a singer: *Her voice has a range of nearly three octaves.*

octet [ok'tet] *nc* a group of eight musicians, eight lines in a poem *etc.*

October [ok'toubə] *n* the tenth month of the year, the month following September: *It happened last October; He will be here in October; He is coming on October 15* (said as 'on October (the) fifteenth' or 'on the fifteenth of October'); *He will be here on the 15th/fifteenth of October.*

octogenarian [oktədʒi'neəriən] *nc* (*formal*) a person between eighty and eighty-nine years old: *My grandfather is an octogenarian.*

octopus ['oktəpəs] *nc* a type of sea-creature with eight tentacles.

oculist ['okjulist] *nc* a doctor who specializes in diseases of the eyes.

'**ocular** *adj* (*formal or tech*: *esp attrib*) of, or related to, the eyes or seeing: *an ocular defect.*

odd [od] *adj* **1** unusual; strange: *What an odd thing to say!; He's wearing very odd clothes; a very odd young man; I don't think he's mad but he is certainly very odd.* **2** (of a number) that cannot be divided exactly by 2: *1, 3, 5 and 7 are odd (numbers); Write down all the odd numbers.* **3** (*usu attrib*) not one of a pair, set *etc*; left over; extra: *an odd shoe; I found an odd knife among our cutlery.* **4** (*attrib*) occasional; free; not busy: *He only does that at odd times/moments; I know you're busy, but have you got an odd minute to help me?* **5** (only used with numbers) a little more than: *'How many books has he got?' 'He must have a hundred odd at least'; She has fifty odd pounds; I've got £5 odd/five pounds odd.*

'**oddity** **1** *nc* (*inf*) a strange person or thing: *He's a bit of an oddity.* **2** *nu* (*formal*) the state of being strange or unusual: *People comment on his oddity.*

'**oddly** *adv* strangely; unusually: *He is behaving very oddly.* – *See also* **oddly enough** *below.*

'**oddments** *n pl* pieces left over from something, *usu* a roll of material: *After she had finished making the dress she had several oddments of material left over.*

'**oddness** *nu* the state of being odd: *the oddness of his comments.*

odds *n pl* **1** chances; probability: *The odds are that he will win;* (*inf*) *It's odds on* (= very likely) *that he will win.* **2** a difference in strength, numbers *etc* in favour of one person, team, army *etc*: *They are fighting against heavy odds* (= The enemy is much stronger than they are). **3** in betting (the statement of) the number of times greater that the money a person wins will be than the amount of money he bets: *Odds of ten to one mean that if a person bets £1 and wins, he will get £11* (= the bet plus the amount won) *back; I would lay odds* (= offer odds) *of ten to one against that happening.* – *See also* **odds** *in phrases below.*

'**oddball** *nc* (*inf*) a person who behaves in a strange way: *A lot of people look on me as a bit of an oddball but I don't care.*

odd jobs *n pl* (*usu* small) jobs of various kinds, often done for other people: *He's unemployed, but earns some money by doing odd jobs for the local farmers; When he retired he at last found time to do various odd jobs around the house.*

ˌ**odd 'job man** *nc* a person employed to do such jobs.

be at 'odds (with someone over something) (*formal*) to be quarrelling, not in agreement *etc* (with a person over a particular matter): *He has been at odds with his brother for years over the money their father left them.*

make no odds to be unimportant: *We haven't got quite as much money as we wanted, but that makes no odds.*

oddly enough (*inf*) it is strange or remarkable (that): *I saw John this morning. Oddly enough, I was just thinking I hadn't seen him for a long time.*

odd man out/odd one out **1** a person or thing that is different from others: *In this test, you have to decide which of these three objects is the odd one out; Which are the odd ones out?* **2** a person or thing that is left over when teams, sets *etc* are made up: *When they chose the two teams, I was the odd man out.*

odds and ends small objects *etc* of different kinds: *There were various odds and ends lying about on the table; We have moved all our furniture to our new house – we just have to collect the odds and ends.*

what's the odds? it's not important; it doesn't matter: *We didn't win the competition but what's the odds?*

ode [oud] *nc* (*usu* in titles of poems) a poem written to a person or thing: *'Ode to a Nightingale' and 'Ode on a Grecian Urn' were written by John Keats.*

odious ['oudiəs] *adj* (*formal*) hateful; disgusting: *an odious personality/smell; She is an odious young* *woman*; *I hate him – he is odious!* **'odiously** *adv*. **'odiousness** *nu*.

odour, (*Amer*) **odor** ['oudə] *nc* (*formal*) a smell (*usu* particularly good or bad): *the sweet odour of roses*; *There is an odour of fish in this boat.*

'odourless *adj* (*formal*) without a smell: *an odourless liquid*; *The liquid is colourless and odourless.*

o'er [o:] *adv, prep* (*liter*) short for **over**: *o'er the sea.*

of [ov] *prep* **1** belonging to: *This farm is the property of my family*; *He broke the leg of the chair*; *a picture of my father's*; *a friend of mine.* **2** away from (a place *etc*); after (a given time): *We must be within five miles of London*; *Within a year of his death, there was civil war in the country.* **3** written, made *etc* by: *the plays of Shakespeare.* **4** belonging to or forming a group: *He is one of my friends*; *This vase is one of a number of objects found recently by archaeologists.* **5** showing; painted, carved *etc* to look like (a person *etc*): *a picture of my father*; *a photograph of my house.* **6** made from; consisting of: *a dress* (*made*) *of silk*; *a collection of pictures.* **7** used to show a part, amount, measurement of something: *a gallon of petrol*; *five bags of coal*; *a pair of shoes*; *all of us*; *a herd of cows.* **8** about; concerning: *an account of his work.* **9** containing: *a box of chocolates*; *a glass of whisky.* **10** used to show a cause: *She died of a fever*; *I'm tired of working*; *He's afraid of the dark.* **11** used to show a loss or removal: *She was robbed of her jewels*; *He cured him of his cold*; *Get rid of it!* **12** (*often formal*) used to show the connection between an action *etc* or the person performing the action *etc* and the object of the action *etc*: *the smoking of a cigarette*; *the children's love of their mother*; (*liter*) *a singer of songs.* **13** (*formal or liter*) indicating the connection between a person performing an action *etc* and the action: *the love of God*; *a man beloved of the gods.* **14** used to show character, qualities *etc*: *a man of courage*; *It's very good of you* (*to do it*); *His opinions are of no importance*; *That fool of a butcher has sent me the wrong meat!* **15** (*Amer*) (of time) a certain number of minutes before (the hour); to: *It's ten minutes of three.* **16** used in names of towns *etc*: *the city of Edinburgh.* **17** (*formal or liter*) used to show the time when something happens: *I go to bed early of an evening.*

off [of] **1** *adv* away (from a place, time *etc*): *He walked off*; *I put it on the table but it fell off*; *Off you go and do that* (= Go away and do it); *I must be off* (= I must leave); *She cut her hair off*; *The holidays are only a week off.* **2** *adv* not being worn: *She took off her coat*; *I can't get these boots off.* **3** *adv, adj* not working; not giving power *etc*: *The light is off*; *Switch off the electricity/light/motor*; *I couldn't find the off button on the television.* **4** *adv, adj* (*pred*) not at work; as a holiday: *He's taking tomorrow off*; *He's off today.* **5** *adv* completely: *Finish off your work.* **6** *adv* (of a price) reduced by a certain amount: *They're selling radios at £20 off.* **7** *adv, adj* not as good as usual, or as it should be: *His work has gone off recently*; (*inf*) *He's having an off day* (= a day on which his work *etc* is not as good as usual). **8** *adv, adj* (*pred*) (of food) rotten: *This milk has gone off – we can't drink it*; *That meat is certainly off.* **9** *adj* (*pred*) (used in a restaurant *etc*) not available: *The steak pie is off.* **10** *adv, adj* (*pred*) out of a vehicle, train *etc*: *The bus stopped and we got off*; *Is everybody off?* **11** *adj* (*attrib*) (of vehicles *etc*) offside: *the off front wheel.* – *prep* **1** away from; down from: *He took a book off the shelf*; *It fell off the table*; *The ship anchored a mile off the coast.* **2** taken away from: *Please cut about five centimetres off my hair*; *There is £10 off the usual price.* **3** not wanting or allowed to have (food *etc*, *usu* because of illness): *The child is off his food*; *His doctor has taken him off alcohol.* **4** out of (a vehicle, train *etc*): *We got off the bus.*

ˌoff-'beat *adj* (*sl*) unusual: *off-beat clothes*; *His clothes are a bit off-beat.*

ˌoff-'chance *nc* (*no pl*) a slight chance: *We waited, on the off-chance* (*that*) *he might come*; *There is an off-chance that he might come.*

ˌoff-'colour, (*Amer*) **ˌoff-'color** *adj* (*inf*: *pred*) not very well: *She's a bit off-colour this morning.*

off-duty *see* **duty**.

ˌoff'hand *adj* acting or speaking so casually that one is being rude: *She was upset by his offhand behaviour*; *I thought he was rather offhand.* – *adv* without thinking about something first: *I can't tell you the answer offhand.*

ˌoff'handedly *adv*. **ˌoff'handedness** *nu*.

'off-licence *nc* (*Brit*) a shop selling alcoholic drinks: *He went down to the off-licence for a bottle of whisky.*

ˌoff'peak *adj* (*usu attrib*) for use, used *etc* at a time when there is little demand, need, use *etc* and therefore *usu* cheaper: *Train fares are cheaper at offpeak times*; *offpeak rates for electricity*; *offpeak electricity.*

'offshoot *nc* something growing out of something else: *an offshoot of a plant*; (*fig*) *an offshoot of an international firm.*

ˌoff'shore *adj* (*usu attrib*) **1** in or on the sea, not far from the coast: *offshore oil-wells.* **2** (of winds) blowing away from the coast, out to sea: *offshore breezes.*

ˌoff'side 1 *adj, adv* (in football, hockey *etc*) in a position (not allowed by the rules) between the ball and the opponents' goal: *The referee disallowed the goal because one of the players was offside.* **2** *adj* (*Brit*: *attrib*) (of a vehicle *etc*) on the side nearest to the centre of the road *ie* (in Britain) the right: *the front offside wheel.*

'offspring – *pl* **'offspring** – *nc* (*formal or liter*) a child; the young (of animals): *He was the offspring of a German prince and an English kitchen-maid*; *How many offspring does a lion usually have?*

ˌoff-'white *ncu, adj* (a colour which is) not quite white, *eg* slightly yellow *etc*: *I don't want to wear a pure white dress – I think I'll buy one that is cream or off-white.*

badly/well off 1 poor or rich: *The family was quite well off.* **2** (*inf*: *with* **for**) having little or a lot (of something): *They're badly off for clothes at the moment.*

be 'off with you! (*old inf*) go away!

in the 'offing (*inf*) about to happen: *He has a new job in the offing.*

off and on/on and off (*inf*) sometimes; occasionally: *I see him off and on at the club.*

off the cuff, off duty, off one's head *see* **cuff, duty, head**.

the off season the period, at a hotel, holiday resort *etc*, when there are few visitors: *It's very quiet here in the off season*; (*attrib*) *off-season rates.*

off the top of one's head *see* **head**.

offal ['ofəl] *nu* the parts of an animal *eg* the heart, liver *etc* which are thought of either as not suitable to be used as food for people or as less important as food than the flesh.

off-beat, off-chance, off-colour *see* **off**.

offend [ə'fend] **1** *vt* (*more formal than* **upset**) to make (someone) feel upset or angry; to hurt (someone's) feelings: *If you don't go to her party she will be offended; His criticism offended her; He was offended by her rudeness.* **2** *vt* (*formal*) to be unpleasant or disagreeable (to someone): *Cigarette smoke offends me.* **3** *vi* (*formal*) (*often with* **against**) to act wrongly according to law, usual customs, religious belief *etc*: *His behaviour offends against good manners; Such an action would offend against God.*

of'fence, (*Amer*) **of'fense 1** *ncu* (any cause of) anger, displeasure, hurt feelings *etc*: *You are giving offence to your friends; That rubbish dump is an offence to the eye.* – *See also* **take offence** *below.* **2** *nc* a crime: *The police charged him with several offences.*

of'fender *nc* (*formal or legal*) a person who offends, *esp* against the law: *The boy was sent to a young offenders' institution* (= a prison for young people).

of'fensive [-siv] *adj* **1** insulting: *an offensive person; He made several offensive remarks; I thought his remarks about his mother were rather offensive.* **2** disgusting: *an offensive smell.* **3** (*very formal*) used to attack: *an offensive weapon.* – *nc* (*formal*) an attack: *They launched an offensive against the invading army.* – *See also* **be on the offensive** *below.*

of'fensively *adv.* **of'fensiveness** *nu.*

be on the offensive (*formal*: *often fig*) to be making an attack: *She always expects people to criticize her and so she is always on the offensive.*

take offence (*with* **at**) to be offended (by something): *He took offence at what she said.*

take the offensive (*formal*: *sometimes fig*) to attack first: *The emperor's troops took the offensive; (fig) She does not wait to be criticized – she always takes the offensive.*

See also **inoffensive**.

offer ['ofə] – *pt, ptp* **'offered** – **1** *vt* to put forward (a gift, payment, a suggestion *etc*) for acceptance or refusal: *She offered the man a cup of tea; He offered her £5 for the picture; He offered an alternative possibility;* (*formal*) *The thieves offered no resistance to the police when they were arrested.* **2** *vti* to say that one is willing (to do something): *He offered to help; I didn't want to help but I thought I ought to offer.* **3** *vt* (*formal*: *sometimes with* **up**) to present or give (something) *usu* to God or a god: *They offered prayers to God; The priest offered up a lamb as a sacrifice to the idol.* – *nc* **1** an act of offering: *They made an offer of help; Tea is cheap at the supermarket this week – it's a special offer.* **2** (*usu with* **for**) an offering of money as the price of something: *They made an offer of £14 000 for the house.* – *See also* **on offer** below.

'offering *nc* **1** (*old or facet*) a gift: *a birthday offering.* **2** a gift (*usu* a sum of money) given during a religious service and used for the work of *eg* the church *etc*: *a church offering.*

on 'offer for sale, often cheaply: *That shop has chairs on offer at £10 each; I bought these cups at the supermarket – they're on offer this week.*

offhand *see* **off**.

office ['ofis] **1** *nc* (*often in pl*) the room or building in which the business of a firm, *esp* clerical or administrative work (*eg* typing letters, keeping accounts *etc*) is done: *Our office is quite close to our factory; The firm's head offices are in London;* (*attrib*) *He sells office equipment; office furniture.* **2** *nc* the *usu* small room in which a particular person works: *the bank manager's office; She shares an office with several other people.* **3** *nc* (*usu in cmpds*) a room or building used for a particular purpose: *Train tickets are bought at the ticket-office; If you have lost your suitcase, ask about it at the lost-property office.* – *See also* **box office** *under* **box**[1], **post office** *under* **post**[2]. **4** *ncu* (*formal*) a position of authority, *esp* in the government or as a government: *Our party has not been in office for years; He held office in the last Labour government; the office of mayor; What office does he hold?* **5** *nc* a department of the government: *the Foreign Office.*

'officer *nc* **1** a person holding a commission in the army, navy or air force: *a naval officer; He is an officer in the army.* **2** (*often in cmpds or, usu with cap, in titles*) a person who carries out a public duty: *a police-officer; the Medical Officer of Health.*

official [ə'fiʃəl] *adj* **1** (*usu attrib*) of or concerning a position of authority: *official powers; official uniform; Public celebrations for the Queen's birthday are held not on the actual day, but on her official birthday in June.* **2** (*neg* **un-**) done or confirmed by people in authority *etc*; not yet publicly announced: *an official decision; the official result of the race; Their engagement is not official yet.* – *nc* a person who holds an office (*def* 4): *a government official.*

officially [ə'fiʃəli] *adv* **1** (*formal*) (*neg* **un-**) as, or because of being, an official: *He attended the ceremony officially.* **2** formally; with ceremony: *The new library was officially opened yesterday, though people had been using it for weeks; They have officially announced their engagement.* **3** (*neg* **un-**) according to what is announced publicly (though not necessarily true in fact): *Officially he is on holiday – actually he is working on a new book.*

officiate [ə'fiʃieit] *vi* (*formal*) to do the duty or service of an office or official position, *esp* at a church service: *The Reverend John Smith will officiate at the wedding.*

officious [ə'fiʃəs] *adj* (*formal derog*) offering help *etc* in order to interfere: *His mother-in-law is so officious that he does not let her visit his house; He showed an officious interest in their affairs.* **of'ficiously** *adv.* **of'ficousness** *nu.*

'office-bearer *nc* a person who holds office (*def* 4) in a society *etc*: *There will be a meeting of the office-bearers of the association tomorrow evening.*

'office-block *nc* a large building with offices (*def* 1) in it: *The centre of the city used to have a lot of private houses but it has been spoiled by the building of huge modern office blocks.*

through the (kind) offices of (*very formal*) with the help of: *I got the job through the kind offices of a friend.*

offing, off-licence, offshoot, offshore, offside *see* **off**.

oft [oft] *adv* (*liter*) often.

often ['ofn] *adv* many times: *I often go to the theatre; How often do you see him?; I should see him more often;* (*inf*) *I'd like to go oftener; We don't often drink wine.*

as often as not quite often: *As often as not, he's late for work.*

every so often sometimes; occasionally: *I meet him at the club every so often.*

more often than not usually; very often: *More often than not, he's drunk when I meet him.*

ogle ['ougl] *vti* (*derog*) (*usu* of a man) to look or stare at (a person, *usu* a woman) because of feelings of admiration or sexual attraction: *He ogles all the pretty women.*

ogre ['ougə] *nc* (*often fig*) in fairy stories, a frightening, cruel and ugly giant: *The children were frightened by the tale of the wicked ogre*; *Her husband is an absolute ogre*; *The children seem to regard their teacher as some kind of ogre.*

oh [ou] *interj* an expression of surprise, admiration *etc*, or used when speaking to a person or attracting his attention: *Oh! What are you doing here?*; *Oh, John, will you come into my room, please?*

See also **o**.

oil [oil] *nu* a *usu* thick liquid that will not mix with water, obtained from plants, animals and minerals: *olive oil*; *whale oil*; *She uses vegetable oil for frying food*; *cooking oil*; *You should put some oil on the hinges of that gate – it doesn't open very easily*; *The car's engine is in need of oil.* – *vt* to put oil on or into (something): *The machine will work better if it's oiled.*

oils *n pl* oil paint: *He paints in oils.*

'oily *adj* **1** of or like oil: *an oily liquid*; *This salad dressing is too oily.* **2** covered with oil: *He cleaned it with an oily rag*; *Don't touch that white wall – your hands are oily!* **3** (*derog*) (of a person, behaviour *etc*) trying to be too friendly or polite: *The waiters in that restaurant are too oily*; *Her mother likes rather oily young men who flatter her.*

'oil colour, (*Amer*) **'oil color** *ncu* oil paint.

'oilfield *nc* a place where mineral oil is found: *There are oilfields in the North Sea.*

,oil-'fired *adj* using oil as a fuel: *oil-fired central heating*; *Is your heating system oil-fired?*

oil paint *ncu* paint made with oil: *Some artists prefer to use oil paint(s).*

oil painting **1** *nc* a picture painted with oil paints. **2** *nu* the activity of painting in oils: *One of his latest hobbies is oil painting.*

'oil-rig *nc* a structure used to drill oil-wells: *The ship sailed past an enormous oil-rig.*

'oilskin **1** *nu* a type of waterproof cloth: *a sheet of oilskin*; (*attrib*) *an oilskin coat.* **2** *nc* a garment made of this: *He was wearing an oilskin when he went out in the boat.*

oil-slick *see* **slick**.

'oil-tanker *nc* a ship used for carrying oil: *An oil-tanker has run aground on some rocks near here.*

'oil-well *nc* a hole drilled into the earth or the sea-bed to obtain petroleum.

strike oil (*often fig*) to find oil under the ground: *After drilling for several months, they finally struck oil*; (*fig*) *We've been looking for a suitable house for years and this time I think we've struck oil* (= found what we have been looking for).

ointment ['ointmənt] *ncu* any greasy substance rubbed on the skin to heal injuries *etc*: *Put some ointment on the cut.*

O.K., okay [ou'kei] *interj, adj, adv* (*inf*) all right: *Will you do it? O.K., I will*; *Is my dress O.K.?*; *He answered the question O.K.*; *That's O.K. with/by me* (= I agree). – *nc* (*inf*) agreement; approval: *He gave the plan his O.K.* – *vt* (*inf*) to agree to or approve of (something): *Their boss okayed the idea.*

old [ould] *adj* **1** advanced in age: *an old man*; *He is in a hospital for old people*; *He is too old to live alone.* – *See also* **the old** *below.* **2** (*pred*) having a certain age: *He is thirty years old*; *Those houses are centuries old.* **3** having existed for a long time: *old customs*; *an old building*; *The houses in this street are very old*; *Those oak trees are very old.* **4** no longer useful; out-of-date: *She threw away those old shoes*; *rather old ideas*; *'Is this dress old?' 'No, I still wear it.'* **5** (*attrib*) belonging to times long ago: *old civilizations like those of Rome and Greece.*

old age *nu* **1** the later part of a person's life: *He wrote most of his poems in his old age.* **2** the state of being old: *You're not ill – all you're suffering from is old age.*

old age pension(er) *see* **pension**.

'old boy/girl *ncs* a former pupil (of a school): *Did you join the old girls' association?*; *The new prime minister is an old boy of our school.*

Old English *nu* the English language as spoken and written up to the twelfth century A.D. – *See also* **Anglo-Saxon**.

,old-'fashioned *adj* (*often derog*) in a style common some time ago: *old-fashioned clothes/ideas*; *Her hairstyle is very old-fashioned.*

old hand *nc* (*inf*) a person who is very experienced (at doing something): *He's an old hand at this sort of job.*

old maid *nc* (*inf derog*) an unmarried woman who is past the usual age of marriage: *She is so scared of being an old maid that she will marry anyone*; *The old maid next door complained about my son's kissing his girlfriend in public.*

'any old (*inf*) any; it doesn't matter which: *Just bring any old book.*

in days of old, in olden times/days, of old (*liter*) long ago: *In olden times, people used to fight with swords.*

old 'boy/'chap/'fellow/'man (*inf*: *usu* only used by older men of the middle and upper classes) an expression used when speaking to another man: *I say, old boy. Can you tell me the way to the station?*

the old old people: *hospitals for the old.*

See also **elder, eldest**.

olive ['oliv] **1** *nc* a type of edible fruit which is used as a garnish, appetizer *etc* and which gives oil used for cooking: *He put an olive in her cocktail*; *There was a dish of stuffed olives on each table in the bar*; (*attrib*) *an olive tree*; (*attrib*) *olive oil.* **2** *nc* the tree on which it grows: *a grove of olives*; (*attrib*) *an olive grove.* **3** *nu, adj* (*also* **olive-green**) (of) the brownish-green or yellowish-green colour of the fruit: *They painted the room olive*; *She wore an olive-green hat.* **4** *nu, adj* (*also* **'olive-wood**) (of) the wood of the tree.

'olive branch *nc* (*fig*) a sign of a wish for peace: *The government is willing to hold out the olive branch to its opponents who have fled from the country.*

Olympic [ə'limpik]: **the Olympic Games** **1** (*hist*) an athletic *etc* contest held in ancient Greece. **2** (*also* **the Olympics**) a sports competition held once every four years for competitors from all parts of the world.

ombudsman ['ombudzmən] *nc* an official appointed to look into complaints *esp* against a government.

omega ['oumigə, (*Amer*) ou'megə] *n* the last letter of the Greek alphabet (Ω, ω).

omelette, omelet ['omlit] *nc* eggs beaten and fried sometimes with vegetables, meat *etc*: *I had an omelette for supper*; *a mushroom omelette.*

omen ['oumən] *nc* a sign of a future event: *I took it as a good omen that the sun began to shine as I went off to start my new job*; *He regards it as a good omen if he sees a black cat*; *In olden times storms were regarded as bad omens.*

ominous ['ominəs] *adj* giving a suggestion or

warning about something bad that is going to happen: *an ominous cloud*; *an ominous silence*; *The government's decision sounds ominous.* **'ominously** *adv.*

omit [ə'mit] – *pt, ptp* **o'mitted** – *vt* (*formal*) **1** to leave out: *You can omit the last chapter of the book.* **2** not to do (something): *I omitted to tell him about the meeting.*

o'mission [-ʃən] (*formal*) **1** *nc* something that has been left out: *I have made several omissions in the list of names.* **2** *nu* the act of omitting: *He noticed the omission of popular music from the radio programme.*

omnibus ['omnibəs] *nc* **1** (*old* or used in names of companies *etc*) a bus: *The old lady remembers going in an omnibus to the seaside*; *South-eastern Omnibuses Ltd.* **2** (*formal*) a large book containing a number of books, stories *etc*: *a Jane Austen omnibus*; (*attrib*) *an omnibus edition of Jane Austen's novels.*

omnipotent [om'nipətənt] *adj* (*formal*) having absolute, unlimited power: *In Greek mythology, the gods were not always omnipotent*; *the omnipotent power of God.* **om'nipotently** *adv.* **om'nipotence** *nu.*

on [on] *prep* **1** touching, fixed to, covering *etc* the upper or outer side of: *The book was lying on the table*; *He was standing on the floor*; *The picture was hanging on the wall*; *The spider was walking on the ceiling*; *She wore a hat on her head*; *You'll see a picture of this on the next page*; (*fig*) *They heaped insults on him*; *The hammer fell on his foot.* **2** in or into (a vehicle, train *etc*): *We were sitting on the bus*; *I got on the wrong bus*; *We can have something to eat on the train.* **3** at or during a certain day, time *etc*: *on Monday*; *on October 26*; *on a cold winter's day*; *He got a surprise on opening the letter*; *On his arrival, he went straight to the manager's office.* **4** about: *He wrote a book on the theatre.* **5** in the state or process of: *Concert tickets are on sale at this office*; *He's still on holiday.* **6** supported by: *She was standing on one leg*; *Is this based on fact? I have it on his authority that this is true.* **7** receiving or taking: *He is on drugs*; *The doctor put her on a diet*; *He cannot afford a car on such low wages.* **8** being a member of (a group or people working together *etc*); taking part in (an activity *etc*): *He is on the committee*; *He's on a tour of Europe*; *Do you have to go on that conference?*; *Which detective is working on this case?* **9** towards: *They marched on the town*; *On our left, we can see the house where William Shakespeare was born.* **10** near or beside (a person, or the side or edge of something): *a village on the river*; *He has a shop on the main road.* **11** expressing the connection between something done, performed *etc*, and the instrument *etc* that is the means of doing it: *He played a tune on the violin*; *There was an excellent play on (the) television*; *The concert was broadcast on the radio*; *I spoke to him on the telephone.* **12** showing the connection between an action, feeling *etc* and its object: *She spent the money on books* (= She bought books); *He took pity on her*; *He's very keen on swimming.* **13** used to show money *etc* being charged for something: *There's a tax on whisky*; *We can't pay the interest on the loan.* **14** (*inf*) being carried by (a person): *When the police found him, the thief still had the stolen jewels on him*; *Do you have a 7p stamp on you?* **15** when (something is or has been done): *On inquiring, I found that the plane had already left*; *On investigation, there proved to be no need to panic.* **16** (*liter*) followed by: *They suffered disaster on disaster.* – **1** *adv* (*esp* of something being worn) so as to be touching, fixed to, covering *etc* the upper or outer side of: *She put her coat/hat on.* **2** *adv* used to show a movement forward, a continuing state *etc*: *She kept on asking questions*; *They moved on*; *He carried on reading*; *From now on your work must improve*; *From then on he was happier.* **3** *adj* (*pred*) in progress: *The game was on.* **4** *adj* (*pred*) going to take place; not cancelled: *Is the party on tonight?*; *Is it still on?* **5** *adv, adj* (of electric light, machines *etc*) working: *The television is on*; *Which is the on switch for the television?*; *Turn/Switch the light on.* **6** *adv, adj* (*pred*) (of films *etc*) able to be seen (*eg* at a cinema): *There's a good film on at the cinema this week*; *They're putting on that film again*; *What's on* (= being shown on the television) *tonight?* **7** *adj* (*pred*: *inf*: *usu with neg*) acceptable; right: *Telling lies just isn't on*; *If you want to borrow £5, you're not on!* **8** *adv, adj* (*pred*) in or into a vehicle, train *etc*: *The bus stopped and we got on*; *Is everyone on?*

'oncoming *adj* (*attrib*) approaching: *You should always face the oncoming traffic when you are walking along a road.*

'ongoing *adj* (*formal*: *attrib*) continuing: *the ongoing struggle against male domination.*

onto *see* **on to**.

'onward *adj* (*attrib*: *esp formal*) moving forward (in place or time): *the onward march of time.*

'onward(s) *adv* moving forward (in place or time): *They marched onward(s)*; *Time moved onward(s).*

and so on *see* **so**.

be 'on to (someone) (*inf*) to have discovered (a person's) trick, secret *etc*: *The thieves realized that the police were on to them.*

farther/further on at a later point on a journey, in a book *etc*: *There is more discussion of this farther on*; *Further on, he met an old man with a long, white beard.*

just on almost exactly: *He arrived just on three o'clock*; *Their new baby weighs just on four kilos.*

later on *see* **late**.

on and off *see* **off**.

on and on (*inf*) (used with certain verbs to emphasize the length of an activity) on (*adv def 2*): *She kept on and on asking questions*; *We walked on and on.*

on 'time promptly; at the right time: *He got here on time.*

'on to/'onto to a position on: *He lifted it onto the table.*

once [wʌns] *adv* **1** a single time: *He did it once*; *I shall help you once but then you must do it by yourself*; *If I could see her once again I would be happy*; *You may see her once more and then she will go away.* **2** at a time in the past: *I once went to Paris*; *I once wanted to be a dancer.* – *See also* **once** *in phrases below.* – *conj* when; as soon as: *Once (it had been) unlocked, the door opened easily.*

all at once *see* **all**.

at 'once immediately; without any delay: *Go away at once!*

(just) for once on (this) one occasion only; as an exception: *He doesn't usually allow people to leave work early but he'll let you do it just for once*; *Why can't you be nice to her for once?*

,give (a person, thing *etc*) the 'once-over (*inf*) to look at, study or examine (a person, thing *etc*) quickly: *I haven't got much time but I'll give your report the once-over.*

once and for all once and finally: *Once and for all, I refuse!*

once in a while occasionally: *I meet him once in a while at the club.*

once or twice a few times; on a few occasions: *I don't really know him – I've only met him once or twice.*

once upon a time (used to begin fairy-tales) at a certain time in the past: *Once upon a time, there was a beautiful princess.*

oncoming *see* **on**.

one [wʌn] **1** *nc* the number or figure 1: *Add one and one; One and one is two (1+1=2).* **2** *nu* the age of 1: *Babies start to talk at one.* – *pron* **1** a single person or thing: *She's the one I like the best; I'll buy that one; 'Which book do you want?' 'The red one'; Which ones do you want?* **2** (*more formal than* **you**) anyone; any person: *One can see the city from here; One should look after one's own family and property;* (*Amer also*) *One should look after his own property.* **3** (*very formal or facet*) I: *One doesn't like that sort of foolish behaviour* (= I don't like it). – *adj* **1** (*usu attrib*) 1 in number: *one person; He took one book; He has only one leg – the other was amputated during the war.* **2** (*pred*) aged 1: *The baby will be one tomorrow.* **3** (*formal*) the same; of the same opinion *etc*: *We are one in our love of freedom; We are of one mind on this matter.*

one- (*in cmpds*) having one (of something): *a one-legged man; a one-parent family.* – *See also* **one-** *in phrases below.*

one'self *pron* (*very formal*) **1** used as the object of a verb, the subject of which is **one** or not stated: *One should wash oneself every morning.* **2** used to emphasize **one**: *One does not oneself believe this.* **3** without help *etc*: *One always has to do these things oneself.*

one-off *nc, adj* (*attrib*) (*inf*) (something) made, intended *etc* for one occasion only: *It's just a one-off arrangement.*

ˌone-'sided *adj* **1** (of a competition *etc*) with one person or side having a great advantage over the other: *a one-sided contest; That match was rather one-sided – one of the players was much older than the other.* **2** seeing, accepting or representing only one aspect of a subject: *a one-sided view of the problem; a one-sided discussion; The discussion was rather one-sided – they talked most of the time and we listened.*

ˌone-'way *adj* **1** (of a road or street) in which traffic can move in one direction only: *a one-way street; one-way traffic; Is this street one-way now?* **2** (*esp Amer*) (of a ticket) valid for travel in one direction only, not back again: *a one-way ticket to New York; Is this ticket only one-way?*

one-year-old *nc* a person or animal that is one year old. – *adj* (*attrib*) (of a person, animal or thing) that is one year old. – *See* **eight-year-old** *under* **eight** *for constructions.*

all one just the same; making no difference: *It's all one to me what she does.*

be at one (*formal*) (*usu with* **with**) to be in agreement: *We are at one with the government in this matter.*

be one and the same (person, thing) to be the same person, thing *etc*: *Her father and the murderer were in fact one and the same (person).*

be ˌone 'up on (a person) (*inf*) to have an advantage over (someone): *We brought out a book on this before our rivals so we're one up on them.*

by oneself *see* **by**.

not be oneself to look or feel different from usual, because of illness, anxiety *etc*: *I'd better go home – I'm not myself today; They are not themselves today.*

one and all everyone; all (of a group): *Good evening, one and all; This was agreed by one and all.*

one after another/the other (of a number of people, things *etc*) in a series; each one after the one before: *He broke six windows one after another.*

one another used as the object of a verb when an action takes place between people *etc*: *They hit one another; They said goodbye to one another.* – *See also* **each other**.

one by one (of a number of people, things *etc*) each one alone; one after the other: *The boss wants to see each member of staff one by one; He examined all the vases one by one.*

one or two (*inf*) a few: *I don't want a lot of nuts – I'll just take one or two.*

See also Appendix 1 *and* **first**.

onerous ['ounərəs] *adj* (*formal*) heavy; hard to bear or do: *an onerous task; The burden is too onerous for you to bear alone.*

ongoing *see* **on**.

onion ['ʌnjən] **1** *nc* a type of vegetable with an eatable bulb which has a strong taste and smell. **2** *ncu* the bulb as food: *We had steak and fried onions for dinner; pickled onions; Will you chop some onions for the sauce?; Put plenty of onion in the stew;* (*attrib*) *onion soup.*

onlooker ['onlukə] *nc* a person who watches something happening: *A crowd of onlookers had gathered round the two men who were fighting.*

only ['ounli] *adj* (*attrib*) **1** without any others of the same type, doing the same thing *etc*: *He has no brothers or sisters – he's an only child; This is the only book of its kind in the world; The three of us were the only ones to say thank you to him.* **2** (*inf*) best: *She assured him that this was really the only way to make bread.* – *adv* **1** not more than: *We have only two cups left; He lives only a mile away; We have only one bedroom;* (*inf*) *We can only take three of you in our car;* (*more formally*) *We can take only three of you in our car.* **2** alone: *Only you can do it; Only he would be so cruel; I ˌonly heard 'John* (= the only person I heard was John). **3** showing the one action done, in contrast to other possibilities: *I ˌonly 'heard John* (= I didn't see him, speak to him *etc*); *I ˌonly 'scolded the child – I ˌdid not 'smack him; He is ˌhere only to 'help, not to do ˌeverything him'self.* **4** not longer ago than: *I saw him only yesterday; It was only last week that I saw her.* **5** showing the one possible action or result of an action: *If you do that, you'll only make him angry; We can only hope* (= All we can do is hope) *he won't come.* – *conj* except that; but: *I'd like to go, only I have to work.*

if only *see* **if**.

'only if, only . . . if used to state that something must happen before something else can or will be allowed to happen: *I'll only come if you promise me that you won't invite Mary; 'Will you come?' 'Only if you promise not to invite Mary.'*

'only too very: *I'll be only too pleased to come; She was only too glad to get rid of that car.*

See also **unique**.

onrush ['onrʌʃ] *ncu* a strong forward movement: *the onrush of the water; There was a sudden onrush* *of spectators towards the football pitch.*

onset ['onset] *nc* (*formal*) a beginning: *the onset of a cold*; *the onset of the disease.*

onslaught ['onslo:t] *nc* (*formal*) a fierce attack: *an onslaught on the enemy troops*; (*fig*) *an onslaught of questions.*

onto *see* **on**.

onus ['ounəs] *nc* (*formal*: *no pl*) the responsibility (for doing something): *The onus is on him to prove his theory.*

onward(s) *see* **on**.

onyx ['oniks] *ncu, adj* (of) a type of precious stone with layers of different colours: *The ashtray is* (*made of*) *onyx*; *an onyx ashtray.*

ooze [u:z] **1** *vi* to flow gently or slowly: *The water oozed through the sand*; *The oil is oozing out of the can*; (*formal fig*) *Their courage began to ooze away.* **2** *vt* (*formal*) to have (something liquid) flowing or coming slowly out: *His arm was oozing blood.* – *nu* **1** liquid, slippery mud: *The river bed was thick with ooze.* **2** (*formal*) a slow, gentle flow: *the ooze of blood from a wound.*

'**oozy** *adj* like ooze.

opacity *see* **opaque**.

opal ['oupəl] *ncu* a type of *usu* bluish-white or milky white precious stone, with slight traces or streaks of various other colours: *There are three opals in her brooch*; (*attrib*) *an opal necklace.*

opaque [ə'peik, (*Amer*) ou-] *adj* (*formal*) not able to be seen through; not transparent: *The glass was filled with an opaque liquid*; *Is the glass completely opaque?*

o'paqueness, opacity [ə'pasəti] *nus*: *She is suffering from opacity of the lenses of her eyes.*

open ['oupən] *adj* **1** allowing things or people to go, or be taken or put, through, in, or out; not shut: *an open door/box*; *The gate is wide open*; *The suitcase is not locked – it's open.* **2** allowing the inside to be seen: *an open book*; *The flowers are open now.* **3** (*usu attrib*) ready for business; able to be used: *The shop is open on Sunday afternoons*; *Now that the workmen have finished, the road is open again*; *After the fog had cleared, the airport was soon open again.* **4** which can be entered, seen *etc* by anyone: *The gardens are open to the public*; *an open competition at the golf club.* **5** (*usu attrib*) (of cloth *etc*) with (wide) spaces between the threads: *This material has a very open weave.* **6** not hidden or kept secret: *The affair is quite open*; *an open show of affection*; *They are quite open about their love for each other.* **7** willing to talk, *esp* about oneself; friendly: *He was very open with me about his work and interests*; *He is a frank, open young man.* **8** (*esp pred*) not finally decided; still being discussed, considered *etc*: *Leave the matter open*; *What the government should do about inflation is an open question*; *Is the vacancy for a typist still open?*; *Is your offer of help still open?* (= still available). **9** (*usu attrib*) empty; with no walls, trees, buildings *etc*: *I like to be out in the open country*; *They're going to build offices in the open space next to our factory.* **10** (*attrib*) without a roof: *an open car.* – *vti* **1** to make or become open: *He opened the door*; *The door opened*; *When she opened her eyes again, the men had gone*; *He opened the box.* **2** (*often with* **with**) to begin: *He opened the meeting with a speech of welcome*; *The meeting opened with a speech from the chairman.* **3** to start, begin business *etc*: *They opened a new shop in the High Street*; *When was the new library opened to the public?*; *The shop opened last week*; *The shop opens at nine o'clock every morning.* – *See also* **open** *in phrases below.*

'**opener** *nc* (*usu in cmpds*) something that opens (something): *a tin-opener*; *a bottle-opener.*

'**opening 1** *nc* a hole; a clear or open space (*def 3*): *an opening in the hedge/fence/forest.* **2** *nc* a beginning: *the opening of the film*; (*attrib*) *The opening scene of the film is set in Paris*; (*attrib*) *the chairman's opening remarks at a meeting.* **3** *nu* the act of becoming or making open (*defs 1–4*): *the opening of a flower/shop/door*; (*attrib*) *the opening night of a play/film* (= the first night on which it is performed/shown). **4** *nc* a ceremony to mark the beginning of business in (a public building *etc*): *We went to the opening of the new theatre.* **5** *nc* (*formal*) an opportunity for work: *There are good openings in the shipping industry*; *There is an opening in this firm for a production manager.*

'**openly** *adv* without trying to hide anything; frankly: *She talked very openly about it*; *They were openly in love with each other.*

'**open-air** *adj* (*attrib*) in the open air; outside: *an open-air meeting.* – *See also* **in the open air** *below.*

ˌ**open-'minded** *adj* willing to consider new ideas; *an open-minded approach to the problem*; *I shall hear what everyone has to say – I am completely open-minded on the subject.* – *See also* **keep/have an open mind** *below.*

ˌ**open-'plan** *adj* (of a building) built with few walls inside: *In this open-plan school, there are no separate classrooms for each class*; *The new primary school is completely open-plan.*

'**open season** *nc* a period of the year in which particular animals, birds, fish *etc* may be legally killed for sport: *When is the open season for pheasants?*

be an open secret to be known to many people although supposed to be a secret: *It's an open secret that he is having an affair with the boss's wife.*

be out in the open to have become generally known: *Although the government tried to keep the matter secret, it's all out in the open now.*

bring (something) out into the open to make (something) public: *This affair has been kept a secret for too long – it's time it was brought out into the open.*

come (out) into the open to make one's opinions known: *At first, he made no criticism of the government, but eventually he came out into the open and attacked its policies.*

in the 'open 1 outside; in the open air: *It's very healthy for children to be able to play in the open.* **2** in the country: *It's lovely to be able to spend the week-ends out in the open, after being in town all week.*

in the open air outside; not in a building: *If it doesn't rain, we'll have the party in the open air.* – *See also* **open-air** *above.*

keep/have an open mind to have a willingness to listen to or accept new ideas, other people's suggestions *etc* (*eg* before making a decision): *It doesn't seem to be a very good plan, but I think we should keep an open mind about it for the time being.* – *See also* **open-minded** *above.*

lay oneself open to *see* **open to** *below.*

open fire *see* **fire**.

open on to *vt fus* (of a door *etc*) to open towards (a garden *etc*): *Our front door opens straight on to the street – we have no front garden.*

open out 1 *vt sep* to unfold or spread out (a map): *The hikers opened out the map to see which route they* *ought to take*; *They opened it out carefully.* **2** *vi* (of flowers) to become open: *The tulips are beginning to open out at last.*

the open sea any area of sea far from land: *The sea was calm close to shore, but once they were out in the open sea, they were faced with large waves and a strong gale blowing.*

'open to 1 likely to receive (criticism *etc*): *If you give him a gift in return for his help, you'll be laying yourself open to charges of corruption.* **2** willing to listen to *etc*: *He's always open to suggestions from any member of staff.* **3** possible or available for: *There are only two possible courses of action open to us* (= There are only two things we can do) *if we want to stop this.*

open up 1 *vt sep* to open (a shop *etc*): *They've opened up a new shop in the High Street*; *I open up the shop at nine o'clock every morning*; *She opened it up yesterday.* **2** *vt sep* to open (a box *etc*) completely: *He opened up the parcel*; *He opened it up quickly.* **3** *vi* (*usu in imperative*) to open the (main) door of a building *etc*: *'Open up!' shouted the policeman. 'We know you are in there!'*

throw open *see* **throw**.

with open arms in a very friendly way: *They received their visitors with open arms.*

opera[1] ['opərə] *ncu* a musical drama in which the dialogue is sung: *The company are performing an opera by Verdi*; *I'm very keen on opera.*

ˌope'ratic [-'ra-] *adj* (*usu attrib*) of, or relating to, opera: *an operatic society*; *an operatic singer.*

ˌope'retta [-'retə] *nc* a short, less serious musical drama.

'opera glasses *n pl* binoculars for use in a theatre.

'opera-house *nc* a theatre in which operas are performed.

opera[2] *see* **opus**.

operate ['opəreit] **1** *vi* (*formal*) (of machines *etc*) to act or work: *The sewing-machine isn't operating properly.* **2** *vi* (*often with* **for** *and* **on**) to do or perform an operation (*def 3*): *The surgeon operated on her for appendicitis*; *Dr Jones is operating this morning.* **3** *vti* (*formal*) to do business; to control or direct (a business): *They operate a small factory in the south of England*; *The firm operates from the south of England.* **4** *vt* (*formal*) to make (a machine *etc*) work: *You must be very clever to operate that machine.*

ˌope'ration 1 *nc* an action or process, *esp* when planned: *The whole operation only took five minutes*; *a rescue operation.* **2** *nu* the process of acting or working: *the operation of a machine*; *Our plan is now in operation.* **3** *nc* the act of cutting open or cutting off a part of the body in order to cure disease: *She had an operation on her eye/for appendicitis.* **4** *nc* (*mil*: *often in pl*) the movement, fighting *etc* of armies: *The general was in command of operations in the north.*

ˌope'rational *adj* (*formal*) ready for action; in good working order: *The machine is fully operational*; *all operational machinery.*

'operative [-rətiv, (*Amer*) -reitiv] *adj* (*formal*: *usu pred*) **1** working; in action: *The airport is operative again after the bad weather.* **2** (of a rule, law) in force; having effect: *Many old laws which are irrelevant to the modern world are still operative.*

'operator *nc* **1** a person who works a machine: *a lift operator.* **2** a person who works in a telephone exchange whose job is to connect people making telephone calls with the people they wish to speak to: *Ask the operator to connect you to that number.*

'operating-table *nc* a special table on which operations are performed: *The patient died on the operating table.*

'operating-theatre *nc* (*sometimes* **theatre**) the room in a hospital in which operations are performed: *She was given an anaesthetic before being taken into the operating-theatre.*

See also **inoperable, inoperative**.

operetta *see* **opera**[1].

ophthalmic [of'θalmik] *adj* (*formal or tech*: *esp attrib*) of or concerning the eye: *an ophthalmic surgeon.*

opiate *see* **opium**.

opinion [ə'pinjən] **1** *ncu* what a person thinks or believes: *My opinions about education have changed.* **2** *nc* a (professional) judgement, *usu* of a doctor, lawyer *etc*: *He wanted a second opinion on his illness.* **3** *nc* (*no pl*) what one thinks of the worth or value of someone or something: *I have a very high opinion of his work.*

(ˌself-)o'pinionated [-nei-] *adj* (*formal*) having very strong opinions which one is unwilling to change: *She's a very (self-)opinionated woman.*

be of the opinion (that) (*formal*) to think: *He is of the opinion that nothing more can be done.*

in 'my, 'your *etc* **opinion** according to what I, you *etc* think: *In my opinion, he's right.*

a matter of opinion 1 something about which different people (may) have different opinions: *Whether it is better to marry young or not is a matter of opinion.* **2** an expression used to show that one does not agree with another person's opinion: *He says the book is excellent but that's a matter of opinion* (= I don't agree with him).

public opinion poll *see* **public**.

opium ['oupiəm] *nu* a drug made from the dried juice of a type of poppy.

opiate ['oupiət] *nc* (*formal*) **1** any drug containing opium, used to make a person sleep: *The doctor gave him an opiate.* **2** (*fig*) anything that calms or dulls the mind or feelings: *The music was an opiate to his tired brain.*

opponent [ə'pounənt] *nc* **1** a person who fights against (someone or something) by force or argument: *an opponent of the government.* **2** a person who competes against someone (in a game): *He beat his opponent by four points.*

See also **oppose, opposition**.

opportunity [opə'tju:nəti] *ncu* a time when the circumstances are right for doing something; a chance to do (something): *I had/got an opportunity to go to Rome*; *He gave me the opportunity of reading his book*; *You've had several opportunities to ask him, so why haven't you?*; *At last the opportunity came for him to leave*; *I don't have much opportunity to go to the cinema these days.* – *See also* **take the opportunity** *below.*

ˌoppor'tune *adj* (*formal*) suitable or right, *esp* coming at the right time: *It seemed an opportune moment to leave the room*; *an opportune remark*; *It was most opportune that a taxi arrived just as I was leaving the house.* **ˌoppor'tunely** *adv.* **ˌoppor'tuneness** *nu.*

ˌoppor'tunist *nc* (*derog*) a person who takes advantage of any opportunity or circumstance which will help him personally: *a political opportunist.* **ˌoppor'tunism** *nu.*

take the opportunity (of doing something) to do (something) at a particularly good or suitable time *esp* when doing something else: *I took the*

opportunity of visiting some old friends while I was in London on business.
See also **inopportune**.

oppose [ə'pouz] *vt* **1** to resist or fight against (someone or something) by force or argument: *We oppose the government on this matter.* **2** to act or compete against (someone or something): *Who is opposing him in the election?*
as op'posed to separate or distinct from; in contrast with: *It happened in the late afternoon, as opposed to the evening.*
be op'posed to (*formal*) not to want something to be done *etc*: *I am strongly opposed to you(r) going abroad.*
See also **opponent, opposition**.

opposite ['opəzit] *adj* **1** (*attrib*) being on the other side of (something): *He lives on the opposite side of (the) town; I was on the opposite side of the street (to him).* **2** completely different: *The two men walked off in opposite directions; He and I are on opposite sides in this argument; His views and mine are completely opposite.* – *prep, adv* on the opposite side of (something) in relation to something else: *He lives in the house opposite (mine); The shop is opposite the station.* – *nc* something that is completely different: *Hate is the opposite of love; Love and hate are opposites.*
opposite number (*inf*) the person who does the same job *etc* as someone in another company, country *etc*: *Our Sales Manager is having discussions with his opposite number in their firm.*

opposition [opə'ziʃən] *nu* **1** the act of resisting or fighting against (someone or something) by force or argument: *There is a lot of opposition to his ideas; His ideas met with a lot of opposition.* **2** the people who are fighting or competing against (someone): *In war and business, one should always get to know one's opposition; (Brit) The Labour Party has formed a government and the Conservative Party is in opposition* (= forming the Opposition).
the Opposition (*Brit*) the political party which is opposed to the governing party: *The Opposition voted against the bill.*
See also **oppose**.

oppress [ə'pres] *vt* (*formal*) **1** to govern cruelly: *The king oppressed his people.* **2** to worry or depress: *The thought of leaving her oppressed me.*
op'pression [-ʃən] *nu*: *The dictator was hated because of his oppression of the peasants; After five years of oppression, the peasants revolted.*
op'pressive [-siv] *adj* **1** oppressing; cruel; hard to bear; *oppressive laws/taxes; The employers regard the new employment laws as oppressive.* **2** (of weather) hot and without wind: *It is always oppressive before a storm; such oppressive weather.*
op'pressively *adj.* **op'pressiveness** *nu.*
op'pressor *nc* (*formal*) a ruler who oppresses his people; a tyrant: *The people have murdered their oppressor.*

opprobrium [ə'proubriəm] *nu* (*formal*) public disgrace or scorn: *His dishonest activities earned him the opprobrium of his colleagues.*

opt [opt] *vti* (*slightly formal*) to choose: *He opted to go home; She opted for a trip to Rome.*
opt out *vi* (*often with* **of**) to choose or decide not to do something or take part in something: *You promised to help us, so you can't opt out (of it) now.*

optician [op'tiʃən] *nc* **1** a person who makes and sells spectacles and optical instruments: *The optician mended my spectacles.* **2** an optician's practice: *Is there an optician near here?*

optic ['optik] *adj* (*formal or tech*: *esp attrib*) of or concerning the eye or one's ability to see: *the optic nerve.*
optical ['optikəl] *adj* (*formal or tech*: *esp attrib*) of or concerning sight or what one sees: *The two objects in the picture appear to be the same size, but this is just an optical illusion* (= they are not actually the same size); *This shop sells microscopes and other optical instruments.*
op'tician's *nc* an optician's practice: *I got this at the optician's.*
optics ['optiks] *n sing* (*tech*) the science of light.

optimal *see* **optimum**.

optimism ['optimizəm] *nu* a state of mind in which one always hopes or expects that something good will happen or that nothing unpleasant will happen: *Even when it was obvious to the others that he was not going to succeed he was full of optimism.*
'optimist *nc.*
ˌopti'mistic *adj* always hoping or believing that something good will happen: *an optimistic person/attitude; I think it is rather optimistic to assume that you'll get an increase in salary.*
ˌopti'mistically *adv.*

optimum ['optiməm], **optimal** ['optiməl] *adjs* (*formal or tech*) best: *the optimum conditions for growth; Conditions for the growth of that plant are optimal in early summer.*

option ['opʃən] *nc* (*more formal than* **choice**) choice: *There are several options open to you; You have no option but to obey him* (= You have to obey him).
'optional *adj* a matter of choice; not compulsory: *Evening dress is optional; Music is optional at our school; Spanish is an optional subject.*

opulent ['opjulənt] *adj* (*formal*) luxurious; rich: *They lived in opulent surroundings; Their surroundings are indeed opulent; (fig) the opulent growth of tropical plants.* **'opulently** *adv.* **'opulence** *nu.*

opus ['oupəs] – *pl* **opera** ['opərə] – *nc* (*formal*: *sometimes abbrev* **op** *when written*) a work, *esp* a musical composition: *They're playing Haydn's opus 76.*

or [oː] *conj* **1** used to show an alternative: *Is that your book or is it mine?; Is your book green, or blue?* **2** because if not: *You had better hurry or you'll be late.*
either ... or *see* **either**.
or else *see* **else**.
or 'so (*inf*) about; approximately: *I bought a dozen or so (books).*
whether ... or *see* **whether**.

oracle ['orəkl] *nc* **1** (*often facet*) a very wise, knowledgeable person: *I don't know the answer to this problem, so I'd better go and ask the oracle.* **2** (*hist*) a holy place where a god was believed to give answers to questions: *the oracle at Delphi.* **3** (*hist*) the answer given by the god. **4** (*hist*) the priest(ess) through whom the oracle spoke.

oral ['oːrəl] *adj* **1** (*formal*) spoken, not written: *an oral examination; Is the examination only oral?* **2** (*tech*: *esp attrib*) of the mouth: *oral hygiene.* **3** (*formal or tech*: *esp attrib*) taken in by the mouth: *an oral contraceptive.* – *nc* a spoken examination: *He passed the written exam, but failed his oral.*
'orally *adv* by the mouth: *medicine to be taken orally.*
See also **aural**.

orange ['orindʒ] **1** *nc* a type of juicy citrus fruit with a thick reddish-yellow skin: *He was eating an* *orange*; *Would you like a piece of orange?* (*attrib*) *an orange drink*; (*attrib*) *an orange tree.* **2** *nu* the colour of this fruit. **3** *ncu* (a glass of) an orange drink: *I'd like an orange, please.* – *adj* **1** of the colour orange: *an orange dress*; *Is the dress orange or red?* **2** (*usu attrib*) with the taste of orange juice: *an orange drink.*

orang-utan ['o:raŋ'u:tan] *nc* a type of large, man-like ape.

oration [ə'reiʃən] *nc* (*formal*) a formal, public speech, *esp* in fine, beautiful language: *He delivered an oration to the people*; *a funeral oration.*

orator ['orətə] *nc* (*formal*) a person who makes public speeches, *esp* very eloquent ones: *the orators of ancient Rome*; *Very few politicians are good orators.*

'oratory ['orə-] *nu* (*formal*) the art of speaking well in public: *I have always admired his oratory.*

orb [o:b] *nc* **1** (*liter*) anything in the shape of a ball *esp* a star, planet *etc.* **2** (*formal*) a (*usu* jewelled) ball with a cross on top carried by a king or queen *eg* at their coronation or on some other very formal occasions.

orbit ['o:bit] *nc* the path in which something moves around a planet, star *etc, eg* the path of the Earth round the Sun or a spacecraft round the Earth: *The spaceship is in orbit round the moon.* – *vt* to go round (the Sun, Earth *etc*) in space: *The spacecraft orbits the Earth every 24 hours.*

orchard ['o:tʃəd] *nc* a garden or other area in which fruit trees are grown: *They have planted an apple orchard*; *a cherry orchard.*

orchestra ['o:kəstrə] *nc* a (*usu* large) group of musicians playing together, led by a conductor: *He plays the violin in an orchestra.*

or'chestral [-'kes-] *adj* (usu attrib) for, or given by, an orchestra: *orchestral music*; *an orchestral concert.*

'orchestrate [-streit] *vt* **1** (*music*) to arrange (a piece of music) for an orchestra: *He had the tune orchestrated.* **2** (*fig formal*) to organize or arrange (something) so as to achieve the best result: *He orchestrated the whole political campaign.*

orchid ['o:kid] *nc* a kind of plant *usu* having brightly-coloured or unusually-shaped flowers: *He sent her a white orchid on her birthday – it was very expensive.*

ordain [o:'dein] *vt* **1** to make (someone), a priest, minister *etc, usu* by a church ceremony: *He was ordained a priest.* **2** (*formal*) to order or command formally: *The king ordained that the prisoners should be freed*; *He felt that he had been ordained by fate to lead his people.*

See also **ordinance, ordination.**

ordeal [o:'di:l] *nc* a difficult, painful experience: *She went through a terrible ordeal when her husband died*; *Being kidnapped was an ordeal for the child.*

order ['o:də] **1** *nc* a statement (by a person in authority) of what someone must do; a command or instruction: *Go home – that is an order*; *He gave me my orders.* **2** *nc* (*often with* **for**) an instruction to make or supply (something): *The factory has received several orders from Germany for these special gates.* **3** *nc* the thing(s) made or supplied: *Your order is nearly ready.* **4** *nu* a tidy or efficient state: *Everything in the house is in* (*good*) *order.* – *See also* **in (good) running/working order** *below.* **5** *nu* (*formal*) a regular system or method of acting or living: *I must have order in my life.* **6** *ncu* the arrangement (of people, things *etc*) in space, time *etc*: *Write the names in any order*; *in alphabetical order*; *Describe the events in chronological order* (= in the order in which they happened); *in order of importance.* **7** *nu* a peaceful condition; the absence of crime: *law and order*; *You must keep order among the children.* **8** *nc* a written instruction to pay money: *a banker's order*; *a postal order.* **9** *nc* (*formal or tech*) a group, kind or class: *This is a list of the various orders of plants*; *This research work demands intelligence of a high order.* **10** *nu* the arrangement of groups or classes in relationship to each other: *the social order.* **11** *nc* a religious society, *esp* of monks: *the Benedictine order.* **12** *nc* (*usu with cap*) (the people belonging to) a special group, membership of which is granted by a king *etc* as an honour: *the Order of the Garter.* – *See also* **order** *in phrases below.* – **1** *vt* to tell (someone) to do something (from a position of authority): *He ordered me to stand up.* **2** *vt* to give an instruction to someone to make or supply (something): *I have ordered some new furniture from the shop.* **3** *vti* to ask someone to supply food *etc* in a hotel, restaurant *etc*: *He ordered a steak*; *Have you ordered yet?* **4** *vt* to arrange or put in order: *Should we order these alphabetically?*; (*formal fig*) *You must try to order your thoughts, then you will be more convincing in an argument.* – *See also* **order** *in phrases below.*

'orderly *adj* **1** (*formal*) in good order; well-arranged: *an orderly room.* **2** well-behaved; quiet: *an orderly queue of people*; *in an orderly manner*; *The prisoners were quiet and orderly.* – *nc* **1** a hospital attendant who does routine jobs: *A hospital orderly took the patient back to the ward from the operating-theatre.* **2** a soldier who carries an officer's orders and messages. **'orderliness** *nu.*

'order-form *nc* a form on which a customer's order is written.

be in, take (holy) orders (*formal*) to be, or become, a priest, minister *etc.*

by 'order (of) (*formal*) because someone in authority has ordered it: *No parking on this side of the street, by order* (*of the police*).

in 'order 1 (*formal*) correct according to what is regularly done, *esp* in meetings *etc*: *It is quite in order to end the meeting now.* **2** in a good efficient state: *Everything is in order for the party.*

in 'order (that) (*formal*) for the purpose of allowing or causing (something) to happen; so that: *He checked all his figures again in order that the report might be as good as possible.*

in 'order to for the purpose of: *I went home in order to change my clothes*; *I left early in order not to be late.*

in (good) running/working order (of a machine *etc*) working well or able to work well: *The car is in good running order.*

made to order made when and how a customer wishes: *curtains made to order.*

on 'order having been ordered but not yet supplied: *We don't have any copies of this book at the moment, but it's on order.*

order about *vt usu sep* (*often derog*) to keep on giving orders (to someone): *I'm tired of him ordering me about all the time.*

out of order 1 not working (properly): *The machine is out of order.* **2** (*formal*) not correct according to what is regularly done, *esp* in meetings *etc*: *The last speaker was out of order in saying that.*

take (holy) orders *see* **be in (holy) orders** *above.*

take orders from (someone) to do what someone tells one to do: *I'm not going to take orders from you!*

a tall order (*inf*) a difficult job or task: *Asking us to finish this by Friday is a bit of a tall order.*

See also **disorder**.

ordinal ['o:dinl]: **ordinal numbers** *n pl* (*formal or math*) the numbers which show order in a series *ie* first, second, third *etc*.

See also **cardinal**.

ordinance ['o:dinəns] *nc* (*formal*) a rule or law: *government ordinances.*

ordinary ['o:dənəri] *adj* **1** (*usu attrib*) usual; as is often seen, done *etc*: *Typing letters isn't my ordinary job – I'm just helping to get this pile of letters finished; He works on Sundays – so it's just an ordinary working day to him; She was behaving in a perfectly ordinary manner.* **2** (*derog*) not unusually good *etc*: *Some people love his poetry but I think it's rather ordinary; She's very beautiful but he is a very ordinary young man.*

'ordinarily *adv* as a general rule; usually: *Ordinarily I wouldn't do this, but I will this time because it is very important.*

out of the ordinary unusual: *I don't consider her behaviour at all out of the ordinary.*

See also **extraordinary**.

ordination [o:di'neiʃən] *ncu* the act of making (a person) a priest, minister *etc*, or the ceremony at which this is done: *The Roman Catholic Church does not allow the ordination of women; We went to his ordination.*

See also **ordain**.

ordnance ['o:dnəns]: **Ordnance Survey (Department)** *nu* (a government department dealing with) the production of official detailed maps of Great Britain and Ireland: *He works for the Ordnance Survey*; (*attrib*) *an Ordnance Survey map.*

ore [o:] *ncu* any mineral, rock *etc* from which a metal is obtained: *iron ore.*

organ[1] ['o:gən] *nc* **1** (*formal or tech*) a part of the body or a plant which has a special purpose *eg* the liver, a leaf: *the reproductive organs*; (*fig*) *Parliament is the main organ of government in Britain.* **2** (*formal*) a means of spreading information, *eg* a newspaper: *an organ of the Communist Party.*

or'ganic [-'ga-] *adj* **1** (*formal or tech*) of or concerning the organs of the body: *organic diseases; There is nothing organic wrong with you.* **2** (*tech*: *esp attrib*) of, found in, or produced by, living things: *Organic compounds all contain carbon.* **3** (*esp attrib*) (of food) grown without the use of artificial fertilizers: *Some people will eat only organic food.*

or'ganically *adv*: *Was this food organically grown?; There's nothing organically wrong with him – all the medical tests proved negative.*

See also **inorganic**.

organ[2] ['o:gən] *nc* **1** a *usu* large musical instrument similar to a piano in which sound is produced by air being forced through pipes: *He plays the organ; He played the tune on the organ.* **2** any similar instrument without pipes: *an electric organ.*

'organist *nc* a person who plays the organ: *the organist in the church.*

organdie ['o:gəndi] *nu, adj* (of) a very fine, thin, stiff muslin material: *Her dress was (made of) organdie; an organdie dress.*

organic *see* **organ**[1].

organism ['o:gənizəm] *nc* a *usu* small living animal or plant: *A pond is full of small organisms.*

organist *see* **organ**[2].

organize, -ise ['o:gənaiz] *vt* **1** to arrange or prepare (something), *usu* requiring some time or effort: *They organized a party/a conference.* **2** (*with* **into**) to make (a group of people *etc*) into a society *etc*: *He organized the workers into a trade union.* **'organizer, -s-** *nc*.

,organi'zation, -s- **1** *nc* a group of people working together for a purpose: *a business organization.* **2** *nu* the act of organizing: *Efficiency depends on the organization of one's work.* **3** *nu* the state of being organized: *This report lacks organization.*

'organized, -s- *adj* **1** able to plan or do (work) well; efficient: *She is very organized in her work; She's a very organized person.* **2** well-arranged: *an organized report.* **3** (*usu attrib*) having been arranged or planned: *an organized protest.*

See also **disorganized, reorganize**.

orgasm ['o:gazəm] *ncu* the climax of sexual excitement.

orgy ['o:dʒi] *nc* **1** (*formal*) a wild party or celebration: *a drunken/sexual orgy.* **2** (*fig derog*) any activity done to too great an extent: *an orgy of shopping/drinking.*

Orient ['o:riənt]: **the Orient** (*liter*) the east (China, Japan *etc*): *the mysteries of the Orient.*

,ori'ental [-'en-] *adj* in or from the east: *oriental art: That dress looks very oriental; Her features are very oriental.* – *nc* (*often derog*: *sometimes with cap*) a person who comes from the east: *There are a lot of Orientals in London.*

orientate ['o:riənteit], (*Amer*) **orient** ['o:riənt] *v refl* **1** to get used to (unfamiliar surroundings, conditions *etc*): *She soon managed to orientate herself in her new environment.* **2** to decide or find out (one's position) in relation to something else: *The hikers tried to orientate themselves before continuing their walk.* **,orien'tation** *nu*.

orienteering [o:riən'tiəriŋ] *nu* the sport of finding one's way across country with the help of a map and compass.

origin ['oridʒin] *ncu* the place or point from which anything first comes or starts; the cause (of something): *the origin(s) of the English language; There are several words of English origin in French; This was the origin of the disagreement.* – *See also* **origins** *below*.

o'riginal [ə'ri-] *adj* **1** existing at the beginning; first: *This part of the house is new but the rest is original; Who were the original inhabitants of Britain?* **2** (able to produce ideas which are) new, fresh or not thought of before: *He produces a lot of original ideas; He has a very original mind; That drawing is very original; She cannot write in an original way.* **3** (*usu attrib*) not copied: *The original painting is in the museum, but there are hundreds of copies.* – *nc* **1** the earliest version: *This is the original – all the others are copies.* **2** a model from which a painting *etc* is made: *She is the original of the famous portrait.*

o,rigi'nality [əridʒi'na-] *nu*: *He has great originality; His writing shows originality.*

o'riginally *adv*: *I liked him originally but I don't now.*

originate [ə'ridʒineit] *vti* (*formal*) to bring or come into being; to start: *Darwin originated the theory of evolution; The theory of evolution originated with Darwin; That style of painting originated in China.*

ˈ**origins** *n pl* a person's place of birth, family, background *etc*: *He tried to hide his origins.*

ornament [ˈoːnəmənt] *ncu* something decorative, *eg* carving *etc* used or intended to make a room, house, building *etc* more beautiful: *There was a china dog along with other ornaments on the mantelpiece; Most modern architects use as little ornament as possible.* – [oːnəˈment] *vt* to decorate, or add ornament(s) to (something): *The church was richly ornamented.* ˌ**ornamenˈtation** *nu.*

ˌ**ornaˈmental** [-ˈmen-] *adj* used for ornament: *an ornamental pool in the garden; Those clocks no longer work – they're purely ornamental.* ˌ**ornaˈmentally** *adv.*

ornate [oːˈneit] *adj* (*often derog*) with a lot of ornament; not plain and simple: *The church has an ornate doorway; That style of furniture is too ornate for my taste.* **orˈnately** *adv.* **orˈnateness** *nu.*

ornithology [oːniˈθolədʒi] *nu* (*tech*) the scientific study of birds and their behaviour: *He is interested in ornithology.* ˌ**ornithoˈlogical** [-ˈlo-] *adj.* ˌ**orniˈthologist** *nc.*

orphan [ˈoːfən] *nc* a child who has lost both parents (rarely only one parent): *That little girl is an orphan; (attrib) an orphan child.* – *v see* **be orphaned** *below.*

ˈ**orphanage** [-nidʒ] *nc* a home for orphans: *He was brought up in an orphanage.*

be ˈorphaned to become an orphan: *She was orphaned when her parents died in a car-crash.*

orthodox [ˈoːθədoks] *adj* **1** (*formal or relig*: *neg* **un-**) (having opinions and beliefs) that are the same as those of most people in one's country, religion *etc*: *The party is worried about those members who do not hold orthodox beliefs; He's a good man but are his views orthodox?; Her behaviour was far from orthodox.* **2** (*with cap*) of the **(Eastern) Orthodox Church**, one branch of the Christian church found *esp* in eastern Europe.

ˈ**orthodoxy** *nu* **1** (*formal*) the state of being orthodox or having orthodox beliefs: *I doubt his orthodoxy; I doubt the orthodoxy of his beliefs.* **2** (*with cap*) the beliefs *etc* of the Orthodox Church.

orthop(a)edics [oːθəˈpiːdiks] *n sing* the branch of medicine which concerns diseases and injuries of the bones: *He specialized in orthopaedics; (attrib) the orthopaedics department of the hospital.*

ˌ**orthoˈp(a)edic** *adj* (*tech or formal*: *esp attrib*): *He consulted an orthopaedic specialist about his sore back.*

oscillate [ˈosileit] *vi* (*tech*) to swing backwards and forwards like the pendulum of a clock; to vary or move between two points, amounts *etc*: *Radio-waves oscillate; (formal fig) He oscillated between two opinions.* ˌ**oscilˈlation** *ncu.*

ostensible [oˈstensəbl] *adj* (*formal*: *attrib*) (of reasons *etc*) apparent, stated or claimed, but not necessarily true: *Illness was the ostensible reason for his absence, but in fact he was just too lazy to come.* **oˈstensibly** *adv.*

ostentatious [ostenˈteiʃəs] *adj* (*formal derog*) behaving, done *etc* in such a way as to be seen by other people and to impress them: *an ostentatious style of living; Their style of living is very ostentatious; She's a very ostentatious person; She made an ostentatious offer of help to impress the other ladies.* ˌ**ostenˈtation,** ˌ**ostenˈtatiousness** *nus.*

ˌ**ostenˈtatiously** *adv* (*formal derog*): *an ostentatiously large house.*

osteopath [ˈostiəpaθ] *nc* a person who treats injuries to bones, muscles *etc* by making sure the bones and parts of the body are in the correct position (not by drugs or surgery): *He refused to go to the orthopaedic department of the hospital – instead he went to an osteopath to have his slipped disc cured.* ˌ**osteˈopathy** [-ˈo-] *nu* (*tech*).

ostracize, -ise [ˈostrəsaiz] *vt* (*formal*) to refuse to accept (someone) in society or a group: *His former friends ostracized him because of his rudeness.* ˈ**ostracism** *nu.*

ostrich [ˈostritʃ] *nc* a type of large bird which cannot fly.

other [ˈʌðə] **1** *adj* (*attrib*), *pron* the second of two: *I have lost my other glove; He lives on the other side of town; I've got one of my gloves but I can't find the other (one).* **2** *adj* (*attrib*), *pron* those people, things *etc* not mentioned, present *etc*; additional; different: *Some of them have arrived – where are the others?; The baby is here and the other children are at school; There must be some other reason for him refusing to help.* **3** *adj* (*attrib*) (*with* **day, week** *etc*) recently past: *I saw him just the other day/morning.*

ˈ**otherwise** *adv* **1** in every other way except this: *She has a big nose but otherwise she is very good-looking.* **2** (*formal*) in a different way; doing, thinking *etc* something else: *He seems to think otherwise; I am otherwise engaged this evening.* – *conj* or else; if not: *Take a taxi – otherwise you won't get there in time.*

each other *see* **each**.

every other *adj* **1** (*less formal than* **alternate**) using, involving *etc* one person or thing in a series, then leaving or not involving the next before going on to the next again: *Leave every other line on the exam paper blank* (= Write on one line, leave the next one blank, then write on the next *etc*); *I work only every other day.* **2** all the others: *I've not read that one but I've read every other book in the library.*

ˌ**no/**ˌ**none ˈother than** the very same person as: *The man who had sent the flowers was none other than the man she had spoken to the night before.*

one after another/the other, one another *see* **one.**

on the other hand *see* **hand**.

ˈ**other than** except: *There was no-one there other than an old woman; There was nothing to do other than (to) wait.*

ˈ**somehow or other** in some way not known or decided; by some means if not by another: *Somehow or other I know she had no intention of coming to the party; I'll finish this job on time somehow or other.*

ˈ**someone/**ˈ**something or other** a person or thing that is not known, that has not been chosen *etc*: *Someone or other broke that window, and I intend to find out who; Someone or other will have to ask him; There must be something or other we can use.*

ˈ**somewhere or other** in one place if not in another; in some place not known or decided: *He must have hidden it somewhere or other.*

See also **another**.

otter [ˈotə] *nc* a type of small, furry, river animal that eats fish.

ouch [autʃ] *interj* an expression of pain: *Ouch! That hurt!*

ought [oːt] – *neg short form* **oughtn't** [ˈoːtnt] – *modal aux* (*usu with* **to**) **1** used to indicate duty or need; should: *You ought to help them; You ought to have gone; He ought not to do that; 'Oughtn't I to* *have done that?' 'No, you oughtn't.'* **2** used to indicate something that one can or could reasonably expect; should: *The weather ought to be fine tomorrow; He ought to have been able to do it; He ought to be home by now – I don't know why he's late.*

ounce [auns] *nc* **1** (*usu abbrev* **oz** *when written*) a unit of weight, one-sixteenth of a pound, 28·35 grammes. **2** (*fig: usu with a neg*) a very small amount; any: *He hasn't an ounce of common sense.*

our [auə] *adj* (*attrib*) belonging to us: *This is our house; Here is our son.*

ours [auəz] *pron* the one(s) belonging to us: *The house is ours; 'Are these your books?' 'No, we put ours on the shelf.'*

our'selves *pron* **1** used as the object of a verb when the person speaking and other people are the object of an action *etc* they perform: *We saw ourselves in the mirror; John and I saw ourselves in the mirror.* **2** used to emphasize **we, us** or the names of the speaker and other people performing an action *etc*: *We ourselves played no part in this.* **3** without help *etc*: *We'll just have to finish the job ourselves.*

by ourselves *see* **by oneself** *under* **by**.

we are not ourselves *see* **not be oneself** *under* **one**.

See also **us, we**.

oust [aust] *vt* (*formal*) to force out (and take the place of): *She ousted him as leader of the party; He was ousted from the post of manager by the younger members of staff.*

out [aut] **1** *adv, adj* (*pred*) not in a building *etc*; from inside a building *etc*; in(to) the open air: *The children are out in the garden; They went out for a walk; The old lady rarely goes out now; When he got home, he found he had been locked out.* **2** *adv* from inside (something): *He opened the desk and took out a pencil.* **3** *adv, adj* (*pred*) away from home, an office *etc*: *We had an evening out; The manager is out.* **4** *adv, adj* (*pred*) far away: *The ship was out at sea; He went out to India.* **5** *adv* loudly and clearly: *He shouted out the answer;* (*fig*) *People should speak out about what they believe.* **6** *adv* completely: *She was tired out; The fire had burnt out.* **7** *adv, adj* (*pred*) not burning: *He put his cigarette out; The fire was out.* **8** *adv, adj* (*pred*) inaccurate; not correct: *The bill was £2 out; The increase in the price of petrol put my calculations out; My calculations seem to be out.* **9** *adv, adj* (*pred*) free, known, available *etc*: *He opened the sack and let the cat out; The secret is out; The autumn issue of the magazine is out.* **10** *adv, adj* (*pred*) (in games) having been defeated: *The batsman is out; The batsman was caught out.* **11** *adv, adj* (*pred*) (*inf*) on strike: *The men came out in protest against their working conditions; The dockworkers are out again.* **12** *adv, adj* (*pred*) (*inf*) no longer in fashion: *Pointed shoes have gone right out; Long hair is definitely out.* **13** *adv, adj* (*pred*) (of the tide) with the water at or going to its lowest level: *The tide is out; The tide is going out.* **14** *adj* (*pred: inf*) unacceptable: *That suggestion is right out.* – *See also* **out of** *below.* – (*in cmpds*) **1** not inside or near, as in **outhouse, outlying**. **2** indicating outward movement, as in **outburst, outgoing**. **3** (*with a verb*) indicating that the action goes further or beyond a normal action, as in **outbid, outshine**.

'outer *adj* (*attrib*) near the edge, outside *etc*; far from (the centre of) something: *Coats are outer clothes; outer space.*

'outermost *adj* (*usu attrib*) nearest the edge, outside *etc*; farthest from (the centre of) something: *the outermost ring on the target.*

'outing *nc* a *usu* short trip or journey, made for pleasure: *We went on an outing to the seaside.*

'outward *adj* (*attrib*) **1** on or towards the outside; able to be seen: *Judging by his outward appearance, he's not very rich; He gave no outward sign of his unhappiness.* **2** (of a journey) away from (a place): *The outward journey will be by sea, but they will return home by air.*

'outwardly *adv* in appearance; on the outside: *Outwardly he is cheerful, but he is really a very unhappy person.*

'outwards *adv* towards the outside edge or surface of (something); away from (the centre) of something: *Moving outwards from the centre of the painting, we see that the figures become smaller.*

'out-and-out *adj* (*attrib*) complete; very bad: *He's an out-and-out liar.*

out-of-date *see* **date**.

ˌout-of-the-'way *adj* difficult to reach or arrive at: *Their farm is very out-of-the-way; an out-of-the-way place.* – *See also* **out of the way** *below.*

before the week, year *etc* **is, was out** before the end of the week, year *etc*: *I'll be back here before the week is out.*

be out, up and about (of a person who has been ill in bed, in hospital *etc*) to be well enough to go out, go to work *etc*: *He was very ill for a while, but he's out and about again; After his accident he was soon up and about.*

be 'out for (*inf*) to be wanting or intending to get: *She is out for a good time* (= enjoyment).

be 'out to (*inf*) to be determined to do (something): *He is out to win the race.*

have it out with *see* **have**.

ins and outs *see* **in**.

'out of 1 from inside (a building *etc*): *She ran out of the room; He took it out of the bag.* **2** not in (something): *Mr Smith is out of the office; Fish can't live out of water; We're not out of danger yet.* **3** free: *How did the lion get out of the cage?; He let the cat out of the box.* **4** from among (a group): *Four out of five people like this song.* **5** having none of something left: *We are out of food; The man was quite out of breath.* **6** used to indicate what something is made from: *He carved a figure out of a piece of wood; He built a clock out of pieces of others that were broken.* **7** because of: *He did it out of curiosity/spite.* **8** from: *He drank the lemonade straight out of the bottle.* **9** used to indicate the result of some action involving the loss of something, persuasion not to do something *etc*: *We'll try to talk him out of doing it; He's been cheated out of his money.* **10** (in games) having been defeated: *They were out of the contest.*

out of date *see* **date**.

out of doors outside; not in a house *etc*: *We like to eat out of doors in summer.*

out of hand *see* **hand**.

'out of it 1 (*inf*) not part of, or wanted in, a group, activity *etc*: *I felt a bit out of it at the party since I was the only one who couldn't dance.* **2** no longer part of, or involved in, something: *The whole scheme was crazy – I'm glad to be out of it.*

out of the way unusual: *There was nothing out of the way about what she said.* – *See also* **out-of-the way** *above and* **in, out of the/someone's way** *under* **way**.

'out with it! (*inf*) say what you want to say or have

to say *etc*: *You obviously know more than you have told us so far – out with it, then!*
See also **outside**.

outback ['autbak] *nu* (in Australia) the country areas away from the coast and cities: *They live in the outback.*

outbid [aut'bid] – *prp* **out'bidding**: *pt, ptp* **out'bid** – *vt* (*formal*) to offer a higher price (at an auction sale) than (someone else): *He outbid me for the picture.*

outboard ['autbo:d]: **outboard motor/engine** a motor or engine fixed on to the outside of a boat.

outbreak ['autbreik] *nc* a sudden beginning (*usu* of something unpleasant): *the outbreak of war; There has been an outbreak of cholera in the town.*

outburst ['autbə:st] *nc* (*fig*) an explosion, *esp* of angry feelings: *a sudden outburst (of rage); She regretted her outburst.*

outcast ['autka:st] *nc* a person who has been driven away from friends, home *etc*: *an outcast from society.*

outclass [aut'kla:s] *vt* to be much better than: *At swimming he outclassed all his friends.*

outcome ['autkʌm] *ncu* the result: *What was the outcome of your discussion?*

outcry ['autkrai] *nc* (*often with* **about** *or* **against**) a show of anger, disapproval *etc, esp* by the general public: *There was a great outcry about the knocking down of the old building.*

out-dated [aut'deitid] *adj* (of ideas, clothes *etc*) old-fashioned; out of date: *out-dated ideas; His ideas on the subject are rather out-dated.*

outdistance [aut'distəns] *vt* (*formal*) to run faster than (someone) in a race: *He soon outdistanced all the others.*

outdo [aut'du:] – *pt* **out'did** [-'did]: *ptp* **out'done** [-'dʌn] – *vt* (*formal*) to do better than: *He worked very hard as he did not want to be outdone by anyone.*

outdoor ['autdo:] *adj* (*attrib*) done, for use *etc* outside, not in a building: *outdoor shoes/activities.*
ˌ**out'doors** *adv* outside; not in a building *etc*: *We spent most of our holiday outdoors; Don't go outdoors if it is raining.*
See also **out of doors** *under* **out**.

outer, outermost *see* **out**.

outfit ['autfit] *nc* a set of clothes, *esp* for a particular occasion: *a wedding outfit.*
'**outfitter** *nc* a person who sells clothes, *esp* for men: *a gents' outfitters.*

outgoing [aut'gouiŋ] *adj* **1** friendly: *She has a very outgoing personality; We need someone outgoing as leader.* **2** (*formal*: *attrib*) going out; leaving: *the outgoing president; the outgoing committee.*

outgrow [aut'grou] – *pt* **out'grew** [-'gru:]: *ptp* **out'grown** – *vt* to grow too big or too old for: *My son has outgrown all his clothes; I used to be very selfish as a child, but I hope I have outgrown that.*

outhouse ['authaus] *nc* a *usu* small building outside a house *etc*; a hut or shed: *He keeps his bicycle in the outhouse.*

outing *see* **out**.

outlandish [aut'landiʃ] *adj* (*derog*) very strange: *Everyone stared at her because of her outlandish clothes; outlandish ideas; He does look rather outlandish in those clothes.*

outlast [aut'la:st] *vt* (*formal*) to last or live longer than: *He outlasted his usefulness as a Prime Minister.*

outlaw ['autlo:] *nc* (*hist*) a criminal, *esp* one who is punished by being refused the protection of the law. – *vt* **1** (*hist*) to make (someone) an outlaw. **2** (*formal*) to forbid officially: *The government has outlawed racial discrimination.*

outlay ['autlei] *ncu* money spent: *For an outlay of £80, you can get a very good hi-fi system.*

outlet ['autlit] *nc* **1** a way or passage outwards, *esp* for water or steam: *That pipe is an outlet from the main water-tank.* **2** a way of releasing energy, strong feeling *etc*: *Playing football is an outlet for energy.*

outline ['autlain] *ncu* **1** the line forming, or showing, the outer edge of something in a drawing *etc*: *He drew the outline of the face first, then drew the eyes, nose and mouth; He drew the face in outline.* **2** a short description of the main details of a book, plan *etc*: *Don't tell me the whole story, just give me an outline.* – *vt* **1** to draw the outline of: *He outlined the figure in ink.* **2** to give a brief description of: *He outlined his plans to his friends.*

outlive [aut'liv] *vt* (*formal*) to live longer than: *He outlived his wife by five years; (fig) She never outlived her disgrace.*

outlook ['autluk] *nc* **1** a view (from a window): *Their house has a wonderful outlook.* **2** a person's view of life *etc*: *He has a strange outlook (on life).* **3** what is likely to happen in the future: *The outlook is gloomy for foreign trade; The weather outlook is not very promising.*

outlying ['autlaiiŋ] *adj* (*attrib*) distant; away from (a city or central area): *The doctor needed a car to reach patients in outlying villages.*

outmoded [aut'moudid] *adj* (*sometimes derog*) old-fashioned; out of date: *outmoded ideas; outmoded styles of clothing; Is marriage outmoded now?*

outnumber [aut'nʌmbə] *vt* to be more (in number) than: *The boys in the class outnumber the girls.*

out-of-date *see* **date**.

out of doors, out-of-the way *see* **out**.

out-patient ['autpeiʃənt] *nc* a person who comes to hospital for treatment but does not stay there overnight: *This department only deals with out-patients; (attrib) an out-patient department.*

outpost ['autpoust] *nc* **1** (*mil*) a group of soldiers, a fort *etc* in front of, or away from, the main army. **2** (*formal*) a distant place: *The island was an outpost of British rule.*

output ['autput] *ncu* (*usu in sing*) **1** the quantity of goods produced by a machine, factory *etc*: *The output of this factory has increased by 20%.* **2** the amount of work done by a person *etc*: *We must improve our output.*

outrage ['autreidʒ] **1** *ncu* a wicked act of great violence: *The citizens complained about the outrages committed by the soldiers.* **2** *nc* an act which hurts people's feelings or makes them angry: *The Local Authority's decision to close the road is a public outrage; It's an outrage against the public.* **3** *nu* (a feeling of) great anger: *a feeling of outrage.* – *vt* to hurt, shock or insult: *She was outraged by his behaviour.*
out'rageous *adj* **1** (*inf*: *often facet*) terrible: *What an outrageous thing to say!; She was wearing an outrageous hat* (= *eg* a very large, bright, ugly hat); *The price of that carpet is outrageous!* **2** causing a feeling of outrage: *The boy was punished for his outrageous behaviour.* **out'rageously** *adv.* **out'rageousness** *nu.*

outright [aut'rait] *adv* **1** completely; honestly: *I told him outright what I thought.* **2** immediately; at one time: *He was killed outright; He bought it outright – he did not pay by instalments.* – *adj* ['autrait] (*attrib*) complete; without any exception or doubt: *He is the outright winner; an outright refusal.*

outrun [aut'rʌn] – *prp* **out'running**: *pt* **out'ran** [-'ran]: *ptp* **out'run** – *vt* (*formal*) to run faster than: *He outran the others and won the race.*

outset ['autset] *nc* (*with* **at** *or* **from**) (*more formal than* **beginning** *or* **start**) the beginning of something: *At the outset of his career, he didn't earn very much money; We have to get quite clear from the outset what our policy is.*

outshine [aut'ʃain] – *pt, ptp* **out'shone** [-'ʃon] – *vt* (*formal or liter*) to be brighter than: *The sun outshines the moon*; (*fig*) *She outshone all the other students.*

outside ['autsaid] *nc* the outer surface: *The outside of the house was painted white; His coat was wool on the outside, fur on the inside.* – ['autsaid] *adj* (*attrib*) **1** of, on, or near the outer part of anything: *the outside door.* **2** not part of (a group, organization *etc*): *We cannot finish it ourselves – we shall need outside help.* **3** not part of one's work: *She works hard but also has a lot of outside interests.* **4** (*inf*) (of a chance, possibility *etc*) very small: *He has an outside chance of winning the race.* – [aut'said] *adv* **1** out of a building *etc*; not in a building *etc*: *He went outside; He is outside in the garden.* **2** on the outside: *The house looked beautiful outside.* – [aut'said] *prep* **1** on the outer part or side of; not inside: *He stood outside the house.* **2** beyond the limits of: *This will have to be done outside working hours*; (*formal*) *The judge said that such a matter was outside his jurisdiction.*

out'sider *nc* **1** (*derog*) a person who is not part of a group *etc*: *Some families do not welcome outsiders.* **2** (in a race *etc*) a runner which is not expected to win: *That horse is an outsider; The race was won by a complete outsider.*

at the ˌout'side (*inf*) at the most: *I shall be there for an hour at the outside.*

ˌoutside 'in turned so that the inside and outside change places: *You're wearing your jersey outside in.* – *See also* **inside out**.

out'side of (*inf*: *esp Amer*) **1** outside: *They live somewhere outside of the town.* **2** except: *Outside of Angela, I can think of no-one who'd be willing to do this work.*

outsize ['autsaiz] *adj* (*euph*: *usu attrib*) (for people who are) bigger than usual: *She is so fat that she has to wear outsize clothes; the outsize department; I wouldn't have said that she was outsize.*

outskirts ['autskə:ts] *n pl* the outer parts or area, *esp* of a town: *I live on the outskirts of London.*

outsmart [aut'sma:t] *vt* (*inf*) to outwit (someone): *The burglar outsmarted the police and escaped.*

outspoken [aut'spoukən] *adj* saying exactly what one thinks: *She's very outspoken about her friends; She's a very outspoken person.* **out'spokenness** *nu.*

outspread [aut'spred] *adj* (*liter*) (of arms *etc*) stretched or spread out widely: *with outspread wings; She ran towards him with arms outspread.*

outstanding [aut'standiŋ] *adj* **1** excellent; very good: *an outstanding student; She is outstanding as a painter.* **2** (*formal*) not yet paid, done *etc*: *He has a lot of work outstanding; You must pay all outstanding bills.*

out'standingly *adv*: *She is outstandingly good at music.*

outstretched [aut'stretʃt] *adj* (*formal or liter*) stretched out; reaching out: *He took her outstretched hand; with arms outstretched.*

outstrip [aut'strip] – *pt, ptp* **out'stripped** – *vt* to go much faster than: *He soon outstripped the other runners*; (*fig*) *He outstripped all the other students.*

outvote [aut'vout] *vt* to defeat (*eg* in a debate *etc*) by a larger number of votes: *The Socialists were outvoted by the Conservatives on their proposal to restrict wage increases to five per cent.*

outward(s), outwardly *see* **out**.

outweigh [aut'wei] *vt* (*formal*) to be greater or more than: *The advantages outweigh the disadvantages.*

outwit [aut'wit] – *pt, ptp* **out'witted** – *vt* to defeat (someone) by being cleverer than he is: *She managed to outwit the police and escape.*

ova *see* **ovum**.

oval ['ouvəl] *adj* shaped like an egg: *an oval table; Her face is oval.* – *nc* (*formal*) an oval shape: *He drew an oval.*

ovary ['ouvəri] *nc* the part of the female body in which eggs are formed: *She cannot have children – there is something wrong with her ovaries; She has had her ovaries removed.*

ovation [ə'veiʃən, (*Amer*) ou-] *nc* (*usu formal*) cheering or applause *etc* to express approval, welcome *etc*: *They gave him a great ovation at the end of his speech; They gave the president a standing ovation* (= They stood and applauded him).

oven ['ʌvn] *nc* a closed box-like space, *usu* part of a cooker which is heated for cooking food: *She put the cake into the oven; Do you have a gas oven?; Bake the ham in a hot oven.*

over ['ouvə] *prep* **1** higher than; above in position, number, authority *etc*: *Hang that picture over the fireplace; He paid over £10 for it; He ruled over the people.* **2** from one side to another, on or above the top of: *They walked over the bridge; He jumped over the gate; She fell over the cat; We won't be safe until we are over the frontier; He spoke to her over his shoulder* (= by turning his head). **3** on top of; covering: *He put his handkerchief over his face.* **4** (*sometimes with* **all**) (found, thrown *etc*) across (an area): *He threw the rubbish* (*all*) *over the floor; You find people like him all over the world; There will be rain over the whole of Scotland.* – *See also* **all over** *under* **all**. **5** about; concerning: *They quarrelled over money.* **6** by means of: *He spoke to her over the telephone; The programme was broadcast over the radio.* **7** during: *Over the years, she grew to hate her husband.* **8** while doing, having *etc*: *He fell asleep over* (*his*) *dinner.* – *adv* **1** higher; moving *etc* above someone or something: *The plane flew over about an hour ago.* **2** used to show movement which shows a new or different side of something: *He rolled over on his back; He rolled over and over down the hill; He turned over the page.* **3** across: *He went over and spoke to them; He handed over the jewels to the police; The officer went over to the enemy* (= joined the enemy). **4** downwards; from an upright position: *He fell over; He was knocked over by a bus.* **5** higher in number *etc*: *This is for people aged twenty and over; These shirts cost £10 and over.* **6** remaining; in addition: *There are two cakes for each of us, and two* (*left*) *over.* **7** through from beginning to end; completely; carefully: *Read it over; Talk it over between you; Think it over.* **8** (*usu with* **not**) very: *He's not over intelligent, that boy.* – *adj* finished: *The programme is over; Their love affair is over now.* – *nc* (in cricket) a certain number of balls bowled from one end of the wicket: *They won by seven overs.* – (*in cmpds*) **1** too (much), as in **overeat, overpopulation**. **2** above; in a higher position or authority, as in **overhead, overlord**. **3** covering, as in **overcoat**. **4** down from an upright position, as in **overturn**. **5** completely, as in **overcome, overwhelm**.

'overly *adv* (*formal*) too; very much: *He wasn't overly worried.*

all over *see* **all**.

be 'over to have recovered from (an illness, disappointment *etc*): *He's over his cold at last.* – *See also* **get over** *under* **get**.

over again once more: *Play the tune over again; There are too many mistakes in this – do the whole thing over again.*

over all *see* **overall** *below*.

over and above (*formal*) in addition to: *Over and above my normal duties, I have on occasion to assist the Sales Manager.*

over and done with finished; no longer important: *He has behaved very wickedly in the past but that's all over and done with now.*

over and over (again) continually repeated: *He sang the same song over and over (again).*

over there in that place: *The book is over there on the table.*

overact [ouvər'akt] *vti* to act in an exaggerated way: *That production of Hamlet was dreadful – they all overacted (their parts).*

overall ['ouvərо:l] *nc* a garment worn over ordinary clothes to protect them from dirt *etc*: *The children had to wear overalls at playschool when they were painting; She wore an overall when cleaning the house.* – *adj* (*attrib*) complete; including everything: *What is the overall cost of the scheme?* – [ouvər'o:l] *adv* (*also* **over all**) complete; including everything: *What will the scheme cost overall?*

'overalls *n pl* a type of trousers or suit made of hard-wearing materials worn *usu* over ordinary clothes by workmen *etc* to protect them from dirt *etc*: *The painter put on his overalls before starting work; I'll need a clean pair of overalls tomorrow.*

overarm ['ouvəra:m] *adj, adv* (of a throw) with the hand and arm moving round above the shoulder: *He bowled overarm; an overarm throw.*

overawe [ouvər'o:] *vt* (*formal*: *usu in passive*) to make silent by fear or astonishment: *He was overawed by the crowds of people.*

overbalance [ouvə'baləns] *vi* to lose balance and fall: *He overbalanced on the edge of the cliff and fell into the sea below.*

overbearing [ouvə'beəriŋ] *adj* (*formal derog*) too sure that one is right; frequently telling people what to do in too proud a way: *I disliked her overbearing manner; She is proud and overbearing.*

overboard ['ouvəbo:d] *adv* over the side of a ship or boat into the water: *He jumped overboard; She fell overboard and was drowned.*

go 'overboard (*inf*: *often derog*) to be very enthusiastic, often too enthusiastic, about someone or something: *She's gone overboard about that new pop-group; The child has gone overboard for that building toy.*

overcast [ouvə'ka:st] *adj* cloudy: *on a slightly overcast day; It is cold and overcast.*

overcharge [ouvə'tʃa:dʒ] *vt* to charge too much: *He overcharged me £2 for the meal; I have been overcharged for these goods.*

overcoat ['ouvəkout] *nc* a *usu* heavy coat worn over all other clothes *esp* in winter: *He wore an overcoat on top of his tweed jacket.*

overcome [ouvə'kʌm] *adj* (*usu pred*) helpless; defeated by exhaustion, emotion *etc*: *She was quite overcome by the heat; overcome with grief; For a minute or two I felt quite overcome.* – *v* – *pt* **ˌover'came** [-'keim] : *ptp* **ˌover'come** – *vti* (*formal*) to defeat or conquer: *After a hard struggle, the army overcame the enemy; She finally overcame her fear of the dark.*

overcrowded [ouvə'kraudid] *adj* having too many people on or in: *overcrowded buses/cities; This area is becoming very overcrowded.*

ˌover'crowding *nu* the state of being overcrowded: *There is a great deal of overcrowding in cities.*

overdo [ouvə'du:] – *pt* **ˌover'did** [-'did] : *ptp* **ˌover'done** [-'dʌn] – *vt* **1** to do, say (something) to too great an extent, in an exaggerated way *etc*: *They overdid the sympathy.* **2** to cook for too long: *The meat was rather overdone.*

ˌover'do it to work too hard: *You've been overdoing it recently – you need a holiday.*

overdose ['ouvədous] *nc* too great an amount (of medicine): *He took an overdose of sleeping-pills.*

overdraft ['ouvədra:ft] *nc* the amount of money by which a bank account is overdrawn: *I have a large overdraft.*

overdrawn [ouvə'dro:n] *adj* (*usu pred*) having taken more money out of one's account than it had in it: *He is overdrawn by £500; His account is overdrawn.*

See also **overdraft**.

overdressed [ouvə'drest] *adj* (*derog*) wearing clothes that are too bright, too expensive or too formal for the occasion: *She was overdressed – everyone else was in jeans; rich, overdressed old women.*

overdue [ouvə'dju:] *adj* (*usu pred*) **1** late: *The train is overdue.* **2** (of bills, work *etc*) not yet paid, done, delivered *etc*, although the date for doing this has passed: *My library books are a week overdue; You must pay a fine for overdue library books.*

overeat [ouvər'i:t] – *pt* **ˌover'ate** [-'et, -'eit; (*Amer*) -'eit]: *ptp* **ˌover'eaten** – *vi* to eat too much: *The children overate at the party and were sick.*

overestimate [ouvər'estimeit] *vt* to estimate, judge *etc* (something) to be greater, larger or more important than it is: *She overestimated the number of people that would be coming; He overestimates his own ability.*

overexcited [ouvərik'saitid] *adj* too excited: *The child would not go to sleep as he was overexcited; overexcited children.*

overflow [ouvə'flou] *vti* to flow over the edge or limits (of): *The river overflowed (its banks); (fig) The crowd overflowed into the next room; (fig formal) My heart is overflowing with happiness.* – ['ouvəflou] *nc* **1** a flowing over of liquid: *I put a bucket under the pipe to catch the overflow; (attrib) an overflow pipe; (fig) We'll use this room to accommodate the overflow from the meeting.* **2** an overflow pipe.

overgrown [ouvə'groun] *adj* **1** (of a garden *etc*) full of or covered with plants that have grown too large or thick: *Our garden is overgrown with weeds; an overgrown garden.* **2** (*usu attrib*) grown too large: *an overgrown puppy; an overgrown tomato plant.*

overhang [ouvə'haŋ] – *pt, ptp* **ˌover'hung** [-'hʌŋ] – *vti* (*formal*) to project or stick out (over something): *Rocks overhung the stream.* – ['ouvəhaŋ] *nc* (*formal or tech*) a piece of rock, part of a roof *etc* that overhangs.

overhaul [ouvə'ho:l] *vt* to examine carefully and repair: *I had my car overhauled at the garage.* – ['ouvəho:l] *nc*: *They gave it a complete overhaul.*

overhead [ouvə'hed] *adv, adj* (*attrib*) above; over one's head: *The plane flew overhead*; *an overhead railway.*

'**overheads** *n pl* the regular expenses of a business *eg* rent, wages, electricity: *They have very high overheads in that industry.*

overhear [ouvə'hiə] – *pt, ptp* ˌ**over'heard** [-'hə:d] – *vti* to hear (what one was not intended to hear): *She overheard two people talking in the next room*; *I could not help overhearing (their conversation).*

overjoyed [ouvə'dʒoid] *adj* (*usu pred*) full of joy; very glad: *She was overjoyed to hear of his safe arrival.*

overland [ouvə'land] *adv*, ['ouvəland] *adj* (*attrib*) (of a journey *etc*) across land: *We travelled overland to Australia*; *an overland route.*

overlap [ouvə'lap] – *pt, ptp* ˌ**over'lapped** – *vti* to extend over and cover a part of: *The pieces of cloth overlapped (each other)*; (*fig*) *The work of the two researchers often overlapped.* – ['ouvəlap] *ncu* the amount by which something overlaps: *an overlap of two centimetres*; *There is bound to be a certain amount of overlap between the two projects.*

overleaf [ouvə'li:f] *adv* (*formal*) on the other side of the page: *See the diagram overleaf.*

overload [ouvə'loud] *vt* **1** to load or fill (something) with too much of something: *The lorry overturned because it had been overloaded.* **2** to put too great an electric current through (an electric circuit): *The lights fused because we had overloaded the electricity supply by switching on too many appliances.*

overlook [ouvə'luk] *vt* **1** (of a house, town, hill *etc*) to look down on (something) from a higher point; to give a view of: *The house overlooked the river.* **2** (*formal*) not to see; to miss: *He overlooked the mistake in the bill.* **3** to take no notice of (of a mistake, fault, crime *etc*); not to punish: *We shall overlook your lateness this time.*

overlord ['ouvəlo:d] *nc* (*hist*) a lord, *esp* one who has authority over other lords: *a feudal overlord.*

overmuch [ouvə'mʌtʃ] *adv* (*formal*) too much: *I don't like it overmuch.*

overnight [ouvə'nait] *adj* (*attrib*), *adv* **1** for or during the night: *an overnight bag*; *He stayed overnight with a friend.* **2** very quick(ly): *He was an overnight success*; *He completely changed overnight.*

overpass ['ouvəpa:s] *nc* a bridge-like part of a road *etc* which passes over another road, a railway *etc*: *an overpass across a motorway.*

overpower [ouvə'pauə] *vt* to defeat or make helpless or captive by a greater strength: *The police overpowered the thieves*; (*fig*) *He was overpowered by grief.*

ˌ**over'powering** *adj* very strong: *an overpowering smell*; *That smell is quite overpowering.* ˌ**over'poweringly** *adv.*

overrate [ouvə'reit] *vt* to think that something is better, stronger, more valuable *etc* than it really is: *She overrated her strength*; *Her beauty is overrated.*

overreach [ouvə'ri:tʃ] *v refl* (*formal*: *sometimes derog*) to try to do or get more than one can: *She overreached herself in trying to get the manager's job.*

overreact [ouvəri'akt] *vi* to react too much: *She overreacts to criticism*; *She overreacted when I said her illness was imaginary.* ˌ**overre'action** [-ʃən] *nu.*

override [ouvə'raid] – *pt* ˌ**over'rode** [-'roud]: *ptp* ˌ**over'ridden** [-'ridn] – *vt* (*formal*) to ignore or set aside: *He overrode their objections.*

overrule [ouvə'ru:l] *vt* (*formal*) to go against, or cancel, a judgement or request that has already been made: *The judge overruled the previous decision.*

overrun [ouvə'rʌn] – *prp* ˌ**over'running**: *pt* ˌ**over'ran** [-'ran]: *ptp* ˌ**over'run** – **1** *vt* (*usu in passive*) to spread over or through (something); to fill, occupy or take possession of (something): *The house was overrun with mice*; *The country was overrun by the enemy soldiers.* **2** *vi* to continue longer than allowed or intended: *The programme overran by five minutes.*

overseas ['ouvəsi:z] *adj* (*attrib*), [ouvə'si:z] *adv* across the sea; abroad: *an overseas voyage*; *He went overseas*; *overseas trade.*

oversee [ouvə'si:] – *pt* ˌ**over'saw** [-'so:]: *ptp* ˌ**over'seen** – *vt* (*formal*) to watch over or supervise: *He oversees production at the factory.*

overseer ['ouvəsiə] *nc* a person whose job is to oversee work, production *etc*: *The overseer reported her for being late.*

overshadow [ouvə'ʃadou] *vt* (*formal*) **1** to make someone seem less noticeable or important by being or doing something much better: *With her beauty and wit she quite overshadowed her sister.* **2** to make (something) less happy: *The threat of war overshadowed the otherwise happy events of that month.*

overshoe ['ouvəʃu:] *nc* (*also* **galosh**) a shoe *usu* made of rubber *etc* and worn over one's shoe as a protection against wet *etc*: *She wore (a pair of) plastic overshoes over her evening shoes.*

overshoot [ouvə'ʃu:t] – *pt, ptp* ˌ**over'shot** [-'ʃot] – *vt* (*inf*) to go farther than (the point one was aiming at): *The aeroplane overshot the runway.*

oversight ['ouvəsait] *nc* (*formal*) a failure to notice (something): *Due to an oversight, we have not paid the bill.*

oversleep [ouvə'sli:p] – *pt, ptp* ˌ**over'slept** [-'slept] – *vi* to sleep longer than one intended: *He overslept and missed the train.*

overspend [ouvə'spend] – *pt, ptp* ˌ**over'spent** [-t] – *vi* to spend too much money: *He overspent on his new house.*

overspill ['ouvəspil] *ncu* the people leaving, or forced to leave, a town when areas of old or poor-quality houses are knocked down: *This town was built to house Glasgow's overspill*; (*attrib*) *an overspill development.*

overstate [ouvə'steit] *vt* (*formal*) to state too strongly; to exaggerate: *She overstated her argument*; *There is no need to overstate your case.* ˌ**over'statement** *ncu.*

overstep [ouvə'step] – *pt, ptp* ˌ**over'stepped** – *vt* to go beyond (the limit *etc* allowed): *He overstepped his authority when he ordered the prisoner to be released.*

overt [ou'və:t] *adj* (*usu attrib*) not hidden or secret; done, said *etc* openly: *overt opposition to a plan.* **o'vertly** *adv*: *His objections were never overtly stated.*

overtake [ouvə'teik] – *pt* ˌ**over'took** [-'tuk]: *ptp* ˌ**over'taken** – *vti* to pass (a car, a person in a car *etc*) while driving *etc*: *He overtook a police-car*;

Don't try to overtake – there's a car coming the other way.

overtax [ouvə'taks] *vt* **1** (*formal*) to put too great a strain on: *He overtaxed his strength.* **2** to force (someone) to pay too much tax: *The Inland Revenue have overtaxed me again*; *He thinks he has been overtaxed.*

overthrow [ouvə'θrou] – *pt* ˌ**over'threw** [-'θru:]: *ptp* ˌ**over'thrown** – *vt* to defeat and force out of power: *The government has been overthrown.* – ['ouvəθrou] *nc* the act of overthrowing (a government *etc*): *After the overthrow of the government, the country was in chaos.*

overtime ['ouvətaim] *nu* **1** time spent in working beyond one's set number of hours *etc*: *He did five hours' overtime this week.* **2** the money paid for this extra time: *He got £20 overtime this week.*

overtones ['ouvətounz] *n pl* (*formal*) suggestions; hints; an additional meaning to what is actually said or written: *Although he made no overt criticism of the government, his speech had revolutionary overtones*; *There were overtones of discontent in his speech.*

overture ['ouvətjuə] *nc* **1** a piece of music played as an introduction to an opera *etc.* **2** (*formal*) a proposal or offer intended to start discussions: *The government is making overtures of peace.*

overturn [ouvə'tə:n] *vti* to (cause to) turn over: *They overturned the boat*; *The car overturned on the icy road.*

overweening ['ouvəwi:niŋ] *adj* (*attrib*: *old or liter*) caused by too much confidence or certainty: *His overweening pride infuriates me.*

overweight [ouvə'weit] *adj* too heavy; too fat: *If I eat too much I soon get overweight*; *Overweight people are usually unhealthy.*

overwhelm [ouvə'welm] *vt* (*often in passive*) to defeat or overcome: *The soldiers were overwhelmed by the enemy*; (*fig*) *He was overwhelmed with work/grief.*

ˌ**over'whelming** *adj* (*usu attrib*) very great; causing a person to be defeated or overcome: *an overwhelming victory*; (*fig*) *an overwhelming amount of work*; (*fig*) *overwhelming grief.*

overwork [ouvə'wə:k] *nu* the act of working too hard: *It's overwork that made him ill.* – *vti* (*formal*) to (cause to) do too much work: *He always overworks – he never seems to rest.*

ˌ**over'worked** *adj* made to work too hard: *His staff are overworked*; *overworked factory workers.*

overwrought [ouvə'ro:t] *adj* (*formal*) too nervous or excited; very tired because of too much work *etc*: *You could tell from the way she burst into tears that she was overwrought*; *in rather an overwrought state.*

ovum ['ouvəm] – *pl* **ova** ['ouvə] – *nc* (*formal or tech*) the egg from which the young of people and animals develop: *The ovum is fertilized by the sperm of the male.*

owe [ou] *vt* (not used with **is, was** *etc* and **-ing**) **1** to be in debt to (someone who has done something for one, or who has paid or lent money *etc*): *I owe (him) £5*; *I owe you for my lunch*; *I owe my success to you.* **2** (*formal*) to give (someone) as a duty: *We owe allegiance to the king.*

'**owing** *adj* (*formal*: *pred*) still to be paid: *There is some money still owing (to us).*

'**owing to** because of: *Owing to the rain, the football has been cancelled.* – *See also* **due to** *under* **due**.

owl [aul] *nc* a type of bird that feeds on small birds and animals and flies at night.

'**owlish** *adj* (*facet*) like an owl; solemn: *Her glasses gave her an owlish appearance*; *She does look rather owlish in those large spectacles.* '**owlishly** *adv.* '**owlishness** *nu.*

own [oun] (not used with **is, was** *etc* and **-ing**) **1** *vt* to have as a possession: *I own a car*; *We do not own a television set*; *We do not own this house – we rent it.* **2** *vi* (*formal*) to admit (that something is true): *I own that I have not been working very hard.* – *adj, pron* (*often used for emphasis*) belonging to (the person stated): *The house is my own*; *It was John's own idea*; *I saw it with my own eyes.*

'**owner** *nc* a person who owns something: *Are you the owner of that car?*; *He is not the owner of the land – he rents it from Sir John Smith.*

'**ownership** *nu* the act of owning or having (something) as one's own: *The police are not certain of the ownership of the car.*

on one's own (*sometimes with* **all**) **1** alone: *He lives on his own.* **2** with no one else's help: *He did it (all) on his own.*

get one's own back (*inf*: *sometimes with* **on**) to revenge oneself: *He has beaten me this time, but I'll get my own back (on him).*

hold one's own *see* **hold**.

own up *vi* (*often with* **to**) to admit that one has done something: *Who did this? Own up!*; *He owned up to having broken the window.*

See also **disown**.

ox [oks] – *pl* '**oxen** – *nc* **1** a castrated bull used (formerly in Britain and still in some countries) to pull carts, ploughs *etc*: *We saw an ox pulling a plough*; *an ox-drawn cart.* **2** (*old*: *esp in pl*) any bull or cow.

oxygen ['oksidʒən] *nu* an element (symbol **O**), a gas without taste, colour or smell, forming part of the air: *Water is a compound of hydrogen and oxygen*; *He died from lack of oxygen.*

'**oxygen mask** *nc* a mask through which a person can breathe oxygen.

'**oxygen tent** *nc* a sort of tent filled with oxygen in which a sick person can be put to help his/her breathing.

oyster ['oistə] *nc* a type of shellfish eaten as food, and from which pearls are got: *We celebrated his birthday by having champagne and oysters*; (*attrib*) *oyster soup.*

'**oyster bed** *nc* a place in the sea where oysters breed or are bred.

the world is his, your *etc* **oyster** he, you *etc* can go anywhere and do anything: *You're talented, young, healthy and wealthy – the world's your oyster!*

ozone ['ouzoun] *nu* **1** (*inf or facet*) fresh (sea) air. **2** a type of oxygen.

Pp

pace [peis] **1** *nc* (*formal*) a step: *He took a pace forward*; *She took three paces back.* **2** *ncu* speed of movement: *He went at a fast pace*; *He could not keep up with the pace of the other runners.* – **1** *vti* to walk backwards and forwards (across): *He paced up and down anxiously*; *She was so nervous that she got up and paced the room.* **2** *vi* (*formal*) to walk slowly with a regular step: *The hikers paced steadily on.* **3** *vt* to set the speed of a race: *He is pacing the rest of the runners.* – *See also* **pace out** *below.*

'**pacemaker** *nc* **1** an electronic device to make the heart beats regular: *He was suffering from a form of heart disease and had to have a pacemaker inserted.* **2** a person who sets the speed of a race.

'**pacesetter** *nc* (*fig*) a person who sets the speed at which new ideas will be adopted, changes made *etc*: *New opportunities are opening before us and our firm will be the pacesetters in this new field.*

keep pace with to go as fast as: *He kept pace with the car on his motorbike*; (*fig*) *It is difficult to keep pace with scientific discoveries.*

pace out *vt sep* to measure by walking along, across *etc* with even steps: *She paced out the room and decided that the carpet would fit.*

put someone *etc* **through his** *etc* **paces** to make someone *etc* show what he *etc* can do: *They put the new horse through its paces*; *The fine weather gave him an opportunity to put his new car through its paces.*

set the pace (*often fig*) to go forward at a particular speed which everyone else has to follow: *He set the pace for most of the race, but was defeated in the end*; (*fig*) *Her experiments set the pace for future research.*

show one's paces to show what one can do: *They made the horse show its paces*; *The new sales manager was able to show his paces at the sales conference.*

pacify ['pasifai] *vt* (*formal*) to make calm or peaceful: *She tried to pacify the quarrelling children.* ˌ**pacifi'cation** [-fi-] *nu*..

'**pacifism** *nu* the belief that all war is wrong and that one must not take part in it: *He was tortured because of his belief in pacifism.*

'**pacifist** *nc* a person who believes in pacifism: *As a pacifist he refused to fight in the war.*

pack [pak] *nc* **1** things tied up together or put in a container, *esp* to be carried on one's back: *He carried his luggage in a pack on his back.* **2** a set of (fifty-two) playing-cards: *He shuffled the pack and dealt it out*; *a pack of cards.* **3** a number or group of certain animals: *a pack of wolves/a wolf-pack*; (*fig*) *They are just a pack of thieves.* **4** (*esp Amer*) a packet: *a pack of cigarettes.* – **1** *vti* to put (clothes *etc*) into a bag, suitcase or trunk for a journey: *I've packed all I need and I'm ready to go*; (*fig*) *He packed the children into the bus.* **2** *vi* to come together in large numbers in a small space: *They packed into the hall to hear his speech.* **3** *vt* (*formal*) to fill (a jury, a meeting *etc*) with people who will vote as one wants: *He packed the meeting with his own supporters.* – *See also* **pack** *in phrases below.*

'**packing** *nu* **1** the act of putting things in bags, cases *etc*: *He has done his packing tonight as he is leaving in the morning.* **2** the materials (paper, string *etc*) used to wrap things for posting *etc*: *He unwrapped the vase and threw away the packing.*

'**pack-horse** *nc* (*hist*) a horse used to carry luggage, goods for sale *etc.*

'**pack-ice** *nu* a mass of large pieces of ice floating on the sea near the North and South Poles.

'**packing-case** *nc* a (large) wooden box in which goods are packed and sent from place to place: *We put our glassware into packing-cases when we moved house.*

packed out (*inf*) containing as many people as possible: *The theatre/meeting was packed out.*

pack in *vt sep* (*inf*) to abandon or stop doing, using *etc*: *It was so difficult I just packed in the whole idea.*

pack it in (*sl*) to stop doing whatever one is doing: *I'm tired of hearing your complaints, so just pack it in!*; *I hate working – I'm going to pack it in and go on holiday.*

pack off *vt sep* (*inf*) to send away, *usu* quickly and without wasting time: *He packed off his children to do their homework*; *They packed the children off to bed early.*

pack up 1 *vt sep* to put into containers in order to take somewhere else: *She spent the weekend packing up the contents of her house.* **2** *vi* (*sl*) to stop working or operating: *We'd only gone five miles when the engine packed up*; *At one point the doctor thought her kidneys were packing up, but she's all right now.*

send (someone) packing *see* **send**.

See also **unpack**.

package ['pakidʒ] *nc* (*esp Amer*) things wrapped up and tied (for posting *etc*); a parcel: *a package of books*; *We received a package from the postman*; (*Amer*) *packages at Christmas.* – *vt* (*Amer*: *sometimes with* **up**) to wrap up into a package: *He packaged* (*up*) *the clothes.*

package deal *nc* an offer or agreement which includes decisions on a number of matters and has to be accepted or refused as a whole: *The miners have accepted a package deal which will eventually give them a lot more money.*

package holiday, package tour *ncs* a holiday or tour for which one pays the organizer a fixed price which includes everything (travel, hotel, food *etc*): *It is cheaper to go on a package holiday but we prefer to make our own arrangements.*

packet ['pakit] *nc* **1** a small *often* flat, *usu* paper or cardboard container, especially one in which food is sold or in which small objects are sent through the post: *a packet of biscuits*; *She bought a packet of tea.* **2** (*Brit inf*) a large amount of money: *He earns a packet*; *That coat must have cost her a packet!*

pact [pakt] *nc* an agreement, *esp* if formal and/or between the representatives of nations: *They made a pact to help each other*; *The three countries signed a non-aggression pact.*

pad[1] [pad] *nc* **1** a soft, cushion-like object made of or filled with a soft material, used to prevent damage by knocking, rubbing *etc*: *She knelt on a pad to clean the floor*; *The dentist put a cottonwool pad between her cheek and her gums.* **2** (*sometimes in cmpds*) sheets of paper fixed together: *a writing-pad*; *a pad of drawing paper.* **3** (*usu in cmpds*) a platform from which rockets are sent off: *a launching-pad.* **4** (*formal*) the soft, thick underside of the paw of certain animals, such as dogs and cats: *The vet examined the dog's pads.* **5** (*sl*) one's home: *Come over to my pad.* – *v* – *pt, ptp* **'padded** – *vt* to put a pad in or on (for protection, to make something big enough *etc*): *He padded the sharp corners with pieces of rubber*; *The shoes were too big so she padded them with cottonwool*; *The shoulders of his jacket are padded.* – *See also* **pad out** *below.*

'padding *nu* material used to make a pad to protect, fill *etc*: *He used old blankets as padding*; (*fig*) *There's a lot of description in the novel but it's mostly padding.*

pad out *vt sep* to fill (something) with a soft material to make it the right size: *The actor's costume was padded out to make him look fat*; (*fig*) *He felt his letter was not long enough, so he padded it out with remarks about the weather.*

pad[2] [pad] – *pt, ptp* **'padded** – *vi* to walk softly: *The dog padded along the road.*

paddle[1] ['padl] *vi* to walk about in shallow water: *The children went paddling in the sea.*

paddle[2] ['padl] *nc* a short, light oar, often with a blade at each end of the shaft, used to move canoes *etc*: *We found the boat but not the paddles.* – *vt* to move with a paddle: *He paddled the canoe along the river.*

'paddle-steamer *nc* a boat driven by paddle-wheels.

'paddle-wheel *nc* a large wheel fitted with flat pieces of wood and attached to the side or stern of a boat which is turned to make it move through the water.

paddock ['padək] *nc* a small field, containing grass and *usu* near a house or stable, in which horses *etc* are often kept: *They keep donkeys in the paddock by the side of their house.*

paddy-field ['padifi:ld] *nc* a field, often flooded with water, in which rice is grown.

padlock ['padlok] *nc* a (*usu* metal) movable lock with a U-shaped bar which can be passed through a ring, chain *etc* and locked: *He has put a padlock on the gate to stop people coming in.* – *vt* to fasten with a padlock: *She padlocks her bike when she leaves it in the street.*

paediatrics, (*Amer*) **pediatrics** [pi:di'atriks] *n sing* the study of the illnesses of children: *Paediatrics is his main interest.*

,paedi'atric *adj* (*formal or tech*: *esp attrib*): *paediatric cough mixture*; *paediatric illnesses.*

,paedia'trician [-ʃən] *nc* a doctor who specializes in treating and studying children's illnesses.

paella [pai'elə] *ncu* a Spanish kind of stew, containing chicken, rice, vegetables *etc.*

pagan ['peigən] *adj* (*usu attrib*) not belonging to any of the major world religions: *pagan tribes*; *pagan gods.* – *nc* a person who does not belong to any of the major world religions.

'paganism *nu.*

page[1] [peidʒ] *nc* one side of a sheet of paper in a book, magazine *etc*: *Please read page ninety-four*; *a three-page letter*; *That book has four hundred and ninety-two pages.*

page[2] [peidʒ] *nc* **1** (in hotels) a boy who takes messages, carries luggage *etc.* **2** (*hist*: *also* **'page-boy**) a boy servant. **3** (*also* **'page-boy**) a small boy chosen to be one of the bride's attendants at a wedding: *The bride had two bridesmaids and a page (-boy).* – *vt* to try to find someone in a public place by calling out his name (often through a loud-speaker system): *I could not see my friend in the hotel, so I had him paged.*

pageant ['padʒənt] *nc* **1** a dramatic performance made up of different, *usu* historical scenes, often performed during a procession: *The village children performed a historical pageant which moved through the streets on several large lorries.* **2** (*fig*: *liter*) any fine show or display: *a pageant of colour.*

'pageantry *nu* (*formal*) splendid and colourful show or display: *I love the pageantry of royal processions.*

pagoda [pə'goudə] *nc* a Chinese temple, built in the shape of a tall tower, each storey of which has its own narrow strip of overhanging roof.

paid *see* **pay**.

pail [peil] *nc* a bucket: *Fetch a pail of water.*

pain [pein] **1** *ncu* hurt or suffering of the body or mind: *I have a pain in my chest*; *The pain in my back is getting worse*; *She cannot bear pain.* **2** *nc* (*inf*) an irritating or annoying person: *She is a real pain!* – *See also* **pain** *in phrases below.* – *vt* (*liter or formal*: *usu with* **it** *as subject*) to cause suffering or upset to (someone): *It pained her to admit that she was wrong.*

pained *adj* (*usu fig*) showing or expressing pain: *He had a pained expression on his face all the time she was singing*; (*fig*) *Don't look so pained!*

'painful *adj* (*more formal than* **sore**) causing pain: *a painful injury*; *Is your finger still painful?*

'painfully *adv.*

'painless *adj* without pain: *painless childbirth*; *Is childbirth ever totally painless?* **'painlessly** *adv.*

'painkiller *nc* (*not a tech term*) a drug *etc* which lessens or removes pain: *None of these painkillers seems to get rid of the pain in my back.*

'painstaking ['peinz-] *adj* going to great trouble and taking great care: *He is a very painstaking student*; *Artists have to be very painstaking.*

be at 'pains/take 'pains (*formal*) to take great trouble and care (to do something): *She was at pains to explain that she had only been out for five minutes*; *He took great pains to make sure we enjoyed ourselves*; *She always takes pains with her work.*

for one's 'pains (*formal or facet*) as a (poor) reward for one's trouble and effort (in doing something): *She looked after him for years, and all she got for her pains was rudeness.*

on 'pain of (*formal or facet*) at the risk of being given (some kind of punishment): *The employees were forbidden, on pain of instant dismissal, to tell anyone about their work*; *on pain of death* (= at the risk of being executed).

a pain in the neck (*derog inf*) a person who is constantly annoying: *People who are always complaining are a pain in the neck!*

paint [peint] *ncu* a colouring substance in the form of liquid or paste: *He bought several litres of green paint to decorate the bedroom*; (*attrib*) *a paint pot*; *The artist's clothes were covered in paint.* – *vti* **1** to spread paint carefully on (wood, walls *etc*): *I can put up wallpaper, but I'm not good at painting*; *He is painting the door/the kitchen.* **2** to make a picture (of something or someone) using paint: *She painted her mother and father in oils*; *She paints very well.*

'painter *nc* **1** a person whose job is to put paint on things, *esp* walls, doors *etc* in houses: *We employed a painter to paint the outside of the house.* **2** an artist who makes pictures in paint: *Who was the painter of this portrait?*

'painting **1** *nu* the act or art of using paint: *Painting is very relaxing.* **2** *nc* a painted picture: *There were four paintings (hanging) on the wall.*

'**paint-box** *nc* a (small) box containing different paints for making pictures.

'**paint-brush** *nc* a brush used for putting on paint.

paint the town (red) to go out and enjoy oneself in a noisy and expensive manner: *He inherited a lot of money and proceeded to paint the town (red) with it!*

pair [peə] *nc* **1** a set of two of the same thing which are (intended to be) used *etc* together: *a pair of shoes*; *These two gloves are not a pair – one is leather and one is wool.* **2** a single thing made up of two parts: *a pair of scissors*; *a pair of pants.* **3** (*inf of people*) two people, animals *etc*, often one of either sex, who are thought of together for some reason: *She has a pair of Dutch rabbits*; *She and her husband are a pair of criminals*; *Our neighbours are a nice enough pair but I don't like them.* – *vt* (*usu with* **with**) to make into a pair: *She was paired with my brother in the tennis match.*

pair off *vi, vt sep* to join together with one other person to make a pair: *The boys and girls all paired off at the party*; *Their parents paired John and Mary off when they were children.*

pajamas *see* **pyjamas**.

Pakistan, Pakistani *see* Appendix 2.

pal [pal] *nc* (*inf*) a friend: *My son brought a pal home for tea.*

'**pally** *adj* (*inf*: *usu pred*: *usu facet*) friendly: *They've suddenly become very pally.*

,**pal** '**up with** – *pt, ptp* **palled** – *vt fus* (*inf*) to become friends with: *He palled up with a French boy.*

palace ['paləs] *nc* (*with cap in names*) a large and magnificent house, *esp* one lived in by a king or queen: *Buckingham Palace*; *The Archbishop of Canterbury officially lives at Lambeth Palace*; (*fig*) *Their house is an absolute palace!*

palatial [pə'leiʃəl] *adj* (*formal or facet*) large and magnificent, as (in) a palace: *They lived in a palatial house in the most expensive part of the city*; *Their new house is positively palatial*; *palatial rooms.*

palaeolithic, paleolithic [paliə'liθik] *adj* (*usu attrib*) of the early Stone Age: *the palaeolithic period*; *palaeolithic remains.*

palate ['palət] *nc* **1** the top of the inside of the mouth: *My mouth is sore – I have an ulcer on my palate.* **2** (*fig*) the ability to tell good wine, food *etc* from bad: *He has a good palate for wine.*

'**palatable** *adj* (*formal*: *neg* **un-**) pleasant when tasted: *a very palatable meal*; *I found that wine most palatable*; (*fig*) *The truth is not always palatable.*

palatial *see* **palace**.

palaver [pə'la:və] *nu* (*inf*) useless talk or fuss: *What's all this palaver about?*

pale[1] [peil] *adj* **1** (of a person, his face *etc*) having less colour than normal: *a pale face*; *She went pale with fear.* **2** (of a colour) closer to white than black; not dark: *pale green.* – *vi* (*formal*) to become pale: *She paled at the bad news.* '**paleness** *nu.*

pale[2] [peil]: **beyond the pale** outside the normal limits of good behaviour, what is acceptable *etc*: *Her behaviour is really beyond the pale!*

Palestine, Palestinian *see* Appendix 2.

palette ['palit] *nc* a small flat piece of wood *etc*, with a hole for the thumb, on which an artist mixes his colours.

paling ['peiliŋ] *nc* a wooden post stuck in the ground to make part of a fence; a fence made of such posts: *The garden was surrounded by wooden palings/a wooden paling.*

palisade [pali'seid] *nc* (*formal*) a fence made of wooden posts, *esp* one used for defence: *A medieval farm was often surrounded by a palisade to keep out wolves.*

pall[1] [po:l] *nc* (*formal*: *usu fig*) the (*usu* dark-coloured) cloth which covers a coffin at a funeral: *a pall of purple velvet*; (*fig*) *A pall of smoke hung over the town.*

pall[2] [po:l] *vi* (*formal*) to become boring or uninteresting: *Loud music soon palls.*

'**pall on** *vt fus* (*formal*) to become boring or uninteresting to (a person): *The little girl was reading, but the book had no pictures and soon palled on her.*

pallet[1] ['palit] *nc* a wooden platform or tray on which goods can be carried by a fork-lift truck: *The books were moved from the warehouse on pallets.*

pallet[2] ['palit] *nc* (*hist*) a straw bed or mattress.

pallid ['palid] *adj* (*formal*: *derog*) unpleasantly pale (*usu* suggesting ill-health): *rather a pallid child*; *He looked pallid and sickly*; *There was nothing to eat but a plate of limp, pallid sandwiches.*

'**pallor** *nu* unpleasant paleness: *an unhealthy pallor.*

pally *see* **pal**.

palm[1] [pa:m] *nc* the inner surface of the hand between the wrist and the fingers: *She held the mouse in the palm of her hand*; *He had a long scar across his palm.*

palm (something) off on (someone) (*inf*) to get rid of (an undesirable thing or person) by giving, selling *etc* to (someone else): *His car was always breaking down so he palmed it off on his brother*; *They palmed off their unwelcome guests on the people next door.*

palm[2] [pa:m] *nc* (*also* '**palm tree**) a kind of tall tree, with broad, spreading leaves, which grows in hot countries: *a coconut palm*; *Dates grow on palms*; (*attrib*) *palm fronds.*

palpable ['palpəbl] *adj* **1** (*very formal*: *usu attrib*) easily noticed; obvious: *palpable lies*; *palpable errors.* **2** (*med*) able to be felt: *The spleen is palpable – it must be enlarged*; *a large palpable lump.* '**palpably** *adv.*

palpitate ['palpiteit] *vi* (*formal*) (of the heart) to beat rapidly: *Her heart was palpitating with fear.*

,**palpi'tations** *n pl* an attack of rapid beating of the heart: *She gets palpitations if she runs upstairs too fast.*

paltry ['po:ltri] *adj* (*old or formal*: *usu attrib*) of little or no value or importance: *a paltry sum (of money).*

pamper ['pampə] *vt* (*more formal than* **spoil**: *often derog*) to treat with great kindness and give a great many special things to (a person): *The child was often ill and was pampered by his parents.*

pamphlet ['pamflit] *nc* a small paper-covered book *usu* giving information, expressing an opinion on a popular subject *etc*: *The bureau publishes a pamphlet on child care*; *political pamphlets.*

pan[1] [pan] *nc* **1** (*usu in cmpds*) a metal pot used for cooking food: *a frying-pan*; *a saucepan.* **2** (*tech*) a shallow hollow in the ground, *esp* one in which salt collects: *a salt pan.*

'**pancake** *nc* a thin cake *usu* made of milk, flour and eggs and fried in a pan *etc*: *We had pancakes and syrup for breakfast*; *She made stuffed pancakes.*

a flash in the pan *see* **flash**.

pan out – *pt, ptp* **panned** – *vt* (*inf*) to turn out (well or badly): *How did the meeting pan out?*

pan[2] [pan] – *pt, ptp* **panned** – *vti* (*tech*) to move (a film or television camera) so as to follow a moving object or show a wide view: *The camera panned slowly across to the other side of the street.*

pan- [pan] (*in cmpds*) all; whole, as in *pan-American.*

panacea [panə'siə] *nc* (*formal*: *usu fig*) a cure for everything: *a panacea for all ills*; (*fig*) *He regards a holiday as a panacea for everybody's problems.*

panache [pə'naʃ] *nu* (*formal*) a dramatic showing of confidence in one's skill and appearance: *The riders carried out their display with panache and enthusiasm.*

panama [panə'maː, (*Amer*) 'panəmaː] *nc* (*often* **panama hat**) a hat made of straw-like material, worn in hot weather: *He always wears a panama (hat) in summer.*

pan-American [panə'merikən] *adj* including the whole of America or all Americans, both North and South.

pancake *see* **pan**[1].

pancreas ['paŋkriəs] *nc* a part of the body which helps in the digestion of food: *He has cancer of the pancreas.*

panda ['pandə] *nc* (*often* **giant panda**) a large black and white bear-like animal, a member of the raccoon family, which lives in the mountains of China.

'**panda car** *nc* in the UK, a small car used by a patrolling policeman.

pandemonium [pandi'mouniəm] *nu* (*formal or facet*) a state of noise and confusion: *There was pandemonium in the classroom before the teacher arrived.*

pander ['pandə]: '**pander to** *vt fus* (*derog*) to give (someone) something that he likes but which is morally wrong or bad: *Some newspapers pander to people's interest in crime and violence.*

pane [pein] *nc* a flat piece of glass: *a window-pane*; *The glazier put in a new pane of glass in the shop window.*

panel ['panl] *nc* **1** a flat, straight-sided piece of wood, fabric *etc* such as is put into a door, wall, dress *etc*: *a door-panel*; *Her skirt is green with panels of white.* **2** (*sometimes with a pl verb*) a group of people chosen for a particular purpose *eg* to judge a contest, take part in a quiz or other game: *I will ask some questions and the panel will try to answer them*; *The panel are all experts in their various subjects.*

'**panelled** *adj* made of or surrounded with panels (*usu* of wood): *a panelled door*; *an oak-panelled dining-room*; *Our doors are panelled and so are difficult to paint.*

'**panelling** *nu* (wood used for) panels covering the walls of a room *etc*: *oak panelling.*

pang [paŋ] *nc* a sudden sharp pain: *He felt a pang of hunger in his stomach*; (*fig*) *He felt a pang of grief/regret.*

panic ['panik] *ncu* (a) sudden great fear, *esp* that spreads through a crowd *etc*: *The fire caused a panic in the city*; *He was filled with panic.* – *v* – *pt, ptp* '**panicked** – *vti* to make or become so frightened that one loses the power to think clearly: *He panicked at the sight of the audience and couldn't think of anything to say*; *His words panicked her into an action she later regretted.*

'**panicky** *adj* inclined to panic: *She gets panicky in an exam*; *in a panicky mood.*

pannier ['paniə] *nc* one of a pair of baskets, bags *etc* carried on either side of the back of a horse, bicycle, motorbike *etc.*

panoply ['panəpli] *nu* (*formal*) all the splendid clothes, equipment *etc* associated with a particular event: *the panoply of a coronation.*

panorama [panə'raːmə] *nc* (*formal*) a wide view, of a landscape *etc*: *There is a wonderful panorama of the city from the top of that hill.*

ˌ**pano'ramic** [-'ra-] *adj* (*formal*: *attrib*) of or like a panorama: *a panoramic view.*

pansy ['panzi] *nc* **1** a kind of small flower. **2** (*sl*: *derog*) a man or boy who looks feminine or behaves in a feminine manner; a male homosexual: *That boy looks a real pansy – his mother always dresses him in velvet trousers.*

pant [pant] **1** *vi* to gasp for breath: *He was panting heavily as he ran.* **2** *vt* to say while gasping for breath: *'Wait for me!' she panted.*

pantechnicon [pan'teknikən, (*Amer*) -kon] *nc* (*formal*) a large van, *esp* one for carrying furniture.

panther ['panθə] *nc* **1** a leopard, *esp* a large one. **2** (*Amer*) a puma.

panties ['pantiz] *n pl* (*inf*) pants (*def 1*) for women: *a pair of nylon panties.*

pantomime ['pantəmaim] *nc* a play performed at Christmas time, *usu* based on a popular fairy tale, with music, dancing, comedy *etc*: *We're taking the children to the pantomime.*

pantry ['pantri] *nc* a room for storing food: *The house had a large kitchen with a pantry opening off it.*

pants [pants] *n pl* **1** a short undergarment worn on the lower part of the body: *a pair of nylon pants.* **2** (*Amer*) trousers.
See also **panties, underpants**.

papa [pə'paː, (*Amer*) 'paːpə] *nc* (*with cap when used as a name*: *old*: *used esp by children*) a father: *You must ask your papa*; *where are you, Papa?*

papacy ['peipəsi] *nu* **1** the position or power of the pope: *The papacy is the central authority of the Roman Catholic church.* **2** government by popes: *the history of the papacy.*

'**papal** *adj* (*usu attrib*) of the pope or the papacy: *papal authority.*

'**papist** *nc* (*offensive*) a Roman Catholic.

paper ['peipə] **1** *nu* the material on which these words are written, made from wood, rags *etc* and used for writing, printing, wrapping parcels, sticking on walls as decoration *etc*: *I need paper and a pen to write a letter*; *She wrapped the book in brown paper*; *wallpaper*; (*attrib*) *a paper bag.* **2** *nc* a single (often printed or typed) piece of this: *There were papers all over his desk.* **3** *nc* a newspaper: *Have you read the paper?* **4** *nc* a group of questions for a written examination: *The Latin paper was very difficult.* **5** *nc* an essay, *esp* one to be read to an audience: *He's giving a paper on tropical diseases.* – *See also* **papers** *below.* – *vt* to cover with paper: *They papered (the walls of) the bedroom in green.*

'**papers** *n pl* documents proving one's identity, nationality *etc*: *The policeman asked to see my papers.*

'**papery** *adj* like paper: *That plant has papery leaves.*

'**paperback** *nc* a book with a paper cover: *Paperbacks are cheaper than hard-backs*; (*attrib*) *They publish paperback novels.*

'**paper-clip** *nc* a small, *usu* metal clip for holding

papers together: *She attached her note to the papers with a paper-clip.*

'**paper-knife** *nc* a knife used for opening envelopes *etc.*

'**paperweight** *nc* a small, heavy object which can be put on top of pieces of paper to keep them in place, but which is often used as an ornament: *a brass paperweight shaped like a ship.*

'**paperwork** *nu* the part of a job which consists of keeping files, writing letters *etc*: *After I came back from holiday I had a lot of paperwork to deal with.*

on 'paper in theory but not in practice: *The idea seemed all right on paper, but they soon found that it didn't work.*

papier-mâché [papiei'maʃei, (*Amer*) peipərmə'ʃei] *nu, adj* (of) a substance consisting of paper mixed together with some kind of glue, which can be made into models, bowls, boxes *etc*: *The mask was (made of) papier-mâché; a papier-mâché model.*

papist *see* **papacy**.

paprika ['paprikə, (*esp Amer*) pə'pri:kə] *nu* a type of red pepper powder used in cooking.

par [pa:] *nu* the normal level, standard, value *etc.*

below par/not up to par 1 not up to the usual standard: *Your work is not up to par this week.* **2** (*inf*) not well: *She had a cold and was feeling below par.*

on a 'par with equal to: *As a writer he is on a par with the great novelists.*

para- [parə] (*in cmpds*) beside; in addition to, as in **paramilitary**.

parable ['parəbl] *nc* a story (*esp* in the Bible) which is intended to teach a lesson: *Jesus told a great number of parables; the parable of the sower.*

parachute ['parəʃu:t] *nc* an umbrella-shaped piece of light, strong cloth *etc* beneath which a person *etc* is tied with ropes so that he *etc* can come slowly down to the ground from a great height: *His parachute was fastened to his back; They made the descent from the plane by parachute; In severe winters food is sometimes dropped by parachute to isolated villages;* (*attrib*) *a parachute-jump.* – *vi* to come down to the ground using a parachute: *The troops parachuted into France.*

'**parachutist** *nc* a person who makes a parachute-jump.

parade [pə'reid] **1** *nc* a line of people, vehicles *etc* moving forward in order often as a celebration of some event: *a circus parade.* **2** *nu* an arrangement of soldiers in a particular order: *The troops are on parade.* **3** *n* (*with cap*) a word used in the names of certain roads or streets: *41 Circus Parade.* – **1** *vi* to march in a line moving forward in order: *They paraded through the town.* **2** *vt* to arrange soldiers in order: *The colonel paraded his soldiers.* **3** *vt* (*inf*) to show or display in an obvious way: *She paraded her new clothes in front of her friends.*

paradise ['parədais] **1** *ncu* a place or state of great happiness: *The Greek islands are a holiday paradise; It's paradise to be by a warm fire on a cold night.* **2** *n* (*with cap*) heaven: *When we die, we go to Paradise.*

paradox ['parədoks] *nc* (*formal*) a statement *etc* that seems to say two things which cannot both be true but which is in fact true: *It is a paradox that a person could be twenty-one years old but have had only five birthdays if he was born on February 29.*

ˌ**para'doxical** *adj.* ˌ**para'doxically** *adv.*

paraffin ['parəfin] *nu* a kind of oil which is used as a fuel: *This heater burns paraffin;* (*attrib*) *a paraffin lamp.*

paragon ['parəgən, (*Amer*) -gon] *nc* (*formal*) a perfect example of a good quality *etc*: *This boy is a paragon of good manners; She is a paragon of virtue.*

paragraph ['parəgra:f] *nc* a part of a piece of writing, marked by beginning the first sentence on a new line and *usu* leaving a short space at the beginning of the line: *For each main idea in your essay, start a new paragraph; There are a couple of paragraphs about football on page three of today's paper.*

Paraguay, Paraguayan *see* Appendix 2.

parallel ['parəlel] *adj* **1** (of straight lines) going in the same direction and always staying the same distance apart: *Railway tracks are parallel lines; The road is parallel to/with the river.* **2** (*formal fig*) alike (in some way): *There are parallel passages in the two books.* – *adv* in the same direction but always about the same distance away: *We sailed parallel to the coast for several days.* – *nc* **1** (*geom*) a line parallel to another: *Draw a parallel to this line.* **2** (*formal fig*) a likeness or state of being alike: *Is there a parallel between the British Empire and the Roman Empire?* **3** (*tech*) a line drawn from east to west across a map *etc* at a fixed distance from the equator: *The border between Canada and the United States follows the forty-ninth parallel.* – *vt* (*usu in passive*) to be equal to: *His stupidity can't be paralleled.*

See also **unparalleled**.

paralysis [pə'raləsis] *nu* a loss of the ability to move: *The paralysis affects both his legs and he cannot walk; He is suffering from paralysis of the lower limbs.*

paralyse, (*Amer*) **paralyze** ['parəlaiz] *vt* to make unable to move: *He is paralysed from the waist down;* (*fig*) *She was paralysed with fear;* (*fig*) *The strike paralysed production at the factory.*

paralytic [parə'litik] *adj* **1** (*old*) suffering from or caused by paralysis. **2** (*sl*) drunk: *He gets paralytic every Saturday night.*

paramilitary [parə'militəri] *adj* (*formal*: *usu attrib*) organized on the same principles as an army: *a terrorist paramilitary organization.*

paramount ['parəmaunt] *adj* (*formal*: *attrib*: *usu with* **importance**) the greatest: *This matter is of paramount importance.*

paranoia [parə'noiə] *nu* (*tech*) a type of mental illness in which a person has fixed and unreasonable ideas that he is very important, or that other people are being unfair or unfriendly to him.

ˌ**para'noiac** [-'no:ik], '**paranoid** [-noid] *nc, adj* (*often used loosely*: *usu pred*) (a person) suffering from paranoia: *The doctor says that he is paranoiac; Our new secretary is paranoid – she thinks that everyone is criticizing her.*

parapet ['parəpit] *nc* a low wall along the edge of a bridge, balcony *etc*: *He leant over the parapet.*

paraphernalia [parəfə'neiliə] *nu* (*formal or facet*: *often derog*) (large) collection of (small) objects, often the tools *etc* for a job or hobby: *Do you really need all that paraphernalia just to take a photograph?*

paraphrase ['parəfreiz] *vt* (*formal*) to repeat (something), in speech or writing, in different words: *He paraphrased the poem in modern English; His whole speech could be paraphrased in a sentence.* – *nc* something which repeats something else in different words: *He made a para-*

phrase of the poem; *He read some paraphrases from the Bible.*

paraplegia [parə'pli:dʒə] *nu* (*tech*) paralysis of the legs and the lower part of the body: *His paraplegia is incurable.*

ˌpara'plegic 1 *nc, adj* (a person) suffering from paraplegia: *He is* (*a*) *paraplegic.* **2** *adj* (*attrib*) of or relating to such a person: *paraplegic sports* (= sports for people suffering from paraplegia).

parasite ['parəsait] *nc* an animal or plant that lives on another animal or plant without giving anything in return: *Fleas are parasites*; *Mistletoe is a parasite*; (*fig derog*) *He is a parasite on society.*

ˌpara'sitic *adj* (*formal*).

parasol ['parəsol] *nc* a light umbrella used as a protection against the sun.

paratroops ['parətru:ps] *n pl* soldiers who are trained to drop by parachute into enemy territory.

'paratrooper *nc.*

parboil ['pa:boil] *vt* to boil (food) so that it is partly cooked: *My mother always parboils potatoes before she roasts them.*

parcel ['pa:sl] *nc* thing(s) wrapped and tied, *usu* to be sent by post: *I got a parcel in the post this morning.*

parcel out – *pt, ptp* **'parcelled**, (*Amer*) **'parceled** – *vt sep* to divide or share (among several people *etc*): *He parcelled the food out between them.*

parcel up – *pt, ptp* **'parcelled**, (*Amer*) **'parceled** – *vt sep* to put into a parcel: *He parcelled up the books and took them to the post office.*

part and parcel *see* **part**.

parch [pa:tʃ] *vt* (*formal*) to make hot and very dry: *The sun parched the earth.*

parched *adj* **1** hot and dry: *Nothing could grow in the parched land*; *The ground was parched.* **2** (*inf*: *pred*) thirsty: *Can I have a cup of tea – I'm parched!*

parchment ['pa:tʃmənt] *ncu* (*usu hist*) a (piece of a) material used for writing on, made from animal skin: *Medieval men often wrote on parchment*; *They found several old parchments in the box.*

pardon ['pa:dn] *vt* **1** (*often formal*) to forgive: *Pardon my asking, but can you help me?* **2** to free (from prison, punishment *etc*): *The king pardoned the prisoners.* – **1** *nu* forgiveness: *He prayed for pardon for his wickedness.* **2** *nc* a (document) freeing from prison or punishment: *He was granted a pardon.* – *interj* used to indicate that one has not heard properly what was said: *Pardon? Could you repeat that last sentence?*

'pardonable *adj* (*neg* **un-**) able to be forgiven: *a pardonable mistake*; *Do you think that such behaviour is pardonable?*

beg someone's pardon to say one is sorry (*usu* for having offended someone else *etc*): *I've come to beg* (*your*) *pardon for being so rude this morning.*

I beg your pardon I'm sorry: *I beg your pardon – what did you say? I wasn't listening.*

pardon me *interj* (*often facet*) expressing a polite apology, *esp* for not agreeing with someone: *Pardon me, but I think you are wrong*; *Pardon me for interrupting you.*

pare [peə] *vt* (*formal*) **1** to cut or trim (*esp* finger- or toe-nails): *She was paring her nails with nail-scissors.* **2** to peel (fruit): *He pared an apple.*

parent ['peərənt] *nc* **1** one of the two persons *etc* (one male and one female) who are jointly the cause of one's birth: *She lived with her parents until she grew up.* **2** a person who has the legal position of a mother or father *eg* by adoption: *an adopted parent.*

'parentage [-tidʒ] *nu* (*formal*) family or ancestry: *a man of unknown parentage.*

parental [pə'rentl] *adj* (*formal*: *attrib*): *parental responsibility.*

'parenthood *nu* the state of being a parent.

parenthesis [pə'renθəsis] – *pl* **pa'rentheses** [-si:z] – *nc* **1** (*gram*) a word or group of words within a sentence, which gives a comment, explanation *etc* and *usu* separates from the rest of the sentence by brackets, dashes *etc*: *I asked John* (*my friend John Smith*) *to come and see me.* **2** (*usu in pl*) a round bracket used to mark the separate part of such a sentence.

parenthetical [parən'θetikəl] *adj* (*formal*: *usu attrib*): *a parenthetical remark.*

in pa'rentheses (*formal*) said, written *etc* as a parenthesis.

See also **bracket**.

parenthood *see* **parent**.

pariah [pə'raiə] *nc* (*formal*) a person driven out of a group or community; an outcast: *Because of his political beliefs he became a pariah in the district*; *In former times divorced people were social pariahs.*

parish ['pariʃ] *nc* a district or area which has a particular church and priest or minister: *Our house is in the parish of St Mary('s)*; (*attrib*) *parish affairs.*

pa'rishioner [-ʃənə] *nc* a person who belongs to a church parish.

parish council *nc* in England, a division of local government which looks after a smaller area than, and which is much more limited in power than, either a county council or a district council.

See also **parochial**.

parity ['parəti] *nu* (*formal*) the state of being equal: *Scottish teachers want parity with those in England.*

See also **disparity**.

park [pa:k] **1** *nc* a public piece of ground with grass and trees: *The children go to the park every morning to play.* **2** *nc* the land surrounding a large country house: *Deer run wild in the park surrounding the mansion.* **3** *n* (*with cap*) a word used in the names of certain roads or streets: *His address is 17 Calder Park.* – **1** *vti* to stop and leave (a motor car *etc*) for a time: *He parked in front of our house*; *Wait a minute while I park the car.* **2** *vt* (*inf*) to put (something) down and leave it for a time: *She parked the baby at her mother's house.*

'parking-lot *nc* (*Amer*) a car park.

'parking-meter *nc* a coin-operated meter beside which a car may be parked for the number of minutes or hours shown on the meter: *Have you got any change for the parking-meter?*

'parkland [-land] *nu* land covered with short grass and with trees (often ornamental): *The castle is surrounded by beautiful parkland.*

parlance ['pa:ləns] *nu* (*formal*) a way of speaking: *in legal parlance.*

parley ['pa:li] *vi* (*old*) to have a conference, discuss *usu* with an enemy. – *nc* (*old*) a meeting or conference between enemies, to arrange peace *etc.*

parliament ['pa:ləmənt] *nc* (*often with cap*) the highest law-making council of a nation – in Britain, the House of Commons and the House of Lords, considered together: *Where does the Australian parliament meet?*; *That was the last sitting of Parliament before we elect a new government*; *an Act of Parliament.*

ˌparliamen'tarian *nc* a person who knows all

about the rules and methods of parliament.

ˌ**parliaˈmentary** [-ˈmen-] *adj* (*usu attrib*): *parliamentary procedure.*

parlour, (*Amer*) **parlor** [ˈpaːlə] *nc* **1** (*old*) a room in a (*usu* small) house used for sitting in and for entertaining guests. **2** (*esp Amer*) room(s) for customers *usu* of firms providing particular services: *a beauty parlo(u)r*; *a funeral parlo(u)r.*

ˈ**parlour-maid** *nc* (*old*) a female servant who opens the door to visitors, serves tea *etc.*

parochial [pəˈroukiəl] *adj* **1** (*derog*) interested only in local affairs; narrow-minded: *The people here are so parochial*; *unimaginative, parochial people.* **2** (*formal*: *usu attrib*) of a parish: *He is very interested in parochial affairs.* **paˈrochialism** *nu* (*derog*).

parody [ˈparədi] *nc* **1** an amusing imitation of a serious author's style of writing: *He writes parodies of John Donne's poems.* **2** (*fig formal*) a very bad imitation: *The story he told was an absolute parody of the truth.* – *vt* to make a parody of (something or someone).

parole [pəˈroul] *nu* (*formal or legal*) the release of a prisoner before the end of his/her sentence, on condition that he/she will have to return to prison on breaking the law again: *He was released on parole*; *He was out on parole when he murdered the girl.*

paroxysm [ˈparəksizəm] *nc* (*formal*) a sudden sharp attack (of pain, rage, laughter *etc*): *The news sent him into paroxysms of fury*; *a paroxysm of coughing.*

parquet [ˈpaːkei, (*Amer*) paːrˈkei] *nu* a type of floor-covering made of pieces of wood arranged in a design: *flooring made of parquet*; (*attrib*) *a parquet floor.*

parricide [ˈparisaid] (*formal or legal*) **1** *nu* the murder of a parent or near relative. **2** *nc* a person who does such a murder.

See also **patricide**.

parrot [ˈparət] *nc* a kind of bird found in warm countries, *esp* in South America, with a hooked bill and *usu* brightly-coloured feathers, that can be taught to imitate human speech: *The old man keeps a parrot in a cage as a pet.*

parry [ˈpari] *vt* (*formal*) to keep off or turn aside (*esp* a blow or a question): *He parried the attack successfully.*

parse [paːz, (*Amer*) paːrs] *vt* (*gram*) to give the correct grammatical name to each word of (a sentence or phrase) and say how they are connected with each other.

parsimonious [paːsiˈmouniəs] *adj* (*formal derog*) too careful in spending money; mean: *He is so parsimonious that he lives in a broken-down old house although he is very wealthy*; *a parsimonious old man.* ˈ**parsimony** *nu.*

parsley [ˈpaːsli] *nu* a kind of herb used in cookery to decorate or add flavour to food: *Add some parsley to the leek soup*; *Garnish the stew with parsley.*

parsnip [ˈpaːsnip] *nc* **1** a kind of plant with a yellowish-white root used as a vegetable. **2** the root.

parson [ˈpaːsn] *nc* **1** the priest, minister *etc* of a parish, *usu* of the Church of England. **2** (*inf*) any priest, minister *etc.*

ˈ**parsonage** [-nidʒ] *nc* the house in which the parson of a parish lives.

part [paːt] *nc* **1** something which, together with other things, makes a whole; a piece: *We spent part of the time at home and part at the seaside*; *the parts of the body*; *a large part of the country.* **2** an equal division: *He divided the cake into three parts*; *a penny is the hundredth part of a pound*; *a twelve-part serial.* **3** a character in a play *etc*: *She played the part of the queen.* **4** the words, actions *etc* of a character in a play *etc*: *He learned his part quickly.* **5** in music, the notes to be played or sung by a particular instrument or voice: *the violin part.* **6** a person's share, responsibility *etc* in doing something: *He played a great part in the government's decision*; *You do your part and I shall do the rest.* – *vti* (*more formal than* **separate**) to separate; to divide: *The lovers were parted by their families*; *They parted (from each other) at the gate*; *The curtains parted and the play began.* – *See also* **part with** *below.*

ˈ**parting 1** *ncu* the act of leaving someone, saying goodbye *etc*: *Their final parting was at the station.* **2** *nc* a line dividing hair brushed in opposite directions on the head.

ˈ**partly** *adv* to a certain extent but not completely: *She was tired, partly because of the journey and partly because of the heat.*

parts *n pl* (*inf or dial*) a district or area: *You won't find tourists in these parts*; *foreign parts* (= countries abroad).

ˈ**part-song** *nc* a song in which singers sing different notes in harmony.

ˌ**part-ˈtime** *adj, adv* not taking one's whole time; for only a few hours or days a week: *She is a part-time secretary*; *It is only a part-time job*; *The new assistant is only part-time*; *She works part-time in a grocer's.*

do one's part (*formal*) to do as much work *etc* as one should at something: *He can be relied upon to do his part.*

for ˈmy *etc* **part** (*formal*) as far as I am *etc* concerned: *He is very worried, but for my part I can't see anything wrong.*

for the ˈmost part (*formal*) usually or generally: *He is quite a good worker for the most part.*

in ˈpart (*formal*) partly: *He agreed that he was in part responsible for the accident.*

part and parcel (*inf*) something which is naturally part: *Doing this is part and parcel of my work.*

part company *vi* **1** (*formal*) to go in different directions: *We parted company at the bus-stop.* **2** to leave each other or end a friendship, partnership *etc*: *My husband and I finally parted company because he was having an affair with another woman.*

the parting of the ways (*fig*) the point at which people must take different decisions, follow different courses of action *etc*: *We have come to the parting of the ways.*

part of speech (*gram*) one of the groups into which words are divided (*eg* noun, verb, adjective *etc*).

ˈ**part with** *vt fus* (*inf*) to give away or be separated from: *He doesn't like parting with money.*

take in good part to accept without being hurt or offended: *He took their jokes in good part.*

take someone's part to support someone (in an argument *etc*): *His mother always takes his part.*

take part in be one of a group of people doing something, to take an active share in (*eg* playing a game, performing a play, holding a discussion *etc*): *She takes part in many student activities*; *He* *never took part in arguments; He was one of many taking part.*

partake [pa:'teik] – *pt* **partook** [-'tuk]: *ptp* **par'taken** – *vi* **1** (*formal*) (*with* **in**) to take part: *They all partook in the final decision.* **2** (*old or liter*) (*with* **of**) to share in: *They partook of a simple meal.*

partial ['pa:ʃəl] *adj* **1** (*formal*) not complete; in part only: *a partial success; on partial payment; His recovery was only partial.* **2** (*pred with* **to**) having a liking for (a person or thing): *He is very partial to cheese.* **3** (*old*) preferring one person or side more than another (in an examination *etc*): *The referee was accused of being partial.*

ˌparti'ality [-ʃi'aləti] *nu* (*formal*) **1** (*with* **for**) a liking for: *He has a partiality for cheese.* **2** the preferring of one person or side more than another: *He could not help showing his partiality for/towards his own team.*

See also **impartial**.

participate [pa:'tisipeit] *vi* (*formal: usu with* **in**) to be one of a group of people actively doing something: *Did you participate in the discussion?*

parˌtici'pation *nu.*

par'ticipant, par'ticipator *ncs* (*formal*) a person who participates (in a particular activity): *the participants in the Olympic Games.*

participial *see* **participle**.

participle ['pa:tisipl] *nc* a form of a verb used with other verbs to form tenses, or as an adjective: *He was eating; He has arrived; a shining light; stolen jewels.*

ˌparti'cipial *adj* (*gram: usu attrib*) of or containing a participle: *a participial phrase.*

particle ['pa:tikl] *nc* **1** (*formal or facet*) a very small piece: *a particle of dust;* (*fig*) *There wasn't a particle of truth in his story.* **2** (*gram*) a short adverbial or prepositional word which functions in a sentence as part of a phrasal verb: *He carried the box in, opened it up, and looked at what was in it.*

particular [pə'tikjulə] *adj* **1** (*attrib*) of a single definite person, thing *etc* thought of separately from all others: *this particular man; this particular problem.* **2** (*attrib*) more than ordinary: *Please take particular care of this letter.* **3** (*sometimes derog*) difficult to please: *He is very particular about his food; She is particular in her way of dressing; a very particular old man.*

par'ticularize, -ise *vti* (*formal*) to speak of the details of (something), naming them one by one: *Would you particularize the items on the bill?; He has a great many faults – I will not particularize them.*

par'ticularly *adv* more than usually: *He was particularly pleased to see his brother.*

par'ticulars *n pl* facts or details: *You must give them all the particulars about the accident.*

in par'ticular more than others: *I liked this book in particular although the others were very interesting too.*

parting *see* **part**.

partisan [pa:ti'zan, (*Amer*) 'pa:rtizən] *adj* (*formal*) giving strong and enthusiastic support or loyalty to a particular cause, theory *etc, esp* without considering other points of view: *He has strong partisan feelings; You must try to listen to both points of view and not be partisan.* – *nc* **1** (*formal*) a strong and enthusiastic supporter of a person, political party, idea or philosophy *etc*: *Every movement has its partisans.* **2** a member of a group organized to fight against an enemy which has occupied their country.

partition [pə'tiʃən] **1** *nc* something that divides, *eg* a light, often temporary, wall between rooms: *The office was divided in two by a wooden partition.* **2** *ncu* (*formal*) the act of dividing; the state of being divided: *the partition of India.* – *vt* to divide: *They partitioned the room* (*off*) *with a curtain.*

partner ['pa:tnə] *nc* **1** a person who shares the ownership of a business *etc* with one or more others: *After several years, she was made a partner in the firm.* **2** one of two people who dance, play in a game *etc* together: *She wanted to dance, but could not find a partner; a tennis partner.* – *vt* to be a partner to (someone): *He partnered his wife in the last dance.*

'partnership **1** *ncu* the state of being or becoming partners: *They entered a business partnership; After training, he entered into partnership with his brother.* **2** *nc* people playing together in a game: *The champions were defeated by the partnership of Jones and Smith in the men's doubles.*

partridge ['pa:tridʒ] – *pls* **'partridges, 'partridge** – **1** *nc* a type of bird which lives mainly on the ground and is often shot for sport: *He shot three partridges and a pheasant; a brace* (= pair) *of partridge.* **2** *ncu* (the flesh of) the bird as food: *We had roast partridge for dinner.*

party ['pa:ti] *nc* **1** a meeting of guests for entertainment, celebration *etc*: *a birthday party; a dinner-party; She's giving/having a party tonight;* (*attrib*) *a party dress.* **2** a group of people with a particular purpose: *a party of tourists; a raiding-party;* (*attrib*) *There are reduced prices for party bookings.* **3** a group of people with the same ideas and purposes, *esp* political: *a political party; the Conservative Party;* (*attrib*) *party politics.* **4** (*formal: with* **to**) a person who takes part in, or knows about and agrees to, an action: *Because he allowed the criminals to hide in his house, he was considered to be* (*a*) *party to the crime.* **5** (*usu legal*) a person or group of people (concerned in an agreement or lawsuit): *He is one of the interested parties; He is one of the parties involved.*

party line *nc* **1** a telephone line shared by two or more people. **2** (*with* **the**) the official ideas and opinions of a political party (on a particular subject): *We must all follow the party line on education.*

party to *see* **party** (*n def 4*).

pass [pa:s] **1** *vti* to move towards and then beyond (something, by going past, through, by, over *etc*): *I pass the shops on my way to work; The bus passed five minutes ago; Pass the rope through the ring; He passed the money across the desk; The procession passed along the corridor.* **2** *vti* to move, give *etc* from one person, state *etc* to another: *They passed the photographs around from one to the other until they had all seen them; The tradition is passed* (*on/down*) *from father to son; His mood soon passed from despair to hope.* **3** *vt* (*fig formal*) to go or be beyond: *This passes my understanding; He passed all expectations and actually won the prize.* **4** *vt* (of vehicles *etc* on a road) to overtake: *The sports car passed me at a dangerous bend in the road.* **5** *vt* (*formal*) to spend (time): *We passed a pleasant hour; They passed several weeks in the country.* **6** *vt* (of an official group, government *etc*) to accept or approve: *They passed my application for permission to build a house; The government has passed a resolution.* **7** *vt* (*legal*) to give or announce (a judgement or sentence): *The magistrate passed judgement on the prisoner.* **8** *vt* (*formal*) to make or express (an opinion or statement): *She passed a very rude remark.* **9** *vi* to end or go away: *His sickness soon passed.* – (*See also* **pass off** *below*). **10** *vt* to (judge to) be successful in (an examination *etc*): *I passed my driving test*; *They usually pass about half the candidates.* – *nc* **1** a narrow path between mountains: *The bandits attacked him as he rode through the mountain pass.* **2** a ticket or card allowing a person to do something, *eg* to travel free or to get in to a building: *You must show your pass before entering.* **3** a successful result in an examination, *esp* when below a distinction, honours *etc*: *There were ten passes and no fails*; (*attrib*) *A pass degree is of a lower standard than an Honours degree.* **4** (in ball games) a throw, kick, hit *etc* of the ball from one player to another: *The centre-forward made a pass towards the goal.* **5** (*sl*) an obvious attempt to make someone (*usu* of the opposite sex) sexually interested in one: *He makes a pass at every girl he meets.*

ˈ**passable** *adj* **1** fairly good: *a passable knowledge of art*; *a passable tennis player*; *He's not a brilliant tennis-player but he's passable.* **2** (*usu pred*) (of a river, road *etc*) able to be passed, travelled over *etc*: *The snow is so deep that the roads are no longer passable.*

ˈ**passably** *adv* fairly well: *He's passably good at mathematics.*

ˈ**passing** *adj* (*usu attrib*) **1** going past: *a passing car.* **2** lasting only a short time: *a passing interest.* **3** (of something said) casual and not made as part of a serious talk about the subject: *He made only a passing reference to Ireland in his speech.* – *See also* **pass** *in phrases below.*

ˈ**passbook** *nc* a book in which records of money put into and taken out a bank account *etc* are officially written.

ˌ**passer-ˈby** – *pl* ˌ**passers-ˈby** – *nc* a person who is going past a place when something happens: *He asked the passers-by if they had seen the accident.*

ˈ**password** *nc* a secret word by which those who know it can recognize each other and be allowed to go past, enter *etc*: *He was not allowed into the army camp because he did not know the password.*

come to pass (*arch*) to happen.

in ˈpassing while doing or talking about something else; without explaining fully what one means: *He told her the story, and said in passing that he did not completely believe it.*

let (something) pass to ignore something rather than take the trouble to argue about it: *I'll let that pass.*

ˈ**pass as/for** *vt fus* to be mistaken for or accepted as: *Some man-made materials could pass as silk*; *His nasty remarks pass for wit among his admirers.*

pass away *vi* (*euph*) to die: *Her grandmother passed away last night.* – *See also* **pass on**.

pass the buck (*inf*) to give the responsibility or blame for something to someone else: *She always passes the buck if she is asked to do anything.*

pass by 1 *vi, vt fus* to go past (a particular place): *I was passing by when the bride arrived at the church*; *She passed by the hospital on the way to the library.* **2** *vt sep* to ignore or take no notice of: *They passed him by when the new jobs were given out.*

pass for *see* **pass as** *above.*

pass off *vi* **1** (of sickness, an emotion *etc*) to go away: *By the evening, his sickness had passed off and he felt better.* **2** (of an event) to happen (with emphasis on the fact that the course of the event was not stopped or spoiled): *The wedding passed off very well in the end.*

pass (something or someone) off as to pretend that (something or someone) is (something or someone else): *He passed the whole embarrassing incident off as a joke*; *He passed himself off as a journalist.*

pass on 1 *vt sep* to give to someone else (*usu* something which one has been given by a third person): *I passed on his message to Mrs Brown*; *Please read this note and pass it on.* **2** *vi* (*euph*) to die: *I am sorry to tell you that mother passed on yesterday.* – *See also* **pass away**.

pass out 1 *vi* to faint: *I feel as though I'm going to pass out.* **2** *vi* to leave or graduate from a college, *esp* military or police. **3** *vt sep* to give to several different people: *The teacher passed out books to her class.*

pass over *vt sep* to ignore or overlook: *This is the third time he's been passed over for that job*; *We'll pass over that remark*; *They passed him over for promotion.*

pass the time of day to have a short, formal conversation on meeting someone *etc*: *He hates her so much that he won't even pass the time of day with her.*

pass up *vt sep* (*inf*) not to accept (a chance, opportunity *etc*): *He passed up the offer of a good job in America to come here*; *He passed the job up without even considering it.*

a pretty pass (*old or facet*) a bad state or condition: *Things have come to/reached a pretty pass when you cannot trust your best friend.*

See also **impassable**.

passage [ˈpasidʒ] **1** *nc* a long narrow way through, *eg* a corridor through a building: *I met her in the passage*; *There was a dark passage leading down to the river between tall buildings.* **2** *nc* a part of a piece of writing or music: *That is my favourite passage from the Bible.* **3** *nu* (*formal*) (*usu* of time) the act of passing: *the passage of time.* **4** *nc* a journey by boat: *He paid for his passage by working as a steward.*

passé [ˈpasei, (*Amer*) paˈsei] *adj* (*formal derog*: *pred*) **1** out of date: *That dress is distinctly passé.* **2** past its best: *She was an excellent singer, but she's a bit passé now.*

passenger [ˈpasindʒə] *nc* a person who travels in any vehicle, boat, aeroplane *etc* (not the driver or anyone working there): *a passenger on a train*; *The driver of the car was killed but the passengers escaped uninjured*; (*attrib*) *a passenger train.*

passing *see* **pass**.

passion [ˈpaʃən] *ncu* very strong feeling, *esp* of anger or love: *He argued with great passion*; *His passion for her soon cooled*; (*inf facet*) *She has a passion for mint chocolates.*

ˈ**passionate** [-nət] *adj* having very strong feelings; intense or emotional: *a passionate woman*; *He is very passionate but his wife is rather frigid*; *passionate hatred.*

See also **impassioned, dispassionate**.

passive [ˈpasiv] *adj* **1** showing no interest, emotion *etc*, or not resisting an attack *etc*: *In spite of their threats the old lady remained passive*; *The villagers showed passive resistance to the enemy* (= They opposed their authority by disobedience *etc*, not by active opposition). **2** (*gram*) of the form of the verb used when the subject receives the action of the verb: *The boy has been bitten by a dog*; *This castle was built in the fourteenth century*. – **1** *nu* the passive form of the verb: *a verb in the passive*. **2** *nc* a verb in the passive. ˈ**passively** *adv*. ˈ**passiveness, pasˈsivity** *nus*.

See also **active, impassive**.

passport [ˈpa:spo:t] *nc* a document of identification which is necessary for foreign travel: *a British passport*; (*fig formal*) *a passport to happiness*.

past [pa:st] *adj* **1** just finished: *the past hour*; *the past year*; *the year that is past*. **2** over, finished or ended, of an earlier time than the present: *The time for discussion is past*; *He thanked me for past kindness*. **3** (*gram*) (of the tense of a verb) indicating action in the past: *In 'He did it', the verb is in the past tense*. – *prep* **1** up to and beyond; by: *He ran past me*. **2** after: *It's past six o'clock*. – *adv* up to and beyond (a particular place, person *etc*): *The soldiers marched past*. – **1** *nc* (*usu in sing*: *sometimes facet*) a person's earlier life or career, *esp* if secret or not respectable: *He came to London to start a new life, and never spoke about his past*; *She is a woman with a past!* **2** *nu* (*gram*) the past tense: *a verb in the past*.

the past the time which was before the present: *In the past, all houses in this area were built of wood or stone*.

a past master someone who is extremely skilful (at an activity which requires skill): *She is a past master at the art of getting her own way*.

pasta [ˈpastə, (*Amer*) ˈpa:-] *nu* a dough used in Italian cooking for making spaghetti, macaroni *etc*.

paste [peist] *nu* **1** a soft, damp mixture, *esp* one made up of glue and water and used for sticking pieces of paper *etc* together: *wallpaper paste*. **2** a mixture of flour, fat *etc* used for making pies, pastry *etc*. **3** a mixture made from some types of food: *almond paste*. **4** a kind of fine glass used in making imitation jewellery: *Her 'diamond' necklace was just paste*.

ˈ**pasty** *adj* (*derog*) (*usu* of the face or complexion) soft, fat and very pale in colour: *He was a fat boy with a pasty face*; *He looks rather pasty*. ˈ**pastiness** *nu*.

ˈ**pasteboard** *nu* cardboard.

pastel [ˈpastəl, (*Amer*) paˈstel] *adj* (*attrib*) (of colours) pale and containing a lot of white: *She always wore pastel shades*; *a soft pastel green*. – *nc* **1** a kind of coloured pencil, made with chalk, which makes a pale, whitish colour. **2** a picture drawn with this kind of pencil.

pasteurize, -ise [ˈpastʃəraiz] *vt* (*tech*) to heat food, *esp* milk, for a time to kill germs in it. ˌ**pasteuriˈzation, -s-** *nu*.

pastille [ˈpastəl, (*Amer*) paˈsti:l] *nc* a small sweet often containing medicine (*usu* for infections of the mouth or throat *etc*): *throat pastilles*.

pastime [ˈpa:staim] *nc* an occupation which one enjoys and takes part in in one's spare time; a hobby: *Playing chess is his favourite pastime*.

pastiness *see* **paste**.

pastor [ˈpa:stə] *nc* (*with cap in titles*) a minister of religion, *esp* of the Protestant church.

ˈ**pastoral** *adj* (*usu attrib*) **1** (*usu liter*) of country life: *a pastoral scene*. **2** of a pastor, or his work: *pastoral responsibilities*.

pastry [ˈpeistri] **1** *nu* flour paste used in making pies, tarts *etc*. **2** *nc* a pie, tart *etc* made with this: *Danish pastries*.

pasture [ˈpa:stʃə] *ncu* a field or area of ground covered with grass for cattle *etc* to eat: *The horses were out in the pasture*; *The farm has 1 000 hectares of pasture*.

pasty[1] *see* **paste**.

pasty[2] [ˈpasti] *nc* a pie containing meat and vegetables in a covering of pastry: *a Cornish pasty*.

pat [pat] *nc* **1** a light, gentle blow or touch, *usu* with the palm of the hand and showing affection: *She gave the child a pat on the head*. **2** (of butter) a small piece; a lump. – *v* – *pt*, *prp* ˈ**patted** – *vt* to strike gently with the palm of the hand, *usu* as a sign of affection: *He walked up to the horse and patted its neck*. – *adv* (*often* **off pat**) memorized, prepared and ready to be said: *He had the answer (off) pat*.

a pat on the back (*inf*) a demonstration of approval or praise: *We all got a pat on the back from the manager for our hard work*.

patch [patʃ] *nc* **1** a piece of material sewn on to cover a hole: *She sewed a patch on the knee of her jeans*. **2** a small piece of ground: *a vegetable patch*. – *vt* to mend (clothes *etc*) by sewing on pieces of material: *She patched the (hole in the) child's trousers*. – *See also* **patch up** *below*.

ˈ**patchy** *adj* not all the same; varying in quality: *Her work is very patchy*; *rather patchy work*. ˈ**patchiness** *nu*.

ˈ**patchwork** *nu* cloth made by sewing small pieces of material together: *I enjoy making patchwork*; *a skirt made of patchwork*; (*attrib*) *a patchwork quilt*.

not a ˈpatch on (*inf*) not nearly as good as: *Her cooking is not a patch on my mother's*.

patch up *vt sep* **1** to mend, *esp* quickly and temporarily: *He patched up the roof with bits of wood*. **2** (*fig*) to settle (a quarrel): *They soon patched up their disagreement*; *They patched it up yesterday*.

pâté [ˈpatei, (*Amer*) pa:ˈtei] *nu* a paste made of meat or fish and herbs, spices *etc*: *We'll start the meal with pâté*.

ˈ**pâté de ˌfoie ˈgras** [-dəfwa:ˈgra:] *nu* pâté made of fat goose liver.

patent [ˈpeitənt, (*Amer*) ˈpa-] *nc* an official licence from the government giving one person or business the right to make and sell a particular article and to prevent others from doing the same: *She took out a patent on her design*; (*attrib*) *a patent process*. – *vt* to obtain a patent for; *He patented his new invention*. – *adj* (*formal*: *attrib*) obvious: *a patent disregard for the truth*.

ˌ**patenˈtee** *nc* a person who has obtained a patent.

ˈ**patently** *adv* (*formal*) obviously; clearly: *It is patently obvious that she is lying*.

patent leather *nu*, *adj* (of) very smooth and shiny leather: *Her shoes were made of patent leather*; *patent leather shoes*.

patent medicines *n pl* medicines that one can buy easily, made up and sold by a particular firm: *He has not gone to the doctor – he is trying to cure his cold with patent medicines*.

paternal [pəˈtə:nl] *adj* (*formal*) **1** of or like a father: *a paternal attitude*; *He is not in love with her – his feelings towards her are almost paternal*. **2** among one's father's relatives: *Her paternal grandmother*.

paˈternity *nu* (*formal or legal*) the fact or state of being a father: *It is impossible to be certain of the paternity of a child by medical means*; (*attrib*) *a paternity suit*.

See also **maternal, fraternal**.

path [pa:θ] – *pl* **paths** [pa:ðz] – *nc* **1** a way made across the ground by the passing of people or animals: *There is a path through the fields*; *a path up the mountain*; *a mountain path*; *a woodland path.* 2 (any place on) the line along which someone or something is moving: *She stood right in the path of the bus*; *Scientists had predicted the path of the whirlwind.*

'pathway *nc* a **path**.

pathetic *see* **pathos**.

pathology [pə'θolədʒi] *nu* the science of diseases. **pa'thologist** *nc*.

,patho'logical [paθə'lo-] *adj* **1** (*tech*: *esp attrib*) concerned with pathology: *a pathological disease.* **2** (*often loosely*) unhealthy or unnatural: *a pathological hatred*; *His hatred of her was almost pathological.* **,patho'logically** *adv.*

pathos ['peiθos] *nu* (*formal*) the quality (of something) that makes a person feel pity: *The play is notable for the pathos of its final scene*; *the pathos of the orphan children.*

pathetic [pə'θetik] *adj* **1** causing pity: *The lost dog was a pathetic sight*; *The lost dog looked so pathetic that we took him home.* **2** (*inf*) weak and useless: *He can dance well, but as a singer he is pathetic!*; *He made a pathetic attempt to answer the question.* **pa'thetically** *adv.*

patient ['peiʃənt] *adj* (*usu pred*) suffering delay, pain, irritation *etc* quietly and without complaining: *It will be your turn soon – you must just be patient!* – *nc* a person who is being treated by a doctor, dentist *etc*: *The hospital had not enough doctors and too many patients.*

'patience *nu* **1** the ability or willingness to be patient: *Patience is a virtue.* **2** a card game *usu* played by one person: *The lonely old lady often plays patience.*

'patiently *adv*: *They waited patiently for the next bus to arrive.*

See also **impatient**.

patio ['patiou] – *pl* **'patios** – *nc* an open paved area attached to a house, on which people sit, eat *etc*: *On hot summer evenings, we often have dinner out on the patio.*

patois ['patwa:] – *pl* **'patois** [-z] – *ncu* (*often derog*) the language spoken by the people of a certain area in informal situations, as opposed to the standard, official, literary language of the country concerned: *Although Alsace is in France, the local patois is a form of German*; *They all speak patois in this village*; *They are talking in patois.*

patrial ['peitriəl] *nc* (*formal or legal*: *Brit*) a citizen of the UK, a British colony or the British Commonwealth, who for certain reasons (*eg* because one of his parents was born in the UK) has the right to enter and stay in the UK. **,patri'ality** [-'a-] *nu.*

patriarch ['peitria:k] *nc* **1** (*formal*) the male head of a family or tribe. **2** (*with cap in titles*) *esp* in the Eastern Orthodox Church, a high-ranking bishop: *the Patriarch of Constantinople.*

,patri'archal *adj* (*formal*) of, like, ruled by *etc* a patriarch or patriarchs: *a patriarchal society/church*; *Their society is patriarchal.*

See also **matriarch**.

patrician [pə'triʃən] **1** *adj* (*liter*) like an aristocrat: *a patrician manner.* **2** *nc, adj* (*hist*) *esp* in ancient Rome, (a person who is) aristocratic.

See also **plebeian**.

patricide ['patrisaid] (*formal or legal*) **1** *ncu* the act of killing one's father: *Patricide is a serious crime.* **2** *nc* a person who does such an act.

See also **parricide**.

patrimony ['patriməni] *ncu* (*legal*) property passed on to a person by his or her father or ancestors: *This farm is part of my patrimony.* **,patri'monial** [-'mou-] *adj.*

patriot ['peitriət] *nc* a person who loves (and serves) his country: *Many terrorists consider themselves to be patriots fighting for freedom.*

patriotic [patri'otik, (*esp Amer*) pei-] *adj* (*neg* **un-**) having or showing great love for one's country: *He is so patriotic that he refuses to buy anything made abroad*; *a patriotic young man.* **,patri'otically** *adv.*

'patriotism ['pa-, (*esp Amer*) 'pei-] *nu* (the showing of) great love for one's country: *Patriotism is essential in a soldier.*

patrol [pə'troul] – *pt, ptp* **pa'trolled** – *vti* to watch or protect (an area) by moving continually around or through it: *Soldiers patrolled the streets*; *Naval ships patrolled the coastal seas*; *We've been patrolling for days but have seen nothing.* – **1** *nc* a group of people *etc* who patrol an area: *They came across several army patrols in the hills*; *Patrols were set up in the streets.* **2** *nu* the act of watching or guarding by patrolling: *The soldiers went out on patrol*; (*attrib*) *He was on patrol duty at the time*; (*attrib*) *a police patrol car.* **3** *nc* a small group of *usu* six or seven Scouts or Guides: *Each Scout troop or Guide company is divided into patrols.*

pa'trolman *nc* **1** (*esp Amer*) a policeman who patrols an area: *The murderer was seen by a couple of patrolmen.* **2** a person who patrols a certain area and who helps motorists in difficulty, *eg* because their cars have broken down.

patron ['peitrən] *nc* **1** a person who supports (often with money) an artist, musician, writer, form of art *etc*: *He is a patron of the local Art Society*; *He's a patron of the arts.* **2** a (regular) customer of a shop *etc*: *The manager of the pub said that he knew all his patrons by sight.*

patronage ['patrənidʒ, (*Amer*) 'pei-] *nu* (*formal*) the support given by a patron: *The artist said that he relied on the patronage of certain rich businessmen*; *When the shop closed, the manager thanked his former customers for their patronage.*

'patronize, -ise ['pa-, (*Amer*) 'pei-] *vt* **1** (*derog*) to behave towards (someone) in a way which is kind and friendly which nevertheless shows that one thinks oneself to be more important, clever *etc* than that person: *He's a nice fellow but he does tend to patronize his assistants.* **2** (*formal*) to visit (a shop, theatre, society *etc*) regularly: *That's not a shop I patronize nowadays.*

'patronizing, -s- *adj* (*derog*): *a patronizing person/manner*; *He is so patronizing to the younger staff.* **'patronizingly, -s-** *adv.*

patron saint *nc* a saint who protects a particular person, group of people, country *etc*: *St Andrew is the patron saint of Scotland.*

patter ['patə] *vi* (of rain, footsteps *etc*) to make a quick, tapping sound: *She heard the mice pattering behind the walls.* – *nu* **1** the sound made in this way: *the patter of rain on the roof.* **2** (*inf*) fast talk, *esp* the fast, persuasive talk of a salesman or the (often amusing) talk of a comedian *etc*: *A conjuror's patter is almost as important as his ability to do tricks.*

pattern ['patən] *nc* **1** (*often in cmpds*) a model or guide for making something: *a paper pattern*; *a dress-pattern.* **2** a repeated decoration or design on wallpaper, dress material *etc*: *The dress is nice but I'm not keen on the pattern on the material.* **3** an example suitable to be copied: *the pattern of good behaviour.* **4** a sample, *eg* of material, showing a design on it: *a book of tweed patterns.* **5** (*fig*) the way in which something is done: *the pattern of economic development in African countries.*

'patterned *adj* with a decoration or design on it; not plain: *patterned wallpaper*; *Is her new carpet plain or patterned?*

paunch [po:ntʃ] *nc* (*usu derog*) a large, round stomach: *As he got older he developed quite a paunch.*

pauper ['po:pə] *nc* (*formal or liter*) a very poor person: *The title of the story is 'The Prince and the Pauper'*; *Her husband died a pauper.*

pause [po:z] *nc* **1** (*more formal than* **stop**) a short stop, break or interval (while doing something): *There was a pause in the conversation*; *He spoke for ten minutes without a pause.* **2** (*music*) the act of making a note or rest slightly longer than normal, or a mark showing that this is to be done. – *vi* (*often with* **for**) to stop talking, working *etc* for a short time: *They paused to have a cigarette*; *They paused for a cup of tea*; *He paused for a moment, and then continued his speech.*

pave [peiv] *vt* to cover (a street, path *etc*) with (*usu* large) flat stones, concrete *etc* to make a flat surface for walking on *etc*: *He wants to dig up the lawn and pave the garden instead.*

'pavement *nc* (*Amer* **'sidewalk**) a paved surface, *esp* a paved footpath along the sides of a road for people to walk on: *One shouldn't ride a bicycle on the pavement.*

'paving-stone *nc* a large flat stone or piece of concrete used for paving.

pave the way for (*fig*) to make it easy or possible for (something to happen): *The scientific discoveries of the eighteenth century paved the way for the Industrial Revolution in Britain.*

pavilion [pə'viljən] *nc* **1** a building on a sports ground in which players change their clothes, store equipment *etc*: *a cricket pavilion.* **2** a large ornamental building: *the Royal Pavilion in Brighton.*

paw [po:] *nc* **1** the foot of an animal with claws or nails: *The dog had a thorn in its paw.* **2** (*sl*) a hand: *Get your paws off those cakes!* – **1** *vti* (*often with* **at**) (of an animal) to touch, hit *etc* (*usu* several times) with a paw or paws: *The cat was pawing (at) the dead mouse.* **2** *vti* (*often with* **at**) (of an animal) to hit (the ground, *usu* several times) with a hoof, *usu* a front hoof: *The horse pawed (at) the ground.* **3** *vt* (*inf*: *sometimes with* **about** *or* **around**) (of a person) to handle or touch clumsily or rudely: *Don't paw my books (about)*; *Stop pawing me!*; *He paws every woman that he sits beside.*

pawn [po:n] *vt* to give (an article of value) to a pawnbroker in exchange for money (which may be repaid at a later time to get the article back): *I had to pawn my watch to pay the bill.* – *nc* **1** in chess, one of the small pieces of lowest rank. **2** a person who is used by another person for his own gain, advantage *etc*: *She was a pawn in his ambitious plans.* – *See also* **in pawn** *below.*

'pawnbroker *nc* **1** a person who lends money in exchange for pawned articles. **2** a pawnbroker's shop.

'pawnbroker's *nc* a pawnbroker's shop: *I got this watch at a pawnbroker's.*

'pawnshop *nc* a pawnbroker's place of business.

in 'pawn having been pawned: *His watch is in pawn.*

pay [pei] – *pt, ptp* **paid** – **1** *vti* (*sometimes with* **for**) to give (money) to (someone) in exchange for goods, services *etc*: *He paid £2 for the book*; *I'll pay you £50 for that*; *I'll pay (for the dinner)*; *I haven't been paid (for that work) yet*; *I paid to get into the cinema.* **2** *vti* to return (money that is owed): *He paid me the £5 he had borrowed*; *It's time you paid your debts*; *When he owes money he always pays.* **3** *vi* (*fig*: *with* **for**) to suffer punishment (for): *You'll pay for that remark!* **4** *vti* to be useful or profitable (to): *It will pay (you) to be careful*; *Crime doesn't pay.* **5** *vt* to give (attention, homage, respect *etc*): *Pay attention to what I am going to say!*; *We've come to pay our respects to him.* **6** *vti* (*with* **in(to)**) to put (money into a bank, an account *etc*): *Are you paying in or withdrawing?*; *I'd like to pay in £50*; *I'll pay this into my account.* – *See also* **pay** *in phrases below.* – *nu* (*more inf than* **salary** *or* **wages**) money given or received for work *etc*; wages: *How much pay do you get for the job?*

'payable *adj* (*usu pred*) which may be or must be paid: *The cheque is payable to me*; *The account is payable at the end of the month.*

pay'ee *nc* (*very formal*) a person to whom money is (to be) paid.

'payment **1** *nc* money *etc* paid: *The radio can be paid for in ten weekly payments of £2.* **2** *nu* the act of paying: *He gave me a book instead of money in payment for my kindness.*

'pay-packet *nc* **1** an envelope containing a person's wages: *The manager handed out the pay-packets.* **2** (*inf*) (the amount of) a person's wages: *He's complaining about the size of his pay-packet.*

'pay-roll *nc* **1** a list of all the workers in a factory *etc*: *We have 450 people on the pay-roll.* **2** the total amount of money to be paid to all the workers: *The thieves stole the pay-roll.*

in someone's 'pay (*inf*: *usu derog*) employed by, or given money by, someone, *usu* for a bad purpose: *The judge was in the pay of a group of important criminals.*

pay back *vt sep* **1** to give back (to someone something that one has borrowed): *I'll pay you the £5 back tomorrow*; *I'll pay you back as soon as I can.* **2** (*inf fig*) to punish: *I'll pay you back for that!*

pay off **1** *vt sep* to pay in full and discharge (workers) because they are no longer needed: *Hundreds of steel-workers have been paid off.* **2** *vi* (*fig*) to have good results: *His hard work paid off.*

pay out **1** *vi, vt sep* to spend or give (money), *eg* to pay bills, debts *etc*: *I'm not willing to pay out large sums of money to repair an old car like this*; *Her father is always paying out to settle her bills.* **2** *vt sep* to cause or allow (rope *etc*) to become slack.

pay through the nose *see* **nose**.

pay up *vi, vt fus* (*inf*) to give (money) to someone, *eg* in order to pay a debt: *You lost the bet, so pay up (what you owe me)*; *You have three days to pay up* (=You must pay up within three days).

pay a visit *see* **visit**.

put paid to to prevent a person from doing (something he planned or wanted to do): *The rain put paid to our visit to the zoo*; *His wife's stupidity put paid to his plans to become the director of the firm.*

pea [pi:] *nc* **1** the round seed of a kind of climbing plant, eaten as a vegetable: *We had roast beef, potatoes and peas for dinner*; (*attrib*) *pea soup.* **2** the plant which produces these seeds: *We planted peas and beans this year.*

pease [pi:z]: **pease pudding** a kind of pudding

made from peas, eaten as part of a main course.

peace [pi:s] *nu* **1** (*sometimes with* **a**) (a time of) freedom from war; (a treaty or agreement which brings about) the end or stopping of a war: *The ambassador was asked whether his country wanted peace or war; Peace was signed in November; After a brief peace, fighting between the two countries began again*; (*attrib*) *a peace treaty.* **2** freedom from disturbance; quietness: *I would work better if I could have a bit of peace and quiet.*

'**peaceable** *adj* liking peace; not fighting, quarrelling *etc*: *He's a fairly peaceable person; He is far from being peaceable.* '**peaceably** *adv.*

'**peaceful** *adj* quiet; calm; without worry or disturbance: *It's very peaceful out here in the country; a peaceful night's sleep.* '**peacefully** *adv.* '**peacefulness** *nu.*

'**peacemaker** *nc* a person who tries to make peace between enemies, people who are quarrelling *etc*: *My brother and sister are always quarrelling, so I have to act as peacemaker.*

'**peace-offering** *nc* something offered or given to make peace: *After they had quarrelled, she took him a cup of tea as a peace-offering.*

'**peacetime** *nu* a time when there is no war: *Even in peacetime, a soldier's life is hard*; (*attrib*) *peacetime operations.*

at '**peace** not at war; not fighting: *The two countries were at peace; At that time, Scotland was at peace with England*; (*fig*) *I feel at peace with the world* (= I have no fears, worries *etc*).

breach of the peace *see* **breach**.

in '**peace** **1** without disturbance: *Why can't you leave me in peace?; I'd like to read this book in peace.* **2** (*formal*) not wanting to fight: *Although they carried guns, they said they came in peace.*

Justice of the Peace *see* **justice**.

keep the peace **1** (*legal*) not to create a disturbance in public: *The judge did not fine him, but bound him over to keep the peace.* **2** to prevent fighting, quarrelling *etc*; not to fight, quarrel *etc*: *She tries to keep the peace between her brothers.*

make peace to agree to end a war: *The two countries finally made peace* (*with each other*).

peace of mind freedom from worry *etc.*

See also **pacify**.

peach [pi:tʃ] **1** *nc* a kind of juicy, soft-skinned fruit: *She doesn't like peaches*; (*attrib*) *a peach tree.* **2** *nu, adj* (of) the orange-pink colour of the fruit: *Would you call that colour peach?; The walls are painted peach.*

peacock ['pi:kok] – *fem* '**peahen** [-hen] – *nc* a kind of large bird, the male of which is noted for its magnificent tail-feathers.

peak [pi:k] *nc* **1** the pointed top of a mountain or hill: *the highest peak in Snowdonia; snow-covered peaks.* **2** the highest, greatest, busiest *etc* point, time *etc*: *He was at the peak of his career*; (*attrib*) *Traffic moves very slowly at peak hours.* **3** the front part of a cap which shades the eyes: *The boy wore a white cap with a green peak.* – *vi* (*formal*) to reach the highest, greatest, busiest *etc* point, time *etc*: *Prices peaked in July and then began to fall.*

peaked *adj* (*attrib*) having a peak: *a peaked cap.*

'**peaky** *adj* (*inf*) looking pale and unhealthy: *You look peaky today. Don't you feel well?; rather a peaky child.*

offpeak *see* **off**.

peal [pi:l] *nc* **1** the ringing of (a set of) bells. **2** a set of (*usu* church) bells. **3** a loud noise: *peals of laughter/thunder.* – *vti* (*formal*) to (cause to) ring or sound loudly: *Thunder pealed through the valley.*

peanut ['pi:nʌt] *nc* (*also* '**groundnut** *or* '**monkey nut**) a type of nut that looks rather like a pea: *She bought some shelled peanuts* (= peanuts with the outer casing removed); *roasted peanuts.*

peanut butter *nu* a paste made from ground, roasted peanuts: *She made a sandwich with bread and peanut butter*; (*attrib*) *a peanut butter sandwich.*

pear [peə] *nc* a type of fruit of the apple family, round at the bottom and narrowing towards the stem or top: *She's very fond of pears*; (*attrib*) *a pear tree*; (*attrib*) *a pear flan.*

'**pear-shaped** *adj* of the shape of a pear: *a pear-shaped woman; She finds it difficult to find clothes to fit her as she is pear-shaped.*

pearl [pə:l] **1** *nc* a valuable, hard, round object formed by oysters and several other shellfish: *The necklace consists of three strings of pearls*; (*attrib*) *a pearl necklace.* **2** *nu, adj* (of) mother-of-pearl: *The handles of these knives are* (*made of*) *pearl; pearl handles.* **3** *nc* (*formal or liter*) something which is like a pearl in value or appearance: *pearls of wisdom/dew.*

pearls *n pl* a pearl necklace: *I think I'll wear my pearls to the dance this evening.*

'**pearly** *adj* (*usu attrib*) **1** (*liter*) like pearls: *pearly teeth.* **2** covered or made with pearls or pearl: *pearly buttons.*

'**pearl-diver,** '**pearl-fisher** *ncs* a person who dives or fishes for pearls.

peasant ['peznt] *nc* a person who lives and works on the land, *esp* in a poor, primitive or underdeveloped area: *Many peasants died during the drought*; (*attrib*) *a peasant farmer.*

'**peasantry** *nu* (*formal or hist*: *usu with* **the**) peasants as a group; the peasants of a particular place: *What part did the peasantry play in the Russian revolution?*

pease *see* **pea**.

peat [pi:t] **1** *nu* a substance consisting of rotted plants found in marshy areas, sometimes cut into blocks, dried and burned as fuel: *Peat is sometimes used as a fertilizer in gardens; In the Scottish Highlands people still burn peat*; (*attrib*) *a peat fire.* **2** *nc* a block of this substance: *He put some peats on the fire.*

'**peaty** *adj* of or like peat.

pebble ['pebl] *nc* a small, *usu* smooth stone: *small pebbles on the beach.*

'**pebbly** *adj*: *a pebbly beach.*

pecan [pi'kan, (*Amer*) pi'ka:n] *nc* **1** (*also* **pe'can nut**) a kind of nut found in North America. **2** (*also* **pe'can-tree**) the tree bearing such nuts.

peccadillo [pekə'dilou] – *pl* ˌ**pecca'dillo(e)s** – *nc* (*formal or facet*) a small, unimportant sin or bad act: *He admitted kissing his secretary, but said that he didn't feel such a peccadillo was sufficient reason for his being dismissed.*

peck [pek] **1** *vt* (of birds) to strike or pick up with the beak, *usu* in order to eat: *The birds pecked at the corn; The sparrows are pecking the lettuces; The bird pecked his hand.* **2** *vti* (*fig*: *usu with* **at**) to eat very little: *She just pecks* (*at*) *her food.* **3** *vt* (*inf*) to kiss quickly and briefly: *She pecked her mother on the cheek as she left.* – *nc* **1** a tap or bite with the beak: *The bird gave him a painful peck on the hand.* **2** (*inf*) a brief kiss: *a peck on the cheek.*

'**peckish** *adj* (*inf*: *usu pred*) rather hungry: *I feel a bit peckish – is it nearly tea-time?*

pectoral ['pektərəl] *adj* (*tech*: *esp attrib*) of or on the breast or chest: *the pectoral muscles.*

peculiar [pi'kju:ljə] *adj* **1** strange; odd: *What is that peculiar smell?*; *peculiar behaviour*; *I find it rather peculiar that she left so suddenly.* **2** (*formal*: *pred with* **to**) belonging to one person, place or thing in particular and to no other: *customs peculiar to France.*

pe͵culi'arity [-'a-] *ncu*: *Just ignore the peculiarity of his pronunciation*; *There are a few peculiarities in his plans for the house*; *These clothes are a peculiarity of the region.*

pe'culiarly *adv*: *He was behaving most peculiarly.*

pecuniary [pi'kju:niəri] *adj* (*very formal*: *usu attrib*) of money: *a pecuniary reward.*
See also **impecunious**.

pedagogy ['pedəgodʒi] *nu* (*very formal*) the science of teaching.

͵peda'gogic(al) *adj* (*very formal*: *usu attrib*): *No-one doubts his pedagogical skill.*

pedal ['pedl] *nc* a lever worked by the foot, as on a bicycle, piano, organ *etc*: *the brake pedal in a car*; *This bike is too big for the child – he cannot reach the pedals.* – *v* – *pt*, *ptp* **'pedalled**, (*Amer*) **'pedaled** – *vti* to move (something) by means of pedals: *He pedalled (his bicycle) down the road*; *He pedalled away as fast as he could.*

pedant ['pedənt] *nc* (*formal derog*) **1** a person who makes a great show of his knowledge. **2** a person who attaches too much importance to minor details.

pe'dantic [-'dan-] *adj*: *He is so pedantic that he never uses simple words if he can think of a difficult word*; *He is so pedantic that he criticizes his wife's English in public.* **pe'dantically** *adv*.

'pedantry *nu*: *His attempts to achieve grammatical correctness in his reports often develop into nothing more than ridiculous pedantry.*

peddle ['pedl] *vti* to go from place to place or house to house selling (small objects): *Gypsies often peddle (goods) from door to door.*

'pedlar, (*also*, *esp Amer*) **'peddler** *nc* a person who peddles: *I bought some clothes-pegs from a pedlar at the door.*

pedestal ['pedistl] *nc* the foot or base of a column, statue *etc*: *During the earthquake, several statues fell off their pedestals and were smashed*; (*fig*) *She puts her husband on a pedestal* (= She treats him with very great, *usu* too great, respect).

pedestrian [pi'destriən] *nc* a person who travels on foot: *Three pedestrians were hit by the car*; (*attrib*) *a pedestrian crossing* (= a place where pedestrians can walk across a road safely). – *adj* (*formal derog*) ordinary; rather boring or unexciting: *He gave a pedestrian account of his travels*; *His essays are always so pedestrian.*

pediatrics *etc see* **paediatrics**.

pedigree ['pedigri:] **1** *nc* a list of the ancestors from whom a person or animal is descended: *Did you get a copy of the dog's pedigree from the breeder?* **2** *nu* (*formal or liter*) distinguished descent or ancestry: *a man of pedigree.* – *adj* (*usu attrib*) (of an animal) pure-bred; from a long line of ancestors of the same breed: *a herd of pedigree cattle*; *All our dogs are pedigree.*

'pedigreed *adj* having a pedigree.

pedlar *see* **peddle**.

pee [pi:] *vi* (*inf*) to urinate. – *nc* (*inf*) an act of urinating: *I must have a pee.*

peek [pi:k] *vi* (*inf*) to look, *esp* quickly and in secret: *He opened the door slightly and peeked out*; *Cover your eyes and don't peek.* – *nc* (*inf*) a quick look: *Take a peek through the window*; *I just had a quick peek at the baby because it was sleeping.*

peel [pi:l] **1** *vt* to take off the skin or outer covering of (a fruit or vegetable): *One usually peels an orange before eating it*; *She peeled the potatoes.* **2** *vi* to be peeled: *Potatoes peel easily.* **3** *vti* (*often with* **off**) to take off or come off in small pieces: *The paint is beginning to peel (off)*; *Do you need a knife to peel off the skin?*; *That new drug made my skin peel*; *After I lay in the hot sun my back* (= the skin on my back) *began to peel.* – *nu* the skin of certain fruits, *esp* oranges, lemons *etc*: *I need more raisins and mixed peel* (= candied orange and lemon peel) *for this cake.*

'peeler *nc* (*usu in cmpds*) a tool *etc* that peels (something): *a potato-peeler.*

'peelings *n pl* the strips or pieces of skin peeled off an apple, potato *etc*: *I always put the potato peelings on the compost heap.*

peep[1] [pi:p] *vi* **1** to look through a narrow opening or from behind something: *She peeped through the window*; (*fig*) *The sun peeped out from behind the clouds.* **2** (*usu with* **at**) to look quickly and in secret: *He peeped at the answers at the back of the book.* – *nc* a quick look (*usu* in secret): *She took a peep at the visitor from behind the door*; *He had a peep at the answers at the back of the book.*

'peep-hole *nc* a hole (in a door *etc*) through which one can look: *The old lady always looks through the peep-hole before opening her front door.*

peep[2] [pi:p] *vi* (*inf*) to make a high pitched sound: *The car horns were peeping.* – *nc* **1** such a sound: *the peep of a car horn.* **2** (*inf*: *usu with a neg*) any noise: *I don't want to hear a peep out of you*; *There was not a peep from the sleeping children.*

peer[1] [piə] *nc* **1** (the status of) in Britain, a member of the House of Lords: *He used to be in the House of Commons but he has been made a peer.* **2** (the status of) a nobleman (in Britain, one from the rank of baron upwards). **3** (*formal*) a person's equal in rank, merit or age: *The child was disliked by his peers*; (*attrib*) *He is more advanced than the rest of his peer group.*

'peerage [-ridʒ] *nc* **1** a peer's title or status: *He was granted a peerage*; *He was raised to the peerage.* **2** (often with *pl* verb when considered as a number of separate individuals) all noblemen as a group: *The Scottish peerage has an interesting history*; *The peerage have as many responsibilities as privileges.*

'peeress *nc* **1** (the status of) the wife or widow of a peer (*def 2*). **2** (the status of) a woman who is a peer (*defs 1, 2*) in her own right.

'peerless *adj* (*liter*: *attrib*) without equal; better than all others: *Sir Galahad was a peerless knight.*

peer[2] [piə] *vi* to look with difficulty: *He peered at the small writing*; *He peered (out) into the darkness*; *She tends to peer when she is not wearing her spectacles.*

peevish ['pi:viʃ] *adj* easily made angry; irritable; frequently complaining: *a peevish old man*; *The child is sulky and peevish.* **'peevishly** *adv*. **'peevishness** *nu*.

peeved *adj* (*inf*: *usu attrib*) angry; annoyed: *She was a bit peeved when they didn't ask her to the party*; *She was peeved about it*; *She is rather peeved with you for not saying goodbye.*

peg [peg] *nc* **1** (*sometimes in cmpds*) a *usu* short, not very thick, piece of wood, metal *etc* used to fasten or mark something: *There were four pegs stuck in* *the ground to show where the house would be built; He fastened the ropes of the tent to the tent-pegs.* **2** a hook on a wall or door for hanging clothes *etc* on: *The children had to hang their clothes on the pegs in the cupboard.* **3** (*also* **'clothes-peg**) a wooden or plastic clip for holding clothes *etc* to a rope while drying. – *v* – *pt, ptp* **pegged** – *vt* **1** to fasten with a peg: *She pegged the clothes on the line.* **2** to fix (prices, incomes *etc*) at a certain level: *The government are trying to prevent inflation by pegging prices.*

be level pegging (*inf*) (of two or more people *etc*) to be doing equally well, have equal scores *etc*: *The two teams at the top of the football league are level pegging at the moment.*

ˌtake (someone) 'down a peg (or two) to make (a proud person) more humble: *She thought she was very clever, but she was taken down a peg when she failed the exam; We must find some way of taking her down a peg or two.*

pejorative [pəˈdʒorətiv] *adj* (*very formal*) showing dislike, disapproval *etc*: *a pejorative remark; Most languages have some pejorative words to describe foreigners, but one should never use them; I did not intend to be pejorative.* **pe'joratively** *adv.* **pe'jorativeness** *nu.*

pelican [ˈpelikən] *nc* a kind of large water-bird with a large beak with a pouch for carrying fish.

pellet [ˈpelit] *nc* a little ball or similarly-shaped object: *a bread pellet; The children threw paper pellets at the teacher; He bought a box of lead pellets for his gun.*

pell-mell [pelˈmel] *adv* quickly and in disorder or great confusion: *The children rushed pell-mell into the room.*

pelmet [ˈpelmit] *nc* a strip of cloth, wood *etc* hiding a curtain rail.

pelt[1] [pelt] **1** *vt* (*usu with* **with**) to throw (things) at: *The children pelted each other with snowballs.* **2** *vi* (*inf*) to run very fast: *He pelted down the road.* **3** *vi* (*often with* **it** *as subject: sometimes with* **down**) (of rain; sometimes also of hailstones) to fall very heavily: *You can't leave now – it's pelting down.*

at full pelt (running) as fast as possible: *They set off down the road at full pelt.*

pelt[2] [pelt] *nc* the (untreated) skin of an animal with fur or wool: *The trapper sold the beaver pelts to the fur-trader.*

pelvis [ˈpelvis] – *pls* **'pelvises**, (*med*) **'pelves** [-viːz] – *nc* the framework of bone around the body below the waist: *Women with narrow pelvises can have difficulty having babies.* **'pelvic** *adj.*

pen[1] [pen] *nc* (*often in cmpds*) a small enclosure, *usu* for animals: *The dog chased the sheep into the pen; a sheep-pen.* – *v* – *pt, ptp* **penned** – *vt* (*formal*) to put or keep in a pen: *The sheep have to be penned (in) every night.*

See also **playpen** *under* **play**.

pen[2] [pen] *nc* an instrument for writing in ink: *My pen needs a new nib; I must fill* (= put ink in) *my pen.* – *v* – *pt, ptp* **penned** – *vt* (*liter or formal*) to write (a letter *etc*): *She penned a quick note to her mother.*

'pen-friend, 'pen-pal *ncs* a *usu* young person (*usu* living abroad) with whom another (*usu* young) person regularly exchanges letters: *My daughter has pen-friends in India and Spain.*

'pen-knife *nc* a pocket-knife with blades which fold into the handle.

'pen-name *nc* a name used by a writer instead of his own name: *Samuel Clemens used the pen-name of Mark Twain.*

pen-nib *see* **nib**.

pen-pal *see* **pen-friend** *above*.

See also **ballpoint** *under* **ball**[1], **fountain pen** *under* **fountain**.

penal [ˈpiːnl] *adj* (*legal or formal: esp attrib*) of legal punishment: *penal laws; penal reform.*

penalize, -ise [ˈpiːnəlaiz] *vt* (*formal*) **1** to punish (someone) for doing something wrong (*eg* breaking a rule in a game, cheating in an examination), *eg* by the loss of points *etc* or by the giving of some advantage to an opponent: *The child was penalized for her untidy handwriting.* **2** to punish (some wrong action *etc*) in this way: *Any attempt at cheating will be heavily penalized.*

penalty [ˈpenlti] *nc* **1** a punishment for doing wrong, breaking a contract *etc*: *They did wrong and they will have to pay the penalty; The death penalty* (= punishment by execution) *has been abolished in this country;* (*attrib*) *There's a penalty clause in this contract which states that we will have to pay £500 if we don't finish the job on time.* **2** in sport *etc*, a disadvantage *etc* that must be suffered for breaking the rules *etc*: *The referee awarded the team a penalty* (= allowed them some advantage because of something wrong that the other team had done); (*attrib*) *a penalty kick* (= in football, a chance to kick the ball towards the goal from a spot in front of the goal without being tackled by members of the other team).

on/under penalty of (death *etc***)** (*legal or formal*) with (death *etc*) as the penalty or punishment.

penance [ˈpenəns] *ncu* (*relig or facet*) punishment that a person suffers willingly to show that he is sorry for something wrong he has done: *He did penance for his sins; I'll finish the work at home tonight as (a) penance for being late this morning.*

pence *see* **penny**.

pencil [ˈpensl] *nc* **1** a long, thin instrument (*usu* of wood) containing a thin stick of graphite or some similar solid substance for writing or drawing: *This pencil needs sharpening/to be sharpened;* (*attrib*) *a pencil drawing.* **2** anything with a similar shape and purpose: *The girl made her eyebrows darker with an eyebrow pencil.* – *v* – *pt, ptp* **'pencilled**, (*Amer*) **'penciled** – *vt* (*sometimes with* **in**) to write or draw with a pencil: *He pencilled an outline of the house; He pencilled in the answers in the spaces provided.*

pendant [ˈpendənt] *nc* **1** an ornament hung from a necklace: *a pendant hanging from a silver chain.* **2** the ornament and the necklace together: *She fastened a gold pendant round her neck.*

pending [ˈpendiŋ] *adj* (*pred: formal*) **1** waiting to be decided: *No agreement has been reached – the matter is still pending.* **2** waiting to be received or sent: *There's a reply pending.* – *prep* (*formal*) **1** waiting for; until: *He was held in prison pending trial.* **2** during: *No information can be given to the press pending the meeting of the directors.*

'pending tray, file *etc* *nc* a tray on a desk *etc* containing letters *etc* which are pending.

pendulous [ˈpendjuləs, (*Amer*) -dʒu-] *adj* (*formal*) hanging down: *pendulous branches; Her breasts are heavy and pendulous.* **'pendulousness** *nu.*

pendulum [ˈpendjuləm, (*Amer*) -dʒu-] *nc* a swinging weight, *eg* that which operates the mechanism of a clock: *The little girl was fascinated by the* *pendulum which swung back and forwards*; (*attrib*) *a pendulum clock.*

penetrate ['penitreit] **1** *vt* to move, go or make a way into, past, or through (something): *He penetrated the security guard surrounding the president*; *The bullet penetrated his left shoulder*; *His voice penetrated the silence*; (*fig*) *Their minds could not penetrate the mystery.* **2** *vti* (*inf*) to be understood or fully realized: *I smelt smoke but it didn't penetrate that the house was on fire*; *It took a long time to penetrate.*

'**penetrating** *adj* **1** (of a voice, sound *etc*) loud and clear; easily heard: *a penetrating voice*; *Her voice is so harsh and penetrating.* **2** (of a glance, stare *etc*) hard and searching, as if trying, or able, to see into a person's mind: *She gave him a penetrating glance*; *Her glance was brief but penetrating.* **3** (*usu attrib*) quick at understanding: *a penetrating mind.*

'**penetratingly** *adv.*

ˌ**pene'tration** *nu* **1** the act of getting or going into, past or through (something): *the penetration of the enemy's defences.* **2** (*formal*) quickness or cleverness in understanding: *This report shows that he is a man of great insight and penetration.*

See also **impenetrable**.

penguin ['peŋgwin] *nc* a large sea-bird which is found in Antarctic regions and which cannot fly.

penicillin [peni'silin] *nu* a kind of antibiotic medicine which kills many harmful bacteria: *The doctor gave her penicillin to cure her throat infection*; (*attrib*) *penicillin injections.*

peninsula [pə'ninsjulə] *nc* (*sometimes found with cap in place-names*) a piece of land that is almost surrounded by water: *Spain and Portugal together form the Iberian Peninsula.*

pe'ninsular *adj* of or like a peninsula.

penis ['pi:nis] *nc* the male sexual organ in humans and many animals.

penitent ['penitənt] *adj* (*formal, facet or relig*) sorry for the wrong things one has done: *a penitent sinner*; *He did break the window but he is penitent now.* – *nc* (*relig*) a penitent person, *esp* one who is doing penance.

ˌ**penitence** *nu.*

ˌ**peni'tentiary** [-'tenʃəri] *nc* (*Amer*) a prison.

See also **impenitent**.

pennant ['penənt], (*also* **pennon** ['penən]) *nc* a small flag, *usu* in the shape of a long narrow triangle: *The boy had fastened a brightly-coloured pennant to the front of his bike.*

penny ['peni] – *pls* **pence** [pens] (*defs 1, 3, 7*), [pins] (*in cmpds, esp def 3*), '**pennies** (*defs 2, 4–6*) – *nc* **1** (also (*formal*) **new penny**: *usu abbrev* **p** [pi:] when following a number in writing and also (*inf*) in speech: **pence** also sometimes used as *inf sing* form) the hundredth part of £1: *It costs seventy-five pence*; *It costs seven and a half pence*; *Oranges, 7p each*; *They only cost one pence each*; (*attrib*) *a two-pence piece.* **2** (*also* (*formal*) **new penny**) a coin of this value: *I need three pennies to get a cup of coffee from the coffee-machine.* **3** (*hist*: *usu abbrev* **d** in *sing* and *pl* when written with numbers) the two-hundred-and-fortieth part of £1: *One shilling equals twelve pence*; *I can remember when a bar of chocolate cost sixpence*; *Chocolate bars, 6d each.* **4** (*hist*) a coin of this value. **5** in the US and Canada, (a coin worth) one cent. **6** in certain countries, a coin of low value. **7** the value of such a coin.

'**penniless** *adj* very poor; with little or no money: *He died and left his widow penniless*; *a penniless old man*; (*facet*) *The banks are all shut so I'm penniless till the morning.*

penny whistle *nc* a type of cheap whistle for playing tunes on: *I'm not very musical, but I can play a few tunes on the penny whistle.*

'**pennyworth** *nc* (*old*) the amount of anything that can be bought for one penny (*esp def 1*).

not cost a penny (*inf*) not to cost anything at all: *I'll do the job for you and it won't cost you a penny.*

the penny drops (*inf*) I *etc* understand: *He didn't understand at first, but eventually the penny dropped.*

a pretty penny (*inf*) a large amount of money: *That car must have cost you a pretty penny.*

spend a penny (*inf euph*) to urinate: *Do you need to spend a penny before we get on the train?*

two a penny (*derog*) very common; of little value: *Books like that are two a penny.*

See also **halfpenny, threepence, twopence** *etc.*

pension ['penʃən] *nc* a sum of money paid regularly to a widow, a person who has retired from work, a soldier who has been seriously injured in a war *etc*: *The retirement pension is usually known as the old age pension*; *Pensions are usually drawn* (= obtained) *at a post office*; (*attrib*) *He pays money into a pension fund each month so that he will have a pension when he retires.*

'**pensionable** *adj* giving the right to have a pension: *a pensionable post*; *pensionable age*; *Is the post pensionable?*

'**pensioner** *nc* a person who receives a pension, *esp* (**old age pensioner**) one who receives a retirement pension: *Old age pensioners are often allowed to travel free on buses.*

pension off *vt sep* (*sometimes derog*) to allow to retire, or to dismiss, with a pension: *They pensioned him off when they found a younger man for the job.*

pensive ['pensiv] *adj* (*formal or liter*) thinking deeply (about something): *He was in a very pensive mood.* '**pensively** *adv.* '**pensiveness** *nu.*

pentagon ['pentəgən, (*Amer*) -gon] *nc* (*geom*) a two-dimensional figure with 5 sides. **pen'tagonal** [-'ta-] *adj.*

pentameter [pen'tamitə] *nc* in poetry, a line with five stressed syllables.

pentathlon [pen'taθlən] *nc* a competition in the Olympic games *etc* which consists of contests in swimming, cross-country riding and running, fencing and pistol-shooting.

penthouse ['penthaus] *nc* a (*usu* luxurious) flat at the top of a building: *That apartment building has a beautiful penthouse*; (*attrib*) *a penthouse flat.*

pent-up [pent'ʌp] *adj* (*usu attrib*) (of emotions *etc*) (becoming) very strong but not (allowed to be) freely or openly expressed: *The boy admitted breaking the windows, but explained that it was his only way of releasing his pent-up anger.*

penultimate [pi'nʌltimət] *adj* (*formal*) the last but one: *the penultimate line of the poem.*

penury ['penjuri] *nu* (*formal*) poverty: *The old man had hardly any money but he was too proud to admit his penury.*

people ['pi:pl] **1** *n pl* persons: *There are a lot of people here*; *There were three people in the room.* **2** *n pl* men and women in general: *People often say such things*; *People will do anything to save their own lives.* **3** *nc* (*liter*) a nation or race: *all the peoples of this world.* **4** *n pl* (*inf*) relatives: *His people come from Scotland.* – *vt* (*liter*) **1** to fill with people, animals *etc*: *God peopled the world.* **2** (of people) to fill (a country *etc*); to inhabit: *The tribes of Israel peopled the deserts.*

the people the ordinary people of a country as opposed to the aristocracy *etc*: *'Power to the People!' is a common revolutionary slogan.*

See also **populace, popular**.

pep [pep] *nu* (*inf*) energy: *full of pep.*

ˌ**pep-pill** *nc* (*not a tech term*) a pill that stimulates the nervous system and makes a person able to work harder, longer *etc*: *Athletes are not allowed to take pep-pills during competitions.*

ˈ**pep-talk** *nc* (*inf*) a talk intended to arouse enthusiasm, or to make people work harder, better *etc*: *Morale was rather low in the factory, so the managing director gave all the staff a pep-talk.*

pepper [ˈpepə] **1** *nu* the dried, powdered berries of a certain plant, used for seasoning food: *white/black pepper*; *This soup has too much pepper in it.* **2** *nc* (*usu attrib*) the plant bearing these berries: *a pepper plant.* **3** *nc* any of several red, yellow, or green, hollow seed-containing fruits used as food: *The main course of the meal consisted of red peppers stuffed with rice.* – *See also* **capsicum**. **4** *nc* any of the plants which bear these. – *vt* **1** to put pepper in or on (some food): *You don't have to pepper the soup.* **2** (*with* **with**) to throw, fire *etc* many, *usu* small, objects at (someone): *He peppered them with bullets.*

ˈ**peppery** *adj* **1** (of food) containing a lot of pepper: *I can't eat this – it's too peppery*; *peppery food.* **2** (*fig*) easily made angry: *The old colonel is a bit peppery now*; *a peppery old man.*

ˈ**peppercorn** *nc* the berry of the pepper plant.

ˈ**pepper-mill** *nc* a small container in which pepper-corns are ground into a powder.

ˈ**peppermint** **1** *nu* a flavouring taken from a type of plant and used in sweets *etc.* **2** *nc* (*sometimes abbrev* **mint**) a sweet flavoured with peppermint: *The little boy had a bag of peppermints.*

per [pəː] *prep* **1** out of: *We have less than one faulty car per thousand completed.* **2** for each: *The dinner will cost £5 per person*; *Beef costs 70p per pound.* **3** in each: *six times per week*; *an average of two children per family.*

per annum [pərˈanəm] (*sometimes abbrev* **p.a.** *when written*) each year: *He earns £10 000 per annum.*

per capita [pəˈkapitə] (*formal*) for each person: *What is the average income per capita in this country?*; (*attrib*) *the per capita income.*

per cent [pəˈsent] (*often written % with figures*) (of numbers, amounts *etc*) stated as a fraction of one hundred: *Twenty-five per cent of one hundred and twenty is thirty*; *25% of the people did not reply to our letters*; *I agree with you one hundred per cent* (= completely). – *See also* **percentage**.

per se [pəːˈsei] (*formal*) in itself: *This reply does not per se mean that he will not help us*; *The fact that he has no alibi does not mean that he is guilty per se.*

perambulator [pəˈrambjuleitə] *nc* (*old or very formal*) a pram.

perceive [pəˈsiːv] *vt* (*formal*: not used with **is, was** *etc* and **-ing**) to be or become aware of (something); to understand; to realize: *She perceived that he was tired*; *He perceived a change in the mood of the crowd*; *He soon perceived that his job would be difficult.*

See also **perception**.

percentage [pəˈsentidʒ] *nc* **1** an amount, number or rate given as a fraction of one hundred: *We've expressed all these figures as percentages.* **2** a part or proportion of something: *a large percentage of the population can't read or write.*

See also **per cent** *under* **per**.

perception [pəˈsepʃən] *nu* (*formal*) **1** the ability to see, understand *etc* clearly: *a man of great perception.* **2** the act of becoming aware: *his gradual perception of the immenseness of the problem.*

perˈceptible *adj* (*formal*) able to be perceived; noticeable: *a perceptible delay*; *The change in her is scarcely perceptible.* **perˈceptibly** *adv.* **perˌceptiˈbility** *nu.*

perˈceptive [-tiv] *adj* (*formal*: *often with* **of** *when pred*) able to see, understand *etc* clearly: *a very perceptive man*; *That was very perceptive of you.* **perˈceptively** *adv.* **perˈceptiveness** *nu.*

See also **imperceptible, perceive**.

perch[1] [pəːtʃ] *nc* **1** a branch *etc* on which a bird sits or stands: *The pigeon would not fly down from its perch*; *There were only two perches in the budgerigar's cage.* **2** any high seat or position: *He looked down from his perch on the roof.* – **1** *vi* (of birds) to go to (a perch); to sit or stand on (a perch): *The bird flew up and perched on the highest branch of the tree*; *These birds perch in trees or on buildings.* **2** *vti* to put, or be, in a high seat or position: *He perched the child on his shoulder*; *The castle was perched on a rock*; *They perched on the fence.*

perch[2] [pəːtʃ] – *pls* **perch**, (*rarely*) ˈ**perches** – *nc* a type of small fresh-water fish. *He caught three perch*; *They cooked the perch over a camp-fire.*

perchance [pəˈtʃaːns] *adv* (*arch*) **1** by chance: *Have you, perchance, seen this person?* **2** perhaps: *Perchance he may come this way.*

percolate [ˈpəːkəleit] **1** *vti* (*formal*) (of a liquid) to pass through some substance or small holes in something: *Rain-water percolates through the soil*; *The best way to make coffee is to percolate boiling water through ground coffee beans.* **2** *vti* (*also inf* **perk** [pəːk]) (of coffee) to make or be made by passing boiling water through ground coffee beans: *I'll go and percolate some coffee*; *Is the coffee percolating yet?* **3** *vi* (*fig*) (of news *etc*) to pass slowly through a group of people: *Gradually the news of her engagement percolated through the whole class*; *The news will percolate through to him eventually.*

ˈ**percolator** *nc* an apparatus for percolating, *esp* a type of pot in which coffee is made by passing boiling water through ground coffee beans in a small container at the top of the pot: *a coffee-percolator.*

percussion [pəˈkʌʃən] *nu* **1** (in an orchestra, the group of people who play) musical instruments in which the sound is produced by striking them *eg* drums, cymbals *etc*: *He plays* (*the*) *percussion in the orchestra*; (*attrib*) *He's in the percussion section*; (*attrib*) *a percussion instrument*; *He's in the percussion.* **2** (*tech*) the striking of one hard object against another: *A cartridge is fired from a gun by means of percussion.*

perˈcussionist *nc* a person who plays percussion instruments in an orchestra *etc.*

perdition [pəˈdiʃən] *nu* (*liter*) **1** everlasting damnation; hell: *He is doomed to perdition for his foul deeds.* **2** complete loss or ruin: *By his foolish arrogance, the general led his army to perdition.*

peremptory [pəˈremptəri] *adj* (*formal derog*) showing that one arrogantly expects to be obeyed at once and without question: *People resented the*

manager's peremptory manner; He is so peremptory that people resent doing what he asks; The duke was in the habit of issuing peremptory commands.
pe'remptorily *adv.* **pe'remptoriness** *nu.*

perennial [pə'reniəl] **1** *nc, adj* (a plant) which lasts for more than two years: *Daffodils are perennial plants; They are perennials.* **2** *adj* (*liter or facet: usu attrib*) continual: *He was tired of her perennial complaints.* **pe'rennially** *adv.*

perfect ['pə:fikt] *adj* **1** without fault or flaw; excellent: *The plane made a perfect landing; It was a perfect day for a picnic; a perfect rose; Your choice of candidate is perfect.* **2** (*usu attrib*) exact: *He drew a perfect circle; a perfect copy.* **3** (*inf: attrib*) (*usu* of something bad) very great; complete: *I looked a perfect fool; He was a perfect stranger; That's perfect nonsense!* **4** (*gram*) (of the tense of a verb) indicating action in the past: *In 'He has done it', the verb is in the perfect tense.* – *ncu* (*gram*) (a verb in) the perfect tense: *These verbs should be in the perfect.* – [pə'fekt] *vt* (*formal*) to make perfect: *He went to France to perfect his French.*

per'fection [-ʃən] *nu* **1** the state of being perfect: *Absolute perfection in a dictionary is rare.* **2** (*formal*) the act of finishing something: *He is working on the perfection of his painting.* – *See also* **to perfection** *below.*

per'fectionist [-ʃə-] *nc* a person who is only satisfied if what he is doing is perfect: *He is a very slow worker because he is such a perfectionist; She's a perfectionist – she will only sell clothes that are perfect in every detail.*

'perfectly *adv* **1** without mistakes or flaws: *She performed the dance perfectly.* **2** very; completely: *He was perfectly happy where he was.*

to per'fection (*formal*) so that (something) is perfect; perfectly (*def 1*): *The chef cooks veal to perfection.*

See also **imperfect**.

perfidious [pə:'fidiəs] *adj* (*liter*) not to be trusted; treacherous: *her perfidious lover; His behaviour was most perfidious.* **per'fidiousness** *nu.*

perfidy ['pə:fidi] *ncu* (*liter*) a treacherous act or acts.

perforate ['pə:fəreit] **1** *vt* to make a hole or holes in, *esp* a line of small holes in paper, so that it may be torn easily: *Sheets of postage stamps are perforated.* **2** *vi* (*tech*) (of an ulcer *etc*) to develop a hole; to burst: *Her appendix perforated before she reached the hospital.*

'perforated *adj*: *perforated paper;* (*tech*) *a perforated ulcer.*

ˌperfo'ration **1** *ncu* (*often in pl*) a small hole, or a number or line of small holes, made in a sheet of paper *etc*: *The purpose of the perforation(s) in a sheet of stamps is to make it easier to tear off the stamps.* **2** *nu* the act of perforating or being perforated: *the perforation of her appendix.*

perforce [pə'fo:s] *adv* (*old or liter*) necessarily: *As we have no horse and carriage, you must perforce return on foot.*

perform [pə'fo:m] **1** *vt* (*more formal than* **do** *or* **carry out**) to do, *esp* with care or as a duty: *The doctor performed the operation; We all have our tasks to perform.* **2** *vti* to act (in the theatre *etc*) or do anything musical, theatrical *etc* to entertain an audience: *She used to perform in Shakespeare; The company will perform a Greek play; She performed on the violin; The animals performed several tricks.*

per'formance **1** *nu* (*formal*) the doing of something: *He is very conscientious in the performance of his duties.* **2** *ncu* the way in which something or someone performs: *The car's performance was not very good; His performance in the exams was not very good.* **3** *nc* something done on stage *etc*: *The company gave a performance of 'Othello'; His last three performances have not been very good.*

per'former *nc* a person who performs, *esp* theatrically or musically.

perfume ['pə:fju:m] *ncu* **1** (*more formal or liter than* **scent**) a sweet smell or fragrance: *the perfume of roses.* **2** a liquid, cream *etc* which has a sweet smell when put on the skin, hair, clothes *etc*: *She loves French perfume(s).* – [pə'fju:m] *vt* **1** (*formal or liter*) to put perfume on or in: *She perfumed her hair.* **2** to give a sweet smell to: *Flowers perfumed the air.*

per'fumery [-'fju:-] *nc* a shop where perfume is sold or a factory where it is made.

perfunctory [pə'fʌŋktəri] *adj* (*formal*) done carelessly, without real interest, only as a duty: *He made a perfunctory inspection of the factory; His reading of my essay was rather perfunctory.*
per'functorily *adv.* **per'functoriness** *nu.*

perhaps [pə'haps] *adv* possibly: *Perhaps it will rain; Perhaps that is the best he can do; He is, perhaps, the best actor in Britain.*

peril ['peril] *ncu* (*formal*) great danger: *He is in peril of his life; You are in great peril; The explorers knew they would face many perils.*

'perilous *adj* (*formal*) very dangerous: *a perilous journey; The journey through the jungle was perilous.* **'perilousness** *nu.*

'perilously *adv* (*formal or facet*) dangerously: *He came perilously close to death; He came perilously close to getting a punch on the nose.*

at one's 'peril (*often facet*) at one's own risk: *If the boss tells you not to do that, then you do it at your peril.*

See also **imperil**.

perimeter [pə'rimitə] *nc* **1** (*formal*) the outside edge of any area: *the perimeter of the city.* **2** (*geom*) the outside line enclosing a figure or shape: *the perimeter of a circle.*

period ['piəriəd] *nc* **1** any length of time: *a period of three days; a period of time; a period of illness; a period of waiting.* **2** the time during which a lesson takes place in a school: *We have two periods of French today; In this school, a period is forty minutes long.* **3** a stage in the Earth's development, an artist's development, in history *etc*: *the Pleistocene period; the Jacobean period;* (*facet*) *I painted this room during my brown period.* **4** the punctuation mark (.), put at the end of a sentence; a full stop. **5** a time of menstruation: *She always feels unwell at the start of her period.* – *adj* (*attrib*) (of furniture, costumes *etc*) of or from the same or appropriate time in history; (*loosely*) antique or very old: *The play was set in the seventeenth century and the actors were wearing period costumes* (= costumes of the seventeenth century); *The house is Georgian* (= built during the period from 1714 to 1830, during the reigns of the first four British kings named George) *and full of period furniture* (= furniture of the Georgian period); *His house is full of period furniture* (= antique furniture).

ˌperi'odic [-'o-] *adj* **1** (*usu attrib*) happening, done *etc* occasionally: *He suffers from periodic fits of depression.* **2** (*also* **ˌperi'odical**: *usu attrib*) happening, done *etc* at regular intervals: *I expect regular periodical reports from you.*

ˌperi'odically *adv.* *We see each other periodically.*
ˌperi'odical [-'o-] *nc* a magazine which is issued regularly (every week, month *etc*). – *adj see* **periodic** (*def 2*).

peripatetic [peripə'tetik] *adj* (*formal*: *esp attrib*) moving from place to place: *a peripatetic salesman/music teacher.*

periphery [pə'rifəri] *nc* (*formal*: *usu in sing with* **the**) the edge (of something): *The shops are on the periphery of the housing estate*; (*fig*) *That's on the periphery of his field of interest.*
pe'ripheral *adj* (*formal*) **1** of little importance: *a matter of peripheral interest.* **2** of, or on, a periphery.

periscope ['periskoup] *nc* a tube containing mirrors, through which a person can look in order to see things which cannot be seen from the position the person is in, *esp* one used in submarines when under water to allow a person to see what is happening on the surface of the sea.

perish ['periʃ] *vi* **1** (*liter*) to die, *esp* in war, accident *etc*: *Many people perished in the earthquake.* **2** (*esp* of rubber) to rot or become hard and brittle: *These elastic bands have perished.*
'perishable *adj* (*esp* of food) likely to go bad quickly: *Butter is perishable*; *perishable goods.*
'perishing *adj, adv* (*Brit inf*) **1** very (cold): *It's perishing (cold) outside.* **2** *adj* (*attrib*: *euph*) used to show anger *etc*: *Get that perishing car out of my way!*
See also **imperishable**.

periwinkle *see* **winkle**.

perjure ['pə:dʒə] *v refl* (*formal or legal*) to tell a lie when one has sworn to tell the truth, *esp* in a court of law: *She perjured herself by saying that the accused man had been with her at the time of the crime.*
'perjury *ncu* (*formal or legal*) the telling of lies after swearing to tell the truth, *esp* in a court of law: *It is a criminal offence to commit perjury.*

perk[1] [pə:k]: **perk up** *vi, vt sep* (*inf*) to recover one's energy or cheerfulness: *I gave her a cup of tea and she soon perked up*; *A cup of tea will soon perk you up.*
perky *adj* (*inf*) lively; cheerful: *I think he has recovered from his cold – he seems quite perky*; *You're in a perky mood.* **'perkily** *adv.* **'perkiness** *nu.*

perk[2] [pə:k] *nc* (*inf*: *usu in pl*) a perquisite: *One of the perks in this job is that the company gives you a car*; *Free coal is one of a miner's perks.*

perk[3] *see* **percolate**.

perm [pə:m] *nc* a permanent wave in a person's hair: *She's had a perm.* – *vt* to give a permanent wave to (hair): *She's had her hair permed.*

permanent ['pə:mənənt] *adj* lasting; not temporary: *After many years of travelling, they made a permanent home in England*; *The paint left a permanent mark on the carpet*; *Is this ink permanent?* (=Will it wash off?). **'permanently** *adv.* **'permanence**, (*formal*) **'permanency** *nus.*
permanent wave *nc* (*usu abbrev* **perm** [pə:m]) a wave or curl put into a person's hair by a special process and *usu* lasting for several months.

permeate ['pə:mieit] *vti* (*formal*) (of a liquid, gas *etc*) to pass or spread into or through (something): *The water had permeated (through/into) the soil*; *The smell of burnt toast permeated the house*; (*fig*) *The new ideas gradually permeated the minds of the people.*
See also **impermeable**.

permit [pə'mit] – *pt, ptp* **per'mitted** – *vt* (*formal*) **1** to agree to (another person's action); to allow or let (someone do something): *Permit me to answer your question*; *Smoking is not permitted.* **2** to make possible: *My aunt's legacy permitted me to go to America.* – ['pə:mit] *nc* a written order allowing a person to do something: *We have a permit to export our product.*
permissible [pə'misəbl] *adj* (*formal*) able to be permitted; allowable: *The prison governor said that what the prisoner had requested was unfortunately not permissible*; *scarcely permissible behaviour.*
permission [pə'miʃən] *nu* a written, spoken *etc* agreement that someone may do something: *She gave me permission to leave*; *I have permission to go*; *He asked her permission to do it.*
permissive [pə'misiv] *adj* (*often derog*) allowing a lot, *usu* too much freedom, *esp* in sexual or moral matters: *permissive parents*; *the permissive society*; *Her parents are far too permissive – they allow her to be away from home all night.* **per'missively** *adv.* **per'missiveness** *nu.*
per'mit of *vt fus* (*very formal*) (of plans, events *etc*) to allow (something): *The scheme does not permit of any changes at this stage.*

permutation [pə:mju'teiʃən] *nc* (*formal*) a particular order in which things are arranged: *We can write down these numbers in various permutations.*

pernicious [pə'niʃəs] *adj* (*formal*: *often with* **to** *when pred*) very harmful: *a pernicious influence*; *Pornography is pernicious to society.* **per'niciously** *adv.* **per'niciousness** *nu.*
pernicious anaemia *nu* a form of anaemia which was formerly fatal.

pernickety [pə'nikəti] *adj* (*inf*) very concerned with small, often unimportant details: *She's very pernickety about her appearance*; *a pernickety old lady.* **per'nicketiness** *nu.*

peroxide [pə'roksaid] *nu* a chemical, hydrogen peroxide (H_2O_2), sometimes used for bleaching hair *etc*: (*attrib*) *She's a peroxide blonde.*

perpendicular [pə:pən'dikjulə] *adj* (*with* **to** *when pred*) **1** standing, rising *etc* straight upwards; vertical: *a perpendicular cliff*; *That wall is not quite perpendicular.* **2** (*math*) at right angles to: *Draw a line perpendicular to the base of the triangle*; *Draw a perpendicular line.* **ˌperpen'dicularly** *adv.*

perpetrate ['pə:pitreit] *vt* (*very formal*) to do (something wrong or bad, *eg* a crime): *If the murderer is allowed to go free, he may perpetrate more crimes.* **ˌperpe'tration** *nu.* **'perpetrator** *nc.*

perpetual [pə'petʃuəl] *adj* (*usu attrib*: *more formal than* **continuous**) lasting for ever or for a long time; occurring repeatedly over a long time: *He lives in perpetual fear of being discovered*; *I cannot stand the perpetual noise in this office.* **per'petually** *adv.*
per'petuate [-eit] *vt* (*formal*) to make (something) continue, or continue to be known, for ever or for a long time: *The monument will perpetuate his name*; *Your silence is perpetuating the quarrel.* **perˌpetu'ation** *nu.*
perpetuity [pə:pə'tʃu:əti]: **in ˌperpe'tuity** (*formal or legal*) for ever: *This land will belong to your family in perpetuity.*

perplex [pə'pleks] *vt* to puzzle or confuse (someone); to make (someone) unable to understand: *She was perplexed by his questions.* **per'plexed** *adj.* **per'plexedly** [-'pleksid-] *adv.*

per'plexity *nu* (*formal*): *She stood there in complete perplexity.*

perquisite ['pə:kwizit] *nc* (*formal*) something given by employers or got by a worker in some other way related to his job, in addition to his wages or salary.
See also **perk**[2].

persecute ['pə:sikju:t] *vt* (*usu with* **for**) to make (someone) suffer, *esp* because of their opinions or beliefs: *They were persecuted for their religion.* **ˌperse'cution** *ncu.* **'persecutor** *nc.*

persevere [pə:si'viə] *vi* to continue to (try to) do something in spite of difficulties: *The job was almost impossible, but he persevered (with it)*; *He persevered in his task*; *I don't think he'll ever be able to speak French, but I'll persevere with him.* **ˌperse'verance** *nu.*

Persian *see* Appendix 2.

persist [pə'sist] *vi* **1** (*often with* **in**) to keep doing, thinking *etc* in spite of opposition or difficulty; to continue asking, persuading *etc*: *It will not be easy to borrow the money but you will succeed if you persist*; *He persisted in believing that the world is flat*; *He persisted in that belief till the day he died*; *He didn't want to tell her, but she persisted (in asking).* **2** to continue to exist: *The idea still persists that the Scots are mean with money.*
per'sistent *adj*: *She was persistent in her demands/denials*; *a persistent young woman*; *a persistent refusal*; *persistent questions.* **per'sistently** *adv.* **per'sistence** *nu.*

person ['pə:sn] – *pl* **people** ['pi:pl], (*formal*) **'persons** – **1** *nc* (*sometimes formal or derog*) a human being: *There's a person outside who wants to speak to you, sir*; (*derog*) *Please remove this person from my office*; (*formal*) *Any person found damaging this train will be liable to a fine of up to £50.* **2** *nc* (*formal*) a person's body: *He never carried money on his person* (= with him; in his pockets *etc*). **3** *nc* (*fig formal*) the form or shape (of something or someone): *Trouble arrived in the person of John.* **4** *ncu* (*gram*) one of *usu* three grammatical categories of pronouns or verbs referring either to (a group including) the speaker (**first person**) or to (a group including) the person spoken to (**second person**) or to some other person or group (**third person**): *This verb is in the third person*; (*attrib*) *'I' and 'we' are first person pronouns.*
'personable *adj* (*formal*: *usu attrib*) good-looking: *a personable young man.*
'personage [-nidʒ] *nc* (*old or facet*) a well-known or important person: *Several famous personages were at the dinner last night.*
'personal *adj* **1** (*usu attrib*) one's own: *This is his personal opinion, not that of his family*; *The matter will have my personal attention*; *This is my personal property*; *I bought the dress in a shop and then added these flowers to give it a personal touch.* **2** private: *for personal reasons*; *This is a personal matter between him and me*; *My reasons are purely personal.* **3** (*attrib*) for a particular person: *I did him a personal favour.* **4** (*attrib*) in person: *The Prime Minister will make a personal appearance.* **5** (making remarks which are) insulting, *esp* about a person's appearance *etc*: *personal remarks*; *personal criticism*; *Don't be personal!*; *My remarks were not intended to be personal.* **6** (*attrib*) of the body: *personal hygiene*; *personal freshness.* – *See also* **in person** *below.*
ˌperso'nality 1 *nc* a person's characteristics (of the mind, the emotions *etc*) as a whole: *She has a most likeable personality*; *He has such a forceful* (= strong) *personality that everyone obeys him.* **2** *nu* strong, distinctive (*usu* attractive) character: *We are looking for someone with personality for the job of publicity officer*; *She is not beautiful but she has so much personality that people find her attractive.* **3** *nc* a well-known person: *a television personality*; (*attrib*) *a personality cult* (= very great, *usu* too great, admiration for a person, *usu* a political leader).
'personalize, -ise (*formal*) *vt* to do, add *etc* (something) to something to make it different from other people's, or to show that it belongs to a certain person: *Notepaper can be personalized by having one's name put on it.*
'personalized, -s- *adj*: *personalized notepaper.*
'personally *adv* **1** in one's own opinion: *Personally, I prefer the other.* **2** doing something oneself, not having or letting someone else do it on one's behalf: *He thanked me personally.*
perˌsonifi'cation [-sonifi-] *ncu* the act of personifying a quality *etc*: *She is the personification of patience/evil.*
personify [pə'sonifai] *vt* (*formal*) **1** (not *usu* used with **is, was** *etc* and **-ing**) to speak of (an idea, quality *etc*) as if it were a person: *Innocence is often personified as a child.* **2** (not used with **is, was** *etc* and **-ing**) to be a perfect example of: *My mother personifies patience.*
personal column *nc* (in a newspaper *etc*) one of the columns in which inquiries, advertisements *etc* by individual members of the public are printed.
personal pronoun *nc* (*gram*) a pronoun which refers to the first, second or third persons: *I am going*; *He hit her. She saw you.*
in person personally; one's self, not represented by someone else: *The Queen was there in person*; *I'd like to thank him in person.*
on one's person *see* **person** (*def 2*).
See also **impersonal, impersonate**.

persona non grata [pə'sounənon'gra:tə] *adj* (*formal*: *pred*) not liked by or acceptable to someone else, *esp* a state or government; not to be allowed to enter or stay in a particular country: *He has been declared persona non grata by the British government*; (*facet*) *I spilt coffee all over that manuscript, so I'm persona non grata with the boss at the moment.*

personnel [pə:sə'nel] *nu* (*formal*: *usu with pl verb*) the people employed in a firm, factory, shop *etc*; the staff: *Our personnel are very highly trained*; (*attrib*) *a personnel manager.*

perspective [pə'spektiv] **1** *nu* (*tech*) the way of drawing solid objects, natural scenes *etc* on a flat surface, so that they appear to have the correct shape, distance from each other *etc*: *Early medieval paintings lacked perspective*; (*attrib*) *I need a perspective drawing, not just a plan.* **2** *nc* (*formal*) a picture or view of something: *This report gives a rather distorted perspective of our company's affairs.*
in/out of perspective 1 (of an object in a painting, photograph *etc*) having, or not having, the correct size, shape, distance *etc* in relation to the rest of the picture: *These houses don't seem to be in perspective in your drawing*; *The drawing of the house is good, but the car is out of perspective.* **2** (*sometimes with* **into** *instead of* **in**) with, or without, a correct or sensible understanding of something's true importance: *Don't worry so much*

– *try to get these problems in(to) perspective*; *Don't let things get out of perspective*; *Keep things in perspective.*

Perspex ® ['pə:speks] *nu, adj* (*also no cap*) (of) a kind of transparent plastic which looks like glass: *The windscreen is (made of) Perspex*; *a Perspex windscreen.*

perspicacious [pə:spi'keiʃəs] *adj* (*formal or ironic*) having a clear or quick understanding: *How perspicacious of you to notice these mistakes!*; *a perspicacious lawyer.* ˌ**perspi'cacity** [-'kasəti] *nu.*

perspire [pə'spaiə] *vi* (*formal*) to lose moisture through the skin when hot; to sweat: *He was perspiring in the heat.*

ˌ**perspi'ration** [pə:spi-] *nu* (*more formal than* **sweat**) the moisture lost when perspiring: *The perspiration was running down his face.*

persuade [pə'sweid] *vt* **1** to make (someone) (not) do something, by arguing with him or advising him: *We persuaded him (not) to go*; *We persuaded him that he should go.* **2** (*formal*: *sometimes with* **of**) to make (someone) certain (that something is the case); to convince: *We eventually persuaded him that we were perfectly serious*; *We persuaded him of our serious intentions.*

per'suasion [-ʒən] **1** *nu* the act of persuading: *He gave in to our persuasion and did what we wanted him to do.* **2** *nc* (*rare and formal*) (a group of people who have) belief, *esp* religious: *He is of the Methodist persuasion.*

per'suasive [-siv] *adj* able to persuade: *He is a persuasive speaker*; *His arguments are quite persuasive.* **per'suasively** *adv.* **per'suasiveness** *nu.*

See also **dissuade**.

pert [pə:t] *adj* (*old*) (of a person or what he says) not showing enough respect; cheeky: *a pert girl/answer*; *She is rather pert.* '**pertly** *adv.* '**pertness** *nu.*

pertain [pə'tein] *vi* (*formal or legal*: *with* **to**) to belong: *These are documents that pertain to my business*; *The lawyer read all the documents pertaining to the case.*

pertinent ['pə:tinənt] *adj* (*formal*: *usu pred with* **to**) connected (to a particular matter); relevant: *That is not pertinent to the matter we are discussing.* '**pertinence** *nu.*

pertinacity [pə:ti'nasəti] *nu* (*very formal*) the state of being obstinate, determined, unwilling to change one's opinion *etc*: *He showed great pertinacity in looking for a job.* ˌ**perti'nacious** [-'neiʃəs] *adj.*

pertinent *see* **pertain**.

perturb [pə'tə:b] *vt* (*formal*) to make (someone) worried or anxious: *His threats didn't perturb her in the least.*

See also **imperturbable**.

Peru *see* Appendix 2.

peruse [pə'ru:z] *vt* (*formal or facet*) to read or look at carefully: *She perused the letter.* **pe'rusal** *ncu.*

Peruvian *see* Appendix 2.

pervade [pə'veid] *vt* (*formal or liter*) (of feelings, smells *etc*) to spread through the whole of (something): *Fear pervaded the city*; *A strange smell pervaded the room.*

per'vasive [-siv] *adj* (*formal*: *usu attrib*): *Terror is a pervasive emotion*; *Some people claim that society is becoming more violent due to the pervasive influence of television.* **per'vasively** *adv.* **per'vasiveness** *nu.*

perverse [pə'və:s] *adj* (*formal*) **1** continuing to do, think *etc* something which one knows, or which one has been told, is wrong or unreasonable: *a perverse child*; *It was perverse of her to do that – she knew it would upset her mother.* **2** deliberately wrong; unreasonable: *perverse behaviour*; *Her conduct was unnecessarily perverse.* **per'versely** *adv.* **per'verseness, per'versity** *nus.*

pervert [pə'və:t] *vt* (*formal*) **1** to change (something) from what is normal or right: *He was charged with attempting to pervert the course of justice.* **2** to lead (someone) to crime or to evil or immoral (*esp* sexually immoral) acts: *The man was accused of trying to pervert children.* – ['pə:və:t] *nc* a person who does perverted (*esp* sexually immoral) acts: *He is a (sexual) pervert and has been convicted of assaulting children.*

per'version [-ʃən] (*formal*) **1** *ncu* (the) act of perverting: *a perversion of justice.* **2** *nc* a perverted act, *esp* one which is sexually immoral: *He is capable of any perversion.*

per'verted *adj* **1** (of behaviour) unnatural, *esp* sexually immoral. **2** (of a person) showing perverted behaviour.

peseta [pə'seitə] *nc* the standard unit of currency in Spain.

peso ['peisou] – *pl* '**pesos** – *nc* the standard unit of currency in many South and Central American countries and in the Philippines.

pessimism ['pesimizəm] *nu* the state of mind of a person who always expects bad things to happen: *The trouble with his pessimism is that it depresses everyone else as well.*

'**pessimist** *nc* a person who thinks in this way: *He is such a pessimist that he always expects the plane he is travelling in to crash.*

ˌ**pessi'mistic** *adj*: *I am pessimistic about my chances of getting the job.* ˌ**pessi'mistically** *adv.*

See also **optimism**.

pest [pest] *nc* **1** a creature that is harmful or destructive, *eg* a mosquito, a rat *etc*: *Greenfly and slugs are two common garden pests.* **2** (*inf*) a troublesome person or thing: *He is always annoying me – he is an absolute pest!*

'**pesticide** [-tisaid] *ncu* (*formal or tech*) a substance that kills animal and insect pests.

pester ['pestə] *vt* (*derog*) to annoy (someone) frequently or continually: *He pestered me with questions*; *She pestered him for money*; *She pestered him to help her.*

pesticide *see* **pest**.

pestilence ['pestiləns] *ncu* (*old or facet*) any type of deadly epidemic disease, *esp* bubonic plague.

ˌ**pesti'lential** [-'lenʃəl] *adj* (*old or facet*: *usu fig*) causing serious disease or (*loosely*) trouble: *That child is pestilential!*

pestle ['pesl] *nc* a tool like a small club, used for pounding things to powder, *esp* in a mortar: *Chemists use a mortar and pestle for mixing drugs*; *He ground the nutmeg to a powder with a mortar and pestle.*

pet[1] [pet] *nc* **1** a tame animal *etc*, *usu* kept in the home: *She keeps a rabbit as a pet*; (*attrib*) *a* ˌ*pet* '*rabbit*/'*goldfish*; (*attrib*) '*pet food*; (*attrib*) *a* '*pet shop.* **2** (*derog*) a favourite person: *a teacher's pet.* **3** (*esp* of children) a delightful or lovely person (used also as a term of affection): *Isn't that baby a pet?*; *Would you like some ice-cream, pet?* – *adj* (*attrib*) favourite; greatest: *What is your pet ambition/hate?* – *v* – *pt, ptp* '**petted** – **1** *vt* to stroke or caress (an animal) in a loving, often too loving, way: *The old lady sat by the fire petting her dog.* **2** *vi* (*inf*) to stroke or caress in a sexual way: *There* *were several couples sitting petting at the back of the cinema.*

'**pet name** *nc* a particular name used to express affection: *His pet name for her was 'Kitten'.*

pet[2] [pet] *nc* (*old or rare: usu in sing with* **a**) a display of bad temper or sulking: *She is in a pet because she can't go to the cinema.*

'**pettish** *adj* (*old or rare*) in a bad temper; sulky. '**pettishly** *adv.* '**pettishness** *nu.*

petal ['petl] *nc* one of the *usu* brightly coloured leaf-like parts of a flower: *This rose has yellow petals edged with pink.*

petard *see* **hoist with one's own petard** *under* **hoist.**

peter ['pi:tə]: **peter out** *vi* to come gradually to an end: *As the river dried up our water-supply petered out; Their enthusiasm and support for the project gradually petered out.*

petite [pə'ti:t] *adj* (of women and girls) small and neat: *a petite brunette; That little girl is very petite.*

petition [pə'tiʃən] *nc* a formal request made to someone in authority and *usu* signed by a large number of people: *We are asking local people to sign a petition against the building of the new motorway; We're getting up a petition.* – *vt* (*formal*) to make such a request: *They petitioned the government for the release of the prisoners.* **pe'titioner** *nc* (*formal*).

petrify ['petrifai] *vt* **1** (*formal or facet*) to make (someone) very frightened; to terrify: *The thought of having to make a speech petrified him.* **2** (*tech*) to turn (something) into stone: *Objects left by tourists had been petrified by the action of chemicals in the water.*

petro- [petrou] (*in cmpds*) of or related to petrol, as in **petrochemical**.

petrochemical [petrə'kemikəl] *nc* (*usu attrib*) any chemical obtained from petroleum or natural gas: *the petrochemical industry.*

petrol ['petrəl] *nu* (*Amer* **gas** *or* **gasoline**) a liquid got from petroleum, used as fuel for motor cars *etc*: *I'll stop at the next garage and buy more petrol; (attrib) a petrol engine.*

petroleum [pə'trouliəm] *nu* oil in its raw, unrefined form, which is found in natural wells below the earth's surface and from which petrol, paraffin *etc* are obtained.

petroleum jelly *nu* a soft substance got from petroleum, used *eg* in ointments.

'**petrol pump** *nc* (*Amer* ˌ**gaso'line pump**) an apparatus at a petrol station which pumps petrol into cars *etc*, and which measures the amount of petrol it pumps.

'**petrol station** *nc* (*esp Amer* '**filling station**: *Amer inf* '**gas station**) a garage where petrol is sold.

petticoat ['petikout] *nc* an underskirt: *a lace-trimmed petticoat.*

pettish *see* **pet**[2].

petty ['peti] *adj* (*derog*) **1** (*usu attrib*) of very little importance; trivial: *He's forever fussing over petty details.* **2** deliberately nasty for a foolish or trivial reason: *petty behaviour; She is so petty that she would not lend me the book although she did not want to read it herself.* '**pettily** *adv.* '**pettiness** *nu.*

petty cash *nu* money used for small, everyday expenses in an office *etc*: *I've sent my secretary out to buy a couple of pens – I just took the money out of petty cash.*

petty officer *nc* (*with caps, and often abbrev* **PO**, *when written in titles*) in the British navy, (a person of) the rank above leading seaman: *He was promoted to petty officer; He is a petty officer; Petty Officer Summers.* – *See also* Appendix 3.

petulant ['petjulənt, (*Amer*) -tʃə-] *adj* (*formal*) easily made angry, often about unimportant things; irritable: *a petulant old lady; She becomes petulant when people disagree with her.* '**petulantly** *adv.* '**petulance** *nu.*

pew [pju:] *nc* a seat or bench in a church.

take a pew (*Brit inf facet: usu in imperative*) to sit down; to take a seat: *Take a pew – I'll be ready to go for a walk with you in a minute!*

pewter ['pju:tə] **1** *nu, adj* (of) a metal made by mixing tin and lead: *That mug is (made of) pewter; a pewter mug.* **2** *nu* dishes *etc* made of pewter: *She's polishing the pewter.*

phallic ['falik] *adj* (*formal*) shaped like a penis, *esp* as a symbol of sexual power, fertility *etc*: *a phallic symbol; I don't know what that carving is supposed to represent, but it looks a bit phallic to me.*

phantasy *see* **fantasy**.

phantom ['fantəm] *nc* (*formal or liter*) a ghost: *The castle is said to be haunted by a weird phantom; (attrib) a phantom horseman.*

pharmacology [fa:mə'kolədʒi] *nu* the scientific study of medicines and drugs and their effects: *He is studying pharmacology; (attrib) the pharmacology department of the hospital.* ˌ**pharma'cologist** *nc.*

pharmacy ['fa:məsi] **1** *nu* the preparation of medicines: *He is studying pharmacy.* **2** *nc* a shop *etc* where medicines are sold or given out: *the hospital pharmacy.*

ˌ**pharma'ceutical** [-'sju:tikəl] *adj* (*tech: esp attrib*) of or about the preparing of medicines and drugs: *the pharmaceutical industry.*

'**pharmacist** *nc* (*Amer* '**druggist**) **1** a person who prepares and sells medicines; a chemist (*def 2*). **2** a pharmacist's shop: *Is there a pharmacist near here?*

'**pharmacist's** *nc* (*Amer* **druggist's**) a pharmacist's shop: *You can buy all sorts of things at a pharmacist's.*

pharynx ['fariŋks] *nc* (*tech*) the back part of the throat. **pharyngal** [fə'riŋgəl], **pharyngeal** [farin'dʒi:əl] *adjs.*

ˌ**pharyn'gitis** [-'dʒaitis] *nu* (*med*) an illness in which the pharynx becomes sore and inflamed.

phase [feiz] *nc* **1** (*more formal than* **stage**) a stage in the development of something: *We are entering a new phase in the war; The child is going through a difficult/silly phase* (= a period of bad, silly *etc* behaviour which will stop when the child is older). **2** one in a series of regular changes in the shape or appearance of something (*esp* the moon or a planet): *the phases of the moon.*

phased *adj* done in stages: *We are planning a phased re-development of this part of the town; The development is carefully phased.*

phase in, out *vt sep* to begin or stop doing, using *etc* (something) in stages: *These new teaching methods will be gradually phased in and the old methods phased out.*

pheasant ['feznt] – *pls* '**pheasants**, '**pheasant** – **1** *nc* a type of long-tailed bird, the male of which has brightly-coloured feathers and certain types of which are often shot for sport: *a brace of pheasant(s); two pheasants.* **2** *ncu* (the flesh of) the bird as food: *We had roast pheasant for dinner.*

phenomenon [fə'nomənən, (*Amer*) -non] – *pl* **phe'nomena** [-nə] – *nc* (*formal*) a natural fact or event that is seen or happens regularly or frequently: *Magnetic attraction is an interesting phenomenon.*

phe'nomenal *adj* (*often used loosely*) very unusual; remarkable: *His knowledge of history is quite phenomenal; a phenomenal amount of money.* **phe'nomenally** *adv.*

phew [fju:] *interj* a word or sound used to express disgust, tiredness, relief *etc*: *Phew! It's hot today!*; *Phew! I thought he was going to ask me something but he didn't.*

phial ['faiəl] *nc* (*formal or liter*: *also* (*old*) **vial** ['vaiəl]) a small glass bottle: *a phial of perfume/poison.*

philander [fi'landə] *vi* (*formal or liter*: *often with* **with**) (*usu* of a man) to have a lot of casual love affairs: *He spent the summer philandering with the young women of the town.*

phi'landerer *nc*: *I am not surprised that she divorced him – he was such a philanderer.*

philanthropy [fi'lanθrəpi] *nu* (*formal*) love for mankind, *usu* as shown by money given to, or work done for, other people: *He shows his philanthropy by helping people who have been in prison.*

philanthropic [filən'θropik] *adj* (*formal*) giving money or other help *etc* to others: *a philanthropic person; a philanthropic act; He is so philanthropic that he gives money to all poor people.*

phi'lanthropist *nc* a philanthropic person.

See also **misanthrope**.

philately [fi'latəli] *nu* (*formal*) the study and collecting of postage-stamps. **ˌphila'telic** [-'te-] *adj.*

phi'latelist *nc* a person who studies and collects postage-stamps.

Philippine, Philippines *see* Appendix 2.

philistine ['filistain, (*Amer*) -stin] *nc, adj* (*formal*) (of) a person who ignores or dislikes good art, literature *etc*: *He loves art and music but his wife is a complete philistine; The poet accused his critics of being philistines; philistine tastes.*

philology [fi'lolədʒi] *nu* **1** (*formal*) the study of ancient or medieval literary texts: *Romance philology.* **2** (*old*) linguistics, *esp* the comparison and study of the development of related languages: *comparative philology.* **ˌphilo'logical** [-'lo-] *adj.* **phi'lologist** *nc.*

philosophy [fi'losəfi] **1** *nu* the search for knowledge and truth, *esp* about the nature of man and his behaviour and beliefs: *moral philosophy.* **2** *nc* a particular system of philosophical doctrines or theories: *Locke's political philosophy*; (*loosely*) *I have a very simple philosophy* (= attitude to life) – *enjoy life!*

phi'losopher *nc* a person who studies philosophy, *esp* one who develops a particular set of doctrines or theories: *Rousseau was a famous philosopher.*

ˌphilo'sophical, ˌphilo'sophic [-'so-] *adjs* **1** (*usu attrib*) of philosophy: *a philosophical discussion; philosophical works.* **2** (of a person) calm; not easily upset or worried: *He's had a lot of bad luck, but he's philosophical about it; He's a very philosophical person.* **ˌphilo'sophically** *adv.*

phi'losophize, -ise *vi* (*formal*) to think about or discuss the nature of man, the purpose of life *etc*: *He spends all his time philosophizing and never does any work.*

natural philosophy *nu* (*old*) physics.

phlegm [flem] *nu* **1** thick, slimy liquid brought up from the throat by coughing: *People with bronchitis produce a lot of phlegm.* **2** (*old or liter*) calmness; lack of emotion.

phlegmatic [fleg'matik] *adj* (*more formal than* **calm**) calm; not easily excited: *She's very phlegmatic – nothing would ever make her panic; a phlegmatic personality.*

phobia ['foubiə] *nc* (*more formal or tech than* **fear**) (*often in nu cmpds*) an intense fear or hatred of something, *usu* without reason: *She has a phobia about birds; She suffers from claustrophobia.*

phoenix ['fi:niks] *nc* (*myth*) a bird that burns itself and is born again from its own ashes.

phone [foun] *nc* (*less formal than* **telephone**) a telephone: *We don't have a phone; We were talking on the phone.* – *vti* (*less formal than* **telephone**) to telephone (a person, message or place): *I'll phone you this evening; Someone phoned when you were out, but he didn't leave any message for you; If you want to catch your train, you'd better phone for a taxi; Can one phone Paris from that call-box?; Please phone your reply to me – a letter would take too long to arrive.*

phone up *vi, vt sep* to (try to) speak to (someone) by means of the telephone: *If you have any problems, just phone me up; He has phoned up all the people concerned; I'll phone up and ask about it.*

phonetic [fə'netik] *adj* (*usu attrib*) **1** relating to the sounds of (a) language: *He's making a phonetic study of the speech of the deaf.* **2** written according to, or used in order to show, the actual sounds (of a word *etc*): *In some text-books, the pronunciation is shown by giving the words a phonetic spelling as well as their normal one, eg fiziks for physics; a phonetic transcription; This dictionary uses the symbols of the International Phonetic Alphabet to show the pronunciations of words.*

phonetician [founə'tiʃən] *nc* (*formal*) an expert in phonetics (*def 1*).

pho'netics *n sing* **1** the study of the sounds of language. **2** (a system of) symbols used to show the pronunciation of words.

phon(e)y ['founi] *adj* (*inf derog*) not genuine; fake; false: *a phoney French accent; He pretends to be English but his accent is rather phoney.* – *nc* a person who is not what he pretends to be: *He's not a real doctor – he's a phoney.*

phonograph ['founəgra:f] *nc* (*Amer*) a record-player.

phosphorus ['fosfərəs] *nu* an element (symbol **P**), a wax-like poisonous substance that gives out a faint light and catches fire easily.

'phosphate [-feit] *ncu* any of several chemical compounds containing phosphorus, *esp* one used as a fertilizer: *He spread some phosphate on the soil; Several phosphates are used as fertilizers.*

photo ['foutou] – *pl* **'photos** – *nc* (*less formal than* **photograph**) a photograph.

photo- [foutou] (*in cmpds*) **1** of or relating to photography, as in **photocopy**. **2** of or relating to light, as in **photosensitive**.

photocopy ['foutəkopi] *nc* a copy of a document *etc* made by a machine which photographs it: *I'll get some photocopies made of this letter so that you can all study it.* – *vt* to make a copy in this way: *Will you photocopy this letter for me, please?*

'photocopier *nc* a machine that makes photocopies.

photoelectric [foutoui'lektrik]: **photoelectric cell** *nc* a cell or other device which produces electricity when light falls on it.

photo-finish [foutou'finiʃ] *nc* the finish of a race in which the runners (*usu* horses) are so close together that a photograph is necessary to see which one has won.

photogenic [foutə'dʒenik] *adj* (*formal*) being a good subject for a photograph; that looks good when photographed: *She is very photogenic*; *a photogenic subject.*

photograph ['foutəgra:f] *nc* (*abbrev* **photo** ['foutou]) a picture taken by a camera, using the action of light on film or plates covered with certain chemicals: *I took a lot of photographs during my holiday.* – *vt* to take a photograph or photographs of (a person, thing *etc*): *He spends all his holidays going round the country photographing old buildings.*

photographer [fə'togrəfə] *nc*: *He is a professional photographer.*

ˌ**photo'graphic** [-'gra-] *adj* (*esp attrib*) of photographs or photography: *He made a photographic record of his journey.*

photography [fə'togrəfi] *nu* the act of taking photographs: *He's very keen on photography.*

photosensitive [foutə'sensitiv] *adj* (*tech*) affected by light: *Photoelectric cells are photosensitive*; *photosensitive film.*

Photostat ® ['foutəstat] *nc* **1** a type of special camera for making photographic copies of documents, plans *etc*: (*attrib*) *a Photostat copy.* **2** (*no cap*: *loosely*) a copy made by one of these: *I'd like a photostat of these plans.*

phrase [freiz] *nc* **1** (*gram*) a small group of words (*usu* without a finite verb) which forms part of an actual or implied sentence: *He arrived after dinner*; *As a result of his hard work, he became very rich*; *'When did you leave?' 'Yesterday morning.'* **2** (*music*) a small group of notes which follow each other to make a definite individual section of a melody: *the opening phrase of the overture.* – *vt* to express (something) in words: *I phrased the invitation very carefully*; *They obviously didn't understand what I was saying, so I tried to phrase my explanations in simple language.*

phraseology [freizi'olədʒi] *nu* (*formal*) the manner of putting words and phrases together to express oneself: *His phraseology shows that he is a foreigner.*

'**phrasing** *nu* **1** phraseology. **2** the act of putting musical phrases together either in composing or playing.

phrasal verb *nc* a phrase, consisting of a simple verb and one or more particles, which together function like a verb: *'Leave out' and 'go away' are phrasal verbs.*

'**phrase-book** *nc* a book (*eg* for tourists) which contains and translates useful words and phrases in a foreign language.

phut [fʌt]: **go phut** (*inf*) (*usu* of something mechanical or electrical) to break or cease to function: *My television has gone phut*; (*fig*) *His plans went phut.*

physical ['fizikəl] *adj* (*usu attrib*) **1** of the body: *Playing football is one form of physical exercise*; *physical strength.* **2** (*formal*) of things that can be seen or felt: *the physical world.* **3** of the laws of nature: *It's a physical impossibility for a man to fly like a bird*; (*fig inf*) *It's a physical impossibility for us to finish this by Christmas.* **4** (*tech*) relating to the natural features of the surface of the Earth: *physical geography.* **5** (*tech*) relating to physics: *physical chemistry.* '**physically** *adv.*

physician [fi'ziʃən] *nc* a doctor who specializes in medical rather than surgical treatment of patients: *My general practitioner transferred me to a physician at the hospital.*

physics ['fiziks] *n sing* the study of natural phenomena such as heat, light, sound, electricity, magnetism *etc* but not *usu* chemistry or biology: *Physics is his main subject at university*; (*attrib*) *a physics lecture.*

'**physicist** [-sist] *nc* a person who studies, or is an expert in, physics.

physiognomy [fizi'onəmi, (*Amer*) -'ognəmi] *ncu* (*very formal or liter*) (the features or expression of) the face.

physiology [fizi'olədʒi] *nu* the study of the way in which living bodies work, *eg* breathing, blood-circulation, food-digestion, plant growth *etc*: *Doctors study physiology*; (*attrib*) *physiology lectures.* ˌ**physi'ologist** *nc.*

ˌ**physi'ological** [-'lo-] *adj* (*tech*: *esp attrib*) of the way in which living bodies work; of physiology: *physiological changes.* ˌ**physio'logically** *adv.*

physiotherapy [fiziə'θerəpi] *nu* the treatment of disease by physical exercise, massage *etc*, not drugs: *People with arthritis often have physiotherapy.* ˌ**physio'therapist** *nc.*

physique [fi'zi:k] *nu* (*formal or facet*) the structure of a person's body: *He has a poor/powerful physique.*

pi [pai] *n* a letter of the Greek alphabet (Π, π), π also being used as a mathematical symbol representing the ratio of the circumference of a circle to its diameter (= 3·14159).

piano [pi'anou] – *pl* **pi'anos** – *nc* a large musical instrument played by pressing keys which make hammers strike metal wires: *She plays the piano very well*; *He played the tune on the piano*; (*attrib*) *a piano stool*; (*attrib*) *piano music.*

pianist ['piənist] *nc* a person who plays the piano.

piˌano-ac'cordion *nc* a type of accordion with a keyboard like that of a piano.

pianoforte [pianou'fo:ti] *nc* (*formal*) a piano.

grand piano a large piano in which the metal wires are stretched horizontally, used *eg* in concert-halls.

upright piano a piano in which the metal wires are stretched vertically, found *eg* in houses.

piccolo ['pikəlou] – *pl* '**piccolos** – *nc* a kind of small, high-pitched flute: *He plays the piccolo*; *Can you play that tune on the piccolo?*

pick[1] [pik] *vt* **1** to choose or select: *Pick the one you like best*; *He picked the winner of the competition* (= He chose the best person in the competition); *He picked the winner of the race* (= The one he chose, *eg* from a list, happened to win the race). **2** (*less formal that* **gather**) to take (flowers from a plant, fruit from a tree *etc*), *usu* by hand: *We went to a farm to pick strawberries*; *The little girl sat on the grass and picked daisies.* **3** to lift (someone or something): *He dropped his book and bent down to pick it up again*; *He stood in front of the mirror picking hairs off/from his jacket*; *He picked up the child and carried it.* **4** to unlock (a lock) with a tool other than a key: *When she found that she had lost her key, she picked the lock with a hair-pin.* – *See also* **pick** *in phrases below.* – *nc* (*no pl*) **1** whatever or whichever a person wants or chooses: *Take your pick of these prizes*; *You can have your pick.* **2** (*inf*) the best one(s) from, or the best part of, (something): *These grapes are the pick of the* bunch; *This girl is a pretty useless secretary, but she was the pick of the applicants.*

'**picker** *nc* (*usu in cmpds*) a person or thing that picks something: *a berry-picker.*

'**pickings** *n pl* (*sl*) money *etc* gained, sometimes dishonestly: *If this business deal goes through, there will be rich pickings for all of us!*

'**pick-me-up** *nc* (*inf*) something which restores a person's energy, cheerfulness, health *etc*: *A cup of tea is a real pick-me-up.*

'**pickpocket** *nc* a person who steals from people's pockets: *He kept his wallet in his hand because he knew there would be pickpockets in the crowd.* – *See also* **pick (someone's) pocket** *below.*

'**pick-up** *nc* **1** the part of a record-player that holds the stylus. **2** a type of small lorry or van. **3** (*sl*) (*usu* of a man) the act of forming a casual and *usu* not permanent friendship with a person of the other sex, *usu* implying a sexual relationship; the person with whom such a friendship is formed: *The girl said she didn't like pick-ups, and she had no intention of being a pick-up.* – *See also* **pick up** *below.*

have a bone to pick with (someone) *see* **bone**.

pick and choose to select or choose very carefully: *When I'm buying apples, I like to pick and choose (the ones I want)*; (*derog*) *Do make up your mind and stop picking and choosing!*

'**pick at** *vt fus* **1** to eat very little of (something): *He was not very hungry, and just picked at the food on his plate.* **2** to keep on touching, scratching or pulling at (something, *esp* a scab): *Do stop picking at that scab or the cut will never heal.*

pick someone's brains (*inf*) to ask (a person) questions in order to get ideas, information *etc* from him which one can use oneself: *You might be able to help me with this problem – can I come and pick your brains for a minute!*

pick a fight *see* **pick a quarrel** *below.*

pick holes in (something) (*fig*) to criticize or find faults in (an argument, theory *etc*): *He sounded very convincing, but I'm sure one could pick holes in what he said.*

pick one's nose to remove hard mucus from the nostrils with one's finger: *It is considered impolite to pick one's nose in public.*

pick off *vt sep* to shoot (*esp* people in a group) one by one: *He picked off the enemy soldiers as they tried to leave their hut.* – *See also* **pick** (*def 3*).

'**pick on** *vt fus* (*inf*) **1** to choose (someone) to do a *usu* difficult or unpleasant job: *Why do they always pick on me to do the washing-up?* **2** to speak to or treat (a person) angrily or critically: *Don't pick on me because we didn't get this finished on time – it wasn't my fault.*

pick out *vt sep* **1** to choose or select: *She picked out one dress that she particularly liked.* **2** to see or recognize (a person, thing *etc*): *He must be among those people getting off the train, but I can't pick him out.* **3** to play (a piece of music), *esp* slowly and with difficulty, *esp* by ear, without music in front of one: *I don't really play the piano, but I can pick out a tune on one with one finger.*

pick someone's pocket to steal something from a person's pocket: *My wallet has gone – someone has picked my pocket!* – *See also* **pickpocket** *above.*

pick a quarrel/fight with (someone) to start a quarrel, argument or fight with (someone) on purpose: *He was angry because I beat him in the race, and he tried to pick a fight with me afterwards.*

pick up 1 *vt sep* to learn gradually, without formal teaching: *I never studied Italian – I just picked it up when I was in Italy.* **2** *vi, vt sep* to let (someone) into a car, train *etc* in order to take him somewhere: *I picked him up at the station and drove him home*; *The bus stopped at the end of the road to pick up passengers*; *The train only picks up at certain stations.* **3** *vt sep* to get (something) by chance: *I picked up a real bargain at the shops today*; *You can pick up quite a lot of gossip in a pub.* **4** *v refl sep* to stand up: *He fell over and picked himself up again.* **5** *vt sep* (*inf*) to collect (something) from somewhere: *I ordered some meat from the butcher – I'll pick it up on my way home tonight.* **6** *vt sep* (of radio, radar *etc*) to receive signals: *We picked up a foreign broadcast last night.* **7** *vt sep* to find; to catch: *We lost his trail but picked it up again later*; *The police picked up the man they wanted outside the cinema.* **8** *vi* (*inf*) to recover (health): *He has been very ill, but he's picking up again now.* **9** *vt sep* (*sl*) (*esp* of a man) to form a casual, not permanent, and *usu* sexual, relationship with a person of the opposite sex: *He picked her up at a party last Saturday.* – *See also* **pick-up** *above and* **pick** (*def 3*).

pick up speed to go faster; to accelerate: *The car picked up speed as it ran down the hill.*

pick one's way to walk carefully (around or between something one wishes to avoid touching *etc*): *She picked her way between the puddles on the pavement.*

See also **unpick**.

pick[2] [pik] *nc* (*also* (*Brit*) '**pickaxe**, (*Amer*) '**pickax**) a tool with a heavy metal head pointed at one or both ends, used for breaking hard surfaces *eg* walls, roads, rocks *etc.*

See also **toothpick**.

pickaback ['pikəbak], **piggyback** ['pigibak] *adv* (*inf*) (of a child) carried on the back: *He carried the boy pickaback.* – *nc* a ride on someone's back: *Give me a pickaback, Daddy.*

pickax(e) *see* **pick**[2].

picket ['pikit] *nc* **1** (any one of) a number of people employed at a factory *etc* who are on strike and who try to persuade workers not to go to work there, not to deliver goods there *etc*: *The men set up a picket to stop lorries getting into the factory*; (*attrib*) *a picket line.* **2** (*mil*) a soldier or a small group of soldiers on special duty, *usu* to guard against a sudden attack by the enemy: *The commander placed pickets at various points round the camp*; (*attrib*) *picket duty.* – **1** *vt* to place a group of soldiers, strikers *etc* somewhere as a picket: *The strikers' leaders decided to picket the factory*; *The commander picketed the camp.* **2** *vti* to act as a picket (at): *In this country, strikers have the legal right to picket*; *The soldiers picketed the camp.*

'**picketer** *nc* a member of a picket (*def 1*).

pickle ['pikl] **1** *nu, nc* (*usu in pl*) a vegetable or vegetables preserved in vinegar, salt water *etc*: *Do you want some pickle(s) on your salad?* **2** *nc* (*usu in sing*) (*fig inf*) trouble; an unpleasant situation: *She got herself into a real pickle.* – *vt* to preserve in vinegar, salt water *etc*: *I think I will pickle these cucumbers.*

picnic ['piknik] *nc* a very informal meal eaten in the open air, *usu* as part of a trip, outing *etc*: *We'll go to the seaside and take a picnic*; *Let's go on a picnic!*; (*attrib*) *a picnic lunch.* – *v* – *pt, ptp* '**picnicked** – *vi* to have a picnic: *We picnicked on the beach.*

pictorial [pik'to:riəl] *adj* (*usu attrib*) **1** having

many pictures: *a pictorial magazine.* 2 consisting of pictures: *a pictorial record of our holiday.*
pi'ctorially *adv.*

picture ['piktʃə] *nc* 1 a painting or drawing: *This is a picture of my mother.* 2 a photograph: *I took a lot of pictures when I was on holiday.* 3 (*Brit inf*) a cinema film: *There's a good picture on at the cinema tonight.* *See also* **the pictures** *below.* 4 what is seen on a television screen: *The picture is not very good tonight – there's some interference from somewhere.* 5 (*no pl*: *with* **the**) a symbol or perfect example (of something): *She looked the picture of health/happiness.* 6 *nc* (*no pl*: *with* **a**) a beautiful sight: *She looked a picture in her new dress.* 7 *nc* (*no pl*) a clear description: *He gave me a good picture of what was happening.* – *vt* to imagine: *I can picture the scene; Just try to picture the scene to yourself.*
'picture-house *nc* (*old*) a cinema.
picture window *nc* a large window through which an attractive view can be seen: *One feature of this house is the picture window in the lounge.*
put (someone)/be in the picture to give or have all the necessary information (about something): *He put me in the picture about what had happened.*
the pictures (*inf*) the cinema: *We went to the pictures last night, but it wasn't a very good film.*

picturesque [piktʃə'resk] *adj* (*more formal than* **pretty** *or* **attractive**) (of places) pretty and interesting: *He lives in a very picturesque village; That little village is most picturesque.*
,pictu'resquely *adv.* **,pictu'resqueness** *nu.*

piddle ['pidl] *vi* (*inf*: *often a child's word*) to urinate: *The puppy piddled on the carpet.*

piddling ['pidliŋ] *adj* (*inf*: *attrib*) unimportant; trivial: *I'm not interested in piddling little details like that.*

pidgin ['pidʒən] *nc* any of a number of languages which consist of a mixture of English, French, Portuguese *etc* and some non-European (*esp* African) language: *Beach-la-mar is a pidgin spoken in parts of the southern Pacific Ocean*; (*attrib*) *a pidgin language*; (*attrib*) *pidgin English.*

pie [pai] *ncu* food baked in a covering of pastry: *a steak/apple pie; Does anyone want some more pie?*
have a finger in the/every pie *see* **finger**.
pie in the sky something good promised for the future but which one is not certain or likely to get: *Many Communists say that the Christian doctrine of heaven is just pie in the sky; He says he will get a well-paid job but it's just pie in the sky.*

piebald ['paibo:ld] *adj* (*usu* of horses) black and white in patches.

piece [pi:s] *nc* 1 a part of anything: *a piece of cake; There are over a hundred pieces in this jigsaw puzzle; He examined the tea-set carefully piece by piece* (= each piece separately); *a fifty-piece orchestra* (= an orchestra with fifty people in it); *an eighteen-piece tea-set.* – *See also* **in pieces** *and* **to pieces** *below.* 2 a single thing or example of something: *a piece of paper; a piece of news.* 3 a composition in music, writing (an article, short story *etc*), drama, sculpture *etc*: *He wrote an informative piece on social reform in the local newspaper; Michelangelo sculpted several pieces for the Pope's tomb.* 4 a coin of a particular value: *a fifty-pence piece.* 5 in chess, draughts and other games, a small shape made of wood, metal, plastic *etc* that is moved according to the rules of the game.
,piece'meal *adv* (*sometimes derog*) a little bit at a time; not as a whole: *He did the work piecemeal.* – *adj* (*usu attrib*) done *etc* in this way: *He has a rather piecemeal way of working.*
'piecework *nu* (*often attrib*) work paid for according to the amount done, not the time taken to do it: *Thank goodness we aren't being paid on a piecework basis!*
give (someone) a piece of one's mind *see* **mind**.
go (all) to pieces (*inf*) (of a person) to collapse physically or nervously: *She went to pieces when her husband died.*
in 'pieces 1 with its various parts not joined together: *The bed is delivered in pieces and the customer has to put it together himself.* 2 broken: *The vase was lying in pieces on the floor.*
a piece of cake (*sl*) something very easy: (*Winning*) *the race was a piece of cake.*
piece together *vt sep* to put (the pieces of something) together: *They tried to piece together the fragments of the broken vase*; (*fig*) *We managed to piece together his story.*
to 'pieces into separate, *usu* small pieces, or into the various parts from which (something) is made: *The hair-drier came to pieces in my hands; It was so old, it just fell to pieces when I touched it; The baby pulled the book to pieces; He took his car engine to pieces.*

pièce de résistance [pjesdəri'zistãs] *nc* (*formal*) the most important or best thing (in a series): *I've designed some beautiful dresses in the past, but this, I think, is my pièce de résistance.*

pied [paid] *adj* (*formal or liter*) (of birds, animals) of two or more colours, *esp* black and white.

pier [piə] *nc* 1 a platform of stone, wood *etc* stretching from the shore into the sea, a lake *etc* used as a landing-place for boats or as a place of entertainment: *The passengers stepped down on to the pier; There's a cafe and a theatre at the end of the pier.* 2 (*tech*) a pillar supporting an arch, bridge *etc.*

pierce [piəs] *vt* 1 (of pointed objects) to go into or through (something): *The arrow pierced his arm*; (*fig*) *A sudden light pierced the darkness*; (*fig*) *The cold wind pierced them to the bone*; (*fig formal*) *Her misery pierced his heart*; (*fig*) *The sound of a woman's screams pierced the air.* 2 to make a hole in or through (something) with a pointed object: *Pierce the lid before attempting to remove it from the jar.*
'piercing *adj* 1 (*usu attrib*) loud; shrill: *a piercing scream.* 2 (of cold weather, winds *etc*) sharp; intense: *a piercing wind; the piercing cold of a winter's night; That wind is piercing.* 3 (*usu attrib*) looking intently or sharply as though able to see through things: *piercing eyes; a piercing glance.*
'piercingly *adv.* **'piercingness** *nu.*

piety *see* **pious**.

piffle ['pifl] *nu, interj* (*inf*) nonsense: *That's just a lot of piffle; 'He's going to be the next managing director.' 'Piffle!'*

pig [pig] *nc* 1 a kind of farm animal whose flesh is eaten as pork, ham and bacon: *He keeps pigs.* 2 (*inf derog*) an unpleasant, greedy or dirty person: *You pig! You've eaten the whole cake!*
'piggy *nc* (*inf*) a child's word for a (little) pig. – *adj* (*inf derog*: *attrib*) like a pig's: *piggy eyes.*
'piglet [-lit] *nc* a baby pig.
piggy-back *see* **pickaback**.
,pig'headed *adj* (*derog*) stubborn: *a pigheaded idiot; He's so pigheaded* (*about everything*) *that you*

can never get him to listen to reason. ˌ**pig'headedness** *nu.*

'**piggy bank** *nc* a box (sometimes but not always in the shape of a pig) in which children can save their money: *He put his 5p in his piggy bank.*

'**pigskin** *nu, adj* (of) a kind of leather made from the skin of a pig: *Her purse was (made of) pigskin; pigskin shoes.*

'**pigsty** *nc* **1** a building in which pigs are kept. **2** (*inf derog*) a dirty, untidy place: *This room is an absolute pigsty!*

pigswill *see* **swill**.

'**pigtail** *nc* (*more inf than* **plait**) a plait (*def 1*) *usu* worn at the back of the head: *She wears her hair in pigtails; The boy pulled the little girl's pigtails; Sometimes she wears her hair in one single pigtail, sometimes in two.*

ˌ**make a 'pig of oneself** (*inf*) to eat greedily; to eat too much: *I really made a pig of myself at dinner last night.*

a pig in a poke (*inf*) something that one buys *etc* without knowing whether it is worth anything or not: *The new car we bought was a pig in a poke.*

pigs might fly said of something very unlikely to happen: *'We might have fine weather for our holiday.' 'Yes, and pigs might fly!'*

pigeon ['pidʒən] *nc* any of several kinds of bird of the dove family: *He keeps pigeons as a hobby – he enters them in races.*

'**pigeon-hole** *nc* a small compartment for letters, papers *etc* in a desk *etc* or *eg* hung on the wall of an office, staffroom *etc*: *He has separate pigeon-holes for bills, for receipts, for letters from friends and so on; Members of staff are advised to look in their pigeon-holes at least once a day.*

ˌ**pigeon-'toed** *adj* (of a person or his manner of walking) with toes turned inwards: *a pigeon-toed person/walk; He is pigeon-toed.*

carrier pigeon, homing pigeon *see* **carry**, *and* **homing** (*def 1*) *under* **home**.

that's (not) my pigeon that is (not) my affair or interest: *You'll have to ask someone else about buying a house – that's not my pigeon!; I'm not interested in these problems – that's his pigeon!*

pigment ['pigmənt] *ncu* **1** any substance used for colouring, making paint *etc*: *People used to make paint and dyes from natural pigments.* **2** a substance in plants or animals that gives colour to the skin, leaves *etc*: *Some people have darker pigment in their skin than others.*

ˌ**pigmen'tation** *nu* colouring (of skin *etc*): *Some illnesses cause a loss of pigmentation.*

pigmy *see* **pygmy**.

pike [paik] – *pl* **pike** (*def 1*), **pikes** (*def 2*) – *nc* **1** a kind of large, fierce freshwater fish: *He went fishing for pike.* **2** (*hist*) a type of weapon like a long spear: *The soldiers were armed with pikes.*

'**pikestaff: as plain as a pikestaff** obvious; very clear: *It's plain as a pikestaff that he was embarrassed.*

pilaff [pi'laf, (*Amer*) -'la:f] *ncu* a dish of rice, meat *etc* seasoned with spices.

pilchard ['piltʃəd] *nc* a kind of small sea-fish, like a herring, used as food: *a tin of pilchards.*

pile[1] [pail] *nc* **1** a (large) number of things lying on top of each other in a tidy or untidy heap; a (large) quantity of something lying in a heap: *There was a neat pile of books in the corner of the room; There was a pile of rubbish at the bottom of the garden.* **2** (*fig inf*: *often in pl*) a large quantity, *esp* of money: *He must have piles of money to own a car like that; He made a pile (of money) betting on horses; He made his pile* (= a lot of money) *from making cars.* – **1** *vt* to make a pile of (something); to put (something) in a pile: *He piled the boxes on the table.* – *See also* **pile up** *below.* **2** *vi* (*inf*) to move (into or out of) *esp* a form of transport, *esp* quickly and in a crowd: *They piled into the bus and drove off; When the train stopped, we all piled out; If you'll all pile in, we'll be off.*

'**pile-up** *nc* (*inf*) an accident or crash involving *usu* several vehicles: *There has been a serious pile-up on the M1, involving three cars and a lorry.*

pile up *vi, vt sep* to make or become a pile; to accumulate: *He piled up the earth at the end of the garden; The rubbish piled up in the kitchen; (fig) His debts soon piled up.*

pile[2] [pail] *nc* (*tech*) a large pillar or stake driven into the ground as a foundation for a building, bridge *etc*: *The entire city of Venice is built on piles.*

'**pile-driver** *nc* (*tech*) a machine for driving piles into the ground.

pile[3] [pail] *ncu* the thick soft surface of carpets and some kinds of cloth *eg* velvet: *The rug has a deep/thick pile; The carpet is threadbare – it has no pile.*

piles [pailz] *n pl* (*not a tech term*) haemorrhoids: *He suffers from piles.*

pilfer ['pilfə] *vti* (*inf*) to steal (small things): *He pilfered enough pieces of wood from the factory to make a chair; He's always pilfering.* '**pilferer** *nc.*

pilgrim ['pilgrim] *nc* a person who travels to a holy place: *Every year thousands of pilgrims visit Jerusalem.*

'**pilgrimage** [-midʒ] *nc* a journey to a holy place: *She went on a pilgrimage to Lourdes; Muslims try to make a pilgrimage to Mecca at least once in their lives.*

Pilipino *see* Appendix 2.

pill [pil] *nc* a small ball or tablet of medicine, to be swallowed: *She needs these pills to help her sleep; sleeping-pills.*

the pill a contraceptive in the form of a pill: *She's (going) on the pill* (= She takes (or is going to take) contraceptive pills); *She told me she was taking the pill.*

pillage ['pilidʒ] *vti* (*old*) to steal from (a person or place) with violence, *esp* in war: *The soldiers pillaged the area.* – *nu* (*old*) the act of stealing with violence: *theft and pillage.*

pillar ['pilə] *nc* **1** an upright post used in building as a support or decoration: *The hall was surrounded by stone pillars.* **2** (*formal or facet*) a person who supports an organization *etc*: *He is a pillar of the church.* **3** (*liter*) anything in the shape of a pillar: *a pillar of smoke.*

'**pillarbox** *nc* (*Brit*) a tall, round, red box found in public places, into which letters are posted to be collected by a postman.

from pillar to post (*inf*) (*usu* of a person in trouble, difficulty *etc*) from one place to another (*usu* looking for help *etc*): *He was driven from pillar to post in search of a job.*

pillion ['piljən] *nc* a passenger seat on a motorcycle: *He drove the motorbike and she sat on the pillion; (attrib) a pillion passenger/seat.*

pillory ['piləri] *vt* (*formal*: *usu in passive*) to mock or laugh at (someone) publicly: *He was pilloried for his strange ideas.*

pillow ['pilou] *nc* a kind of cushion for the head, *esp* on a bed. – *vt* (*liter*) to rest (one's head) on: *He pillowed his head on her breast.*

'pillowcase/'pillowslip *ncs* a cover for a pillow: *They bought linen sheets and pillowcases.*

pilot ['pailət] *nc* **1** a person who flies an aeroplane: *The pilot and crew were all killed in the air crash.* **2** a person who directs a ship in and out of a harbour, river, or coastal waters. – *adj* (*attrib*) experimental: *a pilot scheme* (= one done on a small scale, *eg* to solve certain problems before a larger, more expensive project is started). – *vt* to guide as a pilot: *He piloted the ship down the river*; *My brother piloted the plane.*

'pilot-light *nc* a small gas light *eg* on a gas cooker, which burns continually and is used to light the main gas jets when they are turned on: *I can't light the cooker – the pilot-light has gone out.*

'pilot officer *nc* (*with cap, and often abbrev* **PO**, *when written in titles*) in the British airforce, (a person of) the lowest commissioned rank: *He is a pilot officer*; *He was promoted to pilot officer*; *Pilot Officer Jones.* – *See also* Appendix 3.

pimp [pimp] *vi* (*old or inf*: *with* **for**) to find customers (for a prostitute). – *nc* (*sl*) a man who does this.

pimple ['pimpl] *nc* (*more informal than* **spot**) a small round swelling on the skin: *He had a pimple on his nose.*

'pimpled/'pimply *adjs* (*sometimes derog*) having pimples: *a pimpled/pimply face*; *a pimply youth*; *He is pale and pimply.*

pin [pin] *nc* **1** a short, thin, pointed piece of metal used *eg* to hold pieces of fabric, paper *etc* together, *esp* when making clothes: *While I was trying on the dress a pin scratched me*; *I have not sewn that seam yet – it is held together by pins.* **2** (*usu in cmpds*) a similar but more ornamental object: *a hat-pin.* **3** a wooden or metal peg or nail: *When she broke her hip, she had to have a pin put in it*; *The joiner hammered the panel-pins into the door.* – *v* – *pt, ptp* **pinned** – *vt* **1** (*neg* **un-**) to fasten with a pin: *She pinned the material together*; *She pinned the flower to her dress*; *They pinned down the carpet with tacks*; *Could you pin this brooch on for me please?* – *See also* **pin down** *and* **pin on** *below.* **2** to hold by pressing against something: *The fallen tree pinned him to the ground*; *They pinned him against the wall and hit him several times.* – *See also* **pin down** *below.*

'pincushion *nc* a small cushion or similar object into which pins (*def 1*) are pushed to be kept.

'pinpoint *vt* to place or show very exactly: *He pinpointed the position on the map*; (*fig*) *He pinpointed the cause of the trouble.*

'pin-stripe *nc* (*usu attrib*) a very narrow stripe in cloth: *pin-stripe trousers.*

'pin-up *nc* **1** a picture of an attractive girl (or man), often pinned on a wall: *He has dozens of pin-ups in his room*; (*attrib*) *a pin-up girl.* **2** the girl (or man): *She's the favourite pin-up of the soldiers.*

pin down *vt oblig sep* (*fig*) to make (someone) give a definite answer, statement, opinion or promise: *I can't pin him down to a definite date for his arrival*; *He refused to be pinned down about his opinions on abortion.*

pin one's hopes/faith on (someone) to rely on (someone); to hope or expect (that someone will do or achieve something): *Britain's athletes have not done very well so far this year, but this afternoon we are pinning our hopes on Lorna Smith.*

'pin (something) on (someone) (*inf*) to prove or suggest that (a person) was responsible for (something bad, *esp* a crime): *You can't pin that robbery on me – I've got an alibi!*

pins and needles (*not a tech term*) a tingling feeling in one's hands, arms, feet or legs: *I've got pins and needles in my arm.*

See also **drawing-pin, hairpin, rolling-pin, safety-pin, tie-pin**.

pinafore ['pinəfo:] *nc* **1** a kind of apron covering the clothes above and below the waist: *The children wore pinafores at nursery school.* **2** (*also* **'pinafore dress**: *Amer* **'jumper**) a kind of dress with no sleeves, designed to be worn over a blouse, sweater *etc.*

pince-nez [pẽs'nei] *n pl* (*old*) spectacles which grip the nose instead of being supported over the ears: *My grandmother used to wear* (*a pair of*) *pince-nez.*

pincers ['pinsəz] *n pl* **1** a tool for gripping things tightly: *He pulled the nail out with the pincers*; *He used a pair of pincers.* **2** the claws of lobsters, crabs *etc.*

pinch [pintʃ] **1** *vt* to squeeze or press tightly (flesh), *esp* between the thumb and forefinger: *He pinched her arm.* **2** *vti* to hurt by being too small or tight: *My new shoes are pinching* (*me*). **3** *vt* (*inf*) to steal: *Who pinched my bicycle?* – *nc* **1** an act of pinching; a squeeze or nip: *He gave her a pinch on the cheek.* **2** a very small amount; what can be held between the thumb and forefinger: *a pinch of salt.*

pinched *adj* (*usu pred*) (of a person's face) looking cold, pale or thin because of cold, poverty *etc*: *Her face was pinched with cold*; *She looks rather pinched since her illness*; *She has rather a pinched look these days.*

at a 'pinch/if it comes to the pinch (*inf*) in an emergency; if absolutely necessary: *At a pinch, you could get home on foot*; *If it comes to the pinch, I'll play the piano for you, but I'm not very good.*

feel the pinch (*inf*) to have problems because of lack of money: *Now that my wife has given up her job, we are really feeling the pinch.*

take (something) with a pinch of salt *see* **salt**.

pincushion *see* **pin**.

pine[1] [pain] **1** *nc* (*also* **'pine tree**) any of several kinds of evergreen trees with cones (**'pine-cones**) and needlelike leaves (**'pine-needles**): *Those trees are all pines*; (*attrib*) *a pine wood.* **2** *nu, adj* (of) its wood: *The table is* (*made of*) *pine*; *a pine table.*

pine[2] [pain] *vi* **1** (*often with* **away**) to lose strength, become weak (with pain, grief *etc*): *Since his death she has been pining* (*away*); *Gradually she pined away and died.* **2** (*usu with* **for**) to want (something) very much; to long (for someone or something, or to do something): *He knew that his wife was pining for home*; *She was pining to return to England.*

pineapple ['painapl] **1** *nc* a type of large tropical fruit shaped like a large pine-cone, or the plant which produces it: *Pineapples grow in hot climates.* **2** *nu* this fruit as food: *Would you like some pineapple?*; (*attrib*) *pineapple juice.*

ping [piŋ] *nc* a sharp, ringing sound such as that of a glass being lightly struck, or a stretched wire, thread *etc* being pulled and released: *His knife struck the wine-glass with a loud ping.* – *vi* to make such a sound: *The glass pinged.*

ping-pong ['piŋpoŋ] *nu* **1** (*inf*) the game of table tennis: *Do you play ping-pong?*. **2** (*with cap*: ®) in the US, the equipment used in table tennis.

pinion ['pinjən] *vt* (*formal*) **1** to make it impossible for a person to move by holding or tying his arms: *He was pinioned against the wall.* **2** to hold or tie (a person's arms): *His arms were pinioned behind his back.* – *nc* (*liter*) a bird's wing: *The falcon rose, pinions spread.*

pink[1] [piŋk] **1** *ncu, adj* (of) (any shade of) a colour between red and white: *a dress of pink satin.* **2** *nu* something (*eg* material, paint *etc*) pink in colour: *She was dressed in pink.* **3** *ncu, adj* (of) the colour of healthy skin: *pink cheeks*; *Her cheeks are pink with health.* **'pinkness** *nu.*

'pinkish *adj* fairly pink; close to pink: *The flowers of this plant are pinkish in colour.*

in the 'pink (of 'health) (*inf*) very well; in good health: *I've been ill for a few weeks but I feel in the pink now.*

pink[2] [piŋk] **1** *vt* to cut (cloth *etc*) with **'pinking scissors/shears**, leaving a zigzag edge: *If you pink the edges, they won't fray.* **2** *vi* (of an engine *etc*) to make a knocking or clinking noise due to faulty combination of the fuel: *The car engine was pinking slightly, so he took it to a garage.*

pinnacle ['pinəkl] *nc* **1** a tall thin spire built on the roof of a church, castle *etc.* **2** a high pointed rock or mountain: *It was a dangerous pinnacle to climb.* **3** (*formal or liter*) a high point (of achievement, success *etc*): *He has reached the pinnacle of his career.*

pinpoint *see* **pin**.

pint [paint] *nc* (*often abbrev* **pt** *when written*) a unit for measuring liquids, one-eighth of a gallon (in Britain, 0·57 litre; in the US, 0·47 litre): *a pint of milk/beer*; *They had to give the injured man two pints of blood.*

pioneer [paiə'niə] *nc* **1** a person who goes to a new, often uninhabited or uncivilized (part of a) country to live and work there: *the American pioneers*; (*attrib*) *a pioneer family.* **2** a person who first studies some new subject, or first uses or develops a new technique *etc*: *Lister was one of the pioneers of modern medicine.* – *vt* to be the first to do or make: *Who pioneered the use of vaccine as a cure for polio?*

pious ['paiəs] *adj* having or showing strong religious feelings, reverence for or devotion to God *etc*: *a pious woman/attitude*; *She is a most pious woman.* **'piously** *adv.* **piety** ['paiəti] *nu.*

See also **impious**.

pip[1] [pip] *nc* a seed of a fruit: *an orange/apple pip*; *Take the pips out of the orange before you give it to the child.*

pip[2] [pip] *nc* (*usu in pl with* **the**) a short sharp sound on radio, a telephone *etc*, used *eg* to show the exact time: *He put his watch right by the pips.*

pip[3] [pip]: **pipped at the post** (*inf*) beaten in the very final stages of a race, competition *etc*: *I thought I was going to win the painting competition, but I was pipped at the post by a friend of mine.*

pipe [paip] **1** *ncu* (*sometimes in cmpds*) a tube, *usu* made of metal, earthenware *etc*, through which water, gas *etc* can flow: *a water pipe*; *a drainpipe*; *a length of pipe*; *a long piece of drainpipe.* **2** *nc* a small tube with a bowl at one end, in which tobacco is smoked: *He smokes a pipe*; (*attrib*) *pipe tobacco.* **3** *nc* a musical instrument consisting of a hollow wooden, metal *etc* tube through which the player blows or causes air to be blown in order to make a sound: *He played a tune on a bamboo pipe*; *an organ pipe.* – **1** *vt* to convey gas, water *etc* by a pipe: *Water is piped to the town from the reservoir.* **2** *vti* (*formal*) to play (music) on a pipe or pipes: *He piped a tune.* **3** *vti* (*liter*) to speak in a high voice: *'Hallo,' the little girl piped.* **4** *vt* to decorate (a cake) with icing, cream *etc*: *She piped 'Happy Birthday' on the cake.* **5** *vi* (*liter*) to make the high-pitched sound of a bird: *birds piping in the trees.* – *See* **pipe down, pipe up** *below.*

'piper *nc* a person who plays a pipe or pipes, *esp* the bagpipes: *They had a piper playing at their wedding.*

pipes *n pl* **1** (*usu with* **the**) bagpipes or some similar instrument: *He plays the pipes*; *Irish pipes*; *He was trying to play a waltz on the pipes.* **2** a set of musical pipes joined together to form a single instrument: *the pipes of Pan.*

'piping *nu* **1** the act of playing a musical pipe or pipes: *the piping in of the haggis at a Burns' Supper.* **2** (the act or process of conveying water, gas *etc* by means of) a length of pipe or number of pipes (*def 1*): *lead piping*; *Piping the oil ashore will not be easy.* **3** a narrow cord or piece of material for decorating clothes: *a blue dress with brown piping.* **4** the act of decorating a cake *etc* with icing, cream *etc*; the decoration itself: *pink piping on white icing.* – *adj* **1** (*usu attrib*) (of a sound) high-pitched: *a piping voice.* **2** (*inf*) piping hot (*see below*).

'pipe dream *nc* an idea which can only be imagined, and which would be impossible to carry out: *For most people a journey round the world is only a pipe dream.*

'pipeline *nc* a long line of pipes used for conveying oil, gas, water *etc*: *an oil pipeline across the desert.*

in the 'pipeline (*inf*) in preparation; not yet ready: *Our new orders are still in the pipeline.*

pipe down *vi* (*inf*) to stop talking; to be quiet: *Will you pipe down for a moment?*

pipe up *vi* (*inf*) to say (something); to start speaking: *He soon piped up with a question.*

piping hot (*inf*) very hot: *a piping hot plate of soup*; *Be careful, the soup is piping hot.*

See also **windpipe** *under* **wind**[1].

piquant ['pi:kənt] *adj* (*formal*) sharp in taste; appetizing: *a piquant sauce*; *These spices make the sauce deliciously piquant*; (*fig*) *a piquant* (= exciting or interesting) *situation.* **'piquantly** *adv.*

'piquancy *nu* (*formal*): *the piquancy of a sauce/conversation.*

pique [pi:k] *nu* (*formal*) anger caused by one's pride being hurt: *She walked out of the room in a fit of pique.* – *vt* (*formal*: *usu in passive*) to hurt the pride of (someone): *She was piqued by his lack of interest.*

pirate ['paiərət] *nc* **1** a person who attacks and robs ships at sea: *Their ship was attacked by pirates*; (*attrib*) *a pirate ship.* **2** (*usu attrib*) a person who does something without legal right, *eg* publishes someone else's work as his own or broadcasts without a licence: *a pirate radio-station.* – *vt* to publish, broadcast *etc* without the legal right to do so: *The dictionary was pirated and sold abroad.*

'piracy *nu* the act(s) of a pirate: *He was accused of piracy on the high seas*; *Publishing that book under his own name was piracy.*

pirouette [piru'et] *nc* a dancer's quick turning movement: *The ballerina did/danced a pirouette.* – *vi* to do one or a series of these movements: *She pirouetted across the stage*; *The child pirouetted to show off her new dress.*

Pisces ['paisi:z] *n* a sign of the zodiac, the Fish: *People born between February 20 and March 20 are said to be born under the sign of Pisces.*

piss [pis] *vi* (*vulg*) to urinate: (*fig*) *It's pissing down* (= It's raining hard). – *nu* (*vulg*) urine.
pissed *adj* (*sl*: *usu pred*) drunk: *We all got pissed at the party last night.*
pissed off (*vulg*: *often with* **with**) annoyed; bored; tired: *I'm pissed off with waiting*; *I'm pissed off with this job.*
piss off *vi* (*vulg*: *usu as a command*) to go away: *Why don't you just piss off and leave me alone!*

pistachio [pi'staːʃiou] – *pl* **pis'tachios** – **1** *nc* a greenish nut used as flavouring for food. **2** *nu, adj* (of) its colour or flavour: *The ice-cream/wallpaper is pistachio*; *pistachio ice-cream*; *pistachio green.* **3** *nc* the tree bearing this nut.

pistol ['pistl] *nc* a small gun, held in one hand when fired: *He shot himself with a pistol.*

piston ['pistən] *nc* (*tech*) (in engines, pumps *etc*) a round piece *usu* of metal that fits inside a cylinder and moves up and down or backwards and forwards inside it.

pit[1] [pit] *nc* **1** a large hole in the ground: *The campers dug a pit for their rubbish.* **2** (*often in cmpds*) a place from which minerals are dug, *esp* a coal-mine: *a chalk-pit*; *He works at/down the pit.* **3** (*Brit*) in a theatre, (the people sitting in) the back part of the ground floor: *We watched the play from the pit.* **4** (*often in pl*) a place beside a motor race track for repairing and refuelling racing cars: *The leading car has gone into the pit(s).* – *v* – *pt, ptp* **'pitted** – *vt* (*with* **against**) to set (a person or thing) against another in a fight, competition *etc*: *I had to pit my wits against him*; *He was pitted against a much stronger man.*
'pitted *adj* (*formal*: *usu pred with* **with**) marked with small holes: *The surface of the moon is pitted with craters*; *His face was pitted with scars.*
'pitfall *nc* a possible danger: *She has managed to avoid most of the pitfalls of life.*
the pit of the stomach the hollow in the body below the breastbone: *The stone hit him in the pit of the stomach*; (*fig*) *When he realized what he had done, he had a sick feeling in the pit of his stomach.*

pit[2] [pit] *nc* (*more formal than* **stone**) the hard stone of a peach, cherry *etc.* – *v* – *pt, ptp* **'pitted** – *vt* to remove the stone from (a peach, cherry *etc*).
'pitted *adj* having had the stones removed: *pitted cherries*; *Are these cherries pitted?*

pitch[1] [pitʃ] **1** *vt* to set up (a tent or camp): *They pitched their tent in the field.* **2** *vt* to throw: *He pitched the stone into the river.* **3** *vti* (*formal*: *usu with* **forward, out** *etc*) to (cause to) fall heavily: *He pitched forward.* **4** *vi* (of a ship) to rise and fall violently: *The boat pitched up and down on the rough sea.* **5** *vt* (*music*) to set (a note or tune) at a particular level: *He pitched the tune too high for my voice.* – *See also* **pitch in, pitch into** *below.* – **1** *nc* the field or ground for certain games: *The pitch is too wet to play on*; *a cricket-pitch*; *a football pitch.* **2** *nu* the degree of highness or lowness of a musical note, voice *etc.* **3** *nu* (*formal*) an extreme point or intensity: *His anger reached such a pitch that he hit her.* **4** *nc* (*inf*) the part of a street *etc* where a street-seller or entertainer works: *He has a pitch on the High Street where he sells souvenirs.* **5** *nc* the act of pitching (*def 2*) or the distance something is pitched: *That was a long pitch.* **6** *nu* (of a ship) the act of pitching (*def 4*).
-pitched (*in cmpds*) of a (certain) musical pitch: *a high-pitched/low-pitched voice.*
'pitcher *nc* a person who pitches *esp* (in baseball) the player who throws the ball.
pitched battle *nc* a battle between armies that have been prepared and arranged for fighting beforehand: *They fought a pitched battle outside the town.*
'pitchfork *nc* a large long-handled fork for lifting and moving hay.
pitch in *vi* (*inf*) to (begin to) deal with, do *etc* something: *If everyone pitches in, we'll soon get the job done*; *There's plenty food for everyone, so pitch in.*
pitch into *vt fus* (*inf*) **1** to attack; to start a fight or argument: *He pitched into her about her careless work.* **2** to (begin to) deal with, do *etc* (something): *Everyone pitched into the work/food.*
queer someone's pitch *see* **queer**.

pitch[2] [pitʃ] *nu* a thick black substance obtained from tar: *as black as pitch.*
,pitch-'black, ,pitch-'dark *adjs* as black, or dark, as pitch; completely black or dark: *Outside the house it was pitch-black*; *It's a pitch-dark night.*

pitcher[1] *see* **pitch**[1].

pitcher[2] ['pitʃə] *nc* a large jug: *The girl was carrying a pitcher of water.*

pitchfork *see* **pitch**[1].

piteous *see* **pity**.

pitfall *see* **pit**[1].

pith [piθ] *nu* **1** the white substance between the peel of an orange, lemon *etc* and the fruit itself: *Remove the pith of the orange before you give it to the child.* **2** the soft substance in the centre of the stems of plants. **3** (*fig formal*) the most important part of anything: *the pith of the argument.*
'pithy *adj* (*formal*) short and full of wisdom and good sense: *a pithy saying*; *His speech was short and pithy.* **'pithily** *adv.* **'pithiness** *nu.*

pitiable, pitiful, pitiless *see* **pity**.

pittance ['pitəns] *nc* (*derog*) a very small amount of money: *He works for a (mere) pittance.*

pitter-patter [pitə'patə] *nu* a light, tapping sound: *the pitter-patter of rain on a window.* – *vi* to make such a sound. – *adv* while making this sound: *The mouse ran pitter-patter across the floor.*

pity ['piti] *nc* (*no pl*) **1** a feeling of sorrow for the troubles and sufferings of others: *He felt a great pity for her.* **2** a cause of sorrow or regret: *What a pity (that) she can't come*; *The pity of it is that she won't be there.* – *See* **have pity on, take pity on** *below.* – *vt* (*formal or liter*) to feel pity for (someone): *She pitied him in his unhappiness*; *She is to be pitied.*
piteous ['pitiəs] *adj* (*liter*: *usu attrib*) pitiful (*def 1*): *She gave a piteous cry*; *It was a piteous sight.* **'piteously** *adv.* **'piteousness** *nu.*
'pitiable *adj* pitiful: *He was in a pitiable condition*; *He made a pitiable attempt at passing the exam*; *Her unhappiness was indeed pitiable.* **'pitiably** *adv.*
'pitiful *adj* **1** very sad; causing pity: *a pitiful sight*; *Her poverty was pitiful.* **2** very poor, bad *etc*; causing contempt: *That was a pitiful attempt*; *a pitiful amount of money*; *It is pitiful that he cannot do anything right.* **'pitifully** *adv.* **'pitifulness** *nu.*
'pitiless *adj* (*liter*) without pity: *pitiless cruelty*; *The tyrant is pitiless.* **'pitilessly** *adv.* **'pitilessness** *nu.*
'pityingly *adv* (*sometimes derog*) in a way which shows that one feels pity for someone: *He looked at her pityingly.*
have 'pity on (someone or something) to feel pity for someone (because of something): *Have pity on the old man. Have pity on their innocence*; *He had pity on her.*

take pity on (someone) (not) to do something to or for someone because one feels pity for them: *He took pity on her and lent her the £50 she needed.*

pivot ['pivət] *nc* **1** (*tech*) the pin or centre on which anything balances and turns: *The chair turns on a pivot.* **2** (*fig formal*) a person or thing on which something depends; the central or most important person or thing: *The headmaster is the pivot of the school.* – *v* – *pt, ptp* '**pivoted** – *vi* (*with* **on**) (*tech*) to turn (on): *The door pivoted on a central hinge.*

pixy, pixie ['piksi] *nc* (*myth*) a kind of fairy.

pizza ['pi:tsə] *ncu* a flat piece of dough spread with tomato, cheese *etc* and baked: *Have a/some pizza*; (*attrib*) *a pizza pie.*

pizzicato [pitsi'ka:tou] *adj, adv* (*music*) played by plucking the strings of a musical instrument, not using the bow.

placard ['plaka:d] *nc* a notice printed on some stiff material (*eg* wood or cardboard), and carried, hung *etc* in a public place: *All the protesters were carrying placards denouncing the government's policy*; *Every lamp-post in the district had a placard with a political slogan on it.*

placate [plə'keit, (*Amer*) 'pleikeit] *vt* (*more formal than* **soothe**) to stop (an angry person) feeling angry: *He placated her with an apology.*

place [pleis] **1** *nc* a particular spot or area: *I know a nice, quiet place in the country*; *I spent my holiday in various different places.* **2** *nc* an empty space: *There's a place for your books on this shelf.* **3** *nc* (*often in cmpds*) an area or building with a particular purpose: *a market-place*; *Please state your usual place of business.* **4** *nc* a seat (in a theatre, train, at a table *etc*): *He went to his place and sat down.* **5** *nc* a position in an order, series, queue *etc*: *She got the first place in the competition*; *He came in in first place in the race*; *I had to go to the toilet and lost my place in the queue*; *Will you keep my place, please?* **6** *nc* (*no pl*) a person's position or level of importance in society: *She knows her place and keeps to it*; *You must keep them in their place* (= make sure that they don't act as if they are more important than they are). – *See also* **put (someone) in his place** *below.* **7** *nc* a passage in a book, *esp* the passage one is reading or has just read: *There's something about nationalism in this book, but I can't find the place*; *The wind was blowing the pages of my book and I kept losing my place* (= being unable to find the passage I was reading). **8** *nc* (*no pl*) duty or right: *It is your place to welcome the guests*; *It's not my place to tell him he's wrong.* **9** *nc* a job or position in a team, organization *etc*: *He's got a place in/on his local football team*; *He's hoping for a place on the staff.* **10** *nc* (*inf*) house; home: *Come over to my place*; *She's got a place in town.* **11** *n* (*with cap*: *often abbrev* **Pl.** *when written*) a word used in the names of certain roads, streets or squares: *He lives in Drummond Place.* **12** *nc* (*math*) a number or one of a series of numbers following a decimal point: *The value of pi is 3·14159 correct to five decimal places, or, 3·142 correct to three decimal places.* – *vt* **1** (*more formal than* **put**) to put (in a particular place or position): *He placed it on the table*; *He was placed in command of the army.* **2** (not *usu* used with **is, was** *etc* and **-ing**) to remember (who a person is): *I know I've met her, but I can't quite place her.* **3** to give (an order for goods *etc*): *I placed an order with the firm for fifty machines.*

'**place-name** *nc* the name of a town, hill, valley *etc.*

give place to (*formal*) to be followed and replaced by (something): *The horse gave place to the motor car.*

'**go places** (*inf*) to be successful, *esp* in one's career: *That young man is sure to go places.*

in the '**first,** '**second** *etc* **place** expressions used to show steps in an argument, explanation *etc*: *He decided not to buy the house, because in the first place it was too expensive, and in the second place it was too far from his office.*

in '**place** in the proper position; tidy: *He left everything in place*; *This room's in a terrible mess – I want everything in place by this time tomorrow.*

in '**place of** (*formal*) instead of (something): *We advise discussion in place of argument.*

in someone's '**place** instead of (someone): *John was ill so I went in his place.*

out of place 1 not suitable (to the occasion *etc*): *His clothes are quite out of place at a formal dinner.* **2** not in the proper position; untidy: *Although he had had to run most of the way, he arrived with not a hair out of place.*

put (oneself) in someone else's place to imagine what it would be like to be (someone else): *If you put yourself in his place, you can understand why he is so careful.*

put (someone) in his place to remind (someone), often in a rude or angry way, of his lower social position, or lack of importance, experience *etc*: *He tried to tell her what to do, but she soon put him in his place.*

take place (*formal*) to happen: *What took place after that?*

take someone's place to do something or go somewhere as a replacement for someone else: *He took my place in the queue so that I could go and get something to eat*; *John is too ill to come, so I'm taking his place.* – *See also* **take** (*def 10*).

take the place of to be used instead of, or to be a substitute for, (something): *I don't think television will ever take the place of books.*

See also **displace, misplace.**

placid ['plasid] *adj* calm and not easily disturbed or upset: *a placid child*; *She would have to be placid – she has eight children.* '**placidly** *adv.* '**placidness** *nu.*

plagiarize, -ise ['pleidʒəraiz] *vti* (*formal*) to steal (from) the ideas or writings of someone else: *He plagiarized most of his book from my book*; *He has plagiarized my book.*

'**plagiarism** *ncu*: *The article is full of plagiarisms*; *The plagiarism in this book is obvious.* '**plagiarist** *nc.*

plague [pleig] **1** *ncu* a fatal, infectious disease: *Plagues often broke out in the Middle Ages*; *The people were continually afraid of bubonic plague.* **2** *nc* a large and annoying quantity (of): *a plague of flies.* – *vt* (*inf*: *usu with* **with**) to annoy or pester continually or frequently: *The child was plaguing her with questions.*

plaice [pleis] – *pl* **plaice** – **1** *nc* a type of flat fish: *They were fishing for plaice*; *We caught three plaice.* **2** *nu* its flesh as food: *We had fried plaice for lunch.*

plaid [plad] *nc* a long piece of (*usu* tartan) cloth worn over the shoulder, an item of Scottish national dress sometimes worn with the kilt.

plain [plein] *adj* **1** simple or ordinary; without ornament or decoration: *plain living*; *He likes good, plain food*; *plain sewing*; *Their style of living* *is simple and plain.* **2** easy to understand; clear: *His words were quite plain.* **3** absolutely open or honest; not hiding one's feelings or opinions out of kindness, tact *etc*: *I'll be quite plain with you; He was quite plain about his feelings on the matter; He's a man who believes in plain speaking.* **4** (*pred*) obvious; evident: *It's plain* (*to see*) *you haven't done this before.* **5** not pretty: *a rather plain girl; She is very plain but she is kind and gentle.* – **1** *nc* a large, flat level piece of land: *the plains of central Canada.* **2** *nu* a kind of knitting stitch.

ˈ**plainly** *adv.* ˈ**plainness** *nu.*

plain chocolate *nu* chocolate to which milk has not been added in manufacture.

plain clothes *n pl* ordinary clothes, not a uniform: *Detectives usually wear plain clothes;* (*attrib*) *a plain-clothes job* (= a job for which a policeman does not wear a uniform).

plain sailing *nu* (*fig inf*) progress without difficulty: *Once we have got the money, it will be plain sailing.*

ˌ**plain-ˈspoken** *adj* speaking one's thoughts openly and honestly, not hiding them out of kindness, tact *etc*: *a plain-spoken man; He is too plain-spoken to be popular.*

plaintiff [ˈpleintif] *nc* (*legal*) except in Scots law, a person who starts a legal case against another: *Who is the plaintiff in this case?*

See also **defendant.**

plaintive [ˈpleintiv] *adj* (*formal*) sounding sad or sorrowful: *a plaintive tune/cry; The sound of the bagpipes is rather plaintive.* ˈ**plaintively** *adv.* ˈ**plaintiveness** *nu.*

plait [plat] *nc* **1** a length of hair arranged by folding three (or more) separate bunches of hair together: *She wore her hair in plaits.* **2** a similar arrangement of any material: *a plait of straw.* – *vt* to arrange in this way: *She plaited three strips of leather to make a belt; She plaited her daughter's hair.*

plan [plan] *nc* **1** an idea (of how to do something); a method (of doing something): *If everyone follows the plan, we will succeed; Just stick/keep to the plan; I have worked out a plan for making a lot of money; The government published a five-year plan for economic growth; Our usual plan is to work for a few hours then stop for lunch.* **2** an intention or arrangement (of or for doing something): *My plan is to rob a bank and leave the country quickly; Have you made any plans for your holiday?* (= Is there anything you have decided to do?). **3** (*sometimes in cmpds*) a drawing, diagram *etc* showing a building (sometimes not yet built), town *etc* as if seen from above: *These are the plans of/for our new house; a street-plan.* – *v* – *pt, ptp* **planned** – **1** *vti* (*sometimes with* **on**) to intend (to do something): *We are planning on going to Italy this year; We were planning to go last year but we hadn't enough money; They are planning a trip to Italy.* **2** *vti* to decide how something is to be done; to arrange (something): *We are planning a party; We'll have to plan very carefully if we are to succeed; More people came than we had planned for* (= allowed for when making plans). **3** *vt* to design (a building, town *etc*): *This is the architect who planned the building.*

ˈ**planner** *nc* (*sometimes in cmpds*) a person who plans (*esp def 3*): *a town-planner.*

ˈ**planning** *nu* (*often in cmpds*) the act of planning: *town-planning;* (*attrib*) *You will have to get planning permission* (= official permission from a local authority *etc*) *to build houses there.*

go according to plan to happen as arranged or intended: *The journey went according to plan.*

plan ahead *vi* to plan (something) a (fairly) long time before it will happen *etc*: *If you want to be successful in publishing, you have to plan ahead.*

plane[1] [plein] *nc* **1** (*less formal than* **aeroplane**) an aeroplane. **2** a level or standard: *Man is on a higher plane* (*of development*) *than the apes.* **3** (*geom*) a level surface. – *vi* to move smoothly over the surface (of water *etc*).

plane figure *nc* (*geom*) a flat, two-dimensional figure.

plane[2] [plein] *nc* a carpenter's tool for making a level or smooth surface. – *vt* **1** (*sometimes with* **down**) to make (a surface) level, smooth or lower by using a plane: *The wood will be fine for a small table once I've planed it; The top of the door keeps rubbing on the door-frame – I'll have to plane it down.* **2** to remove (something) with a plane: *I'll plane away the rough bits on this wood.*

plane[3] [plein] *nc* (*also* ˈ**plane tree**) a type of tree with broad leaves.

planet [ˈplanit] *nc* any of the bodies (*eg* the Earth) which move round the Sun or round another star: *Mars and Jupiter are planets, but the Moon is not.*

ˌ**planeˈtarium** [-ˈteəriəm] – *pls* ˌ**planeˈtariums,** ˌ**planeˈtaria** [-riə] – *nc* (a building with) an apparatus which shows the positions and movements of the planets and stars by shining points of light on the dark surface of a domed ceiling representing the sky.

ˈ**planetary** *adj* (*esp attrib*) of the planets: *Astrology is nonsense – I don't believe that there is any planetary influence on a person's life.*

plank [plaŋk] *nc* a long, flat piece of wood: *The floor was made of planks.* – *vt* (*usu with* **with**) to cover or make with planks: *The floor was planked with oak.*

plankton [ˈplaŋktən] *nu* (*tech*) very tiny living creatures floating in seas, lakes *etc*: *Fish feed on plankton.*

planner *see* **plan.**

plant [plaːnt] **1** *nc* anything growing from the ground, having a stem, a root and leaves: *flowering/tropical plants.* **2** *nu* industrial machinery: *engineering plant.* **3** *nc* a factory: *The firm has three plants in Britain.* – **1** *vti* to put (something) into the ground so that it will grow: *We have planted vegetables in the garden; I'll plant a row of turnips.* **2** *vt* (*usu in passive with* **with**) to make (a garden *etc*); to cause (a garden *etc*) to have (plants *etc*) growing in it: *The garden was planted with all sorts of beautiful shrubs; We're going to plant an orchard in that field.* **3** *vt* (*fig*) to put (something) into (a person's mind): *She planted in his mind the idea of going to Paris; He planted doubts in her mind about her son's honesty.* **4** *vt* to place heavily or firmly: *She planted the child* (*down*) *in front of him; He planted himself between her and the door.* **5** *vt* (*sl*) to put (something *usu* illegal or related to a crime) in someone's possession, *esp* as false evidence: *He claimed that the police had planted the weapon on his brother.*

planˈtation [plan-] *nc* **1** a place that has been planted *esp* with trees: *a fir plantation.* **2** a piece of land or estate for growing certain crops, *esp* cotton, sugar, rubber, tea and tobacco: *He owned a rubber plantation in Malaysia.*

ˈ**planter** *nc* (*often in cmpds*) the owner of a plantation (*def 2*): *a tea-planter.*

plantation, planter *see* **plant.**

plaque [pla:k] **1** *nc* a plate of metal, china *etc*, *usu* fixed to a wall, statue *etc* as an ornament or memorial: *His name was inscribed on a brass plaque.* **2** *nu* (*tech*) a deposit of saliva and bacteria which forms on the teeth.

plasma ['plazmə] *nu* (*tech*) the liquid part of blood and certain other fluids produced by the body.

plaster ['pla:stə] **1** *nu, adj* (of) a substance put on walls, ceilings *etc* which dries to form a hard smooth surface: *He mixed up some plaster to repair the wall*; *The ceiling is plaster*; *a plaster wall.* **2** *nu, adj* (*also* **plaster of Paris**) (of) a similar quick-drying substance used for supporting broken limbs, making models *etc*: *She's got her arm in plaster*; *a plaster model.* **3** *ncu* (*also* **'sticking-plaster**) (a piece of) sticky tape (sometimes with a dressing) used to cover a wound *etc*: *You should put a plaster on that cut*; *Have you got any sticking-plaster?* – *vt* **1** to put plaster on: *They plastered the walls.* **2** (*sometimes inf*) to put (a liquid or semi-liquid substance) on (something) thickly: *He plastered hair cream on his hair.* **3** (*sometimes inf*: *usu with* **with**) to cover (something) with a large amount or thick layer of (something): *He plastered his hair with cream.*

'plastered *adj* (*sl*: *usu pred*) drunk: *He got plastered at the party*; *He came home absolutely plastered last night.*

'plasterer *nc* a person whose job is to put plaster on walls, ceilings *etc.*

plaster cast *nc* **1** a model or copy of something made by pouring plaster of Paris into a mould: *a plaster cast of Michelangelo's statue of David.* **2** a covering of gauze and plaster of Paris to support a broken limb: *He had a plaster cast on his leg.*

plastic ['plastik] **1** *nu, adj* (of) any of many chemically manufactured substances which can be moulded when soft, which can often be bent and which do not break easily: *This cup is* (*made of*) *plastic*; *a plastic cup.* **2** *adj* (*esp attrib*: *formal*) easily made into different shapes: *Clay is a plastic substance.* **pla'sticity** [-'stisəti] *nu* (*formal*).

plastic surgery *nu* surgery to repair or replace damaged skin, or to improve the appearance *usu* of the face: *He was so badly burned that he had to have plastic surgery*; *She has had plastic surgery on her nose.* **plastic surgeon** *nc.*

Plasticine ® ['plastisi:n] *nu, adj* (*often no cap*) (of) a coloured substance like clay used for modelling *esp* by children: *Give them some Plasticine to play with*; *a plasticine horse*; *The horse was* (*made of*) *plasticine.*

plate [pleit] **1** *nc* a shallow dish for holding food *etc*: *We ate off china plates*; *The little boy put his penny in the offering plate when it was passed round the church.* **2** *nc* a plateful: *a plate of soup.* **3** *nc* a flat piece *usu* of metal: *The ship was built of steel plates.* **4** *nu* (*esp Brit*) articles made of, or plated with, *usu* gold or silver: *The thieves stole some valuable gold plate.* **5** *nc* a flat piece of metal with words, a design *etc* engraved on it, used in printing: **6** *nc* an illustration in a book, *usu* on glossy paper: *The book has ten full-colour plates.* **7** *nc* (*also* **dental plate**) a piece of plastic that fits in the mouth with false teeth attached to it; dentures. **8** *nc* a sheet of glass *etc* coated with a sensitive film, used in photography.

'plated *adj* **1** (*usu in cmpds*) covered with a thin layer of a different metal: *plated with silver*; *gold-plated dishes.* **2** made of, or covered with, metal plates: *A ship usually has a plated hull.*

'plateful *nc* the complete contents of a plate (*def 1*): *a huge plateful of potatoes.*

'plating *nu* (*often in cmpds*) a thin covering of metal: *The silver-plating is beginning to wear off this old teapot.*

plate glass *nu* a kind of glass made in thick sheets for windows, mirrors *etc*: *The shop front was made of plate glass*; (*attrib*) *a plate-glass window.*

on one's 'plate waiting to be dealt with; occupying one's time: *I'd like to help you but I've got too much on my plate at the moment.*

plateau ['platou, (*Amer*) pla'tou] – *pls* **'plateaus, 'plateaux** [-z] – *nc* **1** an area of high flat land; a mountain with a wide, flat top. **2** (*fig formal*) a steady, unchanging state or condition: *Prices have now reached a plateau.*

platform ['platfo:m] *nc* **1** a raised part of a floor *eg* in a hall (*def 2*), for (important) speakers, entertainers *etc*; the people who sit on this at a meeting: *The orchestra arranged themselves on the platform*; *The Prime Minister addressed the conference from the platform*; *He was on the platform at the political meeting*; (*attrib*) *the platform party.* **2** the raised area between or beside the lines in a railway station: *They waited on the platform for their train to arrive*; *The London train will leave from platform six.* **3** the policy, plans *etc* of a political party or candidate: *He is standing for election on a platform of economic reform.* **4** (*Brit*) the open area at the back of a bus on to which passengers step as they get on the bus.

plating *see* **plate**.

platinum ['platinəm] *nu, adj* (of) an element (symbol **Pt**), a heavy, valuable grey metal, often used in making jewellery: *The brooch is* (*made of*) *platinum*; *a platinum ring.*

platitude ['platitju:d] *nc* (*formal*: *derog*) a statement of something which is obvious or trivial or which has been said (many times) before but which is made as if it were new and important: *He made a very dull speech, full of platitudes.*

,plati'tudinous [-dinəs] *adj* (*very formal*): *platitudinous remarks*; *His speeches are so platitudinous.*

platonic [plə'tonik] *adj* (of a relationship between a man and a woman) without sexual love: *Ours is just a platonic friendship*; *They say that their relationship is platonic.* **pla'tonically** *adv.*

platoon [plə'tu:n] *nc* a section of a company of soldiers.

platter ['platə] *nc* (*Amer or arch*) a kind of large, flat plate: *a wooden platter.*

plaudit ['plo:dit] *nc* (*formal*: *usu in pl*) a sign of applause, praise *etc*: *She gracefully accepted their plaudits.*

plausible ['plo:zəbl] *adj* **1** seeming to be reasonable or true: *a plausible explanation*; *His story seemed plausible enough.* **2** (*usu derog*) (of people) seeming to be honest and truthful, while probably not being so; very good at producing plausible but *usu* dishonest explanations: *He's a very plausible fellow*; *He's just a bit too plausible.* **'plausibly** *adv.* **,plausi'bility** *ncu.*

See also **implausible**.

play [plei] **1** *vi* to amuse oneself: *The child is playing in the garden*; *He is playing with his car*; *The little girl wants to play with her friends.* **2** *vti* to take part in (games or amusements): *He plays football*; *He is playing in goal*; *Here's a pack of cards – who wants to play* (*with me*)*?*; *I'm playing golf with him this evening.* **3** *vti* to act (the part of someone or something in a theatre *etc*): *She's playing Lady Macbeth*; *He is playing to large audiences in London this week.* **4** *vti* (*formal*: *with* **is/was** *etc and* **-ing**) (of a play *etc*) to perform or be performed: *'Macbeth' is playing at the local theatre.* **5** *vti* to (be able to) perform (on a musical instrument): *She plays the piano*; *Who was playing the piano this morning?*; *He plays in an orchestra.* **6** *vt* (*usu with* **on**) to carry out or do (a trick): *He played a (nasty) trick on me.* **7** *vt* (*usu with* **at**) to compete against (someone) in a game *etc*: *I'll play you at tennis.* **8** *vti* (*formal or liter*) (of light) to move, direct or be directed in a flickering movement: *The firelight played across the ceiling.* **9** *vti* to direct or be directed over or towards (something): *The firemen played their hoses on/over the burning house.* **10** *vi* (*with* **with**) to play (*def 1*) with the food in one's plate, *eg* with one's fork (*eg* because one is not hungry): *She was just playing with her food.* **11** *vt* to put down or produce (a playing-card) as part of a card game: *He played the seven of hearts.* – *See also* **play** *in phrases below.* – **1** *nu* recreation; amusement: *A person must have time for both work and play.* **2** *nc* an acted story; a drama: *Shakespeare wrote many great plays.* **3** *nu* the playing of a game: *At the start of today's play, England was beating India by fifteen runs.* **4** *nu* freedom of movement: *There is a certain amount of play in the steering-wheel*; (*fig formal*) *She gave full play to her emotions.* **'player** *nc.*

'playable *adj* (*usu pred*: *neg* **un-**) **1** (of a sport, ground, pitch *etc*) not good enough for a game to be played on it: *Due to the rain, the referee decided the ground was not playable.* **2** (of a ball *eg* in golf) not able to be hit.

'playful *adj* **1** happy; full of the desire to play: *a playful kitten*; *The puppy is very playful.* **2** (*usu attrib*) joking; not serious: *a playful remark.* **'playfully** *adv.* **'playfulness** *nu.*

play-back *see* **play back** *below.*

'playboy *nc* (*often derog*) a rich man who spends most of his time and money on pleasure: *We live in a society of playboys and pleasure-seekers.*

playfellow *see* **playmate** *below.*

'playground *nc* an area in which children can play in a park, outside a school *etc.*

'playgroup *nc* an organized group of children of *usu* less than five years old who play together, looked after by adults: *The little girl is not old enough to go to school but she goes to a playgroup.*

'playing-card *nc* one of a pack of cards used in card games.

'playing-field *nc* (*often in pl*) a field which is specially prepared and used for sport: *Rugby coaching will take place after school at the playing-fields.*

'playmate (*formal*) *nc* (of children) a friend.

play-off *see* **play off**.

'playpen *nc* a small enclosure in which a very young child can play safely: *The baby was sitting happily in his playpen.*

'playschool *nc* a nursery school or playgroup.

'plaything *nc* (*formal*) a toy: *The child has too many playthings*; (*liter fig*) *She thought that he was in love with her but to him she was just a plaything.*

'playtime *nu* a set time for children to play (at school *etc*): *The children go outside at playtime.*

'playwright *nc* (*formal*) a person who writes plays: *He is a famous playwright.*

at 'play playing: *the happy sound of children at play.*

bring/come into play (*formal*) to (cause to) be used or exercised: *He brought the full range of his intellectual powers into play to solve the many problems he was faced with.*

'child's play (*inf*) something that is very easy: *Of course you can do it – it's child's play!*

fair play, foul play *see* **fair, foul**.

in 'play, out of 'play (of a ball) according to the rules of the game, (not) in a position where it can be hit, kicked *etc*: *The football rolled towards the edge of the pitch, but he managed to keep it in play*; *The ball is/went out of play.*

'play at *vt fus* **1** to pretend to do or be something; to do something in a not serious way: *The children were playing at cowboys and Indians*; *He only plays at being a poet – he never actually writes any poetry.* **2** (*inf*: used *esp* when questioning angrily why someone is doing something) to do: *What does he think he's playing at? Why doesn't he do what he is told to do?*

play a waiting game *see* **wait**.

play back *vt sep* to play music, speech *etc* on a record or tape after it has just been recorded: *They recorded the song and then played it back to the singer* (*nc* **'play-back**).

play ball with *see* **ball**.

play one's cards badly, right, well (*inf*) to act stupidly, correctly or cleverly: *If you play your cards right, you could become manager.*

play down *vt sep* to try to make (something) appear less important: *He played down the fact that he had failed the exam.*

play fair to act honestly and in an unbiased way; not to cheat: *You're not playing fair! You've taken all the chocolate biscuits and left me the plain ones.* – *See also* **fair play** *under* **fair**.

play fast and loose with (*inf*) to do what one likes with; to act irresponsibly with: *He played fast and loose with his father's money.*

play for time to delay an action, decision *etc* in the hope or belief that conditions will be better at a later time: *Play for time – tell them we need more information from them before we can make a decision.*

play havoc with to cause a lot of damage to: *The storm played havoc with the farmer's crops*; (*fig*) *The rain played havoc with our holiday arrangements.*

play into someone's hands to do exactly what an opponent or enemy wants one to do: *By accepting the money he has played right into my hands.*

play it by ear (*inf*) to do what a situation requires as and when it is required, without making a fixed plan beforehand: *I don't know how he is going to react at the meeting so we had better just play it by ear.*

play off *vi* (in games) to play a final deciding game after a draw: *The score was 2–2, so they will play off next Saturday* (*nc* **'play-off**).

play (someone) off against (someone) to set one person against another in order to gain an advantage: *He played them off one against the other*; *He played his father off against his mother to get more pocket money.*

play on/(*formal*) **upon someone's feelings, fears** to make use of someone's feelings, fears *etc*: *He played on my sympathy until I lent him £10.*

a play on/(*formal*) **upon words** a joke, clever

saying *etc* based on similarities, associations *etc* between words: *'They went and told the sexton and the sexton tolled the bell' is a play on words.*

play a, no part in (not) to be one of the people who are doing (something): *He played no part in the robbery itself.*

play safe to take no risks: *He probably won't object, but we had better play safe and ask his permission first.*

play second fiddle to (*inf*) to be less important than: *His wife plays second fiddle to his work.*

play the fool *see* **fool**.

play the game (*inf*) to act fairly and honestly: *Reading other people's letters is not playing the game.*

play to the gallery *see* **gallery**.

play up *vi* **1** (*inf*) to be troublesome or disobedient: *The children are playing up today.* **2** (*with* **to**) to flatter or pretend to admire someone for one's own advantage: *He is always playing up to the manager.*

play with fire *see* **fire**.

plea [pliː] *nc* **1** (*legal*) a prisoner's answer to a charge: *He made a plea of (not) guilty.* **2** (*formal*) an urgent request: *The hospital sent out a plea for blood-donors.* **3** (*formal*) an excuse: *He stayed away from work on the plea of illness.*

plead [pliːd] – *pts, ptps* **'pleaded**, (*Amer also*) **pled** – **1** *vt* (*legal*) (of a prisoner) to answer a charge, saying whether one is guilty or not: *'How does the prisoner plead?' 'He pleads guilty.'* **2** *vti* (*legal*) to present a case in court: *My solicitor will plead my case; My solicitor will plead for me.* **3** *vi* (*often with* **with**) to make an urgent request: *He pleaded with me not to go; He pleaded to be allowed to go.* **4** *vt* (*formal*) to give as an excuse: *She pleaded poverty.*

'pleading *adj* asking; begging: *The dog gave me a pleading look.* **'pleadingly** *adv.*

pleasant ['pleznt] *adj* giving pleasure; agreeable: *a pleasant day/person; He seems very pleasant.* **'pleasantly** *adv.*

'pleasantness *nu.*

'pleasantry *ncu* (*formal*) a good-natured joke or jokes: *a conversation full of pleasantry/pleasantries.*

See also **unpleasant**.

please [pliːz] **1** *vt* (not *usu* used with **is, was** *etc* and **-ing**: *formal with* **it** *as subject*) to do what is wanted by (a person); to give pleasure or satisfaction to: *You can't please everyone all the time; It pleases me to read poetry.* **2** *vi* (not used with **is, was** *etc* and **-ing**) to choose (to do something): *He does as he pleases.* – *adv* a word added to an order or request in order to be polite: *Please open the window; Close the door, please; Will you please come with me?*

pleased *adj* (*usu with* **about** (a fact), **with** (a thing)) happy; satisfied: *Are you pleased about your new job?; She was pleased with the dress; He gave a pleased smile.*

'pleasing *adj* (*old or formal*) giving pleasure; attractive: *a pleasing view; It is pleasing to think that they are happy.* **'pleasingly** *adv.*

if you 'please (*old or formal*) please: *Come this way, if you please.*

please yourself (*inf*) do what you choose: *I don't think you should go, but please yourself.*

See also **displease**.

pleasure ['pleʒə] *ncu* something that gives one enjoyment; joy or delight: *the pleasures of country life; I get a lot of pleasure from listening to music; It gives him great pleasure to see the children enjoying themselves.* – *See also* **take pleasure in** *below.*

'pleasurable (*old or liter*) *adj* giving pleasure; agreeable: *a pleasurable pastime.* **'pleasurably** *adv.*

'pleasure-boat/'pleasure-craft *ncs* a boat used for pleasure: *On a fine day the harbour is full of pleasure-boats.*

have had the pleasure (of meeting) (*formal or facet*) to have been introduced to: *'Have you met Mrs Jones?' 'No, I have not had the pleasure.'; I had the pleasure of meeting your daughter yesterday.*

take pleasure in to get enjoyment from doing (something): *He takes great pleasure in annoying me; She takes pleasure in reading aloud to her children.*

pleat [pliːt] *nc* a fold sewn or pressed into cloth *etc*: *a skirt with pleats.* – *vt* to make pleats in: *She pleated the material.*

'pleated *adj* (*usu attrib*): *a pleated skirt.*

plebeian [plə'biːən] *nc, adj* **1** (*formal derog*) (a person) having ordinary or vulgar characteristics, tastes *etc*: *He has such plebeian ideas; His taste in music is so plebeian.* **2** (*hist*) *esp* in ancient Rome, (a person who is) not aristocratic: *In ancient Rome, society was divided into the patricians and the plebeians.*

plebiscite ['plebisait] *nc* (*formal*) a vote of all the people in a country, state *etc* on a particular matter: *The government should hold a plebiscite on that issue.*

plectrum ['plektrəm] *nc* (*tech*) a small piece of plastic, metal *etc* used for plucking the strings of a guitar.

pled *see* **plead**.

pledge [pledʒ] *nc* **1** (*formal or liter*) a promise: *He gave me his pledge.* **2** (*formal*) something given by a person who is borrowing money *etc* to the person he has borrowed it from, to be kept until the money *etc* is returned: *He borrowed £10 and left his watch as a pledge.* **3** (*formal*) a sign or token: *They exchanged rings as a pledge of their love.* – *vt* (*formal*) **1** to promise: *He pledged his support; He pledged himself to help.* **2** to give to someone when borrowing money *etc*; to pawn: *He pledged his house to the finance company.*

plenary ['pliːnəri] *adj* (*very formal*: *usu attrib*) **1** full; complete: *The court has plenary powers.* **2** attended by everyone who should be present: *a plenary session of the congress.*

plenty ['plenti] *pron, adj* (*attrib*) **1** a sufficient amount; enough: *I don't need any more books – I've got plenty; We've got plenty of time to get there; I have plenty things to do today without you creating more work for me.* **2** a large amount (of); a lot (of): *He's got plenty of money.*

'plenteous [-tiəs] *adj* (*old or liter*) plentiful.

'plentiful *adj* existing in large amounts: *Fruit is plentiful at this time of year; a plentiful supply.*

plethora ['pleθərə] *nc* (*formal or facet*: *no pl*) too large a quantity (of anything): *a plethora of policemen.*

pleurisy ['pluərəsi] *nu* (*med*) a serious illness in which the covering of the lungs becomes inflamed: *He is suffering from pleurisy.*

plexus *see* **solar plexus**.

pliable ['plaiəbl] *adj* **1** (*formal or tech*) easily bent: *pliable wire/metal; This material is very pliable;* (*fig*) *She is very pliable* (= easily persuaded); (*fig*) *a pliable mind/person.* **plia'bility** *nu.*

'pliant *adj* pliable. **'pliancy** *nu.*

pliers ['plaiəz] *n pl* a kind of tool used for gripping, bending or cutting wire *etc*: *He used a pair of pliers to pull the nail out*; *Where are my pliers?*

plight[2] [plait] *nc* (*no pl*) a (bad) situation or state: *She was in a sorry plight, as she had lost all her money.*

plimsoll ['plimsəl] *nc* a light, inexpensive, *usu* rubber-soled shoe for sports *etc*: *a pair of plimsolls.*

plinth [plinθ] *nc* in architecture, the (*usu* square) base for a column, statue *etc*: *The statue stood on a marble plinth.*

plod [plod] – *pt, ptp* '**plodded** – **1** *vti* (*often with* **along, down** *etc*) to walk heavily and slowly (along *etc*), (as if) with great effort: *He plodded down the street*; *The policeman plods his beat every day.* **2** *vi* (*fig*) to work slowly but *usu* thoroughly: *She found the work very difficult, but plodded on with it.*

'**plodder** *nc* (*often derog*) a person who works slowly but *usu* thoroughly.

plonk[1] [ploŋk] *nc* (something similar to) the fairly deep sound, *eg* of something dropping into water: *The stone fell into the stream with a plonk.* – *vt* (*inf*: *usu with* **down**) **1** to drop something with this sound; *He plonked his books on the table.* **2** to put something down suddenly: *She plonked herself down in front of the fire.*

plonk[2] [ploŋk] *nu* (*inf*) (*esp* cheap) wine: *Bring a bottle of plonk to the party.*

plop [plop] *nc* (*inf*) (something similar to) the sound of a small object, *esp* a drop of liquid, falling into water *etc*: *The raindrop fell into her teacup with a plop.* – *v* – *pt, ptp* **plopped** – *vi* to fall with this sound: *A stone plopped into the pool.*

plot [plot] *nc* **1** a plan, *esp* for doing something evil; a conspiracy: *There's a plot to assassinate the President.* **2** the story of a play, novel *etc*: *The play has a very complicated plot.* **3** a small piece (of land), *usu* marked off for a special use, *eg* as a gardening area or for building a house on: *We have bought a plot of land to build a house on*; *a housing plot*; *a plot of land*; *a vegetable plot.* – *v* – *pt, ptp* '**plotted** – **1** *vti* to plan to bring about (something evil): *They were plotting the death of the king.* **2** *vt* to make a plan, map, graph *etc* of: *The navigator plotted the course of the ship.*

plough, (*Amer*) **plow** [plau] *nc* a type of farm tool pulled through the top layer of the soil to turn it over: *Ploughs are usually pulled by tractors, not horses, nowadays.* – **1** *vti* to turn over (the earth) with such a tool: *The farmer was ploughing (in) a field.* **2** *vi* (*with* **through**) to travel with difficulty, force a way *etc*: *The ship ploughed through the rough sea*; (*fig derog*) *I've been ploughing through a very dull book.* **3** *vi* (*with* **into**) to crash violently: *A car has ploughed into the side of a stationary lorry in the High Street.*

plough back *vt sep* to put (money, profits *etc*) back (into a business *etc*): *He made a profit last year, but ploughed it back so that he could buy more machinery.*

See also **snow-plough** *under* **snow**.

ploy [ploi] *nc* a method of doing something (often cunningly) in order to obtain a particular result: *She found that threats brought no result, and so decided to use a persuasive ploy*; *The children are off on some ploy of their own.*

pluck [plʌk] *vt* **1** (*more formal or liter than* **pull**) to pull: *She plucked a grey hair from her head*; *She plucked out her grey hairs*; *He plucked at my sleeve*; (*liter*) *He was plucked from the jaws of death.* **2** to pull the feathers off (a chicken *etc*) before cooking it: *Get the butcher to pluck the turkey.* **3** (*liter*) to pick (flowers *etc*): *She plucked a rose from the bush.* **4** to pull hairs out of (in order to improve the appearance of): *She always plucks her eyebrows.* **5** to pull and let go (the strings of a musical instrument): *She plucked (the strings of) her harp.* – *nu* (*slightly inf*) courage: *He had/showed a lot of pluck.*

'**plucky** *adj* (*slightly inf*) courageous: *a plucky young fellow*; *It was very plucky of him to dive in to save the drowning girl.* '**pluckily** *adv.* '**pluckiness** *nu.*

pluck up (the) courage, energy *etc* to gather up one's courage *etc* (to do something): *She plucked up (the) courage to ask a question.*

plug [plʌg] *nc* **1** a device fitted into a mains socket in order to allow an electric current to flow through the appliance to which it is attached by cable; *She changed the plug on the electric kettle.* **2** something which can be fitted into the hole in a bath or sink to prevent the water from running away; *Don't take the plug out – I haven't had my bath yet.* **3** (*inf*) an advertisement, *esp* on a radio or television programme: *He gave their new record a free plug on his programme.* **4** a small piece of tobacco, cut for chewing. – *v* – *pt, ptp* **plugged** – *vt* **1** (*neg* **un-**) to block (a hole) by putting a plug in it: *He plugged the hole in the window with a piece of newspaper.* **2** (*inf*) to advertise (on radio, television *etc*): *They are plugging a new type of car.*

plug away *vi* (*inf*: *often with* **at**) to work very hard (at): *He is plugging away (at his studies) every evening.*

plug in *vi, vt sep* to connect up (an electrical apparatus) by inserting its mains plug into a socket: *Could you plug in the electric kettle, please?*

plum [plʌm] **1** *nc* a type of fruit, *usu* dark-red or purple, with a stone in the centre: *She bought a kilo of plums*; (*attrib*) *a plum tree*; (*attrib*) *plum jam.* **2** *nu, adj* (*usu* '**plum-coloured**) (of) the purple or dark red colour of this fruit: *a plum-coloured dress.* – *adj* (*inf*: *attrib*) very good or highly desirable: *a plum job in advertising.*

'**plummy** *adj* (*derog*) (of a person's voice) snobbish or upper-class: *The children laugh at their teacher's plummy voice*; *Her voice is rather plummy.*

plum cake/pudding *ncus* (a) cake or pudding containing raisins, currants *etc*: *Plum pudding is eaten at Christmas time.*

plumage ['plu:midʒ] *ncu* the feathers of a bird or birds; *The peacock has (a) brilliant plumage.* *See also* **plume**.

plumb [plʌm] *vt* (*formal fig*) to go to (the deepest part of): *She had plumbed the depths of misery.*

'**plumbline** *nc* a string with a lead weight hanging on it, used to make sure that a wall *etc* is exactly vertical, or to find out the depth of water *etc.*

plumber ['plʌmə] *nc* **1** a person who fits and mends domestic water, gas and sewage pipes: *Send for a plumber – we have a leaking pipe.* **2** a plumber's workshop: *Where is the nearest plumber?*

'**plumber's** *nc* a plumber's workshop: *I'll just go round to the plumber's and ask them to send someone round to mend the tap.*

'**plumbing** *nu* **1** the system of pipes in a building *etc*: *We shall have to have the plumbing repaired.* **2** the fitting and repairing *etc* of pipes: *He came and did the plumbing before we started to paint the house.*

plumbline *see* **plumb**.

plume [plu:m] *nc* **1** a large decorative feather: *She* *wore a plume in her hat*; *The coat of arms has three ostrich plumes painted on it.* **2** (*liter*) a (*usu* large) column (of smoke *etc*): *A plume of smoke rose from the burning aircraft.*

plumed *adj* (*usu attrib*) having a plume or plumes: *a plumed hat.*

See also **plumage**.

plummet ['plʌmit] – *pt, ptp* '**plummeted** – *vi* (of a heavy weight) to fall or drop swiftly: *The rock plummeted to the bottom of the cliff*; (*fig*) *Prices have plummeted.*

plummy *see* **plum**.

plump[1] [plʌmp] *adj* pleasantly fat and rounded; well filled out: *plump cheeks*; *plump cushions*; *She is small and plump.* **plumply** *adv.* '**plumpness** *nu.*

plump up *vt sep* to shake out (cushions *etc*): *The nurse plumped up his pillows to make him comfortable.*

plump[2] [plʌmp] (*inf*) **1** *vt* (*sometimes with* **down**) to put (down) heavily: *He plumped his books* (*down*) *on the table.* **2** *vi* (*with* **down**) to sit or fall down heavily: *She plumped down on the sofa.* – *nc* (*inf*: *no pl*) the sound made by something heavy falling into water or on to something soft: *He sat down on the cushion with a plump.*

'**plump for** *vt fus* (*inf*) to choose or decide on: *She finally plumped for a house in the country.*

plunder ['plʌndə] *vti* **1** (*formal or liter*) to rob or steal from (a place): *The soldiers plundered and looted* (*the city*). – *nu* (*formal or liter*) the things stolen: *They ran off with their plunder.* '**plunderer** *nc.*

plunge [plʌndʒ] **1** *vi* to throw oneself down (into deep water *etc*); to dive: *He plunged into the river*; (*fig*) *He plunged into the crowd.* **2** *vt* to push (something) violently or suddenly into: *He plunged a knife into the meat*; (*fig*) *He plunged the room into darkness by switching off the lights.* **3** *vi* (of the neckline of a dress *etc*) to become or be made lower: *Necklines have plunged this year.* – *nc* an act of plunging; a dive: *He took a plunge into the pool.*

'**plunger** *nc* an instrument for clearing blocked pipes by suction: *The toilet is blocked – you'll need a plunger.*

take the plunge to (decide to) start doing something new or difficult: *She was hesitant at first, but soon relaxed after she had taken the plunge.*

pluperfect [plu:'pə:fikt] *adj* (*gram*) (of the tense of a verb) indicating an action which took place before another action in the past which is also referred to, expressed in English by the use of **had** and a past participle: *In the sentence 'He had been to England many times before he came to Scotland', the first verb is in the pluperfect tense.* – *ncu* (a verb in) the pluperfect tense: *a verb in the pluperfect*; *'Had been' is a pluperfect.*

plural ['pluərəl] (*gram*) **1** *nc, adj* (in) the form of a word which expresses more than one: *'Mice' is the plural of 'mouse'*; *a plural noun/verb*; *The noun 'mice' is plural.* **2** *nu* the state of being plural: *Is the verb in the singular or the plural?*

plus [plʌs] *prep* (*math*) used to show addition: *Two plus three equals five* (2+3 = 5). – *nc* **1** (*math*: *also* '**plus sign**) a sign (+) used to show addition or positive quality. **2** (*inf*) something extra which is good; an advantage *etc*: *The fact that you already speak Chinese is a definite plus.* – *adj* (*attrib*) positive or more than zero: *a plus number/quantity*; *The temperature was plus fifteen degrees.* – *adv* (*inf*) and a bit more: *He earns £3000 plus.*

ˌ**plus-'fours** *n pl* baggy trousers reaching to just below the knee, worn *esp* by golfers: *He wears plus-fours*; *He bought a pair of plus-fours.*

See also **minus**.

plush [plʌʃ] *adj* (*attrib*) luxurious: *a plush way of life.*

Pluto *see* Appendix 6.

plutonium [plu:'touniəm] *nu* a radioactive element (symbol **Pu**) used in many nuclear processes.

ply[1] [plai] **1** *vt* (*old or facet*) to work at: *He plies his trade in the village.* **2** *vt* (*old or facet*) to use vigorously: *to ply a needle.* **3** *vt* (*formal*) to keep supplying: *They plied their guests with drink*; (*fig*) *He was plying her with questions.* **4** *vi* (*formal*) (of ships, buses *etc*) to make regular journeys: *The ship plies between England and America.*

ply[2] [plai] (*in cmpds*) having (a certain number of) layers or strands: *three-ply/two-ply wool.*

'**plywood** *nu, adj* (of) a type of material made up of thin layers of wood glued together: *The furniture is* (*made of*) *plywood*; *a plywood box.*

pneumatic [nju'matik] *adj* (*tech*: *esp attrib*) **1** filled with air: *pneumatic tyres.* **2** worked by air: *a pneumatic pump/drill.* **pneu'matically** *adv.*

pneumonia [nju'mouniə] *nu* an illness in which the lungs become inflamed: *You'll catch pneumonia if you stand out in the pouring rain without a hat on*; *We thought that she just had a bad cold but it developed into pneumonia.*

poach[1] [poutʃ] *vt* to cook (*eg* an egg without its shell, a fish *etc*) in boiling liquid, *esp* water or milk: *Would you poach my egg, please – I don't like boiled eggs.*

poached *adj*: *a poached egg.*

poach[2] [poutʃ] *vti* to hunt (game) or catch (fish) illegally on someone else's land: *The farmer caught a man poaching* (*pheasants*) *on his land*; (*derog inf*) *That new firm is trying to poach our best members of staff* (= trying to get them to go and work for them). '**poacher** *nc.*

pocket ['pokit] *nc* **1** a small bag sewn into or on to clothes, for carrying things in: *He stood with his hands in his pockets*; *a coat pocket.* **2** a small bag attached to the corners and sides of a billiard-table *etc* to catch the balls. **3** (*formal or tech*) a small isolated area or group: *a pocket of unemployment/resistance/warm air.* **4** (a person's) income or amount of money available for spending: *a range of prices to suit every pocket*; (*attrib*) *a pocket-handkerchief* (= one for carrying in a clothes pocket); *a pocket-camera*; *a pocket-knife.* – *vt* **1** to put in a pocket (*defs 1, 2*): *He pocketed his wallet*; *He pocketed the red ball.* **2** (*inf*) to steal: *Be careful he doesn't pocket the silver.*

'**pocketful** *nc* the amount contained by a pocket: *a pocketful of ten-pence pieces.*

'**out-of-pocket** *adj* (*attrib*) (of expenses) paid for with one's own money, and owed to one by one's company *etc.* – *See also* **out of pocket** *below.*

'**pocket-book** *nc* a wallet for holding papers or money, carried in the pocket.

'**pocket-money** *nu* money for personal use, *esp* a child's regular allowance: *He has fifty pence a week pocket-money.*

'**pocket-size(d)** *adj* (*usu attrib*) of a size suitable for carrying in a clothes pocket: *a pocket-size*(*d*) *dictionary.*

out of pocket, in pocket having lost/gained money over a business deal *etc*: *His last deal has* *left him out of pocket.* – *See also* **out-of-pocket** *above.*

See also **pickpocket, pick (someone's) pocket** *under* **pick**[1].

pockmark ['pokma:k] *nc* a scar or small dent in the skin caused by smallpox *etc*: *His face was covered with pockmarks.* '**pockmarked** *adj.*

pod [pod] *nc* the long seed-case of the pea, bean *etc.*

podgy ['podʒi], **pudgy** ['pʌdʒi] *adjs* (*inf*) (short and) fat: *A podgy little man came into the shop*; *She has podgy fingers.* '**podginess,** '**pudginess** *nus.*

podiatry [pə'daiətri] *nu* (*Amer*) chiropody.

po'**diatrist** *nc* (*Amer*) a chiropodist.

podium ['poudiəm] *nc* (*formal*) a platform on which a lecturer, musical conductor *etc* stands.

poem ['pouim] *nc* a piece of writing arranged in lines which *usu* have a regular rhythm and often rhyme: *He writes poems.*

poet ['pouit] – *fem* '**poet,** '**poetess** – *nc* a person who writes poems: *John Donne is a famous poet*; *That lady is a well-known poet/poetess.*

poetic [pou'etik] *adj* of, like, or suitable for, a poem: *poetic drama*; *poetic language*; *His language is very poetic.* **po'etically** *adv.*

'**poetry** *nu* **1** poems in general: *He writes poetry.* **2** the art of composing poems: *Poetry comes naturally to some people.* **3** (*formal*) beauty *etc* like that which is found in a poem: *the poetry of motion*; *The dancer's movements were sheer poetry.*

poetic justice *nu* (*formal*) the suitable but accidental punishing of wrong and rewarding of right: *It was poetic justice that the car broke down after he had taken it without permission.*

poetic licence *nu* (*formal*) freedom from the usual order of words, grammar *etc*, as in poetry: *That's not a grammatical mistake – it's poetic licence.*

poet laureate ['loriət] – *pl* **poets laureate** – *nc* (*sometimes with caps*) an official poet attached to the British royal household.

poignant ['poinjənt] *adj* (*usu attrib*) painful and distressing to the feelings: *a poignant farewell*; *poignant memories.* '**poignantly** *adv.* '**poignancy** *nu.*

point [point] **1** *nc* (*sometimes in cmpds*) the sharp end of anything: *the point of a pin*; *a knife/sword point*; *at gunpoint* (= threatened by a gun). **2** *nc* (*often found with cap in place-names*) a piece of land that projects into the sea *etc*: *The ship came round Lizard Point.* **3** *nc* a small round dot or mark (•): *a decimal point*; *five point three six* (= 5·36); *In punctuation, a point is another name for a full stop.* **4** *nc* an exact place or spot: *When we reached this point on the road we stopped to rest.* **5** *nc* an exact moment: *At this point in the day I usually have a cup of coffee*; *Her husband walked in at that point.* **6** *nc* (*usu in cmpds*) a place on a scale *esp* of temperature: *What is the boiling-point of water?* **7** *nc* a division on a compass *eg* north, south-west *etc*: *They came from all points of the compass* (= from everywhere). **8** *nc* a mark in scoring a competition, game, test *etc*: *He has won by five points to two.* **9** *nc* a particular matter for consideration or action: *The first point we must decide is, where to meet*; *They arranged everything point by point*; *He made* (= stated) *some very good points*; *a five-point plan*; *You have missed the point* (= not understood the central meaning) *of my argument*; *That's the whole point* (= the main consideration); *The point is, (that) we'll be too late anyway*; *The joke was so long that I thought he'd never get to the point*; *We're wandering away from the point* (= We're discussing irrelevant matters). **10** *ncu* (a) purpose or advantage: *What's the point of going to the seaside in winter?*; *There's not much point (in) asking me – I don't know.* **11** *nc* a personal characteristic or quality: *We all have our good points and our bad ones.* **12** *nc* an electrical socket in a wall *etc* into which a plug can be put: *Is there only one electrical point in this room?* – **1** *vt* to aim (something) in a particular direction: *He pointed the gun at her.* **2** *vti* to call attention to something or someone *esp* by stretching the index finger in the direction of the thing *etc*: *He pointed (his finger) at the door*; *He pointed to a sign*; *It's rude to point!* **3** *vt* to fill worn places in brickwork *etc* with mortar: *We are having the walls pointed.* – *See also* **point out** *below.*

'**pointed** *adj* **1** having a sharp end: *a pointed nose*; *pointed shoes*; *His nose is long and pointed.* **2** (of something said) meant for, although not addressed to, a particular person *etc*: *That's a very pointed remark*; *His remark was rather pointed.* '**pointedly** *adv.*

'**pointer** *nc* **1** a long stick used to indicate places on a large map *etc.* **2** an indicator on a dial: *The pointer is on/at zero.* **3** a kind of dog trained to indicate birds, game *etc* by pointing with the nose. **4** (*inf*) a hint; a suggestion: *Give me some pointers on how to do it.*

'**pointless** *adj* having no meaning or purpose: *a pointless speech*; *a pointless journey*; *His remarks were rather pointless.* '**pointlessly** *adv.*

points *n pl* **1** a movable section of rails which allow a train to cross over other lines or pass from one line to another: *The points had to be changed before the train could continue.* **2** the solid tips of a pair of a certain type of ballet shoes: *She can dance on her points.*

'**point duty** *nu* the directing of traffic (by a traffic policeman): *There's a policeman on point duty outside the station.*

be beside the point *see* **beside**.

be on the point of (doing something) to be about to do something: *I was on the point of going out when the telephone rang.*

be ˌto the 'point (*formal*) to be connected with what is being discussed; to be relevant: *Her speech was very much to the point.*

a case in point (*formal*) an example illustrating the matter being discussed: *As we are talking about education, let me tell you of a case in point.*

come to the point **1** (*also* **get to the point**) to reach the most important consideration in a conversation *etc*: *He talked and talked but never came to the point.* **2** (*only with* **it** *as subject*) to arrive at the moment when something must be done: *He always promises to help, but when it comes to the point he's never there.*

in point of fact actually; in reality: *He says he can ride, but in point of fact he has never been on a horse before.*

make a point of (doing something) to be especially careful to do something: *I'll make a point of asking her today.*

make one's point to state an opinion *etc* so clearly and persuasively that it has been understood and accepted: *You've made your point – we'll do what you suggest.*

the point of no return the stage in a process *etc* after which there is no possibility of stopping or going back.

a point of order (*formal*) a question asked in a

meeting as to whether the business is being done according to the rules: *I would like to raise a point of order.*

point of view *see* **view**.

point out *vt sep* to indicate or draw attention to: *He pointed out his house to her*; *I pointed out* (= drew attention to the fact) *that we needed more money.*

point one's toes to stretch the foot out, shaping the toes into a point, when dancing *etc*: *She pointed her toes daintily.*

point-blank [point'blaŋk] *adj* (*usu attrib*), *adv* (of a shot) (fired) at very close range: *a point-blank shot*; *He fired point-blank at her*; *at point-blank range*; (*fig*) *He asked her point-blank* (= abruptly and without warning) *how old she was.*

poise [poiz] *vt* (*more formal than* **balance**) to balance: *She poised the bundle carefully on her head*; *He poised himself on the diving-board.* – *nu* **1** balance and control in bodily movement; gracefulness: *Good poise is important for a dancer.* **2** dignity and self-confidence: *She showed great poise at the interview*; *He lost his poise for a moment.*

poised *adj* **1** (*pred*) staying in a state of balance and stillness: *The car looked as if it was poised on the edge of the cliff*; *The bird was poised in mid-air over its nest.* **2** having the body in a state of tension and readiness to act: *The animal was poised ready to leap*; *The runners stood poised on the starting line*; (*fig*) *We're all poised* (= ready) *for action.*

poison ['poizn] *ncu* any substance which causes death or illness when taken into the body: *She killed herself by taking poison*; (*attrib*) *poison gas*; (*formal fig*) *Selfishness is a poison that is spreading through society.* – *vt* **1** to kill or harm with poison: *He poisoned his wife.* **2** to put poison into (food *etc*): *He poisoned her coffee.* **3** (*formal fig*) to corrupt (a person's mind *etc*): *He poisoned her mind with evil ideas.* '**poisoner** *nc.*

'**poisoned** *adj* **1** containing or affected by, poison: *a poisoned drink*; *Her drink was poisoned.* **2** (*not a tech term*) (of a part of the body) infected: *a poisoned knee*; *That cut is poisoned.*

'**poisonous** *adj* containing or using poison: *That fruit is poisonous*; *a poisonous snake*; (*formal fig*) *poisonous words.* '**poisonously** *adv.*

ˌ**poison-'pen letter** *nc* an anonymous letter saying wicked things about a certain person *etc.*

poke [pouk] (*slightly inf*) **1** *vt* to push something (*eg* a finger or a stick) into something; to prod: *He poked a stick into the hole*; *He poked her in the ribs with his elbow.* **2** *vt* to make (a hole) by doing this: *She poked a hole in the sand with her finger.* **3** *vti* to (cause to) protrude or project: *She poked her head in at the window*; *His foot was poking out of the blankets.* – *See also* **poke about/around** *below.* – *nc* an act of poking; a prod or nudge: *He gave me a poke in the arm.*

'**poker** *nc* a (*usu* metal) rod for stirring up a fire.

'**poky, pokey** *adjs* (*derog*) (of a room *etc*) small, with not enough space: *He lives in a poky little flat*; *This bedroom is too poky for me.*

poke about/around *vi* (*inf*) to look or search for something among other things: *He was poking about in the attic*; *He poked around for his pen in my desk.*

poke fun at to laugh at unkindly: *The children often poked fun at him because of his stammer.*

poke one's nose into (*inf*: *offensive*) to interfere with other people's business: *He is always poking his nose into my affairs.*

poker[1] ['poukə] *nu* a kind of card game *usu* played for money.

ˌ**poker-'faced** *adj* wearing an expression that does not show any hint of one's feelings: *a poker-faced chess player.*

poker[2], **poky** *see* **poke**.

Poland *see* Appendix 2.

polar, polarity, polarize *see* **pole**[1].

Polaroid ® ['pouləroid] *nu* (*usu attrib*) a transparent substance used in glass to reduce the glare of sunlight: *Polaroid sunglasses.*

Polaroid camera ® *nc* a type of camera that will take, develop and print photographs in a few seconds.

pole[1] [poul] *nc* **1** (*usu with cap*) the north or south end of the Earth's axis: *the North/South Pole.* **2** the points in the heavens opposite the Earth's North and South Poles, around which stars seem to turn. **3** either of the opposite ends of a magnet: *The opposite poles of magnets attract each other.* **4** either of the opposite terminals of an electric battery: *the positive/negative pole.* – *See also* **be poles apart** *below.*

'**polar** *adj* (*usu attrib*) of the earth's North or South Pole or the region around it: *a polar bear* (= a type of bear found near the North Pole); *the polar ice-cap*; *the polar region.*

po'larity [-'la-] *nu* **1** the state of having two opposite poles: *magnetic polarity.* **2** (*fig*) the tendency to develop in two opposite directions: *the polarity of political opinion.*

'**polarize, -ise** *vt* (*formal*) to cause (people, *etc*) to be drawn into two opposing groups: *Political violence tends to increase hostility on both sides, and so polarize public opinion.*

the Pole Star *n* the star nearest to the North Pole (*def 2*).

be poles apart (*inf*) to be as different or as far apart as possible: *They are poles apart in their attitude to education.*

pole[2] [poul] *nc* a long, thin, rounded piece of wood, metal *etc*: *a telegraph pole* (= a pole supporting telegraph wires); *a tent pole.*

'**pole-vault** *ncu* (in athletics *etc*) a type of jump made with the help of a pole: *He's very good at the pole-vault.*

Pole *see* Appendix 2.

polecat ['poulkat] *nc* **1** a kind of large weasel. **2** (*Amer*) a skunk.

police [pə'liːs] *n pl* the men and women whose job is to prevent crime, keep order, see that laws are obeyed *etc*: *Call the police!*; *The police are investigating the matter*; (*attrib*) *the police force* (= the police); (*attrib*) *a police officer* (= a policeman). – *vt* (*formal*) to supply (a place) with police: *We cannot police the whole area.*

po'lice dog *nc* a dog trained to work with policemen (in tracking criminals, finding drugs *etc*).

po'liceman, po'licewoman *ncs* a member of the police.

po'lice station *nc* the office or headquarters of a local police force: *The man was charged with murder at the police station*; *The lost dog was taken to the police station.*

police state *nc* (*derog*) a country or government controlled by secret police who detect and eliminate opposition to the government.

policy[1] ['poləsi] *ncu* a planned or agreed course of action *usu* based on particular principles: *I don't agree with the government's policies on education*;

according to Conservative policy.
See also **politic**.

policy[2] ['poləsi] *nc* a (written) agreement with an insurance company: *He took out* (= arranged) *an insurance policy on his house.*

polio ['pouliou] (short for **poliomyelitis** [poulioumaiə'laitis]) *nu* (*med*) a disease of the spinal cord often causing paralysis: *He had polio as a child and he has had a limp ever since.*

polish ['poliʃ] **1** *vti* to make or become smooth and shiny by rubbing: *She polished her shoes; This table doesn't polish very well.* **2** *vt* (*formal fig*) to improve the style of; to make more refined: *If you polish the article, we will print it in the newspaper; His manners need polishing.* – *See also* **polish off** *below.* – *nu* **1** smoothness and shininess: *There's a wonderful polish on this old wood.* **2** a kind of liquid, or other substance used to make something smooth and shiny: *a tin of furniture polish; silver polish.* **3** (*formal fig*) fine manners, behaviour *etc*; refinement: *a man of charm and polish.* **'polished** *adj* (*neg* **un-**).
polish off *vt sep* (*inf*) to finish: *She polished off the last of the food.*

Polish *see* Appendix 2.

polite [pə'lait] *adj* having or showing good manners; courteous: *a polite child; a polite suggestion; You should teach children to be polite (to adults).* **po'litely** *adv.* **po'liteness** *nu.*
See also **impolite**.

politic ['politik] *adj* (*formal: sometimes facet*) wise: *a politic decision; a politic person; He considered it politic to escape before further trouble developed.*

politics ['politiks] *n sing or pl* the science or business of, or ideas about, or affairs concerning, government: *Politics was one of his university subjects; He wants to make politics his career; What are his politics?* (= his political opinions).
po'litical *adj* of, or concerning, politics: *for political reasons; political aims/studies; His reasons for doing that were purely political.* – *See also* **political asylum, political prisoner** *below.* **po'litically** *adv.*
,poli'tician [-'tiʃən] *nc* a person whose job is politics; a member of parliament: *At the moment he is a lawyer but he wants to become a politician.*
political asylum *nu* protection given by a government to a foreigner who has left his own country for political reasons: *He asked for political asylum.*
political prisoner *nc* a person who has been imprisoned for political reasons and not for any crime.

polka ['polkə, (*Amer*) 'poulkə] *nc* (a piece of music for) a type of quick, lively dance: *They danced the/a polka; The band played a polka.*

poll [poul] *nc* **1** an election: *They organized a poll to elect a president.* **2** the number of votes: *There has been a heavy poll* (= a large number of votes). **3** (*also* **o'pinion poll**) a test of public opinion by asking people questions: *A recent poll shows a change in public opinion.* – *vt* to receive a number of votes: *The Labour candidate polled fifty per cent of the votes.*
'polling-booth *nc* a small place or stall where one can mark one's voting-paper.
'polling-station *nc* a place where one goes to vote: *They are using the local school as a polling-station.*
go to the polls to hold an election: *The British public will go to the polls on October 11.*

pollen ['polən] *nu* the powder inside a flower which fertilizes other flowers: *Bees carry pollen from flower to flower.*
pollinate ['poləneit] *vt* (*formal*) to make (a plant) fertile by carrying pollen to it from another flower: *Insects pollinate the flowers.* **,polli'nation** *nu.*

pollute [pə'lu:t] *vt* to make (something) dirty: *Chemicals are polluting the air; Our water has been polluted by water from that factory;* (*formal fig*) *His mind was polluted by wicked thoughts.*
pol'lution [-ʃən] *nu* the process of polluting or state of being polluted: *We must try to prevent the pollution of our country.*

polo ['poulou] *nu* a game like hockey, played on horseback.
'polo-neck *nc, adj* (*attrib*) (a garment *esp* a sweater) with a high, close-fitting part around the neck: *She wears a polo-neck to keep her throat warm; a polo-neck shirt/jersey.*

poltergeist ['poltəgaist, (*Amer*) 'poul-] *nc* a kind of ghost that moves furniture, throws objects through the air *etc.*

poly- [poli] (*in cmpds*) many or much, as in **polysyllable**.

polygamy [pə'ligəmi] *nu* (*formal*) the state or custom of having more than one wife or husband at the same time: *Few modern societies allow polygamy.* **po'lygamist** *nc.* **po'lygamous** *adj.*

polyglot ['poliglot] *adj* (*formal*) written in, or using, many languages: *a polyglot translation.*

polygon ['poligən, (*Amer*) -gon] *nc* (*geom*) a two-dimensional figure with many angles and sides. **po'lygonal** [-'li-] *adj.*

polysyllable ['polisiləbl] *nc* (*formal*) a word of three or more syllables: *He uses a polysyllable wherever possible.*
,polysyl'labic [-'la-] *adj*: *He always uses polysyllabic words.*

polytechnic [poli'teknik] *nc* a school or college in which technical subjects, *eg* engineering and building, are taught: *He studies at the polytechnic; He has left school and now attends a polytechnic.*

polythene ['poliθi:n] *nu, adj* (of) any of several types of plastic that can be moulded when hot: *It's (made of) polythene; a polythene bag.*

pomegranate ['pomigranət] *nc* a type of fruit with a thick skin and many seeds.

pomp [pomp] *nu* (*formal*) solemn stateliness and magnificence, *eg* at a ceremonial occasion: *The Queen arrived with great pomp and ceremony.*
'pompous *adj* (*derog*) too grand and officious in manner or speech; self-important: *a pompous little man; He is so pompous that everyone dislikes him.* **'pompously** *adv.* **'pompousness, pom'posity** [-'po-] *nus.*
pomp and circumstance great magnificence and solemnity.

pompom ['pompom], **pompon** ['pompon] *ncs* a small ball of cut wool, silk *etc* used as a decoration on clothes, furniture *etc*: *The child wore a hat with a pompom.*

pomposity *see* **pomp**.

poncho ['pontʃou] – *pl* **'ponchos** – *nc orig* a S American garment, made of, or made like, a blanket with a hole for the head: *The girl wore a poncho over her jeans and sweater.*

pond [pond] *nc* a small lake or pool: *a duck pond; The little girl fell into the village pond.*

ponder ['pondə] *vti* (*formal*) to consider carefully: *He pondered the suggestion; He was pondering on* *the difficulty of his task; He pondered for a few minutes and then left.*

'**ponderous** *adj* (*formal*) heavy; awkward: *ponderous movements; His way of walking is very slow and ponderous;* (*fig*) *His style of writing is rather ponderous.* '**ponderously** *adv.* '**ponderousness** *nu.*

See also **imponderable**.

pontiff ['pontif] *nc* (in the Roman Catholic church) a bishop, *esp* the Pope.

pon'tifical *adj* (*formal*) **1** (*attrib*) of or belonging to a pontiff: *pontifical dignity.* **2** (*derog*) appearing to have great authority; pompous: *a pontifical manner/statement; His comments were so pontifical.*

pon'tificate [-keit] *vi* (*formal*: *derog*) to speak in a pompous manner: *He pontificates about everything; He is always pontificating on the vices of modern society.*

pontoon[1] [pon'tu:n] *nc* (*tech*) one of the flat-bottomed boats used to support a temporary roadway (a **pontoon bridge**) across a river *etc.*

pontoon[2] [pon'tu:n] *nu* a kind of card-game: *Let's play pontoon; a game of pontoon.*

pony ['pouni] *nc* a small horse: *The child was riding a brown pony;* (*attrib*) *She belongs to a pony club and goes riding there on Saturdays.*

'**pony-tail** *nc* (a kind of hairstyle with) the hair tied in a bunch at the back of the head.

'**pony-trekking** *nu* the sport or pastime of riding cross-country in small groups: *This summer we are going pony-trekking; After a day's pony-trekking we were all stiff and sore.*

poodle ['pu:dl] *nc* a breed of dog whose curly hair is often clipped in a decorative way.

poof [pu:f] *nc* (*offensive sl*) a male homosexual.

pooh [pu:] *interj* used to show scorn, contempt or disgust.

,**pooh-'pooh** *vt* (*inf*) to treat (an idea *etc*) with scorn: *She pooh-poohed the suggestion.*

pool[1] [pu:l] *nc* **1** (*more formal than* **puddle**) a small area of still water: *The rain left pools in the road.* **2** a similar area of any liquid: *a pool of blood/oil.* **3** a deep part of a stream or river: *He was fishing (in) a pool near the river-bank.* **4** a swimming-pool: *They spent the day at the pool.*

pool[2] [pu:l] *nc* a stock or supply: *We put our money into a general pool; a typing pool* (= a number of typists who do general typing work in an office). – *vt* to put together for general use: *We pooled our money and bought a holiday house which we could all use; We should pool our resources.*

('football) pools *n pl* organized gambling on the results of football matches: *My father does the (football) pools every week.*

pool[3] [pu:l] *nu* a type of game played on a billiard- or pool-table: *They were playing pool;* (*attrib*) *a pool game.*

poor [puə] *adj* **1** having little money or property: *His family is very poor; She is too poor to buy a new coat; the poor nations of the world.* **2** not good; of poor quality: *His work is very poor; rather a poor effort.* **3** (*attrib*) deserving pity: *Poor fellow!* '**poorness** *nu.*

'**poorly** *adv* not well; badly: *a poorly written piece of work.* – *adj* (*old inf or dial*: *usu pred*) not healthy; ill: *He is very poorly.*

the poor poor people: *He gave away a lot of his money to the poor.*

See also **impoverish, poverty**.

pop[1] [pop] (*inf*) **1** *nc* a sharp, quick, explosive noise, such as that made by a cork as it comes out of a bottle: *The paper bag burst with a loud pop.* **2** *nu* fizzy drink: *a bottle of pop.* – *v* – *pt, ptp* **popped** – **1** *vti* to (make something) make a pop: *Champagne corks were popping; He popped the balloon.* **2** *vi* to spring upwards or outwards: *The wooden cuckoo pops out of the clock on a spring; His eyes nearly popped out of his head in amazement.* – *See also* **pop up** *below.* **3** *vi* (*inf*) to go quickly and briefly somewhere: *I popped next door to see my friend; He popped out to buy a newspaper.* **4** *vt* (*inf*) to place or put quickly: *He popped the letter into his pocket.*

'**popcorn** *nu* a kind of maize that bursts open when it is heated, and is eaten either sweetened or salted.

pop the question (*inf often facet*) to propose marriage: *He thought that he would pop the question that evening.*

pop up *vi* (*inf*) to appear: *I never know where he'll pop up next.*

pop[2] [pop] *adj* (*attrib*: short for **popular**) **1** (of music) written, played *etc* in a modern style: *pop music.* **2** of, or related to, pop music: *a pop group; a pop singer; pop records.*

pop[3] [pop] *nc* (*inf*: *with cap when used as a name*) a name for one's father: *I'll have to ask Pop to lend me some money.*

pope [poup] *nc* (*usu with cap*) (the status of) the bishop of Rome, head of the Roman Catholic church: *A new Pope has been elected.*

'**popery** *nu* (*offensive*) Roman Catholicism.

See also **papacy**.

popinjay ['popindʒei] *nc* (*old derog*) a person who is conceited, *esp* about his clothes and appearance.

poplar ['poplə] *nc* (*also* '**poplar tree**) a kind of tall, narrow tree: *The wind has blown down that poplar.*

poplin ['poplin] *nu, adj* (of) a kind of strong cotton cloth: *Her summer coat is (made of) poplin; a poplin dress.*

poppy ['popi] *nc* a type of plant with large, *usu* red, flowers: *poppies growing in a corn field.*

poppycock ['popikok] *nu* (*old*) nonsense: *Don't talk such poppycock!*

populace ['popjuləs] *nu* (*formal*) the people (of a country *etc*): *The government informed the populace of its decisions.*

popular ['popjulə] *adj* **1** liked by most people: *a popular decision; a popular person; She is very popular with children.* **2** (*formal*: *attrib*) believed by most people: *a popular theory.* **3** (*formal*: *attrib*) of the people in general: *the popular vote.* **4** (*attrib*) easily read, understood *etc* by most people: *a popular history of Britain.*

'**popularly** *adv* amongst, or by, most people: *The Duke of Wellington was popularly known as the Iron Duke; A copper bracelet is popularly supposed to cure rheumatism.*

,**popu'larity** [-'la-] *nu* the state of being popular (*def 1*): *His popularity increased with each book he published.*

'**popularize, -ise** *vt* (*formal*) to make popular or widely known: *She did much to popularize the wearing of make-up.*

populate ['popjuleit] *vt* (*usu in passive*) to fill with people: *The poorer parts of the country are thinly populated; That part of the world used to be populated by wandering tribes.*

,**popu'lation** *ncu* the people living in a particular country, area *etc*: *the population of London; the Indian population; a rapid increase in population.*

'**populous** *adj* (*formal*) full of people: *London is the most populous area of Britain*; *Our cities are becoming too populous.*
See also **depopulate**.

porcelain ['po:səlin] *nu, adj* (of) a kind of fine china: *That dish is (made of) porcelain*; *a porcelain figure.*

porch [po:tʃ] *nc* **1** a covered entrance to a building: *They waited in the porch until it stopped raining.* **2** (*Amer*) a veranda.

porcupine ['po:kjupain] *nc* a kind of gnawing animal covered with long prickles (called quills), and larger than a hedgehog.

pore[1] [po:] *nc* (*formal or tech*) a tiny hole, *esp* of a sweat gland in the skin: *Blackheads are caused by blocked pores.*
'**porous** *adj* (*formal or tech*) allowing liquid to pass through: *porous clay*; *Is that substance porous?*

pore[2] [po:]: '**pore over** *vt fus* to study with great attention: *He pored over his books.*

pork [po:k] *nu* the flesh of a pig used as food: *a slice of pork*; *roast pork*; (*attrib*) *a pork sausage.*
pork pie *nc* a *usu* small pie containing minced pork.

pornography [po:'nogrəfi] *nu* (*sl abbrev* **porn** [po:n]) literature, pictures, films *etc* that are indecent in a sexual way: *He makes a great deal of money out of pornography*; *Pornography of all kinds used to be illegal in many countries*; *The kind of porn he sells is more obscene than most*; (*attrib*) *porn shops*; (*attrib*) *porn magazines.*
pornographic [po:nə'grafik] *adj*: *pornographic literature*; *That new magazine is pornographic.*

porous *see* **pore**[1].

porpoise ['po:pəs] *nc* a type of blunt-nosed sea animal of the dolphin family.

porridge ['poridʒ] *nu* a food made from oatmeal boiled in water or milk: *We had porridge for breakfast.*

port[1] [po:t] *nc* **1** (*usu* without an article) a harbour: *The ship came into port*; *We reached port next morning.* **2** a town with a harbour: *the port of Hull.*

port[2] [po:t] *nu* (*naut*) the left side of a ship or aircraft: *The helmsman steered the ship to port*; (*attrib*) *the port wing.*

port[3] [po:t] **1** *ncu* a type of strong, dark-red, sweet kind of wine *orig* from Portugal: *We had port after dinner but they had brandy*; *a small glass of port*; *The wine-shop stocks several different ports.* **2** *nc* a glass of port: *Would you like a sherry or a port?*

portable ['po:təbl] *adj* (*slightly formal*) able to be carried, or moved easily from place to place: *a portable radio*; *Is that machine portable?*

portal ['po:tl] *nc* (*liter*) an entrance or doorway, *usu* large and magnificent: *the portals of the palace.*

portcullis [po:t'kʌlis] *nc* (*hist*) a wooden or iron grating that can be lowered to close a gateway: *the portcullis of the castle.*

portend [po:'tend] *vt* (*liter or facet*) to give warning of; to foretell: *The stars portend great changes in human affairs*; *What does his present behaviour portend?*
portent ['po:tent] (*liter or facet*) **1** *nc* something *usu* strange and remarkable that warns of some future happening: *strange signs and portents.* **2** *nu* significance or warning: *an event of grim portent.*
por'tentous [-təs] *adj* (*liter or facet*: *usu attrib*): *a portentous sign*; *a portentous event*; *a portentous speech.* **por'tentously** *adv.*

porter[1] ['po:tə] *nc* **1** a person whose job is to carry luggage in a railway station *etc*: *The old lady could not find a porter to carry her suitcase from the train.* **2** a person whose job is to carry things *eg* in rough country where there is no other form of transport: *He set off into the jungle with one companion and three porters.* **3** a doorman or attendant in a hotel *etc*: *The hotel porter will show you to your room*; *a hospital porter.*

porter[2] ['po:tə] *nu* (*old*) a kind of strong, dark beer.

portfolio [po:t'fouliou] – *pl* **port'folios** – *nc* **1** a case for carrying papers, drawings *etc*; the contents of such a case: *He carried a leather portfolio*; *The art student showed the tutor his portfolio.* **2** the post or job of a government minister: *a minister without portfolio* (= without responsibility for any particular department of government).

porthole ['po:thoul] *nc* a small, *usu* round, window in a ship: *We had a porthole in our cabin.*

portico ['po:tikou] – *pl* '**portico(e)s** – *nc* in architecture, a row of columns supporting a roof, *usu* forming a porch to a building.

portion ['po:ʃən] *nc* **1** (*formal*) a part: *Read this portion of the book.* **2** (*more formal than* **share**) a share: *Her portion of the money amounted to £100.* **3** (*more formal than* **helping**) an amount of food *usu* for one person: *a portion of salad.*
portion out *vt sep* (*formal*) to divide into portions or shares: *The money was portioned out between the three children.*

portly ['po:tli] *adj* (*formal or liter*) stout and dignified: *a portly gentleman*; *He is red-faced and portly.* '**portliness** *nu.*

portmanteau [po:t'mantou] – *pls* **port'manteaus, port'manteaux** [-z] – *nc* (*esp old*) a large bag or case for one's clothes *etc* when travelling.

portrait ['po:trət] *nc* **1** a drawing, painting, photograph *etc* of a person: *She had her portrait painted by a famous artist.* **2** (*formal or liter*) a written description of a person, place *etc*: *Thomas Hardy's novels are well-known for their portraits of country life.*
'**portraiture** [-tʃə] *nu* (*formal*) the art of making portraits: *the development of photographic portraiture.*

portray [po:'trei] *vt* (*formal*) **1** to make a portrait of (someone or something): *In this painting, the king is portrayed sitting on his throne*; *Dickens portrays the society of his time.* **2** to act the part of: *Hamlet is portrayed in our production by a Russian actor.*
portrayal [po:'treiəl] *ncu*: *I never enjoy the portrayal of wickedness on the stage*; *Chaucer's portrayals of medieval characters.*

Portugal, Portuguese *see* Appendix 2.

pose[1] [pouz] *nc* **1** a position or attitude of the body: *He sat in a relaxed pose*; *The model was asked to adopt various poses for the photographer.* **2** (*derog*) a false manner or way of behaving assumed in order to impress others; a pretence: *His indignation was only a pose.* – *vi* **1** to position oneself *eg* for a photograph to be taken: *She posed in the doorway*; *The model had to pose in a fur coat for the magazine photographs.* **2** (*with* **as**) to pretend to be: *He posed as a doctor.*
poseur [pou'zə:] *nc* (*formal derog*) a person who uses poses (*def 2*) to impress others: *He can be quite amusing – but he is such a poseur that he irritates me.*
strike a pose *see* **strike**.

pose[2] [pouz] *vt* (*formal*) to set or offer (a question or problem) for answering or solving: *He posed a difficult question*; *This poses a problem.*

'**poser** *nc* (*inf*) a difficult question or problem: *That's quite a poser!*

poseur *see* **pose**[1].

posh [poʃ] *adj* (*inf: often derog*) of a superior type or class: *He comes from a posh family; posh clothes; She speaks with a posh accent; What a posh car!; She thinks she is too posh to speak to us.*

position [pəˈziʃən] *nc* **1** a way of standing, sitting *etc*: *He lay in an uncomfortable position.* **2** a place or situation: *The house is in a beautiful position.* **3** (*more formal than* **job**) a job; a post: *He has a good position with a local bank.* **4** a point of view: *Let me explain my position on employment.* **5** a set of circumstances: *I'm not in a position to* (= I can't) *do anything about that.* – *vt* (*formal*) to put or place: *He positioned the lamp in the middle of the table.*

be in, out of position to be (not) in the right place: *Is everything in position for the photograph?*

positive [ˈpozətiv] *adj* **1** (*formal or tech*) meaning or saying 'yes': *a positive answer; The pregnancy test is positive – you are definitely pregnant.* **2** (*formal: usu attrib*) definite; leaving no doubt: *positive proof; This is proof positive of his wickedness.* **3** (*usu pred*) certain or sure: *I'm positive he's right.* **4** (*inf: attrib*) complete or absolute: *His work is a positive disgrace.* **5** (*formal*) optimistic and prepared to make plans for the future: *Take a more positive attitude to life; Do try to be more positive – you give up too easily.* **6** (*gram*) not showing any comparison; not comparative or superlative. **7** (*math: attrib*) greater than zero: *2+ is a positive number.* **8** (*tech: esp attrib*) having fewer electrons than normal: *In an electrical circuit, electrons flow to the positive terminal.* – **1** *nc* (*tech*) a photographic print, made from a negative, in which light and dark are as normal. **2** *ncu* (*gram*) (an adjective or adverb of) the positive degree: *This is a good book; He did it carefully.*

'**positively** *adv* **1** in a positive way: *He stated quite positively that he was innocent.* **2** (*inf*) absolutely; completely: *He is positively the nastiest person I know.*

'**positiveness** *nu.*

posse [ˈposi] *nc* (*esp Amer*) a group or body of policemen *etc*: *The sheriff sent a posse to arrest the cattle-thief.*

possess [pəˈzes] *vt* **1** (*more formal than* **have**: not used with **is, was** *etc* and **-ing**) to own or have: *How much money does he possess?* **2** (*formal or liter*) (of an emotion *etc*) to take hold of; to control the mind of: *Fury suddenly possessed her.*

pos'sessed *adj* (*usu pred: formal or liter*) controlled, *esp* by the devil, evil spirits *etc*: *Witches and mad people were once thought to be possessed (by evil spirits); He fought like a man possessed* (= like a madman).

pos'session [-ʃən] **1** *nc* something which is owned by a person, country *etc*: *She lost all her possessions in the fire; Britain and her foreign possessions* (= territory controlled by Britain). **2** *nu* the state of possessing or being possessed: *the possession of money and property; the possession of one's soul by the devil.*

pos'sessive [-siv] *adj* **1** (*gram*) showing that someone or something possesses an object *etc*: *'Yours', 'mine', 'his', 'hers', 'theirs' are possessive pronouns; 'Your', 'my', 'his', 'their' are possessive adjectives.* **2** (*derog*) acting as though things and people are one's personal possessions: *a possessive mother; His wife is so possessive that she gets very angry if he speaks to another woman.* – *ncu* (*gram*) a possessive word; (a word in) the possessive case.

pos'sessively *adv*: *His wife was clinging possessively to his arm.* **pos'sessiveness** *nu.*

pos'sessor *nc* (*more formal than* **owner**): *He is the proud possessor of a new car.*

See also **dispossess, self-possessed.**

possible [ˈposəbl] *adj* **1** able to happen or be done: *It's possible (that)* (= perhaps) *the train's late; We'll come as soon as possible; I'll do everything possible; We need all possible help; She did the only possible thing in the circumstances.* **2** (*attrib*) satisfactory; acceptable: *I've thought of a possible solution to the problem.*

ˌ**possi'bility** *ncu* something that is possible; the state of being possible; (a) likelihood: *Mountaineers must always take into consideration the possibility of bad weather; There isn't much possibility of that happening; There's a possibility of war; Failure is still a possibility; The scheme has great possibilities* (= looks as if it may be a very good one); *'We could meet tomorrow.' 'Yes, that's a possibility.'*

'**possibly** *adv* **1** perhaps: *'Will you have time to do it?' 'Possibly.'; I may possibly be late.* **2** in a way or manner that is possible: *I'll come as fast as I possibly can; I can't possibly eat any more; Could you possibly* (= Please would you) *lend me your pen?*

See also **impossible**.

post[1] [poust] *nc* (*sometimes in cmpds*) a long piece of wood, metal *etc, usu* fixed upright in the ground: *The notice was nailed to a post; a gate-post* (= the post to which a gate is attached); *winning-post* (= the post marking the end of a race-track). – *vt* (*formal*) **1** to fix (a notice *etc*) to a wall *etc*: *They posted a sign on the wall.* **2** to announce publicly by means of such a notice: *The soldier was posted (as) missing.*

be first past the post (*sometimes fig*) to win a race.

keep (somebody) posted (*inf*) to give regular information to (a person): *He always keeps me posted about what he's doing.*

post[2] [poust] **1** *nu* (the system of collecting, transporting and delivering) letters, parcels *etc*: *I sent the book by post; Please send a reply by return of post* (= by the next collection from the postbox); *Your letter may have got lost in the post; Has the post arrived yet?; Is there any post for me?* **2** *n* (*with cap*) a word often used in the titles of newspapers: *the Baberton Post.* – *vt* to send (a letter *etc*) by post: *He posted the parcel yesterday.*

'**postage** [-tidʒ] *nu* (the money paid for) the sending of a letter *etc* by post: *The postage was 50 pence; It will cost 50 pence (for) postage.*

'**postal** *adj* (*attrib*) of, or concerning, the system of sending letters *etc*: *the postal service.*

'**postage stamp** *nc* (*more formal than* **stamp**) a small printed label fixed to a letter, parcel *etc* to show that postage has been paid.

postal order *nc* a printed document bought at a post office, which can be exchanged at another post office for the amount of money paid for it: *He paid by postal order; He sent me a postal order.*

postbox [ˈpousboks] *nc* (*also* '**letterbox,** '**mailbox,** '**pillar box**) a box into which letters *etc* are put to be collected (and sent to their destination).

postcard [ˈpouskaːd] *nc* a card on which a message may be sent by post, often with a picture on one side (a **picture postcard**): *She sent me a* *postcard when she was on holiday in France.*

postcode ['pouskoud] *nc* (*Amer* '**zip code**) a set of letters and numbers added to the address on a letter to make delivery easier: *What is the postcode for London?*

ˌ**post-'free** *adj* (*attrib*), *adv* without charge for sending by post: *You can send it post-free.*

ˌ**post(-)'haste** *adv* (*liter*) very quickly: *He travelled post(-)haste to London.*

postman ['pousmən] *nc* (*Amer* '**mailman**) a person whose job is to (collect and) deliver letters *etc*: *Has the postman been this morning yet?*

postmark ['pousma:k] *nc* a mark put on a letter at a post office, showing the date and place of posting, and cancelling the postage stamp: *I cannot read the postmark on this letter.*

postmaster ['pousma:stə] – *fem* **postmistress** ['pousmistris] – *nc* the manager of a post office: *She complained to the postmaster about the damaged parcel.*

Postmaster General – *pl* **Postmasters General** – *nc* the minister in charge of the government department that deals with the postal service.

'**post office** *nc* an office for receiving and dispatching letters, parcels *etc*: *I am going to the post office to post this parcel*; *Where is the nearest post office?* – *See also* **general post office**.

post-paid [pous'peid] *adj, adv* with the postage already paid: *He sent the parcel post-paid*; *A post-paid envelope was provided for his reply.*

post[3] [poust] *nc* **1** (*more formal than* **job**) a job: *He has a post in the government*; *a teaching-post.* **2** a place of duty: *The soldier remained at his post.* **3** a settlement, camp *etc esp* in a distant or unpopulated area: *a trading-post*; *a British military post.* – *vt* (*formal*) to send (someone) somewhere on duty: *He was posted to India*; *He was posted abroad.*

post[4] [poust]: **the first/last post** (*mil*) the morning/evening bugle-call.

post- [poust] (*in cmpds*) after, as in **post-graduate**.

postage, postal, postbox, postcard, postcode *see* **post**[2].

postdate [pous'deit] *vt* to mark with a date later than the date of signing: *He postdated the cheque.*

ˌ**post'dated** *adj*: *a postdated cheque.*

poster ['poustə] *nc* a large notice or advertisement for sticking on a wall *etc*: *Have you seen any posters advertising the circus?*; *Her room is decorated with colourful posters.*

post restante [poust'restãt, (*Amer*) poustre'sta:nt] *ncu, adv* (a direction to) the department of a post office to which letters can be addressed, and where they can be kept until someone calls for them: *While he is touring in France his letters are to be addressed to the poste restante in Paris*; (*attrib*) *the post restante counter at the post office*; *Could you send the letter to me poste restante?*

posterior *nc* (*euph or facet*) the buttocks: *He slapped her posterior.* – *adj* (*formal or tech*) coming, or situated behind: *in a posterior position.*

posterity [po'sterəti] *nu* people coming after; future generations: *The treasures must be kept for posterity.*

post-free *see* **post**[2].

post-graduate [pous'gradjuət, (*Amer*) -dʒuət] *adj* (*often attrib*) (of studies *etc*) done *etc* after a (first) university degree: *post-graduate work*; *He is studying for a post-graduate degree/diploma.* – *nc* a student involved in post-graduate studies.

post(-)haste *see* **post**[2].

posthumous ['postjuməs] *adj* **1** happening, coming *etc* after someone's death: *a posthumous award*; *the posthumous publication of his book.* **2** (of a child) born after its father has died: *a posthumous son*; *The child was posthumous – he was born three months after his father was killed in battle.*

'**posthumously** *adv*: *The soldier received a military medal posthumously.*

postman, postmark, postmaster, postmistress *see* **post**[2].

post mortem [pous'mo:təm] *nc* (*often* ˌ**post'mortem**) **1** a medical examination of a dead body in order to find out the cause of death: *The post mortem revealed that she had died of poisoning.* **2** (*facet*) an examination or investigation of an event *etc*, *usu* to find out why it did not succeed: *After each game they lost, they always had a post mortem.*

post-natal [pous'neitl] *adj* (*formal or tech*: *esp attrib*) concerned with, or happening, in the period after birth: *Babies always suffer a post-natal weight loss*; *post-natal depression.*

post office, post-paid *see* **post**[2].

postpone [pəs'poun] *vt* to cancel until a future time: *The football match has been postponed (till tomorrow) because of the bad weather.* **post'ponement** *ncu.*

postscript ['pousskript] *nc* a part added to a letter after the writer has signed it: *She added a postscript.*

postulate ['postjuleit] *vt* (*formal*) to take for granted; to assume: *Certain facts must be postulated.*

posture ['postʃə] **1** *nu* the way in which a person places or holds his body when standing, sitting, walking *etc*: *Good posture is important for a dancer.* **2** *nc* a position or pose: *He knelt in an uncomfortable posture.* – *vi* (*formal*: *usu derog*) to put oneself into showy poses or attitudes: *He enjoys posturing in front of an audience.*

postwar [poust'wo:] *adj* (*usu attrib*) of, or belonging to, the time after a war: *postwar austerity.*

posy ['pouzi] *nc* a small bunch of flowers: *a posy of primroses.*

pot [pot] **1** *nc* (*sometimes in cmpds*) any one of many kinds of deep container used in cooking, for holding food, liquids *etc* or for growing plants: *This pot is too small*; *a cooking pot*; *a plant pot*; *a chamberpot.* **2** *nc* the amount held by such a container: *They've eaten a whole pot of jam*; *She made a pot of tea.* **3** *nu* (*now old sl*) marijuana. **4** *nc* (*inf*) a fat stomach: *He's getting a pot.* – *v* –*pt, ptp* '**potted** – *vt* to plant in a pot: *Those plants must be potted in early spring.*

pots *n pl* (*sl*) a lot: *He's got pots of money.*

'**potted** *adj* (*attrib*) **1** (of food) pressed into a pot or jar in order to preserve it: *potted meat.* **2** contained in a pot: *a potted plant.* **3** *inf* (of a book *etc*) a shortened version: *a potted history of Britain.*

pot belly *nc* (*inf*) a fat stomach. ˌ**pot-'bellied** *adj.*

'**pot-boiler** *nc* (*derog*) a book or other work by a writer, artist *etc*, produced for the sake of money only.

'**pothole** *nc* **1** a hole or cave made in rock by the action of swirling water. **2** (*fig*) a hole worn in a road-surface.

'**potholer** *nc* a person who explores potholes (*def 1*) as a sport (called **potholing**): *We went potholing last weekend.*

'**pot-shot** *nc* an easy or casual shot that doesn't

need careful aim: *He took a pot-shot at a bird on the fence.*

go to pot (*inf*) to become bad; to get worse and worse: *He was under a terrible strain and his work went completely to pot.*

take pot luck (*inf*) to have a meal as someone's guest without their having prepared special food: *Do come and eat with us, if you don't mind taking pot luck.*

potassium [pə'tasiəm] *nu* a silvery-white element (symbol **K**).

potato [pə'teitou] – *pl* **po'tatoes** – **1** *nc* a type of plant with round underground stems (called **tubers**) which are used as a vegetable. **2** *ncu* the tuber or tubers: *She bought 2 kilos of potatoes*; (*attrib*) *potato soup*; *Would you like some potato?*

potato crisp *nc* (*usu* **crisp**: *Amer* **potato chip**: *usu in pl*) a thin, crisp, fried slice of potato: *a packet of (potato) crisps.*

sweet potato *see* **yam**.

pot-boiler *see* **pot**.

potent ['poutənt] *adj* (*formal or facet*) powerful; strong: *a potent drink*; *He has a potent imagination*; *This cocktail is rather potent.*

'potency *nu* (*formal*) power; strength.

'potentate [-teit] *nc* (*liter*) a person with power; a prince or ruler: *an Eastern potentate.*

potential [pə'tenʃəl] *adj* (*attrib*) possible; that may develop into the thing specified: *That hole in the road is a potential danger*; *Your child is a potential actor.* – *nu* the possibility, or likelihood, of successful development (in a particular way): *The land has great farming potential*; *He shows potential as a teacher*; *Their child shows great potential.*

po'tentially *adv.*

See also **impotent**.

pothole *etc see* **pot**.

potion ['pouʃən] *nc* (*liter or facet*) a drink containing *eg* medicine or poison, or having a magic effect: *The old woman claimed to cure diseases by the use of herbal potions*; *What a foul-tasting potion they served at that party*; *a love-potion.*

pot luck *see* **pot**.

pot-pourri [poupu'ri:] **1** *ncu* a mixture of dried flower-petals *etc* that gives off a sweet smell. **2** *nc* (*formal fig*) a mixture: *a pot-pourri of old tunes.*

potter[1] ['potə] *nc* a person who makes plates, cups, vases *etc* out of clay and fires them in an oven (called a **kiln**).

'pottery 1 *nu* articles made of fired clay: *He collects old pottery*; *He is learning how to make pottery.* **2** *nc* a place where articles of fired clay are made: *He is working in the pottery.* **3** *nu* the art of making such articles: *He is learning pottery at an evening class*; (*attrib*) *pottery classes.*

potter[2] ['potə] *vi* (*often with* **about**) to wander about doing small jobs or doing nothing important: *He likes to potter (about) in the garden*; *I spent the afternoon pottering (about).*

potty[1] ['poti] *adj* (*inf*) mad; crazy: *He must be potty to do that!*; *You're driving me potty!*; *a slightly potty old man*; *He's potty about her.*

potty[2] ['poti] *nc* (*inf*) a child's chamberpot.

pouch [pautʃ] *nc* **1** (*old or in cmpds*) a small bag: *a tobacco-pouch.* **2** something bag-like: *This animal stores its food in two pouches under its chin*; *People sometimes get pouches under their eyes as they get older.* **3** the pocket of skin in which the young of certain kinds of animal, *eg* the kangaroo, are reared.

pouffe, pouf [pu:f] *nc* a large firm kind of cushion that can be used as a seat: *The child sat on a pouffe by her mother's knee.*

poulterer *see* **poultry**.

poultice ['poultis] *nc* a *usu* hot, soft mixture spread on a bandage *etc* and placed on the skin to cure inflammation *etc*: *She tried to make the boil on her arm burst by putting a hot poultice on it.*

poultry ['poultri] *nu* farmyard birds, *eg* hens, ducks, geese, turkeys: *They keep poultry*; (*attrib*) *a poultry farm.*

'poulterer *nc* **1** a person who sells poultry (and game) as food: *We ordered a turkey from the poulterer.* **2** a poulterer's shop.

poulterer's *nc* a poulterer's shop: *Call at the poulterer's and collect the turkey.*

pounce [pauns] *vi* to jump suddenly, in order to seize or attack: *The cat waited beside the bird-cage, ready to pounce.* – *See also* **pounce on** *below.* – *nc* an act of pouncing; a sudden attack: *The cat made a pounce (at the bird).*

'pounce on *vt fus* to leap upon (*eg* one's prey) in order to attack or grab it: *The tiger pounced on its victim*; (*fig*) *He pounced on the book he had been looking for*; (*fig*) *She pounced on the weak point in his argument.*

pound[1] [paund] *nc* **1** (*also* **pound sterling**: *usu abbrev* **£** *when written with a number*) the standard unit of British currency, 100 (new) pence (in old money, 20 shillings): *It costs £10/ten pounds*; *a £10 note/ten-pound note.* **2** (*usu abbrev* **lb(s)** *when written with a number*) a measure of weight, 16 ounces (0·454 kilograms): *It weighs fourteen pounds/14 lbs*; *a five-pound/5 lb weight.*

-pounder (*in cmpds*) **1** something weighing a certain number of pounds: *I went fishing for trout and caught a ˌthree-ˈpounder.* **2** a big gun that fires a shot weighing a specified number of pounds: *a ˌtwenty-four ˈpounder.*

pound[2] [paund] *nc* an enclosure or pen into which stray animals are put: *a dog-pound.*

pound[3] [paund] **1** *vi* (*with* **at** *or* **on**) to hit or strike heavily; to thump: *He pounded at the door*; *The children were pounding on the piano.* **2** *vi* to walk or run heavily: *He pounded down the road.* **3** *vt* to break up (a substance) into powder or liquid: *She pounded the dried bread into crumbs.*

pour [po:] **1** *vti* to (cause to) flow in a stream: *She poured the milk into a bowl*; *Who would like to pour the tea?*; *Water poured down the wall from the broken pipe*; (*fig*) *People were pouring out of the factory.* **2** *vi* (*only with* **it** *as subject*) to rain heavily: *It was pouring this morning.*

See also **downpour** *under* **down**[1].

pout [paut] *vi* to push the lips out *usu* as a sign of displeasure: *She pouted sulkily.* – *nc* this expression of the face.

poverty ['povəti] *nu* the condition of being poor: *They lived in extreme poverty*; *the poverty of the soil*; *His written work shows poverty of imagination.*

See also **impoverish**.

POW *see* **prisoner of war** *under* **prison**.

powder ['paudə] **1** *ncu* (*often in cmpds*) any substance made up of fine particles: *soap powder*; *milk-powder* (= a dehydrated form of milk); (*attrib*) *in powder form.* **2** *nu* (*often in cmpds*) a special kind of substance in this form, used as a cosmetic *etc*: *face-powder*; *talcum powder.* **3** *nu* (*old*) gun-powder: *powder and shot.* **4** *nc* (*esp old*) a dose of medicine in the form of powder: *The doctor gave me some powders to take.* – *vt* to put powder on (one's face or body): *She went into the* *bedroom to powder her nose.*

'powdered *adj* **1** (*usu attrib*) in the form of fine particles of dust: *powdered chocolate.* **2** covered with powder: *Her face was thickly powdered*; *her heavily powdered complexion.*

'powdery *adj* **1** like powder: *powdery snow*; *The snow is dry and powdery.* **2** covered with powder: *powdery hands*; *My hands are powdery – I've been putting talcum powder on the baby.*

'powder puff *nc* a piece of very soft material used to apply face-powder or talcum powder to the skin.

'powder room *nc* (*euph*) a ladies' cloakroom or toilet in a restaurant, hotel *etc.*

power ['pauə] **1** *ncu* (an) ability: *A witch has magic power*; *A cat has the power of seeing in the dark*; *I haven't the power to help you*; (*formal*) *I'll help you if it is within my power* (= if I can); *God has infinite power.* **2** *nu* (*sometimes in cmpds*) strength, force or energy: *A rabbit has great power in its back legs*; *muscle power*; *water-power*; *horse-power*; (*attrib*) *a power tool* (= a tool operated by electricity *etc*, not by hand). **3** *nu* authority or control: *Several rival groups were fighting for power*; *How much power does the Queen have?*; *I have him in my power* (= under my control and dependent on my mercy) *at last*; *power politics* (= political negotiation with the support of military force); *student power* (= control of university administration by students). – *See also* **be in power** *below.* **4** *nc* a right belonging to *eg* a person in authority: *The police have the power of arrest*; *What powers does a headmaster have in dealing with rebellious staff?* **5** *nc* (*inf*) a person with great authority or influence: *He is quite a power in the government.* **6** *nc* a strong and influential country: *the Western powers.* **7** *nc* (*math*) the result obtained by multiplying a number by itself a given number of times: *$2 \times 2 \times 2$ or 2^3 is the third power of 2, or 2 to the power of 3.*

'powered *adj* (*often in cmpds when attrib*) supplied with mechanical power: *The machine is powered by electricity*; *an electrically-powered machine.*

'powerful *adj* having great strength, influence *etc*: *a powerful engine*; *He's powerful in local politics*; *He has become too powerful*; (*facet*) *a powerful smell.*

'powerfully *adv*: *He is powerfully built* (= He is very muscular).

'powerfulness *nu.*

'powerless *adj* (*formal*) having no power: *He is powerless to act*; *a powerless president.* **'powerlessness** *nu.*

high-powered *see* **high**.

'power cut *nc* a break in the electricity supply: *We had a power cut last night.*

,power-'driven *adj* worked by electricity or other mechanical means, not by hand.

'power point *nc* a socket on a wall *etc* into which an electric plug can be fitted: *This room has too few power points.*

'power station *nc* a building where electricity is produced.

be in power (of a political party) to be the governing party: *When were the Conservatives last in power?*

do a/the power of good, harm *etc* to do a lot of good, harm, evil *etc*: *A weekend in the country will do you the power of good*; *A mistake like that can do a power of harm.*

the ,powers that 'be (*facet*) the people in authority: *I have been sacked because the powers that be have decided that I am inefficient.*

See also **empower, potent**.

pow-wow ['pauwau] *nc* **1** (*inf facet*) a conference or discussion. **2** (*hist*) a conference with or among American Indians.

pox [poks] (*in cmpds*) a disease causing spots on the skin which often leave scars: *smallpox*; *chickenpox.*

practicable ['praktikəbl] *adj* (*formal*) able to be used or done: *a practicable theory/plan*; *It just isn't practicable!*

'practicably *adv.* **'practicableness, ,practica'bility** *nus.*

See also **impracticable**.

practical ['praktikəl] *adj* **1** concerned with practice (*def 1*): *There are some practical difficulties*; *He has a practical* (= useful, though not of a high academic standard) *knowledge of the language*; *His knowledge is practical rather than theoretical.* **2** (of a thing, idea *etc*) useful; effective: *You must try to find a practical answer to the problem*; *That wasn't a very practical thing to do*; *That course of action does not sound very practical.* **3** (*neg* **un-**) (of a person) able to do or deal with things well or efficiently: *He can look after himself – he's a very practical child*; *You must try to be practical.*

,practi'cality [-'ka-] *ncu* (*formal*): *There are various practicalities that we must discuss.*

'practically *adv* **1** almost: *The room was practically full.* **2** (*formal*) in a practical way: *Practically, it's more difficult than you think.*

practical joke *nc* a *usu* irritating joke consisting of an action done to someone, rather than a story told: *He nailed my chair to the floor as a practical joke*; *He played a practical joke on me.*

See also **impractical**.

practice ['praktis] **1** *nu* the actual doing of something, as opposed to the theory or idea: *In theory the plan should be successful, but in practice there are a lot of difficulties.* **2** *ncu* (*formal*) the usual way(s) of doing things; (a) habit or custom: *It was his usual practice to rise at 6.00 a.m.*; *He was accused of dishonest practices*; *It is normal practice for travel agents to make a charge for their services.* **3** *ncu* the repeated performance or exercise of something in order to learn to do it well: *She needs a lot of practice (at it)*; *They have sports practices every day after school.* **4** *nc* a doctor's or lawyer's business: *He has a practice in Edinburgh.* – *v* (*Amer*) *see* **practise**.

be in/out of practice (not) having had a lot of practice (*def 3*) recently: *I haven't played the piano for months – I'm very out of practice.*

make a practice of (doing something) to do something habitually: *He makes a practice of arriving late at parties.*

put into practice to do (something), as opposed to thinking, planning *etc*: *He never gets the chance to put his ideas into practice.*

sharp practice *see* **sharp**.

practise, (*Amer*) **practice** ['praktis] **1** *vti* to do exercises to improve one's performance in a particular skill *etc*; to have a lot of practice (*def 3*): *She practises the piano every day*; *You must practise more if you want to enter the competition.* **2** *vt* (*formal*) to make (something) a habit: *He practises self-control.* **3** *vti* to do or follow (a profession, *usu* medicine or law): *He practises (law) in London.*

'practised *adj* (*attrib*) skilled through much practice (*def 3*): *a practised performer/*

performance; *a practised liar.*

practitioner *see* **general practitioner**.

pragmatic [prag'matik] *adj* (*formal*) concerned with matters of fact, rather than ideas and theories; practical (*def 1*): *a pragmatic person/decision*; *He is rather pragmatic.* **prag'matically** *adv.*

'pragmatism *nu* (*formal*) the state or quality of being (too) concerned with matters of fact, practical results *etc.*

'pragmatist *nc* (*formal*) a person who is pragmatic.

prairie ['preəri] *nc* in N America, an area of flat, treeless, grass-covered land: *the Canadian prairies*; (*attrib*) *prairie farming.*

praise [preiz] *vt* **1** to express admiration or approval of; to commend: *He praised her beauty and her singing.* **2** (*relig*) to glorify (God) by singing hymns *etc*: *Praise the Lord!* – *nu* the expression of approval or honour: *He has received a lot of praise for his musical skill.*

'praiseworthy *adj* (*formal*) deserving praise: *Giving one's time and money to charity is very praiseworthy*; *a praiseworthy action.*

pram [pram] *nc* (short for **pe'rambulator**: *Amer* **'baby buggy/carriage**) a kind of small carriage on wheels for carrying a baby, pushed by its mother *etc*: *She pushed the pram along the street.*

prance [pra:ns] *vi* (*formal or liter*) to dance or jump about, *esp* of horses: *The soldiers' horses pranced along in the procession*; (*fig*) *He pranced into the room in his fine new clothes.*

prank [praŋk] *nc* (*esp old*) a trick; a practical joke: *He was always playing pranks on his brothers and sisters.*

prate [preit] *vi* (*formal derog*) to talk foolishly and *usu* pompously: *He's always prating about the behaviour of young people.*

prattle ['pratl] *vi* (*derog*) to talk or chatter about unimportant things or like a child: *She prattled* (*on*) *about nothing.* – *nc* (*derog*) childish talk; chatter.

prawn [pro:n] *nc* a type of edible shellfish like the shrimp: *We had prawns for the first course*; (*attrib*) *prawn cocktail.*

pray [prei] **1** *vti* to speak reverently to God or a god in order to express thanks, make a request *etc*: *Let us pray*; *She prayed to God to help her*; (*usu fig*) *Everybody is praying for rain*; (*fig*) *I hope and pray that he gets here in time.* **2** *vt* (*old or liter*) to ask earnestly: *Let me go, I pray you!* – *interj* (*esp old*) used to add politeness or sarcasm to a request, question *etc*: *Pray sit down!*; *What right have you to say that, pray?*

'prayer *ncu* (an) act of praying: *He spent his time in prayer*; *a book of prayer*; *The child said his prayers*; (*fig*) *My prayers have been answered* (= I've got what I desired); *a prayer for mercy.*

'prayers *n pl* a religious service in which requests are made, thanks given *etc*, to God: *The school has prayers every morning.*

pre- [pri:] (*in cmpds*) before, as in **prewar**.

preach [pri:tʃ] **1** *vti* to give a talk (called a sermon), *usu* during a religious service, about religious or moral matters: *The vicar preached* (*a sermon*) *on/about pride.* **2** *vi* (*derog fig*) to speak to someone as though giving a sermon: *Don't preach at/to me!* **3** *vt* (*formal*) to advise: *He preaches caution.* **'preacher** *nc.*

preamble [pri:'ambl] *nc* (*formal*: *often derog*) a spoken or written introduction *eg* to a speech or a document: *He introduced the main speaker in a long, extremely boring preamble.*

prearranged [pri:ə'reindʒd] *adj* arranged or agreed previously: *At a prearranged signal, they all rose to their feet*; *The password was prearranged.*

precarious [pri'keəriəs] *adj* (*formal*) insecure; risky or dangerous: *The house stood in a precarious position on the edge of the cliff*; (*fig*) *Acting is a precarious career.* **pre'cariously** *adv.* **pre'cariousness** *nu.*

precaution [pri'ko:ʃən] *ncu* care taken to avoid accidents, disease *etc*: *They took every precaution to ensure that their journey would be safe and enjoyable*; *If you want to avoid accidents you must take precautions.*

pre'cautionary *adj* (*formal*): *We must take precautionary measures so that the disease will not spread*; *These measures are strictly precautionary.*

precede [pri'si:d] *vti* (*formal*) to go, happen *etc* before: *She preceded him into the room*; *He is mentioned in this chapter and also in the one that precedes.*

precedence ['presidəns] *nu* (the right of) going before in order of importance *etc*: *This matter should be given precedence over others at the moment*; *Does an earl come before a duke in order of precedence?*; *An earl takes precedence over a duke.*

ˌprecedent ['presidənt] *nc* (*formal*) a past action, *esp* a legal decision, which may act as a guide or rule in the future: *If you allow this pupil to go unpunished, it will set* (= provide) *a precedent*; *In deciding the case in this way, the judge was following a precedent set in 1910.*

pre'ceding *adj*: *on the preceding page.*

See also **unprecedented**.

precept ['pri:sept] *nc* (*formal*) a rule to guide one's actions: *moral precepts*; *He always followed the precept 'Do as you would be done by'* (= Always treat others in the way that you would wish to be treated yourself).

precinct ['pri:siŋkt] *nc* **1** (*formal*: *often in pl*) an area of ground within walls or boundaries: *the city precincts*; *the cathedral precincts.* – *See also* **precincts** *below.* **2** (*esp Amer*) an administrative district: *a police precinct.*

'precincts *n pl* (*formal*) the area surrounding a particular place: *within the precincts of the station.*

pedestrian/shopping precinct *nc* an area of shops where no cars are allowed.

precious ['preʃəs] *adj* of great value: *precious jewels*; *My children are very precious to me.*

precious metal *ncu* a valuable metal such as gold, silver or platinum.

precious stone *nc* a jewel; a gem: *diamonds, emeralds and other precious stones.*

precious few/little (*inf*) very few/little: *Precious few people would agree with you*; *I've precious little money left.*

precipice ['presipis] *nc* (*more formal than* **cliff**) a steep cliff.

precipitous [pri'sipitəs] *adj* (*formal*) very steep: *a precipitous path*; *The mountain road is very precipitous.*

precipitate [pri'sipiteit] *vt* (*formal*) **1** to make something happen (more quickly or sooner): *The assassination of the president precipitated a war.* **2** (*usu fig*) to throw violently: *He precipitated his country into ruin*; *He precipitated himself into the fight.* – [-tət] *adj* (*formal derog*) (too) hurried: *a precipitate decision*; *His decision was rather precipitate.* – [-teit] *ncu* (*tech*) the substance that settles at the bottom of a liquid: *A precipitate gathered at the bottom of the bottle.*

pre'cipitately [-tət-] *adv*: *Take your time to decide – don't do anything precipitately.*

pre,cipi'tation *nu* **1** (*very formal*) (too) great hurry. **2** (*formal or tech*) (the amount of) rainfall, snow *etc*: *The annual precipitation is greater in the west than the east.* **3** (*tech*) the act of forming a precipitate.

precipitous *see* **precipice**.

précis ['preisi:, (*Amer also*) prei'si:] – *pl* **'précis** [-z] – *nc* a summary of a piece of writing: *The students were asked to write a précis of a newspaper article.*

precise [pri'sais] *adj* **1** exact: *Give me his precise* (= actual) *words!*; *precise* (= clear and detailed) *instructions*; *a precise* (= accurate) *translation*; *Your directions were not precise enough.* **2** (*formal*) careful to be accurate and exact in manner, speech *etc*: *a precise person*; *He is always very precise.*

pre'ciseness *nu*.

pre'cisely *adv* **1** exactly: *at midday precisely*; *Precisely what do you mean?*; *He spoke very precisely* (= carefully and clearly). **2** used to express complete agreement: *'So you think we should wait until tomorrow?' 'Precisely.'*

pre'cision [-'siʒən] *nu* exactness; accuracy: *He spoke with great precision*; (*attrib*) *precision tools* (= tools used for obtaining very accurate results).

See also **imprecise**.

preclude [pri'klu:d] *vt* (*formal*) to prevent; to make impossible: *She explained the matter very clearly, so as to preclude all misunderstandings.*

precocious [prə'kouʃəs] *adj* (*sometimes derog*) (*usu* of children or their speech, actions *etc*) unexpectedly mature, advanced or well-developed: *All child actors seem to be precocious*; *What precocious behaviour for a three-year-old child!* **pre'cociously** *adv*. **pre'cociousness, pre'cocity** [-'kosəti] *nus*.

preconceived [pri:kən'si:vd] *adj* (*formal*: *attrib*) (of ideas *etc*) formed before any actual experience or knowledge has been gained: *He started married life with too many preconceived ideas.*

,precon'ception [-'sepʃən] *nc* (*formal*) an idea or opinion formed before one has actual knowledge: *I had formed no preconception about the nature of my new work.*

See also **conceive**.

precursor [pri'kə:sə] *nc* (*formal or facet*) a person or thing that goes before, *esp* as a sign of something to come: *A sudden cold wind was the precursor of the approaching storm*; *He was the precursor of that form of drama.*

predate [pri:'deit] *vt* to be earlier than, or precede, in date: *His university career predated mine.*

predator ['predətə] *nc* (*formal or tech*) a bird, *eg* a hawk, or animal, *eg* a lion, that attacks and kills others for food.

'predatory *adj* living by attacking and feeding on others: *a predatory animal*; (*formal fig*: *derog*: *usu attrib*) *predatory lawyers/women.*

predecease [pri:di'si:s] *vt* (*esp legal*) to die before (someone): *His money will be inherited by his niece if his sister predeceases him.*

predecessor ['pri:disesə, (*Amer*) 'pre-] *nc* (*formal*) **1** someone who has had a particular job or position before: *He was my predecessor as manager.* **2** an ancestor: *My predecessors came from Scotland.*

predestine [pri:'destin] *vt* (*formal*) (*esp* of fate, God *etc*) to decide, fix or ordain beforehand: *Our victory was predestined*; *He was predestined to be a leader.*

pre,desti'nation *nu* (*esp relig*) the belief that God has decided in advance everything that will happen: *Do you believe in predestination?*

predetermine [pri:di'tə:min] *vt* (*formal*: not *usu* used with **is, was** *etc* and **-ing**) to settle or decide in advance: *A man's bodily health is partly predetermined by that of his parents.*

predicament [pri'dikəmənt] *nc* an unfortunate or difficult situation: *We found ourselves in a terrible predicament*; *What an embarrassing predicament!*

predicate ['predikət] *nc* (*gram*) what is said about the subject of a sentence: *We live in London*; *Isn't he a nuisance?*; *The president of the republic died.*

pre'dicative [-'dikətiv] *adj* (*gram*) (of an adjective) (always) part of the predicate; not preceding the noun to which it refers: *The boy was afraid*; *The house was ablaze.*

See also **attributive** *under* **attribute**.

predict [pri'dikt] *vt* (*formal*) to say in advance; to foretell: *He predicted a change in the weather*; *It is difficult to predict which political party will win the election.*

pre'dictable *adj* (*neg* **un-**: *formal*) able to be foretold: *a predictable decision/reaction*; *His anger was predictable*; *She has a rather unpredictable temperament.*

pre'diction [-ʃən] *ncu* (*formal*): *I'm making no predictions about the result of the race*; *A change of government is one of my predictions for next year*; *Accurate prediction of next month's weather is impossible.*

predilection [pri:di'lekʃən] *nc* (*formal or facet*) a particular liking for something; a preference: *I have a predilection for bananas*; *He has a distinct predilection for blondes.*

predispose [pri:di'spouz] *vt* (*formal*: not used with **is, was** *etc* and **-ing**) to incline (a person) in advance to react in a certain way: *His friendliness predisposed us to trust him*; *Clear writing and correct spelling will predispose the examiners in your favour*; *His general unhealthiness predisposes him to* (= makes him liable to get) *colds.*

,predispo'sition [-'ziʃən] *ncu* (*formal*) a mental or physical state that inclines a person in a certain direction: *She has a predisposition to infections.*

predominate [pri'domineit] *vi* (*formal*: *with* **over**) **1** to be the stronger or greater in amount, size, number *etc*: *In this part of the country industry predominates* (*over agriculture*). **2** to have control over: *Ignorance often predominates over knowledge.*

pre'dominant *adj* stronger, more numerous, more noticeable *etc*: *The English language has always been predominant in America*; *The predominant cause of the war was economic failure.*

pre'dominantly *adv*. **pre'dominance** *nu*.

pre-eminent [pri:'eminənt] *adj* (*formal*: *usu pred*) better or worse than all others; outstanding: *Of all her good qualities, her kindness is pre-eminent.*

pre-'eminently *adv*. **pre-'eminence** *nu*.

preen [pri:n] *vt* (of birds) to arrange (the feathers): *The sea-gulls were preening themselves/their feathers*; (*fig*: *usu derog*) *The woman was preening herself in front of the mirror.*

prefabricated [pri:'fabrikeitid] *adj* (*tech*: *usu attrib*) (of a building *etc*) made of parts manufactured in advance and ready to be put together: *prefabricated bungalows.*

prefab ['pri:fab, (*Amer also*) pri:'fab] *nc* (*Brit*

old) a *usu* small prefabricated house.

preface ['prefəs] *nc* an introduction to a book *etc*: *The preface explained how to use the dictionary.* – *vt* (*formal*) to start (a speech *etc*) with a preface: *He prefaced his speech with a few words of welcome.*

'**prefatory** [-təri] *adj* (*very formal*: *attrib*) forming a preface: *a few prefatory words before the speech.*

prefect ['pri:fekt] *nc* **1** one of a number of senior pupils having special powers in a school *etc.* **2** in some countries, an administrative official.

'**prefecture** [-tjuə, (*Amer*) -tʃər] *nc* **1** an administrative area under a prefect (*def 2*): *a French prefecture.* **2** the official home of such a prefect.

prefer [pri'fə:] – *pt, ptp* **pre'ferred** – *vt* **1** (not used with **is, was** *etc* and **-ing**) to like better: *Which do you prefer – tea or coffee?*; *Would you prefer to go alone?*; *I prefer reading to watching television*; *She would prefer to come with you rather than stay here.* **2** (*formal*) to make (a claim, charge *etc*) officially: *He has preferred charges against the manufacturers of the faulty goods.*

'**preferable** ['pre-] *adj* (*pred*) more desirable: *Is it preferable to write or make a telephone call?*

'**preferably** *adv.*

'**preference** ['pre-] *ncu* (a) choice of, or (a) liking for, one thing rather than another: *My preference is for wild flowers rather than cultivated ones*; *He likes most music but he has a preference for classical music*; *I chose this in preference to* (= rather than) *that*; *What are your preferences?* (= What do you prefer?); *This candidate has the best qualifications and should be given preference over the others.*

preferential [prefə'renʃəl] *adj* (*formal or facet*: *attrib*) showing or giving preference: *He got preferential treatment.*

pre'ferment *ncu* (*old*) promotion in one's job *etc.*

prefix ['pri:fiks] *nc* a syllable or syllables put *eg* at the beginning of another word to change its meaning: *dislike*; *unemployed*; *remake*; *ineffective.*

pregnant ['pregnənt] *adj* **1** carrying unborn young in the womb: *a pregnant cow*; *Is she pregnant?*; *She is six months pregnant.* **2** (*formal fig*: *usu attrib*) full of meaning: *a pregnant remark.*

pregnancy **1** *nu* the state of being pregnant (*esp def 1*): *Pregnancy can have a strange effect on appetite.* **2** *nc* an instance of being pregnant (*def 1*): *She has had three pregnancies in four years.*

prehensile [pri'hensail] *adj* (*tech*) able to take hold of something: *Most monkeys have prehensile tails.*

prehistoric [pri:i'storik] *adj* (*usu attrib*) of, or belonging to, the time before recorded history: *a prehistoric monster*; *prehistoric pottery.*

prejudge [pri:'dʒʌdʒ] *vt* (*formal*) to judge; to make a decision about something before hearing all the facts: *We must try not to prejudge the issue.*

prejudice ['predʒədis] *ncu* (*often derog*) (an) opinion or feeling for or *esp* against something, formed unfairly or unreasonably *ie* without proper knowledge: *He has a prejudice against modern poetry*; *The jury must listen to his statement without prejudice*; *These people are full of ignorance and prejudice*; *Is racial prejudice* (= dislike of people because of their race) *increasing in this country?* – *vt* to cause (someone) to feel prejudice for or against something: *I'm prejudiced in favour of punctual people*; (*formal*) *His life in the army had prejudiced him against laziness and lack of discipline.* **2** to harm or endanger (a person's position, prospects *etc*) in some way: *Your illegible handwriting will prejudice your chances of passing the exam.*

'**prejudiced** *adj* (*often derog*) having or showing prejudice: *a prejudiced attitude to people of other races*; *Don't be so prejudiced.*

ˌ**prejudicial** [-'diʃəl] *adj* (*with* **to**: *formal*) harmful: *Smoking is prejudicial to health.*

to the 'prejudice of/withˌout 'prejudice to (*formal*) with or without possible harm or danger to (a person's rights, position, prospects *etc*): *You ought to be able to criticize your firm without prejudice to your chances of promotion.*

prelate ['prelət] *nc* (*old or formal*) a bishop, archbishop or other clergyman of high rank.

preliminary [pri'liminəri] *adj* (*formal*) coming before, and preparing for, something: *The chairman made a few preliminary remarks before introducing the speaker.* – *nc* (*usu in pl*) something done, said *etc* in preparation for something else: *After the usual preliminaries the meeting was opened.*

prelude ['prelju:d] *nc* (*formal or facet*) **1** an event *etc* that goes before, and acts as an introduction to, something: *This disagreement was the prelude to a series of terrible quarrels.* **2** a piece of music played as an introduction to the main piece.

premarital [pri:'maritl] *adj* (*formal*: *attrib*) happening *etc* before marriage: *Should premarital sexual relations be encouraged?*

premature [premə'tʃuə, (*Amer*) pri:-] *adj* happening *etc* before the right or expected time: *a premature birth/baby*; *The baby was three weeks premature*; *a premature decision*; *His resignation was rather premature – he does not have another job.*

ˌ**prema'turely** *adv.*

premeditated [pri'mediteitid] *adj* (*formal or legal*) thought out in advance; planned: *This was a case of premeditated murder*; *Was this crime premeditated?* **preˌmedi'tation** *nu.*

premier ['premiə, (*Amer*) 'pri:-] *adj* (*attrib*: *formal*) first or leading: *Italy's premier industrialist.* – *nc* a prime minister: *the French premier.*

première ['premieə, (*Amer*) pri'miər] *nc* the first performance of a play, film *etc*: *the British première of a new German opera.*

premise, premiss ['premis] *nc* (*formal*) a known fact, or an assumption, from which a conclusion is formed: *Acting on the premise that people like to travel in comfort, he designed a new type of train.*

premises ['premisiz] *n pl* (a part of) a building and the area of ground belonging to it: *These premises are used by the local football team.*

premium ['pri:miəm] *nc* a regular, *usu* annual payment on an insurance policy. – *See also* **be at a premium** *below.*

Premium Bond *nc* (*Brit*) a government bond that gives the holder a chance of a prize in draws held regularly.

be at a premium to be wanted by a lot of people and be therefore difficult to get: *Tickets for the football match were at a premium.*

premonition [premə'niʃən] *nc* (*formal*) a feeling that something (*esp* something unpleasant) is going to happen: *a premonition of disaster*; *I had a premonition about the accident.*

prenatal [pri:'neitl] *adj* (*formal or tech*: *esp attrib*) occurring *etc* before birth: *prenatal injury.* *See also* **antenatal**.

preoccupy [pri'okjupai] *vt* (*formal*) to engage or occupy (a person's mind *etc*) or the attention of (someone) completely: *Thoughts of death were continually preoccupying her*; *His mind was pre-*

occupied with plans for the summer.
pre,occu'pation *ncu: her preoccupation with death.*
pre'occupied *adj* deep in thought, with something completely filling one's mind: *He spoke to her, but she seemed preoccupied; in rather a preoccupied mood.*

prep *see* **preparation** *under* **prepare**.

prepaid *see* **prepay**.

prepare [pri'peə] *vti* to make or get ready: *The teacher prepared his students for their examination; Have you prepared your speech for Thursday?; My mother prepared a meal; He prepared to go out; Prepare yourself for a shock – I have some bad/surprising news for you; You must prepare for the future by finding a well-paid job.*
preparation [prepə'reiʃən] **1** *nu* the act of preparing: *You can't pass an exam without preparation.* **2** *nu* (*usu abbrev* **prep** [prep]) study for a lesson at school, college *etc*; homework: *Does your teacher give you a lot of prep(aration)?* **3** *nc* (*formal*) something that has been prepared, *esp* as a medicine or cosmetic: *The chemist gave her a preparation to cure her spots.*
preparatory [-'parə-] *adj* (*formal*: *usu attrib*) acting as an introduction or in order to prepare for something: *Political leaders have agreed to meet for preparatory talks about an end to the war.* – *See also* **preparatory to** *below.*
pre'pared *adj* (*neg* **un-**) made ready: *Everything is prepared; a prepared* (= written beforehand) *speech.*
pre'paratory school [-'parə-] *nc* a private school which educates children in preparation for a public or other senior school (*abbrev* **'prep school** ['prep-]).
be prepared (for something, to do something *etc***)** (of a person) to be (*esp* mentally) ready for something, to do something *etc*: *We must be prepared for a disappointment; I was prepared for this to happen; I'm not prepared* (= willing) *to lend him more money; The motto of the Boy Scouts is 'Be Prepared!'.*
pre'paratory to [-'parə-] (*formal*) before; in preparation for: *I packed a few sandwiches preparatory to leaving/to my departure.*

prepay [pri:'pei] – *pt, ptp* **,pre'paid** – *vti* to pay in advance: *The reply to the telegram had been prepaid.* **,pre'payment** *nu.*

preponderance [pri'pondərəns] *nu* (*often with* **a**: *formal or facet*) a greater weight, strength or number: *There was a preponderance of young people in the audience.* **pre'ponderant** *adj.* **pre'ponderantly** *adv.*

preposition [prepə'ziʃən] *nc* (*gram*) a word put before a noun or pronoun to show how it is related to another word: *through the window; in the garden; written by me.*
,prepo'sitional *adj* (*gram*) of, with or acting as, a preposition: *a prepositional phrase.*

prepossessing [pri:pə'zesiŋ] *adj* (*formal*: *neg* **un-**) pleasant, attractive: *He's not a very prepossessing young man; This is not a very prepossessing place; I do not find him at all prepossessing; What an unprepossessing-looking person!*

preposterous [pri'postərəs] *adj* (*formal*) very foolish; ridiculous: *That's a preposterous idea!; That suggestion is preposterous.* **pre'posterously** *adv.*

prerequisite [pri:'rekwizit] *nc, adj* (*formal*) (something that is) necessary for something else to be done or happen: *An interest in other people is (a) prerequisite for a writer.*

prerogative [prə'rogətiv] *nc* (*formal or facet*) a special right or privilege belonging to a person because of his rank, position *etc*: *Does the Queen have the prerogative of pardoning condemned criminals?; Is it the Prime Minister's prerogative to choose the date of the next election?;* (*facet*) *It is a woman's prerogative to change her mind.*

presage ['presidʒ] *vt* (*formal or liter*) to foretell; to give warning of: *This trouble presages war.*

Presbyterian [prezbi'tiəriən] *adj* (of a church) having business *etc* managed by ministers and elders (sometimes called **'presbyters** [-təz]). – *nc* a member of such a church. **,Presby'terianism** *nu.*
'presbytery [-təri] *nc* **1** a group of presbyters, *ie* the representatives of a group of churches within an administrative area: *the presbytery of Edinburgh.* **2** (in the Roman Catholic Church) a priest's house.

prescribe [prə'skraib] *vt* **1** to advise or order (the use of): *The doctor prescribed a complete rest; My doctor prescribed some pills for my cold; Here is a list of books prescribed by the examiners for the exam.* **2** (*formal*) to establish as a rule: *The law prescribes certain penalties for this offence.*
pre'scription [-'skrip-] **1** *nc* a doctor's (*usu* written) instructions for the preparing and taking of a medicine: *He gave me a prescription to give to the chemist.* **2** *nu* the act of prescribing: *He is against the prescription by doctors of drugs to drug-addicts; These drugs can be got from a chemist only on prescription* (= if prescribed by a doctor).
pre'scriptive [-'skriptiv] *adj* (*formal*) establishing as a rule: *prescriptive rights; Dictionaries should be descriptive, not prescriptive.*

presence ['prezns] *nu* **1** the state, or fact, of being present: *His presence at the discussion showed that he was interested;* (*formal*) *The committee requests your presence at Thursday's meeting.* **2** (*formal*) a striking impressive manner: *The old duchess certainly has presence.*
in (someone's) presence/in the presence of (someone) while (someone) is present: *Don't talk about it in my mother's presence; This document must be signed in the presence of a witness.*
presence of mind calmness and the ability to act sensibly (in an emergency *etc*): *He showed great presence of mind in the face of danger.*
See also **absence** *under* **absent**.

present[1] ['preznt] *adj* **1** (*usu pred*) being here, or at the place, occasion *etc* mentioned: *My father was present on that occasion; Who else was present at the wedding?; Now that the whole class is present, we can begin the lesson.* **2** (*attrib*) existing now: *the present moment; our present difficulties; the present prime minister; I have nothing to say on the present* (= now being discussed) *subject.* **3** (*gram*) (of the tense of a verb) indicating action now: *In the sentence 'She wants a chocolate', the verb is in the present tense.* – *ncu* (a verb in) the present tense: *Is this verb in the present or the past?*
'presently *adv* **1** soon: *He will be here presently.* **2** (*esp Amer*) at the present time: *The manager is presently on holiday.*
the present the time now: *Forget the past – think more of the present and the future!*
at 'present at the present time: *He's away from home at present.*
for the 'present as far as the present time is

concerned: *You've done enough work for the present.*
See also **absent**.

present[2] [pri'zent] **1** *vt* to give, *esp* formally or ceremonially: *He presented her with a medal; The child presented a bunch of flowers to the Queen; He was presented with a gold watch when he retired.* **2** *vt* (*formal*) to introduce: *May I present my wife (to you)?* **3** *vt* (*drama etc*) to arrange the production of (a play, film *etc*): *The Elizabethan Theatre Company present 'Hamlet', by William Shakespeare.* **4** *vt* to offer (ideas *etc*) for consideration, or (a problem *etc*) for solving: *The situation presents a problem; He was presented with a difficult choice; She presents* (= expresses) *her ideas very clearly.* **5** *v refl* (*often facet*) to appear: *An idea presented itself in his mind; He presented himself at the dinner table half an hour late.* **pre'senter** *nc*.

pre'sentable *adj* suitable to be seen, introduced *etc*: *You don't look very presentable in those clothes; a very presentable young man.*

,presen'tation [pre-] **1** *nu* (*sometimes attrib*) the act of presenting: *the presentation of the prizes; a presentation ceremony; a presentation gold watch; after the presentation of the winners to the Queen; The presentation of a new play is always a welcome event.* **2** *nu* the manner in which written work *etc* is presented or set out: *The presentation of your written work is poor. Try to make it neater.* **3** *nc* a performance, or set of repeated performances, of a play, opera *etc*: *This is the best presentation of 'Macbeth' that I've ever seen.*

present arms (*mil*) to hold a rifle upright in front of one, as a salute: *As the Queen drove past, the guards presented arms.*

present[3] ['preznt] *nc* a gift: *She was given a great many presents when she had her baby; a wedding present; birthday presents.*

presentiment [pri'zentimənt] *nc* (*formal*) a feeling that something (*usu* bad) is about to happen; a foreboding: *He felt/had a strong presentiment of disaster.*

presently *see* **present**[1].

preserve [pri'zə:v] *vt* **1** (*formal*) to keep safe from harm: (*May*) *Heaven preserve us from danger!* **2** to keep in existence: *They have managed to preserve many old documents.* **3** to treat (food), *eg* by cooking it with sugar, so that it will not go bad: *What is the best method of preserving raspberries?* – **1** *nc* (*formal fig*) an activity, kind of work *etc* in which only certain people are allowed to take part: *Government used to be a preserve of the nobility.* **2** *nc* a place where game animals, birds *etc* are protected: *a game preserve.* **3** *ncu* (*formal or old*) (a type of) jam: *a jar of preserve; blackberry jam and other preserves.*

,preser'vation [pre-] *nu* the action of preserving or the state or process of being preserved: (*formal*) *The preservation of peace will be his main concern; The books are in a poor state of preservation.*

pre'servative [-vətiv] *ncu* (*formal or tech*) something that preserves, *esp* that prevents food *etc* from going bad: *a chemical preservative.*
See also **conserve**.

preside [pri'zaid] *vi* (*formal or facet*: *with* **at** *or* **over**) to be the chairman of a meeting *etc*: *The prime minister presided at/over the meeting;* (*fig*) *Grandmother presided at the dinner table.*

presidency ['prezidənsi] *nu* **1** (*formal*) the rank or office of a president: *His ambition is the presidency.* **2** the period of time for which somebody is president: *during the presidency of Dwight D. Eisenhower.*

president ['prezidənt] *nc* (*with cap in titles*) **1** the leading member of a club, association *etc*: *She was elected president of the Music Society.* **2** the leader of a republic: *the President of the United States.*

presidential [prezi'denʃəl] *adj* (*attrib*): *a presidential election.*

press [pres] **1** *vti* to use a pushing motion (against): *He pressed the switch down; Press the bell twice!; The child pressed his face against the shop window; He pressed against her in the crowd; The children pressed close to their mother.* **2** *vt* to squeeze; to flatten: *The grapes are pressed to extract the juice; She pressed the flower between the pages of a book.* **3** *vt* (*formal*) to urge: *He pressed her to enter the competition; He pressed me for an answer.* **4** *vt* (*formal*) to insist on: *I don't feel like pressing the matter; The printers are pressing their claim for higher pay; I said that I thought he was wrong, but I didn't press the point* (= try to convince him). **5** *vt* to iron: *Your trousers need to be pressed; I must press my skirt.* – **1** *nc* an act of pressing (*defs 1, 2, 5*): *He gave her hand a press; You had better give your shirt a press.* **2** *nc* (*also* **'printing-press**) a printing machine. **3** *nu* newspapers in general: *It was reported in the press;* (*attrib*) *a press agent;* (*attrib*) *a press photographer.* **4** *n sing or pl* the people who work on newspapers and magazines; journalists: *The press is/are always interested in the private lives of famous people.* **5** *nc* (*formal*) a crowd: *There was a terrible press in the corridor.* **6** *nc* (*usu in cmpds*) a device or machine for pressing: *a wine-press; a flower-press.*

pressed *adj* **1** (*attrib*) squeezed or flattened: *pressed flowers; pressed beef.* **2** (*pred*: *inf*) busy, or in a hurry: *I'm rather pressed at the moment.* **3** (*neg* **un-**: *esp in cmpds*) ironed: *well-/badly-pressed clothes; His shirts never look pressed.*

'pressing *adj* urgent: *a pressing invitation/problem; The problem is rather pressing.* **'pressingly** *adv*.

'press conference *nc* a meeting in which information is given to journalists: *The prime minister held a press conference.*

'press-cutting *nc* an article cut out of a newspaper or magazine: *She collected press-cuttings about film-stars.*

be hard pressed (*inf*) to be in difficulties or under a strain: *He's hard pressed financially.*

be 'pressed for (something) (*inf*) to be short of (time, money *etc*): *Do hurry up – I'm a bit pressed for time.*

'press for *vt fus* to try to get; to keep demanding: *The miners are pressing for higher wages.*

press forward/on *vi* to continue (in spite of difficulties): *They pressed forward through the crowd; She pressed on with her work.*

press (someone or something) into service (*formal or facet*) to make use of (a person or thing) in an emergency: *Even the children were pressed into service to prepare for the wedding.*

'press (something) on (someone) (*formal*) to urge (a person) to accept (a thing): *She pressed the money on him.*
See also **compress, depress, pressure**.

pressgang ['presgaŋ] *nc* (*hist*) a group of men employed to seize men and force them into the army or navy. – *vt* (*inf*: *with* **into**) to force (someone) to do something: *He was pressganged into helping.*

pressure ['preʃə] **1** *nu* (the amount of force exerted by) the action of pressing: *She felt the pressure of his hand on her arm*; *You should apply pressure to his cut to stop the bleeding*; *A barometer measures atmospheric pressure*; *tyre pressure* (= degree of inflation); *The patient has high blood pressure.* **2** *ncu* (a) strain or stress; (an) oppressive or overwhelming quality: *She is suffering from pressure of work*; *The pressures of family life are sometimes too much for her.* **3** *nu* strong persuasion; compulsion or force: *He agreed to resign only under pressure*; *She always works well under pressure* (= when compelled by necessity); *I'm under pressure* (= being urged) *to buy my wife a new coat*; *He will agree to do it if we put pressure* (= use force) *on him.*

'**pressurize, -ise** *vt* **1** (*tech*) to fit (an aeroplane *etc*) with a device that keeps air pressure normal: *The cabins have all been pressurized.* **2** (*formal*) to force (someone to do something): *He was pressurized into giving up his job.*

'**pressure cooker** *nc* a type of saucepan in which food is cooked quickly by steam kept under great pressure.

'**pressure group** *nc* a group of people who try to get the government *etc* to take notice of certain matters: *The local teachers formed a pressure group.*

bring pressure to bear on (*formal*) to try to force (someone to do something): *They brought pressure to bear on the government to lower taxes.*

prestige [pre'stiːʒ] *nu* reputation or influence due to success, rank *etc*: *The success of his writing brought him great prestige.* **pre'stigious** [-'stidʒəs] *adj* (*formal*).

presume [prə'zjuːm] **1** *vti* to believe that something is true without proof; to take for granted: *When I found the room empty, I presumed that you had gone home*; *The picture was presumed to be by Rembrandt*; *He has, I presume, paid the money back?*; *'Has he gone?' 'I presume so.'* **2** *vi* (*formal*) to be bold enough (to act without the right, knowledge *etc* to do so): *I wouldn't presume to advise someone as clever as you*; *Do you presume to tell us what our duty is?* – *See also* **presume on** *below.*

pre'sumably *adv* I presume: *Presumably you know him*; *He has presumably arrived.*

pre'sumption [-'zʌmp-] **1** *nc* something presumed: *She married again, on the presumption that* (= in the belief that) *her first husband was dead.* **2** *nu* (*formal derog*) unsuitable boldness, *eg* in one's behaviour towards another person: *She disliked his presumption.*

pre'sumptuous [-'zʌmptjuəs, (*Amer*) -'zʌmptʃuəs] *adj* (*derog*) showing presumption (*def 2*): *presumptuous behaviour*; *It was presumptuous of you to ask for an invitation to the party.* **pre'sumptuousness** *nu.*

pre'sume on *vt fus* to take advantage of; to make use of in an unjustified way: *He is presuming on your good nature.*

See also **assume.**

presuppose [priːsə'pouz] *vt* (*formal*: not used with **is, was** *etc* and **-ing**) to imply: *To be a concert pianist presupposes years of hard work.*

pretend [pri'tend] *vti* **1** to make believe that something is true, in play: *Let's pretend that this room is a cave!*; *Pretend to be a lion!*; *He wasn't really angry – he was only pretending.* **2** to try to make it appear (that something is true), in order to deceive: *He pretended that he had a headache*; *She was only pretending to be asleep*; *I pretended not to understand*; (*formal*) *He pretended surprise* (= to be surprised).

pre'tence, (*Amer*) **pre'tense** [-s] *ncu* (an) act of pretending: *Don't be upset – his anger was only a pretence!*; *Under the pretence of friendship, he persuaded her to get into his car.*

pre'tender *nc* (*hist or old*) a person who claims something, *esp* to be king: *a pretender to the title*; *a pretender to the throne.*

pre'tension [-ʃən] (*formal*) **1** *nc* (*esp in pl*) a claim: *I have no pretensions to musical skill.* **2** *nu* (*derog*) self-importance: *He lacks all pretension, in spite of his great popularity as a writer.*

pre'tentious [-ʃəs] *adj* (*neg* **un-**: *derog*) having, or showing, pretension (*def 2*): *He is a pretentious writer*; *His plays are pretentious and silly*; *They live in a rather pretentious-looking house.* **pre'tentiously** *adv.* **pre'tentiousness** *nu.*

false pretences *n pl* (*legal*) acts or behaviour intended to deceive: *He got the money by/on/under false pretences.*

preternatural [priːtə'natʃərəl] *adj* (*very formal*) beyond what is natural; abnormal: *The child has a preternatural grasp of mathematics.* ˌ**preter'naturally** *adv.*

pretext ['priːtekst] *nc* a reason given in order to hide the real reason; an excuse: *He left early, on the pretext of having another appointment.*

pretty ['priti] *adj* **1** (not *usu* of boys and never of men) pleasing or attractive to see or listen to: *a pretty girl/tune*; *She is dark and pretty.* **2** (*ironic*) fine: *This is a pretty mess!* – *adv* (*inf*) fairly: *That's pretty good*; *He's pretty old now.*

'**prettily** *adv.* '**prettiness** *nu.*

a pretty kettle of fish *see* **kettle.**

pretty much the same, alike *etc* (*inf*) more or less the same, alike *etc*: *The houses are all pretty much alike.*

'**pretty well** (*inf*) nearly: *I've pretty well finished.*

prevail [pri'veil] *vi* **1** (*with* **over** *or* **against**: *esp liter*) to win or succeed (against an enemy *etc*): *With God's help we shall prevail over sin and wickedness*; *Truth must prevail in the end.* **2** (*formal*) to be most usual or common: *This mistaken belief still prevails in some parts of the country.* – *See also* **prevail on** *below.*

pre'vailing *adj* (*formal*: *attrib*) **1** most frequent: *The prevailing winds are from the west.* **2** common or widespread at the present time, or at the time mentioned: *the prevailing mood of discontent among young people.*

prevalent ['prevələnt] *adj* (*formal*) common; widespread: *Lung diseases used to be prevalent among miners*; *a prevalent misconception.*

prevalence ['prevələns] *nu*: *the prevalence of certain ideas.*

pre'vail on, upon *vts fus* (*formal*) to persuade: *Can I prevail on you to stay for supper?*

prevaricate [pri'varikeit] *vi* (*formal*) to avoid telling the truth: *I asked him what had happened, but he prevaricated.*

preˌvari'cation *ncu*: *lies and prevarications.*

prevent [pri'vent] *vt* (*more formal than* **stop**) to stop (someone doing something or something happening): *He prevented me from going*; *Her illness prevented my going*; *Rain prevented the football match.*

pre'vention [-ʃən] *nu* the act of preventing: *a*

society for the prevention of road accidents.

pre'ventive [-tiv] *adj* (*formal or tech*: *esp attrib*) that helps to prevent illness *etc*: *preventive medicine*; *preventive dentistry.*

preview ['pri:vju:] *nc* a viewing of a performance, exhibition *etc* before it is open to the public: *There will be a preview of the exhibition on the night before it opens.*

previous ['pri:viəs] *adj* **1** (*more formal than* **earlier**: *attrib*) earlier in time or order: *on a previous occasion*; *the previous owner of the house.* **2** (*pred*: *very formal or facet*) too quick or hasty: *Your congratulations are rather previous – I don't know if I've got the job yet!* '**previously** *adv.*

'**previous to** before: *They told their families about their engagement previous to publishing it in the newspaper.*

prey [prei] – *pl* **prey** – *ncu* a bird or animal, birds or animals, that is/are hunted by other birds or animals for food: *The lion carried off its prey/ate some of its prey*; *The tiger's prey ran off into the jungle.*

be a 'prey to to be a sufferer from: *He is a prey to anxiety.*

beast/bird of prey an animal, *eg* the lion, or a bird, *eg* the eagle, that kills and eats others.

'**prey on, upon** *vts fus* (*formal*) to attack as prey: *Hawks prey upon smaller birds*; (*fig*) *Fears preyed on her mind.*

price [prais] *nc* **1** the amount of money for which a thing is or can be bought or sold; the cost: *The price of the book was £5*; *4p was the price of my bus ticket*; (*facet*) *Everyone has his price* (= can be bribed). **2** (*fig*) what one must give up or suffer in order to gain something: *Loss of freedom is often the price of success.* – *vt* **1** to mark a price on: *I haven't priced these articles yet.* **2** (*inf*) to find out the price of: *He went into the furniture shop to price the beds.*

'**priceless** *adj* **1** too valuable to have a price: *priceless jewels*; *Those diamonds are priceless.* **2** (*inf*) very funny: *I heard a priceless story today*; *That story is priceless.*

'**pricey** *adj* (*inf*) very expensive: *Meat is getting pricey nowadays.*

at a 'price at a high price: *We can get dinner at this hotel – at a price!*

at the 'price of (*formal*) paying (something) as a price: *He became a very powerful man, but at the price of his self-respect.*

beyond/without price priceless (*def 1*): *Good health is beyond price.*

price something/oneself out of the market to charge so much for something, or for one's services, that no one can afford to pay: *If you ask as much as that for your house, you will price it out of the market.*

prick [prik] *vt* to pierce slightly or stick a sharp point into: *She pricked her finger on/with a pin*; *He pricked a hole in the paper.* – *nc* **1** (a pain caused by) an act of pricking: *You'll just feel a slight prick in your arm*; *He gave her a prick with a pin.* **2** (*often in cmpds*) a tiny hole made by a sharp point: *a pin-prick.* **3** (*vulg sl*) a penis.

prick (up) one's ears **1** (of an animal) to raise the ears in excitement, attention *etc*: *The dog pricked up its ears at the sound of the doorbell.* **2** (*inf fig*) (of people) to start to pay attention: *He pricked up his ears at the mention of food.*

prickle ['prikl] *nc* **1** a sharp point growing on a plant or animal: *A hedgehog is covered with prickles.* **2** (*fig formal*) a feeling of being pricked: *a prickle of fear.*

'**prickly** *adj* **1** covered with prickles: *Holly is a very prickly plant*; *Holly is prickly.* **2** pricking; stinging: *a prickly sensation*; *This rash feels rather prickly.* '**prickliness** *nu.*

pride [praid] **1** *nu* a feeling of (justifiable) pleasure and satisfaction at one's achievements, possessions, family *etc*: *She looked with pride at her handsome sons*; *The ancient Greeks believed that the gods punished men for their pride.* **2** *nu* personal dignity: *Anyone who wears such terrible clothes has no pride*; *His pride was hurt by her criticism.* **3** *nc* a group (of lions or of peacocks): *a pride of lions.*

be the 'pride and 'joy of to be the object of the pride of: *He was the pride and joy of his parents/his parents' pride and joy.*

the 'pride of the finest thing in (a certain class, collection *etc*): *The pride of our collection is this painting by Carpaccio.*

pride of place the most important place: *They gave pride of place at the exhibition to a painting by Canaletto*; *Pride of place went to a small Chinese vase.*

'**pride oneself on,** (*formal*) **upon** to take pride in, or feel satisfaction with (something one has done, achieved *etc*): *He prides himself on his driving skill.*

take pride in (something) to feel pride about: *I take pride in my family's achievements*; *You should take more pride in* (= care more for) *your appearance.*

See also **proud**.

priest [pri:st] – *fem* '**priestess** (*def 2*) – *nc* **1** (in the Christian Church, *esp* the Roman Catholic, Orthodox and Anglican churches) a clergyman. **2** (in non-Christian religions) an official who performs sacrifices *etc* to the god(s).

'**priesthood** *nu* (*formal*) **1** priests in general: *the Anglican priesthood.* **2** the office or position of a priest: *He was called to the priesthood.*

prig [prig] *nc* (*derog*) a person who is too satisfied with his/her own behaviour, beliefs *etc*; a smug person: *He is such a prig that he thinks he is better than anyone else.* '**priggish** *adj.* '**priggishly** *adv.* '**priggishness** *nu.*

prim [prim] *adj* (*derog*) (of a person, behaviour *etc*) too formal and correct: *a prim manner*; *rather a prim old lady*; *The old lady is rather prim and was embarrassed by the workman's jokes.* '**primly** *adv.* '**primness** *nu.*

prima ['pri:mə]: ˌ**prima** ˌ**balle'rina** *nc* the leading female dancer in a ballet company.

ˌ**prima 'donna** [-'donə] *nc* **1** a leading female opera singer. **2** (*derog*) a person, *esp* a woman, who is over-sensitive and difficult to please: *Our new boss is rather a prima donna.*

primacy *see* **prime**[1].

primaeval *see* **primeval**.

primary *see* **prime**[1].

primate[1] ['praimeit] *nc* an archbishop.

See also **primacy** *under* **prime**[1].

primate[2] ['praimət] *nc* (*tech*) a member of the highest order of mammals, *ie* man, monkeys, apes, lemurs.

prime[1] [praim] *adj* (*attrib*) **1** first or most important: *the prime minister*; *The matter is of prime importance.* **2** best: *prime meat*; *in prime condition.* – *nu* (*formal or facet*) the best part (of a person's *etc* life, *usu* early middle age): *He is in his prime*; *She's past her prime*; *in the prime of life*; *The apple trees are in their prime now.*

ˈ**primacy** *ncu* (*formal*) the state or condition of being first or supreme, *esp* the position of an archbishop.

ˈ**primary** *adj* (*attrib*) **1** (*formal*) first or most important: *his primary concern.* **2** of the first level or stage: *a primary school.* – **1** *ncu* a primary school. **2** *nc* (*Amer*) the first stage in an election, in which the voters of each party nominate candidates.

ˈ**primarily** [(*Amer*) praiˈme-] *adv* (*formal*) chiefly; in the first place: *I wrote the play primarily as a protest, and only secondarily as entertainment*; *His job, primarily, is to deal with the firm's foreign correspondence.*

primary colours *n pl* (of pigments, but not of light) those colours from which all others can be made, *ie* red, blue and yellow.

ˈ**primary school** *nc* a school for children in the first stages of education: *She has two children at primary school and one at secondary school.*

primary stress **1** *ncu* (an example of) the strongest of the degrees of stress that may be applied to a syllable of a word when pronouncing it: *The first syllable of the word 'football' carries (a) primary stress.* **2** *nc* a mark used to indicate the position of this stress in a word: *In the entry for 'primary school' above, there is a primary stress before the 'p'.*

prime minister *nc* the chief minister of a government.

prime mover *nc* the original force that sets something in motion: *He was the prime mover in the protest against the new motorway.*

prime number *nc* (*math*) a number that can only be divided without a remainder by itself and 1, *eg* 3, 5, 7, 31.

See also **premier, secondary.**

prime[2] [praim] *vt* **1** (*tech*) to prepare (something) by putting something into or on it: *He primed* (= put gunpowder into) *his gun*; *You must prime* (= treat with primer) *the wood before you paint it.* **2** (*fig*) to prepare (someone) by giving him information: *She was well primed with the facts before the meeting.*

ˈ**primer** **1** *nc* (*esp old*) a book that gives information about a subject (*usu* as an introduction to it): *a Latin primer.* **2** *nu* (*tech*) a substance put on a surface to prime it before painting: *a tin of metal/wood primer.*

primeval, primaeval [praiˈmiːvəl] *adj* (*liter*: *attrib*) of or belonging to the first ages of history: *primeval forests.*

primitive [ˈprimətiv] *adj* **1** (*esp attrib*) belonging to the earliest times: *primitive stone tools*; *primitive civilizations.* **2** simple or rough: *We were living in rather primitive conditions in a tent*; *He made a primitive boat out of some pieces of wood*; *Conditions in the campsite were rather primitive.* – *nc* **1** an artist of the period before the Renaissance. **2** an artist of the 19th or 20th century who painted in a very simple style. **3** a painting or sculpture of either of these periods: *I've just bought a couple of French primitives.*

primrose [ˈprimrouz] **1** *nc* a kind of pale yellow spring flower common in woods and hedges. **2** *nu, adj* (*also* **primrose yellow**) (of) its colour: *The walls were painted in pale primrose*; *primrose walls.*

prince [prins] *nc* (*with cap in titles*) **1** (the status of) a male member of a royal family, *esp* the son of a king or queen. **2** (the status of) the ruler of some states or countries: *Prince Rainier of Monaco.*

ˈ**princely** *adj* (*attrib*) **1** (*formal*) of a prince: *his princely duties.* **2** (*formal or facet*) magnificent; splendid: *a princely gift*; *a princely sum of money*; *My salary isn't exactly princely.*

princess [prinˈses, (*Amer*) ˈprinsəs] *nc* (*with cap in titles*) **1** (the status of) the wife or widow of a prince: *Princess Mary.* **2** (the status of) a woman of the same rank as a prince in her own right.

ˌ**princiˈpality** [-ˈpa-] *nc* a state or country ruled by a prince: *the principality of Monaco.*

principal [ˈprinsəpəl] *adj* (*attrib*: *more formal than* **chief**) most important: *Shipbuilding is one of Britain's principal industries.* – **1** *nc* the head of a school, college or university. **2** *nc* a leading actor, singer or dancer in a theatrical production: *He started in the chorus and now he's one of the principals.* **3** *nu* (*formal*) the amount of money in a bank *etc* on which interest is paid.

ˈ**principally** *adv* mostly; chiefly: *I am principally concerned with teaching English.*

principal clause *nc* (*gram*) a main clause.

principality *see* **prince.**

principle [ˈprinsəpəl] *nc* **1** a general truth, rule or law: *the principle of gravity*; *the principles of economy.* **2** the theory by which a machine *etc* works: *the principle of the jet engine.* – *See also* **in principle, on principle** *below.*

ˈ**principles** *n pl* one's own personal rules or standards of behaviour: *It is against my principles to borrow money.*

in ˈprinciple in general, as opposed to in detail: *I think it is a good idea in principle, but I must know all the details before I finally agree.*

on ˈprinciple because of one's principles or moral standards: *He refused to do it on principle.*

See also **unprincipled.**

print [print] **1** *nc* (*often in cmpds*) a mark made by pressure: *a footprint*; *a fingerprint.* **2** *nu* printed lettering: *I can't read the print in this book.* **3** *nc* a photograph made from a negative: *I entered three prints for the photographic competition.* **4** *nc* a printed reproduction of a painting or drawing: *There was an eighteenth century print above the fireplace.* **5** *ncu* material(s) with a printed design: *Prints are popular this season*; (*attrib*) *print curtains.* – *See also* **be in/out of print** *below.* – **1** *vt* to mark (letters *etc*) on paper (by using a printing press *etc*): *The invitations will be printed on white paper.* **2** *vt* to publish (a book, article *etc*) in printed form: *His new novel will be printed next month.* **3** *vt* to produce (a photographic image) on paper: *He develops and prints his own photographs.* **4** *vt* to mark designs on (cloth *etc*): *When the cloth has been woven, it is dyed and printed.* **5** *vti* to write, *usu* using capital letters: *I can't read his writing, so I asked him to print the information*; *Please print neatly!*

ˈ**printable** *adj* (*usu pred*: *neg* **un-**) suitable to be printed or published: *Only half of what he said was printable.*

ˈ**printer** *nc* **1** a person who prints books, newspapers *etc.* **2** a printer's factory.

ˈ**printer's** *nc* a printer's factory: *We've sent the book to the printer's.*

ˈ**printing-press** *nc* (*also* **press**) a machine for printing (*defs 1, 2*).

ˈ**print-out** *ncu* the printed information given by a computer.

be in/out of print (of books) available/unavailable to be bought from the publisher: *That particular book has been out of print for years.*

prior[1] ['praiə] *adj* (*formal*: *attrib*) **1** already arranged for the same time: *I could not go to the meeting as I had a prior engagement.* **2** more important: *She gave up her job as she felt her family had a prior claim on/to her attention.*

pri'ority [-'o-] **1** *nu* (*formal*) the right to be or go first: *An ambulance must have priority over other traffic*; *You must give priority to ambulances.* **2** *nc* something that must be considered or done first: *Our* (*first*) *priority is to feed the hungry.*

'prior to (*formal*) before: *Prior to working in America, he had travelled in Europe for several years.*

prior[2] ['praiə] – *fem* **'prioress** – *nc* the head of a priory.

'priory *nc* a building in which a community of monks or nuns live.

prise, (*esp Amer*) **prize** [praiz] *vt* to use force to dislodge (something) from its position: *He prised open the lid with a knife*; *She prised the shell off the rock.*

prism ['prizm] *nc* **1** (*geom*) a solid figure whose sides are parallel and whose two ends are the same in shape and size. **2** (*esp tech*) a figure like this, *usu* with triangular ends made of glass, which breaks up a beam of white light into the colours of the rainbow.

pris'matic [-'ma-] *adj* (*formal or tech*) **1** of or like a prism. **2** (of colours) bright and varied.

prison ['prizn] *nc* **1** a building in which criminals are kept; a jail: *He was sent to prison*; *He is in prison*; *There has been rioting in the prison.* **2** any place where someone is kept against his or her will: *She could no longer walk and her room became a prison.*

'prisoner *nc* anyone who has been captured and is held against his will as a criminal, in a war *etc*: *The prisoners escaped from jail.* – *See also* **take/keep prisoner** *below.*

prisoner of war – *pl* **prisoners of war** – *nc* (*often abbrev* **POW**) a member of the armed forces captured in a war.

take, keep, hold (someone) prisoner to (capture and) confine (a person) against his will: *Many soldiers were killed and the rest taken prisoner*; *She was kept/held prisoner in a locked room.*

pristine ['pristi:n] *adj* (*formal*: *attrib*) in the original unspoiled state: *They restored the old palace to its pristine magnificence.*

private ['praivət] *adj* **1** of, for, or belonging to, one person or group, not to the general public: *The headmaster lives in a private apartment in the school*; *The door was marked 'private'*; *It is my private* (= personal) *opinion that he is lazy*; *This information is to be kept strictly private* (= must be given to no-one else); *You shouldn't listen to private conversations.* **2** having no public or official position or rank: *It is your duty as a private citizen to report this matter to the police*; *a private member* (= a member of parliament who is not a minister). – *See also* **in private** *below.* – *nc* (*with cap, and often abbrev* **Pte**, *when written in titles*) in the British army, (a person of) the lowest rank of ordinary soldier: *He is a private in the Scots Guards*; *Private Craig.*

privacy ['privəsi, (*Amer*) 'prai-] *nu* the state of being away from other people's sight or interest: *He built a high wall around his garden to preserve his privacy*; *in the privacy of your own home.*

'privately *adv.*

private enterprise *nu* the management and financing of industry *etc* by individual persons or companies and not by the state.

private means *n pl* money that does not come from one's work but from investment, inheritance *etc*: *She is a woman of private means.*

in 'private with no-one else listening or watching; not in public: *May I speak to you in private?*

See also **privy**[1].

privation [prai'veiʃən] *ncu* (*formal*) poverty; hardship; want: *They were living in conditions of terrible privation*; *We suffered some privations during the war.*

See also **deprivation** *under* **deprive**.

privet ['privit] *nu* (*usu attrib*) a type of bush often grown to form hedges: *a privet hedge.*

privilege ['privəlidʒ] *ncu* (a) favour or right available, or granted, to only one person, or to a small number of people: *Senior students are usually allowed certain privileges*; (*formal*) *It is a privilege* (= an honour) *to meet you*; *He was born into a world of wealth and privilege* (= social and educational advantage). **'privileged** *adj.*

See also **underprivileged**.

privy[1] ['privi]: **privy council** *nc* a group of statesmen appointed as advisers to a king or queen.

be 'privy to (*old or formal*) to know about (something not generally known): *Were you privy to their decision?*

privy[2] ['privi] *nc* (*old*) a toilet.

prize[1] [praiz] *nc* **1** a reward for good work *etc*: *He was awarded a lot of prizes at school.* **2** (*sometimes attrib*) something won in a competition *etc*: *I've won first prize!*; *a prize* (= having won, or worthy of, a prize) *bull*; (*ironic*) *I've made a prize fool of myself!* – *vt* (*formal*) to value (something) highly: *He prized my friendship above everything else.*

'prize-fight *nc* a boxing-match fought for money. **'prize-fighter** *nc.* **'prize-fighting** *nu.*

prize[2] *see* **prise**.

pro[1] [prou] short for **professional, prostitute**.

pro[2] [prou]: **pros and cons** [prouzən'konz] the arguments for and against: *Let's hear all the pros and cons before we make a decision.*

pro- [prou] (*in cmpds*) in favour of: **ˌpro-'British**.

probable ['probəbl] *adj* that may be expected to happen or be true; likely: *the probable result*; *It seems probable that he will come*; *Such an event is possible but not probable.*

'probably *adv*: *I'll probably telephone you this evening.*

ˌproba'bility 1 *nu* the state or fact of being probable; likelihood: *There isn't much probability of that happening*; *There's little probability of success.* **2** *nc* an event, result *etc* that is probable: *Let's consider the probabilities.*

in all probability most probably; most likely: *In all probability we shall arrive before them.*

See also **improbable**.

probate ['proubeit] (*legal*) **1** *nu* the legal process of examining a will and establishing that it is valid. **2** *nc* the official copy of a will.

probation [prə'beiʃən, (*Amer*) prou-] *nu* **1** the system allowing people who have broken the law to go free on condition that they commit no more crimes and report regularly to a social worker (called a **pro'bation officer**). **2** (in certain jobs) a period of time during which a person is carefully watched to see that he is capable of the job: *After leaving college, teachers have to do a year's probation* *before they are fully qualified.* – See also **on probation** *below.*

pro'bationary *adj* (*formal*: *usu attrib*): *a probationary period*; *a probationary nurse.*

pro'bationer *nc* a person on probation.

be/put on probation to (cause to) undergo a period of probation: *New members of staff are on probation for a year*; *Juvenile offenders are usually put on probation.*

probe [proub] *nc* **1** (*tech*) a long thin instrument used by doctors to examine a wound *etc.* **2** (*formal fig*) an investigation: *a police probe into illegal activities.* – **1** *vi* (*with* **into**) to examine carefully; investigate: *He probed into her private life.* **2** *vti* to examine (as if) with a probe: *The doctor probed the wound*; *He probed about in the hole with a stick.*

probity ['proubəti] *nu* (*formal*) honesty; goodness of character: *You can rely on his probity.*

problem ['probləm] *nc* **1** a difficulty; a matter about which it is difficult to decide what to do: *Life is full of problems*; (*attrib*) *a problem child* (= a child whose behaviour causes problems). **2** a question to be answered or solved: *The teacher set the boys three mathematical problems for homework.*

ˌproble'matic(al) [-'ma-] *adj* (of something in the future) doubtful; uncertain: *The future of the school is problematic(al)*; *a problematic issue.*

proboscis [prə'bosis] *nc* (*tech*) **1** the nose of some animals, *esp* the trunk of an elephant. **2** the trunk-like mouth of some insects.

procedure [prə'siːdʒə] *ncu* (*formal*) the order or method of doing something: *according to normal legal procedure*; *They followed the usual procedure(s).* **pro'cedural** *adj.*

proceed [prə'siːd] *vi* **1** (*formal*) to go on; to continue: *They proceeded along the road*; *They proceeded with their work.* **2** (*formal*) to follow a course of action: *I'd like to start teaching again, but I don't know how to proceed* (= what actions to take). **3** (*more formal than* **begin**) to begin (to do something): *They proceeded to ask a lot of questions.* **4** (*with* **from**: *formal*) to be the result of; to originate in: *Fear often proceeds from ignorance.* **5** (*with* **against**: *legal*) to take legal action (against): *The police decided not to proceed against her.*

pro'ceedings *n pl* **1** the things said and done at a meeting of a society *etc*: *The secretary made a note of the proceedings.* **2** a legal action: *We shall start proceedings against him if the bill is not paid.*

proceeds ['prousiːdz] *n pl* money or profit made (from a sale *etc*): *They gave the proceeds of the sale to charity.*

process ['prouses, (*Amer*) 'pro-] *nc* **1** a method or way of manufacturing things: *We are using a new process to make glass.* **2** a series of events that produce change or development: *The process of growing up can be difficult for a child*; *Food is absorbed into the body by various digestive processes*; *A year in France will complete his educational process.* **3** a course of action undertaken: *Carrying him down the mountain was a slow process.* – *vt* (*tech*) to deal with (something) by the appropriate process: *Have your photographs been processed?* (= developed and printed); *The information is being processed* (= analysed by a computer).

'processed *adj* (of food) treated in a special way: *processed cheese/peas.*

in the 'process of in the course of: *He is in the process of changing jobs*; *These goods were damaged in the process of manufacture*; *In the process of making the beds, she discovered the lost toy*; *I was looking for your house, and got lost in the process.*

procession [prə'seʃən] *nc* a line of people, vehicles *etc* moving forward, *esp* in order for a ceremonial purpose: *The procession moved slowly through the streets of London.*

proclaim [prə'kleim, (*Amer*) prou-] *vt* (*formal*) to announce or state publicly: *He was proclaimed the winner*; *A holiday was proclaimed*; (*fig liter*) *The state of his clothes proclaimed his poverty.*

ˌprocla'mation [proklə-] **1** *nc* an official, *usu* ceremonial, announcement made to the public: *a royal proclamation.* **2** *nu* the act of proclaiming: *the proclamation of the king's abdication.*

procrastinate [prə'krastineit] *vi* (*formal*) to put off or delay doing something: *He is always procrastinating.* **proˌcrasti'nation** *nu.* **pro'crastinator** *nc.*

procreate ['proukrieit] *vt* (*formal*) to produce (children or young). **ˌprocre'ation** *nu.*

procurator-fiscal [prokjureitə'fiskəl] *nc* (*legal*) in Scotland, the prosecuting officer of a district.

procure [prə'kjuə] **1** *vt* (*formal or facet*) to get or obtain: *He managed to procure a car.* **2** *vti* (*legal*) to provide (a prostitute *etc*) for sexual pleasure: *He made money by procuring (prostitutes) for rich men.*

prod [prod] – *pt, ptp* **'prodded** – **1** *vti* to push with something pointed; to poke: *He prodded her arm with his finger*; *Stop prodding me!*; *She prodded at the dog with her umbrella.* **2** *vt* (*fig*) to urge or encourage (someone to do something): *He prodded her into action.* – *nc* an act of prodding: *She gave him a prod.*

prodigal ['prodigəl] *adj* (*liter*) spending (money) too extravagantly; wasteful: *He was prodigal with his money.* – *nc* (*liter*) a prodigal person. **'prodigally** *adv.* **ˌprodi'gality** [-'ga-] *nu.*

prodigy ['prodidʒi] *nc* (*formal*) something strange or wonderful, *esp* a person who is unusually clever at something: *a child prodigy* (= an amazingly clever or talented child); *volcanoes and other prodigies of nature.*

pro'digious [-'didʒəs] *adj* (*old or liter*: *usu attrib*) **1** strange or wonderful: *a prodigious sight.* **2** very big; enormous: *a prodigious sum of money.* **pro'digiously** *adv.*

produce [prə'djuːs] *vt* **1** to bring out: *She produced a letter from her pocket.* **2** to give birth to: *A cow produces one or two calves a year.* **3** to cause or bring about: *His joke produced a shriek of laughter from the children.* **4** to make or manufacture: *The factory produces furniture.* **5** to give or yield: *The country produces enough food for the population.* **6** to arrange (a theatre performance, or the making of a film, television programme *etc*): *The play was produced by Henry Dobson.* – ['prodjuːs] *nu* something that is produced (*def 5*), *esp* crops, eggs, milk *etc* from farms: *agricultural/farm produce.*

pro'ducer *nc* **1** a person who produces a play, film, *etc*, but is *usu* not responsible for instructing the actors. **2** (*formal*) someone or something that produces: *Canada is a producer of wheat.*

product ['prodəkt] *nc* **1** a result: *The plan was the product of hours of thought.* **2** something manufactured: *The firm manufactures metal products.* **3** (*math*) the result of multiplying one number by another: *The product of 9 and 2 is 18.*

pro'duction [-'dʌkʃən] **1** *nu* (*sometimes in cmpds*) the act or process of producing something: *The* *production of the new evidence astonished the court*; *car-production*; *The production of the film cost a million dollars.* **2** *nu* the amount produced, *esp* of manufactured goods: *The new techniques increased production.* **3** *nc* a particular performance, or set of repeated performances, of a play, opera or ballet: *I prefer this production of 'Hamlet' to the one I saw two years ago.*

pro'ductive [-'dʌktiv] *adj* (*neg* **un-**: *formal*) **1** producing a lot; fruitful: *productive land.* **2** (*fig*) giving (good) results: *productive ideas*; *Our discussion was not very productive.*

productivity [prodək'tivəti] *nu* the rate or efficiency of work *esp* in industrial production: *We must increase productivity.*

pro'ductive of (*very formal*) tending to produce: *Such a policy can be productive only of further industrial troubles.*

profane [prə'fein, (*Amer*) prou-] *adj* (*formal*) showing contempt for God or holy things: *profane talk*; *Please do not be so profane.* **pro'fanely** *adv.*

pro'fanity [-'fa-] (*formal*) **1** *nu* lack of respect for God or holy things: *an age of profanity.* **2** *ncu* word(s) showing contempt for God; swear-words: *He uttered a string of profanities on discovering that the car would not start.*

profess [prə'fes] *vt* (*formal*) **1** to state or declare openly: *He professed his belief in her innocence.* **2** (not *usu* used with **is, was** *etc* and **-ing**) to claim or pretend (to be): *He professed to be an expert.*

pro'fession [-ʃən] **1** *nc* an occupation or job that needs special knowledge, *eg* medicine, law, teaching, engineering *etc.* **2** *nu* the people who have such an occupation: *the legal profession.* **3** *nc* (*formal*) an open statement or declaration: *a profession of faith in God.*

pro'fessional [-ʃə-] *adj* (*neg* **un-**) **1** (*usu attrib*) of a profession: *professional skill.* **2** of a very high standard: *a very professional performance*; *As an actor, he is so professional!* **3** earning money by performing, or giving instruction, in a sport or other activity that is a pastime for other people; not amateur: *a professional musician*; *a professional golfer*; *He turned* (= became) *professional last year.* – *nc* (*inf abbrev* **pro** [prou]) a person who is professional (*defs 2, 3*): *He's a real professional/pro!*; *a golf professional/pro.*

pro'fessionally *adv.*

professor [prə'fesə] *nc* (*with cap, and often abbrev* **Prof.**, *when written in titles*) **1** a teacher of the highest rank in a university; the head of a university department: *He is a professor of English at Leeds*; *Professor Jones.* **2** (*Amer*) a university teacher. **ˌprofes'sorial** [profə'so:-] *adj* (*formal*).

pro'fessorship *nc* the post of a professor: *He has got a professorship at Oxford.*

proffer ['profə] – *pt, ptp* **'proffered** – *vt* (*formal*) to offer: *May I proffer some advice?*

proficient [prə'fiʃənt] *adj* (*formal*) skilled; expert: *She is proficient in typing*; *a most proficient typist.*

pro'ficiently *adv.*

pro'ficiency *nu*: *He showed great proficiency in (speaking) French.*

profile ['proufail] *nc* **1** the view of a face, head *etc* from the side; a side view: *She has a beautiful profile*; *He painted her in profile* (= from the side). **2** a short description of a person's life, work *etc*: *The newspaper published a profile of the new member of parliament.*

profit ['profit] **1** *ncu* money which is gained in business *etc*, *eg* from selling something for more than one paid for it: *I made a profit of £1 000 on my house*; *How much profit did you make?*; *He sold it at a great profit*; *The firm has made large profits from exports.* **2** *nu* advantage; benefit: *A great deal of profit can be gained from living abroad.* – *v* – *pt, ptp* **'profited** – *vi* (*with* **from** *or* **by**) to gain profit(s) from: *The business profited from its exports*; (*fig*) *I am profiting by my mistakes.*

'profitable *adj* (*neg* **un-**) giving profit: *The deal was quite profitable*; *a profitable experience.* **'profitably** *adv.*

ˌprofi'teer *vi* (*derog*) to make large profits, *esp* unfairly, *eg* in wartime. – *nc* a person who does this.

profligate ['profligət] *adj* (*old or liter*: *often derog*) **1** (of a person) living an immoral life: *He punished his profligate son*; *He is wicked and profligate.* **2** (of spending *etc*) too extravagant: *a profligate way of life.* – *nc* (*derog*) a profligate person.

'profligacy [-gəsi] *nu.*

profound [prə'faund] *adj* (*formal*) **1** (*fig*: *usu attrib*) deep: *profound sleep*; *She sat in profound thought*; *profound happiness.* **2** showing great knowledge or understanding: *a profound remark*; *His comments were very profound.* **pro'foundly** *adv.* **pro'fundity** [-'fʌn-] *ncu.*

profuse [prə'fju:s] *adj* (*formal*) (too) plentiful; excessive: *He offered profuse apologies*; *He was very profuse in his thanks.* **pro'fusely** *adv.*

pro'fusion [-ʒən] *nu* (*formal*) (*sometimes with* **a**) (too) great abundance: *a profusion of flowers.*

progenitor [prə'dʒenitə] *nc* (*old*) an ancestor.

progeny ['prodʒəni] *n pl* (*formal or facet*) children: *He managed to get his numerous progeny into the car.*

prognosticate [prəg'nostikeit] *vt* (*very formal*) to foretell; to forecast: *All the signs prognosticate a bad winter.* **progˌnosti'cation** *ncu.*

programme, (*Amer*) **program** ['prougram] *nc* **1** (a booklet or paper giving the details of) the planned items or events in an entertainment, ceremony *etc*: *According to the programme, the show begins at 8.00*; *What is on the programme for tonight's concert?* **2** a plan or scheme: *a political programme*; *a programme of social reform.* **3** (*Brit and Amer* **'program**) a set of information, instructions *etc* put into a computer.

'program *v* – *prp* **'programming** (*Amer also* **'programing**): *pt, ptp* **'programmed** (*Amer also* **'programed**) – *vti* to give information, instructions *etc* to (a machine, *esp* a computer, so that it can do a particular job): *Do you know how to program a computer?*

'programmer *nc* a person who prepares a program for a computer.

progress ['prougres, (*Amer*) 'pro-] *nu* **1** movement forward; advance: *the progress of civilization.* **2** improvement: *Progress has been made in the treatment of many serious illnesses*; *The students are making (good) progress.* – *See also* **in progress** *below.* – [prə'gres] *vi* **1** (*formal or facet*) to go forward: *We had progressed only a few miles when the car broke down.* **2** (*formal*) to improve: *Your French is progressing.*

pro'gression [-ʃən] *nu* (*formal*) movement forward: *the slow progression of the mourners*; (*fig*) *the progression of one's thoughts.*

pro'gressive [-siv] *adj* **1** (*usu attrib*) moving forward, advancing, *esp* by stages: *the progressive deterioration of her health.* **2** using, or favouring, new methods: *progressive education*; *The new* *headmaster is very progressive.* **3** (*gram*) (of a tense of a verb) indicating continuing action: *In 'I am sitting' and 'he was laughing', the verbs are in progressive tenses or forms.* – *ncu* (a verb in) the progressive tense or form: *'Am sitting' is a progressive.*

pro'gressively *adv.* **pro'gressiveness** *nu.*

in 'progress happening; taking place: *There is a meeting in progress; Work is in progress on this scheme.*

prohibit *vt* (*formal*) **1** to forbid: *Smoking is prohibited.* **2** to prevent: *We were prohibited from travelling by the bad weather.*

prohibition [proui'biʃən] **1** *nu* (*formal*) the act of prohibiting: *We demand the prohibition by the government of the sale of this drug.* **2** *nc* (*formal*) a rule, law *etc* forbidding something: *The headmaster issued a prohibition against bringing knives into school.* **3** *nu* (*sometimes with cap*) the forbidding by law of the making and selling of alcoholic drinks, *esp* in the United States in the 1920s.

pro'hibitive [-tiv] *adj* **1** prohibiting: *prohibitive laws.* **2** (*fig*: of prices, costs *etc*) so high that it is almost impossible to buy: *The price of houses is prohibitive nowadays; prohibitive prices.*

project ['prodʒekt] *nc* **1** a plan or scheme: *a building project.* **2** a piece of study or research: *I am doing a project on Italian art.* – [prə'dʒekt] (*formal*) **1** *vt* to throw outwards, forwards or upwards: *The missile was projected into space; The light projected his shadow on to the wall.* **2** *vi* to stick out: *A sharp rock projected from the sea.* **3** *vt* to plan or propose: *A new dictionary has been projected.*

pro'jectile [-tail, (*Amer*) -tl] *nc* something that is thrown, *usu* as a weapon: *The projectile was fired into space.* **pro'jection** [-ʃən] *ncu.*

pro'jector *nc* a machine for projecting films on to a screen: *a movie projector.*

proletarian [proulə'teəriən] *adj, nc* (*liter or formal*) (a member) of the ordinary working people: *a proletarian society; As a proletarian, I would say this is wrong.*

ˌprole'tariat [-ət] *nu* proletarians as a whole: *the opinions of the proletariat.*

proliferate [prə'lifəreit] *vi* (*formal*) to grow or increase rapidly: *This kind of plant proliferates in a warm climate.* **proˌlife'ration** *nu.*

prolific [prə'lifik] *adj* (*formal*: *usu attrib*) producing a lot; abundant: *prolific plant growth; a prolific writer.*

prolix ['prouliks, (*Amer*) prou'liks] *adj* (*very formal*) using too many words; long and dull: *a prolix speaker/speech.*

prologue ['proulog] *nc* an introduction, *esp* to a play: *The prologue was spoken by one of the actors; The meeting was a prologue to official discussions.*

prolong [prə'loŋ] *vt* to make longer: *We prolonged our holiday until September; Please do not prolong the discussion unnecessarily.*

pro'longed *adj* (*sometimes derog*) very long: *after prolonged discussion; The discussion was rather prolonged.*

prolongation [prouloŋ'geiʃən] *ncu.*

prom [prom] *nc* **1** (*inf*) short for **promenade**. **2** short for **promenade concert**.

promenade [promə'na:d, (*Amer*) -'neid] *nc* **1** (*inf abbrev* **prom** [prom]) a level road for the public to walk along, *usu* beside the sea: *They went for a walk along the promenade.* **2** (*old*) a walk (for pleasure); a stroll: *They went for a promenade along the beach.* – *vti* (*old or facet*) to (cause to) walk or stroll, *esp* with the intention of attracting notice: *She promenaded along the street in her new clothes; She promenaded her children through the park.*

promenade concert *nc* a concert at which part of the audience is not seated.

prominent ['prominənt] *adj* **1** standing out; projecting: *a prominent nose/chin; Her front teeth are rather prominent.* **2** (*usu attrib*) easily seen: *The church tower is a prominent landmark.* **3** (*fig*: *usu attrib*) famous; distinguished: *a prominent politician.* **'prominently** *adv.* **'prominence** *ncu.*

promiscuous [prə'miskjuəs] *adj* (*formal derog*) having many sexual relationships: *a promiscuous person; She has many men friends but is not at all promiscuous.* **pro'miscuously** *adv.* **promiscuity** [promi'skju:əti] , **pro'miscuousness** *nus.*

promise ['promis] **1** *vti* to say, or give one's assurance (that one will, or will not, do something *etc*): *I promise* (*that*) *I won't be late; I promise not to be late; I won't be late, I promise* (*you*)*!* **2** *vt* to say or give one's assurance that one will give: *He promised me a new coat; He promised her his help.* **3** *vti* (*formal*) to show signs of future events or developments: *Those clouds promise rain; She promises to be a brilliant musician; This situation promises well for the future.* – **1** *nc* (a statement of) something promised: *He made a promise; I'll go with you – that's a promise!* **2** *nc* a sign of something that is going to happen: *There's a promise of spring in the air.* **3** *nu* a sign of future success: *She shows great promise in her work.*

'promising *adj* showing a lot of promise (*def 3*); likely to be very good: *She's a very promising pianist; Her work is very promising.* **'promisingly** *adv.*

promontory ['proməntəri] *nc* a piece of land that projects from the coastline.

promote [prə'mout] *vt* **1** to raise (to a higher rank or position): *He was promoted to* (*the position of*) *head teacher.* **2** to encourage, organize, or help the progress of (a particular cause *etc*): *He worked hard to promote peace/this scheme/the cause of homeless people.* **3** to encourage the buying of; to advertise: *We are promoting a new brand of soap-powder.* **pro'moter** *nc.*

pro'motion [-ʃən] **1** *ncu* the raising of a person to a higher rank or position: *He has just been given* (*a*) *promotion.* **2** *nu* the encouragement (of a cause, charity *etc*): *the promotion of world peace.* **3** *nu* the activity of advertising a product *etc*: *He is against the promotion of cigarettes.* **4** *nc* a particular advertising campaign: *a sales promotion.*

prompt[1] [prompt] *adj* acting, or happening, without delay or punctually: *We received a prompt reply; They were prompt in their response; He was prompt to offer assistance; I'm surprised that she's late. She's usually so prompt.*

'promptly *adv* **1** immediately: *He promptly accepted my offer.* **2** punctually: *They arrived promptly at two o'clock.*

'promptness *nu* **1** quickness or readiness to act *etc*: *Promptness to obey is a quality of every good soldier; Thank you for your promptness in replying to my letter.* **2** punctuality: *My boss insists on promptness.*

at one/two *etc* **o'clock prompt** punctually at one/two *etc* o'clock.

prompt[2] [prompt] **1** *vt* to persuade (a person) to do something: *She prompted him to ask for higher wages; What prompted you to say that?* **2** *vti* to remind (*esp* an actor) of the words that he is to say: *Several actors forgot their words and had to be prompted; Who is going to prompt at tonight's performance?* **'prompter** *nc*.

promulgate ['proməlgeit] *vt* (*formal*) to announce publicly, or make widely known (a law *etc*): *A new law was promulgated.* **ˌpromul'gation** *nu*.

prone [proun] *adj* **1** lying flat, *esp* face downwards: *He lay prone on the floor; in a prone position.* **2** (*with* **to**) inclined to; likely to experience *etc*: *He is prone to illness/accidents; She's the most accident-prone person I know.*

prong [proŋ] *nc* a spike of a fork: *The prongs of this fork have not been washed properly.*

pronged *adj* having prongs: *a pronged instrument.*

pronged (*in cmpds*) having or involving a (certain number or type of) prong(s): *a ˌtwo-pronged 'fork.*

pronoun ['prounaun] *nc* a word used instead of a noun or a phrase containing a noun: *'He', 'it', 'who', and 'anything' are pronouns.* **pronominal** [prə'nominl] *adj*.

pronounce [prə'nauns] *vt* **1** to speak (words or sounds, *esp* in a certain way): *He pronounced my name wrongly; How do you pronounce 'flaccid'?; The 'b' in 'lamb' and the 'k' in 'knob' are not pronounced.* **2** (*formal*) to announce officially or formally: *He pronounced judgement on the prisoner; He pronounced the picture to be genuine.*

pro'nounceable *adj* (*neg* **un-**) able to be pronounced.

pro'nounced *adj* noticeable; definite: *He walks with a pronounced limp; He is a man of pronounced ideas; His stammer is growing more pronounced.*

pro'nouncement *nc* (*formal*) a statement; an announcement: *The judge made a pronouncement about the case.*

proˌnunci'ation [-nʌnsi-] *ncu* the act, or a way, of saying a word *etc*: *She had difficulty with the pronunciation of his name; She tried several pronunciations.*

pronto ['prontou] *adj* (*sl*) quickly: *I want it done pronto!*

proof [pru:f] **1** *ncu* (a piece of) evidence, information *etc* that shows definitely that something is true: *He gave proof of his innocence; We still have no proof that he is innocent; As (a) proof of his love, he spent all his money on a ring for her.* **2** *nc* a first copy of a printed sheet, that can be corrected before the final printing and publication: *She was correcting the proofs of her novel.* **3** *nc* (*phot*) the first print from a negative. **4** *nu* (*tech*) the standard of strength of whisky and other spirits: *This brandy is below proof.* – *adj* (**pred** *with* **against**) able to keep out or resist (something): *He was proof against her arguments; The animal's hide seemed to be proof against his bullets.*

-proof (*in cmpds*) able to withstand or avoid (something): *waterproof covering; The car was fitted with bullet-proof glass; leakproof* (= not able to leak) *batteries.*

See also **prove**.

prop[1] [prop] *nc* (*sometimes in cmpds*) a support: *a clothes-prop* (= a pole that supports a washing-line); (*fig*) *He acted as a prop to his mother after his father died.* – *v* – *pt, ptp* **propped** – *vt* to support (something), *eg* by leaning it against something else: *He propped his bicycle against the wall.*

prop up *vt sep* to support (something) in an upright position, or stop it from falling: *We had to prop up the roof with a wooden post; He propped himself up against the wall.*

prop[2] [prop] (*tech*) short for **propeller**.

prop[3] [prop] short for **property** (*def 4*): *stage props.*

propaganda [propə'gandə] *nu* (*sometimes attrib*: *often derog*) the activity of spreading particular ideas, opinions *etc* according to an organized plan, *eg* by a government; the ideas *etc* spread in this way: *Who is in charge of propaganda?; a propaganda campaign; political propaganda; propaganda films/leaflets.*

ˌpropa'gandist *nc* (*derog*) a person who works to spread propaganda, *eg* for a political party.

propagate ['propəgeit] **1** *vt* (*formal*) to spread: *The aim of newspapers is to propagate news and ideas.* **2** *vti* to (make plants) produce seeds: *April is the time to propagate seeds.* **ˌpropa'gation** *nu*.

propel [prə'pel] – *pt, ptp* **pro'pelled** – *vt* (*tech*) to drive forward, *esp* mechanically: *The boat is propelled by a diesel engine;* (*facet*) *The teacher propelled the child out of the classroom.*

pro'peller *nc* (*tech abbrev* **prop**) a device, consisting of revolving blades, used to drive a ship or an aircraft.

pro'pulsion [-'pʌlʃən] *nu* (*formal or tech*) the process of driving, or being driven forward: *jet-propulsion.*

proˌpelling-'pencil *nc* a type of pencil consisting of a metal or plastic case containing a lead that is pushed forward by a screwing mechanism.

propensity [prə'pensəti] *nc* (*formal*) a natural inclination or tendency: *He has a propensity to criticize; He also has a propensity for making mistakes.*

proper ['propə] *adj* **1** (*attrib*) right, correct, or suitable: *He couldn't think of the proper words to say; That isn't the proper way to clean the windows; You should have done your schoolwork at the proper time – it's too late to start now;* (*formal*) *This is not a proper time for joking.* **2** (*inf*: *attrib*) complete or thorough: *Have you made a proper search?;* (*inf*) *That child is a proper nuisance!* **3** (*sometimes derog*) (too) respectable or well-mannered: *Such behaviour isn't quite proper; She's a rather proper young lady.* **4** (*formal*: *placed immediately after noun*) strictly (the thing named), not the wider meaning or concept: *in the city proper* (= not including the surrounding suburbs).

'properly *adv* **1** correctly or rightly: *She can't pronounce his name properly; You behaved quite properly; Spiders can't properly be called insects.* **2** completely or thoroughly: *I didn't have time to read the book properly;* (*inf*) *You've confused me properly!*

proper noun/name *nc* (*gram*) a noun or name which names a particular person, thing or place (beginning with a capital letter): *'John', 'the Chambers Dictionary', 'New York' are proper nouns.*

See also **improper, propriety**.

property ['propəti] **1** *nu* something that a person owns: *That book is my property; This dictionary is my personal property, not the common property of all the office staff.* **2** *ncu* land or buildings that a person owns: *He has property/properties in London and Scotland.* **3** *nc* (*formal*) a quality (*usu* of a substance): *Hardness is a property of diamonds.* **4** *nc* (*usu abbrev* **prop** [prop]) an article or small piece of furniture used by an actor in a play.

prophecy ['profəsi] **1** *nu* the power of foretelling

the future: *She had the gift of prophecy.* 2 *nc* something that is foretold: *He made many prophecies about the future that were never fulfilled.*

'prophesy [-sai] *vt* to foretell (the future): *He prophesied (that there would be) a very cold winter.*

'prophet [-fit] – *fem* **'prophetess** – *nc* 1 a person who (believes that he) is able to foretell the future. 2 (*relig*) a person who tells people what God wants, intends *etc*: *the prophet Isaiah.*

pro'phetic [-'fe-] *adj* of or concerning prophecy: *prophetic words*; *Her words proved prophetic.* **pro'phetically** *adv.*

prophylactic [profi'laktik, (*Amer*) prou-] *nc, adj* (*formal or tech*) (a substance, device *etc*) preventing disease.

,prophy'laxis [-'laksis] *nu* medical treatment to prevent disease.

propinquity [prə'piŋkwəti] *nu* (*very formal*) nearness of place, time or relationship.

propitiate [prə'piʃieit, (*Amer*) prou-] *vt* (*very formal*) to calm the anger of: *The people made sacrifices to propitiate the gods.* **pro,piti'ation** *nu.*

pro'pitious [-ʃəs] *adj* (*neg* **un-**: *formal*) favourable; advantageous: *propitious circumstances*; *The circumstances are far from propitious.*

proportion [prə'po:ʃən] 1 *nc* a part (of a total amount): *Only a small proportion of the class passed the exam.* 2 *ncu* the (correct) quantity, size, number *etc* (of one thing compared with that of another): *The proportion of women to men at the meeting was small*; *For this dish, the butter and flour should be in the proportion of three to four* (= *eg* 300 grammes of butter with every 400 grammes of flour); *Your essay lacks proportion – you've concentrated too much on some topics and neglected others.* – *See also* **proportion** *in phrases below.*

pro'portions *n pl* size or measurements: *a man of huge proportions.*

pro'portional *adj* 1 of, or relating to, proportion. 2 being in the correct proportion or relationship: *proportional representation* (= a system by which each political party is represented in a government in proportion to the number of people who voted for it). **pro'portionally** *adv.*

pro'portionate [-nət] *adj* (*formal*) being in correct proportion: *Are her wages really proportionate to the amount of work she does?* **pro'portionately** *adv.*

be, get *etc* **in proportion (to)** to (cause to) have a correct relationship (to each other or something else): *Her ambition is in proportion to her skill*; *In drawing a person, it is difficult to get all the parts of the body in proportion.*

be, get *etc* **out of (all) proportion (to)** to (cause to) have an incorrect relationship (to each other or something else): *An elephant's tail seems out of (all) proportion to the rest of its body*; *Her eyes and nose look out of proportion*; *His interest in stamp-collecting has grown out of (all) proportion* (= it consumes too great a part of his time, money, interest *etc*); *You've got this affair out of proportion* (= You think it is more important than it really is).

in 'proportion to in relation to; in comparison with: *You spend far too much time on that work in proportion to its importance.*

sense of proportion the ability to judge what is important and what is not: *Don't get so worried about such a trivial matter – you're losing your sense of proportion.*

propose [prə'pouz] 1 *vt* (*more formal than* **suggest**) to offer (a plan, someone's name for a job *etc*) for consideration; to suggest: *I proposed starting early*; *I proposed my friend for the job*; *Who proposed this scheme?* 2 *vt* to intend: *He proposes to build a new house.* 3 *vi* to make an offer of marriage: *He proposed (to me) last night and I accepted him.*

pro'posal 1 *nc* something proposed or suggested; a plan: *Both presidents have proposals for peace between their two countries.* 2 *nc* an offer of marriage: *She received three proposals.* 3 *nu* (*formal*) the act of proposing or suggesting: *the proposal of a new education system.*

proposition [propə'ziʃən] *nc* 1 a proposal or suggestion: *He made an interesting proposition.* 2 a thing or situation that must be done or dealt with: *That's rather a difficult proposition.* 3 (*inf euph*) an indecent proposal; a request for sexual relations. – *vt* to make (such) a suggestion to: *If you wear that skirt, you'll be propositioned by every man you meet!*

propound [prə'paund] *vt* (*formal*) to state, and offer for consideration (an idea or a problem *etc*): *He propounded his theory about education.*

proprietor [prə'praiətə] – *fem* **pro'prietress**, (*old*) **pro'prietrix** [-triks] – *nc* an owner, *esp* of a shop, hotel *etc.*

pro'prietary *adj* (*usu attrib*) owned or produced by a particular firm *etc*, *ie* carrying its name: *a proprietary brand of soap-powder/shoe-polish.*

proprietary name *nc* a trademark.

propriety [prə'praiəti] *nu* (*formal*) 1 correct behaviour; decency: *She behaved with propriety.* 2 fitness or suitability; rightness: *I am not certain of the propriety of his plan.*

pro'prieties *n pl* (*with* **the**: *formal or facet*) the details of correct behaviour: *One must be careful to observe the proprieties.*

See also **impropriety** *under* **improper, proper**.

propulsion *see* **propel**.

prosaic [prə'zeiik, (*Amer*) prou-] *adj* (*formal derog*) dull; uninteresting: *a prosaic speaker/speech*; *I find his ideas rather prosaic.* **pro'saically** *adv.*

proscribe [prə'skraib, (*Amer*) prou-] *vt* 1 (*formal*) to state officially that (something) is dangerous or forbidden: *Doctors have declared this drug harmful and proscribed its use.* 2 (*hist*) to outlaw: *The king proscribed all those who had rebelled against him.*

pro'scription [-'skrip-] *ncu.*

pro'scriptive [-'skriptiv] *adj* (*formal*) proscribing (*def 1*): *proscriptive laws.*

prose [prouz] *nu* writing that is not in verse; ordinary written or spoken language: *a fine example of English prose*; (*attrib*) *nineteenth century prose style.*

See also **prosaic**.

prosecute ['prosikju:t] *vt* 1 to bring a legal action against (someone): *He was prosecuted for theft.* 2 (*formal*) to continue (an investigation *etc*): *He prosecuted his enquiries.*

,prose'cution 1 *nu* (*formal*) the act of prosecuting (an inquiry *etc*). 2 *ncu* (*legal*) (an) act of prosecuting or process of being prosecuted: *He faces prosecution for drunken driving*; *There are numerous prosecutions for this offence every year.* 3 *n sing or n pl* (*legal*: *sometimes attrib*) the person/people bringing a legal action, including the lawyer(s) representing them: *First the prosecution stated its case, then the defence*; *prosecution witnesses.*

public prosecutor *nc* a lawyer who prosecutes on behalf of the state.

prospect [(*Brit and Amer*) 'prospekt] *ncu* **1** an outlook for the future; a view of what one may expect to happen: *He didn't like the prospect of going abroad*; *He has a job with good prospects.* **2** (*formal*) a view or scene: *a prospect of trees and fields.* – [prə'spekt, (*Amer*) 'prospekt] *vi* to make a search, *eg* for gold or other minerals: *He is prospecting for gold.*

prospective [(*Brit and Amer*) prə'spektiv] *adj* (*attrib*) likely or expected; future: *They want to sell their house, and already have a prospective buyer*; *He is the prospective Liberal candidate for this district.*

prospector [prə'spektə, (*Amer*) 'prospektər] *nc* a person who prospects for gold *etc.*

prospectus [(*Brit and Amer*) prə'spektəs] *nc* a booklet giving information about a school, organization *etc*: *We have received prospectuses from several schools.*

prosper ['prospə] *vi* to do well; to succeed: *His business is prospering.*

pro'sperity [-'spe-] *nu* success; wealth: *We wish you happiness and prosperity.*

'prosperous *adj* successful, *esp* in business: *a prosperous businessman*; *He has become very prosperous.* **'prosperously** *adv.*

prostitute ['prostitju:t] *nc* a person who has sexual intercourse for payment. – **1** *vt* (*formal*) to put (something) to a wrong use: *He prostituted his talents on worthless work.* **2** *v refl* (*old*) to offer (oneself) as a prostitute. **ˌprosti'tution** *nu.*

prostrate ['prostreit] *adj* (*formal*) **1** lying flat, *esp* face downwards; prone: *She was prostrate on the floor*; *He gazed with alarm at her prostrate figure.* **2** completely exhausted or overwhelmed: *He is quite prostrate with grief.* – [prə'streit] (*formal*) **1** *v refl* to throw (oneself) flat on the floor, *esp* in respect or reverence: *They prostrated themselves before the emperor.* **2** *vt* to exhaust or overwhelm: *They were prostrated by the long journey and the heat.*

pro'strated *adj* (*formal*): *She is prostrated with grief.* **pro'stration** *nu.*

protagonist [prə'tagənist, (*Amer*) prou-] *nc* (*formal or liter*) **1** a chief character in a play *etc*: *Macduff is one of the protagonists in Shakespeare's 'Macbeth'.* **2** a leader or champion of a movement, cause *etc*: *one of the protagonists of sexual equality.*

protect [prə'tekt] *vt* (*with* **from** *or* **against**) to guard or defend from danger; to keep safe: *She protected the children from every danger*; *Which type of helmet protects the head best?*; *He wore a woollen scarf to protect himself against the cold.*

pro'tection [-ʃən] **1** *nu* the act of protecting or state of being protected: *She returned under the protection of a policeman*; *He ran to his mother for protection*; *This type of lock gives extra protection against burglary.* **2** *nc* something that protects: *The trees were a good protection against the wind.*

pro'tective [-tiv] *adj* giving, or intended to give, protection: *protective clothing*; *She felt protective towards her children.*

pro'tector *nc* a person or thing that protects or guards.

pro'tectorate [-tərət] *nc* a country that is partly governed and defended by another: *The island is a British protectorate.*

protégé ['protəʒei, (*Amer*) 'prou-] – *fem* **'protégée** – *nc* (*formal*) a person who is helped in his career by someone important or powerful: *He was a protégé of the Prime Minister.*

protein ['prouti:n] *ncu* (*tech*) any of a large number of substances present in milk, eggs, meat *etc*, which are necessary as part of the food of human beings and animals: *Our blood contains proteins*; *Eat plenty of protein!*

pro tem [prou'tem] (short for **pro tempore** [prou'tempəri]) (*formal*) temporarily; for the time being: *He is president of the society pro tem.*

protest [prə'test] **1** *vi* to express a strong objection: *They are protesting against the new law*; *I protest!* **2** *vt* (*esp formal or liter*) to state or declare definitely *esp* against opposition: *She protested that she had meant no harm*; *He protested his innocence.* – ['proutest] *nc* a strong statement or demonstration of objection or disapproval: *He made no protest*; (*attrib*) *a protest march.*

ˌprote'station [protə-] *nc* (*formal*) a solemn statement or declaration: *He made many protestations of loyalty.*

pro'tester *nc* a person who protects (*def 1*).

Protestant ['protəstənt] *nc, adj* (a member) of any of the Christian churches that separated from the Roman Catholic church at or after the Reformation.

'Protestantism *nu* the beliefs, teachings *etc* of the Protestant churches.

proto- [proutou] (*in cmpds*) first or earliest, as in **prototype**.

protocol ['proutəkol] *nu* (*formal*) correct (diplomatic) procedure: *We must arrange the meeting according to protocol.*

proton ['prouton] *nc* (*tech*) a particle with a positive electrical charge, forming part of the nucleus of an atom.

protoplasm ['proutəplazəm] *nu* (*tech*) the half-liquid substance that is found in all living cells.

prototype ['proutətaip] *nc* the first or original model from which others are copied: *the prototype of a new aircraft.*

protracted [prə'traktid, (*Amer*) prou-] *adj* (*formal*) lasting a long time, often longer than necessary: *protracted talks.* **pro'traction** [-ʃən] *nu.*

protractor [prə'traktə, (*Amer*) prou-] *nc* an instrument for drawing and measuring angles.

protrude [prə'tru:d, (*Amer*) prou-] *vi* (*formal*) to stick out; to project: *His teeth protrude.*

pro'truding *adj*: *He has protruding teeth*; *Her front teeth are rather protruding.* **pro'trusion** [-ʒən] *ncu.*

protuberance [prə'tju:bərəns, (*Amer*) prou-] *nc* (*very formal*) a swelling; a bulge: *a protuberance on the trunk of a tree.*

pro'tuberant *adj* (*very formal*): *a protuberant stomach.*

proud [praud] *adj* **1** (*sometimes with* **of**) feeling (justifiable) pleasure or satisfaction at one's achievements, possessions, connections *etc*: *He was proud of his new house*; *She was proud of her son's achievements*; *He felt proud to be British*; *He's proud of being chosen for the team*; *It was a proud moment for him* (= a moment that made him proud) *when he received his prize.* **2** (*usu derog*) having a (too) high opinion of oneself; arrogant: *She was too proud to talk to us.* **3** wishing to be independent: *She was too proud to accept help.* **4** (*liter*) splendid or impressive: *The assembled fleet was a proud sight.* **'proudly** *adv.*

do (someone) proud (*inf*) to give (a person) good treatment or entertainment: *We always do*

them proud when they come to dinner.
See also **pride**.

prove [pru:v] **1** *vt* to show (something) to be true or correct: *He proved that she was innocent; This fact proves his guilt; He was proved guilty; Can you prove your theory?* **2** *vi* to turn out, or be found, to be: *His suspicions proved (to be) correct; This tool proved very useful.*
'proven (*Brit legal*) *adj* proved.

provender ['provəndə] *nu* (*liter*) food for animals, *esp* horses and cows.

proverb ['provə:b] *nc* a well-known saying that gives good advice or expresses a supposed truth: *Two common proverbs are 'Many hands make light work' and 'Don't count your chickens before they're hatched!'*
pro'verbial *adj* **1** of or like a proverb: *a proverbial truth; the cat's proverbial nine lives.* **2** well-known: *The warm-heartedness of the Italians is proverbial.*
pro'verbially *adv.*

provide [prə'vaid] **1** *vt* to give or supply: *He provided a bottle of wine for their dinner; He provided them with a bed for the night.* **2** *vi* to supply or prepare what is necessary: *He is unable to provide for his family.*
pro'vided, pro'viding *conjs* if; on condition (that): *We can buy it provided/providing (that) we have enough money.*
See also **provision**.

providence ['providəns] *ncu* (*relig*) (an event showing) God's care for all creatures: *We must trust to divine providence; He was saved by a special providence.*
'provident *adj* (*old*) careful in providing for the future; thrifty: *a provident housewife.* **'providently** *adv.*
ˌprovi'dential [-'denʃəl] *adj* (*formal: often pred*) fortunate; as if coming from or sent by God: *Her arrival was providential; It is providential that you were there.* **ˌprovi'dentially** *adv.*

province ['provins] *nc* **1** a division of a country, empire *etc*: *Britain was once a Roman province.* **2** (*fig formal*) the area of one's duties, knowledge *etc*: *Cooking is not my province; That question is outside my province.*
pro'vincial [-'vinʃəl] *adj* **1** (*usu attrib*) of or concerning the provinces: *provincial theatres; He speaks with a provincial accent.* **2** (*attrib*) of a province (*def 1*): *a provincial governor.* **3** (*derog*) (of people, behaviour *etc*) with narrow interests and opinions; rough or unsophisticated: *a provincial person/attitude; He is so provincial!* – *nc* (*usu derog*) a person from the provinces.
pro'vincialism [-'vinʃə-] *nu* (*derog*) provincial (*def 3*) behaviour.
pro'vincially *adv.*
the provinces all parts of a country outside the capital: *Do you live in London or the provinces?*

provision [prə'viʒən] **1** *nu* the act of providing: *The government are responsible for the provision of education for all children.* **2** *nc* an agreed arrangement: *according to the provisions made last year.* **3** *nc* (*legal*) a rule or condition: *There are certain provisions in the will.* – *See also* **make provision for** *below.* – *vt* (*formal*) to supply with food: *enough food to provision an army.*
pro'visional *adj* temporary; appointed, arranged *etc* only for the present time: *a provisional government; The arrangement is only provisional.*
pro'visionally *adv.*
pro'visions *n pl* (a supply of) food: *We got our provisions at the village shop.*
make provision for to provide what is necessary for: *You should make provision for your old age.*
See also **provide**.

proviso [prə'vaizou] – *pl* **pro'visos** (*Amer also* **pro'visoes**) – *nc* (*formal*) a condition decided in advance: *He agreed to come, with the proviso that he could leave early.*

provoke [prə'vouk] *vt* **1** to make angry or irritated: *Are you trying to provoke me?* **2** to cause or result in (trouble, laughter *etc*): *His words provoked laughter among the audience.* **3** to cause (a person *etc*) to react in an angry way: *His rudeness provoked her to slap him on the face; He was provoked into hitting her.*
provocation [provə'keiʃən] **1** *nu* the act of provoking or state of being provoked: *He did it under provocation.* **2** *nc* something that provokes: *She gets angry at the slightest provocation.*
pro'vocative [-'vokətiv] *adj* **1** likely to cause anger: *a provocative statement; Her comments were rather provocative.* **2** likely to cause interest, *esp* sexual interest: *a provocative dress/perfume; She is rather provocative.* **pro'vocatively** *adv.*
pro'voking *adj* (*esp old*) annoying or irritating: *He is so provoking!* **pro'vokingly** *adv.*

provost ['provəst] *nc* (*with cap in titles*) **1** the head of a cathedral. **2** the head of some university colleges. **3** in Scotland, the head of a burgh council.
Lord Provost *nc* in Scotland, the provost of certain large towns.

prow [prau] *nc* the front part of a ship; the bow.

prowess ['prauis] *nu* (*formal*) skill or ability: *He is showing great prowess as an athlete.*

prowl [praul] *vi* to move about stealthily in order to steal, attack someone *etc*: *I can hear someone prowling about in the garden; Tigers were prowling in the jungle.* **'prowler** *nc.*
be on the prowl (*inf*) to be prowling: *The police are on the prowl for criminals.*

proximity [prok'siməti] *nu* (*formal*) nearness: *It is only when you live in close proximity to/with someone that you discover his real personality.*

proxy ['proksi] *ncu* **1** (the function of) a person who acts or votes for another: *I have a proxy to vote on my behalf; She voted by proxy.* **2** (a document giving) the authority to act or vote for someone else.

prude [pru:d] *nc* (*derog*) a person who is too modest, *eg* who dislikes any mention of sex: *She's a terrible prude!*
'prudery *nu* the behaviour of a prude. **'prudish** *adj.*

prudent ['pru:dənt] *adj* (*formal*) wise and careful: *a prudent person/attitude; It was prudent of you to save money.* **'prudently** *adv.*
'prudence *nu* (*formal*) wisdom and caution: *She acted with great prudence.*
See also **imprudent**.

prudery, prudish *see* **prude**.

prune[1] [pru:n] *vt* **1** to trim (a tree *etc*) by cutting off unnecessary twigs and branches: *He pruned the roses.* **2** (*fig*) to remove unnecessary parts from (a piece of written work *etc*): *You must prune the article before it is published.*

prune[2] [pru:n] *nc* a dried plum: *We had prunes for breakfast.*

prurient ['pruəriənt] *adj* (*very formal: usu attrib*) showing too much interest in, or curiosity about, sex: *He has a prurient mind.* **'prurience** *nu.*

pry [prai] *vi* (*with* **into**: *derog*) to try to find out about something that is secret, *esp* other people's affairs: *He is always prying into my business.*

psalm [sa:m] *nc* a sacred song, *esp* one from the Book of Psalms in the Bible: *to sing a psalm.*
'psalmist *nc* a person who writes psalms.

psalter ['so:ltə] *nc* a book of psalms.

pseudo- [sju:dou] (*in cmpds*) false: *ˌpseudo-ˌscientific 'books.*

pseudo ['sju:dou] *adj* (*inf*) false; fake: *His foreign accent is pseudo.*

pseudonym ['sju:dənim] *nc* a false name used by an author: *'Mark Twain' was the pseudonym used by Samuel Clemens.*

psyche ['saiki] *nc* (*psych*) the human soul, spirit or mind: *the influence of the psyche on human behaviour.*

psychedelic [saikə'delik] *adj* **1** (*usu attrib*) (of drugs) causing excitement, hallucinations *etc*: *LSD is a psychedelic drug.* **2** (of colours, music *etc*) having an exciting effect, like psychedelic drugs: *The room was painted in psychedelic colours; Her new dress is rather psychedelic.*

psychiatry [sai'kaiətri, (*Amer also*) si-] *nu* the treatment of mental illness.
psychiatric [saiki'atrik] *adj* of, or needing, such treatment: *a psychiatric hospital; a psychiatric patient.*
psy'chiatrist *nc* **1** a person who treats mental illness. **2** a psychiatrist's practice: *She's at the psychiatrist.*
psy'chiatrist's *nc* a psychiatrist's practice.

psychic(al) ['saikik(əl)] *adjs* **1** of the mind or soul. **2** of influences and forces that act on the mind and senses but have no physical cause: *psychic research* (= the study of such things as ghosts, the ability to know other people's thoughts *etc*). **3** (only in the form **'psychic**: *inf*) (of a person) sensitive to these influences: *She always knows what is going to happen in the future – she must be psychic.*

psycho- [saikou] (*in cmpds*) (of) the mind, as in **psychoanalyse**.

psychoanalyse, (*Amer*) **psychoanalyze** [saikou-'anəlaiz] *vt* to treat (a person suffering from mental illness) by discussing events in his/her past life which may have caused it: *She is being psychoanalysed.*
ˌpsychoa'nalysis [-'naləsis] *nu.*
ˌpsycho'analyst [-list] *nc* a person who gives this treatment.

psychology [sai'kolədʒi] *nu* **1** the study or science of the human mind: *Psychology was one of his university subjects.* **2** (*loosely*) the mental processes of a person *etc*: *I can't understand the psychology of such a man.*
ˌpsycho'logical [-'lo-] *adj* of the mind, or of psychology: *The accident had a psychological as well as physical effect on him; a psychological topic; Her fear of birds is psychological.* **ˌpsycho'logically** *adv.*
psy'chologist *nc* a person whose work is to study the human mind.
psychological warfare *nu* a way of attacking an enemy by trying to influence his beliefs, state of mind *etc.*
the psychological moment (*sometimes facet*) the right or appropriate moment: *If you ask her to marry you at the psychological moment, she will say yes.*

psychopath ['saikəpaθ] *nc* (*tech*) a person whose mind and emotions are very unbalanced, *usu* making him/her aggressive and likely to commit crimes: *The man who murdered those children must be a psychopath.*
ˌpsycho'pathic *adj* (*tech*) of or suffering from mental or emotional illness.

psychosis [sai'kousis] – *pl* **psy'choses** [-si:z] – *nc* (*tech*) any of several types of mental illness.
psy'chotic [-'kotik] *adj* (*tech*: *esp attrib*): *a psychotic condition.*

psychosomatic [saikəsə'matik] *adj* (*tech*) of or concerning the relationship between mind and body: *psychosomatic illness* (= a physical illness caused by a mental state); *His sore stomach is psychosomatic.*

psychotherapy [saikə'θerəpi] *nu* (*tech*) the treatment of disease by psychological means, *eg* hypnosis or psychoanalysis.

pub [pʌb] short for **public house**: *I'll meet you in the pub down the road.*

puberty ['pju:bəti] *nu* (*formal or tech*) the time when a child's body becomes sexually mature: *In Victorian times many children died before reaching puberty.*

pubic ['pju:bik]: **pubic hair** *nu* the hair that grows around the genitals.

public ['pʌblik] *adj* (*esp attrib*) of, for, or concerning, the people (of a community or nation) in general: *a public library; a public meeting; Public opinion* (= the attitude of people in general) *turned against him; The public announcements are on the back page of the newspaper; This information should be made public* (= generally announced) *and not kept secret any longer; This affair will soon be (a matter of) public knowledge* (= generally known); *A well-loved public figure* (= a well-known person) *died today. – See also* **in public** *below.*
pu'blicity [-'blisə-] *nu* **1** advertising: *There is a lot of publicity about the dangers of smoking.* **2** the state of being widely known: *Film stars usually like publicity.*
'publicize, -ise [-saiz] *vt* to make widely known; to advertise: *We are publicizing a new product.*
public bar *nc* a bar, in a public house, which is *usu* less comfortable or less luxurious than a lounge bar.
public convenience *see* **convenience**.
public holiday *nc* a day on which all (or most) shops, offices and factories are closed for a holiday.
public house *nc* (*usu abbrev* **pub** [pʌb]) a house where alcoholic drinks are sold to the public; an inn.
public relations *n pl* or *n sing* (*often abbrev* **PR**) **1** the attitude, understanding *etc* between a firm, government *etc* and the public: *Our firm has good public relations; Public relations is to be the main topic of discussion at our next meeting.* **2** (*usu attrib*) a department of a firm *etc* which works to improve relationships with the public: *She has a job in public relations; a public relations officer* (sometimes abbrev **PRO**).
public school *nc* **1** (*Brit*) a boarding-school, *usu* established a long time ago, and mostly financed by private money, *esp* pupils' fees: *Eton and Harrow are two of England's most famous public schools;* (*attrib*) *a public-school education.* **2** (*Amer*) a school run by the government.
public spirit *nu* a desire to do things for the good of the community: *He shows a great deal of public*

spirit. ˌ**public-ˈspirited** *adj.*

public transport *nu* the bus, tram and train services provided by a state or community for the public: *We can get there by public transport.*

in ˈpublic in front of other people, not in private: *They are always quarrelling in public.*

the public 1 people in general: *This swimming pool is open to the public every day.* **2** (*with an adjective etc following or replacing* **the**) a particular section of people: *the reading public* (= people who read books); *An author must consider his public* (= the people who read his books).

ˌ**public ˈopinion poll** a way of finding out public opinion by questioning a certain number of people.

See also **publication.**

publican [ˈpʌblikən] *nc* the keeper of a public house: *Publicans are protesting about the increase in the cost of beer.*

publication [pʌbliˈkeiʃən] **1** *nu* the act of publishing or announcing publicly: *the publication of a new novel; the publication of the facts.* **2** *nc* something that has been published *eg* a book or magazine: *There are a lot of publications about gardening.*

See also **publicity** *under* **public.**

publish [ˈpʌbliʃ] *vt* **1** to prepare, print and produce for sale (a book *etc*): *His new novel is being published this month.* **2** (*formal*) to make known: *They published their engagement.*

ˈ**publisher** *nc* a person who publishes books *etc.*

ˈ**publishing** *nu* the business of publishing books *etc*: *He has a job in publishing;* (*attrib*) *a publishing-house.*

See also **publication.**

puce [pju:s] *nu, adj* (of) a brownish-purple colour.

puck [pʌk] *nc* a rubber disc used instead of a ball in ice-hockey.

pucker [ˈpʌkə] *vti* (*often with* **up**) to make or become wrinkled: *She puckered* (*up*) *her forehead; Her dress puckered* (*up*) *at the waist.* – *nc* a wrinkle or fold.

pudding [ˈpudiŋ] **1** *ncu* (*inf abbrev* **pud** [pud]) any of several types of soft foods made with eggs, flour, milk *etc*: *sponge pudding; rice pudding.* **2** *nu* (*inf abbrev* **pud** [pud]) the sweet course of a meal; dessert: *What's for pudding?* (= What are we having as dessert?) **3** *ncu* any of several types of sausages: *black pudding.*

ˈ**pudding-plate** *nc* a shallow, rather than flat, dish, in which pudding *etc* is served.

puddle [ˈpʌdl] *nc* a small, *usu* dirty, pool (of water): *It had been raining, and there were puddles in the road.*

pudgy *see* **podgy.**

puerile [ˈpjuərail] *adj* (*formal derog*) childish; silly: *puerile behaviour; His conduct was rather puerile.* ˌ**pueˈrility** [-ˈri-] *nu.*

puff [pʌf] *nc* **1** (*slightly liter*) a small blast of air, wind *etc*; a gust: *A puff of wind moved the branches.* **2** (*esp attrib or in cmpds*) any of various kinds of soft, round, light or hollow objects: *She powdered her nose with a powder puff; jam puffs* (= cakes made with puff pastry); *puff sleeves* (= sleeves shaped like soft balls); *A puff-ball is a poisonous type of fungus.* – **1** *vti* to blow in small blasts: *Stop puffing cigarette smoke into my face!; He puffed at his pipe; We no longer see steam trains puffing* (= moving along giving out puffs of smoke) *through the countryside.* **2** *vti* (*inf*) to breathe quickly, after running *etc*: *He was puffing as he climbed the stairs.* – *See also* **puff out, puff up** *below.*

puffed *adj* (*pred: inf*) short of breath; breathing quickly: *I'm puffed after running so fast!*

ˈ**puffy** *adj* swollen, *esp* unhealthily: *a puffy face/ankle; Her face is rather puffy.*

puff pastry *nu* a light, flaky type of pastry.

puffed up (*inf*) **1** swollen: *Her face is all puffed up;* (*attrib*) *The boxer has a very puffed-up eye.* **2** (*derog*) conceited: *That puffed-up little man!*

puff out *vt sep* to cause to swell or expand: *The bird puffed out its feathers; He puffed out his cheeks.*

puff up *vi* (*inf*) to swell: *Her eye puffed up after the wasp stung her.* – *See also* **puffed up.**

pug [pʌg] *nc* a kind of small dog with a flat nose.

ˌ**pug-ˈnose** *nc* a short, turned-up nose, like that of a pug. ˌ**pug-ˈnosed** *adj.*

pugilism [ˈpju:dʒilizm] *nu* (*old or formal*) the sport of boxing.

ˈ**pugilist** (*old or formal*) *nc* a boxer.

pugnacious [pʌgˈneiʃəs] *adj* (*formal or facet*) quarrelsome; fond of fighting. **pugˈnaciously** *adv.*

pugˈnaciousness, pugˈnacity [-ˈnasə-] (*formal or facet*) *nus* readiness to fight.

puke [pju:k] *vti* (*inf*) to vomit: *That child puked all over me.*

pukka [ˈpʌkə] *adj* (*facet*) superior; posh: *They live in rather a pukka part of town.*

pulchritude [ˈpʌlkritju:d] *nu* (*very formal or facet*) beauty: *feminine pulchritude.*

pull [pul] **1** *vti* to (try to) move something *esp* towards oneself *usu* by using force: *He pulled the chair towards the fire; She pulled the door open; She pulled at the door but couldn't open it; Stop pulling! You're hurting my arm!; That naughty boy keeps pulling the girls' hair; Don't pull your sweater out of shape; Help me to pull my boots off; The horse was pulling a cart along the road; This railway engine can pull twelve carriages.* **2** *vi* (*with* **at** *or* **on**) in *eg* smoking, to suck at: *He pulled at his cigarette.* **3** *vi* to row: *He pulled towards the shore.* **4** *vi* (of a driver or vehicle) to steer or move in a certain direction: *The car pulled in at the garage; I pulled in to the side of the road and stopped; The train pulled out of the station; The motorbike pulled out to overtake; The bus pulled over to let the traffic pass; He pulled off the road.* – *See also* **pull up** *below.* – *See also* **pull** *in phrases below.* – **1** *nc* an act of pulling: *I felt a pull at my sleeve; He took a pull at his beer/pipe.* **2** *nu* a pulling or attracting force: *magnetic pull;* (*fig liter*) *He still feels the pull of the sea.* **3** *nu* (*inf*) influence: *He thinks he has some pull with the headmaster.*

pull (something) apart/to pieces to tear or destroy (something) completely by pulling: *He began to pull the furniture apart/to pieces.*

pull down *vt sep* to destroy or demolish (buildings): *They pulled down the old shop and built a supermarket; They pulled it down last year.*

pull a face/faces (at) to make strange expressions with the face *eg* to show disgust, or to amuse: *The children were pulling faces at each other; He pulled a face when he smelt the fish.*

ˌ**pull a ˈfast one (on)** (*inf*) to deceive (someone): *He certainly pulled a fast one on me.*

pull a gun *etc* **on** to produce and aim a gun *etc* at (a person).

pull someone's leg *see* **leg.**

pull a muscle to strain a muscle.

pull off *vt sep* (*inf*) to succeed in doing

(something): *He's finally pulled it off!*; *He's pulled off a good business deal.* – *See also* **pull** (*defs 1, 4*).

pull on *vt sep* to put on (a piece of clothing) hastily: *She pulled on a sweater*; *He pulled on his shoes*; *He pulled them on hurriedly.*

pull oneself together (*inf*) to control oneself; to regain one's self-control: *At first she was terrified, then she pulled herself together.*

pull one's punches *see* **punch**.

pull one's socks up *see* **sock**.

pull strings *see* **string**.

pull the wool over someone's eyes *see* **wool**.

pull through *vt sep, vi* (*inf*) to (help to) survive an illness *etc*: *He is very ill, but he'll pull through*; *The expert medical treatment pulled him through.*

pull up *vi* (of a driver or vehicle) to stop: *He pulled up at the traffic lights.* – *See also* **pull** (*def 1*).

pull one's weight (*inf*) to take one's fair share of work, duty *etc*: *Some of the workers are not pulling their weight.*

pullet ['pulit] *nc* a young hen.

pulley ['puli] *nc* a wheel over which a rope *etc* can pass in order to lift heavy objects.

pullover ['pulouvə] *nc* a knitted garment for the top part of the body; a sweater: *He wore a green pullover over his brown shirt.*

pulmonary ['pʌlmənəri] *adj* (*tech*: *esp attrib*) of, or affecting, the lungs: *pulmonary diseases.*

pulp [pʌlp] *nu* **1** the soft, fleshy part of a fruit. **2** a soft mass of other matter, *eg* of wood *etc* from which paper is made: *wood-pulp*; (*fig inf*) *I'll beat him to* (*a*) *pulp if I catch him!* – *vt* to make into pulp: *The fruit was pulped and bottled.*

'**pulpy** *adj* of or like pulp.

pulpit ['pulpit] *nc* a raised box or platform in a church, where the priest or minister stands, *esp* to preach the sermon: *a carved stone pulpit.*

pulse[1] [pʌls] *nc* the regular beating of the heart: *The doctor felt/took her pulse* (= counted the heartbeats by feeling the artery in the wrist). – *vi* (*esp liter*) to throb.

pulsate [pʌl'seit, (*Amer*) 'pʌlseit] *vi* (*esp formal or liter*) to beat or throb: *He felt the blood pulsating in his head as he grew angrier.* **pulsation** [(*Brit and Amer*) pʌl'seiʃən] *ncu.*

pulse[2] [pʌls] *ncu* (*tech*) (a type of vegetable producing) edible seeds that grow in pods, such as beans, peas, lentils *etc*: *Vegetarians often use various kinds of pulses in their cooking.*

pulverize, -ise ['pʌlvəraiz] *vt* (*tech or formal*: *sometimes facet*) to make or crush into dust or powder: *The machine pulverized the rock and extracted the gold*; (*fig*) *He pulverized his opponent with his arguments.* ˌ**pulveri'zation, -s-** *nu.*

puma ['pju:mə] *nc* (*also* **cougar** ['ku:gə]) a type of wild animal like a large cat, found in America.

pumice ['pʌmis] *nu* a light kind of solidified lava.

'**pumice stone** *ncu* (a piece of) this type of stone, used for cleaning and smoothing the skin *etc*: *If you rub your elbows with pumice stone it will remove the hard skin from them.*

pummel ['pʌml] – *pt, ptp* '**pummelled**, (*Amer*) '**pummeled** – *vt* (*formal*) to beat again and again with the fists: *She pummelled his chest as he picked her up.*

pump[1] [pʌmp] *nc* (*sometimes in cmpds*) **1** a machine for making water *etc* rise from under the ground: *Every village used to have a* (*water-*)*pump from which everyone drew their water.* **2** a machine or device for forcing liquid or gas into, or out of, something: *a bicycle pump* (for forcing air into the tyres). – *vt* **1** to raise or force with a pump: *Oil is being pumped out of the ground.* **2** (*inf*) to get information from (someone) by asking (*usu* indirect) questions: *He tried to pump me about the exam.*

pump up *vt sep* to inflate (tyres *etc*) with a pump.

pump[2] [pʌmp] *nc* any of several types of light shoe for *eg* dancing, gymnastics *etc*: *a pair of dancing pumps.*

pumpkin ['pʌmpkin] **1** *nc* a kind of large, round, thick-skinned yellow fruit, eaten as food: *He grows pumpkins.* **2** *nu* its flesh as food: *Have some pumpkin*; (*attrib*) *a pumpkin pie.*

pun [pʌn] *nc* a type of joke in which words are used that have a similar sound, but a different meaning: *One example of a pun would be 'A pun is a punishable offence'.* – *v* – *pt, ptp* **punned** – *vi* to make a pun: *He is always punning.*

'**punster** *nc* (*old*) a person who makes puns.

punch[1] [pʌntʃ] *ncu* a kind of drink made of spirits or wine, water, sugar *etc*: *He made a punch for the party*; *rum punch.*

punch[2] [pʌntʃ] *vti* to hit with the fist: *He punched him on the nose*; *I'd like to punch his face!*; *He's a boxer who can really punch hard.* – **1** *nc* a blow with the fist: *He gave him a punch.* **2** *nu* (*inf*) the quality of strength or impact in speech, writing *etc*: *His writing has tremendous punch.*

'**punch-drunk** *adj* (*often fig*) (of a boxer) dizzy from being continually hit.

'**punch line** *nc* the funny sentence or phrase that ends a joke: *He always laughs before he gets to the punch line.*

'**punch-up** *nc* (*inf*) a fight (using fists): *They had a punch-up with the police.*

pull one's punches (*usu fig and often in neg*) to use less force in attacking than one is really capable of: *He didn't pull his punches when he criticized her work.*

punch[3] [pʌntʃ] *nc* a tool or device for making holes in something: *Could I borrow the punch to make holes in this paper?*; *Will this punch make holes in leather?* – *vt* to make holes in (something) with such a tool: *The bus conductor punched my ticket*; *He punched a hole in the leather.*

Punch [pʌntʃ] *n* the name of a comic figure in a puppet-show (traditionally known as a ˌ**Punch and 'Judy show**).

as pleased as Punch very pleased.

punctilious [pʌŋk'tiliəs] *adj* (*formal*) paying great attention to correctness of details *esp* in one's behaviour: *a punctilious attitude*; *He is most punctilious.* **punc'tiliously** *adv.* **punc'tiliousness** *nu.*

punctual ['pʌŋktʃuəl] *adj* **1** (*pred*) arriving *etc* on time; not late: *He's always punctual for an appointment*; *Please be punctual.* **2** (*attrib*) taking care always to be on time: *She's a very punctual person.* ˌ**punctu'ality** [-'a-] *nu.*

'**punctually** *adv* on time: *He arrived punctually.*

punctuate ['pʌŋktʃueit] *vt* **1** to divide up sentences *etc* by commas, full stops, colons *etc.* **2** (*fig formal*) to interrupt repeatedly: *His speech was punctuated by bursts of applause.*

ˌ**punctu'ation** *nu* **1** the act of punctuating. **2** the use of punctuation marks: *The child can write quite well, but his punctuation is terrible.*

ˌ**punctu'ation mark** *nc* (*esp in pl*) any of the symbols used for punctuating, *eg* comma, full stop, question mark *etc.*

puncture ['pʌŋktʃə] *vti* to make or get a small hole

in: *He punctured the lid of the jar with a nail*; *The glass on the road punctured my new tyre.* – **1** *nc* a hole in a tyre: *My car has had two punctures this week.* **2** *nc* (*formal*) a small hole in another surface, *eg* skin: *A mosquito can make a puncture in one's skin.* **3** *nu* the act of puncturing.

pundit ['pʌndit] *nc* (*sometimes derog*) an expert: *The pundits disagree about the state of the economy.*

pungent ['pʌndʒənt] *adj* (*formal*) (of a taste or smell) sharp and strong: *a pungent smell of smoke*; *That smell is rather pungent*; (*fig*) *a pungent remark.* '**pungently** *adv.*

punish ['pʌniʃ] *vt* **1** to cause (someone) to suffer for a crime or fault: *He was punished for stealing the money.* **2** to give punishment for: *The teacher punishes disobedience.* **3** (*inf*: *often fig*) to treat roughly: *He really punished his rival at golf.*

'**punishable** *adj* (of offences *etc*) able or likely to be punished: *Driving without a licence is a punishable offence*; *This crime is punishable by death in some parts of the world.*

'**punishment 1** *nu* the act of punishing or process of being punished. **2** *ncu* suffering, or a penalty, imposed for a crime, fault *etc*: *He was sent to prison for two years as* (*a*) *punishment.*

punitive ['pju:nətiv] *adj* (*formal or facet*) giving punishment or suffering: *Punitive measures will be taken against any offenders*; *That level of taxation is really punitive.*

punnet ['pʌnit] *nc* a type of small basket in which fruit *etc* is sold: *a punnet of strawberries.*

punster *see* **pun**.

punt [pʌnt] *nc* a type of flat-bottomed boat with square ends, moved by pushing against the bottom of the river *etc* with a pole. – *vi* to travel in a punt: *They punted up the river.*

punter ['pʌntə] *nc* (*inf*) a person who bets on horses *etc*; a gambler.

puny ['pju:ni] *adj* (*derog*) small and weak: *a puny child*; *Her husband is small and puny*; (*fig*) *a puny effort.* '**punily** *adv.* '**puniness** *nu.*

pup [pʌp] *nc* **1** (*also* **puppy** ['pʌpi]) a young dog: *a sheepdog pup(py).* **2** (*also* **puppy** ['pʌpi]: *old derog*) a conceited or rude young man: *Insolent young puppy!* **3** the young of certain other animals: *a seal pup.*

pupa ['pju:pə] – *pl* '**pupae** [-pi:] – *nc* (*tech*) the form that an insect takes when it is changing from a larva (*eg* a caterpillar) to its perfect form (*eg* a butterfly); a chrysalis.

pupil[1] ['pju:pl] *nc* a person who is being taught by a teacher or tutor: *The school has 2000 pupils*; *He is a pupil of one of the best music teachers in Europe.*

pupil[2] ['pju:pl] *nc* the round opening in the middle of the eye through which the light passes.

puppet ['pʌpit] *nc* **1** a doll that can be moved *eg* by wires or rods, or by putting the hand inside the body: *He has three puppets dressed as animals*; *a glove puppet.* **2** (*fig and often attrib*) a person or group that is completely under the control of another: *The king is a puppet of the most powerful aristocratic family*; *a puppet ruler/government.*

'**puppetry** *nu* the art of making puppets and producing puppet shows.

'**puppet-show** *nc* a play *etc* performed by puppets.

puppy *see* **pup**.

purchase ['pə:tʃəs] *vt* (*formal*) to buy: *I purchased a new house.* – **1** *nc* anything that has been bought: *She carried her purchases home in a bag.* **2** *nu* the act of buying: *The purchase of a car should never be a hasty matter.* **3** *nu* (*tech*) firmness in holding or gripping: *He tried to get more purchase on the rope.*

'**purchaser** *nc* a buyer.

'**purchase tax** *ncu* a tax on the buying of certain articles: *a purchase tax on musical instruments.*

pure ['pjuə] *adj* **1** (*usu attrib*) not mixed with anything *esp* dirty or less valuable: *pure gold*; *pure milk.* **2** (*formal*) clean, *esp* morally: *a pure young girl*; *pure thoughts*; *She is chaste and pure.* **3** (*attrib*) complete; absolute: *a pure accident*; *pure nonsense.* **4** without faults: *His French is very pure*; *Foreigners often speak a very pure kind of English.* **5** (of sounds) clear; keeping in tune: *a pure note.*

'**pureness**, '**purity** *nus.*

'**purely** *adv* **1** (*formal*) in a pure manner. **2** wholly; entirely: *He won the prize purely on his own merit.* **3** only, merely: *He wrote it purely as an exercise.*

'**purify** [-fai] *vt* (*tech*) to make pure: *What is the best way to purify the air?* ˌ**purifi'cation** [-fi-] *nu.*

'**purist** *nc* a person who insists on absolute correctness: *My father is a purist about grammar.*

'**purism** *nu.*

ˌ**pure-'blooded** *adj* (*esp attrib*) of unmixed race: *a pure-blooded Englishman.*

ˌ**pure-'bred** *adj* (of animals) of unmixed breed; thoroughbred: *a pure-bred Arab horse*; *Is that horse pure-bred?*

pure and simple (*used after a noun*) nothing but: *It was an accident pure and simple.*

pure mathematics/science mathematics/science in theory, as opposed to practice.

See also **impure**.

purée ['pjuərei, (*Amer*) pju'rei] *ncu* any of several types of food made into a soft pulp: *For this recipe you need two spoonfuls of potato purée*; *I made a purée of the fruit in my liquidizer.*

purge [pə:dʒ] *vt* **1** (*formal*: *usu fig*) to make (something) clean by clearing it of everything that is bad, not wanted *etc*: *You must purge your mind of all wicked thoughts*; (*polit*) *It is time to purge the party* (*of everybody thought to be disloyal*). **2** (*old*) to empty (the bowels). – *nc* an act of purging a political party *etc*: *Several members of the administration lost their jobs in the last purge.*

purgative ['pə:gətiv] *ncu, adj* (a medicine) which clears waste matter out of the body: *He took a purgative*; *purgative medicine.*

purgatory ['pə:gətəri] *nu* **1** (*esp* in the Roman Catholic teaching) a place or state after death in which a soul is made pure before it goes to heaven. **2** (*inf fig or facet*) any state of suffering or unpleasantness: *Living in this climate is absolute purgatory.*

purification, purify, purism, purist *see* **pure**.

puritan ['pjuəritən] *nc* **1** (*derog*) a person who is morally strict and disapproves of many kinds of enjoyment: *He is too much of a puritan to go to the theatre.* **2** (*with cap*: *hist*) in England and America, a member of a religious group wanting to make religion simpler *esp* by abolishing ceremony from church services.

ˌ**puri'tanical** [-'ta-] *adj* of a puritan: *puritanical behaviour*; *She can be rather puritanical about matters of sex.*

purity *see* **pure**.

purl [pə:l] *nu* a kind of knitting stitch: *This part is done in purl and plain.* – *vti* to knit (this stitch): *Purl three* (*stitches*).

purloin [pə'loin] *vt* (*formal or facet*) to steal: *He was accused of purloining the firm's property.*

purple ['pə:pl] **1** *nu, adj* (of) a dark colour made by mixing blue and red. **2** *nu* something (*eg* paint, material *etc*) purple in colour: *She was dressed in purple.*

purport ['pə:po:t] *nu* (*formal*) meaning: *I did not understand the purport of his remarks.* – [pə'po:t] *vi* (*formal*) to seem or appear, *esp* if not really so: *This letter purports to be from my brother.*

purpose ['pə:pəs] **1** *ncu* the reason for doing something; the aim to which an action *etc* is directed: *What is the purpose of your visit?*; *What is your purpose in asking that question?*; *Is there much purpose in remaining here?* **2** *nc* the use or function of an object: *What is the main purpose of this dictionary?*; *The purpose of this lever is to stop the machine in an emergency*; *a multi-purpose tool* (= a tool with many uses). **3** *nu* determination: *a man of purpose.* – *See also* **on purpose** *below.*

'**purposeful** *adj* having a definite purpose: *with a purposeful look on his face*; *He looks very purposeful.* '**purposefully** *adv.*

'**purposeless** *adj* (*formal*: *usu attrib*) having no purpose: *purposeless destruction*; *a purposeless life.*

'**purposely** *adv* intentionally: *He did it purposely to attract my attention*; *I purposely did not tell him about my new job.*

,**purpose-'built** *adj* made or built for a particular need or purpose: *People who use wheelchairs sometimes live in purpose-built houses*; *Their new car was purpose-built.*

on 'purpose intentionally: *Did you break the cup on purpose?*

serve a purpose (*formal*) to be useful in some way: *Keep that bag – it may serve a purpose*; *This is not the tool I wanted but it will serve my purpose* (= do what I need) *very well.*

to no purpose (*formal*) with no useful results: *We have discussed the problem several times but to no purpose.*

to the 'purpose (*formal*) relevant; to the point: *His reply was not really to the purpose.*

purr [pə:] *vi* to make the low, murmuring sound of a cat when it is pleased: *The cat was purring by the fire*; (*fig*) *My mother purred with delight when she heard of my brother's success.* – *nc* such a sound.

purse [pə:s] *nc* **1** a small bag for carrying money: *I looked in my purse for some change.* **2** (*Amer*) a handbag. – *vt* to close (the lips) tightly: *She pursed her lips as she thought about it.*

'**purser** *nc* the officer in charge of a ship's money, supplies *etc.*

pursue [pə'sju:] *vt* (*formal*) **1** to follow *esp* in order to catch or capture; to chase: *They pursued the thief through the town.* **2** to occupy oneself with (studies, enquiries *etc*); to continue: *He is pursuing his studies at the University.*

pur'suance *nu* (*very formal or legal*) the process of performing or carrying out (a duty *etc*): *in the pursuance of his duty.*

pur'suer *nc.*

pursuit [pə'sju:t] **1** *nu* the act of pursuing: *in our pursuit of happiness*; *The thief ran down the street, with a policeman in hot pursuit* (= energetically chasing him). **2** *nc* an occupation or hobby: *holiday pursuits.*

purulent *see* **pus**.

pus [pʌs] *nu* a thick, yellowish liquid that forms in infected wounds *etc.*

purulent ['pjuəjulənt] *adj* (*very formal or tech*) containing or producing pus: *a purulent wound*; *The wound is purulent.*

push [puʃ] **1** *vti* to press against something, in order to (try to) move it further away: *He pushed the door open*; *Push the red button to stop the elevator*; *She pushed him away*; *He pushed her out of the room*; *She pushed him off the wall*; *He pushed against the door with his shoulder*; *She tried to push her way through the crowd*; *The queue can't move any faster, so stop pushing!*; *I had a good view of the race till someone pushed in front of me.* – *See also* **push over** *below.* **2** *vt* (*inf derog*) to try to make (someone) do something; to urge on, *esp* foolishly: *She pushed him into applying for the job*; *Some parents are inclined to push their children.* **3** *vt* to put (something or someone) forward for notice, consideration *etc*: *He doesn't push his ideas enough.* **4** *v refl* to make (oneself) go further, do more *etc* than normal: *They pushed themselves to their limit to finish the work in time.* **5** *vt* (*sl*) to sell (addictive drugs) illegally: *He was arrested for pushing drugs.* – **1** *nc* a movement of pressure against something; a thrust: *She gave him a push.* **2** *nc* an effort, attempt: *They made a final push and reached the top of the mountain.* **3** *nu* (*inf*) energy and determination: *He has enough push to do well in his job.*

'**pusher** *nc* **1** (*derog*) a person who pushes himself forward; an ambitious and forceful person. **2** (*sl*) a person who sells addictive drugs illegally.

'**pushing,** '**pushy** *adj* (*derog*) rudely pushing oneself forward; determined to get what one wants: *a pushing young man*; *He is too pushy.*

'**push-bike** *nc* (*inf*) a bicycle that does not have a motor.

'**push-chair** *nc* (*Brit*) a small wheeled chair for a child, pushed by its mother *etc*: *The child does not have to be put in a pram any more – she is old enough to sit in a push-chair.*

'**push-over** *nc* (*sl*) a very easy job or task: *The thieves thought the robbery would be a push-over.* – *See also* **push over**.

be 'pushed for (*inf*) to be short of; not to have enough of: *I'm a bit pushed for time/money.*

be pushing forty, fifty *etc* (*inf*) to be nearly forty, fifty *etc* in age: *She's very agile and she must be pushing seventy.*

give/get the push (*sl*) to dismiss (someone)/be dismissed from a job *etc*: *He was the manager of that firm but he got the push.*

push along *vi* (*inf*) to leave or go away: *I'll have to be pushing along now.*

push around *vt oblig sep* (*inf*) to treat (someone) roughly: *He pushes his younger brother around*; (*fig*) *I don't let anyone push me around.*

push off *vi* (*inf*) to go away: *I wish you'd push off!*

push on *vi* (*inf*) to go on; to continue: *I'm late, I'll have to push on*; *Push on with your work.*

push over *vt sep* to cause to fall; to knock down: *He pushed me over.*

pusillanimous [pju:si'lanəməs] *adj* (*formal*) cowardly. ,**pusilla'nimity** *nu.*

puss [pus], **pussy** ['pusi] *nc* (*inf*) a cat.

'**pussyfoot** *vi* (*inf*: *usu derog*) to behave in a wary or timid way: *Stop pussyfooting, and come to a decision!*

pustule ['pʌstju:l, (*Amer*) 'pʌstʃu:l] *nc* (*tech or formal*) a small spot or pimple containing pus: *This ointment should cure the pustules on the young man's face.*

put [put] – *prp* '**putting**: *pt, ptp* **put** – *vt* **1** to place in a certain position or situation: *He put the plate in the cupboard*; *Did you put any sugar in my coffee?*;

He put his arm round her shoulders; *I'm putting a new lock on the door*; *Put the matter out of your mind!* (= Forget it); *You're putting too much strain on that rope*; *When did the Russians put a man into space?*; *You've put me in a bad temper* (= made me angry); *I'll try to put things right* (= improve the situation) *by apologizing*; *We must put an end to* (= stop) *this vandalism*; *Can you put* (= translate) *this sentence into French?* **2** to submit or present (a proposal, question *etc*): *I put several questions to him*; *She put her ideas before the committee*; *I put it* (= suggested) *to him that he was not being quite honest.* **3** to express in words: *He put his refusal very politely*; *Children have such a funny way of putting things!*; *How do you put* (= say) *that in German?* **4** (*inf*) to write down: *I'm trying to write a letter to her, but I don't know what to put.* **5** (*naut*) to sail in a particular direction: *We put out to sea*; *The ship put into harbour for repairs*; *They put about* (= turned) *and sailed for home.* – *See also* **put** *in phrases below.*

'put-on *adj* (*without hyphen when pred*) pretended; not genuine: *She spoke in a put-on foreign accent*; *That accent is put on.* – *See also* **put on** *below.*

a ˌput-up 'job (*inf*) something done to give a false appearance, in order to cheat or trick someone: *The trial was just a put-up job.*

put about *vt sep* (*formal*) to spread (news *etc*): *They put* (*it*) *about that she was married.* – *See also* **put** (*def 5*).

put across/over *vt sep* to convey or communicate (ideas *etc*) to others: *He's very good at putting his ideas across*; *He has a great deal of information but he does not put it across very well.*

put aside *vt sep* **1** to abandon (work *etc*) temporarily: *She put aside her needlework*; *She put it aside.* **2** to save or preserve for the future: *He tries to put aside a little money each month.*

put a sock in it *see* **sock**.

put away *vt sep* to return (something) to its proper place, *esp* out of sight: *She put her clothes away in the dresser*; *She put them away.*

put back *vt sep* to return (something) to its proper place: *Did you put my keys back?*

put by *vt sep* to save or preserve for the future: *I have put by some money for emergencies.*

put down *vt sep* **1** to lower (one's hand *etc*): *The teacher asked the pupil to put his hand down.* **2** to place on the floor or other surface, out of one's hands: *Put that knife down immediately!* **3** (*formal*) to subdue (a rebellion *etc*): *The revolt was quickly put down.* **4** (*inf*) to humiliate or snub: *She is always putting her husband down.* **5** to kill (an animal) painlessly when it is old or very ill: *The dog was getting deaf and blind so we had it put down*; *The poor cat was in pain and had to be put down.*

put (someone) down for (something) to write (a person's name) on a list *etc* for a particular purpose: *You have been put down for the one hundred metres' race.*

put (something) down to (something) to attribute (*eg* a way of behaving) to a particular circumstance: *I put her rudeness down to anxiety.*

put one's feet up to take a rest by lying down or sitting with one's feet supported on something: *I look forward to getting home and putting my feet up.*

put forth *vt sep* (*old*) (of plants *etc*) to produce (leaves, shoots *etc*). – *See also* **put out** *below.*

put forward *see* **bring forward** *under* **forward**.

put in *vt sep* **1** to insert or install: *We're having a new bath put in*; *The plumber put it in yesterday.* **2** to do (a certain amount of work *etc*): *He put in an hour's piano practice today.*

ˌput 'in for *vt fus* to apply for, or claim: *Are you putting in for that job/grant?*

put off **1** *vt sep* to switch off (a light *etc*): *Please put the light off!* **2** *vt sep* to delay; to postpone: *He put off leaving/his departure till Thursday.* **3** *vt sep* to cancel an arranged meeting *etc* with (a person): *I had to put the Browns off because I had 'flu.* **4** *vt oblig sep* to cause (a person) to feel disgust or dislike: *The cheese looked nice but the smell put me off.*

put (someone) off (something) to cause (a person) to feel disgust *etc* for: *The conversation about illness put me off my dinner.*

put on *vt sep* **1** to switch on (a light *etc*): *Put the light on!* **2** to dress oneself in: *Which shoes are you going to put on?* **3** to add or increase: *The car put on speed*; *I've put on weight* (= become fatter). **4** to present or produce (a play *etc*): *They're putting on 'Hamlet' next week.* **5** to provide (*eg* transport): *They always put on extra buses between 8.00 and 9.00 a.m.* **6** to make a false show of; to feign: *She said she felt ill, but she was just putting it on*; *He put on a Spanish accent.* – *See also* **put-on** *adj.*

'put (something) on (something) to bet (a sum of money *etc*) on (a horse *etc*): *I've put a pound on that horse to win.*

put out *vt sep* **1** to extend (a hand *etc*): *He put out his hand to steady her.* **2** (of plants *etc*) to produce (shoots, leaves *etc*). – *See also* **put forth** *above.* **3** (*less formal than* **extinguish**) to extinguish (a fire, light *etc*): *The fire brigade soon put out the fire.* **4** (*less formal than* **issue**) to issue: *They put out a distress call.* **5** (*inf*) to cause bother or trouble to: *Are we putting you out?*; *Don't put yourself out for my sake!* **6** to annoy: *I was put out by his decision.* **7** to strain or dislocate (a joint in the body): *He put his shoulder out trying to move the piano.*

put over *see* **put across**.

put through *vt sep* **1** to arrange (a deal, agreement *etc*): *Has he managed to put that deal through?* **2** to connect by telephone: *Could you put me through to the manager?*; *I'm trying to put you through*; *I want to put through a call to London.*

put to death *see* **death**.

put together *vt oblig sep* to construct: *The vase broke, but I managed to put it together again* (= mend it).

put up *vt sep* **1** to raise (a hand *etc*). **2** (*less formal than* **erect**) to build; to erect: *They're putting up some new houses.* **3** to fix (a notice *etc*) on a wall *etc*: *He put the poster up.* **4** to increase (a price *etc*): *They're putting up the fees again.* **5** to offer or show (resistance *etc*): *He's putting up a brave fight.* **6** to provide (money) for a purpose: *He promised to put up the money for the scheme.* **7** to provide a bed *etc* for (a person) in one's home: *Can you put us up next Thursday night?*

ˌput (someone) 'up to (doing something) to persuade (a person) to do something: *Who put you up to writing that letter?*; *Did he put you up to it?*

put 'up with *vt fus* (*less formal than* **bear** *or* **tolerate**) to bear patiently; to tolerate: *I cannot put up with all this noise.*

putative ['pjuːtətiv] *adj* (*very formal*: *attrib*) supposed; generally accepted: *the putative father of the child.*

putrefy ['pjuːtrəfai] *vti* (*formal*) to make or go bad or rotten: *The meat soon putrefied in the heat.*

ˌputreˈfaction [-ˈfak-] *nu.*

putrescent [pju:ˈtresnt] *adj* (*very formal*) going bad or rotten: *putrescent fruit*; *The fruit is putrescent.* **puˈtrescence** *nu.*

putrid [ˈpju:trid] *adj* (smelling) rotten: *putrid fish*; *a putrid smell*; *This meat is putrid.*

putt [pʌt] *vti* (in golf) to send a ball gently forward when aiming for the hole. – *nc* a stroke that does this.

ˈ**putter** *nc* a golf-club used for putting.

putty [ˈpʌti] *nu* a type of paste made from ground chalk and oil, used to fix glass in windows *etc.*

puzzle [ˈpʌzl] **1** *vt* to present (someone) with a difficult problem; to be difficult for (someone) to understand; to perplex, baffle or bewilder: *The question puzzled them*; *I was puzzled by his attitude*; *What puzzles me is how he got here so soon.* **2** *vi* (*esp with* **over** *or* **about**) to think long and carefully about, and try to solve (a problem *etc*): *I puzzled over the letter for hours.* – *See also* **puzzle out** *below.* – *nc* **1** a problem that causes a lot of thought: *Her decision was a puzzle to him.* **2** (*often in cmpds*) a kind of game or toy to test one's thinking, knowledge or skill: *a jig-saw puzzle*; *a crossword puzzle.*

ˈ**puzzler** *nc* (*inf*) a difficult question or problem: *That's quite a puzzler!*

ˈ**puzzling** *adj* difficult to understand; perplexing: *Her words were puzzling*; *rather puzzling comments.*

puzzle out *vt sep* to solve (a problem *etc*): *He managed to puzzle out the code.*

pygmy, pigmy [ˈpigmi] *nc* a member of an African race of very small people.

pyjamas, (*Amer*) **pajamas** [pəˈdʒa:məz] *n pl* a suit for sleeping, consisting of trousers and a jacket: *He does not wear pyjamas*; *He has three pairs of pyjamas.*

pylon [ˈpailən, (*Amer*) -lon] *nc* **1** a tall steel tower for supporting electric power cables. **2** a guiding mark at an airfield.

pyramid [ˈpirəmid] *nc* **1** (*geom*) a solid shape *usu* with a square or triangular base, and sloping triangular sides meeting in a point. **2** something built in this shape, *esp* such a thing built as a tomb in ancient Egypt.

pyre [ˈpaiə] *nc* a pile of wood on which a dead body is ceremonially burned: *a funeral pyre.*

Pyrex ® [ˈpaireks] **1** *n* (*usu attrib*) a registered trademark for a type of glass used in cooking-dishes *etc* which will not break when heated: *a Pyrex dish.* **2** *nu* Pyrex dishes: *We got a lot of Pyrex as wedding presents.*

pyro- [pairou] (*in cmpds*) fire, as in **pyrotechnics**.

pyrotechnics [pairəˈtekniks] *n pl* **1** (a display of) fireworks. **2** (*fig formal*) a brilliant display in a speech, musical performance *etc.*

python [ˈpaiθən] *nc* a type of large non-poisonous snake that twists around its prey and crushes it.

Qq

quack[1] [kwak] *nc* the cry of a duck. – *vi* to make such a sound: *The ducks quacked noisily as they swam across the pond.*

quack[2] [kwak] *nc* (*derog*) a person who pretends that he has skill and knowledge (*esp* in medicine) that he does not really possess: *The man claimed to have found a cure for cancer, but doctors said he was just a quack*; (*attrib*) *quack medicines.*

quad [kwod] short for **quadrangle, quadruple**.

quadrangle [ˈkwodraŋgl] *nc* (*inf abbrev* **quad** [kwod]) a four-sided open space surrounded by buildings, *esp* in a school, college *etc*: *The students walked in the quadrangle before they went to their English lecture.*

quadrilateral [kwodriˈlatərəl] *nc* (*geom*) a two-dimensional figure with four straight sides.

quadruped [ˈkwodruped] *nc* (*tech*) a four-footed animal: *An elephant is a quadruped.*

quadruple [kwoˈdru:pl] *adj* (*formal*) **1** four times as much or as many: *Their firm has an annual profit quadruple that of ours.* **2** (*esp attrib*) made up of four parts, made by four people *etc*: *a quadruple alliance* (= an alliance made by *eg* four countries). – *vti* to make or become four times as great: *Our profits have quadrupled in the past year.* – *nu* four times the (usual) amount: *He is paid quadruple for working in these terrible conditions.*

quadruplet [kwoˈdru:plit] *nc* (*also abbrev* **quad** [kwod]) one of four children born at the same time to one mother: *She was expecting triplets but she's had quads.*

quadruplicate [kwəˈdru:plikət]: **in quaˈdruplicate** (*formal*) in four identical copies: *Please fill out this form in quadruplicate.*

quaff [kwof, (*Amer*) kwa:f] *vti* (*liter*) to drink up (something) eagerly: *He quaffed a glass of wine.*

quagmire [ˈkwagmaiə] *nc* an area of soft marshy ground.

quail[1] [kweil] *vi* (*formal*: *with* **at**) to draw back (from someone) in fear: *The little boy quailed at the sound of his mother's angry voice.*

quail[2] [kweil] – *pls* **quail, quails** – **1** *nc* a small bird of the partridge family. **2** *ncu* (the flesh of) the bird as food: *We had stuffed quail for dinner as a treat.*

quaint [kweint] *adj* pleasantly odd or strange, *esp* because of being old-fashioned: *quaint customs/clothes*; *I find those thatched houses very quaint.* ˈ**quaintly** *adv.* ˈ**quaintness** *nu.*

quake [kweik] **1** *vi* (*often facet*) (of people) to shake or tremble, *esp* with fear: *The boys stood quaking outside the headmaster's room.* **2** (*formal*) (of the ground) to shake: *The ground quaked under their feet.* – *nc* **1** a shake or shudder (*esp* of fear). **2** (*inf*) an earthquake.

qualify [ˈkwolifai] **1** *vti* to (cause to) become able or suitable for: *A degree in English does not qualify you to teach English*; *A degree in English does not qualify you for this job*; *To qualify for a grant of money, you need to be earning less than £2500 a year.* **2** *vi* (*with* **as**) to show that one is suitable for a profession or job *etc*, *esp* by passing a test or examination: *I hope to qualify as a doctor.* **3** *vti* (*with* **for**) to allow, or be allowed, to take part in a competition *etc*, *usu* by reaching a satisfactory standard in an earlier test or competition: *Every football fan hopes that his national team will qualify for the World Cup*; *That team is not playing in the European Cup matches – it did not qualify.* **4** *vt* to change or add something to (something one has said or written) in order to make it less strong: *That's very good – no, I'll qualify that – it's quite good.* **5** *vt* (*gram*) (of an adjective) to describe, or add to the meaning of (a noun, a pronoun or an equivalent phrase): *In 'red books', the adjective 'red' qualifies the noun 'books'.*

ˌqualifiˈcation [-fi-] **1** *ncu* (the act of gaining) a skill, achievement *etc* (*eg* an examination pass) that makes (a person) able or suitable to do a job *etc*: *What qualifications do you need for this job?* **2** *nc* something that gives (a person) the right to do (something). **3** *ncu* (the changing or adding of) something that makes what one has said or written less strong; (the adding of) a restriction or limitation to something one has said or written: *I think this is an excellent piece of work – with certain qualifications.*

ˈqualified *adj* (*neg* **un-**) **1** having the necessary qualification(s) to do (something): *a qualified engineer*; *You are not qualified to judge him.* **2** (*formal*: *usu attrib*) with some limitations or restrictions: *qualified praise* (= praise that includes some criticisms).

ˈqualifying *adj* (*attrib*) in which players, teams *etc* attempt to qualify for a competition *etc*: *Our team was beaten in the qualifying round.*

quality [ˈkwoləti] **1** *ncu* the extent to which something has features which are good or bad, wanted or unwanted *etc*, *esp* features which are good, desirable *etc*: *We produce several different qualities of paper*; *In this firm, we look for quality* (= good quality) *rather than quantity*; (*attrib*) *quality goods.* **2** *nc* some (*usu* good) feature which makes a person or thing special or noticeable: *Kindness is a human quality which everyone admires.* **3** *nu* (*arch or facet*) (people who belong to) the upper class or nobility: *Many of the quality were at the gathering*; *people of quality.*

qualm [kwa:m] *nc* (*formal*) a feeling of uncertainty about whether one is doing right: *I have qualms about reading other people's letters, but I must find out what they are saying about me*; *She had no qualms about reporting her husband's crime to the police.*

quandary [ˈkwondəri] *nc* a state of uncertainty; a situation in which it is difficult to decide what to do: *I'm in a bit of a quandary about whether to go to the police or deal with him myself.*

quantify [ˈkwontifai] *vt* (*formal*) to estimate or state the amount of (something): *The destruction and misery of war is hard to quantify*; *We think our efforts have been successful but it is difficult to quantify the results.*

quantity [ˈkwontəti] *ncu* the size, weight, number *etc* of something, *esp* a large size *etc*: *What quantity of paper do you need?*; *I buy these things in quantity*; *I only need a small quantity of cement for this job*; *He buys large quantities of tinned food every month.*

quantity surveyor *nc* a person who is responsible for estimating the quantities of building materials needed for constructing something, and their probable cost.

an unknown quantity 1 a person or thing whose characteristics, abilities *etc* cannot be predicted: *We do not know how he will react – he's an unknown quantity.* **2** (*math*) a symbol, *eg x*, representing an unknown amount in an equation *etc.*

quarantine [ˈkworənti:n] **1** *nu* the keeping away from other people or animals of people or animals that might be carrying an infectious disease: *Britain has a system of quarantine*; (*attrib*) *quarantine regulations.* **2** *nu* the state of being kept away from other people or animals for this reason: *My dog was in quarantine for six months.* **3** *nc* the period of time during which this is done: *The quarantine for a dog entering Britain from abroad is six months.* – *vt* to put (a person or animal) in quarantine: *We were quarantined because in the plane we sat next to someone who later was discovered to have smallpox.*

quarrel [ˈkworəl] *nc* an angry disagreement or argument: *I've had a quarrel with my girl-friend.* – *v* – *pt, ptp* **ˈquarrelled**, (*Amer*) **ˈquarreled** – *vi* (*with* **with**) **1** to have an angry argument (with someone): *I've quarrelled with my girl-friend*; *My girl-friend and I have quarrelled.* **2** (*formal*) to disagree (with something): *I wouldn't quarrel with your analysis of the situation.*

ˈquarrelsome *adj* inclined to quarrel: *Those children are so quarrelsome*; *quarrelsome children.*

ˈquarrelsomeness *nu.*

pick a quarrel *see* **pick**[1].

quarry[1] [ˈkwori] *nc* a place, *usu* a very large hole in the ground, from which stone is got for building *etc*: *The lorries carry stone from the quarry to the building site.* – *vti* to dig (stone) in a quarry.

quarry[2] [ˈkwori] *nc* **1** a hunted animal or bird: *The hounds bayed as they got close to their quarry.* **2** someone or something that is hunted, chased or eagerly looked for: *The policeman followed his quarry right across the town and watched him go into a pub*; *The thief followed his quarry into a dark street and attacked him.*

quart [kwo:t] *nc* (*sometimes abbrev* **qt** *when written*) a measure of liquids, a quarter of a gallon (1·136 litres): *a quart of milk.*

quarter [ˈkwo:tə] **1** *nc* one of four equal parts of something which together form the whole (amount) of the thing: *There are four of us, so we'll cut the cake into quarters*; *It's* (*a*) *quarter* (= a quarter of an hour) *past/*(*Amer*) *after four*; *In the first quarter of this year, we made a profit of £2 000*; *The shop is about a quarter of a mile away*; *A quarter of tea, please* (= a quarter of a pound); *It'll take you about an hour and a quarter/two and a quarter hours to get there*; (*attrib*) *a quarter stone of potatoes.* **2** *nc* in the US and Canada, (a coin worth) twenty-five cents, the fourth part of a dollar: *That candy will cost you a quarter.* **3** *nc* a district or part of a town, *esp* where a particular group of people live: *He lives in the Chinese quarter/poor quarter of the town.* **4** *nc* (*formal*) a person or people: *No help came to the man from any quarter.* **5** *nc* (*sometimes abbrev* **qr** *when written*) a measure of weight, a quarter of a hundredweight, in Britain 28 pounds (12·7 kg), in the US 25 pounds (11·34 kg). **6** *nc* a direction; (the part of the Earth corresponding to) a point of the compass: *People were coming at me from all quarters.* **7** *nu* (*formal*) mercy shown to an enemy: *No quarter was given by either side in the battle* (= no prisoners were taken; the soldiers fought to the death). **8** *nc* the leg of a *usu* large animal, or a joint of meat which includes a leg: *a quarter of beef*; *a bull's hindquarters.* **9** *nc* the shape of the moon at the end of the first and third weeks of its cycle; the first or fourth week of the cycle itself. **10** *nc* (*Amer*) one of four equal periods of play in some games. **11** *nc* (*Amer*) a period of study at a college *etc*, *usu* 10 to 12 weeks in length. – *vt* **1** to cut into four equal parts: *We'll quarter the cake* *and then we'll all have an equal share.* **2** to divide (something) by four: *If we each do the work at the same time, we could quarter the time it would take to finish the job.* **3** to give (*esp* a soldier) somewhere to stay: *The soldiers were quartered* (*on people*) *all over the town.* **4** (*loosely*) to cut (something) into four parts which are not exact quarters. **5** (*hist*) to cut (a criminal's body) into four parts: *Traitors used to be sentenced to be hanged, drawn and quartered.*

'quarterly *adj* (*attrib*) happening *etc* once every three months: *a quarterly journal*; *He makes quarterly payments.* – *adv* once every three months: *We pay our electricity bill quarterly.* – *nc* a magazine *etc* which is published once every three months: *He reads all the literary quarterlies.*

'quarters *n pl* a place to stay *esp* for soldiers: *The soldiers were given quarters in the villagers' houses*; *Married quarters* (= *usu* houses near army barracks *etc*) *are provided for those soldiers with families.*

'quarter-deck *nc* (*hist*) the part of the upper deck of a ship between the stern and the mast nearest it.

ˌquarter-'final *nc* (*often in pl*) the third-last round in a competition: *Rangers beat Clyde in the quarter-finals, and will play against Celtic in the semi-finals.*

ˌquarter-'finalist *nc* a person, team *etc* competing in a quarter-final.

'quartermaster *nc* (*mil*) an officer whose job is to provide soldiers with food, transport, a place to live *etc.*

at close quarters **1** close together: *The soldiers were fighting with the enemy at close quarters.* **2** very near: *The enemy were at close quarters.*

quartet [kwoː'tet] *nc* **1** a group of four singers or people playing musical instruments: *the Amadeus Quartet*; *My brother and I play in a quartet.* **2** a piece of music written for such a group: *We played a Mozart quartet.*

quartz [kwoːts] *nc, adj* (of) a kind of hard substance found in rocks, often in the form of crystals: *There's a great deal of quartz in those mountains*; *quartz crystal.*

quasar ['kweisaː] *nc* (*tech*) a star-like object (not really a star) which gives out light and radio waves.

quash [kwoʃ] *vt* **1** (*legal and formal*) to say that (a jury's or judge's decision) is not valid: *The boys were convicted of theft, but the conviction was later quashed.* **2** (*formal*) to stop or put an end to (a revolt *etc*): *The captain soon quashed the sailors' mutiny.*

quasi- [kweisai] (*in cmpds*: *formal*) **1** (*derog*) not really; only apparently: *a ˌquasi-scienˌtific 'study.* **2** almost; not completely: *a ˌquasi-ofˌficial po'sition.*

quaver ['kweivə] (*formal*) **1** *vi* (*esp* of a sound or a person's voice) to shake or tremble: *The old man's voice quavered*; *The child's voice quavered as he tried to sing the high notes.* **2** *vt* to say or sing (something) in a shaky voice: *He quavered out his thanks with difficulty.* – *nc* **1** (*esp* of a sound or a person's voice) a shaking or trembling: *There was a quaver in the old man's voice.* **2** (*music*) a note of a certain length. – *See also* Appendix 4.

quay [kiː] *nc* a solid, *usu* stone, landing-place, where boats are loaded and unloaded: *She stood on the quay to welcome the boat's passengers*; *The boat is moored at the quay.*

'quayside *nc* the side or edge of a quay: *The boat was tied up at the quayside*; *We walked along the quayside.*

queasy ['kwiːzi] *adj* **1** feeling as if one is about to be sick: *I feel rather queasy on this boat.* **2** easily upset: *I have rather a queasy stomach.* **'queasiness** *nu.*

queen [kwiːn] *nc* **1** (*with cap in titles*) (the status of) a woman who rules a country, who inherits her position by right of birth: *the Queen of Scotland*; *Queen Elizabeth II*; *Most girls have longed at some time to be a queen.* **2** (*with cap in titles*) (the status of) the wife of a king: *The king and his queen were both present*; *Anne Boleyn was one of Henry VIII's queens.* **3** a woman who is in some way important, excellent or special: *a beauty queen*; *a movie queen*; (*formal*) *She is the acknowledged queen of the Women's Guild*; (*fig*) *Isn't there some town that is known as the queen of the Mediterranean?* **4** a playing-card with a picture of a queen on it: *I have two aces and a queen.* **5** an important chess-piece: *a bishop, a king and a queen.* **6** (*biol*) the egg-laying female of certain kinds of insect (*esp* bees, ants and wasps). **7** (*sl*: *usu derog*) a male homosexual.

'queenly *adj* (*formal*) of, like or suitable for, a queen: *queenly dignity*; *She is tall and queenly.* **'queenliness** *nu.*

queen mother *nc* (*often with caps*) (the status of) the mother of the reigning king or queen, who was herself once a queen: *The Queen Mother is considered by everyone to be a very gracious lady.*

turn queen's evidence *see* **turn king's evidence** *under* **king**.

queer [kwiə] *adj* **1** odd, strange or unusual: *She's wearing a very queer hat*; *queer behaviour*; *I think it is very queer that she disappeared so suddenly*; *My wife keeps hearing queer noises in the middle of the night.* **2** (*inf*) sick; unwell: *I do feel a bit queer – perhaps I ate too many oysters*; *He has taken rather a queer turn* (= He is feeling unwell). **3** (*inf*: *usu pred*) slightly mad: *I think he's a bit queer in the head.* **4** (*sl offensive*: *usu pred*) (of a man) homosexual: *Just because he is not married does not mean that he is queer.* – *nc* (*sl offensive*) a male homosexual: *The queer tried to seduce the young man.*

'queerly *adv.* **'queerness** *nu.*

be in 'Queer Street (*inf*) to be in debt or be having difficulties because of a lack of money: *The firm is in Queer Street because of all the strikes.*

queer someone's pitch (*inf*) to spoil (a person's) plans; to make it impossible for (a person) to do something: *He had persuaded her to go and live with him but her sister queered his pitch by telling her that he was married.*

quell [kwel] *vt* (*formal*) **1** to put an end to (a rebellion *etc*) by force: *The general quelled the rebellion*; *The headmistress quelled the noisy pupils with a stern look.* **2** to put an end to, or take away (a person's fears *etc*): *Her father succeeded in quelling the child's fear of the dark.*

quench [kwentʃ] *vt* (*formal*) **1** to drink enough to take away (one's thirst): *I had a glass of lemonade to quench my thirst.* **2** to put out (a fire): *The firemen were unable to quench the fire.*

querulous ['kwerələs] *adj* (*formal derog*) making complaints; complaining: *a querulous person*; *querulous remarks*; *in querulous tones*; *That child is so querulous!* **'querulously** *adv.* **'querulousness** *nu.*

query ['kwiəri] *nc* (*more formal than* **question**) **1** a question: *I am sorry that I am unable to answer your queries*; *In answer to your query about hotel* *reservations I am sorry to tell you that we have no vacancies.* **2** a question mark: *You have omitted the query.* – *vt* **1** to question (a statement *etc*): *I think the waiter has added up the bill wrongly – you should query it*; *I query his ability to do the job* (= I do not think he is able for the job). **2** (*liter*) to ask: *'What time does the train leave?' she queried.*

quest [kwest] *nc* (*formal or liter*) a search: *the quest for gold*; *the quest for truth.*

question ['kwestʃən] **1** *nc* something which is said, written *etc* which asks for an answer from someone: *'Where are you going?' is a question.* **2** *nc* a problem or matter for discussion: *the energy question*; *There is the question of how much to pay him*; *The question is really one of how to overcome these problems.* **3** *nc* a single problem in a test or examination: *We had to answer four questions in three hours.* **4** *ncu* criticism; doubt; discussion: *This whole project is still open to question*; *He is, without question, the best man for the job.* **5** *nc* a suggestion or possibility: *There is no question of our dismissing him.* – *vt* **1** to ask (a person) questions: *I'll question him about what he was doing last night.* **2** to regard (something) as being doubtful: *I question if you can do it*; *I question whether he will come*; *He questioned her right to do that.*

'questionable *adj* **1** (*usu pred*) doubtful; uncertain: *It is questionable whether we will finish this in time.* **2** (*usu attrib*) probably not true, honest, respectable: *questionable behaviour.* **'questionably** *adv.* **'questionableness** *nu.*

'questioning *adj* **1** (*usu attrib*) asking many questions: *a questioning mind.* **2** showing that a question is being asked: *a questioning tone of voice*; *Her tone was questioning rather than complaining.*

'questioningly *adv.*

'question mark *nc* a mark, (**?**), used in writing to indicate a question: *Where are you going?*

'question-master *nc* a person who asks the questions in *eg* a quiz.

ˌquestion'naire [-'neə] *nc* a written list of questions to be answered by a large number of people to provide information for a survey or report: *We issued a questionnaire to find out which people were most likely to buy dictionaries.*

beg the question *see* **beg**.

call (something) in(to) question (*formal*) to raise doubts about (something); to dispute (something): *I will not have you call into question the government's good intentions*; *The company's ability to survive has been called in question.*

in 'question (*formal*) being talked about: *The matter in question can be left till next week.*

out of the question not to be thought of as possible; not to be done: *It is quite out of the question for you to go out tonight*; *Going on holiday tomorrow is out of the question – you haven't finished your work.*

See also **unquestionable**.

queue [kjuː] *nc* a line of people waiting (for something or to do something): *a queue for the bus.* – *vi* to stand in a queue: *We had to queue to get into the cinema*; *We had to queue for the cinema*; *During the war people had to queue for meat.*

queue up *vi* (*often with* **for**) to form, or stand in, a queue: *People are queuing up for tickets for the concert*; *They queued up to get into the theatre.*

quibble ['kwibl] *vi* **1** (*with* **over**) to avoid discussing or agreeing to an important part of something by bringing up unimportant, trivial objections, arguments *etc*: *He agreed with the treaty in principle but quibbled over the details.* **2** (*with* **at** *or* **about**) to argue about or object to (something): *He quibbled at the price.* – *nc* **1** an unimportant, trivial objection or argument: *quibbles over some of the details.* **2** an argument or objection: *There was a quibble over the price.*

quick [kwik] *adj* **1** done, said, finished *etc* in a short time: *a quick trip into town*; *The train journey was not as quick as usual.* **2** moving, or able to move, with speed: *He's a very quick walker*; *With a quick movement of his foot, he pressed the alarm button*; *I made a grab at the dog, but it was too quick for me* (= it escaped). **3** doing (something), able to do (something), or done, without delay; prompt; lively: *He is quick to respond to a call for help*; *a quick answer*; *a quick eye for mistakes*; *He's very quick at arithmetic*; *Her quick wits* (= Her alertness and promptness in acting *etc*) *saved the situation*; *She has a quick wit* (= She is witty); *He has a quick temper* (= He easily gets angry). – *adv* (*inf or in cmpds*) quickly: *quick-frozen food*; (*inf*) *Come as quick as you can.* – *nc* (*formal*) a very tender part of the body, *esp* under the nails.

'quickly *adv*: *He quickly realized that he was wrong*; *He walked quickly*; *Quickly – there's someone coming!*

'quicken *vti* to make or become quicker: *He quickened his pace*; *His pace quickened.*

'quickness *nu.*

'quicklime *nu* lime which has not been mixed with water.

'quicksand *ncu* (*often in pl*) (an area of) loose, wet sand that sucks in anyone or anything that stands on it.

'quicksilver *nu* (*old*) mercury.

'quickstep *nc* (a piece of music for) a type of fast ballroom dance: *Can you do the quickstep?*; *The next dance will be a quickstep.*

ˌquick-'tempered *adj* easily made angry: *a quick-tempered young man*; *He is quick-tempered and rather violent.*

ˌquick-'witted *adj* thinking very quickly: *a quick-witted policeman*; *Policemen must be quick-witted to catch criminals.* **ˌquick-'wittedly** *adv.* **ˌquick-'wittedness** *nu.*

cut (someone) to the quick *see* **cut**.

the quick and the dead (*arch*) the living and the dead.

quid [kwid] – *pl* **quid** – *nc* (*Brit sl*) a pound (£1): *Can you lend me a quid?*; *He paid five quid for it.*

quiescent [kwi'esnt] *adj* (*formal*) not in an active state: *a quiescent volcano*; *The volcano is quiescent now.* **qui'escence** *nu.*

quiet ['kwaiət] *adj* **1** not making very much, or any, noise; without very much, or any, noise: *Tell the children to be quiet*; *It's very quiet out in the country*; *The car's engine is very quiet*; *He is a very quiet man*; *the quiet purr of the car engine.* **2** free from worry, excitement *etc*: *I live a very quiet life*; *Country life is too quiet for me.* **3** without much movement or activity; not doing anything very active; not busy: *the quiet waters of a lake*; *We'll have a quiet afternoon watching television*; *The shop was very quiet this morning.* **4** (of colours) not bright: *I think we should have a nice quiet colour in the bedroom.* **5** not expressed aloud: *quiet resentment.* – *nu* a state, atmosphere, period of time *etc* which is quiet: *In the quiet of the night*; *All I want* *is peace and quiet*; *a period of quiet after a storm*; *the quiet of the countryside*. – *vti* (*esp Amer*: *often with* **down**) to quieten.

'quieten 1 *vti* (*esp Brit*: *often with* **down**) to make or become quiet: *I expect you to quieten down when I come into the classroom.* **2** *vt* to remove or lessen (a person's fears, doubts *etc*).

'quietly *adv*: *He moved quietly and quickly*; *She lives very quietly*; *The river flowed quietly by*; *She spoke quietly.*

'quietness *nu*.

'quietude [-tju:d] *nu* (*formal*) quietness.

keep quiet about (something) to say nothing about (something); to keep (something) secret: *I'd like you to keep quiet about the fact that the child's father is in prison.*

on the 'quiet (*inf*) secretly; without letting anyone find out: *We thought he was working in the other room, but he was just having a cigarette on the quiet.*

quill [kwil] *nc* **1** a large feather, *esp* the feather of a goose, made into a pen: *In former times people used quills to write with*; (*attrib*) *a quill pen.* **2** one of the sharp spines of certain animals (*eg* the porcupine).

quilt [kwilt] *nc* a bedcover filled with down, feathers *etc*: *The child's bed had a pink quilt over the blankets.*

'quilted *adj* (of clothes) made of two layers of material with padding or stuffing between them: *a quilted jacket*; *Her evening skirt is quilted.*

quin [kwin] short for **quintuplet**.

quince [kwins] *nc* a fruit with a sharp taste, used in making jam *etc*: (*attrib*) *quince jelly.*

quinine ['kwini:n, (*Amer*) 'kwainain] *nu* a bitter-tasting drug got from the bark of a type of tree, used as a medicine, *esp* for malaria.

quintet [kwin'tet] *nc* **1** a group of five singers or people playing musical instruments: *A string quintet is usually formed of two violins, two violas and a cello.* **2** a piece of music written for such a group: *Schubert's 'Trout' Quintet.*

quintuplet [kwin'tju:plit] *nc* (*also inf abbrev* **quin** [kwin]) one of five children born to one mother at the same time: *With the introduction of new fertility drugs, quins have become more common.*

quip [kwip] *nc* a quick, witty remark: *He is very good at making clever quips.* – *v* – *pt, ptp* **quipped** – *vi* (*formal*) to make a quip or quips.

quirk [kwə:k] *nc* **1** a strange or unusual feature of a person's character or behaviour: *Throwing biscuit crumbs over his shoulder is just one of his little quirks.* **2** a *usu* strange or unexpected happening (caused by fate): *By a strange quirk of fate he never met his father till the day he died.*

'quirky *adj* (of people) having quirks. **'quirkiness** *nu*.

quisling ['kwizliŋ] *nc* (*derog or offensive*) a person (*esp* a person who holds some official position of authority) who helps or co-operates with an enemy country that has taken over his country.

quit [kwit] – *pts, ptps* **'quitted, quit** – **1** *vt* (*inf*) to stop (doing something): *Quit whining, will you*; *Will you quit that!* **2** *vti* (*inf*) to leave, or resign from, one's job: *I'm going to quit teaching*; *I'm going to quit next week.* **3** *vti* (*Brit*) to leave a rented house, flat *etc*: *We've been given notice to quit.*

'quitter *nc* (*inf*) a person who gives up easily or who does not finish a task he has started if he meets with difficulties *etc*.

be 'quit of (*inf*) to be rid of; not to have any more: *His wife has left him but he is glad to be quit of her*; *I am glad to be quit of that job.*

be 'quits (with someone) to be even with (someone), neither owing them anything nor being owed anything by them: *He's paid me back what he owes me, so we are quits now*; *You hit him and he hit you back, so you are quits*; *He hit me and I hit him back, so I am quits with him.*

call it quits (*inf*) to agree with someone that neither person owes the other person anything: *This fight has been going for years – why don't you two call it quits and be friends?*

quite [kwait] *adv* **1** completely; entirely: *This is quite impossible*; *You are being quite unreasonable.* **2** fairly; rather; to a certain extent: *It's quite warm today*; *He's quite a good artist*; *I quite like the idea but I do have a few criticisms.* – *interj* (*formal*) (*often with* **so**) exactly; indeed; I agree: *'He has been working for this firm for a long time.' 'Quite so.'*; *'I think he is being unfair to her.' 'Quite.'*

quiver[1] ['kwivə] *vti* (*formal*) to (cause to) tremble or shake: *The bird's wings quivered*; *The child quivered with cold/fear*; *The bird quivered its wings.* – *ncu* (*formal*) a quivering sound, movement *etc*: *the quiver of a bird's wings*; *There was a slight quiver in his voice as he spoke.*

quiver[2] ['kwivə] *nc* a *usu* long, narrow case for carrying arrows in.

quixotic [kwik'sotik] *adj* (*formal*) having noble but foolish and unrealistic aims which cannot be carried out: *a quixotic gesture.*

quiz [kwiz] – *pl* **'quizzes** – *nc* a game or competition in which (*usu* a small number of) people's knowledge is tested by asking questions, *usu* for the amusement of an audience: *He took part in a television quiz and won several prizes*; *The child is trying to answer a quiz in the newspaper*; (*attrib*) *a quiz game.* – *v* – *pt, ptp* **quizzed** – *vt* (*often with* **about**) to ask (a person) questions: *He tried to quiz me about the other applicants for the job*; *Don't try to quiz me about my reasons for leaving.*

'quizzical *adj* (of *eg* a look) as if asking a question, *esp* humorously or mockingly: *He gave her a quizzical look*; *His expression was quizzical.*

'quizzically *adv*.

'quiz-master *nc* a question-master.

quoits [koits, (*Amer*) kwoits] *n sing* a game in which rings of metal, rope *etc*, called **quoits**, are thrown on to one or more small rods or hooks.

quorum ['kwo:rəm] *nc* (*formal*) the smallest number of members necessary at a meeting before any business can be done: *We can't have a meeting of the society – we haven't a quorum.*

quota ['kwoutə] *nc* (*formal*) the part, share or amount (of something) that each person or group of people among a number of people or groups of people, may or must produce, receive, do *etc*: *No boat was allowed to catch more than its quota of fish.*

quote [kwout] **1** *vti* (*often with* **from**) to repeat the exact words of (a person) exactly as they were said or written: *To quote a well-known saying/To quote Donne, 'No man is an island'*; *By way of illustration, I shall quote from Gray's 'Elegy'.* **2** *vt* to name (a price): *What price would you quote me for that painting?* **3** *vt* to mention or state (something) *usu* in support of an argument: *I could quote you several examples of that.*

'quotable (*formal or facet*) *adj* worth quoting;

likely to be quoted: *There are several very quotable phrases in that poem*; *His speeches are very quotable.*

quo'tation **1** *nc* a person's exact words, as repeated by someone else: *I will illustrate my point with a quotation from Shakespeare/Gray's 'Elegy'.* **2** *nc* a price (for a job *etc*): *We have received quotations from three firms for this job.* **3** *nu* the act of quoting (something).

quo'tation marks marks (" " or ' ') used to show that a person's words are being repeated exactly: *He said 'I'm going out.'*

Rr

rabbi ['rabai] *nc* (*with cap in titles*) a Jewish priest or teacher of the law: *That man is a rabbi*; *Rabbi Perlman.*

rabbit ['rabit] **1** *nc* a type of small long-eared burrowing animal, found living wild in fields or sometimes kept as a pet: *Rabbits have small, round, furry tails*; (*attrib*) *rabbit fur.* **2** *nu* the meat of the rabbit, used as food: *We had rabbit for dinner.* **3** *nu, adj* (*usu pred*) (of) the fur of the rabbit, often used in making coats *etc*: *The collar of her jacket is (made of) rabbit.*

'rabbit-hutch *nc* a small (*usu* wooden) cage in which pet rabbits are kept.

'rabbit-warren *nc* a system of burrows in which wild rabbits live.

rabbit on *vi* (*inf derog*: *often with* **about**) to talk at great length (about something): *What is he rabbiting on about?*

rabble ['rabl] *nc* (*no pl*) a noisy, disorderly crowd: *What a rabble there was at his party last night – they broke up all the furniture.*

'rabble-rouser *nc* a person who makes rabble-rousing speeches.

'rabble-rousing *adj* arousing, or intended to arouse, the feelings, anger *etc* of the lowest class of society: *a rabble-rousing speech.*

the rabble the lowest class of people: *His speeches are designed to appeal to the rabble.*

rabid ['rabid] *adj* **1** (of dogs *etc*) mad; suffering from rabies: *a rabid dog*; *That dog is rabid.* **2** (*derog*) very (sometimes violently) enthusiastic: *a rabid supporter of the local football team*; *a rabid nationalist.*

rabies ['reibi:z] *nu* (*also* (*tech*) **hydrophobia** [haidrə'foubiə]) a disease that causes madness (and *usu* death) in dogs and other animals (including humans).

raccoon, racoon [rə'ku:n, (*Amer*) ra-] *nc* a type of small, furry, N American animal, with a striped, bushy tail.

race[1] [reis] *nc* **1** a competition to find who or which is the fastest (person, horse, car *etc*): *a horse race*; *Johnny's running in the next race.* **2** (*inf*) a rush; a need to hurry or run: *It'll be a bit of a race to catch that train.* **3** (*fig*) an activity done in competition with someone else, in which speed is important: *The arms race is the competition between countries in building up their stocks of weapons.* – *See also* **the races** *below.* – **1** *vti* (*often with* **against**) to (cause to) run in a race: *I'm racing my horse at Epsom*; *The horse is racing against five others.* **2** *vt* (*inf*) to have a competition with (someone) to find out who is the fastest: *I'll race you to that tree.* **3** *vti* (*inf*) to go, take, transport *etc* quickly: *He raced along the road on his bike*; *He raced the manuscript to the printers.*

'racer *nc* (*inf*) a car, bicycle *etc* built for competitive racing.

'race-card *nc* a list of all the competitors and races on a particular day (*esp* at a horse- or dog-racing meeting).

'racecourse *nc* (a place with) a course over which horse races are run.

'race-horse *nc* a horse bred (and *usu* used) for racing.

'racetrack *nc* (a place with) a course over which races are run by cars, dogs, athletes *etc* (not *usu* horses).

'racing-car *nc* a car specially designed and built for racing.

a race against time a desperate attempt to do (something) before a certain time: *We'll try to get this finished by May, but it'll be a race against time.*

race[2] [reis] **1** *nc* any one section of mankind, having a particular set of characteristics which make it different from other sections: *the Negro race*; *the white races*; (*attrib*) *race relations* (= relations between people of different races). **2** *nu* the fact of belonging to any of these various sections: *the problem of race*; (*attrib*) *the race question.* **3** *nc* (*loosely*) a group of people who share the same culture, language *etc*: *the Anglo-Saxon race.* **4** *ncu* (*old*) family; ancestors; descent: *a man of noble race*; *He comes from a noble race of leaders.*

racial ['reiʃəl] *adj* (*usu attrib*) **1** of, or having to do with, a particular race (*def 1*): *racial characteristics/similarities.* **2** of, or having to do with, race (*def 2*): *racial discrimination/hatred.*

'racialism ['reiʃə-], **'racism** *nus* (*derog*) **1** (policies or actions based on) the belief that some races of men are better than others. **2** prejudice (against someone) on the grounds of (his) race.

'racialist ['reiʃə-], **'racist** *ncs* (*derog*) a person who believes in and/or shows his support of such prejudiced theories. – *adjs* (*derog*) showing prejudice on the basis of race: *racist attitudes.*

the human race mankind.

of mixed race having ancestors (*esp* parents) from two or more different human races.

the races a meeting for horse-racing: *I'm going to the races today.*

rack[1] [rak] *nc* **1** (*sometimes in cmpds*) a frame or shelf in or on which objects (*eg* letters, plates, luggage *etc*) are put until they are wanted or needed: *Put these tools back in the rack*; *Put your bag in the luggage-rack*; *a toast-rack.* **2** (*hist*: *usu in sing with* **the**) an instrument for torturing people by pulling their arms in one direction and their legs in the other. – *vt* (*usu in passive*) to fill completely with something extremely painful or emotionally disturbing: *His body was racked with fever*; *Her voice was racked by sobs.*

rack[2] [rak]: **rack one's brains** to exert one's brains greatly (in trying to think of something): *He racked his brains for the answers.*

rack[3] [rak]: **go to rack and ruin** to get into a state of neglect and decay: *The castle has gone to rack and ruin now.*

racket[1], **racquet** ['rakit] *nc* (*sometimes in cmpds*) a wooden or metal frame strung with catgut or nylon, used in tennis and certain other games: *a tennis-racket/squash-racket/badminton racket.*

racket[2] ['rakit] *nc* (*inf*) **1** (*no pl*) a great deal of noise: *Tell the children to stop banging those drums! That's a dreadful racket they are making.* **2** a dishonest way of making money: *He is in the drug racket.*

ˌracke'teer *nc* (*derog*) a person who makes money by dishonest means, often by threatening people with violence: *He's a racketeer who makes money out of selling heroin to drug addicts.*

raconteur [rakon'təː] *nc* (*formal*) a person who tells stories in an amusing or entertaining way: *The old sailor is an amazing raconteur – he tells fascinating stories about his life at sea.*

racoon *see* **raccoon**.

racquet *see* **racket**[1].

racy ['reisi] *adj* lively, and often slightly indecent: *a racy style of writing*; *Don't buy that book for your mother – it's too racy for her.* **'racily** *adv.* **'raciness** *nu.*

radar ['reidaː] *nu* a method of showing the direction and distance of an object by means of radio waves which bounce off the object and return to their source: *Ships use radar to avoid colliding with each other in fog*; *Bats use a kind of radar to stop themselves from flying into things.*

radial ['reidiəl] *adj* (*formal or tech*: *esp attrib*) spreading out from the centre of a circle, like rays: *The spokes in a bicycle wheel are arranged in a radial pattern.* **'radially** *adv.*

radiant ['reidiənt] *adj* **1** showing great joy: *a radiant smile*; *The bride looks radiant.* **2** (*tech*: *attrib*) sending out rays of heat, light *etc*: *a radiant heater.* **3** (*tech*: *attrib*) carried, sent *etc* in the form of, or by means of, rays of heat, light *etc*: *radiant heat.* **'radiantly** *adv.*

'radiance *nu* brightness: *the radiance of her smile. See also* **radiate**.

radiate ['reidieit] (*formal*) **1** *vti* to send out rays of (light, heat *etc*): *A fire radiates heat*; (*fig*) *She's a person who radiates peace and contentment.* **2** *vi* (*with* **from**) to go out (from something) or be sent out by (something) in rays, or in many directions from a central point: *Heat radiates from a fire*; (*fig*) *All the roads radiate from the centre of the town.*

ˌradi'ation *nu* rays of light, heat *etc* or of any radioactive substance: *He died from a massive dose of radiation.*

'radiator *nc* **1** one type of apparatus for heating a room by circulating water which has been heated by gas, electricity *etc.* **2** an apparatus in a car which, with a fan, cools the engine.

radical ['radikəl] *adj* **1** (*usu attrib*) relating to the basic nature of something: *There are radical faults in the design of this car. It will have to be re-designed.* **2** (*usu attrib*) thorough; complete; extreme: *There will be some radical changes in this department*; *Our methods need a radical overhaul.* **3** (*polit*: *sometimes with cap*) wanting or involving great or extreme political, social or economic changes: *Our party favours radical policies*; *He's fairly radical in his opinions.* – *nc* (*esp polit*: *sometimes with cap*) a person who has radical opinions or who wants radical changes (in something).

'radically *adv.* **'radicalness** *nu.*

'radicalism *nu* (*esp polit*: *sometimes with cap*) the principles and beliefs of a radical; the state of being a radical.

radio- [reidiou] (*in cmpds*) of, or relating to, rays or radiation, as in **radioactive**.

radio ['reidiou] – *pl* **'radios** – *ncu* (an apparatus for) the sending and receiving of human speech, music *etc*: *a pocket radio*; *The concert is being broadcast on radio*; *I heard on the radio that it's going to snow tonight*; (*attrib*) *a radio programme*; (*attrib*) *radio waves.* – *v* – *3rd pers sing prt* **'radios**: *pt, ptp* **'radioed** – *vti* to send (a message) by radio: *When someone on the island is ill, we have to radio* (*to*) *the mainland for a doctor*; *An urgent message was radioed to us this evening.*

'radiogram [-gram] *nc* (*slightly old*) an apparatus consisting of a radio and record-player.

radioactive [reidiou'aktiv] *adj* **1** (of some substances, *eg* uranium) giving off rays which can be dangerous, but which can also be used in *eg* medicine: *radioactive metals*; *Is that element radioactive?* **2** containing radioactive substances: *radioactive waste/dust.*

ˌradioac'tivity *nu* **1** the state of being radioactive. **2** the giving off of radioactive rays: *Radioactivity can be very dangerous.*

radiogram *see* **radio**.

radiograph ['reidiəgraːf] *nc* (*tech*) a photograph taken by means of X-rays or other rays; an X-ray photograph.

ˌradi'ographer [-'o-] *nc* a person who makes these: *She is a radiographer at the local hospital.*

ˌradi'ography [-'o-] *nu* the making of radiographs: *She is studying radiography*; (*tech*) *the radiography of the skull.*

radiology [reidi'olədʒi] *nu* **1** the branch of medicine involving the use of radioactive substances and radiation in the diagnosis (and treatment) of diseases: *He specialized in radiology*; (*attrib*) *the radiology department.* **2** the scientific study of (the use of) radioactive substances and radiation.

ˌradi'ologist *nc* a person who studies or practises radiology: *Doctors who diagnose disease by means of X-rays are called radiologists*; *He is an industrial radiologist.*

radiotherapy [reidiou'θerəpi] *nu* the treatment of disease by X-rays and other forms of radiation: *He has cancer of the stomach and he is being treated by means of radiotherapy*; (*attrib*) *the radiotherapy department*; (*attrib*) *radiotherapy treatment.*

radish ['radiʃ] *nc* **1** a plant with a red-skinned white root. **2** the root itself eaten raw in salads.

radium ['reidiəm] *nu* a radioactive metallic element (symbol **Ra**), used in treating certain diseases.

radius ['reidiəs] – *pl* **'radii** [-diai] (*defs 1, 2*), **'radiuses** (*def 1*) – *nc* **1** (*usu in sing*) the area within a given distance from a central point: *They searched within a radius of one mile from the school.* **2** (*geom*) a straight line from the centre of a circle to its circumference.

raffia ['rafiə] *nu* (strips of) fibre from the leaves of a type of palm tree, used for making mats, baskets *etc*: *a sun hat made of raffia*; (*attrib*) *raffia tablemats.*

raffle ['rafl] *nc* a way of raising money by selling numbered tickets, one or more of which win a prize: *I won this doll in a raffle in aid of church funds*; (*attrib*) *raffle tickets.* – *vt* to give (something) as the prize in a raffle: *They raffled a bottle of whisky to raise money for cancer research.*

raft [raːft] *nc* **1** a number of logs, planks *etc* fastened together and used as a boat: *The boys made a raft and went sailing on the lake.* **2** (*formal*) a large floating mass (of vegetation *etc*).

rafter ['raːftə] *nc* a sloping beam supporting the roof of a house: *The old cottage has beautiful oak rafters; There was a side of bacon hanging from the rafters of the farm kitchen.*

rag[1] [rag] *nc* **1** (*inf*) a piece of old, torn or worn cloth: *I'll polish my bike with this old rag.* – See also **rags** *below.* **2** (*inf derog*) a newspaper or magazine of low quality: *I would never read that rag!* – *adj* (*attrib*) made of rags or cloth: *a rag doll; a child's rag book.*

ragged ['ragid] *adj* **1** (*formal*) dressed in old, worn or torn clothing: *a ragged beggar; The children were thin and ragged.* **2** torn: *a beggar dressed in ragged clothes; Her clothes are dirty and ragged.* **3** rough or uneven; not straight or smooth: *I don't like using sheets of paper with ragged edges; The scissors must have been blunt – the edge of this material is very ragged.* **4** (*inf*) not perfect; not very good: *The musicians gave a pretty ragged performance.* **'raggedly** *adv.* **'raggedness** *nu.*

rags *n pl* old, worn or torn clothes: *The beggar was dressed in rags.*

'rag-bag *nc* (*usu fig and derog*) a bag for storing odd scraps of material: *His latest book seems to be a rag-bag of old-fashioned ideas.*

glad rags *see* **glad**.

the 'rag trade (*inf*) the business of designing, making or selling clothes: *She has just finished art college and she is looking for a job in the rag trade.*

rag[2] [rag] – *pt, ptp* **ragged** – *vt* (*inf: esp Brit*) to tease; to play tricks on (someone): *The other boys ragged him about his new girl-friend.* – *nc* (*sometimes with cap*) an occasion on which students dress up in strange clothes, play tricks on people *etc*, in order to raise money for charity: *The students' rag begins this week;* (*attrib*) *rag week.*

rag[3] [rag]: **lose one's rag** (*Brit inf*) to lose one's temper: *The teacher really lost his rag when the children started to laugh.*

ragamuffin ['ragəmʌfin] *nc* (*formal derog*) a ragged, dirty person, *esp* a child: *She said that she did not want her children to play with the ragamuffins from the council housing estate.*

rage [reidʒ] **1** *ncu* (*more formal than* **anger**) (a fit of) violent anger: *He flew into a rage; He shouted with rage.* **2** *nu* (*formal*) violence; great force: *the rage of the sea during a storm.* – *vi* **1** (*usu with* **at** *or* **against**) to act or shout in great anger; to show great anger: *He raged at his secretary; She was raging (on) about what a fool he is.* **2** (of wind, storms *etc*) to be violent; to blow with great force: *The storm raged all night.* **3** (of battles, arguments *etc*) to be carried on with great violence: *The battle raged for two whole days.* **4** (*formal*) (of diseases *etc*) to spread quickly and be caught by many people: *Fever was raging in/through the town.*

'raging *adj* (*attrib*) **1** violent: *a raging storm.* **2** very painful or extreme: *raging toothache; a raging fever.*

(all) the rage (*inf*) very much in fashion: *Fur hats are (all) the rage this winter.*

raglan ['raglən] *adj* (*attrib*) **1** (of a sleeve) attached to a jersey *etc* by a seam which runs from the neck to the armpit: *I prefer raglan sleeves.* **2** (of a jersey *etc*) having such sleeves: *a white raglan sweater.*

ragtime ['ragtaim] *nu* a type of music originating with the American Negroes in the 1920s: *They play ragtime;* (*attrib*) *a ragtime melody/band.*

raid [reid] *nc* **1** a sudden, short and *usu* unexpected attack: *The enemy made a raid on the docks;* (*fig*) *The boys made a raid on the food cupboard.* **2** an unexpected visit by the police (to catch a criminal, get back stolen goods *etc*): *The police carried out a raid on the gambling den.* – *vt* **1** to make a raid on (someone or something): *The police raided the gambling club.* **2** (*fig*) to take things from (somewhere): *I'm hungry – let's raid the larder.*

'raider *nc* (*esp hist*) a person, ship *etc* that takes part in a raid: *The raiders burned down all the houses.*

rail[1] [reil] *nc* **1** (*often in cmpds*) a (*usu* horizontal) bar of metal, wood *etc* used in fences *etc*, or for hanging things on: *Don't lean over the (guard-)rail, or you may fall off; a curtain-rail; a towel-rail.* **2** (*usu in pl*) a long bar of steel which forms the track on which trains *etc* run. – *vt* (*usu with* **in** *or* **off**) to surround with a rail or rails: *The children's playground has been railed in so that the children do not wander on to the main road; We'll rail that bit of ground off to stop people walking on it.*

'railing *nc* (*usu in pl*) a fence or barrier of (*usu* vertical) metal or wooden bars: *They've put railings up all round the park.*

'railroad *nc* (*Amer*) a railway. – *vt* (*inf*) to do, or cause (a person) to do, (something) by unfair means or with great haste: *The bill was railroaded through Congress; The congressmen were railroaded into passing the bill.*

'railway, (*Amer*) **'railroad** *nc* **1** a track with (*usu* more than one set of) two (or sometimes three) parallel steel rails on which trains run: *They're building a new railway;* (*attrib*) *a railway station.* **2** (*sometimes in pl*) the whole organization which is concerned with the running of trains, the building of tracks *etc*: *He has a job on the railway; The railways are very badly run in some countries.*

by 'rail by or on the railway: *Some goods are sent by rail.*

off the rails (*inf: Brit*) not sensible; slightly mad: *I think he has gone a bit off the rails with some of these suggestions.*

rail[2] [reil] *vi* (*formal: with* **against** *or* **at**) to speak angrily or bitterly (to, or about, a person or thing): *He railed at his wife about her extravagance.*

raiment ['reimənt] *nu* (*arch*) clothing: *The king was clad in gold raiment.*

rain [rein] **1** *ncu* water falling from the clouds in liquid drops: *We've had a lot of rain today; I do like walking in the rain; We had flooding because of last week's heavy rains.* **2** *nc* (*formal*) a great number of things falling like rain: *A rain of arrows fell on the soldiers.* – **1** *vi* (*only with* **it** *as subject*) to cause rain to fall: *I think it will rain today.* **2** *vti* (*formal or facet*) to (cause to) fall like rain: *Arrows rained down on the soldiers; The enemy rained arrows on the soldiers;* (*fig inf*) *It looks like it's been raining birthday cards today!* (= Someone seems to have got a lot of birthday cards today!) **3** *vt* (*formal*) to give a great deal of (something): *The grateful people rained thanks/presents on the soldiers.*

'rainy *adj* (*usu attrib*) **1** having (many) showers of rain: *a rainy day; the rainy season.* **2** likely to produce rain: *rainy skies.* **'raininess** *nu.*

'rainbow *nc* the coloured arch sometimes seen in the sky opposite the sun when rain is falling.

'raincoat *nc* a light waterproof coat worn to keep out the rain.

'raindrop *nc* a single drop of rain.

'rainfall *ncu* the amount of rain that falls in a certain place in a certain time: *We haven't had much rainfall this year*; *Do you know the annual rainfalls of these countries?*

(keep, save *etc* **something) for a rainy day** to keep (something, *esp* money) until one needs it or in case one may need it: *I don't spend my whole salary. I put some in the bank for a rainy day.*

rain cats and dogs (*inf*) to rain very hard: *It's raining cats and dogs – the streets are flooded.*

the rains (in tropical countries) the rainy season.

(as) right as rain (*inf*) perfectly all right; completely well: *Your daughter has a slight cold. Keep her in bed and she'll be (as) right as rain in a couple of days.*

raise [reiz] *vt* **1** (*more formal than* **lift**) to move or lift (something) to a high(er) position: *Raise your right hand and repeat the oath*; *Raise the flag.* **2** to make (the price or value of something) higher: *If you paint your flat, that will raise the value of it considerably.* **3** to make (something) higher: *We'll raise that wall a couple of feet*; *The extra effort raised his blood pressure well above normal.* **4** to grow (crops) or breed (animals) for food: *We don't raise pigs on this farm.* **5** to look after and train (a child) while it is growing: *She has raised a large family.* **6** to state (a question, objection *etc* which one wishes to have discussed): *Has anyone in the audience any points they would like to raise?* **7** to collect (something) together; to gather: *We'll never manage to raise enough money to have the church roof repaired*; *The revolutionaries managed to raise a small army.* **8** to cause (something): *His remarks raised a few smiles.* **9** (*formal*) to make (something) rise or appear: *These shoes have raised blisters on my feet*; *The car raised a cloud of dust.* **10** (*formal*) to build (something, *usu* a monument): *They've raised a statue to Robert Burns/in memory of Robert Burns.* **11** to give (a shout *etc*): *They raised an outcry in protest at their low wages.* **12** (*inf*) to make contact with (someone) by radio: *I can't raise the mainland. Their radio must be out of order.* – *nc* (*inf: also, esp Brit,* **rise**) an increase in wages or salary: *I'm going to ask the boss for a raise.*

raise a person's hopes to make a person more hopeful than he was: *I don't want to raise your hopes too much, but I have heard that you're going to be promoted.*

raise hell/Cain/the roof *etc* (*inf*) to make a great deal of noise: *She raised hell when she discovered what the children had done*; *The children raised the roof when the comedian came on to the stage.*

raise someone's spirits to make (a person) less unhappy: *His spirits were raised by the news that his son was coming home.*

raise (someone) to the peerage to make (a person) a noble.

raise one's voice *see* **voice**.

See also **rise**.

raisin ['reizən] *nc* a dried grape: *She put raisins and sultanas in the cake.*

raison d'être [reizõ'detr, (*Amer*) -zoun-] *nc* (*formal*) the reason for, or the purpose of, the existence of (a person or thing): *Much as I enjoy the job, I don't look on writing dictionaries as my raison d'être.*

rajah ['ra:dʒə] *nc* (*with cap in titles*) (the status of) an Indian king or prince.

rake[1] [reik] *nc* **1** a tool which consists of a *usu* metal bar with teeth at the end of a long handle, used for smoothing earth, gathering *eg* leaves together *etc.* **2** any similar tool: *a croupier's rake in a casino.* **3** (*no pl*) the act of raking (something): *I'll need to give that bit of the garden a rake before I plant the seeds.* – *vt* **1** (*often with* **up, together** *etc*) to smooth (earth) or gather (leaves *etc*) with a rake: *I'll rake these leaves up later*; *It's your turn to rake the garden.* **2** (*often with* **out**) to remove the ashes from (a fire) with a poker *etc.* **3** (*formal*) to fire guns at (a target) from one end of it to the other: *The soldiers raked the entire village with machine-gun fire*; (*fig*) *He raked the whole valley with his binoculars.* – *See also* **rake through, rake up**.

'rake-off *nc* (*sl*) a *usu* dishonest or slightly immoral share of profits: *The man agreed to arrange for the company to get the contract, but demanded a rake-off (from the profits).*

rake in the money/rake it in (*sl*) to make a great deal of money: *A lot of people buy things in their shop, so they must be raking in the money.*

rake through *vt fus* to make a thorough search for something in (something): *I'm raking through these boxes of old clothes in case there is anything valuable in them.*

rake up *vt sep* to find out and tell or remind people about (something, *usu* something unpleasant that would be better forgotten): *The newspaper reporters raked up a story about the politician stealing £20 from a shop when he was a boy.*

rake[2] [reik] *nc* (*old*) a man who lives an immoral life.

rake[3] [reik] *nu* (*tech*) the extent to which something slopes: *The rake of the ground means that the path will not be level.* – *vti* (*tech*) to (cause to) slope: *The radiator has been raked to give the car a better appearance.*

'rakish *adj* slanting, showing that one is independent, confident, adventurous *etc*: *She wore her hat at a rakish angle.* **'rakishly** *adv.* **'rakishness** *nu.*

rally ['rali] *vti* **1** to come or bring together again: *The general tried to rally his troops after the defeat*; *The troops rallied round the general.* **2** to come or bring together for a joint action or effort: *The supporters rallied to save the club from collapse*; *The politician asked his supporters to rally to the cause.* – *See also* **rally round** *below.* **3** to get or give strength (to a person, thing *etc*); to (cause to) recover one's health: *She rallied from her illness*; *The pound rallied just before the foreign exchange market closed*; (*formal*) *The Bank of England tried to rally the pound.* – *nc* **1** a *usu* large gathering of people for some purpose: *a Scouts' rally*; *They held a rally to call for peace.* **2** a meeting (*usu* of cars or motorcycles) for a competition, race *etc*: *a car rally*; *He won last week's rally.* **3** an improvement in health after an illness. **4** (in tennis *etc*) a (*usu* long) series of shots before the point is won or lost: *The Wimbledon crowd applauded the long and exciting rally.*

rally round *vi, vt fus* to come together for a joint action or effort, *esp* of support: *When John's business was in difficulty, his friends all rallied round (to help) him.*

ram [ram] *nc* **1** a male sheep: *a ram and several ewes.* **2** something heavy, *esp* a part of a machine, used for ramming. – *v* – *pt, ptp* **rammed** – **1** *vti* (*often with* **into** *or* **against**) (of ships, cars *etc*) to run into, and cause damage to (something): *The destroyer rammed the submarine; His car rammed into/against the car in front of it.* **2** *vt* to push (something) down, into, on to *etc* (something) with great force: *We rammed the soil flat before we built the hut; We rammed the fence-posts into the ground.*

'ramrod *nc, adj* (of) a person who is very strict and upright (physically and morally).

ram (something) down someone's throat (*inf*) to (try to) force (a person) to believe or accept (a statement, idea *etc, esp* one he is unwilling to believe or accept).

ram (something) home to say (something) with great stress in order to (try to) force (a person) to accept it, understand it *etc*: *The speaker rammed home his point with a few blunt words about strikes; You certainly rammed that home.*

See also **battering-ram** *under* **batter**[1].

ramble ['rambl] *vi* **1** to go for a long walk or walks, *usu* in the countryside, for pleasure. **2** (*often with* **about**) to speak in an aimless or confused way (about something): *As the old man lay dying he kept rambling (about the experiences of his boyhood in Africa).* – *See also* **ramble on** *below.* – *nc* a long walk, *usu* in the countryside, taken for pleasure: *We're going for/on a ramble on Saturday.*

'rambler *nc* **1** a climbing plant (*usu* a rose). **2** a person who goes walking in the country for pleasure.

'rambling *adj* **1** (*derog*) (of speeches *etc*) aimless and confused; not keeping to the topic: *He gave a long, rambling speech which bored the audience; His speech was interesting but rather rambling.* **2** (of towns, streets, houses *etc*) built (as if) without any plan, stretching in various directions: *a rambling old town; Their house is large and rambling.* **3** (of plants, *usu* roses) climbing. – *nu* **1** the activity of going on long walks in the countryside for pleasure: *I enjoy rambling.* **2** the act of talking in an aimless or confused way.

ramble on *vi* (*derog: usu with* **about**) to talk for a long time in an aimless or confused way (about something): *The lecturer rambled on although the students were not listening.*

ramification [ramifi'keiʃən] *nc* (*formal or facet*) **1** a part or section of a complex subject, plot (*eg* of a play) *etc*: *I could not understand all the ramifications of the plot.* **2** a consequence (of an action, decision *etc*), *esp* indirect and one of many: *This new agreement with all its ramifications will mean widespread revisions in every department.*

ramp [ramp] *nc* a sloping surface between places, objects *etc* which are at different levels (up or down which cars, wheelchairs *etc* can be moved): *The car drove up the ramp from the quay to the ship; They should have ramps in this building – people in wheelchairs cannot use the stairs.*

rampage [ram'peidʒ] *vi* (*usu with* **about, through** *etc*) to rush about angrily, violently or in excitement: *The elephants rampaged through the jungle; The gang of thugs rampaged through the city.*

be/go on the rampage ['rampeidʒ] to rush about angrily, violently or in excitement, often causing great destruction: *The escaped elephant was on the rampage for two days;* (*fig inf*) *The boss is on the rampage because people keep coming in late.*

rampant ['rampənt] *adj* **1** (*formal*) very common and uncontrolled: *Vandalism is rampant in the city; rampant antisemitism.* **2** (placed immediately after noun) in heraldry, standing erect on the left hind leg: *That flag has a lion rampant on it.*

rampart ['rampa:t] *nc* (*often in pl*) a mound or wall for defence: *The soldiers watched from the ramparts.*

ramrod *see* **ram**.

ramshackle ['ramʃakl] *adj* (*derog*) badly made; falling to pieces or likely to fall to pieces: *a ramshackle hut/car; Their country cottage is a bit ramshackle.*

ran *see* **run**.

ranch [ra:ntʃ] *nc* a farm, *esp* one in N America for rearing cattle or horses. – *vi* to own, manage, or work on, a ranch: *He ranches in Texas.*

'rancher *nc* a person who owns, manages, or works on, a ranch.

rancid ['ransid] *adj* (*formal*) (of food, *esp* butter) tasting or smelling bad: *In hot weather, butter soon becomes rancid; rancid fat.* **'rancidness** *nu.*

rancour, (*Amer*) **rancor** ['raŋkə] *nu* (*formal*) a *usu* long-lasting feeling of anger, dislike or hatred: *In spite of my apologies, she still has a feeling of rancour (against me); There has always been a feeling of rancour between the two families.* **'rancorous** *adj.* **'rancorously** *adv.*

rand [rand] – *pl* **rand(s)** – *nc* the standard unit of S African currency.

random ['randəm] *adj* done *etc* without any particular plan or system; irregular: *The opinion poll was based on a random sample of adults; The officer was killed by a random bullet; The sample was totally random.* **'randomly** *adv.*

at 'random without any particular plan or system: *The police were stopping cars at random and checking their brakes; Choose any number at random.*

randy ['randi] *adj* (*inf*) full of sexual desire: *The nude photographs made him feel randy; a randy young man.* **'randily** *adv.* **'randiness** *nu.*

rang *see* **ring**[2].

range [reindʒ] **1** *nc* a *usu* large selection or variety (of things for sale in a shop, of ideas, interests *etc*): *We like to offer the public a wide range of books; He has a very wide range of interests; This computer has a whole range of applications.* **2** *ncu* the distance over which an object can be sent or thrown, sound can be heard, an aeroplane can travel *etc*: *What is the range of this missile?; We are within range of/beyond the range of/out of range of their guns.* **3** *nc* the amount between certain limits: *I'm hoping for a salary within the range £4 000 to £5 000; the range of a person's voice* (= the distance between the top and bottom notes that a person can sing *etc*). **4** *nc* (*usu* of mountains) a row or series: *a mountain range.* **5** *nc* (*usu in sing*) in the US, land, *usu* without fences, on which cattle *etc* can graze. **6** *nc* (*often in cmpds*) a place where a person can practise shooting, archery *etc*: *a rifle-range.* **7** *nc* a large, old-fashioned kitchen stove with a flat top. – **1** *vt* to put (people, things *etc*) in a row or rows: *The two armies were ranged on opposite sides of the valley.* **2** *vi* (*with* **between,** *or* **from** *and* **to**) to vary between certain limits: *Weather conditions here range between bad and dreadful/from bad to dreadful.* **3** *vti* (*liter or fig: often with* **over** *or* **through**) to go, move, walk *etc*: *He loves ranging (over) the hills and mountains; His studies range over a number of topics (see also* **wide-ranging**). **4** *vi* to stretch or extend (often in a straight line): *His kingdom ranged from the River Humber to the River Trent.* **5** *vt* (*usu refl: formal or liter*) to belong to, or consider (a person) as belonging to, a group: *I range myself with/among his admirers.*

'ranger *nc* (*with cap in titles*) **1** a person who looks after (in Britain) a forest or park belonging to the Queen or King, or (in the US) a public forest. **2** (*Amer*) a soldier who is a member of a specially trained force; a commando.

rank[1] [raŋk] **1** *nc* a line or row (*esp* of soldiers or taxis): *The officer ordered the front rank to fire*; (*fig*) *He's joined the ranks of the unemployed.* **2** *nc* (in the army, navy *etc*) a person's position of importance: *He was promoted to the rank of sergeant/colonel* – *See also* Appendix 3. **3** *nc* a (social) class: *the upper ranks of society.* **4** *nu* importance in society: *a man of rank.* – **1** *vt* (not used with **is, was** *etc* and **-ing**) to put or consider (people, things *etc*) in order of importance: *I rank horses higher than donkeys.* **2** *vi* (not *usu* used with **is, was** *etc* and **-ing**) to have a place in a group, relative to one's importance: *He ranks among our greatest writers*; *Apes rank above dogs in intelligence.*

(the) other ranks ordinary soldiers, as opposed to officers.

the rank and file 1 ordinary people: *the rank and file in a Trade Union do not always agree with their officials*; (*attrib*) *a rank-and-file movement.* **2** (*mil*: *also* **the ranks**) ordinary soldiers, as opposed to officers.

rank[2] [raŋk] *adj* **1** (*formal*) (of plants, gardens *etc*) (filled with plants that are) growing too thickly and untidily: *rank weeds*; *a garden rank with weeds.* **2** complete; very much (of): *a rank outsider.* **3** (*usu attrib*) very bad; extreme: *rank bad behaviour*; *rank stupidity.* **4** (*formal*: *usu attrib*) having a strong unpleasant taste or smell: *rank bacon/tobacco.* **'rankness** *nu.*

rankle ['raŋkl] *vti* to cause (a person) to feel annoyance or bitterness (*usu* for a long time): *The unkind remark rankled in Mary's mind for days.*

ransack ['ransak, (*Amer*) ran'sak] *vt* **1** to search thoroughly (in something): *She ransacked the whole house to find her keys/for her keys.* **2** (*formal*) to steal (almost) everything from a building, town *etc*: *The army ransacked the conquered city.*

ransom ['ransəm] **1** *nc* a sum of money *etc* paid for the freeing of a prisoner: *They paid a ransom of £20 000.* **2** *nu* the freeing of a prisoner in exchange for such a sum of money *etc*: *They paid £20 000 for his ransom.* – *vt* (*formal*) **1** to pay money *etc* to free (someone). **2** to keep (a person) as a prisoner until a sum of money *etc* is paid for his release.

hold (a person) to ransom to keep (a person) as a prisoner until a sum of money *etc* is paid for his release: *The bandits held the president's daughter to ransom.*

a king's ransom (*fig*) a vast amount of money: *She would not marry him for a king's ransom*; *He's not exactly paid a king's ransom.*

rant [rant] *vi* (*usu* **rant on** *or* **rant and rave**) to talk angrily (about something): *He's still ranting and raving about the damage to his car*; *He was ranting (on) about how badly he'd been treated.*

rap [rap] *nc* (the sound of) a quick, brief knock: *He gave/heard a sudden rap on the door.* – *v* – *pt, ptp* **rapped** – *vti* to hit or knock (on something) quickly and briefly: *The teacher rapped the child's fingers with a ruler*; *He rapped on the table and called for silence.*

rap out *vt sep* to say quickly: *He rapped out his orders.*

take the rap (for something) (*sl*) to take the blame, punishment *etc* for a crime, mistake *etc.*

rapacious [rə'peiʃəs] *adj* (*formal*) greedy (*esp* for money); eager to seize as much as possible: *rapacious invaders*; *The raiders were rapacious and ruthless.* **ra'paciously** *adv.* **ra'paciousness, ra'pacity** [-'pasə-] *nus.*

rape [reip] *nu* **1** the crime of having sexual intercourse with a woman against her will: *He has been found guilty of rape*; *The rape of the young girl shocked everyone.* **2** (*liter or formal fig*) the act of causing great damage, destruction, loss of property *etc* (in a city *etc*): *the rape of the countryside.* – *vt* **1** to force a woman to have sexual intercourse against her will: *She claims that he raped her although he denies it.* **2** (*liter or formal fig*) to cause great damage, destruction, loss of property *etc* in (a city *etc*).

'rapist *nc* a man who rapes (a woman): *The women in the crowd booed as the rapist left the court after the trial.*

rapid ['rapid] *adj* (*more formal than* **quick**) quick; fast: *He had a rapid rise to fame*; *He made some rapid calculations*; *The doctor thought that the patient's pulse was rather rapid.* **'rapidly** *adv.* **ra'pidity, 'rapidness** *nus.*

'rapids *n pl* a place in a river where the water flows quickly, often having dangerous rocks in mid-stream: *The canoeist was drowned when going over the rapids.*

rapier ['reipiə] *nc* a type of long thin sword.

rapist *see* **rape**.

rapport [ra'po:] *nu* (*formal*: *sometimes with* **a**) a close emotional connection with, or understanding of (a person, situation *etc*): *Having known each other for a long time, they have (an) excellent rapport*; *She has divorced her husband – there was no longer any rapport between them.*

rapt [rapt] *adj* (*formal*: *usu attrib*) fascinated (*usu* in admiration): *He listened to the speaker with rapt attention*; *She wore a rapt expression.*

rapture ['raptʃə] *nu* (*formal*) great delight.

'rapturous *adj* showing great delight: *They gave him a rapturous welcome*; *The applause was rapturous.* **'rapturously** *adv.*

in/into 'raptures (*often facet*: *with* **over** *or* **about**) greatly delighted: *She was in raptures about her beautiful new house*; *She went into raptures about his new car.*

rare ['reə] *adj* **1** not done, found, seen *etc* very often; uncommon: *a rare postage-stamp/flower*; *It is rare for a person in his position to make such a mistake.* **2** (of meat) only slightly cooked: *a rare steak*; *I like my steak rare.* **3** (*inf*: *attrib*) very good: *We had rare fun at the seaside.* **'rareness** *nu.*

rarefied, rarified ['reərəfaid] *adj* (of air, atmosphere *etc*) thin; not supplying enough oxygen for normal breathing: *the rarefied air of the high mountains.*

'rarely *adv* not often: *We rarely go to bed before midnight*; *I rarely meet him now.*

'rarity 1 *nu* (*formal*) the state of being rare (*def 1*). **2** *nc* something which is rare (*def 1*): *This stamp is quite a rarity.*

raring ['reəriŋ]: **raring to go** (*inf*) very keen to begin, go *etc*: *He always arrives early, full of energy and raring to go.*

rascal ['ra:skəl] *nc* a cheeky or naughty person, *esp* a child: *Her youngest child is a cheeky little rascal*; *That little rascal has broken my window.* **'rascally** *adj.*

rase *see* **raze**.

rash[1] [raʃ] *adj* acting, or done, with little caution or thought: *a rash person*; *a rash action/statement*; *It was rather rash of you to leave your present job without first finding another.* **'rashly** *adv.* **'rashness** *nu.*

rash[2] [raʃ] *nc* **1** a redness or large number of red spots on the skin: *Eating strawberries brings me out/makes me come out in* (= makes me develop) *a rash*; *That child has a rash – is it measles?* **2** (*fig*) a large number (of *usu* unpleasant things) happening at once: *A rash of thefts and burglaries.*

rasher ['raʃə] *nc* a thin slice (of bacon or ham): *I'll have two rashers of bacon and an egg for breakfast.*

rasp[1] *see* **raspberry**.

rasp[2] [ra:sp] **1** *nc* (*tech*) a very rough file. **2** *nu* (*also* **'rasping**) a harsh, rough, unpleasant sound: *the rasp of sandpaper on wood.* – **1** *vt* to say (something) in a harsh, rough, unpleasant voice: *'Stand still!' he rasped. – See also* **rasp out** *below.* **2** *vi* (of sounds, voices *etc*) to be harsh, rough and unpleasant: *His voice rasped on her ears.* **3** *vt* to rub (something) with a rasp.

'rasping *adj* (of a sound, voice *etc*) harsh, rough and unpleasant: *the rasping sound of metal scraping against stone*; *She looks beautiful but her accent is rather rasping.*

rasp out *vt sep* to say (something) in a rasping voice: *The sergeant major rasped out an order to his troops.*

raspberry ['ra:zbəri] *nc* **1** (*also* (*inf, esp dial*) **rasp** [ra:sp]) a type of edible red berry: *We had raspberries and cream for dessert*; (*attrib*) *raspberry jam.* **2** (*also* **'raspberry bush**) the bush which bears it.

rasping *see* **rasp**[2].

rat [rat] *nc* **1** a small animal with a long tail, like a mouse but larger: *There are rats in the old lady's cellar*; *The rats have eaten holes in those bags of flour.* **2** (*inf derog*) a person, *usu* a man, whom one dislikes very much: *He's a real rat – he's going out with another woman while his wife is in hospital.* – *v* – *pt, ptp* **'ratted** – *vi* (*sl*: *often with* **on**) **1** to break (an agreement, promise *etc*). **2** to betray (one's friends, colleagues *etc*): *The police know we're here. Someone must have ratted* (*on us*).

'ratty *adj* **1** of or like a rat. **2** (*inf*) not in a good mood; (easily made) angry: *The boss is feeling a bit ratty this morning*; *in rather a ratty mood.* **'rattily** *adv.* **'rattiness** *nu.*

'rat race *nc* (*inf*) a fierce, unending competition for success, wealth *etc* in business, society *etc*: *He grew tired of the rat race and retired to live in the country.*

smell a rat (*inf*) to have a feeling that something is not as it should be, but is wrong or bad: *The police set up a trap, but the thieves smelt a rat and drove away.*

ratable *see* **rate**.

rat-a-tat-tat [ratətat'tat], **rat-tat** [rat'tat] *nc* a sound of knocking, *esp* on a door, or a similar sound: *Suddenly there was a rat-a-tat-tat at/on the door*; *the rat-tat of machine-gun fire.*

ratchet ['ratʃit] *nc* (*tech*) **1** a bar which fits into the notches of a toothed wheel so as to cause the wheel to turn in a given direction. **2** (*also* **'ratchet-wheel**) the toothed wheel. **3** the mechanism including the bar and toothed wheel together.

rate [reit] *nc* **1** the number of occasions within a given period of time when something happens or is done: *a high* (*monthly*) *accident rate in a factory.* **2** the number or amount of something (compared to something else); a ratio: *There was a failure rate of one pupil in ten in the exam.* **3** the speed with which something happens or is done: *He works at an incredible rate*; *the rate of increase of export levels.* **4** the level (of pay), cost *etc* (of or for something): *What is the rate of pay for this job?*; *They're paid at a higher rate than we are.* **5** (*Brit*: *usu in pl*) a sum of money paid by the owner of a house, shop *etc* (the amount being calculated on the basis of the property's value) to the local authority to pay for public services such as the water supply, libraries, the removal of rubbish *etc*: *I see the rates have gone up again this year* (= the sum of money to be paid by each ratepayer has increased); *the water rate* (= the sum paid for the supply of water). – (not used with **is, was** *etc* and **-ing** (*defs 1, 3*)) **1** *vti* to consider that something has, or to be considered as having, a particular value, quality *etc*: *I don't rate this book* (*very highly*); *This book doesn't rate very highly.* **2** *vt* (*Brit*: *usu in passive*) to calculate the value of (a house, shop *etc*), according to which rates must be paid: *Our house is rated at £250.* **3** *vti* to consider (someone or something), or be considered, as (something): *He is rated* (*as*)/*He rates as a good and kind man*; *In my experience, he rates as the most bad-tempered man I know.*

'rating **1** *ncu* (*Brit*) (the calculation of) the rates to be paid on a property. **2** *nc* (*usu in pl*) the position of importance, popularity *etc* (of a person, thing *etc*): *This television programme has had some very bad ratings recently.* **3** *nc* (*esp Brit*) an ordinary sailor, as opposed to an officer.

rat(e)able value *nc* (*Brit*) the value of a house, shop *etc*, used to calculate the rates to be paid on it: *The rateable value of our house has increased since we installed central heating.*

'ratepayer *nc* the person who owns a house, shop *etc* on which rates are paid.

at any rate *see* **any**.

at this, at that rate if this or if that is the case; if this or if that continues: *He says that he isn't sure whether we'll be allowed to finish, but at that rate we might as well not start.*

rate of exchange the relative values of the currencies of two or more countries: *I want to change some pounds into francs – what is the rate of exchange?*

See also **first-rate, second-rate, third-rate** *under* **first, second, third**.

rather ['ra:ðə] *adv* **1** to a certain extent; slightly; a little: *It's rather cold today*; *That's a rather silly question/rather a silly question*; *I've eaten rather more than I intended/rather too much.* **2** (*often with* **than**) more willingly; preferably: *I'd rather do it now than later*; *Can we do it now rather than tomorrow?*; *I'd rather not do it at all*; *I would leave rather than agree to that*; *I would/had rather you didn't do that* (= I would prefer you not to do that); *Wouldn't you rather stay another night?*; *Rather than risk leaving any mistakes, I'd check the whole thing again.* **3** (*often with* **than**) more exactly; more correctly: *He agreed, or rather he didn't disagree*; *One could say he was foolish rather than wicked*; *I would say it was a terrible book rather than a good one.* **4** (*formal*: *sometimes with* **than**) on the contrary: *It isn't a good book. It is, rather, an absolutely terrible book.* – *interj* (*Brit*) yes, indeed; very much: *Are you enjoying yourself?' 'Rather!'*

ratify ['ratifai] *vt* (*formal*) to approve and agree to (something) formally and officially, *usu* in writing: *The new peace treaty was ratified at a meeting in Paris.* ˌ**ratifi'cation** *nu.*

rating *see* **rate**.

ratio ['reiʃiou] – *pl* '**ratios** – *nc* the amount or proportion of one thing compared to another: *Mix sand and cement in the ratio of two (parts) to one*; *There is a ratio of two girls to one boy in this class.*

ration ['raʃən] *nc* a measured amount of food *etc* allowed during a particular period of time: *During the war, everyone had a ration of butter*; *The butter ration was two ounces per week.* – *See also* **rations** *below.* – *vt* **1** to allow only a certain amount of (food *etc*) to a person or animal during a particular period of time: *During the war, butter was rationed to two ounces per person per week.* **2** to allow (a person) only such an amount: *People were rationed to two ounces of butter per week.* – *See also* **ration out** *below.*

'**rations** *n pl* **1** the amount of food allowed to a person (*esp* a soldier) for one day. **2** (*inf*) food *eg* for a journey.

'**ration-book** *nc* a book containing coupons which may be exchanged for things which are rationed.

ration out *vt sep* to give or allow a ration of (food *etc*), *eg* to a number of people, over a period of time: *During the war meat had to be rationed out*; *She rationed out the sweets to the children.*

rational ['raʃənl] *adj* **1** able to think, form opinions and judgements *etc*: *Man is a rational animal*; *Man is rational*; *Are men more rational than women?* **2** sensible; reasonable; logical; not (over-)influenced by emotions *etc*: *I don't believe in ghosts. There must be a rational explanation for those noises*; *Do try to be rational*; *Her behaviour isn't rational.* '**rationally** *adv.* ˌ**ration'ality** *nu.*

ˌ**ratio'nale** [-'na:l, (*Amer*) -'nal] *nc* (*formal*: *usu in sing*) the reason for, or principle behind, doing something (in a particular way) or believing something: *I don't see the rationale behind these decisions.*

'**rationalize, -ise** *vt* **1** to invent a reasonable explanation (*usu* for oneself) of (a feeling or action) so as not to feel guilty about it: *He rationalized her behaviour by telling himself that she was nervous.* **2** to organize work in *eg* a factory, so as to make it efficient and economical: *Our entire production system has recently been rationalized.* ˌ**rationali'zation, -s-** *ncu.*

See also **irrational**.

rat-tat *see* **rat-a-tat-tat**.

rattle ['ratl] **1** *vti* to (cause to) make a series of short, sharp noises by knocking (things) together: *The cups rattled as he carried the tray in*; *The strong wind rattled the windows*; *The car rattled along the road.* **2** *vi* (*inf*: *usu with* **along**) to move quickly: *The car was rattling along at top speed.* **3** *vt* (*inf*) to upset and confuse (a person): *She was rattled by the stupid questions she was asked*; *Don't let him rattle you – he likes annoying people.* – *See also* **rattle** *in phrases below.* – **1** *ncu* (something which makes) a series of short, sharp noises: *She heard the rattle of cups*; *There are a lot of rattles in this car.* **2** *nc* a child's toy, or a wooden instrument, which makes a noise of this sort: *The baby waved its rattle happily.* **3** *nc* the bony rings of a rattlesnake's tail.

'**rattler** *nc* (*inf*) a rattlesnake.

'**rattling** *adj* (*attrib*) **1** consisting of a series of short, sharp noises: *a rattling noise.* **2** (*inf*) fast; lively: *The car travelled at a rattling pace.* – *adv* (*old inf*) very; extremely: *a rattling good story.*

'**rattly** *adj* (*inf*) that rattles: *a rattly car/noise*; *It sounds rather rattly.*

'**rattlesnake** *nc* a type of poisonous American snake with bony rings in its tail which rattle.

'**rattletrap** *nc* (*derog sl*) a shaking, rickety vehicle *etc.*

rattle off *vt sep* (*inf*) to say (something) quickly and *usu* without any feeling or expression: *The boy rattled off the poem as if he was reading a telephone directory.*

rattle on *vi* (*often with* **about**) to talk quickly and at length (about something): *He rattled on all evening about his new job.*

rattle through *vt fus* (*inf*) to say or do (something) quickly: *The teacher rattled through his explanation so quickly that no-one could understand him.*

ratty *see* **rat**.

raucous ['ro:kəs] *adj* (*formal*) hoarse or harsh (and *usu* loud): *He spoke in a raucous voice*; *Her voice is rather raucous.* '**raucously** *adv.* '**raucousness** *nu.*

raunchy ['ro:ntʃi] *adj* (*sl*: *esp Amer*) slightly obscene or coarse: *a raunchy joke/book.* '**raunchiness** *nu.*

ravage ['ravidʒ] *vt* (*formal*) to cause great damage or destruction in, or to steal everything of value from (a town, country *etc*): *The enemy ravaged all the villages near the coast*; (*fig*) *Sorrow had ravaged her beauty.*

'**ravages** *n pl* the damaging effects (of war, weather, time *etc*): *The ravages of time affected her beauty* (= She became much less beautiful as she became older).

rave [reiv] *vi* **1** to talk wildly because, or as if, one is mad: *The invalid has a high fever – he's been raving*; (*inf*) *What are you talking about? You're raving!* **2** (*inf*: *often with* **about** *or* **over**) to talk very enthusiastically (about something): *He's been raving about this new record he's heard.* – *adj* (*attrib*: *inf*) very enthusiastic: *a rave review of a play.*

'**raving** *adj* (*attrib*), *adv* talking, behaving *etc* as if mad: *a raving lunatic*; *He's raving mad.*

'**ravings** *n pl* (*derog*) wild talk, said because, or as if, one is mad: *I'm not going to listen to his ravings.*

raven ['reivən] *nc* a large black bird of the crow family.

ˌ**raven-'haired** *adj* (*formal or liter*) (*usu* of women) having black and glossy hair: *a raven-haired beauty*; *Spanish women are sometimes raven-haired.*

ravenous ['ravənəs] *adj* (*sometimes facet*) very hungry: *The children were ravenous after they had played football*; *The ravenous men ate berries in the jungle to keep alive.* '**ravenously** *adv.* '**ravenousness** *nu.*

ravine [rə'vi:n] *nc* a deep narrow valley.

raving(s) *see* **rave**.

ravioli [ravi'ouli] *nu* small envelopes of pasta containing minced meat.

ravish ['raviʃ] *vt* **1** (*formal*: *usu in passive*) to cause great delight: *I was ravished by her beauty.* **2** (*old or formal*) to rape (a woman): *She was ravished by her captors*; (*fig*) *The beautiful city was ravished, and all its treasures stolen.*

'**ravishing** *adj* (*usu* of women) superb; delightful; very lovely: *a ravishing beauty*; *She looks ravishing tonight.* '**ravishingly** *adv.*

raw [ro:] *adj* **1** not cooked: *raw onions/meat*; *We cannot have dinner yet – the meat is still raw.* **2** (*attrib*) not prepared or refined; in the natural state: *raw cotton*; *What are the raw materials used to make plastic?*; (*fig*) *raw data for use by the computer.* **3** (*inf*) with the skin rubbed and sore: *My heel is raw because my shoe doesn't fit correctly.* **4** untrained; inexperienced: *raw recruits*; *The new policeman is very capable but he's still a bit raw.* **5** (*inf*) cold and wet: *a raw day*; *It's raw today.*

'rawness *nu.*

'rawhide *nu, adj* (of) untanned leather: *a whip made of rawhide*; *a rawhide whip.*

in the 'raw 1 in the natural state; exactly as it is, without anything to make it look nicer: *You see nature in the raw in the jungle.* **2** (*inf*) (of a person) naked.

a raw deal (*inf*) unfair treatment: *His secretary thinks she got a raw deal, since everyone got an increase in salary except her.*

raw material *see* **raw** (*def 2*).

ray [rei] *nc* **1** a narrow beam (of light, heat *etc*): *the sun's rays*; *X-rays*; *heat-rays*; *a ray of light.* **2** (*fig*) a slight amount (of something): *There is a ray of hope for him.*

See also **radial, radiant, radiate**.

rayon ['reion] *nu, adj* (of) a type of artificial silk: *The scarf is (made of) rayon*; *a rayon scarf.*

raze, (*rare*) **rase** [reiz] *vt* (*formal*) to destroy (something) completely, *esp* by fire: *The houses were razed to the ground.*

razor ['reizə] *nc* an instrument for shaving, having a sharp cutting edge, blade (a **razor-blade**), or electrically-powered revolving cutters.

,razor-'sharp *adj* as sharp as a razor: *a razor-sharp cutting edge*; (*fig*) *His wit was razor-sharp.*

re [ri:] *prep* (*formal*: *usu* only in business letters) about; concerning: *Dear Sir, Re your letter of the 12th, I must point out that we have no vacancies.*

're *see* **be**.

reach [ri:tʃ] **1** *vt* to arrive at (a place, age *etc*): *We'll never reach London before dark*; *Money is not important when you reach my age*; *The noise reached our ears*; (*fig*) *Has the total reached a thousand pounds yet?*; (*fig*) *Have they reached an agreement yet?* **2** *vt* to (be able to) touch or get hold of (something): *My keys have fallen down this hole and I can't reach them.* **3** *vi* (*with* **for**) to try to touch, get hold of or take (something) by stretching out one's hand: *He reached (across the table) for another cake.* – *See also* **reach out** *below.* **4** *vt* to make contact with (a person); to communicate with (a person): *If anything happens you can always reach me by phone.* **5** *vi* to stretch or extend: *My property reaches from here to the river*; (*fig*) *His influence reached as far as the next town.* **6** *vt* (*inf*: *often with* **down, over** *etc*) to stretch out one's hand and get (something) (for someone): *Can you reach me (down) that book?*; *Reach me over the dictionary, will you?* – *See also* **reach out** *below.* **7** *vt* (*formal*) to have an effect on the feelings, emotions *etc* of (a person): *Her tears couldn't reach him.* – **1** *nu* (*often with* **of**) the distance that can be travelled easily: *My house is within (easy) reach (of London).* **2** *ncu* (*no pl*) the distance one can stretch one's arm: *I keep medicines on the top shelf, out of the children's reach*; *I keep medicines out of reach of the children*; *I keep the biscuits on the top shelf beyond the children's reach*; *I always like to have a pencil within easy reach* (= where it can be reached easily); *My keys are down that hole, just out of reach*; *The boxer has a very long reach.* **3** *nc* (*usu in pl*) a straight part of a river, canal *etc* (*eg* between two bends or two locks): *the lower reaches of the Thames.*

reach out *vt sep, vi* (*also* **reach across/over** *vi*) (*often with* **for**) to try to touch, grasp or take (something) by stretching out one's hand: *He reached across/out/over for the last cake*; *He reached out his hand and took the last cake.* – *See also* **reach** (*def 3*).

react [ri'akt] *vi* **1** (*formal*) to behave, think or act in a certain way because of something that has been said, done *etc*: *How did he react when you called him a fool?*; *He reacts badly to criticism*; *He always reacts by shouting at me*; *How does the metal react in great heat?* **2** (*with* **against**) to behave, think or act in a certain way because one dislikes, wishes to change *etc* something that has been said or done: *Students who wear strange clothes and have long hair are often reacting against the way they had to dress as children.* **3** (*with* **to**) to be affected, *usu* badly, by (a drug *etc*): *I react very badly to penicillin.*

re'action [-ʃən] **1** *nc* (*formal*) the act of reacting (against, to *etc* something): *What was his reaction to your remarks?*; *Their behaviour is just a reaction against society*; *I have a bad reaction to penicillin*; *I'd like to ask you for your reactions to these suggestions* (= what you think about them). **2** *nu* (*formal*) in politics *etc*, (a desire for, or an attempt to achieve) a return to things as they were; opposition to change and progress: *reaction against the new developments in the industry.* **3** *nc* (*formal*) a change of opinions, feelings *etc* (*usu* against someone or something): *The new government was popular at first, but then a reaction set in* (= happened). **4** *ncu* (*chem*) a process of change which occurs when two or more substances are put together: (*a*) *nuclear reaction*; *a chemical reaction between iron and acid.*

re'actionary [-ʃə-] *adj* (*derog*) (of a person or policies) opposed to change and progress or favouring a return to things as they were: *The reactionary old men try to prevent the young men from bringing in new ideas.* – *nc* (*derog*) a person who supports such policies.

re'actor *nc* (*also* **nuclear reactor**) an apparatus in which nuclear energy is produced which can be used as a source of power, *eg* when converted into electricity.

reactivate [ri:'aktiveit] *vt* to activate again: *They've reactivated the old system.*

reactor *see* **react**.

read [ri:d] – *pt, ptp* **read** [red] – **1** *vti* to look at and understand (printed or written words or other signs): *Have you read this letter?*; *I don't like to be interrupted when I'm reading*; *Can your little girl read yet?*; *Can anyone here read Chinese?*; *I've never been taught to read music*; (*fig*) *I can read her thoughts/mind.* **2** *vti* to learn (something) by reading: *I read in the paper today that the government is going to cut taxes again*; *Have you read about the bank-robbery?* **3** *vti* to read (something) aloud, *usu* to someone else: *I read my daughter a story before she goes to bed*; *I read to her before she goes to bed.* **4** *vti* to pass one's time by reading (books *etc*) for pleasure *etc*: *I don't have much time to read these days*; *I've read a lot about ancient civilizations.* **5** *vt* (*Brit formal*) to study (a subject) at a university *etc*: *He's reading French at Oxford.* **6** *vt* to look at or be able to see (something) and get information from it: *I can't* *read the clock without my glasses*; *The nurse read the thermometer*; *The gypsy read my palm* (= described my character, told me what would happen to me in the future *etc*, by studying the lines on my hand). **7** *vi* (*formal*) to be written or worded; to say: *His letter reads as follows: Dear Sir, . . .* **8** *vti* (*formal*) to think that (a statement, action *etc*) has a particular meaning; to seem to have a particular meaning: *I read this to mean that he won't help us*; *This letter reads to me as if he won't help us*; *Don't read more into the speech than was intended.* – *See also* **read in. 9** *vi* (*formal*) (of a piece of writing *etc*) to make a (good, bad *etc*) impression on someone: *This report reads well, but it doesn't have much information in it.* **10** *vt* (of dials, instruments *etc*) to show a particular figure, measurement *etc*: *The thermometer reads −5° C.* **11** *vt* to (cause a word, phrase *etc* to) be replaced by another, *eg* in a document or manuscript: *There is one error on this page. For 'two yards', read 'two metres'*; *'Two yards long' should read 'two metres long'.* – *See also* **read** *in phrases below.* – *nc* (*inf*: *usu in sing*) **1** the act of reading: *Would you like to have a read at that, and see what you think of it?* **2** a period of reading: *I like a good read before I go to sleep.*

'readable *adj* (*neg* **un-**) **1** (*usu pred*) easy or pleasant to read: *I don't usually enjoy poetry but I find these poems very readable.* **2** (*less formal than* **legible**) able to be read: *You don't need to type your report, but at least make sure your handwriting is readable.* **'readableness, ˌreada'bility** *nus.*

'reader *nc* **1** a person who reads (books, magazines *etc*): *He's an avid reader* (= He reads a lot; He enjoys reading). **2** a person who reads a particular newspaper, magazine *etc*: *The editor asked readers to send any complaints about the newspaper to him.* **3** a reading-book, *esp* for children or for learners of a foreign language: *a Latin reader.* **4** (*Brit*: *with cap in titles*) a type of senior university or college lecturer: *He's (the) Reader in linguistics at the local university.*

'readership *nc* **1** the (number of) people who read a newspaper, magazine *etc*: *The new editor said that his main aim was to increase the paper's readership.* **2** (*Brit*) the position of being a reader (*def 4*): *He has a readership in linguistics.*

'reading 1 *ncu* the act of reading, sometimes as a form of entertainment for others: *You'll hurt your eyes with all that reading*; *a poetry reading.* **2** *nu* the ability to read; the way in which a person reads: *The boy is good at reading*; *The boy's reading is good.* **3** *nc* the figure, measurement *etc* on a dial, instrument *etc*: *The reading on the thermometer was −5° C.* **4** *nc* (*formal*) a person's understanding or interpretation (of a situation *etc*): *It all depends on one's reading of this section of the agreement.* **5** *nc* any one of three stages through which a bill has to pass in Parliament or Congress before it is accepted. **6** *nc* a section *eg* of the Bible which is read *eg* at home or in church: *The first reading is from the Gospel according to St Mark*; *a bible-reading.* **7** *nc* a particular version of a section of a manuscript *etc*: *We have three readings for this passage of Homer.*

reading- (*in cmpds*) **1** for the purpose of reading: *reading-glasses*; *a reading-room in a library.* **2** for learning to read: *a reading-book.*

'read-out – *pl* **'read-outs** – *ncu* data produced by a computer, *eg* on magnetic or paper tape, or the part of the computer where it appears.

read back *vt sep* to read (something) aloud to someone who has said it first: *The manager dictated the letter to his secretary, and then asked her to read it back to him.*

read between the lines (*fig*) to look for or find information (*eg* in a letter) which is not actually stated: *He doesn't say so, but reading between the lines, I don't think he likes the idea.*

read in *vt sep* to look for or find (meanings, *eg* in a speech or letter) which the speaker or writer did not intend: *You're reading rather a lot in. I'm sure he didn't mean that at all.*

read (something) into (something) to read (something) in: *You're reading more into his speech than he intended.*

read off *vt sep* to read (something) from a dial, instrument *etc*: *The engineer read off the temperatures one by one.*

read on *vi* to continue to read; to read further: *He paused for a few moments, and then read on.*

read out *vt sep* to read (something) aloud: *Read out the answers to the questions.*

read over/through *vt sep* to read (something) from beginning to end: *I'll read over your manuscript, and let you know if I find any mistakes.*

read up *vt sep,* **read up on** *vt fus* to learn (something) by study: *I must read up on this/read this up before my exam.*

take (something) as read [red] to assume (something) without checking it, doing it *etc*: *Can we take it as read that this has all been checked or do we need to do it ourselves now?*

readdress [riːə'dres] *vt* to change the address on a letter *etc*: *This letter is for the person who used to live here – I'll readdress it and send it to him.*

readily, readiness *see* **ready**.

reading *see* **read**.

readjust [riːə'dʒʌst] (*formal*) **1** *vi* (*with* **to**) to change one's way of life, habits *etc* again in order to fit in with new conditions: *Some soldiers find it hard to readjust to civilian life when they leave the army.* **2** *vt* to make right or correct again; to change, move *etc* (something) again in order to make it more comfortable, better *etc*: *Every time I drive the car, I have to readjust the seat because my wife moves it when she drives.* **ˌrea'djustment** *ncu.*

ready ['redi] *adj* **1** (*pred*: *neg* **un-**) prepared; able to be used *etc* immediately or when needed; able to do (something) immediately or when necessary: *I've packed our cases, so we're ready to leave*; *Is tea ready yet?*; *Your coat has been cleaned and is ready (to be collected).* **2** (*pred*: *neg* **un-**) willing: *I'm always ready to help.* **3** quick: *You're too ready to find faults in other people*; *He always has a ready answer.* **4** (*pred*) likely to do (something); about to do (something): *My head feels as if it's ready to burst.* **'readiness** *nu.*

'readily *adv* (*formal*) **1** willingly: *I'd readily help you.* **2** without difficulty: *I can readily answer all your questions.*

ready cash *nu* (*inf*) ready money.

ˌready-'made *adj* (*esp* of clothes) made in standard sizes, and for sale to anyone who wishes to buy, rather than being made for one particular person: *a ready-made suit*; *His jackets are all ready-made.*

ready money *nu* (*inf*) coins and banknotes: *I want to be paid in ready money, not by cheque.*

ready reckoner *nc* a book of tables giving the answers to calculations required in day-to-day business.

ˌ**ready-to-'wear** *adj* (of clothes) ready-made.
at the ready (of rifles *etc*) in the position ready for firing: *The soldiers stood with their guns at the ready.*
in readiness (*formal*) ready; prepared (for something): *I want everything in readiness before he arrives/for his arrival.*
the ready (*sl*) ready money.

real [riəl] *adj* **1** which actually exists; not imagined: *The police were surprised to see that the man's fears were real; That's not a real monster – it's a man dressed up as one.* **2** not imitation; genuine: *These chairs are covered in real leather, not plastic; Is that diamond real?; He has a real* (= sincere) *love of art.* **3** (*attrib*) actual; in fact: *He may own the factory, but it's his manager who is the real boss;* (*inf*) *He's a real idiot to leave his job.* **4** (*attrib*) great: *a real surprise/problem.* – *adv* (*inf*: *esp Amer*) very; really: *This is a real nice house.*
'realism *nu* **1** in art and literature, the showing or describing of things as they really are. **2** the habit of taking a sensible, unemotional view of life.
'realist *nc* a person who sees, or claims to see, life as it is, without being affected by emotion *etc*: *He says that I am a pessimist but I think I am a realist.*
ˌ**rea'listic** *adj* (*neg* **un-**) **1** showing things as they really are: *a realistic painting; That drawing is so realistic.* **2** taking a sensible, practical view of life: *I'd like to think we'd sell five of these a day, but it would be more realistic to say two; I cannot give you a realistic idea of what a house like that would cost.*
ˌ**rea'listically** *adv.*
reality [ri'aləti] (*formal*) **1** *nu* that which is real and not imaginary: *All science is basically a search for reality.* **2** *nu* the state of being real. – *See also* **bring (someone) back to reality** *below.* **3** *nc* (*often in pl*) a fact; something which is true of (a situation *etc*): *Death and sorrow are two of the grim realities of human existence.* **4** *nu* the state of showing things as they really are: *The film showed life in the poor areas with great reality.* – *See also* **in reality** *below.*
'really *adv* **1** in fact: *He looks a fool but he is really very clever.* **2** very: *That's a really nice hat!* – *interj* an expression of surprise, protest, doubt *etc*: *'I'm going to be the next manager.' 'Oh really?'; Really! I find your attitude deplorable.*
Realtor ®, **realtor** [-to:] *nc* (*Amer*) an estate-agent, *esp* one who is a member of the National Association of Real Estate Boards.
'real estate *nu* (the buying and selling of) land and houses.
bring (someone) back to reality to get (a person) to see the true facts (of a situation *etc*); to get (a person) to stop dreaming, putting forward foolish ideas *etc*: *My wife has forgotten that electricity is not cheap, but these bills will bring her back to reality.*
for 'real (*esp Amer*: *sl*) genuine; true: *He says he's got a new bike, but I don't know if that's for real.*
in re'ality really; actually: *He pretends to be busy, but in reality he has very little to do.*
See also **unreal**.

realign [ri:ə'lain] (*formal*) **1** *vi, v refl* to group together on a different basis; to come together in new groups: *The political parties have realigned* (*themselves*)*, and one has left the coalition government.* **2** *vt* to put into a straight line or parallel lines: *The garage man realigned the wheels of our car today.* ˌ**rea'lignment** *ncu.*

realism, reality *etc see* **real**.

realize, -ise ['riəlaiz] *vt* **1** (not used with **is, was** *etc* and **-ing**) to know; to understand: *I realize that I can't have everything I want; I suddenly realized that all my calculations were wrong; I realized my mistake.* **2** to make real; to make (something) come true: *He realized his ambition to become an astronaut.* **3** (*in passive*) to become fact; to happen: *My worst fears* (= The things I was most afraid would happen) *were realized.* **4** (*formal*) to get money for (something); to be exchanged for a certain sum of money: *He realized £20 000 on the sale of his house; His house realized £20 000.*
ˌ**rea'lizable, -s-** *adj* (*formal*) able to be realized: *realizable assets.*
ˌ**reali'zation, -s-** *ncu* the act of realizing (something): *the realization of his mistake/hopes.*

really *see* **real**.

realm [relm] *nc* **1** (*formal or liter*) a kingdom. **2** (*formal fig*) an area of activity, interest *etc*: *She's well known in the realm of sport.*

realtor *see* **real**.

ream [ri:m] *nc* a measure for paper, equal to 480 sheets.
reams *n pl* (*inf*) large quantities (of paper, writing *etc*): *He wrote reams in his English exam.*

reap [ri:p] *vti* to cut and gather (corn *etc*): *The farmer is reaping the wheat;* (*fig*) *He's reaping the rewards of his hard work.*
'reaper *nc* a person or machine that reaps (corn *etc*).

reappear [ri:ə'piə] *vi* to appear again: *The boy disappeared behind the wall, and reappeared a few yards away.* ˌ**reap'pearance** *ncu.*

reappraisal [ri:ə'preizl] *ncu* (*formal*) the act of looking at a situation *etc* to decide whether decisions *etc* that have been made need to be changed *etc*: *a reappraisal of the government's policy on education.*
ˌ**reap'praise** *vt* (*very formal*) to make a reappraisal of (something): *We must reappraise the firm's accounting system.*

rear[1] [riə] *nc* **1** (*more formal than* **back**) (a position at or behind) the back part (of something): *There is a second bathroom at the rear of the house; There is a garden to the rear of the house; The enemy attacked the army in the rear;* (*attrib*) *the rear wheels of a car;* (*attrib*) *the rear end of the car.* – *See also* **bring up the rear** *below.* **2** (*inf euph*) the buttocks: *The horse kicked him in the rear.*
ˌ**rear-'admiral** *nc* (*with cap, and often abbrev* **R. Adm.**, *when written in titles*) in the British navy, (a person of) the rank above commodore: *He was promoted to rear-admiral; He is a rear-admiral; Rear-Admiral Naylor.*
'rearguard *n sing or n pl* (the group of) soldiers who protect the rear of an army (*eg* when it is retreating).
bring up the rear *see* **bring**.

rear[2] [riə] **1** *vt* to feed and care for (a family, animals *etc* while they grow up): *She has reared six children; He rears cattle.* **2** *vi* (*esp* of a horse) to rise up on the hind legs: *The horse reared in fright as the car passed.* **3** *vt* to raise (the head *etc*): *The snake reared its head;* (*fig*) *This problem has reared its* (*ugly*) *head once again* (= has appeared once again).
rear up *vi* **1** (*esp* of horses) to rear. **2** (*fig*) (of problems *etc*) to appear.

rearm [ri:'a:m] *vti* to give or get weapons again,

esp weapons of a new type. **re'armament** [-məmənt] *nu.*

rearrange [riːə'reindʒ] *vt* to change the position (of something): *We'll rearrange the chairs/room.* **ˌrear'rangement** *ncu.*

reason ['riːzn] **1** *nc* something which makes something happen, describes why it happened, should happen or is going to happen *etc*: *What is the reason for this noise?*; *What is your reason for going to London?*; *There is no reason not to do it*; *The reason (why) I am going is that I want to.* **2** *nu* (*formal*) the power of the mind to think, form opinions and judgements *etc*: *Only man has reason – animals do not.* – (*formal*) **1** *vi* to (be able to) think, form opinions and judgements *etc*: *Man alone has the ability to reason.* **2** *vt* to argue; to suggest or decide (something) after some thought: *Since the allies had not yet appeared, the general reasoned that they had met the enemy forces.* – *See also* **reason with** *below.*

'reasonable *adj* **1** sensible: *That seems a reasonable suggestion*; *It is only reasonable to listen to what others have to say.* **2** willing to listen to argument; acting with good sense: *a reasonable person*; *You will find him very reasonable.* **3** fair; correct; which one should or could accept: *Is £5 a reasonable price for this book?*; *£5 seems reasonable enough*; *These chairs are very reasonable* (= fairly priced); *The dentist's fees are very reasonable.* **4** (*attrib*) satisfactory; equal to what one might expect or want: *There was a reasonable number of people at the meeting.* **'reasonableness** *nu.*

'reasonably *adv* in a reasonable way; to a reasonable extent: *He behaved very reasonably*; *The car is very reasonably priced*; *The meeting was reasonably well attended.*

'reasoning *ncu* the act or process of reaching a decision, conclusion *etc*: *I don't understand his reasoning at all.*

have 'reason to (believe, think *etc***)** (*formal*) to feel justified in (believing *etc* something): *I have (good) reason to think that he is lying.*

it stands to reason (that) anyone who thinks about (a subject) will come to the conclusion (that something is true, probable *etc*): *If you go on smoking sixty cigarettes a day, it stands to reason that you'll get lung cancer.*

listen to reason to allow oneself to be persuaded to do something more sensible than what one was going to do; to pay attention to common sense: *He was so angry, he was going to resign but I got him to listen to reason.*

lose one's reason (*formal*) to become mad or insane.

'reason with *vt fus* to argue with (a person) in order to persuade him to be more sensible: *We tried to reason with the worried mother but she went out alone in the storm to look for the child.*

rhyme or reason *see* **rhyme**.

see reason to (be persuaded to) be more sensible than one is or has been.

within reason within the limits of good sense: *I'll do anything/go anywhere within reason.*

See also **unreasonable, unreasoning**.

reassemble [riːə'sembl] (*formal*) **1** *vt* to put (things) together after taking them apart: *The mechanic took the engine to pieces, then reassembled it.* **2** *vi* to come together again: *The tourists went off sight-seeing, then reassembled for their evening meal.*

reassure [riə'ʃuə] *vt* to take away (a person's) doubts or fears: *The woman was worried about the dangers of taking aspirins, but her doctor reassured her.*

ˌreas'surance **1** *nu* the process of reassuring (someone) or being reassured. **2** *ncu* something which makes a person feel reassured: *She wants reassurance*; *Despite his reassurances, I'm still not happy.*

ˌreas'suring *adj* causing (a person) to feel reassured: *the doctor's reassuring remarks*; *I found his remarks very reassuring.* **ˌreas'suringly** *adv.*

rebate ['riːbeit] *nc* a part of a payment, tax *etc* which is given back to the person paying it, or a sum of money by which the payment, tax *etc* is reduced: *People who have low incomes sometimes qualify for a rent rebate*; *Everyone got a tax rebate today.*

rebel ['rebl] *nc* **1** a person who opposes or fights against people in authority, *eg* a government: *The rebels killed many soldiers*; (*attrib*) *rebel troops.* **2** (*loosely*) a person who does not accept the rules of normal behaviour *etc*: *My son is a bit of a rebel.* – [rə'bel] *v* – *pt, ptp* **re'belled** – *vi* (*often with* **against**) to fight (against people in authority, *eg* a government): *The people rebelled against the dictator*; (*loosely*) *Teenagers often rebel against their parents' way of life.*

rebellion [rə'beljən] *nc* **1** an open or armed fight against people in authority, *eg* a government: *The dictator ordered his troops to put down the rebellion.* **2** a refusal to obey orders *etc* or to accept the rules of normal behaviour *etc.*

rebellious [rə'beljəs] *adj* (*formal*) rebelling or likely to rebel: *rebellious troops*; *The boys are at a rebellious age.* **re'belliously** *adv.* **re'belliousness** *nu.*

rebound [ri'baund] *vi* (*formal*) to bounce back: *The ball rebounded off the wall.*

on the 'rebound ['riːbaund] **1** as (something) bounces back: *He caught the ball on the rebound.* **2** (*inf*) soon after, and as the result of suffering, a great disappointment, *esp* the end of a love affair: *His fiancée left him, and he married the girl next door on the rebound.*

re'bound on/(*formal*) **upon** *vt fus* (of actions *etc*) to have a *usu* bad or unfortunate effect on the person performing the action *etc*: *The lies you tell sometimes rebound on you.*

rebuff [ri'bʌf] *nc* (*formal*) an unkind or unfriendly refusal or rejection (of a request, offer of help, friendship *etc*): *He met with/suffered many rebuffs.* – *vt* (*formal*) to reject or refuse (a request, offer of help *etc*) in an unkind or unfriendly way: *He rebuffed all attempts at friendship.*

rebuke [rə'bjuːk] *vt* (*formal*) to speak severely to (a person), *eg* because he has done wrong: *The boy was rebuked by his teacher for cheating.* – *nc* (*formal*) (stern) words spoken to a person, *eg* because he has done wrong.

rebut [ri'bʌt] – *pt, ptp* **re'butted** – *vt* (*formal or legal*) to prove (something that has been said) wrong: *The prosecution's arguments were rebutted by the defence lawyers.*

re'buttal *nc* (*formal or legal*) a statement proving that something that has been said is wrong.

recalcitrant [rə'kalsitrənt] *adj* (*very formal*) not willing to accept discipline, rules *etc*: *a recalcitrant child*; *Do try not to be so recalcitrant.* **re'calcitrance** *nu.*

recall [ri'koːl] *vt* **1** to order (a person *etc*) to return: *He had been recalled to his former post.* **2** (*more formal than* **remember**) to remember: *I don't* *recall when I last saw him.* – **1** *nc* an order to return. **2** *nu* the act of recalling (someone): *the recall of soldiers to duty.* **3** *nu* ['ri:ko:l] the ability to remember and repeat what one has seen, heard *etc*: *He has total recall.*

beyond recall [ri'ko:l] unable to be changed, stopped *etc*: *The matter is beyond recall.*

recant [ri'kant] *vi* (*formal*) **1** to reject one's (*usu* religious or political) beliefs publicly: *He was burned as a heretic because he refused to recant.* **2** to admit that something one has said is wrong: *The management accused him of making a wrong decision but he refused to recant.*

recantation [ri:kan'teiʃən] (*formal*) **1** *ncu* the act of recanting. **2** *nc* a statement in which one rejects one's beliefs *etc*.

recapitulate [ri:kə'pitjuleit] *vti* (*formal*: *also* (*inf*) **recap** ['ri:kap] – *pt, ptp* **'recapped**) to go over again (the chief points of a statement, argument *etc*): *Can I just recap the details of the plan?*; *I've forgotten some of the points you raised – could you recap?*

'reca,pitu'lation *ncu* (*formal*: *also* (*inf*) **recap** ['ri:kap]).

recapture [ri'kaptʃə] *vt* **1** to capture again (someone or something that has escaped, been lost *etc*): *The soldiers recaptured the city.* **2** to produce a copy or imitation of (something); to convey (the feeling of something in or from the past): *In this film, we try to recapture the atmosphere of Victorian London.* – *nc* (*no pl*) the act of recapturing or being recaptured: *Many people were killed in the recapture of the city.*

recede [ri'si:d] *vi* (*formal*) **1** to go or move back: *When the rain stopped, the floods receded*; (*fig*) *His hair is receding*; (*fig*) *His hair has receded since I last saw him*; (*fig*) *Our profits have receded this year.* **2** to become distant: *As the ship sailed out to sea, the coast receded behind us.*

re'ceding *adj* (*usu attrib*): *a receding hair-line*; *a receding chin.*

receipt [rə'si:t] **1** *nu* (*formal*) the act of receiving or being received: *Please sign this form to acknowledge receipt of the money*; *We are in receipt of your payment.* **2** *nc* a written note saying that money *etc* has been received: *Do you need a receipt for what you have paid/bought?*

re'ceipts *n pl* the money that has been received *eg* in a business: *Our receipts this year are higher than last year's.*

See also **receive**.

receive [rə'si:v] **1** *vt* (*more formal than* **get**) to get or be given (something): *He received a letter*; *She received their thanks*; *They received a good education*; *You will receive a nasty shock when you have to pay for your own food!* **2** *vt* (*formal*) to have a formal meeting with (someone): *The Pope received the Queen in the Vatican.* **3** *vti* (*formal*) to act as host or hostess to guests: *She receives (visitors) on Mondays.* **4** *vt* (*formal*) to allow (someone) to join (something): *He was received into the group.* **5** *vt* (*formal*) to greet (a person, thing *etc*) in some way: *The news was received in silence*; *The townspeople received the heroes with great cheers.* **6** *vti* to accept and pay for stolen goods, *esp* with the intention of reselling them: *He was jailed for receiving (stolen diamonds).*

re'ceiver *nc* **1** the part of a telephone which is held to one's ear. **2** an apparatus for receiving wireless or television signals. **3** a person who receives stolen goods: *He was the receiver of stolen diamonds.* **4** a person who is appointed to take control of the business of someone who has gone bankrupt: *The receiver has been called in.* **5** a stereo amplifier with a built-in radio.

Received Pronunciation (*often abbrev* **RP** [a:'pi:]) the particular pronunciation of British English which is regarded by many as being least regionally limited, most socially acceptable, and most 'standard'.

See also **receipt, reception, recipient**.

recent ['ri:snt] *adj* (*usu attrib*) happening, done *etc* not long ago: *Things have changed in recent weeks/because of recent events*; *The change in management is quite recent.*

'recently *adv*: *He came to see me recently*; *Recently I have been rather unwell.*

receptacle [rə'septəkl] *nc* (*formal*) a container of some kind: *A dustbin is a receptacle for rubbish.*

reception [rə'sepʃən] **1** *ncu* the act of receiving or being received: *We have a special room for the reception of patients*; *His speech got a good reception.* **2** *nc* a formal party or social gathering to welcome guests: *a wedding reception.* **3** *nu* the quality of radio or television signals: *Radio reception is poor in this part of Scotland.*

re'ceptionist *nc* a person who is employed (*eg* in a hotel, office *etc*) to answer the telephone, attend to guests, clients *etc*: *Please give the receptionist your name, and she will inform me of your arrival.*

See also **receive**.

receptive [rə'septiv] *adj* (*formal*) (of people, their minds *etc*: *usu with* **to** *when pred*) quick to understand and accept new ideas *etc*: *He has a receptive mind*; *The management is very receptive to proposals for improving working conditions.*

re'ceptively *adv*.

See also **receive**.

recess [ri'ses, 'ri:ses (*in cmpds* ri'ses)] **1** *nc* (*sometimes in cmpds*) an enlargement of a room, like a large cupboard without a door, formed by part of the wall being built further back than the rest of the wall: *We can put the bed in that recess*; *a bed-recess.* **2** *ncu* the time during which Parliament or the law-courts do not work: *Parliament is in recess.* **3** *nc* (*Amer*) a short period of free time between school classes.

recesses *n pl* (*often fig*) the inner parts of something; the parts of something which are difficult to reach: *the dark recesses of a cave*; *the recesses of a person's mind.*

recession [rə'seʃən] *nc* (*formal*) a temporary fall in (a country's or the world's) business activities: *a trade recession.*

recipe ['resəpi] *nc* **1** a set of instructions on how to prepare and cook (a cake, food *etc*): *a recipe for scones*; (*attrib*) *a recipe book.* **2** (*fig*) a way of achieving (something): *a recipe for success.*

recipient [rə'sipiənt] *nc* (*very formal*) a person who receives (something): *the recipient of a letter*; *the recipient of bad news.*

See also **receive**.

reciprocal [rə'siprəkəl] *adj* (*formal*: *usu attrib*) **1** given to and received from (a person *etc*): *reciprocal aid/affection.* **2** (*gram*) (of pronouns) expressing a relationship between two people, things *etc*: *John and Mary love each other/one another.* **re'ciprocally** *adv*.

re'ciprocate [-keit] (*formal*) **1** *vt* to feel about, do to *etc* (a person) as he feels about, does to *etc* you: *I reciprocate his dislike.* **2** *vti* to do *etc* (something) as repayment for something: *A favour deserves to* *be reciprocated.* **reˌcipro'cation, reciprocity** [resi'prosəti] *nus.*

recite [rə'sait] **1** *vti* to repeat (a poem *etc*) aloud from memory: *I used to be able to recite all the main speeches from 'Hamlet'.* **2** *vt* (*inf*) to make a detailed statement about, or a list of (something): *He loved to recite his grievances; At every opportunity he will recite his reasons for wanting to leave.*

re'cital 1 *nc* a public performance (of music or songs) *usu* by one person or a small number of people: *a recital of Chopin's waltzes.* **2** *nc* (*inf*) a detailed statement about or a list of (something): *a recital of his grievances.* **3** *nu* the act of reciting (something).

ˌreci'tation [resi-] **1** *nc* a poem *etc* which is recited: *a recitation from Shakespeare.* **2** *nu* the act of reciting.

reckless ['rekləs] *adj* very careless; acting or done without any thought of the consequences: *a reckless driver; reckless driving; He is very reckless when he is drunk;* (*formal*) *He dashed out, reckless of the danger.* **'recklessly** *adv.* **'recklessness** *nu.*

reckon ['rekən] **1** *vt* (*often in passive*: not used with **is, was** *etc* and **-ing**) to have an opinion about (someone or something): *He is reckoned (to be/as/as being) the best pianist in Britain.* **2** *vti* (*inf*: *esp Amer*) to think; to have decided; to intend: *I reckon I might/will come; Is he reckoning on coming?* **3** *vt* (*formal*: *with* **among**: not *usu* used with **is, was** *etc* and **-ing**) to consider that (someone) belongs to a group: *I reckon him among my friends.* – *See also* **reckon** *in phrases below.*

'reckoning 1 *nu* calculation; counting: *By my reckoning, we must be about eight kilometres from the town.* **2** *nc* (*usu in sing*) the settling of debts, grievances *etc*: *You may think you've got away with your crimes, but one day there will be a reckoning.*

day of reckoning the time when one has to pay for, or be punished for, one's mistakes: *Your day of reckoning will come when the boss finds out that you've borrowed money from the firm; His day of reckoning came when the headmaster found that he'd broken a window.*

ready reckoner *see* **ready**.

reckon on/(*formal*) **upon** *vt fus* to depend on or expect (someone or something): *I was reckoning on meeting him tonight.*

reckon up *vt sep* to count or calculate (something): *When you reckon up the cost of eating in a restaurant it makes you decide to eat at home.*

'reckon with *vt fus* to be prepared for (something); to expect (something); to expect trouble, difficulties *etc* from (a person *etc*): *I didn't reckon with all these problems; He's a man to be reckoned with.*

reckon without *vt fus* to expect not to have (something); to expect not to have (trouble, difficulties *etc* from someone); to make plans *etc* without taking (someone or something) into consideration: *I was reckoning without all the problems which keep coming up; He was reckoning without her mother's interference.*

reclaim [ri'kleim] *vt* **1** to ask for (something one owns which has been lost, stolen *etc* and found by someone else): *A wallet has been found and can be reclaimed at the manager's office.* **2** to make (waste land) fit for use; to get back (land) from under the sea *etc* by draining *etc.* **ˌrecla'mation** [reklə-] *nu.*

recline [rə'klain] (*formal*) **1** *vi* to lean or lie on one's back or side: *The invalid was reclining lazily on the sofa.* **2** *vt* to lean or lay (one's head *etc*) in a resting position: *He reclined his head on the pillow.*

reclining chair an armchair with a back which can be made to slope backwards.

recluse [rə'kluːs] *nc* (*formal*) a person who lives alone and avoids other people: *There is no point in asking him to go to a party – he is too much of a recluse.*

recognize, -ise ['rekəgnaiz] *vt* (not used with **is, was** *etc* and **-ing** (*defs 1, 2, 5*)) **1** to see, hear *etc* (a person, thing *etc*) and know who or what that person, thing *etc* is, because one has seen or heard him, it *etc* before: *I recognized his voice/handwriting; I recognized him by his voice.* **2** to admit (something); to agree (that something is true): *He recognized that he had made mistakes;* (*formal*) *Everyone recognized his skill.* **3** (*formal*) to show that one approves of and is grateful for (something): *They recognized the boy's courage by giving him a medal.* **4** (*formal*) to be willing to have social or political relations with (a person, country *etc*): *Many countries were unwilling to recognize the new republic.* **5** (*formal*) to accept (someone or something) as valid, well-qualified *etc*: *I don't recognize the authority of this court.* **ˌrecog'nizable, -s-** *adj* (*neg* **un-**). **ˌrecog'nizably, -s-** *adv.*

ˌrecog'nition [-'niʃən] *nu* the act or state of recognizing or being recognized: *They gave the boy a medal in recognition of his courage; the recognition of a new republic; I said hello to him but there was no recognition in his eyes/he showed no recognition; He received no recognition for the part he played in the war.*

'recognized, -s- *adj* (*neg* **un-**) accepted as valid, well-qualified *etc*: *He's a recognized authority on beetles.*

recoil [rə'koil] *vi* **1** (*with* **at** *or* **from**) to move back or away (from something or someone), *usu* quickly, in horror or fear: *He recoiled at/from the sight of the murdered child.* **2** (*tech*) (of guns when fired) to jump back. – ['riːkoil] *ncu* the act of recoiling.

recollect [rekə'lekt] *vt* (*more formal than* **remember**) to remember: *I don't recollect having seen him before; I recollect the first day I met her.*

ˌrecol'lection [-ʃən] (*more formal than* **remembering** *or* **memory**) **1** *nu* the act of recollecting; the ability to recollect. **2** *nc* something that is remembered: *My book is called 'Recollections of Childhood'; I have no recollection of doing that.*

recommend [rekə'mend] *vt* **1** to advise (someone to do something): *I recommend you to take a long holiday; I recommend (that) you take a long holiday; I recommend a long holiday.* **2** to suggest that (a person, thing *etc*) is particularly good, particularly suitable for a certain job, purpose *etc*: *I can recommend these cakes; He recommended her (to me) for the job.* **3** to make (something) desirable or pleasing: *This flat has very little to recommend it; This applicant for the job has very little to recommend him.*

ˌrecommen'dation *ncu*: *I gave her the job on his recommendation; They refused to accept my recommendations.*

recompense ['rekəmpens] *nu* (*formal*) a reward given to someone because he has done well; money *etc* given to someone because he has suffered inconvenience, loss *etc*: *The miner was given a large sum of money as recompense for his injuries.* – *vt* (*formal*) to give (someone) money *etc* for doing well, having suffered an inconvenience *etc*: *The nobleman recompensed his followers for their loyalty*; *May I recompense you for any inconvenience caused?*

reconcile ['rekənsail] *vt* 1 (*formal*: *often with* **with**) to cause (people) to become friendly again, *eg* after they have quarrelled: *Why won't you be reconciled (with him)?* 2 (*often with* **with**) to bring (two or more different aims, points of view *etc*) into agreement: *The unions want high wages and the bosses want high profits – it's almost impossible to reconcile these two aims.* 3 (*with* **to**) to (make someone) accept (a situation, fact *etc*) patiently: *Her mother didn't want the marriage to take place but she is reconciled to it now*; *Only time will reconcile her to the death of her husband*; *I am reconciled to the idea of retirement.*

'recon,cili'ation [-sili-] *ncu* (*often with* **between** *or* **with**) (an) act of reconciling or being reconciled: *There has been a reconciliation between her and her husband*; *There is no sign of reconciliation.*

recondition [ri:kən'diʃən] *vt* to put (something) in good condition again by cleaning it, repairing it *etc*.

,recon'ditioned *adj*: *A reconditioned television set is cheaper than a new one.*

reconnaissance [rə'konəsəns] *ncu* (*formal or mil*) (the act of making) a study (of land, enemy troops *etc*) to obtain information, *eg* before a battle: *These soldiers are engaged in reconnaissance*: (*attrib*) *a reconnaissance operation.*

reconnoitre, (*Amer*) **reconnoiter** [rekə'noitə] *vti* (*formal or mil*) to make a reconnaissance of (land, enemy troops *etc*).

reconsider [ri:kən'sidə] *vti* (*formal*) to think about (something) again and possibly change one's opinion, decision *etc*: *Please reconsider your decision to go*; *I know that you have decided to go away, but please reconsider.* **'recon,side'ration** *nu*.

reconstitute [ri:'konstitju:t] *vt* (*formal*) 1 to put or change (something) back to its original form *eg* by adding water: *The dried milk must be reconstituted before use.* 2 to form or make up in a different way: *The board of directors of the firm was reconstituted, with many members being given different posts.* **re,consti'tution** *nu*.

reconstruct [ri:kən'strʌkt] *vt* to create a complete description or idea (of something) on the basis of certain facts, with the idea of seeing how it originally happened *etc*: *Let us try to reconstruct the crime.*

,recon'struction [-ʃən] *ncu*: *the reconstruction of a crime.*

record ['reko:d, -kəd, (*Amer*) -kərd] 1 *nc* a written report of facts, events *etc*: *Historical records show that Macbeth did in fact exist*; *I wish to keep a record of everything that is said at this meeting.* – *See also* **off the record, on record** *below*. 2 *nc* a round flat piece of (*usu* black) plastic on which music *etc* is recorded: *I'm looking for a record of Beethoven's Sixth Symphony.* – *See also* **disc**. 3 *nc* (in races, games, or almost any activity) the best performance so far; something which has never yet been beaten: *He holds the record for the 1 000 metres*; *The record for the high jump was broken/beaten this afternoon*; *He claimed to have eaten fifty sausages in a minute and asked if this was a record*; (*attrib*) *a record score*; (*attrib*: *often loosely*) *He did it in record time* (= very fast). 4 *nc* a description of one's life, character or achievements *etc*, whether written or not: *This school has a very bad record* (= its pupils do not pass exams *etc*): *He admitted he had a criminal record* (= that he had been convicted of a crime at some time in his life). 5 *n* (*with cap*) a word often used in the titles of newspapers: *the Weekly Record.* – [rə'ko:d] 1 *vt* to write a description of an event, facts *etc* so that they can be read in the future: *It is recorded in the Bible that Jesus cured people's illnesses*; *The decisions will be recorded in the minutes of the meeting.* 2 *vti* to put (the sound of music, speech *etc*) on a record or tape so that it can be listened to in the future: *I've recorded the whole concert*; *Don't make any noise when I'm recording*; *My tape-recorder isn't recording for some reason.* 3 *vti* to sing (a song), play (music) *etc* which is recorded on a record or tape: *I don't think Mario Lanza ever recorded that song*; *She hasn't been recording for several years now.* 4 *vt* (of a dial, instrument *etc*) to show (a figure *etc*) as a reading: *The thermometer recorded 30° C yesterday*; *Temperatures of 30° C were recorded yesterday.* 5 *vt* to give or show (something), *esp* in writing: *Everyone should record his vote in an election*; *I'd like to record my appreciation of your efforts.*

re'corder *nc* 1 a type of musical wind instrument, made of wood, plastic *etc*. 2 a judge in certain courts. 3 a person who records something. – *See also* **tape-recorder** *under* **tape**.

re'cording 1 *nu* the process of making a record (of something), *esp* on a record or on tape: *The recording of this song only took half an hour.* 2 *nc* the sound record made in this way: *This is a recording of Beethoven's Fifth Symphony.*

'record-player *nc* an electrical instrument which reproduces the sounds recorded on records.

off the record (of information, statements *etc*) not intended to be repeated or made public: *The Prime Minister admitted off the record that the country was going through a serious crisis.*

on 'record written down or recorded for future reference: *I wish to go/be put on record as disagreeing with all these decisions*; *This is the coldest winter on record* (= since records were started).

recount [ri'kaunt] *vt* (*formal*) to tell (a story *etc*) in detail: *He recounted his adventures.*

re-count [ri:'kaunt] *vt* to count (something) again. – ['ri:kaunt] *nc* a second count: *Sometimes in an election there has to be a re-count of votes*; *He demanded a re-count.*

recoup [ri'ku:p] *vt* (*formal*) to get back all or part of what one has lost (*eg* money): *One book made great losses, but the firm recouped these losses from the profits on other books.*

recourse [rə'ko:s]: **have re'course to** (*formal*) to make use of (something) *eg* in an emergency or in a case of necessity: *When the negotiations failed, the union said they would need to have recourse to strike action.*

recover [rə'kʌvə] 1 *vi* (*often with* **from**) to become well again; to return to good health *etc*: *He is recovering from a serious illness*; *The country is recovering from an economic crisis*; *He has been very ill but he is now recovering.* 2 *vt* to get or find again: *The police have recovered the stolen jewels.* 3 *vt* (*formal*) to get (money *etc*) from someone because one has suffered damage or loss: *He recovered the cost of the repairs to his car from the person who caused the damage.* 4 *vti* to get control of (one's actions, emotions *etc*) again: *The actor almost fell over but quickly recovered (his balance)*;

He was very upset by her behaviour but managed to recover his composure (= become calm again); *He was very upset but recovered (himself) in time to give a speech.*

re'coverable *adj* (*formal*): *Is the cost of the repairs recoverable?*; *recoverable expenses.*

re'covery *ncu* (an) act or process of recovering (from) something or being recovered: *The patient made a remarkable recovery after his illness*; *the recovery of stolen property*; (*attrib*) *The broken-down car was being towed by a recovery vehicle*; *the recovery of his composure.*

re-cover [riːˈkʌvə] *vt* to put a new cover on (something): *This chair needs to be re-covered.*

re-create [riːkriˈeit] *vt* to describe (something); to make a picture, copy or representation, or give a description of (something in the past): *In this film, we try to re-create the atmosphere of Victorian England.* **ˌre-cre'ation** *ncu.*

recreation [rekriˈeiʃən] *ncu* (a) pleasant activity which one enjoys doing in one's spare time (*eg* a sport, hobby): *I have little time for recreation*; *I wouldn't consider digging the garden a recreation.*

ˌrecre'ational *adj.*

ˌrecre'ation ground *nc* a piece of land for playing sports, games *etc* on.

recrimination [rəkrimiˈneiʃən] (*formal*) **1** *nc* (*often in pl*) an accusation made by a person who has himself been accused of something, against the person who made the accusation: *His hasty words will lead to recriminations if he is later proved wrong.* **2** *nu* the act of making such an accusation.

re'criminatory [-nə-] *adj* (*formal*) involving recrimination(s): *recriminatory remarks*; *His comments were unnecessarily recriminatory.*

recruit [rəˈkruːt] *nc* **1** a person who has (just) joined the army, air force *etc.* **2** a person who has (just) joined a society, group *etc*: *Our party needs new recruits before the next election*; *Mr Jones is the latest recruit to the ranks of those calling for racial equality.* – *vti* to cause (someone) to join the army, a society *etc*: *If we are going to win the war, we must recruit more troops*; *Can't you recruit more members to the music society?* **re'cruitment** *nu.*

rectangle [ˈrektaŋgl] *nc* (*geom*) a two-dimensional, four-sided figure with opposite sides equal and all its angles right angles. **rec'tangular** [-gjulə] *adj.*

rectify [ˈrektifai] *vt* (*formal*) to put right or correct (a mistake *etc*): *We shall rectify the error as soon as possible.* **ˌrecti'fiable** *adj.* **ˌrectifi'cation** [-fi-] *nu.*

rectitude [ˈrektitjuːd] *nu* (*very formal*) (of a person) honesty; correctness of behaviour: *a person of high moral rectitude.*

rector [ˈrektə] *nc* (*with cap in titles*) **1** in the Church of England and certain other churches, a clergyman in charge of a parish; in the Roman Catholic Church, the head priest of a parish or of a religious house. **2** in Scotland, the headmaster of certain secondary schools. **3** *esp* in Scotland, a senior university official elected by the students; occasionally in other countries, the head of a university or college.

rec'torial [-ˈtoː-] *adj* (*attrib*) of a rector: *rectorial duties.*

'rectorship *nc* **1** the position of rector: *The rectorship is vacant.* **2** the time during which a person is a rector: *How long did his rectorship last?*

'rectory *nc* the house of a rector (*def 1*).

rectum [ˈrektəm] *nc* (*tech*) the lower part of the alimentary canal, through which waste substances pass from the intestines: *The surgeon has operated on her rectum.*

recumbent [rəˈkʌmbənt] *adj* (*very formal*: *usu attrib*) lying down: *The archaeologists found a statue of a recumbent woman*; *in a recumbent position.*

recuperate [rəˈkjuːpəreit] *vi* (*formal*) to recover, *eg* after an illness: *He went to the country to recuperate.* **reˌcupe'ration** *ncu.*

re'cuperative *adj* (*formal*: *usu attrib*) causing recovery of health: *the recuperative powers of certain substances.*

recur [riˈkəː] – *pt, ptp* **re'curred** – *vi* (*formal*) to happen again; to come back again: *This is a problem which keeps recurring*; *His illness is likely to recur.*

re'currence [-ˈkʌ-, (*Amer*) -ˈkəː-] *ncu* (*formal*): *He has had several recurrences of his illness*; *The recurrence of his mental illness was a surprise to everyone.*

re'current [-ˈkʌ-, (*Amer*) -ˈkəː-] *adj* (*formal*) happening often or regularly: *a recurrent illness/problem*; *His illness is likely to be recurrent.*

red [red] *adj* **1** of the colour of blood: *a red car/dress*; *Her cheeks were red*; *The paint is red.* **2** (of hair or fur) of a colour which varies between a golden brown and a deep reddish-brown: *I prefer red squirrels to grey squirrels*; *Her hair is red.* **3** (of eyes) bloodshot; with the veins showing, causing the white part of the eye to look red; having red lids: *Her eyes were red with crying*; *She has an eye infection – her eyes are red and itchy.* **4** (*inf*: *usu attrib*: *sometimes with cap*: *sometimes derog*) communist: *Red China.* – **1** *ncu* the colour of blood, or a similar shade: *The room was painted in a variety of reds and blues* (= different shades of red and blue). **2** *ncu* something (*eg* material, paint *etc*) which is red: *She was dressed in red* (= red clothes); *He missed a red* (= one of the red balls in *eg* billiards). **3** *nc* (*inf*: *often with cap*: *derog*: *often offensive*) a communist or socialist: *His aim is to get the Reds out of Parliament*; *I don't want my daughter to marry a Red.* – *See also* **red** *in phrases below.*

'redden 1 *vti* to make or become red or redder: *Her cheeks reddened as she realized her mistake*; *The paint is too orange – let's redden it a bit.* **2** *vi* to blush: *She reddened as she realized her mistake.*

'reddish *adj* slightly red; close to red: *I would like a reddish dress*; *Her hair is reddish.*

'redness *nu*: *the redness of her cheeks*; *The redness of her hair doesn't look natural*; *the redness of her eyes.*

ˌred-'blooded *adj* (*usu attrib*) active; manly; full of strong, *usu* sexual, desires: *a red-blooded male.*

ˌred'brick uni'versity *nc* (*sometimes derog*) any of the universities founded in England in the late nineteenth century, *usu* contrasted with Oxford and Cambridge: *He didn't get into Cambridge – he's going to one of the redbrick universities.*

red cabbage 1 *nc* a type of cabbage with deep purple leaves: *We are growing red cabbages this year.* **2** *nu* its leaves, used as food: *We had red cabbage with the roast pheasant.*

'redcoat *nc* (*hist*) a type of British soldier.

'redcurrant *nc* **1** a type of garden bush grown for its small red fruit: *We planted two redcurrants by the kitchen window*; (*attrib*) *a redcurrant bush.* **2** its fruit: *We had redcurrants for dessert*; (*attrib*) *redcurrant mousse*; (*attrib*) *redcurrant jam.*

red deer – *pl* **red deer** – *nc* a type of deer with red (*def 2*) fur, found in Europe and Asia.

'redhead *nc* a person, *usu* female, with red (*def 2*) hair: *His new girlfriend is a beautiful redhead.*

red herring *nc* **1** a subject, idea *etc* introduced into a discussion *etc* to take people's attention away from the main topic: *Mentioning racialism in a discussion on education is a complete red herring.* **2** a false clue, intended to mislead someone.

ˌred-'hot *adj* **1** (of metal *etc*) so hot that it is glowing red: *red-hot steel*; *This iron is red-hot.* **2** (*inf fig*) very enthusiastic: *a red-hot socialist*; *He's red-hot at geography.*

Red Indian *nc* (*rare*) a N American Indian. – *adj* (*rare*) of a Red Indian or Red Indians: *Red Indian carvings.*

ˌred-'letter day *nc* a day which will always be remembered because something particularly pleasant or important happened on it: *The day I won a prize on the football pools was a real red-letter day.*

red pepper *see* **pepper**.

'redskin *nc* (*inf derog*) a N American Indian.

red tape *nu* (*derog*) (the strict attention to and following of) annoying and unnecessary rules and regulations: *I need a new passport, but because of all the red tape, I won't get it in time for my holiday.*

red wine *see* **wine**.

be in the red (*inf*) to be in debt: *I am/My bank account is in the red.*

'catch (someone) ˌred-'handed to find (a person) in the act of doing wrong: *The police caught the thief red-handed.*

paint the town red (*inf*) to enjoy oneself (*esp* in town) in a lively, noisy, sometimes drunken, way.

the Red Army the army of the USSR.

ˌred-'carpet treatment great respect and honour given to important guests or visitors, from the practice of rolling out a red carpet for important guests to walk on: *The Prime Minister was given the red-carpet treatment when he visited the town.*

the Red Cross a world-wide organization which helps people who are wounded, homeless *etc* in time of war, disaster *etc.*

a red rag to a bull (*inf*) something which is certain to make (a person) angry: *Criticizing the Liberal Party in front of him is like a red rag to a bull.*

see red (*inf*) to become angry: *When he started criticizing my work, I really saw red.*

redeem [rə'di:m] *vt* (*formal*) **1** to buy back (something that has been pawned): *I'm going to redeem my gold watch.* **2** to set (a person) free by paying a ransom, *esp fig* (of Jesus Christ) to free (a person) from sin: *We have all been redeemed by Jesus Christ.* **3** to make up or compensate for (something bad or wrong): *His willingness to work redeemed him in her eyes.*

Re'deemer *n* (*often with* **the**) Jesus Christ.

redemption [rə'dempʃən] *nu*: *the redemption of man by Christ.*

past/beyond redemption (*formal or facet*) too bad to be redeemed or improved: *He is so wicked that he is past redemption*; *His schoolwork is so bad that it is beyond redemption.*

redeeming feature something which compensates (for something which is bad or wrong): *It's an ugly house – its one redeeming feature is its position on the hill.*

redeploy [ri:di'ploi] *vti* (*very formal*) to move (soldiers, workmen *etc*) to another place where they will be more useful. **ˌrede'ployment** *nu.*

redirect [ri:di'rekt] *vt* (*formal*) to put (a person's) new address on, and post (a letter *etc*), *eg* because he has moved to a new house.

re-do [ri:'du:] – *pt* **re-did** [ri:'did] : *ptp* **re-done** [ri:'dʌn] – *vt* to do (something) (to something) again: *This page will have to be re-done* (= rewritten).

redolent ['redələnt] *adj* (*formal*) **1** (*with* **of** *or* **with**) smelling strongly (of something): *The room was redolent of tobacco.* **2** (*with* **of** *or* **with**) suggesting (something) very strongly: *a street redolent of Victorian England.* **'redolence** *nu.*

redouble [ri'dʌbl] *vti* to make (something) twice as great: *He redoubled his efforts*; *Their efforts have redoubled.*

redoubtable [rə'dautəbl] *adj* (*formal or facet*: *usu attrib*) (of a person) brave; bold; causing fear or respect: *a redoubtable general*; *He is the most redoubtable admiral in the navy*; *His mother-in-law is a most redoubtable lady.*

redress [rə'dres] *vt* (*very formal*) to set right or compensate for (something wrong that has been done): *The company offered the man a large sum of money to redress the harm which they had done him.* – *See also* **redress the balance** *below.* – *nu* (*very formal*) the act of redressing or being redressed; money *etc* which is paid as compensation (for something wrong which has been done): *He went to his lawyer to seek redress for his dismissal.*

redress the balance (*very formal*) to make things (more nearly) equal again: *The general claimed that the enemy had many more missiles than our allies and that the government must find a way of redressing the balance.*

redskin *see* **red**.

reduce [rə'dju:s] **1** *vt* (*more formal than* **make less**) to make (something) less, smaller *etc*: *The shop reduced its prices*; *The train reduced speed*; *The doctor told him to reduce* (*his*) *weight.* **2** *vi* (*inf*) to lose weight by dieting: *I must reduce to get into that dress.* **3** *vt* (*formal*: *with* **to**) to change (a person, thing *etc*) into another and *usu* worse state, form, condition *etc*: *The bombs reduced the city to ruins*; *She was so angry, she was almost reduced to tears* (= she almost cried); *The officer was reduced to the ranks* (= he was demoted and became an ordinary soldier). **4** *vt* (*with* **to**: *usu in passive*) to force (a person) to do (something less pleasant or desirable than normal): *During the famine, many people were reduced to eating grass and leaves.* **re'ducible** *adj* (*formal*).

re'duction [-'dʌk-] *ncu*: *The government promised a reduction in prices later in the year*; *the reduction of prices in the supermarkets*; *During the sale, the shop advertised great price reductions.*

reduced circumstances (*euph*) the condition of having much less money than before: *The old lady was once quite rich but is now living in reduced circumstances.*

redundant [rə'dʌndənt] *adj* **1** (*usu pred*) (of workers) no longer employed because there is no longer any job for them where they used to work: *Fifty men have just been made redundant at the local factory*; *angry protests by redundant workers.* **2** expressing an idea which is already conveyed by another word which is also used: *In 'the final end of the quarrel', 'final' is redundant because 'end' already conveys the idea of finality*; *a redundant word.*

re'dundancy *ncu*: *There have been a lot of redundancies at the local factory recently*; *the* *redundancy of 'final' in 'the final end'*; (*attrib*) *redundancy money* (= compensation paid to a person when he is made redundant).

reduplicate [ri'dju:plikeit] *vt* (*very formal*) to repeat or copy (an action *etc*), *esp* unnecessarily: *Let's decide who does what, so that we don't reduplicate each other's work.* **re͵dupli'cation** *nu.*

reed [ri:d] *nc* **1** a kind of tall, stiff grass growing on wet or marshy ground: *reeds along a river-bank.* **2** a thin piece of cane or metal in certain wind instruments (*eg* the oboe, clarinet) which vibrates and makes a sound when the instrument is played.

reef [ri:f] *nc* a line of rocks *etc* just above or below the surface of the sea: *The ship got stuck on a reef.*

reefer ['ri:fə] *nc* **1** (*sl*) a cigarette containing marijuana. **2** a reefer-jacket.

'reefer-jacket *nc* a type of short coat made of thick, warm material.

reek [ri:k] *nc* (*no pl*: *more inf and derog than* **smell**) a strong, *usu* unpleasant smell: *the reek of tobacco smoke.* – *vi* (*more inf and derog than* **smell**: *with* **of**) **1** to smell strongly (of something): *He reeks of tobacco smoke.* **2** (*fig*) to show or suggest a great deal (of something bad or unpleasant): *This scheme reeks of racism.*

reel [ri:l] *nc* **1** a round wheel-shaped or cylindrical object of wood, metal *etc* on which thread, film, fishing-lines *etc* can be wound: *When you've used up all that thread would you give the empty reels to my child – he likes to play with them.* **2** the quantity of film, thread *etc* wound on one of these: *Is that reel of film finished yet?* **3** (the music for) a type of lively Scottish, Irish or American dance: *The fiddler played a reel*; *The children danced a reel.* – **1** *vi* to stagger; to sway; to move in an unsteady way: *The drunk man reeled along the road*; (*fig*) *My brain was reeling with all the information that he gave me.* **2** *vi* to appear to move, sway *etc*: *The room began to reel and then I fainted.*

reel in *vt sep* to pull (*eg* a fish out of the water) by winding the line to which it is attached on to a reel.

reel off *vt sep* to say or repeat (something) quickly and easily, without pausing: *He reeled off the list of names/the parts of the verb 'to be'*; *He reeled it off without thinking.*

re-elect [ri:i'lekt] *vt* to elect (someone) again: *They have re-elected him to Parliament.* **͵re-e'lection** [-ʃən] *nu.*

re-enter [ri:'entə] *vti* to enter (something) again: *The spaceship will re-enter the Earth's atmosphere tomorrow.*

͵re-'entry *ncu*: *Re-entry will take place tomorrow afternoon at two o'clock*; *Previous re-entries have resulted in disaster.*

refectory [rə'fektəri] *nc* a dining-hall for monks, students *etc.*

refer [rə'fə:] – *pt, ptp* **re'ferred** – (*with* **to**) **1** *vi* (*more formal than* **mention**) to talk or write (about something); to mention (something): *He doesn't like anyone referring to his wooden leg*; *I referred to your theories in my last book.* **2** *vi* to relate to, concern, or apply to (a person, thing *etc*): *My remarks refer to your last letter*; *Does this refer to me?* **3** *vt* (*formal*) to send or pass (a person, problem *etc*) to (a person *etc*) for discussion, information, a decision *etc*: *The dispute was referred to the arbitration board*; *I'll refer you to the managing director*; *For details, I refer you to the speech I made last week.* **4** *vi* (*formal*) to look for information (in something): *The speaker often referred to his notes*; *If I'm not sure how to spell a word, I refer to a dictionary.*

referee [refə'ri:] *nc* **1** a person who controls boxing, football *etc* matches, makes sure that the rules are not broken *etc*: *The referee sent two of the footballers off the field*; (*fig*) *The government acted as referee in the dispute between the management and the trade union.* **2** a person who is willing to provide a note about one's character, ability *etc*, *eg* when one applies for a new job: *The lecturer agreed to act as (a) referee for the student.* – *v* – *pt, ptp* **͵refe'reed** – *vti* to act as a referee (in) (*def 1*): *I've been asked to referee (a football match) on Saturday.*

reference ['refərəns] **1** *ncu* (*formal*) (an) act of referring (to something); a mention (of something): *He made reference to your remarks at the last meeting*; *He made several references to your remarks*; *With reference to your request for information, I regret to inform you that I am unable to help you.* **2** *nc* a note about one's character, ability *etc*, *eg* when one applies for a new job: *Our new secretary had excellent references from her previous employers.* **3** *nc* an indication in a book, report *etc*, showing where one got one's information or where further information can be found: *References are given in full at the end of this article*; *Have you checked the references in that book you're editing?*

'reference book *nc* a book which is not usually read from beginning to end but which is consulted occasionally for information, *eg* a dictionary or encyclopaedia.

'reference library *nc* a library of books to be looked at for information but not borrowed.

terms of reference (*formal*) (a statement which describes) the exact work *etc* to be carried out by *eg* a committee: *It was not within our terms of reference to make such inquiries.*

See also **cross-refer, cross-reference** *under* **cross**[2].

referendum [refə'rendəm] – *pls* **͵refe'rendums**, (*formal*) **͵refe'renda** [-də] – *nc* the act of giving the people of a country *etc* the chance to state their opinion about some important matter by voting for or against it: *The British government held a referendum on whether or not to join the Common Market.*

refill ['ri:fil] *nc* (something which contains) the amount of some material needed to fill up some object which becomes empty through use: *I must go and buy some refills for my pen*; (*inf*) *Can I get you a refill?* (= another drink). – [ri:'fil] *vt* to fill (something) up again: *He refilled his pipe.*

refine [rə'fain] *vt* to make a substance (*eg* sugar) pure by taking out dirt, waste substances *etc*: *Oil is refined before it is used*; (*fig formal*) *We have refined our techniques considerably since the work began.*

re'fined *adj* (*neg* **un-**) **1** (of a person, his speech *etc*) very polite; well-mannered; elegant: *a very refined lady*; *She is so refined that she uses a finger bowl at meal-times.* **2** having been refined: *refined sugar/methods.*

re'finement **1** *nu* good manners, good taste, polite speech *etc*: *He is a man of great refinement.* **2** *ncu* (an) improvement: *We have added several refinements/a great deal of refinement to our techniques over the last year.*

re'finery *nc* a place where sugar or oil *etc* is refined.

refit [ri:'fit] – *pt, ptp* ˌ**re'fitted** – **1** *vt* to repair or fit new parts to (a ship): *They are refitting the liner.* **2** *vi* (of a ship) to be repaired or have new parts fitted: *The ship is refitting just now.* – ['ri:fit] *ncu* the act of refitting (a ship) or of being refitted: *The ship went into the dock for a refit; The ship is under refit.*

reflect [rə'flekt] **1** *vti* to send back (light, heat *etc*): *The white sand reflected the sun's heat.* **2** *vti* (of a mirror *etc*) to give an image of (someone or something): *She was reflected in the mirror/water;* (*fig formal*) *The style of this poem reflects my mood when I wrote it.* **3** *vt* (*formal*) to be caused by (something): *The price increases reflect greater demand for the goods.* **4** *vi* (*formal: sometimes with* **on** *or* **upon**) to think carefully: *Give him a minute to reflect (on what he should do).* **5** *vti* (*formal: with* **on** *or* **upon**) to bring (praise, blame *etc*) on (someone): *Her behaviour reflects (badly)* (= brings blame) *on her mother; Her behaviour reflects credit* (= brings praise) *on her mother.*

re'flected *adj*: *The moon shines by reflected light.*

re'flecting *adj* (*attrib*) able to reflect (light *etc*): *a reflecting surface.*

reflection, reflexion [rə'flekʃən]: *She looked at her reflection in the water; This poem is a reflection of my mood at the time I wrote it; After/On reflection* (= After thinking about it), *I feel I made the wrong decision; The books are called 'Reflections of a Politician' and 'Reflections on Life in England'; Your bad behaviour is a reflection on me.*

re'flective [-tiv] *adj* **1** (*formal*) thoughtful: *in a reflective mood; He seems rather reflective today.* **2** reflecting: *Reflective number-plates are easier to read in the dark; The paint is reflective.*

re'flectively *adv.*

re'flector *nc* something, *esp* of glass or metal, that reflects light, heat *etc.*

reflex ['ri:fleks] *nc, adj* (*attrib*) (an action which is) automatic or not intended: *The doctor tapped the patient's knee in order to test his reflexes; Jerking one's leg when one's kneecap is hit lightly is a reflex action.*

reflexion *see* **reflect**.

reflexive [rə'fleksiv] *adj* (*gram*) **1** (of a pronoun) showing that the object of a verb is the same (person, thing *etc*) as the subject: *In 'He cut himself' and 'She looked at herself in the mirror', 'himself' and 'herself' are reflexive pronouns.* **2** (of a verb) (always) used with a reflexive pronoun: *In 'He abandoned himself to despair', 'abandoned' is a reflexive verb.*

reform [rə'fo:m] **1** *vt* to improve or remove faults from (a person, behaviour, an organization *etc*): *The criminal's wife stated that she had made great efforts to reform her husband.* **2** *vi* to give up bad habits, improve one's behaviour *etc*: *He admitted that he had been a criminal, but said that he intended to reform.* – **1** *nu* the act of improving: *the reform of our political system.* **2** *nc* an improvement (in some part of the social or political system *etc*): *He intends to make several reforms in the prison system.*

ˌ**refor'mation** [refə-] *ncu.*

re'formatory *nc* (*old: esp Amer*) a school for reforming young people who break the law.

re'formed *adj* (*neg* **un-**) improved, *esp* in behaviour: *His wife claimed that he was now a reformed man/character; He is reformed now.*

re'former *nc* a person who wishes to bring about improvements: *one of the reformers of our political system.*

the Reformation the 16th-century religious movement which led to the forming of the Protestant churches.

refrain[1] [rə'frein] *nc* a line of words or music repeated regularly in a song, *esp* at the end of or after each verse: *This song has a simple refrain, so you can all join in and sing it.*

refrain[2] [rə'frein] *vi* (*formal: with* **from**) not to do (something): *You are asked to refrain from smoking/from (drinking) alcohol.*

refresh [rə'freʃ] *vt* to give new strength and energy to (a person *etc*); to make (a person *etc*) feel less hot, tired *etc, eg* after or during a period of hard work: *This glass of cool lemonade will refresh you; When I'm studying, I refresh myself from time to time with a cup of coffee.* – *See also* **refresh someone's memory** *below.*

re'freshing *adj* **1** giving new strength and energy to (a person *etc*); making (a person) feel less hot, tired *etc*: *a refreshing drink; A glass of cold water is very refreshing.* **2** particularly pleasing because different from normal: *For a politician, his speeches show a refreshing lack of pompousness; It is refreshing to hear such an honest speech.*

re'freshingly *adv.*

re'freshments *n pl* food and drink served *eg* at a meeting: *Light refreshments are available in the other room.*

re'fresher course *nc* a course of study or training intended to increase or bring up to date a person's knowledge of or skill in a subject he already knows: *The education department decided to send all teachers on a refresher course every seven years.*

refresh someone's memory to think about, read *etc* the facts or details (of something) again so that they are clear in one's mind: *I'd better refresh my memory/Let me refresh your memory about the details of our plans in case anyone asks any awkward questions.*

refrigerator [rə'fridʒəreitə] *nc* (*Brit inf also* **fridge** [fridʒ]: *Amer also* **'icebox**) a machine which keeps food cold and so prevents it from going bad: *Butter and milk should be kept in the refrigerator.*

re'frigerate *vt* (*formal*) to keep (food) cold to prevent it from going bad: *In hot weather, milk must be refrigerated; Butchers refrigerate meat.*

reˌ**frige'ration** *nu.*

refuel [ri:'fjuəl] – *pt, ptp* **re'fuelled**, (*Amer also*) **re'fueled** – **1** *vt* to supply (an aeroplane *etc*) with more fuel: *The plane has to be refuelled every thousand miles.* **2** *vi* to take on more fuel: *The plane stopped to refuel.*

refuge ['refju:dʒ] *ncu* (*formal*) (a place which gives) shelter or protection from danger, trouble *etc*: *The outlaw sought refuge in the church; Monasteries were refuges for outlaws.*

ˌ**refu'gee** *nc* a person who seeks shelter (*esp* from religious or political persecution) in another country: *During the war, many refugees fled to Britain;* (*attrib*) *a refugee camp.*

refund [ri'fʌnd] *vt* (*formal*) to pay back: *When the concert was cancelled, the people who had bought tickets had their money refunded.* – ['ri:fʌnd] *nc* the paying back of money: *They demanded a refund.*

refuse[1] [rə'fju:z] **1** *vti* not to do what one has been asked, told or expected to do: *He refused to help me; She refused to believe what I said; When I asked him to leave, he refused.* **2** *vt* not to accept (something): *He refused my offer of help; They refused our invitation; She refused the money.* **3** *vt* (*formal*) not to give (permission *etc*): *I was* *refused admittance to the meeting; They refused permission to go ahead with the project.*

re'fusal *ncu*: *I was surprised at his refusal to help me; When we asked for her permission, we were met with/by a blunt refusal; When we sent out the wedding invitations, we had several refusals; Refusal to do as she asks will make her very angry.*

first refusal the opportunity to buy, accept *etc* or refuse (something) before it is offered, given, sold *etc* to someone else: *If you ever decide to sell your caravan, will you give me (the) first refusal?; Can I have first refusal on your house when you sell it?*

refuse[2] ['refju:s] *nu* (*formal*: *esp Brit*) rubbish; waste material from *eg* a kitchen: *What do you do with the garden refuse?*

'refuse collector *nc* (*formal*) a dustman.

refute [rə'fju:t] *vt* (*very formal*) to prove that (a person, statement *etc*) is wrong: *You can easily refute his argument.* **re'futable** *adj.* **ˌrefu'tation** [refju-] *ncu.*

See also **irrefutable**.

regain [ri'gein] *vt* **1** to get (something) back again: *The champion was beaten in January but regained the title in March; He was obviously very shocked but he soon regained his composure* (= became calm again). **2** (*formal*) to get back to (a place): *The swimmer was swept out to sea, but managed to regain the shore.*

regal ['ri:gəl] *adj* (*formal*) of, like, or suitable for, a king or queen: *regal splendour; She was looking positively regal.* **'regally** *adv.*

See also **royal**.

regale [ri'geil] (*formal or facet*) *vt* **1** (*with* **with**) to entertain or amuse (someone) by one's conversation *etc*: *He regaled his friends with stories about his adventures in France.* **2** (*with* **with** *or* **on**) to entertain (a person) with food and drink: *They were regaled with a great feast/regaled on fine food.*

regalia [rə'geiliə] *nu or n pl* (*formal*) **1** objects (*eg* the crown and sceptre) which are a sign of royalty, used *eg* at a coronation. **2** any ornaments, ceremonial clothes *etc* which are worn as a sign of a person's importance or authority: *When the Queen came to the city, she was met by the mayor dressed in (his) full regalia; What does his regalia consist of?*

regard [rə'ga:d] *vt* (not used with **is, was** *etc* and **-ing** (*defs 1-3*)) **1** (*with* **as**) to consider (someone or something) to be (something): *He is regarded as a nuisance by his neighbours; I regard his conduct as (being) totally unacceptable.* **2** (*formal*: *often in passive*) to think of (something or someone) as being very good, important *etc*; to respect (someone): *He is very highly regarded by his friends.* **3** (*formal*: *with* **with**) to have a good, bad *etc* opinion (about someone or something): *I regard him with horror; He regards his wife's behaviour with amusement; He regards their new plans with some misgiving* (= doubt). **4** (*formal or facet*) to look at (someone or something): *He regarded me quizzically over the top of his glasses.* **5** (*very formal*) to pay attention to (advice *etc*): *You should regard his warnings/advice.* – *nu* **1** (*formal*) thought; attention: *He ran into the burning house, without regard for his safety.* **2** sympathy; care; consideration: *He shows no regard for other people.* **3** (*formal*) the *usu* good opinion that people have (of a person); respect: *I hold him in high regard.* – *See also* **regards** *below.*

re'garding *prep* (*more formal than* **about**) about; concerning: *Have you any suggestions regarding this project?*

re'gardless *adv* (*inf*) not thinking or caring about costs, problems, dangers *etc*: *There may be difficulties but I shall carry on* (= continue) *regardless.* – *See also* **regardless of** *below.*

re'gards *n pl* greetings; good wishes: *Give my regards to your mother; He sent her his regards.*

as regards (*formal*) as far as (something) is concerned; turning our attention to (something): *That answers your first question. As regards your second question, I feel that it is ridiculous.*

re'gardless of (*formal*) without thinking or caring about (something); in spite of (something): *I will carry out my plan, regardless of the consequences.*

with re'gard to (*formal*) about; concerning: *I have no complaints with regard to his work; That answers your first question. With regard to your second question, I feel that it needs no answer.*

See also **disregard**.

regatta [rə'gatə] *nc* a meeting for yacht or (*usu* small) boat races.

regent ['ri:dʒənt] *nc* a person who governs in place of a king or queen: *The prince was only two years old when the king died, so his uncle was appointed regent.*

'regency **1** *nu* the position of a regent. **2** *ncu* (the period of) rule by a regent: *During his regency, there was a war with Spain.*

régime, regime [rei'ʒi:m] *nc* (*formal or facet*) a (system of) government: *a Communist régime; Under the new régime in our office, no-one is allowed to leave early.*

regimen ['redʒimən] *nc* (*very formal*) a set of rules about diet, exercise *etc* which must be followed for the sake of one's health: *For his health's sake the doctor has put him on a very strict regimen.*

regiment ['redʒimənt] *nc* a body of soldiers commanded by a colonel: *He is in command of one of the Highland regiments.* – [-ment] *vt* (*often derog*) to organize or control (people) very strictly, *usu* too strictly: *Children in schools are no longer regimented as they used to be; She tries to regiment us into doing exactly as she says.*

ˌregi'mental [-'men-] *adj* (*usu attrib*) of a regiment: *They have a dog as the regimental lucky mascot; He is regimental sergeant-major.*

ˌregimen'tation *nu* (*derog*) very strict, *usu* too strict, control: *I dislike the regimentation at that school.*

region ['ri:dʒən] *nc* **1** a part of a country, the world *etc*: *The Midlands is a region of England that I know very well.* **2** the larger of the two administrative units of local government in Scotland: *(the) Lothian Region; Scotland is divided into several regions.* – *See also* **in the region of** *below.*

'regional *adj* (*usu attrib*) of a region: *a regional council.* **'regionally** *adv.*

in the 'region of (*formal*) near(ly): *I have a pain in the region of my heart; The cost of the new building will be somewhere in the region of £50 000.*

See also **county, district**.

register ['redʒistə] *nc* **1** (a book containing) a written list, record *etc* (of events, people *etc*): *a school attendance register; a register of births, marriages and deaths.* **2** the distance between the highest and lowest notes of a person's voice, an instrument *etc*: *What is the register of a trumpet?* **3** in linguistics, a style of speech (suitable for, and used in, a particular situation): *a formal register;*

It is important to mark registers for learners of a language; (*attrib*) *a register label.* – **1** *vt* to write (something) or cause (something) to be written in a register: *to register the birth of a baby.* **2** *vi* to write one's name, or have one's name written, in a register *etc* (*eg* at a hotel): *In many countries, foreigners have to register with the police*; *to register as a voter.* **3** *vt* to obtain a certificate (after paying a sum of money) showing that (a letter, parcel *etc*) has been posted: *If you register this parcel, you will receive compensation* (= a sum of money) *if it is damaged or lost.* **4** *vt* (of an instrument, dial *etc*) to show (a figure, amount *etc*): *The thermometer registered minus five* (*degrees*) *last night.* **5** *vt* (*formal*) to express or state (a complaint *etc*): *You must register your complaint with the manager.* **6** *vt* (*formal*) (of a person, his face *etc*) to show (one's feelings *etc*): *His face registered surprise.* **7** *vti* (*inf*: *sometimes with* **with**) to be realized (by someone): *I saw the smoke but somehow it didn't register* (*with me*) *that the house was on fire.* **ˌregiˈstration** *ncu.*

ˈregistered *adj* (*usu attrib*): *a registered letter*; *registered post/mail.*

ˌregiˈstrar [-ˈstraː] *nc* **1** a person whose duty it is to keep a register (*esp* of births, marriages and deaths). **2** (*Brit*) one of the grades of hospital doctors: *The registrar had to send for the senior registrar and the consultant because the patient was so ill.*

ˈregistry *nc* an office or place where registers are kept.

ˈregister office/ˈregistry office an office where records of births, marriages *etc* are kept and where marriages may be performed: *They were not married in church but in the local registry office.*

ˌregiˈstration number (*also* **ˈlicence number**) the letters and numbers which a car, bus *etc* has on a plate at the front and rear: *Did you make a note of the registration number of the car which killed the old lady?*

See also **cash register** *under* **cash**.

regress [riˈgres] *vi* (*formal*) to go back to a less perfect, less desirable, less advanced *etc* state or condition: *He was getting better when he went to the mental hospital but he is regressing now.* **reˈgression** *nu.*

regret [rəˈgret] – *pt, ptp* **reˈgretted** – *vt* (*more formal than* **be sorry**) to be sorry about (something): *I regret my foolish behaviour*; *I regret that I missed the concert*; *I regret missing the concert*; *I regret to have to do this, but I have no choice*; (*formal*) *I regret to inform you that your application for the job was unsuccessful.* – *ncu* a feeling of sorrow *eg* because a person has not done something which he wishes he had done, or because he has done something that he wishes he had not: *I have no regrets/I feel no regret about what I did*; *It was with deep regret that I heard the news of his death.*

reˈgretful *adj* feeling regret: *She gave a regretful smile*; *I feel rather regretful that the affair ended like that.*

reˈgretfully *adv* with regret: *Regretfully, we have had to turn down your offer.*

reˈgrettable *adj* (*formal*) that should be regretted: *This is a most regrettable mistake*; *It is most regrettable that he behaved like that.* **reˈgrettably** *adv.*

regular [ˈregjulə] *adj* **1** (*attrib*) usual; normal: *This isn't his regular route to town*; *Saturday is his regular day for shopping*; *That isn't our regular postman, is it?* **2** occurring, acting *etc* with equal amounts of space, time *etc* between: *They placed guards at regular intervals round the camp*; *a regular heart-beat*; *Is his pulse regular?*; *Are his bowel movements regular?*; *Her periods* (= menstruation) *are not very regular.* **3** (*usu attrib*) involving doing the same things at the same time each day *etc*: *a man of regular habits*; *He keeps* (= goes to bed and gets up at) *regular hours.* **4** (*usu attrib*) frequent: *He's a regular visitor.* **5** (*usu attrib*) permanent; lasting for a long time: *He's looking for regular work/a regular job.* **6** (*formal*) accepted as right or correct: *I don't think your method of dealing with complaints is quite regular.* **7** (*gram*) (of a noun, verb *etc*) following one of the usual grammatical patterns of the language: *'Walk' is a regular verb, but 'go' is an irregular verb.* **8** the same on both or all sides or parts: *a girl with regular features*; *A square is a regular figure*; *Her features are small and regular.* **9** (*Brit inf*) very much of (something): *He's a regular scoundrel*; *That child is a regular little monster.* **10** having bowel movements at suitably frequent intervals: *A little bran every day will help to keep you regular.* **11** of ordinary size: *I don't want the large size of packet – just give me the regular one.* – *nc* **1** a soldier in the regular army. **2** (*inf*) a regular customer (*eg* at a bar): *The barman gave free drinks to the regulars at Christmas.*

ˌreguˈlarity [-ˈla-] *nu* the state of being regular, or done, said *etc* regularly: *He makes the same stupid suggestions with great regularity.*

ˈregularize, -ise *vt* (*formal*) to make lawful or correct (something which has not been so up to that time): *They have decided to regularize their living together by getting married.* **ˌregulariˈzation, -s-** *nu.*

ˈregularly *adv* **1** at regular times, places *etc*: *His heart was beating regularly.* **2** frequently: *He comes here fairly regularly.*

ˈregulate [-leit] *vt* **1** (*formal*) to control (a person, thing *etc*), often by means of rules: *We must regulate our spending*; *Traffic lights are used to regulate traffic.* **2** to adjust (a piece of machinery *etc*) so that it works at a certain rate, produces a certain amount of something *etc*: *This radiator can be regulated* (= adjusted to give a certain amount of heat) *by this small dial at the side*; *Can you regulate this watch so that it keeps time accurately?*

ˌreguˈlation **1** *nc* a rule or instruction: *There are certain regulations laid down as to how this job should be done, and these must be obeyed*; (*attrib*) *Please use envelopes of the regulation size.* **2** *nu* (*formal*) the act of regulating or state of being regulated: *the regulation of a piece of machinery.*

ˈregulator [-lei-] *nc* a thing that regulates (a piece of machinery *etc*): *There is a regulator on this radiator.*

the regular army the part of the armed forces of a country made up of regular soldiers.

regular soldier a professional full-time soldier.

See also **irregular**.

regurgitate [riˈgəːdʒiteit] *vti* (*formal*) to bring back (food) into the mouth after it has been swallowed: *He has indigestion – he keeps regurgitating* (*food*); *The baby has regurgitated all of its food.* **reˌgurgiˈtation** *nu.*

rehabilitate [riːəˈbiliteit] *vt* (*formal*) to bring (a criminal or someone who has been ill) back to a normal life, normal standards of behaviour *etc* by treatment or training: *Many people feel that attempts should be made to rehabilitate criminals instead of putting them in prison; Those doctors tried to rehabilitate soldiers who had limbs amputated during the war.*

'reha,bili'tation *nu*: *the rehabilitation of criminals/polio victims*; (*attrib*) *a rehabilitation centre.*

rehash ['ri:haʃ] *nc* (*inf derog*) a speech, book *etc* which uses subject matter which has been used before: *Everything he publishes now is simply a rehash of what he wrote ten years ago.* – *vt* (*inf derog*) to use (subject matter which has been used before) in a speech, book *etc*: *That student has just rehashed the lecture I gave yesterday.*

rehearse [rə'hə:s] **1** *vti* to practise (a play, piece of music *etc*) before performing it in front of an audience: *You must rehearse the love scene again.* **2** *vt* (*very formal*) to tell (of), list, or describe (a series of facts, events *etc*): *He rehearsed all the events of the day.*

re'hearsal *ncu*: *This opera will need a lot of rehearsal; There is a rehearsal tonight.*

dress rehearsal *nc* a final rehearsal (of a play, opera *etc*) in which the actors or singers wear their costumes *etc*: *I hope the first performance will be better than the dress rehearsal.*

rehouse [ri:'hauz] *vt* (*formal*) to provide (a person) with a new or different house: *Conditions in the flats were so bad that the tenants demanded to be rehoused.*

reign [rein] *nc* the time during which a king or queen rules: *in the reign of Queen Victoria*; (*fig*) *Many revolutions develop into nothing better than a reign of terror.* – *vi* **1** (*often with* **over**) to rule, as a king or queen: *The king reigned (over his people) for forty years.* **2** (*fig formal*) to be present or exist: *Silence reigned at last.*

reimburse [ri:im'bə:s] *vt* (*formal*: *often with* **for**) to pay (a person) an amount of money to cover expenses, losses *etc*: *Your train fare will be reimbursed; You will be reimbursed (for) the cost of your journey.* **,reim'bursement** *ncu.*

rein [rein] *nc* (*usu in pl*) one of two straps attached to a bridle for guiding a horse: *You must hold the reins tightly or the horse will run away; Because of a broken rein the jockey was unable to control the horse.*

reins *n pl* **1** a set of straps for keeping a young child close to oneself *eg* when walking in the street: *The mother had to put reins on the toddler – otherwise he would have run on to the road.* **2** (*fig formal*) (a means of) control or government: *The President is the Head of State, but who actually holds the reins of power?; I've been asked to take the reins while the manager is on holiday.*

give (free) rein to (something) (*formal*) to allow (oneself, one's mind *etc*) great freedom to act, think *etc* as one pleases: *In writing that novel she gave free rein to her imagination.*

keep a tight rein on (a person, thing *etc***)** (*formal*) to keep strict control of (a person, thing *etc*): *He tries to keep a tight rein on his daughter; I have to keep a tight rein on my wife's spending.*

rein in *vi, vt sep* to stop or restrain (a horse *etc*) by pulling on its reins: *He reined in the horse; He reined it in; He reined in as he approached the busy road.*

reincarnation [ri:inka:'neiʃən] (*formal*) **1** *nu* the rebirth of the soul in another body after death: *Do you believe in reincarnation?* **2** *nc* an example of this: *My uncle claims to be a reincarnation of Julius Caesar.*

reindeer ['reindiə] – *pl* **'reindeer** – *nc* a kind of large deer found in Northern Europe, Asia and America: *a herd of reindeer; Do you eat reindeer?*

reinforce [ri:in'fo:s] *vt* (*formal*) to make (something) stronger, by adding men, material *etc* to it: *I've reinforced the elbows of this jacket with leather patches; The army will need to be reinforced.*

,rein'forcement *nu*: *the reinforcement of the elbows of this jacket.*

,rein'forcements *n pl* men added to an army *etc* in order to strengthen it: *As the enemy attacks increased, the general called for reinforcements.*

reinstate [ri:in'steit] *vt* (*formal*: *often with* **in**) to put (a person) back in a position (*eg* of power, importance) he once had: *The manager was dismissed but was later reinstated (in his job).* **,rein'statement** *nu.*

reiterate [ri:'itəreit] *vt* (*very formal*) to repeat (something) *usu* several times: *He reiterated his remarks on the economic crisis in every speech he made.*

re,ite'ration *ncu* (*formal*): *This is just a reiteration of what he said last week; He tried to emphasize his point by constant reiteration.*

reject [rə'dʒekt] *vt* to refuse to accept: *She rejected his offer of help; He asked her to marry him, but she rejected him; This machine accepts 10 pence pieces but rejects foreign coins; His application was rejected.* – ['ri:dʒekt] *nc* a person, thing *etc* which is rejected because he/it is faulty, wrong or not good enough: *This pipe is cheap because it's a reject.*

re'jection [-ʃən] *ncu*: *He was upset by her rejection of his offer; the rejection of my application; He keeps applying for jobs but constant rejections have discouraged him.*

rejoice [rə'dʒois] *vi* (*formal*) to feel or show great happiness: *They rejoiced at/over the news of the victory.*

re'joicing *ncu* (*formal*: *often in pl*) the act of feeling or showing great joy; celebrations: *There was great rejoicing at the news of the victory; The rejoicings over the birth of the baby lasted well into the night.*

rejoinder [rə'dʒoində] *nc* (*formal*) an answer or remark, *esp* one made in reply to something stated by someone else *eg* in an argument: *He is very good at making witty rejoinders.*

re'join *vti* (*formal*) to say (something) as a rejoinder: *'You are not always right,' she rejoined.*

rejuvenate [rə'dʒu:vəneit] *vt* (*formal or facet*) to make (a person) (feel) young again: *I find that a game of golf rejuvenates me after a week's work; Marrying a young wife seems to have rejuvenated him.* **re,juve'nation** *nu.*

relapse [rə'laps] *vi* (*formal*) to return to a former bad or undesirable state (*eg* ill health, bad habits): *He swore that he would never steal again, but soon relapsed into a life of crime.* – *nc* (*formal or tech*) a falling back or return to a former bad or undesirable state, *esp* ill health: *The patient seemed to be recovering but suddenly had/suffered a relapse.*

relate [rə'leit] **1** *vt* (*more formal than* **tell**) to tell (a story *etc*): *He related all that had happened to him.* **2** *vt* (*formal*: *with* **to** *or* **with**) to show the connection or relationship that exists between (facts, events *etc*): *In his biography he relates the queen's love of power to the fact that she had never married.* **3** *vi* (*formal*: *with* **to** *or* **with**) to have a connection or relationship: *Does crime relate to poverty?*; *Her wicked behaviour relates to her unhappy childhood.* **4** *vi* (*with* **to**) to be about or concerned with: *Have you any information relating to the effect of penicillin on mice?*

re'lated *adj* (*neg* **un-**: *often with* **to**) **1** belonging to the same family (as): *I'm related to the Prime Minister*; *The Prime Minister and I are related.* **2** connected: *other related topics.*

re'lation *nc* **1** a person who belongs to the same family as another person, either by birth or because of marriage: *When I married my wife, all her relations became my relations by marriage.* **2** (*with* **between**) a relationship (between facts, events *etc*): *I can find no relation between crime and poverty.*

re'lations *n pl* the contact, communications *etc* which exist between people, countries *etc*: *They established friendly/diplomatic relations with their former enemies.*

re'lationship 1 *nc* the friendship, contact, communications *etc* which exist between people, countries *etc*: *He finds it very difficult to form lasting relationships with girls.* **2** *nc* the fact that, or the way in which, facts, events *etc* are connected: *Is there any relationship between crime and poverty?*; *What is the relationship of crime to poverty?* **3** *nu* the state of being related by birth or because of marriage.

relative ['relətiv] *nc* a relation (*def 1*): *All his relatives attended the funeral.* – *adj* **1** (*formal*) compared with something else or each other: *the relative speeds of a car and a train*; *She is living in relative poverty* (= compared to other people); *Relative to our house, his house is a palace.* **2** (*very formal*: *with* **to**) which relates to (something): *Have you any information relative to the effect of penicillin on mice?*

relatively ['relətivli] *adv* when compared to someone or something else: *He seems relatively happy now*; *This is relatively unimportant*; *Relatively speaking this is a fairly unimportant problem.*

relative pronoun *nc* a pronoun which relates a clause to a preceding noun: *the man whose son we just met*; *the man that we met*; *the place where we stayed last year*; *the girl who sang the song.*

relative clause *nc* a clause which contains or could contain a relative pronoun: *the girl who sang the song*; *the man we met yesterday.*

in re'lation to (*formal*) about; concerning: *In relation to the complaint you have made there is nothing we can do to improve the quality of these goods.*

with re'lation to (*formal*) about; concerning: *We have received some reports with relation to the new sales campaign.*

See also **public relations (officer)** *under* **public**.

relax [rə'laks] *vti* **1** to make or become less tense or worried; to rest (someone or something) completely: *The doctor told him that he must relax*; *He gave him a drug to make him relax*; *Relax, will you!* (= Stop worrying!); (*formal*) *That drug will relax your muscles.* **2** to make or become less strict or severe: *The rules were relaxed because of the Queen's visit*; (*formal*) *The strict army discipline tends to relax a bit before Christmas.*

ˌrelax'ation [ri:lak-] *ncu*: *I play golf for relaxation*; *Golf is one of my favourite relaxations.*

re'laxing *adj* (of a climate) making people less energetic than usual.

relax one's grip/hold (on something) to hold (something) less tightly: *I relaxed my grip for a second and the boat dragged the rope out of my hand.*

relay [ri'lei] – *pt, ptp* **re'layed** – *vt* (*formal*) to receive and pass on (news, a message, a television programme *etc*): *Could you relay the news of the poet's death?* – ['ri:lei] **1** *ncu* (the sending out of) a radio, television *etc* signal or programme which has been received (from another place). **2** *nc* a relay race: *The British team won the relay*; (*attrib*) *a relay team.* **3** *nc* a set of people *etc* who (come and) replace others who are doing some job, task *etc*: *A relay of firemen tried to put out the blazing fire.* – *See also* **in relays** *below.*

'relay race *nc* a race between teams of runners, swimmers *etc*, in which the members of the team run, swim *etc* one after another, each covering one part of the total distance to be run, swum *etc.*

in 'relays in groups which perform (some job, task *etc*) one after another, one group starting when another group stops: *During the flood, firemen and policemen worked in relays to rescue people who were trapped.*

release [rə'li:s] *vt* **1** to set (a prisoner *etc*) free; to allow (a prisoner *etc*) to leave: *He was released from prison yesterday*; (*fig formal*) *I am willing to release him from his obligations to me.* **2** (*more formal than* **let go**) to stop holding *etc* (something); to allow (something) to move, fall *etc*: *He released* (*his hold on*) *the rope.* **3** to move (a catch, brake *etc*) which prevents something else from moving, operating *etc*: *He released the safety-catch on his gun/the handbrake of his car.* **4** to make (news *etc*) known publicly; to allow (news *etc*) to be made known publicly: *News has just been released of an explosion in a chemical factory.* **5** to offer (a film, record *etc*) to the general public: *Their latest record will be released next week.* **6** to stop (a person *etc*) suffering from (something unpleasant): *The patient asked the doctor to give him something that would release him from his pain.* – **1** *ncu* the act of releasing or being released: *After his release, the prisoner returned to his home town*; *the release of the safety-catch*; *the release of a film*; (*attrib*) *the release catch*; *a release from prison.* **2** *nc* something that is released: *This record is their latest release*; *The Government issued a press release* (= a statement giving information about something, sent or given to newspapers, reporters *etc*). **3** *nc* an order, document *etc* allowing (a prisoner *etc*) to be released: *The prime minister signed her release.*

relegate ['religeit] *vt* **1** (*formal*: *often with* **to**) to put (someone) down (to a lower grade, position, group *etc*): *The local football team has been relegated* (*to the Second Division*). **2** (*very formal*) to leave or give (a job, task *etc*) to someone else to do: *He has relegated the task of dismissing her to me.*

ˌrele'gation *nu.*

relent [rə'lent] *vi* to become less severe or unkind; to agree (to allow someone) to do something after refusing at first: *At first she wouldn't let them go to the cinema, but in the end she relented.*

re'lentless *adj* (*formal*) without pity; not allowing anything to keep one from what one is doing or trying to do: *The police fight a relentless battle against crime*; *The police force are relentless in their fight against crime.* **re'lentlessly** *adv.* **re'lentlessness** *nu.*

relevant ['reləvənt] *adj* (*often with* **to**) connected with, or saying something important about, what is being spoken about or discussed: *I don't think* *his remarks are relevant (to our discussion); Any relevant information should be given to the police.* **'relevance** *nu.*

See also **irrelevant.**

reliable, reliance *etc see* **rely**.

relic ['relik] *nc (formal)* **1** something left from a past time: *relics of an ancient civilization; (facet) That old lady is a relic of Victorian times.* **2** *(esp hist: often in pl)* something connected with, *esp* the bones of, a dead person *(esp* a saint): *He claimed to be selling relics of Christ.*

relief [rə'li:f] **1** *nu* a lessening or stopping of pain, worry, boredom *etc*: *When one has a headache, an aspirin often brings/gives relief; He gave a sigh of relief; It was a great relief to find nothing had been stolen.* **2** *nu* help *(eg* food) given to people in need of it: *famine relief; (attrib) A relief fund has been set up to send supplies to the refugees.* **3** *nc (inf)* a person who takes over some job or task from another person, *usu* after a given period of time: *The bus-driver was waiting for his relief; (attrib) a relief driver.* **4** *nu (formal)* the act of freeing (a town *etc)* from siege: *the relief of Mafeking; (attrib) the relief forces.* **5** *nu (tech)* a way of carving *etc* in which the design is raised above the level of its background: *a carving in relief.*

re'lieve [-v] **1** *vt* to lessen or stop (a person's pain, worry, boredom *etc*): *To relieve his toothache, he rubbed whisky on his gums; The doctor gave him some drugs to relieve the pain; This will help to relieve the hardship of the refugees.* **2** *vt* to take over (a job or task) from someone: *You stand guard first, and I'll relieve you in two hours.* **3** *v refl (euph)* to urinate: *The old lady was upset when she saw him relieving himself in the street.* **4** *vt (formal: with* **of**: *usu in passive)* to dismiss (a person) from his job or position: *He was relieved of his post/duties.* **5** *vt (formal: with* **of**) to take (something) from someone: *May I relieve you of that heavy case?; (facet) The thief relieved several people of their wallets and purses.* **6** *vt (formal)* to come to the help of (a town *etc* which is under siege or attack).

re'lieved *adj* no longer anxious or worried: *I was relieved to hear you had arrived safely.*

relieve one's feelings to cry, shout, swear *etc* in order to make oneself feel better when one feels angry, upset *etc*: *He relieved his feelings by banging the door; She relieved her feelings by throwing plates at her husband.*

religion [rə'lidʒən] **1** *nu* a belief in, or the worship of, a god or gods. **2** *nc* a particular system of belief or worship: *Christianity and Islam are two different religions; (fig) Football is his religion.*

re'ligious *adj* **1** *(attrib)* of religion: *religious education.* **2** following the rules, forms of worship *etc* of a religion: *a religious man; He is very religious.* **3** *(formal)* taking great care; doing things as well as possible: *He was religious in his efforts; He made religious attempts to get in touch with her.* **re'ligiousness** *nu.*

re'ligiously *adv* regularly; with great care: *He religiously saves the metal caps from milk bottles.*

See also **irreligious**.

relinquish [rə'liŋkwiʃ] *vt (formal)* to give up (something): *The dictator was forced to relinquish control of the country.*

relish ['reliʃ] *vt* **1** *(usu in neg)* to enjoy; to like (the thought of) doing something: *I don't relish having to tell him that I've crashed his car.* – **1** *nu* pleasure; enjoyment: *He ate the food with great relish; I have no relish for playing golf.* **2** *ncu* (something, *eg* a sauce or pickles, which is added to food in order to give it more) flavour: *This sauce will add relish to these sandwiches; a variety of relishes.*

reluctant [rə'lʌktənt] *adj* unwilling: *I am reluctant to leave this job but another firm has offered me a higher salary; He was reluctant to accept the medal for his bravery; the reluctant receiver of a medal for bravery.* **re'luctantly** *adv.*

re'luctance *nu*: *I don't understand his reluctance to go.*

rely [rə'lai]: **rely on**/*(formal)* **upon** *vt fus* **1** to depend on or need (something or someone): *The people on the island relied on the supplies that were brought from the mainland.* **2** to trust (someone) to do something; to be certain that (something will happen): *We can't rely on him coming in time; He can be relied on.*

re'liable [-'lai-] *adj (neg* **un-**) able to be trusted: *Is he reliable?; Is this information reliable?; I received the information from a reliable source.*

re,lia'bility *nu.*

re'liably [-'lai-] *adv (formal)* from a reliable source; by a reliable person: *I am reliably informed that the Prime Minister is going to resign.*

re'liance [-'lai-] *nu (with* **on**/*(formal)* **upon**) the act or state of relying on (a person, thing *etc*): *a country's reliance on aid from other countries; a child's reliance on its mother.* **re'liant** *adj.*

See also **self-reliant**.

remain [rə'mein] *vi* **1** (not used with **is, was** *etc* and **-ing**: *more formal than* **be left**) to be left when (something) has been lost, taken away *etc*: *Only two tins of soup remained; Very little remained of the cinema after the fire; A great many things still remain to be done.* **2** *(more formal than* **stay**) to stay; not to leave: *I shall remain here.* **3** (not *usu* used with **is, was** *etc* and **-ing**: *more formal than* **be still**) to be still (the same); to continue to be (something): *The problem remains unsolved; Despite all attempts to educate them, these tribesmen remain head-hunters.*

re'mainder [-də] *nc (pl rare, usu only in mathematics)* the amount or number of (people, things *etc*) that is left when the rest has/have gone, been taken away *etc*: *I've corrected most of the essays – the remainder will get done tomorrow.*

re'mains *n pl* **1** what is left after part (of something) has been taken away, eaten, destroyed *etc*: *the remains of a meal.* **2** *(euph)* a dead body: *We will bury the/his remains this afternoon.*

See also **remnant, rest**[2].

remake ['ri:meik] *nc* something which is made again: *a remake of an old film.* – [ri:'meik] *vt* to make *(eg* a film) again.

remand [rə'ma:nd] *vt (formal)* to send (a person who has been accused of a crime) back to prison until more evidence can be collected: *The judge has remanded him; He has been remanded for six months.*

re'mand home *nc* a place to which a judge may send a child or young person who has broken the law, either on remand or as punishment.

on re'mand having been remanded.

remark [rə'ma:k] *nc* a comment; something said: *The chairman made a few remarks, then introduced the speaker; I wish he would stop passing remarks* (= making rude comments) *about me.* – *vti* to say; to comment (on something): *'It will soon be summer,' he remarked; He remarked that it would soon be summer; He remarked on the similarity of their replies.*

re'markable *adj* (*neg* **un-**) unusual; worth mentioning; extraordinary: *What a remarkable coincidence!*; *He really is a remarkable man*; *It is quite remarkable how alike the two children are.*
re'markably *adv*: *Their replies were remarkably similar.*
worthy of remark (*formal*) worth noticing or mentioning.

remedy ['remədi] *nc* (*more formal than* **cure**) a cure for an illness or something bad: *My mother had a home-made remedy for toothache*; (*fig*) *One remedy for laziness is a good beating.* – *vt* (*formal*) to put (something) right; to correct (a fault *etc*): *These mistakes can be remedied.*
remedial [rə'mi:diəl] *adj* (*formal*: *usu attrib*) able to, or intended to, put (something) right; to correct or cure (something): *She teaches remedial reading*; *remedial education* (= special education for children who have great difficulty with reading, writing, arithmetic *etc*).

remember [ri'membə] *vt* (not *usu* used with **is, was** *etc* and **-ing** (*defs, 1, 3*)) **1** to keep (a person, fact *etc*) in the mind, or to bring (a person, fact *etc*) back into the mind after forgetting for a time: *I remember you – we met three years ago*; *I remember hearing Churchill speak at a meeting in the town*; *Remember to meet me tonight*; *Do you remember how we used to fish for tadpoles?*; *I don't remember where I hid it.* **2** (*formal*) to reward or make a present to (a person): *He remembered her in his will.* **3** (*formal*: *with* **to**) to pass (a person's) good wishes (to someone): *Remember me to your parents.*
re'membrance (*formal*) **1** *nu* the act of remembering or reminding: *a statue erected in remembrance of the dead.* **2** *nc* something which reminds (a person) of something or someone: *This brooch is a remembrance of my grandmother*; *He gave remembrances to all his employees.*
See also **memory, remind, reminiscent**.

remind [rə'maind] *vt* **1** (*with* **to** *or* **of**) to tell (someone) that there is something he or she ought to do, remember *etc*: *Remind me to post that letter*; *She reminded me of my promise.* **2** (*with* **of**) to make (someone) think about (a person, thing *etc*) (*usu* because of some similarity to the person, thing *etc*): *She reminds me of her sister*; *Her eyes remind me of stars.*
re'minder *nc* something that reminds (a person) to do something: *If this bill isn't paid by the end of the month, send Mr Smith a reminder* (= a letter which reminds him to pay the bill).
See also **remember**.

reminiscent [remə'nisnt] *adj* **1** (*pred*: *with* **of**) making (a person) think about (a person, place *etc*) (*usu* because of some similarity to the person, place *etc*); having a similarity to (a person, place *etc*): *That artist's style is reminiscent of van Gogh*; *These buildings are reminiscent of barns.* **2** thinking about past events *etc*: *When he drinks a lot, he becomes reminiscent*; *in a reminiscent mood.*
ˌremi'nisce *vi* (*often with* **about**) to think and talk about things remembered from the past: *reminiscing about one's childhood*; *When he gets drunk he reminisces.*
ˌremi'niscence *ncu*: *She bored everyone with her reminiscences of childhood.*

remiss [rə'mis] *adj* (*formal*: *pred*: *usu with* **in** *or* **of**) careless: *It was remiss of me to forget your birthday*; *You have been remiss in your duties.*

remission *see* **remit**.

remit [rə'mit] – *pt, ptp* **re'mitted** – *vt* (*very formal*) **1** to send (money) *usu* in payment for something: *Please remit payment as soon as possible.* **2** to send (a report, problem *etc*) to someone for discussion or a decision: *You will have to remit this problem to a higher authority.* **3** (*legal*) to cancel (a debt, punishment, fee *etc*): *The prisoner's sentence was remitted.*
re'mission [-ʃən] **1** *ncu* (of a disease *etc*) a lessening in force or effect: *There has been some remission of the cancer*; *Remissions in that form of cancer are not unknown.* **2** *ncu* a shortening (of a person's) prison sentence: *The remission of the murderer's sentence shocked everyone*; *Remissions for murderers are unpopular.* **3** *nu* (*very formal*) the act of remitting (something).
re'mittance (*formal*) **1** *nu* the sending (of money) *usu* in payment for something: *the remittance of the correct sum of money.* **2** *nc* the money sent: *We received your remittance.*
See also **unremitting**.

remnant ['remnənt] *nc* a small piece or amount (of something) or a small number (of things) left over from a larger piece, amount or number: *The shop is selling remnants of cloth at half price*; *the remnant of the army.*

remonstrate ['remənstreit, (*Amer*) ri'monstreit] *vt* (*formal*: *with* **with** *and* **about**) to make a protest: *I remonstrated with him about his treatment of his friend.* **remonstrance** [ri'monstrəns] *nc.*

remorse [rə'mo:s] *nu* (*formal*) regret about something wrong or bad which one has done: *He was filled with remorse.*
re'morseful *adj* (*formal*) feeling remorse: *She felt remorseful about her cruel treatment of her father*; *a remorseful remark.* **re'morsefully** *adv.*
re'morseless *adj* (*formal*) cruel; without pity: *He was remorseless in his treatment of his prisoners*; *a remorseless tyrant.* **re'morselessly** *adv.*

remote [rə'mout] *adj* **1** (*often with* **from**) far away in time or place; far from any (other) village, town *etc*: *They live in a remote village in the North of Scotland*; *a farmhouse remote from civilization.* **2** not closely related: *a remote cousin*; *His remarks could not have been more remote from what we were talking about.* **3** very small or slight: *There is only a remote chance of success*; *He hasn't the remotest idea what is going on*; *Your chances of winning are remote.* **4** (of a person's manner) not friendly; not showing interest: *He always seems so remote when I talk to him*; *a remote manner.* **re'moteness** *nu.*
re'motely *adv* (even) to a very slight extent: *What he said wasn't remotely relevant to the subject of discussion*; *He's remotely related to me.*
remote control the control of *eg* a switch, a model aeroplane from a distance, by means of radio waves *etc*: *The model plane is operated by remote control*; (*attrib*) *a remote control model plane.*

remould ['ri:mould] *nc* a used tyre which has been made like new again: *We could not afford new tyres and so we bought remoulds.*

remove [rə'mu:v] **1** *vt* (*more formal than* **take away**) to take (a person, thing *etc*) away from, out of *etc* the place he, it *etc* is in or on: *Will someone please remove all this rubbish!*; *He removed all the evidence of his crimes*; *I can't remove this stain from my shirt*; (*fig*) *The manager's remarks did little to remove the workers' fears*; (*formal fig*) *He has been removed from his post as minister of education.* **2** *vt* (*formal*) to take off (a piece of clothing):

Women used to be asked to remove their hats in cinemas so that the people behind could see the screen. **3** *vi* (*Brit formal*) to move to a new house *etc*: *He has removed to London.* – *nc* (*formal*) one step or degree (from something): *The president's behaviour was only one remove from tyranny* (= it was almost tyranny).

re'movable *adj*: *a removable stain*; *Is this stain removable?*

re'moval *ncu* the act of removing or the state of being removed, *esp* the moving of furniture *etc* to a new home: *After his removal from power, the dictator was sent into exile*; *Our removal is to take place on Monday*; (*attrib*) *a removal(s) firm/van.*

re'moved *adj* **1** (*often with* **far**) separated or distant (from something): *a house far removed from the town*; (*fig*) *What he said today is far removed from what he said yesterday.* **2** (of cousins) separated by one, two *etc* generations: *A person's first cousin once removed is either the child of his first cousin or the first cousin of one of his parents.*

re'mover *nc* a person or thing that removes (something): *a stain remover*; *a firm of furniture removers.*

remunerate [rə'mju:nəreit] *vt* (*very formal*) to pay (someone) for something he has done: *You will be remunerated for the work which you have done.*

re,mune'ration *ncu* (*formal*) the payment made to a person for something he has done.

re'munerative [-rətiv] *adj* (*formal*) bringing a good profit or having a good salary: *Writing dictionaries is not very remunerative*; *She has found more remunerative employment.*

Renaissance [rə'neisəns, (*Amer*) 'renəsa:ns] *n* (*with* **the**) the revival of arts and literature in Europe in the 14th to 16th centuries. – *adj* (*attrib*) of the Renaissance: *Renaissance art.*

rend [rend] – *pt, ptp* **rent** [rent] – *vti* (*arch*) to tear: *He rent his garments*; *His garments rent*; *It rent his heart to witness her sorrow.*

rent *nc* (*arch*) a tear.

render ['rendə] *vt* (*formal*) **1** to cause to become: *His remarks rendered me speechless.* **2** to give or produce (a decision, a bill, thanks *etc*): *He gave them a reward for services rendered* (= for the help they had given him); *Let us render thanks to God.* **3** to translate (something): *The teacher rendered the passage from Homer into English.* **4** to perform (the rôle of a character in a play, a piece of music *etc*): *The piano solo was well rendered.* **5** to melt and purify (fat).

'rendering *ncu* (*formal*): *The pianist gave a beautiful rendering of the sonata.*

rendition [ren'diʃən] *nc* (*very formal or facet*) the rendering of a piece of music *etc*, or the way in which it is rendered: *The pianist gave an excellent rendition of the sonata*; *a rendition of a passage of Greek poetry.*

rendezvous ['rondivu:] – *pl* **'rendezvous** [-vu:] – *nc* (*formal*) **1** an agreement to meet (someone) somewhere: *They had made a rendezvous to meet at midnight.* **2** the place where such a meeting is to be: *The summer-house is the lovers' usual rendezvous.* **3** the meeting itself: *The rendezvous took place at midnight.* **4** a place where a certain group of people meet or go regularly: *This pub is the rendezvous for the local artists and poets.* – *v* – *pt, ptp* **'rendezvoused** [-vu:d] – *vi* to meet at an appointed place.

rendition *see* **render**.

renegade ['renigeid] *nc* (*formal*: *usu derog*) a person who leaves the religious, political *etc* group to which he belongs and joins an enemy or rival group: *a renegade from the Labour Party*; (*attrib*) *The leader of the revolutionaries was a renegade priest.*

renew [rə'nju:] *vt* **1** to begin (to do) (something) again: *He renewed his efforts*; *The leader of the opposition party renewed his attacks on the Government's policies.* **2** to cause (*eg* a licence) to continue for another or longer period of time: *My television licence has to be renewed in October*; *I must renew my golf club membership*; *Have you renewed your subscription to the magazine?* **3** to make new or fresh or as if new again: *The wood panels on the doors have all been renewed*; *I must renew the water in the fish-tank.* **re'newable** *adj.*

re'newal *ncu* the act of renewing (something): *the renewal of a licence*; *How many renewals have we had so far?*

re'newed *adj* (*attrib*): *with renewed effort*; *with renewed energy.*

rennet ['renit] *nu* a substance used for curdling milk *etc.*

renounce [ri'nauns] *vt* (*formal*) **1** to give up (a title, claim, intention *etc*) *esp* formally or publicly: *He renounced his claim to the throne.* **2** to say *esp* formally or publicly that one will no longer do, eat, use *etc* (something), or speak to, associate with *etc* (someone): *I have renounced violence/alcohol*; *He renounced his family.*

renunciation [rinʌnsi'eiʃən] *nu.*

renovate ['renəveit] *vt* (*formal or tech*) to make (something) as good as new again: *to renovate an old building.* **'renovator** *nc.*

,reno'vation *ncu* (*often in pl*): *Have they completed the renovations?*; *the renovation of the building.*

renown [rə'naun] *nu* (*formal*) fame: *a person of great renown.*

re'nowned *adj* (*formal*: *with* **as** *or* **for**) famous: *He is renowned as an artist/for his paintings*; *a renowned actress.*

rent[1] [rent] *ncu* money paid, *usu* regularly, for the use of a house, shop, land *etc* which belongs to someone else: *The rent for this flat is £20 a week.* – *vt* to pay or receive rent for the use of a house, shop, land *etc*: *We rent this flat from Mr Smith*; *Mr Smith rents this flat to us.* – *See also* **rent out** *below.*

'rental 1 *nc* money paid as rent: *The rental of that television is £5 a week*; *Rentals have increased recently.* **2** *nu* the act of renting.

,rent-'free *adv* without payment of rent: *He lives there rent-free.* – *adj* for which rent does not need to be paid: *a rent-free flat*; *The flat is rent-free.*

rent out *vt sep* to allow (someone) to use a house, land *etc* which one owns, in exchange for money: *I own a cottage in the country which I rent out to tourists.*

rent[2] *see* **rend**.

renunciation *see* **renounce**.

reorganize, -ise [ri:'o:gənaiz] *vti* to change the way in which (something) is organized, done *etc*; to put (things *etc*) in a different order: *We'll have to reorganize our filing system/the books on this shelf.*

re,organi'zation, **-s-** *nu.*

rep [rep] short for **representative** (*n*) and **repertory**.

repaid *see* **repay**.

repair [ri'peə] **1** *vt* (*more formal than* **mend** *or* **fix**) to mend (something); to make (something) that is damaged or has broken down work again; to restore (something) to good condition: *repair a* *broken lock/torn jacket.* **2** *vt* (*formal*) to put right or make up for (something wrong that has been done): *Nothing can repair the harm done by your foolish remarks.* **3** *vi* (*with* **to**: *old*) to go: *He repaired to his house.* – **1** *ncu* (*often in pl*) the act of repairing (something damaged or broken down): *I put my car into the garage for repairs*; *The bridge is under repair* (= being repaired). **2** *nu* a condition or state: *The road is in good/bad repair*; *The house is in a good state of repair.* **3** *nc* (*formal*) a mended part or place: *This coat has so many repairs in it, it's not fit to wear.*

re'pairable *adj* (*neg* **un-**: *usu pred*) able to be mended: *Is the car repairable?*

reparable ['repərəbl] *adj* (*formal*) able to be put right.

ˌrepa'ration [repə-] *nu* (*formal*: *esp legal*) **1** the act of making up for (something wrong that has been done): *reparation of wrong-doing.* **2** money paid for this purpose: *He has received some reparation for the damage.*

re'pairman [-man] *nc* a man who repairs (televisions *etc*).

See also **disrepair, irreparable**.

repartee [repa:'ti:] *nu* (the making of) quick, witty replies; conversation having many of these: *He's good at repartee.*

repast [rə'pa:st] *nc* (*old, formal or facet*) a meal.

repatriate [ri:'patrieit, (*Amer*) -'pei-] *vt* (*formal*) to send (someone) back to his own country: *He has no work permit and so the British Government are repatriating him.* **reˌpatri'ation** *nu*.

repay [ri'pei] – *pt, ptp* **repaid** [ri'peid] – *vt* **1** (*more formal than* **pay back**) to pay back: *When are you going to repay the money you borrowed?* **2** to do or give (something) to someone in return for something he has done: *I must find a way of repaying his kindness.* **re'payment** *ncu*.

re'payable *adj* (*pred*: *formal*) which must be repaid: *money repayable within ten years.*

repeal [rə'pi:l] *vt* (*formal or legal*) to make (a law *etc*) no longer valid. – *nu* (*formal or legal*) the act of repealing (a law *etc*).

repeat [rə'pi:t] *vt* **1** to say or do (something) again: *Would you repeat these instructions, please?*; *The salesman claimed that the offer could not be repeated.* **2** to say (something one has heard) to someone else, sometimes when one ought not to: *Please do not repeat what I've just told you.* **3** to say (something) one has learned by heart: *repeat a poem.* – *See also* **repeat oneself** *below.* – *nc* something (*eg* a passage of music, a television programme) which is repeated: *I'm tired of seeing all these repeats on television*; (*attrib*) *a repeat performance.*

re'peatable *adj* (*usu pred*: *neg* **un-**) **1** fit to be told to other people: *What he said when I told him he was a fool is simply not repeatable.* **2** able to be repeated: *These bargains are not repeatable.*

re'peated *adj* (*attrib*) said, done *etc* many times: *In spite of repeated requests, he still hasn't sent us his report.*

re'peatedly *adv* (*more formal than* **often**) many times: *I've asked him for it repeatedly.*

repetition [repə'tiʃən] *ncu* (*formal*) the act of repeating or being repeated: *May I ask for a repetition of the remarks you made yesterday*; *I don't want ever to see a repetition of this behaviour again*; *The only way to get him to understand anything is by repetition.*

repetitious [repə'tiʃəs] , **repetitive** [rə'petətiv] *adjs* (*formal*: *often derog*) repeating (something) too often: *His speeches are very repetitive*; *I am tired of his repetitious speeches*; *His work is of a very repetitive nature.* **ˌrepe'titiously, re'petitively** *advs.* **repe'titiousness, re'petitiveness** *nus.*

re'peat oneself to say the same thing more than once: *Listen carefully because I don't want to have to repeat myself*; *The old man keeps repeating himself.*

repel [rə'pel] – *pt, ptp* **re'pelled** – **1** *vt* (*formal*) to resist or fight (an enemy) successfully; to force (an enemy) to stop attacking: *The soldiers on the hill repelled the invaders and drove them back to their ships.* **2** *vt* (*formal*) to cause a feeling of dislike or disgust: *She was repelled by his filthy hair and clothes.* **3** *vti* (*tech*) to force (something) to move away: *Like poles of magnets repel* (*each other*).

re'pellent *ncu* something that repels insects *etc*: *If you don't want to be stung, rub on some insect repellent.* – *adj* (*formal*) causing a feeling of dislike or disgust: *His appearance was repellent*; *a dirty, repellent old tramp.*

repulse [rə'pʌls] *vt* (*formal*) **1** to repel (an enemy). **2** to refuse to accept (a person's) help, advice *etc*; to behave in an unfriendly manner towards a person who wishes to be friendly: *She repulsed his offers of assistance.* – *ncu* the act of repulsing or state of being repulsed.

repulsion [rə'pʌlʃən] *nu* (*formal*) (a feeling of) great dislike or disgust: *I feel a great repulsion for racialist policies like theirs.*

repulsive [rə'pʌlsiv] *adj* that causes a feeling of great dislike or disgust: *She was horrified by his repulsive features/suggestions*; *He is repulsive!* **re'pulsively** *adv.* **re'pulsiveness** *nu.*

repent [rə'pent] *vti* **1** (*usu relig*) to be sorry that one has done (something bad): *The preacher called on the people to repent.* **2** (*very formal*) to wish that one had not done (something): *He repented* (*of*) *his generosity.* **re'pentance** *nu* (*formal*).

re'pentant *adj* (*neg* **un-**: *formal*): *He was not at all repentant for having attacked the old lady*; *a repentant criminal.*

repercussion [ri:pə'kʌʃən] *nc* (*formal*: *usu in pl*) the *usu* bad effect or result of something that has happened: *This apparently unimportant event had great repercussions throughout the world.*

repertoire ['repətwa:] *nc* (*formal*) the list of songs, plays *etc* that a performer, singer, group of actors *etc* is able or ready to perform: *The song which you have requested is not in my repertoire.*

repertory ['repətəri] **1** *nu* (*also inf* **rep** [rep]) the state of belonging to a repertory company: *She has spent the last two years in repertory.* **2** *nc* (*formal*) a repertoire.

'repertory theatre a theatre with a more or less permanent company of actors, a **'repertory company**, which performs a series of plays.

repetition, repetitious, repetitive *see* **repeat**.

rephrase [ri:'freiz] *vt* to say (something) again, using different words: *Perhaps you'll understand better if I rephrase my question.*

replace [rə'pleis] *vt* **1** to put, use *etc* (a person, thing *etc*), or to be put, used *etc*, in place of another: *I must replace that broken lock*; *Has anyone been chosen to replace you when you leave?*; *He replaced the cup he broke with a new one*; *Cars have replaced horses as the normal means of transport*; *Horses have been replaced by cars.* **2** (*formal*) to put (something) back where it was: *Please replace the books in their correct positions on the shelves.* **re'placeable** *adj.*

re'placement *ncu*: *I must find a replacement for my secretary – she's leaving next week*; *The replacement of this rare vase will take some time.* *See also* **irreplaceable**.

replay [riː'plei] *vt* to play (a football match *etc*) again (*eg* because neither team won): *The match ended in a draw – it will have to be replayed.* – ['riːplei] *nc* a replayed football match *etc*: *The replay will take place next Saturday.*

replenish [rə'pleniʃ] *vt* (*formal*) to fill (something) up again; to fill up (one's supply of something) again: *We must replenish our stock of coal.* **re'plenishment** *nu.*

replete [rə'pliːt] *adj* (*formal*: *pred*) full; filled (with something); having a great deal (of something): *a workshop replete with the latest tools and gadgets*; *I feel rather replete after that large meal.*

replica ['replikə] *nc* an exact copy, *esp* of a work of art: *a replica of a statue carved by Michelangelo.*

reply [rə'plai] **1** *vti* (*more formal than* **answer**: *often with* **to**) to answer: *'I don't know,' he replied*; *Should I reply to his letter?*; *She replied that she had never seen the man before.* **2** *vi* (*formal*) to do something as an answer to some other action: *The enemy replied to our fire* (= They fired back at us); *They replied to our attack with an even more forceful attack.* **3** *vi* (*with* **for**) to make a speech of thanks in answer to a speech of welcome: *I've been asked to reply for the guests at the dinner this evening.* – (*more formal than* **answer**) **1** *nc* an answer: *'I don't know,' was his reply*; *I'll write a reply to his letter.* **2** *nu* the act of answering: *What did he say in reply (to your question)?*

report [rə'poːt] **1** *nc* a statement or description of what has been said, seen, done *etc*: *a company's financial report* (= a statement of its profits *etc*); *a child's school report* (= the list of the child's examination results *etc*); *a report on a conference*; *a road report* (= a description of the state of the roads because of *eg* snow, fog, ice, accidents). **2** *nu* (*formal*) rumour; general talk: *According to report, the manager is going to resign.* **3** *nc* (*formal*) a loud noise, *esp* of a gun being fired. – **1** *vti* (*vi sometimes with* **on**) to give a statement or description of what has been said, seen, done *etc*: *A serious accident has just been reported*; *He reported on the results of the conference*; *Our spies report that troops are being moved to the border*; *Troops are reported to be only ten miles from the border*; *His speech was reported in the 'Edinburgh Herald'*; *She reports for the 'Edinburgh Herald'* (= She is a reporter who works for that paper). **2** *vt* to make a complaint about (someone); to say that (someone) has done wrong: *The boy was reported to the headmaster for swearing at a teacher.* **3** *vt* to tell (someone, *usu* someone in authority) that something has happened: *He reported the theft to the police.* **4** *vi* (*with* **for** *or* **to**) to go (somewhere) and tell (someone) that one is there, ready for work *etc*: *The boys were ordered to report to the police-station every Saturday afternoon*; *So many people have 'flu that hardly any policemen reported for duty.* – *See also* **report back** *below.*

re'portedly *adv* (*formal*) according to report, rumour *etc*: *He is reportedly going to resign tomorrow.*

re'porter *nc* a person who writes articles and reports for a newspaper: *Several reporters and photographers rushed to the scene of the fire.*

re'port card *nc* a child's school report.

reported speech *nu* (*gram*) indirect speech.

report back *vi* (*sometimes with* **to**) to come again and report (to someone); to send a report (to someone): *Don't forget to report back here after you have finished these jobs*; *He was asked to study the matter in detail and report back to the committee.*

repose [rə'pouz] *nu* (*formal*) rest; calm; peacefulness: *Her face looks very sad in repose.*

reprehensible [repri'hensəbl] *adj* (*formal*) deserving blame: *a reprehensible action*; *It was thoroughly reprehensible of him to steal from his mother.*

ˌrepre'hensibly *adv*: *You behaved most reprehensibly.*

represent [reprə'zent] *vt* **1** to speak or act on behalf of (a person or a group of people): *You have been chosen to represent our association at the conference*; *As he was unable to be at the meeting, he asked his assistant to represent him.* **2** to be a sign, symbol, picture *etc* (of someone or something): *In this play, the man in black represents Death and the young girl Life*; *That line at the bottom of the painting represents the sea*; *Letters and combinations of letters represent sounds.* **3** to be a good example of (something): *What he said represents the feelings of many people.* **4** (*formal*: *often with* **as**) to say or claim wrongly that (someone or something) is something; to describe (someone or something) wrongly or incorrectly: *He represents himself as an expert on dictionaries*; *He is not the fool he is sometimes represented to be.* **5** to correspond to, be the result of *etc*: *These few pages represent several hours' work*; *This price rise represents an increase of five per cent.* **6** (*formal*) to show, explain or say (something) to someone: *He represented the difficulties to the rest of the committee*; *The lawyer represented to the court that his client was innocent.*

ˌrepresen'tation **1** *nu* (*formal*) the act of representing or being represented: *Our firm has adequate representation in Europe.* **2** *nc* a person, or thing that repesents (someone or something): *The man in black is a representation of Death in this play*; *These primitive statues are intended as representations of gods and goddesses.* **3** *nc* (*formal*: *often in pl*) a strong appeal, demand or protest: *The people made strong representations to the Local Authority to have the motorway built further away from their homes.*

ˌrepre'sentative [-tətiv] *adj* (*formal*) **1** (*often with* **of**: *neg* **un-**) being a good example (of something); typical: *We need opinions from a representative sample of people*; *Is this poem representative of his work?* **2** carried on by elected people: *representative government.* – *nc* **1** (*also inf* **rep** [rep]) a person who represents a business; a travelling salesman: *Our representative will call on you this afternoon.* **2** a person who represents a person or group of people: *A Member of Parliament is the representative of the people in his constituency.*

the House of Representatives the lower house of the US Congress and of the state governing assemblies.

repress [rə'pres] *vt* (*formal*) to keep (an impulse, a desire to do something *etc*) under control: *He repressed a desire to hit the man*; *She repressed her tears*; *Her artistic talent had been repressed because her mother wanted her to study science.* **re'pression** [-ʃən] *nu.*

re'pressive [-siv] *adj* (*formal*) severe; harsh: *The dictator took repressive measures to prevent the revolt continuing*; *The new régime is very repressive.* **re'pressiveness** *nu.*

See also **oppress, suppress**.

reprieve [rə'pri:v] *vt* **1** to pardon (a criminal) or delay his punishment: *The murderer was sentenced to death, but later reprieved.* **2** (*fig*) to give (someone *etc*) a period of freedom from trouble, difficulty *etc*: *A Government loan of £100 000 reprieved the shipyard.* – *nc* the act of pardoning (a criminal) or delaying his punishment; the order to do this: *The murderer was granted/given a reprieve*; (*fig*) *We have had a reprieve – the firm is not going to close down after all.*

reprimand [repri'ma:nd, (*Amer also*) 'reprimand] *vt* (*formal*) (*esp* of a person in authority) to speak or write angrily or severely (to someone) because he has done wrong: *The soldier was severely reprimanded for being drunk.* – ['reprima:nd] *nc* (*formal*) angry or severe words made to someone (by someone in authority) because he has done wrong: *He was given a severe reprimand.*

reprint [ri:'print] **1** *vt* to print more copies of (a book *etc*): *We are reprinting his new novel already.* **2** *vi* (of a book *etc*) to have more copies made: *The book is reprinting at the moment.* – ['ri:print] *nc* **1** a copy of a book *etc* made by reprinting the original without any changes. **2** the copies of a book *etc* made at one time by reprinting the original: *This book is now in its third reprint.*

reprisal [rə'praizəl] *ncu* (*formal*) (the act of doing) something bad done to someone who has done something bad to one: *The attack was a reprisal for the enemy's attack the previous day*; *The enemy had been expecting reprisals for their attack*; *They attacked the enemy camp in reprisal for an attack the enemy had made earlier.*

reproach [rə'proutʃ] *vt* to tell (a person) that he has done wrong, caused some harm *etc* (*usu* with a suggestion of sadness and disappointment rather than anger): *She reproached me for not telling her*; *She reproached me with the failure of her plans*; *There is no need to reproach yourself – you did the best you could.* – **1** *nu* the act of reproaching: *a look of reproach.* **2** *nc* words said to a person one is reproaching: *He didn't deserve your reproaches.*

re'proachful *adj* showing or expressing reproach: *a reproachful look*; *reproachful words*; *Don't look so reproachful!* **re'proachfully** *adv.*

reprobate ['reprəbeit] *nc* (*formal or facet*) a person of bad or immoral habits: *Her father is a real reprobate but he's rather charming.* – *adj* (*very formal*) bad or immoral.

reproduce [ri:prə'dju:s] **1** *vt* to make or produce a copy of (something); to make or produce (something) again: *Good as the films are, they somehow fail to reproduce the atmosphere of the festival*; *A record-player reproduces the sound which has been recorded on a record.* **2** *vi* (of humans, animals and plants) to produce (young, seeds *etc*): *How do fish reproduce?*

ˌrepro'duction [-'dʌk-] **1** *nu* the act or process of reproducing: *He is studying reproduction in rabbits.* **2** *nc* a copy (of a work of art *etc*): *These paintings are all reproductions.*

ˌrepro'ductive [-'dʌktiv] *adj* (*attrib*) of or for reproduction: *the reproductive organs of a rabbit.*

reproof [rə'pru:f] (*formal*) **1** *nu* the act of telling (someone) that he has done wrong: *a look of reproof.* **2** *nc* words of criticism said to someone who has done something wrong: *He has received several reproofs for bad behaviour.*

reprove [rə'pru:v] *vt* (*formal*) to tell (a person) that he has done wrong: *The teacher reproved the boys for coming late to school.*

re'proving *adj* (*usu attrib*): *a reproving look.* **re'provingly** *adv.*

reptile ['reptail] *nc* any of the group of cold-blooded animals to which snakes, lizards, crocodiles *etc* belong.

rep'tilian [-'ti-] *adj* (*formal or tech*) of or like reptiles.

republic [rə'pʌblik] *nc* (a country with) a form of government in which there is no king or queen, the power of government, law-making *etc* being given to one or more elected representatives (*eg* a president, members of a parliament *etc*): *The United States is a republic – the United Kingdom is not.*

re'publican 1 *adj* of a republic: *a republican form of government.* **2** *adj, nc* (a person) who supports a republican form of government: *He is not a monarchist – he is a republican.* **3** *adj, nc* (*with cap*) (a member or supporter) of the **Republican Party**, one of the two chief political parties in the US: *He is a Democrat but she is a Republican.*

repudiate [rə'pju:dieit] *vt* (*formal*) **1** to deny or reject (something); to say that one has not done (something), is not responsible for (something) *etc*: *He repudiated the suggestion that he was a racialist*; *He repudiated the argument.* **2** to refuse to pay (something): *He repudiated his debts.* **3** to say publicly that one will no longer associate with, talk to, be friendly with *etc* (a person): *He repudiated his son.* **reˌpudi'ation** *nu.*

repugnant [rə'pʌgnənt] *adj* (*formal*: *often with* **to**) causing a feeling of great dislike or disgust: *His opinions are repugnant to me*; *repugnant behaviour.*

re'pugnance *nu* (*formal*): *the repugnance of his opinions*; *I feel a great repugnance for these opinions/to cleaning up this disgusting mess.*

repulse, repulsion, repulsive *see* **repel**.

reputation [repju'teiʃən] *ncu* **1** the opinion which people in general have about a person *etc*, a person's abilities *etc*: *That firm has a good/bad reputation*; *He has the reputation of being a difficult man to please*; *He has made a reputation for himself* (= He has become well-known) *as an expert in computers*; *He has made quite a reputation for himself.* **2** (*formal*) the good opinion or respect which people in general have for a person *etc*: *He is a person of some reputation in the town.* – See also **live up to one's reputation** *below.*

'reputable *adj* (*formal*) respectable; well thought of: *Is that a reputable firm?*; *Yes, it is quite reputable.*

reputed [ri'pju:tid] *adj* (*formal*) believed to be (something): *He is reputed to be very wealthy*; *the reputed author of the article.*

reputedly [ri'pju:tidli] *adv* in the opinion of most people: *He is reputedly very wealthy.*

by re'pute [ri'pju:t] (*formal*) reputedly: *He is by repute a very wealthy man.*

live up to one's reputation to behave in the way that people say one behaves; to do what people expect one to do: *He has the reputation of being a fool, and he is really living up to it.*

of re'pute [ri'pju:t] (*formal*) well thought of and respected by many people: *He is a man of some repute in this town.*

See also **disrepute**.

request [ri'kwest] **1** *ncu* (*slightly formal*) the act of asking (for something): *I did that at his request*; *After frequent requests, he eventually agreed to sing*;

(*attrib*) *a request stop* (= a place where buses *etc* stop only when asked to do so). **2** *nc* something asked for: *The next record I will play is a request.* – *vt* (*more formal than* **ask**) to ask (for) something: *People using this library are requested not to talk*; *May I request that you work more quietly?*; *Many people have requested this next song.*

by re'quest (of) when or because one is asked to do something (by someone): *I'm singing this next song by request (of Mrs Anne Smith).*

on re'quest when requested: *Buses only stop here on request.*

requiem ['rekwiem] *nc* (a piece of music written for) a mass for the souls of the dead: (*attrib*) *a requiem mass.*

require [rə'kwaiə] *vt* (not used with **is, was** *etc* and **-ing**) **1** (*more formal than* **need**) to need: *Is there anything else you require?* **2** (*formal*) to ask, force or order (someone) to do something: *You are required by law to send your children to school*; *I will do everything that is required of me.*

re'quirement *nc* (*formal*) something that is needed, asked for, ordered *etc*: *It is a legal requirement that all cars have brakes which work*; *Our firm will be able to supply all your requirements.*

requisite ['rekwizit] *adj* (*very formal*: *attrib*) required; necessary: *Before you get a passport you have to fill in the requisite forms.* – *nc* (*formal or facet*) something which is necessary or used for some purpose: *toilet requisites.*

ˌrequi'sition [-'ziʃən] *vt* **1** (of an army *etc*) to demand or take (supplies, shelter *etc*): *The soldiers requisitioned the farmers' horses/houses.* **2** to order (supplies) *usu* in writing by sending a list of what one needs to a person who will place the order on behalf of a number of people: *The teachers were told that there was now a new system for requisitioning exercise-books.* – **1** *nc* a *usu* written demand or request (for supplies): *Have you sent in your library requisition yet?* **2** *nu* the act of demanding, requesting or taking supplies *etc*, *eg* by an army: *the requisition of our house as a military hospital.*

rescind [rə'sind] *vt* (*legal*) to cancel (an order, law *etc*): *The Home Secretary has rescinded the court's decision.*

rescue ['reskju:] *vt* to get or take (a person) out of a dangerous situation, captivity *etc*: *The lifeboat was sent out to rescue the sailors from the sinking ship*; (*fig*) *The government has rescued the firm from bankruptcy by giving them a grant.* – *ncu* the act of rescuing or state of being rescued: *The lifeboat was involved in four rescues last week*; *The lifeboat went/came to the rescue of the sailors on the sinking ship*; *After his rescue, the man told the reporters what it was like to be in the hands of the terrorists.*

'rescuer *nc.*

research [ri'sə:tʃ, (*esp Amer*) 'ri:sə:(r)tʃ] *ncu* a close and careful (*usu* scientific) study to (try to) find out (new) facts or information: *He is engaged in cancer research*; *He's doing research in linguistics*; (*attrib*) *a research student*; *My researches have shown that there was a civilization here 4 000 years ago.* – [(*Brit and Amer*) ri'sə:(r)tʃ] *vti* (*vi with* **into**) to carry out such a study: *He's researching (into) Old English poetry.* **re'searcher** [ri'sə:tʃə, (*Amer also*) 'ri:sə:rtʃər] *nc.*

resemble [rə'zembl] *vt* (*slightly formal*: not used with **is, was** *etc* and **-ing**) to be like or look like (someone or something): *He doesn't resemble either of his parents.*

re'semblance *ncu*: *There is some resemblance between him and his father*; *They do show some resemblances.*

resent [ri'zent] *vt* to feel annoyed about (something) because one thinks it is unfair, not right, insulting *etc*: *I resent his interfering/interference in my affairs*; *I resent having to take work home every evening.*

re'sentful *adj* (*often with* **about** *or* **at**) having or showing a feeling of resentment; *She feels resentful that her sister married before she did*; *a resentful attitude.* **re'sentfully** *adv.* **re'sentfulness** *nu.*

re'sentment *nu* a feeling of annoyance about an action *etc* which one feels is unfair, not right, insulting *etc*, or against the person who performs this action *etc*: *He has a feeling of resentment against the police*; *He feels resentment against the police*; *He feels resentment at the way he was treated by the police.*

reserve [rə'zə:v] *vt* **1** (*more formal than* **book**) to ask for or order (something) to be kept for the use of a particular person, often oneself: *The restaurant is busy on Saturdays, so I'll phone up today and reserve a table.* **2** to keep (something) for the use of a particular person or group of people, or for a particular use: *These seats are reserved for the use of committee members only*; *Some of the profits will be reserved to buy new machinery.* – **1** *nc* (*formal*) something which is kept for later use or for use when needed: *The farmer kept a reserve of food in case he was cut off by snow during the winter.* **2** *nc* a piece of land used for a special purpose *eg* for the protection of animals: *a wild life/a game reserve.* **3** *nu* (*formal*) the habit of not saying very much, not showing what one is feeling, thinking *etc*; shyness: *She behaves with reserve until she knows you very well.* **4** *nc* (*often in pl*) soldiers, sailors *etc* who do not belong to the regular full-time army, navy *etc* but who are called into action when needed *eg* during a war: *The reserves have been called up*; *the Royal Naval Volunteer Reserve.* **5** *nc* a reservation (*def 4*).

ˌreser'vation [rezə-] **1** *nu* (*formal*) the act of reserving (something): *the reservation of a room.* **2** *nc* something (*eg* a hotel room, a table in a restaurant) which has been reserved: *Have you a reservation, Sir?* **3** *ncu* doubts; uncertainty: *He agreed to the plans but with certain reservations* (= he wanted certain changes in the plans); *I had reservations about his appointment*; *We accepted his story with some reservation(s).* **4** *nc* a piece of land set aside for a particular purpose; *an Indian reservation in the United States.*

re'served *adj* not saying very much; not showing what one is feeling, thinking *etc*: *She is very reserved*; *She has a reserved manner/nature.*

have, keep *etc* **(something) in reserve** (*formal*) to have or keep (something) in case or until it is needed: *If you go to America please keep some money in reserve for your fare home.*

See also **unreserved**.

reservoir ['rezəvwa:] *nc* **1** a place, *usu* a man-made lake, where water for drinking *etc* is stored. **2** (*formal*) a great store or amount (of something): *a reservoir of information.*

resident ['rezidənt] *nc* a person who lives or has his home (in a particular place): *a resident of Edinburgh*; *The residents' association complained to the local authority about the state of the roads.* – *adj* **1** (*pred*) living or having one's home (in a place): *He is now resident abroad.* **2** (*usu attrib*) living, having to live, or requiring a person to live, in the place where he works: *a resident caretaker*; *This job is a resident post.*

reside [rə'zaid] *vi* (*formal*) **1** to live or have one's home (in a place): *He resides at 31 Highlow Avenue*; *He now resides abroad.* **2** (*very formal*) (*with* **in**) (of power, authority *etc*) to be present or placed (in someone); to belong (to someone): *All authority in that country resides in the President.*

'residence (*formal*) **1** *nc* a house or other building where one lives, *esp* an impressive or large building where someone important lives: *This is Lord Bone's residence.* **2** *nu* the act of living (in a place). **3** *nu* the period of time one lives in a place: *during his residence in Spain.* – *See also* **in residence, take up residence** *below.*

'residency *nc* (*formal*) the residence of the governor *etc* in a colony *etc.*

ˌresi'dential [-'denʃəl] *adj* **1** (of an area of a town *etc*) containing houses rather than factories, shops *etc*: *This district is mainly residential*; *He lives in a residential area.* **2** requiring a person to live in the place he works: *a residential post*; *a residential course of study*; *Is the job residential?* **3** (*attrib*: *formal*) of or relating to (a person's) residence in a place: *Before one can get married, one must satisfy the residential qualifications* (= one must stay a certain number of weeks in a place).

in 'residence (*formal*) (*esp* of someone important) staying in a place, sometimes to perform some official duties: *The Queen is in residence here this week.*

take up residence (*formal*) to go and live (in a place, building *etc*): *He has taken up residence in France.*

See also **non-resident**.

residue ['rezidju:] *nc* (*formal or tech*) what remains or is left over (when a part has been taken away, used *etc*): *Heat the dish until the water evaporates, then examine the residue.*

residual [rə'zidjuəl, (*Amer*) -dʒu-] *adj* (*formal or tech*: *usu attrib*) remaining; left over: *There are still a few residual problems to be discussed.*

resign [rə'zain] **1** *vti* to leave (a job *etc*): *If he criticizes my work again I'll resign*; *He resigned from the committee/as secretary of the committee*; *He resigned his post.* **2** *v refl* (*with* **to**) to accept (a situation, fact *etc*) with patience and calmness: *He has resigned himself to never being able to walk again.*

resignation [rezig'neiʃən] **1** *ncu* the act of resigning. **2** *nc* a letter *etc* stating that one is resigning: *You will receive my resignation tomorrow morning.* **3** *nu* (the state of having or showing) patient, calm acceptance (of a situation, fact *etc*): *He accepted his fate with resignation.*

re'signed *adj* (*often with* **to**) having or showing patient, calm acceptance (of a fact, situation *etc*): *He is/seems resigned to his fate*; *He gave a resigned smile.*

re'signedly [-nid-] *adv* (*formal*) in a resigned way: *'I suppose we'll have to wait for hours,' he said resignedly.*

resilient [rə'ziliənt] *adj* **1** (*formal*) (of people) quickly recovering from bad luck, illness *etc*: *Children are so resilient that they are not unhappy for long*; *a very resilient young lady.* **2** (*tech*) (of an object, substance *etc*) quickly returning to its original shape after being bent, twisted *etc*: *a resilient substance*; *Is that substance resilient?* **re'silience, re'siliency** *nus.*

resin ['rezin] *ncu* a sticky substance produced by certain trees (*eg* firs, pines) and some other plants.

'resinous *adj* like or containing resin: *Pine-cones are resinous.*

resist [rə'zist] *vt* **1** to fight against (someone or something), *usu* successfully: *The soldiers resisted the enemy attack*; *He tried to resist arrest*; (*fig*) *It's hard to resist temptation.* **2** (*with* **can/could** *in neg*) to be able to stop (oneself) doing, taking *etc* (something): *I couldn't resist kicking him when he bent down*; *I just can't resist strawberries.* **3** (*chem*) to be (almost) unaffected or undamaged by (something): *a metal that resists rust/acids.*

re'sistance *nu* **1** the act of resisting (a person, idea *etc*): *The army offered little resistance/put up a strong resistance to the enemy*; *His suggestion met with some resistance*; (*attrib*) *a resistance movement/group* (= people who continue to fight against an enemy who has taken over a country). **2** the ability or power to be (almost) unaffected or undamaged by something: *This breed of cattle shows (a) great resistance to disease.* **3** (*tech*) the force that one subject, substance *etc* exerts against the movement of another object *etc.* **4** (*tech*) the ability of a substance to turn an electric current passing through it into heat.

re'sistant *adj* (*in cmpds, or pred with* **to**) (almost) unaffected or undamaged by something: *This breed of cattle is resistant to disease*; *heat-resistant table-mats.*

the Resistance the resistance movement in a particular country (*esp* during the Second World War): *the French Resistance.*

See also **irresistible**.

resolution [rezə'lu:ʃən] **1** *nc* a firm decision (to do something): *New Year resolutions* (= traditionally, decisions to improve one's habits, made at New Year). **2** *nc* (*formal*) an opinion or decision formally expressed by a group of people, *eg* at a public meeting: *The meeting passed/adopted/rejected a resolution in favour of/against allowing women to join the society*; *The resolution that women be allowed to join the society was carried.* **3** *nu* (*formal*) resoluteness: *You must behave with resolution.* **4** *nu* (*very formal*) the act of resolving (a problem, question *etc*): *the resolution of our problems.*

'resolute [-lu:t] *adj* (*formal*: *usu pred*) doing what one has decided to do, in spite of opposition, criticism *etc*: *You must be resolute and do what you think best.* **'resolutely** *adv.* **'resoluteness** *nu.*

resolve [rə'zolv] *vt* **1** (*more formal than* **decide**) to make a firm decision (to do something): *I've resolved to stop smoking.* **2** (*more formal than* **decide**) to pass (a resolution): *It was resolved that women should be allowed to join the society.* **3** (*formal*) to take away (a doubt, fear *etc*) or produce an answer to (a problem, difficulty *etc*): *The problem will resolve itself eventually*; *Have you resolved your problems yet?* **4** (*tech*) to break up (a problem, chemical *etc*) into parts. – (*formal*) **1** *nu* determination to do what one has decided to do: *He showed great resolve.* **2** *nc* a firm decision: *It is his resolve to become a director of this firm.*

resolved [rə'zolvd] *adj* (*neg* **un-**: *pred*: *formal*) determined: *I am resolved to go and nothing will stop me.*

See also **irresolute, solve, solution**.

resonant ['rezənənt] *adj* (*formal*) **1** (of sounds) loud; echoing; continuing for a long time because of echoes *etc.* **2** (of voices) deep and easy to hear at a distance. **3** (of rooms, walls *etc*) causing sounds to be louder or longer because of echoes *etc.* **'resonance** *nu.*

'resonate [-neit] *vti* (*formal*) to have or cause resonance. **'resonating** *adj.* **'resonator** *nc.*

See also **resound**.

resort [rə'zoːt] *vi* (*formal*: *with* **to**) to begin to use, do *etc* (something) as a way of solving a problem *etc* when other methods have failed: *He couldn't persuade people to do what he wanted, so he resorted to threats of violence.* – *nc* a place visited by many people (*esp* for holidays): *Brighton is a popular (holiday) resort.*

as a/in the last resort when all other methods *etc* have failed: *If we can't get the money in any other way, I suppose we could, as a last resort, sell the car.*

resound [rə'zaund] *vi* (*formal*) **1** to sound loudly or for a long time, *eg* because of echoes: *The audience's cheers resounded through the hall*; (*liter fig*) *His fame resounded throughout the country.* **2** to be filled with sound: *The hall resounded with the cheers of the audience.*

re'sounding *adj* (*attrib*) **1** loud; echoing: *resounding cheers.* **2** (*fig*) very great; complete: *a resounding victory/success.* **re'soundingly** *adv.*

See also **resonant**.

resource [rə'zoːs] **1** *nc* (*formal*) (*usu in pl*) a person, thing *etc* which gives help, support *etc* when needed; a supply of (something): *We have used up all our resources.* **2** *nc* (*usu in pl*) the wealth of a country, or the supply of materials *etc* which bring this wealth: *This country is rich in natural resources*; *Oil is an important natural resource.* **3** *nu* the ability to find ways of solving difficulties, problems *etc*: *He showed great resource in solving his problems*; *He is full of resource.*

re'sourceful *adj* (*formal*) good at finding ways of solving difficulties, problems *etc*: *He is very resourceful*; *a resourceful young man.* **re'sourcefully** *adv.* **re'sourcefulness** *nu.*

re'sources *n pl* (*formal*) means, money, property *etc*: *This firm hasn't got the resources for such a project.*

leave (someone) to his own resources to leave (a person) to amuse himself, or to find his own way of solving a problem *etc*: *After they had finished interviewing him they left him to his own resources.*

respect [rə'spekt] **1** *nu* admiration; good opinion: *He is held in great respect by everyone*; *He has no respect for politicians*; *With all due respect, I must disagree with what you have just said.* **2** *nu* consideration; thoughtfulness; willingness to obey *etc*: *He shows no respect for the law/his parents*; *We must have respect for/pay respect to the wishes of our customers.* **3** *nc* a particular detail, feature *etc* (of something): *These two poems are similar in some respects.* – *See also* **respect** *in phrases below.* – *vt* **1** to show or feel admiration for (someone): *I respect you for what you did.* **2** to show or have consideration or thoughtfulness for, a willingness to obey *etc*: *One should respect other people's feelings/property.*

re'spectable *adj* **1** deserving respect; having a good reputation or character; decent: *a respectable married woman*; *She has become very respectable since marrying him.* **2** (of behaviour) correct; acceptable: *Wearing a bikini to go to church is not considered respectable*; *respectable behaviour.* **3** (of clothes) good enough or suitable to wear: *You can't go out in those torn trousers – they're not respectable*; *respectable clothes.* **4** (*inf*) large, good *etc* enough; fairly large, good *etc*: *Four goals is a respectable score*; *That score is quite respectable.* **re'spectably** *adv.* **re,specta'bility** *nu.*

re'spectful *adj* having or showing respect. **re'spectfully** *adv.* **re'spectfulness** *nu.*

re'specting *prep* (*formal*) about; concerning: *Respecting your salary, we shall come to a decision later.*

re'spective [-tiv] *adj* (*attrib*) belonging to *etc* each person or thing mentioned: *Peter and George went to their respective homes* (= Each went to his own home).

re'spectively [-tiv-] *adv* referring to each person or thing mentioned, in the order in which they are mentioned: *Peter, James and John were first, second and third, respectively* (= Peter was first, James was second *etc*).

re'spects *n pl* (*formal*) greetings; good wishes: *He sends his respects to you.*

in re'spect of (*formal*) as far as (something) is concerned: *This report is fine in respect of information but the spelling is dreadful.*

pay one's respects (to someone) to visit (a person) as a sign of respect to him: *I've come to pay my respects to your father*; *to pay one's last respects to someone who has died* (= to go to someone's funeral).

with re'spect to (*formal*) about; concerning: *With respect to your requests, we regret that we are unable to assist you in this matter.*

See also **disrespectful**.

respire [rə'spaiə] *vi* (*very formal*) to breathe.

,respi'ration [respə-] *nu* (*formal*) breathing.

respirator ['respəreitə] *nc* **1** a sort of mask worn over the mouth and nose to purify the air breathed in *eg* by firemen in a smoke-filled room. **2** a piece of apparatus used to help very ill or injured people breathe when they are unable to do so naturally.

respiratory ['respərətəri] *adj* (*formal or tech*: *esp attrib*) related to breathing: *respiratory diseases*; *respiratory infection.*

artificial respiration *see* **artificial**.

respite ['respait, (*Amer*) -pit] *ncu* (*formal*) a pause or rest; a temporary stopping of something unpleasant, difficult *etc*: *The patient said that he never had any respite from the pain*; *We had a brief respite from poverty.*

resplendent [rə'splendənt] *adj* (*formal*: *usu pred*) very bright or splendid in appearance: *The ladies were resplendent in their brightly-coloured silk gowns and their jewellery.* **re'splendently** *adv.* **re'splendence** *nu.*

respond [rə'spond] *vi* (*often with* **to**) **1** (*more formal than* **answer**) to answer: *He didn't respond to my question.* **2** to do (something) as a reaction to something that has been done *etc*: *I smiled at her, but she didn't respond.* **3** to show a *usu* good reaction *eg* to some course of treatment: *His illness did not respond to treatment by drugs.* **4** (of vehicles *etc*) to be guided easily by controls: *The pilot said the plane did not respond to the controls.*

re'sponse [-s] **1** *ncu* (*more formal than* **answer**) a reply or answer: *Our letters have never met with any response*; *In response to your inquiries, we regret to inform you that we cannot help you in this matter.* **2** *ncu* an action, feeling *etc* as a reaction to something that has been done *etc*: *My suggestions met with little response/brought some very odd responses.* **3** *nc* (*relig*) any of the parts of the liturgy of certain churches which is said by the congregation rather than the priest.

re,sponsi'bility [-sə-] 1 *nc* something which a person has to look after, do *etc*: *He takes his responsibilities very seriously.* 2 *nu* the state of being responsible or having important duties for which a person is responsible: *a sense of responsibility; A manager's job is a position of great responsibility.*

re'sponsible [-səbl] *adj* 1 (*pred*) having a duty to see that something is done *etc*, and likely to have to report to (a particular person) when it has not been done *etc*: *We'll make one person responsible for buying the food for the trip; He is responsible to the manager for the way his staff behave.* 2 (*usu attrib*) (of a job *etc*) having many duties *etc* for which a person is responsible *eg* the making of important decisions: *The job of manager is a very responsible post.* 3 (*usu with* **for**) being the cause of something: *Who is responsible for the stain on the carpet?* 4 (of a person) able to be trusted; sensible: *We need a responsible person for this job; Is he reliable and responsible?* 5 (*usu with* **for**) (of a person) not able to control oneself; not aware of what one is doing: *The lawyer said that at the time of the murder, his client was not responsible for his actions.*

re'sponsibly [-sə-] *adv* in a trustworthy or serious way: *Do try to behave responsibly.*

re'sponsive [-siv] *adj* (*neg* **un-**) 1 (of a person) quick to react, *eg* to show interest, sympathy *etc*: *a responsive person; I always find her very responsive.* 2 (*pred*: *usu with* **to**) reacting well (to something done *etc*): *This disease is responsive to treatment with drugs.* 3 (*usu attrib*) made as a response: *a responsive smile.* **re'sponsively** *adv.* **re'sponsiveness** *nu.*

See also **irresponsible**.

rest[1] [rest] 1 *ncu* a (*usu* short) period of not working *etc* after, or between periods of, great effort; (a period of) freedom from worries *etc*: *Digging the garden is hard work – let's stop for a rest; Let's have/take a rest; I need a rest from all these problems – I'm going to take a week's holiday; Since she's been ill she needs a lot of rest.* 2 *nu* sleep: *He needs a good night's rest.* 3 *nc* (*often in cmpds*) something which holds or supports (something): *a book-rest; a headrest on a car seat.* 4 *nu* (*formal*) a state of not moving: *The machine is at rest.* – 1 *vti* to (allow to) stop working *etc* in order to get new strength or energy: *We've been walking for four hours – let's stop and rest; The riders stopped to rest their horses; Stop reading for a minute and rest your eyes; Let's stop walking for a while and rest our legs.* 2 *vi* to sleep; to lie or sit quietly in order to get new strength or energy, or because one is tired: *Mother is resting at the moment.* 3 *vti* to (make or allow to) lean, lie, sit *etc* on or against something: *Her head rested on his shoulder; She rested her head on his shoulder.* 4 *vti* (*formal*) to have or give as a basis or support: *The whole argument rests on his assumption that there is no God; He rested his argument on that one assumption.* 5 *vi* to relax, be calm *etc*: *I will never rest until I know the murderer has been caught.* 6 *vti* (*formal*) to (allow to) remain looking at someone or something: *Her eyes rested on the jewels: She rested her gaze on the jewels.* 7 *vti* (*formal*) to (allow to) depend on (a person): *Our hopes now rest on him, since all else has failed; We rested our trust on him.* 8 *vi* (*formal*: *with* **with**) to be (a person's) right, duty *etc* (to do something): *Unfortunately, it rests with me to tell you the sad news; The choice rests with you.* 9 *vi* (*formal*: *with* **with**) to be found (in or with a person): *Power in this country rests with the people.* 10 *vi* (*formal*) (of dead people) to be buried: *He now rests with his ancestors.*

'restful *adj* 1 bringing rest: *a restful holiday; The holiday was uneventful but restful.* 2 (of colours, music *etc*) causing a person to feel calm and relaxed: *Some people find blue a very restful colour; After a hard day's work, I like to sit and listen to some slow, quiet, restful music; This room is very restful.* 3 relaxed: at rest: *The patient seems more restful now; in a restful mood.* **'restfully** *adv.* **'restfulness** *nu.*

'restless *adj* 1 always moving; showing signs of worry, boredom, impatience *etc*: *a restless child;* (*liter*) *the restless sea; The invalid seems very restless tonight; He's been doing the same job for years now and he's beginning to get restless.* 2 (*attrib*) during which a person does not manage to sleep (much) or relax: *a restless night.* **'restlessly** *adv.* **'restlessness** *nu.*

'rest-room *nc* (*Amer euph*) a toilet in a shop, theatre, factory *etc* for the use of the public, staff *etc.*

at 'rest (*formal*) 1 free from pain, worry *etc.* – *See also* **set someone's mind at rest** *below.* 2 (*euph*) dead: *He is at rest after his long, painful illness.*

come to rest to stop moving: *The ball came to rest under a tree.*

God rest his soul a wish that a dead person's soul may be at peace.

lay (someone) to rest (*formal euph*) to bury (someone) in a grave: *She was laid to rest in the village where she was born.*

let the matter rest (*formal*) to stop discussing, worrying about, investigating, complaining about *etc* (a problem, something that has been done *etc*): *You have made a mistake and been punished for it, so we'll let the matter rest there.*

rest assured (*formal*) to be certain: *You may rest assured that we will take your views into consideration.*

rest one's case (*legal*) to finish putting forward arguments, evidence *etc* for the defence or prosecution of a person.

set someone's mind at rest to take away a person's worries (about something): *Let me put your mind at rest – we have no intention of building a motorway near this village.*

See also **unrest**.

rest[2] [rest]: **the rest** 1 what is left when part of something is taken away, finished *etc*: *the rest of the meal.* 2 all the other people, things *etc*: *Jack went home, but the rest of us went to the cinema.*

restaurant ['restront, (*Amer*) -tərənt] *nc* a place where meals may be bought and eaten.

restaurateur [restərə'tə:] *nc* (*formal*) the owner or manager of a restaurant.

'restaurant-car *nc* a carriage on a train in which meals are served to travellers.

restitution [resti'tju:ʃən] *nu* (*formal*) the act of giving back to a person *etc* what was lost or taken away, or the giving of money *etc* to pay for damage, loss or injury: *When the war ended the defeated country was forced to make restitution to the victors for the destruction they had caused.*

restive ['restiv] *adj* 1 (*formal*) unwilling to accept control, delay *etc*; beginning to show displeasure, impatience, boredom *etc*: *When the singer was late the audience grew restive; rather a restive group of* *people.* 2 (*loosely*) restless; always moving: *He doesn't like his new job – he's become rather restive*; *She's in a restive mood.* 3 (of a horse *etc*) difficult to control; unwilling to move forwards. **'restively** *adv.* **'restiveness** *nu.*

restore [rə'sto:] *vt* (*formal*) 1 to repair (a building, a painting, a piece of furniture *etc*) so that it looks as it used to or ought to: *He is employed to restore paintings.* 2 to bring back to a normal or healthy state: *The patient was soon restored to health.* 3 to bring or give (something) back: *The police chief said that his men would do everything necessary to restore law and order*; *The police restored the stolen cars to their owners.* 4 to bring or put (a person) back to a position, rank *etc* he once had: *The manager was asked to resign but was later restored to his former job.*

ˌresto'ration [restə-] *ncu*: *the restoration of a person to his former job*; *The building was closed for restorations.* – *See also* **the Restoration** *below.*

re'storative [-rətiv] *nc, adj* (*formal*) (a food, medicine *etc*) that restores (a person's health, strength *etc*): *The French regard that liqueur as a restorative.*

re'storer *ncu* (*often in cmpds*) a person or thing that restores (something): *a furniture restorer*; *hair-restorer* (= something that claims to bring back hair to bald heads).

the Restoration the return of Charles II as king of Great Britain and Ireland in 1660, after a period of republican rule under Oliver Cromwell: (*attrib*) *Restoration poetry.*

restrain [rə'strein] *vt* 1 (*more formal than* **prevent**) to prevent (a person, animal *etc* from doing something); to control (a person, animal *etc*): *He was so angry he could hardly restrain himself*; *He had to be restrained from hitting the man.* 2 (*formal*) to control or prevent (a feeling *etc*): *He restrained his anger with difficulty.* 3 (*formal*) to put (a person) in prison *etc* or in a strait-jacket *etc*: *He is mentally ill and violent – he has to be restrained.* 4 (*formal*) to limit or restrict (something): *His ambition/activities must be restrained somehow.*

re'strained *adj* (*neg* **un-**) controlling, or able to control, one's emotions; *It was very restrained of you not to hit him*; *He was very restrained – he didn't lose his temper in spite of their insults*; *in a very restrained mood.*

re'straint [-t] 1 *nu* the act of restraining or state of being restrained: *He showed great restraint when they called him a liar*; *The lunatic was placed under restraint in a mental hospital.* 2 *nc* (*formal*) something which limits or restricts (something): *Lack of money and lack of machinery are two restraints on the growth of this firm.* 3 *nu* the avoidance of exaggeration, language which is too shocking *etc* in literature *etc*: *He described in full the horrors of war, but did so with restraint.*

restrict [rə'strikt] *vt* 1 (*often with* **to**) to keep (a person, thing *etc*) within certain limits: *I try to restrict myself/my smoking to five cigarettes a day*; *During these experiments, entry to this room is restricted to authorized personnel only.* 2 to make (something) less than usual, desirable *etc*: *After the accident, the driver said his view of the road had been restricted by a high hedge*; *He feels this new law will restrict his freedom.*

re'stricted *adj* (*neg* **un-**: *formal*) 1 limited: *a restricted space*; *The space provided is too restricted.* 2 (*usu attrib*) to which entry has been restricted to certain people: *The battlefield was a restricted zone.* 3 (*attrib*) in which certain restrictions (*eg* a speed limit) apply: *a restricted area.*

re'striction [-ʃən] *ncu*: *Even in a free democracy a person's behaviour is obviously subject to certain restrictions*; *The government placed restrictions on the number of foreign cars that could be imported*; *He dislikes their restriction of his freedom of choice.*

re'strictive [-tiv] *adj* (*formal*) restricting or intended to restrict (something): *I find living in the country too restrictive*; *rather a restrictive way of life.* **re'strictively** *adv.*

restrictive practice (*often in pl*: *formal*) some form of activity in trade or industry which keeps prices high, prevents the most efficient use of men and machinery *etc*: *That firm has been found guilty of restrictive practices.*

result [rə'zʌlt] 1 *ncu* anything which is due to something already done: *His deafness is the result of a car accident*; *He went deaf as a result of an accident*; *We've had some excellent results with our sales campaign*; *He worked hard, but without result.* 2 *nc* the answer to a sum *etc*: *Add all these figures and tell me the result.* 3 *nc* the final score (in a football match *etc*): *What was the result of Saturday's match?* 4 *nc* (*often in pl*) the list of people who have been successful in a competition, of subjects a person has passed or failed in an examination *etc*: *He had very good exam results*; *The results will be published next week.* – *vi* (*formal*) 1 (*often with* **from**) to be caused (by something): *We will pay for any damage which results* (*from our experiments*). 2 (*with* **in**) to cause or have as a result: *The experiment resulted in the discovery of a cure for cancer*; *The match resulted in a draw.*

re'sultant *adj* (*attrib*), (*formal*) (something) which is the result (of something): *He worked hard and deserved his resultant successes.*

resume [rə'zju:m] 1 (*formal*) *vti* to begin again after stopping: *After tea, the meeting resumed*; *We'll resume the meeting after tea.* 2 *vt* (*very formal*) to go back to or into (a position *etc*); to take back again: *At the end of his speech, he resumed his seat* (= he sat down again); *He has resumed possession of the castle.*

resumption [rə'zʌmpʃən] *ncu*: *the resumption of war.*

résumé ['reizumei, (*Amer*) 're-, rezu'mei] *nc* (*formal*) a short statement of the most important details (of a story, report *etc*).

resumption *see* **resume**.

resurgence [ri'sə:dʒəns] *nu* (*formal*) the act of coming again into a state of activity *etc* (after a period of inactivity *etc*): *the resurgence of nationalistic feeling among the Scots.* **re'surgent** *adj* (*attrib*).

resurrection [rezə'rekʃən] 1 *nu* (*fig*: *often facet*) the act of resurrecting (something): *the resurrection of certain New Year customs.* 2 *nc* the act of becoming alive again after death. – *See also* **the Resurrection** *below.*

ˌresur'rect [-'rekt] *vt* (*fig*: *often facet*) to bring back (a custom, story *etc*) into general use: *Our village has resurrected the custom of dancing round the maypole*; *Those trade unionists have resurrected the old story about the rich capitalists and the poor workers.*

ˌthe Resurrection 1 the resurrection of Jesus. 2 the resurrection of all dead people on the Day of Judgement.

resuscitate [rə'sʌsəteit] *vt* (*formal*) to bring (a

person) back to consciousness: *They resuscitated the swimmer who had almost drowned.* **reˌsusci'tation** *nu.*

retail[1] ['ri:teil] **1** *vt* to sell (goods) (*usu* in small quantities) to the person who is going to use them (rather than to someone who is going to sell them to someone else). **2** *vi* (of goods) to be sold in this way: *These books retail at £1.* – *nu* (*usu attrib*) the sale of goods in this way: *a retail price.* – *adv* by retail; in small quantities or at retail prices: *This shop sells goods retail.*

'retailer *nc* a person who sells goods retail; a shopkeeper.

See also **wholesale**.

retail[2] [ri'teil] *vt* (*formal*) to tell (a story *etc*) in great detail.

retain [rə'tein] *vt* **1** (*more formal than* **keep**) to continue to have, use, remember *etc*; to keep in one's possession, memory *etc*: *He finds it difficult to retain information*; *He retained the use of his legs till the day he died*; *These dishes don't retain heat very well.* **2** (*formal*) to pay (a person, *esp* a lawyer) a sum of money to do a particular job, or so that one can ask for his services when needed: *We retained (the services of) an excellent lawyer.* **3** to hold (something) back or keep (something) in its place: *This wall was built to retain the water from the river in order to prevent flooding.*

re'tainer *nc* **1** a sum of money paid (to a person, *esp* a lawyer) to retain him: *We pay him a retainer to act as adviser to us.* **2** (*old*) a servant (to a family), *eg* a butler, gardener, cook: *His grandfather had several retainers.*

See also **retention**.

retake [ri:'teik] – *pt* **ˌre'took** [-'tuk] : *ptp* **ˌre'taken** – *vt* **1** to capture (something) again: *The soldiers set out to retake the villages that the enemy had captured the day before.* **2** to film (part of a film *etc*) again: *We'll need to retake the last scene.* – ['ri:teik] *nc* (*inf*) the filming of part of a film again: *This is the fourth retake of this scene.*

retaliate [rə'talieit] *vi* (*formal*) to do something unpleasant (to a person) in return for something unpleasant he has done to one: *If you insult him, he will retaliate*; *If we attack now, they may retaliate against us.*

reˌtali'ation *ncu* (*formal*): *The attack was carried out in retaliation for the enemy attack the previous week.*

re'taliatory [-ətəri] *adj* (*formal*) done or intended as a retaliation: *a retaliatory attack*; *Their action was simply retaliatory.*

retard [rə'ta:d] *vt* (*formal*) **1** to make (something) slower or later: *Strikes only serve to retard this country's economic progress.* **2** to make (a person's mental or physical development) slower or less than normal: *The injury to his head seems to have retarded his thought processes.* **ˌretar'dation** [ri:ta:-] *nu.*

re'tarded *adj* having a physical or *usu* mental development which is slower or less than normal: *a mentally retarded child*; *He has been retarded since birth.*

retch [retʃ] *vi* to make the muscular actions and sound of vomiting, *usu* without actually vomiting: *The sight of the dead body without a head made him retch.*

retention [rə'tenʃən] *nu* (*formal*) the act of retaining: *the retention of information*; *the retention of heat*; *the retention of Mr Smith as adviser.*

re'tentive [-tiv] *adj* (*formal*) able to retain: *a retentive memory* (= a memory which is able to retain information); *retentive soil* (= soil which holds water and does not dry out quickly); *His mind is very retentive.*

retexture [ri:'tekstʃə] *vt* to treat (a coat, blanket *etc*) with chemicals which bring back the original firmness of the material which has been lost in dry-cleaning it: *I'd like this coat to be cleaned and retextured, please.*

rethink [ri:'θiŋk] – *pt, ptp* **ˌre'thought** [-'θo:t] – *vt* to consider (a plan *etc*) again and come to a different decision about it: *The Government was asked to rethink its policy on taxation.* – ['ri:θiŋk] *nc* (*inf*) the act of rethinking: *We'll have to have a rethink about this project.*

reticent ['retisənt] *adj* (*formal*) not willing to say much (about something); not usually speaking very much: *He's very reticent about what the manager said to him*; *a reticent person.* **'reticence** *nu.*

retina – *pls* **'retinas, 'retinae** [-ni:] – *nc* (*tech*) the part of the back of the eye that receives the image of what is seen.

retinue ['retinju:] *nc* (*formal or facet*) the servants, officials *etc* who travel with a person of importance, or who appear with him on important occasions *etc*: *the king and his retinue*; *the film-star and her retinue.*

retire [rə'taiə] **1** *vti* to (cause to) stop working permanently, *usu* because of age: *He retired at the age of sixty-five*; *In order to save the younger men's jobs, some of the older workers were retired early.* **2** *vi* (*formal*) to go to bed: *We always retire at midnight.* **3** *vi* (*formal or facet*) to leave; to go away (to somewhere): *When he doesn't want to talk to anyone, he retires to his garden shed and locks the door*; (*formal*) *The ladies retired to the lounge while the men stayed in the dining-room and smoked.* **4** *vi* (*formal*) (of soldiers *etc*) to move back: *The enemy attack was so strong that the soldiers were forced to retire to safer positions.*

re'tiral *ncu* (*formal*) (an) act of retiring from work: *He died shortly after his retiral*; *There have been several retirals from the firm this month.*

re'tired *adj* having stopped working: *My father is retired now*; *a retired university professor.*

re'tirement *ncu* **1** the act of retiring from work: *There have been several retirements this year*; *It is not long till his retirement*; *He has gone into retirement* (= He has retired). **2** a person's life after retiring from work: *He's enjoying his retirement.*

re'tiring *adj* (*formal*) shy; not liking to be with people, to be noticed *etc*: *She's a very shy, quiet, retiring person*; *She is too retiring to enter for a beauty contest.*

retook *see* **retake**.

retort [rə'to:t] *vi* to make a quick and clever or angry reply: *'You're not very clever yourself,' he retorted.* – *nc* a quick and clever or angry reply.

retrace [ri'treis] *vt* (*formal*) **1** to go back along (a path *etc*) one has just come along: *She lost her keys somewhere on the way to the station, and had to retrace her steps until she found them.* **2** to describe or form a mental picture of something a person has done: *The police asked the woman to retrace her actions before the accident occurred.*

retract [rə'trakt] *vti* (*formal*) **1** to admit that one should not have said something, or that what one said *etc* was wrong, offensive *etc*: *The speaker was told to retract (his insulting remarks).* **2** to pull (something), or be able to be pulled, into (the body *etc*): *A cat can retract its claws*; *A cat's claws can retract.* **re'traction** [-ʃən] *ncu.*

re'tractable *adj* (*formal*) able to be pulled up or in: *An aeroplane has retractable wheels*; *Are the wheels retractable?*

retread [riː'tred] *vt* to make a new tread on (an old or worn tyre). – ['riːtred] *nc* a retreaded tyre: *We can't afford new tyres – we'll have to buy retreads.*

retreat [rə'triːt] *vi* **1** (of soldiers) to move back or away from a battle (*usu* because the enemy is winning): *After a hard struggle, they were finally forced to retreat*; (*fig facet*) *After being severely criticized at the meeting, he retreated to his office*; (*fig*) *After a week's work, I like to retreat to the country to relax.* – **1** *ncu* the act of retreating (from a battle, danger *etc*): *After the retreat, the soldiers rallied once more.* **2** *nc* (*no pl*: *usu with* **the**) a signal to retreat: *The bugler sounded the retreat.* **3** *nc* (*formal*) (a place to which a person can go for) a period of rest, religious meditation *etc*: *He has gone to a retreat to pray.*

beat a (hasty) retreat *see* **beat.**

retribution [retri'bjuːʃən] *nu* (*formal or relig*) deserved punishment: *He cannot escape retribution for his sins*; *Retribution is bound to overtake him* (= He is bound to be punished).

retrieve [rə'triːv] **1** *vt* (*formal*) to get back (something which was lost *etc*): *My hat blew away, but I managed to retrieve it*; (*fig*) *He must do something to retrieve his reputation*; (*fig*) *All our plans have gone wrong, but we may still manage to retrieve the situation.* **2** *vti* (of *usu* trained dogs) to search for and bring back (birds or animals that have been shot by a hunter): *The spaniel retrieved the pheasant his master had shot*; *Does your dog retrieve?*

re'trieval *nu* (*formal*) the act or possibility of retrieving: *the retrieval of stolen goods*; *The situation is now beyond retrieval.*

re'triever *nc* a breed of dog trained to find and bring back birds and animals that have been shot: *The golden retriever is an excellent hunting dog.*

See also **irretrievable.**

retrograde ['retrəgreid] *adj* (*formal*: *usu attrib*) being, or causing (something) to be, in a worse, less desirable *etc* state than it was before: *The re-introduction of hanging as a punishment for murder would be thought of by many people as a retrograde step.*

retrospect ['retrəspekt]: **in 'retrospect** (*formal*) when considering or looking back on what has happened: *It seemed a good idea when we started six months ago, but in retrospect I can see that we should never have agreed to do it.*

ˌretro'spective [-tiv] *adj* (*formal*) **1** (of a law *etc*) applying to the past as well as to the present and to the future: *The new tax laws were made retrospective.* **2** (*usu attrib*) looking back on past events: *in retrospective mood.* **ˌretro'spectively** *adv.*

return [rə'təːn] **1** *vi* to come or go back: *He returns home tomorrow*; *He will return to London tomorrow*; *He returned from Paris yesterday*; *He expects us to have finished this before he returns*; *The pain has returned*; *He has returned to his evil way of life.* **2** *vt* to give, send, put *etc* (something) back where it came from: *He returned the book to its shelf*; *Don't forget to return the books you borrowed.* **3** *vi* (*with* **to**) to (continue to) talk about (something) later: *I'll return to this topic in a minute.* **4** *vt* to do (something) which has been done to oneself: *He returned the blow* (= He hit the person who hit him); *She returned the compliment* (= She said something complimentary to the person who had said something complimentary about her). **5** *vt* to elect (someone) to be a Member of Parliament: *He has been returned to Parliament as member for London Central.* **6** *vt* (*legal*) (of a jury) to give (a verdict): *The jury returned a verdict of not guilty.* **7** *vt* (in tennis *etc*) to hit (a ball) back to one's opponent: *She returned his serve.* – **1** *ncu* the act of returning: *On our return, we found the house had been burgled*; *the return of a ball in tennis*; (*attrib*) *a return journey.* **2** *nc* (*often in pl*) profit: *We're hoping for a good return on our investment*; *Our returns are not as good as we had hoped.* **3** *nc* a statement of income (for calculating a person's income tax), or of other official facts and figures: *Have you filled in a tax return this year?* **4** *nc* (*Brit*) a return ticket: *Do you want a single or a return?*; *A day return is valid for a return journey made on a particular day*; *A weekend return is valid for a return journey made between Friday and Monday.*

re'turnable *adj* (*usu pred*: *formal*) **1** able to be returned: *This form is returnable to any of our offices*; *These lemonade bottles are non-returnable.* **2** which must be returned: *This form is returnable by the end of this month.*

return match *nc* a second match played between the same (teams of) players: *We played the first match on our football pitch – the return match will be on theirs.*

return ticket *nc* a ticket which allows a person to travel to a place and back again to where he started from.

by return (of post) (*formal*) (of a letter *etc*) to be returned immediately; (sent) by the very next post: *Please send me your reply by return of post.*

in re'turn (for) as an exchange (for something): *We'll send them whisky and they'll send us vodka in return*: *They'll send us vodka in return for whisky.*

many happy returns (of the day) an expression of good wishes (said to a person on his birthday): *He visited his mother on her birthday to wish her many happy returns.*

point of no return *see* **point.**

reunion [riː'juːnjən] **1** *nc* a meeting of people who have not met for some time: *We attended a reunion of former pupils of school*; *We have annual reunions.* **2** *nu* the act of reuniting or state of being reunited: *the reunion of old friends.*

reunite [riːju'nait] *vti* (*often with* **with**) to bring or come together after being separated: *The family was finally reunited after the war*; *The children were reunited with their parents.*

rev [rev] – *pt, ptp* **revved** – (*inf*: *often* **rev up**) **1** *vti* to increase the speed of revolution of (a car engine *etc*): *He revved the engine* (*up*). **2** *vi* (of a car engine *etc*) to have an increased speed of revolution: *Don't let the engine rev* (*up*).

revs *n pl* (*inf*) revolutions (of a car engine *etc*): *thirty revs a second.*

reveal [rə'viːl] *vt* (*slightly formal*) **1** to make known: *All their secrets have been revealed*; *He will never reveal his methods.* **2** to show; to allow (someone) to see (something): *He scraped away the top layer of paint, revealing a second painting beneath it*; *That dress would reveal more of me than I am willing to show.*

re'vealing *adj* allowing or causing something to be known or seen: *a revealing book/dress*; *That dress is too revealing.*

See also **revelation**.

reveille [ri'vali, (*Amer*) 'revəli] *ncu* a bugle call at daybreak to waken soldiers: *The bugler sounded (the) reveille.*

revel ['revl] – *pt, ptp* **'revelled**, (*Amer*) **'reveled** – *vi* (*formal*: *with* **in**) to take great delight in something: *He revels in danger*; *He revels in doing dangerous tasks.* – *nc* (*formal or facet*: *usu in pl*) noisy, lively enjoyment (*usu* of a group of people): *midnight revels.*

'reveller *nc.*

'revelry *nu, nc* (*in pl*) (*formal or facet*) noisy, lively enjoyment: *Their revelry upset the old lady*; *midnight revelries.*

revelation [revə'leiʃən] (*formal or facet*) **1** *nu* the act of revealing (secrets, information *etc*): *the revelation of the true facts.* **2** *nc* something which is made known or seen, *esp* something which is not expected: *It was quite a revelation to me to see the boss drunk at the party*; *Such revelations shocked my mother.*

revelry *see* **revel**.

revenge [rə'vendʒ] *nu* **1** harm done to another person in return for harm which he has done (to oneself or to someone else): *The man told the manager he would get/have his revenue on the company for dismissing him*; *His revenge was to burn down the factory.* **2** the desire to do such harm: *The man said he had burned down the factory out of revenge/in revenge for being dismissed.* – **1** *vt* to do harm to another person in return for harm done (to oneself or someone else): *He revenged his father's death.* **2** *v refl* (*with* **on**) to get revenge (on someone): *He revenged himself on his enemies.*

be revenged/take revenge (*usu with* **on**) to get revenge: *He was so angry with her he took revenge on her cat.*

See also **avenge, vengeance**.

revenue ['revinju:] *nu* (*formal*) money which comes to a person *etc* from any source or sources (*eg* property, shares), *esp* the money which comes to a government from taxes *etc*: *Much of the government's revenue comes from income tax.*

the Inland Revenue *see* **inland**.

reverberate [rə'və:bəreit] *vi* (*formal*) (of a sound) to echo and re-echo: *The noise reverberated round the hall.* **re͵verbe'ration** *ncu.*

revere [rə'viə] *vt* (*very formal*) to feel or show great respect for (someone): *Students revere the older professor.*

reverence ['revərəns] *nu* great respect: *He was held in reverence by those who worked for him*; *Young people nowadays show little reverence for the church.*

Reverend ['revərənd] *n* (*usu abbrev* **Rev.** *when written*: *often with* **the**) a title given to a clergyman: (*the*) *Rev. John Brown*; (*very formal*) *the Rev. Mr Brown.*

reverent ['revərənt] *adj* (*formal*) showing great respect: *A reverent silence followed the professor's lecture*; *His attitude to his tutor is almost reverent.*

'reverently *adv.*

reverential [revə'renʃəl] *adj* (*formal*) showing great respect. **͵reve'rentially** *adv.*

See also **irreverent**.

reverie ['revəri] (*formal*) **1** *nu* a state of pleasant dreamy thought: *He was lost in reverie.* **2** *nc* (*usu in pl*) such a thought; a day-dream: *pleasant reveries.*

reverse [rə'və:s] **1** *vti* to move backwards or in the opposite direction to normal: *He reversed the car into the garage*; *The car reversed into a lamp-post*; *The direction of movement of this machine can be reversed by pressing this button.* **2** *vt* to put (something) into the opposite position, state, order *etc*: *We'll reverse (the order in which we deal with) the items on the agenda, and take item two first*; *This jacket can be reversed* (= worn inside out). **3** *vt* to change (a decision, policy *etc*) to the exact opposite: *The previous government was in favour of high taxation, but this policy has been reversed by this government*; *The man was found guilty, but the judges in the appeal court reversed the decision* (= declared him innocent). – **1** *nu* the opposite of (something): *What he said to you is exactly the reverse of what he told me yesterday*; *'Are you hungry?' 'Quite the reverse – I've eaten far too much!'* **2** *nc* (*formal*) a defeat; a piece of bad luck: *This firm has suffered a few minor reverses but is now making good profits.* **3** *ncu* (a mechanism *eg* one of the gears of a car *etc* which makes something move in) a backwards direction or a direction opposite to normal: *He put the car into reverse*; (*attrib*) *a reverse gear.* **4** *nc* the back of a coin, medal *etc*: (*attrib*) *the reverse side of a coin.*

re'versal *ncu* (*formal*) the act of reversing or being reversed: *a reversal of his previous decision.*

re'versed *adj* in the opposite state, position, order *etc*: *Once he worked for me. Now our positions are reversed and I work for him.*

re'versible *adj* **1** able to be reversed. **2** (of clothes) able to be worn with either side out: *a reversible cape*; *Is that raincoat reversible?*

reverse the charges to make a telephone call (a **reverse-charge call**) which is paid for by the person who receives it instead of by the caller: *When she phoned her parents she reversed the charges as she did not have any money.*

reversion *see* **revert**.

revert [rə'və:t] *vi* (*formal*: *with* **to**) **1** to come or go back to something talked about earlier: *Shall we revert to our previous topic?* **2** to go back to a former, *usu* worse, state or condition: *Soon after the missionaries left, the tribesmen reverted to their old beliefs.* **3** (*legal*) (of an object, title *etc*) to return or be returned to its previous owner or to (a member of) his family. **re'version** [-ʃən, (*Amer*) -ʒən] *nu.*

review [rə'vju:] *nc* **1** a written report on a book, play *etc* giving the person's opinion of its value *etc*: *Have you read the review of his latest novel?* **2** (*with cap in titles*) a magazine which contains such reports, along with other articles on interesting events *etc.* **3** a (second or additional) study or consideration of facts, events *etc*: *We'll have a review of the situation/of our progress at the end of the month.* **4** an inspection of troops *etc.* – *vt* to make or have a review of (someone or something): *The book was reviewed in yesterday's paper*; *The Queen reviewed the troops*; *We'll review the situation at the end of the month.*

re'viewer *nc* a person who reviews (something): *Who was the reviewer of the biography of Churchill?*

revile [rə'vail] *vt* (*old*) to say unpleasant things about (someone or something).

revise [rə'vaiz] **1** *vt* to (examine in order to) correct faults and make improvements (in a book *etc*): *This dictionary has been completely revised.* **2** *vti* to study one's previous work, notes *etc* in preparation for an examination *etc*: *You'd better start revising (your Latin) for your exam.* **3** *vt* (*formal*) to change (one's opinion *etc*).

revision [rə'viʒən] **1** *nu* the act of revising: *The* *revision of that book took several years.* **2** *nc* a book *etc* that has been revised: *That book is a revision of his earlier work.*

revive [rə'vaiv] *vti* **1** to come, or bring, back to consciousness, strength, health *etc*: *They attempted to revive the woman who fainted; She soon revived; The flowers seemed to be dying, but revived in water;* (*fig*) *We need something to revive our hopes.* **2** to come or bring back to use, to an active state *etc*: *This old custom has recently been revived in some parts of the country.*

re'vival **1** *ncu* the act of reviving or state of being revived: *the revival of the invalid; the revival of our hopes.* **2** *nc* (a time of) new or increased interest (in something): *a religious revival.* **3** *ncu* (the act of producing) an old and almost forgotten play on the stage: *I am tired of these revivals on television.*

re'vivalist *nc* a person who creates or helps to create a religious revival.

revoke [rə'vouk] *vt* (*formal*) to change (a decision); to make (a law *etc*) no longer valid: *The chairman revoked his previous decision.* **revocation** [revə'keiʃən] *nu.*

revolt [rə'voult] **1** *vi* (*often with* **against**) to rebel (against a government *etc*): *The army revolted against the dictator.* **2** *vt* to disgust: *His habits revolt me.* – **1** *nu* the act of rebelling: *The peasants rose in revolt.* **2** *nc* a rebellion: *the Peasants' Revolt.*

re'volted *adj* (*usu pred*) having a feeling of disgust: *I feel quite revolted at the idea of walking about naked.*

re'volting *adj* causing a feeling of disgust: *revolting habits; This pudding is revolting.* **re'voltingly** *adv.* **re'voltingness** *nu.*

See also **revolution, revulsion**.

revolution [revə'lu:ʃən] **1** *ncu* (the act of making) a successful, violent attempt to change or remove (a government *etc*): *the American Revolution.* **2** *nc* a complete change in ideas, methods *etc*: *There's been a complete revolution in the way things are done in this office; the Industrial Revolution* (= the economic, industrial and social changes in Britain in the late eighteenth and early nineteenth centuries, caused by the great increase in the use of (large) machinery in industry). **3** *nc* a complete circle or turn round a central point, axis *etc* (*eg* as made by a record turning on a record-player, a wheel turning on an axle or the Earth moving round the Sun). **4** *ncu* the act of turning or moving round a central point, axis *etc*: *the revolution of the Earth round the Sun.*

ˌrevo'lutionary *adj* **1** involving or causing great changes (in ideas, methods *etc*): *a revolutionary new process for making paper; His methods are quite revolutionary.* **2** (*usu attrib*) of a revolution (*def 1*): *He was sentenced to thirty years' imprisonment for revolutionary activities.* – *nc* a person who takes part in, or is in favour of, (a) revolution: *The dictator imprisoned the revolutionaries.*

ˌrevo'lutionize, -ise *vt* (*formal*) to cause great changes in (ideas, methods *etc*): *This new machinery will revolutionize the paper-making industry.*

See also **rev, revolt, revolve**.

revolve [rə'volv] *vti* to move, roll or turn (in a complete circle) around a central point, axis *etc*: *A wheel revolves on its axle; This disc can be revolved; The Moon revolves (a)round the Earth; The Earth revolves* (= moves in a circle) *about the Sun and also revolves* (= spins) *on a line drawn from the North Pole to the South Pole.*

re'volver *nc* a type of pistol: *She shot him with a revolver.*

re'volving *adj* (*usu attrib*) which revolves: *a revolving stage in a theatre; revolving doors.*

See also **revolution**.

revue [rə'vju:] *nc* an amusing, not very serious, theatre show *usu* with songs, short plays *etc*, often based on recent events, important or popular people *etc.*

revulsion [rə'vʌlʃən] *nu* **1** (*often with* **against**) disgust; great dislike: *a feeling of revulsion; a revulsion against war.* **2** (*often with* **a**) a sudden change of feeling, opinion *etc*, *esp* from love to hate.

See also **revolt**.

reward [rə'wo:d] **1** *ncu* something given in return for or got from work done (*usu* for someone else), good behaviour *etc*: *He was given a gold watch as a reward for his services to the firm; He doesn't want any money – he says that his pleasure at being able to help is reward enough; Apart from the salary, teaching children has its own particular rewards.* **2** *nc* a sum of money offered for finding or helping to find a criminal, lost or stolen property *etc*: *A reward of £50 has been offered to the person who finds the diamond brooch.* – *vt* (*often with* **for**) to give a reward to someone for something: *He was rewarded for his services; His services were rewarded.*

re'warding *adj* (*neg* **un-**) giving pleasure, satisfaction *etc*: *a rewarding job; She finds looking after children very rewarding.*

reword [ri:'wə:d] *vt* to say or write (something) with different words: *This letter will have to be reworded.*

rhapsody ['rapsədi] *nc* music, poetry or speech which shows strong feeling or excitement.

go into rhapsodies over (something) to talk very enthusiastically about (something): *She went into rhapsodies over her new hat.*

rhetoric ['retərik] *nu* (*formal*) **1** the art of speaking and writing well, *esp* to persuade people: *He studied rhetoric.* **2** language which is full of unnecessarily long, formal or literary words and phrases, and which is also often insincere: *Politicians' speeches are often full of rhetoric.*

rhe'torical [-'to-] *adj.*

rhetorical question *nc* a question which the speaker answers himself, or which does not need an answer.

rheumatism ['ru:mətizəm] *nu* a disease which causes stiffness and pain in one's joints (*eg* in one's hips, knees, fingers *etc*): *She has rheumatism in her fingers – she finds it difficult to type.*

rheu'matic [-'ma-] **1** *nc, adj* (a person who is) suffering from rheumatism: *a rheumatic old man; He is a rheumatic.* **2** *adj* of or caused by rheumatism: *rheumatic pains.*

rheu'matics [-'ma-] *n pl* (*inf*) (pain caused by) rheumatism: *His rheumatics are bothering him today.*

rheumatic fever a kind of serious infectious disease of children causing fever, painful swelling of the joints and possible damage to the heart.

rhino ['rainou] – *pl* **'rhinos** – short for **rhinoceros**.

rhinoceros [rai'nosərəs] – *pls* **rhi'noceroses**, (*sometimes*) **rhi'noceros** – *nc* a type of large thick-skinned animal with one or two horns on its nose: *The hunter was charged by a herd of* *rhinoceros(es)*; *Two rhinoceroses were drinking from a shady pool.*

Rhodesia, Rhodesian *see* Appendix 2.

rhododendron [roudə'dendrən] *nc* a type of flowering shrub with thick evergreen leaves and large flowers.

rhubarb ['ru:ba:b] *nu* **1** a large-leaved garden plant, the stalks of which can be cooked and eaten: *He grows rhubarb by the side of the house.* **2** the stalks as food: *We had rhubarb and custard for dessert*; *(attrib) rhubarb jam.*

rhyme [raim] **1** *nc* a short poem: *a book of rhymes for children.* **2** *nu* poetry: *To amuse his colleagues he wrote his report in rhyme.* **3** *nc* a word which is like another in its final sound(s): *Beef and leaf are rhymes.* **4** *nu* (the use of) a pattern of words which are like each other in their final sound(s) *eg* at the ends of lines in a poem. – *vi* (*often with* **with**) (of words) to be rhymes: *Beef rhymes with leaf.*

rhyme or reason (*always in neg*) sense; system; reason: *This system of classifying books seems to be without rhyme or reason/seems to have neither rhyme nor reason.*

rhythm ['riðəm] **1** *ncu* a regular, repeated pattern of sounds, stresses or beats in music, speech (*esp* poetry) *etc*: *Just listen to the rhythm of those drums*; *The music those tribesmen are playing contains some incredibly complicated rhythms.* **2** *ncu* a regular, repeated pattern of movements: *The rowers lost their rhythm and the boat lost speed.* **3** *nu* an ability to sing, move *etc* with rhythm: *That girl will be a great dancer – she's got natural rhythm.*

'rhythmic, 'rhythmical *adjs* of or with rhythm: *rhythmic movement*; *The dancing was very rhythmical.* **'rhythmically** *adv.*

rib [rib] *nc* **1** any one of the bones which curve round and forward from the backbone, enclosing the heart and lungs: *He broke a rib when he fell off his motorcycle.* **2** one of the curved pieces of wood which are joined to the keel to form the framework of a boat. **3** a vertical raised strip in knitted or woven material, or the pattern formed by a number of these. **4** any of a number of things similar in shape, use *etc* to a rib (*defs 1, 2*) *eg* one of the supports for the fabric of an aeroplane wing or of an umbrella. – *v* – *pt, ptp* **ribbed** – *vt* (*inf*: *slightly old*) to tease (someone): *They ribbed him about the book of poetry he had written.*

ribbed *adj* having ribs (*esp def 3*): *a ribbed pattern.*

'ribbing *nu* **1** a pattern or arrangement of ribs. **2** (*inf*) teasing: *She had to put up with a lot of ribbing when she had her hair permed.*

ribald ['ribəld] *adj* (*formal*) rude; vulgar: *ribald jokes*; *His stories are always rather ribald.* **'ribaldry** *nu.*

ribbon ['ribən] *ncu* a long narrow strip of material used in decorating clothes, tying hair *etc*: *The little girl had a blue ribbon in her hair*; *He bought four metres of red ribbon.*

rice [rais] *nu* **1** a plant, grown in well-watered ground in tropical countries: *He grows rice.* **2** the seeds of the plant, which are cooked and eaten: *We had rice and stewed apples for pudding*; *We had curried lamb and rice for supper.*

rich [ritʃ] *adj* **1** wealthy; having a lot of money, possessions *etc*: *a rich man/country*; *He is so rich that he does not have to work.* **2** (*formal*: *pred with* **in**) having a lot of (something): *This part of the country is rich in coal.* **3** (*formal*: *attrib*) valuable; large: *a rich reward.* **4** (of cakes *etc*) containing a lot of fat, eggs *etc*: *This sauce is too rich for me*; *a rich fruit cake.* **5** (*formal*) (of clothes, material *etc*) very beautiful and expensive. **6** (*formal*) (of colours and sounds) deep and strong: *a rich purple*; *Her voice is low and rich.* **7** (of soil) producing good crops. **8** (*inf*) amusing; ironic: *He accused me of lying? That's rich – he never tells the truth himself!*

'riches *n pl* wealth.

'richly *adv* **1** (*formal*) in a rich manner: *The king was richly dressed.* **2** with riches: *He was richly rewarded.*

'richness *nu* the state of being rich (*except def 1*).

the rich rich people.

richly deserved very much deserved: *His punishment was richly deserved.*

strike it rich *see* **strike**.

rickety ['rikəti] *adj* not well built; unsteady; likely to fall over or collapse: *a rickety table*; *This chair is rather rickety.*

rickshaw ['rikʃo:] *nc* in Japan *etc*, a small two-wheeled carriage pulled by a man.

ricochet ['rikəʃei] – *pt, ptp* **'ricocheted** [-ʃeid] – *vi* to hit something and bounce away at an angle: *The bullet ricocheted off the wall.*

rid [rid] – *ptp* **'ridding**: *pt, ptp* **rid** – *vt* (*old or formal*: *with* **of**) to remove someone or something from (a person, thing *etc*); to free (a person, thing *etc*) from (a worry, problem *etc*): *I can't see how to rid myself of these irritating people*; *He rid the town of rats.*

be, get 'rid of (someone or something) to have removed/remove (someone or something); to free oneself from (a problem, worry *etc*); to make (someone or something) go away: *I thought I'd never get rid of these stains/weeds/people/debts.*

,good 'riddance ['ridəns] (*sometimes with* **to**) I am happy to have got rid of (someone or something): *I've thrown out all those old books, and good riddance (to the lot of them)!*

ridden *see* **ride**.

riddle[1] ['ridl] *nc* a puzzle *usu* in the form of a question, which describes an object, person *etc* in a mysterious or misleading way: *Can you guess the answer to this riddle?*; *The answer to the riddle 'What flies for ever, and never rests?' is 'The wind'.*

riddle[2] ['ridl] *nc* a sort of tray with holes or wire mesh in the bottom, allowing powder and small objects to pass through, but not larger objects, and used therefore to separate *eg* stones from sand or soil. – *vt* **1** (*inf*) to make (something) full of holes: *They riddled the car with bullets.* **2** to pass (*eg* soil) through a riddle.

ride [raid] – *pt* **rode** [roud] : *ptp* **ridden** ['ridn] – **1** *vi* (*often with* **in** *or* **on**) to travel or be carried in a car, train *etc* or on a bicycle, horse *etc*: *He rides to work every day on an old bicycle*; *The little boy waved to the horsemen as they rode past.* **2** *vt* to (be able to) ride on and control a horse, bicycle *etc*: *Can you ride a bicycle?* **3** *vti* to take part in (a horse-race *etc*): *He's riding (in) the first race.* **4** *vi* to go out regularly on horseback (*eg* as a hobby): *My daughter rides every Saturday morning.* **5** *vi* (of a ship) to float at anchor. – *See also* **ride out, ride up** *below.* – *nc* **1** a journey on horseback, on a bicycle *etc*: *He likes to go for a long ride on a Sunday afternoon.* **2** (*inf*) a *usu* short period of riding on or in something: *Can I have a ride on your bike?*

'rider *nc* **1** a person who rides. **2** (*formal*) something added to what has already been said or written, *eg* an extra clause added to a document: *He added the rider that he hoped they would be happy.*

'riding-school *nc* a place where people are taught to ride horses.

let (something) ride (*inf*) to do nothing about (something); to let (something) continue as it is: *I can foresee a lot of problems with his plans, but we'll let that ride for the time being.*

ride out *vt sep* **1** (of a ship) to keep afloat throughout (a storm *etc*): *to ride out a storm.* **2** (*fig*) to survive until (a period of difficulty) is past: *I think we'll ride out the crisis.*

ride up *vi* (of a skirt *etc*) to move gradually up out of its correct position: *I can't wear this skirt when I go to town, as it rides up when I walk.*

take (someone) for a ride (*inf*) to trick, cheat or deceive (someone): *He doesn't actually work for a charity at all, so the people who have sent him money have been taken for a ride.*

ridge [ridʒ] *nc* **1** a long narrow piece of ground *etc* raised above the level of the ground *etc* on either side of it. **2** a long narrow row of hills. **3** anything like a ridge in shape: *A ridge of high pressure is a long narrow area of high pressure as shown on a weather map.* **4** the top edge of something where two sloping surfaces meet, *eg* on a roof.

ridiculous [rə'dikjuləs] *adj* very silly; deserving to be laughed at: *That's a ridiculous suggestion*; *You look ridiculous in that hat!*; *That's a ridiculous price for a hat* (= *eg* It is much too expensive). **ri'diculously** *adv.* **ri'diculousness** *nu.*

ridicule ['ridikju:l] *vt* (*formal*) to laugh at (a person or thing) because he, it *etc* appears very silly; to make (a person or thing) seem silly: *The child was ridiculed by the schoolchildren because he wore thick spectacles*; *They ridiculed him because he was wearing one brown shoe and one black shoe.* – *nu* (*formal*) laughter at someone or something which seems very silly; the act of making someone or something seem very silly: *Despite the ridicule of his neighbours he continued to build a space-ship in his garden.*

rife [raif] *adj* (*formal*: *pred*) (often of bad or unpleasant things) very common: *Disease and hunger are rife in that country.*

riff-raff ['rifraf] *nu* (*derog*) worthless people: *The boy's father said he didn't like the riff-raff he was associating with.*

rifle ['raifl] *nc* a gun with a long barrel, fired from the shoulder: *The soldiers are being taught to shoot with rifles.* – (*inf*) **1** *vti* to search through (something) thoroughly in order to steal something from it: *The thief rifled (through the contents of) the desk drawers.* **2** *vt* to steal (something): *The spy rifled the documents.*

'rifle-range 1 *nc* a place for rifle practice. **2** *nu* the distance over which a rifle can fire a bullet.

rift [rift] *nc* **1** (*formal or tech*) a split or crack, *eg* in the ground. **2** (*formal*) a disagreement between friends: *They used to be friends but there has been a rift between the two families recently.*

rig [rig] – *pt, ptp* **rigged** – *vt* **1** (*derog*) to manage or control illegally or dishonestly: *They rigged the election so that their candidate won*; *The butler stole the jewels but rigged the theft so that it seemed that a burglar had done it.* **2** to fit (a ship) with ropes and sails. – *See also* **rig out, rig up** *below.* – *nc* **1** an oil-rig. **2** any special equipment, tools *etc* for some purpose. **3** the arrangement of sails *etc* of a sailing-ship.

'rigging *nu* the ropes *etc* which control a ship's masts and sails.

rig out *vt sep* (*inf*) to dress (oneself, someone else): *She was rigged out in rather odd clothes* (*nc* **'rig-out**).

rig up *vt sep* to build (something) *usu* quickly with whatever material is available: *They rigged up a rough shelter with branches and mud.*

right [rait] *adj* **1** (*attrib*) on or related to the side of the body which in most people has the more skilful hand, or to the side of a person or thing which is toward the east when that person or thing is facing north (opposite to **left**): *When I'm writing, I hold my pen in my right hand*; *My right shoe is the shoe I put on my right foot*; *The right bank of a river is the bank which is on the right when one is looking in the same direction as the river is flowing.* **2** correct: *Put that book back in the right place*; *Is that the right answer to the question?*; *Is this answer right?* **3** (*usu pred*) morally correct; good: *It's not right to let thieves keep what they have stolen.* **4** suitable; appropriate: *He's not the right man for this job*; *We'll have to choose the right time to ask him*; *The time isn't right.* – **1** *nc* (*often in pl*) something a person is, or ought to be, allowed to have, do *etc*: *Everyone has the right to a fair trial*; *You must stand up and fight for your rights*; *You have no right to be here*; *civil rights* (= the rights of a citizen to political and religious freedom, justice *etc*). **2** *nu* that which is correct or good: *Who's in the right in this argument?* **3** *nu* the right side, part or direction: *Turn to the right*; *Take the second road on the right.* **4** *nu* (*sometimes with cap*) in politics, the people, group, party or parties holding the more traditional, conservative beliefs, *usu* in favour of *eg* capitalism, the monarchy *etc* and against (extreme) socialism *etc*: *the parties of the Right*; *He's on the right of the Labour Party.* **5** *nc* in boxing, (a punch with) one's right hand: *He hit him with his right*; *a right to the jaw.* – *See also* **rights** *below.* – *adv* **1** exactly: *He was standing right here.* **2** immediately: *I'll go right after lunch*; *I'll come right down* (= I'll come down at once). **3** close: *He was standing right beside me.* **4** completely; all the way: *The bullet went right through his arm*; *He walked right along the pier and back again.* **5** to the right: *Turn right.* **6** (*inf*) correctly: *Have I done that right?*; *These shoes don't fit right.* **7** in a suitable or agreeable way: *Don't worry – everything may turn out right in the end.* – *vt* **1** to bring, put or come back to the correct, *usu* upright, position: *The boat tipped over, but righted itself again*; *They managed to right the boat.* **2** (*formal or liter*) to put an end to and make up for something wrong that has been done: *He's like a medieval knight, going about the country looking for wrongs to right.* – *interj* I understand; I'll do what you say *etc*: *'I want you to type some letters for me.' 'Right, I'll do them now.'*

righteous ['raitʃəs] *adj* **1** (*formal*: *attrib*) caused by justifiable anger at something wrong that has been done: *righteous indignation.* **2** (*neg* **un-**: *old*) living a good moral life: *a righteous man.* **3** (*neg* **un-**: *old*) good; morally right: *a righteous action.* **'righteously** *adv* (*old*). **'righteousness** *nu* (*old*). – *See also* **self-righteous**.

'rightful *adj* (*attrib*) proper; correct; which ought to be or has a right to be (something): *He is the rightful king of this country.*

'rightfully *adv* because one has the right (to be, have *etc* something): *It rightfully belongs to me,* *although she has it at the moment.*

'rightly *adv* **1** it is right, good or just that (something is the case): *He was severely punished for his stupidity and rightly so*: *Rightly or wrongly she refused to speak to him* (= I am not willing or able to say whether she was right or not). **2** correctly; accurately: *They rightly assumed that he would refuse to help.*

'rightness *nu* the state of being good or morally correct: *They believe in the rightness of their cause.*

righto, right-oh [rait'ou] *interj* (*inf*: *esp Brit*) right: *Right-oh! I'll come now.*

rights *n pl* the legal right given in return for a sum of money to produce *eg* a film from a book: *He's sold the film rights of his new book to an American company.*

'right angle *nc* an angle of ninety degrees, like any of the four angles in a square.

'right-angled *adj* having a right angle: *a right-angled triangle.*

'right-hand *adj* (*attrib*) **1** at the right; to the right of something else: *If you want a pair of scissors, look in the top right-hand drawer of my desk.* **2** towards the right: *a right-hand bend in the road*. – *See also* **right-hand man** *below.*

ˌright-'handed *adj* **1** (of people) using the right hand more easily than the left, *eg* for writing: *When writing, right-handed people hold their pen or pencil in their right hand.* **2** for use by people of this kind. **ˌright-'handedness** *nu.*

ˌright-of-'way *nc* a road or path over private land along which the public have the right to walk *etc*: *You can't build a wall across this path – it's a right-of-way.* – *See also* **right of way** *below.*

ˌright-'wing *adj* in politics, (having opinions which are) more traditional and conservative, *usu* favouring *eg* capitalism, the monarchy *etc* or opposed to (extreme) socialism *etc*: *He has right-wing opinions*; *He is very right-wing.*

ˌright-'winger *nc* a person who has right-wing opinions, or who supports a right-wing political party or the right wing (*see below*) of a political party.

all right *see* **all.**

by 'right(s) rightfully: *By rights, I ought to be in charge of this department.*

get, keep on the right side of (someone) to make (someone) feel, or continue to feel, friendly or kind towards oneself: *If you want a pay rise, you'd better get on the right side of the boss.*

get (something) right to understand, do, say *etc* (something) correctly: *Did I get the answer right?*; *The movements in this dance are quite difficult, so you won't get them right at your first attempt.*

go right to happen as expected, wanted or intended; to be successful or without problems: *Nothing ever goes right for him.*

in one's own right 1 not because of someone else; independently: *She is a baroness in her own right* (= because she has inherited the title or has received it as an honour, not because she is married to a baron). **2** because of one's own ability, work *etc*: *She's married to a writer, but is a novelist in her own right.*

keep (someone) right to prevent (someone) from making mistakes: *This book of instructions will keep you right.*

not in one's right mind, not (quite) right in the head (slightly) mad: *He can't be in his right mind – making incredible suggestions like that!*

put (someone) right 1 to tell (someone) the truth, the correct way of doing something *etc*: *I used to think he was a fool but John put me right about him.* **2** to make (someone) healthy again: *I had an upset stomach, but that medicine soon put me right.*

put (something) right 1 to repair (something); to remove faults *etc* in something: *There is something wrong with this kettle – can you put it right?* **2** to put an end to or change (something that is wrong): *He hasn't been paid for the last job he did, but we can soon put that right.* **3** to put (a watch, clock *etc*) to the correct time.

put/set (something) to rights (*formal*) to put (something) into the correct order, place *etc*, or into a good or desirable state: *The room was in a dreadful mess, and it took us the whole day to set it to rights.*

right as rain *see* **rain**.

right away immediately; at once: *He wants me to type these letters right away.*

ˌright-hand 'man a person's most trusted and useful assistant.

Right Honourable (*attrib*: *often abbrev* **Rt Hon.** *when written*) in the UK, a title used before the name of certain noblemen, cabinet ministers in the British government, Lord Mayors *etc*: *the Right Honourable James Smith.* – *See also* **honourable** *under* **honour**.

right now immediately; at once: *He wants that done right now.*

right of way 1 the right of the public to use a path that goes across private property. – *See also* **right-of-way** *above.* **2** the right of one car *etc* to move first *eg* when crossing a cross-roads, or going round a roundabout: *It was your fault that our cars crashed – I had right of way.*

right wing the members of a political party who hold more traditional, conservative, right-wing (*see above*) opinions: *He's on the right wing of the Labour Party.*

serve (someone) right to be what a person deserves (*usu* something bad): *If you fall and hurt yourself, it'll serve you right for climbing up there when I told you not to.*

rigid ['ridʒid] *adj* (*formal*) **1** completely stiff; not able to be bent (easily): *An iron bar is rigid*; *Is that substance rigid enough?* **2** not able to be moved: *This shelf is quite rigid*; *a rigid structure.* **3** (of a person) very strict; not willing to change rules, standards *etc*: *a rigid headmaster*; *You are too rigid – you must learn to compromise.* **4** (of rules *etc*) strict; not to be changed: *rigid discipline*; *These laws are too rigid.* **'rigidly** *adv.* **'rigidness, ri'gidity** *nus.*

rigmarole ['rigməroul] *nc* (*facet*: *pl rare*) a long, complicated series of actions, instructions *etc*, often rather pointless, boring or irritating: *I have just finished telling him how to do it, and now you come along and I've got to go through the whole rigmarole again.*

rigour, (*Amer*) **rigor** ['rigə] *nu* (*formal*) strictness; harshness *eg* in punishing people: *the rigour of the punishment.* **2** (*also* **'rigours** *n pl*) (of weather *etc*) the state of being very bad or unpleasant, or the hardship caused by this: *the rigour(s) of life in the Arctic Circle.*

'rigorous *adj* (*formal*) harsh; unpleasant; strict: *rigorous punishment.* **'rigorously** *adv.* **'rigorousness** *nu.*

rim [rim] *nc* an edge or border: *the rim of a wheel*; *the rim of a cup.*

'**rimless** *adj* without a rim: *rimless spectacles*; *His new spectacles are rimless.*

rimmed *adj* (*often in cmpds*) having a rim or rims of a certain type: *horn-rimmed spectacles*; *red-rimmed eyes* (= eyes which are red because one has been crying).

rime [raim] *nu* thick white frost.

rind [raind] *nu* (*often in compds*) a thick, hard outer layer or covering, *esp* the outer surface of cheese or bacon, or the peel of fruit: *Do you eat the rind of cheese?*; *bacon-rind*; *lemon-rind.*

ring[1] [riŋ] *nc* **1** a small circle *esp* of gold, silver or other metal, worn on the finger *etc*: *a wedding ring*; *She wears a diamond ring.* **2** (*often in cmpds*) a circle of metal, wood *etc* used for holding (something), keeping (something) tidy *etc*: *a napkin ring*; *a key-ring.* **3** anything which is like a circle in shape: *The children formed a ring round their teacher*; *The hot teapot left a ring* (= a mark in the shape of a ring) *on the polished table.* **4** an enclosed space for boxing matches, circus performances *etc*: *The elephants entered the ring*; *the circus-ring*; *The crowd cheered as the boxer entered the ring.* **5** a small group of people formed for business or criminal purposes: *a drugs ring.* – *v* – *pt, ptp* **ringed** – *vt* **1** (*formal*) to form a ring round someone or something: *Tents and caravans ringed the lake.* **2** to put, draw *etc* a ring round something: *He has ringed all your errors.* **3** to put a ring on (the leg of a bird) as a means of identifying it.

ringed *adj* having a ring or rings round it: *a ringed bird.*

'**ringlet** [-lit] *nc* a long curl of hair: *She wore her hair in ringlets.*

'**ring finger** *nc* the finger on which the wedding ring is worn (*usu* the third finger of the left hand): *She is wearing an engagement ring on her ring finger.*

'**ringleader** *nc* (*often derog*) the leader of a group of people who are doing something wrong: *The police arrested the ringleaders of the rioters.*

'**ringmaster** *nc* a person who is in charge of performances in a circus ring.

'**ring road** *nc* (*Brit*) a road that goes round a town or through its suburbs, allowing traffic to keep away from the centre of the town: *If you want to avoid the city centre go by the ring road.*

ˌ**ringside** '**seat** *nc* **1** a seat close to a boxing or circus ring. **2** (*fig*) (a seat *etc* which allows) a clear view (**ringside view**) of anything: *The two of them were having a furious argument, and there I was in a ringside seat/and I had a ringside seat/view.*

run/make rings round (someone) (*inf*) to be very much better (at doing something) than someone else; to beat (someone) easily: *The government/football team ran rings round their opponents.*

See also **earring** *under* **ear**.

ring[2] [riŋ] – *pt* **rang** [raŋ]: *ptp* **rung** [rʌŋ] – **1** *vti* to (cause to) sound: *The doorbell rang*; *He rang the doorbell*; *The telephone rang as I left the room.* **2** *vi* to make a noise like a bell: *The blacksmith's hammer rang on the anvil.* **3** *vt* (*esp Brit*: *often with* **up**) to telephone (someone): *I'll ring you* (*up*) *tonight.* – *See also* **ring up** *below.* **4** *vi* (*often with* **for**) to ring a bell (*eg* in a hotel) to tell someone to come, to bring something *etc*: *She rang for the maid.* **5** *vi* (of certain objects) to make a sound: *The glass rang as she hit it with a metal spoon.* **6** *vi* (*formal*: *with* **to** *or* **with**) to be filled with sound: *The hall rang to/with the sound of laughter*; (*fig*) *The country rang with his praises.* **7** *vi* (*often with* **out**) to make a loud, clear sound: *His voice rang out*; *A shot rang out.* **8** *vi* (of ears) to hear a buzzing or ringing sound in one's head: *My ears are ringing.* – *See also* **ring** *in phrases below.* – **1** *ncu* the act or sound of ringing: *the ring of a bell/a telephone/laughter.* **2** *nc* (*inf*: *no pl*: *esp Brit*) a telephone call: *I'll give you a ring.* **3** *nc* (*no pl*) a suggestion, impression or feeling: *His story has a ring of truth about it/a sad ring to it.*

ring a bell (*inf*) to have been seen, heard *etc* before, but not remembered in detail: *His name rings a bell, but I don't remember where I've heard it before.*

ring back *vi, vt oblig sep* to telephone (someone who has telephoned): *If he is busy at the moment, he can ring me back*; *He'll ring back tomorrow.*

ring down, up the curtain **1** to give the signal for lowering or raising the curtain in a theatre. **2** (*fig formal*) to start or end (a project *etc*): *We have decided to ring down the curtain on that deal – it is not economic.*

ring off *vi* to end a telephone call.

ring the changes to use, do *etc* a small number of things in a variety of ways: *I only have three shirts and two ties, but I ring the changes with them.*

ring true to sound or seem to be true or false: *His story does not ring true.*

ring up *vt sep* to record (the price of something sold) on a cash register: *You have rung up £5 and this sweater cost only £3.*

rink [riŋk] *nc* **1** (*usu* '**ice-rink**) (a building containing) an area of ice, for ice-skating, curling, ice hockey *etc.* **2** (a building containing) a smooth floor for roller-skating.

rinse [rins] *vt* (*often with* **out**) **1** to wash (clothes *etc*) in clean water to remove soap *etc*: *After washing the towels, rinse them* (*out*). **2** to clean (a cup, one's mouth *etc*) by filling with clean water *etc* and then emptying the water out: *This cup isn't very dirty – just rinse it* (*out*) *to remove the tea-leaves*; *The dentist asked me to rinse my mouth out.* – *nc* **1** the act of rinsing: *Give the cup a rinse.* **2** a liquid used for changing the colour of a person's hair: *a blue rinse.*

riot ['raiət] *nc* **1** a noisy disturbance or disorder by a *usu* large group of people: *The protest march developed into a riot.* **2** (*no pl*: *formal*) an impressive show (of colour *etc*): *In summer, when the flowers bloom, the garden is a riot of colour.* **3** (*no pl*: *inf*) a very amusing person, play *etc*: *He's a riot at a party.* – *vi* to form or take part in a riot: *When the police stopped the protest march, the marchers rioted.* '**rioter** *nc.*

'**riotous** *adj* **1** (*very formal*) starting, or likely to start, a riot: *a riotous assembly*; *The crowd is growing more and more riotous.* **2** (*usu attrib*) very active, noisy and cheerful: *a riotous party.* **3** (*attrib*) filled with gambling, parties, drinking alcohol *etc*; *riotous living.* **4** (*formal*) very impressive in colour, amount *etc*: *the riotous colour of flowers in a garden.* '**riotously** *adv.* '**riotousness** *nu.*

ˌ**read the** '**riot act** (*fig*) to tell (a person) angrily that they have done wrong and warn them that their bad behaviour must stop: *The teacher read the riot act when he found the boys cheating in their exams.*

run riot to act, speak *etc* in an uncontrolled way: *When the teacher left the room the children ran riot.*

rip [rip] – *pt, ptp* **ripped** – *vti* **1** to make or get a hole or tear (in material, clothes *etc*) by pulling, tearing *etc*: *He ripped his shirt on a branch*; *His shirt ripped.* **2** to remove (something) by pulling, *usu* causing (something) to break or tear: *The roof of the car was ripped off in the crash*; *The electricians had to rip up the floorboards*; *He ripped open the envelope*; *The sack caught on a branch and ripped open.* – *nc* a tear or hole: *There's a rip in my shirt.*

let it rip (*inf*) to allow a car, engine *etc* to go at full speed, power *etc.*

ripe [raip] *adj* **1** (*neg* **un-**) (of fruit, grain *etc*) ready to be gathered in or eaten: *ripe apples/corn*; *These plums are not ripe.* **2** (*formal*: *pred*: *sometimes with* **for**) suitable, right or ready: *We'll do it when the time is ripe*; *After five years of the tyrant's rule, the country was ripe for revolution.* **3** (of cheese) having a good or strong flavour *etc*, *eg* because of having been kept for a long time before being used: *This Brie* (= a kind of French cheese) *is ripe*; *ripe Camembert* (= a kind of French cheese).

'ripeness *nu.*

'ripen *vti* to make or become ripe or riper: *The sun ripened the corn*; *The corn ripened in the sun*; *Our tomatoes have not ripened this year.*

ripe (old) age a very old age: *He lived to the ripe (old) age of ninety-five.*

riposte [ri'post] *nc* (*very formal*) a quick answer made in reply to something that has been said (*eg* in an argument).

ripple ['ripl] *nc* **1** a little wave or movement on the surface of water *etc*: *He threw the stone into the pond, and watched the ripples spread across the water.* **2** a soft sound rhat rises and falls quickly and gently: *A ripple of laughter spread across the room.* – *vti* (*formal*) to cause or have ripples: *The grass rippled in the wind*; *The wind rippled the grass.*

rise [raiz] – *pt* **rose** [rouz]: *ptp* **risen** ['rizn] – *vi* **1** (*more formal than* **go up**) to become greater, larger, higher *etc*; to increase: *Food prices are still rising*; *When the sun shines in, the temperature in this room rises rapidly*; *If the river rises much more, there will be a flood*; *Her voice rose* (= became louder) *to a scream*; *Bread rises when it is baked*; *He could feel his anger rising*; *His spirits rose* (= He became more cheerful) *at the news.* **2** to move upwards: *Smoke was rising from the chimney*; *The birds rose into the air*; *Fish rise to the surface of a river to catch flies*; *The curtain rose to reveal an empty stage.* **3** (*more formal than* **get up**) to get up from bed, *esp* after a night's sleep: *He rises every morning at six o'clock.* **4** (*formal*) to stand up: *The children all rose when the headmaster came in*; *When the old man slipped and fell, he found he was too weak to rise again*; *The horse rose on its hind legs.* **5** (of the sun *etc*) to appear above the horizon: *The sun rises in the east and sets in the west.* **6** to stretch or slope upwards: *There was a beautiful view across the valley to the hills which rose in the distance*; *If you look at a map, you can see that the ground rises at this point.* **7** (*formal*: *often* **rise up**: *often with* **against**) to rebel: *The people rose (up) in revolt against the dictator.* **8** to move to a higher rank, a more important position *etc*: *He began as a salesman, but rose to become the managing director*; *He rose to the rank of colonel.* **9** (of a river) to begin or appear: *The Rhone rises in the Alps.* **10** (of wind) to begin; to become stronger: *Don't go out in the boat – the wind has risen.* **11** to be built: *Office blocks are rising all over the centre of the town.* **12** to be or become better than (something): *His speeches never rise above the level of childish nonsense.* **13** (of hair, *esp* an animal's fur) to become straight and stiff *eg* because of fear, anger *etc*: *The two dogs faced each other, their hackles rising.* **14** (of a committee, Parliament *etc*) to finish a meeting, session *etc*: *The House of Commons did not rise until 2.30 a.m. today.* **15** (*formal*) to come back to life: *Jesus has risen.* – *See also* **rise** *in phrases below.* – **1** *ncu* (the) act of rising: *He had a rapid rise to fame*; *the rise of the sun*; *a rise in prices*; *We are tired of the constant rise in prices.* **2** *nc* an increase in salary or wages: *She asked her boss for a rise.* **3** *nc* a slope or hill: *The house is just beyond the next rise.* **4** *nc* the beginning and early development (of something): *the rise of the Roman Empire.*

'rising 1 *nu* the act of rising: *the rising of the sun.* **2** *nc* (*usu hist*) a rebellion: *The king executed those who took part in the rising against him.* – *adj* (*attrib*) **1**: *the rising sun*; *rising prices.* **2** becoming adult: *the rising generation.* **3** becoming important, famous *etc*: *a rising young politician.*

early, late riser a person who gets out of bed early or late in the day.

give 'rise to (*formal*) to cause: *This plan has given rise to various problems.*

rise above *vt fus* (*formal*) to ignore or not be affected by: *I know that you feel bad about having a stammer but you will just have to try and rise above it.*

rise to the bait, 'rise to it (*inf*) to do what someone has been trying to make one do by means of suggestions, hints, attractions *etc*: *I hinted that if he went to the party, he might meet Joan, but he didn't rise to the bait*; *I could see he was trying to make me angry, but I didn't rise to it.*

rise to the occasion (*formal*) to be able to do what is required in an emergency *etc*: *He had never been asked to run a meeting before, but he rose to the occasion magnificently.*

take/get a rise out of (someone) (*inf*) to make (a person) angry *etc* by teasing or annoying him; (*loosely*) to tease or make fun of (someone): *Just ignore him when he makes fun of your nose – he's just trying to take a rise out of you.*

See also **arise, raise**.

risk [risk] *ncu* (a person, thing *etc* which causes or could cause) danger or possible loss or injury: *He thinks we shouldn't go ahead with the plan because of the risks involved/because of the risk of failure*; *He's a good/safe risk* (= not likely to cause loss, failure *etc*); *He's a bad risk* (= not to be trusted or relied on). – *vt* **1** to expose (something) to danger; to lay (something) open to the possibility of loss: *He would risk his life for his friend*; *He risked all his money on betting on that horse.* **2** to take the chance of (something bad happening): *He was willing to risk death to save his friend*; *This scheme could lose a lot of money, but I'm willing to risk it*; *I'd better leave early as I don't want to risk being late* (= I don't want to be late) *for the play*; *I don't want to risk being late – I might get the sack.*

'risky *adv* possibly causing or bringing loss, injury *etc*: *Publishing is a risky business*; *I am not going to steal apples – it's too risky.*

at (a person's) own risk with the person agreeing to accept any loss, damage *etc* involved: *Cars may be parked here at their owner's risk* (= The owners of the car park will not pay for any damage *etc* to parked cars).

at 'risk (*formal*) in danger; likely to suffer loss, injury *etc*: *Heart disease can be avoided if people at risk take medical advice.*

at the 'risk of (*formal*) with the possibility of (loss, injury *etc*): *He saved the little girl at the risk of his own life*; *At the risk of offending you, I must tell you that I disapprove of your behaviour.*

run/take the risk (of doing something) to do (something which involves a risk): *He's not willing to run the risk of losing his money/of helping us*; *I took the risk of buying that jumper for you in the sales – I hope it fits.*

take risks/take a risk to do (something) which might cause loss, injury *etc*: *One cannot be successful in business unless one is willing to take risks*; *If you drive after drinking all that whisky you'll be taking a risk – the police might catch you.*

risotto [rə'zotou] – *pl* **ri'sottos** – *ncu* (a dish of) rice cooked with onions, cheese *etc*: *We had risotto for supper*; *There are several different risottos/kinds of risotto*; *That restaurant specializes in risotto.*

risqué ['ri:skei, (*Amer*) ri'skei] *adj* (*formal*) (of a story, joke *etc*) slightly rude or indecent: *His jokes are rather risqué*; *His risqué stories embarrassed her.*

rissole ['risoul] *nc* a fried cake or ball of chopped meat, fish *etc*: *beef rissoles*; *turkey rissoles.*

rite [rait] *nc* (*formal*) a solemn ceremony, *esp* a religious one: *marriage rites*; *witchcraft rites.*

ritual ['ritʃuəl] (*formal*) **1** *nc* (*often in pl*) a particular set of traditional or fixed actions *etc* used in a religious *etc* ceremony: *Many Christian churches have impressive rituals*; (*facet*) *Last thing every night, he goes through the ritual of choosing which socks, shirt and tie he will wear the next day.* **2** *nu* all the rituals of a church *etc*: *the ritual of the Roman Catholic church.* **3** *nu* the use of rituals in a religious *etc* ceremony: *Most of these ceremonies involve a great deal of ritual.* – *adj* (*attrib*) forming (part of) a ritual or ceremony: *a ritual dance/sacrifice.*

rival ['raivəl] *nc* a person *etc* who tries to compete with another; a person who wants the same thing as someone else: *Our company intends to give a better service to its customers than any of its rivals*; *As a work of reference for students of English, this dictionary is without a rival*; *The two brothers are rivals for the girl next door – they both want to marry her*; (*attrib*) *rival companies*; (*attrib*) *rival teams.* – *v* – *pt, ptp* **'rivalled**, (*Amer*) **'rivaled** – *vt* (*formal*) to (try to) be as good as someone or something else: *He rivals his brother in his skill as a chess-player*; *Nothing rivals football for excitement and entertainment.*

'rivalry *ncu* the state of or an instance of being rivals: *the rivalry/rivalries between business companies.*

See also **unrivalled**.

river ['rivə] *nc* (*sometimes found with cap in place-names*) a large stream of water flowing across country: *The Thames is a river*; *the river Thames*; *the Hudson River*; (*fig formal*) *She wept a river of tears*; (*attrib*) *a river animal.*

'river-bed *nc* the ground over which a river runs.

'riverside *nc* the ground along or near the side of a river: *He has a cottage on the riverside*; (*attrib*) *a riverside cottage.*

sell down the river *see* **sell**.

rivet ['rivit] *nc* a sort of metal nail; a bolt for fastening plates of metal together *eg* when building the sides of a ship. – *v* – *pt, ptp* **'riveted** – *vt* **1** to fasten (something) with rivets: *They riveted the sheets of metal together*; (*fig*) *He stood riveted to the spot with fear.* **2** to attract or fix (one's attention *etc*) on something: *His eyes were riveted on the television.* **'riveter** *nc.*

rivulet ['rivjulit] *nc* (*formal*) **1** a small stream or brook. **2** a small flow of liquid: *rivulets of sweat*; *rivulets of rain running down the window.*

road [roud] **1** *nc* a long, narrow piece of ground specially prepared (*usu* with a hard level surface) for people, vehicles *etc* to travel on: *There are a lot of holes in this road*; *There has been an accident on the Glasgow to Edinburgh road*; (*attrib*) *a road map*; (*attrib*) *road safety.* **2** *n* (*with cap*: *often abbrev* **Rd** *when written*) a word used in the names of certain roads or streets: *His address is 24 Burnham Road*; *He lives in Marston Road.* **3** *nc* (*inf*) a route; the correct road(s) to follow in order to arrive somewhere: *We'd better look at the map because I'm not sure of the road.* **4** *nc* (*fig formal*) a way of getting (something) or behaviour *etc* which leads to (something): *the road to peace*; *He's on the road to ruin.*

'roadblock *nc* a barrier put across a road (*eg* by the police) in order to stop or slow down traffic: *The police set up a roadblock in order to catch the kidnappers.*

'road-hog *nc* a person who drives carelessly or selfishly, causing trouble and annoyance to other drivers.

'roadside *nc* the ground or land beside or along a road: *flowers growing by the roadside*; (*attrib*) *a roadside café.*

'roadway *nc* (*no pl*) the part of a road on which cars *etc* travel: *People shouldn't walk on the roadway.*

'roadworks *n pl* the building or repairing of a road: *Traffic is moving very slowly today because there are roadworks at the cross-roads*; *Roadworks ahead!*

'roadworthy *adj* good enough or safe to be used on the road: *Is this car roadworthy?*; *a roadworthy vehicle.* **'roadworthiness** *nu.*

by 'road in a lorry, car *etc*: *We'll send the furniture by road rather than by rail*; *We came by road.*

in/out of the/someone's road (*inf*: *Brit, esp Scottish*) in or out of the (or someone's) way: *Get out of my road!*

roam [roum] *vti* (*formal*) to walk from place to place (over or across something) without any fixed plan or purpose: *He roamed from town to town*; *He roamed* (*over*) *the hills.* **'roamer** *nc.*

roan [roun] *adj, nc* (a horse) with a reddish-brown coat with spots of grey or white on it.

roar [ro:] **1** *vti* to give a loud deep cry; to say or shout (something) loudly: *The lions roared*; *The injured man roared in pain*; *The sergeant roared* (*out*) *his commands*; *The sergeant roared at the soldiers.* **2** *vi* to laugh loudly: *The audience roared* (*with laughter*) *at the man's jokes.* **3** *vi* to make a loud deep sound: *The cannons/thunder roared.* **4** *vi* (*often with* **along, away, past** *etc*) to make a loud deep sound while moving: *The lorry roared past*; *He roared away on his motorbike.* – **1** *nc* a loud deep cry: *He gave a roar of pain/laughter*; *She was frightened by the lion's roars.* **2** *nu* a loud, deep sound: *the roar of thunder/cannons/traffic.*

do a roaring trade (*inf*) to have a very successful business; to sell a lot of (something): *She and her friends have started selling home-made cakes and biscuits, and they're doing a roaring trade.*

roaring drunk (*inf*) very drunk.

roast [roust] *vti* **1** to cook or be cooked in an oven, or over or in front of a fire *etc*: *They roasted the chestnuts in front of the fire*; *The beef was roasting in the oven.* **2** (of coffee-beans) to heat or be heated before grinding. – *adj* (*attrib*) roasted: *roast beef/chestnuts.* – *ncu* **1** meat which has been roasted: *That's a lovely roast*; *Have some more roast.* **2** (a piece of) meat for roasting: *She bought a roast at the butcher's.*

'**roasting** *adj* (*inf*) very hot: *It's roasting outside*; *a roasting summer day.*

rob [rob] – *pt, ptp* **robbed** – *vt* **1** to steal from (a person, place *etc*): *He robbed a bank/an old lady*; *I've been robbed! My purse has been stolen.* **2** (*formal fig*: *with* **of**) to cause (a person) not to get what he ought to get: *He worked on the project for twenty years, but death robbed him of his reward.*

'**robber** *nc*: *The bank robbers got away with nearly £25 000.*

'**robbery** *ncu* the act of robbing: *Robbery is a serious crime*; *He was charged with having committed four robberies.*

daylight robbery (*inf*) the charging of prices which are too high: *Asking £5 for a book like that is daylight robbery!*

robe [roub] *nc* **1** (*often in pl*: *sometimes in cmpds*) a long, loose piece of clothing: *Many Arabs still wear robes*; *a baby's christening-robe.* **2** (*usu in pl*) a long, loose piece of clothing worn as a sign of a person's rank or importance *eg* on official occasions: *a judge's robes*; *The Lord Mayor was dressed in robes of scarlet cloth.* **3** (*esp Amer*) a loose piece of clothing worn casually in the house *etc*; a dressing-gown: *She wore a robe over her nightdress*; *a bath-robe*; *a beach-robe.*

robed *adj* (*formal*: *often with* **in**) wearing robes (of a particular type, colour *etc*): *The judges were robed* (*in black*).

robin ['robin] *nc* **1** a small European bird with a red breast. **2** an American thrush with an orange-red breast.

robot ['roubot] *nc* a machine which behaves, works, and often looks like a human being: *Science fiction stories often mention robots that can talk.*

robust [rə'bʌst] *adj* **1** strong; healthy: *a robust child*; *He is never ill – he is so robust.* **2** (*formal*) rough; vigorous and sometimes rather rude: *a robust style of writing/sense of humour*; *His prose is so robust.* **ro'bustly** *adv.* **ro'bustness** *nu.*

rock[1] [rok] **1** *ncu* (a large lump or mass of) the solid parts of the surface of the Earth: *The ship struck a rock and began to sink*; *The children climbed over the rocks along the seashore*; *He built his house on rock*; *Those cliffs are solid rock.* **2** *nc* a large stone: *The climber was killed by a large rock which fell on him.* **3** *nu* (*esp Brit*) a type of hard sweet (*def 1*) made in sticks: *Edinburgh rock*; *This stick of rock has the name of the town all the way through it.* – *See also* **on the rocks** *below.*

'**rockery** *nc* a heap of rocks or stones in a garden with earth between them in which *usu* small plants and flowers, *esp* rock-plants, are grown: *We have planted heather in our rockery*; (*attrib*) *rockery plants.*

'**rocky** *adj* **1** full of rocks; made of rock: *a rocky coastline*; *It is difficult to walk here – it is very rocky.* **2** (*usu attrib*) like rock: *This is made of concrete but has been given a rocky appearance.* '**rockiness** *nu.*

ˌ**rock-'bottom** *nu* the lowest level possible (of prices, poverty *etc*): *Prices have reached rock-bottom*; *His depression has reached rock-bottom*; (*attrib*) *rock-bottom prices.*

'**rock-garden** *nc* a rockery.

'**rock-plant** *nc* any plant which grows among rocks *eg* on mountains, often also grown in rockeries.

ˌ**rock-'salt** *nu* common salt as found in large solid masses *eg* in mines.

on the rocks (*inf*) **1** (of a marriage) in(to) a state where the husband and wife wish to separate or be divorced: *Their marriage is* (*going*) *on the rocks.* **2** (of a *usu* alcoholic drink) served with ice cubes: *I'll have a Scotch on the rocks, please.* **3** (of a business firm) in(to) a state of great financial difficulty, having no, or not enough, money: *The firm is on the rocks.*

rock[2] [rok] **1** *vti* to (cause to) swing gently backwards and forwards or from side to side while still standing at a given point: *The mother rocked the cradle*; *The mother rocked the baby to sleep in the cradle*; *This cradle rocks.* **2** *vt* to swing or shake (a baby) gently and rhythmically in one's arms *eg* until it falls asleep. **3** *vti* to shake or move violently: *The earthquake rocked the building*; *The building rocked.*

'**rocker** *nc* **1** one of *usu* two curved supports on which a cradle, rocking-chair *etc* rocks. **2** a rocking-chair.

'**rocky** *adj* (*inf*) which rocks or shakes: *a rocky table*; *This chair's a bit rocky.* '**rockiness** *nu.*

'**rocking-chair** *nc* a chair which rocks backwards and forwards on rockers.

'**rocking-horse** *nc* a toy horse which rocks backwards and forwards on rockers.

off one's rocker (*sl*) mad; crazy: *If you think he'll lend you £100, you must be off your rocker.*

rock[3] [rok] *nu* (*also* **rock music**) music or songs with a strong, heavy beat and *usu* a simple melody: *The only music she likes is rock*; (*attrib*) *a rock band.*

ˌ**rock'n''roll** *nu* (*also* ˌ**rock-and-'roll**) a simpler, earlier form of rock music: *Elvis Presley played a lot of rock'n'roll.*

rocket ['rokit] *nc* **1** a tube containing materials which, when set on fire, give off a jet of gas which drives the tube forward, *usu* up into the air, used *eg* as a firework, for signalling, or for launching a spacecraft. **2** a spacecraft launched in this way: *The Americans have sent a rocket to Mars.* – *v* – *pt, ptp* '**rocketed** – *vi* to rise or increase very quickly: *Bread prices have rocketed over the past year.*

rocky *see* **rock**[1], **rock**[2].

rod [rod] *nc* (*sometimes in cmpds*) a long thin stick or piece of wood, metal *etc*: *a fishing-rod*; *a divining-rod*; *The wheels of the toy car were fixed on to metal rods.*

rode *see* **ride**.

rodent ['roudənt] *nc* (*tech*) any of a number of types of animal with large front teeth for gnawing, *eg* squirrels, beavers, rats *etc.*

rodeo ['roudiou] – *pl* '**rodeos** – *nc esp* in the US, a show or contest of riding, lassoing *etc* by cowboys *etc.*

roe[1] [rou] *nu* the eggs of fish: *We had cod roe for supper.*

roe[2] [rou]: '**roe deer** – *pls* '**roe deer,** '**roe deers** – *nc* a small deer found in Europe and Asia: *a herd of roe deer*; *two roe deers.*

rogue [roug] *nc* **1** (*derog*) a dishonest person: *I wouldn't buy a car from a rogue like him.* **2** a person, *esp* a child who is playfully mischievous or naughty: *She's a lovely child, but she can be a little rogue sometimes.* **'roguery** *nu.*

'roguish *adj* (*usu attrib*) mischievous: *She had a roguish look on her face.* **'roguishly** *adv.* **'roguishness** *nu.*

rôle, role [roul] *nc* **1** a part played by an actor or actress in a play *etc*: *He is playing a very difficult rôle – he has to pretend to be mad.* **2** (*formal*) the actions or functions of a person in some activity: *The police asked the boy what his rôle had been in the robbery*; *He played the rôle of peacemaker in the dispute.*

roll[1] [roul] **1** *nc* (*sometimes in cmpds*) anything flat (*eg* a piece of paper, a carpet) rolled or formed into the shape of a tube or wound round a tube *etc*: *a roll of wallpaper*; *a toilet-roll* (= a roll of toilet paper). **2** *nc* a small round or long piece of baked bread dough, often used for sandwiches: *a cheese roll* (= a roll with a filling of cheese). **3** *nc* (*usu in sing*) the act of rolling: *Our dog loves a roll on the grass.* **4** *nu* (of a ship) the act of moving or rolling from side to side: *She said that the roll of the ship made her feel ill.* **5** *ncu* a long low sound: *the roll of thunder.* **6** *nc* a thick mass of something which goes round something: *There were rolls of fat round his neck.* **7** *nc* a series of quick beats (on a drum). – **1** *vti* to move (something) by turning over like a wheel or ball: *The ball/coin/pencil rolled under the table*; *He rolled the ball towards the puppy*; *The ball rolled away.* **2** *vti* to move (something) on wheels, rollers *etc*: *The children pushed the cart up to the top of the hill, then let it roll back down again*; *If you put wheels on that case, you could roll it along instead of carrying it.* **3** *vti* (of things which are flat *eg* a piece of paper, a carpet) to form a tube or cylinder by winding (something) round itself or round a tube, stick, cylinder *etc*: *If you want to lift the floor-boards, you'll have to roll the carpet back*; *It won't roll back very easily.* **4** *vti* (of a person, animal *etc* lying on the ground *etc*) to turn over: *The doctor asked the patient to roll (over) on to his side*; *The dog rolled on to its back.* **5** *vt* to make (something), or form (something) into the shape of a ball or cylinder, by rolling: *He rolled the clay into a ball (between his hands)*; *He rolled a cigarette.* **6** *vti* to cover (a person, thing *etc*) with something by rolling: *Roll the fish in batter*; *When the little girl's dress caught fire, they rolled her in a coat/she rolled in a coat to put out the flames.* **7** *vt* to make (something) flat or flatter by rolling something heavy over it: *You ought to roll your lawn*; *She rolled the pastry flat.* **8** *vi* (of a ship) to move or rock from side to side while travelling forwards: *The storm made the ship roll.* **9** *vi* to make a series of low sounds: *The thunder rolled.* **10** *vti* to produce a sound in a series of rapid beats or taps: *The drums rolled*; *Scottish people often roll their r's* (= pronounce the 'r' sound by tapping the tip of the tongue rapidly against the gum above the upper front teeth). **11** *vti* to move (one's eyes) round in a circle: *The child's eyes rolled in fear*; *The child rolled his eyes.* **12** *vi* (*usu with* **along** *etc*) to travel in a car *etc*: *We were rolling along merrily when suddenly we had a burst tyre.* **13** *vi* (of waves, rivers *etc*) to move gently and steadily: *The waves rolled in to the shore.* – *See also* **roll** *in phrases below.*

'roller *nc* **1** any of a number of tube-shaped objects, or machines having one or more such objects, for flattening, crushing, printing *etc*: *A garden roller is used for flattening lawns*; *A road-roller is used for flattening the surface of a road.* **2** a small tube-shaped object on which hair is wound to curl it: *I always put rollers in my hair to make it curly.* **3** a small solid wheel or cylinder on which something can be rolled along: *This machine is fitted with rollers so that it can be moved easily.* **4** a long large wave on the sea.

'rolling *adj* (*attrib*) (of land, country *etc*) with low hills and valleys, without steep slopes: *rolling landscape.*

'roller-skate *nc* a skate with wheels instead of a blade: *He was given a pair of roller-skates for his birthday.* – *vi* to move on roller-skates: *You shouldn't roller-skate on the pavement.*

'rolling-pin *nc* a wooden, glass *etc* roller for flattening out dough.

'rolling stock *nu* the engines, wagons *etc* that run on a railway.

be 'rolling in (something) (*inf*) to have large amounts of something, *usu* money: *He doesn't have to worry about money – he's rolling in it.*

roll in *vi* (*inf*) to come in or be got in large numbers or amounts: *They've started selling home-made cakes, and the money is just rolling in.*

roll on *vi* **1** (of times, days *etc*) (*usu* as a wish) may (a given time) come soon: *Roll on the day when I can afford to buy a car.* **2** (of time) to pass or go by: *Time is rolling on and we haven't finished this job.*

roll up 1 *vt sep* to form (something) into a roll: *We'll need to roll up the carpet*; *He rolled up his sleeves* (= He rolled his sleeves up from the cuffs in order to leave his arms bare). **2** *vi* (*inf*) to arrive: *John rolled up ten minutes late.* **3** *vi* (*usu in imperative*) (*usu* to a crowd *eg* in a market, at a fair) to come near: *Roll up! Roll up! Come and see the bearded lady.*

sausage-roll *see* **sausage**.

See also **unroll**.

roll[2] *nc* a list of names, *eg* of the members of a club, pupils in a school *etc*: *There are nine hundred pupils on the roll.*

'roll-call *ncu* an act of calling names from a list, *usu* to make sure that no-one is missing *eg* in a prison or school class, or the time when this is done: *We have a roll-call twice a day*; *I'll speak to him after roll-call.*

rollicking ['rolikiŋ] *adj* (*attrib*) noisy and gay; full of fun: *a rollicking party*; *We had a rollicking time at the party.*

Roman ['roumən] *adj* **1** connected with Rome, *esp* ancient Rome and the empire of which it was the capital: *a Roman fort*; *These coins are Roman.* **2** (*no cap*) (of printing type) written in ordinary upright letters, as these definitions are: *That should be printed in roman type, not in italics.* **3** (*sometimes derog*) connected with the Roman Catholic Church: *Roman rites.* – **1** *nc* a person belonging to Rome, *esp* to ancient Rome or the ancient Roman Empire: *The Romans built many roads in Britain.* **2** *nu* (*no cap*) roman type: *The definitions in this dictionary are written in roman.*

Roman alphabet the alphabet in which Western European languages such as English are written.

Roman Catholic (*also* **Catholic**) (a member) of the Christian church which recognizes the Pope as its head: *He's (a) Roman Catholic.*

Roman Catholicism (*also* **Catholicism**) the beliefs, government *etc* of the Roman Catholic church.

Roman numerals I, II, III *etc*, as opposed to the

Arabic numerals 1, 2, 3 *etc.*

romance [rə'mans] **1** *nc* the relationship, actions *etc* of people who are in love: *They didn't want anyone to know about their romance*; *It was a beautiful romance, but it didn't last.* **2** *nc* a story about such a relationship, actions *etc*, *esp* one in which the people, events, relationships *etc* are more exciting, interesting, beautiful *etc* than in normal life: *She writes romances*; *There's nothing my mother likes better than a good romance.* **3** *nu* the sort of love and excitement usually described in a romance: *Although she had a husband who loved her, she felt her life was lacking in romance*; *He has no romance in his soul.* **4** *nc* (*liter*) an exciting story of adventure, *esp* one about knights, heroes *etc eg* in the Middle Ages.

ro'mantic [-tik] *adj* **1** (*usu attrib*: *neg* **un-**) (of a story) describing the relationship, actions *etc* of people who are in love: *a romantic novel.* **2** (of a person, thing *etc*) causing or feeling love, *esp* the beautiful love described in a romance: *Her husband is very romantic – he brings her flowers every day*; *romantic music*; *Dimly lit restaurants are very romantic.* **3** (of a person or his thoughts) involving ideas about love and excitement which are foolish and unlike real life: *Her head is full of foolish romantic notions*; *a foolish, romantic young girl*; *She thought it would be romantic to be a film-star.* **ro'mantically** *adv.*

ro'manticize, -ise [-tisaiz] *vti* (*formal*) to make (something) seem romantic (*def 3*): *She leads such a dull life that she tends to romanticize it*; *Oh don't believe what she says – she's apt to romanticize.*

the Romance languages the languages which developed from Latin, *eg* French, Spanish, Italian.

Romania, Romanian *see* Appendix 2.

Romany ['roumәni] **1** *nc* a gipsy. **2** *n* the language of gipsies. – *adj* **1** (*usu attrib*) of Romanies: *a Romany camp/caravan.* **2** of Romany.

romp [romp] *vi* **1** to play in a lively way, *esp* by running about, jumping *etc*: *The children and their dog were romping about on the grass.* **2** to do (something) quickly and easily: *Some people find these problems difficult but he just romps through them.* – *nc* the act of romping: *The children had a romp in the grass.*

'rompers *n pl* (*also* **'romper-suit** *nc*) a short suit for a baby: *The baby was wearing rompers/a pair of rompers*; *She made her grandchild a romper-suit.*

romp home (*inf*) to win easily: *The horse romped home*; *After scoring the first goal, the team romped home to an easy victory.*

rood [ru:d] *nc* (*liter*) a cross carrying the image of Christ, *esp* in a church.

roof [ru:f] *nc* the top covering of a building, car *etc*: *The roof of the garage was made of asbestos.* – *vt* to cover with a roof: *The garages will be roofed with asbestos.*

'roofing *nu* materials for a roof: (*attrib*) *roofing tiles.*

go through the roof/hit the roof (*inf*) to become very angry: *When he saw all the mistakes his secretary had made, he really hit the roof*; *Your father will go through the roof when you tell him you have crashed his car.*

raise the roof *see* **raise**.

roof of the mouth the upper part of the mouth: *I have an ulcer on the roof of my mouth.*

rook [ruk] *nc* **1** a kind of crow. **2** (*usu* **'castle**) a chess-piece.

'rookery *nc* a breeding-place of rooks.

room [ru:m (*in cmpds* rum, (*Amer*) ru:m)] **1** *nc* (*often in cmpds*) one part of a house or building, *usu* used for a particular purpose: *This house has six rooms*; *a bedroom*; *a dining-room.* – *See also* **rooms** *below.* **2** *nu* the space or area in which a person, thing *etc* is or could be put *etc*; *This large bed takes up a lot of room*; *Is there room for this book on that shelf?*; *There's no room for you in our car*; *We'll move the bookcase into the corner to make room for the television.* **3** *nu* (*with* **for**) the state in which something could be done or allowed: *There is room for improvement in his work* (=His work could be improved).

-roomed (*in cmpds*) having (a certain number or type of) rooms: *a four-roomed house* (*usu* = a house with four rooms plus a kitchen and a bathroom).

'roomful *nc* the number of people *etc* or amount of something which is, or can be kept, in a room: *a roomful of people.*

rooms *n pl* a set of rented rooms for living in, which are part of someone's house or a boarding-house.

'roomy *adj* (*inf*) having plenty of room: *roomy cupboards*; *Their new house is nice and roomy.*

'room-mate *nc* a person who shares a room with another person *eg* in a hostel for students, nurses *etc.*

'room service *nu* the serving of food *etc* to people in their room(s) in a hotel *etc*: *Ask for room service if you want breakfast in your room.*

roost [ru:st] *nc* a branch *etc* on which a bird rests at night. – *vi* (of birds) to sit or sleep on a roost: *Starlings roost on trees and buildings.*

'rooster *nc* (*esp Amer*) a farmyard cock.

come home to roost (of a *usu* bad action) to have an unpleasant effect on the person who did the action: *All his lies have come home to roost.*

rule the roost to be the person in a group, family *etc* whose orders, wishes *etc* are obeyed: *If you look at that family, there's no doubt that it's the grandmother who rules the roost.*

root[1] [ru:t] *nc* **1** the part of a plant that grows under the ground and draws food and water from the soil: *Trees often have deep roots*; *Carrots and turnips are edible roots*; (*fig*) *Our roots* (= Our family origins) *are in the north.* – *See also* **take root** *below.* **2** the base of something growing in the body: *the roots of one's hair/teeth.* **3** (*fig formal*) cause; origin: *Love of money is the root of all evil*; *We must get at the root of the trouble*; (*attrib*) *the root cause of the trouble.* **4** (*gram*) a word or part of a word from which other words have been built up: *'Love' is the root of 'lovely' and 'loveliness'*; *The word 'cordial' comes from a Latin root.* – *vti* to (make something) grow roots: *These plants aren't rooting very well*; *He rooted the plants in compost.*

'rooted *adj* (*formal*) strong; firmly established: *These customs are rooted in tradition*; *I have a rooted objection to that kind of behaviour.* – *See also* **be rooted in** *below.*

cube root *see* **cube**.

root beer *nu* (*Amer*) a kind of non-alcoholic drink made from certain plant roots: *You can't have wine or beer in this restaurant – only root beer.*

'root crop *nc* plants with roots that are grown for food: *The farm has three fields of root crops.*

be 'rooted in (*formal*) to have as a cause; to originate in: *His difficulties are rooted in his lack of education.*

root out/up *vt sep* **1** to pull up or tear out by the roots: *The gardener began to root out/up the weeds.* **2** (*fig*) to destroy completely: *We must do our best to root out disease and poverty.*

square root *see* **square**.

take root to grow firmly; to become established: *The plants soon took root*; (*fig*) *The new business took root.*

See also **uproot**.

root[2] [ru:t] *vi* **1** (of animals) to poke about in the ground in search of food: *The pigs were rooting about for food.* **2** (*inf*) to search (for something) by turning things over *etc*: *She rooted about in the cupboard.*

rope [roup] *ncu* (a) thick cord, made by twisting together lengths of hemp, nylon *etc*: *He tied it with a (piece of) rope*; (*fig*) *a rope of pearls.* – *vt* **1** to tie or fasten with a rope: *He roped the suitcase to the roof of the car.* **2** to catch with a rope; to lasso: *to rope a calf.* – *See also* **rope in, rope off** *below.*

'ropy *adj* (*inf*) not very good: *The food's a bit ropy*; *I've had flu – I still feel ropy*; *in a ropy condition.*

ˌrope-'ladder *nc* a ladder made of rope: *They had to climb up a rope-ladder on to the boat.*

know the ropes *see* **know**.

rope in *vt sep* (*inf*) to include (someone); to persuade (someone) to join in doing something: *We roped him in to help.*

rope off *vt sep* to put a rope around or across (a place) in order to prevent (other) people going in: *The end of the room was roped off for the most important guests.*

rosary ['rouzəri] **1** *nc* a string of beads representing prayers, used in the Roman Catholic Church: *She carried a rosary of silver and pearls.* **2** *nu* the group of prayers represented: *She said the rosary every day.*

rose[1] [rouz] **1** *nc* a kind of brightly-coloured, *usu* sweet-scented flower, *usu* with sharp thorns: *He gave her a bouquet of roses*; (*attrib*) *a rose-garden.* **2** *nu, adj* (of) a pink colour: *Her dress was of a pale rose*; *a rose(-coloured) dress.* **3** *nc* (*formal*) a device put on the end of a hose or watering-can to make the water spray in small drops.

rosette [rə'zet, (*Amer*) rou-] *nc* a badge or decoration in the shape of a rose, *usu* made of coloured ribbon: *He wore a blue rosette to show that he was supporting the team whose colour was blue.*

'rosy *adj* **1** rose-coloured; pink: *rosy cheeks*; *cheeks rosy with health.* **2** (*fig*) hopeful; optimistic: *His future looks rosy*; *a rosy future.* **'rosily** *adv.* **'rosiness** *nu.*

rose window *nc* (in Gothic architecture) a window in the shape of a rose.

'rosewood *nu, adj* (of) a kind of dark wood used in making furniture of the highest quality: *made of rosewood*; *a rosewood cabinet.*

look at/see something through rose-coloured spectacles/glasses (*fig*) to have a very ideal, optimistic view: *She looks at marriage through rose-coloured spectacles.*

rose[2] *see* **rise**.

rosemary ['rouzməri] **1** *nc* a kind of evergreen, sweet-smelling bush: *He grows rosemary in his herb garden*; (*attrib*) *a rosemary bush.* **2** *nu* its leaves used as a herb to flavour food when cooking: *Add some rosemary when cooking lamb.*

rosette *see* **rose**[1].

rosin ['rozin] *nu* the hardened resin of some trees, used on the bows of stringed musical instruments.

roster ['rostə] *nc* (*formal*) a list showing the work, duties *etc* that people are to do: *Look up your name on the roster and see what your duties are*; *a duty roster.*

rostrum ['rostrəm] – *pls* **'rostrums, 'rostra** [-trə] – *nc* a platform on which a public speaker stands: *He mounted the rostrum and began his speech.*

rosy *see* **rose**[1].

rot [rot] – *pt, ptp* **'rotted** – *vti* to make or become bad or decayed: *The fruit is rotting on the ground*; *Water will rot unpainted woodwork.* – *nu* **1** decay: *The house is suffering from rot.* **2** (*inf*) nonsense: *Don't talk rot!*

'rotten *adj* **1** (of meat, fruit *etc*) having gone bad; decayed: *rotten vegetables*; *These apples are rotten.* **2** (*inf*) bad; mean: *What rotten luck!*; *It was a rotten thing to do*; *Don't be rotten – let her go with you!* **'rottenness** *nu.*

'rotter *nc* (*old sl*) a worthless, bad person: *He's an absolute rotter.*

rota ['routə] *nc* (*formal*) a list showing duties that are to be done in turn, and the names of the people who are to do them: *I've made out a rota for the washing-up.*

rotary ['routəri] *adj* (*formal or tech*: *esp attrib*) turning like a wheel: *a rotary movement.*

rotate [rə'teit, (*Amer*) 'routeit] *vti* to turn like a wheel: *He rotated the handle*; *The engine rotated slowly*; *While he is training he rotates from department to department.* **ro'tation** *ncu.*

rotation of crops, 'crop rotation a system by which crops are grown on a different area of land each year.

rote [rout]: **by 'rote** by memory; by heart: *Children used to learn lessons by rote.*

rotor ['routə] *nc* (*tech*) the rotating part of an engine, *esp* the blades of a helicopter: *The rotor began to turn*; (*attrib*) *a rotor-blade.*

rotten, rotter *see* **rot**.

rotund [rə'tʌnd, (*Amer*) rou-] *adj* (*formal*) round; plump: *a rotund figure*; *He is jolly and rotund.* **ro'tundly** *adv.* **ro'tundity, ro'tundness** *nus.*

rouble ['ru:bl] *nc* the standard unit of Russian currency: *It cost ten roubles.*

roué ['ru:ei, (*Amer*) ru:'ei] *nc* (*old*) a disreputable man; a rake: *He is a gambler and a roué.*

rouge [ru:ʒ] *nu* a pink powder or cream used to give colour to the cheeks: *She uses rouge.*

rough [rʌf] *adj* **1** not smooth: *Her skin felt rough*; *rough hands.* **2** uneven: *a rough path*; *the path is rough and rocky.* **3** harsh; unpleasant: *a rough voice*; (*fig*) *She's had a rough* (= difficult) *time since her husband died.* **4** noisy and violent: *His behaviour was very rough.* **5** stormy: *The sea was rough*; *rough waves*; *rough weather.* **6** not complete or exact; approximate: *a rough drawing*; *a rough idea*; *This estimate is very rough.* – (*inf*) **1** *nc* a person with rough behaviour; a hooligan or bully: *a gang of roughs.* **2** *nu* uneven or uncultivated ground, *esp* on a golf course: *I lost my ball in the rough.* – *See also* **rough it, rough out** *below.*

'roughly *adv.* **'roughness** *nu.*

'roughage [-fidʒ] *nu* (*formal*) substances in food, *eg* bran or fibre, which help digestion: *You should eat a lot of roughage to keep your bowels regular.*

'roughen *vti* to make or become rough: *Anger roughened his voice*; *The sea roughened as the wind grew stronger.*

'roughcast *nu* a mixture of plaster and small stones used to cover outside walls.

rough diamond *nc* (*fig*) a good person who is not

well-mannered, polite *etc*: *He's rather a rough diamond.*

be 'rough on (someone) (*inf*) to be hard luck or unfortunate for (someone): *It's rough on her, to have to stay behind when her husband goes to Paris.*

cut up rough *see* **cut up** *under* **cut**.

ˌride 'roughshod over (*inf*) to treat (someone) without any regard for his/her feelings: *He is so ambitious that he rides roughshod over everyone.*

ˌrough-and-'ready *adj* **1** not carefully made or finished, but good enough: *She gave us a rough-and-ready meal*; *His speech at the dinner was a bit rough-and-ready.* **2** (of people) friendly enough but without politeness *etc*: *He's rather rough-and-ready but you'll like him*; *rather a rough-and-ready old man.*

ˌrough-and-'tumble *ncu* a (*usu* friendly) fight; a scuffle: *The children were having a rough-and-tumble in the garden*; *He enjoys the rough-and-tumble of the playgroup.*

'rough it *vi* (*inf*) to live primitively, without the usual comforts of life: *We had no money for a hotel so we had to rough it and camp out.*

rough out *vt sep* to draw or explain a rough sketch *etc* or idea: *I roughed out a diagram*; *He roughed out the plan to the others.*

take the rough with the smooth (*fig*) to accept the disadvantages of a person, situation *etc* with the advantages: *I don't like living in the town, but with a new job you have to take the rough with the smooth.*

roulette [ru'let] *nu* a game of chance, played with a ball on a revolving wheel: *a game of roulette*; (*attrib*) *a roulette wheel/table.*

round [raund] *adj* **1** shaped like a circle or globe: *a round hole*; *a round stone*; *The stone is round.* **2** (*fig*) rather fat; plump: *a round face*; *Her face is round and jolly.* **3** (*attrib*) moving in a circle: *a round trip* (= a trip to several towns, countries *etc* and back to the starting-place). **4** (*attrib*) (of numbers) complete; exact: *a round dozen.* – *adv* **1** in the opposite direction: *He turned round.* **2** in a circle: *They all stood round and listened*; *A wheel goes round*; (*fig*) *All* (*the*) *year round.* **3** from one person to another: *They passed the letter round*; *The news went round that they had won.* **4** from place to place: *We drove round for a while.* **5** in circumference: *The tree measured two metres round.* **6** (*inf*) to a particular place, *usu* a person's home: *Are you coming round* (*to our house*) *tonight?* – *prep* **1** on all sides of: *Trees grew round the pond*; *a wall round the garden*; *He looked round the room.* **2** passing all sides of (and returning to the starting-place): *They ran round the tree*; *They walked round the town.* **3** changing direction at: *He came round the corner*; *They had to drive round the fallen tree.* **4** in or to all parts of: *The news spread/was* (*all*) *round the town.* – *nc* **1** something round (and *usu* flat) in shape: *a round of pastry.* **2** something complete: *a round of toast* (= a complete slice of bread); *a round of drinks* (= one for everyone present); *a round of golf.* **3** a regular journey one takes to do one's work: *a postman's round*; (*fig*) *one's daily round* (= of work, duties *etc*). **4** a burst of cheering, shooting *etc*: *They gave him a round of applause*; *The soldier fired several rounds.* **5** a single bullet, shell *etc*: *five hundred rounds of ammunition.* **6** a stage in a competition *etc*: *The winners of the first round will go through to the next.* **7** (*music*) a type of song sung by several singers singing the same tune starting in succession: *They sang an Elizabethan round.* – *See also* **rounds** *below.* – *vi* to go round: *The car rounded the corner.* – *See also* **round** *in phrases below.*

'rounded *adj* curved; like part of the line forming a circle: *a rounded arch*; *the blade of a gouge is rounded.*

'rounders *nu* a kind of game, using a bat and ball: *The children were playing rounders.*

'roundly *adv* (*formal*) (of one's way of speaking) plainly, often rudely: *He told her roundly what he thought of her.*

'roundness *nu.*

rounds *n pl* a doctor's visits to his patients: *The doctor is* (*out*) *on his rounds.*

'all-round *adj* (*attrib*) complete: *He was an all-round success.*

ˌall-'rounder *nc* in games *etc*, a person who can play any position *eg* who can bat as as well as bowl in cricket. – *See also* **all round** *below.*

'roundabout *nc* **1** a revolving machine on which one can ride for pleasure; a merry-go-round: *The children wanted to go on the roundabout.* **2** a circular piece of ground where several roads meet, and round which traffic must travel: *Drive on till you get to the roundabout, then turn left.* – *adj* (*usu attrib*) not direct: *We arrived by a roundabout route.*

round figures/numbers *n pl* the nearest convenient or easily remembered numbers: *Tell me the cost in round figures* (*ie* £20 rather than £19·87 or £5 000 rather than £5 123).

'Roundhead *nc* (*hist*) a member of the parliamentary party in the English Civil War: *the Roundheads and the Cavaliers*; (*attrib*) *the Roundhead armies.*

ˌround-'shouldered *adj* with stooping shoulders: *He's very round-shouldered.*

round-up *see* **round up**.

all round surrounding: *There were people all round him.* – *See also* **all-round** *and* **all-rounder** *above.*

bring (someone) round *see* **bring**.

come round *see* **come**.

go round *see* **go**.

in the 'round (*formal*) visible from all sides: *Sculpture should be seen in the round*; *theatre in the round* (= where the audience sits all round the stage).

round about 1 surrounding: *She sat with her children round about her.* **2** near: *There are not many houses round about.* **3** approximately: *There must have been round about a thousand people there.*

round off *vt sep* **1** to make something smooth *etc*: *He rounded off the sharp corners with a file.* **2** (*fig*) to complete successfully; to make a successful ending (to): *He rounded off his career by becoming president*; *He rounded the meal off with a glass of port.*

'round on *vt fus* (*formal*) to attack (*usu* in words); to turn on: *He rounded on her, demanding to know where she had been.*

round up *vt sep* to collect together: *The farmer rounded up the sheep* (*nc* **'round-up**).

See also **around, about**.

rouse [rauz] **1** *vti* (*formal*) to awaken: *I'll rouse you at 6 o'clock*; *She roused from a deep sleep.* **2** *vt* to stir or excite: *Her interest was roused by what he said.*

'rousing *adj* stirring; exciting: *a rousing speech*; *The music was very rousing.*

See also **arouse**.

rout [raut] *vt* (*formal*) to defeat completely: *The*

army was routed. – *nc* a complete defeat: *the rout of the enemy.*

route [ru:t] *nc* a way of getting somewhere; a road: *Our route took us through the mountains; Which is the best route from here to Switzerland? We followed the route exactly.* – *vt* to arrange a route for; to send by a certain route: *Heavy traffic was routed round the outside of the town.*

'route march *nc* a long march for soldiers in training: *They were sent on a route march.*

See also **en route**.

routine [ru:'ti:n] *ncu* a regular, fixed way of doing things: *to follow one's daily routine; One must have routine in one's life; Children's routines vary.* – *adj* (*sometimes derog*) regular; ordinary: *routine work; This work is too routine for my taste; It is dull and routine.*

rove [rouv] *vti* (*liter*) to wander; to roam: *He roved* (*across*) *the hills.*

'rover *nc* (*liter*) a wanderer: *a gipsy rover.*

'roving *adj* (*liter: attrib*) wandering: *a roving mind.*

have a roving eye (*inf*) to be interested in women (apart from one's wife).

row[1] [rou] *nc* a line: *a row of houses; They were sitting in a row; They sat in the front row in the theatre* (= the line of seats nearest the stage).

row[2] [rou] **1** *vti* to move (a boat) through the water using oars: *He rowed* (*the dinghy*) *up the river.* **2** *vt* to carry in a rowing-boat; to transport by rowing: *He rowed them across the lake.* – *nc* a trip in a rowing-boat: *They went for a row on the river.*

'rower *nc* a person who rows; an oarsman.

'rowing-boat, 'row-boat *nc* a boat which is moved by oars.

row[3] [rau] *nc* **1** (*more inf than* **quarrel**) a (noisy) quarrel: *They had a terrible row; a family row.* **2** (*more inf than* **noise**) a (continuous) loud noise: *They heard a row in the street.*

rowan ['rauən] *nc* (*also* **'rowan tree**) a kind of tree with bright red berries, also called the mountain ash: *We have a rowan by our garden gate.*

rowdy ['raudi] *adj* noisy and rough: *rowdy children/behaviour; Their party became more and more rowdy.* – *nc* (*inf*) a noisy, rough person: *a gang of rowdies.*

'rowdily *adv.* **'rowdiness** *nu.*

'rowdyism *nu* rowdy behaviour.

royal ['roiəl] *adj* (*usu attrib*) **1** of, concerning, given by *etc* a king, queen *etc*: *the royal family; His Royal Highness, Prince Charles; a royal decree.* **2** (*formal fig*) magnificent; splendid: *a royal feast; royal entertainment.* **'royally** *adv.*

'royalist *nc* a person who supports a king or queen: *The republicans fought the royalists.*

'royalty **1** *nc* a payment made to a writer, recording artist *etc* for every book, record *etc* sold: *He has received thousands of pounds in royalties on/for his last novel.* **2** *nu* royal people in general: *The commands of royalty must be obeyed; She is entertaining royalty this evening.* **3** *nu* (*formal*) the state of being royal: *respect for the king's royalty.*

royal blue *nu, adj* (of) a bright, darkish blue: *a dress of royal blue;* (*attrib*) *a royal-blue dress.*

See also **regal**.

rub [rʌb] – *pt, ptp* **rubbed** – *vti* to move (something) against the surface of something else with a certain amount of pressure: *He rubbed his eyes; The horse rubbed its head against my shoulder; The tree branch is rubbing against the window.* – *See also* **rub** *in phrases below.* – *nc* an act of rubbing: *He gave the teapot a rub with a polishing cloth.*

rub along (*fig inf: with* **with**) to get on fairly well with (someone); to be fairly friendly with: *I rub along all right with my relations.*

rub down *vt sep* to clean or make smooth by rubbing: *Your horse needs rubbing down; Rub down the wall before you paint it.*

rub in *vt sep* **1** to make (a substance) go into the surface of something by rubbing: *She rubbed cream in to her hands; She rubbed it in firmly.* **2** (*inf*) to keep reminding someone of (something unpleasant): *I know I've lost my job – you don't have to keep rubbing it in!*

rub out *vt sep* to remove (a mark, writing *etc*) with a rubber; to erase: *He rubbed out what he had written and started again; He rubbed it out.*

rub shoulders with (*fig*) to mix or associate with: *He rubs shoulders with some very strange people in his job.*

rub up *vt sep* **1** to polish: *She rubbed up the silver until it shone.* **2** (*fig inf*) to refresh one's memory of; to remind oneself of: *I'm rubbing up my French before I go on holiday.*

rub (someone) (up) the wrong way (*fig inf*) to annoy or irritate someone: *He's always rubbing me* (*up*) *the wrong way.*

rubber[1] ['rʌbə] **1** *nu, adj* (of) a strong elastic substance made from the juice of certain plants (or an artificial substitute for this): *Tyres are made of rubber; rubber boots.* **2** *nc* (*also* **ˌindia-'rubber** *or* **e'raser**) a piece of rubber used to rub out pencil *etc* marks: *You will need a pencil, a ruler and a rubber.* **3** *nc* (*Amer inf*) a condom.

'rubbery *adj* (*often derog*) like rubber: *The food was rubbery; rubbery meat.*

rubber band *see* **elastic band**.

rubber stamp *nc* an instrument with rubber figures, letters *etc* which is used to stamp a name, date *etc* on books or papers.

rubber[2] ['rʌbə] *nc* in cards *etc*, an odd number of games, *usu* three or five: *They played a rubber of bridge.*

rubbish ['rʌbiʃ] *nu* **1** waste material; things that have been or are to be thrown away: *Our rubbish is taken away twice a week;* (*attrib*) *a rubbish bin/bag.* **2** nonsense: *Don't talk rubbish!*

'rubbishy *adj* (*derog*) worthless: *rubbishy jewellery.*

rubble ['rʌbl] *nu* **1** broken stones, plaster *etc* from a ruined or demolished building: *After the explosion, there was nothing left of the house but rubble.* **2** small stones used in building: *The walls were built of two layers of brick filled with rubble.*

rubicund ['ru:bikənd] *adj* (*liter: usu attrib*) with a red or rosy face: *a smiling, rubicund old man.*

ruby ['ru:bi] **1** *nc* a kind of deep red precious stone: *a ring set with rubies;* (*attrib*) *a ruby necklace.* **2** *nu, adj* (*also* **ruby red**) (of) its colour: *The wine was a rich ruby;* (*attrib*) *a ruby-red dress; The dress was ruby red.*

ruck [rʌk] *nc* a wrinkle or crease: *She smoothed the rucks out of the sheet on the bed.*

rucked up wrinkled; caught up: *Her dress was rucked up at the back.*

rucksack ['rʌksak] *nc* a type of bag carried on the back by walkers, climbers *etc*: *He set off with his rucksack on his back.*

ructions ['rʌkʃənz] *n pl* (*formal or facet*) disturbance or confusion; noisy argument or anger: *If* *you don't behave yourself there will be ructions!*; *There will be ructions if his wife finds out about his affair with his secretary.*

rudder ['rʌdə] *nc* **1** a flat piece of wood, metal *etc* fixed vertically to the back of a boat for steering: *He was at/took the rudder.* **2** a similar device on an aircraft.

ruddy ['rʌdi] *adj* **1** (of the face) rosy and showing good health: *a ruddy-faced woman*; *Her face is wrinkled and ruddy.* **2** (*attrib*) red: *The fire gave off a ruddy glow.*

rude [ru:d] *adj* **1** not polite; showing bad manners: *rude children/behaviour*; *Don't be rude (to me)!* **2** (*old*) roughly made: *They built a rude shelter.* **3** (*attrib*) sudden: *a rude awakening*; *a rude surprise.* **4** (*attrib*) vigorous; flourishing: *in rude health.* **5** vulgar; indecent: *rude gestures*; *rude pictures*; *That gesture was rather rude.* **'rudely** *adv.* **'rudeness** *nu.*

rudiments ['ru:dimənts] *n pl* the first simple facts or rules of anything: *She's learning the rudiments of cooking.*

ˌrudi'mentary [-'men-] *adj* (*formal*) primitive or undeveloped: *a rudimentary knowledge of the subject*; *rudimentary medical treatment*; *Her knowledge of cooking is rudimentary.*

rue [ru:] – *prp* **'ru(e)ing**: *pt, ptp* **rued** – *vt* (*old or liter*) to regret; to be sorry for: *I rue the day I met him.*

'rueful *adj* (*formal*) regretful; sorrowful: *He had a rueful expression*; *Her smile was rather rueful.* **'ruefully** *adv.* **'ruefulness** *nu.*

ruff [rʌf] *nc* **1** (*hist*) a linen *etc* frill worn round the neck in the 16th century. **2** a thick band of feathers or hair on a bird's or animal's neck: *The parrot had a blue ruff (round its neck).*

ruffian ['rʌfiən] *nc* a violent, brutal person: *He was attacked by a gang of ruffians.*

ruffle ['rʌfl] **1** *vt* to make wrinkled or uneven, *esp* hair, feathers *etc*: *The wind ruffled her hair*; *The bird ruffled its feathers in anger.* **2** *vti* (*fig*) to make or become irritated or annoyed: *He is easily ruffled*; *She ruffles at the slightest annoyance.* – *nc* a frill on one's clothes, *esp* at the neck or wrist: *lace ruffles.*

rug [rʌg] *nc* **1** a mat for the floor; a small carpet: *a woollen rug in front of the fire*; *a hearth-rug* (= for putting in front of the fire). **2** (*also* **'travelling-rug**) a thick blanket for keeping one warm when travelling: *Put that rug over your knees.*

Rugby, rugby ['rʌgbi] *nu* (*also* **Rugby/rugby football**: *inf abbrev* **rugger** ['rʌgə]) a kind of football using an oval ball which can be carried: *Rugby is played a lot in Wales*; (*attrib*) *a rugby match.*

rugged ['rʌgid] *adj* **1** (of rocks, hills *etc*) rough; uneven: *rugged mountains*; *The countryside around there is very rugged.* **2** strong; tough: *a rugged character*; *He had rugged good looks*; *He is tall and rugged.* **'ruggedly** *adv.* **'ruggedness** *nu.*

rugger ['rʌgə] (*inf*) short for **Rugby/rugby (football)**: *Do you play rugger?*; (*attrib*) *a rugger match.*

ruin ['ru:in] *nu* **1** a broken, collapsed or decayed state: *the ruin of a city/civilization/career.* **2** (*formal*) a cause of collapse, decay *etc*: *Drink was his ruin.* **3** financial disaster; complete loss of money: *The company is facing ruin.* – See also **ruins, in ruins** *below.* – *vt* **1** to cause ruin to: *The scandal ruined his career*; *Loss of trade is ruining the business*; *The storm has ruined the garden.* **2** (*inf*) to spoil; to treat too indulgently: *You are ruining that child!* **ˌrui'nation** *ncu.*

'ruined *adj* **1** (*attrib*) collapsed; decayed: *ruined houses.* **2** (*usu pred*) completely spoiled: *My dress is ruined!*

'ruinous *adj* (*formal or facet*) likely to bring ruin: *ruinous prices*; *The cost of a glass of whisky in that pub is ruinous.* **'ruinously** *adv.*

'ruins *n pl* collapsed and decayed buildings: *The ruins of the abbey look very beautiful.*

in 'ruins in a ruined state: *The town lay in ruins*; (*fig*) *His life was in ruins.*

rule [ru:l] **1** *nu* government: *under foreign rule.* **2** *nc* a regulation or order: *school rules*; *You must follow the rules.* **3** *nu* what usually happens or is done; a general principle: *He is an exception to the rule that fat people are usually happy.* **4** *nc* a general idea which one has as a standard to guide one's actions: *I make it a rule never to be late for appointments.* **5** *nc* (*formal or tech*) a marked strip of wood, metal *etc* for measuring: *He measured the windows with a rule.* – **1** *vti* to govern: *The king ruled (the people) wisely.* **2** *vt* (*often legal*) to make an official decision (about): *The chairman ruled him out of order*; *The judge ruled that the witness should be heard.* **3** *vt* (*formal*) to draw (a straight line): *He ruled a line across the page.* – See also **rule off, rule out** *below.*

ruled *adj* having straight lines drawn across: *ruled paper.*

'ruler *nc* **1** a person who governs: *the ruler of the state.* **2** an instrument (*usu* a long narrow piece of wood, plastic *etc*) for drawing straight lines: *I can't draw straight lines without a ruler.*

'ruling *adj* (*usu attrib*) **1** governing: *the ruling party.* **2** most important; strongest: *His ruling interest is music.* – *nc* (*formal*) an official decision: *The judge gave his ruling on the matter.*

as a 'rule usually: *I don't go out in the evening as a rule.*

rule off *vt sep* to draw a line in order to separate: *He ruled off the rest of the page.*

rule of thumb a method of doing something, based on experience rather than theory or careful calculation: *I usually work by rule of thumb.*

rule out *vt sep* to leave out; not to consider: *We mustn't rule out the possibility of bad weather.*

work to rule *see* **work**.

See also **overrule**.

rum[1] [rʌm] **1** *nu* a type of alcoholic drink, a spirit made from sugar cane: *a bottle of rum.* **2** *nc* a glass of rum.

rum[2] [rʌm] *adj* (*slightly old*) strange; odd: *That was a rum thing to do*; *How rum of him to do that!*

Rumania, Rumanian *see* Appendix 2.

rumba ['rʌmbə] *nc* (a piece of music for) a South American dance: *Can you dance the rumba?*; *The band played a rumba.*

rumble ['rʌmbl] *vi* to make a low grumbling sound: *Thunder rumbled in the distance*; *The wheels rumbled over the tracks.* – *nc* this kind of sound: *the rumble of thunder.*

rumbustious [rʌm'bʌstʃəs] *adj* (*formal or facet*) noisy and cheerful; boisterous: *rumbustious behaviour.*

ruminant ['ru:minənt] *nc, adj* (*tech*) (of) an animal that chews the cud, *eg* a cow.

'ruminate [-neit] *vi* (*formal*) **1** to be deep in thought: *He was ruminating about/on/over the problem.* **2** to chew the cud. **ˌrumi'nation** *nu.*

rummage ['rʌmidʒ] *vi* to search by turning things

out or over: *He rummaged in the drawer for a clean shirt*; *She rummaged through the papers on his desk.* – *nc* a thorough search.

rummy ['rʌmi] *nu* a kind of card game: *Shall we have a game of rummy? Do you play rummy?*

rumour, (*Amer*) **rumor** ['ru:mə] **1** *nc* a piece of news or story passed from person to person, which may not be true: *I heard a rumour that you had got a new job.* **2** *nu* general talk or gossip: *Rumour has it that they are getting married.* – *vt* (*formal*: *usu in passive*) (of talk or gossip) to say: *He is rumoured to have left the country*; *It is rumoured that they are getting married.*

rump [rʌmp] *nc* (of animals and *facet* of people) the buttocks: *He slapped the cow on the rump*; (*attrib*) *rump steak.*

rumple ['rʌmpl] *vt* to make untidy; to crease: *Don't rumple my hair!*; *You've rumpled your shirt.*

'rumpled *adj* untidy, *esp* creased or wrinkled: *rumpled bedclothes.*

rumpus ['rʌmpəs] *nc* a noisy disturbance; an uproar: *There was a terrible rumpus in the kitchen*; *There will be a rumpus when my mother finds out that I'm getting married.*

run [rʌn] – *prp* **'running**: *pt* **ran** [ran]: *ptp* **run** – **1** *vi* (of a person or animal) to move quickly, faster than walking: *He ran down the road.* **2** *vi* to move smoothly: *Trains run on rails*; (*fig*) *His life ran smoothly.* **3** *vi* (of water *etc*) to flow: *Rivers run to the sea*; *Is the water running in the bathroom?* **4** *vti* (of a machine *etc*) to work or operate: *The engine is running*; *He ran the motor to see if it was working.* **5** *vt* to organize or manage: *He runs the business very efficiently.* **6** *vi* to race: *Is your horse running this afternoon?* **7** *vi* (of buses, trains *etc*) to travel regularly: *The buses run every half hour*; *The trains are running late/on time.* **8** *vi* to last or continue; to go on: *The programme runs for two hours*; *The play ran for six weeks.* **9** *vt* to own and use, *esp* of cars: *He runs a Rolls Royce.* **10** *vi* (of colour) to spread: *When I washed my new dress the colour ran.* **11** *vt* (*inf*) to drive (someone); to give (someone) a lift: *He ran me to the station.* **12** *vt* to move (something): *She ran her fingers through his hair*; *He ran his eyes over the letter*; (*fig*) *Excitement ran through the audience.* **13** *vi* (in certain phrases) to be or become: *The river ran dry*; *My blood ran cold* (= I was afraid). – **1** *ncu* the act of running: *He set off at a run*; *He went for a run before breakfast.* **2** *nc* a trip or drive: *It was a beautiful day so we went for a run in the country.* **3** *nc* a length of time (for which something runs): *The play had a six-month run*; *He's had a run of bad luck.* **4** *nc* a ladder (in a stocking *etc*): *I've got a run in my tights.* **5** *nu* the free use of (a place): *He gave me the run of his house.* **6** *nc* demand for or from: *There's been a run on tickets for the play*; *a run on the bank*; *a run on the pound.* **7** *nc* in cricket, a batsman's act of running from one end of the wicket to the other, representing a single score: *He scored/made 50 runs for his team.* **8** *nc* (*often in cmpds*) an enclosure or pen *esp* for fowls: *a chicken-run.*

'runner *nc* **1** a person who runs: *There are five runners in this race.* **2** the long narrow part on which a sledge *etc* moves: *He polished the runners of the sledge.* **3** a long narrow tablecloth, stair-carpet *etc*: *a table-runner*; *a stair-runner.* **4** a long stem of a plant which puts down roots: *strawberry runners.*

'running *nu* **1** the act of moving fast, flowing *etc*: *I could hear the running of feet/water.* **2** the act of managing, organizing *etc*: *He took over the running of the business from his father.* – *adj* (*attrib*) **1** of or for the act of running: *running shoes.* **2** continuous: *a running commentary on the football match.* **3** giving out pus: *a running sore.* – *adv* one after another; continuously: *We travelled for four days running.*

'runny *adj* (*inf*) liquid; watery: *My egg is runny – it wasn't boiled long enough*; *The child has a cold – he has a runny nose.*

'runaway *nc* a person, animal *etc* that runs away: *The police caught the two runaways*; (*attrib*) *He was knocked down by a runaway horse.* – *See also* **run away** *below.*

,run-'down *adj* (*usu pred*) tired or exhausted because one has worked too hard: *He felt run-down so he had a holiday.*

,runner-'up *nc* a person, thing *etc* that is second in a race or competition: *My friend won the prize and I was the runner-up.*

,run-of-the-'mill *adj* ordinary; not special: *It was just a run-of-the-mill visit*; *This kind of work is very run-of-the-mill.*

'runway *nc* a wide path from which aircraft take off and on which they land: *The plane landed on the runway.*

'also-ran *nc* (*inf*) a person, horse *etc* that runs in a race but does not come first, second or third: *My horse was one of the also-rans*; (*fig*) *She married someone else – I was one of the also-rans.*

in, out of the running having (no) chance of success: *She's in the running for a new job.*

in the long run *see* **long**.

on the run escaping; running away: *He's on the run from the police.*

run across *vt fus* (*inf*) to meet: *I ran across an old friend.*

run after *vt fus* (*inf*) to chase: *The dog ran after a cat.*

run aground *vi* (of a ship) to become stuck on rocks, the bottom of a shallow river *etc*: *The ship ran aground on a sandbank.*

run along *vi* (*inf*) to go away: *Run along now, children!*

run away *vi* **1** to escape: *He ran away from school*; *He ran away from prison.* **2** (*with* **with**) to steal: *He ran away with all her money.* **3** (*with* **with**) to go too fast *etc* to be controlled: *The horse ran away with him*; (*fig*) *Her enthusiasm ran away with her.* – *See also* **runaway** *above.*

run down **1** *vi* (of a clock, battery *etc*) to finish working: *My watch has run down – it needs rewinding.* **2** *vt sep* (of a vehicle or driver) to knock down: *I was run down by a bus*; *He ran down a pedestrian.* **3** *vt sep* (*fig*) to speak badly of: *He is always running me down.*

run errands to do jobs (for): *He runs errands for his mother.*

run for *vt fus* (*esp Amer*) to stand for election for: *He is running for president.*

run for it (*inf*) to try to escape: *Quick – run for it!*

run in **1** *vt sep*, *vi* to get (a new engine *etc*) working properly: *I only bought the car last month, so I am still running it in*; *The car is still running in.* **2** *vt sep* (*sl*) to arrest: *The policeman ran him in for dangerous driving.*

run into *vt fus* **1** (*inf*) to meet: *I ran into her in the street.* **2** *vi*, *vt sep* to crash into or collide with: *The car ran into a lamp-post*; *I ran my bike into the back of a bus.*

run its course (*formal*) to develop or happen in the usual way: *The fever ran its course.*

run off 1 *vt sep* to print: *I want 500 copies run off at once.* **2** *vi* (*with* **with**) to steal or take away: *He ran off with all my money*; (*fig*) *He ran off with my wife.*

run out 1 *vi* (of a supply) to come to an end; to finish: *The food has run out.* **2** *vi* (*with* **of**) to have no more: *We've run out of money.* **3** *vt* in cricket, to put a batsman out by getting the ball to the end of the wicket before he reaches it when he is making a run: *He was run out by the wicket-keeper.* **4** *vi* (*inf*: *with* **on**) to leave or abandon someone: *His wife ran out on him.*

run over 1 *vt sep* (of a vehicle or driver) to knock down or drive over: *Don't let the dog out of the garden or he'll get run over.* **2** *vt fus* to repeat for practice: *Let's run over the plan again.*

run riot *vi* to act wildly: *The crowd ran riot in the streets.*

run short *see* **short**.

run a temperature (of a person or animal) to have a high temperature: *He must be ill – he's running a temperature.*

run the gauntlet *see* **gauntlet**.

run through *vt fus* to look at, deal with *etc*, one after another: *He ran through the names on the list*; *He ran through their instructions.*

run to *vi* (*inf*) to have enough money for: *We can't run to a new car this year.*

run (someone or something) to earth (*inf*) to find after long and hard searching: *I finally ran the information I wanted to earth in an old book.*

run to seed *see* **seed**.

run up *vt sep* **1** to hoist (a flag): *They ran up the British flag.* **2** (*inf*) to make quickly or roughly: *I can run up a dress in a couple of hours.* **3** to make (money) increase; to accumulate: *He ran up an enormous bill.*

run wild *vi* **1** to behave without control or discipline: *They let their children run wild.* **2** (of plants) to grow all over, without control: *The garden was running wild.*

See also **outrun, overrun**.

rune [ru:n] *nc* any of the letters of an early alphabet used in northern Europe about 200-600 AD. **'runic** *adj.*

rung[1] [rʌŋ] *nc* a step on a ladder: *The child tried to climb the ladder but fell off the third rung.*

rung[2] *see* **ring**.

runny *see* **run**.

runt [rʌnt] *nc* (*derog*) a small person or animal that has not grown fully: *a little runt of a man*; *There's a runt in every litter.*

runway *see* **run**.

rupee [ru'pi:] *nc* the standard unit of currency in India, Pakistan and Sri Lanka *etc.*

rupture ['rʌptʃə] *nc* **1** (*tech*) a tearing of the wall of the stomach *etc*; a hernia: *to have a rupture.* **2** (*very formal*) a breaking: *a rupture in our friendship.* – **1** *v refl* to cause a rupture (*def 1*): *He ruptured himself lifting a heavy weight.* **2** *vti* (*formal*) to break or tear: *He ruptured a blood-vessel*; *A pipe ruptured with the cold.*

rural ['ruərəl] *adj* (*usu attrib*) of the country: *a rural area/way of life.*

ruse [ru:z] *nc* (*derog*) a clever trick or plan: *He thought up a cunning ruse to get me to give him money.*

rush[1] [rʌʃ] **1** *vti* to (make someone or something) hurry or go quickly: *He rushed into the room*; *She rushed him to the doctor*; *He rushed the photographs to the newspaper.* **2** *vt* (*formal*) to attack suddenly: *They rushed the guard at the door.* – **1** *nc* a sudden quick movement: *They made a rush for the door.* **2** *nu* a hurry: *I'm in a dreadful rush.*

'rush hour *nc* a period when there is a lot of traffic on the roads, *usu* when people are going to or leaving work: *I got caught in the rush hour this morning.*

rush[2] [rʌʃ] *nc* a tall grass-like plant growing in or near water: *They hid their boat in the rushes.*

rusk [rʌsk] *nc* a kind of biscuit like hard toast: *Rusks are good for babies when their teeth are growing.*

russet ['rʌsit] **1** *nu, adj* (of) a reddish-brown colour: *the russet of the autumn leaves*; *a russet scarf.* **2** *nc* a type of apple of this colour.

Russian ['rʌʃən]: **Russian tea** *nu* a kind of tea served with lemon: *a glass of Russian tea.*

Russia, Russian *see* Appendix 2.

Russo- [rʌsou] (*in cmpds*) of Russia: *a Russo-American treaty.*

rust [rʌst] **1** *nu* the reddish-brown substance which forms on iron and steel, caused by air and moisture: *The car was covered with rust.* **2** *nu, adj* (of) a reddish-brown colour: *a deep rust*; (*attrib*) *rust(-coloured) material.* – *vti* to cause or become covered with (rust): *The rain has rusted the gate*; *There's a lot of old metal rusting in the garden.*

'rustproof *adj* that will not (allow) rust: *rustproof paint*; *Has this metal been made rustproof?*

'rusty *adj* **1** covered with rust: *a rusty old bicycle*; *This car is rather rusty.* **2** (*inf*: *usu pred*) not as good as it was because of lack of practice: *My French is rusty.* **'rustily** *adv.* **'rustiness** *nu.*

rustic ['rʌstik] *adj* (*usu attrib*) **1** of the country: *rustic life.* **2** roughly made: *a rustic fence*; *rustic garden furniture.* **3** (*liter*) simple; unsophisticated: *the rustic beauty of Nature.* – *nc* (*liter*) a countryman; a peasant: *the hard-working rustics.*

ru'sticity [-səti] *nu.*

rustle ['rʌsl] *vti* **1** to (make something) make a soft, whispering sound: *The wind rustled in the trees*; *She rustled her papers.* **2** (*Amer*) to steal (cattle *etc*): *They were caught rustling cows.*

'rustler *nc* (*Amer*) a person who steals cattle *etc*: *a gang of rustlers.*

rustle up *vt sep* (*sl*) to get or make quickly: *He rustled up some food and clean clothes.*

rut[1] [rʌt] *nc* a deep track made by a wheel *etc* in soft ground: *The road was full of ruts.*

'rutted *adj* (*often in cmpds*) having ruts: *a deeply-rutted path.*

in(to) a rut having a fixed, monotonous, firmly established way of life: *I felt that I was (getting) in a rut, so I changed my job.*

rut[2] [rʌt] *nu* a male animal's period of sexual excitement.

'rutting season *nu* the time when this occurs.

ruthless ['ru:θlis] *adj* without pity: *a ruthless attack*; (*fig*) *ruthless ambition*; *a ruthless tyrant*; *He is so ruthless that he would do anything to be promoted.* **'ruthlessly** *adv.* **'ruthlessness** *nu.*

rye [rai] **1** *nu* a kind of cereal: *The farm grows wheat and rye.* **2** *nu* rye whisky, a kind of whisky made wholly or partly from rye: *a glass of rye.* **3** *nc* a glass of rye.

rye bread *nu* a kind of bread made with flour made from rye.

Ss

's[1] *see* **be, have**.

's[2] [s, z, iz] *prep* a word used to show possession; *Dick's* [diks] *book*; *John's* [dʒonz] *book*; *Margo's* ['ma:gouz] *book*; *George's* ['dʒo:dʒiz] *book*.

Sabbath ['sabəθ] *n* (*usu with* **the**) a day of the week regularly set aside for religious services and rest – among the Jews, Saturday; among most Christians, Sunday: *Some devout people will not even read a novel on the Sabbath*; (*attrib*) *the Sabbath day*.

sabbatical [sə'batikəl] *ncu* a period of freedom from teaching duties, given to a university teacher so that he or she can travel or study: *After seven years teaching, a lecturer is allowed one term's sabbatical*; (*attrib*) *a sabbatical term*; (*attrib*) *sabbatical leave*; *Dr Morris is on sabbatical this year*.

saber *see* **sabre**.

sable[1] ['seibl] **1** *nc* a kind of small animal found in Arctic regions, valued for its glossy fur. **2** *nu, adj* (of) its fur: *Artists' brushes are sometimes made of sable*; *a sable coat*.

sable[2] ['seibl] *adj* (*liter*: *usu attrib*) black or very dark: *the sable night*.

sabot ['sabou] *nc* a wooden shoe or clog of the kind worn *eg* by some French country people: *He bought a pair of sabots when he was on holiday*.

sabotage ['sabəta:ʒ] *nu* the deliberate destruction in secret of machinery, roads, bridges *etc*, by *eg* enemies in wartime, by dissatisfied workers *etc*: *The machinery had been wrecked so efficiently that the police were sure it was a case of sabotage*. – *vt* (*formal*) to destroy, damage or cause (something) to fail by sabotage: *The police were sure that someone had been paid to sabotage the machinery*.

ˌsabo'teur [-'tə:] *nc* a person who sabotages (something): *The soldiers said that the three men they shot were saboteurs*.

sabre, (*Amer*) **saber** ['seibə] *nc* a type of curved sword, used by cavalry.

sac [sak] *nc* (*formal or tech*: *sometimes in cmpds*) in plants or animals, a bag or bag-like container, often containing a liquid: *The air that one breathes in goes into the air-sacs in one's lungs*; *The poison of venomous snakes is held in small sacs in their heads*.

saccharin(e) ['sakərin] *nu* a very sweet substance used instead of sugar by some people *eg* those who want to slim.

sachet ['saʃei, (*Amer*) sa'ʃei] *nc* a (small) sealed packet containing a product in liquid or powder form (*eg* shampoo, sugar *etc*): *If you want only a small quantity of shampoo, you can buy a sachet instead of a bottle*.

sack[1] [sak] *nc* **1** a large bag of coarse cloth, strong paper or plastic, for holding *eg* grain, flour, coal *etc*: *The potatoes were put into sacks*. **2** a sackful: *The sack of potatoes weighed forty kilogrammes*; *Tell the coalman to leave three sacks for me*.

'sackful *nc* the amount contained in a sack: *We use about a sackful of coal every week*.

'sacking *nu* a type of coarse cloth for making sacks *etc*.

'sackcloth *nu* a type of coarse cloth formerly worn as a sign of mourning or of sorrow for sin.

sack[2] [sak] *vt* (*inf*) to dismiss (a person) from his job: *One of the workmen was sacked for drunkenness*; *The football team has lost every game this season, so it has sacked its manager*.

get the sack (*inf*) to be sacked: *I'll get the sack if I arrive at the office late!*

give (someone) the sack (*inf*) to sack (someone): *They gave Jones the sack for being drunk on duty*.

sack[3] [sak] *vt* (*formal or liter*) (of a victorious army *etc*) to steal everything of value from (a captured town *etc*) *usu* with violence: *After they captured Troy, the Greeks sacked the city*. – *nc* (*formal or liter*: *no pl*) the act of sacking (a captured town *etc*): *Many important works of art were lost or destroyed during the sack of the city*.

sacrament ['sakrəmənt] *nc* in the Christian church, a ceremony regarded as especially sacred, *eg* Holy Communion, marriage, or baptism.

ˌsacra'mental [-'men-] *adj* (*relig*: *esp attrib*) belonging to, or being (like), a sacrament: *the sacramental bread and wine used in Holy Communion*.

sacred ['seikrid] *adj* **1** of God or a god; (that must be treated with great respect because) connected with religion or with God or a god: *The Bible contains the sacred writings of the Christian religion, the Koran those of Islam*; *Temples, mosques, churches and synagogues are all sacred buildings*; *sacred music/art*; *The cat was considered sacred in ancient Egypt*. **2** (of a promise, duty *etc*) which must be kept, carried out, done *etc eg* because of respect for someone: *He considered it a sacred duty to fulfil his dead father's wishes*. – See also **sacred to** below. **'sacredly** *adv*. **'sacredness** *nu*.

nothing is sacred (to him, them *etc***)** he, they *etc* have no respect for anything: *That man is making fun of the Queen – is nothing sacred (to him)?*

'sacred to 1 dedicated to (a dead person): *On the gravestone was written 'Sacred to the memory of James Smith'*. **2** dedicated to, or closely associated with, a god: *The cat was sacred to the goddess Bast in ancient Egypt*.

sacrifice ['sakrifais] **1** *ncu* the act of offering something (*eg* an animal that is specially killed) to a god: *Before the battle, the commanders ordered the sacrifice of two bullocks to the god of war*; *The commanders ordered the priests to make sacrifices*; *A lamb was offered in sacrifice*. **2** *nc* the thing that is offered in this way: *They offered a pig as a sacrifice*. **3** *ncu* the act of giving away, losing or allowing oneself not to have something of value, *eg* in order to gain something more important or to benefit another person: *His parents sold their car and made other sacrifices to pay for his education*; *Was the sacrifice of so many men's lives in the war really justified?*; *At the sacrifice of his own comfort, he allowed the guest to use his bed*. – **1** *vti* to offer (something) as a sacrifice: *He sacrificed a sheep in the temple*. **2** *vt* to give away, lose, or allow oneself not to have (something) for the sake of something or someone else: *He sacrificed his life trying to save the children from the burning house*; *Many women have to sacrifice their own careers to their husbands' work*; *He doesn't seem to realize how much I have sacrificed for him*.

ˌsacri'ficial [-'fiʃəl] *adj* (*formal*: *usu attrib*) of (a) sacrifice: *sacrificial victims*. **ˌsacri'ficially** *adv*.

sacrilege ['sakrəlidʒ] *ncu* the act of using a holy thing or place in an evil way or of doing something bad to a holy thing or place: *Robbing a church is considered (a) sacrilege*; (*facet*) *Some people think that putting water in whisky is sacrilege.*

'sacri'legious [-'lidʒəs] *adj* of (a) sacrilege: *He will be punished for his sacrilegious act.* **ˌsacri'legiously** *adv.* **ˌsacri'legiousness** *nu.*

sacrosanct ['sakrəsaŋkt] *adj* (*formal or facet*) that must never be harmed, changed or interfered with *eg* because holy or sacred: *Few people still regard the bond of marriage as sacrosanct*; *sacrosanct privileges/rights*; (*fig*) *My week-ends are sacrosanct – I never take work home with me from the office.*

sad [sad] *adj* **1** unhappy or causing unhappiness: *He is still very sad about his sister's death*; *She's sad because her son is ill*; *He has a sad face/expression*; *What a sad time that family has had recently!*; *It was sad that his books were never successful during his lifetime*; *The complete failure of his foolish business scheme left him sadder and wiser.* **2** (*attrib*) (*esp* of a state or condition) very bad; disgraceful: *The paintwork in this house is in a sad state.*

'sadness *nu.*

'sadden *vti* to make or become sad: *She was saddened by her son's ingratitude*; *Suddenly, his face saddened.*

'sadly *adv* **1** in a sad way: *He stared sadly at the ruins of his house.* **2** to a disgraceful extent; in a bad way: *The garden has been sadly neglected.*

saddle ['sadl] *nc* **1** a seat for a rider used on the back of a horse, on a bicycle *etc*: *The bicycle saddle is too high for this child.* **2** a certain joint of meat cut from the back of an animal: *a saddle of beef/mutton.* – *vt* (*neg* **un-**) to put a saddle on (a horse, camel *etc*): *He saddled his horse, mounted, and rode away.* – *See also* **saddle (someone) with (something), saddle up** *below.*

'saddler *nc* a person who makes saddles and harness for horses.

in the 'saddle (*fig*) in a position of power or control: *The new manager had not been in the saddle long when the trouble occurred.*

saddle up *vi, vt sep* to put a saddle on (a horse *etc*): *He saddled up and rode away.*

'saddle (someone) with (something) (*inf*) to give (a person) something annoying, difficult *etc* to deal with: *I can't do very much shopping when I'm saddled with the children*; *He saddled his parents with his debts.*

sadism ['seidizəm] *nu* (*formal or tech*) pleasure got from cruelty to others: *Teachers have occasionally beaten pupils purely out of sadism.*

'sadist *nc* a person who is guilty of sadism: *Only a sadist could hurt a child so cruelly.*

sa'distic [sə-] *adj* of a sadist or sadism: *sadistic behaviour*; *He is rather sadistic.* **sa'distically** *adv.*

safari [sə'fa:ri] *ncu* an expedition or tour, *esp* in Africa, for hunting or observing animals: *A safari was organized to the lion reserve*; *When we were in Africa we went on many safaris*; *We often went out on safari.*

sa'fari park *nc* a large area of land reserved for wild animals, in which they can move freely and be seen by the public who *usu* drive through the park in cars.

safe[1] [seif] *adj* **1** (*neg* **un-**: *with* **from**) protected, or free (from danger *etc*): *It is impossible to keep children safe from all dangers*; *In its burrow, a rabbit is usually safe from attack.* **2** (*neg* **un-**) (of a place *etc*) providing good protection: *You should have put your money in a safe place*; *Is this place safe enough?* **3** (*attrib*) unharmed; not injured; *The missing child has been found safe and well.* **4** (*neg* **un-**) not likely to cause harm: *These pills are not safe for children*; *Will the fire be safe without a fireguard in front?* **5** (of a person) trustworthy, reliable, and not likely to take risks: *He's a very safe driver*; *He's a very fast driver but he's safe enough.* **6** not involving any risk: *That's a safe choice*; *You're money will be safe enough.* – *See also* **play safe** *at* **play**. **7** (*polit*) (of a parliamentary seat, constituency *etc*) having a large majority in favour of a particular party: *Bluetown is a safe Tory seat.*

'safely *adv* without harm or risk: *He got home safely*; *We can safely leave him to deal with the matter.*

'safeness *nu.*

'safety *nu* (*sometimes in cmpds or attrib*) the state of being safe (*defs 1-6*): *I worry about the children's safety on these busy roads*; *Your valuable pictures should be transferred to a place of safety*; *You had better lock the door for safety's sake*; *safety-belt.*

ˌsafe-'conduct *ncu* (a document, passport *etc* given to a person which gives him) the right to travel without arrest *etc*, *esp* in time of war: *The commander granted the journalist (a) safe-conduct to the frontier.*

'safeguard *nc* anything that prevents danger or gives security or protection: *Always tell your neighbours when you are going away, as a safeguard against burglary.* – *vt* to protect: *Put a good lock on your door to safeguard your property.*

ˌsafe-'keeping *nu* care; protection: *He gave me his watch for safe-keeping*; *Her jewellery was in the safe-keeping of the bank.*

'safety-belt *nc* a fixed belt in a car or aircraft used to keep a passenger from being thrown out of the seat in an accident, crash *etc*; a seat-belt: *A driver should always fasten his safety-belt before starting out on a journey.*

'safety lamp *nc* a type of lamp used in mines that does not set fire to any inflammable gases there.

'safety-pin *nc* a pin that has a cover over its point when it is closed: *When the zip broke, he had to fasten his trousers with a couple of safety-pins.*

'safety valve *nc* **1** a valve *eg* on a pressure cooker that opens if the pressure of the steam in it becomes too great. **2** a harmless outlet for feelings, *eg* of anger, excitement *etc*: *Don't stop the children quarrelling – it's a safety valve for their emotions.*

ˌbe on the 'safe side to avoid risk or danger: *I don't think we'll need much money but I'll take my cheque-book just to be on the safe side.*

play safe *see* **play**.

safe and sound unharmed: *He returned safe and sound.*

See also **save**.

safe[2] [seif] *nc* **1** a heavy metal chest or box in which money, jewellery, documents *etc* can be locked away safely: *There is a small safe hidden behind that picture on the wall.* **2** a type of cupboard in which meat *etc* can be kept to protect it from flies: *We do not have a fridge but we have a meat safe.*

saffron ['safrən] **1** *nu* a yellow colouring and flavouring substance used in cooking: *We added some saffron to the rice.* **2** *nu, adj* (of) an orange-yellow colour: *Many Buddhist monks wear saffron robes.*

sag [sag] – *pt, ptp* **sagged** – *vi* **1** to bend, sink, hang down *etc* in some part *esp* in the middle: *There were so many books on the shelf that it sagged in the middle; I think the hem of your skirt is sagging on the left side.* **2** to become weaker, less firm *etc*: *Our muscles start to sag as we get older.* – *nc* a dip caused by sagging: *There's quite a sag in the middle of the bed.*

saga ['sa:gə] *nc* **1** a medieval Icelandic or Norwegian prose story of heroes, kings *etc*: *King Harald's Saga is the story of Harald Hardrada, King of Norway.* **2** a word sometimes used in the title of a novel or series of novels about several generations of a family: *Galsworthy wrote 'The Forsyte Saga'.* **3** (*inf*) a long, detailed story: *I expected he told you the saga of his troubles.*

sagacious [sə'geiʃəs] *adj* (*very formal or facet*) showing intelligence, wisdom, good judgement or cunning: *Cats are extremely sagacious animals; The old priest was learned and sagacious; Locking yourself out of your own house is not a sagacious thing to do.* **sa'gaciously** *adv.*

sagacity [sə'gasəti] *nu* (*formal or facet*) the quality of being sagacious: *an animal of remarkable sagacity.*

sage[1] [seidʒ] **1** *nu* a plant whose leaves are used as flavouring in cooking: *Sage and onion are used for stuffing roast duck.* **2** *nu, adj* (*also* **sage green**) (of) the colour of sage; greyish-green: *a sage (green) dress.*

sage[2] [seidʒ] *nc* (*liter or facet*) a wise man: *His library was full of books written by the sages of past centuries.* – *adj* (*liter: attrib*) wise: *a sage old country woman; I thanked him for his sage advice.* **'sagely** *adv.*

Sagittarius [sadʒi'teəriəs] *n* a sign of the zodiac, the Archer: *People born between November 22 and December 20 are said to be born under the sign of Sagittarius.*

sago ['seigou] *nu* a starchy substance in the form of small round grains obtained from inside the trunk of certain palm trees, used in *eg* pudding: *We have sago for lunch every Tuesday;* (*attrib*) *sago pudding.*

said [sed] *adj* (*attrib: formal: usu with* **the**) mentioned earlier in a statement *etc*: *The said motorist was fined £50; We'll wait until the said person arrives.* – *v see* **say**.

sail [seil] *nc* **1** a sheet of strong cloth spread to catch the wind, by which a ship is driven forward: *A small yacht usually has two sails.* **2** a journey in a ship: *We had a sail up the coast in his yacht; Is it a week's sail from Liverpool to New York?* **3** an arm of a windmill: *Windmills have four wooden sails.* – **1** *vi* (of a ship) to be moved by sails: *The yacht sailed round the headland.* **2** *vti* to steer or navigate a ship or boat (*eg* as a sport): *He sailed the boat out to the island; Do you sail?* **3** *vi* to go somewhere in a ship or boat (with or without sails): *I've never sailed through the Mediterranean; I've never sailed before – I've always gone by air.* **4** *vi* (of a ship or its passengers) to begin a voyage: *The ship sails today; My aunt sailed (from Portsmouth) today (for Gibraltar).* **5** *vt* to travel on (the sea *etc*) in a ship: *He had sailed the North Sea many times.* **6** *vi* to move steadily and easily through the air *etc*: *Small clouds sailed across the sky;* (*fig*) *He sailed through his exams.* **7** *vi* (*facet or derog*) to move in a proud or impressive way: *She sailed into the room.*

'sailing 1 *nu* the activity or sport of navigating a ship or boat that has sails: *Sailing is one of his hobbies.* **2** *nc* a *usu* regular journey made by a ship: *Are there sailings every day from Liverpool to the Isle of Man?*

sailing- (*in cmpds*) having a sail or sails: *sailing-ships; sailing-boats.*

'sailor *nc* a member of a ship's crew whose job is helping to sail a ship.

'sailcloth *nu* strong cloth, *usu* canvas, used to make sails.

in full sail with all the sails spread: *The ship was in full sail.*

set sail to set out on a sea-voyage: *We set sail from Dover for Ostend.*

saint [seint, (*before a name*) snt] *nc* **1** (*relig: with cap in names: often abbrev* **St**, *esp when used in the names of places, plants etc*) a title given *esp* by the Roman Catholic and Orthodox churches to a very good or holy person after his death *usu* after he has performed, or is believed to have performed, miracles: *Saint Matthew was a tax-collector before he became Christ's follower; He lives in St John's Road; St Andrews is a town in Scotland.* **2** (*inf fig*) a very good, kind person: *You really are a saint to invite us all to stay with you!*

'saintly *adj* of, or like, a saint; very good or holy: *He led a saintly life; a saintly face/expression.* **'saintliness** *nu.*

'saint's day *nc* a day on which a particular saint is honoured.

See also **sanctify**.

sake [seik]: **for the 'sake of 1** in order to benefit (someone or something): *I came late to his lecture, and he began it again just for my sake; He bought a house in the country for the sake of his wife's health.* **2** for the purpose of; because of a desire for: *She changed into old clothes for the sake of comfort; For the sake of peace, he said he agreed with her.*

for God's/goodness' sake *see* **god, good**.

salable *see* **sale**.

salacious [sə'leiʃəs] *adj* (*formal*) (of a story, picture *etc*) dealing with or describing sexual activity in a rather obscene way; likely to cause obscene thoughts or sexual desire: *Just because a book is slightly salacious in places, there is no reason to say that it is not literature; salacious photographs.* **sa'laciously** *adv.* **sa'laciousness** *nu.*

salad ['saləd] *ncu* (a dish of) mixed raw vegetables *etc*, *usu* cut up and often seasoned with oil, vinegar, pepper *etc*: *In Britain, salad is often made with lettuce and tomato; We like to eat a lot of salads in the summer.*

fruit salad *nu* a mixture of chopped fruits *usu* eaten as a dessert.

salad cream *nu* a type of mayonnaise *usu* sold in bottles.

salad dressing *nu* a sauce for putting on salad, *usu* consisting of oil and vinegar and sometimes spices.

salami [sə'la:mi] *nu* a type of strongly-seasoned *usu* Italian sausage.

salary ['saləri] *nc* a fixed, regular *usu* monthly payment for work, *usu* to a person in a profession, in a managerial position *etc*: *the salary of a university teacher; Secretarial salaries in London are quite high.*

'salaried *adj* (*formal: neg* **un-**) **1** (of a person) receiving a salary: *the salaried staff of the museum; Is he salaried?* **2** (of a job) paid by salary: *a salaried position; The post is salaried.*

See also **fee, wage**.

sale [seil] **1** *ncu* the act of giving something to someone in exchange for money: *He got £17 000* *from the sale of his house; The shop assistant said she had made two sales that morning; Sales of electric heaters have increased.* 2 *nu* (*sometimes with* **a**) a public need or desire for, and therefore willingness to buy, a particular product: *There is no sale for cotton dresses in the autumn; Her pictures always found a good sale among the summer tourists.* 3 *nc* (*often in pl*) in a shop *etc*, an offer of goods at lowered prices for a short time: *I bought my dress in a sale; I got it at the sales; the January sales.* 4 *nc* an event at which goods are sold *eg* by auction: *an auction sale; Our school is having a book sale next week.* – *See also* **for sale, on sale** *below.*

'sal(e)able *adj* (*neg* **un-**) fit to be sold; easy to sell: *This type of book is just not saleable; Victorian clocks are highly saleable.*

'saleroom *nc* a room or building where public auctions are held: *His furniture was taken to the saleroom.*

'salesman ['seilz-] – *fem* **'saleswoman** – *nc* a person who sells, or shows, goods to customers in a shop *etc.*

'salesmanship ['seilz-] *nu* (*sometimes derog*) the art of persuading people to buy things.

'sales-talk (*sometimes derog*) what is said by a salesman to persuade a person to buy some object: *He tried to tell me all the marvellous things the car could do, but I'm never interested in sales-talk – I like to test things for myself.*

for 'sale intended to be sold: *I would buy that house if it was for sale; Have you any pictures for sale?*

on 'sale offered, or available, for buying: *There are some nice apples on sale in that shop; The book has been published but won't be on sale till next week.*

sale of work an event at which needlework and other articles *usu* made by members of an association are sold to raise money for some purpose: *There will be a sale of work at the church next Saturday to raise money to repair the church roof.*

See also **sell.**

salient ['seiliənt] *adj* (*formal*: *attrib*) main; chief; most noticeable: *What were the salient points of his speech?*

saline ['seilain] *adj* (*formal*: *esp tech*) salty or containing salt: *Water in which salt has been dissolved is called a saline solution.*

saliva [sə'laivə] *nu* the liquid that forms in the mouth to help digestion: *When a lot of saliva forms in our mouths, we say our mouths are watering.*

salivate ['saliveit] *vi* (*formal or facet*) to produce saliva, *esp* in excessively large amounts: *She was salivating so much that the dentist had difficulty in examining her teeth; The dog salivated at the sight of the meat.* **ˌsali'vation** *nu.*

sallow ['salou] *adj* (of the colour of a face) of an abnormal or unhealthy pale yellowish colour: *She has dark hair and a sallow complexion; Her skin is rather sallow.* **'sallowness** *nu.*

sally ['sali] *nc* 1 (*mil*) a sudden act of rushing out (*eg* from a fort) to make an attack: *The defenders' sally took the troops surrounding the town by surprise.* 2 (*liter or very formal*) a joke or funny remark: *They all laughed at his witty sally.*

sally forth *vi* 1 (*liter or very formal*) (of soldiers) to rush out (of a fort *etc*) in order to make an attack: *They sallied forth against the enemy.* 2 (*facet*) to go out (*eg* for a walk): *We sallied forth one morning to visit the museum.*

salmon ['samən] – *pl* **'salmon** – 1 *nc* a type of large fish with orange-pink flesh: *Salmon always swim upstream to lay their eggs.* 2 *nu* its flesh used as food: *We had smoked salmon for lunch.* 3 *nu, adj* (of) the colour of its flesh: *Her curtains were a salmon shade.*

salon ['salon, (*Amer*) sə'lon] *nc* 1 (*formal or used in shops etc*) (*sometimes in cmpds*) a name sometimes given to a place where hairdressing *etc* is done: *a beauty-salon; My hairdresser has opened a new salon.* 2 (*hist*) one of a *usu* regular series of gatherings of famous and fashionable people at the house of *usu* a famous lady: *He used to attend her Friday salons.*

saloon [sə'lu:n] *nc* 1 (*sometimes in cmpds*) a large public room on a ship: *the dining-saloon.* 2 (*Amer* **se'dan**) a motor car with enclosed seating space for driver and at least three passengers: *Most motor cars are saloons.* 3 (*Brit*) a saloon-bar. 4 (*Amer*) a bar where alcoholic drinks are sold: *The police searched in all the saloons for the man they thought was the thief.*

saˌloon-'bar *nc* (*Brit*) a quieter and more comfortably furnished part of a public house, *usu* forming a separate room in it.

salt [so:lt] 1 *nu* (*also* **common salt**) sodium chloride (**NaCl**), a white substance frequently used for seasoning, and either mined from the earth (**rock-salt**) or obtained from sea water (**sea-salt**): *The soup needs more salt;* (*attrib*) *salt mines.* 2 *nc* (*tech*) any other substance formed, like common salt, from a metal or a chemically similar substance and an acid: *Silver nitrate is a salt.* 3 *nc* (*liter inf*) a sailor, *esp* an experienced one: *an old salt.* – *adj* 1 containing salt; tasting of salt; salty: *Sea-water is salt; salt water/butter;* 3 (*attrib*) preserved with salt: *salt pork.* – *vt* to put salt on or add salt to (something): *Have you salted the potatoes?*

'salted *adj* (*usu attrib*: *neg* **un-**) 1 containing salt: *salted butter.* 2 preserved with salt: *salted herring.*

'saltness *nu.*

'salty *adj* containing or tasting of salt: *Tears are salty; salty water.* **'saltiness** *nu.*

'bath salts *n pl* a *usu* perfumed mixture of certain salts added to bath water to make one's bath more enjoyable.

'salt-cellar *nc* a small container for salt, used at table during meal-times.

'smelling salts *n pl* a strong-smelling perfumed liquid containing ammonia, formerly used to revive a person who has fainted *etc.*

salt away *vt sep* (*inf*) to store up (money) for future use: *He has a pile of money salted away.*

the salt of the earth a very good or worthy person: *She would do anything to help someone in trouble – people like that are the salt of the earth/she is the salt of the earth.*

take (something) with a grain/pinch of salt to receive (a statement, news *etc*) with a slight feeling of disbelief: *I took his story with a pinch of salt.*

worth one's salt (*often in neg*) deserving the pay that one gets: *If he can't even do that, he's not worth his salt.*

saltpetre, (*Amer*) **saltpeter** [so:lt'pi:tə] *nu* a nitrogen salt used in gunpowder *etc.*

salubrious [sə'lu:briəs] *adj* (*very formal or facet*) (of a climate, place *etc*) likely to make people healthy: *His health improved in the salubrious air of the mountains;* (*fig facet*) *The pubs he goes to are not very salubrious.* **sa'lubriousness** *nu.*

salutary ['saljutəri] *adj* (*formal*: *usu attrib*) (of advice, a warning *etc*) preventing (further) harm; having a good effect: *My illness was a salutary warning* (*to me*) *and I immediately stopped smoking cigarettes*; *His angry words had a salutary effect on her – she behaved more sensibly from then on.*

salute [sə'lu:t] **1** *vti* (*esp* in the armed forces) to raise the (*usu* right) hand to the forehead to show respect to (a person, flag *etc*): *They saluted their commanding officer*; *The officers saluted as the soldiers marched past.* **2** *vt* (in the army, navy *etc*) to honour (an important person) by firing *eg* large guns: *They saluted the Queen by firing one hundred guns.* **3** *vt* (*formal or liter*) to greet (a person) with words, a kiss or some other gesture: *He saluted her with a cheerful wave.* – *nc* an act of saluting: *The officer gave a salute*; *The Queen's birthday was honoured by a 21-gun salute*; (*formal or liter*) *He waved to her and she returned the salute.*

ˌ**salu'tation** [salju-] *ncu* (*formal or liter*) an act of greeting; a spoken or written greeting: *He bowed his head to me in salutation*; *My neighbour passed by with his customary salutation.*

salvage ['salvidʒ] *vt* **1** to save (something) from loss or destruction in a fire, shipwreck *etc*: *He managed to salvage his books and pictures from the burning house*; *Most of the furniture was ruined but we managed to salvage a few chairs once the firemen had put the fire out*; (*fig*) *The company was in financial difficulties but a new managing director was appointed in the hope that he would be able to salvage it.* – *nu* **1** (*usu attrib*) the act of salvaging a ship, cargo, property *etc*: *a salvage company.* **2** payment for this: *Anyone who helps to save a ship's cargo is entitled to be paid salvage.* **3** property *etc* which has been salvaged: *Was there any salvage from the wreck?* **4** (the keeping of) waste material that can be used again *eg* after being processed in a factory: *You should keep your waste paper for salvage.*

salvation [sal'veiʃən] *nu* **1** (*relig*) (someone or something which causes) the freeing of a person from sin or the saving of his soul from hell and damnation: *Christians hope and pray for salvation*; *Christians consider Jesus Christ to be the salvation of the world.* **2** (*formal*) the cause or means of keeping someone from danger, destruction *etc*: *The prompt arrival of the police was his salvation*; *This delay was the salvation of the army.*

salve [salv, (*Amer*) sav] *ncu* (*sometimes in cmpds*) (an) ointment to heal or soothe: *Putting lip-salve on your lips stops them becoming cracked and sore.* – *vt* to calm or soothe (one's conscience): *He tried to salve his conscience by buying expensive presents for the child he had neglected.*

salver ['salvə] *nc* a small tray, often made of silver: *He received a silver salver as a retirement present from his firm.*

same [seim] *adj* (*usu with* **the**) **1** alike; very similar: *The houses in this road are all the same*; *They all look the same* (*to me*); *Is my hat the same as yours?*; *You have the same eyes as your brother* (*has*). **2** identical; not different: *My friend and I are the same age*; *Our interests and hobbies have always been the same*; *The two families decided to share the same house*; *I am of the same opinion as you*; *He went to the same school as me*; *Are you going to the same meeting as I am?*; *He went back to the same place where he had found the ring*; *Is that the same girl who/that came last week?*; *He and I had the very same idea.* **3** unchanged: *We have had the same postman for ten years*; *My opinion is still the same*; *It is the same as it always was.* **4** mentioned before: *A man asked me the time, and later I saw the/this/that same man catching a bus*; *I arrived home on April 12, and that same day I broke my leg.* – *pron* (*usu with* **the**) the same thing: *He sat down and we all did the same*; *He may believe us if we all say the same*; *I'll never think the same of her again* (= I'll never have the same opinion of, feelings *etc* about her). – *adv* (*usu with* **the**) in the same way: *I don't feel the same about you as I did.*

'**sameness** *nu* the state of being similar: *His books all had a certain sameness* (*about them*).

all/just the same nevertheless; in spite of this: *There are some mistakes in your essay, but it's quite good all the same*; *I'm sure I locked the door, but, all the same, I think I'll go and check.*

at the same time 1 together; at once: *We were all shouting at the same time.* **2** nevertheless; still: *Mountain-climbing is fun, but at the same time we must not forget the danger.*

be all the same to (*inf*) to make no difference to, or be a matter of no importance to, someone: *I'll leave now, if it's all the same to you*; *He can do what he likes – it's all the same to me.*

be one and the same *see* **one**.

much the same not very much changed: *'How is your mother?' 'Much the same* (*as she was*).*'*

the same as always/ever not at all changed: *I was in London last week – it was the same as ever.*

same here (*inf*) I think, feel *etc* the same: *'This job bores me.' 'Same here.'*

(and) the same to you I wish you the same thing as you have wished me: *'Merry Christmas!' 'And the same to you!'*

sample ['sa:mpl] *nc* a part taken from a whole, or one thing taken from a number, to show the quality of the rest: *The salesman brought some samples of his firm's products*; (*attrib*) *The doctor gave her a sample tube of ointment to try*; *Is this a sample of his usual work?* – *vt* to try or test a sample of (something): *He sampled my cake.*

'**sampler** *nc* **1** (*often in cmpds*) a person who tests a product by sampling: *a tea-sampler.* **2** a piece of cloth embroidered by a person to show his or her skill.

sanatorium [sanə'to:riəm] – *pls* ˌ**sana'toriums,** ˌ**sana'toria** [-riə] – *nc* **1** (*Amer also* ˌ**sani'tarium**) a hospital, *esp* for people with certain diseases of the lungs or for people who are recovering from an illness: *That large house is now a sanatorium for people suffering from tuberculosis.* **2** a place or room in a school, college *etc* for those who are ill.

sanctify ['saŋktifai] *vt* (*relig*) to make (someone or something) sacred, holy or free from sin: *We pray that God will sanctify our hearts.* ˌ**sanctifi'cation** [-fi-] *nu.*

See also **saint**.

sanctimonious [saŋkti'mouniəs] *adj* (*formal derog*) trying to appear full of holiness or goodness: *He had a sanctimonious expression on his face*; *He is actually very wicked although he always appears very sanctimonious.* ˌ**sancti'moniously** *adv.* ˌ**sancti'moniousness** *nu.*

sanction ['saŋkʃən] (*formal*) **1** *nu* permission or approval given by *eg* a person in authority: *No soldier may leave the camp without the sanction of his commanding officer*; *If we do not protest against these crimes it will look as if we give them our sanction.* **2** *nc* (*usu in pl*) a penalty or punishment for not keeping a law, rule of conduct *etc*, imposed *eg* by one or more countries against another country in order to force it to change a course of action *etc*: *Should sanctions be applied against all countries that do not give their citizens equal rights?* – *vt* (*formal*) to permit or agree to (something): *We cannot sanction the use of corporal punishment in schools.*

sanctity ['saŋktəti] *nu* (*formal*) the quality of being sacred: *Many people feel that the sanctity of human life is disregarded by those who approve of abortion.*

sanctuary ['saŋktʃuəri] **1** *nc* (*liter*) a holy or sacred place, *eg* a temple or church: *The sanctuary of the god Apollo.* **2** *ncu* (a place of) safety from *eg* arrest or violence: *In earlier times a criminal could use a church as a sanctuary*; Most countries refuse to give sanctuary to people who hijack aeroplanes. **3** *nc* an area of land in which the killing of birds, wild animals *etc* is forbidden: *That island is a bird sanctuary.*

sand [sand] *nu* **1** a large amount of tiny particles of crushed or worn rock, shells *etc*, found on beaches, in deserts *etc*: *Sand is used in the making of glass, and also in concrete.* **2** an area or expanse of sand, *esp* on a beach: *We lay on the sand and sunbathed.* – *See also* **sands** *below.* – *vt* to smooth (a surface) with sandpaper or something similar: *The floor should be sanded before you varnish it.*

sands *n pl* (*often found with cap in place-names*) an area or stretch of sand *esp* on a beach: *a sheltered beach with beautiful sands*; *Camber Sands.*

'sandy *adj* **1** filled or covered with sand: *a sandy beach*; *My hands are all sandy*; *sandy fingers.* **2** (of hair) yellowish-red in colour; *She has fair skin and sandy hair*; *Her hair is not golden – it's sandy.*

'sandiness *nu.*

sandbank ['sanbaŋk] *nc* a bank of sand formed by tides and currents.

sandcastle ['sanka:sl] *nc* a pile of sand, sometimes made to look like a castle, built *esp* by children on beaches, in sandpits *etc*: *The little girl spent all morning happily building sand castles and then knocking them down.*

sand-dune *see* **dune**.

sandpaper ['sanpeipə] *nu* a type of paper with a layer of sand glued to it, used for smoothing and polishing: *He rubbed the rough surface of the wood with sandpaper.* – *vt* to make (a surface) smooth with sandpaper: *He sandpapered the table.*

sandpit ['sanpit] *nc* a shallow pit *usu* in a garden containing sand for children to play in: *The children were building a castle in the sandpit.*

sandshoes ['sanʃu:z] *n pl* soft light shoes, often with rubber soles, for wearing on the beach *etc*: *a pair of sandshoes.*

sandstone ['sanstoun] *nu* a soft type of rock made of layers of sand pressed together, sometimes used in building.

sand-storm ['sansto:m] *nc* a storm of wind, carrying with it clouds of sand: *We were caught in a sandstorm in the desert.*

sandal ['sandl] *nc* a type of light shoe, the sole of which is held on to the foot by straps: *I'm going to buy a pair of sandals this afternoon*; *He always wears sandals in the summer.*

sandwich ['sanwidʒ, (*Amer*) -witʃ] *nc* **1** two slices of bread or a roll with any kind of food between: *He made some cheese sandwiches.* – *vt* to place or press (someone or something) between two objects *etc*; *On the train, I was sandwiched between two large women and could hardly move*; *His car was sandwiched between two lorries.*

sane [sein] *adj* **1** healthy in mind; not mad: *Sometimes he does not seem quite sane*; *in a perfectly sane state of mind.* **2** sensible: *He's a very sane person*; *His opinions/judgements are always sane.*

'sanely *adv* in a sane manner: *We can trust him to deal with it sanely*; *He seemed to me to be acting quite sanely.*

'saneness *nu.*

'sanity ['sa-] *nu* the state or quality of being sane: *When I have so many jobs to do all at once, I begin to fear for my sanity*; *I doubt the sanity of such a plan.* *See also* **insane**.

sang *see* **sing**.

sangfroid [sã'frwa:] *nu* (*formal or facet*) the ability to remain calm and not become excited *eg* when in danger or difficulty: *He received the bad news with his usual sangfroid.*

sanguine ['saŋgwin] *adj* (*formal*) cheerful and full of hope: *He seemed quite sanguine about his chances of success*; *a very sanguine attitude to life.* **'sanguinely** *adv.* **'sanguineness** *nu.*

sanitarium [sani'teəriəm] – *pls* **ˌsani'tariums, ˌsani'taria** – *nc* (*Amer*) a sanatorium.

sanitary ['sanitəri] *adj* **1** (*attrib*) of or concerning conditions or arrangements that encourage good health and prevent disease, *esp* the removal of human waste from lavatories *etc*: *The toilets and other sanitary arrangements in this school must be improved*; *A sanitary engineer deals with the means of supplying pure water to buildings and of removing human waste etc.* **2** (*formal*) free from dirt and germs: *The conditions in that camp are not very sanitary*; *not very sanitary conditions.*

ˌsani'tation *nu* (*formal or tech*) the arrangements for protecting health, *esp* the removal of human waste from toilets: *When new housing is being built, sanitation is one of the first things to consider.* *See also* **insanitary**.

sanity *see* **sane**.

sank *see* **sink**.

sap[1] [sap] *nu* the liquid in trees, plants *etc*: *The sap flowed out when he broke the stem of the flower.*

sap[2] [sap] – *pt, ptp* **sapped** – *vt* (*formal*) to weaken or destroy (a person's strength, confidence, courage *etc*): *The disease slowly sapped his strength*; *The constant delays had sapped his confidence.*

sapling ['sapliŋ] *nc* a young tree: *Saplings were planted beside the new road.*

sapphire ['safaiə] **1** *nc* a kind of dark-blue precious stone: *a gold brooch set with a sapphire*; (*attrib*) *a sapphire ring.* **2** *nu, adj* (*liter*) (of) the colour of sapphires: *a sapphire sky.*

sarcasm ['sa:kazəm] *nu* (the use of) unpleasant remarks intended to hurt a person's feelings, *esp* ironic remarks which mean the opposite of what they appear to mean: *'Setting fire to the kitchen was a really clever thing to do,' said her husband with biting sarcasm.*

sar'castic [-'kas-] *adj* containing, or using, sarcasm: *a sarcastic comment/person*; *His remarks were rather sarcastic.* **sar'castically** *adv.*

sardine [sa:'di:n] *nc* a young pilchard or other similar fish, often packed in oil in small tins, and used as food: *She opened a tin of sardines*; *The train was so full that we were packed like sardines* (= as close together as sardines in a tin).

sardonic [sa:'donik] *adj* (*formal*) mocking or scornful: *a sardonic laugh/smile*; *He had a sardonic expression on his face*; *His smile was rather sardonic.* **sar'donically** *adv.*

sartorial [sa:'to:riəl] *adj* (*formal or facet*: *attrib*) of men's clothes, *esp* if made by a tailor: *sartorial elegance.*

sash[1] [saʃ] *nc* a broad band of cloth worn round the waist, or over one shoulder: *She wore a white dress with a red sash at the waist*; *A sash with her title written on it is usually presented to the winner of a beauty competition.*

sash[2] [saʃ] *nc* (*sometimes in cmpds*) a (*usu* sliding) frame fitted with a pane or panes of glass and forming part of a window: *the upper/lower sash*; *a sash-window.*

sat *see* **sit**.

Satan ['seitən] *n* the Devil; the spirit of evil: *There is a proverb which says that Satan finds mischief for idle hands to do.*

satanic [sə'tanik, (*Amer*) sei-] *adj* (*formal*: *usu attrib*) of, or like, the Devil; very wicked: *The candlelight showed his satanic features*; *The police found out about his satanic schemes.*

satchel ['satʃəl] *nc* a small bag for schoolbooks *etc*: *The little boy took his pet mouse to school in his satchel.*

sated ['seitid] *adj* (*formal*: *usu pred*) (of a person or his appetite) having had (more than) enough (food *etc*): *I feel sated after that huge meal*; *Its appetite sated, the lion left its prey half-eaten*; (*fig*) *He was sated with success/pleasure.*
See also **satiate**.

satellite ['satəlait] *nc* **1** a smaller body that revolves around a planet: *The Moon is a satellite of the Earth.* **2** a man-made object fired into space to travel round *usu* the Earth as an aid to weather-forecasting, for the transmission of television programmes round the world *etc*: *a weather satellite.* **3** a state *etc* controlled by a more powerful neighbouring state: *Russia and her satellites*; (*attrib*) *a satellite state.*

satiate ['seiʃieit] *vt* (*formal*) to satisfy (a person or appetite) fully, *esp* with more food *etc* than is necessary: *He was satiated with rich food and luxurious living*; *This book arouses rather than satiates one's interest in moths and butterflies.*

satiety [sə'taiəti] *nu*.
See also **sated, insatiable**.

satin ['satin] *nu, adj* (of) a closely woven type of silk with a shiny surface: *The baby's skin was as smooth as satin*; *a satin dress.*

satire ['sataiə] *ncu* (a piece of) writing *etc* that makes someone look foolish or makes people laugh at him *eg* because of his faults, foolish actions, odd beliefs *etc*: *The play was a satire on university life*; *Satire is often a form of protest against injustice.*

sa'tirical [-'ti-] *adj* **1** of satire: *satirical writing*; *His article was satirical.* **2** mocking: *He seems to be in a satirical mood*; *His smile was satirical.*

'satirist [-ti-] *nc* a person who writes or performs satire(s).

'satirize, -ise [-ti-] *vt* to make (a person *etc*) look foolish or make people laugh at him by using satire: *Do politicians mind being satirized every week in this television programme?*

satisfy ['satisfai] *vt* (not used (*def 3*)/not *usu* used (*def 1, 2*) with **is, was** *etc* and **-ing**) **1** to give (a person) enough of what he wants or needs to take away his hunger, curiosity *etc*: *I ate an apple but that didn't satisfy my hunger*; *I told him enough to satisfy his curiosity*; *The meal satisfied him.* **2** to please (a person): *Some people are very difficult to satisfy.* **3** to fulfill (requirements *etc* for a job etc): *Your qualifications seem to satisfy the conditions/requirements.* **4** to convince (a person): *He wanted to satisfy himself that the machine was properly mended.*

ˌsatis'faction [-'fakʃən] **1** *nu* the act of satisfying or state of being satisfied: *He thinks of nothing but the satisfaction of his own desires.* **2** *ncu* (*no pl*) (something which gives) pleasure or contentment: *Your success gives me great satisfaction*; *I had the satisfaction of knowing that I had beaten him in the examination*; *It is a great satisfaction to me that he has a good job.* – *See also* **to my, his** *etc* **satisfaction** *below.* **3** *nu* (*formal*) something given to a person because of harm, damage *etc* done to him: *He eventually obtained satisfaction for his unfair treatment.* **4** *nu* (*old*) an opportunity to get revenge (*usu* in a fight) *eg* because one has been insulted: *You should demand satisfaction for the insult.*

ˌsatis'factory [-'faktəri] *adj* (*neg* **un-**) giving satisfaction; good enough to satisfy: *Your work is not satisfactory*; *The condition of the sick man is satisfactory*; *I had a highly satisfactory evening at the opera*; *You have not given a satisfactory excuse for your behaviour.*

ˌsatis'factorily [-'faktə-] *adv*: *Our negotiations are progressing satisfactorily.*

'satisfied *adj* **1** (*sometimes with* **with**) pleased: *I'm satisfied with his progress*; *a satisfied customer.* **2** (*usu pred*) convinced: *I was satisfied that he was guilty.*

'satisfying *adj* pleasing: *The story had a satisfying ending*; *It is satisfying to be proved right.* **'satisfyingly** *adv.*

to my, his *etc* **satisfaction** (*formal*) satisfactory; in a satisfactory way: *Is the meal to your satisfaction?*; *You have not done the work to my satisfaction.*
See also **dissatisfy**.

saturate ['satʃəreit] *vt* **1** to make (something) very wet: *After planting these seeds, saturate the earth round them.* **2** (*usu in ptp*) to fill completely: *The air was saturated with the perfume of the flowers*; (*fig*) *He is saturated with knowledge*; *The market has been saturated with paintings like that – no one wants them now.* **satu'ration** *nu*.

satu'ration point *nc* (*formal or facet*) the point at which no more of something can be added: *I can't learn any more history today – I've reached saturation point.*

Saturday ['satədei] *n* the seventh day of the week, the day following Friday: *I'll see you on Saturday*; *There was a meeting last Saturday*; *I go to the pub on Saturdays* (= every Saturday, or only on a Saturday but not necessarily every Saturday); (*attrib*) *on Saturday morning.*

Saturn *see* Appendix 6.

sauce [so:s] **1** *ncu* (a kind of) *usu* thick liquid that is poured over other food in order to add moisture and flavour: *ice cream with hot chocolate sauce*; *tomato sauce*; *The cook was an expert at making sauces.* **2** *nu* (*inf*: *slightly old*) (*usu* amusing) slightly rude or disrespectful remarks *esp* by a child to an adult: *That's enough of your sauce!*

'saucy *adj* (*inf*: *slightly old*) **1** (*esp* of a child or of something said by a child to an adult) slightly rude or disrespectful (but *usu* amusing): *a saucy remark/child*; *Don't be saucy!* **2** showing little respect for normal sexual convention in an amusing way; causing sexual desire in an amusing way: *She wore her hat at a saucy angle*; *This* night-dress is rather saucy. **'saucily** *adv.* **'sauciness** *nu.*

'sauce boat *nc* a long shallow jug in which sauce is served at table.

'saucepan [-pən, (*Amer*) -pan] *nc* a deep pan *usu* with a long handle for boiling or stewing food.

saucer ['so:sə] *nc* **1** a small shallow dish for placing under a cup: *Could you bring me another cup and saucer?* **2** anything like a saucer in shape, *eg* the disc of a radio telescope.

flying saucer *see* **fly**[2].

saucy *see* **sauce**.

Saudi, Saudi Arabia, Saudi Arabian *see* Appendix 2.

sauerkraut ['sauəkraut] *nu* a German dish of cabbage cut fine and pickled in salt.

sauna ['so:nə] *nc* (a building or room equipped for) a Finnish form of steam bath: *They have a sauna in their house; They had a refreshing sauna.*

saunter ['so:ntə] *vi* (*often with* **along, off, past** *etc*) to walk or stroll about without much purpose or hurry: *He sauntered along the street looking in the shop windows; I was working in the garden when he sauntered by.* – *nc* (*inf*) a walk or stroll: *We had a saunter in the park.*

sausage ['sosidʒ] **1** *nu* minced meat seasoned and pushed into a tube of animal gut or a similar material, and formed into sections: *garlic sausage.* **2** *nc* one section of this: *We're having sausages for lunch.*

'sausage-meat *nu* minced meat of the kind used for making sausages.

,sausage-'roll *nc* (*Brit*) a piece of sausage meat cooked in a roll of pastry: *They had sausage-rolls at the children's party.*

sauté ['soutei, (*Amer*) sou'tei] *adj* (*usu attrib*) fried lightly and quickly: *sauté potatoes.* – *v* – *pt, ptp* **'sauté(e)d** – *vt* to fry (food) in this way: *Sauté the onions for a few minutes; She usually sautés the potatoes.*

savage ['savidʒ] *adj* **1** (*old*: *usu attrib*) uncivilized: *savage tribes; The inhabitants were still in the savage state.* **2** fierce and cruel: *The elephant can be quite savage; The fox made a savage attack on the hens; her bitter and savage remarks; He was in a savage mood.* – *vt* to attack: *He was savaged by wild animals.* – *nc* **1** (*old*) a person in an uncivilized state: *During his travels he met many tribes of savages.* **2** (*formal: derog*) a person who behaves in a cruel, uncivilized way: *I hope the police catch the savages who attacked the old lady.*

'savagely *adv.* **'savageness** *nu.*

'savagery (*formal*) **1** *nu* cruelty or fierceness: *She had been attacked with horrifying savagery.* **2** *nu* the uncivilized state: *The British had progressed far beyond the state of savagery when the Romans arrived.* **3** *nc* a cruel act: *the shocking savageries of the invading army.*

savanna(h) [sə'vanə] *nc* a grassy plain with few trees: *the savanna(h)s of Central America.*

save[1] [seiv] **1** *vt* to rescue or bring (someone or something) out of danger: *He saved his friend from drowning; The doctors managed to save his life; The house was burnt but he saved the pictures.* **2** *vti* to keep (money *etc*) for future use: *He's saving (his money) to buy a bicycle; They're saving for a house; Save – don't spend!; He had a piece of chocolate left and decided to save it for/till later.* – *See also* **save up** *below.* **3** *vt* to prevent the using or wasting of (money, time, energy *etc*) or to allow (a person) not to do something: *Make a list before you go shopping if you want to save (yourself) time; Frozen foods save a lot of trouble; I'll telephone and that will save me writing a letter; Making my own clothes saves me pounds every month; I'd have been saved the bother of coming if I'd known you were away.* – *See also* **save on** *below.* **4** *vt* in football *etc*, to prevent the opposing team from scoring a goal: *The goalkeeper saved six goals.* **5** *vt* (*relig*) to free (a person or his soul) from the power of sin and evil: *Jesus came to save the world.* **6** *vt* (*arch except in certain phrases*) to protect: *God save the Queen.* – *nc* (in football *etc*) an act of preventing the opposing team from scoring a goal: *The goalkeeper made some good saves.*

'saver *nc* (*often in cmpds*) a person or thing that saves, avoids waste *etc*: *He's a saver rather than a spender; The telephone is a great time-saver.*

'saving *nc* a way of saving money *etc* or the amount saved in this way: *Travelling by train in the middle of the week can mean a saving of several pounds; It's a great saving to be able to travel free on the buses.*

'savings *n pl* money saved up: *He keeps his savings in the Post Office.*

saviour, (*Amer*) **savior** ['seivjə] *nc* **1** (*usu with cap*) a person or god who saves people from sin, hell *etc*, *esp* (*with cap*) in the Christian religion, Jesus Christ: *our Lord and Saviour.* **2** (*liter*) a person who rescues a person *etc* from danger *etc*: *He was the saviour of his country.*

saving grace *nc* a good quality that makes (someone or something) less bad than he, it *etc* would have been: *His speeches are boring but they have the saving grace of being short.*

'savings account *nc* an account in a bank or post office on which interest is paid.

'savings bank *nc* a bank that receives small savings and gives interest.

save one's face *see* **face**.

'save on *vt fus* to stop or prevent the wasting of (something, *esp* a form of fuel or power): *Cooking all the vegetables in one pot would save on gas; I think we should try to save on electricity/petrol.*

save up *vi, vt sep* to save: *He's been saving up for a new bike.*

See also **safe, salvation**.

save[2] [seiv], **saving** ['seiviŋ] *preps, conjs* (*arch*) except: *All save him had gone; Saving Monday, every day was sunny; We have no news save that the ship reached port safely.*

savour, (*Amer*) **savor** ['seivə] *ncu* (*formal*) (a) taste or flavour: *Cheese dishes should have a slight savour of mustard; The wine has lost its savour;* (*fig*) *At my age, life begins to lose its savour.* – *vt* (*formal*) to eat (food), drink (wine *etc*) (*usu* slowly) in order to enjoy or appreciate its taste or quality: *He slowly savoured the delicious soup;* (*fig*) *She savoured the news with growing delight.* – *See also* **savour of** *below.*

'savoury *adj* having a *usu* salty or sharp, but not sweet, taste or smell: *He made a savoury omelette with leeks and cheese;* (*fig*) *I heard a savoury bit of gossip today.* – *nc* (*Brit*) something tasting of or made with salt, cheese, pâté, pickles *etc* served with *eg* alcoholic drinks: *At the party, savouries were served with the drinks.*

'savouriness *nu.*

'savour of *vt fus* (*formal*) to have a suggestion or impression of (a *usu* bad quality, idea *etc*): *Their action savours of rebellion.*

See also **unsavoury**.

saw[1] *see* **see**.

saw[2] [so:] *nc* a tool for cutting, having a blade, band or disc of thin steel with a toothed edge: *He used a saw to cut through the branch.* – *v* – *pt* **sawed**: *ptps* **sawn, sawed** – *vti* to cut with a saw: *He sawed the log in two*; *Can you saw?*; *He has sawn through the table.* – *See also* **saw off, saw up** *below.*

'sawdust *nu* a dust of tiny fragments of wood, made by sawing: *Sawdust is sometimes scattered on floors to help clean them.*

'sawmill *nc* a place in which wood is mechanically sawn.

ˌsawn-off 'shotgun *nc* a shotgun, the barrel of which has been shortened by cutting with a saw: *The bank-robbers carried sawn-off shotguns.*

saw off *vt sep* to cut (a piece) from something by sawing: *He had sawn the branch off.*

saw up *vt sep* to saw (wood *etc*) into pieces: *He sawed the tree up for firewood.*

saxophone ['saksəfoun] *nc* a type of musical instrument with a curved metal tube, played by blowing: *He plays the saxophone*; *I can play a few tunes on the saxophone.*

saxophonist [sak'sofənist] *nc* a person who plays the saxophone.

say [sei] – *3rd pers sing prt* **says** [sez]: *pt, ptp* **said** [sed] – *vt* **1** to speak or utter (words): *What did you say?*; *She said 'Yes'*; *'Thank you,' he said*; *He didn't say anything.* **2** to tell, state or declare (a fact, opinion *etc*): *They say (that) they are leaving*; *In her letter she said how she had enjoyed meeting me*; *I've nothing more to say*; *You may not think she's stupid but I say she is*; *It says in this book that women are more intelligent than men*; *She is said to be very beautiful.* **3** to repeat (prayers, poetry *etc*): *I listened to him saying the poetry he had learnt*; *The child says her prayers every night.* **4** to form or have an opinion, guess, or estimate: *I can't say* (= I don't know) *when he'll return*; *'How long will she be away?' 'I couldn't say.'* – *nc* the right or opportunity to state one's opinion, *esp* when something is being decided: *I haven't had my say yet*; *You've already said/had your say*; *Hasn't she a/any say in the matter?*; *We have no say in the decision*; *She ought to have the final say about whether we go or not* (= She ought to be the one who decides).

'saying *nc* something often said, *esp* a proverb *etc*: *There's some truth in the old saying, 'Don't try to run before you can walk'*; *'Waste not, want not,' as the saying goes.*

go without saying *see* **go**.

have (something, nothing *etc***) to say for oneself** to be able/unable to explain one's actions *etc*: *Your work is very careless – what have you to say for yourself?*; *You've been caught stealing apples – have you anything to say for yourself?*

I say! words expressing surprise or protest or used to attract someone's attention: *I say! What a surprise!*; *I say! Be careful! You're hurting me!*; *I say! Look at those birds!*

it's 'said/they 'say expressions used in reporting rumours, news that is not yet definite *etc*: *It's said her health is very poor*; *They say he hasn't much money.*

I ˌwouldn't say 'no to (something) (*inf*) I would like (something): *I wouldn't say no to an ice-cream.*

(let's) say 1 roughly; approximately; about: *You'll arrive there in, (let's) say, three hours.* **2** if we suppose: *Let's say he started at 9.00 a.m., when will he arrive?*

say the word (*inf*) I'm ready to obey your wishes: *If you'd like to go with me, say the word.*

'so' you, they *etc* **'say** used to express slight disbelief: *'Is that really what happened?' 'So they say'.*

so to say *see* **so**.

that is to say in other words; I mean: *He was here last Thursday, that's to say the 4th of June.*

there's no saying it is impossible to guess: *There's no saying what will happen next.*

they say *see* **it's said** *above.*

you can say that again! (*inf*) you're absolutely right!: *'He's crazy.' 'You can say that again!'*

See also **said, unsaid**.

scab [skab] **1** *nc* a crust formed over a sore or wound: *A scab forms over a wound, then dries and falls off as the wound heals.* **2** *nu* any of several diseases of animals or plants. **3** *nc* (*sl*: *derog*) a workman who refuses to join a strike: *The strikers said they would make life unpleasant for the scabs when the strike was over.* **'scabby** *adj.*

scabbard ['skabəd] *nu* a case in which the blade of a sword is kept; a sheath: *He drew his sword out of its scabbard.*

scabies ['skeibi:z] *nu* a type of itchy, contagious skin disease: *He is suffering from scabies.*

scaffold ['skafəld] *nc* a raised platform *esp* for use when putting a criminal *etc* to death: *A large crowd had gathered round the scaffold to see the man executed.*

'scaffolding *nu* a framework of metal poles and wooden planks which form platforms used by men at work on (the outside of) a building: *Scaffolding has been put up round the building so that it can be cleaned.*

scald [sko:ld] *vt* **1** to hurt (a part of the body) with hot liquid or steam: *He scalded his hand with boiling water*; *She is always scalding herself.* **2** in cooking, to heat (*eg* milk) to just below boiling-point: *Scald the milk before you make the custard.* – *nc* a hurt caused by hot liquid or steam: *Burns and scalds can often be treated with cold water.*

'scalding *adj* (of a liquid) hot enough to scald: *The water was scalding.* – *adv* enough to scald: *It's scalding hot.*

scale[1] [skeil] **1** *nc* a set of regularly spaced marks made on something (*eg* a thermometer or a ruler) for use as a measure; a system of numbers, measurement *etc*: *This thermometer has two scales marked on it, one in Fahrenheit and one in Centigrade*; *Clinical thermometers in Britain use the Fahrenheit rather than the Centigrade scale.* **2** *nc* a series or system of items of increasing or decreasing size, value *etc*: *a wage/salary scale*; *Are doctors high on the social scale?* **3** *nc* (*music*) a group of notes going up or down in order: *In singing, or playing an instrument, it is important to practise scales.* **4** *ncu* the size of measurements on a map, model, plan *etc* compared with the real size of the country, object, area *etc* that is shown by it: *In a map drawn to the scale 1:50 000, one centimetre represents half a kilometre*; *This model differs in scale from that one.* **5** *ncu* the size or amount of an activity or business: *These guns are being manufactured on a large scale* (= in large amounts); *The business had to be reduced in scale* (= made smaller).

scale down, up *vt sep* to decrease or increase (*eg*

wages) by a certain percentage or according to a certain scale: *The wages for workers of all grades will be scaled up by five per cent.*

scale[2] [skeil] *vt* to climb (a ladder, cliff *etc*): *The prisoner scaled the prison walls and escaped.*

scale[3] [skeil] *nc* any of the small thin plates or flakes that cover the skin of fishes, reptiles *etc*: *A herring's scales are silver in colour.* – *vt* to remove the scales from (*eg* a fish): *Have you scaled the herring?*

'scaly *adj* **1** (of fish *etc* or their bodies) covered with scales: *She dislikes fish and other scaly creatures; This fish is very scaly.* **2** having a surface that peels or flakes: *In certain skin diseases, a person's skin becomes very dry and scaly; Her skin has a scaly appearance.* **'scaliness** *nu.*

scales [skeilz] *n pl* a *usu* small weighing-machine: *Are your kitchen scales accurate?; a set of scales; He weighed himself on the bathroom scales.*

turn the scales at (*inf*) (*esp* of a boxer *etc*) to be of a certain weight: *He turns the scales at 140 pounds.*

scallop, *also* **scallop** ['skoləp] *nc* a type of shellfish that has a pair of hinged, fan-shaped shells, and can be used as food.

'scalloped *adj* (*usu attrib*) (of the edge of a garment *etc*) cut into curves and notches: *The collar of the blouse has a scalloped edge.*

scallywag ['skaliwag] *nc* (*inf*) (*esp* of a child) someone who is naughty or who has done something wrong: *That little scallywag has pulled the heads off all those flowers.*

scalp [skalp] *nc* **1** the skin of the part of the head usually covered by hair: *When you wash your hair, rub the shampoo well into your scalp.* **2** the skin and hair of the top of the head: *Some North American Indians used to cut the scalps from their prisoners.* – *vt* **1** to cut the scalp from: *The Indians killed and scalped him.* **2** (*inf fig*) to cut (a person's hair) very short: *The barber scalped me*

scalpel ['skalpəl] *nc* a small knife with a thin blade, used in surgical operations.

scaly *see* **scale**[3].

scamp [skamp] *nc* a mischievous person, *esp* a child: *He's a little scamp.*

scamper ['skampə] *vi* to run quickly and lightly: *The mouse scampered away when it saw me; The children were scampering about happily on the beach.* – *nc* (*inf*) the act of running about, or a period of doing this, *esp* in a playful way: *The dogs had a scamper in the field.*

scampi ['skampi] **1** *n pl* small, slender lobsters found in European seas. **2** *nu* (a dish, plate *etc* of) these, as food: *The scampi is excellent; fried scampi.*

scan [skan] – *pt, ptp* **scanned** – **1** *vt* (*formal or liter*) to look at or examine carefully: *He scanned the horizon for any sign of a ship.* **2** *vt* to look at or study (something) quickly but not thoroughly or in detail: *She drank her tea and scanned the newspaper for news of the murder.* **3** *vt* (*tech*) to pass radar beams, electronic beams, X-rays *etc* over (an area, person *etc*): *The area was scanned for signs of enemy aircraft; This apparatus scans patients' brains for tumours.* **4** *vt* to examine the metre or rhythm of (line of poetry) and mark the accented syllables or beats in it: *They were given four lines of Latin verse to scan.* **5** *vi* (of a line of poetry) to fit correctly into a particular rhythm or metre: *The second line of that verse doesn't scan properly.*

'scanner *nc* a machine, person *etc* that scans something.

'scansion [-ʃən] *nu* (*tech*) **1** the art of scanning poetry: *Scansion is often set as a test for students of Latin and Greek.* **2** the manner in which poetry fits into a particular rhythm or metre: *The scansion of this verse depends on some words being wrongly accented.*

scandal ['skandl] **1** *nc* something that is considered shocking or disgraceful: *This book describes the scandal of the British opium trade during the nineteenth century; (fig) The price of meat is a scandal.* **2** *nc* an outburst of public horror or indignation caused by something shocking or disgraceful: *Her love affair caused a great scandal amongst the neighbours; They kept the matter secret, in order to avoid a scandal.* **3** *nu* gossip or unkind talk about other people: *Do tell me all the latest scandal; You shouldn't listen to such scandal.*

'scandalize, -ise *vt* (*formal*) to shock or horrify: *Their behaviour used to scandalize the neighbours; He was scandalized by that obscene film.*

'scandalous *adj* **1** shocking or disgraceful: *The whole world should hear about his scandalous treatment of his wife; That shop charges scandalous prices* (= prices that are much too high); *Such immorality is scandalous.* **2** (*attrib*) (of stories *etc*) containing scandal: *scandalous tales.*

'scandalously *adv* in a disgraceful way: *Her pay is scandalously low.*

'scandalmonger *nc* (*derog*) a person who spreads gossip or scandal: *Some newspaper writers are just scandalmongers.*

Scandinavia, Scandinavian *see* Appendix 2.

scanner, scansion *see* **scan**.

scant [skant] *adj* (*formal*: *usu attrib*) (of experience, knowledge, attention *etc*) hardly enough; not very much: *He gave the matter scant attention; He has had scant experience in this field.*

'scantily *adv* in a scanty way: *It is too cold to go out so scantily dressed.*

'scanty *adj* small in size or amount; hardly enough: *scanty clothing; The potato crop was rather scanty this year.* **'scantiness** *nu.*

scapegoat ['skeipgout] *nc* a person who is blamed or punished for the sins or mistakes of others: *Although the manager of the football team was not to blame, he was made a scapegoat for the team's failure, and was forced to resign.*

scapula ['skapjulə] *nc* (*formal or tech*) the shoulder-blade: *They are X-raying his scapula.*

scar [ska:] *nc* the mark that is left by a wound or sore: *He has a scar on his arm where the dog bit him; Smallpox leaves terrible scars; (fig) The tragedy left a scar on her mind.* – *v* – *pt, ptp* **scarred**. – *vt* to mark with a scar: *He recovered from the accident but his face was badly scarred; (fig) The children were scarred by their experiences during the war.*

scarce [skeəs] *adj* (*pred*) not many in number; not as much as people need or want: *Paintings by this artist are very scarce; Plums are scarce because of the bad summer.* – *See also* **make oneself scarce** *below.* **'scarceness** *nu.*

'scarcely *adv* **1** only just; not quite: *Speak louder please – I can scarcely hear you; They have scarcely enough money to feed themselves; He had scarcely gone before they started talking about him; Scarcely had he arrived when they were asking him to leave again.* **2** used to suggest that something is unlikely or unreasonable: *You can scarcely expect me to* *work when I'm ill*; *She's scarcely the right person for the job.*

'scarcity 1 *nu* lack of normal or sufficient supplies: *In times of scarcity, we must do our best to avoid waste.* **2** *nc* a lack or shortage of a particular thing: *a scarcity of work/jobs*; *In wartime there are always scarcities.*

make oneself scarce (*inf*) to run away or stay away, *esp* in order to avoid trouble or difficulty: *As soon as his mother-in-law arrived, he made himself scarce.*

scare [skeə] *vt* **1** to startle or frighten (a person or animal): *You'll scare the baby if you shout.* **2** (*with* **into** *or* **out of**) to make (someone) do or not do something: *His warning scared her into obeying him*; *Their threats scared him out of telling the police.* – *nc* **1** a feeling of fear or alarm: *The noise gave me a scare.* **2** a feeling of fear or panic among a large number of people: *A rabies scare was started by the rumour of a case of the disease in Birmingham.*

scared *adj* frightened (by a person, thing *etc*): *I'm scared of spiders*; *I was too scared to open the door*; *I'm scared!*; *rather a scared little girl.*

'scary *adj* (*inf*) causing fear: *a scary story*; *The dark room was very scary!*

'scarecrow *nc* a figure set up *eg* in a field, to scare away birds and stop them eating the seeds *etc*: *The scarecrow was made of two crossed sticks, and wore a ragged jacket and hat.*

'scaremonger *nc* (*derog*) a person who spreads alarming rumours: *The Prime Minister told the people to pay no attention to scaremongers.*

scare away/off *vt sep* to make (someone or something) go away or stay away because of fear: *The birds were scared away by the dog*; *We keep a cat to scare the mice off.*

scare stiff/out of one's wits/to death (*inf*) to make (a person) very scared: *The thought of him as Prime Minister scares me stiff*; *He scared me out of my wits.*

scarf [ska:f] – *pls* **scarves** [ska:vz], **scarfs** – *nc* **1** a long strip of *eg* knitted wool to wrap round one's neck *eg* in cold weather: *I always wear a woollen scarf in winter.* **2** (*Brit*) a headscarf: *She wore a scarf to protect her hair from the wind.*

scarlet ['ska:lit] *nu, adj* (of) a bright red colour: *scarlet poppies*; *She blushed scarlet.*

scarlet fever *nu* an infectious fever *usu* with a sore throat and red rash: *He's got scarlet fever.*

scarves *see* **scarf**.

scathing ['skeiðiŋ] *adj* **1** (of *eg* remarks or criticism) cruel, bitter, or hurtful: *She was upset by his scathing comments about her work.* **2** (of a person) criticizing in a cruel or hurtful way: *He was very scathing about her book.* **'scathingly** *adv.*

scatter ['skatə] **1** *vti* to (make something or someone) go or rush in different directions: *The sudden noise scattered the birds*; *The crowds scattered when the bomb exploded.* **2** *vt* to throw (things) loosely in different directions: *I always scatter some crumbs on the ground for the birds*; *The load from the overturned lorry was scattered over the road.*

'scattered *adj* occasional; not close together: *There are some scattered farms on these hills*; *Scattered showers are forecast for this morning*; *The few houses in the valley are very scattered.*

'scattering *nc* a small amount scattered here and there: *There was a scattering of snow on the ground this morning.*

'scatterbrain *nc* (*inf*) a forgetful or unreliable person: *I asked him to post the letter, but he's such a scatterbrain that he'll probably forget.*

'scatterbrained *adj* being, or of, a scatterbrain: *a scatterbrained person*; *scatterbrained behaviour*; *He's so scatterbrained!*

scatty ['skati] *adj* (*inf*) **1** (*usu pred*) mad or crazy: *All this work is driving me scatty.* **2** forgetful; unreliable: *She's rather scatty – she probably won't remember to come to the party*; *in rather a scatty mood.*

scavenger ['skavindʒə] *nc* **1** a bird, animal *etc* that feeds on decaying flesh, vegetable matter *etc*: *Vultures are scavengers.* **2** (*old*: *Brit*) a person who cleans the street and picks up rubbish.

'scavenge *vti* to search for useful or usable objects, food *etc* amongst rubbish *etc*: *The children were given so little to eat that they were forced to go scavenging in dustbins for scraps of food.*

scenario [si'na:riou] – *pl* **sce'narios** – *nc* a written outline or summary of a play, film, opera *etc*: *a film scenario.*

scene [si:n] *nc* **1** the place where something real or imaginary happens: *A murderer sometimes revisits the scene of his crime*; *The police got quickly to the scene of the accident*; *The scene of this opera is laid/set in Switzerland.* **2** an incident, event or happening which is seen or remembered: *In this book the author recalls scenes from his childhood*; *There were horrifying scenes as people tried to escape from the blazing theatre.* **3** a show of strong feeling, *esp* of anger; a quarrel: *I was very angry but I didn't want to make a scene*; *We had a terrible scene about the housekeeping money.* **4** a view of a landscape *etc*: *The sheep grazing on the hillside made a peaceful scene.* **5** one part or division of a play, opera *etc*: *The balcony scene in Romeo and Juliet is Scene 2 of Act II.* **6** (the painted boards, furniture *etc* forming) the setting or background for (a part of) a play *etc*: *The scene is a kitchen*; *Scene-changing must be done as quickly as possible.* **7** (*pl rare*) a particular area of activity: *There have been several changes on the business scene*; *the academic/drug scene.* **8** (*sl*: *no pl*) an area of interest; an activity which a person enjoys: *Nude sunbathing is not my scene.*

'scenery *nu* **1** the painted background for a play *etc* on a stage: *The scenery looked rather old and shabby.* **2** the general appearance of a landscape *etc*: *There is some beautiful scenery in the Scottish Highlands.*

'scenic *adj* **1** of scenery, real or theatrical: *Some of the scenic effects in the film were very clever*; *Come to Switzerland and enjoy its scenic beauties!* **2** having beautiful scenery (*def 2*): *a scenic highway/route.* **'scenically** *adv.*

behind the scenes out of sight of the audience or public: *The stage manager was giving instructions behind the scenes*; (*fig*) *It would be interesting to know what goes on behind the scenes at the White House.*

come on the scene to arrive: *We were enjoying ourselves till you came on the scene*; *Now that a baby has come on the scene she has stopped working.*

on the scene at the place where something is happening or has happened: *The doctor was on the scene very quickly after the accident.*

set the scene to explain to someone where the action of a play *etc* is taking place, what has happened up to a particular point *etc*: *Before we go on to study Act Two, perhaps one of you could set the* *scene for us and remind us of what happened in Act One.*

scent [sent] *vt* (not used with **is, was** *etc* and **-ing** (*defs 1, 2*)) **1** to smell (something); to discover (something) by the sense of smell: *The dog scented a cat.* **2** to suspect or have a feeling (that something, *usu* bad, has happened or will happen); *As soon as he came into the room I scented trouble.* **3** (*formal*) to cause to smell pleasantly: *The roses scented the air.* – **1** *ncu* a (*usu* pleasant) smell: *This rose has a delightful scent*; *When you're choosing which flower to plant, appearance and scent should both be considered.* **2** *nc* a trail consisting of the smell which a person or animal has left and by which he, it *etc* may be tracked or followed: *The dogs picked up the man's scent and then lost it again.* **3** *ncu* (*Brit*) a liquid or cream with a pleasant smell, for use on the body; perfume: *She wears too much scent.* **4** *nu* (*esp* of dogs) the ability to smell (things) and follow scents (*def 2*): *A dog has keen scent.*

'scented *adj* (*neg* **un-**) made sweet-smelling with perfume: *scented writing-paper*; *Is this soap scented?*

put/throw (someone) off the scent to give (a person) wrong information so that he will not find the person, thing *etc* he is looking for: *She told the police a lie in order to throw them off the scent.*

scepter *see* **sceptre**.

sceptic (*Amer also* **skeptic**) ['skeptik] *nc* (*formal*) a person who is unwilling to believe a theory, idea, statement *etc*: *Most people now accept this theory, but there are a few sceptics.*

'sceptical *adj* (*formal*: *often with* **about**) unwilling to believe; showing doubt and disbelief: *They say apples clean your teeth, but I'm sceptical about that myself*; *He listened to me with a sceptical expression.* **'sceptically** *adv.*

'scepticism [-sizəm] *nu* (*formal*) a doubting or questioning attitude: *I regard his theories with scepticism.*

sceptre, (*Amer*) **scepter** ['septə] *nc* the ornamental rod carried by a king or queen on ceremonial occasions as a sign of his or her power: *The Queen was carrying the sceptre and the orb.*

schedule ['ʃedju:l, (*Amer*) 'sked-] *nc* **1** a statement of details, *esp* of time of activities, events *etc* or of things to be done: *He planned his work schedule for the following month*; *What is on the schedule this morning?* **2** (*formal*) a form or paper in which details are to be written: *Please complete Schedule A.* – *vt* (*formal*) to plan or arrange the time of (an event *etc*): *The meeting is scheduled for 9.00 a.m. tomorrow*; *The Prime Minister is scheduled to arrive at noon.*

according to schedule as planned: *The work is going according to schedule.*

ahead of, behind, on schedule before, later than, or by, the arranged time: *The plane is two hours behind schedule*; *They finished the work on schedule.*

scheme [ski:m] *nc* **1** a plan or systematic arrangement; a way of doing something: *I'm trying to plan the colour scheme for the sitting-room*; *In this sort of social work voluntary helpers are part of the scheme*; *There are various schemes for helping immigrants to learn English*; *They are working on a scheme to prevent trouble at football grounds.* **2** (*often in pl*) a (*usu* secret) dishonest plan: *He planned to steal the money, but his schemes were discovered.* **3** in Scotland, a set of houses *etc* owned by, and rented from, a local authority; a local authority housing-estate: *They live in the new housing-scheme.* – *vi* (*often with* **against** (a person) *or* **for** (something)) to make (*esp* dishonest) schemes: *He was punished for scheming against the King*; *He schemed to get himself elected as president*; *They have all been scheming for my dismissal.*

'schemer *nc* (*derog*) a person who has (*usu* secret) dishonest plans: *He's a dangerous schemer.*

'scheming *adj* (*derog*) having or making (*usu* secret) dishonest plans: *a scheming woman*; *his scheming personality*; *He is so honest and she is so scheming.*

schism ['skizəm] *ncu* (*very formal*) (the) act of breaking away from the main group, *esp* in the Christian church: *The Church has been weakened by schism*; *There have been frequent schisms.*

schizophrenia [skitsə'fri:niə] *nu* a form of insanity in which the patient becomes severely withdrawn from reality, has delusions *etc.*

ˌschizo'phrenic [-'fre-] *nc, adj* (a person) suffering from schizophrenia: *She is schizophrenic*; *She has a schizophrenic personality*; *She is a schizophrenic.*

scholar ['skolə] *nc* **1** a person of great knowledge and learning: *He is a fine classical scholar.* **2** a person who has been awarded a scholarship: *As a scholar, you will not have to pay college fees.* **3** (*old*) a schoolchild or student.

'scholarly *adj* **1** having or showing knowledge: *a scholarly person*; *He is so scholarly.* **2** showing great knowledge, detailed study, accuracy *etc*: *a scholarly book*; *This work is most scholarly.* **'scholarliness** *nu.*

'scholarship **1** *nu* knowledge, learning and the use of scholarly methods of working: *a man of great scholarship*; *This book has been written with admirable scholarship.* **2** *nc* a sum of money awarded to a good student to enable him to go on with further studies: *She won a scholarship to go to university*; *She was awarded a travel scholarship.*

scho'lastic [-'las-] *adj* (*formal*: *usu attrib*) of schools or education: *his brilliant scholastic achievements*; *universities and other scholastic institutions.*

school[1] [sku:l] **1** *ncu* (attendance at) a place for teaching *esp* children, or the process of education at such a place: *Which school do you go to?*; *I don't go to school – I'm at university*; *She goes to the school down the road*; *He's not at university – he's still at school*; (*Amer*) *He's still in school*; *What did you learn at/in school today?*; *Do you like school?*; *I fell over on my way to school*; *School begins at 8.30 every morning*; *He went straight home after school*; *At what age do children start/leave school?*; (*attrib*) *What are your plans for the school holidays?* – *See also* **boarding-school, day school**. **2** *nc* the pupils of a school: *The behaviour of this school in public is sometimes not very good.* **3** *nc* a series of meetings for instruction *etc*: *She runs a sewing school*; *This university has a summer school every year for foreigners.* **4** *nc* a department of a university or college dealing with a particular subject: *the History/Mathematics school*; *the School of Mathematics.* **5** *nc* (*Amer*) a university or college. **6** *nc* a group of people with the same ideas, opinions or methods of working: *a painter of the school of Raphael*; *the Platonic school of philosophy*; *There are two schools of thought about the treatment of this disease.* – *vt* (*formal*) to train (a person *etc*) through practice: *We must school* *ourselves to be patient*; *He had been schooled by experience.*

'**schooling** *nu* (*formal*) instruction in school: *He had no proper schooling until he was twelve.*

'**schoolbag** *nc* a bag for carrying books *etc* to and from school: *She had a schoolbag on her back.*

'**schoolbook** *nc* a book for use in school.

'**schoolboy,** '**schoolgirl** *ncs* a boy or girl who goes to school: *Schoolboys should not have to wear uniforms*; (*attrib*) *schoolboy jokes.*

school bus *nc* **1** a *usu* small bus owned by a school: *The school held a concert to raise money for a new school bus.* **2** a bus which takes children to and from school.

'**schoolchild** – *pl* '**schoolchildren** – *nc* a child who goes to school.

'**school-day** *nc* a day on which children go to school: *When I was a child, I classified the days of the year into three groups – school-days, week-ends and holidays*; *On a school-day I got up at seven o'clock.*

'**schooldays** *n pl* the time of a person's life during which he goes to school: *Were your schooldays happy?*

'**schoolfellow** *nc* (*slightly old*) a person who is or was taught at the same school, *esp* in the same class: *I met an old schoolfellow of yours.*

'**school-leaver** *nc* a school-pupil who is about to leave, or has just left, school *eg* because he has finished his course of education there.

'**schoolmaster** – *fem* '**schoolmistress** – *nc* a person who teaches in a school.

'**schoolmate** *nc* (*slightly old*) a schoolfellow, *esp* a friend.

'**school-teacher** *nc* a person who teaches in a school.

school[2] [sku:l] *nc* a number of certain kinds of fish, whales or other water animals of one kind swimming about together: *a school of porpoises.* See also **shoal**.

schooner ['sku:nə] *nc* **1** a type of fast sailing-ship with two or more masts. **2** (*Brit*) a type of sherry glass. **3** (*Amer*) a type of beer glass.

sciatica [sai'atikə] *nu* (*tech*) an illness which causes severe pain in the upper part of the leg: *She suffers from sciatica*; (*inf*) *She has a touch of sciatica.*

science ['saiəns] **1** *nu* knowledge gained by observation and experiment and carefully arranged so that it can be studied: *Science demands that theories must be tested by careful experiment and calculation.* **2** *nc* a branch of such knowledge *eg* biology, chemistry, physics, electrical engineering, psychology *etc*: *Is geography one of the arts or one of the sciences?* **3** *nu* these sciences considered as a whole: *My daughter prefers science to languages or art*; (*attrib*) *science subjects.*

ˌ**scien'tific** [-'ti-] *adj* **1** (*attrib*) of science: *new scientific discoveries*; *scientific work.* **2** (*neg* **un-**) careful; following the rules of science: *His methods were not very scientific*; *scientific methods.*

ˌ**scien'tifically** [-'ti-] *adv* (*neg* **un-**) in a scientific way: *This theory has been scientifically proved.*

'**scientist** *nc* a person who studies one or more branches of science.

science fiction *nu* stories dealing with future times on Earth or in space: *The only fiction he reads is science fiction*; (*attrib*) *a science-fiction story.*

scimitar ['simitə] *nc* (*hist*) a type of short, curved sword, the blade of which gets wider towards the point.

scintillating ['sintileitiŋ] *adj* (*formal or facet*) (of a person, talk *etc*) witty; very clever and amusing: *She was in a scintillating mood*; *scintillating wit*; *His speech wasn't exactly scintillating.*

scissors ['sizəz] *n pl* a type of cutting instrument with two blades joined together in the form of an X: *Scissors are used especially for cutting paper and cloth*; *Can you lend me a pair of scissors?*

scoff[1] [skof] *vi* (*sometimes with* **at**) to jeer or express scorn: *You've no right to scoff*; *She scoffed at my poem.*

scoff[2] [skof] *vti* (*sl*) to eat rapidly or greedily: *They were sitting round the table scoffing*; *Who has scoffed all the biscuits?*

scold [skould] *vti* to criticize or blame (a person) loudly and angrily: *She scolded the child for coming home so late*; *Don't scold!*

'**scolding** *nc* a stern or angry rebuke: *I got a scolding for doing careless work.*

scollop *see* **scallop**.

scone [skon, (*Amer*) skoun] *nc* a kind of small, flat cake made of flour and fat: *We had scones and jam for tea.*

scoop [sku:p] *nc* **1** (*often in cmpds*) any of several types of tool with a hollow spoon-like part and a handle, used for lifting, serving *etc* (sugar, grain, water *etc*): *a grain scoop*; *an ice-cream scoop.* **2** (*inf*) a piece of news *etc* that one newspaper prints before others: *The reporter was sure that he had a scoop for his paper.* **3** (*inf*) a large profit or large sum of money gained: *He got a scoop with these shares he bought.* – *vt* **1** to move (something) with, or as if with, a scoop: *He scooped the crumbs together with his fingers.* **2** (*inf*) to get as a scoop (*defs 2 and 3*): *She scooped the football pools.*

'**scoopful** *nu* the amount of something held in a scoop: *a scoopful of ice-cream.*

scoop out *vt sep* to get or dig out with a scoop or with a scooping movement: *She scooped some ice-cream out on to his plate*; *He scooped out a hole in the sand with his hands.*

scoop up *vt sep* to pick up with a scoop or with a scooping movement: *She scooped up the pebbles in her hands.*

scoot [sku:t] *vi* (*sl*: *often with* **along, away, past** *etc*) to move (away) fast: *He scooted down the road*; *Go away! Scoot!*

'**scooter** *nc* **1** a type of small motor-bicycle: *He had a crash on his scooter.* **2** a child's two-wheeled toy vehicle propelled by the foot: *Scooters should not be used on the pavement.*

scope [skoup] *nu* **1** (*often with* **for**) the opportunity or chance to do, use or develop (something): *The job gave his abilities and talents full scope*; *There's no scope for originality in this job*; *Children should be kept busy and not given scope for mischief.* **2** the area or extent of an activity, piece of work *etc*: *Many words are outside the scope of this dictionary*; *Few things are beyond the scope of a child's imagination.*

scorch [sko:tʃ] *vti* to burn slightly: *She scorched her dress with the iron*; *That material will scorch easily if it is too near the fire*; *The sun had scorched the grass.* – *nc* (*sometimes in cmpds*) a mark made *eg* on cloth by scorching: *She could not wash away the mark of the scorch*; *scorch-marks.*

'**scorcher** *nc* (*inf*) a very hot day: *Yesterday was an absolute scorcher.*

'**scorching** *adj* (*inf*) very hot: *scorching weather*; *a scorching day.* – *adv* (*inf*) very (hot): *It's scorching hot outside.*

score [skoː] – *pls* **scores**, (*def 3*: after a number or a word signifying a quantity) **score** – *nc* **1** the number of points, goals *etc* gained in a game, competition *etc*: *The final score at the football match was 3–2*; *The cricket score is 3 for 59*; *After the first round of darts he had a score of 45.* **2** a written piece of music showing all the parts for instruments and voices: *Have you a copy of the score of this opera?* **3** a set or group of twenty: *There was barely a score of people there*; *We sell these pencils in scores.* – *See also* **scores** *below.* **4** a scratch or cut (in the surface of something): *There's a bad score on that table.* – **1** *vti* to gain (points, goals *etc*) in a game *etc*: *He scored two goals before half-time*; *In the cricket match, Brown is 20 not out, but White has not yet scored.* **2** *vt* (*sometimes with* **off** *or* **out**) to remove (*eg* a name) from *eg* a list by putting a line through it: *Please could you score my name off* (*the list*)*?*; *Is that word meant to be scored out?* **3** to keep score: *Will you score for us, please?* **4** *vt* to cut or scratch (the surface of something): *The typewriter has scored the table.* **5** *vt* (*music*) to write a score (*def 2*): *Who scored this piece?*

'**scorer** *nc* **1** a person who scores points, goals *etc*: *Our team scored two goals – Smith and Brown were the scorers.* **2** a person who writes down the score during *eg* a cricket match.

'**score-board** *nc* a *usu* large board on which the score is shown at a cricket match, a quiz-programme *etc*.

keep (the) score to record the score in a game *etc* as it is made: *Who's keeping score for the darts match?*

on 'that score for that reason: *He's perfectly healthy, so you don't need to worry on that score.*

'**score off** *vt fus* to make (a person) appear foolish, *esp* in conversation: *He's always scoring off his wife in public.* – *See also* **score** (*v def 2*).

scores (of) 1 (*loosely*) very many: *She received scores of letters about her radio programme.* **2** several score.

settle old scores to get revenge from someone for past wrongs: *I have some old scores to settle with you.*

scorn [skoːn] *nu* **1** contempt or disgust: *His cowardly behaviour filled her with scorn*; *He looked at my drawing with scorn.* **2** (*formal*) someone or something that is despised: *He was the scorn of the other boys because he could not swim.* – *vt* **1** to show contempt for; to despise: *They scorned my suggestion.* **2** (*formal*) to consider (an action) unworthy of oneself: *He scorns asking for help/to ask for help.*

'**scornful** *adj* **1** (*often with* **of**) feeling or showing scorn (for something): *a scornful expression/remark*; *He was scornful of the danger.* **2** (of a person) making scornful remarks (about something): *He was rather scornful about your book*; *Don't be so scornful!*; *a very scornful attitude.* '**scornfully** *adv.* '**scornfulness** *nu.*

Scorpio ['skoːpiou] *n* a sign of the zodiac, the Scorpion: *People born between October 23 and November 21 are said to be born under the sign of Scorpio.*

scorpion ['skoːpiən] *nc* an animal of the same class as spiders, that has a tail with a sting.

Scotch [skotʃ] **1** *nu* Scotch whisky, the type of whisky distilled in Scotland: *Have some Scotch!* **2** *nc* a glass of Scotch: *a Scotch and water*; *two Scotches, please.*

Scotch broth *nu* a type of soup made with barley and chopped vegetables.

Scotch tape ® *nu* (*Amer*) a kind of (transparent) adhesive tape: *He mended the torn page with Scotch tape.*

Scot, Scotch, Scotland, Scotsman, Scotswoman, Scottish *see* Appendix 2.

scotch [skotʃ] *vt* (*formal*) **1** to state or show that (a rumour *etc*) is false: *The rumour that the prince was engaged to be married was quickly scotched by an official denial from the palace.* **2** to spoil or put an end to (a plan *etc*): *They scotched his attempt to become the chairman.*

scot-free [skot'friː]: **escape/get off/go scot-free** to be or remain unhurt or unpunished: *The older of the two boys was fined but the younger got off scot-free*; *The car was badly damaged in the accident, but the driver escaped scot-free.*

scoundrel ['skaundrəl] *nc* a very wicked person; a rogue: *She knew he was a scoundrel even before she married him.*

scour[1] ['skauə] *vt* to clean (a pan *etc*) by hard rubbing or scrubbing: *She scoured the blackened saucepan.* – *nc* an act of scrubbing thoroughly: *These tiles could do with a scour.*

'**scourer** *nc* (*often in cmpds*) a person or thing that scours (pots *etc*): *a pot-scourer.*

scour[2] ['skauə] *vt* to make a thorough search of (an area *etc*) looking for a thing or person: *They scoured the woods for the child.*

scourge [skəːdʒ] *nc* **1** (*fig formal*) a cause of great suffering to many people: *Vaccination has freed us from the scourge of smallpox*; *The Huns were the scourge of Europe in the fifth century.* **2** (*arch*) a whip made of strips of leather.

scout [skaut] *nc* **1** (*mil*) a person, aircraft *etc* sent out to bring in information, observe the enemy *etc*: *The scouts reported that there were Indians nearby.* **2** (*with cap*: *sometimes* **Boy Scout**) a member of the Scout Movement, an organization of boys formed to develop alertness and strong character. – *vi* to act as a scout (*def 1*): *A party was sent ahead to scout*; (*inf*) *I'll scout about for a good place to eat.*

Girl Scout *see* **Girl Guide** *under* **girl**.

scowl [skaul] *vi* to wrinkle the brow in displeasure or anger or to look at someone in this way: *He scowled furiously* (*at her*); *What are you scowling about?* – *nc* an angry or sulky expression on the face: *She had a scowl on her face.*

Scrabble ® ['skrabl] *n* a kind of word-building game: *She's an expert at Scrabble*; *Do you play Scrabble?*

scrabble ['skrabl] *vi* (*usu with* **about** *or* **around**) to make scratching noises or movements: *He could hear mice scrabbling about under the floorboards*; *He was scrabbling about looking for the money he had dropped on the floor.*

scraggy ['skragi] *adj* (*derog*) unattractively thin: *She has a rather scraggy neck*; *She's tall and scraggy*; (*in cmpds*) *a scraggy-looking dog.* '**scragginess** *nu.*

scram [skram] – *pt, ptp* **scrammed** – *vi* (*inf*: *usu in imperative*) to go away: *Scram!*; *I told him to scram and he scrammed.*

scramble ['skrambl] **1** *vi* to crawl or climb quickly, using arms and legs: *They scrambled up the slope*; *He scrambled over the rocks.* **2** *vi* to move, or do (something) hastily and inelegantly: *He scrambled to his feet*; *He scrambled out of his clothes and jumped into the river.* **3** *vi* (*with* **for**) to rush, or struggle with others, to get (something): *The boys scrambled for the ball.* **4** *vt* to mix up or distort the sounds of (a telephone message *etc*) so that it can only be received and understood with a special receiver: *The telephone conversation had been scrambled.* – *nc* **1** (*sometimes with* **for**) an act of scrambling; an undignified or inelegant rush or struggle: *There was a scramble to get into the shop on the first day of the bargain sales; There was a scramble for the best bargains.* **2** a motorcycle race over rough country: *The route for the scramble went up a steep farm track.*

'**scrambler** *nc* a device for scrambling telephone messages.

scrambled egg(s) *nu, n pl* beaten eggs cooked with milk and butter until thick: *Have some scrambled egg!; The scrambled eggs are delicious.* *See also* **unscramble**.

scrap[1] [skrap] **1** *nc* a small piece or fragment: *a scrap of paper; a scrap of material.* **2** *nc* (*usu in pl*) a piece of food left over after a meal: *They finished eating their meal and gave the scraps to the dog.* **3** *nu* waste articles that are only valuable for the material they contain which can be processed and used again: *The old car was sold as scrap; He collects metal scrap;* (*attrib*) *scrap metal.* **4** *nc* a picture *etc* bought or cut out of a magazine *etc* for sticking into a scrapbook: *She has a large collection of scraps.* – *v* – *pt* **scrapped** – *vt* to throw away or discard: *They scrapped the old television set and bought a new one;* (*fig*) *She decided to scrap the whole plan.*

'**scrappy** *adj* made up of bits and pieces and not making a satisfactory whole: *a scrappy meal; He wrote a very scrappy essay; Her letter was a bit scrappy.* '**scrappily** *adv.* '**scrappiness** *nu.*

'**scrapbook** *nc* a book with blank pages on which to stick pictures *etc*: *The actor kept a scrapbook for all his pictures and newspaper cuttings about his career.*

'**scrap heap** *nc* a heap of waste material, unwanted objects *etc*: *Throw the junk on the scrap heap!;* (*fig*) *Sometimes old people feel that they're unwanted and on the scrap heap.*

scrap[2] [skrap] *nc* (*inf*) a fight: *He tore his jacket in a scrap with another boy.* – *v* – *pt* **scrapped** – *vi* (*inf*) to fight: *The dogs were scrapping over a bone.*

scrape [skreip] **1** *vti* to rub against something sharp or rough, *usu* causing damage: *He drove too close to the wall and scraped his car; My car scraped along the wall;* I scraped my elbow on the ground when I fell. **2** *vt* to clean or clear (something) by rubbing with something sharp: *He scraped his boots clean; She scraped the mixing-bowl before washing it; She scraped out the jam jar.* **3** *vti* to rub (something) against something else, so making a harsh noise: *I hate to hear knives scraping on plates or chairs scraping on the floor; Stop scraping your feet!* **4** *vi* to move along something while just touching it: *The boat scraped against the landing-stage.* **5** *vt* to make (a hole *etc*) by scraping: *The dog scraped a hole in the sand.* **6** *vti* to remove or be removed by scraping: *He scraped the dirt from his boots; We ought to scrape the old paint off* (*the door*)*; The paint will scrape off quite easily; She scraped out the remains of the pudding on to my plate.* **7** *vt* to pull (*eg* hair) together tightly: *She wears her hair scraped back/scraped into a knot.* – *See also* **scrape** *in phrases below.* – *nc* **1** an act or sound of scraping: *He pushed back his chair with a loud scrape.* **2** a mark or slight wound made by scraping: *How did you get that scrape on your knee?* **3** (*inf*) a difficulty that may lead to disgrace or punishment: *That child is always getting into scrapes.*

'**scraper** *nc* a tool or instrument for scraping, *esp* one for scraping paint and wallpaper off walls *etc.*

scrape a living to earn just enough money to live: *He doesn't earn much money but he manages to scrape a living by selling a few of his paintings.*

scrape along *vi* to manage to live in spite of difficulties: *We don't have much money but we scrape along somehow.*

scrape the bottom of the barrel (*fig*) to (be obliged to) use the least valuable, efficient, reliable person or thing available for some purpose: *I know we're short of players for the game on Saturday but including John would really be scraping the bottom of the barrel.*

scrape through *vi, vt fus* to only just avoid failing (an examination *etc*): *He scraped through his exams; He took the test and just scraped through.*

scrape together/up *vt sep* to manage (with difficulty) to find (enough money, people *etc* to do something): *His parents scraped up enough* (*money*) *to buy him a bicycle; I'll try to scrape a team together for tomorrow's game.*

scrappy *see* **scrap**[1].

scratch [skratʃ] **1** *vti* to pull or push something with a sharp point or rough surface across something, so damaging or hurting it or making lines or marks on it: *The cat scratched my hand; Don't pick up the cat – she may scratch!; You've scratched the table with your toy cars.* **2** *vt* to injure (oneself or a part of the body) through such a process, *usu* by accident: *How did you scratch your leg?; I scratched myself on a rose bush.* **3** *vti* to rub (a part of the body) to relieve itching: *The dog is always scratching* (*itself*)*; You should try not to scratch insect bites.* **4** *vt* to make (a hole, mark *etc*) by scratching: *The cat has scratched a hole in the flower bed; He scratched his name on the rock with a sharp stone.* **5** *vt* to remove, dig up *etc* by scratching: *The witch threatened to scratch his eyes out; Your cat has scratched up my flowers.* – *See also* **scratch out** *below.* **6** *vti* (*inf*) to withdraw from a game, competition, race *etc*: *That horse has been scratched; He was feeling too ill to compete and decided to scratch.* – *nc* **1** a mark, injury or sound made by scratching: *He fell into a thorn bush and was covered with scratches; The table was covered in scratches; His dog just gives a scratch at the door when it wants to come in.* **2** (*fig*) a slight wound: *I hurt myself, but it's only a scratch.* **3** (*pl rare*) an act of scratching (*eg* to relieve itching): *The cat's having a scratch.* **4** (*no pl: without* **a** *or* **the**) in certain races or competitions, the starting point for people with no handicap or advantage: *The runners without a handicap start at scratch;* (*attrib*) *A golf player who is too good to be allowed a handicap is called a scratch player.*

'**scratchy** *adj* **1** (of materials *etc*) likely to scratch: *This wool is rather scratchy; a scratchy material.* **2** making a scratching noise: *a scratchy pen.* **3** (of writing *etc*) untidy, as though done by scratching. '**scratchiness** *nu.*

scratch about *vi* (of birds *etc*) to scratch the ground *etc* looking for food *etc*: *The birds were scratching about* (*for food*) *in the snow.*

scratch out *vt sep* to delete (a word *etc*) by drawing a line or lines untidily through it: *A name was written in the book, but it had been scratched out.*

a scratch team, crew *etc* a team *etc* put together quickly from whichever players *etc* are available: *Most of the players are ill – this is just a scratch team.*
scratch the surface to deal too slightly with a subject: *We started to discuss the matter, but only had time to scratch the surface.*
start from scratch to start (an activity *etc*) from nothing, from the very beginning, or without preparation or the advantage of previous experience: *He now has a very successful business but he started from scratch; He decided to start writing the novel again from scratch.*
up to scratch at or to the required or satisfactory standard: *Your work does not come up to scratch; His health is not up to scratch; Do you think the new employee will come up to scratch?*

scrawl [skro:l] *vti* (*derog*) to write or draw untidily or hastily: *I scrawled a hasty note to her; The baby has scrawled all over my book.* – *nc* (*derog*) untidy or bad handwriting: *His writing is just a scrawl; I hope you can read this scrawl.*

scrawny ['skro:ni] *adj* (*derog*) thin, bony and wrinkled: *She was beautiful when she was young but now she is beginning to look scrawny; She has a scrawny neck.* **'scrawniness** *nu.*

scream [skri:m] **1** *vti* to cry or shout in a loud shrill voice because of fear or pain or with laughter; to make a loud shrill noise: *The child fell down and started screaming (with pain); He was screaming in agony; 'Look out!' she screamed; We screamed with laughter; She screamed abuse at me; The baby screamed itself sick* (= screamed until it was sick); *He drove round the corner with tyres screaming.* **2** *vi* (*fig inf*) (of colours) to have an unpleasant effect if placed together: *These two reds scream at each other.* – **1** *nc* a loud, shrill cry or noise: *She gave a scream of anger/pain/laughter; The car stopped suddenly with a scream of tyres; a scream of brakes.* **2** *nc* (*inf*) a cause of laughter: *The play was a scream; She's an absolute scream.*
screamingly funny (*inf*) extremely funny.

scree [skri:] *ncu* (*tech or formal*) (an area of) loose stones lying on a rocky slope: *They found it difficult to walk along the scree.*

screech [skri:tʃ] *vti* to make a harsh, shrill cry, shout or noise: *The peacocks screeched in the garden; She screeched (abuse) at him; The car screeched to a halt.* – *ncu* a loud, shrill cry or noise: *She gave a screech when she saw the mouse; screeches of laughter; The taxi stopped with a screech of brakes.*

screed [skri:d] *nc* (*inf*: *often in pl*) a long (often boring) report, letter *etc*: *She wrote me a screed all about her holiday; I don't know why he wants another report from me – I've already written screeds about the conference for him.*

screen [skri:n] *nc* **1** (*sometimes in cmpds*) a flat, movable, often folding, covered framework for preventing a person *etc* from being seen, for decoration, or for protection from heat, cold *etc*: *Screens were put round the patient's bed; There was a tapestry fire-screen standing in the fire-place.* **2** (*often in cmpds*) anything that protects a person *etc* from being seen or from cold, heat, danger *etc*: *He hid behind the screen of bushes;* (*fig*) *His job was a screen for his spying activities; The soldiers attacked under cover of a smoke-screen.* **3** the *usu* white sheet-like object or surface on which films, slides *etc* are shown or projected, or the part of a television *etc* on which pictures appear: *He projected his film on to the wall as he had no screen; a cinema/television/radar screen.* – *See also* **the screen** *below.* – *vt* **1** (*formal*) to hide, protect or shelter (a person *etc*): *The tall grass screened him from view; He used his family life to screen him from police investigations.* – *See also* **screen off** *below.* **2** to make a cinema film of (a story *etc*): *Several of Dickens's novels were screened in the 1930s.* **3** to show (a film) in a cinema or on television: *This film hasn't been screened for twenty years.* **4** to test (a person) or examine his past activities, so as to judge his ability to do a job, or his loyalty, reliability *etc*: *He was well screened before he took the job.* **5** to test (a person, or group of persons) for a disease: *Women should be regularly screened for cancer.*
'screenplay *nc* the script of a film, including the dialogue, descriptions of the characters, stage-directions *etc.*
'screen test *nc* a test of a person's ability to act in cinema films.
the screen cinema or television films: *You can see him on the screen quite often;* (*attrib*) *screen actors.*
screen off *vt sep* to separate or hide (something) with, or as if with, a screen: *Part of the room was screened off; The vegetable garden was screened off by a row of bushes.*

screw [skru:] *nc* **1** a type of nail which has a head with a slot in it and a groove or ridge running spirally down its shaft, that is driven into something by a firm twisting action: *I need four strong screws for fixing the cupboard to the wall.* **2** an action of turning or twisting a screw *etc*: *He tightened it by giving it another screw.* **3** (*vulg*) an act of, or partner in, sexual intercourse. **4** (*Brit*) a small twisted piece of paper containing something: *a screw of tobacco; He brought some salt in a screw of paper.* – **1** *vti* to fix or fasten, or be fixed or fastened, with a screw or screws: *He screwed the handle to the door; He screwed down the floorboards; I can't get the clock off the wall – it's screwed on; The handle screws on with these two screws.* – *See also* **screw up** *below.* **2** *vti* to fix, fasten, or remove, or be fixed, fastened or removed, with a twisting movement: *The lid should be screwed on tight; Make sure that the hook is fully screwed in; He managed to screw the lid off.* **3** *vt* (*vulg*) to have sexual intercourse with (a woman).
'screwy *adj* (*Brit*: *sl*) crazy or mad: *Is he a bit screwy?; The whole plan is screwy; a screwy scheme.*
'screwdriver *nc* a kind of tool for turning screws to put them in or get them out.
screw propeller *nc* a type of propeller with spiral blades, used in ships and aircraft.
ˌhave a 'screw loose (*inf*) (of a person) to be a bit mad: *She must have a screw loose.*
ˌhave one's head screwed on (the right way) (*inf*) to be a sensible person: *You can rely on her – she has her head screwed on (the right way).*
put the screws on (*inf*) to use force or pressure in dealing with a person: *If he won't give us the money, we'll have to put the screws on (him).*
screw up *vt sep* **1** to fasten with screws: *The windows are screwed up so that they won't open.* **2** to twist or wrinkle (the face or features): *The baby screwed up its face and began to cry; She screwed her nose up in disgust.* **3** to crumple (a piece of paper *etc*): *She screwed up the letter.*
screw up one's courage to make oneself brave enough to do something: *He screwed up his courage to ask her to marry him.*

See also **unscrew**.

scribble ['skribl] **1** *vti* to write quickly or carelessly: *He scribbled a message*; *She's always scribbling in her notebook.* **2** *vi* to make untidy or meaningless marks with a pencil *etc*: *That child has scribbled all over the wall.* – **1** *nu* untidy, careless handwriting: *Does he call that scribble handwriting?* **2** *nc* a mark *etc* made by scribbling: *childish scribbles.* '**scribbler** *nc.*

scribe [skraib] *nc* (*hist*) **1** a clerk or secretary; a person who copies manuscripts. **2** a teacher of the law among Jews.

scrimp [skrimp]: **scrimp and save** to be mean or very careful with money: *She scrimps and saves for her sons' education.*

script [skript] **1** *nc* the text of a play, talk *etc*: *Have the actors all got their scripts?* **2** *nu* handwriting: *I received a letter from him in his neat script.* **3** *nc* a system of writing: *Japanese children have to learn several different scripts.*

'**scriptwriter** *nc* a person who writes the texts for radio or television programmes.

scripture ['skriptʃə] **1** *nc* the sacred writings of a religion: *The service included readings from Buddhist and Hindu scriptures.* **2** *n* the Bible: *According to Scripture, everyone is descended from two people, Adam and Eve.* '**scriptural** *adj.*

the Scriptures the Bible.

scroll [skroul] *nc* a roll of paper or parchment with writing on it, now *usu* having a formal or ceremonial purpose: *The successful candidates were presented with scrolls stating that they had gained their degrees.*

scrotum ['skroutəm] *nc* (*tech*) the pocket of skin enclosing the testicles.

scrounge [skraundʒ] *vti* (*inf*: *often facet*) to get (what one wants or needs) by begging from someone else: *He's always scrounging*; *You're not going to scrounge any more money from me!*; *Do you mind if I scrounge some coffee?* '**scrounger** *nc.*

scrub[1] [skrʌb] – *pt*, *ptp* **scrubbed** – **1** *vti* to rub (something) hard in order to clean it: *She's scrubbing the floor*; *I hate scrubbing*; *Have you scrubbed the pan clean?* – *See also* **scrub out** *below.* **2** *vt* to remove (something) by scrubbing: *She scrubbed the mess off the carpet.* **3** *vt* (*inf*) to cancel (a plan *etc*): *We planned to go but had to scrub the idea.* – *nc* an act of scrubbing: *These pans need a good scrub.*

'**scrubbing-brush** *nc* a brush with short stiff bristles for scrubbing.

scrub out *vt sep* to clean the inside of (*eg* a bowl) by scrubbing: *Please scrub the bath out!*

scrub[2] [skrʌb] *nu* (land covered with) low bushes: *miles of scrub.*

scruff [skrʌf]: **the scruff of the neck** the back of the neck by which an animal can be grasped or lifted: *She picked up the cat by the scruff of the neck*; (*fig*) *He took the boy by the scruff of the neck and pushed him out of the room.*

scruffy ['skrʌfi] *adj* (*inf*) dirty and untidy: *a scruffy person*; *Their house is a bit scruffy*; *My son always looks scruffy.*

scrum [skrʌm] *nc* in rugby football, a struggle for the ball by the rival forwards hunched tightly round it.

scrumptious ['skrʌmpʃəs] *adj* (*inf*: *used esp by children*) delicious: *a scrumptious cake*; *This ice-cream is scrumptious.*

scruple ['skru:pl] *ncu* (*formal*) a feeling of hesitation or doubt about doing something because one thinks or knows that it would or might be wrong, unkind *etc* to do it: *He had no scruples about accepting the money*; *I have a slight scruple about deceiving my mother*; *He borrows my money without scruple.*

scrupulous ['skru:pjuləs] *adj* (*formal*) careful in attending to every small detail, *esp* in matters of honesty; taking care to do nothing wrong, dishonest *etc*: *He is absolutely scrupulous in his handling of the association's accounts*; *He is unfortunately not always scrupulous about how he achieves his aims*; *scrupulous honesty/cleanliness*; *He paid scrupulous attention to his instructions.* '**scrupulously** *adv.* '**scrupulousness** *nu.*

See also **unscrupulous**.

scrutiny ['skru:təni] *ncu* (*formal*) (a) careful, detailed examination or inspection: *All the fruit undergoes a careful scrutiny before it is sold in the shops*; *Famous people live their lives under continuous public scrutiny.*

'**scrutinize, -ise** *vt* (*formal or facet*) to examine carefully: *He scrutinized the document carefully to make sure that there were no errors in it*; *He scrutinized the bank-notes with a magnifying-glass.*

scud [skʌd] – *pt* '**scudded** – *vi* (*formal or liter*) to move lightly and swiftly: *Clouds were scudding across the sky*; *The wind sent bits of rubbish scudding along the street.*

scuff [skʌf] **1** *vti* to walk without lifting one's feet properly: *Don't scuff* (*your feet*) – *it's very irritating!* **2** *vt* to rub the polished surface off (shoes *etc*) in this or some other way: *You've scuffed the toes of your new shoes.*

scuffle ['skʌfl] *nc* a confused fight *usu* between a few people using their fists, feet *etc*: *The two men quarrelled and there was a scuffle.* – *vi* **1** to be involved in such a fight: *They scuffled together on the floor.* **2** to make pattering or shuffling noises: *I could hear mice scuffling in the attic.*

scull [skʌl] *nc* a short, light oar. – *vti* to move (a boat) with a pair of these or with an oar worked at the stern of the boat.

scullery ['skʌləri] *nc esp* in large, old houses, a room for rough kitchen work, such as cleaning pots, pans *etc.*

sculptor ['skʌlptə] – *fem* '**sculptress** – *nc* an artist who carves or models figures or designs in stone, clay, wood *etc*: *Michelangelo was a famous Italian painter and sculptor.*

sculpt *vti* to carve (statues *etc*): *He sculpted the statue out of sandstone.*

'**sculpture** [-tʃə] **1** *nu* the art of modelling or carving figures, shapes *etc*: *He went to art school to study painting and sculpture.* **2** *ncu* (a piece of) work done by a sculptor or sculptress: *He made a beautiful sculpture of her head*; *These statues are all examples of ancient Greek sculpture.* – *vt* to carve: *The figure is to be sculptured out of marble.*

'**sculptured** [-tʃəd] *adj* (*attrib*: *liter or formal*) as beautiful as if carved by a sculptor: *Everyone admired the actor's handsome, sculptured features.*

scum [skʌm] *nu* **1** (a quantity of) dirty foam that forms on the surface of a liquid: *The pond was covered with* (*a*) *scum*; *Boil the bones in water, removing the scum from time to time.* **2** (*derog*) the worst and most worthless part of anything, *esp* bad, worthless people: *People of that sort are the scum of the earth*; *Scum like him should be put up against a wall and shot!* '**scummy** *adj.*

scupper ['skʌpə] *vt* (*inf*) to ruin: *He was late for the* *examination and scuppered his chances of winning the scholarship.*

'**scuppered** *adj* (*pred*: *inf*) ruined; having problems or difficulties: *If they publish their book before we publish this one, we're scuppered.*

scurf [skə:f] *nu* small dry flakes of dead skin *esp* on the scalp; dandruff: *Some shampoos help to get rid of scurf.*

'**scurfy** *adj* full of scurf: *a scurfy scalp*; *His skin is scurfy.*

scurrilous ['skʌriləs, (*Amer*) 'skə:-] *adj* (*formal*) (of a joke, a piece of writing *etc*) insulting or abusive: *This magazine is constantly making scurrilous attacks on politicians*; *a scurrilous poem.* '**scurrilously** *adv.* '**scurrilousness** *nu.* **scur'rility** [-'ri-] *ncu.*

scurry ['skʌri, (*Amer*) 'skə:ri] *vi* (*usu with* **along, away, off** *etc*) to hurry; to run with short, quick steps: *It began to rain and we scurried home*; *The mouse scurried away into its hole.* – *nu* (*sometimes with* **a**) an act or a noise of hurrying: *I heard a scurry of feet in the passage*; *There was a great scurry for ice-cream during the interval of the play.*

scurvy ['skə:vi] *nu* a disease caused by lack of fresh fruit and vegetables: *Sailors used to suffer from scurvy until oranges were carried on board.*

scuttle[1] ['skʌtl] *vi* to hurry with short, quick steps: *I poked the spider and it scuttled away.*

scuttle[2] ['skʌtl] short for **coal-scuttle**.

scuttle[3] ['skʌtl] *vt* (*naut*) (of a ship's crew) to make a hole in (the ship) in order to sink it: *The sailors scuttled the ship to prevent it falling into the hands of the enemy.*

scythe [saið] *nc* a tool with a long, curved blade and a long handle, for cutting tall grass, hay *etc.* – *vi* to cut (grass *etc*) with a scythe: *He ought to scythe the hay*; *Are you good at scything?*

se *see* **per se** *under* **per**.

sea [si:] **1** *nu* (*often with* **the**) the mass of salt water covering most of the Earth's surface: *About threequarters of the Earth is covered by sea*; *Is the sea here warm enough for swimming?*; *This bird flies many miles over land and sea*; *The sea is many kilometres deep in parts*; (*attrib*) *A whale is a type of large sea animal.* **2** *nc* (*often found with cap in place-names*) a particular area of sea; a large expanse of water smaller than an ocean: *the Baltic Sea*; *The North Sea separates Britain from Europe*; *These fish are found in tropical/warm seas.* **3** *nc* (*sometimes in pl*) a particular state of the sea: *There's a rough sea today*; *You've got a calm sea for the trip*; *The ship encountered mountainous seas.* **4** *nc* (*fig*) a great expanse, amount or number: *He looked down from the stage at the sea of faces.* – *See also* **sea** *in phrases below.*

'**seaward** *adj* (*attrib*) facing, going *etc* towards the sea: *There is a beautiful view on the seaward side of the house.*

'**seaward(s)** *adv* towards the sea; away from the land: *The yacht left the harbour and sailed seawards.*

'**seabed** *nu* (*usu with* **the**) the ground under the sea: *The wrecked ship was lying on the seabed.*

'**seaboard** *nc* the seacoast: *the eastern seaboard of the United States.*

sea breeze *nc* a breeze blowing from the sea towards the land.

'**seacoast** *nu* (*usu with* **the**) the land next to the sea: *We drove along the seacoast.*

'**sea dog** *nc* (*liter*) an (old) sailor.

'**seafaring** *adj* (*formal or liter*: *attrib*) of work or travel on ships: *There is nothing better than the seafaring life*; *a seafaring man.*

'**seafood** *nu* shellfish: *Seafood makes me ill*; (*attrib*) *seafood restaurants.*

'**seafront** *nc* a promenade or part of a town with its buildings facing the sea: *They run an hotel on the seafront.*

'**sea-going** *adj* (of a ship) (designed and equipped for) travelling on the sea, rather than sailing on rivers, along coasts *etc*: *a sea-going yacht*; *Is his new boat sea-going?*

'**seagull** *nc* a gull.

'**sea level** *nu* the level of the surface of the sea used as a base from which the height of land can be measured: *The town is three hundred metres above sea level.*

'**sea-lion** *nc* a type of large seal found in the Pacific ocean: *Sea-lions roar and the male has a mane.*

'**seaman** – *pl* '**seamen** – *nc* a sailor, *esp* a member of a ship's crew who is not an officer: *merchant seamen*; *the Seamen's Union.*

'**seamanship** *nu* (*formal*) the art of navigating and looking after ships at sea: *I know nothing about seamanship.*

'**seaport** *nc* a port on the seacoast.

'**seascape** *nc* (*formal*) a picture of a scene at sea: *The artist painted a splendid seascape.*

'**seashell** *nc* the (empty) shell of a sea creature: *She makes necklaces from seashells.*

'**seashore** *ncu* the land close to the sea: *Let's go down to the seashore and swim.*

'**seasick** *adj* (*often pred*) ill because of the motion of a ship at sea: *Were you seasick on the voyage?*; *Do you get* (= become) *seasick?* '**seasickness** *nu.*

'**seaside** *nu* (*usu with* **the**) a place beside the sea: *We like to go to the seaside in the summer*; (*attrib*) *seaside cottages/entertainment.*

sea wall *nc* a wall to stop the sea from flowing on to the land.

'**seawater** *nu* water from the sea: *There is now a special process for making seawater drinkable.*

'**seaweed** *nu* plants growing in the sea: *The beach was covered with seaweed.*

'**seaworthy** *adj* (*formal*: *neg* **un-**) (of a ship) suitably built and in good enough condition to sail at sea. '**seaworthiness** *nu.*

at 'sea 1 on a ship and away from land: *He has been at sea for four months.* **2** (*inf*) puzzled or bewildered: *Can I help you? You seem all/completely/rather at sea.*

by 'sea in a ship: *He travelled to New York by sea.*

get one's sea legs (*inf*) to become accustomed to the motion of a ship: *I felt seasick at first, but I soon got my sea legs.*

go *etc* **to sea** to become a sailor: *He wants to go to sea*; *He left home and ran away to sea.*

the high seas *see* **high**.

the open sea *see* **open**.

put to sea to leave the land or a port: *They planned to put to sea the next day.*

sail the Seven Seas (*liter*) to sail to all parts of the world.

seal[1] [si:l] *nc* **1** a piece of wax or other material bearing a design, attached to a document to show that it is genuine and legal: *The king's seal was attached to the document.* **2** a piece of wax *etc* used to seal a parcel *etc* or attached to a parcel *etc* in such a way that it will break if the parcel is opened. **3** a stamp made of metal or other material, and engraved with a design, used to impress the design on such pieces of wax (*esp def*

1): *He wore a ring with a seal bearing his initials.* **4** (something that makes) a tight join or a complete closure or covering: *Paint and varnish act as protective seals for woodwork.* – *vt* **1** to mark with a seal: *The document was signed and sealed.* **2** (*neg* **un-**) to close completely, *eg* by means of an adhesive or adhesive tape: *He licked and sealed the envelope*; *Some parcels are cheaper to send if they are not sealed*; *All the air is removed from a can of food before it is sealed.* – *See also* **seal in** *below.* **3** (*formal*) to settle or decide: *The bargain was sealed*; *This mistake sealed his fate.*

sealed *adj* (*usu attrib*) (of instructions, orders *etc*) placed in a sealed envelope, only to be opened in certain circumstances: *He gave his lawyer sealed instructions about what to do if he died.*

'sealing-wax *nu* a type of wax for sealing letters *etc*: *a stick of sealing-wax.*

my, our *etc* **lips are sealed** (*often facet*) I, we *etc* have promised not to speak about the matter: *I won't tell what your mum has for your birthday – my lips are sealed.*

seal in *vt sep* to enclose (something) within a container *etc* so that it cannot escape: *The full flavour of the coffee will remain sealed in until the tin is opened.*

seal of approval official approval: *Doctors have now given this new drug their seal of approval.*

seal off *vt sep* to prevent all approach to, or exit from, (an area): *The police have sealed off the area where the murdered girl was found.*

set one's seal to to give one's authority or agreement to: *The Prime Minister has finally set his seal to the proposals for Parliamentary reforms.*

seal[2] [siːl] *nc* any of several types of sea animal, some furry, living partly on land and valuable for their skin and oil.

'sealskin *nu, adj* (of) the fur of the furry type of seal: *sealskin boots*; *The boots are (made of) sealskin.*

seam [siːm] *nc* **1** the line formed by the sewing together of two pieces of cloth *etc*: *When making a garment, you need to pin the seams before sewing them.* **2** the line where two things meet or join, *eg* the line between two planks of a ship: *Water was coming in through the seams of the boat.* **3** a thin line or layer of coal, iron ore *etc* in the earth: *a coal seam.* – *vt* to sew a seam in (a garment *etc*): *I've pinned the skirt together but I haven't seamed it yet.*

seamed *adj* (of a garment) having a seam or seams: *seamed stockings.*

'seamless *adj* (of a garment) having no seams, made from a single piece of material: *seamless stockings/tights*; *Are those stockings seamless?*

'seamstress *nc* (*old*) a woman who earns her living by sewing.

the seamy side (of life) the roughest, most unpleasant side or aspect of human life: *As a social worker, you certainly see the seamy side of life.*

seaman *see* **sea**.

séance ['seiãns] *nc* a meeting of people trying to obtain messages from the spirits of dead people: *She claims to have spoken to the emperor Napoleon at a séance.*

sear [siə] *vt* (*formal*) **1** (*esp fig*) to burn severely: *The material was seared by the hot iron*; (*fig*) *He was seared to the heart* (= very badly hurt) *by her infidelity.* **2** to dry up; to wither: *The hot sun seared the grass.* **'searing** *adj.*

search [səːtʃ] **1** *vti* (*often with* **for**) to seek or look for something by careful examination of a place *etc*: *I've searched all over the house and I still can't find that money*; *Have you searched through your pockets thoroughly?*; *I've been searching for that book for weeks*; *I've searched the town for nails of the right size.* – *See also* **search out** *below.* **2** *vt* (of the police *etc*) to examine (*eg* a house, a person's pockets and clothes) looking for *eg* stolen goods, weapons, drugs *etc*: *He was taken to the police station, searched and questioned.* – *nc* (*often with* **for**) an act of searching; an attempt to find something: *His search did not take long*; *The search for the missing man is continuing today.* – *See also* **in search of** *below.* **'searcher** *nc.*

'searching *adj* (*usu attrib*) trying to find out the truth by careful examination or observation: *He gave me a searching look*; *She asked some searching questions.* **'searchingly** *adv.*

'searchlight *nc* a strong light with a beam that can be turned in any direction, used *eg* to see enemy aeroplanes in the sky.

'search party *nc* a group of people looking for a missing person: *When they failed to return from their climbing expedition, a search party was sent out.*

'search warrant *nc* a warrant giving legal permission to the police to search a house *etc, eg* for stolen goods: *The man demanded to see the police officer's search warrant before he would allow him into the house.*

in 'search of searching for (something or someone): *We went in search of a restaurant*; *This play is called 'Six Characters in Search of an Author'.*

search me! (*inf*) I really don't know!: *'Why does the manager want to see us?' 'Search me!'*

searing ['siəriŋ] *adj* (*attrib*) (of a pain *etc*) extremely severe, as if caused by burning.

season ['siːzn] *nc* **1** one of the main divisions of the year according to the regular variation of the weather, length of day *etc*; any large part of a year which has particular characteristics: *The four seasons are spring, summer, autumn and winter*; *The monsoon brings the rainy season.* **2** the usual, proper or suitable time for something: *the football season*; *the planting season.* – *See also* **in season** *below.* **3** a period of time during which something is done: *a season of concerts.* – *vt* **1** to add salt, pepper, mustard *etc* to (food) to improve its flavour: *She seasoned the meat with plenty of pepper*; (*fig*) *His talk was always seasoned with humour.* **2** to let (wood) be affected by rain, sun *etc* until it is ready for use: *The wood was left out in the open to season it.*

'seasonable *adj* (*neg* **un-**) (of weather) of the kind that is to be expected for a particular time of year: *seasonable October weather.*

'seasonal *adj* (of work, games *etc*) done at a particular season only: *She gets seasonal work as a waitress in a seaside hotel*; *seasonal sports*; *Hotel work is often seasonal.*

'seasoned *adj* experienced; trained to endure harsh conditions, criticism *etc*; *seasoned troops*; *seasoned political campaigners.*

'seasoning *ncu* something used to season food: *The soup needs more seasoning*; *Salt, pepper and mustard are used as seasonings.*

season ticket *nc* a ticket (*usu* for travel) that can be used repeatedly during a certain period: *He has a three-month season ticket for his bus journey to work.*

close season *see* **close**.

in 'season (of food) available, ripe and ready for

eating: *This type of plum is in season at the end of August.*
off season, open season *see* **off, open.**
out of season not in season.

seat [siːt] *nc* **1** something for sitting on, *eg* a chair, bench *etc*: *Are there enough seats for everyone?*; *He was using an upturned bucket as a seat.* **2** a sitting position: *He got up from his seat on the floor.* **3** (*sometimes in cmpds*) the part of a chair *etc* on which the body sits: *This chair-seat is broken.* **4** (*inf euph*) the buttocks: *I've got a sore seat after all that horse riding.* **5** the part of a garment covering the buttocks: *He has a hole in the seat of his trousers.* **6** a place (*eg* in a theatre *etc*) in which a person has a right to sit: *I've got two seats for the play.* **7** membership of a group of people that meets to administer, control or run (some organization *etc*): *a seat in Parliament*; *He won/lost his seat in the last election*; *She has resigned her seat on the town council*; *He has a seat on the board of this company.* **8** a place that is the centre of some activity, organization *etc*: *The seat of government in Britain is Westminster*; *Universities are seats of learning.* **9** (*formal*) a large house and estate: *The family's country seat is in Buckinghamshire.* – *vt* **1** to cause (a person) to sit down: *I seated him/myself in the armchair.* **2** (of a room, vehicle *etc*) to have seats for (a certain number): *This bus seats forty-five people*; *Our table seats eight.*
-seater (*in cmpds*) having seats for (a certain number of people *etc*): *The bus is a thirty-seater.*
'seating *nu* the supply or arrangement of seats: *She arranged the seating for the lecture*: (*attrib*) *seating arrangements.*
'seat belt *nc* in a car, aeroplane *etc*, a safety-belt which will hold a person in his seat in an accident *etc*: *You should always put on a seat belt even for a short trip*; *Fasten your seat belts, please.*
be seated! (*formal*) sit down.
take a seat (*more formal than* **sit down**) to sit down: *Please take a seat!*
take one's seat (*formal*) to sit down in the place that one has a right to, or is supposed to, sit in (at a theatre, meeting *etc*): *If the audience will take their seats, the concert can begin.*

secateurs [sekə'təːz] *n pl* (*Brit*) a tool like a pair of scissors used by gardeners for pruning bushes *etc*: *a pair of secateurs.*

secede [sə'siːd] *vi* (*formal*: *often with* **from**) to withdraw from a group, society *etc*: *The American Civil War began when some of the southern states seceded (from the United States).* **secession** [sə'seʃən] *ncu.*

secluded [si'kluːdid] *adj* not able to be seen, talked to *etc* by other people; far away from other people, disturbance *etc*: *A secluded country cottage*; *Their farmhouse is very secluded*; *In some parts of the world, women are kept secluded.*
se'clusion [-ʒən] *nu* the state of being secluded; privacy: *She did not weep till she was in the seclusion of her own room*; *In the summer we live in seclusion in the country.*

second[1] ['sekənd] *adj* **1** (*usu attrib*) next after, or following, the first in time, place *etc*: *February is the second month of the year*; *Our second son is unmarried*; *She finished the race in second place*; *King Henry the Second*; *You're the second person to have done that today.* **2** (*attrib*) additional or extra: *They have a second house in the country.* **3** (*usu attrib*) lesser in importance, quality *etc*: *He plays in the school's second orchestra*; *She's a member of the school's second swimming team.* – *See also* **second to none** *below.* **4** (*attrib*: *music*) playing, singing *etc* at a lower pitch: *He plays with the second violins in the orchestra*; *He's one of the second tenors.* – *adv* next after the first: *He came second in the exam/race.* – *nc* **1** a second person, thing *etc*: *She's arriving on the second of June*; *You're the second to make that mistake.* **2** a person who supports and helps a person who is fighting in a boxing match, duel *etc*: *The second sponges and manages the boxer between rounds*; *The seconds arranged the time and place of the duel.* **3** (*often with cap*) a degree with second-class honours: *He got a second in French and English.* – *vt* to agree with (something said by a previous speaker), *esp* to do so formally (as part of a debate *etc*) in order to allow a vote to be taken: *He proposed the motion and I seconded it*; *'I suggest that we leave now.' 'I second that!'*
'secondary *adj* (*attrib*) **1** coming after, and at a more advanced level than, primary: *secondary education.* **2** lesser in importance: *That's a secondary matter*; *This matter is of secondary importance.* – *ncu* a secondary school.
'seconder *nc* a person who seconds *eg* a motion in a debate, a nomination in an election *etc.*
'secondly *adv* in the second place: *I have two reasons for not buying the house – firstly, it's too big, and secondly it's too far from town.*
'seconds *n pl* goods that are not of the best quality: *These wine glasses are seconds.*
secondary colours *n pl* colours got by mixing primary colours: *Orange and purple are secondary colours.*
secondary school *ncu* a school where subjects are taught at a more advanced level than at primary school: *A child usually goes to secondary school at about the age of twelve.*
secondary stress **1** *ncu* a stress weaker than primary stress. **2** *nc* a mark used to indicate the position of this stress in a word.
ˌsecond-'best *nu, adj* next after the best; not the best: *She wore her second-best hat*; *I want your best work. Your second-best is not good enough*; *He did marry her eventually but he regarded her as second-best – he would have preferred to marry her sister.* – *See also* **come off second best** *below.*
second childhood *ncu* (*derog*) the return to childish habits and behaviour that occurs in some elderly people: *He's in his second childhood.*
ˌsecond-'class *adj* **1** of or in the class next after or below the first; not of the very best quality: *a second-class restaurant*; *He gained a second-class honours degree in French.* **2** (for) travelling in a part of a means of transport that is not as comfortable or luxurious as some other part: *a second-class passenger*; *His ticket is second-class.* **3** (*attrib*) (of citizens) not having full (political) rights, privileges *etc*: *In some countries, coloured people are treated as second-class citizens.* **4** (of mail) sent at a cheaper rate, and *usu* delivered more slowly than first-class mail: *second-class post.* – *adv*: *I'll be travelling second-class*; *I sent the letter second-class.* – *See also* **first-class** *under* **first.**
second cousin *nc* the child of a first cousin of either of a person's parents.
second floor *nc* (*with* **the**) the floor that is two floors (*Amer* one floor) above the ground floor: *We live on the second floor*; (*attrib*) *a second-floor flat.*
ˌsecond-'hand *adj* previously used by someone

else: *second-hand clothes/bicycles*; *Are all her clothes second-hand?*; (*fig derog*) *The book is full of second-hand ideas.* – *See also* **at second hand** *below*.

ˌ**second-in-com'mand** – *pl* ˌ**seconds-in-com'mand** – *nc, adj* (*pred*) in an *esp* military group, (the person) next below the commander in seniority: *He's my second-in-command*; *I'm second-in-command in the garrison.*

second lieutenant *nc* (*with caps, and often abbrev* **2/Lt**, *when written in titles*) in the British army, (a person of) the rank below lieutenant: *He is a second lieutenant*; *Second Lieutenant Jones.*

second nature *nu* a firmly fixed habit: *It was second nature to/with him to think carefully before spending even 10p.*

ˌ**second-'rate** *adj* (*derog*) inferior: not of the best quality: *He has a second-rate mind*; *The play was pretty second-rate.*

second sight *nu* the power of seeing into the future or into other mysteries: *They asked a woman with second sight where the dead body was.*

second thoughts *n pl* a change of opinion, decision *etc*; an opinion reached after thinking again about something: *I'm having second thoughts about selling the piano*; *On second thoughts, I'd rather stay here.*

at second hand through or from another person: *I heard the news at second hand.* – *See also* **second-hand** *above.*

be a second (someone) to have the qualities, ability *etc* of (someone): *He's not a very good pianist, but his parents think he's a second Mozart.*

come off second best to be the loser in a struggle: *That cat always comes off second best in a fight.*

every second week, month *etc* (on or during) alternate weeks, months *etc*: *The manager only comes into the shop every second day* (= He comes in one day, not on the next, then he comes in on the following day, and so on).

get one's second wind *see* **wind**[1].

in the second place *see* **place**.

second person (*gram*) *see* **person**.

second to none better than every other (person, thing *etc*) of the same type; (*loosely*) very good: *His roast pheasant is second to none*; *As a portrait painter, he is second to none.*

See also **two** *and* Appendix 1.

second[2] ['sekənd] *nc* **1** the sixtieth part of a minute: *He ran the race in three minutes and forty-two seconds*; *a ten-second delay.* **2** (*geog or geom*) the sixtieth part of the minute of a degree: *an angle of 14° 5′ 16″* (fourteen degrees, five minutes and sixteen seconds). **3** (*inf*) a short time: *I'll be there in a second.*

'**second hand** *nc* a *usu* very thin hand on a watch, clock *etc*, which records the time in seconds.

second[3] [si'kond, (*Amer*) 'sekənd] *vt* (*formal*: *with* **from** *or* **to**) to transfer (a person) to some place temporarily *usu* to do a special job: *He has been seconded to the London office.*

se'condment *ncu* (*formal*: *with* **from** *or* **to**): *He is on secondment from/to our head office*; *Secondments from head office are rare.*

secret ['si:krit] *adj* hidden from, unknown to, or not told to, other people: *a secret agreement*; *He kept his illness secret from his wife*; *I know a secret place where he can hide.* – *nc* **1** a fact, purpose, method *etc* that is, or must be kept, secret: *The date of their marriage is a secret*; *industrial secrets*; *I was in on* (= I knew about) *the secret from the beginning*; *His reason for coming was kept a secret.* – *See also* **in secret, keep a secret** *below.* **2** a hidden, or secret, explanation of something or method of doing something: *I wish I knew the secret of her success*; *One of the secrets of good health is regular exercise*; *the secrets of engineering.*

'**secrecy** *nu* **1** the state of being secret: *the secrecy of his plans.* **2** the act of keeping, or ability to keep, (something) secret: *I rely on your secrecy*; *It was done with great secrecy.*

'**secretive** [-tiv] *adj* (*usu derog*) inclined to conceal one's activities, thoughts *etc*: *a secretive person*; *secretive behaviour*; *That child is so secretive.*

'**secretively** *adv.* '**secretiveness** *nu.*

'**secretly** *adv* in such a way that others do not know, see *etc*: *He secretly copied the numbers down in his notebook*; *Secretly, between you and me, I wish that she would go away.*

secret agent *nc* a spy.

secret police *nu* a police force whose activities are kept secret and which is concerned mostly with political crimes.

Secret Service *nc* (*sometimes no cap*) the government department dealing with spying *etc* and, *eg* in the US, with protecting the President: *He says he travels abroad to sell books but I think he works for the Secret Service.*

in 'secret secretly: *He told me about it in secret*; *This must all be done in secret*; *He married her in secret.*

keep a secret not to tell (something secret) to anyone else: *You can't trust her to keep a secret.*

let (someone) into a secret to tell (someone) something which is secret: *I'll let you into a secret – I am going to be married.*

secretary ['sekrətəri] *nc* **1** a person employed to write letters, keep records and make business arrangements *etc* for another person: *He dictated a letter to his secretary*; *Please see my secretary if you want to apply for extra holidays.* **2** a (sometimes unpaid) person who writes official letters, keeps records and deals with other administrative matters for an organization *etc* or who is in charge of the people who do so: *The secretary read out the minutes of the society's last meeting.* **3** (*with cap*) in Britain, a Secretary of State: *the Foreign Secretary.* **4** (*with cap*) in the US, a person in charge of a large government department: *The Secretary of the Treasury.*

ˌ**secre'tarial** [-'teə-] *adj* (*usu attrib*) of a secretary or his/her duties: *She has been trained in secretarial work*; *She's at secretarial college*; *We need more secretarial help.*

ˌ**secre'tariat(e)** [-riət] *nc* (the building containing) the offices of a large, *usu* international, political or administrative organization.

Secretary of State 1 in Britain, a cabinet minister holding one of the more important positions: *the Secretary of State for Defence.* **2** in the US, the Secretary (*def 4*) concerned with foreign affairs.

secrete [si'kri:t] *vt* **1** (*formal or tech*) (of a gland or similar organ of the body) to separate (a fluid) from the blood, store it, and give it out: *The liver secretes bile.* **2** (*formal*) to hide (something): *He secreted the money under his mattress.*

se'cretion [-ʃən] **1** *nu* (*formal or tech*) the process of secreting a fluid. **2** *nc* (*formal or tech*) a substance produced by this process: *Saliva and urine are secretions.* **3** *nu* (*formal*) the act of hiding something: *the secretion of the stolen diamond.*

sect [sekt] *nc* a group of people within a larger, *esp* religious, group, having views different from those of the rest of the group: *the various sects of the Christian church.*

sec'tarian (*often derog*: *often attrib*) *adj* **1** of a sect or sects; concerned with the narrow interests of a sect or sects: *sectarian loyalties.* **2** caused by membership of a sect: *a sectarian murder.* – *nc* a member of a sect, or a person who cares only for the interests of his sect.

sec'tarianism *nu* **1** concern only for the interests of a sect: *While continuing to be loyal to our own church, we must avoid all sectarianism.* **2** the tendency to form sects: *Sectarianism has split the Protestant church into hundreds of small groups.*

section ['sekʃən] *nc* **1** a part or division: *He divided the orange into sections; There is disagreement in one section of the community; She has been transferred to the accounts section of the business; She cut a large section from the cake; The building was delivered in sections and assembled on the site.* **2** (*tech*) a thin slice (of *eg* body tissue) for examination under a microscope: *The pathologist examined the section of cancerous tissue.* **3** a view of the inside of anything when, or as if, it is cut right through or across: *The architect's model was of a section through the house; a section of the stem of a flower.*

'sectional *adj* (*formal*: *usu attrib*) **1** made *etc* in sections: *sectional tent-poles.* **2** of, or (caused by) belonging to a section or sections of a community *etc*: *sectional interests.* **3** of a section: *a sectional model.*

sector ['sektə] *nc* **1** one part of an area that has been divided into parts for military operations, occupation by a foreign power *etc*: *The sector of Germany occupied by the Russians after the war has become East Germany; the eastern sector of Berlin.* **2** (*geom*) a section of a circle whose sides are a part of the circumference and two straight lines drawn from the centre to the circumference.

'private, 'public sector *nc* that part of industry and business that is privately owned or owned by the government respectively: *Wages for workers in the public sector don't always keep up with those for workers in the private sector.*

secular ['sekjulə] *adj* (*formal*: *often attrib*) not spiritual or religious: *secular art/music.*

secure [si'kjuə] *adj* **1** (*often with* **against** *or* **from**) safe; free from danger, loss *etc*: *Is your house secure against/from burglary?; Will my money be secure if it is invested in this firm?;* (*fig*) *He was secure in the knowledge that he had done well in the exam;* (*fig*) *I don't feel at all secure about my future in this firm.* **2** (*more formal than* **firm** *or* **fastened**) firm, fastened, or fixed: *Don't pull that rope – it's not secure!; Is that lock/window/door secure?* **3** certain; definite; not likely to be lost: *She has had a secure offer of a job; He has a secure job; His promotion/election is secure.* – *vt* **1** (*formal with* **against** *or* **from** (something bad) *or very formal with* **to** (someone)) to guarantee or make safe: *Keep your jewellery in the bank to secure it against theft;* (*fig*) *Order your tickets early to secure against disappointment!; By his will, possession of the house is secured to his children.* **2** (*more formal than* **fasten**) to fasten or make firm: *Secure all the doors and windows before leaving; He secured the boat with a rope.* **3** (*formal*) to obtain or get (often with difficulty): *I've secured us two front seats for the circus; She secured a promise from him that he would pay.* **se'curely** *adv.*

se'curities *n pl* certificates, or other evidence of ownership of property, shares *etc*: *She had a few worthless securities.*

se'curity **1** *nu* the state of being, or making (a person, thing *etc*) safe, secure, free from danger *etc*: *Many children have never experienced the security of a happy home; The police told them to leave the country, or their security could not be guaranteed; This alarm system will give the factory some security against/from theft; After the police caught the murderer, the villagers were able to live in security once more; There has to be tight security at a prison;* (*attrib*) *It is the job of the security forces to prevent and deal with outbreaks of violence – See also* **security risk** *below.* **2** *ncu* something valuable given or promised as a guarantee of repayment of money borrowed: *He borrowed the money on the security of his house; What can you give me as security? He deposited the securities in the bank. – See also* **securities** *above.*

se'curity risk *nc* a person considered not safe to be given a job involving knowledge of secrets because he might give such secret information to an enemy, competitor *etc.*

See also **insecure**.

sedan [si'dan] *nc* **1** (*Amer*) a covered car for four or more people. **2** (*hist*: *also* **se'dan-chair**) an enclosed seat for one person carried on two poles by two men.

sedate[1] [si'deit] *adj* (of a person or his manner *etc*) calm, serious and dignified: *She became more sedate as she grew older; a sedate, middle-aged woman.* **se'dately** *adv.* **se'dateness** *nu.*

sedative ['sedətiv] *nc, adj* (a medicine, drug *etc*) having a soothing or calming effect: *She has to take sedatives to calm her nerves; This medicine will have a sedative effect.*

sedate[2] [si'deit] *vt* (*formal or tech*) to give (a person) a sedative: *After the accident the doctor gave her some pills to sedate her.*

se'dation [-'dei-] *nu* (*formal or tech*) the use of sedatives to calm a patient: *The patient is under sedation.*

sedentary ['sedntəri] *adj* (*formal*: *usu attrib*) (of a job, way of living *etc*) requiring or involving much sitting and little exercise: *He has a sedentary job in a tax office; Now that she's old, she leads a very sedentary life.* **'sedentariness** *nu.*

sediment ['sedimənt] *nu* the material that settles at the bottom of a liquid: *In a bottle of red wine, there is a certain amount of sediment; Her feet sank into the sediment on the river bed.*

,sedi'mentary [-'men-] *adj* **1** (*tech*) (of rocks) formed from layers of sediment: *Limestone is a sedimentary rock.* **2** (*formal*) of or forming sediment.

sedition [sə'diʃən] *nu* (*formal or legal*) (talk or actions intended to encourage) rebellion against the government or those in authority: *His speech was considered to be incitement to sedition; He was arrested on a charge of sedition.*

se'ditious *adj* (*formal or legal*: *usu attrib*) (of a speech, action, person *etc*) encouraging rebellion: *seditious acts.*

seduce [si'dju:s] *vt* **1** to succeed in tempting (a *usu* less experienced person) into having sexual intercourse: *She was seduced at the age of fifteen by an older man.* **2** (*formal*) to persuade or attract (a person) into doing, thinking *etc* (something, *esp* something foolish or wrong): *Politicians try to seduce us into thinking they can solve the country's* *problems*; *She was seduced by the attractions of the big city.*

se'ducer *nc* a person who seduces (*def 1*) another person.

se'duction [-'dʌk-] **1** *nu* the act of seducing or process of being seduced: *the seduction of a young girl by a middle-aged man*; (*fig, formal*): *Television advertising aims at the seduction of our minds through our senses.* **2** *nc* (*formal*) something that tempts or attracts: *the seductions of life in the big city.*

seductive [si'dʌktiv] *adj* tempting, attractive or charming: *her seductive charms*; *a seductive melody*; *Her smile was meant to be seductive.*

sedulous ['sedjuləs, (*Amer*) -dʒu-] *adj* (*very formal*) (of a person or his efforts *etc*) steady, earnest and persistent: *He worked with sedulous concentration.* **'sedulously** *adv.* **'sedulousness** *nu.*

see[1] [si:] – *pt* **saw** [so:]: *ptp* **seen** – (not used with **is, was** *etc* and **-ing** (*defs 1–4, 6, 10*)) **1** *vi* to have the power of sight: *After six years of blindness, he found he could see.* **2** *vti* to (be able to) notice or be aware of (something) by means of the eye: *I can see her in the garden*; *She was seen going out of the house*; *I've never seen a bird like that before*; *Watch him and you'll see how he shoes the horse*; *I saw that the door was open*; *As you see, I'm busy*; *Can you see into the room?*; *I'm too small to see over the fence.* **3** *vt* to have or form a thought or picture of (something) in the mind: *I see many difficulties ahead*; *I can't see her being a good mother.* **4** *vti* to understand: *I don't see what you mean*; *At last she understood, and said 'Oh, I see!'*; *She didn't see the point of the joke*; *I can see that my idea was a bad one*; *I can't see the advantage of doing that*; *As far as I can see, she'll arrive next Friday*; *The way I see it, you are in the wrong.* **5** *vti* to investigate: *I'll go and see what the children are doing*; *'What are their plans?' 'I'll see.'*; *He had been told that the door was locked but wanted to see for himself*; *Leave this here and I'll see what I can do for you.* **6** *vt* to look at: *Did you see that play on television?*; *They went to see the Taj Mahal.* **7** *vt* to meet or consult (a person): *I'll see you at the usual time*; *I'm seeing my doctor tomorrow.* **8** *vt* to accompany (a person) to a place, or watch while they go there: *I'll see you home*; *He saw the children across the road.* **9** *vt* to experience: *He has seen a lot of trouble*; *This spade has seen plenty of use.* **10** *vi* to consider: *Let me see, I think we should turn left here.* **11** *vt* to make certain: *See that he finishes his schoolwork by seven o'clock.* – *See also* **see** *in phrases below.*

'see-through *adj* transparent; allowing a person's body *etc* to be seen through it: *a see-through blouse/night-dress*; *Her blouse was completely see-through.*

(I'll) be 'seeing you (*inf*) goodbye.

'see about *vt fus* to attend to, or deal with (a matter): *I'll see about this tomorrow*; *Will you see about putting the children to bed?*

see fit *see* **fit**[1].

see here! a phrase used, *usu* in anger, when telling a person what he ought (not) to do or have done: *See here! when I ask for tea, I don't expect to be given coffee!*

seeing that since; considering that: *Seeing that he's ill, he's unlikely to come.*

see off *vt usu sep* **1** to accompany (a person starting on a journey) to the airport, railway station *etc* from which he is to leave: *He saw me off at the station.* **2** (*inf*) to chase away: *There were some children stealing my apples but my dog soon saw them off.*

see out *vt oblig sep* **1** to lead or accompany (a person) to the door or exit of a building *etc*: *The maid will see you out.* **2** (*inf*) to last longer than: *These old trees will see us all out.*

see over *vt fus* to visit and inspect (*eg* a house that is for sale): *We'll see over the house on Friday.*

see red *see* **red**.

see things *see* **things**.

see through 1 *vt oblig sep* to give support to (a person, plan *etc*) until the end is reached: *She had a lot of difficulties, but his family saw her through*; *Will this money see you through till the end of the week?*; *I'd like to see the job through.* **2** *vt fus* not to be deceived by (a person, trick *etc*): *We soon saw through him and his little plan.*

'see to *vt fus* to attend to or deal with (someone or something): *I must see to the baby*; *I can't come now – I've got this job to see to.*

'see to it that (*formal*) to ensure or make certain that: *See to it that this never happens again!*

see you later (*inf*) goodbye.

I, we *etc* **will see** I, we *etc* shall wait and consider the matter later: *'May I have a new bicycle?' 'We'll see.'*; *'Did he agree?' 'He says he'll see.'*

you 'see 1 a phrase used when giving an explanation: *I can't meet you tomorrow – I'm going away, you see.* **2** a phrase used to draw attention to the correctness of what one has said: *You see! I told you he would/wouldn't help us.*

See also **unseen**.

see[2] [si:] *nc* the district over which a bishop or archbishop has authority.

seed [si:d] **1** *nc* the (part of) the fruit of a tree, plant *etc* from which a new plant may be grown: *Figs are full of seeds*; *I bought a packet of sunflower seeds.* **2** *nu* a quantity of seeds for sowing *etc*: *We need another bag of grass seed.* **3** *nc* the beginning from which anything grows: *There was already a seed of doubt in her mind.* **4** *nc* (in a sporting competition *etc*) a seeded player: *He is Hungary's No. 3 seed.* **4** *nu* (*liter, esp* in the Bible) children or descendants: *Jacob and his seed.* – **1** *vi* (of a plant) to produce seed: *A plant seeds after it has flowered.* **2** *vt* in golf, tennis *etc*, to arrange (good players) in a competition so that they do not compete against each other till the later rounds.

'seeded *adj* having been seeded (*def 2*): *a seeded player.*

'seedless *adj* having no seeds: *seedless grapes*; *Are these oranges seedless?*

'seedling [-liŋ] *nc* a young plant just grown from a seed: *Don't walk on the lettuce seedlings!*

'seedy *adj* **1** (*inf*) full of seeds: *A pomegranate is a seedy fruit.* **2** (*derog*) shabby: *a rather seedy hotel*; *in a seedy part of town*; *These houses look rather seedy.* **3** (*usu pred*) ill or unhealthy: *He's still looking/feeling a bit seedy.* **'seediness** *nu.*

'seedbed *nc* ground prepared for growing seeds: *The seeds should be sown in a carefully prepared seedbed.*

'seedbox/'seedtray *ncs* a shallow box in which seedlings can be grown.

go to seed 1 (of a person) to become careless about one's clothes and appearance: *Don't let yourself go to seed when you reach middle age!* **2** (of a place) to become rather shabby and uncared for: *This part of town has gone to seed in the past twenty years.*

go/run to seed (of a plant) to produce seeds after

flowering: *The broccoli has gone to seed – we can't use it as a vegetable.*

seek [si:k] – *pt, ptp* **sought** [so:t] – **1** *vti* (*formal: sometimes with* **for**) to try to find, get or achieve: *He sought employment in London: They are seeking (for) a solution to the problem; You should seek your lawyer's advice; She's seeking fame in the world of television; The police are still seeking the men involved in last week's robbery; Seek and you may find!* **2** *vt* (*formal or liter*) to go to: *The cattle sought the shade of the big oak tree; When it started to rain, we sought shelter in the doorway of a shop.* **3** *vt* (*formal*) to try (to do something): *These men are seeking to destroy the government.*

seek out *vt sep* (*formal or liter*) to find by searching: *He sought out all his old friends; There's enough trouble in the world without seeking it out.*

'sought after (*formal*) wanted; asked for: *This book is much sought after; a much sought-after book.*

seem [si:m] *vti* (not used with **is, was** *etc* and **-ing**) to have the appearance or give the impression of being or doing: *A thin person always seems (to be) taller than he really is; She seems kind; He seemed to hesitate for a minute; The clock seems to be wrong; It would seem* (= It seems) *that they have quarrelled; 'He has just fallen in the water.' 'So it seems.'; There seem to be no difficulties to be discussed; I can't seem to please him; I seem not to be able to please him.*

'seeming *adj* (*formal; attrib*) existing in appearance, though not *usu* in reality: *a seeming success; her seeming indifference.*

'seemingly *adv* **1** apparently; according to report: *Seemingly, what happened was that he swerved to avoid a cat.* **2** only in appearance: *He is seemingly very intelligent, but in fact he isn't.*

'seemly *adj* (*old or liter: neg* **un-**) (of behaviour *etc*) suitable, proper or decent: *His show of anger was not at all seemly; seemly conduct.* **'seemliness** *nu.*

seen *see* **see**[1].

seep [si:p] *vi* (of liquids) to flow slowly *eg* through a very small opening: *There was a hole in the boat, and water was seeping in; Blood seeped out through the bandage round his head; (fig) All his confidence seeped away.*

'seepage [-pidʒ] *nu* (*formal or tech*) **1** the act of seeping: *We've lost a lot of liquid through seepage.* **2** fluid that has seeped out: *Put a bucket there to collect the seepage.*

seer [siə] *nc* (*old*) a prophet.

seesaw ['si:so:] *nc* **1** a long flat piece of wood, metal *etc*, balanced on a central support so that one end of it goes up as the other goes down, used as a plaything by children, who sit *usu* in equal numbers at each end: *He fell off the seesaw in the park.* **2** (*usu fig*) an up-and-down, or backwards-and-forwards, motion: (*attrib*) *a seesaw movement; (fig) the seesaw of politics.* – *vi* (*formal*) to move like a seesaw: *The boat seesawed on the crest of the wave;* (*fig*) The values of the dollar and the mark are seesawing wildly on the money market.

seething ['si:ðiŋ] *adj* **1** (*formal: with* **with** *when pred*) very crowded: *Every weekend this beach is a seething mass of people; The beach is seething with people.* **2** (*formal: pred: usu with* **with**) very excited or agitated: *The whole community was seething with excitement/anger.* **3** (*inf pred*) very angry: *He was seething when he left the meeting.*

seethe *vi* (*liter*) (of water *etc*) to surge and foam: *The sea seethed among the rocks.*

segment ['segmənt] *nc* **1** a part or section: *He divided the orange into segments.* **2** (*geom*) a part of *eg* a circle cut off by a straight line. – [seg'ment, (*Amer*) 'segment] *vti* (*geom*) to split into segments: *Draw a line which segments the circle.*

segmented [seg'mentid, (*Amer*) 'segmentid] *adj* divided into segments: *An insect has a segmented body.*

segregate ['segrigeit] *vt* (*formal*) to separate (a person, group *etc*) from others; to keep (people, groups *etc*) apart from each other: *At the swimming-pool, the sexes are segregated; It is that government's policy to segregate black people from white.*

ˌsegre'gation [-ʃən] *nu* (*formal*): *racial segregation.*

seismic ['saizmik] *adj* (*tech: esp attrib*) of earthquakes: *There were a lot of seismic disturbances throughout the world last year.*

'seismograph [-məgra:f] *nc* an instrument that records, and measures the strength of, earthquake shocks.

seis'mology [-'molədʒi] *nu* the science or study of earthquakes. **ˌseismo'logical** [-'lo-] *adj.* **seis'mologist** *nc.*

seize [si:z] **1** *vt* to take or grasp (something) suddenly, *esp* by force: *She seized the gun from him; He seized her hand and dragged her away; He seized her by the arm; The kidnappers seized the child as he was on his way to school; (fig) He seized the opportunity of working in India.* **2** *vt* to take into one's possession, *esp* by force or by law: *The police raided his house and seized quantities of the drug heroin.* **3** *vi* to seize up (*see below*). **4** *vt* (*liter*) (of a feeling, illness *etc*) to overcome (a person): *Fury seized him; She was seized with jealousy.*

'seizure [-ʒə] **1** *nu* the act of seizing (*def 2*): *The arrest of the political prisoners was followed by the seizure of their property.* **2** *nc* (*old*) a sudden attack of illness, *esp* a heart attack: *He has had a seizure and has lost the power of speech.*

'seize on/(*formal*) **upon** *vt fus* to accept (an idea, suggestion *etc*) with enthusiasm: *I suggested a cycling holiday, and he seized on the idea.*

seize up *vi* (of machinery *etc*) to get stuck and stop working: *The car seized up yesterday.*

seldom ['seldəm] *adv* rarely; not often: *I've seldom experienced such rudeness; They seldom, if ever, go out in the evening; She seldom or never writes to us; This happens very seldom.*

select [sə'lekt] *vt* (*more formal than* **choose**) to choose or pick (the person, thing *etc* that is preferred) from among a number: *They selected a diamond engagement ring; She selected a blue dress from the wardrobe; You have been selected to represent us on the committee; Has the cricket team been selected?* – *adj* **1** (*usu attrib*) picked or chosen carefully: *The book is a select collection of poetry from various authors; A select group of their friends was invited to the wedding.* **2** (of a school, club *etc*) intended only for carefully chosen (*usu* rich or upper-class) people: *She belongs to a very select club; He went to a very select school; That school is very select.* – *See also* **select committee** *below.* **se'lectness** *nu.*

se'lection [-ʃən] **1** *nu* the act or process of selecting or being selected: *What is your method of selection in choosing boys for the choir?; (attrib) a selection committee.* **2** *nc* a collection or group of things that have been selected or from which a choice can be made: *a selection of verses/fruit.*

se'lective [-tiv] *adj* having the power of choice and using it, *esp* carefully: *She has plenty of money, so can afford to be selective when buying clothes; She is very selective about clothes.* **se'lectively** *adv.* **se'lectiveness** *nu.*

se'lector *nc* a person who chooses (someone or something, *esp* athletes or a team for a competition *etc*): *The selectors have announced the cricket team to meet Australia.*

select committee *nc* in Britain, a group of Members of Parliament chosen to report and advise on some matter.

self [self] – *pl* **selves** [selvz] – **1** *nc* a person's own body and personality: *We call the good and bad sides of our personality our better and worse selves; All the personal characteristics and qualities that combine to form the self.* **2** *nu* (*formal*) one's own personal interests or advantage: *He always thinks first of self.*

'selfish *adj* (*neg* **un-**: *derog*) thinking of one's own pleasure or good and not considering other people: *a selfish person/attitude; He's very selfish with his money – he gives very little to his wife.* **'selfishly** *adv.* **'selfishness** *nu.*

'selfless *adj* (*formal*) utterly unselfish, and tending to consider the good of others before one's own: *a selfless person/act; As a soldier, he showed selfless devotion to duty.* **'selflessly** *adv.* **'selflessness** *nu.*

self- [self] (*in cmpds*) **1** showing that the person or thing acting is acting upon himself or itself, as in **self-respect**. **2** showing that the thing is acting automatically, as in **self-closing doors**. **3** by oneself, as in **self-imposed, self-made**. **4** in, within *etc* oneself or itself, as in **self-centred, self-contained**.

self-addressed [selfə'drest] *adj* (*usu attrib*) addressed to oneself: *I enclose a stamped, self-addressed envelope for your reply.*

self-appointed [selfə'pointid] *adj* (*usu attrib*) having chosen to do, be *etc* something oneself, not having been chosen or asked by others: *He is the self-appointed judge of the good taste and morality of the plays performed in this town.*

self-assertive [selfə'səːtiv] *adj* (*derog*) too inclined to draw attention to oneself, or to state one's wishes, opinions *etc* too forcefully: *He is usually a very quiet person, but he becomes very self-assertive when he discusses politics; a very self-assertive young woman.* ˌ**self-as'sertion** [-ʃən] ˌ**self-as'sertiveness** *nus.*

self-assurance [selfə'ʃuərəns] *nu* self-confidence. ˌ**self-as'sured** *adj.*

self-centred [self'sentəd] *adj* (*usu derog*) interested only in one's own affairs; selfish: *She's too self-centred to take any interest in my troubles.* ˌ**self-'centredness** *nu.*

self-closing [self'klouziŋ] *adj* which close automatically: *self-closing doors.*

self-coloured, (*Amer*) **self-colored** [self'kʌləd] *adj* of one colour all over: *a self-coloured carpet; Are the curtains self-coloured or patterned?*

self-confessed ['selfkənfest] *adj* (*formal*: *attrib*) fully admitting one's fault: *He's a self-confessed liar/alcoholic.*

self-confidence [self'konfidəns] *nu* belief or trust in one's own powers: *You need plenty of self-confidence to be a good airline pilot.* ˌ**self-'confident** *adj.* ˌ**self-'confidently** *adv.*

self-conscious [self'konʃəs] *adj* too easily becoming shy or embarrassed when in the presence of others: *She'll never be a good teacher – she's too self-conscious.* '**self-'consciously** *adv.* ˌ**self-'consciousness** *nu.*

self-contained [selfkən'teind] *adj* (*Brit*) (of a flat *etc*) complete in itself, not sharing the kitchen, bathroom, front door *etc* with other flats *etc.*

self-control [selfkən'troul] *nu* control of oneself, one's emotions and impulses: *He behaved with admirable self-control although he must have been very angry.*

self-defence, (*Amer*) **self-defense** [selfdi'fens] *nu* defence of one's own body, property *etc* against attack: *He killed his attacker in self-defence.*

self-denial [selfdi'naiəl] *nu* (*formal*) the practice or habit of refusing to satisfy one's own desires *eg* in order to help others: *He should practise a little self-denial in his eating habits; Self-denial will be necessary if we are to pay for the children's education.*

self-drive [self'draiv] *adj* (of a car *etc*) to be driven by the person hiring it.

self-educated [self'edʒukeitid] *adj* educated by one's own efforts: *Livingstone was too poor to go to school, so was largely self-educated; a self-educated man.*

self-effacing [selfi'feisiŋ] *adj* (*formal*) not trying to attract people's notice or attention; modest: *a self-effacing person/personality; She is shy and self-effacing.* ˌ**self-ef'facement** *nu.*

self-employed [selfim'ploid] *adj* working for oneself and not employed by someone else: *A person who works in his own shop is self-employed; a self-employed dressmaker.*

self-esteem [selfi'stiːm] *nu* (*formal*) a person's good opinion of, or respect for, himself: *My self-esteem suffered when I failed the exam.*

self-evident [self'evidənt] *adj* (*formal*) clear enough to need no proof: *The existence of God is not self-evident; It is self-evident that we need food to stay alive.*

self-explanatory [selfik'splanətəri] *adj* needing no explanation: *I think the pictures in the instruction manual are self-explanatory; self-explanatory instructions.*

self-expression [selfik'spreʃən] *nu* the expression of one's own personality and feelings *eg* in art or poetry: *Painting is a form of self-expression.*

self-government [self'gʌvəmənt] *nu* government by the people of the country without outside control.

self-important [selfim'poːtənt] *adj* (*derog*) having too high an opinion of one's own importance; pompous: *What a conceited, self-important little man!; a self-important little man.* ˌ**self-im'portance** *nu.*

self-imposed [selfim'pouzd] *adj* (*formal*: *usu attrib*) (of *eg* a job, task *etc*) imposed by a person on himself: *She doesn't really need to clean the house every day – it's a self-imposed labour.*

self-indulgent [selfin'dʌldʒənt] *adj* (*derog*) too ready to satisfy one's own desires: *These self-indulgent people who sit watching television and eating sweets; self-indulgent habits/behaviour.* ˌ**self-in'dulgence** *nu.*

self-inflicted [selfin'fliktid] *adj* (*formal*) (of wounds *etc*) done to oneself: *The doctors proved that the man's injuries were self-inflicted.*

self-interest [self'intrəst] *nu* (*formal*: *derog*) consideration only for one's own aims and advantages: *He acted out of self-interest.*

selfish, selfless *see* **self**.

self-made [self'meid] *adj* owing wealth or important position to one's efforts, not to advantages given by birth, education *etc*: *He is a self-made man.*

self-opinionated [selfə'pinjəneitid] *adj* (*formal*: *derog*) refusing to believe that one's opinions may be wrong, or to take notice of other people's views: *an obstinate, self-opinionated man.*

self-pity [self'piti] *nu* pity for oneself: *He's so full of self-pity, he can't see anyone else's problems.*

self-portrait [self'po:trit] *nc* a person's portrait or description of himself: *Rembrandt painted several self-portraits*; *The man described in this passage is a self-portrait of the author.*

self-possessed [selfpə'zest] *adj* calm in manner or mind, and able to act confidently in an emergency: *a calm, self-possessed person*; *She is so self-possessed.* ˌ**self-pos'session** [-ʃən] *nu.*

self-preservation ['selfprezə'veiʃən] *nu* (*formal*) the natural inclination towards the protection of oneself from harm, danger *etc*: *Self-preservation is our strongest instinct.*

self-raising [self'reiziŋ] *adj* (of flour) already containing an ingredient to make cakes *etc* rise.

self-reliant [selfri'laiənt] *adj* having or showing confidence in one's own abilities: *She has always depended on her husband for advice, and has never learnt to be self-reliant*; *a very self-reliant young woman.* ˌ**self-re'liance** *nu.*

self-respect [selfri'spekt] *nu* respect for oneself and concern for one's reputation: *Well-known personalities should have more self-respect than to take part in television advertising.* ˌ**self-re'specting** *adj.*

self-righteous [self'raitʃəs] *adj* (*derog*) having too high an opinion of one's own goodness, and intolerant of other people's faults: *'I'm never late for work,' he said in a self-righteous voice.* ˌ**self-'righteously** *adv.* ˌ**self-'righteousness** *nu.*

self-sacrifice [self'sakrifais] *nu* the act of giving up or sacrificing one's own desires, interests *etc* in order to help others: *With great self-sacrifice, she gave up the holiday to care for her sick aunt.* '**self-'sacrificing** *adj.*

selfsame ['selfseim] *adj* (*formal*: *attrib*) the very same: *This doll is the self-same one that I saw in the shop window.*

self-satisfied [self'satisfaid] *adj* (*derog*) too easily pleased with oneself and one's achievements: *'Our house is the cleanest in the row,' she said in her self-satisfied way*; *She always looks so self-satisfied.* '**self-ˌsatis'faction** [-'fakʃən] *nu.*

self-service [self'sə:vis] *nu* the arrangement (*eg* in a shop, restaurant *etc*) by which customers themselves collect the goods that they want to buy. – *adj* (of a shop *etc*) having this arrangement: *Is this petrol-station self-service?*; *a self-service restaurant.*

self-styled ['selfstaild] *adj* (*attrib*: *often derog*) (of a person) using a title or name chosen by himself: *Those self-styled freedom-fighters are nothing but terrorists.*

self-sufficient [selfsə'fiʃənt] *adj* (of a person or country) not dependent on other people, or other countries for help, imports *etc*: *How can such a small island be self-sufficient?*; *a self-sufficient community.* ˌ**self-suf'ficiency** *nu.*

self-supporting [selfsə'po:tiŋ] *adj* (*usu pred*) (of a person, business organization *etc*) having an income that is enough to pay all expenses: *We plan to live abroad as soon as all our children are self-supporting*; *Three years after its establishment, the business was self-supporting.*

self-taught [self'to:t] *adj* (*usu pred*) taught by oneself without help from others: *As a musician, he is completely self-taught.*

self-willed [self'wild] *adj* (*derog*) determined to do, or have, what one wants: *I can't control that child – he's so self-willed*; *a self-willed little brat.*

sell [sel] – *pt, ptp* **sold** [sould] – **1** *vti* to give something in exchange for money: *They sold their pictures to an art dealer*; *Who sold you that car?*; *The house was sold for £20 000*; *He sold it at a profit*; *I'd like to know what the table is worth, although I'm not thinking of selling*; *I've got some books to sell.* **2** *vt* to have or keep (goods) for sale: *The village shop sells postage-stamps*; *Does the farmer sell milk and eggs?* **3** *vi* to be sold: *These apples are selling at 40 pence a kilo*; *The picture sold for £200 000*; *His book sold well*; *The shop stopped stocking those pens because they didn't sell.* **4** *vt* to cause to be sold: *Manufacturers claim that attractive packaging is what sells a product.* **5** *vt* (*inf*) to tell (something *usu* untrue) to (a person) and persuade him to believe it: *He sold me a story/line about how he had lost his money on the train.* **6** *v refl* (*inf*) to present (oneself) in an attractive way *eg* when applying for a job: *He knows how to sell himself.* **7** *vt* (*derog*) to give oneself, one's help *etc* in a bad way or for some bad purpose in return for money: *He was willing to sell his vote* (= vote in a particular way if paid to do so); *She has to sell herself* (= be a prostitute) *to buy food for the children.* – *See also* **sell** *in phrases below.* – *nc* (*inf old*) something that is not as good as it was expected, claimed *etc* to be; a disappointment: *What a sell!*

ˌ**sell-out** *nc* (*inf*) **1** an event, *esp* a concert, for which all the tickets are sold: *His concert was a sell-out.* **2** a betrayal: *The gang realized it was a sell-out and tried to escape.* – *See also* **be sold out, sell out** *below.*

be 'sold on (*inf*) to be enthusiastic about: *I'm sold on the idea of a holiday in Canada.*

be sold out 1 to be no longer available, because all have been sold: *The second-hand records are all sold out.* **2** (*sometimes with* **of**) to have no more (of something) available to be bought: *The concert is sold out*; *We are sold out of children's socks.* – *See also* **sell-out, sell out.**

sell down the river (*inf*) to betray: *The gang found that they had been sold down the river by one of their associates.*

sell off *vt sep* to sell (goods) quickly and cheaply: *They're selling off their old stock.*

sell out 1 *vi, vt sep* (*sometimes with* **of**) to sell all of one's stock or supply of something: *We have sold out of children's socks*; *We sold out our entire stock*; *We had a stock of those plates, but we've sold out.* **2** *vi* to be all sold: *The second-hand records sold out within minutes of the sale starting.* **3** *vi, vt sep* (*inf*: *usu with* **to**) to join or assist (an enemy): *The newspaper published evidence that an important politician had sold out to the enemy.* **4** *vi, vt sep* (*sometimes with* **to**) to sell one's share in a business: *I got tired of filling in complicated tax-forms, so I sold out and went to live in the country.* – *See also* **be sold out, sell-out** *above.*

sell-up *vi, vt sep* to sell a house, business *etc*: *He has sold up his share of the business*; *I'm thinking of selling up and retiring.*

See also **sale.**

Sellotape ® ['selәteip] *nu* (*also no cap*) a type of transparent adhesive tape, used *eg* for sticking pieces of paper together.

selvage, selvedge ['selvidʒ] *nc* (*usu with* **the**) the firm edge of a woven piece of cloth.

selves *see* **self**.

semantic [si'mantik] *adj* (*usu attrib*) of semantics, or of the meaning of words and sentences: *We are going to attempt to make a semantic analysis of this sentence.*

se'mantics *n sing* the science of the meaning of words: *He is studying semantics.*

semaphore ['seməfo:] *nu* a system of signalling with flags held in each hand: *He signalled the message to them in semaphore*; (*attrib*) *a semaphore message.*

semblance ['sembləns] *ncu* (*formal or facet*) an appearance or likeness: *I have to coach them into some semblance of a football team by Saturday*; *There was not even a semblance of cheerfulness in her voice.*

semen ['si:mən] *nu* in the male animal, the fluid containing the sperm: *He is having his semen tested to see if he is infertile.*

semi- [semi] (*in cmpds*) **1** half, as in **semiquaver**. **2** partly, as in **semi-conscious**.

semibreve ['semibri:v] *nc* (*music*) a note of a certain length. – *See also* Appendix 4.

semicircle ['semisə:kl] *nc* a half circle: *The chairs were arranged in a semicircle round the speaker.*

ˌsemi'circular [-'sə:kju-] *adj.*

semicolon [semi'koulən, (*Amer*) 'semikoulən] *nc* the punctuation mark (;) used *esp* to separate parts of a sentence which have more independence than clauses separated by a comma, *esp* ones in a series: *He wondered what to do. He couldn't go back*; *he couldn't borrow money*; *he couldn't even telephone his mother.*

semi-conscious [semi'konʃəs] *adj* partly conscious: *The doctors allowed the police to try to question the semi-conscious man*; *He was semi-conscious when they took him to hospital*; *in a semi-conscious state.* **ˌsemi-'consciousness** *nu.*

ˌsemi-'consciously *adv* without fully thinking or being aware of what one is doing: *He was so interested in the conversation that he was semi-consciously spooning salt into his cup of tea instead of sugar.*

semi-detached [semidi'tatʃt] *adj* (of a house) joined to another house on one side but separate on the other: *He lives in a semi-detached bungalow*; *Their new house is semi-detached.*

semi-final [semi'fainl] *nc* (*often in pl*) a match, round *etc* immediately before the final: *She reached the semi-finals of the competition.*

ˌsemi-'finalist *nc* a person, team *etc* competing in a semi-final: *The four semi-finalists will play their two matches tomorrow.*

seminar ['semina:] *nc* a class at which students and a tutor discuss or study a particular subject: *She is attending a seminar on ancient Greek vases*; *The professor is giving a seminar tomorrow.*

seminary ['seminəri] *nc* **1** a training college for Roman Catholic priests. **2** (*old*) a girls' school: *She went to a young ladies' seminary.*

semi-official [semiə'fiʃəl] *adj* (of announcements *etc*) having some, but not complete, official authority: *He has semi-official approval for his proposed scheme*; *Their engagement is only semi-official – her parents have not yet given their permission.*

semi-precious [semi'preʃəs] *adj* (of a stone) having some value, but not considered a gem: *garnets and other semi-precious stones.*

semiquaver ['semikweivə] *nc* (*music*) a note of a certain length. – *See also* Appendix 4.

semitone ['semitoun] *nc* half a tone in the musical scale: *F sharp is a semitone above F natural.*

semolina [semə'li:nə] *nu* hard particles of wheat sifted from flour and used *eg* in milk pudding: *a packet of semolina*; (*attrib*) *semolina pudding.*

senate ['senət] *nc* **1** a lawmaking body, *esp* the upper house of the parliament in some countries (*eg* Australia or the United States). **2** the governing council in some British universities. **3** (*hist*) in ancient Rome, the chief legislative and administrative body.

'senator *nc* **1** (*with cap, and sometimes abbrev* **Sen.**, *in titles*) a member of a senate (*def 1*): *This is Senator Smith, one of the senators from Ohio.* **2** a member of a senate (*def 3*).

'senate-house *nc* the place where a senate meets.

send [send] – *pt, ptp* **sent** [sent] – *vt* **1** to cause or order (a person) to go, or (a thing) to be carried, to a place or person, without going oneself: *He was sent to the chemist's to collect the medicine*; *The teacher sent the disobedient boy to the headmaster*; *I've sent him back to bed as he was feverish*; *She sent me this book*; *He sent a telegram to his parents.* **2** to cause (someone or something) to move rapidly or with force: *His blow sent me right across the room*; *He sent the ball right into the goal*; (*fig*) *The sudden excitement sent the patient's temperature up*; (*fig*) *The increase in supply has sent the price of coffee down.* **3** to cause (a person or animal) to go into a certain, *usu* bad, state: *The pain sent the dog mad*; *The music seems to send them crazy*; *It sent them into a frenzy*; *The news sent them into a panic.* **4** (*slightly old sl*: *often facet or ironic*) to rouse (a person) to a state of great excitement or emotion: *He sends me.* – *See also* **send** *in phrases below.*

'sender *nc* a person who sends *eg* a letter: *On the envelope was a note*: *'If undelivered, return to sender'.*

send-off, send-up *see* **send off, send up** *below.*

send (someone) about his business *see* **send (someone) packing** *below.*

send away for *vt fus* to order (goods) by post: *I've sent away for some things that I saw in the catalogue.*

send down *vt sep* to expel (a student) from a university.

send (someone or something) flying *see* **fly**[2].

'send for *vt fus* to ask (somebody) to come, or order (goods) to be delivered: *She was very ill, and her son was sent for*; *I've sent for some meat from the butcher's*; *You'll have to send for a plumber to mend that pipe*; *I'll send for a taxi.*

send in *vt sep* to offer or submit (something) *eg* for a competition: *Let's send in our names for the essay competition!*; *He sent in three drawings for the competition*; *Suggestions for the next meeting must be sent in by Friday.*

send off *vt sep* **1** to dispatch (by post): *Have you sent off that letter yet?* **2** to accompany (a person) to the place, or be at the place, where he will start a journey: *A great crowd gathered at the station to send the football team off* (*nc* **'send-off**).

send off for *vt fus* to send away for: *I must send off for that dress I saw advertised in the Sunday newspaper.*

send on *vt sep* **1** to re-address (a letter *etc*) and post it to a person who is not at his usual address: *Do you want your mail sent on while you're on holiday?* 2 to send (*eg* a person, luggage *etc*) ahead, or in advance: *She sent them on to find a hotel while she waited with the luggage*; *She didn't want to carry her heavy cases, so she sent them on ahead of her.*

send out *vt sep* 1 to distribute *eg* by post: *A notice has been sent out to all employees*; *They've already sent out to all employees*; *They've already sent out the invitations to the wedding.* 2 (*eg* of plants) to produce: *This plant has sent out some new shoots.*

send (someone) packing/send (someone) about his business (*inf*) to send (a person) away firmly and without politeness: *He tried to borrow money from me again, but I soon sent him packing.*

send up *vt sep* (*inf*) to ridicule (something), *esp* through satire or parody: *In his latest play, he sends up university teachers*; *Don't send him up – he's easily embarrassed* (*nc* **'send-up**).

senile [(*Brit and Amer*) 'siːnail] *adj* (*formal*) showing the feebleness or childishness of old age: *It is not safe to leave her alone in the house for long as she is becoming senile*; *a senile old woman.* **se'nility** [sə'ni-] *nu.*

senior ['siːnjə] 1 *nc, adj* (a person who is) older in years or higher in rank or authority: *John is senior to me by two years*; *He is two years my senior*; *senior army officers*; *The young doctor consulted his senior about the patient's condition*; *Senior pupils need not wear full school uniform*; *One of the seniors took the sick pupil home.* 2 *adj* (*with cap*: *placed immediately after a name*: *often abbrev* **Snr, Sr** *or* **Sen.** *when written*) used to indicate the father (or *rare* the mother) of a person who has the same name, if both the father and son (or mother and daughter) are alive: *I'm referring to John Jones Senior, not John Jones Junior.*

ˌseni'ority [-ni'o-] *nu* the state of being senior: *The officers sat at the table in order of seniority.*

sensation [sen'seiʃən] 1 (*more formal or tech than* **feeling**) *nu* the ability to feel through the sense of touch: *Cold can cause a loss of sensation in the fingers and toes.* 2 *nc* (*more formal than* **feeling**) a feeling: an effect on the senses: *He had a sensation of floating/faintness.* 3 *nc* a general feeling, or a cause, of excitement or horror: *The news/murder caused a sensation*; *His arrest was the sensation of the week*; *The song/singer became a sensation.* 4 *nu* the causing of such feelings: *There is far too much sensation in political discussion nowadays.*

sen'sational *adj* 1 (*usu attrib*) causing great excitement or horror: *a sensational robbery*; *a sensational piece of news.* 2 (*inf*) very good: *The film was sensational*; *She was wearing an absolutely sensational dress.* 3 (*derog*) intended or intending to create feelings of excitement, horror *etc*: *a sensational novelist/newspaper*; *That magazine is too sensational for me.* **sen'sationally** *adv.*

sen'sationalism *nu* (*derog*) the practice of deliberately trying to excite and shock people: *the sensationalism of the press/television.* **sen'sationalist** *nc.*

sense [sens] 1 *ncu* one of the five powers (hearing, taste, sight, smell, touch) by which a person or animal feels or notices: *Dogs have a better sense of hearing than humans*; *My sister has no sense of smell*; *We learn by means of the senses.* 2 *nu* (*usu with* **a** *or* **my, his, her** *etc*) a feeling (of something): *He has a continual sense of failure*; *Have you no sense of shame/duty/responsibility?*; *He has an exaggerated sense of his own importance.* 3 *nu* (*usu with* **a** *or possessive adjs*) an awareness of, or ability to appreciate or understand, (something): *He has a well-developed musical sense*; *She has no sense of humour*; *I'll never find the right house – I've a poor sense of direction.* 4 *nu* wisdom or good judgement: *Use your sense! You can rely on him – he has plenty of sense*; *There's no sense in waiting any longer*; *Where's the sense in learning Latin?*; *What's the sense of that?* 5 *nc* a meaning: *This word can be used in several senses*; *Do you mean 'funny' in the sense of 'odd'?* 6 *nu* something which can be understood or which is meaningful: *Talk sense! I can't understand you*; *That sentence doesn't make sense* (= cannot be understood); *Why would he say one thing to you and the exact opposite to me? It doesn't make sense!* (= It seems very odd, foolish *etc*); *Can you make sense of her letter?* (= Can you understand or interpret it?) – *vt* (not *usu* used with **is, was** *etc* and **-ing**) to feel, become aware of, or realize: *He sensed her disapproval*; *He sensed that she disapproved.*

'senseless *adj* 1 (*usu pred*) stunned or unconscious: *After the accident he lay senseless for many hours*; *The blow knocked him senseless.* 2 (*usu attrib*) foolish or purposeless: *What a senseless thing to do!*

'senselessly *adv* in a senseless (*esp def 2*) way or state.

'senselessness *nu* the state of being senseless (*esp def 2*).

'senses *n pl* (*usu with* **my, his, her** *etc*) a person's normal, sane or conscious state of mind: *How can he do such a crazy thing? He must be out of his senses!*; *He must have taken leave of his senses* (= become slightly mad); *He was knocked unconscious and when he came to his senses* (= became conscious) *again, he was lying in a hospital bed*; *He is behaving stupidly, but his wife may be able to bring him to his senses* (= make him behave sensibly); *Is he in his right senses?*

'sensory *adj* (*tech: usu attrib*) of, or connected with, a sense: *sensory nerves*; *The eyes, ears and nose are sensory organs.*

in a 'sense in a certain way, or to a certain extent, but not complete: *What you said was right in a sense, but the problem is rather more complex than you seem to think.*

sixth sense an ability to feel or realize something apparently not by means of any of the five senses: *He couldn't hear or see anyone, but a sixth sense told him that he was being followed.*

See also **common sense** *under* **common**.

sensibility [sensi'biləti] *nu* (*formal*) 1 (*sometimes with* **to**) the state of having (too great) a tendency to be affected by pleasant or unpleasant things: *sensibility to praise*; *a man of great sensibility.* 2 an awareness of, or an ability to create, art, literature *etc* which shows very high standards of beauty and good taste: *She is a writer of great sensibility.*

ˌsensi'bilities *n pl* (*formal*) feelings that can be easily affected *esp* in a bad way *eg* offended or hurt by criticism *etc*: *Do try not to offend her sensibilities.*

sensible ['sensəbl] *adj* 1 wise; having or showing good judgement: *She's a sensible, reliable person*; *a sensible suggestion*; *Was it sensible to do that?* 2 (*sometimes derog*) (of clothes *etc*) practical rather than attractive or fashionable: *Bring sensible clothes for camping*; *She wears flat, sensible shoes.* 3

(*old, formal or liter*: *pred with* **of** *or* **to**) aware: *I am sensible of the danger.*

'sensibly *adv* in a sensible way: *He sensibly brought a spare pair of shoes.*

sensitive ['sensitiv] *adj* **1** (*usu with* **to** *when pred*) strongly or easily affected (by something): *A sensitive skin is easily damaged by a cold wind or a hot sun*; *Photographic film is sensitive to light*; *A barometer is sensitive to changes in atmospheric pressure.* **2** (*usu with* **about** *or* **to**) having or showing a tendency to be easily hurt or offended: *He's sensitive about his large nose*; *She is very sensitive to criticism.* **3** (*formal*) having or showing an awareness of, or an ability to produce, artistic beauty and good taste: *a sensitive writer*; *He gave a sensitive performance of the sonata.* **'sensitively** *adv.* **'sensitiveness, ˌsensi'tivity** *nus.* *See also* **insensitive**.

sensory *see* **sense**.

sensual ['sensjuəl] *adj* **1** (*formal*) of the senses and the body rather than the mind: *sensual pleasures*; *The pleasure was purely sensual.* **2** (*often derog*) having, showing, or suggesting a fondness for bodily pleasures, *esp* sexual activity: *He has always been a very sensual person*; *a sensual face*; *His lips are full and sensual.* **'sensually** *adv.* **ˌsensu'ality** [-'a-] *nu.*

sensuous ['sensjuəs] *adj* (*formal*) affecting the senses pleasantly: *I find his music very sensuous*; *Her sculptures have a sensuous quality.* **'sensuously** *adv.* **'sensuousness** *nu.*

sent *see* **send**.

sentence ['sentəns] *nc* **1** (*gram*) a number of words forming a complete statement, question or command: *'I want it', 'Why do you want it?', 'Give it to me!' are sentences.* **2** a punishment imposed by a lawcourt or the judge's announcement of this: *Has the judge delivered the sentence yet?*; *The convicted man was given a sentence of three years' imprisonment*; *He is under sentence of death.* – *vt* (*usu with* **to**) to condemn (a person) to a particular punishment: *He was sentenced to death*; *The judge sentenced him to one year's imprisonment.*

pass sentence (*esp legal*) to sentence (someone): *Have you anything to say before I pass sentence* (*on you*)*?*

sententious [sen'tenʃəs] *adj* (*formal*: *derog*) too full of wise or self-righteous comments: *a sententious person*; *a sententious piece of writing*; *Do not be so sententious.* **sen'tentiously** *adv.* **sen'tentiousness** *nu.*

sentient ['senʃənt] *adj* (*very formal or facet*: *attrib*) that has feeling or consciousness: *a sentient being.*

sentiment ['sentimənt] **1** *nu* (a *usu* excessive show of) tender feeling or emotion: *A wedding is usually an occasion for sentiment and nostalgia*; *His books are too full of sentiment*; *a song full of patriotic sentiment.* **2** *nc* (*often in pl*: *old*: *often facet*) a thought or opinion (expressed in words): *What are your sentiments on this matter?*; *those charming little sentiments that you find printed in birthday cards.*

ˌsenti'mental [-'men-] *adj* **1** (*derog*: *sometimes with* **about**) having, showing or causing too much tender feeling: *a sentimental person*; *a sentimental film about a little boy and a donkey.* **2** of the emotions or feelings: *Although the ring was not expensive, it has sentimental value, as my husband gave it to me.* **ˌsenti'mentally** *adv.* **ˌsentimen'tality** [-'ta-] *nu.*

ˌsenti'mentalism [-'men-] *nu* (*often derog*) (too) great delight in sentiment or sentimentality. **ˌsenti'mentalist** *nc.*

ˌsenti'mentalize, -ise [-'men-] *vti* (*derog*) to be sentimental about (a person, event *etc*), ignoring what is unpleasant or cruel: *This book sentimentalizes war.*

sentinel ['sentinl] *nc* (*liter or old*) a sentry.

sentry ['sentri] *nc* a soldier or other person on guard to stop anyone who has not a right to enter, pass *etc*: *The entrance was guarded by two sentries*; (*attrib*) *He is on sentry duty.*

'sentry-box *nc* a small shelter for a sentry: *There are two sentry-boxes outside Buckingham Palace.*

separate ['sepəreit] **1** *vt* (*sometimes with* **into** *or* **from**) to place, take, keep or force apart: *He separated the tenpence pieces from the fivepence pieces*; *He separated the money into two piles*; *I can't separate the three parts of the tentpole*; *The Atlantic Ocean separates America from Britain*; *A policeman tried to separate the men who were fighting.* **2** *vi* to leave one another and go in different directions: *We all walked along together and separated at the cross-roads.* **3** *vi* (of a husband and wife) to start living apart from each other by choice: *Did you know that John and Jane have separated?* **4** *vi* to come off or apart: *If you boil tomatoes, their skins will separate easily.* – *See also* **separate** *in phrases below.* – [-rət] *adj* **1** divided; not joined: *The house is divided into three separate apartments*; *He sawed the wood into four separate pieces*; *The garage is quite separate from the house.* **2** different or distinct: *If possible, a teenage brother and sister should have separate bedrooms*; *We have two separate problems to consider*; *This happened on two separate occasions*; *I like to keep my job and my home life separate.* **'separateness** *nu.*

'separable *adj* (*formal*: *sometimes with* **from**) that can be separated. **ˌsepara'bility** *nu.*

'separately [-rət-] *adv* in a separate way; not together: *The two sets of books were packed separately*; *She and her husband are living separately.*

'separates [-rəts] *n pl* (*usu* used in shops) garments (*eg* jerseys, skirts, trousers, blouses, shirts) that can be worn together in varying combinations, not being part of *eg* a suit.

ˌsepa'ration 1 *nu* the act of separating or the state or process of being separated: *There is no good reason for the separation of the sexes during the years spent at school*; *She could not bear the thought of separation from her children.* **2** *nc* a period of being separated: *They were together again after a separation of three years.* **3** *ncu* a (legal) arrangement by which a husband and wife remain married but live separately: *They did not want to divorce, but decided on* (*a*) *legal separation.*

'separatist [-rə-] *nc* (*usu derog*) a person who leaves, or urges separation from, an established political state, church *etc.* **'separatism** *nu.*

'separator [-rei-] *nc* a machine for separating, *esp* milk from cream.

separate off *vt sep* to make or keep (a part or parts) separate: *Part of the office is separated off for the use of the manager*; *His room is separated off from the rest of the office.*

separate out *vt sep* to make or keep (things) separate or distinct: *You're confusing two ideas – you should try to separate them out in your mind*; *Try to separate out all the good apples and/from all the bad ones.*

separate up (*often with* **into**) *vt sep* to divide:

The house has been separated up into different flats. *See also* **inseparable**.

sepia ['si:piə] *nu, adj* **1** (of) a brown colour: *a sepia photograph.* **2** (of) a paint of this colour: *He drew the portrait in sepia; a sepia print.*

September [səp'tembə] *n* the ninth month of the year, the month following August: *He is coming in September; He is coming on September 23* (said as 'on September (the) twenty-third' or 'on the twenty-third of September'); *He is coming on the 23rd/twenty-third of September; She died last September.*

septic ['septik] *adj* (of a wound *etc*) full of or caused by germs that are poisoning the blood: *Clean that cut properly in case it goes septic; a septic finger; septic poisoning.*

septic tank *nc* a tank in which sewage is partially purified by the action of bacteria.

See also **antiseptic**.

septuagenarian [septjuədʒi'neəriən, (*Amer*) -tʃuə-] *nc* (*formal*) a person from seventy to seventy-nine years old.

sepulchre, (*Amer*) **sepulcher** ['sepəlkə] *nc* (*arch or liter*) a tomb: *The tomb where the body of Jesus Christ lay is called the Holy Sepulchre.*

se'pulchral [-'pʌl-] *adj* (*formal*) **1** (*usu attrib*) of tombs or burials: *sepulchral monuments.* **2** gloomy or dismal: *a deep, sepulchral voice.*

sequel ['si:kwəl] *nc* (*sometimes with* **to**) **1** a result or consequence: *There was an unpleasant sequel to that incident.* **2** a story that is a continuation of an earlier story: *She wrote a story about a boy called Matthew and has now written a sequel (to it).*

sequence ['si:kwəns] *nc* (*formal*) a series of events, or a set of things, following one another in a particular order: *Where does 'Macbeth' come in the chronological sequence of Shakespeare's plays?; He described the sequence of events leading to his dismissal from the firm; I want you to describe all the events of that morning in sequence* (= in the order in which they happened); *a sequence of numbers; a dance sequence; There is a frightening sequence in the film* (= section of the film) *where the hero is climbing a cliff.*

sequestered [si'kwestəd] *adj* (*liter*) lonely or secluded: *He leads a sequestered life; Their cottage is on a sequestered part of the coast.*

sequin ['si:kwin] *nc* a small, round, shining ornament sewn on a dress *etc*: *Her dress was covered in sequins.*

seraph ['serəf] – *pls* **'seraphim** [-fim], **'seraphs** – *nc* an angel of the highest rank.

se'raphic [-'ra-] *adj* (*formal*) of or like an angel: *The child has a seraphic nature; a seraphic smile; Her smile was seraphic.*

Serbo-Croat *see* Appendix 2.

serenade [serə'neid] *nc* a piece of music (suitable to be) played or sung in the open air at night, *esp* by a lover under a lady's window. – *vt* to entertain (a person) with a serenade: *The girl stood on her balcony and was serenaded by her lover.*

serene [sə'ri:n] *adj* **1** (of a person or his mood *etc*) happy and peaceful: *She's one of those serene people who never seem to get worried or angry; She is calm and serene.* **2** (*liter*) (of weather *etc*) calm: *a serene summer day.* **se'renely** *adv.* **se'reneness, se'renity** [-'re-] *nus.*

serf [sə:f] *nc* (*hist*) a person who was bought and sold with the land on which he worked.

'serfdom *nu* the slave-like condition of a serf.

serge [sə:dʒ] *nu, adj* (of) a type of strong, *usu* woollen, cloth: *The schoolgirls wore tunics of brown serge; brown serge tunics.*

sergeant ['sa:dʒənt] *nc* (*with cap, and often abbrev* **Sgt**, *when written in titles*) **1** in the British army or air force, (a person of) the rank above corporal: *He is a sergeant; He was promoted to sergeant; Sergeant Brown.* **2** (a police officer of) the rank next above constable or patrolman.

ˌsergeant-'major *nc* (*with cap, and often abbrev* **Sgt-Maj.**, *when written in titles*) in the British army, (a person of) the highest rank of non-commissioned officer: *Sergeant-Major Brown.* *See also* Appendix 3.

serial *see* **series**.

series ['siəri:z] – *pl* **'series** – *nc* a number of *usu* similar things done, produced *etc* one after another: *The child's leg was straightened after a series of operations; She made a series of brilliant scientific discoveries; This university has produced a series of fine mathematicians; Are you watching the television series* (= series of television programmes) *on Britain's castles?; This publishing firm is planning a new series of school textbooks.*

'serial [-riəl] *adj* **1** (*usu attrib*) of or in a series: *Banknotes are all printed with a serial number, each note having a different number.* **2** (*attrib*) (of a story *etc*) published or broadcast in parts: *Are you following that new serial story in the magazine?* – *nc* a serial story, play *etc*: *I always listen to the radio serial on Sunday evenings.*

'serialize, -ise [-riə-] *vt* to publish or broadcast (a story *etc*) as a serial: *Several of Charles Dickens's novels have been serialized on television.* **ˌseriali'zation, -s-** *ncu.*

serious ['siəriəs] *adj* **1** grave or solemn; looking as if one is thinking deeply about something: *He's a quiet, serious boy; You're looking very serious; She always has a serious expression.* **2** (*often with* **about**) intending to do what one says one will do; sincere: *Is he serious about wanting to be a doctor?; He wasn't joking. He was quite serious; You must make a serious attempt to improve your work.* **3** intended to make people think and not purely for amusement or entertainment: *He reads very serious books; The play was amusingly written, but its subject was a serious one.* **4** causing worry; likely to have dangerous results: *He has a serious head injury; The situation is becoming serious.* **5** (*usu attrib*) of great artistic or literary merit and *usu* written, composed *etc* in classical (*def 2*) style: *serious literature; He prefers serious music to pop music and dance music.* **'seriousness** *nu.*

'seriously *adv* **1** in a serious way; to a serious extent: *He looked seriously at her; Is he seriously thinking of being an actor?; She is seriously ill.* **2** (as a question) Are you serious?; Do you mean what you say?: *'I'm thinking of getting a new job.' 'Seriously?'*

take (someone or something) seriously 1 to regard (a person or his statement *etc*) as in earnest: *The child took me seriously; You mustn't take his jokes/promises seriously.* **2** to regard (a matter) as a subject for concern or serious thought: *He refuses to take anything seriously.*

sermon ['sə:mən] *nc* a serious talk, *esp* one given in church based on or discussing a passage in the Bible: *The text for this morning's sermon is taken from the fifth chapter of the Gospel according to Saint Matthew.*

serpent ['sə:pənt] *nc* (*old or liter*) a snake.

'serpentine [-tain, (*Amer*) -ti:n] *adj (liter)* winding or full of twists and bends: *a serpentine river.*

serrated [sə'reitid, (*Amer*) 'sereitid] *adj* notched as the edge of a saw is: *The leaves of the elm tree have serrated edges; A bread-knife is often serrated.*

serried ['serid] *adj* (*liter*: *usu attrib*) crowded; set close together: *serried ranks of soldiers.*

serum ['siərəm] (*tech*) **1** *nu* watery fluid from the body, *esp* the fluid that separates from blood when it clots and which helps fight disease. **2** *ncu* such a fluid taken sometimes from a human being, *usu* from an animal, that has been made immune to a disease, and injected into a human being or animal to help him or it to fight the disease or to become immune to it: *Diphtheria vaccine is a serum.*

servant ['sə:vənt] *nc* **1** a person who is hired to work for another, *esp* in helping to run a house: *Only the largest and wealthiest households can afford servants nowadays; The servants' quarters were at the top of the castle.* **2** a person employed by the government, or in the administration of a country *etc*: *a public servant; civil servants.*
See also **serve, service**.

serve [sə:v] **1** *vti* to work for a person *etc eg* as a servant: *He served his master for forty years; (formal) All his life, he has done nothing but serve.* **2** *vti* to distribute portions of food *etc* or supply goods to people: *The manager of the restaurant has trained the waitress to serve (customers) correctly at table; She served the soup to the guests; 'Can we start the meal?' 'Who is going to serve?'; Which shop assistant served you (with these goods)?; Would you like to serve in a shop?* **3** *vti* (*formal*) to be suitable for a purpose: *This box will serve my purpose/needs; Pieces of stone and bone served the Stone Age people for every sort of tool; This upturned bucket will serve as a seat.* **4** *vti* to perform duties, *eg* as a member of the armed forces: *He served (his country) as a soldier for twenty years; He served under Admiral Vernon at the battle of Portobello; I served on the committee for five years.* **5** *vt* to undergo (a prison sentence): *He served (a sentence of) six years for armed robbery.* **6** *vti* in tennis and similar games, to start the play by throwing up the ball *etc* and hitting it *eg* over the net to one's opponent or towards a wall, depending on the game played: *He served the ball into the net; Is it your turn to serve?* **7** *vt* (*legal*: *often with* **on**) to deliver (a warrant, writ *etc*) to the person named on it: *A summons has been served on him to appear in court.* – *nc* the act of serving (*def 6*): *That was an excellent serve.*

'server *nc* **1** (*usu in pl*) a utensil used in serving food *etc*: *a pair of salad servers.* **2** a person who serves (*def 6*).

'serving *nc* (*more formal than* **helping**) a portion of food served to one person for one course of a meal: *I had two servings of pie.*

it ˌserves you *etc* **'right** you *etc* deserve your misfortune *etc*: *He has done no work so it will serve him right if he fails his exam.*

serve an apprenticeship to spend a (fixed) period of time as an apprentice: *Our plumber served his apprenticeship in one of the large plumbing firms in town; (fig) I served my apprenticeship as a teacher in a large grammar school.*

serve out *vt sep* to distribute or give (a portion of food *etc*) to each of a number of people: *She served out the pudding; You haven't served the ice-cream out fairly!*

serve up *vi, vt sep* to start serving (a meal): *Is it time to serve up (the meal)?*

service ['sə:vis] **1** *nu* the process of attending to or serving customers in a hotel, shop *etc*: *At most hotels, a certain percentage is added to the bill for service; (attrib) a service charge; You get very slow service in that shop.* **2** *ncu* (*sometimes formal*) the act of doing something, or something done, for, or to help, a person: *Could you do me a service by collecting my milk from the shop?; He was rewarded for his service to refugees; I'm not ill enough to need the services of a doctor; The local electrician gives (a) prompt service.* – *See also* **be of service** *below.* **3** *nu* the condition or work of a servant: *In the last century, many young women went into service; She had been in service as a kitchen maid; He has given faithful service to the church for many years.* **4** *ncu* a check made of all parts of *eg* a car, machine *etc* to ensure that it is in a good condition: *When did your car last have a service?; Bring your car/electric blanket in for service.* **5** *nc* a regular public supply of something *eg* transport: *There is a good bus/train service into the city; The postal service is very poor here.* **6** *nc* a religious ceremony, *eg* a regular meeting for worship (in church): *He attends a church service every Sunday; the marriage service; What time does the service start?* **7** *nc* in tennis and similar games, the act or manner of serving the ball; a person's turn to serve: *He has a strong service; Is it your service now?* **8** *nc* a department of public or government work: *the Civil Service; the Health Service.* **9** *nc* (*often in pl*) one of the three fighting forces, the army, navy or air force: *Which of the services were you in?; The British navy is called the Senior Service.* **10** *nu* employment in one of these: *A period of military service used to be compulsory for men.* **11** *nc* (*usu in cmpds*) a set of dishes: *a dinner/tea service.* – *vt* to check (a car, machine *etc*) thoroughly to ensure that it works properly: *Have you had your car/washing-machine serviced recently?*

'serviceable *adj* (*neg* **un-**) **1** useful; capable of being used: *This tractor is so old it is barely serviceable now; This isn't exactly what I needed, but I suppose it is serviceable.* **2** designed for a practical purpose rather than for decoration; hard-wearing; that will last long and give good service: *He walks to school every day, so he must have serviceable shoes; Her clothes are always serviceable rather than fashionable.*

'serviceman – *fem* **'servicewoman** – *nc* a person in one of the armed services.

active service *nu* duties performed by members of the armed services in fighting the enemy in wartime: *He was on active service in France.*

'service station *nc* a petrol station with facilities for servicing cars *etc.*

at your, his *etc* **service** (*often facet*) ready to help or be of use: *I'm at your service if you want my help; My bicycle is at your service.*

be of service to (*formal*) to help: *Can I be of service to you?*

do service as (*formal or liter*: *sometimes facet*) to be used as: *He pulled down the piece of newspaper that did service as a curtain.*

have seen good service to have been well used: *This bicycle has seen good service.*

serviette [sə:vi'et] *nc* a table napkin: *a paper serviette.*

servile ['sə:vail] *adj* (*formal derog*) (of a person or his behaviour) obedient or respectful in an excessively or unpleasantly slave-like way; slavish: *servile obedience/flattery*; *He is so servile that she despises him.* '**servilely** *adv.* **ser'vility** [-'vi-] *nu.*

servitude ['səːvitjuːd] *nu* (*formal*) the state of being a slave, or of being forced to work hard for others and being deprived of freedom: *Their lives were spent in servitude*; *penal servitude* (= servitude as punishment for a crime).

session ['seʃən] *nc* **1** a meeting, or period for meetings of a court, council, parliament *etc*: *This was decided by the town council at its last session*; *The judge will give his summing up at tomorrow's court session*; *The autumn session of Parliament begins in October.* **2** a period of time spent on a particular activity: *a filming session.* **3** a university or school year or (*esp Amer or Scottish*) one part of this: the *session 1978-9*; *the summer session.* **4** (*inf*) a discussion or argument: *I had a session with him this morning.*

in 'session (*formal*) (of a court *etc*) meeting: *There must be silence while the court is in session*; *Parliament is not in session during the summer months.*

set [set] – *prp* '**setting**: *pt, ptp* **set** – **1** *vt* (*slightly formal*) to put or place: *She set the tray down on the table*; *She set the fallen chair the right way up.* **2** *vt* to put plates, knives, forks *etc* on (a table) for a meal: *Please would you set the table for me?* **3** *vt* to settle or arrange (a date, limit, price *etc*) for something: *Has the date for the competition been set?*; *I'm setting a limit of three hours on the time you may spend on this essay*; *It's difficult to set a price on a book when you don't know its value.* **4** *vt* to give a person (a task *etc*) to do or (an example *etc*) to follow: *The witch set the prince three tasks*; *The teacher set a test/examination for her pupils*; *Who set this exam/paper?* (= Who chose or prepared the questions?); *He ought to set a better example to his children*; *He should set them a good example*; *He set the pace for the other walkers.* **5** *vt* (*slightly formal*) to cause (people *etc*) to start doing something: *His behaviour set people talking/complaining*; *The sight of him set her heart beating fast.* **6** *vi* (of the sun *etc*) to disappear below the horizon: *It gets cold when the sun sets*; *That star sets very early in summer.* **7** *vi* to become firm or solid: *Has the concrete/jelly set?* **8** *vt* to adjust (a clock or its alarm, or some other instrument) so that it is ready to perform its function: *He set the alarm for 7.00 a.m.*; *Have you set the mousetrap?* **9** *vti* to fix (the hair when wet) in waves or curls: *Is your hairdresser good at setting?*; *I help my wife to set her hair.* **10** *vt* to arrange or fix (something) in the surface of something, *eg* jewels in a ring or other adornment: *Rubies and emeralds were set into the crown*; *A mosaic panel was set into the wall.* **11** *vt* to put (broken bones) into the correct position for healing: *They set his broken arm.* **12** *vt* to arrange the type for the printing of a book *etc*: *This edition has been set in large type*; *Have the printers set the type yet?* **13** *vt* to compose music for (words, a poem *etc*): *Many of Burns's poems were set to music*; *The words have been set to a well-known tune*; *Beethoven set some Scottish songs.* **14** *vt* (*music*) to put at a certain pitch: *The song has been set too high for me.* – *adj* **1** (*usu attrib*) fixed or arranged previously: *There is a set procedure for doing this*; *Are the meals at set times in this hotel?* **2** (*attrib*) (of a speech) written beforehand: *He delivered a set speech.* **3** (*attrib*) (of a purpose *etc*) deliberate: *You said that with the set intention of insulting me.* **4** (*attrib*) stiff; fixed: *He has a grim, set expression on his face*; *He had a set smile on his face* (= He was only pretending to be pleased or amused). **5** not changing or developing: *He has very set ideas.* – *See also* **be set in one's ways** *below.* **6** (*formal*: *pred*: *with* **to**) ready, prepared or intending (to do something): *The Labour Party is set to introduce new tax laws soon.* – *See also* **all set, get set** *below.* **7** (*pred*: *with* **with**) having something set (*def 10*) in it: *She wore a gold ring set with diamonds.* – *nc* **1** a group of things used together or belonging together in some way: *I like your new teaset, particularly the cups*; *a set of carving tools*; *Have you a complete set of (the novels of) Jane Austen?*; *There is a set of rules that you must follow if you're going mountain-climbing.* **2** an apparatus for receiving radio or television signals: *a television/radio set.* **3** a group of people who meet or associate: *the young/academic/musical set*; *He used to be with a very wild/fast set.* **4** the process of fixing a person's hair into waves *etc*: *He charges £4 for a shampoo and set.* **5** an arrangement of scenery for a scene in a play or film: *There was a very impressive set in the final act*; *a film set.* **6** (*formal*: *usu in sing*) the angle or poise of *eg* a person's head: *He admired the delicate set of the child's head.* **7** a group of six or more games in tennis: *She won the first set and lost the next two.*

'**setting** *nc* **1** a background or scene: *The story develops against a Mediterranean setting*; *This castle is the perfect setting for a murder*; *The setting for the play is a Spanish village.* **2** an arrangement of jewels in *eg* a ring or other ornament: *Her ring had three sapphires in an eighteenth-century setting*; *I like old-fashioned settings better than modern ones.* **3** music composed for a poem *etc*: *Who composed this setting?*; *his settings of English folk songs.*

setback *see* **set back** *below.*

set book, text *etc nc* a book *etc* which a student must study as part of his course: *'Macbeth' is one of our set texts this year.*

set phrase *nc* a phrase which always occurs in one form, and which cannot be changed: *'Of no fixed abode' is a set phrase.*

'**set-square** *nc* a triangular instrument with one right angle, used in geometrical drawing *etc.*

'**setting-lotion** *nu* a lotion that is used in setting the hair.

ˌ**set-'to** *nc* (*inf*) an argument or fight: *There was a set-to between two of the office staff.*

'**set-up** *nc* (*inf*) an arrangement; the way in which something is organized: *There are several families living together in that house – it's a funny set-up.* – *See also* **set up** *below.*

all set (*often with* **to**) ready or prepared (to do something); just on the point (of doing something): *We were all set to leave when the phone rang*; *Are we all set? Let's go, then!*

be/become set in one's ways to be unwilling to change one's habits, routine *etc*: *The firm is rather old-fashioned because the managing director is very set in his ways.*

be 'set on/(*formal*) **upon** to want (to do something) very much; to be determined (to do something): *He was set on going to university.*

get 'set (*usu in imperative*) (of runners in a race) to get ready to start running: *Get ready! Get set! Go!*

set about *vt fus* **1** to begin: *She set about planning her holiday*; *How will you set about this task?* **2** (*formal*) to attack: *When I refused to give him money, he set about me with a stick.*

set (someone) against (someone) (*formal*) to cause (a person) to dislike (another person): *She set the children against their father.*

set (something) alight *see* **alight**[2].

set apart *vt sep* (*formal*: *usu with* **from**) **1** to place separately: *Their house was set apart from the others in the street.* **2** to cause (a person or thing) to be or seem different: *His academic brilliance set him apart from the other children.*

set aside *vt sep* **1** to keep (something) for a special use or purpose: *He set aside some cash for use at the weekend.* **2** (*formal*) to reject: *I warned them not to do it, but my objections were set aside.*

set back *vt usu sep* **1** to delay the progress of: *His illness set him back a bit at school* (*nc* **'setback**). **2** (*inf*) to cause (a person) a lot of expense: *The new carpet must have set you back a few pounds.* **3** (*sometimes with* **from**) to put (something) at a slight distance from something: *The house was set back from the road and partly hidden by trees.*

set down *vt sep* **1** (of a bus *etc*) to stop and let (passengers) out: *The bus set us down outside the post-office.* **2** to write: *He tried to write his essay, but found it difficult to set his thoughts down.*

set eyes on *see* **lay eyes on** *under* **eye**.

set 'fire/'light to (something) *see* **fire, light**.

set forth (*old*: *formal or liter*) **1** *vi* to start a journey: *What time did he set forth?* **2** *vt sep* to exhibit or explain: *The goods were set forth for display*; *His opinions are clearly set forth in this document.*

set free *see* **free**.

set one's heart on *see* **heart**.

set in *vi* (of weather, seasons, feelings *etc*) to begin or become established: *Winter has set in early*; *Boredom soon set in among the children.*

set someone's mind at rest *see* **rest**.

set off **1** *vi* (*sometimes with* **on**) to start a journey: *We set off to go to the beach*; *We set off on our journey.* **2** *vt usu sep* (*slightly inf*) to cause (someone or something) to start doing something: *She had almost stopped crying, but his harsh words set her off again.* **3** *vt sep* to make (something) more beautiful; to look well with (something): *The frame sets off the picture well.* **4** *vt sep* to explode (bombs *etc*) or ignite (fireworks *etc*): *You should let your father set off all the fireworks.*

set on *see* **set upon** *below*.

set (something or someone) on (someone) to cause (*eg* dogs) to attack (a person): *He set his dogs/men on me.*

set (something) on fire *see* **fire**.

set (oneself) to do something to try to do something in a determined way: *He set himself to discover the truth.*

set out **1** *vi* to start a journey: *He set out to explore the countryside*; *When are we setting out on our trip?* **2** *vi* to intend: *I didn't set out to prove him wrong.* **3** *vt sep* to exhibit, display or explain: *The goods are set out in the shop window*; *He always sets his ideas out very clearly.*

set sail, set the scene, set someone's teeth on edge *see* **sail, scene, edge**.

set to *vi* to start to do something (vigorously): *They set to, and finished the work the same day.*

set a trap *see* **trap**.

set up **1** *vt sep* (*less formal than* **establish**) to establish: *When was the organization set up?*; *A committee of inquiry has been set up.* **2** *vi, vt usu sep* to (help a person to) start working in a business *etc*: *He set (himself) up as a bookseller*; *His father set him up in business.* **3** *vt sep* to arrange or construct: *He set up the apparatus for the experiment*; *The type for the book is being set up.* **4** *vt oblig sep* (*slightly inf*) to improve the health or spirits of (a person): *The holiday has really set us up again.*

set up camp to erect tents *etc*: *They set up camp in a field.*

set up house to establish one's own home: *He'll soon be earning enough to set up house on his own.*

set up shop to start a shop: *He set up shop as a chemist*; (*fig*) *She set up shop as a singing teacher.*

'set upon *vt fus* (*also* **'set on**: *usu in passive*: *formal*) to attack: *He set upon me in the dark*; *He was set upon by thieves.*

set(t) [set] *nc* a block of stone used in street paving.

settee [se'ti:] *nc* a sofa.

setter ['setə] *nc* any of several breeds of dog that can be trained to point with the head towards game.

settle ['setl] **1** *vt* to place (someone or oneself) in a position of rest or comfort: *He settled his mother in a corner of the train compartment*; *I settled myself in the armchair.* **2** *vi* to come to (a position of) rest: *The robin flew down and settled on the fence*; *She blew away the dust that had settled on the book.* **3** *vti* to soothe; to make or become quiet and calm: *I gave him a pill to settle his stomach/nerves*; *After a week of storms, the weather settled.* **4** *vti* to go and live (in a particular place) *eg* as a colonist: (*formal*) *What parts of Canada did the French settle?*; *Many Scots settled in New Zealand*; *When did you settle in New York?* **5** *vt* (*sometimes with* **with**) to reach a decision or agreement about (something): *Until we know the full value of the picture, we can't settle the price*; *My parents are relieved that my future has at last been settled*; *Have you settled with the builders when they are to start work?*; *The dispute between management and employees is still not settled.* **6** *vt* to pay (a bill): *We still have that electricity bill to settle.*

'settlement **1** *nu* the act of settling (a dispute *etc*): *At present there is no hope of settlement in this dispute.* **2** *nc* an agreement: *The two sides have at last reached a settlement.* **3** *nu* the process of colonizing a land *etc*: *When did the settlement of Carolina begin?* **4** *nc* a small community: *There was an Iron Age settlement on top of this hill.* **5** *nc* a colony or group of colonists: *Trading took place between the settlement and the native population.* **6** *nc* (*formal or legal*) money *etc* given to a person for his use: *She received a settlement when she got married.* – *See also* **settle (something) on (someone)** *below*.

'settler *nc* a person who settles in a country that is being newly populated: *They were among the early settlers on the east coast of America.*

settle down **1** *vi, vt sep* to (cause to) become quiet, calm and peaceful: *He waited for the audience to settle down before he spoke*; *Settle down, children!*; *She settled the baby down at last.* **2** *vi, v refl sep* to make oneself comfortable: *She settled (herself) down in the back of the car and went to sleep.* **3** *vi* to begin to concentrate on something, *eg* work: *He settled down to (do) his schoolwork.* **4** *vi* to (begin to) work, live *etc* in a quiet, calm *etc* way: *He is settling down well in his new school/job*; *Isn't it time you got married and settled down?*

'settle for *vt fus* to accept (something that is not completely satisfactory): *We wanted two single* *rooms at the hotel, but had to settle for a room with two beds instead.*

settle in *vi* to arrange possessions *etc* satisfactorily after moving into a new house; to become used to one's new surroundings when starting a new job *etc*: *We move house on Friday, but we'll take another week to settle in.*

'settle on *vt fus* to agree about or decide (something): *They at last settled on a plan after much arguing.*

'settle (something) on (somebody) (*formal or legal*) to give (money, property *etc*) to (a person) for his use: *He settled £2 000 a year on his daughter.* – *See also* **settlement** (*def 6*).

settle up *vi* to pay (a bill): *He asked the waiter for the bill, and settled up.*

settle up with *vt fus* to pay money owed to (somebody): *We shall have to settle up with the travel agent tomorrow.*

'settle with *vt fus* **1** to do something unpleasant to (someone who has done wrong to one): *He has told everyone I'm a liar and a cheat – I'll settle with him later!* **2** to settle up with.

See also **unsettle**.

seven ['sevn] **1** *nc* the number or figure 7. **2** *nu* the age of 7. – *adj* **1** (*usu attrib*) 7 in number. **2** (*pred*) aged 7. – *See* **eight** *for constructions.*

seven- (*in cmpds*) having seven (of something): *a ˌseven-sided 'figure.*

'seventh 1 *nc* one of seven equal parts. **2** *nc, adj* (the) last of seven (people, things *etc*); (the) next after the sixth. – *See* **eighth** *under* **eight** *for constructions.*

'seven-year-old *nc* a person or animal that is seven years old. – *adj* (*attrib*) (of a person, animal or thing) that is seven years old. – *See* **eight-year-old** *under* **eight** *for constructions.*

at sixes and sevens *see* **six**.

See also Appendix 1.

seventeen [sevn'tiːn] **1** *nc* the number or figure 17. **2** *nu* the age of 17. – *adj* **1** (*attrib*) 17 in number. **2** (*pred*) aged 17. – *See* **eighteen** *for constructions.*

seventeen- (*in cmpds*) having seventeen (of something): *a ˌseventeen-page re'port.*

ˌseven'teenth 1 *nc* one of seventeen equal parts. **2** *nc, adj* (the) last of seventeen (people, things *etc*); (the) next after the sixteenth. – *See* **eighteenth** *under* **eighteen** *for constructions.*

ˌseven'teen-year-old *nc* a person or animal that is seventeen years old. – *adj* (*attrib*) (of a person, animal or thing) that is seventeen years old. – *See* **eighteen-year-old** *under* **eighteen** *for constructions.*

See also Appendix 1.

seventy ['sevnti] **1** *nc* the number or figure 70. **2** *nu* the age of 70. – *adj* **1** (*attrib*) 70 in number. **2** (*pred*) aged 70. – *See* **eighty** *for constructions.*

seventy- (*in cmpds*) having seventy (of something): *a ˌseventy-year 'lease.*

'seventies *n pl* **1** the period of time between a person's seventieth and eightieth birthdays. **2** the range of temperatures between seventy and eighty degrees. **3** the period of time between the seventieth and eightieth years of a century. – *See* **eighties** *under* **eighty** *for constructions.*

'seventieth 1 *nc* one of seventy equal parts. **2** *nc, adj* (the) last of seventy (people, things *etc*); (the) next after the sixty-ninth. – *See* **eightieth** *under* **eighty** *for constructions.*

'seventy-year-old *nc* a person or animal that is seventy years old. – *adj* (*attrib*) (of a person, animal or thing) that is seventy years old. – *See* **eighty-year-old** *under* **eighty** *for constructions.* *See also* Appendix 1.

sever ['sevə] (*formal*) *vt* **1** to put an end to (communication, friendship *etc*): *After the quarrel, he completely severed his relations with his family.* **2** to cut or break off: *His arm was severed (from his body) in the accident.*

'severance *nu* (*formal*) the act of severing or state of being severed: *The disagreement led to the severance of his connections with the firm.*

several ['sevrəl] *adj* (*usu attrib*) **1** more than one or two, but not a great many: *Several weeks passed before he got a reply to his letter.* **2** (*formal*) different; separate: *The boys went their several ways.* – *pron* some or a few: *Several of them are ill; When I opened the box of eggs, I found that several were broken.*

'severally *adv* (*old or formal*) separately or singly: *All the problems must be severally considered before we can make a decision.*

severe [sə'viə] *adj* **1** (*formal*) (of something bad or unpleasant) serious; extreme: *severe shortages of food; He had a severe illness at the age of twelve; His headache must be quite severe, or else he wouldn't have complained about it; Our team suffered a severe defeat.* **2** strict or harsh: *a severe mother; severe criticism; That punishment was rather severe, wasn't it?* **3** (*formal*) (of the weather *etc*) very cold, stormy *etc*: *Severe weather conditions hindered the rescuers.* **4** (of style in dress *etc*) very plain and without decoration, ornament *etc*: *She has a severe hairstyle; That dress looks rather severe on you.*

se'verely *adv*: *He was severely ill; She was severely punished; a severely-dressed old lady.*

se'verity [-'ve-] *nu* (*often formal*): *The school is well known for its discipline and severity; the severity of the punishment; the severity of the weather; I don't like the severity of his style of painting; the severity of her dress.*

sew [sou] – *pt* **sewed**; *ptp* **sewn** – *vti* to make, stitch or attach with thread, *eg* by means of a needle: *She is busy sewing a shirt; This material is difficult to sew; She sewed the two pieces together; Can you sew?; Have you sewn my button on yet?*

'sewer *nc* a person who sews: *She's a good sewer.*

'sewing *nu* **1** the skill or activity of sewing: *I was taught sewing at school;* (*attrib*) *sewing lessons.* **2** clothes *etc* that are being, or have to be, sewn: *She sat down with a pile of sewing.*

'sewing-machine *nc* a machine for sewing: *She makes all her clothes on an old-fashioned sewing-machine.*

sew up *vt sep* to fasten completely or mend by sewing: *I've cut out the dress, but I haven't sewn it up yet; I must sew up this hole in my skirt; The surgeon sewed up the wound.*

sewn up (*inf*) completely settled or arranged: *Is the agreement all sewn up?; We've definitely got the contract – it's all sewn up.*

sewer[1] ['sjuə] *nc* an underground pipe or channel for carrying water and waste matter from the drains of buildings and streets for disposal or treatment.

'sewage [-idʒ] *nu* waste matter (carried away in sewers): *How do they deal with sewage at their cottage?;* (*attrib*) *He's an expert on sewage disposal.*

'sewerage [-ridʒ] *nu* the system of sewers in a town *etc.*

'**sewage farm** *nc* a place where sewage is treated and disposed of.

sewer[2] *see* **sew**.

sex [seks] **1** *nc* either of the two classes (male and female) into which human beings and animals are divided according to the part they play in producing children or young: *the male/female sex*; *What sex is the baby/dog?*; *Why should the sexes learn different subjects at school?*; *It is illegal to refuse a job to a woman on the grounds of her sex.* **2** *nu* the fact of belonging to either of these two groups: *It is illegal to discriminate on the grounds of sex*; (*attrib*) *sex discrimination.* **3** *nu* sexual activities and relationships *usu* between males and females: *He thinks about nothing but sex*; *Is there a lot of sex in that book?*; *She thinks that there is too much sex and violence in television plays.* **4** *nu* (*inf*) sexual intercourse: *Sex between unmarried people is often condemned as immoral*; *Her mother does not know that she is having sex with her boyfriend.*

-sexed (*in cmpds*) having sexual feelings to a stated extent: *She's a highly-sexed young woman*; *I'm sure that dog is oversexed* (= has too strong sexual feelings); *Do you think he's undersexed?*

'**sexist** *nc, adj* (*often derog*) (a person) showing contempt for the other sex: *sexist attitudes*; *That was a very sexist remark*; *It is sexist to say that women should not work*; *He is a sexist.*

'**sexless** *adj* **1** (*tech*) neither male nor female. **2** (*derog*) not sexually interesting or attractive: *She's one of those rather sexless women*; *I find him a bit sexless.*

sexual ['sekʃuəl] *adj* **1** (*attrib*) concerned with the production of young or children: *the sexual organs.* **2** of sex (*def 3*): *sexual activity*; *sexual enjoyment*; *Their relationship is purely sexual – they have no deep love for one another.* '**sexually** *adv.*

'**sexy** *adj* (*inf*) **1** sexually attractive: *I think she's very sexy*; *a sexy dress.* **2** concerned with sex (*defs 3, 4*): *a sexy film*; *His latest novel is very sexy.*

'**sex appeal** *nu* the quality of being attractive to people of the other sex: *That actress has sex appeal.*

sexual intercourse *nu* the activity between a man and woman which involves the insertion of the man's penis into the woman's vagina: *He says that he cannot be the father of her child because he has never had sexual intercourse with her.*

See also **asexual**.

sexagenerian [seksədʒi'neəriən] *nc* (*formal*) a person from sixty to sixty-nine years old.

sextant ['sekstənt] *nc* an instrument used in ships *etc* for calculating the position of the ship *etc* by means of measuring *eg* the height of the sun above the horizon.

sextet [seks'tet] *nc* **1** a group of six singers or musicians: *She plays the oboe and is a member of a wind sextet.* **2** a piece of music composed for such a group: *String sextets are usually written for two violins, two violas and two cellos.*

sexton ['sekstən] *nc* in certain church denominations, a person who looks after a church and often has various other responsibilities, *eg* bellringing, gravedigging *etc.*

shabby ['ʃabi] *adj* **1** (of clothes *etc*) looking old and worn; not smart and fresh: *shabby curtains*; *He always wears such shabby clothes*; *This sunshine makes the room look very shabby.* **2** (of people) wearing old or dirty clothes: *a shabby old man*; *He used to be so smart but he looks shabby now.* **3** (*formal fig*) (of behaviour) unworthy or mean: *That was a shabby thing to do*; *I think his behaviour was rather shabby.* '**shabbily** *adv.* '**shabbiness** *nu.*

shack [ʃak] *nu* (*often derog*) a roughly-built hut: *a wooden shack*; *They don't really have a holiday cottage – it's just a shack.*

shack up together *vi* (*sl*) (of *eg* a man and woman not married to each other) to live together: *They couldn't afford a wedding so they just shacked up together.*

shack up with *vt fus* (*sl*) to live with (someone one is not married to): *He has been shacking up with his secretary for years.*

shackles ['ʃaklz] *n pl* a pair of iron rings joined by a chain that are put on a prisoner's wrists, ankles *etc*, to limit movement: *His captors put shackles on him*; (*fig*) *Early Christian missionaries thought they were freeing native populations from the shackles of ignorance and superstititon.*

'**shackle** *vt* to put shackles on (a prisoner *etc*): *He was shackled to* (= attached by shackles to) *the bedpost*; (*fig*) *We are so shackled by the rules of politeness that we cannot walk away from a person who will not stop talking to us.*

shade [ʃeid] **1** *nu* slight darkness caused by the blocking of some light: *The group of trees provided some shade from the sun*; *I prefer to sit in the shade rather than the sun.* **2** *nu* the dark parts of a picture: *A portrait looks lifeless with no light and shade.* **3** *nc* (*usu in cmpds*) something that screens or shelters someone or something from light or heat: *She was holding a large sunshade over her head*; *Some spectators at the cricket match were wearing eye-shades*; *It's time we bought a (lamp)shade for that electric light.* **4** *nc* a variety of a colour; a slight difference: *Her dress was a pretty shade of green*; *There are an amazing number of different shades of white*; *The word 'peculiar' has several shades of meaning.* **5** *nc* a slight amount: *The weather is a shade better today.* **6** *nc* (*myth*: *liter*) a ghost, *esp* one in the underworld: *He visited the underworld and met the shades of many heroes.* – **1** *vt* (*sometimes with* **from**) to shelter (someone or something) from light or heat: *He put up his hand to shade his eyes*; *These plants don't like much sunshine, so I'm growing bushes here to shade them (from the sun).* **2** *vti* to make (*eg* parts of a picture) darker: *When drawing a landscape you should shade the foreground most heavily.* – *See also* **shade in** *below.* **3** *vi* (*with* **into**) to change very gradually *eg* from one colour to another: *The sky was a deep blue in the east, shading into yellow, then red, towards the west.* **4** *vt* to put a shade (*def 3*) round: *He put his hands over his eyes to shade them from the bright sunlight.*

shades *n pl* (*sl*: *esp Amer*) sunglasses.

'**shading** *nu* (in a picture *etc*) the marking that shows the darker parts: *Very fine shading can be used in a portrait instead of lines to show the shape of the features.*

'**shady** *adj* **1** sheltered or giving shelter from heat or light: *a shady tree*; *This corner of the garden is pleasantly shady.* **2** (*inf derog*) dishonest: *He's a rather shady person*; *The whole business was rather shady.* '**shadiness** *nu.*

put (someone or something) in the shade to cause (a person, a piece of work *etc*) to seem unimportant: *His piano-playing puts me and my playing in the shade*; *She is so beautiful that she puts her sister in the shade.*

shade in *vt sep* to mark the dark parts of (a picture *etc*): *I've done the outlines of the drawing,* *but I haven't yet shaded it in.*

'shades of (someone or something)! that reminds me of (a particular person or thing)!: *Shades of school! We were all treated at the conference as if we were children.*

shadow ['ʃadou] **1** *ncu* (a patch of) shade on the ground *etc* caused by an object blocking the light (*eg* of the sun): *Shadows lengthen in the evening; By 6.00 p.m. this part of the garden is in shadow; We are in the shadow of that building;* (*fig*) *We were all so happy till the shadow of his illness fell across our lives.* **2** *nu, nc* (*in pl with* **the**) darkness or partial darkness caused by lack of (direct) light: *In many of Vermeer's paintings of people, the light comes from the left, so that the right side of their faces is in shadow; The child was afraid that wild animals were lurking in the shadows at the corner of his bedroom.* **3** *nc* a dark patch or area: *You look tired – there are shadows under your eyes.* **4** *nc* (*no pl*) a very slight amount: *There's not a shadow of doubt that he stole the money; Is there a shadow of a suspicion that she has been lying?* **5** *nc* a very close companion or over-obedient follower: *I want a friend, not a shadow!; The child is his mother's shadow.* – *vt* **1** to hide or darken (something) with shadow: *A broad hat shadowed her face.* **2** (*inf*) to follow (a person) closely, *esp* as a detective, spy *etc*: *We shadowed him for a week.*

'shadowy *adj* (*formal*) **1** full of shadows: *in the shadowy corners of the shop; The inside of the cave was shadowy and mysterious.* **2** dark and indistinct: *A shadowy figure went past in the darkness.* **'shadowiness** *nu.*

Shadow Cabinet *nc* in Britain, the leaders of the opposition in parliament, each chosen to take a particular office when there is a change of government.

worn to a shadow made thin and weary through *eg* hard work: *She was worn to a shadow after months of nursing her sick husband.*

shaft [ʃa:ft] *nc* **1** the long straight part or handle of a tool, weapon *etc*: *the shaft of a golf-club.* **2** one of two poles on a cart *etc* to which a horse is harnessed: *The horse stood patiently between the shafts.* **3** (*often in cmpds*) a long revolving bar transmitting motion in an engine: *the crankshaft; the driving-shaft.* **4** (*often in cmpds*) a long, narrow space, sloping or vertical, made for *eg* a lift in a building *etc* or to provide entry to a mine *etc*: *a liftshaft; a mineshaft.* **5** a ray or beam of light *etc*: *A shaft of sunlight brightened the room.* **6** (*liter*) an arrow: *He was wounded by an enemy shaft;* (*fig*) *a victim of the shafts of love.* **7** (*tech*) the main vertical part of a column, pillar *etc*: *The shaft of the pillar developed a crack.*

shaggy ['ʃagi] *adj* (covered with hair, fur *etc* that is) rough and untidy in appearance: *The dog had a shaggy coat; a shaggy dog; You must get your hair cut – it's looking rather shaggy.* **'shaggily** *adv.* **'shagginess** *nu.*

shake [ʃeik] – *pt* **shook** [ʃuk]: *ptp* **shaken** – **1** *vti* to (cause to) tremble or move with jerks from side to side, up and down, backwards and forwards: *Shake the medicine bottle before use; In his anger, he grabbed the child and shook him violently; The dog shook itself; The explosion shook the building; It shook the picture off the wall; Every time a lorry passes, this house shakes; We were shaking with laughter/fear; Her voice shook as she told me the sad news.* **2** *vt* to shock, disturb or weaken: *I was very shaken by the news; I used to think he was reliable, but my confidence in him has been shaken;* (*facet*) *That shook you!* (= That surprised you, didn't it!). – *nc* **1** an act of shaking: *He gave the bottle a shake; He gave the child a shake.* **2** (*usu in cmpds*) a drink made by shaking or stirring the ingredients together vigorously: *a chocolate milk-shake; an ice-cream shake.*

'shaker *nc* an instrument for shaking or mixing: *a cocktail shaker.*

'shaking *nc* an act of shaking or state of being shaken, shocked *etc*: *They got a terrible shaking in the car crash.*

'shaky *adj* (*often inf*) **1** weak or trembling with age, illness *etc*: *He's getting rather shaky nowadays; a shaky voice; shaky handwriting.* **2** unsteady or likely to collapse: *Don't sit on that chair! It's rather shaky.* **3** (*sometimes with* **at** *when pred*) not very good, accurate *etc*: *He's a bit shaky at arithmetic; My arithmetic has always been very shaky; I'd be grateful if you would correct my rather shaky spelling.* **'shakily** *adv.* **'shakiness** *nu.*

'shakedown *nc* (*inf*) a temporary or makeshift bed, made *eg* of cushions and blankets on the floor.

'shake-up *nc* (*inf*) a disturbance or reorganization: *a political shake-up.* – *See also* **shake up** *below.*

in a couple of shakes (*slightly old*) very soon: *I'll be back in a couple of shakes.*

no great shakes (*inf*) not very good or important: *He has written a book, but it's no great shakes.*

shake one's fist at (someone) to hold up one's fist as though threatening to punch (a person): *He shook his fist at me when I drove into the back of his car.*

shake hands *see* **hand**.

shake one's head to move one's head round to left and right to mean 'No': *'Are you coming?' I asked. She shook her head.*

shake off *vt sep* to rid oneself of (something unwanted): *By running very hard he managed to shake off his pursuers; He soon shook off the illness.*

shake out *vt sep* to cause to spread or unfold by shaking: *She shook out the dress and hung it up after she removed it from the suitcase.*

shake up *vt sep* (*inf*) to disturb or rouse (people) so as to make them more energetic: *The new headmistress will shake the school up.* – *See also* **shake-up** *above.*

shale [ʃeil] *nu* a type of rock from which oil is sometimes obtained.

shall [ʃəl, ʃal] – *neg short form* **shan't** [ʃa:nt] – *modal aux* **1** (*esp Brit*) used to form future tenses of other verbs when the subject is **I** or **we**: *I shall be glad when this work is finished; We shall be leaving tomorrow; Shall we see you next week?* **2** used to show the speaker's intention or willingness that something should happen: *I shan't be late tonight; He shall have a bicycle if he passes his exam; I'm determined that they shall never do that again.* **3** used in questions with **I** and **we**, also (*formal*) with **you, he, she, it** and **they** when asking what to do, or about a decision *etc*: *Shall I* (= Ought I to) *tell him, or shan't I?; Shall we* (= Let's!) *go now?; Shall you* (= Have you decided to) *dismiss the man?* **4** (*formal*) used, *esp* in laws, rules *etc*, as a form of command or to insist that something be done: *You shall go if I say you must; We have decided that you shall stay; House-owners shall keep their gardens in a neat and orderly state.*

ˈ**shall have 1** used to refer to something which will be completed by some time in the future, when the subject of the verb is **I** or **we**: *I shall have finished this by tomorrow.* 2 (*formal*) used, *esp* in laws *etc*, as a form of command or to insist that something be done by some time in the future: *All foreign residents shall have reported to the nearest police station by September 30.*

See also **should, will, would**.

shallot [ʃəˈlot] *nc* a kind of onion: *I'm going to make a sauce with shallots and red wine.*

shallow [ˈʃalou] *adj* **1** not deep: *shallow water*; *a shallow pit*; *That dish is too shallow to serve soup in.* **2** (*derog*) (of a person, his mind *etc*) showing no ability to think seriously or feel deeply: *She has a rather shallow personality*; *I've read some of his books – they're very shallow.* – *vi* (*formal or tech*) (of water) to become shallow: *The channel shallows just here.* ˈ**shallowness** *nu.*

ˈ**shallows** *n pl* a place where the water is shallow: *There are dangerous rocks and shallows near the island.*

sham [ʃam] (*derog*) **1** *nc* something that is pretended, not genuine: *The whole trial was a sham.* **2** *nu* the act or state of pretending: *I'm tired of all this sham – why don't you say what you really think?* – *adj* (*derog*) pretended, artificial or false: *a sham fight*; *Are those diamonds real or sham?* – *v* – *pt, ptp* **shammed** – *vti* (*sometimes derog*) to pretend (to be in some state): *He shammed sleep/anger*; *He shammed dead*; *I think she's only shamming.*

shamble [ˈʃambl] *vi* (*often with* **along, away, past** *etc*) to walk slowly and awkwardly, (as if) not lifting one's feet properly off the ground: *The old man shambled wearily along the street*; *He shambled off.*

shambles [ˈʃamblz] *n sing* (*inf*) a confused mess; (something in) a state of disorder: *His room was a shambles*; *The organization of this office is a complete shambles*; *The meeting was a total shambles*; *We have just moved into our new house, so we're in a bit of a shambles at the moment.*

shame [ʃeim] **1** *nu* (*often with* **at**) an unpleasant feeling caused by awareness of one's own or someone else's guilt, fault, foolishness or failure: *I was full of shame at my rudeness*; *He felt no shame at having behaved in the way he had.* **2** *nu* the ability to experience this feeling: *This is the third time in a week that you've come home drunk – have you no shame?* **3** *nu* dishonour or disgrace: *The news that he had accepted bribes brought shame on his whole family.* **4** *nc* (*no pl*: *with* **a**) a cause of disgrace or a matter for blame: *It's a shame to treat a child so cruelly.* **5** *nc* (*no pl*: *with* **a**: *slightly inf*) a pity: *It's a shame to sit indoors on such a beautiful day*; *What a shame that he didn't get the job!* – *vt* **1** (*often with* **into**) to force or persuade (someone) to do something by making him ashamed: *He was shamed into paying his share.* **2** to cause (someone) to have a feeling of shame: *He wouldn't help us, so we shamed him by doing it without him*; *His cowardice shamed his parents.*

ˈ**shameful** *adj* disgraceful: *shameful behaviour*; *I think his conduct was absolutely shameful!* ˈ**shamefully** *adv.* ˈ**shamefulness** *nu.*

ˈ**shameless** *adj* (*derog*) **1** (*usu attrib*) doing something, done *etc* without shame; blatant: *She's the most shameless liar I've ever met*; *his shameless deception of his wife.* **2** having no modesty: *She's always chasing after men – she's completely shameless!*; *The shameless creature!* ˈ**shamelessly** *adv.* ˈ**shamelessness** *nu.*

ˈ**shaming** *adj* giving cause to feel shame: *It's a shaming thought that while people are dying of hunger, we throw food away*; *It's very shaming to think that he had no friends or relations with him when he died.*

ˈ**shamefaced** *adj* showing shame or embarrassment: *He was very shamefaced about it*; *She made a shamefaced confession.*

for ˈ**shame!** (*old*) you ought to feel shame!: *For shame to beat a child!*

put (someone or something) to shame to make (a person) feel ashamed of his work or to make (the work) seem to be of poor quality by showing greater excellence: *She works so hard that she puts me to shame*; *Your beautiful drawing puts mine to shame.*

to my, his *etc* ˈ**shame** it is a cause of shame to me, him *etc* that: *To my shame, my daughter always beats me at chess.*

See also **ashamed**.

shampoo [ʃamˈpuː] – *pl* **shampoos** – **1** *ncu* (a type of) soapy liquid or other substance for washing the hair and scalp or for cleaning carpets, upholstery *etc*: *This is a special (type of) shampoo for greasy hair*: *We haven't enough carpet shampoo.* **2** *nc* an act of washing *etc* with shampoo: *I've been giving my hair a shampoo*; *I had a shampoo and set at the hairdresser's.* – *v* – *3rd pers sing prt* **shamˈpoos**: *pt, ptp* **shamˈpooed** – *vt* to wash (hair) or clean (carpets *etc*) with shampoo: *How often do you shampoo your hair?*; *We shampooed the rugs yesterday.*

shandy [ˈʃandi] **1** *nu* a mixture of beer and lemonade or ginger beer: *Can the little boy have some shandy?* **2** *nc* a glass of shandy: *I'll have a shandy please.*

shank [ʃaŋk] *nc* **1** (*usu in pl*: *usu facet and derog*) the leg, *esp* the part between the knee and foot: *his long thin shanks.* **2** (*tech*) the long straight part of *eg* a nail or screw.

shan't *see* **shall**.

shanty[1] [ˈʃanti] *nc* (*derog*) a roughly-built hut or shack.

ˈ**shanty town** *nc* (*often derog*) an area of shanties, inhabited by poor people, *eg* on the edge of a large city.

shanty[2], (*rare*) **chanty** [ˈʃanti] *nc* a type of song formerly sung by sailors *eg* while working on a ship: *The choir sang a sea shanty.*

shape [ʃeip] **1** *ncu* the external form or outline of anything: *No-one is quite the same shape as anybody else – we are all (of) different shapes and sizes*; *What shape is his head?*; *The house is built in the shape of a letter L*; *The mountain is like a lion in shape*; *Shape must be taken into consideration when you're planning your garden*; *He's just a machine in human shape*; (*fig facet*) *Help arrived in the shape of a passing motorist*; *A lively introduction would give your essay more shape.* – *See also* **out of shape, take shape** *below.* **2** *nc* an indistinct form: *I saw a large shape in front of me in the darkness*; *The ship was just a dark shape in the fog.* **3** *nu* (*inf*) condition or state: *What sort of shape is he in after his accident?*; *I want to get into (good) shape for the race*; *You're in better physical shape than I am.* **4** *nc* a mould (for a jelly *etc*) or pattern round which something is shaped: *The little girl spent hours in the sandpit, happily filling shapes with sand.* – **1** *vt* to make (something) into a certain shape; to mould, form or model: *She shaped the* *dough into three separate loaves; The potter carefully shaped the vase.* **2** *vt* (*formal*) to influence the nature of (something) strongly: *This event shaped his whole life: His early life shaped his attitude to women.* **3** *vi* (*sometimes with* **up**) to develop or become formed: *Our holiday plans are gradually shaping; The team is shaping* (*up*) *well.*

shaped *adj* (*often in cmpds*) having a certain shape: *That cloud is shaped like a fish; A rugby ball is egg-shaped.*

'shapeless *adj* (*usu derog*) lacking shape: *She wears a rather shapeless, baggy coat; This pullover's getting rather loose and shapeless.* **'shapelessness** *nu.*

'shapely *adj* (*esp* of a person's body, or part of it) well-formed and having an attractive shape: *Her figure was tall and shapely; She has long, shapely legs.* **'shapeliness** *nu.*

get/knock (something) into shape (*inf*) to put (something) into the desired condition: *I must try to knock the team into shape; A couple of days' work will get the garden into shape.*

in 'any shape (or form) at all: *I don't accept bribes in any shape or form.*

out of shape not in the proper shape: *I sat on my hat and it's rather out of shape.*

take shape to develop or grow into a definite form: *My book/garden is gradually taking shape; We have been moving furniture around ever since we moved into our new house, and the house is at last taking shape.*

See also **misshapen**.

share [ʃeə] **1** *nc* one of the parts of something that is divided among several people *etc*: *They divided the money into equal shares; We all had a share of the cake; Who has eaten my share of the sweets?; We each paid our share of the bill for the meal.* **2** *ncu* (*no pl*) the part played by a person in something done *etc* by several people *etc*: *I had no share in the decision; You must accept your share of responsibility for the failure of the firm; He took no share in the work.* **3** *nc* one of the equal parts into which the capital of a business firm is divided: *He bought four hundred shares in the business and sold them later at a big profit.* – **1** *vt* (*usu with* **among, between, with**) to divide among a number of people or give other people a share of (something): *We shared the money between us; The teacher shared the tasks among the children; She shared her piece of cake with me.* – *See also* **share out** *below.* **2** *vti* to have, use *etc* (something that another person has or uses); to allow someone to use (something one has or owns): *The students have their own bedrooms, but they share a sitting-room; The little boy hated sharing his toys* (*with other children*)*; Children should learn to share; He shares my interest in early music and my dislike of pop music; I don't share his opinions.* **3** *vti* (*vi with* **in**) to do or deal with (something) with someone else: *He wouldn't let her share the cost of the taxi; We all shared in his happiness when he won the scholarship.*

'shareholder *nc* a person who owns shares in a business company.

share-out *see* **share out** *below.*

go shares with (*inf*) to share expenses, profits *etc* with (a person): *I went shares with him in the cost of the meal.*

share and share alike (to own, use, pay for *etc* something) with everyone having an equal share: *We divided the money between us, share and share alike; The motto of this community is 'Share and share alike'.*

share out *vt sep* to divide (something) between several people *etc*: *She shared the pudding out* (*nc* **'share-out**: *a share-out of money*).

shark [ʃa:k] *nc* **1** a type of large, fierce, flesh-eating fish: *Bathing is not allowed in this bay because of the sharks.* **2** (*inf*) a swindler or a greedy, dishonest person: *He says that lawyers are all sharks – charging high fees and doing very little.*

sharp [ʃa:p] *adj* **1** having a thin edge that can cut or a point that can pierce: *a sharp sword; We'll need a sharp knife to cut this bread; These roses have sharp thorns; You can't write neatly if your pencil isn't sharp.* **2** (of pictures, outlines *etc*) clear and distinct: *the sharp outline of the mountain; That photograph isn't very sharp.* **3** (of changes in direction *eg* bends and turns in a road) sudden and quick; forming an angle smaller than a right angle: *I didn't realize that that right-hand bend was so sharp; Drivers found the sharp left turn very difficult.* **4** (*usu attrib*) (of pain *etc*) keen, acute or intense as though biting or piercing: *He gets a sharp pain after eating; She experienced a sharp pang of disappointment.* **5** (of flavour *etc*) sour, bitter or strong: *Lemons have a sharp taste; This cheese tastes rather sharp.* **6** (*often with* **with** *when pred*) severe or sarcastic: *Don't be so sharp with the child!; She got a sharp reproach from me; His sharp words hurt her.* **7** alert or quick to notice or understand: *Birds have sharp eyes and dogs have sharp ears; Your son's very sharp, isn't he?; Keep a sharp lookout for the enemy.* **8** (*usu attrib*) (of a cry *etc*) shrill and sudden: *The cat scratched him and he gave a sharp cry.* **9** (*sometimes inf*) (of weather *etc*) cold and harsh: *sharp east winds; It's a bit sharp today, isn't it?* **10** (*music*) raised a semitone; too high in pitch: *F sharp* (= F♯)*; a sharp note; That last note was rather sharp.* **11** (*usu attrib*) quick: *a short, sharp shower of rain.* – *adv* **1** (*inf*) (used immediately after a stated time) punctually: *Come at six* (*o'clock*) *sharp.* **2** (*inf*) with an abrupt change of direction: *Turn sharp left here.* **3** (*music*) at too high a pitch: *You're singing sharp.* – *nc* (*music*) **1** a sharp note: *sharps and flats.* **2** a sign (♯) to show that a note is to be raised a semitone.

'sharpen *vti* to make or grow sharp: *He sharpened his pencil; The picture sharpened as he adjusted the film-projector.*

'sharpener *nc* (*usu in cmpds*) an instrument for sharpening: *a pencil-sharpener.*

'sharply *adv* in a sharp manner: *a sharply-pointed piece of glass; Opinions are sharply* (= distinctly and definitely) *divided on this matter; The road turned sharply to the left; He rebuked her sharply.*

'sharpness *nu.*

sharp practice *nu* (*derog*) dishonesty or cheating: *There has been some sharp practice over this contract.*

'sharpshooter *nc* a soldier or other person who can shoot accurately with a rifle: *A sharpshooter was stationed at the window and had killed six of the enemy already.*

ˌsharp-'sighted/ˌsharp-'eyed *adjs* having good, keen sight: *You have to be sharp-sighted to be a bird-watcher; a sharp-eyed detective.*

ˌsharp-'witted *adj* intelligent and alert: *a sharp-witted boy.*

look sharp (*inf*) to be quick or to hurry: *Bring me the books and look sharp* (*about it*)*!*

a sharp tongue (*derog*) the tendency to be bad-tempered or sarcastic in speech: *He could bear his wife's sharp tongue no longer*; *He has rather a sharp tongue.*

shatter [ˈʃatə] **1** *vti* to break in small pieces, *usu* suddenly or forcefully: *The stone shattered the window*; *The window shattered*; (*fig formal*) *Her illusions were shattered by the experience.* **2** *vt* (*usu in passive*) to be very upset: *She was shattered by the news of his death.* **3** *vt* (*inf*) to make very tired: *Climbing the hill absolutely shattered me.*

ˈshattered *adj*: *the shattered window*; *I am absolutely shattered by what you have said*; (*inf*) *After digging the garden, I felt absolutely shattered.*

shave [ʃeiv] **1** *vti* (*vt sometimes with* **off**) to cut away (hair) from (*usu* oneself) with a razor: *He only shaves once a week*; *She always shaves her legs*; *He shaved off his beard*; *He asked the barber to shave him.* **2** *vt* (*sometimes with* **off**) to scrape or cut away (the surface of wood *etc*) or to remove (something) from the surface of wood in this way: *The joiner shaved a thin strip off the edge of the door.* **3** *vt* to touch lightly or just avoid touching in passing: *The car just shaved the corner before crashing.* – *nc* (the result of) an act of shaving: *This razor gives a good shave*; *I'd better go and have a shave if your mother's coming.*

ˈshaven *adj* (*often in cmpds*) shaved: *a shaven head*; *He was dark and clean-shaven.*

ˈshavings *n pl* (*often in cmpds*) very thin strips *esp* of wood: *The cups and saucers were carefully packed in wood shavings.*

ˈshaving-brush *nc* a small round brush for putting lather on the face before shaving.

ˈshaving-cream, ˈshaving-soap *ncus* (a type of) cream or soap used to make a lather *eg* on the face before shaving.

a close shave *see* **close call/shave** *under* **close**[1].

shawl [ʃoːl] *nc* a piece of fabric, often knitted, used as a covering for the shoulders *etc*: *The baby was wrapped in a woollen shawl*; *The old lady wore a black shawl.*

she [ʃiː] *pron* (used only as the subject of a verb) **1** a female person or animal, or a thing (such as a ship) thought of as female, that has already been spoken about: *When the girl saw us, she asked the time.* **2** (*formal*) any female person: *She who runs the fastest will be the winner.* – *nc* a female person or animal: *Is a cow a he or a she?*

she- (*in cmpds*) female: *a she-wolf.*

See also **her, hers, herself**.

sheaf [ʃiːf] – *pl* **sheaves** [ʃiːvz] – *nc* a bundle (of corn, papers *etc*) *usu* tied or held together in some way: *a sheaf of notes*; *He seems unable to give a lecture without sheaves of notes.*

shear [ʃiə] – *pt* **sheared**: *ptps* **sheared** (*not defs 2 and 3*), **shorn** [ʃoːn] – **1** *vt* to clip or cut wool from (a sheep): *They usually shear the sheep in June.* **2** *vt* (*formal*: *usu in passive*: *often with* **off**) to cut (hair) off: *All her curls have been shorn off.* **3** *vt* (*formal or facet*: *usu in passive*: *esp with* **of**) to cut hair from (someone): *He has been shorn* (*of all his curls*); (*liter fig*) *Who would have guessed that the famous and respected general would soon be shorn of all his former glory?* **4** *vti* (*formal or tech*: *often with* **off** *or* **through**) to cut or (cause to) break: *A tree fell down and sheared* (*through*) *the telephone cable*; *A piece of the steel girder sheared off.*

shears *n pl* a cutting-tool with two blades, like a large pair of scissors: *He cut the hedge with garden shears*; *a pair of shears.*

sheath [ʃiːθ] – *pl* **sheaths** [ʃiːθs, ʃiːðz] – *nc* **1** a case for a sword or blade. **2** a long close-fitting covering: *The rocket is encased in a metal sheath for protection.* **3** a *usu* rubber covering for the penis, used as a contraceptive; a condom.

sheathe [ʃiːð] *vt* (*formal or liter*) to put into, or cover with, a sheath (*defs 1 and 2*): *He sheathed his sword.*

sheaves *see* **sheaf**.

shed[1] [ʃed] *nc* (*often in cmpds*) a kind of *usu* small, often wooden or metal building for working in, or for storage: *He has built a wooden shed at the foot of his garden*; *a coalshed*; *a bicycle-shed*; *a garden shed.*

shed[2] [ʃed] – *prp* ˈ**shedding**: *pt*, *ptp* **shed** – *vt* (*formal*) **1** to cast or send out (light *etc*): *The torch shed a bright light on the path ahead.* **2** to throw or cast off (clothing, skin, leaves *etc*): *Many trees shed their leaves in autumn*; *How often does a snake shed its skin?* **3** to let out or produce (tears): *I don't think many tears were shed when she left.*

shed blood (*formal*) **1** to be killed or wounded: *Too many young men have shed their blood for their country.* **2** to cause wounding and killing: *Surely the governments of the two countries can settle their quarrel without shedding any more innocent blood?* (= causing the deaths of innocent people).

shed light on (*fig*) to make (a reason, subject *etc*) clearer: *This letter sheds light on the reasons for his actions at the time.*

See also **bloodshed** *under* **blood**.

she'd *see* **have, would**.

sheen [ʃiːn] *nu* shine or glossiness: *the sheen of satin*; *Her hair always has such a sheen.*

sheep [ʃiːp] – *pl* **sheep** – *nc* **1** a kind of animal related to the goat, whose flesh is used as food and from whose wool clothing is made: *a flock of sheep.* **2** (*fig*: *usu in pl*) a person who imitates unthinkingly the behaviour of others: *Some advertisers seem to think that all women are sheep.*

ˈsheepish *adj* embarrassed because of having done something wrong or foolish: *He looked rather sheepish about what he had done*; *His face had a sheepish expression.* **ˈsheepishly** *adv.* **ˈsheepishness** *nu.*

black sheep *see* **black**.

ˈsheep-dip *nu* a liquid used for disinfecting sheep.

ˈsheepdog *nc* a dog (of a kind often) trained to work with sheep.

ˈsheepskin *ncu, adj* (of) (leather prepared from) the skin of a sheep, *usu* with the wool left on it: *a pile of sheepskins*; *The rug is* (*made of*) *sheepskin*; *a sheepskin jacket.*

sheer[1] [ʃiə] *adj* **1** (*attrib*) complete; absolute: *Her singing was a sheer delight*; *Such behaviour is sheer foolishness*; *It all happened by sheer chance.* **2** very steep; vertical: *From the top of the cliff, there is a sheer drop to the sea*; *The cliff is absolutely sheer.* **3** (*usu attrib*) (of cloth) very thin; transparent: *sheer nylon.* – *adv* (*formal*) straight up or down; vertically: *The land rises sheer out of the sea at that point.*

sheer[2] [ʃiə]: **sheer off/away** *vi* to turn aside or swerve: *The speed-boat seemed to be heading straight towards some swimmers but sheered off at the last moment.*

sheet [ʃiːt] *nc* **1** a broad piece of linen, cotton *etc* cloth *eg* for a bed: *The hotel puts clean sheets on all the beds every day.* **2** a large, thin, *usu* flat, piece (of paper, glass, metal, ice *etc*): *Begin the answer to each question on a fresh sheet of paper*; *sheets of* *corrugated iron*; (*attrib*) *sheet metal*; (*fig*) *sheets of flames*; (*fig*) *The rain fell in sheets.*

'**sheeting** *nu* **1** cloth used for making sheets. **2** a lining or covering of sheets of wood or metal: *copper sheeting.*

ˌ**sheet-'lightning** *nu* the kind of lightning which, because it is reflected and spread by cloud, appears in broad flashes rather than narrow streaks.

sheik(h) [ʃeik, (*Amer*) ʃiːk] *nc* an Arab chief.

'**sheik(h)dom** *nc* a state ruled by a sheik(h).

shelf [ʃelf] – *pl* **shelves** [ʃelvz] – *nc* **1** a board for laying things on, *usu* fixed in a cupboard or on a wall: *Put those books on the top shelf*; *I'm having some shelves put on the kitchen walls.* **2** a ledge or flat piece of rock sticking out from a cliff or mountain: *He waited all night on a narrow shelf (of rock) until the rescuers arrived in the morning.*

shelve [ʃelv] **1** *vt* to put (a problem *etc*) aside, *usu* for consideration, completion *etc* later: *The project has been shelved for the moment.* **2** *vt* to put up shelves in (a cupboard *etc*): *One wall of the study has been completely shelved.* **3** *vi* (of land) to slope smoothly and gradually: *The land shelves gently towards the sea.*

'**shelving** [-viŋ] *nu* (a framework, or pieces of wood *etc*, shaped for use as) shelves: *We have put up shelving in the library.*

on the shelf (*inf*) (of an unmarried woman) no longer likely to attract a man enough for him to want to marry her: *Some girls seem to think they're on the shelf if they're not married by the age of eighteen.*

shell [ʃel] **1** *ncu* (*often in cmpds*) the hard outer covering of a shellfish, egg, nut *etc*: *an eggshell*; *the hard shell of an animal*; *While I was breaking the egg, a bit of shell fell into the cake mixture*; *A tortoise can pull its head and legs under its shell.* **2** *nc* the outer covering or framework of anything, *esp* if the contents are missing: *After the fire, all that was left was the burned-out shell of the building*; *By this time the shell of the boat was complete*; (*fig*) *He lost all interest in life and became a mere shell of a man.* **3** *nc* a metal case filled with explosives and fired from a gun *etc*: *A shell exploded right beside him.* – *vt* **1** to remove from its shell or pod: *You have to shell peas/peanuts before eating them.* **2** to fire explosive shells at: *The army shelled the enemy mercilessly.*

'**shellfish** – *pl* '**shellfish** – *nc* any of several kinds of sea animal covered with a shell (*eg* oyster, crab): *Do you like shellfish?*; *He thinks that shellfish make him ill.*

'**shell-shock** *nu* any of several types of nervous or mental illness caused by war experiences: *He was sent home suffering from shell-shock.*

come out of one's shell to become more confident and less shy: *She was very quiet and reserved when she first went to school, but she's coming out of her shell a bit now.*

shell out *vi*, *vt sep* (*inf derog*) to pay out (money): *I was the one who had to shell out for the food*; *I had to shell out five pounds*; *I refuse to shell out any more money on a project that's bound to fail.*

she'll *see* **will**.

shelter ['ʃeltə] **1** *nu* (*formal*) protection against wind, rain, enemies *etc*: *We gave the old man shelter for the night*; *shelter from the wind and rain.* – *See also* **take shelter** *below.* **2** *nc* (*often in cmpds*) a building *etc* designed to give such protection: *a bus-shelter*; *an air-raid shelter* (= a place constructed underground into which people can go to be protected from air-raids). – **1** *vi* to be in, or go into, a place of shelter: *He sheltered from the storm.* **2** *vt* to give protection: *That line of trees shelters my garden*; *He was accused of sheltering criminals.*

'**sheltered** *adj* protected from harm and unpleasantness of all kinds: *a sheltered existence*; *He has had very little experience of life as his childhood was rather sheltered.*

take shelter to shelter (*def 1*): *The rain was quite heavy and he took shelter in a doorway.*

shelve, shelves *see* **shelf**.

shepherd ['ʃepəd] – *fem* (*old or liter*) '**shepherdess** – *nc* a person who looks after sheep: *The shepherd and his dog gathered in the sheep*; *He is employed as a shepherd.* – *vt* (*often with* **around, in, out** *etc*) to guide or lead, *usu* in too careful or restricting a way: *He shepherded me through a maze of corridors*; *The tourists were shepherded around by a young woman dressed in a grey uniform*; *We were shepherded into a coach.*

shepherd's pie *ncu* a dish of minced meat with mashed potatoes on the top: *We had (a) shepherd's pie for supper*; *Do you like shepherd's pie?*

sherbet ['ʃəːbit] **1** *nu* (powder for making) a kind of fizzy drink: *The little boy bought a packet of sherbet*; (*attrib*) *sherbet powder.* **2** *nc* a glass of sherbet: *I'd love a sherbet.*

sheriff ['ʃerif] *nc* **1** in the US, the chief law officer of a county, concerned with maintaining peace and order. **2** the judge of the main local courts of the Scottish legal system. **3** the chief representative of the king *etc* in an English county, whose duties are mainly administrative.

sherry ['ʃeri] **1** *ncu* a kind of strong wine, made in Spain and often drunk before a meal: *Have some sherry*; *Is this a sweet sherry or a dry sherry?*; (*attrib*) *a sherry glass.* **2** *nc* a glass of sherry: *I'd like a sherry, please.*

she's *see* **be, have**.

shield [ʃiːld] *nc* **1** (*often hist*) a broad piece of metal, wood *etc*, carried to protect oneself against weapons: *The knight's shield saved him from being killed by his enemy's lance.* **2** something or someone giving, or used for, protection: *There was a thick steel plate in front of the furnace which acted as a heat shield*; *The terrorists prevented the police from shooting at them by using some of their prisoners as shields.* **3** (*with cap in titles*) a trophy shaped like a shield presented as a prize in a sporting competition *etc*: *My son has won the John Smith Junior Archery Shield.* – *vt* (*often with* **from**) **1** (*more formal or tech than* **protect**) to protect from something harmful *etc*: *Lead aprons shield people from radiation*; (*fig*) *He shields her from criticism.* **2** to prevent from being seen clearly: *That group of trees shields the house from the road.*

shift [ʃift] **1** *vti* (*slightly inf*) to change the position or direction (of): *We'll have to shift the furniture before we paint the room*; *We spent the whole evening shifting furniture around*; *The wind shifted to the west overnight*; *I left it on the table. If it's not there now, someone must have shifted it.* **2** *vt* (*slightly inf*) to transfer: *Don't try to shift the blame on to me.* **3** *vt* (*less formal than* **remove**) to get rid of; to remove: *This detergent shifts stains.* – **1** *nc* (*slightly inf*) a change (of position *etc*): *a shift of direction/emphasis.* **2** *nc or n pl* a group of people who begin work on a job when another group stop work: *The night shift does the heavy work.* **3** *ncu* the period during which such a group works: *an eight-hour shift*; (*attrib*) *shift work*; *The men in this factory work in shifts.* **4** *nc* a kind of loose-fitting dress.

'shiftless *adj* (*formal derog*) inefficient, lazy, or without a set purpose: *He's a rather shiftless individual – he's had four jobs in six months*; *I wish my son was not quite so shiftless.* **'shiftlessness** *nu.*

'shifty *adj* (*derog*) not to be trusted; looking cunning and dishonest: *I don't trust him – he has a very shifty look*; *He looks rather shifty.* **'shiftily** *adv.* **'shiftiness** *nu.*

shift for oneself (*formal*) to do as well as one can; to manage without help: *I may be old and my legs may be a bit shaky, but I can still shift for myself.*

shift one's ground *see* **ground**.

shilling ['ʃiliŋ] *nc* **1** in Britain, (the value of) a coin worth one-twentieth of £1, or twelve old pence (12d), the word still being used occasionally for the same coin which is now worth five new pence (5p): *He gave the little boy a shilling*; *That book cost me 10 shillings.* **2** in certain E African countries, (the value of) a coin worth 100 cents.

shilly-shally [ʃili'ʃali] *vi* (*derog*) to hesitate in making up one's mind: *Stop shilly-shallying and say something definite!*

shimmer ['ʃimə] *vi* to shine with a quivering or unsteady light: *The sequins on her dress shimmered.* – *nu* such a light: *the shimmer of sequins.*

shin [ʃin] *nc* the front part of the leg below the knee: *He kicked him on the shins*; *I banged my shin on the coffee table.* – *v* – *pt, ptp* **shinned** – *vi* (*inf*: *usu with* **up**) to climb (a tree *etc*) by alternate movements of both arms and both legs: *He shinned up the tree/rope*; *He took hold of the drainpipe and shinned up on to the roof.*

shindig ['ʃindig] *nc* (*sl*) a noisy, and *usu* large, party.

shindy ['ʃindi] *nc* (*inf*) a noisy protest or disturbance: *The meeting became a bit of a shindy with people shouting at each other.*

kick up a shindy (*inf*) to make such a protest or disturbance: *He is going to kick up a shindy about the council's plan to build a road through his garden.*

shine [ʃain] – *pt, ptp* **shone** [ʃon, (*Amer*) ʃoun] – (*defs 1, 2, 4*), **shined** (*def 3*) – **1** *vti* to (cause to) give out light; to direct such light towards someone or something: *The light shone from the window*; *The policeman shone his torch*; *The light was shining in* (= towards) *his eyes and he could not see*; *He shone a torch on* (= towards) *the body.* **2** *vi* to be bright with reflected light: *She polished the silver spoons till they shone*; (*fig*) *Her eyes shone with happiness.* **3** *vt* to cause to shine; to polish: *He tries to make a living by shining shoes.* **4** *vi* (*inf*: *often with* **at**) to be very good (at something): *He shines at games*; *You really shone in this afternoon's football match.* – (*sometimes in cmpds*) **1** *nu* (*sometimes with* **a**) brightness caused by the giving out of light or reflection of light; the state of being well polished: *He likes a good shine on his shoes*; *a ray of sunshine.* **2** *nc* an act of polishing: *I'll just give my shoes a shine*; *Give the silver a good shine!*

'shining *adj* **1** very bright and clear; producing or reflecting light; polished: *a bright, shining star*; *The cutlery was all clean and shining.* **2** (*formal*: *attrib*) greatly to be admired: *He is a shining example to us all.*

'shiny *adj* glossy; reflecting light; (looking as if) polished: *a shiny cover on a book*; *a shiny nose*; *The seat of his trousers was thin and shiny.* **'shininess** *nu.*

(come) rain or shine whether the weather is good or bad; whatever happens: *We'll definitely come to Tuesday's meeting, rain or shine.*

take a shine to (*inf*) to become fond of: *The boss took a shine to the new girl.*

shingle ['ʃiŋgl] *nu* coarse gravel, consisting of rounded stones, on the shores of rivers, the sea *etc*: *It's not a very nice beach – there's too much shingle and not enough sand*; (*attrib*) *a shingle beach.*

shingles ['ʃiŋglz] *n sing* a kind of infectious disease causing a rash of painful blisters that spreads in a band round the waist or other part of the body: *She's not at work – she's got shingles*; *People suffering from shingles are often in pain.*

shiny *see* **shine**.

ship [ʃip] *nc* **1** a large boat for journeys on sea, lake, or river: *He's going by ship – he doesn't like flying*; *The ship sank and all the passengers and crew were drowned.* **2** (*in cmpds*) any of certain types of transport that fly: *an airship*; *a spaceship.* – *v* – *pt, ptp* **shipped** – *vt* to send or transport (*usu* things) by ship: *The books will go to London by rail, and will then be shipped to Nigeria.*

'shipment 1 *nc* a load of goods sent, *esp* by ship: *a shipment of wine from Portugal.* **2** *nu* the act or process of shipping: *Our firm specializes in the shipment of goods abroad.*

'shipper *nc* a person who arranges for goods to be shipped: *a firm of shippers*; *Will you arrange for your shipper to collect the books from our warehouse?*

'shipping *nu* **1** ships taken as a whole: *The harbour was full of shipping.* **2** transport by ship: *The shipping of goods overseas is very expensive*; (*attrib*) *a shipping-agent* (= a person in charge of a shipowner's business in a port).

'shipbuilder *nc* a person whose business is the construction of ships: *a firm of shipbuilders.* **'shipbuilding** *nu.*

'ship canal *nc* a canal large enough for sea-going ships: *the Manchester Ship Canal.*

ship chandler, ship's chandler ['tʃa:ndlə] *nc* a person who sells supplies for ships.

'shipmate *nc* (*usu facet or liter*) a fellow sailor: *When we were on that Mediterranean cruise we grew tired of our shipmates*; *He and his shipmates mutinied.*

'shipowner *nc* the owner of (a share in) a ship or ships: *He married the daughter of a wealthy Greek shipowner.*

ˌship'shape *adj* (*usu pred*) in good order; neat: *She left everything shipshape in her room when she went away.*

'shipwreck 1 *ncu* the accidental sinking or destruction of a ship: *There were many shipwrecks on this part of the coast before the lighthouse was built*; *The owners were insured against shipwreck.* **2** *nc* a wrecked ship: *The children were playing on an old shipwreck on the shore.* – *vt*: *We were shipwrecked off the coast of Africa.*

'shipwright *nc* a person employed in building or repairing ships.

'shipyard *nc* a place where ships are built or repaired.

ship off *vt sep* to send away: (*inf*: *often derog*) *The children have been shipped off to boarding-school.*

ship water (of a boat) to let water in over the side: *The boat shipped water and nearly capsized.*

shire ['ʃaiə, (*in cmpds usu*) -ʃə] *nc* a county (now used mainly in *cmpds* in British place-names):

Lancashire; *Berkshire*; *Aberdeenshire no longer exists since the introduction of the new regional system of administration in Scotland.*

shirk [ʃə:k] *vti* to avoid doing, accepting responsibility for *etc* (something one ought to): *She was obviously trying to shirk the responsibility of making a decision*; *He's shirking again.* **'shirker** *nc.*

shirt [ʃə:t] *nc* **1** a kind of garment for men worn on the upper part of the body, *usu* with a collar, sleeves and buttons down the front: *I don't think a pink shirt goes well with a green tie*; *a casual shirt*; *a short-sleeved shirt.* **2** a similar garment for a woman; a type of blouse: *She wore black jeans and a white shirt.*

ˌshirt'waister *nc* a dress with a top like a shirt.

in one's ˌshirt-'sleeves without a jacket or coat: *I don't like wearing a jacket when I'm working – I prefer to wear a jersey or work in my shirt-sleeves.* *See also* **T-shirt** *under* **T**.

shirty ['ʃə:ti] *adj* (*inf*) angry; bad-tempered: *He was a little bit shirty with her when she asked him to repeat all his instructions*; *He's in a rather shirty mood.*

shit [ʃit], **shite** [ʃait] (*vulg*) **1** *nu* the solid waste material that is passed out of the body through the anus; faeces: *I wish people would train their dogs not to leave shit all over the pavements.* **2** *nc* the act of passing this substance from the body: *I need a shit.* **3** *ncu* used offensively for someone or something that a person thinks is worthless: *Everything he said was a load of shit*; *She's a conceited little shit.* – *v* – *prps* **'shitting** ['ʃi-], **'shiting** ['ʃai-]: *pts, ptps* **shit, shat** [ʃat] – *vi* (*vulg*) to pass faeces from the body. – *interj* (*vulg*) an expression of disgust, pain, anger *etc*: *Shit! I've cut my finger*; *Oh, shite! I've broken my shoelace.*

shiver[1] ['ʃivə] *vi* to quiver or tremble (with cold, fear *etc*). – *nc* an act of shivering: *'The castle is haunted,' he said with a shiver*; *Judging from the shivers of the children it must be cold outside.*

'shivery *adj* inclined to shiver: *I feel shivery when I have a fever*; *The mention of ghosts gave her a shivery feeling.*

the shivers (*inf*) a feeling of horror: *The thought of working for him gives me the shivers.*

shiver[2] ['ʃivə] *nc* a small piece (of glass *etc*); a splinter: *When the dish smashed, there were shivers of glass all over the floor.*

shoal[1] [ʃoul] *nc* a great number of fish swimming together in one place: *The fishing-boats were searching for large shoals of fish*; (*fig*) *People were arriving in shoals* (= in large numbers at a time).

shoal[2] [ʃoul] *nc* a shallow place in the sea *etc*; a sandbank: *The boats had to follow a narrow channel of deep water through the shoals.* – *vi* (of the sea) to become shallow.

shock[1] [ʃok] **1** *ncu* (something which causes) a severe emotional disturbance: *The news was a shock to all of us*; *They were white with shock.* **2** *nc* (*often* **electric shock**) the effect on the body of an electric current: *He got a slight shock when he touched the live wire.* **3** *nc* a sudden blow coming with great force: *When the lorry crashed into the cottage, the shock brought the ceiling down*; *the shock of an earthquake.* **4** *nu* (*tech*) a medical condition caused by a severe mental or physical shock: *He was taken to hospital suffering from shock after the crash.* – *vt* to give a shock to; to upset or horrify: *Everyone was shocked by his death*; *The amount of violence shown on television shocks me.*

'shocker (*inf*) *nc* a person or thing that is offensive, unpleasant *etc*: *What a shocker that woman is!*; *This headache is a real shocker.*

'shocking *adj* **1** causing horror or dismay: *shocking news.* **2** (*inf*) very bad: *a shocking cold*; *His work has been really shocking recently.*

'shockingly *adv* **1** (*inf*) very: *shockingly expensive.* **2** very badly: *He treated her shockingly*; *It was shockingly translated.*

'shock-absorber *nc* a device (in an aeroplane, motor car *etc*) for reducing the effect of bumps.

'shock tactics *n pl* a course of action in which suddenness and force are used to achieve a purpose: *He decided that shock tactics were needed to calm the hysterical girl, so he slapped her hard several times.*

shock[2] [ʃok] *nc* (*inf*) a bushy mass (of hair) on a person's head: *a shock of untidy red hair.*

shod *see* **shoe**.

shoddy ['ʃodi] *adj* (*slightly inf*: *derog*) **1** of poor material or quality (but often intended to seem to be good): *shoddy furniture*; *His workmanship is rather shoddy.* **2** mean and contemptible: *a shoddy trick*; *I thought his behaviour extremely shoddy.* **'shoddily** *adv.* **'shoddiness** *nu.*

shoe [ʃu:] *nc* **1** an outer covering for the foot, not reaching above the ankle: *a new pair of shoes*; *He took off his shoes and put on his slippers.* **2** (*also* **horse-shoe**) a curved piece of iron nailed to the hoof of a horse: *The horse cast a shoe* (= One of its shoes dropped off). **3** (*sometimes in cmpds*) an extra piece attached to a machine *etc* where there is rubbing, *eg* the part of a brake that touches the wheel *etc*: *a brake-shoe.* **4** anything like a shoe in shape or use, *eg* used to protect something. – *v* – *prp* **'shoeing**: *pts, ptps* **shod** [ʃod], **shoed** – *vt* to put a shoe or shoes on (a horse *etc*).

shod [ʃod] *adj* (*old, tech or liter*) with a shoe or shoes on: *You need to be properly shod before going out in the rain*; *This part of the machine is shod with iron.*

'shoehorn *nc* a curved piece of horn, metal *etc* used to make a shoe slip on easily over the heel.

'shoelace, (*Amer*) **'shoestring** *nc* a kind of string or cord for fastening a shoe. – *See also* **on a shoestring** *below.*

'shoemaker *nc* a person who makes, repairs, or sells shoes.

in (someone's) shoes in someone's place: *I wouldn't like to be in your shoes when they find out what you've done!*

on a 'shoestring with or using very little money: *We organized this party on a shoestring and had very little food to spare*; *He has to live on a shoestring.*

shone *see* **shine**.

shoo [ʃu:] *interj* an exclamation used when chasing a person, animal *etc* away: *'Shoo!' she shouted, chasing the pigeons away from her seeds.* – *v* – *3rd pers sing prt* **shoos**: *pt, ptp* **shooed** – *vt* (*often with* **away, off** *etc*) to chase (a person, animal *etc*) away (as if) by shouting 'shoo': *She shooed the pigeons away*; *A crowd of children gathered round, but he shooed them away.*

shook *see* **shake**.

shoot [ʃu:t] – *pt, ptp* **shot** [ʃot] – **1** *vti* (*often with* **at**) to send or fire (bullets, arrows *etc*) from a gun, bow *etc*: *The enemy were shooting at us*; *I go shooting every Saturday*; *Can you shoot straight?* **2** *vi* (of a gun, bow *etc*) to fire bullets, arrows *etc*: *Does this gun shoot straight?* **3** *vt* to hit or kill with a bullet, arrow *etc*: *He went out to shoot pigeons*; *He* *was sentenced to be shot at dawn.* **4** *vt* (*fig*) to direct (something) swiftly, suddenly and with force: *He shot a question at me*; *She shot them an angry glance.* **5** *vti* (*often with* **in, out, over, through** *etc*) to move swiftly: *He shot out of the room*; *The winner shot past the post*; *The pain shot up his leg*; *When the car crashed, the driver was shot through the window.* **6** *vti* to take (*usu* moving) photographs (for a film): *That film was shot in Spain*; *We will start shooting next week.* **7** *vi* (*often with* **at**) to kick or hit (a ball) at a goal in order to try to score: *'Shoot!' shouted the crowd as he ran towards the goal.* **8** *vti* to kill (game birds *etc*) for sport: *He goes there in August to shoot (grouse).* – *See also* **shoot up** *below.* – *nc* new growth on a plant: *The deer were eating the young shoots on the trees.*

shooting-star *see* **meteor**.

shoot down *vt sep* (*often fig*) to hit (*eg* a plane) with *eg* a shell and cause it to crash into the ground: *They shot down six of the enemy's planes.*

shoot (the) rapids to pass through rapids: *They shot the rapids in a canoe.*

shoot up *vi* to grow or increase rapidly: *Prices have shot up*; *After last week's rain, the weeds have shot up.*

See also **shot**.

shop [ʃop] *nc* **1** a place where goods are sold: *a baker's shop*; *a fruit shop.* **2** (*often in cmpds*) a workshop, or a place where any kind of industry is carried on: *a machine-shop.* – *v* – *pt, ptp* **shopped** – **1** *vi* (*often* **go shopping**) to visit shops for the purpose of buying: *We shop on Saturdays*; *She goes shopping once a month.* **2** *vt* (*sl*) to betray, *esp* to the police: *He shopped his fellow criminals to the police.*

'shopper *nc* **1** a person who is shopping: *The street was full of shoppers.* **2** a large bag used when shopping: *She put everything in a large shopper.*

'shopping *nu* **1** the activity of buying goods in shops: *Have you a lot of shopping to do?*; (*attrib*) *a shopping-list.* **2** the goods bought: *He helped her carry her shopping home*; (*attrib*) *a shopping-basket/bag.*

'shop assistant *nc* (*Amer* **'salesclerk, clerk**) a person employed in a shop *usu* to help in serving customers.

shop floor *nc* the workers in a factory or workshop, as opposed to the management.

'shopkeeper *nc* a person who runs a shop of his own: *Many shopkeepers complain about the number of hours they have to spend calculating VAT.*

'shoplifter *nc* a person who steals goods from a shop: *Many shops employ people to guard against shoplifters.* **'shoplifting** *nu.*

'shopping centre *nc* a place, often a very large building, where there is a large number of different shops.

'shop-soiled *adj* slightly dirty or spoilt *eg* as a result of being handled while on display: *shop-soiled goods*; *These handkerchiefs are to be sold cheap, as they are shop-soiled.*

shop steward *nc* in a factory *etc*, a worker elected by the other workers as their official representative: *The shop stewards called the men out on strike.*

go shopping *see* **shop** *vi.*

set up shop *see* **set**.

shop around *vi* to compare prices, quality of goods *etc* at several shops before buying anything: *This isn't exactly what I want, so I think I'll shop around a bit before I make any decision.*

talk shop *see* **talk**.

shore[1] [ʃo:] *nc* land bordering on the sea or on any large area of water: *Let's go for a walk along the shore*; *When the ship reached Gibraltar the passengers were allowed to go on shore.*

See also **ashore**.

shore[2] [ʃo:]: **shore up** *vt sep* to support with props *etc*; to prop up: *The fire damaged the building so badly that it had to be shored up*; (*fig*) *The government shored up the business with extra money.*

shorn *see* **shear**.

short [ʃo:t] *adj* **1** not long in extent: *a short street*; *You look nice with your hair short*; *Do you think my dress is too short?*; *He finished the work in a very short time*; *When it comes to their own past failings, people have very short memories* (= they easily forget their own past faults). **2** not tall; smaller than usual: *a short man*; *He's short and fat.* **3** not lasting a long time; brief: *a short film.* **4** not as much as it should be: *The baker was reported for giving short weight*; *When I checked my change, I found it was 4p short.* **5** (*pred*: *usu with* **of**) not having enough (money *etc*): *Most of us are short of money these days*; (*inf*) *I'd like to lend you the money, but I'm a bit short myself this week.* – *See also* **go short, run short, short of** *below.* **6** (*often pred with* **with**) rude; curt; sharp in manner: *He was very short with me.* **7** (of pastry) made so that it is crisp and crumbles easily. – *adv* **1** suddenly; abruptly: *He stopped short when he saw me.* **2** not as far as intended: *The shot fell short.* – *See also* **short of, short on** *below.* – *nc* (*inf*) **1** a short circuit. **2** a short film: *There are a couple of shorts on before the main film.* **3** (*inf*: *usu in pl*) a small strong, alcoholic drink (*eg* of spirits as opposed to beer, cider *etc*): *I only drink shorts at a party – at home I drink beer.* – *See also* **shorts** *below.* – *vti* (*inf*) to cause or suffer a short circuit: *The fuse has blown again – something in the television must be shorting.*

'shortage [-tidʒ] *ncu* a lack; the state of not having enough: *There is a shortage of water when it does not rain enough*; *Shortage of manpower is the chief cause of the delay at the factory.*

'shorten *vti* to make or become shorter: *The dress is too long – we'll have to shorten it*; *I think we ought to shorten the letter.*

'shortening *nu* (*esp Amer*) fat used for making pastry: *How much shortening do you need for this recipe?*; *Sift the flour and add the shortening.*

'shortly *adv* **1** soon: *He will be here shortly*; *Shortly after that, the police arrived.* **2** curtly; abruptly: *He answered me rather shortly, I thought.*

'shortness *nu*: *He must have been in a hurry, to judge from the shortness of his letter.*

shorts *n pl* short trousers: *I like looking at girls in shorts*; *He'll be needing a new pair of shorts soon.*

'shortbread *nu* a kind of crisp, crumbling biscuit made with flour and butter: *You can buy various different types of shortbread.*

ˌshort-'change *vt* (*inf*) to cheat (a buyer) by giving him too little change from a note or large coin.

short circuit *nc* (*tech*) the *usu* accidental missing out by an electric current of a part of an electrical circuit *eg* in a television or radio, sometimes causing blowing of fuses, sparking and fire.

ˌshort-'circuit *vti* (*tech*) to have or cause a short circuit.

'shortcoming *nc* (*more formal than* **fault**) a fault: *He's always criticizing other people for their shortcomings*; *This system has its shortcomings, but on the whole we're satisfied with it.*

'shortcut *nc* **1** a quicker way between two places: *I can show you a shortcut to the motorway; I'm in a hurry – I'll take a shortcut across the field.* **2** a quicker way to achieve a result, do something *etc*: *There is no shortcut to success.*

'shorthand *nu* **1** a method of writing rapidly, *usu* using strokes, dots *etc* to represent speech sounds and groups of sounds: *My daughter is learning shorthand and typing at school.* **2** writing of this kind: *The note is written in shorthand, and I can't read shorthand.*

ˌshort-'handed *adj* (*pred*) having fewer workers than are necessary or usual: *With three people off ill, we're a bit short-handed this week.*

shorthand typist *nc* a person who is able to take down letters *etc* in shorthand as they are dictated to him or her, and type them out afterwards.

'short-list *nc* (*Brit*) a list of candidates for a job *etc* selected from the total number of applicants: *I was on the short-list for the post, but one of the other people got the job.* – *vt* (*Brit*) to put on a short-list: *We've short-listed three of the twenty applicants.*

ˌshort-'lived [-'livd, (*Amer*) -'laivd] *adj* living or lasting only for a short time: *short-lived plants/insects*; *All his schemes were very short-lived*; *short-lived enthusiasm.*

short odds *n pl* in betting, odds showing that the person betting is likely to win.

ˌshort-'range *adj* (*attrib*) **1** not reaching a long distance: *short-range missiles.* **2** not covering or taking into consideration a long period of time: *a short-range weather forecast.*

ˌshort-'sighted *adj* **1** seeing clearly only things that are near: *I don't recognize people at a distance without my glasses on, because I'm rather short-sighted*; *A lot of short-sighted people have the same problem.* **2** (of a person, action *etc*) taking no account of what is likely to happen in the future: *I later regretted my short-sighted refusal to consider his plan.* **ˌshort-'sightedly** *adv.* **ˌshort-'sightedness** *nu.*

ˌshort-'tempered *adj* easily made angry: *My husband is very short-tempered in the mornings*; *He's a rather short-tempered man.*

ˌshort-'term *adj* (*usu attrib*) **1** concerned only with the near future: *short-term plans.* **2** lasting only a short time: *a short-term loan.*

short wave *see* **wave(band)** *under* **wave**.

by a short head by a very small amount: *The horse won by a short head.*

cut short *see* **cut**.

for 'short as an abbreviation: *His name is Victor, but we call him Vic for short.*

give (someone or something) short shrift to waste little time or consideration on someone or something, *usu* in an unpleasant or unfriendly way: *He came to me with some crazy plan, but I gave him/it very short shrift!*

go short (*often with* **of**) to cause or allow oneself not to have enough of something, *eg* in order to allow someone else to have some: *If you can lend me some bread, I'd be grateful, but I don't want you to go short*; *I don't want you to go short of bread.*

in 'short (often used after listing complaints, reasons *etc*) in a few words: *In short, I didn't like the film at all.*

in short supply not available in sufficient quantity: *Fresh vegetables are in short supply in winter.*

little/nothing short of (almost) the same as, or as bad as (something else): *Charging prices like that is little short of robbery*; *To do that would be nothing short of suicide!*

the long and the short of it *see* **long**.

make short work of to settle, or dispose of, very quickly: *The children made short work of the cream cakes.*

run short 1 (of a supply) to become insufficient: *Our money is running short.* **2** (*with* **of**) not to have enough: *We're running short of money.*

sell (someone or something) short to belittle (a person or thing): *Tell them about your achievements – don't sell yourself short.*

short and sweet (*ironic*): *His reply was short and sweet: 'Get out!' he shouted.*

'short for an abbreviation of: *'Vic' is short for 'Victor'*; *'Phone' is short for 'telephone'.*

'short of 1 not as far as or as much as: *The shell fell short of the target We were aiming to raise £1 000, but unfortunately we came/fell short of our target*; *Our total came to just short of £1 000*; *We stopped five miles short of London.* – *See also* **short** (*adv def 2*). **2** without doing something as bad, unpleasant *etc* as (something else): *He couldn't think how he would get the money, short of stealing it*; *Short of murdering her, I'd do anything to get rid of her.* – *See also* **stop short of/at** *under* **stop**.

short on (*inf*) lacking in (a particular thing, quality *etc*): *The book is rather short on illustrations, but has some useful information*; *She's a nice person, if a bit short on good looks* (= even though she's not very pretty).

shot [ʃot] **1** *nc* a single act of shooting: *He fired one shot.* **2** *nc* the sound of a gun being fired: *He heard a shot from the house.* **3** *nc* (*inf*) a throw, hit, turn *etc* in a game or competition: *It's your shot*; *Can I have a shot?*; *He played some very good shots in that tennis match*; *Good shot – well played!* **4** *nc* (*inf*) an attempt (at doing something): *I don't know if I can do that, but I'll have a shot* (*at it*). **5** *nu* something which is shot or fired, *esp* small lead bullets used in cartridges: *lead shot.* **6** *nc* a photograph, *esp* a scene in a film. **7** *nc* (*inf*) an injection: *The doctor gave me an anti-tetanus shot.* **8** *nc* a marksman: *He's a good shot.* – *adj* (*with* **with** *when pred*) (of silk *etc*) showing changing colours, streaked or mixed with: *shot silk*; *The sky was shot with gold.* – *v see* **shoot**.

'shotgun *nc* a type of rifle which fires shot: *The farmer was carrying a double-barrelled shotgun.*

shotgun marriage/wedding *nc* a forced marriage: *I think theirs was a shotgun wedding – the bride was certainly pregnant at the time.*

get 'shot of (*sl*) to get rid of: *It's not easy to get shot of unwanted guests.*

like a 'shot very quickly; eagerly: *He accepted my invitation like a shot.*

a shot in the arm (*fig*) the addition of new ideas, money *etc* to a failing business *etc* in the hope of reviving it: *This loan is a shot in the arm for the economy.*

a shot in the dark (*inf*) a guess based on little or no information: *The detective admitted that his decision to check the factory had just been a shot in the dark.*

should [ʃud] – *neg short form* **shouldn't** ['ʃudnt] – *modal aux* **1** *pt of* **shall**: *I thought I should never see you again.* **2** used to state that something ought (not) to happen, be done *etc*: *You shouldn't do things like that*; *You should hold your knife in your right hand.* **3** used to state that something is (not) likely to happen *etc*: *If you leave now, you should* *arrive there by six o'clock.* **4** used after certain expressions of sorrow, surprise *etc*: *It's surprising that you should say that*; *It is unfortunate that you should decide to leave at this time.* **5** (*formal*) used, after **if** or with the subject following the modal, to state a condition referring to a possible future event: *If anything should happen to me, I want you to remember everything I have told you today*; *Should anything ever happen to me, all my money will be yours.* **6** (*esp Brit*: **I** *or* **we**) used to state that a person wishes something was possible: *I should love to go to France,* (*if only I had enough money*). **7** used to refer to an event *etc* which is rather surprising: *I was just about to get on the bus when who should come along but John, the very person I was going to visit.*

'should have 1 used to state that something ought (not) to have happened, been done *etc* at some time in the past: *You should have come to the party last night.* **2** used to state that something is (not) likely to happen *etc* before some time in the future: *I should have finished this by tomorrow night.* **3** used after certain expressions of sorrow, surprise *etc* when referring to something which has happened: *It is most unfortunate/surprising that he should have chosen that moment to leave.* **4** (*formal*) used, after **if** or with the subject following the modal, to state a condition referring to a possible future event: *If anything should have happened to her, I'll make him sorry for what he did.* **5** (*esp Brit*: *with* **I** *or* **we**) used to state that a person wishes that something had been possible: *I should have loved to have been there* (*but unfortunately I wasn't able to be*). **6** used to refer to something rather surprising which has happened: *Who should have been there before me but John!*

shoulder ['ʃouldə] *nc* **1** the part of the body between the neck and the upper arm: *The bullet hit him in the shoulder*; *He was carrying the child on his shoulders.* **2** anything that resembles a shoulder in shape or position: *the shoulder of the hill.* **3** the part of a garment that covers the shoulder: *The shoulder of a coat.* **4** the upper part of the foreleg of an animal. – *See also* **shoulder** *in phrase below.* – *vt* **1** to lift on to the shoulder: *He shouldered his pack and set off on his walk.* **2** to bear the full weight of (something): *He must shoulder his responsibilities.* **3** to push with the shoulder, or make (one's way) by doing this: *He shouldered his way through the crowd.*

'shoulder-blade *nc* the broad flat bone of the back of the shoulder; the scapula: *He broke his shoulder-blade when he fell.*

give (someone) the cold shoulder *see* **cold**.

the hard shoulder the strip of ground covered with a hard material which runs along the side of a motorway *etc*, on which cars *etc* may stop when in difficulty *etc*: *He felt rather ill so he pulled over on to the hard shoulder and stopped the car.*

head and shoulders above *see* **head**.

put one's shoulder to the wheel (*inf*) to begin to work very hard: *We'll have to put our shoulders to the wheel if we are going to finish this by Christmas.*

shoulder to shoulder close together; side by side: *They marched along, shoulder to shoulder*; (*fig*) *We'll fight this battle shoulder to shoulder, and we'll show the management that they can't treat their staff like slaves.*

shouldn't *see* **should**.

shout [ʃaut] *nc* **1** a loud cry or call: *He heard a shout.* **2** a loud burst (of laughter, cheering *etc*): *A shout went up from the crowd when he scored a goal.* – *vti* (*often with* **at** *or* **to**) to say (something) very loudly: *He shouted the message across the river*; *I'm not deaf, so there's no need to shout*; *He shouted to him to warn him not to go in*; *I don't care how angry you are – don't shout at* (= shout in an angry way at) me.

shout down *vt sep* to make it impossible for a speaker to be heard (*eg* at a meeting) by shouting, jeering *etc* very loudly: *The meeting had to be abandoned because certain people in the audience were determined to shout down all the speakers.*

shout out *vi, vt sep* to shout (something): *The teacher scolded the child for shouting out* (*the answers*) *in class.*

shove [ʃʌv] *vti* (*inf*) to thrust; to push with force; to push aside: *I shoved the papers hurriedly in a drawer*; *I'm sorry for bumping into you – somebody shoved me*; *Do stop shoving!*; *He shoved his way through the crowd.* – *nc* a push: *He gave the table a shove and moved it closer to the wall.*

shove off *vi* (*inf*: *esp in the imperative*: *sometimes offensive*) to go away: *Shove off and leave me alone!*; *Will you please just shove off!*; *I think I'll shove off now.*

shovel ['ʃʌvl] *nc* **1** a kind of broad tool like a spade, but often with a short handle, used for scooping up and moving coal, gravel *etc*: *He cleared the snow from his path with a shovel.* **2** a shovelful: *He put a shovel of coal on the fire.* **3** (the shovel-like part of) a type of machine used for digging, removing rubbish *etc*. – *v* – *pt, ptp* **'shovelled**, (*Amer*) **'shoveled** – *vt* **1** to move (as if) with a shovel, *esp* in large quantities: *He shovelled snow from the path*; (*fig*) *Don't shovel your food into your mouth like that!*

'shovelful *nc* the amount (of something) that can be held, carried *etc* on a shovel: *a shovelful of coal.*

show [ʃou] – *pt* **showed**: *ptps* **showed, shown** – **1** *vt* to allow or cause to be seen: *Show me your new dress*; *You have to show your membership card before you get into the meeting*; *His work is showing signs of improvement.* **2** *vi* to be able to be seen: *Your underskirt is showing*; *The tear in your dress hardly shows*; *There was a faint light showing through the gap in the curtains.* **3** *vti* to offer or display, or to be offered or displayed, for the public to look at: *This picture is now showing at the local cinema*; *They are showing a very interesting film*; *His paintings are being shown at the local art gallery.* **4** *vt* to point out or point to: *He showed me the road to take*; *He showed me the place on his map*; *Show me the one you want*; *Show me the man who did it.* **5** *vt* (*often with* **(a)round**) to guide or conduct: *Please show this lady to the door*; *They showed him round* (*the factory*); *The guide showed the visitors around* (*the castle*). **6** *vt* to demonstrate: *Will you show me how to do it?*; *He showed me a very clever trick.* **7** *vt* to prove: *The incident showed the stupidity of his attitude*; *Is there any way of showing the relationship between these two facts?*; *That just goes to show* (= is evidence of) *how ignorant he is.* **8** *vt* (*formal or liter*) to give or offer (someone) kindness *etc*: *He showed him no mercy.* **9** *vi* (*inf*: *esp Amer*) to show up (*def 4*): *I waited for hours but he didn't show.* – *See also* **show** *in phrases below.* – **1** *nc* (*sometimes in cmpds*) an entertainment, public exhibition, performance *etc*: *a horse-show*; *a flower show*; *the new show at the theatre*; *a TV show.* **2** *nc* a display or act of showing: *a show of strength.* **3** *nc* (*no pl*) an act of pretending to be, do *etc* (something): *He made a show of working* (= pretended to work), *but he wasn't really concentrating.* **4** *nu* appearance, behaviour *etc* which is very, *esp* unnecessarily, splendid or formal: *They just did it for show, in order to make themselves seem more important than they are.* **5** *nc* (*no pl*) an effort or attempt (at doing something); a person's performance: *He put up rather a good show at the chess competition, considering he was just a beginner.* – *See also* **on show** *below.*

'showing *nc* **1** an act of exhibiting: *He gave a showing of his work.* **2** (*formal*: *no pl*) the way in which a person or thing performs: *He made a rather poor showing at the interview*; *On his past showing, he's not likely to pass the exam.* **3** (*formal*) a statement or argument: *On your own showing* (= to judge from your own words), *you ought to punish him.*

'showy *adj* (*formal*) giving an (often false) impression of value by a bright and striking outward appearance: *a showy hat*; *a rather showy person*; *His clothes are too showy for my liking.* **'showiness** *nu.*

'show-business (*inf abbrev* **'showbiz** [-biz]) *nu* the entertainment industry, *esp* the branch of the theatre concerned with variety shows, comedy *etc* rather than serious drama, opera *etc*: *He's in show-business*; (*attrib*) *a show-business personality.*

'showcase *nc* a glass case for displaying objects in a museum, shop *etc*: *There was a beautiful selection of diamond rings in the jeweller's showcases.*

'showdown *nc* (*inf*) an open quarrel *etc* ending a period of hidden rivalry *etc*: *Their feelings in the matter were so strong that a showdown was inevitable.*

'showground *nc* an area where shows (*def 1*) are held: *The showground is used for exhibitions when the show is not being held.*

'show-jumping *nu* a competitive sport in which horses and their riders have to jump a series of artificial fences, walls *etc.*

'showman *nc* **1** a person who owns or manages an entertainment, a stall at a fair *etc.* **2** (*inf*) a person skilled in displaying things (his own abilities *etc*) in such a way as to attract attention: *He said he had to be a bit of a showman in order to attract customers.*

'showmanship *nu* the ability to be, or act of being, a showman (*def 2*): *Showmanship is important to a conjurer.*

'show-off *nc* (*inf*) a person who tries to impress others with his ability to do things *etc*: *She's a terrible show-off – She insisted in speaking to him in French although he can speak English perfectly well.* – *See also* **show off** *below.*

'showroom *nc* a room where objects for sale *etc* are displayed for people to see: *a car showroom*; (*attrib*) *I saw it in the showroom window.*

ˌgive the 'show away to make known a secret, trick *etc*: *She tried to hide but gave the show away by giggling noisily.*

good show! (*Brit*: *slightly old*) that's good; I'm pleased: *Good show! I'm glad he is able to come*; *So you're finished that already! Good show!*

on show being displayed in an exhibition, showroom *etc*: *There are over five hundred paintings on show here.*

show one's face *see* **face**.

a show of hands *see* **hand**.

show off 1 *vt sep* to show or display for admiration: *He showed off his new car by taking it to work*; *She is just showing off her knowledge of French.* **2** *vi* (*inf derog*) to try to impress others with one's possessions, ability to do something *etc*: *She is just showing off – she wants everyone to know how well she speaks French.* – *See also* **show-off** *above.*

show up 1 *vt sep* to make obvious (faults *etc*): *This kind of light really shows up the places where I've mended this coat.* **2** *vt sep* (*inf*) to reveal the faults, mistakes *etc* of (a person): *Mary was so neat that she really showed me up.* **3** *vi* to stand out clearly: *The scratches showed up badly on the photograph.* **4** *vi* (*inf*) to appear or arrive: *I waited for hours, but she never showed up.*

to 'show for (something) having been got as a profit, advantage *etc*: *I've worked for this firm for twenty years and what have I got to show for it? Nothing!*; *I've nothing to show for all my work.*

shower ['ʃauə] *nc* **1** a short fall (*usu* of rain): *I got caught in a shower on my way here.* **2** anything resembling such a fall of rain : *a shower of sparks*; *a shower of bullets*; (*fig*) *a shower of questions.* **3** (*also* **'shower-bath**) a bath in which water is sprayed down on the bather from above: *I'm just going to have/take a shower.* **4** the equivalent used for such a bath: *We're having a shower fitted in the bathroom.* **5** the place where such equipment is set up: *Our shower has a tiled floor.* **6** (*Brit derog*) a group of lazy, foolish, untidy *etc* people: *Now listen, you shower of idiots! I want this whole job done again, and this time do it correctly!* **7** (*Amer*) a party at which gifts are given (to someone about to be married *etc*): *The neighbours held a shower for the girl*; (*attrib*) *a shower party.* – **1** *vti* to pour down in large quantities (on): *They showered confetti on the bride*; (*fig*) *We were showered with invitations.* **2** *vi* to bathe in a shower: *He showered quickly before he got dressed.*

'showery *adj* raining from time to time: *showery weather*; *It's a bit showery today.*

shower-bath *see* **shower** (*n def 3*).

'showerproof *adj* (of material, a coat *etc*) which will not be soaked by a light shower of rain: *Is this coat showerproof?*; *Showerproof material would be no protection against a heavy thunder-storm.*

shown *etc see* **show**.

shrank *see* **shrink**.

shrapnel ['ʃrapnəl] *nu* **1** small pieces of metal from an explosive shell, bomb *etc*: *His leg was torn open by shrapnel.* **2** such a bomb or bombs: *They're firing shrapnel at us.*

shred [ʃred] *nc* a long, narrow strip (*esp* very small) torn or cut off: *The lion tore his coat to shreds*; (*fig*) *There's not a shred of evidence for that assertion.* – *v* – *pt, ptp* **'shredded** – *vt* to cut or tear into shreds: *They shredded the cabbage to make cole-slaw.*

shrew [ʃru:] *nc* **1** a type of small mouse-like animal with a long, pointed nose. **2** (*old or liter*) a quarrelsome or scolding woman: *Shakespeare wrote a play called 'The Taming of the Shrew'.*

'shrewish *adj* (*old or liter*: *derog*) (of women) ill-tempered; quarrelsome: *a shrewish woman*; *She is mean and shrewish.*

shrewd [ʃru:d] *adj* showing good practical judgement: *a shrewd man*; *He is very shrewd*; *a shrewd choice.* **'shrewdly** *adv.* **'shrewdness** *nu.*

shriek [ʃri:k] *vti* to give out, or say with, a high scream or laugh: *She shrieked if she saw a spider*; *She was shrieking with laughter.* – *nc* such a scream or laugh: *She gave a shriek as she felt someone grab her arm*; *shrieks of laughter.*

shrift *see* **give (someone or something) short shrift** *under* **short**.

shrill [ʃril] *adj* high-pitched and piercing: *the shrill cry of a child*; *Her voice is very shrill.* **'shrilly** *adv.* **'shrillness** *nu.*

shrimp [ʃrimp] *nc* **1** a kind of small long-tailed shellfish: *The children were fishing for shrimps.* **2** (*inf*: *often derog*) a small person: *He is quite tall but his brother is just a shrimp.* – *vi* to (try to) catch shrimps: *We're going shrimping tomorrow.*

shrine [ʃrain] *nc* **1** a holy or sacred place: *Many people visited the shrine where the saint lay buried.* **2** a *usu* highly-decorated case for holding holy objects: *This shrine contains the bones of Saint Francis.*

shrink [ʃriŋk] – *pt* **shrank** [ʃraŋk]: *ptp* **shrunk** [ʃrʌŋk] – **1** *vti* to (cause material, clothes *etc* to) become smaller: *My jersey shrank in the wash*; *Do they shrink the material before they make it up into clothes?*; (*fig*) *Business at his shop has shrunk to nothing in the past few weeks.* **2** *vi* (*often with* **back**) to move back in fear, disgust *etc* (from): *She shrank back from the man.* **3** *vi* to try to avoid or wish to avoid (something unpleasant): *I shrank from telling him the terrible news.*

'shrinkage [-kidʒ] *nu* the act of shrinking, or the amount by which something shrinks: *I have made the skirt larger to allow for shrinkage.*

shrunken ['ʃrʌŋk(ən)] *adj* (*formal*) having been made or become smaller: *The cannibals had decorated their huts with shrunken heads*; *He had become old and shrunken since I had last seen him.*

shrivel ['ʃrivl] – *pt, ptp* **'shrivelled**, (*Amer*) **'shriveled** – *vti* to make or become dried up, wrinkled and withered: *A person's skin shrivels with age*; *The flowers shrivelled because of the heat.*

shrivel up *vi, vt sep* to shrivel: *The flowers shrivelled up*; *The heat shrivelled up the flowers.*

shroud [ʃraud] *nc* **1** a cloth wrapped around a dead body: *This cloth is said to be Christ's shroud.* **2** something that covers and encloses like cloth: *The mountain was hidden in a shroud of mist.* – *vt* (*usu in passive*: *often fig*) to cover or hide: *The whole incident was shrouded in mystery.*

shrouds *n pl* the ropes from the top of a ship's mast(s) to the ship's sides: *The sailors climbed the shrouds.*

shrub [ʃrʌb] *nc* a small bush or woody plant: *He has planted a lot of bushes and shrubs in his garden.*

'shrubbery *nc* a place, *usu* a part of a garden, where shrubs are grown.

shrug [ʃrʌg] – *pt, ptp* **shrugged** – *vti* to show doubt, lack of interest *etc* by raising (the shoulders): *When I asked him if he knew what had happened, he just shrugged* (*his shoulders*). – *nc* an act of shrugging: *She gave a shrug of disbelief.*

shrug off *vt sep* to dismiss, get rid of or treat as unimportant: *She shrugged off all criticism and calmly went on with the project.*

shrunk, shrunken *see* **shrink**.

shudder ['ʃʌdə] *vi* to tremble from fear, disgust, cold *etc*: *The thought of having to look at the dead body made me shudder.* – *nc* an act of trembling in this way: *She gave a shudder of horror.*

shuffle ['ʃʌfl] **1** *vti* to move (one's feet) along the ground *etc* without lifting them: *Do stop shuffling* (*your feet*)! **2** *vi* (*often with* **along, past** *etc*) to walk in this way: *The old man shuffled along the street.* **3** *vti* to mix (playing-cards *etc*): *It's your turn to shuffle* (*the cards*). – *nc* an act of shuffling: *The old man walked with a shuffle*; *He gave the cards a shuffle.*

'shuffler *nc.*

shun [ʃʌn] – *pt, ptp* **shunned** – *vt* (*formal*) to avoid or keep away from: *When he got out of prison, he was shunned by all his former friends.*

shunt [ʃʌnt] *vt* **1** to move (a train, carriages *etc*) on to another track, *esp* a siding: *The coaches were shunted on to the branch line.* **2** (*fig inf*) to move (something) out of the way: *The poor child was always being shunted off to his grandmother's house.*

shut [ʃʌt] – *prp* **'shutting**: *pt, ptp* **shut** – **1** *vt* to move (a door, window, lid *etc*) so that it covers or fills an opening; to move (a drawer, book *etc*) so that it is no longer open: *Shut that door, please!*; *He shut the drawer and locked it*; *Shut your eyes and don't look*; *Shut your books now, and I'll ask you some questions about what you've been reading.* **2** *vi* to become closed: *The window shut with a bang.* **3** *vti* to close and *usu* lock (a building *etc*) *eg* at the end of the day or when people no longer work there; to become closed and *usu* locked at such a time: *The shops all shut at half past five*; *She shut the shop and went home*; *There's a rumour that the factory is going to be shut.* – *See also* **shut down, shut up** *below.* **4** *vt* (*often with* **away, in, out** *etc*) to keep in or out of some place or keep away from someone by shutting something: *The dog was shut inside the house*; *We shut the dog in at night, and shut the cat out*; *He shut himself in his room and refused to come out.* **5** *vt* to hurt or damage (something) by shutting something: *He shut his finger in the door* (= He caught his fingers between the door and the door frame).

shut down *vi, vt sep* (of a factory *etc*) to close or be closed, for a time or permanently: *There is a rumour going round that the factory is going to* (*be*) *shut down* (*nc* **'shut-down**).

shut off *vt sep* **1** to stop an engine working, a liquid flowing *etc*: *Is there any way of shutting off that part of the motor?*; *I'll need to shut the gas off before I repair the fire.* **2** to keep away (from); to make separate (from): *He shut himself off from the rest of the world.*

shut up **1** *vi, vt sep* (*inf*) to (cause to) stop speaking: *Tell them to shut up!*; *That'll shut him up!* **2** *vt sep* to close and lock: *It's time to shut up the shop.* **3** *vt sep* to shut in: *He shut himself up in his room.*

shutter ['ʃʌtə] *nc* **1** (*usu in pl*) one of *usu* two *usu* wooden covers over a window: *He closed the shutters.* **2** the moving cover over the lens of a camera, which opens when a photograph is taken: *When the shutter opens, light is allowed into the camera and reacts with the film*; (*attrib*) *a shutter speed of one-sixtieth of a second* (= the shutter opens for one-sixtieth of second). – *vt* (*usu in passive*) to close with shutters: *The windows will need to be shuttered because there's a storm coming.*

'shuttered *adj*: *shuttered windows.*

shuttle ['ʃʌtl] *nc* **1** in weaving, a piece of equipment for carrying the thread backwards and forwards across the other threads. **2** a piece of machinery for making loops in the lower thread in a sewing-machine. **3** (*inf*) an air, train or other transport service *etc* which operates constantly backwards and forwards between two places: *They operate a shuttle between the supermarket and the town centre*; (*attrib*) *a shuttle service*; (*fig*: *attrib*) *shuttle diplomacy* (= done by a person travelling backwards and forwards between two or more places).

'shuttlecock *nc* a rounded cork *etc*, with feathers *etc* fixed in it, used in the game of badminton.

shy[1] [ʃai] – *compar* **'shyer** *or* **'shier**: *superl* **'shyest** *or* **'shiest** – *adj* **1** lacking confidence in the presence of others, *esp* strangers; not wanting to attract attention: *She is too shy to go to parties*; *She's a very shy girl.* **2** (*with* **of**) drawing back from (an action, person *etc*): *He is shy of giving his opinion*; *She is shy of strangers.* **3** (of a wild animal) easily frightened; timid: *Deer are very shy animals.* – *vi* (*with* **at**) (of a horse) to jump or turn suddenly aside in fear: *The horse shied at a paper bag caught in the hedge.*

'shyly *adv.* **'shyness** *nu.*

fight shy of *see* **fight**.

shy[2] [ʃai] *vt* (*old*) to toss or throw (a ball *etc*). – *nc* (*old*) a throw (at something).

'coconut shy *nc* a stall in a fair *etc* at which people throw balls at coconuts and try to knock them off tall stands.

sibilant ['sibilənt] *nc, adj* (*formal or tech*) (of, like or with) a hissing sound or sounds: *a sibilant whisper*; *The sounds represented by the letters 's' and 'sh' are sibilants.*

sick [sik] *adj* **1** (*usu pred*: *sometimes in cmpds*) vomiting or inclined to vomit: *He has been sick* (= has vomited) *several times today*; *I think I'm going to be sick*; *I feel sick*; *That pudding made me sick* (*see also* **make (someone) sick** *below*); *She's inclined to be seasick/airsick/car-sick* (= is likely to feel sick when travelling in a boat/plane/car). **2** (*esp Amer*: *Brit usu attrib*) ill: *He is a sick man*; (*Amer*) *The doctor told me that my husband is very sick and may not live very long.* **3** (*pred with* **of**) very tired (of); wishing to have no more (of): *I'm sick of doing this*; *I'm sick and tired of hearing about it!* **4** (*usu pred*) affected by strong, unhappy or unpleasant feelings: (*liter*) *He was sick at heart*; (*inf*) *I was really sick at making that bad mistake.* – *See also* **homesick** *under* **home**. **5** in bad taste: *a sick joke*; *His remarks were rather sick*; *sick humour.* – *nu* (*inf*) vomit: *The bedclothes were covered with sick.*

'sicken 1 *vi* (*often with* **for**) to become sick: (*liter*) *He rapidly sickened and died*; *He is sickening for something* (= becoming ill with some disease). **2** *vt* (*inf*) to disgust: *The very thought sickens me.*

'sickening *adj* (*inf*) causing sickness, disgust or weariness; very unpleasant or annoying: *There was a sickening crunch*; *The weather is really sickening!* **'sickeningly** *adv.*

'sickly *adj* **1** tending to be often ill: *She is rather sickly*; *a sickly child.* **2** suggesting sickness; pale; feeble: *a sickly complexion*; (*fig*) *a sickly yellow*; *She looks sickly.*

'sickness 1 *nu* (*sometimes in cmpds*) the state of being sick or ill: *There seems to be a lot of sickness in the town*; *He's suffering from sickness and diarrhoea*; *seasickness*; *Some people develop altitude sickness when climbing high mountains.* **2** *nc* (*old*) an illness; a disease.

'sick-bay *nc* a room *etc* set aside for ill or injured people in a ship, boarding-school *etc*: *The wounded sailors were carried to the sick-bay.*

'sick-bed *nc* (*liter*) a bed in which a person is lying ill.

'sick-leave *nu* time taken off from work *etc* because of sickness: *He has been on sick-leave for the last three days.*

'sick list *nc* the list of people in some place, organization *etc* who are ill: *How many are on the sick list today?*

'sickroom *nc* (*formal or liter*) a room where a person is, or people are, ill: *Hygiene is very important in a/the sickroom.*

make (someone) sick (*inf*) to make (someone) feel very annoyed, upset *etc*: *It makes me sick to see him waste money like that.* – *See also* **sick** (*def 1*).

the sick (*formal*: *old or liter*) ill people: *He spent his life visiting the sick.*

'sickness benefit money given *usu* by the government, to a person who is unable to work because of illness.

worried sick (*inf*) very worried: *I'm worried sick about it.*

sickle ['sikl] *nc* a tool with a curved blade for cutting grain *etc*: *He used a sickle to cut the long grass growing round his trees.*

side [said] *nc* **1** (the ground beside) an edge, border or boundary line: *He walked round the side of the field*; *He was standing by the side of the road*; *He was standing on the far side of the river* (= the side farthest from me); *He lives on the same side of the street as me.* **2** a surface of something: *a cube has six sides.* **3** one of the two of such surfaces which are not the top, bottom, front, or back: *There is a label on the side of the box*; *There's a door at the side of the house*; (*attrib*) *a side-door.* **4** either surface of a piece of paper, cloth *etc*: *Don't waste paper – write on both sides!* **5** the right or left part of the body (*esp*, of people, between the armpit and hip): *My side is sore*; *I've got a pain in my side*; *He bought a side of beef.* **6** a part or division of a town *etc*: *He lives on the north side of the town.* **7** (*often in cmpds*) a slope (of a hill): *a mountain-side*; *the side of the valley.* **8** a point of view; an aspect: *We must look at all sides of the problem.* **9** a party, team *etc* which is opposing another: *Whose side are you on?*; *Which side is winning?* – *See also* **pick sides** *below.* **10** the set of relatives, ancestors *etc* a person has through his father or his mother: *He takes after his father's side* (*of the family*); *He is related to the Prime Minister on his mother's side.* – *See also* **side** *in phrases below.* – *adj* (*attrib*) additional, but less important: *a side issue.* – *v see* **side with** *below.*

-side (*in cmpds*) (the ground *etc* beside) the edge of something: *He walked along the dockside/quayside*; *a roadside café.*

-sided (*in cmpds*) having (a certain number or type of) sides: *a ˌfour-sided 'figure.*

'sidelong *adj* (*usu attrib*), *adv* from or to the side; not directly: *a sidelong glance*; *He glanced sidelong at her.*

'sideways *adj* (*usu attrib*) *adv* to or towards one side: *He moved sideways*; *a sideways movement.*

'siding *nc* a short line of rails on which trucks *etc* are moved from the main line: *The trucks were shunted into a siding near to the station.*

'sideboard *nc* a *usu* large piece of furniture, *usu* in a dining-room, for holding dishes *etc.*

'sideburns *n pl* the *usu* short hair grown on the side of a man's face in front of the ears.

'sidecar *nc* a type of small, *usu* single-wheeled vehicle fixed to the side of a motorcycle with a seat for a passenger: *His wife travels in the sidecar.*

'side effect *nc* an additional (often bad) effect of a drug *etc*: *I have to take these pink pills to help me sleep, and these blue ones to counteract the side effects of the pink ones.*

'sidekick *nc* (*sl derog*) a partner, assistant or special friend: *He has some sort of sidekick he calls his 'Financial Adviser'.*

'sidelight *nc* **1** a light fixed to the side, or at the side of the front or back, of a car, boat *etc*: *He switched his sidelights on when it began to get dark.* **2** something which gives information about or helps to explain a puzzling subject: *The story provides an interesting sidelight on the world of finance.*

'sideline *nc* **1** (*fig*) a business *etc* carried on outside one's regular job or activity: *He runs a mail-order business as a sideline.* **2** the line marking one of the long edges of a football pitch *etc.*

'sidelines *n pl* (*fig*) the position or point of view of a person not actually taking part in a sport, argument *etc*: *He threw in the occasional suggestion from the sidelines.*

ˌside-'on *adv, adj* (*attrib*) with the side of something towards (an attacker *etc*): *They turned the boat in order to meet their attackers side-on*; *a side-on crash.*

'side-road *nc* a small, minor road: *He turned down a side-road and drove towards the farm.*

'side-saddle *adv* (of a woman on horseback) with both legs on one side of the saddle: *Women who wear skirts on horseback normally ride side-saddle.*

'sideshow *nc* (*often in pl*) a stall with some form of amusement or game at a fair, beside a circus *etc*: *I don't really like circuses – I only go for the sideshows.*

'sidestep – *pt, ptp* **'sidestepped** – **1** *vi* to step to one side: *He sidestepped as his attacker tried to grab him.* **2** *vt* to avoid by stepping to one side: *He sidestepped his attacker*; (*fig*) *I feel you are sidestepping the problem.*

'side-street *nc* a small, minor street: *The man ran down a side-street and disappeared.*

'sidetrack *vt* (*fig*) to turn (a person) aside from what he was about to do: *I intended to write letters this evening, but was sidetracked into going to the pictures instead.*

'sidewalk *nc* (*Amer*) a pavement or footpath.

'side-whiskers *n pl* (*old*) long hair grown on the side of a man's face.

choose sides *see* **pick/choose sides** *below.*

from all sides from every direction: *People were running towards him from all sides.*

on all sides all around: *They were trapped – with enemies on all sides.*

on the 'short, 'long, 'tight *etc* **side** (*inf*) rather too short, long, tight *etc*: *This shirt is a bit on the small side for me.*

on the 'side (*sl*) in another way than through one's ordinary occupation: *He is earning quite a lot on the side as a singer.*

pick, choose sides to select the people for each team *etc* before a game: *The children had many ways of picking sides*; *Let's pick sides and start the game.*

side by side beside one another; close together: *They walked along the street side by side.*

'side with *vt fus* (*often with* **against**) to give support to (a person, group *etc*) in an argument *etc*: *Don't side with him against us!*

take sides to choose to support a particular opinion, group *etc* against another: *Everybody in the office took sides in the dispute*; *Don't take sides against us!*

sidle ['saidl] *vi* to go or move, *esp* sideways, in a manner not intended to attract attention or as if one is shy or uncertain: *The little boy sidled up to me*; *He sidled out of the room.*

siege [siːdʒ] *nc* an attempt to capture a fort or town by keeping it surrounded by an armed force until it surrenders: *the siege of Paris*; *The town is under siege.*

lay siege to to besiege; to begin a siege of: *They laid siege to the town.*

siesta [si'estə] *nc* (*usu facet or when referring to people in Spain or South and Central America*) a short sleep or rest, *esp* one taken in the early afternoon after the midday meal: *It's too hot to work – I think I'll lie out in the sun and have a siesta.*

sieve [siv] *nc* a container with a bottom full of very small holes, used to separate liquids from solids or small, fine pieces from larger ones *etc*: *He poured the soup through a sieve to remove all the lumps.* – *vt* to pass (something) through a sieve: *You'd better sieve that flour to remove the lumps in it.* – *See also* **sift**.

have a head/memory like a sieve to be very forgetful: *I'd better write the date of the meeting in my diary – I've got a head like a sieve.*

sift [sift] *vt* **1** to separate by passing through a sieve *etc*: *Sift the flour before making the cake.* **2** to examine closely: *He sifted the evidence carefully.*

sigh [sai] *vi* **1** to take a long, deep-sounding breath showing tiredness, sadness, longing *etc*: *He thought of the long distance he still had to travel and sighed*; *She sighed with exasperation.* **2** (*formal or liter*) (of wind) to make a sound like this. – *vt* to say, or express, with sighs: *'I've still got several hours' work to do,' he sighed*; *He sighed his reluctant agreement to the proposal.* – *nc* an act of sighing: *a sigh of discontent.*

heave a sigh to sigh: *She heaved a sigh of relief when she found her purse.*

'sigh for *vt fus* (*liter*) to regret: *He sighed for his lost opportunities.*

sight [sait] **1** *nu* the act or power of seeing: *The blind man had lost his sight in the war*; *His sight has improved since his operation*; *Birds have a keen sense of sight.* **2** *nu* the area within which things can be seen by someone: *I waited a whole hour at the bus stop before a bus at last came into sight*; *He looked up the street but the car was out of sight* (= had disappeared) *round the corner*; *The boat was within sight of land* (= Land could be seen from the boat); (*fig*) *The end of our troubles is in sight.* **3** *nc* (*usu pl*) something worth seeing: *She took her visitors to see the sights of London.* **4** *nc* a view or glimpse: *I would like a sight of those papers.* **5** *nc* something seen that is unusual, ridiculous, shocking *etc*: *She's quite a sight in that hat.* **6** *nc* (on a gun *etc*) an apparatus to guide the eye in taking aim: *Where is the sight on a rifle?* – *See also* **sight** *in phrases below.* – *vt* **1** (*formal*: not used with **is, was** *etc* and **-ing**) to get a view of; to see suddenly: *We sighted the coast as dawn broke.* **2** to look at (something) through the sight of a gun: *He sighted his prey and pulled the trigger.*

'sight-reading *nu* reading or playing from music that one has not seen before: *He is a good pianist, but he is no good at sight-reading.*

'sight-seeing *nu* visiting the chief buildings, places of interest *etc* of an area: *They spent a lot of their holiday sightseeing in London*; (*attrib*) *a sight-seeing tour.* **'sight-seer** *nc.*

a sight (*sl*) a great deal; a great many: *He got a sight more money than he expected.*

a sight for sore eyes (*inf*) a most welcome sight: *You're a sight for sore eyes!*

at/on 'sight as soon as seen, without previous

practice: *playing music at sight*; (*very formal*) *a bill payable at sight.*

catch sight of to get a brief view of; to begin to see: *He caught sight of her as she came round the corner.*

in/out of sight *see* **sight** (*def 2*).

keep sight of to remain close enough to see (something): *He kept sight of her as she walked along the street*; (*fig*) *We must keep sight of our original intention.*

lose sight of to stop being able to see: *She lost sight of him in the crowd.*

See also **unsightly**.

sign [sain] *nc* **1** a mark used to mean something; a symbol: + *is the sign for addition.* **2** (*often in cmpds*) a notice set up to give information (a shopkeeper's name, the direction of a town *etc*) to the public: *a road-sign*; *an inn-sign.* **3** a movement (*eg* a nod, wave of the hand) used to mean or represent something: *He made a sign to me to keep still.* **4** a piece of evidence suggesting that something is present or about to come: *There were no signs of life at the house and he was afraid they were away*; *Mist in the morning is a sign of good weather.* – **1** *vti* to write one's name (on): *Sign at the bottom, please*; *He took out his pen to sign a cheque.* **2** *vt* to write (one's name) on a letter, document *etc*: *He signed his name on the document.* **3** *vi* to make a movement of the head, hand *etc* in order to show one's meaning: *She signed to me to say nothing.* – *See also* **sign** *in phrases below.*

'signboard *nc* a board with a notice: *In the garden was a signboard which read 'House for Sale'.*

'signpost *nc* a post with a sign on it, showing the direction and distance of places: *We saw a signpost which told us we were 80 kilometres from London.*

sign away *vt sep* to give away or transfer, by signing one's name: *She signed away her money to her daughter.*

sign in/out *vi* to record one's arrival (*esp* at work) or departure by writing one's name: *We have to sign in when we arrive at the office*; *He signed in at the hotel when he arrived.*

sign off (*inf*) **1** *vi* to stop work: *Because of the bad weather, we signed off at four o'clock.* **2** *vi* (of a radio channel *etc*) to stop broadcasting: *Radio 3 signed off at midnight.* **3** *vt sep* to sign a certificate of (someone's) unfitness to work: *The doctor has signed me off for a month.*

sign on *vti* to engage (oneself) for work *etc*: *He signed on a new crew in London*; *Every week more people sign on at the Labour Exchange.*

sign up **1** *vi* to join an organization or make an agreement to do something *etc* by writing one's name: *I have signed up for a place on the outing next week.* **2** *vt* to engage for work by making a legal contract: *The football club have signed up two new players for this season.*

signal ['signəl] *nc* **1** a sign (*eg* a movement of the hand, a light, a sound), *esp* one arranged beforehand, giving a command, warning or other message: *He gave the signal to advance*; (*fig*) *His arrival was the signal for the party to begin.* **2** a machine *etc* used for this purpose: *a railway signal.* **3** (*tech*) the wave, sound received or sent out by a radio set *etc.* – *v* – *pt, ptp* **'signalled**, (*Amer*) **'signaled** – **1** *vti* to make signals (to): *He was signalling urgently to me*; *The policeman signalled the driver to stop.* **2** *vt* to send (a message *etc*) by means of signals: *They were signalling orders from the shore.*

'signal-box *nc* the building in which a railway signalman works: *There is a signal-box next to the station.*

'signalman *nc* **1** a person who operates railway signals: *The signalman waved to the driver as the train passed the signal-box.* **2** a person who sends signals in general: *He is a signalman in the army.*

signature ['signətʃə] **1** *nc* a signed name: *That is his signature on the cheque.* **2** *nu* an act of signing one's name: *Signature of this document means that you agree with us.* **3** *nc* (*music*: *usu* **ˌkey-'signature, 'time-signature**) signs placed at the beginning of a piece or section of written music to identify its key and time.

'signatory [-təri, (*Amer*) -to:ri] *nc* (*formal*) a person who has signed an agreement to do something: *He was one of the signatories of the peace treaty.*

'signature tune *nc* a piece of music used to identify and often to introduce a particular person, television programme *etc*: *The programme was introduced as usual by its signature tune.*

signet-ring ['signitriŋ] *nc* a ring bearing a small, flat stone *etc* carved with the owner's initials *etc*: *He wore a signet-ring set with a small emerald and carved with a horse's head.*

signify ['signifai] *vt* (*formal*) **1** to be a sign of; to mean: *His frown signified disapproval*; *That sign on the map signifies a church with a tower.* **2** to show; to make known by a sign, gesture *etc*: *He signified his approval with a nod.*

significance [sig'nifikəns] *nu* (*slightly formal*) meaning or importance: *a matter of great significance.*

significant [sig'nifikənt] *adj* (*slightly formal*) having a lot of meaning or importance: *He has told us all the significant facts*; *There was no significant change in the patient's condition*; *The difference in their ages is not significant.*

significantly [sig'nifikəntli] *adv* (*slightly formal*) **1** in a significant manner: *He patted his pocket significantly.* **2** to an important degree: *Sales-levels are significantly lower than last year, which is very disappointing.*

See also **insignificant**.

silage *see* **silo**.

silence ['sailəns] **1** *ncu* (a period of) absence of sound or of speech: *There was silence in the room while everyone read the newspapers*; *A sudden silence followed his remark*; *There was a long silence before anyone spoke.* **2** *nu* failure to mention, tell something *etc*: *Your silence on this subject is disturbing.* – *See also* **in silence** *below.* – *vt* (*formal*) to cause to be silent: *The arrival of the teacher silenced the class*; *the government's attempts to silence their critics.* – *interj* be silent!

'silencer *nc* a piece of equipment fitted to a gun, or (*Amer* **'muffler**) in an engine, for making noise less: *The gun was fitted with a silencer and the shot could not be heard.*

'silent [-t] *adj* **1** free from noise: *It was a silent, windless night*; *The house was empty and silent.* **2** not speaking: *a silent man*; *He was silent on that subject.* **3** not making any noise: *This lift is quite silent.* **'silently** *adv.*

in 'silence without saying anything: *The children listened in silence to the story.*

silhouette [silu'et] *nc* **1** an outline drawing of a person *esp* seen from the side and *usu* filled in with black: *A silhouette in a silver frame hung on the wall.* **2** (*formal*) a dark image, *esp* a shadow, seen against the light: *The woman's silhouette appeared on the drawn blind of her lighted window.* – *vt* (*formal*) (of a light) to show up an object as a silhouette: *The trees on the top of the hill were silhouetted against the setting sun.*

silk [silk] *nu, adj* **1** (of) very fine, soft threads made by silkworms: *She sewed it with thread made from silk*; *silk thread.* **2** (of) thread, cloth *etc* made from this: *a silk dress*; *The dress was* (*made of*) *silk.*

'silken *adj* (*old or liter*) **1** made of silk: *a silken gown.* **2** silky.

'silky *adj* soft, fine and rather shiny like silk: *The dog had long, silky hair*; *This shampoo will make your hair soft and silky.* **'silkiness** *nu.*

'silkworm *nc* the caterpillar of certain moths, which makes silk.

sill [sil] *nc* a ledge of wood, stone *etc* at the foot of an opening, such as a window or a door: *The windows of the old house were loose, and the sills were crumbling.*

See also **window-sill** *under* **window**.

silly ['sili] *adj* foolish; not sensible: *Don't be so silly!*; *You are all silly little girls!*; *That was a silly thing to say.* **'silliness** *nu.*

silo ['sailou] – *pl* **'silos** – *nc* an airtight pit or tall round tower used for storing grain or silage: *The corn was kept in a silo until it was needed.*

'silage [-lidʒ] *nu* food (grass *etc*) kept for feeding farm animals in winter, stored in a silo.

silt [silt] *nu* fine sand and mud left behind by flowing water: *The banks of the river were formed by silt brought down from the hills.*

silt up *vi, vt sep* to (cause to) become blocked by mud *etc*: *The harbour had gradually silted up, so that large boats could no longer use it.*

silver ['silvə] *nu* **1** an element (symbol **Ag**), a precious grey metal which is used in making jewellery, ornaments *etc*: *The tray was made of solid silver.* **2** money made of silver or a metal alloy used instead of it: *He pulled a handful of silver from his pocket.* **3** anything made of, or looking like, silver *esp* knives, forks, spoons *etc*: *Burglars broke into the house and stole all our silver.* – *adj* **1** made of, of the colour of, or looking like, silver: *a silver brooch*; *silver stars/paint.* **2** (*attrib*) (of a wedding anniversary, jubilee *etc*) twenty-fifth: *We celebrated our silver wedding* (*anniversary*) *last month*; *Queen Elizabeth II's silver jubilee occurred in 1977.*

'silvery *adj* (*usu attrib*) **1** like silver, *esp* in colour: *The door-handle was made of a silvery metal.* **2** (*liter*) (of sound) clear, high-pitched and musical: *A flute has a sweet, silvery sound.*

silver foil/paper *nu* a common type of wrapping material, made of metal and having a silvery appearance: *Chocolate bars are sold wrapped in silver paper*; *He wrapped the chicken in* (*silver*) *foil before putting it in the oven.*

'silverside *nu* (*Brit*) the upper and better side of a round of beef: *Two kilos of silverside, please.*

'silversmith *nc* a person who makes and/or sells silver articles: *This bowl is the work of an expert silversmith.*

similar ['similə] *adj* (*often with* **to**) alike in many (often most) ways; having a resemblance: *Your situation is similar to mine*; *Our jobs are similar.*

simi'larity [-'la-] *nu.*

'similarly *adv* in the same, or a similar, way: *My brother was taught to read by my mother, and similarly, so was I.*

simile ['siməli] *ncu* a form of expression using 'like' or 'as', in which one thing is compared to another which it only resembles in one or a small number of ways: *'Her hair was like silk' is an example of simile*; *'A mind sharp as a needle' was the simile that he used.*

simmer ['simə] **1** *vti* to (cause) to cook gently at or just below boiling point: *The stew simmered on the stove*; *Simmer the ingredients in water for five minutes*; (*formal fig*) *His resentment simmered for weeks.* **2** *vi* (of a person) to go on feeling annoyance, resentment *etc* without saying much: *All day she was simmering with impatience, longing for the evening to come.*

simmer down *vi* (*inf*: *usu in imperative*) to calm down: *Do simmer down – there's no point in being angry*; *She'll soon simmer down.*

simper ['simpə] **1** *vi* to smile in a silly manner: *I don't like her – she simpers and giggles too much.* **2** *vt* to say with a simper: *She simpered her thanks for their congratulations.* – *nc* a silly smile: *'Thank you,' she said with a simper.*

simple ['simpl] *adj* **1** not difficult; easy: *This job will be quite simple*; *a simple task.* **2** not complicated or involved: *a simple choice*; *The matter is not as simple as you think*; *a simple shape.* **3** not fancy or unusual; plain: *a simple dress/design*; *His tastes are very simple*; *He leads a very simple life*; *I like simple, everyday objects.* **4** (*attrib*) pure; mere: *the simple truth*; *That remark of his was simple rudeness.* **5** (*attrib*: *old*) of humble rank: *a simple peasant.* **6** trusting and easily cheated: *She is too simple to see through his lies*; *She's just a simple soul – she has never learnt to distrust people.* **7** weak in the mind; not very intelligent: *I'm afraid he's a bit simple, but he's good with animals*; *He's a rather simple boy.*

'simpleton [-tən] *nc* a foolish person: (*derog*) *Those simpletons at the stationer's have given me the wrong size of paper.*

simplicity [sim'plisəti] *nu* the state of being simple (not *defs 4, 5*): *The beauty of this idea is its simplicity*; *He answered with a child's simplicity.*

ˌsimplifi'cation [-plifi'kei-] (*formal*) **1** *ncu* (an) act of making simpler: *The simplification of the language in their book is not an easy task*; *You could make some simplifications to the text.* **2** *nc* a simpler form: *This plan is a simplification of the original.*

'simplified *adj* (*attrib*) made less difficult or complicated: *simplified language/tasks.*

'simplify [-plifai] *vt* to make simpler: *Can you simplify your language a little? – it's difficult to understand.*

simplistic *adj* (*formal*: *usu derog*) tending to over-simplify: *His approach to the whole problem is rather simplistic, and tends to ignore several important points*; *He proposed a very simplistic solution to the problem.*

'simply *adv* **1** only: *I do it simply for the money.* **2** absolutely: *simply beautiful.* **3** in a simple manner: *She was always very simply dressed.*

simple fracture *nc* a fracture in which the bone does not pierce the skin.

ˌsimple-'minded *adj* of low intelligence; stupid.

ˌsimple-'mindedness *nu.*

See also **pure and simple** *under* **pure**.

simulate ['simjuleit] *vt* (*formal*) to cause (something) to appear to be the case, be real *etc*: *He simulated illness*; *This machine simulates the take-off and landing of an aircraft.*

'simulated *adj* (*formal or tech*: *usu attrib*) artificial; having the appearance of: *simulated leather*; *a simulated accident.*

ˌ**simu'lation** (*formal*) **1** *ncu* (an) act of simulating. **2** *nc* something made to resemble something else: *a simulation by computer of the effects of wind on a tall building.*

simultaneous [siməl'teiniəs, (*Amer*) sai-] *adj* happening, or done, at exactly the same time: *The group of dancers had rehearsed the dance until their movements were absolutely simultaneous; He fell, and there was a simultaneous gasp from the crowd.*
ˌ**simul'taneously** *adv.*
simultaneous translation *ncu* (a) translation of a speaker's words into other languages while he is speaking.

sin [sin] *ncu* wickedness, or a wicked act, *esp* one that breaks a religious law: *It is thought to be a sin to envy the possessions of other people; No-one is entirely free from sin; Lying and cheating are both sins;* (*fig*) *It's a sin that all that good food should go to waste!;* (*fig*) *Arriving late is a sin in his eyes.* – *v* – *pt, ptp* **sinned** – *vi* (*formal*) to do wrong; to commit a sin, *esp* in the religious sense: *Forgive me, Father, for I have sinned.* '**sinner** *nc.*
'**sinful** *adj* wicked. '**sinfully** *adv.* '**sinfulness** *nu.*

since *conj* **1** (*often with* **ever**) from a certain time onwards: *I have been at home* (*ever*) *since I returned from Italy.* **2** at a time after: *Since he agreed to come, he has become ill.* **3** because: *Since you are going, I will go too.* – *adv* **1** (*usu with* **ever**) from that time onwards: *We fought and I have avoided him ever since;* (*formal*) *I have since avoided him.* **2** (*formal*) at a later time: *We have since become friends.* **3** (*inf*) ago: *The matter has been settled long since; His wife died a year since.* – *prep* **1** from the time of (something in the past) until the present time: *Have you seen him since his arrival?; She has been very unhappy ever since her quarrel with her boyfriend; He's never spoken to me since then.* **2** at a time between (something in the past) and the present time: *I've changed my address since last year; I've become converted to his ideas since* (= as a result of) *hearing him speak.* **3** (*inf*) from the time of (the invention, discovery *etc* of): *the greatest invention since the wheel; the best thing since sliced bread.*

sincere [sin'siə] *adj* **1** true; genuine: *a sincere desire; sincere friends; Her concern for our welfare never strikes me as quite sincere.* **2** not trying to pretend or deceive: *a sincere person; He has always been absolutely frank and sincere.*
sin'cerely *adv*: *I sincerely hope that you will succeed.*
sin'cerity [-'se-] *nu* the state of being sincere: *The sincerity of his comments was obvious to all.*
yours sincerely *see* **your**.

sinecure ['sinikjuə] *nc* a job for which one is paid but in which one has little or no work to do: *His position on the board of management is something of a sinecure, I believe.*

sinew ['sinju:] *ncu* (*formal or liter*) (a) strong cord or fibre that joins a muscle to a bone; (a) tendon.
'**sinewy** *adj* (*formal*) **1** having sinews, *esp* well-developed ones; strong, tough vigorous *etc*: *sinewy arms.* **2** (of meat) tough and stringy; containing too many sinews.

sinful *see* **sin**.

sing [siŋ] – *pt* **sang** [saŋ]: *ptp* **sung** [sʌŋ] **1** *vti* to make (musical sounds) with one's voice: *He sings very well; They were singing an ancient Irish tune; She sang a Scottish song; Do you sing bass or baritone?; I could hear the birds singing in the trees.* **2** *vi* (*liter*) to make a sound resembling a musical note: *The kettle sang on the stove; The noise was still singing in her head.*
'**singer** *nc* a person who sings, *eg* as a profession: *Are you a good singer?* (= Do you sing well?); *She wants to train as a singer; He's a trained singer.*
'**singing** *nu* (*often attrib*) the art or activity of making musical sounds with one's voice: *Do you do much singing nowadays?; a singing lesson/teacher; She has a good singing voice.*
'**singsong** *nc* (*Brit*) an informal period of singing entered into by a group of people for their own pleasure: *Let's have a singsong.* – *adj* (*usu attrib*) (of one's speaking voice) going up and down in pitch to a greater extent than normal: *He talks in a singsong voice/way.*
sing out *vi* (*inf*) to shout or call out: *Sing out when you're ready to go.*
sing someone's praises (*inf*) to speak with enthusiasm about someone's ability *etc*: *The boss is always singing his praises.*
See also **song**.

Singapore, Singaporean *see* Appendix 2.

singe [sindʒ] – *prp* '**singeing**: *pt, ptp* **singed** – *vti* to (cause to) burn on the surface; to scorch: *She singed her woollen dress by pressing it with too hot an iron.*

single ['siŋgl] *adj* **1** (*attrib*) one only: *The spider hung on a single thread; Give me a/one single reason why I should lend you money!* **2** (*attrib*) for one person only: *a single bed/mattress.* **3** unmarried: *a single person; She won't be single much longer – she's getting married on Saturday.* **4** (*attrib*) of the basic unit of measurement in size *etc*: *a single whisky.* **5** (*attrib*) for or in one direction only: *a single ticket/journey/fare.* – *nc* (*inf*) **1** a gramophone record with only one tune or song on each side: *This group have just brought out a new single.* **2** a one-way ticket: *Can I have a single to Manchester, please?* – *See also* **single out** *below.*
'**singleness** *nu.*
'**singles 1** *ncu* in tennis *etc*, a match or matches with only one player on each side: *The men's singles are being played this week;* (*attrib*) *a singles match.* **2** *n pl* (*inf esp Amer*) unmarried (*usu* young) people: *a bar for singles;* (*attrib*) *a singles holiday/club.*
'**singly** *adv* one by one; separately: *They came all together, but they left singly.*
ˌ**single-'bedded** *adj* (*usu attrib*) containing one single bed: *a single-bedded room.*
ˌ**single-'breasted** *adj* (*usu attrib*) (of a coat, jacket *etc*) overlapping only slightly at the front, and having only one row of buttons: *a single-breasted tweed suit.*
single combat *nu* (*formal*) fighting by oneself against a single opponent or enemy: *The two armies each chose a champion, and the men chosen then met in single combat.*
ˌ**single-'decker** *nc* a bus *etc* having only one deck or level: *They sometimes put a single-decker on this route;* (*attrib*) *a single-decker bus.*
ˌ**single-'figure** *adj* (*attrib*) in single figures: *single-figure inflation.*
single figures *n pl* the numbers between 1 and 9 inclusive, *esp* the higher ones: *Inflation will be down to single figures next year.*
ˌ**single-'handed** *adj* (*usu attrib*), *adv* working *etc* by oneself, without help: *He runs the restaurant single-handed; single-handed efforts.*
ˌ**single-'minded** *adj* (of a person) having one aim or purpose only: *He is single-minded about his*

work; *a single-minded attitude/devotion to duty.* ˌ**single-ˈmindedly** *adv.* ˌ**single-ˈmindedness** *nu.*

not a single not (even) one: *There's not a single person that I can trust*; *There isn't a single reason why I should help you!*; *I haven't a single pair of shoes without holes in!*

single out *vt sep* to choose or pick out for special treatment: *He was singled out to receive special thanks for his help.*

singsong *see* **sing**.

singular [ˈsiŋgjulə] **1** *nc, adj* (*gram*) (in) the form of a word which expresses only one: *'Foot' is the singular of 'feet'*; *a singular noun/verb*; *The noun 'foot' is singular.* **2** *nu* (*gram*) the state of being singular: *Is this noun in the singular or the plural?* **3** *adj* (*formal*: *usu attrib*) exceptional: *He had a singular success with his last play.* **4** *adj* (*formal*: *usu attrib*) unusual or strange: *I find talking to him a singular experience.* ˌ**singuˈlarity** [-ˈla-] *nu.*

ˈ**singularly** *adv* (*formal*) unusually: *The idea was singularly unpleasant*; *I find him singularly attractive/repulsive.*

Sinhala, Sinhalese *see* Appendix 2.

sinister [ˈsinistə] *adj* suggesting, or warning of, evil: *sinister happenings*; *a sinister stranger*; *His disappearance is extremely sinister*; *His beard makes him look rather sinister.*

sink [siŋk] – *pt* **sank** [saŋk]: *ptp* **sunk** [sʌŋk] – **1** *vti* to (cause to) go down below the surface of water *etc*: *The torpedo sank the battleship immediately*; *The ship sank in deep water.* **2** *vi* to go down or become lower (slowly): *The sun sank slowly behind the hills*; *Her voice sank to a whisper*; *He sank thankfully into a chair.* **3** *vi* to pass gradually into (sleep *etc*): *He sank into a deep sleep.* **4** *vti* to (cause to) go deeply (into something): *The ink sank into the paper*; *He sank his teeth into an apple*; *They sank the foundations deep into the earth.* – *See also* **sink in** *below.* **5** *vi* (*liter or formal*) (of one's spirits *etc*) to become depressed or less hopeful: *My heart sinks when I think of the difficulties ahead.* **6** *vt* (*inf*) to invest (money): *He sank all his savings in the business.* – *nc* a kind of basin with a drain and a water supply connected to it, fitted *esp* in a kitchen: *He washed the dishes in the sink.*

ˈ**sinker** *nc* a small weight fixed on a fishing-line *etc.*

ˈ**sunken** *adj* (*often formal*) **1** (*attrib*) sunk under water: *a sunken ship.* **2** (*attrib*) below the level of the surrounding area: *a sunken garden.* **3** having lost flesh and become hollow: *sunken cheeks*; *His face was pale and his cheeks were sunken.*

ˈ**sink unit** *nc* a fitting for a kitchen *etc* with a sink, draining-board and cupboards underneath: *They have had the old kitchen sink removed and a modern sink unit installed.*

be sunk (*sl*) to be defeated, in a hopeless position *etc*: *If he finds out that we've been disobeying him, we're sunk.*

sink in *vi* **1** to be fully understood: *The news took a long time to sink in.* **2** to be absorbed: *The surface water on the paths will soon sink in.*

sink our, your *etc* **differences** to forget mutual disagreements *etc*: *For the next six months, we're going to sink our differences and work together.*

sinner *see* **sin**.

sinuous [ˈsinjuəs] *adj* (*formal or liter*) **1** bending in and out: *The snake moves in a sinuous manner.* **2** (of a movement or the person making it) graceful and bending easily: *The dance was slow and sinuous.*

ˈ**sinuously** *adv.* ˈ**sinuousness** *nu.*

sinus [ˈsainəs] *nc* (*usu in pl*) an air-filled hollow in the bones of the skull, connected with the nose: *His sinuses frequently become blocked in the winter*; (*attrib*) *He suffers from sinus trouble.*

sip [sip] – *pt, ptp* **sipped** – *vti* to drink in very small mouthfuls: *She sipped her gin and tonic slowly.* – *nc* a very small mouthful: *She took a sip of the medicine and spat it out.*

siphon, (*rare*) **syphon** [ˈsaifən] *nc* **1** a bent pipe or tube through which liquid can be drawn off from one container to another at a lower level: *He used a siphon to get some petrol out of the car's tank.* **2** (*also* ˈ**soda-siphon**) a glass bottle with such a tube, used for soda water: *Put the soda-siphon by the whisky bottle.* – *vt* (*with* **off, into** *etc*) to draw (off) through a siphon: *He siphoned off some water for tests*; *They siphoned the petrol into a gallon can.*

siphon off *vt sep* (*inf derog*) to take (part of something) away gradually and illegally: *He siphoned off some of the club's funds for his own use.*

sir [səː] *nc* **1** (*formal*: with cap when written in letters) a polite form of address (spoken or written) to a man: *Excuse me, sir!*; *He started his letter 'Dear Sirs, With reference to your letter of April 2, . . .'* **2** (*with cap*) in the UK, the title of a knight or baronet: *Sir Francis Drake.*

sire [ˈsaiə] *nc* **1** (*esp arch*: *usu in sing*) a form of address used to a king: *At your service, sire!* **2** (of an animal, *esp* a horse: *arch* of people) a male parent. – *vt* (of an animal, *esp* a horse: *arch* of people) to be the male parent of: *That stallion has sired three champions.*

siren [ˈsaiərən] *nc* **1** a kind of instrument that gives out a loud hooting noise, often as a warning signal: *a factory siren*; *a siren warning of a bomb raid.* **2** (*myth*) a nymph whose sweet singing attracted sailors towards dangerous rocks. **3** (*fig*: *often derog*) a dangerously attractive woman: *She's a siren who breaks hearts as easily as eggshells.*

sirloin [ˈsəːloin] *ncu* a joint of beef cut from the upper part of the back: *Two pounds of sirloin, please*; (*attrib*) *a sirloin steak.*

sisal [ˈsaisəl] *nu, adj* (of) a type of fibre from a kind of Central American plant, used in making ropes *etc.*

sissy [ˈsisi] *nc* (*inf derog*: *Brit also* **cissy** [ˈsisi]) a womanish boy or man: *He is always so neatly dressed that the other boys call him a sissy.* – *adj* (*inf derog*) (of a boy or man) womanish; not manly.

sister [ˈsistə] *nc* **1** the title given to a female child to describe her relationship to the other children of her parents: *She's my sister*; *my father's sister.* **2** (*with cap in titles*) a type of senior nurse, *esp* one in charge of a hospital ward: *She's a sister on Ward 5.* **3** (*with cap in names*) a female member of a religious group: *Sister Ursula*; *The sisters in this order have taken a vow of silence.* **4** (*sometimes attrib*) a (female) fellow member of any group, *esp* a socialist or women's rights organization: *We must fight for equal opportunities, sisters!*; *sister revolutionaries.* – *adj* (*attrib*) closely similar in design, function etc: *sister ships.*

ˈ**sisterhood** **1** *nc* a group of women formed for religious or charitable purposes. **2** *nu* the state of being a sister.

ˈ**sisterly** *adj* like a sister in being kind and loving: *sisterly kindness*; *Her manner towards me is very sisterly.* ˈ**sisterliness** *nu.*

ˈ**sister-in-law** – *pl* **sisters-in-law** – *nc* **1** the sister

of one's husband or wife. **2** the wife of one's brother.
See also **half-sister** *under* **half**.

sit [sit] – *prp* **sitting**: *pt, ptp* **sat** [sat] – **1** *vti* to (cause to) rest on the buttocks; to (cause to) be seated: *He likes sitting on the floor*; *They sat me in the chair and started asking questions.* **2** *vi* to lie or rest; to have a certain position: *The parcel is sitting on the table*; (*liter*) *The great house sits on the hill.* **3** *vi* (*with* **on**) to be an official member of (a board, committee *etc*): *He sat on several committees.* **4** *vi* (of birds) to perch: *An owl was sitting in the tree by the window.* **5** *vt* to undergo (an examination): *I've got an exemption from the English exam, but I'll have to sit the French one.* **6** *vi* (of birds) to rest on eggs in order to hatch them: *The female of certain types of geese only sits for about two weeks.* **7** *vi* to take up a position, or act as a model, in order to have one's picture painted or one's photograph taken: *She is sitting for a portrait/photograph*; *She quite often sits for that artist.* **8** *vi* (of a committee, parliament *etc*) to be in session: *Parliament sits from now until the Christmas break.* – *See also* **sit** *in phrases below.*

'**sitter** *nc* (*inf*) **1** a person who poses for a portrait *etc*. **2** a baby-sitter: *We can't get a sitter tonight.*

'**sitting** *nc* **1** a period of continuous action, meeting *etc*: *I read the whole book at one sitting*; *The committee were prepared for a lengthy sitting.* **2** a period of posing for an artist *etc*: *The painting will probably take three sittings.*

'**sit-down** *adj* (*attrib*) **1** (of a strike) in which the workers remain in the factory *etc* but refuse to work. **2** (*inf*) (of a meal) for which one sits down at a table.

'**sit-in** *nc* an occupation of a building *etc* by protesters: *The students staged a sit-in for higher grants.* – *See also* **sit in** *below.*

sitting duck *nc* someone or something likely to be attacked and unable to put up a strong defence: *He wants to criticize someone, and I'm afraid his secretary is a sitting duck.*

'**sitting-room** *nc* a room used mainly for sitting in.

sitting target *nc* (*usu fig*) someone or something that is in an obvious position to be attacked: *If they're reducing staff, he's a sitting target.*

be sitting pretty (*inf*) to be in a very good position: *These problems don't worry you – you're sitting pretty.*

sit back *vi* to rest and take no part in an activity: *He just sat back and let it all happen.*

sit down *vi, vt sep* to (cause to) take a seat, take a sitting position: *Let's sit down over here*; *He sat the child down on the floor.*

sit in *vi* **1** (*with* **on**) to be present at (a meeting *etc*) without being an actual member: *The inspector sat in on the trainee teacher's lesson.* **2** to hold a sit-in: *The students seem tired of sitting in.*

sit out **1** *vi, vt sep* to remain seated during a dance: *Let's sit* (*this one*) *out.* **2** *vt sep* to remain inactive and wait until the end of: *They'll try to sit out the crisis*; *We'll sit it out to the very end.*

sit tight *vi* (*inf*: *usu fig*) to keep the same position or be unwilling to move or act: *The best thing to do is to sit tight and see if things improve.*

sit up **1** *vi, vt sep* to (cause to) rise to a sitting position: *Can the patient sit up?*; *The nurse sat the patient up against his pillows.* **2** *vi* to sit with one's back straight: *Do sit up in your chair and stop slouching!* **3** *vi* to remain awake, not going to bed: *I sat up until 3 a.m. waiting for you!* **4** (*fig inf*) to pay attention: *That'll make them all sit up!*

site [sait] *nc* (*often in cmpds*) a place where a building, town *etc* is, was, or is to be, built: *He's got a job on a building-site*; *The site for the new factory has not been decided*; *a bombsite.* – *vt* (*formal*) to select a place for (a building *etc*); to put (a building) in a place: *Where are they going to site the new school?*

situation [sitju'eiʃən] *nc* **1** circumstances; a state of affairs: *an awkward situation.* **2** (*formal*) the place where anything stands or lies: *The house has a beautiful situation beside a lake.* **3** (*formal*) a job: *the situations-vacant columns of the newspaper.*

'**situated** *adj* (*formal*) to be found; placed: *The new school is situated on the north side of town.*

six [siks] **1** *nc* the number or figure 6. **2** *nu* the age of 6. – *adj* **1** (*usu attrib*) 6 in number. **2** (*pred*) aged 6. – *See* **eight** *for constructions.*

six- (*in cmpds*) having six (of something): *a* ˌ*six-cylinder* '*engine.*

sixth **1** *nc* one of six equal parts. **2** *nc, adj* (the) last of six (people, things *etc*); (the) next after the fifth. – *See* **eighth** *under* **eight** *for constructions.*

'**sixpence** [-pəns, (*Amer*) -pens] *ncu* (*hist Brit*) (a coin, silver in colour, worth) six old pence (6d) (= $2\frac{1}{2}$p).

'**sixpenny** [-pəni, (*Amer*) -peni] *adj* (*hist Brit*: *attrib*) worth or costing sixpence: *a sixpenny ice-cream.*

'**six-year-old** *nc* a person or animal that is six years old. – *adj* (*attrib*) (of a person, animal or thing) that is six years old. – *See* **eight-year-old** *under* **eight** *for constructions.*

at sixes and sevens (*inf*) in confusion; completely disorganized: *On the day before the wedding, the whole house was at sixes and sevens.*

knock (someone) for six (*Brit inf*) to overcome or defeat completely; to take totally by surprise: *The news just knocked me for six!*

See also Appendix 1.

sixteen [siks'ti:n] **1** *nc* the number or figure 16. **2** *nu* the age of 16. – *adj* **1** (*usu attrib*) 16 in number. **2** (*pred*) aged 16. – *See* **eighteen** *for constructions.*

sixteen- (*in cmpds*) having sixteen (of something): *a* ˌ*sixteen-page* '*booklet.*

ˌ**six'teenth** **1** *nc* one of sixteen equal parts **2** *nc, adj* (the) last of sixteen (people, things *etc*); (the) next after the fifteenth. – *See* **eighteenth** *under* **eighteen** *for constructions.*

ˌ**six'teen-year-old** *nc* a person or animal that is sixteen years old. – *adj* (*attrib*) (of a person, animal or thing) that is sixteen years old. – *See also* **eighteen-year-old** *under* **eighteen** *for constructions.*

See also Appendix 1.

sixty ['siksti] **1** *nc* the number or figure 60. **2** *nu* the age of 60. – *adj* **1** (*usu attrib*) 60 in number. **2** (*pred*) aged 60. – *See* **eighty** *for constructions.*

'**sixties** *n pl* **1** the period of time between one's sixtieth and seventieth birthdays. **2** the range of temperatures between sixty and seventy degrees. **3** the period of time between the sixtieth and seventieth years of a century. – *See* **eighties** *under* **eighty** *for constructions.*

'**sixtieth** **1** *nc* one of sixty equal parts. **2** *nc, adj* (the) last of sixty (people, things *etc*); (the) next after the fifty-ninth. – *See* **eightieth** *under* **eighty** *for constructions.*

sixty- (*in cmpds*) having sixty (of something): *a* ˌ*sixty-page* '*supplement.*

'**sixty-year-old** *nc* a person or animal that is sixty years old. – *adj* (*attrib*) (of a person, animal or thing) that is sixty years old. – *See* **eighty-year-old** *under* **eighty** *for constructions.*
See also Appendix 1.

size[1] [saiz] **1** *nu* largeness: *an area the size of a football pitch*; *the size of an industry*; *The size of the problem alarmed us.* **2** *nc* one of a number of classes in which shoes, dresses *etc* are grouped according to measurements: *I take size 5 in shoes*; *Do you have any smaller sizes in this style?*

'**sizeable,** (*rarer*) '**sizable** *adj* fairly large: *He has a sizeable estate in Ireland*; *His income is quite sizeable, now that he has been promoted.*

size up *vt sep* (*slightly inf*) to form an opinion about the worth, nature, *etc* of (a person, situation *etc*): *I'm not very good at sizing people up quickly*; *He sized up the situation and acted immediately.*

size[2] [saiz] *nu* a weak kind of glue. – *vt* to cover with size: *The walls must be sized before you paper them.*

sizzle ['sizl] *vi* (of (things cooking in) hot fat *etc*) to make a hissing sound: *Sausages were sizzling in the pan.*

skate[1] [skeit] *nc* **1** a boot with a steel blade fixed to it for moving on ice *etc*: *I can move very fast across the ice on skates.* **2** a roller-skate. – **1** *vi* to move on skates: *She skates beautifully.* **2** *vt* to move over, along *etc* by skating: *He skated the length of the rink without stopping.* – *See also* **skate over** *below.*

'**skater** *nc.*

'**skating-rink** *nc* an area of ice set aside or designed for skating on.

get one's skates on (*Brit inf*) to hurry up: *I'd better get my skates on if I want to get to the cinema by nine o'clock.*

skate over *vt fus* (*inf*) to pass over (a subject, difficulty *etc*) quickly, trying to avoid taking it into consideration: *He always skates over the problems attached to his plans.*

skate[2] [skeit] – *pls* **skate, skates** – **1** *nc* a kind of large, flat fish. **2** *nu* its flesh, used as food: *One and half kilos of skate, please.*

skein [skein] *nc* a length of wool or thread, loosely coiled: *Would you hold this skein of wool while I roll it into a ball?*

skeleton ['skelitn] *nc* **1** the bony framework of an animal or person: *The archaeologists dug up the skeleton of a dinosaur.* **2** (*fig*: *often liter*) any framework or outline: *the steel skeleton of a building.*

'**skeletal** *adj* **1** (*tech*) of a skeleton. **2** (*formal*: *usu pred*) like a skeleton; extremely thin: *The inhabitants of the prison looked positively skeletal.*

skeleton key *nc* a key from which the inner part has been filed away so that it can open many different locks.

skeleton staff, crew *etc nc* a set of staff *etc* reduced to a minimum: *There will only be a skeleton staff working over Christmas.*

skeleton in the cupboard/(*Amer*) **closet** a closely kept secret concerning a hidden cause of shame: *Aunt Mary's affair with the milkman is the skeleton in the family cupboard.*

skeptic *see* **sceptic**.

sketch [sketʃ] *nc* **1** a rough plan, drawing or painting: *He made several sketches before starting the portrait.* **2** a short (written or spoken) account without many details: *The book began with a sketch of the author's life.* **3** a short play, dramatic scene *etc*: *a comic sketch.* – **1** *vt* to draw, describe, or plan without completing the details: *Many artists sketch their subjects before putting paint to canvas*; *He sketched the history of the project so far.* **2** *vi* to make rough drawings, paintings *etc*: *She sketches purely as a hobby.*

'**sketchy** *adj* **1** incompletely done or carried out: *He made a sketchy search for the bill among his papers but didn't have time to look thoroughly.* **2** slight or incomplete: *a sketchy knowledge of French*; *His knowledge of French is decidedly sketchy.* '**sketchily** *adv.* '**sketchiness** *nu.*

'**sketch-book** *nc* a book for drawing sketches in.

skew [skju:]: **on the skew** (*formal*) at a slant: *That picture is on the skew.*

skewer ['skjuə] *nc* a long pin of wood or metal for keeping meat together while roasting: *Put the cubes of meat on a skewer.* – *vt* to fasten or fix, with a skewer, or with something sharp: *Skewer the chicken securely.*

ski [ski:] *nc* one of a pair of long narrow strips of wood *etc* that are attached to the feet for gliding over snow, water *etc.* – *v* – *prp* '**skiing**; *pt, ptp* **skied** [ski:d] – *vi* to travel on or use skis *esp* as a leisure activity: *He skis in Austria every winter*; *He often goes skiing.*

ski- (*in cmpds*) of or for the activity of skiing: *children's ski-suits*; *He performed an impressive ski-jump*; *a ski-lift* (= a moving rope with seats for taking skiers to the top of the slope).

'**skier** *nc*: *The slope was crowded with skiers.*

'**skiing** *nu*: *Skiing is her favourite sport*; (*attrib*) *a skiing holiday.*

skid [skid] – *pt, ptp* '**skidded** – *vi* to slide accidentally sideways: *His back wheel skidded and he fell off his bike.* – *nc* **1** an accidental slide sideways: *The road was wet and my car went into a skid.* **2** a wedge *etc* put under a wheel to check it on a steep place. **3** a log or plank *etc* on which things can be moved by sliding.

put the skids under (someone) (*inf*) to cause (someone) to hurry: *Tell him he's fired unless he finishes the work by Friday – that'll put the skids under him!*

skiff [skif] *nc* a small light boat.

skill [skil] **1** *nu* cleverness at doing something, resulting either from practice or from natural ability: *She has great skill with a needle*; *This job requires quite a lot of skill.* **2** *nc* a job or activity that requires training and practice; an art or craft: *Some teenagers seem to leave school without even the basic skills of reading and writing*; *Bookbinding is a skill that takes years to learn.*

'**skilful**, (*Amer*) '**skillful** *adj* having, or showing, skill: *a skilful surgeon*; *It was very skilful of you to repair my bicycle*; *a skilful mechanic.* '**skilfully** *adv.* '**skilfulness** *nu.*

skilled *adj* **1** (*with* **in** *or* **at** *when pred*: *neg* **un-**) (of a person *etc*) having skill, *esp* skill gained by training: *a skilled craftsman*; *Only the skilled eye of an expert could spot the faked picture*; *She is skilled at all types of dressmaking*; *a man highly skilled in the art of restoring pictures.* **2** (*attrib*) (of a job *etc*) requiring skill: *a skilled trade.*

skillet ['skilit] *nc* **1** a small metal pan with a long handle used in cooking. **2** (*Amer*) a frying-pan: *The pancake has stuck to the skillet.*

skim [skim] – *pt, ptp* **skimmed** – **1** *vt* to remove (floating matter, *eg* cream) from the surface of (a liquid): *Skim the fat off the gravy*; *Skim the jam before you pour it into the jars.* **2** *vti* (*formal or liter*) to move lightly and quickly over (a surface): *The* *skier skimmed across the snow*; *The birds skimmed the waves.* **3** *vti* to read (something) quickly, missing out parts: *If you skim* (*through*) *the play too quickly, you'll forget the plot.*

skim milk *nu* milk from which the cream has been skimmed: *She is on a diet – she will drink only skim milk.*

skimp [skimp] **1** *vi* (*with* **on**) to spend, use, give *etc* too little or only just enough: *She skimped on everything to send her son to college.* **2** *vti* to do (a job *etc*) imperfectly: *He was always skimping his work.*

ˈ**skimpy** *adj* (*inf*) **1** too small: *He ate a skimpy breakfast.* **2** (of clothes) too short or tight: *That dress looks rather skimpy on you.* ˈ**skimpily** *adv.* ˈ**skimpiness** *nu.*

skin [skin] *ncu* **1** (*often in cmpds*) the natural outer covering of an animal or person: *She couldn't stand the feel of wool against her skin*; *A snake can shed its skin*; *There was a pile of sheepskins in the corner of the shop*; *Her jacket is made of sealskin*; (*attrib*) *The medical student wanted to specialize in skin diseases*; (*attrib*) *She went to a skin specialist about her rash.* **2** (*often in cmpds*) a thin outer layer, as on a fruit: *a banana-skin*; *onion-skins.* **3** a (thin) film or layer that forms on a liquid: *Boiled milk often has a skin on it.* – *v* – *pt, ptp* **skinned** – *vt* to remove the skin from: *He skinned and cooked the rabbit*; (*inf*) *I fell over and skinned* (= grazed) *my elbow.*

ˌ**skin-ˈdeep** *adj* (*formal or liter*: *pred*) on the surface only: *His sorrow was skin-deep*; *Beauty is skin-deep.*

ˈ**skin-diving** *nu* diving and swimming under water with simple equipment (a mask, flippers *etc*) and not wearing a protective suit.

ˈ**skinflint** *nc* (*inf derog*) a very mean person.

ˈ**skin-ˈtight** *adj* (*usu attrib*) fitting as tightly as one's skin: *His skin-tight jeans seemed permanently in danger of splitting*; *Her new sweater is skin-tight.*

by the skin of one's teeth very narrowly; only just: *We escaped by the skin of our teeth.*

get under someone's skin (*inf*) to annoy and upset someone greatly: *Don't let his comments get under your skin.*

skinny [ˈskini] *adj* (*inf*: *often derog*) very thin: *He's rather a skinny baby*; *Most fat girls long to be skinny.* ˈ**skinniness** *nu.*

skint [skint] *adj* (*Brit sl*: *pred*) without money: *I'm absolutely skint, so I can't go to the cinema.*

skip[1] [skip] – *pt, ptp* **skipped** – **1** *vi* to go along with a hop on each foot in turn: *The little girl skipped up the path.* **2** *vi* to jump over a rope that is being turned under the feet and over the head (as a children's game): *Two little girls turned the rope and the others skipped.* **3** *vti* (*inf*) to miss out (a meal, part of a book *etc*): *I skipped lunch and went shopping instead*; *Skip chapter two*; *I skipped to the last chapter.* – *nc* a hop on one foot in skipping: *The child went along with little skips of happiness.*

ˈ**skipping-rope** *nc* a rope used in skipping (*def 2*).

skip[2] [skip] *nc* a large container for holding or carrying rubbish, building materials *etc*: *Hire a skip to get rid of those old fireplaces.*

skipper [ˈskipə] *nc* (*inf*) the captain of a ship, aeroplane or team. – *vt* (*inf*) to act as skipper of: *Who skippered the team?*

skirmish [ˈskəːmiʃ] *nc* (*formal*) **1** a fight between small parties of soldiers: *He was killed in a street skirmish between government troops and rebels.* **2** a short, sharp contest or disagreement: *There was a skirmish between the Prime Minister and the Leader of the Opposition in Parliament today.* – *vi* (*formal*) to take part in a skirmish: *The two sides have been skirmishing for years.*

skirt [skəːt] *nc* **1** a garment, worn by women, that hangs from the waist: *Was she wearing trousers or a skirt?* **2** the lower part of a dress, coat *etc*: *a dress with a flared skirt.* – *vti* (*formal*) to lie on, or pass along, the edge of (something): *We skirted the field so as not to damage the crops*; *The footpath skirts the forest*; (*fig*) *In his speech he seemed to skirt* (*round*) (= avoid mentioning) *all the main problems.*

ˈ**skirting(-board)** *ncu* the narrow board next the floor round the walls of a room: *The mice have made a hole in the skirting(-board).*

skit [skit] *nc* a short piece of writing or a dramatic scene making fun of a person, an event, a kind of literature *etc*: *The skit on politicians was the funniest part of the show.*

skittish [ˈskitiʃ] *adj* (*slightly inf*) (too) frisky or lively: *a skittish young horse*; *She was being rather skittish at the party.*

skittle [ˈskitl] *nc* a bottle-shaped, *usu* wooden object used as a target for knocking over in the game of skittles.

ˈ**skittles** *n sing* a game in which the players try to knock down a number of skittles with a ball: *a game of skittles*; *Do you play skittles?*; (*attrib*) *a skittles match.*

skive [skaiv] *vi* (*often with* **off**: *sl*) to avoid work *esp* by going, or keeping, away from the place where one should be working: *He's not ill – he's just skiving*; *I saw him skiving off at two o'clock today.*

skulk [skʌlk] *vi* to wait about or keep oneself hidden (often for a bad purpose): *Someone was skulking in the bushes.*

skull [skʌl] *nc* the bony case that encloses the brain: *He's fractured his skull.*

ˈ**skullcap** *nc* a cap that fits closely to the head.

ˌ**skull and ˈcrossbones** *nc* (*no pl*: *usu with* **the**: *hist*) (a design displayed on) a pirate's flag.

skunk [skʌŋk] *nc* a small North American animal which defends itself by squirting out an unpleasant-smelling liquid.

sky [skai] *ncu* (*often with* **the** *and sometimes in pl*) the part of space above the earth, in which the sun, moon *etc* can be seen; the heavens: *The sky was blue and cloudless*; *The weather may clear – I can see a patch of blue sky*; *We had grey skies and rain throughout our holiday*; *You should be able to see the comet clearly in the night sky.*

ˌ**sky-ˈblue** *adj, nu* (of) the light blue colour of cloudless sky: *She wore a sky-blue dress.*

ˈ**sky-diving** *nu* the sport of jumping from aircraft and waiting for some time before opening one's parachute. ˈ**sky-diver** *nc.*

ˌ**sky-ˈhigh** *adv, adj* very high: *The car was blown sky-high by the explosion*; *sky-high prices.*

ˈ**skylark** *nc* the common lark, which sings while flying high in the sky. – *vi* (*slightly old*: *sometimes with* **about**) to have fun in a rough, mischievous way: *Stop skylarking about!*

ˈ**skylight** *nc* a window in a roof or ceiling: *The attic had only a small skylight and was very dark.*

ˈ**skyline** *nc* the outline of buildings, hills *etc* seen against the sky: *the New York skyline*; *I could see something moving on the skyline.*

ˈ**skyscraper** *nc* a high building of very many storeys, *esp* in the US.

praise (someone) to the skies to praise (someone) very highly.

the sky's the limit (*inf*) there is no upper limit *eg* to the amount of money that may be spent: *Choose any present you like – the sky's the limit!*

slab [slab] *nc* a thick slice or thick flat piece of anything, *usu* square or rectangular in shape: *concrete slabs*; *a stone slab*; (*sometimes inf*) *a slab of cake/chocolate/cheese.*

slack[1] [slak] *adj* **1** loose; not firmly stretched: *Leave that rope slack*; *a slack knot* **2** not firmly in position: *He tightened a few slack screws*; *These nuts are slack* **3** not strict; careless: *He is very slack about getting things done*; *She was shocked at the slack discipline in the school.* **4** (*inf*) in industry *etc*, not busy; inactive: *The summer is the slack season for umbrella-makers*; *Business has been rather slack lately.* – *nu* (*slightly inf*) the loose part (of a rope *etc*): *Take up the slack*; *There's still a lot of slack left.*

'slacken *vti* (*sometimes with* **off** *or* **up**) **1** to make or become looser: *You can start slackening off the rope now*; *She felt his grip on her arm slacken.* **2** to make or become less busy, less active or less fast: *The car slackened speed as it left the motorway*; *Work slackens off in the summer*; *The doctor told him to slacken up if he wanted to avoid a heart-attack.*

'slacker *nc* (*inf derog*) a person who works less hard than he should.

'slackly *adv* **'slackness** *nu.*

slacks *n pl* (*slightly old*) trousers, not part of a suit, *usu* loose-fitting, worn informally by men or women: *I bought some new slacks*; *a pair of slacks.*

slack[2] [slak] *nu* small pieces of coal and coal dust.

slag [slag] *nu* waste left over from metal smelting.

slain *see* **slay**.

slake [sleik] *vt* (*liter*) to satisfy or make less strong (thirst, anger *etc*).

slalom ['sla:ləm] *nc* a race, *usu* on skis or in canoes, in which skill is required to avoid obstacles: *He won the slalom three times*; (*attrib*) *a slalom course.*

slam [slam] – *pt, ptp* **slammed** – **1** *vti* to shut with violence *usu* making a loud noise: *He slammed the door angrily*; *The door suddenly slammed* (*shut*); *He slammed the door in my face* (= just as I was going to enter). **2** *vti* (*inf*) to strike against something violently *esp* with a loud noise: *She slammed the cup and saucer on to the table*; *The car slammed into the wall.* – *nc* (the noise made by) an act of closing violently and noisily: *The door closed with a slam.*

slander ['sla:ndə] *ncu* (the act of making) an untrue spoken, not written, statement about a person with the intention of damaging that person's reputation: *That story about her is nothing but a wicked slander!*; *a piece of downright slander*; (*legal*) *What are the penalties for slander?* – *vt* to make such statements about (a person *etc*).

'slanderous *adj.* **'slanderously** *adv.*

slang [slaŋ] *nu* words and phrases (often in use for only a short time) used very informally in everyday speech and writing, and not for formal or polite use, *eg* words used mainly by, and typical of, a particular group: *army slang*; *teenage slang*; *Cockney rhyming slang*; *'A stiff' is slang for 'a corpse'*; (*attrib*) *'Kick the bucket' is a slang expression for 'die'.* – *vt* (*inf*) to speak rudely and angrily to or about (someone); to abuse: *I got furious when he started slanging my mother.*

'slangy *adj* (*inf*): *Some of his expressions are rather slangy.*

slanging match *nc* (*inf*) an angry quarrel or argument in which rude expressions are used by both sides.

slant [sla:nt] **1** *vi* to be, lie *etc* at an angle, away from a vertical or horizontal position or line; to slope: *The house is very old and all the floors and ceilings slant a little*; *From here the road slants away to the left.* **2** *vt* to give or present (news, a talk, television programme *etc*) in a special way so that emphasis is put on a certain aspect, or favour given to a certain point of view: *They slanted the programme to appeal to the younger members of the audience*; *The report on the strike had been slanted to draw sympathy away from the miners.* – *nc* **1** a sloping line or direction: *The roof has a steep slant.* – *See also* **at a slant/on a slant** *below.* **2** a way of looking at things: *Our magazine has a new slant on fashion.*

'slanted *adj* (*derog*) (of a news report *etc*) presented so as to favour one particular point of view *etc*; biased: *a very slanted report*; *The programme on China was rather slanted.*

'slanting *adj* (*usu attrib or in cmpds*): *He has backward-slanting writing*; *slanting eyes.*

at a slant/on a slant lying *etc* at an angle; slanting: *The ship suddenly rolled violently and the whole cabin was at a slant.*

slap [slap] *nc* a blow with the palm of the hand or anything flat: *They started to quarrel and she gave him a slap on the cheek*; *The child got a slap from his mother for being rude.* – *vt* to give a slap to: *Don't slap that child!*; *He slapped my face*; *He slapped me on the back and congratulated me on my promotion.* – *adv* (*inf*) suddenly and directly: *The car ran slap into the wall.*

,slap'dash *adj* (*derog*) careless and hurried: *He does everything in such a slapdash manner*; *Your work has been very slapdash recently.*

,slap-'happy *adj* (*inf*) cheerfully careless; carefree: *I don't know how she makes such marvellous food, because she cooks in a very slap-happy way*; *Her housekeeping methods are very slap-happy.*

'slapstick *nu* (*esp drama*) a kind of humour which depends for its effect on very simple practical jokes *etc*: *Throwing custard pies turns a play into slapstick*; (*attrib*) *slapstick comedy.*

'slap-up *adj* (*inf*: *attrib*) (of a meal *etc*) splendid; excellent: *The firm gave its employees a slap-up dinner in the local hotel.*

slap down *vt sep* (*inf*) to dismiss or dispose of (opposition *etc*) abruptly: *My suggestion was immediately slapped down.*

a slap in the face (*inf*) an insult or rebuff: *The miners' decision to strike was a slap in the face for the government.*

slash [slaʃ] **1** *vt* to make long cuts in (cloth *etc*): *He slashed his victim's face with a razor.* **2** *vi* (*with* **at**) to strike out violently at (something): *He slashed at the bush angrily with a stick.* **3** *vt* (*inf*) to reduce greatly: *A notice in the shop window read 'Prices slashed!'* – *nc* **1** a long cut or slit: *There was a slash in her skirt from waistband to hem.* **2** a sweeping blow: *He gave the horse a vicious slash with a stick.*

slat [slat] *nc* a thin strip of wood, metal *etc.*

'slatted *adj* having, or made with, slats: *a slatted door.*

slate[1] [sleit] **1** *ncu* (a piece of) a type of easily split rock of a dull blue-grey colour, used for roofing *etc*: *Slates fell off the roof in the wind*; *The house is roofed with Welsh slate*; (*attrib*) *a slate roof.* **2** *nc* (*hist*) a small writing-board made of this, used by schoolchildren. – *vt* to cover (a roof *etc*) with slate: *They have almost finished building the house but they haven't slated the roof.*

ˌ**slate-ˈblue**/ˌ**slate-ˈgrey** *nus, adjs* (of) the blue-grey colour of slate.

a clean slate *see* **clean**.

slate[2] [sleit] *vt* (*inf*) to say harsh things to or about: *The new play was slated by the critics.*

ˈ**slating** *nc* (*inf*): *She got a slating from the manager about her unpunctuality.*

slattern [ˈslatən] *nc* (*old*) a woman of dirty or untidy appearance or habits. ˈ**slatternly** *adj.*

slaughter [ˈslo:tə] *nu* **1** the killing of people or animals in large numbers, cruelly and *usu* unnecessarily: *Many people protested at the annual slaughter of seals.* **2** the killing of animals for food: *Methods of slaughter must be humane.* – *vt* **1** to kill (animals) for food: *Thousands of cattle are slaughtered here every year.* **2** to kill in a cruel manner, *esp* in large numbers: *The entire population was slaughtered in one of the most terrible crimes of the war.* **3** (*inf*) to criticize unmercifully or defeat very thoroughly: *The playwright was slaughtered by the press; Our team absolutely slaughtered the other side.*

ˈ**slaughter-house** *nc* a place where animals are killed in order to be sold for food; an abattoir.

slave [sleiv] *nc* **1** a person who works for a master to whom he belongs: *In the nineteenth century many Africans were sold as slaves in the United States; I refuse to be treated like a slave by you!* **2** (*facet*) a person who works very hard for someone else: *He has a slave who types his letters and organizes his life for him.* **3** (*formal*) a person who is unable to resist the influence of (an emotion, a habit *etc*): *He is a slave to drink; We're the slaves of habit.* – *vi* (*inf: sometimes with* **away**) to work very hard, often for another person: *She slaves to keep her family in clothes; I've been slaving away for you all day while you sit and watch television.*

ˈ**slavery** *nu* **1** the state of being a slave: *The tribe was sold into slavery.* **2** the system of ownership of slaves: *Slavery still exists in some parts of the world; the abolition of slavery.* **3** (*inf*) very hard and badly-paid work: *Her job is sheer slavery.*

ˈ**slavish** *adj* (*formal derog*) **1** (acting or thinking) exactly according to instructions or to rules: *She had made a slavish attempt to do everything she was told.* **2** (of an imitation *etc*) exact in every detail: *The building is a slavish copy of a Georgian masterpiece.*

ˈ**slavishly** *adv* (*formal derog*): *She had followed her instructions slavishly; She quotes her husband's opinions slavishly.*

ˈ**slavishness** *nu.*

ˈ**slave-driver** *nc* **1** (*hist*) a man in charge of slaves. **2** a person who expects too much work from his employees, pupils *etc. My son's teacher is a real slave-driver – she gives him so much homework.*

slaver [ˈslavə] *vi* to let saliva run out of one's mouth: *The invalid could not help slavering; Some types of dog slaver more than others.* – *nu* saliva running from the mouth.

slay [slei] – *pt* **slew** [slu:] *ptp* **slain** [slein] – *vt* (*arch or liter*) to kill: *Cain slew his brother Abel.*

sleazy [ˈsli:zi] *adj* (*inf derog*) dirty and neglected: *a sleazy block of flats; This area is rather sleazy.*

sledge [sledʒ] *nc* (*also, esp Amer,* **sled** [sled]) a vehicle, *usu* with runners, made for sliding upon snow. – *vi* to ride on a sledge: *After the snowfall we went sledging; The children were sledging down the hill.*

sledge-hammer [ˈsledʒhamə] *nc* a large heavy hammer: *He hammered the fence-post into the ground with a sledge-hammer.*

sleek [sli:k] *adj* **1** (of hair, an animal's fur *etc*) smooth, soft and glossy: *The dog has a lovely sleek coat; Her hair is sleek and healthy.* **2** well fed and cared for: *a sleek Siamese cat lay by the fire.* **3** (*sometimes derog*) elegant and well-dressed: *She was having lunch with a sleek young man in an expensive jacket.* ˈ**sleekly** *adv.* ˈ**sleekness** *nu.*

sleep [sli:p] – *pt, ptp* **slept** [slept] – *vi* **1** to rest with the eyes closed and in a state of natural unconsciousness: *Goodnight – sleep well!; The children slept soundly* (= well) *after all the excitement; I always sleep badly when I'm away from home; I can't sleep – my mind is too active; Did you manage to sleep through all that noise last night?; The baby's sleeping at last; We shall be sleeping in our new house for the first time tonight; The children usually sleep at their grandmother's house during the week.* **2** (*liter euph*) to be dead: *He sleeps with his ancestors in this graveyard.* – *ncu* (a) rest in a state of natural unconsciousness: *It is bad for you to have too little sleep, since it makes you tired; I had only four hours' sleep last night; I'll feel better after a good night's sleep; He had a short sleep and woke up feeling refreshed; The doctor gave him an injection which put him into a deep sleep; Did you realize you were talking in your sleep last night?*

ˈ**sleeper** *nc* **1** a person who sleeps: *Nothing occurred to disturb the sleepers; She is a light/heavy sleeper* (= She is roused easily/with difficulty from sleep). **2** (*Brit*) one of the heavy beams of wood or metal across which railway lines are laid. **3** a berth or compartment for sleeping, on a railway train: *I'd like to book a sleeper on the London train.* **4** a train made up of sleeping-cars.

ˈ**sleepless** *adj* without sleep: *She was sleepless* (= unable to sleep) *with worry; He spent a sleepless night worrying about the situation.*

ˈ**sleepy** *adj* **1** inclined to sleep; drowsy: *I feel very sleepy after that long walk; She took the sleepy children off to bed.* **2** (*esp attrib*) not (seeming to be) alert: *She always has a sleepy expression; a young man with rather a sleepy manner.* **3** (of places *etc*) very quiet; lacking entertainment and excitement: *a sleepy town; This village is too sleepy for me.* ˈ**sleepily** *adv.* ˈ**sleepiness** *nu.*

ˈ**sleeping-bag** *nu* a kind of large warm bag for sleeping in, used by campers *etc.*

ˈ**sleeping-car** *nc* a railway coach with berths or beds.

sleeping partner *nc* (*Amer* **silent partner**) a partner in a business who takes no part in managing it.

ˈ**sleeping-pill**/ˈ**sleeping-tablet** *nc* a kind of pill that can be taken to make one sleep: *She tried to commit suicide by swallowing an overdose of sleeping-pills.*

ˈ**sleepwalk** *vi* to walk about while asleep: *She was sleepwalking again last night.* ˈ**sleepwalker** *nc.*

ˈ**sleepyhead** *nc* (*inf*) (used *esp* to a child) a person who is sleepy or not paying attention: *Wake up, you sleepyheads!*

get (off) to sleep to manage to go to sleep; to cause or persuade (a person *etc*) to go to sleep: *I can't get to sleep because of the noise outside; It took me three hours to get the baby off to sleep last night.*

go to sleep **1** to pass into a state of being asleep: *The baby has finally gone to sleep.* **2** (of limbs) to become numb: *I've been leaning on my arm so long that it's gone to sleep.*

lose sleep over (*inf*) to worry about: *Don't lose any sleep over the problem!*

put to sleep 1 (*inf*) to cause (a person or animal) to become unconscious by means of an anaesthetic; to anaesthetize: *The doctor will give you an injection to put you to sleep.* **2** (*euph*) to kill (an animal) painlessly, *usu* by the injection of a drug: *As she was so old and ill my cat had to be put to sleep.*

sleep around *vi* (*inf often derog*) to be in the habit of having sexual intercourse with a number of different people; to be promiscuous: *She finally got married and stopped sleeping around.*

sleep in *vi* **1** to sleep at one's place of work: *She employs a gardener who lives in the village, but the maid is required to sleep in.* **2** (*Brit inf*) to sleep late in the morning; to oversleep: *I slept in by mistake and was very late for work.*

sleep like a log/top (*inf*) to sleep very well: *After my hard day's work I slept like a log.*

sleep off *vt sep* to recover from (something) by sleeping: *She's in bed sleeping off the effects of the party; I have a slight infection, but I think I'll manage to sleep it off.*

'sleep on *vt fus* (*inf*) to put off making a decision about (something) overnight: *I'll sleep on it and let you know tomorrow.*

sleep out *vi* to sleep away from one's place of work: *She has a housekeeper who sleeps out.*

sleep together *vi* (*euph*) (of two people) to have, or be in the habit of having, sexual intercourse: *Do you think John and Jane are sleeping together?*

'sleep with *vt fus* (*euph*) to have, or be in the habit of having, sexual intercourse with: *Many unmarried girls sleep with their boyfriends nowadays; His wife has a lot of male friends but I don't think she ever sleeps with any of them.*

See also **asleep**.

sleet [sli:t] *nu* rain mixed with snow or hail: *That isn't snow – it's just sleet.* – *vi* (*inf: only with* **it** *as subject*) to hail or snow, with a mixture of rain: *It seems to be sleeting outside.*

sleeve [sli:v] *nc* **1** the part of a garment that covers the arm: *He tore the sleeve of his jacket; a dress with long/short sleeves; He rolled up his sleeves and got to work in the garden.* **2** (*also* **'record-sleeve**) a stiff envelope for a gramophone record, *usu* with information *etc* about the record printed on it. **3** (*tech*) something, *eg* a tubular part in a piece of machinery, that covers as a sleeve does.

-sleeved (*in cmpds*) having (a certain kind of) sleeve(s): *a long-sleeved dress.*

'sleeveless *adj* (*usu attrib*) without sleeves: *a sleeveless dress.*

have/keep (something) up one's sleeve to keep (a plan *etc*) secret for possible use at a later time: *I'm keeping this idea up my sleeve for the time being.*

sleigh [slei] *nc* a *usu* large sledge pulled by a horse *etc.*

sleight-of-hand [slaitəv'hand] *nu* (*formal*) skill and quickness of hand in performing card tricks etc: *Conjurors depend on sleight-of-hand in performing most of their tricks; (fig) The Prime Minister mustn't think he can fool the unions with his sleight-of-hand.*

slender ['slendə] *adj* (*formal*) **1** thin, slim or narrow: *The girl was pretty and slender; a wine glass with a slender stem.* **2** slight or small: *His chances of winning are extremely slender; He can't afford a car on his slender income.*

slept *see* **sleep**.

sleuth [slu:θ] *nc* (*old or facet*) a person who tracks down criminals; a detective.

slew[1] [slu:] *vti* to (cause to) turn or swing in a certain direction: *The car skidded and slewed across the road.*

slew[2] *see* **slay**.

slice [slais] *nc* **1** a thin broad piece (of something): *a slice of bread/cake; How many slices of meat would you like?* **2** (*inf*) a part or share: *Who got the largest slice of the profits?* **3** (*usu in cmpds*) a kitchen utensil with a wide flat blade for lifting, cutting, turning or serving fish, bacon *etc*: *a fish-slice.* **4** in golf *etc*, a shot that slices the ball. – **1** *vt* to cut into slices: *He sliced the sausage/cucumber.* **2** *vti* to cut (as) with a sharp blade or knife: *Could you slice me a piece of ham, please?; The blade slipped and sliced off the tip of his forefinger; A sheet of steel slipped off the lorry and sliced through the bonnet of the car behind.* **3** *vt* in golf *etc*, to hit (a ball) in such a way that it curves away to the right (or in the case of a left-handed player, to the left).

sliced *adj* (*neg* **un-**) cut into slices: *a sliced loaf; sliced pineapple; thinly-sliced cucumber.*

'slicer *nc* (*often in cmpds*) a tool, machine *etc* for slicing: *a bacon-slicer; a cheese-slicer.*

slick[1] [slik] *adj* (*often derog*) clever *esp* in a sly or dishonest way; smart: *slick salesmen; Their methods of selling are a bit too slick for me; That was a very slick move!* **'slickly** *adv.* **'slickness** *nu.*

slick down *vt sep* (*inf*) to make (hair *etc*) smooth: *His hair was slicked down with hair-cream.*

slick[2] [slik] *nc* (*also* **'oil-slick**) a broad band of oil floating on the surface of the sea *etc*: *They used detergents to break up the slick; An oil-slick is threatening the Cornish coast.*

slide [slaid] – *pt, ptp* **slid** [slid] – **1** *vti* to (cause to) move or pass along smoothly: *He slid the drawer open; The cups and plates slid to the floor as the table was tipped over; The children were sliding on the ice; Children must not slide in the school corridors.* **2** *vti* to move quietly or secretly: *I slid hurriedly past the window; He slid the book quickly out of sight under his pillow.* – *nc* **1** an act of sliding: *The children were enjoying having a slide on the icy pavement; Some rocks suddenly went into a slide down the mountainside.* **2** a slippery track, or a specially constructed apparatus with a smooth sloping surface, on which people or things can slide: *The children were taking turns on the slide in the playground.* **3** a small transparent photograph for projecting on to a screen *etc*: *They showed us their holiday slides; The lecture was illustrated with slides.* **4** a glass plate on which objects are placed to be examined under a microscope. **5** (*also* **'hair-slide**) a (decorative) hinged fastening for the hair.

'slide-rule *nc* an instrument used for calculating, like a ruler in shape and having a central section which slides up and down between the outer sections.

sliding door *nc* a type of door that slides across an opening rather than swinging on a hinge.

sliding scale *nc* a scale of wages, charges *etc* which can be changed as conditions change.

let (something) slide (*inf*) to neglect and not to bother about (something): *I tend to let things slide during the holidays.*

slight [slait] *adj* **1** (*usu attrib*) small; not great; not serious or severe: *a slight breeze*; *She showed slight irritation at my remark*; *The improvement is only slight*; *We have a slight problem.* **2** (of a person) slim and delicate-looking: *It seemed too heavy a load for such a slight woman*; *She's dark-haired and slight*; *a man of slight build.* – *vt* (*formal*) to treat as unimportant or to fail to show proper respect for (a person): *I didn't mean to slight him.* – *nc* (*formal*) an insult through failure to show respect or interest: *He did not speak to her and she felt the slight deeply.*

'**slightest** *adj* (*attrib*; *often in negative sentences, questions etc*) least possible; any at all: *I haven't the slightest idea* (= I don't know at all) *where he is*; *He left home without the slightest regret*; *If you have the slightest doubt, don't sign the contract*; *Do you really think he has the slightest intention of apologizing?*; (*inf*) *I'm just the slightest bit uneasy about the situation*; *The slightest difficulty seems to upset her*; *He'll tell you his life history with only the slightest encouragement.* – *See also* **in the slightest** *below.*

'**slighting** *adj* (*usu attrib*: *formal*) insulting; disrespectful: *He made rather a slighting remark about her parents.* '**slightingly** *adv.*

'**slightly** *adv* **1** to a small extent: *I'm still slightly worried about it*; *I know him slightly.* **2** slenderly: *The missing girl is described as fair and slightly built.*

in the '**slightest** (*in negative sentences, questions etc*) at all: *You haven't upset me in the slightest*; *That doesn't worry me in the slightest*; *'Am I disturbing you?' 'No, not in the slightest.'* – *See also* **slightest** *above.*

slily *see* **sly**.

slim [slim] *adj* **1** not thick or fat; thin: *She has a slim, graceful figure*; *Taking exercise is one way of keeping slim.* **2** not good; slight: *There's still a slim chance that we'll find the child alive.* – *v* – *pt, ptp* **slimmed** – *vi* to use means (such as eating less) in order to become slimmer: *I mustn't eat bread, biscuits or cakes – I'm trying to slim*; *You haven't eaten very much – are you slimming?*

'**slimming** *adj* having the effect of making a person (seem) slimmer: *The style of this dress is very slimming*; *Black is a slimming colour.* – *nu* (*often in cmpds*) the process or practice of trying to become slimmer: *Slimming can be dangerous – it should be done carefully*; *She's on a slimming-diet*; *Do slimming-pills really help you to slim?*

'**slimness** *nu.*

slime [slaim] *nu* thin, slippery mud or other matter that is soft, sticky and half-liquid: *Snails leave a trail of slime*; *There was a layer of slime at the bottom of the pond.*

'**slimy** *adj* **1** covered with, consisting of, or like, slime: *Snakes look slimy but actually they're quite dry*; *The squashed banana had made a slimy mess on the floor.* **2** (*inf*) humble in an unpleasantly insincere way; obsequious: *The new cashier has rather a slimy manner*; *I'd prefer him if he were less slimy.* '**sliminess** *nu.*

sling [sliŋ] *nc* **1** a type of bandage hanging from the neck or shoulders to support an injured arm: *He had his broken arm in a sling.* **2** a band of cloth *etc* worn over the shoulder for supporting a rifle *etc* on the back. **3** a looped arrangement of ropes, chains *etc* for supporting, hoisting, carrying and lowering heavy objects. **4** (*hist*) a type of weapon consisting of a leather strap with a string attached to each end, used for hurling stones *etc.* – *v* – *pt, ptp* **slung** [slʌŋ] – *vt* **1** (*inf*) to throw violently: *The boy slung a stone at the dog*; (*fig*) *You'll be slung out (of the house) if you behave like that.* **2** to support, hang or swing by means of a strap, sling *etc*: *Several pieces of equipment had been slung from the roof on ropes*; *He stood up and slung his gun over his shoulder*; *He had a camera and binoculars slung round his neck.*

'**slingshot** *nc* (*Amer*) a catapult.

slink [sliŋk] – *pt, ptp* **slunk** [slʌŋk] – *vi* to move as if wanting to avoid attention: *The dog slunk off after being beaten*; *He slunk into the kitchen when no-one was looking and stole a cake.*

'**slinky** *adj* (*inf*) **1** (of a dress *etc*) clinging attractively to the body: *a slinky evening dress.* **2** having a slim, attractive figure: *a slinky blonde*; *You look very slinky in that outfit.*

slip[1] [slip] – *pt, ptp* **slipped** – **1** *vi* to slide accidentally and lose one's balance or footing: *I slipped and fell on the path.* **2** *vi* to slide, or drop, out of the right position or out of control: *The plate slipped out of my grasp*; *The razor slipped and he cut his chin.* **3** *vi* to drop in standard: *She has slipped in my estimation since I read her last report*; *I'm sorry about my mistake – I must be slipping!* **4** *vi* to move quietly *esp* without being noticed: *She slipped out of the room*; *The months were slipping by fast.* **5** *vt* to escape from: *The dog had slipped its lead and disappeared*; (*fig*) *I'm so sorry I forgot to give you the message – it completely slipped my mind/memory.* **6** *vt* to put or pass (something) with a quick, light movement: *She slipped the letter back in its envelope*; *I slipped a coat over my shoulders*; *Perhaps you slipped your purse into a drawer by mistake*; *She slipped a pound-note into his hand.* – *See also* **slip** *in phrases below.* – **1** *nc* an act of slipping: *Her sprained ankle was a result of a slip on the path.* **2** *nc* a *usu* small mistake: *Everyone makes the occasional slip.* **3** *nc* a kind of undergarment worn under a dress; a petticoat: *She was wearing a pink nylon slip.* **4** *nc* (*also* '**slipway**) a sloping platform next to water used for building and launching ships. **5** *nu* (*sometimes in pl with* **the**) in cricket, the position of a fielder standing behind and to the (right) side of the batsman: *He was caught at first slip/in the slips*; (*attrib*) *a slip fielder.*

'**slipper** *nc* a loose, soft kind of shoe for wearing indoors, *eg* with nightclothes and dressing-gown.

'**slippery** *adj* **1** so smooth as to cause slipping: *The path is slippery – watch out!*; *slippery mud.* **2** not trustworthy: *He's rather a slippery character.*

'**slipperiness** *nu.*

'**slip-knot** *nc* a knot that slips along the cord round which it is tied and can be pulled tight.

'**slip-on** *nc, adj* (a type of shoe) able to be put on without fastenings: *I'd like to buy a pair of slip-ons*; *slip-on shoes.* – *See also* **slip on** *below.*

slipped disc *nc* a displacement of one of discs between the vertebrae in the spine, *usu* causing considerable pain: *He has got a slipped disc.*

'**slip road** *nc* a road for joining or leaving a motorway.

'**slipshod** *adj* (*formal derog*) (of work, *etc*) untidy; careless: *The survey was carried out in a very slipshod manner and will have to be done again*; *The teacher told him his work was slipshod.*

slip-up *see* **slip up** *below.*

slipway *see* **slip** (*n def 4*).

give (someone) the slip (*inf*) to escape from or avoid (someone) in a secretive manner: *The crooks gave the policemen the slip.*

let slip 1 to miss (an opportunity *etc*): *I let the*

chance slip, unfortunately. **2** to say (something) unintentionally: *He let slip that his mother had been criticizing me; She let slip some remark about my daughter.*

slip a disc to get a slipped disc: *He slipped a disc when he lifted that heavy box.*

slip into *vt fus* to put on (clothes) quickly: *She slipped into her nightdress.*

slip off **1** *vt sep* to take (clothes) off quickly: *Slip off your shoe.* **2** *vi* to move away noiselessly or hurriedly: *We'll slip off when no-one's looking.*

slip on *vt sep* to put on (clothes) quickly: *She got out of bed and slipped on her dressing-gown.*

slip (someone) something (*inf*) to pass money *etc, usu* intended as a bribe, to a person: *I slipped the barman a pound-note to serve us first.*

slip up *vi* to make a mistake; to fail to do something: *They certainly slipped up badly over the new appointment.* (*nc* **'slip-up**).

slip[2] [slip] *nc* a strip or narrow piece of paper, *esp* a small printed form for filling in: *Fill in your name and address on this slip*; (*in cmpds*) *When you want to take a day off work you must get your leave-slip signed by the boss; She wrote down his telephone number on a slip of paper.*

a slip of a girl/child *etc* (*formal*) a small, slim, young person: *She carried the coal up by herself, and she's just a slip of a girl.*

slipper, slippery *see* **slip**[1].

slit [slit] – *prp* **'slitting**: *pt, ptp* **slit** – *vt* to make a long cut in: *She slit the envelope open with a knife.* – *nc* a long cut; a narrow opening: *She made a slit in the material with a large pair of scissors; The castle had slits on either side of the main door through which arrows could be fired at attackers.*

slither ['sliðə] *vi* to slide or slip while trying to walk (*eg* on ice or mud): *The dog was slithering about on the ice.*

sliver ['slivə] *nc* a long thin piece or slice of something: *He cut his finger on a sliver of broken glass; I'd like just a sliver of cake, please.*

slobber ['slobə] *vti* to let (saliva) dribble from the mouth.

'slobbery *adj* unpleasantly wet.

slog [slog] – *pt, ptp* **slogged** – (*inf*) **1** *vt* to hit hard (*usu* without aiming carefully): *A man tried to attack her in the street and she slogged him with her handbag.* **2** *vi* to make one's way with difficulty: *We slogged on up the hill.* **3** *vi* to work very hard: *She has been slogging all week at her history, as she has an exam next week.* – (*inf*) **1** *ncu* (a period of) hard work: *Working for exams is a hard slog; months of hard slog.* **2** *nc* a hard blow: *He gave the ball a slog.*

slogan ['slougən] *nc* an easily-remembered and frequently repeated phrase which is used in advertising *etc*: *We are trying to invent a slogan to advertise our product on television; When was the slogan 'Safety First' invented?*

sloop [slu:p] *nc* (*hist*) a one-masted sailing boat.

slop [slop] – *pt, ptp* **slopped** – *vti* (*slightly inf*) to (cause liquid to) splash, spill, or move around violently in a container: *She slopped some milk on to the floor from the jug she was carrying; Some water slopped over the side of the pail; The water was slopping about in the bucket.*

slops *n pl* (*slightly inf: sometimes derog*) **1** waste liquid (*eg* dregs from tea-cups *etc*). **2** tasteless, semi-liquid food: *All the time I was ill, they wouldn't give me anything to eat but slops.*

'sloppy *adj* (*inf: often derog*) **1** semi-liquid; tending to slop: *sloppy food; This porridge is sloppy.* **2** careless and untidy; messy: *His work is sloppy; sloppy old clothes.* **3** very sentimental: *a sloppy love-story; That film is rather sloppy.* **'sloppily** *adv.* **'sloppiness** *nu.*

'slop basin/bowl *nc* a bowl into which to pour slops (*def 1*).

slop about/around *vi* (*inf*) **1** to move about in, or play with, anything wet or sloppy: *The children were slopping about in the puddles.* **2** (*with* **in**) to go about dressed in an untidy way: *I like to slop around in old clothes at the weekend.*

slope [sloup] **1** *ncu* a position or direction that is neither level nor upright; an upward or downward slant: *My wardrobe won't fit in here because of the slope of the ceiling; The floor is on a slight slope.* **2** *nc* a surface with one end higher than the other: *The house stands on a gentle slope.* – *vi* to be in a position which is neither level nor upright: *The field slopes steeply towards the road.*

slope off *vi* (*sl*) to go away, *esp* secretively and without warning: *When I next looked round for him, he had taken his chance and sloped off.*

slot [slot] *nc* **1** a small narrow opening, *esp* one to receive coins: *I put the correct money in the slot, but the machine didn't start.* **2** (*inf*) a (*usu* regular) position (in *eg* the schedule of television/radio programmes): *The early-evening comedy slot.* – *v* – *pt, ptp* **'slotted** – *vt* (*with* **in** *or* **into**: *inf*) to fit (something) into a small space: *He slotted the last piece of the puzzle into place; If you're a good typist, I'm sure we could slot you in somewhere in the firm; I managed to slot in my tea-break between two jobs.*

'slot machine *nc* a machine, *esp* one containing cigarettes, sweets *etc* for sale, worked by putting a coin in a slot.

sloth [slouθ] **1** *nu* (*old or formal*) laziness, *esp* as a habit. **2** *nc* a kind of South American animal that lives in trees and moves very slowly.

'slothful *adj* (*formal*) lazy: *He scolded the slothful boy; He regretted that he had been so slothful as a youth.* **'slothfully** *adv.* **'slothfulness** *nu.*

slouch [slautʃ] *vt* (*derog*) to sit, move or walk in an unattractive way with shoulders rounded and head hanging: *He slouched sulkily out of the room; He was slouching in an armchair.* – *nc* (*derog: usu in sing*) this way of sitting, moving *etc*: *We could see him approaching with his usual slouch.*

slough [slau] (*formal: sometimes with* **off**) **1** *vt* (of snakes *etc*) to get rid of (a dead outer skin). **2** *vi* (of dead skin *etc*) to fall off: *Some of her skin sloughed off after she had been badly burned.* – *nc* (*formal or liter: often fig*) a swamp: *He was in a deep slough of depression.*

Slovak *see* Appendix 2.

Slovenian *see* Appendix 2.

slovenly ['slʌvnli] *adj* untidy, careless or dirty: *a slovenly woman; Her work has been rather slovenly recently.* **'slovenliness** *nu.*

slow [slou] *adj* **1** not fast; not moving quickly; taking a long time: *a slow train; This symphony has two fast movements and one slow movement; The service at that restaurant is very slow; The old lady was becoming rather slow and unsteady on her feet; He was very slow to offer help.* **2** (*usu pred*) (of a clock *etc*) showing a time earlier than the actual time; behind in time: *My watch is five minutes slow.* **3** not clever; not quick at learning: *a slow child; Her daughter is quite clever, but her son is rather slow; He's particularly slow at arithmetic.* **4** (*usu pred*) not lively or interesting; dull: *I think* *she finds life in the country a little slow.* – *vti* to make, or become slower: *The car slowed to take the corner*; *The thick snow slowed her progress.*

'**slowly** *adv*: *He slowly opened his eyes*; *He drove home slowly*; *Slowly but surely we're reaching the end of this job*; *He spoke slowly and deliberately.*

'**slowness** *nu.*

'**slowcoach** *nc* (*inf*) a person who is slow in movement: *Hurry up, you slowcoach!*

slow motion *nu* movement which is slower than normal or actual movement *esp* as a special effect in films: *Let's watch that sequence again, in slow motion.*

go slow *see* **go**.

slow down/up *vi, vt sep* to make or become slower: *The police were warning drivers to slow down because of the fog*; *The snow was slowing up the traffic.*

sludge [slʌdʒ] *nu* soft, slimy mud, grease or other matter which settles at the bottom of a liquid: *The river-bed is covered with thick sludge.*

slug[1] [slʌg] *nc* a kind of animal like a snail but with no shell: *I saw a lot of black slugs in the garden after the rain.*

'**sluggard** [-gəd] *nc* (*old*) a person who is slow and lazy in habits.

'**sluggish** *adj* moving slowly; not active or alert: *a sluggish river*; *a sluggish heartbeat*; *I always feel rather sluggish in the mornings*; *a person of very sluggish habits.* '**sluggishly** *adv.* '**sluggishness** *nu.*

slug[2] [slʌg] *nc* a piece of metal, *esp* (*inf*) an irregularly shaped lump used as a bullet, or (*tech*) a strip with type along one edge, used in printing. – *v* – *pt, ptp* **slugged** – *vt* (*inf*) to strike (a person) heavily *usu* causing unconsciousness: *The unconscious man had been slugged on the back of the neck with a heavy object.*

sluice [slu:s] *nc* **1** (*often* '**sluice-gate**) a sliding gate for controlling a flow of water in an artificial channel: *We shall have to open the sluice.* **2** the channel or the water which flows through it. – **1** *vt* (*often with* **down** *or* **out**) to clean with a strong flow of water: *He sluiced out the cattle troughs*; *We sluiced down the walls and the floor.* **2** *vi* (*formal*) to pour or flow.

slum [slʌm] *nc* (*often attrib*) a group of houses, blocks of flats, street *etc* where the conditions are dirty and overcrowded and the building(s) *usu* in a bad state: *That new block of flats is rapidly turning into a slum*; *a slum dwelling*; *slum housing/property*; *slum clearance* (= the demolishing of slums and rehousing of the inhabitants); (*fig*) *This room is a slum – please tidy it!* – *See also* **the slums** *below.* – *vi* (*inf*) to adopt a lower standard (*eg* of tidiness, social behaviour *etc*) than is usual for oneself: *We're slumming (it) in the kitchen while the painters are re-decorating the sitting-room.*

'**slummy** *adj* (*inf*): *This area is really rather slummy.*

the slums the area(s) of a town *etc* where there are slums: *As a social worker, she does a lot of work in the slums.*

slumber ['slʌmbə] *vi* (*formal*) to sleep. – *ncu* (*formal or facet: sometimes in pl with sing meaning*) sleep: *She was in a deep slumber*; *several hours of dreamless slumber*; *I didn't want to disturb your slumbers.*

slump [slʌmp] *vi* **1** to fall or sink suddenly and heavily: *He slumped wearily into a chair.* **2** (of prices, stocks, trade *etc*) to become less; to lose value suddenly: *Business has slumped*; *That company's shares slumped last month.* – *nc* **1** a sudden fall in value, trade *etc*: *a slump in prices.* **2** a time of very bad economic conditions, with serious unemployment *etc*; a depression: *There was a serious slump in the 1930s*; *Economists are forecasting a slump.*

slung *see* **sling**.

slunk *see* **slink**.

slur [slə:] – *pt, ptp* **slurred** – *vt* **1** to pronounce indistinctly: *The drunk man slurred his words.* **2** (*music*) to play or sing (notes) in a smoothly connected way: *In this phrase the notes are slurred.* – **1** *nc* (*formal*) an injury unfairly done to a person's reputation: *Although he was acquitted at the trial, the slur to his reputation was permanent*; *He is merely trying to cast a slur on me by saying that.* **2** a damaging or insulting remark or suggestion: *She decided to ignore the slur implied in his comment.* **3** an act of slurring (words *etc*). **4** (*music*) a smooth connection between notes.

slurred *adj*: *His speech was rather slurred, and I thought he might be drunk*; *a slurred note.*

slush [slʌʃ] *nu* **1** melting snow: *The streets are covered with slush.* **2** (*inf derog*) (something said or written showing) weak sentimentality: *I think most romantic novels are just slush!* '**slushy** *adj.* '**slushiness** *nu.*

slut [slʌt] *nc* a dirty, untidy woman. '**sluttish** *adj.*

sly [slai] *adj* **1** (*derog*) cunning or deceitful: *He sometimes behaves in rather a sly manner*; *I don't trust that girl – she's sly.* **2** playfully mischievous: *He made a sly reference to my foolish mistake.* '**slyly**, '**slily** *advs.* '**slyness** *nu.*

on the '**sly** secretly, without informing others: *I think he's helping himself to the firm's stationery on the sly.*

smack[1] [smak] *vt* to strike smartly and loudly; to slap: *He was smacked by his mother for being rude to her*; *She smacked the child's hand/bottom*; *She smacked his hand away.* – *ncu* (the sound of) a blow of this kind; a slap: *It does children no harm to give them an occasional smack when they're naughty*; *He could hear the smack of the waves against the side of the ship.* – *adv* directly and with force: *He ran smack into the door.*

a smack on the cheek (*inf*) a quick, loud kiss on the cheek: *He gave her a quick smack on the cheek and said goodbye.*

smack one's lips (*usu fig*) to bring one's lips together with a sharp noise, to show an eager appetite: *He smacked his lips at the sight of the feast*; *This new scandal will make them smack their lips!*

smack[2] [smak] *vi* (*with* **of**: *usu formal fig*) to taste of: *The whole affair smacks of prejudice.* – *nc* (*usu fig: no pl*) a particular taste: *There's a smack of corruption about this affair.*

smack[3] [smak] *nc* a small fishing boat.

small [smo:l] *adj* **1** little in size, degree, importance *etc*; not large or great: *She was accompanied by a small boy of about six*; *The boy seemed rather small for his age*; *There's only a small amount of sugar left*; *He owns a small grocery business*; *There are a few small points I'd like to discuss with you*; *She cut the meat up small for the baby.* **2** (*attrib*) not doing something on a large scale: *He's a small businessman* (= He has a small business); *the small farmers*; *a small tradesman*; *I'm only a small eater* (= I haven't a large appetite). **3** (*attrib*: *used with nus*: *formal*) little; not much: *You have small* *reason to be satisfied with yourself*; *It's small wonder* (= It's not surprising) *that he hated his parents.* **4** (of the letters of the alphabet) not capital: *The teacher showed the children how to write a capital G and a small g.*

small ads *n pl* (*inf*) advertisements in the personal columns of a newspaper.

ˈ**small arms** *n pl* weapons small and light enough to be carried by a man: *They found a hoard of rifles and other small arms belonging to the rebels.*

small beer *see* **beer**.

small change *nu* coins of small value: *a pocketful of small change.*

ˈ**small fry** *see* **fry**[2].

ˈ**smallholder** *nc* (*Brit*) a person owning or renting a smallholding.

ˈ**smallholding** *nc* (*Brit*) a piece of land *usu* under fifty acres in size, bought or rented for cultivation.

small hours *n pl* the hours immediately after midnight: *He woke up in the small hours*; *She works into the small hours every night.*

ˌ**small-ˈminded** *adj* having, or showing, narrow interests or intolerant and unimaginative opinions: *those small-minded people who take no interest in the arts*; *Am I just being small-minded in objecting to nudity on television?*

ˈ**smallpox** *nu* a type of serious infectious disease in which there is a severe rash of large, pus-filled spots that *usu* leave scars: *Vaccination against smallpox is no longer thought necessary in Britain.*

small screen *nc* (*no pl*) television, not the cinema: *This play is intended for the small screen.*

ˈ**small-time** *adj* (*attrib*) (of a thief *etc*) not working on a large scale: *a small-time crook/thief.*

ˈ**small talk** *nu* (polite) conversation about very unimportant matters: *I refuse to go to the party and indulge in small talk all evening.*

feel/look small to feel or look foolish or insignificant: *He criticized her in front of her colleagues and made her feel very small.*

in a small voice in a tone that is quiet or subdued, *esp* as a result of guilt or fear: *'Who spilt the paint on the floor?' 'I did', said John in a small voice.*

in a small way 1 with little money or stock: *He is an antique-dealer in a small way.* **2** quietly, without extravagance: *We celebrated in a small way at home.*

look small *see* **feel small** *above*.

the small of the back the narrow part of the back at, and just below, the waist: *Kidney infections sometimes cause pain in the small of the back.*

smallholding, smallpox *see* **small**.

smarmy [ˈsmaːmi] *adj* (*inf derog*) over-respectful and inclined to use flattery; obsequious: *I think he's rather smarmy*; *I can't bear his smarmy manner.*

ˈ**smarminess** *nu*.

smart [smaːt] *adj* **1** neat and well-dressed; fashionable: *You're looking very smart today*; *a smart suit.* **2** (*sometimes derog*) clever and quick in thought and action: *We need a smart boy to help in the shop*; *I don't trust some of those smart salesmen*; (*ironic*) *That was a smart thing to do – you've gone and burnt the stew!*; *If you think you're so smart, can't you suggest some way out of this mess?* **3** (*formal*) brisk; sharp: *She gave him a smart slap on the cheek.* – *vi* **1** (of part of the body) to be affected by a sharp stinging feeling: *The thick smoke made his eyes smart.* **2** to feel annoyed, resentful *etc* after being insulted *etc*: *He is still smarting from your remarks.* – *ncu* the stinging feeling left by a blow or the resentful feeling left by an insult: *He could still feel the smart of her slap/insult.*

ˈ**smarten** (*often with* **up**) *vti* to make or become smarter: *They've smartened up the building by painting the doors and window-frames*; *He has smartened up a lot in appearance lately*; *He thought he'd better smarten himself a bit before meeting her mother.*

ˈ**smartly** *adv*: *The soldiers stood smartly to attention*; *He was smartly rebuked for his bad behaviour*; *She is always smartly dressed.*

ˈ**smartness** *nu*.

ˈ**smart-Alec(k), ˈsmart-Alick** [-alik] *nc* (*derog sl*) a person who thinks he is cleverer than others: *those smart-Alecks in the government*; (*attrib*) *a smart-Aleck remark/suggestion.*

smash [smaʃ] *vti* **1** (*sometimes with* **up**) to (cause to) break in pieces or be ruined: *The plate dropped on the floor and smashed into little pieces*; *This unexpected news had smashed all his hopes*; *He had an accident and smashed up his car*; *He became violent and started to smash the furniture up*; *The firemen had to smash their way into* (= break doors *etc* in order to enter) *the burning building.* – *See also* **smash-up** *below.* **2** to strike with great force; to crash: *The car smashed into a lamp-post*; *He smashed his fist down on the table in fury.* – *nc* **1** (the sound of) a breakage; a crash: *A plate fell to the ground with a smash*; *There has been a bad smash on the motorway*; (*fig*) *I'm afraid that firm is heading for a smash.* **2** (*inf*) a strong blow: *He gave his opponent a smash on the jaw.* **3** in tennis *etc*, a hard downward shot.

ˈ**smasher** *nc* (*inf*) something very fine or splendid: *His new car's a smasher!*; *Did you see that girl? What a smasher!*

ˈ**smashing** *adj* (*inf*) marvellous; splendid: *What a smashing idea!*; *a smashing new bike*; *Your girlfriend's smashing!*

ˌ**smash-and-ˈgrab (raid/robbery)** *nc* a robbery in which the window of a shop is smashed and goods grabbed from behind it: *There was a smash-and-grab robbery at the jeweller's last night*; *a spate of smash-and-grabs.*

smash hit *nc* (*inf*) a song, show *etc* that is a great success: *This play was a smash hit in New York.*

ˈ**smash-up** *nc* (*inf*) an act or instance of smashing (*def 1*): *Several cars were involved in the smash-up.*

smattering [ˈsmatəriŋ] *nc* a very slight knowledge of a particular subject: *He has a smattering of French.*

smear [smiə] *vt* **1** to spread (something sticky or oily) over a surface: *The little boy smeared jam on the chair*; *My hands were smeared with grease from the engine.* **2** *vti* to make or become blurred; to smudge: *He brushed against the newly painted notice and smeared the lettering*; *The lettering has smeared a little.* **3** *vt* to try to discredit (a person *etc*) by slandering him: *He has been spreading false stories in an attempt to smear us.* – *nc* **1** a mark made by smearing: *There was a smear of paint on her dress*; *He had a smear of blood on his face.* **2** a piece of slander: *a vicious smear*; (*attrib*) *a smear campaign by the press.* **3** (*tech*) a sample of cells *etc* obtained from a part of the body, *eg* the cervix, and spread out for examination under a microscope.

ˈ**smeary** *adj* (*inf*): *The wall was covered with smeary fingerprints*; *This poster has just been printed and the ink is still smeary* (= likely to smear).

ˈ**smear test** *nc* (*tech*) an examination, under a

microscope, of a smear (*def 3*): *She has had a smear test to make sure that she does not have cancer of the cervix.*

smell [smel] **1** *nu* the sense or power of being aware of things through one's nose: *My sister never had a good sense of smell.* **2** *ncu* the quality that is noticed by using this power: *a pleasant smell*; *There's a strong smell of gas*; *These flowers have very little smell.* **3** *nc* an act of using this power: *Have a smell of this!* – *v* – *pts, ptps* **smelled, smelt** [smelt] – **1** *vti* (not used with **is, was** *etc* and **-ing**) to notice by using one's nose: *I smell gas*; *I thought I smelt (something) burning*; (*fig*) *He could smell danger*; *I've got a cold and I can't smell very well.* **2** *vi* (not *usu* used with **is, was** *etc* and **-ing**) to give off a smell: *How that river smells!*; *The roses smelt beautiful*; *Her hands smelt of fish.* **3** *vti* to examine by using the sense of smell: *Let me smell those flowers*; *Do you think this meat is bad? Smell (it)!* – *See also* **smell out** *below.*

-smelling (*in cmpds*) having a (particular kind of) smell: *a nasty-smelling liquid*; *sweet-smelling roses.*

'smelly *adj* (*inf*) having a bad smell: *smelly fish*; *That dog is rather smelly today.* **'smelliness** *nu.*

smelling-salts *see* **salt**.

smell out *vt sep* **1** to find (as if) by smelling: *We buried the dog's bone, but he smelt it out again.* **2** to fill (a place) with a very strong, unpleasant smell: *That cheese is smelling the room out.*

smelt[1] [smelt] *vt* (*tech*) to melt (ore) in order to separate metal from waste.

smelt[2] *see* **smell**.

smile [smail] *vti* to show pleasure, amusement *etc* by turning up the corners of the mouth: *He smiled warmly* (= kindly) *at her as he shook hands*; *They all smiled politely at the joke*; *He asked her what she was smiling at*; *She has little to smile about*; *She smiled and waved when she saw him*; *Smile at the camera, please!*; *He smiled broadly/widely* (= with the mouth stretched wide); *He smiled* (= was amused) *to think he had once thought her shy*; (*liter*) *He smiled his appreciation.* – *See also* **smile on** *below.* – *nc* an act of smiling, or the resulting facial expression: *'How do you do?' he said with a smile*; *the happy smiles of the children*; *She gave an amused smile*; *He gave her a smile of recognition*; *She has an attractive smile* (= She looks attractive when she smiles); (*inf derog*) *This news will soon wipe the smile off his face* (= make him less contented).

'smiling *adj* (*usu attrib*): *a smiling expression*; *a happy, smiling face.*

be all smiles to be, or look, very happy: *He was all smiles when he heard the good news.*

'smile on *vt fus* (*liter*) to be favourable to: *Fate smiled on us.*

smirch [smə:tʃ] *vt* (*old*: *often fig*) to stain; to make dirty: *He has smirched his reputation*; *His face was smirched with grime.*

smirk [smə:k] *vi* (*often derog*) to smile in a self-satisfied or foolish manner: *He sat there smirking after the teacher had praised him.* – *nc* (*often derog*) a smile of this sort: *What has he got that silly smirk on his face for?*

smite [smait] – *pt* **smote** [smout]: *ptp* **'smitten** ['smitn] – *vt* (*arch or facet*: *often fig*) to strike or hit hard: *His conscience smote him after he had lied to the child.*

'smitten *adj* (*pred, usu with* **with**: *arch or facet*): *He's smitten with flu*; *He seems to be strongly smitten* (= in love) (*with her*).

smith [smiθ] *nc* **1** a blacksmith. **2** (*in cmpds*) a person whose job is to work with a particular metal, or make a particular type of article: *a goldsmith*; *a silversmith*; *a gunsmith.*

'smithy *nc* the workshop of a blacksmith.

smithereens [smiðə'ri:nz]: **(in)to smithereens** (in)to tiny fragments: *The vase was smashed to smithereens.*

smitten *see* **smite**.

smock [smok] *nc* a loose, shirt-like garment sometimes worn over other clothes to protect them: *Smocks, especially worn with trousers, are very fashionable for women these days*; (*in cmpds*) *The children must wear painting-smocks for their art lessons.*

smog [smog] *nu* fog mixed with smoke and fumes from factories, houses, vehicles *etc*: *London has less of a problem with smog than it used to, since smokeless zones were introduced.*

smoke [smouk] **1** *nu* the cloudlike gases and particles of soot given off by something which is burning: *Smoke was coming out of the chimney*; *Smoke poured out of the windows of the burning house*; *He puffed cigarette smoke into my face.* **2** *nc* (*inf*) an act of smoking (a cigarette *etc*): *I came outside for a smoke.* – **1** *vi* to give off smoke: *This fire smokes sometimes when the wind is in a certain direction.* **2** *vti* to draw in and puff out the smoke from (a cigarette *etc*): *I don't smoke, but he smokes cigars*; *He's smoking in the garden.* **3** *vt* to dry, cure, preserve (ham, fish *etc*) by hanging it in smoke. **4** *vt* to darken (ornamental glass) with smoke. – *See also* **smoke out** *below.*

smoked *adj* (*attrib*) treated with smoke: *smoked cheese*; *A kipper is a smoked herring*; *This factory specializes in smoked glass.*

'smokeless *adj* (*usu attrib*) **1** allowing no smoke: *Our part of the town is a smokeless zone.* **2** burning without smoke: *smokeless fuel.*

'smoker *nc* **1** (*sometimes in cmpds*) a person who smokes cigarettes *etc*: *When did you become a smoker?*; *He's a pipe-smoker.* **2** (*inf*) a railway carriage or compartment in which smoking is allowed: *Is this carriage a smoker or a non-smoker?* – *See also* **non-smoking carriage/compartment** *below.*

'smoking *nu* (*sometimes in cmpds*) the habit of smoking cigarettes *etc*: *He has given up cigarette-smoking at last*; *Smoking can damage your health*; *Didn't you see the notice saying 'No Smoking'?*

'smoky *adj* **1** filled with, or giving out (too much) smoke: *The atmosphere in the room was thick and smoky*; *That's a rather smoky fire.* **2** (*formal or liter*) like smoke in appearance *etc*: *Her eyes were a smoky blue.* **'smokiness** *nu.*

'smokescreen *nc* **1** a cloud of smoke used to conceal the movements of troops *etc.* **2** (*fig*) something intended to conceal one's activities *etc*: *He adopts other people's attitudes as a smokescreen for his real beliefs.*

go up in smoke **1** to be completely destroyed by fire: *The whole house went up in smoke.* **2** (*inf fig*) to vanish very quickly leaving nothing behind: *All his plans have gone up in smoke.* **3** (*inf fig*) to lose one's temper: *He'll go up in smoke when he hears about this.*

non-smoking carriage/compartment (*inf abbrev* **ˌnon-'smoker**) a carriage or compartment in which smoking cigarettes *etc* is not allowed.

smoke out *vt sep* to drive (an animal *etc*) into the open by filling its burrow, hiding-place *etc* with smoke: *They decided to smoke the fox out.*

smolder *see* **smoulder**.

smooth [smu:ð] *adj* **1** having an even surface; not rough: *Her skin is as smooth as satin*; *a soft, smooth hairstyle*; (*liter fig*) *Our path in life will not always be smooth.* **2** without lumps: *Mix the ingredients to a smooth paste*; *Add the milk to the flour and beat the mixture till smooth.* **3** (of movement) without breaks, stops or jolts: *Did you have a smooth flight from New York?*; *This lift has a very smooth operation*; *The train came to a smooth halt.* **4** without problems or difficulties: *a smooth journey*; *Nothing occurred to disturb the smooth routine of his life*; *His progress towards promotion was smooth and rapid.* **5** (*often derog*) (too) agreeable and pleasant in manner *etc*: *I don't trust those smooth salesmen.* – *vt* **1** (*often with* **down, out** *etc*) to make (something) smooth or flat: *She smoothed back her hair from her forehead*; *She smoothed (down) the icing on the cake with a knife*; *She tried to smooth the creases out*; (*formal fig*) *He promised to smooth her path towards promotion.* **2** (*with* **into** *or* **over**: *formal*) to rub (a liquid substance *etc*) gently over (a surface): *Smooth the moisturizing cream into/over your face and neck.* – *See also* **smooth away, smooth over** *below.*

'smoothly *adv*: *The plane landed smoothly*; *The meeting went very smoothly.* **'smoothness** *nu.*

,smooth-'faced / ,smooth-'spoken / ,smooth-'tongued *adjs* (*derog*) (*usu* of a dishonest person) pleasant in manner, or persuasive and plausible in speech: *That smooth-faced hypocrite!*; *I wouldn't trust him – he was too smooth-spoken for me*; *a smooth-tongued liar.*

smooth away *vt sep* (*often fig*) to cause to disappear by smoothing: *I think we'll be able to smooth away these little difficulties.*

smooth over *vt sep* to make (problems *etc*) seem less important: *It's no good trying to smooth over the quarrel – they've been enemies for years.*

smote *see* **smite**.

smother ['smʌðə] **1** *vti* to kill or die from lack of air, caused *esp* by a thick covering over the mouth and nose; to suffocate: *He smothered his victim by holding a pillow over her face*; *The baby had been lying with its face against the pillow and had smothered*; (*fig*) *She's the kind of mother who smothers her children with too much love.* **2** *vt* to prevent (a fire) from burning by covering it thickly: *He threw sand on the fire to smother it*; (*fig*) *He managed to smother his anger and act as though nothing had happened.* **3** *vt* (*facet*) to cover (too) thickly; to overwhelm: *When he got home his children smothered him with kisses.* **4** *vt* (*formal or liter*) to prevent the growth or development of (opposition *etc*): *Complaints were smothered before anyone in authority heard them.*

smoulder, (*Amer*) **smolder** ['smouldə] *vi* to burn slowly or without flame: *A piece of coal had fallen out of the fire and the hearthrug was smouldering*; (*liter fig*) *His anger went on smouldering for years*; (*liter fig*) *His eyes smouldered with hate.*

smudge [smʌdʒ] *nc* a smear or a blurred mark: *There's a smudge of ink on your nose*; *The child's letter was full of blots and smudges.* – *vti* to make or become blurred or smeared: *Don't smudge my painting*; *The ink has smudged*; *The child's face was smudged with tears.*

'smudgy *adj.* **'smudginess** *nu.*

smug [smʌg] *adj* (*derog*) well satisfied, or too obviously pleased, with oneself: *I don't like that smug little man*; *He had a smug smile on his face because he had been proved right*; *There are several mistakes in your work, so you've got nothing to be smug about!* **'smugly** *adv.* **'smugness** *nu.*

smuggle ['smʌgl] **1** *vti* to bring (goods) into, or send them out from, a country illegally, or without paying duty: *He was caught smuggling (several thousand cigarettes through the Customs)*; *There is a great danger of rabies reaching Britain if people continue to smuggle animals into the country, ignoring the quarantine regulations.* **2** *vt* (*inf*) to send or take secretly: *I smuggled some food out of the kitchen.*

'smuggler *nc* a person who smuggles: *These caves were used by eighteenth-century smugglers for storing contraband goods.*

'smuggling *nu*: *the laws against smuggling*; (*in cmpds*) *drug-smuggling.*

smut [smʌt] **1** *nc* a spot of dirt or soot: *The passing steam trains left smuts of soot on her washing.* **2** *nu* (*inf*) vulgar or indecent talk *etc*: *There is too much smut on television nowadays!*

'smutty *adj* **1** covered with smuts; dirty; grimy: *a smutty face.* **2** (of a conversation, film *etc*) indecent; vulgar: *He could not be prevented from telling smutty stories*; *That show is too smutty to take the children to.* **'smuttiness** *nu.*

snack [snak] *nc* a light, hasty meal: *I usually have a large meal in the evening and only a snack at lunchtime*; (*attrib*) *We had a snack lunch in the pub.*

'snack bar *nc* a café *etc* where snacks are served, or a counter, kiosk *etc* where snacks can be bought: *We had lunch in the snack bar*; *He bought a sandwich at a snack bar and ate it in the park.*

snaffle ['snafl] *vt* (*inf facet*) to take without permission, or dishonestly: *I managed to snaffle several cakes from the table to eat later*; *Who has snaffled my pencil?*

snag [snag] *nc* **1** a difficulty or drawback: *We did not realize at first how many snags there were in our plan.* **2** a place on a garment where a thread has been torn or pulled out of place: *His clothes were full of snags after he had pushed his way through the prickly bushes.* – *v* – *pt, ptp* **snagged** – *vt* to catch or tear on a sharp or rough point sticking out of something: *She snagged her tights on the rough edge of the table.*

snail [sneil] *nc* a kind of soft-bodied small crawling animal with a coiled shell: *The garden is full of slugs and snails*; *Snails leave a silvery trail as they move along.*

at a 'snail's pace very slowly: *The old man walked along at a snail's pace*; *She knits beautiful jumpers – but she does them at a snail's pace.*

snake [sneik] *nc* any of a group of legless reptiles with long bodies that move along on the ground with a twisting movement, many of which have a poisonous bite: *Do all snakes have forked tongues?*; *He was bitten on the heel by a snake and nearly died.* – *vti* (*liter*) to move like a snake: *He snaked his way through the narrow tunnel*; *The path snaked away into the distance across the hillside.*

'snake-bite *ncu* the wound resulting from the bite of a snake: *What is the best emergency treatment for (a) snake-bite?*; *He died of a snake-bite.*

'snake-charmer *nc* a person who can handle snakes and make them perform rhythmical movements.

snakes and ladders *n sing* a game played with counters on a board that is printed with ladders, along which counters can progress, and snakes, along which they must go back: *The children were* *playing snakes and ladders.*

snake in the grass (*inf derog*) a person who cannot be trusted: *Beware of him – he's a real snake in the grass.*

snap [snap] **1** *vi* (*with* **at**) to make a biting movement; to try to grasp with the teeth: *The dog snapped at his ankles*; *Their dog is inclined to snap.* **2** *vti* to break with a sudden sharp noise: *The branch suddenly snapped*; *He snapped the stick in half*; *The handle of the cup snapped off.* **3** *vti* to (cause to) make a sudden sharp noise, in moving *etc*: *The lid snapped shut*; *He snapped the book shut.* **4** *vti* to speak in a sharp *esp* angry way: *'Mind your own business!' he snapped*; *There's no need to snap (at me) just because you happen to be in a bad mood*; *He snapped out a command.* **5** *vt* (*inf*) to take a photograph of: *He snapped the children playing in the garden.* – **1** *nc* (the noise of) an act of snapping: *There was a loud snap as his pencil broke*; *He shut the book with a snap.* **2** *nc* (*inf*) a photograph; a snapshot: *He wanted to show us his holiday snaps.* **3** *nu* a kind of simple card game in which each player lays his cards down in turn, and tries to be the first one to shout 'Snap!' when two cards of the same sort, number *etc* are laid one on top of the other: *The children were having a noisy game of snap*; *They were playing snap.* **4** *nc* a name used for certain types of biscuit: *ginger snaps*; *brandy snaps.* – *adj* (*attrib*) done, made *etc* quickly: *We took a snap vote on the issue*; *a snap decision.*

'snappish *adj* (*old*) snappy (*def 1*): *She was inclined to be snappish in the mornings*; *a snappish old man.* **'snappishly** *adv.* **'snappishness** *nu.*

'snappy *adj* **1** irritable; inclined to snap: *He is always rather snappy on a Monday morning*; *They have a snappy little dog.* **2** (*inf*: *esp pred*) quick; prompt: *You'll have to be snappy if you're catching that bus!* **3** (*inf*: *usu attrib*) smart: *He's certainly a snappy dresser* (= He dresses smartly). **'snappily** *adv.* **'snappiness** *nu.*

'snapdragon *nc* a kind of garden plant whose flower when pinched opens and closes like a mouth.

'snapshot *nc* a photograph taken quickly and without a lot of equipment: *That's a good snapshot of the children playing in the garden.*

cold snap *see* **cold**.

make it snappy (*inf*) hurry up: *I want an answer, and make it snappy!*

snap one's fingers to make a sharp noise by moving the thumb quickly across the top joint of the middle finger, as an informal gesture *eg* to attract someone's attention, mark the rhythm in music *etc*: *He snapped his fingers to attract the waiter's attention.*

snap someone's head/nose off (*inf*) to answer or interrupt rudely and impatiently: *There's no need to snap my head off!*

snap out of it (*inf*) to make oneself quickly stop being miserable, depressed *etc*: *I was getting very depressed so I decided to snap out of it and go on holiday*; *Come on – snap out of it!*

snap up *vt sep* to grab eagerly: *I saw this bargain in the shop and snapped it up straight away.*

snare [sneə] *nc* **1** a trap made with a noose of string, wire *etc*, for catching an animal: *He set a snare for rabbits.* **2** (*formal or liter*) a temptation or danger: *Pride is a snare we must all try to avoid.* – *vt* to catch with a snare: *He snared a couple of rabbits.*

snarl[1] [sna:l] *vti* (of a dog *etc*) to growl angrily, showing the teeth: *The dog snarled at the burglar*; (*fig*) *'Get out!' the man snarled (at her).* – *nc* an angry sound of this kind: *With a snarl, the dog leapt at him.*

snarl[2] [sna:l]: **snarl up** *vt sep* (*inf*) to cause to become confused, tangled *etc* and stop working, moving *etc* smoothly: *A loose screw had fallen into the machinery and snarled it up* (*nc* **'snarl-up**).

snatch [snatʃ] **1** *vti* (*vi with* **at**) to (try to) seize or grab suddenly: *The monkey snatched the biscuit out of my hand*; *She snatched at her hat as the wind carried it away*; *He snatched his coat up and ran out of the house.* **2** *vt* to take quickly, when one has time or the opportunity: *She managed to snatch an hour's sleep*; (*old inf*) *He snatched a kiss when no-one was looking.* – *nc* **1** an attempt to seize: *The thief made a snatch at her handbag.* **2** a short piece or extract *eg* from music, conversation *etc*: *He was humming a snatch (of song/music) from the new show*; *He overheard a snatch of conversation between the manager and his secretary.*

sneak [sni:k] **1** *vi* (*sometimes derog*) to go quietly and secretly, *esp* for a dishonest purpose: *He must have sneaked into my room when no-one was looking and stolen the money*; *She sneaked off* (= went away) *without telling anyone.* **2** *vi* (*inf derog*) (used *esp* by children) to behave in a disloyal way, *esp* to tell tales or inform on others: *The children were sure someone had sneaked on them to the teacher.* **3** *vt* (*inf*) to take secretly: *I want to sneak a look at his book*; *He sneaked the letter out of her drawer.* – *nc* (*inf*) a mean, deceitful person, *esp* a telltale: *That girl's a sneak – she told the teacher I hadn't done my homework.*

'sneakers *n pl* (*Amer, or Brit inf*) soft shoes with soles made of rubber, rope *etc*: *He was wearing blue jeans and sneakers*; *I need a new pair of sneakers.*

'sneaking *adj* (*attrib*) (of a *usu* unwanted or shameful feeling) slight but not easy to suppress: *I had a sneaking suspicion that she was enjoying being ill*; *She knew he was wicked but she had a sneaking admiration for his courage.*

'sneaky *adj* (*inf derog*): *I think she has behaved in a very sneaky way*; *It was a bit sneaky of him to tell the teacher about me.* **'sneakiness** *nu.*

'sneak thief *nc* (*formal*) a thief who gets in through unlocked doors *etc* without breaking in.

sneer [sniə] **1** *vi* to raise the top lip at one side in a kind of smile that expresses scorn: *What are you sneering for?* **2** *vi* (*with* **at**) to show contempt for (something) by such an expression or by scornful words *etc*: *He sneered at our attempts to improve the situation and said it was useless.* **3** *vt* to say with contempt: *'You haven't a chance of getting that job,' he sneered.* – *nc* a scornful expression, words *etc* that express contempt: *She examined his work with a sneer on her face that indicated that she was not impressed.*

'sneering *adj* (*attrib*): *a sneering comment.*

sneeze [sni:z] *vi* to blow out air suddenly, violently and involuntarily through the nose: *She had a cold and couldn't stop sneezing*; *The pepper made him sneeze.* – *nc* an act of sneezing: *She suddenly gave a loud sneeze.*

not sneeze at (*inf*) not to ignore (a chance, opportunity *etc*): *I certainly wouldn't sneeze at the opportunity of working abroad*; *This is a bargain that isn't to be sneezed at.*

snicker ['snikə] *vi* (*inf derog*) to giggle or laugh quietly and unpleasantly, *eg* at someone's misfortune; to snigger.

snide [snaid] *adj* (*derog*) sneering or critical in a sly, not open, manner: *He made a snide remark about her relationship with the boss*; *I thought that remark was really rather snide.*

sniff [snif] **1** *vi* to draw in air through the nose with a slight noise: *Why don't you blow your nose instead of sniffing all the time?* **2** *vti* to do this in an attempt to smell something: *The dog sniffed at the lamp-post*; *The dog sniffed me all over*; *He sniffed suddenly, wondering if he could smell smoke* – *See also* **sniff out** *below.* **3** *vt* to say in a complaining or tearful way: *'I'm not appreciated in this office,' she sniffed.* – *nc* an act of sniffing: *She gave a sniff of contempt and walked off.*

'**sniffle** *vi* (*inf*) to sniff repeatedly, as when one has a cold or is crying: *I wish she could get rid of that cold – she's been sniffling all week.* – *nc* (*inf*) (the sound of) an act of sniffling.

sniff out *vt sep* (*inf*) to discover or detect (by using the sense of smell): (*fig*) *I'll see if I can sniff out the cause of the trouble.*

not sniff at (*inf*) not to ignore (a chance, opportunity *etc*): *They're making you an offer that is certainly not to be sniffed at* (= is worth accepting).

snigger ['snigə] *vi* (*derog*) to laugh quietly in an unpleasant manner *eg* at someone else's misfortune: *When the teacher sat on a drawing-pin, several of the pupils sniggered.* – *nc* an act of sniggering: *The children were having a quiet snigger in the corner.*

snip [snip] – *pt, ptp* **snipped** – *vt* to cut sharply, *esp* with a single quick action, with scissors *etc*: *She finished off her sewing and snipped the thread*; *I snipped off two inches of thread.* – *nc* **1** a cut with scissors: *With a snip of her scissors she cut a hole in the cloth.* **2** a small piece cut off: *The floor was covered in snips of paper.* **3** (*inf*) a bargain: *It's a snip at £1!*

'**snippet** [-pit] *nc* a little piece, *esp* of information, gossip *etc*: *a snippet of news.*

snipe [snaip]: **snipe at** *vt fus* to shoot at (someone) from a hidden position: *The rebels had occupied a block of flats and were sniping at the government troops from the windows*; (*fig*) *As a politician he is quite used to being sniped at in the newspapers.*

'**sniper** *nc*: *The soldier was shot by a sniper as he walked down the street.*

snippet *see* **snip**.

snivel ['snivl] – *pt, ptp* '**snivelled**, (*Amer*) '**sniveled** – *vi* (*inf derog*) to whine or complain tearfully: *By this time the child was tired, and snivelled the rest of the way home.*

'**snivelling** *adj* (*attrib*: *derog*) weak; inclined to whine and complain: *That snivelling fool!*

snob [snob] *nc* (*derog*) a person who admires people of high rank or social class, and despises those in a lower class *etc* than himself: *Being a snob, he was always trying to get to know members of the nobility.*

'**snobbery** *nu* (*derog*) behaviour, talk *etc* that is typical of a snob: *She couldn't bear her mother's snobbery*; *social snobbery*; *I'm bored with the intellectual snobbery of people who despise all jazz on principle.*

'**snobbish** *adj* (*derog*): *She always had a snobbish desire to live in an area of expensive housing*; *People are often snobbish without being aware of it.* '**snobbishly** *adv.* '**snobbishness** *nu.*

snooker ['snu:kə] *nu* a kind of game played on a billiard-table with fifteen red balls and seven balls of other colours: *Do you play snooker?*; *Let's have a game of snooker*; (*attrib*) *a snooker match.*

snoop [snu:p] *vi* (*derog*: *often with* **around** *or* **into**) to make secretive investigations into things that do not concern oneself: *There were several suspicious-looking people snooping round the house*; *Why were you snooping around in my room?*; *She's always snooping into other people's business.*

snooze [snu:z] *vi* (*inf*) to doze or sleep lightly: *His grandfather was snoozing in his armchair.* – *nc* a short period of light sleep: *I think I'll just have a snooze for half an hour.*

snore [sno:] *vi* to make a noise like a snort while sleeping, when one is breathing in: *He was obviously asleep because he was snoring loudly.* – *nc* an act of snoring: *The sleeper in the armchair suddenly gave a loud snore.*

snorkel ['sno:kəl] *nc* a tube with the end(s) above water for allowing an underwater swimmer to breathe or a submarine to take in air.

snort [sno:t] *vi* **1** (*usu* of animals) to force air noisily through the nostrils, breathing either in or out: *The horses snorted impatiently.* **2** (of people) to make a similar noise, showing disapproval, anger, contempt, amusement *etc*: *She snorted at the very suggestion that she was tired.* – *nc* an act of snorting: *a snort of impatience*; *She gave a snort of laughter.*

snot [snot] *nu* (*inf*) the sticky or slimy fluid produced by the lining of the nose; mucus.

'**snotty** *adj* (*inf*: *esp attrib*) like, or covered with, snot: *a snotty nose.*

snout [snaut] *nc* the projecting mouth and nose part of certain animals, *esp* of a pig: *The pigs pushed their snouts through the bars of their pen*; *This type of dog has a long thin snout.*

snow [snou] *ncu* frozen water vapour that falls to the ground in soft white flakes: *We woke up one morning to find a thick covering of snow on the ground*; (*in cmpds*) *We were caught in a heavy snow-shower*; *About 15 centimetres of snow had fallen overnight*; (*formal*) *Many animals died in last winter's heavy snows* (= falls of snow); *The children love playing in the snow.* – *vi* (*only with* **it** *as subject*) to cause snow to fall: *It's snowing heavily*; *It looks as if it's going to snow.*

'**snowy** *adj* **1** full of, or producing a lot of, snow: *He looked out of the window at the snowy scene*; *The weather has been very snowy recently.* **2** (*liter*) white like snow: *the old man's snowy* (*white*) *hair.* '**snowiness** *nu.*

'**snowball** *nc* a ball of snow pressed hard together, *esp* made by children for throwing, as a game. – **1** *vti* to throw snowballs (at): *Several children were snowballing* (*one another*) *outside.* **2** *vi* (of a problem, project *etc*) to get bigger and bigger as it proceeds: *This whole business has snowballed recently.*

'**snow-bound** *adj* prevented from moving, progressing, functioning *etc*, because of snow: *The guests were snow-bound in the hotel and had to stay an extra week*; *snow-bound cars/traffic.*

'**snow-capped** *adj* (*liter*: *usu attrib*) (of mountains *etc*) having tops which are covered with snow: *snow-capped peaks.*

'**snow-capped**/(*liter*) '**snow-clad** *adjs* (*usu attrib*) covered with snow: *snow-covered fields*; *snow-clad trees.*

'**snowdrift** *nc* a bank of snow blown together by the wind: *There were deep snowdrifts at the side of* the road; *The sheep were found buried in a snowdrift.*

'snowdrop *nc* a kind of small white flower growing from a bulb in early spring.

'snowfall 1 *nc* a fall or shower of snow that settles on the ground: *There was a heavy snowfall last night.* **2** *nu* the amount of snow that falls in a certain place: *The snowfall last year was much higher than the average annual snowfall for this area.*

'snowfield *nc* a wide area always covered in snow on high mountains *etc.*

'snowflake *nc* one of the soft, light flakes composed of groups of crystals, in which snow falls: *A few large snowflakes began to fall from the sky.*

'snowline *nc* the level or height on a mountain above which there is always snow: *The climbers reached the snowline at about midday.*

'snowman [-man] *nc* a figure shaped like a human being made out of snow: *The children had built a snowman in the garden.*

'snow-plough *nc* (*Amer* **'snow-plow**) a kind of large vehicle for clearing snow from roads *etc.*

'snow-shoe *nc* a frame with a network of leather straps stretched across it, for wearing on the foot, to prevent a walker from sinking in the snow: *a pair of snow-shoes.*

'snowstorm *nc* a heavy fall of snow *esp* accompanied by a strong wind.

ˌsnow-'white *adj* white like snow: *clean, snow-white sheets*; *His hair had become snow-white since I had last met him.*

snowed in/up cut off, or prevented from going away from home *etc*, by snow: *Last winter we were snowed up for a week – the children couldn't even get to school*; *We were snowed in at home for several days.*

snowed under overwhelmed *eg* with a great deal of work: *Last week I was absolutely snowed under with work.*

snub [snʌb] – *pt, ptp* **snubbed** – *vt* to treat, or speak to, in a cold, scornful way; to insult: *She snubbed him rudely when he tried to speak*; *He snubbed me by not replying to my question.* – *nc* an act of snubbing; an insult: *He considered it a deliberate snub when she didn't invite him to her party.* – *adj* (of the nose) short and slightly turned up at the end: *a snub nose*; *She's quite good-looking, but her nose is rather snub.*

snuff[1] [snʌf] *nu* powdered tobacco for sniffing up into the nose: *He took a pinch of snuff.* – *vi* (*esp* of animals) to sniff.

'snuffbox *nc* a small box for holding snuff: *She gave him an antique gold snuffbox for Christmas.*

snuff[2] [snʌf] *vt* to snip off the burnt part of the wick of (a candle or lamp).

snuff it (*Brit sl*) to die: *I was sorry to hear that he'd snuffed it.*

snuff out *vt sep* **1** to extinguish the flame of (a candle *etc*): *He snuffed out the candle by squeezing the wick between his thumb and forefinger.* **2** to (cause to) come to a sudden end: *Opposition was quickly snuffed out.*

snuffle ['snʌfl] *vi* (*inf*) to make sniffing noises, or breathe noisily, *esp* as the result of a cold: *He had a bad cold and had been snuffling and coughing for a week.* – *nc* (*inf*) an act of snuffling.

snug [snʌg] *adj* **1** warm, comfortable; sheltered from the cold: *a snug room*; *The house is small but snug*; *The children are snug in bed.* **2** (of clothes *etc*) fitting closely: *This jacket is a nice snug fit.* **3** not large, but large enough: *He gets quite a snug income in his job.*

'snuggle *vi* (*inf*: *often with* **down** *or* **up**) to curl one's body up *esp* closely against another person, for warmth *etc*: *She snuggled down among the blankets*; *She snuggled up to her mother and went to sleep.*

'snugly *adv* **1** tightly and neatly: *The gun fitted snugly into my pocket.* **2** comfortably or warmly: *The little girl had a woollen scarf wrapped snugly round her neck.* **'snugness** *nu.*

so [sou] *adv* **1** (used in several types of sentence to express degree) to this extent, or to such an extent: *'The snake was about so long,' he said, holding his hands about a metre apart*; *Don't get so worried!*; *She was so pleased with his progress in school that she bought him a new bicycle*; *My mother lives so very far away that we hardly ever see her*; *Surely your husband isn't so mean as to refuse you housekeeping money?*; (*formal*) *Would you be so good as to* (= Please would you) *open the door for me?*; (*inf*) *They couldn't all get into the room, there were so many of them* (= There were too many of them to get into the room); *He isn't so much ill as depressed* (= He's depressed rather than ill); *He departed without so much as* (= without even) *a goodbye*; *His novels are just so much* (= nothing but) *rubbish*; *I can do only so much* (= a certain amount of) *work and no more*; *The exam wasn't quite so bad as I thought it would be*; *You've been so* (= very) *kind to me!*; *Thank you so much!*; *Everything has gone so well!*; (*inf*) *He's ever so nice!*; *You are so obstinate!* **2** (used to express manner) in this/that way: (*formal*) *As you hope to be treated by others, so you must treat them*; (*formal*) *Remain sitting just so, while I take the photograph*; *He likes everything to be (arranged) just so* (= in one particular and precise way); (*liter*) *So it is that* (= That is why) *men come to consider themselves superior to women*; (*formal*) *I was putting the children to bed, and while I was so engaged, the doorbell rang*; *It so happens that I have to go to an important meeting tonight.* **3** (used in place of a word, phrase *etc* previously used, or something previously stated) as already indicated: *'Are you really leaving your job?' 'Yes, I've already told you/said so'*; *'Is she arriving tomorrow?' 'Yes, I hope so'*; *'They're going to increase my salary next month.' 'So I should hope!'*; *'Are you tired?' 'Yes.' 'I thought so.'*; *If you haven't read the notice, please do so now*; *Are you going now? Because if so, I'd like to come with you*; *'Is that so* (= true)*?' 'Yes, it's really so'*; *It just isn't so*; *It can't be so!*; (*inf*: used *esp* by children) *'You're mean!' 'I am not!' 'You are so!'* (= Yes, you are!); *My wife has a headache, or so she says*; *'Was your father angry?' 'Yes, even more so than I was expecting – in fact, so much so that he refused to speak to me all day!*; *He was angry, and rightly so* (= he was right to be angry). **4** (used immediately before a modal auxiliary, or **be, do, have**, followed by a noun or pronoun) in the same way; also: *'I hope we'll meet again.' 'So do I.'*; *She has a lot of money and so has her husband.* **5** (used immediately before a pronoun that is the subject of modal auxiliary, **be, do** or **have** to express agreement or confirmation) indeed: *'You said you were going shopping today.' 'So I did, but I've changed my mind.'*; *'You'll need this book tomorrow, won't you?' 'So I will.'*; *'You seem to be very cheerful today.' 'So I am.'* – *conj* (and) therefore: *John had a bad cold, so I took him to the doctor*; *You'll never *persuade him, so don't try to; 'So you think you'd like this job, then?' 'Yes.'; And so they got married and lived happily ever after.*

'so-and-so – *pl* (*def 2*) **'so-and-sos** – **1** *n* an unnamed, unidentified person: *If I said I would meet so-and-so, I would do it.* **2** *nc* (*derog*) used as a substitute for an offensive term for a person or thing: *I've had another letter from those so-and-sos at the bank!; That so-and-so of a headmaster has muddled up the timetable!; She's an absolute so-and-so!*

ˌso-'called *adj* (*derog: usu attrib*) wrongly described or named in such a way: *Your so-called friends have gone without you!*

ˌso-'so *adj* (*inf: pred*) neither very good nor very bad: *His health is so-so.*

and 'so on/forth and more of the same kind of thing: *He reminded me of what I owed him and so on.*

just/quite so precisely; exactly: *'We can't expect any results till Friday.' 'Just so.'*

or so *see* **or**.

'so as to 1 in order to: *He sat at the front so as to be able to hear; He listened carefully so as not to miss anything that was said.* **2** in such a way to: *Try not to make a noise so as to upset your grandfather again.*

so far, so good all is well up to this point: *So far, so good – we've checked the equipment, supplies and the vehicle and they're in good order.* – *See also* **so far, so far as** *under* **far**.

so much for *see* **much**.

'so that 1 with the purpose that; in order that: *I'll wash this dress so that you can wear it.* **2** with the result that: *He got up very late, so that he missed the bus and was late for work.*

so to say/speak if one may use such an expression; in a way; it could be said: *The dog is, so to speak, a member of this family.*

so what? *see* **what**.

soak [souk] **1** *vti* to (let) stand in a liquid: *She soaked the clothes overnight in soapy water; Your trousers are soaking in the sink.* – *See also* **soak off, soak out** *below.* 2 *vt* to make very wet: *That shower has completely soaked my clothes.* **3** *vi* (*with* **in, into, through** *etc*) (of a liquid) to penetrate: *That spilt ink has soaked into the carpet; Wipe the orange-juice off the rug before it soaks in; The blood from his wound has soaked right through the bandage.* – *See also* **soak up** *below.* **4** (*sl*) to take large amounts of money from: *Their aim is to soak the rich.* – *nc* (*old inf*) a person who is in the habit of drinking too much alcohol: *He's an old soak.*

soaked *adj* (*often with* **through**: *pred*): *She got soaked (through) in that shower; My books are soaked through; I'm soaked to the skin!*

-soaked (*in cmpds*): *rain-soaked/blood-soaked clothing.*

'soaking *adj* very wet: *You shouldn't have gone out in the rain – your clothes are soaking; She took off her soaking garments.*

soaking wet soaking; very wet: *I've washed my hair and it's still soaking wet;* (*attrib*) *You can't go outside with soaking-wet hair!*

soak off *vt sep* to remove by soaking: *A good way to get a stamp off an envelope is to soak it off.*

soak out *vi, vt sep* to (cause *eg* dirt to) disappear by soaking: *I've got a dirty mark on my dress, but I may be able to soak it out.*

soak up *vt sep* to draw in or suck up; to absorb: *He used a large piece of blotting-paper to soak up the ink; You'd better soak that spilt coffee up with a cloth before it stains the carpet;* (*fig*) *That child absolutely soaks up information!*

soap [soup] *ncu* a mixture containing oils or fats and other substances, *esp* formed into small regularly-shaped pieces and used in washing: *He found a bar of soap and began to wash his hands; Can you lend me a piece of soap?; Which (type of) soap do you recommend for people with sensitive skins?* – *vt* to rub with soap: *She soaped the baby all over.*

'soapy *adj* **1** covered with, or full of, soap: *She rinsed her soapy hands; My hands are soapy; soapy water.* **2** like soap: *This chocolate has a soapy taste; It tastes soapy.* **3** (*inf*) over-polite and inclined to flatter: *He has a rather soapy manner; He's a bit soapy – I don't like him.* **'soapiness** *nu.*

'soap-flakes *n pl* thin flakes of soap used for washing clothes: *I prefer soap-flakes to detergents for washing woollens; a packet of soap-flakes.*

'soap opera *nc* (*derog*) a radio or television serial broadcast weekly, daily *etc*, *esp* one that continues from year to year, that concerns the daily life, troubles *etc* of the characters in it.

'soapsuds *n pl* soapy water, *esp* when frothy: *She was standing at the sink doing the washing, with soapsuds up to her elbows.*

'soft soap *nu* (*inf*) persuasive flattery or cajoling: *You'll have to use some soft soap to persuade him.*

ˌsoft-'soap *vt* (*inf*): *We'll have to soft-soap him into agreeing to do it.*

soar [so:] *vi* to fly high into the air: *Seagulls soared above the cliffs;* (*fig*) *Prices have soared recently;* (*fig*) *The singer's voice soared easily to the top notes.*

sob [sob] – *pt, ptp* **sobbed** – **1** *vti* to weep noisily: *I could hear her sobbing in her bedroom; The child sobbed himself to sleep* (= sobbed until he fell asleep). **2** *vt* to say, while weeping: *'I can't find my mother,' sobbed the child.* **3** *vi* (*formal*) to breathe in sharply and noisily; to gasp loudly: *She was not used to running and was soon sobbing for breath.* – *nc* the loud gasp for breath made when one is weeping *etc*: *The more she wept the louder her sobs became; She gave a sob of relief.*

'sob-story *nc* (*inf derog*) a story of misfortune *etc* told in order to gain sympathy: *She asked me to lend her five pounds, telling me a sob-story about her purse being stolen and her children needing food.*

sober ['soubə] *adj* **1** (*often pred*) not drunk: *He was still sober when he left; in a far from sober state.* **2** (*formal*) serious in mind: *a sober mood.* **3** (*formal: usu attrib*) (of colour) not bright: *She wore a sober (grey) dress.* **4** (*formal*) moderate; not overdone or too emotional: *a sober description; His account of the accident was factual and sober.* – *vti* (*inf*) to sober up.

'sobering *adj* (*usu attrib*): *a sobering experience/thought.*

'soberly *adv.*

'soberness *nu* the quality which a thing, person *etc* has when sober: *soberness of mind.*

sober up *vi, vt sep* (*inf*) to make or become (more) sober: *You'll have to sober up if you want to be able to drive home.*

sobriety [sə'braiəti] *nu* (*formal*) the state of being sober, *esp* in the sense of not drunk.

so-called *see* **so**.

soccer ['sokə] short for **Association football**.

sociable ['souʃəbl] *adj* (*neg* **un-**) fond of the company of others; friendly: *He's a cheerful, sociable man; We recently moved house and our new neighbours haven't been very sociable to us.*

'**sociably** *adv.* ˌ**socia'bility,** '**sociableness** *nus.*

social ['souʃəl] *adj* **1** concerning or belonging to the way of life and welfare of people in a community: *social problems*; *The problems are social rather than medical.* **2** (*attrib*) concerning the system by which such a community is organized: *social class.* **3** (*formal or tech*) living in communities: *Ants are social insects.* **4** concerning the gathering together of people for the purposes of recreation or amusement: *a social club*; *a social evening/gathering*; *His reasons for calling were purely social.*

'**socialism** *nu* the belief or theory that a country's wealth (its land, mines, industries, railways *etc*) should belong to the people as a whole, not to private owners.

'**socialist** *nc* (*sometimes with cap*) a person who believes in and/or practises socialism. – *adj* (*sometimes with cap*) of or concerning socialism: *socialist policies/governments.*

'**socialite** *nc* (*often derog*) a person who always mixes in the highest social circles.

'**socialize, -ise** *vi* (*often facet*) to mix socially (*eg* with guests at a party *etc*): *Why don't you go and socialize instead of standing here in the corner?*

'**socially** *adv* in a social (*esp def 4*) way: *I've seen him at various conferences, but we've never met socially*; *It seems to be accepted that a bus-driver is socially inferior to a doctor.*

social science *ncu* (any branch of) the study of people in society: *Sociology, economics and anthropology are social sciences.*

social security *nu* **1** the system (paid for by the community as a whole) which provides insurance for unemployment, old age, illness *etc*: *He's on* (= living by means of) *social security*; (*attrib*) *social security payments.* **2** the money paid out by this system: *He gets £10 social security per week.*

social services *n pl* (the facilities *etc* provided by) the local government departments which deal with pensions, the unemployed, welfare work *etc*: *The social services are paid for by the rates.*

'**social work** *nu* work which deals with the care of people in a community, *esp* of the poor, under-privileged *etc.* '**social worker** *nc.*

society [sə'saiəti] **1** *nu* mankind considered as a whole: *He was a danger to society.* **2** *ncu* a particular group or part of mankind considered as a whole: *middleclass society*; *modern western societies.* **3** *nc* a group of people joined together for a purpose; an association or club: *a model railway society*; *Morningside Photographic Society.* **4** *nu* the class of people who are wealthy, fashionable or of high rank in any area: *high society*; (*attrib*) *a society party.* **5** *nu* (*formal*) company or companionship: *I enjoy the society of young people.*

sociology [sousi'olədʒi] *nu* the science, or group of sciences, that studies man as a member of human groups. ˌ**socio'logical** [-'lo-] *adj.* ˌ**socio'logically** *adv.* ˌ**soci'ologist** *nc.*

sock [sok] *nc* **1** a (*usu* wool or nylon) covering for the foot and ankle, sometimes reaching to the knee, worn inside a shoe, boot *etc.*

put a 'sock in it! (*sl*) be quiet!

pull one's 'socks up to make an effort to do better: *You'd better pull your socks up if you want to succeed in this business!*

socket ['sokit] *nc* a specially-made or specially-shaped hole or set of holes into which something is fitted: *We'll need to have a new electric socket fitted into the wall for the television plug*; *The top of the thigh-bone fits into a socket at the hip.*

sod[1] [sod] *nc* a *usu* square or rectangular piece of earth with grass growing on it; a turf: *Some sods have been removed to make a place for the bonfire.*

sod[2] [sod] *nc* (*Brit offensive sl*) a term of abuse for a person: *When I got to the door, those sods had locked it!* – *interj* (*Brit offensive sl*) an exclamation of irritation *etc*: *Sod it! I've dropped that screw!*

soda ['soudə] **1** *nu* the name given to several substances formed with sodium, *esp* one (washing soda or **sodium carbonate**) in the form of crystals, used for washing, or one (baking soda or **sodium bicarbonate**) used in baking. **2** *nu* soda-water: *whisky and soda.* **3** *nc* (*Amer*) a drink made with flavoured soda-water and *usu* ice-cream.

'**soda fountain** *nc* (*Amer*) a counter or bar in a shop *etc* from which fizzy drinks, ice-cream *etc* are served.

'**soda-water** *nu* water through which the gas carbon dioxide has been passed, making it fizzy.

sodden ['sodn] *adj* very wet; soaked through: *He took off his sodden boots*; *The garden is sodden after all that rain.*

sodium ['soudiəm] *nu* an element (symbol **Na**) from which many substances are formed, including common salt (**sodium chloride**).

sodium bicarbonate/carbonate *see* **soda**.

sofa ['soufə] *nc* a kind of long seat, stuffed and with a back and arms: *Three people were sitting on the sofa in our living-room.*

soft [soft] *adj* **1** not hard or firm; easily changing shape when pressed: *a soft cushion*; *The mattress on my bed is too soft.* **2** pleasantly smooth to the touch: *This soap will make your skin soft and clear*; *The dog has a soft, silky coat.* **3** not loud: *a soft voice*; *The music was soft and soothing.* **4** (*usu attrib*) (of colour) not bright or harsh: *a soft pink.* **5** (*inf*: *usu pred*) not strict (enough): *You are too soft with him.* **6** (*attrib*) (of a drink) not alcoholic: *At the party they were serving soft drinks as well as wine and spirits.* **7** (*formal or liter*) without a clear, sharp outline: *soft shadows.* **8** (*inf*) childishly weak, timid or silly: *That man's just a big soft baby!*; *Don't be so soft – the dog won't hurt you.* **9** (of water) containing few chemical salts, and so easily forming bubbles when soap is added: *Soft water is more pleasant to drink than hard water*; *The water in this part of Scotland is very soft.* **10** (of the letters *c* and *g*) pronounced as in *city* and *gentle*: *The 'g' in 'gender' is soft.* **11** (*attrib*) (of an addictive drug) less harmful than *eg* heroin, cocaine *etc.* '**softly** *adv.* '**softness** *nu.*

soften ['sofn] *vti* to make or become soft or softer, less strong or less painful: *The thick walls softened the noise of the explosion*; *Soften the butter by placing it near the hot stove.* – *See also* **soften up** *below.*

ˌ**soft-'boiled** *adj* (of eggs) slightly boiled, so that the yolk is still soft: *May I have two soft-boiled eggs tomorrow morning?*; *She likes her eggs soft-boiled.*

ˌ**soft-'hearted** *adj* kind-hearted and generous: *She was always too soft-hearted to send us to bed early*; *He had been given some money by a soft-hearted aunt.*

soft pedal *nc* the pedal on a piano *etc* which deadens slightly the vibrations from the strings.

ˌ**soft-'pedal** – *pt, ptp* ˌ**soft-'pedalled,** (*Amer*) ˌ**soft-'pedaled** – *vti* (*inf*) not to make evident or acknowledge the importance *etc* of (something): *The government is soft-pedalling (on) the wages issue until after the election.*

ˌ**soft-ˈspoken** *adj* having a gentle voice or manner: *She was a small, soft-spoken woman with a shy smile; She is quiet and soft-spoken.*

soft soap *see* **soap**.

ˈ**software** *nu* the paper or card input and output of a system of computers, as opposed to the machines themselves (ˈ**hardware**).

ˈ**softwood** *nu* the wood of a cone-bearing tree *eg* a pine: (*attrib*) *softwood furniture.*

be/go soft in the head (*inf*: *often facet*) to be/become mentally weak: *That's the second time I've made that mistake – I must be going soft in the head!*

have a ˈsoft spot for (*inf*) to have a weakness for (someone or something) because of great affection: *He's always had a soft spot for his youngest son.*

soften up [ˈsofn] *vt sep* (*usu fig inf*) to weaken or make less able to resist something which follows: *He sent his aunt a bunch of flowers to soften her up before asking for a loan.*

soggy [ˈsogi] *adj* (*slightly inf*: *usu derog*) very wet and soft: *In the centre of the puddle was a piece of soggy cardboard; the cake was rather soggy.* ˈ**sogginess** *nu.*

soil[1] [soil] *nu* **1** the upper layer of the earth, in which plants grow: *to plant seeds in the soil; a handful of soil.* **2** (*liter*) territory: *He was born on Irish soil.*

soil[2] [soil] *vt* (*formal*) to dirty or stain, *esp* with faeces: *Don't soil your dress with these dusty books!; That little boy has soiled his trousers.*

sojourn [ˈsodʒəːn, (*Amer*) ˈsou-, souˈdʒəːrn] *vi* (*very formal or liter*) to stay for a time. – [ˈsodʒəːn, (*Amer*) ˈsou-] *nc* (*very formal or liter*) a short stay.

solace [ˈsoləs] *nu* (*formal or liter*) something that makes pain or sorrow easier to bear; comfort: *He found solace (for his grief) in working in the garden.*

solar [ˈsoulə] *adj* (*tech*: *attrib*) having to do with, powered by, or influenced by, the sun: *the solar year; a solar heating system.*

ˌ**solar-ˈpowered** *adj.*

solar system *nc* the Sun or any star and the planets which move round it.

solar plexus [souləˈpleksəs] *nc* (*tech*: *usu in sing with* **the**) (a set of nerves found just behind) the pit of the stomach.

sold *see* **sell**.

solder [ˈsouldə, (*Amer*) ˈsodər] *nu* melted metal or alloy used to join one piece of metal to another. – *vti* to join (two or more pieces of metal) with solder: *He soldered the broken wire back on to the transistor; I'd like to learn how to solder.*

ˈ**soldering-iron** *nc* a type of tool for providing the heat needed when soldering.

soldier [ˈsouldʒə] *nc* a member (*usu* male) of an army, often one who is not an officer: *The boy wants to be a soldier when he grows up; The British soldiers were led by a very young officer.* – *vi* (*formal*) to serve as a soldier: *He had soldiered in France in his youth.*

ˈ**soldierly** *adj* (*formal*) like a soldier: *He has a fine, soldierly bearing; He's tall and soldierly in appearance.*

soldier on *vi* to keep going despite difficulties *etc*: *There have been several power-cuts in the office, but we are trying to soldier on (despite them).*

sole[1] [soul] *nc* **1** the underside of the foot, the part on which one stands and walks. **2** the flat surface of a boot or shoe that covers this part of the foot, not *usu* including the heel: *There's a hole in the sole of my shoe.* – *vt* to put a sole on (a shoe *etc*): *These shoes need to be soled and heeled.*

sole[2] [soul] – *pls* **sole, soles** – **1** *nc* a type of small, flat fish: *They were fishing for sole; three soles.* **2** *nu* its flesh as food: *We had sole for supper.*

sole[3] [soul] *adj* (*formal*: *attrib*) **1** only; single: *my sole purpose/reason; the sole objection to his plan.* **2** not shared; belonging to one person or group only: *This publisher has bought the sole rights to his next book.*

ˈ**solely** *adv* (*formal*) only: *She is solely responsible for the crisis; His attempt to sail the Atlantic was made solely for reasons of enjoyment.*

solemn [ˈsoləm] *adj* **1** (*more formal than* **serious**) serious and earnest: *a solemn question; a solemn child; He looked very solemn as he announced the bad news.* **2** (*usu attrib*) stately; having formal dignity: *a solemn procession; a solemn occasion.* ˈ**solemnly** *adv.* ˈ**solemnness** *nu.*

solemnity [səˈlemnəti] *nu* (*formal*) **1** the state of being solemn: *the solemnity of the occasion.* **2** (*often in pl*: *formal*) a solemn ceremony: *After the solemnities at the church, there was a large wedding reception.*

ˈ**solemnize, -ise** [ˈsoləmnaiz] *vt* (*very formal*) to perform (*esp* a marriage) with religious ceremonies: *Their marriage was solemnized in church.*

sol-fa [solˈfaː, (*Amer*) soul-] *nu* in music, a series of syllables representing, and to be sung to, the notes of a scale.

solicit [səˈlisit] **1** *vt* (*very formal*) to ask (for): *May I solicit a favour?; People working for charities are permitted to solicit (money from) the public.* **2** *vi* (*formal or euph*) (of prostitutes) to make advances to men: *She solicits in a different area of the city every night.* **soˌliciˈtation** *ncu.*

soˈlicitor *nc* a lawyer who prepares legal documents and briefs, gives legal advice, and (in the lower courts only) speaks on behalf of his clients.

soˈlicitous *adj* (*formal*) very anxious or concerned, *usu* on another person's behalf: *He was very solicitous about your father's health; He made solicitous enquiries about you.* **soˈlicitously** *adv.*

soˈlicitude [-tjuːd] *nu* (*formal*) anxiety or uneasiness of mind, *esp* when more than necessary: *Her solicitude about my health was almost embarrassing.*

solid [ˈsolid] *adj* **1** not easily changing shape; not in the form of liquid or gas: *Water becomes solid when it freezes; The pond has frozen solid; solid substances.* **2** not hollow: *The tyres of the earliest cars were solid; They had solid tyres.* **3** (*often fig*) firm and strongly made (and therefore sound and reliable): *That's a solid piece of furniture; That table looks nice and solid; His argument is based on good solid facts/reasoning;* (*facet*) *This scandal has shocked the solid citizens of Manchester; He's a solid, steady worker; His party is hoping for a solid majority at this election.* **4** (*attrib*) completely made of one substance: *This bracelet is made of solid gold; a solid silver spoon; We dug till we reached solid rock.* **5** without breaks, gaps or flaws: *The policemen formed themselves into a solid line; We have the solid* (= unanimous) *support of our fellow trade-union members; They are solid in their determination to strike.* **6** (*geom*: *attrib*) having height, breadth and width: *A cube is a solid figure; solid geometry* (= the study of solid figures). **7** (*attrib or placed immediately after noun*) consecutive; without a pause: *I've been working for six solid hours/six hours solid.* – *nc* **1** a substance that is solid: *Butter is a solid but milk is a liquid.* **2** (*geom*) a shape that has length, breadth and height.

ˌsoliˈdarity [-ˈdarə-] *nu* the uniting of the interests, feelings or actions (of a group): *We must try to preserve our solidarity (of purpose).*

soˈlidify [-difai] *vti* (*formal or tech*) to make or become solid: *The extreme cold has solidified the water in the pipes; The water has solidified because the temperature is below freezing-point.*

soˌlidifiˈcation [-difi-] *nu.*

soˈlidity, ˈsolidness *nus.*

ˈsolidly *adv* **1** firmly; strongly: *solidly-built houses.* **2** continuously: *I worked solidly from 8.30 a.m. till lunchtime.* **3** unanimously: *We're solidly in agreement with your suggestions.*

ˌsolid-ˈstate *adj* (*tech*: *usu attrib*) (of radios, record-players *etc*) using transistors *etc* rather than valves.

soliloquy [səˈliləkwi] *nc* a speech made to oneself, *esp* on the stage: *Hamlet's soliloquies are very famous.*

soˈliloquize, -ise *vi* (*formal or liter*) (*esp* of a character on stage) to speak to oneself.

solitaire [soliˈteə, (*Amer*) ˈsoliteər] *nu* any of several kinds of game *eg* with cards, that can be played by one person.

solitary [ˈsolitəri] *adj* **1** (*formal*: *usu attrib*) alone; without companions: *a solitary traveller*; (*fig*) *a solitary tree.* **2** (*formal*) living or being alone, by habit or preference: *She was a solitary person; The child is rather solitary by nature.* **3** (*in negative sentences, questions etc*: *attrib*) single: *not a solitary example; Is there a solitary reason why I should help you?* – *nu* (*inf*) short for **solitary confinement**.

ˈsolitude [-tjuːd] *nu* (*formal*) the state of being alone: *He likes solitude; He lives in solitude.*

solitary confinement *nu* imprisonment in a cell by oneself: *He was sentenced to six months' solitary confinement; He is in solitary confinement.*

solo [ˈsoulou] – *pl* **ˈsolos** – *nc* something (*eg* a musical piece for one voice or instrument, a dance or other entertainment) in which only one person takes part: *a cello/soprano solo.* – *adj* (*attrib*) **1** in which only one takes part: *a solo flight in an aeroplane.* **2** (of a motorcycle) without a sidecar. – *adv* by oneself: *The flying-instructor told her she was to fly solo the next day.*

ˈsoloist *nc* a person who plays, dances, sings *etc* a solo.

solstice [ˈsolstis] *nc* the time of the greatest length of daylight (**summer solstice**, around June 21 in the northern hemisphere) or shortest length of daylight (**winter solstice**, around December 21 in the northern hemisphere).

soluble [ˈsoljubl] *adj* (*formal or tech*) **1** able to be dissolved or made liquid: *This dye is soluble in water.* **2** (of a problem, difficulty *etc*) able to be solved: *Do you think the problem is soluble?*

solution [səˈluːʃən] **1** *nc* an answer to a problem, difficulty or puzzle: *the solution to a crossword.* **2** *nu* (*formal*) the act of finding such an answer: *Solution of the problem proved more difficult than we had hoped.* **3** *nc* (*sometimes tech*) a liquid with something dissolved in it: *a solution of salt and water; an adhesive solution.*

See also **dissolve, insoluble, solve, solvent**.

solve [solv] *vt* **1** to discover the answer to (a problem *etc*): *The mathematics teacher gave the children some problems to solve.* **2** to clear up or explain (a mystery, crime *etc*): *That crime has never been solved.* **3** to find a way round or out of (a difficulty): *I think I've managed to solve the question of what to buy my mother for her birthday.*

ˈsolvable *adj.*

See also **insoluble, soluble**.

solvent [ˈsolvənt] *adj* (*formal or facet*: *usu pred*) able to pay all one's debts: *He has given up his business – he was finding it increasingly difficult to remain solvent; I won't be solvent till I get paid.* – *ncu* something in which another substance will dissolve: *You'll need a solvent, for example petrol, to get the oil off your sleeve; He rubbed some solvent on to the greasy mark.*

ˈsolvency *nu* (*formal*) the state of being able to pay all one's debts.

See also **insolvent**.

Somali, Somalia, Somalian *see* Appendix 2.

sombre, (*Amer usu*) **somber** [ˈsombə] *adj* (*formal*) **1** dark (and gloomy): *Black is a sombre colour; She was dressed in sombre black for the funeral; The furniture looked sombre and old-fashioned.* **2** grave; serious: *His expression was sombre as he listened to the report of the accident; He was in a sombre mood.* **ˈsombrely** *adv.* **ˈsombreness** *nu.*

some [sʌm] **1** *pron, adj* (*attrib*) an indefinite amount or number (of): *I can see some people walking across the field; You'll need some money if you're going shopping; It's all right – I got some (more) at the bank; 'Have you anything to read?' 'Yes, there are some old magazines in the cupboard.'; Some of the ink was spilt on the carpet.* **2** *pron, adj* (*attrib*) (said with emphasis) a certain, or small, amount or number (of): *'Has she any experience of the work?' 'Yes, she has some.'; That book has sold very well, but we still have some unsold copies left in the shop; Only some parts of the book were written by me – my colleague did the rest; Some people like the idea and some don't.* **3** *pron, adj* (*attrib*) (said with emphasis) at least one/a few/a bit (of): *You must have some reason for saying what you did!; Surely there are some people who agree with me?; I don't need much leisure from work, but I must have some.* **4** *pron, adj* (*attrib*) certain: *He wouldn't listen to my advice – some people think they know everything!; He's quite kind in some ways; Some* (= certain people) *might say he was lazy.* **5** *adj* (*attrib*) a large, considerable or impressive (amount or number of): *Personally, I think he has some cause for complaint; I spent some time trying to convince her;* (*inf*) *I'll have some problem sorting out these papers!;* (*inf*) *You had some nerve, telling the boss he was stupid!;* (*inf ironic*) *Some pal you were, running away when I was in difficulties!;* (*inf ironic*) *'Have you nearly finished the work?' 'Some hope!* (= No!)*'.* **6** *adj* (*attrib*) an unidentified or unnamed (thing, person *etc*): *She was hunting for some book that she's lost; I'll deal with that problem some other day – I'm too tired now; Have I offended you in some way?; Some untidy person (or other) has dropped cigarette ash on the carpet; He had some silly idea about going for a midnight swim.* **7** *adj* (*attrib*) (used with numbers) about; at a rough estimate: *There were some thirty people at the reception.* – *adv* (*Amer*) somewhat; to a certain extent: *I think we've progressed some.*

ˈsomebody *pron* someone.

ˈsomeday, ˈsome day *advs* at an unknown time in the future: *We'll manage it someday.*

ˈsomehow *adv* in some way not known for certain: *I'll get there somehow; Somehow, I know he'll succeed.*

ˈsomeone *pron* **1** an unknown or unnamed person: *There's someone at the door – would you* *answer it?*; *We all of us know someone who needs help*; *When someone telephones, remember to ask for his/(inf) their name.* 2 (*inf*) a person of importance: *He thinks he is someone*; *At last I'm someone.*

'**something** *pron* 1 a thing not known or not stated: *Would you like something to eat?*; *Do you get angry when you lose something?*; *I've got something to tell you*; *Something queer is going on.* 2 a thing of importance: *I think you may 'have something there* (= you may be right, have said, or thought of, something correct or important); *There's something in what you say*; *'He has injured his leg, but it's not broken.' 'That's something!'*

'**sometime** *adv* at an unknown time in the future or the past: *We'll go there sometime next week*; *They went sometime last month*; *Sometime, we'll take a trip to Venice.* – *adj* (*attrib*: *very formal or liter*) (a) former: *John Smith, sometime priest of this parish, died last week.*

'**sometimes** *adv* occasionally: *He sometimes goes to Edinburgh*; *He goes to Edinburgh sometimes*; *Sometimes he seems very forgetful.*

'**somewhat** *adv* (*formal*) rather; a little: *He is somewhat sad*; *The news puzzled me somewhat*; *'How is he?' 'Somewhat better, thank you.'*

'**somewhere** *adv* (*Amer* '**someplace**) (in or to) some place not known or not named: *They live somewhere in London*; *I won't be at home tonight – I'm going somewhere for dinner*; *Britain's climate can't be very pleasant for visitors who have come from somewhere warm.*

be/have something to do with to be connected with: *Calculus has/is something to do with mathematics, hasn't/isn't it?*

get somewhere *see* **get**.

make something of (something) to understand (something): *I apologize for the untidiness of my letter, but I hope you can make something of it.*

make something of oneself to become important or successful in some way: *He's a clever boy – I hope he'll make something of himself.*

'**mean something** to have meaning; to be significant: *Do all these figures mean something?*; *It means something to her* (= She understands it, its importance, significance *etc*).

or something used when the speaker is uncertain or being vague: *Her name is Mary or Margaret or something*; *I like to knit or something while I watch television.*

see something of to see (*esp* a person) occasionally: *I hope we'll see something of you now that you live nearby.*

some such (*slightly derog*) more or less of that sort: *They're going to the Isle of Man, or some such place.*

'**something like** 1 about: *We have something like five hundred people working here.* 2 (*inf*) rather like: *A zebra is something like a horse with stripes.*

'**something of,** '**somewhat of** (*formal*) to a certain extent: *She's something of an idiot.*

something tells me I have reason to believe; I suspect: *Something tells me she's lying.*

See also **somehow/someone/something/somewhere or other** *under* **other**.

somersault ['sʌməso:lt] *nc* a leap or roll in which a person turns with his feet going over his head. – *vi* to make such a leap or roll.

something, sometime(s), somewhat, somewhere *see* **some**.

somnambulist [som'nambjulist] *nc* (*formal or tech*) a person who walks in his sleep.

son [sʌn] *nc* a male child (when spoken of in relation to his parents): *He is the son of the manager*; (*liter fig*) *one of England's most famous sons.*

'**son-in-law** – *pl* '**sons-in-law** – *nc* a daughter's husband.

sonata [sə'na:tə] *nc* a piece of music with three or more movements, *usu* written for a solo instrument: *a flute sonata.*

song [soŋ] 1 *nc* something (to be) sung: *He wrote this song for his wife to sing.* 2 *nu* (*formal*) singing: *He burst into song* (= suddenly began singing). 3 *nu* the sound(s) made by a bird: *the song of the nightingale*; *birdsong.*

'**songbird** *nc* any of the types of bird which have a pleasant song.

'**songster** *nc* (*liter* of birds: *usu facet* (*fem* '**songstress**) of people) a singer.

'**songwriter** *nc* a person who writes songs (*usu* pop songs) for a living.

for a 'song (*inf*) for a very small amount of money: *He bought the lamp for a song.*

See also **sing**.

sonic ['sonik] *adj* (*tech*: *esp in cmpds*) of, or using, sound waves: *sub-sonic speeds* (= speeds which are slower than the speed of sound).

sonic boom *nc* a sudden loud noise heard when an aircraft which is travelling faster than the speed of sound passes overhead.

See also **supersonic**.

sonnet ['sonit] *nc* a type of poem with fourteen lines of ten or eleven syllables each: *Milton's/Shakespeare's sonnets.*

sonorous ['sonərəs] *adj* (*formal*) 1 giving out a clear deep sound: *a sonorous bell*; *His voice was deep and sonorous.* 2 sounding important: *sonorous phrases.* '**sonorously** *adv.*

soon [su:n] *adv* 1 in a short time from now or the time mentioned: *They'll be here sooner than you think*; *I hope he arrives soon*; *Soon the children will be grown up and ready to leave home.* 2 early: *It's too soon to tell*; *I would have phoned you sooner if I could.* 3 willingly: *I would (just) as soon go as stay*; *I would sooner stand than sit.*

as soon as (not later than the moment) when: *You may have a biscuit as soon as we get home*; *As soon as he had done it, he knew it was a mistake.*

no sooner . . . than when . . . immediately: *No sooner had we set off than we realized we'd left the dog behind.*

no sooner said than done (of a request, promise *etc*) immediately fulfilled: *She asked him to get her a drink of water. This was no sooner said than done.*

sooner or later eventually: *He'll come home sooner or later, I suppose.*

the sooner the better as quickly as possible: *'When shall I tell him?' 'The sooner the better!'*

speak too soon to say something that takes a result *etc* for granted before it is certain: *I don't want to speak too soon, but I know she'll win that scholarship.*

soot [sut] *nu* the black powder left after the burning of coal *etc*: *We'll have to get a chimney-sweep to clear the soot out of the chimney*; *as black as soot.*

'**sooty** *adj* 1 covered with soot. 2 of the colour of soot. '**sootiness** *nu.*

soothe [su:ð] *vt* (*slightly formal*) 1 to calm, comfort or quieten (a person, his feelings *etc*): *She was so upset that it took half an hour to soothe her.* 2 to ease (pain *etc*): *The medicine soothed the child's tooth-*

ache. **'soothing** *adj.* **'soothingly** *adv.*

sooty *see* **soot**.

sop [sop] *nc* something given to quieten or soothe someone who is displeased or disappointed: *He failed to get the job, but he was offered a more junior post as a sop (to his pride).*

'soppy *adj* (*inf derog*) foolishly sentimental: *What a soppy film that was!*; *The boy said he thought all girls were soppy.*

sops *n pl* soft, wet food, *esp* bread dipped into milk or other liquid.

sopping wet (*inf*) soaked through: *Your coat is sopping wet after that rain*; (*attrib*) *sopping-wet hair.*

sophisticated [sə'fistikeitid] *adj* (*neg* **un-**) **1** (of a person) having a great deal of experience and worldly wisdom, knowledge of how to dress elegantly *etc*: *a sophisticated young man*; *She has become very sophisticated since she went to live in London.* **2** suitable for, or typical of, sophisticated people: *The joke was too sophisticated for the child to understand*; *This film will appeal to sophisticated tastes*; *sophisticated clothes/hairstyles.* **3** (of machines, processes *etc*) highly-developed, elaborate and produced with a high degree of skill and knowledge: *sophisticated photographic techniques*; *This process is highly sophisticated.* **so,phisti'cation** *nu.*

soporific [sopə'rifik] *adj* (*formal*: *sometimes derog*) causing sleep: *I find his voice very soporific*; *a soporific drug.*

sopping, soppy *see* **sop**.

soprano [sə'pra:nou] – *pl* **so'pranos** – *nc* **1** (a singer having) a singing voice of the highest pitch for a woman: *She is a fine soprano*; *Her soprano is excellent*; (*attrib*) *a soprano voice.* **2** in music, a part written for a voice at this pitch: *In this piece of music, the soprano is quite difficult*; (*attrib*) *the soprano part.* – *adv* with a soprano voice: *She sings soprano.*

See also **mezzo-soprano**.

sorcery ['so:səri] *nu* **1** the use of power gained from evil spirits. **2** witchcraft or magic in general.

'sorcerer – *fem* **'sorceress** – *nc* a person who practises sorcery.

sordid ['so:did] *adj* (*formal or derog*) **1** (of a place *etc*) dirty, mean and poor: *a very sordid neighbourhood*; *This room starts looking very sordid if it's not kept tidy.* **2** (of a person's behaviour *etc*) showing low standards or ideals *etc*; not very pleasant or admirable: *The whole affair was rather sordid*; *He probably had his own sordid reasons for behaving like that.* **'sordidly** *adv.* **'sordidness** *nu.*

sore [so:] *adj* **1** (*less formal than* **painful**) painful: *My leg is very sore*; *I have a sore leg*; *The cut on my knee is still sore.* **2** (*inf*: *usu pred*) suffering pain: *She's still sore after her fall*; *I am still a bit sore after my operation.* **3** (*sl*: *esp Amer*: *usu pred*) irritated, annoyed or offended: *He is still sore about what happened.* – *nc* a painful, injured or diseased spot on the skin: *His hands were covered with horrible sores.*

'sorely *adv* (*formal*) badly; acutely: *I'm sorely in need of new shoes*; *He misses her sorely.*

'soreness *nu.*

a sore point a subject which it annoys or offends one to speak about: *Gambling has been a sore point with him since he lost a fortune betting on horses.*

sorrow ['sorou] *ncu* (*formal*) (something which causes) pain of mind or grief: *It was a great sorrow to her that she never saw him again*; *He felt great sorrow when she died.* – *vi* (*old liter*) to feel sorrow or mourn: *The people sorrowed greatly when he died.*

'sorrowful *adj* (*sometimes formal*) showing or feeling sorrow: *sorrowful people*; *a sorrowful expression*; *The dog sat looking sorrowful and forlorn as they packed their cases.* **'sorrowfully** *adv.* **'sorrowfulness** *nu.*

sorry ['sori] *adj* **1** (*pred*) used when apologizing or expressing regret: *I'm sorry (that) I forgot to return your book*; *I'm (very/so) sorry if I misled you*; *Did I give you a fright? I'm sorry*; *He said he was sorry to cause her inconvenience*; *I'm sorry that your mother's ill*; *I'm sorry about this delay.* **2** (*pred*) apologetic or full of regret: *I think he's really sorry for his bad behaviour*; *She's sorry now that she didn't buy one of those dresses when they were being sold cheap*; *I'm sure you were sorry to hear about his death.* **3** (*formal*: *attrib*) unsatisfactory; poor; wretched: *This house is in a sorry state*; *a sorry state of affairs.* – *interj* **1** used when apologizing: *Did I tread on your toe? Sorry!*; *Sorry, I didn't see you standing behind me*; *Don't be so angry with me – I've said sorry, haven't I?* **2** (used when asking a person to repeat what he has said) I beg your pardon?: *Sorry (, what did you say)?*

be/feel sorry for to pity: *I'm/I feel really sorry for that poor woman.*

sort [so:t] *nc* (*often loosely*) a class, type or kind: *People of that sort always do things like that*; *Which/what sort of flowers do you like best?*; (*derog*) *What sort of husband are you – going to the pub and getting drunk every night?*; *I like this sort of book/*(*inf*) *these sort of books*; *I like all sorts of books*; *She was wearing a sort of* (= something rather like a) *crown*; *That's a silly sort of remark* (= a silly remark) *to make!* – *vt* to separate into classes or groups, putting each item in its place: *She sorted the buttons into large ones and small ones*; *The postman sorted the letters according to their destinations.* – *See also* **sort out** *below.*

'sorter *nc* a person or machine that separates and arranges, *esp* letters, postcards *etc.*

not a bad sort (*inf*) quite a nice person: *The headmaster's not a bad sort when you get to know him.*

of a 'sort/of 'sorts of a (*usu* poor) kind: *She threw together a meal of sorts but we were still hungry afterwards.*

out of sorts (*inf*) **1** slightly unwell: *I felt a bit out of sorts after last night's heavy meal.* **2** not in good spirits or temper: *He's been a little out of sorts since they told him to stay at home.*

'sort of (*inf*) rather; in a way; to a certain extent: *He was sort of peculiar!*; *I feel sort of worried about him.*

sort out *vt sep* **1** to separate (one lot or type of) things from a general mixture: *I'll try to sort out some books that he might like.* **2** to correct, improve, solve *etc*: *You must sort out your business affairs before you are forced to close down.* **3** (*sl*) to attend to, *usu* by punishing or reprimanding: *I'll soon sort you out, you evil little man!*

sortie ['so:ti] *nc* **1** (*mil*) a sudden raid or attack by the defenders of a place against those who are trying to capture it; an attacking mission: *This aeroplane has flown fifteen sorties in as many days.* **2** a short trip or expedition: *We planned a sortie into unexplored territory*; (*facet*) *This is my first sortie into town since I had flu.*

SOS [esou'es] *nc* a call for help or rescue, often in code and *usu* from a distance: *Send an SOS to the mainland to tell them that we are sinking!*

so-so *see* **so**.

sot [sot] *nc* (*old*) a person who is continually drunk.

sotto voce [sotou'voutʃi] *adj, adv* (*formal*) in a low voice, so as not to be overheard: *All through the talk, he made a stream of sotto voce comments on what the speaker was saying*; *He spoke sotto voce.*

soufflé ['su:flei, (*Amer*) su:'flei] *ncu* a kind of frothy cooked dish, made with whisked whites of egg: *I made a cheese soufflé*; *Would you like some soufflé?*

sought *see* **seek**.

soul [soul] **1** *nc* the spirit; the non-physical part of a person, which is often thought to continue in existence after he or she dies: *People often discuss whether animals and plants have souls.* **2** *nc* (*inf*) a person: *She's a wonderful old soul*; *You mustn't tell a soul* (= anyone) *about this*; (*formal*) *a parish of about 500 souls.* **3** *nc* (*formal or liter*) (of an enterprise *etc*) the organizer or leader: *He is the soul of the whole movement.* **4** *nu* soul music.

'**soulful** *adj* full of (*usu* sad, wistful *etc*) feeling: *a soulful expression*; *That dog always looks soulful.* '**soulfully** *adv.*

'**soulless** *adj* **1** (of a person) without fine feeling or nobleness. **2** (of life, a task *etc*) dull or very unimportant.

'**soul-destroying** *adj* (of a task *etc*) very dull, boring, repetitive *etc.*

'**soul music** *nu* (*also* **soul**) a type of music, descended from American Negro gospel songs, which has great emotion in its words and melodies.

'**soul-searching** *nu* the examination of one's own conscience to find out *eg* whether one's motives are genuine: *He went through a lot of soul-searching before he finally decided to leave the priesthood.*

heart and soul *see* **heart**.

keep body and soul together to keep alive: *He doesn't eat enough to keep body and soul together.*

the life and soul of the party *see* **life**.

the soul of a perfect example of: *She's the soul of honour/discretion.*

sound[1] [saund] *adj* **1** strong or in good condition: *The foundations of the house are not very sound*; *He's 87, but he's still sound in mind and body*; *The doctor says I have a sound constitution.* **2** (*usu attrib*) (of sleep) deep: *A night's sound sleep made me feel much better*; *She's a very sound sleeper.* **3** (*usu attrib*) full; thorough: *a sound basic training.* **4** accurate; free from mistakes: *a sound piece of work*; *My spelling is not very sound*; *He's a very sound mathematician.* **5** having or showing good judgement or good sense: *His advice is always very sound*; *That's not a very sound suggestion!*; *John would be a sound person to ask about this.* **6** (of a motive, reason *etc*) trustworthy, well-meaning, well-justified *etc*: *He has behaved rather foolishly, but his motives were quite sound*; *That was scarcely a sound reason for being absent from work.* '**soundly** *adv.* '**soundness** *nu.*

sleep sound to sleep soundly: *How can he sleep sound in his bed with that crime on his conscience?*

sound asleep sleeping deeply: *The baby is sound asleep.*

See also **unsound**.

sound[2] **1** *nu* the impressions transmitted to the brain by the sense of hearing: *He opened the door and was met by a barrage of sound*; (*attrib*) *sound waves.* **2** *nc* something that is, or can be, heard: *The sounds were coming from the garage.* **3** *nc* (*no pl*) the impression created in the mind by a piece of news, a description *etc*: *I didn't like the sound of her hairstyle at all!* **4** *nu* (*rare*: *often liter*) the distance within which something can be heard; earshot: *within* (*the*) *sound of Bow Bells.* – **1** *vti* to (cause something to) make a sound: *Sound the bell!*; *The bell sounded.* **2** *vt* to signal (something) by making a sound: *Sound the alarm!* **3** *vi* (not used with **is, was** *etc* and **-ing**) (of something heard or read) to make a particular impression; to seem; to appear: *Your singing sounded very good*; *That sounds like a train*; *The two words sound alike, but are spelt differently*; *That newspaper article sounds true enough*; *It sounds as if* (= I think) *she may be leaving soon.* **4** *vt* to pronounce: *In the word 'pneumonia', the letter p is not sounded.* **5** *vt* to examine by tapping and listening carefully: *She sounded the patient's chest.* – *See also* **sound off** *below.*

-sounding (*in cmpds*) having a sound, or giving an impression, of a particular kind: *im'portant-sounding.*

'**soundless** *adj.* '**soundlessly** *adv.*

'**sound barrier** *nc* (*tech*) the difficulty, met at around the speed of sound, in increasing the speed of an aircraft.

'**sound effects** *n pl* sounds other than dialogue or music, used in films, radio *etc.*

'**sounding-board** *nc* a means of making one's opinions *etc* more widely known: *The editor was accused of using his newspaper as a sounding-board for his political views.*

'**soundproof** *adj* not allowing sound to pass in, out, or through: *The walls are soundproof*; *a soundproof room.* – *vt* to make (walls, a room *etc*) soundproof.

'**sound-track** *nc* (a recording of) the music (and, rarely, some of the dialogue) from a film: *I've just bought the sound-track of that new film.*

sound off *vi* (*derog sl*) to speak loudly and freely, *esp* while complaining: *She was sounding off about the price of tea.*

sound[3] [saund] *vt* to measure the depth of (water *etc*).

'**sounding** **1** *ncu* (a) measurement of depth of water *etc.* **2** *nc* a depth measured. **3** *ncu* (an) act of trying to find out views *etc*: *Have you taken any soundings on the likely public reaction to your proposals?*

sound out *vt sep* to try to find out someone's thoughts and plans *etc*: *Will you sound out your father on this?*; *I sounded out his views in my letter.*

sound[4] [saund] *nc* (*usu found with cap in place-names*) a narrow passage of water connecting two seas or between an island and the mainland *etc*: *the Sound of Jura.*

soup [su:p] *ncu* a liquid food made from meat, vegetables *etc*: *She made some chicken soup*; *various* (*types of*) *soups.*

'**soup-plate** *nc* a type of plate in which a single portion of soup is served.

'**soup-spoon** *nc* a type of spoon used when eating soup.

in the soup (*sl*) in serious trouble: *If she's found out about it, we're all in the soup!*

soup up *vt sep* (*sl*) to tune (an engine) so as to make it go faster than normal.

sour ['sauə] *adj* **1** having a taste or smell similar in nature to that of lemon juice or vinegar: *Unripe* *apples are/taste very sour*; *a sour taste*; *sour grapes.* **2** having a similar taste as a stage in going bad: *sour milk*; *This milk is slightly sour.* **3** (of a person, his character *etc*) discontented, bad-tempered or disagreeable: *She was looking very sour this morning*; *Her face had a sour expression.* – *vt* to make or become sour: *This hot weather has soured all the milk*; (*formal fig*) *She had been soured by bad luck.* **'sourly** *adv.* **'sourness** *nu.*

source [soːs] *nc* **1** the place, person, circumstance, thing *etc* from which anything begins or comes: *They have discovered the source of the trouble*; *What was the source of the journalist's information?* **2** the spring from which a river flows: *the source of the Nile.*

souse [saus] *vt* (used *esp* in cooking) to plunge into or soak with water or other liquid (*esp* herrings *etc* in salt water or vinegar).

south [sauθ] *nu* **1** the direction to the right of a person facing the rising sun, or any part of the earth lying in that direction. *He stood facing towards the south*; *The rain is coming over from the south*; *They live in a village to the south of* (= further south than) *Aberdeen*; *She lives in the south of France.* **2** (*often with cap*: *also* **S**) one of the four main points of the compass: *We set a course 15° W of S* (= fifteen degrees west of south). – *See also* **the South** *below.* – *adj* (*attrib*) **1** in the south: *She works on the south coast.* **2** from the direction of the south: *a south wind.* – *adv* towards the south: *This window faces south.*

southerly ['sʌðəli] *adj* (*usu attrib*) **1** (of a wind *etc*) coming from the south: *a southerly wind.* **2** looking, lying *etc* towards the south: *in a southerly direction.*

southern ['sʌðən] *adj* of the south or the South: *My accent is southern English*; *Your speech sounds southern to me.*

southerner ['sʌðənə] *nc* a person who lives, or was born, in a southern region or country.

southernmost ['sʌðənmoust] *adj* being furthest south: *the southernmost point on the mainland*; *the southernmost of the islands.*

'southward *adj* (*usu attrib*) towards the south: *in a southward direction.*

'southward(s) *adv* towards the south: *We are moving southwards.*

'southbound *adj* (*usu attrib*) travelling southwards: *southbound traffic.*

ˌsouth-'east/ˌsouth-'west *nus* the direction midway between south and east or south and west, or any part of the earth lying in that direction. – *adjs* (*attrib*) **1** in the south-east or south-west: *the south-east coast.* **2** from the direction of the south-east or south-west: *a south-east wind.* – *advs* towards the south-east or south-west: *The gateway faces south-west.*

ˌsouth-'easterly/ˌsouth-'westerly *adjs* (*usu attrib*) **1** (of a wind *etc*) coming from the south-east or south-west: *a south-easterly wind.* **2** looking, lying *etc* towards the south-east or south-west: *a south-westerly direction.*

ˌsouth-'eastern/ˌsouth-'western *adjs* of the south-east or south-west: *a south-western dialect*; *His father's accent is south-eastern.*

the South (in Britain) the southern part of England, *esp* the south-eastern part.

South Africa, South African *see* Appendix 2.

the Southern Lights *see* **aurora**.

the South Pole the southern end of the imaginary line through the earth, round which it turns.

souvenir [suːvə'niə, (*Amer*) 'suːvəniər] *nc* something (bought, kept or given) which reminds one of a place, person or occasion: *a souvenir of one's holiday/first boyfriend/twenty-first birthday party.*

sou'wester [sau'westə] *nc* a waterproof hat with a wide flap at the back of the neck.

sovereign ['sovrin] *nc* **1** (*formal*) a king or queen. **2** (*hist*) a British gold coin, *orig* worth £1. – *adj* (*very formal*) **1** supreme or highest: *our sovereign lord, the King*; *sovereign power*; *The Queen's will is sovereign in this matter.* **2** (*attrib*) (of a country) self-governing: *a sovereign state.*

'sovereignty *nu* (*very formal*) independent power: *to recognize the sovereignty of a country.*

soviet ['souviət] *adj* (*often with cap*) of the USSR. – *nc* (*Amer*: *usu in pl*) one of the people, *esp* one of the leaders, of the USSR. – *See also* Appendix 2.

Soviet Union *see* Appendix 2.

sow[1] [sou] – *pt* **sowed**: *ptp* **sown, sowed** – *vt* **1** to scatter over, or put in, the ground: *I sowed lettuce in this part of the garden.* **2** to plant seed over: *This field has been sown with wheat.* **3** (*formal fig*) to spread (trouble *etc*): *They went round the country sowing discontent among the ordinary people.*

sow[2] [sau] *nc* a female pig.

soya bean ['soiəbiːn], **soybean** ['soibiːn] *nc* a type of bean, processed and used as a substitute for meat *etc.*

soy(a) sauce *nu* a sauce made from soya beans, used in Chinese *etc* cooking.

spa [spaː] *nc* (*with cap in names*) a town *etc* where people go to drink or bathe in the water from a natural spring: *Cheltenham Spa*; (*attrib*) *a spa holiday in Austria.*

space [speis] **1** *nc* a gap; an empty or uncovered place: *I couldn't find a space for my car*; *Please leave a larger space between words when you write.* **2** *nu* room; the absence of objects; the area available for use: *Have you enough space to turn round?*; *The children need more space for playing football*; *Is there space for one more?* **3** *nu* (*often* **outer space**) the region outside the Earth's atmosphere, in which all stars and other planets *etc* are situated: *travellers through space.* – *vt* (*also* **space out**) to set (things) apart from one another: *He spaced the rows of potatoes half a metre apart.*

'spacing *nu* the amount of distance left between objects, words *etc* when they are set or laid out: *His spacing of the lines on the page was very irregular.*

spacious ['speiʃəs] *adj* providing or having plenty of room: *a spacious living-room/layout*; *Their dining-room is very spacious.* **'spaciously** *adv.* **'spaciousness** *nu.*

spatial ['speiʃəl] *adj* (*tech or very formal*) of, or relating to, space (*defs 2, 3*): *the spatial relationships between objects.*

'space-age *adj* (*attrib*) extremely up-to-date and advanced: *space-age technology.*

'spacecraft *nc* a vehicle *etc*, manned or unmanned, for travelling in space.

'spaceman [-man] *nc* a crew member in a spaceship.

'spaceship *nc* a spacecraft, *esp* a manned one.

'spacesuit *nc* a suit designed to be worn by spacemen.

(with)in the space of (a minute, hour *etc***)** in as little as (a minute, hour *etc*): *She contradicted herself twice in the space of five minutes.*

spade[1] [speid] *nc* a tool with a broad blade and a handle, used for digging.

'**spadework** *nu* (*fig*) hard work done at the beginning of a project *etc*, serving as a basis for the future.

call a spade a spade to say plainly and clearly what one means, not softening anything by trying to use polite words.

spade[2] [speid] *nc* one of the playing-cards of the suit spades.

spades *n pl* (sometimes treated as *n sing*) one of the four card suits: *the ten of spades.*

spaghetti [spəˈgeti] *nu* an Italian food made of wheat paste formed into long strands which soften when boiled: *We had spaghetti and tomato sauce.*

Spain *see* Appendix 2.

span[1] [span] *nc* **1** a bridge's or arch's length between its supports: *The first span of the bridge is one hundred metres long.* **2** the full time for which anything lasts: *Seventy or eighty years is the normal span of a man's life.* **3** (*old*) the distance from the tip of the thumb to the tip of the little finger when the hand is spread out (about 23 cm (= 9 ins)) in the average adult male. – *v* – *pt, ptp* **spanned** – *vt* (*formal or liter*) to stretch across: *A bridge spans the river*; (*fig*) *His career spans three decades.*

See also **wingspan** *under* **wing**.

span[2] *see* **spick and span.**

spangle [ˈspaŋgl] *nc* a thin glittering piece of metal used as an ornament, *usu* on a garment. – *vt* (*usu in passive*) to sprinkle with spangles or small bright objects: *Her dress was brightly spangled.*

'**spangled** *adj* (*attrib*).

Spaniard *see* Appendix 2.

spaniel [ˈspanjəl] *nc* a breed of dog with large ears which hang down.

See also **cocker spaniel**.

Spanish *see* Appendix 2.

spank [spaŋk] *vt* to strike or slap with the flat of the hand, *esp* on the buttocks, *usu* as a punishment: *The child was spanked for his disobedience.* – *nc* a slap with the hand, *esp* on the buttocks: *His mother gave him a spank on the bottom.*

'**spanking** *nc* a series of spanks: *Your father'll give you a good spanking when he gets home.* – *adj* (*attrib*) fast: *The yacht was moving at a spanking pace across the bay.*

spanner [ˈspanə] *nc* a type of tool used for tightening or loosening nuts, bolts *etc.*

throw a spanner in the works to frustrate or ruin (a plan, system *etc*).

spar[1] [spa:] *nc* a strong, thick pole of wood or metal, *esp* one used as a ship's mast *etc.*

spar[2] [spa:] – *pt, ptp* **sparred** – *vi* **1** to box, *usu* for practice only. **2** (*usu with* **with**) to have an argument, *usu* a friendly one: *They've been sparring* (*with each other*) *for months now.*

'**sparring-partner** *nc* **1** a person with whom a boxer practises. **2** (*inf*) a person with whom one enjoys a lively argument: *His sparring-partner in the debate was an old friend of his.*

spare [speə] *vt* **1** to manage without: *I can't spare her today – I need everyone I can get*; *No-one can be spared from this office.* **2** to afford or set aside for a purpose: *I can't spare the time for a holiday*; *I'd like to speak to you if you can spare me a minute or two*; *Just now I can't spare the money to buy you football boots.* **3** (*old or formal*) to treat with mercy; to avoid injuring *etc*: *The attackers spared the lives of all those who were old or ill, but killed the rest*; *'Spare us!' they begged.* **4** to avoid causing grief, trouble *etc* to (a person): *Break the news gently in order to spare her as much as possible*; *He works extremely hard from morning till night – he never spares himself.* **5** (*usu in neg*) to avoid using, spending *etc*: *He spared no expense or effort in his desire to help us.* **6** to avoid troubling (a person with something); to save (a person trouble *etc*): *I answered the letter myself in order to spare you the bother*; *Spare us all these boring details – we're not interested!*; *Order your clothes from this catalogue, and spare yourself the trouble of going shopping.* – *adj* **1** (*usu attrib*) extra; not actually being used: *She always carried a spare pair of socks when hiking*; *We haven't a spare* (*bed*)*room for guests in our house.* **2** (*attrib*) (of time *etc*) free for leisure *etc*: *What do you do in your spare time?*; *He spends all his spare time playing football*; *Read this when you have a spare minute.* **3** thin: *He was a small, spare man*; *He was tall and spare.* – *nc* a spare part (for a car *etc*); an extra wheel *etc*, kept for emergencies: *Your tyre's flat – do you have a spare?*; *They sell spares at that garage.*

'**spareness** *nu* the state of being thin.

'**sparing** *adj* careful or economical: *Be sparing in your use of pepper*; *a sparing use of cosmetics.*

'**sparingly** *adv.*

spare part *nc* a part for a machine *etc*, used to replace an identical part if it breaks *etc.*

spare rib *nc* a rib of pork with only a small amount of meat left on it

(and) to 'spare in larger numbers or quantities than is needed; extra: *Go to the exhibition if you have time to spare*; *I haven't much money to spare*; *She has enough and to spare.*

See also **unsparing**.

spark [spa:k] *nc* **1** a tiny red-hot piece thrown off by something burning, or when two very hard (*eg* metal) surfaces are struck together: *Sparks were being thrown into the air from the burning building.* **2** (*tech*) an electric current jumping across a gap: *A spark from a faulty light-socket had set the house on fire.* **3** a trace (*eg* of life, humour): *He had failed to rouse the slightest spark of enthusiasm in his pupils.* – **1** *vi* to give off sparks. **2** *vt* (*often with* **off**) to start (a row, disagreement *etc*): *This dispute has sparked* (*off*) *a major discussion on pay policy.*

'**sparking-plug**, (*Amer*) '**spark-plug** *nc* (*tech*) a part of a car engine that produces a spark to set on fire the explosive gases.

a 'bright spark (*inf*: *usu derog*: *often ironic*) an intelligent person: *He's a real bright spark – he's made a mess of the whole plan!*

sparkle [ˈspa:kl] **1** *ncu* an effect like that made by little sparks: *There was a sudden sparkle as her diamond ring caught the light*; *the sparkle of sunlight on the water.* **2** *nu* liveliness or brightness: *She has lots of sparkle.* – *vi* **1** to glitter, as if throwing off tiny sparks: *The snow sparkled in the sunlight.* **2** to be lively or witty: *She really sparkled at that party.*

'**sparkler** *nc* **1** (*sl*) a diamond or other jewel: *He bought her a huge sparkler when they got engaged.* **2** a type of small firework, held in the hand, which gives off showers of sparks.

'**sparkling** *adj* (*attrib*) **1** (of wines) giving off bubbles of gas: *Would you like one of the sparkling white wines with the meal?* **2** lively: *sparkling humour/wit.*

sparrow [ˈsparou] *nc* a common type of small brown bird related to the finch family.

sparse [spa:s] *adj* (*slightly formal*) thinly scattered: *sparse vegetation*; *The illustrations in that book are rather sparse.* '**sparsely** *adv.* '**sparseness** *nu.*

spartan ['spa:tən] *adj* (*formal*) (of conditions of life *etc*) hard, simple and without luxury: *He led a spartan existence in a cottage without electricity or water*; *a spartan meal*; *His upbringing has been spartan and severe.*

spasm ['spazəm] *nc* **1** a sudden uncontrollable jerking of the muscles: *A spasm of pain twisted his face for a moment.* **2** a strong short occurrence or burst (of anger, work *etc*): *She had a sudden spasm of energy and did all the washing in one morning.*

spas'modic [-'modik] *adj* consisting of sudden, short periods of activity; happening *etc* now and again, but not regularly: *He made spasmodic attempts to do some work.* **spas'modically** *adv.*

spastic ['spastik] *nc, adj* (a person) suffering from brain damage that causes extreme muscle spasms and/or muscular paralysis: *Their youngest child is* (*a*) *spastic*; *a spastic child.*

spat *see* **spit**.

spate [speit] *nc* (*usu fig*) a flood or sudden rush: *a spate of new books for Christmas.*

in 'spate (of a river) flowing very fast because of having more water than normal, often due to flooding.

spatial *see* **space**.

spats [spats] *n pl* cloth or leather leggings covering the instep and ankle: *a pair of white leather spats.*

spatter ['spatə] *vt* **1** to scatter or sprinkle (something liquid): *The frying-pan spattered fat all over the kitchen.* **2** (*usu with* **with**) to splash (someone or something, with mud, liquid *etc*): *The passing cars spattered her with water from the puddles.*

spatula ['spatjulə, (*Amer*) -tʃu-] *nc* **1** a kind of tool, used (by artists and cooks) for mixing or spreading, with a broad blunt blade: *Spread the icing on the cake with a spatula.* **2** a similarly-shaped, but smaller, instrument (*usu* of wood) used by a doctor to flatten the tongue when examining the throat.

spawn [spo:n] *nu* (*sometimes in cmpds*) the eggs of fish, frogs *etc*: *In the spring, the pond is full of frog-spawn.* – **1** *vi* (of frogs, fish *etc*) to produce spawn: *Hundreds of salmon come up this river each year to spawn.* **2** *vt* (*formal derog*) to produce or give rise to (something) in large quantities: *The new Government department has spawned huge numbers of useless documents.*

speak [spi:k] – *pt* **spoke** [spouk]: *ptp* **'spoken** ['spoukən] – **1** *vti* to say (words) or talk: *He can't speak*; *He spoke a few words to us.* **2** *vi* (*often with* **to** *or* (*Amer*) **with**) to talk or converse: *Can I speak to you for a moment?*; *We spoke for hours about it*; *He never speaks of his dead wife*; *I'll have to speak to him* (= reprimand him) *about his terrible behaviour.* **3** *vt* to (be able to) talk in (a language): *She speaks Russian*; *Can you speak English?* **4** *vt* to tell or make known (one's thoughts, the truth *etc*): *I always speak my mind.* **5** *vi* to make a speech: *The Prime Minister spoke on the state of the nation.* **6** *vi* (*formal*: *with* **of**) to be evidence (for the existence of a certain state of affairs *etc*): *Everything about him speaks of money.* – *See also* **speak** *in phrases below.*

'speaker *nc* **1** a person who is or was speaking: *We could not see the speaker, as he was on the other side of the wall.* **2** (*with cap*) the person who presides over meetings of the House of Commons. **3** (*sometimes* **ˌloud'speaker**) the device in a radio, record-player *etc* which converts the electrical impulses into audible sounds: *Our record player needs a new speaker.*

'speaking *adj* (*attrib*) **1** involving speech: *a speaking part in a play.* **2** used in speech: *a pleasant speaking voice.*

'spoken *adj* (*attrib*) produced by speaking: *He made marvellous speeches – he was a master of the spoken word.*

-spoken (*in cmpds*) speaking in a particular way: *ˌplain-'spoken*; *ˌsmooth-'spoken.*

be on 'speaking terms (with) to be friendly enough with (someone) to speak to him: *She's not on speaking terms with me since I broke her favourite ornament.*

generally speaking in general: *Generally speaking, men are stronger than women.*

in a manner of speaking *see* **manner**.

so to speak *see* **so**.

'speak for *vt fus* to give an opinion *etc* on behalf of (someone else): *I myself don't have any objections to your suggestions, but I can't speak for Liz and Frank.*

speak for itself/themselves to have an obvious meaning; not to need explaining: *The situation speaks for itself*; *The facts speak for themselves.*

speak out *vi* to say boldly what one thinks: *I don't like to make a fuss, but I feel the time has come to speak out.*

speak the same language (as) to have a good mutual understanding (with someone), similar tastes and thoughts: *John and I like each other well – we speak the same language.*

speak too soon *see* **soon**.

speak up *vi* to speak (more) loudly: *Speak up! We can't hear you!*

to 'speak of worth mentioning: *He has no talent to speak of.*

to 'speak to (*inf*) well enough to have a conversation with: *I don't know him to speak to.*

See also **speech, outspoken, unspeakable**.

spear [spiə] *nc* **1** a type of long-handled weapon, *usu* with an iron or steel point on the end: *He was armed with a spear and a round shield.* **2** a long pointed shoot or leaf: *asparagus/broccoli spears.* – *vt* to pierce or kill with a spear: *He went out in a boat to spear fish.*

'spear-gun *nc* a weapon which fires steel darts, used for hunting fish *etc* underwater.

'spearhead *nc* (*formal or liter*) the leading part of an attacking force. – *vt* (*formal or liter*) to lead (a movement, an attack *etc*): *The cavalry spearheaded the charge towards the enemy lines.*

'spearmint *nu* (*usu attrib*) a common variety of the mint plant, grown for flavouring *etc*: *spearmint flavour*; *spearmint chewing-gum.*

spec [spek]: **on 'spec** (*inf*) taking a chance in the hope of achieving something *etc*: *I didn't have an appointment, but I went along on spec and they were able to give me one.*

special ['speʃəl] *adj* **1** out of the ordinary; unusual or exceptional: *a special occasion*; *a special friend*; *I bought something* (*extra*) *special for supper.* **2** (*attrib*) appointed, arranged, designed *etc* for a particular purpose: *a special messenger*; *a special train*; *a special tool for drilling holes.* **3** (*formal*: *attrib*) belonging to or limited to one person or thing: *his own special talents.* – *nc* (*slightly inf*) something which is special (*def 2*): *There's a special* (= a special train) *due through here at 5.20*; *They're doing a television special on the life and work of John Donne.*

'**specialism 1** *nc* an activity *etc* in which someone specializes: *His specialism is brain disorders.* **2** *nu* the act of specializing.

'**specialist** *nc* a person who makes a very deep study of one branch of a subject or field: *Dr Brown is a heart specialist; She's a specialist on the Renaissance.*

speciality [speʃi'aləti], (*Amer*) **specialty** *nc* **1** a special product for which one is well-known: *Brown bread is this baker's speciality.* **2** a special activity, or subject about which one has special knowledge: *There are many specialities in medicine; His speciality is gynaecology.*

'**specialize, -ise** *vi* (*usu with* **in**) to give one's attention (to), work (in), or study (a particular job, subject *etc*): *The stamp-collector decided to specialize in Canadian stamps.* ˌ**speciali'zation, -s-** *nu.*

'**specialized, -s-** *adj* **1** (of knowledge, skills *etc*) of the accurate detailed kind obtained by specializing: *He has specialized knowledge of this subject, and has written a book about it.* **2** involving specialization: *a highly specialized task/job; The work is highly specialized.*

'**specially** *adv* **1** with one particular purpose: *I picked these flowers specially for you; I came home early specially to watch that television programme; a splendid cake, specially made for the occasion.* **2** particularly; exceptionally: *He's a nice child, but not specially clever.*

nothing special 1 no particular thing: *'What are you planning to do this evening?' 'Nothing special.'* **2** not particularly good: *Her paintings are quite good, but they're nothing special.*

See also **especial**.

species ['spiːʃiːz] – *pl* **species** – *nc* **1** a group (of animals *etc*) whose members are so similar or closely related as to be able to breed together or be fertilized by each other: *There are several species of zebra.* **2** (*formal*) a kind or sort: *Satire is a species of humour.*

specify ['spesifai] *vt* **1** to name as wanted or demanded (in an agreement *etc*): *When they were discussing plans for the house, he specified a kitchen of twice the normal size.* **2** to make particular or definite mention of: *He specified three types of mistake which had occurred.*

specific [spə'sifik] *adj* **1** giving all the details clearly: *specific instructions; My orders were quite specific; Be more specific about when you want us to come.* **2** particular; exactly stated or described: *Each of the bodily organs has its own specific function; Is there anything specific that you'd like to ask me about?; What is the specific treatment for this kind of poisoning?*

spe'cifically *adv*: *I told you quite specifically not to do that; This dictionary is specifically intended for foreign learners of English.*

ˌ**specifi'cation** [-fi-] **1** *nc* (*often in pl*) something specified in a building plan, a contract *etc*: *I'll send the specifications for the building tomorrow.* **2** *nu* (*formal*) the act of specifying.

specimen ['spesimin] *nc* **1** something used as a sample (of a group or kind of something, *esp* an object to be studied or to be put in a collection): *We looked at specimens of different types of rock under the microscope; The bank manager will need a specimen of your signature;* (*facet*) *What a fine specimen of manhood he is!* **2** a urine sample: *The doctor asked for a specimen for testing.* **3** (*derog*) a person: *He's an ugly-looking specimen!*

specious ['spiːʃəs] *adj* (*formal*) seeming to be good, sound, just *etc* but in reality not so at all: *a specious claim/argument; That argument strikes me as very specious.*

speck [spek] *nc* **1** a small spot or stain: *a speck of ink.* **2** a tiny piece (*eg* of dust).

speckle ['spekl] *nc* a little spot on a different-coloured background: *The eggs were pale blue with dark green speckles.*

'**speckled** *adj* marked with speckles: *Many birds lay speckled eggs.*

specs [speks] (*inf*) short for **spectacles**.

spectacle ['spektəkl] *nc* (*formal*) a sight, *esp* one that is very impressive or wonderful: *The royal wedding was a great spectacle.*

spec'tacular [-'takju-] *adj* (*neg* **un-**) **1** making a great show or display: *a spectacular performance; This sunset is spectacular – come and look!* **2** impressive; dramatic: *a spectacular recovery.* **spec'tacularly** *adv.*

spectacles ['spektəklz] *n pl* (*inf abbrev* **specs** [speks]) glasses which a person wears to help his eyesight: *a pair of spectacles; I've lost my specs.*

spectator [spek'teitə, (*Amer*) 'spekteitər] *nc* a person who watches (an event): *Fifty thousand spectators came to the match;* (*attrib*) *a spectator sport* (= a sport which is easy and enjoyable to watch).

spec'tate *vi* to be a spectator (at an event): *I'm not actually playing in the football match – I'm only spectating.*

spectre, (*Amer usu*) **specter** ['spektə] *nc* (*formal or liter*) a ghost.

'**spectral** *adj* (*formal or liter: usu attrib*) ghostly or like a ghost: *Spectral figures emerged from the fog.*

spectrum ['spektrəm] – *pls* '**spectrums**, (*tech or formal*) '**spectra** [-trə] – *nc* (*usu in sing with* **the**) **1** (*loosely*) the visible spectrum. **2** (*fig*) the full range (of something): *The actress's voice was capable of expressing the whole spectrum of emotion.* **3** (*tech*) the entire range of radiation of different wavelengths produced *eg* by passing a beam of light through a prism, part of which (the **visible spectrum**) is normally visible to the naked eye and forms *eg* the colours of the rainbow: *Ultraviolet light forms part of the invisible area of the spectrum.* **4** (*tech*) a similar range of frequencies of sound (the **sound spectrum**).

speculate ['spekjuleit] *vi* (*formal*) **1** (*often with* **on** *or* **about**) to make guesses: *He's only speculating – he doesn't know; I've been speculating on my future; There's no point in speculating about what's going to happen.* **2** (*often with* **in**) to buy and sell (shares *etc*), hoping to make a profit and risking a loss: *He tried speculating in mining shares and lost a lot of money.*

ˌ**specu'lation** (*formal*) **1** *nc* a theory arrived at by speculating; a guess: *Your speculations were all quite close to the truth.* **2** *nu* the act of speculating: *When the police came to see the headmaster, there was great speculation amongst the pupils as to what was happening.* **3** *ncu* (a) risky investment of money for the sake of making a possible profit: *Speculation is a dangerous way of trying to make a fortune; He lost a great deal of money as a result of his speculations in the stock market.*

'**speculative** [-lətiv, (*Amer*) -leitiv] *adj* (*formal*) **1** of, or reached by, speculation: *a speculative prediction; These estimates are purely speculative; speculative buying of shares.* **2** (of a person) inclined to speculate: *She was of a speculative turn of mind.*

'**speculator** *nc* a person who speculates (in shares *etc*).

sped *see* **speed**.

speech [spi:tʃ] **1** *nu* (the act of) saying words, or the ability to say words: *Speech is one method of communication between people*; *His illness deprived him of the power of speech.* **2** *nu* the words said: *His speech is full of insults and cynicism.* **3** *nu* manner or way of speaking: *His speech is very slow.* **4** *nc* a formal talk given to a meeting *etc*: *an after-dinner speech*; *parliamentary speeches.* **5** *nc* a group of lines in a play that are spoken by an actor at one time: *He forgot one of his speeches.*

'**speechless** *adj* unable to speak, often because of surprise, shock *etc*: *Her daring left us all speechless with envy*; *He looked at her in speechless amazement.* '**speechlessly** *adv.* '**speechlessness** *nu.*

'**speech day** *nc* a day at the end of a school year, when speeches are made and prizes are given out.

speech therapy *nu* the treatment of speech and language disorders. **speech therapist** *nc.*

See also **speak**.

speed [spi:d] **1** *ncu* rate of moving: *a slow speed*; *The car was travelling at high speed.* **2** *nu* quickness of moving: *You'll need a lot more speed if you're going to beat me*; *The car was travelling at speed* (= quickly). – *v* – *pt, ptp* **sped** [sped] (*def 1*), '**speeded** (*defs 1, 2*) – **1** *vti* to (cause to) move or progress quickly; to hurry: *The car sped/speeded along the motorway*; *Plenty of fresh air and exercise will speed his recovery.* **2** *vi* (*usu* with **is, was** *etc* and **-ing**) to drive very fast in a car *etc*, faster than is allowed by law: *The policeman said that I had been speeding in a thirty-mile-per-hour area.* – *See also* **speed up** *below.*

'**speeding** *nu* driving at (an illegally) high speed: *He was fined for speeding*; (*attrib*) *a speeding offence.*

'**speedy** *adj* (*slightly inf*) done, carried out *etc* quickly: *a speedy answer*; *Their reaction was speedy*; *a speedy journey.* '**speedily** *adv.* '**speediness** *nu.*

speedometer [spi'domitə] *nc* an instrument (on a car *etc*) to measure how fast one is travelling.

'**speedway** **1** *nu* a type of motorcycle racing. **2** *nc* the track used for it.

speed up – *pt, ptp* '**speeded** – **1** *vi* to increase speed: *The car speeded up as it left the town.* **2** *vt sep* to quicken the rate of: *We are trying to speed up production.*

spell[1] [spel] – *pt, ptp* **spelt** [-t], **spelled** – **1** *vt* to name or give in order the letters of (a word): *How do you spell 'necessary'?*; *I asked him to spell his name for me.* **2** *vi* (of letters) to form (a word): *C-a-t spells 'cat'.* **3** *vi* to (be able to) spell words correctly: *I can't spell!* **4** *vt* (*liter or formal fig*) to mean or amount to: *This spells disaster.*

'**speller** *nc* a person who spells, *esp* well or badly: *He's a good/bad speller.*

'**spelling** *nu*: *She writes interestingly, but her spelling is terrible*; (*attrib*) *The teacher gave the children a spelling lesson/test.*

spell out *vt sep* **1** to say the letters of (a word) in order: *Could you spell that word out for me?* **2** (*often ironic*) to give a highly detailed explanation of (something): *He's a bit stupid – you'll have to spell it out for him.*

spell[2] [spel] *nc* **1** a set of words which, when spoken, is supposed to have magical power: *The witch recited a spell and turned herself into a swan.* **2** (*usu in sing with* **the**) a strong influence: *the spell of music*; *He was completely under her spell.*

'**spellbound** *adj* (*often pred*) charmed or held as if by magical power: *We watched spellbound as the clowns went through their routine*; *The conjuror held* (= kept) *the audience spellbound.*

spell[3] [spel] *nc* **1** (*slightly inf*) a turn (at work): *Shortly afterwards I did another spell at the machine.* **2** a period of time during which something (*esp* a certain type of weather) lasts: *a spell of cold weather/bad health.* **3** (*slightly inf*) a short time: *We stayed in the country for a spell and then came home.* – *vt* (*inf*) to take the place of (someone) for a time in doing a task *etc*: *We'll take turns at driving – I'll spell you when you get tired.*

spelt *see* **spell**[1].

spend [spend] – *pt, ptp* **spent** [-t] – **1** *vti* to use up or pay out (money): *He spends more than he earns.* **2** *vt* to pass (time): *I spent a week in Spain this summer.* **3** *vt* (*formal*) to use up or exhaust: *The storm spent itself*; *I spent a lot of effort on that drawing!*

spent [spent] *adj* **1** (*usu attrib*) having lost force or power; used: *a spent bullet*; *a spent match.* **2** (*formal or liter*: *usu pred*) exhausted: *By the time we had done half of the job we were all spent.*

'**spendthrift** *nc* (*usu derog*) a person who spends money freely and carelessly: *He didn't want his daughter to marry that lazy spendthrift.*

sperm [spə:m] – *pls* **sperms, sperm** – **1** *nu* the fluid in a male animal *etc* that fertilizes the female egg. **2** *nc* one of the fertilizing cells in this fluid.

spew [spju:] *vti* (*inf or fig liter*) to vomit: *The thought makes me spew!*; *The red mouth of the volcano was spewing boulders and molten rock.*

sphere [sfiə] *nc* **1** a solid object with a surface on which all points are an equal distance from the centre, like *eg* most types of ball. **2** (*formal*) a range (of influence, activity *etc*): *These things aren't really in my sphere.* **3** (*formal*) a group in society: *He moves in the highest literary spheres.* **4** (*liter*: *often in pl*) a star or planet.

spherical ['sferikəl] *adj* (*esp tech or formal*) completely round, like a ball: *It is now known that the world is not flat, but spherical*; *a spherical object.*

spice [spais] **1** *ncu* a *usu* strong-smelling, sharp-tasting vegetable substance used to flavour food (*eg* pepper or nutmeg): *We add cinnamon and other spices*; *This cake needs some more spice.* **2** *nu* anything that adds liveliness or interest: *Her arrival added spice to the party.* **3** *nc* (*no pl*: *formal*) a suggestion or flavour: *a remark with a spice of malice.* – *vt* **1** to flavour with spice: *The curry had been heavily spiced.* **2** (*with* **with**) to add (wit *etc*) to, in order to give variety or liveliness to: *His speech was spiced with witty comments.*

spiced *adj* containing spice(s) (*def 1*): *a spiced biscuit*; *The dish was heavily spiced.*

'**spicy** *adj* **1** tasting or smelling of spices: *a spicy cake*; *He complained that the sausages were too spicy for him.* **2** (*inf*) lively and sometimes slightly indecent: *He told us several spicy stories about people we all knew.* '**spiciness** *nu.*

spick and span [spikn'span] *adj* (*usu pred*) neat, clean and tidy: *In half an hour she had the whole house spick and span.*

spicy *see* **spice**.

spider ['spaidə] *nc* a kind of small creature with eight legs and no wings, which spins a web.

'**spidery** *adj* like a spider, *esp* in being thin and

angular: *spidery handwriting*; *His drawings are rather spidery.*

spiel [ʃpi:l] *nc* (*inf derog*) a long rambling story, *esp* one used as an excuse or to persuade someone to do something: *He came in with a long spiel about why he was late.*

spike [spaik] *nc* **1** a hard, thin, pointed object (of wood, metal *etc*): *The yard was surrounded by a railing with long spikes on top.* **2** a pointed piece of metal attached to the sole of a shoe *etc* to prevent slipping. – *See also* **spikes** *below.* – *vt* (*inf*) to add an alcoholic liquor to: *She had a strong suspicion that someone had spiked her orange juice with vodka.*

spiked *adj.*

spikes *n pl* running-shoes which have spikes (*def 2*) in the soles: *He wore a pair of spikes.*

'**spiky** *adj* **1** having spikes, or points similar to spikes: *the spiky coat of a hedgehog.* **2** easily offended; irritable: *He's sometimes rather spiky.*

'**spikiness** *nu.*

spike someone's guns to spoil an opponent's plans by making it impossible to carry them out.

spill[1] [spil] – *pt, ptp* **spilt** [-t] , **spilled** – *vti* to (cause something to) fall or run out (*usu* accidentally): *He spilt milk on the floor*; *Potatoes spilled out of the burst bag.*

spill blood (*formal*) to (cause people to) be killed or wounded: *This quarrel must be settled before any blood is spilt.*

spill the beans (*inf*) to give away a secret: *By Monday it was evident that someone had spilled the beans to the newspapers.*

spill[2] [spil] *nc* a thin strip of wood or twisted paper for lighting a pipe, candles *etc.*

spilt *see* **spill**[1].

spin [spin] – *prp* '**spinning**: *pt, ptp* **spun** [spʌn] – *vti* **1** to (cause to) go round and round rapidly: *The revolving door spun round and round*; *She spun round in surprise*; *He spun the revolving door round and round.* **2** to form threads from (wool, cotton *etc*) by drawing out and twisting: *The old woman was spinning (wool) in the corner of the room.* **3** (of a spider) to produce (silk) in order to make (a web): *I watched the spider spinning its web.* – *nc* **1** a whirling or turning motion: *The car struck the patch of ice and went into a spin.* **2** (*inf*) a ride, *esp* on wheels: *After lunch we went for a spin in my new car.*

'**spinner** *nc* a person or thing that spins, *esp* (*inf*) a spin-drier.

ˌ**spin-'drier** *nc* a machine which dries clothes by spinning them round and round and forcing the water out of them.

'**spinning-wheel** *nc* a machine for spinning thread, driven by the hand or foot, consisting of a wheel which drives a spindle.

spin out *vt sep* to cause to last a (*usu* unnecessarily) long or longer time: *He spun out his speech for an extra five minutes.*

spin a yarn to tell a long story, *esp* one that is not true: *He managed to spin a yarn of some sort to account for his lateness.*

spinach ['spinidʒ, (*Amer*) -nitʃ] *nu* **1** a kind of plant whose young leaves are eaten as a vegetable: *He grows spinach in his garden.* **2** the leaves as food: *We had steak and spinach for dinner.*

spinal *see* **spine**.

spindle ['spindl] *nc* **1** the pin, *usu* wooden, by means of which thread is twisted in spinning. **2** a thin pin on which something turns (*eg* the one in the middle of the turntable of a record-player): *I can't turn on the radio any more, because the spindle of the control knob has broken.*

'**spindly** *adj* (*inf derog*) very long and thin, *esp* if lacking strength: *My plants are getting spindly from lack of light*; *Her boyfriend is six feet tall, and has long, spindly legs.* '**spindliness** *nu.*

spine [spain] *nc* **1** the line of linked bones running down the back of humans and many animals; the backbone: *She had damaged her spine when she fell.* **2** something like a backbone in shape or function: *the spine of a range of hills*; *the spine of a book.* **3** a thin, stiff, pointed part growing on an animal (*eg* a hedgehog) or a plant (*eg* a thistle).

'**spinal** *adj* (*usu attrib*) of or concerned with the backbone: *a spinal injury.*

'**spineless** *adj* **1** (*tech*) having no spine; invertebrate: *spineless creatures.* **2** (*inf derog*) (of a person) weak and easily frightened or made to change one's mind: *He's too spineless ever to disagree with what his wife says*; *that spineless husband of hers!*

'**spiny** *adj* full of, or covered with, spines (*def 3*): *a spiny cactus.*

spinal cord *nc* (*esp tech*) a cord of nerve cells running up through the backbone: *He damaged his spinal cord when he fell off his horse.*

spinet [spi'net, (*Amer*) 'spinit] *nc* a type of small harpsichord.

spinner *see* **spin**.

spinney ['spini] *nc* (*Brit*) a small clump of trees: *The children were playing in the spinney by the side of the house.*

spinster ['spinstə] *nc* a woman who is not married, *esp* (*sometimes derog*) one who is past the usual age for marrying.

'**spinsterhood** *nu* the state of being a spinster.

'**spinsterish** *adj* (*derog*) of or like a spinster in being fussy, too precise *etc.*

spiny *see* **spine**.

spiral ['spaiərəl] *adj* (*usu attrib*) **1** coiled round like a spring, with each coil the same size as the one below: *a spiral staircase.* **2** winding round and round, *usu* tapering to a point: *a spiral shell.* – *nc* **1** an increase or decrease, or rise or fall, becoming more and more rapid (*eg* in prices or in the value of money). **2** (*often liter*) a spiral line or object: *A spiral of smoke rose from the chimney.* – *v* – *pt, ptp* '**spiralled**, (*Amer*) '**spiraled** – *vi* to go or move in a spiral, *esp* to increase more and more rapidly: *Prices have spiralled in the last six months.*

'**spirally** *adv.*

spire ['spaiə] *nc* a tall, pointed tower, *esp* one built on the roof of a church: *The cathedral is crowned by a spire seventy metres high.*

spirit ['spirit] **1** *ncu* a principle or emotion which makes someone act: *the spirit of reform*; *The spirit of kindness seems to be lacking in the world nowadays*; *He was only trying to help – he didn't act in any unkind spirit*; *You'll all need to show far more team spirit* (= loyalty to the team) *if you want to win that match.* **2** *nc* a person's mind, will, personality *etc* thought of as distinct from the body, or as remaining alive *eg* as a ghost when the body dies: *I can't come to the meeting in person, but I'll be with you in spirit* (= I'll be thinking of you); *Our great leader may be dead, but his spirit still lives on, influencing our daily thoughts and decisions*; *A medium is a person who tries to make contact with the spirits of the dead, on behalf of the living*; (*attrib*) *the spirit world*; (*liter*) *Evil spirits* (= influences) *have taken possession of him.* **3** *nc* the real or intended meaning: *He acted according to the spirit of the law.* **4** *nu* liveliness; courage: *He acted with spirit.* **5** *nu* purified alcohol: *She put some (surgical) spirit on the spot on her face. – See also* **spirits** *below.*

'spirited *adj* (*usu attrib*) full of courage or liveliness: *a spirited attack/description.* **'spiritedly** *adv.*

-spirited (*in cmpds*) showing (a particular kind of) spirit (*def 1*) or spirits: *a ˌmean-spirited re'mark; ˌhigh-spirited ˌyoung 'men.*

'spiritless *adj* (*formal*) without liveliness, courage *etc*: *He seems a rather spiritless person; His performance was somewhat spiritless.*

'spirits *n pl* **1** a person's mood: *He's in good/high/low spirits* (= He's happy/very cheerful/depressed); *His spirits rose as the weather improved; This news may raise his spirits.* **2** strong alcoholic drink, *eg* whisky, gin, vodka *etc*: *The grocer sells wine and spirits.*

'spiritual [-tʃul] *adj* (*usu attrib*) of one's spirit or soul, or of one's religious beliefs: *one's spiritual, rather than material, needs.* – *nc* (*usu* **Negro spiritual**) an emotional, religious song with a strong rhythm, of the type developed by the American Negroes while in slavery.

ˌspiritu'ality [-tʃu'a-] *nu* (*formal*) the state of being concerned with the soul.

'spiritualism [-tʃulizm] *nu* the belief that the spirits of dead people can talk to those who are still alive.

'spiritualist [-tʃulist] *nc* (*sometimes with cap*) a believer in spiritualism.

'spiritually *adv.*

'spirit level *nc* a tool consisting of a bar containing a glass tube of liquid, for testing whether a surface is level.

out of spirits (*formal or liter*) feeling depressed: *He is out of spirits today.*

spirit away *vt sep* to carry away or remove secretly and suddenly, as if by magic: *The actress left the hotel by a back door and was spirited away before the reporters discovered the plan.*

take (something) in the right spirit not to be offended by: *He took the joke/criticism in the right spirit.*

See also **dispirited**.

spit[1] [spit] *nu* (*also* **spittle** ['spitl]) (*inf*) the liquid that forms in the mouth. – *v* – *prp* **'spitting**: *pt, ptp* **spat** [spat] – **1** *vti* to throw out (spit) from the mouth: *He spat a cherry-stone into the fire; He spat in the gutter as an indication of contempt; The angry cat arched its back and spat at the dog.* **2** *vi* (*inf*) to rain slightly: *I thought the rain had stopped, but it's still spitting.* **3** *vt* to send (out) with force: *The fire spat (out) sparks.*

spitting image *nc* (*inf: no pl*) an exact likeness (of someone): *He's/They are the spitting image of his/their father!*

spit[2] [spit] *nc* a type of sharp-pointed metal bar on which meat is roasted.

spit[3] [spit] *nc* a long narrow point of land or sand sticking out into the sea.

spite [spait] *nu* ill-will or desire to hurt or offend: *She neglected to give him the message out of spite.* – *vt* to annoy, offend or frustrate, because of spite: *He only did that to spite me!*

'spiteful *adj*: *a spiteful remark/person; You're being very spiteful.* **'spitefully** *adv.* **'spitefulness** *nu.*

in 'spite of 1 taking notice of: *He went in spite of his father's orders.* **2** although something has or had happened, is or was a fact *etc*: *In spite of all the rain that had fallen, the ground was still pretty dry.*

spittle *see* **spit**.

splash [splaʃ] **1** *vt* to make wet with drops of liquid, mud *etc, esp* suddenly and accidentally: *A passing car splashed my coat (with water).* **2** *vti* to (cause to) fly about in drops: *Water splashed everywhere; The children were splashing water about in the bath.* **3** *vi* to fall or move with splashes (*def 1*): *The children were splashing in the sea.* **4** *vt* (*inf: usu derog*) to display *etc* in a place, manner *etc* that will be noticed: *Posters advertising the concert were splashed all over the wall; The scandal was splashed across the newspapers.* – *nc* **1** a scattering of drops of liquid or the noise made by this: *He fell in with a loud splash.* **2** a mark made by splashing: *There was a splash of mud on her dress.* **3** a bright patch: *a splash of colour.*

make a splash to attract a lot of notice, *esp* deliberately: *He has made quite a splash in his new career as an actor.*

splay [spleɪ]: **ˌsplay-'footed** *adj* having feet (**splay feet**) which are turned outwards more than normal when walking or standing.

spleen [spliːn] **1** *nc* an organ of the body, close to the stomach, which causes changes in the blood. **2** *nu* (*arch or very formal*) ill-humour, anger or bad temper: *a fit of spleen.*

splendid ['splendid] *adj* **1** brilliant, magnificent, very rich and grand *etc*: *She arrived in a splendid golden coach drawn by white horses; He looked splendid in his robes.* **2** very good or fine: *a splendid piece of work.* **'splendidly** *adv.* **'splendour** [-də], **'splendidness** *nus.*

splice [splais] *vt* **1** (*naut*) to join (two pieces of rope) by weaving the strands of one into the other. **2** to join (two pieces of film, recording tape *etc*) end to end. – *nc* a join in a rope, film *etc* made in these ways.

splint [splint] *nc* a piece of wood *etc* used to keep a broken arm or leg in a fixed position while it heals: *The doctor put the boy's broken leg in a splint; The young nurse is learning how to put a broken arm in splints.*

'splinter *nc* a small sharp broken piece of wood *etc*: *The rough plank gave her a splinter in her finger; The surgeons removed a bomb splinter from his leg.* – *vti* to split into splinters: *The heavy blow splintered a panel of the door; The door splintered under the heavy blow.*

'splinter group *nc* a group (*esp* a political group) formed by breaking away from a larger one: *He's a member of a left-wing splinter group formed by ex-supporters of the Radical Party.*

split [split] – *prp* **'splitting**: *pt, ptp* **split** – **1** *vti* to cut or (cause to) break lengthwise: *to split firewood; The skirt split all the way down the back seam.* **2** *vti* to divide or (cause to) disagree: *The issue of nationalization split the voters into two opposing groups.* – *nc* a crack or break: *There was a split in one of the sides of the box;* (*fig*) *a split in the ranks of the Labour Party. – See also* **the splits** *below.*

split infinitive *nc* in English, an infinitive with an adverb between 'to' and the verb, considered substandard by many people: *Be sure to carefully dry it.*

ˌsplit-'level *adj* (*usu attrib*) built, made *etc* on more than one level (*usu* two levels): *a split-level dining-room/cooker.*

split personality *ncu* (*not a tech term*) a mental

condition in which the sufferer has two or more personalities, with different attitudes and types of conduct; a form of schizophrenia: *He has a split personality*; *She suffers from split personality.*

split second *nc* a fraction of a second: *For a split second she thought she saw a face at the window, and then it vanished*; (*attrib*) *split-second timing.*

splitting headache *nc* (*inf*) a very bad headache: *Turn down the radio – I've a splitting headache.*

split hairs *see* **hair**.

the splits the gymnastic exercise of sitting down on the floor with one leg straight forward and the other straight back: *to do the splits.*

splutter ['splʌtə] (*slightly inf*) **1** *vi* to make spitting sounds and throw out drops of moisture *etc*: *The sausages spluttered in the pan.* **2** *vti* (*fig*) to speak quickly and confusedly because of excitement, surprise *etc*: *She had unfortunately overheard what he had said and was spluttering with indignation.* – *nc* (*usu in sing*): *The sausages/speaker gave a splutter.*

spoil [spoil] – *pts, ptps* **spoiled, spoilt** [-t] – **1** *vt* to damage or ruin; to make bad or useless: *If you touch that drawing you'll spoil it*; *If you eat too much just now, you'll spoil your appetite.* **2** *vt* to give (a child *etc*) too much of what he wants and possibly to make his character, behaviour *etc* worse by doing so: *They spoil that child dreadfully and she's becoming unbearable!* **3** *vi* (of food) to become bad, be burned *etc*: *All the time they were arguing, dinner was spoiling in the oven.* – *nu* (*formal or liter*) something which is obtained by stealing: *By the time the police arrived, the thieves had got away with their spoil.*

spoils *n pl* (*formal or liter*) the profits or rewards (of an enterprise, a position of power *etc*): *the spoils of war*; *the spoils of success.*

'spoilsport *nc* a person who spoils, or refuses to join in, the fun of others: *I'm sorry to be a spoilsport, but it's time the children were in bed.*

be 'spoiling for (*inf*) to be eager for (*esp* a fight).

spoke[1] [spouk] *nc* one of the ribs or bars from the centre to the rim of the wheel of a bicycle, cart *etc.*

put a spoke in someone's wheel to put difficulties in the way of what someone is doing: *It's time someone put a spoke in his wheel – he always seems to get what he wants.*

spoke[2], **spoken** *see* **speak**.

spokesman ['spouksmən] – *fem* **'spokeswoman** – *nc* a person who speaks on behalf of a group of others: *Who is the spokesman for your party?*

sponge [spʌndʒ] **1** *nc* a type of sea animal, or its soft skeleton, which has many holes and is able to suck up and hold water. **2** *ncu* a piece of such a skeleton or a substitute, used for washing the body *etc.* **3** *ncu* a sponge pudding or cake: *We had jam sponge for dessert.* **4** *nc* an act of wiping *etc* with a sponge: *Give the table a quick sponge over, will you?* – **1** *vt* to wipe or clean with a sponge: *She sponged the child's face*; *I'll sponge that jacket for you – there are a few dirty marks on it.* **2** *vt* (*sometimes with* **up, away** *etc*) to wipe, soak (up) or remove with a sponge (*def 2*): *She sponged the mess up off the table.* **3** *vi* (*inf derog*: *with* **off** *or* **on**) to get a living, money *etc* (from someone else): *He's been sponging off/on us for years*; *He's always sponging.*

'sponger *nc* (*inf derog*) a person who lives by sponging on others: *The politician maintained that many of the people who live off social security benefits are just spongers who don't like work.*

'spongy *adj* soft and springy or holding water like a sponge: *The football pitch is too spongy for play*; *spongy ground.* **'spongily** *adv.* **'sponginess** *nu.*

'sponge cake, sponge pudding *ncus* (a) very light cake or pudding made from flour, eggs and sugar *etc.*

sponge rubber *nu* foam rubber.

sponsor ['sponsə] *vt* **1** to take on the financial responsibility for (a person, project *etc*), often as a form of advertising or for charity: *My church is sponsoring a divinity student at University*; *The firm sponsors several golf tournaments.* **2** to promise (a person) that one will pay a certain sum of money to a charity *etc* if that person completes a set task (*eg* a walk, swim *etc*): *Are you willing to sponsor me on a 24-mile walk?* **3** to make oneself responsible for (the introduction of a law *etc*): *Who is sponsoring the bill in Parliament?* – *nc* a person, firm *etc* that acts in this way.

'sponsorship *nu* (the money given as) the act of sponsoring.

spontaneous [spən'teiniəs] *adj* **1** said, done *etc* of one's own free will without pressure from others: *a spontaneous invitation*; *His offer was quite spontaneous.* **2** (*formal*) natural; not forced: *spontaneous behaviour*; *the spontaneous growth of a certain industry/firm.* **spon'taneously** *adv.* **spon'taneousness, spontaneity** [spontə'neiəti, -'niːəti] *nus.*

spoof [spuːf] *nc* (*inf*) a ridiculous imitation (of a type of film, book *etc*), intended to be humorous: *The actors performed a brilliant spoof on Shakespearean tragedy*; (*attrib*) *a spoof Western.*

spook [spuːk] *nc* (*inf*) a ghost. – *vt* (*inf*: *esp Amer*) to frighten: *A snake came out from the bushes and spooked his horse.*

'spooky *adj* (*inf*) eerie and suggesting the presence of ghosts: *a spooky house*; *It's very spooky walking through the graveyard at night.* **'spookiness** *nu.*

spool [spuːl] *nc* **1** a type of cylindrical holder on or in which thread, photographic film *etc* is wound: *How can I wind this film back on to its spool?* **2** the amount of thread, film *etc* held by such a holder: *She used three spools of thread in one week.*

spoon [spuːn] *nc* **1** (*often in cmpds*) an instrument shaped like a shallow bowl with a handle for lifting food (*esp* soup or pudding) to the mouth, or for stirring tea, coffee *etc*: *a teaspoon/soup-spoon.* **2** a spoonful: *I take three spoons of sugar in my tea.* – *vt* to lift or scoop up with a spoon: *She spooned food into the baby's mouth.*

'spoonful *nc* the amount held by a spoon: *three spoonfuls of sugar.*

ˌspoon-'feed – *pt, ptp* **ˌspoon-'fed** – *vt* **1** to feed with a spoon. **2** (*derog*) to teach or treat (a person) in a way that does not allow him to think or act for himself: *Some of these students expect to be spoon-fed with information rather than finding it themselves.*

See also **dessertspoon** *under* **dessert, soupspoon** *under* **soup, tablespoon** *under* **table, teaspoon** *under* **tea**.

spoonerism ['spuːnərizəm] *nc* a slip in speaking that changes the position of the first sounds of words: *'Shoving leopard' for 'loving shepherd' is a spoonerism.*

spoor [spuə] *nc* (*rare or tech*) footprints or tracks left by an animal.

sporadic [spə'radik] *adj* (*formal*: *usu attrib*) happening here and there or now and again: *sporadic gunfire.* **spo'radically** *adv.*

spore [spo:] *nc* a tiny seedlike cell from which ferns and other types of non-flowering plant grow.

sporran ['sporən] *nc* in the Scottish national dress, a type of leather *etc* purse worn hanging in front of the kilt.

sport [spo:t] **1** *nu* games or competitions involving physical activity organized for the entertainment of the people taking part and/or of spectators: *She's very keen on sport of all kinds.* **2** *nc* a particular game or amusement of this kind: *Hunting, shooting and fishing are not sports I enjoy; the sport of motor-racing.* **3** *nc* (*inf*) a good-natured and obliging person: *He's a good sport to agree to do that for us!* **4** *nu* (*old*) fun; amusement: *Don't be angry! I wasn't serious – I only did it for sport; He's not very clever, and he provides the other boys with a great deal of sport. – See also* **make sport of** *below.* – *vt* (*facet*) to wear, *esp* in public: *He was sporting a very colourful pink tie.*

'**sporting** *adj* **1** (*attrib*) of, or concerned with, sports: *This should be one of the best sporting occasions of the year!; a sporting personality; the sporting world.* **2** (*neg* **un-**) showing fairness and kindness or generosity, *esp* if unexpected: *Well, that's very sporting of you!; a sporting gesture. – See also* **a sporting chance** *below.*

'**sportingly** *adv* in a sporting (*def 2*) manner: *He sportingly let me start first.*

sports *adj* (*attrib*: *Amer also* **sport**) designed, or suitable, for sport: *a sports centre; sports equipment.*

'**sporty** *adj* (*inf*: *sometimes derog*) (of a person) who takes part in (*usu* several) sports: *He plays cricket, football, squash and rugby – he's a real sporty type; She looks rather sporty.*

'**sports car** *nc* a small, fast car with only two seats.

'**sports jacket** *nc* a type of jacket for men, designed for casual wear: *His brother was wearing a dark suit but he was wearing a sports jacket and flannels.*

'**sportsman** ['spo:ts-] – *fem* '**sportswoman** – *nc* **1** a person who takes part in sports: *He is a very keen sportsman.* **2** a person who shows a spirit of fairness and generosity in sport: *He's a real sportsman who doesn't seem to care if he wins or loses.*

'**sportsmanlike** ['spo:ts-] *adj* (*neg* **un-**) showing qualities of fairness and generosity: *That was a very sportsmanlike gesture; His behaviour on the football pitch has always been very sportsmanlike.*

'**sportsmanship** ['spo:ts-] *nu* the state or quality of being sportsmanlike.

'**sportswear** *nu* clothing designed for playing sports in.

make sport of (*formal*) to make fun of or ridicule (a person, efforts *etc*): *They made sport of his attempts to start a conversation with one of the girls.*

a sporting chance a reasonably good chance: *He should start the race about ten metres back to give you a sporting chance; If our train is on time, we have a sporting chance of getting home before midnight.*

spot [spot] *nc* **1** a small mark or stain (made by mud, paint *etc*): *She was trying to remove a spot of grease from her skirt.* **2** a small, round mark of a different colour from its background, used to make a pattern on cloth *etc*: *His tie was navy blue with white spots.* **3** a pimple or red mark on the skin caused by an illness *etc*: *On the very day of the party, she developed a spot on her chin; She had measles and was covered in spots; Chickenpox spots can be very unpleasant.* **4** a place or small area, *esp* the exact place (where something happened *etc*): *We found a sheltered spot by the river to have our picnic; There was a large number of detectives gathered at the spot where the body had been found.* **5** (*inf*) a spotlight: *He positioned the spot so that it shone on the front of the stage.* **6** (*inf*) a small amount: *Can I borrow a spot of sugar?* **7** (*inf*) a regular performance or appearance (on radio, TV, in the theatre *etc*), *esp* a short one: *He has a five-minute spot on Radio 4 once a week.* – *v* – *pt, ptp* '**spotted** – *vt* (*inf*: not used with **is, was** *etc* and **-ing**) **1** to catch sight of: *She spotted him eventually at the very back of the crowd.* **2** to recognize or pick out: *No-one watching the play was able to spot the murderer; We spotted the winner of the beauty contest the moment she appeared.*

'**spotless** *adj* **1** very clean: *Her house is absolutely spotless; a spotless kitchen.* **2** (*formal or facet*) completely free from dishonesty, wickedness, or anything else which is undesirable: *a spotless character; His reputation is spotless* '**spotlessly** *adv.* '**spotlessness** *nu.*

'**spotted** *adj* marked or covered with spots: *Her dress was spotted with grease; a spotted tie.*

-spotter (*in cmpds*: *inf*) a person whose hobby is collecting the numbers of (planes, trains *etc*): *a* '*train-spotter.*

'**spotty** *adj* (*inf*) (of people) covered with spots: *She's almost over her bout of chickenpox, but she's still a bit spotty; a spotty face/young man.* '**spottiness** *nu.*

spot check *nc* an inspection made without warning, *esp* on items chosen at random from a group: *We only found out about the flaw during a spot check on goods leaving the factory.*

'**spotlight** *nc* (a lamp for projecting) a circle of light that is thrown on to a small area, *esp* on to an actor or on a small part of a theatre stage: *The painting is beautifully lit by a small spotlight;* (*fig*) *The spotlight of the investigation has been turned on his financial affairs.* – *v* – *pt, ptp* '**spotlit**, (*def 2*) '**spotlighted** – *vt* **1** to light with a spotlight: *The stage was spotlit.* **2** to show up clearly or draw attention to: *The incident spotlighted the difficulties with which we were faced.*

in a '**spot** (*inf*) in trouble: *His failure to return the papers on time put her in a spot.*

knock spots off *see* **knock**.

on the spot (*inf*) **1** at once: *she liked it so much that she bought it on the spot;* (*attrib*) *an on-the-spot decision.* **2** in the exact place referred to; in the place where one is needed: *He felt he was the best person to deal with the crisis as he was on the spot; It was a good thing you were on the spot when he had his heart attack;* (*attrib*) *our on-the-spot reporter.* **3** (*esp with* **put**) in a dangerous, difficult or embarrassing position: *The interviewer's questions really put the Prime Minister on the spot.*

spot on (*inf*) very accurate or exactly on the target: *His description of Mary was spot on!*

spouse [spaus] *nc* (*old, legal or facet*) a husband or wife.

spout [spaut] **1** *vt* to throw out or be thrown out in a jet: *Water spouted from the hole in the tank; The urn suddenly began to spout coffee; The whale spouted (water) high into the air.* **2** *vti* (*inf*: *usu derog*) to talk or say (something) loudly and dramatically: *He started to spout poetry, of all things!; She was spouting about duty and loyalty and all that rubbish.* – *nc* **1** the part of a kettle, teapot, jug, water-pipe *etc* through which the liquid it contains is poured out. **2** a jet or strong flow (of water *etc*).

up the spout (*sl*) ruined, defeated, damaged beyond repair *etc*: *My plans are/My car is completely up the spout.*

sprain [sprein] *vt* to twist (a joint, *esp* the ankle or wrist) in such a way as to tear or stretch the ligaments. – *nc* a twisting of a joint in this way: *The only injury to her ankle was a bad sprain, despite the distance she had fallen.*

sprang *see* **spring**.

sprat [sprat] *nc* a type of small fish rather like the herring, used as food.

sprawl [spro:l] *vi* (*often derog*) **1** to sit, lie or fall with the arms and legs spread out widely and carelessly: *Several tired-looking people were sprawling in armchairs.* **2** (of a town *etc*) to spread out in an untidy and irregular way: *The housing-scheme sprawled (out) over the slope of the hill.* – *nc* **1** an act of sprawling: *He was lying in a careless sprawl on the sofa.* **2** (*liter*) an untidy and irregular area (of houses *etc*): *She lost her way in the grimy sprawl of back streets.*

sprawled *adj* (*pred*) spread untidily and irregularly: *His papers were (lying) sprawled all over the desk*; *The dead man's body had fallen sprawled (out) across the floor.*

'sprawling *adj* (*attrib*): *the huge, sprawling city of Los Angeles.*

spray[1] [sprei] **1** *ncu* a fine mist of small flying drops (of water *etc*) such as that given out by a waterfall: *We were drenched with spray whenever we went up on to the deck of the ship*; (*in cmpds*) *sea-spray*; *The perfume came out of the bottle in a fine spray.* **2** *nc* a device with many small holes, or other instrument, for producing a fine mist of liquid: *She used a spray attached to the bath-taps to rinse her hair*; (*in cmpds*) *a perfume spray.* **3** *ncu* (*sometimes in cmpds*) a liquid for spraying: *He bought a can of fly-spray to kill the flies in his kitchen.* – **1** *vti* to (cause liquid to) come out in a mist or in fine jets: *The water sprayed all over everyone*; *She sprayed water on the sheets before trying to iron them.* **2** *vt* to cover with a mist or with fine jets of liquid: *He sprayed the roses to kill pests.*

spray[2] [sprei] *nc* **1** a small branch of a tree or plant, with its leaves and flowers: *a spray of apple-blossom.* **2** a small bunch of flowers *etc* arranged to look like this, for wearing as a decoration on clothes: *She wore a spray in her button-hole*; *The bride carried a spray of roses.*

spread [spred] – *pt, ptp* **spread** – **1** *vti* to (cause to) go (often more widely or more thinly) over a surface: *She spread honey thickly on her toast*; *The butter has been in the fridge and won't spread easily.* **2** *vt* to cover (a surface with something): *She spread the bread with jam.* **3** *vti* to (cause to) reach a wider area, affect a larger number of people *etc*: *The stain spread gradually over the wall*; *The news spread through the village very quickly*; *When she had flu she was warned to stay in the house so as not to spread the infection.* **4** *vt* to distribute over a wide area, period of time *etc*: *The exams were spread over a period of ten days, so he had plenty of time to study between each one.* **5** *vt* to open out: *He spread the map on the table.* – *See also* **spread out** *below.* – **1** *nu* the process of reaching a wider area, affecting more people *etc*: *the spread of information/television*; *the spread of crime among schoolchildren.* **2** *nu* something to be spread on bread *etc*: *cheese spread*; *Have some chicken spread.* **3** *nc* (*inf*) a (large) meal laid out: *She had organized a wonderful spread for us as she thought we'd be hungry.* **4** *nc* (*inf*) an article, advertisement *etc* in a magazine *etc*, *usu* occupying a large area: *a two-page spread.* **5** *nc* (*no pl*) the space or time covered (by something) or the extent of spreading: *a spread of several miles*; *Her children's ages cover a spread of nearly twenty years.*

,spread-'eagled *adj* (*usu pred*) with arms and legs spread out: *We found the body lying spread-eagled on the floor.*

spread out 1 *vti* to extend or stretch out: *The fields spread out in front of him*; *He spread out the rug on the grass.* **2** *vt* to distribute over a wide area or period of time: *She spread the leaflets out on the table*; *She spread out her trips to town over six weeks.* **3** *vi* to scatter and go in different directions, in order to cover a wider area: *They spread out when they entered the field and began to search the ground.*

spree [spri:] *nc* (*slightly inf*) a cheerful, careless period of doing something: *They went on a spending spree to London.*

on the/a spree (*slightly inf*) enjoying such a spell of activity: *He went out on the/a spree.*

sprig [sprig] *nc* a small piece of a plant; a twig: *a sprig of heather.*

sprightly ['spraitli] *adj* cheerful and quick-moving: *a sprightly old lady*; *She seems very sprightly after her holiday.* **'sprightliness** *nu.*

spring [spriŋ] – *pt* **sprang** [spraŋ]: *ptp* **sprung** [sprʌŋ] – **1** *vi* (*more formal than* **jump**) to jump, leap or move swiftly (*usu* upwards): *She sprang into the boat*; *A piece of the clock sprang out when he took the back off.* **2** *vi* (*formal*) to arise or result from: *His bravery springs from his love of adventure.* **3** *vti* to (cause a trap to) close violently: *The trap must have sprung when the hare stepped in it*; *He sprang the trap.* – *See also* **spring** *in phrases below.* – **1** *nc* a coil of wire or other similar device which can be compressed or squeezed down but returns to its original shape when released: *a watch-spring*; *the springs in a chair*; (*attrib*) *a spring clip.* **2** *ncu* (*sometimes with cap*) the season of the year when plants begin to grow, February or March to April or May in cooler northern regions: *We sometimes have snow in spring*; *We had snow last spring*; *We should be finished by the spring* (= the spring of this year or next year); *in the spring of 1975*; *Spring is my favourite season*; *Winters and springs are very wet in this part of the world*; (*attrib*) *spring flowers.* **3** *nc* (*more formal than* **jump**) a leap or sudden movement: *The lion made a sudden spring on its prey.* **4** *nu* the ability to stretch and spring back again: *There's a lot of spring in this floor*; (*fig*) *He had a spring in his walk.* **5** *nc* a small stream flowing out from the ground: *This stream comes from a spring in the woods*; (*attrib*) *spring water.*

'springy *adj* **1** able to spring back into its former shape: *springy grass*; *The grass is very springy.* **2** having spring: *a springy step*; *These floorboards are springy.* **'springiness** *nu.*

sprung [sprʌŋ] *adj* having springs: *a sprung mattress*; *Is the mattress sprung?*

'springboard *nc* a springy type of diving-board from which a person can jump high before diving or a board on which gymnasts jump before vaulting: *You should practise diving off the springboard*; (*fig*) *His election to the town council provided a springboard for wider political activities.*

spring cleaning *nu* thorough cleaning of a house *etc esp* in spring: *I am very disorganized – I do my* *spring cleaning in September.*

spring tide *nc* the very high and low tide when the moon is full or new.

'**springtime** *nu* the season of spring: *Lambs are born in the springtime*; (*attrib*) *springtime fashions.*

spring a leak (of a ship *etc*) to develop a hole through which water begins to enter: *Our rowing-boat has sprung a leak.*

spring back *vi* to return suddenly to a former, *usu* normal, shape or position: *When using a bow and arrow, you should wear a wristguard to protect your wrist when the bowstring springs back.*

'**spring (something) on (someone)** (*inf*) to tell or propose (something) suddenly to (a person), so that he is surprised: *He sprang the news of his divorce on me.*

spring up *vi* to develop or appear suddenly: *Weeds seemed to have sprung up all over the garden*; *New buildings are springing up everywhere.*

sprinkle ['spriŋkl] *vt* to scatter something over something else in small drops or bits: *He sprinkled salt over his food*; *He sprinkled his food with salt*; *They have a special apparatus for sprinkling the roses with water*; (*fig*) *Her golden hair is now sprinkled with grey.*

'**sprinkler** *nc* an apparatus for sprinkling *eg* water over a lawn.

'**sprinkling** *nc* a small amount or a few: *a sprinkling of snow*; *There were mostly women at the meeting but there was a sprinkling of men.*

sprint [sprint] **1** *nc* a run or running race performed at high speed over a short distance: *He had a quick sprint round the track*; *Who won the 100 metres sprint?* **2** *nu* the pace of this: *He ran up the road at a sprint.* – *vti* to run at full speed *esp* (in) a race: *He sprinted (for) the last few hundred metres.*

'**sprinter** *nc* a person who is good at sprinting: *He is France's best sprinter.*

sprite [sprait] *nc* (*liter*: *often in cmpds*) an elf or fairy: *a water-sprite.*

sprocket ['sprokit] *nc* one of a set of teeth on the rim of a wheel that fit into the holes or links of a chain *etc.*

sprout [spraut] **1** *vti* to (cause to) develop leaves, shoots *etc*: *Potatoes should be eaten before they start sprouting*; (*formal*) *How do you sprout this type of bean?*; *The trees are sprouting new leaves.* **2** *vt* (of animals, birds *etc*) to develop *eg* horns, produce *eg* feathers: *The young birds are sprouting their first feathers.* – **1** *nc* a new shoot or bud: *bean sprouts.* **2** (*usu in pl*) a Brussels sprout.

sprout up *vi* (of plants or *inf* of children) to grow: *That fruit bush has sprouted up fast*; *At the age of fourteen he really began to sprout up.*

spruce[1] [spru:s] *adj* (*inf*) neat and smart: *You're looking very spruce today*; *a spruce outfit/young man.*

spruce up *vti* (*inf*) to make oneself or somebody else smarter: *I'll go and spruce up before going out*; *She brushed his jacket and spruced him up*; *Spruce yourself up a bit!*

spruce[2] [spru:s] – *pls* **spruces, spruce** – **1** *nc* (*also* '**spruce tree**) a type of fir tree: *a plantation of spruce.* **2** *nu, adj* (of) its wood.

sprung *see* **spring**.

spry [sprai] *adj* (*formal*) lively or active: *He's eighty years old, but very spry*; *a spry old gentleman.* '**spryly** *adv.* '**spryness** *nu.*

spud [spʌd] *nc* (*sl*) a potato: *Have you peeled the spuds?*

spume [spju:m] *nu* (*liter*) foam or froth: *Clouds of white spume rose from the crashing waves.*

spun *see* **spin**.

spunk [spʌŋk] *nu* (*inf*) courage: *That boy has plenty of spunk.*

spur [spə:] *nc* **1** a small instrument with a sharp point or points that a rider wears on his heels and digs into the horse's sides to make it go faster. **2** (*formal*) anything that urges a person to make greater efforts: *He was driven on by the spur of ambition*; *Encouragement is always a spur to achievement.* **3** a claw-like point at the back of a bird's, *esp* a cock's leg. **4** (*formal*) something looking like a spur, *eg* a small range of mountains running off from a larger range: *That line of hills is one of the southern spurs of the Pyrenees.* – *v* – *pt, ptp* **spurred** – *vt* to prick a horse's sides with spurs to make it go faster: *They spurred their horses and galloped away.*

on the spur of the moment suddenly; without previous planning: *We decided to go to Paris on the spur of the moment.*

spur on *vt sep* to urge a horse to go faster, using spurs, or a person to make greater efforts: *He spurred his horse on*; *The thought of the prize spurred her on.*

spurious ['spjuəriəs] *adj* (*formal*) fake or false; not genuine: *a spurious signature/document*; *The evidence in this case is rather spurious.*

spurn [spə:n] *vt* (*formal*) to reject scornfully: *He spurned my offers of help.*

spurt [spə:t] *vi* (of a liquid) to spout or gush: *Blood spurted from the wound*; *The pipe had a hole in it and water was spurting out.* – *nc* a sudden gush or burst: *a spurt of blood*; *With a sudden spurt of energy, he raced to the top of the hill.*

put a spurt on/put on a spurt (*inf*) to run or go faster *eg* towards the end of a race: *He put a sudden spurt on and passed the other competitors.*

sputter ['spʌtə] *vi* to make spitting and hissing noises: *The bacon was sputtering under the grill*; *He sputtered with rage.*

sputum ['spju:təm] *nu* (*tech*) saliva and mucus from the nose, throat *etc.*

spy [spai] *nc* a secret agent or person employed to gather information secretly *esp* about the military affairs of other countries: *She was arrested as a spy*; (*fig*) *industrial spies.* – **1** *vi* to be a spy: *He had been spying for the Russians for many years.* – *See also* **spy on** *below.* **2** *vt* (*often liter*) to see or notice: *She spied a human figure on the mountain-side.*

'**spyglass** *nc* a small telescope.

'**spyhole** *nc* a peep-hole.

'**spy on** *vt fus* to watch (a person *etc*) secretly: *The police had been spying on the gang for several months*; (*inf*) *Our next-door neighbours are always spying on us.*

spy out the land to investigate or examine (*eg* an area of land, a matter *etc*) before proceeding further: *Scouts were sent ahead of the party to spy out the land.*

See also **espionage**.

squabble ['skwobl] *vi* to quarrel noisily, *usu* about something unimportant: *The children are always squabbling over the toys.* – *nc* a noisy quarrel: *The children had a squabble about who would ring the door-bell.*

squad [skwod] *nc* **1** a small group of soldiers drilled or working together: *The men were divided into squads to perform different duties.* **2** a group of people, *esp* a working-party: *a squad of workmen.*

squadron ['skwodrən] *nc* a division of a regiment, a section of a fleet, or a group of aeroplanes.
ˌ**squadron-'leader** *nc* (*with caps, and often abbrev* **Sqn-Ldr,** *when written in titles*) in the British air force, (a person of) the rank below wing commander: *He is a squadron-leader*; *He was promoted to squadron-leader*; *Squadron-Leader Ash.* – *See also* Appendix 3.

squalid ['skwolid] *adj* (*derog*) very dirty or filthy: *The houses are squalid and overcrowded*; *squalid living conditions*; (*fig*) *mean, squalid behaviour.*
'**squalor** [-lə] *nu*: *They lived in poverty and squalor.*

squall [skwo:l] *nc* **1** a sudden violent wind, *eg* bringing rain: *The ship was struck by a squall.* **2** (*inf*) a harsh cry or scream: *the baby's squalls.* – *vi* (*inf*) to cry harshly: *I can't bear babies that squall all the time.*
'**squally** *adj* (*inf*) with many squalls or gusts of wind: *squally weather*; *a squally day*; *It's a bit squally today.* '**squalliness** *nu.*

squalor *see* **squalid**.

squander ['skwondə] *vt* to waste: *He squandered all his money on gambling*; (*formal*) *He is squandering his time playing cards when he should be studying.*

square [skweə] **1** *nc* a four-sided two-dimensional figure with all sides equal in length and all angles right angles. **2** *nc* (*sometimes in cmpds*) something in the shape of this: *A scarf for the head is sometimes called a headsquare.* **3** *nc* an open place in a town, with the buildings round it. **4** *n* (*with cap*: *often abbrev* **Sq.** *when written*) a word used in the names of such places: *His address is 21 Sloan Square*; *He met her in Leicester Square.* **5** *nc* the resulting number when a number is multiplied by itself: *3×3, or 3^2=9, so 9 is the square of 3.* **6** *nc* (*sl derog*) a person who is not modern in ideas, style of dress *etc*: *My parents are real squares!* – *adj* **1** (*sometimes in cmpds*) having the shape of a square or right angle: *Roman camps were normally square*; *I need a square piece of paper*; *I prefer a table with rounded rather than square corners*; *He has a short, square body/a square chin*; (*facet*) *We call children square-eyed if they watch too much television*; *a tall, square-shouldered man.* **2** (*formal*: *pred*) positioned *etc* at right angles, or straight or level: *The picture isn't square in its frame.* **3** (*pred*: *inf*) (of business dealings, scores in games *etc*) level, even, fairly balanced *etc*: *If I pay you an extra £1.50 shall we be* (*all*) *square?*; *My account with the butcher is square* (= paid) *up to April 2*; *That gang/team beat us last time, but we'll soon get/be square with them*; *Their scores are* (*all*) *square* (=equal). **4** measuring a particular amount on all four sides: *This piece of wood is two metres square.* **5** (*sl derog*) old-fashioned: *She's a bit square*; *square ideas about clothes.* – *adv* **1** at right angles, or in a square shape: *The carpet is not cut square with the corner*; (*in cmpds*) *a square-built man.* **2** firmly and directly: *She hit him square on the point of the chin.* – **1** *vt* to give a square shape to or make square: *He squared* (= straightened) *his shoulders and looked very determined.* **2** *vt* (*inf*) to settle, pay *etc* (an account, debt *etc*): *I must square my account with you.* **3** *vti* (*inf*) to (cause to) fit or agree: *His story doesn't square with the facts*; *How can he square his action with his principles/conscience?* **4** *vt* to multiply a number by itself: *Two squared is four.*
squared *adj* **1** (*attrib*) marked or ruled with squares: *squared paper.* **2** having been squared.
'**squarely** *adv* directly and firmly: *He stood squarely in front of me*; *She looked squarely at me.*
square brackets *n pl* brackets of this shape: **[ ]**.
square centimetre, metre *etc nc* (*often abbrev* **cm^2** *etc when written*) an area equal to a square in which each side is one centimetre, metre *etc*: *If the door is 3 metres high and $1^1/_2$ metres wide, its area is $4^1/_2$ square metres.*
square meal *nc* a good nourishing meal: *Her children never seem to get a square meal.*
square root *nc* the number which, multiplied by itself, gives the number that is being considered: *The square root of 16 is 4* ($\sqrt{16}=4$).
fair and square directly: *He hit him fair and square on the jaw.*
go back to square one (*inf*) to start again at the beginning: *If this experiment fails, we'll have to go back to square one.*
a square deal (*inf*) an honest bargain, transaction *etc*: *You always get a square deal in that shop.*
square up (with) *vi, vt fus* (*inf*) to settle (an account): *I'll pay for the meal and we can square up/you can square up with me afterwards.*

squash [skwoʃ] **1** *vti* (*slightly inf*) to press, squeeze or crush: *He tried to squash too many clothes into his case*; *The tomatoes got squashed* (*flat*) *at the bottom of the shopping-bag*; *Fifty children were squashed into one classroom*; *We all squashed into the room to hear his talk.* **2** *vt* (*inf*) to repress or subdue (a person) *eg* with a scornful remark: *It's impossible to squash him.* **3** *vt* to defeat (a rebellion *etc*). –**1** *nc* (*inf*: *in sing with* **a**) a state of being squashed or crowded: *There was a great squash in the doorway*; *I managed to get all the books into the shelf, but it was rather a squash.* **2** *ncu* (a particular flavour of) a drink containing the juice of crushed fruit: *Squashes are quite easy to make*; *Have some orange squash!* **3** *nu* (*also* **squash rackets**) a type of game played in a walled court with rackets and a rubber ball. **4** *ncu* (*Amer*) (a) marrow.
'**squashy** *adj* (*inf*) soft or easily squashed: *The rain makes the fruit very squashy*; *a squashy ball.*

squat [skwot] – *pt, ptp* '**squatted** – *vi* **1** to sit down on the heels or in a crouching position: *The beggar squatted all day in the market place*; *He squatted down to talk to the child.* **2** to settle on land or in a building without the right to do so: *A large family has been squatting in the empty house.* – *adj* (*derog*) short and fat; dumpy: *a squat little man*; *an ugly, squat building*; *He is small and squat.*
'**squatter** *nc* a person who squats (*def 2*) on land or in a building.

squaw [skwo:] *nc* a North American Indian woman or wife.

squawk [skwo:k] *nc* a loud harsh cry made *eg* by an excited or angry bird: *The hen gave a squawk when she saw the fox*; (*facet*) *My sister uttered a squawk of pain.* – *vi* to make a sound of this sort: *The hen squawked and ran away.*

squeak [skwi:k] *nc* a shrill cry or sound: *the squeaks of the mice/puppies.* – *vi* to make a shrill cry or sound: *The door-hinge is squeaking.*
'**squeaky** *adj* making squeaks: *squeaky shoes.* '**squeakily** *adv.* '**squeakiness** *nu.*
a narrow squeak a narrow escape: *Phew! That was a narrow squeak.*

squeal [skwi:l] *nc* a long, shrill cry: *The children welcomed him with squeals of delight*; *a squeal of laughter/pain.* – *vi* **1** to give a cry of this sort: *The puppy squealed with pain.* **2** (*sl*) to act as informer:

One member of the gang squealed and they were all arrested.

squeamish ['skwi:miʃ] *adj* (*usu pred*) **1** slightly sick: *I start feeling squeamish as soon as I get on a boat.* **2** easily shocked or made to feel sick: *He's squeamish about wounds and blood.*

squeeze [skwi:z] **1** *vt* to press (something) together or from all sides tightly: *The baby likes to have a soft rubber ball to squeeze between his fingers; He squeezed her hand affectionately; Stop squeezing me!; He squeezed the clay into a ball.* **2** *vti* to force (*eg* oneself) *eg* into or through a narrow space: *The dog squeezed himself/his body into the hole; I squeezed through the gap; We were all squeezed into the back seat of the car; The room was crowded but I managed to squeeze in.* – *See also* **squeeze up** *below.* **3** *vt* to force something, *eg* liquid, out of something by pressing: *Can't you squeeze more juice out of that lemon?; She squeezed the oranges (into a jug); She squeezed the water out of her swimming-suit; (fig) We might be able to squeeze some more money/information out of him.* – *nc* **1** an act of squeezing: *He gave his sister an affectionate squeeze.* **2** a condition of being squeezed: *We all three got into the telephone box, but it was a squeeze.* **3** a few drops produced by squeezing: *You only need a small squeeze of dish-washing liquid.* **4** (*inf*) a time of financial restriction: *an economic squeeze.*

'**squeezer** *nc* (*usu in cmpds*) an instrument for squeezing: *a lemon squeezer.*

squeeze up *vi* to move closer together: *Could you all squeeze up on the bench and make room for me to sit down?*

squelch [skweltʃ] *nc* the sucking sound made by movement in a thick, sticky substance *eg* mud: *He walked through the mud with a series of squelches.* – *vi* to make squelches, *eg* by walking through mud, marsh *etc*: *He squelched across the marsh.*

squib [skwib] *nc* a type of small firework that jumps around on the ground and hisses.

a damp squib something which is expected to be exciting, effective *etc* but which completely fails to work: *The debate turned out to be a damp squib as none of the important speakers turned up.*

squid [skwid] – *pls* **squid, squids** – *nc* a type of sea creature with ten tentacles.

squiggle ['skwigl] *nc* (*inf*) a scribbled, twisting line: *His writing is just a series of illegible squiggles.*

'**squiggly** *adj.*

squint [skwint] *vi* **1** to have the physical defect of having the eyes turning towards or away from each other or to cause the eyes to do this: *The child squints; You squint when you look down at your nose.* **2** (*with* **at, up at, through** *etc*) to look with half-shut or narrowed eyes: *He squinted up at the sun; He squinted through the telescope.* – *nc* **1** a squinting position of the eyes: *The child is going to have an eye-operation to correct her squint.* **2** (*sl*) a glance or look at something: *Let me have a squint at that photograph.* – *adj* (*usu pred*), *adv* (placed *etc*) crookedly or not straight: *Your hat is squint; You've stuck the stamp on squint.*

squire ['skwaiə] *nc* **1** (*old*: *with cap in titles*) an English gentleman owning a large amount of land in the country district: *the local squire; Squire Jones.* **2** (*hist*) a young man who attended a knight in preparation for becoming one himself. – *vt* (*old or facet*) to escort (a lady): *He squired her to the dance.*

squirm [skwə:m] *vi* **1** to twist the body or wriggle: *He lay squirming on the ground with pain; The child squirmed out of his grasp.* **2** (*inf*) to be very embarrassed or ashamed: *I squirmed when I thought of how rude I'd been.*

squirrel ['skwirəl, (*Amer*) 'skwə:rəl] *nc* a type of animal of the rodent family, *usu* either reddish-brown or grey, with a large bushy tail.

squirt [skwə:t] *vti* to (make a liquid *etc*) shoot out in a narrow jet: *The elephant squirted water over itself; Water squirted from the hose; He squirted me with his water pistol.* – *nc* (*sl derog*) an unimportant but nasty person: *That little squirt!*

Sri Lanka *see* Appendix 2.

stab [stab] – *pt, ptp* **stabbed** – *vt* to wound or pierce with a pointed instrument or weapon: *He stabbed him (through the heart/in the chest) with a dagger; He stabbed the knife into her back; (fig formal) I was stabbed with remorse.* – *See also* **stab at** *below.* – *nc* an act of stabbing or a piercing blow: *In the fight, he received a stab in the shoulder; (fig) He felt a stab of pain/conscience.*

'**stabbing** *adj* (*usu attrib*) (of pain *etc*) very acute as though caused by a stab: *He complained of a stabbing pain just before he collapsed.*

have a stab at (doing) something (*inf*) to try (to do) something: *I must have a stab at mending this machine.*

'**stab at** *vt fus* to make poking or stabbing movements in the direction of: *The soldiers kept stabbing at them with their bayonets.*

stab (someone) in the back (*fig*) to behave treacherously towards someone: *He always pretended to be her friend but he stabbed her in the back by applying for her job when she was in hospital.*

a stab in the back a treacherous act: *The government's refusal to allow a pay-rise is a stab in the back.*

stable[1] ['steibl] *adj* (*neg* **un-**) **1** (*more formal than* **steady**: *usu pred*) firm and steady or well-balanced: *This chair isn't very stable.* **2** firmly established and likely to last: *a stable government; How stable is the present government?* **3** (of a person or his character) unlikely to become unreasonably upset or hysterical: *She's the only stable person in the whole family; She is not stable enough to be a schoolteacher.* **4** (*tech*) (of a substance) not easily decomposed.

stability [stə'bi-] *nu* the quality of being stable: *He has great stability of character; There are doubts about the stability of these cars.*

'**stabilize, -ise** [-bi-] *vt* (*formal*) to make (more) stable: *He put a wedge of paper under the table to stabilize it; People with epilepsy and similar diseases can take pills to stabilize their condition.*

ˌ**stabili'zation, -s-** *nu.*

'**stabilizer, -s-** [-bi-] *nc* a device on a ship or aeroplane or (*in pl*) on a child's bicycle that keeps it steady and stops it rolling or tipping: *You should buy a bike with stabilizers for your five-year-old child.*

See also **instability**.

stable[2] ['steibl] *nc* **1** a building in which horses are kept. **2** (*in pl*) a horse-keeping establishment: *He runs the riding stables.* **3** a number of horses, *esp* race-horses, kept by one owner. – *vt* to put or keep (a horse) in a stable: *He looked for an inn where he could sleep and stable his horse.*

staccato [stə'ka:tou] *adj* (*usu attrib*), *adv* **1** (*music*) with each note played separately, with a short, clear sound: *a staccato passage; Play these notes staccato.* **2** (of speaking) (done) in a jerky manner: *She spoke in staccato tones.*

stack [stak] *nc* **1** a large, *usu* neatly shaped, pile *eg* of hay, straw, wood *etc*: *a haystack*; *The rifles were put into a stack.* **2** a set of shelves for books *eg* in a library. – *vt* to arrange in a large, *usu* neat, pile: *The planks of wood were stacked neatly against the wall*; *Stack the books up against the wall.*

stacks of (*inf*) a large quantity of: *I've got stacks of letters to write.*

stadium ['steidiəm] – *pls* '**stadiums,** '**stadia** [-diə] – *nc* a large sports-ground or racecourse *usu* with seats for spectators: *The athletics competitions were held in the new Olympic stadium.*

staff[1] [sta:f] *nc* **1** (*old*) a stick on which a person can support himself in walking *etc*: *He carried a wooden staff.* **2** a rod carried in ceremonies by someone in authority: *The mayor carried his staff of office.*

staff[2] [sta:f] *nc or n pl* **1** a group of people employed in running a business, school *etc*: *The school has a large teaching staff*; *The staff are annoyed about the changes in the timetable*; *How long has she been on the staff of the library/a member of the library staff?* **2** (*mil*) a group of officers helping a commanding officer: *the general and his staff*; (*attrib*) *a staff sergeant/officer.* – *vt* to supply (a school *etc*) with staff: *Most of our offices are staffed by volunteers.*

'**staffroom** *nc* a sitting-room for the staff of *eg* a school: *A meeting will be held in the staffroom*; (*attrib*) *staffroom gossip/politics.*

staff[3] [sta:f], **stave** [steiv] – *pl* **staves** – *nc* (*music*) a set of lines and spaces on which music is written or printed.

stag [stag] *nc* a male deer, *esp* a red deer.

'**stag party** *nc* a party without women: *He had a stag party the night before his wedding.*

stage[1] [steidʒ] *nc* a platform *esp* for performing or acting on, *eg* in a theatre: *Wagner's operas need a large stage.* – *See also* **the stage** *below.* – *vt* **1** to prepare and produce (a play *etc*) in a theatre *etc*: *This play was first staged in 1928.* **2** to organize (an event *etc*): *The protesters are planning to stage a demonstration outside the Houses of Parliament*; *He wants to stage a come-back as a filmstar.*

'**staging** *nu* **1** wooden planks *etc* forming a platform *eg* on builders' scaffolding: *The staging collapsed.* **2** the way in which a play *etc* is presented on a stage: *The staging was good, but the acting poor.*

'**stagy** *adj* (*inf derog*) theatrical or of or like actors: *He speaks in a rather stagy way.*

stage direction *nc* an order to an actor playing a part to do this or that: *a stage direction to enter from the left.*

'**stage fright** *nu* the nervousness felt by an actor *etc* when in front of an audience, *esp* for the first time: *The young actress was suffering from stage fright and could not utter a word.*

'**stagehand** *nc* a workman employed to help with scenery *etc.*

ˌ**stage-'manage** *vt* **1** to be the stage manager of (a play *etc*). **2** (*fig*) to be in charge of the organization of (*eg* a military operation, a large-scale robbery *etc*): *The police failed to arrest the man who had stage-managed the escape of the prisoners.*

stage manager *nc* a person who is in charge of scenery and equipment for plays *etc.*

'**stage-struck** *adj* (*often derog*) having a great desire to be an actor: *He wants his daughter to go to university but she is stage-struck*; *a stage-struck teenager.*

stage whisper *nc* a loud whisper that is intended to be heard by the audience.

the stage the profession of an actor; theatrical work, productions *etc*: *He chose the stage as a career*; *Would you like to go on the stage?*; *He has worked for the stage as a designer.*

stage[2] [steidʒ] *nc* **1** a period or step in the development of something: *The plan is in its early stages*; *Most teenagers go through a rebellious stage*; *At this stage, we don't know how many people have survived the air crash*; *a three-stage development programme.* **2** part of a journey: *The first stage of our journey to Cyprus will be the flight from London to Gibraltar.* **3** a section of a bus route, or a bus stop marking these sections: *It costs 10 pence to travel three stages.* **4** one of the separable sections of a rocket: *a three-stage rocket.*

'**stagecoach** *nc* (*hist*) a horse-drawn public coach taking passengers over a regular route.

stagger ['stagə] **1** *vi* to sway, move or walk unsteadily: *The drunk man staggered along the road*; *The blow sent him staggering across the room.* **2** *vt* (*inf*) to astonish: *I was staggered to hear he had died.* **3** *vt* to arrange (people's hours of work, holidays *etc*) so that they do not begin and end at the same times: *Our management has decided to stagger our working-hours.*

'**staggering** *adj* causing unsteadiness, shock or astonishment: *He received a staggering blow on the side of the head*; *staggering events*; *There has been a staggering increase in crime recently*; *That piece of news is staggering.*

staging *see* **stage**[1].

stagnant ['stagnənt] *adj* **1** (of water) standing still rather than flowing and therefore *usu* dirty: *a stagnant pool*; *That water is stagnant.* **2** dull or inactive: *This country is suffering from a stagnant economy*; *Our economy is stagnant.*

stagnate [stag'neit, (*Amer*) 'stagneit] *vi* **1** (of water) to be or become stagnant. **2** to become dull and inactive through lack of change, development, stimulation *etc*: *Some women find that their minds stagnate when they cannot go out to work.*

stag'nation *nu.*

stagy *see* **stage**[1].

staid [steid] *adj* (*sometimes derog*) (of a person or his manner *etc*) (over-)serious or old-fashioned: *A person of staid appearance/habits*; *Her choice of clothes is very staid.*

stain [stein] **1** *vti* to leave a (permanent) dirty mark or coloured patch on *eg* a fabric: *The coffee I spilt has stained the carpet*; *Does blackberry juice stain or can it be washed off?*; (*liter fig*) *The great king's name was stained with acts of cruelty.* **2** *vi* to become marked in this way: *Silk stains easily.* **3** *vt* to dye or colour (*eg* wood): *The wooden chairs had been stained brown.* – **1** *nc* a dirty mark on a fabric *etc* that is difficult or impossible to remove: *His overall was covered with paint-stains*; (*liter fig*) *There is not the slightest stain upon her reputation.* **2** *nu* a type of dye or colouring for wood *etc*: *I need some more stain for the floor.*

stained glass *nu* glass into which colour has been fixed by a special process, used in church windows *etc*: *The church is famous for its stained glass*; (*attrib*) *stained-glass windows.*

stainless steel *nu, adj* (of) a metal alloy composed of steel and chromium that does not rust: *a sink made of stainless steel*; *stainless steel knives/cutlery.*

stair [steə] *nc* (any one of) a number of steps, *usu* inside a building, going from one floor to another:

Although the house is old, the stair and floors are in good condition; He fell down the stairs; The top stair creaks when you step on it.

'staircase, 'stairway *ncs* a series or flight of stairs often with a rail for the hand on one or both sides: *A dark and narrow staircase led up to the top floor.*

'stair rod *nc* a rod of metal, wood *etc* placed in the angle between two stairs to keep the carpet in position.

stake[1] [steik] *nc* a strong stick or post, *usu* with one or both ends pointed, that can be pushed into the ground *eg* to support a young tree *etc*, or as an upright support for fencing *etc*. – *vt* to fasten or support (something) with a stake: *He planted and staked all the new trees.*

the stake (*hist*) the post to which a person was tied to be burnt to death as a punishment: *Many men and women went to/died at/were burnt at the stake for heretical religious beliefs.*

stake a claim (*usu fig*) to assert or establish one's ownership or right to something: *You ought to stake your claim to the property.*

stake out *vt sep* to mark the boundary of (a piece of territory *etc*) with stakes: *They are staking out the ground for a new football pitch.*

stake[2] [steik] *nc* a sum of money risked in betting: *He and his friends enjoy playing cards for high stakes.* – *See also* **at stake** *below.* – *vt* to bet or risk (money or something of value): *I'm going to stake £2 on that horse; I'm sure my idea is correct – I'll stake my life/reputation on it.*

at 'stake 1 to be won or lost: *A great deal of money is at stake.* **2** in great danger: *The peace of the country/Our children's future is at stake.*

have a 'stake in (something) to have an investment in (a business *etc*) or an interest or concern in something: *He has a stake in several companies; We all have a stake in the future of the world.*

stalactite ['staləktait, (*Amer*) stə'laktait] *nc* a spike of limestone hanging from the roof of a cave *etc* formed by the dripping of water containing lime.

stalagmite ['staləgmait, (*Amer*) stə'lagmait] *nc* a spike of limestone rising from the floor of a cave, formed by water dripping from the roof.

stale [steil] *adj* **1** (of food *etc*) not fresh and therefore dry and tasteless: *stale bread; The beer is stale.* **2** no longer interesting because done, heard *etc* too often before: *stale news; His ideas are stale and dull.* **3** (*usu pred*) (of a person) no longer able to work *etc* well because of too much study, training, practice *etc*: *If she practises the piano for more than two hours a day, she will grow stale.*

stalemate ['steilmeit] *nu* **1** (*chess*) a position in which a player cannot move without putting his king in danger. **2** (*fig*) in any contest, dispute *etc*, a position in which neither side can win: *The recent discussions ended in stalemate.*

stalk[1] [sto:k] *nc* the stem of a plant or of a leaf, flower or fruit: *If the stalk is damaged, the plant may die; When cutting flowers, cut the stalks as long as possible; cherry stalks.*

stalk[2] [sto:k] **1** *vi* to walk stiffly and proudly, *eg* in anger: *He stalked out of the room after she had criticized his work.* **2** *vti* (*liter*) (of some evil force) to move menacingly through a place: *Disease and famine stalk (through) the country.* **3** *vti* in hunting, to move gradually as close as possible to game, *eg* deer, trying to remain hidden: *Have you ever stalked deer/been deer-stalking?; He has gone stalking today.*

'stalker *nc* a person who stalks game.

stall[1] [sto:l] *nc* **1** a three-sided compartment for one animal in a cowshed, stable *etc*: *cattle stalls.* **2** (*sometimes in cmpds*) a small shop with an open front or a counter or table on which goods are displayed for sale: *He bought a newspaper at the bookstall on the station; On market day, the town square is full of traders' stalls.* **3** in a church, a partly enclosed seat for *eg* (a member of) the clergy or choir.

stalls *n pl* (*often with* **the**) in a theatre, the seats on the ground floor: *I've booked three seats in the stalls; I always sit in the stalls;* (*attrib*) *a stalls seat.*

stall[2] [sto:l] **1** *vi* (of a car *etc* or its engine) to stop suddenly through lack of power, braking too quickly *etc*: *The car stalled when I was halfway up the hill.* **2** *vi* (of an aircraft) to lose speed while flying and so go out of control: *The plane stalled just after take-off and crashed on to the runway.* **3** *vt* to cause (a car *etc*, or aircraft) to do this: *Use the brake gently or you'll stall the engine.* – *nc* a dangerous loss of flying speed in an aircraft, causing it to drop: *The plane went into a stall.*

stall[3] [sto:l] *vi* (*inf*) to avoid making a definite decision in order to give oneself more time: *They're stalling for time; The town council is stalling over the proposals for a new swimming pool.*

stallion ['staljən] *nc* a fully-grown male horse, *esp* one kept for breeding.

stalwart ['sto:lwət] *adj* **1** (*often liter*) strong and sturdy: *a man of stalwart build; The prince was tall and stalwart.* **2** (*usu attrib*) firm and loyal: *stalwart support; a stalwart supporter of the cause.* – *nc* (*often inf*) a firm and loyal supporter (of a political party *etc*): *Most of the party's stalwarts were at the meeting.*

stamen ['steimən] *nc* (*tech*) one of the thread-like spikes in the middle of a flower that bear the pollen.

stamina ['staminə] *nu* (*formal or facet*) strength or power to endure fatigue *etc*: *Long-distance runners require plenty of stamina; I haven't got the stamina to cope with young children.*

stammer ['stamə] *nc* (*usu in sing with* **a**) the speech defect of being unable to produce easily certain sounds when they occur at the beginning of words, so that such sounds are repeated: *'You m-m-must m-m-meet m-m-my m-m-mother' is an example of a stammer; That child has a bad stammer.* – *vti* to speak with a stammer or in a similarly uncontrolled way because of *eg* fright, nervousness *etc*: *Clever people, especially men, quite often stammer; He was stammering with fright; 'Wh-what do you w-want?' stammered the frightened girl; He stammered an apology.*

'stammerer *nc* a person who has a stammer.

stammer out *vt sep* to say (something) with a stammer; to stammer (something): *He stammered his explanation out with difficulty; He stammered out an explanation.*

stamp [stamp] **1** *vti* to bring (the foot) down with force (on the ground): *He stamped his foot with rage; She was stamping with fury; He threw his sister's doll on the floor and stamped on it.* **2** *vt* to print or mark (a design, words *etc*) on to (a surface): *He stamped the date at the top of his letter; The oranges were all stamped with the exporter's name;* (*fig formal*) *His experiences had stamped his features with a look of despair;* (*fig formal*) *His behaviour at that time stamped him as a person of courage.* **3** *vt* to stick a postage stamp on (a letter *etc*): *I've addressed the envelope but haven't stamped it.* – *nc* **1** an act of stamping (*def 1*): *'Give it to me!' she shouted with an angry stamp of her foot.* **2** (*sometimes in cmpds*) the object with which a design *etc* is stamped on a surface: *He marked the date on the form with a rubber date-stamp.* **3** a postage stamp: *He stuck the stamps on the parcel*; *He collects foreign stamps.* **4** a design *etc* made by stamping (*def 2*): *All the goods bore the manufacturer's stamp*; (*fig*) *All his work has the stamp of quality.* **5** (*usu in sing*: *fig formal*) a kind or quality: *He and his brother are men of a different stamp.*

'stamp duty *nu* a tax on *eg* legal papers, paid by using specially stamped paper or by putting on a stamp.

'stamping-ground *nc* (*often facet*) a place where *eg* certain wild animals or a person or people can usually be found: *The auction rooms are his stamping-ground*; *He's gone off to a new stamping-ground – he's looking for a new girlfriend.*

stamp out *vt sep* **1** to put out or extinguish (a fire) by stamping on it: *She stamped the remains of the fire out*; *The fire has been stamped out.* **2** to crush or subdue (a rebellion *etc*): *The new king stamped out all opposition to his rule.*

stampede [stam'pi:d] *nc* a sudden wild rush (of frightened animals or (*often facet*) of a large number of people): *a stampede of buffaloes*; *The school bell rang for lunch and there was a stampede for the door.* – **1** *vti* to (cause to) rush in a stampede: *The noise stampeded the elephants/made the elephants stampede.* **2** *vt* (*inf*) to force (a person) into a rash or hasty action or decision: *Don't be stampeded into buying a house that you don't like!*

stance [sta:ns] *ncu* (*formal*) a person's position or manner of standing, *eg* in playing golf, cricket *etc*: *His stance is good.*

stanch [sta:ntʃ], **staunch** [sto:ntʃ] *vt* (*formal*) to stop (the flow of *eg* blood from a wound): *He tried to staunch the flow of blood by tying a bandage round his leg.*

stand [stand] – *pt*, *ptp* **stood** [stud] – **1** *vi* to be in an upright position, not sitting or lying: *His leg was so painful that he could hardly stand*; *There were no chairs, so she had to stand*; *After the storm, few trees were left standing*; *The village has changed greatly and few of the original buildings still stand.* **2** *vi* (*often with* **up**) to rise to the feet: *He pushed back his chair and stood up*; *Some people like to stand (up) when the National Anthem is played.* **3** *vi* to remain motionless: *The train stood for an hour outside Newcastle.* **4** *vi* to remain unchanged: *This law has stood for many centuries*; *The arrangement still stands.* **5** *vi* to be in or have a particular place: *A grandfather clock stood in the corner*; *That chair usually stands by the wall*; *There is now a factory where our house once stood.* **6** *vi* (*formal*) to be in a particular state, condition or situation: *He stands in terrible danger*; *As matters stand* (= In the present situation) *we can do nothing to help*; *How do you stand financially?*; *He stands well with* (= is approved of by) *the manager*; *No playwright can rival Shakespeare – he stands alone.* **7** *vi* to accept or offer oneself for a particular position *etc*: *He is standing as Parliamentary candidate for North Edinburgh*; (*formal*) *He stood sponsor for the scheme*; (*formal*) *She stood godmother to her nephew.* **8** *vt* to put in a particular position, *esp* upright: *He picked up the fallen chair and stood it beside the table.* **9** *vt* to undergo (a test, legal trial *etc*) or endure (something unpleasant): *These houses have stood the test of time* (= have lasted well); *He will stand (his) trial for murder* (= will be tried for murder); *She was dreading her husband's funeral, but she stood it very well*; *I can't stand her/her rudeness any longer.* **10** *vt* (*inf*) to pay for (a meal *etc*) for (a person): *Let me stand you a drink!* – *nc* **1** a position or place in which to stand ready to fight, resist attack *etc*, or an act of resisting: *The guard took up his stand* (= went to his post) *at the gate*; (*fig*) *We must take/make a firm stand against the lowering of educational standards*; *I shall make a stand for what I believe is right.* **2** (*sometimes in cmpds*) an object, *esp* a piece of furniture, for holding or supporting something: *He hung his coat on the coat-stand*; *The sculpture had been removed from its stand for cleaning.* **3** a stall or other structure where goods are displayed for sale or advertisement: *Only the larger publishing firms had a stand at the book fair.* **4** a large structure beside a football pitch, race course *etc* with rows of seats for spectators: *The stand was crowded.* – *See also* **grandstand**. **5** (*Amer*) a witness box in a law court: *The accused took* (= entered) *the stand.*

'standing *adj* (*attrib*) permanent or remaining permanently in readiness: *She has a standing order at the grocer's for two pints of milk a day*; *His supposed ill-health is a standing joke*; *The general's standing orders must be obeyed*; *The standing committee meets every month.* – *nu* **1** duration or time of lasting: *an agreement of long standing.* **2** social position, rank or reputation: *a diplomat of high standing*; *He has a high standing among his fellow musicians.*

'stand-by – *pl* **'stand-bys** – **1** *nu* readiness for action: *Two fire-engines went directly to the fire, and a third was on stand-by* (= ready to go if ordered). **2** *nc* something that can be used in an emergency *etc*: *Fruit is a good stand-by when children get hungry between meals.* – *adj* (*attrib*) (of an airline passenger or ticket) costing or paying less than the usual fare, as the passenger does not book a seat for a particular flight, but waits for the first free seat: *There are several stand-by passengers waiting to go to London.* – *adv* travelling in this way: *It costs a lot less to travel stand-by.* – *See also* **stand by** *below.*

'stand-in *nc* a person who takes someone else's job *etc* for a temporary period, *esp* in making films: *When the dangerous stunts are filmed, they use a stand-in in case the star hurts himself.* – *See also* **stand in** *below.*

'standing-room *nu* space for standing only, not sitting: *There was standing-room only on the bus.*

'stand-up *adj* (*attrib*) **1** (*often fig*) (of a fight) with both contestants standing up and hitting each other: *The argument developed into a stand-up fight.* **2** (of a collar) intended to stand upright, not lie flat. – *See also* **stand up** *below.*

make one's hair stand on end to frighten one very greatly: *The horrible scream made his hair stand on end.*

,one-night 'stand 1 a stay of one night at a place, *eg* for a touring theatrical company: *They toured Germany doing a series of one-night stands.* **2** (*vulg*) (a partner in) a sexual liaison lasting only for a single night: *He regarded her as a one-night stand.*

stand aside *vi* to move to one side or withdraw out of someone's way: *He stood aside to let me past.*

stand back *vi* to move backwards or away: *A*

crowd gathered round the injured man, but a policeman ordered everyone to stand back.

stand by 1 *vi* to watch something happening without doing anything: *I couldn't just stand by while he was hitting the child.* **2** *vi* to be ready to act: *The police are standing by in case of trouble.* **3** *vt fus* to support or maintain: *She stood by him throughout his trial; I stand by my principles.* – *See also* **stand-by** *above.*

stand clear of (something) to move away from (something) *eg* for safety: *Stand clear of the train doors!*

stand down *vi* to withdraw *eg* from a contest: *Two of the candidates have stood down.*

stand fast/firm to refuse to yield: *I'm standing firm on/over this issue.*

'stand for *vt fus* **1** to be a candidate for election to (*eg* the British parliament): *He stood for Parliament/one of the London constituencies.* **2** to be an abbreviation for: *HQ stands for Headquarters.* **3** to represent: *I hate commercialism and all it stands for.* **4** (*more inf than* **tolerate**) to tolerate: *I won't stand for her rudeness.*

stand one's ground *see* **ground.**

stand in *vi* (*usu with* **for**) to take another person's place, job *etc* for a time: *Could you stand in for me as chairman of the meeting?; The leading actor was ill and another actor stood in for him.* – *See also* **stand-in** *above.*

stand on one's own (two) feet to manage one's own affairs without help: *I won't always be here to help you – it's time you learned to stand on your own feet.*

stand out *vi* **1** to be noticeable because exceptional: *They were all pretty, but she stood out among them.* **2** (*formal*) to go on resisting or to refuse to yield: *The garrison stood out (against the besieging army) as long as possible.*

stand over *vt fus* to supervise (a person) closely: *I have to stand over him to make him do his schoolwork.*

stand to *vi* (*esp mil*) to prepare for action: *The troops were ordered to stand to in case of attack.*

stand to win, gain, lose *etc* to be likely to win or lose (a contest, sum of money *etc*): *If the dispute is settled in her favour, she stands to gain £20 000.*

stand up *vt sep* (*sl*) not to keep a promise to meet (*eg* a girlfriend): *You've stood me up three times this week!* – *See also* **stand-up** *above.*

stand up for *vt fus* to support or defend (*eg* a person) in a dispute *etc*: *I thanked him for standing up for me/my proposals.*

stand up to *vt fus* to show resistance to: *He stood up to the bigger boys who tried to bully him; These chairs have stood up to very hard wear.*

standard ['standəd] **1** *nc* something used as a basis of measurement: *The kilogram is the international standard of weight.* **2** *nc* a basis for judging quality or a level of excellence aimed at, required or achieved: *You can't judge an amateur artist's work by the same standards as you would judge that of a trained, professional artist; She sets high standards of behaviour for herself and her children; His performance did not reach the required standard; This school has a high academic standard; The standard of work done by these builders is poor; Her work is of a high standard.* **3** *nc* a flag or carved figure *etc* fixed to a pole and carried *eg* at the front of an army going into battle: *The Roman standards were in the shape of eagles; The socialist standard is the Red Flag.* **4** *n* (*with cap*) a word often used in the titles of newspapers: *the Western Standard.* – *adj* (accepted as) normal or usual: *The Post Office likes the public to use a standard size of envelope; £1 is the standard charge for this service; Are these fittings standard on this type of car?*

,standardi'zation, -s- *nu* (*formal*) the act of standardizing or process of being standardized: *There was little standardization of English spelling until the nineteenth century.*

'standardize, -ise *vt* (*formal*) to make or keep (products *etc*) of one size, shape *etc*: *All parts of this sewing machine are standardized, so that it is very simple to get replacements for them.*

'standard-bearer *nc* a person who carries a standard or banner.

standard lamp *nc* a lamp on a tall support, which stands on the floor.

be up to/below standard to (fail to) achieve the required standard: *Her work is well up to standard.*

standard of living the level of comfort and welfare achieved in any particular society: *Scandinavia has a higher standard of living than Britain.*

stand-offish [stand'ofiʃ] *adj* (*derog*) (of a person or his manner *etc*) unfriendly: *The neighbours were rather stand-offish when we first moved into this house; stand-offish people.*

standpipe ['standpaip] *nc* a vertical pipe in which water is kept under pressure, *eg* in a street.

standpoint ['standpoint] *nc* a position from which a person views or considers something: *From my standpoint the new car-parking arrangements are very convenient.*

standstill ['standstil]: **be at, come to, reach a standstill** to remain without moving; to stop, halt *etc*: *The traffic was at a standstill; Production at the factory has come to a standstill.*

stank *see* **stink.**

stanza ['stanzə] *nc* (*liter*) a group of lines making up a part of a poem; a verse.

staple[1] ['steipl] *nc* **1** a chief product of trade or industry: *Paper is one of the staples of Sweden.* **2** a chief or main item (of diet, reading *etc*): *Bananas form the staple of their diet.* – *adj* (*attrib*) main or chief: *Romantic novels are her staple reading.*

staple[2] ['steipl] *nc* **1** a U-shaped type of nail. **2** a similarly-shaped piece of wire that is driven through sheets of paper *etc* to fasten them together. – *vt* to fasten or attach (paper *etc*) with staples: *He stapled the two letters together/the drawing to the board.*

'stapler *nc* an instrument for stapling papers *etc.*

star [sta:] *nc* **1** the fixed bodies in the sky, which are really distant suns: *The Sun is a star, and the Earth is one of its planets.* **2** (*loosely*) any of the bodies in the sky appearing as points of light: *The sky was cloudless and full of stars.* **3** (*often in pl*) any of these heavenly bodies considered as able to influence a person's destiny, fortune *etc*: *Many newspapers have a column on the stars, telling you your fortune for the next day; What star were you born under?* **4** an object, shape or figure with a number of pointed rays, *usu* five or six, often used as a means of marking quality *etc*: *The Star of David has six points; The teacher stuck a gold star on the child's neat exercise book; A four-star hotel is better than a three-star hotel.* **5** a leading actor or actress or other well-known performer *eg* in sport *etc*: *She wants to be a film/television star; a football star;* (*attrib*) *She has had many star rôles in films;* (*attrib*) *The singer got star billing* (=prominent display of her name on posters *etc*) *for her part in the show*. – *v* – *pt, ptp* **starred** – **1** *vt* to mark with a star or asterisk: *I've read the catalogue and starred the items I want you to order.* **2** *vi* to play a leading rôle in a play, film *etc*: *She has starred in two recent films.* **3** *vt* (of a film *etc*) to have (a certain actor *etc*) as its leading performer: *This film, starring Sir Alec Guinness, will be shown next week.*

'**stardom** *nu* the state of being a famous performer: *He's a good actor, but he'll never achieve stardom.*

'**starless** *adj* (of the sky, night *etc*) clouded with no stars visible: *a starless night*; *The sky was starless.*

'**starlet** [-lit] *nc* a young (film) actress on her way to becoming a star.

'**starry** *adj* full of or shining like stars: *a starry sky/night*; *Her eyes were bright and starry.* – *See also* **starry-eyed** *below.*

'**starfish** *nc* a type of small sea creature with five points as arms.

'**stargazer** *nc* (*facet*) an astronomer or astrologer or (*derog*) a dreamy, impractical person. '**stargazing** *nu.*

'**starlight** *nu* the light from the stars.

'**starlit** *adj* (*usu attrib*) bright with stars: *a starlit night.*

ˌ**starry-'eyed** *adj* **1** having eyes shining with happiness. **2** (*derog*) too naïve and idealistic: *He's one of those starry-eyed people who want to reform the world*; *She is too starry-eyed.*

star turn *nc* the most successful or spectacular performance or item (in a show *etc*): *The acrobats were the star turn of the evening.*

see stars (*inf*) to see flashes of light as a result of a hard blow on the head: *I banged my head on the car door and saw stars.*

the Stars and Stripes the flag of the United States of America.

thank one's lucky stars (*inf*) to be grateful for one's good luck: *I thanked my lucky stars that he hadn't noticed my mistake.*

See also **stellar**.

starboard ['sta:bəd] *nu* (*tech*) the right side of a ship or aircraft, from the point of view of a person looking towards the bow or front: *Rocks were sighted to starboard*; (*attrib*) *the starboard bow/wing.*

starch [sta:tʃ] *nu* **1** a white food substance found *esp* in flour, potatoes *etc*: *Bread contains a great deal of starch.* **2** a powder prepared from this, used for stiffening clothes: *Starch was once used regularly by housewives for stiffening shirt collars and cuffs.* – *vt* to stiffen (clothes) with starch: *She starched the dress to make the skirt stick out more.*

'**starchy** *adj* **1** like or containing starch: *cake, biscuits and other starchy foods.* **2** (*derog*) too formal in manner or prim in attitude: *Her parents are rather starchy*; *She gave him a starchy smile.* '**starchiness** *nu.*

stardom *see* **star**.

stare [steə] *vti* (*often with* **at**) to look at (something) with a fixed gaze: *They stared at her clothes in amazement*; *Don't stare – it's rude!*; *The dead body lay on its back and its eyes were open and staring*; *He stared her straight in the eye* (= looked directly at her). – *nc* a staring look: *He fixed her with an insolent stare* (= looked intently and insolently at her).

stare (someone) in the face 1 (*fig inf*) to be easy to see or obvious: *The pencil I lost/The answer to the problem was staring me in the face.* **2** (of something unpleasant) to seem to be inevitable: *Ruin stared him in the face.*

stare out *vt sep* to stare at (a person, animal *etc*) for longer than he/it can stare at oneself: *People used to be taught that a wolf would not attack them if they stared it out.*

starfish, stargazer *see* **star**.

stark [sta:k] *adj* **1** (*formal*) (of *eg* a landscape, scenery, artistic style *etc*) bare, harsh or simple in a severe way: *a stark, rocky landscape*; *The scenery and lighting for the play are stark and simple*; *his stark descriptions of the horrors of the Vietnam War.* **2** (*attrib*) complete, utter or sheer: *His plan is a piece of stark idiocy.*

stark crazy/mad (*inf*) completely mad: *He must be stark mad!*

stark naked (of a person) completely naked: *The children were playing on the beach stark naked.*

starlet, starlight, starlit, starless *see* **star**.

starling ['sta:liŋ] *nc* a type of small bird with glossy dark feathers.

starry *see* **star**.

start[1] [sta:] **1** *vi* to leave or begin a journey: *We shall have to start at 5.30 a.m. in order to get to the boat in time.* **2** *vi* (*sometimes with* **on**), *vt* to begin: *He starts working at six o'clock every morning*; *She started to cry*; *She starts her job at the shop next week*; *Haven't you started* (*on*) *your meal yet?*; *This is not good weather for starting on a journey*; *What time does the play start?* **3** *vti* to (cause an engine *etc* to) begin to work: *I can't start the car*; *The car won't start*; *The clock stopped but I started it again.* **4** *vt* to cause something to begin or begin happening *etc*: *One of the students decided to start a college magazine*; *What started you taking an interest in archaeology?* – *nc* **1** the beginning of an activity, scheme, journey, race *etc*: *I told him right at/from the start that his idea would not succeed*; *The runners lined up at the start*; *He stayed in the lead after a good start*; *I shall have to make a start on* (= begin doing) *that work.* **2** (*no pl*) in a race *etc*, the advantage of beginning before or further forward than others, or the amount of time, distance *etc* gained through this: *The youngest child in the race got a start of five metres*; *The driver of the stolen car already had twenty minutes' start/a start of twenty minutes before the police began the pursuit.*

'**starter** *nc* **1** a person, horse *etc* that actually runs *etc* in a race: *After several withdrawals, there were only seven starters.* **2** a person who gives the signal for the race to start: *He did not see the starter's signal.* **3** a device in a car *etc* for starting the engine: *He pulled the starter but nothing happened.*

'**starting-point** *nc* the point from which something begins: *The anonymous letter was the starting-point of the police investigation.*

for a 'start (used in argument *etc*) in the first place, or as the first point in an argument: *You can't have a new bicycle because for a start we can't afford one.*

get off to a good, bad start to start well or badly in a race, business *etc*: *The new scheme got off to a good start.*

get 'started on (something) (*inf*) to start doing *etc* or talking about (something): *I'd better get started on* (*making*) *the supper.*

start back *vi* to begin a return journey: *We ought to start back soon.*

start off 1 *vi* to begin a journey: *It's time we started* *off.* **2** *vt sep* to cause or allow something to begin, someone to start doing something *etc*: *The money lent to him by his father started him off as a bookseller; She had stopped crying, but his remark started her off again.*

start out *vi* to begin a journey; to start off: *To arrive there in the afternoon we shall have to start out at dawn.*

start up *vi, vt sep* to (cause to) begin or begin working *etc*: *The machine suddenly started up; Her eye trouble has started up again; What started it up again?; He has started up a new boys' club in the town.*

to 'start with 1 at the beginning: *He was very nervous to start with.* **2** (used in argument *etc*) as the first point in an argument: *There are many reasons why he shouldn't get the job. To start with, he isn't qualified.*

See also **non-starter**.

art[2] [sta:t] *vi* **1** (*more formal than* **jump**) to jump or jerk suddenly *eg* because of fright, surprise *etc*: *The sudden noise made me start; She started up from her chair in alarm.* **2** to rise or spring suddenly: *The pain made tears start from her eyes.* – *nc* **1** (*more formal than* **jump**) a sudden movement of the body: *He gave a start of surprise.* **2** a shock: *What a start the news gave me!*

start back *vi* to jump or step backwards suddenly *eg* in fright: *He started back in terror when he saw the snake.*

artle ['sta:tl] *vt* to give a shock or surprise to: *The sound startled me; The announcement is bound to startle many people.*

arve [sta:v] **1** *vti* to (cause to) die, or suffer greatly, from hunger: *In a bad winter, many birds and animals starve (to death); They were accused of starving their prisoners.* **2** *vi* (*inf*) to be very hungry: *Can't we have supper now? I'm starving.* **3** *vt* to deprive: *As a child, he was starved of love.*

star'vation *nu* a starving state: *They died of starvation;* (*attrib*) *a starvation diet.*

starve out *vt sep* (of a besieging army *etc*) to force (a city, garrison *etc*) to surrender, by preventing supplies of food from reaching it.

ate[1] [steit] **1** *nc* (*usu in sing*) the condition in which a thing or person is: *the bad state of the roads; The room was in an untidy state; His nerves are in a bad state; It is difficult to know what her state of mind* (= attitude) *is; He inquired about her state of health; What is the present state of affairs* (= present situation) *in their marriage?; What a state you're in!* (= How upset, angry, dirty *etc* you are!); *He was in no fit state/not in a fit state/not in any fit state to drive the car.* – *See also* **get into a state** *below.* **2** *ncu* (*often with cap*) a country considered as a political community, or, as in the United States, one division of a federation: *The Prime Minister visits the Queen once a week to discuss affairs of state; Which industries belong to the state?; The care of the sick and elderly is considered partly the responsibility of the state; In America, the law varies from state to state;* (*attrib*) *The railways were once privately owned, but are now under state control;* (*in cmpds*) *state-owned/-run/-aided industries* (= industries owned, managed or supported financially by the government). **3** *nu* (*often attrib*) ceremonial dignity and splendour: *The Queen, wearing her robes of state, drove in a horse-drawn coach to Westminster;* (*attrib*) *state occasions/banquets.* – *See also* **lie in state** *below.*

stately *adj* (*formal*) noble, dignified and impressive in appearance or manner: *The duchess was a woman of stately appearance; She is tall and stately; a stately house/mansion.* **'stateliness** *nu.*

'stateroom *nc* a large cabin in a ship.

'statesman ['steits-] *nc* a person who plays an important part in the government of a state: *Churchill was a great statesman.*

'statesmanlike ['steits-] *adj* showing the qualities of a good statesman: *his statesmanlike solution of the problem; His handling of the situation was most statesmanlike.*

'statesmanship ['steits-] *nu* skill in directing the affairs of a state: *Many people admired Winston Churchill's statesmanship.*

get into a state (*inf*) to become very upset or anxious: *Don't come home late, or Mother will get into a state!*

lie in state (of a corpse) to be laid in a place of honour for the public to see, before burial.

state[2] [steit] *vt* (*more formal than* **say**) to say or announce clearly, carefully and definitely: *You have not yet stated your intentions; He stated on the application form that he was a British citizen.*

'stated *adj* (*usu attrib*) fixed, settled or announced: *The trains run at stated intervals from this station.*

'statement 1 *nu* the act of stating: *The statement of such an obvious fact is surely unnecessary.* **2** *nc* something that is stated: *The prime minister will make a statement tomorrow on the international crisis; Several conflicting statements have been issued.* **3** *nc* a written statement of how much money a person has, owes *etc*: *Your bank statement will tell you how much money is in your account; We received a statement from the plumber saying how much we owed him.*

static ['statik] *adj* (*formal or tech*) still; not moving: *The latest weather report says that the ridge of high pressure will remain static for a few more days.* – *nu* (*tech*) atmospheric disturbances causing poor reception of radio or television programmes: *We couldn't hear the programme because of static.* – *See also* **static (electricity)** *below.*

static (electricity) *nu* electricity that accumulates on the surface of objects (*eg* hair, nylon garments *etc*) that will not conduct it.

station ['steiʃən] *nc* **1** a place with a ticket office, waiting rooms *etc*, where trains, buses or coaches stop to allow passengers to get on or off: *You have to go to the bus station if you want to get a bus going out of town; You'll be able to buy a newspaper on/at the station to read in the train;* (*attrib*) *She got a cup of tea at the station buffet.* **2** a local headquarters or centre of work, duty *etc* of some kind: *How many fire-engines are kept at the fire station?; Most cities have their own local radio station; Where is the police station?; military/naval stations.* **3** (*formal*) a post or position (*eg* of a guard or other person on duty): *The watchman remained at his station all night; The dog took up its station beside its master.* **4** (*old or very formal*) a person's rank or position in society: *He came from a humble station in life.* – *vt* (*formal or facet*) to put (a person, oneself, troops *etc* in a place or position to perform some duty): *He stationed himself at the corner of the road to keep watch; The regiment is at present stationed in Northern Ireland.*

'stationary *adj* (*slightly formal*) standing still, not moving: *a stationary vehicle; The bus remained stationary.*

stationer ['steiʃənə] *nc* **1** a person that sells

stationery. 2 a stationer's shop: *Is there a stationer near here?*

'stationer's *nc* a stationer's shop: *Can you buy stamps at a stationer's?*

'stationery *nu* paper, envelopes, pens and other articles used in writing *etc*: *As a journalist you must spend a great deal of money on stationery.*

statistics [stə'tistiks] **1** *n pl* figures giving information about something: *There were 4,050 deaths and 350,000 injuries on the roads last year, but the statistics for the previous year were worse*; *Have you studied the recent divorce statistics?* **2** *n sing* the study of such figures: *He is studying statistics.*

sta'tistical *adj* (*usu attrib*) of statistics: *He made a statistical survey of crime in the neighbourhood.*

sta'tistically *adv.*

statistician [stati'stiʃən] *nc* a person who is an expert in statistics.

See also **vital statistics** *under* **vital**.

statue ['statju:] *nc* a sculptured figure of a person, animal *etc* in bronze, stone, wood *etc*: *A statue of Nelson stands at the top of Nelson's Column*; *The children stood as still as statues.*

ˌstatu'esque [-'esk] *adj* (*formal or facet*) like a statue in dignity, *etc*: *She was tall and statuesque*; *a statuesque blonde.*

ˌstatu'ette [-'et] *nc* a small statue: *A statuette of Napoleon stood on the mantelpiece.*

stature ['statʃə] *nu* (*formal*) **1** height of body: *a man of gigantic stature.* **2** importance or reputation: *a musician of international stature.*

status ['steitəs, (*Amer also*) 'sta-] *ncu* (*usu in sing*) **1** (*legal or formal*) the position of a person as a member of a group entitled to certain rights *etc*: *If she marries a foreigner, will her status as a British citizen be affected?*; *What is the legal status of gipsies?* **2** a person's rank or position in society, *esp* as seen by other people: *Does a doctor have a higher status than a teacher?*; *Actors have a higher status than they used to have*; *She lost status by marrying him.*

'status symbol *nc* a possession, which people are supposed to get in order to show their high social position: *A house with a swimming-pool is a status symbol among business executives.*

the status quo [kwou] (*formal or legal*) the situation as it now is, or as it was before a particular change: *The committee voted not to change the status quo with regard to hospital visiting*; *They decided to return to the status quo before 1976 when the new scheme was introduced.*

statute ['statju:t] *nc* (*legal or formal*) a written law of a country: *the statutes of this realm*; *You are required by statute to do this.*

'statutory *adj* (*legal or formal*: *often attrib*) of, or required by, a statute: *the statutory penalty for this offence.*

staunch[1] [sto:ntʃ] *adj* firm, trusty or steadfast: *a staunch believer/supporter.*

'staunchly *adv.* **'staunchness** *nu.*

staunch[2] *see* **stanch**.

stave[1] [steiv] *nc* **1** (*formal*) one of the side pieces of a cask or tub. **2** (*music*) a staff. **3** (*old liter*) a stanza or verse of a poem or song.

stave in – *pts, ptps* **staved, stove** – *vt sep, vi* to crush or drive a hole in (something) or to become crushed or holed: *In the car crash, the driver's chest was stove in by the steering wheel*; *The car hit a lamp-post and its side stove in.*

stave off – *pts, ptps* **staved, stove** – *vt sep* to delay or keep (something) away: *They ate some berries to stave off their hunger*; *They staved off their hung by eating some berries.*

stay[1] [stei] **1** *vi* to remain (in a place) for a time, e while travelling, or as a guest *etc*: *We stayed thr nights at that hotel/with a friend/in Paris*; *Are y staying in town overnight?*; *Aunt Mary is coming stay for a fortnight*; *Would you like to stay f supper?*; *Stay and watch that television programn if you think it's worth staying for.* **2** *vi* to remain (a particular position, place, state or condition *The doctor told her to stay in bed*; *He never sta long in any job*; *Stay away from the office till yo cold is better*; *The child complained that her soc would not stay up*; *Stay where you are – do move!*; *I wish you would stay still*; *In 1900, peop didn't realize that motor cars were here to stay.* **3** *v* (*arch*) to (cause to) stop, pause or wait: *He near struck her, but prudence stayed his hand*; *Stay! Y must not attempt such a thing!* – *See also* **stay** *phrases below.* – *nc* a period of staying (in a pla *etc*): *We had an overnight stay/a two days' stay London.* – *See also* **stay of execution** *below.*

'stayer *nc* (*inf*) a person, racehorse *etc* that ca continue going, working *etc* without getting tire *He isn't a particularly fast runner, but he's a staye*

'stay-at-home *nc* (*inf*) a person who prefers th quietness of his home to new places or exper ences: *She likes to go to parties but her husband is stay-at-home.*

'staying-power *nu* the ability to continue doir something without getting tired, bored *etc*: *H has never been able to work long at one job – he has staying-power.*

stay behind *vi* to remain in a place after othe have left it: *They all left the office at five o'cloc but he stayed behind to finish some work/to wait f me.*

stay in *vi* to remain in one's house *etc* and not g out of doors: *I'm staying in tonight to wat television.*

stay of execution (*legal*) a permitted delay in th obeying of an order of the court: *He was granted stay of execution for a year.*

stay out *vi* to remain out of doors and not retur to one's house *etc*: *The children mustn't stay o after 9 p.m.*

stay put (*inf*) to remain where placed: *Once child can crawl, he won't stay put for long.*

stay the course to continue going to the end of (race, period of training *etc*): *The race/training w strenuous, and few people managed to stay th course.*

stay up *vi* not to go to bed: *The children wanted stay up and watch television*; *Don't stay up for m* (= until I return), *as I shall be home late.*

stay[2] [stei] *nc* (*old liter*) a support: *His wife ha always been his prop and stay.*

stays *n pl* (*old*) a corset: *In the old days mo women wore stays.*

stead [sted]: **in someone's stead** (*formal*) place of (a person): *He could not go, so he foun someone to go in his stead.*

stand (someone) in good stead (*formal*) to b useful to (a person) in a time of need: *H knowledge of French stood him in good stead when h lost his money in France.*

See also **instead**.

steadfast ['stedfa:st] *adj* (*formal*) firm; unchang ing: *He felt uneasy before the child's steadfast gaze a steadfast friend/religious faith*; *He remaine steadfast* (= loyal) *to his friend.*

'**steadfastly** *adv*: *He steadfastly refused to yield.* '**steadfastness** *nu.*

steady ['stedi] *adj* **1** (*neg* **un-**) firmly fixed, balanced or controlled: *The table isn't steady*; *You need a steady hand to be a surgeon.* **2** (*usu attrib*) regular or even: *The plants should be kept at a steady temperature*; *He was walking up the hill at a steady speed/pace.* **3** unchanging or constant: *He has always been a steady supporter of our cause*; *steady devotion/faith*; *Our profits have remained steady.* **4** (*inf*: *usu attrib*) (of a person) sensible and hardworking in habits *etc*: *Most parents would like their daughters to marry steady young men.* – *vti* to make or become steady: *He stumbled but managed to steady himself*; *These pills will steady your nerves*; *His pulse gradually steadied.*

'**steadily** *adv*: *His work is improving steadily.* '**steadiness** *nu.*

go steady (of a girl and boy not yet engaged to be married) to go out together regularly; to have a steady relationship: *They are going steady*; *He's going steady with his friend's sister.*

steady (on)! *interj* (*inf*) don't be so angry, upset *etc*!: *Steady on! You mustn't shout at her – she's only a child!*

steak [steik] *ncu* a slice of meat (*usu* beef) or fish (often cod) for *eg* frying or stewing: *We're having steak/cod steaks for dinner.*

steal [stiːl] – *pt* **stole** [stoul]: *ptp* **stolen** ['stoulən] – **1** *vti* to take (another person's property), *esp* secretly, without permission or legal right: *Thieves broke into the house and stole money and jewellery*; *The dog stole a leg of mutton from the kitchen/cook*; *He was expelled from the school for stealing (money).* **2** *vt* (*formal or liter*) to obtain or take (*eg* a look, a nap *etc*) quickly or secretly: *He stole a glance at her*; *She managed to steal a few hours' sleep.* **3** *vi* (*formal or liter*) to move quietly: *He stole quietly into the room*; *She didn't see him and he stole away without saying anything.*

stealth [stelθ] *nu* (*formal*) a secret manner of acting: *The child would not give back the doll, but her mother removed it from her by stealth.*

'**stealthy** *adj* (*formal*) acting, or done, with stealth: *He took a stealthy glance at his watch.* '**stealthily** *adv.* '**stealthiness** *nu.*

steam [stiːm] *nu* **1** the gas or vapour that rises from hot or boiling water or other liquid: *Steam rose from the plate of soup/the wet earth in the hot sun*; *A cloud of steam rose from the kettle*; (*attrib*) *A sauna is a type of steam bath.* **2** (*often attrib or in cmpds*) power or energy obtained from this: *The machinery is steam-driven/driven by steam*; *before the days of steam*; *Diesel fuel has replaced steam on the railways*; *steam power*; *steam engines/trains.* – **1** *vi* to give out steam: *A kettle was steaming on the stove.* **2** *vi* (of a ship, train *etc*) to move by means of steam: *The train steamed into the station*; *The ship steamed across the bay.* **3** *vt* to cook by steam: *The pudding should be steamed for four hours.*

'**steamer** *nc* a steamboat or steamship: *He travelled by steamer from Liverpool to the Isle of Man.*

'**steamy** *adj* of, or full of, steam: *She found that the steamy atmosphere of the laundry made her hair straight*; *The kitchen's a bit steamy.* '**steaminess** *nu.*

'**steamboat,** '**steamship** *ncs* a ship driven by steam: *When did steamships replace sailing ships?*

'**steam engine** *nc* a moving engine for pulling a train, or a fixed engine, driven by steam: *Who invented the steam engine?*

ˌ**steam-'pudding** *ncu* (a) pudding often containing suet, cooked by steaming: *He enjoys steam-pudding(s).*

steam roller *nc* a type of vehicle driven by steam, with wide and heavy wheels for flattening the surface of newly-made roads *etc.* – *vt* (*with hyphen*: *inf*) to crush or force as if with a steam roller: *All their objections were steam-rollered*; *The bill was steam-rollered through* (= forced through its various stages in) *Parliament.*

full steam ahead at the greatest speed possible: *The ship was moving full steam ahead*; (*fig*) *The building programme was going full steam ahead.*

get/be (all) steamed up (*inf*) to get very upset or angry: *It is useless to get all steamed up about it.*

get up steam to increase the pressure of steam in an engine *etc*: *The train has to get up steam again after a stop*; (*fig inf*) *I was just getting up steam to get to the summit of the mountain.*

let off steam 1 (of an engine) to release steam into the air. **2** (*inf*) to release or get rid of excess energy, emotion *etc*: *The children were letting off steam by running about in the playground*; *A noisy quarrel can be a way of letting off steam.*

run out of steam (*fig inf*) to lose energy, or become exhausted: *He ran out of steam shortly before the end of the race.*

steam off/open *vts sep* to remove (*eg* a stamp from an envelope) or open (an envelope) by holding it in steam: *She held the letter over the kettle to steam it open.*

steam up *vi, vt sep* to (cause to) become covered with steam: *Kitchen windows steam up/become steamed up easily.*

under one's own steam (*inf*) by one's own efforts, without help from others: *John gave me a lift in his car, but Mary arrived under her own steam.*

steed [stiːd] *nc* (*old, liter or facet*) a horse for riding: *his noble steed.*

steel [stiːl] **1** *nu, adj* (of) a very hard alloy of iron and carbon, used for making tools *etc*: *tools of the finest steel*; *steel knives/chisels*; *Is this cutlery Sheffield steel?*; (*fig*) *He had a grip of steel* (= a very strong grip); (*in cmpds*) *women's shoes with steel-tipped heels.* **2** *nc* (*old liter*) a weapon, *esp* a sword: *Take care, or you'll feel the point of my steel!* **3** *nc* a bar of steel on which knives *etc* may be sharpened. **4** *nc* (*hist*) a piece of steel against which a flint is struck to make sparks. – *vt* to harden and strengthen (oneself, one's nerves *etc*) in preparation for doing, or resisting, something: *He steeled himself to meet the attack/to tell his wife the truth*; (*liter*) *She had steeled her heart against any plans he might make.*

'**steely** *adj* (*usu liter*) hard, cold, strong or bright like steel: *steely eyes*; *a steely look/gaze*; *Her eyes are blue and steely.* '**steeliness** *nu.*

steel band *nc* a West Indian type of band with instruments made from old petrol drums *etc.*

steel blue *nu, adj* (of) a deep blue or greyish blue colour: *steel blue eyes*; *eyes of steel blue.*

steel grey *nu, adj* (of) a greyish blue colour.

steel wool *nu* a pad, ball *etc* of steel shavings used for scouring (pans *etc*) and polishing: *You'll have to use steel wool to get the dried milk off that pan.*

'**steelworks** *n pl or n sing* a factory where steel is made: *He is an engineer at the local steelworks.*

steep[1] [stiːp] *adj* **1** (of *eg* a hill, stairs *etc*) rising with a sudden rather than a gradual slope: *The hill was too steep for me to cycle up it*; *a steep path*; *steep* *steps*; *It's a steep climb to the top of the mountain.* **2** (*inf*) (of a price asked or demand made) unreasonable or too great: *He wants rather a steep price for his house, doesn't he?*; *It's a bit steep to ask her to feed and look after the children while you go to the cinema.* **'steepness** *nu*.

'steeply *adv* in a steep or sudden way: *The path/prices rose steeply.*

steep[2] [sti:p] **1** *vti* (*more inf than* **soak**) to soak thoroughly in liquid *eg* in order to remove dirt: *Clothes will wash better if you steep them first* (*in water*); *The clothes are steeping.* **2** *vt* (*formal fig*: *often in passive*) to fill (a person) with a quality, a thorough knowledge of something *etc*: *They have been steeped in prejudice/in French literature since their childhood.*

steeple ['sti:pl] *nc* a high tower of a church *etc*, *usu* having a spire.

'steeplechase *nc* a race on horseback or on foot across open country, over hedges *etc*, or over a course on which obstacles (*eg* fences, hedges *etc*) have been made: *The race called the Grand National is a steeplechase.*

'steeplejack *nc* a person who climbs steeples, tall chimneys *etc*, to make repairs.

steer[1] [stiə] *nc* a young ox raised to produce beef.

steer[2] [stiə] *vti* to guide or control the course of (*eg* a ship, car *etc*): *He steered the car skilfully through the narrow streets*; *He went below deck while I steered out of the harbour*; *This ship/car steers well* (= is easy to steer); *We steered a hazardous course between the rocks*; *He took his mother's arm and steered her towards the door*; (*fig*) *She managed to steer the conversation towards the subject of her birthday party*; (*fig*) *Who is steering this bill through Parliament?* – *See also* **steer clear of** *below*.

'steerage [-ridʒ] *nu, adv* (*old*) (in) the part of a ship nearest the rudder, formerly reserved for passengers paying the lowest fare: *They travelled steerage to New York.*

'steering *nu* the equipment or apparatus for steering a ship or car *etc*: *The steering is faulty.*

'steering-wheel *nc* the wheel in a car for steering it, fixed to the **'steering-column**, or the wheel on a ship that is turned to control the rudder.

steer clear of to avoid: *I want to steer clear of trouble if possible*; *You should steer clear of her – she is not trustworthy.*

stellar ['stelə] *adj* (*tech or formal*: *esp attrib*) of stars: *stellar clusters*; *stellar bodies.*

stem[1] [stem] *nc* **1** the part of a plant that grows upward from the root, or the part from which a leaf, flower or fruit grows; a stalk: *Poppies have long, hairy, twisting stems*; *Daffodil stems are straight and thick.* **2** the narrow part of various objects, *eg* of a wine-glass between the bowl and the base: *He broke the stem of the wine-glass/of his tobacco-pipe.* **3** (*gram*) the main part of a word to the end of which parts are added to change the meaning, grammatical function *etc*: *In the words 'cordiality' and 'cordially', 'cord-' is the root and 'cordial-' the stem.* **4** the upright piece of wood or metal at the bow of a ship: *As the ship touched the rock, she shook from stem to stern.* – *v* – *pt, ptp* **stemmed** – *vi* (*formal*: *with* **from**) to be caused by: *a feeling of hate that stems from envy.*

-stemmed (*in cmpds*) having a (particular kind of) stem: *a thick-stemmed plant*; *He smoked a short-stemmed pipe.*

stem[2] [stem] – *pt, ptp* **stemmed** – *vt* (*formal or liter*) to stop the flow of (*eg* blood); to staunch: *He could not stem the bleeding.*

stench [stentʃ] *nc* a strong, bad smell: *The room was filled with the stench of stale tobacco smoke and spilt beer.*

stencil ['stensl] *nc* **1** a thin piece of metal or card in which a design *etc* has been cut which can be reproduced on another surface, *eg* paper, by printing or inking over the metal *etc*: *He used a stencil to do the lettering on the poster.* **2** a piece of waxed paper into which words have been cut by a typewriter, to be reproduced by a similar process: *Have you cut the stencil for the circular yet?* – *v* – *pt, ptp* **'stencilled** – *vti* to produce (a design, pattern *etc*) by using a stencil: *A repeating pattern had been stencilled on to the cloth*; *Show me how to stencil.*

stenography [stə'nogrəfi] *nu* (*Amer or old Brit*) the art, or any method, of writing in shorthand.

ste'nographer *nc* (*Amer or old Brit*) a shorthand typist.

stentorian [sten'to:riən] *adj* (*very formal or liter*) (of a voice) very loud and powerful: *in stentorian tones.*

step [step] *nc* **1** one movement of the foot in walking, running, dancing *etc*: *He took a step forward*; *She came along the street with hurried steps.* **2** the distance covered by this: *He moved a step or two nearer*; (*inf*) *Come to the park with me – it's only a short step* (= a short distance) *away.* **3** the sound made by someone walking *etc*: *I thought I heard* (*foot*)*steps.* **4** (*usu in sing*) the sound or appearance of a person's way of walking: *He has a long, striding step*; *Blind people can recognize the step of people they know well.* **5** a particular movement with the feet, *eg* in dancing: *The dance has some complicated steps.* **6** a flat surface, or one flat surface in a series, *eg* on a stair or stepladder, on which to place the feet or foot in moving up or down: *The bottom step of the ladder needs repairing*; *A flight of steps led down to the cellar*; *Steps had been cut in the rock*; *Mind the step!*; *She was sitting on the doorstep.* **7** a stage in progress, development *etc*: *Mankind made a big step forward with the invention of the wheel*; (*inf*) *His present job is a step up from* (= higher in grade than) *his previous one.* **8** an action or move (towards accomplishing an aim *etc*): *That would be a foolish/sensible step to take*; *I shall take steps to* (= act so as to) *prevent this happening again.* – *v* – *pt, ptp* **stepped** – *vi* to make a step, or to walk: *He opened the door and stepped out*; *He stepped down from the train on to the platform*; *She stepped briskly along the road.*

steps *n pl* a stepladder: *May I borrow your steps? Mine are broken*; *a pair of steps.*

'stepladder *nc* a ladder with a hinged support at the back and flat steps, not rungs.

'stepping-stones *n pl* large stones placed in a shallow stream *etc*, on which a person can step when crossing.

a false step a mistake: *He has made a false step.*

in, out of step (of two or more people walking together) with or without the same foot going forward at the same time: *They were walking/marching in step*; *Keep in step!*; *He got out of step*; (*fig*) *He feels that he is out of step with* (= unable to share the interests of) *people of his own age.*

step aside *vi* to move to one side: *He stepped aside to let me pass*; (*fig*) *He's getting too old for the job, and should step aside for a younger man.*

step by step gradually: *He improved step by step.*

step in *vi* to intervene: *The children began to*

quarrel, and I thought it was time I stepped in.
'step on it (*inf*) to hurry, *esp* by driving a car faster: *We'll have to step on it!*
step out *vi* to walk with a long(er) and (more) energetic stride: *Once he reached the mountain ridge, he was able to step out.*
step up *vt sep* to increase: *The firm must step up production this year.*
watch one's step (*inf*) to be careful, *esp* over one's own behaviour: *He was rebuked for his rudeness and told to watch his step in future.*

step- [step] (*in cmpds*) showing a relationship not by blood but by a second or later marriage.
'step-father, 'step-mother *ncs* the second or later husband of a person's own mother or wife of a person's own father.
'step-sister, 'step-brother *ncs* a daughter or son of a person's step-father or step-mother.
'step-son, 'step-daughter, 'step-child *ncs* a son or daughter from a previous marriage of a person's wife or husband.

steppe [step] *nc* a dry, grassy, *esp* treeless plain, as in the south-east of Europe and in Asia.

stereo ['steriou] *adj* (*usu attrib*) short for **stereophonic**: *a stereo record/recording.* – **1** *ncu* (*inf*) stereophonic equipment, *esp* a record-player: *Have you got (a) stereo?* **2** *nu* stereophonic sound or stereoscopic vision: *Has the opera been recorded in stereo?*; *The film was made in stereo.*

stereophonic [steriə'fonik] *adj* (*often abbrev* **stereo** ['steriou]: *usu attrib*) **1** (of recorded or broadcast sound) giving the effect of coming from different directions, and *usu* requiring two loud-speakers placed apart from each other: *a stereophonic broadcast*; *stereophonic sound.* **2** (of equipment, apparatus *etc*) intended for recording or playing such sound.

stereoscopic [steriə'skopik] *adj* (*tech*: *esp attrib*) (of films, pictures *etc*) filmed, shown *etc* by an apparatus taking or showing two photographs at different angles, so that a three-dimensional image is produced: *stereoscopic vision*; *a stereoscopic image.*

stereotype ['steriətaip] *nc* (*formal*) an idea, image, phrase *etc* that has become fixed and unchanging: *He is the stereotype of an army colonel*; (*attrib*) *stereotype images.*
'stereotyped *adj* (*often derog*) (of *eg* opinions, phrases *etc*) fixed and unchanging: *the usual stereotyped opinions about racial characteristics*; *The actor left the television series for fear of becoming stereotyped.*

sterile ['sterail] *adj* **1** (of soil, plants, humans and other animals) unable to produce crops, seeds, children or young: *When a husband and wife fail to have children, doctors may find that one or the other is sterile*; *a sterile male*; (*fig formal*) *sterile* (= producing no useful result) *arguments/discussions/researches.* **2** free from germs: *A surgeon's equipment must be absolutely sterile*; *a sterile operating table.*
ste'rility [-'ri-] *nu* the state of being sterile (*esp def 1*).
'sterilize, -ise [-ri-] *vt* **1** to make (a person *etc*) sterile: *A woman can be sterilized by means of a surgical operation if she wishes.* **2** to kill germs in (*eg* milk) or on (*eg* surgical instruments) by boiling: *Have the scissors been sterilized?*
ˌsterili'zation, -s- *nu.*

sterling ['stəːliŋ] *nu* British money, *esp* in international trading *etc*: *Sterling fell (in value) on the international market.* – *adj* (*attrib*) **1** (of silver) of a certain standard of purity: *Is the spoon sterling silver?* **2** (*fig*) (of a person or his qualities *etc*) worthy and admirable: *He has many sterling qualities.* – *See also* **pound sterling** *under* **pound**[1].
the sterling area a group of countries whose currencies have close connections with sterling and which use the pound sterling in foreign trade: *Which countries are within the sterling area?*

stern[1] [stəːn] *adj* harsh, severe or strict: *Their teacher looked rather stern*; *These men must have stern prison sentences*; *stern discipline*; *Her face wore a stern expression*; (*liter*) *the stern mountain landscape.* **'sternly** *adv.* **'sternness** *nu.*

stern[2] [stəːn] *nc* (*naut*) the back part of a ship.

stethoscope ['steθəskoup] *nc* an instrument by which a doctor can listen to the beats of the heart, the breathing *etc.*

stevedore ['stiːvədoː] *nc* a person who loads and unloads ships; a docker.

stew [stjuː] *vti* **1** to cook (meat, fruit *etc*) by slowly boiling and simmering: *He stewed the mutton*; *She stewed apples*; *The meat was stewing in the pan.* **2** (*inf*) (*of tea*) to leave or remain too long in the teapot before drinking: *The tea must be stewed by now.* – *ncu* (a dish of) stewed meat *etc*: *I've made some beef stew*; *She's good at (making) stews.*
be/get in a stew (*old*) to be or become very anxious and worried: *My mother will get in a stew if we're late home.*
stew in one's own juice (*inf*) to suffer as a result of one's own stupidity *etc*: *If she doesn't like her new job she'll just have to stew in her own juice – she shouldn't have left her previous one.*

steward ['stjuəd] – *fem* **'stewardess** – *nc* **1** a passenger's attendant on ship or aeroplane: *If you would like a private cabin, please ask the cabin steward*; *an air stewardess.* **2** a person who helps to arrange, and is an official at, races, dances, entertainments *etc*: *a race steward.* **3** a person who supervises the supply of food and stores in a club, on a ship *etc*: *a college steward.* **4** a person who manages an estate or farm for another person.
shop steward *see* **shop**.

stick[1] [stik] – *pt, ptp* **stuck** [stʌk] – **1** *vt* (*slightly inf*) to push or thrust (something sharp or pointed) into or through something: *He stuck his knife into the butter*; *She stuck a pin through the papers to hold them together.* **2** *vi* (*slightly inf*) (of something pointed) to be thrust or pushed into or through something (and remain fixed there): *Two arrows were sticking in his back*; *His elbow keeps sticking into me.* **3** *vti* to fasten or be fastened by glue, gum *etc*: *He licked the flap of the envelope and stuck it down*; *Please stick two sevenpenny stamps on this parcel*; *These labels don't stick very well*; *He stuck (the broken pieces of) the vase together again*; (*fig inf*) *His brothers used to call him Bonzo and the name has stuck* (= he is still called Bonzo). **4** *vt* (*usu in passive*), *vi* to (cause to) be or become fixed and unable to move: *The car stuck in the mud*; *The cupboard door stuck and I couldn't open it*; (*inf*) *I'll help you with your mathematics exercise if you're stuck* (= if you can't do it); (*inf*) *She's stuck* (= has to stay) *at home all day with the children.* **5** *vt* (*sl*) to put (something) somewhere: *Stick your coat over there!* **6** *vt* (*inf*) to bear or endure: *I can't stick her/her rudeness any longer.* – *See also* **stick** *in phrases below.*
'sticker *nc* an adhesive label or sign bearing *eg* a

design, political message *etc*, for sticking *eg* on a car's window *etc*: *The car sticker read 'Blood-donors needed'.*

'sticky *adj* **1** able, or likely, to stick or adhere to other surfaces: *He mended the torn paper with sticky tape*; *sticky sweets*; *His hands were sticky with jam.* **2** (*inf*) (of a situation or person) difficult: *It's a very sticky situation*; *My mother is a bit sticky about letting me go out in the evening.* **'stickily** *adv*. **'stickiness** *nu*.

sticking-plaster *see* **plaster** (*def 3*).

'stick-in-the-mud *nc* (*inf derog*) a person who never does anything new: *She has become a terrible stick-in-the-mud since she got married.*

be/get 'stuck with (*sl*) to be unable to escape from, or avoid (a burden, task *etc*): *She doesn't want to get stuck with* (*looking after*) *her husband's mother permanently.*

come to a sticky end (*inf*) to have an unpleasant death: *He'll come to a sticky end if he isn't more careful!*

get stuck in (*sl*) **1** to start working hard (at a job *etc*): *It's time we got stuck in.* **2** to start eating: *Dinner's ready – get stuck in!*

stick around *vi* (*sl*) to remain (in a place), *usu* in the hope of some future advantage *etc*: *If you stick around, we might have a job for you in a week or two.*

'stick at *vt fus* **1** to hesitate, or refuse, *eg* to do (*esp* something wrong): *He probably wouldn't stick at murder to get what he wants.* **2** to persevere with (work *etc*): *He must learn to stick at his job.*

stick by *vt fus* to support or be loyal to (a person): *His friends stuck by him when he was in trouble.*

stick it out (*inf*) to endure a situation for as long as necessary: *Will you manage to stick it out?*

stick on *vt sep* to stick (an adhesive label, stamp *etc*) on something: *He locked his case and stuck a label on.*

stick out 1 *vi*, *vt sep* (*more informal than* **project**) to (cause to) project: *He stuck his foot out and tripped her*; *His front teeth stick out.* **2** *vi* to be noticeable: *She has red hair that always sticks out in a crowd.*

stick out for *vt fus* (*inf*) to refuse to accept less than: *The men are sticking out for a fifteen per cent pay rise.*

stick one's neck out (*inf*) to take a risk: *I may be sticking my neck out here but I'm willing to volunteer for the job.*

'stick to/with *vt fus* not to abandon: *We've decided to stick to our previous plan*; *If you stick to* (= remain loyal to) *me, I'll stick to you*; *He stuck with* (= remained in) *the firm for twenty years.*

stick together 1 *vi*, *vt sep* to (cause to) be fastened together: *We'll stick the pieces together*; *These stamps are sticking together.* **2** *vi* (of friends *etc*) to remain loyal to each other: *They've stuck together all these years.*

stick up for *vt fus* to speak in defence of (a person *etc*): *When my father is angry with me, my mother always sticks up for me.* – *See also* **stuck-up**.

stick with *see* **stick to** *above*.

See also **non-stick, unstuck**.

stick[2] [stik] *nc* **1** a branch or twig from a tree: *Throw a stick for the dog to fetch*; *They were sent to find sticks for firewood.* **2** (*often in cmpds*) a long thin piece of wood *etc* shaped for a special purpose, *eg* one out from a branch as a support for a person when walking: *She always walks with a stick nowadays*; *a walking-stick/hockey-stick*; *a drumstick*; *candlesticks.* **3** a long piece: *a stick of rhubarb/sealing-wax*; *He was sucking a stick of toffee.*

get (hold of) the wrong end of the stick to misunderstand a situation, something said *etc*: *I got the wrong end of the stick and thought you wouldn't be coming till tomorrow.*

stickler ['stiklə] *nc* (*inf*: *with* **for**) a person who attaches great importance (to a particular matter): *He's a stickler for punctuality.*

sticky *see* **stick**[1].

stiff [stif] *adj* **1** rigid or firm, and not easily bent, folded *etc*: *He walks with a stiff leg* (= without bending the knee) *since he injured his knee*; *a sheet of stiff paper*; *The fashion for stiff petticoats is returning*; *The body of the dead cat was stiff and cold.* **2** moving, or moved, with difficulty, pain *etc*: *I can't turn the key – the lock is stiff*; *I woke up with a stiff neck*; *I felt stiff the day after the climb.* **3** (of a cooking mixture *etc*) thick, and not flowing: *She beat the cream till it was stiff*; *a stiff dough.* **4** (*inf*) difficult to do: *a stiff English examination*; *That exam was a bit stiff*; *a stiff climb up the mountain.* **5** strong: *I need a stiff* (= strong, alcoholic) *drink*; *A stiff breeze has got up.* **6** (of a person or his manner *etc*) formal and unfriendly: *He was rather stiff with me*; *I received a stiff note from the bank manager.* – *nc* (*sl*) a corpse.

'stiffen *vti* to make or become stiff(er): *You can stiffen cotton with starch*; *He stiffened when he heard the unexpected sound.*

'stiffening *nu* material used to stiffen something: *The collar has some stiffening in it.*

'stiffly *adv* in a stiff way or manner: *He bowed stiffly.* **'stiffness** *nu*.

bore, scare (someone) stiff (*inf*) to bore or frighten (a person) very much: *His driving scares me stiff*; *I was bored stiff at the lecture.*

stifle ['staifl] **1** *vti* to prevent, or be prevented, from breathing (easily) *eg* because of bad air, an obstruction over the mouth and nose *etc*; to suffocate: *He was stifled to death when smoke filled his bedroom*; *I'm stifling in this heat!* **2** *vt* to extinguish or put out (flames): *He flung a blanket over her burning nightdress to stifle the flames.* **3** *vt* to suppress (a yawn, a laugh *etc*): *She was getting sleepy/bored, and tried to stifle a yawn.*

'stifling *adj* so hot, stuffy *etc* that breathing is difficult: *a stifling atmosphere*; *stifling heat*; *It's stifling in here.*

stigma ['stigmə] *nc* a mark of disgrace: *There is no stigma nowadays attached to being mentally ill.*

'stigmatize, -ise [-taiz] *vt* (*formal*) to describe (a person) in scornful words: *He did not want to be stigmatized as ignorant/cowardly.*

stile [stail] *nc* a step, or set of steps, for climbing over a wall or fence.

stiletto [sti'letou] – *pl* **sti'lettos** – *nc* a dagger or other instrument with a narrow pointed blade.

stiletto heel *nc* a high, very thin heel on a lady's shoe.

still[1] [stil] *adj* **1** without movement or noise: *The city seems very still in the early hours of the morning*; *Please stand/sit/keep still while I brush your hair!*; *a still* (= windless) *day*; *still* (= not quickly-flowing) *waters.* **2** (*attrib*) (of drinks) not fizzy: *still orange juice.* – **1** *nu* (*liter*) silence or calmness: *in the still of evening.* **2** *nc* a photograph selected from a cinema film: *The magazine contained some stills from the new film.* – *vt* (*liter*) to make calm or quiet: *He was unable to still her fears.*

stillness *nu* the quality of being still: *the stillness of the water.*

stillborn *adj* dead when born: *a stillborn baby; The child was stillborn.*

still life *ncu* (an example of) representation by an artist of something that is not living, *eg* a bowl of fruit, vase of flowers *etc*, *esp* in a painting: *Three of his still lifes are in the exhibition; I enjoy painting still life;* (*attrib*) *still-life pictures.*

hold still to keep still; not to move: *Hold still till I fasten these buttons for you.*

ill[2] [stil] *adv* **1** up to and including the present time, or the time mentioned previously: *Are you still working for the same firm?; By Saturday he had still not/still hadn't replied to my letter; Do you make your own dresses still?* **2** nevertheless; in spite of that: *Although the doctor told him to rest, he still went on working; This picture is not valuable – still, I like it.* **3** (used with a comparative) to a greater degree; even: *He seemed very ill in the afternoon and in the evening looked still worse.*

ill[3] [stil] *nc* an apparatus or place in which a type of spirit *eg* whisky is distilled, often illegally.

ilted ['stiltid] *adj* (*derog*) (of a person's style of speech, writing *etc*) over-formal or unnatural: *The answer 'It is I' to the question 'Who is there?' nowadays seems rather stilted, and most people say 'It's me'; He spoke in rather stilted English.*

ilts [stilts] *n pl* **1** a pair of poles with supports for the feet, on which a person may stand and so walk raised off the ground: *Can you walk on stilts?; a pair of stilts.* **2** tall poles fixed under a house *etc* to support it *eg* if it is built on a steep hillside or over water: *a house on stilts.*

imulant ['stimjulənt] *nc* (*formal or tech*) something *eg* a medicine, drink *etc* that makes a person more alert or a part of his body more active: *Tea, coffee and alcohol are all stimulants; This drug is a heart stimulant;* (*fig*) *A visit to the art gallery is the best stimulant I know.*

imulate ['stimjuleit] *vt* to rouse or make (*eg* a person) more alert, active *etc*: *The discussion stimulated her; After listening to the violin concerto, he felt stimulated to practise the violin again.*

stimulating *adj* rousing; very interesting: *Coffee has a stimulating effect; a very stimulating lecture; I found his talk very stimulating.*

stimu'lation *nu*: *Housewives often complain that their minds get no stimulation.*

imulus ['stimjuləs] – *pl* **'stimuli** [-liː] – *nc* **1** (*tech*) something that causes a reaction in a living thing: *Light is the stimulus that causes a flower to open.* **2** (*formal*) something that rouses or encourages a person *etc* to action or greater effort: *Many people think that children need the stimulus of competition to make them work better in school.*

ing [stiŋ] *nc* **1** a part of some plants, insects *etc*, *eg* nettles and wasps, that can prick and inject an irritating or poisonous fluid into the wound: *Do bees always leave their stings in the wound?* **2** an act of piercing with this part: *Some spiders can give a poisonous sting.* **3** (*often in cmpds*) the wound, swelling, or pain caused by this: *She had a bee sting on her lip; You can soothe a wasp sting by putting vinegar on it.* **4** (*formal*) any sharp pain, or the power of causing this: *He felt the sting of the whip;* (*fig*) *Her words had a sting in them.* – *v* – *pt, ptp* **stung** [stʌŋ] – **1** *vti* to wound or hurt by means of a sting: *The child was badly stung by nettles;* (*fig*) *I was stung by his remark; Do those insects sting?* **2** *vi* (of a wound, or a part of the body) to smart or be painful: *The salt water made his eyes sting.* **3** *vt* to drive or provoke (a person) to act: *She was stung into making an angry reply.* **4** *vt* (*sl*) to charge (a person) too much, or a great deal of, money for something: *If you get the car repaired at that garage, they'll sting you for £40.*

stingy ['stindʒi] *adj* (*inf derog*) mean or ungenerous: *My father's very stingy* (*with his money/about giving me money*); *We get very stingy portions of food for school dinners.* **'stingily** *adv.* **'stinginess** *nu.*

stink [stiŋk] – *pt* **stank** [staŋk]: *ptp* **stunk** [stʌŋk] – *vi* (*inf derog*) to have a very bad smell: *That meat stinks; The house stinks of cats;* (*fig*) *The whole contract stinks* (*of corruption*). – *nc* **1** (*inf derog*) a very bad smell: *What a stink!* **2** (*sl*) trouble: *Sacking that man will cause quite a stink; He will raise a stink* (= cause trouble) *if he finds out about that.*

stink out *vt sep* (*inf*) to fill (a place) with a stink: *The fish has stunk the whole house out.*

stint [stint] *vt* (*often refl and in neg*) to give or allow only a small amount of something: *He complains of poverty, but he doesn't seem to stint himself with regard to food and wine.* – *nc* a person's fixed amount of work, duty *etc*: *I've done my stint of housework for today; a daily stint.*

without stint (*formal*) without limit; not grudgingly: *He praised him without stint.*

See also **unstinting**.

stipend ['staipend] *nc* a salary paid for services (*esp* to a clergyman).

stipple ['stipl] *vt* to engrave, paint, draw *etc* using dots or dabs of colour *etc* rather than lines or masses of colour.

stipulate ['stipjuleit] *vt* (*formal*) to state as a necessary condition for an agreement: *I stipulated that, if I did the job, I must be paid immediately; You must stipulate how many hours you can work.*

stipu'lation *nc* (*formal*) something stipulated; a condition: *The money was paid to her on the stipulation that it was to be used for the children's education; You can have the money but there are several stipulations.*

stir [stəː] – *pt, ptp* **stirred** – **1** *vt* to cause a liquid *etc* to be mixed *esp* by the constant circular movement of a spoon *etc*, in order to mix it: *He put sugar and milk into his tea and stirred it; She stirred the sugar into the mixture.* **2** *vti* to move, either slightly or vigorously: *The breeze stirred* (= gently moved) *her hair; He stirred in his sleep;* (*inf*) *Come on – stir yourselves!* **3** *vt* (*liter*) to arouse or excite (a person or his feelings): *He/His sympathy was stirred by her story.* – *nc* a fuss or disturbance: *The news caused quite a stir.*

'stirring *adj* (*attrib*) exciting: *a stirring tale.*

stir up *vt sep* to cause (trouble *etc*): *He was trying to stir up trouble at the factory.*

See also **bestir**.

stirrups ['stirəps, (*Amer*) 'stəː-] *n pl* a pair of metal loops hanging on straps from a horse's saddle, to support a rider's feet: *He put his feet into the stirrups; a pair of stirrups.*

stitch [stitʃ] **1** *nc* a loop made in thread, wool *etc* by a needle in sewing or knitting: *She sewed the hem with small, neat stitches; Bother! I've dropped a stitch* (= let a loop slip off the knitting needles). **2** *ncu* (a type of stitch as part of) a particular pattern in sewing, knitting *etc*: *The cloth was edged with neat blanket stitches; The jersey was knitted in stocking stitch.* **3** *nc* a sharp pain in a person's side caused by *eg* running: *I've got a stitch.* – *vti* to sew or put stitches into something: *She stitched the two pieces together*; *A button fell off, but I stitched it on again*; *She was stitching busily.*

'**stitching** *nu* stitches: *The stitching is very untidy.*

he, she *etc* **hasn't got a stitch on/isn't wearing a stitch** (*inf*) he or she is completely naked.

in stitches (*inf*) laughing a great deal: *His stories kept us in stitches* (= caused us to laugh a lot) *all night*; *We were in stitches at the comedian's jokes*; *He had us in stitches with his stories.*

stitch up *vt sep* to close by stitching: *Could you stitch up the hole in my shirt?*; *The doctor stitched up the wound.*

stoat [stout] *nc* a type of animal similar to a weasel, sometimes called the ermine when in its white winter fur.

stock [stok] **1** *ncu* (*often in pl*) a store of goods in a shop, warehouse *etc*: *The new stocks of bathing-suits don't arrive in the shops till March*; *Buy while stocks last!*; *He is selling off* (= selling quickly and cheaply) *his stock*; *The tools you require are in/out of stock* (= available/not available). **2** *nc* a supply of something: *We bought a large stock of food for the camping trip*; *She has a stock of interesting stories about her youth.* **3** *nu* farm animals: *He would like to purchase more (live) stock.* **4** *ncu* (*econ*: *often in pl*) money lent to the government or to a business company at a fixed interest: *government stock*; *He has £9 000 in stocks and shares.* **5** *nu* a person's family or ancestry: *He comes of old pioneer stock.* **6** *nu* liquid obtained by boiling meat, bones *etc* and used for making soup *etc.* **7** *nc* the handle of a whip, rifle *etc.* – *adj* (*attrib*) common; usual: *My feet are so narrow that I can never get shoes in a shop that only has stock sizes*; *When I asked about him at the hospital I received the stock reply that he was as well as could be expected*; *a stock remark/joke/question.* – *vt* **1** to keep a supply of (something) for sale: *Does this shop stock writing paper?* **2** to supply (a shop, farm *etc*) with goods, animals *etc*: *He cannot afford to stock his farm.*

'**stockist** *nc* a person who stocks certain goods: *These boots can be obtained from your local stockist.*

stocks *n pl* **1** the wooden framework upon which a ship is supported when being built, repaired *etc*: *The ship is still on the stocks/left the stocks only last year.* **2** (*hist*) a wooden frame, with holes for the ankles (and wrists) in which a criminal is fastened as a punishment: *The stocks still stand just outside the village.* – *See also* **stock** (*defs 1, 4*).

'**stockbroker** *nc* a person who buys and sells stocks and shares for others.

'**stock-cube** *nc* a small cube of dried stock (*def 6*) for making soup *etc*: *I haven't time to make chicken stock – I'll use a chicken stock-cube.*

'**stock exchange** *nc* a place where stocks (*def 4*) *etc* are bought and sold: *the latest prices on the stock exchange*; *He works on the stock exchange*; (*attrib*) *stock exchange dealings.*

ˌ**stock-in-'trade** *nu* (*usu fig*: *often derog*) the necessary equipment *etc* for a particular trade *etc*: *These tools were part of a shoemaker's stock-in-trade*; (*fig*) *Sarcasm is too often part of a teacher's stock-in-trade.*

'**stock market** *nc* a stock exchange, or the dealings on that: (*Dealing on*) *the stock market was slow today.*

'**stockpile** *nc* a supply of goods or materials accumulated *eg* by a government in case of war or other emergency. – *vt* to accumulate (a supply of this sort): *Housewives started to stockpile brea when they heard that the bakers were going on strike*

'**stockroom** *nc* a room where goods are stored c kept in reserve, *eg* in a shop, factory *etc.*

ˌ**stock-'still** *adj* (*pred*), *adv* motionless: *He sto absolutely stock-still.*

'**stock-taking** *nu* a regular check of the goods in shop, warehouse *etc*: *Several losses were recorde during the annual stock-taking.*

stock up *vi, vt sep* (*often with* **on** *or* **with**) t accumulate a supply of (something): *The bo were stocking up on chocolate and lemonade for the walk*; *There is likely to be a shortage of sugar, so w had better stock up (our supplies).*

take stock 1 to make a list of goods in stock. (*often with* **of**) to form an opinion (about situation *etc*): *Before you decide on a new career yo should try to take stock*; *He had no time to take stoc of the situation.*

See also **livestock, laughing-stock** *under* **live laugh.**

stockade [sto'keid] *nc* a fence of strong posts pu up round an area for defence: *The camp wa surrounded by a stockade.*

stoc'kaded *adj* surrounded by a stockade: *stockaded settlement.*

stockbroker *see* **stock.**

stocking ['stokiŋ] *nc* (*often in pl*) a pair close-fitting coverings for the legs and fee reaching to or above the knee: *a pair of knitte woollen stockings*; *Most women prefer tights stockings nowadays*; *I have lost a stocking.*

stockist, stockpile, stockroom *see* **stock.**

stocky ['stoki] *adj* (of a person *etc*) short, ofte rather stout and *usu* strong: *He's a stocky litt boy*; *The boxer was rather stocky.* '**stockiness** *nu*

'**stockily** *adv* (*usu in cmpds*) in a stocky way: *stockily-built man.*

stodge [stodʒ] *nu* (*inf derog*) heavy, solid and *us* rather indigestible food: *He loves suet puddin and other kinds of stodge.*

'**stodgy** *adj* (*inf derog*) **1** (of meals *etc*) consistin of stodge: *School meals are often stodgy*; *He lik steam-puddings and other stodgy food.* **2** (of peopl books *etc*) dull and without liveliness: *He has sense of humour – he is a very stodgy young man*; *H will not go to a dance – he is too stodgy.* '**stodgines** *nu.*

stoic ['stouik] *nc* (*formal or facet*) a person wh bears pain or misfortune without complaining showing any sign of feeling it: *He was a stoic – did not cry out when he was burned alive*; *I'm not o of those stoics who suffer in silence!* '**stoical** *ad* '**stoically** *adv.*

'**stoicism** [-sizəm] *nu* (*formal*) the practice bearing pain *etc* without complaining: *his adm able stoicism in the face of illness.*

stoke [stouk] *vt* to put coal or other fuel on (a fir *eg* in the furnace of a boiler *etc*: *The men stoked t fires/furnaces/boilers/engine.*

'**stoker** *nc* a person, or device, that stokes furnace *etc.*

stoke up 1 *vi, vt sep* to stoke: *Have they stoked u (the fires)?* **2** *vi* (*inf*: *sometimes with* **with**) to e plenty: *You ought to stoke up (with food) befo going up the mountain.*

stole[1] [stoul] *nc* **1** (*formal*) a narrow strip of *eg* si round the neck and hanging down in front, wo by clergymen. **2** a woman's garment of simil shape, made of *eg* fur: *She wore a mink stole ov her evening dress.*

stole[2], **stolen** *see* **steal**.

stolid ['stolid] *adj* (*usu derog*) (of a person *etc*) not easily excited, unimaginative and rather dull: *He is a very interesting person but his wife is rather stolid; a stolid schoolgirl; a stolid-looking girl.*
sto'lidity, 'stolidness *nus.*
'stolidly *adv* in a stolid manner: *The town councillors stolidly opposed any attempt at reform.*

stomach ['stʌmək] *nc* **1** the bag-like part of the body into which food passes when swallowed, and where most of it is digested: *Food passes down the gullet to the stomach.* **2** (*loosely*) the part of the body between the chest and thighs: *a pain in the stomach.* – *vt* (*usu in questions or negative statements: inf*) to endure or tolerate: *I can't stomach her rudeness.*
'stomach-ache *nc* a pain in the stomach.
have no stomach for (*formal*) not to have any desire, enough courage *etc* for (something): *I had no stomach for the fight.*
See also **gastric**.

stomp [stomp] *vi* (*inf*) to stamp or tread heavily: *She stomped angrily out of the room.*

stone [stoun] – *pl* **stones,** (*def 6 also*) **stone** – **1** *nu, adj* (*often in cmpds*) (of) the material of which rocks are composed: *limestone; sandstone; a stone house; stone walls; In early times, men made tools out of stone;* (*fig*) *You must have a heart of stone to refuse to help the child.* **2** *nc* a piece of this, of any shape or size: *He threw a stone at the dog; desolate moorland covered with stones.* **3** *nc* (*usu in cmpds*) a piece of this shaped for a special purpose: *a tombstone; a millstone; paving-stones; a grindstone.* **4** *nc* a gem or jewel: *She lost the stone out of her ring; diamonds, rubies and other types of stones.* **5** *nc* (*sometimes in cmpds*) the hard shell containing the nut or seed in some fruits *eg* peaches and cherries: *a cherry-stone; He ate the plum and spat out the stone.* **6** *nc* (*sometimes abbrev* **st.** *when written*) a measure of weight still used in Britain, equal to 14 pounds (6·35 kilogrammes): *She weighs 9½ stone; He lost two stone(s) when he was ill.* **7** *nc* a piece of hard material that forms in the kidney, bladder *etc* and causes pain: *She had a stone removed from her kidney.* – *vt* **1** (*formal*) to throw stones at, *esp* as a ritual punishment: *Saint Stephen was the first Christian martyr to be stoned to death by a crowd.* **2** to remove the stones from (fruit): *She washed and stoned the cherries.*
stoned *adj* (*pred: sl*) **1** very drunk: *You were absolutely stoned last night.* **2** under the influence of drugs.
'stonily *adv* in an unsympathetic manner: *He listened stonily to her excuses.*
'stony *adj* **1** full of, or covered with stones: *stony soil; a stony path/beach; It's very stony around here.* **2** (*mainly fig*) like stone in coldness, hardness *etc*: *He gave me a stony* (=hostile) *stare/look; Her expression was cold and stony.* – *See also* **stony-broke** *below.* **'stoniness** *nu.*
'Stone Age *n* (*with* **the**) the early period in history when tools, weapons *etc* were made of stone: *This pottery was made by people living in the Stone Age;* (*attrib*) *Stone Age houses.*
ˌstone-'cold, ˌstone-'dead, ˌstone-'deaf *adjs* completely cold, dead, or deaf: *He's almost stone-deaf; Your soup is stone-cold; stone-cold soup.*
ˌstone'wall *vti* (*formal*) to obstruct or impede progress intentionally, *eg* of parliamentary business by talking: *I tried to get her to tell me what was wrong but she stonewalled me.*
'stoneware *nu, adj* (of) a hard type of pottery made of clay containing pieces of stone, or articles of this: *You have some nice stoneware; a stoneware jug.*
'stonework *nu* construction done in stone, *esp* the stone parts of a building: *The stonework needs to be cleaned.*
ˌstony-'broke, stony *adjs* (*inf*) having absolutely no money: *I'm stony-broke till Saturday.*
leave no stone unturned to try every possible means: *The police left no stone unturned to* (*try to*) *find the child.*
a 'stone's throw a very short distance: *They live only a stone's throw away from here.*
ˌstone-cold 'sober (*inf*) completely sober and not under the influence of alcohol.

stood *see* **stand**.

stooge [stu:dʒ] *nc* **1** a comedian's assistant, who is made the object of all his jokes. **2** (*inf derog*) a person who is used by another to do a *usu* humble or unpleasant job: *A powerful criminal often employs a stooge to do his work for him.* – *vi* (*inf derog*) to act as a stooge: *I don't want to spend my life stooging for other people.*

stool [stu:l] *nc* **1** (*sometimes in cmpds*) a seat without a back: *a piano-stool; a kitchen stool; a three-legged stool.* **2** *ncu* (*formal or tech: often in pl*) a discharge of faeces from the bowels: *His stools are perfectly normal; The doctor asked for a sample of his stool.*
'stool-pigeon *nc* (*inf derog*) an informer or spy *esp* for the police.
fall between two stools to lose both of two possibilities by hesitating between them or trying for both: *That book falls between two stools – it is neither fiction nor biography.*

stoop [stu:p] **1** *vti* (*more formal than* **bend**) to bend the body forward and downward: *The doorway was so low that he had to stoop* (*his head*) *to go through it; She stooped down to talk to the child.* **2** *vi* (*fig*) to lower one's (moral) standards by doing something: *Surely he wouldn't stoop to cheating!* – *nc* (*no pl*) a stooping position of the body, shoulder *etc*: *Many people develop a stoop as they grow older.*
stooped *adj* in a stooping position: *stooped shoulders; a stooped old man; He is stooped with age.*

stop [stop] – *pt, ptp* **stopped** – **1** *vti* (*less formal than* **cease** *or* **halt**) to (make something) cease moving, or come to a rest, halt *etc*: *He stopped the car and got out; This train does not stop at any stations between here and Birmingham; He stopped for a few minutes to look at the map; He signalled with his hand to stop the bus.* **2** *vt* (*less formal than* **prevent**) to prevent (a person *etc*) from doing something: *We must stop* (*him*) *from going; Can't you stop her doing such stupid things?; I was going to say something rude but stopped myself just in time.* **3** *vti* (*less formal than* **cease**) to discontinue or cease *eg* doing something: *Why have you stopped work*(*ing*)*?; That woman just can't stop talking; It has stopped snowing; The rain has stopped; Her pain has stopped.* **4** *vt* to block or close (a hole *etc*): *He stopped his ears with his hands when she started to shout at him.* **5** *vt* (*music*) to close (a hole, *eg* on a flute) or press down (a string on a violin *etc*) in order to play a particular note: *You can play a chord by stopping two strings simultaneously.* **6** *vt* (of a bank) to refuse payment of (a cheque): *The bank stopped* (*payment of*) *her cheque.* **7** *vi* (*inf or Brit dial*) to stay: *Will you be stopping long at the hotel?*

– *See also* **stop** *in phrases below.* – *nc* **1** an act of stopping or state of being stopped: *We made only two stops on our journey; Work came to a stop for the day.* **2** a place for *eg* a bus to stop: *a bus stop; Which stop shall I catch the bus at?* **3** in punctuation, a full stop: *You've forgotten to put a stop at the end of this sentence.* **4** (*music*) a device on a flute *etc* for covering the holes in order to vary the pitch, or knobs for bringing certain pipes into use on an organ: *He pulled out the stops.* **5** (*esp in cmpds*) a device, *eg* a wedge *etc*, for stopping the movement of something, or for keeping it in a fixed position: *a door-stop.*

'stoppage [-pidʒ] **1** *ncu* (an) act of stopping or state or process of being stopped: *The building was at last completed after many delays and stoppages; Stoppage of this artery usually leads to a heart attack.* **2** *nc* (*more formal or tech than* **block**) something that blocks *eg* a tube or passage in the body: *Colds usually cause a stoppage in the nose.*

'stopper *nc* an object, *eg* a cork, that is put into the neck of a bottle, jar *etc* to close it: *Put the stopper back in!*

'stopping *nc* (*inf*) a filling in a tooth: *I have toothache – one of my stoppings has come out.*

'stopcock *nc* a tap and valve for controlling flow of liquid through a pipe.

'stopgap *nc* a person or thing that fills a gap in an emergency: *He was made headmaster as a stopgap till a new man could be appointed;* (*attrib*) *a stopgap prime minister;* (*attrib*) *We must take stopgap measures while we elect a new president.*

stop-over *see* **stop over** *below.*

stop press *nu* the most recent news inserted in a specially reserved space in a newspaper that is already being printed; the space itself: *It was reported in the stop press.*

'stopwatch *nc* a watch with a hand that can be stopped and started, used in timing a race *etc.*

put a stop to (something) to make sure that (a thing) does not continue: *We must put a stop to his disobedience.*

stop at nothing to be willing to do anything unworthy, in order to get something: *He'll stop at nothing to get what he wants.*

stop dead to stop completely: *I stopped dead when I saw him.*

stop in *vi* (*inf or Brit dial*) to remain at home: *I'll stop in tonight.*

stop off *vi* (*inf*) to make a halt on a journey *etc*: *We stopped off at Edinburgh to see the castle.*

stop out *vi* (*inf or Brit dial*) not to return home: *He stopped out all night.*

stop over *vi* (*inf*) to make a stay of a night or more: *We're planning to stop over in Amsterdam* (*nc* **'stop-over**).

stop short of to be unwilling to go beyond a certain limit in one's conduct: *He wouldn't stop short at murder if his children were starving.*

stop up 1 *vt sep* to block: *My nose is stopped up; Some rubbish got into the drain and stopped it up.* **2** *vi* (*inf or Brit dial*) to stay out of bed: *He stopped up till 2 a.m.*

See also **non-stop, unstop.**

storage *see* **store.**

store [sto:] *nc* **1** (*sometimes in pl*) a supply of *eg* goods from which things are taken when required: *They took a store of dried and canned food on the expedition; The quartermaster is the army officer in charge of stores.* **2** (*usu in sing*) a (large) collected amount or quantity: *this fine castle with its store of beautiful paintings and furniture; He has a store of interesting facts in his head.* **3** (*sometimes in pl*) a place where a supply of goods *etc* is kept; a storehouse or storeroom: *It's in the store(s).* **4** (*sometimes in pl and or cmpds*) a shop: *The post office here is also the village store; The Army and Navy Stores are/is in the next street; a department store; a chain store* (*see under* **chain**). – *See also* **in store** *below.* – *vt* **1** to put into a place for keeping: *We stored our furniture in the attic while the tenants used our house.* **2** (*often in passive*) to stock (a place *etc*) with goods *etc*: *The museum is stored with interesting exhibits.* – *See also* **store up** *below.*

'storage [-ridʒ] *nu* the act of storing or state of being stored: *We've put our furniture into storage at a warehouse; How much will you have to pay the warehouse for storage?*

'storehouse, 'storeroom *ncs* a place or room where goods *etc* are stored: *There is a storeroom behind the shop.*

in, into cold storage of goods, which are (to be) stored in storerooms in which they can be refrigerated: *The shipment of butter was put into cold storage.*

in 'store 1 kept or reserved for future use: *Keep some chocolate in store for the walk!* **2** coming in the future: *There's trouble in store for her!; If you've never been to York, that's a treat in store* (= a future pleasure) (*for you*).

set (great) store by to value highly (*eg* a person's approval, opinion *etc*): *She sets great store by her husband's approval.*

store up *vt sep* to collect and keep (for future need): *I don't know why she stores up all those old magazines; She stored up the joke to tell her husband later.*

storey, story ['sto:ri] *nc* one of the floors or levels in a building: *an apartment block of seventeen storeys.*

-storeyed, -storied (*in cmpds*) having (a particular number of) storeys: *A two-storied house is one with a ground floor and one floor above it.*

stork [sto:k] *nc* a type of wading bird with long beak, neck and legs.

storm [sto:m] *nc* **1** (*often in cmpds*) a violent disturbance in the air causing wind, rain, thunder *etc*: *a rainstorm; a snowstorm; a windstorm; a thunderstorm; I've never been in a storm at sea; The roof was damaged by the storm.* **2** a violent outbreak of feeling *etc*: *A storm of anger greeted his speech; a storm of applause/weeping.* – (*formal*) **1** *vi* (*with* **at**) to shout very loudly and angrily: *He stormed at her; She stormed and raged.* **2** *vi* to move or stride in an angry manner: *He stormed into/out of the room.* **3** *vt* (of soldiers *etc*) to attack with great force, and capture (a building *etc*): *They stormed the castle.*

'stormy *adj* **1** having a lot of strong wind, heavy rain *etc*: *a stormy day; stormy weather/winds; a stormy voyage; It is too stormy to sail today.* **2** full of anger or uncontrolled feeling: *He was in a stormy mood; a stormy discussion; her stormy personality; Today's meeting was rather stormy.* **'stormily** *adv.* **'storminess** *nu.*

'stormbound *adj* prevented by storms from continuing with a voyage, receiving regular supplies *etc*: *ships stormbound in the Channel; The island was stormbound for a week; stormbound ships.*

'stormtrooper *nc* a soldier specially trained for violent and dangerous attacks.

a storm in a teacup a fuss made over an unimportant matter: *We thought that they had decided not to get married but their quarrel was just a storm in a teacup.*

take (someone or something) by storm (*esp fig*) to capture (a fort *etc*) by means of a sudden violent attack: *The invaders took the city by storm*; (*fig*) *The singer took the audience by storm* (= caused them to applaud enthusiastically).

story[1] ['sto:ri] *nc* **1** an account of an event, or series of events, real or imaginary: *the story of the disaster*; *In this book he tells the story of his life/the Russian ballet*; *He went to the police with his story*; *Don't talk to journalists – they're just looking for a good story!*; *What sort of stories do boys aged 10 like reading?*; *adventure/murder/love stores*; (*in cmpds*) *a story-book*; *He's a good story-teller.* **2** (*euph*) (used *esp* to children) a lie: *Don't tell stories!*

the story goes (that) people say (that): *The story goes that he beats his wife*; *He's been married before or so the story goes.*

a tall story an obviously untrue story that is intended to be believed.

story[2] *see* **storey**.

stout[1] [staut] *adj* **1** (*liter*: *usu attrib*) strong or thick: *a stout stick.* **2** (*formal or liter*: *usu attrib*) brave and resolute: *The defenders put up a stout resistance*; *stout opposition.* **3** (*euph*) (of a person) fat: *He's getting stout*; *a stout old lady.*

,stout-'hearted *adj* (*liter*) brave: *stout-hearted men.*

stout[2] [staut] **1** *nu* a dark, strong type of beer: *a bottle of stout.* **2** *nc* a glass of stout.

stove[1] [stouv] *nc* an apparatus using coal, gas, electricity or other fuel, used for cooking, or for heating a room: *a gas/electric (cooking) stove*; *Put the saucepan on the stove.*

stove[2] *see* **stave**[1].

stow [stou] *vt* (*esp naut*) to pack something neatly and *esp* out of sight: *The sailor stowed his belongings in his locker*; *The ship's hold was stowed with valuable cargo.* – *See also* **stow away** *below.*

'stowaway *nc* a person who stows away (*def 1*): *She was a stowaway on a ship to America.*

stow away 1 *vi* to hide oneself on a ship, aircraft *etc* before its departure, in order to travel on it without paying the fare: *He stowed away on a cargo ship for New York.* **2** *vt sep* to put or pack in a (secret) place until required: *My jewellery is safely stowed away in the bank.*

straddle ['stradl] *vt* to stand or sit with legs on either side of (*eg* a path, a chair *etc*): *He straddled the path/stood with his legs straddling the path*; *He sat facing the back of the chair, (his legs) straddling the seat.*

straggle ['stragl] *vi* (*formal*) **1** to grow or spread untidily: *His beard straggled over his chest.* **2** to walk too slowly to remain with a body of *eg* marching soldiers, walkers *etc*: *They straggled along behind the others.*

'straggler *nc* a person who walks too slowly during a walk, march *etc* and gets left behind the main group: *A car was sent to pick up the stragglers.*

'straggly *adj* (*inf*) straggling untidily: *straggly hair*; *a straggly plant.* **'straggliness** *nu.*

straight [streit] *adj* **1** not bent or curved: *a straight line*; *straight* (=not curly) *hair*; *That line is not straight.* **2** (of a person, his behaviour *etc*) honest, frank and direct: *Give me a straight answer!*; (*inf*) *You're not being straight with me.* **3** (*pred*) properly or levelly positioned: *Your tie isn't straight*; *The picture isn't straight.* **4** (*pred*: *often inf*) correct and tidy: *I'll never get this house straight!*; *The police made him repeat his story to make sure they had the facts straight*; *I was wrongly quoted in the newspaper and want to put the record straight* (= give the correct words); *Now let's get this straight!* (= get the facts right!). **5** (of drinks) not mixed: *He wants a straight gin*; *He likes his vodka straight.* **6** (of a face, expression *etc*) not smiling or laughing: *You should keep a straight face/your face straight while you tell a joke.* **7** (*drama*) (of an actor) playing normal rather than eccentric characters, or (of a play) of the ordinary type – not a musical or variety show. – *adv* **1** in a straight, not curved, line; directly: *His route went straight across the desert*; *She can't steer straight*; *You'll get to the museum if you keep straight on.* **2** immediately, without any delay: *He went straight home after the meeting.* **3** (*inf*) honestly or fairly: *You're not playing* (= behaving) *straight.* – *nc* (*with* **the**: *no pl*) the straight part of something, *eg* of a racecourse: *He's in the final straight.*

'straighten *vti* to make or become straight: *He straightened his tie*; *The road curved and then straightened.*

'straightness *nu.*

straight'forward *adj* **1** without difficulties or complications; simple: *a straightforward job*; *a straightforward case of jealousy*; *This job is not as straightforward as it first seems to be.* **2** (of a person, his manner *etc*) frank and honest: *a nice straightforward boy*; *She is so straightforward compared with her brother.* **straight'forwardly** *adv.* **straight'forwardness** *nu.*

straight talking *nu* frank and honest conversation: *The time has come for some straight talking.*

go straight (*inf*) (of a former criminal) to lead an honest life: *He got out of prison last year, and now he is going straight.*

straight away, (*old*) **,straight'way** *adv* immediately: *Do it straight away!*

straighten out/up *vi, vt sep* to make or become straight: *Their house is just where the lane straightens out*; *He was bending over his work, but straightened up when he saw me*; *She straightened the room up*; *He's trying to straighten out the facts.*

a straight fight (*polit*) an election contest involving only two candidates.

straight off (*inf*) straight away: *I knew straight off that she was telling a lie.*

straight out (*inf*) frankly: *I told her straight out that she was talking nonsense.*

strain[1] [strein] **1** *vti* to exert oneself or a part of the body to the greatest possible extent: *He strained his ears to hear the whisper*; *He strained every muscle to lift the stone*; *The dog will hurt its neck if it strains* (= pulls forward) *so much at its lead*; *He strained to reach the rope*; (*usu facet*) *I'd be glad if you could help me, but don't strain yourself.* **2** *vt* to injure (a muscle *etc*) through too much use, exertion *etc*: *He has strained a muscle in his leg*; *You'll strain your eyes by reading in such a poor light.* **3** *vt* (*formal*) to force or stretch (*eg* patience, authority, a word's meaning *etc*) too far: *You were straining your authority by giving them permission to do that.* **4** *vt* to put (*eg* a mixture) through a sieve *etc* in order to separate solid matter from liquid: *She strained the coffee*; *Have you strained the potatoes?* – *See also* **strain off** *below.* – **1** *nu* force exerted: *Can nylon ropes take more strain than the old kind of rope?* **2** *ncu* (something *eg* too much work *etc* that causes) a state of anxiety and fatigue: *The strain of nursing her dying husband was too much for her; She is suffering from strain.* **3** *ncu* (an) injury *esp* to a muscle caused by too much exertion: *He is suffering from muscular strain.* **4** *nc* too great a demand: *These constant delays are a strain on our patience.*

strained *adj* (of a person's manner, behaviour *etc*) not natural, easy or relaxed: *a strained smile; There were strained relations* (= unfriendly feelings) *between them for several weeks after the quarrel; She looks rather strained today.*

ˈstrainer *nc* (*sometimes in cmpds*) a sieve or other utensil for separating solids from liquids: *a coffee-/tea-strainer.*

strain off *vt sep* to remove (liquid) from *eg* vegetables by using a sieve *etc*: *When the potatoes were cooked, she strained off the water.*

strain[2] [strein] *nc* **1** (*more tech than* **kind** *or* **type**) a kind or breed (of animals, plants *etc*): *He has been trying to breed a new strain of cattle; a virus of unidentified strain.* **2** a tendency in a person's character: *I'm sure there's a strain of madness in her; There's a strain of madness in her family.* **3** (*formal or liter*: *often in pl*) (the sound of) a tune: *I heard the strains of a hymn coming from the church.* **4** (*formal or liter*) a particular mood or manner in writing, talking *etc*: *He writes in a happier strain about his childhood; He continued to speak in the same strain.*

strait [streit] *nc* **1** (*often in pl*) a narrow strip of sea between two pieces of land: *the straits of Gibraltar; the Bering Strait.* **2** (*in pl*: *formal*) difficulty; (financial) need: *The defenders were reduced to terrible straits during the siege and finally ate each other; She has been in great straits (financially) since her husband died.*

ˈstrait-jacket *nc* a type of jacket with long sleeves tied behind to hold back the arms of *eg* a violent and insane person who is being restrained.

ˌstrait-ˈlaced *adj* (*derog*) strict and severe in attitude and behaviour: *Her parents are rather strait-laced; strait-laced attitudes.*

straitened [ˈstreitnd]: **in straitened circumstances** (*formal euph*) having very little money: *They used to be very wealthy but they live in straitened circumstances now.*

strand[1] [strand] *nc* (*liter except in place-names*) the shore or beach of a sea or lake: *Children played on the strand.*

be stranded 1 (of a ship) to go aground: *The ship was stranded on the rocks during a violent storm.* **2** (*also* **be left stranded**) to be left helpless without *eg* money or friends: *He was left stranded in Yugoslavia when he lost his money and passport; When we heard that we had missed the plane we realized that we were stranded in a strange city.*

strand[2] [strand] *nc* a thin thread, *eg* one of those twisted together to form rope, string, knitting-wool *etc*, or a long thin lock of hair: *She pushed the strands of hair back from her face.*

strange [streindʒ] *adj* **1** not known, seen *etc* before; unfamiliar or foreign: *What would you do if you found a strange man in your house?; Whenever you're in a strange country, you should take the opportunity of learning some of the language; The town is strange to me; I'm still strange to the customs here.* **2** unusual, odd or queer: *She had a strange look on her face; The dog was making a strange noise; She looks a bit strange today.* **ˈstrangeness** *nu.*

ˈstrangely *adv* in an odd way: *The man's face was strangely familiar. – See also* **strangely enough** *below.*

ˈstranger *nc* **1** a person who is unknown to oneself: *I've met her once before, so she's not a complete stranger (to me).* **2** (*inf*) a visitor: *I can't tell you where the post office is – I'm a stranger here myself.*

be a ˈstranger to (*liter or formal*) to have no experience of (a condition, quality *etc*): *He is no stranger to misfortune* (= has had a lot of misfortune); *He is a stranger to fear* (= is very brave); (*euph*) *He is a stranger to the truth* (= He tells lies).

strange to say/tell/relate surprisingly: *Strange to say, he did pass his exam after all.*

strangely enough it is strange (that): *He lives next door, but strangely enough I rarely see him; 'Did you recognize him?' 'Strangely enough, yes.'*

strangle [ˈstraŋgl] *vt* to kill by gripping or squeezing the neck tightly, *eg* by tightening a cord *etc* round it: *It was said that he had strangled his wife with a nylon stocking; This top button is nearly strangling me!;* (*fig*) *High taxation is gradually strangling the country's economy.*

ˈstrangled *adj* (*liter*: *usu attrib*) (of a cry, sob, scream *etc*) half-suppressed.

ˌstranguˈlation [-gju-] *nu* the act of strangling or state of being strangled: *The murder victim had been killed by strangulation.*

ˈstranglehold *nc* (*no pl*: *often fig*) a tight grip or control over something that prevents it moving freely, developing *etc*: *The trade unions seem to have the government in a stranglehold.*

strap [strap] *nc* **1** (*often in cmpds*) a narrow strip of leather, cloth, or other material, *eg* with a buckle for fastening something (*eg* a suitcase, wristwatch *etc*) or by which to hold, hang or support something (*eg* a camera, rucksack *etc*): *I need a new watch-strap; luggage straps; shoulder straps (of a bra).* **2** a short looped strip of leather *etc*, hanging from the roof of a train, by which a standing passenger can support himself. – *v* – *pt, ptp* **strapped** – *vt* **1** to beat (*eg* a schoolchild) on the hand with a leather strap: *He was strapped for being rude to the teacher.* **2** (*often with* **on, to** *etc*: *neg* **un-**) to fasten with a strap *etc*: *The two pieces of luggage were strapped together; The robbers strapped him to a tree; He strapped on his new watch.*

ˈstrapping *adj* large, tall and strong: *She's a big strapping girl; The farmer's son is tall and strapping.*

strap in *vt sep* to confine with a strap, *eg* by fastening a safety-belt in a car: *I won't start this car till you've strapped yourself in; Have you strapped the child in?*

strap up *vt sep* to fasten or bind with a strap, or other form of binding: *His injured knee was washed and neatly strapped up* (= bandaged); *He has broken a rib and the doctor has strapped it up.*

strata *see* **stratum**.

stratagem [ˈstratədʒəm] *ncu* (*formal*) (the use of) a trick or plan *eg* for deceiving an enemy: *several bold stratagems; Stratagem and deceit are his speciality; He achieved his aim by stratagem.*

strategy [ˈstratədʒi] *nu* **1** the art of planning a campaign or large military operation: *naval/military strategy.* **2** the art of managing an affair cleverly: *By careful strategy he gradually managed to persuade the committee to agree.*

straˈtegic [-ˈtiː-] *adj* (*usu attrib*) of (successful) strategy: *The army made a strategic withdrawal/retreat; As a town councillor he's in a strategic position for influencing the education plans.* **straˈtegically** *adv.*

ˈstrategist *nc (formal)* a person who is an expert in (*esp* military) strategy.

stratify *etc see* **stratum**.

stratosphere [ˈstratəsfiə] *nc (no pl: usu with* **the***)* (*tech*) the layer of the earth's atmosphere between 10 and 60 kilometres above the earth.

stratum [ˈstra:təm, (*Amer*) ˈstrei-] – *pl* **ˈstrata** [-tə] – *nc* **1** (*tech*) a layer of rock: *This stratum of the earth's crust belongs to the Jurassic period* (= one of the earth's earliest geological periods). **2** (*fig formal*) a level or class in society: *In a hospital ward you will meet people from all the different social strata.*

stratify [ˈstratifai] *vt (often in passive)* to form in layers or levels: *You can see how the rock in these cliffs has been stratified; Medieval society was stratified by the feudal system.* **ˈstratified** *adj.* **ˌstratifiˈcation** [-fi-] *nu.*

straw [stro:] **1** *nu* the cut stalks of corn *etc,* having many uses, *eg* as bedding for cattle *etc,* making mats and other goods *etc*: *The cows need fresh straw;* (*attrib*) *She wore a straw sunhat.* **2** *nc* a single stalk of corn: *There's a straw in your hair; Their offer isn't worth a straw!* (= It is completely worthless!). **3** *nc* a paper or plastic tube through which to suck a drink into the mouth: *He was sipping orange juice through a straw.*

straw poll/vote *nc* a vote taken unofficially *eg* within a trade union to get some idea of the general opinion.

clutch at straws *see* **clutch**.

the last straw an additional and intolerable circumstance in a disagreeable situation: *The hotel was expensive, the food poor, and the bad weather was the last straw.*

a man of straw (*liter*) a person without any real power or influence: *Some of these politicians are just men of straw.*

strawberry [ˈstro:bəri] *nc* **1** a type of small juicy red fruit: *Strawberries are delicious with sugar and cream;* (*attrib*) *strawberry jam.* **2** the plant which bears such fruit.

stray [strei] *vi (formal)* to wander, *esp* from the right path, place *etc*: *The shepherd went to search for some sheep that had strayed; It's annoying to talk to people who keep straying from the point;* (*old relig*) *We have strayed from God's ways* (= become sinful). – *nc* a cat, dog *etc* that has strayed and has no home: *She loves cats and is always bringing strays home.* – *adj (attrib)* **1** wandering or lost: *stray cats and dogs.* **2** occasional, or not part of a general group or tendency: *This is only a stray example; The weather was beautiful except for one or two stray showers.*

See also **astray**.

streak [stri:k] *nc* **1** a long, irregular mark or stripe different in colour from the surrounding surface *etc*: *The aeroplane left a white streak of vapour in the blue sky; There was a streak of blood on her cheek; a streak of lightning.* **2** (*fig*) a trace of some quality in a person's character *etc*: *She has a streak of obstinacy/selfishness in her.* – **1** *vt (usu in passive)* to mark with streaks: *Her dark hair was streaked with grey; The child's face was streaked with tears.* **2** *vi (inf)* to move very fast, like a streak of lightning: *The runner streaked round the racetrack.*

ˈstreaky *adj* marked with streaks: *streaky bacon* (= bacon with fat and lean in layers). **ˈstreakily** *adv.* **ˈstreakiness** *nu.*

be on a winning streak to have a series of successes in gambling *etc*: *I think I'll go on playing cards for a while – I'm on a winning streak.*

stream [stri:m] *nc* **1** a small river or brook: *He managed to jump across the stream.* **2** (*sometimes in cmpds*) a flow of *eg* water, air *etc*: *A stream of water was pouring down the gutter; A cold airstream is covering the north of Britain; A stream of people was coming out of the cinema; He got into the wrong stream* (= lane) *of traffic; He uttered a stream of abuse/curses.* **3** (*often in cmpds*) the current of a river *etc*: *He was swimming upstream/downstream/against the stream.* **4** in schools, one of the classes into which children of the same age are divided according to ability: *He's a clever boy – he has always been in the A-stream.* – **1** *vi* to flow: *Tears streamed down her face; The wound was streaming with blood; Workers streamed out of the factory gates; Her hair streamed out in the wind.* **2** *vti* to divide school children into classes according to ability: *Many people disapprove of streaming (children) in schools.*

ˈstreamer *nc* a long narrow banner, or narrow paper ribbon: *The aeroplane dragged a streamer that read 'Come to the Festival'; The bus taking the children to the picnic was decorated with balloons and streamers.*

ˈstreamline *vt* to make (a business *etc*) more efficient, *eg* by simplifying: *We must steamline our methods.*

ˈstreamlined *adj (usu attrib)* **1** (of a plane, car, ship *etc*) shaped so as to move faster and more efficiently: *the newest, most streamlined aircraft.* **2** modern and efficient: *a beautiful streamlined kitchen.*

street [stri:t] **1** *nc* a road with houses, shops *etc* on one or both sides, in a town or village: *Where is the main shopping street?; I met her in the street.* **2** *n (with cap: often abbrev* **St** *when written)* a word used in the names of certain roads: *Her address is 4 Shakespeare St; She lives in Shakespeare Street.*

ˈstreetcar *nc (esp Amer)* a tramcar.

ˈstreetwalker *nc (inf)* a prostitute.

be *etc* **on the street** (*inf*) to be homeless: *We'll find ourselves on the street if we don't pay the rent.*

be streets ahead of/better than (*inf*) to be much better than: *Your work is streets ahead of hers.*

be up (someone's) street (*inf*) to be exactly suitable for (a person): *That job is just up her street.*

go on the streets (*sl*) to become a prostitute.

not to be in the same street as (*inf*) to be completely different, *usu* worse, in quality than: *Her clothes are not in the same street as yours; She's not in the same street as you when it comes to organizing meetings.*

strength, strengthen *see* **strong**.

strenuous [ˈstrenjuəs] *adj* energetic; requiring effort or energy: *It's a strenuous climb to the top of the mountain; He made strenuous efforts to save her; That long walk will be too strenuous for the old man.*

ˈstrenuously *adv* in a strong or vigorous way: *He strenuously denied the accusation.*

stress [stres] *ncu* **1** the worry or pressure experienced by a person in particular circumstances, or the state of anxiety caused by this: *Not all of us can cope with the stresses of modern life; I apologize if, in the stress of the moment, I was rude to you; The child's headaches may be caused by stress.* **2** (*tech*) force exerted by (parts of) bodies on each other: *It is vital for bridge-designers to know about stress.* **3** force or emphasis placed, in speaking, on particular syllables or words: *In the word 'widow' we put stress on the first syllable.* – *vt* to emphasize (a syllable *etc*, or a fact *etc*): *Should you stress the last syllable in 'violin'?; He stressed that they must arrive punctually/the necessity of being punctual.*

'stress-mark *nc* a mark (') used to show where the stress comes in a word *etc*: *'bookworm; de'signer.*

lay/put stress on (*formal*) to emphasize (a fact *etc*): *He laid stress on this point; He puts too much stress on dressing neatly; She did not lay enough stress on the importance of arriving early.*

See also **primary stress, secondary stress,** *under* **prime, second**.

stretch [stretʃ] **1** *vti* to make or become longer or wider *esp* by pulling or by being pulled: *She stretched the piece of elastic to its fullest extent; The painter stretched the canvas tightly over the frame; His scarf was so long that it could stretch across the room; This material stretches; The sweater stretched* (= became and remained bigger) *when it was washed; The dog yawned and stretched (itself); He stretched (his arm/hand) up as far as he could, but still could not reach the shelf; Ask someone to pass you the jam instead of stretching across the table for it;* (*fig*) *To say he was ill is stretching the truth – he was merely drunk.* **2** *vt* (*often in passive*) to cause (a person) to exert himself: *He feels that he isn't being stretched by the work.* **3** *vi* (of land *etc*) to extend: *The plain stretched ahead of them for miles.* – *See also* **stretch out** *below.* – *nc* **1** an act of stretching or state of being stretched: *He got out of bed and had a good stretch; You couldn't call her beautiful – not by any stretch of the imagination* (= however hard you try to think her so). **2** a continuous extent, of *eg* a type of country, or of time: *I always think this is a pretty stretch of country; a stretch of bad road; They still remembered him, even after a stretch of twenty years.* – *See also* **at a stretch** *below.*

'stretcher *nc* a light folding bed with handles for carrying the sick or wounded: *The injured man was carried to the ambulance on a stretcher.*

'stretchy *adj* (of materials *etc*) able to stretch: *a stretchy bathing-costume; This material is stretchy.*

at a 'stretch continuously: *He can't work for more than three hours at a stretch.*

be at full stretch to be using all one's powers, energy *etc* to the limit in doing something: *They're at full stretch trying to complete the work in time.*

stretch one's legs to go for a walk for the sake of exercise: *I need to stretch my legs.*

stretch out *vt sep, vi* in moving the body, to straighten or extend: *She stretched out a hand for the child to hold; He stretched (himself) out on the grass; She stretched out on the bed.*

stretch a point to go further, in giving permission, than the rules allow: *The children are only allowed two sweets a day but we might stretch a point today.*

strew [stru:] – *pt* **strewed**: *ptp* **strewn** – *vt* (*liter or facet except in ptp*) to scatter: *Rubbish was strewn about on the ground; The ground was strewn with rubbish.*

stricken ['strikən] *adj* (*esp liter except in cmpds*) deeply affected, overwhelmed or afflicted: *In his youth he was stricken with a crippling disease;* (*in cmpds*) *the grief-stricken parents of the dead child; Panic-stricken crowds rushed from the burning theatre; He knew from her stricken* (= very worried) *face that there was bad news.*

See also **strike, stroke**[1].

strict [strikt] *adj* **1** (of a person or law *etc*) severe, stern, and compelling obedience: *This class needs a strict teacher; His parents were very strict with him; The school rules are unnecessarily strict; He had strict orders to take the letter straight to the hospital; He told me this in the strictest confidence* (= secrecy). **2** exact or precise: *What does 'strategy' mean, in the strict military sense?; If the strict truth were known, he was drunk, not ill.*

'strictness *nu.*

'strictly *adv* in a strict way: *He was strictly brought up by his parents; He was not always strictly* (= exactly) *truthful.*

strictly speaking if we must be completely accurate, act according to rules *etc*: *Strictly speaking, he should be punished for this; Strictly speaking, the cyclist was responsible for the accident.*

stricture ['striktʃə] *nc* (*often in pl*: *very formal*) an unfavourable remark or criticism: *In spite of these strictures, the critic thought the book good; It seems unkind to pass strictures on* (= to criticize unfavourably) *a friend's work.*

stride [straid] – *pt* **strode** [stroud]: *ptp* (*rare*) **stridden** ['stridn] – *vi* to walk with long steps: *He strode along the path; He strode off in anger; The stream was so narrow that we could stride* (= walk with one step) *across it.* – *nc* **1** (the space covered by) a long step: *He was only a stride away from her when he stopped; He walked with long strides.* **2** (*no pl*) a manner of striding: *He has an easy, swinging stride.*

make great strides to progress well: *He's making great strides in his piano-playing.*

take (something) in one's stride to accept or cope with (a matter) successfully without worrying about it: *She takes difficulties in her stride.*

See also **astride**.

strident ['straidənt] *adj* (*formal*) (of a sound, *esp* a voice) loud and harsh: *He could hear her strident tones in the next room; Her voice is rather strident.*

'stridently *adv.* **'stridency** *nu.*

strife [straif] *nu* (*formal*) conflict, fighting or quarrelling: *a country torn by strife; This century has been a time of widespread industrial strife* (= disagreements between employers and workers in industries).

strike [straik] – *pt* **struck** [strʌk]: *ptps* **struck**, (*arch or liter except in cmpds*) **stricken** ['strikən] – **1** *vt* (*more formal than* **hit**) to hit, knock or give a blow to (someone or something): *He struck me in the face with his fist; Why did you strike him?; The stone struck me a blow on the side of the head; His head struck the table as he fell; The tower of the church was struck by lightning; The morning sun was striking the hilltops.* – *See also* **strike at** *below.* **2** *vi* (*formal*) to attack: *The enemy troops struck at dawn; We must prevent the disease striking again.* **3** *vt* to produce (sparks or a flame) by rubbing: *He struck a match/light; He struck sparks from the stone with his knife.* **4** *vi* (of workers) to stop work as a protest, or in order to force employers to give better pay: *The men decided to strike for higher wages/for better conditions/against the dismissal of a colleague.* **5** *vt* (*formal*) to discover or find: *After months of prospecting they finally struck gold/oil; If we walk in this direction we may strike the right path.* **6** *vti* to (make something) sound: *He struck a note* *on the piano/violin*; *The clock struck twelve*; (*fig*) *His speech struck a note of sadness when he mentioned those who had died in the war.* **7** *vt* to impress, or give a particular impression to (a person): *I was struck by the resemblance between the two men*; *This discussion strikes me as* (= seems to me to be) *pointless*; *How does the plan strike you?*; *It/The thought struck me* (= I suddenly thought) *that she had come to borrow money.* **8** *vt* to mint or manufacture (a coin, medal *etc*): *A 25-pence piece was struck in honour of the Queen's Jubilee.* **9** *vi* (*formal*) to go in a certain direction: *He left the path and struck* (*off*) *across the fields.* **10** *vt* to lower or pull down (tents, flags *etc*): *They struck camp* (= packed up their tents) *and continued their journey. – See also* **strike** *in phrases below. –* *nc* **1** an act of striking (*def 4*): *a miners' strike*; *a post-office workers'/postal strike*; (*in cmpds or attrib*) *The trade union had a strike fund from which strike-pay was provided for striking workers.* **2** a discovery of oil, gold *etc*: *He made a lucky strike.*

'striker *nc* **1** a person who strikes (*def 4*): *The strikers held a meeting and decided to call off* (= discontinue or cancel) *the strike.* **2** in football, a forward player.

'striking *adj* noticeable or impressive: *She's a striking woman*; *She is tall and striking*; *She always wears striking clothes.* **'strikingly** *adv.*

be (out) on strike (of workers) to be striking: *The electricity workers have been out on strike for several weeks now.*

call a strike (of a trade union leader *etc*) to ask workers to strike: *They will call a strike if they don't get more money.*

come out on strike (of workers) to strike: *The coalminers are coming out on strike for higher wages.*

ˌcome, ˌbe within 'striking distance of to come or be close enough to hit or attack (something): *The enemy was within striking distance of our city's walls*; (*fig*) *He didn't come within striking distance of passing the exam* (= He didn't nearly pass the exam).

strike an agreement *see* **strike a bargain**.

'strike at *vt fus* to attempt to strike, or aim a blow at (a person *etc*): *He struck at the dog with his stick.*

strike an attitude/pose to place oneself in a particular *usu* rather showy pose, as an actor does, or to express an opinion *etc* strongly and *usu* insincerely: *He's always striking attitudes.*

strike a balance to reach a satisfactory state of compromise between two undesirable extremes: *As a teacher she finds it difficult to strike a balance between too much and too little discipline.*

strike a bargain/agreement to make a bargain; to reach an agreement: *We struck a bargain with each other.*

strike a blow for to make an effort on behalf of (a cause *etc*): *A blow was struck for women's rights today.*

strike dead, blind, dumb *etc* (*esp old or relig*) to make (a person) die, become blind or dumb *etc* suddenly: *God will strike you dead if you tell lies*; (*fig*) *I was struck dumb with amazement.*

strike down *vt sep* (*formal*: *usu fig*) to hit or knock (a person) so that he falls down: *He was struck down by* (= was killed by or afflicted with) *a terrible disease.*

strike fear/terror *etc* **into** (*formal*) to fill (a person) with fear *etc*: *The sound struck terror into them/their hearts.*

strike home (*formal*) (of a blow, insult *etc*) to reach the place where it will hurt most: *His fist/bitter remark struck home.*

strike it rich (*inf*) to make a lot of money: *He did not make much money in his new business at first but he finally struck it rich.*

strike (it) lucky (*inf*) to have good luck in a particular matter: *We certainly struck lucky in choosing that school.*

strike off *vt sep* to remove or erase (*eg* a doctor's name) from a professional register *etc* for misconduct: *He/His name was struck off.*

strike out 1 *vt sep* to erase or cross out (a word *etc*): *He read the essay and struck out a word here and there.* **2** *vi* to start fighting: *He's a man who strikes out with his fists whenever he's angry.* **3** *vi* to swim strongly: *He struck out towards the land.*

strike a pose *see* **strike an attitude** *above.*

strike terror into *see* **strike fear into** *above.*

strike up 1 *vi, vt sep* to begin to play a tune *etc*: *The band struck up* (*with*) *'The Red Flag'.* **2** to begin (a friendship, conversation *etc*): *He struck up an acquaintance with a girl on the train.*

See also **stricken, stroke**[1].

string [striŋ] **1** *ncu* (*sometimes in cmpds*) (a piece of) long narrow cord made of threads twisted together, or tape, for tying, fastening *etc*: *I need a piece of string to tie this parcel up*; *She bought a ball of string*; *The puppet's strings got entangled*; *Please untie my apron-strings for me!* **2** *nc* (*less formal than* **fibre**) a fibre *etc, eg* on a vegetable: *Remove the strings from the beans/artichokes before cooking.* **3** *nc* a piece of wire, gut *etc* on a musical instrument, *eg* a violin: *His A-string broke*; (*attrib*) *a string orchestra* (= an orchestra consisting entirely of stringed instruments). **4** *nc* a series or group of things threaded on a cord *etc*: *a string of beads/onions.* **5** *nc* a number of things coming one after another: *He uttered a string of curses. – v – pt, ptp* **strung** [strʌŋ] – *vt* **1** to put (beads *etc*) on a string *etc*: *The pearls were sent to a jeweller to be strung*; (*fig*) *I can hardly string two words together in French.* **2** to put a string or strings on (*eg* a bow or stringed instrument): *The archer strung his bow and aimed an arrow at the target.* **3** to remove strings from (vegetables *etc*): *You should wash and string the beans.* **4** (*often with* **up, together** *etc*) to tie and hang with string *etc*: *The farmer shot two crows and strung them* (*up*) *on the fence. – See also* **string along, string out** *below.*

strings *n pl* (*often with* **the**) (in an orchestra, the group of people who play) stringed musical instruments played with a bow, *ie* violins, violas, 'cellos and double basses: *The conductor said the strings were too loud.*

'stringy *adj* (*derog*) (*esp* of meat or vegetables) having a lot of strings or tough fibres: *a stringy bit of meat*; *This meat is stringy.* **'stringiness** *nu.*

stringed instruments *n pl* musical instruments that have strings *eg* violins, guitars *etc.*

have (someone) on a string (*inf*) to have (a person) under one's control: *He seems to have his poor mother on a string.*

pull strings (*inf*) to use one's influence or that of others to gain an advantage: *His father had to pull strings to get him that job.*

pull the strings (*inf*) to be the person who is really, though *usu* not apparently, controlling the actions of others: *The Government pulls the strings when the Bank of England decides to change the bank rate.*

string along (*old sl*) **1** *vi* (*with* **with**) to be a girlfriend/boyfriend/companion to: *She has been stringing along with him for years.* 2 *vt sep* to keep (a person) attached to oneself without being seriously committed to him/her: *You're just stringing me along till you find a girl you like better.*

string out *vt sep* (*esp in passive*) to spread or stretch into a long line: *The runners were strung out along the course.*

strung up (*inf*) very nervous: *She's a bit strung up about her exam*; (*attrib*) *in rather a strung-up state.*

with no strings attached (*inf*) without any conditions: *The money was lent to them with no strings attached* (= without instructions or conditions about how it was to be spent).

See also **unstrung**.

stringent ['strindʒənt] *adj* (*formal*) (of rules *etc*) very strict, or strongly enforced: *There should be much more stringent laws against the dropping of rubbish in the streets*; *The laws against stealing used to be very stringent.* '**stringently** *adv.*

'**stringency** *nu* (*formal*) 1 the quality of being strict. 2 (*econ*: *often attrib*) scarcity of money for lending *etc*: *The government are demanding stringency measures.*

stringy *see* **string**.

strip [strip] – *pt, ptp* **stripped** – 1 *vt* to remove the covering from (something): *He stripped the old wallpaper off the wall*; *He stripped the branch* (*of its bark*) *with his knife.* 2 *vti* to undress: *She stripped the child* (*naked*) *and put him in the bath*; *He stripped and dived into the water*; *They were told to strip to the waist* (= remove all the clothes from the top half of their bodies). 3 *vt* to remove the contents of (a house *etc*): *The house/room was stripped bare/stripped of its furnishings*; *They stripped the house of all its furnishings.* 4 *vt* (*formal*) to deprive (a person) of something: *He was stripped of his possessions/rights*; *The officer was stripped of his rank for misconduct.* – *See also* **strip down, strip off** *below.* – *nc* 1 a long narrow piece of (*eg* cloth, ground *etc*): *a strip of paper*; *Each house has its own strip of lawn*; *The wallpaper was hanging in strips from the wall.* 2 a strip cartoon. 3 a footballer's shirt, shorts, socks *etc*: *The team has a red and white strip.*

'**stripper** *nc* (*inf*) a woman who does strip-tease.

strip cartoon *nc* a row of drawings, *eg* in a newspaper or comic paper, telling an (amusing) story.

'**strip-club** *nc* a club in which strip-tease is regularly done.

'**strip-lighting** *nu* lighting by long tubes rather than bulbs.

'**strip-show** *nc* a theatrical entertainment that includes strip-tease.

ˌ**strip-'tease** *nu* the act, by a woman, of removing her clothes one by one as a theatrical entertainment: (*attrib*) *a strip-tease show.*

strip down *vt sep* 1 to remove *eg* wallpaper, paint *etc* from (walls, doors *etc*): *The woodwork should be stripped down*; *Strip the doors down before you put the new paint on.* 2 to remove parts from (an engine *etc*) in order to repair or clean it: *He stripped the engine down and then couldn't put it together again.*

strip off *vi, vt sep,* to remove clothes or a covering from a thing or person: *He stripped* (*his clothes*) *off and had a shower*; *The doctor stripped his bandage off.*

stripe [straip] *nc* 1 a band of colour *etc* different from the background on which it lies: *The wallpaper was grey with broad green stripes*; *A zebra has black and white stripes.* 2 (*mil*) a (*usu* V-shaped) badge worn on a uniform sleeve to show rank.

striped *adj* having stripes: *a striped shirt*; *blue-and-white-striped curtains*; *Her new dress is red-and-white striped.*

'**stripy** *adj* (*usu attrib*) covered with stripes: *A tiger has a stripy coat.*

stripling ['stripliŋ] *nc* (*liter or sometimes facet*) a boy or youth not yet fully grown: *A young stripling like you should have plenty of energy!*

stripper *see* **strip**.

strive [straiv] – *pt* **strove** [strouv]: *ptp* **striven** ['strivn] – *vi* (*formal*) to try very hard or struggle: *He always strives to please his teacher*; *All his life he has striven against injustice.*

strode *see* **stride**.

stroke[1] [strouk] 1 *nc* an act of hitting, or the blow given: *He felled the tree with one stroke of the axe*; *The slave was given five strokes of the whip.* 2 *nc* a sudden occurrence of something: *He was killed by a stroke of lightning*; *By an unfortunate stroke of fate, the train was late*; *What a stroke of luck to find that money!* 3 *nc* (*sometimes fig*) the sound made by a clock striking the hour: *She arrived on the stroke of* (= punctually at) *ten.* 4 *nc* a movement or mark made in one direction by a pen, pencil, paintbrush *etc*: *He erased the name with a stroke of the pen*; *He carefully shaded the portrait with short, even strokes*; *'4/1', in words, is 'four-stroke-one'.* 5 *nc* a single pull of an oar in rowing, or a hit with the bat in playing cricket: *He rowed with vigorous strokes*; *He played a cautious stroke.* 6 *ncu* (*often in cmpds*) a movement of the arms and legs in swimming, or a particular method of swimming: *He swam with slow, strong strokes*; *Can you do breaststroke/backstroke?* 7 *nc* (*no pl*) an effort or action: *I haven't done a stroke* (*of work*) *all day.* 8 *nc* (*no pl*) a clever achievement: *Your idea is a stroke of genius*; *That was a masterly stroke!* 9 *nc* a sudden attack of illness which damages the brain, causing paralysis, loss of feeling in the body *etc*: *He is unable to speak properly as a result of a stroke.*

at a 'stroke with a single effort: *He solved the problem at a stroke.*

See also **strike**.

stroke[2] [strouk] *vt* to rub (*eg* a furry animal) gently and repeatedly in one direction, *esp* as a sign of affection: *He stroked the cat/her hair/her cheek*; *The dog loves being stroked.* – *nc* an act of stroking: *He gave the dog a stroke.*

stroll [stroul] *vi* to walk or wander without hurry: *He strolled along the street.* – *nc* an act of strolling: *I went for a stroll round the town.*

strong [stroŋ] *adj* 1 firm, sound, or powerful *eg* in body or mind, and therefore not easily broken, destroyed, attacked, defeated, resisted, or affected by weariness, illness *etc*: *strong furniture*; *a strong castle*; *a strong wind*; *She's a strong swimmer*; *He has a very strong will*; *With his strong personality he ought to succeed*; *He has never been very strong* (= healthy); *He is not strong enough to lift that heavy table*; *The wind is too strong to fly your kite*; *These shoes are not strong enough for a child.* 2 very noticeable; very intense: *The colour of the walls is too strong*; *a strong smell*; *I have a strong impression that she's lying*; *I took a strong dislike to him*; *I have strong feelings about people smoking.* 3 containing a large amount of the flavouring ingredient: *strong tea/coffee*; *This cocoa* *is too strong.* **4** (*gram*) (of a verb) forming the past tense by changing the vowel rather than by adding **-d, -ed,** or **-t**: *You say 'I swam' not 'I swimmed' because 'swim' is a strong verb.* **5** (of a group, force *etc*) numbering a particular amount: *An army 20 000 strong was advancing towards the town.*

strength [streŋθ] *nu* **1** the quality of being strong: *He underestimated the enemy's strength; He got his strength back slowly after his illness; I hadn't the strength to resist him; Is your tea the right strength?* **2** the number of people *etc* in a force, organization *etc*, considered as an indication of its power or effectiveness: *The protesters were present at the meeting in great strength* (= in large numbers); *The force is below strength* (= contains too few people)/*must be brought up to strength* (= increased to the appropriate number). – *See also* **on the strength of** *below.*

strengthen ['streŋθən] *vti* to make or become strong or stronger: *He did exercises to strengthen his muscles; The wind strengthened; The pound has strengthened against the dollar* (= The value of the pound has increased in relation to the dollar).

'strongly *adv* in a strong way: *He smelt strongly of alcohol; I strongly suspect that he's going mad.*

'strongbox *nc* a safe or box for valuables, money *etc.*

strong drink *nu* (*formal or facet*) alcoholic liquors: *His parents brought him up to disapprove of strong drink.*

'stronghold *nc* **1** a fort, fortress or castle *etc.* **2** a place where a cause *etc* is strongly supported: *The town council is a stronghold of conservatism.*

strong language *nu* (*formal or facet*) swearing or abuse: *The workman used strong language and embarrassed the old lady.*

ˌstrong-'minded *adj* having a determined mind: *You must be strong-minded to study when the sun is shining; a strong-minded young woman.*

'strong point *nc* a quality *etc* in which a person excels: *His ability to talk to strangers is one of his strong points.*

strongroom *nc* a room specially constructed for keeping valuable articles, with thick walls and a heavy steel door *etc.*

strong-willed *see* **will**.

be going strong *see* **go**.

on the 'strength of relying on: *On the strength of this offer of money, we plan to start building soon.*

strong-arm tactics/methods *etc* the use of violent methods to solve a problem *etc.*

strop [strop] *nc* a strip of *eg* leather on which a razor is sharpened. – *v* – *pt, ptp* **stropped** – *vt* to sharpen (a razor) on a strop.

stroppy ['stropi] *adj* (*derog inf*) obstinate and bad-tempered: *He's feeling stroppy today; He gets stroppy if you disagree with him; He is in a stroppy mood.*

strove *see* **strive**.

struck *see* **strike**.

structure ['strʌktʃə] **1** *nu* the way in which something is arranged or organized: *A flower has quite a complicated structure; the structure of a human body/of society in Britain.* **2** *nc* (*more formal than* **building**) a building, or something that is built or constructed: *The Eiffel Tower is one of the most famous structures in the world.*

'structural *adj* (*formal*) of structure: *You must get permission before making structural alterations to your house; In the disease of cancer, structural changes occur in the body's cells; The damage is not structural.*

'structurally *adv* in a structural way: *These houses are not structurally sound.*

struggle ['strʌgl] *vi* **1** to twist violently when trying to free oneself: *The child struggled in his arms; A bird was caught in the net and was struggling to get free.* **2** to make great efforts or try hard: *All his life he has been struggling with illness/against injustice/for reform.* **3** to move with difficulty: *He struggled out of the hole/up from the chair/through the mud.* – *See also* **struggle along** *below.* – *nc* an act of struggling, or a fight: *The struggle for independence was long and hard; They yielded at last, but not without a struggle.*

struggle along *vi* (*inf*) to have only just enough money to live: *They managed to struggle along somehow.*

strum [strʌm] – *pt, ptp* **strummed** – *vti* (*sometimes derog*) to play *esp* noisily and unskilfully on a piano or stringed instrument: *He strummed his guitar; She was strumming away on the piano; He keeps strumming the same tune.*

strung *see* **string**.

strut[1] [strʌt] – *pt, ptp* **'strutted** – *vi* (*derog* when used of a person) to walk in a stiff, proud way: *The cock strutted about the farmyard; He was strutting along looking very pleased with himself.*

strut[2] [strʌt] *nc* (*tech*) a bar or column taking pressure or supporting weight in the direction of its length: *Struts will have to be fixed against the walls to stop the building from collapsing.*

strychnine ['strikni:n] *nu* a poison used in small quantities as a medicine: *He poisoned his wife with strychnine.*

stub [stʌb] *nc* **1** a stump or short remaining end of *eg* a cigarette, pencil *etc*: *The ashtray contained seven cigarette stubs.* **2** the counterfoil or retained section of a cheque *etc*: *Remember to fill in the amount on the stub as well as on the cheque.* – *v* – *pt, ptp* **stubbed** – *vt* to hurt (*esp* a toe) by striking it against something hard: *She stubbed her toe(s) against the bedpost.* – *See also* **stub out** *below.*

'stubby *adj* (*slightly derog*) being a stub, or short and thick like a stub: *a stubby tail; stubby fingers; Her fingers are short and stubby.*

stub out *vt sep* to extinguish (a cigarette or cigar) by pressing it against a hard surface: *He stubbed out his cigarette in the ashtray.*

stubble ['stʌbl] *nu* **1** the stubs or ends of corn left in the ground when the stalks are cut: *Mice ran among the stubble.* **2** short coarse hairs growing *eg* on an unshaven chin: *A grey stubble covered his chin.*

'stubbly *adj* being stubble; like stubble: *a stubbly beard; stubbly grass; His face is a bit stubbly – he needs a shave.*

stubborn ['stʌbən] *adj* (*usu derog*) obstinate, or unwilling to yield, obey *etc*: *a stubborn child; Donkeys are often considered stubborn; He is too stubborn to take my advice; his stubborn opposition/resistance to the plans; a stubborn skin disease* (= a skin disease that is difficult to cure); *His skin disease proved rather stubborn* (= it was difficult to cure).

stubby *see* **stub**.

stucco ['stʌkou] *nu, adj* (of) a kind of plaster used for covering walls, moulding ornaments round ceilings *etc.* – *v* – *3rd pers sing prt* **'stuccoes** *or* **'stuccos**: *pt, ptp* **'stuccoed** – *vt* (*usu in passive*) to cover (walls *etc*) with stucco.

stuck *see* **stick**[1].

stuck-up [stʌk'ʌp] *adj* (*inf derog*) proud and conceited: *What a stuck-up family they are!*; (*pred*) *She is too stuck up to speak to a workman.*

stud[1] [stʌd] *nc* a collection of horses and mares kept for breeding.

put out to stud to use (a male horse) for breeding purposes: *That horse does not race any more – he has been put out to stud.*

stud[2] [stʌd] *nc* **1** a knob, or nail with a large head, put into the surface of something as a protection or decoration *etc*: *There were metal studs on the soles of his football boots*; *a belt decorated with studs.* **2** a type of button with two heads for fastening a collar: *a collar stud.* – *v* – *pt, ptp* **'studded** – *vt* (*liter fig*) to cover with studs: *The sky was studded with stars*; *The lawn was studded with daisies*; *Her engagement ring was studded with diamonds.*

student ['stju:dənt] *nc* **1** an undergraduate or graduate studying for a degree at a university *etc*: *university students*; *He is a medical student*; *She is a music student*; (*attrib*) *She is a student nurse*; (*attrib*) *a student teacher*; (*attrib*) *student grants* (= amounts of money given to students by the government). **2** (*esp Amer*) a boy or girl at school. **3** (*formal*) a person studying a particular thing: *a student of politics*; *a student of human behaviour.*

studio ['stju:diou] – *pl* **'studios** – *nc* **1** the workroom of an artist or photographer: *The painter had a large studio with a window facing north.* **2** (*often pl*) a building or place in which cinema films are made: *This film was made at Ramrod Studios*; *a film studio.* **3** a room from which radio or television programmes are broadcast: *a television studio*; *We're returning you to John Jones in the studio.*

studious ['stju:diəs] *adj* (*formal*) **1** spending much time in careful studying: *She has always been a studious girl*; *She is so studious that she will certainly pass her exams.* **2** (*attrib*) careful and deliberate: *his studious avoidance of unpleasant subjects.*

'studiously *adv*. **'studiousness** *nu*.

study ['stʌdi] *vti* **1** to give time and attention to gaining knowledge of a subject: *What subject is he studying?*; *He is studying French*; *He is studying for a degree in mathematics*; *She is studying for her music exams*; *She's studying to be a teacher.* **2** to look at or examine (a thing *etc*) carefully: *He studied the railway timetable*; *She was studying the road-map carefully*; (*formal*) *He studied her face to see if she had been weeping*; *He has been studying the problem/situation for several months.* – **1** *ncu* the act of devoting time and attention to gaining knowledge: *He spends all his evenings in study*; *She has made a study of the habits of bees*; *He interrupted his studies to attend his sister's wedding.* **2** *nc* something that is (to be) studied or observed closely: *The Journal of Roman Studies.* **3** *nc* (the title of) a musical or artistic composition intended as an experiment or exercise: *a book of studies for the piano*; *The picture was entitled 'A Study in Grey'.* **4** *nc* a room in a house *etc*, in which to study, read, write *etc*: *Father is writing letters at his desk in his study*; *The headmaster wants to speak to the senior pupils in his study.*

'studied *adj* (*formal*: *often derog*) (of behaviour *etc*) **1** intentional or planned: *a studied insult.* **2** too careful, and obviously not genuine: *studied politeness*; *He spoke with studied ease.*

a brown study *see* **brown**.

See also **unstudied**.

stuff[1] [stʌf] **1** *nu* (*slightly inf*) material or substance: *Many shoes nowadays are made of plastic or similar stuff*; *What is that black oily stuff on the beach?*; *The doctor gave me some good stuff for removing warts*; *This paper is very poor stuff*; *Show them what stuff you're made of!* (= how brave, strong *etc* you are). **2** *nu* (*often inf*) (unimportant) matter, things, objects *etc*: *We've got quite a lot of stuff* (= books *etc*) *about the French Revolution*; *She asked me to remove his stuff* (= possessions) *from the room.* **3** *ncu* (*esp arch*) (a kind of) cloth: *beautiful stuffs imported from India*; *a dress of coarse stuff.*

do one's stuff (*inf*) to perform in the expected way, or show what one can do: *They watched him while he did his stuff on the trapeze.*

know one's stuff (*inf*) to have skill and knowledge in one's chosen subject, job *etc*: *He's a good lecturer as he really knows his stuff.*

stuff and nonsense! (*slightly old*) that's nonsense!: *You're too tired to work? Stuff and nonsense!*

that's the stuff! (*inf*) that's just what is wanted!

stuff[2] [stʌf] *vt* **1** to pack or fill tightly, often hurriedly or untidily: *His drawer was stuffed with papers*; *She stuffed the fridge with food*; *He stuffed the papers into the drawer*; *She stuffed newspapers up the chimney*; (*inf*) *The children have been stuffing themselves with cakes.* – *See also* **stuff up** *below.* **2** to fill (*eg* a turkey, chicken *etc*) with stuffing before cooking: *The cook stuffed the chicken with sausage meat*; *She stuffed the leg of pork with apple and breadcrumbs.* **3** to fill the skin of (a dead animal) to preserve the appearance it had when alive: *They stuffed the golden eagle which he shot*; *She asked him to stuff her dead cat.*

'stuffing *nu* **1** material used for stuffing *eg* toy animals: *The teddy-bear had lost its stuffing.* – *See also* **knock the stuffing out of** *below.* **2** a mixture containing *eg* breadcrumbs, spices, sausage-meat *etc*, used for stuffing chickens *etc*: *What kind of stuffing did you put in the turkey?*

stuffed shirt *nc* (*inf derog*) a pompous person: *He never looks as though he is enjoying himself – he is such a stuffed shirt.*

knock the stuffing out of (*inf*) to make (someone) weak, less strong *etc*: *His last illness knocked the stuffing out of him*; *The death of his wife knocked the stuffing out of him.*

stuff up *vt sep* to block: *He stuffed the hole up with some newspaper*; *They don't use the fireplace and so they've stuffed up the chimney*; *I've got a cold and my nose is stuffed up.*

stuffy ['stʌfi] *adj* **1** (of a room *etc*) too warm, and lacking fresh air: *Why do you sit in this stuffy room all day?*; *It's so stuffy in here that I feel sleepy.* **2** (*inf derog*) formal and dull: *Must we visit those stuffy people?*; *I hate visiting her – she is so stuffy*; *The firm's annual dinner is rather a stuffy occasion.*

'stuffily *adv*. **'stuffiness** *nu*.

stultify ['stʌltifai] *vt* (*formal*) to make (efforts *etc*) appear useless or foolish: *The government's attempts at improving the country's economy were stultified by strikes.*

stumble ['stʌmbl] *vi* **1** to strike the foot against something and lose one's balance, or nearly fall: *He stumbled* (*over the edge of the carpet*) *and fell.* – *See also* **stumble across** *below.* **2** to walk unsteadily: *He stumbled along the track in the dark.* **3** to make mistakes, or hesitate in speaking, reading aloud *etc*: *He stumbles over his words when speaking in public.*

'stumbling-block *nc* a difficulty that prevents progress: *The scheme would be excellent, but its cost is the main stumbling-block.*

'stumble across/on *vt fus* to find (something) by chance: *I stumbled across this book today in a shop; When writing a biography of Napoleon she stumbled across some hitherto unknown facts.*

stump [stʌmp] *nc* **1** the part of a tree left in the ground after the trunk has been cut down: *He sat on a stump and ate his sandwiches;* (*in cmpds*) *a tree-stump.* **2** (*inf*) the part of a limb, tooth, pencil *etc* remaining after the main part has been cut off, worn away *etc*: *He opened his mouth to reveal a few rotten stumps* (*of teeth*). **3** in cricket, one of the three upright sticks forming the wicket: *A bowler should aim at the stumps.* – **1** *vi* to walk with heavy, stamping steps: *He stumped angrily out of the room.* **2** *vt* (*inf*) to puzzle or baffle completely: *The problem stumped her; I'm stumped!* **3** *vt* in cricket, to get (a batsman who is not in his crease) out by hitting his stumps with the ball. – *See also* **stump up** *below.*

'stumpy *adj* (*inf*) being a stump; short and thick like a stump: *The cat had a stumpy tail;* (*derog*) *She's rather short and stumpy.*

stump up *vi, vt fus* (*inf*) to pay (a sum of money), often unwillingly: *We all stumped up £1 for his present; We're always being asked to stump up.*

stun [stʌn] – *pt, ptp* **stunned** – *vt* **1** to make unconscious or knock senseless *eg* by a blow on the head: *The blow stunned him.* **2** to shock or astonish: *He was stunned by the news of her death; She was stunned to discover that her husband had left home.*

'stunner *nc* (*inf*) a person, *esp* a woman, or thing of overwhelming beauty or attractiveness: *What a stunner!; His latest girlfriend is a real stunner.*

'stunning *adj* (*inf*) marvellous: *You look stunning today; a stunning dress.*

stung *see* **sting**.

stunk *see* **stink**.

stunt[1] [stʌnt] *vt* to prevent or check full growth or development: *It is thought that smoking by a pregnant mother may stunt the baby's growth.*

'stunted *adj* not well grown or developed: *a small, stunted tree.*

stunt[2] [stʌnt] *nc* something (daring or spectacular) done to attract attention *etc*: *The firm put an airship in the sky as an advertising stunt; One of his stunts was to cross the Niagara Falls blindfold on a tightrope.*

'stuntman [-man] *nc* a person who takes the place of an actor in film sequences involving *eg* athletic skill and danger: *The film actor insisted on jumping off the bridge himself instead of getting a stuntman to do it.*

stupefy ['stju:pifai] *vt* (*formal*) to bewilder, confuse or amaze: *The rabbit was stupefied by the car's headlights; I was completely stupefied by her behaviour.*

ˌstupe'faction [-'fakʃən] *nu* (*formal*): *He stared at her in complete stupefaction.*

stupendous [stju'pendəs] *adj* (*formal or facet*) astonishing or tremendous: *They have made a stupendous discovery; The response to our appeal for money has been stupendous.*

stupid ['stju:pid] *adj* **1** foolish; slow at understanding: *It's stupid to dust the bedroom before you make the bed; a stupid mistake; Don't be stupid!; He isn't as stupid as he looks; He is a very stupid young man.* **2** (*formal*: *usu pred*) in a bewildered or dazed state: *He was* (*feeling*) *stupid from lack of sleep; stupid with tiredness.* – *nc* (*inf derog*: *usu* used when speaking to a person) a stupid person: *You've done it wrong again, stupid!* **'stupidly** *adv.*

stu'pidity *ncu*: *an act of sheer stupidity; This is just another of the Government's stupidities.*

stupor ['stju:pə] *nu* (*formal*) a half-conscious, dazed or bewildered condition caused by *eg* alcohol, drugs, shock *etc*: *He was sitting in a drunken stupor; She was in a stupor after she heard about the death of her husband.*

sturdy ['stə:di] *adj* **1** strong and healthy: *They have two sturdy sons; He is small but sturdy.* **2** firm and well-made: *sturdy furniture; The chair which he made at school is quite sturdy.* **'sturdily** *adv.* **'sturdiness** *nu.*

sturgeon ['stə:dʒən] – *pls* **'sturgeon, 'sturgeons** – *nc* a type of large fish from which caviare is obtained.

stutter ['stʌtə] *vti* to stammer: *He stutters sometimes when he's excited; 'I've s-s-seen a gh-gh-ghost,' he stuttered.* – *nc* (*no pl*) a stammer: *He has a stutter.*

'stutterer *nc* a person who has a stammer.

sty[1] [stai] *nc* a pigsty.

sty[2], **stye** [stai] – *pls* **sties, styes** – *nc* a small inflamed swelling on the eyelid.

style [stail] **1** *nc* (*sometimes in cmpds*) a manner or way of doing something, *eg* writing, speaking, painting, building *etc*: *a formal style of writing/speaking; She paints in an old-fashioned style; You'll find several different styles of architecture in this street; What kind of style are you going to have your hair cut in?; I'd like a new hairstyle.* **2** *nc* (*sometimes in cmpds*) a fashion in clothes *etc*: *Have you seen the latest Paris styles?; I don't like the new style of shoe.* **3** *nu* (*formal*) elegance in dress, behaviour *etc*: *She certainly has style.* – *vt* **1** to arrange (hair) in a certain way: *I'm going to have my hair cut and styled.* **2** (*esp* used in shops *etc*) to design in a certain style: *These chairs are styled for comfort.* **3** (*formal*) to call (a person *etc*) by a certain title: *Many Italian women have the right to style themselves 'countess'.*

'stylish *adj* elegant or fashionable: *stylish clothes/furniture; She's very stylish.* **'stylishly** *adv.* **'stylishness** *nu.*

'stylist *nc* (*esp* used in shops *etc*) a person who arranges or designs a style *esp* in hairdressing: *a men's/women's hair-stylist.*

sty'listic *adj* (*formal*) of a style of writing *etc*: *He has a few stylistic faults.* **sty'listically** *adv.*

'stylize, -ise *vt* (*formal*) in art, to represent something in a conventional *usu* simplified way. **styli'zation, -s-** *nu.*

'stylized, -s- *adj* (*formal*) represented in this way: *The carpet had a pattern of stylized flowers; All her designs are rather stylized.*

live/do something *etc* **in style** to live, or do something, in a luxurious, elegant way without worrying about the expense: *The bride arrived at the church in style, in a horse-drawn carriage.*

stylus ['stailəs] – *pls* **styluses, styli** [-li:] – *nc* **1** a gramophone needle. **2** a cutting tool used in making gramophone records.

suave [swa:v] *adj* (*sometimes derog*) (of a man or his manner) pleasant, elegant, polite and agreeable *esp* in a rather insincere way: *a suave young man; suave manners; a man of suave appearance; The* *manager of the store is very suave.* '**suavely** *adv.* '**suaveness,** '**suavity** *nus.*

sub [sʌb] *nc* (*inf*) short for several words *eg* **submarine, subscription** *etc*: *He's the commander of a sub*; *Several people still haven't paid their subs.*

subaltern ['sʌbltən, (*Amer*) sə'boːltərn] *nc* (*Brit*) a commissioned officer in the army under the rank of captain. – *See also* Appendix 3.

subatomic [sʌbə'tomik] *adj* (*tech*) **1** (of particles) forming an atom. **2** (of changes, processes *etc*) happening within the atom.

subcommittee [sʌbkə'miti] *nc* a committee having powers given to it by a larger committee: *The committee of the architects' association appointed a subcommittee to arrange the annual dance.*

subconscious [sʌb'konʃəs] *adj, nc* (*no pl*) (of) those activities of the mind of which we are not aware: *I suspect that his generosity arose from a subconscious desire for praise*; *His desire to hurt his mother was completely subconscious*; *We can't control the activities of the subconscious.* **sub'consciously** *adv.*

subcontinent [sʌb'kontinənt] *nc* a mass of land so large as to be almost the size of a continent, forming part of a larger mass of land: *the Indian Subcontinent* (= India, Pakistan and Bangladesh).

subcontractor [sʌbkən'traktə, (*Amer*) sʌb'kontraktər] *nc* a person who undertakes work for a contractor and is therefore not directly employed by the person who wants such work done: *The building contractor has employed several subcontractors to build the block of flats.*

subdivide [sʌbdi'vaid] *vti* to divide into smaller parts or divisions: *Each class of children is subdivided into groups according to reading ability.*

ˌsubdi'vision [-'viʒən] **1** *nu* the act of subdividing or process of being subdivided: *Growth in a living thing happens by means of the division and subdivision of cells.* **2** *nc* a part formed by subdividing: *This office is a subdivision of the Education Department.*

subdue [səb'djuː] *vt* (*formal*) to conquer, overcome or bring under control: *After months of fighting the rebels were subdued*; *His fears returned and he could not subdue them.*

sub'dued *adj* (*neg* **un-**) quiet; not bright or lively: *They talked in subdued voices*; *He seems subdued today*; *The rooms were painted in subdued colours.*

subject ['sʌbdʒikt] *adj* (*attrib*: *formal*) (of countries *etc*) not independent, but dominated by another power: *subject nations/tribes/states.* – *See also* **be subject to** *below.* – *nc* **1** a person who is under the rule of a monarch or a member of a country that has a monarchy *etc*: *We are loyal subjects of the Queen*; *He is a British subject.* **2** someone or something that is talked about, written about *etc*: *We discussed the price of food and similar subjects*; *What was the subject of the debate?*; *His mother is the subject of several of his poems*; *The teacher tried to think of a good subject for their essay*; *I've said all I can on that subject.* – *See also* **change the subject** *below.* **3** a branch of study or learning in school, university *etc*: *What are your favourite subjects at school?*; *He is taking exams in seven subjects*; *Mathematics is his best subject.* **4** (*formal*) a thing, person or circumstance suitable for, or requiring, a particular kind of treatment, reaction *etc*: *I don't think her behaviour is a subject for laughter/blame*; *This is certainly a subject for further investigation.* **5** (*gram*) in English, the word(s) representing the person or thing that *usu* does the action shown by the verb, and with which the verb agrees: *The cat sat on the mat*; *He hit her because she broke his toy*; *He was hit by the ball.* – [səb'dʒekt] *vt* (*formal*) **1** (*usu with* **to**) to bring (a person, country *etc*) under control: *They have subjected all the neighbouring states* (*to their rule*); *He tries to subject his whole family to his will.* **2** (*with* **to**) to cause (a person, thing *etc*) to suffer, undergo or submit to: *He was subjected to severe criticism*; *He subjected his victim to cruel treatment*; *They were subjected to the curiosity of the public*; *These tyres are subjected to various tests/heavy pressure before leaving the factory.*

subjection [səb'dʒekʃən] *nu* (*formal*) the act of subjecting, or state or process of being subjected: *The Romans became supreme through the gradual subjection of surrounding peoples*; *We have no right to keep people in subjection simply because of the colour of their skins.*

subjective [səb'dʒektiv] *adj* (*formal*) (of a person's attitude *etc*) arising from, or influenced by, his own thoughts and feelings only; not objective or impartial: *He took a subjective view of the problem*; *You must try not to be too subjective if you are on a jury in a court of law.* **sub'jectively** *adv.*

'**subject matter** *nu* the subject discussed in an essay, book *etc*: *Your subject matter is good, but your spelling and style must be improved.*

be 'subject to (*formal*) **1** to be liable or likely to suffer from, or have a tendency towards (something): *He is subject to colds/infection*; *The programme is subject to alteration.* **2** to depend on: *These plans are subject to your approval.*

change the subject to start talking about something different: *I mentioned the money to her, but she changed the subject.*

See also **object**[1]**, objective.**

sub judice [sʌb'dʒuːdisi] (*formal or legal*) under consideration by the courts and therefore not to be publicly discussed or remarked on: *The matter is still sub judice and therefore must not be discussed on a radio programme.*

subjugate ['sʌbdʒugeit] *vt* (*very formal*) to conquer; to make obedient: *They succeeded in subjugating all the surrounding kingdoms*; *She dominated him and subjugated his will completely.* **ˌsubju'gation** *nu.*

subjunctive [səb'dʒʌŋktiv] *adj* (*gram*) (of a verb) in the mood or form that is used in *eg* conditions, wishes, indefinite forms of speech *etc.* – *ncu* (*gram*) (a verb in) the subjunctive mood, now rare in English except in a few common phrases: *If only I were young again!*; *If it were so, he would have told us*; *God save the Queen*; *Politeness be hanged!*; *Far be it from me* (= I don't wish) *to criticize*; *Be that as it may* (= in spite of that), *he is still to blame*; *Come what may* (= whatever happens), *I shall go there tomorrow*; *Latin subjunctives*; *The verb is in the subjunctive.*

sublet [sʌb'let] – *prp* **ˌsub'letting**: *pt, ptp* **ˌsub'let** – *vt* to let (a house, room *etc* of which one is the tenant) to another person: *The tenant wants to sublet some of the rooms as offices.* – *nc* a let of this kind: *This flat is a sublet.*

sub-lieutenant [sʌblef'tenənt, (*Amer*) -luː-] *nc* (*with caps, and often abbrev* **Sub-Lt.**, *when written in titles*) in the British navy, (a person of) the rank below lieutenant: *He is only a sub-lieutenant*; *Sub-Lieutenant Green.* – *See also* Appendix 3.

sublimate ['sʌblimeit] *vt* (*formal or tech*) to turn (an emotion or impulse) into one considered to be of higher or nobler quality: *She was unconsciously sublimating her sexual desires in her enthusiasm for hard work.*

sublime [sə'blaim] *adj* (*usu attrib*) **1** (*formal*) of overwhelming greatness, grandeur, beauty *etc*: *sublime truths.* **2** (of *eg* ignorance, indifference *etc*) very great: *his sublime indifference to her pain.*

su'blimity [-'bli-] *nu.*

su'blimely *adv*: *sublimely beautiful*; *sublimely unaware of the danger.*

subliminal [səb'liminəl] *adj* (*formal*) (of *eg* television advertising) presented to the senses so briefly that only the subconscious part of the mind has time to receive an impression.

submarine ['sʌbməri:n] *nc* (*often abbrev* **sub**) a ship that can travel under the surface of the sea. – [sʌbmə'ri:n] *adj* (*formal*) existing, or intended for use *etc*, under the surface of the sea: *submarine vegetation/pipe-lines.*

submerge [səb'mə:dʒ] *vti* (*formal*: *often fig*) to cover with, or sink under, water or other liquid: *I watched the submarine gradually submerging*; *The main point of the discussion is being submerged by unimportant details.*

sub'merged *adj* (*formal*) sunk beneath the surface: *Submerged rocks are a great danger to shipping*; *submerged* (= hidden) *aspects of his personality.*

sub'mergence, sub'mersion [-ʃən, (*Amer*) -ʒən] *nus* (*formal*).

submission, submissive *see* **submit**.

submit [səb'mit] – *pt, ptp* **sub'mitted** – (*formal*) **1** *vti* to yield to control or to a particular kind of treatment by another person *etc*: *I refuse to submit (myself) to his control*; *She was unwilling to submit her house to rough treatment by tenants*; *Why did he submit to such cruelty?*; *The rebels were ordered to submit* (= stop resisting). **2** *vt* to offer (a plan, proposal *etc*) for discussion *etc*: *The committee members were asked to submit proposals on this matter*; *Competitors for the painting competition must submit their entries by Friday.* **3** *vt* (*esp legal*: not *usu* used with **is, was** *etc* and **-ing**) to suggest: *I submit that the witness is lying.*

su'bmission [-ʃən] **1** *nu* the act of submitting: *Keep on resisting – you will gain nothing by submission*; (*formal*) *12 June is the date for the submission of his thesis.* **2** *nu* (*esp formal and liter*) humbleness or obedience: *She yielded with quiet submission.* **3** *nc* (*formal*: *esp legal*) an idea, theory *etc* that is suggested *esp* in a court of law: *My submission is that he killed his wife in a fit of jealousy.*

sub'missive [-siv] *adj* (*formal*) obedient and humble: *Children used to be taught always to be meek and submissive to their parents*; *a quiet, submissive manner.* **sub'missively** *adv.* **sub'missiveness** *nu.*

subnormal [sʌb'no:məl] *adj* (*tech or formal*) below the normal level or standard: *subnormal temperatures*; *The child is considered severely subnormal* (= far below normal in intelligence).

subordinate [sə'bo:dinət] *adj* (*formal*) lower in rank, power, importance *etc*: *A colonel is subordinate to a brigadier*; *These questions are subordinate to the main problem*; *She's too ambitious to remain in a subordinate job for long.* – *nc* (*formal*: *often derog*) a person who is subordinate: *The surgeon asked his subordinate to make notes on the patient's medical history.* – [-neit] *vt* (*very formal*) to regard or treat as less important: *She constantly subordinated her own wishes to the children's welfare.*

su,bordi'nation *nu* (*formal*) the act of subordinating or state of being subordinated.

subordinate clause *nc* (*gram*) a dependent clause introduced in a sentence by a conjunction, relative or interrogative pronoun *etc*, and acting as a noun, adjective or adverb: *I don't know who she is*; *The book that's on the table is mine*; *She's crying because you were unkind.*

See also **insubordinate**.

suborn [sə'bo:n] *vt* (*formal*: *esp legal*) to persuade (a person) to do something illegal, *eg* give false evidence in a court of law: *He was charged with suborning witnesses.*

subpoena [sə'pi:nə] *nc* (*legal*) an order to a person to appear in a court of law. – *vt* (*legal*) to order (a person) by subpoena to appear in court: *He was subpoenaed by the defence as a witness.*

subscribe [səb'skraib] **1** *vti* (*formal*) to give money, with other people, to a charity or other cause: *He subscribes to a lot of charities*; *We each subscribed fifty pence towards the present/to buy her a present.* **2** *vi* (*with* **to**) to promise to receive and pay for a series of issues of (a magazine *etc*): *I've been subscribing to that magazine for four years.* **3** *vi* (*formal*: *with* **to**) to agree with, or support (an idea, statement *etc*): *I don't subscribe to the notion that most young people are lazy.*

sub'scriber *nc* a person who subscribes to a charity or a magazine *etc*: *We apologize to our subscribers for the delay in publication.*

subscription [səb'skripʃən] **1** *nu* the act of subscribing: *The new children's playground was provided by public subscription.* **2** *nc* a sum of money that is subscribed *eg* for receiving a magazine, for a membership of a club *etc*: *May I remind all members that their subscriptions are due this month?*

subsection ['sʌbsekʃən] *nc* a (numbered) section or paragraph within a section or paragraph of a document *etc*: *This is mentioned in section B, subsection 5.*

subsequent ['sʌbsikwənt] *adj* (*attrib*: *formal*) following or coming after: *His misbehaviour and subsequent dismissal from the firm was reported in the newspaper*; *He died during the subsequent year.* – *See also* **subsequent to** *below.*

'subsequently *adv* afterwards: *He escaped from prison but was subsequently recaptured.*

'subsequent to (*formal*) after: *The child became ill subsequent to an injection.*

subservient [səb'sə:viənt] *adj* (*formal usu derog*) (too) respectful or slave-like: *subservient waiters*; *He has a rather subservient attitude to those in authority*; *He is always subservient to the owner of the firm.* **sub'servience** *nu.*

subside [səb'said] *vi* (*formal or tech*) **1** (of land, streets, buildings *etc*) to sink lower: *When a building starts to subside, cracks usually appear in the walls.* **2** (of floods) to become lower and withdraw: *Gradually the water subsided.* **3** (of a storm, noise or other disturbance) to become quieter: *They stayed anchored in harbour till the wind subsided*; *By the morning his fever had subsided a little.* **4** (*facet*) to sit down with the appearance of sinking: *He subsided thankfully into an armchair.*

subsidence ['sʌbsidəns, (*Amer*) səb'saidəns] *nu* (*formal or tech*) the process of subsiding: *The road has had to be closed because of subsidence.*

subsidiary [səb'sidjəri] *adj* (*formal*) **1** (*with* **to** *when pred*) adding to, or making a contribution towards, something larger, more important *etc*: *Several subsidiary streams flow into the river*; *This question is subsidiary to the previous question.* **2** (of a firm, company *etc*) controlled by another, larger firm. – *nc* something that is subsidiary: *this firm and its subsidiaries.*

subsidy ['sʌbsidi] *ncu* (a sum of) money paid by a government *etc* to an industry *etc* that needs help, or to farmers *etc* to keep the price of their products low: *Which industries are supported by government subsidy?*; *Food subsidies are necessary for keeping down the price of dairy products and bread.*

'subsidize, -ise *vt* to give a subsidy to: *The production of wheat is subsidized by the government.*

subsist [səb'sist] *vi* (*very formal*) **1** (*with* **on**) to stay alive by means of (a particular food *etc*): *They subsist mainly on eggs, bread and milk.* **2** to exist: *The living things on the earth could not subsist on Mars.*

sub'sistence *nu* (*very formal*) (the means of) existence: *Their subsistence comes from the sea* (= They live by fishing); *What is his means of subsistence?* (*attrib*) *These people are living at subsistence level* (= They have barely enough food to keep alive).

subsoil ['sʌbsoil] *nu* (*tech*) the layer of earth beneath the surface soil.

substance ['sʌbstəns] **1** *nc* (*slightly formal*) a material: *Rubber is a tough, stretchy substance obtained from the juice of certain plants.* **2** *nc* (*tech*) an element, compound or mixture. **3** *nu* (*formal*) thickness or solidity: *Walls in some new houses have very little substance*; (*fig*) *His speech had no substance.* **4** *ncu* (*formal*: *no pl*) the main argument or general meaning of a speech *etc*: *What was the substance of his speech?*; *In substance, he was saying that the scheme was a waste of money.* **5** *nu* (*formal or liter*) wealth or property: *He appears to be a man of substance.*

See also **substantial**.

substandard [sʌb'standəd] *adj* (*formal*) below the (officially) approved standard: *substandard accommodation/working conditions*; *The housing is substandard.*

substantial [səb'stanʃəl] *adj* **1** solid or strong: *I like a nice, substantial writing-table*; *That old house is still quite substantial.* **2** large: *a substantial sum of money*; *That meal was quite substantial.* **3** (*formal or tech*) able to be seen and felt: *A child can easily confuse the real substantial world with the world of his imagination.* **4** (*formal*) more or less complete: *We are in substantial agreement*; *This was the substantial truth.*

subs'tantially *adv* **1** considerably: *The money you gave me helped substantially towards paying for our holiday.* **2** more or less completely: *Our opinions are substantially the same*; *The statement is substantially true.*

substantiate [səb'stanʃieit] *vt* (*formal*) to give the facts that are able to prove or support (a claim, theory *etc*): *He cannot substantiate his claim/accusation.*

substantive ['sʌbstəntiv] *nc* (*formal gram*) a noun.

substitute ['sʌbstitju:t] *vti* to put (a thing, person *etc*) in, or to take, the place of someone or something else: *I substituted your name for mine on the list*; *In manufacturing, cheaper materials are constantly being substituted for the better, more expensive kind*; *If you cannot go yourself, please find someone to substitute for you.* – *nc* a person or thing used or acting instead of another: *Guesswork is no substitute for investigation*; *Soya beans are widely used as a substitute for meat*; *She is not well enough to play in the tennis match, so we must find a substitute*; (*attrib*) *I was substitute headmaster for a term.*

ˌsubsti'tution *nc* the act of substituting, or process of being substituted.

substratum [sʌb'stra:təm, (*Amer*) -'strei-] – *pl* **sub'strata** [-tə] – *nc* (*tech*) an underlying layer.

subsume [səb'sju:m] *vt* (*very formal*: not used with **is, was** *etc* and **-ing**) to include within a larger group, category *etc*: *The old accounts department was subsumed into the new financial department.*

subterfuge ['sʌbtəfju:dʒ] *ncu* (*formal derog*) (the use of) a trick or plan for avoiding a difficulty *etc*: *I'm tired of his plots and subterfuges*; *I had to resort to subterfuge to get him to do what I wanted.*

subterranean [sʌbtə'reiniən] *adj* (*formal or liter*: *esp attrib*) lying, situated or constructed underground: *subterranean passages.*

subtitle ['sʌbtaitl] *nc* **1** a second or explanatory title to a book. **2** on a cinema film *etc*, a translation of foreign speech appearing at the bottom of the screen: *I found it difficult to read the subtitles.*

subtle ['sʌtl] *adj* (*neg* **un-**: *formal*) **1** faint or delicate in quality, and therefore difficult to describe or explain: *There is a subtle difference between 'unnecessary' and 'not necessary'*; *These flowers have a subtle perfume*; *a subtle flavour*; *The flavour of this dessert is very subtle.* **2** clever or cunning: *He has a subtle mind*; *By subtle means, he managed to persuade her*; *You will have to be very subtle if you want to give the old lady a gift of money – she is very independent.*

subtlety ['sʌtlti] *nu* (*formal*) **1** the quality of being subtle: *The subtlety of the change*; *his subtlety as an actor.* **2** something *eg* a difference that is subtle: *In this dictionary there is no room to include all the subtleties of meaning for each word.*

'subtly *adv* in a subtle way: *Her appearance had subtly changed.*

subtract [səb'trakt] *vti* to take one number or quantity from another: *If you subtract 5 from 8, 3 is left*; *In their first year at school, most children learn to add and subtract.* **sub'traction** [-ʃən] *nu.*

subtropical [sʌb'tropikəl] *adj* (belonging to those areas) close to the tropical zone: *a subtropical climate*; *subtropical regions*; *The vegetation there is subtropical.*

suburb ['sʌbə:b] *nc* (*often in pl with* **the**) an area of houses on the outskirts of a city, town *etc*: *Edgbaston is a suburb of Birmingham*; *They decided to move out to the suburbs.*

su'burban *adj* **1** (*attrib*) of suburbs: *suburban housing.* **2** (*derog*) narrow and unoriginal in attitudes, tastes, interests *etc*: *suburban attitudes*; *Her house was decorated in a rather suburban style*; *Her tastes are very suburban.*

su'burbia [-biə] *nu* (*usu derog*) the suburban environment: *She wants to live in London – she does not want to live in suburbia.*

subvert [səb'və:t] *vt* (*very formal*) to overthrow or ruin completely (*eg* a person's morals, loyalty, arguments, a government). **sub'version** [-ʃən, (*Amer*) -ʒən] *nu.*

sub'versive [-siv] *adj* (*formal*) likely to destroy or overthrow (government, discipline in a school *etc*): *That boy is a subversive influence in this class*; *Their actions were subversive.*

subway ['sʌbwei] **1** *nc* an underground passage *eg* for pedestrians, under a busy road: *It's safer to cross by the subway.* **2** *ncu* an underground railway in a city: *Don't wait for a bus – go by subway; The subway has been modernized.*

succeed [sək'si:d] **1** *vi* (*often with* **in**) to manage to do what one is trying to do; to achieve one's aim or purpose: *He succeeded in persuading her to do it; He's happy to have succeeded* (= done well) *in his chosen career; She tried three times to pass her driving-test, and at last succeeded; Our new teaching methods seem to be succeeding.* **2** *vti* (*sometimes with* **to**) (*usu formal* except when of kings *etc*) to follow next in order, and take the place of someone or something else: *He succeeded his father as manager of the firm/king; The cold summer was succeeded by a stormy autumn; If the duke has no children, who will succeed* (*to the title/dukedom*)*?*

success [sək'ses] **1** *nu* (the prosperity gained by) the achievement of an aim or purpose: *He has achieved great success as an actor/in his career; I'm delighted with the success of our efforts; I had no success trying to buy tickets for the concert.* **2** *nc* a person or thing that succeeds or prospers: *She's a great success as a teacher; His first two novels were both successes.*

suc'cessful [-'ses-] *adj* (*neg* **un-**) having success: *Were you successful in finding a new house?; The successful applicant for this job will be required to start work next month; a successful novelist; a successful career.* **suc'cessfully** *adv.*

succession [sək'seʃən] **1** *nu* the right of succeeding to a throne as king, to a title *etc*: *The Princess is fifth in* (*order of*) *succession* (*to the throne*). **2** *nc* a number of things following after one another: *a succession of failures/victories/bad harvests.* – *See also* **in succession** *below.* **3** *nu* (*formal*) the act or process of following and taking the place of someone or something else: *His succession as headmaster was not in any doubt.*

successive [sək'sesiv] *adj* (*formal*: *attrib*) following one after the other: *He won three successive matches.*

suc'cessively [-'sesiv-] *adv* (*formal*): *He joined the school staff in 1950 and became successively head of the mathematics department and headmaster.*

suc'cessor [-'se-] *nc* a person who follows, and takes the place of another: *Who will be appointed as the manager's successor/successor to the manager?*

in suc'cession one after another: *five wet days in succession.*

succinct [sək'siŋkt] *adj* (*formal*) (of something written or said) using as few words as possible; brief and precise: *I admire his succinct style of writing; His speech was clear and succinct.* **suc'cinctly** *adv.* **suc'cinctness** *nu.*

succour ['sʌkə] *vt* (*liter*) to help (a person) in time of need. – *nu* (*liter*) help or aid given to a person in need, danger *etc*: *to give succour to the poor.*

succulent ['sʌkjulənt] *adj* **1** (*formal*) (of fruit or other food *eg* meat) juicy and delicious: *a succulent peach; That steak looks succulent.* **2** (*tech*) (of plants) having thick stems and leaves that are full of moisture. – *nc* (*tech*) a plant of this type: *A cactus is a type of succulent.*

'succulence *nu* (*formal*).

succumb [sə'kʌm] *vi* (*formal or facet*) to yield: *She succumbed to temptation and ate the chocolate; My father is ill with flu, but the rest of us haven't succumbed* (= become ill) *yet.*

such [sʌtʃ] *adj* (*used immediately before* **a** *or a noun*) **1** of the same kind as that already mentioned or being mentioned: *That man dropped some rubbish on the street – such people should be severely punished; Animals that gnaw, such as mice, rats, rabbits and weasels are called rodents; His sculptures should be kept in such a place as an art gallery or museum; He came from Bradford or some such place; She asked to see Mr Johnson but was told there was no such person there; I've seen several such buildings; I've never done such a thing before; doctors, dentists and such people; Such is the present situation.* **2** of the great degree already mentioned or being mentioned: *If you had telephoned her, she wouldn't have got into such a state of anxiety; She never used to get such bad headaches* (*as she does now*). **3** (*formal when pred*) of the great degree, or the kind, to have a particular result: *He shut the window with such force that the glass broke; She's such a good teacher that the headmaster asked her not to leave the school;* (*formal*) *His anger was such that he lost control of himself;* (*formal*) *Their problems are such as to make it impossible for them to live together any more.* **4** (*slightly inf*) used for emphasis: *The news gave me such a shock! They have been such good friends to me!* – *pron* such a person or thing, or such persons or things: (*formal*) *Such of us as* (= Those of us who) *knew him will regret his death; I have only a few photographs, but can show you such as I have; This isn't a good book as such* (= if one judges it as a book) *but it has some interesting pictures; He is an important man, and likes to be treated as such;* (*inf*) *milk, butter, cheese and such.*

'suchlike *adj, pron* (*derog*) (things) of the same kind: *I don't like books about love, romance and suchlike* (*things*).

'such-and-such *adj, pron* used, in discussing unreal or hypothetical situations, to refer to an unnamed person or thing: *Let's suppose that you go into such-and-such a shop and ask for such-and-such.*

ˌsuch as it 'is, they 'are (*ironic*) though it scarcely deserves the name: *You can borrow our lawnmower, such as it is.*

suck [sʌk] **1** *vti* to draw liquid *etc* into the mouth: *As soon as they are born, young animals learn to suck milk from their mothers; Sometimes a mother has difficulty in getting her baby to suck* (*at the breast*)*; Is it true that some types of bats suck human blood?; He was noisily sucking* (*the juice from*) *an orange; She sucked up the lemonade through a straw.* **2** *vti* to hold something between the lips or inside the mouth, as though drawing liquid from it: *I told him to take the sweet out of his mouth, but he just went on sucking; Did you suck your thumb when you were a child?; He sucked the end of his pencil thoughtfully.* **3** *vt* (*usu with* **up, down** *etc*) to pull or draw in a particular direction with a sucking or similar action: *The vacuum cleaner sucked up all the dirt from the carpet; A plant sucks up moisture from the soil; The little boy was sucked down into the marsh.* – *See also* **suck up** *below.* – *nc* (*inf*) an act of sucking: *I gave him a suck of my lollipop.*

'sucker *nc* **1** (*esp in cmpds*) a person or thing that sucks: *She's still a thumbsucker; Are these insects bloodsuckers?* **2** an organ on an animal, *eg* an octopus, by which it sticks to objects. **3** a curved pad or disc (of rubber *etc*) that can be pressed on to a surface and stick there. **4** a side shoot coming from the root of a plant. **5** (*inf derog*) a person who is easily fooled or impressed: *those suckers who believe any advertisement; I'm a sucker for that kind* *of advertisement*; *He's a sucker for small blonde women.*

suck up *vi* (*inf derog*: *often with* **to**) to try to gain a person's favour by flattery *etc*: *He's just trying to suck up* (*to you*).

suckle ['sʌkl] *vt* (*old or formal*) (of a woman or female animal) to give milk from the breasts or teats to (a baby or young): *She was suckling the child.*

suction ['sʌkʃən] *nu* (*tech*) **1** the act of sucking: *Leeches draw blood out of an animal by suction.* **2** the process of creating a vacuum by reducing air pressure *eg* on part of the surface of a liquid substance so that it can be drawn up into a tube *etc*, or between two surfaces, *eg* a rubber disc and a wall, so that they stick together: *A vacuum cleaner works by suction*; (*attrib*) *suction pads.*

Sudan, Sudanese *see* Appendix 2.

sudden ['sʌdn] *adj* happening *etc* quickly and unexpectedly: *The enemy made a sudden attack*; *His decision to get married is rather sudden!*; *There was a sudden bend in the road.* '**suddenness** *nu.*

'**suddenly** *adv*: *He suddenly woke up*; *Suddenly he realized that she had a gun.*

all of a sudden suddenly or unexpectedly: *All of a sudden the lights went out.*

suds [sʌdz] *n pl* (*inf*) soapsuds.

sue [suː] **1** *vti* to start a law case against a person *etc*: *He is suing the other driver in the crash* (*for £3 000 damages*); *Are you going to sue?* **2** *vi* (*with* **for**: *legal or formal*) to ask or beg for (something): *She is suing for divorce*; *They have decided to sue for peace at last.*

See also **suit** (*n defs 3, 4*).

suede, suède [sweid] *nu, adj* (of) leather from a sheep or lamb *etc* with a soft, rough surface: *Suede is difficult to keep clean*; *suede shoes.*

suet ['suːit] *nu* the hard fat from around the kidneys of an ox or sheep: *Christmas puddings usually contain suet*; (*attrib*) *suet puddings.*

suffer ['sʌfə] **1** *vti* to undergo, endure or bear pain, misery *etc*: *He suffered terrible pain from his injuries*; *The crash killed him instantly – he didn't suffer at all*; *He suffered terribly when his mother died*; (*esp formal or old*) *I'll make you suffer* (= I'll see that you're punished) *for this insolence.* **2** *vt* (*formal*) to undergo or experience (*eg* a process, a kind of treatment *etc*): *The army suffered enormous losses/terrible defeat.* **3** *vi* to be neglected: *I like to see you enjoying yourself, but you mustn't let your work suffer.* **4** *vi* (*with* **from**) to have or to have often (a particular illness, complaint *etc*): *She suffers from stomach-aches/cold feet.* **5** *vt* (*formal*) to tolerate or bear: *He would not suffer any interference with his plan*; *I'll suffer this rudeness no longer!* **6** *vt* (*old liter*) to allow or permit: *She suffered him to lead her to a chair.*

'**suffering** *ncu* (a feeling of) pain or misery: *The shortage of food caused widespread suffering*; *She keeps complaining about all her sufferings.*

on '**sufferance** ['sʌfrəns] (*formal*) with permission but without welcome: *He's here on sufferance.*

suffer fools gladly (*usu in neg*) to be sympathetic and patient with foolish people: *He's an irritable man and doesn't suffer fools gladly.*

See also **insufferable**.

suffice [sə'fais] *vti* (*very formal*: not used with **is, was** *etc* and **-ing**) to be enough, or good enough, for a purpose or person: *Two bottles of wine will suffice* (*for lunch*); *His written work will hardly suffice to please the examiner*; *Will £5 suffice you till Monday?*

sufficiency [sə'fiʃənsi] *nc* (*no pl*: *with* **a**: *very formal*) a large enough quantity: *a sufficiency of food.*

sufficient *adj* (*more formal than* **enough**) enough: *We haven't got sufficient food to feed all these people*; *Has he sufficient authority to allow them to do this?*; *£10 will be sufficient*; *Will this be sufficient for your needs?* **suf'ficiently** *adv.*

suffice it to say (*very formal*) I need only say: *Suffice it to say that the manager is on the whole pleased with the work.*

See also **insufficient**.

suffix ['sʌfiks] *nc* a small part added to the end of a word or stem that changes the meaning and often grammatical function: *goodness*; *quickly*; *advisable*; *misty*; *yellowish.*

suffocate ['sʌfəkeit] *vti* to kill, die, cause distress to (a person or animal) or feel distress, through lack of air or the prevention of free breathing: *She suffocated her baby with a pillow*; *A baby may suffocate if it sleeps with a pillow*; *The smoke was suffocating him*; *May I open the window? I'm suffocating.* ˌ**suffo'cation** *nu.*

'**suffocating** *adj* making breathing difficult: *suffocating fumes*; *The air is suffocating.*

suffrage ['sʌfridʒ] *nu* (*very formal*) **1** consent given by voting: *He was chosen by universal suffrage.* **2** the right to vote: *Women did not get full suffrage till 1928.*

ˌ**suffra'gette** [-'dʒet] *nc* (*hist*) one of the women who worked and fought for women's suffrage in the early part of the twentieth century.

suffuse [sə'fjuːz] *vt* (*formal*) (of *eg* colour, light, tears *etc*) to cover: *Her eyes were suffused with tears*; *A blush suffused his face and neck.* **suf'fusion** [-ʒən] *nu.*

sugar ['ʃugə] *nu* the sweet substance that is obtained from sugar-cane, sugar-beet, or from the juice of certain other plants, and used in cooking and for sweetening tea, coffee *etc*: *I haven't enough sugar to make jam*; *Do you take sugar in your tea?* – *vt* to sweeten or sprinkle with sugar: (*inf*) *Have you sugared my tea?*; *She sugared the strawberries well.*

'**sugared** *adj* **1** sweetened with sugar, or covered with sugar or icing: *sugared almonds*; *The drinks are sugared.* **2** (*liter*: *attrib*: *often derog*) (too) sweet: *She spoke in sugared tones.*

'**sugary** *adj* **1** tasting of sugar, or containing a lot of sugar: *Most children eat too many sugary foods*; *This dessert is too sugary.* **2** (*fig derog*) too sweet or sentimental: *a sugary story/film*; *That piece of music is rather sugary.* '**sugariness** *nu.*

sugar-beet *see* **beet**.

'**sugar-cane** *ncu* (one stem of) a type of tall grass from whose juice sugar is obtained.

ˌ**sugar-'coated** *adj* covered with icing: *sugar-coated biscuits/pills*; *These biscuits are very sweet – they're sugar-coated.*

'**sugar daddy** *nc* (*inf derog*) an elderly man who has a young girlfriend to whom he gives generous presents: *She doesn't have to work – she has a wealthy sugar daddy.*

'**sugar lump** *nc* a small cube of sugar, used for sweetening tea *etc*: *How many sugar lumps do you like in your tea?*

'**sugar tongs** *n pl* an instrument for lifting sugar lumps: *Use the sugar tongs to put the sugar lump in your tea*; *a pair of sugar tongs.*

suggest [sə'dʒest, (*Amer also*) səg-] *vt* **1** to put (an idea *etc*) before another person *etc* for consideration; to propose: *He suggested a different plan; I suggest doing it a different way; She suggested to me one or two suitable people for the committee; I suggest that we have lunch now.* **2** to put (an idea *etc*) into a person's mind; to hint: *Are you suggesting that I'm too old for the job?; His attitude suggests that he isn't really interested; Everything in the house suggested newly-acquired wealth; An explanation suddenly suggested itself to me.*

sug'gestible *adj* (*formal*) (of a person or his mind *etc*) easily influenced by suggestions: *He's a suggestible child, and is easily led into mischief by the naughtier children; She is so suggestible that if she hears that someone is ill she becomes ill too.*

sug'gestion [-tʃən] **1** *nu* the act of suggesting: *They thanked him for his suggestion of the scheme; She acted at/on my suggestion* (= did what I suggested). **2** *nc* something that is suggested; a proposal or idea: *Has anyone any other suggestions to make?; What a clever suggestion!* **3** *nu* (*formal*) the process of influencing a person's opinion without his being aware that this is happening, *eg* by hypnotism: *An advertisement showing a beautiful girl using a particular soap is using suggestion to persuade us to buy it.* **4** *nc* (*usu in sing*) a slight trace or sign: *There was a suggestion of boredom in his tone.*

sug'gestive [-tiv] *adj* **1** (*esp* of remarks, glances *etc*) suggesting something particular, *esp* of a sexually improper nature: *He made suggestive remarks to her; That remark was rather suggestive.* **2** (*formal*: *with* **of**) giving an impression of (something): *The scene was suggestive of an Eastern bazaar.*

suicide ['su:isaid] **1** *ncu* the/an act of killing oneself deliberately: *She committed suicide; Every year there are several suicides amongst students taking examinations.* **2** *nc* (*formal or legal*) a person who kills himself deliberately.

ˌsui'cidal *adj* **1** inclined to suicide: *She is very depressed and sometimes feels suicidal; She has had a suicidal tendency since childhood.* **2** extremely dangerous, or likely to lead to death or disaster: *He was driving at a suicidal speed; a suicidal decision; Driving so fast is suicidal.* **ˌsui'cidally** *adv.*

suit [su:t] *nc* **1** a set of clothes *usu* all of the same cloth *etc*, made to be worn together, *eg* a jacket, trousers (and waistcoat) for a man, or a jacket and skirt or trousers for a woman: *He was wearing a tweed suit with a checked pattern.* **2** (*in cmpds*) a piece of clothing for a particular purpose: *a bathing-suit/diving-suit.* **3** (*esp legal*) a case in a law court; an act of suing: *He won/lost his suit; She brought a suit for damages against him.* **4** (*liter or old*) a formal request, *eg* a proposal of marriage to a lady: *He knew that his suit was hopeless.* **5** one of the four sets of playing-cards – spades, hearts, diamonds, clubs. – **1** *vt* to satisfy the needs of, or be convenient for (a person *etc*): *The arrangements did not suit us; The work/climate suits me very well; It doesn't suit me to work on Saturdays.* **2** *vt* (of clothes, styles, fashions *etc*) to be right or appropriate for (a person *etc*): *Long hair suits her; That dress doesn't suit her; This music suits my present mood.* **3** *vt* (*formal*: *often with* **to**) to adjust or make (something) appropriate, fit or suitable: *He suited his speech to his audience.*

'suited *adj* **1** (*neg* **un-**: *formal*: *often with* **to** *or* **for**) fitted, or appropriate to or for: *He should have behaved in a manner better suited to the occasion; They seem well suited* (= well matched) *as dancing partners; I don't think he's suited to/for this work.* **2** (*in cmpds*) wearing a particular kind of suit: *a fat, tweed-suited gentleman.*

'suitor *nc* (*hist or old*) a man who tries to gain the love of a woman: *The princess rejected her suitors one by one.*

'suitcase *nc* a case with flat sides for clothes *etc*, used by a person when travelling: *He hastily packed his (clothes in his) suitcase.*

be (someone's) strong suit (*formal*) to be the thing in which a person is expert or excels: *Being agreeable to ladies is his strong suit.*

follow suit (*formal*) to do just as someone else has done: *He went to bed and I followed suit after a few minutes.*

suit one's actions to one's words (*liter or formal*) to do immediately what one is promising or threatening to do: *The father said he would smack the child if she disobeyed and he suited his actions to his words.*

suit (someone) down to the ground (*inf*) (of *eg* an arrangement, fashion *etc*) to suit (a person) completely: *The job/dress suits her down to the ground.*

suit oneself (*inf*) to do what one wants to do, without considering other people *etc*: *I never know what time my husband will come home for his supper – he just suits himself; You can suit yourself whether you come or not.*

suitable ['su:təbl] *adj* (*neg* **un-**) **1** right or appropriate for a purpose or occasion: *I haven't any suitable shoes for the wedding; Those shoes are not suitable for walking in the country; Many people applied for the job but not one of them was suitable; no suitable candidate.* **2** convenient: *Is the time of the interview suitable for you?; We must find a suitable day for our meeting.* **ˌsuita'bility, 'suitableness** *nus.*

'suitably *adv*: *You're not suitably dressed; He tried to appear suitably pleased at the news.*

suite [swi:t] *nc* a number of things forming a set: *He has rented a suite of rooms on the ground floor; a suite of furniture; He has composed a suite of music for the film.*

sulfur *see* **sulphur**.

sulk [sʌlk] *vi* (*derog*) to show anger or resentment by being silent: *He's sulking because his mother won't let him have an ice-cream.*

'sulky *adj* (*derog*) sulking, or tending to sulk: *He's in a sulky mood; She's a rather sulky girl; She is bad-tempered and sulky.* **'sulkily** *adv.* **'sulkiness** *nu.*

the sulks the state of being sulky: *He's in the sulks today; She had a fit of the sulks because her father made her go to bed early.*

sullen ['sʌlən] *adj* (*derog*) **1** silent and bad-tempered: *a sullen young man; He wore rather a sullen expression; He looks rather sullen.* **2** (*liter fig*) (of the sky) dark and gloomy. **'sullenly** *adv.* **'sullenness** *nu.*

sully ['sʌli] *vt* (*esp liter fig*) to make dirty, or spoil the purity of: *She felt sullied by his touch; He had sullied her virtue.*

sulphur, (*Amer*) **sulfur** ['sʌlfə] *nu* a light yellow non-metallic element (symbol **S**) found in the earth, which burns with a blue flame giving off a choking smell and is used in matches, gunpowder *etc*.

'**sulphate** [-feit] *ncu* any of several substances containing sulphur, oxygen and some other element: *sulphate of lime and other sulphates; copper sulphate.*

sultan ['sʌltən] *nc* (the status of) a ruler in certain Muslim countries.

sultana [-'taːnə] *nc* (the status of) the mother, wife, sister or daughter of a sultan.

sultana[1] [səl'taːnə] *nc* a type of small, seedless raisin.

sultana[2] *see* **sultan**.

sultry ['sʌltri] *adj* **1** (*derog*) (of weather) hot but cloudy, and likely to become stormy: *a hot, sultry day; I think it's going to rain – it's so sultry.* **2** (of a person, *esp* a woman) passionate: *a sultry brunette; She looks glamorous and sultry.* '**sultriness** *nu*.

sum [sʌm] *nc* **1** the amount or total made by two or more things or numbers added together: *The sum of 12, 24, 7 and 11 is 54.* **2** a quantity of money: *It will cost an enormous sum to repair the swimming pool.* **3** a problem in arithmetic: *My children are better at sums than I am.* **4** (*no pl*) the general meaning of something said or written: *He told me a long story, the sum of which was that he hadn't had time to do the work.*

ˌ**summing-'up** – *pl* ˌ**summings-'up** – *nc* (*legal*) a summary given by a judge of the evidence and arguments in a case: *The judge will deliver his summing-up this afternoon.* – *See also* **sum up** *below*.

sum total *nc* (*no pl*) the complete or final total: *The sum total of the cost/damage cannot be calculated.*

sum up – *pt, ptp* **summed** – *vi, vt sep* to give the main or important points of (a discussion *etc*): *He summed up the various arguments against the proposal.* – *See also* **summing-up** *above*.

summary ['sʌməri] *nc* a shortened form of a statement, story *etc* giving only the main points: *A summary of his speech was printed in the newspaper; He gave me a quick summary of the events leading to the quarrel.* – *adj* (*formal*: *usu attrib*) done *etc* quickly, without wasting time or considering details: *Any worker who does not obey the regulations faces summary dismissal* (= will be dismissed immediately): *Army deserters were dealt with through the summary justice of a court-martial.* '**summarily** *adv*.

'**summarize, -ise** *vt* to make, or be, a summary of (something): *He summarized the arguments; His statement summarizes the situation.*

summer ['sʌmə] *ncu* the warmest season of the year, May or June till August in cooler northern regions: *This plant has a blue flower in summer; I went to Italy last summer;* (*attrib*) *Where are you going for your summer holidays?;* (*attrib*) *We like to go for walks in the long summer evenings; The summers are very hot here; Summer is my favourite season; It happened in the summer of 1937; This has to be completed by the summer* (= the summer of this year).

'**summery** *adj* like, or appropriate for, summer: *summery weather; It's very summery today; thin, summery clothes.*

'**summerhouse** *nc* a small building or shelter for sitting in, in a garden.

'**summer school** *ncu* a course of instruction held *eg* at a university during the summer holidays: *He applied to attend* (*a*) *summer school.*

'**summertime** *nu* the season of summer: *The countryside looks its best in summertime.*

'**summer time** *nu* time one hour ahead of time as reckoned by the position of the sun, adopted in Britain in 1916 for the summer months: *In Britain we usually change to summer time in March.*

summit ['sʌmit] *nc* **1** (*more formal than* **top**) the highest point (of a mountain *etc*): *They reached the summit at midday;* (*fig*) *At the age of thirty he was at the summit of his powers as a composer.* **2** (*polit*: *usu attrib*) the highest level of international negotiation, at which heads of state meet for discussion: (*attrib*) *a summit conference/meeting.*

summon ['sʌmən] *vt* to order (a person) to come or appear: *He was summoned to appear in court on a charge of careless driving; The head teacher summoned her to his room; A meeting was summoned immediately.*

'**summons** – *pl* '**summonses** – *nc* (*legal*) an order to appear in court: *He received a summons from the police court.* – *vt* to issue a summons to (a person): *The judge summonsed her.*

sump [sʌmp] *nc* (*tech*) **1** the part of a motor-engine that contains the oil. **2** a small pit into which water drains and out of which it can be pumped.

sumptuous ['sʌmptʃuəs] *adj* (*formal*) expensive and splendid: *The king wore sumptuous robes; The furnishings in the palace are sumptuous.*

sun [sʌn] **1** *n* (*with* **the** *and sometimes with cap*) the round body in the sky that gives light and heat to the earth: *The Sun is nearly 150 million kilometres away from the Earth.* **2** *nc* any of the fixed stars: *Do other suns have planets revolving round them?* **3** *nu* (*often with* **the**) light and heat from the sun; sunshine: *We sat in the sun; This room gets plenty of sun in the morning; The sun has faded the curtains.* – *v* – *pt, ptp* **sunned** – *v refl* to expose (oneself) to the sun's rays: *He's sunning himself in the garden.*

'**sunless** *adj* without sun, or lacking sunlight: *a sunless day; He lived in a dark, sunless basement flat; This room faces north and is completely sunless.*

'**sunny** *adj* **1** filled with sunshine: *sunny weather; a sunny room; This room is very sunny.* **2** (*usu attrib*) cheerful and happy: *The child has a sunny nature.* '**sunniness** *nu*.

'**sunbathe** *vi* to lie or sit in the sun, *esp* wearing few clothes, in order to get a suntan: *She was sunbathing in a bikini in the back garden.*

'**sunbeam** *nc* (*liter*) a ray of the sun: *The first sunbeams were showing behind the hill.*

'**sunburn** *nu* the brown or red colour of the skin caused by exposure to the sun's rays: *After lying in the hot sun all day she was suffering from sunburn.*

'**sunburned,** '**sunburnt** *adjs* having sunburn: *sunburnt faces; Her back is sunburned.*

'**sundial** *nc* an instrument for telling time from the shadow of a rod or plate on its surface cast by the sun: *The house had an old-fashioned garden with a sundial.*

'**sundown** *nu* (*esp Amer*) sunset.

'**sunflower** *nc* a type of large yellow flower with petals like rays of the sun, from whose seeds we get oil: *a field of sunflowers;* (*attrib*) *sunflower oil.*

'**sunglasses** *n pl* glasses of dark-coloured glass or plastic to protect the eyes in bright sunlight: *You should wear sunglasses when driving your car in bright sunlight.*

'**sunlamp** *nc* an apparatus giving out rays that have the same effect as those of the sun, used for medical treatment or to give an artificial suntan:

Her skin disease has improved since she started using a sunlamp.

'sunlight *nu* the light of the sun: *The cat was sitting in a patch of sunlight.*

'sunlit *adj* (*often attrib*) lighted up by the sun: *The picture shows a sunlit scene in a garden.*

'sunrise *ncu* the rising of the sun in the morning, or the time of this: *He watched the sunrise*; *She left the house at sunrise.*

'sunset *ncu* the setting of the sun, or the time of this: *The sky was filled with the red glow of the sunset*; *They planned to go on walking until sunset.*

'sunshade *nc* a type of umbrella for sheltering a person from the sun; a parasol.

'sunshine *nu* **1** the light of the sun: *The children were playing in the sunshine.* **2** (*fig*) cheerfulness or happiness: *Her little grandchild has brought some sunshine into her life again.*

'sunstroke *nu* a serious illness caused by being in very hot sunshine for too long: *He sunbathed for too long and got sunstroke.*

'suntan *nc* a brown colour of the skin caused by exposure to the sun: *I'm trying to get a suntan*; *They came back from Greece with lovely suntans.*

'suntan cream/lotion/oil *nus* substances for rubbing into the skin to prevent it from burning in the sun.

catch the sun (*inf*) to become sunburnt: *You've certainly caught the sun today! Your nose is red!*

under the sun (*inf*) in the whole world: *I'm sure that he must have visited every country under the sun.*

sundae ['sʌndei] *nc* a portion of ice-cream served with fruit, syrup *etc*: *I'd like a fruit sundae.*

Sunday ['sʌndi] *n* the first day of the week, the day following Saturday, kept for rest and worship among Christians: *We'll meet on Sunday*; *I went to London last Sunday*; *I go to church on Sundays* (= every Sunday, or only on a Sunday but not necessarily every Sunday); (*attrib*) *on Sunday afternoon.*

Sunday best/clothes *n pl* the smart, formal garments that a person wears for going to church or for other special occasions: *She was all in her Sunday best.*

'Sunday school *nc* a school attended by children on Sundays in a church *etc*, for religious instruction: *Where is the nearest Sunday school?*; *The child goes to Sunday school every Sunday*; (*attrib*) *a Sunday-school teacher.*

a month of Sundays (*inf*) a very long time: *I could never finish all this work in a month of Sundays.*

sundial, sundown *see* **sun**.

sundry ['sʌndri] *adj* (*formal or liter*: *attrib*) several or various: *We had sundry other matters to discuss.* – *See* **all and sundry** *below.*

'sundries *n pl* (*usu old*) a term used for the various small articles, items *etc* that are not named separately, *eg* in a list of laundry *etc.*

all and sundry everybody: *This announcement concerns all and sundry.*

sunflower *see* **sun**.

sung *see* **sing**.

sunglasses *see* **sun**.

sunk, sunken *see* **sink**.

sunlamp, sunlight *etc see* **sun**.

sup [sʌp] – *pt, ptp* **supped** – **1** *vt* to eat or drink a small mouthful of, *esp* soup from a spoon: *He supped his broth slowly.* **2** *vi* (*arch or facet*) to eat one's supper or evening meal: *Haven't you supped yet?*

super[1] ['su:pə] *adj* **1** (*inf*) extremely good, nice *etc*: *She's got a super new dress*; *You look super in your new clothes!*

super[2] *see* **superintendent** *under* **superintend**.

super- [su:pə] (*in cmpds*) more or greater than usual, as in **superhuman, supertax**.

superabundant [su:pərə'bʌndənt] *adj* (*formal or facet*: *usu attrib*) very abundant or more than enough: *superabundant crops/enthusiasm.*

ˌsupera'bundance *nu* (*formal or facet*) the condition of being superabundant: *The children had a superabundance of energy.*

superannuate [su:pə'ranjueit] *vt* to retire a person from employment because of old age, *esp* with a pension: *At what age are teachers superannuated?*

ˌsuper'annuated *adj* (*facet*) (of an article *etc*) old and hardly fit for use: *a superannuated bicycle/raincoat.*

'superˌannu'ation *nu* (*often attrib*) retirement, or the allowance or pension paid to a retired person: *What are the superannuation arrangements in the Civil Service?*

superb [su'pə:b] *adj* magnificent or excellent: *a superb view*; *She's a superb singer*; *That meal was superb.* **su'perbly** *adv.*

supercilious [su:pə'siliəs] *adj* (*formal derog*) contemptuous or disdainful: *He gave her a supercilious look and walked away*; *He was very supercilious when I said I didn't know how to drive a car.*

ˌsuper'ciliously *adv.* **ˌsuper'ciliousness** *nu.*

superficial [su:pə'fiʃəl] *adj* (*formal*) **1** on, or affecting, the surface only: *The wound is only superficial*; *It isn't surprising that you mistook one man for the other, as they have a superficial likeness.* **2** (*sometimes derog*) not thorough: *He has only a superficial knowledge of the subject*; *His interest in the subject is purely superficial*; *The doctor decided, after a superficial examination of the patient, that she must go straight to hospital.* **3** (*derog*) (of a person) incapable of deep thought or feeling: *I thought her rather superficial*; *She's rather a superficial person.*

'superˌfici'ality [-ʃi'a-] *ncu.*

ˌsuper'ficially *adv*: *Superficially these two paintings look identical.*

superfluous [su'pə:fluəs] *adj* (*formal and sometimes facet*) beyond what is needed or wanted: *Why don't you go for a walk if you have so much superfluous energy?*; *I knew what to do already, so his advice was superfluous.* **su'perfluously** *adv.*

superfluity [su:pə'flu:əti] *nc* (*formal or facet*) a superfluous quantity: *These children have a superfluity of possessions.*

superhuman [su:pə'hju:mən] *adj* **1** (*formal*) divine, or beyond what is human: *a superhuman being*; *superhuman powers*; *He thinks he is superhuman.* **2** greater than would normally be expected of a human being: *a man of superhuman strength*; *He made a superhuman effort to control his anger*; *His strength is superhuman.*

superimpose [su:pərim'pouz] *vt* (*formal*) to lay or plan (one thing) on top of another: *The new city was superimposed on the ruins of the old one*; *This photographic effect is obtained by superimposing one photograph on another.* **'superˌimpo'sition** [-pə'ziʃən] *nu.*

superintend [su:pərin'tend] *vt* to supervise: *An adult should be present to superintend the children's activities.*

ˌsuperin'tendence *nu* (*formal*) the work of superintending: *He placed his estate under the superintendence of a manager.*

ˌ**superinˈtendent** *nc* 1 a person who superintends something, or is in charge of an institution, building *etc*: *the superintendent of a hospital.* 2 (*inf abbrev* **super**: *with cap, and often abbrev* **Supt**, *when written in titles*) (a police officer of) the rank above chief inspector: *He was promoted to superintendent; He is a superintendent; Superintendent Kennedy.*

superior [suˈpiəriə] *adj* 1 (*usu with* **to** *when pred*) higher in rank, better, or greater, than: *Is a captain superior to a commander in the navy?; He was told how to address his superior officer; This carpet is far superior (to that one) in quality; The enemy attacked us in superior numbers* (= with forces larger or stronger than ours); *With his superior strength he managed to overwhelm his opponent.* 2 (*usu attrib*: *formal*) high, or above the average, in quality: *a superior wine; superior workmanship.* 3 (*often derog*) (of a person or his attitude) contemptuous or disdainful: *Don't be so superior!; He looked at her with a superior smile/air.* – *nc* a person who is better than, or higher in rank than, another or others: *The servant was dismissed for being rude to her superiors; She considers her husband (to be) her superior in intelligence.*

suˌperiˈority [-ˈo-] *nu* the quality of being superior: *the superiority of this cloth to that; her superiority as an artist.*

superlative [suˈpəːlətiv] *adj* 1 (*gram*) (of an adjective or adverb) of the highest degree of comparison: *'Biggest' is a superlative adjective.* 2 (*formal*) of the highest degree or quality: *He played the piece of music with superlative skill; His cooking is superlative.* – *ncu* (*gram*) (an adjective or adverb of) the superlative degree: *'Best' and 'worst' are the superlatives of 'good' and 'bad'; That adverb is in the superlative; She is the prettiest girl in the room; They're all tall, but he is the tallest; That's the most delightful news I've heard for ages; We'll go by different roads to see who will arrive (the) soonest; Who did it (the) most quickly?*

superman [ˈsuːpəman] *nc* an imagined man of the future with amazing powers: *a race of supermen.*

supermarket [ˈsuːpəmaːkit] *nc* a large, self-service store selling food and other goods.

supernatural [suːpəˈnatʃərəl] *adj* (of *eg* matters concerning ghosts *etc*) beyond what is natural or physically possible: *supernatural happenings; a creature of supernatural strength; These events seem supernatural.*

the supernatural supernatural things, influences, events *etc*: *Do you believe in the supernatural?*

supernumerary [suːpəˈnjuːmərəri] *adj* (*very formal*: *usu attrib*) over and above, or in excess of the usual, or necessary, number: *supernumerary staff.*

supersede [suːpəˈsiːd] *vt* (*formal*) to take the place of (a thing or person), or replace (a thing or person) with something or someone else: *Transport of goods by road is gradually superseding transport by rail; These methods have long ago been superseded by more modern ones.*

supersonic [suːpəˈsonik] *adj* faster than the speed of sound: *These planes are designed to travel at supersonic speeds; Is that aircraft supersonic?*

superstition [suːpəˈstiʃən] 1 *nu* (the state of fear and ignorance resulting from) the belief in magic, witchcraft and other things that cannot be explained by reason: *Some people feel that religion is just a form of superstition.* 2 *nc* an example of this type of belief: *There is an old superstition that those who marry in May will have bad luck.*

ˌ**superˈstitious** *adj* of, or affected by, superstition: *superstitious beliefs; She has always been very superstitious.* ˌ**superˈstitiously** *adv.*

superstructure [ˈsuːpəstrʌktʃə] *nc* (*tech*) a structure above or on something else, *eg* the upper part of a building or ship: *The base of the building is concrete, and the superstructure mainly glass.*

supertax [ˈsuːpətaks] *nu* (*inf*) an extra tax on large incomes; surtax: *How much can you earn before you pay supertax?*

supervise [ˈsuːpəvaiz] *vt* to direct, control or be in charge of (work, workers *etc*): *She supervises (the work of) the typists.*

ˌ**superˈvision** [-ˈviʒən] *nu* the act or work of supervising or state of being supervised: *The firm's accounts are under the personal supervision of the manager; These children should have more supervision.*

ˈ**supervisor** *nc* a person who supervises: *She is a supervisor in a biscuit factory; If you are having difficulty with your university thesis you should consult your supervisor.*

supine [ˈsuːpain, (*Amer*) suːˈpain] *adj* (*formal*) 1 lying on the back: *He lay/was supine on the bed; a supine figure.* 2 inactive, or lacking energy and interest: *In his present supine state he's unlikely to make a quick decision; He is too supine to make any plans by himself.* ˈ**supinely** *adv.*

supper [ˈsʌpə] *ncu* a meal, sometimes a very small meal, taken at the end of the day: *Our suppers have been getting later recently; I only want a small supper; Would you like some supper?; Do stay for supper!; She has invited me to supper.*

ˈ**supper-time** *nu* the time in the evening when people eat supper: *I'll be back at supper-time.*

supplant [səˈplaːnt] *vt* (*formal*) to take the place of (someone or something), *esp* unjustly or unfairly: *That row of fine old houses was pulled down and supplanted by ugly modern buildings; The new baby supplanted his older sister in his mother's affections.*

supple [ˈsʌpl] *adj* bending easily: *She has always taken a lot of exercise and her body has remained very supple; He admired the graceful, supple movements of the dancers.* ˈ**suppleness** *nu.*

supplement [ˈsʌpləmənt] *nc* 1 an addition made to supply something lacking, or to correct errors *etc*: *A supplement to the dictionary is to be published next year.* 2 (*with cap in titles*) a special part of a magazine, newspaper *etc* published in addition to the main part: *The Times Literary/Educational Supplement.* – [-ment] *vt* to make, or be, an addition to (something): *His grandmother sometimes supplemented his pocket money with a fifty-pence piece; Her earnings supplemented his income; She supplements her diet with vitamin pills; The old man supplements his pension by doing odd jobs for people.*

ˌ**suppleˈmentary** [-ˈmen-] *adj* (*formal*) added to supply what is lacking; additional: *This question is supplementary to the previous question; A supplementary volume has been published containing the index; She is breast-feeding her baby but he needs supplementary bottle feeds as she doesn't have enough milk.*

suppliant [ˈsʌpliənt] *nc, adj* (*very formal or liter*) (a person) acting or begging humbly and earnestly: *They knelt as suppliants at his feet, begging for mercy; She stretched out her hands in a suppliant gesture.*

supplication [sʌpli'keiʃən] *ncu* (*very formal or liter*) (an) earnest prayer or entreaty: *They made supplication(s) to the king to spare their lives.*

supply [sə'plai] *vt* to give or provide (something that is wanted or needed): *Who is supplying the rebels with guns and ammunition?*; *Extra paper will be supplied by the teacher if it is needed*; *The town is supplied with water from a reservoir in the hills*; *The shop was unable to supply what she wanted.* – **1** *nu* the act or process of supplying: *The supply of uniforms to the hospital staff is under the control of the matron.* – *See also* **be in short supply** *below.* **2** *nc* (*often in pl*) an amount or quantity that is supplied; a stock or store: *She left a supply of food for her husband when she went away for a few days*; *Who will be responsible for the expedition's supplies?*; *The shopkeeper said he would be receiving new supplies of food soon.*

supply teacher *nc* a teacher who temporarily fills another's post.

be in short supply (of goods *etc*) to be scarce: *Cabbages/Good joiners are in short supply.*

support [sə'po:t] *vt* **1** to bear the weight of, or hold (a thing *etc*) upright, in place *etc*: *That chair won't support him/his weight*; *He limped home, supported by a friend on either side of him*; *She stood up, supporting herself on the arms of the chair.* **2** to give help, or approval to (a thing, person *etc*): *He has always supported our cause*; *His family supported him in his decision*; *I don't support the idea that teenagers are lazy.* **3** to provide evidence for the truth or genuineness of (a theory, statement, claim *etc*): *New discoveries have been made that support his theory*; *The* (*evidence of the*) *other witness supports his statement.* **4** to supply (a person) with the means of living: *He has a wife and four children to support.* **5** (*old formal*) to endure or bear: *I can support this situation no longer.* – **1** *nu* the act of supporting or state of being supported: *That type of shoe doesn't give the foot much support*; *The plan was cancelled because of lack of support*; *Her job is the family's only means of support*; *I would like to say a word or two in support of his proposal.* **2** *nc* something that supports: *One of the supports of the bridge collapsed*; (*no pl*) *Her wages were the family's only support.*

sup'porter *nc* a person who helps or supports (a person, cause *etc*): *His supporters were mainly young people*; *a crowd of football supporters.*

sup'porting *adj* (*attrib*) (of an actor, rôle *etc*) secondary to the leading actor, rôle *etc*: *He has had many supporting rôles*; *a supporting cast.*

suppose [sə'pouz] *vt* (not *usu* used with **is, was** *etc* and **-ing** (*defs 1, 2, 4*)) **1** to think probable; to believe or guess: *I supposed, mistakenly, that you already knew about her death*; *Who do you suppose* (= Guess who) *telephoned today?*; *'I suppose you'll be going to the meeting?' 'Yes, I suppose so/No, I don't suppose so.'*; *Do you suppose it will rain today?*; *'Surely her statement can't be correct?' 'No, I suppose not.'* **2** to accept (a particular circumstance) as true for the sake of argument: *Let's suppose we each had £100 to spend – what would we buy with it?* **3** (*only in the imperative*) used to make a suggestion or give an order in a polite way: *Suppose we have lunch now!*; *Suppose you make us a cup of tea!* **4** (*formal*) to imply or presume the existence of (something): *His request supposes a willingness on their side which they don't in fact have.* – *See also* **be supposed to** *below.*

sup'posed [-zid] *adj* (*attrib*: *formal*: *often ironic*) accepted as a fact: *His supposed illness was nothing more than a slight cold.* **sup'posedly** [-zid-] *adv.*

sup'posing (*often with* **that**) if: *Supposing* (*that*) *she doesn't come, what shall we do?*

supposition [sʌpə'ziʃən] *ncu* (*formal*) the act of supposing, or that which is supposed: *Argue from facts, not from supposition!*; *He bases his theory on a false supposition*; *On the supposition that you would be unable to go, I cancelled the arrangements.*

be sup'posed to (**be/do** *etc*) **1** to have the reputation of (being *etc*): *He's supposed to be the best doctor in the town.* **2** to be expected or obliged to (do something *etc*): *You're supposed to make your own bed every morning*; (*inf*) *He's not supposed* (= not allowed) *to do that.*

suppress [sə'pres] *vt* (*formal*) **1** to crush, defeat, or put a stop to (*eg* a rebellion): *The rebels were quickly suppressed.* **2** to keep back or stifle: *She suppressed a laugh*; *He tried to suppress a yawn.* **3** to prevent from being published, known *etc*: *The newspaper has suppressed the name of the girl who was raped*; *The politician tried to suppress that piece of information.*

sup'pression [-ʃən] *nu* (*formal*): *the suppression of the rebels*; *the suppression of a smile*; *the suppression of the true facts.*

supreme [su'pri:m] *adj* (*formal*) **1** (*with* **the**) the highest, greatest, or most powerful: *the supreme ruler.* **2** (*usu attrib*) the greatest possible: *an act of supreme courage*; *He treated them with supreme contempt.* **su'premely** *adv.*

supremacy [su'preməsi] *nu* (*formal*) the state of being the greatest or most powerful: *How did Rome maintain her supremacy over the rest of the world for so long?*; *Few people dispute Shakespeare's supremacy as a playwright.*

surcharge ['sə:tʃa:dʒ] *nc* an extra amount of money charged: *We paid for our holiday abroad in advance but we had to pay a surcharge because of the devaluation of the pound.*

sure [ʃuə] **1** (*pred*: *neg* **un-**) having no doubt; certain: *I'm sure that I gave him the book*; *I'm not sure where she lives/what her address is*; *'There's a bus at two o'clock.' 'Are you quite sure?'*; *I thought the idea was good, but now I'm not so sure*; *You shouldn't have told him anything until you were sure of the/your facts* (= convinced that you knew the truth); *I'll help you – you can be sure of that!*; *I'm not sure of/about his ability to cope with this.* **2** (*pred*) unlikely to fail (to do or get something): *He's sure to win*; *You're sure of a good dinner if you stay at that hotel.* **3** (*attrib*) reliable or trustworthy: *I know a sure way to cure hiccups*; *a safe, sure method*; *He has a sure aim with a rifle.* – *See also* **sure** *in phrases below.* – *adv* (*inf*: *esp Amer*) certainly; of course: *Sure I'll help you!*; *'Would you like to come?' 'Sure!'*

'surely *adv* **1** used in questions, exclamations *etc* to indicate what the speaker considers probable: *Surely she's finished her work by now!*; *You don't believe what she said, surely?*; *Surely I've read this book already!* **2** without doubt, hesitation, mistake or failure: *She knew that he was unhappy as surely as if he had told her*; *Slowly but surely we're achieving our aim.* **3** (in answers) certainly; of course: *'May I come with you?' 'Surely!'*

'sureness *nu.*

ˌsure-'footed *adj* not likely to slip or stumble: *Deer are very sure-footed animals*; *Goats are also sure-footed.*

as 'sure as used in various *inf* phrases meaning 'without fail' or 'without doubt': *As sure as fate/anything/eggs are eggs, he'll be late again.*

be 'sure to/(*inf*) **and** don't fail to (do something *etc*): *Be sure to/and switch off the television.*

be/feel sure of oneself to be confident: *He's never very sure of himself amongst people he doesn't know.*

for 'sure definitely or certainly: *We don't know for sure that he's dead; We haven't heard for sure that the college has a place for him.*

make sure to act so that, or check that, something is certain or sure: *Arrive early at the cinema to make sure of (getting) a seat!; I think he's coming today but I'll telephone to make sure (of that/that he is).*

sure enough in fact, as was expected: *I thought it would rain, and sure enough it did.*

to be 'sure (*old or dial*) certainly; of course: *He's a nice person, to be sure, but not very clever.*

surety ['ʃuərəti] *ncu* (*old or formal*) (something that is) a guarantee, *eg* of the repayment of a loan: *She gave him her gold necklace in surety of the loan; What sureties can you offer?; If you want a loan from the bank you will need some surety.*

stand surety (*formal or legal*) to take responsibility if another person fails *eg* to pay a debt, appear in a law court *etc*: *He stood surety for her.*

surf [sə:f] *nu* the foam made as waves break on rocks or on the shore: *The children were playing in the white surf.*

'surfing *nu* (*also* **'surf-riding**) the sport of riding on a surfboard.

'surfboard *nc* a board on which a bather rides towards shore on the surf.

surface ['sə:fis] *nc* **1** the outside part (of anything): *More than two-thirds of the earth's surface is covered with water; This road has a very uneven surface.* **2** (*with* **the**) the top of a liquid *eg* the sea, or of the ground: *Three-quarters of an iceberg is hidden beneath the surface; (attrib) Should surface workers* (= miners who do not work underground) *get the same pay as underground workers?* **3** (*with* **the**) the outward or external appearance of, or first impression made by, a person or thing: *On the surface he seems cold and unfriendly, but he's really a kind person; On the surface his offer seems very generous but there may be a hidden disadvantage.* – (*formal*) **1** *vt* to put a surface on (a road *etc*): *The road has been damaged by frost and will have to be surfaced again.* **2** *vi* (of a submarine, diver *etc*) to come to the surface: *He watched the submarine surfacing.*

surface mail *nu* mail sent by ship, train *etc* and not by aeroplane: *Surface mail takes much longer, but is cheaper, than air mail.*

surfeit ['sə:fit] *nc* (*usu in sing with* **a**: *formal or facet*) (the feeling of sickness or discomfort resulting from having) too much of anything, *esp* food or drink: *You're probably suffering from a surfeit of coffee; We had a surfeit of spaghetti in Italy.*

surge [sə:dʒ] *vi* (*formal or liter*) (of *eg* water or waves) to move forward with great force: *The waves surged over the rocks; The dam broke and water surged through the gap; The crowd surged forwards.* – *nc* (*formal or liter*) a surging movement, or a sudden rush or onset (*eg* of pain or other feeling): *The stone hit his head and he felt a surge of pain; a sudden surge of anger.*

surgeon ['sə:dʒən] *nc* **1** a doctor who treats injuries or diseases by operations in which the body sometimes has to be cut, *eg* to remove a diseased part: *He was the surgeon who operated on my father; The surgeon had to amputate* (= cut off) *her leg; The surgeon took out the child's tonsils because she kept having sore throats.* **2** a doctor in the army or navy.

surgery ['sə:dʒəri] **1** *nu* the practice or art of treating disease or injuries by operation: *He wants to specialize in surgery.* **2** *nc* a doctor's or dentist's room in which he examines patients.

surgical ['sə:dʒikəl] *adj* (*usu attrib*) of, or by means of, surgery: *He has finished his surgical training; Surgical instruments must be absolutely clean; He is in need of surgical treatment.*

surly ['sə:li] *adj* bad-tempered or rude: *a surly fellow; He answered her question in a surly manner; He is always surly.* **'surliness** *nu.*

surmise [sə'maiz] *vt* (*formal*) to guess or suppose: *I surmised that you would need this book.* – ['sə:maiz, (*Amer also*) sər'maiz] *nc* (*formal*) a guess: *My surmise was correct.*

surmount [sə'maunt] *vt* (*formal*) to overcome or deal with (problems, obstacles *etc*) successfully: *He surmounted these obstacles without trouble.*

surname ['sə:neim] *nc* a person's family name: *The common way of addressing people is by their surnames, preceded by Mr, Mrs, Miss, Dr etc; Smith is a common British surname.*

surpass [sə'pa:s] *vt* (*formal*) to be, or do, better than (someone or something else) or to exceed (something): *He surpasses all his rivals; His performance surpassed my expectations.* **sur'passed** *adj* (*neg* **un-**).

surplus ['sə:pləs] *ncu* the amount left over when what is required has been used *etc*: *This shop stocks army surplus* (= goods intended for, but not required by, the army); *Canada produces a surplus of raw materials; (attrib) surplus stocks; (attrib) You should get rid of some of your surplus fat by taking more exercise; The country had a trade surplus* (= exported more than it imported) *last month.*

surprise [sə'praiz] *ncu* (the feeling or emotion caused by) something sudden or unexpected: *His statement caused some surprise; She gave them a surprise by arriving early; Your letter was a pleasant surprise; There were some nasty surprises waiting for her when she returned; He stared at her in surprise; To my surprise the door was unlocked; (attrib) He paid them a surprise visit.* – *See also* **take by surprise** *below.* – *vt* **1** to cause (a person) to feel surprise: *The news surprised me.* **2** to lead (a person), by means of surprise, into doing something: *Her sudden question surprised him into betraying himself.* **3** (*formal*) to find, come upon, or attack, without warning: *She came home early and surprised a burglar; They surprised the enemy from the rear.*

sur'prised *adj* showing surprise: *his surprised face; His expression was rather surprised.* – *See also* **be surprised** *below.*

sur'prising *adj* likely to cause surprise: *surprising news; It is not surprising that he resigned – he earned a very low salary.*

sur'prisingly *adv*: *Surprisingly, he failed his exam; Surprisingly, she has married again.*

be sur'prised to feel surprise: *I'm surprised (that) you arrived so early; You behaved very badly – I'm surprised at you!; I was surprised to see/at seeing him there; I shouldn't be surprised if he won.*

take by surprise 1 (*formal*) to catch (a person) unawares: *The news took me by surprise.* 2 (*mil*) to capture (*eg* a stronghold, fort *etc*) by a sudden, unexpected attack: *We took the enemy camp by surprise.*

surrealism [sə'riəlizəm] *nu* a modern artistic movement that attempts to show the activities of the subconscious or unconscious mind *eg* by representing objects, events *etc* as though occurring in a dream.

sur'realist *nc* a person who paints *etc* in this way.

sur,rea'listic *adj* painted or represented in this way: *a surrealistic painting of the countryside in winter*; *His work is too surrealistic for me – I like things to look like what they are.*

surrender [sə'rendə] 1 *vi* to yield (to an enemy *etc*): *The general refused to surrender to the enemy*; *We shall never surrender!* 2 *vt* to give up or abandon: *In 1558 the English were forced to surrender the port of Calais to the French*; *He surrendered all claim to the throne*; (*formal*) *You must surrender your old passport when applying for a new one.* 3 *vi, v refl* (*liter*: *with* **to**) to allow (oneself) to be overwhelmed by (a feeling or emotion): *He surrendered (himself) to despair/grief.* – *ncu* (an) act of surrendering: *The garrison was forced into surrender*; *The terms of the agreement meant a complete surrender of his authority and power.*

surreptitious [sʌrəp'tiʃəs, (*Amer*) sə:rəp-] *adj* (*formal or facet*) (of actions or activities) done secretly: *He gave her a surreptitious glance*; *He is acting in rather a surreptitious manner*; *His manner of entering the room was rather surreptitious.*

,surrep'titiously *adv.*

surround [sə'raund] *vt* 1 to be, or come, all round (something): *Britain is surrounded by sea*; *Enemy troops surrounded the town*; *Mystery surrounds his death.* 2 to enclose: *He surrounded the castle with a high wall*; (*fig*) *He likes to surround himself with amusing people.* – *nc* (*inf*) a border, *eg* the area of floor-space between the edge of a carpet and the wall: *Don't forget to polish the surround!*

sur'rounding *adj* (*usu attrib*) lying or being all round: *The village and its surrounding scenery are very pretty*; *the town and the countryside surrounding.*

sur'roundings *n pl* 1 the countryside *etc* that is round a place: *a pleasant hotel in delightful surroundings.* 2 the conditions *etc* in which a person, animal *etc* lives: *He was happy to be at home again in his usual surroundings.*

surtax ['sə:taks] *ncu* (*not a tech term*) an additional tax on high income *etc*: *How much can you earn before you start paying surtax?*

surveillance [sə'veiləns] *nu* (*formal*) constant supervision, or a close watch kept (on *eg* a person suspected of criminal activities): *He is being kept under surveillance*; *All those who were in contact with the person who has smallpox are being kept under surveillance in case they develop symptoms.*

survey [sə'vei] *vt* 1 (*formal*) to look at, or view, in a general way: *He surveyed his neat garden with satisfaction.* 2 to examine carefully or in detail: *The police are surveying the evidence.* 3 (*tech*) to measure, and estimate the position, shape *etc* of (a piece of land *etc*): *They have started to survey the country that the new motorway will pass through.* 4 (*tech*) to make a formal or official inspection of (a house *etc* that is being offered for sale): *Most people have a house surveyed before offering a price for it.* – ['sə:vei] *nc* 1 a general view or detailed examination: *After a brief survey of the damage he telephoned the police*; *He wrote a survey of crime in Glasgow.* 2 (*tech*) a careful measurement of land *etc*, or a map made using such measurement: *He plots archaeological sites for the Ordnance Survey of Great Britain.*

sur'veyor *nc* a person who surveys buildings or land officially: *He is training to be a surveyor*; *The surveyor says the roof of that house is in need of repair.*

survive [sə'vaiv] 1 *vti* to remain alive in spite of (a disaster *etc*): *Few birds managed to survive the winter last year*; *He didn't survive long after the accident.* 2 *vt* (*formal*) to live longer than (another person): *He died in 1940 but his wife survived him by another twenty years*; *He is survived by his wife and two sons.*

sur'vival 1 *nu* the state of surviving: *the problem of survival in sub-zero temperatures*; (*attrib*) *survival equipment.* 2 *nc* a custom, belief *etc* that remains from earlier times: *This custom is a survival from the 13th century.*

sur'viving *adj* (*usu attrib*) remaining alive: *She has no surviving relatives.*

sur'vivor *nc* a person who survives a disaster *etc*: *There were no survivors of the air crash.*

susceptible [sə'septəbl] *adj* (*formal*) 1 easily affected by emotions or feelings (*esp* of love): *a susceptible young man*; *Young children have highly susceptible natures*; *He is always falling in love – he's very susceptible.* 2 (*with* **to**) liable to be affected by: *She's very susceptible to colds*; *He's too susceptible to flattery.*

su,scepti'bility *nu* (*formal*): *his youth and susceptibility*; *her susceptibility to infection.*

suspect [sə'spekt] *vt* (not used with **is, was** *etc* and **-ing**) 1 to think (a person *etc*) guilty: *Whom do you suspect (of the crime)?*; *I suspect him of killing the girl*; *The milk jug has been overturned, and I suspect the cat.* 2 to distrust: *I suspected her motives/air of honesty.* 3 to think (something) probable: *I suspect that she's trying to hide her true feelings*; *I began to suspect a plot/trap.* – ['sʌspekt] *nc* a person who is thought guilty: *There are three possible suspects in this murder case.* – *adj* (*formal*) not trustworthy: *The evidence for this theory is suspect*; *rather suspect evidence*; *I think his statement is suspect.*

suspicion [sə'spiʃən] 1 *ncu* the process of suspecting or being suspected; the/a feeling causing a person to suspect: *Suspicion between a husband and wife can be very harmful*; *They regarded each other with suspicion*; *A fraud has been discovered and three people are under suspicion*; *I have a suspicion that she is not telling the truth*; *His activities aroused my suspicion(s).* – *See also* **be above suspicion** *below.* 2 *nc* (*formal or facet*) a slight quantity or trace: *She added a suspicion of garlic to the stew*; *There was a suspicion of triumph in his tone.*

suspicious [sə'spiʃəs] *adj* 1 having or showing suspicion: *I'm always suspicious of men like him*; *I have a suspicious nature*; *He gave me a suspicious glance.* 2 causing or arousing suspicion: *If you see anything suspicious, telephone the police immediately*; *suspicious circumstances.* **su'spiciousness** *nu.*

suspiciously [sə'spiʃəsli] *adv*: *He was suspiciously late coming home*; *She glanced at him suspiciously.*

be above suspicion (*formal*) to be too highly respected ever to arouse suspicion: *A country's* *police force should be above suspicion.*

See also **unsuspected**.

suspend [sə'spend] *vt* **1** (*formal*) to hang: *The pieces of meat were suspended from the ceiling on hooks.* **2** (*formal or tech*: *usu in passive*) to keep (particles *etc*) from falling or sinking: *A beam of sunlight lit up the particles of dust that were suspended in the air.* **3** to stop or discontinue temporarily: *All business in the city will be suspended until after the funeral*; *The trial is to be suspended while new evidence is considered.* **4** to prevent (a person) temporarily from continuing his (professional) activities or having his usual privileges: *Two footballers were suspended after yesterday's match*; *The doctor has been suspended from duty.* **5** (*formal*) to postpone or delay: *You should suspend judgement* (= wait before forming an opinion) *until you have more information.*

su'spenders *n pl* **1** a pair, or set, of elastic straps for holding up socks or stockings. **2** (*Amer*) braces for holding up trousers.

su'spense [-s] *nu* a state of uncertainty and anxiety: *We waited in suspense for the result of the competition*; *He could not stand the suspense any longer and went to find out who had won.*

su'spension [-ʃən] **1** *nu* the act of suspending or state of being suspended: *This incident led to his suspension from his job.* **2** *ncu* (*tech*) in a motor vehicle *etc*, the system of springs *etc* supporting the frame on the axles: *This car has good suspension/has recently had a new suspension fitted.* **3** *nc* (*tech*) a mixture of a liquid with solid particles that do not sink, but remain suspended.

suspension bridge *nc* a type of bridge that has its roadway suspended from cables supported by towers.

suspicion, suspicious *etc see* **suspect**.

sustain [sə'stein] *vt* (*formal*) **1** to bear (the weight of): *The branches could hardly sustain the weight of the fruit.* **2** to give help or strength to: *The thought of seeing her again sustained him throughout his ordeal*; *You have eaten too little to sustain you for the journey.* **3** to maintain or keep (something) going: *He was not a good enough actor to be able to sustain the part/rôle.* **4** to suffer or undergo (attack, injuries *etc*): *The fort sustained repeated attacks*; *He sustained head injuries and a broken leg when he fell off the ladder.* **5** (*legal*) to show (a claim *etc*) to be just or true: *His claim was sustained by the court.*

su'staining *adj* (*formal or facet*) (of food *etc*) giving strength: *You ought to eat a sustaining breakfast before a day's walking*; *A cup of coffee is not sustaining enough.*

sustenance ['sʌstənəns] *nu* (*formal or facet*) (the amount of nourishment in) food or drink: *There isn't much sustenance in a cup of coffee*; *Let me give you some sustenance before you go!*

svelte [svelt] *adj* (*formal*) (*esp* of a woman) slender; graceful: *She is svelte and elegant*; *a svelte, elegant figure.*

swab [swob] *nc* **1** a piece of cotton wool *etc*, used by doctors for several purposes: *The nurse handed the surgeon a swab to clean the patient's wound*; *He used a swab to take a specimen of mucus from the patient's throat.* **2** a specimen of mucus *etc*, to be examined for bacteria, taken with a swab: *The doctor said that he thought that I had a throat infection and took a swab.* **3** (*esp naut*) a mop for cleaning or drying decks or floors. – *v* – *pt*, *ptp* **swabbed** – *vt* to wash or wipe (*esp* a deck) with a swab.

swab down *vt sep* to wash (a deck): *The sailors were swabbing down the deck.*

swaddle ['swodl] *vt* **1** (*usu old*) to wrap or bind (a baby) tightly with strips of cloth. **2** (*formal or facet*) to wrap up (a person) tightly and almost completely: *She was swaddled in furs.*

'swaddling-clothes *n pl* (*old*) bands of cloth used for wrapping a baby.

swag [swag] **1** *nu* (*old sl*) stolen goods: *The burglar hid the swag.* **2** *nc* in Australia, a tramp's bundle.

swagger ['swagə] *vi* (*derog*) to walk in a way that shows over-confidence or conceit: *I saw him swaggering along the street in his new suit.* – *nc* a swaggering way of walking.

Swahili *see* Appendix 2.

swain [swein] *nc* (*liter or arch*) a young country boy, *esp* one who is a lover.

swallow[1] ['swolou] *vti* **1** to allow (food *etc*) to pass down the throat to the stomach: *He swallowed the whisky at one gulp*; *Try to swallow the pill whole!*; *His throat was so painful that he could hardly swallow.* – *See also* **swallow up** *below.* **2** (*inf*) to accept (*eg* a lie or insult) without question or protest: *You'll never get her to swallow that story!*; *Surely you're not going to swallow an insult like that!* – *nc* an act of swallowing: *He drank his tea at one swallow.*

swallow one's pride to behave humbly, *eg* by making an apology.

swallow up *vt sep* (*fig*) to swallow completely: *She was swallowed up by the crowd*; *His wife's clothes bills swallowed up his wages.*

swallow[2] ['swolou] *nc* a type of insect-eating bird with long wings and a divided tail that goes to warmer climates in winter.

'swallow dive *nc* a type of dive in which the arms are held stretched wide until the diver is about to enter the water.

swam *see* **swim**.

swamp [swomp] *ncu* (an area of) wet, marshy ground: *These trees grow best in swamp(s)*; *The rain has turned the garden into a swamp.* – *vt* to cover or fill (*eg* a boat) with water: *A great wave broke over the ship and swamped the deck*; (*fig*) *I'm swamped with work*; (*fig*) *They were swamped with replies to their advertisement.*

'swampy *adj* (of land) covered with swamp; marshy: *swampy ground*; *My feet are wet – it's swampy here.* **'swampiness** *nu.*

swan [swon] *nc* a large, *usu* white, water-bird of the duck family, with a long graceful neck: *The swans were swimming on the lake in the park.*

'swan song *nc* (*formal or facet*) the last work or performance of *eg* a poet, musician *etc* before his death or retirement.

swan around, off *vi* (*inf derog*) to go travelling in a leisurely and rather irresponsible way: *He swans around doing nothing while his wife works*; *His job seems to allow him to go swanning off to Italy from time to time.*

swank [swaŋk] *vi* (*derog sl*) to behave or talk in a conceited way: *She's always swanking about how clever/rich she is.* – *nc* (*derog sl*) a person who swanks: *She's a terrible swank.*

'swanky *adj* (*derog sl*) very smart: *a swanky new car*; *swanky parties.*

swap *see* **swop**.

swarm [swo:m] *nc* **1** a great number (of insects or other small creatures) in movement together, *esp* bees following a queen bee: *a swarm of ants.* **2** (*often in pl*: *inf*) a great number or crowd: *There were swarms of people on the beach.* – *vi* **1** (of bees) to follow a queen bee in a swarm: *Look at all those bees – they must be swarming.* **2** (*fig*) to move in great numbers: *When the bell rang the children swarmed out of the school.* **3** (*inf*) to be full of moving crowds: *The Tower of London swarmed/was swarming with tourists.*

swarm up *vt fus* to climb (a tree, wall *etc*) using arms and legs: *The sailors swarmed up the rigging.*

swarthy ['swo:ði] *adj* (*sometimes derog*) (of a person) having a dark skin: *a dark-haired, swarthy gipsy*; *He is dark and swarthy.*

swashbuckling ['swoʃbʌkliŋ] *adj* (*liter*: *usu attrib*) (of *eg* a pirate *etc*) bold, adventurous and boastful: *a swashbuckling hero.*

swastika ['swostikə] *nc* a cross with the ends bent at right angles, adopted as the badge of the Nazi party in Germany before the Second World War.

swat [swot] – *pt, ptp* **'swatted** – *vt* to crush (a fly *etc*) by slapping it with something flat: *He swatted the fly with a folded newspaper.* – *nc* an act of swatting: *He gave the wasp a swat.*

swath [swoθ], **swathe**[1] [sweið] *nc* (*esp old*) a line of corn or grass cut, or left uncut, by the scythe, mowing-machine *etc.*

swathe[2] [sweið] *vt* (*formal or facet*) to wrap or bind: *Her head was swathed in bandages/a towel*; *She was swathed in silk.*

sway [swei] *vti* **1** to (cause to) move from side to side or up and down with a swinging or rocking action: *She swayed her hips from side to side as she walked*; *The branches swayed gently in the breeze*; *The drunk man swayed as he walked along the road.* **2** to influence (a person's opinion, action *etc*): *A good lawyer knows how to sway a jury*; *She's too easily swayed one way or the other by her emotions.* – *nu* **1** the motion of swaying: *He felt the sway of the deck under his feet.* **2** (*liter*) power, rule or control: *For more than a century, England was under the sway of the Tudors.*

hold sway (*formal*) to have control or influence; to rule: *Rome held sway over a huge empire for several hundred years*; *The older members of the committee still hold sway.*

swear [sweə] – *pt* **swore** [swo:]: *ptp* **sworn** [swo:n] – *vti* **1** to state, declare, or promise solemnly with an oath, or very definitely and positively: *The witness must swear to tell the truth*; *He swore an oath of loyalty*; *He swore eternal love to her*; *'Will you swear never to reveal the secret?' 'I swear'*; *I could have sworn* (= I'm sure) *she was here a minute ago*; *She swore that she had obeyed my instructions.* **2** to use the name of God and other sacred words, or obscene words, for emphasis or abuse; to curse: *I could hear her swearing at her husband*; *Don't swear in front of the children!* – *See also* **swear by, swear in, swear to** *below.*

sworn [swo:n] *adj* (*attrib*) **1** (of friends, enemies *etc*) (determined, as if) having taken an oath always to remain so: *He is a sworn opponent of private education*; *They are sworn enemies.* **2** (of evidence, statements *etc*) given by a person who has sworn to tell the truth: *The prisoner has made a sworn statement.*

'swear-word *nc* a word used in cursing: *'Damn' is a mild swear-word.*

'swear by 1 to appeal to (*eg* God) as a witness of one's words: *I swear by all the saints that I'm completely innocent.* **2** (*inf*) to put complete trust in (a certain remedy *etc*): *She swears by aspirin for all the children's illnesses.*

swear in *vt sep* to introduce (a person) into a post or office formally, by making him swear an oath: *The new Governor is being sworn in next week*; *They swore the jury in yesterday.*

'swear to *vt fus* to make a solemn statement, with an oath, about (something): *I'll swear to the truth of what he said*; *I think he was here this morning, but I wouldn't like to swear to it.*

sweat [swet] *nu* **1** (*less formal than* **perspiration**) the moisture given out through the skin: *He was dripping with sweat after running so far in the heat*; *I think the child's recovering from his fever – his hair is wet with sweat.* **2** (*sometimes with* **a**) moisture that forms in drops on any surface, *eg* through condensation: *Hot food placed inside a plastic bag will cause* (*a*) *sweat to form on the inside surface of the bag.* **3** (*inf*) (*with* **a**) a state of nervousness or worry: *He was in a sweat in case his enemies should find him.* **4** (*inf*) (*sometimes with* **a**) hard work or effort: *It was a sweat trying to finish the work in time.* – *vi* **1** to give out sweat: *Vigorous exercise makes you sweat*; *He was sweating in the heat.* **2** to give out moisture: *Sometimes cheese sweats in hot weather*; *The walls are sweating with damp*; *Newly plastered walls sweat a bit.* **3** (*inf*) to work hard: *I was sweating* (*away*) *at my work from morning till night.* – *See also* **sweat** *in phrases below.*

'sweater *nc* any kind of knitted pullover or jersey.

'sweaty *adj* (*inf*) **1** wet or stained with, or smelling of, sweat: *sweaty clothes/bodies*; *His feet are sweaty.* **2** (*usu attrib*) (of work *etc*) likely to cause a person to sweat: *Gardening is sweaty work.*

'sweatiness *nu.*

sweated labour *nu* the labour of people who are overworked and underpaid: *These goods are produced by sweated labour.*

'sweatshop *nc* (*inf derog*) a workshop, factory *etc* in which people work very hard for too little pay.

in a cold sweat (coldness and dampness of the skin when a person is in) a state of shock, fear *etc*: *I was in a cold sweat*; *The horrible sound brought me out in a cold sweat.*

sweat blood (*inf*) to work very hard; to use a great deal of effort: *I sweated blood to finish that essay last night.*

sweat it out (*inf*) to endure or bear a difficult or unpleasant situation: *He'll just have to sweat it out by himself.*

sweat out *vt sep* to rid oneself of (*eg* a cold) by sweating: *He tried to sweat his cold out by taking aspirins.*

Swede, Sweden, Swedish *see* Appendix 2.

swede [swi:d] **1** *nc* a kind of large yellow turnip. **2** *ncu* its root as food.

sweep [swi:p] – *pt, ptp* **swept** [swept] – **1** *vti* (*often fig*) to clean (a room *etc*) using a brush or broom: *The floor needs sweeping*; *The room has been swept clean*; *The dust has all been swept away*; (*fig*) *They swept the sea of enemy mines.* – *See also* **sweep out, sweep up** *below.* **2** *vt* (*often fig*) to move (something) as though with a brush: *She swept the crumbs off the table with her hand*; *He swept the papers into his case*; *The wave swept him overboard*; *She swept her guests into the sitting-room*; *He swept us along with his enthusiasm*; *Don't get swept away by* (= become over-enthusiastic about) *the idea!*; *She swept aside* (= rejected or dismissed) *my objections.* **3** *vt* (*often liter*) to move quickly over: *Her fingers swept the strings of her harp*; *She looked anxiously for him, her eyes sweeping the room*; *The disease/craze is sweeping the country.* **4** *vi* to move swiftly or in a proud manner: *High* *winds sweep across the desert; The invading army swept through the country; She swept into my room without knocking on the door.* **5** *vi* (*formal or liter*) (of *eg* hills or other features of the landscape *etc*) to curve or extend: *The hills sweep down to the sea; A broad driveway sweeps up to the house.* – *nc* **1** an act of sweeping, or process of being swept, with a brush *etc*: *She gave the room a sweep.* **2** (*no pl*) a sweeping movement: *He watched the sweep of their oars as they rowed away; He indicated the damage with a sweep of his hand.* **3** (*formal or liter*: *no pl*) the range or extent of a sweeping movement: *She stared hard at my brooch as it came within the sweep of her gaze.* **4** (*formal or liter*) a curve, stretch or extent: *The wide sweep of the bay.* **5** a chimney sweep. **6** a sweepstake.

'sweeper (*in cmpds*) a person or thing that sweeps: *I shouldn't like to be a road-sweeper; May I borrow your carpet-sweeper?; This ship is called a minesweeper.*

'sweeping *adj* **1** (*usu attrib*) that sweeps: *a sweeping gesture.* **2** (of changes *etc*) very great: *a sweeping victory; sweeping reforms; The reforms proved more sweeping than he had intended.* **3** (*derog*) (of a statement *etc*) made without consideration of all the facts; too general: *I disapprove of his sweeping statements/generalization about the bad state of the world; That statement is too sweeping.*

'sweepings *n pl* (*inf*) rubbish *etc* gathered together by sweeping: *the sweepings from the floor of the restaurant.*

swept *adj* (*esp in cmpds*) being swept, or having been swept: *Her hair was swept back into a knot; a sweptback/an upswept hairstyle; windswept hair/hills.*

'sweeping-brush *nc* a type of brush with a long handle that is used for sweeping floors *etc*.

at one/a sweep by one action, at one time: *He sacked half of his employees at one sweep.*

make a clean sweep *see* **clean**.

sweep (someone) off his feet to affect (a person) with strong emotion or enthusiasm: *She was swept off her feet by* (= fell violently in love with) *him.*

sweep out *vt sep* to sweep (a room *etc*) thoroughly; to clean by sweeping: *The cleaner sweeps the classroom out every evening.*

sweep the board to be very successful, *orig* in gambling: *The young singer swept the board at the musical competition.*

'sweep (something) under the carpet to avoid facing, or dealing with, an unpleasant situation *etc*, by pretending it does not exist: *The government is trying to sweep these facts under the carpet.*

sweep up *vt sep* to gather together or remove (dirt *etc*) by sweeping: *She swept up the crumbs/mess.*

sweepstake ['swi:psteik] *nc* a system of gambling *eg* on a horse-race, in which the person who holds a ticket for the winning horse gets all the money staked by the other ticketholders: *We run* (= organize) *a sweepstake in our firm in aid of charity.*

sweet [swi:t] *adj* **1** tasting like sugar; not sour, salty or bitter: *as sweet as honey; Children eat too many sweet foods; These strawberries are very sweet; Do you prefer sweet wines to dry wines?;* (*in cmpds*) *sweet-tasting oranges.* **2** tasting fresh and pleasant: *young, sweet carrots; These peas are sweet and tender.* **3** (of smells) pleasant or fragrant: *The sweet smell of flowers filled the house;* (*in cmpds*) *sweet-smelling roses.* **4** (of sounds) agreeable or delightful to hear: *She has a sweet voice; the sweet song of the nightingale; Her voice is sweet and low.* **5** attractive or charming: *What a sweet little baby!; She has a sweet face/smile; She looks sweet in that dress.* **6** kindly and agreeable: *She's a sweet girl; The child has a sweet nature;* (*in cmpds*) *a sweet-tempered child;* (*inf*) *It was sweet of you to send me a birthday present.* – **1** *nc* (*Amer* **'candy**) a small piece of sweet food *eg* chocolate, toffee *etc*: *He bought a packet of sweets; She offered him a sweet; That child eats far too many sweets.* **2** *ncu* (a dish or course of) sweet food near or at the end of a meal; (a) pudding or dessert: *What are we having for sweet?; The sweet was ice-cream with chocolate sauce; I don't want any sweet.* **3** (*inf*: *with* **my**: used as an endearment) dear; darling: *Hallo, my sweet!*

'sweeten **1** *vti* to make or become sweet or sweeter: *Did you sweeten* (= put sugar in) *my tea?; The fruit gradually ripened and sweetened.* **2** *vt* (*inf*) to persuade, or make (a person) more agreeable, with flattery or gifts: *I bought her a bunch of flowers to sweeten her.*

'sweetener *nc* **1** something that sweetens, *eg* a substance used for sweetening food: *Saccharin is an artificial sweetener, often used instead of sugar.* **2** (*inf*) a bribe: *£10 will act as a sweetener on the official.*

'sweetly *adv* in an attractive, charming, agreeable or kindly manner: *She sang/smiled very sweetly.*

'sweetness *nu*.

'sweetheart *nc* **1** (*slightly old*) a boyfriend or girlfriend: *Has she a sweetheart?* **2** used as an endearment for any beloved person, *eg* a child: *Goodbye, sweetheart!*

'sweetmeat *nc* (*old*) a sweet, candy *etc*.

sweet pea *nc* a type of climbing plant with sweet-smelling flowers.

sweet potato *see* **yam**.

be 'sweet on (*slightly old inf*) to love, or be in love with (a girl or boy): *She's sweet on him.*

a sweet tooth *see* **tooth**.

the 'sweets of (something) (*liter*) the delights of (*eg* life, success *etc*): *He was enjoying the sweets of victory.*

swell [swel] – *pt* **swelled**: *ptp* **swollen** ['swoulən] – *vti* to make or become larger, greater or thicker: *The insect bite made her finger swell; Her ankles swelled in the heat; The continual rain had swollen the river; I invited her to join us on the excursion in order to swell the numbers;* (*liter*) *Her heart swelled with pride as she looked at her children;* (*liter*) *The sound of the organ swelled through the church.* – *See also* **swell out, swell up** *below.* – *nc* **1** (*usu in sing*) a rolling condition of the sea, *usu* after a storm: *The sea looked fairly calm but there was a heavy swell.* **2** (*formal or liter*: *no pl*) an increase in sound: *the swell of the music; a swell of sound.* **3** (*old sl*) an important or fashionable person: *You do look a swell!* – *adj* (*sl*: *esp Amer*) used as a term of approval: *a swell idea; That's swell!*

'swelling *nc* a swollen area, *esp* on the body as a result of injury, disease *etc*: *She had a large swelling on her arm where the wasp had stung her.*

swollen ['swoulən] *adj* increased in size, thickness *etc*, through swelling: *a swollen river; Her eyes were red and swollen with weeping; He had a badly swollen ankle after falling down the stairs.*

,swollen-'headed *adj* (*derog*) too pleased with oneself; conceited: *a swollen-headed young man;*

He's very swollen-headed about his success.

swell out *vi, vt sep* to (cause to) bulge: *The sails swelled out; Her cheeks swelled out; The wind swelled the sails out.*

swell up *vi* (of a part of the body) to swell: *The toothache made her face swell up; Her ankles have swollen up.*

swelter ['sweltə] *vi* (*inf*) (of a person *etc*) to be uncomfortably hot: *I'm sweltering in these thick clothes/this heat!*

'**sweltering** *adj* (*inf*) (of weather *etc*) very hot: *a sweltering day; It's sweltering today.*

swept *see* **sweep**.

swerve [swəːv] *vi* to turn away (from a line or course), *esp* quickly: *The car driver swerved to avoid the dog;* (*formal*) *She never swerved once from her purpose/path of duty.* – *nc* an act of swerving: *The sudden swerve rocked the passengers violently in their seats.*

swift[1] [swift] *adj* (*esp formal or liter*) fast or quick: *You'll need a swift horse to take you there; Our methods are swift and efficient; His face showed a swift change of expression; He is swift to take offence* (= is easily offended); (*in cmpds*) *a swift-footed* (= able to run fast) *animal.* '**swiftly** *adv.* '**swiftness** *nu.*

swift[2] [swift] *nc* a type of bird rather like a swallow.

swig [swig] – *pt, ptp* **swigged** – *vt* (*inf*) to drink (*esp* alcohol): *He's in the bar swigging whisky/beer.* – *nc* (*inf*) a long gulp or act of swigging: *He took a swig from the bottle; a swig of whisky.*

swill [swil] *vti* **1** (*sometimes derog*) to (cause to) flow around: *He swilled the wine about in his mouth; Water was swilling around in the bottom of the boat; Greasy water was swilling around in the sink.* **2** (*inf derog*) to drink greedily: *Who has been swilling all the milk?* – **1** *nc* (*sometimes derog*) a rinse: *He brushed his teeth and then gave his mouth a swill; She gave the cups a swill in dirty water.* **2** *nc* (*inf*) a drink: *He had a good swill of brandy.* **3** *nu* (*also* '**pigswill**) semi-liquid food given to pigs.

swill out *vt sep* to rinse: *She poured away the dirty water and then swilled the bowl out with fresh water.*

swim [swim] – *prp* '**swimming**: *pt* **swam** [swam]: *ptp* **swum** [swʌm] – **1** *vi* to move through water using arms and legs or fins, tails *etc*: *The children aren't allowed to go sailing until they've learnt to swim; I'm going/I've been swimming; She likes swimming on her back; He swam into the cave; We watched the fish swimming about in the aquarium.* **2** *vt* to cross (a river *etc*), compete in (a race), cover (a distance *etc*) by swimming: *He has already swum the river/two races today/three lengths of the swimming-pool; She can't swim a stroke* (= at all). **3** *vi* to seem to be moving round and round, as a result of dizziness, blurred vision *etc*: *His head was swimming; Everything began to swim before his eyes; He opened his eyes and her face swam into focus.* – *nc* an act of swimming: *Did you enjoy your swim?; We went for a swim in the lake.*

'**swimmer** *nc* a person who swims or who can swim: *She's no swimmer* (= She can't swim very well); *He's a good/strong swimmer.*

'**swimming** *adj* (*sometimes derog*: *with* **in** *or* **with**) covered with, or floating in, a liquid: *meat swimming in/with grease.*

'**swimmingly** *adj* (*old inf*) easily and successfully: *The party went swimmingly.*

'**swimming-bath,** '**swimming-pool** *ncs* an indoor or outdoor pool for swimming in.

swimming-costume *see* **swimsuit** *below.*

'**swimming-trunks** *n pl* short pants worn by boys and men for swimming.

'**swimsuit,** '**swimming-costume** *ncs* a (woman's) garment worn for swimming.

be in the swim (*inf*) to be involved in, or aware of, the latest fashion or trend of affairs, business *etc.*

swindle ['swindl] *vt* to cheat: *That shopkeeper has swindled me!; He swindled me of £1.50; She has already swindled several pounds out of me.* – *nc* an act or example of swindling; a fraud: *They tried to organize an insurance swindle by deliberately setting fire to their house; Our new car was a swindle – it has never worked properly.*

'**swindler** *nc* a person who swindles: *You swindler!*

swine [swain] – *pls* **swine** (*defs 1, 2*), **swines** (*def 2*) – *nc* **1** (*arch*) a pig. **2** (*inf derog*) a person who behaves in a cruel or contemptible way towards others: *Her husband is an absolute swine; You swine!; The swines murdered my husband.*

'**swinish** *adj* (*inf derog*) typical of a person who is a swine: *swinish behaviour; It was swinish of him to behave like that.*

'**swineherd** *nc* (*hist*) a man or boy who looks after swine (*def 1*).

swing [swiŋ] – *pt, ptp* **swung** [swʌŋ] – **1** *vti* to (cause to) move or sway in a curve (from side to side or forwards and backwards) from a fixed point: *You should swing your arms when you walk; The children were swinging on a rope hanging from a tree; The door suddenly swung open; He swung the child on to his back;* (*inf*) *You'll swing* (=be hanged) *for this!* – *See also* **swing to** *below.* **2** *vi* (*formal*) to walk with a long, relaxed, but fast stride: *He swung happily along the road.* **3** *vti* to turn suddenly: *He swung round and stared at them; He swung the car into the lane;* (*fig*) *They are hoping to swing the voters in their favour.* – *nc* **1** an act, period, or manner, of swinging: *He was having a swing on the rope; Most golfers would like to improve their swing* (= the way the club moves before and after hitting the ball). **2** (*no pl*) a swinging movement: *the swing of a kilt.* **3** (*no pl*) a strongly marked dancing rhythm: *The music should be played with a swing.* **4** a change in public opinion *etc*: *There was a big swing away from the government in the northern counties.* **5** a seat for swinging, hung on ropes or chains from a supporting frame, a branch of a tree *etc*: *There are swings in the park for the children.*

'**swinging** *adj* (*inf*) fashionable and exciting: *the swinging city of London.*

swing bridge *nc* a type of bridge that swings open to let ships pass.

swing door *nc* (*often in pl*) a door that swings open in both directions.

be in full swing to be going ahead, or continuing, busily or vigorously: *The work/party was in full swing.*

get into the swing (of things) (*inf*) to begin to understand, and fit into, a routine or rhythm of work *etc*: *He took a few days to get back into the swing of things after his illness.*

go with a swing (*inf*) (of an organized event *etc*) to proceed or go easily and successfully: *The reception went with a swing.*

swing to *vi, vt oblig sep* to close: *The gate swung to; Will you swing the gate to?*

swingeing ['swindʒiŋ] *adj* (*formal*: *usu attrib*) very severe: *You will have to pay a swingeing fine if you* *are arrested; swingeing taxation.*

swinish *see* **swine**.

swipe [swaip] *vti* (*inf*) to hit hard: *She swiped the tennis ball over the net; He swiped at the wasp but didn't hit it.* – *nc* (*inf*) a hard hit: *She gave the child a swipe across the face.*

swirl [swə:l] *vti* (*formal or liter*) to (cause to) move quickly, with a whirling or circling motion: *The leaves were swirled along by the wind; They watched the snow swirling past the window.* – *nc* a whirling or circling motion or shape: *the swirl of the dancers' skirts; a pattern of swirls and zig-zags.*

swish [swiʃ] *vti* to (cause to) move with a hissing or rustling sound: *He swished the stick about in the air; Her long skirt swished (along) the floor as she walked.* – *nc* an act, or the sound, of swishing: *The horse gave a swish of its tail;* (*formal or liter*) *We could hear the swish of leaves against the windows.*

Swiss *see* Appendix 2.

switch [switʃ] *nc* **1** (*sometimes in cmpds*) a small lever, handle or other device *eg* for putting or turning an electric current on or off: *The switch is down when the power is on and up when it's off; He couldn't find the lightswitch.* **2** (*more inf than* **change**) an act of turning or changing: *After several switches of direction they found themselves on the right road; a switch of support from one political party to another; When did you make the switch from gas to electricity in this house?* **3** a thin stick: *He cut a switch from a hazel tree.* – *vti* **1** to (cause to) turn: *He switched the lever to the 'off' position.* – *See also* **switch on/off** *below.* **2** (*more inf than* **change**) to (cause to) change: *Having considered that problem, they switched their attention to other matters; He decided to switch to a vegetarian diet; I don't like this radio play – let's switch to another programme.* – *See also* **switch over** *below.*

'switchback *nc* a railway *eg* in an amusement park, or a road that has many ups and downs (and sudden turns): *Let's go along the switchback;* (*attrib*) *a switchback road.*

'switchboard *nc* a board with many switches for controlling electric currents *etc*, or for making connections by telephone, *eg* within a large office *etc*: *He asked the girl at the switchboard to connect him* (= on the telephone) *with the manager.*

switchover *see* **switch over**.

be switched on (*sl*) **1** to be aware of and in sympathy with all the activities and developments that are up to date and fashionable: *My grandmother's really switched on – she enjoys pop music.* **2** to take drugs for stimulation; to be under the influence of such drugs.

switch on/off *vt sep* to put or turn on/off (an electric current/light *etc*): *He switched on the light; You should always switch off the electricity before going on holiday.*

switch over *vi, vt sep* to (cause to) change: *We're switching over from coal-gas to North Sea gas soon; Our cookers are being switched over to North Sea gas; When are they switching them over?* (*nc* **'switchover**).

Switzerland *see* Appendix 2.

swivel ['swivl] *nc* (*often in cmpds*) a type of joint between two parts of an object that enables one part to turn without the other: *There's a swivel between the two parts of the chain; a swivel-joint; a swivel-chair* (= a chair that can be turned round on its base). – *v* – *pt, ptp* **'swivelled** – *vti* to (cause to) move round (as though) on a swivel: *He swivelled his chair round to face the desk; He swivelled round when he heard the noise.*

swizz [swiz] *nc* (*inf*) a swindle, fraud or disappointment: *What a swizz!*

swollen *see* **swell**.

swoon [swu:n] *vi* (*esp old or liter*) to faint: *She swooned into his arms; The teenagers swooned as the pop-singer appeared on the stage.* – *nc* (*esp old or liter*) a fainting fit: *She lay in a swoon.*

swoop [swu:p] *vi* (*sometimes liter*) to rush or fly downwards: *The owl swooped down on its prey; The aeroplane swooped and rose again.* – *nc* (*sometimes liter*) an act of swooping: *With a sudden swoop the hawk attacked the field mouse; the swoop of the aircraft.*

at one fell swoop all at the same time; in a single movement or action: *The new manager got rid of several unwanted employees at one fell swoop.*

swop, swap [swop] – *pt, ptp* **swopped, swapped** – *vti* (*inf*) to exchange one thing for another: *He swopped his rubber ball with another boy for a toy pistol; They often swopped books (with each other); I like your pen better than mine – would you like to swop?* – *nc* (*inf*) an exchange: *That seems a fair swop.*

sword [so:d] *nc* (*esp hist*) a weapon with a long blade that is sharp on one or both edges: *He drew his sword (from its sheath) and killed the man.*

'sword-play *nu* the activity of fencing: *He watched the skilful sword-play between the two men.*

'swordsman ['so:dz-] – *fem* **'swordswoman** – *nc* a man who can fight or fence with a sword: *a good/poor swordsman; He's no swordsman* (= has no skill with a sword).

cross swords (*fig*) to quarrel or disagree: *I have crossed swords with him several times about this matter; I try not to cross swords with my boss but he is a most unreasonable man.*

swore, sworn *see* **swear**.

swot [swot] – *pt, ptp* **'swotted** – *vi* (*inf*) to study hard, *esp* by memorizing *eg* for an examination: *She stayed indoors and swotted (for her exam).* – *nc* (*inf*: *usu derog*) a person who studies hard or is clever at school work.

swot up *vt sep* (*inf*) to memorize (a subject *etc*), *esp* for an examination: *I must swot up my history dates/French irregular verbs.*

swum *see* **swim**.

swung *see* **swing**.

sycamore ['sikəmo:] **1** *nc* (*also* **'sycamore tree**) a name given to several different types of tree, the maple, plane, or a type of fig-tree. **2** *nu, adj* (of) its wood.

sycophant ['sikəfant] *nc* (*formal derog*) a person who flatters someone in order to gain some advantage for himself: *The king's advisers were nothing but a crowd of sycophants.* **,syco'phantic** *adj.*

syllabi *see* **syllabus**.

syllable ['siləbl] *nc* a word or part of a word *usu* containing a vowel sound: *'Cheese' has one syllable, 'but-ter' two and 'mar-ga-rine' three;* (*fig*) *Don't breath a syllable of this!* (= Don't tell anyone about this).

syl'labic [-'la-] *adj* (*formal*) of, or in, syllables: *The inhabitants of ancient Crete used a form of Greek which they wrote in syllabic form.*

syllabus ['siləbəs] – *pls* **'syllabuses, 'syllabi** [-bai] – *nc* a programme or list, *eg* of a course of lectures, or of courses of study: *He carefully read the examination syllabus.*

sylph [silf] *nc* **1** (*myth*) a type of fairy supposed to inhabit the air. **2** a slender, graceful woman.

'sylph-like *adj* slender and graceful: *a sylph-like figure*; *She is tall and sylph-like.*

symbol ['simbəl] *nc* **1** a thing that is regarded as representing or standing for another: *The cross is the symbol of Christianity*; *The colour white is a symbol of purity*; *The dove is the symbol of peace.* **2** a sign used as a short way of stating something *eg* in mathematics, chemistry *etc*: *O is the symbol for oxygen.*

sym'bolic [-'bo-] *adj* **1** of, or using, symbols: *This author's style of writing is highly symbolic*; *symbolic writing.* **2** (*pred with* **of**) representing: *In the Christian religion, bread and wine are symbolic of Christ's body and blood.* **sym'bolically** *adv.*

'symbolism *nu* the practice of expressing a meaning by the use of symbols: *religious symbolism.*

'symbolize, -ise *vt* to be a symbol of (something) or represent (something) by a symbol: *A ring symbolizes everlasting love*; *Different qualities are symbolized by different colours, as jealousy by green, death by black, royalty by purple.*

symmetry ['simitri] *nu* (*formal*) the state in which two parts, on either side of a dividing line, are equal in size, shape and position: *An extra part was added to the house in 1850, which spoilt the symmetry of its front.*

sym'metrical [-'me-] *adj* (*formal*) having symmetry: *The two sides of a person's face are never completely symmetrical*; *a symmetrical shape.* **sym'metrically** *adv.*

sympathy ['simpəθi] *nu* **1** a feeling of pity or sorrow for a person in trouble: *When her husband died, she received many letters of sympathy*; *He touched her hand to express his sympathy.* **2** (*also* **'sympathies** *n pl*) the state or feeling of being in agreement with, or of being able to understand, the attitude or feelings of another person: *I have no sympathy with such a stupid attitude*; *The other unions are in sympathy with* (= agree with) *the railwaymen in their claim for more pay*; *My sympathies are with her husband* (= I feel sorry for him, not her).

,sympa'thetic [-'θetik] *adj* (*neg* **un-**) showing or feeling sympathy: *She was very sympathetic when I failed my exam*; *I'm not sympathetic towards these new teaching methods*; *He gave her a sympathetic smile.*

'sympathize, -ise *vi* (*with* **with**) to show or feel sympathy to (a person *etc*): *I find it difficult to sympathize with him when he complains so much*; *I approve of his determination and energy, though I can't sympathize with his ideas.*

symphony ['simfəni] *nc* a *usu* long piece of music for an orchestra *usu* of many different instruments, *usu* in three or four movements or parts: *Beethoven wrote nine symphonies.*

sym'phonic [-'fo-] *adj* (*formal or tech*) of, or like, a symphony: *the symphonic form.*

symposium [sim'pouziəm] – *pl* **sym'posiums, sym'posia** [-ziə] – *nc* (*formal*) a collection of essays on a single subject by different writers; a conference where a particular subject is discussed: *a symposium on nationalism*; *The university is holding a symposium on new forms of energy.*

symptom ['simptəm] *nc* **1** something that is a sign (of a particular disease *etc*): *A red rash is one of the symptoms of measles.* **2** a sign (of a *usu* bad state or condition): *The drunkenness in this area is a symptom of the despair felt by the people here.*

,sympto'matic [-'matik] *adj* (*formal or tech*: *usu pred with* **of**) being a symptom of: *These quarrels are symptomatic of the state of tension between them.*

synagogue ['sinəgog] *nc* (the building used by) a gathering of Jews meeting together for worship: *He attends the synagogue regularly.*

synchronize, -ise ['siŋkrənaiz] *vti* (*formal or tech*) to (cause to) happen at the same time, go at the same speed *etc*, as something else: *In the film, the movements of the actors' lips did not synchronize with the sounds of their words*; (*sometimes facet*) *We'll meet back here again in ten minutes' time – but let's synchronize our watches* (= turn the hands to the same time) *first.* **,synchroni'zation, -s-** *nu.*

syncopate ['siŋkəpeit] *vt* (*music*) to alter the rhythm of (music) by putting the accent on beats not usually accented, *eg* the second and fourth beats in a bar of four beats. **,synco'pation** *nu.*

syndicate ['sindikət] *nc* **1** a council or number of persons who join together to manage a piece of business: *That publishing firm is under the control of a syndicate.* **2** a group of newspapers under the same management. **3** (*tech*) an agency that supplies articles, photographs *etc* for publication at the same time in newspapers *etc* in different places. – [-keit] *vt* (*tech*) to sell or use (a picture, article *etc*) for publication in a number of newspapers.

synod ['sinəd] *nc* a meeting or council of clergymen: *a synod of bishops.*

synonym ['sinənim] *nc* (*tech*) a word having the same, or very nearly the same, meaning as another: *'Ass' and 'donkey' are synonyms – so are 'brave' and 'courageous' and 'hide' and 'conceal'.*

sy'nonymous [-'no-] *adj* (*sometimes with* **with**) having the same meaning: *'Ass' and 'donkey' are synonymous.*

synopsis [si'nopsis] – *pl* **sy'nopses** [-si:z] – *nc* (*formal*) a short account or summary (*eg* of the plot of a book, speech *etc*): *He read the synopsis of the book that was printed on its back cover.*

syntax ['sintaks] *nu* (*gram*) (the rules for) the correct arrangement of words in a sentence: *German syntax is almost as difficult for learners as Latin syntax*; *The sentence 'He took away it' contains a mistake in syntax.*

syn'tactic, syn'tactical *adjs* of, or relating to, syntax: *'Syntactic Structures' is a very important book in linguistics.*

synthesis ['sinθəsis] – *pl* **'syntheses** [-si:z] – *ncu* (*formal or tech*) (something produced through) the process of combining separate parts, *eg* chemical elements or substances, into a whole: *Plastic is produced by synthesis*; *His recent book is a synthesis of several of his earlier ideas.*

'synthesize, -ise *vt* (*formal or tech*) to make (*eg* a drug) by synthesis: *Some hormones can be synthesized.*

synthetic [sin'θetik] **1** *nc, adj* (a substance) produced artificially by synthesis: *nylon and other synthetic materials/synthetics.* **2** *adj* (*formal or facet*: *derog*) not genuine or natural: *His Irish accent was as synthetic as his smile*; *synthetic sympathy.*

syphilis ['sifəlis] *nu* a type of serious infectious disease that is caught through sexual intercourse.

,syphi'litic [-tik] **1** *nc, adj* (a person who is) suffering from syphilis. **2** *adj* of or caused by syphilis.

syphon *see* **siphon**.

Syria, Syrian *see* Appendix 2.

syringe [si'rindʒ] *nc* an instrument for sucking up or squirting out liquids, having *eg* a rubber bulb or a piston and a needle for giving injections. – *vt* to clean or wash using a syringe: *He had to have his ears syringed.*

syrup ['sirəp, (*Amer*) 'səː-] *nu* **1** water or the juice of fruits boiled with sugar and made thick and sticky. **2** a purified form of treacle: *He spread some syrup on his bread.*

'**syrupy** *adj* **1** of, or like, syrup: *a syrupy mixture*; *The liquid was thick and syrupy.* **2** (*fig derog*) too sweet and sentimental: *That film was too syrupy*; *a syrupy musical.*

system ['sistəm] **1** *nc* an arrangement of many parts that work together: *a railway system*; *the solar system*; *the digestive system.* **2** *nc* a person's body, considered as an arrangement of working parts: *Take a walk every day – it's good for the system!* **3** *nc* a way of organizing something according to certain ideas, principles *etc*: *a system of government/education.* **4** *nc* a plan or method: *What is your system for washing the dishes?* **5** *nu* the quality of being efficient and methodical: *I find that her working methods lack system.*

ˌ**syste'matic** [-'matik] *adj* using a system; methodical: *He investigated the matter with systematic thoroughness*; *They have made a systematic* (= organized and deliberate) *attempt to ruin his reputation.* ˌ**syste'matically** *adv.*

'**systematize, -ise** [-mətaiz] *vt* (*formal*) to organize (something) into, or according to, a system: *We ought to try to systematize the collected evidence/our methods.*

the system (*sometimes facet*) the established order or arrangement of things *eg* in a business, in society *etc*: *We mustn't upset the system!*

Tt

T [tiː]: '**T-shirt** (*also* '**tee shirt**) *nc* a light shirt with short sleeves and no collar: *The little boys always wore shorts and T-shirts in the summer.*

to a 'T, (*also* **to a 'tee**) (*inf*) exactly; very well: *This job suits me to a T.*

ta [taː] *interj* (*Brit*) (used *esp* by or to young children) thank you: *She's only twenty months old, but she knows when to say 'please' and 'ta'.*

tab [tab] *nc* **1** a small flat piece of some material attached to, or part of, something larger which stands up so that it can be seen, held, pulled *etc*: *You open the packet by pulling the tab*; *He collects the metal tabs from beer-cans.* **2** a strip of material attached to a piece of clothing by which it can be hung up: *There aren't any coat-hangers so you'll have to hang your jacket up by the tab.* **3** (*usu* '**name-tab**) a piece of material with a person's name or some other mark on it, attached to a piece of clothing so that its owner can be identified: *All pupils must have name-tabs on all articles of clothing.*

keep tabs on (*inf*) to keep a check on; to watch: *I like to keep tabs on what is happening at home when I'm on holiday*; *The boss tries to keep tabs on all of us in the office.*

pick up the tab (*Amer inf*) to pay the bill (for): *He insisted on picking up the tab for the meal.*

tabby ['tabi] *nc* (*also* '**tabby-cat**) a *usu* grey or brown cat with darker stripes, *esp* a female one: *Her tabby(-cat) was sitting in front of the fire.*

table ['teibl] **1** *nc* (*sometimes in cmpds*) a piece of furniture consisting of a flat, horizontal surface on legs used *eg* to put food on at meals, or for some games: *Put all the plates on the table*; *a billiard-table.* **2** *nc* a statement of facts or figures arranged in columns *etc*: *The results of the experiments can be seen in table 5.* – *See also* **timetable** *under* **time**. **3** *nc* the people sitting at a table: *The whole table heard what he said.* **4** *nu* (*old or liter*) food as served on a table: *the pleasures of the table*; *our friends keep an excellent table.* – *vt* (*formal*) **1** to put forward for discussion: *The government tabled a motion.* **2** to make into a table (*def 2*) or list: *He tabled the times of arrival.*

'**tablecloth** *nc* a cloth for covering a table, *usu* for a meal: *an embroidered tablecloth.*

table d'hôte [taːblə'dout] *adv, adj* (*usu pred*) (of a meal) with a limited choice of dishes and a fixed price: *The meals in this hotel are all table d'hôte*; *Are we going to eat à la carte or table d'hôte?*

'**table linen** *nu* tablecloths, napkins *etc*: *They gave us table linen as a wedding present.*

table napkin *see* **napkin**.

'**tablespoon** *nc* **1** a large spoon, used *eg* for serving food. **2** a tablespoonful: *Add a tablespoon of sugar.*

'**tablespoonful** *nc* the amount that will fill a tablespoon: *two tablespoonfuls of jam.*

'**table tennis** *nu* a game played on a table with small bats and a light ball: *Let's have a game of table tennis*; *Do you play table tennis?*

at 'table (*old or liter*) (sitting) around a table, having a meal: *There were eight of us at table that night.*

lay/set the table to put a tablecloth, plates, knives, forks *etc* on a table for a meal: *The meal is ready – will you lay the table?*

turn the tables on (someone) *see* **turn**.

See also **dressing-table** *under* **dress** *and* **tabular**.

tableau ['tablou, (*Amer also*) ta'blou] – *pl* **tableaux** [-z] – *nc* a group of people forming a silent, motionless scene *usu* representing historical *etc* events: *The entertainment consisted of a series of tableaux of important events in the town's history.*

tablecloth, tablespoon, tablespoonful *see* **table**.

tablet ['tablit] *nc* **1** (*sometimes in cmpds*) a pill: *Take these tablets for your headache*; *a sleeping-tablet* (= a tablet to make one sleep). **2** a flat piece or bar (of soap *etc*): *I bought a tablet of soap.* **3** a piece of *usu* stone with a flat surface on which words are engraved *etc*: *They put up a marble tablet in memory of his father.*

tabloid ['tabloid] *nc* (*sometimes derog*) (a newspaper) with a relatively small size of page and *usu* pictures, cartoons *etc* and news given in a short and simple form.

taboo, tabu [tə'buː] – *pls* **ta'boos, ta'bus** – *nc, adj* (*usu pred*) (something) forbidden for religious reasons or because it is against social custom: *Incest is usually considered (a) taboo*; *Alcohol is (a) taboo in Muslim societies.*

tabular ['tabjulə] *adj* (*formal*: *usu attrib*) in the form of a table (*def 2*); set out in columns and rows: *He wrote down the results of his experiments in tabular form.*

'**tabulate** [-leit] *vt* (*formal*) to arrange (information) in tabular form: *He tabulated the distances they had travelled.* ˌ**tabu'lation** *nu.*

tacit ['tasit] *adj* (*formal*: *usu attrib*) understood but not actually stated: *They had a tacit agreement to help each other when necessary.* '**tacitness** *nu.*

'**tacitly** *adv* (*formal*): *It was tacitly agreed that they should each pay half of the bill.*

taciturn ['tasitə:n] *adj* (*formal*) not inclined to talk; quiet: *a taciturn child*; *He's a very kind man, but very taciturn, which sometimes makes him seem unfriendly.* '**taciturnly** *adv.* ˌ**taci'turnity** *nu.*

tack [tak] *nc* **1** (*sometimes in cmpds*) a short nail with a broad flat head: *I need some tacks to attach this picture to the wall*; *a carpet-tack.* **2** in sewing, a large, temporary stitch used to hold material together while it is being sewn together properly: *When the dress was finished, she took out the tacks.* **3** in sailing, a movement diagonally against the wind: *We sailed on an easterly tack.* **4** (*fig*) a direction or course: *After they moved, their lives took a different tack.* – **1** *vt* (*with* **down, on** *etc*) to fasten with tacks: *I tacked the carpet down*; *She tacked the material together.* – *See also* **tack on** *below.* **2** *vi* (of sailing-boats) to move diagonally (backwards and forwards) against the wind: *The boat tacked into harbour.*

get down to brass tacks *see* **brass**.

tack on *vt sep* (*inf*: *sometimes derog*: *sometimes with* **to**) to add (something) to (the end of) something: *That last speech in the play doesn't seem to have any purpose – it has just been tacked on at the end to please the producer.*

tackle ['takl] **1** *nc* an act of tackling: *a rugby tackle.* **2** *nu* equipment, *esp* for fishing: *fishing tackle.* **3** *nu* ropes, pulleys *etc* for lifting heavy weights: *lifting tackle.* **4** *nu* in sailing, the ropes, rigging *etc* of a boat. – **1** *vt* to try to grasp or seize (someone): *The policeman tackled the thief.* **2** *vt* to deal with or try to solve (a problem); to ask (someone) about a problem: *He tackled the problem*; *She tackled the teacher about her child's work.* **3** *vti* in football, hockey *etc*, to (try to) take the ball *etc* from a player on the other team: *He tackled his opponent*; *He tackles well.*

tacky ['taki] *adj* (*inf*) sticky: *Be careful – the paint is still tacky*; *tacky paint.* '**tackiness** *nu.*

tact [takt] *nu* care and skill in one's behaviour to people, in order to avoid hurting or offending them: *a person of great tact*; *He showed tact in dealing with difficult customers.*

'**tactful** *adj* showing tact: *a tactful person*; *tactful behaviour*; *It wasn't very tactful of you to ask about her husband – he left her last year.* '**tactfully** *adv.* '**tactfulness** *nu.*

tactless *adj* without tact: *a tactless person/remark*; *She didn't mean to hurt you – she's just tactless.* '**tactlessly** *adv.* '**tactlessness** *nu.*

tactics ['taktiks] *n pl* (*sometimes in sing*) the art of arranging troops, warships *etc* during a battle, in order to win or gain an advantage over one's opponents: *The generals discussed their tactics*; (*fig*) *They planned their tactics for the election/game/meeting.*

'**tactical** *adj* (*formal*: *often attrib*) of or concerned with tactics or successful planning: *a tactical advantage.* '**tactically** *adv.*

tac'tician [-'tiʃən] *nc* (*formal*) a person who is good at tactics or successful planning.

tadpole ['tadpoul] *nc* a young frog or toad in its first stage of development.

taffeta ['tafitə] *nu, adj* (of) a thin, stiff, shiny cloth: *a dress of white taffeta*; *a taffeta skirt.*

tag [tag] **1** *nc* (*often in cmpds*) a label: *a price-tag on a piece of clothing in a shop*; *a name-tag.* **2** *nc* a saying or quotation that is often repeated: *a well-known Latin tag.* **3** *nu* (*also* **tig** [tig]) a child's game in which one child chases the others and tries to catch or touch one of them, who then becomes the chaser: *They were playing tag in the street.* – *v* – *pt, ptp* **tagged** – *vt* **1** to put a tag (*def 1*) on something: *All the clothes have been tagged.* **2** to catch or touch (a person) in the game of tag.

tag along *vi* (*inf*: *sometimes derog*: *often with* **behind** *or* **with**) to follow or go (with someone), often when one is not wanted: *We never get away from him – everywhere we go, he insists on tagging along (with us)!*

tag on 1 *vt sep* (*usu with* **at** *or* **to**) to attach (something) to something: *These comments weren't part of his speech – he just tagged them on at the end.* **2** *vi* (*often derog*: *with* **to**) to follow (someone) closely: *The child always tags on to his elder brother.*

tail [teil] *nc* **1** the part of an animal, bird or fish that sticks out behind the rest of its body: *The dog wagged its tail*; *A fish swims by moving its tail.* **2** anything which has a similar function or position: *the tail of an aeroplane/comet*; *We'll never get into the cinema – we're at the tail of the queue.* – *vt* (*inf*) to follow closely: *The detectives tailed the thief to the station.* – *See also* **tail away, tail off** *below.*

-tailed (*in cmpds*) having a (certain size, type *etc* of) tail: *a black-tailed duck*; *a long-tailed dog.*

tails 1 *n pl* a tail-coat: *He was wearing tails.* **2** *n, adv* (on) the side of a coin that does not have the head of the sovereign *etc* on it: *He tossed the coin and it came down tails.* – *interj* a call showing that a person has chosen that side of the coin when tossing a coin to make a decision *etc.* – *See also* **heads or tails** *under* **head**.

tail-coat *nc* (*usu abbrev* **tails**) a type of coat with a long divided tail worn as part of a man's formal dress.

ˌ**tail-'end** *nc* (*inf often derog*: *usu with* **the**) the very end or last part: *They were at the tail-end of the procession*; *I didn't hear the whole story – I just heard the tail-end of it.*

'**tail-light** *nc* the (*usu* red) light on the back of a car, train, bicycle *etc*: *He followed the tail-lights of the bus.*

'**tail wind** *nc* a wind coming from behind: *We sailed home with a tail wind.*

tail away *see* **tail off** *below.*

tail off *vi* **1** to become fewer, smaller or weaker (at the end): *A lot of people came to see the exhibition when it opened, but the crowds tailed off after a couple of weeks*; *His interest tailed off towards the end of the film.* **2** (*also* **tail away**) (of voices *etc*) to become quieter or silent: *He realized what he was saying was nonsense, and his voice tailed off into silence*; *He tailed off when the headmaster entered the room*; *His voice tailed away into silence.*

turn tail *see* **turn**.

tailor ['teilə] *nc* **1** a person who cuts and makes suits, overcoats *etc*: *He has his clothes made by a London tailor.* **2** a tailor's shop: *There's a tailor in the High Street.* – *vt* **1** to make and fit (suits, coats etc): *He has his suits tailored in London.* **2** (*formal fig*) to make (something) fit the circumstances; to adapt: *He tailored his way of living to his income.*

'tailored *adj* (*usu attrib*) made by a tailor: *She wears tailored suits.*

'tailor's *nc* a tailor's shop: *Can you buy socks at a tailor's?*

,tailor-'made *adj* **1** (*esp* of women's clothes) made by a tailor to fit a person exactly: *I prefer tailor-made clothes; I like my clothes tailor-made.* **2** (*fig: often pred*) very well suited or adapted for some purpose: *This tool is tailor-made for this job; His new job seems tailor-made for him.*

taint [teint] *vt* (*formal or liter*) **1** to spoil (something) by touching it or bringing it into contact with something bad or rotten: *The meat has been tainted.* **2** (*fig*) to affect (someone or something) with something evil or immoral; to corrupt: *He has been tainted by his contact with criminals.* – *nc* (*formal or liter*) a mark or trace of something bad, rotten or evil: *the taint of decay.*

'tainted *adj* (*formal or liter: often with* **with** *when pred*) spoiled or corrupted: *tainted food; The whole nation is tainted with evil and corruption.*

Taiwan, Taiwanese *see* Appendix 2.

take [teik] – *pt* **took** [tuk]: *ptp* **taken** – (not used with **is, was** *etc* and **-ing** (*def 8*): not *usu* used with **is, was** *etc* and **-ing** (*defs 6, 11, 19*)) **1** *vt* (*often with* **down, out** *etc*) to reach out for and grasp, hold, lift, pull *etc*: *He took my hand; Will you take the baby while I look for my keys; He took her in his arms and kissed her; He took the book down from the shelf; He took the man by the arm, and led him away; He opened the drawer and took out a gun; I've had a tooth taken out; Take whichever one you like; Take a card.* **2** *vt* (*often with* **away, in, off, out** *etc*) to carry, conduct or lead to another place: *I took the books (back) to the library; He's taking me to America with him; The bus will take you to the centre of town; Could you take her into my office, please?; The police came and took him away; He escaped from the mental hospital, but was caught and taken back; I took the dog out for a walk; He took her out for dinner* (= He took her to a restaurant and paid for the meal). **3** *vt* to do or perform some action: *I think I'll take a walk; Will you take a look at my sick child; He decided to take a bath.* **4** *vt* to get, receive, buy, rent *etc*: *I'm taking French lessons; These strawberries look nice – I'll take three kilos; We take the local newspaper; We took a house in London for the summer.* **5** *vt* (*sometimes with* **back**) to agree to have; to accept: *He took my advice* (= He did what I suggested); *They refused to take responsibility for the accident; The hotel doesn't take dogs; I won't take that (insult) from you!; I won't take less than £500 for that car; I'm afraid we can't take back goods bought in a sale.* **6** *vt* to need or require: *How long does it take you to go home?; It took a lot of courage to leave his job; It takes time to do a difficult job like this.* **7** *vt* to travel by (bus *etc*): *I'm taking the next train to London; I was in a hurry so I took a taxi.* **8** *vt* to have enough space for: *The car takes five people; The shelf won't take any more books.* **9** *vt* to make a note, record *etc*: *He took a photograph of the castle; The nurse took the patient's temperature; All the students were taking notes at the lecture; The tailor took his measurements; The policeman took my name and address.* – *See also* **take down** *below.* **10** *vt* to remove, use, occupy *etc* with or without permission: *Someone's taken my coat; He took all my money; That fellow has taken my seat!; Take my car if yours has broken down; This quotation was taken from Shelley.* **11** *vt* to consider (as an example): *Lots of people I know drink too much alcohol. Take John for example.* **12** *vt* to capture or win: *The soldiers took the city; He took the first prize.* **13** *vt* (*often with* **away, from, off**) to make less or smaller by a certain amount: *Take (away) four from ten, and that leaves six; He took 60p off the price.* **14** *vt* to suppose or think (that something is the case): *Do you take me for an idiot?* (= Do you think I am an idiot?); *I take him to be a friend of yours; I take it (that) you won't be coming with us.* **15** *vt* to eat or drink: *Take these pills; I can't take alcohol; Do you take sugar in your tea?* **16** *vt* to conduct, lead or run; to be in charge or control of: *John can't come so will you take the class/lecture/meeting this evening?* **17** *vt* (*used only with certain adverbs*) to consider or react or behave to (something) in a certain way: *He took the news calmly;* (*formal*) *He took it ill/amiss that he was not consulted before the decision was made.* **18** *vt* (*with certain nouns and* **in**) to feel: *He took pleasure/pride/a delight/an interest in his work.* **19** *vt* to go down or go into (a road): *Take the second road on the left; Take first left and second right.* **20** *vi* (of an inoculation *etc*) to be effective: *They had to wait for the inoculation to take.* – *See also* **take** *in phrases below.* – **1** *nu* (*inf*) the amount of money taken in a shop *etc*; takings: *What was the take today?* **2** *nc* the filming of a single scene in a cinema film: *After five takes, the director was satisfied.*

taker *nc* a person who takes (something) *esp* one who accepts an offer or takes a bet: *I offered my friends the use of my car, but there were no takers.*

takings *n pl* the amount of money taken at a concert, in a shop *etc*: *He took the day's takings to the bank.*

take-away *nc* (*Amer and Scottish* **carry-out**: *Amer* **take-out**: *inf*) **1** food prepared and bought in a restaurant but taken away and eaten somewhere else *eg* at home: *I haven't time to prepare a meal this evening, so I'll go and buy a take-away;* (*attrib*) *a take-away meal.* **2** a restaurant where such food is prepared and bought: *a Chinese take-away.*

take-off *see* **take off** *below.*

take-out *nc* (*Amer*) a take-away.

take-over *see* **take over** *below.*

be taken aback, be taken ill *see* **aback, ill**.

be taken up with to be busy or occupied with: *He's very taken up with his new job.* – *See also* **take up with** *below.*

be 'taken with/by to find pleasing or attractive: *He was very taken with the village and its inhabitants.*

have (got) what it takes *see* **have**.

take account of *see* **account**.

take advantage of *see* **advantage**.

'take after *vt fus* to be like (someone, *esp* a parent or relation) in appearance or character: *She takes after her father.*

take aim, take apart *see* **aim, apart**.

take (something) as read *see* **read**.

take back 1 *vt oblig sep* to make (someone) remember or think about (something): *Meeting my old friends took me back to my childhood.* **2** *vt sep* to admit that what has been said is not true; to retract (something that has been said): *Take back* *what you said about my sister!* – *See also* **take** (*v def 5*).

take a bet, take the biscuit *see* **bet, biscuit.**

take the bull by the horns *see* **bull.**

take (someone) by surprise *see* **surprise.**

take care, take a/one's chance, take charge *see* **care, chance, charge.**

take a corner to go round a corner: *The car took the corner too quickly and crashed.*

take a degree to study for and obtain a degree (*def 4*): *He took a degree in chemistry.*

take a dislike to *see* **dislike.**

take down *vt sep* to make a note or record of: *He took down her name and address*; *He took down the details in a note book.* – *See also* **take** (*v def 1*).

take effect *see* **effect.**

take an examination/test to have one's knowledge or ability tested formally, often in writing.

take exception (to), (not) take one's eyes off, take a fancy (to), take (one's) fancy *see* **exception** *under* **except, eye, fancy.**

take (someone) for to believe (mistakenly) that (someone) is (someone or something else): *I took you for your brother*; *I took him for an intelligent person.* – *See also* **take** (*def 14*).

take for granted, take fright, take a gamble, take heart, take heed, take a hint, take hold of *see* **grant, fright, gamble, heart, heed, hint, hold** (*n def 1*).

ˌ**take-home** ˈ**pay** the amount of a person's wages that they have left to spend after tax, insurance *etc* have been taken away.

take in *vt sep* **1** to include: *Greater London takes in the county of Middlesex.* **2** to give (someone) shelter: *He had nowhere to go, so I took him in.* **3** (*fig*) to understand and remember: *I didn't take in what he said.* **4** to make (clothes) smaller: *I lost a lot of weight, so I had to take all my clothes in.* **5** (*inf*) to deceive or cheat: *I was told the picture was very valuable, but I soon found out I'd been taken in*; *He took me in with his story.* – *See also* **take** (*v def 2*).

take in good part, take (someone) in hand, take into account *see* **part, hand, account.**

take it (*with* **can/could**) to be able to bear suffering, trouble, difficulty *etc*: *Tell me the bad news. Don't worry, I can take it.*

take it from me (that) you can believe me when I say (that): *Take it from me – this company is heading for bankruptcy.*

take it into one's head (to) to decide (to): *She took it into her head to go to Spain.*

take a joke, take one's leave, take the liberty of, take liberties with, take a liking to, take one's mind off, take notice, take an oath *see* **joke, leave**[2]**, liberty, like**[2]**, mind, notice, oath.**

take off 1 *vt sep* to remove (clothes *etc*): *He took off his coat/bandage/mask*; *I don't know how much this costs – someone has taken the price-tag off.* **2** *vi* (of an aircraft) to leave the ground: *The plane took off for Rome* (*nc* ˈ**take-off**). **3** *vt oblig sep* not to work during (a period of time): *I'm taking tomorrow morning off.* **4** *vt sep* (*inf*) to imitate someone (often unkindly): *He used to take off his teacher to make his friends laugh* (*nc* ˈ**take-off**).

take offence, take the offensive *see* **offence.**

take on 1 *vt sep* to agree to do (work *etc*); to undertake: *He took on the job.* **2** *vt sep* to employ: *They are taking on five hundred more men at the factory*; *They will take more on next year.* **3** *vt sep* (*with* **at**) to challenge (someone) to a game *etc*: *I'll take you on at tennis.* **4** *vt sep* to get; to assume: *When we learnt all about the poet, his writing took on a completely new meaning.* **5** *vt sep* to allow (passengers) to get on or in: *The bus only stops here to take on passengers – you can't get off here.* **6** *vi* (*inf*) to be upset: *Don't take on so!*

take the opportunity, take orders *see* **opportunity, order.**

take out insurance *see* **insurance.**

take it out of (*inf*) to tire or exhaust: *The long walk really took it out of me.*

take it out on (*inf*) to be angry with or unpleasant to (someone) because one is angry, disappointed *etc* oneself: *I know you're upset, but there's no need to take it out on me!*

take over 1 *vt sep* to take control (of): *He has taken the business over* (*nc* ˈ**take-over**). **2** *vt sep, vi* (*often with* **from**) to do (something) after someone else stops doing it: *He drove as far as Paris, then I took over* (*from him*); *He retired last year, and I took over his job.*

take pains, take part, take pity, take place, take a risk, take a/one's seat, take stock *see* **pain, part, pity, place, risk, seat, stock.**

take a test *see* **take an examination** *above.*

take one's time *see* **time.**

ˈ**take to** *vt fus* **1** to find acceptable or pleasing: *I soon took to her children/idea.* **2** to begin to do (something) regularly: *He took to smoking a pipe.*

take to heart, take to one's heels, take (the) trouble, take umbrage, take (someone) unawares *see* **heart, heel, trouble, umbrage, unaware.**

take up *vt sep* **1** to use or occupy (space, time *etc*): *I won't take up much of your time*; *His clothes took up most of the wardrobe.* **2** to begin doing, playing *etc*: *He has taken up the violin*; *He has taken up teaching.* **3** to shorten (clothes): *My skirts were too long, so I had them taken up.* **4** (*old*) to lift or raise; to pick up: *He took up the book.*

take up arms *see* **arm**[2].

take (someone) up on (an offer *etc*) to accept (a person's offer *etc*): *'Why don't you come and stay with us one day?' 'I might take you up on that.'*

take (something) upon oneself to take responsibility (for): *I took it upon myself to make sure she arrived safely.*

take up with *vt fus* (*inf*) to become friendly with; to associate with: *She has taken up with some very strange people.* – *See also* **be taken up with** *above.*

take (something) up with (someone) (*formal*) to discuss (*esp* a complaint): *I shall take the matter up with my MP.*

take (someone's) word (for it) *see* **word.**

See also **intake, partake.**

talc [talk] *nu* **1** a kind of soft mineral that feels like soap. **2** talcum: *She put some talc on the baby after it had had its bath.*

talcum [ˈtalkəm] *nu* (*also* ˈ**talcum powder**: *often abbrev* **talc**) a kind of fine, *usu* perfumed, powder made from talc, used on the body: *She got out of her bath, dried herself, and rubbed on some talcum powder.*

tale [teil] *nc* **1** (*more formal than* **story**) a story: *He told me the tale of his travels.* **2** an untrue story; a lie: *He told me he had a lot of money, but that was just a tale.*

telltale *see* **tell.**

old wives' tale *see* **wife.**

tell tales *see* **tell.**

talent [ˈtalənt] *nc* **1** a special ability or cleverness; a skill: *He has a talent for drawing; Singing and dancing are just two of his many talents.* 2 (*hist*) a measure of weight, or the value of this weight of gold or silver.

'**talented** *adj* (*neg* **un-**) naturally clever or skilful; having or showing great ability: *a talented pianist; She is the most talented member of the family.*

talisman ['talizmən, (*Amer*) -lis-] *nc* (*formal*) an object which is supposed to have magic powers to protect its owner; a charm: *He had a rabbit's foot which he wore round his neck as a talisman; I don't believe in talismans.*

talk [to:k] 1 *vi* to speak; to have a conversation or discussion: *He refused to talk to me; We talked about it for hours; Cats can't talk; My parrot can talk* (= imitate human speech); *We talked together for a few minutes;* (*formal*) *I must talk with him.* 2 *vi* (*inf*) to gossip: *You can't stay here – people will talk!* 3 *vi* to give information: *He was tortured but he refused to talk.* 4 *vt* to talk about: *They spent the whole time talking philosophy.* – 1 *nc* (*sometimes in pl*) a conversation or discussion: *We had a long talk about it; The Prime Ministers met for talks on their countries' economic problems.* 2 *nc* a lecture: *The doctor gave us a talk on family health.* 3 *nu* (*inf*) gossip: *There's a lot of talk about them in the village; Her behaviour causes a lot of talk among the neighbours.* 4 *nu* useless discussion; statements of things a person says he will do but which will never actually be done: *He says he's going to tell his boss what he thinks of him, but that's just talk; There's too much talk and not enough action.*

talkative ['to:kətiv] *adj* talking a lot: *a talkative person; You're not very talkative this morning.*

'**talker** *nc*: *My parrot is a good talker; She's a terrible talker* (= She talks a lot or too much).

'**talkie** [-ki] *nc* (*inf: usu in pl*) a cinema film with sound, *esp* one of the first such films: *Al Jolson was the star of the first talkie.*

'**talking-point** *nc* something to talk about; a subject, *esp* an interesting one: *Football is the main talking-point in my family.*

ˌ**talking-'to** *nc* (*inf*) a talk given to someone in order to scold, criticize or blame them: *I'll give that child a good talking-to when he gets home!*

'**baby talk** words used by or to very young children.

be all talk (*inf*) (of a person) to talk a lot about what he is going to do, but not actually to do anything: *He says he's going to write a book, but he's all talk – he'll never really do it.*

small talk *see* **small**.

talk back *vi* (*often with* **to**) to answer rudely: *Don't talk back to me!*

talk big (*inf*) to talk as if one is very important; to boast: *He's always talking big about his job.*

talk down to *vt fus* to speak to (someone) as if he/she is much less important, clever *etc*: *Now that she is at university, she talks down to all her relatives; Children dislike being talked down to.*

'**talking of** (*inf*) while we are on the subject (of): *Talking of food, what time are we having dinner?*

talk (someone) into/out of (doing) to persuade (someone) (not) to do (something): *He talked me into changing my job; She tried to talk her husband out of going.*

the talk of the town someone or something that everyone (in society) is talking about: *Their divorce is the talk of the town.*

talk over *vt sep* to discuss: *We talked over the whole idea; We must talk it over.*

talk round 1 *vt usu sep* to persuade: *I managed to talk her round.* 2 *vt fus* to talk about (something) for a long time without reaching the most important point: *We did not come to a decision about who should get the job although we talked round it for hours.*

talk sense/nonsense to say sensible, or ridiculous, things: *'The firm has gone bankrupt!' 'Don't talk nonsense – of course it hasn't'; I do wish you would talk sense.*

talk shop to talk about one's work: *We agreed not to talk shop at the party.*

tall [to:l] *adj* 1 (of people and thin or narrow objects such as buildings or trees) higher than normal: *a tall man; She is not as tall as her sister; Your son is very tall for his age* (= taller than most boys of his age). 2 (*pred*) (of people) having a particular height: *John is only four foot tall.*

'**tallness** *nu.*

'**tallboy** *nc* (*Amer* '**highboy**) a piece of furniture with drawers; a high chest of drawers.

a tall order something very difficult to do: *Finding somewhere for fifty children to stay tonight is rather a tall order.*

a tall story a story which is hard to believe: *He says the Queen has invited him to Buckingham Palace, but that's just one of his tall stories.*

tallow ['talou] *nu, adj* (of) a substance made of animal fat melted down, and used to make candles, soap *etc*: *It's* (*made of*) *tallow;* (*attrib*) *a tallow candle.*

tally ['tali] *nc* an account: *He kept a tally of all the work he did.* – *vi* (*often with* **with**) to agree or match: *Their stories tally; His story tallies with mine.*

talon ['talən] *nc* the claw of a bird of prey: *The hawk seized the rabbit in its talons.*

tambourine [tambə'ri:n] *nc* a kind of small, one-sided drum with tinkling metal discs in the rim, held in the hand and shaken or beaten against some part of the body: *She sings in a folk group, and sometimes plays the tambourine.*

tame [teim] *adj* 1 (of animals) used to living with people; not wild or dangerous: *He kept a tame bear as a pet; Don't worry about his pet eagle – it's quite tame.* 2 dull; not exciting: *My job is very tame; rather a tame way of life.* – *vt* to make tame (*def 1*): *It is impossible to tame some animals;* (*fig*) *He said he would tame her when she was his wife.*

'**tameable** *adj* (*neg* **un-**) able to be tamed.

'**tamely** *adv.* '**tameness** *nu.*

'**tamer** *nc* (*often in cmpds*): *a lion-tamer.*

tam-o'-shanter [tamə'ʃantə] *nc* (*usu abbrev* **tammy** ['tami]) a round, flat, woollen cap: *The Scottish football supporters were wearing tartan tam-o'-shanters.*

tamper ['tampə] *vi* (*with* **with**: *derog*) to interfere or meddle (with something) *usu* in such a way as to damage, break, alter *etc* it: *Don't tamper with the engine or it will break down; The car-crash was no accident – the brakes had been tampered with.*

tampon ['tampon] *nc* a piece of cottonwool *etc* inserted in a wound *etc* to stop bleeding or absorb blood.

tan [tan] – *pt, ptp* **tanned** – 1 *vt* to make an animal's skin into leather (by treating it with tannin or other chemicals). 2 *vti* to (cause a person's skin) to become brown in the sun: *She always tans quickly; She was tanned by the sun.* – 1 *nu, adj* (of) a light brown colour: *I should like some shoes in tan; tan shoes.* 2 *nc* sun-tanned skin: *He came back* *from holiday with a wonderful tan; Her tan has begun to fade.*

tanned *adj* sunburnt: *tanned skin; She was very tanned when she came back from holiday.*

'tanner *nc* a person whose job is to tan leather: *He works as a tanner.*

'tannery *nc* a place where leather is tanned: *He works in a tannery.*

tannin ['tanin] *nu* any of several substances got from plants, used in tanning, dyeing *etc.*

andem ['tandəm] *nc* a long bicycle with two seats and two sets of pedals, one behind the other: *You don't see many tandems nowadays;* (*attrib*) *a tandem bicycle.* – *adv* (*usu* of two people on a tandem) one behind the other: *They rode tandem.*

ang [taŋ] *nc* (*often liter*) a strong or sharp taste, flavour or smell: *The air had a salty tang; the tang of wood smoke.*

angent ['tandʒənt] *nc* (*geom*) a line that touches a curve but does not cut it.

go off at a tangent to go off suddenly in another direction or on a different line of thought, action *etc*: *It is difficult to have a sensible conversation with her, as she keeps going off at a tangent.*

angerine [tandʒə'riːn] *nc* a type of small orange that has a sweet taste and is easily peeled.

angible ['tandʒəbl] *adj* **1** (*formal*: *often attrib*) real or definite: *The handkerchief was tangible evidence that she had been in the room.* **2** (*very formal*) able to be felt by touch: *the tangible qualities of sculpture.*

'tangibly *adv.* **'tangibility** *nu.*

See also **intangible**.

angle ['taŋgl] *nc* an untidy, confused or knotted state: *The child's hair was in a tangle; I'll never be able to straighten out these tangles in the string.* – *vti* to make or become tangled: *Don't tangle my wool when I'm knitting; My wool always seems to tangle.*

'tangled *adj* in a tangle: *tangled hair/branches; Her hair is always tangled.*

'tangle with *vt fus* (*inf*) to become involved in a quarrel or struggle with (a person *etc*): *I tangled with him over politics; I wouldn't like to tangle with a lion.*

See also **untangle**.

ango ['taŋgou] – *pl* **'tangos** – *nc* (music for) a type of South American dance. – *v* – *3rd pers sing prt* **'tangos**: *pt, ptp* **'tangoed** – *vi* to perform this dance: *She tangos very well.*

ank [taŋk] *nc* **1** a large container for liquids or gas: *How mang litres does your car's petrol tank hold?; a hot-water/cold-water tank.* **2** a heavy steel-covered vehicle armed with guns and moving on caterpillar wheels.

'tanker *nc* **1** a ship or large lorry for carrying oil. **2** an aircraft used to transport fuel.

ankard ['taŋkəd] *nc* a large drinking-mug of metal, glass *etc*: *a beer tankard.*

anker *see* **tank**.

anner, tannery, tannin *see* **tan**.

Tannoy ® ['tanoi] *nc* a type of communication system with loudspeakers, used *eg* at railway stations, airports *etc* for making announcements: *An announcement was made over the Tannoy; We'll have to install a Tannoy* (*system*) *in the factory.*

antalize, -ise ['tantəlaiz] *vt* (*formal or facet*) to tease or torment (a person *etc*) by making him want something he cannot have and by keeping it just beyond his reach: *He was tantalized by her beauty, but lacked the courage to speak to her.*

'tantalizing, -s- *adj* (*formal or facet*): *He was aware of tantalizing smells from the kitchen; Her beauty was tantalizing.*

tantamount ['tantəmaunt]: **tantamount to** (*formal*) having the same effect as; equivalent to: *His refusal to appear in court to answer the charges is tantamount to an admission of guilt.*

tantrum ['tantrəm] *nc* a fit of extreme rage, with the person *eg* shouting and stamping his feet: *Small children have occasional tantrums when they don't get what they want; That child is always throwing tantrums.*

Tanzania, Tanzanian *see* Appendix 2.

tap[1] [tap] *nc* a quick touch or light knock or blow: *I heard a tap at the door; She felt a tap on her shoulder.* – *v* – *pt, ptp* **tapped** – *vti* (*often with* **at, on** *or* **with**) to give a light knock (on or with something): *He tapped the table with his pencil; He tapped his pencil on the table; This music sets your feet tapping!; He tapped at/on the window.*

'tap-dancing *nu* a type of dancing performed with special shoes that make a tapping noise.

'tap-dancer *nc.*

tap[2] [tap] *nc* (*Amer* **'faucet**) any of several types of device (*usu* with a handle and valve that can be shut or opened) for controlling the flow of liquid or gas from a pipe, barrel *etc*: *Most washbasins have hot and cold taps; He ran the cold tap; You mustn't leave the taps running; Turn the tap off/on!; Where is the gas tap?; He fitted a tap to the beer barrel.* –*v* – *pt, ptp* **tapped** – *vt* **1** to get liquid from (a barrel *etc*) by piercing it or opening a tap: *This barrel hasn't been tapped yet.* **2** to get liquid from the trunk of (a tree): *Rubber trees are tapped.* **3** to start using (a source, supply *etc*): *The country has many rich resources that have not been tapped.* **4** (*sl*: *usu with* **for**) to get money *etc* from (a person): *We could tap him for a loan of a few pounds.* **5** (*inf*) to attach a device to (someone's telephone wires) in order to be able to listen to their telephone conversations: *I suspected that my phone was being tapped.*

on 'tap 1 of beer *etc* ready to be drawn off from the cask. **2** ready for immediate use: *You're lucky to live near a library and have all that information on tap*

tape [teip] **1** *ncu* (a piece of) a narrow strip or band of cloth used for tying *etc*: *In the drawer were bundles of letters tied with tape; She sewed some new tapes on to the mattress cover.* **2** *nc* a piece of this or something similar, *eg* a string, stretched above the finishing line on a race track: *The two girls reached the tape together.* **3** *ncu* (*sometimes in cmpds*) a narrow strip of paper, plastic, metal *etc* used for sticking materials together, recording sounds *etc*: *He sealed the parcel with adhesive tape; I need some insulating tape for electrical repair work; I recorded the concert on tape; I've got some tapes of ballet music; The interview was recorded on videotape.* **4** *nc* a tape-measure. – *vt* **1** to fasten or seal with tape: *The kidnapped girl's hands were tied and her mouth taped with adhesive plaster.* **2** to record (the sound of something) on tape: *He taped the concert.*

'tape-measure, 'measuring-tape *ncs* a length of *eg* plastic, cloth or metal tape, marked with centimetres, metres *etc* for measuring: *You can't make clothes without a measuring-tape; He measured the shelf with a metal tape-measure.*

'tape-recorder *nc* a machine which records sounds on magnetic tape and reproduces them when required. **'tape-record** *vt.* **'tape-recording** *nc.*

have (got) (someone or something) taped (*esp Brit*: *inf*) to understand (something, *esp* a person's character and abilities) very clearly: *He was trying very hard to impress me, but I soon had him taped.*

have got (something) taped (*Brit inf*) to have got (a matter) arranged as one wants: *I'm to start a new job next month – I've got it all taped.*

red tape *see* **red**.

taper ['teipə] *nc* **1** a long, thin type of candle: *We had red tapers on the table at Christmas-time.* **2** a long, waxed wick or spill: *He lit the gas fire with a lighted taper.* – *vti* (*sometimes with* **off**) to make or become narrower or slimmer at one end: *The leaves taper (off) to a sharp point; The joiner tapered the chair legs.*

'tapered, 'tapering *adjs* becoming narrower or slimmer at one end: *She has elegant hands with tapering fingers; Pillars and columns are usually tapered towards the top.*

tapestry ['tapəstri] **1** *ncu* (a piece of) cloth into which a picture or design has been sewn or woven, hung on a wall for decoration or used to cover *eg* the seats of chairs: *Four large tapestries hung on the walls; I like chairs covered with tapestry.* **2** *nu* the art of sewing such cloth: *She teaches tapestry and weaving at the art college.*

tapioca [tapi'oukə] *nu* a type of food obtained from the underground part of the cassava plant: *a packet of tapioca*; (*attrib*) *tapioca pudding.*

tar [ta:] *nu* any of several kinds of thick, black, sticky material obtained from wood, coal *etc* and used *eg* in roadmaking. – *v* – *pt, ptp* **tarred** – *vt* to cover with tar: *The road surface is sticky as it has just been tarred.*

'tarry *adj* of or like tar; covered with tar: *Your shoes are tarry; There are tarry marks on his clothes.*

be tarred with the same brush/stick (*derog*) to have the same faults (as someone else): *My brothers are both tarred with the same brush – they're both extremely lazy.*

See also **tarmac**.

tarantula [tə'rantjulə, (*Amer*) -tʃu-] *nc* any of several types of large hairy spider, some poisonous.

tardy ['ta:di] *adj* (*formal or liter*: *with* **in** *when pred*) slow in coming, happening *etc*: *his tardy admission of guilt; tardy offers of help; He was rather tardy in offering to help us.* **'tardily** *adv.* **'tardiness** *nu.*

target ['ta:git] *nc* **1** a marked board or other object aimed at in shooting practice, competitions *etc* with a rifle, bow and arrow *etc*: *His shots hit the target every time.* **2** any object at which shots, bombs *etc* are directed: *Their target was the ammunitions factory*; (*attrib*) *The bombs all fell within the target area.* **3** a person, thing *etc* against which unfriendly comment or behaviour is directed: *The minister for education was the target of angry criticism in Parliament today.* **4** a result, achievement *etc* aimed at: *Our profits were £12 000, surpassing our target of £10 000*; (*attrib*) *The target figure was (set at) £10 000.*

tariff ['tarif] *nc* **1** a list of prices or charges *eg* in a hotel: *A copy of the tariff is placed in each bedroom.* **2** (a list of) taxes to be paid on imported or exported goods: *the customs tariff.*

tarmac ['ta:mak] **1** (*Amer* **Tarmac** ®) tarmacadam or a similar substance. **2** *nc* (*no pl*: *with* **the**) the surface of a road, runway at an airpor[t] *etc*: *The plane was waiting on the tarmac.*

tarmacadam [ta:mə'kadəm] *nu* a mixture o[f] small stones and tar used to make road surface[s] *etc.*

tarnish ['ta:niʃ] *vti* to (cause a metal to) becom[e] dull and stained: *Damp can tarnish metals; Silver[,] copper and brass tarnish easily*; (*fig*) *His reputatio[n] was tarnished by remarks made in his former wife'[s] autobiography.* – *nu* something on the surface o[f] metal which causes it to have a dull, staine[d] appearance: *Rub the spoon well to remove th[e] tarnish!*

'tarnished *adj* (*neg* **un-**).

tarpaulin [ta:'po:lin] *ncu* (a sheet of) a kind o[f] strong waterproof material: *The goods on the truck were protected by a tarpaulin; He covered his ca[r] with a sheet of tarpaulin.*

tarry[1] *see* **tar**.

tarry[2] ['tari] *vi* (*old or liter*) **1** to linger or stay: *W[e] did not tarry long in that town.* **2** to be slow or late i[n] coming *etc*: *Do not tarry on the way home.*

tart[1] [ta:t] *adj* **1** sharp or sour in taste: *These berrie[s] taste rather tart; tart apples.* **2** (of a remark *etc*) brief and sarcastic: *a tart reply; Her reply wa[s] rather tart.* **'tartly** *adv.* **'tartness** *nu.*

tart[2] [ta:t] *ncu* a pie containing *eg* fruit or jam: *a[n] apple tart; Do you want a piece of rhubarb tart?*

tart[3] [ta:t] *nc* (*inf*: *offensive*) a prostitute or [a] woman who seems to behave like one.

tart up *vt sep* (*sl*: *often derog*) to make (a person[,] thing *etc*) more attractive, *esp* in a showy o[r] tasteless (*def 2*) way: *She was tarting herself up i[n] front of the mirror; Their house was nicer before [it] was tarted up.*

tartan ['ta:tən] **1** *nu* (woollen or other cloth wove[n] with) a pattern of different coloured lines an[d] broader stripes, crossing each other at righ[t] angles, *orig* used by clans of the Scottish Highlands: *I've bought a few metres of tartan to make a skirt; These jackets are available in plain colour o[r] in tartan.* **2** *nc* any one pattern of this sort, *usu* associated with a particular clan *etc*: *the Camero[n] tartan.*

tartar[1] ['ta:tə] *nc* (*inf*) a fierce person who is hard t[o] please: *The new headmaster is a real tartar!*

tartar[2] ['ta:tə] *nu* **1** a hard substance that forms on the teeth: *The dentist scraped the tartar off the boy's teeth.* **2** a substance that forms inside wine casks.

cream of tartar *nu* a white powder obtained from tartar (*def 2*), used in baking.

task [ta:sk] *nc* (*formal*) a piece of *esp* hard work; a duty that must be done: *She washed the dishes and finished the other household tasks; She dreaded the task of telling her mother that she was leaving home.*

'task-force *nc* **1** (*mil*) a combined land, air and sea force under one commander, with a special task to perform. **2** a group of people similarly combined for a special job: *The police have set up a special task-force to deal with terrorism.*

'taskmaster *nc* any person who sets and supervises the work of others, *esp* in a strict and unsympathetic way: *The new manager is a hard taskmaster.*

take (someone) to task (*formal*) to blame or criticize (a person): *She took him to task for his rudeness to her mother.*

tassel ['tasəl] *nc* a decoration, consisting of a hanging bunch of threads tied firmly at one end and loose at the other end, put *eg* on a cushion, a hat, a shawl *etc*: *a cushion with a tassel at each corner.*

'**tasselled** *adj* (*formal or liter*) decorated with tassels: *a tasselled hat.*

taste [teist] (not used with **is, was** *etc* and **-ing** (*defs 1, 3, 4*)) **1** *vti* to be aware of, or recognize, the flavour of something: *I can taste ginger in this cake*; *Sometimes when you are ill, you can't taste (your food) properly.* **2** *vti* to test or find out (the flavour or quality of food *etc*) by eating or drinking a little of it: *Please taste this and tell me if it is too sweet*; *I'll taste and see if this stew needs more salt.* **3** *vi* (*often with* **of**) to have a particular flavour or other quality that is noticed through the act of tasting: *This milk tastes sour*; *The sauce tastes of garlic.* **4** *vt* to eat (food) *esp* with enjoyment: *The man said he hadn't tasted food for days*; *I haven't tasted such a beautiful curry for ages.* **5** *vt* (*fig*) to experience: *He had tasted the delights of country life and never again wanted to live in the town.* – **1** *nu* (*often with* **the**) one of the five senses, the sense by which we are aware of flavour: *I find that having a cold affects my (sense of) taste*; *This herb is very bitter to the taste.* **2** *ncu* the quality or flavour of anything that is known through this sense: *This wine has an unusual taste*; *I like to try new tastes occasionally*; *Put some salt in the soup to give it more taste.* **3** *nc* (*often inf*) an act of tasting or a small quantity of food *etc* for tasting: *Do have a taste of this cake!*; *I'd like a small taste*; (*fig*) *I've already had a taste of his temper!* **4** *ncu* (*usu in sing*) a liking or preference: *I've always had a taste for medieval music*; *She has a queer taste in books*; *Their tastes in drink are certainly expensive!*; *She has expensive taste in clothes.* **5** *nu* the ability to judge what is suitable in behaviour, dress *etc* or what is fine and beautiful: *She shows good taste in clothes*; *Her clothes are always in good taste*; *He's a man of taste and experience*; *That joke was in bad/poor/doubtful taste* (= was rude or offensive). – *See also* **to my, his** *etc* **taste** *below.*

'**tasteful** *adj* showing good judgement or taste: *a tasteful flower arrangement*; *Her jewellery is always very tasteful.* '**tastefully** *adv.* '**tastefulness** *nu.*

'**tasteless** *adj* **1** lacking flavour: *tasteless food.* **2** showing a lack of good taste or judgement: *a tasteless piece of writing*; *It was tasteless of you to behave like that.* '**tastelessly** *adv.* '**tastelessness** *nu.*

'**taster** *nc* (*often in cmpds*) a person whose job is to taste and judge the quality of something, *esp* wine or tea: *He's a wine-taster.*

-tasting (*in cmpds*) **1** having a (particular kind of) taste: *a sweet-tasting liquid.* **2** (an event) at which (something) is tasted (*def 2*): *We went to a wine-tasting (evening) last Saturday.*

'**tasty** *adj* (*inf*) having a good, *esp* savoury, flavour: *a tasty snack*; *These sandwiches are tasty*; (*fig*) *a tasty bit of gossip.* '**tastiness** *nu.*

'**taste buds** *n pl* the groups of cells on the tongue that are sensitive to flavour.

to my, his *etc* **taste** (in a way that is) pleasing to me, him *etc*: *The furniture was at last arranged to her taste*; *A walking holiday would not be to his taste.*

to 'taste (used in recipes *etc*) in whatever quantity is desired: *Add salt and pepper to taste.*

See also **distaste**.

ta-ta [ta'ta:] *interj* (*inf*) (often used to or by young children) good-bye: *Say ta-ta to Gran.*

tatters ['tatəz] *n pl* (*often liter*) torn and ragged pieces: *A few tatters of clothing still covered the dead body.*

'**tattered** *adj* ragged or torn: *a tattered cloak*; *a tattered copy of a book*; *This book is rather tattered.*

in 'tatters in a torn and ragged condition: *His clothes were in tatters*; (*fig*) *The government's policy is in tatters.*

tattle ['tatl] *nu* (*old or inf*) gossip: *This newspaper contains nothing but worthless tattle.* – *vi* (*old or inf*) to gossip: *She's always tattling about her neighbours.* '**tattler** *nc.*

See also **tittle-tattle**.

tattoo[1] [tə'tu:, (*Amer*) ta-] – *3rd pers sing prt* **tat'toos**: *pt, ptp* **tat'tooed** – *vt* to make coloured patterns or pictures on part of a person's body by pricking the skin and putting in dyes: *He wants to have his arms tattooed*; *The design he chose was tattooed on his arm.* – *n* – *pl* **tat'toos** – *nc* a design tattooed on the skin: *His arms were covered with tattoos.*

tat'tooed *adj*: *a tattooed man.*

tattoo[2] [tə'tu:, (*Amer*) ta-] – *pl* **tat'toos** – *nc* **1** (*no pl*: *with* **the**: *hist*: *mil*) a signal made by the beating of drums *etc* to call soldiers back to their quarters at night: *The tattoo was sounded.* **2** a rhythm beaten on a table *etc*, *eg* with the tips of the fingers, *eg* as a mark of impatience or while thinking: *He beat a tattoo on the table while waiting for the waiter to bring the bill.* **3** an outdoor military display given at night, with music *etc*: *the Edinburgh Military Tattoo.*

tatty ['tati] *adj* (*inf derog*) shabby and untidy: *tatty clothes*; *You look a bit tatty in these clothes.*

taught *see* **teach**.

taunt [to:nt] *vt* to tease, or say unpleasant things to, (a person) in a cruel way: *The children at school taunted him for being dirty*; *She taunted him with having a drunkard for a father.* – *nc* cruel, unpleasant remarks: *He did not seem to notice their taunts.*

'**taunting** *adj.* '**tauntingly** *adv.*

Taurus ['to:rəs] a sign of the zodiac, the Bull: *People born between April 21 and May 20 are said to be born under the sign of Taurus.*

taut [to:t] *adj* **1** (*more formal than* **tight**) pulled tight: *It is difficult to keep the string round a parcel taut while you tie a knot in it.* **2** (of nerves *etc*) in a state of emotional strain: *The sound of the doorbell gave a sudden shock to her taut nerves and she screamed*; *Her nerves are rather taut.*

'**tauten** *vti* to make or become taut: *The ropes were tautened*; *She saw his jaw muscles tauten.*

tautology [to:'tolədʒi] *ncu* (*tech or formal*) (an example of) a form of repetition in which the same thing is said in two different ways: *'God is eternal and he will last for ever' is an example of tautology.*

ˌ**tauto'logical** [-'lo-] *adj.*

tavern ['tavən] *nc* (*arch or liter*: *sometimes used with cap in names*) an inn or public house: *The travellers stopped at a tavern for a meal and a mug of ale*; *Our local pub is called the 'Village Tavern'.*

tawdry ['to:dri] *adj* (*formal derog*) very (*usu* too) bright and showy but of poor quality: *tawdry clothes/jewellery*; *That hat looks rather tawdry.* '**tawdriness** *nu.*

tawny ['to:ni] *adj* (*usu* of animals' fur *etc*) yellowish-brown: *the lion's tawny mane*; *Her eyes are tawny.*

tax [taks] **1** *ncu* money, *eg* a percentage of a person's income or of the price of goods *etc* taken by the government to help pay for the running of the state: *Every year, I pay more income tax*; *I lose half my income in tax*; *There is a heavy tax on tobacco*; (*attrib*) *The tax system is very unfair.* 2 *nc* (*no pl*: *with* **a**: *formal*) a strain or burden: *The continual noise was a tax on her nerves.* – *vt* 1 to make (a person) pay (a) tax; to put a tax on (goods *etc*): *He is taxed on his own and his wife's income*; *Alcohol is heavily taxed.* 2 (*formal or facet*) to put a strain on: *Have a rest – don't tax your strength!* – *See also* **tax someone with something** *below.*

'**taxable** *adj* (*neg* **un-**) liable to be taxed: *taxable income/goods*; *Is all your income taxable?*

tax'ation *nu* the act or system of taxing: *The government may abolish direct taxation, or the taxation of incomes, and depend entirely on indirect taxation, or the tax on goods etc*; *Many people feel that taxation should be abolished, but no one has found a suitable alternative.*

'**taxing** *adj* (*formal*) mentally or physically difficult: *This isn't a very taxing job*; *She found her new job too taxing.*

ˌ**tax-'free** *adj, adv* without payment of tax: *Pensioners may earn a certain amount per week tax-free*; *Income from National Savings is tax-free*; *tax-free income.*

'**taxpayer** *nc* a citizen who pays taxes: *Taxpayers' money is frequently wasted through inefficient government.*

'**tax (someone) with (something)** (*formal*) to accuse (a person) of (a fault or wrong act): *I taxed him with dishonesty*; *She taxed him with having told a lie.*

taxi ['taksi] – *pls* '**taxis,** '**taxies** – *nc* (*also* '**taxi-cab**: (*Amer*) **cab**) a car, *usu* fitted with a taximeter, that can be hired with its driver, *esp* for short journeys: *He telephoned for a taxi*; *I took a taxi from his hotel to the station*; *I don't like buses – I'll go by taxi.* – *v* – *3rd pers sings prt* '**taxies,** '**taxis**: *prps* '**taxiing,** '**taxying**: *pt, ptp* '**taxied** – *vi* 1 (of an aeroplane) to move slowly along the ground before beginning to run forward for take-off: *The plane taxied along the runway.* 2 (*rare*) to travel in a taxi: *I taxied across London.*

'**taximeter** *nc* (*tech*: *usu abbrev* **meter**) an instrument *usu* fitted to taxis to show the fare owed for the distance travelled.

'**taxi rank** *nc* a place where taxis stand until hired: *There is a taxi rank at the railway station.*

taxidermy ['taksidə:mi] *nu* the art of preparing and stuffing the skins of animals *etc.*

'**taxidermist** *nc*: *She took her dead cat to a taxidermist to be stuffed.*

taximeter *see* **taxi**.

taxpayer *see* **tax**.

tea [ti:] 1 *nu* a type of plant grown in Asia, *esp* India, Ceylon and China, or its dried and prepared leaves: *He has a tea-plantation in Sri Lanka*; *I bought half a kilo of tea.* 2 *nu* a drink made by adding boiling water to these: *She made a pot of tea*; *Have a cup of tea!* 3 *nu* a drink looking or made like tea: *beef/herbal tea.* 4 *nc* a cup *etc* of tea: *Two teas, please!* 5 *ncu* a small meal in the afternoon (**afternoon tea**) or a larger one in the early evening, at which tea is often drunk: *She invited him to tea*; *Will you have tea with us this afternoon?*; *The child ate his tea quickly*; *This hotel specializes in afternoon teas*; *What would you like for tea?*

high tea *see* **high**.

'**tea bag** *nc* a small bag or sachet of thin paper containing tea, on to which boiling water is poured in a pot or cup.

'**tea-break** *nc* (*inf*) a pause during the working day for drinking tea *etc*: *What time is tea-break?*; *There are two tea-breaks during the day.*

tea caddy *see* **caddy**.

'**tea chest** *nc* a tall box of thin wood in which tea is packed for export, often used also for packing things in when moving house.

tea-cosy *see* **cosy**.

'**teacup** *nc* a cup, *usu* of medium size, in which tea is served.

'**teacupful** *nc* an amount that is enough to fill a teacup: *The recipe requires two teacupfuls of flour.*

'**tea-leaf** *nc* (*usu in pl*) one of the small leaves of tea in a teapot or teacup when tea has been made, drunk *etc*: *One good reason for using tea-bags is that you don't get tea-leaves in your cup.*

'**tea-party** *nc* an afternoon party at which tea is *usu* served: *She is giving a tea-party this afternoon*; *My little girl has been invited to a tea-party.*

'**teapot** *nc* a pot with a spout used for making and pouring tea.

'**tearoom** *nc* a restaurant where tea, coffee, cakes *etc* are served.

'**tea-set,** '**tea-service** *ncs* a set of cups, saucers and plates, sometimes with a teapot and milk-jug.

'**teaspoon** *nc* 1 a small spoon for use with a teacup: *I need a teaspoon to stir my tea.* 2 a teaspoonful: *a teaspoon of salt.*

'**teaspoonful** *nc* an amount that fills a teaspoon: *Put two teaspoonfuls of baking powder into the cake mixture.*

'**tea-time** *nu* the time in the late afternoon or early evening at which people take tea (*def 5*): *He said he would be back at tea-time*; *Hurry up and wash your hands, children – it's tea-time.*

'**tea-towel** *nc* a cloth for drying dishes after they have been washed *eg* after a meal.

be (someone's) cup of tea (*inf*: *usu in neg*) to be the sort of thing that (a person) likes: *Long walks are not my cup of tea.*

a storm in a teacup *see* **storm**.

teach [ti:tʃ] – *pt, ptp* **taught** [to:t] – *vti* to give knowledge, skill or wisdom to a person; to instruct or train (a person): *Miss Brown taught my daughter last year*; *Who teaches French in the school?*; *She teaches us mathematics*; *Who taught you (to play) the violin?*; *I'll teach you (how to do) this trick*; *Why can't the public be taught that it is wrong to drop litter in the street?*; *How many hours a week do you teach?*; *She has decided to teach* (= be a teacher); *Experience has taught him nothing*; (*fig*) *A good beating will teach you to tell the truth in future.* – *See also* **teach** *in phrases below.*

'**teachable** *adj* (*often pred*) 1 (*neg* **un-**) able or willing to learn: *The child was not considered teachable.* 2 capable of being taught to someone: *I doubt if such a skill is teachable.*

'**teacher** *nc* a person who teaches, *esp* in a school: *There are only four teachers at this school*; *What's the name of the chemistry teacher?*; *Christians regard Jesus as their teacher.*

teaching 1 *nu* the work of a teacher: *Teaching is a tiring but satisfying job*; (*attrib*) *the teaching staff of a school.* 2 *nu* guidance or instruction: *As a result of her mother's teaching, she never wasted any food.* 3 *nc* (*usu in pl*) something that is taught: *It is one of the teachings of Christ that we should not take revenge against those who hurt us.*

teach school (*Amer*) to be a teacher in a school:

My daughter wants to teach school when she grows up.

I, that *etc* **will teach (someone) to be, do** *etc* **(something bad)** to punish a person, or be a person's punishment, for doing something bad: *I'll teach you to be rude to me!*; *That'll teach you to disobey me.*

teacup *see* **tea**.

teak [ti:k] **1** *nc* a type of tree that grows in India, Malaysia, Burma *etc.* **2** *nu, adj* (of) its very hard wood: *The table is (made of) teak*; *teak furniture.*

team [ti:m] *nc* **1** a group of people forming a side in a game: *He's a member of the school football team.* **2** a group of people working together: *A team of doctors worked all night to save her life.* **3** two or more animals working together *eg* pulling a cart, plough *etc*: *a team of horses/oxen.*

team spirit *nu* willingness of each member of a team or group to work together with loyalty and enthusiasm: *A few people in this school seem to lack team spirit.*

'team-work *nu* cooperation between those who are working together on a task *etc*: *A newspaper editor depends on good team-work among his staff.*

team up *vi* (*usu with* **with**) to join with another person in order to do something together: *They decided to team up*; *They teamed up with another family to rent a house for the summer.*

teapot *see* **tea**.

tear[1] [tiə] *nc* (*often in pl*) a drop of liquid coming from the eye, as a result of emotion (*esp* sadness) or because something (*eg* smoke) has irritated it: *Tears rolled down her cheeks as she watched him go*; *The sad play reduced me to tears* (= made me cry); *Her tears had no effect on him*; *tears of joy/laughter/rage*; *As soon as I start chopping onions, my eyes fill with tears*; (*fig*) *No-one shed any tears over* (= no-one was sorry about) *his departure from our office.*

'tearful *adj* **1** inclined to cry or weep; with much crying or weeping: *She was very tearful*; *a tearful farewell.* **2** covered with tears: *tearful faces.*

'tearfully *adv.* **'tearfulness** *nu.*

'tear gas *nu* a kind of gas causing blinding tears, used against *eg* rioters: *The police threw a canister of tear gas into the crowd.*

'tear-jerker *nc* (*inf*) a sentimental play, film story *etc*, intended to make people cry: *Films about children and animals are often tear-jerkers.*

'tear-stained *adj* marked with tears: *a tear-stained face.*

burst into tears to begin to cry or weep: *When I asked her if she had taken the money, she just burst into tears.*

in 'tears crying or weeping: *She was in tears over the broken doll.*

tear[2] [teə] – *pt* **tore** [to:]: *ptp* **torn** [to:n] – **1** *vt* (*sometimes with* **off** *etc*) to make a split or hole in (something), intentionally or unintentionally, with a sudden or violent pulling action or to remove (something) from its position by such an action or movement: *He tore the photograph into pieces*; *He tore it in half*; *You've torn a hole in your jacket*; *I tore it on a nail*; *I tore the letter open*; *She tore a corner off the newspaper*; *I tore the picture out of a magazine*; (*fig*) *She tore her clothes off and dived into the water to save the child.* – *See also* **tear up** *below.* **2** *vi* to become torn: *Newspapers tear easily.* **3** *vi* (*inf: often with* **off, away** *etc*) to rush: *He tore off after the bus*; *He tore along the road.* **4** *vt* (*formal*) to cause severe suffering to: *The child's misery tore my heart*; *The country was torn by disaster and war.* – *See also* **tear** *in phrases below.* – *nc* a hole or split made by tearing: *There's a tear in my dress.*

'tearaway *nc* (*inf derog*) an undisciplined, uncontrollable young person: *The old lady complained that she was being disturbed by a crowd of young tearaways on motorbikes.*

be torn between (one thing and another) to have a very difficult choice to make between (two things): *He was torn between obedience to his parents and loyalty to his friends.*

tear a strip off (someone) (*inf*) to rebuke (a person) very angrily: *He tore a strip off his secretary for arriving at the office half an hour late.*

tear at *vt fus* to pull violently or attack with tearing movements: *The animal's claws tore at his body.*

tear (oneself) away (*often with* **from**) to leave a place, activity *etc* unwillingly: *I couldn't tear myself away from the television.*

tear one's hair (*inf*) to be in despair with impatience and frustration: *Their inefficiency makes me tear my hair.*

a tearing hurry (*inf*) a great hurry: *I'm in a tearing hurry to get home tonight*; *Where are you going in such a tearing hurry?*

tear up *vt sep* **1** to remove (something) from a fixed position by violence: *The wind tore up several trees.* **2** to tear into pieces: *She tore up the letter.*

that's torn it! (*inf*) that has spoilt everything!; that's most unfortunate!: *That's torn it! We've missed the last train home.*

tease [ti:z] **1** *vt* to annoy or irritate on purpose: *He's teasing the cat.* **2** *vti* to annoy or laugh at (a person) playfully: *His schoolfriends tease him because he's so small*; *They tease him about his size*; *Take no notice of them – they're only teasing.* – *nc* a person who enjoys teasing others: *He's a terrible tease!*

'teaser *nc* **1** a puzzle or difficult problem: *This question is rather a teaser.* **2** a person who teases.

'teasingly *adv* in a teasing manner.

teaspoon *see* **tea**.

teat [ti:t] *nc* **1** the part of a female animal's breast or udder through which milk passes to the young; the nipple. **2** (*Amer* **'nipple**) a rubber object shaped like this attached to a baby's feeding-bottle: *This teat doesn't have a big enough hole in it – the baby isn't getting any milk.*

technical ['teknikəl] *adj* **1** (*usu attrib*) having, or relating to, a particular science or skill, *esp* of a mechanical or industrial kind: *a technical college*; *This process needs a high level of technical skill*; *We have incorporated all the latest technical advances in our machinery in this factory.* **2** (having many terms) relating to a particular art or science: *'Myopia' is a technical term for 'short-sightedness'*; *The instructions were a bit technical.* **3** (*usu attrib*) according to strict laws or rules: *a technical defeat.*

ˌtechni'cality [-'ka-] **1** *nc* a technical detail or technical term: *I don't understand all the technicalities of this process*; *Their instructions were full of technicalities.* **2** *nc* a (trivial) detail or problem, *eg* caused by (too) strict obedience to laws, rules *etc*: *I'm not going to be put off by mere technicalities.* **3** *nu* (*formal*) the state of being technical (*def 2*): *the technicality of instructions.*

'technically *adv* **1** in a technical way: *He described the machine in simple terms, then rather more technically.* **2** as far as skill and technique are concerned: *The pianist gave a very good performance technically, although she seemed to lack feeling for the music.* **3** according to strict obedience to laws or rules: *Technically (speaking), you aren't allowed to do that, but I don't suppose anyone will object.*

tech'nician [-'niʃən] *nc* a person who has been trained to do something which involves some skill, *eg* with a piece of machinery: *The machine has broken down, but one of our technicians will repair it; a dental technician.*

technique [tek'ni:k] *ncu* (*slightly inf*) the way in which a (*usu* skilled) process is, or should be, carried out: *They admired the pianist's faultless technique; There are various techniques that have to be learned before one can do this job properly.*

technology [tek'nolədʒi] **1** *nu* (the study of) science applied to practical, (*esp* industrial) purposes: *the local college of science and technology.* **2** *ncu* the technical skills and achievements of a particular time in history *etc*: *These people have reached only a very low level of technology; It has been claimed that the technologies shown by some early civilizations could only have been learned from people from another planet.* ˌ**techno'logical** [-'lo-] *adj*. **tech'nologist** *nc*.

teddy ['tedi] *nc* (*also* '**teddy bear**) a child's stuffed toy bear: *The child takes her teddy to bed every night.*

tedious ['ti:diəs] *adj* (*derog*: *more formal than* **boring**) boring and continuing for a long time: *a tedious speech/speaker; I find this job very tedious.* '**tediously** *adv*. '**tediousness** *nu*.

'**tedium** *nu* (*formal*) boredom; tediousness: *the tedium of a long journey.*

tee[1] [ti:] *nc* **1** the small area of level ground from which a golf-ball is driven for the first shot at each green: *They walked to the next tee.* **2** the peg or small pile of sand on which the golf-ball is placed for driving off: *I use plastic tees.* – *vt* to place (a golf-ball) on a tee: *He teed the ball.*

tee up *vi* to tee a golf-ball: *He teed up for the first hole.*

tee[2]: **tee shirt, to a tee** *see* **T-shirt, to a T** *under* **T**.

teem [ti:m] *vi* **1** (*with* **with**) to be full of: *The pond was teeming with fish; His mind is teeming with clever ideas; Her kitchen is teeming with germs.* **2** (*inf: sometimes with* **down**) to rain heavily: *It teemed (with rain) all night; The rain was teeming down.*

teens [ti:nz] *n pl* **1** the years of a person's life between the ages of thirteen and nineteen: *She's in her teens.* **2** the numbers from thirteen to nineteen: *I can't remember the number of his house, but it's in the teens.*

'**teenage** [-eidʒ] *adj* (*usu attrib*) of, or suitable for, people in their teens: *teenage children/clothes/behaviour.*

'**teenager** [-eidʒə] *nc* a person in his or her teens: *This club is for teenagers and people in their early twenties.*

teeny ['ti:ni] *adj* (*also* **teeny-weeny** [ti:ni'wi:ni]: *often with* **little**: *inf*) tiny: *There's a teeny little insect crawling up your neck.*

teeter ['ti:tə] *vi* (*sometimes with* **about, along** *etc*) to stand or move while having difficulty remaining upright or balanced: *He was teetering (about) on the edge of the cliff; She went teetering along the road in her high-heeled shoes.*

teeth, teethe, teething *see* **tooth**.

teetotal [ti:'toutl] *adj* never taking alcoholic drink: *The whole family is teetotal; I never ask my teetotal friends to parties.*

tee'totaller, (*Amer*) **tee'totaler** *nc* a person who is teetotal.

telecommunications ['telikəmju:ni'keiʃənz] *n pl* (*tech*) the science of sending messages, information *etc* by telephone, telegraph, radio, television *etc.*

telegram ['teligram] *nc* a message sent by telegraph: *Since we couldn't go to their wedding, we sent a telegram of congratulations to the reception; He received a telegram saying that his mother had died.*

telegraph ['teligra:f] **1** *nu* a system of sending messages using either wires and electricity or radio: *Send it by telegraph.* **2** *nc* (*tech*) an instrument for this: *Send the message on the telegraph.* – *vt* **1** to send (a message) by telegraph: *He telegraphed the time of his arrival.* **2** to inform by telegraph: *He telegraphed us to say when he would arrive.*

te'legrapher [-'le-], **te'legraphist** [-'le-] *ncs* (*tech*) a person who operates a telegraph: *a skilled telegrapher/telegraphist.*

ˌ**tele'graphic** [-'gra-] *adj* **1** of a telegraph: *a telegraphic message/address.* **2** with unnecessary information, words *etc* omitted, (as if) for sending by telegraph.

te'legraphy [-'le-] *nu* (*tech*) the process, science or skill of sending messages by telegraph.

'**telegraph pole** *nc* a high, wooden pole which supports telegraph wires.

'**telegraph wire** *ncu* (a) wire by which telegraph messages are sent: *The birds perched on the telegraph wires.*

telepathy [tə'lepəθi] *nu* the communication of ideas, thoughts *etc* directly from one person's mind to another person's mind without the use of hearing, sight *etc*: *He knew just what I was thinking – it must have been telepathy.*

telepathic [teli'paθik] *adj*: *telepathic communication; He must be telepathic.* **tele'pathically** *adv*.

te'lepathist *nc* a person who studies or practises telepathy.

telephone ['telifoun] *nc* (*often abbrev* **phone** [foun]) an instrument for speaking to someone from a distance, using either an electric current which passes along a wire or radio waves: *He spoke to me on the telephone; Can I contact you by telephone?*; (*attrib*) *What is your telephone number?* – (*often abbrev* **phone** [foun]) *vti* **1** to (try to) speak to (someone) by means of the telephone: *I'll telephone you tomorrow; A man telephoned when you were out, but he didn't leave his name.* **2** to send (a message) or ask for (something) by means of the telephone: *I'll telephone for a taxi; Please telephone your reply to me as soon as possible.* **3** to reach or make contact with (another place) by means of the telephone: *Can you telephone Paris from here?; Can one telephone from England to Australia?*

te'lephonist [-'le-] *nc* a person who operates a telephone switchboard in a telephone exchange.

te'lephony [-'le-] *nu* (*tech*) the process or method of communication by means of the telephone.

'**telephone booth**, (*Brit*) '**telephone box** *nc* (*also* '**call-box**) a small room or compartment containing a telephone for public use: *There's a telephone box on the corner of the street.*

'**telephone directory** *nc* a book containing a list of the names, addresses and telephone numbers of all the people in a particular area who have telephones: *Look up the number in the telephone directory.*

'telephone exchange *nc* a central control through which telephone calls are directed.

on the telephone 1 having a telephone: *I can't contact them – they are not on the telephone.* **2** talking to someone by means of the telephone: *He was on the telephone for hours.*

telephoto [teli'foutou]: **telephoto lens** *nc* a photographic lens used for taking photographs from a long distance away.

teleprinter ['teliprintə] *ncu* (*tech*) telegraph system or instrument by which messages are sent out at one place, and received and printed at another: *We got the message by teleprinter.*

telescope ['teliskoup] *nc* a kind of tube containing lenses through which distant objects appear closer or longer: *He looked at the ship through his telescope.* – *vti* **1** to push or be pushed together so that one part slides inside another, like the parts of a closing telescope: *The fishing-rod telescopes into its handle*; (*fig*) *The crash telescoped the railway coaches*; (*fig*) *He telescoped 200 years of history into one lesson.*

,tele'scopic [-'sko-] *adj* **1** of, like, or containing, a telescope: *a telescopic sight on a rifle.* **2** made in parts which can slide inside each other: *a telescopic radio aerial.*

television ['teliviʒən] (*often abbrev* **TV** [ti:'vi:]) **1** *nu* ((*inf*) **telly** ['teli]) the sending of pictures from a distance, and the reproduction of them on a screen: *Baird invented* (*the*) *television*; *We saw it on television*; (*attrib*) *a television serial.* **2** *nc* (*also* **'television set**: *inf* **telly** ['teli]) an apparatus with a screen for receiving these pictures: *Have you got a television?*

'televise [-vaiz] *vt* to send a picture of (something) by television: *The football match was televised.*

telex ['teleks] (*also with cap*) **1** *nu* a system of sending messages by teleprinters: *I shall send you the information by telex.* **2** *nc* a teleprinter attached to this system: *Can you operate a telex?* **3** *nc* a message sent or received by this system: *Did you receive our telex?* – *vti* (*also with cap*) to send (a message) in this way: *We'll telex the information to you*; *As soon as we know we'll telex* (*you*).

tell [tel] – *pt, ptp* **told** [tould] **1** *vt* (*often with* **to** *or* **about**) to inform or give information to (a person) about (something): *He told me where to go*; *He told John what had happened*; *He told the whole story to John*; *He told John about it*; *'John is leaving next week.' 'So I've been told.'* **2** *vt* to order or command; to suggest or warn: *I told him to go away*; *I told you not to climb trees, because I knew you would fall and hurt yourself.* **3** *vt* to say or express in words: *She always tells lies*; *She never tells the truth*; *He told the children a story.* **4** *vt* (*sometimes with* **by** *or* **from**: *less formal than* **distinguish**) to distinguish; to see (a difference); to know or decide: *Can you tell the difference between them?*; *I can't tell which is which*; *I can't tell one from the other*; *How can you tell whether the meat is cooked or not?*; *You can tell by/from the colour of the meat.* – *See also* **tell apart** *under* **apart. 5** *vi* to give away a secret: *You mustn't tell or we'll get into trouble.* **6** *vi* to be effective; to be seen to give (good) results: *Good teaching will always tell*; *Experience tells.* – *See also* **tell** *in phrases below.*

'teller *nc* **1** (*usu in cmpds*) a person who tells (stories): *a story-teller.* **2** a person whose job is to receive and pay out money to the public in a bank. **3** a person who counts votes at an election: *We don't yet know who is to be our MP – the tellers have not finished counting the votes.*

'telling *adj* (*formal*) having a great effect: *a telling argument*; *Her remarks were most telling.*

'tellingly *adv.*

telling-off *see* **tell off**.

'tell-tale *nc* (*inf derog*) a person who tells tales: *The teacher didn't notice I was cheating until that rotten little tell-tale told her.* – *adj* (*attrib*) giving information (often which a person would not wish to be known): *He has all the tell-tale signs of drug addiction*; *They pretended they hadn't hit the child, but there were tell-tale bruises on its body.*

all told altogether; including everything or everyone: *This has been a very successful day all told*; *There was an audience of nine all told.*

I 'told you so I told or warned you that this would happen, had happened *etc*, and I was right: *'He's made a complete mess of this.' 'I told you so, but you wouldn't believe me.'*

take a telling (not) to do what one is told, warned *etc* (not) to do: *I warned you not to climb trees, but you just won't take a telling, will you?*

tell off *vt sep* (*inf*) to scold: *The teacher used to tell me off for not doing my homework* (*nc* **,telling-'off**: *He gave me a good telling-off*).

'tell on *vt fus* **1** (*formal* **tell upon**) to have a bad effect on: *Smoking began to tell on his health*; *The strain of looking after her invalid mother is obviously telling upon her.* **2** (*inf*) to give information about (a person, *usu* if they are doing something wrong): *I'm late for work – don't tell on me!*

tell tales (*often with* **about**) to give away secret or private information about the (*usu* wrong) actions of others: *You must never tell tales.* – *See also* **tell-tale** *above.*

tell the time to (be able to) know what time it is by looking at a clock *etc* or by any other means: *He's too young to* (*be able to*) *tell the time*; *He can tell the time from the position of the sun*; *Could you tell me the time, please?*

tell (someone) where to get off *see* **get.**

there's no telling it is impossible to know: *There's no telling what he'll do if you make him angry!*

you never can tell it is possible: *It might rain – you never can tell*; *You might be a millionaire one day – you never can tell.*

you're telling me! (*inf*) certainly; that is definitely true: *'It's cold today.' 'You're telling me* (*it is*)*!'*

telly ['teli] (*inf*) short for **television.**

temerity [ti'merəti] *nu* (*formal*) rashness or boldness: *He had the temerity to ask me for money.*

temper ['tempə] **1** *nc* (*no pl*) a state of mind; a mood or humour: *She has an even temper* (= She is not easily upset or made angry); *He's in a bad temper* (= He is angry or likely to become angry about unimportant things). **2** *nc* a tendency to become (unpleasant when) angry: *He has a terrible temper.* **3** *nc* (*no pl*) a state of anger: *She's in a temper.* **4** *nu* (*tech*) the amount of hardness in metal, glass *etc*: *the temper of steel.* – *vt* **1** (*tech*) to bring metal *etc* to the right degree of hardness by heating and cooling: *The steel must be carefully tempered.* **2** (*formal fig*) to soften or make less severe: *One must try to temper justice with mercy.*

-tempered (*in cmpds*) having a (certain) state of mind: *good-tempered*; *mean-tempered*; *sweet-tempered.*

fly into a temper *see* **fly**[2].

keep one's temper not to lose one's temper: *He was very annoyed but he kept his temper.*

lose one's temper to show anger: *He lost his temper and shouted at me.*

temperament ['tempərəmənt] *nc* (*formal*) a person's natural way of thinking, behaving *etc*: *She has such a sweet temperament*; *She is of a nervous temperament.*

ˌ**tempera'mental** [-'men-] *adj* **1** emotional; excitable; showing quick changes of mood: *a temperamental actress*; *He is very calm but his wife is very temperamental.* **2** of, or caused by, (a person's) temperament: *temperamental attitudes*; *Their differences of opinion are mostly temperamental.*

ˌ**tempera'mentally** [-'men-] *adv*: *She is temperamentally unsuited to be doing this job*; *She behaved very temperamentally yesterday.*

temperance ['tempərəns] *nu* (*formal*) **1** temperate behaviour: *I believe in temperance in all things.* **2** the taking of little or no alcohol: *Some people believe in strict temperance*; (*attrib*) *a temperance society.*

'**temperate** [-rət] *adj* **1** (*formal*) moderate; showing self-control; not extreme in temper, behaviour, eating, drinking *etc*: *a man of temperate habits*; *You ought to be more temperate in your behaviour.* **2** (of climate) neither too hot nor too cold: *Britain lies in a temperate zone*; *The climate is temperate there.* '**temperately** *adv.* '**temperateness** *nu.*

See also **intemperate**.

temperature ['temprətʃə] **1** *nu* the amount or degree of cold or heat: *The temperature in this room is too high*; *The food must be kept at a low temperature.* **2** *nc* a level of body heat that is higher than normal: *She had a temperature and wasn't feeling well.*

take someone's temperature to measure a person's body heat, using a thermometer: *The nurse took his temperature.*

tempest ['tempist] *nc* (*liter*) a violent storm, with very strong winds: *A tempest arose and they were drowned at sea.*

tempestuous [tem'pestjuəs] *adj* **1** (*formal*) (of a person, behaviour *etc*) violently emotional; passionate: *tempestuous feelings*; *a tempestuous argument*; *They had a tempestuous love affair*; *Their relationship was tempestuous.* **2** (*liter*) very stormy; of or like a tempest: *tempestuous winds.* **tem'pestuously** *adv.* **tem'pestuousness** *nu.*

template/templet ['templət] *nc* a thin flat piece of metal, plastic *etc* cut in a certain shape, used as a pattern (by drawing or marking round it).

temple[1] ['templ] *nc* a building in which people worship, *usu* as part of a non-Christian religion: *a Greek/Hindu temple.*

temple[2] ['templ] *nc* (*formal or liter*) either of the flat parts of the head at the side of the forehead: *The stone hit him on the temple, and he fell to the ground.*

templet *see* **template**.

tempo ['tempou] – *pls* '**tempos**, (*music*) '**tempi** [-pi:] – *nc* the speed at which a piece of music should be or is played: *at a fast/slow tempo*; (*fig*) *the tempo of life.*

temporal ['tempərəl] *adj* (*formal*) **1** of or belonging to this world or this life only; not eternal or relating to a person's soul or spirit: *A king has temporal power*; *His power is only temporal.* **2** (*gram*) relating to time or tense: *a temporal clause/conjunction.*

temporary ['tempərəri] *adj* lasting, acting, used *etc* for a (short) time only: *a temporary job*; *This is only a temporary solution to the problem*; *He made a temporary repair to his burst tyre*; *The improvement will probably be only temporary.* '**temporarily** *adv.* '**temporariness** *nu.*

temporize, -ise ['tempəraiz] *vi* (*formal*) not to take a definite decision or action (in order to give oneself more time); to speak or act vaguely in order to avoid deciding or promising anything: *I've been waiting for weeks for him to give me a definite answer but every time I see him, he just temporizes.*

tempt [tempt] *vt* to (try to) persuade or attract (someone) to do something; to make (someone) want to do (something): *The devil tempted him* (*to kill her*); *The sunshine tempted them* (*to go*) *out.* – *See also* **be tempted** *below.*

temp'tation **1** *nu* the act of tempting: *the temptation of Christ* (*by the devil*). **2** *nu* (*sometimes with* **a**) the state or feeling of being tempted: *I can't resist the temptation of all that food!* **3** *nc* something that tempts: *He was surrounded by temptations.*

'**tempter** – *fem* '**temptress** – *nc* (*liter*) a person who tempts, *esp* (*with cap*) the Devil.

'**tempting** *adj* attractive: *That cake looks tempting*; *a tempting display of food.* '**temptingly** *adv.*

be '**tempted (to do something)** to think that it would be pleasant, interesting *etc* to do (something): *I'm rather tempted to go to the party to see what happens.*

ten [ten] **1** *nc* the number or figure 10. **2** *nu* the age of 10. – *adj* **1** (*usu attrib*) 10 in number. **2** (*pred*) aged 10. – *See* **eight** *for constructions.*

ten- (*in cmpds*) having ten (of something): *a* ˌ*ten-pound* '*fine.*

'**tenner** *nc* (*inf*) (a banknote worth) £10 or $10: *It cost me a tenner*; *Have you got change of a tenner?*

tenth **1** *nc* one of ten equal parts. **2** *nc, adj* (the) last of ten (people, things *etc*); (the) next after the ninth. – *See* **eighth** *under* **eight** *for constructions.*

'**tenfold** [-fould] *adj, adv* (*formal or liter*) ten times as much or as great: *There has been a tenfold increase in output*; *Output has increased tenfold.*

ˌ**ten-pin** '**bowling** *nu* a game in which a ball is rolled at ten skittles in order to knock down as many as possible.

'**ten-year-old** *nc* a person or animal that is ten years old. – *adj* (*attrib*) (of a person, animal or thing) that is ten years old. – *See* **eight-year-old** *under* **eight** *for constructions.*

ten to one very probably: *Ten to one, he'll apologize to you tomorrow.*

See also Appendix 1.

tenable ['tenəbl] *adj* (*formal*: *neg* **un-**) **1** (of a theory, attitude of mind *etc*) able to be defended: *His theories seem to be quite tenable*; *a tenable theory.* **2** (*pred with* **for**) (of a job or position) able to be held or occupied: *This post is tenable for one year.*

tenacious [tə'neiʃəs] *adj* (*formal*) **1** (*usu attrib*) keeping a firm hold: *a tenacious grip.* **2** determined; obstinate: *a tenacious person*; *He is so tenacious that he will never stop trying to persuade her to marry him.* **te'naciously** *adv.* **te'naciousness, te'nacity** [-'nasə-] *nus.*

tenant ['tenənt] *nc* a person who pays rent to another for the use of a house, building, land *etc*: *a council tenant*; *That man is one of Sir Arthur's tenants*; (*attrib*) *tenant farmers.*

'**tenancy** (*formal*) **1** *nu* the renting of a house, farm *etc* by a tenant: *He has the tenancy of the farm next to us.* **2** *nc* the period during which this is held: *a tenancy of five years.*

'**tenanted** *adj* (*neg* **un-**: *formal*) occupied; lived in: *a tenanted house*; *Is the house tenanted?*

tend[1] [tend] *vt* (*old*) to take care of; to look after: *A shepherd tends his sheep*; *Doctors tend patients.*

'**tender** *nc* **1** (*usu in cmpds*) a person who looks after something: *a bartender.* **2** a small boat which carries stores or passengers to and from a larger boat. **3** a railway wagon attached to a steam-engine to carry coal *etc.*

tend[2] [tend] *vi* (not *usu* used with **is, was** *etc* and **-ing**) **1** to be likely (to do something); to do (something) frequently: *Plants tend to die in hot weather if you don't water them*; *He tends to get angry when people disagree with him.* **2** (*formal*: *with* **to(wards)**) to move, lean or slope in a certain direction: *This bicycle tends to(wards) the left*; (*fig*) *His political opinions tend to(wards) the left.*

'**tendency** *ncu* (*formal*: *with* **to(wards)**) likelihood; inclination: *He has a tendency to forget things*; *He has a worrying tendency towards left-wing extremism.*

tender[1] ['tendə] *adj* **1** soft; not hard or tough: *The meat is tender*; *tender pieces of meat*; *tender green beans.* **2** sore; painful when touched: *His injured leg is still tender*; *a tender area of skin*; (*fig*) *a tender subject* (= one which will cause sorrow, anger *etc* if talked about). **3** (*often attrib*) loving; gentle: *a tender heart*; *tender words*; *She was very tender towards the children.* '**tenderness** *nu.*

'**tenderize, -ise** to make (*esp* meat) tender (*def 1*): *He tenderized his steak by beating it with a sort of wooden mallet.*

'**tenderly** *adv* in a loving and gentle manner: *He kissed her tenderly.*

ˌ**tender-'hearted** *adj* kind and sympathetic; easily made to feel pity. ˌ**tender-'heartedness** *nu.*

a/the tender age (*formal or facet*) a/the young age: *She was left an orphan at a tender age*; *She had her first job at the tender age of eight.*

tender[2] ['tendə] **1** *vt* (*formal*) to offer: *He tendered his resignation/apologies.* **2** *vi* (*usu with* **for**) to make an offer to do work *etc*: *The firm tendered for the contract to build a new hotel.* – *nc* an offer to do a job of work at a particular price: *We will give the contract to the firm which submits the lowest tender.*

legal tender *nu* coins or notes which are legally acceptable when offered in payment: *Farthings are no longer legal tender.*

tender[3] *see* **tend**[1].

tendon ['tendən] *nc* (*tech*) a strong cord joining a muscle to a bone *etc*: *He has damaged a tendon in his leg.*

tendril ['tendril] *nc* (*formal or tech*) a thin, curling part of some kinds of climbing plant which attaches itself to a support: *The tendrils of the vine twisted round the fence*; (*fig*) *a tendril of hair.*

tenement ['tenəmənt] *nc* in Scotland, a large building divided into flats: *He was born in a tenement in Glasgow*; (*attrib*) *a tenement building.*

tenet ['tenit] *nc* (*formal*) a belief or opinion, *esp* religious: *I have a firm belief in the tenets of my church.*

tenner *see* **ten**.

tennis ['tenis] *nu* (*also* **lawn tennis**) a game for two or four players who use rackets to hit a ball to each other over a net stretched across a tennis-court: *Let's play* (*a game of*) *tennis*; (*attrib*) *a tennis-player*; (*attrib*) *a tennis match.*

'**tennis-court** *nc* a specially-marked area on which tennis is played.

'**tennis-racket** *nc* a racket with which one plays tennis.

tenon *see* **mortise**.

tenor[1] ['tenə] *nc* **1** (a man with) a singing voice of the highest normal pitch for an adult male: *He is a tenor*; *He has a good tenor*; (*attrib*) *a tenor voice.* **2** in music, a part written for a voice at this pitch: *The tenor is more difficult than the bass*: (*attrib*) *the tenor part.* – *adv* with a tenor voice: *Do you sing tenor or bass?*

tenor[2] ['tenə] *nu* (*formal*) **1** the general course: *the tenor of a person's life*; *His life runs on an even tenor.* **2** the general meaning: *Much of what he said was beyond her comprehension but she understood the tenor of his remarks.*

ten-pin bowling *see* **ten**.

tense[1] [tens] *nc* (*gram*) a form of a verb that shows the time of its action in relation to the time of speaking: *a verb in the past/future tense*; *How many tenses are there in English?*

tense[2] [tens] *adj* **1** strained; nervous: *The crowd was tense with excitement*; *a tense situation*; *She seems very tense today*; *She is a very tense person.* **2** (*formal*) tightly stretched: *Are the ropes tense?* – *vti* to make or become tense: *He tensed his muscles*; *The muscles in his arms suddenly tensed.*

'**tensely** *adv.* '**tenseness** *nu.*

'**tensile** [-sail, (*Amer*) -sl] *adj* (*tech or formal*: *often attrib*) **1** able to be stretched: *tensile wire.* **2** of stretching; when stretched: *the greater the tensile strength of a wire, the greater the weight it will support without breaking.*

'**tension** [-ʃən] **1** *nu* (*often formal or tech*) the state of being stretched, or the degree to which something is stretched: *He lessened the tension of the rope.* **2** *nu* (*tech*) in knitting *etc*, the number of stitches to the inch: *The jumper she knitted was too small as she had not checked the tension*; *The tension of that jumper should be twelve stitches to the inch.* **3** *ncu* mental strain; anxiety: *She is suffering from the tension of waiting to discover if he had won or not*; *nervous tension*; *He cannot endure the tensions of modern life.*

See also **intense**.

tent [tent] *nc* a movable shelter made of canvas or other material, supported by poles or a frame and fastened to the ground with ropes and pegs: *When we go on holiday, we usually sleep in a tent*; *There are some tents and some caravans on that campsite.*

tentacle ['tentəkl] *nc* (*tech*) a long, thin, flexible arm-like or horn-like part of an animal, used to feel, grasp *etc*: *An octopus has eight arm-like tentacles*; *A snail has two tentacles on its head.*

tentative ['tentətiv] *adj* (*formal*) **1** not final or complete; not definite: *We have made a tentative arrangement to meet next month*; *the arrangement is only tentative*; *We have made a tentative offer – we shall confirm it as soon as possible.* **2** uncertain or hesitating: *He made a tentative movement*; *His attempts to walk are still rather tentative.* '**tentatively** *adv.* '**tentativeness** *nu.*

tenterhooks ['tentəhuks]: **be on tenterhooks** (*inf*: *often with* **about** *or* **over**) to be uncertain and anxious about what is going to happen: *He was on tenterhooks about the result of the exam; We were all on tenterhooks waiting to hear the result of the general election.*

tenth *see* **ten**.

tenuous ['tenjuəs] *adj* (*formal*: *usu fig*) thin or weak: *There seems to be only a very tenuous connection between what he promises and what he does; Any relationship between them is very tenuous.*

tenure ['tenjə] (*very formal*) **1** *nu* (the conditions relating to) the holding of property or of a position or job; the right to hold a job (*esp* a teaching job) permanently: *He has legal tenure (of the property); This post has security of tenure* (= the person is on the permanent staff of the organization); (*esp Amer*) *He hopes to get tenure* (= a permanent university post) *at Columbia University this year.* **2** *nc* the period of time during which property, a position *etc* is held: *a tenure of three years.*

tepid ['tepid] *adj* (*sometimes derog*) **1** slightly or only just warm; lukewarm: *tepid water; I wanted to have a hot bath – but this water is tepid.* **2** (*fig*) not very enthusiastic: *a tepid welcome; His congratulations were rather tepid.* **'tepidly** *adv.* **'tepidness, te'pidity** *nus.*

tercentenary [təːsən'tiːnəri, (*Amer also*) tər'sentineri] *nc* (*formal*) a three-hundredth anniversary: *This year marks the tercentenary of the birth of one of our greatest poets.*

term [təːm] *nc* **1** a (*usu* limited) period of time: *a term of imprisonment; a term of office.* **2** a division of a school or university year: *The autumn/Michaelmas term.* **3** a word or expression: *Myopia is a medical term for short-sightedness.*

terms *n pl* **1** the rules or conditions of an agreement or bargain: *They had a meeting to arrange terms for a cease-fire; Tell them they must surrender on our terms – there will be no negotiation.* **2** fixed charges (for work, service *etc*): *The firms sent us a list of their terms.* **3** a relationship between people: *They are on bad/friendly terms; We are on equal terms* (= Neither of us has an advantage); *We're not on speaking terms* (= We are not friendly enough to speak to each other). – *vt* (*formal*) to name or call: *That kind of painting is termed 'abstract'.*

come to terms 1 (*often with* **with**) to reach an agreement or understanding: *The opposing armies finally came to terms; They came to terms with the enemy.* **2** (*with* **with**) to find a way of living with or tolerating (some personal trouble or difficulty): *He managed to come to terms with his illness.*

in 'terms of using (something) as a terminology, a means of expression, a means of assessing value *etc*: *He thought of everything in terms of money; Give the answer in terms of a percentage.*

terms of reference (*formal*) (a statement giving) the exact work to be done, enquiries to be made *etc*, *eg* by a committee: *That kind of inquiry does not come within our terms of reference.*

See also **terminology**.

terminate ['təːmineit] *vti* (*formal*) to bring or come to an end or limit: *She terminated the conversation; The meeting terminated at 5 o'clock; Your employment has been terminated; Their engagement has been terminated.*

'terminal *adj* (*esp attrib*) (of an illness) bringing death; fatal: *a terminal disease; She is in the terminal stages of cancer; This ward is for terminal cases* (= people who are fatally ill). – *nc* **1** a building containing the arrival and departure areas for passengers at an airport: *an air terminal;* (*attrib*) *the terminal buildings.* **2** a building in the centre of a city or town where passengers can buy tickets for air travel *etc* and can be transported by bus *etc* to an airport: *an air terminal.* **3** a *usu* large station at either end of a railway line, or one for long-distance buses: *a bus terminal.* **4** (*tech*) in an electric circuit, a point of connection to a battery *etc*: *the positive/negative terminal.*

'terminally *adv.*

ˌtermi'nation *nu* (*formal*) ending: *the termination of hostilities in a war.*

'terminus [-nəs] – *pls* **'terminuses, 'termini** [-niː] – *nc* an end, *esp* of a railway or bus route: *I get off at the terminus.*

See also **interminable**.

terminology [təːmi'nolədʒi] *ncu* (*formal*) the special words or phrases used in a particular art, science *etc*: *legal terminology; Every science has its own terminology.* **ˌtermino'logical** *adj.*

terminus *see* **terminate**.

termite ['təːmait] *nc* a pale-coloured wood-eating kind of insect, like an ant.

terrace ['terəs] **1** *nc* (one of a number of) raised level banks of earth *etc*, like large steps, on the side of a hill *etc*: *Vines are grown on terraces on the hillside; It's cheaper to watch a football match from the terraces than from the stand.* **2** *nc* a row of houses connected to each other: *Edinburgh has many beautiful terraces.* **3** *n* (*with cap*: *often abbrev* **Ter(r)**. *when written*) a word used in the names of certain roads or streets: *His address is 6 Sloan Terrace; He lives in Sloan Terrace.* **4** *nc* (*Amer*) a patio. – *vt* to make into a terrace or terraces: *The hillside has been terraced to make new vineyards.*

'terraced *adj* (*usu attrib*) forming part of a terrace: *The house-agents advertised a terraced villa for sale.*

terracotta [terə'kotə] *nu, adj* **1** (of) a brownish-red mixture of clay and sand used to make vases, small statues *etc*: *This vase is (made of) terracotta; a terracotta vase.* **2** (of) its colour: *a dress in various shades of terracotta; terracotta silk.*

terra firma [terə'fəːmə] *nu* (*usu facet*) land as opposed to water or air: *I'm glad to be on terra firma again after spending six days on a boat.*

terrain [tə'rein] *nu* (*formal or tech*) a stretch of land, *esp* with regard to its physical features: *rocky terrain; This is difficult terrain (to travel across).*

terrible ['terəbl] *adj* **1** (*inf*) very bad: *a terrible singer; She's a terrible gossip* (= She gossips a great deal): *That music is terrible!* **2** causing great pain, suffering, hardship *etc*: *War is terrible; It was a terrible disaster.* **3** causing great fear or horror: *the noise of the guns was terrible; His face was terrible to see; A terrible sight met his eyes.*

'terribly *adv* **1** (*inf*) very: *She is terribly clever.* **2** in a terrible way: *Does your leg hurt terribly?*

terrier ['teriə] *nc* (*often in cmpds*) any of several breeds of small dog: *a fox-terrier;* (*attrib*) *a terrier dog/bitch.*

terrify ['terifai] *vt* to make very frightened: *She was terrified by his appearance.*

terrific [tə'rifik] *adj* (*inf*) **1** marvellous; wonderful: *a terrific party.* **2** very great, powerful *etc*: *He gave the ball a terrific kick.*

terrifically [tə'rifikəli] *adv* (*inf*) very (much): *terrifically amusing; She enjoyed herself terrifically.*

'terrified *adj*: *The terrified little girl screamed for her mother.*

'**terrifying** *adj.*

territory ['teritəri] **1** *ncu* a stretch of land; a region: *They explored the territory around the North Pole.* **2** *ncu* the land under the control of a ruler or state: *British territory.* **3** *nc* an area in which a salesman *etc* works: *His territory is the north of England.* **4** *nu* (*formal fig*) an area of interest, knowledge *etc*: *Ancient history is outside my territory.*

ˌ**terri'torial** [-'to:-] *adj* of or belonging to a territory, *esp def 2*: *territorial rights/claims.*

territorial waters *n pl* the sea close to a country, considered to belong to it.

terror ['terə] **1** *nu* (*sometimes with* **a**) very great fear: *She screamed with/in terror*; *She has a terror of spiders.* **2** *nc* something which makes one very afraid: *The terrors of war.* **3** *nc* (*inf*) a troublesome person, *esp* a child: *That child is a real terror!*

'**terrorism** *nu* the actions or methods of terrorists: *international terrorism.*

'**terrorist** *nc* a person who tries to frighten people or governments into doing what he/she wants by using or threatening violence: *The plane was hijacked by terrorists*; *Terrorists have kidnapped the prime minister's daughter and are demanding the release of some of their friends who are in prison*; (*attrib*) *terrorist activities.*

'**terrorize, -ise** *vt* (*formal*) to make very frightened by using or threatening violence: *They terrorized the local people*; *A lion escaped from the zoo and terrorized the whole town.* ˌ**terrori'zation, -s-** *nu.*

'**terror-stricken** *adj* (*formal*) feeling very great fear: *The children were terror-stricken when the bombs landed near their school*; *terror-stricken women and children.*

terse [tə:s] *adj* (*formal*) **1** (of a speech *etc*) brief and concise; with no unnecessary words: *a terse statement*; *Her reply was terse and rather rude.* **2** (*usu pred*) (of a person) speaking in such a way; curt: *She was terse in her reply.* '**tersely** *adv.* '**terseness** *nu.*

tertiary ['tə:ʃəri] *adj* (*formal or tech*: *esp attrib*) of or at a third level, degree, stage *etc*: *Tertiary education follows secondary education.*

terylene ® ['terəli:n] *nu, adj* (of) a kind of man-made fibre used for making clothes *etc*: *The sheets are* (*made of*) *terylene*; *terylene sheets.*

test [test] *nc* **1** a set of questions or exercises intended to find out a person's ability, knowledge *etc*; a short examination: *They took an arithmetic test*; *I'm sitting my driving test next week.* **2** something done to find out whether a thing is good, strong, efficient *etc*: *Tests were carried out on the new aircraft*; *a blood test.* **3** an event, situation *etc* that shows how good or bad something is: *Climbing the mountain was a test of his courage*; *The rough road was a test of his new car's springs.* – *See also* **put to the test** *below.* **4** a way to find out if something exists or is present: *a test for radioactivity.* **5** a test match. – *vti* to carry out a test or tests on (someone or something): *The students were tested on their French*; *The teacher tested the students' knowledge of grammar*; *They tested the new aircraft*; *He tested the ice with his foot to see if it would support him*; *He tested* (*the air*) *for radioactivity*; *Perhaps I need glasses – I'd better have my eyes tested.*

'**test drive** *nc* a drive in a car one is *eg* thinking of buying in order to find out how good or bad it is. ˌ**test-'drive** *vt.*

'**test match** *nc* in cricket, (one of) a series of matches between teams from two countries.

'**test pilot** *nc* a pilot who tests new aircraft.

'**test-tube** *nc* a glass tube closed at one end, used in chemical tests or experiments.

put (someone or something) to the test to test: *He put her courage to the test.*

testament ['testəmənt] *nc* (*legal*) a written statement *esp* of what one wants to be done with one's personal property after one dies: *This is his last will and testament.*

Old Testament, New Testament the two main parts of the Bible.

testicle ['testikl] *nc* (*usu in pl*) one of the two glands in the male body in which sperm is produced.

testify ['testifai] **1** *vi* (*legal*: *often with* **against** *or* **on behalf of**) to give evidence, *esp* in a law court: *He agreed to testify on behalf of the accused man*; *Can wives testify against their husbands in a court of law?* **2** *vti* (*formal*: *often with* **to**) to show or give evidence of; to state that (something) is so: *I will testify to her kindness*; *Her actions testify her willingness to help.*

testimonial [testi'mouniəl] *nc* (*formal*) **1** a (written) statement saying what one knows about a person's character, abilities *etc*: *When applying for a job, one usually needs a testimonial from one's last employer.* **2** a gift to show respect or thanks: *She was given flowers as a testimonial.*

'**testimony** *ncu* (*legal*) the statement(s) made by a person or people who testify in a law-court; evidence: *The jury listened carefully to his testimony.*

testis ['testis] – *pl* '**testes** [-ti:z] – *nc* (*tech*) a testicle.

testy ['testi] *adj* (*formal derog*) irritable; easily made angry: *a testy person*; *testy behaviour*; *He is always testy in the morning.* '**testily** *adv.* '**testiness** *nu.*

tetanus ['tetənəs] *nu* (*also* '**lockjaw**) a type of serious disease, caused by an infected wound *etc*, in which certain muscles (*esp* of the jaw) become stiff: *The old man contracted tetanus.*

tetchy ['tetʃi] *adj* (*formal derog*) irritable; easily made angry: *tetchy behaviour*; *a tetchy old man*; *Don't be so tetchy!* '**tetchily** *adv.* '**tetchiness** *nu.*

tête-à-tête [teita:'teit] *nc, adv* (*formal or facet*) (having) a private conversation *usu* between two people: *They had a cosy tête-à-tête by the fire*; *They dined tête-à-tête.*

tether ['teðə] *nc* a rope or chain for tying an animal to a post *etc*: *He put the horse on a tether*; *He put a tether on his horse.* – *vt* to tie with a tether: *He tethered the goat to the post*; (*fig formal*) *he was tethered to a woman whom he no longer loved.*

at the end of one's tether emotionally exhausted because of worry, anger *etc*; having no more patience: *Her mother is ill, her husband has lost his job and now her son has been arrested for murder – you can see why she's at the end of her tether.*

text [tekst] **1** *nu* in a book, the written or printed words, as opposed to the illustrations, notes *etc*: *First the text was printed, then the drawings added.* **2** *nc* a written or printed version of a speech, play *etc*: *He studied Shakespeare's texts.* **3** *nc* a passage from the Bible about which a sermon is preached: *He preached on a text from St John's gospel.*

textual ['tekstjuəl, (*Amer*) -stʃu-] *adj* (*formal*: *esp attrib*) of or in a text: *textual errors/changes.*

'**textbook** *nc* a book used in teaching, giving the main facts about a subject: *a history textbook.*

textile [(*Brit and Amer*) 'tekstail] *nc* (*more formal* *than* **cloth**) a cloth or fabric made by weaving: *woollen textiles*; (*attrib*) *the textile industry.*

texture ['tekstjuə] *ncu* **1** the way something feels when touched, eaten *etc*: *the texture of wood, stone etc*; *the texture of a baby's skin.* **2** (*formal*) the way that a piece of cloth looks or feels, caused by the way in which it is woven: *the loose texture of this material.*

Thai, Thailand *see* Appendix 2.

than [ðən, ðan] *conj, prep* a word used in comparisons: *It is easier than I thought*; *I sing better than he does*; *He sings better than me*; (*formal*) *He sings better than I*; *This one is even worse than that one*; *I know you better than* (*I do*) *her.*

thank [θaŋk] *vt* (*often with* **for**) to express appreciation or gratitude to (someone) for a favour, service, gift *etc*: *He thanked me for the present*; *I enjoyed helping you – you don't have to thank me*; *She thanked him for inviting her to the theatre.*

'**thankful** *adj* grateful; relieved and happy: *I am thankful for my good fortune*; *He was thankful that the journey was over*; *She gave a thankful sigh when she arrived at her destination.* '**thankfully** *adv.* '**thankfulness** *nu.*

'**thankless** *adj* (*usu attrib*) for which no-one is grateful: *Collecting taxes is a thankless task.* '**thanklessly** *adv.* '**thanklessness** *nu.*

thanks *n pl* (*often with* **for**) expression(s) of gratitude: *Give thanks to God for all His gifts*; *I really didn't expect any thanks for helping them.* – *interj* (*inf*: *often with* **for**) thank you: *Thanks* (*very much*) *for your present*; *'Do you want to come with us?' 'No, thanks.'*; *'Would you like a biscuit?' 'Yes, thanks.'*

'**thanksgiving** *nu* the act of giving thanks, *esp* to God, *eg* in a church service: *a service of thanksgiving.*

Thanks'giving *n* (*also* **Thanks'giving Day**) in the US, a special day of the year (the fourth Thursday in November) for giving thanks to God.

no thanks to (*inf*) in spite of (a person's help, lack of help *etc*): *We eventually managed to finish the job, no thanks to him and his stupid ideas.*

thank God, goodness, Heavens *see* **god, good, heaven.**

'**thanks to** because of: *Thanks to the bad weather, our journey was very uncomfortable*; *Thanks to your generous donation, we can rebuild our laboratory.*

'**thank you** (*often with* **for**: often used when (not) accepting something one has been offered) I thank you: *Thank you* (*very much*) *for your present*; *'Would you like another piece of cake?' 'Thank you. I'd love a piece'*; *'Would you like a biscuit?' 'No, thank you'.*

vote of thanks *see* **vote.**

that [ðat] – *pl* **those** [ðouz] – *adj* used to indicate a person, thing *etc* spoken of before, not close to the speaker, already known to the speaker and listener *etc*: *Don't take this book – take that one*; *At that time, I was living in Italy*; *Who made that rude noise?*; *I don't like those paintings of his*; (*inf*) *I don't like those kind of paintings*; *When are you going to return those books you borrowed?*; *When are you going to pay me back that £10 you borrowed?* – *pron* used to indicate a thing *etc*, or (in *pl* or with the verb **be**) people, spoken of before, not close to the speaker, already known to the speaker and listener *etc*: *What is that you've got in your hand?*; *Who is that?*; *That is the managing director*; *I've never seen that before*; *That is something completely different*; *All those who want a copy of this report, please sign their names on this list*; *Those present at the meeting included the mayor and mayoress and the local member of parliament.* – [ðət, ðat] *relative pron* (*pl* **that**: *usu* omitted when it is the object of the verb or preposition in its clause) used to refer to a person, thing *etc* mentioned in a preceding clause in order to distinguish it from others: *Where is the parcel that arrived this morning?*; *Who was it that told you he was coming?*; *Everyone* (*that*) *I have asked agreed with me*; *Who is the man* (*that*) *you were talking to?*; *Those books* (*that*) *you lent me were very useful.* – [ðət, ðat] *conj* **1** (often omitted) used to report what has been said *etc* or to introduce other clauses giving facts, reasons, results *etc*: *I know* (*that*) *you didn't do it*; *Did you say* (*that*) *you were at the meeting?*; *The book is so boring* (*that*) *I've never finished it*; *I told him* (*that*) *I would do it*; *I was surprised* (*that*) *he had gone.* **2** used to introduce expressions of sorrow, wishes *etc*: *That I should be accused of murder!* (= I am surprised, sad, shocked *etc* that I could be accused of murder!); (*liter*) *Oh, that I were with her now!* (= I wish I was with her now!). – [ðat] *adv* (*inf*) so; to such an extent: *I didn't realize she was that ill*; *His book isn't all that good* (= not very good; not as good as you, he *etc* have suggested).

like that in that way: *Don't hold it like that – you'll break it!*

not that, now that, so that *see* **not, now, so.**

that's a (good) boy, girl, dog *etc* (*inf*) an expression used to praise or encourage a child, animal *etc*: *That's a girl. You drink up all your milk.*

that's that an expression used to show that a decision has been made, that something has been completed, made impossible *etc*: *He has said that we can't do it, so that's that*; *'The car has broken down.' 'That's that then. We won't reach Glasgow tonight.'*

thatch [θatʃ] *nu* straw, rushes *etc* used as a roofing material for houses: *Thatch is not often used nowadays.* – *vt* to cover the roof of (a house) with thatch: *Not many people nowadays know how to thatch cottages.*

thatched *adj* covered with thatch: *thatched cottages*; *The barn is thatched.*

thaw [θo:] *vti* **1** (of ice, snow *etc*) to melt or make or become liquid: *The snow thawed quickly*; *The sun thawed the ice on the pond*; *It is thawing* (= the weather has become warm enough to thaw the snow/ice). **2** (of frozen food *etc*) to make or become unfrozen: *How long will the meat take to thaw?*; *Frozen food must be thawed before cooking.* **3** (*formal fig*) to make or become friendly, less severe *etc*: *As they talked, be began to thaw.* – *nc* (*usu in sing*) (the time of) the melting of ice and snow at the end of winter, or the change of weather that causes this: *The thaw has come early this year*; *I can feel a thaw in the air.*

thaw out *vi, vt sep* to thaw (*defs 2, 3*): *We thawed out the frozen meat*; (*inf fig*) *He tried to thaw out in front of the fire*; (*inf fig*) *A couple of sherries will thaw out the guests and get them chatting to each other.*

the [ðə, ði] *adj* (definite article. The form [ðə] is used before words beginning with a consonant *eg* the house [ðə haus] or consonant sound *eg* the union [ðə 'ju:njən]; the form [ði] is used before words beginning with a vowel *eg the apple* [ði 'apl] or vowel sound *eg the honour* [ði 'onə]). **1** used to refer to a person, thing *etc* mentioned previously, described in a following phrase, known to the people involved, or for any other reason assumed to be understood by the reader or listener as referring to a particular person, thing *etc*: *Where is the book I put on the table?*; *The book you want is on that shelf – I think it's the big red one in the middle*; *We've eaten all the food we brought*; *Who was the man you were talking to?*; *Switch the light off, please*; *I saw her on the night of the party*; *The last time I saw him, he said he was going to Canada*; *The children* (= My, our *etc* children) *are out in the garden*; *'How's the headache* (= your headache) *now?' 'It's much better, thank you.'*; *He offered me a large cake or a small cake, so obviously I took the large one*; *This type of music was very popular in the 'sixties.* **2** used with a singular noun or an adjective to refer to all members of a group, class type *etc* or to a general type of object, group of objects *etc*: *The horse is a beautiful animal*; *Who invented the wheel?*; *The French are said to be good cooks*; *Take care of the wounded and the dying*; *He expects me to do the impossible* (= things that are impossible); *I never listen to the radio*; *I spoke to him on the telephone*; *The life of an artist is not an easy one*; *He plays the piano/violin very well*; *The sea was calm*; *The wind was howling through the trees.* **3** used to refer to unique objects *etc*, *esp* in titles and names: *The top of that desk is badly scratched*; *I can see the moon*; *the Duke of Edinburgh*; *the tenth Earl of Lincoln*; *King George the First*; *His boat is called 'The Adventurer'*; *the North Sea*; *the Atlantic* (*Ocean*); *the* (*river*) *Thames*; *the Alps*; *the Sudan*; *the Netherlands*; *He works for the GPO*; *'My name is John Smith'. 'You're not the* (= [ði:]) *John Smith, are you? The famous artist?'*; *He is the only person who could do that.* **4** used after a preposition with words referring to a unit of quantity, time *etc*: *My car does forty miles to the gallon* (= It will travel forty miles for every gallon of petrol it uses); *In this job, we are paid by the hour* (= we receive a certain sum of money for each hour we work). **5** used with superlative adjectives and adverbs to denote a person, thing *etc* which is or shows more of something than any other: *Of all our friends, he is the most amusing*; *He is the kindest man I know*; *No matter what we do, the way he would do it is always the best way*; *Have you heard the latest* (*news*)*? John is leaving the company*; *We like him* (*the*) *best of all.* **6** (*often with* **all**) used with comparative adjectives to show that a person, thing *etc* is better, worse *etc*: *He has had a week's holiday and looks* (*all*) *the better for it*; *If you annoy him, he's all the less likely to help us.*

the . . ., the . . . (*with compar adjs or advs*) used to show the connection or relationship between two actions, states, processes *etc*: *The harder you work, the more you earn*; *The older they are, the quieter they become*; *The more one reads, the less one seems to know*; *The younger, the better* (= The younger they are, the better it will be).

theatre, (*Amer*) **theater** ['θiətə] **1** *nc* a place where plays, operas *etc* are publicly performed: *London has more theatres than any other British city*; *I like to attend our local theatre as often as possible.* **2** *nu* plays in general; any theatre: *Are you going to the theatre tonight?*; *I'm very fond of the theatre.* **3** *nc* (*also* **'operating-theatre**) a room in a hospital where surgical operations are performed: *Take the patient to the theatre*; (*attrib*) *a theatre nurse.* **4** *nc* (*formal*) an area in which something, *esp* a war or battle, happens: *the theatre of war.* – *See also* **the theatre** *below.*

the'atrical [-'a-] *adj* **1** (*usu attrib*) of theatres or acting: *a theatrical performance/career.* **2** (*derog*) (behaving) as if in a play; over-dramatic: *She's very theatrical*; *theatrical behaviour.* **the'atrically** *adv.* **the,atri'cality** [θiatri'ka-] *nu.*

the'atricals [-'a-] *n pl* dramatic performances: *He's very interested in amateur theatricals.*

the theatre 1 the profession of actors: *He's in the theatre* (= He is an actor). **2** drama: *His special interest is the theatre.*

thee [ði:] *pron* (*arch* or *dial*, or (*relig*) used when addressing God: used as the object of an actual or implied verb or preposition, and sometimes as the subject of a verb, when addressing one person *etc*) you: *Shall I go with thee?*; *I saw thee open the door.*

See also **thou, thy(self)**.

theft [θeft] *ncu* (an act of) stealing: *the theft of a picture*; *There have been several thefts in this area*; *He was jailed for theft.*

See also **thief**.

their [ðeə] *adj* (*attrib*) belonging to them: *This is their car*; *Take a note of their names and addresses.*

theirs [ðeəz] *pron* a person, thing *etc* belonging to them: *a friend of theirs*; *The child is theirs*; *Is that yours or theirs?*

See also **them(selves), they**.

theism ['θi:izəm] *nu* (*formal*) the belief in the existence of God or a god.

'theist *nc.* **the'istic** *adj.*

them [ðəm, ðem] *pron* (used as the object of an actual or implied verb or preposition or (*inf*) as the subject of an implied verb) **1** people, animals, things *etc* already spoken about, being pointed out *etc*: *I don't need these shoes. Do you want them?*; *Let's invite them to dinner*; *He gave them some food*; *What will you do with them?*; *'Who did she come with?' 'Them.'*; *'Who did it?' 'Them.'* (= They did it). **2** (*not formal*: *esp Brit*: *usu* used to refer to **someone, anyone** *etc*): *If anyone brings their children with them, I'll be very annoyed.*

them'selves *pron* **1** used as the object of a verb or preposition when people, animals *etc* are the object of actions they perform: *They hurt themselves*; *They looked at themselves in the mirror.* **2** used to emphasize *they, them* or the names of people, animals *etc*: *They themselves did nothing wrong*; *John and Mary themselves played no part in this.* **3** without help *etc*: *They decided to do it themselves.* **4** (*esp Brit*: *not formal*) used as the object of a verb or preposition to refer to **someone, anyone** *etc*: *If anyone has to blame themselves, it's her.*

by themselves *see* **by oneself** *under* **by**.

they are not themselves *see* **not be oneself** *under* **one**.

See also **their, they**.

theme [θi:m] *nc* **1** (*formal*) the subject of a discussion, essay *etc*: *The theme for tonight's talk is education.* **2** in a piece of music, the main melody, which may be repeated often.

'theme song, 'theme tune *nc* a song or a piece of music that is associated with, and *usu* played at the beginning and end of, a film, television or radio programme or which is associated with a particular character on stage *etc*: *The programme* *has a very good theme tune; They played the comedian's theme song.*

themselves *see* **them**.

then [ðen] *adv* **1** at that time in the past or future: *I was at school then; If you're coming next week, I'll see you then.* **2** (*with preps*) that time in the past or future: *Come back at six o'clock – John should be here by then; I'll need the posters before then; I have been ill since then; Until then, he had never asked for money; We'll see you next week. Goodbye till then!* **3** after that: *I had a drink, (and) then I went home.* **4** in that case: *He might not give us the money and then what would we do?; What would we do then?* **5** often used *esp* at the end of sentences in which an explanation, opinion *etc* is asked for, or which show surprise *etc*: *What do you think of that, then?; That was a bit of a shock, then, wasn't it!; Well, then. What do you think you are doing?* **6** also; in addition: *I have two brothers, and then I have a cousin in Wales.* – *conj* in that case; as a result: *If you're tired, then you must rest; If the sides of the triangle are equal, then the angles must be equal; 'The paper isn't on your desk.' 'Then it must be in one of the drawers.'* – *adj* (*formal*: *attrib*) at that time (in the past): *the then Prime Minister.*

(every) now and then, now then *see* **now**.

then and there/there and then (*inf*) at that very time or moment: *He asked me then and there; She began to take all her clothes off right there and then.*

thence [ðens] *adv* (*old, liter, or formal*) from that place: *He was taken thence to prison.*

theodolite [θiˈodəlait] *nc* (*tech*) a type of instrument for measuring angles, used in surveying land.

theology [θiˈolədʒi] *nu* the study of God and religious belief. ˌ**theoˈlogical** [-ˈlo-] *adj.* ˌ**theoˈlogically** [-ˈlo-] *adv.*

ˌ**theoˈlogian** [-ˈloudʒiən] *nc* a person who studies, or is an expert in, theology.

theorem [ˈθiərəm] *nc esp* in mathematics, something that has been or must be proved to be true by careful reasoning: *a geometrical theorem.*

theory [ˈθiəri] **1** *ncu* an idea or explanation which has not yet been proved to be correct: *There are many theories about the origin of life; I think I know why he resigned, but, of course, it's only a theory; Your suggestions seem all right in theory, but have we enough money to carry them out?; In theory, I agree with you, but I feel that your ideas would not work in practice.* **2** *nc* the main principles and ideas in an art, science *etc* as opposed to the practice of actually doing it: *A musician has to study both the theory and practice of music.* ˌ**theoˈretical** [-ˈreti-] *adj.* ˌ**theoˈretically** [-ˈreti-] *adv.*

ˈ**theorize, -ise** *vi* (*formal*: *often with* **about**) to make theories: *He did not know what had happened, so he could only theorize about it.* ˈ**theorist** *nc.*

therapy [ˈθerəpi] *nu* (*sometimes in cmpds*) the (methods of) treatment of disease, disorders of the body *etc*: *He is having heat therapy for his sore shoulder; She is studying speech therapy; She is studying psychotherapy.* ˈ**therapist** *nc.*

therapeutic [θerəˈpjuːtik] *adj* (*formal or tech*) of or concerning the healing and curing of disease: *the therapeutic properties of herbs; therapeutic treatment/exercises; Massaging can be very therapeutic for stiff muscles.*

therapeutics [θerəˈpjuːtiks] *n sing* (*tech*) the branch of medicine concerned with the treatment and cure of disease: *He specialized in therapeutics;* (*attrib*) *Where is the therapeutics department?*

there [ðeə, (*def 2 usu*) ðə] *adv* **1** (at, in, or to) that place: *He lives there; Don't go there; He lives not far from there; 'Where should I put this?' 'Over there on that shelf.'* **2** (with the subject of the sentence *usu* following the verb: *usu* with **something, nothing** *etc* or a word preceded by **a, any, some** *etc* as subject) used to introduce sentences, *esp* with **be, seem** *etc* in which a state, fact *etc* is being announced: *There has been an accident at the factory; There don't seem to be any mistakes in this; There seems to be something wrong with the engine; I don't want there to be any mistakes in this; There's nothing wrong, is there?; Is there anywhere near here we could get a meal?* **3** at that time; at that point in a speech, argument *etc*: *There he paused for a moment; There I cannot agree with you; Don't stop there – tell me what happened next!* **4** (with the subject of the sentence following the verb except when it is a pronoun) used at the beginning of a sentence, *usu* with **be** or **go**, to draw attention to, or point out, someone or something: *There goes John!; There goes the bus!; There she goes now!; There's the bell; There's the book I want; There it is!* **5** (*placed immediately after noun*) used for emphasis or to point out someone or something: *That book there is the one you need.* – *interj* **1** used to calm or comfort: *There, there. Don't cry; There, now. Things aren't as bad as they seem.* **2** used when a person has been shown to be correct, when something bad happens, or when something has been completed: *There! I told you he would do it!; There! That's that job done; There! I said you would hurt yourself!*

there- (*in cmpds*) **1** (at) that place, time *etc*, as in **thereabouts**. **2** then, as in **thereafter**. **3** that, as in **therein**.

ˌ**thereaˈbout(s)** (*inf*) *adv* approximately in that place, of that number, at that time *etc*: *a hundred or thereabouts; at three o'clock or thereabouts; I'll see you at the station or thereabouts.*

thereˈafter *adv* (*formal*) afterwards; from that time on: *Thereafter he devoted himself to looking after the poor.*

thereˈby *adv* (*formal*) by that means: *He was extremely rude to her last year and thereby lost her friendship.*

therefore [ˈðeəfoː] *adv* (*more formal than* **so**) for that reason: *He worked hard, and therefore he was able to save money; He was therefore able to buy a new car.*

thereˈin *adv* (*very formal*) in it: *the box and the documents therein.*

thereˈon *adv* (*very formal*) on it: *I have witnessed the document and the signature thereon.*

thereˈto *adv* (*very formal*) to it: *This is the document and these are the names of the witnesses thereto.*

ˌ**thereuˈpon** *adv* (*formal*) because of that; then: *I thereupon left the house.*

all there *see* **all**.

get there *see* **get**.

there and then *see* **then**.

there's a (good) boy, girl *etc* (*inf*) an expression used to praise or encourage a child, animal *etc*: *You finish your soup now – there's a good boy.*

thermal [ˈθəːməl] *adj* (*formal or tech*: *esp attrib*) of heat: *thermal springs* (= natural springs of warm or hot water); *thermal units.*

thermo- (*in cmpds*) relating to heat, as in **thermometer**.

thermometer [θə'momitə] *nc* an instrument (*usu* a thin, glass tube with *eg* mercury in it) used for measuring temperature, *esp* body temperature: *The nurse took his temperature with a thermometer*; *She put the thermometer in his mouth.*

Thermos (flask) ® ['θə:məs(fla:sk)] *nc* a type of vacuum-flask: *He had some tea in a Thermos (flask).*

thermostat ['θə:məstat] *nc* an apparatus which automatically controls the temperature of a room, of water in a boiler *etc* by switching a heater or heating system on or off.

ˌthermo'static *adj* (*tech*: *esp attrib*) using a thermostat: *thermostatic control.* **ˌthermo'statically** *adv.*

thesaurus [θi'so:rəs] *nc* a book which gives information (*eg* a dictionary or encyclopedia) *esp* one which lists words and their synonyms: *If you can't think of the word you want, try and find it in a thesaurus.*

these *see* **this**.

thesis ['θi:sis] – *pl* **'theses** [-si:z] – *nc* **1** a long written essay, report *etc*, often done for a university degree: *a doctoral thesis*; *He is hoping to get a postgraduate degree in English literature and is writing a thesis on the works of John Milton.* **2** (*formal*) a statement of an idea or point of view: *He argued his thesis well.*

they [ðei] *pron* (used only as the subject of a verb) **1** persons, animals or things already spoken about, being pointed out *etc*: *They are in the garden*; *They didn't come*; *Are there no cakes left? Have they all been eaten?*; *They did it!* **2** (*esp Brit*: *not formal*: *usu* used to refer to **someone, anyone** *etc*) used instead of **he, he or she** *etc* when the person's sex is unknown or when people of both sexes are being referred to: *If anyone does that, they are to be severely punished.*

See also **their, them(selves)**.

they'd *see* **have, would**.

they'll *see* **will**.

they're *see* **be**.

they've *see* **have**.

thick [θik] *adj* **1** having a relatively large distance between opposite sides; not thin: *thick paper*; *a thick book*; *thick walls*; *a thick pane of glass*; *This glass is not thick enough*; *The walls of old houses are usually very thick.* **2** having a certain distance between opposite sides: *It's two inches thick*; *a two-inch-thick pane of glass.* **3** (of liquids, mixtures *etc*) containing solid matter; not flowing (easily) when poured: *thick soup*; *thick oil*; *This sauce is too thick – add some milk.* **4** made of many single units placed very close together; dense: *a thick forest*; *thick hair*; *Her hair is long and thick.* **5** difficult to see through: *thick fog*; *The mist is very thick here.* **6** (*pred*: *with* **with**) full of, covered with *etc*: *The room was thick with dust*; *The air was thick with smoke.* **7** (*inf*) (of speech) not clear: *He was drunk and his speech was thick*; *I could not understand his thick speech – he has a very strong accent.* **8** (*inf*) stupid: *Don't be so thick!*; *I'm tired of teaching thick pupils.* – *See also* **thick** in phrases *below.* – *nu* (*fig*) the thickest, most crowded or active part: *in the thick of the forest*; *in the thick of the fight.*

'thickly *adv.* **'thickness** *nu.*

'thicken *vti* to make or become thick or thicker: *We'll add some flour to thicken the soup*; *The fog thickened and we could no longer see the road.*

'thickening *nu* **1** something used to thicken: *She used flour as thickening for the soup.* **2** the process of making or becoming thicker: *He noticed the gradual thickening of her waist.*

ˌthick-'headed *adj* (*inf*) **1** (*derog*) stupid: *He's so thick-headed, he does everything the wrong way*; *a thick-headed young man.* **2** unable to think clearly because of a cold, alcohol *etc*: *After drinking so much at the party I felt rather thick-headed.*

ˌthick'set *adj* **1** (of a person's body) broad and strong: *He was short and thickset*; *a small, thickset man.* **2** (*usu attrib*) closely planted together: *a thickset hedge.*

ˌthick-'skinned *adj* not easily hurt by criticism or insults: *You won't upset her – she's very thick-skinned*; *Thick-skinned people are not easily offended.*

a bit thick (*inf*) more than a person can tolerate; not just or fair: *He expected me to do his work for him – that's a bit thick, isn't it?*

as thick as thieves (*inf*) very friendly: *They didn't like each other at first, but they're as thick as thieves now.*

thick and fast frequently and in large numbers: *The bullets/insults were flying thick and fast.*

through thick and thin (*inf*) whatever happens; in spite of all difficulties: *They were friends through thick and thin.*

thicket ['θikit] *nc* a group of trees or bushes growing closely together: *He hid in a thicket.*

thief [θi:f] – *pl* **thieves** [θi:vz] – *nc* a person who steals: *The thief got away with all my money*; *Someone has stolen my pen – which of you is the thief?* – *See also* **as thick as thieves** *under* **thick**.

thieve [θi:v] *vti* (*formal or facet*) to steal: *He is always thieving my pencils*; *Why don't you give up thieving?*

See also **theft**.

thigh [θai] *nc* the part of the leg between the knee and hip: *She doesn't wear trousers – her thighs are too fat*; *The muscles in my thighs are sore after climbing that hill.*

thimble ['θimbl] *nc* a kind of metal or plastic cap to protect the finger and push the needle when sewing.

'thimbleful *nc* (*sometimes facet*) a very small quantity (of a liquid): *a thimbleful of whisky.*

thin [θin] *adj* **1** having a short distance between opposite sides: *thin paper*; *a thin layer of paint*; *She rolled the pastry thin*; *The walls of these houses are too thin – we can hear our next-door neighbours talking*; *You will be very cold in that thin coat.* **2** (of people or animals) not fat: *That horse is too thin – it does not get enough to eat*; *She thinks that only thin people are attractive*; *He is pale and thin since his illness*; *She looks thinner since her illness.* **3** (*sometimes derog*) (of liquids, mixtures *etc*) not containing any solid matter; rather lacking in taste; (tasting as if) containing a lot of water or too much water: *thin soup*; *thin beer*; *This gravy is too thin.* **4** not set closely together; not dense or crowded: *a thin population*; *His hair is getting rather thin.* **5** not convincing or believable: *I'm not surprised that she didn't believe you – that was rather a thin excuse*; *He wore a false beard so that they wouldn't recognize him but it was rather a thin disguise*; *That excuse is wearing* (= becoming) *rather thin.* – *v* – *pt, ptp* **thinned** – *vti* to make or become thin or thinner: *He used water to thin the paint*; *The crowd thinned after the parade was over.*

'thinly *adv.* **'thinness** *nu.*

thin air *nu* (*fig*) nowhere: *He disappeared into*

thin air; *The magician seemed to produce coins out of thin air.*

ˌ**thin-ˈskinned** *adj* sensitive; easily hurt or upset: *Be careful what you say – she's very thin-skinned*; *Thin-skinned people are difficult to live with because they are so easily offended.*

thin on the ground rare: *Real experts are thin on the ground.*

thin out *vi, vt sep* to make or become less dense or crowded: *The trees thinned out near the river*; *I must thin out the turnips – they are much too close together.*

a thin time (*inf*) a difficult or not very pleasant time, *eg* because of a lack of money: *They are having a thin time living in London on such a small salary*; *She's had rather a thin time of it since her husband died.*

thine *see* **thy**.

thing [θiŋ] *nc* **1** (*sometimes derog*) an object; something that is not living: *What is that thing on the table?*; *What do you use that thing for?* **2** (*inf*) (*usu* with an adjective expressing some opinion), a person, *esp* a person one likes: *She's a nice old thing*; *You stupid thing! Why did you do that?* **3** any fact, quality, idea *etc* that one can think of or refer to: *Music is a wonderful thing*; *You must remember one thing – always be polite*; *You can always trust him to say the right thing* (= say something suitable in the situation); *I hope I haven't done the wrong thing* (= something I should not have done); *He has decided to do that, and there's not a thing we can do about it* (= we cannot stop him doing it); *That was a stupid thing to do* (= stupid action); *'Can you see anything?' 'No, not a thing.'*

things *n pl* (*inf*) things, *esp* clothes, that belong to someone: *You can put your things in the cupboard*; *Take all your wet things off.*

first thing (in the morning *etc***)** (*inf*) early in the morning just after getting up, starting work *etc*: *I'll do it first thing (in the morning)*; *I'll send the report to you first thing tomorrow morning.* – *See also* **last thing** *below.*

for ˈone thing . . . for aˈnother (thing) used to introduce the first reason (for (not) doing something): *I can't go – for one thing, I have no money, and for another, I have too much work.*

have a ˈthing about (*inf*) to be especially fond of, keen on, annoyed by, frightened by *etc*: *I've got a thing about men in uniform*; *She's got a thing about spiders.*

hear things *see* **see things** *below.*

last thing (at night *etc***)** late at night, just before stopping work, going to bed *etc*: *She always has a cup of tea last thing at night*; *Last thing before going to bed, I have a good wash.* – *See also* **first thing** *above.*

make a ˈthing of (*inf*) to make a fuss about: *Don't make a thing of leaving early, it's not important.*

(just) one of those things something that must be accepted: *Being ill on holiday was just one of those things.*

a near thing the act or state of just avoiding an accident, punishment *etc*: *I managed to avoid running the child over, but it was a near thing*; *That was a near thing – he almost caught us cheating!*

ˈ**see, ˈhear things** (*usu* with **is, was** *etc* and **-ing**) to see or hear something that is not there: *'That man has two heads!' 'Don't be silly – you're seeing things!'*; *I keep hearing things – it's very frightening.*

the thing (*old inf*) the proper or right thing (to do, be *etc*): *I'm afraid her behaviour is not quite the thing.*

the thing is . . . the important fact or question is; the problem is: *The thing is, is he going to help us?*; *The thing is, I haven't any money.*

thingummy [ˈθiŋəmi] *nc* (*inf*: *also* ˈ**thingummy-jig** [-dʒig], ˈ**thingummy-bob** [-bob]) used for a person or thing when the correct word or name is forgotten or not known: *the thingummy that works the engine*; *I asked thingummy-jig about it.*

think [θiŋk] – *pt, ptp* **thought** [θoːt] – **1** *vi* (*often with* **about**) to have or form ideas in one's mind: *Can babies think?*; *What are you thinking about?*; *I was thinking about my mother.* **2** *vti* (*often with* **about** *or* **of**) to have or form opinions in one's mind; to believe: *He thinks (that) the world is flat*; *I was just thinking (to myself) how silly this is*; *What do you think of his poem?*; *What do you think about his suggestion?*; *He thinks (that) we ought to go*; *He thought me very stupid*; *'Is he coming?' 'I think so.'*; *I don't think so* (= I think that is not so); (*formal*) *I think not* (= I don't think so); *I don't think you should do that* (often used as a mild warning not to do something). – *See also* **think of** *below.* **3** *vti* (*often with* **about** *or* **of**) to intend or plan (to do something), *usu* without making a final decision: *I must think what to do*; *I was thinking of/about going to London next week*; *I have often thought of leaving this job.* – *See also* **think of** *below.* **4** *vti* (*formal*: not used with **is, was** *etc* and **-ing**) to imagine or expect: *I never thought to see you again*; *Little did he think that I would be there as well*; *'No doubt he was caught.' 'One would have thought so, but in fact he wasn't.'* – *See also* **think** *in phrases below.* – *nc* (*no pl*: *with* **a**: *usu with* **about**) the act of thinking: *Go and have a think about it and you can tell me what you have decided in the morning.*

ˈ**thinker** *nc* a person who thinks, *esp* deeply and constructively: *He's a great thinker, and several books have been written about him.*

ˈ**thinking** *adj* (*attrib*) who think deeply and constructively: *All thinking people will agree with me.*

thinking-cap *see* **put on one's thinking-cap** *below.*

-thought-out (*in cmpds*) planned: *This was a* ˌ*well-thought-out camˈpaign.* – *See also* **think out** *below.*

I, he *etc* **can't think (something)** I, he *etc* do not know or cannot imagine (something): *I can't think where I put it*; *I couldn't think what had happened.* – *See also* **think of** *below.*

I should/would have thought (*esp Brit*) used to express surprise at something one has been told *etc*: *Is she only thirty-five? I would have thought she was much older.*

I should/would think I think, expect or believe: *I should think we'll be finished by the end of the week.*

I should think so/not that is (not) what one should do *etc*; certainly (not): *'I've come to apologize for being rude to you.' 'I should think so, too!'*; *'I never drink when I'm going to be driving.' 'I should think not!'*

ˌ**put** ˌ**on one's** ˈ**thinking-cap** (*inf*) to think about, and try to solve, a problem *etc*: *We've got to find some way of improving our sales figures, so we'd better all put on our thinking-caps.*

think better of **1** to think again and decide not to; to reconsider: *He was going to ask for more money, but he thought better of it.* **2** to think that someone would not be so bad *etc* as to do (something): *I thought better of you than to suppose you would do that.*

think fit *see* **fit**[1].

think highly, well, badly *etc* of (a person, thing *etc*) to have a good, or bad, opinion of: *She thought highly of him and his poetry.*

think little of/not think much of to have a very low opinion of: *He didn't think much of what I had done; He thought little of my work.*

think nothing of, think nothing of it *see* **nothing**.

'**think of** *vt fus* **1** to remember to do (something); to keep in one's mind; to consider: *He has a lot of things to think of before he leaves; You think of everything* (= You remember and do everything that needs to be done); *Have you thought of the cost involved?* **2** (*with* **can** *or* **could** *in neg*) to remember: *I couldn't think of her name when I met her at the party.* **3** (*with* **would, should, not, never** *etc*) to be willing to do (something): *I would never think of being rude to her; He couldn't think of leaving her; Such a thing is not to be thought of.* **4** to have a particular idea; to suggest: *That's a brilliant idea. I wonder why no-one thought of it before; I can't think of any way of doing this more efficiently.*

think out *vt sep* to plan; to work out in the mind: *He thought out the whole operation.* – *See also* **thought-out** *above.*

think over *vt sep* to think about (something) carefully; to consider all aspects (of an action, decision *etc*): *He thought it over, and decided not to go.*

think twice (*often with* **about**) to hesitate before doing (something); to decide not to do (something one was intending to do): *I said I would help him, but then I thought twice about it; I would think twice before going, if I were you.*

think up *vt sep* to invent; to devise: *He thought up a new process.*

think the world of (someone) to be very fond of (someone): *He thinks the world of his wife.*

See also **thought, unthinkable**.

third [θɔ:d] **1** *nc* one of three equal parts. **2** *nc, adj* (the) last of three (people, things *etc*); (the) next after the second. – *See* **eighth** *under* **eight** *for constructions.* **3** *nc* (*often with cap*) a degree with third-class honours: *He got a third in English and Latin.* – *adv* in the third position: *John came in first in the race, and I came third.*

'**thirdly** *adv* in the third place: *Firstly, I haven't enough money; secondly, I'm too old; and thirdly, it's raining.*

ˌ**third-'class** *adj, adv* of or in the class next after or below the second.

third degree *nc* a severe method of questioning people, sometimes using torture *etc*: *The police gave him a third degree.*

third party *nc* (*formal*) a third person who is not directly involved in an action, contract *etc*: *Was there a third party present when you and she agreed to the sale of the house?*

third person (*gram*) *see* **person**.

ˌ**third-'rate** *adj* (*derog*: *often attrib*) of very bad quality: *a third-rate performance; a third-rate actress; I thought that performance third-rate.*

in the third place *see* **place**.

the Third World the developing countries, those not part of or aligned with the two main powers: *the needs of the Third World.*

See also Appendix 1.

thirst [θɔ:st] *nu* **1** a feeling of dryness (in the mouth) caused by a lack of water or moisture: *I have a terrible thirst.* **2** (*formal*: *with* **for**) a strong and eager desire for something: *the thirst for knowledge.* – *vi* **1** (*formal*: *with* **for**) to have a great desire for: *He's thirsting for revenge.* **2** (*arch*) to be thirsty.

'**thirsty** *adj* **1** suffering from thirst: *I'm so thirsty – I must have a drink; the thirsty walkers.* **2** (*attrib*) causing a thirst: *Digging the garden is thirsty work.* **3** (*formal*: *pred with* **for**) eager; wanting or desiring: *He's thirsty for power.* '**thirstily** *adv.* '**thirstiness** *nu.*

thirteen [θɔ:'ti:n] **1** *nc* the number or figure 13. **2** *nu* the age of 13. – *adj* **1** (*usu attrib*) 13 in number. **2** (*pred*) aged 13. – *See* **eighteen** *for constructions.*

thirteen- (*in cmpds*) having thirteen (of something): *a* ˌ*thirteen-*ˌ*year cam'paign.*

ˌ**thir'teenth** **1** *nc* one of thirteen equal parts. **2** *nc, adj* (the) last of thirteen (people, things *etc*); (the) next after the twelfth. – *See* **eighteenth** *under* **eighteen** *for constructions.*

ˌ**thir'teen-year-old** *nc* a person or animal that is thirteen years old. – *adj* (*attrib*) (of a person, animal or thing) that is thirteen years old. – *See* **eighteen-year-old** *under* **eighteen** *for constructions.*

See also Appendix 1.

thirty ['θɔ:ti] **1** *nc* the number or figure 30. **2** *nu* the age of 30. – *adj* **1** (*usu attrib*) 30 in number. **2** (*pred*) aged 30. – *See* **eighty** *for constructions.*

'**thirties** *n pl* **1** the period of time between one's thirtieth and fortieth birthdays. **2** the range of temperatures between thirty and forty degrees. **3** the period of time between the thirtieth and fortieth years of a century. – *See* **eighties** *under* **eighty** *for constructions.*

'**thirtieth** **1** *nc* one of thirty equal parts. **2** *nc, adj* (the) last of thirty (people, things *etc*); (the) next after the twenty-ninth. – *See* **eightieth** *under* **eighty** *for constructions.*

thirty- (*in cmpds*) having thirty (of something): *a* ˌ*thirty-pound* '*fine.*

'**thirty-year-old** *nc* a person or animal that is thirty years old. – *adj* (*attrib*) (of a person, animal or thing) that is thirty years old. – *See* **eighty-year-old** *under* **eighty** *for constructions.*

See also Appendix 1.

this [ðis] – *pl* **these** [ði:z] – *adj* **1** used to indicate a person, thing *etc* nearby or close in time: *This book is better than that (one); Can I see this new car of yours?*; (*inf*) *I'm very fond of these kind of biscuits.* **2** (*inf*) used in stories to indicate a person, thing *etc* that one is describing or about to describe: *Then this man arrived.* – *pron* used for a thing *etc* or (*in pl* or with the verb **be**) a person nearby or close in time: *Read this – you'll like it; This is my new car; This is my friend John Smith.* – *adv* (*inf*) so; to this degree: *We've come this far; I didn't think it would be this easy.*

like this in this way: *It would be quicker if you did it like this.*

this afternoon, evening, morning in or during the afternoon, evening or morning of the day on which one is speaking: *I went to the office this morning; This evening, I shall go to the theatre.*

this minute (*inf*) **1** at one: *come here this minute!* **2** a moment ago: *I was talking to him just this minute.*

this month, week, year in or during the month, week in which one is speaking: *I've been late for* *work three times this week; He is getting married this year.*

thistle ['θisl] *nc* a type of prickly plant with purple flowers, which grows in fields *etc*.

thither ['ðiðə, (*Amer*) 'θi-] *adv* (*old or liter*) to that place: *They hurried thither as fast as they could.*
hither and thither *see* **hither**.

tho' [ðou] short for **though**.

thong [θoŋ] *nc* **1** a piece of leather used to fasten something: *His shoes were tied with leather thongs.* **2** the long, thin part of a whip: *The thong touched the horse's neck.*

thorax ['θo:raks] *nc* (*tech*) **1** in a human or animal body, the chest. **2** in an insect's body, the middle section.

thorn [θo:n] *nc* a hard, sharp point sticking out from the stem of certain plants: *She pricked her finger on a thorn.*
'thorny *adj* **1** full of or covered with thorns: *a thorny branch; Rose trees are often thorny.* **2** (*often attrib*) difficult, causing trouble *etc*: *This is rather a thorny problem.*
a thorn in one's flesh/side something or someone that continually irritates: *His sister is a thorn in his flesh.*

thorough ['θʌrə, (*Amer*) 'θə:rou] *adj* **1** (of a person) very careful; attending to every detail: *He's a very thorough worker; Our new accountant is rather slow but very thorough.* **2** (of a task *etc*) done with a suitably high level of care, attention to detail *etc*: *He's done a thorough job; His work is always very thorough.* **3** (*attrib*) complete; absolute: *a thorough waste of time; He's a thorough nuisance.*
'thoroughly *adv* **1** with great care, attending to every detail: *She doesn't do her job very thoroughly.* **2** completely: *He's thoroughly stupid/bored.*
'thoroughness *nu* care; attention to detail.
'thoroughbred *nc, adj* (an animal, *esp* a horse) bred from pedigree parents of the best strain: *He was riding a thoroughbred (horse)*; (*fig*) *This car is a real thoroughbred.*
'thoroughfare [-feə] **1** *nc* a public road or street: *Don't park your car on a busy thoroughfare.* **2** *nu* (the right of) passage through: *A sign on the gate said 'No Thoroughfare', because the road belonged to a private estate.*
'thorough-going *adj* (*attrib*) complete and utter: *a thorough-going villain/mess.*

those *see* **that**.

thou [ðau] *pron* (*arch* or *dial*, or (*relig*) used when addressing God) **1** (used as the subject of a verb when addressing one person) you: *Thou hast* (= You have) *finished.* **2** (used with a noun in addressing one person, *esp* when calling them something unpleasant) you: *Thou rascal, I shall kill thee!*
See also **thee, thy(self)**.

though [ðou] *conj* (*rare abbrev* **tho'**) **1** despite the fact that; although: *He went out, (even) though it was raining; Strange though it may seem, he arrived early; I don't know him very well, though I've known him a long time.* **2** (*old*) if or even if: *I wouldn't marry her though she was the last girl in the world.* – *adv* however: *I wish I hadn't done it, though.*
as 'though as if: *You sound as though you've caught a cold.*

thought [θo:t] *v see* **think**. – **1** *nc* something that one thinks; an idea: *I had a sudden thought; She seemed to be able to read my thoughts; She kept her thoughts a secret.* **2** *nu* the act of thinking; consideration: *He gave the subject a lot of thought; After a great deal of thought we decided to emigrate to America*; (*attrib*) *the thought processes.* **3** *nu* general opinion: *recent scientific thought.*
'thoughtful *adj* **1** (appearing to be) thinking deeply: *You look thoughtful; in a thoughtful mood.* **2** thinking of other people; consideration: *She's a very thoughtful person; It was very thoughtful of you to bring me breakfast in bed.* **'thoughtfully** *adv.* **'thoughtfulness** *nu.*
'thoughtless *adj* (*derog*) not thinking about other people; showing no thought, care or consideration; inconsiderate: *thoughtless words; She upsets people by being thoughtless; She's a very thoughtless young woman to upset her parents like that.* **'thoughtlessly** *adv.* **'thoughtlessness** *nu.*
second thoughts *see* **second**.

thousand ['θauzənd] – *pls* **'thousand** (*defs 1, 3*), **'thousands** (*defs 2, 3*) – *nc* **1** (preceded by **a**, a number, or a word signifying a quantity) the number 1000: *a thousand; one thousand; two thousand; several thousand.* **2** the figure 1000. **3** a thousand pounds or dollars: *This cost us several thousand(s).* – *adj* (preceded by **a**, a number, or a word signifying a quantity: *usu attrib*) 1000 in number: *a few thousand people; I have a couple of thousand pounds in the bank.*
thousand- (*in cmpds*) having a thousand (of something): *a ˌthousand-mile 'journey across Europe.*
'thousandth **1** *nc* one of a thousand equal parts. **2** *nc, adj* (the) last of a thousand (people, things *etc*) or (the person, thing *etc*) in an equivalent position.
one in a thousand (*inf*) a very special person or thing: *He's one in a thousand!*
thousands of **1** several thousand: *He's got thousands of pounds in the bank.* **2** (*loosely*) lots of: *I've read thousands of books.*
See also Appendix 1.

thrall [θro:l]: **hold (someone) in thrall** (*old*) to keep (someone) amazed or enchanted: *Her beauty held him in thrall.*
See also **enthral(l)**.

thrash[1] [θraʃ] **1** *vt* to strike with blows: *The child was soundly thrashed.* **2** *vi* (*usu with* **about, around** *etc*) to move about violently: *The wounded animal thrashed about on the ground.* **3** *vt* (*inf*) to defeat easily, by a large margin: *Our team was thrashed eighteen-nil.*
'thrashing *nc* a physical beating: *He needs a good* (= hard) *thrashing!*; (*inf fig*) *I'll give you a thrashing at tennis next week.*
thrash out *vt sep* to discuss (a problem *etc*) thoroughly and solve it: *They thrashed it out between them, and finally came to an agreement.*

thrash[2] *see* **thresh**.

thread [θred] **1** *ncu* a thin strand of cotton, wool, silk *etc*, *esp* when used for sewing: *a needle and some thread; coloured threads; I shall need some red thread to sew this dress.* **2** *nc* the spiral ridge around a screw: *This screw has a worn thread.* **3** *nc* the connection between the various events or details (in a story, account *etc*): *I've lost the thread of what he's saying.* – *vt* **1** to pass a thread (*def 1*) through: *I cannot thread this needle; How do you thread the needle on this sewing-machine?; The child was threading beads.* **2** to make (one's way) through: *She threaded her way through the crowd with difficulty.*

'threadbare *adj* (of material) worn thin; shabby: *a threadbare jacket*; *Her clothes looked poor and threadbare.*

hang by a thread (*fig*) to be in a very precarious, dangerous state: *His life is hanging by a thread.*

threat [θret] *nc* **1** a warning that one is going to hurt or punish (someone): *He will certainly carry out his threat to try to kill you.* **2** a sign of something dangerous or unpleasant which may be, or is, about to happen: *There is a threat of rain in the air.* **3** (*with* **to**) a source of danger (for): *His presence is a threat to our plan/success.*

'threaten *vti* to make or be a threat (to): *She threatened to kill herself*; *He threatened me with violence/with a gun*; *Her nervousness threatens to ruin the whole idea*; *A storm was threatening* (= was likely to happen).

three [θri:] **1** *nc* the number or figure 3. **2** *nu* the age of 3. – *adj* **1** (*usu attrib*) 3 in number. **2** (*pred*) aged 3. – *See* **eight** *for constructions.*

three- (*in cmpds*) having three (of something): *a three-page letter.*

'threefold [-fould] *adj, adv* (*formal or liter*) three times as much or as great: *a threefold increase*; *He repaid her threefold.*

'threesome *nc* a group of three: *The children went about in a threesome.*

ˌthree-di'mensional *adj* (*abbrev* **3-D**) having three dimensions, *ie* height, width and depth.

threepence ['θrepəns, 'θrʌpəns] *nu* (*hist Brit*) the sum of three pence (*def 3*): *It costs threepence.*

threepenny ('θrepəni, 'θrʌpni] *adj* (*hist Brit*: *attrib*) worth or costing threepence: *a threepenny bar of chocolate.*

threepenny bit/piece *nc* (*hist Brit*) a coin worth threepence.

ˌthree-'ply *nc, adj* (*usu attrib*) **1** (wool *etc*) which has three strands wound together: *I need some three-ply (wool) to knit this cardigan.* **2** (wood *etc*) which has three layers glued together.

three-'quarter *adj* (*attrib*) not quite full-length: *a three-quarter (-length) coat*; *a three-quarter portrait.*

'threescore *adj* (*old or liter*: *attrib*) sixty: *Threescore years and ten* (= seventy years).

'three-year-old *nc* a person or animal that is three years old. – *adj* (*attrib*) (of a person, animal or thing) that is three years old. – *See* **eight-year-old** *under* **eight** *for constructions.*

See also **third** *and* Appendix 1.

thresh [θreʃ], (*rare*) **thrash** [θraʃ] *vti* to beat (the stalks of corn) in order to extract the grain: *They are threshing (the corn) in the barn.*

threshold ['θreʃould] *nc* **1** (*formal*) (a piece of wood or stone under) a doorway forming the entrance to a house *etc*: *He paused on the threshold before ringing the doorbell*; *Don't stand on the threshold – come in!* **2** (*fig*) beginning: *She is on the threshold of a brilliant career*; *He has a very low threshold of pain* (= He feels pain more easily than most people).

threw *see* **throw**.

thrice [θrais] *adv* (*arch or liter*) three times: *He asked her thrice*; *Thrice two is six.*

thrift [θrift] *nu* (*formal*) careful spending of money, or using of food or other resources, so that one can save or have some left in reserve; economy: *Her thrift meant that they were able to live well on little money*; *She is noted for her thrift but her husband is very extravagant*; *The government is advising thrift as a means of improving the present economic situation.*

'thrifty *adj* showing thrift: *She has to be thrifty because her husband does not earn very much money*; *She is a very thrifty housewife*; *a thrifty attitude towards money.* **'thriftily** *adv.* **'thriftiness** *nu.*

thrill [θril] *vti* (*often in passive*) to (cause someone to) feel excitement: *We were thrilled to hear that she had had a baby*; *She was thrilled at/by the invitation.* – *nc* **1** an excited feeling: *a thrill of pleasure/expectation.* **2** something which causes this feeling: *Meeting the Queen was a great thrill.*

'thriller *nc* an exciting novel or play, *usu* about crime, detectives *etc*: *I always take a thriller to read on the train*; *I would like to go to the theatre tonight – there's a thriller by Agatha Christie on.*

thrive [θraiv] *vi* to grow strong and healthy: *Children thrive on milk*; (*fig*) *She is working very hard but she seems to thrive on it*; (*fig*) *The business is thriving.*

'thriving *adj* (*attrib*) successful: *a thriving industry.*

thro' [θru:] (*rare Brit or old Amer*) short for **through**.

throat [θrout] **1** *nc* the back part of the mouth connecting the openings of the stomach, lungs and nose: *She has a sore throat*; *He made a coughing noise in his throat.* **2** *nu* the front part of the neck: *Her dress had a ribbon at the throat*; *She wore a silver brooch at her throat.*

-throated (*in cmpds*) having a (certain type of) throat: *a ˌred-throated 'bird*; *a ˌdeep-throated 'voice.*

'throaty *adj* (of a voice) coming from far back in the throat; deep and hoarse: *She has a very throaty voice for a woman*; *She sounded rather throaty on the phone.* **'throatily** *adv.* **'throatiness** *nu.*

jump down someone's throat *see* **jump**.

ram (something) down someone's throat *see* **ram**.

stick in one's throat (*fig inf*) to be impossible to believe, accept *etc*: *Opening other people's letters really sticks in my throat*; *I don't usually criticize other people's behaviour but the way she carries on really sticks in my throat.*

throb [θrob] – *pt, ptp* **throbbed** – *vi* **1** (*liter or fig*) (of the heart) to beat: *Her heart throbbed with excitement.* **2** to beat regularly like the heart: *The engine was throbbing gently.* **3** to beat regularly with pain; to be very painful: *His head is throbbing (with pain)*; *My sore finger is throbbing.* – *nu* a regular beat: *the throb of the engine/her heart/her sore finger.*

throes [θrouz]: **death throes** (*formal often fig*) the final spasm(s) before death: *It was terrible to watch the death throes of the injured animal*; (*fig*) *We are witnessing the death throes of civilization as we know it.*

in the 'throes of (*formal or facet*) in the (difficult) process of: *The country is in the throes of a minor revolution*; *We are in the throes of a severe snow storm.*

thrombosis [θrom'bousis] *ncu* (*tech*) the forming of a clot in a blood-vessel: *He has a thrombosis in one of the veins in his leg*; *You should not stay in bed too long after an operation – you might get thrombosis of the leg*; *She died of cerebral thrombosis.*

throne [θroun] **1** *nc* the ceremonial chair of a king, queen *etc*, pope or bishop. **2** *nu* (*sometimes with cap*) the king or queen: *He swore allegiance to the throne.* – *vt* (*very formal*) to install (someone) as a king, queen *etc*: *The new king will be throned today.*

come to the throne to become king or queen: *Queen Elizabeth came to the throne in 1952.*

See also **accede to the throne** *under* **accede**, *and* **enthrone**.

throng [θroŋ] *nc* (*formal or liter*) a crowd: *Throngs of people gathered to see the queen*; *a throng of people.* – (*formal*) **1** *vt* to crowd or fill: *People thronged the streets to see the president*; *The streets were thronged with people*; *The town was thronged with tourists.* **2** *vi* to move in a crowd: *The audience thronged into the theatre.*

throttle ['θrotl] *nc* (in engines, the lever attached to) the valve controlling the flow of steam, petrol *etc*: *The car went faster as he opened the throttle.* – *vt* to choke (someone) by gripping the throat: *'How did he kill her?' 'He throttled her.'*; (*inf*) *This tight scarf is throttling me!*; *Trade was being throttled by the government.*

through [θru:] *prep* (*rare Brit or old Amer short form* **thro'**: *Amer short form* **thru**) **1** into from one direction and out of in the other: *The water flows through a pipe*; *The road goes under the river through a tunnel.* **2** from side to side or end to end of: *He walked* (*right*) *through the town.* **3** from the beginning to the end of: *She read through the magazine*; *He sat through the concert although he did not enjoy it.* **4** because of: *He lost his job through his own stupidity.* **5** by way of: *He got the job through a friend*; *He is related to her through his mother's family.* **6** (*Amer*) from . . . to (inclusive): *I go to work Monday thru/through Friday.* – *adv* into and out of; from one side or end to the other; from beginning to end: *He went straight/right through*; *The police were preventing people from going along that road but they let me through*; (*fig inf*) *Although I was worried about the exam, I got through okay.* – *adj* **1** (*attrib*) (of a bus or train) that goes all the way to one's destination, so that one doesn't have to change (buses or trains): *There isn't a through train to London – you'll have to change at Birmingham.* **2** (*pred*: *inf*) finished: *Are you through yet?*; *When he sacked me, he just said 'You're through!'.* – *See also* **be through, through with** *below.*

through'out *prep* **1** in all parts of: *They searched throughout the entire house.* **2** from start to finish of: *She complained throughout the journey.* – *adv* in every part: *The house was furnished throughout*; *The house is carpeted throughout.*

through traffic *nu* vehicles which are passing straight through (a town, city *etc*), not stopping.

all through 1 from beginning to end of: *The baby cried all through the night.* **2** in every part of: *Road conditions are bad all through the country.*

be 'through (doing something) (*inf*) to have finished or completed (something): *I'm through talking to her*; *I'll be through writing in a few minutes.*

get through (to) *see* **get**.

go through *see* **go**.

put through *see* **put**.

soaked, wet through very wet: *It suddenly started to rain, and I was soaked through by the time I got home*; *His coat was wet through.*

through and through completely: *He was a gentleman through and through.*

'through with (*inf*) finished with: *Are you through with the newspaper yet?*; *I'm through with working*; *I'm through with him.*

throw [θrou] – *pt* **threw** [θru:]: *ptp* **thrown** – **1** *vti* to send (something or someone) through the air with force; to hurl or fling: *He threw the ball to her/threw her the ball*; *They were throwing stones at a tree*; *You throw, and I'll catch*; (*fig*) *This has thrown everything into confusion*; (*fig*) *He threw himself to/on the ground.* – *See also* **throw about/around, throw away** *below.* **2** *vt* (of a horse) to make its rider fall off: *My horse threw me.* **3** *vt* (*tech*) to make (pottery) on a potter's wheel: *His hobby is throwing pots.* **4** *vt* to puzzle or confuse: *He was completely thrown by her question.* **5** *vt* (in wrestling, judo *etc*) to wrestle (one's opponent) to the ground. **6** *vt* (*inf*) to lose (a contest) deliberately: *He threw the fight because he had been bribed.* **7** *vt* to construct hurriedly or temporarily: *The army threw a bridge/road across the river.* – *See also* **throw** *in phrases below.* – *nc* **1** an act of throwing (*defs 1, 5*): *That was a good throw!* **2** the distance something is thrown: *She achieved a throw of sixty metres in the javelin event.*

'throwback *nc* (*often inf*) an example of a creature *etc* from an earlier age: *He looks like a throwback from/to the Stone Age*; *All of the rest of the family have red hair but she is dark-haired – she must be a throwback.*

throw about/around *vt sep* to throw in(to) various places; to scatter: *He threw his papers about*; (*fig*) *He throws his money around on expensive luxuries.*

throw away *vt sep* **1** to get rid off: *He always throws away his old clothes.* **2** to lose through lack of care, concern *etc*: *Don't throw your chance of promotion away by being careless.*

throw cold water on *see* **cold**.

throw doubt on to suggest or hint that (something) is not true: *The latest scientific discoveries throw doubt on the original theory.*

throw down the gauntlet (*inf*) to challenge (to a fight, competition *etc*), *orig* by throwing a glove at one's opponent's feet.

throw an eight, a six *etc* to throw one or more dice and obtain such a total.

throw a fit to have a fit, seizure *etc*: *She threw a fit on the floor*; (*fig inf*) *My mother nearly threw a fit when she discovered where I'd been.*

throw in *vt sep* (*inf*) to include or add as a gift or as part of a bargain: *When I bought his car he threw in the radio and a box of tools*; (*fig*) *He threw in a rude remark.*

throw in one's hand (*inf*) to give up or abandon (what one is doing): *He threw in his hand after only one week at the job.*

throw in one's lot with (someone) to join (someone): to share (someone's) life, work *etc*: *I tried to work on my own, then I threw in my lot with my brother.*

throw in the towel/sponge (*inf*) to give up or abandon: *He worked on the problem for hours, then finally threw in the towel.*

throw light on (*fig*) to help to solve or give information on (a mystery, puzzle, problem *etc*): *Can anyone throw any light on the problem?*

throw oneself into to begin (doing something) with great energy: *She threw herself into her work with enthusiasm*; *When her husband left she threw herself into looking after the children.*

throw off *vt sep* **1** to get rid off: *She finally managed to throw off her cold*; *They were following us but we threw them off.* **2** to take off very quickly: *He threw off his coat and sat down.*

throw on *vt sep* (of clothes *etc*) to put on very quickly: *He threw on a jacket and ran after her.*

'**throw oneself on** (*liter*) to rely on or give oneself up to: *He threw himself on the mercy of the judge.*

throw open *vt sep* **1** to open suddenly and widely: *He threw open the door and walked in.* **2** to allow anyone to enter, take part *etc*: *The house/competition was thrown open to the public.*

throw out *vt sep* **1** (*inf*) to get rid of by throwing (*def 1*) or by force: *He was thrown out of the meeting*; (*fig*) *The committee threw out the proposal.* **2** to say something casually or as an offer: *He threw out a remark/a challenge.* **3** to cause to become inaccurate: *This new factor has thrown out all my previous calculations.* **4** to cause to stick out: *He threw out his chest and sang.*

throw over *vt sep* (*fig inf*) to leave, abandon (a girl-friend, boy-friend *etc*): *She threw him over for someone with more money.*

throw a party to hold, organize *etc* a party: *They threw a party for her birthday.*

throw together *vt sep* **1** to bring (people) together (by chance): *They were thrown together by their interest in skiing*; *She tries to throw those two young people together – she wants them to marry.* **2** (*inf*) to put together in a hurry: *She threw a meal together*; *She threw her clothes together and put them in a suitcase.*

throw up **1** *vi* (*sl*) to vomit: *She had too much to eat, and threw up on the way home.* **2** *vt sep* (*inf*) to give up or abandon: *He threw up his job.* **3** *vt sep* (*often derog*) to build hurriedly: *They threw up a temporary building.*

throw one's voice to make one's voice appear to come from somewhere else, *eg* the mouth of a ventriloquist's dummy.

throw one's weight about (*inf derog*) to use one's power in an unsubtle way; to be bossy or domineering: *He's always throwing his weight about.*

thru [θru:] (*Amer*) short for **through**.

thrush[1] [θrʌʃ] *nc* a common type of singing bird with a brown back and spotted breast.

thrush[2] [θrʌʃ] *nu* a type of infection affecting the mouth and throat: *The baby has white spots on her throat – I think it's thrush.*

thrust [θrʌst] – *pt, ptp* **thrust** – *vti* (*formal*) to push suddenly and violently: *He thrust his spade into the ground*; *She thrust forward through the crowd.* – **1** *nc* (*formal*) a sudden violent forward movement: *The army made a sudden thrust through Africa.* **2** *nu* (*tech*) a force pushing forward: *the thrust of the engines*; *These engines have a thrust of 20000 pounds.*

thrust on/(*formal*) **upon** to bring (something or someone) forcibly to someone's notice, into someone's company *etc*: *He thrust £100 on me*; *She is always thrusting herself on other people*; (*fig*) *Fame was thrust upon him.*

thud [θʌd] *ncu* a dull sound like that of something heavy falling to the ground: *He dropped the book with a thud*; *the constant thud of bombs exploding in the distance.* – *v* – *pt, ptp* '**thudded** – *vi* to move or fall with such a sound: *He thudded down the stairs*; *The tree thudded to the ground.*

thug [θʌg] *nc* a violent, brutal person: *He was attacked by thugs*; *Where are the young thugs who robbed the old man?*

thumb [θʌm] *nc* **1** the short thick finger of the hand, set at a different angle from the other four. **2** the part of a glove covering this finger: *This glove has a hole in the thumb.* – *vti* (*often with* **through**) to turn over (the pages of a book) with the thumb or fingers: *She was thumbing through the dictionary*; *He thumbed through the telephone directory.*

'**thumb-nail** *nc* the nail on the thumb: *I have broken my thumb-nail.* – *adj* (*attrib*) small or brief but complete: *a thumb-nail sketch.*

'**thumbscrew** *nc* (*hist*) an instrument of torture which crushed the thumbs.

ˌ**thumbs-'up** *nu* a sign expressing a wish for good luck, success *etc*: *He gave me the thumbs-up*; (*attrib*) *a thumbs-up sign.*

'**thumbtack** *nc* (*Amer*) a drawing-pin: *She hung the picture on the wall with thumbtacks.*

well-thumbed *see* **well**.

be all fingers and thumbs *etc see* **finger**.

rule of thumb *see* **rule**.

thumb a lift to ask for or to get a lift in someone's car *etc* by signalling to the driver with one's thumb: *He thumbed a lift outside the hospital*; *I can't afford to go by train – I hope to thumb a lift.*

under someone's thumb controlled or greatly influenced by someone: *She is completely under her husband's thumb.*

thump [θʌmp] *nc* (*inf*) (the sound of) a heavy blow or hit: *They heard a thump on the door*; *He gave him a thump on the head.* – *vti* (*inf*) to hit, move or fall with, or make, a dull, heavy noise: *He thumped him on the back*; *His heart thumped*; *The bag thumped on to the floor.*

'**thumping** *adj* (*old inf*: *attrib*) very great: *a thumping mistake.* – *adv* (*old inf*) very: *a pair of thumping great boots.*

thunder ['θʌndə] *nu* (*often in cmpds*) the deep rumbling sound heard in the sky after a flash of lightning: *a clap/peal of thunder*; *a thunderclap/thunderstorm*; (*fig*) *the thunder of horses' hooves.* – **1** *vi* (*only with* **it** *as subject*) (of thunder) to sound, rumble *etc*: *It thundered all night.* **2** *vi* to make a noise like thunder: *The tanks thundered over the bridge*; *He thundered down the stairs.*

'**thundering** *adj* (*old inf*: *attrib*) very great: *a thundering idiot.* – *adv* (*old inf*) very: *a thundering great error.*

'**thunderous** *adj* (*formal*) like thunder: *a thunderous noise*; *The noise was thunderous.* '**thunderously** *adv.*

'**thundery** *adj* warning of, or likely to have or bring, thunder: *thundery clouds/weather*; *a thundery day*; *It feels thundery.*

'**thunderbolt** *nc* **1** a flash of lightning immediately followed by thunder. **2** (*fig formal*) a sudden great surprise: *Her arrival was a complete thunderbolt.*

'**thunderstruck** *adj* overcome by surprise; astonished: *He stood thunderstruck when we told him the news*; *She had a thunderstruck expression on her face.*

Thursday ['θə:zdi] *n* the fifth day of the week, the day following Wednesday: *She came on Thursday*; *She will go next Thursday*; *He goes on Thursdays* (= every Thursday, or only on a Thursday but not necessarily every Thursday); (*attrib*) *Thursday evening.*

thus [ðʌs] *adv* (*old or formal*) (referring to something mentioned immediately before or after) in this or that way or manner: *He spoke thus*; *Thus, he was able to finish the work quickly.*

thus far (*old or formal*) to this or that degree, extent or distance: *We have managed all right thus far.*

thwack [θwak] *nc* (*inf*) (the noise made by) a blow

or hit with something flat: *He gave him a thwack with the flat of his sword*; *He struck the water with a thwack.* – *vt* (*inf*) to hit, or make a noise, like this: *He thwacked the horse with his hand.*

thwart [θwo:t] *vt* (*formal*) **1** to stop or hinder (someone) from doing something: *He doesn't like to be thwarted.* **2** to prevent (something being done by someone): *All his attempts to become rich were thwarted.*

thy [ðai] *adj* (*attrib*: *arch* or *dial*, or (*relig*) used when addressing God: used only before a consonant or consonant sound: used only when addressing one person) your: *thy father*; *thy union.*

thine [ðain] *pron* (*arch* or *dial*, or (*relig*) used when addressing God: used only when addressing one person) yours: *Thine is the glory.* – *adj* (*attrib*: *arch* or *dial*, or (*relig*) used when addressing God: used only before a vowel or vowel sound: used only when addressing one person) yours: *Thine anger is great*; *thine honour.*

thy'self *pron* (*arch* or *dial*, or (*relig*) used when addressing God: used only when addressing one person) **1** used as the object of a verb or preposition when a person addressed as 'thou' is the object of an action he or she performs: *Look at thyself.* **2** used to emphasize **thou** or **thee**. **3** without help *etc.*

See also **thee, thou**.

thyme [taim] *nu* a type of sweet-smelling herb used to season food.

thyroid (gland) ['θairoid] *nc* a large gland in the neck which controls the body's energy: *There is something wrong with her thyroid – she is putting on a lot of weight*; *She has an enlarged thyroid gland.*

thyself *see* **thy**.

tiara [ti'a:rə] *nc* a jewelled ornament for the head, similar to a crown.

tibia ['tibiə] *nc* (*tech*) the larger of the two bones between the knee and ankle: *His leg is in plaster – he has broken his tibia.*

tic [tik] *nc* a nervous, involuntary movement or twitch of a muscle, *esp* of the face: *She has a nervous tic below her left eye.*

tick[1] [tik] *nc* **1** a (*usu* soft) regular sound, *esp* that of a watch, clock *etc.* **2** (*inf*) a moment: *Wait a tick!*; *I'll be with you in two ticks.* – *vi* to make a sound like this: *Your watch ticks very loudly!*

tick[2] [tik] *nc* a mark (√) used to show that something is correct, has been noted *etc*: *He put a tick by her name on the list.* – *vt* (*often with* **off**) to put this mark beside an item or name on a list *etc*: *She ticked everything off on the list.*

tick (someone) off, give (someone) a ˌticking-'off (*inf*) to scold someone (*usu* mildly): *The teacher gave me a ticking-off for being late.*

tick over *vi* to run quietly and smoothly at a gentle pace: *The car's engine is ticking over*; (*fig inf*) *Our sales are ticking over nicely at the moment.*

tick[3] [tik] *nc* a type of small, blood-sucking insect: *Our dog has ticks*; (*in cmpds*) *sheep-ticks.*

tick[4] [tik]: **on tick** (*Brit inf*) on credit, promising to pay later: *He bought the books on tick.*

ticket ['tikit] *nc* (*often in cmpds*) **1** a (*usu* printed) piece of card or paper which gives the holder a certain right, *eg* of travel, entering a theatre *etc*: *a bus-ticket*; *a cinema-ticket*; *Could you get me some tickets for tonight's show?* **2** (*inf*) a notice advising of a minor motoring offence: *She got a ticket for speeding*; *a parking-ticket.* **3** a card or label stating the price *etc* of something: *a price-ticket*; *I don't know the price of this dress – the ticket has fallen off.* **4** (*Amer*) a list of candidates put up by a particular party at an election: *Mr Lopez is on the Democratic ticket.*

just the ticket (*slightly old inf*) exactly right, ideal *etc*: *A cup of hot tea is just the ticket on a cold day.*

ticking ['tikiŋ] *nu* a type of material, often striped, which is used to make covers for mattresses, pillows *etc.*

tickle ['tikl] **1** *vt* to touch (sensitive parts of someone's skin) lightly, often making the person laugh: *He tickled me/my feet with a feather.* **2** *vi* (of a part of the body) to feel as if it is being touched in this way: *My nose tickles.* **3** *vt* (*inf*) to amuse: *The funny story tickled him.* – *nc* **1** an act or feeling of tickling (*defs 1, 2*). **2** a feeling of irritation of the nerves, *esp* in the throat (making one cough): *He got a tickle in his throat and could not help coughing during her speech.*

'ticklish *adj* **1** (*usu pred*) easily made to laugh when tickled: *Are you ticklish?* **2** (*inf*) not easy to manage; difficult: *a ticklish problem/situation*; *This problem proved rather ticklish.*

be tickled pink (*inf*) to be very pleased (by something): *He was tickled pink when she asked him for his autograph.*

tickle one's fancy (*inf*) to attract one mildly in some way: *The amusing toy tickled his fancy, so he bought it for his daughter.*

tidal *see* **tide**.

tidbit *see* **titbit**.

tiddler ['tidlə] *nc* (*inf*) a small fish: *He went fishing but caught only tiddlers.*

tiddly ['tidli] *adj* (*inf*) slightly drunk: *She got tiddly on brandy*; *We were served by a tiddly barmaid.*

tiddly-winks ['tidliwiŋks] *n sing* a game in which small flat (*usu* plastic) discs are made to jump into a cup *etc*: *We often play tiddly-winks – it's a good game.*

tide [taid] *ncu* the regular, twice-a-day ebbing and flowing movement of the sea: *It's high/low tide*; *The tide is coming in/going out*; (*fig*) *the tide of public opinion.*

-tide (*in cmpds*: *arch or liter*) (a) time or season: *'Christmastide*; *'Eastertide.*

'tidal *adj* (*esp attrib*) of or affected by tides: *tidal currents*; *a tidal river.*

tidal wave *nc* an enormous wave in the sea, caused by an earthquake *etc.*

'tidemark *nc* (*usu fig inf*) a mark showing the highest level that the tide has reached: *They pulled their boat above the tidemark*; *There's a tidemark round your neck where you haven't washed!*

tide (someone) over (*inf*) to help (someone) for a time: *He gave me £10 to tide me over until I could get to the bank.*

tidings ['taidiŋz] *n pl* (*old or liter*) news: *They brought tidings of a great victory.*

tidy ['taidi] *adj* **1** (*neg* **un-**) in good order; neat: *a tidy room/person*; *She is always neat and tidy*; *Her hair never looks tidy.* **2** (*inf*: *attrib*) fairly big: *a tidy sum of money.* – *vt* (*sometimes with* **up, away** *etc*) to put in good order; to make neat: *He tidied (away) his papers*; *She was tidying the room (up) when her mother arrived.* **'tidily** *adv.* **'tidiness** *nu.*

tie [tai] – *prp* **'tying**: *pt, ptp* **tied** – **1** *vt* (*often with* **to, on** *etc*) to fasten with a string, rope *etc*: *He tied the horse to a tree*; *She tied on her apron*; *I have tied a label on that parcel*; *The parcel was tied with string*; (*fig*) *She has been tied to* (= unable to leave) *the house for weeks, looking after her invalid father*; (*fig inf*) *I don't like this job – I hate being tied to a desk*; *His new job ties him rather.* **2** *vt* to fasten by knotting; to make a knot in: *They tied the rope to a tree*; *She tied a ribbon round her hair*; *He tied his shoelaces.* **3** *vi* to be joined by a knot *etc*: *The belt of this dress ties at the front.* **4** *vi* to score the same number of points *etc* (in a game, competition *etc*): *They tied with Newtown United in the competition*; *Three people tied for first place.* – *nc* **1** a strip of material worn tied round the neck under the collar of a shirt: *He wore a shirt and tie.* **2** (*formal*) something that joins: *The wall was strengthened with metal ties*; (*fig*) *the ties of friendship.* **3** (*inf*) something that limits one's freedom *etc*: *Young children are a tie.* **4** an equal score or result (in a game, competition *etc*); a draw (*n def 1*): *The result was a tie.* **5** (*sometimes in cmpds*) a game or match to be played: *a football cup-tie* (= in which a cup is to be won).

tied house/cottage *nc* a house or cottage reserved for the person doing a particular job, which he has to move out of when he leaves the job: *Many farm workers live in tied houses.*

'tie-on *adj* (*attrib*) designed to be fastened to something by strings *etc*: *a tie-on label.*

'tie-pin *nc* an ornamental clasp fixed to a tie (*n def 1*) to keep it in place: *She gave him a silver tie-pin for Christmas.*

be tied up 1 (*inf*: *sometimes with* **with**) to be busy; to be involved (with): *I can't come to the party this evening – I'm a bit tied up tonight*; *I can't discuss this matter just now – I'm tied up with other things.* **2** (*with* **with**) connected with: *His state of depression isn't just because of his job – it's tied up with his home life.*

tie (someone) down 1 to limit someone's freedom *etc*: *The baby ties her down a bit*; *Her work tied her down.* **2** to make (someone) come to a decision: *He managed to tie them down to a definite date for the meeting.*

tie in/up *vi* (*fig*: *often with* **with**) to be linked or joined (logically): *This doesn't tie in* (*with what he said before*); *These statements don't tie up.*

See also **untie**.

tier [tiə] *nc* (*formal*) a row of seats, *esp* when there are other rows above and below: *They sat in the front/first tier*; *The seats were arranged in tiers.*

tiff [tif] *nc* (*inf*) a slight quarrel (*usu* between people who know each other well): *She's had a tiff with her boy-friend.*

tig *see* **tag** (*n def 3*).

tiger ['taigə] – *fem* **'tigress** – *nc* a large wild animal of the cat family, with a striped coat.

tight [tait] *adj* **1** fitting very or too closely: *I couldn't open the box because the lid was too tight*; *My trousers are too tight*; *We all got into the car, but it was a tight squeeze/fit* (= the car was really too small to hold all of us). **2** stretched to a great extent; not loose: *He made sure that the ropes were tight.* **3** (*usu attrib*) (of control *etc*) strict and very careful: *She keeps a tight rein on her emotions.* **4** not allowing much time: *We hope to finish this next week but the schedule's a bit tight*; rather a tight timetable. **5** (*inf*: *usu pred*) (of people) not generous (with money); mean: *He's tight with his money.* **6** (*inf*: *often pred*) slightly drunk; tipsy: *He got tight on champagne.* **7** (*pred*) (of money) scarce; difficult to obtain: *Money is a bit tight just now – we can't afford to go on holiday.* – *adv* (*also* **'tightly**) closely; with no extra room or space: *The bags were packed tight/tightly packed*; *tightly-packed bags.*

-tight (*in cmpds*) sealed so as to keep (something) in or out, as in **airtight, watertight**.

'tighten *vti* to make or become tight or tighter: *He tightened the ropes*; *She tightened her stomach muscles*; *The sail tightened in the wind.*

'tightish *adj* (*inf*: *often pred*) rather tight: *This dress is tightish around the hips.*

'tightly *see* **tight** *adv.*

'tightness *nu.*

tights *n pl* a close-fitting (*usu* nylon or woollen) garment covering the feet, legs and body to the waist: *She only wears tights when she has a skirt on – she wears socks under trousers*; *Ballet-dancers wear woollen tights to keep their legs warm when practising*; *She bought three pairs of tights.*

,tight-'fisted *adj* (*inf*) mean and ungenerous with money: *a tight-fisted employer*; *He's too tight-fisted to give his wife a birthday present.*

,tight-'lipped *adj* with lips firmly closed, refusing to say anything, explain *etc*, often in anger: *a tight-lipped refusal*; *She was tight-lipped with anger.*

'tightrope *nc* a tightly-stretched rope or wire on which acrobats balance.

a tight corner/spot a difficult position or situation: *His refusal to help put her in a tight corner/spot.*

tighten one's belt (*fig inf*) to make sacrifices and reduce one's standard of living: *If the economy gets worse, we shall just have to tighten our belts.*

tigress *see* **tiger**.

tilde ['tildə] *nc* **1** a mark (˜) sometimes found over the letter **n** in Spanish to indicate a certain sound, *eg* **señor** [sen'jor], or over **a** or **o** in Portuguese to show that the vowel is nasalized. **2** the same mark, often used in dictionaries *etc* to indicate that (the stem of) a word has been missed out to save space, *eg* **tight** *adj* (*inf*) slightly drunk: *He got ~ on champagne.*

tile [tail] *nc* **1** a piece of baked clay used in covering roofs, walls, floors *etc*: *We have put tiles on the wall behind the bath*; *Some of the tiles were blown off the roof during the storm.* **2** a similar piece of plastic material used for covering floors *etc*: *What did you use to stick the tiles to the kitchen floor?* – *vt* to cover with tiles: *We had to have the roof tiled.*

tiled *adj* covered with tiles: *a tiled floor*; *The kitchen is tiled.*

be (out) on the tiles (*inf*) to be away from home drinking, dancing *etc*: *He was out on the tiles last night!*

till[1] [til] *prep, conj* to the time of or when: *I'll wait till six o'clock*; *I didn't know till* (= before) *now that you were ill*; *Go on till you reach the station.* *See also* **until**.

till[2] [til] *nc* (in a shop *etc*) a container or drawer in which money is put and registered: *He rang up* (= registered) *50 pence on the till.*

till[3] [til] *vt* (*old*) to prepare (land) for the growing of crops, *esp* with a plough; to cultivate: *They tilled the fields.*

tiller ['tilə] *nc* the handle or lever used to turn the rudder of a boat: *He was at the tiller* (= was steering the boat).

tilt [tilt] **1** *vti* to go or put (something) into a sloping or slanting position: *He tilted his chair backwards*; *The lamp tilted and fell.* **2** *vi* (*hist*: *with* **at**) to fight on horseback with a lance *etc*; to joust: *At a tournament, the knights tilted* (*at each other*); (*fig* *formal) The newspapers are continually tilting at politicians.* – *nc* a slant; a slanting position: *The ship lay at a tilt; The table is at a slight tilt.*

(at) full tilt (at) full speed: *He rushed down the street at full tilt; He rushed round the corner and ran full tilt into* (= collided with full force with) *the headmaster.*

timber ['timbə] **1** *nu* wood, *esp* for building: *Houses used to be built of timber.* **2** *nu* trees suitable for this: *a hundred acres of good timber*; (*attrib*) *a timber forest.* **3** *nc* a wooden beam used in the building of a house, ship *etc*: *The timbers are weak.*

timbre [tẽbr, (*Amer.*) 'timbər] *nc* (*formal or music*) the quality of a (musical) sound or voice: *Her voice had a pleasant timbre.*

time [taim] **1** *nu* the hour of the day: *What time is it?*; *Can your child tell* (= read from a clock *etc*) *the time yet?*; *What time was it when he left?* **2** *nu* the passage of days, years, events *etc*: *time and space*; *She felt less unhappy as time passed*; *Time will tell* (= As time passes, the truth will become evident). **3** *ncu* (*often in cmpds*) a point at which, or period during which, something happens: *at the time of his wedding*; *in the time of Queen Anne*; *breakfast-time.* **4** *ncu* (*usu in sing*) the quantity of minutes, hours, days *etc, eg* spent in, or available for, a particular activity *etc*: *You've taken/been a long time writing that letter*; *This won't take much time to do*; *Take your time over it!* (= Spend as long as you want doing it!); *His time for running a mile was 4½ minutes*; *I enjoyed the time I spent in Paris*; *I haven't had time to do it yet*; *I can't spare the time for that now. I'll have more time later*; *You have only a short time to decide*; *At the end of the exam, the supervisor called 'Your time is up!'* (= 'Your allowed time is over!'). **5** *nc* (*no pl*) a suitable moment or period: *Now is the time to ask him*; *The morning is the time for work*; *Will this evening be a good time to mention it?* **6** *nc* one of a number of occasions: *He's been to France four times*; *How many times have you read it? I'll forgive you this time, but another time you'll be punished!* **7** *nc* a period characterized by a particular quality in a person's life, experience *etc*: *He went through an unhappy time when she died*; *We had some good times together*; *Are you having a good time?* (= enjoying yourself?); *I had a difficult time persuading him.* **8** *nu* (*music*) the number of beats in a bar and their length: *quadruple time.* **9** *nu* (*music*) the speed at which a piece of music should be played; tempo: *in slow time.* – *vt* **1** to measure the time taken by (a happening, event *etc*) or by (a person, in doing something): *He timed the journey*; *He timed her as she swam a mile.* **2** to choose a particular time for: *You timed your arrival beautifully!*

'timeless *adj* **1** (*formal*) not belonging to, or typical of, any particular time: *His style of writing is timeless*; *timeless works of art.* **2** (*liter*) never-ending: *the timeless beauty of Venice*; *The beauty of the city is timeless.* **'timelessly** *adv.* **'timelessness** *nu.*

'timely *adj* coming at the right moment: *his timely arrival*; *Your arrival was most timely.* **'timeliness** *nu.*

times 1 *n pl* a period; an era: *in Elizabethan times*; *We live in difficult times*; (*The*) *times* (= the present times) *are hard.* **2** *n pl* (*math*) used to mean multiplied by: *Four times two is eight.* **3** *n* (*with cap*) a word often used in the titles of newspapers: *the Rutherglen Times.*

'timing *nu* (*esp drama*) the speed of dialogue, reaction *etc* between actors: *All comedians should have a good sense of timing*; *His timing is perfect!*

'time bomb *nc* a bomb that has been set to explode at a particular time.

'time-honoured *adj* (*formal*: *attrib*) (of a custom *etc*) respected because it has lasted a long time: *the time-honoured custom of giving presents at Christmas.*

'time limit *nc* a fixed length of time during which something must be done and finished: *The examination has a time limit of three hours.*

'timepiece *nc* (*old*) a watch or clock.

'time-signal *nc* (on the radio *etc*) a signal for giving the exact time: *I put my watch right by the time-signal.*

'timetable *nc* a list of the times of trains, school classes *etc.*

'timeworn *adj* (*liter sometimes derog*) worn through long use; old: *timeworn customs*; (*facet*) *timeworn excuses.*

all in good time soon enough: *The work will be finished all in good time*; *'Haven't you finished yet?' 'All in good time'* (= Don't hurry me!).

all the time continually: *The baby cried all the time.*

at 'times occasionally; sometimes: *At times I can't understand him.*

be behind time (*slightly formal*) to be late: *The train is behind time.*

do time (*sl*) to be in prison: *He's doing time in Pentonville.*

for the time being meanwhile: *I am staying at home for the time being.*

from time to time occasionally; sometimes: *From time to time he brings me a present.*

have no time for to despise: *I have no time for people of that sort.*

have the time of one's life (*inf*) to enjoy oneself very much; to have a wonderful time: *They are having the time of their lives in London.*

in good time (*inf*) early enough; before a set time (for an appointment *etc*): *We arrived in good time for the concert.*

in time 1 early enough: *He arrived in time for dinner*; *Are we in time to catch the train?* **2** (*with* **with**) at the same speed or rhythm: *They marched in time with the music.*

keep time to sing, play, dance *etc* in the same rhythm: *You must keep time with the conductor.*

make good time to travel as quickly or more quickly than one had expected or hoped: *We got caught in a traffic jam in Glasgow, but we made good time on the rest of the journey.*

no time (at all) (*inf*) a very short time indeed: *He arrived in no time*; *The journey took no time* (*at all*).

one, two *etc* **at a time** singly, or in groups of two *etc*: *They came into the room three at a time.*

on time at the right time: *The train left on time*; *He was on time for his appointment.*

save, waste time to avoid spending time; to spend time unnecessarily: *Take my car instead of walking, if you want to save time*; *We mustn't waste time discussing unimportant matters.*

take one's time to do (something) as slowly as one wishes, often more slowly than someone else wishes: *Take your time – there's no hurry*; *I wish he would hurry up – he's rather taking his time about making a decision.*

ˌ**time and 'motion study** (*also* **'work study**) the study of the way work is done in factories *etc*, and the possibility of its being done more efficiently.

time and (time) again again and again; repeatedly: *I asked her time and (time) again not to do that.*

time is getting on time is passing; it is getting late: *Time is getting on – we ought to be leaving soon.*

time out of mind (*very formal*) during the whole time within human memory.

See also **untimely**.

timid ['timid] *adj* (*slightly formal*) easily frightened; nervous; shy: *A mouse is a timid creature*; *Don't be so timid – ask your employer for an increase in salary.* **'timidly** *adv.* **ti'midity, 'timidness** *nus.*

timorous ['timərəs] *adj* (*liter*) very timid: *a timorous creature.*

timpani, tympani ['timpəni] *n pl* kettledrums. **'timpanist, 'tympanist** *nc* a person who plays the timpani.

tin [tin] **1** *nu* an element (symbol **Sn**), a silvery-white metal: *Is that box made of tin or steel?* **2** *nc* (*Amer and often Brit* **can**) a container, *usu* for food, made of **'tin-plate**, thin sheets of iron covered with tin or other metal: *a tin of fruit*; *He bought a tin of tomatoes*; *a biscuit-tin.* – *adj* made of tin or tinplate: *a tin plate.* – *v* – *pt, ptp* **tinned** – *vt* (*rare*: *usu* **can**) to pack in tins: *a fruit-tinning factory.*

tinned *adj* (of food) sealed in a tin for preservation *etc*: *tinned peaches*; *tinned foods*; *Are the peaches fresh or tinned?*

'tinny *adj* (*derog inf*) **1** (*usu pred*) (of something metal) not strong or solidly made: *Modern cars are so tinny.* **2** (*usu attrib*) (of sound) thin and high-pitched: *a tinny voice.*

'tinfoil *nu* tin or other metal in the form of very thin, paper-like sheets, used for wrapping *etc*: *The sandwiches will keep if you wrap them in tinfoil*; *I'm going to bake the ham in tinfoil.*

'tin-opener *nc* (*Amer* **'can-opener**) any of several types of tool or device for opening tins of food.

tin-plate *see* **tin** (*def 2*) above.

tincture ['tiŋktʃə] **1** *ncu* (*formal or tech*) a medicine *etc* mixed in alcohol: *tincture of iodine.* **2** *nc* (*rare*) a slight tinge: *a tincture of green in the water.* – *vt* (*rare or liter*: *usu in passive*) to colour slightly; to tinge: *The clouds were tinctured with pink.*

tinder ['tində] *nu* (*formal*) dry material easily set on fire.

'tinder-box *nc* (*hist*) a box containing tinder and a flint for striking a spark, used to light a fire *etc.*

tinge [tindʒ] *nc* (*formal or liter*) a trace, or slight amount, of a colour: *He hair had a tinge of red*; *His face had an unhealthy grey tinge*; (*fig*) *The music had a tinge of sadness.* – *vt* (*formal or liter*) to tint; to colour slightly: *Dawn tinged the sky with pink*; (*fig*) *Her laughter was tinged with anger.*

tingle ['tiŋgl] *vi* to feel a prickling sensation: *The cold wind made my face tingle*; *My fingers were tingling with cold*; (*fig*) *She was tingling with excitement.* – *nc* this feeling.

tinker ['tiŋkə] *nc* a person, *usu* who travels around like a gypsy, who mends kettles, pans *etc.* – *vi* (*sometimes derog*: *often with* **about** *or* **around**) to fiddle, or work in an unskilled way, with machinery *etc*: *He enjoys tinkering around* (*with car engines*); *Who's been tinkering* (= meddling) *with the television set?*

tinkle ['tiŋkl] *vti* (*formal or liter*) to (cause to) make a sound of, or like, the ringing of small bells: *The doorbell tinkled*; *The rain tinkled on the metal roof.* – *nc* (*formal or liter*) this sound: *The bell gave a tinkle*; *I heard the tinkle of breaking glass.*

tinny *etc see* **tin**.

tinsel ['tinsəl] *nu* a sparkling, glittering substance used for decoration: *The Christmas tree was decorated with tinsel.* **'tinselly** *adj.*

tint [tint] *nc* a variety, or shade, of a colour: *There were green tints in her eyes.* – *vt* to give a tint to; to colour slightly: *She had her hair tinted red.*

tiny ['taini] *adj* very small: *a tiny insect*; *a tiny little girl*; *The amount is tiny.*

tip[1] [tip] *nc* the small or thin end, point or top of something: *Only the tip of an iceberg shows above the water*; *the tips of my fingers*; *His nose is pink at the tip.* – *v* – *pt, ptp* **tipped** – *vt* (*usu in passive*) to put, or form, a tip on: *The spear was tipped with an iron point.*

tipped *adj* (*usu in cmpds*: *neg* **un-**) having a tip of a particular kind: *filter-tipped cigarettes*; *a white-tipped tail.*

ˌ**tip-'top** *adj* (*inf*: *usu attrib*) excellent: *The horse is in tip-top condition.*

be on the tip of one's tongue to be almost, but *usu* not, spoken or said: *Her name is on the tip of my tongue* (= I can't quite remember it); *It was on the tip of my tongue to tell him* (= I almost told him).

tip[2] [tip] – *pt, ptp* **tipped** – **1** *vti* (*sometimes with* **up**) to (make something) slant: *The boat tipped to one side*; *The back part of the truck can be tipped up to empty the load.* – *See also* **tip over** *below.* **2** *vt* (*slightly inf*) to empty (something) from a container, or remove (something) from a surface, with this kind of motion: *He tipped the water out of the bucket*; *Tip the rubbish into the dustbin!*; *She tipped the money on to the table from her purse*; *I tipped the cat off the chair* (= I removed the cat from the chair by tilting the chair); *You can tip those books off the table.* **3** *vt* to dump (rubbish): *People have been tipping their rubbish in this field.* – *nc* (*Brit*) a place where rubbish is thrown: *a refuse/rubbish tip*; (*fig inf*) *Your room is a tip!* (= is very untidy!).

tip over *vt sep, vi* to knock or fall over; to overturn: *He tipped the lamp over*; *She put the jug on the edge of the table and it tipped over.*

tip the scale(s) **1** to be the deciding factor in a result *etc*: *The politeness of this applicant tipped the scales in his favour and he got the job.* **2** (*with* **at**) to weigh a particular amount: *The boxer tipped the scales at 180 lbs.*

tip[3] [tip] *nc* a gift of money given to a servant, waiter, taxidriver *etc*, for personal service: *I gave him a generous tip.* – *v* – *pt, ptp* **tipped** – *vt* to give such a gift to: *He paid the bill and tipped the waiter 20 pence.*

tip[4] [tip] *nc* (*slightly inf*) a piece of useful information; a hint: *He gave me some good tips on/about gardening*; *I received a tip* (= a piece of advice on betting) *for this afternoon's race.*

'tip-off *nc* (*inf*) a hint; a useful bit of information: *The police were given a tip-off about the murderer by a member of the criminal world.* – *See also* **tip off** *below.*

tip off *vt sep* (*inf*) to give information or a hint to; to warn: *He tipped me off about her arrival.* – *See also* **tip-off** *above.*

tip (someone) the wink (*inf*) to give (someone) information privately or secretly: *He tipped me the wink that the house was for sale.*

tip[5] ['tip] – *pt, ptp* **tipped** – *vt* (*slightly inf*) to touch or strike lightly: *She just tipped the ball with her tennis racket.* – *nc* (*slightly inf*) an act of striking lightly; a light blow: *I didn't smack the child – I just gave her a tip.*

tipple ['tipl] *vi* (*inf*) to drink alcohol (often): *He's always tippling; I think he tipples.* – *nu* (*inf*) a person's favourite alcoholic drink: *My tipple is rum.* '**tippler** *nc.*

tipsy ['tipsi] *adj* (*inf: often pred*) slightly drunk: *She always gets tipsy on sherry.* '**tipsily** *adv.* '**tipsiness** *nu.*

tiptoe ['tiptou] *vi* to walk on the toes, *usu* in order to be quiet: *He tiptoed past her bedroom door.*

walk, stand *etc* **on tiptoe(s)** to walk, stand *etc* on the toes: *He stood on tiptoe(s) to reach the shelf.*

tirade [tai'reid] *nc* (*formal or facet*) a long angry speech: *She delivered a tirade against politicians.*

tire[1] *see* **tyre**.

tire[2] ['taiə] *vti* to make, or become, physically or mentally in want of rest, because of lack of strength, patience, interest *etc*; to weary: *Walking tired her; His conversation tired her; You will tire the invalid if you talk to her for too long; She tires easily.* – *See also* **tire out** *below.*

tired *adj* **1** wearied; exhausted: *She was too tired to continue; a tired child.* **2** (*pred with* **of**) no longer interested in; bored with: *I'm tired of (answering) stupid questions!* '**tiredness** *nu.*

'**tireless** *adj* (*formal*) never becoming weary or exhausted; never resting: *a tireless worker; tireless energy/enthusiasm; She was tireless in her attempts to help the poor.* '**tirelessly** *adv.* '**tirelessness** *nu.*

'**tiresome** *adj* (*more formal than* **annoying**) troublesome; annoying: *The grass needs cutting again. How tiresome!; a tiresome person; It was tiresome of him to arrive so late.* '**tiresomely** *adv.* '**tiresomeness** *nu.*

'**tiring** *adj* causing (physical) tiredness: *I've had a tiring day; The journey was very tiring.*

tire out *vt sep* to tire or exhaust completely: *The hard work tired her out.*

See also **untiring**.

tissue ['tiʃu:] *ncu* **1** (*formal or tech*) (one of the kinds of) substance of which the organs of the body are made: *nervous tissue; muscle tissue; the tissues of the body.* **2** (a piece of) thin soft paper used for wiping the nose *etc*: *He bought a box of tissues* (= paper handkerchiefs) *for his cold;* (*formal*) *a roll of soft toilet tissue* (= toilet-paper). **3** (*liter*) (a kind of) delicate woven fabric: *gold tissue;* (*fig*) *His story is a tissue of lies.*

tissue paper *nu* very thin paper, used for packing, wrapping *etc*: *She wrapped her dress in tissue paper.*

tit[1] [tit] *nc* any of several kinds of small bird: *a blue tit.*

tit[2] [tit]: **tit for tat** [tat] (*inf*) blow for blow; repayment of injury with injury: *He tore my dress, so I spilt ink on his suit. That's tit for tat.*

tit[3] [tit] *nc* **1** (*sl*) a teat. **2** (*vulg*) a woman's breast: *What enormous tits she has!*

titbit ('titbit), **tidbit** ['tidbit] *nc* a tasty little piece of food: *He gave the dog a titbit;* (*fig*) *a titbit of gossip.*

tithe [taið] *nc* (*hist*) a tenth part of a person's income or produce, paid as a tax to the church.

titillate ['titileit] *vt* (*formal or facet*) to excite: *to titillate the senses.* ˌ**titil'lation** *ncu.*

'**titillating** *adj* (*formal or facet*) exciting, *esp* sexually: *titillating pictures; He finds pornographic pictures titillating.*

titivate ['titiveit] *vti* (*inf*) to decorate or make smart: *She was titivating (herself) in front of the mirror; This old hat needs to be titivated.*

title ['taitl] *nc* **1** the name of a book, play, painting, piece of music *etc*: *The title of the painting is 'A Winter Evening'.* **2** a word put before a person's name to show rank, honour, occupation *etc*: *Sir John; Lord Henry; Captain Smith; Professor Brown; Dr (Doctor) Peter Jones.* **3** (*legal*) a legal right or claim to money, property *etc*: *He has no title to the estate.*

'**titled** *adj* having a title that shows noble rank: *a titled lady; I did not realize that he was titled.*

titular ['titjulə, (*Amer*) -tʃu-] *adj* (*formal: attrib*) having the title of an office *etc* but not the actual authority or duties: *He is the titular head of the organization.*

'**title deed** *nc* a document that proves legal ownership: *I have the title deeds of the house.*

'**title page** *nc* the page at the beginning of a book on which are the title, the author's name *etc.*

'**title rôle** *nc* the rôle or part in a play of the character named in the title: *He's playing the title rôle in 'Hamlet'.*

titter ['titə] *vi* (*more inf than* **giggle**) to giggle: *He tittered nervously.* – *nc* (*more inf than* **giggle**) a giggle: *She gave a nervous titter.*

tittle-tattle ['titltatl] *nu* (*inf: sometimes derog*) gossip or chatter: *There's been a lot of tittle-tattle about his relationship with his secretary – but he's not having an affair with her.*

titular *see* **title**.

tizzy ['tizi]: **be in, get into a tizzy** (*inf*) to be or become very nervous or upset: *She was in a terrible tizzy when she lost her purse; She gets into such a tizzy when visitors come to stay.*

TNT [ti:en'ti:] *nu* a type of explosive material: *The bridge was blown up with TNT.*

to [tə, tu] *prep* **1** towards; in the direction of: *He's going to London; I cycled to the station; The road from Cockbridge to Tomintoul is blocked by snow; We travelled from place to place; The book fell to the floor;* (*fig*) *We've changed from gas to electricity; The children are going to* (= to live with) *their grandmother for the holidays; I went to* (= I attended) *the concert/lecture/play.* **2** as far as: *His story is a lie from beginning to end; It is five miles from my house to hers.* **3** until: *He teaches from midday to 4 o'clock; Did you stay to the end of the concert?; He bears the scars of the attack to this day* (= He still has the scars). **4** sometimes used to introduce the indirect object of a verb: *He sent it to us; Who did you send invitations to?;* (*formal*) *To whom did you give it?; You're the only person I can talk to.* **5** used in expressing various relations: *He put his ear to the door; Listen to me!; Did you reply to his letter?; What did you say to his offer?; How did he react to your suggestion?; He yielded/submitted/gave way to my wishes; Where's the key to* (= for) *this door?; There seems to be no answer to the problem; He sang to (the accompaniment of) his guitar; You must apply the glue to both surfaces.* **6** into a particular state or condition: *She tore the letter to pieces; He boiled the fruit to a pulp.* **7** used in expressing comparison or proportion: *He's junior to me; Your skill is superior to mine; Compared to her sister, she isn't particularly pretty; We won the match by 5 goals to 2; The odds are 10 to*

1 against. **8** showing the purpose or result of an action *etc*: *He came quickly to my assistance*; *To my horror, he took a gun out of his pocket*; *I discovered to my surprise that the room was empty.* **9** [tə] used before an infinitive *eg* after various verbs (but not *aux* **do** or a *modal aux* and adjectives, or in other constructions: *I want to go!*; *He asked me to come*; *Try to work harder!*; *I intended to do it*; *I'll have to leave now*; *He told me what to say*; *He worked hard to* (= in order to) *earn a lot of money*; *These buildings were designed to* (= so as to) *resist earthquakes*; *To tell the truth* (= It must be admitted that) *he did his best*; *He didn't live to* (= long enough to) *see his great-grand-children*; *She opened her eyes to find* (= and found) *him standing beside her*; *I wasn't ready to go*; *Are you willing to do it?*; *He was happy to tell her the news*; *It's difficult to decide*; *I arrived too late to see him*; *To tell* (= telling) *the truth is often difficult*; *It is impolite to talk with your mouth full.* **10** used instead of a complete infinitive: *He asked her to stay but she didn't want to.* – [tu:] *adv* **1** into a closed or almost closed position: *He pulled/pushed the door to.* **2** used in phrasal verbs and compounds: *He came to* (= regained consciousness); *The ship hove to* (= stopped); *a lean-to* (= built against another building) *hut*; *They set to* (= They began).

to and fro [tu:ən'frou] (*formal*) backwards and forwards: *They ran to and fro in the street.*

toad [toud] *nc* a kind of reptile, like a large frog.

'toady *vi* (*inf derog*: *with* **to**) to flatter someone and do everything he/she wishes: *He is always toadying to the boss.* – *nc* (*inf derog*) a person who does this.

'toadstool *nc* any of several kinds of mushroom-like fungi, often poisonous: *He ate a toadstool thinking it was mushroom and died of poisoning.*

toast[1] [toust] *vt* to make (bread *etc*) brown in front of a fire or other direct heat; *We toasted slices of bread for tea*; (*fig inf*) *They toasted* (= warmed) *their feet in front of the fire.* – *nu* bread that has been toasted: *He always has two pieces of toast for breakfast.*

'toasted *adj* heated by direct heat, *eg* under a grill: *toasted cheese*; *Do you like your bread toasted?*

'toaster *nc* an electric machine for toasting bread: *We don't have a toaster – we toast bread under the grill.*

'toasting-fork *nc* a fork with a long handle, used to toast bread in front of a fire.

'toastrack *nc* a small stand in which slices of toast can be served: *Put the toastrack and the butter on the breakfast table.*

toast[2] [toust] *vt* to drink ceremonially in honour of, or to wish success to (someone or something): *We toasted the bride and bridegroom/the new ship.* – *nc* **1** an act of toasting: *Let's drink a toast to our friends!* **2** the wish conveyed, or the person *etc* honoured, by such an act: *Our toast is 'The bride and groom – may they have long life and happiness!'*; (*fig*) *After his victory, the general was the toast of the whole country* (= he was praised and honoured by everyone).

'toastmaster *nc* a person who announces the toasts at a ceremonial dinner *etc*: *The toastmaster announced the toast to the Queen.*

tobacco [tə'bakou] – *pl* **tobaccos** – *ncu* (a type of plant that has) leaves that are dried and used for smoking in pipes, cigarettes, cigars *etc*, or as snuff: *He bought some pipe tobacco – he doesn't smoke cigarettes*; *Tobacco is bad for your health*; *mild/strong tobaccos.*

to'bacconist [-nist] *nc* **1** a person who sells tobacco, cigarettes *etc.* **2** a tobacconist's shop: *There's a tobacconist at the corner of the street.*

to'bacconist's *nc* a tobacconist's shop: *You can buy cigars and cigarettes at a tobacconist's.*

toboggan [tə'bogən] *nc* a kind of light sledge. – *vi* to go on a toboggan: *They tobogganed down the hill*; *We went tobogganing.*

today [tə'dei] *nc* (*usu in sing*), *adv* **1** (on) this day: *Today is Friday*; *Here is today's newspaper*; *Do you think she will arrive today?*; *I'm working today.* **2** (at) the present time: *the people of today*; *Life is easier today than a hundred years ago.*

toddle ['todl] *vi* (*esp* of a very young child) to walk unsteadily: *The child toddled into the garden.*

'toddler *nc* a very young child (who has just begun to be able to walk): *She has a young baby and a toddler.*

toddy ['todi] *ncu* a drink made of spirits, sugar, hot water *etc*: *Let's have a (glass of) toddy!*; *He had a hot toddy to cure his cold.*

to-do [tə'du:] *nc* (*inf*) a fuss; a commotion: *What a to-do!*; *She made a dreadful to-do about missing the train.*

toe [tou] *nc* **1** one of the five finger-like end parts of the foot: *A child should have straight toes*; *These tight shoes hurt my toes.* **2** the front part of a shoe, sock *etc*: *There's a hole in the toe of my sock.*

-toed (*in cmpds*) having (a certain kind or number of) toe(s): *a ˌthree-toed 'sloth.*

'toe-cap *nc* a piece that covers the toe of a boot or shoe: *His boots had metal toe-caps.*

'toe-hold *nc* a place for one's foot (when climbing something): *He got a toe-hold in the rock*; (*fig formal*) *He had a toe-hold in the business.*

'toenail *nc* the nail that grows on one's toes: *He was cutting his toenails.*

be on one's toes (*fig inf*) to be ready; to be prepared for action: *We are all on our toes and just waiting for the order to start.*

from top to toe *see* **top**.

toe the line (*fig inf*) to act according to the rules: *He isn't allowed to do as he likes in that firm – they make him toe the line.*

toffee ['tofi] *ncu* (a piece of) a kind of sticky sweet made of sugar and butter: *Have a (piece of) toffee.*

toga ['tougə] *nc* (*hist*) the loose outer garment worn by a citizen of ancient Rome.

together [tə'geðə] *adv* **1** with someone or something else; in company: *They travelled together*; *The houses stood together.* **2** at the same time: *They all arrived together.* **3** so as to be joined or united: *He nailed/fitted/stuck the pieces of wood together*; *Families always get together at a wedding.* **4** by action with one or more other people: *Together we persuaded him.* – *See also* **together with** *below.*

to'getherness *nu* (*often facet*) the state of being close together: *Their evenings round the fire gave them a feeling of togetherness.*

for hours, days *etc* **together** for hour after hour, day after day *etc*, without a break: *As a sailor, he is away from home for months together.*

to'gether with in company with: in addition to: *My knowledge, together with his money, should be very useful.*

toggle ['togl] *nc* a small piece of wood held by a loop of string, used as a button: *Her coat was fastened with toggles.*

togs [togz] *n pl* (*inf*) clothes: *She was wearing new* *togs*; *Remember to bring your swimming togs!*

(all) togged up (*inf*) carefully dressed; dressed up: *She was (all) togged up in a leather outfit.*

toil [toil] *vi* (*formal*) **1** (*often with* **at**) to work hard and long: *He toiled all day in the fields*; *She was toiling at her work.* **2** to move with great difficulty: *He toiled along the road with all his luggage.* – *nu* hard work: *He slept well after his hours of toil.*

'toilworn *adj* (*liter*) wearied by hard work: *her toilworn face*; *She is old and toilworn.*

in the toils of *see* **toils**.

toilet ['toilit] **1** *nc* (a room containing) a receptacle for the body's waste matter, *usu* with a supply of water for washing this away; a lavatory: *Do you want to go to the toilet?*; *Where is the ladies' toilet?*; *Have you cleaned the toilet?*; (*attrib*) *toilet cleaner*; (*attrib*) *a toilet-seat.* **2** *nu* (*old*) the process of washing and dressing oneself, arranging one's hair, make-up *etc*: *She spent an hour on her toilet.*

'toilet-paper *nu* paper for use in a toilet (*def 1*).

'toilet-roll *nc* a roll of toilet-paper.

'toilet-water *nu* a type of perfumed liquid for the skin.

toils [toilz]: **in the 'toils of** in the snare or trap of: *He was caught in the toils of the law.*

toilworn *see* **toil**.

token ['toukən] *nc* **1** a mark or sign: *Wear this ring, as a token of our friendship*; (*attrib*) *They called a one-day token* (= symbolizing their attitude, intentions *etc*) *strike in protest against their colleague's dismissal.* **2** a card or piece of metal, plastic *etc*, for use instead of money: *The shopkeeper will exchange these tokens for goods to the value of £5*; *a book-token* (= a voucher that can be used to buy a book).

by the same token (*formal*) also; in addition: *By the same token, we should like to thank your wife.*

in 'token of (*formal*) as a token of: *Please accept this gift in token of our gratitude.*

told *see* **tell**.

tolerate ['toləreit] *vt* (*more formal than* **put up with**) to bear or endure; to put up with: *I couldn't tolerate his rudeness*; *How can you tolerate that conceited girl?*; *I won't tolerate that kind of behaviour.*

'tolerable *adj* (*formal*) **1** able to be borne or endured: *The heat was barely tolerable*; *scarcely tolerable living conditions.* **2** (*sometimes facet*) quite good: *The food was tolerable*; *There are few tolerable hotels here.* **'tolerableness** *nu.*

'tolerably *adv* (*formal or old*): *He's tolerably* (= fairly) *well*; *She's tolerably good-looking.*

'tolerance *nu* **1** the ability to be fair and understanding to people whose ways, opinions *etc* are different from one's own: *We should always try to show tolerance to other people*; *racial/religious tolerance.* **2** (*usu with* **a**) the ability to resist the effects of *eg* a drug, hardship *etc*: *If you take a drug regularly, your body gradually acquires a tolerance of it.*

'tolerant *adj* showing tolerance: *I'm a tolerant person on the whole*; *He's very tolerant towards his neighbours.* **'tolerantly** *adv.*

ˌtole'ration *nu* **1** the act of tolerating: *His toleration of her behaviour amazed me.* **2** tolerance, *esp* in religious matters: *The government passed a law of religious toleration.*

See also **intolerable**.

toll[1] [toul] *vti* to ring (a bell) slowly, as for a funeral: *The church bell tolled solemnly*; *It is the sexton's job to toll the bell.*

toll[2] [toul] *nc* **1** a tax charged for crossing a bridge, driving on certain roads *etc*: *All cars pay a toll of fifteen pence*; (*attrib*) *a toll bridge.* **2** (*formal*) an amount of loss or damage suffered, *eg* as a result of disaster: *Every year there is a heavy toll of human lives on the roads*; *The storm took its toll* (= caused a lot of damage).

Tom [tom]: **any/every Tom, Dick or/and Harry** [dik, 'hari] anybody at all: *But you can't go on holiday with any Tom, Dick or Harry you happen to meet!*

tomahawk ['toməho:k] *nc* (*hist*) a kind of small axe once used as a weapon by the North American Indians.

tomato [tə'ma:tou, (*Amer*) -'mei-] – *pl* **to'matoes** – *nc* **1** (*often attrib*) a type of fleshy, juicy fruit, *usu* red, used in salads, sauces *etc*: *We had a salad of lettuce, tomatoes and cucumbers*; *tomato purée/sauce.* **2** the plant which bears these.

tomb [tu:m] *nc* a hole or vault in the ground in which a dead body is put; (*loosely*) a grave: *He was buried in the family tomb.*

'tombstone *nc* an ornamental stone placed over a grave on which the dead person's name *etc* is engraved.

tombola [tom'boulə] *nc* a kind of lottery with money or prizes to be won: *We had a tombola at the church fête*; (*attrib*) *a tombola stall.*

tomboy ['tomboi] *nc* (*inf*) a girl who likes rough games and activities: *She's a real tomboy!*

tomcat ['tomkat] *nc* a male cat.

tome [toum] *nc* (*formal or facet*) a large, heavy and *usu* learned book: *She wrote a tome about Roman religion.*

tomfool [tom'fu:l] *nc* (*usu attrib*: *inf*) an absolute fool: *That tomfool of a chairman!*; *his tomfool behaviour.*

ˌtom'foolery *nu* (*inf*) stupidity: *Stop this tomfoolery at once!*

tommygun ['tomigʌn] *nc* (*inf*) a submachine gun.

tommyrot [tomi'rot, (*Amer*) 'tomirot] *nu* (*inf derog*) nonsense: *That's all tommyrot!*

tomorrow [tə'morou] *nc* (*usu in sing*), *adv* **1** (on) the day after today: *Tomorrow is Saturday*; *The news will be in tomorrow's newspaper*; *I'm going away tomorrow.* **2** (*liter*) (in) the future: *tomorrow's world*; *Tomorrow we die.*

tom-tom ['tomtom] *nc* a kind of (African or North American Indian) drum *usu* beaten with the hands.

ton [tʌn] *nc* **1** a unit of weight, (*Brit*) 2240 lb, (*Amer*) 2000 lb; a **metric ton** (*also* **tonne** [tʌn]) is 2204·6 lb (1000 kilogrammes): *It weighs a ton and a half*; *a three-ton weight.* **2** a unit of space in a ship (100 cubic feet). **3** (*inf*) a speed of 100 miles per hour: *He did a/the ton on his motorbike.*

'tonnage [-nidʒ] *nu* the space available in a ship, measured in tons (*def 2*).

-tonner (*in cmpds*) a ship, or lorry that can carry (a certain number of) tons: *a ˌten-'tonner*; *a ˌtwenty-thousand-'tonner.*

tons *n pl* (*inf*) a lot: *I've got tons of letters to write.*

tonal *see* **tone**.

tone [toun] **1** *ncu* (the quality of) a sound, *esp* a voice: *He spoke in a low/angry/gentle tone*; *He told me about it in tones of disapproval*; *a tone of command*; *a quiet tone of voice*; *I heard the sweet tones of a clarinet*; *That singer/violin/piano has very good tone*; (*fig*) *The general tone of the meeting was friendly.* **2** *nc* (*more formal than* **shade**) a shade of colour: *various tones of green.* **3** *nu* firmness of body or muscle: *Your muscles lack tone – you need exercise.* **4** *nc* (*music*) one of the larger intervals in an octave *eg* between C and D. – *vi* (*sometimes with* **in**) to fit in well; to blend: *The brown carpet tones (in) well with the curtains.*

'tonal *adj* (*music*) of tones.

'toneless *adj* without tone (*def 1*); with no variation in sound, expression *etc*: *She spoke in a toneless voice*; *Her voice is rather toneless.*

'tonelessly *adv.*

ˌtone-'deaf *adj* unable to distinguish between musical sounds: *She can't sing – she's tone-deaf.*

tone down *vi, vt sep* to make or become softer, less harsh *etc*: *The bright colour of the bricks will soon tone down*; *He toned down some of his criticisms.*

tone up *vt sep* to give strength to; to put in good condition: *The exercise toned up his muscles.*

See also **intonation**.

tongs [toŋz] *n pl* (*often in cmpds*) an instrument for holding and lifting objects: *sugar-tongs*; *coal-tongs*; *a pair of tongs.*

tongue [tʌŋ] **1** *nc* the fleshy organ inside the mouth, used in tasting, swallowing, speaking *etc*: *The doctor looked at her tongue.* **2** *ncu* (*sometimes in cmpds*) the tongue of an animal used as food: *How do you cook an ox-tongue?*; *a slice of tongue.* **3** *nc* (*formal*) something with the same shape as a tongue: *A tongue of land stuck out into the sea*; *a tongue of flame.* **4** *nc* (*formal*) a language: *English is his mother-tongue/native tongue*; *a foreign tongue.*

'tongue-tied *adj* finding it difficult to speak because of shyness, embarrassment *etc*: *The child stood, tongue-tied, in front of the teacher*; *a shy, tongue-tied little girl.*

'tongue-twister *nc* a phrase or sentence that is difficult to say quickly: *She sells sea shells.*

hold one's tongue *see* **hold**.

put/stick one's tongue out (at someone) to stick one's tongue out of one's mouth towards someone, as a sign of contempt: *Don't be so rude – you musn't stick out your tongue at people!*

speak *etc* **with/have one's tongue in one's cheek** to say something that one does not intend literally or seriously: *He said it with his tongue in his cheek.*

tonic ['tonik] **1** *ncu* (a) medicine that gives strength or energy: *The doctor prescribed a (bottle of) tonic*; (*fig*) *The sea-air was a tonic.* **2** *nu* (*also* **'tonic-water**) water containing quinine, often drunk with gin *etc*: *I'd like a gin and tonic.* **3** *nc* (*music*) the keynote of a scale. – *adj* of tones or sounds: *tonic sol-fa* (= a system of writing down music).

tonight [tə'nait] *nc* (*usu in sing*), *adv* (on) the night of this present day: *Here is tonight's weather forecast*; *I'm going home early tonight*; *Will she arrive tonight?*

tonnage, tonne *see* **ton**.

tonsil ['tonsil] *nc* (*usu in pl*) either of two lumps of tissue at the back of the throat: *He had to have his tonsils (taken) out.*

ˌtonsil'litis [tonsi'laitis] *nu* painful inflammation of the tonsils: *She had/was suffering from tonsillitis.*

tonsure ['tonʃə] **1** *nc* the part of a monk's head that has been shaved: *He had a tonsure.* **2** *nu* the shaving of the top part of a monk's head.

too [tu:] *adv* **1** to a greater extent, or more, than is required, desirable or suitable: *The children are being too noisy*; *He has too much money*; *She arrives late far too often*; *He's too fat for his clothes*; *It's much too cold to play outside*; (*inf*) *I'm not feeling too well* (= I'm feeling rather ill). **2** in addition; also; as well: *My husband likes cycling, and I do, too* (= so do I); (*formal*) *I too* (= as well as he) *like cycling*; *I enjoy swimming and I like cycling too* (= as well as swimming). **3** (*loosely*) moreover; what is more: *She wants a fur coat, and her husband is buying her one, too!*

took *see* **take**.

tool [tu:l] *nc* **1** an instrument for doing work, *esp* by hand: *hammers, saws and other tools*; *garden tools* (= spade, fork *etc*); *the tools of his trade*; (*fig*) *Advertising is a powerful tool.* **2** (*formal*) a person used by another for selfish or dishonest reasons: *He was a tool (in the hands) of the secret police.*

tooled *adj* (*tech*: *esp attrib*) (*esp* of leather) marked with designs made by a heated tool: *tooled leather bookbindings.*

toot [tu:t] *nc* (*inf*) a quick blast of a trumpet or other wind instrument, or of a motor-horn. – *vti* (*inf*) to blow or sound a horn *etc*: *He tooted (on) the horn.*

tooth [tu:θ] – *pl* **teeth** [ti:θ] – *nc* **1** any of the hard, bone-like objects that grow in the mouth and are used for biting and chewing: *He has had a tooth out at the dentist's.* **2** something that looks or acts like a tooth: *the teeth of a comb/saw/cogwheel.* – *See also* **tooth** *in phrases below.*

teethe [ti:ð] *vi* (of a baby) to grow one's first teeth: *He cries a lot because he's teething.*

toothed *adj* (*usu attrib*) having teeth: *a toothed wheel.*

'toothless *adj* without teeth: *a toothless old woman*; *He's old and toothless now.*

'toothy *adj* showing a lot of teeth: *a toothy grin*; *She looks toothy in that photograph.*

'toothache *nu* (*sometimes with* **a**) a pain in a tooth: *He has/is suffering from toothache.*

'toothbrush *nc* a brush for cleaning the teeth.

'toothpaste *nu* a kind of paste used to clean the teeth: *a tube of toothpaste.*

'toothpick *nc* a small sharp piece of wood, plastic *etc* for picking out food *etc* from between the teeth.

'toothpowder *nu* a kind of powder used to clean the teeth.

be, get *etc* **long in the tooth** (*inf sometimes derog*) (of a person or animal) to be, become *etc*, old: *I'm getting a bit long in the tooth to climb mountains*; *He's a bit long in the tooth to think of marrying again.*

a fine-tooth comb a comb with the teeth set close together, for removing lice, dirt *etc* from hair *etc*: *You'll need a fine-tooth comb for your dog's fur*; (*fig*) *She went through her cupboards with a fine-tooth comb* (= She searched her cupboards very thoroughly) *but couldn't find the letter.*

in the 'teeth of (*formal*) against; in opposition to: *They were walking in the teeth of a gale*; *in the teeth of opposition.*

set one's teeth on edge *see* **edge**.

show one's teeth to show one's anger and power to resist; to act decisively *etc*: *The government soon showed its teeth to the rebels.*

a sweet tooth (*inf*) a liking for sweet food: *My friend has a sweet tooth.*

tooth and nail fiercely and with all one's strength: *They fought tooth and nail.*

top[1] [top] (*often in cmpds*) **1** *ncu* the highest part of anything: *the top of the hill*; *The mountain-tops are covered with snow*; *the top of her head*; (*attrib*) *The book is on the top shelf*; (*attrib*) *He got top* (= higher than anyone else) *marks in the exam*;

(*attrib*) *Were you driving the car in top gear?*; *He had reached the top* (= the most senior position) *of his profession.* **2** *nc* (the person in) the position of the cleverest in a class *etc*: *He's* (*at*) *the top of the class*; *She's top in French.* **3** *nc* the upper surface: *the table-top.* **4** *nc* a lid: *I've lost the top to this jar*; *a bottle-top.* **5** *nc* (*inf*) a (woman's) garment for the upper half of the body; a blouse, sweater *etc*: *I bought a new skirt and top.* – *v* – *pt, ptp* **topped** – *vt* **1** to cover on the top: *She topped the cake with cream.* **2** to rise above; to surpass: *Our exports have topped £100 000.* **3** to remove the top of: *She topped and tailed the gooseberries.* – See also **top up** *below.*

'topless *adj* **1** having no top. **2** (*liter*) very high: *topless towers.* **3** (of a dress, or woman wearing such a dress) leaving the breasts exposed: *a topless evening dress*; *topless waitresses*; *She was completely topless.*

'topmost *adj* (*often liter*) the very highest: *the topmost peak of the Alps.*

'topping *ncu* something that forms a covering on top of something, *esp* food: *Whipped egg and milk make* (*an*) *excellent topping for fruit*; *a tart with a topping of cream.*

'topcoat *nc* an overcoat.

top hat *nc* (*inf abbrev* **topper** ['topə]) a man's tall hat, worn as formal dress.

ˌtop-'heavy *adj* having the upper part too heavy for the lower: *That pile of books is top-heavy – it'll fall over!*; *That looks a bit top-heavy.*

'top-knot *nc* a knot of hair worn on top of the head: *She wore her hair in a top-knot.*

ˌtop-'secret *adj* very secret: *top-secret information*; *This information is top-secret.*

at the top of one's voice very loudly: *They were shouting at the top(s) of their voices.*

be/feel *etc* **on top of the world** to feel very well and happy: *She's on top of the world – she's just got engaged to be married.*

be top dog (*inf*) to be the most important or powerful person: *He always likes to be top dog in any group.*

the big top the large tent in which a circus performs.

blow one's top *see* **blow**[2].

from top to bottom completely: *They've painted the house from top to bottom.*

from top to toe completely; from head to foot: *She was dressed in green from top to toe.*

on 'top (of) above: *He put his clothes in the wardrobe and his suitcase on top*; *He put his books on top of hers*; (*fig*) *He arrived home late and on top of* (= in addition to) *that, he was very rude.*

top gear *see* **gear**.

the top of the ladder/tree (*fig inf*) the highest point in one's profession: *He has reached the top of the ladder/tree.*

top up *vt sep* to fill (a cup *etc* that has been partly emptied) to the top: *Let me top up your glass/drink*; *I'm going to top up the petrol tank*; *Will you top it up?*

top[2] [top] *nc* a kind of toy that spins.

sleep like a top to sleep very well: *The child slept like a top after a day on the beach.*

topaz ['toupaz] *ncu* a kind of precious stone, of various colours: *Her necklace was a topaz set in silver*; (*attrib*) *a topaz ring.*

topcoat *see* **top**[1].

topi, topee ['toupi, (*Amer*) tou'pi:] *nc* a helmet-like hat worn in hot countries as protection against the sun: *He wore a topi on his journey through the tropical jungle.*

topiary ['toupiəri] *nu* the art of cutting trees, bushes and hedges into ornamental shapes: *He tried to cut the bush in the shape of a swan but he was not very successful at topiary.*

topic ['topik] *nc* (*more formal than* **subject**) something spoken or written about; a subject: *various topics of conversation*; *They discussed the weather and other topics.*

'topical *adj* of interest at the present time: *The themes of Shakespeare's plays seem topical even today*; *a topical subject.* **'topically** *adv.*

topless, topmost *see* **top**[1].

topography [tə'pogrəfi] *nu* (*tech*) (the description of) the features or nature of the land in a particular area: *He studied the topography of the town and its surroundings.* **ˌtopo'graphical** [topə'gra-] *adj.* **ˌtopo'graphically** [topə'gra-] *adv.*

topper short for **top hat**.

topping *see* **top**[1].

topple ['topl] *vti* (*often with* **over**) to (make something) fall: *The trees slowly toppled to the ground*; *He toppled the pile of books*; *The child toppled over*; *That strike finally toppled the government.*

topsyturv(e)y [topsi'tə:vi] *adj, adv* (*inf*) upside down; in confusion: *It's a topsy-turvy world!*; *Everything was turned topsyturvy.*

torch [to:tʃ] *nc* **1** (*Amer* **'flashlight**) a small portable light worked by an electric battery: *He shone his torch into her face.* **2** (*hist*) a piece of wood *etc* set on fire and carried as a light.

'torchlight *nu* (*usu attrib*) the light of a torch or torches: *a torchlight procession.*

tore *see* **tear**[2].

toreador ['toriədo:] *nc* a bull-fighter, *esp* one on horseback.

torment ['to:ment] (*formal*) **1** *ncu* (a) very great pain, suffering, worry *etc*: *He was in torment*; *the torments of the prisoners.* **2** *nc* something that causes this: *Her shyness was a torment to her.* – [to:'ment] *vt* to cause pain, suffering, worry *etc* to: *She was tormented with worry/toothache*; *The children tormented her*; (*inf*) *Don't torment the child!*

tor'mentor [-'men-] *nc* a person who torments.

torn *see* **tear**[2].

tornado [to:'neidou] – *pl* **tor'nadoes** – *nc* a violent whirlwind that can cause great damage: *The village was destroyed by a tornado.*

torpedo [to:'pi:dou] – *pl* **tor'pedoes** – *nc* a long, cylindrical type of missile fired at ships *eg* from submarines or aircraft, that travels through the sea towards its target: *an enemy torpedo.* – *v* – *3rd pers sing prt* **tor'pedoes**: *pt, ptp* **tor'pedoed** – *vt* to attack, damage or destroy with torpedoes: *The ship was torpedoed.*

torpid ['to:pid] *adj* (*formal*) slow and dull; lacking energy: *Everybody felt torpid in the heat of the sun*; *in a torpid state.* **'torpidly** *adv.*

'torpor [-pə], **tor'pidity** *nus.*

torrent ['torənt] *nc* a rushing stream: *A torrent of water/lava poured down the mountain*; *The rain fell in torrents*; (*fig*) *She attacked him with a torrent of abuse.*

torrential [tə'renʃəl] *adj* of, or like, a torrent: *torrential rain*; *The rain was torrential.*

torrid ['torid] *adj* **1** (*formal or tech*) (of weather or land) very hot: *the torrid zone* (= the area of the world on either side of the equator); *It is dry and* *torrid in that part of the world.* **2** (*formal or facet*) passionate: *a torrid love affair.*

torsion ['to:ʃən] *nu* (*formal or tech*) the act of twisting or state of being twisted: *The metal was tested under torsion.*

torso ['to:sou] – *pl* **'torsos** – *nc* the body, excluding the head and limbs: *He had a strong torso.*

tortoise ['to:təs] *nc* a kind of four-footed, slow-moving reptile covered with a hard shell.

'tortoiseshell 1 *nu, adj* (of) the brown and yellow mottled shell of a kind of sea turtle, used in making combs and other articles: *A hairbrush backed with tortoiseshell; a tortoiseshell comb.* **2** *adj* of the colour of this shell: *a tortoiseshell cat.*

tortuous ['to:tʃuəs] *adj* (*formal*) full of twists; roundabout; not straightforward: *tortuous paths; The mountain road is steep and tortuous;* (*fig*) *tortuous methods.*

torture ['to:tʃə] *vt* to treat (someone) cruelly or painfully, as a punishment, or in order to make him/her confess something, give information *etc*: *He tortured his prisoners;* (*fig*) *She was tortured by rheumatism/jealousy.* – **1** *nu* the act or practice of torturing: *The king would not permit torture.* **2** *ncu* (something causing) great suffering: *They had to undergo terrible tortures in the prisoner-of-war camp; the torture of waiting to be executed.*

Tory ['to:ri] *nc, adj* (a member or supporter) of the Conservative party: *He's a Tory; a Tory government.*

toss [tos] **1** *vt* to throw into or through the air: *He was tossed by an angry bull; She tossed the ball up into the air; The children tossed a ball about;* (*inf*) *He tossed the book on to the desk.* **2** *vt* to jerk (the head), indicating impatience *etc*: *The horse tossed his head.* **3** *vi* (*often with* **about**) to throw oneself restlessly from side to side: *She tossed about all night, unable to sleep.* **4** *vi* (of a ship) to be thrown about: *The boat tossed wildly in the rough sea.* **5** *vti* to throw (a coin) into the air and decide a matter according to (a correct guess about) which side falls uppermost: *They tossed a coin to decide which of them should go first; We'll toss for the first ride on the new bicycle; I'll toss you* (= with you) *for it!* – *See also* **toss up** *below.* – *nc* an act of tossing: *'Go away!' she said with a toss of her head; The decision depends on the toss of a coin.* – *See also* **win/lose the toss** *below.*

argue the toss (*inf*) to dispute a decision: *I won't argue the toss with you.*

it's a toss-up (whether) (*inf*) it is a matter of uncertainty (whether): *It's a toss-up whether we shall get there in time.* – *See also* **toss up** *below.*

toss off *vt sep* (*inf*) **1** to drink quickly: *He tossed off a pint of beer.* **2** to produce quickly and easily: *He tossed off a few verses of poetry.*

toss up *vi* (*inf*) to toss a coin to decide a matter: *We tossed up (to decide) whether to go to the play or the ballet.* – *See also* **it's a toss-up** *above.*

win/lose the toss guess rightly or wrongly which side of the coin will fall uppermost: *He won the toss so he started the game of cards first.*

tot[1] [tot] *nc* (*inf*) **1** a small child: *a tiny tot.* **2** a small amount of alcoholic drink: *a tot of whisky.*

tot[2] [tot] – *pt, ptp* **'totted** – **tot up** *vt sep* (*inf*) to add up: *He totted up the figures on the bill; Could you tot up the cost of the meal and let me know how much I owe you?; If you write down the figures I'll tot them up.*

total ['toutəl] *adj* (*usu attrib*) whole; complete: *What is the total cost of the holiday?; The car was a total wreck.* – *nc* the whole amount *ie* of various sums added together: *The total came to/was £10.* – *v* – *pt, ptp* **'totalled** – *vt* to add up or amount to: *The doctor's fees totalled £20.* – *See also* **total up** *below.*

to'tality [-'ta-] *nu* (*formal*) completeness: *The problem must be studied in its totality.*

totalitarian [toutali'teəriən] *adj* (*formal or tech*) of a system or government by a single party which allows no rivals: *a totalitarian government.*

'totalizator, -s- [-laizeitə] *inf abbrev* **tote** [tout]) *nc* (*very formal*) a machine that calculates the amount of money to be paid to people who bet on winning race-horses.

'totally *adv* completely: *I was totally unaware of his presence; She has totally changed her appearance.*

total up *vi, vt sep* to add up (to): *He totalled up (the amount he had sold) at the end of the week.*

tote[1] *see* **total**.

tote[2] [tout] *vt* (*inf*: *often with* **about, around** *etc*) to carry: *He was toting a pile of books about with him; I don't want to tote this heavy bag around all day.*

totem ['toutəm] *nc* (an image of) an animal or plant used as the badge or sign of a tribe, among North American Indians *etc.*

'totem pole *nc* a large wooden pole on which totems are carved and painted.

totter ['totə] *vi* to move unsteadily as if about to fall: *The building tottered and collapsed; He tottered down the road;* (*fig*) *The empire was tottering.*

'tottery *adj* (*inf*) shaky; unsteady: *That wardrobe looks a bit tottery; a tottery old lady.*

touch [tʌtʃ] **1** *vti* to be in, come into, or make, contact with something else: *The branch was so long that it touched the window; Their shoulders touched; He touched the water with his foot; Can you touch your nose with your tongue?* **2** *vti* to feel (lightly) with the hand: *He touched her cheek; Somebody touched me on the arm; You mustn't touch!* **3** *vt* to affect the feelings of; to make (someone) feel pity, sympathy *etc*: *His story touched them; I was touched by her generosity.* **4** *vt* (*liter*) to mark slightly with colour; to tinge: *The sky was touched with pink.* **5** *vt* (*usu in negative*: *inf*) to be concerned with; to have anything to do with: *I wouldn't touch a job like that.* **6** *vt* (*usu in neg*: *inf*) to be as good as; to reach the same standard as: *There's no-one to touch him at chess.* – *See also* **touch** *in phrases below.* – **1** *nc* an act or sensation of touching: *I felt a touch on my shoulder; The controls of the machine operate at a touch* (= very easily, without pressure). **2** *nu* (*often with* **the**) one of the five senses, the sense by which we feel things: *the sense of touch; The stone felt cold to the touch.* **3** *nc* (*usu fig*) a mark or stroke made with a paintbrush *etc* to improve the appearance of something: *The painting still needs a few finishing touches; She put a vase of flowers on the table and added other elegant touches to the room.* **4** *ncu* artistic skill or style: *That pianist has (a) marvellous touch; He hasn't lost his touch as a writer.* **5** *nu* (in football) the ground outside the edges of the pitch (which are marked out with **'touchlines**): *He kicked the ball into touch.* – *See also* **in touch with, out of touch with** *below.*

touched *adj* (*inf*: *pred*) slightly mad: *He's a bit touched.*

'touching *adj* moving; causing emotion: *a touch-*

ing story; *His concern for his mother is most touching.* – *prep* (*old*) concerning: *Touching our conversation of yesterday, I may be able to lend you the money.*

'touchingly *adv* in a moving way, so as to cause emotion: *Her face was touchingly childlike.*

'touchy *adj* (*inf*) easily annoyed or offended: *You're very touchy today*; *in rather a touchy mood.* **'touchily** *adv.* **'touchiness** *nu.*

touch-down *see* **touch down** *below.*

'touchstone *nc* (*formal fig*) a test or standard of the quality of something: *His loyalty was the touchstone by which we measured others!*

in 'touch (with) in communication (with); able to talk to: *I have kept in touch with my school-friends*; *I'll get in touch with you again about this matter*; *Good-bye! We'll be in touch!*

lose touch (with) to stop communicating (with): *If you don't write regularly, you will soon lose touch with him*; *I used to see him quite often but we have lost touch.*

out of touch (with) 1 not in communication (with): *We have been out of touch for years.* **2** not sympathetic or understanding (towards): *Older people sometimes seem out of touch with the modern world.*

a touch (*inf*) a small quantity or degree: *The soup needs a touch of salt*; *a touch of imagination*; *He's a touch nervous today.*

,touch-and-'go: it's touch-and-go (whether) it's very uncertain (whether): *It was touch-and-go whether he would survive the operation.*

touch down *vi* **1** (of aircraft) to land: *The plane should touch down at 2 o'clock.* **2** in rugby football, to put the ball on the ground behind the opposite team's goal line (*nc* **'touch-down**).

touch (someone) for (something) (*inf*) to persuade (a person) to lend (money): *I touched him for £5.*

touch off *vt sep* to make (something) explode: *a spark touched off the gunpowder*; (*fig*) *His remark touched off an argument.*

'touch on *vt fus* to speak of (a subject) casually; to mention: *He spoke about social conditions, touching on housing and education.*

touch up *vt sep* to improve *eg* paintwork, a photograph *etc* by small touches (*n def 3*): *He took a brush and touched up the paintwork*; *The photograph had been touched up.*

touch wood (*used as an interjection*) to touch something made of wood superstitiously, in order to avoid bad luck: *None of the children has ever had a serious illness, touch wood!*

tough [tʌf] *adj* **1** strong; not easily broken, worn out *etc*: *Plastic is a tough material*; *These shoes aren't tough enough for my son.* **2** (*derog*) (of food *etc*) difficult to chew: *This meat is very tough*; *a tough piece of beef.* **3** (of people) strong; able to bear hardship, illness *etc*: *She's a tough old lady*; *She must be tough to have survived such a serious illness.* **4** (*inf derog*) rough and violent: *There are some really tough children in this street*; *It's a tough neighbourhood*; *He's too tough for you to play with.* **5** difficult to deal with or overcome: *a tough problem*; *tough opposition*; *The competition was really tough.* – *See also* **get tough with** *below.* – *nc* (*inf*) a rough, violent person; a bully: *a crowd of toughs.*

'toughness *nu.*

'toughen *vti* (*sometimes with* **up**) to make or become tough (*defs 1 and 3*): *The steel was toughened by a special process*; *A year in the army will toughen him up.*

tough customer *nc* (*inf*) a person who is difficult to deal with: *I couldn't persuade him – he's a real tough customer.*

tough luck *nu, interj* bad luck: *That was tough luck*; *Tough luck!*

get 'tough with (someone) (*inf*) to deal forcefully with or refuse to yield to (a person): *When he started to argue, I got tough with him.*

toupee ['tu:pei, (*Amer*) tu:'pei] *nc* a small wig or piece of false hair, *usu* for men, worn to cover a bald patch: *Does he wear a toupee?*

tour [tuə] *nc* **1** a journey to several places and back: *They went on a tour of Italy*; *a bus/cycle tour to Australia.* **2** a visit around a particular place: *He took us on a tour of the house and gardens.* **3** (*formal*) an official period of time of work *usu* abroad: *He did a tour of duty in Fiji.* – *vti* to go on a tour (around): *We spent our holidays touring* (*Britain*); *They are touring in France.*

'tourism *nu* the industry dealing with tourists *ie* hotels, catering *etc*: *Tourism is an important part of our economy*; *This island's main industry is tourism.*

'tourist *nc* (*often attrib*) a person who travels for pleasure: *London is usually full of tourists*; (*attrib*) *the tourist industry*; (*attrib*) *The Tower of London is one of the city's chief tourist attractions.*

tour de force [tuədə'fo:s] *nc* (*formal*) something done with great skill, strength *etc*: *His performance on the violin was a real tour de force.*

tourism, tourist *see* **tour**.

tournament ['tuənəmənt] *nc* **1** a competition, *esp* in chess, tennis *etc*, in which many players compete in many separate games: *I'm playing in the next tennis tournament.* **2** (*hist*) a competition in which knights wearing armour fought on horseback: *King Arthur held a tournament.*

tourniquet ['tuənikei, (*Amer*) -kit] *nc* (*tech*) a bandage, or other device, tied very tightly round an injured arm or leg to prevent too much blood being lost: *He applied a tourniquet to her leg.*

tousle ['tauzl] *vt* (*esp* of hair) to make untidy; to tangle: *The wind tousled her hair.* **'tousled** *adj.*

tout [taut] *vti* (*inf*: *with* **for**) to go about in search of buyers, jobs, support, votes *etc*: *The taxi-driver drove around touting for custom*; *The political candidates visited the area to tout for votes*; *I had to tout my paintings about for months before I got any buyers.* – *nc* (*esp in cmpds*) **1** (*sometimes derog*) a person who touts: *a ticket-tout* (= a person who sells tickets for football matches *etc* at high prices). **2** a person who gives information to people who bet on horse-races: *a race-course tout.*

tow[1] [tou] *vt* to pull (a ship, barge, car, trailer *etc*) by a rope, chain or cable: *The tugboat towed the ship out of the harbour*; *The car broke down and had to be towed to the garage.* – *ncu* (an) act of towing or process of being towed: *Give us a tow!*; *They took the yacht in tow* (= fixed a rope *etc* to it and started to tow it); *A notice on the back of the vehicle read 'On Tow'* (= being towed); (*fig inf*: *often derog*) *He always has a girlfriend in tow* (= with him).

'towline/'tow-rope *ncs* a rope *etc* used in towing.

'towpath *nc* a path beside a canal along which the horses that used to tow barges walked.

tow[2] [tou] *nu* the coarse fibres of flax or hemp often used for making ropes.

towards, (*more formal*) **toward** [tə'wo:d(z), (*Amer*) to:rd(z)] *prep* **1** (moving, facing *etc*) in the direction of: *He walked toward the door*; *She* *turned towards him.* **2** in relation to: *What are your feelings towards him?*; *His attitude towards his son is very strange.* **3** as a contribution or help to: *Here's £1 towards the cost of the journey.* **4** (of time) near: *He'll arrive towards six o'clock*; *Towards night-time, the weather worsened.*

See also **untoward**.

towel ['tauəl] *nc* (*often in cmpds*) a piece of any of several types of absorbent cloth or paper for drying oneself, dishes *etc* after washing *etc*: *After her swim she dried herself with a towel*; *a roll of paper kitchen towels*; *Pass me a tea-towel and I'll dry the dishes*; *a bath-towel.* – *v* – *pt, ptp* **'towelled**, (*Amer*) **'toweled** – *vt* (*formal*) to rub with a towel: *He towelled his hair vigorously.*

'towelling *nu* a kind of rough cloth from which towels *etc* are made: *Her dressing-gown is made of towelling*; *bathroom curtains made of towelling*; (*attrib*) *a towelling dressing-gown.*

tower ['tauə] *nc* (*sometimes in cmpds*) a tall, narrow (part of a) building, *esp* (of) a castle: *You can see the tower of the castle from here*; *the Tower of London*; *a church-tower.* – *vi* (*formal or facet*) to rise high: *The mountain towered into the sky*; *She is so small that he towers above her* (= is much taller than her).

'towering *adj* (*attrib*) **1** (*formal or liter*) very high: *towering cliffs.* **2** (of rage, fury *etc*) very violent or angry: *He was in a towering rage.*

'tower-block *nc* a very high block of flats, offices *etc*: *They live in a tower-block.*

a tower of strength (*fig*) someone who is a great help or encouragement: *He was a tower of strength to me when my father died.*

towline *see* **tow**[1].

town [taun] **1** *nc* (*sometimes without* **a**) a group of houses, shops, schools *etc*, that is bigger than a village but smaller than a city: *We live in the Yorkshire town of Beverley*; *I'm going into town* (= to the main shopping area) *to buy a dress*; *He spends his weekends out of town* (= away from the city or town). **2** *nc* the people who live in such a group of houses *etc*: *The whole town turned out to greet the heroes.* **3** *nu* (*usu with* **the**) towns in general as opposed to the countryside: *Do you live in the country or the town?*

town centre *nc* the main shopping and business area of a town: *You can get a bus from the town centre.*

town clerk *nc* a secretary and legal advisor to a town.

town council *nc* **1** in England, a parish council or part of a district council, representing an area which has kept its historical title of 'town', the chairman of the council being called 'mayor': *He has been elected to the town council.* **2** (*formerly*) the governing body of a town. **town councillor** *nc.*

town crier *nc* (*hist*) a person whose job is to make public announcements in a town.

town hall *nc* the building in which the official business of a town is done.

town planning *nu* the planning of the future development of a town: *He works in town planning*; (*attrib*) *the town-planning department.*

'townsfolk, 'townspeople *n pl* the people living in a town.

'township *nc* in Africa, Australia *etc*, a *usu* rather small or primitive town.

'townsman – *fem* **'townswoman** – *nc* (*old*) a person who lives in a town.

go out on the town (*inf*) to have a good time eating, drinking, dancing *etc*: *Let's go out on the town tonight!*

go to town (*inf*) to do something very thoroughly or with great enthusiasm or expense: *He really went to town on (preparing) the meal.*

man about town *see* **man**.

towpath, tow-rope *see* **tow**[1].

toxic ['toksik] *adj* (*formal or tech*) poisonous: *toxic substances*; *This chemical is toxic.*

ˌtoxi'cology [-'kolədʒi] *nu* (*tech*) the study of poisons. **ˌtoxi'cologist** *nc.*

'toxin [-n] *nc* (*tech*) any of several poisonous substances that are produced naturally by plants, animals, bacteria *etc*: *the toxins in toadstools.*

toy [toi] *nc* (*often attrib*) an object made for a child to play with: *He got lots of toys for Christmas*; *a toy soldier.* – *adj* (*attrib*) (of a dog) of a very small variety of a particular breed: *They have a toy poodle/spaniel.* – *vi* (*with* **with**) to play with in an idle way: *He wasn't hungry and sat toying with his food*; *He toyed with* (= considered lightheartedly) *the idea of writing a book.*

trace [treis] *nc* **1** a mark or sign left by something: *There were traces of egg on the plate*; *Traces of the struggle could be seen on the ground*; *There's still no trace of the missing child*; *He has disappeared without (a) trace* (= completely). **2** a small amount: *Traces of poison were found in the cup*; *There was a trace of jealousy in her voice.* – *vt* **1** to follow or discover by means of clues, evidence *etc*: *The police have traced him to London*; *The source of the infection has not yet been traced*; *Several ancient Roman army camps have been traced with the help of air photographs*; *I can't trace* (= find) *that letter.* **2** to make a copy of (a picture *etc*) by putting transparent paper over it and drawing the outline *etc*: *I traced the map.*

'tracing *nc* a copy made by tracing (*def 2*): *I made a tracing of the diagram.*

'trace elements *n pl* (*tech*) elements that are needed in small quantities for the growing and developing of animal and plant life.

'tracing-paper *nu* thin transparent paper used for tracing (*def 2*).

trachea [trə'kiːə, (*Amer*) 'treikiə] *nc* (*tech*) the windpipe: *He is suffering from inflammation of the trachea.*

track [trak] *nc* (*sometimes in cmpds*) **1** a mark left, *esp* a footprint *etc*: *They followed the lion's tracks.* **2** a path or rough road: *a mountain track*; *a sheep-track* (= a pathway made by sheep walking on it). **3** (*also* **'racetrack**) a course on which runners, cyclists *etc* race: *They ran five times round the track*; *a running track*; (*attrib*) *the 100 metres sprint and other track events.* **4** a railway line: *The track went through a tunnel.* – *See also* **track** *in phrases below.* – *vt* to follow (*eg* an animal) by the marks, footprints *etc* that it has left: *They tracked the wolf to its lair.* – *See also* **track down** *below.*

'tracker dog *nc* a dog used to hunt criminals *etc*: *The police went after him with tracker dogs.*

'track-suit *nc* a warm suit worn by athletes *etc* when exercising, or before and after performing.

be on someone's track/be on the track of (someone or something) to be following, pursuing, or looking for (someone or something): *I'm on the track of a valuable painting*; *She was close on his tracks*; *The police are already on the track of the murderer.*

in one's tracks (*inf*) where one stands or is: *He stopped dead in his tracks.*

keep/lose track of (*inf*) (not) to keep oneself informed about (the progress or whereabouts of): *I find it difficult to keep track of my old friends; I've lost track of what is happening.*

make tracks (for) (*inf*) to depart, or set off (towards): *We ought to be making tracks (for home).*

off the beaten track (*inf*) (of a house *etc*) away from towns, roads, other houses *etc*: *We live a long way off the beaten track.*

a ˌone-track ˈmind (*inf*) a mind with only one, *usu* sexual, idea: *He's got a one-track mind – he's always thinking about women.*

track down *vt sep* to pursue or search for (someone or something) until it is caught or found: *I managed to track down an old copy of the book.*

tract [trakt] *nc* **1** (*formal*) a piece of land: *a tract of wooded country.* **2** (*tech*) a system formed by connected parts of the body: *the digestive tract.* **3** (*formal*) a short essay or booklet, *eg* on a religious subject: *a philosophical tract.*

traction [ˈtrakʃən] *nu* (*sometimes in cmpds*) the action of pulling or state of being pulled: *steam-traction; The doctors put her leg in traction* (= attached it to a system of weights *etc* to pull it into the correct position) *when she broke it;* (*attrib*) *a traction engine* (= a type of engine for pulling heavy loads).

tractor [ˈtraktə] *nc* a motor vehicle for pulling *esp* agricultural machinery: *I can drive a tractor.*

trad [trad] *nu* (*inf*) short for **traditional (jazz)**, the style of jazz music first played in the 1920s and 1930s.

trade [treid] **1** *nu* the buying and selling of goods: *Japan does a lot of trade with Britain; Trade between the two countries is declining;* (*attrib*) *Britain's trade figures* (= statistics of imports and exports) *for March were quite good.* **2** *ncu* (a) business, occupation, or job: *He is a carpenter by trade; His sons all followed different trades; He's in the jewellery trade.* – **1** *vi* (*often with* **in** *or* **with**) to buy and sell: *They made a lot of money by trading; They trade in fruit and vegetables; They don't often trade with China.* **2** *vt* (*inf*) to exchange: *They were persuaded to trade information (for money); I traded my watch for a bicycle.* – *See also* **trade in** *below.*

ˈtrader *nc* (*sometimes in cmpds*) a person who trades: *All the local traders complained to the town council about the increase in rates; a fur trader.*

ˈtrademark, ˈtradename *ncs* an officially registered mark or name belonging to a particular company, and not to be used by anyone else, that is put on all goods made by that company.

ˈtradesman [ˈtreidz-] *nc* **1** a shopkeeper. **2** a workman in a skilled job: *My husband cannot mend the television-set – I'll have to send for a tradesman.*

trade(s) union *nc* a group of workers of the same trade who join together to bargain with employers for fair wages, better working conditions *etc.* **trade(s) unionism** *nu.*

trade(s) unionist *nc* a member of a trade(s) union.

ˈtrade wind *nc* a wind that blows towards the equator (from the north-east and south-east).

ˈtrading-post *nc* a place, *usu* in an undeveloped country, where goods are traded: *After five days in the jungle we reached a trading-post.*

ˈtrading-stamp *nc* a stamp or ticket *etc* given to a customer when he buys something, and which can be exchanged later for money or goods.

trade in *vt sep* to give (something) as part-payment for something else: *We decided to trade in our old car and get a new one* (*nc* **ˈtrade-in**).

ˈtrade on *vt fus* (*derog*) to take *usu* unfair advantage of: *He traded on her kindness.*

tradition [trəˈdiʃən] **1** *nu* (the process of passing on from generation to generation) customs, beliefs, stories *etc*: *These songs have been preserved by tradition; According to tradition, the castle is haunted.* **2** *nc* a custom, belief, story *etc* that is passed on: *It is one of our family traditions for eldest sons to be called John.* **traˈditional** *adj.* **traˈditionally** *adv.*

traˈditionalism *nu* (*formal*) belief in the importance of, and liking for, tradition. **traˈditionalist** *nc.*

See also **trad**.

traffic [ˈtrafik] *nu* **1** (*often attrib and in cmpds*) vehicles, aircraft, ships *etc* moving about: *There's a lot of traffic on the roads/on the river; air-traffic; traffic problems.* **2** (*derog*) trade, *esp* illegal or dishonest: *the drug traffic; the traffic in stolen pictures.* – *v* – *pt, ptp* **ˈtrafficked** – *vi* (*derog with* **in**) to deal or trade in, *esp* illegally or dishonestly: *They were trafficking in smuggled goods.*

ˈtrafficker *nc* (*derog*) a *usu* illegal or dishonest dealer: *a trafficker in drugs.*

ˈtraffic island *nc* a small raised pavement in the middle of a road for pedestrians to stand on as they cross.

ˈtraffic lights *n pl* lights of changing colours for controlling traffic at road crossings *etc*: *Turn left at the traffic lights.*

ˈtraffic warden *nc* a person whose job is to control the parking of cars *etc* in towns: *You will have to pay a fine if the traffic warden sees that you have parked near a pedestrian crossing.*

tragedy [ˈtradʒədi] **1** *ncu* (a) drama about unfortunate events with a sad outcome: *'Hamlet' is one of Shakespeare's tragedies; Shakespeare wrote both tragedy and comedy.* **2** (*fig*) *nc* an unfortunate or sad event: *His early death was a great tragedy for his family.*

tragedian [trəˈdʒiːdiən] – *fem* **tragedienne** [trədʒiːdiˈen] – *nc* (*old*) an actor/actress of tragic roles.

ˈtragic *adj* **1** sad; unfortunate: *I heard of the tragic death of her son; The driver of the car made a tragic mistake.* **2** of tragedy or tragedies (*def 1*): *a tragic hero.*

trail [treil] **1** *vti* to drag, or be dragged, along loosely: *He trailed his fingers through the water; Garments were trailing from the suitcase; The bird trailed its broken wing; An aeroplane flew across the sky trailing white vapour.* **2** *vi* (*inf*) to walk slowly and *usu* wearily: *He trailed down the road; A few walkers were trailing behind the main group.* **3** *vt* to follow the track of: *The herd of reindeer was being trailed by a pack of wolves.* **4** *vi* (*formal*) (of a plant) to grow with a spreading or straggling action: *There is ivy trailing all over the wall.* – *nc* **1** a track (of an animal): *The trail was easy for the hunters to follow.* **2** a path through a forest or other wild area: *a mountain trail.* **3** a line, or series of marks, left by something as it passes: *There was a trail of blood across the floor;* (*fig*) *He left a trail of debts.*

ˈtrailer *nc* **1** a vehicle pulled behind a motor car:

We carry our luggage in a trailer. 2 (*Amer*) a caravan (*def 1*). 3 a short film advertising a complete film.

blaze a trail *see* **blaze**[2].

train[1] [trein] *nc* 1 a railway engine with its carriages and/or trucks: *I caught the train to London.* 2 a part of a long dress or robe that trails behind the wearer: *The bride wore a dress with a train.* 3 (*old*) the attendants who follow or accompany an important person: *He was in the Duke's train.* 4 a connected series: *I can't follow* (= understand) *your train of thought*; *Then began a train of events which ended in disaster.* 5 a line of animals carrying people or baggage: *a mule train*; *a baggage train.*

'train-bearer *nc* (*usu old*) a person who carries the train of someone's dress, robe *etc*: *The Queen had four train-bearers.*

train[2] [trein] 1 *vti* to prepare, be prepared, or prepare oneself, through instruction, practice, exercise *etc*, for a sport, job, profession *etc*: *I was trained as a teacher*; *He's training to be an electrician*; *You'll have to train hard before the next match*; *The race-horse was trained by my uncle*; *He trained the dog to come when he whistled*; *You've trained your children* (= taught them how to behave) *very well*; *These soldiers were trained for mountain warfare.* 2 *vt* to point or aim (a gun, telescope *etc*) in a particular direction: *He trained the gun on/at the soldiers.* 3 *vt* to make (a tree, plant *etc*) grow in a particular direction: *I am going to try to train this vine along the east wall of the garden.*

trained *adj* (*often in cmpds*: *neg* **un-**) having had teaching: *She's a trained nurse*; *She is trained to look after children*; *a well-trained dog.*

,trai'nee *nc* a person who is being trained (*def 1*): *He's a trainee with an industrial firm*; (*attrib*) *a trainee teacher.*

'trainer *nc* a person who prepares people or animals for sport, a race *etc*: *Our trainer makes us do a lot of practice*; *He's an animal trainer at the circus.*

'training *nu* 1 preparation for a sport: *He has gone into training* (= started to train) *for the race.* 2 the process of learning (the practical side of) a job: *It takes many years of training to be a doctor.*

traipse, trapse, trapes [treips] *vi* (*inf*) to walk along idly, wearily, or looking untidy: *I saw her traipsing along the street in a skirt that was too long for her*; *I'm tired of traipsing round the shops.*

trait [treit] *nc* (*formal*) a particular quality of a person's character: *Patience is one of his good traits.*

traitor ['treitə] – *fem* (*rare*) **'traitress** – *nc* 1 a person who changes to the enemy's side or gives away information to the enemy: *He was a traitor to his country.* 2 a person who betrays someone's trust: *Even my best friend proved a traitor.*

'traitorous *adj* (*formal*) of or like a traitor; treacherous: *his traitorous behaviour*; *I could not believe that he could be so traitorous.* **'traitorously** *adv.*

turn traitor to become a traitor.

trajectory [trə'dʒektəri] *nc* (*tech*) the curved path of something travelling through the air: *a bullet's trajectory.*

tram [tram] *nc* (*also* **'tramcar**: *Amer* **'streetcar**) a long car running on rails and *usu* driven by electric power, for carrying passengers *esp* along the streets of a town.

'tramline *nc* a rail, *usu* one of a pair, along which a tram travels.

'tramway *nc* a system of tracks for trams.

tramp [tramp] 1 *vi* to walk with heavy footsteps: *He tramped up the stairs.* 2 *vti* to walk *usu* for a long distance: *He tramped the streets looking for a place to stay*; *She loves tramping over the hills.* – 1 *nc* a person with no fixed home or job, who travels around on foot and *usu* lives by begging: *He gave his old coat to a tramp.* 2 *nc* a long walk *eg* in the country: *We went for a tramp over the hills.* 3 *nu* the sound of heavy footsteps: *We heard the tramp of soldiers.* 4 *nc* (*derog sl*) a prostitute or promiscuous woman: *He is a very nice man but he married a real tramp.* 5 *nc* (*also* **'tramp steamer**) a small cargo-boat with no fixed route.

trample ['trampl] *vti* to tread heavily (on): *The horses trampled the grass* (*underfoot*); *Cigarette ash had been trampled into the carpet*; (*fig*) *He trampled on her feelings* (= hurt her feelings badly).

trampoline ['trampəli:n] *nc* a horizontal framework across which a piece of canvas *etc* is stretched, attached by springs, for gymnasts *etc* to jump on: *Children love jumping on trampolines.*

tramway *see* **tram**.

trance [tra:ns] *nc* a sleep-like or half-conscious state: *The hypnotist put her into a trance*; *He sat staring in front of him as if in a trance.*

tranquil ['traŋkwil] *adj* (*formal*) quiet; peaceful: *a tranquil scene/state*; *Life in the country is not always tranquil.* **'tranquilly** *adv.* **tran'quillity** *nu.*

'tranquillizer, -s- *nc* a drug *esp* a pill to calm the nerves or cause sleep: *He took a tranquillizer.*

trans- [trans, tranz] (*in cmpds*) across or through, as in **transatlantic**.

transact [tran'sakt] *vt* (*formal*) to do or carry out (business): *I transacted some business in London.*

tran'saction [-ʃən] 1 *nc* a particular piece of business; a business deal: *business transactions.* 2 *nu* the act of transacting: *The transaction of the deal took several days.*

tran'sactions [-ʃənz] *n pl* (*formal*) (records of) the things said and done at the meetings of a learned society: *Volume 3 of the Transactions of the Philosophical Society.*

transatlantic [tranzət'lantik] *adj* (*usu attrib*) 1 crossing the Atlantic ocean: *a transatlantic liner*; *transatlantic flights/telephone calls.* 2 being on, or belonging to, the other side of the Atlantic ocean; American: *our transatlantic friends*; *a transatlantic accent.*

transcend [tran'send] *vt* (*formal or liter*) 1 to be greater or better than; to surpass: *The power of God transcends all human knowledge.* 2 to overcome (difficulties *etc*): *We shall transcend all obstacles.*

,transcen'dental [-'den-] *adj* (*formal*: *usu attrib*) going beyond normal human experience or knowledge: *transcendental meditation.*

transcontinental ['tranzkonti'nentl] *adj* (*usu attrib*) crossing a continent: *a transcontinental railway.*

transcribe [tran'skraib] *vt* 1 to copy, or write out, in full: *He transcribed two paragraphs from the book into his notebook*; *She made shorthand notes which she later transcribed*; *The conversations were recorded on tape and then transcribed.* 2 (*music*) to adapt or arrange (a piece of music) for a particular instrument or group of instruments *etc*: *The sonata has been transcribed for the violin.*

transcript ['transkript] *nc* something that has been transcribed; a written copy: *I was not present at the meeting – I'd like a transcript of her speech.*

transcription [tran'skripʃən] 1 *nu* the act of

transcribing. 2 *nc* a transcript.

transept ['transept] *nc* in a church that is built in the form of a cross, the part that is at right angles to the main part (the nave).

transfer [trans'fəː] – *pt, ptp* **trans'ferred** – (*formal*) 1 *vt* to remove to another place: *He transferred the letter from his briefcase to his trouser pocket.* 2 *vti* to (cause to) move to another place, job, vehicle *etc*: *I'm transferring/They're transferring me to the Edinburgh office*; *At Glasgow I transferred to another train.* 3 *vt* (*formal or legal*) to give to another person, *esp* legally: *I intend to transfer the property to my son.* – ['transfəː] 1 *ncu* the act of transferring: *The manager arranged for his transfer to another football club.* 2 *nc* a design, picture *etc* that can be transferred from one surface to another, *eg* from paper to material as a guide for embroidery: *She would like a transfer of some trees*; *a flower transfer.*

trans'ferable *adj* (*formal*: *pred*) that can be transferred from one place or person to another: *This ticket is not transferable* (= may not be used except by the person to whom it is issued).

transference ['transfərəns, (*Amer*) trans'fəːrəns] *nu* (*formal*) the act of transferring from one person or place to another: *thought-transference.*

transfigure [trans'figə, (*Amer*) -gjər] *vt* (*formal*) to change the appearance of something, *esp* so that it seems beautiful or glorious: *Her face was transfigured with joy.* **trans,figu'ration** *ncu.*

transfix [trans'fiks] *vt* (*formal*) to cause (someone) to be unable to move, through surprise, fear *etc*: *He was transfixed with amazement.*

transform [trans'foːm] *vt* (*more formal than* **change**) to change the appearance or nature of completely: *He transformed the old kitchen into a beautiful sitting-room*; *She is quite a plain girl but her face is transformed when she smiles*; (*fig*) *His marriage has transformed him.*

,transfor'mation (*more formal than* **change**) 1 *nu* the act of transforming or process of being transformed: *the transformation of water into ice.* 2 *nc* a change: *The event caused a transformation in her character.*

trans'former *nc* an apparatus for changing electrical energy from one voltage to another.

transfuse [trans'fjuːz] *vt* (*formal*) to transfer (the blood of one person) into the veins of another.

trans'fusion [-ʒən] 1 *nc* a quantity of blood transferred from one person to another: *She was given a blood transfusion.* 2 *nu* (*formal*) the act or process of transferring blood from one person to another.

transgress [trans'gres] (*very formal or liter*) *vti* to break (a law, rule *etc*): *He transgressed the law*; *He has transgressed against all the rules.*

trans'gression [-ʃən] (*formal or liter*) 1 *nu* the act of breaking rules *etc*: *Transgression of the law will be punished.* 2 *nc* a fault, crime, sin *etc*: *Forgive us our transgressions.*

transient ['tranziənt, (*Amer*) -ʃənt] *adj* (*formal*) lasting for a short time only; passing quickly: *a transient feeling/mood*; *His feeling of depression was transient.* **'transience** *nu.*

transistor [tran'sistə] *nc* 1 (*tech*) a small electronic device that controls the flow of an electric current. 2 (*also* **transistor radio**) a portable radio that uses these: *She took her transistor everywhere with her.*

tran'sistorized, -s- *adj* (*tech*) having transistors: *a transistorized television set.*

transit ['transit] *nu* the carrying or movement of goods, passengers *etc* from place to place: *The goods have been lost in transit*; (*attrib*) *a transit lounge in an airport.*

'transit camp *nc* a camp for soldiers *etc* who are in transit from one place to another.

'transit visa *nc* a visa which allows a person to pass through a country but not to stop in it.

transition [tran'ziʃən] *ncu* (*more formal than* **change**) (a) change from one place, state, subject *etc* to another: *The transition from child to adult can be difficult*; *a sudden transition from grief to joy.*

tran'sitional *adj* (*formal*: *usu attrib*) of or concerning transition: *a transitional stage/period.*

transitive ['transitiv] *adj* (*gram*) (of a verb) having an object: *He hit the ball*; *Open the door!* See also **intransitive**.

transitory ['transitəri] *adj* (*formal or liter*) lasting only for a short time; transient: *Pessimists say that happiness is transitory*; *transitory joy.* **'transitorily** *adv.* **'transitoriness** *nu.*

translate [trans'leit] *vti* to put (something said or written) into another language: *He translated the book from French into English*; *I can't understand Greek. Will you translate for me?*

trans'lation 1 *nu* the act of translating: *The translation of poetry is difficult.* 2 *nc* a version of a book, something said *etc*, in another language: *He gave me an Italian translation of the Bible.*

trans'lator *nc* a person who translates: *He works as a translator.*

translucent [trans'luːsnt] *adj* (*formal or tech*) allowing light to pass through, but not transparent: *translucent silk*; *The material is translucent.* **trans'lucence, trans'lucency** *nus.*

transmit [tranz'mit] – *pt, ptp* **trans'mitted** – 1 *vt* (*formal or tech*) to pass on: *He transmitted the message*; *Insects can transmit disease.* 2 *vti* (of a television or radio station) to send out (signals, programmes *etc*): *The programme will be transmitted at 5.00 p.m.*; *They've stopped transmitting on that frequency.*

trans'mission [-ʃən] (*formal or tech*) 1 *nu* the act of transmitting: *the transmission of disease/radio signals.* 2 *nc* a radio or television broadcast: *a news transmission.*

trans'mitter *nc* an apparatus for transmitting, or a person who transmits, *esp* radio signals: *a radio transmitter.*

transparent [trans'peərənt] *adj* 1 able to be seen through: *Glass is transparent but wood is opaque*; *That material is completely transparent*; *The box has a transparent lid.* 2 (*formal*: *usu attrib*) obvious; evident: *transparent lies*; *transparent honesty.* **trans'parently** *adv.*

trans'parency [-'pa-] 1 *nu* the state of being transparent: *the transparency of the water.* 2 *nc* a photograph printed on transparent material and seen by shining light through it or projecting it on to a screen; a slide: *I took some transparencies of the cathedral.*

transpire [tran'spaiə] (*formal*) 1 *vti* (*usu with* **it** *as subject*) to become known: *It transpired that he had been in Paris for the weekend*; *He had been in Paris – or so it later transpired.* 2 *vi* (*loosely*) to happen: *He told me what had transpired.*

transplant [trans'plaːnt] 1 *vt* to remove (an organ of the body) and put it into another person or animal: *Doctors are able to transplant kidneys.* 2 *vt* to remove (skin) and put it on another part of the body: *Her face was badly burned and she had to have skin transplanted.* **3** *vti* to plant (a growing plant), or be planted, in another place: *We transplanted the rose-bush (into the back garden); It didn't transplant successfully.* – ['transpla:nt] *nc* **1** an operation in which an organ or skin is transplanted: *He had to have a kidney transplant.* **2** an organ, skin, or a plant that is transplanted: *The transplant was rejected by the surrounding tissue.*

ˌ**transplan'tation** [transpla:n-] *nu.*

transport [trans'po:t] *vt* **1** (*more formal than* **carry** *or* **take**) to carry (goods, passengers *etc*) from one place to another: *The goods were transported by air; A bus transported us from the airport to the city.* **2** (*hist*) to send (a convicted prisoner) to a prison in a colony: *Convicts used to be transported to Australia.* **3** (*formal or liter*) to overcome with strong feelings: *She was transported with grief.* – ['transpo:t] *nu* the process of transporting or being transported: *the transport of goods and passengers; air* (= by aeroplane) *transport; road transport; My husband is using my car, so I have no (means of) transport; I can take you in my car if you require transport to the meeting.*

trans'portable *adj* (*formal*) able to be transported: *Are the goods easily transportable?; transportable goods.*

ˌ**transpor'tation** *nu* **1** (*formal*) transport. **2** (*hist*) the punishment of prisoners by sending them to a prison in a colony: *He was sentenced to seven years' transportation.*

trans'porter *nc* someone or something that transports, *esp* a heavy vehicle for carrying large goods.

transpose [trans'pouz] *vt* **1** (*formal*) to make (two things) change places: *He transposed their names on the list.* **2** (*music*) to change (a piece of music) into a different key: *He transposed the song into the key of F.* ˌ**transpo'sition** [-'zi-] *nu.*

transverse ['tranzvə:s] *adj* (*formal or tech*: *usu attrib*) placed, lying, built *etc* across, or at right angles: *transverse beams in the roof.* ˌ**trans'versely** *adv.*

transvestite [tranz'vestait] *nc* a person who likes to dress in the clothes of the opposite sex.

trap [trap] *nc* **1** (*sometimes in cmpds*) a device for catching animals: *He set a trap to catch the bear; a mousetrap.* **2** a plan or trick for taking a person by surprise: *She led him into a trap; He fell straight into the trap.* **3** (*hist*: *esp Brit*) a carriage with two wheels: *a pony-trap.* **4** (*tech*) a bend in a pipe, which is kept full of water, for stopping the escape of air, gas *etc.* **5** (*offensive sl*) a mouth: *Keep your trap shut!* – *v* – *pt, ptp* **trapped** – *vt* to catch in a trap or by a trick: *He lives by trapping animals and selling their fur; She trapped him into admitting that he liked her.*

'**trapper** *nc* a person who traps animals and sells their fur.

'**trap-door** *nc* a small door, or opening, in a floor or ceiling: *A trap-door in the ceiling led to the attic.*

trapes *see* **traipse**.

trapeze [trə'pi:z, (*Amer*) tra-] *nc* a horizontal bar hung on two ropes, on which gymnasts or acrobats perform tricks, exercises *etc*: *They performed on the trapeze; (attrib) a trapeze artist.*

trapper *see* **trap**.

trappings ['trapiŋz] *n pl* (*formal*) clothes or ornaments suitable for a particular occasion or person: *all the trappings of royalty.*

trapse *see* **traipse**.

trash [traʃ] *nu* (*inf derog*) something worthless; rubbish: *Throw it away! It's just trash; That magazine is nothing but a load of trash.*

'**trashy** *adj* (*inf derog*: *usu attrib*) worthless; like rubbish: *trashy jewellery/novels/music.* '**trashiness** *nu.*

'**trashcan** *nc* (*Amer*) a dustbin.

trauma ['tro:mə] *nu* (*formal or tech*) the condition caused by a physical or emotional shock: *He was suffering from trauma.*

traumatic [-'ma-] *adj* (*formal or tech*: *sometimes used loosely*) of or concerning (a) trauma: *a traumatic experience; Her first love affair proved rather traumatic.*

travel ['travl] – *pt, ptp* '**travelled**, (*Amer*) '**traveled** – **1** *vti* to go from place to place; to journey: *I travelled to Scotland by train; He travelled the country on foot; He has to travel a long way to school.* **2** *vi* to move: *Light travels in a straight line.* **3** *vi* to visit places, *esp* foreign countries: *He has travelled a great deal.* – *nu* the act of travelling: *Travel to and from work can be very tiring; rail* (= by train) *travel; air travel.*

'**travelled** *adj* (*usu in cmpds*) having travelled (*def 3*) a certain amount: *The children are already well-travelled; a much-travelled man.*

'**traveller** *nc* **1** (*esp formal or liter*) a person who travels: *a weary traveller.* **2** a travelling representative of a business firm.

'**travelogue**, (*Amer*) '**travelog** *nc* a film, article, talk *etc* about travels.

'**travels** *n pl* the visiting of foreign countries *etc*: *She's off on her travels again; 'Gulliver's Travels' is the title of a book by Swift.*

'**travel agency**, '**travel bureau** *ncs* a place where one can arrange journeys, book tickets *etc*: *We went to the travel agency to book our holidays.*

'**travel agent** *nc* a person in charge of, or working in, a travel agency.

traveller's cheque *nc* (*sometimes without* **a**) a cheque issued by a bank, which can be cashed in another country for currency of that country: *We always take traveller's cheques when we go abroad; Can we pay by traveller's cheque?*

traverse [trə'və:s] *vt* (*old*) to go across or through: *They traversed the mountains.*

travesty ['travəsti] *nc* a ridiculous or comical imitation: *The modern version of the song is a travesty of the original; The trial was a travesty of justice.*

trawl [tro:l] *nc* a wide-mouthed, bag-shaped net used to catch fish in the sea. – *vti* to fish (the sea-bed *etc*) by dragging a trawl across the seabed: *They are trawling (the Atlantic) for cod.*

'**trawler** *nc* a fishing-boat used in trawling: *a Russian trawler; (attrib) a trawler captain.*

tray [trei] *nc* (*sometimes in cmpds*) a flat piece of wood, metal *etc* with a low edge, for carrying dishes *etc*: *She brought in the tea on a tray; a tea-tray.*

treacherous ['tretʃərəs] *adj* **1** betraying or likely to betray; traitorous: *a treacherous person/act; He thinks that she is his friend, but she is treacherous.* **2** dangerous: *a treacherous path; The roads are treacherous in winter.* '**treacherously** *adv.* '**treacherousness** *nu.*

'**treachery** *ncu* (an) act of betraying someone; disloyalty: *His treachery led to the capture and imprisonment of his friend; He was punished for his various treacheries.*

See also **traitor**.

treacle ['tri:kl] *nu* (*Amer* **mo'lasses**) a thick, dark, sticky liquid produced from sugar: *Toffee is sometimes made with treacle*; (*attrib*) *treacle toffee.*

tread [tred] – *pt* **trod** [trod]: *ptp* **trodden** ['trodn] – **1** *vi* (*usu with* **on**) to place one's feet on: *He threw his cigarette on the ground and trod on it*; *He accidentally trod on her foot.* **2** *vt* (*formal*) to walk on, along, over *etc*: *He trod the streets looking for a job.* **3** *vt* to crush by putting one's feet on: *They trod the flowers into the ground*; *He trod the cigarette ash into the carpet*; *We watched them treading the grapes.* **4** *vt* (*formal*) to wear (a path) by walking: *The sheep trod a path through the grass.* – **1** *nc* a way of walking or putting one's feet: *I heard his heavy tread.* **2** *ncu* the grooved and patterned surface of a tyre: *The tread has been worn away*; *The tyres have good treads.* **3** *nc* the horizontal part of a step or stair on which the foot is placed.

'**treadmill** *nc* (*fig*) a tiring and boring routine: *the treadmill of factory work.*

tread on someone's toes (*inf*) to offend or upset (someone): *I would like to help to organize the fête but I am afraid to suggest it in case I tread on someone's toes.*

tread water to keep oneself afloat in an upright position by moving the legs (and arms): *The swimmer trod water before beginning the long swim to the shore.*

treadle, treddle ['tredl] *nc* a pedal that drives a machine, *eg* a sewing-machine.

treason ['tri:zn] *nu* (*also* **high treason**) disloyalty to, or betrayal of, one's own country, ruler or government, *eg* by helping a foreign power to conquer it, or by giving secret information away: *They were convicted of (high) treason.*

'**treasonable** *adj* (*formal or legal*) consisting of, or involving, treason: *a treasonable statement*; *treasonable acts*; *That action is treasonable.*

treasure ['treʒə] **1** *ncu* a store of money, gold, jewels *etc*: *The miser kept a secret hoard of treasure*; *the treasures of the East*; (*attrib*) *a treasure chest.* **2** *nc* (*fig*) something very valuable: *the treasures of Italian art*; (*inf*) *Our babysitter is a real treasure!* – *vt* (*formal*) **1** to value; to think of as very valuable: *I treasure the hours I spend in the country.* **2** to keep (something) carefully because one values it: *I treasure the book you gave me*; (*fig*) *I treasure the memory of our visit to Paris.*

'**treasured** *adj* (*usu attrib*) regarded as precious; valued: *The photograph of her son is her most treasured possession.*

'**treasurer** *nc* the person in a club, society *etc*, who looks after the money: *He has been elected treasurer of our music society.*

'**treasure-trove** [-trouv] *nu* treasure or money that is found *eg* buried in the earth, whose owner is unknown: *The gold coins that he dug up in the field were declared to be treasure-trove.*

the Treasury the government department that deals with the country's money.

treat [tri:t] **1** *vt* to deal with, or behave towards (a thing or person), in a certain manner: *The soldiers treated me very well*; *They treated me as one of the family*; *You treat my house as if it were a hotel!*; *They treated the situation as an emergency*; *The police are treating his death as a case of murder.* **2** *vt* to try to cure (a person or disease, injury *etc*): *They treated her for a broken leg*; *The doctor treated her rheumatism.* **3** *vt* to put (something) through a process: *The woodwork has been treated with a new chemical.* **4** *vt* to buy (a meal, present *etc*) for (someone): *I'll treat you to lunch*; *She treated herself to a new hat*; *If you haven't enough money for the cinema, I'll treat you!* **5** *vt* (*formal*) to write or speak about; to discuss: *She treats this subject fully in her book.* **6** *vi* (*with* **with**: *formal*) to negotiate (with another nation *etc*): *They decided to treat with the enemy (for peace).* – *nc* something that gives pleasure, *eg* an arranged outing, or some special food: *He took them to the theatre as a treat*; *It was a (real) treat to visit them!*; *She cooked their favourite meal as a treat.*

'**treatment** *ncu* (an) act or manner of treating: *Their treatment of me was very kind*; *This chair seems to have received rough treatment*; *This patient/disease requires urgent treatment*; *One of the best treatments for a cold is a drink of hot whisky*; *the treatment of wood with chemicals*; (*formal*) *I do not like her treatment of Scottish history in her new book.*

treatise ['tri:tiz, (*Amer*) -s] *nc* (*formal*) a long, detailed, formal piece of writing on some subject: *He wrote a treatise on methods of education.*

treaty ['tri:ti] *nc* a formal agreement between states or governments: *They signed a peace treaty*; *Under the terms of the treaty that ended the war, the island was given back to France.*

treble[1] ['trebl] *nu, adj* (something that is) three times as much, many *etc* as something else, or as the normal: *These children have the treble handicap of poverty, parental neglect and bad schooling*; *He earns treble what* (= three times as much as) *I do*; *She took treble the normal dose of sleeping-pills.* – *vti* to make, or become, three times as much: *He trebled his earnings*; *His income has trebled.* '**trebly** *adv.*

See also **triple**.

treble[2] ['trebl] *nc* **1** (a singer, *usu* a boy, having) a high-pitched singing voice: *The trebles sing the following passages*; (*attrib*) *a treble voice.* **2** in music, a part written for a voice at this pitch: *The treble is rather difficult*; (*attrib*) *the treble part.* – *adv* with a treble voice: *He sings treble.*

treddle *see* **treadle**.

tree [tri:] *nc* the largest kind of plant, with a thick, firm, wooden stem (called a trunk) and branches: *Is that an ash tree?*; *We have three apple trees growing in our garden*; *The old oak tree has been cut down*; *The mountain slopes were covered with trees*; *These trees will have to be felled* (= cut down).

'**treetop** *nc* (*often formal or liter*) the top of a tree: *the birds in the treetops.*

'**tree-trunk** *nc* the trunk of a tree.

at the top of the tree at the top of one's profession: *He's at the top of the publishing tree now.*

family tree *see* **family**.

trek [trek] – *pt, ptp* **trekked** – *vi* to make a long, hard journey: *They are trekking through the mountains*; (*fig inf*) *She trekked wearily up the stairs*; (*fig inf*) *I've been trekking round the shops looking for a present for her.* – *nc* a long, hard journey: *a trek through the mountains*; (*fig inf*) *a trek round the supermarket.*

trellis ['trelis] *nc* a network of strips, *usu* of wood, used to support climbing plants *etc*: *The roses grew up a trellis.*

tremble ['trembl] *vi* to shake *eg* with cold, fear, weakness *etc*: *She trembled with cold*; *His hands trembled as he lit a cigarette*; *The bridge trembled as the train went over it*; *I tremble* (= I am afraid) *to think what will happen.* – *nc* a shudder; a tremor: *a* 'tremble of fear; The walls gave a sudden tremble as the lorry passed by.*

be/go in fear and trembling (of) (*esp facet*) to be very afraid: *I was in fear and trembling in case you made a mistake; They go in fear and trembling of their father.*

tremendous [trə'mendəs] *adj* (*often used loosely*) very large; very great: *That required a tremendous effort; He is very strong and has tremendous muscles; The response to our appeal was tremendous; We got a tremendous surprise when she arrived.*

tre'mendously *adv* very: *It's tremendously interesting; He's tremendously strong.*

tremor ['tremə] *nc* (*formal or tech*) a shaking or quivering: *Earth tremors* (= slight earthquakes) *were felt in Sicily yesterday; There was a tremor in her voice as she spoke of her dead father.*

tremulous ['tremjuləs] *adj* (*formal*) trembling; showing fear: *a tremulous voice; Her voice sounded rather tremulous.* **'tremulousness** *nu.*

trench [trentʃ] *nc* a long narrow ditch dug in the ground, *esp* as a protection for soldiers against gunfire: *The soldiers returned to the trenches; an irrigation trench;* (*attrib*) *trench warfare.* – *vti* (*formal*) to dig trenches (in).

trenchant ['trentʃənt] *adj* (*very formal*) (of a remark *etc*) sharp, cutting; effective: *trenchant wit; His remarks were rather trenchant.*

trend [trend] *nc* a general direction or tendency: *The trend of modern opinion is away from corporal punishment; fashion trends; She follows all the latest trends in fashion; He claims that it was he who set* (= started, made) *the trend towards long hair; an upward trend in share prices.*

'trendy *adj* (*inf*) following the latest fashions: *trendy people/clothes; Her mother tries to be trendy.*

trepidation [trepi'deiʃən] *nu* (*formal*) fear or nervousness: *She was in a state of trepidation before her exam.*

trespass ['trespəs] *vi* **1** to enter illegally: *You are trespassing (on my land).* – *See also* **trespass on/upon** *below.* **2** (*old*) to sin: *He trespassed against God.* – **1** *nu* the act of trespassing: *The police charged him with trespass.* **2** *nc* (*old*) a sin: *Forgive us our trespasses.*

'trespasser *nc* a person who trespasses (*esp def 1*): *There was a notice on the gate, saying 'Trespassers will be prosecuted'.*

'trespass on/upon *vt fus* (*formal*) to intrude into (a person's time, privacy *etc*): *I don't want to trespass on your time.*

tress [tres] *nc* (*liter: usu in pl*) a lock of hair: *her long golden tresses.*

trestle ['tresl] *nc* a wooden support with legs: *The platform was on trestles;* (*attrib*) *a trestle table.*

trews [tru:z] *n pl* trousers made of tartan cloth: *Scottish soldiers wear a kilt or trews; He was wearing a pair of trews.*

tri- [trai, tri] (*in cmpds*) three, as in **tricycle**.

trial ['traiəl] *nc* **1** an act of testing or trying; a test: *Give the new car a trial; The disaster was a trial of his courage.* – *See also* **on trial** *below.* **2** a legal process by which a person is judged in a court of law: *Their trial will be held next week;* (*attrib*) *a trial witness.* – *See also* **on trial** *below.* **3** a (source of) trouble or anxiety: *My son is a great trial (to me); the trials of one's life.*

trial run *nc* a rehearsal, first test *etc* of anything, *eg* a play, car, piece of machinery *etc.*

on 'trial 1 the subject of a legal action in court: *She's on trial for murder.* **2** undergoing tests or examination: *We've had a new television installed, but it's only on trial.*

trial and error the trying of various methods, alternatives *etc* until the right one happens to appear or be found: *He found the best way of driving through London by trial and error; They didn't know how to put in a central-heating system, but they managed it by trial and error.*

See also **try**.

triangle ['traiaŋgl] *nc* **1** a two-dimensional figure with three sides and three angles. **2** a musical instrument consisting of a triangular-shaped metal bar that is struck with a small hammer: *Children enjoy playing the triangle.*

tri'angular [-gju-] *adj* in the shape of a triangle: *a triangular road-sign; It is triangular in shape.*

tribe [traib] *nc* **1** a race of people, or a family, who are all descended from the same ancestor: *the tribes of Israel.* **2** a group of families, *esp* of a primitive or wandering people, ruled by a chief: *the desert tribes of Africa.*

'tribal *adj* (*usu attrib*) of a tribe or tribes: *tribal lands/customs; the tribal system.*

'tribalism *nu* (*formal*) **1** the system of tribes: *Tribalism still exists in many parts of the world.* **2** the feeling of belonging to a tribe: *Their attitude is strongly affected by tribalism; religious tribalism.*

'tribesman ['traibz-] *nc* a man who belongs to a tribe: *an African tribesman.*

tribulation [tribju'leiʃən] *ncu* (*formal or liter: sometimes facet*) (a) great sorrow or trouble: *He suffered great tribulation(s); the tribulations of growing old.*

tribunal [trai'bju:nl] *nc* (*formal*) a group of people appointed to give judgement, *esp* on official decisions: *He took the matter to a rent tribunal* (= a court that judges whether a particular rent is just).

tribune ['tribju:n] **1** *nc* (*hist*) a high official elected by the ordinary people of ancient Rome to defend their rights. **2** *n* (*with cap*) a word sometimes used in the titles of newspapers: *the Burnside Tribune.*

tributary[1] ['tribjutəri] *nc, adj* (a stream) flowing into a river: *The River Thames has many tributaries/tributary streams.*

tributary[2] *see* **tribute**.

tribute ['tribju:t] **1** *ncu* (an) expression of praise, thanks *etc*: *Many tributes of flowers were laid on his grave; This statue has been erected as (a) tribute to a great man; We must pay tribute to his great courage.* – *See also* **be a tribute to** *below.* **2** *ncu* (*esp hist*) (a sum of) money paid regularly by one nation or ruler to another in return for protection or peace: *Many Greek cities had to send (a) yearly tribute to Athens.*

'tributary *nc, adj* (*formal or hist*) (a person or nation) paying tribute (*def 2*): *a tributary nation; Rome and her tributaries.*

be a 'tribute to to be the (praiseworthy) result of: *The success of the scheme is a tribute to his hard work.*

trice [trais]: **in a 'trice** (*old or facet*) in a very short time; almost immediately: *He returned in a trice.*

trick [trik] *nc* **1** something which is done, said *etc* in order to cheat or deceive someone, and sometimes to frighten them or make them appear stupid: *The message was just a trick to get her to leave the room; It was a nasty trick to pretend that you had lost his ticket.* **2** a clever or skilful action (to amuse *etc*: *The magician performed some clever tricks; He* *taught the monkey to do tricks.* **3** (*inf*: *no pl*) the way (of doing a particular job *etc*); the knack: *He hasn't got the trick of driving this car yet.* **4** (*inf*) a habit: *He has a trick of scratching his nose when he's angry.* **5** (in a card game) a group of cards, one played by each player, which makes up one part of the game and is won by one player or team: *I won five tricks in that last game.* – *adj* (*attrib*) intended to deceive or give a certain illusion: *trick photography* (= when a photograph shows something that is not true, real *etc*, *eg* two images of one person in the same picture).

'trickery *ncu* (*formal*) (an) act of deceiving or cheating: *She could not stand his trickery/trickeries.*

'trickster *nc* (*old or formal*) a person who deceives or cheats.

'tricky *adj* (*inf*) difficult: *a tricky problem/job*; *a tricky person to deal with*; *This is a bit tricky.* **'trickily** *adv.* **'trickiness** *nu.*

do the trick (*inf*) to do or be what is necessary: *I need a piece of paper. This old envelope will do the trick!*; *I had a very bad headache but I feel better now – that aspirin did the trick.*

play a trick/tricks on to do something which is amusing to oneself because it deceives or frightens (someone else), or makes them appear stupid: *He played a trick on her by hiding and then jumping out from behind a wall as she passed*; *Don't play tricks on me – I want to know the truth.*

a trick of the trade (*sometimes derog*) one of the ways of being successful in a job *etc*: *Remembering the customers' names is one of the tricks of the trade.*

up to one's tricks (*inf*: *often derog*) behaving in one's usual (deceitful, amusing *etc*) way: *He's up to his old tricks again – he's been getting money from people by pretending to be blind.*

trickle ['trikl] *vi* to flow in small amounts: *Rain trickled down the window*; *Blood was trickling down her face*; (*fig*) *A few people trickled into the street to see what was happening.* – *nc* a small amount (of a liquid) which is flowing: *a trickle of water*; (*fig*) *At first there was only a trickle of people but soon a crowd arrived.*

trickster, tricky *see* **trick**.

tricycle ['traisikl] *nc* (*inf abbrev* **trike** [traik]) a kind of cycle with three wheels, *esp* of a size suitable for small children: *My older children have bicycles but my two-year-old daughter has a tricycle.* *See also* **bicycle**.

trident ['traidənt] *nc* (*hist*) a type of spear with three prongs: *Neptune* (= a Roman god) *is usually portrayed carrying a trident.*

trifle ['traifl] **1** *nc* (*formal*) anything of very little value: *£100 is a trifle when one is very rich.* **2** *ncu* (a dish of) a sweet pudding made of sponge-cake, fruit, cream *etc*: *There's fruit salad or trifle for dessert*: *I'm making a trifle for dessert.*

'trifling *adj* (*formal derog*) unimportant: *a trifling amount of money*; *trifling details*; *The sum of money involved is trifling.*

'trifle with *vt fus* (*formal*) to act towards (someone or their feelings) without enough respect: *Don't trifle with me!*; *I won't be trifled with*; *He was trifling with her affections.*

trig [trig] (*inf*) short for **trigonometry**.

trigger ['trigə] *nc* **1** a small lever on a gun, which is pulled to make the gun fire: *He aimed the rifle at her but did not pull the trigger.* **2** (*formal*) anything which starts a series of actions or reactions: *The announcement of these men's dismissals acted as a trigger for a series of strikes all over the country.* – *vt* (*often with* **off**) to start (a series of events): *The attack triggered* (*off*) *a full-scale war*; *Don't upset him – it will trigger off an asthmatic attack.*

'trigger-happy *adj* (*inf*) too ready or likely to use guns (or general violence): *One group of trigger-happy soldiers can cause a war*; *I hope that they don't elect him president – he is so trigger-happy that he will certainly start a war.*

trigonometry [trigə'nomətri] *nu* (*inf abbrev* **trig** [trig]) the branch of mathematics which deals with the relationship between the sides and angles of triangles.

trike [traik] (*inf*) short for **tricycle**.

trilby ['trilbi] *nc* (*also* **trilby hat**) a type of soft felt hat for men.

trill [tril] *nc* (*music*) a sound made by continuing to play or sing two notes very close together one after the other: *She sang/played a difficult trill.* – *vti* **1** (*music*) to sing (something) with a trill: *He trilled the note.* **2** (*liter*) (of birds) to sing (a song *etc*): *Birds were trilling* (*their song*) *in the bushes.*

trilogy ['trilədʒi] *nc* a group of three plays, novels *etc* by the same author which are parts of the same story or are written about the same subject.

trim [trim] – *pt, ptp* **trimmed** – *vt* **1** to cut the edges or ends of (something) in order to make it shorter and/or neat: *He's trimming the hedge*; *She had her hair trimmed*; (*fig*) *We've trimmed the book from 100000 words to 80000.* **2** to decorate (a dress, hat *etc*, *usu* round the edges): *She trimmed the sleeves with lace.* **3** to arrange (the sails of a boat *etc*) suitably for the weather conditions. – *nc* a haircut: *She went to the hairdresser's for a trim.* – *See also* **in (good) trim** *below.* – *adj* neat and tidy: *a trim appearance*; *She always looks neat and trim.* **'trimly** *adv.* **'trimness** *nu.*

'trimming **1** *ncu* something added as a decoration: *lace trimming*; (*loosely*) *roast chicken with all the trimmings.* **2** *nc* pieces cut off; ends or edges: *He cut a circle out of a piece of paper and threw away the trimmings.*

in (,good) 'trim in good condition: *The engine seems in good trim*; *Her figure's in very good trim after all those exercises.*

trinket ['triŋkit] *nc* (*sometimes derog*) a small (*usu* cheap) ornament or piece of jewellery: *That shop sells postcards and trinkets*; *I have a few pieces of good jewellery but the rest are just trinkets.*

trio ['tri:ou] – *pl* **'trios** – *nc* **1** a group of three (people or things): *A trio of soldiers was coming down the road.* **2** (a piece of music for) three players: *A trio was playing in the hotel lounge*; *They played a trio by Mozart.*

trip [trip] – *pt, ptp* **tripped** – **1** *vti* (*often with* **up** *or* **over**) to (cause to) catch one's foot and stumble or fall: *She tripped and fell*; *He tripped her* (*up*) *with his foot*; *She tripped over the carpet.* **2** *vi* (*liter or facet*: *with* **along** *etc*) to walk with short, light steps: *She tripped happily along the road.* – *nc* a (*usu* short) journey or tour: *She went on/took a trip to Paris.*

'tripper *nc* (*usu derog*) a person who has made a journey for pleasure: *The seaside resort was full of trippers*; *day-trippers.*

'trip-wire *nc* a wire which sets off a mechanism of some kind, *esp* a bomb, when someone trips over it.

trip up *vi, vt sep* (*inf*) to (cause to) make mistakes: *He tripped her up with a difficult question*; *She spoke well but kept tripping up over foreign words.*

tripartite [trai'pa:tait] *adj* (*very formal: often attrib*) of or concerning three countries, governments *etc*: *a tripartite agreement.*

tripe [traip] *nu* **1** parts of the stomach of a cow or sheep, used as food: *a plate of tripe and onions.* **2** (*inf*) nonsense; rubbish: *Don't talk tripe!*

triple ['tripl] *adj* (*attrib*) **1** three times (as big, much *etc* as usual): *He received triple wages for all his extra work*; *a triple whisky.* **2** made up of three (parts *etc*): *a triple agreement.* – *vti* to make or become three times as much, big *etc*; to treble: *He tripled his income*; *His income tripled in ten years.* – *nu* three times the (usual) amount: *If you work the bank holiday, you will be paid triple.*

'**triplet** [-lit] *nc* **1** one of three children or animals born to the same mother at the same time: *She's just had triplets.* **2** (*music*) a group of three notes played in the time usually given to two. **3** a group of three rhyming lines in a poem: *There are two triplets in each verse.*

See also **treble**[1].

triplicate ['triplikət]: **in 'triplicate** (*formal or facet*) on three separate copies (of the same form *etc*): *Fill in the form in triplicate.*

tripod ['traipod] *nc* a stand with three legs, *esp* for a camera.

trite [trait] *adj* (*formal derog*) (of a remark, saying *etc*) already said in exactly the same way so often that it no longer has any worth, effectiveness *etc*: *I wanted to tell her that I was sorry that her husband had died but my letter sounded so trite*; *His poetry is full of trite descriptions of nature.* '**tritely** *adv.* '**triteness** *nu.*

triumph ['traiʌmf] **1** *nc* (*more formal than* **victory**) a great victory or success: *The battle ended in a triumph for the Romans*; *His portrayal of 'Othello' was one of his greatest triumphs.* **2** *nu* a state of happiness, celebration, pride *etc* after a success: *They went home in triumph.* – *vi* (*more formal than* **win**: *often with* **over**) to win a victory: *The Romans triumphed* (*over their enemies*).

tri'umphal *adj* (*formal: usu attrib*) **1** having to do with (a) triumph: *a triumphal battle.* **2** built, done, used *etc* in celebration of a triumph: *A triumphal arch was built to celebrate the victory.*

tri'umphant *adj* (glad and excited because of) having won a victory, achieved something difficult *etc*: *the triumphant army*; *He gave a triumphant shout*; *She looked so triumphant that I knew she had won.* **tri'umphantly** *adv.*

trivia ['triviə] *n pl* (*formal or facet: derog*) unimportant matters or details: *I haven't time to worry about such trivia.*

'**trivial** *adj* (*derog*) **1** of very little importance: *trivial details*; *This matter is too trivial to worry about.* **2** (*esp* of people) only interested in unimportant things; not at all serious: *She's a very trivial person.* '**trivially** *adv.*

ˌ**trivi'ality** [-'a-] (*formal derog*) **1** *nu* the state of being trivial: *He was surprised by the triviality of her anxieties.* **2** *nc* something which is trivial: *He is always worrying about some triviality or other.*

trod, trodden *see* **tread**.

troll [troul] *nc* an imaginary creature of human-like form, very ugly and evil-tempered, *usu* a dwarf or a giant: *The child was reading a book of stories about trolls.*

trolley ['troli] *nc* (*often in cmpds*) **1** a type of small cart for carrying things *etc* at a station, in a supermarket *etc*: *She quickly filled the trolley with groceries*; *These suitcases are too heavy to carry – we need a trolley*; *This airport doesn't have enough luggage-trolleys.* **2** (*also* '**tea-trolley**, (*Amer*) '**teacart**) a small cart, *usu* consisting of two or three trays fixed on a frame, used for serving tea, food *etc*: *She brought the tea in on a trolley.*

'**trolley-bus** *nc* a bus which is driven by power from an overhead wire to which it is connected.

trollop ['troləp] *nc* (*derog*) a careless, untidy woman, *esp* (*orig*) a prostitute: *You look a real trollop in those clothes.*

trombone [trom'boun] *nc* a type of brass musical wind instrument, on which the pitch of notes is altered by sliding a tube in and out: *He plays the trombone*; *He played a tune on his trombone.*

trom'bonist *nc* a person who plays the trombone.

troop [tru:p] *nc* **1** a group of ordinary soldiers, *esp* cavalry or with vehicles: *He rode in my troop.* – *See also* **troops** *below.* **2** (*inf: slightly facet*) a crowd or collection (of people or animals): *A troop of visitors arrived.* – *vi* (*inf: slightly facet: with* **along, over, into** *etc*) to go in a group: *They all trooped into his office.*

'**trooper** *nc* (*old*) an ordinary soldier, *esp* in the cavalry *etc*: *A trooper arrived at the gallop.*

troops *n pl* soldiers: *Foreign troops landed in France.*

'**troopship** *nc* a ship for carrying soldiers.

trophy ['troufi] *nc* **1** a prize (*eg* a cup or medal) for winning in a sport *etc*: *He won a silver trophy for shooting.* **2** something which is kept in memory of a victory, success *etc*: *hunting trophies* (= heads, horns, skins *etc* of animals that have been hunted and killed).

tropic ['tropik] *nc* (*with cap in titles*) either of two imaginary circles running round the earth at about 23 degrees north (**Tropic of Cancer**) or south (**Tropic of Capricorn**) of the equator.

'**tropics** *n pl* the hot regions between or (*loosely*) near these lines: *The ship is heading for the tropics.*

'**tropical** *adj* **1** of the tropics: *tropical countries*; *tropical climates*; *The climate there is tropical.* **2** growing *etc* in hot countries: *tropical plants.* '**tropically** *adv.*

trot [trot] – *pt, ptp* '**trotted** – **1** *vi* (of a horse) to move with fairly fast, bouncy steps, faster than a walk but slower than a canter or gallop: *The horse trotted down the road*; (*fig*) *The child trotted along beside his mother.* **2** *vti* (of a rider) to cause (a horse) to move, or to move on a horse, at a trot: *The soldiers trotted* (*their horses*) *into the barracks.* – *nu* the pace at which a horse or rider *etc* moves when trotting: *They rode at a trot*; (*fig*) *The old man set off at a quick trot.*

'**trotter** *nc* (*usu in pl*) a pig's foot, used as food: *We had pigs' trotters for dinner.*

on the 'trot (*inf*) **1** one after the other: *He ate four ice-creams on the trot.* **2** continually moving about; busy: *My job keeps me on the trot.*

trot out *vt fus* (*inf derog*) to bring out (*usu* to show to someone): *He is always trotting out the same excuses for being late.*

trouble ['trʌbl] **1** *ncu* (something which causes) worry, difficulty, work, anxiety *etc*: *He never talks about his troubles*; *We've had a lot of trouble with our children*; *I had a lot of trouble finding the book you wanted*; *I don't want to put you to* (= cause you) *a lot of trouble*; *She went to a lot of trouble* (= She spent a lot of time, attention and work) *to make sure we enjoyed ourselves*; *I should like to stay with you, but please do not go to a lot of trouble for me*; *It was good of you to take the trouble* (= give yourself the inconvenience, work *etc*) *to help us*; *The patient has trouble breathing – I think he's dying.* – *See also* **get (someone) into trouble, take trouble** *below.* **2** *ncu* (*euph*) disturbances; rebellion, fighting *etc*: *It occurred during the time of the troubles in Cyprus.* **3** *nu* illness or weakness (in a particular part of the body): *He has heart trouble*; *He has some kind of chest trouble*; *She has kidney trouble.* – **1** *vt* (*formal*) to cause worry, anger or sadness to: *He was troubled by her behaviour*; *She was troubled by the news of her sister's illness.* **2** *vt* (*formal*) used as part of a very polite and formal request: *May I trouble you to close the window?* (= Would you close the window?); *Could I trouble you for a light?* (= Please light my cigarette, give me a match *etc*). **3** *vi* to make any effort: *He didn't even trouble to tell me what had happened.*

'troubled *adj* (*neg* **un-**) **1** (*formal*) worried or anxious: *He is obviously a troubled man.* **2** (*usu liter*) disturbed and not peaceful: *troubled sleep*; *troubled waters.*

'troublesome *adj* (*formal*) causing worry or difficulty: *These are troublesome times*; *troublesome children/tasks*; *Nothing is too troublesome for her to do for others.*

'troublemaker *nc* (*derog*) a person who continually (and *usu* deliberately) causes worry, difficulty or disturbance to other people: *A lot of people have left the firm because of her – she is a real troublemaker.*

'trouble-shooter *nc* (*esp Amer*) a person whose job is to solve difficulties (*eg* in a firm's business): *Our overseas branch is having a dispute with the local government authorities – we'll have to send out a trouble-shooter.*

get (someone) into trouble to (cause to) get into difficulties, *esp* because of doing something wrong or illegal: *He is always getting into trouble with the police*; *He got his little brother into trouble*; *His quick temper was always getting him into trouble*; (*euph*) *That man got my sister into trouble* (= pregnant).

take the trouble *see* **trouble** (*n def 1*).

take trouble to work hard and carefully when doing something: *He has taken a lot of trouble with/over this painting.*

trough [trof] *nc* **1** a long, low, open container for animals' food or water: *a drinking-trough for the cattle.* **2** a low part between two waves (in the sea *etc*): *The boat went down into a trough.* **3** (*tech*) an area of low pressure in the atmosphere, *usu* causing rain.

trounce [trauns] *vt* (*formal or facet*) to beat or defeat completely: *They were trounced by the enemy army*; *Our football team was trounced.*

troupe [tru:p] *nc* a performing group (of actors, dancers *etc*): *a circus troupe*; *a troupe of acrobats.*

'trouper *nc* **1** a member of a group of this kind. **2** (*inf*) a hard-working colleague, *usu* one who has been doing a particular job for a long time: *He's a wonderful old trouper.*

trousers ['trauzəz] *n pl* an outer garment for the lower part of the body, covering each leg separately: *He wore (a pair of) black trousers*; *She was dressed in trousers and a sweater.*

trouser- (*in cmpds*) of trousers: *a* '*trouser-button*; *That dog has torn my* '*trouser-leg.*

trousseau ['tru:sou] – *pls* **'trousseaus, 'trousseaux** [-z] – *nc* (*formal*) a bride's set of new clothes, traditionally bought for her wedding, honeymoon *etc*: *She spent a lot of money on her trousseau.*

trout [traut] – *pl* **trout** – **1** *nc* a type of freshwater fish of the salmon family: *He caught five trout.* **2** *nu* its flesh, used as food: *Have some more trout!*

trove *see* **treasure**.

trowel ['trauəl] *nc* **1** a tool like a small shovel, used in gardening: *He filled the flowerpot with earth, using a trowel.* **2** a tool with a flat blade, for spreading mortar, plaster *etc.*

troy [troi]: **troy weight** *nu* (*tech*) a system of units used in weighing gold, jewels *etc.*

truant ['truənt] *nc* someone who stays away from school *etc* without permission: *The truants were caught and sent back to school*; (*attrib*) *a truant schoolboy.*

'truancy *nu* *Truancy is a great problem in some schools.*

play truant to be a truant and stay away from school *etc*: *He was always playing truant (from school).*

truce [tru:s] *nc* a (*usu* temporary) rest from fighting, agreed to by both sides: *They called a truce while they discussed the possibility of ending the war*; *a Christmas truce.*

truck[1] [trʌk] *nc* **1** a railway vehicle (*usu* without a roof) for carrying goods: *The engine was pulling several (goods-)trucks.* **2** (*esp Amer*) a lorry: *He drives a truck*; (*attrib*) *a truck-driver*; *He took three truckloads* (= the amount carried by a truck) *of cement to the building-site.*

truck[2] [trʌk]: **have no truck with** (*formal*) to have nothing to do with; not to take part in: *My father would have no truck with politics*; *I shall have no truck with such people.*

truculent ['trʌkjulənt] *adj* (*formal derog*) (of a person) aggressive and inclined to argue rather than do as one is told: *He is a very truculent person*; *in a truculent mood*; *That child is so truculent.* **'truculently** *adv.* **'truculence** *nu.*

trudge [trʌdʒ] *vi* (*often with* **along, around, up** *etc*) to walk with slow, tired steps: *He trudged wearily up the hill*; *I hate trudging round the shops.* – *nc* (*usu in sing*) such a walk or way of walking: *Can you manage the long trudge up the hill?*

true [tru:] *adj* **1** (*neg* **un-**) telling of something that really happened; not invented; agreeing with fact; not wrong: *a true story*; *That is a true statement*; *Is it true that you did not steal the ring?*; *Do you think his story could be true?*; *It is true that we have enough money to live on.* **2** (*neg* **un-**: *attrib*) accurate: *This photograph doesn't give you a true idea of the size of the building*; *They don't have a true idea of its importance.* **3** (*neg* **un-**) faithful; loyal: *He has been a true friend*; *He was true to his promise.* **4** properly so called: *A spider is not a true insect*; *At last we have found the true* (= actual) *thief*; *He is the true* (= by right) *heir.* **5** in the correct position; well-fitting: *The doorpost is not quite true*; (*fig formal*) *He has found his true position in life.* **'trueness** *nu.*

'truism *nc* (*formal sometimes derog*) a statement, idea *etc* which it is unnecessary to make or express, as it is so obviously true: *He spoke of the unhappiness of the hungry and other such truisms*; *I am tired of listening to his truisms.*

'truly *adv* **1** really: *I truly believe that this decision is the right one.* **2** in a true manner: *He loved her truly.*

come true (of a dream, hope *etc*) to really happen: *Her dreams finally came true.*

true to type being or acting exactly like other

things or people of the same type, or exactly as one would have predicted: *This wealthy woman, true to type, married a wealthy man*; *At the party she behaved true to type and flirted with all the men.*

See also **truth**.

truffle ['trʌfl] *nc* a type of round fungus which grows underground and is used as (a flavouring for) food: *Truffles are delicious but extremely expensive.*

truism, truly *see* **true**.

trump[1] [trʌmp] *nc* in some card games, any card of a suit which has been declared to rank higher than the other suits: *This time, hearts are trumps*; (*attrib*) *a trump card.* – *vti* to defeat (an ordinary card) by playing a card from the trump suit: *He trumped (my king) with a heart.*

play one's trump card (*fig*) to use something powerful and influential which one saves in order to use when really necessary: *When they refused to allow him into the football match he finally played his trump card, saying he was the manager's brother.*

turn up trumps (*inf*) to behave or do one's work well when things are difficult, *esp* unexpectedly: *When I lost my job my friends really turned up trumps, helping me with my rent and so on.*

trump[2] [trʌmp]: **trump up** *vt fus* (*inf derog*) to invent or make up (false evidence, accusations *etc*): *He said that the police had trumped up a charge against him.*

'trumped-up *adj* (*inf derog*: *attrib*): *a trumped-up charge.*

trumpet ['trʌmpit] *nc* **1** a brass musical wind instrument with a high, clear tone: *He plays the trumpet*; *He played a tune on his trumpet.* **2** (*usu in sing*) the cry of an elephant: *The elephant gave a loud trumpet.* – *vi* (*esp* of an elephant) to make a noise like a trumpet: *The elephant trumpeted wildly.*

'trumpeter *nc* a person who plays the trumpet.

'trumpet-call *nc* a signal, *esp* a call to action, played on a trumpet.

blow one's own trumpet (*inf*) to boast, praise oneself greatly *etc*: *He really isn't very clever but he is always blowing his own trumpet.*

truncated [trʌŋ'keitid, (*Amer*) 'trʌŋkeitid] *adj* (*formal or facet*) shortened by cutting off a part, *esp* the end: *a truncated version of the play.*

truncheon ['trʌntʃən] *nc* a short heavy stick, carried *esp* by British policemen for use in self-defence *etc*: *The thief claimed that the policeman injured him badly by hitting him with his truncheon.*

trundle ['trʌndl] *vti* (*with* **along, through** *etc*) to (cause to) roll slowly and heavily along on wheels: *He trundled the wheelbarrow down the garden*; *The huge lorry trundled along the road*; (*inf*); *We were trundling along in the car when I saw him.*

trunk [trʌŋk] *nc* **1** the main stem (of a tree): *The trunk of this tree is five metres thick.* **2** a large box or chest for packing or keeping clothes *etc* in: *He packed his trunk and sent it to Canada by sea*; *We store our old clothes in a trunk in the attic.* **3** an elephant's long nose: *The elephant sucked up water into its trunk.* **4** the body (not including the head, arms and legs) of a person (and certain animals): *He had a powerful trunk, but thin arms*; *The police have found the trunk of a dead woman.* **5** (*Amer*) a boot (*def 2*): *Put your baggage in the trunk.*

trunks *n pl* (*often in cmpds*) short trousers or pants worn by boys or men, *esp* the type used for swimming: *swimming-trunks*; *He wore only a pair of bathing-trunks.*

'trunk call *nc* (*Brit*) a long-distance telephone call: *I wish to make a trunk call from London to Aberdeen.*

trunk road *nc* a main road between large towns *etc.*

truss [trʌs] *nc* **1** (*formal*) a bundle (of hay or straw): *The barn was full of trusses of hay.* **2** (*often tech*) a system of beams *etc* joined together to support something: *a roof-truss.* **3** a supporting belt or bandage for a person who has a hernia: *He has to wear a truss since his operation.* – *vt* (*often with* **up**) to tie or bind tightly: *She trussed the chicken and put it in the oven*; *The burglars trussed up the guards.*

trust [trʌst] **1** *vti* (*often with* **in**) to have confidence or faith; to believe: *She trusted (in) him*; *She trusted in his ability to look after her.* **2** *vt* to give (something to someone), believing that it will be used well and responsibly: *I can't trust him with my car*; *I can't trust my car to him.* **3** *vi* (*formal or facet*) to hope or be confident (that): *I trust (that) you had/will have a good journey.* – **1** *nu* (*with* **in**) belief or confidence in the power, reality, truth, goodness *etc* of a person or thing: *Try to have trust in him*; *The firm has a great deal of trust in your ability*; *trust in God.* **2** *nu* charge or care; responsibility: *The child was placed in my trust.* **3** *ncu* (*formal*) (the giving of) a task *etc* given to a person by someone who believes that they will do it, look after it *etc* well: *The Queen believed that the government of her kingdom was a sacred trust*; *He holds a position of trust in the firm.* **4** *ncu* arrangement(s) by which something (*eg* money) is given to a person to use in a particular way, or to keep until a particular time: *The money was to be held in trust for his children*; *He established a trust for the education of orphans*; (*attrib*) *a trust fund.* **5** *nc* a group of business firms working together: *The companies formed a trust.*

,trus'tee *nc* a person who keeps and takes care of something (*esp* money or property) for someone else: *He was appointed a trustee of the estate until the heir was old enough to manage it himself.*

'trustful *adj* full of trust (*def 1*). **'trustfully** *adv.* **'trustfulness** *nu.*

'trustworthy *adj* (*neg* **un-**) worthy of trust: *Is your friend trustworthy?*; *a trustworthy colleague.* **'trustworthiness** *nu.*

'trusty *adj* (*old, formal or facet*: *attrib*) able to be trusted or depended on: *a trusty sword*; *a trusty friend.* **'trustily** *adv.* **'trustiness** *nu.*

take (something or someone) on trust to accept or believe (someone or something) without checking: *He always takes his friends on trust*; *He took it on trust that he would be made president.*

See also **distrust, entrust**.

truth [tru:θ] – *pl* **truths** [tru:ðz, tru:θz] – **1** *nu* (*sometimes with* **the**) trueness; the state of being true: *I am certain of the truth of his story*; *'What is truth?' asked the philosopher*; *He worships truth and beauty*; *The police disputed the truth of his statement.* **2** *nu* (*with* **the**) the true facts: *I don't know, and that's the truth!*; *Tell the truth about it.* **3** *nc* (*neg* **un-**: *formal*) a true fact: *He told her several truths about himself* – *See also* **home truth** *under* **home**.

'truthful *adj* (*neg* **un-**) **1** (of a person) telling the truth: *She's a truthful child*; *She is honest and truthful.* **2** (*formal*: *usu attrib*) true: *a truthful* account of what happened. **'truthfully** *adv.* **'truthfulness** *nu.*

tell the truth to confess or make a true statement: *The man told the truth and admitted he murdered his wife; It is sometimes more difficult to tell the truth than it is to tell a lie.*

to tell the truth really; actually: *To tell the truth I forgot it was your birthday last week.*

See also **true**.

try [trai] **1** *vi* (*less formal than* **attempt**: *with* **to, for** *or* (*less formal*) **and**) to attempt or make an effort (to do, get *etc*): *He tried to answer the questions; He tried for a scholarship; We'll try for* (= attempt to get to) *the shore; Let's try and climb that tree!; You might at least try!* **2** *vt* to test; to make an experiment (with) in order to find out whether something will be successful, satisfactory *etc*: *She tried washing her hair with a new shampoo; He tried the door* (= turned the handle to find out if it would open) *but it was locked; Have you tried* (= tasted) *the local beer?; I'd like to try* (= taste) *some Greek food; I think we'll try Germany for our holiday this year.* – *See also* **try out** *below.* **3** *vt* (*usu in passive*) to judge (someone or their case) in a court of law: *The prisoners were tried for murder; The case was tried in secret.* **4** *vt* (*formal*) to test the limits of; to strain: *You are trying my patience; Her unhappy experience tried her faith.* – *nc* **1** (*slightly inf*) an attempt or effort: *Have a try* (*at the exam*). *I'm sure you will pass.* **2** in rugby football, an act of putting the ball on the ground behind the opponents' goal-line: *Our team scored three tries.*

tried *adj* (*neg* **un-**: *attrib*) tested and proved to be good, efficient *etc*: *a tried and trusted remedy for colds.*

'trier *nc* (*inf*) a person who keeps on trying, who does not give up: *He may not be very good, but he's a trier.*

'trying *adj* **1** difficult; causing strain or anxiety: *It's a very trying time for her, with her father being ill; Having to stay such a long time in hospital must be very trying.* **2** (*derog*) (of people) stretching one's patience to the limit; annoying: *She's a very trying woman!; That child is so trying!*

'try-on *nc* (*inf derog*) an attempt to deceive: *He pretended to be blind and begged for money from the old lady, but she realized it was a try-on; This is just another of his try-ons.* – *See also* **try on** *below.*

try one's hand at (*inf*) to see if one can do (something): *He tried his hand at farming; I think I'll try my hand at swimming.*

try on *vt sep* **1** to put on (clothes *etc*) to see if they fit: *She tried on a new hat; I've bought a dress but I haven't tried it on yet.* **2** (*inf*: *usu with* **it**) to attempt to do (something); to indulge in (a certain kind of behaviour) *etc* in order to see whether it will be allowed: *Take no notice of the child's behaviour – he's just trying it on.* – *See also* **try-on** *above.*

try out *vt sep* to test (something) by using it: *He tried out the bicycle; We are trying out new teaching methods; I think I'd like that washing-machine but I'd like to try it out before I buy it.*

See also **trial**.

tryst [trist] *nc* (*arch or liter*) an arrangement to meet someone, *esp* a lover, at a certain place (called a **'trysting-place**): *a lover's tryst.*

tsar, czar, tzar [za:] *nc* (*with cap in titles*) (the status of) any of the former emperors of Russia: *He was crowned tsar; Tsar Nicholas.*

tsarina, czarina, tzarina [za:'ri:nə] *nc* (*with cap in titles*) **1** (the status of) the wife or widow of a tsar. **2** (the status of) a woman who was an empress of Russia in her own right.

tsetse ['tsetsi] *nc* (*also* **'tsetse-fly**) a kind of African fly which causes dangerous diseases in men and animals.

T-shirt *see* **T**.

tub [tʌb] *nc* **1** (*often in cmpds*) a round (*usu* wooden) container for keeping water, washing clothes *etc*: *a huge tub of water; a rain-water tub; My grandmother washed clothes in a wash-tub.* **2** (*inf or Amer*: *usu in sing*) a bath: *He was sitting in the tub; It's time for my tub.* **3** a small round (*esp* plastic or cardboard) container for ice-cream *etc*: *The child was eating a tub of chocolate ice-cream in the cinema.* **4** (*inf derog*) a boat: *You'll never cross the Atlantic in that ancient tub.*

'tubby *adj* (*inf*) rather fat: plump: *a tubby child; She was rather tubby as a child but she is very slim now.*

tuba ['tju:bə] *nc* a large brass musical wind instrument giving a low-pitched range of notes: *He plays the tuba; He played the tune on the tuba.*

tubby *see* **tub**.

tube [tju:b] *nc* **1** a long, low cylinder-shaped object through which liquid can pass; a pipe: *The water flowed through a rubber tube; a glass tube.* **2** an organ of this kind in animals or plants: *the bronchial tubes.* **3** (*esp with* **the**: *inf*) an underground railway (*esp* in London): *I go to work on the tube/by tube; (attrib) a tube train/station.* **4** a container for a semi-liquid substance *eg* paint, which is got out by squeezing: *I must buy a tube of toothpaste; a tube of tomato puree.* **5** a cathode-ray tube: *Our television tube has broken.*

'tubeless *adj* (of a tyre) having no inner tube.

'tubing *nu* (material for) a length or system of tubes (*def 1*): *metal tubing; two metres of tubing.*

'tubular [-bjulə] *adj* (*formal or tech*: *esp attrib*) **1** made of, or consisting of tubes: *tubular steel; tubular furniture.* **2** shaped like a tube: *a tubular shape; the container is tubular in shape.*

tuber ['tju:bə] *nc* (*tech*) a swelling on the stem or root of a plant, in which food is stored: *Potatoes are the tubers of the potato plant.*

tuberculosis [tjubə:kju'lousis] *nu* (*often abbrev* **TB** [ti:'bi:]) an infectious disease *usu* affecting the lungs: *He suffers from/has tuberculosis.*

tu'bercular *adj* (*formal or tech*: *esp attrib*) of, suffering from, or affected with, tuberculosis: *tubercular lungs; He has a tubercular cough.*

tubing, tubular *see* **tube**.

tuck [tʌk] **1** *nc* a fold sewn into a piece of material: *Her dress had tucks in the sleeves; This dress is too large at the waist – I must put a tuck in it.* **2** *nu* (*slightly old inf*) sweets, cakes *etc*: *Schoolboys used to spend their money on tuck; (attrib) a tuck shop.* – *vt* (*with* **in** *or* **into**) to push, stuff *etc*: *He tucked his shirt into his trousers.*

tuck in **1** *vt sep* to gather bedclothes *etc* closely round: *I said goodnight and tucked him in.* **2** *vi* (*inf*) to eat greedily or with enjoyment: *They sat down to breakfast and started to tuck in straight away.*

tuck into *vt fus* (*inf*) to eat eagerly: *He tucked into his tea.*

tuck up *vt sep* to tuck in (*def 1*): *It's late. You should be tucked up in bed.*

Tudor ['tju:də] *adj* of (the style or time of) the English kings and queens of the period 1485-1603: *the Tudor period; Tudor architecture.*

Tuesday ['tju:zdi] *nc* the third day of the week, the

day following Monday: *He came on Tuesday*; *He will arrive next Tuesday*; *He goes on Tuesdays* (= every Tuesday, or only on a Tuesday but not necessarily every Tuesday); (*attrib*) *Tuesday evening.*

tuft [tʌft] *nc* a small bunch or clump (of grass, hair, feathers, wool *etc*): *She sat down on a tuft of grass*; *The bird had a tuft of feathers on top of its head.*

'tufted *adj* (*usu attrib*) having or growing in tufts: *a tufted carpet*; *tufted grass.*

tug [tʌg] – *pt, ptp* **tugged** – *vti* (*often with* **at**) to pull (something) sharply and strongly: *He tugged* (*at*) *the door but it wouldn't open*; *The child tugged at his mother's coat*; *She tried to tug my hand away*; *She tried to tug the book away from me.* – *nc* **1** a strong, sharp pull: *He gave the rope a tug.* **2** a tug-boat.

'tug-boat *nc* a small boat with a very powerful engine, for towing larger ships.

ˌtug-of-'war *nc* a competition in which two people or teams pull at opposite ends of a rope, trying to pull their opponents over a centre line.

tuition [tju'iʃən] *nu* (*more formal than* **teaching**) teaching, *esp* private: *He gives music tuition/tuition in music*; (*attrib*) *tuition fees.*
See also **tutor**.

tulip ['tju:lip] *nc* a kind of plant with brightly-coloured cup-shaped flowers, grown from a bulb: *tulips and daffodils and other Spring flowers.*

tulle [tju:l] *nu, adj* (of) a type of cloth made of thin silk or rayon net: *a dress made of tulle*; *a tulle dress.*

tum *see* **tummy**.

tumble ['tʌmbl] **1** *vti* (*with* **down, over** *etc*) to (cause to) fall, *esp* in a helpless or confused way: *She tumbled down the stairs*; *I tumbled over the cat*; *The box suddenly tumbled off the top of the wardrobe*; (*fig*) *The children tumbled into/out* (= got in/out in a disorganized group) *of the car*; (*formal*) *Many types of electric clothes-driers tumble the clothes as they dry.* **2** *vi* (*usu with* **to**: *inf*) to understand or realize (suddenly): *All at once he tumbled to my plan*: *He has been deceiving her for many years but she has still not tumbled to it* (= realized that he has been deceiving her). – *nc* (*inf*) a fall: *She took a tumble* (= She fell) *on the stairs.*

'tumbler *nc* **1** a large drinking glass: *a tumbler of whisky.* **2** a tumblerful.

'tumblerful *nc* the amount contained by a tumbler: *two tumblerfuls of water.*

'tumbledown *adj* (*usu attrib*) (of a building) falling to pieces: *a tumbledown old house.*

ˌtumble-'drier *nc* a machine for drying clothes by tumbling them around and blowing hot air into them.

tummy ['tʌmi] *nc* (*inf*: *also* (*facet*) **tum**) a (*esp* child's) word for stomach (*def 2*): *She has a pain in her tummy*; (*attrib*) *a tummy-ache.*

tumour, (*Amer*) **tumor** ['tju:mə] *nc* an abnormal (dangerous) mass of tissue growing on or in the body: *a brain tumour*; *The surgeon removed a tumour from her bladder.*

tumult ['tju:mʌlt] *nc* (*liter*) a great noise (*usu* made by a crowd): *He could hear a great tumult in the street.*

tu'multuous [-tʃuəs] *adj* (*formal or liter*: *usu attrib*) with great noise or confusion: *The crowd gave him a tumultuous welcome*; *tumultuous applause.* **tu'multuously** *adv.*

in 'tumult (*formal or liter*) in a state of great confusion or excitement: *His mind was in tumult.*

tuna(-fish) ['tʃu:nə(fiʃ), (*Amer*) 'tu:nə(-)] – *pls* **'tuna, 'tuna-fish, 'tunas** – (*also* **tunny(-fish)** ['tʌni(fiʃ)] – *pls* **'tunnies, 'tunny, 'tunny-fish**) – **1** *nc* a kind of large sea-fish of the mackerel family. **2** *nu* its flesh, used as food: *a plate of tuna*; (*attrib*) *a tuna salad.*

tundra ['tʌndrə] *ncu* (*tech*: *usu with* **the**) (an area of) treeless plains in Arctic regions: *They travelled across the tundra.*

tune [tju:n] *nc* musical notes put together in a particular (melodic and pleasing) order; a melody: *He played a tune on the violin*; *She wrote the words of the song and he wrote the tune.* – *See also* **in tune, out of tune** *below.* – *vt* **1** to adjust (a musical instrument, or its strings *etc*) to the correct pitch: *The orchestra tuned their instruments*; *He has come to tune the piano.* – *See also* **tune up** *below.* **2** to adjust a radio so that it receives a particular station: *The radio was tuned to a German station.* – *See also* **tune in** *below.* **3** to adjust (an engine, non-musical instrument *etc*) so that it runs well: *He had the engine of his motorbike tuned at the garage.*

'tuneful *adj* **1** having a good, clear, pleasant *etc* tune: *I like tuneful music*; *That song is very tuneful.* **2** full of music: *a tuneful show.* **'tunefully** *adv.* **'tunefulness** *nu.*

'tuneless *adj* (*esp attrib*) without a good *etc* tune; unmusical: *tuneless music*; *The child was singing in a tuneless voice.* **'tunelessly** *adv.* **'tunelessness** *nu.*

'tuner *nc* **1** (*also* **pi'ano-tuner**) a person whose profession is tuning pianos. **2** the dial on a radio *etc* used to tune in to the different stations. **3** a radio which is part of a stereo system.

'tuning-fork *nc* a piece of metal with two prongs, which gives out a certain fixed note when struck and is used in tuning pianos *etc.*

call the tune (*inf*) to be the person who gives the orders: *He calls the tune in this office.*

change one's tune (*inf*) to change one's attitude, opinions *etc*: *He said he liked travelling by train, but after six hours standing in the corridor he changed his tune.*

in 'tune 1 (of a musical instrument) having been adjusted so as to give the correct pitches: *Are your instruments in tune?*; *Is the violin in tune with the piano?* **2** (of a person's singing voice) at the same pitch as that of other voices or instruments: *Someone in the choir isn't* (*singing*) *in tune*; (*fig*) *The sunny weather was in tune with his happy mood.*

out of tune not in tune.

to the 'tune of (*inf*) amounting to the sum or total of: *He received bills to the tune of £20.*

tune in *vi, vt sep* (*often with* **to**) to tune a radio (to a particular station or programme): *We usually tune* (*the radio*) *in to the news.*

tune up *vi* (of an orchestra *etc*) to tune instruments: *The orchestra stopped tuning up just before the conductor came on stage.*

tunic ['tju:nik] *nc* **1** a soldier's or policeman's jacket. **2** (*hist*) a loose garment reaching to or nearly to the knees, worn *esp* in ancient Greece and Rome. **3** a similar type of modern garment: *a gym tunic* (= a type of short dress worn by schoolgirls as part of their uniform).

Tunisia, Tunisian *see* Appendix 2.

tunnel ['tʌnl] *nc* a (*usu* man-made) underground passage, *esp* one cut through a hill or under a river: *The road goes through a tunnel under the River Tyne*; *a railway tunnel*; *The prisoners dug a* *tunnel under their cell and so managed to escape; Moles make underground tunnels.* – *v* – *pt, ptp* **'tunnelled**, (*Amer*) **'tunneled** – *vi* to make a tunnel: *They escaped from prison by tunnelling under the walls.*

tunny(-fish) *see* **tuna(-fish)**.

tuppence, tuppenny *see* **two**.

turban ['tə:bən] *nc* **1** a long piece of cloth worn wound round the head, *esp* by men belonging to certain of the races and religions of Asia. **2** a woman's hat similar to this: *Mrs Smith wore a silk turban.*

turbine ['tə:bain] *nc* a type of motor, operated by the action of water, steam, gas *etc*: *a steam turbine*; (*attrib*) *a turbine engine.*

turbo- [tə:bou] (*in cmpds*) having a turbine engine: *a turbojet* (*aircraft*).

turbot ['tə:bət] – *pls* **'turbot, 'turbots** – **1** *nc* a kind of large, flat fish: *He caught several turbot.* **2** *nu* its flesh, used as food: *fried turbot.*

turbulent ['tə:bjulənt] *adj* (*formal or liter*) violently disturbed or confused: *turbulent water*; *The seas are turbulent*; (*fig*) *the turbulent years of war*; (*fig*) *a turbulent mob.* **'turbulently** *adv.* **'turbulence** *nu.*

turd [tə:d] *nc* (*vulg*) a lump of (animal's) excrement: *a dog turd.*

tureen [tə'ri:n] *nc* a large dish from which soup or vegetables are served at table: *He served the soup from a large tureen*; *a soup tureen.*

turf [tə:f] – *pl* **turfs** [-fs], **turves** (*formal*) [-vz] – **1** *nu* rough grass (*esp* on moorland) and the earth it grows out of: *He walked across the springy turf.* **2** *ncu* (a *usu* square piece of) grass and earth: *We laid turf in our garden to make a lawn*; *We have ordered several turfs of a new type of grass to make our lawn.* **3** *nu* (*inf*: *with* **the**) horse-racing and everything concerned with it: *He's very interested in the turf.* – *vt* **1** (*formal*) to cover with turf(s): *We are going to turf that part of the garden.* **2** (*inf*: *esp Brit*) to throw: *Turf that book over here*; *We turfed him out of the house*; *I turfed out all my old clothes.*

'turf accountant (*formal*) *nc* a bookmaker.

turgid ['tə:dʒid] *adj* (*formal*: *derog*) (of language) sounding important but meaning very little; pompous: *He writes turgid verse*; *His prose is rather turgid.* **'turgidly** *adv.* **'turgidness, tur'gidity** *nus.*

Turk, Turkey *see* Appendix 2.

turkey ['tə:ki] **1** *nc* a kind of large farmyard bird. **2** *nu* its flesh used as food, eaten *esp* at Christmas or (in the US) Thanksgiving: *We had turkey for dinner.*

Turkish ['tə:kiʃ]: **Turkish bath** *nc* a room filled with hot air or steam in which people are massaged, made to sweat *etc.*

Turkish delight *nu* a kind of sticky, jelly-like sweet: *He bought me a box of Turkish delight.*

See also Appendix 2.

turmeric ['tə:mərik] *nu* a powder made from the underground stem of an Indian plant, often used in making curry.

turmoil ['tə:moil] *ncu* (*formal or facet*) a state of wild confused movement or disorder: *The crowd/His mind was in* (*a*) *turmoil.*

turn [tə:n] **1** *vti* to (make something) move or go round; to revolve: *The wheels turned*; *What makes the wheels of that machine turn round?*; *He turned the handle*; *She turned the pages of her book.* **2** *vi* to face or go in another direction: *He turned and walked away*; *She turned towards him*; *She turned round when she heard his voice.* **3** *vi* to change direction: *The road turned to the left*; (*fig*) *His thoughts turned to supper.* **4** *vt* to direct; to aim or point: *He turned his gaze on her*; *He turned his attention to his work.* **5** *vt* to go around: *They turned the corner.* **6** *vti* (*with* **in(to)**) to (cause something to) become or change to: *You can't turn lead into gold*; *His love turned to hate*; *At what temperature does water turn into ice?*; *In the fairy story the witch turned the prince into a frog.* **7** *vti* to (cause to) change colour to: *Her hair turned white*; *The shock turned his hair white.* **8** *vti* (of milk) to make or become sour: *The hot weather turned the milk*; *Milk soon turns in summer.* **9** *vt* to make into a circular shape (on a lathe or a potter's wheel): *He turned the wood/a candlestick on a lathe.* **10** *vi* (*with* **on**) to move or swing around a point or pivot: *The gate turned on its hinge*; (*fig*) *He turned on his heel and left.* **11** *vi* (*with* **on**) to depend: *This is the point of disagreement on which the whole affair turns.* **12** *vi* (of leaves) to change colour: *The leaves begin to turn in September.* **13** *vt* (*inf*) to pass the age or time of: *She must have turned forty*; *It's turned three o'clock.* – *See also* **turn** *in phrases below.* – *nc* **1** an act of turning: *He gave the handle a turn*; *The dancer executed a perfect turn.* **2** (*tech*) a winding or coil: *There are eighty turns of wire on this aerial.* **3** (*also* **'turning**) a point where one can change direction, *eg* where one road joins another: *Take the third turn*(*ing*) *on/to the left*; (*fig formal*) *His life took a new turn*(*ing*). **4** one's chance or duty (to do, have *etc* something shared by several people): *It's your turn to choose a record*; *You'll have to wait your turn in the bathroom*; *He took a turn at the machine*; *a turn of duty.* – *See also* **take turns** *below.* **5** one of a series of short circus or variety acts, or the person or persons who perform it: *The show opened with a comedy turn.* **6** (*old inf*) a short walk: *He took a turn along the beach.* **7** (*inf*) a nervous shock; a fit of dizziness: *It gave her quite a turn*; *She had a nasty turn while she was out shopping.* – *See also* **turn** *in phrases below.*

'turner *nc* (*usu in cmpds*) a person who turns (something) on a lathe: *a metal-turner.*

'turning *see* **turn** (*n def 3*).

'turncoat *nc* (*derog*) a person who betrays his party, principles *etc*, or (*esp* treacherously) changes his loyalties.

-turned-out (*in cmpds*) dressed: *a very ˌwell-turned-out young 'man.*

'turning-point *nc* a place where a turn (*def 3*) is made: *the turning-point in the race*; (*fig*) *a turning-point in his life.*

'turnkey [-ki:] *nc* (*hist*) a person who keeps the keys in a prison.

'turn-out *nc* the number of people who have come to a meeting, celebration, event *etc*: *There was a good turn-out at the election.* – *See also* **turn out** (*def 4*) *below.*

'turnover *nc* (*no pl*) **1** the total value of sales in a business during a certain time: *The firm had a turnover of £50 000 last year.* **2** the rate at which money or workers pass through a business: *a regular turnover of money*; *a fast turnover of workers.*

'turnpike *nc* **1** (*Amer*) an express highway, *esp* one on which a toll must be paid. **2** (*hist*) a gate across a road, which was opened when the traveller paid a toll.

'turnstile *nc* a revolving gate which allows only one person to pass at a time, *usu* after payment of entrance fees *etc*: *There is a turnstile at the entrance to the football ground.*

'turntable *nc* **1** the revolving part of a record-player on which the record rests while it is being played: *He put another record on the turntable so that people could dance to the music.* **2** (*tech*) a revolving platform for turning a railway engine round.

'turn-up *nc* **1** a piece of material which is folded up at the bottom of a trouser-leg: *Trousers with turn-ups are not fashionable at the moment.* **2** (*also* **a turn-up for the book**: *inf*) something which happens unexpectedly: *He's won a lot of money – what a turn-up (for the book)! – See also* **turn up** *below.*

at every turn (*formal or liter*) everywhere, at every stage *etc*: *She encountered difficulties at every turn.*

by 'turns in turn (*see below*).

do (someone) a good turn to do something helpful for someone: *He did me several good turns.*

done to a turn (*inf*) cooked to exactly the right degree: *The meat was done to a turn.*

in 'turn, by turns one after another, in regular order: *They answered the teacher's questions in turn.*

not turn a hair (*inf*) to be calm and unsurprised: *He didn't turn a hair when she told him she had spent all his money.*

on the turn 1 (of the tide *etc*) in the process of turning: *The tide is on the turn.* **2** (*inf*) (of milk *etc*) on the point of going sour: *This cream is on the turn.*

out of turn out of the correct order: *He answered a question out of turn* (= when it was not his turn to do so); (*facet*) *I'm sorry if I spoke out of turn* (= impertinently).

take a turn for the better, worse (of things or people) to become better or worse: *His fortunes have taken a turn for the better*; *Her health has taken a turn for the worse.*

take turns (of two or more people) to do something one after the other, not at the same time: *We took turns at pushing the pram*; *They took turns to look after the baby.*

turn a blind eye (*inf*: *usu with* **to**) to pretend not to see or notice (something): *Because he works so hard, his boss turns a blind eye when he comes in late.*

turn (and turn) about one after the other, each taking his turn (*n def 4*): *They drove the car turn (and turn) about.*

turn a deaf ear (*usu with* **to**) to refuse to listen (to): *He turned a deaf ear (to her requests).*

turn against *vt fus* to become dissatisfied with or hostile to (people or things that one previously liked *etc*): *He turned against his friends.*

turn (someone) against (someone or something) to cause (a person) to become dissatisfied or hostile to (a person or thing): *She turned him against his family by constantly criticizing them.*

turn away *vi, vt sep* to move or send away: *He turned away in disgust*; *The police turned away the crowds*; *The police turned them away.*

turn back *vi, vt sep* to (cause to) go back in the opposite direction: *He got tired and turned back*; *The travellers were turned back at the frontier*; *The police turned them back.*

turn one's back on to leave for ever; to have no more to do with: *He has turned his back on his past way of life.*

turn down *vt sep* **1** to say 'no' to; to refuse: *He turned down her offer/request.* **2** to reduce (the level of light, noise *etc*) produced by (something): *Please turn down (the volume on) the radio – it's far too loud!*; *The lights in the auditorium were turned down before the concert performance.*

turn one's hand to to (have the ability to) do a job *etc*: *He can turn his hand to anything, from painting to engineering.*

turn someone's head to make someone conceited *etc*: *Success has turned his head.*

turn in (*inf*) **1** *vi* (*Brit*) to go to bed: *I usually turn in at about 11 o'clock.* **2** *vt sep* to hand over (a person or thing) to people in authority: *They turned the escaped prisoner in to the police.*

turn king's/queen's evidence *see* **king**.

turn loose to set free: *He turned the horse loose in the field.*

turn off *vt sep* **1** to cause (water, electricity *etc*) to stop flowing: *I've turned off the water/the electricity.* **2** to turn (a tap, switch *etc*) so that something stops: *I turned off the tap.* **3** to cause (something) to stop working by switching it off: *He turned off the light/the oven.* **4** (*sl*) to create feelings of dislike, repulsion, disgust *etc* in (someone): *People with loud voices turn me off*; *I was turned off by the callous treatment of her family.*

turn of mind way of thinking: *She has a very logical turn of mind.*

turn of phrase way of expressing things: *He has a very blunt turn of phrase.*

the turn of the month, year, century the end of one month or year or century and the beginning of the next: *He hasn't been to Leeds since the turn of the year.*

turn on 1 *vt sep* to make water, electric current *etc* flow: *He turned on the water/the gas.* **2** *vt sep* to turn (a tap, switch *etc*) so that something works: *I turned on the tap.* **3** *vt sep* to cause (something) to work by switching it on: *He turned on the radio.* **4** *vt sep* (*sl*) to create feelings of excitement, interest, lust, pleasure *etc* in (someone): *Music really turns me on.* **5** *vt fus* to attack: *The dog turned on him. – See also* **turn** (*v defs 10 and 11*).

turn out 1 *vt oblig sep* to send away; to make (someone) leave: *His parents threatened to turn him out* (= make him leave home) *if he ever got into trouble with the police.* **2** *vt sep* to make or produce: *The factory turns out ten finished articles an hour*; (*fig*) *The school turns out well-behaved young women.* **3** *vt sep* to empty or clear: *I turned out the cupboard.* **4** *vi* (of a crowd) to come out; to get together for a (public) meeting, celebration *etc*: *A large crowd turned out to see the procession. – See also* **turn-out** *above.* **5** *vt sep* to turn off (*def 3*): *Turn out the light!* **6** *vi* to happen or prove to be: *He turned out to be right*; *It turned out that he was right*; *The weather turned out (to be) fine*; *You said we shouldn't trust him, and you were right, as it turns out.*

turn over *vt sep* **1** (*fig*) to think about: *She turned it over in her mind.* **2** (*often with* **to**) to give (something) up (to): *He turned the money over to the police.*

turn someone's stomach, make someone's stomach turn (*inf*) to make someone feel sick: *The smell turned my stomach.*

turn tail (*liter*) to turn and run away: *When the enemy appeared over the hill, the soldiers turned tail and fled.*

turn the corner *see* **corner**.

turn the tables (*often with* **on**) to reverse a situation *etc* and put (someone) in a totally different position, *esp* one where he has lost his previous advantage: *I'll turn the tables on you one day, and I will be the boss.*

turn to *vi* to get down to (hard) work: *She turned to and scrubbed the floor.* – *See also* **turn** (*v defs 3 and 4*).

turn turtle *see* **turtle**.

turn up 1 *vi* (*inf*) to appear or arrive: *He turned up at our house.* **2** *vi* (*inf*) to be found: *Don't worry – it'll turn up again.* **3** *vt sep* to increase (the level of noise, light *etc*) produced by (something): *Turn up* (*the volume on*) *the radio*; *The lights in the auditorium were turned up again at the end of the concert performance.* **5** *vt sep* to fold up and sew: *to turn up a hem.* **6** *vt sep* (*inf*) to discover (facts) *etc*: *The police have apparently turned up some new evidence.* – *See also* **turn-up** (*def 1*).

a turn-up for the book *see* **turn-up** (*def 2*).

turnip ['tə:nip] **1** *nc* a type of plant with a large round root: *a field of turnips.* **2** *nu* the root used as food: *Would you like some turnip!*

turnkey, turnpike, turnstile, turntable *see* **turn**.

turpentine ['tə:pəntain] *nu* (*often* (*inf*) *abbrev* **turps** [tə:ps]) a type of oil obtained from certain trees and used for thinning certain kinds of paint, cleaning paint-brushes *etc.*

turquoise ['tə:kwoiz] **1** *ncu* a kind of greenish-blue precious stone: *The ring was set with a turquoise*; (*attrib*) *a turquoise ring.* **2** *nu*, *adj* (of) its colour: (*a*) *pale turquoise* (*dress*).

turret ['tʌrit, (*Amer*) 'tə:rit] *nc* **1** a small tower on a castle or other building: *a fortress often has turrets.* **2** (*also* '**gun-turret**) a small tower-like structure on which guns are attached *esp* on a ship: *a war-ship with twin* (*gun-*)*turrets.*

'**turreted** *adj* having turrets (*def 1*): *a turreted castle.*

turtle *nc* a kind of large tortoise, *esp* one living in water.

'**turtle-neck** *nc* (a garment, *esp* a sweater, with) a high round neck: *He was wearing a turtle-neck*; (*attrib*) *a turtle-neck sweater.*

turtle soup *nu* soup made from the flesh of a type of turtle.

turn turtle (of a boat *etc*) to turn upside down; to capsize: *The boat turned turtle in the rough sea.*

turtle-dove ['tə:tldʌv] *nc* a kind of dove, noted for its sweet song and its affection for its mate.

turves *see* **turf**.

tusk [tʌsk] *nc* one of a pair of large curved teeth which project from the mouth of certain animals *eg* the elephant, walrus, wild boar *etc.*

tussle ['tʌsl] *nc* (*inf*) a struggle or fight: *He had a tussle with his conscience*; *We had a bit of a tussle over the price of the house.*

tussock ['tʌsək] *nc* (*formal*) a clump of grass.

tut(-tut) (*sometimes* [tʌt('tʌt)]) *interj* used in writing to represent the sound used to express disapproval, mild annoyance *etc.*

tutor ['tju:tə] *nc* **1** a teacher of a group of students in a college or university. **2** a privately-employed teacher: *His parents employed a tutor to teach him Greek.* **3** a book which teaches a subject, *esp* music: *I bought a violin tutor.* – *vt* (*often with* **in**) to teach (a person about a subject): *He tutored the child in mathematics.*

tu'torial [-'to:-] *adj* (*usu attrib*) of or concerning a tutor: *a tutorial post.* – *nc* a lesson by a tutor at a college or university: *We have lectures and tutorials in history.*

See also **tuition**.

tutu ['tu:tu:] *nc* a female ballet dancer's short stiff skirt: *The ballerina only wears a tutu when she's dancing on stage – when she's practising she wears a leotard.*

tuxedo [tʌk'si:dou] – *pl* **tu'xedos** – *nc* (*Amer*: *inf abbrev* **tux**) a dinner-jacket or dinner-suit.

twaddle ['twodl] *nu* (*inf derog*) nonsense: *Don't talk such twaddle!*

twain [twein] *nu* (*arch or liter*) two: *Never the twain shall meet!*

in 'twain (*arch or liter*) in two (pieces): apart: *His heart was torn in twain.*

twang [twaŋ] *nc* **1** a sound of or like a tightly-stretched string breaking or being plucked: *The string broke with a sharp twang.* **2** (*inf*: *often derog*) a way of speaking in which the voice seems to come through the nose; a nasal tone of voice: *He speaks with an American twang.* – *vti* to make a twang (*def 1*): *He twanged his guitar*; *The wire twanged.*

tweak [twi:k] *vt* to pull with a sudden jerk: *He tweaked her hair.* – *nc* a sudden sharp pull: *He gave her nose a playful tweak.*

twee [twi:] *adj* (*inf derog*) too pretty, sweet, sentimental *etc*: *a terribly twee dress/person*; *The verses in that birthday card are terribly twee.*

tweed [twi:d] *nu*, *adj* (of) a kind of woollen cloth with a rough surface: *His suit was* (*made of*) *tweed*; *a tweed jacket.*

tweeds *n pl* clothes, *esp* a suit, made of tweed: *She wore tweeds.*

tweezers ['twi:zəz] *n pl* a tool for gripping or pulling hairs, small objects *etc*: *She used a pair of tweezers to pluck her eyebrows*; *I need some tweezers to get the splinter out of your finger.*

twelve [twelv] **1** *nc* the number or figure 12. **2** *nu* the age of 12. – *adj* **1** (*usu attrib*) 12 in number. **2** (*pred*) aged 12. – *See* **eight** *for constructions.*

twelve- (*in cmpds*) having twelve (of something) *a ˌtwelve-week de'lay.*

'**twelfth** [-fθ] **1** *nc* one of twelve equal parts. **2** *nc*, *adj* (the) last of twelve (people, things *etc*); (the) next after the eleventh. – *See* **eighth** *under* **eight** *for constructions.*

Twelfth Night, (*Amer*) '**Twelfth Night** *n* the twelfth day after Christmas (January 5 or 6, according to custom).

'**twelve-month** *nc* (*old or liter*) a year: *a twelve-month since* (= a year ago).

'**twelve-year-old** *nc* a person or animal who is twelve years old. – *adj* (*attrib*) (of a person, animal or thing) that is twelve years old. – *See* **eight-year-old** *under* **eight** *for constructions.*

See also Appendix 1.

twenty 1 *nc* the number or figure 20. **2** *nu* the age of 20. – *adj* **1** (*usu attrib*) 20 in number. **2** (*pred*) aged 20. – *See* **eighty** *for constructions.*

'**twenties** *n pl* **1** the period of time between one's twentieth and thirtieth birthdays. **2** the range of temperatures between twenty and thirty degrees. **3** the period of time between the twentieth and thirtieth years of a century. – *See* **eighties** *under* **eighty** *for constructions.*

'**twentieth 1** *nc* one of twenty equal parts. **2** *nc*, *adj* (the) last of twenty (people, things *etc*); (the) next after the nineteenth. – *See* **eightieth** *under* **eighty** *for constructions.*

twenty- (*in cmpds*) having twenty (of something): *a ˌtwenty-pound ˈfine.*

ˈtwenty-year-old *nc* a person who is twenty years old. – *adj* (*attrib*) (of a person or thing) twenty years old. – *See* **eighty-year-old** *under* **eighty** *for constructions.*

See also Appendix 1.

twerp, twirp [twəːp] *nc* (*inf derog*) a foolish person: *Silly twerp!*

twice [twais] *adv* **1** two times: *I've been to London twice.* **2** two times the (amount of): *She has twice the* (*amount of*) *courage he has; She has twice his courage.* **3** two times as good *etc* as: *He is twice the man you are.*

think twice about (doing) something to be very careful about considering (doing) something: *We thought twice about travelling in bad weather; I wouldn't think twice about sacking him.*

twiddle [ˈtwidl] *vt* (*inf*) to twist (something) round and round: *He twiddled the knob on the radio; She sat twiddling her pencil.*

twiddle one's thumbs (*inf fig*) to do nothing: *He spent six months twiddling his thumbs while he waited for a job.*

twig[1] [twig] *nc* a small branch of a tree: *The ground was covered with broken twigs.*

twig[2] [twig] – *pt, ptp* **twigged** – *vti* (*slightly old inf*) to understand (a joke, situation) *etc*: *It took me a long time to twig* (*that joke*): *Hasn't he twigged yet* (*that she's going out with his brother*)?

twilight [ˈtwailait] *nu* **1** (the time of) the dim light just before the sun rises or just after it sets: *the evening twilight.* **2** (*fig formal*) the time when the full strength or power of something is decreasing: *in the twilight of his life.*

twill [twil] *nu* a kind of strong woven cloth: *trousers made of cotton twill;* (*attrib*) *twill trousers.*

twin [twin] *nc* **1** one of two children or animals born of the same mother at the same time: *She gave birth to twins; She had just had twins;* (*attrib*) *They have twin daughters; They married twin sisters.* **2** (*fig*) one of two similar or identical things: *Her dress is the exact twin of mine;* (*attrib*) *a bedroom with twin beds.*

ˌtwin-ˈbedded *adj* (*usu attrib*) (of a room) having two single beds rather than a double bed.

ˌtwin-ˈengined *adj* having a pair of engines: *a twin-engined aircraft.*

ˈtwinset [-set] *nc* a matching sweater and cardigan: *She wore a twinset.*

twine [twain] *nu* a strong kind of string made of twisted, threads: *He tied the parcel with twine; He tied up the tomatoes with green garden twine.* – *vti* (*neg* **un-**: *with* **together, round** *etc*: *formal or liter*) to twist: *She twined her arms round him; The ivy twined round the tree; She twined ribbons into her hair.*

See also **entwine**.

twinge [twindʒ] *nc* a sudden sharp pain: *He felt a twinge* (*of pain*) *in his neck;* (*fig*) *a twinge of regret.*

twinkle [ˈtwiŋkl] *vi* **1** to shine with a small, slightly unsteady light: *The stars twinkled in the sky.* **2** (of eyes) to shine in this way *usu* to express amusement: *His eyes twinkled mischievously.* – **1** *nc* (*usu in sing*) an expression of amusement (in one's eyes): *He seemed very serious but he had a twinkle* (*in his eye*). **2** *nu* the act of twinkling (*def 1*): *the twinkle of the stars.*

in the ˈtwinkling of an ˈeye/in a ˈtwinkling in a moment; immediately: *He arrived in the twinkling of an eye.*

twirl [twəːl] *vti* to (cause to) turn round (and round); to spin: *She twirled her hair round her finger; The dancers twirled gaily.* – *nc* an act of twirling: *She did a quick twirl to show off her dress.*

twirp *see* **twerp**.

twist [twist] **1** *vti* to turn round (and round): *He twisted the knob; The road twisted through the mountains.* **2** *vti* to wind around or together: *He twisted the pieces of string* (*together*) *to make a rope; A piece of rope has twisted* (*itself*) *round the propeller.* **3** *vt* to force out of the correct shape or position: *The heat of the fire twisted the metal; He twisted her arm painfully; She twisted her ankle when she fell;* (*fig*) *The newspaper report twisted his words/what he had said.* – **1** *ncu* the act of twisting: *He gave her arm a twist.* **2** *nc* a twisted piece of something: *He lit his pipe with a twist of paper; He added a twist of lemon to her drink; a twist of tobacco.* **3** *nc* a turn, coil *etc*: *There's a twist in the rope; The accident happened at the twist in the road.* **4** *nc* (*fig*) a change in direction (of a story *etc*): *the story had a strange twist at the end.*

ˈtwisted *adj* bent out of shape: *a twisted branch;* (*fig*) *a twisted report;* (*fig*) *His mind is all twisted; a twisted sense of humour.*

ˈtwister *nc* (*inf derog*) a dishonest or deceiving person: *He's nothing but a twister.*

twist someone's arm (*inf*) to make someone do something: *'Will you have a drink?' 'Well, if you're twisting my arm, I'll have a whisky.'*

twist (someone) (a)round one's little finger (*inf*) to make (someone) do what one wants: *She can twist her father* (*a*)*round her little finger.*

See also **untwist**.

twit[1] [twit] *nc* (*inf derog*) a fool or idiot: *Stupid twit!*

twitch [twitʃ] *vti* **1** to (cause to) move jerkily: *His hands were twitching; The rabbit's nose twitched; Can you twitch your ears?* **2** to give a little pull or jerk to (something): *He twitched her sleeve; He twitched nervously at his collar.* – *nc* a twitching movement: *His foot gave a sudden twitch.*

ˈtwitchy *adj* (*inf*) nervous: *You're a bit twitchy* (*about something*)*; in a twitchy state.*

twitter [ˈtwitə] *nu* a light, repeated chirping sound, *esp* made by (small) birds: *He could hear the twitter of sparrows.* – *vi* to make such a noise: *The birds were twittering in the trees;* (*fig usu derog*) *She twittered* (*on*) *for hours about her children.*

two [tuː] **1** *nc* the number or figure 2. **2** *nu* the age of 2. – *adj* **1** (*usu attrib*) 2 in number. **3** (*pred*) aged 2. – *See* **eight** *for constructions.*

two- (*in cmpds*) having two (of something): *a ˌtwo-door ˈcar.*

ˌtwo-ˈfaced *adj* (*inf*) deceitful: *a two-faced person.*

ˌtwofold [-fould] **1** *adj, adv* (*formal or liter*) twice as much or as great: *He repaid the money twofold; a twofold return for one's money.* **2** *adj* (*formal*) with or in two parts: *The answer is twofold; a twofold reply.*

ˌtwo-ˈhanded *adj, adv* (to be used, played *etc*) with two hands: *a two-handed stroke.*

twopence/tuppence [ˈtʌpns, (*Amer*) ˈtuːpens] *nu* (*hist Brit*) the sum of two pence (*def 3*): *It cost twopence/tuppence.*

twopenny/tuppenny [ˈtʌpni, (*Amer*) ˈtuːpeni] *adj* (*hist Brit*: *attrib*) worth or costing twopence: *a twopenny stamp.*

twosome *nc* (a game *etc* for) two people; a couple: *They usually travel in a twosome; They played a twosome at tennis.*

ˌtwo-ˈtime *vt* (*sl*) to deceive (a boyfriend or girlfriend) by having a relationship with another person. 'two-timing *adj* (*attrib*).

ˌ**two-'way** *adj* (*attrib*) able to act, operate, be used *etc* in two ways or directions: *two-way traffic*; *a two-way radio.*

'**two-year-old** *nc* a person or animal that is two years old. – *adj* (*attrib*) (of a person, animal or thing) that is two years old. – *See* **eight-year-old** *under* **eight** *for constructions.*

in 'two (broken) in two pieces: *The magazine was torn in two.*

put two and two together (*inf*) to realize or work out from what one sees, hears *etc*: *You won't be able to keep your marriage a secret – people will soon put two and two together.*

See also **double, second, twice**, *and* Appendix 1.

tycoon [tai'kuːn] *nc* (*sometimes derog*) a rich and powerful businessman: *Several tycoons arrived in their private aeroplanes*; *an oil tycoon.*

tying *see* **tie**.

tympani, tympanist *see* **timpani**.

type[1] [taip] *nc* **1** a kind, sort; variety: *What type of house would you prefer to live in?*; *They are marketing a new type of washing powder*; *I would prefer a different type of education for my children*; (*inf*) *I prefer a beach type holiday to any other kind.* **2** (*inf*) a (*usu* male) person: *He's quite a pleasant type, really.*

'**typecast** *adj* (of an actor) always given the same kind of character to play: *He has become typecast as a policeman.* – *v* – *pt, ptp* '**typecast** – *vt* to cast (an actor) in this way.

See also **typical, typify**.

type[2] [taip] **1** *ncu* (a particular variety of) metal blocks with letters, numbers *etc* used in printing: *His job is to set the type for the printing of the newspaper*; *Can we have the headline printed in a different type?* **2** *nu* printed letters, words *etc*: *I can't read the type – it's too small.* – *vti* to write (something) using a typewriter: *Can you type?*; *I'm typing a letter.*

'**typing, typewriting** *nu* writing produced by a typewriter: *fifty pages of typing.*

'**typist** *nc* a person whose job is to type: *She works as a typist*; *She is a typist in a publishing firm.*

'**typeface** *nc* a set of letters for printing, cut in a particular style: *What typeface would you like this printed in?*

'**typescript 1** *nc* a typed copy (of a book *etc*): *the typescript of a novel.* **2** *nu* the writing produced by a typewriter: *The letter is easier to read in typescript than in handwriting.*

'**typesetter** *nc* a person or machine that sets printing type.

'**typewriter** *nc* a machine with keys for printing letters on a piece of paper: *a portable/an electric typewriter.*

ty'pographer *nc* (*tech*) a person who is skilled in typography.

typography [tai'pogrəfi] *nu* (*tech*) the art or style of printing: *If you are looking for a job in publishing it would be useful to have some knowledge of typography.* ˌ**typo'graphic** [-'gra-] *adj.* ˌ**typo'graphically** [-'gra-] *adv.*

typhoid (fever) ['taifoid] *nu* a dangerous type of infectious disease, caused by germs in food or drinking water: *He died of typhoid (fever)*; *The cook has typhoid and she has infected many of the hotel guests.*

typhoon [tai'fuːn] *nc* (*formal*) a violent sea-storm occurring in the East: *They were caught in a typhoon in the China seas.*

typhus ['taifəs] *nu* a dangerous type of infectious disease, spread by lice: *He died of typhus*; *She is suffering from typhus.*

typical ['tipikəl] *adj* (*neg* **un-**: *sometimes derog*: *sometimes with* **of**) having or showing the usual characteristics (of): *He is a typical Englishman*; *They're typical civil servants*; *This is a typical English country house*; *This mountain scenery is typical of Scotland*; *It was typical of her to say that*; *'I suppose he forgot his umbrella again?' 'Yes. 'Typical!'* '**typically** *adv.*

typify ['tipifai] *vt* (*formal*) to be a very good example of (someone who has): *To children he typified old-fashioned attitudes*; *She typifies the bored, intelligent housewife*; *Vandalism at football matches typifies the modern disregard for law and order.*

typing, typist, typography *see* **type**[2].

tyrant ['tairənt] *nc* a cruel and unjust ruler: *The people suffered under foreign tyrants*; *The emperor is a tyrant.*

tyrannical [ti'ranikəl], **tyrannous** ['tirənəs] *adjs* (*formal*) of or like a tyrant: *a tyrannical ruler*; *He is cruel and tyrannical*; *tyrannous behaviour*; *His actions were tyrannous.* **ty'rannically**, '**tyrannously** *advs.*

tyrannize, -ise ['ti-] *vti* (*formal*) to rule or treat (a person or people) cruelly and unjustly: *He tyrannizes his family*; *He tyrannized over the whole country.*

'**tyranny** ['ti-] *ncu* an action, or the method of ruling, of a tyrant: *People will always resist tyranny*; *People will remember the tyrannies of his reign.*

tyre, (*Amer*) **tire** ['taiə] *nc* a thick, rubber, *usu* air-filled strip around the edge of the wheel of a car, bicycle *etc*: *Lend me a bicycle pump – this bike has a flat tyre*; *The tyres of this car don't have enough air in them.*

tzar, tzarina *see* **tsar**.

Uu

u [juː]: ˌ**U-'turn** *nc* a turn, in the shape of the letter U, made by a motorist *etc* in order to reverse his direction: *No U-turns are allowed on motorways*; *He made a swift U-turn and went back the way he had come.*

ubiquitous [ju'bikwitəs] *adj* (*formal or facet*: *usu attrib*) present, or seen, everywhere: *There's that ubiquitous beer advertisement*; *The ubiquitous John Jones was at the party, of course.* **u'biquity, u'biquitousness** *nus.*

udder ['ʌdə] *nc*, (*inf*) '**udders** *n pl* the bag-like part of a cow, goat *etc*, with teats that supply milk for their young or for humans: *The cow has a diseased udder*; *the cow's udders.*

Uganda, Ugandan *see* Appendix 2.

ugh! [ə:(x), ʌ(x)] *interj* expressing disgust: *Ugh! The cat has been sick!*

ugly ['ʌgli] *adj* **1** unpleasant to look at: *She is rather an ugly young woman*; *He is old and ugly*; *That modern building is so ugly!* **2** unpleasant, nasty or dangerous: *ugly black clouds*; *An ugly situation developed outside the factory gates when fighting broke out*; *The crowd was in an ugly mood*; *The scene in the street grew more and more ugly as the crowd began to fight with the police*; (*inf*) *Keep away from him – he is an ugly customer* (= he is dangerous or difficult to deal with). '**ugliness** *nu*.
ugly duckling *nc* a member of a family who at first lacks beauty, cleverness *etc*, but later becomes the most beautiful or successful.

ukulele, ukelele [ju:kə'leili] *nc* a small, *usu* four-stringed guitar: *He plays the ukelele*; *He played a tune on his ukulele*.

ulcer ['ʌlsə] *nc* a kind of sore that does not heal easily, on the skin or inside the body: *a mouth/stomach ulcer*; *Her legs were covered with ulcers*.

ulterior [ʌl'tiəriə] *adj* (*formal derog*: *attrib*) (of the purpose or motive of a person's action) hidden; not openly stated at first: *She had an ulterior motive in bringing me the book – she wanted to borrow money*.

ultimate ['ʌltimət] *adj* (*formal*) last or final.
'**ultimately** *adv* (*formal*) in the end: *We hope ultimately to be able to buy a house of our own*; *Ultimately, our aims are the same as yours*.

ultimatum [ʌlti'meitəm] – *pl* ˌ**ulti'matums** – *nc* (*formal*) a final demand made by one person, nation *etc* to another, with a threat to stop peaceful discussion and declare war *etc* if the demand is ignored: *An ultimatum has been issued to him to withdraw his troops from our territory*.

ultra- [ʌltrə] (*in cmpds*) **1** beyond, as in **ultraviolet**. **2** (*sometimes derog*) very or excessively: *He's ultra-cautious when he drives a car*; *She is ultra-smartly dressed*.

ultrasonic [ʌltrə'sonik] *adj* (*tech*: *esp attrib*) (of sound waves *etc*) beyond the range of human hearing: *ultrasonic vibrations*; *medical techniques using ultrasonic waves*.

ultraviolet [ʌltrə'vaiəlit] *adj* (of light) consisting of rays from the invisible part of the spectrum beyond the purple, that have an effect on the skin, *eg* causing suntan.

umbilical [ʌm'bilikəl]: **umbilical cord** *nc* the cord that attaches an unborn baby to its mother.

umbrage ['ʌmbridʒ]: **take umbrage** (*old or facet*) to feel, and show that one is, offended by another person's action *etc*: *He took umbrage because I forgot to introduce him to my mother*.

umbrella [ʌm'brelə] *nc* **1** an apparatus for protecting a person from the rain, made of a folding covered framework attached to a stick with a handle: *Take an umbrella – it's going to rain*; *The wind blew my umbrella inside out*. **2** (*fig*) (political) authority or protection: *This action was taken under the umbrella of the United Nations*; *Primary education comes under the umbrella of local government*.

umpire ['ʌmpaiə] *nc* in cricket, tennis *etc*, a person who supervises a game, makes sure that it is played according to the rules, and decides doubtful points: *Tennis players usually have to accept the umpire's decision*; (*fig*) *If the industrial dispute cannot be settled, an umpire will be appointed to arbitrate between the two sides*. – *vti* to act as umpire: *Have you umpired a tennis match before?*; *Who is going to umpire?*

unable [ʌn'eibl] *adj* (*pred*: *often formal*) without enough strength, power, skill, opportunity, information *etc* to be able (to do something): *I am unable to get out of bed*; *They are unable to give you permission*; *Are the children unable to add these numbers correctly?*; *I shall be unable to meet you for lunch today*; *We are as yet unable to say when the train will arrive*.
See also **inability, disable**.

unaccountable [ʌnə'kauntəbl] *adj* (*formal*) that cannot be explained: *his unaccountable absence*; *His mistake is quite unaccountable*; *for some unaccountable reason*.
ˌ**unac'countably** *adv* (*formal*) in a way that cannot be explained: *He was unaccountably late/ill*.

unadulterated [ʌnə'dʌltəreitid] *adj* (*formal or facet*) pure, or not mixed with anything else: *a feeling of unadulterated hatred*; *Your drink is quite unadulterated*.

unaffected [ʌnə'fektid] *adj* (*formal*) **1** (*pred*) (of a person, his feelings *etc*) not moved or affected: *The child seemed unaffected by his father's death*. **2** (*pred*) (of an arrangement *etc*) not altered: *It has been raining heavily, but this evening's football arrangements are unaffected*. **3** (of a person) having a straightforward manner, without artificiality or pretence: *She's a pleasant, unaffected person*; *She is very wealthy but she is friendly and unaffected*. **4** (of a show of feeling) sincere or genuine: *He laughed with unaffected joy*; *His happiness was unaffected*.

unafraid [ʌnə'freid] *adj* (*formal*: *pred*) not afraid: *She remained unafraid throughout the terrifying experience*.

unalloyed [ʌnə'loid] *adj* (*liter*) (of joy, pleasure *etc*) pure, and unmixed with *eg* sadness, anxiety *etc*: *Her happiness was unalloyed*; *unalloyed bliss*.

unanimous [ju'naniməs] *adj* having, or showing, complete agreement: *The whole school was unanimous in its approval of the headmaster's plan*; *Money was to be provided for the playground through the unanimous decision of the town councillors*; *a unanimous vote*. **u'nanimously** *adv*.
una'nimity [ju:nə-] *nu* (*formal*) complete agreement: *An English jury has to reach unanimity in deciding its verdict*.

unanswerable [ʌn'a:nsərəbl] *adj* (*formal*) (of *eg* a line of reasoning, or a point made by a person in an argument) that cannot be proved false or denied: *Their argument is unanswerable*; *an unanswerable case against him*.

unapproachable [ʌnə'proutʃəbl] *adj* (of a person) formal and unfriendly: *The other teachers find the new headteacher a bit unapproachable*; *She is a stern, unapproachable person*.

unarmed [ʌn'a:md] *adj* without weapons or other means of defence: *Policemen in Britain are normally unarmed*; *The gangster shot an unarmed policeman*; *Judo is a type of unarmed fighting*.

unashamedly [ʌnə'ʃeimidli] *adv* (*formal or liter*) showing no shame or embarrassment: *She was weeping unashamedly*.

unassuming [ʌnə'sju:miŋ] *adj* (of a person or his personality) modest: *a quiet, unassuming man*; *You would never guess that he holds an important position in the firm – he is so unassuming*.

unattached [ʌnə'tatʃt] *adj* not married or engaged to be married: *A woman sometimes gives up hope of* *marriage if she is still unattached at the age of thirty; She frequently invites unattached young ladies to dinner to meet her son.*

unattended [ʌnəˈtendid] *adj* (*formal*: *often pred*) not under the care or supervision of anybody: *It is foolish of you to leave your luggage unattended on the railway platform; It is dangerous to leave small children unattended in the house.*

unauthorized, -s- [ʌnˈoːθəraizd] *adj* (*very formal*: *often attrib*) not having the permission of the people in authority: *unauthorized use of the firm's equipment.*

unavailing [ʌnəˈveiliŋ] *adj* (*formal*) (of efforts *etc*) useless, or made *etc* in vain: *his unavailing cries for help; They tried to free him but their efforts were unavailaing.*

unaware [ʌnəˈweə] *adj* not aware or not knowing: *I was unaware of the man's presence; She was unaware that the man was in the room.*

ˌunaˈwares *adv* unintentionally; without knowing: *She dropped her hat unawares; She hurt the child unawares.*

take (someone) unawares to surprise or startle (someone): *He came into the room so quietly that he took me unawares; The news took us unawares.*

unbalanced [ʌnˈbalənst] *adj* **1** (*often attrib*) without the proper amount of attention being given to everything: *If we don't hear both sides of the argument, we'll get an unbalanced view of the situation.* **2** (*often pred*) disordered in the mind; not quite sane: *Living alone can sometimes make people a bit unbalanced; The murderer was completely unbalanced.*

unbar [ʌnˈbaː] – *pt, ptp* **ˌunˈbarred** – *vt* to open (a door, gate, entrance *etc*) by moving the bars that are keeping it closed: *He unlocked and unbarred the door.*

unbearable [ʌnˈbeərəbl] *adj* too painful, unpleasant *etc* to bear or to tolerate: *I am suffering from unbearable toothache; I find such rudeness quite unbearable; That child is quite unbearable.*

unˈbearably *adv*: *unbearably painful; unbearably rude.*

unbecoming [ʌnbiˈkʌmiŋ] *adj* (*formal*) **1** (of clothes) not suited to the wearer: *She wore a most unbecoming dress; That style of dress is rather unbecoming.* **2** (of behaviour) unworthy of a person or unsuitable in a certain situation: *unbecoming conduct; His show of anger was unbecoming to a member of the Royal Family; It would be unbecoming for me to accept the money.* **ˌunbeˈcomingly** *adv.*

unbelief [ʌnbiˈliːf] *nu* (*formal*) lack of (*esp* religious) faith or belief: *He goes to church in spite of his unbelief.*

ˌunbeˈlievable [-v-] *adj* too bad, good *etc* to be believed in: *unbelievable rudeness; Her good luck is unbelievable!* **ˌunbeˈlievably** *adv.*

ˌunbeˈliever [-v-] *nc* (*liter or facet*) a person who does not follow a certain religion: *My husband's a Christian, but I'm an unbeliever.*

ˌunbeˈlieving [-v-] *adj* (*formal*: *less common than* **disbelieving**) doubting or disbelieving: *He looked at the feast with unbelieving eyes; Do not look so unbelieving.* **ˌunbeˈlievingly** *adv.*

See also **disbelieve**.

unbend [ʌnˈbend] – *pt, ptp* **unˈbent** [-t] – *vi* to behave in a friendly, informal way: *At the office party even the manager unbends a little.*

unˈbending *adj* (*formal*) strict or severe; not relaxed: *The new headmaster has an unbending attitude towards school discipline; his unbending ideas about discipline; a rather formal, unbending manner/atmosphere.*

unbidden [ʌnˈbidn] *adj* (*liter*: *usu pred*) without being invited: *The tears came unbidden to her eyes.*

unbolt [ʌnˈboult] *vt* to open the bolt of (*eg* a door): *The shop-keeper unbolted the door and let the customers enter.*

unborn [ʌnˈboːn] *adj* **1** (*usu attrib*) (of a baby) still in the mother's womb: *When she was involved in a car accident the doctor was worried in case her unborn baby had been injured.* **2** (*formal*) coming in the future: *unborn generations; generations as yet unborn.*

unbound [ʌnˈbaund] *adj* **1** (of hair) hanging loosely. **2** (of books) in loose sheets.

unbounded [ʌnˈbaundid] *adj* (*formal or liter, esp when pred*) unlimited or very great: *She dreams of unbounded wealth; I admire her unbounded enthusiasm; She has courage unbounded.*

unbridled [ʌnˈbraidld] *adj* (*liter*: *usu attrib*) uncontrolled: *unbridled ambition; unbridled passion.*

unbuckle [ʌnˈbʌkl] *vt* to undo the buckle or buckles of: *He unbuckled his belt.*

unburden [ʌnˈbəːdn] *vti* (*liter or formal*) to relieve (oneself, one's mind *etc*) of feelings that are hard to bear, by freely telling one's troubles, secrets *etc*: *He unburdened his heart to me about his marriage difficulties; The friendly atmosphere encouraged him to unburden (himself of his troubles); He unburdened his troubles on me.*

unbutton [ʌnˈbʌtn] *vt* to unfasten the buttons of: *She unbuttoned her coat.*

uncalled-for [ʌnˈkoːldfoː] *adj* (of actions, remarks *etc*) unnecessary and *usu* rude: *Some of his comments are a bit uncalled-for; I resented his uncalled-for criticisms.*

uncanny [ʌnˈkani] *adj* strange or mysterious: *an uncanny noise/silence; Like a cat, he has an uncanny sense of direction; She looks so like her sister that it's quite uncanny.* **unˈcannily** *adv.*

uncared-for [ʌnˈkeədfoː] *adj* neglected; not well looked after: *The garden has an uncared-for appearance; The child looks uncared-for.*

unceasing [ʌnˈsiːsiŋ] *adj* (*formal*: *often attrib*) never stopping: *his unceasing efforts to help the sick and wounded.* **unˈceasingly** *adv.*

uncertain [ʌnˈsəːtn] *adj* **1** (*usu pred*) (of a person) not sure; not definitely knowing: *I'm uncertain of my future plans; The government is uncertain what is the best thing to do; They are uncertain what to do next; The actor was still uncertain of his words/of his ability to play the part.* **2** not definitely known or settled: *My plans are still uncertain; The uncertain weather delayed our departure; The dog is of uncertain temper.* **unˈcertainly** *adv.*

uncharted [ʌnˈtʃaːtid] *adj* (*formal*) **1** of which a detailed map has never been made: *an uncharted route through the desert; That area of the Asian continent is as yet uncharted.* **2** not shown on a chart or map.

uncivil [ʌnˈsivl] *adj* (*formal*) rude: *He apologized for being uncivil to her; It was most uncivil of him to leave the meeting while she was speaking; an uncivil remark/act.* **unˈcivilly** *adv.*

See also **incivility**.

uncle [ˈʌŋkl] *nc* (*with cap in names*) the brother of a person's father or mother, or the husband of an aunt: *He's my uncle; Hallo, Uncle Jim!*

unclean [ʌnˈkliːn] *adj* (*formal*: *esp relig*) (*eg* of food) not pure: *The Jews are not allowed to eat* *pork, as pigs are considered unclean.*

uncoil [ʌn'koil] *vti* to straighten from a coiled position: *The snake uncoiled (itself).*

uncommitted [ʌnkə'mitid] *adj (formal)* having made no promise or agreement to do something, *eg* support a particular party, side in a dispute *etc*: *Several countries manage to remain politically uncommitted; uncommitted nations/politicians.*

uncommon [ʌn'komən] *adj* rare; unusual: *This type of animal is becoming very uncommon; Her eyes were an uncommon shade of green.*

un'commonly *adv* very; unusually: *an uncommonly clever person.*

uncompromising [ʌn'komprəmaiziŋ] *adj (formal: usu attrib)* keeping firmly to a particular attitude, policy *etc* and refusing to yield: *She has always been an uncompromising enemy of pornography; You should not adopt such an uncompromising attitude.*

unconcern [ʌnkən'səːn] *nu (formal)* lack of interest or anxiety: *He received the news of his failure with apparent unconcern.* **ˌuncon'cerned** *adj.* **'unconˌcernedly** [-nid-] *adv.*

unconditional [ʌnkən'diʃənl] *adj (formal: usu attrib)* complete and absolute, and not dependent on certain terms or conditions: *The victorious side demanded unconditional surrender.* **ˌuncon'ditionally** *adv.*

unconfirmed [ʌnkən'fəːmd] *adj (formal)* (of *eg* a rumour *etc*) not yet shown or proved to be true: *There are unconfirmed reports of another earthquake in China; Early reports that the president is dead are as yet unconfirmed.*

unconscionable [ʌn'konʃənəbl] *adj (old or facet: attrib)* completely unreasonable: *You take an unconscionable time to get up in the morning!*

unconscious [ʌn'konʃəs] *adj* **1** senseless or stunned, *eg* because of an accident: *She was unconscious for three days after the crash; in an unconscious state.* **2** *(pred: with* **of***)* not aware: *She was quite unconscious of her own beauty; He was unconscious of having said anything rude.* **3** unintentional: *She spoke with unconscious wit; Her prejudice is quite unconscious.* – *nu (often with* **the***: tech)* the deepest level of the mind, the processes of which are revealed only through *eg* psychoanalysis: *the secrets of the unconscious.*

un'consciously *adv* unintentionally, or without being aware: *She unconsciously addressed me by the wrong name.* **un'consciousness** *nu.*

uncouple [ʌn'kʌpl] *vt* to disconnect (*eg* railway wagons).

uncouth [ʌn'kuːθ] *adj (formal derog)* (of a person or his behaviour) clumsy, awkward or rough: *a large, uncouth man; uncouth behaviour; I cannot think why she married him – he is so uncouth!*

uncover [ʌn'kʌvə] *vt* to remove the cover from: *He uncovered the dead body; (fig) His criminal activities were finally uncovered.*

uncrowned ['ʌnkraund]: **uncrowned king** a person who is considered by most people to be the best or most successful in a particular area of activity: *He's the uncrowned king of the criminal world; He's the uncrowned king of jazz.*

unctuous ['ʌŋktjuəs, *(Amer)* -tʃu-] *adj (formal derog)* (of a person or his manner *etc*) making a false, unpleasant show of willingness, earnestness, sympathy *etc*: *I almost prefer a shop assistant to be rude rather than unctuous; I dislike his unctuous manner.*

uncurl [ʌn'kəːl] *vti* to straighten from a curled position: *The hedgehog slowly uncurled (itself).*

uncut [ʌn'kʌt] *adj (often attrib)* **1** (of a book, film *etc*) not shortened: *The film is being shown in the uncut version.* **2** (of a diamond or other precious stone) not yet cut into shape for using in jewellery *etc*: *uncut jewels.* **3** *(tech)* (of a book) having the pages not yet separated by cutting.

undaunted [ʌn'doːntid] *adj (formal or liter)* fearless; not discouraged: *In spite of his injuries he continued the fight undaunted; He was undaunted by his failure to succeed first time.*

undecided [ʌndi'saidid] *adj (pred)* **1** (of a person) unable to make a decision about something: *I'm undecided about my plans/what to do.* **2** (of a matter) not settled: *The date of the meeting is still undecided.*

undeniable [ʌndi'naiəbl] *adj (formal)* not able to be denied; obviously true: *His statement is undeniable; Let me tell you a few undeniable facts.*

ˌunde'niably *adv (formal)*: *undeniably true; Undeniably, he knew about the plan.*

under ['ʌndə] *prep* **1** in or to a position lower than, or covered by: *Your pencil is under the chair; Look under the bed!; Strange plants grow under the sea; He dived under the water; He got out from under the car.* **2** less than, or lower in rank than: *Children under five should not cross the street alone; His salary is under £2 000; all army officers under the rank of colonel; You can do the job in under an hour.* **3** subject to the authority of: *As a foreman, he has about fifty workers under him.* **4** beneath the weight of: *The car will collapse under all that luggage; (fig formal) She was ready to sink under her misery.* **5** used to express various states: *The fort was under attack; The business improved under the new management; (formal) The matter is under consideration/discussion; Some war criminals are still living in South America under false names; That library book is catalogued under 'crime'; Under this agreement, he is permitted to return to his own country.* – *adv* in or to a lower position, rank *etc*: *The swimmer surfaced and went under again; children aged seven and under.*

under- *(in cmpds)* **1** beneath, as in **underline**. **2** too little, as in **underpay**. **3** lower in rank: *the ˌunder-'manager.* **4** less in age than: *a nursery for ˌunder-ˌfives* (= children aged four and under).

underarm ['ʌndəraːm] *adj, adv* (of an action in tennis, cricket *etc*) with the arm kept below the level of the shoulder: *He bowled underarm; an underarm throw.*

undercarriage ['ʌndəkaridʒ] *nc (tech)* the landing-gear of an aircraft: *The pilot had some difficulty in lowering the undercarriage.*

underclothes ['ʌndəklouðz, *(Amer)* -klouz] *n pl* underwear: *Have you packed my vest and other underclothes?*

'underclothing *nu (formal)* underclothes: *Take some clean underclothing!; The police said that the dead girl's underclothing had been found some distance from the body.*

undercover [ʌndə'kʌvə] *adj (attrib)* working or done in secret: *an undercover job; He is an undercover agent for the Americans.*

undercurrent ['ʌndəkʌrənt, *(Amer)* -kəː-] *nc* a movement or flow under the water surface: *Don't swim there – there is a strong undercurrent; (fig formal) The men seem to be working normally after the strike, but there are still undercurrents of dissatisfaction.*

undercut [ʌndə'kʌt] – *pt, ptp* **ˌunder'cut** – *vt* to sell goods *etc* at a lower price than (a competitor): *Japanese car-exporters are able to undercut British motor manufacturers.*

underdeveloped [ʌndədi'veləpt] *adj* (*formal*) **1** not well grown: *an underdeveloped body*; *Because of lack of protein his muscles are underdeveloped.* **2** (of a country *etc*) not having efficient modern agriculture and industry or a high standard of living: *the underdeveloped countries*; *Those areas of the world are still underdeveloped.*

underdog ['ʌndədog] *nc* (*usu with* **the**) a weak person who is dominated by someone else, or who is the loser in a struggle: *He always likes to help the underdog*; *He is so much smaller and weaker than the other boys in his class that he is always the underdog.*

underdone [ʌndə'dʌn] *adj* (*usu derog*) (of food) not completely cooked: *This meat is underdone – it is completely raw in the middle*; *underdone meat.*

underestimate [ʌndər'estimeit] *vt* to estimate (a thing, a person *etc*) at less than his or its real amount, value, strength *etc*: *I always underestimate the length of time I'll take to do something*; *Never underestimate your opponent!*; *I underestimated his strength/ability.*

under-exposed [ʌndərik'spouzd] *adj* (*tech*) not exposed long enough to light: *This film is under-exposed.*

underfed [ʌndə'fed] *adj* not given enough to eat: *the underfed peoples of the world*; *That child looks underfed.*

underfoot [ʌndə'fut] *adv* on the ground under the feet of anyone walking: *It is not actually raining just now but it is very wet underfoot.*

undergarment ['ʌndəga:mənt] *nc* (*formal*) an article of clothing worn under the outer clothes: *vests, pants, petticoats and other undergarments.*

undergo [ʌndə'gou] – *pt* ˌ**under'went** [-'went]: *ptp* ˌ**under'gone** [-'gon] – *vt* (*formal*) **1** to experience or endure: *They underwent terrible hardships*: *I wouldn't like to undergo that experience again.* **2** to go through (a process): *The car is undergoing tests/repairs*; *She has been undergoing medical treatment.*

undergraduate [ʌndə'gradjuət] *nc* a student who has not taken his first degree: *2 000 undergraduates will be taking their final exams this month*; (*attrib*) *undergraduate humour.*

underground [ʌndə'graund] *adj* (*usu attrib*) **1** below the surface of the ground: *underground passages*; *underground railways.* **2** (of *esp* political organizations) secret, and working against the ruling power: *an underground political movement.* – *adv* **1** (to a position) under the surface of the ground: *Rabbits live underground*; *The badger's tracks disappeared underground.* **2** into hiding: *He will go underground if the police start looking for him.* – ['ʌndəgraund] *nc* **1** (*Amer* **'subway**) an underground railway: *She hates travelling by/on the underground.* **2** a secret organization working against the ruling power: *He's a member of the underground.*

undergrowth ['ʌndəgrouθ] *nu* low bushes or large plants growing among trees: *She tripped over in the thick undergrowth.*

underhand [ʌndə'hand] *adj* (*formal*) sly or dishonest: *He used underhand methods to get himself elected*; *an underhand scheme.*

ˌ**under'handed** *adj* underhand.

underlie [ʌndə'lai] – *pt* ˌ**under'lay** [-'lei]: *ptp* ˌ**under'lain** [-'lein] – *vt* (*formal*) **1** to form the basis of: *His essay is badly written, but the idea underlying it is good.* **2** to be the hidden cause or source of: *The desire to be liked underlies most of his behaviour.*

ˌ**under'lying** *adj*: *an underlying cause/meaning.*

underline [ʌndə'lain] *vt* **1** to draw a line under: *He wrote down the title of his essay and underlined it*; *We underline those words that we wish to stress as in 'I'll never go there again!'* **2** (*formal*) to emphasize or stress: *In his speech he underlined several points.*

underling ['ʌndəliŋ] *nc* (*derog*) a person in an unimportant position working for someone else: *one of Hitler's underlings*; *I wanted to speak to the manager but he sent one of his underlings.*

undermentioned [ʌndə'menʃənd]: **the undermentioned** (*very formal*) those named or mentioned below or in the text following: *The undermentioned (people) have passed the examination.*

undermine [ʌndə'main] *vt* (*formal*) **1** to make (*eg* a building) insecure by digging away or destroying the base or foundations: *The river is undermining the edge of the golf course*; *The road was being undermined by a stream.* **2** to weaken (*eg* a person's health or authority): *Constant hard work had undermined his health*; *He undermines my authority by allowing the children to do things that I've forbidden.*

underneath [ʌndə'ni:θ] *prep, adv* at or to a lower position (than); beneath: *She was standing underneath the light*; *Have you looked underneath the bed?*; *He curled himself up underneath the blankets*; *She picked up the pillow and looked underneath*; *He seems bad-tempered, but he's a nice man underneath.* – *nc* (*inf*) the part or side beneath: *Have you ever seen the underneath of a bus?*

undernourished [ʌndə'nʌriʃt, (*Amer*) -'nə:-] *adj* (*formal*) suffering from lack of food or nourishment: *undernourished children*; *The refugees are obviously undernourished.*

underpaid *see* **underpay**.

underpants ['ʌndəpants] *n pl* a short undergarment worn (*usu* by men) over the buttocks: *a clean pair of underpants.*

underpass ['ʌndəpa:s] *nc* a road or path built to pass under another road, railway *etc*: *It is easier to cross that busy road by means of the underpass.*

underpay [ʌndə'pei] – *pt, ptp* ˌ**under'paid** – *vt* (*formal*) to pay (a person) too little: *They claim that they are underpaid and overworked*; *Do you think that is enough money for the gardener? I don't want to underpay him.*

underprivileged [ʌndə'privilidʒd] *adj* (*formal*) (of a person *etc*) not having the social, financial and educational advantages that many others have: *underprivileged children*; *Children with only one parent are not necessarily underprivileged.*

underrate [ʌndə'reit] *vt* (*formal*) to estimate (a thing, person *etc*) at less than its or his real value, strength *etc*: *I have to admit that I underrated him*; *Do not underrate his ability.*

undersell [ʌndə'sel] – *pt, ptp* ˌ**under'sold** [-'sould] – *vt* (*formal*) to sell goods at a lower price than (a competitor): *This firm claims that it is never knowingly undersold* (= that it knows of no other firm that sells the same articles more cheaply); *They try to undersell all the other car manufacturers.*

undersigned [ʌndə'saind]: **the undersigned** (*formal*) the person or persons whose names are signed below: *We, the undersigned, agree to these arrangements.*

undersized [ʌndə'saizd] *adj* (*sometimes derog*) of less than the usual size: *an undersized child*; *He is rather undersized.*

underskirt ['ʌndəskə:t] *nc* a skirt of light, thin material, worn under a dress or another skirt.

undersold *see* **undersell.**

understand [ʌndə'stand] – *pt, ptp* ˌ**under'stood** [-'stud] – (not used with **is, was** *etc* and **-ing**) **1** *vti* to see or know the meaning of (something): *I can't understand his absence*; *She could not understand his failure to attend the meeting*; *It is difficult to understand why he is not here*; *Speak slowly to foreigners so that they'll understand you*; *He did seem to understand what you were saying!*; *Do you understand Spanish/this sentence?*; *Why are you leaving? I don't understand.* **2** *vt* to know (*eg* a person) thoroughly: *She complained that her husband never understood her*; *She understands children/dogs.* **3** *vt* (*often formal*) to learn or realize (something), *eg* from information received: *At first I didn't understand how ill she was*; *I understood that you were planning to leave today*; *They understood him to say that he would telephone*; *Are we to understand that you disagree?* **4** *vt* (*often formal,*) to assume (something) as part of an agreement: *It is understood that, as the children's nurse, she will have one free day a week.* **5** *vt* (*gram*) to take (something) as meant though not expressed: *In the sentence 'I took some chocolate and John a cake', the verb 'took' is understood after 'John'.* – *See also* **understand** *in phrases below.*

ˌ**under'standable** *adj* that can be understood: *His anger is quite understandable*; *understandable grief.*

ˌ**under'standing** *adj* (of a person) good at knowing how other people feel; sympathetic: *an understanding person*; *Try to be more understanding!* – **1** *nu* the power of thinking clearly: *a man of great understanding.* **2** *nu* the ability to sympathize with another person's feelings: *His kindness and understanding were a great comfort to her.* **3** *nc* (*usu in sing*) a (state of) informal agreement (*eg* to marry): *John and Jane have had an understanding for some years*; *The two men have come to/reached an understanding after their disagreement.* – *See also* **on the understanding that** *below.*

give (someone) to understand that (*formal*) to cause (someone) to think that: *I was given to understand that you were coming at two o'clock.*

make (oneself) understood to make one's meaning or intentions clear: *He tried speaking German to them, but couldn't make himself understood.*

on the understanding that on the condition that: *They divorced on the understanding that the husband could see the children every weekend.*

under'stand one another to realize one another's intentions: *Now that we understand one another, we can make plans.*

understate [ʌndə'steit] *vt* (*formal*) to state less than the truth about (something): *They understated the number of dead after the earthquake*; *She has understated her difficulties.*

ˌ**under'statement** *ncu*: *It's an understatement to say he's foolish – he's quite mad*; *Understatement is sometimes a wise policy.*

understood *see* **understand.**

understudy ['ʌndəstʌdi] *vti* to study (a part in a play, opera *etc*) so as to be able to take the place of (another actor, singer *etc*): *He is understudying Romeo*; *She is to understudy the leading lady.* – *nc* a person who understudies: *He was ill, so his understudy had to take the part.*

undertake [ʌndə'teik] – *pt* ˌ**under'took** [-'tuk], *ptp* ˌ**under'taken** – *vt* (*formal*) **1** to accept (a duty, task, responsibility *etc*): *He undertook the job willingly*; *Who will undertake responsibility for this work?*; *You have already undertaken too much.* **2** to promise (*eg* to do something): *He has undertaken to appear at the police court tomorrow*; *I can undertake that you will enjoy the play.*

'**undertaker** [-teikə] *nc* a person who organizes funerals: *The undertaker is coming at twelve to remove the body.*

ˌ**under'taking** *nc* (*formal*) **1** a task or piece of work that is being attempted, or that a person has promised to do: *a business undertaking*; *I didn't realize what a large undertaking this job would be.* **2** a promise: *He made an undertaking that he would pay the money back.*

undertone ['ʌndətoun] *nc* (*formal*) **1** a low, quiet tone of voice: *He spoke in an undertone.* **2** a partly hidden quality, meaning, feeling *etc*: *There were undertones of cruelty in his words.*

undertook *see* **undertake.**

undervalue [ʌndə'valju:] *vt* (*formal*) to value (something) below its real worth: *He undervalued his own contribution to the work.*

underwear ['ʌndəweə] *nu* clothes worn under the outer clothes: *Pants and other bits of underwear hung on the washing line*; *She washed her skirt, blouse and underwear.*

underwent *see* **undergo.**

underworld ['ʌndəwə:ld] *nc* (*usu with* **the**) **1** (*usu with cap*: *myth*) the place where the spirits of dead people go: *Orpheus tried to rescue Eurydice from the Underworld.* **2** the part of the population that gets its living from crime *etc*: *A member of the underworld told the police where the murderer was hiding*; (*attrib*) *underworld contacts.*

underwrite [ʌndə'rait] – *pt* ˌ**under'wrote** [-'rout]: *ptp* ˌ**under'written** [-'ritn] – *vt* in insurance, to agree to pay compensation for (a real or possible loss), *esp* in shipping: *The loss of the tanker has been underwritten by Lloyds.*

'**underwriter** [-raitə] *nc* a person who insures, *esp* shipping: *the underwriters at Lloyds.*

undesirable [ʌndi'zairəbl] *adj* (*formal*: *often attrib*) **1** not wanted: *These pills can have some undesirable effects.* **2** (*derog*) (of a person or his habits *etc*) unpleasant or objectionable: *his undesirable friends*; *undesirable behaviour/habits.* – *nc* (*inf derog*) a person who is undesirable: *This café is a meeting place for drug-peddlers and other undesirables.*

undid *see* **undo.**

undistinguished [ʌndi'stiŋgwiʃt] *adj* (*formal derog*) (of work, a performance *etc*) of poor or low quality: *a rather undistinguished performance of the concerto*; *His latest book is undistinguished.*

undo [ʌn'du:] – *pt* **un'did** [-'did]: *ptp* **un'done** [-'dʌn] – *vt* **1** to unfasten or untie: *I can't undo this button*; *Could you undo the knot in this string?*; *His shoelaces are undone.* **2** to reverse, or destroy, the effect of: *The evil that he did can never be undone*; *That one mistake undid all the good work of the past three months.* **3** (*usu in passive*: *old*) to ruin *eg* the reputation, morals, finances, career *etc* of (a person): *He knew that he would be undone if there was a public scandal.*

un'doing *nu* (*formal*) (the cause of) ruin or disaster: *Extravagance was his undoing*; *He hesi-*

tated, to his undoing (= and this caused his undoing).

un'done [-'dʌn] *adj* (*often pred*) (of work, a task *etc*) not done, or not finished: *I don't like going to bed leaving jobs/work undone.*

undoubted [ʌn'dautid] *adj* (*formal*: *attrib*) not doubted or denied: *the undoubted excellence of the work*; *his undoubted skill/talent.*

un'doubtedly *adv* definitely: *'Is he mistaken?' 'Undoubtedly!'*

See also **indubitably**.

undreamed-of [ʌn'dri:mdov], **undreamt-of** [ʌn'dremtov] *adj* (*liter*: *usu attrib*) never even imagined; completely unexpected: *His success brought him undreamt-of fame/wealth.*

undress [ʌn'dres] **1** *vt* to take the clothes off (a person): *She undressed the child*; *Undress yourself and get into bed.* **2** *vi* to undress oneself: *I undressed and went to bed.*

undue [ʌn'dju:] *adj* (*formal*: *attrib*) too great; more than is necessary: *You show undue caution in distrusting him.*

un'duly *adv* (*formal*): *You were unduly severe with the child.*

undulate ['ʌndjuleit, (*Amer*) -dʒu-] *vi* (*formal or liter*) to move, or look, like waves: *The countryside undulated gently.*

,undu'lation *ncu* (*formal or liter*) (a) movement or form like that of a wave or waves: *the gentle undulation(s) of the countryside.*

unduly *see* **undue**.

undying [ʌn'daiiŋ] *adj* (*formal*: *usu attrib*) lasting for ever: *undying gratitude.*

unearned [ʌn'ə:nd] *adj* **1** (of income) gained through investments and not through work: *How much tax do you pay on unearned income?*; *He pays a high rate of taxation because most of his income is unearned.* **2** (*formal*: *usu attrib*) not deserved: *unearned praise/criticism.*

unearth [ʌn'ə:θ] *vt* (*formal*) to discover (something) or remove it from a place where it is put away or hidden: *The children unearthed this shoe while digging in the sand*; *I'll unearth those letters from my trunk if you want to see them*; *During his studies, he unearthed several new facts about the history of the place.*

unearthly [ʌn'ə:θli] *adj* **1** supernatural, mysterious or frightening: *an unearthly sight*; *We heard unearthly groans coming from the cave*; *The loud shrieks sounded unearthly.* **2** (*inf*: *attrib*) outrageous or unreasonable: *He telephoned at the unearthly* (= very early) *hour of 6.30 a.m.*

uneasy [ʌn'i:zi] *adj* (of a person or a situation *etc*) troubled, anxious or unsettled: *When her son did not return, she grew uneasy*; *I'm uneasy about his future*; *an uneasy truce/peace*; *They spent an uneasy day waiting for news.*

un'ease *nu* (*liter*) uneasiness.

un'easily *adv* in an uneasy or embarrassed way: *He glanced uneasily at her.*

un'easiness *nu* the state of being uneasy: *I could not understand her apparent uneasiness.*

unemployed [ʌnim'ploid] *adj* not having, or not able to find, work: *He has been unemployed for three months*; *There are many unemployed teachers.* – *n pl* (*often with* **the**) people who are unemployed: *The numbers of (the) unemployed are still increasing.*

,unem'ployment *nu* **1** the state of being unemployed: *If the factory is closed, many men will face unemployment.* **2** the numbers of people without work: *There is serious unemployment in Scotland*; *Unemployment has reached record figures this year.*

,unem'ployment benefit/pay *nus* money paid to an unemployed person through insurance: *Are you entitled to unemployment benefit?*

unending [ʌn'endiŋ] *adj* (*often formal*) never finishing; never ending: *their unending struggle for survival*; *His list of complaints seems unending.*

unequal [ʌn'i:kwəl] *adj* **1** (*formal*) not equal in quantity, quality *etc*: *They got unequal shares of/an unequal share in the money*; *two sticks of unequal length*; *an unequal division of labour*; *The division of the wealth was rather unequal.* **2** (*with* **to**: *formal or facet*) not having enough strength or ability (for): *I feel unequal to the task.* **un'equally** *adv.*

un'equalled *adj* (*formal*) without equal; not surpassed: *He was unequalled as a performer of Chopin's music*; *a landscape unequalled for beauty*; *his unequalled talent.*

See also **inequality**.

unerring [ʌn'ə:riŋ] *adj* (*formal*: *usu attrib*) (always) accurate: *He threw the spear with unerring aim*; *She has unerring taste and judgement in choosing her clothes.* **un'erringly** *adv.*

uneven [ʌn'i:vn] *adj* **1** not even: *an uneven heartbeat/road surface*; *The road surface here is very uneven.* **2** (of work *etc*) not all of the same quality: *His work is very uneven*; *of uneven quality.*

un'evenness *nu.*

un'evenly *adv* in an uneven or unequal way: *The teams are unevenly matched.*

unexceptionable [ʌnik'sepʃənəbl] *adj* (*formal*) in which there is nothing to criticize or object to: *His speech was unexceptionable*; *unexceptionable behaviour.*

unexpected [ʌnik'spektid] *adj* not expected, *eg* because sudden: *his unexpected death*; *His promotion was quite unexpected.*

unfailing [ʌn'feiliŋ] *adj* (*formal*) **1** constant: *Her unfailing courage inspired us all*; *Her enthusiasm seems unfailing.* **2** (*usu attrib*) reliable or infallible: *Such a situation is an unfailing test of a person's friendship.*

un'failingly *adv* (*formal*) constantly: *He is unfailingly polite.*

unfair [ʌn'feə] *adj* not fair or just: *He has received unfair treatment*; *His work has been subjected to unfair criticism*; *The punishment was rather unfair*; *It was unfair of you to punish one child and not the other.* **un'fairly** *adv.* **un'fairness** *nu.*

unfaithful [ʌn'feiθful] *adj* not loyal and true; used *esp* of a husband or wife who has (a) lover(s): *She has divorced him because he was unfaithful to her*; *an unfaithful husband.*

unfasten [ʌn'fa:sn] *vt* to undo (something that is fastened): *He unfastened (the buttons of) his jacket*; *Could you unfasten my necklace for me?*

unfathomable [ʌn'faðəməbl] *adj* (*liter*) **1** too deep or great to measure: *unfathomable space*; *the unfathomable love of God.* **2** too mysterious to understand: *his unfathomable ways*; *The mystery has remained unfathomable.*

unfeeling [ʌn'fi:liŋ] *adj* (*formal*) hard-hearted or unsympathetic: *He behaved in a cold, unfeeling way when she was ill*; *a stern unfeeling man*; *He is so strict and unfeeling.* **un'feelingly** *adv.*

unfeigned [ʌn'feind] *adj* (*formal*) sincere: *unfeigned enthusiasm*; *Her joy was unfeigned.* **un'feignedly** [-nid-] *adv.*

unfit [ʌn'fit] *adj* **1** not good enough; not in a

suitable state: *He has been ill and is quite unfit to travel*; *These houses are unfit for human habitation*; *houses in their present unfit state.* **2** (of a person, dog, horse *etc*) not as strong and healthy as is possible: *You become unfit if you don't take regular exercise*; *In my present unfit state I couldn't climb that hill.* **un'fitness** *nu.*

un'fitted *adj* (*formal*: *pred*) (of a person) not suitable for, or able to do, (something) because of one's personality, physique *etc*: *The boy is unfitted for this sort of job.*

unflagging [ʌn'flagiŋ] *adj* (*formal*) not tiring or losing vigour: *her unflagging energy*; *Her enthusiasm seems unflagging.*

unflappable [ʌn'flapəbl] *adj* (*inf*) able to remain calm in a crisis: *We need an unflappable person for this job*; *She seems completely unflappable.*

unflinching [ʌn'flintʃiŋ] *adj* (*formal*: *usu attrib*) not yielding *etc* because of pain, danger, difficulty *etc*: *his unflinching courage/determination.* **un'flinchingly** *adv.*

unfold [ʌn'fould] **1** *vt* to open and spread out (a map *etc*): *He sat down and unfolded his newspaper.* **2** *vti* (*formal*) to (cause to) be revealed or become known: *She gradually unfolded her plan to them*; *As the trial went on, the story behind the murder slowly unfolded (itself).*

unforgettable [ʌnfə'getəbl] *adj* never able to be forgotten, because of beauty, or horror *etc*: *an unforgettable moment/scene*; *He was one of those unforgettable characters*; *The experience was unforgettable.* **ˌunfor'gettably** *adv.*

unfortunate [ʌn'fo:tʃənət] *adj* **1** unlucky: *He has been very unfortunate*; *an unfortunate happening.* **2** regrettable: *That was an unfortunate remark*; *He has an unfortunate habit of giggling all the time.*

un'fortunately *adv*: *I'd like to help but unfortunately I can't*; *Unfortunately I have not enough money to travel abroad.*

unfounded [ʌn'faundid] *adj* (*formal*) not based on facts or reality: *unfounded fears*; *The rumours are completely unfounded.*

unfrequented [ʌnfri'kwentid] *adj* (*formal or liter*) rarely visited: *an unfrequented spot*; *a part of the country as yet unfrequented.*

unfruitful [ʌn'fru:tful] *adj* (*formal*) unsuccessful; producing no results: *I spent two unfruitful hours at the library*; *My search proved unfruitful.*

See also **fruitless**.

unfurl [ʌn'fə:l] *vti* (*formal*) to unfold and spread out: *They slowly unfurled the sail*; *The flag unfurled and blew in the breeze.*

ungainly [ʌn'geinli] *adj* (*formal derog*) awkward, clumsy or ungraceful: *an ungainly person*; *ungainly movements*; *She is rather large and ungainly.* **un'gainliness** *nu.*

ungodly [ʌn'godli] *adj* **1** (*old*) wicked or sinful: *ungodly people/behaviour*; *He is wicked and ungodly.* **2** (*inf*) (*esp* of the time) unreasonable: *She has to get up at the ungodly* (= very early) *hour of 5.00 a.m.*

ungovernable [ʌn'gʌvənəbl] *adj* (*formal*: *usu attrib*) (of feelings, passions *etc*) uncontrollable: *ungovernable passion/rages*; *He has an ungovernable temper.*

ungracious [ʌn'greiʃəs] *adj* (*formal*) rude; impolite: *She accepted the money in a rather ungracious manner*; *It was rather ungracious of you to refuse his invitation.* **un'graciously** *adv.*

ungrateful [ʌn'greitful] *adj* (*derog*) not showing thanks for kindness: *It will look very ungrateful if you don't write and thank him*; *an ungrateful young man.*

See also **ingratitude**.

unguarded [ʌn'ga:did] *adj* (*formal*) **1** without protection: *The castle gate was never left unguarded*; *an unguarded castle gate.* **2** careless: *an unguarded remark*; *In an unguarded moment, he mentioned the thing that he had intended to keep secret.*

unhappy [ʌn'hapi] *adj* **1** sad or miserable: *He had an unhappy childhood*; *She seems an unhappy person*; *She has been very unhappy since he went away.* **2** (*usu attrib*) regrettable: *He has an unhappy knack of always saying the wrong thing.*

un'happiness *nu.*

un'happily *adv* **1** in a sad or miserable way: *He stared unhappily at her angry face.* **2** (*formal*) unfortunately: *Unhappily, I shan't be able to see you tomorrow.*

unhealthy [ʌn'helθi] *adj* **1** not healthy: *an unhealthy person/plant*; *A home where the parents fight constantly is an unhealthy environment for a child*; *crowded, unhealthy conditions*; *He is fat and unhealthy – he doesn't take enough exercise.* **2** (*inf*) dangerous: *The situation was getting unhealthy*; *the unhealthy nearness of the enemy.* **un'healthily** *adv.* **un'healthiness** *nu.*

unheard [ʌn'hə:d]: **un'heard-of** *adj* so exceptional as never to have been known before: *unheard-of behaviour*; *You can't do that – it's unheard-of!*

go unheard (*formal*) to be ignored: *I asked him to help me but my words went unheard.*

unhinge [ʌn'hindʒ] *vt* to cause (a person, his mind *etc*) to become unbalanced: *His wife's death seems to have unhinged him.*

unholy [ʌn'houli] *adj* (*attrib*) **1** (*liter*) disrespectful or irreverent: *shrieks of unholy laughter.* **2** (*inf facet*) outrageous or unreasonable: *She made an unholy fuss*; *an unholy din.*

unhook [ʌn'huk] *vt* **1** to take or release (something) from a hook: *He unhooked the picture from the wall.* **2** to unfasten the hooks of: *He unhooked her dress for her.*

uni- [(*Brit and Amer*) ju:ni] (*in cmpds*) one, or a single, as in **unilateral**.

unicorn ['ju:niko:n] *nc* (*myth*) an animal like a horse, but with one straight horn on the forehead.

unidentified [ʌnai'dentifaid] *adj* (*formal*) not identified: *The man killed in the accident is still unidentified*; *an unidentified victim.*

unidentified flying object (*often abbrev* **UFO** [ju:ef'ou, (*inf*) 'ju:fou]) an object from outer space, *eg* a flying saucer.

unification *see* **unify**.

uniform ['ju:nifo:m] *adj* (*formal*) the same always or everywhere; not changing or varying: *He mentioned his plan to several people, and met a uniform reaction*; *The sky was a uniform grey*; *It was uniform in colour.* – *ncu* (a set of) clothes worn by *eg* soldiers, children at a particular school *etc*: *Full uniform must be worn*; *They were in school uniform*; *The new uniforms will arrive tomorrow.*

'uniformed *adj* (*eg* of police) wearing a uniform, not plain clothes: *the uniformed branch of the police.*

ˌuni'formity *nu* (*very formal*) the condition of being uniform: *The houses in the street had no uniformity of appearance.*

'uniformly *adv* (*very formal*) in a uniform way: *The essays were uniformly dull.*

unify ['ju:nifai] *vt* (*formal*) to combine (several things, parts, people *etc*) into a single whole: *The country consisted of several small states and was unified only recently*; *A repeated tune has a unifying effort on the different parts of a musical work.*

ˌ**unifi'cation** [-fi-] *nu* (*very formal*) the process of unifying or being unified: *Many Christians claim that they are seeking the unification of the church.*

unilateral [ju:ni'latərəl] *adj* (*formal or tech*) on, affecting, done by *etc* one side only: *The cutting of this nerve results in a unilateral paralysis of the facial muscles*; *As Britain refused to grant it to her, Rhodesia made a unilateral declaration of independence*; *The response was unilateral.* ˌ**uni'laterally** *adv.*

unimpeachable [ʌnim'pi:tʃəbl] *adj* (*formal*) that is so good, trustworthy *etc* that it cannot be doubted or disapproved: *unimpeachable evidence/conduct*; *His behaviour was unimpeachable*; *Her taste in furniture is unimpeachable.*

uninformed [ʌnin'fo:md] *adj* (*formal*) ignorant: *You shouldn't try to speak on matters about which you're uninformed*; *an uninformed opinion.*

uninhibited [ʌnin'hibitid] *adj* expressing feelings *etc* freely and without embarrassment: *uninhibited people/behaviour*; *He is completely uninhibited.*

uninitiated [ʌni'niʃieitid]: **the uninitiated** (*formal or facet*) those who have no/little experience or knowledge of something: *I shall explain the rules of the game for the benefit of the uninitiated.*

uninspired [ʌnin'spaiəd] *adj* (*formal derog*) dull; boring: *an uninspired speech*; *Her lecture was uninspired.*

ˌ**unin'spiring** *adj* (*formal derog*): *I found his lecture very uninspiring*; *an uninspiring teacher.*

unintelligible [ʌnin'teligəbl] *adj* (*formal*) not able to be understood: *unintelligible writing/words*; *Her speech was completely unintelligible.*

uninterested [ʌn'intristid] *adj* not having or showing any interest: *I told him the news but he seemed uninterested*; *an uninterested attitude.*
See also **disinterested**.

uninterrupted [ʌnintə'rʌptid] *adj* **1** continuing without pause: *four hours of uninterrupted rain*; *Work continued uninterrupted.* **2** (*usu attrib*) (of a view) not blocked by anything: *We have an uninterrupted view of the sea.*

uninvited [ʌnin'vaitid] *adj* (*usu attrib*) **1** without an invitation: *uninvited guests.* **2** (*formal*) not required or encouraged: *His uninvited interference.*

union ['ju:njən] **1** *ncu* (*formal*) the act of uniting or process of being united: *Union between the two countries would be impossible*; *the union of Scotland with England in 1707.* **2** *ncu* (*formal*) the state of being united, *eg* in marriage, friendship *etc*: *The dog and cat live in perfect union*; *They married in 1932 but it was not a happy union.* **3** *nc* states, countries *etc* forming a single political group: *The Union of Soviet Socialist Republics* (*see also* Appendix 2). **4** *nc* a club or association: *trade unions*; *the Mother's Union*; *university unions.*

ˌ**Union 'Jack** [-'dʒak] *nc* (*usu with* **the**) the national flag of the United Kingdom.

unique [ju:'ni:k] *adj* being the only one of its kind, or having no equal: *As a writer he has his own unique style*; *An actor with a unique sense of timing*; *His style is unique.*

unisex ['ju:niseks] *adj* (*usu attrib*) (of clothes *etc*) in a style that can be worn by both men and women: *unisex clothes*; *a unisex hairstyle.*

unison ['ju:nisn] *nu* **1** (*music*) an identical note, or series of notes produced by several voices singing, or instruments playing, together: *For several bars, all the voices are in unison*; (*fig*) *'No!' they shouted in unison.* **2** (*formal*) agreement: *The two groups acted in unison.*

unit ['ju:nit] *nc* **1** (*sometimes formal*) a single thing, individual *etc* within a group or class: *The house is divided into about twelve different apartments or living units*; *an army unit*; *The teaching of good behaviour belongs within the family unit.* **2** an amount or quantity that is used as a standard in a system of measuring or of coinage: *The kilogram(me) is the unit of weight in the metric system*; *The dollar is the standard unit of currency in America.* **3** the smallest whole number, 1, or any number between 1 and 9: *In the number 23, 2 is a ten, and 3 is a unit.* **4** (*often in pl*) a piece of furniture, equipment *etc* often designed so that other pieces can be added: *storage units*; *kitchen units.*

unite [ju'nait] **1** *vti* (*more formal than* **join together**) to join together, or to make or become one: *England and Scotland were united under one parliament in 1707*; *The crisis of war united the whole country*; *He was relieved to be united with his friends again*; *The two associations are planning to unite.* **2** *vi* (*formal*) to act together: *Let us unite against the common enemy*; *They united to find a solution to the problem.*

u'nited *adj* **1** (*usu attrib*) joined into a political whole: *the United States of America* (*see also* Appendix 2). **2** joined together by love, friendship *etc*: *They're a very united pair/family.* **3** (*usu attrib*) made as a result of several people *etc* working together for a common purpose: *Let us make a united effort to increase the output of this factory.*

United Kingdom *see* Appendix 2.

unity ['ju:nəti] (*formal*) **1** *nu* the state of being united or in agreement: *Their motto is 'unity is strength'*; *When will men learn to live in unity with each other?* **2** *nu* singleness, or the state of being one complete whole: *Unity of design in his pictures is this artist's main aim.* **3** *nc* something that is arranged to form a single and complete whole: *This play is not a unity, but a series of unconnected scenes.*

universe ['ju:nivə:s] *nu* (*often with* **the**) everything – earth, planets, sun, stars *etc* – that exists anywhere: *Somewhere in the universe there must be another world like ours.*

ˌ**uni'versal** *adj* affecting, including *etc* the whole of the world or all or most people: *There was universal rejoicing at his victory*; *English may become a universal language that everyone can learn and use*; *The drought was universal that year.* ˌ**uni'versally** *adv.* ˌ**univer'sality** [-'sa-] *nu* (*formal*).

university [ju:ni'və:səti] *nc* (*with cap in names*) (the buildings or colleges of) a centre of advanced education and research, that has the power to grant degrees: *Scotland has eight universities*; *Stirling University is situated on a lake*; *a degree from the University of London*; *He'll have four years at university after he leaves school*; (*attrib*) *He is a university teacher*; (*attrib*) *a university student.*

unjust [ʌn'dʒʌst] *adj* not just; unfair: *an unjust trial*; *Your suspicions are unjust*; *He was very unjust to her.*

unkempt [ʌn'kempt] *adj* (*formal or old*) untidy:

He had an unkempt appearance; He is dirty and unkempt.

unkind [ʌn'kaind] *adj* cruel or harsh: *You were very unkind to her; an unkind comment.*

unknowingly [ʌn'nouiŋli] *adv* without being aware: *She had unknowingly given the patient the wrong medicine.*

un'known *adj* **1** not known: *her unknown helper; The driver of the car is as yet unknown.* **2** not famous; not well-known: *That actor was almost unknown before he played that part; an unknown singer.*

an unknown quantity *see* **quantity**.

unknown to me, him *etc* without me, him *etc* knowing: *Unknown to me, she was on a plane to New York.*

unlace [ʌn'leis] *vt* to undo the lace in (a shoe *etc*).

unleash [ʌn'li:ʃ] *vt* **1** to release (*eg* a dog) from its leash. **2** (*formal*) to give free expression to (rage *etc*): *The full force of his rage was unleashed against me.*

unless [ən'les] *conj* **1** if not: *Don't come unless I telephone; Unless I'm mistaken, I've seen that man before.* **2** except when: *The directors have a meeting every Friday, unless there is nothing to discuss.*

unlike [ʌn'laik] *adj* (*pred*) **1** different (from): *I never saw twins who were so unlike (each other).* **2** not typical or characteristic of: *It is unlike Mary to be so silly.*

unlikely [ʌn'laikli] *adj* not likely or probable: *an unlikely explanation for his absence; In the unlikely event of my winning the prize, I'll share the money with you; She's unlikely to arrive before 7.00 p.m.; It is unlikely that she will come.*

unload [ʌn'loud] *vti* to remove (cargo) from (*eg* a ship, vehicle *etc*): *The men were unloading the ship; They unloaded fishboxes on to the jetty; Vehicles may park here when loading and unloading.*

unlock [ʌn'lok] *vt* to open (something locked): *Unlock this door, please!; Could you unlock my suitcase?*

unlooked-for [ʌn'luktfo:] *adj* (*formal*: *often attrib*) not expected: *unlooked-for success; The praise was unlooked-for.*

unloose [ʌn'lu:s] *vt* (*often liter*) **1** to unfasten or make (something) loose: *He unloosed his belt/his grasp of her arm.* **2** to set (something) free from being tied up, harnessed, restrained *etc*: *Unloose the horses!; Drink unloosed their tongues.*

un'loosen *vt* (*often liter*) to unfasten or make loose: *He unloosened his belt.*

unlucky [ʌn'lʌki] *adj* not lucky or fortunate: *By some unlucky chance the train was late; I am unlucky – I never win at cards; He's always unlucky in love.*

un'luckily *adv* unfortunately: *He should be playing the piano in a concert, but unluckily he has hurt his hand.*

unmade [ʌn'meid] *adj* (*esp* of a bed) not yet made: *an untidy house with unmade beds; The beds were still unmade at lunchtime.*

unman [ʌn'man] – *pt, ptp* **un'manned** – *vt* (*liter*) to cause (a man) to lose self-control and yield to *eg* grief: *The sight of his sick child unmanned him for a minute; He was completely unmanned by the death of his wife.*

unmanly [ʌn'manli] *adj* (*derog*) (of a man or boy, or his behaviour) weak and cowardly: *unmanly tears; His behaviour was unmanly.*

unmanned[1] *see* **unman**.

unmanned[2] [ʌn'mand] *adj* (of *eg* an aircraft or spacecraft) automatically controlled and therefore without a crew: *unmanned flights to Mars; The craft was unmanned.*

unmannerly [ʌn'manəli] *adj* (*formal*) rude or impolite: *an unmannerly person/act; It was most unmannerly of you to refuse her invitation in that way.*

unmask [ʌn'ma:sk] *vt* (*liter*) to reveal or show (a person, or activity *etc*) in his or its true character: *The traitor was at last unmasked; He had unmasked a plot against the government.*

unmatched [ʌn'matʃt] *adj* (*formal*) without equal: *unmatched skill; He is unmatched as a singer of Schubert's songs.*

unmentionable [ʌn'menʃənəbl] *adj* (*often facet*: *usu attrib*) too shocking to be talked about: *He did some unmentionable things to his wife.*

un'mentionables *n pl* (*facet*) underwear: *underpants and other unmentionables.*

unmistakable [ʌnmi'steikəbl] *adj* very clear; impossible to mistake: *His meaning was unmistakable; She heard the unmistakable sound of her husband's footsteps.*

unmitigated [ʌn'mitigeitid] *adj* (*formal*: *often attrib*) absolute; lacking anything that might improve the situation *etc*: *He is an unmitigated nuisance; It was an unmitigated disaster.*

unmoved [ʌn'mu:vd] *adj* (*pred*) not affected or moved in feelings, determination *etc*: *He was unmoved by her sobbing; He remained unmoved in his determination.*

unnatural [ʌn'natʃərəl] *adj* **1** strange or queer: *an unnatural silence; Her reaction was unnatural; an unnatural laugh; Did her behaviour seem unnatural in any way?* **2** (*derog*: *esp* of sexual activity) contrary to what is considered natural: *unnatural practices; She considered her husband's sexual demands unnatural.* **3** (*old liter*) cruel: *his unnatural treatment of his father.* **un'naturally** *adv.*

unnecessary [ʌn'nesəsəri] *adj* **1** (*pred*) not necessary: *It is unnecessary to waken him yet.* **2** (*attrib*) that might have been avoided: *Your mistake caused a lot of unnecessary work in the office.*

unˌneces'sarily *adv*: *He was unnecessarily rude.*

unnerve [ʌn'nə:v] *vt* (*formal*) to frighten or weaken the courage of (a person): *He was unnerved by the accident, and for a long time refused to drive the car.*

un'nerving *adj* (*formal*): *an unnerving experience; I found the silence unnerving.*

unobtrusive [ʌnəb'tru:siv] *adj* (*formal*) not too obvious or noticeable: *The house was elegant in an unobtrusive way; a quiet, unobtrusive girl; She is quiet and unobtrusive.*

ˌunob'trusively *adv* (*formal*): *unobtrusively dressed.*

unoccupied [ʌn'okjupaid] *adj* (*formal*) **1** empty or vacant: *The room/seat was unoccupied; an unoccupied table.* **2** not busy: *I paint in my unoccupied hours/when I'm otherwise unoccupied.*

unpack [ʌn'pak] **1** *vt* to take out (things that are packed): *He unpacked his clothes; She unpacked the doll carefully from its box.* **2** *vti* to take (clothes *etc*) out of (a case *etc*): *Have you unpacked (your case)?*

unparalleled [ʌn'parəleld] *adj* (*very formal*) so remarkable as to be otherwise unknown: *This procedure is unparalleled; unparalleled foolishness.*

unpick [ʌn'pik] *vt* to take out stitches from

(something sewn or knitted): *She unpicked the seam of the dress.*

unpleasant [ʌn'pleznt] *adj* disagreeable: *an unpleasant task; an unpleasant smell; He was rather unpleasant to me.* **un'pleasantly** *adv.*

un'pleasantness *nu* (*euph*) ill-feeling; disagreement: *There has been some unpleasantness between them.*

unpopular [ʌn'popjulə] *adj* generally disliked: *an unpopular person/law; He was unpopular at school.* **un,popu'larity** [-'la-] *nu.*

unpractical [ʌn'praktikəl] *adj* (of a person) not good at practical tasks: *She's so unpractical that she can't even change an electric plug; a completely unpractical person.*

See also **impracticable, impractical**.

unprecedented [ʌn'presidentid] *adj* (*very formal*) never known to have happened before: *Such an action by a prime minister is unprecedented; The air crash caused an unprecedented number of deaths.*

unpretentious [ʌnpri'tenʃəs] *adj* (*formal*) not trying to look or seem important: *In spite of his fame, he lives in an unpretentious house; He is a very famous singer but he is completely unpretentious.*

unprincipled [ʌn'prinsəpld] *adj* (*formal derog*) lacking a sense of right and wrong; wicked: *an unprincipled rascal; unprincipled behaviour; He is totally unprincipled.*

unprofessional [ʌnprə'feʃənl] *adj* (*formal*) **1** (of a person's conduct) not according to the (*usu* moral) standards required in his profession: *The doctor was dismissed from his post for unprofessional conduct; His behaviour was quite unprofessional.* **2** (of a piece of work *etc*) not done with the skill of a trained person: *This bandage looks a bit unprofessional; an unprofessional piece of work.*

unqualified [ʌn'kwolifaid] *adj* **1** not having the necessary qualifications (*eg* for a job): *unqualified teachers/nurses; He is unqualified for the job; She is unqualified to do that job.* **2** (*formal*) complete; without limits: *He deserves our unqualified praise; His praise of her was not entirely unqualified.*

unquestionable [ʌn'kwestʃənəbl] *adj* (*formal*) that cannot be doubted; completely certain: *unquestionable proof; a writer of unquestionable ability; His right to the property is unquestionable.*

un'questionably *adv* (*formal*) certainly: *Unquestionably, he deserves to be punished.*

un'questioning *adj* (*formal*) (done *etc*) without any disagreement or protest: *unquestioning obedience/belief; Their faith in their leader was unquestioning.*

unquiet [ʌn'kwaiət] *adj* (*liter*: *usu attrib*) anxious uneasy: *Our son never gave us an unquiet moment; unquiet minds.*

unquote [ʌn'kwout] used with **quote** in place of quotation marks when a person's words are being dictated by telephone *etc*: *He said* (*quote*) *there is no truth in this statement* (*unquote*); (*loosely*: *facet*) *He and Mary* (*quote*) *are just good friends* (*unquote*).

unravel [ʌn'ravəl] – *pt* **un'ravelled**, (*Amer*) **un'raveled** – **1** *vt* (*more formal than* **untangle**) to take (*eg* string, thread *etc*) out of its tangled condition; to disentangle: *She could not unravel the tangled thread.* **2** *vti* (*esp* of a knitted fabric): to undo or become undone: *My knitting* (*got*) *unravelled when it fell off the needles.* **3** *vt* to solve (a problem, mystery *etc*): *Is there no-one who can unravel this mystery?*

unreal [ʌn'riəl] *adj* not existing in fact: *He lives in an unreal world imagined by himself; The countryside seemed unreal covered in snow; After such a terrible shock, you will feel that everything is a bit unreal.* **,unre'ality** [ʌnri'a-] *nu.*

unreasonable [ʌn'ri:zənəbl] *adj* **1** not guided by good sense or reason: *His conduct/attitude is unreasonable; It is unreasonable to expect children to work so hard.* **2** excessive, or too great: *That butcher charges unreasonable prices; He makes unreasonable demands on my time; The demands for higher wages are quite unreasonable.*

un'reasoning *adj* (*formal*: *usu attrib*) not guided by, or using, reason: *He had an unreasoning dislike of the child.*

unremitting [ʌnrə'mitiŋ] *adj* (*formal*: *usu attrib*) never ceasing: *unremitting efforts to help the poor.*

unrequited [ʌnrə'kwaitid] *adj* (*liter*) (of love) not felt in return by the loved person: *the pain of unrequited love; His passion for her was unrequited.*

unreserved [ʌnri'zə:vd] *adj* **1** (of a seat *etc*) not reserved: *the unreserved area of the theatre auditorium; These seats are unreserved.* **2** (*formal*) complete: *The committee gave his suggestion its unreserved approval; Their approval was completely unreserved.* **3** (*formal*) frank: *She had a cheerful, unreserved nature; Her sister is very shy but she is friendly and unreserved.*

,unre'servedly [-vid-] *adv* (*formal*) **1** completely: utterly: *We are unreservedly delighted/relieved about the result.* **2** frankly: *She spoke unreservedly.*

unrest [ʌn'rest] *nu* (*formal*) a state of trouble or discontent, *esp* among a group of people: *political unrest.*

unrivalled, (*Amer*) **un'rivaled** [ʌn'raivəld] *adj* (*formal*) having no equal or rival: *his unrivalled ability; She is unrivalled as a Shakespearian actress.*

unroll [ʌn'roul] *vti* to open from a rolled position: *He unrolled the mattress; Take care that the bandage doesn't unroll.*

unruly [ʌn'ru:li] *adj* uncontrollable or disorderly: *unruly teenagers; unruly behaviour; The schoolboys are unruly and rude.* **un'ruliness** *nu.*

unsaid [ʌn'sed] *adj* (*formal*: *pred*) not said: *My remark was unkind – consider it unsaid; Remarks of that sort are better left unsaid.*

unsavoury [ʌn'seivəri] *adj* (*formal derog*) very unpleasant or disgusting: *There are some unsavoury stories about that man; The tales I have heard about him are rather unsavoury.*

unscathed [ʌn'skeiðd] *adj* (*formal*: *usu pred*) not harmed: *She was lucky to escape unscathed from the car crash.*

unscramble [ʌn'skrambl] *vt* to decode (a message) or make clear the words of (a telephone message).

unscrew [ʌn'skru:] *vt* to remove or loosen (something) by taking out screws, or with a twisting or screwing action: *He unscrewed the cupboard door; Can you unscrew this lid?*

unscrupulous [ʌn'skru:pjuləs] *adj* (*formal derog*) having no conscience or scruples; wicked: *He is an unscrupulous rogue; He is totally unscrupulous – he would steal money from anyone; She is ambitious and unscrupulous – she would do anything to be promoted.*

unseat [ʌn'si:t] *vt* (*very formal*) to remove (a person) from an official position, *esp* a seat in parliament: *He was unseated at the last election.*

unseemly [ʌn'si:mli] *adj* (*formal*) not suitable:

improper: *He is guilty of unseemly conduct*; *His behaviour was unseemly.*

unseen [ʌn'siːn] *adj* not seen: *She came into the room unseen*; *the unseen hand of God.* – *nc* a passage in a foreign language to be translated without previous preparation: *I couldn't do the unseen.*

unsettle [ʌn'setl] *vt* to disturb or upset: *Will a change of schools unsettle the child?*

un'settled *adj* **1** (of weather) changeable: *unsettled weather*; *The weather is unsettled.* **2** anxious or restless: *I feel very unsettled*; *in an unsettled mood.*

unsheathe [ʌn'ʃiːð] *vt* (*formal or liter*) to draw (a sword) from the sheath or scabbard.

unsightly [ʌn'saitli] *adj* (*formal*) ugly: *those unsightly modern buildings*; *That new block of flats is so unsightly.*

unsound [ʌn'saund] *adj* (*formal*) **1** not in good condition: *That building is unsound*; *an unsound building*; *The foundations of this building are unsound.* **2** incorrect and therefore unreliable: *His argument/theory is unsound*; *unsound reasoning.*

of unsound mind (*esp legal*) insane: *The coroner's verdict was that he had committed suicide while of unsound mind.*

unsparing [ʌn'speəriŋ] *adj* (*formal*) giving generously: *She was unsparing in her love for him*; *She was unsparing in her efforts to help him.*

unspeakable [ʌn'spiːkəbl] *adj* (*derog*) that cannot be expressed in words, *esp* because too bad to describe: *his unspeakable cruelty/rudeness*; *His conduct was unspeakable.*

un'speakably *adv*: *He was unspeakably rude*; *The house is unspeakably filthy.*

unstinting [ʌn'stintiŋ] *adj* (*formal*) very generous: *unstinting help*; *unstinting praise*; *They were unstinting in their praise.* **un'stintingly** *adv.*

unstop [ʌn'stop] *vt* to remove a blockage from (*eg* a drain): *The plumber has unstopped the blocked kitchen drain.*

unstuck [ʌn'stʌk]: **come unstuck 1** to stop sticking: *The label has come unstuck.* **2** (*inf*) to fail: *Our plans have come unstuck.*

unstudied [ʌn'stʌdid] *adj* (*liter*: *often attrib*) natural; effortless: *her unstudied charm.*

unsung [ʌn'sʌŋ] *adj* (*liter*) (of *eg* achievements) not praised: *His achievements went unsung*; *the unsung heroes.*

unsuspected [ʌnsə'spektid] *adj* (*often attrib*) not imagined or known to exist: *He had unsuspected talents.*

ˌunsu'specting *adj* (*formal*) not aware of (coming) danger: *This product is being sold to an unsuspecting public*; *He stole all her money and she was completely unsuspecting.*

untangle [ʌn'taŋgl] *vt* to take (*eg* string, thread *etc*) out of its tangled condition; to disentangle: *She tried to untangle the wool that her cat had been playing with.*

unthinkable [ʌn'θiŋkəbl] *adj* (*formal*) too outrageous to be considered: *It would be unthinkable to ask him to do that*; *unthinkable dangers.*

un'thinking *adj* (*usu attrib*) showing lack of thought or consideration: *those unthinking people who scatter rubbish in the streets*; *His unthinking words had hurt her deeply.*

untie [ʌn'tai] *vt* to loosen or unfasten: *He untied the string from the parcel*; *He untied his shoelaces.*

until [ən'til] *prep, conj* to the time of or when: *I waited until the end of the morning*; *He was here until one o'clock*; *I won't know until I get a letter from him.*

See also **till**.

untimely [ʌn'taimli] *adj* (*formal or liter*: *usu attrib*) **1** happening too soon: *Mozart's untimely death at the age of 37.* **2** not suitable in the circumstances: *his untimely interference.*

untiring [ʌn'taiəriŋ] *adj* (of a person or his efforts *etc*) never stopping or ceasing because of weariness: *She has been quite untiring in her work for the community*; *his untiring efforts/energy.* **un'tiringly** *adv.*

See also **tireless**.

unto ['ʌntu] *prep* (*arch*) to.

untold [ʌn'tould] *adj* **1** (*usu pred*) not told: *His story remained untold.* **2** (*attrib*: *liter*) too great to be counted, measured: *untold millions.*

untoward [ʌntə'woːd] *adj* (*formal*: *usu attrib*) inconvenient or unfortunate: *untoward events/circumstances*; *The circumstances are untoward.*

untrue [ʌn'truː] *adj* **1** not true; false: *The statement is untrue*; *an untrue account.* **2** (*old*) disloyal, or unfaithful: *She suspected her husband of being untrue to her.*

un'truth [-θ] (*formal*) **1** *nu* lack of truth: falseness: *The untruth of his statement is obvious.* **2** *nc* (*euph*) a lie or false statement: *His autobiography contains outrageous untruths.*

untwist [ʌn'twist] *vti* to straighten from a twisted position: *He untwisted the wire*; *Her hands nervously twisted and untwisted.*

unusual [ʌn'juːʒuəl] *adj* not usual; rare; uncommon: *an unusual shade of blue*; *It is unusual for it to snow here in June*; *He has an unusual job.*

un'usually *adv*: *She is unusually cheerful today*; *It is unusually warm today.*

unutterable [ʌn'ʌtərəbl] *adj* (*formal*: *usu attrib*) **1** (of a feeling) too strong to be expressed: *To his unutterable horror, the ground began to shake.* **2** too bad to describe: *What unutterable rudeness!*

unvarnished [ʌn'vaːniʃt] *adj* (*formal or facet*: *attrib*) (of facts, truth *etc*) plain and direct: *I'll tell you the whole unvarnished truth.*

unveil [ʌn'veil] (*formal*) **1** *vti* to remove a veil (from *eg* a face): *After the marriage ceremony, the bride unveils* (*her face*). **2** *vt* to uncover (a new statue *etc*) ceremonially: *The prime minister was asked to unveil the new portrait of himself at the House of Commons.*

unvoiced [ʌn'voist] *adj* (*formal*) not expressed in words: *his unvoiced thoughts/opinion*; *His opinions remain unvoiced.*

unwary [ʌn'weəri] *adj* (*formal*) not cautious: *If you are unwary he will cheat you*; *unwary people.*

un'warily *adv.* **un'wariness** *nu.*

the unwary people who are unwary: *Most television advertising is just a trap for the unwary.*

unwelcome [ʌn'welkəm] *adj* received unwillingly or with disappointment: *unwelcome news/guests*; *I felt that we were unwelcome.*

unwell [ʌn'wel] *adj* (*usu pred*) not in good health: *He felt unwell this morning.*

unwieldy [ʌn'wiːldi] *adj* (*derog*) large and awkward to carry or manage: *A wardrobe is an unwieldy thing to move*; *He rides an unwieldy old-fashioned bicycle*; *That piece of furniture is too unwieldy for this small house*; (*fig*) *This organization has become too large and unwieldy.*

un'wieldiness *nu.*

unwilling [ʌn'wiliŋ] *adj* not willing; reluctant: *He's unwilling to accept the money*; *I was an unwilling witness of their quarrels.* **un'willingness** *nu.*

un'willingly *adv*: *He did agree to go, but rather unwillingly.*

unwind [ʌn'waind] – *pt, ptp* **un'wound** [-'waund] – **1** *vti* to take or come out of a coiled or wound position: *He unwound the bandage from his ankle*; *A watch-spring starts tightly coiled and gradually unwinds.* **2** *vi* (*fig*) to relax after a period of tension: *Give me a chance to unwind!*

unwise [ʌn'waiz] *adj* (*formal*) not wise; foolish: *an unwise suggestion*; *It was rather unwise of you to agree to do that.* **un'wisely** *adv.*

unwitting [ʌn'witiŋ] *adj* (*formal*: *attrib*) **1** not knowing: *I was the unwitting cause of her accident.* **2** not intended: *an unwitting insult.*

un'wittingly *adv* (*formal*) unintentionally: *I was unwittingly cruel to her.*

unwonted [ʌn'wountid] *adj* (*formal*: *attrib*) unusual; not customary: *He received my idea with unwonted enthusiasm.*

unworthy [ʌn'wəːði] *adj* **1** (*usu attrib*) shameful or disgraceful: *That was an unworthy act/thought.* **2** (*often pred with* **of**) not deserving: *Such a remark is unworthy of notice*; *He's unworthy to have the same name as his father.* **3** (*pred with* **of**) less good than should be expected from (*eg* a person): *Behaviour of this sort is unworthy of him*; *This piece of work is unworthy of you.* **un'worthily** *adv.* **un'worthiness** *nu.*

unwound *see* **unwind**.

unwrap [ʌn'rap] – *pt, ptp* **un'wrapped** – *vt* to open (something wrapped or folded): *He unwrapped the gift.*

unwritten [ʌn'ritn] *adj* (*usu attrib*) **1** not recorded in writing: *He used mainly unwritten sources for his collection of country songs.* **2** (of a law or rule) not officially stated in writing, but based on custom and generally accepted: *Unwritten laws are often those that concern basic human rights.*

unzip [ʌn'zip] – *pt, ptp* **un'zipped** – *vt* to undo the zip of: *Will you unzip this dress please?*

up [ʌp] *adv, adj* **1** to, or at, a higher or better position: *He was just pulling his trousers up*; *Is the elevator going up?*; *The office is up on the top floor*; *She looked up at him*; *The aircraft was 4 000 metres up*; *The sun is up already*; *The price of coffee is up again*; *Our football team was two goals up at half-time*; *In most types of writing, the down strokes are thicker than the up strokes.* **2** erect: *Sit/Stand up*; *He got up from his chair.* **3** out of bed: *What time do you get up?*; *I'll be up all night finishing this work*; *She has been ill in bed but is up again now.* **4** to a more important place: *I'm going up to London tomorrow.* **5** to a university *esp* Oxford or Cambridge: *He is going up to Cambridge next term.* **6** to the north: *I've never been up as far as Edinburgh*; *What time is the next up train?* **7** to the place or person mentioned or understood: *A taxi drove up and she got in*; *He came up* (*to me*) *and shook hands.* **8** into the presence, or consideration, of a person, group of people *etc*: *He brought up the subject during the conversation*; *His case will come up in the police court next week*; *The problem will be coming up again at the next meeting.* **9** to an increased degree *eg* of loudness, speed *etc*: *Please turn the radio up a little!*; *Speak up! I can't hear you*; *The work will have to be speeded up*; *Hurry up!* **10** used to indicate completeness; thoroughly or finally: *Has the child eaten up all his food?*; *You'll end up in hospital if you don't drive more carefully*; *He locked up the house*; *Help me wash up the dishes!*; *She wrapped it up in brown paper*; *I've used up the whole supply of paper*; *He tore up her letter*; *At the end of the exam, the teacher called 'Your time is up!'* – *prep* **1** to or at a higher level on: *He climbed up the tree*; *They live up the hill.* **2** (at a place) along: *They walked up the street*; *Their house is up the road.* **3** towards the source of (a river): *When do the salmon start swimming up the river?* – *v* – *pt, ptp* **upped** – (*inf*) **1** *vt* to increase (a price *etc*): *They upped the price that they wanted for their house.* **2** *vi* to stand up or act with determination: *She upped and hit him*; *He upped and complained to the manager.*

'upward *adj* (*attrib*) going up or directed up: *They took the upward path*; *an upward glance.*

'upward(s) *adv* (facing) towards a higher place or level: *He was lying on the floor face upwards*; *The path led upwards.* – *See also* **upward(s) of** *below.*

ˌup-and-'coming *adj* (*attrib*) (of *eg* a person starting a career) progressing well: *an up-and-coming young doctor.*

ˌup'grade *vt* (*formal*) to increase the importance of, or improve the quality of: *His job has been upgraded and his salary has been increased.*

ˌup'hill *adv* up a slope: *We travelled uphill for several hours.* – *adj* **1** (*usu attrib*) sloping upwards; ascending: *an uphill road/journey*; *It's uphill all the way.* **2** (*fig*: *attrib*) difficult: *Training this team will be an uphill job*; *This will be an uphill struggle.*

ˌup'stairs *adv* on or to an upper floor: *His room is upstairs*; *She went upstairs to her bedroom.* – *n* – *pl* **up'stairs** – *nc* (*inf*: *with* **the**) the upper floor(s): *The ground floor needs painting, but the upstairs is nice*; (*attrib*) *an upstairs sitting-room.*

up'stream *adv* towards the upper part or source of a stream, river *etc*: *Salmon swim upstream to lay their eggs.*

up-to-date *see* **date**.

be on the ˌup-and-'up (*inf*) to be progressing very successfully, *esp* financially: *The firm is on the up-and-up now.*

be/come *etc* **'up against** to be faced with (difficulties *etc*): *I'm up against a problem*; *You may come up against several difficulties.*

be ˌup a'gainst it (*inf*) to be in difficulties: *She's really up against it!*

be up and about (*inf*) to be out of bed: *I've been up and about for hours*; *Is she up and about again after her accident?*

be/come 'up for to be presented or offered for (*eg* discussion, judgement, sale *etc*): *The matter will be coming up for discussion again*; *Their house is up for sale.*

be 'up on (*inf*) to be better or more than: *His performance was up on last week's*; *Imports are up on last year's.*

be 'up to 1 (*inf*) to be busy or occupied with (an activity *etc*): *What is he up to now?*; *I'm sure that man is up to no good* (= is planning to do something bad or evil). **2** (*inf*) to be capable of: *She wasn't up to cooking a meal*; *He isn't quite up to the job.* **3** to reach the standard of: *This work isn't up to your best.* **4** to be the duty or privilege of: *It's up to you to decide*; *The final choice is up to him.*

be 'up (with) (*inf*) to be wrong (with): *Something's up!*; *What's up with her?*

be (ˌwell) 'up in/on (something) to know a lot about (a subject): *Are you well up on mythology?*; *He is well up in astrology.*

ups and downs (*inf*) times of good and bad luck: *We all have our ups and downs.*

'up to as far, or as much, as: *He counted up to 100*; *Up to now, the work has been easy*; *Save up to 25 per*

cent on your train fare by travelling midweek!
up to date *see* **date**[1].
'upward(s) of (*formal*) more than: *There were upwards of a hundred people at the meeting.*
See also **upside down**.

upbraid [ʌp'breid] *vt* (*formal or old*) to reproach, rebuke or scold: *She upbraided him for his laziness.*

upbringing ['ʌpbriŋiŋ] *ncu* (an example of) the process of rearing and giving moral training to a child: *Some parents care very little about the upbringing of their children*; *He had a stern upbringing.*

update [ʌp'deit] *vt* to make (something) suitable for the present time by adapting it to recent ideas *etc*: *Dictionaries constantly need to be updated.*

upgrade *see* **up**.

upheaval [ʌp'hi:vəl] *nc* a great change or disturbance: *We should move house, but I couldn't bear the upheaval*; *The late eighteenth century was a time of social upheaval.*

upheld *see* **uphold**.

uphill *see* **up**.

uphold [ʌp'hould] – *pt, ptp* **up'held** [-'held] – *vt* (*formal*: not *usu* used with **is, was** *etc* and **-ing** (*defs 1, 3*)) **1** to support (a person's action): *His family upholds (him in) his present action.* **2** to confirm (*eg* a claim, legal judgement, *etc*): *The decision of the judge was upheld by the appeal court.* **3** to maintain (*eg* a custom): *The old traditions are still upheld in this school.*

upholster [ʌp'houlstə] *vt* to fit (seats) with springs, stuffing, covers *etc*: *He upholstered the chair.*
up'holstered *adj*: *upholstered chairs.*
up'holsterer *nc* a person who makes, repairs, or sells upholstered furniture.
up'holstery *nu* **1** the business or process of upholstering: *She goes to classes in upholstery*; (*attrib*) *upholstery classes.* **2** the springs, coverings *etc* of *eg* a chair: *luxurious upholstery.*

upkeep ['ʌpki:p] *nu* (the cost of) the process of keeping *eg* a house, car *etc* in a good condition: *The upkeep of a car can cost several hundred pounds per annum*; *She can no longer afford the upkeep of this house.*

uplands ['ʌpləndz] *n pl* (*old or found with cap in place-names*) a hilly or mountainous region: *the Southern Uplands.*

uplift [ʌp'lift] *vt* (*formal or old*) to improve the moral or emotional state of (a person): *He felt uplifted by the music.* – ['ʌplift] *ncu* (*formal or old*) the process of being uplifted: *His words gave us an uplift.*

upmost ['ʌpmoust] *adj, adv* (*formal*) uppermost.

upon [ə'pon] *prep* (*formal or liter*) on: *He sat upon the floor*; *Please place it upon the table*; *He died upon the same day*; *Upon arrival, they went in search of a hotel.*
once upon a time *see* **once**.
upon my word! (*old*) an exclamation indicating surprise *etc.*

upper ['ʌpə] *adj* (*attrib*) higher in position, rank *etc*: *the upper floors of the building*; *He has a scar on his upper lip*; *The part of the arm between the elbow and shoulder is called the upper arm*; *the upper classes of the school*; *the upper* (= nearer the source) *reaches of the Thames.* – *See also* **get/have the upper hand of/over** *below.* – *nc* (*usu in pl*) the part of a shoe above the sole: *There's a crack in the upper.*
'uppermost *adj* (*often liter*: *attrib*) highest: *in the uppermost room of the castle.* – *adv* in the highest place or position: *Thoughts of him were uppermost in her mind*; *The canoe capsized and floated keel uppermost.*
upper class *nc* (*with* **the**: *sometimes in pl*), *adj* (*sometimes derog*) (of) the highest rank of society; (of) the aristocracy: *The upper classes can no longer afford to have many servants*; *His accent is very upper-class*; *He speaks with an upper-class accent.*
upper house *nc* (*sometimes with caps*) a second, *usu* smaller, administrative and legislative body within a country's parliamentary system: *The House of Lords is the Upper House of the British Parliament.*
get/have the upper hand (of/over someone) (*inf*) to have or win an advantage over: *I've got the upper hand over you*; *Our team managed to get the upper hand in the end.*

upper-crust ['ʌpəkrʌst] *adj* (*inf derog*: *usu attrib*) of the upper classes: *an upper-crust accent*; *His accent sounds rather upper-crust.*

uppercut ['ʌpəkʌt] *nc* in boxing *etc*, a blow aimed upwards, *eg* to the chin.

uppish ['ʌpiʃ] *adj* (*inf derog*) proud or haughty: *He's getting very uppish*; *an uppish young woman.*

upright ['ʌprait] **1** *adj, adv* standing straight up; erect or vertical: *He placed the books upright in the bookcase*; *She got off the bed and stood upright*; *a row of upright posts.* **2** *adj* (*formal*) (of a person) just and honest: *an upright, honourable man*; *He has not always been upright in his business affairs.* – *nc* **1** an upright post *etc* supporting a construction: *When building the fence, place the uprights two metres apart.* **2** (*inf*) an upright piano (*see under* **piano**).
'uprightly *adv* (*formal*) honestly: *He behaved uprightly.*
'uprightness *nu* (*formal*) honesty: *uprightness of character.*

uprising ['ʌpraiziŋ] *nc* (*formal or old*) a rebellion or revolt: *The Hungarian uprising was quickly suppressed.*

uproar ['ʌpro:] **1** *ncu* (an outbreak of) noise, shouting *etc*: *The Prime Minister's speech was followed by (an) uproar*; *The whole town was in (an) uproar after the football team's victory.*
up'roarious *adj* (*often attrib*) very noisy, *esp* with much laughter: *uproarious applause*; *The team were given an uproarious welcome*; *The applause was uproarious.* **up'roariously** *adv.*

uproot [ʌp'ru:t] *vt* to pull (a plant *etc*) out of the earth with the roots: *I uprooted the weeds and burnt them*; (*fig*) *My husband has had jobs in many parts of the world, so we are used to being uprooted and settling down in a new place.*

upset [ʌp'set] – *pt, ptp* **up'set** – *vt* **1** (*slightly formal*) to overturn: *He upset a glass of wine over the table*; *I've upset a cup of coffee all over my skirt.* **2** to disturb or put (something) out of order: *Bananas always upset my digestion*; *His illness has upset all our arrangements.* **3** to distress: *His friend's death upset him very much*; *Try not to upset yourself about losing your job.* – *adj* disturbed or distressed: *He's suffering from an upset stomach*; *Is he very upset about failing his exam?* – ['ʌpset] *nc* (*inf*) a disturbance: *He has a stomach upset*; *I couldn't bear the upset of moving house again.*
'upset (price) *nc* the price at which the bidding starts at an auction sale or the price below which a seller (of a house *etc*) is not willing to sell: *The upset (price) of the house was £25 000 but it sold for £37 000.*

upshot ['ʌpʃot]: **the upshot** (*inf*) the result or end (of a matter): *What was the final upshot of that affair?*

upside down [ʌpsai'daun] *adv* **1** with the top part underneath: *The plate was lying upside down on the floor.* **2** into confusion: *The burglars turned the house upside down.* – *adj* (*attrib*) having the top part underneath: *an upside-down cake.*

upstage [ʌp'steidʒ] *adv* (*drama*) away from the front of the stage: *The actor moved upstage to the left.* – *adj* (*inf derog*) snobbish or haughty: *He was rather upstage with me*; *an upstage manner.* – *vt* (*inf*) to take people's interest or attention away from (someone or something): *With her skin-tight orange trousers, she upstaged all the other girls at the party.*

upstairs *see* **up**.

upstanding [ʌp'standiŋ] *adj* (*formal*: *attrib*) strong and healthy; frank and honest: *a fine upstanding young man/character.*

be upstanding (*formal*: used ceremonially) to stand up respectfully, *usu* to drink a toast *eg* to the sovereign: *Be upstanding for Her Majesty the Queen!*

upstart ['ʌpsta:t] *nc* (*inf derog*) a person who has risen quickly to wealth or power but seems to lack dignity or ability: *I shall leave the firm if that little upstart becomes manager*; (*attrib*) *irresponsible, upstart politicians.*

upstream *see* **up**.

uptake ['ʌpteik]: **quick, slow on the uptake** quick or slow to understand: *She's inexperienced, but very quick on the uptake.*

upward, upwards *see* **up**.

uranium [ju'reiniəm] *nu* radioactive element (symbol **U**).

Uranus *see* Appendix 6.

urban ['ə:bən] *adj* (*formal*: *usu attrib*) of, consisting of, or living in, a city or town: *He dislikes urban life*; *urban traffic.*

urbane [ə:'bein] *adj* (*formal*: *often derog*) (too) smoothly polite: *I dislike him intensely – he is too smooth and urbane*; *an urbane young man.* **urbanity** [ə:'banəti] *ncu.*

urchin ['ə:tʃin] *nc* (*esp old*) a mischievous, *usu* dirty or ragged, child, *esp* a boy: *He was chased by a crowd of street urchins.*

Urdu *see* Appendix 2.

urge [ə:dʒ] *vt* **1** to try to persuade or request earnestly (someone to do something): *He urged her to drive carefully*; *'Come with me,' he urged.* **2** (*formal*) to try to convince a person of (*eg* the importance of, or necessity for, some action): *He urged* (*on them*) *the necessity for speed.* – *See also* **urge on** *below.* – *nc* a strong impulse or desire: *I felt an urge to hit him*; *He had a sudden urge to go to Italy*; *She gets these sudden urges.*

urge on *vt sep* to drive or try to persuade (a person *etc*) to go on or forwards: *He tried to urge the donkey on*; *He urged himself on in spite of his weariness.*

urgent ['ə:dʒənt] *adj* needing immediate attention: *The refugees are in urgent need of help*; *There is an urgent message for the doctor*; *It is extremely urgent that they should be rescued from the mountain before dark.* **'urgently** *adv.*

'urgency *nu* need for immediate action, speed *etc*: *This is a matter of great urgency.*

urine ['ju:rin] *nu* the waste fluid passed out of the body of animals from the bladder: *There was a smell of urine from the baby's nappy.*

urinal ['ju:rinəl, (*Brit also*) ju'rainəl] *nc* (*formal*) a receptacle in a public lavatory for men to urinate into.

'urinary *adj* (*formal*): *a urinary infection.*

'urinate ['juərineit] *vi* (*formal*) to pass urine from the bladder: *He embarrassed the old lady by urinating in the street.*

urn [ə:n] *nc* **1** a tall vase or other container, *esp* for holding the ashes of a dead person: *a stone-age burial urn.* **2** (*often in cmpds*) a large metal container with a tap, in which tea or coffee is made *eg* in a canteen *etc*: *a tea-urn.*

Uruguay, Uruguayan *see* Appendix 2.

us [ʌs] *pron* (used as the object of an actual or implied verb or preposition or (*inf*) as the subject of an implied verb) the speaker or writer plus one or more other people: *He woke us*; *She gave us a present*; *A plane flew over us*; (*inf*) *'Who did it?' 'Us.'* (= We did it); *'Who did she come with?' 'Us.'* *See also* **our(selves), we.**

usage ['ju:zidʒ, (*Amer*) -sidʒ] **1** *nu* (*formal or liter*) treatment: *subjected to rough usage.* **2** *ncu* (*formal or liter*) (a) custom or habit: *ancient traditions and usages.* **3** *ncu* the generally accepted way in which a language is used, or a way in which a particular word *etc* is used: *Meanings of words change and develop through usage*; *Is the usage 'one pence' incorrect?*

use[1] [ju:z] *vt* **1** to employ (something) for a purpose: *I always use scissors to cut up meat*; *What did you use to open the can?*; *Use your common sense!*; *He used his job as a screen for his spying activities.* **2** to consume: *Did you use all the milk?*; *We're using far too much electricity.* **3** (*formal*) to treat (a person) in a particular way: *She felt that she had been badly used.*

'usable *adj* that can be used: *Are any of these clothes usable?*; *These are all usable instruments.*

used *adj* **1** (*pred*) employed or put to a purpose: *This road is not used any more.* **2** (*usu attrib*) not new: *used cars.*

'user *nc* (*sometimes in cmpds*) a person who uses something: *road-users*; *electricity users.*

used to (something) ['ju:stu] accustomed to: *She isn't used to such hard work*; *I'm not used to being treated like this.*

used to ['ju:stu] – *neg short forms* (*esp Brit*) **usedn't to, usen't to** ['ju:sntu] – (only found in *pt* and with *aux* **did**) (I, he *etc*) was in the habit of (doing something); (I, he *etc*) was (usually) in a particular position, state *etc*: *I used to swim every day*; *She used not to be so forgetful*; *She didn't use(d) to do it, did she?*; *They used to play golf, didn't they?*; *Didn't you use(d) to live near me?*; (*esp Brit formal*) *Used he to do that?*; *Did he used to do that?*; *There used to be a butcher's shop there, didn't there?*; *Didn't there use(d) to be a church at the corner of the street?*

See also **use**[2], **usual, utility, utilize.**

use[2] [ju:s] **1** *nu* the act of using or state of being used: *The use of force to persuade workers to join a strike cannot be justified*; *The telephone number 999 is for use in emergencies.* **2** *ncu* the/a purpose for which something may be used: *This little knife has plenty of uses*; *Can you find a use for these empty boxes?*; *I have no further use for these clothes.* **3** *nu* (often in questions or with negatives) value or advantage: *Is this coat* (*of*) *any use to you?*; *It's no use offering to help when it's too late.* **4** *nu* the power of using: *She lost the use of her right arm as a result of the accident.* **5** *nu* permission, or the right, to use: *They let us have the use of their car while they were away.* – *See also* **use** *in phrases below.*

'useful *adj* helpful or serving a purpose well: *a useful tool/dictionary; She made herself useful by doing the washing for her mother; Here are the names of some people who might be useful to you.* – *See also* **come in useful** *below.*

'usefully *adv* in a useful way: *He spent the day usefully in repairing the car.*

'usefulness *nu* the quality of being useful: *Since the fashions changed, this skirt has lost its usefulness.*

'useless *adj* having no use or no effect: *Why don't you throw away those useless things?; We can't do it – it's useless to try.*

be in use, out of use to be used or not used: *How long has the gymnasium been in use/out of use?*

come into use to begin to be used: *When did umbrellas come into use?*

come in useful to become useful: *My French came in useful on holiday.*

go out of use to be no longer used: *When did trams go out of use in this city?*

have no use for (someone/something) (*inf*) to despise: *I have no use for such silliness/silly people.*

it's no use it's impossible or useless: *He tried in vain to do it, then said 'It's no use'.*

make (good) use of (something), put (something) to (good) use: *He makes use of his training; He puts his training to good use in that job.*

use(d)n't *see* **use**[1].

usher ['ʌʃə] – *fem* ˌ**ushe'rette** [-'ret] – *nc* a person who shows people to their seats in a theatre *etc*: *He was one of the ushers at the wedding.* – *vt* to lead or escort: *The waiter ushered him to a table.*

usher in *vt sep* **1** to conduct (a person) into a house, room *etc*: *The door was opened and he was ushered in.* **2** (*liter fig*) to introduce or bring (a period, era *etc*) into existence: *The succession of the new emperor ushered in an era of terror.*

usual ['juːʒuəl] *adj* done, happening *etc* most often; customary: *Are you going home by the usual route?; There are more people here than usual; We shall have the usual difficulty persuading people to help; Is behaviour like this usual in a child?; Such behaviour is quite usual with children of that age; As usual, he was late.*

'usually *adv* on most occasions: *We are usually at home in the evenings; Usually we finish work at 5 o'clock.*

usurp [ju'zəːp] *vt* (*hist or formal*) to take (another person's power, position *etc*) without the right to do so: *The king's uncle tried to usurp the throne; I shall not allow him to usurp my authority.*

ˌ**usur'pation** [juːzəː-] *nu*. **u'surper** *nc*.

usury ['juːʒuri] *nu* (*usu derog*) the practice of lending money at an (excessively) high rate of interest.

'usurer *nc* (*derog*) a moneylender who demands a very high rate of interest.

utensil [ju'tensl] *nc* an instrument or vessel used in everyday life: *pots and pans and other kitchen utensils.*

uterus ['juːtərəs] *nc* (*formal or tech*) the womb: *She is suffering from cancer of the uterus.*

utility [ju'tiləti] **1** *nu* (*very formal*) usefulness: *Some kitchen gadgets have only a limited utility.* **2** *nc* (*formal*) a useful public service, *eg* the supply of water, gas, electricity *etc.*

uˌ**tili'tarian** *adj* useful rather than ornamental: *Our plates and glasses are rather utilitarian; utilitarian articles.*

utilize, -ise ['juːtilaiz] *vt* (*formal*) to find a useful purpose for (something): *The extra money is being utilized to buy books for the school library; You must utilize all available resources.* ˌ**utili'zation, -s-** *nu*.

utmost ['ʌtmoust] *adj* (*formal*: *attrib*) **1** most distant: *the utmost ends of the earth.* **2** greatest possible: *Take the utmost care!*

do one's utmost to make the greatest possible effort: *She has done her utmost to help him.*

Utopia [juː'toupiə] *n* an imaginary country that has a perfect social and political system.

U'topian *adj* (of *eg* plans for benefiting mankind) desirable, but idealistic and impossible: *Utopian schemes.*

utter[1] ['ʌtə] *adj* (*attrib*) complete or total: *There was utter silence; utter darkness; I was amazed by his utter lack of tact.*

'utterly *adv* completely or totally: *She was utterly unaware of her danger.*

'uttermost *adj* (*liter*) utmost.

utter[2] ['ʌtə] *vt* **1** (*formal*) to produce (sounds, *eg* cries, words *etc*) with the mouth: *She uttered a sigh of relief; He uttered a cry of despair; She didn't utter a single word of encouragement.* **2** (*legal*) to issue (counterfeit money *etc*): *He was convicted of uttering a false cheque.*

'utterance (*formal*) **1** *nu* the act of expressing something, or the process of being expressed, in words: *He had no time to give utterance to his thoughts.* **2** *nc* something that is said: *blasphemous utterances.*

uttermost *see* **utter**[1].

U-turn *see* **U**.

Vv

v *see* **versus**.

V- [viː] (*in cmpds*) shaped like a V: *a* ˌ*V-neck(ed)* '*pullover* (= a pullover with a neckline in the shape of a V).

V-sign ['viːsain] *nc* a sign, made with the index and middle fingers in a V shape, used to indicate either victory (with the palm of the hand facing away from oneself) or (*Brit vulg*) strong dislike, scorn *etc* (with the palm of the hand facing towards oneself).

vac [vak] (*inf*) short for **vacation**: *the summer vac.*

vacant ['veikənt] *adj* **1** empty or unoccupied: *a vacant chair; There are no vacant rooms in this hotel; Are there any rooms vacant?* **2** showing no thought, intelligence or interest: *a vacant stare;* (*inf*) *He looks rather vacant* (= not very intelligent).

'vacancy 1 *nc* an unoccupied post: *We have a vacancy for a typist.* **2** *nu* (*formal*) the condition of being vacant; emptiness: *The vacancy of his expression made me doubt if he was listening.*

'vacantly *adv* absent-mindedly; without concentration: *He stared vacantly out of the window.*

vacate [və'keit, (*Amer*) vei-] *vt* (*formal*) to cease to occupy: *Hotel guests are requested to vacate their rooms by midday on the day of departure.*

vacation [vəˈkeiʃən, (*Amer*) vei-] *nc* (*esp Amer*) a holiday: *a summer vacation.* – *vi* (*Amer*) to take a holiday: *He vacationed in Paris last year.*

on vacation (*esp Amer*) not working; having a holiday: *He is on vacation*; *She has gone to Italy on vacation.*

vaccine [ˈvaksiːn] *ncu* a substance made from the germs that cause a particular disease, *esp* smallpox, and given to a person or animal to prevent him from catching that disease: *Vaccines are prepared in various ways*; *a good supply of vaccine.*

ˈvaccinate [-ksi-] *vt* to protect (a person *etc*) against a disease by putting vaccine into his blood: *Has your child been vaccinated against smallpox?*

ˌvacciˈnation [-ksi-] *ncu* (an) act of vaccinating or process of being vaccinated: *I'm to have a vaccination tomorrow*; *Vaccination was introduced in the eighteenth century.*

vacillate [ˈvasileit] *vi* (*formal*: *often derog*) to change from one opinion, alternative *etc* to another, being unable to decide between them: *Oh, do stop vacillating and make up your mind!*; *He vacillated between accepting and not accepting.* **ˌvacilˈlation** *ncu.*

vacuous [ˈvakjuəs] *adj* (*formal derog*) showing lack of intelligence; stupid: *His face had a vacuous expression*; *He looks decidedly vacuous.*

vacuum [ˈvakjum] *nc* **1** a space from which (almost) all air or other gas has been removed. **2** (*fig formal*) a situation from which all normal guiding signs, information, help *etc* have been removed: *She was brought up in a vacuum, isolated from the normal world.* **3** (*inf*) short for **vacuum cleaner**. – *vti* to clean (something) using a vacuum cleaner: *She vacuumed the carpet.*

vacuum cleaner *nc* a machine that cleans carpets *etc* by sucking dust *etc* into itself.

ˈvacuum-flask *nc* (*often abbrev* **flask**) a container with double walls that have a vacuum between them to keep the contents from losing or gaining heat: *a vacuum-flask of hot coffee.*

vagabond [ˈvagəbond] *nc, adj* (*attrib*) (*old*: *usu derog*) (a person) having no settled home, or roving from place to place, *esp* in an idle or disreputable manner: *rogues and vagabonds*; *You must give up your vagabond ways!*

vagary [ˈveigəri, (*Amer also*) vəˈgeəri] *nc* (*formal*: *often in pl*) a piece of odd or unexpected behaviour: *the vagaries of the weather*; *the vagaries of human nature.*

vagina [vəˈdʒainə] *nc* (in the female of humans and other mammals) the passage connecting the genital area to the womb. **vaˈginal** *adj.*

vagrant [ˈveigrənt] *nc* (*formal or legal*) a person who has no fixed home; a tramp: *He was arrested as a vagrant because he was sleeping on park benches.*

ˈvagrancy *nu* (*formal or legal*) the state of being a vagrant: *Vagrancy is a crime in some countries.*

vague [veig] *adj* **1** not clear, distinct or definite: *Through the fog we saw the vague outline of a ship*; *She has only a vague idea of how this machine works*; *My plans are somewhat vague at the moment.* **2** (of people) imprecise, or impractical and forgetful: *He's a rather vague old man*; *He is always very vague when making arrangements.*

ˈvagueness *nu.*

ˈvaguely *adv* **1** in a vague manner: *I remember him very vaguely.* **2** (*loosely*) slightly: *She felt vaguely irritated*; *I feel vaguely uneasy.*

vain [vein] *adj* **1** (*derog*) having too much pride in one's appearance, achievements *etc*; conceited: *She's very vain about her good looks*; *rather a vain young woman.* **2** (*usu attrib*) unsuccessful: *He made a vain attempt to reach the drowning woman.* – *See also* **in vain** *below.* **3** (*attrib*) empty; meaningless: *vain threats*; *vain promises.*

ˈvainly *adv* unsuccessfully: *Vainly he tried to find someone to marry him*; *He searched vainly for the treasure.*

vanity [ˈvanəti] **1** *nu* excessive admiration of oneself; conceit: *Vanity is her chief fault.* **2** *nu* (*formal*) worthlessness or pointlessness: *the vanity of human ambition.* **3** *nc* something, *eg* a piece of behaviour, that is vain: *I'm tired of all your little vanities!*

ˈvanity case *nc* a small case for carrying cosmetics: *She had as luggage two suitcases and a vanity case.*

in ˈvain with no success: *He tried in vain to open the locked door*; (*formal*) *It was in vain that we tried to find his mother.*

take someone's name in vain (*formal or facet*) to use someone's (*esp* God's) name in an insulting or blasphemous way: *Who has been taking His name in vain?*; *Someone has been taking my name in vain.*

valance [ˈvaləns] *nc* a short length of material hanging round the frame of a bed: *I would like a bedspread with a valance attached.*

vale [veil] *nc* (*liter or found with cap in place-names*) a valley: *the vale of sorrow*; *the Vale of Evesham.*

valediction [valiˈdikʃən] *ncu* (*liter or formal*) (a) farewell: *He raised his hat in valediction.*

ˌvaleˈdictory *adj* (*liter or formal*: *usu attrib*) saying farewell: *a valedictory salute.*

valency [ˈveilənsi] *nc* (*tech*) the combining power of an atom or group: *In water (H_2O), oxygen shows valency two.*

valentine [ˈvaləntain] *nc* a sweetheart chosen, or a card, love-letter *etc* sent, on St Valentine's Day, February 14: *Will you be my valentine?*; *He sent her a valentine*; (*attrib*) *a valentine card.*

valet [ˈvalit, ˈvalei] *nc* a manservant who looks after his master's clothes *etc*: *His valet laid out his evening suit.*

valiant [ˈvaliənt] *adj* (*formal or liter*) (of a person, his actions *etc*) brave, courageous or heroic: *valiant deeds*; *He was valiant in battle.* **ˈvaliantly** *adv.*

valid [ˈvalid] *adj* **1** (*formal*) (of reasons, arguments *etc*) soundly-based; reasonable or acceptable: *That is not a valid excuse*; *I do not find your objection valid.* **2** legally effective; having legal force: *He has a valid passport*; *This railway ticket is valid for three months.* **ˈvalidly** *adv.*

ˈvalidate [-deit] *vt* (*very formal*) to confirm, prove, or give a sound basis to: *Do these results validate his theory?* **ˌvaliˈdation** *nu.*

vaˈlidity, ˈvalidness *nus* (*formal*): *I am not questioning the validity of his statement*; *the validity of his passport.*

See also **invalid**[1].

valise [vəˈliːz, (*Amer*) -s] *nc* (*Amer*) a type of soft bag in which clothes and personal items are carried when travelling.

Valium ® [ˈvaliəm] – *pls* **ˈValium, ˈValiums** – **1** *nu* a name of a type of tranquillizer: *The doctor has prescribed Valium for her.* **2** *nc* a tablet of this: *Take a couple of Valium and you will be calmer.*

valley [ˈvali] *nc* (*sometimes found with cap in place-names*) a stretch of flat, low land between hills or mountains, *usu* drained by a river and its tributaries: *a beautiful green valley between the mountains; the valley of the river; He lives in a place called Happy Valley.*

valour ['valə] *nu* (*formal*) courage or bravery, *esp* in battle: *He displayed his valour on the battlefield.*

value ['vaIju:] **1** *nu* worth, importance or usefulness: *His special knowledge was of great value during the war; He puts little value on qualifications; She sets little value on wealth* (= She thinks wealth is unimportant). **2** *ncu* price: *What is the value of that stamp?; the market values of various shares.* **3** *ncu* purchasing power: *Is the value of the dollar much less now than it was ten years ago?; Are those coins of any value?* **4** *nu* fairness of exchange (for one's money *etc*): *This holiday has been excellent value (for money); You get value for money at this supermarket!* **5** *nc* (*music*) the length of a musical note: *In Appendix 4, you will discover that the value of a crotchet is half the value of a minim.* **6** *ncu* (*tech*) power of resistance *etc*: *What is the value of this resistor/capacitor?* **7** *nc* the number or quantity represented by a symbol in algebra: *In this equation, the value of x is 4. – See also* **values** *below.* – *vt* **1** to suggest a suitable price for: *This painting has been valued at £20 000.* **2** (not used with **is, was** *etc* and **-ing**) to regard as good or important: *He values your advice very highly.*

'**valuable** *adj* having considerable value: *Is the watch valuable?; a valuable painting.*

'**valuables** *n pl* things of special value: *She keeps her jewellery and other valuables in a locked drawer.*

ˌ**valu'ation 1** *ncu* (an) act of valuing: *They had a valuation done on their house last month.* **2** *nc* an estimated price: *The valuation on their property was £40 000.*

'**valuator** [-eitə], '**valuer** *ncs* a person who has been trained to estimate the value of property, antiques *etc*.

'**valued** *adj* regarded as valuable or precious: *What is your most valued possession?; This piece of my jewellery is the most valued.*

'**valueless** *adj* (*derog*) having no value; worthless: *The necklace is completely valueless; a valueless trinket.*

'**values** *n pl* standards or principles: *People have very different sets of moral values.*

ˌ**value-'added tax** (*often abbrev* **VAT** [vi:ei'ti:, vat]) *nu* a tax calculated on the basis of the increase in value of a product at each stage of its manufacture or marketing, or charged on certain services *etc*: *Must I pay VAT on meals eaten in a restaurant?*

See also **evaluate, invaluable**.

valve [valv] *nc* **1** a device for allowing a liquid or gas to pass through an opening in one direction only: *the valve of a bicycle tyre.* **2** a structure with the same effect in an animal body: *Valves in the heart control the flow of blood in the human body.* **3** a type of electronic component found in many, *esp* older, types of television, radio *etc*. **4** a device for varying the length of the tube, and, therefore, the pitch, in a brass musical instrument. **5** one of the parts into which the shell of some sea animals is divided.

vamp[1] [vamp] *nc* (*derog*) a woman who seduces and exploits men: *a red-haired vamp.* – *vt* (*derog*) to act (towards) like such a woman: *She tries to vamp all the men.*

vamp[2] [vamp] *vti* (*inf*) to play (a simple type of accompaniment *etc*): *He vamped (a few bars) on the piano while she sang.*

vampire ['vampaiə] *nc* a dead person who is imagined to rise from the grave at night and suck the blood of sleeping people.

van[1] [van] short for **vanguard**.

van[2] [van] *nc* a vehicle for carrying goods on roads or railways: *He drives a van; (attrib) a van-driver; a vanload* (= the amount carried by a van) *of waste paper.*

vandal ['vandəl] *nc* a person who purposely and pointlessly damages or destroys public buildings or other property: *Vandals have damaged this telephone kiosk; Vandals have painted slogans on this wall.*

'**vandalism** *nu* the behaviour of a vandal: *All the telephones are out of order owing to vandalism.*

'**vandalize, -ise** *vt* (*formal*): *The lift in our block of flats has been vandalized.*

vane [vein] *nc* **1** short for **weathervane**. **2** any of the blades of a windmill, propeller, fan *etc*.

vanguard ['vanga:d] *nc* (*no pl*: *often abbrev* **van** [van]) **1** the part of an army going in front of the main body. **2** (*fig*) the leaders in any movement: *We can boast we're in the vanguard of the movement for reform!*

vanilla [və'nilə] *nu* (*often attrib*) a flavouring obtained from a tropical orchid, and used in ice-cream and other foods: *vanilla ice-cream; Flavour the dessert with vanilla essence.*

vanish ['vaniʃ] *vi* to become no longer visible, *esp* suddenly: *The magician vanished in a cloud of smoke; The ship vanished over the horizon; (fig) Our hopes suddenly vanished.*

vanity *see* **vain**.

vanquish ['vaŋkwiʃ] *vt* (*liter or formal*) to defeat or conquer: *The enemy was vanquished at last; You must vanquish your fears.*

vantage ['va:ntidʒ]: '**vantage point** *nc* (*formal*) a position from which one has a clear view: *That hill will provide an excellent vantage point; (fig) From the vantage point of someone who has ten years' experience, it is easy to see what mistakes are being made.*

vapid ['vapid] *adj* (*formal derog*) dull; uninteresting: *She's a rather vapid talker; Why did he marry her? She is so vapid!* **va'pidity** *ncu*.

vapour, (*Amer*) **vapor** ['veipə] **1** *nu* the gas-like form into which a substance can be changed by heating: *water vapour; alcohol vapour.* **2** *ncu* (*formal*) mist, fumes or smoke in the air: *Near the marshes the air was filled with a strange-smelling vapour.*

'**vaporize, -ise** *vti* (*formal or tech*) to (cause to) change into a gas-like state.

'**vaporizer, -s-** *nc* a device for sending liquid out in a fine spray.

'**vapour trail** *nc* a white trail left in the sky by a high-flying aircraft.

variable, variance, variant, variation *see* **vary**.

varicose ['varikəs]: **varicose veins** *n pl* a condition in which veins, *usu* of the leg, are swollen and painful: *She has had to have an operation for varicose veins; I've had varicose veins since my baby was born.*

variegated ['veərigeitid] *adj* (*formal or tech*) (of leaves *etc*) varied in colour; speckled or mottled with different colours: *plants with variegated colours; I would prefer a selection of plants which were variegated.*

See also **vary**.

variety [və'raiəti] **1** *nu* the quality of being of many different kinds or of being varied: *There's a great deal of variety in this job; He wants variety – he doesn't want to have just one girlfriend.* **2** *nc* (*no pl*: *with* **a**) a mixed collection or range: *The children got a variety of toys on Christmas day; He offered a variety of excuses.* **3** *nc* a sort or kind: *They grow fourteen different varieties of rose here; many varieties of cauliflower.* **4** *nu* a type of mixed theatrical entertainment including dances, songs, short sketches *etc*: *I much prefer straight plays to variety*; (*attrib*) *a variety show.*
See also **vary**.

various ['veəriəs] *adj* **1** (*formal when pred*) different; varied: *His reasons for leaving were many and various.* **2** (*attrib*) several: *Various people have told me about you; I have heard various reasons for his leaving.* '**variously** *adv.*

varnish ['va:niʃ] *nu* **1** a *usu* clear sticky liquid which gives protection and glossy surface to wood, paint *etc*: *a tin of varnish.* **2** the glossy surface given by this liquid: *Be careful or you'll take the varnish off the table!* – *vt* to cover with varnish: *Don't sit on that chair – I've just varnished it.*
See also **unvarnished**.

varsity ['va:səti] (*inf*: not used in names) short for **university**.

vary ['veəri] *vti* to make, be or become different: *It is possible to vary the pitch of a guitar string by tightening it; Her daily routine never varies; These apples vary in size from small to medium.*
'**variable** *adj* **1** that may be varied: *The speed of the windscreen wipers is variable; a variable speed.* **2** (of *eg* winds, weather *etc*) liable or likely to change: *variable winds; The winds here tend to be variable.* – *nc* something that varies, *eg* in quantity, value, effect *etc*: *Have you taken all the variables into account in your calculations?*
'**variably** *adv.* ˌ**varia'bility** *nu.*
'**variant** *nc, adj* (*attrib*: *formal*) (something) which has a different form or version from the normal: *This plant is a variant of the common type; Johnson is the most usual spelling of the name, but the variant form Johnston is commonly found in Scotland.*
ˌ**vari'ation 1** *ncu* the extent to which a thing changes: *Farther from the sea, the variation in temperature is greater; In the desert there are great variations in temperature.* **2** *nc* one of a series of musical elaborations made on a basic theme or melody: *Brahms' variations on Haydn's 'St Anthony's Chorale'.*
'**varied** *adj*: *He had had a very varied career; His excuses were many and varied.*
be at 'variance (*formal*) to be in disagreement: *The two men's views were at variance; This statement is completely at variance with what I was told earlier.*
See also **invariable**.

vase [va:z, (*Amer*) veis] *nc* a type of jar or jug used mainly as an ornament or for holding cut flowers: *a vase of flowers; a Grecian vase.*

vasectomy [və'sektəmi] *nc* (*tech*) a small surgical operation that can be done to produce sterility in a man: *Her husband has decided to have a vasectomy as they don't want any more children.*

Vaseline ® ['vasəli:n] *nu* a type of soothing ointment made from petroleum: *Put some Vaseline on your lips to keep them smooth.*

vassal ['vasəl] *nc* (*hist*) under the feudal system, a person who holds land from a landowner, for which he gives the landlord certain services.

vast [va:st] *adj* (*usu attrib*) of very great size or amount: *A vast desert lay before us; He inherited a vast fortune.* '**vastness** *nu.*
'**vastly** *adv* to a very great degree: *He is vastly superior to me.*

vat [vat] *nc* a large vessel or tank, *esp* one for holding fermenting spirits.

VAT *see* **value-added tax** *under* **value**.

vaudeville ['vo:dəvil] *nu* (*formal*) the type of theatre show in which there is a variety of short acts: music-hall: *There are very few theatres now where vaudeville is performed*; (*attrib*) *a vaudeville act/comedian.*

vault[1] [vo:lt] *nc* **1** (a room, *esp* a cellar, with) an arched roof or ceiling: *the castle vaults.* **2** an underground room, *esp* for storing valuables: *The thieves broke into the bank vaults.* **3** a burial chamber, often for all the members of a family: *He was buried in the family vault.*
'**vaulted** *adj* (*usu attrib*) **1** (of a roof or ceiling) arched. **2** (of a building *etc*) having an arched roof or ceiling.

vault[2] [vo:lt] *nc* a leap aided by the hands or by a pole: *With a quick vault he was over the fence and away.* – *vti* to leap (over): *He vaulted (over) the fence.*
'**vaulting-horse** *nc* an apparatus used by gymnasts for vaulting over.
See also **pole-vault** *under* **pole**[2].

vaunt [vo:nt] *vt* (*very formal or old*) to boast about (*eg* one's success).

VD *see* **venereal disease**.

've *see* **have**.

veal [vi:l] *nu* the flesh of a calf, used as food: *We had veal for dinner*; (*attrib*) *veal cutlets.*

vector ['vektə] *nc* (*tech*) (a straight line drawn from a given point to represent) a quantity, *eg* a velocity or a force, that has both size and direction.

veer [viə] *vi* to change direction suddenly; *The car veered across the road to avoid hitting a small boy; The wind has veered round to the East*; (*fig formal*) *He kept veering between despair and happiness.*

vegetable ['vedʒtəbl] *nc* (*often attrib*) **1** a plant or part of a plant, other than a fruit used as food: *We grow potatoes, artichokes and other vegetables; Apples and strawberries are fruit not vegetables; Many people overcook vegetables; vegetable oils; a vegetable diet.* **2** (*tech*) a plant: *Grass is a vegetable, gold is a mineral and a human being is an animal; the vegetable kingdom; vegetable dyes.* **3** (*sometimes derog*) a person whose brain has become almost incapable of working, because of injury, damage *etc*: *As a result of the accident he will be a vegetable for the rest of his life; I'm tired of being a housewife – I don't want to become a vegetable.*
ˌ**vege'tarian** [vedʒi-] *nc* (*often attrib*) a person who does not eat meat of any kind: *Has he always been a vegetarian?; This is a vegetarian dish; He is on a vegetarian diet; There is a good vegetarian restaurant nearby.* ˌ**vege'tarianism** *nu.*
vegetate ['vedʒiteit] *vi* (*inf derog*) to live an idle, boring and pointless life: *I would like to get a job – I don't want to vegetate.*
ˌ**vege'tation** [vedʒi-] *nc* plants in general; plants of a particular region or type: *Jungle vegetation; tropical vegetation.*

vehement ['vi:əmənt] *adj* (*formal*) violent or passionate: *He made a vehement plea for reform;*

The argument was long and vehement. **'vehemently** *adv.* **'vehemence** *nu.*

vehicle ['viəkl] *nc* **1** any means of transport on land, *esp* on wheels, *eg* a car, bus, bicycle *etc.* **2** (*formal*) a means of conveying something, *eg* information: *The daily papers, TV and radio are vehicles for the spread of news.*

vehicular [vi'hikjulə] *adj* (*formal: usu attrib*) consisting of vehicles: *Vehicular traffic on this bridge is forbidden.*

veil [veil] *nc* a piece of thin cloth worn over the face or head to hide, cover, or protect it: *Some women wear veils for religious reasons, to prevent strangers from seeing their faces; A bee-keeper wears a veil to avoid being stung;* (*fig formal*) *There was a veil of mist over the mountains;* (*fig formal*) *He carries on these activities under a veil of secrecy.* – *vt* to cover with a veil.

veiled *adj* **1** wearing, or covered by, a veil: *a veiled lady; The bride was veiled.* **2** (only slightly) disguised: *a veiled threat; His hints were scarcely veiled.*

vein [vein] *nc* **1** any of the tubes that carry the blood back to the heart. **2** a similar-looking line on a leaf. **3** a thin layer of a mineral: *a vein of gold in quartz.* **4** (*formal or liter*) a trait or characteristic in a personality: *He has a vein of stubbornness.* **5** a manner or style: *He continued talking in the same light-hearted vein.*

venous ['vi:nəs] *adj* (*tech*) of the veins: *The blood that is passing through the veins is called venous blood.*

veld, veldt [velt] *nu* in South Africa, grass-covered land with few, or no, trees.

vellum ['veləm] *nu* fine parchment made from the skin of calves, kids or lambs.

velocity [və'losəti] *nu* **1** (*tech*) speed in a given direction: *the velocity of a body that is falling vertically.* **2** (*loosely*) speed.

velour(s) [və'luə] *nu, adj* (of) a material similar to velvet: *a hat made of velour; a velour hat.*

velvet ['velvit] *nu, adj* (of) a type of cloth made from silk *etc* with a soft, thick surface: *skin as soft as velvet; The lawn looked like green velvet; a velvet jacket;* (*fig*) *The cat crept forward on its velvet paws.* **'velvety** *adj.*

,velve'teen [-'ti:n] *nu, adj* (of) a material similar to, but cheaper than, velvet: *a dress made of velveteen; a velveteen dress.*

venal ['vi:nl] *adj* (*very formal derog*) (of a person) willing to accept bribes to do something dishonest.

vendetta [ven'detə] *nc* a fierce, often violent, long-lasting dispute or feud: *There has been a bitter vendetta between the two families for many years.*

vendor ['vendə] *nc* (*in cmpds or legal*) a person who sells: *A street vendor is a person who sells goods in the streets; A peanut vendor is a person who sells peanuts; Is the vendor always held responsible if goods are faulty?*

'vending-machine *nc* an automatic coin-operated machine, selling *eg* cigarettes, hot drinks *etc*: *There is a vending-machine in the office and it sells tea, coffee and soup.*

veneer [və'niə] **1** *nu* thin, fine-quality wood, often used to give a smooth surface to a material of poorer quality: *a table made of plywood covered in teak veneer.* **2** *nc* a covering of this: *The table had been given an oak veneer.* **3** *nc* (*fig formal*) a surface appearance: *His veneer of good manners hid his brutality.* – *vt* (*formal*) to cover with veneer.

ve'neered *adj.*

venerate ['venəreit] *vt* (*formal*) to respect; to honour greatly: *In some countries, old people are venerated more than in others.*

'venerable *adj* (*formal: usu attrib*) worthy of great respect because of age or for special goodness: *a venerable old man.*

,vene'ration *nu* (*formal*): *His pupils regarded him with veneration.*

venereal [və'niəriəl]: **venereal disease** (*often abbrev* **VD** [vi:'di:]) *ncu* any of various contagious diseases transferred by sexual intercourse: *Some venereal diseases can affect the children of affected mothers; She is suffering from a form of venereal disease.*

Venetian [və'ni:ʃən]: **Venetian blind** *nc* a window blind made of thin, movable, horizontal strips of wood, metal or plastic: *We have put up Venetian blinds to stop our neighbours looking in our front windows.*

Venezuela, Venezuelan *see* Appendix 2.

vengeance ['vendʒəns] *nu* (*esp formal or liter*) harm done in return for injury received; revenge: *He soon had his opportunity for vengeance.* – *See also* **seek vengeance** *below.*

'vengeful *adj* (*formal or liter*) eager for vengeance.

seek vengeance (*formal*) to look for a means of getting revenge.

with a 'vengeance (*inf*) in a very great or unexpected degree; violently; thoroughly: *If the plans for the redevelopment scheme are approved, they'll start knocking houses down with a vengeance.*

See also **avenge, revenge**.

venial ['vi:niəl] *adj* (*formal: usu attrib*) (of a sin) pardonable; not serious: *He is guilty of a venial sin.*

venison ['venisn] *nu* the flesh of deer, used as food: *We had roast venison for dinner;* (*attrib*) *venison stew.*

venom ['venəm] *nu* **1** the poison produced by some snakes, scorpions *etc*, transmitted by biting or stinging: *the venom of a cobra.* **2** (*formal*) great ill-feeling, anger *etc*: *He spoke the words with considerable venom; There was venom in his reply.*

'venomous *adj* **1** (of snakes *etc*) poisonous: *venomous reptiles.* **2** (*formal derog*) (of people, their words *etc*) full of ill-feeling: *a venomous speech; He was venomous in his reply.* **'venomously** *adv.*

venous *see* **vein**.

vent[1] [vent] *nc* a slit in the back or side of a coat, jacket *etc*: *His sports-jacket has a vent in the back.*

vent[2] [vent] *nc* (*sometimes in cmpds*) a hole to allow air, smoke *etc* to pass out or in: *an air-vent; The tent has two vents on each side.* – *vt* to give expression or an outlet to (an emotion *etc*): *He was angry with himself and vented his rage on his son by beating him violently.*

give 'vent to to express (an emotion *etc*) freely: *He gave vent to his anger in a furious letter to the newspaper.*

ventilate ['ventileit] *vt* **1** to allow fresh air to enter (*eg* a room). **2** (*formal*) to open up discussion on (a subject) or talk about it in public: *This topic should be ventilated more often.*

,venti'lation *nu* the act or means of ventilating or the state of being ventilated: *There was no window in the room, and no other* (*means of*) *ventilation.*

'ventilator *nc* a device for ventilating a room *etc.*

ventricle ['ventrikl] *nc* (*tech*) a small cavity, *esp* in the brain or heart.

ventriloquist [ven'trilǝkwist] *nc* a professional entertainer who can speak so that his voice seems to come from some other person or place, *esp* from a dummy which he controls. **ven'triloquism** *nu.*

venture ['ventʃǝ] *nc* an undertaking or scheme that involves some risk: *his latest business venture.* – (*esp formal or liter*) **1** *vi* to dare to go: *Every day the child ventured further into the forest.* **2** *vt* to dare (to do (something), *esp* to say (something)): *He ventured to kiss her hand*; (*facet*) *I ventured* (*to remark*) *that her skirt was too short*; *May I venture* (*to make*) *a suggestion?* **3** *vt* to risk: *He decided to venture all his money on the scheme.*

'**venturesome** *adj* (*formal*) daring.

'**venture on** *vt fus* (*formal*) to take the risk of starting on: *You should never have ventured on such a journey/enterprise.*

See also **adventure**.

venue ['venju:] *nc* the scene of an action or event, *eg* a sporting event: *Which ground is the venue for next week's football match?*

Venus, Venusian *see* Appendix 6.

veranda(h) [vǝ'randǝ] *nc* (*Amer* **porch**) a kind of covered balcony with a roof extending beyond the main building supported by light pillars.

verb [vǝ:b] *nc* the word or phrase (phrasal verb) that gives the action, or asserts something, in a sentence, clause *etc*: *I saw him*; *He ran away from me*; *I have a feeling*; *What is this?*

'**verbal** *adj* **1** of, or concerning, verbs: *verbal endings such as '-fy', '-ize'.* **2** (*formal*: *often attrib*) consisting of, or concerning, spoken words: *verbal/non-verbal communication*; *a verbal warning/agreement*; *You should get the agreement in writing – at the moment it's only verbal.*

'**verbally** *adv* in or by speech, not writing: *I replied to the invitation verbally.*

verbatim [vǝ'beitim] *adj* (*usu attrib*), *adv* exactly as spoken or written: *He repeated my speech verbatim*; *a verbatim report.*

verbiage ['vǝ:biidʒ] *nu* (*very formal or facet derog*) (the use of) many unnecessary words: *His speeches are full of ridiculous verbiage.*

verbose [vǝ'bous] *adj* (*formal*: *derog*) (of a person or a statement *etc*) using too many words: *He is so verbose that I would not ask him to be an after-dinner speaker*; *a boring, verbose account of his travels abroad.* **ver'bosity** [-'bo-] *nu.*

verdant ['vǝ:dǝnt] *adj* (*liter*) green with grass and/or leaves.

verdict ['vǝ:dikt] *nc* **1** the decision of a jury at the end of a trial: *The jury brought in a verdict of guilty.* **2** an opinion or decision reached after consideration: *The competitors are still waiting for the verdict of the judges*; *What is your verdict on his new house?*

verge [vǝ:dʒ] *nc* the (grass) edging of a garden bed, a road *etc*: *It's illegal to drive on the grass verge.* – *vi* (*fig*: *with* **on**) to be on the border (of): *This idea of his verges on the idiotic!*; *She is verging on insanity.*

be on the 'verge of (doing) something to be just about to do something: *She was so unhappy that she was on the verge of* (*committing*) *suicide.*

verger ['vǝ:dʒǝ] *nc* an official in church who shows people to their seats *etc.*

verify ['verifai] *vt* (*formal*) to confirm the truth or correctness of (something): *Can you verify her statement?* '**verifiable** *adj.* ,**verifi'cation** [-fi-] *nu.*

verily ['verili] *adj* (*arch*: *esp* in the Bible) truly.

verisimilitude [verisi'militju:d] *nu* (*very formal or old*) similarity to truth or reality.

veritable ['veritǝbl] *adj* (*formal or facet*: *attrib*) genuine or real: *a veritable triumph*; *a veritable feast.* '**veritably** *adv.*

verity ['verǝti] *nu* (*very formal*) truth.

vermicelli [vǝ:mi'tʃeli] *nu* a type of pasta similar to spaghetti but much thinner.

vermilion [vǝ'miljǝn] *nu, adj* (of) a bright red colour.

vermin ['vǝ:min] *nu* undesirable or troublesome pests such as fleas, rats, or mice: *Farmers are always having trouble with various types of vermin*; (*fig offensive*) *It is vermin such as these men that are trying to destroy society.*

vermouth ['vǝ:mǝθ, (*Amer*) vǝr'mu:θ] **1** *nu* a type of drink containing white wine flavoured with certain herbs: *She had a glass of vermouth before dinner.* **2** *nc* a glass of vermouth: *He ordered two vermouths.*

vernacular [vǝ'nakjulǝ] *adj* (*usu attrib*) colloquial or informally conversational: *vernacular speech/language.* – *nc* the common informal language of a country *etc* as opposed to its formal or literary language: *They spoke to each other in the vernacular of the region.*

verruca [vǝ'ru:kǝ] *nc* a wart, *esp* on the foot.

versatile ['vǝ:sǝtail] *adj* **1** (of people *etc*) able to turn easily and successfully from one task, activity or occupation to another: *a versatile entertainer*; *He will easily get another job – he is so versatile.* **2** (of a material *etc*) capable of being used for many purposes: *I like my clothes to be versatile*; *a versatile tool.* ,**versa'tility** [-'ti-] *nu.*

verse [vǝ:s] **1** *nc* a number of lines of poetry, grouped together and forming a separate unit within the poem, song, hymn *etc*: *This song has three verses.* **2** *nc* a short section in a chapter of the Bible. **3** *nu* poetry, as opposed to prose: *He expressed his ideas in verse.*

versed *adj* (*pred with* **in**: *formal*) having knowledge, experience or skill (in a particular subject, art *etc*): *He was already versed in Greek.* – *See also* **well-versed**.

version ['vǝ:ʃǝn, (*Amer*) -ʒǝn] *nc* **1** an account from one point of view: *The boy gave his version of what had occurred.* **2** a translation: *the 1611 Authorized Version of the Bible.*

versus ['vǝ:sǝs] *prep* (*often abbrev* **v** *or* **vs** *when written*) against: *the England v Wales rugby match.*

vertebra ['vǝ:tibrǝ] – *pl* '**vertebrae** [-bri:] – *nc* (*tech*) any of the bones of the spine: *She has a broken vertebra.*

'**vertebrate** [-brǝt] *nu, adj* (*tech*) (an animal) having a backbone: *Insects are not vertebrates.*

vertex ['vǝ:teks] – *pl* '**vertices** [-tisi:z] – *nc* (*tech*) the point of a cone, pyramid or angle.

vertical ['vǝ:tikǝl] *adj* standing straight up at right angles to the earth's surface, or to a horizontal plane or line; upright: *At a certain point in his evolution, man adopted a vertical stance*; *The hillside looked almost vertical.* '**vertically** *adv.*

vertigo ['vǝ:tigou] *nu* (*tech*) dizziness, *esp* as brought on by fear of heights: *Keep her back from the edge of the cliff – she suffers from vertigo.*

verve [vǝ:v] *nu* (*formal*) lively or energetic quality: *The musical performance lacked verve*; *The little girl is full of verve and vitality.*

very ['veri] *adv* (*used with an adjective or another adverb*) to a great degree: *He's very clever*; *She's a* *very nice girl*; *You came very quickly*; *What a very pleasant day it's been!*; *I haven't very much* (= I have only a little) *money*; *I'm not feeling very well* (= I feel ill); *She isn't a very good teacher.* 2 (*used with a superl or* **own**) absolutely; in the highest degree: *The very first thing you must do is ring the police*; *He won't arrive till 3.00 p.m. at the very earliest*; *She has a car of her very own.* – *adj* 1 (*often with* **the**: *attrib*) exactly or precisely the thing, person *etc* mentioned: *You're the very man I want to see*; *That's the very thing* (*I need*)*!*; *At that very minute the door opened*; *He gave me the very same message as he gave you*; *Those were his very words.* 2 extreme: *at the very end of the party*; *at the very top of the tree.* 3 used for emphasis in other ways: *Our very homes* (= Even our homes) *are in danger*; *The very suggestion* (= The mere suggestion without the reality) *of a sea voyage makes her feel seasick*; *Fancy him asking to borrow money – the very idea!* (= what cheek!).

very well used to express (reluctant) agreement to a request *etc*: *'Please be home before midnight.' 'Very well.'* – *See also* **very** (*def 1*).

vespers ['vespəz] *n pl* the evening service in certain churches.

'vesper *adj* (*attrib*): *a vesper hymn.*

vessel ['vesl] *nc* 1 (*formal*) a container, *usu* for liquid: *a plastic vessel containing acid.* 2 a ship: *a 10 000-ton grain-carrying vessel.*

See also **blood-vessel**.

vest [vest] *nc* 1 (*esp Brit*) a kind of sleeveless shirt worn under a shirt, blouse *etc*: *He was dressed only in* (*a*) *vest and underpants.* 2 (*esp Amer*) a waistcoat: *jacket, vest and trousers*; (*attrib*) *a vest pocket.*

ˌvested 'interest *nc* (*sometimes derog*: *usu in sing*) a biased and *usu* personal interest (in continuing or suggesting a particular scheme *etc*): *She has a vested interest in suggesting that we sell our shares in the company, since she would make a huge profit if we did.*

'vest (something) in (someone or something) (*formal*) to grant (authority, power *etc*) to (a person *etc*): *Certain powers have been vested in this committee.*

See also **invest**.

vestibule ['vestibju:l] *nc* (*old or formal*) an entrance hall: *I'll meet you in the vestibule of the theatre.*

vestige ['vestidʒ] *nc* (*formal*) a trace: *After the explosion, not a vestige of the building remained.*

vestigial [və'stidʒəl] *adj* (*formal*) surviving only as a trace: *A Manx cat has a vestigial tail.*

vestment ['vestmənt] *nc* (*often in pl*) a garment worn by the clergy during a religious service: *a priest's vestments.*

vestry ['vestri] *nc* a room in or near a church used by the clergy as a dressing-room and for small meetings.

vet[1] *see* **veterinary**.

vet[2] [vet] – *pt, ptp* **'vetted** – *vt* (*inf*) to investigate carefully (and pass as satisfactory): *Every member of staff has been vetted by our security department before he starts work here.*

veteran ['vetərən] *nc* 1 a person who is (old and) experienced as a soldier *etc* or in some other occupation: *This 1000 metres race is for veterans only*; (*attrib*) *a veteran footballer/entertainer.* 2 (*Amer*) a person who has been in the army *etc*: *war veterans.*

veteran car *nc* any car built before December 31, 1904. – *See also* **vintage car** *under* **vintage**.

veterinary [vetə'rinəri] *adj* (*tech*: *usu attrib*) of, or concerning, the treatment of diseases in animals: *veterinary medicine*; *veterinary care.*

veterinary surgeon *nc* (*Amer* **veterinarian** [vetəri'neəriən]: *Brit usu abbrev* **vet** [vet]) a doctor for animals.

veto ['vi:tou] – *3rd pers sing prt* **'vetoes**: *pt, ptp* **'vetoed** – *vt* (*formal*) to forbid, or refuse to consent to: *They vetoed your suggestion*; *He vetoed our proposal that the school remain open.* – *n* – *pl* **'vetoes** – *nc* (*also* **power of veto**) the power or right to refuse or forbid: *the chairman's* (*power of*) *veto.*

vex [veks] *vt* (*esp old or formal*) to annoy or distress (a person): *There were no other problems to vex us*; *His behaviour vexed her.*

vex'ation (*esp old or formal*) 1 *nu* the state of being vexed. 2 *nc* a cause of annoyance or trouble: *minor worries and vexations.*

vex'atious [-'seiʃəs] *adj* (*esp old or formal*) annoying or troublesome: *a vexatious change in arrangements.*

vexed *adj* (*esp old or formal*: *usu pred*) annoyed or upset: *I'm very vexed at your selfishness.*

a vexed question a problem that is discussed a great deal, without being solved.

via ['vaiə] *prep* by way of: *We went to Exeter via London*; (*inf*) *The news reached me via my aunt.*

viable ['vaiəbl] *adj* (*formal or tech*) 1 (of *eg* a scheme) capable of working successfully: *Do you really think that this is a viable plan/proposition?* 2 capable of living and surviving: *At what stage is a foetus viable?* **ˌvia'bility** *nu.*

viaduct ['vaiədʌkt] *nc* a *usu* long bridge carrying a road or railway over a valley *etc.*

vial *see* **phial**.

vibrate [vai'breit, (*Amer*) 'vaibreit] *vti* to (cause to) shake, tremble, or move rapidly back and forth: *The different notes of a stringed musical instrument are made by vibrating the strings*; *Every sound that we hear is making part of our ear vibrate*; *The engine has stopped vibrating*; (*fig*) *The whole hall was vibrating with excitement.*

'vibrant *adj* (*formal*) 1 vibrating: *a vibrant chord/voice*; (*fig*) *vibrant with excitement.* 2 bright and strong: *a vibrant shade of red*; *That colour is too vibrant for this room.* 3 (of people) full of energy: *a vibrant personality*; *She is always energetic and vibrant.*

vi'bration [(*Brit and Amer*) -'brei-] *ncu* (an) act of vibrating: *This building is badly affected by the vibration of all the heavy traffic that passes*; *a series of vibrations.* – *See also* **vibrations**.

vi'brations [(*Brit and Amer*) -'brei-] *n pl* (*sl abbrev* **vibes** [vaibz]) emotions or feelings sensed by one person from another, or from a place *etc*: *She kept getting very hostile vibrations from his father all through the meal*; *This town has bad vibes for me.*

vi'brator [(*Amer*) 'vaibreitər] *nc.*

vicar ['vikə] *nc* a clergyman of the Church of England.

'vicarage [-ridʒ] *nc* the house of a vicar.

vicarious [vi'keəriəs, (*Amer*) vai-] *adj* (*formal*: *usu attrib*) 1 (of suffering *etc*) endured on another person's behalf: *vicarious suffering/punishment.* 2 (of pleasure *etc*) experienced or enjoyed not personally, but through the medium of other people: *vicarious satisfaction/pleasures.* **vi'cariously** *adv.*

vice[1], (*Amer usu*) **vise** [vais] *nc* a kind of strong tool for holding an object firmly, *usu* between two metal jaws: *The carpenter held the piece of wood in a vice*; *He has a grip like a vice.*

vice[2] [vais] **1** *nc* a serious moral fault: *Continual lying is a vice.* **2** *nc* a bad habit: *Smoking is not one of my vices.* **3** *nu* immorality, *esp* involving sexual or other crimes: *a campaign against vice*; (*attrib*) *the police vice squad.*

vice- [vais] (*in cmpds*: *often with cap*) second in rank and acting as deputy for: *the ˌVice-ˈPresident*; *the ˌvice-ˈchairman*; *the ˌVice-ˈConsul.*

viceroy [ˈvaisroi] *nc* (*with cap in titles*) a person who governs a country in the name of his sovereign: *the Viceroy of India.* **ˌviceˈregal** [-ˈri:gl] *adj.*

vice versa [vaisiˈvə:sə] (of two things or people) the other way round: *John dislikes Mary and vice versa* (= Mary dislikes John); *Dogs often chase cats but not usually vice versa* (= cats don't usually chase dogs).

vicinity [viˈsinəti] *nc* (*formal*) a neighbourhood or local area: *Are there any cinemas in the/this vicinity?*; *This isn't a very pleasant vicinity.*

in the viˈcinity of (*formal*) near to: *There is a playground in the vicinity of the house*; *I didn't want to remain long in his vicinity* (= near him).

vicious [ˈviʃəs] *adj* evil; cruel; likely to attack or cause harm: *Keep back from that dog – it's vicious*; *his vicious treatment of the children*; *That was a vicious blow*; *She is spiteful and vicious.* **ˈviciously** *adv.* **ˈviciousness** *nu.*

vicious circle *nc* (*inf*) a bad situation whose results make it worse: *He works hard, gets tired, gets behind with his work, and has to work harder still – it's a vicious circle.*

victim [ˈviktim] *nc* a person who receives ill-treatment, injury *etc*: *a murder victim*; *The murderer's victims were all women*; *Supplies are being sent to the victims of the disaster*; *A few years ago, she was the victim of a road accident*; *He was the victim of a cruel campaign in the press.*

ˈvictimize, -ise *vt* to make (a person) suffer in some undeserved way: *He claims that he was victimized by his fellow-workers because he did not go on strike.* **ˌvictimiˈzation, -s-** *nu.*

victor [ˈviktə] *nc* (*formal*) the person who wins a battle or other contest.

vicˈtorious [-ˈto:-] *adj* (*formal*) successful or winning: *the victorious army*; *Which team was victorious?* **vicˈtoriously** *adv.*

ˈvictory *ncu* (a) defeat of an enemy or rival: *Our team has had two defeats and has gained eight victories*; *At last they experienced the joy of victory.*

Victorian [vikˈto:riən] *adj* **1** of the reign of Queen Victoria (1837-1901): *Victorian writers*; *Victorian households/furniture.* **2** (*derog*) (of an attitude towards morals *etc*) strict and conservative: *a Victorian attitude to sex.* – *nc* a person living in Queen Victoria's reign: *The Victorians were great engineers and industrialists.*

victorious, victory *see* **victor**.

victuals [ˈvitlz] *n pl* (*old or facet*) food (for human beings).

ˈvictualler *nc* (*formal*) a person or business that supplies food and (**licensed victualler**) alcoholic drink.

video- [vidiou] (*in cmpds*) of television, as in **videotape**.

videotape [ˈvidiouteip] *nu* recording tape carrying pictures and sound. – *vt* to record (something) using videotape.

vie [vai] – *prp* **ˈvying** [ˈvaiiŋ]: *pt, ptp* **vied** – *vi* (*often with* **with**) to compete with: *The two parents vied with each other in their attempts to gain the children's love*; *They vied for her affection.*

Vietnam, Vietnamese *see* Appendix 2.

view [vju:] **1** *nc* (an outlook on to, or picture of) a scene: *Your house has a fine view of the hills*; *He painted a view of the harbour*; (*fig*) *Let us take an overall view of the subject.* **2** *nc* an opinion: *Tell me your view/views on the subject*; *She has strong views about smoking.* **3** *nc* an act of seeing or inspecting: *We were given a private view of the exhibition before it was opened to the public.* **4** *n* (*with cap*) a word used in the names of certain roads or streets: *His address is 4 Humber View.* – *See also* **view** *in phrases below.* – *vt* (*formal*) **1** to look at, or regard (something): *She viewed the scene with astonishment*; (*fig*) *They viewed his actions as unnecessary*; (*fig*) *He views the whole thing as a joke.* **2** to inspect: *The house may be viewed between 2.00 and 4.00 p.m.*

ˈviewer *nc* **1** a person who watches television: *This programme has five million viewers.* **2** a device with a magnifying lens, and often with a light, used in viewing transparencies.

ˈviewpoint *nc* a point of view: *I am probably looking at it from a different viewpoint.*

from, in(to), out of view from, in(to), out of *etc* a position from which (someone or something) can be seen: *He disappeared from view*; *She came suddenly into (my) view*; *The mountain is just out of view*; *He slapped his wife in full view of* (= right in front of) *the children*; *I'm keeping every possibility in view* (= not forgetting any possibility); *The time is already in view when the children must leave home*; *What reforms have you in view?* (= do you plan or visualize).

in ˈview of (*formal*) taking into consideration; because of: *In view of the Committee's criticisms of him, he felt he had to resign.*

on ˈview being shown or exhibited: *There's a marvellous collection of prints on view at the gallery.*

point of view a way or manner of looking at a subject, matter *etc*: *You must consider everyone's point of view before deciding.*

take a serious, kindly *etc* **view of** to adopt a serious, kindly *etc* attitude to: *Fortunately the headmaster took a benevolent view of his behaviour.*

with a ˈview to (*formal*) with the aim of: *He's started walking to work with a view to cutting down expenses.*

vigil [ˈvidʒil] *nc* (*formal*) a time of keeping awake and watching: *They were tired out by their long vigil.*

ˈvigilance *nu* (*formal*) watchfulness or readiness for danger: *He watched her with the vigilance of a hawk.* **ˈvigilant** *adj.*

keep vigil (over) (*formal*) to keep watching (over someone or something): *Two of them slept while the third kept vigil*; *The dog kept vigil over his sleeping master.*

See also **invigilate, vigilante**.

vigilante [vidʒiˈlanti] *nc* a member of a self-appointed group that administers what it regards as justice in an unsettled country, or watches over the morals or welfare of a community: *Parents have formed groups of vigilantes to look out for the murderer*; *Local vigilantes have been fighting against the terrorists.*

vigour, (*Amer*) **vigor** ['vigə] *nu* (*formal*) strength and energy: *He is a young lad with plenty of vigour; He began his new job with enthusiasm and vigour;* (*fig*) *The music was full of vigour.*
'vigorous *adj*: *He was tall and vigorous; a vigorous dance; They made a vigorous attempt to stop me.*
'vigorously *adv*.

vile [vail] *adj* (*formal or facet*) horrible; wicked; disgusting: *a vile person; That was a vile thing to say!;* (*facet*) *What a vile colour!;* (*facet*) *The food tasted vile.* **'vilely** *adv*. **'vileness** *nu*.
vilify ['vilifai] *vt* (*very formal*) to say vile things about; to abuse: *He was vilified by the press for his part in the unpopular decision.*
ˌvilifi'cation [vilifi-] *nu* (*formal*) abuse uttered in the act of vilifying.

villa ['vilə] *nc* a type of detached or semi-detached (*usu* luxury) house, *usu* in the country or suburbs, or used for holidays at the seaside: *They have a villa in the South of France.*

village ['vilidʒ] *nc* **1** a group of houses *etc* which is smaller than a town: *They live in a little village in the West of England;* (*attrib*) *a village school.* **2** the people who live in such a group of houses: *The whole village turned out to see the celebrations.*
'villager *nc* a person who lives in a village.

villain ['vilən] *nc* (*esp in drama etc*) a person who is wicked or of very bad character: *the villain of the play/story;* (*fig*) *The children have been teasing the cat, the little villains!* **'villainous** *adj*.
'villainy *ncu* (*formal*) (an instance of) wickedness: *His villainy/villainies were well known; a piece of villainy.*
the villain of the piece (*formal or facet*) the person or thing responsible for some evil: *Who is the real villain of the piece in this scandal?*

villein ['vilein, (*Amer*) -lən] *nc* (*hist*) a slave in the feudal system.

vim [vim] *nu* (*inf*) energy or vigour: *She does seem full of vim today.*

vindicate ['vindikeit] *vt* (*formal*) to justify or clear from blame *etc*: *My judgement/action was completely vindicated by later events.* **ˌvindi'cation** *nu*.

vindictive [vin'diktiv] *adj* (*formal*) determined to have revenge, or to hurt others: *She was often cruel and vindictive; a vindictive remark.*

vine [vain] *nc* **1** a type of climbing plant which bears grapes. **2** any climbing or trailing plant.
'vineyard ['vin-] *nc* an area which is planted with grape vines: *We spent the summer touring the French vineyards.*
See also **vintage, vintner**.

vinegar ['vinigə] *nu* a sour liquid made from wine, beer *etc*, used in seasoning or preparing food: *Mix some oil and vinegar as a dressing for the salad.*

vintage ['vintidʒ] *ncu* (*often fig and attrib*) (a wine from) the grape-harvest of a certain (particularly good) year: *He has a lot of excellent vintages in his cellar; What vintage is this wine?; a vintage year* (= a year in which good wine was produced); *vintage port* (= port from a vintage year); (*derog*) *Her clothes are 1950s vintage; vintage Edwardian furniture; This play is absolutely vintage Chekhov* (= shows Chekhov at his best and most typical).
vintage car *nc* a car built between 1919 and 1930 or (*loosely*) between 1905 and 1940. – *See also* **veteran car** *under* **veteran**.

vintner ['vintnə] *nc* (*esp old*) a person who sells wine.

viola [vi'oulə] *nc* a type of musical instrument very similar to, but slightly larger than, the violin: *She plays the viola in the school orchestra; She played the tune on her viola.*

violate ['vaiəleit] *vt* (*formal*) **1** to break (a promise, a law *etc*): *They have violated the law against murder.* **2** to treat (a sacred place, *eg* a temple) without respect: *Thieves have violated the emperor's tomb.* **3** (*sometimes facet*) to disturb roughly (*eg* someone's privacy or peace): *You are violating the peace of the countryside.* **4** to rape (a female).
ˌvio'lation *ncu*. **'violator** *nc*.

violent ['vaiələnt] *adj* **1** having, using, or showing, great force: *There was a violent storm at sea; a violent earthquake; He was usually drunk and often violent; He has a violent temper; violent behaviour.* **2** (*attrib*) caused by force: *a violent death.*
'violently *adv*.
'violence *nu* great roughness and force, often causing severe physical injury or damage: *I was amazed at the violence of his temper; She was terrified by the violence of the storm.*

violet ['vaiəlit] **1** *nc* a kind of small bluish-purple flower. **2** *nu, adj* (of) a bluish-purple colour.
See also **ultraviolet**.

violin [vaiə'lin] *nc* a type of musical instrument with four strings, played with a bow: *She played the violin in the school orchestra; Can you play that on the violin?*
ˌvio'linist *nc* a violin player: *She is a leading violinist.*

violoncello [vaiələn'tʃelou] full form of **cello**.
ˌviolon'cellist full form of **cellist**.

viper ['vaipə] *nc* an adder.

virago [vi'ra:gou] – *pl* **vi'ragos** – *nc* (*liter*) a fierce, bad-tempered woman.

viral *see* **virus**.

virgin ['və:dʒin] *nc* (*often fig attrib*) a person, *esp* a woman, who has had no sexual intercourse: *She was still a virgin when she married; virgin soil/forest* (= soil/forest in its natural, unspoilt, unused state).
'virginal *adj* of a virgin: *Her face had a virginal look.*
vir'ginity *nu* the state of being a virgin.
virgin birth *ncu* birth, *esp* that of Christ, from a virgin, without a human father.
the (Blessed) Virgin (Mary) the mother of Christ.

Virgo ['və:gou] *n* a sign of the zodiac, the Virgin: *People born between August 23 and September 22 are said to be born under the sign of Virgo.*

virile ['virail] *adj* (of a man) sexually potent; strong and manly: *He is young and virile; virile young men.*
vi'rility [-'ri-] *nu* manliness or masculinity; sexual potency.

virtual ['və:tʃuəl] *adj* (*attrib*) not actual, but having the effect of being actual: *He influenced all the king's policies, and so was the virtual ruler of the country; the virtual collapse of the business.*
'virtually *adv* more or less, though not strictly speaking; in effect: *He was virtually penniless; We were virtually cut off from the town by snow.*

virtue ['və:tʃu:] **1** *nc* a good moral quality: *Honesty is a virtue.* **2** *nc* a good quality: *One of the virtues of this material is its hard-wearing nature; The house is small, but it has the virtue of being easy to clean.* **3** *nu* (*formal*) goodness of character *etc*: *She is a person of great virtue.* **4** *nu* (*old or formal euph*) chastity or virginity: *She had lost her virtue at an early age.* – *See also* **by virtue of** *below*.
'virtuous *adj* (*formal*) morally good: *She is a*

virtuous young woman; She is pure and virtuous. **'virtuously** *adv.* **'virtuousness** *nu.*

by virtue of (*formal*) because of : *By virtue of the position he held, he was able to move about freely; She is allowed to do as she wishes by virtue of the fact that she is the manager's daughter.*

virtuoso [vəːtʃu'ousou] – *pl* **ˌvirtu'osos** – *nc* (*formal*) a person who knows a great deal about *eg* music, painting, *esp* a skilled performer: *He's a virtuoso on the violin*; (*attrib*) *a virtuoso pianist/performance.*

ˌvirtu'osity [-'o-] *nu* (*formal*) great skill in one of the fine arts: *I am impressed by the virtuosity of that musician.*

virtuous *etc see* **virtue.**

virulent ['virələnt] *adj* (*formal*) **1** (*often attrib*) (of a disease) dangerous: *a virulent type of 'flu.* **2** (of hatred *etc*) bitter or violent: *In his speech he made a virulent attack on one of the government ministers; His speech against the opposition was spiteful and virulent.* **'virulently** *adv.*

'virulence *nu*: *the virulence of the infection; the virulence of his attack.*

virus ['vaiərəs] *nc* any of various types of germs that are smaller than known bacteria, can grow on body cells and are a cause of disease: *Different viruses can cause influenza, mumps, smallpox etc*; (*attrib*) *He is suffering from a virus infection.*

'viral *adj* (*tech*) caused by a virus: *a viral infection; He is suffering from viral pneumonia; I think your sore throat must be viral.*

visa ['viːzə] *nc* a mark or stamp put on a passport by the authorities of a country to show that the bearer may travel to, or in, that country: *I have applied for a visa for the United States.*

visage ['vizidʒ] *nc* (*liter*) a person's face: *By his pale visage I knew that he was ill.*

vis-à-vis [viːzaː'viː, (*Amer*) -zə-] *prep* (*formal*) in relation to: *What is your country's position vis-à-vis the Common Market?; his ambition vis-à-vis his ability.*

viscosity *see* **viscous.**

viscount *nc* (*with cap in titles*) (the status of) a nobleman next in rank below an earl: *Viscount Hailes of Baberton; He is a viscount.*

'viscountess *nc* (*with cap in titles*) **1** (the status of) the wife or widow of a viscount: *Viscountess Hailes.* **2** (the status of) a woman of the same rank as a viscount.

viscous ['viskəs] *adj* sticky, not flowing easily. **vi'scosity** [-'sko-], **'viscousness** *nus.*

vise *see* **vice**[1].

visible ['vizəbl] *adj* (*slightly formal*) able to be seen: *The house is visible through the trees; There's been a visible change in her since she got married; The scar on her face is scarcely visible now.* **'visibly** *adv.*

ˌvisi'bility *nu* the range of distance over which things may be (clearly) seen: *Visibility is poor today; Visibility in the foggy conditions was down* (= reduced) *to twenty yards in places.*

See also **invisible, visual.**

vision ['viʒən] **1** *nc* (*esp relig*) something seen in the imagination or in a dream: *God came to Elijah in a vision; He had a vision of Britain as a prosperous country leading the world*; (*fig*) *She was a vision of loveliness* (= She was very beautiful); (*facet*) *When it began to snow, I had visions of you abandoning the car and walking home.* **2** *nu* the ability to see or plan into the future: *She was a woman of considerable vision; Politicians should be men of vision.* **3** *nu* (*formal*) the ability to see or the sense of sight: *A severe headache can affect one's vision; My vision is getting worse as I grow older; He is slowly losing his vision.* **4** *nu* (*inf*) the picture on a television set: *This customer's set still has good sound, but he's complaining of poor vision.*

'visionary *adj* (*very formal or liter*) **1** existing or practicable only in the imagination: *visionary schemes/plans.* **2** (of a person) having impractical or fanciful thoughts, ideas *etc.* – *nc* (*formal or liter*) a visionary person: *The early scientists were often considered to be visionaries.*

See also **visual.**

visit ['vizit] **1** *vti* to go to see (a person or place): *We visited my parents at the weekend; When are you due to visit the dentist next?; They visited the ruins at Pompeii while they were on holiday; We visit* (*each other*) *quite often nowadays.* **2** *vti* to stay in (a place) or with (a person) for a time: *Many birds visit* (*Britain*) *only during the summer months.* **3** *vt* (*very formal or arch*) to inflict: *He visited his anger upon everyone around him.* **4** *vt* (*formal or arch*: *usu in passive*) to punish or torment: *The people were visited with a plague of rats.* – *nc* an act of going to see someone or something for pleasure, socially, professionally *etc*, or going to stay for a time: *We went on a visit to my aunt's; the children's visit to the museum; They're here on a six-week visit.*

ˌvisi'tation *nc* (*formal or arch*) **1** a visit by a superior officer, or by a supernatural being: *The shepherds had a visitation from an angel during the night.* **2** an attack (of a disease, plague *etc*).

'visitor *nc* a person who visits, socially or professionally: *I'm expecting visitors from America; We're having visitors next week; a health visitor.*

'visiting-card *nc* (*esp old*) a small card bearing one's name and address, left with a person whom one visits.

'visitors' book *nc* a book in which the names and often addresses of visitors are written: *Did you sign the visitors' book when you went round the castle?*

pay a visit to visit (*defs 1 and 2*): *It's a long time since we paid them a visit; I may pay a visit to my aunt; I will pay you a visit next week; They paid a visit to America last year.*

visit with *vt fus* (*Amer*) to visit (*defs 1 and 2*): *She is visiting with her parents.*

visor ['vaizə] *nc* **1** (*esp hist*) the part of a helmet covering the face: *the knight's visor.* **2** the peak of a cap *etc*: *The visor of his cap prevented the strong sunlight from hurting his eyes.* **3** (*tech*) a movable flap which folds down against the windscreen of a car *etc* to act as a sunshade.

vista ['vistə] *nc* (*formal*) a view that is long rather than broad, *eg* through an avenue of trees: *The driveway had been designed to provide approaching visitors with a fine vista of the house*; (*fig*) *Exciting new vistas* (= prospects or possibilities) *open up before us.*

visual ['viʒuəl] *adj* (*formal*) of sight or the process of seeing: *strange visual effects; The effect is purely visual; He is suffering from a visual disturbance.* **'visually** *adv.*

'visualize, -ise *vt* (*formal*) to form a clear picture of (something) in the mind: *Can you visualize how big this firm could be in ten years' time?; I know his name, but I can't visualize him* (= remember his appearance).

visual aids *n pl* pictures, films *etc* that are used as aids to learning: *Primary school teachers use a lot of visual aids.*

See also **visible, vision**.

vital ['vaitl] *adj* **1** essential; of the greatest importance: *Speed is vital to the success of our plan; We must try to ensure that vital food supplies are maintained; It is vital that we arrive at the hospital soon.* **2** (*formal or arch*: *attrib*) of, or necessary for, life: *Has he injured any of the vital organs?* **3** lively and energetic: *a vital person/personality; She is vital and attractive.*

ˌvi'tality [-'ta-] *nu* liveliness and energy: *a girl of tremendous vitality.*

'vitalize, -ise *vt* (*formal*) to give energy and vigour to: *He has vitalized the whole workforce with his enthusiasm.*

'vitals *n pl* (*arch*) the organs of the body which are essential to life.

vital statistics *n pl* **1** (*inf facet*) a woman's chest, waist and hip measurements: *If you enter the beauty contest you will have to give your vital statistics.* **2** statistics concerning births, marriages, deaths and other matters to do with population figures.

vitamin ['vitəmin, (*Amer*) 'vai-] *nc* (*sometimes attrib*) any of a group of substances necessary for healthy life, different ones occurring in different natural things such as raw fruit, dairy products, fish, meat *etc*: *A healthy diet is full of vitamins; Vitamin C is found in fruit and vegetables*; (*attrib*) *They don't get enough vitamins in their diet, so they have to take vitamin pills* (= pills containing vitamins).

vitiate ['viʃieit] *vt* (*very formal*) to spoil; to make impure or faulty: *This error vitiated her entire theory.* **ˌviti'ation** *nu.*

vitreous ['vitriəs] *adj* (*tech*: *esp attrib*) made of or like glass: *vitreous china.*

vitrify ['vitrifai] *vti* (*tech or formal*) to make or become (like) glass. **'vitrified** *adj.*

vitriolic [vitri'olik] *adj* (*formal derog*) extremely bitter or violent: *In his speech, he made a vitriolic attack on the nationalists; His speech was cruel and vitriolic.*

vituperative [vi'tju:pərətiv, (*Amer*) vai-] *adj* (*formal or facet*) (of language) very abusive or insulting: *He was very vituperative about her ability as an actress; vituperative criticism.* **viˌtupe'ration** *nu.*

viva ['vaivə], **viva voce** [vaivə'vousi] *nc* an oral examination: *We had a written exam yesterday and a viva today.*

vivacious [vi'veiʃəs] *adj* lively and bright: *She is a very vivacious person; She has a vivacious manner; She is vivacious and attractive.* **vi'vaciously** *adv.* **vi'vacity** [-'vasə-], **vi'vaciousness** *nus.*

vivid ['vivid] *adj* **1** (of colours *etc*) brilliant; very bright: *The door was painted a vivid yellow; The trees were vivid in their autumn colours.* **2** clear; striking: *I have many vivid memories of that holiday; a vivid image/description; My memory of that is still very vivid.* **3** (of the imagination) active; lively: *She has a vivid imagination; His imagination is more vivid than most people's.* **'vividly** *adv.* **'vividness** *nu.*

vivisection [vivi'sekʃən] *nu* (*formal or tech*) the performance of surgical experiments on living animals: *She loves animals and hates vivisection; Vivisection is essential in medical research.* **ˌvivi'sect** *vt.*

vixen ['viksn] *nc* **1** a female fox: *The vixen was followed by her cubs.* **2** (*derog*: *usu old*) an ill-tempered woman: *She is a real vixen.*

vocabulary [və'kabjuləri] **1** *nu* words in general: *This book contains some difficult vocabulary.* **2** *ncu* (the stock of) words known and used *eg* by one person, or within a particular trade or profession: *He has a vocabulary of about 20 000 words; These words are found only in the criminal vocabulary; the specialized vocabulary of nuclear physics.* **3** *nc* a list of words in alphabetical order with meanings *eg* added as a supplement to a book dealing with a particular subject: *This edition of Shakespeare's plays has a good vocabulary at the back.*

vocal ['voukəl] *adj* (*formal*) **1** (*often attrib*) of, or concerning, the voice: *vocal music* (= music to be sung). **2** (of a person) talkative; keen to make one's opinions heard by other people: *He's always very vocal at staff meetings; Does the vocal minority truly represent the silent majority?* **vo'cally** *adv.*

vo'calic [-'ka-] *adj* (*tech*) of a vowel or vowels.

'vocalist *nc* (*formal*) a singer: *a female vocalist.*

vocal cords *n pl* folds of membrane in the larynx that produce the sounds used in speech, singing *etc* when vibrated.

vocation [və'keiʃən, (*Amer*) vou-] **1** *nu* a feeling of having been called (by God), or born *etc*, to do a particular type of work: *He had a sense of vocation about his work; In order to be a doctor you must have a sense of vocation.* **2** *nc* the work done, profession entered *etc* (as a result of such a feeling): *Nursing is her vocation; Many people regard teaching as a vocation*: (*loosely facet*) *It is her vocation in life to make as much money as possible.*

vo'cational *adj* (*formal*) (of training, preparation *etc*) of, or for, a vocation: *Nursing is vocational work; a degree in medicine is vocational.*

vociferous [və'sifərəs, (*Amer*) vou-] *adj* (*formal often derog*) loud; noisy: *vociferous complaints; She was vociferous in her criticism of him.* **vo'ciferously** *adv.* **vo'ciferousness** *nu.*

vodka ['vodkə] **1** *nu* an alcoholic spirit made from rye or sometimes from potatoes: *a bottle of vodka; Would you like some vodka?* **2** *nc* a glass of vodka: *a vodka and orange.*

vogue [voug] *nc* (*formal or facet*) a fashion: *the current vogue for high-heeled shoes; We're returning to the vogues of the 1950s; Short hair is again the vogue*; (*attrib*) *Let's hope that 'ongoing situation' will not be a vogue expression for much longer.*

in vogue (*formal or facet*) fashionable: *The French style of trousers is very much in vogue just now.*

voice [vois] **1** *nc* the sounds from the mouth made in speaking or singing: *He has a very deep voice; I didn't recognize John's voice on the telephone; He spoke in a quiet/loud/angry/kind voice; Her speaking voice is low but she has a soprano singing voice; a choir of two hundred voices* (= singers). **2** *ncu* (*esp formal and liter*) the voice regarded as the means of expressing opinion: *My voice* (= opinion) *has little effect in these discussions; We have little voice* (= power of expressing opinion) *in the affairs of the society; The voice of the people should not be ignored; He is regarded as the voice of* (= spokesman for) *the moderates*; (*fig*) *I should have listened to the voice of reason/conscience.* **3** *nc* (*gram*) the form of a verb that shows whether the subject of a sentence performs, or suffers, the action of the verb: *In 'He struck John,' the verb is in the active voice, but in 'John was struck by him,' the verb is in the passive voice.* – *See also* **voice** *in* *phrases below.* – *vt* **1** (*formal*) to express (feelings *etc*): *He voiced the discontent of the whole group; I dared not voice my dissatisfaction.* **2** (*tech*) to produce the sound of (*esp* a consonant) with a vibration of the vocal cords as well as with the breath: *'Th' should be voiced in 'this' but not in 'think'.* **voiced** *adj* (*neg* **un-**).

'voiceless *adj.*

at the top of one's voice *see* **top**.

be in good voice to have one's voice in good condition for singing or speaking: *The choir was in good voice tonight.*

give 'voice to (*formal*) to express (an opinion *etc*).

lose one's voice to be unable to speak *eg* because of having a cold, sore throat *etc*: *When I had 'flu I lost my voice for three days.*

raise one's voice to speak more loudly than normal *esp* in anger: *I don't want to have to raise my voice to you again.*

with one voice (*formal*) simultaneously or unanimously: *They asked for his resignation with one voice.*

See also **vocal**.

void [void] *adj* **1** (*also* **null and void**) (*legal or formal*) not valid or binding: *The treaty has been declared void; Their marriage was declared null and void.* **2** (*formal*: *pred with* **of**) lacking entirely: *a statement void of meaning.* – *nc* (*formal*) a huge empty space, *esp* (*with* **the**) outer space: *The rocket shot up into the void;* (*fig*) *Her death left a void in her husband's life.*

See also **devoid**.

volatile ['volətail] *adj* **1** (*tech*) (of a liquid *etc*) changing quickly to vapour. **2** (*loosely*) likely to explode: *a highly volatile substance.* **3** (*formal*) changeable; unstable: *There is rather a volatile political situation in that part of the world; She is excitable and volatile; a volatile personality.*

vol-au-vent ['voləvã, (*Amer*) volou'vã] *nc* a small pie made of puff pastry, filled with meat, fish *etc.*

volcano [vol'keinou] – *pl* **vol'canoes** – *nc* a *usu* conical hill or mountain with an opening through which molten rock, ashes *etc* periodically erupt, or have erupted in the past, from inside the earth: *That mountain is an extinct* (= no longer active) *volcano; The village was destroyed when the volcano erupted.*

vol'canic [-'ka-] *adj* (*often attrib*) of, like, or produced by, a volcano: *volcanic rock.*

vole [voul] *nc* any of several types of small animal with gnawing teeth.

volition [və'liʃən, (*Amer*) vou-]: **of one's own volition** (*formal*) willingly, or without being forced: *No one told him to do it. He did it of his own volition.*

volley ['voli] *nc* **1** in tennis, the hitting of a ball before it bounces: *The spectators round the tennis court applauded the long volley.* **2** a burst of firing *etc*: *a volley of shots; We were subjected to a volley of questions/curses.* – **1** *vti* to hit (a ball *etc*) before it bounces: *He volleyed the ball back to his opponent.* **2** *vt* to fire a rapid burst of (bullets, shells, questions *etc*).

'volleyball *nu* a game in which a ball is volleyed over a high net, using the hands: *Do you play volleyball?; Let's have a game of volleyball!;* (*attrib*) *a volleyball team.*

volt [voult] *nc* (*often abbrev* **V** *when written*) the unit used in measuring the force driving electricity through a circuit, or (*loosely*) the strength of an electric current.

'voltage [-tidʒ] *ncu* (a) force measured in volts: *Low voltage reduces the current, causing the lights to burn dimly; These transistors have different working voltages.*

'voltmeter *nc* (*tech*) a meter which measures volts.

volte-face [volt'fas] *nc* (*formal*) a sudden and complete change of opinion: *The government appears to have made a complete volte-face on this issue.*

voluble ['voljubl] *adj* (*formal*) very talkative: *He became very voluble on the subject; a voluble woman.* **'volubly** *adv.* **ˌvolu'bility** *nu.*

volume ['voljum] **1** *nc* (*formal*) a book: *This library contains over a million volumes.* **2** *nc* (*often abbrev* **vol.** *when written*) one of a series of connected books: *Where is volume fifteen of the encyclopedia?; I have lost vol. IV.* **3** *nu* (*often tech*) the amount of space occupied by something, expressed in cubic measurement: *What is the volume of the petrol tank?; The volume of water in the water tank is 440 cubic centimetres; Find the volume of a box measuring 10 centimetres by 6 centimetres by 5 centimetres.* **4** *ncu* amount: *The volume of trade is declining; A large volume of work remains to be done.* **5** *nu* level of sound *eg* on a radio, television *etc*: *Turn up the volume on the radio.*

speak volumes to have a great deal of meaning: *She said nothing but her face spoke volumes.*

voluminous [və'lu:minəs] *adj* (*formal or facet*) **1** great in quantity: *It will take months to examine his voluminous correspondence.* **2** large and full: *a voluminous dress; The skirt of that dress is incredibly voluminous.*

voluntary ['voləntəri] *adj* **1** done, given *etc* by choice, not by accident or because of being forced: *All the society's money comes from voluntary contributions; Their action was completely voluntary – nobody asked them to do that.* **2** (*attrib*) run, financed *etc* by such actions, contributions *etc*: *He does a lot of work for a voluntary organization.* – *nc* a piece of organ music of a type normally played at the end and/or beginning of a church service.

voluntarily ['voləntərəli, volən'terəli] *adv.*

See also **involuntary**.

volunteer [volən'tiə] **1** *vi* to offer oneself for a particular task, of one's own free will: *He volunteered to act as messenger; She volunteered for a dangerous mission; I asked if anyone would help me, but no-one volunteered.* **2** *vt* (*formal*) to offer (*eg* an opinion, information *etc*): *Two or three people volunteered suggestions.* – *nc* a person who offers to do, or does, something (*esp* who joins the army) of his own free will: *There are not enough ambulance drivers and so ambulances are being driven by volunteers; We are asking for volunteers to dig the school garden; If we can get enough volunteers we shall not force people to join the Army;* (*attrib*) *a volunteer force.*

voluptuous [və'lʌptʃuəs] *adj* (*formal or facet*) producing sensual pleasure: *voluptuous music; a woman with a voluptuous* (= large and sexually attractive) *figure; Her breasts are large and voluptuous.* **vo'luptuousness** *nu.*

vomit ['vomit] *vti* to throw out (the contents of the stomach or other matter) through the mouth; to be sick: *The patient was vomiting repeatedly; Whenever the ship started to move she felt like* *vomiting; If the patient starts to vomit blood, call the doctor!*; (*liter fig*) *The volcano vomited molten rock and ash.* – *nu* food *etc* ejected from the stomach: *Don't let the patient swallow his vomit – make him sit up*; *blood-stained vomit.*

voodoo ['vu:du:] *nu* a type of witchcraft originally practised by certain Negro races in the West Indies: *These tribes used to practise voodoo.*

voracious [və'reiʃəs] *adj* (*formal*) greedy or difficult to satisfy: *She has a voracious appetite*; *Her appetite seems voracious*; (*fig*) *a voracious reader.* **vo'raciously** *adv.* **vo'racity** [-'rasə-], **vor'aciousness** *nus.*

vortex ['vo:teks] – *pls* **'vortices** [-tisi:z], **'vortexes** – *nc* (*liter*) a whirlpool or whirlwind.

vote [vout] *nc* (*sometimes without* **a**) (the right to give) a formal indication of a wish or opinion, *eg* in a ballot or by raising a hand *etc*, *esp* at an election or in a debate: *In Britain, the vote* (= the right to vote at elections) *was given to women over twenty-one in 1928*; *Nowadays everyone over eighteen has a vote*; *I shall cast* (= give) *my vote for/against that candidate/proposal*; *A vote was taken to decide the matter*; *The matter was decided by vote*; *The result of the vote was a win for the Liberals.* – **1** *vi* to cast or record one's vote: *I'm going to the polling booth to vote*; *She voted for the Conservative candidate*; *I always vote Labour* (= for the Labour party); *I shall vote against the restoration of capital punishment.* **2** *vt* to authorize, by a vote, the provision of (something) *eg* to someone, for a purpose *etc*: *They were voted £1 000 to help them in their research.* **3** *vt* (*inf*) to declare; to pronounce: *The evening was voted a huge success by everyone.*

'voter *nc* a person who votes or has the right to vote: *Each political party is wondering how best to impress the voters.*

put (something) to the vote to decide (a matter) by voting: *There is disagreement about whether we should close the school – let us put it to the vote.*

a vote of confidence a vote taken to establish whether the government or other body or person in authority still has the majority's support for its/his policies.

a vote of thanks an invitation, *usu* in the form of a short speech, to an audience *etc* to show gratitude to a speaker *etc* by applauding *etc*: *Mrs Smith proposed a vote of thanks to the organizers of the fête.*

vouch [vautʃ] (*with* **for**) **1** to say or declare that one is sure that something is fact or truth: *I can vouch for his honesty*; *Will you vouch for the truth of the statement.* **2** to guarantee the honesty *etc* of (a person): *My friends will vouch for me.*

'voucher *nc* a piece of paper which confirms that a sum of money has been, or will be, paid: *a sales voucher*; *a luncheon voucher.*

vouchsafe [vautʃ'seif] *vt* (*very formal or arch*) to be good enough to give or grant; to condescend to give: *He vouchsafed no reply*; *He refused to vouchsafe any information.*

vow [vau] *nc* a solemn promise, *esp* one made to God: *The monks have made/taken a vow of silence*; *marriage vows*; *He refused to break his vow.* – *vt* **1** to make a solemn promise (that): *He vowed that he would die rather than surrender.* **2** (*formal*) to threaten: *He vowed revenge on all his enemies.* **3** (*formal or old*) to declare (that): *She vowed that he was the most unpleasant person she had ever met.*

vowel ['vauəl] *nc* **1** in English and many other languages, the letters *a, e, i, o, u*. **2** (*also* **vowel sound**) any of the sounds represented by these five letters or by *y*, or by combination of these with each other and/or *w*.

See also **vocalic** *under* **vocal**.

voyage ['voiidʒ] *nc* a *usu* long journey, *esp* by sea: *The voyage to America used to take many weeks.* – *vi* (*esp liter*) to make such a journey: *They voyaged for many months.*

'voyager *nc* (*old or liter*) a person making a voyage, or who has made several voyages.

vs *see* **versus**.

V-sign *see* **V-**.

vulgar ['vʌlgə] *adj* **1** (*derog*) not generally socially acceptable, decent or polite; ill-mannered or coarse: *She uses vulgar expressions*; *He made a vulgar gesture*; *Such behaviour is regarded as vulgar.* **2** (*esp old*: *usu attrib*) of the common or ordinary people: *the vulgar tongue/language.* **'vulgarly** *adv.*

'vulgarism *nc* (*formal*) an expression which is not to be used in polite conversation: *'Fuck' is a vulgarism.*

vul'garity [-'ga-] *ncu* (an example of) coarseness, bad taste *etc*, in *eg* speech, behaviour *etc*: *the vulgarity of his language*; *the vulgarity of his table manners.*

vulgar fraction *nc* a fraction expressed in the form $^2/_3$, $^{47}/_{100}$ *etc*, rather than in decimals.

vulnerable ['vʌlnərəbl] *adj* (*formal*) unprotected against attack; liable to be hurt or damaged: *The enemy's position is vulnerable*; *In his teens, a child is at a very vulnerable* (= sensitive) *stage*; *a vulnerable young girl.* **ˌvulnera'bility** *nu.*

See also **invulnerable**.

vulture ['vʌltʃə] *nc* a type of large bird of prey feeding chiefly on dead bodies.

vulva ['vʌlvə] *nc* (*tech*) the opening of the genitals in a female.

vying *see* **vie**.

Ww

wad [wod] *nc* **1** a mass of loose material used to protect things in packing, keep them jammed in place *etc*: *He stuffed up the hole with a wad of newspaper*; *She used a wad of cottonwool to stop her nose bleeding.* **2** a large bundle (*esp* of bank-notes): *He took a wad of five-pound notes from his wallet.*

'wadding *nu* material used in packing *etc*, *eg* cottonwool or straw.

waddle ['wodl] *vi* (*derog* when used of people) to take short steps and move from side to side in walking (as a duck does): *The ducks waddled across the road*; *The fat old lady waddled down the street.* – *nc* (*derog* when used of people: *no pl*) a clumsy, rocking way of walking: *Pregnant women often have a distinct waddle.*

wade [weid] **1** *vti* to go or walk (through water, mud *etc*) with some difficulty: *He waded across the pool towards me*; (*fig*) *I waded my way across the* *floor, which was knee-deep in sawdust*; (*fig*) *I've finally managed to wade through that boring book I had to read.* 2 *vt* to cross (a river *etc*) by wading: *We'll wade the stream at its shallowest point.*

'wader *nc* **1** any of several types of bird that wade in search of food. **2** (*usu in pl*) a type of high waterproof boot used by anglers *etc.*

wade in *vi*, **wade into** *vt fus* (*inf*) to attack (people, a task *etc*) with enthusiasm and without hesitation: *He waded into the discussion without thinking*; *He really waded into the child for lying to him.*

wafer ['weifə] *nc* **1** a type of very thin biscuit, often eaten with ice-cream: *an ice-cream wafer*; (*attrib*) *a wafer biscuit.* **2** a thin disc of bread used at Holy Communion in some denominations of the Christian Church.

ˌwafer-'thin *adj* extremely thin: *a wafer-thin piece of metal*; *Those cucumber sandwiches are wafer-thin.*

waffle[1] ['wofl] *nc* (*esp Amer*) a kind of light, crisp cake made from batter.

waffle[2] ['wofl] *vi* (*inf derog*) to talk on and on foolishly, pretending that one knows something which one does not: *If you ask him a question, he'll only waffle, and you won't get a satisfactory answer*; *This lecturer will waffle on for hours.* – *nu* talk of this kind: *His speech was pure waffle. He has no idea what he's talking about.*

waft [woft, (*Amer*) waft] *vti* (*formal or liter*) to (cause to) float or drift lightly: *The smoke wafted gently across the valley*; *The wind wafted the leaves through the window.*

wag[1] [wag] – *pt, ptp* **wagged** – **1** *vti* (*esp* of a dog's tail) to (cause to) move to and fro, *esp* from side to side: *The dog wagged its tail with pleasure*; *You can tell he likes you because his tail is wagging.* **2** *vi* (*inf*) (of people's tongues) to move; to gossip: *Her strange behaviour has set the neighbours' tongues wagging.* – *nc* a single wagging movement: *The dog's tail gave a feeble wag.*

wag[2] [wag] *nc* (*old inf*) a person who is always joking; a wit: *He's quite a wag – he tells very funny stories.*

wage[1] [weidʒ] *vt* (*formal*) to carry on or engage in (*esp* a war): *The North waged war on/against the South.*

wage[2] [weidʒ] *nc* (*also* **'wages** *n pl*) a regular, *usu* weekly rather than monthly, payment for work done, given to or received by a person, *esp* one who is not in a profession, in a managerial position *etc*: *He spends all his wages betting on horses*; *What is his weekly wage?*

'wage-packet *nc* **1** the packet in which wages are paid: *The cashier puts the workmen's money in wage-packets.* **2** wages: *Due to heavier taxation, my wage-packet has been getting smaller.*

wager ['weidʒə] *nc* (*formal*) a bet: *We made a wager that he would win*; *Their wager was fifty pounds.* – *vti* (*formal*) to bet (something) on the chance of something happening: *I'll wager* (*ten dollars*) *that I can jump further than you.*

waggle ['wagl] *vti* (*inf*) to (cause to) move from side to side: *She waggled her hips as she walked down the street*; *His beard waggled as he ate.* – *nc* (*inf*: *no pl*) such a movement: *the waggle of her hips.*

wagon, waggon ['wagən] *nc* **1** a type of four-wheeled vehicle for carrying heavy loads: *a hay wagon.* **2** (*Brit*) an open railway carriage for goods: *a goods wagon.* **3** (*Amer*: *often in cmpds*) a trolley for carrying food: *a tea-wagon.*

'wagoner *nc* the driver of a wagon.

'wagonload *nc* the amount carried by a wagon: *a wagonload of hay.*

waif [weif] *nc* (*formal*) a stray, uncared-for child: *a poor little waif.*

waifs and strays (*old or facet*) people (*usu* children) without homes or possessions: *In the old days, houses for accommodating homeless children were called homes for waifs and strays.*

wail [weil] *vi* (*formal*) to utter sorrowful or complaining cries: *The child is wailing over its broken toy*; (*fig*) *I heard a siren wailing.* – *nc* (*formal*) a long cry of *usu* sorrow: *wails of grief*; (*fig*) *I heard the wail of a police siren.*

See also **bewail**.

wainscot ['weinskət] *nc* (*esp old*) a wooden lining applied to (the lower part of) the walls of rooms.

'wainscoting, 'wainscotting *nu* (materials for making) wainscots: *There are mice in the wainscoting.*

waist [weist] *nc* **1** (the measurement round) the narrow part of the human body between the ribs and hips: *She has a very small waist*; *What size* (*of*) *waist do you have?*; (*attrib*) *What is your waist measurement?* **2** the narrow middle part of something similar, *eg* a violin, guitar *etc.* **3** the part of an article of clothing which goes round one's waist: *Can you take in the waist of these trousers?*

'waisted *adj* shaped to fit round the waist: *a waisted jacket*; *Her new jacket is waisted.*

waistband ['weisband] *nc* the part of a pair of trousers, skirt *etc* which goes round the waist: *The waistband of this skirt is too tight.*

waistcoat ['weiskout] *nc* (*Amer* **vest**) a short, *usu* sleeveless jacket worn immediately under the outer jacket: *a three-piece suit consists of trousers, jacket and waistcoat.*

wait [weit] *vi* **1** to remain or stay (in the same place or without doing anything): *Wait* (*for*) *two minutes* (*here*) *while I go inside*; *Wait until I tell you*; *I'm waiting for John* (*to arrive*); *I refuse to wait around here any longer*; *He's waiting for the next train*; (*fig*) *He's just waiting for an opportunity to leave.* – *See also* **wait up** *below.* **2** (*with* **for**: *inf fig*) to expect: *I was just waiting for that pile of dishes to fall!* **3** (*formal*: *often with* **on**) to serve dishes, drinks *etc* (at table): *This servant will wait on your guests*; *He waits at table.* – *nc* an act of waiting; a delay: *There was a long wait before they could board the train.*

'waiter – *fem* **'waitress** – *nc* a person who serves people with food *etc* at table: *She is a waitress in a seaside café*; *Which waiter served you in the restaurant?*

'waiting-list *nc* a list of the names of people who are waiting for something: *She is on the waiting-list for the publishing course*; *They have put us on the waiting-list for a council house.*

'waiting-room *nc* a room in which people may wait (*eg* at a station, doctor's surgery *etc*).

wait for *see* **wait** (*defs 1 and 2*).

wait up *vi* (*sometimes with* **for**) to stay out of bed at night waiting (for someone to come home): *I'll be late, so don't wait up* (*for me*); *The parents waited up till their daughter came in.*

See also **await**.

waive [weiv] *vt* (*formal*) **1** to give up or not insist upon; to abandon (*eg* a claim or right): *He waived his claim to all the land north of the river.* **2** not to demand or enforce (a fine, penalty *etc*): *The judge* *waived the sentence and let him go free.*

wake[1] [weik] – *pt* **woke** [wouk], (*rare*) **waked**: *ptp* **woken** ['woukən], (*rare*) **waked** – 1 *vti* to bring or come back to consciousness after being asleep: *He woke to find that it was snowing*; *Go and wake the others, will you?* – *See also* **wake up** *below.* 2 *vt* (*formal*) to cause (something) to be thought about or experienced, either for the first time or after a long interval: *The music woke memories of holidays in Spain*; *Her handicaps woke great feelings of sympathy in everyone around her.*

'**wakeful** *adj* (*formal*) 1 not asleep; not able to sleep: *a wakeful child*; *The children are wakeful.* 2 (*usu attrib*) (of a night) in which one gets little sleep: *We spent a wakeful night worrying about her.*

'**wakefully** *adv.* '**wakefulness** *nu.*

'**waken** *vti* to wake: *What time are you going to waken him?*; *I wakened early.*

'**wake (someone) to (something)** (*formal*) to make (someone) aware, or to become aware, of (something): *His narrow escape woke him to/He woke to the dangers of driving too fast in fog.*

wake up *vi, vt sep* 1 to wake: *I have to leave very early in the morning and I'm afraid that I won't wake up in time*; *Wake up! You're late*; *Try and wake him up, will you?*; *The baby woke up in the middle of the night.* 2 (*inf*) to become aware of: *It is time you woke up to the fact that your wife is being unfaithful.*

See also **awake**.

wake[2] [weik] *nc* a strip of smooth-looking or foamy water left behind a ship.

in the 'wake of immediately behind or after: *Our tiny boat was caught in the wake of the huge ship*; (*formal fig*) *He resigned in the wake of accusations that he had stolen from the company.*

wake[3] [weik] *nc* in certain areas, an act of watching over the body of a dead person overnight before their burial, and the eating, drinking and celebration which accompanies this.

wakeful, waken *see* **wake**[1].

walk [wo:k] 1 *vti* (of people or animals) to (cause to) move on foot at a pace slower than running, never having both or all the feet off the ground at once: *He walked across the room and sat down*; *How long will it take to walk to the station*; *I can't walk – I've hurt my leg*; *Don't run – walk!*; *He walked the horse up and down in front of the judges*; *She walks her dog in the park every morning.* 2 *vi* (*also* **go walking**) to travel on foot for pleasure: *We're going walking in the Highlands for our holidays.* 3 *vt* to move on foot along: *It's dangerous to walk the streets of New York alone after dark*; *He's walking the streets – he has no job and no home.* 4 *vt* (*inf*) to walk with (someone): *I'll walk you home*; *He walked her to the bus stop.* – *See also* **walk** *in phrases below.* – 1 *nc* (the distance covered during) an outing or journey on foot: *She wants to go for/to take a walk*; *I think I'll take a walk*; *Will you take the dog for a walk?*; *It's a long walk to the station*; *It's two hours' walk to the town*; *The city is a forty-mile walk from here.* 2 *nc* a way or manner of walking: *I recognised her walk.* 3 *nc* a route for walking: *There are many pleasant walks in this area.* 4 *n* (*with cap: often abbrev* **Wk** *when written*) a word used in the names of certain roads or streets: *His address is 17 Middle Meadow Walk.*

'**walker** *nc* a person who goes walking for pleasure: *We met a party of walkers as we were going home.*

'**walkabout** *nc* (*inf*) a walk around among the crowds of ordinary people by a famous person, a member of the Royal Family *etc.*

,**walkie-'talkie** *nc* (*inf*) a portable two-way radio: *The soldiers spoke to each other on the walkie-talkie.*

'**walking-stick** *nc* a stick used (*esp* as an aid to balance) when walking: *The old lady has been using a walking-stick since she hurt her leg.*

'**walk-on** *adj* (*attrib*) (of a part in a play *etc*) in which an actor has no lines to say: *He had a walk-on part in Hamlet.*

'**walk-out** *nc* an act of walking out, *esp* at the beginning of a strike: *The workers staged a mass walk-out in protest against the sacking of a workmate.* – *See also* **walk out** *below.*

'**walkover** *nc* (*inf*) 1 an easy victory: *It was a walkover! We won 8–nil.* 2 (a round of) a competition where only one competitor appears or is entered, and he automatically wins: *The tennis competition was a walkover for me because my opponent did not appear*; *I was given a walkover to the next round of the badminton competition – my opponent was ill and did not come.*

'**walkway** *nc* a path *etc* for pedestrians only: *There is a moving walkway at that airport.*

at/to a 'walk at or to the normal speed at which one walks, or to a slow speed: *The horse slowed to a walk*; *You don't have to run – you'll get there easily at a walk.*

walk all over (someone) (*inf derog*) to pay no respect to (a person's) rights, feelings *etc*: *He'll walk all over you if you let him.*

walk away with (*inf*) *vt fus* to win (prizes *etc*) easily: *Of course you'll win – you'll walk away with all the prizes.*

walk off 1 *vi* to walk away: *He walked off down the road.* 2 *vt sep* to get rid of (*eg* a headache) by walking: *He's gone to try to walk off his hangover.*

walk off with *vt fus* (*inf*) 1 to win easily: *He walked off with all the prizes at the school sports.* 2 to steal: *The thieves have walked off with my best silver and china.*

walk of life (*formal*) a way of earning one's living; an occupation or profession: *People from all walks of life went to the minister's funeral.*

walk on air (*inf*) to feel extremely happy *etc*: *She's walking on air since he asked her to marry him.*

walk out *vi* to leave (a factory *etc*) on strike: *The entire work-force has walked out (on strike) in protest against the new agreement.* – *See also* '**walk-out** *above.*

walk out on *vt fus* (*derog*) to abandon: *He's walked out on his wife/responsibilities.*

wall [wo:l] *nc* 1 something built of stone, brick, plaster, wood *etc* and used to separate off or enclose something: *There's a wall at the bottom of the garden*: *The Great Wall of China*; *He climbed over the wall into our orchard and stole the apples*; *a garden wall*; (*attrib*) *Ivy is a wall plant.* 2 any of the sides of a building or room: *One wall of the room is yellow – the rest are white*; *This secret must not be discussed outside these four walls*; (*attrib*) *The only clock in the room is a wall clock.* 3 a surface which forms the outside of something: *There is something wrong with the wall of his heart*; *the wall of a plant cell.* 4 (*formal*) something which forms a barrier: *a wall of defenders*; (*fig*) *We were met by a wall of silence.* – *See also* **wall** *in phrases below.* – *vt* (*often with* **in**) to enclose (something) with a wall: *We're going to wall the garden*; *We've walled in the playground to prevent the children getting out.* – *See also* **wall up** *below.*

walled *adj*: *a walled city.*

walled- (*in cmpds*) having (a certain type or number of) wall(s): *a ˌhigh-walled ˈgarden.*

ˈwallflower *nc* **1** a type of sweet-smelling spring plant having yellow, orange or brownish-red flowers. **2** (*inf*) a person (*usu* a woman) who remains sitting at a dance because no-one asks him or her to dance: *Go and dance with Miss Smith – she's such a wallflower.*

ˈwallpaper *nu* paper used to decorate interior walls of houses *etc*: *My wife wants to put wallpaper on the walls but I would rather paint them.* – *vti* to put such paper on: *I am going to wallpaper this afternoon; I have wallpapered the front room.*

ˌwall-to-ˈwall *adj* (*often attrib*) (*usu* of carpet) covering the entire floor of a room *etc*: *I prefer wall-to-wall carpeting to polished floors.*

go to the wall to be defeated in (*esp* business) competition: *Several small firms went to the wall in the past financial year.*

have one's back to the wall to be in a desperate situation: *The army in the south have their backs to the wall, and are fighting a losing battle.*

up the wall (*inf*) crazy: *This business is sending/driving me up the wall!; He's going up the wall about the mess they've made of his garden!*

wall up *vt sep* to shut (a person) up permanently inside a wall, often alive: *Many years ago, people were sometimes sentenced to death by being walled up.*

wallet [ˈwolit] *nc* **1** a small (*usu* folding) case made of soft leather, plastic *etc*, carried in the pocket and used for holding (*esp* paper) money, personal papers *etc*: *He has lost all his money – his wallet has been stolen.* **2** a similar case containing other things: *a plastic wallet containing a set of small tools.*

wallop [ˈwoləp] *vt* (*inf*) to strike (something or someone) hard: *He walloped the desk with his fist; I'll wallop you if you do that again!* – *nc* (*inf*) a heavy or powerful blow: *He gave John a wallop right on the chin.*

ˈwalloping *adv* (*inf*) very (big): *a walloping great bruise.* – *adj* (*inf*: *attrib*) very big: *a walloping bruise.*

wallow [ˈwolou] *vi* to roll about with enjoyment: *The hippopotamus wallowed in the mud; She wallowed in the hot bath*; (*fig*) *They wallowed in the sunshine/luxury*; (*fig*) *He's wallowing in self-pity* (= He is enjoying feeling sorry for himself). – *nc* an act of wallowing: *to have a wallow in the mud; I enjoyed my wallow in the hot bath.*

walnut [ˈwoːlnʌt] **1** *nc* a type of tree whose wood is used for making furniture *etc*: (*attrib*) *a walnut tree.* **2** *nc* the nut produced by this tree. **3** *nu, adj* (of) the wood of the tree: *a walnut table; The table is (made of) walnut.*

walrus [ˈwoːlrəs] – *pls* **ˈwalruses, ˈwalrus** – *nc* a type of large sea animal with huge tusks, related to the seal.

waltz [woːlts] *nc* (a piece of music for) a type of slow ballroom dance performed by couples: *The band is playing a waltz; She has requested a waltz; I prefer waltzes to modern dances*; (*attrib*) *waltz music.* – **1** *vti* to dance a waltz (with): *Can you waltz?; He waltzed round the room with his partner; He waltzed her merrily round the room.* **2** *vi* (*inf*) to move cheerfully or with confidence: *He waltzed into the room and told us that he was getting married the next day.*

wan [won] *adj* (*formal*) pale and sickly-looking: *She still looks wan after her illness; a wan little face.*

ˈwanly *adv.* **ˈwanness** *nu.*

wand [wond] *nc* a long slender rod *eg* as used by conjurors, (*myth*) fairies *etc*, often thought to have magic powers: *In the story, the fairy waved her magic wand and the frog became a prince.*

wander [ˈwondə] **1** *vti* to go, move, walk *etc* (about, in or on) from place to place with no definite destination in mind: *Groups of nomads wander across the desert; I'd like to spend a holiday wandering through France; They wander the jungle, searching for food; The mother wandered the streets looking for her child.* **2** *vi* to go astray or move away from the proper place or home: *Our dog has a tendency to wander*; (*fig*) *His mind wanders*; (*fig*) *I realized that my attention was wandering.* – *nc* (*sometimes inf*) an act of wandering: (*inf*) *He's gone for a wander round the shops.*

ˈwanderer *nc.*

ˈwanderlust *nu* the wish to travel: *He's always travelling – his wanderlust will never be satisfied.*

wane [wein] *vi* **1** (of the moon) to appear to become smaller as less of it becomes visible. **2** (*formal*) to become less: *His influence is waning; The daylight is waning.*

on the wane (*formal*) becoming less: *His power is on the wane.*

See also **wax**[2].

wangle [ˈwaŋgl] *vt* (*inf*) to obtain or achieve (something) by trickery: *He got us seats for the concert – I don't know how he wangled it; Could you wangle a job for me?*

want [wont] (not *usu* used with **is, was** *etc* and **-ing** (*defs 1, 2*): not used with **is, was** *etc* and **-ing** (*defs 3, 4*)) **1** *vt* to be interested in having or doing, or to wish to have or do (something); to desire: *Do you want a cigarette?; I want to go to London this weekend; She wants to know where he is; We want to see the manager!; She wants to go home; She wants a job; She wants her mummy.* **2** *vi* (*inf*) to desire to go or come: *The dog wants out for a walk; The cat wants in.* **3** *vt* (*inf*) to need: *This wall wants a coat of paint; Your kids want a smack!* **4** *vti* (*formal or liter*) to lack: *This house wants none of the usual modern features but I do not like it; The people will want* (= be poor) *no longer.* – *See also* **be ˈwanting, want for** *below.* – **1** *nc* (*sometimes inf*) something desired: *The child has a long list of wants.* **2** *nu* (*formal*) poverty: *They are waging a war on want; They have lived in want for many years.* **3** *nc* (*no pl*) a lack: *There's no want of opportunities these days.*

ˈwanted *adj* **1** being searched for by the police because of having committed a criminal act: *He is a wanted man; He is wanted for murder.* **2** (*neg* **un-**: *esp pred*) (of people) needed; cared for: *Old people must be made to feel wanted.*

be found wanting (in) (*formal*) to be seen to be lacking (certain things): *When it came to the time when courage was necessary, he was found wanting; You won't find her wanting in charm.*

be ˈwanting (*formal or liter*) to be lacking: *Some desirable features are wanting, but on the whole I like the house.* – *See also* **want** (*v def 4*).

ˈwant for *vt fus* to lack: *She's never wanted for money or possessions; She wants for nothing* (= She has everything she could wish for).

wanton [ˈwontən] *adj* **1** (*formal*: *usu attrib*) without reason; motiveless: *wanton cruelty; the wanton destruction of property.* **2** (*formal or liter*) (of a person) immoral or not chaste: *wanton young* *women*; *His wife was lazy and wanton.* – *nc* (*old or liter*) a person (*usu* a woman) who is wanton in morals: *No wonder that he divorced her – she is a wanton.*

'wantonly *adv.* **'wantonness** *nu.*

war [wo:] *ncu* (an) armed struggle, *esp* between nations: *Their leader has declared war on Britain*; *The larger army will win the war*; *The Christians are waging* (= carrying on) *war against the heathens*; *the horrors of war*; *He served in the two World Wars*; (*attrib*) *He is guilty of war crimes*; (*fig*) *We must all contribute to the war against cancer.* – *See also* **war** *in phrases below.* – *v* – *pt, ptp* **warred** – *vi* (*formal*) to fight: *The two countries have been warring constantly for generations.*

'warlike *adj* (*neg* **un-**) fond of, or likely to begin, war: *a warlike nation*; *The tribe is fierce and warlike.*

'warrior ['wo-] *nc* (*liter* or in primitive societies) a soldier or skilled fighting man: *The chief of the tribe called his warriers together*; (*attrib*) *a warrior prince.*

'war correspondent *nc* a newspaper reporter who writes articles on a war or wars.

'war-cry *nc* (*often fig*) a shout used in battle as an encouragement to the soldiers: *'For king and country' was the war-cry of the troops as they faced the enemy*; (*fig*) *'Equality with men' is the war-cry of many modern women.*

'war-dance *nc* a dance performed by some peoples (*eg* (*hist*) North American Indians) before going to war.

'warfare *nu* fighting, as in a war: *He refused to fight, because he has religious objections against warfare.*

'warhead *nc* the explosive section of a missile, torpedo *etc*: *nuclear warheads.*

'warhorse *nc* **1** a horse used in battle. **2** (*inf*) a veteran soldier, politician *etc*: *that well-loved old warhorse, eighty-year-old General Brown.*

'warlord *nc* a very powerful military leader.

war memorial *see* **memorial**.

'warmonger *nc* (*derog*) a person who encourages war(s), often for personal reasons: *He was accused of being a warmonger by refusing to agree to the enemy's terms.*

'warpaint *nu* **1** paint applied to the face *etc* by some peoples (*eg* (*hist*) North American Indians) before going into battle. **2** (*inf facet*) women's cosmetics: *She must be going out – she's got her warpaint on.*

'warship *nc* a ship used in war or defence: *the warships of the Royal Navy.*

'wartime *nu* the time during which a country, a people *etc* is at war: *The economy is often thought to expand in wartime*; (*attrib*) *a wartime economy.*

be at 'war to be taking part in an armed struggle (with): *My country is at war with yours*; *Our countries are at war.*

civil war *see* **civil**.

cold war *see* **cold**.

declare war (on) to announce the beginning of a war (against): *The North has declared war* (*on the South*); (*fig*) *The government have declared war on inflation.*

go to war 1 (of countries) to begin a war: *The United States went to war with Mexico in 1846.* **2** (of a soldier) to depart for the scene of the fighting: *James went off to war six years ago and we've never heard of him since.*

have been in the wars (*inf facet*) to have been injured (*usu* slightly): *He came back from the rugby match looking as if he'd really been in the wars.*

make/wage war (on) (*formal*) to have an armed struggle with (a country *etc*): *They are waging war on Britain*; (*fig*) *We must wage war on poverty.*

on the 'warpath 1 (*hist*) of North American Indians, setting off to fight. **2** (*inf fig*) in a very angry mood: *The boss is on the warpath this morning, so be careful!*

war of nerves (*often fig*) a war, contest *etc* in which each side tries to win by making the other nervous, *eg* by bluff, rather than by actually fighting: *That game of chess was a war of nerves*; *Our competitors are conducting a war of nerves against us by trying to make us lose our confidence.*

warble ['wo:bl] *vti* to sing (something) in a trembling voice, as some birds do: *The bird was warbling* (*his song*) *on a high branch*; (*fig*) *The old lady's voice came warbling across the room.* – *nc* (*no pl*) an act, or the sound, of warbling: *the warble of a bird in summer.*

'warbler *nc* any of several kinds of small singing bird.

ward [wo:d] *nc* **1** a room with a bed or beds for patients in a hospital *etc*: *He is in a surgical ward of the local hospital*; *a private ward.* **2** (the people living in) any of the areas into which a city *etc* is divided for the purpose of local government elections: *He's contesting Edinburgh South ward*; *My ward is not in favour of these measures.* **3** a person who is under the legal control and care of someone who is not his or her parent or (a **ward of court**) of a court: *He has sent his ward to boarding-school*; *She was made a ward of court so that she could not marry until she was eighteen.*

'warder *nc* a person who guards prisoners in a jail: *He shot a warder and escaped from jail.*

warden ['wo:dn] *nc* **1** the person in charge of an old people's home, a student residence *etc*: *The warden has reported that two students are missing from the hostel.* **2** (*also* **'traffic warden**) a person who controls parking and the flow of traffic in an area: *If the warden finds your car parked there you will be fined*; *That's not a policeman directing traffic – that's a traffic warden.* **3** a person who has been appointed to look after the civil population in case of *eg* air raids (an **'air-raid warden**). **4** (*also* **'game warden**) a person who guards a game reserve.

warder *see* **ward**.

wardrobe ['wo:droub] *nc* **1** a cupboard in which clothes may be hung: *Hang your suit in the wardrobe.* **2** (*usu in sing*) a stock of clothing: *She bought a complete new wardrobe in Paris.*

-ward(s) [wəd(z)] (*in cmpds*) in a (certain) direction, as in **backward(s), homeward(s)**.

-ware [weə] (*in cmpds*) manufactured articles (made of a particular material): *silverware/glassware.*

wares *n pl* (*esp old*) articles for sale: *a tradesman peddling his wares.*

warehouse *nc* a building in which goods are stored: *a furniture warehouse.*

warfare, warhead, warhorse, warlike, warlord *see* **war**.

warm [wo:m] *adj* **1** moderately hot: *Are you warm enough, or shall I close the window?*; *Open a window – I'm too warm!*; *warm sunshine*; *a warm summer's day.* **2** (of clothes) keeping the wearer moderately hot: *a warm jumper*; *This coat is not* *very warm.* **3** (*often attrib*) welcoming, friendly, enthusiastic *etc*: *We received a warm welcome*; *She gave them a warm smile*; *a warm reception.* **4** (*usu attrib*) tending to make one fairly hot: *This is warm work!* **5** (of a scent or trail) fresh: *If the trail is still warm the hounds might catch the fox*; (*fig*) *The policeman might still catch the murderer – the trail is still warm.* **6** (of colours, *esp* the pale ones) enriched by a certain quantity of red or pink, or (of red *etc*) rich and bright: *a warm red*; *I don't want white walls – I want something warmer.* **7** (*pred*) (in guessing-games *etc*) close to finding the answer, hiding-place *etc*: *You are getting warm.* – **1** *vt* to make moderately hot: *He warmed his hands in front of the fire*; *Warm the plates before you serve the food.* **2** *vi* (*formal*: *with* **to**) to become friendly (towards) or enthusiastic (about): *She warmed to his charm*; *The audience warmed to the talented comedian.* – *See also* **warm up** *below.* – *nc* (*inf*: *no pl*) an act of warming: *Give your hands a warm in front of the fire.*

'**warmly** *adv*: *The sun was shining warmly*; *Dress warmly – it's cold outside*; *She thanked him warmly*; *He congratulated her warmly.*

warmness *nu.*

'**warmth** [-θ] *nu* the state of being warm: *the warmth of the fire*; *the warmth of the sun*; *Food and warmth are the refugees' most urgent needs*; *There is little warmth in this thin coat*; *The soloist was delighted by the warmth of the applause*; *The warmth of her smile made me feel welcome.*

ˌ**warm-'blooded** *adj* **1** (*tech*) having a blood temperature greater than that of the surrounding atmosphere: *warm-blooded animals such as man.* **2** (*liter or facet*) enthusiastic; passionate: *When I was young and warm-blooded, I was passionate about many things that don't interest me now.*

warm front *see* **front** (*def 5*).

ˌ**warm'hearted** *adj* kind and affectionate: *a warmhearted old lady*; *a warmhearted action*; *She is generous and warmhearted.* ˌ**warm'hearted-ness** *nu.*

warm up *vi, vt sep* to make or become moderately warm: *Your feet will soon warm up once you get indoors*; *The room will soon warm up*; *Have a cup of coffee to warm you up.*

warmonger *see* **war**.

warn [wo:n] **1** *vti* to tell (a person) in advance (about a danger *etc*): *The radio warned of severe snowfalls ahead*; *Black clouds warned us of the approaching storm*; *They warned her that she would be ill if she didn't diet*; *I did warn you (about this)!* **2** *vt* to advise (someone against doing something): *I was warned about/against speeding by the policeman*; *They warned him not to be late.*

'**warning** **1** *nc* an event, or something said or done, that warns: *He gave her a warning against driving too fast*; *She ignored the policeman's warning*; *The headmaster let the boy off with a warning, telling him he would be punished if he did such a thing again*; *His heart attack will be a warning to him not to work so hard.* **2** *nu* advance notice or advance signs: *Did she give you (any) warning of her move to England?*; *He had little or no warning of the car's approach*; *The firm's collapse came without warning.* – *adj* (*attrib*) giving a warning: *She received a warning message.*

'**warningly** *adv*: *She looked warningly at the naughty boy.*

warp[1] [wo:p] **1** *vti* to make or become twisted out of shape: *The door has been warped by all the rain we've had lately*; *This book has been lying in the sun and the cover has warped*; (*fig formal*) *The whole story was warped by the newspapers.* **2** *vt* to cause to think or act in an abnormal way: *His experiences had warped his judgement/mind.* – *nc* (*no pl*) the shape into which something is twisted by warping: *The rain has given this wood a permanent warp.*

warped *adj*: *warped wood*; *This plank is warped*; *a warped mind.*

warp[2] [wo:p] *nc* (*usu with* **the**) one of the two sets of threads crossing each other at right angles in a loom during weaving (the other being the **weft** [weft] or **woof** [wu:f, (*Amer usu*) wuf]).

warpaint *see* **war**.

warrant ['worənt] *vt* **1** (*formal*) to justify: *A slight cold does not warrant your staying off work.* **2** (*old*) to state confidently or (be willing to) bet that: *I'll warrant he's gone riding instead of doing his work.* – *nc* something that gives authority, *esp* a legal document giving the police the authority for searching someone's premises, arresting someone *etc*: *The police have a search warrant – they're going to search his house for the jewels*; *a warrant for someone's arrest.*

'**warrantable** *adj* (*usu pred*: *neg* **un-**: *formal*) justifiable: *Do you consider his interference warrantable?* '**warrantably** *adv.*

warren ['worən] *nc* **1** (*also* '**rabbit-warren**) a place where many rabbits have their burrows: *The rabbit escaped from the dog by running back to its warren*; (*fig derog*) *That block of flats is a real warren* (= a building or area where many people live close together). **2** (*fig*) a maze or network (of passages *etc*): *The lower floors of this building are a warren of corridors.*

warrior, warship *see* **war**.

wart [wo:t] *nc* a small hard growth on the skin: *He has warts on his fingers.*

warts and all including all the faults, disadvantages or unattractive parts: *They've adopted our system of government, warts and all*; *When you marry someone you must accept him warts and all.*

wartime *see* **war**.

wary ['weəri] *adj* (*formal*: *often with* **of**) cautious or on one's guard (about or concerning): *a wary animal*; *Be wary of lending money to him*; *She's very wary of upsetting him, as he has a violent temper.* '**warily** *adv.* '**wariness** *nu.*

See also **unwary**.

was *see* **be**.

wash [woʃ] **1** *vti* to clean (a thing or person, *esp* oneself) with (soap and) water or other liquid: *Many people wash their cars on Sundays*; *How often do you wash your hair?*; *She sent the child to wash his face and hands before tea*; *You wash (the dishes) and I'll dry*; *This soap powder washes whiter!*; *We can wash* (= wash ourselves) *in the stream near the campsite*; *Do you think he ever washes (himself)?* **2** *vi* to be able to be washed without being damaged: *This jumper doesn't wash very well.* **3** *vi* to become clean after having been washed: *These sheets are still dirty – they haven't washed very well.* **4** *vti* to flow (against, over *etc*): *The waves washed (against) the ship with a gentle rhythm.* **5** *vt* (*with* **away, along** *etc*) to sweep (away *etc*) by means of water: *The floods have washed away hundreds of houses.* **6** *vi* (*inf*: *esp in neg*) to be accepted or bear examination: *Your statement just won't wash (with the committee), because what you say is obviously untrue.* – *See also*

wash out, wash up *below.* – **1** *nc* (*no pl*) an act of washing: *He's just gone to have a wash*; *Could you give the paintwork a wash?* **2** *nc* (*usu in sing*) things to be washed or being washed: *She's doing a huge wash*; *Your sweater is in the wash*; *I must do a wash today, as I have no clean clothes left.* **3** *nu* (*with* **the**) the flowing or lapping (of waves *etc*): *the wash of waves against the rocks.* **4** *nc* (*often in cmpds*) a liquid with which something is washed: *a mouth-wash.* **5** *nc* a thin coat (of water-colour paint *etc*), *esp* in a painting: *The background of the picture was a pale blue wash.* **6** *nc* (*no pl*) the waves caused by a moving boat *etc*: *The rowing boat was tossing about in the wash from the ship('s propellers).*

'washable *adj* able to be washed without being damaged: *Is this dress washable?*; *a washable material.*

'washer *nc* **1** (*sometimes in cmpds*) a person or thing (*eg* a machine) that washes: *They've just bought an automatic dish-washer.* **2** a flat ring of rubber, metal *etc* to keep nuts or joints tight: *Our tap needs a new washer.*

'washing 1 *ncu* (an) act of cleaning by water: *Are you going to do a washing today?*; *I don't mind washing, but I hate ironing*; (*attrib*) *The washing facilities at the campsite were rather primitive.* **2** *nu* clothes washed or to be washed: *Put your dirty shirt in with the washing*; *I'll hang the washing out to dry.*

'washcloth *nc* a cloth used for washing (*Amer esp* oneself): *I need a new washcloth for the kitchen floor*; *I have forgotten to pack my washcloth and soap.*

'wash-day *see* **washing-day** *below.*

,washed-'out *adj* **1** (*inf*: *usu pred*) completely lacking in energy *etc*: *I feel washed-out today.* **2** (of garments *etc*) pale, having lost colour as a result of washing: *She wore a pair of old, washed-out jeans.*

,washed-'up *adj* (*inf*: *pred*) defeated, finished, failed *etc*: *You're all washed-up in advertising, so find yourself another job!* – *See also* **wash up** *below.*

'washerwoman *nc* (*esp old*) a woman who is paid to wash clothes.

,washhand 'basin *nc* a basin in which to wash one's face and hands: *We are having a new washhand basin installed in the bathroom.*

'wash-house *nc* (*esp old*) a public or communal building in which clothes may be washed.

'washing-day, wash-day *nc* a (regular) day on which clothes are washed: *Monday is her washing-day*; *I hate wash-day(s).*

'washing-machine *nc* an electric machine for washing clothes: *She has an automatic washing-machine.*

'washing-powder *nu* a powdered detergent used when washing clothes.

washing soda *nu* crystals formed with sodium, used for washing; sodium carbonate.

,washing-'up *nu* (*Brit inf*) dishes *etc* cleaned or to be cleaned after a meal *etc*: *I'll help you with the washing-up*; (*attrib*) *washing-up liquid* (= a liquid detergent used when washing dishes *etc*); (*attrib*) *a washing-up bowl.*

'washout *nc* (*inf*) (an idea, project, person *etc* which is) a complete failure: *Today's outing has been a washout*; *She was a complete washout as a secretary.* – *See also* **washed-out** *above and* **wash out** *below.*

'washroom *nc* (*Amer*) a lavatory or toilet.

'washstand *nc* (*esp old*) a piece of furniture on which are placed a jug, basin *etc* for washing oneself.

come out in the wash 1 to work out satisfactorily in the end: *Never mind, these problems will all come out in the wash.* **2** (of a stain, colour *etc*) to be removed by washing: *Will that dirty mark come out in the wash?*

in the wash *see* **wash** (*n def 2*) *and* **come out in the wash** *above.*

wash one's hands of *see* **hand**.

wash out *vt sep* to ruin, prevent *etc, esp* by rain: *Heavy rain washed out twenty football matches today in southern England.* – *See also* **washed-out** *and* **washout** *above.*

wash up 1 *vi, vt sep* (*Brit*) to wash dishes *etc* after a meal: *I'll help you wash up*; *We've washed the plates up.* **2** *vi* (*Amer*) to wash one's hands and face. **3** *vt sep* (*often in passive*) to bring up on to the shore: *The ship was washed up on the rocks*; *A lot of rubbish has been washed up on the beach.* – *See also* **washed-up** *above.*

wasn't *see* **be**.

wasp [wosp] *nc* a type of winged insect having a sting and a slender waist.

'waspish *adj* (*formal derog*) (of a person) unpleasant in manner, temper *etc*: *a nasty, waspish young woman*; *She is spiteful and waspish.* **'waspishly** *adv.* **'waspishness** *nu.*

waste [weist] *vt* to fail to use (something) fully or in the correct or most useful way: *The amount of food which he wastes is very small*; *You're wasting my time with all these stupid questions*; *I'm not wasting my energy walking home – I'm going to go by bus.* – *See also* **waste away** *below.* – **1** *nu* material which is or has been made useless: *The waste from this process is collected and thrown away*; *industrial waste from the factories*; *Where do you put your kitchen waste?*; (*attrib*) *waste material*; (*attrib*) *a waste bin* (= a container for waste). **2** *ncu* (*no pl*) (the) act of wasting: *The waste of time and money is incredible!*; *That was a waste of an opportunity.* **3** *nc* (*formal or liter*: *often in pl*) a huge stretch of unused or infertile land, or of water, desert, ice *etc*: *the Arctic wastes.*

'wastage [-tidʒ] *nu* loss by wasting; the amount wasted: *They're reducing the total number of jobs by not replacing those people who leave, and calling it 'natural wastage'*; *When you are putting wallpaper on a room you must allow for wastage*; *Of the total amount, roughly 20% was wastage.*

'wasteful *adj* involving or causing waste: *This process is rather wasteful*; *Throwing away that bread is wasteful.* **'wastefully** *adv.* **'wastefulness** *nu.*

'waster (*inf*), **wastrel** (*liter*) *ncs* a person who wastes (*esp* money).

waste land *nu* unoccupied, unused land within the area of a town *etc*: *He is going to build houses on that piece of waste land by the railway.*

'wasteland *nc* (*formal or liter*) an area of empty, desolate and barren land.

waste paper *nu* paper which is thrown away as not being useful: *People keep dropping waste paper and so the streets are full of litter*; *Offices usually have a great deal of waste paper.*

wastepaper basket ['weispeipə] *nc* a basket or other (small) container for waste paper: *Put those old letters in the wastepaper basket.*

waste pipe ['weispaip] *nc* a pipe to carry off waste material, or water from a sink *etc*: *The kitchen waste pipe is blocked.*

go/run to waste to (be allowed to) be wasted: *All this good land is going to waste simply because there's nobody to farm it.*

lay waste (*formal or liter*) to destroy or ruin (a town, country *etc*) by force: *The invaders laid waste a huge area of excellent farmland.*

waste away *vi* to decay; to lose weight, strength and health *etc*: *He is wasting away because he has a terrible disease.*

watch [wotʃ] **1** *nc* (*sometimes in cmpds*) a small instrument for telling the time by, worn on the wrist or carried in the pocket of a waistcoat *etc*: *He wears a gold watch*; *a wrist-watch.* **2** *nc* a period of standing guard during the night: *I'll take the watch from two o'clock till six.* **3** *nc* (*formal or old*) a person who stands guard during the night: *The watch has reported lights moving to the south-east.* **4** *nc or n pl* in the navy *etc*, a group of officers and men who are on duty at a given time: *The night watch come(s) on duty soon.* – **1** *vti* to look at (someone or something): *Watch what I do, and copy it*; *He was watching her carefully*; *'Did you see what he did?' 'No, I wasn't watching'*; *Would you like to watch the tennis match?*; *He is watching television.* **2** *vi* (*with* **for**) to keep a lookout (for): *They've gone to watch for the ship coming in*; *Could you watch for the postman?* **3** *vti* to be careful of (someone or something): *Watch (that) you don't fall off!*; *Watch him! He's dangerous*; *Watch! That tree is going to fall on top of you!* **4** *vt* to guard or take care of: *Watch the prisoner and make sure he doesn't escape*; *Please watch the baby while I go shopping.* **5** *vt* to wait for (a chance, opportunity *etc*): *Watch your chance, and then run.* – *See also* **watch** *in phrases below.* **ˈwatcher** *nc.*

ˈwatchful *adj* (*formal*) alert and cautious; *watchful eyes*; *If you are watchful you will not be robbed.* **ˈwatchfully** *adv.* **ˈwatchfulness** *nu.*

ˈwatchdog *nc* a dog which guards someone's property *etc*: *We leave a watchdog in our office at night to scare away thieves.*

ˈwatchmaker *nc* a person who makes and repairs watches, clocks *etc.*

ˈwatchman *nc* (*often* **night watchman**) a man employed to guard a building *etc* against thieves, *esp* at night: *The bank-robbers shot the (night) watchman.*

ˈwatchnight service *nc* a religious service which ends just after midnight, *usu* held on Christmas Eve or New Year's Eve.

ˈwatchtower *nc* (*esp hist*) a tower on which a lookout is posted.

ˈwatchword *nc* (*liter or formal*) a motto or slogan used by members of a group of people who think (or act) alike: *Let freedom be our watchword!*

be on the watch for to stay alert in order to notice; to look out for: *The staff are always on the watch for shoplifters.*

keep a watch on to continue to observe (someone or something) closely: *The police are keeping a watch on his movements.*

keep watch to be on guard: *He kept watch while the other soldiers slept.*

keep (a) watch over to observe continuously: *The mother kept watch over the sick child all night.* – *See also* **watch over** *below.*

ˈwatch it! (*inf*) be careful!: *Watch it! Next time you do that you'll be sacked!*

watch one's step (*usu inf fig*) to be careful what one does or says: *He's in a foul mood, so watch your step and don't say anything wrong!*

watch out *vi* (*often with* **for**) to be careful (of): *Watch out (for the cars)!*; *Watch out! The police are coming!*

ˈwatch over *vt fus* (*formal*) to guard or take care of: *The mother bird is watching over her young.* – *See also* **keep (a) watch over** *above.*

water [ˈwoːtə] *nu* a colourless, transparent liquid compound of hydrogen and oxygen (H_2O), having no taste or smell, which turns to steam when boiled and to ice when frozen: *She drank two glasses of water*; *'Are you going swimming in the sea?' 'No, the water's too cold'*; *The boat is leaking – it's full of water*; *Each bedroom in the hotel is supplied with hot and cold running water* (= a washbasin with hot and cold taps); (*attrib*) *The plumber had to turn off the water supply in order to repair the pipe*; *The goods were transported by water* (= by boat). – **1** *vt* to supply with water: *He watered the plants*; *Would you water the horses?* **2** *vi* (*often inf*) (of the mouth) to produce saliva: *His mouth watered at the sight of all the food*; (*fig*) *This latest scandal will make their mouths water!* **3** *vi* (of the eyes) to fill with tears: *The dense smoke made his eyes water*; *My eyes are watering because of that cold wind.*

ˈwaters *n pl* **1** (*liter*) a body of water such as the sea, a river *etc*: *He crossed the stormy waters in this wooden boat.* **2** the water, containing minerals, found at a spa and thought to be health-giving: *People used to go to Harrogate to take the waters.*

ˈwatery *adj* **1** (*often derog*) like water: *a watery fluid*; (*derog*) *This soup is watery.* **2** (of eyes) full of water or fluid: *The baby had watery eyes when he had measles*; *His eyes are watery – has he got a cold?*; (*liter*) *He had a watery grave* (= He drowned). **3** (*usu derog*) (of a colour) pale: *a sky of watery blue.* **ˈwateriness** *nu.*

ˈwater-bed *nc* a bed whose mattress is a water-filled bag.

ˈwater-bottle *nc* a bottle for containing water: *The mountaineer took a drink from his water-bottle.*

ˈwaterborne *adj* (*esp attrib*) carried or transmitted by water: *waterborne traffic*; *Typhoid is a waterborne disease.*

ˈwater butt *nc* a large barrel for rainwater.

ˈwater-closet *nc* (*formal*: *usu abbrev* **WC** [dʌbljuˈsiː] when written or spoken) a lavatory.

ˈwater-colour *nc* **1** a type of paint which is thinned down with water instead of with oil. **2** a painting made using this type of paint: *Turner painted many famous water-colours.*

ˈwatercress *nu* a herb related to mustard, which grows in water and is often used in salads.

ˈwaterfall *nc* a natural fall of water from a height such as a rock or a cliff: *There are several beautiful waterfalls in those mountains.*

ˈwaterfowl *ncu or n pl* a bird or birds which live on or beside water.

ˈwaterfront *nu* land at the edge of the sea *etc*, *esp* that part of a town which faces the sea or a lake: *He lives on the waterfront.*

ˈwaterhole *nc* a spring or other place where water can be found in a desert or other dry country: *They watched the elephant drinking from the waterhole.*

ˈwatering-can *nc* a container used when watering plants: *She keeps a watering-can for watering her indoor plants.*

ˈwater level *nc* the level of the surface of a mass of water: *The water level in the reservoir is sinking/rising.*

'waterlogged *adj* (of ground) soaked in water: *I cannot dig this garden – it is waterlogged; waterlogged fields.*

'water main *nc* a large underground pipe carrying a public water supply: *Traffic had to be diverted from the High Street because of a burst water main.*

'watermark *nc* **1** the limit to which water normally rises at high tide or falls at low tide: *the high/low watermark.* **2** (*tech*) a mark in paper to show its size or its manufacturer: *You can see the watermark in the paper if you hold it against the light.* **3** (*tech*) a mark in the paper of a stamp, bank-note *etc* to prevent forgery: *The bank-clerk realized that the pound notes were forged – they had no watermark.*

'water-melon 1 *nc* one of the two types of melon, having green skin and red flesh. **2** *nu* its flesh used as food.

'watermill *nc* a mill driven by water.

'water-pistol *nc* a toy pistol which fires a stream of water.

'waterproof *adj* not allowing water to soak through: *waterproof material; Is that coat waterproof?* – *nc* a coat made of waterproof material: *She was wearing a waterproof.* – *vt* to make (something) proof against water: *He tried to waterproof his jacket.*

'watershed *nc* **1** an area of high land from which rivers flow in different directions into different basins. **2** (*formal*) a point at which one phase stops and another begins, or at which events take a different turn *etc*: *We have reached a watershed in our economic progress.*

'water-skiing *nu* the sport of skiing on water, *usu* towed by a motor-boat. **'water-ski** *vi.*

'watertight *adj* **1** (having joints *etc*) made in such a way that water cannot pass through. **2** (*formal*) without a flaw; that cannot be found fault with or misunderstood: *a watertight excuse; His alibi is watertight.*

'waterway *nc* a channel, *eg* a canal or river, along which ships can sail: *inland waterways.*

'waterwheel *nc* a wheel moved by water to work machinery *etc.*

'water-wings *n pl* an inflated device for keeping a person afloat in water, *esp* when learning to swim: *The child wore a pair of water-wings.*

'waterworks 1 *n pl or n sing* a place in which water is purified and stored before distribution to an area. **2** *n pl* (*inf*) tears: *Turn off the waterworks, will you!*

be in, get into hot water *see* **hot.**

high, low water *see* **high, low.**

hold water (*formal*) to be correct or accurate and bear examination: *His explanation doesn't hold water.*

in(to) deep water in(to) trouble or danger: *I got into deep water during that argument.*

keep one's head above water *see* **head.**

like 'water (*inf*) very freely or in great quantities: *He spent money like water.*

pass water (*very formal euph*) to urinate.

throw cold water on *see* **cold.**

water down *vt sep* to dilute: *This milk has been watered down;* (*fig*) *He watered down his comments so that they became less offensive; He watered them down.*

watt [wot] *nc* (*often abbrev* **W** *when written*) a unit of power, *esp* of heat or light: *a two-kilowatt fire; a forty-watt light bulb.*

'wattage [-tidʒ] *nu* (*tech*) power in watts: *What is the wattage of the bulb in the living-room?*

wave [weiv] *nc* **1** a moving ridge, larger than a ripple, moving on the surface of water: *The waves were beating on the shore;* (*fig*) *a wave of depression.* **2** a vibration travelling *eg* through the air: *radio waves; sound waves; light waves.* **3** a curve or curves in the hair: *She can't get her hair to keep a wave; Are those waves natural?* **4** a (*usu* temporary) rise or increase (of *eg* emotion, pain, crime, prosperity): *The police cannot cope with the recent crime wave; a wave of violence; Waves of nausea kept passing over her; The pain came in waves.* **5** an act of waving (*defs 3, 4*): *She recognized me, and gave me a cheerful little wave; The queen acknowledged the waves from the children.* – **1** *vti* to (cause to) move backwards and forwards or flutter: *The flags waved gently in the breeze.* **2** *vti* (*esp* of hair) to (cause to) curve first one way then the other: *She's had her hair waved; Her hair waves naturally.* **3** *vti* to make a gesture (of greeting *etc*) with (*eg* the hand): *She waved to me across the street; Everyone was waving handkerchiefs in farewell.* **4** *vt* to express (something) in this way: *They waved goodbye/a farewell.*

'wavy *adj* (*esp* of hair) full of waves: *She has wavy hair; Her hair is wavy but her sister's hair is straight.* **'waviness** *nu.*

'wave(band) *nc* a range of wavelengths on which *eg* radio signals are broadcast: *the medium/long/short wave(band);* (*attrib*) *a medium-wave radio.*

'wavelength *nc* the distance from any given point on one (radio *etc*) wave to the corresponding point on the next.

on the (same) wavelength (as) to have the same attitude of mind, opinions, sympathies *etc* as someone: *She and her mother are not on the same wavelength; I can't understand her – I'm just not on her wavelength.*

wave aside *vt sep* to dismiss (a suggestion *etc*) without paying much attention to it: *'Of course it won't rain!' she said, waving my objection aside.*

waver ['weivə] *vi* to be unsteady or uncertain as to which direction to take, *esp* when deciding something: *He always wavers instead of making a decision immediately; He wavered between accepting and refusing.*

wax[1] [waks] *nu* **1** the sticky, fatty substance of which bees make their cells; beeswax. **2** the sticky, yellowish substance formed in the ears. **3** a manufactured, fatty substance used in polishing, to give a good shine: *Use wax to polish the table;* (*attrib*) *wax polish.* **4** (*also* **'candle-wax**) a similar substance made from paraffin, used in making candles, models *etc*, that melts when heated: *Candles are made by pouring melted wax into a mould; How will I remove this red candle-wax from the table?;* (*attrib*) *a wax taper;* (*attrib*) *a wax model.* **5** sealing-wax. – *vt* to smear, polish or rub with wax (*def 3*).

'waxen (*formal or liter*), **'waxy** *adjs.*

'waxwork *nc* a wax model (*usu* of a well-known person).

'waxworks 1 *n pl* an exhibition of figures (*usu* of well-known people) made of wax: *We took the children to the waxworks.* **2** *n sing* a building housing such an exhibition.

wax[2] [waks] *vi* **1** (of the moon) to appear to grow in size as more of it becomes visible. **2** (*formal or facet*) (of someone's or something's importance, power *etc*) to increase: *As his power waxed the queen's authority waned; They began to wax* (= become) *cheerful after several bottles of wine.* *See also* **wane**.

way [wei] **1** *nc* an opening or passageway: *This is the way in/out; There's no way through.* **2** *nc* (*often in cmpds*) a route, direction *etc*: *Which is the way to Princes Street?; Which way do we go for Manchester?; His new house is on the way between Glasgow and Edinburgh; Will you be able to find your/the way to my house?; I don't mind calling at your house – it's on my way* (= it is on the route that I am taking); *The errand took me out of my way* (⇒ away from my route); *a motorway; a railway.* **3** *n* (*with cap*) a word used in the names of certain roads or streets: *His address is 21 Melville Way; He lives in Melville Way.* **4** *nc* (*no pl*) a distance: *It's a very long way from here to Australia; The nearest shops are only a short way away.* **5** *nc* a method or manner: *There are many ways of writing a book; What is the easiest way to write a book?; I know a good way of doing it; She answered in a very polite way; He's got a funny way of talking; This is the quickest way to chop onions; Do it the way you were taught.* **6** *nc* an aspect or side of something: *In some ways this job is quite difficult – in other ways it's simple; There are many ways in which this book will prove useful; In a way* (= From a certain point of view) *I think she has made a mistake.* **7** *nc* a characteristic of behaviour; a habit: *He has some rather unpleasant ways; He has a way of suggesting that he's the only one who does any work.* **8** *nc* (*usu in sing*) used with many verbs to give the idea of progressing or moving: *He pushed his way through the crowd; I managed to limp my way back home; The path wound its way across the hill; They soon ate their way through the food.* – *See also* **make one's way** *below.* – *adv* (*inf*: *esp Amer*) by a long distance or time; far: *The winner finished the race way ahead of the other competitors; Hurry up and get undressed, kids – it's way past your bedtime.*

out-of-the-way *see* **out**.

right-of-way *see* **right**.

'wayfarer *nc* (*old or liter*) a traveller, *esp* on foot.

,way-'out (*slightly old sl*) unusual, *esp* in being very modern: *way-out clothes; That music is too way-out for me.*

'wayside *nc* (*formal or old with* **the**) the side of a road, path *etc*: *We can stop by the wayside somewhere and have a picnic;* (*attrib*: *esp old*) *a wayside inn;* (*fig*) *Those firms which have not progressed to using computers have fallen by the wayside* (= have failed).

be/get on one's way to start or continue a walk, journey *etc*: *Well, thanks for the cup of tea, but I must be on my way now.* – *See also* **way** (*def 2*).

by the way incidentally, in passing, while I remember *etc*: *By the way, I'm leaving on Thursday; By the way, did you know he was getting married?*

by 'way of (*formal*) **1** by the route passing or through; via: *We went to Edinburgh by way of York.* **2** for, or as if for, the purpose of: *He did it by way of helping me; She said it by way of (an) insult.*

get/have one's own way to do, get *etc* what one wants: *That child always cries if he doesn't get his (own) way; You can't always have your own way.*

get into/out of the way of (doing) something to become accustomed to (not) doing; to get into/out of the habit of doing: *They got into the way of waking up early when they were on holiday; I can't get into the way of this new job; I have got out of the way of working in an office.*

give way *see* **give**.

go a long way to(wards) to help greatly in (achieving something): *These measures go a long way towards solving the problem.*

go out of one's way to do more than is really necessary: *He went out of his way to help us.*

have a way with (someone *etc***)** to be good at dealing with or managing (someone or something): *He has quite a way with the ladies; She has a way with children.*

have a way with one (*formal or facet*) to have an attractive manner: *'He's very charming.' 'Yes, he certainly has a way with him!'*

have everything/it (all) one's own way to get one's own way in everything/something: *He likes to have everything his own way; Oh, have it your own way – I'm tired of arguing.*

have it both ways (*usu with a neg*) to get the benefit from two actions, situations *etc*, each of which excludes the possibility of the other: *'She wants to divorce him, but she doesn't want to lose the importance she gets from being married to him.' 'Well, she can't have it both ways.'*

in a bad way (*inf*) unwell: *The patient is in a bad way;* (*fig*) *The nation's economy is in a bad way.*

in, out of the/someone's way (not) blocking someone's progress, or occupying space that is needed by someone: *We had to stop the car because there was a fallen tree in the/our way; Don't leave your bicycle where it will get in the way of pedestrians; Will I be in the/your way if I work at this table?; 'Get out of my way!' he said rudely; He moved out of the way to let her pass; Please would you move your car out of my way?* – *See also* **out of the way** *under* **out**.

lose one's way to stop knowing where one is, or in which direction one ought to be going: *I lost my way when I was driving through Birmingham; The child lost his way in the woods.*

make one's way 1 (*formal*) to go: *They made their way towards the centre of the town; We made our way up the path; You should make your way to the coast.* **2** to get on in the world: *He has made his own way – his father has not helped him at all.*

make way (for) to stand aside and leave room (for): *The crowd parted to make way for the ambulance; Make way, please!*

no way (*sl*) absolutely not: *'Are you going?' 'No way!'*

out of the way *see* **out** and **in, out of the/someone's way** *above.*

pay one's way to pay one's own expenses; never to owe money.

put (someone) out of the way (*inf*) to get rid of (someone), *esp* by killing or imprisoning him.

under way moving, in progress *etc*: *The ship got under way;* (*fig*) *Her plans are under way.*

way of life a manner of spending one's life: *I enjoy working on a farm – it's a pleasant way of life.*

ways and means methods, *esp* of providing money: *You must use any ways and means you can think of;* (*attrib*) *the government's ways and means committee.*

waylay [wei'lei] – *pt, ptp* **way'laid** – *vt* (*formal*) to ambush (someone): *He was waylaid by a crowd of angry demonstrators;* (*fig inf*) *The kids waylaid me, and wouldn't let me go until I gave them their pocket-money.*

wayward ['weiwəd] *adj* (*formal*) undisciplined,

self-willed or rebellious: *a home for wayward children; He is obstinate and wayward.*

WC *see* **water-closet** *under* **water**.

we [wiː] *pron* (used only as the subject of a verb) the word used by a speaker or writer in mentioning himself or herself together with other people: *We are going home tomorrow.*
See also **our(selves), ours, us**.

weak [wiːk] *adj* **1** lacking in physical strength: *Her illness has made her very weak; She has a weak heart.* **2** not strong in character: *I'm very weak when it comes to giving up cigarettes; He always agrees with everyone – he's too weak to disagree.* **3** (of a liquid) diluted or not strong in solution: *She gave him a cup of weak tea; This coffee is too weak; a weak solution of acid.* **4** (of an argument *etc*) not convincing: *His story sounded weak even to his own ears; He gave rather a weak alibi.* **5** (of a joke) poor or not particularly funny. **6** (of a verb) following the regular pattern of grammatical endings: *'Walk' and 'talk' are weak verbs, but 'go' and 'come' are strong verbs.* **'weakly** *adv.*

'weaken *vti* to (cause to) become weak, *esp* in physical strength or character: *The table weakened under the strain; His strength has weakened; The strain of the last few days has weakened him considerably; I was determined not to let her have the dress but I weakened and gave it to her.*

'weakling [-liŋ] *nc* (*often derog*) a weak person, animal, or plant: *She married a weakling.*

'weakness 1 *nu* the state of being weak: *the weakness of her tired muscles; the weakness of his character.* **2** *nc* something weak or faulty; a defect: *Hardly anyone is without weaknesses of character; Smoking is one of my weaknesses.* – *See also* **have a weakness for** *below.*

ˌweak-'kneed *adj* (*sometimes derog*) (easily) overcome by, or showing, fear: *Don't be so weak-kneed – just tell her you're not going with her; He was weak-kneed with fear; I've had enough of your weak-kneed excuses.*

ˌweak-'minded *adj* **1** having little intelligence: *The murderer was discovered to be weak-minded; He's just a poor, weak-minded old man.* **2** too easily persuaded: *Don't be so weak-minded – don't go if you don't want to; a weak-minded attitude towards the children.* **ˌweak-'mindedness** *nu.*

have a 'weakness for (*inf*) to have a liking for: *She has a weakness for plain chocolate biscuits; He has a weakness for blondes.*

the weaker sex (*old or facet*) women.

weal [wiːl] *nc* a raised mark on the skin caused by *eg* a blow with a whip: *The child had great weals all over her body after her father had beaten her with his belt.*

wealth [welθ] **1** *nu* riches: *He is a man of great wealth; His wealth has not made him happy.* **2** *nc* (*no pl*: *with* **of**) a great quantity (of): *She has a wealth of knowledge about china.*

'wealthy *adj* (*more formal than* **rich**) having much money and/or many possessions; rich: *She is a wealthy young widow; He has inherited a great deal of money and is now very wealthy.*

wean [wiːn] *vt* to cause (a child or young animal) to become used to food other than the mother's milk: *Is she never going to wean that child?; The baby has been weaned on to solid foods;* (*fig*) *We must wean Mary from this bad habit.*

weapon ['wepən] *nc* any instrument or means which is used for one's own defence or for attacking others: *Rifles, arrows, atom bombs and tanks are all weapons; The police are looking for the murder weapon;* (*fig*) *His own obvious honesty is his most powerful weapon against those who indulge in corrupt practices;* (*fig*) *Surprise is our best weapon.*

wear [weə] – *pt* **wore** [woː]: *ptp* **worn** [woːn] – **1** *vt* to be dressed in or carry on (a part of) the body: *She wore a white silk dress; He wore all his medals on Remembrance Sunday; Does she usually wear spectacles?; She wears tights, not stockings; She wore black shoes; Was she wearing earrings?* **2** *vt* to arrange (*esp* one's hair) in a particular way: *She wears her hair in a pony-tail; I don't like the way she wears her hair.* **3** *vt* (*formal*) to have or show (a particular facial expression): *His face wore a look of utter boredom; She wore an angry expression.* **4** *vt* (*inf*: *esp in negative sentences, questions etc*) to accept or approve of (a proposal *etc*): *Suggest it to him and see if he'll wear it; They'll never wear that!* **5** *vi* (*often* **wear thin**) to become thinner *etc* because of use: *This carpet has worn in several places; This sweater is wearing thin at the elbows;* (*fig*) *My patience is wearing thin* (= I shall not be patient for much longer). **6** *vt* to make (a bare patch, a hole *etc*) by rubbing, use *etc*: *I've worn a hole in the elbow of my jacket.* **7** *vi* (*with* **badly, well** *etc*) to stand up to use: *This material doesn't wear very well;* (*fig inf*) *She may be sixty-five, but she's worn well.* – *See also* **wear** *in phrases below.* – *nu* **1** use as clothes *etc*: *I use this suit as everyday wear; Those shoes don't look as though they'll survive much wear.* **2** (*often in cmpds*) articles for use as clothes: *casual wear; sportswear; leisurewear.* **3** (*sometimes* **wear and tear**) damage due to use: *The hall carpet is showing signs of wear.* **4** ability to withstand use: *There's plenty of wear left in it yet.*

'wearable *adj* (*neg* **un-**) fit to be worn: *These shoes are no longer wearable; My only wearable coat is at the cleaners.*

'wearer *nc* a person who is dressed in (clothes): *This is the type of dress that makes the wearer feel and look exceptionally elegant.*

'wearing *adj* exhausting: *I find working in this office extremely wearing; I find my male assistant extremely wearing* (*on the nerves*)*; I've had rather a wearing day.*

worn [woːn] *adj* (*often in cmpds*) **1** having been worn or used: *a scarcely-worn coat.* **2** damaged as a result of use: *a badly-worn carpet.*

worn-out *see* **worn out** *below.*

wear away *vi, vt sep* to make or become damaged due to use: *The steps have been worn away over the years; The stonework has worn away in places.*

wear down *vt sep* (*fig*) to lessen (someone's resistance): *They gradually wore him down, and finally he changed his mind.*

wear off *vi* (of effects *etc*) to become less or improve: *The effect of the anaesthetic began to wear off; His headache wore off; The pain is wearing off.*

wear out *vi, vt sep* to (cause to) become unfit for further use: *My socks have worn out; I've worn out my socks.*

worn out 1 so damaged by use as to be unfit for further use: *These shoes are worn out;* (*attrib*) *a worn-out sweater;* (*fig derog*: *attrib*) *worn-out excuses/phrases.* **2** very tired: *His wife is worn out after looking after the children;* (*attrib*) *a worn-out mother.*

weary ['wiəri] *adj* (*more formal than* **tired**) tired; with strength or patience exhausted: *She gave a weary sigh; He looks weary after today's meeting; I* *am weary of his stupid jokes.* – *vti* (*formal*) to (cause to) become tired or impatient: *They wearied of his constant talking*; *That long walk has wearied me.*

'wearily *adv.* **'weariness** *nu.*

'wearisome *adj* (*formal derog*) causing weariness: *a wearisome journey*; *I find his conversation wearisome.* **'wearisomely** *adv.* **'wearisomeness** *nu.*

weasel ['wi:zl] *nc* a type of small flesh-eating animal with a long slender body: *The rabbit was attacked by a weasel.*

weather ['weðə] *nu* (*often with* **the**) conditions in the atmosphere, *esp* as regards heat or cold, wind, rain, snow *etc*: *What was the weather like yesterday?*; *I think we're going to have stormy weather*; *There's been some rainy weather recently*; (*attrib*) *a weather report*; *the weather forecast.* – **1** *vti* to affect or be affected by exposure to the air, resulting in drying, change of colour, shape *etc*: *The wind and sea have weathered the rocks to a smooth, even surface*; *The rocks have been weathered smooth.* **2** *vt* to survive (something) safely: *The ship weathered the storm although she was badly damaged*; (*fig*) *I think we've weathered moving house reasonably well.*

'weatherbeaten *adj* showing effects of exposure to the weather: *a tanned and weatherbeaten face*; *He looks weatherbeaten after working on the farm.*

'weathercock, 'weathervane *nc* a piece of metal (often in the form of a farmyard cock), placed on top of a building, which turns to show the direction of the wind.

keep a weather eye (open) to remain alert or watchful: *You should keep a weather eye open for signs of difficulties ahead*; *You should keep a weather eye on him – I don't trust him.*

make heavy weather of (something) to find it very (often unnecessarily) difficult to do (something): *He made heavy weather of (climbing) the last few hundred feet of the mountain*; *She's making heavy weather of typing that letter.*

under the weather (*inf*) in poor health; unwell: *I'm feeling a little under the weather this week.*

weave [wi:v] – *pt* **wove** [wouv] (*defs 1, 2*), **weaved** (*def 3*): *ptp* **woven** ['wouvən] (*defs 1, 2*), **weaved** (*def 3*) – **1** *vti* to make (articles) by crossing strands in a pattern, often at right-angles to each other: *The old woman was weaving (tweed) on her loom.* **2** *vt* (*liter*) to construct (a story), *usu* verbally: *He wove a fascinating tale of knights in shining armour.* **3** *vti* to move backwards and forwards or from side to side: *The car weaved in and out of the stream of traffic*; *The boxer weaved about all over the ring*; *The drunk man weaved his way home.*

'weaver *nc* a person who weaves (*def 1*).

get weaving (*inf*) to start working or moving quickly: *We'll have to get weaving if we want to catch that train.*

web [web] *nc* **1** a type of trap for flies *etc* made of fine silk threads, spun by a spider *etc*: *a spider's web*; (*fig formal*) *a web of deceit and trickery.* **2** the skin between the toes of a waterfowl.

webbed *adj* (of ducks' *etc* feet) joined between the toes by a web (*def 2*).

'webbing *nu* a rough woven fabric made from hemp, used in making belts, furniture, upholstery *etc.*

'web-'footed, ˌweb-'toed *adj* having webbed feet.

wed [wed] – *pts, ptps* **'wedded, wed** – *vti* (*liter or facet*) to marry: *Andrew and Sara are due to wed in the spring*; (*fig*) *He's wedded to the business, and won't leave it.*

'wedding *nc* a marriage ceremony: *The wedding will take place on Saturday*; (*attrib*) *Her mother baked the wedding-cake*; (*attrib*) *She often talks of her wedding-day*; (*attrib*) *Is she wearing a wedding-ring?* (= a ring given by the groom to his bride).

we'd *see* **have, would**.

wedge [wedʒ] *nc* **1** a piece of wood or metal, thick at one end and sloping to a thin edge at the other, used in splitting wood *etc* or in fixing something tightly in place: *She used a wedge under the door to prevent it swinging shut.* **2** something similar in shape: *He had a banana and a wedge of cheese for lunch.* – *vti* to fix or become fixed by, or as if by, a wedge or wedges: *His foot wedged in the narrow crack*; *He is so fat that he got wedged in the doorway*; *The salesman wedged his foot in the door as the housewife tried to close it*; (*fig*) *He wedged himself in among the people at the door.*

the thin end of the wedge a small beginning (*usu* of something bad) that will certainly lead to greater (and worse) things: *This demand is only the thin end of the wedge – soon they'll want more and more.*

wedlock ['wedlok] *nu* (*formal or old*) the state of being married.

born out of wedlock (of a child) illegitimate.

Wednesday ['wenzdi] *n* the fourth day of the week, the day following Tuesday: *He will arrive on Wednesday*; *She will come next Wednesday*; *They go on Wednesdays* (= every Wednesday, or only on a Wednesday but not necessarily every Wednesday); (*attrib*) *Wednesday evening.*

wee [wi:] *adj* (*inf or dial*) small or tiny: *a wee house*; *That coat is too wee for her now.*

weed [wi:d] *nc* any wild plant, *esp* when growing among cultivated plants or where it is not wanted: *The garden is full of weeds*; *Look at all those weeds in our rose garden – I must pull them out.* – *vti* to remove weeds (from): *It took me four hours to weed the garden*; *I would not employ anyone just to weed – I really want someone to dig.*

'weedy *adj* (*inf derog*) (*usu* of a person) thin, frail, weak-looking *etc*: *Her son is thin and weedy*; *Her boyfriend is rather a weedy creature.*

'weedkiller *ncu* a chemical *etc* used to kill weeds: *Which weedkiller do you use?*; *How much weedkiller should I apply?*

weed out *vt sep* (*inf*) to remove (things which are unwanted) from a group or collection: *We'll weed out all the unsuitable candidates and then interview the rest.*

week [wi:k] *nc* **1** any sequence of seven days, *esp* from Sunday to Saturday inclusive: *Wednesday is in the middle of the week*: *It's been (three) weeks since I last saw her*; *a three-week delay.* **2** the five days from Monday to Friday inclusive: *He can't go during the week, but he'll go on Saturday or Sunday*; *It takes three working weeks to finish each copy*; *You can fly from Edinburgh to Copenhagen during the week, but not at the weekend.* **3** the amount of time spent working during any given period of seven days: *He works a six-day, forty-eight-hour week.*

'weekly *adj* (*attrib*) happening, published *etc* once a week: *a weekly magazine.* – *adv* once a week: *The newspaper is published weekly.* – *nc* a publication coming out once a week: *Is this newspaper a weekly or a daily?*

'weekday *nc* any day except a Saturday or Sunday: *Our office is only open on weekdays*; (*attrib*) *weekday flights from Glasgow to Stockholm.*

,week'end *nc* the period from the end of one normal working week until the beginning of the next (*ie* Saturday and Sunday, or Friday evening to Sunday evening): *We spent a lovely weekend in Edinburgh*; (*attrib*) *a weekend trip/ticket.* – *vi* (*rare*) to spend a weekend: *We weekended in London.*

this week *see* **this**.

today, Friday *etc* **week** (*inf*) a week from today, Friday *etc*: *I am going on holiday today week.*

a week last Friday *etc* the Friday *etc* before last: *She died a week last Tuesday.*

a week today, tomorrow, (on/next) Friday *etc* a week from today, tomorrow, Friday *etc*: *I'm going away a week tomorrow*; *Could we meet a week (on/next) Monday?*

week in, week out *see* **day in, day out** *under* **in**.

weep [wi:p] – *pt, ptp* **wept** [wept] – *vti* (*formal or liter*) to shed (tears): *She wept when she heard the terrible news*; *They wept tears of happiness*; *The child wept with disappointment.*

weeping willow *see* **willow**.

weft *see* **warp**[2].

weigh [wei] **1** *vt* to find the heaviness of (something) by balancing it on a scale with something of equal heaviness: *He weighed himself on the bathroom scales*; *You must have your luggage weighed at the airport.* **2** *vt* to be equal to in heaviness: *This parcel weighs one kilo*; *How much/What does this box weigh?* **3** *vti* (*often liter or formal*: *often with* **down**) to be a heavy burden to: *She was weighed down with two large suitcases*; *The burden of his responsibility weighs heavily on his shoulders*; *You'd think that every care in the world was weighing him down!* **4** *vt* to judge or consider (arguments *etc*): *The lawyer weighed all the arguments for and against his client's case*; *You must weigh all the advantages of resigning against all the disadvantages.* **5** *vi* (*formal*) to be considered of importance: *The witness's statement weighed heavily in his favour, and he was declared not guilty.*

weight [weit] **1** *nu* the amount which a person or thing weighs: *Her weight has been steady at fifty kilos for the last ten years*; *He's put on a lot of weight* (= got a lot heavier) *over the years*; *Is she losing weight – she looks a lot thinner?* **2** *nc* a piece of metal *etc* of a standard weight: *a seven-pound weight.* **3** *nc* (*no pl*) burden; load: *The supports of that bridge have to bear a great weight*; (*fig*) *She looks very tired under the weight of all that responsibility*; (*fig*) *You have taken a weight off my mind.* **4** *nu* (*formal*) importance: *Her opinion carries a lot of weight*; *How much weight will be attached to his decision?* – *vt* **1** to attach, or add, a weight or weights to: *The plane is weighted at the nose so that it balances correctly in flight.* **2** (*often with* **down**) to hold down by attaching weights: *They weighted (down) the balloon to prevent it from flying away*; (*fig*) *She was weighted down by two huge shopping-baskets.* – *adj* (*pred*) of heaviness: *ten pounds weight* (= rather than pounds sterling).

'weighting *nc* an amount added to one's salary to allow for the high cost of living in a given area: *London weighting.*

'weightless *adj* (*tech esp pred*) not affected by the earth's gravity pull: *The astronauts became weightless after passing out of the earth's atmosphere.* **'weightlessness** *nu.*

'weighty *adj* **1** (*formal*) important: *a weighty argument in favour of staying at home.* **2** (*formal or facet*) heavy: *a weighty box*; (*facet*) *a weighty gentleman.* **'weightily** *adv.* **'weightiness** *nu.*

'weighbridge *nc* a machine for weighing vehicles with their loads.

'weigh-in *nc* the act of weighing in before a fight, after a race *etc*: *At the weigh-in the British boxer was found to be too heavy.* – *See also* **weigh in** *below.*

'weighing-machine *nc* a (public) machine for weighing people, loads *etc*: *I weighed myself on the weighing-machine at the railway station.*

pull one's weight *see* **pull**.

throw one's weight about *see* **throw**.

weigh anchor to lift a ship's anchor in preparation for sailing.

weigh down *see* **weigh** (*def 3*).

weigh in *vi* **1** to find one's weight before a fight, after a horse-race *etc.* **2** (*often with* **with**) to join in a discussion, project with enthusiasm: *She weighed in with a long list of complaints*; *Mr Smith has weighed in with an offer of help.* – *See also* **weigh-in** *above.*

weigh out *vt sep* to measure out by weighing: *He weighed out six kilos of sand into one-kilo bags.*

weigh up *vt sep* to calculate or assess a probability *etc*: *He weighed up his chances of success*; *She weighed the situation up and decided she could win easily*; *She's good at weighing up people.*

weir [wiə] *nc* a dam across a river, with a (*usu* small) drop on one side.

weird [wiəd] *adj* **1** unnatural or uncanny: *The old woman told weird stories*; *They heard a weird scream in the old house.* **2** (*inf*) odd or very strange: *She looks weird in those bright clothes*; *She wears weird clothes*; *He has a weird way of looking at people.* **'weirdly** *adv.* **'weirdness** *nu.*

welcome ['welkəm] *adj* greeted with, causing *etc* gladness and happiness: *She will make you very welcome* (= be glad to see you and treat you with hospitality); *He is a welcome visitor at our house*; *A rise in salary will be very welcome*; *The holiday made a welcome change for us all.* – *See also* **be welcome to** *below.* – *nc* a greeting: *They gave us a very friendly welcome*; *We received a very warm welcome.* – *vt* to receive or greet with pleasure and gladness: *We were warmly welcomed by our hosts*; *She will welcome the chance to see you again.* – *interj* used to express gladness at someone's arrival: *Welcome to Britain!*

'welcoming *adj* giving a welcome: *She gave us a welcoming smile.* **'welcomingly** *adv.*

be 'welcome to to be gladly given permission to (have, do or accept something): *You're welcome to stay as long as you wish*; (*ironic*) *You're welcome to marry him – I don't want him.*

you're 'welcome! (*esp Amer*) that's quite all right, no thanks are necessary: *'Thanks so much for all your help!' 'You're welcome!'*

weld [weld] *vti* to join (together) (pieces of metal) by pressure and often using heat, electricity *etc*: *The metal plates were welded together to make a strong joint*; (*formal fig*) *The different sections of the organization were welded together to form a strong whole.* – *nc* a joint made by welding.

'welder *nc* a person who welds: *He is a welder at the local steelworks.*

welfare ['welfeə] *nu* **1** mental and physical health; living conditions: *The Social Services department* *are looking after the child's welfare; the welfare of the army*; (*attrib*) *A welfare worker called at their house to make sure that the children were being looked after properly.* 2 (*inf*) payments made by the government to assist people in need through unemployment *etc*: *He's been living on welfare since he lost his job two months ago*; (*attrib*) *welfare payments.*

welfare state *nc* (*often with caps and* **the**) a country which runs insurance schemes for its inhabitants, supplying them with free medical care, pensions, sickness and unemployment benefit *etc.*

well[1] [wel] *nc* **1** (*usu in cmpds* when not for water) a lined shaft made in the earth so as to obtain water, oil, natural gas *etc*: *They have no indoor water supply – they get their water from a well at the foot of their field*; *He has an oil-well on his land.* **2** any similar walled space, *eg* the space round which a staircase winds, a lift-shaft *etc*: *He fell down the stair-well and broke his neck*; *The house is on fire – smoke is coming up the well of the stair.* – *vi* (*often with* **up** *or* **out**) (of water from the earth or of tears) to flow freely: *The tears welled up, and she began to cry*; *Water welled out from the broken pipe.* *See also* **oil-well**.

well[2] [wel] – *compar* **better** ['betə]: *superl* **best** [best] – **1** *adj* (*less formal than* **healthy**: *usu pred*: *no compar or superl when attrib*) healthy: *He didn't feel very well after the operation*; *I don't feel at all well*; *She doesn't look very well today*; *She's been ill but she's quite well now*; *Well babies are usually happy babies.* **2** (*pred*) in a satisfactory state or condition: *All is well now.* **3** (*pred*: *formal or liter*) fortunate; desirable: *It was well that you saw him coming.* – *adv* **1** in a good, correct, successful, suitable *etc* way: *He did his job extremely well*; *He's done well to become a millionaire at thirty*; *She plays the piano rather well*; *Mother and baby are both doing well* (= they are both healthy); *How well did he do in the exam?* **2** with good reason; with justice: *You may well look ashamed – that was a cruel thing to do*; *You can't very well refuse to go – you have no real excuse.* **3** (*formal*) with approval or praise: *He speaks well of you.* **4** (*inf*) used (*with eg* **damn, jolly, blooming** *etc*) for emphasis: *You can damn well do it yourself, you idiot!* **5** thoroughly: *You must examine that car well before you buy it.* **6** to a great or considerable extent: *He is well over fifty years old.* – *See also* **well** *in phrases below.* – *interj* **1** used to express surprise *etc*: *Well! I'd never have believed it!* **2** used when re-starting a conversation, starting an explanation *etc*: *Do you remember John Watson? Well, he's become a teacher.*

well- (*in cmpds*) **1** in a good, satisfactory *etc* way *etc*, as in **well-behaved, well-groomed**. **2** very much, as in **well-known, well-read**.

ˌ**well-ad'vised** *adj* (*usu pred*) wise: *You would be well-advised to sell now.*

ˌ**well-ap'pointed** *adj* (*formal*: used *esp* by house-agents *etc*) (of a flat, house *etc*) thoroughly equipped: *a well-appointed residence*; *Their new flat is very well-appointed.*

ˌ**well-'balanced** *adj* (*formal*) **1** sane and stable: *a well-balanced person*; *You can trust her judgement – she is so well-balanced.* **2** having the correct amount of all the necessary foods: *To be healthy you must have a well-balanced diet*; *The child's diet is not very well-balanced.*

ˌ**well-be'haved** *adj* behaving correctly: *well-behaved children*; *She is quiet and well-behaved.*

ˌ**well-'being** *nu* (*formal*) welfare: *She is always very concerned about her mother's well-being.*

ˌ**well-'bred** *adj* (*formal*) (of a person) having good manners: *a well-bred young lady*; *She is too well-bred to be rude to him.*

ˌ**well-'built** *adj* (of a person, *usu* a man) muscular: *He is tall and well-built*; *well-built young men.*

ˌ**well-dis'posed** *adj* (*formal*: *pred*) feeling kind (towards): *She's always well-disposed towards those poorer than herself.*

ˌ**well-'earned** *adj* thoroughly deserved: *a well-earned rest*; *Her holiday was well-earned.*

ˌ**well-'educated** *adj* educated to a good standard.

ˌ**well-'fed** *adj* correctly and adequately fed: *well-fed children*; *The cat looks sleek and well-fed.*

ˌ**well-'founded** *adj* (*formal*: *often pred*) justified: *Your suspicions were well-founded*; *well-founded doubts.*

ˌ**well-'groomed** *adj* (of a person) of smart, tidy appearance: *a well-groomed young woman*; *She is well-groomed and elegant.*

ˌ**well-'heeled** *adj* (*inf*) having plenty of money; rich: *He is well-heeled but mean*; *He married a well-heeled widow.*

ˌ**well-in'formed** *adj* (*formal*) having, or being based on, good and reliable information: *I make a point of being well-informed*; *a well-informed article on China.*

ˌ**well-in'tentioned** *adj* meant to be helpful, kind *etc*: *His remarks were well-intentioned, but were misunderstood*; *The poor people were offended by her well-intentioned gifts.*

ˌ**well-'known** *adj* familiar or famous: *a well-known local beauty-spot*; *a well-known TV personality*; *He was well-known some years ago.*

ˌ**well-'mannered** *adj* polite.

ˌ**well-'meaning** *adj* (of a person) or (*also* ˌ**well-'meant**) their actions *etc*; having good intentions: *She is well-meaning but she usually upsets people*; *a well-meaning old lady*; *Their actions were well-meant but they made her angry*; *a well-meant attempt to help.*

'**well-nigh** *adv* (*formal*) almost: *It was well-nigh six o'clock when they arrived*; *He was well-nigh dead when we found him.*

ˌ**well-'off** *adj* **1** (*more informal than* **rich**) rich: *He is very well-off*; *a well-off young lady.* **2** (*inf*) in a fortunate position: *You do not know when you are well-off.*

ˌ**well-pro'portioned** *adj* having the correct, attractive proportions: *a well-proportioned young man*; *This room is well-proportioned.*

ˌ**well-'read** [-'red] *adj* (*formal*) (clever from) having read many books *etc*; intelligent: *a well-read young woman*; *He is very well-read.*

ˌ**well-'rounded** *adj* **1** (*often facet*) (of a person) pleasantly plump: *I wouldn't call you fat – you're just well-rounded.* **2** (*usu attrib*) (of one's education, experience *etc*) suitably wide and varied: *This school provides a well-rounded education*; *a well-rounded personality.*

ˌ**well-'spoken** *adj* (of a person) speaking with a pleasing and generally acceptable accent, in a grammatically correct way *etc*: *She is educated and well-spoken*; *We are looking for a well-spoken girl to be our telephone receptionist.*

ˌ**well-'thought-of** *adj* (*usu pred*) greatly admired and respected: *She is very well-thought-of as a teacher.*

ˌ**well-thought-'out** *adj* (*usu attrib*) (of an idea *etc*) having every detail carefully decided upon: *a well-thought-out scheme.*

ˌ**well-'thumbed** *adj* (of a book, its pages *etc*) creased because of considerable use.

ˌ**well-'timed** *adj* (*formal or facet*) done, said *etc*, at a suitable or fortunate time: *a well-timed action; Your arrival was well timed.*

ˌ**well-to-'do** *adj* (*formal or facet*) having enough money to live comfortably: *She's very well-to-do; a well-to-do family.*

ˌ**well-'versed** *adj* (*formal*: *pred with* **in**) knowledgeable (about a given subject): *She's well-versed in the use of this machine.*

'well-wisher *nc* a person who wishes success *etc* to a person or cause: *She received a good luck card from an unknown well-wisher.*

ˌ**well-'worn** *adj* that has been worn or used often, or too often: *a well-worn jacket; Those shoes look well-worn*; (*fig derog*) *a well-worn excuse.*

as 'well (*inf*) in addition; too: *If you will go, I'll go as well.*

as 'well as in addition to: *She works in a restaurant in the evenings as well as doing a full-time job during the day.*

be doing well *see* **well** (*adv def 1*).

be just as well (that) it is fortunate or advantageous (that); it is no cause for regret (that): *It's just as well that you didn't go – the meeting was cancelled.*

be (just) as well to to be advisable or sensible: *It would be as well to go by train – the roads are very icy; You would be as well to look for a new job.*

be well out of (*inf*) to be lucky because one has got out of an unfortunate situation *etc*: *You're well out of that firm – the police have arrested the owner for fraud.*

do well out of (*inf*) to make a profit or get some other advantage from: *You did well out of that deal.*

very well (*formal*) fine, okay, in that case *etc*: *Have you finished? Very well, you may go now.*

well done! used in congratulating a person: *I hear you won the competition. Well done!*

well enough fairly, but not particularly, well.

well met (*formal or old*) meeting by chance at an appropriate or fortunate time: *That was well met – I was just coming to see you.*

well up (in) (*inf*) knowing a great deal (about): *He's very well up in antiques, you know.*

See also **good, ill**.

we'll *see* **will**.

wellingtons ['weliŋtənz] *n pl* rubber boots loosely covering the calves of the legs: *He was wearing wellingtons because it was snowing heavily; The child needs a new pair of wellingtons.*

welsh [welʃ] *vi* (*derog*: *often with* **on**) to cheat by dodging payment or not carrying out an obligation: *He welshed on his employer.*

Welsh, Welshman, Welshwoman *see* Appendix 2.

welt [welt] *nc* **1** a band or strip fastened to an edge of an article of clothing for strength or for ornament. **2** a weal.

welter ['weltə] *nc* (*no pl*) (*formal or facet*) a huge confused mass: *He gave us a welter of useless information.*

wench [wentʃ] *nc* (*arch or facet*) a girl.

wend [wend]: **wend one's way** (*formal*) to move along slowly: *She wended her way gradually through the streets.*

went *see* **go**.

wept *see* **weep**.

were, we're, weren't *see* **be**.

west [west] *nu* **1** the direction in which the sun sets or any part of the earth lying in that direction: *They travelled towards the west; The rain is coming from the west; We stayed in a village west of* (= further west than) *Aberdeen; She works in the west of Scotland.* **2** (*often with cap*: *also* **W**) one of the four main points of the compass: *The ship's navigator set a course 15° W of N* (= fifteen degrees west of north). – *See also* **the West** *below.* – *adj* (*attrib*) **1** in the west: *She's in the west wing of the hospital.* **2** from the direction of the west: *There was a west wind blowing.* – *adv* towards the west: *The cliffs face west, out to sea.*

'westerly *adj* (*usu attrib*) **1** (of a wind, breeze *etc*) coming from the west: *a westerly wind.* **2** looking, lying *etc* towards the west: *They were coming from a westerly direction.*

'western *adj* of the west or the West: *a western political system; This philosophy is western in origin.* – *nc* a film or novel about the Wild West (*see below*): *Most westerns are about cowboys and Red Indians.*

'westernmost *adj* being furthest west: *the westernmost point on the mainland.*

'westward *adj* (*usu attrib*) towards the west: *in a westward direction.*

'westward(s) *adv* towards the west: *We journeyed westwards for two weeks.*

go west (*sl*) to become useless; to be destroyed: *I'm afraid this jacket has finally gone west; That's all hopes of winning gone west.*

the West 1 Europe and North and South America. **2** (*polit*: *sometimes without* **the**) America and the countries of Western Europe: *talks on nuclear disarmament between East and West.*

the West End the fashionable district, *esp* including the high-class theatre area, in the west of Central London: *We spent an enjoyable evening in the West End*; (*attrib*) *a West End theatre.*

West Indian, West Indies *see* Appendix 2.

the Wild West the western United States, before the establishment of law and order: *in the days of the Wild West; cowboys of the Wild West*; (*attrib*) *a Wild West stagecoach.*

wet [wet] *adj* **1** containing, soaked in, or covered with, water or another liquid: *We got soaking wet when it began to rain; His shirt was wet through with sweat* (*see also* **wet through** *below*); *I'm not going out in the rain – I don't want to get wet; Go and dry your wet hair; The car skidded on the wet road.* **2** rainy: *It's a horrible, wet day; wet weather; It was wet yesterday.* **3** (*inf derog*) cowardly or having a weak personality: *Her boyfriend is really wet!; a wet young man.* – *v* – *prt* **'wetting**: *pts, ptps* **wet, 'wetted** – *vt* to make wet: *She wet her hair and then put shampoo on it; The baby has wet* (= urinated on) *himself/his nappy/the bed.* – *nu* (*inf*) moisture: *What's this wet on the table?*

'wetness *nu.*

'wettish *adj* rather wet: *a wettish stain on the carpet; It's wettish today.*

wet blanket *nc* (*inf*) a cause of discouragement, *esp* a depressing companion: *Don't ask him to the party – he's such a wet blanket.*

'wet-nurse *nc* (*old*) a woman employed to breast-feed someone else's baby. – *vt* (*inf derog*) to look after (someone) with too much care: *Don't expect me to wet-nurse you like your mother does – you're a man now; Some people think the government wet-nurses the trade unions.*

'**wetsuit** *nc* a rubber suit for wearing in cold conditions when diving *etc.*

in the 'wet in(to) the rain, or other wet conditions: *You don't think I'm going out there in the wet, do you?*

wet through soaked to the skin.

we've *see* **have**.

whack [wak] *vti* (*inf*) to strike smartly, making a loud sound: *His father whacked him for misbehaving*; *The tree's branches whacked against the window.* – *nc* **1** (*inf*) this sound. **2** (*inf*) a blow: *His father gave him a whack across the ear.* **3** (*sl*) a share: *How much does my whack come to?*; *You've had a fair whack of that cake.*

whacked (*inf*: *usu pred*) tired; exhausted: *I've been working all day and I'm whacked*; *I feel whacked.*

'**whacking** *adj* (*inf*), *adv* (*inf*) very (large): *a whacking great car.* – *nc* a beating.

whale [weil] *nc* a type of very large mammal which lives in the sea. – *vi* (*also* **go whaling**) to catch whales.

'**whaler** *nc* a ship, or a person, engaged in whale fishing.

'**whalebone** *nu* (*usu attrib*) a light bendable substance got from the upper jaw of certain whales: *a whalebone corset*; *made of whalebone.*

'**whale oil** *nu* oil obtained from the fatty parts of a whale.

have a whale of a time (*inf*: *slightly old*) to enjoy oneself very much: *We had a whale of a time at the party.*

wharf [wo:f] – *pls* **wharfs, wharves** [wo:vz] – *nc* a platform alongside which ships are moored for loading and unloading.

what [wot] **1** *pron, adj* used in questions *etc* when asking someone to point out, state *etc* one or more persons, things *etc* which do not belong to a particular group: *What street is this?*; *What's your name/address/telephone number?*; *What time is it?*; *What (kind of) bird is that?*; *What idiot has been telling you all this nonsense?*; *What stupid game is he playing now?*; *What is he reading?*; *What did you say?*; *What is this cake made of?*; (*formal*) *Of what does this mixture consist?*; *'What do you want to be when you grow up?' 'A doctor.'*; *Tell me what you mean*; *I asked him what clothes I should wear*; *Show me what to do.* **2** *relative pron* the thing(s) that: *Did you find what you wanted?*; *These tools are just what I need for this job*; *What that child needs is a good spanking!* **3** *adj, relative pron* any (things or amount) that; whatever: *I'll lend you what clothes you need*; *Please lend me what you can*; *What (little) money he has, he spends on drink.* **4** *adj, adv, pron* used in exclamations of surprise, anger *etc*: *What clothes she wears!*; *What a fool he is!*; *What naughty children they are!*; *What a silly book this is!*; *What (on earth/in the world/ever) is happening?*; *You did what?*; *'I've just won £10.' 'What?'*

what'ever 1 *adj, relative pron* any (thing(s) or amount) that: *Show me whatever you have*; *I'll lend you whatever books you need.* **2** *adj, pron* no matter what: *Whatever happens, I'm going*; *You have to go on, whatever difficulties you meet*; *Whatever (else) you do, don't say that!* **3** *adj* (*placed immediately after noun*) whatsoever; at all: *I had nothing whatever to do with that.* **4** *pron* (*also* **what ever**) used in questions or exclamations to express surprise *etc*: *Whatever will he say when he hears this?*

'**whatnot** *nu* (*inf*) such things: *He told me all about publishing and whatnot.*

'**what's-his, -her, -its** *etc* **-name** *n* (*inf*) used in referring vaguely to a person or thing whose name one cannot remember: *Where does what's-his-name live?*

ˌ**whatso'ever** [-sou-] *adj* (*in negative sentences, questions etc*: *placed immediately after noun*) at all: *That's nothing whatsoever to do with me*; *He has no talent whatsoever for this job.*

guess what!/(do) you know what? (*inf*) I've something to tell you: *Guess what! The boss is getting married.*

I know what/I('ll) tell you what (*inf*) I've got an idea: *I'll tell you what – let's go swimming!*

know what's what to be able to tell what is important: *He'll make a sensible decision – he knows what's what.*

or whatever (*inf*) or something of that sort: *You can practise singing while you wash the dishes, clean the house or whatever.*

so what? (*inf*) what of it?; does it really matter?: *'He doesn't like you.' 'So what?'*

'**what about?** (*inf*) used in asking whether the listener would like (to do) something: *What about a glass of milk?*; *What about going to the cinema?*

what . . . for 1 (*more inf than* **why**) why(?): *What did he do that for?* **2** for what function or purpose(?): *What is this switch for?*; *He asked what it was for.*

what 'have you (*inf*) and similar things; and so on: *There are a lot of clothes, books and what have you for sale in her shop.*

'**what if?** what will or would happen if . . . ?: *What if he comes back?*; *What if she finds out that you've lost her book?*

what is more *see* **more**.

what . . . like? used when requiring or asking for information about the qualities of someone or something: *'What does it look like?' 'It's small and square.'*; *'What's her mother like?' 'Oh, she's quite nice.'*; *'What does this sound like?' 'A bit too loud.'*; *We may go – it depends (on) what the weather's like.*

ˌ**what 'of it?** (*inf*) used in replying, to suggest that what has been done, said *etc* is not important: *'You've offended him.' 'What of it?'*

what the (*inf*) used with several words *eg* **hell, devil** *etc* in question or exclamations to express anger or surprise: *What the hell do you think you're doing?*; *What the devil shall we do now?*

what with (*inf*) because of: *What with having no exercise and being overweight, he had a heart attack.*

See also **which**.

wheat [wi:t] *nu* a type of grain from which flour, much used in making bread, cakes *etc*, is obtained: *The farmer grows a lot of wheat*; *Is the wheat ripe yet?*

'**wheaten** *adj* (*attrib*) made of wheat: *a wheaten loaf.*

wheedle ['wi:dl] *vt* (*slightly inf*) to persuade (someone) (often by using flattery *etc*) to do (something) or give one (something): *They wheedled what they wanted out of him*; *She wheedled her father into lending her some money.*

wheel [wi:l] *nc* **1** (*sometimes in cmpds*) a circular frame or disc turning on a rod or axle, on which vehicles *etc* move along the ground: *A bicycle has two wheels, a tricycle has three, and most cars have four*; *One of the car wheels came off*; *a bicycle-wheel*; *a cartwheel.* **2** any of several things similar in shape and purpose: *a potter's wheel*; *He was* *found drunk at the wheel* (= steering-wheel) *of his lorry.* – **1** *vt* to cause to move on wheels: *He wheeled his bicycle along the pavement.* **2** *vti* (*with* **round**) to (cause to) turn quickly: *He wheeled round and struck me angrily*; *He wheeled his chair round to face me.* **3** *vi* (of birds) to fly in circles: *The vultures were wheeling above the dead animal.*

wheeled *adj* (*formal*) having wheels: *a wheeled vehicle.*

-wheeled (*in cmpds*) having (a particular type or number of) wheel(s): *a ˌfour-wheeled ˈvehicle.*

ˈwheelbarrow *nc* a small wooden, metal or plastic carrier with one wheel (or sometimes a ball) at the front, and two legs and two handles at the back: *You'll need a wheelbarrow to move that manure to the back garden*; *a child's wheelbarrow.*

ˈwheelchair *nc* a chair with (*usu* four) wheels, used for moving from place to place by invalids who have lost the use of their legs or who are very weak: *He has been in a wheelchair since he was in a riding accident*; *It is difficult to get a wheelchair into some public buildings.*

ˈwheelhouse *nc* the shelter in which a ship's steering-wheel is placed.

ˈwheelwright *nc* a craftsman who makes wheels and wheeled carriages.

See also **flywheel, freewheel.**

wheeze [wiːz] (*slightly inf*) **1** *vi* to breathe with a hissing sound and with difficulty: *Climbing all these steep stairs makes me gasp and wheeze*; *People with asthma often wheeze.* **2** *vt* to say (something) while breathing in this way: *'Pass me my pills,' he wheezed.* – *nc* (*slightly inf*) such a sound: *a wheeze in his chest*; *the wheezes of the baby.*

ˈwheezy *adj* (*inf*): *He's rather wheezy tonight – he has a cold*; *wheezy breathing.* **ˈwheezily** *adv* **ˈwheeziness** *nu.*

whelk [welk] *nc* a type of small edible shellfish with a spiral shell: *They bought some whelks from a seaside stall and ate them.*

whelp [welp] *nc* (*formal*) a puppy, lion cub *etc.* – *vi* (*formal or tech*) (of a female dog *etc*) to give birth to young: *When is she due to whelp?*

when [wen] *adv* at what time(?): *When did you arrive?*; *When did you last see him?*; *When will you see her again?*; *I know when you left*; *I asked him when exactly the incident had occurred*; *He told me when to jump.* – [wən, wen] *conj* **1** (at or during) the time at which: *I fell when I was coming in*; *It happened when I was abroad*; *When you see her, give her this message*; *When I've finished, I'll telephone you*; *When I'd read the newspaper I went to bed.* **2** in spite of the fact that; considering that: *Why do you walk when you have a car?*; *How did you get there on time when you left here so late?* – [wən, wen] *relative pron* at which: *At the time when I saw him, he was well.*

whence [wens] *adv* (*formal or old*) from what place or circumstance (?): *Whence did you appear?*; *He asked whence such an idea had arisen.* – *relative pron* (*formal or old*) ((to) the place) from which: *He's gone back* (*to the country*) *whence he came*; *He has reddish hair, whence comes his nickname 'Carrots'.*

whenˈever *adv, conj* **1** at any time that: *Come and see me whenever you want to.* **2** at every time that: *I go to the theatre whenever I get the chance*; *Whenever* (*it's*) *possible, the children play outside in the fresh air.*

ˌwhensoˈever [-sou-] *adv, conj* (*arch*) whenever.

where [weə] *adv* (to or in) which place (?): *Where are you going* (*to*)*?*; *Do you know where we are?*; *Where* (*on earth/in the world/ever*) *is he?*; *Where does he get his ideas from?*; *He knows where you live*; *We asked where to find a good restaurant.* – *relative pron* ((to or in) the place) to or in which: *It's nice going on holiday to a place where you've been before*; *This is the town where I was born*; *I couldn't see him from the place where I was sitting*; *Go where he tells you to go*; *It's still where it was*; *I can't see him from where I am.*

ˌwhereaˈbouts *adv* near or in what place(?): *Whereabouts is it?*; *I don't know whereabouts it is.*

ˈwhereabouts *n sing or n pl* the place where a person or thing is: *I don't know his whereabouts.*

whereˈas *conj* when in fact; but on the other hand: *He thought I was lying, whereas I was telling the truth*; *He's tall whereas I'm short.*

whereˈby *relative pron* (*formal*) by which: *That was the means whereby he got here before us.*

ˈwherefore [-foː]: **the why(s) and (the) wherefore(s)** all the reasons (for an action *etc*) or details (of a situation *etc*).

ˌwheresoˈever [-sou-] *adv* (*arch*) wherever.

ˌwhereuˈpon *conj* (*formal*) at or after which time, event *etc*: *He insulted her, whereupon she slapped him.*

wherˈever *relative pron* **1** no matter where: *I'll follow you wherever you may go*; *Wherever he is he will be thinking of you.* **2** (to or in) any place that: *Go wherever he tells you to go*; *I'll telephone you from wherever I get to by tomorrow evening*; *Wherever* (*it's*) *possible, the headmaster will adjust the timetable to meet the needs of individual pupils or teachers.* – *adv* (*also* **where ever**) used in questions or exclamations to express surprise *etc*: *Wherever did you go?*; *Wherever did she get that hat?*

ˈwherewithal [-wiðoːl] *nu* (*facet*: *with* **the**) the means, *esp* money, of doing something: *I don't have the wherewithal to go on holiday.*

whet [wet] – *pt, ptp* **ˈwhetted** – *vt* **1** (*formal or tech*) to sharpen (a tool) by rubbing it on or with a stone: *He whetted the knives on a grindstone.* **2** to make (one's appetite) keen or acute: *The sight of all the lovely food whetted her appetite*; (*fig*) *Having that one piano lesson whetted my appetite for more.*

ˈwhetstone *nc* a stone for sharpening the blades of knives *etc.*

whether [ˈweðə] *conj* if: *I don't know whether it's possible.*

whether ... or introducing alternatives: *Can you tell me whether or not the train has left?*; *He can't decide whether to go or not*; *Whether you like the idea or not, I'm going ahead with it*; *You must decide whether you're going or staying.*

whey [wei] *nu* the watery part of milk separated from the curd (the thick part), *esp* in making cheese.

which [witʃ] **1** *adj, pron* used in questions *etc* when asking someone to point out, state *etc* one or more persons, things *etc* that belong to a particular known group: *Which* (*colour*) *do you like best?*; *Which route will you travel by?*; (*formal*) *At which station should I change trains?*; *Which girl do you prefer?*; *Which of the two girls do you like better?*; *Tell me which* (*books*) *you would like*; *Let me know which train you'll be arriving on*; *I can't decide which to choose.* **2** *relative pron* (used to refer to a thing or things mentioned in a preceding clause to distinguish it or them from others: able to be replaced by **that** except when following a preposition: able to be omitted except when following a preposition or when the subject of a clause) (the) one(s) that: *This is the book which/that was on the table*; *This is the book (which/that) you wanted*; *Have you anything (which/that) you'd like to sell?*; *A scalpel is a type of knife which/that is used by surgeons*; *The chair (which/that) you are sitting on is an antique*; (*formal*) *The documents for which they were searching have been recovered.* **3** *adj, relative pron* used, preceded by a comma, to introduce a further comment on something, or on a previous part of the sentence: *This church, which will soon have to be pulled down, is very old*; *My new car, which I paid several thousand pounds for, is not running well*; *He said he could speak Russian, which was untrue*; (*formal*) *I called him by the wrong name, for which mistake I apologize*; *My father may have to go into hospital, in which case he won't be going on holiday.* **4** *adj, relative pron* any (thing(s) or person(s)) that; whichever: *Take which (dresses) you want from my wardrobe.*

which'ever *adj, relative pron* **1** any (one(s)) that: *I'll take whichever (books) you don't want*; *The prize will go to whichever of them writes the best essay.* **2** no matter which (one(s)): *Whichever way I turned, I couldn't escape.*

which is which (?) which is one and which is the other (?): *Mary and Susan are twins and I can't tell which is which*; *'The brothers are called John and David.' 'Which is which?'*

See also **who**.

whiff [wif] *nc* a sudden puff (of air, smoke, smell *etc*): *a whiff of petrol*; *a whiff of cigar smoke.*

while [wail] *conj* (*also, more formal or liter,* **whilst** [wailst]) **1** during the time that: *Don't telephone me while I'm at the office*; *I saw him while I was out walking*; *It began to rain while we were out.* **2** (*formal*) although: *While I sympathize, I can't really do very much to help*; *While I realize that you are doing your best I really do not think this work is good enough.* – *nc* (*no pl*) a space of time: *It took me quite a while*; *It will take a long while to get here.*

while away *vt sep* to pass (time) without boredom: *He whiled away the time by reading*; *He whiled the time away talking to me.*

worth one's while worth one's time and trouble: *It's not worth your while reading this book, because it isn't accurate*; (*inf*) *If you do this job for me I'll make it worth your while* (= I'll see that you are paid or get some other advantage). – *See also* **worthwhile** *under* **worth**.

whim [wim] *nc* (*often derog*) a sudden desire or change of mind: *This whole project could be cancelled at the managing director's whim*; *I am tired of that child's whims.*

'whimsical [-zikəl] *adj* (*formal*) **1** quaintly humorous: *a whimsical story.* **2** odd or fanciful: *The book was full of whimsical inventions.* **'whimsically** *adv.* **ˌwhimsi'cality** [-'ka-] *nu.*

'whimsy [-zi] *ncu* (*formal or liter*) (an example of) quaint, fanciful humour.

whimper ['wimpə] **1** *vi* to cry with a low, shaky or whining voice: *I heard a puppy whimpering*; *The child began to whimper as his mother went out of the door.* **2** *vt* to say or utter something in this way: *He whimpered that he was sorry*; *He whimpered an excuse*; *'You're hurting me,' he whimpered.* – *nc* a cry of this kind: *The dog gave a little whimper of fear.*

whine [wain] **1** *vi* to utter a complaining cry or a cry of suffering: *That dog whines all day because it's left alone in the house.* **2** *vi* to make a similar noise: *I could hear the engine whine.* **3** *vti* (*inf derog*) to complain in a feeble way or unnecessarily: *Stop whining about how difficult this job is!*; *She's always whining her complaints at me.* – *ncu* such a noise: *the whine of a dog in pain*; *the whine of an engine*; *I am tired of her whines.*

'whiningly *adv.*

whinny ['wini] *vi* to make the cry of a horse: *The horse whinnied when it saw its master.* – *nc* such a cry: *I heard the horse's whinnies.*

whip [wip] *nc* **1** a long cord or strip of leather attached to a handle, used for punishing people, driving horses *etc*: *He carries a whip but he would never use it on the horse*; (*in cmpds*) *a whiplash* (= the lash or cord of a whip). **2** (*often with cap*) in parliament, a member chosen by his party to make sure that no one fails to vote in important ballots: *The government was defeated because some of its MPs refused to obey the whip and voted against the government.* **3** a notice sent out by a parliamentary whip, calling on members to vote: *A three-line whip, ie a notice which is underlined three times, is the most urgent type.* – *v* – *pt, ptp* **whipped** – **1** *vt* to strike with a whip: *He whipped the horse to make it go faster*; *The criminals were whipped.* **2** *vt* to beat (cream *etc*): *Whip the cream stiffly before decorating the cake with it.* **3** *vti* (*formal or liter*) to strike as if with a whip: *The huge waves whipped (against) the shore.* **4** *vti* to move fast *esp* with a twisting motion like a whip: *Suddenly he whipped round and saw me*; *He whipped out a revolver and shot her*; *She whipped my plate away before I'd finished eating.* – *See also* **whip up** *below.*

whipped *adj* (*attrib*) (of cream *etc*) beaten: *I use whipped cream for that pudding.*

whiplash injury *nc* a neck injury caused by the sudden jerking forwards and backwards of the head, common in car accidents: *My neck was sore for weeks after a whiplash injury.*

'whipping-boy *nc* (*formal or liter: fig*) someone punished because of someone else's mistakes: *Our manager always has to have a whipping-boy for his mistakes.*

whipping cream *nu* cream (suitable) for whipping: *You must use whipping cream if you want to decorate a cake with it.*

'whip-round *nc* (*inf*) a collection of money: *We're having a whip-round for George's birthday.*

have the whip hand (over someone) to have control, or hold an advantage (over someone): *He has the whip hand in all these situations.*

whip up *vt sep* **1** to whip (*usu def 2*): *Whip up the cream, will you?*; *I'm whipping up eggs for the dessert.* **2** (*inf*) to produce or prepare quickly: *I'll whip up a meal in no time.* **3** to cause with effort; to excite or rouse: *You must try to whip up some enthusiasm for the project*; *I cannot whip up any support.*

whipper-snapper ['wipəsnapə] *nc* (*old or facet: often derog*) a (*usu* young) boastful but unimportant person: *That young whipper-snapper tried to tell me what to do and I've been here fifty years.*

whippet ['wipit] *nc* a type of racing dog like a small greyhound.

whir(r) [wəː] – *pt, ptp* **whirred** – *vi* to make, or move with, a buzzing sound, *esp* as of something turning through the air: *The propellers whirred loudly as we prepared to take off.* – *nu* such a sound: *the whirr of insects*; *I heard the whirr of helicopter blades.*

whirl [wəːl] *vti* (*usu with* **round, away** *etc*) to move rapidly (round, away *etc*): *She whirled round, startled, when I called her name*; *The wind whirled my hat away before I could grab it.* – *nc* **1** (*no pl*) an excited confusion: *a whirl of activity*; *She's terribly busy in her high-class social whirl*; *My head's in a whirl – I can't believe it's all happening!* **2** a rapid turn: *With an angry whirl she turned round to face him.*

'whirlpool *nc* a circular current in a river or sea, caused by opposing tides, winds or currents.

'whirlwind *nc* a violent circular current of wind with a whirling motion: *Our house was destroyed by a whirlwind*; *This room is so untidy that it looks as though a whirlwind has been through it.*

whirr *see* **whir(r)**.

whisk [wisk] *vt* **1** (*slightly inf*: *usu with* **away, off** *etc*) to sweep, or cause to move, rapidly: *The fireman whisked the families out of the burning building*; *He whisked the dirty dishes off the table*; *He whisked her off to the doctor.* **2** to beat (eggs, cream *etc*) with a fork or whisk. – *nc* **1** (*slightly inf*) a rapid, sweeping motion: *The cow gave a whisk of her tail.* **2** a kitchen tool made of wire *etc*, for beating eggs, cream *etc*.

whiskers ['wiskəz] *n pl* (*old*: *also* (*rare*) **'whisker** *nc*) **1** a man's moustache, beard and/or sideburns: *He has shaved off his whiskers.* **2** the long hairs between the nose and the mouth of a cat *etc*.

'whiskered, 'whiskery *adjs*.

escape, miss (something) *etc* **by a whisker** to barely manage to escape *etc*: *The government won by a whisker.*

whisky, (*Irish and Amer*) **whiskey** ['wiski] **1** *ncu* a type of alcoholic drink made from grain: *A great deal of whisky is made in Scotland*; *Do you like whisky with water?*; *Many different whiskies are produced in Scotland.* **2** *nc* a glass of whisky: *I ordered two beers and a whisky.*

whisper ['wispə] **1** *vti* to speak or say (something) very softly: *He whispered (it) to her so that no-one else would hear*; *You'll have to whisper or he'll hear you*; *She whispered a reply*; *'Don't tell him,' she whispered.* **2** *vt* (*usu with* **it** *as subject*) to spread (a rumour): *It's whispered that Mackenzie's are going to cut their prices next week.* **3** *vi* (*liter*) (of trees *etc*) to make a soft sound by moving gently in the wind: *The leaves whispered in the breeze.* – *nc* **1** a very quiet sound, *esp* something said: *They spoke in whispers.* **2** a rumour: *I've heard a whisper about his business affairs*; *We heard a whisper that he was married.*

'whisperer *nc*.

stage whisper *see* **stage**.

whist [wist] *nu* a type of card game: *Do you play whist?*; *I beat them at whist.*

whistle ['wisl] **1** *vi* to make a shrill, often musical, sound by forcing one's breath between the lips or teeth: *He whistled happily as he rode along on his bike*; *Can you whistle?*; *He whistled to attract my attention.* **2** *vi* to make such a sound with a device designed for this: *The electric kettle's whistling.* **3** *vt* to produce (a tune *etc*) by making such a sound either with one's lips and teeth or with a musical instrument designed to make a similar sound: *He whistled a happy tune*; *He whistled a tune on his penny-whistle.* **4** *vti* to call to (a person or animal) by whistling either with one's lips and teeth or with an instrument designed to make a similar sound: *The policeman whistled us to stop*; *He whistled a waiter over to their table*; *He whistled to his dog.* **5** *vi* to make a shrill sound in passing through the air: *The bullet whistled past his head.* **6** *vi* (of the wind) to blow with a shrill sound: *The wind was whistling in the chimney.* – **1** *ncu* the sound made by whistling: *He gave a loud whistle to his friend across the road.* **2** *nc* a musical instrument designed to make a whistling noise: *He plays the penny-whistle.* **3** *nc* an instrument used by policemen, referees *etc* to make a whistling noise: *The policeman blew his whistle as the thief ran away*; *The gym-teacher blew her whistle and the class stood still*; *The referee blew his whistle at the end of the game.*

'whistle-stop *adj* (*attrib*) having a lot of very brief stops: *a whistle-stop tour of England.*

'whistle for (something) (*sl*) to ask for (something) with no hope of getting it: *If you want me to give you fifty pounds, you can whistle for it.*

whit [wit] *nc* (*usu with a negative*) a very small particle or amount: *His family doesn't care a whit about him.*

Whit *see* **Whitsun**.

white [wait] *adj* **1** of the colour of the paper on which these words are printed: *white snow*; *The bride wore a white dress*; *All the walls of the room are white.* **2** having light-coloured skin, through being of European *etc* descent: *the first white man to explore Africa*; *She is white and he is coloured.* **3** abnormally pale, because of fear, illness *etc*: *He went white with the shock of hearing that his wife had been killed in the air-crash*; *When I saw her white face I knew she was going to faint.* **4** with milk in it: *A white coffee, please.* – **1** *ncu* (any shade of) the colour of the paper on which these words are printed: *White and black are opposites.* **2** *nc* (*sometimes with cap*) a white-skinned person: *Many countries have experienced racial trouble between blacks and whites.* **3** *ncu* (*also* **'egg-white**) the clear fluid in an egg, surrounding the yolk: *This recipe says to separate the yolks from the whites.* **4** *ncu* something (*eg* material, paint *etc*) white in colour: *Can you get me some more white for the ceiling?*; *She always dresses in red and white.* **5** *nc* (of an eye) the white part surrounding the pupil and iris: *The whites of her eyes are bloodshot.*

'whiten *vti* to make or become white or whiter: *When she washed the dirty sheets she used a little bleach in the water to whiten them.*

'whiteness *nu*.

'whitening *nu* a substance used to make certain things (*eg* tennis shoes) white again.

'whitish *adj* fairly white; close to white: *She wore a whitish dress*; *The walls are whitish.*

off-white *see* **off**.

ˌwhite-'collar *adj* (*attrib*) (of workers, jobs *etc*) not manual: *White-collar workers are usually thought to be better paid than manual workers.*

white elephant *nc* something which is useless or which causes much trouble while doing little good: *That enormous wardrobe your mother gave us has been nothing but a white elephant.*

white flag *nc* a sign of truce or of surrender: *Don't shoot at that ship – it's flying the white flag.*

white horse *nc* (*inf*: *usu in pl*) a wave that has a crest of white foam: *The sea is very rough today – look at all those white horses!*

ˌwhite-'hot *adj* (of metals) so hot that they have turned white: *a white-hot poker*; *Don't touch that – it's white-hot!*

white lie *nc* a not very serious lie: *I'd rather tell* my mother a white lie than tell her the truth and upset her.

white magic *nc* magic performed without the help of the Devil, often for good purposes. – *See also* **black magic** *under* **black**.

white paper *nc* a statement printed on white paper, issued by government for the information of parliament.

white pudding *see* **pudding** (*def 3*).

'whitewash *nu* **1** a mixture of *usu* lime and water, used for whitening (*usu* outside) walls of buildings: *Could you mix me another bucket of whitewash for the wall of this cottage?* **2** (*derog*) something which hides a mistake, crime *etc*: *The government's explanation of the affair was just pure whitewash.* – *vt* **1** to cover with whitewash: *We whitewashed our country cottage.* **2** (*derog*) to cover up faults *etc* in (*eg* conduct): *They whitewashed the entire business.* **'whitewashed** *adj.*

white wine *see* **wine**.

whitebait ['waitbeit] *n sing or n pl* any of several types of small white fish fried and used as food.

whither ['wiðə] *relative pron* (*arch or liter*) to which (place): *Is this the place whither he came?*; *Go whither you want.* – *adv* (*arch or liter*) to which place (?): *Whither did he go?*; *He asked whither I was going.*

whiting ['waitiŋ] – *pls* **'whiting, whitings** – **1** *nc* a type of small fish related to the cod. **2** *nu* its flesh used as food: *Would you like some whiting?*

whitlow ['witlou] *nc* an inflammation of the finger or toe, *esp* near the nail.

Whitsun, Whit ['wit(sn)] *n* the week beginning with **Whit Sunday** (or **ˌWhit'sunday**), the seventh Sunday after Easter: *I'm taking a week's holiday at Whitsun*; (*attrib*) *Whit week.*

whittle ['witl] *vti* (*formal or old*) to cut or shape (*eg* a twig) with a knife.

whittle away *vt sep*, **whittle away at** *vt fus* (*usu fig*) to cut away gradually; to reduce: *These bills are whittling away at our savings*; *They have whittled away a fortune.*

whittle down *vt sep* (*fig*) to cut down gradually: *We've whittled down the list of applicants to a few whom we wish to interview*; *Can you whittle it down further?*

whizz [wiz] (*inf*) **1** *vi* to make a hissing sound like an arrow flying through the air: *The fireworks whizzed, banged and crackled.* **2** *vti* to move rapidly: *We whizzed (him) along to the hospital immediately after the accident.*

'whizz-kid *nc* (*inf: sometimes derog*) a very bright person who gains quick promotion: *an electronics whizz-kid*; *The new headmaster is a real whizz-kid.*

who [huː] *pron* (used as the subject of an actual or implied verb, or (*inf*) as the object of an actual or implied verb or preposition) what person(s) (?): *Who is that woman in the green hat?*; *Who did that?*; *Who got the job?*; *Who won?*; *'I saw John Smith yesterday.' 'Who?'*; *Who did you choose for the team?*; *Who did you give it to?*; *Who else did you dance with besides Mary?*; *Do you know who all these people are?*; *I don't know who he gave it to*; *Who (on earth/in the world/ever) told you that?* – *relative pron* **1** (used to refer to a person or people mentioned in a preceding clause to distinguish him or them from others: used as the subject of a verb, or (*inf*) as the object of a verb or preposition: *usu* replaceable by **that**: able to be omitted when not the subject of a clause) (the) one(s) that: *The man who/that telephoned was a friend of yours*; *The people (who/that) you were talking to are Swedes*; *This is the man who/that was in the library yesterday*; *A doctor is a person who looks after people's health*; *Anyone who/that does that must be mad.* **2** used, preceded by a comma, to introduce a further comment on a person or people: *His mother, who by that time was tired out, gave him a smack.* – *See also* **whom** *below.*

who'ever *relative pron* **1** any person or people that: *Whoever gets the job will have a lot of work to do.* **2** no matter who: *Whoever rings, tell him/them I'm out.* – *pron* (*also* **who ever**) used in questions to express surprise *etc*: *Whoever said that?*

whom [huːm] *pron* (used as the object of a verb or preposition in formal speech) what person(s) (?): *Whom do you want to see?*; *Whom did you give it to?*; *To whom shall I speak?* – *relative pron* (used as the object of a verb or preposition in formal speech) **1** (used to refer to a person or people mentioned in a preceding clause, to distinguish him or them from others: able to be omitted or replaced by **that** except when following a preposition) (the) one(s) that: *The man (whom/that) you mentioned is here*; *Today I met some friends (whom/that) I hadn't seen for ages*; (*formal*) *This is the man to whom I referred*; *This is the man (whom/that) I gave it to.* **2** used, preceded by a comma, to introduce a further comment on a person or people: *My father, whom I'd like you to meet one day, is interested in your work.* **3** any person or people that: *Ask whom you like to the party.*

ˌwhoso'ever *pron* (*arch*) whoever.

know who's who to know which people are important: *I think I know who's who in that firm.*

See also **whose, which, that**.

whoa! [wou] *interj* (to horses or (*inf*) people) stop!

whole [houl] *adj* **1** (*attrib*) including everything and/or everyone; complete: *The whole staff collected the money for your present*; *The whole building is in danger of collapsing*; *a whole pineapple.* **2** (placed immediately after noun or pronoun) not broken; in one piece: *She swallowed the biscuit whole.* **3** (*arch or liter*) healthy: *Those who were ill have been made whole again.* – *nc* (*no pl: formal*) **1** a single unit: *The different parts were joined to form a whole.* **2** the entire thing: *The whole of one week was spent in sunbathing on the beach.*

'wholeness *nu.*

'wholly *adv* (*formal*) completely or altogether: *Your idea isn't wholly practical*; *I am not wholly convinced that you are right.*

ˌwhole'hearted *adj* (*often attrib*) sincere and enthusiastic: *His plan had my wholehearted support.*

'wholemeal *nu* (*usu attrib*) flour made from the entire wheat grain or seed: *wholemeal flour/bread.*

on the whole taking everything into consideration: *I think our trip was very successful on the whole*; *On the whole I am quite satisfied with the experiment.*

wholesale ['houlseil] **1** *adj, adv* buying and selling goods on a large scale, *usu* from a manufacturer and to a retailer: *a wholesale business*; *He buys the materials wholesale.* **2** *adj* (*attrib*) on a large scale: *the wholesale slaughter of innocent people.*

'wholesaler *nc* a person who buys and sells goods wholesale (*def 1*).

See also **retail**.

wholesome ['houlsəm] *adj* **1** healthy: causing good health: *wholesome food*; *wholesome exercise*; *Milk is very wholesome.* **2** (*formal or old*) morally healthy: *She's a nice, wholesome young girl*; *It isn't wholesome to be reading such books.* '**wholesomely** *adv.* '**wholesomeness** *nu.*

whom *see* **who**.

whoop [wu:p, (*Amer also*) hu:p] *nc* **1** (*slightly inf*) a loud cry of delight, triumph *etc*: *She gave a whoop of joy.* **2** the noisy sound made when breathing in after coughing when one has whooping-cough. – *vi* (*slightly inf*) to give a loud cry of delight, triumph *etc.*

'**whooping-cough** ['hu:-] *nu* an infectious disease with violent bouts of coughing followed by a whoop when the breath is drawn in again.

whopper ['wopə] *nc* (*old inf*) anything very large, *esp* a lie: *He caught a whopper of a fish*; *That was a whopper of a lie*; *'He told me he could swim ten kilometres.' 'What a whopper!'*

whore [ho:] *nc* (*offensive*) a prostitute.

whorl [wə:l, wo:l] *nc* any one turn in a spiral shell.
whorled *adj* having whorls.

whose [hu:z] *adj, pron* **1** belonging to which person (?): *Whose is this jacket?*; *Whose (jacket) is this?*; *Whose car did you come back in?*; (*formal*) *In whose house did this incident happen?*; *Tell me whose (pens) these are.* **2** of whom or which (the): *Show me the boy whose father is a policeman*; *Which is the book whose pages are torn?*

why [wai] *adv* for which reason (?): *'Why did you hit the child?'*; *'He hit the child.' 'Why?'*; *Why haven't you finished?*; *'I haven't finished.' 'Why not?'*; *'Let's go to the cinema.' 'Why not?'* (= Let's!); *Tell me why you came here.* – *relative pron* for which: *Give me one good reason why I should help you!*

the why(s) and (the) wherefore(s) *see* **wherefore** *under* **where**.

wick[1] [wik] *nc* the twisted threads of cotton *etc* in a candle, lamp *etc*, which draw up the oil or wax into the flame.

wick[2] [wik]: **get on someone's wick** (*sl*) to annoy someone greatly: *His constant complaining gets on my wick!*

wicked ['wikid] *adj* **1** evil; sinful: *He is a wicked man*; *That was a wicked thing to do*; *The wicked old woman murdered the children*; *It is wicked to make other people suffer.* **2** (*inf*) very bad: *a wicked accident*; *wicked weather.* '**wickedly** *adv.* '**wickedness** *nu.*

wicker ['wikə] *adj* (*attrib*) (of *eg* a table or basket) made of twigs, rushes *etc* woven together: *a wicker basket.*

'**wickerwork** *nu* articles made in this way.

wicket ['wikit] *nc* (in cricket) **1** a set of three upright wooden rods at which the bowler aims the ball. **2** the ground between two sets of these rods: *The wicket has dried out well.* **3** the ending of a batsman's period of batting: *They scored fifty runs for (the loss of) one wicket.*

'**wicket-keeper** *nc* (in cricket) the fielder who stands immediately behind the wicket.

wide [waid] *adj* **1** having or being a great (or greater than average) distance from side to side or sometimes from top to bottom: *He admired the city's wide streets*; *Her eyes were wide with surprise*; *The space is not wide enough to build a house in*; *This jacket is too wide for me.* **2** (*pred*) being (a certain distance from one side to the other: *This material is three metres wide*; *How wide is it?* **3** (*usu attrib*) great or large: *He won by a wide margin.* **4** (of interests or experience) great; covering a large and varied range of subjects *etc*: *She has a wide experience of teaching the mentally handicapped*; *Her experience is not as wide as his.* – *adv* with a great distance from top to bottom or side to side: *He opened his eyes wide.*

'**widely** *adv.*

'**widen** *vti* to make, or become, wide or wider: *They have widened the road*; *The lane widens here*; *Her eyes widened in surprise.*

'**wideness** *nu.*

width [widθ] **1** *ncu* size from side to side: *What is the width of this material?*; *This fabric comes in three different widths.* **2** *nc* a piece of cloth which is the full width it was when woven: *I need three widths of cloth four metres long.* **3** *nu* the state of being wide.

wide-apart *see* **wide apart** *below.*

wide-awake *see* **wide awake** *below.*

wide-open *see* **wide open** *below.*

ˌ**wide-'ranging** *adj* (of interests *etc*) covering a large number of subjects *etc.*

'**widespread** *adj* spread over a large area or among many people: *widespread hunger and disease*; *The belief that he is wicked is widespread.*

give a wide berth (to) to avoid by a large margin: *The ships gave each other a wide berth*; (*fig*) *He always gives her a wide berth because he doesn't like her.*

wide apart a great (or greater than average) distance away from one another: *He held his arms wide apart in welcome*; (*attrib*) *wide-apart eyes.*

wide awake fully awake: *She was wide awake*; (*attrib*) *a wide-awake look.*

wide open fully open: *The door was wide open*; (*attrib*) *a wide-open window*; *Her eyes are wide open but she seems to be asleep.*

widow ['widou] *nc* a woman whose husband is dead: *She was left* (= became) *a widow at the age of thirty*; *My brother's widow has married again.* – *vt* (*usu in passive*) to cause to become a widow or widower: *She/He was widowed in 1943.*

'**widower** *nc* a man whose wife is dead.

width *see* **wide**.

wield [wi:ld] *vt* **1** (*formal or liter*) to use: *He can certainly wield an axe*; *He wielded his sword with courage.* **2** to have and use: *He wields a great deal of authority.*

See also **unwieldy**.

wife [waif] – *pl* **wives** [waivz] – *nc* the woman to whom someone is married: *Come and meet my wife*; *She's the wife of a local businessman*; *He is looking for a wife.*

'**wifely** *adj* (*formal or facet*: *usu attrib*) of a wife: *one's wifely duties.*

old 'wives' tale a superstitious and misleading story: *He thinks that herbal medicine is just a collection of old wives' tales.*

See also **fishwife, housewife, midwife**.

wig [wig] *nc* an artificial covering of hair for the head: *Does she wear a wig?*

See also **bigwig**.

wiggle ['wigl] *vti* (*slightly inf*) to (cause to) move irregularly from side to side: *She wiggled through the tight gap between the chairs*; *She wiggles her hips as she walks.*

'**wiggly** *adj* (*inf*) not straight; going up and down, from side to side *etc*: *a wiggly line.*

wigwam ['wigwam, (*Amer*) -wa:m] *nc* a North

American Indian tent made of skins *etc*, *usu* cone-shaped.

wild [waild] *adj* **1** (*often attrib*: *sometimes in cmpds*) (of animals) not tamed: *There are wild horses; wolves and other wild animals; Are these goats tamed or wild?; wildfowl.* **2** (of land) not cultivated. **3** (*usu attrib*) uncivilized or lawless: *They are wild, terrifying people who will murder without a thought.* **4** very stormy; violent: *a wild night at sea; The weather has been very wild recently*; (*fig*) *He went into a wild rage.* **5** mad, crazy, insane *etc*: *He was wild with hunger; She was wild with anxiety; She had wild eyes.* **6** rash: *a wild hope.* **7** not accurate or reliable: *That was a wild guess; £40 000 is a wild estimate of what the house is worth; That guess is a bit wild.* **8** (*Brit inf*) very angry: *She was wild with him for being late.* **'wildly** *adv.*

'wildness *nu.*

'wildcat *adj* (*attrib*) (of an industrial strike) sudden and unofficial.

'wildfire: spread like wildfire (of *eg* news) to spread extremely fast: *The news of the invasion spread like wildfire.*

'wildfowl *n pl* **1** wild birds, *esp* water birds such as ducks, shot as game. **2** wild ducks, geese *etc*.

'wildfowler *nc* a person who shoots birds, *esp* water birds, as a sport. **'wildfowling** *nu.*

ˌwild-'goose chase *nc* an attempt to catch or find something one cannot possibly obtain (*esp* because it does not exist or is not there): *A false clue sent us north on a wild-goose chase, while the criminal escaped southwards.*

'wildlife *nu* wild animals, birds, insects *etc* collectively: *He is interested in preserving the wildlife of the region.*

in the 'wild (of an animal) in its natural surroundings: *The giraffe grew up in the wild, but he's quite tame now.*

run wild *see* **run.**

sow one's wild oats *see* **oats.**

the wilds (*often derog*) the uncultivated areas (of a country *etc*): *They're living out in the wilds of Australia somewhere; We used to live in the wilds but we live in London now.*

the Wild West *see* **west.**

wilderness ['wildənəs] **1** *ncu* (a) desert or wild area of a country *etc*: *The whole region is just (a) dry wilderness, where no plants grow.* **2** *nc* (*formal*) an empty or unhappy place, state *etc*: *Her life became a barren wilderness after her husband died.*

wiles [wailz] *n pl* (*sometimes derog*) persuasive manners or ways: *She used her wiles to get her own way.*

'wily *adj* (*formal*) crafty, cunning, sly *etc*: *a wily old fox; He is too wily for the police to catch him.*

'wiliness *nu.*

wilful *see* **will.**

will [wil] **1** *nu* the mental power by which one controls one's thought, actions and decisions: *Do you believe in freedom of the will?* **2** *ncu* (control over) one's desire(s) or wish(es); determination: *It was done against her/their will; He has no will of his own – he always does what the others want; Children often have strong wills; He has lost the will to live.* – *See also* **at will, with a will** *below.* **3** *nu* (*formal*: *sometimes in cmpds*) feelings towards other people: *I bear you no ill-will.* **4** *nc* (a legal paper having written on it) a formal statement about what is to be done with one's belongings, body *etc* after one's death: *Have you made a will yet?*; (*legal*) *his last will and testament.* – *modal aux* – *short forms* **I'll** [ail], **you'll** [ju:l], **he'll** [hi:l], **she'll** [ʃi:l], **it'll** ['itl], **we'll** [wi:l], **they'll** [ðeil]: *neg short form* **won't** [wount] – **1** used to form future tenses of other verbs: *We'll go at six o'clock tonight; They will be very angry; Will we see you again next week?; Things will never be the same again.* **2** used in requests or commands: *Will you come into my office for a moment, please?; Will you please stop talking!; Shut the window, will you, please?* **3** used to show willingness: *I'll do that for you if you like; I won't do it!* **4** used to state that something happens regularly, is quite normal *etc*: *Accidents will happen.* **5** used to show that something is possible: *This bucket will hold five gallons of water.* **6** used to show that something is probable: *That will be John knocking at the door now.* **7** used to express a wish or hope: *You will be polite to Mother, won't you?* – *vt* **1** to (try to) influence (someone or something) by exercising one's will: *We're all willing you to win; I willed him to live.* **2** (*legal*) to give (property *etc*) to (other people) in one's will (*def 4*): *He willed her an allowance of £500 per month.* **3** (*old*) to command or order (that something should happen): *The emperor wills it, so it must be done.*

'wilful *adj* (*formal derog*) **1** obstinate; determined to get one's own way: *a wilful child; He is bad-tempered and wilful.* **2** (*often attrib*) intentional: *wilful damage to property.* **'wilfully** *adv.*

'wilfulness *nu.*

-willed (*in cmpds*) having a (certain kind of) will (*def 1*): *ˌweak-'willed/ˌstrong-'willed.*

'willing *adj* ready to agree (to do something): *a willing helper; She's willing to help in any way she can.* **'willingly** *adv.* **'willingness** *nu.*

'willpower *nu* the power or determination to do something: *She succeeded by sheer willpower; I don't have the willpower to stop smoking.*

at 'will as, or when, one chooses: *The soldiers fired at will; You are free to leave the house at will.*

will have 1 used to refer to things which are expected to have happened, been done *etc* by some time in the future: *I will have finished this by four o'clock.* **2** used to refer to events which are expected to have happened, been done *etc* by the time of speaking: *I'm sure John will have finished by now.*

with a 'will (*formal*) eagerly and energetically: *They set about (doing) their tasks with a will.*

with the best will in the world (*usu followed by a negative statement*) however hard one tries or wishes to do something: *With the best will in the world, I couldn't do that job, because I don't know anything about electronics.*

See also **shall, should, unwilling, would.**

willies ['wiliz]: **give (someone) the willies, get the willies** (*sl*) to give or get an uncomfortable, eerie or fearful feeling: *This dark, mysterious house gives me the willies!*

willow ['wilou] **1** *nc* (*also* **'willow tree**) a type of tree with long, slender branches, a common variety being the **weeping willow**, whose branches hang down to the ground. **2** *nu, adj* (of) its wood, used in making *eg* cricket bats.

'willowy *adj* (*formal*) slender and graceful: *She is tall and willowy; a willowy, red-haired girl.*

willy-nilly [wili'nili] *adv* whether one wishes it or not: *You must go, willy-nilly.*

wilt [wilt] *vi* **1** (of flowers) to droop: *The plants are wilting because they haven't been watered.* **2** (of people) to lose energy and begin to collapse: *We* *were wilting in the terrific heat.*

wily *see* **wiles**.

win [win] – *prp* ˈ**winning**: *pt, ptp* **won** [wʌn] – **1** *vti* to obtain (a victory) in a contest; to succeed in coming first in (a contest), *usu* by one's own efforts: *He won a fine victory in the election*; *Who won the war?*; *Which side won the football match?*; *He won the bet*; *She won (the quiz) by four points*; *He won (the race) in a fast time.* **2** *vt* to obtain (a prize, not necessarily first prize) in a competition *etc, usu* by luck: *They won the money on the football pools last week*; *I didn't win first prize but I won £5 in the crossword-puzzle competition.* **3** *vt* to obtain (something) by one's own efforts: *He won her respect over a number of years*; *The workers won concessions on pay conditions.* **4** *vt* (*formal or old*) to reach (a place) by effort: *The swimmer finally won the shore.* – *nc* a victory or success: *She's had two wins and two second places out of four races*; *They had a big win on the football pools.*

ˈ**winner** *nc.*

ˈ**winning** *adj* **1** (*attrib*) victorious or successful: *the winning driver in the race.* **2** (*old or formal*: *usu attrib*) attractive or charming: *She has winning ways*; *a winning smile.*

ˈ**winningly** *adv* charmingly.

ˈ**winning-post** *nc* (*also* **post**) in horse-racing, a post marking the place where a race finishes. – *See also* **post**[1].

win over *vt sep* to succeed in gaining the support and sympathy of: *At first he refused to help us but we finally won him over*; *You will have to win over the whole committee.*

win the day (*often fig*) to gain a victory; to be successful: *Common sense will win the day.*

win through *vi* (*often with* **to**) to succeed in getting (to a place, the next stage *etc*): *The soldiers won through to the coast despite heavy losses*; *It will be a struggle, but we'll win through in the end.*

wince [wins] *vi* to shrink or start back quickly (in pain or in anticipation of pain), often screwing up the face, narrowing the eyes *etc*: *He winced as the dentist touched his broken tooth*; (*fig*) *I wince every time I remember how rude I was to him.*

winch [wintʃ] *nc* a type of powerful machine for hoisting or hauling heavy loads. – *vt* (*usu with* **up, in** *etc*) to hoist (up) or haul (in) using a winch.

wind[1] [wind] **1** *ncu* (an) outdoor current of air: *The wind is strong today*; *There wasn't much wind yesterday*; *Cold winds blow from the north*; *the four* (= east, west, north and south) *winds.* **2** *nu* (*inf*) breath: *Climbing these stairs takes all the wind out of me.* **3** *nu* air or gas in the stomach or intestines: *His stomach pains were due to wind.* **4** *nu* (*inf derog*) unimportant, meaningless talk: *He's all wind – he never actually does anything.* – *vt* to cause to be out of breath: *He was winded by the heavy punch to the stomach/by the long climb.* – *adj* (*attrib*) **1** (of a musical instrument) operated or played using air pressure, *esp* a person's breath. **2** (of a section of an orchestra *etc*) playing wind instruments: *a wind ensemble.*

ˈ**windward** *nu* (*no article*: *naut*) the side (of a boat *etc*) towards which the wind blows: *The storm is two miles to windward.* – *adj* (*usu attrib*) *the windward side of the cabin.* – *adv*: *He moved windward.*

ˈ**windy** *adj* **1** exposed to the wind: *a windy corner.* **2** having strong winds: *a windy day*; *It's rather windy today.* ˈ**windiness** *nu.*

ˈ**windbag** *nc* (*inf derog*) a very talkative person: *He's such an old windbag.*

ˈ**windbreak** *nc* something, *eg* a group of trees, which shelters (a person or thing) from wind.

ˈ**windcheater** *nc* (*Amer* ˈ**windbreaker,** ˈ**Windbreaker** ®) a type of close-fitting jacket for protecting oneself against the wind.

ˈ**windfall** *nc* **1** a piece of fruit blown from a tree: *When they had no money, they lived by eating windfalls.* **2** any unexpected gain or success: *He had a small windfall yesterday – he won fifty pounds in a raffle.*

ˈ**windmill** *nc* a machine, using sails to work by wind power, for grinding corn or pumping water.

ˈ**windpipe** *nc* the passage for air between mouth and lungs.

ˈ**windscreen** *nc* (*Amer* ˈ**windshield**) a transparent (*usu* glass) screen above the dashboard of a car.

ˈ**windsock** *nc* a device, attached to a high pole, for indicating the direction and speed of wind on an airfield.

ˈ**windswept** *adj* (*formal or liter*) exposed to the wind and showing the effects of it: *You look really windswept with your hair blown about and clothes in a mess*; *a windswept landscape.*

cast/throw (caution *etc*) **to the wind(s)** to abandon (caution *etc*), often recklessly: *She cast caution to the winds and bought a new dress although she could not afford it.*

get, have, put the ˈ**wind up** (*inf*) to (cause to) become nervous or anxious: *She got the wind up when she realized how close we were to the edge*; *We'll pretend to be the police – that will put the wind up them!*

get/have ˈ**wind of** (*inf*) to get a hint of or hear indirectly about: *The police got wind of an attempt to rob the bank, so they surrounded the building.*

get one's second wind to recover one's natural breathing after breathlessness: *Once she got her second wind, she found it easier to run the next few laps*; (*fig*) *I've been awake for twenty hours, but I'm beginning to get my second wind, so I don't feel tired.*

in the wind about to happen: *Government officials seem to think that a change of policy is in the wind.*

like the ˈ**wind** very quickly: *The horse galloped away like the wind.*

See also **woodwind** *under* **wood**.

wind[2] [waind] – *pt, ptp* **wound** [waund] – **1** *vt* (*often with* **round**) to wrap (something) round (something) in coils: *He wound the rope around his waist and began to climb*; *He was winding a bandage round her leg.* **2** *vt* to make (something) into a ball or coil: *Will you wind this wool for me?* **3** *vi* (of a road *etc*) to twist and turn; to be full of bends and turns: *The road winds up the mountain*; *The path winds through the forest*; *The road winds along the lake.* **4** *vt* to tighten the spring of (a clock, watch *etc*) by turning a knob, handle *etc*: *Wind the clock before you go to bed*; *I forgot to wind my watch.* – *See also* **wind up** *below.*

ˈ**winder** *nc* a lever or instrument for winding, on a clock or other mechanism.

ˈ**winding** *adj* (of a road, river *etc*) curving, full of bends *etc*: *a winding road*; *Drive carefully on that road – it's very winding.*

wind down *vi* **1** (of a clock *etc*) to slow down and stop, because its spring has become uncoiled. **2** (of a person) to relax and become free from tension: *It took several days of her holiday to wind* *down after the pressures of her work.*

wind up 1 *vt sep* to turn, twist or coil; to make into a ball or coil: *My ball of wool has unravelled – could you wind it up again?* **2** *vt sep* to wind a clock, watch *etc*: *She wound up the clock and set the alarm.* **3** *vi, vt sep* (*inf*) to (cause to) end: *The meeting finally wound up at about four o'clock; I think it's time to wind the meeting up.* **4** *vi* (*inf*) to end up: *He will wind up in jail; We always wind up by going for a drink.* – *See also* **be/get wound up** *below.*

be/get wound up (*inf*) to be, or get, in a very excited or anxious state: *He gets very wound up about going to the dentist; Try not to get so wound up about your exams; She is very wound up about her interview.*

window ['windou] *nc* **1** an opening in the wall of a building *etc* which is fitted with a frame of wood, metal *etc* containing a sheet or sheets of glass or similar material which can *usu* be clearly seen through, and which can *usu* be opened: *He opened the kitchen window to let the smell out/let some air in; Could you open the car window?; He is cleaning the windows.* **2** the space just inside such an opening: *She stood/sat in the window, looking out on the garden; We have a small table in the window.*

'windowless *adj* not having a window: *a windowless attic.*

'window-box *nc* a box in which plants may be grown on a window-ledge: *We don't have a garden but I grow herbs in a window-box.*

'window-dressing *nu* **1** the arranging of goods in a shop window: *Who is in charge of window-dressing in the store?* **2** (*derog*) the giving to something of an appearance which makes it seem more favourable, good *etc* than it really is: *The encyclopaedia is almost the same as it was, but they've modernized a few obvious things as window-dressing.*

'window-frame *nc* the wooden or metal frame of a window.

'window-ledge *nc* a ledge at the bottom of a window (*usu* on the outside): *She stood on the window-ledge to clean the windows.*

'window-pane *nc* one of the sheets of glass in a window: *That house has very small window-panes.*

'window seat *nc* **1** a seat next to the window (in a train, plane *etc*): *I'll sit by the aisle – you have the window seat.* **2** (*usu with hyphen*) a seat built into the recess of a bay window *etc*: *My little girl likes to sit on the window-seat and read.*

'window-shopping *nu* looking at things in shop windows, but not actually buying anything: *I really intended just to go window-shopping but I bought a new dress.*

'window-sill *nc* a ledge at the bottom of a window (inside or outside): *I keep my washing-up liquid on the window-sill by the kitchen sink.*

windpipe *etc see* **wind**[1].

wine [wain] *ncu* a type of alcoholic drink made from the fermented juice of grapes or other fruit, either red (**red wine**), pink (**rosé** ['rouzei, (*Amer*) [rou'zei]), or golden (**white wine**) in colour: *He drank two bottles of red wine; Will you have white wine or rosé?; Do you prefer French wine to Italian wine?; We stock a wide range of inexpensive wines.*

'wine-coloured *adj* of a dark, rich, red colour: *She wore a wine-coloured dress; The velvet curtains are wine-coloured.*

'wine-press *nc* a machine in which grapes are pressed in making wine.

wing [wiŋ] *nc* **1** one of the arm-like limbs of a bird or bat, which it *usu* uses in flying, or one of the similar limbs of an insect: *The eagle spread his wings and flew away; The bird cannot fly as it has an injured wing; These butterflies have beautiful red and brown markings on their wings; A penguin uses its wings when swimming; An ostrich has wings but it cannot fly.* **2** a similar structure jutting out from the side of an aeroplane: *the huge wings of a jet.* **3** a section built out to the side of a (*usu* large) house: *Grandmother lives in the East Wing; They live in only one wing of the castle – they rent out the rest.* **4** any of the corner sections of a motor vehicle body: *The front wing of the car was damaged in the accident.* **5** (*often with cap*) a section of a political party or of politics in general: *the Left/Right wing.* **6** a side-piece on the back of some armchairs, acting as a headrest. **7** one side of a football *etc* field: *He made a great run down the left wing.* **8** in rugby and hockey, a player who plays mainly down one side of the field. – *See also* **winger**. **9** in the British air force, a group of three squadrons of aircraft. – **1** *vt* to wound in the wing, or in the arm or shoulder: *He only winged the animal, and it was able to run off into the trees.* **2** *vti* (*liter*) to fly quickly and gracefully: *The eagle winged his way across the valley;* (*fig*) *She sent the message winging across the Atlantic.*

winged *adj* having wings (*def 1*): *a winged creature.*

winged- (*in cmpds*) having (a certain type or number of) wing(s): *a ,four-winged 'insect.*

'winger *nc esp* in Association football, a player who plays mainly down one side of the field. – *See also* **wing** (*n def 8*).

'wingless *adj.*

wings *n pl* **1** (*with* **the**) the sides of a theatre stage: *She waited in the wings.* **2** the badge of a qualified pilot: *to get/be given one's wings.*

wing chair *nc* a chair with a high back with wings (*def 6*) projecting forwards from the top.

wing commander *nc* (*with cap in titles*) in the British air force, (a person of) the rank below squadron leader: *He is a wing commander; He was promoted to wing commander; Wing Commander Paterson.* – *See also* Appendix 3.

'wingspan *nc* (*usu in sing*) the distance from the tip of one wing to the tip of the other when outstretched (of birds, aeroplanes *etc*): *This glider has a fifty-foot wingspan.*

on, (*formal*) **upon the wing** (*liter*) flying, *esp* away: *The autumn has come, and the birds are on the wing for warmer countries.*

take (someone) under one's wing to take (someone) under one's protection and/or guidance: *The older girl took the younger one under her wing and looked after her at school.*

take wing (*liter*) to fly away: *The bird took wing and flew to warmer lands.*

the wings *see* **wings** (*def 1*) *above.*

wink [wiŋk] *vi* **1** to shut and open an eye quickly (*esp* in informal friendly greeting, to show that something is a secret *etc*): *He winks at all the girls who pass; Her father winked at her and said 'Don't tell your mother that I was home late.'* **2** (*liter*) (of *eg* lights) to flicker and twinkle: *As I stood on the hill I could see the lights of the town winking far below.* – *nc* an act of winking: *'Don't tell anyone I'm here,' he said with a wink.*

forty winks (*inf*) a short sleep: *Father often has forty winks in his armchair after Sunday lunch.*

tip (someone) the wink *see* **tip**[4].

winkle[1] ['wiŋkl] *vt* (*inf*: *with* **out**) to force (something out of something) gradually and with difficulty: *He winkled the stone out from inside his shoe*; (*fig*) *You must try to winkle more money out of him*; (*fig*) *He tried to winkle some secret information out of her.*

winkle[2] ['wiŋkl] *nc* (*also* **'periwinkle** ['peri-]) a type of small shellfish, shaped like a small snail, eaten as food: *He bought some winkles at a stall down by the seafront.*

winning *etc see* **win**.

winnow ['winou] *vt* (*esp liter*: *sometimes with* **out**) to separate the chaff from (the grain) by wind.

winsome ['winsəm] *adj* (*old or liter*) charming: *a winsome lass/smile*; *She is pretty and winsome.* **'winsomely** *adv.* **'winsomeness** *nu.*

winter ['wintə] *ncu* the coldest season of the year, November or December till January or February in cooler northern regions: *We often have snow in winter*; *It was very cold last winter*; *We must finish before the winter* (= the winter of this year); *in the winter of 1915*; *The winters are bitterly cold in this part of the world*; *Winter is my favourite season*; (*attrib*) *When are you taking your winter break?*; (*attrib*) *They like to sit round a warm fire in the winter evenings.* – *vi* to spend winter (in a particular place): *They wintered in America*; *Where do swallows winter?*

'wintry *adj* like winter in being very cold: *a wintry day*; *wintry weather*; *It's wintry today*; (*fig formal*) *a wintry greeting*; (*fig formal*) *Her smile was rather wintry.* **'wintriness** *nu.*

winter sports *n pl* sports played in the open air on snow and ice, *eg* skiing, tobogganing *etc*: *He is keen on winter sports*; (*attrib*) *a winter sports resort.*

'wintertime *nu* the season of winter: *Many trees lose their leaves in wintertime.*

wipe [waip] **1** *vti* to clean or dry by rubbing with a cloth, paper *etc*: *Would you wipe the table for me?*; *She wiped the washing-up bowl*; *I'll wash the dishes if you wipe* (= dry) *them.* **2** *vt* (*often with* **away, off, up** *etc*) to remove by rubbing with a cloth, paper *etc*: *The child wiped her tears away with her handkerchief*; *Wipe that writing off the blackboard*; *Please wipe up that spilt milk.* – *nc* an act of cleaning by rubbing: *Give the table a quick wipe.*

'wiper *nc* (*also* **'windscreen wiper**) a moving arm for clearing rain *etc* from a vehicle's windscreen.

wipe out *vt sep* **1** to clean the inside of (something) with a cloth *etc*: *Could you wipe out the washhand basin?* **2** (*fig*) to remove; to get rid of: *You must try to wipe out the memory of these terrible events.* **3** to destroy completely: *They wiped out the whole regiment in one battle.*

wipe up 1 *vt sep see* **wipe** (*def 2*). **2** *vi, vt sep* to dry (dishes): *It is your turn to wipe up*; *I've wiped up the dishes.*

wire ['waiə] **1** *nu* metal drawn out into long strands of a particular thickness (commonly, somewhere between the thicknesses of string or thread): *He'll need some wire to connect the battery to the rest of the circuit*; (*attrib*) *a wire fence.* **2** *nc* a single strand of this: *Connect one wire to each terminal on the electric bell*; *There must be a loose wire in my radio somewhere.* **3** *nc* (*inf*: *with* **the**) the metal cable used in telegraphy: *The message came over the wire this morning.* **4** *nc* (*inf*) a telegram: *Send me a wire if I'm needed urgently.* – *vt* **1** (*often with* **up**) to fasten, connect *etc* with wire: *The house has been wired up, but the electricity hasn't been connected yet*; *How long will they take to wire the garage?* **2** (*inf*) to send a telegram to: *Wire me if anything important happens.* **3** (*inf*) to send (a message) by telegram: *You can wire the details to my brother in New York.*

'wireless *ncu* (*old*) (a) radio: *They bought a new wireless yesterday*; *Did you hear the weather forecast on the wireless this morning?*; (*attrib*) *a wireless programme.*

'wiring *nu* the (system of) wires used in connecting up a circuit *etc*: *The wiring in this house is old and dangerous*; *There's a lot of wiring in that radio.*

'high wire *nc* (*usu with* **the**) a high tightrope: *The circus audience watched the acrobats on the high wire*; (*attrib*) *a high-wire artist.*

,wire-'netting *nu* a material with wide mesh woven of wire, used in fencing *etc*: *We made a chicken coop with wood and wire-netting*; *I'm putting wire-netting over the raspberry bushes to keep the birds off them.*

wiry ['waiəri] *adj* (of a person, his body *etc*) slim but strong: *He has a wiry frame*; *He is thin and wiry.*

wise [waiz] *adj* **1** (*formal*) having a great deal of knowledge, from book-learning or experience or both, and able to use it well: *Confucius was one of the wisest teachers of all time*; *a wise old man*; *He's very wise in matters of this sort.* **2** well-advised, sensible *etc*: *You would be wise to do as he suggests*; *It would be wise to do as he says – he has a very nasty temper*; *I don't think that was a wise decision*; *Do you think that was a wise suggestion?* – *See also* **be wise to, put (someone) wise** *below.*

wisdom ['wizdəm], *nu*: *Wisdom comes only with experience*; *I doubt the wisdom of his decision* (= I don't think he was wise to decide) *to let the child travel alone.*

'wisely *adv*: *He nodded wisely*; *He never behaves wisely.*

'wisdom tooth ['wizdəm-] *nc* any one of the four back teeth cut after childhood, *usu* about the age of twenty.

'wisecrack *nc* (*inf*: *sometimes derog*) a joke: *He and his bride are tired of wisecracks about newly-married people.*

'wise guy *nc* (*ironic inf*) a person who (shows that he) thinks that he is smart, knows everything *etc.*

be 'wise to (*inf*) to be aware of or know the purpose of: *He thinks I'm going to give him some money, but I'm wise to his plan*; *I used to trust him but I'm wise to him now.*

none the wiser not knowing any more than before: *She didn't know what the meeting was about before she went, and now she's still none the wiser.*

put (someone) wise (*inf*: *often with* **to**) to let someone know or give someone information (about): *Before he makes a mistake, you'd better put him wise to the current situation*; *He thought that he was going to be in charge but I soon put him wise.*

-wise [waiz] (*in cmpds*) **1** in respect of or as regards: *This new idea may prove to be difficult costwise.* **2** in a (particular) way: *The stripes run crosswise.* *See also* **likewise, otherwise, unwise**.

wish [wiʃ] (not *usu* used with **is, was** *etc* and **-ing** (*defs 3, 4*)) **1** *vi* (*with* **for**) to have and/or express a desire: *I keep wishing for a chance to do something different*; *There's no point in wishing for a miracle.* **2** *vi* (*also* **make a wish**) to express a desire (*esp* in thought): *She closed her eyes and wished/made a wish.* **3** *vt* (*only with a clause as object*) to express the desire for (something): *He wished that she would go away; I wish that I had never met him.* **4** *vt* (*often with an infinitive as object*: *formal*) to require (to do or have something): *Do you wish to sit down, sir?; We wish to book some seats for the theatre; Do you wish breakfast (to be) brought to your room, madam?; I'll cancel the arrangement if you wish.* **5** *vt* to say that one hopes for (something for someone): *I wish you the very best of luck; We wished him all the best* (= the best of luck). – *nc* **1** a desire or longing, or the thing desired: *It's always been my wish to go to South America some day; The committee has expressed the wish that you resign.* **2** an expression of desire: *The fairy godmother granted him three wishes; Did you make a wish?* **3** (*usu in pl*) an expression of hope for something (*usu* good) for someone: *He sends you his best wishes/every good wish for the future.*

'wishbone *nc* a V-shaped bone in the breast of poultry *etc*.

,wishful 'thinking *nu* the belief that something unlikely will happen merely because one wishes that it should: *His belief that she will marry a poor man like him is only wishful thinking; I keep thinking that he might leave but I know that it's only wishful thinking.*

'wishing-well *nc* a well which is supposed to have the power of granting any wish made when one is beside it: *People throw coins into the wishing-well in the castle and make wishes.*

wish (someone) joy of (*usu ironic*) to wish that (something) will be a pleasure or advantage to someone: *You can take this horrible plant away – I wish you joy of it!; You can have this job with pleasure – I wish you joy of it!*

wish (something) on (to) (someone) to give something unpleasant or unwanted to someone: *I wouldn't wish my brother as a husband on my worst enemy!*

See also **well-wisher** *under* **well**[2].

wishy-washy ['wiʃiwoʃi] *adj* (*inf derog*) **1** (of a colour) weak, not definite *etc*: *I don't like that shade of blue – it's too wishy-washy; Those are very wishy-washy colours – I would like a bright colour.* **2** (of a person) not decisive or strong in manner: *He's so wishy-washy that I can't get him to express an opinion on anything!; an uninteresting, wishy-washy young woman.*

wisp [wisp] *nc* (*formal or liter*) a small tuft or thin strand: *A wisp of hair escaped from her hat; A wisp of smoke curled up from the chimney.*

'wispy *adj*: *wispy hair; Her hair is rather wispy.*

wistful ['wistful] *adj* thoughtful and rather sad, (as if) longing for something with little hope: *The dog looked into the butcher's window with a wistful expression on his face; Don't look so wistful – you wouldn't like these chocolates if you had them.* **'wistfully** *adv*. **'wistfulness** *nu*.

wit[1] [wit]: **to 'wit** (*old or legal*) that is to say: *We make one charge only against the accused – to wit, that he did murder Mrs Jones on the night of the 25th June.*

wit[2] [wit] **1** *nu* humour; the ability to express oneself in an amusing way, or its results: *His plays are full of wit and charm; I admire his wit.* **2** *nc* a person who expresses himself in a humorous way, tells jokes *etc*: *She mistakenly thinks that she's the world's greatest wit.* **3** *nu* (*formal*) common sense, inventiveness *etc*: *He relies entirely on his native* (=inborn) *wit; He did not have the wit to defend himself.* – *See also* **wits** *in phrases below*.

'witless *adj* (*formal*) crazy, stupid *etc*: *She was scared witless; a witless young woman.*

-witted (*in cmpds*) having understanding or intelligence of a certain kind: *,quick-/,sharp-'witted.*

'witticism [-sizəm] *nc* (*formal*) a witty remark *etc*.

'witty *adj* clever and amusing: *She is such a witty person; He made several witty remarks; She is popular at parties because she is so witty.* **'wittily** *adv*. **'wittiness** *nu*.

at one's wits' end (*inf*) utterly confused and desperate: *I'm at my wits' end with this terribly complicated situation.*

have/keep one's wits about one to be cautious, alert and watchful: *You have to keep your wits about you in a dangerous situation.*

live by one's wits (*formal*) to live by cunning rather than by hard work: *He does not work – he lives by his wits.*

(frighten/scare one) out of one's wits (to frighten someone) greatly, (almost) to the point of madness: *The sight of the gun in his hand scared me out of my wits; I was frightened out of my wits by the sight of the dead body.*

See also **half-wit** *under* **half**.

witch [witʃ] *nc* **1** a woman who is supposed to have powers of magic, *usu* through working with the devil: *The harmless old woman was burnt as a witch because people thought that she had killed the cows; The child drew a picture of a witch riding on a broomstick; Witches are thought to cast spells.* **2** (*derog*) an unpleasant woman.

'witchcraft *nu* magic (such as that) practised by a witch: *Quite a lot of people practise witchcraft nowadays.*

'witch-doctor *nc* in some African tribes, a person whose profession is to cure illness and keep away evil magical influences.

'witch-hunt *nc* a search for, and persecution of, people whose views are regarded as being against the best interests of the country where they live: *The McCarthy witch-hunt in the United States from 1950-54 sought out members of the Communist Party.*

with [wið] *prep* **1** in the company of; beside; among; including: *I was walking with my father; She was dancing with my husband; He was playing with the other children; Do they enjoy playing with each other?; He used to play football with* (= as a member of) *the Arsenal team; Put this book with the others; Mix the sugar with the eggs; With the petrol, the holiday cost us £200.* **2** by means of; using: *Mend it with this glue; Sew the cloth with this thread; Polish the table with this; Cut it with a knife; She had been strangled with a nylon stocking.* **3** used in expressing the idea of filling, covering *etc*: *Fill this jug with milk; He was covered with mud; I'm overwhelmed with work; The road was blocked with snow.* **4** in the same direction as: *The dead body was drifting with the current.* **5** at the same time or rate as: *His bad temper increased with age; Wisdom comes with experience.* **6** against: *They quarrelled with each other; He fought with my brother and injured him.* **7** used to express separation: *He was reluctant to part with her; I've finished with these tools.* **8** used to express comparison: *Compared with her sister, she's not clever; His statement today doesn't agree with what he said yesterday.* **9** (used in descriptions of things, actions *etc*) having, showing, giving *etc*: *a man with a limp; a woman with a beautiful face; a girl* *with long hair; a stick with a handle; He did it with ease; Treat this book with care; 'You'll be late,' he said with a frown.* **10** as the result of: *He is shaking with fear; He was white with terror.* **11** because of (having): *With £20 000 in the bank you can feel quite secure; I won't be able to go on holiday with my mother being ill.* **12** in spite of (having): *I like this job with all its disadvantages; With all his money he is still unhappy.* **13** in the care of: *Leave your bag with me; I left my case with the porter.* **14** in relation to; in the case of; concerning: *Be careful with that!; I'm very angry with her; What's wrong with you?; What shall I do with these books?; I can do nothing with this child* (= I cannot get him to do anything I suggest or influence him in any way). **15** used after adverbs *etc* in exclamations expressing a wish: *Down with* (= Let's get rid of) *fascism!; Away with school uniforms!; Into the dustbin with all this junk!; Up with Manchester United!*

be 'with (someone) (*inf*) **1** to understand (someone): *Are you with me so far?* **2** to support (someone): *I'm with you all the way in your effort to be elected.*

'with it (*sl: sometimes facet*) fashionable: *He's very with it; Although he's middle-aged he tries to be with it;* (*attrib*) *a with-it dress.*

with 'that (*formal*) at that point: *'Goodbye,' he said, and with that, we left.*

See also **within, without.**

withdraw [wið'dro:] – *pt* **with'drew** [-'dru:]: *ptp* **with'drawn** – **1** *vti* (*sometimes formal*) to (cause to) move back or away: *The army withdrew from the firing-line; The colonel withdrew his troops;* (*fig*) *He withdrew his support for the plan;* (*fig*) *They withdrew from the competition.* **2** *vt* to take back (something one has said): *She withdrew her previous remarks, and apologized; He later withdrew the charges he made against her.* **3** *vt* to take away or remove (money from a bank account *etc*): *I withdrew all my savings and went abroad; He has withdrawn £200 from his account.*

with'drawal *ncu*: *The withdrawal of troops took place gradually; the withdrawal of his support; the withdrawal of legal charges; She has made several withdrawals from her bank account.*

with'drawn *adj* (*formal*) (of a person, his manner *etc*) not responsive or friendly; very reserved; not liking the company of people: *She hasn't many friends – she's a very withdrawn child; She's been quiet and withdrawn since her husband died.*

wither ['wiðə] *vti* (of plants *etc*) to (cause to) fade, dry up, or decay: *The plants withered because they had no water; The hot sun has withered all my plants.*

'withering *adj* (*usu fig*) causing to wither: *She gave him a cold, withering* (= scornful) *glance; Her look was withering.*

withers ['wiðəz] *n pl* the ridge between the shoulder bones of a horse.

withhold [wið'hould] – *pt, ptp* **with'held** [-'held] – *vt* to refuse to give: *He's withholding his approval until after next week's meeting.*

within [wi'ðin] *prep* (*more formal than* **inside**) inside (the limits of): *She'll be here within an hour; I could hear sounds from within the building; His actions were within the law* (= legal). – *adv* (*formal*) inside: *Car for sale. Apply within.*

without [wi'ðaut] *prep* **1** in the absence of; not having: *They went without you; I could not live without him; Without her, he would die; How can you live without hope?; We cannot survive without water; He will come without doubt* (= certainly). **2** not: *He drove away without saying goodbye; You can't walk along this street without meeting someone you know.* **3** (*formal or legal: rare*) outside (the limits of): *without the terms of the agreement.* – *adv* (*arch or liter*) outside: *Your carriage is without, my lady.*

do without *see* **do.**

go without, go without saying *see* **go.**

withstand [wið'stand] – *pt, ptp* **with'stood** [-'stud] – *vt* (*very formal*) to oppose or resist (successfully): *They withstood the attackers for forty-eight hours, and then surrendered; He withstood the torture bravely.*

See also **notwithstanding.**

witness ['witnəs] **1** *nc* a person who has seen or was present at an event *etc* and so has direct knowledge of it: *Someone must have seen the accident but the police can find no witnesses; He always beat his wife when there were no witnesses around.* **2** *nc* a person who gives evidence, *esp* in a law court: *a witness for the defence/prosecution.* **3** *nc* a person who adds his signature to a document to show that he considers another signature on the document to be genuine: *You cannot sign your will without witnesses.* **4** *ncu* (*formal*) (something that provides) proof or evidence: *His anxiety was a witness to his love for her.* – *See also* **bear witness** *below.* – **1** *vt* (*formal*) to see and be present at: *This lady witnessed an accident at three o'clock this afternoon.* **2** *vt* (*legal*) to sign one's name to show that one knows that (something) is genuine: *He witnessed my signature on the new agreement; She witnessed the documents by signing her name below mine.* **3** *vti* (*legal or very formal: rare*) to give or be evidence or proof (that); to testify (that): *My wife will witness that I was at home all evening.*

'witness-box/'witness-stand *nc* the stand from which a witness gives evidence in a court of law.

bear witness (*formal*) to give or be evidence: *She will bear witness to his honesty; They will bear witness that he is honest; His scars bore witness to the torture he had suffered.*

witticism, witty *etc see* **wit**[2].

wittingly ['witiŋli] *adv* (*formal: usu in neg*) knowingly: *I would never wittingly hurt you; He would not wittingly ruin your chances.*

See also **unwitting.**

wives *see* **wife.**

wizard ['wizəd] *nc* **1** a man who is said to have magic powers: *a fairy-story about a wizard.* **2** (*inf*) a person who is exceptionally good at something: *She is a wizard at making pastry; He is a financial wizard.*

wizened ['wiznd] *adj* (*formal or liter*) **1** (of trees *etc*) dried up and/or withered: *These apples are wizened.* **2** (of people) looking like this: *a wizened old man.*

wobble ['wobl] *vi* (*slightly inf*) to rock unsteadily from side to side: *The ladder wobbled dangerously when he reached the top; The bicycle wobbled slightly and the child fell off.* – *ncu* (*slightly inf*) a slight rocking, unsteady movement: *This wheel has a bit of a wobble.*

'wobbly *adj* (*inf*) unsteady; not firm: *This bike has a wobbly wheel; This ladder is wobbly; I felt a bit wobbly when I got out of bed.* **'wobbliness** *nu.*

woe [wou] *ncu* (*liter or facet*) (a cause of) grief or misery: *He has many woes; He told a tale of woe.*

'woeful *adj* (*formal*) **1** miserable; unhappy: *He wore a woeful expression*; *He looks rather woeful.* **2** (*attrib*) to be regretted; disgraceful: *his woeful ignorance.* **'woefully** *adv.* **'woefulness** *nu.*

'woebegone [-bigon] *adj* (*liter or formal*) sad-looking: *She looks rather woebegone now her friend has gone away*; *a woebegone expression.*

woke, woken *see* **wake**[1].

wolf [wulf] – *pl* **wolves** [wulvz] – *nc* **1** a type of wild animal of the dog family, *usu* found hunting in packs: *We could hear the wolves howling.* **2** (*inf derog*) a man who is constantly pursuing women for sexual purposes: *He keeps paying her compliments and she doesn't realize what a wolf he is.* – *vt* (*inf derog*: *often with* **down**) to eat greedily: *He wolfed* (*down*) *his breakfast and hurried out*; *Please don't wolf your food.*

'wolfish *adj* like a wolf. **'wolfishly** *adv.* **'wolfishness** *nu.*

'wolf-cub *nc* **1** a young wolf (*def 1*). **2** (*with cap*: *old*) a Cub Scout, a member of the junior branch of the Scout movement.

'wolf-whistle *nc* a whistle (impolitely) made by a man to express his admiration of a woman's physical appearance: *She blushed at the wolf-whistles from the workmen as she passed by.*

cry wolf *see* **cry**.

keep the wolf from the door to keep away hunger or want: *The job may not be very exciting, but the money will help to keep the wolf from the door.*

woman ['wumən] – *pl* **women** ['wimin] – **1** *nc* an adult human female: *His sisters are both grown women now*; *She wasn't very pretty as a girl but she grew into a beautiful woman*; *The women and children left the sinking ship first.* **2** *nu* (*no article*: *formal*) adult human females considered as a whole: *Woman is an unpredictable creature.* **3** *nc* (*inf usu derog*) a girl-friend or mistress: *What does this current woman of yours look like?* **4** *nc* (*inf*) a female domestic daily helper: *We have a woman who comes in to do the cleaning.* **5** *n* (*inf*) a word sometimes used in speaking informally (*esp* angrily), or giving commands, to a woman: *Do what you're told, woman!*

-woman (*in cmpds*) sometimes used instead of **-man** when the person performing an activity is a woman, as in **chairwoman**.

'womanhood *nu* (*formal*) **1** the state of being a woman: *She will reach womanhood in a few years' time.* **2** human females considered as a whole: *a fine example of modern womanhood.*

'womanish *adj* (*esp attrib*: *derog*) (of a man or his behaviour *etc*) like, or typical of, a woman: *his womanish weakness.*

'womanize, -ise *vi* (*inf derog*) (of a man) to pursue numerous women for sexual purposes: *If you stopped drinking and womanizing and spent more time studying, you'd pass your university exams.*

'womanizer, -s- *nc* (*inf derog*): *I'm not surprised she divorced him – he's a real womanizer.*

'womankind, womenkind ['wimin-] *nus* (*formal*) women generally.

'womanly *adj* (*formal*) (showing qualities) natural or suitable to a woman: *a womanly figure*; *womanly charm*; *She does not consider it womanly to wear trousers.* **'womanliness** *nu.*

'womenfolk ['wimin-] *n pl* (*often inf*) female people, *esp* female relatives: *None of the womenfolk went to the funeral.*

woman of the world a sophisticated woman who is familiar with most situations and aware of how to react to them: *Her father thinks she is simple and innocent but she is a woman of the world.*

womb [wu:m] *nc* the part of the female body in which the young of mammals are developed and kept until birth; the uterus: *She felt the unborn baby move in her womb*; *The surgeon had to remove her womb as it was diseased.*

women *etc see* **woman**.

won *see* **win**.

wonder ['wʌndə] **1** *nu* (*formal or liter*) the state of mind produced by something unexpected or extraordinary: *He was full of wonder at the amazing sight*; *The child stared with wonder at the Christmas tree.* **2** *nc* something strange, unexpected or extraordinary: *the seven wonders of the world*; (*often ironic*) *You work late so often that it's a wonder you don't take a bed to the office!* **3** *nu* (*often with* **the**) the quality of being strange or unexpected: *The wonder of the discovery is that it was only made ten years ago*; *It is not surprising that he got the job – the wonder is that they are paying him so much.* – **1** *vti* (not used with **is, was** *etc* and **-ing**) to be surprised: (*formal*) *I sometimes wonder at your ignorance!*; (*formal*) *It's past six o'clock – I wonder that he hasn't arrived yet*; *His behaviour isn't to be wondered at – he's just had a bad shock*; *Caroline is very fond of John – I shouldn't wonder if she married* (= I expect she will marry) *him.* **2** *vi* (*with* **about**) to feel curiosity or doubt (about): *Have you ever wondered about his reasons for wanting this money?* **3** *vt* (*usu with a clause as object*) to feel curiosity about or a desire to know: *I wonder what the news is*; *'John was there again yesterday.' 'I wonder why.'*

'wonderful, (*old*) **'wondrous** *adjs* (*often used loosely*) arousing wonder; extraordinary, *esp* in excellence: *That was a wonderful opportunity*; *She gave me a wonderful present*; *It is wonderful to hear that she is having a baby*; *My mother is a wonderful person.* **'wonderfully** *adv.*

'wonderingly *adv* (*formal*) with great curiosity and amazement: *The children gazed wonderingly at the fascinating puppets.*

'wonderment *nu* (*formal*) wonder (*def 1*).

'wonderland [-land] *nc* (*usu in sing*: *often liter*) a land or place full of wonderful things: *a winter wonderland.*

no wonder (*inf*) it isn't surprising (that): *No wonder you couldn't open the door – it was locked!*; *'He says he feels sick.' 'No wonder, after eating all that ice-cream!'*

wonky ['woŋki] *adj* (*inf*) working badly, badly-made, badly-formed *etc*: *The television's gone wonky again*; *a wonky machine.*

wont [wount] *nc* (*formal or liter*: *no pl*) a habit or custom: *He took a walk yesterday, as is his wont when he wants to think.*

won't *see* **will**.

woo [wu:] – *3rd pers sing prt* **woos**: *pt, ptp* **wooed** – *vt* **1** (*old or liter*) (of a man) to seek (someone) as a wife; to court: *He wooed the daughter of the king.* **2** to seek to persuade *etc* (a person) or to gain (*eg* success): *He's being wooed by Bloggs and Company with offers of a huge salary, because they want him to become a director.* **'wooer** *nc.*

wood [wud] **1** *nu, adj* (of) the material of which the trunk and branches of trees are composed: *My desk is made of wood*; *Teak and ebony are hard,* *attractive-looking types of wood; wood panelling; The flooring looked as if it was wood, but it was really plastic;* (*attrib*) *a wood fire/stove* (= a fire or stove that burns wood); *She gathered some wood for the fire.* 2 *nc* (*often in pl*) a group of growing trees: *They went for a walk in the woods; There is a wood behind our house; a beech wood.* 3 *nc* a golf-club whose head is made of wood: *Use a wood for this shot.*

'wooded *adj* (of land) covered with trees: *a wooded hillside.*

'wooden *adj* 1 made of wood: *a wooden cabinet; three wooden chairs; Hand me that wooden pole; That's not plastic – it's wooden.* 2 (of a person, his face, his manner *etc*) stiff; dull; without liveliness or charm: *The actress gave rather a wooden performance; She is a bit wooden in front of a television camera.* **'woodenly** *adv.* **'woodenness** *nu.*

'woody *adj* (*inf*) 1 covered with trees: *I like woody countryside; It's too woody here – I prefer open fields.* 2 (of a smell *etc*) of or like wood.

'woodcut *nc* an engraving cut on wood or an impression from it.

'woodcutter *nc* a person whose job is felling trees.

'woodland *nu* land covered with woods: *a beautiful stretch of woodland.*

'woodpecker *nc* a type of bird which pecks holes in the bark of trees, searching for insects.

'wood-pigeon *nc* a type of bird of the pigeon family, found mainly in woods.

'woodwind [-wind] *nu* (in an orchestra, the group of people who play) wind instruments made of wood: *The woodwind is far too quiet!;* (*attrib*) *a woodwind instrument.*

'woodwork *nu* 1 art of making things from wood; carpentry: *He did woodwork as a subject at school.* 2 the wooden part of any structure: *Dry rot has affected almost all the woodwork in the house.*

'woodworm – *pls* **'woodworm, woodworms** – 1 *nc* the larva of a certain type of beetle, which bores into wood and destroys it: *I can't find a single woodworm in this plank; My chair is full of woodworm.* 2 *nu* the effects of the larva: *Woodworm has affected all the timbers in the roof.*

out of the wood(s) out of danger: *We're not out of the wood(s) yet by a long way.*

touch wood *see* **touch**.

woof *see* **warp**[2].

wool [wul] *nu, adj* (of) the soft hair of sheep and some other animals, often made into yarn *etc* for knitting or into fabric for making clothes *etc*: *I wear wool in winter – it keeps you warmer than other materials do;* (*in cmpds*) *Her ball of knitting-wool fell on to the floor;* (*attrib*) *the wool trade; a wool blanket; This suit is wool and nylon.*

'woollen *adj* 1 made of wool: *She wore a woollen hat; Is that sweater woollen?* 2 (*attrib*) dealing in, producing *etc* goods made of wool: *woollen manufacturers; woollen merchants.*

'woollens *n pl* clothes (*esp* jumpers *etc*) made of wool: *Woollens should always be hand-washed in warm, not hot, water.*

'woolly *adj* (*inf*) 1 made of, or like, wool: *a woolly jumper/rug; This sweater is too woolly; She has woolly hair.* 2 (*also* **ˌwoolly-'headed**) (of a person) vague or hazy: *I felt a bit woolly after I hit my head; She's too woolly-headed to be in charge of a department.* – *nc* (*inf*) a knitted garment: *winter woollies.*

'woolliness *nu.*

cottonwool *see* **cotton**[1].

dyed-in-the-wool *see* **dye**.

steel wool *see* **steel**.

'wool-gathering *nu* absentmindedness or day-dreaming: *I am tired of his constant wool-gathering – I wish he would concentrate on his work.*

pull the wool over someone's eyes to deceive someone: *She tried to pull the wool over his eyes with some ridiculous excuse.*

woozy ['wu:zi] *adj* (*inf*) dazed, dizzy, half-asleep *etc* (through drink, drugs, lack of sleep *etc*): *I felt rather woozy after I came round from the anaesthetic; in rather a woozy state.* **'woozily** *adv.* **'wooziness** *nu.*

word [wə:d] 1 *nc* the smallest unit of language (whether written, spoken or read) which can be used independently (when written, *usu* found with a space on either side): *This example is made up of words, 'this' being the first, 'example' being the second etc: a two-word compound.* 2 *nc* (*no pl*) a (brief) conversation: *I'd like a (quick) word with you in my office.* 3 *nu* news: *When you get there, send word that you've arrived safely; Have you heard any word of John lately?* 4 *nc* (*usu with* **my, your, his** *etc*) a solemn promise: *He gave her his word that it would never happen again.* 5 *nc* (*no pl*: *with* **the**) a rumour: *The word is that he's gone back to Australia.* – *See also* **the Word** *below.* – *vt* to express in written or spoken language: *How are you going to word the letter so that it doesn't seem rude?*

'wording *nu* the manner of expressing something in words, the choice of words *etc*: *The wording of the letter was rather hostile.*

'wordy *adj* (*derog*) containing too many words: *He made a very wordy speech; You will have to shorten that essay – it is too wordy.* **'wordily** *adv.* **'wordiness** *nu.*

'word-blindness *nu* dyslexia.

ˌword-'perfect *adj* repeated, or able to repeat (something), precisely in the original words: *a word-perfect performance; He wants to be word-perfect by next week's rehearsal.*

break, keep one's word to keep or fail to keep one's promise: *If you break your word he will never trust you again; You must keep your word if you promised to take the children to the cinema.*

by word of mouth by one person telling another in speech, not in writing: *She gets a lot of information from the newspapers, and some by word of mouth.*

eat one's words *see* **eat**.

get a word in edgeways (*inf*: *usu in neg*) to break into a conversation *etc* and say something: *She couldn't get a word in edgeways – those two kept shouting at each other.*

have a word in someone's ear to tell someone something confidentially: *Have a word in his teacher's ear and tell her that he is worrying about his school-work.*

have words (*inf*) to argue or row: *He's in a foul mood – I think they've been having words.*

in a word to sum up briefly: *In a word, I don't like him.*

the last word *see* **last**[1].

put in/say a good word (*usu with* **for**) to say something pleasant to someone (about someone else): *John's going to put in a good word for me in the hope that his boss will give me a job.*

say the word *see* **say**.

take (someone) at his word to believe

(someone) without question and act accordingly: *When she said that she would like them to visit her they took her at her word and arrived the following week.*

take someone's word for it to assume that what someone says is correct (without checking): *I'll have to take his word for it that the train leaves at 10 o'clock – I haven't got a timetable; You'll have to take the child's word for it that he did the work by himself.*

the Word in the Christian religion, the teachings and writings of the Bible.

word for word in the exact, original words; verbatim: *That's precisely what he told me, word for word*; (*attrib*) *a word-for-word repeat of what he said last week.*

word of honour *see* **honour**.

wore *see* **wear**.

work [wɔːk] **1** *nu* physical or mental effort made in order to achieve or make something: *This machine can do the work of three men; He's put in a lot of work on this project for very little profit.* **2** *nu* employment: *She's been out of work since the factory closed; I cannot find work in this town.* **3** *nu* a task or tasks; the thing that one is working on: *You must excuse me, but I have (a great deal of) work to do; My husband has so much to do that he often has to bring (his) work home from the office to finish in his spare time.* **4** *nc* a painting, book, piece of music *etc*: *the works of Van Gogh/Shakespeare/Mozart; This work was composed in 1816.* **5** *nu* the manner in which a person does his job *etc*, or the standard of whatever is produced by it: *His work has shown a great improvement lately.* **6** *nu* one's place of employment: *He left (his) work at 5.30 p.m.; I don't think I'll go to work tomorrow – I don't feel well; The bus broke down, so I got to work very late; I won't be at work on Tuesday as I'm going to the dentist.* – **1** *vti* (*sometimes with* **at** *or* **on**) to (cause to) make mental or physical efforts in order to achieve or make something: *She works at the factory three days a week; He always works his employees very hard; I've been working on/at a new project.* **2** *vi* to be employed: *Are you working these days?; 'Is she still working?' 'No, she left to have a baby.'* **3** *vti* to (cause to) operate (in the correct way): *He has no idea how that machine works/how to work that machine; That machine doesn't work, but this one's working all right; I can't get this electric hair-drier to work – it must be broken.* **4** *vi* to be practicable and/or successful: *If my scheme works, we'll be rich!* **5** *vt* (*with* **across, down, up** *etc*) to make (one's way) slowly and carefully with effort or difficulty: *She worked her way up the rock face*; (*fig*) *He gradually worked his way up* (= was promoted) *in the firm until he was managing director.* **6** *vti* to get into, or put into, a stated condition or position, slowly and gradually: *The wheel worked loose because of the vibrations; He gradually worked the nail out of his shoe.* **7** *vt* to put (oneself) into a given state: *She worked herself into a fury.* – *See also* **work up** *below.* **8** *vt* (*usu with* **in**: *often in passive*) to make (things) from (a given metal *etc*): *The ornaments had been worked in gold.* **9** *vt* (*less formal than* **knead**) to knead, massage *etc*: *Work the dough for ten minutes, and then leave it to rise.* **10** *vi* (of muscles *etc*) to move uncontrollably: *The corners of his mouth were working as he tried hard not to laugh.* **11** *vt* to produce (results or effects): *This latest treatment has worked wonders on my rheumatism.* – *See also* **work** *in phrases below.*

-work (*in cmpds*) **1** (the art of making) goods of a particular material: *He learns woodwork at school; This shop sells basketwork.* **2** parts of something, *eg* a building, made of a particular material: *The stonework/woodwork/paintwork needs to be renewed.*

'workable *adj* able to be carried out; practicable: *a workable plan; I don't think this scheme is workable.* **worka'bility** *nu.*

'worker *nc* **1** (*often in cmpds*) a person who works or who is employed in an office, a (certain type of) factory *etc*: *office-workers; car-workers.* **2** a person who works with his hands; a manual worker: *The workers are asking for the same wages as the typists in the factory.* **3** (*inf*) a person who works hard: *He's a real worker.*

'working *nu*, **'workings** *n pl* the (method(s) of) operation: *He gave a detailed explanation of the workings of the factory; Our highly-skilled engineering staff guarantees the smooth working of all our machines.*

works (*inf*) **1** *n sing* (*often in cmpds*) a factory *etc*: *The steel works is closed for the holidays.* **2** *n pl* the mechanism (of a watch, clock or other machinery): *The works are all rusted – that's why it's stopped.* **3** *n pl* (*formal*) deeds, actions *etc*: *She's devoted her life to good works.*

'work-basket, 'work-box *etc nc* a basket, box *etc* for holding thread, needlework *etc.*

work-day *see* **working day** *below.*

,worked-'up *adj* (*pred*) excited, nervous, annoyed *etc*: *He became/got very worked-up about the whole problem.* – *See also* **work up** *below.*

'workhouse *nc* (*hist*) a place where people who were extremely poor and homeless lived and worked.

working class *n sing or n pl* (*with* **the**), *adj* (*sometimes derog*) (of) the section of society who work with their hands, doing manual labour: *She is proud to belong to the working class; Some members of the working class earn more than teachers; Many children of working-class parents go to university nowadays; His attitudes are very working-class.*

working day, 'work-day *nc* **1** a day on which one goes to work, and is not on holiday: *Tomorrow's another working day – I'm going to bed early tonight.* **2** the period of actual labour in a normal day at work: *My working day starts at 8.30 a.m. and it's eight hours long.*

working hours *n pl* the times of day between which one is at work: *Normal working hours are 9 a.m. to 5 p.m.*

'working-party *nc* **1** (*also* **'work-party**) a group of people gathered together (*usu* voluntarily) to perform a particular physical task: *They organized a work-party to clear the canal of weeds.* **2** a group of people appointed to look at or investigate something: *The council set up a working-party to examine the different proposals for educating the handicapped.*

working week *nc* the five days from Monday to Friday inclusive when people go to work: *This job will probably take five working weeks.*

'workman *nc* a man who does manual work: *the workmen on a building site.*

'workmanlike *adj* **1** suitable to a good workman: *a workmanlike attitude.* **2** well performed: *a workmanlike job.*

'workmanship *nu* the skill of a qualified workman; skill in making things: *He admired the workmanship of the cabinet-maker.*

'workmate *nc* (*inf*) one of the people who work in the same factory or other place of employment as oneself: *Her workmates teased her about being the boss's favourite.*

'workout *ncu* (*inf*) a period of hard physical exercise for the purpose of keeping fit *etc*: *They had a workout in the gym.*

work-party *see* **working-party** *above.*

'workshop *nc* **1** a room or building, *esp* in a factory *etc* where construction and repairs are carried out: *He injured his hand while operating one of the machine tools in the workshop.* **2** a course of study or (*esp* experimental) work for a group of people on a particular project: *an actors' workshop*; *a poetry/history workshop.*

'workshy [-ʃai] *adj* (*inf derog*) lazy, and avoiding doing any work: *He is not really looking for a job – he is workshy*; *She gets very annoyed with workshy people.*

work study *see* **time and motion study** *under* **time**.

work-to-rule *see* **work to rule** *below.*

all in the day's work not causing extra or unusual effort or trouble: *She thanked him for attending to her problem so kindly, but he assured her that it was all in the day's work.*

at work working: *He's writing a novel and he likes to be at work (on it) by eight o'clock every morning.* – *See also* **work** (*n def 6*).

get/set to work to start work: *Could you get to work painting that ceiling?*; *I'll have to set to work on this mending this evening.* – *See also* **work** (*n def 6*).

give (someone) the works (*inf*) to give someone the full treatment: *They've certainly given her the works at the hairdresser's – she's had her hair cut, tinted and permed.*

go out to work *see* **go**.

go to work on (something) to begin work on (something): *We're thinking of going to work on an extension to the house.*

have one's work cut out (*inf*) to be faced with a difficult task: *You'll have your work cut out to beat the champion.*

in working order (of a machine *etc*) operating correctly: *Some of the machines were broken but now they're all in working order.*

make short work of *see* **short**.

out of work having no employment: *He's been out of work for months*; (*attrib*) *an out-of-work teacher.*

work of art a painting, sculpture *etc*: *The Royal Gallery houses many works of art.*

work off *vt sep* to get rid of (something unwanted or unpleasant) by taking physical exercise *etc*: *He worked off his anger by running round the garden six times*; *He tried to work off some of his excess weight by doing exercises every day.*

work one's fingers to the bone (*fig*) to work extremely hard: *His mother worked her fingers to the bone to send him to university.*

work one's passage to pay one's fare (*usu* on a ship) not in cash, but by unpaid work on board.

work out 1 *vt sep* to solve or calculate correctly: *I can't work out how many should be left.* **2** *vi, vt sep* to (cause to) happen successfully: *Don't worry – it will all work out in the end.* – *See also* **work** (*v def 6*).

work to rule to work strictly according to the rules laid down for one's job, with the deliberate intention of slowing down work because of an industrial dispute: *Train services were severely disrupted when the train drivers began working to rule.* (*nc* **ˌwork-to-'rule**).

work up 1 *vt sep* to excite or rouse gradually: *She worked herself up into a fury*; *He's worked his mother up into a state of nervous exhaustion.* – *See also* **worked-up** *above.* **2** *vt sep* to raise or create: *I just can't work up any energy/appetite/enthusiasm today.* **3** *vi* (*with* **to**) to get (oneself) into a state of readiness for (doing) something: *Start off with the easy exercises and work up to the difficult ones.* – *See also* **work** (*v def 5*).

world [wəːld] **1** *n* (*with cap and/or* **the**) the planet Earth: *every country of the world.* **2** *nc* (*no pl*: *with* **the**: *rarely with pl verb*) the people who live on the planet Earth: *The whole world is waiting for the results of these talks*; *Half the world live(s) below the poverty line.* **3** *nc* any planet *etc*: *people from other worlds.* **4** *nc* (*usu in sing*) a state of existence (mental or physical): *Many people believe that after death, one enters the next world* (= where people's souls go after death); *He lives in another world* (= He is not aware of what is going on around him). **5** *nc* an area of life or activity: *the insect world*; *the world of the international businessman*; *the literary world.* **6** *nc* (*no pl*) a great deal: *The holiday did him a/the world of good.* **7** *nc* (*no pl*: *with* **the**: *often formal*) the lives and ways of ordinary people: *He's been a monk for so long that he knows nothing of the (outside) world.*

'worldly *adj* (*formal*: *neg* **un-**, *usu* of people) of or belonging to this world; not spiritual: *worldly wisdom/happiness*; *He does not care about worldly pleasures*; *Monks are not at all worldly.* **'worldliness** *nu.*

'worldly-wise *adj* (*formal or liter*: *usu pred*) showing the wisdom of those who are experienced in the ways of the world.

ˌworld'wide *adj, adv* (extending over or found) everywhere in the world: *a worldwide sales network*; *Their products are sold worldwide.*

the best of both worlds the advantages of both the alternatives in a situation *etc* in which one can normally only expect to have one: *She has a well-paid, full-time job as well as a husband and two children – she has the best of both worlds in fact.*

dead to the world *see* **dead**.

for all the world exactly, quite *etc*: *It looked for all the world as if he was going to win*; *He looked for all the world as though he had slept in his clothes.*

man of the world *see* **man**.

the New World America, *esp* North America.

the Old World Europe, Africa and Asia.

on top of the world *see* **top**[1].

out of this world (*inf*) unbelievably marvellous: *His cooking is just out of this world!*; *The concert was out of this world.*

think the world of *see* **think**.

what in the world(?) (*often derog*) used for emphasis when asking a question: *What in the world have you done to your hair?*; *What in the world did you do that for?*

woman of the world *see* **woman**.

the world is his, your *etc* **oyster** *see* **oyster**.

worm [wəːm] *nc* **1** a kind of small creeping animal with a ringed body and no backbone; an earthworm. **2** (*derog*) a weak and worthless person: *He was a worm to leave his wife and family without any means of support.* – *See also* **worms** *below.* – **1**

vti (*inf*: *often* **worm one's way**) to make (one's way) slowly or secretly: *He wormed his way to the front of the crowd*; (*derog*) *He gradually wormed his way into her affections.* **2** *vt* to treat for, or rid of, worms: *Have you wormed the dog?* **3** *vt* (*inf*: *usu with* **out of**) to obtain (information *etc*) slowly and using persuasion or threats (from someone): *It took me hours to worm the true story out of him.*

worms *n sing* a disease in which a type of worm infests the intestines: *That dog has worms.*

worn, worn-out *see* **wear**.

worry[1] ['wʌri, (*Amer*) 'wəːri] **1** *vti* to (cause to) feel anxious: *His dangerous driving always worries me*; *His mother is worried about his education*; *There's no need to worry just because he's late.* **2** *vt* to annoy: *Don't worry me just now – I'm busy!* **3** *vt* (*formal*) to shake or tear with the teeth *etc* as a dog does its prey *etc*: *That dog's been worrying my slippers again – they're torn to shreds!*; *The dog worried the rabbit.* – *ncu* (a cause of) anxiety: *That boy is a constant (source of) worry to his mother!*; *Try to forget your worries*; *The worry of trying to bring up three children has been too much for her.*

'worried *adj* (*neg* **un-**): *a worried look/mind*; *She looks tired and worried.*

worse [wəːs] *adj* **1** bad to a greater extent: *Yours is worse than mine*; *His chances of winning are worse than mine*; *He has a worse garden than I have*; *The weather's much worse than it was yesterday.* **2** (*pred*) not so well: *I feel worse today than I did last week.* **3** more unpleasant: *Waiting for exam results is worse than sitting the exams.* – *adv* not so well: *He sings worse now than he did before*; *He sings worse than me.* – *pron* someone or something which is bad to a greater extent than the other (of two people, things *etc*): *He's the worse of the two.*

'worsen *vti* to (cause to) grow worse: *His illness has worsened*; *This new outbreak of fighting has worsened the situation.*

go from bad to worse *see* **bad**.

none the worse for not in any way harmed by: *The child was lost in the supermarket but fortunately was none the worse for his experience*; *The baby's none the worse for being left out in the cold.*

the 'worse for worse because of: *He looks (all) the worse for his three years in prison.*

the worse for wear (*fig*: *inf*) tired (and untidy *etc*): *You look a bit the worse for wear after last night's party.*

worse off worse in some way, *esp* poorer: *You're no worse off (for money) these days than I am.*

See also **bad, ill, worst**.

worship ['wəːʃip] – *pt, ptp* **'worshipped**, (*Amer*) **'worshiped** – **1** *vt* to pay great honour to: *The Greeks used to worship several gods*; *They worship the Christian God.* **2** *vt* (*inf*) to love or admire very greatly: *She absolutely worships her children.* **3** *vi* (*formal*) to take part in a religious service: *This is the church where we used to worship.* – **1** *nu* (*formal*) religious services: *a place of worship.* **2** *n* (*with cap*: *with* **His, Your** *etc*) a title used when speaking to or of a mayor or an English Justice of the Peace: *Please be seated, Your Worship.* **3** *nu* love and honour (often religious): *the worship of gods*; (*fig*) *the worship of money.*

'worshipful *adj* (*often with cap*) a word sometimes used in the titles of a mayor, an English Justice of the Peace, or certain associations: *the Worshipful the Mayor of Oxbridge*; *the Right Worshipful Mr Jones.*

'worshipper *nc* (*sometimes in cmpds*) a person who worships: *The church was full of devout worshippers*; (*fig*) *They are sun-worshippers.*

worst [wəːst] *adj* bad, wicked *etc* to the greatest extent: *That is the worst book I have ever read*; *She is the worst singer I know.* – *adv* in the worst way or manner: *She sings worst (of all).* – *pron* the thing, person *etc* which is most bad, unfortunate, wicked *etc*: *Tell me the worst!*; *She is/They are the worst I've ever known for getting people's names wrong*; *He is at his worst first thing in the morning.*

do one's worst to do the most evil *etc* thing that one can: *Do your worst – you'll never manage to defeat me*; *He can do his worst – I shall not do as he asks.*

get the worst of to be affected more unpleasantly *etc* than someone else by; to lose: *John got the worst of his fight with Peter*; *If you argue with him, you'll get the worst of it.*

if the worst comes to the worst if the worst possible thing happens: *If the worst comes to the worst and your business fails, you can always sell your house.*

the ˌworst of it 'is (that) the most unfortunate *etc* aspect of the situation is (that): *It's a terrible situation but the worst of it is, I didn't even know she was married!*

See also **bad, ill, worse**.

worsted ['wustid] *nu, adj* (of) a type of firm woollen fabric: *This jacket is (made of) worsted*; *a worsted jacket.*

worth [wəːθ] *nu* (*sometimes formal*) value, importance *etc*: *These books are of little or no worth*; *a person of little worth*; *She sold fifty dollars' worth of tickets.* – *adj* (*pred*) **1** equal in value to: *Each of these stamps is worth a penny*; *The old man's worth a fortune* (= he possesses a great deal of money). **2** good enough for: *His suggestion is worth considering*; *The exhibition is well worth a visit.*

'worthless *adj* of no value or merit: *These stamps are worthless*; *totally worthless old coins.* **'worthlessly** *adv.* **'worthlessness** *nu.*

'worthy [-ði] *adj* **1** (*formal*: *attrib*) good and deserving: *I shall willingly give money to a worthy cause.* **2** (*pred with* **of**) deserving (of): *She was not worthy of the honour given to her.* **3** (*pred with* **of**) typical of, suited to, or in keeping with: *a performance worthy of a champion.* **4** (*formal*: *usu pred with an infinitive*) of great enough importance *etc*: *She was not thought worthy to be presented to the king.* – *nc* (*formal or facet*: *often ironic*) a highly respected, *esp* a local, person: *one of the village worthies.*

'worthily *adv.* **'worthiness** *nu.*

worth'while *adj* deserving attention, time and effort *etc*: *That is a worthwhile cause*; *I wouldn't think it worthwhile to ask him to join the club – he'll only refuse.*

for all one is worth using all one's efforts, strength *etc*: *When the boat sank, he swam towards the shore for all he was worth.*

for what it is worth used to suggest that what is being said is doubtful or does not deserve consideration: *For what it's worth, John told me that quite the opposite was true*; *For what it's worth, I like it even if nobody else does.*

worth one's while *see* **while**.

would [wud] – *short forms* **I'd** [aid], **you'd** [juːd], **he'd** [hiːd], **she'd** [ʃiːd], **it'd** ['itəd], **we'd** [wiːd], **they'd** [ðeid]: *neg short form* **wouldn't** ['wudnt] – *modal aux* **1** *pt* of **will**: *He said he *would be leaving at nine o'clock the next morning*; *I asked if he'd come and mend my television set*; *I asked him to do it, but he wouldn't*; *As children we used to go to Cumberland for holidays, but sometimes we'd go to the Isle of Man for a change*; *The salesman said that the car would hold six people easily*; *'I heard a scream just now.' 'Oh, that would be me, tripping over the cat!'* **2** used in speaking of something that will, may or might happen (*eg* if a certain condition is met): *She would certainly go if you begged her to*; *If I asked her to the party, would she come?*; *Would he be willing to deliver these books for me, do you think?*; *I'd be happy to help you.* **3** used to express a preference, opinion *etc* politely: *I would do it this way, but you may like to do it a different way*; *It'd be a shame to stay indoors on such a beautiful day*; *I'd prefer to go to Birmingham tomorrow rather than today.* **4** used, said with emphasis, to express annoyance at something that often happens, is typical *etc*: *She would borrow my best dress just when I need it!*; *I've lost my car-keys – that would happen!* – *vt* (*arch*) to wish or desire (that something should happen): (*I*) *would* (*that*) *he were gone!*

'would-be *adj* (*attrib*: *often derog*) trying, hoping, or merely pretending, to be: *He's a would-be pilot, and he's come to ask for a job*; *She's married a would-be poet who doesn't have enough money to support her.*

would have 1 used to refer to things that a person was expecting to have happened, been done *etc* by the time of speaking: *I thought you would have finished this by now.* **2** used to state something a person was (or was not) going to do but did not do (or did) because of something or someone else, or something a person has done only because of someone or something else: *I would have come to the party but my aunt arrived unexpectedly*; *I would have had this finished by now if you hadn't interrupted me so often*; *I wouldn't have done it if she hadn't asked me to.*

would like *see* **like**.

would rather *see* **rather**.

would you used to introduce a polite request to someone to do something: (*Please*) *would you read this letter to see if I've made any spelling mistakes?*

wound[1] *see* **wind**[2].

wound[2] [wu:nd] *nc* **1** (*sometimes in cmpds*) a physical hurt or injury: *The wound that he had received in the war still gave him pain occasionally*; *He received a bad wound in the leg when he was shot at*; *How long will the wound in his arm take to heal?*; *He died from a gun-wound*; *He received two bullet-wounds in the head.* **2** (*formal*) a mental or emotional hurt or injury: *Her refusal to have dinner with him was a wound to his vanity.* – *vt* **1** to hurt or injure physically: *He didn't manage to kill the animal, but only wounded it*; *He was wounded in the battle.* **2** (*formal*) to hurt (someone's feelings): *When they rejected his plan, his pride was badly wounded*; *She wounded me with her angry words.*

'wounded *adj* having been injured, *esp* in war *etc*: *They moved the wounded man gently*; *Is he dead or just wounded?* – *n pl* (*often with* **the**) wounded people, *esp* soldiers: *The wounded were carried from the battlefield*; *'How many wounded are there?'*

wove, woven *see* **weave**.

wraith [reiθ] *nc* (*liter*) a ghost.

wrangle ['raŋgl] *vi* (*derog*) to quarrel or argue angrily: *The two boys are always wrangling about/over something*; *Oh, do stop wrangling, you two!* – *nc* (*derog*) an angry argument: *a long legal wrangle over someone's will.*

wrap [rap] – *pt, ptp* **wrapped** – *vt* **1** to roll or fold (round something or someone): *He wrapped his handkerchief round his bleeding finger.* **2** (*often with* **up**) to cover by folding or winding something round: *She wrapped the book* (*up*) *in brown paper*; *She wrapped the baby up in a warm shawl.* – *nc* (*rare*) a shawl or other covering for a woman's shoulders: *You should wear a warm wrap with that thin evening dress.*

'wrapper *nc* (*often in cmpds*) a paper cover for a sweet, parcel, packet of cigarettes *etc*: *Please don't drop sweet-wrappers in the street.*

'wrapping 1 *nu* something used to wrap or pack something in: *What kind of wrapping should I use for this present?* **2** *nc* (*sometimes in cmpds*) something used to cover or pack something: *sweet-wrappings.*

keep something under wraps (*inf*) to keep something secret: *They're keeping the new design under wraps until the first of August.*

wrapped up in (*inf*) giving all one's affection or attention to: *She's very wrapped up in her work/thoughts these days*; *She's become so wrapped up in that child.*

See also **unwrap**.

wrath [roθ, (*Amer*) raθ] *nu* (*formal or liter*) violent anger: *The wrath of her father terrified the young girl*; *the wrath of God.* **'wrathful** *adj.* **'wrathfully** *adv.*

wreak [ri:k]: **wreak havoc** (*formal or liter*) to cause widespread destruction and chaos: *The storm wreaked havoc in the villages along the coast.*

wreak vengeance/one's revenge (on) (*formal or liter*) to take one's revenge (on): *Ten years later, he wreaked vengeance on his former captors.*

wreath [ri:θ] – *pl* **wreaths** [ri:θs, ri:ðz] – *nc* **1** a (*usu* circular) garland of flowers or leaves, placed at a grave as a tribute, or put on someone's shoulders or head after his/her victory (a **'victory wreath**), or used as a decoration: *We put a wreath of flowers on her mother's grave*; *We hung a holly wreath on the door at Christmas.* **2** (*formal or liter*) a drift or curl of smoke, mist *etc*: *Wreaths of smoke rose from the chimney*; *The hills were covered in wreaths of mist.*

wreathe [ri:ð] *vt* (*formal or liter*: *usu in passive*) to cover: *The hills were wreathed in mist*; (*fig*) *Their faces were wreathed in smiles.*

wreck [rek] *nc* **1** a very badly damaged ship: *The divers found a wreck on the sea-bed.* **2** (*inf*) a car *etc* which is ruined or in a very bad condition: *He's driving around in an old wreck because he can't afford anything better.* **3** (*inf*) a person who is in a very poor (mental or physical) state: *By the time the exams finished, she was a complete nervous wreck*; *I feel a wreck after cleaning the house.* **4** (*liter*: *no pl*) the act of (a ship's) being destroyed, sunk *etc*: *I do not know how the wreck of the Hesperus happened* (= how the Hesperus came to be very badly damaged). – *vt* to destroy or damage very badly: *The ship was wrecked on rocks in a storm*; *My car was completely wrecked in the accident*; *My son has wrecked my car*; (*inf*) *The telephone boxes have been wrecked by vandals*; (*fig*) *You have wrecked my plans.*

'wreckage [-kidʒ] *nu* the remains of something wrecked: *After the accident, the wreckage* (*of the cars*) *was removed from the motorway.*

wrecked *adj.*

'wrecker *nc* (*sometimes inf derog*) a person who destroys or damages: *The car was so badly damaged that we took it to the wrecker's yard*; *The wreckers have changed this parliamentary bill beyond recognition.*

See also **shipwreck** *under* **ship**.

wren [ren] *nc* a type of very small bird.

wrench [rentʃ] *vt* **1** (*with* **out** *etc*) to pull with a violent movement: *He wrenched the gun out of my hand*; *I wrenched the door open.* **2** (*more formal than* **twist** *or* **sprain**) to sprain or damage the muscles in: *She wrenched her ankle when she fell down the steps.* – *nc* **1** a violent pull or twist: *He gave the door-handle a wrench and it came off in his hand.* **2** a type of strong tool for turning nuts, bolts *etc.* **3** (*no pl*) something (*esp* a departure) which causes sadness *etc*: *Having to leave this beautiful old house will be a terrible wrench.*

See also **monkey-wrench** *under* **monkey**.

wrest [rest] *vt* (*formal*) to take (away) by force and with difficulty: *He wrested the weapon from his opponent's grasp*; (*liter fig*) *They wrested their living from the soil.*

wrestle ['resl] **1** *vti* to struggle physically (with someone), often as a sport: *Fred Johnson is wrestling* (*with*) *Paddy O'Reilly at the Sparta Club tonight*; *The children wrestled on the floor.* **2** *vi* (*formal*: *with* **with**) to struggle (with a problem *etc*): *He's been wrestling with his conscience, and doesn't know whether he should tell his fiancée about his past*; *I've been wrestling with these figures for ages but get a different answer each time I add them up.*

'wrestler *nc* a person who takes part in the sport of wrestling: *Wrestlers are often very strong men.*

wretch [retʃ] *nc* (*old or formal*) **1** a miserable, unhappy creature: *The poor wretch has no family or friends.* **2** (*derog*) a worthless person: *That wretch has stolen my wallet!*

wretched ['retʃid] *adj* **1** (*formal*) very miserable: *They live in a wretched little house*; *I feel wretched about hurting her*; *She looks wretched – has she been ill?* **2** (*old*) (of a person) worthless. **'wretchedly** *adv.* **'wretchedness** *nu.*

wriggle ['rigl] *vti* (*slightly inf*) to twist to and fro: *She wriggled* (*her arm*) *free of her jacket*; *The worm wriggled* (*its way*) *across the path*; *The child kept wriggling in his seat*; (*fig*) *How are you going to wriggle out of this awkward situation?* – *nc* (*slightly inf*) a wriggling movement.

-wright [rait] (*in cmpds*) a person who makes (something), as in **shipwright, wheelwright, playwright.**

wring [riŋ] – *pt, ptp* **wrung** [rʌŋ] – *vt* **1** (*often with* **out**) to force (water) from (material) by twisting or by pressure: *He wrung the water from his soaking-wet shirt*; *She wrung out the clothes and hung them up to dry*; (*fig*) *The police wrung a confession out of the murderer.* **2** (*formal*) to clasp and unclasp (one's hands) in an agitated manner, *eg* in grief: *She wrung her hands in fear.* **3** (*formal or liter*) to distress, affect with sorrow *etc*: *The sight of the orphan child wrings one's heart.*

'wringer *nc* an old-fashioned machine with two rollers for forcing water from wet clothes: *She had a wringer attached to the kitchen sink.*

wringing wet (*inf*) soaked through: *The clothes are wringing wet*; (*attrib*) *Take off those wringing-wet clothes.*

wrinkle ['riŋkl] *nc* **1** (*less formal than* **crease**) a small crease on a surface: *He ironed the wrinkles out of his shirt.* **2** a small crease on the skin (*usu* on one's face): *Her face is full of wrinkles now*; *She has wrinkles round her eyes.* – *vti* (*less formal than* **crease**) to (cause to) become full of wrinkles or creases: *The heat from the fire wrinkled the cover of the book.*

'wrinkled, 'wrinkly *adjs* full of wrinkles: *a wrinkled skirt*; *a wrinkled face*; *Her face is brown and wrinkled.*

wrist [rist] *nc* the (part of the arm at the) joint between hand and forearm: *The policeman put the handcuffs on my wrists*; *I can't play tennis – I've hurt my wrist.*

'wrist-watch, (*formal*) **'wristlet-watch** [-lit-] *nc* a watch worn on the wrist: *She wore a small gold wrist-watch.*

writ [rit] *nc* (*legal*) a document by which one is summoned, or required to do something.

write [rait] – *pt* **wrote** [rout]: *ptp* **written** ['ritn] – *vti* **1** to draw (letters or other forms of script) on a surface, *esp* with a pen or pencil on paper: *They wrote their suggestions on a sheet of paper*; *He didn't look up from his desk, but continued writing*; *She continued to write*; *The child has learned to read and write*; *Please write in ink.* **2** to compose the text of (a book, poem *etc*): *She wrote a book on sociology*; *He writes for a living.* **3** (*sometimes with* **to**) to compose (a letter), and *usu* post it: *He has written* (*a letter*) *to me complaining about the car which I sold him*; *I wrote to you last week but you did not reply.* – *See also* **write** *in phrases below.*

'writer *nc* a person who writes, *esp* for a living: *Dickens was a famous English writer*; *In one of the letters which you published last week, the writer complained of high prices.*

'writing *nu* letters or other forms of script (whether hand- or machine-written) giving the written form of (a) language: *The Chinese use a different kind of writing from ours in Britain*; *I can't read your writing*; *He asked for a guarantee in writing*; (*attrib*) *a writing system.*

'writings *n pl* the collected books, poems, correspondence *etc* written by a particular (*usu* famous) person: *the writings of George Bernard Shaw.*

written ['ritn] *adj* (*attrib*) expressed in writing (by hand or machine): *a written guarantee*; *a written promise.*

write-off *see* **write off** *below.*

writer's cramp *nu* cramp in the muscles of the hand and arm, caused by writing for long periods: *I've got writer's cramp after writing that long essay.*

'write-up *nc* (*inf*) a review or written criticism (*esp* of a play or other public performance) in a newspaper *etc*: *The concert got a very bad write-up in the 'News'*; *If he likes the play he'll give you a good write-up.*

'writing-paper *nu* (*usu* good-quality) paper for writing letters *etc* on: *I'll have to buy some writing-paper and envelopes.*

write down *vt sep* to record in writing: *She wrote down every word he said*; *I can't remember what he said – I didn't write it down.*

write in *vi* to write a letter (*esp* to a newspaper, radio or TV programme *etc*): *Several readers have written in to say that they like our magazine*; *I think I'll write in to the newspaper and complain about this article*; *She wrote in for advice on how to grow roses.* – *See also* **write** (*def 1*).

write off 1 *vt sep* to regard as lost for ever: *They wrote off the whole amount that had been spent on the* *new project; We'll have to write off the printing costs of that book or it will never make a profit.* 2 *vt sep* (*inf*) to destroy completely or damage beyond repair: *He wrote his car off in a bad accident.* (*nc* **'write-off**: *His car's a write-off*). 3 *vi* to send (for something) by writing a letter: *She wrote off for information on life insurance.*

write out *vt sep* to copy or record in(to) writing: *You'll have to write the letter out again, more neatly than before; Write this out in your neatest handwriting.*

write up *vt sep* to bring (a record) up to date: *He wrote up the records of the week's takings in the accounts book.*

See also **handwriting, songwriter, underwrite, unwritten**.

writhe [raið] *vi* (*formal*) to twist violently to and fro, *esp* in pain or discomfort: *She was writhing in agony when I found her at the foot of the mountain; She writhed about when I tickled her, but she couldn't get away.*

wrong [roŋ] *adj* 1 (not of a person) having an error or mistake(s); incorrect: *The child gave the wrong answer; That answer is wrong; We took the wrong direction.* 2 (*pred*) (of a person) incorrect in one's answer(s), opinion(s) *etc*; mistaken: *I disagree – I think you're wrong in saying that they will win; He was quite wrong in thinking that I was guilty.* 3 (*pred*) not good, not morally correct *etc*: *It is completely wrong to make any differences between white and black people; It is wrong to steal.* 4 (of a person) not suitable: *He's the wrong man for the job.* 5 out of order; not working *etc* properly; not in a right or proper condition: *There's something wrong with this engine; What's wrong* (= what is the matter) *with that child – why is she crying?; What's wrong with the engine – why has it broken down? – adv* (*esp inf*) incorrectly or badly: *You've done this sum wrong – you'll have to do it again; I think I may have spelt her name wrong. – See also* **wrongly** *below. – ncu* (*formal*) that which is not morally correct: *the rights and wrongs of a complicated situation; He does not know right from wrong. – vt* (*formal or liter*) to give a personal insult, or do something morally incorrect, to (a person): *You wrong my by accusing me of such a terrible thing!; He wronged that girl by promising to marry her and then leaving her.*

'wrongful *adj* (*formal*: *often attrib*) not lawful or fair: *wrongful dismissal.* **'wrongfully** *adv.* **'wrongfulness** *nu.*

'wrongly *adv* 1 incorrectly: *The letter was wrongly addressed.* 2 it is not right, good or just that (something is the case): *Rightly or wrongly, she refused to speak to him* (= I am not willing or able to say whether she was right or not in refusing to speak to him).

'wrongdoer *nc* (*formal*) a person who does wrong or illegal things: *The wrongdoers must be punished.* **'wrongdoing** *nu.*

do (someone) wrong (*formal or liter*) to insult (someone), treat (someone) unfairly *etc*: *You do him wrong to suggest that he would betray you.*

do wrong to act incorrectly: *You did wrong to refuse his demands.*

go wrong 1 to go astray, badly, away from the intended plan *etc*: *Everything has gone wrong for her in the past few years.* 2 to stop functioning properly: *The machine has gone wrong – I can't get it to stop!* 3 to make a mistake: *Where did I go wrong in that sum?*

in the wrong guilty of an error or injustice: *She is completely blameless. You're the one who's in the wrong!*

put (someone) in the wrong (*formal*) to cause (someone) to seem to be in the wrong: *Whenever he explains to anyone why we didn't arrive, he always puts me in the wrong.*

wrote *see* **write**.

wrought [ro:t] *adj* (*old or formal*: *pred*) made, *esp* by hand: *These old iron gates were wrought by the local blacksmith.*

wrought iron *nu, adj* (of) a type of iron containing only small amounts of other materials, which rusts less and welds more easily than steel: *These railings are* (*made of*) *wrought iron*; (*attrib*) *wrought-iron railings.*

wrung *see* **wring**.

wry [rai] *adj* (*usu attrib*) 1 (*formal*) slightly mocking or bitter; ironic: *He gave a wry smile; He has rather a wry sense of humour.* 2 (*rare*) twisted or turned to one side: *a wry neck.* **'wryly** *adv.* **'wryness** *nu.*

Xx

X-rays [eks'reiz] *n pl* rays which can pass through many substances impossible for light to pass through, and which produce, on photographic film, a shadow picture (called an X-ray) of the object through which they passed.

ˌX-'ray *nc* 1 a photograph taken using X-rays: *We'll take an X-ray of your chest*; (*attrib*) *an X-ray photograph*; (*attrib*) *an X-ray machine; The doctor is reading my chest X-ray* (= studying it to see if there are any abnormalities). 2 a medical examination using X-rays: *I'm going to the hospital for an X-ray. – vt* to take a photograph of (something) using X-rays: *You must have your neck X-rayed; They X-rayed my arm to see if it was broken.*

xenophobia [zenə'foubiə] *nu* (*formal*) intense fear or dislike of foreigners or strangers. **ˌxeno'phobic** *adj.*

Xerox ® ['ziəroks] *nc* 1 a type of photographic process used for copying documents. 2 a copying-machine using this process. 3 a photocopy (of something) made by such a process. – *vt* to photocopy (something) using this process.

Xmas ['krisməs] (*inf*) short for **Christmas**.

xylophone ['zailəfoun] *nc* a musical instrument consisting of wooden or metal slats of various lengths, which produce different notes when struck by wooden hammers: *He played the xylophone in the school concert; He played a tune on the xylophone.*

Yy

yacht [jot] *nc* a boat or small ship, usually with sails, often with an engine, built and used for racing or cruising: *We spent our holidays on a friend's yacht*; (*attrib*) *a yacht race.*

'yachting *nu* sailing in a yacht: *They enjoy yachting*; *We often go yachting.*

'yachtsman ['jots-] *nc* a person who sails a yacht: *a keen yachtsman.*

'yacht club *nc* a club for yacht-owners.

yack, yak[1] [jak] – *pts, ptps* **yacked, yakked** – *vt* (*derog sl*) to talk continuously: *She never stops yacking/yakking!*

yak[2] [jak] – *pls* **yaks, yak** – *nc* a type of long-haired ox, found in Tibet.

yam [jam] *nc* (*also* **sweet potato**) any of several kinds of potato-like tropical plants used as food.

yank [jaŋk] *nc* (*inf*) a sudden sharp pull; a jerk: *She felt/gave a yank on the rope.* – *vti* (*inf*) to pull suddenly and sharply: *She yanked the child out of the mud*; *She yanked on the string.*

Yank [jaŋk] *nc* 1 (*derog sl*: *not Amer*) a person from the United States of America: *There are always a lot of Yanks in London*; (*attrib*) *a Yank tourist.* 2 short for **Yankee** (*def 1*).

Yankee ['jaŋki] *nc* 1 (*inf*) a person, *orig esp* a soldier, from the northern states of America: *In the American Civil War, the Yankees fought the Confederates*; (*attrib*) *a Yankee soldier.* 2 a Yank (*def 1*).

yap [jap] – *pt, ptp* **yapped** – *vi* 1 (of a puppy or small dog) to give a high-pitched bark: *The puppy yaps at everyone.* 2 (*inf derog*) (of a person) to talk continually in a shrill voice, often about very little: *She's been yapping away for hours.* – *nc* a short, high-pitched bark: *The puppy gave a yap as I entered the room.*

yard[1] [ja:d] *nc* (*often abbrev* **yd** *when written*) a unit of length equal to 3 feet (0·9144 metre): *The garden is ten yards wide*; *six yards of velvet*; *a four-yard length of velvet.*

'yardage [-didʒ] *nu* the length (or, rarely, the area or volume) of something measured in yards: *What is the yardage of this piece of cloth/of your back garden?*

'yardstick *nc* 1 (*formal*) a standard for comparison: *He used his father's behaviour as a yardstick for his own.* 2 a stick exactly a yard long, used for measuring.

yard[2] [ja:d] *nc* 1 an area of (enclosed) ground near a building: *Our house has a garden at the front and a yard at the back*; *a courtyard.* 2 (*often in cmpds*) an area of enclosed ground used for a special (business) purpose: *a shipyard*; *a dockyard.*

yarn[1] [ja:n] *nu* wool, cotton *etc* spun into thread: *knitting-yarn*; *a length of yarn.*

yarn[2] [ja:n] *nc* 1 (*esp old*) a story or tale: *He often told us interesting yarns about his travels.* 2 (*inf euph*) an untrue story; a lie: *He said he was very rich, but that was just a yarn.*

spin a yarn *see* **spin**.

yashmak ['jaʃmak] *nc* a veil worn by Moslem women, covering the face below the eyes: *She was wearing a yashmak.*

yawl [jo:l] *nc* a type of small fishing- or sailing-boat.

yawn [jo:n] *vi* 1 to open the mouth wide and take a breath (involuntarily) when tired or bored: *He yawned and fell asleep*; *She yawned all during his lecture.* 2 (of a hole, gap *etc*) to be or become wide open: *The chasm yawned beneath him.* – *nc* an act of yawning: *He gave a yawn of sheer boredom*; *Seeing the yawns of the children, she sent them to bed.*

'yawning *adj* (*attrib*: *formal or facet*) wide open: *a yawning hole in the road*; *a yawning gap in our lives*; *yawning holes in his socks.*

ye[1] [ji:] *pron* (*arch or dial*: used *usu* when addressing more than one person) 1 (used *esp* as the subject of a verb) you: *Whom do ye see?* 2 used with a noun or phrase when addressing someone, *esp* when calling them something unpleasant: *O ye of little faith!*

ye[2] [ji:] *adj* (*definite article*: *arch or facet*) the: *Ye Olde Englishe Tea Shoppe.*

yea [jei] *interj* (*arch*) yes.

yeah [jeə] *interj* (*inf*) yes.

year [jiə] *nc* 1 the period of time the Earth takes to go once round the Sun, about 365 days: *We lived here for five years, from November 1968 to November 1973*; *a two-year delay.* 2 the period from January 1 to December 31, being 365 days, except in a leap year, when it is 366 days: *in the year 1945.* – *See also* **years** *below.*

'yearling [-liŋ] *nc* an animal which is a year old: *The sheep were all yearlings*; (*attrib*) *a yearling horse.*

'yearly *adj* (*attrib*) happening *etc* every year: *We pay a yearly visit to my uncle.* – *adv* every year: *The premium on my insurance policy decreases yearly.*

years *n pl* 1 age: *He is wise for his years.* 2 (*loosely*) a very long time: *They take years to serve anyone in this shop.*

financial year *see* **finance**.

fiscal year *see* **fiscal**.

leap year *see* **leap**.

'year-book *nc* a book of information which is updated and published every year: *a students' year-book.*

all (the) year round, long *etc* throughout the whole year: *The weather is so good here that we can swim all (the) year round.*

this year *see* **this**.

year in, year out *see* **day in, day out** *under* **in**.

yearn [jə:n] *vi* (*liter or formal*) to feel a great desire; to long: *She yearned for her home*; *He yearned to ask her to marry him.*

yeast [ji:st] *nu* a substance which causes fermentation, used in making beer, bread *etc*: *That bread is rising too much – you've put too much yeast in it.*

'yeasty *adj* (tasting or smelling) of yeast: *There's a yeasty smell from the brewery*; *These buns taste yeasty.*

yell [jel] *nc* (*slightly inf*) a loud, shrill cry; a scream: *a yell of pain/warning*; *He gave a loud yell.* – (*slightly inf*) 1 *vi* to make such a noise: *He yelled at her to be careful.* 2 *vt* to shout loudly or scream (something): *She yelled a warning to us*; *'Stop!' they yelled.*

yellow ['jelou] *adj* 1 of the colour of gold, butter, the yolk of an egg *etc*: *She wore a pale yellow dress*; *yellow sands.* 2 (*derog sl*) cowardly: *a yellow traitor.* – *ncu* 1 (any shade of) the colour of gold, butter, the yolk of an egg *etc*: *He admired the yellows, pinks and reds of the flowers*; *Yellow is my* *favourite colour.* 2 something (*eg* material, paint *etc*) yellow in colour. – *vti* to make or become yellow: *It was autumn and the leaves were beginning to yellow*; *The newspaper had been yellowed by sunlight.*

'yellowish *adj* rather yellow; close to yellow: *a yellowish flower*; *the yellowish pages of the old book.*

'yellowness *nu.*

yellow pages *n pl* (the section of) a telephone directory in which entries are arranged according to the business of the firms or individuals concerned.

yelp [jelp] *vi* (of a dog *etc*) to give a sharp, sudden cry: *The dog yelped with pain.* – *nc* a sharp, sudden cry: *The dog gave a yelp of pain.*

Yemen, Yemeni *see* Appendix 2.

yen[1] [jen] – *pl* **yen** – *nc* the standard unit of Japanese currency: *It cost 50 000 yen.*

yen[2] [jen] *nc* (*inf*: *usu in sing*) a desire: *He had a yen for a holiday/a yen to go abroad.*

yeoman ['joumən] – *pl* **'yeomen** – *nc* **1** (*esp hist*) a farmer who owns and works his own land. **2** (*mil*) a member of the yeomanry.

'yeomanry *nu* **1** (*hist*) the class of land-owning farmers: *the peasantry, the yeomanry and the aristocracy.* **2** a troop of cavalrymen (now supplied with tanks *etc*) serving voluntarily in the British Army.

Yeoman of the Guard the company who guard the Tower of London and act as bodyguard to the British monarch on certain ceremonial occasions.

yes [jes] *interj* used to express agreement or consent: *Yes, that is true*; *Yes, you may go.* – *n* – *pl* **'yesses** – *nc* an expression of agreement or consent: *Answer with a yes or a no*; *How many yesses were there?*

'yes-man [-man] – *pl* **'yes-men** [-men] – *nc* (*inf derog*) a person who always agrees with the person in authority: *The President is surrounded by yes-men.*

yesterday ['jestədi] *nc* (*usu in sing*), *adv* (on) the day before today: *Yesterday was a beautiful day*; *He went home yesterday.*

yesteryear ['jestəjiə] *nu* (*esp liter*) the past, *esp* the recent past: *an exhibition entitled 'Cars of Yesteryear'.*

yet [jet] *adv* **1** (*only in negatives and direct or indirect questions*: *formal or liter when not in final position*) up till now; by now: *He hasn't telephoned yet*; *Have you finished yet?*; *I wonder if she's started yet*; *They haven't yet arrived*; *We're not yet ready.* **2** (*usu in final position*: *formal or liter when immediately following the modal aux*) at some time in the future; before the matter *etc* is finished; still: *He may come yet*; *She may yet make a success of it.* **3** (*with* **another** *or* **more**) used for emphasis to indicate the latest in a series: *He's made yet another mistake/yet more mistakes.* **4** (*with a compar adj*: *formal or liter*) even: *a yet worse/yet more terrible experience*; *yet greater progress.* – *conj* (*often liter or formal*) but; however; nevertheless: *I have failed, yet I shall try again*; *He's pleasant enough, (and) yet I don't like him.*

as yet up to the time referred to, *usu* the present: *I haven't had a book published as yet*; *As yet, Shakespeare had not become famous.*

,not . . . nor 'yet (*liter or relig* with the subject following the verb in the second clause): not . . . neither: *She was not beautiful, nor yet was she pleasant.*

yew [ju:] **1** *nc* (*also* **'yew tree**) a type of evergreen tree with dark leaves and red berries. **2** *nu, adj* (of) its wood: *furniture made of yew*; *a yew cabinet.*

Yid [jid] *nc* (*offensive when used by non-Jews*) a Jew.

'Yiddish *n, adj* (of) a language based on German and Hebrew, with elements of several other modern languages, spoken by many Jews: *He was speaking (in) Yiddish*; *Do you understand Yiddish?*; *a Yiddish dictionary.*

yield [ji:ld] **1** *vti* (*formal*) to give up; to surrender: *The city yielded to the armies of the king*; *He yielded to the other man's arguments*; *He yielded all his possessions to the state.* **2** *vi* (*formal*) to submit (to force or pressure); to give way: *At last the door yielded.* **3** *vt* (*tech*) to produce naturally, grow *etc*: *How much milk does that herd of cattle yield?*; *That field yielded a good crop of potatoes last year.* – *nc* (*tech*: *usu in sing*: *sometimes in cmpds*) the amount produced by natural means: *a cow's milk-yield*; *the annual yield of wheat.*

yippee [ji'pi:] *interj* (*inf*) used to show excitement, delight *etc.*

yob, yobbo ['job(ou)] – *pls* **yobs, 'yobbos** – *nc* (*sl derog*) a rough, dirty, bad-mannered (*usu* young) person: *a bunch of yobs*; *Our windows were broken by a bunch of yobbos.*

yodel ['joudl] – *pt, ptp* **'yodelled**, (*Amer*) **'yodeled** – *vti* to sing (a melody *etc*), changing frequently from a normal to a very high-pitched voice and back again: *The Swiss used to yodel (tunes) to each other across the mountains.* – *nc* (*usu in sing*) an act of yodelling.

'yodeller *nc.*

yoga ['jougə] *nu* **1** (*loosely*) any of several systems of physical exercises based on a Hindu system of philosophy and meditation: *She practises yoga*; (*attrib*) *yoga exercises.* **2** the philosophy (*usu* including the meditation and exercises).

'yogi [-gi] *nc* (*sometimes with cap*) (the title of) a person who practises and/or teaches the yoga philosophy.

yog(h)urt, yoghourt ['jogət, (*Amer*) 'jou-] **1** *nu* a type of semi-liquid food made from fermented milk: *a carton of yoghourt*; *yoghourt flavoured with raspberries.* **2** *nc* a carton of yoghourt.

yoke [jouk] *nc* **1** (*esp hist*) a wooden frame placed over the necks of oxen to hold them together when they are pulling a cart *etc.* **2** (*esp hist*) a frame placed across a person's shoulders, for carrying buckets *etc*: *Two buckets of milk hung from a yoke across his shoulders.* **3** (*usu in sing*: *liter*) something that weighs people down, and/or forces them to obey or do something: *the yoke of slavery.* **4** (*tech*) the part of a garment that fits over the shoulders and round the neck: *a black dress with a white yoke.* – *vt* (*esp hist*) to join together by putting a yoke (*def 1*) on: *He yoked the oxen to the plough.*

yokel ['joukəl] *nc* (*derog*) an unsophisticated (*usu* male) person from the country: *You can't expect these yokels to understand politics*; *Why did she marry that yokel?*

yolk [jouk] *ncu* (*also* **'egg-yolk**) the yellow part of the egg of a bird or reptile: *The child will only eat the yolk of an egg – she won't eat the white.*

yon [jon] *adj* (*attrib*: *liter or dial*) yonder: *yon building.*

yonder ['jondə] *adj* (*attrib*), *adv* (*old, dial or liter*) in or at that (place) over there: *He lives (over) yonder*; *yonder village.*

yore [jo:]: **days of yore** (*liter*) times past or long ago: *They fought for the king in days of yore.*

you [ju:] *pron* **1** (used as the subject or object of a real or implied verb, or as the object of a real or implied preposition) the person(s) *etc* spoken or written to: *You look well!*; *I asked you a question*; *Do you all understand?*; *You're an idiot, Brian!*; *Who did it? You?* (= Did you do it?); *Did he come with you?*; *Who did he come with? You?* **2** used with a noun when calling someone something *esp* something unpleasant: *You idiot! Why did you do that?*; *You stupid fools!*
See also **ye, your(self)**.
you'd *see* **have, would**.
you'll *see* **will**.
young [jʌŋ] *adj* in the first part of life, growth, development *etc*; not old: *a young person*; *Young babies sleep a great deal*; *The young elephant stood beside its mother*; *A young cow is called a calf*; *His mother died when he was very young*; *He is too young to go to school*; (*fig*: *formal or facet*) *The evening is still young*. – *n pl* the group of animals or birds produced by parents: *Most animals will fight to defend their young*: *Birds feed their young on insects*.
'youngster *nc* (*inf*) a young person: *A group of youngsters were playing football*.
the young young people in general: *She doesn't understand the present-day problems of the young*.
See also **youth**.
your [jo:, (*Amer*) juər] *adj* (*attrib*) belonging to you: *your house/car*.
yours [jo:z, (*Amer*) juərz] *pron* something belonging to you: *This book is yours*; *Yours is on that shelf*.
your'self – *pl* **your'selves** [-'selvz] – *pron* **1** used as the object of a verb or preposition when the person(s) spoken or written to is/are the object(s) of an action he/they perform(s): *Why are you looking at yourselves in the mirror?*; *You can dry yourself with this towel*. **2** used to emphasize **you**: *You yourself can't do it, but you could ask someone else to do it*. **3** without help *etc*: *You can jolly well do it yourself!*
by yourself/yourselves *see* **by oneself** *under* **by**.
you are not yourself/yourselves *see* **not be oneself** *under* **one**.
yours (faithfully, sincerely, truly) expressions written before one's signature at the end of a letter: *Should I put 'Yours faithfully' or 'Yours sincerely'?*
See also **you**.
you're *see* **be**.
youth [ju:θ] – *pl* **youths** [ju:ðz] – **1** *nu* (*formal*) (the state of being in) the early part of life: *Enjoy your youth!*; *He spent his youth in Scotland*. **2** *nc* (*sometimes derog*) a boy of fifteen to twenty years old approximately: *I was stopped by a youth in the street*; *That long-haired youth has no manners*. **3** *nu* young people in general: *Some people say that today's youth has no sense of responsibility*.
'youthful *adj* **1** young: *The boy looked very youthful*. **2** energetic, active, young-looking *etc*: *a very youthful old gentleman*; *a youthful grandmother*. **3** (*formal or liter*) of youth: *youthful pleasures*. **'youthfully** *adv*. **'youthfulness** *nu*.
'youth hostel *nc* a place for young people, *esp* hikers, on holiday, where cheap and simple accommodation is provided. **'youth hosteller** *nc*.
See also **young**.
you've *see* **have**.
yowl [jaul] *nc* a sad cry or howl: *They heard the yowl of a cat*. – *vi* to make this noise: *The dog yowled mournfully*.
yo-yo, Yo-yo ® ['joujou] *nc* a type of toy, consisting of a pair of discs made of wood, metal *etc* with a groove between them round which a piece of string is tied, the toy being made to run up and down the string: *going up and down like a yo-yo*.
yuan [ju'an] – *pl* **yu'an** – *nc* the standard unit of currency in the People's Republic of China.
Yugoslav, Yugoslavia, Yugoslavian *see* Appendix 2.
yule [ju:l] *n* (*old*: *often with cap*) Christmas.
'yule-log *nc* (*often with cap*) a log of wood burnt at Christmas.
'yuletide *nu* (*often with cap*: *sometimes attrib*) the Christmas season: *a yuletide greeting*.

Zz

Zaire, Zairean *see* Appendix 2.
Zambia, Zambian *see* Appendix 2.
zany ['zeini] *adj* (*inf*) crazy: *a zany comedy*; *That was a really zany thing to do*; *She's a bit zany*.
zeal [zi:l] *nu* (*formal*) enthusiasm or keenness: *She shows great zeal for her work*.
zealot ['zelət] *nc* (*hist or formal*: *now often derog*) a single-minded, determined supporter of a political cause, religion *etc*; a fanatic: *right-wing zealots*.
zealous ['zeləs] *adj* (*formal*) enthusiastic; keen: *He is a zealous supporter of our cause*; *He was most zealous in performing his duties*. **'zealously** *adv*.
zebra ['zi:brə] – *pl* **'zebras, 'zebra** – *nc* a kind of striped animal of the horse family, found wild in Africa: *two zebras*; *a herd of zebra*.
zebra crossing *nc* a place, marked in black and white stripes, where traffic stops for pedestrians to cross a street: *We must teach the children to use the zebra crossings*.
zenith ['zeniθ] *nc* the highest point: *The sun reaches its zenith at midday*; (*fig*) *He is at the zenith of his career*.
zephyr ['zefə] *nc* (*liter*) a light, soft breeze: *Gentle zephyrs breathed through the woods*.
zeppelin ['zepəlin] *nc* (*hist*) a type of airship used by the Germans in the First World War.
zero ['ziərou] – *pl* **'zeros** – (*formal or tech*) **1** *nc* the number or figure 0: *Three plus zero equals three*; *The figure 100 has two zeros in it*; *zero degrees Fahrenheit*. **2** *nu* the point on a scale (*eg* on a thermometer) which is taken as the standard on which measurements may be based: *The temperature was 5 degrees above/below zero*. **3** *nu* the exact time fixed for something to happen, *eg* an explosion, the launching of a space-craft *etc*: *It is now 3 minutes to zero*.
'zero hour *nu* the time at which a military operation *etc* is fixed to begin: *Zero hour is at midnight*.
absolute zero *see* **absolute**.
See also Appendix 1.

zest [zest] *nu* **1** (*formal*) keen enjoyment; relish: *She joined in the games with great zest.* **2** (used in cooking) the peel of an orange or lemon: *Add the zest of a lemon.*

'zestful *adj* (*formal*) keen; full of enjoyment: *a zestful approach to life.* **'zestfully** *adv.*

zigzag ['zigzag] *adj* (*attrib*) (of a line, road *etc*) having sharp bends or angles from side to side: *a zigzag path through the woods.* – *v* – *pt, ptp* **'zigzagged** – *vi* to move in a zigzag manner: *The road zigzagged through the mountains*; *The motor bike was zigzagging in and out of the traffic.*

zinc [ziŋk] *nu* a bluish-white metallic element (symbol **Zn**).

zip[1] [zip] **1** *nc* (*also* **'zipper**) a zip fastener. **2** *nu* a whizzing sound: *They heard the zip of a flying bullet.* **3** *nu* (*inf*) energy; vitality: *She's always full of zip.* – *v* – *pt, ptp* **zipped** – **1** *vti* (*often with* **up**) to fasten with a zip fastener: *She zipped up her trousers*; *This dress zips at the back.* **2** *vi* to make, or move with, a whizzing sound: *A bullet zipped past his head.*

zip fastener *nc* (*usu* **zip** *or* **'zipper**) a device for fastening clothes *etc*, in which two rows of metal or nylon teeth are made to fit each other when a sliding tab is pulled along them: *I prefer a zip (fastener) to buttons.*

See also **unzip**.

zip[2] [zip]: **zip code** *nc* in the US, a postal code, having the form of a five-figure number, placed at the end of an address.

Zodiac ['zoudiak] *n* (*with* **the**) an imaginary strip across the sky, divided into twelve equal parts called the **signs of the Zodiac**, each sign being named after a group of stars and corresponding (in astrology) to a different part of the year.

zombie ['zombi] *nc* (*inf derog*) a slow-moving person of very little intelligence: *There's no use asking him to do anything – he's just a zombie.*

zone [zoun] *nc* **1** an area or region, *usu* of a country, town *etc*, *esp* one marked off for a special purpose: *a no-parking zone*; *a traffic-free zone*; *a smokeless zone.* **2** any of the five bands into which the Earth's surface is divided according to temperature: *The tropical zone is the area between the Tropic of Capricorn and the Tropic of Cancer.*

zoo [zuː] *nc* **1** (short for **zoological garden**) a place where wild animals are kept for the public to see, and for study, breeding *etc*: *Let's take the children to the zoo.* **2** a collection of animals kept in such a place.

zoology [zu'olədʒi] *nu* the scientific study of animals: *He is studying zoology at university*; (*attrib*) *a zoology lecture.* ˌ**zoo'logical** [-'lo-] *adj.* ˌ**zoo'logically** [-'lo-] *adv.* **zo'ologist** *nc.*

zoological garden *nc* full form of **zoo**.

zoom [zuːm] *nu* a loud, low-pitched buzzing noise: *the zoom of (an) aircraft.* – *vi* **1** (*often with* **past, over, up** *etc*) to make, or move very quickly with, this kind of noise: *The motorbike zoomed past us*; *She zoomed off into the house.* **2** (*inf*) to increase quickly or to a high level: *Prices have zoomed in the last five years.*

zoom lens *nc* a type of camera lens which can make a distant object appear gradually closer without moving the camera: *I filmed it with a zoom lens.*

zoom in *vi* (*usu with* **on**) to direct a camera (on to an object *etc*) and use a zoom lens to make it appear to come closer: *Film the whole building first, then zoom in on the door.*

zucchini [zu'kiːniː] – *pls* **zuc'chini, zuc'chinis** – *nc* (*esp Amer*) a courgette: *We had stuffed zucchini for supper*; *a kilo of zucchini.*

Appendix 1

Numbers, Fractions and Numerical Expressions

Numbers

Cardinal Numbers		Ordinal Numbers	
0	nothing; zero; nought; oh; nil; love (*See note (i) below*)		
1	one	1st	first
2	two	2nd	second
3	three	3rd	third
4	four	4th	fourth
5	five	5th	fifth
6	six	6th	sixth
7	seven	7th	seventh
8	eight	8th	eighth
9	nine	9th	ninth
10	ten	10th	tenth
11	eleven	11th	eleventh
12	twelve	12th	twelfth
13	thirteen	13th	thirteenth
14	fourteen	14th	fourteenth
15	fifteen	15th	fifteenth
16	sixteen	16th	sixteenth
17	seventeen	17th	seventeenth
18	eighteen	18th	eighteenth
19	nineteen	19th	nineteenth
20	twenty	20th	twentieth
21	twenty-one	21st	twenty-first
22	twenty-two	22nd	twenty-second
23	twenty-three	23rd	twenty-third
30	thirty	30th	thirtieth
35	thirty-five	35th	thirty-fifth
40	forty	40th	fortieth
50	fifty	50th	fiftieth
60	sixty	60th	sixtieth
70	seventy	70th	seventieth
80	eighty	80th	eightieth
90	ninety	90th	ninetieth
100	a/one ˈhundred	100th	(one) ˈhundredth
101	a/one ˌhundred and ˈone	101st	(one) ˌhundred and ˈfirst
134	a/one ˌhundred and ˌthirty-ˈfour	134th	(one) ˌhundred and ˌthirty-ˈfourth
200	two ˈhundred	200th	two ˈhundredth
207	two ˌhundred and ˈseven	207th	two ˌhundred and ˈseventh
300	three hundred	300th	three hundredth
400	four hundred	400th	four hundredth
1000	a/one ˈthousand	1000th	(one) ˈthousandth
1001	a/one ˌthousand and ˈone	1001st	(one) ˌthousand and ˈfirst
1101	one ˌthousand, one ˌhundred and ˈone	1101st	one ˌthousand, one ˌhundred and ˈfirst
10 000	ten thousand	10 000th	ten thousandth
17 843	ˌseventeen ˌthousand, ˌeight ˌhundred and ˌforty-ˈthree	17 843rd	ˌseventeen ˌthousand, ˌeight ˌhundred and ˌforty-ˈthird
100 000	a/one hundred thousand	100 000th	(one) hundred thousandth
1 000 000	a/one million	1 000 000th	(one) millionth
3 157 984	ˌthree ˌmillion, ˌone ˌhundred and ˌfifty-ˌseven ˌthousand, nine ˌhundred and ˌeighty-ˈfour	3 157 984th	ˌthree ˌmillion, ˌone ˌhundred and ˌfifty-ˌseven ˌthousand, ˌnine ˌhundred and ˌeighty-ˈfourth
1 000 000 000/1 000 000 000 000	a/one billion (*See* **billion** in Dictionary.)	1 000 000 000th/1 000 000 000 000th	(one) billionth (*See* **billion** in Dictionary.)

Notes

(*i*) Information on the use of the various terms for 0 can be found in the sections on fractions and numerical expressions below. In general, the use of **zero** is more common in the US than in the UK.

(*ii*) **One hundred, one thousand** *etc* are more formal than **a hundred, a thousand** *etc*. The ordinal forms with **one** are more formal, more emphatic or more precise than those without **one**.

(*iii*) There are two ways of writing numbers of four or more digits: in numbers above 999, a comma may be inserted after every third digit from the right, as in 1,000 or 10,000 or 1,000,000; alternatively, in numbers above 9999, a slight space may be left after every third digit from the right, *eg* 1000, but 10 000, 1 000 000. The latter form is more common in scientific works, the former in writing of a more general or less technical nature.

No comma or space should be inserted in the following cases:

- years (1979);
- page numbers (p 1347);
- house numbers (1023 Northside Street);
- car numbers (JV 2679);
- telephone numbers (Baberton 835706; a space is, however, left in an all-figure number between the area code and the individual's number, as in 751 4679);
- line numbers in literary works (*The Song of Roland*, line 3851);
- manuscript *etc* numbers (ms 15793).

Roman Numerals

I	1	XIII	13	XL	40	CD	400
II	2	XIV	14	XLIX	49	CDXLIX	449
III	3	XV	15	L	50	D	500
IV	4	XVI	16	LX	60	DC	600
V	5	XVII	17	LXX	70	DCC	700
VI	6	XVIII	18	LXXX	80	DCCC	800
VII	7	XIX	19	XC	90	CM	900
VIII	8	XX	20	XCI	91	M	1000
IX	9	XXI	21	C	100	MI	1001
X	10	XXV	25	CX	110	MC	1100
XI	11	XXIX	29	CC	200	MCMLXXIX	1979
XII	12	XXX	30	CCC	300	MM	2000

Notes

(*i*) Lower-case letters (*eg* i, v, l *etc*) are sometimes found instead of the capitals shown here, *esp* in the introductory pages of books or additional notes as in these appendices.

(*ii*) In reading and writing Roman numerals, the following general rules apply:

(1) letters of the same value standing as a group are to be added together
eg CCC = C+C+C = 300; III = I+I+I = 3.

(2) a letter or group of letters to the right of another letter or group of letters of a greater value is to be added to it
eg XI = X+I = 10+1 = 11;
CX = C+X = 100+10 = 110.

(3) a letter to the left of another letter of a greater value is to be subtracted from it
eg XC = C−X = 100−10 = 90.
Where such a group appears to the right of a letter or group of letters of a greater value, it is to be added to that group
eg CCXC = C+C+(C−X) = 100+100+(100−10) = 290.

Hence MCMLXXIX = M+CM+LXX+IX
= 1000+(1000−100)+(50+10+10)+(10−1)
= 1000+900+70+9 = 1979.

Fractions

Vulgar Fractions

$\frac{1}{2}$ a half; one-half
$\frac{1}{4}$ a quarter; one-quarter
$\frac{1}{3}$ a third; one-third
$\frac{5}{7}$ five-sevenths
$\frac{31}{100}$ thirty-one hundredths
$4\frac{3}{16}$ four and three-sixteenths
$\frac{20}{7}$ twenty over seven
$\frac{7}{387}$ seven over three hundred and eighty-seven *or* seven three hundred and eighty-sevenths

Decimal Fractions

0·25	(nought) point two five	$(= \frac{25}{100})$
0·576	(nought) point five seven six	$(= \frac{576}{1000})$
3·468	three point four six eight	$(= 3\frac{468}{1000})$
6·007	six point nought nought seven	$(= 6\frac{7}{1000})$

Notes

(*i*) The number above the line in a vulgar fraction is called the **numerator** ['nju:məreitə]; the number below the line is called the **denominator** [di'nomineitə].

(*ii*) When spelt out, fractions should be hyphenated except when one part of the fraction already has a hyphen in it *eg* **seven-thirtieths** but **twenty-three thirtieths**.

(*iii*) Fractions with **one** are more formal or more precise than ones with **a**. **One** is therefore preferred with fractions which are obviously intended to be precise *eg* **one forty-seventh**, whereas **a** is normal with fractions which are used with a less exact intention *eg* **a quarter**.

(*iv*) **Over** is used in fractions with numerators greater than their denominators, and sometimes in fractions whose denominators have relatively long spoken forms.

Numerical Expressions

Times of Day

12.00 twelve o'clock; twelve (a.m./p.m.); midday; midnight; noon; twelve noon.
1.00 one o'clock; one a.m./p.m.

1.15 one fifteen (a.m./p.m.); (a) quarter past one.
1.30 one thirty (a.m./p.m.); half past one; (*inf*) half one.
1.45 one forty-five (a.m./p.m.); (a) quarter to two.

1.05 five past one; (*formal*) five minutes past one; one five (a.m./p.m.); (*formal*) one oh five (a.m./p.m.).
1.10 ten past one; (*formal*) ten minutes past one; one ten (a.m./p.m.).
1.25 twenty-five past one; (*formal*) twenty-five minutes past one; one twenty-five (a.m./p.m.).
1.35 twenty-five to two; (*formal*) twenty-five minutes to two; one thirty-five (a.m./p.m.).

1.04 four minutes past one; one four (a.m./p.m.); (*formal*) one oh four (a.m./p.m.).
1.58 two minutes to two; one fifty-eight (a.m./p.m.).

The (*Amer*) forms are essentially the same as the (*Brit*) forms given above, except that
(*i*) a colon is used instead of a full stop *eg* 1:30 a.m.
(*ii*) **after** and **of** are *usu* used in place of **past** and **to**.
(*iii*) **one, two** *etc* **thirty** is more common than **half past one, two** *etc*.

Twenty-four Hour Clock

These forms are used in timetables, military orders *etc*.

0800	(oh) eight hundred hours	(= 8.00 a.m.)
1130	eleven thirty	(= 11.30 a.m.)
1200	twelve hundred hours	(= midday)
1445	fourteen forty-five	(= 2.45 p.m.)
2204	twenty-two oh four	(= 10.04 p.m.)
2400	twenty-four hundred hours	(= midnight)

Dates

There are several ways of saying and writing dates in English. Some of these are given in the examples under **January, February** *etc* in the text. A fuller list is given below.

Spoken forms

on April (the) twenty-third, nineteen seventy-nine;
on the twenty-third of April, nineteen seventy-nine.

Written forms

(1) standing alone, *eg* as dates on letters:
23 April 1979; 23rd April '79; April 23, 1979; (*Brit*) 23/4/79; (*Amer*) 4/23/79.
(2) standing within a sentence *etc*:
on the twenty-third of April, 1979; on April (the) 23rd, 1979; on 23 April 1979; on April 23, 1979.

Note also

1900 nineteen hundred.
1901 nineteen hundred and one; nineteen (oh) one.
1910 nineteen (hundred and) ten.
2000 two thousand.
2000 BC [biː'siː].
AD 69, 69 AD [ei'diː] (AD is more commonly used with the earlier years of the Christian era, but it is also possible with later years, *eg* 1900 AD.)

Measurement

Our office is twenty foot/feet (wide) by thirty-three foot/feet (long) (*written as* 20 ft×33 ft).
The wall is about ten foot/feet high.
He is five foot/feet eight (inches) (tall).
She is/Her measurements are thirty-six, twenty-five, thirty-five (*written as* 36-25-35; = 36 inches round the bust, 25 inches round the waist and 35 inches round the hips.)

Weight

He weighs ten stone two (pounds) (*Brit*).
He weighs one hundred and forty-two pounds (*Amer*).

Distance

London to Edinburgh is three hundred and seventy miles.

Temperature

Water freezes at nought degrees Centigrade (0°C).
Last night the temperature fell to seven degrees below zero (−7°C)/twenty degrees (20°F).
It was eighty-six (86°F)/thirty (30°C) in the shade this morning.

Money

The tickets are/cost £1 each.
The lemonade is/costs 20p a glass.
It costs one pound fifty (pence).
I paid three (pounds) fifty (pence) for it.
That will cost you a/one dollar fifty.

Telephone Numbers

Each digit of a telephone number is *usu* spoken separately, except in the case of two identical digits occurring together, which are *usu* said as 'double four', 'double six' *etc.* The digits are *usu* spoken in groups of two or three, with slight pauses between the groups.

Baberton 0517	(= Baberton oh five one seven).
Baberton 4417	(= Baberton double four one seven).
Baberton 4447	(= Baberton double four four seven *or* four double four seven).
031-644 4379	(= oh three one, six double four, four three seven nine).
664 4339	(= double six four *or* six six four, four double three nine).

Note

In (*Amer*) usage, **zero** or **nought** are *usu* used instead of **oh**.

Numerical Expressions in Sport

Football

The score was two all (*written as* 2-2).
We won (the match) three two/by three goals to two (3-2).
We won three nil (3-0).

Rugby

We beat them twenty-six sixteen/by twenty-six points to sixteen (26-16).

American Football

We beat them twenty-one zero/by twenty-one points to zero (21-0).

Tennis

The scoring in the first game was fifteen love (*written as* 15-0), thirty love (30-0), thirty fifteen (30-15), thirty all (30-30), forty thirty (40-30), deuce (40-40), advantage Black, game to Black. Black won the first set six three/by six games to three (6-3), and eventually won the match by three sets to one (3-1).

Cricket

Sussex beat Hampshire by an innings and eighty runs/by two wickets. The score is seventy-seven for three. They were all out for a hundred and fifty-two (runs).

Appendix 2

Geographical Names, Nationalities and Languages

Countries and Nationalities

The languages given in brackets in the list below are the main languages spoken in the countries concerned.

Country/Continent/Region	Adjective(s)	Noun(s)
Africa ['afrikə]	African	African
1 Algeria [al'dʒiəriə] (French, Arabic)	Algerian	Algerian
(North/South) America [ə'merikə] *See also* the United States	(North/South) American	(North/South) American
the Antarctic [an'ta:ktik]	Antarctic (*usu attrib*)	
2 Arabia [ə'reibiə] (Arabic) *see* Note 1	Arab ['arəb] (*usu attrib*), Arabian, (Arabic ['arəbik])	Arab, Arabian
3 Argentina [a:dʒən'ti:nə] (Spanish)	Argentinian [-'tiniən]	Argentinian
Asia ['eiʃə, (*esp Amer*) -ʒə]	Asian	Asian
4 Australia [o'streiljə] (English)	Australian	Australian
5 Austria ['ostriə] (German)	Austrian	Austrian
the Balkans ['bo:lkənz] *see* Note 2	Balkan	
6 Bangladesh [baŋglə'deʃ] (Bengali)	Bangladesh (*attrib*), Bangladeshi [-ʃi]	Bangladeshi

7	Belgium ['beldʒəm] (Flemish, French)	Belgian	Belgian
8	Bolivia [bə'liviə] (Spanish)	Bolivian	Bolivian
9	Brazil [brə'zil] (Portuguese)	Brazilian	Brazilian
	Britain *see* the United Kingdom		
10	Bulgaria [bʌl'geəriə] (Bulgarian)	Bulgarian	Bulgarian
11	Burma ['bə:mə] (Burmese)	Burmese [bə:'mi:z, (*Amer also*) -'mi:s]	Burmese (*pl* Burmese: *usu* used in *pl*)
12	Cambodia [kam'boudiə]; Kampuchea [kampu'tʃiə]; *formerly* Khmer Republic [kmeə] (Khmer)	Cambodian, Khmer	Cambodian, Khmer
13	Canada ['kanədə] (English, French)	Canadian [kə'neidiən]	Canadian
	Ceylon *see* Sri Lanka		
14	Chile ['tʃili] (Spanish)	Chilean	Chilean
15	China ['tʃainə] (Chinese)	Chinese [tʃai'ni:z, (*Amer also*) -'ni:s]	Chinese (*pl* Chinese: *usu* used in *pl*)
16	Cuba ['kju:bə] (Spanish)	Cuban	Cuban
17	Cyprus ['saiprəs] (Turkish, Greek)	Cypriot ['sipriət], Cyprian ['sipriən]	Cypriot
18	Czechoslovakia [tʃekəslə'vakiə] (Czech, Slovak)	Czech [tʃek], Czechoslovakian, Czechoslovak [tʃekə'slouvak]	Czech, Czechoslovakian
19	Denmark ['denma:k] (Danish)	Danish ['deiniʃ]	Dane [dein]; Danish (*n pl*)
20	Egypt ['i:dʒipt] (Arabic)	Egyptian [i'dʒipʃən]	Egyptian
	Eire *see* the Irish Republic		
	England *see* the United Kingdom		
21	Ethiopia [i:θi'oupiə] (Amharic)	Ethiopian	Ethiopian
	Europe ['juərəp]	European [juərə'piən]	European
	European Economic Community *see* Note 3		
22	Finland ['finlənd] (Finnish, Swedish)	Finnish ['finiʃ]	Finn [fin]; Finnish (*n pl*)
	Formosa *see* Taiwan		
23	France [fra:ns] (French)	French [frentʃ]	'Frenchman, -woman; French (*n pl*)
24	(the Federal Republic of) Germany; West Germany ['dʒə:məni] (German)	(West) German	(West) German
25	the German Democratic Republic; East Germany ['dʒə:məni] (German)	(East) German	(East) German
26	Ghana ['ga:nə] (English)	Ghanaian [ga:'neiən]	Ghanaian
	Great Britain *see* the United Kingdom		
27	Greece [gri:s] (Greek)	Greek [gri:k]	Greek
	Holland *see* the Netherlands		
28	Hong Kong [hoŋ'koŋ] (English, Chinese)	'Hong Kong (*attrib*)	
29	Hungary ['hʌŋgəri] (Hungarian)	Hungarian [hʌŋ'geəriən]	Hungarian
	the Iberian Peninsula [ai'biəriən] *see* Note 4	Iberian	
30	Iceland ['aislənd] (Icelandic)	Icelandic [ais'landik]	'Icelander
31	India ['indiə] (Hindi, English)	Indian	Indian
32	Indonesia [ində'ni:ziə, (*esp Amer*) -ʒə] (Bahasa Indonesia)	Indonesian	Indonesian
33	Iran [i'ra:n, (*Amer usu*) i'ran] (Persian)	Iranian [i'reiniən]	Iranian
34	Iraq [i'ra:k, (*Amer*) i'rak] (Arabic)	Iraqi [-ki]	Iraqi
	Ireland *see* the Irish Republic *and* the United Kingdom		
35	the Irish Republic ['aiəriʃ], Eire ['eərə], (Southern) Ireland ['aiələnd] (Irish (Erse), English)	(Southern) Irish	'Irishman, -woman; (Southern) Irish (*n pl*)
36	Israel ['izreil, (*esp Amer*) -riəl] (Hebrew, Arabic)	Israeli [iz'reili]	Israeli
37	Italy ['itəli] (Italian)	Italian [i'taljən]	Italian
38	Japan [dʒə'pan] (Japanese)	Japanese [dʒapə'ni:z, (*Amer also*) -'ni:s]	Japanese (*pl* Japanese: *usu* used in *pl*)
39	Jordan ['dʒo:dn] (Arabic)	Jordanian [dʒo:'deiniən]	Jordanian

	Kampuchea *see* Cambodia		
40	Kenya ['kenjə, (*esp Amer*) 'ki:njə] (English, Swahili)	Kenyan	Kenyan
	Khmer Republic *see* Cambodia		
41	North Korea [kə'riə] (Korean)	North Korean	North Korean
42	South Korea [kə'riə] (Korean)	South Korean	South Korean
43	Kuwait [ku'weit, (*Amer also*) ku'wait] (Arabic)	Kuwaiti [-ti]	Kuwaiti
44	Lebanon ['lebənən] (Arabic)	Lebanese [lebə'ni:z, (*Amer also*) -'ni:s]	Lebanese (*pl* Lebanese: *usu* used in *pl*)
45	Libya ['libiə] (Arabic)	Libyan	Libyan
46	Luxemb(o)urg ['lʌksəmbə:g] (French)	Luxemb(o)urg (*attrib*)	Luxemb(o)urger
47	Malawi [mə'la:wi] (English)	Malawi (*attrib*), Malawian	Malawian
48	Malaysia [mə'leiziə, (*esp Amer*) -ʒə] (Malay)	Malaysian	Malaysian
49	Mexico ['meksikou] (Spanish)	Mexican	Mexican
50	Mongolia [moŋ'gouliə] (Mongolian)	Mongolian, Mongol ['moŋgəl]	Mongolian, Mongol
51	Morocco [mə'rokou] (Arabic, French, Spanish)	Moroccan	Moroccan
52	Mozambique [mouzam'bi:k] (Portuguese)	Mozambique (*attrib*), Mozambiquean [-kən]	Mozambiquean
53	Nepal [ni'po:l] (Nepali)	Nepalese [nepə'li:z, (*Amer also*) -'li:s], Nepali [-li]	Nepali; Nepalese (*pl* Nepalese: *usu* used in *pl*)
54	the Netherlands ['neðələndz] (*n sing*), Holland ['holənd] (Dutch)	Dutch [dʌtʃ]	'Dutchman, -woman; Dutch (*n pl*)
55	New Zealand [nju:'zi:lənd] (English)	New Zealand (*attrib*)	New Zealander
56	Nigeria [nai'dʒiəriə] (English)	Nigerian	Nigerian
57	Norway ['no:wei] (Norwegian)	Norwegian [no:'wi:dʒən]	Norwegian
58	Pakistan [pa:ki'sta:n, pa-, (*Amer also*) paki'stan] (Urdu, English)	Pakistan (*attrib*), Pakistani [-ni]	Pakistani
	Palestine ['paləstain] *see* Note 5	Palestinian [palə'stiniən]	Palestinian
59	Paraguay ['parəgwai, (*Amer also*) -gwei] (Spanish)	ˌPara'guayan	Paraguayan
60	Peru [pə'ru:] (Spanish)	Peruvian [-viən]	Peruvian
61	the Philippines ['filipi:nz] (Pilipino, English)	Philippine (*attrib*), Filipino [fili'pi:nou]	Filipino (*pl* -s)
62	Poland ['poulənd] (Polish)	Polish ['pouliʃ]	Pole [poul]; Polish (*n pl*)
63	Portugal ['po:tʃugəl] (Portuguese)	Portuguese [po:tʃu'gi:z, (*Amer also*) -'gi:s]	Portuguese (*pl* Portuguese: *usu* used in *pl*)
64	Rhodesia [rə'di:ʃə, -ziə, -ʒə, (*Amer*) rou-] *see* Zimbabwe-Rhodesia	Rhodesian	Rhodesian
65	Romania [rə'meiniə], Rumania [ru-] (Romanian, Rumanian)	Romanian, Rumanian	Romanian, Rumanian
	Russia *see* the Soviet Union		
66	Saudi Arabia [saudiə'reibiə] (Arabic)	Saudi Arabian, Saudi ['saudi]	Saudi Arabian, Saudi
	Scandinavia [skandi'neiviə] *see* Note 6	Scandinavian	Scandinavian
	Scotland *see* the United Kingdom		
67	Singapore [siŋ(g)ə'po:] (Malay, Chinese, Tamil, English)	Singaporean [siŋ(g)ə'po:riən]	Singaporean
68	Somalia [sə'ma:liə] (Somali)	Somalian	Somalian
69	South Africa ['afrikə] (Afrikaans, English)	South African	South African
70	the Soviet Union ['souviət, (*Amer also*) 'sov-] (Union of Soviet Socialist Republics, Russia ['rʌʃə]) (Russian)	Russian, Soviet	Russian, (*Amer*) Soviet
71	Spain [spein] (Spanish)	Spanish ['spaniʃ]	Spaniard ['spanjəd]; Spanish (*n pl*)

72	Sri Lanka [sri'laŋkə] (*formerly* Ceylon [si'lon]) (Sinhala *or* Sin(g)halese)	Sri Lankan, Sinhalese [sin(h)ə'li:z, siŋ(g)ə-, (*Amer also*) -'li:s], Singhalese [siŋ(g)ə'li:z, sin(h)ə-, (*Amer also*) -'li:s], *formerly* Ceylonese [selə'ni:z, (*Amer usu*) si:-, (*Amer also*) -'ni:s]	Sri Lankan; Sin(g)halese, *formerly* Ceylonese (*pls* Sin(g)halese, Ceylonese: *usu* used in *pl*)
73	Sudan [(*Brit usu*) su'da:n, (*Amer usu*) su'dan] (Arabic)	Sudanese [su:də'ni:z, (*Amer also*) -'ni:s]	Sudanese (*pl* Sudanese: *usu* used in *pl*)
74	Sweden ['swi:dn] (Swedish)	Swedish ['swi:diʃ]	Swede [swi:d]; Swedish (*n pl*)
75	Switzerland ['switsələnd] (French, German, Italian)	Swiss [swis]	Swiss (*pl* Swiss: *usu* used in *pl*)
76	Syria ['siriə] (Arabic)	Syrian	Syrian
77	Taiwan [(*Brit and Amer*) tai'wa:n]; *formerly* Formosa [fo:'mousə] (Chinese)	Taiwanese [taiwa:'ni:z, (*Amer also*) -'ni:s]; *formerly* Formosan	Taiwanese (*pl* Taiwanese: *usu* used in *pl*); *formerly* Formosan
78	Tanzania [tanzə'niə] (Swahili, English)	Tanzanian	Tanzanian
79	Thailand ['tailand] (Thai)	Thai	Thai
80	Tunisia [tju'nisiə, (*Amer*) tu:'ni:ʒə *or* -'niʒə] (Arabic)	Tunisian	Tunisian
81	Turkey ['tə:ki] (Turkish)	Turkish ['tə:kiʃ]	Turk [tə:k]; Turkish (*n pl*)
82	Uganda [ju'gandə] (Swahili, English)	Ugandan	Ugandan
	the Union of Soviet Socialist Republics *see* the Soviet Union		
83	the United Kingdom (of Great Britain and Northern Ireland); (Great) Britain ['britn]	British ['britiʃ]	Briton ['britn] (*rare*); 'Britisher (*Amer*); British (*n pl*)
	England ['iŋglənd] (English)	English ['iŋgliʃ]	'Englishman, -woman; English (*n pl*)
	(Northern) Ireland ['aiələnd] (English)	Irish ['aiəriʃ]	'Irishman, -woman; Irish (*n pl*)
	Scotland ['skotlənd] (English, Gaelic)	Scottish ['skotiʃ], (*not usu used by Scots*) Scotch [skotʃ], Scots [skots]	'Scotsman, -woman; Scot; Scottish (*n pl*); Scotch (*n pl: not used by Scots*)
	Wales [weilz] (*n sing*) (English, Welsh)	Welsh [welʃ]	'Welshman, (*rare*) -woman; Welsh (*n pl*)
84	the United States (of America [ə'merikə]) (*n sing*); America (English)	American	American
85	Uruguay ['juərəgwai, (*Amer also*) -gwei] (Spanish)	ˌUru'guayan	Uruguayan
86	Venezuela [veni'zweilə (*Amer also*) -'zwi:lə] (Spanish)	Venezuelan	Venezuelan
87	Vietnam [viet'nam, (*esp Amer*) -'na:m, (*Amer also*) viət-] (Vietnamese)	Vietnamese [vietnə'mi:z, (*Amer also*) viət-, (*Amer also*) -'mi:s]	Vietnamese (*pl* Vietnamese: *usu* used in *pl*)
	Wales *see* the United Kingdom		
88	West Indies ['indiz, (*Amer*) -di:z] (English)	West Indian	West Indian
89	the Arab Republic of Yemen ['jemən] (Arabic)	Yemeni [-ni]	Yemeni
90	the People's Democratic Republic of Yemen ['jemən] (Arabic)	Yemeni [-ni]	Yemeni
91	Yugoslavia [ju:gə'sla:viə] (Serbo-Croat, Slovenian, Macedonian)	Yugoslavian, Yugoslav ['ju:gəsla:v]	Yugoslavian, Yugoslav
92	Zaire [za:'iə, (*Amer also*) 'zaiər] (French)	Zairean [za:'iəriən, (*Amer also*) 'zaiəriən]	Zairean
93	Zambia ['zambiə] (English)	Zambian	Zambian
	Zimbabwe-Rhodesia [zim'babwirə'di:ʃə, -ziə, -ʒə, (*Amer*) -rou-] (English) (*See* Note 7)	Zimbabwe-Rhodesian	Zimbabwe-Rhodesian

Notes

(1) Arabia comprises Saudi Arabia, the Arab Republic of Yemen, the People's Democratic Republic of Yemen, Kuwait, and certain other states.
(2) The Balkans, or Balkan Peninsula, consist of Yugoslavia, Bulgaria, Romania, Albania, Greece, and part of Turkey.
(3) The European Economic Community (EEC), also known as the Common Market, comprises France, Germany, Italy, the United Kingdom, Belgium, the Netherlands, Luxembourg, the Irish Republic and Denmark.
(4) The Iberian Peninsula consists of Spain and Portugal.
(5) Although no longer a state, Palestine is included in this list because of its frequent occurrence in the news media.
(6) The Scandinavian Peninsula comprises Sweden and Norway, but the region Scandinavia includes Denmark, and often Iceland and Finland also.
(7) The name of the state of Rhodesia was changed to Zimbabwe-Rhodesia in 1979.

Examples of Usage

London is in England/the United Kingdom; *France is in Europe*; *The Netherlands is in Europe*; *Where are the West Indies?*; *He is flying to Spain/South America tomorrow.*

He is Chinese; *They are British citizens*; *This country was once a French colony* (= a colony belonging to France); *an American colony* (= a colony in America); *Can you name six European countries?*; *This is a French wine*; *Is this cheese French or Italian?*; *Have we got a Spanish agent?* (= an agent in Spain *or* an agent who is Spanish); *the Hong Kong government* (*Adjs* marked (*attrib*) in the above list, but not those marked (*usu attrib*), *usu* refer to a state rather than to a person's nationality; hence, one says *the Pakistan government*, but *Pakistani children*, not *Pakistan children*).

He is a Bulgarian/Frenchman/Greek/Dane/Japanese; *The Finns/Finnish/Chinese/Greeks are very hospitable*; *Finns/Greeks/Austrians/New Zealanders are very friendly people* (This construction is possible only with nouns which add an **-s** to form the plural, or with nouns ending in **-men/-women**); *They are both Poles*; *Few Scotsmen wear kilts nowadays* (This construction is not used with nouns ending in **-(i)sh**); *Many Danes speak English.*

Counties and Regions of the United Kingdom

Common written abbreviations of the English counties are given in brackets after each county. The form **Salop** is also used in speech. There are no commonly used abbreviations for Welsh and Northern Irish counties or Scottish regions.

England

Avon ['eivən]
Bedfordshire ['bedfədʃə] (Beds.)
Berkshire ['ba:kʃə] (Berks.)
Buckinghamshire ['bʌkiŋəmʃə] (Bucks.)
Cambridgeshire ['keimbridʒʃə] (Cambs.)
Cheshire ['tʃeʃə] (Ches.)
Cleveland ['kli:vlənd]
Cornwall ['ko:nwəl] (Corn.)
Cumbria ['kʌmbriə]
Derbyshire ['da:biʃə] (Derbys.)
Devon ['devən]
Dorset ['do:sit] (Dors.)
Durham ['dʌrəm] (Dur.)
Essex ['esiks]
Gloucestershire ['glostəʃə] (Glos.)
Hampshire ['hampʃə] (Hants.)
Hereford and Worcester ['herifədən'wustə]
Hertfordshire ['ha:tfədʃə] (Herts.)
Humberside ['hʌmbəsaid]
Isle of Wight [wait] (I. of W.)
Kent [kent]
Lancashire ['laŋkəʃə] (Lancs.)
Leicestershire ['lestəʃə] (Leics.)
Lincolnshire ['liŋkənʃə] (Lincs.)
County of London ['lʌndən]
County of Manchester ['mantʃistə]
Merseyside ['mə:zisaid]
Norfolk ['no:fək] (Norf.)
Northamptonshire [no:'θamptənʃə] (Northants.)
Northumberland [no:'θʌmbələnd] (Northd.)
North Yorkshire ['jo:kʃə] (North Yorks.)
Nottinghamshire ['notiŋəmʃə] (Notts.)
Oxfordshire ['oksfədʃə] (Oxon.)
Shropshire ['ʃropʃə] (Salop ['saləp])
Somerset ['sʌməsit] (Som.)
South Yorkshire ['jo:kʃə] (South Yorks.)
Staffordshire ['stafədʃə] (Staffs.)
Suffolk ['sʌfək] (Suff.)
Surrey ['sʌri]
Sussex ['sʌsiks]
Tyne and Wear ['tainən'wiə]
Warwickshire ['worikʃə] (Warwicks.)
West Midlands ['midləndz]
West Yorkshire ['jo:kʃə] (West Yorks.)
Wiltshire ['wiltʃə] (Wilts.)

Wales

Clwyd ['kluid]
Dyfed ['dʌvid]
Gwent [gwent]
Gwynedd ['gwinəð]
Mid Glamorgan [glə'mo:gən]
Powys ['pauis]
South Glamorgan [glə'mo:gən]
West Glamorgan [glə'mo:gən]

Northern Ireland

Antrim ['antrim]
Armagh [a:'ma:]
Down [daun]
Fermanagh [fə'manə]
Londonderry ['lʌndəndəri]
Tyrone [ti'roun]

Scotland

Borders ['bo:dəz]
Central ['sentrəl]
Dumfries and Galloway [dʌm'fri:sən'galəwei]
Fife [faif]
Grampian ['grampiən]
Highland ['hailənd]
Lothian ['louðiən]
Orkney ['o:kni]
Shetland ['ʃetlənd]
Strathclyde [straθ'klaid]
Tayside ['teisaid]
Western Isles

States of the United States of America

The first abbreviated form given in brackets after each state is that recommended by the U.S.Post Offic Department for use with zip codes. This is followed by other common written abbreviations for the states

Alabama [alə'bamə] (AL; Ala.)
Alaska [ə'laskə] (AK; Alas.)
Arizona [ari'zounə] (AZ; Ariz.)
Arkansas ['a:kənso:] (AR; Ark.)
California [kali'fo:niə] (CA; Cal., Calif.)
Colorado [kolə'ra:dou] (CO; Colo.)
Connecticut [kə'netikət] (CT; Conn., Ct.)
Delaware ['deləweə] (DE; Del.)
District of Columbia [kə'lʌmbiə] (DC; D.C.)
Florida ['floridə] (FL; Fa., Fla.)
Georgia ['dʒo:dʒə] (GA; Ga.)
Hawaii [hə'waii:] (HI)
Idaho ['aidəhou] (ID; Id.)
Illinois [ilə'noi] (IL; Ill.)
Indiana [indi'anə] (IN; Ind.)
Iowa ['aiouə] (IA; Ia.)
Kansas ['kanzəs] (KS; Kan., Kans., Ks.)
Kentucky [ken'tʌki] (KY; Ken., Ky.)
Louisiana [lu:i:zi'anə] (LA; La.)
Maine [mein] (ME; Me.)
Maryland ['meəriland] (MD; Md.)
Massachusetts [masə'tʃusits] (MA; Mass.)
Michigan ['miʃigən] (MI; Mich.)
Minnesota [mini'soutə] (MN; Minn.)
Mississippi [misi'sipi] (MS; Mi., Miss.)
Missouri [mi'zuəri] (MO; Mo.)
Montana [mon'tanə] (MT; Mont.)
Nebraska [nə'braskə] (NE; Neb., Nebr.)
Nevada [nə'va:də] (NV; Nev.)
New Hampshire ['hampʃə] (NH; N.H.)
New Jersey ['dʒə:zi] (NJ; N.J.)
New Mexico ['meksikou] (NM; N.M., N.Mex.)
New York [jo:k] (NY; N.Y.)
North Carolina [karə'lainə] (NC; N.C.)
North Dakota [də'koutə] (ND; N.D., N. Dak.)
Ohio [ou'haiou] (OH; O.)
Oklahoma [ouklə'houmə] (OK; Okla.)
Oregon ['origən] (OR; Ore., Oreg.)
Pennsylvania [pensil'veiniə] (PA; Pa., Penn.)
Rhode Island [roud] (RI; R.I.)
South Carolina [karə'lainə] (SC; S.C.)
South Dakota [də'koutə] (SD; S.D., S.Dak.)
Tennessee [tenə'si:] (TN; Ten., Tenn.)
Texas ['teksəs] (TX; Tex.)
Utah ['ju:to:] (UT; Ut.)
Vermont [və'mont] (VT; Vt.)
Virginia [və'dʒiniə] (VA; Va.)
Washington ['woʃiŋtən] (WA; Wash.)
West Virginia [və'dʒiniə] (WV; W. Va.)
Wisconsin [wis'konsin] (WI; Wis.)
Wyoming [wai'oumiŋ] (WY; Wy., Wyo.)

Other Geographical Names

Aberdeen [abə'di:n]
Adelaide ['adəleid]
the Amazon ['aməzən]
Amsterdam [amstə'dam]
Antwerp ['antwə:p]
Athens ['aθinz]
the Atlantic (Ocean) [ət'lantik]
the Baltic (Sea) ['bo:ltik]
Belfast ['belfast]
Birmingham ['bə:miŋəm]
Boston ['bostən]
Brussels ['brʌsəlz]
Cairo ['kaiərou]
Calcutta [kal'kʌtə]
Cambridge ['keimbridʒ]
Canberra ['kanbərə]
Canterbury ['kantəbəri]
Cardiff ['ka:dif]
the Caribbean (Sea) [kari'bi:ən]
Chicago [ʃi'ka:gou]
the Clyde [klaid]
Copenhagen [koupən'heigən]
Corsica ['ko:sikə]
the Danube ['danju:b]
Detroit [də'troit]
Dover ['douvə]
Dublin ['dʌblin]
Edinburgh ['edinbərə]
Folkestone ['foukstən]
Geneva [dʒi'ni:və]
Glasgow ['glazgou]
Gloucester ['glostə]
the Hague [heig]
Harwich ['haridʒ]
the Hebrides ['hebridi:z]
the Himalayas [himə'leiəz]
Leicester ['lestə]
Lisbon ['lizbən]
Liverpool ['livəpu:l]
London ['lʌndən]
Los Angeles [los'andʒili:z]
Madrid [mə'drid]
Malta ['mo:ltə]
Manchester ['mantʃistə]
the Mediterranean (Sea) [meditə'reiniən]
Melbourne ['melbən]
the Mersey ['mə:zi]
Minneapolis [mini'apəlis]
Montreal [montri'o:l]
Moscow ['moskou, (*Amer*) -kau]
Munich ['mju:nik]
Naples ['neiplz]
New Orleans [nju:'o:liənz]
New York [nju:'jo:k]
Ottawa ['otəwə]
Oxford ['oksfəd]
the Pacific (Ocean) [pə'sifik]
Paris ['paris]

Peking [piː'kiŋ]
Philadelphia [filə'delfiə]
the Pyrenees [piri'niːz]
the Rhine [rain]
Rome [roum]
the Sahara (Desert) [sə'haːrə]
Salisbury ['soːlzbəri]
San Francisco [sanfrən'siskou]
Sydney ['sidni]
the Thames [temz]
Tokyo ['toukjou]
Warsaw ['woːsoː]
Washington ['woʃiŋtən]
Wellington ['weliŋtən]
Worcester ['wustə]

Languages

The numbers indicate the countries in the first table of this appendix in which each language is spoken.

Afrikaans [afri'kaːns, (*Amer also*) -'kaːnz] 69
Amharic [am'harik] 21
Arabic ['arəbik] 1, 2, 20, 34, 36, 39, 43, 44, 45, 51, 66, 73, 76, 80, 89, 90
Bahasa Indonesia [bə'haːzəində'niːziə, (*esp Amer*) -ʒə] 32
Bengali [beŋ'goːli] 6
Bulgarian [bʌl'geəriən] 10
Burmese [bəː'miːz, (*Amer also*) -'miːs] 11
Chinese [tʃai'niːz, (*Amer also*) -'niːs] 15, 28, 67, 77
Czech [tʃek] 18
Danish ['deiniʃ] 19
Dutch [dʌtʃ] 54
English ['iŋgliʃ] 4, 13, 26, 28, 31, 40, 47, 55, 56, 58, 61, 64, 67, 69, 78, 82, 83, 84, 88, 93
Erse [əːs] 35
Finnish ['finiʃ] 22
Flemish ['flemiʃ] 7
French [frentʃ] 1, 7, 13, 23, 46, 51, 75, 92
Gaelic ['geilik, 'ga-] 83
German ['dʒəːmən] 5, 24, 25, 75
Greek [griːk] 17, 27
Hebrew ['hiːbruː] 36
Hindi ['hindi] 31
Hungarian [hʌŋ'geəriən] 29
Icelandic [ais'landik] 30
Irish ['aiəriʃ] 35
Italian [i'taljən] 37, 75
Japanese [dʒapə'niːz, (*Amer also*) -'niːs] 38
Khmer [kmeə] 12
Korean [kə'riən] 41, 42
Macedonian [masə'douniən] 91
Malay [mə'lei] 48, 67
Mongolian [moŋ'gouliən] 50
Nepali [ni'poːli] 53
Norwegian [noː'wiːdʒən] 57
Persian ['pəːʃən] 33
Pilipino [pili'piːnou] 61
Polish ['pouliʃ] 62
Portuguese [poːtʃu'giːz (*Amer also*) -'giːs] 9, 52, 63
Romanian [rə'meiniən], Rumanian [ru-] 65
Russian ['rʌʃən] 70
Serbo-Croat [səːbou'krouat], (*Amer usu*) Serbo-Croatian [səːrboukrou'eiʃən] 91
Sinhala ['sin(h)ələ], Sinhalese [sin(h)ə'liːz, siŋ(g)ə-, (*Amer also*) -'liːs] Singhalese [siŋ(g)ə'liːz, sin(h)ə-, (*Amer also*) -'liːs] 72
Slovak ['slouvak, (*Amer usu*) 'slouvaːk] 18
Slovenian [slə'viːniən] 91
Somali [sə'maːli] 68
Spanish ['spaniʃ] 3, 8, 14, 16, 49, 51, 59, 60, 85, 86
Swahili [swə'hiːli] 40, 78, 82
Swedish ['swiːdiʃ] 22, 74
Tamil ['tamil] 67
Thai [tai] 79
Turkish ['təːkiʃ] 17, 81
Urdu ['uəduː, 'əː-] 58
Vietnamese [vietnə'miːz, (*Amer also*) viət-, (*Amer also*) -'miːs] 87
Welsh [welʃ] 83

Examples of Usage
He speaks French/Arabic/Tamil; *He is a Thai/Finnish speaker*; *Russian/Chinese is not an easy language to learn*; *a grammar of English*; *a grammar of the Dutch language*; *an Arabic lesson*; *Japanese grammar*; *It is written in Danish.*

Appendix 3

Ranks in the British Armed Forces

Men's Services

Royal Navy	Army	Royal Air Force
	Officers	
Admiral of the Fleet	Field Marshal	Marshal of the Royal Air Force
Admiral	General	Air Chief Marshal
Vice Admiral	Lieutenant-General	Air Marshal
Rear Admiral	Major-General	Air Vice Marshal
Commodore	Brigadier	Air Commodore
Captain	Colonel	Group Captain
Commander	Lieutenant-Colonel	Wing Commander
Lieutenant-Commander	Major	Squadron Leader
Lieutenant	Captain	Flight Lieutenant
Sub-Lieutenant	Lieutenant	Flying Officer
Acting Sub-Lieutenant	Second Lieutenant	Pilot Officer

Non-Commissioned Officers

Fleet Chief Petty Officer	Warrant Officer 1st Class	Warrant Officer
	Warrant Officer 2nd Class	
Chief Petty Officer	Staff Sergeant	Flight Sergeant
		Chief Technician
Petty Officer	Sergeant	Sergeant
	Corporal	Corporal

Other Ranks

Leading Seaman		(Junior Technician)
Able Seaman	Lance Corporal	Senior Aircraftman
		Leading Aircraftman
Ordinary Seaman	Private	Aircraftman
(Junior Seaman)		

Officers in the Women's Services

Women's Royal Naval Service	Women's Royal Army Corps	Women's Royal Air Force
Commandant	Brigadier	Air Commandant
Superintendent	Colonel	Group Officer
Chief Officer	Lieutenant-Colonel	Wing Officer
First Officer	Major	Squadron Officer
Second Officer	Captain	Flight Officer
Third Officer	Lieutenant	Flying Officer
		Pilot Officer

Note
Ranks of (approximately) the same status have been placed opposite each other in the above lists.

Appendix 4

Musical Notation

The Common Clefs

The two most commonly used clefs are the **G clef** or **treble clef** and the **F clef** or **bass clef**. These are always fixed in the same position on the staff, and show the position of G and F respectively.

G or treble clef

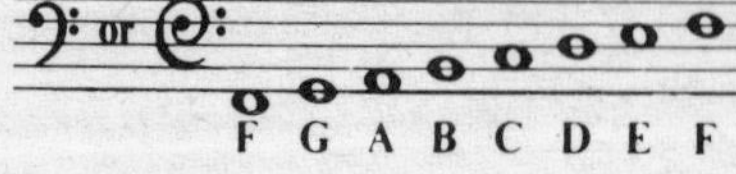

F or bass clef

The Values of the Notes

Each note shown below is twice the length of the note which follows it.

breve (*Amer also* double whole note)

semibreve (*Amer* whole note)

minim (*Amer* half note)

crotchet (*Amer* quarter note)

quaver (*Amer* eighth note)

semiquaver (*Amer* sixteenth note)

demisemiquaver (*Amer* thirty-second note)

hemidemisemiquaver (*Amer* sixty-fourth note)

Appendix 5

Weights and Measures

In the lists below, the weights and measures in bold type are those most commonly found in everyday use.

The Metric System

In the weights and measures of the metric system, the following pronunciations apply:

milli- ['mili-]
centi- ['senti-]
deci- ['desi-]
deca- ['dekə-]
hecto- ['hektou-]
kilo- ['kilou-] (but note that **kilometre** is *usu* [ki'lomitə])

Weight

10 **milligrams** (mg)	=	1 centigram (cg)
10 cg	=	1 decigram (dg)
10 dg	=	1 **gram** (g) (= 0·035 oz)
10 g	=	1 decagram (dag)
10 dag	=	1 hectogram (hg)
10 hg	=	1 **kilogram** (kg) (= 2·2 lb)
1000 kg	=	1 **tonne** *or* **metric ton** (= 2204·62 lb)

Length

10 **millimetres** (mm)	=	1 **centimetre** (cm) (= 0·394 in)
10 cm	=	1 decimetre (dm)
10 dm	=	1 **metre** (m) (= 39·37 in)
10 m	=	1 decametre (dam)
10 dam	=	1 hectometre (hm)
10 hm	=	1 **kilometre** (km) (= 0·62 mile)

Square Measure

100 square millimetres (mm^2)	=	1 square centimetre (cm^2) (= 0·115 in^2)
100 cm^2	=	1 square metre (m^2) (= 1·196 yd^2)
100 m^2	=	1 are
100 ares	=	1 hectare (ha) (= 2·47 acres)
100 ha	=	1 square kilometre (km^2).

Cubic Measure

1000 cubic centimetres (cm^3 *or* cc)	=	1 cubic decimetre (dm^3)
1000 dm^3	=	1 cubic metre (m^3)

Capacity

10 millilitres (ml)	=	1 centilitre (cl)
10 cl	=	1 decilitre (dl)
10 dl	=	1 **litre** (l) (= 1·76 pints (UK), 2·11 pints (US), 1 dm^3)
10 l	=	1 decalitre (dal)
10 dal	=	1 hectolitre (hl)
10 hl	=	1 kilolitre (kl) (= 220 gallons (UK), 264·18 gallons (US))

Note

In the measures listed above, the form **deka-** is sometimes found instead of **deca-**, *esp* in the US.

The British and American Measures

Avoirdupois Weight

In the UK,

		1 **ounce** (= 28·35 g)
16 ounces (oz)	=	1 **pound** (lb) (= 0·454 kg)
14 lb(s)	=	1 stone (st)
2 st(s)	=	1 quarter (qr)
4 qr(s) (112 lb)	=	1 (long) **hundredweight** (cwt) (= 50·8 kg)
20 cwt (2240 lb)	=	1 (long) **ton** (= 1016 kg)

In the US,

25 lb(s)	=	1 qr
4 qr(s) (100 lb)	=	1 (short) cwt (= 45·36 kg)
20 cwt (2000 lb)	=	1 (short) ton (= 907·2 kg)

Notes:
(*i*) The **stone** is not used in the US.
(*ii*) The terms **long hundredweight/ton** and **short hundredweight/ton** are rare, and used only when necessary to distinguish between the *UK* and *US* units.

Length

		1 **inch** (= 2·54 cm)
12 inches (in(s))	=	1 **foot** (ft) (= 30·48 cm)
3 ft	=	1 **yard** (yd) (= 0·91 m)
22 yd(s)	=	1 chain (ch)
10 ch(s)	=	1 furlong (fur)
8 fur(s) (1760 yd)	=	1 **mile** (= 1·61 km)

Square Measure

		1 square inch (= 6·45 cm^2)
144 square inches (in^2)	=	1 square foot (ft^2) (= 0·093 m^2)
9 ft^2	=	1 square yard (yd^2) (= 0·836 m^2)
4840 yd^2	=	1 **acre** (= 4047 m^2)
640 acres	=	1 square mile (= 259 ha)

Cubic Measure

		1 cubic inch (= 16·39 cm^3)
1728 cubic inches (in^3)	=	1 cubic foot (ft^3) (= 0·028 m^3)
27 ft^3	=	1 cubic yard (yd^3) (= 0·765 m^3)

Capacity

In the UK,

		1 fluid ounce (= 28·41 cm^3 *or* cc)
5 fluid ounces (fl oz(s))	=	1 gill
4 gills (20 fl oz)	=	1 **pint** (pt) (= 0·57 litres)
2 pt(s)	=	1 quart (qt)
4 qt(s)	=	1 **gallon** (gal) (= 4·54 litres)

In the US,

		1 fl oz (= 29·6 cm^3 *or* cc)
16 fl oz(s)	=	1 pint (= 0·47 litre)
8 pt(s)	=	1 gallon (= 3·79 litres)

Appendix 6

The Solar System

The planets of the solar system are listed below in order of distance from the Sun.

Mercury ['mə:kjuri]
Venus ['vi:nəs]
Earth [ə:θ]
Mars [ma:z]
Jupiter ['dʒu:pitə]
Saturn ['satən]
Uranus [ju'reinəs, 'juərənəs]
Neptune ['neptju:n]
Pluto ['plu:tou]

Note also

Martian ['ma:ʃn] *nc, adj* (a hypothetical inhabitant) of Mars.
Venusian [vi'nju:ziən] *nc, adj* (a hypothetical inhabitant) of Venus.

Appendix 7

The English Alphabet

Aa [ei]
Bb [bi:]
Cc [si:]
Dd [di:]
Ee [i:]
Ff [ef]
Gg [dʒi:]
Hh [eitʃ]
Ii [ai]
Jj [dʒei]
Kk [kei]
Ll [el]
Mm [em]
Nn [en]
Oo [ou]
Pp [pi:]
Qq [kju:]
Rr [a:]
Ss [es]
Tt [ti:]
Uu [ju:]
Vv [vi:]
Ww ['dʌblju:]
Xx [eks]
Yy [wai]
Zz [(*Brit*) zed, (*Amer*) zi:]

Appendix 8

Abbreviations and Symbols

Abbreviations

Notes

(*i*) No pronunciation is given for abbreviations which consist of a single letter, nor for abbreviations which, when spoken, are pronounced in the same way as the full form of the word(s) concerned (*eg* **amt** is to be pronounced as 'amount', **Adm.** as 'Admiral'). For abbreviations which are spoken as a series of letters, only a stress pattern is given (*eg* **PhD** ˌ--'-). For abbreviations which are pronounced as words, a full transcription is provided (*eg* **Benelux** ['benilʌks]).

(*ii*) There is now a tendency to spell abbreviations, *esp* of scientific terms, university or college degrees, and the names of organizations, without full stops between the letters. The full stops have generally been left out in the list below, but it should be understood that in most cases both forms (with or without full stops) are equally correct.

A (in degrees *etc*) Associate: ampere(s): (*UK*) used to mark a cinema film at a showing of which any child under 14 should be accompanied by an adult: of the highest, or a high, class: (in **A-bomb**) atomic: (*UK*: in **A-level** examination) advanced.
A1 *see* Dictionary.
AA [ˌ-'-] (*UK*) Automobile Association: Alcoholics Anonymous: (*UK*) used to mark a cinema film to a showing of which no child under 14 may be admitted.
AB [ˌ-'-] able seaman: (*US*) Bachelor of Arts.
abbr., abbrev. abbreviated: abbreviation.
AC, ac [ˌ-'-] alternating current.
a/c account.
ACAS ['eikas] (*UK*) Advisory, Conciliation and Arbitration Service.
acc., acct. account.
AD [ˌ-'-] *anno Domini* [anou'dominai] (L) in the year of our Lord (*eg* AD 1900, 1900 AD).
ad *see* Dictionary.
ad lib *see* Dictionary.
Adm. Admiral.
admin [ad'min] administration.
advt. advertisement.
AFL - CIO [ˌ--'- ˌ--'-] (*US*) American Federation of Labor and Congress of Industrial Organizations.
AGM [ˌ--'-] annual general meeting.
AID [ˌ--'-] (*US*) Agency for International Development.
AM [ˌ-'-] (*US*) Master of Arts.
Am. America(n).
a.m. [ˌ-'-] *ante meridiem* [antimə'ridiəm] (L) before noon.
AMA [ˌ--'-] American Medical Association.
Amer. America(n).
amp *see* Dictionary.
amt amount.
anon *see* Dictionary.

ans. answer.
app. appendix.
appro. ['aprou] approval.
approx. approximate(ly).
Apr. April.
apt. apartment.
arr. arrival: arrive(s).
Assoc. Association.
Aug. August.
Av(e). Avenue.
B (on lead pencils) black: (in degrees) Bachelor.
2B [ˌ–'–] (on lead pencils) very black.
b born.
BA [ˌ–'–] Bachelor of Arts: British Airways.
B and B, b and b [ˌ––'–] bed and breakfast.
Bart (*UK*) Baronet.
BB [ˌ–'–] Boys' Brigade.
BBC [ˌ––'–] British Broadcasting Corporation.
BC [ˌ–'–] Before Christ (*eg* 55 BC).
BCom(m) [bi:'kom] Bachelor of Commerce.
BD [ˌ–'–] Bachelor of Divinity.
BEd [bi:'ed] Bachelor of Education.
Benelux ['benilʌks] *Be*lgium, the *Ne*therlands and *Lux*embourg.
bk book.
BL [ˌ–'–] Bachelor of Law.
BLitt [bi:'lit] Bachelor of Letters.
Blvd Boulevard.
BMA [ˌ––'–] British Medical Association.
BMus [bi:'mʌs] Bachelor of Music.
b.o., B.O. [ˌ–'–] body odour.
Boul. Boulevard.
BPhil [bi:'fil] Bachelor of Philosophy.
BR [ˌ–'–] British Rail.
Br. Brother.
Brig. Brigadier.
Brit. British.
Bro. Brother.
BS [ˌ–'–] (*US*) Bachelor of Science.
BSc [ˌ––'–] Bachelor of Science.
BSI [ˌ––'–] British Standards Institution.
BST [ˌ––'–] British Summer Time: British Standard Time.
Bt Baronet.
C centigrade: Celsius: Conservative: one hundred (*see* Appendix 1).
c cent(s): *circa* ['sə:kə] (L) about: cubic: centi- (*see* Appendix 5).
CA [ˌ–'–] Chartered Accountant.
cal calorie(s).
Cantab. ['kantab] of Cambridge (University).
CAP [ˌ––'–] Common Agricultural Policy.
Capt. Captain.
Card. Cardinal.
Cath. Catholic.
CBI [ˌ––'–] Confederation of British Industry.
cc cubic centimetre(s).
CD [ˌ–'–] *Corps Diplomatique* (Fr) Diplomatic Corps.
Cdr Commander.
Cdre Commodore.
Cert. Certificate.
cf. [ˌ–'–] *confer* (L) compare.
ch., chap. chapter.
CIA [ˌ––'–] (*US*) Central Intelligence Agency.
CID [ˌ––'–] (*UK*) Criminal Investigation Department.
C-in-C [ˌ––'–] Commander-in-Chief.
cm centimetre(s).
CNAA [ˌ–––'–] (*UK*) Council for National Academic Awards.
CO [ˌ–'–] Commanding Officer.
Co. Company: County.
c/o care of (= at the address of).
c.o.d. [ˌ––'–] cash on delivery.
co-ed *see* **co-educational** *in* Dictionary.
C of E [ˌ––'–] Church of England.
Col. Colonel.
col. column.
Com. Commander: Commodore.
Comdr. Commander.
comp. compare.
con. [kon] *contra* ['kontra] (L) against.
cont., contd continued.
co-op *see* **co-operative society** *under* **co-operate** *in* Dictionary.
Corp. Corporal: (*Amer*) Corporation.
Coy (*esp mil*) Company.
Cpl Corporal.
CPO [ˌ––'–] Chief Petty Officer.
c.p.s. [ˌ––'–] cycle(s) per second.
Cres(c). Crescent.
CSE [ˌ––'–] (*UK*) Certificate of Secondary Education.
cu., cub. cubic.
cv [ˌ–'–] curriculum vitae.
cwt hundredweight(s).
D fifty (*see* Appendix 1): (*US*) Democrat(ic).
3-D *see* **three-dimensional** *under* **three** *in* Dictionary.
d died: deci- (*see* Appendix 5): (*UK, until 1971*) *denarius, denarii* (L) penny, pence.
DA [ˌ–'–] (*US*) District Attorney.
da- deca- (*see* Appendix 5).
dB, db decibel(s).
DC, dc [ˌ–'–] direct current.
DD [ˌ–'–] Doctor of Divinity.
DDT [ˌ––'–] dichlorodiphenyltrichloroethane (= an insecticide).
Dec. December.
deg. degree(s).
Dep., Dept., dep., dept. department: deputy.
dep. depart(s): departure.
Dip. Diploma.
Dip. Ed. [dip'ed] Diploma in Education.
DIY [ˌ––'–] do-it-yourself.
DJ [ˌ–'–] disc-jockey.
DLitt [di:'lit] Doctor of Letters.
DM Deutsche Mark(s).
DMus [di:'mʌs] Doctor of Music.
DNA [ˌ––'–] deoxyribonucleic acid(s) (= substances found in plant and animal chromosomes and carrying in coded form instructions for passing on hereditary characteristics).
Dnr dinar(s).
do *see* **ditto** *in* Dictionary.
doz. dozen.
DPhil [di:'fil] Doctor of Philosophy.
Dr Doctor: drachma(e).
DSc [ˌ––'–] Doctor of Science.
DSO [ˌ––'–] (*UK*) Distinguished Service Order.
DV [ˌ–'–] *Deo volente* ['di:ouvo'lenti:] (L) if God is willing.
E east.
E and OE [ˌ–––'–] errors and omissions excepted.
Ed. Editor.
ed., edit. edited (by): edition.
EEC [ˌ––'–] European Economic Community (*see* Appendix 2).
EFL [ˌ––'–] English as a foreign language.
EFTA ['eftə] European Free Trade Association.
eg, e.g. [ˌ–'–] *exempli gratia* [ig'zempli: 'greiʃiə] (L) for example.
Emp. Emperor: Empress.

encl. enclosure(s).
ENE east-north-east.
Eng. English: England.
Ens. Ensign.
ENT [ˌ--ˈ-] Ear, Nose and Throat.
EP [ˌ-ˈ-] extended play (record).
EPNS [ˌ---ˈ-] electroplated nickel silver.
ER [ˌ-ˈ-] *Elizabeth Regina* [riˈdʒainə] (L) Queen Elizabeth.
ESE east-south-east.
ESL [ˌ--ˈ-] English as a second language.
ESP [ˌ--ˈ-] extra-sensory perception.
esp. especially.
Esq. *see* **Esquire** *in* Dictionary.
est. established.
et al [etˈal] *et alii/aliae/alia* (L) and (the) others.
etc. *see* **et cetera** *in* Dictionary.
ext. extension.
F (in degrees *etc*) Fellow: Fahrenheit.
f and the following line, page *etc.*
FAO [ˌ--ˈ-] Food and Agriculture Organization.
FBI [ˌ--ˈ-] (*US*) Federal Bureau of Investigation.
Feb. February.
ff and the following lines, pages *etc.*
fig. figure.
fl. oz. fluid ounce(s) – *pl also* **ozs**.
Flt.Lt. Flight Lieutenant.
fn. footnote.
FO Flying Officer.
FP [ˌ-ˈ-] former pupil.
Fr franc(s).
Fr. Father.
fr franc(s).
Fri. Friday.
ft. foot, feet.
G (*US*) used to mark a cinema film to showings of which children under 17 may be admitted.
g gram(me)(s).
gal(l). gallon(s) – *pl also* **gals.**
GB [ˌ-ˈ-] Great Britain.
gbh [ˌ--ˈ-] grievous bodily harm.
GCE [ˌ--ˈ-] (*UK*) General Certificate of Education.
Gdns Gardens.
Gen. General.
GHQ [ˌ--ˈ-] General Headquarters.
GI *see* Dictionary.
Gld guilder(s).
gm gram(me)(s).
GMT [ˌ--ˈ-] Greenwich Mean Time.
govt government.
GP [ˌ-ˈ-] general practitioner: (*US*) used to mark cinema films to showings of which children under 17 may be admitted under parental guidance.
Gp. Capt. Group Captain.
GPO [ˌ--ˈ-] General Post Office.
H (on lead pencils) hard.
2H [ˌ-ˈ-] (on lead pencils) very hard.
h hecto- (*see* Appendix 5).
ha hectare.
HB [ˌ-ˈ-] (on lead pencils) hard black.
HGV [ˌ--ˈ-] heavy goods vehicle.
hi-fi *see* Dictionary.
HMS [ˌ--ˈ-] (*UK*) Her/His Majesty's Ship (used for warships only).
HMSO [ˌ---ˈ-] (*UK*) Her/His Majesty's Stationery Office.
HNC [ˌ--ˈ-] (*UK*) Higher National Certificate.
HND [ˌ--ˈ-] (*UK*) Higher National Diploma.
Hon. Honourable: Honorary.
Hons Honours.
Hon. Sec. Honorary Secretary.
HP [ˌ-ˈ-] hire-purchase: (*or* **hp**) horsepower.
HQ [ˌ-ˈ-] headquarters.
hr hour.
HRH [ˌ--ˈ-] Her/His Royal Highness.
Hz hertz.
I one (*see* Appendix 1).
ib., ibid. *ibidem* [iˈbaidem] (L) in the same place.
ie, i.e. [ˌ-ˈ-] *id est* [idˈest] (L) that is: that means.
IMF [ˌ--ˈ-] International Monetary Fund.
in inch(es) – *pl also* **ins.**
Inc. (*US*) Incorporated.
incl. including.
inf. *infra* [ˈinfrə] (L) below.
Inst. Institute.
inst. instant (= of this month, *eg* your letter of 13th inst.).
IOU *see* Dictionary.
IQ [ˌ-ˈ-] Intelligence Quotient (= the measure of a person's intelligence).
IRA [ˌ--ˈ-] Irish Republican Army.
ITV [ˌ--ˈ-] (*UK*) Independent Television.
J joule(s).
Jan. January.
Jnr Junior.
JP [ˌ-ˈ-] (*UK*) Justice of the Peace.
Jr Junior.
Jul. July.
Jun. June: Junior.
k kilo- (*see* Appendix 5).
KC [ˌ-ˈ-] (*UK*) King's Council (= a high-ranking barrister or advocate).
kg kilogram(me)(s).
kilo kilogram(me).
km kilometre(s).
KO, ko [ˌ-ˈ-] knock out.
kph [ˌ--ˈ-] kilometres per hour.
kr krona, kronor: krone, kroner.
Kt Knight.
kW, kw kilowatt(s).
kWh, kwh kilowatt-hour(s).
L Lake: Liberal: learner (driver): 50 (*see* Appendix 1).
l line: litre(s): lira, lire.
LA [ˌ-ˈ-] Los Angeles.
Lab. Labour.
lab *see* Dictionary.
lat. latitude.
lb *libra(e)* (L) pound(s) – *pl also* **lbs**.
lbw [ˌ--ˈ---] leg before wicket.
L/Cpl Lance Corporal.
Lib. Liberal.
Lieut. Lieutenant.
Lieut.-Col. Lieutenant-Colonel.
Lieut.-Gen. Lieutenant-General.
LittD [litˈdiː] Doctor of Letters.
ll lines.
LlB [ˌ--ˈ-] Bachelor of Laws.
loc. cit. *loco citato* [ˈloukousaiˈteitou] (L) at the same place, in the same book *etc* as the last reference.
log [log] logarithm.
long. longitude.
LP [ˌ-ˈ-] long-playing record.
Lr lira, lire.
LSD [ˌ--ˈ-] lysergic acid diethylamide (= a drug which causes hallucinations *etc*).
L.S.D. [ˌ--ˈ-] (*also* **£.s.d.**) *librae, solidi, denarii* (L) pounds, shillings, and pence.
Lt. Lieutenant.
Lt.-Col. Lieutenant-Colonel.
Ltd. *see* **limited** *under* **limit** *in* Dictionary.
Lt.-Gen. Lieutenant-General.

LW long wave.
M (in degrees, titles *etc*) Member, Master: a thousand (*see* Appendix 1).
m metre(s): mile(s): milli- (*see* Appendix 5).
MA [ˌ–ˈ–] Master of Arts.
Maj. Major.
Mar. March.
Marq. Marquis.
max. maximum.
MBE [ˌ––ˈ–] Member of the Order of the British Empire.
MC [ˌ–ˈ–] Master of Ceremonies.
MCC [ˌ––ˈ–] (*UK*) Marylebone [ˈmarələbən] Cricket Club.
MCP [ˌ––ˈ–] male chauvinist pig (*see* **male chauvinist** *under* **chauvinism**).
MD [ˌ–ˈ–] Doctor of Medicine.
Messrs [ˈmesəz] *Messieurs* (Fr) gentlemen, used as plural of Mister (*eg* Messrs Brown and Smith).
mg milligram(me)(s).
mi. mile(s).
MI5 [ˌ––ˈ–] a department of the British Intelligence Service.
min. minimum: minute (time).
misc. miscellaneous.
ml millilitre(s): mile(s) – *pl also* **mls.**
MLitt [emˈlit] Master of Letters.
mm millimetre(s).
Mme Madame.
Mmes Mesdames, used as *formal pl* of **Mrs.**
mod cons *see* Dictionary.
MOH [ˌ––ˈ–] Medical Officer of Health.
Mon. Monday.
MOT [ˌ––ˈ–] (UK) Ministry of Transport.
MP [ˌ–ˈ–] Member of Parliament: Military Police.
mpg, mph [ˌ––ˈ–] mile(s) per gallon, mile(s) per hour.
Mr Mister.
Mrs *see* Dictionary.
MS(S), ms(s) manuscript(s).
Ms *see* Dictionary.
MSc [ˌ––ˈ–] Master of Science.
Mt Mount: Mountain.
mth month.
MW medium wave.
N north.
NATO [ˈneitou] North Atlantic Treaty Organization.
NB, nb [ˌ–ˈ–] *nota bene* [noutəˈbeni] (L) note well.
NCO [ˌ––ˈ–] non-commissioned officer.
2nd, 22nd, 32nd *etc* second, twenty-second, thirty-second *etc.*
NE north-east.
NHS [ˌ––ˈ–] (*UK*) National Health Service.
NNE north-north-east.
NNW north-north-west.
No., no. *numero* (L) number.
Nov. November.
nr near.
NT New Testament.
NW north-west.
NY New York.
NZ New Zealand.
O (*UK*: in **O-level** examination) ordinary.
OAP [ˌ––ˈ–] Old Age Pensioner/Pension.
OBE [ˌ––ˈ–] Officer of the Order of the British Empire.
Oct. October.
OECD [ˌ–––ˈ–] Organization for Economic Co-operation and Development.
OHMS [ˌ–––ˈ–] (*UK*) On Her/His Majesty's Service.
O.K. *see* Dictionary.
ONC [ˌ––ˈ–] (*UK*) Ordinary National Certificate.
OND [ˌ––ˈ–] (*UK*) Ordinary National Diploma.
ono or nearest offer.
Op., op. Opus.
op. cit. *opere citato* [ˈopəri:saiˈteitou] (L) in the same book *etc* as mentioned in the last reference.
OPEC [ˈoupek] Organization of Petroleum-Exporting Countries.
OT Old Testament.
OXFAM [ˈoksfam] *Ox*ford Committee for *Fam*ine Relief.
Oxon. [ˈoksən] of Oxford (university).
oz ounce(s) – *pl also* **ozs.**
p (new) penny, pence: page.
p.a. per annum.
par(a). paragraph.
p. and p. (*Brit*) postage and packing.
PAYE [ˌ–––ˈ–] (*UK*) Pay As You Earn (Income Tax).
PC [ˌ–ˈ–] (*UK*) Police Constable.
pc [ˌ–ˈ–] postcard.
pd paid.
PE [ˌ–ˈ–] physical education.
Pes. peseta(s).
PG = **GP** (*US cinema*).
PhD [ˌ––ˈ–] Doctor of Philosophy.
Pl. Place.
PM Prime Minister.
p.m. *post meridiem* [poustməˈridiəm] (L) in the afternoon.
PO [ˌ–ˈ–] Post Office: Petty Officer: Pilot Officer: postal order.
pop. population.
POW [ˌ––ˈ–––] prisoner of war.
pp pages: *per pro*(*curationem*) (L) signed on behalf of.
PR [ˌ–ˈ–] public relations.
Pres. President.
PRO [ˌ––ˈ–] public relations officer.
pro. professional.
Prof. Professor.
Prot. Protestant.
pro tem. [ˈprouˈtem] *pro tempore* [ˈprouˈtempəri] (L) for the time being.
PS [ˌ–ˈ–] postscript.
PT [ˌ–ˈ–] physical training.
pt pint(s) – *pl also* **pts.**
PTA [ˌ––ˈ–] Parent/Teacher Association.
Pte (*Brit mil*) Private.
PTO [ˌ––ˈ–] please turn over.
Pty Proprietary.
PVC [ˌ––ˈ–] polyvinyl chloride (= a plastic).
Q queue.
QC [ˌ–ˈ–] (*UK*) Queen's Counsel (= a high-ranking barrister or advocate).
QED, qed [ˌ––ˈ–] *quod erat demonstrandum* (L) which was to be shown or proved.
qqv *quae vide* (L) see these items, entries *etc.*
qr quarter(s) – *pl also* **qrs.**
qt quart(s) – *pl also* **qts.**
qv *quod vide* (L) see this item, entry *etc.*
R *rex* [reks] (L) King: *regina* [riˈdʒainə] (L) Queen: (*US*) used to mark cinema films to showings of which children under 17 are not admitted unless accompanied by an adult: rupee(s) – *pl also* **Rs**: rand(s).
® registered trade mark.
RA [ˌ–ˈ–] (*UK*) Royal Academy.
RAC [ˌ––ˈ–] (*UK*) Royal Automobile Club.
RADA [ˈra:də] (*UK*) Royal Academy of Dramatic Art.

RAF [ˌ--ˈ-; *sometimes* raf] (*UK*) Royal Air Force.
RC [ˌ-ˈ-] Roman Catholic.
Rd Road: rand(s).
3rd, 23rd, 33rd *etc* third, twenty-third, thirty-third *etc.*
RE [ˌ-ˈ-] religious education.
recd received.
ref. reference.
Rep (*US*) Republican.
rep *see* Dictionary.
retd retired.
Rev., Revd Reverend.
rev *see* Dictionary.
RI [ˌ-ˈ-] religious instruction.
RIP [ˌ--ˈ-] *requiescat in pace* (L) may he/she rest in peace.
RN [ˌ-ˈ-] Royal Navy.
RNA [ˌ--ˈ-] ribonucleic acid(s) (= substances found in living cells where they play an important part in the development of proteins).
Rom. Cath. Roman Catholic.
RP [ˌ-ˈ-] Received Pronunciation (*see* Dictionary).
rpm, rps [ˌ--ˈ-] revolution(s) per minute, revolution(s) per second.
RSM [ˌ--ˈ-] Regimental Sergeant-Major.
RSPCA [ˌ--ˌ--ˈ-] (*UK*) Royal Society for the Prevention of Cruelty to Animals.
RSVP [ˌ---ˈ-] *Répondez s'il vous plaît* (Fr) please reply.
Rt Hon. (*UK*) Right Honourable.
S south.
s second(s): shilling(s).
sae [ˌ--ˈ-] stamped addressed envelope.
SALT [so:lt] Strategic Arms Limitation Talks.
Sat. Saturday.
sc. *scilicet* [ˈsailiset] (L) namely: that is to say.
SCE [ˌ--ˈ-] Scottish Certificate of Education.
Sch schilling(s).
sci fi [ˈsaifai] science fiction.
scil. *scilicet* [ˈsailiset] (L) namely: that is to say.
sd *sine die* [ˈsaini:ˈdaii:, ˈsineˈdi:ei] (L) indefinitely.
SE south-east.
SEATO [ˈsi:tou] South-east Asia Treaty Organization.
Sec., Secy Secretary.
sec second(s) – *pl also* **secs.**
SEN [ˌ--ˈ-] (*UK*) State Enrolled Nurse.
Sen. Senator: senior.
Sept. September.
SF [ˌ-ˈ-] science fiction.
Sgt Sergeant.
SI [ˌ-ˈ-] Système International (d'Unités) (Fr) (= the international system of units of measurement, based on the metre, kilogram *etc*).
Snr Senior.
SNP [ˌ--ˈ-] Scottish National Party.
Soc. Society.
SOS *see* Dictionary.
Sq. Square.
sq. square.
Sr Senior.
SRN [ˌ--ˈ-] State Registered Nurse.
SSE south-south-east.
SSW south-south-west.
St Saint: Strait.
St. Street.
st. stone(s) (weight) – *pl also* **sts.**
1st, 21st, 31st *etc* first, twenty-first, thirty-first *etc.*
STD [ˌ--ˈ-] (*UK*) subscriber trunk dialling [= the system of making telephone calls in which people can call each other up without the help of the operator).
Sun. Sunday.
Supt Superintendent.
SW south-west: short wave.
TB [ˌ-ˈ-] tuberculosis.
TEFL [ˈtefəl *or* ˌ---ˈ-] teaching English as a foreign language.
tel. telephone.
temp. temperature: temporary.
Ter(r). Terrace.
TESL [ˈtesəl *or* ˌ---ˈ-] teaching English as a second language.
Th., Thurs. Thursday.
4th, 26th, 38th *etc* fourth, twenty-sixth, thirty-eighth *etc.*
TNT *see* Dictionary.
TT [ˌ-ˈ-] teetotal: tuberculin tested (= tested for the presence of a certain bacillus).
Tu., Tues. Tuesday.
TUC [ˌ--ˈ-] (*UK*) Trades Union Congress.
TV [ˌ-ˈ-] television.
U (*UK*) used to mark cinema films to showings of which children under 14 may be admitted when not accompanied by an adult.
UDI [ˌ--ˈ-] Unilateral Declaration of Independence.
UFO [ˌ--ˈ-] unidentified flying object (*eg* a spaceship).
UHF [ˌ--ˈ-] ultra high frequency.
UK [ˌ-ˈ-] United Kingdom (of Great Britain and Northern Ireland).
ult. *ultimo* (L) of last month (*eg* your letter of 15th ult.).
UN [ˌ-ˈ-] United Nations.
UNCTAD [ˈʌŋktad] United Nations Commission for Trade and Development.
UNESCO [juˈneskou] United Nations Educational, Scientific and Cultural Organization.
UNICEF [ˈju:nisef] United Nations Children's Fund.
UNO [ˌ--ˈ-] United Nations Organization.
US [ˌ-ˈ-] United States.
USA [ˌ--ˈ-] United States of America: United States Army.
USAF [ˌ---ˈ-] United States Air Force.
USN [ˌ--ˈ-] United States Navy.
USS [ˌ--ˈ-] United States Ship/Steamer.
USSR [ˌ---ˈ-] Union of Soviet Socialist Republics.
V volt(s).
v versus: *vide* [ˈvaidi:] (L) see: verse.
VAT [ˌ--ˈ-; *also* vat] Value-added Tax.
VC [ˌ-ˈ-] Victoria Cross.
VD [ˌ-ˈ-] venereal disease (*see* Dictionary).
VHF [ˌ--ˈ-] very high frequency.
vid. *vide* [ˈvaidi:] (L) see.
VIP [ˌ--ˈ-] Very Important Person.
viz *videlicet* [viˈdi:liset] (L) namely.
vol volume.
vs versus.
VSO [ˌ--ˈ-] Voluntary Service Overseas.
W west: watt(s).
WC [ˌ---ˈ-] water closet.
W/Cdr Wing-Commander.
Wed. Wednesday.
WHO [ˌ----ˈ-] World Health Organization.
wk week.
WNW west-north-west.
WRAC [ˌ---ˌ--ˈ-] (*UK*) Women's Royal Army Corps.
WRAF [ˌ---ˌ--ˈ-] (*UK*) Women's Royal Air Force.
WRNS [ˌ---ˌ--ˈ-; *also* renz] (*UK*) Women's

Royal Naval Service.
WSW west-south-west.
X used to mark cinema films to showings of which children under 18, (*US* 17), are not admitted: 10 (*see* Appendix 1).
Xmas *see* Dictionary.
Y yen.
yd yard(s) – *pl also* **yds.**
YHA [ˌ––ˈ–] Youth Hostels Association.
YMCA [ˌ–––ˈ–] Young Men's Christian Association.
Yn yen.
Yr year.
YWCA [ˌ–––ˈ–] Young Women's Christian Association.
ZIP (*US*) *see* **zip**[2] *in* Dictionary.

Symbols

+	plus.
−	minus.
×	multiplied by, times.
÷	divided by.
=	equals.
<	is less than.
>	is greater than.
∴	therefore.
∵	because.
∞	infinity.
α	alpha.
β	beta.
γ	gamma.
δ	delta.
π	pi.
ω	omega.
$\sqrt{8}$	the square root of 8.
$\sqrt[3]{9}$	the cube root of 9.
$\sqrt[4]{20}$	the fourth root of 20.
x^2	*x* squared.
x^3	*x* cubed.
x^4	*x* to the power of four, *x* to the fourth power.
90°	ninety degrees.
2′	two feet: two minutes.
2″	two inches: two seconds.
&	and.
&c	et cetera.
£	pound(s).
$	dollar(s).

Appendix 9

Some Common Affixes and Combining Forms

A number of combining forms (*ie* elements such as **aero-, -bound, micro-, ultra-, -ward(s)** which form compound words) are to be found in the main text of the dictionary, and are therefore not included in the lists below.

Prefixes and Initial Combining Forms

Since the pronunciation of many of the prefixes given below varies from one word to another (*eg* **atheist** [ˈeiθiːist], **anarchy** [ˈanəki], **anonymous** [əˈnoniməs]), no pronunciation has been given for most of the items in this list. For the correct way to pronounce a particular affix in a given word, the reader is referred to the pronunciation of that word given in the main text of the dictionary. The only exceptions to this are certain combining forms whose pronunciations are not given elsewhere in the dictionary and which are therefore provided here.

a-[1], **an-**[1] not; without: *anarchy*; *atheist*; *anonymous.*
a-[2] 1 in; on: *amid*; *ashore.* 2 in the state or process of: *asleep*; (*old or liter*) *he came a-running.*
a-[3], **ab-, abs-** away from: *avert*; *abdicate*; *abstain.*
a-[4], **ad-, af-, ag-, al-, an-**[2], **ap-, ar-, as-, at-** to; towards; at: *aspire*; *advance*; *affix*; *aggressive*; *allure*; *annex*; *appear*; *arrive*; *assault*; *attend.*
ambi- both; two: *ambidextrous*; *ambiguous.*
amphi- 1 round about: *amphitheatre.* **2** both: *amphibious.*
anthrop(o)- of or like man: *anthropoid*; *anthropology.*
be- 1 away from; off: *behead.* **2** used to form transitive verbs with various meanings from intransitive verbs, nouns, and adjs: *bemoan*; *befriend*; *befit.* **3** around; on all sides: *beset.* **4** used to intensify the meaning of a verb: *bestir.*
bene- good; well: *benevolent.*
biblio- of books: *bibliography.*
by- 1 of lesser importance; subsidiary: *by-election*; *by-product.* **2** around: *by-pass.* **3** (in the) past: *bygone.* **4** near; beside: *bystander.*
centi- *see* Appendix 5.
co-, col-, com-, con-, cor- together; with: *cohere*; *collect*; *combine*; *connect*; *correspond.*
contra- opposite; against: *contradict.*
de- 1 away from: *decapitate*; *deodorant.* **2** the negative or opposite of: *decipher*; *decode.*
deca-, deci-, deka- *see* Appendix 5.
demi- [ˈdemi-] half; partly: *demisemiquaver* (*see* Appendix 4); *demigod.*
di- two: *diphthong.*
dia- through; across: *diagonal*; *diameter.*
dis- 1 the negative or opposite of: *dislike*; *discourteous.* **2** away from: *dishonour*; *dispossess.*
e-, ex-[1] from; out of: *emerge*; *exodus*; *expel.*
em-, en- 1 in; into: *embed*; *enlist.* **2** to cause to be, have *etc*: *enrich*; *empower.*
equi- equal: *equidistant.*
ex-[2] [eks-] former: *ex-wife.*
fore- 1 before; in front of: *foreground*; *foreleg.* **2** before (time): *foretell.*
gastr(o)- of the stomach: *gastro-enteritis.*
geo- of the Earth: *geology.*
haemo-, (*Amer*) **hemo-** of blood: *haemorrhage.*
hecto- *see* Appendix 5.

hepta- seven: *heptagon.*
hexa- six: *hexagon.*
hyper- more than normal; over; beyond: *hyperactive*; *hypercritical.*
hypo- under: *hypodermic.*
ig-, il-[1], **im-**[1], **in-**[1], **ir-**[1] not: *ignoble*; *illiterate*; *immortal*; *incapable*; *irrational.*
il-[2], **im-**[2], **in-**[2], **ir-**[2] in; into: *illuminate*; *imbibe*; *income*; *irrigate.*
infra- [ˈinfrə-] below: *infra-red.*
intro- within; inwards: *introspection*; *introvert.*
kilo- *see* Appendix 5.
mal-, male- bad; badly: *maladjusted*; *malevolent.*
milli- *see* Appendix 5.
ob-, op- against; in the way of: *obstruct*; *oppose.*
octa-, octo- eight: *octagonal*; *octopus.*
omni- all; every: *omnipotent.*
ortho- correct: *orthodox.*
penta- five: *pentagon.*
per- through: *pervade.*
peri- around: *perimeter*; *periphrastic.*
physio- 1 of the body: *physiotherapy.* **2** of living things: *physiology.*
quadr(i)- four: *quadrilateral*; *quadruplet.*
quin- five: *quintet.*
re- 1 again: *re-do*; *remould.* **2** back: *repatriate.* **3** away: *remove.*
retro- back: *retrograde*; *retrospective.*
sept- seven: *septet.*
sex- six: *sextet.*
sub- 1 below: *submarine.* **2** less than: *subhuman.* **3** subordinate; lower in rank than: *sub-lieutenant.* **4** a part or division of: *subspecies*; *subgroup.* **5** denoting (the performance or performer of) an action or part of an action repeating an action or done for someone performing the same or a similar action: *subdivide*; *subcontractor.*
syn- together: *synthesis.*
tele- at a distance: *telephone.*
theo- of God or a god: *theology.*
un- 1 not: *unhappy*; *untruth.* **2** the reverse of: *untie*; *unpack.*

Suffixes and Final Combining Forms

-ability [-əˈbiləti], **-ibility** [-iˈbiləti], **-ubility** [-juˈbiləti] denoting the state of being, or something which is, **-able, -ible** or **-uble**: *probability*; *edibility*; *solubility*; *readability.*
-able [-əbl], **-ible** [-ibl], **-uble** [-jubl] **1** able to be –; fit for: *eatable*; *edible*; *soluble.* **2** that must be –: *payable.* **3** in keeping with: *fashionable.* **4** that may cause or give rise to: *objectionable.* **5** worthy of: *desirable*; *respectable.*
-acy *see* **-cy.**
-age [-idʒ] denoting a quality, state, action *etc*: *breakage*; *shrinkage*; *wastage*; *bondage*; *tonnage.*
-al, -ial [-(i)əl] **1** relating to: *naval*; *postal*; *editorial*; *political.* **2** having a quality, state *etc*: *comical*; *central.* **3** denoting an action: *arrival*; *withdrawal.*
-an, -ian [-(i)ən] **1** of or belonging to: *Canadian*; *Moroccan*; *Anglican*; *Christian.* **2** an expert in, or a person concerned with, a noun in **-ic, -ics, -y**: *magician* [-ʃən]; *politician* [-ʃən]; *phonetician* [-ʃən]; *historian.* – *See note on pronunciation below.*
-ana, -iana [-(i)ˈanə] denoting things relating to: *Victoriana.*
-ance, -ence [-əns] denoting a quality, state, action *etc*: *assistance*; *repentance*; *persistence.*
-ant, -ent [-ənt] **1** denoting the person performing an action: *assistant*; *student.* **2** denoting a quality, state, action *etc*: *different*; *repentant.*
-ar [-ə] **1** *see* **-er**[1]. **2** denoting a quality, or relationship to: *angular*; *solar*; *molecular.*
-arian [-ˈeəriən] (denoting a person) having a certain belief, habit *etc*: *disciplinarian*; *vegetarian.*
-ary [-əri, (*Amer usu*) -eri] related to: *budgetary*; *monetary*; *granary* [(*Amer*) -əri].
-ate[1] [-ət] **1** used to denote a group: *electorate.* **2** showing a quality *etc*: *passionate.*
-ate[2] [-eit] **1** used to denote certain salts: *carbonate*; *phosphate.* **2** to cause to become: *activate.*
-ation *see* **-ion.**
-cide [-said] **1** a person who kills: *patricide.* **2** the act of killing: *homicide.*
-cy, -acy [-(ə)si] denoting a quality, state *etc*: *bankruptcy*; *secrecy*; *supremacy.*
-d *see* **-ed.**
-dom [-dəm] **1** used to denote a state or status: *freedom*; *dukedom.* **2** used to denote an area ruled by: *kingdom.* **3** used to denote an event: *martyrdom.*
-ed[1], **-d**[1] [-(i)d, -t], **-t** [-t] used to form the past tenses and past participles of verbs: *walked*; *loved*; *slept*; *married*; *eroded.* – *See note on pronunciation below.*
-ed[2], **-d**[2] [-(i)d, -t] used to form adjectives showing a quality or state: *bearded*; *red-haired*; *foul-mouthed*; *knock-kneed*; *long-legged* [-gid]; *short-sighted*; *hunch-backed.* – *See note on pronunciation below.*
-ee [-iː] **1** a person to whom something is done, given *etc*: *payee*; *employee*; *nominee.* **2** a person who does, wants *etc* something: *absentee*; *refugee.*
-eer [-ˈiə] **1** a person involved with something in any of several ways: *charioteer*; *profiteer*; *mountaineer.* **2** to act in one of these ways: *profiteer.*
-en[1], **-ren** [-(r)ən] used to form plurals of certain nouns: *oxen*; *children.*
-en[2], **-n**[1] [-ən] to (cause to) become: *blacken*; *whiten*; *harden*; *flatten.*
-en[3], **-n**[2], **-ne** [-(ə)n] used to form the past participles of certain verbs: *beaten*; *taken*; *gone*; *borne.*
-en[4] [-ən] made of: *wooden*; *woollen.*
-ence *see* **-ance.**
-ent *see* **-ant.**
-er[1], **-r**[1] [-ə] **1** (*also* **-ar, -or**) a person or thing that performs some action: *speaker*; *runner*; *poker*; *cooker*; *liar*; *sailor.* **2** a person who is involved in some trade or profession: *carpenter*; *hatter*; *footballer*; *painter.* **3** a person who studies or is an expert in something: *philosopher.* **4** a person who belongs to a place: *Londoner*; *New Yorker.* **5** a person or thing that has, is, shows *etc* something: *teenager.*
-er[2], **-r**[2] [-ə] used to form the comparative of adjectives and some adverbs: *faster*; *blacker*; *whiter*; *redder*; *bigger*; *sillier.*
-ery [-əri, (*Amer sometimes*) –eri], **-ry** [-ri] **1** used to denote a state or condition: *bravery*; *slavery.* **2** a collection of things of one type: *cutlery*; *crockery*; *confectionery* [(*Amer*) -eri]. **3** a place in which something is done: *brewery*; *bakery.* **4** the art or practice of: *cookery*; *carpentry.*

-es *see* **-s.**

-ese [-iːz, (*Amer also*) -iːs] **1** (a person or language) of a country *etc*: *Portuguese*; *Japanese.* **2** (*derog*) the style or jargon of: *journalese.*

-ess [-is] used to form feminine nouns: *lioness*; *countess*; *duchess.*

-est [-ist] used to form the superlatives of some adjectives and adverbs: *biggest*; *smallest*; *fastest*; *silliest.*

-ette [-ˈet] **1** used to form feminine nouns: *usherette.* **2** used to form diminutives: *cigarette.*

-fold [-fould] times as much or as many: *fourfold.*

-ful [-ful] **1** full of; having the quality of; causing: *delightful.* **2** the quantity held by a full – : *cupful*; *bucketful.*

-fy, -ify [-(i)fai] to make: *purify*; *liquefy.*

-gon [-gən] an angle or corner: *polygon*; *hexagon.*

-hood [-hud] the quality or state of: *manhood*; *boyhood.*

-ial *see* **-al.**

-ian *see* **-an.**

-iana *see* **-ana.**

-ible, -ibility *see* **-able, -ability.**

-ic [-ik] **1** used to denote certain acids: *phosphoric*; *nitric.* **2** connected with: *atomic*; *poetic*; *historic.*

-ical [-ikl] connected with: *historical.*

-ician *see* **-an.**

-ide [-aid] used to denote certain chemical compounds: *nitride*; *oxide.*

-ie *see* **-y**[2].

-ify *see* **-fy.**

-ing [-iŋ] **1** used to form present participles of verbs, and nouns denoting an action: *going*; *coming*; *reading.* **2** used to form nouns denoting a state derived from an activity: *learning.*

-ion, -sion, -tion, -ation, -ition, -ution [-ʃən, -ʒən, -ˈeiʃən, -ˈiʃən, -ˈ(j)uːʃən] **1** used to denote the act of doing something or process of having something done: *completion*; *invasion*; *introduction*; *conversation*; *initiation*; *pollution.* **2** used to denote a state: *tension.* **3** used to denote a power or ability: *comprehension.* **4** used to denote something which does some action *etc*: *insulation.* **5** used to denote the result of some action *etc*: *expression*; *intention*; *complication.* – *See note on pronunciation below.*

-ise *see* **-ize.**

-ish [-iʃ] **1** rather; quite; to some extent: *blackish*; *smallish.* **2** about: *eight-o'clockish*; *fortyish* (of a person's age). **3** (a person or language) of a place *etc*: *Spanish*; *Scottish.* **4** like: *childish*; *girlish*; *foolish.*

-ism [-izəm] **1** used to denote a system of philosophy, beliefs *etc*: *Communism*; *Marxism.* **2** used to denote a quality: *heroism.* **3** used to denote a practice or activity: *terrorism*; *cannibalism.* **4** used to denote a characteristic (*esp* of language): *archaism*; *Anglicism.*

-ist [-ist] **1** a believer in some philosophical *etc* system: *Marxist.* **2** a person who carries out some activity: *terrorist*; *motorist*; *publicist*; *tobacconist.*

-ite [-ait] **1** (a person) born in or belonging to: *Israelite* (= belonging to the ancient kingdom of Israel, not the modern state); *socialite.* **2** used to denote certain chemical compounds: *nitrite.*

-itis [-ˈaitis] a disease or illness; inflammation of: *gastro-enteritis*; *tonsillitis.*

-ity *see* **-ty.**

-ive [-iv] used to form adjectives denoting qualities: *impressive*; *explosive*; *offensive.*

-ize, -ise [-aiz] **1** to make: *equalize*; *publicize*; *modernize.* **2** to perform some activity: *criticize.*

-less [-lis] free from; not having or causing: *penniless*; *useless*; *harmless*; *toothless.*

-let [-lit] used to form diminutive nouns: *booklet*; *piglet*; *leaflet.*

-like [-laik] similar to: *manlike*; *warlike.*

-ling [-liŋ] **1** young or small: *duckling.* **2** (*usu derog*) a person showing certain qualities, in a certain relationship *etc*: *hireling*; *underling.*

-logy [-lədʒi] used to denote a branch of science *etc*: *biology*; *geology.*

-ly [-li] **1** used to form adverbs: *quickly*; *slowly.* **2** used to denote a quality: *manly.*

-man [-man, -mən], **-men** [-men, -mən] **1** used to denote a person or people who perform(s) some activity: *postman*; *fireman.* **2** a person or people from a country: *Frenchman.* – *See note on pronunciation of compounds on page xviii.*

-ment [-mənt] used to denote a state, means of doing something, substance involved *etc*: *nourishment*; *banishment*; *payment*; *recruitment.*

-most [-moust] used to denote the furthest position in some direction: *westernmost*; *outermost*; *inmost.*

-ness [-nis] used to denote a state or quality: *blackness*; *kindness.*

-oid [-oid] (a person or thing) like or in the form of: *humanoid.*

-or *see* **-er**[1].

-ory [-əri, (*Amer*) -oːri] used to form an adjective denoting a quality: *compulsory*; *auditory.*

-ous [-əs] used to denote a quality: *porous*; *perilous*; *religious.*

-phile [-fail] used to denote a person with a (too) great love of something: *Anglophile.*

-philia [-ˈfiliə] (too) great love of: *Anglophilia.*

-ry *see* **-ery.**

-s [-s, -z], **-es** [-(i)z] **1** used to form plurals: *books*; *dogs*; *churches*; *ponies*; *concertos.* **2** used to form the 3rd person present tense of verbs: *walks*; *runs*; *catches*; *marries.* – *See note on pronunciation below.*

-ship [-ʃip] used to denote a state: *friendship*; *ownership.* **2** used to denote ability, skill, learning: *musicianship*; *scholarship.*

-some [-səm] full of; causing: *troublesome.*

-ster [-stə] used to denote membership of a group, profession, *etc*: *gangster.*

-th [-θ] **1** used to form adjectives and nouns from numbers: *fourth*; *hundredth.* **2** used to denote a state: *warmth.*

-ty, -ity [-(ə)ti] used to denote a state or quality: *cruelty*; *stupidity.*

-uble, -ubility *see* **-able, -ability.**

-ution *see* **-ion.**

-y[1] [-i] used to denote a quality: *meaty*; *beefy.*

-y[2], **-ie** [-i] **1** used to denote a diminutive: *piggy*; *doggy.* **2** used to form familiar forms of certain names: *Johnny*; *Rosie.*

Notes

(*i*) **-(e)d** is pronounced [-id] after the sounds [t] and [d], [-t] after [p, t, k, f, θ, ʃ, tʃ], and [-d] after other consonants and all vowels.

(*ii*) **-(e)s** is pronounced [-iz] after [s, z, ʃ, ʒ, tʃ, dʒ], [-s] after [p, t, k, f, θ] and [-z] after other consonants and all vowels.

(*iii*) **-sion** is pronounced [-ʒən] following a vowel and [-ʃən] following a consonant; **-ssion** and **-tion** are pronounced [-ʃən]; **-cian** is pronounced [-ʃən]; **-tian** is often pronounced [-tʃən] and **-sian** is *usu* [-ʃən].

Exceptions to these general rules, *eg* **-legged**, are given transcriptions in the main text of the dictionary.